BROMLEY'S FAMILY LAW

Tenth edition

N V LOWE

*LLB (Sheffield) of the Inner Temple, Barrister; Professor of Law
at Cardiff University*

G DOUGLAS

LLB (Manchester), LLM (London) Professor of Law at Cardiff University

OXFORD
UNIVERSITY PRESS

OXFORD
UNIVERSITY PRESS

Great Clarendon Street, Oxford OX2 6DP

Oxford University Press is a department of the University of Oxford.
It furthers the University's objective of excellence in research, scholarship,
and education by publishing worldwide in

Oxford New York

Auckland Cape Town Dar es Salaam Hong Kong Karachi
Kuala Lumpur Madrid Melbourne Mexico City Nairobi
New Delhi Shanghai Taipei Toronto

With offices in

Argentina Austria Brazil Chile Czech Republic France Greece
Guatemala Hungary Italy Japan Poland Portugal Singapore
South Korea Switzerland Thailand Turkey Ukraine Vietnam

Oxford is a registered trade mark of Oxford University Press
in the UK and in certain other countries

Published in the United States
by Oxford University Press Inc., New York

British Library Cataloguing in Publication Data

Data available

Library of Congress Cataloging in Publication Data

Data available

Typeset by RefineCatch Limited, Bungay, Suffolk
Printed in Great Britain
on acid-free paper by
Ashford Colour Press Ltd, Gosport, Hants

ISBN 978–0–406–95951–5

5 7 9 10 8 6 4

PREFACE

The tenth edition of any book is a cause for celebration, but for this particular work it is especially significant since 2007 will also mark the fiftieth anniversary of the publication of the first edition, and indeed of the first book on 'family law'.

How different family law was half a century ago. Then, divorce was still squarely based on matrimonial fault (and was discussed in the first edition of this work in three separate chapters). Spousal maintenance, too, was dependent upon fault, while ancillary relief after divorce was confined to secured and unsecured maintenance, settlement of the wife's property and variation of ante-nuptial and post-nuptial settlements. There was no power to transfer property between spouses, and attempts to do so via s 17 of the Married Women's Property Act 1882 and the application of trusts were still developments of the future. The issue of status remained all-important, both in respect of marriage, annulment and divorce and, in relation to children, as to their legitimacy or illegitimacy (there was a separate chapter on illegitimate children). In contrast, there was virtually no discussion of children's welfare and no mention at all of what we now refer to as the public law relating to children (that is, the removal of children from their families into local authority care). Another topic notably absent from the first edition was domestic violence. Overall, the first edition was a masterly survey of what was then hard black letter law (the multidisciplinary dimension of family law was very much an issue of the future both in theory and practice) governing family issues and disputes, but is interestingly far removed from the treatment of family law provided in this edition. Even since the publication of the ninth edition in 1998 developments have been legion, and it is to these that we now turn.

There has, first of all, been a very active programme of legislative reform affecting family law. Perhaps the most fundamental change since the last edition is that brought about by the Civil Partnership Act 2004 which came into force in December 2005 and which allows same-sex couples to enter into a formal and legally recognised civil partnership (a development that simply could not have been imagined 50 years ago). Adoption law has at last been reformed by the Adoption and Children Act 2002, which also came into force in December 2005. That Act also made important changes to the acquisition of parental responsibility by unmarried fathers (i.e. upon being registered as the child's father), to the definition of 'harm' in the welfare checklist and to the ability to review the implementation of local authority care plans. It also made provision for enhanced residence orders and special guardianship. Interesting changes to the powers to make and enforce contact orders are to be introduced by the confusingly named Children and Adoption Act 2006, in part as a response to the growing dissatisfaction with the current law by fathers (another development which would not have been contemplated 50 years ago).

Important changes to the law of domestic violence were made by the Domestic Violence, Crime and Victims Act 2004, while s 58 of the Children Act 2004 importantly limits the right of parents to administer corporal punishment to their children. This latter Act (about to be amended by the Childcare Act 2006) makes important changes to the organisation of local authority services. Significant changes to child support were made by the Child Support, Pensions and Social Security Act 2000, though the scheme is still struggling and will be fundamentally amended again.

Another key Act is the Human Rights Act 1998, which was implemented in October 2000 and which has obvious importance for family law. Indeed a declaration of incompatibility under s 4 made in relation to the Matrimonial Causes Act 1973 s 11(c) (which confines marriages to a male and a female)[1] in part led to the enactment of yet another piece of legislation, the Gender Recognition Act 2004. Rather more negatively, but nonetheless of profound effect, has been the abandonment of plans to implement the radical reform of divorce law as contained in the Family Law Act 1996, and one can only speculate as to how and when divorce law might now be reformed.

Internationally, one significant development has been the creation and implementation of the Brussels Regulations, marking the first occasion that the European Union has made a direct impact on family law. From the family lawyer's perspective, the most important of the Regulations is Brussels II, which originally came into force in March 2001 but was then revised with effect from March 2005. This Regulation governs jurisdiction, recognition and enforcement of judgments in matrimonial matters and in matters of parental responsibility. It is evident that more Regulations are likely to be made.

Accompanying this extensive legislative reform has been a plethora of case law, including numerous decisions by the House of Lords. Among the key decisions since the last edition are *White v White* (2000), which set out a new path for distributing assets after divorce and upon which clarification is made by *Miller v Miller* (2006) and *McFarlane v McFarlane* (2006); *Ghaidan v Godin Mendoza* (2004) and *Fitzpatrick v Sterling Housing Association* (2000) on the position of same-sex partners in relation to tenancies; *Bellinger v Bellinger* (2003) on a transsexual's capacity to marry; *M v Secretary of State for Work and Pensions* (2006) on whether a same-sex partner should be recognised when calculating child support liability; *R (Kehoe) v Secretary of State for Work and Pensions* (2005) on human rights and child support; *Lancashire County Council v A* (2000) and *Re O and N, Re B* (2003) on the application of the statutory threshold under s 31 of the Children Act 1989; *Re S (Minors) (Care Order Implementation of Care Plan)* (2002) on the ability to review the implementation of local authority care plans over children; *Re G (Interim Care Order: Residential Assessment)* (2006) on the ambit of s 38(6) of the 1989 Act; *Barrett v Enfield London Borough Council* (1999) and *W v Essex County Council* (2000) on suing local authorities for negligence; *D v East Berkshire Community NHS Trust* (2005) on suing medical practitioners for negligent misdiagnosis of child abuse; *R(G) v Barnet London Borough Council* (2004) on the duty towards children in need; *Re Moynihan* (2000) and *Re R (IVF: Paternity of Child)* (2005) on paternity issues; *Dawson v Wearmouth* (1999) on naming a child; *R (Williamson) v Secretary of State for Education and Employment)* (2005) on corporal punishment of children in schools; *Re H (Abduction: Rights of Custody)* (2000) on the meaning of 'rights of custody' in the 1980 Hague Abduction Convention and *Re J (Child Returned Abroad: Custody Rights)* (2005) on the application of the welfare principle in abduction cases not governed by an international instrument.

Of course, developments in family law are not confined to statutory changes and case law, but include changes in practice, notable among which is the increasing emphasis

---

[1] See *Bellinger v Bellinger* [2003] UKHL 21, [2003] 2 AC 467. The Act was also the result of the European Court of Human Rights decision in *Goodwin v United Kingdom* (2002) 35 EHRR 18.

placed on mediation and alternative dispute resolution mechanisms and control of court proceedings (in this regard, account should be taken of the Protocol for Judicial Case Management in Public Law Children Act Cases and the President's Private Law Programme). Increasing emphasis is also being placed on the active involvement of children in legal proceedings affecting them.

To accommodate these developments we have made some changes to the structure of the book. In particular, we have significantly extended the introductory chapter; made radical changes to Chapters 2 to 4, replacing them with chapters on the Formation and Recognition of Adult Partnerships, the Personal and Property Consequences of Marriage, Civil Partnership and Cohabitation and on the Family Home. The chapter on Divorce and Dissolution (Chapter 6) has been written in the light of the decision not to go ahead with the reform provided for by the Family Law Act 1996. We have added a new chapter (Chapter 11) on the Voice of the Child and re-ordered some of the earlier chapters on children with Chapter 7 now on Parents and Children, Chapter 8 on Parental Responsibility, Chapter 9 on Guardianship and Chapter 10 on the Welfare Principle. Chapter 13 on International Child Abduction has been expanded to take into account Brussels II. Chapter 14 on Children and Local Authorities has been significantly reorganised and Chapter 15 on Adoption rewritten in the light of the Adoption and Children Act 2002.

This is the first edition to be published by Oxford University Press and we are pleased to record our thanks to the staff there for their patience, support and understanding. An especial debt of gratitude is owed to Sharon Willicombe of Cardiff Law School who has dedicated a good part of the last twelve months to typing and re-typing the many versions of the text. We could not have completed this edition without her help.

We have sought to take account of developments in the law up to 1 May 2006 and we have assumed the enactment of the Childcare Bill and the Children and Adoption Bill. We have also sought to include later developments where possible.

This tenth edition is dedicated to the memory of our parents, Marshall and Beryl Lowe and Jack and Doris Douglas, and in Nigel Lowe's case also to his anonymous bone marrow donor and to the team at the Bristol Stem Cell Transplant Unit, without whose help his contribution would not have been possible.

Nigel Lowe
Gillian Douglas
15 May 2006

CONTENTS

CONTENTS

TABLE OF STATUTES

TABLE OF CASES

1

INTRODUCTION

A THE NATURE AND SCOPE OF FAMILY LAW

1 THE MEANING OF 'FAMILY'

The word 'family' is one which it is difficult, if not impossible to define.[1] In one sense it can mean all persons related by blood or marriage or, since 2005, civil partners;[2] in another it may include all the members of a household, including parents and children with perhaps other relations, lodgers and even servants. But these definitions are unsatisfactory for our purposes. The fact that two persons can claim descent from a common ancestor may not, of itself, affect their legal relations at all. Similarly, the legal relationship between the head of a household and lodgers and servants is contractual and therefore lies outside the scope of this book. Moreover, intimate or caring relationships may be regarded as constituting a 'family' even though there are no blood or status ties between the parties.

Some elucidation of the concept of 'family', at least within European society, can be gleaned from the jurisprudence derived from the European Convention on Human Rights. Article 8(1) of the Convention guarantees to everyone 'the right to respect for his private and family life, his home and his correspondence' and Art 12 provides that 'Men and women of marriageable age have the right to marry and to found a family . . .'. The position is slightly complicated because Art 8 refers to 'family life' rather than 'the family' *per se*, but case law of the European Commission and European Court of Human Rights establishes that, for the purposes of the Convention, the relationship between spouses will always amount to a 'family',[3] although it has not yet been held that cohabitation between unmarried partners does so. It is clear that the relationship between a mother and her child will also always be regarded under the Convention as constituting a 'family' even if the child is born outside wedlock.[4] However, the Court has distinguished between married and unmarried fathers, and between unmarried mothers and unmarried fathers, holding that family life arises between a married father and his child automatically,[5] but that unmarried fathers must show more than the blood tie to establish a family life with their

---

[1] See further A Diduck *Law's Families* (2003); B Hale, D Pearl, E Cooke and P Bates *The Family, Law and Society: Cases and Materials* (2002, 5th edn) ch 1; A Diduck and F Kaganas *Family Law, Gender and the State: Text Cases and Materials* (2006, 2nd edn) ch 1.

[2] The Civil Partnership Act 2004, which came into force on 5 December 2005, creates a legal status broadly equivalent to marriage, for same-sex partners; see further Ch 2. Unless otherwise stated, references to spouses or marriage include civil partners and civil partnership.

[3] *Berrehab v Netherlands* (1988) 11 EHRR 322.   [4] *Marckx v Belgium* (1979) 2 EHRR 330.

[5] *Johnston v Ireland* (1986) 9 EHRR 203.

child.[6] Cohabitation outside marriage with the mother, even if it terminates before the child is born, may suffice[7] and the father need not cohabit with the mother at all, provided that he can demonstrate a sufficient interest in and commitment to the child.[8] Once such a relationship is shown, it will not matter that the parent is a homosexual or transsexual.[9] But the Court has not yet regarded same-sex partnerships as giving rise to 'family life'[10] and has upheld the right of a state to discriminate against homosexuals, as within its margin of appreciation, in restricting who may adopt.[11] Indeed, one could probably conclude that the Court now lags behind many European states, including the United Kingdom, in its treatment of relationships outside marriage and its concept of the family, although, as we will see, the incorporation of the European Convention on Human Rights into domestic law has done much to spur both judicial and legislative reform in widening legal recognition of what constitutes a family.

For our purposes, we regard the family as a basic social unit constituted by at least two people, whose relationship may fall into one of three categories. Most families will consist of three or more members falling into at least two different categories.

First, the relationship may be that of two persons in a marital relationship (including civil partners), or who are living together in a manner similar to spouses.[12] The percentage of non-married men and women under the age of 60 cohabiting outside marriage in Great Britain increased between 1986 and 2004 from 11% to 24% for men and from 13% to 25% for women.[13] This growth has forced the law to adapt to this change in social behaviour.[14] If an extra-marital union—between either heterosexual or same-sex partners—comes to an end by separation or death, the parties and their children may need the same protection as spouses and their children, and consequently the legal position of cohabitants has to a certain extent been assimilated to that of married persons. Secondly, a family may be constituted by a parent living with one or more children. Thirdly, brothers and sisters or other persons related by blood or marriage may be regarded as forming a family. The relationship, however, has only very limited effects on their legal position, and these arise principally on the death of another member of the family.[15]

2 THE FUNCTIONS OF FAMILY LAW

In this context the law has three distinct but related functions.

(a) Definition and alteration of status

Historically this was the law's main role because it was concerned primarily with the

---

[6] *G v Netherlands* (1993) 16 EHRR CD 38.   [7] *Keegan v Ireland* (1994) 18 EHRR 342.

[8] *Lebbink v Netherlands* [2004] 2 FLR 463 (father regularly visited the child and baby-sat).

[9] *Salgueiro da Silva Mouta v Portugal* [2001] 1 FCR 653; *X, Y and Z v United Kingdom* (1997) 24 EHRR 143.

[10] Although in *Karner v Austria* [2003] 2 FLR 623, it was held that the right to succeed to a tenancy of a home shared by a same-sex couple was protected under Art 8 by the right to respect for one's home.

[11] *Fretté v France* [2003] 2 FLR 9.

[12] Whether the basic conjugal model should continue to shape our definition of the family, and its legal recognition, is a matter open to debate: see A Diduck 'Shifting Familiarity' (2005) Current Legal Problems 235; L Glennon 'Displacing the "conjugal family" in legal policy—a progressive move?' [2005] CFLQ 141.

[13] ONS, *Social Trends* 36 (2006) p 27.   [14] See further below pp 99–105.

[15] For example, claims to a tenancy under the Rent Act 1977 or the Housing Act 1985, succession rights, and claims under the Fatal Accidents Act 1976: see Ch 19.

rights which one member of the family could claim over another or over the latter's property. In the case of a man and woman living together, these arose only if they were married, and their legal relationship still depends largely on their status. Similarly, there were virtually no rights and duties with respect to children unless they were legitimate (which in turn depended on whether their parents were married). Questions of status are also important in public law, for on them may turn such matters as a person's nationality and right to live in the United Kingdom and claims to contributory social security benefits.

Akin to the courts' power to define status is their power to alter it. Among the most important aspects of this is their jurisdiction to grant divorces and make adoption orders, because a marriage can be dissolved and a child can be legally adopted only by judicial process.

It might have been argued at one time that the law was moving away from a focus on determining people's rights by virtue of their status, and that greater freedom was being given to them to shape and agree the legal consequences of their personal relationships for themselves.[16] But the introduction of a new legal status of 'civil partnership' for same-sex couples,[17] the automatic acquisition of parental responsibility by unmarried fathers so long as they are named on the child's birth certificate[18] and the fact that extra-marital cohabitation already attracts certain legal consequences[19] suggests that relationship status is still an important source of legal rights.

(b) Normative role

Linked to status is the question of normativity. The types of relationship which attract legal recognition are not selected at random but as a policy choice. The grant of rights and duties marks out both the nature and the functions of the relationship which the state approves and promotes. The legal recognition of marriage, and the lack of equivalent recognition for cohabitation, for example, should be seen as a deliberate decision to encourage intimate relationships to be fitted within the framework of marriage law. The extension of legal recognition to same-sex couples who become 'civil partners' represents a decision to indicate that such partnerships are also approved and regarded as acceptable by the state. Usually, legal recognition will follow social acceptance, but in the case of same-sex relationships, part of the impetus for reform has been based on the view that human rights law requires an end to the discrimination previously suffered by gay and lesbian people. Article 14 of the European Convention on Human Rights, although not a free-standing right, does require that the enjoyment of the rights and freedoms set out in the Convention are secured 'without discrimination on any ground such as sex, race' etc. The European Court of Human Rights has held that discrimination based on sexual orientation may be a breach of this article taken with Art 8.[20]

---

[16] As Sir Henry Maine famously put it: 'the movement of the progressive societies has hitherto been a movement from Status to Contract', *Ancient Law* (1931, at 141).

[17] Civil Partnership Act 2004.

[18] Children Act 1989, s 4(1)(a), discussed below p 414.

[19] The question of what, if any, further rights and responsibilities should attach to cohabitation is being explored by the Law Commission.

[20] *Salgueiro da Silva Mouta v Portugal* [2001] 1 FCR 653.

(c) Remedial role

The courts may be required to resolve disputes between members of the family, to provide protection for weaker members, and to manage the consequences of the termination of the family unit, for example, on a divorce.

The protection of the weaker members of the family has two aspects: physical and economic. The former usually raises the more urgent problems and the courts can give protection to the victims of domestic violence by making non-molestation orders and orders excluding a party from the matrimonial home. As a last resort they may order a child to be taken into the care of a local authority. The economic protection of a member of the family usually assumes importance when the family unit ceases to exist, either through separation or death, and the courts have extensive powers to make orders for financial provision on both these events.

Even though the termination of the family unit may leave the members adequately provided for, justice may nonetheless require the redistribution of their capital assets, and the courts have power to make orders for this purpose on the breakdown of a marriage and, to a more limited extent, on the death of a member of the family. Similarly, if a person dies intestate, his property will have to be distributed, and the law of intestate succession is essentially a part of family law because it provides for the division of a deceased person's property amongst members of his family.

During the past century English family law has shown a steady movement away from the former of these functions to the latter, and today its remedial role is of much greater importance than that of conferring rights. The result has been to give individual judges much greater discretion, for while Parliament and appellate courts can lay down general principles for, say, the resolution of disputes relating to children or the award of financial relief, their application will vary enormously according to the circumstances of each family.

B   TRENDS IN FAMILY LAW

1 EQUALISATION OF MEN AND WOMEN

As family law developed during the nineteenth and especially the twentieth centuries, certain major trends became apparent. The first of these was an equalisation in the positions of men and women. The abolition of the position of the husband as possessor of his wife (and owner of her property) was addressed in the nineteenth century as a major element in the move to women's emancipation which culminated in their obtaining the franchise.[21] (Although the last vestige of this common law favouring of men was removed only in 1991 by the House of Lords when they held that a husband may be convicted for rape of his wife.)[22] Accompanying the recognition of the position of the woman as *wife* was a corresponding move to give the woman as *mother* the same rights over her

---

[21] L Holcombe *Wives and Property* (1983); D Stetson *A Woman's Issue: the Politics of Family Law Reform in England* (1982).

[22] *R v R* [1992] 1 AC 599, HL.

legitimate[23] children as the father had traditionally possessed. One of the most significant steps in this development was the enactment of s 1 of the Guardianship of Infants Act 1925, which provided that in proceedings before a court, neither the father nor the mother should be regarded as having a claim superior to the other in respect of the custody or upbringing of the child.[24] But again, the process has been a lengthy one; it was not until 1973 that parents were given equal rights to determine their children's upbringing, by s 1 of the Guardianship Act 1973; and only under the Children Act 1989 was the rule abolished that a father is sole guardian of his legitimate children during his lifetime.

This recognition of equality has had further consequences for women which they may not have found so palatable. There has been an increasing view that women, who, after all, now expect to work in paid employment throughout most of their lives, rather than remain at home as housewives and child-carers, should be financially independent of their former partners. A 'clean break' between ex-spouses, whereby the man is no longer expected to support his former wife, has become the favoured disposition of finance and property on a divorce, justified further by a view that those who no longer share married status with each other should not be 'shackled' together by economic bonds either.[25]

2 SHIFT IN EMPHASIS FROM PAST FAULT TO FUTURE NEEDS

Another crucial trend has been the extent to which the law has withdrawn from seeking to pass judgment on the misconduct of family members towards each other, as a justification for making an order to settle their future legal positions and relationships.[26] Instead, increasing attention has been focused upon the likely needs of the parties in the aftermath of the breakdown of their relationship. This trend has been fostered by a recognition of the difficulty for a court in ascribing blame for this when it is dependent upon the evidence which a party chooses to place before it. The whole story may never be brought out which would, in theory at least, enable the court to form a valid judgment as to fault. This has been particularly true of divorces, where virtually all suits are undefended. Facts may be highlighted in a party's case in order to fit the constraints of the law, but may bear little relation to their true significance in leading to the breakdown as far as the parties themselves are concerned.[27]

The futility of ascribing blame has also been recognised. A decision that a spouse is responsible for the failure of the marriage does not contribute positively to arriving at a settlement of the financial position where, for example, that 'guilty' spouse is going to continue to care for the couple's children, and hence will need to remain in the former

---

[23] The mother of a child born outside marriage was, and remains, solely entitled automatically to exercise parental responsibility for that child; the father may now acquire shared parental responsibility with her under s 4 of the Children Act 1989.

[24] See S Cretney ' "What Will the Women Want Next?" The Struggle for Power Within the Family 1925–1975' (1996) 112 LQR 110, for a description of the political lobbying and history which lay behind its enactment.

[25] *Ashley v Blackman* [1988] Fam 85; *C v C (Financial Provision: Personal Damages)* [1995] 2 FLR 171.

[26] K O'Donovan 'Love's Law: Moral Reasoning in Family Law' in Morgan and Douglas (eds) *Constituting Families: A Study in Governance* (1994) 40.

[27] Stone has shown how, even in the days of Parliamentary divorce, evidence was concocted and colluded in: see *Road to Divorce: England 1530–1987* (1990) Part X.

matrimonial home, with the former husband correspondingly being kept out of his share of this capital asset.

3 SHIFT OF ATTENTION FROM ADULTS TO CHILDREN

There has been a significant shift in the attention of law makers and the courts away from the adults to the children in the family. This seems to be a counterpart to the other trends we have discussed. Adults are presumed capable of looking after themselves and therefore of not requiring the same degree of protection from the law and the courts that those who are vulnerable may need. The most vulnerable family members are, of course, the children. As divorce has become more common, the economic, psychological, health and educational consequences of the marriage break-up for the children have been more closely researched and the findings, although not clear-cut, have been sufficiently worrying to prompt greater concern that the law and legal processes at least should not add to any deficit which might be suffered. Changes in the thinking about how children develop psychologically have also fed through into legal proceedings, so that adoption and child care proceedings, as well as disputes between parents when their relationship breaks up, have become informed and infused by the desire to ensure that legal outcomes are the best available for the child. At the same time, a growing willingness to recognise children's developing rights to autonomy has resulted in a concern to provide mechanisms to enable them to express their wishes and feelings about what should happen to them, both within legal proceedings and more generally when decisions about their future are being taken. The desire to place children at the centre of legal attention has not been confined to this country, but is a worldwide phenomenon, culminating in the drafting and opening for signature of the United Nations Convention on the Rights of the Child in 1989.

4 GROWING RECOGNITION OF COHABITATION OUTSIDE MARRIAGE AND OF SAME-SEX PARTNERSHIPS

The large increase in the number of couples living together outside marriage has already been noted. There are various reasons for this development. Some couples cannot marry, because one of them is in the process of obtaining a divorce (or, occasionally, is unable to do so). Some wish to avoid the financial responsibilities attached to marriage. Others wish to postpone the assumption of the legal incidents of marriage and regard cohabitation as a form of trial marriage or merely 'a pre-marital experience'. Some drift into cohabitation as their relationship becomes more intimate. Some regard marriage as irrelevant and may cohabit because they reject 'the traditional marriage contract and the assumption of the roles which necessarily seem to go with it'.[28]

Until comparatively recently, cohabitation outside marriage gave the parties no rights over and above those possessed by, say, a brother and sister living together. Indeed, they might have found themselves, legally speaking, in a worse position because their relationship, involving, as it did, 'fornication', might deprive them of rights which they might

---

[28] M Freeman and C Lyon *Cohabitation without Marriage* (1983) p 51. For a much fuller discussion of the question see A Barlow et al, *Cohabitation, Marriage and the Law: social change and legal reform in the 21st century* (2005); and (2004) *Law and Policy* Issue 1 on Cohabitation.

otherwise have. If, for example, a woman contributed a sum towards the purchase of a house in which she was to live with her brother in consideration of his undertaking to have it conveyed into their joint names, she could enforce the contract; if, however, she entered into a similar agreement with a man with whom she was going to cohabit, the illicit purpose of the transaction probably made it unenforceable. Extra-marital sexual inter-course was regarded as immoral, and consequently any agreement entered into with this object in view was liable to be struck down as contrary to public policy. For example, in *Diwell v Farnes*[29] the Court of Appeal expressed the view that any attempt by a woman to claim an interest in a house bought by the man with whom she had been living by spelling out an agreement that they should buy it as a joint venture was doomed to failure, because such a contract would be unenforceable as founded on an immoral consideration.

A complete change in the courts' attitude came a decade or so later. In 1972 the Court of Appeal held that the property rights of cohabitants who intended to marry as soon as they were free to do so should be determined in the same way as the rights of spouses.[30] Three years later they held that a cohabitant could rely on a contractual licence to give her a right to occupy a house bought by her former partner.[31] In the same year they reached the more controversial decision that a cohabitant could claim the transmission of a statutory tenancy under the Rent Act as a member of the deceased tenant's family.[32]

At the same time Parliament started to give claims to cohabitants which could scarcely have been imagined even 25 years before. By enabling a de facto dependant to apply for an order, the Inheritance (Provision for Family and Dependants) Act 1975 gave a cohabitant the right to claim provision after her (or his) partner's death which she did not have during his lifetime.[33] The Administration of Justice Act 1982 amended the Fatal Accidents Act 1976 so as to enable a cohabitant to maintain an action under that Act for the death of her (or his) partner. The Housing Acts include persons who 'live together as husband and wife' among those who can claim a tenancy on the tenant's death. Part IV of the Family Law Act 1996 enables a court to grant an occupation or non-molestation order to cohabit-ants who are defined as 'two persons who are neither married to each other nor civil partners of each other but are living together as husband and wife or as if they were civil partners'. Similarly, the Social Security Contributions and Benefits Act 1992 defines a 'couple' as, inter alia, 'a man and woman who are not married to each other but are living together as husband and wife' for the purpose of establishing entitlement to certain social security benefits.

The judicial and parliamentary attitude towards extra-marital cohabitation merely reflects the attitude of society generally. But it is not without its critics.[34] Convincing arguments can be put forward on both sides. The strongest reason for giving rights to

---

[29] [1959] 2 All ER 379 at 384 (per Ormerod LJ) and 388 (per Willmer LJ) CA: see also *Gammans v Ekins* [1950] 2 KB 328, CA.

[30] *Cooke v Head* [1972] 2 All ER 38, CA.

[31] *Tanner v Tanner* [1975] 3 All ER 776, CA; below p 189.

[32] *Dyson Holdings Ltd v Fox* [1976] QB 503, CA; below, p 1101.

[33] Express recognition of cohabitation was made by the Law Reform (Succession) Act 1995 s 2: see below, p 1108.

[34] See particularly R Deech 'The Case against Legal Recognition of Cohabitation' in J Eekelaar and S Katz (eds) *Marriage and Cohabitation in Contemporary Societies: Areas of Legal, Social and Ethical Change* (1980). Cf. C Barton *Cohabitation Contracts: Extra Marital Partnerships and Law Reform* (1985) pp 73–5; Baroness Hale of Richmond, 'Unmarried Couples in Family Law' [2004] Fam Law 419.

cohabitants is that, as many unmarried couples are virtually indistinguishable from married ones, the parties (or the survivor) and their children may be as much in need of legal protection as spouses if the union breaks down as a result of separation or is brought to an end by death. This argument is particularly strong if the parties were unable to marry each other for some reason. Against this can be raised a number of counter-arguments. The first is a purely moral one and reflects the old common law position: extra-marital cohabitation is wrong and consequently no legal rights should be granted to those who engage in it. The second reason for not according rights to cohabitants rests on the indisputable premise that it is in the interests of society generally that the relationship that a couple enter into should be as stable as possible, particularly if they have children. As marriage implies an emotional and legal commitment, marital relationships, it is argued, should be more stable than extra-marital ones. Consequently, by giving to the unmarried rights previously possessed only by the married, the law is weakening the institution of marriage and thus undermining the family. The force of this argument depends on whether the assumption about the comparative stability of marriage is correct, and evidence is beginning to be produced which does lend it some support.[35] Finally, it is argued that the law should not force the parties to accept the obligations of marriage they have consciously chosen to reject, or confer on them the attendant rights, particularly when it is possible for them, in part at least, to regulate their own legal relationship by contract.[36]

English law has adopted a typical compromise and has assimilated the legal position of cohabitants to that of spouses only in isolated fields. This inconsistency no doubt reflects the ambivalence of society generally to the question of cohabitation, as well as the number of different reasons that couples have for living together outside marriage. As the number of cohabiting couples increases, the problems resulting from the breakdown of their relationship and the attendant loss of home and support will become more common and more acute. Whatever the difficulties, the introduction of a coherent policy is essential.

The position has become even more acute because there has been a major shift in the attitude towards same-sex partnerships in the past decade. The trend began with the courts seeking to assimilate the position of homosexual partners with that of heterosexuals in the realm of tenancy law, holding first that such a partner could succeed to a tenancy held by his or her deceased partner as a member of the deceased tenant's family,[37] and then, after the Human Rights Act 1998 came into force, that the legislation should be construed so that such a person could succeed as if he or she were the spouse of the deceased.[38] Meanwhile, after two private member's bills were introduced into Parliament and withdrawn on the government undertaking to bring forward its own legislation, the Civil Partnership Act was eventually passed in 2004, enabling same-sex couples to achieve

---

[35] See the discussion by F Robertson Elliot *Gender, Family and Society* (1996) pp 13–19 and 25–7; M Maclean and J Eekelaar *The Parental Obligation* (1997) pp 19–21.

[36] But if cohabitants can so regulate their legal position, why should not spouses be able to do so as well (eg by contracting out of their mutual duty of support)?

[37] *Fitzpatrick v Sterling Housing Association Ltd* [2001] 1 AC 27, HL. See A Diduck, 'A Family by any other Name . . . Or Starbucks™ Comes to England' (2001) 28 Journal of Law and Society 290. See further below pp 1101–2.

[38] *Ghaidan v Godin-Mendoza* [2004] UKHL 30, [2004] 2 AC 557. Lord Millett dissented. See R Probert, 'Same-Sex Couples and the Marriage Model' (2005) 13 Fem LS 135. See further below pp 101–2.

a recognised legal status with virtually all the same rights and duties as spouses.[39] It has become harder to argue that heterosexual cohabitants should be denied additional rights and protection in the light of such a profound change in social and legal attitudes, and the further consequence is that it will be impossible to treat same-sex cohabitants any differently from heterosexual cohabitants if, as seems likely, the proposals for reform of the law governing cohabitants forthcoming from the Law Commission are duly enacted.[40]

5 PRIVATE ORDERING

Alongside the withdrawal of the law from attempting to pass judgment on the moral failings of those in family relationships, there has been an equally strong drive to discourage the use of legal proceedings to 'resolve' family disputes, by promoting a 'settlement culture'.[41] There are several reasons for this. Historically, couples and their families may have sought to avoid legal proceedings because of the scandal and stigma attached to them, and to seek to arrive at compromises satisfactory to all concerned without attracting the attention of the hoi polloi in open court hearings. The extent to which this could be done depended upon the outcome sought: clearly, a quiet separation, with financial support for the wife privately agreed between two families, was more easily achieved than a divorce, which could not be obtained without the glare of publicity, until the 1970s. Yet private negotiations ran the risk that, if discovered, any change in legal status being sought would be denied, on the basis that the parties had acted 'collusively' to conceal relevant matters from the court, and it remains the case that the parties cannot 'oust the jurisdiction of the court' by striking a financial bargain which prohibits them from later asking a court to produce a different outcome.[42] The purpose of retaining this state scrutiny over family relationships is probably twofold: first, to protect weaker parties from exploitation, and secondly, to uphold public order and public policy.

Nonetheless, the desirability of arriving, in private, at a solution agreeable to both sides came to be recognised by courts, lawyers and finally the government. Legal costs can be reduced by avoiding trial (since it is the actual hearing which is the most expensive part of litigation), and this may in turn reduce public expenditure on courts and legal aid and save court time.[43] The 'win–lose' essence of adversarial legal proceedings may antagonise and add to the general unhappiness and bitterness associated with the breakdown of a relationship, and this may be emotionally and psychologically damaging to any children affected.[44] Court orders and legal rules are blunt instruments for dealing with complex human problems, and the legal process is ill-equipped to provide the full range of support needed by family members going through crises and change. They may be particularly

---

[39] See below pp 41–3 and passim.

[40] See Law Commission Consultation Paper No 179, *Cohabitation: The Financial Consequences of Relationship Breakdown* (2006).

[41] S Cretney, G Davis and J Collins *Simple Quarrels* (1994) p 211.

[42] Matrimonial Causes Act 1973 s 34 below, p 952; Child Support Act 1991 s 9(4).

[43] For further consideration of the issue of costs, see below p 1056.

[44] Law Com No 192, *The Ground for Divorce* (1990) paras 2.16, 2.19–2.20; Lord Chancellor's Department, *Looking to the Future: Mediation and the Ground for Divorce* Cm 2424 (1993) paras 5.11–5.15 and Cm 2799 (1995) paras 2.22–2.25. For empirical research, see in particular J Pryor and B Rodgers, *Children in Changing Families: Life after Parental Separation* (2001); L Trinder et al, *Making contact: How parents and children negotiate and experience contact after divorce* (2002).

inappropriate where there is a need to preserve and foster a relationship notwithstanding a change in legal status. For example, a court may be able to determine the legal parentage of a child, or who should inherit under a will or intestacy, but may be less competent to assess whether children will benefit from continued contact with their absent parent after a divorce, and still less be able to ensure that such contact takes place. Recognition of this legal impotence has coincided with a political preference for less state intervention in the privacy of the family, manifested in an emphasis, in the Children Act 1989, upon parents having responsibility for their children, and consequently being trusted to take decisions for and about them without undue scrutiny by a court. Finally, the breadth of discretion, which, of necessity, is entrusted to courts to determine issues which turn on a myriad of individual facts, makes it hard to predict the outcome of litigation, and acts as an incentive to parties to try to minimise uncertainty by arriving at their own agreement. Ironically, at the same time this broad discretion forces legal advisers to attempt to second-guess what courts may do, by relying on either reported precedents, or practice within their local area, and to use such knowledge to persuade clients that a particular outcome is the most likely to be obtained, and hence may as well be agreed without waiting for the court to produce a ruling.[45]

For all these reasons, the law now offers firm encouragement to families in dispute to resort to means other than the courts to arrive at settlements. Lawyer-led negotiations remain the prevailing device for achieving these.[46] Many family lawyers developed a more 'conciliatory', non-adversarial approach to their clients' problems in the 1970s and 1980s, to a great extent through the establishment of what was then called the Solicitors Family Law Association,[47] which has a code of practice for its members which emphasises the need to minimise conflict between family members during legal processes. Some lawyers have also begun to practise 'collaborative law', whereby the lawyers for both sides undertake not to act for their clients if the case proceeds to court, thus encouraging them to work with the clients to achieve a settlement.[48]

Alongside this trend, 'alternative dispute resolution' through mediation or conciliation has been introduced both as a part of the legal process, and as an adjunct to it.[49] Mediation and conciliation may be defined as processes whereby a neutral third party acts as a facilitator of discussion between the parties in dispute, helping them to arrive at their own agreed resolution. Many schemes offering these services are focused particularly on disputes relating to children, and in these, the facilitator is most likely to have social work training. But many lawyers are also trained mediators and they offer the service as another aspect of their provision for family clients. Mediation has developed both outside of the courts, so that it is available to couples who may not have begun any legal proceedings as well as those who are engaged in them, and within the courts as an essential step in the legal procedure. Such 'in court' processes may be moderated by either a CAFCASS officer,[50]

[45] R Mnookin and L Kornhauser 'Bargaining in the Shadow of the Law: The Case of Divorce' (1979) 88 Yale LJ 950.

[46] See especially, S Cretney et al *Simple Quarrels* (1994) and J Eekelaar, M Maclean and S Beinart, *Family Lawyers: The Divorce Work of Solicitors* (2000).

[47] Now known as 'Resolution'. For its code of practice, see http://www.resolution.org.uk/code_practice.php.

[48] See further below p 286.   [49] For discussion of these see below pp 282–6 and 988–9.

[50] See below p 11.

if the dispute concerns children (when it tends to be referred to as conciliation), or a district judge, in the case of financial and property disputes.[51] Where a litigant seeks legal aid, this will not be granted until the suitability of the case for mediation has first been established. If the case is deemed suitable, a refusal to engage in mediation may result in the litigant being denied legal aid.[52]

6 MULTI-DISCIPLINARY AND SPECIALIST APPROACHES TO FAMILY PROBLEMS

As the law and legal process have become increasingly regarded as inappropriate to respond to and deal with family problems, attention has turned to other disciplines and other mechanisms outside or alongside law to fill the gap.[53] A key feature of family law today is the extent to which non-legal professionals are involved in its practice and administration. This operates in several different ways. It is perhaps traditional for accountants and tax advisers to be involved in the provision of financial advice and assistance to wealthy divorcees. A more recent development has been the removal, in many instances, of the calculation, collection and enforcement of child maintenance from the jurisdiction of the courts, which, as noted above, are generally given wide discretion in their handling of family matters, to a governmental agency, the Child Support Agency, staffed by civil servants applying a strict formula to the calculation of the maintenance obligation upon non-resident parents.[54] Social work professionals, working both within the courts and in local authority social services departments, are largely responsible for the handling of child protection, albeit with some court control. The creation of a unified service, CAFCASS (Children and Family Court Advisory and Support Service), in 2001[55] brought together court welfare officers, who had been trained as probation officers, guardians ad litem, social workers who usually had local authority child care experience, and lawyers and social workers who had previously been attached to the Official Solicitor's office, to provide advice to the family courts, and to represent the interests, and sometimes the voices, of children who are the subjects of litigation.

Paediatricians, psychologists, psychoanalysts and psychiatrists play an important role in the diagnosis and treatment of child abuse and neglect, and in the provision of support for children facing trauma during and after family breakdown. The legal process makes use of their expertise as expert witnesses to help determine both the occurrence or likelihood

---

[51] See below p 988.

[52] Access to Justice Act 1999 s 8(3); Community Legal Service *Funding Code Part II Procedures* (2005), Section 7—Referral for Family Mediation.

[53] For opposing views on the inter-action of different disciplines within the legal process, see M Murch and D Hooper *The Family Justice System* (1992); M Murch 'The cross-disciplinary approach to family law—are we trying to mix oil with water? in Pearl (ed) *Frontiers of Family Law* (1995); M King and C Piper *How the Law Thinks About Children* (2nd edn, 1995), M King and J Trowell *Children's Welfare and the Law: The Limits of Legal Intervention* (1992), drawing upon Teubner's theory of 'autopoeisis'.

[54] Child Support Act 1991. Whether this has been a successful innovation is explored below, pp 929–51.

[55] Under the Criminal Justice and Court Services Act 2000. Note that the Children Act 2004 s 34 devolved CAFCASS functions relating to Wales to the National Assembly of Wales and these functions are carried out by 'Welsh family proceedings officers' rather than 'CAFCASS officers'. See further below p 484.

of abusive acts and the best mode of dealing with their aftermath for the child.[56] The rise of mediation and attempts to provide support for adults undergoing relationship break-down[57] are further instances of non-legal approaches to what was once regarded as a strictly legal subject.

C THE DEVELOPMENT OF THE FAMILY COURT SYSTEM

Sometimes a question of family law arises in a case of contract or tort or in a criminal prosecution. For example, it may be necessary to determine whether a woman can claim damages in respect of her husband's death or whether the accused's spouse is a compel-lable witness. Each of these cases will, of course, be tried in the ordinary civil or criminal courts and no special problem arises. What we are concerned with here are the courts which hear and determine cases raising issues solely of family law, for example the annul-ment or dissolution of marriage, settling with whom a child is to live, and the making of financial provision. As we explain, there has been a gradual grafting onto the basic court hierarchy of a system of linked courts, exercising the same or similar jurisdiction, staffed by judges and magistrates specially trained to deal with family matters. Thus, it can be suggested that family law in England and Wales is now administered by a family court 'system', if not yet a discrete 'family court', the arguments for which we consider after explaining the current arrangements.

1 THE CURRENT COURT SYSTEM

In broad terms there are three levels of courts with original jurisdiction to hear family cases. In order of superiority, they are the High Court, county court and magistrates' court. The former two are entirely staffed by professional judges. The latter courts are mainly staffed by unpaid 'lay' persons known as magistrates or justices. Lay tribunals comprise three magistrates. Provision is also made for the appointment of full-time pro-fessional judges now known as district judges (magistrates' courts) [formerly known as 'stipendiary magistrates']. All lay magistrates' courts have the services of a justices' clerk, who is a trained lawyer[58] and whose function, inter alia, is to advise the bench on matters of law.[59]

(a) The High Court

In the High Court, family law disputes are handled by the Family Division which was first created by the Administration of Justice Act 1970, s 1. Before that Act, family law work was divided between the old Probate, Divorce and Admiralty Division, which had exclusive jurisdiction over divorce, and the Chancery Division, which had a general supervisory

---

[56] Mr Justice Wall (ed) *Rooted Sorrows: Psychoanalytic Perspectives on Child Protection, Assessment, Therapy and Treatment* (1997). For a short overview of the problems arising from reliance upon experts, see C Cobley and T Sanders, 'Expert Witnesses on Trial' www.ccels.cf.ac.uk/literature/issue/2004/cobley.pdf.

[57] See below pp 282–6, 300–1. [58] A clerk must be a barrister or solicitor of at least seven years' standing.

[59] See *Practice Direction (Justices: Clerk to Court)* [2000] 1 WLR 1886.

jurisdiction over children. The current jurisdiction is set out in Sch 1 to the Supreme Court Act 1981 and broadly covers all types of family law disputes.

Judges sitting on the Family Division (which is headed by the President and comprises a total of 18 puisne judges)[60] are mainly, but not exclusively, drawn from the specialist Family Law Bar and spend a substantial part of their judicial time sitting in family law cases. They are immensely experienced in dealing with family disputes.

(b) County courts

During the 160-plus years since their creation, county courts have steadily acquired expanded jurisdiction to hear family matters to the extent that they now handle the vast majority of the business. Crucially, jurisdiction to hear divorce and other matrimonial causes, first extended to the county courts by the Matrimonial Causes Act 1967, which empowered the Lord Chancellor to designate any county court as a divorce court to hear any *undefended* matrimonial cause, was widened by the Matrimonial and Family Proceedings Act 1984 to empower divorce county courts to hear *all* matrimonial causes, both defended and undefended, and all other applications under the Matrimonial Causes Act 1973,[61] and now all civil partnership causes.[62] County courts have long had jurisdiction over property claims under the Married Women's Property Act 1882[63] and adoption.[64] They have jurisdiction to hear claims under the Inheritance (Provision for Family and Dependants) Act 1975, applications concerning children under the Children Act 1989 and domestic violence applications made under the Family Law Act 1996 Part IV. County courts also have jurisdiction to make declarations of status under the Family Law Act 1986, Part III.

(c) Magistrates' courts

Like county courts, the jurisdiction of magistrates' courts to hear family matters has steadily expanded. Originally resulting from their jurisdiction to administer criminal law, magistrates acquired expanding jurisdiction to make maintenance orders between spouses and for children[65] and, following the creation of the juvenile court in 1908 (renamed the 'youth court' in 1991)[66] had important jurisdiction over both child offenders and children

---

[60] In addition, suitable persons can be appointed to sit as a Deputy High Court judge under the Supreme Court Act 1981, s 9 and hence are known as 'Section 9 judges'.

[61] Matrimonial and Family Proceedings Act 1984 s 33 and s 34.

[62] Ie actions for the dissolution or annulment of a civil partnership or for the legal separation of civil partners: s 32 of the 1984 Act as amended by the Civil Partnership Act 2004, Sch 27, para 91.

[63] First conferred by the Guardianship of Infants Act 1886.

[64] First conferred by the Adoption of Children Act 1926 and now by the Adoption and Children Act 2002.

[65] This was first given by the Matrimonial Causes Act 1878, s 4 under which a criminal court, before which a married man had been convicted of an aggravated assault upon his wife, had the power to make an order that she should no longer be bound to cohabit with him if it felt that her future safety was in peril. The court could also order a husband to pay maintenance to a wife in whose favour such a separation order was made and vest in her the legal custody of any children of the marriage under the age of 10 years. This jurisdiction was eventually overhauled by the Domestic Proceedings and Magistrates' Courts Act 1978. However, by that time most maintenance claims were brought in the context of divorce. Further, the task of administering child support passed to the Child Support Agency created by the Child Support Act 1991, see Ch 17.

[66] Criminal Justice Act 1991, s 70.

at risk of abuse.[67] The lasting legacy of the latter is that all public law cases concerning children (that is, those involving local authorities) brought under the Children Act 1989 must be commenced at the magistrates' level.

Apart from its public law child jurisdiction, magistrates are empowered to hear private law applications concerning children (that is, applications between private individuals, usually the parents) under the Children Act 1989 and declarations of parentage under the Family Law Act 1986, s 55A. They can also hear adoption applications under the Adoption and Children Act 2002 and domestic violence cases under the Family Law Act 1996, Part IV. They do not, however, have jurisdiction to hear divorce or other matrimonial causes nor applications to dissolve civil partnerships or other civil partnership causes nor do they have jurisdiction over property matters.

2 HOW THE CURRENT SYSTEM IS USED

(a) Jurisdictional issues

Unless specifically prescribed, parties are free to choose in which court to make an application. Accordingly, actions for protection against domestic violence,[68] free-standing private law applications concerning children[69] and adoption applications[70] can be brought at any level of first instance court. However, all matrimonial causes (that is, petitions for divorce, nullity and judicial separation and the equivalent actions in relation to civil partnerships) together with all the ancillary issues relating to children, property (including the matrimonial or family home) and money must be brought in the county court.[71] Furthermore as magistrates have no jurisdiction over property, free-standing applications must be brought in one of the two higher courts and a similar restriction applies to declarations of marital or partnership status.[72] Conversely, all public law applications involving children must be commenced in the magistrates' court.[73] In certain other areas, such as international child abduction or actions for recognition and enforcement under Council Regulation (EC) No 2201/2003,[74] jurisdiction is confined to the High Court.[75] The High Court also has special power to deal with children under its wardship and inherent jurisdictions.[76]

---

[67] Views on the appropriate treatment of juvenile offenders have vacillated (see G Douglas 'The Child's Right to Make Mistakes: Criminal Responsibility and the Immature Minor' in Douglas and Sebba (eds) *Children's Rights and Traditional Values* (1998) 264 at pp 270–6). At one time the Children and Young Persons Act 1969 gave magistrates the option of dealing with young offenders through care proceedings alongside child victims of abuse but this option was abolished by the Children Act 1989.

[68] See the Family Law Act 1996, Part IV.

[69] Viz those not related to any other proceedings, such as divorce. Applications are made under the Children Act 1989.

[70] See the Adoption and Children Act 2002.

[71] See the Matrimonial and Family Proceedings Act 1984, s 33(3) (Matrimonial Causes), s 36A(6) (added by the Civil Partnership Act 2004, Sch 27, para 92) (civil partnership causes).

[72] Family Law Act 1986, s 55 (marital status); Civil Partnership Act 2004, ss 181 and 188 (civil partnership status).

[73] Children (Allocation of Proceedings) Order 1991, Art 3(1).

[74] Regulation concerning jurisdiction and the recognition and enforcement of judgments in matrimonial matters and the matters of parental responsibility repealing Regulation (EC) No 1347/2000—the so-called revised Brussels II Regulation. See below p 32.

[75] See the Child Abduction and Custody Act 1985 ss 4 and 16 and the Family Proceedings Rules 1991, ch 5.

[76] See Ch 16.

(b) Workload of the different courts [77]

The 2004 *Judicial Statistics*[78] gives some idea of the relative workload of the different court levels. For example, of 107,349 private law applications for orders relating to children, 17,463 (16%) were made to magistrates' courts; 89,560 (83%) to county courts and 326 (less than 1%) to the High Court. A not dissimilar proportional workload can be seen in adoption with 1,353 (28%) applications being made to the magistrates' court, 3,464 (72%) to the county court and only 5 (less than 1%) being made to the High Court. The vast majority of domestic violence applications are made to the county court. In 2001, for example,[79] 27,810 (98%) of applications were made to the county court[80] as opposed to 372 (1%) made to magistrates' courts and 100 (less than 1%) to the High Court. In contrast, of the 22,051 public applications in relation to children made in 2004, 14,485 (66%) were dealt with by magistrates, 7,434 (33%) by the county court and only 222 (1%) by the High Court. In addition to these applications, county courts handled virtually all of the 167,193 petitions for divorce,[81] including any applications for ancillary relief, making 15,612 maintenance orders in respect of children and 21,873 lump sum and property adjustment orders.

From this summary, it can be seen that the major workload of private family law cases is handled by county courts with magistrates' courts dealing with a significant minority of cases concerning children (but including the majority of public law cases concerning children) and the High Court handling relatively few, mainly difficult or significant cases relating to all types of family disputes.

3 INCREASING SPECIALISATION IN FAMILY MATTERS

The consequential differences in courts' powers which piecemeal accretions of jurisdiction had brought about presented a significant obstacle to the efficiency and efficacy of the courts to handle family problems. The successful creation of the Family Division of the High Court, together with the emerging specialisms in the lower courts, demonstrated that a more coherent system staffed by experts in the field could provide a better service to those involved in proceedings. When the law relating to children was fundamentally reformed by the Children Act 1989, the opportunity was taken to develop a more coherent, and flexible, system which at the same time would create a judiciary specially trained to handle family problems. The primary aim was to ensure that any court, regardless of its level in the court hierarchy, would be able to offer the same remedies in respect of a family problem. This enabled litigants to choose which court to utilise, and facilitated the efficient disposal of cases by permitting transfer of proceedings to other courts where this is desirable on grounds of speed or convenience to the parties. A similar approach was taken when the law on domestic violence was reformed.[82]

---

[77] This is currently under review, see *Focusing Judicial Resources Appropriately—The Right Judge for the Right Code* (CP 25/05), noted at [2006] Fam Law 5.

[78] (2005) Cm 6565.

[79] (2002) Cm 5551. This was the last time the figures were broken down by court.

[80] In 2004 county courts received 27,605 applications; see Table 5.7 of the 2004 *Judicial Statistics*.

[81] There were also 492 petitions for nullity and 742 for judicial separation.   [82] See Ch 5.

(a) County courts

At the county court level most family cases are heard by what are effectively specialist divisions. All matrimonial causes (that is, actions for divorce, nullity of marriage and separation, together with actions for ancillary relief of maintenance, property division and children) must be commenced in a 'divorce county court' (i.e. a county court specially designated for this purpose) or in the Principal Registry in London (which is a divorce county court for this purpose).[83] A similar strategy has been devised for hearing civil partnership causes in what have been designated 'civil partnership proceedings county courts'.[84] With the implementation of the Children Act 1989 in October 1991, two centres were created, the 'family hearing centres' and 'care centres'.[85] The former are competent to hear private law applications concerning children under Parts I and II of the Children Act 1989. These centres are not competent, however, to hear public law cases, which applications have to be heard by the care centres. However, care centres and, in London, the Principal Registry of the Family Division (which for these purposes is both a family hearing and care centre) have full jurisdiction in both private and public law cases. Only 'designated family judges' and 'nominated care judges', that is, circuit judges specified by the Lord Chancellor[86] who have undertaken specialist training, have jurisdiction to hear cases at these centres. The thinking behind this development is that the concentration of family work in these centres ensures that specialist judges can be effectively employed to deal with cases expeditiously and that continuous hearings can be assured, thus avoiding the need for lengthy adjournments.[87] With effect from October 2001, a new class of county court was created, namely, an 'adoption centre',[88] which, as the name implies, deals exclusively with adoptions and in 2005 'intercountry adoption centres', which handle adoption applications with a foreign element.[89] The overall aim of these centres is to reduce delay and efficiency in adoption court proceedings. Despite the proliferation of these centres, specialisation is not complete, since non-designated courts have jurisdiction to hear domestic violence proceedings even when these involve children.

(b) Magistrates' courts

Like county courts, magistrates' courts were reorganised at the time of the Children Act 1989 with the creation of 'family proceedings courts'.[90] These are staffed by magistrates drawn from the 'family panel'[91] and have sole jurisdiction to hear family proceedings at

---

[83] See the Matrimonial and Family Proceedings Act 1984, ss 33 and 34, and the Children (Allocation of Proceedings) Order 1991, Art 2(a)(i).

[84] See the Matrimonial and Family Proceedings Act 1984 s 36A–D added by the Civil Partnership Act 2004, Sch 27, and the Children (Allocation of Proceedings) Order 1991, Art 2(a)(ii), added by SI 2005/2797.

[85] See generally, the Children (Allocation of Proceedings) Order 1991, art 2(b) and (c) and *Practice Direction: Family Proceedings (Allocation to Judiciary) Directions 1999* [1999] 2 FLR 799 and Lord Chancellor's *Direction: Family Proceedings (Allocation to Judiciary)(Amendment) Directions 2002* [2002] 2 FLR 692.

[86] Acting under Courts and Legal Services Act 1990 s 9 and *Practice Direction (Family Proceedings: Allocation to Judiciary)* [1991] 4 All ER 764.

[87] See P Harris and D Scanlan *The Children Act 1989, A Procedural Handbook* (1995, 2nd edn) para 10.10.

[88] See originally, the President's Direction—*Adoption proceedings—A New Approach* and see now the Children (Allocation of Proceedings) Order 1991 art 2(d) (added by SI 2005/2797).

[89] See the Children (Allocation of Proceedings) Order 1991, Art 2(e) (added by SI 2005/2797).

[90] Children Act 1989 s 92(1). They were formerly known as the 'domestic proceedings courts'.

[91] See Family Proceedings (Constitution) Rules 1991, as amended, and Family Proceedings Courts (Constitution) (Metropolitan Area) Rules 1991, as amended.

this level. 'Family proceedings' are defined by the Magistrates' Courts Act 1980, s 65, as amended, and include proceedings under the Domestic Proceedings and Magistrates' Courts Act 1978, the Children Act 1989, the Adoption and Children Act 2002 and Part IV of the Family Law Act 1996.[92] A magistrates' court sitting as a 'family proceedings court' must consist of not more than three magistrates (including, so far as is practicable, both a man and a woman) drawn from a special 'family panel'.[93] Membership of the panel requires induction training and a course of basic training after a justice has commenced sitting. Magistrates are subject to appraisal in accordance with the Magistrates' National Training Initiative. Those chairing courts are required to undertake additional training. The general training aims inter alia to inculcate knowledge of the Children Act 1989 and its philosophy, whilst Chairmanship training must also equip justices to be more productive in conducting court hearings and to be able to articulate reasons for their decisions.[94] Provision is also made for combined family panels comprising justices from more than one petty sessions area[95] and studies have in the words of one commentary[96] 'reinforced the view that family proceedings courts should be concentrated at fewer centres to maintain the expertise of the justices and the court staff'.

4   TRANSFERRING PROCEEDINGS BETWEEN COURTS

To ensure efficiency, the Matrimonial and Family Proceedings Act 1984 provides that certain proceedings may be transferred from the High Court to a county court and vice versa. The High Court may accordingly order family proceedings in that court (other than those under the Children Act 1989 or Adoption and Children Act 2002) to be transferred to a county court if satisfied that the nature of the issues of fact or law raised makes them more suitable for trial in a county court (for example, because these issues are not complex, difficult or grave, or the residence of witnesses makes trial there more convenient), they should be dealt with there.[97] Conversely, a county court may order any family proceedings pending before it (other than those under the Children Act or Adoption and Children Act) to be transferred to the High Court if the complexity, difficulty or gravity of the issues justifies such action.[98]

The transfer of cases dealing with children is subject to different rules. Certain 'specified

---

[92] For the full definition of 'family proceedings', see the Magistrates' Courts Act 1980 s 65, as amended. Until the commencement of the Children Act 1989 such proceedings were known as 'domestic proceedings'. Proceedings for the enforcement of orders and for the variation of periodical payments do not generally come within the definition of family proceedings unless the court otherwise orders.

[93] Magistrates' Courts Act 1980 ss 66–68, as amended by the Children Act 1989 Sch 11.

[94] See R White, P Carr and N Lowe, *Children Act in Practice* (3rd edn) at 4.12.

[95] Magistrates' Courts Act 1980, s 68.

[96] White, Carr and Lowe, op cit, at 4.12 relying inter alia on the *Scoping Study on Delay in Children Act Cases* (Lord Chancellor's Dept, 2002) paras 91ff and J Hunt *Professionalising Lay Justice—The Role of the Court Clerk in Family Proceedings* (Lord Chancellor's Dept, 2002).

[97] Matrimonial and Family Proceedings Act 1984 s 39; Children (Allocation of Proceedings) Order 1991 Art 5.

[98] Matrimonial and Family Proceedings Act 1984 s 39; Children (Allocation of Proceedings) Order 1991 Art 5. In particular the court must have regard to the capital value of assets involved, substantial allegations of fraud, deception or non-disclosure, and substantial contested allegations of conduct.

proceedings'[99] must be commenced in the magistrates' court, while others are 'self-regulating' in the sense that, if other proceedings, such as divorce, are already pending in a particular court, actions concerning the children of the family must be dealt with in the same court. Apart from these, applications under the Act may be brought at High Court, county court, or magistrates' court level. To speed up the hearing of cases and to match the appropriate degree of judicial expertise to the complexity of the case, there is provision for proceedings to be transferred from one court level to another, and also *between* courts of the same level.[100]

5 PROMOTING LIAISON BETWEEN COURTS

The Children Act 1989 also promoted increased liaison between court administrators and the judiciary at all levels, facilitated by the creation of two committees[101] in each court area. The first, the Family Court Business Committee, was concerned with availability of resources, priorities in relation to other litigation, and sound practice in transferring cases between courts. The second, the Family Court Forum,[102] provided for the exchange of concerns and information between the various agencies and professions involved in administering the Children Act. Both bodies were chaired by the designated family judge and serviced by the court administrator for the particular area. The work of these bodies is gradually being taken over by local family justice councils.

At the time of writing there are 42 such councils in England and Wales. A major further development took place with effect from April 2005 when Her Majesty's Court Service began operating.[103] All 650 Crown, county and magistrates' courts in England and Wales are now administered by this single service. The service works in partnership with 52 Courts Boards which each have local representation. These Boards scrutinise, review and make recommendations about how local courts are run.

6 PROMOTING THE EFFECTIVENESS OF THE FAMILY JUSTICE SYSTEM

One of the innovations associated with the implementation of the Children Act 1989 was the creation of the Children Act Advisory Committee which was charged with monitoring the operation of the legislation. This Committee did valuable work. It produced five Annual Reports and its Final Report in 1997 contained a useful summary of all its previous recommendations and of the action taken. Together with its Final Report, the Committee also produced a 'Handbook of Best Practice in Children Act Cases' which was intended as a comprehensive reference tool for use by all those involved in public and private law Children Act proceedings.

When the Committee was wound up in 1997 some of its work was taken up by what became the Children Act Sub-Committee chaired by Wall J (as he then was). That

---

[99] Those concerning care proceedings, principally care and related proceedings: see Children (Allocation of Proceedings) Order 1991 Art 3 and below, p 493.

[100] See generally the Children (Allocation of Proceedings) Order 1991.

[101] See generally Butterworths *Family Law* Services 3A [11] ff and Harris and Scanlan, op cit, paras 10.11–10.12.

[102] Originally called the Family Court Services Committee.   [103] See [2005] Fam Law 410.

Committee reported to the Advisory Board on Family Law (created in 1997 primarily to advise the Lord Chancellor on the implementation of the Family Law Act 1996). Two major achievements of the Sub-Committee were the production of Reports on 'Parental Contact in cases where there is Domestic Violence' and, especially influential, on 'Making Contact Work'.[104]

Both the Board and its Sub-Committee were wound up in 2001 and for a time there was no overseeing body. However, that was rectified by the creation in 2002 of the Family Justice Council[105] which is administered by the Department for Constitutional Affairs. The Council's primary role is to promote an inter-disciplinary approach to the needs of family justice and through consultation and research to monitor the effectiveness of the system and advise on reforms necessary for continuous improvement. Unlike the bodies it has replaced, the Council's remit extends to the whole process of family justice. As well as a national Council, there are also local family justice councils (see above).

7 INCREASED PROFESSIONALISM

The implementation of the Children Act 1989 coincided with the general development of training for the judiciary through the expansion of the activities of the Judicial Studies Board.[106] All judges and magistrates who were to have functions under the Act were given specialist training as to both the terms and procedures of the legislation and the wider context in which children cases should be understood. This innovation heralded a much more professional approach to the acquisition of expertise by the judiciary, and all new circuit judges, district judges and magistrates now undergo training, in family as well as civil and criminal matters, before taking up appointments to the Bench. Training to cope with new initiatives, and refresher training at periodic intervals, is compulsory.

Together with the requirement to undergo training, new obligations and ways of working were imposed on the magistrates' courts in particular, in order to bring them into conformity with the higher courts, so that they could exercise the common jurisdiction introduced by the Children Act. For the first time, a requirement of advance disclosure of written evidence was imposed, with an expectation that magistrates will have read the papers in advance of the hearing. Magistrates, as well as judges, must give reasons for their decisions, and a failure to provide adequate reasons is a ground for appeal.[107]

8 A MORE MANAGERIAL APPROACH

The Children Act also introduced elements of greater 'court control' over the process of family litigation, by requiring courts to set timetables for the determination of the litigation, and emphasising the importance of judicial directions to the parties in the collection and sharing of written evidence and instruction of expert witnesses.[108] The aims were to

---

[104] A Report to the Lord Chancellor by the Advisory Board on Family Law; Children Act Sub-Committee, 2002.

[105] On which see 'The Work of the Family Justice Council' [2005] Fam Law 65.

[106] See *Judicial Studies Board Report 1995–97* (1997).

[107] Family Proceedings Courts (Children Act 1989) Rules 1991 r 21(5)–(6); *W v Hertfordshire County Council* [1993] 1 FLR 118 and *Re W (A Minor)(Contact)* [1994] 1 FLR 843.

[108] See eg Children Act 1989 ss 11 and 32. This duty now extends to adoption proceedings, see s 109 of the Adoption and Children Act 2002.

speed up litigation and to control costs. However, as we discuss in Chapter 10, the early expectations at the time of the 1989 Act that private law cases would generally be disposed in 16 weeks and public law cases within 12 weeks proved wildly optimistic.[109] Consequently a new initiative to control public law Children Act cases was introduced in November 2003 in the form of a Protocol for Judicial Case Management in Public Law Children Act Cases[110] which set a 40-week target for the completion of such cases. Unlike the general timetable provisions set out in the Children Act 1989 (referred to above) which are solely directed to the courts, the Protocol addresses all the participants in the process and sets out, in a detailed 'route map', what action is to be taken by whom and when.

Following implementation of the Protocol a complementary, albeit less detailed, Direction was issued by the then President of the Family Division, Dame Elizabeth Butler-Sloss, namely the Private Law Programme (2005), in relation to private law applications made under Part II of the Children Act 1989. According to the Programme 'the welfare of the child will be safeguarded by the application of the overriding objective of the family justice system in 3 respects: 1. Dispute resolution at a First Hearing 2. Effective court control including monitoring outcomes against aims 3. Flexible facilitation and referrals (matching resources to families'. Guidance on how these aspects are to be achieved are provided in the Programme.[111]

In determining financial and property issues in divorce cases, following the successful 'Ancillary Relief Pilot Scheme' a streamlined procedure was introduced on a nationwide basis in 2000 including the holding of a financial dispute resolution appointment ('FDR') at which privileged meeting parties are encouraged, with the rigorous encouragement of the district judge giving directions, to clarify and explore the scope for early settlement of the issues in dispute.[112]

The more 'managerial' role embodied in each of the above schemes reflects the continuing emphasis, noted above, upon the settlement rather than the adjudication of disputes.

9 TOWARDS A FAMILY COURT?

What has been put in place as a result of these developments is not yet a Family Court, but rather a system of family courts operating as distinct divisions within the civil court structure, exercising a common, or very similar, jurisdiction in certain areas of family law. This approach to reform took the heat out of a long-standing debate concerning the desirability of establishing a discrete Family Court to deal with all aspects of family litigation. Family Courts have existed in the United States for some time and have been introduced in Australia and New Zealand.[113] Impetus for their introduction in this country was provided by the Report of the Committee on One-parent Families (the Finer

---

[109] See the comments by Baroness Hale in *Re G (Interim Care Order: Residential Assessment)* [2005] UKHL 68, [2005] 3 WLR 1166 at [58], discussed further below at p 475.

[110] [2003] 2 FLR 719, discussed in more detail below at p 758.

[111] For comments on the early effectiveness of the Programme, see 'The President's New Focus' [2006] Fam Law 65 at 66–7.

[112] See the Family Proceedings (Amendment No 2) Rules 1999, SI 1999/3491, which apply to all applications for ancillary relief filed after 5 June 2000. See below p 988.

[113] See Brown 'The Legal Background to the Family Court' [1966] BJ Crim 139 (USA); the Family Law Act 1975 s 21 (Australia); the Family Courts Act 1980 s 4 (New Zealand).

Report) in 1974.[114] In 1983 the Lord Chancellor's Department issued a consultation paper, which was in turn overtaken by the establishment of a review committee which published its own consultation paper in 1986.[115] After nearly two decades of inactivity, interest in a Family Court has been renewed with the publication of the Department of Constitutional Affairs in February 2005 of a Consultation Paper 'A Single Civil Court?' and a further paper in response to the consultation in October 2005.[116]

Even with the reforms already introduced, proceedings relating to members of the same family may take place in a number of courts simultaneously. For example, a wife, having taken proceedings for maintenance in a magistrates' court, may then seek a divorce in a divorce county court; at the same time a child of the family may have been made a ward in the High Court.[117] This fragmented and overlapping jurisdiction causes confusion, complicates proceedings, and leads to inconvenience, unnecessary cost and unreasonable delay.[118] Creating a single court would obviate these difficulties. However, to be effective a single Family Court must have sole jurisdiction in all family matters and apply a uniform law: the court's powers must not depend on the tribunal before which proceedings are brought. This raises another major issue: should there be an entirely new court, or could a Family Court be created out of the High Court and county courts?[119] Further, does the lay magistracy have a part to play in a Family Court? The Finer Committee believed that they had, 'not only as a source of manpower, but as an equally indispensable source of lay experience and outlook which is a traditional feature in the administration of family law in England and Wales'.[120] A further advantage of including magistrates amongst the members of the tribunal is that they, like circuit judges, sit locally, and it is essential that litigants should have ready access to a local court and that most cases should be dealt with expeditiously and cheaply.

Following the 2005 Consultation exercise Ministers apparently concluded that the creation of a single Family Court with unified jurisdiction is both feasible and desirable and adopted that as a long-term objective.[121] The single Family Court is envisaged to encompass all the jurisdictions currently shared between the High Court, county court and magistrates' family proceedings courts. One effect of this proposal is that magistrates, i.e. both district judges (magistrates' courts) and lay justices, would acquire matrimonial jurisdiction and consequently be able to deal with divorces and associated ancillary relief.

---

114 Cmnd 5629 Pt 4, s 13 and s 14 on which see S Cretney *Family Law in the Twentieth Century—A History* 746 ff.

115 A useful summary of the contents of the paper is to be found in [1986] Fam Law 247.

116 *Focusing judicial resources appropriately* (DCA, 2005).

117 As occurred in *Re C (Wardship and Adoption)* (1979) 2 FLR 177, CA. See also Hoggett 'Family Courts or Family Law Reform?' (1986) 6 Legal Studies 1, 3–5.

118 See the Lord Chancellor's Department's Consultation Paper (1986). Hoggett, loc cit p 5; M Murch et al *The Overlapping Family Jurisdictions of Magistrates Courts and County Courts—Research Report* (1987).

119 See the three options put forward by the Review Committee. (The third contemplates the retention of the existing courts with a revised jurisdiction to eliminate overlapping.)

120 Report para 4.348. But their role has undoubtedly diminished since 1974. See also the proposals of the Association of Magisterial Officers [1986] Fam Law 250.

121 See 'A Single Family Court' [2005] Fam Law 935.

D THE INTERNATIONALISATION OF FAMILY LAW

The time has long since passed when the study of family law can sensibly be confined to purely domestic issues and jurisprudence. In part this is because there are many more cases involving an international element, be it the involvement of spouses or partners of different nationalities or the ownership of property abroad, or of foreign families living here.[122] One result of the growing phenomenon of cross-border families has been increasing international attempts both to create basic rights regulating the family and to provide international solutions to common problems. This has meant that the UK's legal systems have become subject to international pressure both to conform to global or European norms and to co-operate in transnational ventures to control world-wide problems. Furthermore, familiarity with different legal systems has given new opportunities for rethinking domestic law. In short, as we said in the last edition, one of the most important developments in family law has been the growing significance of international law in the shaping of new thinking about families, and in new legislation regulating them.

Beginning with the Universal Declaration of Human Rights (1948), which, in Article 16(3), provides that the family 'is the natural and fundamental group unit of society and is entitled to protection by society and the State' there has been increasing attention paid to mechanisms for enhancing the position of the family.[123] In some ways this might be regarded as strange, given that the difficulty of defining the family, alluded to above, is even greater in a global context where many different family forms are to be found. There is also a tension, increasingly recognised, between laying down norms for 'family' rights, and providing rights for individual members of families. There may be conflicts of interest between the two. For example, how far should the importance of recognising the family as an entity entitled to protection take priority over the potential need to protect individuals from abuse or exploitation by other family members? The American Convention on Human Rights (1969) attempts, perhaps not wholly successfully, to deal with this problem by heading its Art 17 'Rights of the Family' and then including within that Article the rights of individuals within the family. Nonetheless, international efforts to support families, and to protect family members, have grown apace. These have manifested themselves in a variety of international instruments.

---

[122] According to statistics produced by Eurostat (ed) *People in Europe* (Luxembourg, 2002) p 12, 15% of those entering into marriage within Europe are of different nationalities, often of different European States, and the same is true of other relationships, be they same-sex or heterosexual. Within the EU (that is, before its enlargement) more than 5% of citizens, about 9 million people, did not have citizenship of the State in which they lived, and of these, almost 6 million citizens of the Union lived in another Member State.

[123] H Sokalski 'The International Year of the Family: New Frontiers for Families' in N Lowe and G Douglas (eds) *Families across Frontiers* (1996) 1; G Douglas 'The Significance of International Law for the Development of Family Law in England and Wales' in C Bridge (ed) *Towards the Millennium: Essays for P M Bromley* (1997) 85.

1 UNITED NATIONS CONVENTION ON THE RIGHTS OF THE CHILD[124]

At the global level, the most important of these may be seen as the United Nations Convention on the Rights of the Child of 1989, now signed by over 200 states, including the United Kingdom in 1991. This Convention sets out a variety of rights which must be safeguarded by signatory states through their internal laws. While focusing upon the rights of the child, both within the family, and in relation to the state, it marks an important stage in the international recognition of the family as a distinct unit. Its preamble, for example, states that signatories are:

'*Convinced* that the family ... [is] the fundamental group of society and the natural environment for the growth and well-being of all its members and particularly children ... [and] should be afforded the necessary protection and assistance so that it can fully assume its responsibilities within the community . . .'

Although the United Kingdom is bound internationally by the Convention, because it has not been internally incorporated, it is not binding domestically.[125] Even so, it is increasingly referred to in domestic case law[126] and regulations governing the appointment and function of the Children's Commissioner for Wales provide that in exercising those functions the Commissioner must 'have regard' to the UN Convention.[127] While it might not be directly binding upon the courts, like all signatories, the United Kingdom is required to submit reports (within two years of ratification) to a Committee on the Rights of the Child on their progress in implementing the terms of the Convention, and is thus subject to some degree of scrutiny by the international community.[128] Signing the Convention also leaves governments open to both internal and international criticism should they be seen to be failing in fulfilling their international obligations.[129] For some[130] this scrutiny is simply not good enough. The Committee charged with overseeing compliance with the Convention is, it is argued, under-resourced and over-stretched and in any event many countries are slow to produce their initial reports and their periodic reports. Nevertheless, notwithstanding this perhaps justifiable criticism the Convention should not be written

---

[124] For a definitive study of the international rights of the child, see G Van Bueren *The International Law on the Rights of the Child* (1995). For further assessments see M Freeman 'The End of the Century of the Child' (2000) 53 Current Legal Problems 505 and D Fottrell *Revisiting Children's Rights: 10 years of the UN Convention on the Rights of the Child* (2000).

[125] Though as Ward LJ said in *Re P (A Minor)(Residence Order: Child's Welfare)* [2000] Fam 15 at 42, the Convention commands and receives respect.

[126] It was, for example, referred to in 26 cases reported in Family Law Reports between 1999 and 2005 but in only five cases reported before 1999.

[127] Viz Children's Commissioner for Wales (Appointment) Regulations 2001.

[128] See United Nations Concluding Observations of the Committee on the Rights of the Child: United Kingdom of Great Britain and Northern Ireland CRC/C/15Add34 (1995) which, as A Bainham has said in *Children—The Modern Law* (3rd edn), was less than glowing about the UK Government's record under the Convention (singling out in particular child poverty, permitting corporal punishment of children and the lack of children's rights in the educational sphere). The second report, see United Nations Committee on the Rights of the Child, Thirty First Session Concluding Observations: United Kingdom of Great Britain and Northern Ireland (2002), substantially repeated their criticisms.

[129] Compare Department of Health, *The UK's First Report to the UN Committee on the Rights of the Child* (1994) with Children's Rights Development Unit, *UK Agenda for Children* (1994).

[130] See eg Freeman, op cit.

off simply as an international gesture of no significance. One often overlooked effect is its
influence in shaping subsequent international instruments, some of which have very much
greater bite.

Obtaining worldwide agreement to a set of wide-ranging norms which can be implemented nationally is obviously a difficult task, and runs the risk that such norms will be
pitched at a fairly minimal or very general level to attract maximum adherence. It may be
more fruitful to develop agreed standards at a regional level where there is greater cultural,
economic and political similarity between states. There are several Conventions operating
at this level,[131] and the one of greatest significance to the United Kingdom is the European
Convention on Human Rights particularly since its incorporation into domestic law by
the Human Rights Act 1998.

2 EUROPEAN CONVENTION ON HUMAN RIGHTS

Although the United Kingdom was one of the original signatories to the European Convention for the Protection of Human Rights and Fundamental Freedoms (having ratified
it in 1951) and, since 1966, has allowed individuals to take their complaints to the
European Court of Human Rights in Strasbourg, the Convention remained solely an
international obligation until its incorporation by the Human Rights Act 1988 which came
into force in October 2000. Nevertheless even before this it played an increasingly significant part in the legislative development of English domestic law.[132] That significance has
accelerated after the implementation of the 1988 Act, though perhaps not as much as some
anticipated.[133]

So far as family law is concerned, the two key Articles of substantive relevance are Art 8,
which provides that everyone has the right to respect for his private and family life, his
home and his correspondence, and Art 12, which provides that men and women of
marriageable age have the right to marry and to found a family according to the national
laws governing the exercise of this right. Three other Articles of substantive relevance are
Art 3 relating to the right not to be tortured or be subject to inhuman and degrading
treatment or punishment, Art 5 which provides for the right to liberty and security
of person, Art 14 which provides that the enjoyment of the rights prescribed by the
Convention shall be secured without discrimination, and, of major procedural relevance,
Art 6, under which in the determination of civil rights everyone is entitled to a fair and
public hearing within a reasonable time.

We consider the impact of these provisions throughout the book, but at this introductory stage it will be helpful to outline the basic scheme of the 1998 Act. What this Act

---

[131] See, for example, the American Convention on Human Rights referred to above (although one might
query how far the two American continents can be regarded as sharing cultural and economic standards) and
the African Charter on Human and People's Rights (1981).

[132] It was certainly influential, for example in the drafting of the new Children Act 1989, see eg G Douglas
'The Family and the State under the European Convention on Human Rights' (1988) 2 Int J Law and Fam 76
and, more generally, P Duffy 'English Law and the European Convention on Human Rights' (1980) 29
ICLQ 585.

[133] There was, for example, speculation as to the compatibility of the paramountcy of the child's welfare
principle and the status of unmarried fathers; the lawfulness of secure accommodation orders and about the
inability of the courts to oversee local authority care plans, all of which survived Human Rights challenges
(although in fact in some respects the law has since been changed).

does in general, apart from incorporating into domestic law the terms of the Convention, is to:

(a) oblige all domestic courts at all levels to take Convention case law into account when deciding a question relating to a Convention right;

(b) provide that, so far as it is possible to do so, primary and subordinate legislation must be read and given effect to in a way that is compatible with Convention rights;

(c) empower the higher courts to make declarations of incompatibility if satisfied that a statutory provision is incompatible with a Convention right;

(d) make it unlawful for public authorities to act in a way that is incompatible with a Convention right save where the authorities are obliged to do so by primary legislation;

(e) permit persons to bring proceedings against a public authority acting or proposing to act in a way made unlawful by the 1998 Act;

(f) empower the courts to give an appropriate remedy, including damages in respect of any act (or proposed act) of a public authority which is (or would be) found to be unlawful.

The 1998 Act is without prejudice to the right of any individual alleging a violation of a Convention right to apply to the European Court of Human Rights in Strasbourg after exhausting local remedies.[134]

So far as (a) is concerned, s 2 only requires case law[135] to be taken into account but the jurisprudence is not binding in any strict sense of precedent, and indeed it is open to the English courts to go further than the European Court of Human Rights.[136]

The requirement to construe, so far as practicable, legislation in a manner that is compatible with the Convention is provided by s 3. As Hale LJ said,[137] 'the 1998 Act was carefully designed to promote the search for compatibility rather than incompatibility'. However, while s 3 entitles the courts to depart from earlier domestic precedents insofar as they are thought to be incompatible with Convention rights, there are limits to this power; in particular it does not entitle the courts to legislate. As Lord Nicholls stressed in *Re S (Minors)(Care Order: Implementation of Care Plan), Re W (Minors)(Care Order: Adequacy of Care Plan)*,[138] 'Interpretation of statutes is a matter for the courts, the enactment of statutes and the amendment of statutes, are matters for Parliament'.

Once it has been concluded that it is not possible to read and give effect to legislation in a way that is compatible with the Conventions, then, but only then,[139] under s 4 is it open to the High Court and the appellate courts[140] to make a formal declaration of incompatibility. Such declarations do not in themselves affect the validity of the legislation in

---

[134] See Art 25.
[135] Ie judgments of the European Court of Human Rights and opinions of the former Commission including decisions on admissibility: s 2(1)(a)–(d).
[136] See eg *Fitzpatrick v Sterling Housing Association Ltd* [2001] AC 27, HL, and *Ghaidan v Mendoza* [2004] UKHL 30, [2004] 2 AC 557, HL, discussed at p 102.
[137] *Re W and B, Re W (Care Plan)* [2001] EWCA Civ 757, [2001] 2 FLR 582 at [50].
[138] [2002] UKHL 10, [2002] AC 291 at [39].
[139] See *Wilson v First Country Trust Ltd (No 2)* [2003] UKHL 40, [2004] 2 AC 816.
[140] Human Rights Act 1998, s 4(5).

question but the expectation is that the offending provision(s) will consequently be amended.[141] This sanction is slightly weaker than if the Strasbourg court holds the State to have violated the Convention, which obligates that State to remedy its offending domestic law.[142] Section 4 declarations have so far been rarely made but one example is *Bellinger v Bellinger*[143] in which the House of Lords declared s 11(c) of the Matrimonial Causes Act 1973 (which required the parties to the marriage to be respectively male and female) to be incompatible with Arts 8 and 12.[144] It seems that declarations can only be made in respect of specific provisions; it is not therefore possible to make a declaration of incompatibility against the scheme of a whole Act.[145]

Another significant function of the Act is that of enabling individuals to enforce their Convention rights against a public authority, which for these purposes includes local authorities and the courts.[146] The scheme of the Act in this respect was well described by Lord Nicholls in *Re S*[147]:

'Sections 7 and 8 of the Human Rights Act 1998 have conferred extended powers on the courts. Section 6 makes it unlawful for a public authority to act in a way which is incompatible with a Convention right. Section 7 enables victims of conduct made unlawful by Section 6 to bring court proceedings against the public authority in question. Section 8 spells out, in wide terms, the relief a court may grant in those proceedings. The court may grant such relief or remedy, or make such order, within its powers as it considers just and appropriate. Thus, if a local authority conducts itself in a manner which infringes the Article 8 rights of a parent or child, the court may grant appropriate relief on the application of a victim of the unlawful act'.

3 OTHER CONVENTIONS AND INTERNATIONAL INSTRUMENTS OF INFLUENCE [148]

The Conventions so far discussed may be seen as operating inter alia at the political level, the intention being to educate States to improve their human rights records. But other international instruments are more focused on specific family law issues and problems of common concern. Some aim to harmonise laws in particular areas while others provide a mechanism for handling or control of inter-state family problems. Until recently, there have been two main sources of these types of instruments, namely, the Council of Europe and the Hague Conference on International Private Law, but another institution has now come into play, namely, the European Union. We end this chapter with a brief introductory resumé of the contributions in the family law field of each of these institutions.

---

[141] Human Rights Act 1998, s 10.   [142] See Art 53 of the Convention.

[143] [2003] UKHL 21, [2003] 2 Ac 467, see below p 47. For a general list of cases in which declarations of incompatibility have been made, see the Appendix to Lord Steyn's judgment in *Ghaidan v Mendoza*, ibid.

[144] See further below at p 47.

[145] *Re W and B, Re W (Care Plan)* above at [50], per Hale LJ impliedly upheld by the House of Lords on appeal in *Re S* above at [41] per Lord Nicholls.

[146] Human Rights Act 1998, s 6(3) which states that a 'public authority' includes (a) a court or tribunal, and (b) any person certain of whose functions are functions of a public nature.

[147] In *Re S*, above at [45]. For further discussion of ss 7 and 8 see below at p 814.

[148] For general reference see C Hamilton and A Perry *Family Law in Europe* (2nd edn), Section E.

(a) The Council of Europe

Apart from its key role in relation to the maintenance of the European Court of Human Rights, the Council of Europe[149] has pursued an active programme of work in the family law field principally aimed at harmonising laws and practices at the European level.[150]

Through its Parliamentary Assembly, Committee of Ministers and Conferences, the Council has produced a number of Recommendations (which are best described as statements of international aspirations, such as the Recommendation on Violence in the Family (1985)[151] that legislation on corporal punishment of children be reviewed) and Conventions intended to promote common policy among its member states. Some of the earlier Conventions, such as the 1967 European Convention on the adoption of children, which aimed to provide a uniform approach to certain aspects of adoption, and the 1975 European Convention on the Legal Status of Children Born out of Wedlock, which aimed to reduce discrimination against children whose parents are not married have become dated and have been the subject of internal review by the Council culminating in its 2002 publication of a 'White Paper' on Principles Concerning the Establishment and Legal Consequences of Parentage.[152] Of more lasting consequence (though somewhat over-shadowed by the 1980 Hague Abduction Convention) is the 1980 European Convention on Recognition and Enforcement of Decisions Concerning Custody of Children and on Restoration of Custody of Children, the prime role of which is to provide a uniform approach to international child abduction.

Two more recent Conventions are the 1996 European Convention on the Exercise of Children's Rights, which is intended to complement the UN Convention on the Rights of the Child by providing more detailed provisions concerning procedures for enabling children to exercise the rights guaranteed in the UN Convention and the 2003 European Convention on Contact Concerning Children which aims to provide both harmonising general principles to be applied to contact orders and a scheme to deal with trans-frontier contact issues. We discuss these last three Conventions in greater detail in later chapters.

(b) The Hague Conference

Like the Council of Europe, the Hague Conference[153] has pursued an active programme of work in the family law field. Traditionally, it has been associated with private international law, promoting internationally agreed rules of jurisdiction and consequent recognition and enforcement. But increasingly its instruments have become very much relevant to the mainstream family lawyer. Although of principal concern in this work are a trilogy

[149] The Council of Europe is not to be confused with the European Union. It is a larger body comprising in excess of 40 member states drawn from the whole continent of Europe and includes Russia and Turkey. It was founded in 1949.

[150] For a general discussion of the Council's work see eg M Killerby 'The Council of Europe's Contribution to Family Law (Past, Present and Future)' in N Lowe and G Douglas (eds) *Families Across Frontiers* (1996) 13. See also 'Achievements and documents in Family Law', available on the Council of Europe's website.

[151] Recommendation No R 85(4). Other Recommendations of note include that relating to Parental Responsibilities (1984) and on mediation (1998).

[152] CJ-FA (2001) 16 Rev.

[153] The Conference has a long history, formally beginning with an international conference called by the Dutch government in 1893. For its work generally see K Lipstein 'One Hundred Years of Hague Conference on Private International Law' (1993) 42 ICLQ 553. Unlike the Council of Europe, membership of the Hague Conference is global. Currently there are 65 Member States.

of Conventions dealing with different aspects of child law, its work in the field of maintenance[154] and marriage and divorce[155] should not be overlooked.

The trilogy of Conventions affecting children are, in chronological order, the 1980 Hague Convention on the Civil Aspects of International Child Abduction, the 1993 Hague Convention on Protection of Children and Co-operation in Respect of Intercountry Adoption and the 1996 Hague Convention on Jurisdiction, Applicable Law, Recognition, Enforcement and Co-operation in Respect of Parental Responsibility and Measures for the Protection of Children. The Abduction Convention, to which there are, at the time of writing, 75 Contracting States, provides rules governing the return of and access to children wrongfully removed to or retained in another Contracting State. The Intercountry Adoption Convention, to which there are, at the time of writing, 68 Contracting States, provides an international regulatory framework governing the adoption of a child from one country by adopters of another. These latter highly successful instruments are discussed respectively in Chapters 13 and 15.

The 1996 Child Protection Convention,[156] which has not yet been ratified by the United Kingdom nor any other EU State,[157] in broad terms provides for common jurisdictional rules and consequent provisions for the recognition and enforcement of judgments concerned with child protection. 'Protection' for these purposes is a wide term referring to both private and public law measures taken by judicial and administrative bodies to safeguard children. In particular it governs[158] the attribution, exercise, termination and delegation of parental responsibility,[159] rights of custody and access, guardianship, curatorship and analogous institutions, the designation and functions of any person or body having charge of the child's person or property, representing or assisting the child; placing the child in foster or institutional care or the provision of care by *Kafala*[160] or an analogous institution; public authority supervision of the care of a child and the administrative conservation or disposal of the child's property.[161] It specifically does not include[162] establishing or contesting a parent-child relationship, adoption, names, emancipation,

---

[154] Ie the 1973 Conventions on the Law Applicable to Maintenance Obligations and the Recognition and Enforcement of Decisions Relating to Maintenance Obligations.

[155] On which note the 1970 Convention on Recognition of Divorce and Legal Separation and 1973 Convention on the Celebration and Recognition of the Validity of Marriages.

[156] This in fact is the third Convention on the Protection of Children; the first was drawn up and signed in 1902 and the second in 1961. That latter Convention will be superseded by the 1996 Convention. For detailed discussion of the 1996 Convention see N Lowe, M Everall and M Nicholls *International Movement of Children, Law, Practice and Procedure*, (2004) ch 24.

[157] In fact most Member States of the EU have signed, but ratification is delayed because of the UK-Spanish dispute over Gibraltar, see 'The Hague Family Law Conventions' [2005] IFL 105 at 106. It has been in force since 2002 and at the time of writing there are 11 Contracting States.

[158] See Art 3 which provides illustrative but not definitive examples.

[159] On which there are detailed provisions (see Arts 16 and 17) including the provisions (see Art 16(3) and (4) that where parental responsibility exists under the law of the State of the child's habitual residence it will continue to exist notwithstanding a change of that residence to another State but where the law of the State of the child's new habitual residence automatically confers responsibility on a person who does not already have it, the latter law will prevail. The net effect of these provisions therefore is that they affect *domestic* substantive law on the allocation of parental responsibility.

[160] *Kafala* is an Islamic concept akin to fostering but short of adoption.

[161] Though note under Art 55, reservations may be entered with respect to measures directed at protecting the child's property.

[162] Art 4 which provides a definitive list of exclusions.

maintenance, trusts or succession, social security, general public measures on health or education, measures taken as a result of penal offences committed by children; and the right of asylum and immigration decisions.

Notwithstanding these exemptions, the importance of the 1996 Convention lies in part on the width of its application. For example, it plugs a gap in the 1993 Intercountry Adoption Convention by applying both to *Kafala* (which is important to Islamic states) and to fostering. It also has the potential advantage of its practical global reach. As well as providing jurisdictional rules etc the Convention contains important provisions with regard to co-operation and the exchange of information and has some particularly useful provisions for safeguarding rights of access.[163]

One disadvantage of the Convention is that it is one of a number concerning custody and particularly access which add to the complexity concerning the interrelationship between the international instruments.[164]

(c) The European Union and the Brussels Regulations

How the EU became involved with family law issues[165]

Although the European Union has long had some potential to impact upon family law matters, until recently it did so only peripherally.[166] All that changed with the implementation in March 2001 of Council Regulation (EC) No 1347/2000 of 29 May 2000 on Jurisdiction and the Recognition and Enforcement of Judgments in Matrimonial Matters and in Matters of Parental Responsibility for Children of Both Spouses,[167] commonly referred to as 'Brussels II'. Like all EC Regulations, Brussels II was directly applicable.[168]

The overall inspiration for Brussels II was what was then the 1968 Brussels Convention on Jurisdiction and Enforcement of Judgments in Civil and Commercial Matters,[169] but which is now a Regulation[170] coming into force ironically exactly one year *after* Brussels II, on 1 March 2002. Brussels I provides a general framework for recognition and enforcement of civil and commercial judgments, including maintenance, but expressly excluding matters of status and rights of property arising from marriage.[171] As the Explanatory Report on the 1968 Convention[172] explained, although the ideal solution would have been

---

[163] Under Art 35, discussed below at p 687.

[164] On which see the concerns expressed by N Lowe 'New International Conventions Affecting the Law Relating to Children—A Cause for Concern?' [2001] IFL 171.

[165] See generally N Lowe 'The Growing Influence of the European Union on International Family Law—A View from the Boundary' (2003) 56 Current Legal Problems 439, C McGlynn 'The Europeanisation of family law' (2001) 13 CFLQ 36, J Basedow 'The Communitarization of the Conflict of Laws Under the Treaty of Amsterdam' (2000) 37 CMLR 687, K Boele-Woelki and R Van Ooik 'The Communitarisation of Private International Law' in *Yearbook of Private International Law*, Volume 4 (Amsterdam, 2002) p.1 and H Stalford, 'Regulating family life in post-Amsterdam Europe' (2003) 28 EL Rev 39.

[166] See, for example, the discussion in C Hamilton and K Standby *Family Law in Europe* (1st edn) 580–597.

[167] OJ 2000 L160, 19–29.   [168] Art 249 EC.

[169] This Convention was incorporated into English law by the Civil Jurisdiction and Judgments Act 1982.

[170] Viz Council Regulation (EC) No. 44/2001 of 22 December 2000, OJ 2001 L12/1 on Jurisdiction and the Recognition and Enforcement of Judgments in Civil and Commercial Matters (but note that insofar as it governs relationships with Denmark, the 1968 Convention remains in force, as does the 1988 Lugano Convention on Jurisdiction and the Enforcement of Judgments in Civil and Commercial Matters which basically applies Brussels I as between Member States and (now) Iceland, Norway, Poland and Switzerland.

[171] See below, Ch 18, p 1075.   [172] The Jenard Report, [1979] OJ C 59 at 10.

to apply the Convention to *all* civil and commercial matters, so-called family matters[173] were excluded because it was considered too difficult to unify the jurisdictional rules of even the then six Member States. In this regard, the Report singled out divorce as 'a problem which is complicated by the extreme divergences between the various systems of law'.[174]

When Brussels I was being drafted, what was then the EEC had no particular interest in regulating family matters, since its primary focus was economic. However, with the progression towards the completion of the internal market, the EC widened its area of concern. As the Borras Report (the Explanatory Report on the Brussels II Convention) explained,[175]

'European integration was mainly an economic affair to begin with and for that reason the legal instruments established were designed to serve an economic purpose. However, the situation has changed fundamentally . . . integration is now no longer purely economic and is coming to have an increasingly profound effect on the life of the European citizen. . . . The issue of family law therefore has to be faced as part of the phenomenon of European integration.'

Brussels II was made possible by the Treaty on European Union which opened up new channels for judicial co-operation in civil matters under what were then Arts K.3(2)c and K.1(6).[176]

It was, however, the Treaty of Amsterdam that in the context of family law provided the most dramatic development, namely, the basis upon which the Brussels II Convention was transformed into a Regulation and upon which future Regulations dealing with Family Law issues will be based. The Amsterdam Treaty brought judicial co-operation in civil matters squarely into the Community framework, inasmuch as Art K1 and 3 (which were formerly part of the Third Pillar (viz Justice and Home Affairs) of the EU under the TEU), were removed to form a Community Pillar by the Treaty of Amsterdam and are now Arts 61–69 of the EC Treaty.

Subsequent to Amsterdam, the European Council at its meeting held in Tampere in October 1999 expressed its determination[177] to develop the Union as an area of freedom, security and justice by making full use of the possibilities offered by the Treaty of Amsterdam. To this end it set out the so-called 'Tampere milestones' which included the notion that 'enhanced mutual recognition of judicial decisions and judgments and the necessary approximation of legislation would facilitate cooperation between authorities and the judicial protection of individual rights'. In other words, the underlying rationale is that the free movement of judgments would facilitate the free movement of people within the Union. The Council accordingly endorsed the principle of mutual recognition as the 'cornerstone of judicial co-operation in civil . . . matters within the Union'.[178] It also asked

[173] In point of fact, as the Jenard Report, *ibid*, pointed out, the Convention does not refer to 'Family Law' as such since inter alia 'family law in the six Member States of the Community is not a concept distinct from questions of status or capacity'.
[174] At the time of the report divorce was prohibited in Italy—but this was changed in 1970, see Law of 1 December 1970 No. 878, since amended by the Law of 1 August 1978 No. 436 and then Law of 6 March 1987, No. 84. In fact divorce is permitted throughout the Union except for Malta, with Ireland being the last Member State to permit it in 1996. Spain permitted divorce in 1978.
[175] 1998 OJ C221/27, para 1.   [176] Now Arts 61–69 EC.   [177] Bulletin, EU 10–1999 at para 1.2.
[178] Ibid at para 1.10, 33.

the Council and the Commission to adopt, by the end of 2000, a programme of measures to implement this principle.

Issues of competence

The EC does not have unlimited law making competence. So far as family law is concerned, the current EC basis rests essentially on Art 65 which opens with the words:

'Measures in the field of judicial cooperation in civil matters having cross border implications ... and insofar as necessary for the proper functioning of the internal market, shall include. ...'

The prevailing view[179] is that Art 65 limits EC competence to cross-border issues affecting the proper functioning of the internal market. Accordingly, it is said that the EC lacks competence in matters of substantive family law. This might not be quite as straightforward as it looks, for there is inherent difficulty in drawing a firm line between a cross-border issue, and one of pure domestic substantive law. Nor should one overlook Art 308, which provides that 'If action by the Community should prove necessary to attain ... one of the objectives of the Community and this Treaty has not provided the necessary powers, the Council shall, acting unanimously on a proposal from the Commission, and after consulting the European Parliament, take the appropriate measures', though that is unlikely to be considered to give general latitude to make substantive law provision.

The water is further muddied by the Charter of Fundamental Rights of the European Union. This Charter contains a number of Articles of direct relevance to family law,[180] in particular Art 7 which provides for the right to respect for private and family life, Art 9, the right to marry and found a family, and Art 24 which deals with the rights of the child.[181] Unlike Arts 7 and 9, which are taken from Arts 8 and 12 of the European Convention on Human Rights, Art 24 is based on the 1989 UN Convention on the Rights of the Child (or New York Convention, as it is referred to in the Annotated Notes to the Charter).[182]

Article 24 contains three provisions:

(1) giving children the right to such protection and care as is necessary for their well-being and to express their views freely (such views to be taken into account on matters which concern them in accordance with their age and maturity);

(2) that in all actions the child's best interests must be a primary consideration; and

[179] See eg M Jänterä-Jareborg 'Unification of international family law in Europe—a critical perspective', *Perspectives for the Unification and Harmonisation of Family Law in Europe* CEFL Series No. 4 (ed. K Boele-Woelki, Antwerp, 2003).

[180] For which see generally C. McGlynn 'Families and the European Charter of Fundamental Rights: progressive change or entrenching the status quo?' (2001) 26 EL Rev 582 and the references there cited, and, by the same author, 'Rights for Children?: The Potential Impact of the European Union Charter of Fundamental Rights' (2002) 8 European Public Law 387.

[181] Note also Art 33 concerning family and professional life and which inter alia deals with the right to protection from dismissal for a reason connected with maternity and the right to paid maternal leave and to parental leave following the birth or adoption of a child.

[182] See 'Charter of Fundamental Rights of the European Union. Explanations relating to the complete text of the Charter', prepared at the instigation of the Presidium, December 2000.

(3) giving children the right to maintain on a regular basis a personal relationship and direct contact with both parents unless it is contrary to their interests.[183]

These provisions undeniably embody sound family law principles but where do they fit into EC competence? The Charter is said to have been 'solemnly declared' but has not (yet) been incorporated into a Treaty and is thought to have declaratory force only.[184] Importantly, as Art 51(2) states, 'The Charter does not establish any new power or task for the Community or the Union, or modify powers and tasks defined by the Treaties'. Notwithstanding this clear statement the Commission have already relied on the Charter[185] to include the child's right of continued contact and a right to be heard in the revised Brussels II Regulation.

Arguments about EC competence are not confined to whether it extends to questions of substantive law. It is also a matter of debate whether even in the context of cross-border cases competence extends to matters of public law.

The Brussels II Regulations

Background to the original Regulation.[186] It will be recalled that the inspiration for Brussels II was Brussels I, which provides a general framework for recognition and enforcement of judgments but which expressly excludes matters of status. Once the Community's interest expanded beyond the purely economic, it was perhaps inevitable that this exclusion would be revised. In fact the formal proposal that it should be revised was made by Germany in 1992.

Germany was specifically concerned with problems of recognition and enforcement of divorce, annulment and legal separation, particularly in regard to France, but in 1995 Spain and France proposed that questions relating to children should also be included, in part because a divorce judge would normally have competence to deal with such litigation so that it would be unduly complicated to have different rules dealing with these issues, and in part to raise the profile of the Community. The Council of Ministers instructed work to go ahead on this basis. Negotiations proved protracted and it was not until May 1998 that what was then a Convention, was presented to the Council of Ministers for signing. Even then the Convention was not expected to be implemented for some time, but

---

[183] Based on Art 9(3) of the UN Convention. It might be noted, however, that the European Charter is stronger than the UN in that it confers a right on the child, rather than directing State Parties to respect that right.

[184] See inter alia 'Communication From the Commission on the Legal Nature of the Charter of Fundamental Rights of the European Union' Com (2000) 644 Final (11 October 2000) and, the memorandum presented to the Select Committee on the European Union by the Foreign and Commonwealth Office— included in their 8th Report, Session 1999–2000. In *R (Howard League For Penal Reform) v Secretary of State for the Home Office* [2002] EWHC 2497 (Admin) at paras [45]–[52], [66]–[68], [2003] 1 FLR 484 and *R (A et al) v East Sussex County Council (No. 2)* [2003] EWHC 167 (Admin), paras [68]–[74], [80], [93], [103], [106], Munby J referred to the Charter, which he considered as 'not at present legally binding in our domestic law and is therefore not a source of law in the strict sense. But it can, in my judgment, properly be consulted insofar as it produces, reaffirms or elucidates the content of those human rights that are generally recognised throughout the European family of nations, in particular the nature and scope of those fundamental rights that are guaranteed by the Convention.'

[185] See the proposal dated 3.5.2002 Com (2002) 222 Final, at p 7.

[186] See P McEleavy, 'The Brussels II Regulation: How the European Community has moved into Family Law' (2002) 51 ICLQ 883 at 891 et seq, who provides a detailed account of the provenance of the Regulation.

as we have discussed, the Treaty of Amsterdam enabled the Commission to present a proposal for a Regulation to be based on the text of the Convention. That proposal was adopted by the Council on 29 May 2000 and came into force in all Member States, except Denmark,[187] (Ireland and the UK having opted in) on 1 March 2001. It was the conversion of the Convention into a Regulation that caught many by surprise, particularly as it was the first EC instrument directly affecting mainstream family law.

The scope of the original Brussels II.[188] In outline the Regulation applied to:

'(a) civil proceedings relating to divorce, legal separation or marriage annulment; and

(b) civil proceedings relating to parental responsibility for the children of both spouses on the occasion of the matrimonial proceedings referred to in (a).'

The application to children was limited: it had no application to issues arising in non-matrimonial proceedings nor to issues arising in matrimonial proceedings unless the children concerned were those of both spouses. Parental responsibility was not defined.

The basic strategy of the Regulation was to provide exclusive but separate rules of jurisdiction in relation to matrimonial proceedings and children and then a scheme of recognition and enforcement. In the case of the United Kingdom, judgments relating to parental responsibility only became enforceable when, upon application they were registered for enforcement. There was no provision for a Central Authority to administer the Regulation.

Criticism of the original Regulation. The original Regulation was heavily criticised. In relation to the jurisdictional rules for divorce, nullity and separation, the Regulation provided a number of bases but without a hierarchy. That in itself was necessarily complicated and moreover the so-called solution under Art 11 to give absolute priority to the first jurisdiction seised effectively encouraged a race to gain jurisdiction which was not in keeping with modern family thinking to encourage mediation. There was also a regrettable absence of provision to decline jurisdiction in favour of a more appropriate forum or to permit prorogation of jurisdiction by agreement.

So far as its scope was concerned, it was unfortunate that the Regulation only applied to children of both spouses involved in matrimonial proceedings, since divorces increasingly concern step-children.

Background to the revised Regulation. Barely was the ink dry on the final version of Brussels II, when, in July 2000, France presented a fresh initiative aimed at facilitating, through the abolition of *exequator* (an enforcement procedure), the exercise of cross-border rights of access.[189] Since, as originally conceived, the scope of the proposed Regulation was to be

---

[187] See Art 1(3).

[188] See P Beaumont and G Moir 'Brussels II: A New Private International Law Instrument in Family Matters for the European Union on the European Community?', (1995) 20 EL Rev 268, M Jänterä-Jareborg 'Marriage Dissolution in an Integrated Europe' in *Yearbook of Private International Law* Vol 1–1999 (Eds. Šarcěvić and Volken), Shannon with Kennedy 'Jurisdictional and Enforcement Issues in Proceedings Concerning Parental Responsibility under the Brussels II Convention' [2000] IFL 111, Th. M. de Boer 'Jurisdiction and Enforcement in International Family Law: A Labyrinth of European and International Legislation' *Netherlands International Law Review*, XLIX, 307–351, 2002 and P McEleavy 'The Brussels II Regulation: How the European Community has moved into Family Law' (2002) 51 ICLQ 883.

[189] Initiative of the French Republic with a view to adopting a Council Regulation on the mutual enforcement of judgments on rights of access to children, OJ 2000 C234/7.

limited to judgments granting rights of access for a period of not less than one day in proceedings caught by Art 1(1)(b) of the Brussels II Regulation and would be by way of derogation from Art 21 thereto, this proposed Regulation was dubbed 'Brussels IIA', or 'II Bis'.

The French proposal was followed by the Council's own initiative, to extend the Regulation to all decisions on parental responsibility. Their initial proposal was made in September 2001 with a revised proposal being made in May 2002 (which then incorporated the French proposal).[190] Controversially, the Commission's proposal contained radical provisions about child abduction but eventually this was settled, ironically, by a Danish-brokered compromise (ironic because the Danes are not party to Brussels II or its successor) towards the end of 2002 and after a further year of negotiation (albeit conducted in a more co-operative atmosphere) the new version was finally agreed and formally adopted on 27 November 2003.

What the revised Brussels II Regulation does. The revised Brussels II[191] came fully into force in March 2005. As its name implies, it repealed the original Brussels II Regulation, but like its predecessor the revised Regulation provides exclusive and separate rules of jurisdiction in relation to matrimonial proceedings and in respect of matters of parental responsibility for children and for a consequent scheme of recognition and enforcement.

The revised Regulation has made no changes to that part dealing with matrimonial proceedings and so remains open to the criticism that it has no settled hierarchy of jurisdictional bases. We discuss this aspect of the Regulation further in Chapter 2. So far as children are concerned, it has made numerous changes meeting most, if not all, the criticisms levelled at the original Regulation. It now applies to *all* civil matters relating to the attribution, exercise, delegation, restriction, and termination of parental responsibility. It provides fundamentally revised and rational rules of jurisdiction primarily based on the child's habitual residence but permitting both (a limited) prorogation of jurisdiction by agreement and jurisdiction to be transferred to a court better able to hear the case. It provides important rules applying to abduction and to trans-border access issues and finally it creates a Central Authority to administer the Regulation. We discuss the application of the revised Regulation in relation to children in Chapter 13.

What future Regulations might there be? Mention was made earlier of the so-called 'Tampere Milestones' following which the Council, at its December 2001 meeting, drew up a detailed schedule of work to be undertaken which included rights of property arising out of a marital relationship and separation of an unmarried couple, and wills and succession.[192] It is also clear that action will be undertaken on the so-called Rome III dealing

---

[190] See respectively Proposal for a Council Regulation concerning jurisdiction and the recognition and enforcement of judgments in matrimonial matters and in matters of parental responsibility repealing Regulation (EC) No. 1347/2000 and amending Regulation (EC) No. 44/2001 in matters relating to maintenance. Brussels, 3.5.2002 COM (2002) 222 Final. But note, in the event, no provision was made to amend the Brussels I Regulation in respect of maintenance.

[191] Council Regulation (EC) No 2201/2003 of 27 November 2003 concerning jurisdiction and the recognition and enforcement of judgments in matrimonial matters and in matters of parental responsibility, repealing Regulation (EC) No 1347/2000.

[192] See Draft programme of measures for implementation of the principle of mutual recognition of decisions in civil and commercial matters [2001] OJ C12 (15 January).

with applicable law on divorce etc. In short, there will be a number of further Brussels Regulations in the family law area.

Will European family law be eventually harmonised? As previously discussed, it is outside the general competence of the EU to reform substantive family law but there have been some initiatives to consider whether it is possible to harmonise at least parts of family law. To this end note might be taken of the Commission of European Family Law[193] which has so far produced suggested principles for divorce and maintenance of spouses after divorce.[194] It is currently working on parental responsibility.[195]

---

[193] This Commission was established by an international group of scholars in 2001. The main objective of the Commission is to launch a pioneering theoretical and practical exercise in relation to the harmonisation of substantive family and succession law in Europe.

[194] See K Boele-Woelki, F Ferrand, C González Beilfuss, M Jänterä-Jareborg, N Lowe, D Martiny and W Pintens *Principles of European Family Law Regarding Divorce and Maintenance Between Former Spouses* (2004).

[195] *European Family Law in Action Vol III: Parental Responsibilities* (eds K Boeli-Woelki, B Braat and I Curry-Sumner, 2005).

2

FORMATION AND
RECOGNITION OF
ADULT PARTNERSHIPS

A INTRODUCTION

This chapter examines how the law on entry into marriage has developed and what are the current requirements for a valid marriage. It then considers the equivalent rules enacted for same sex couples entering into a 'civil partnership'. Finally, it contrasts these with cohabitation outside marriage and explains how and when such a relationship will be given limited legal status.

While traditionally and historically, marriage was the only acceptable form in which an intimate adult relationship could be given legal recognition, the latter part of the twentieth century saw a fracturing of social mores and an increased willingness amongst people living in the United Kingdom both to enter into more diverse forms of relationship and to attach legally enforceable consequences to these. Today, perhaps the major debate in family policy concerns how far such diversity should be accepted and embraced or, by contrast, rejected and controlled. The current focus of attention is upon the extent to which relationships other than heterosexual, state-sanctioned marriage should be recognised. But it would be wrong to imagine that this kind of debate is new. The legal recognition of adult relationships has always occupied the minds of policy-makers, from the concerns of the medieval Catholic church over the extent of the prohibitions on marriage between those who might be very distantly related, either by blood or marriage, to each other, to the worries of the English upper classes in the eighteenth century over the problem of 'clandestine marriage' and the loss thereby of their landed estates to the rogue seducers of their daughters.[1] A bar on remarriage of the divorced, still a moral issue for the Anglican church in the matter of the marriage of the Prince of Wales in 2005, and uncertainty over how far to recognise polygamous unions sanctioned by other religions, were continuing subjects of debate over the past one hundred years. All such issues show how the question of legal recognition of relationships marks out the very foundation of state control over family life and serves to set the boundaries for what forms of intimate behaviour will be tolerated or facilitated by society. The power of the State in this issue may be controlled by the recognition in human rights law of the right to 'marry and found a family', contained,

---

[1] See C Brooke, *The Medieval Idea of Marriage* (1989) Ch 6; L Stone, *Uncertain Unions, Marriage in England 1660–1753* (1992); S Cretney, *Family Law in the Twentieth Century: A History* (2003) Part 1.

inter alia, in Art 12 of the European Convention on Human Rights, and the ambit of this right needs to be discussed.

Marriage is declining in popularity, although it is likely that most people will marry at some point in their lives. In 2001, the number of marriages entered into in England and Wales was the lowest recorded since 1897, at 249,227.[2] The number has grown slightly since then, to 267,700 in 2003. Of these, 158,560 were first marriages for both parties, while 41% of the total were remarriages. Meanwhile, the age at which people marry is rising, with an average (mean) age at first marriage for men of 31.2 years, and for women of 28.9 years.[3]

One of the reasons for the decline in marriage has been the growth in cohabitation outside marriage.[4] There has been a very significant growth in the number of people cohabiting outside marriage in the past 30 years in Great Britain. The percentage of non-married men and women under the age of 60 cohabiting in Great Britain increased between 1986 (the earliest year data are available on a consistent basis) and 2004; from 11% to 24% for men and from 13% to 25% for women.[5] The proportion of divorced women cohabiting, formerly much higher than that of single women, is now the same, at 31%. The figures for men are similar—rising from one in eight single men cohabiting in 1986, to one in four in 1998, a doubling in 12 years. Divorced men have cohabited at even higher rates, with the proportion remaining stable at about 40% throughout the period. The peak age for cohabitation for both men and women is in their mid to late 20s.[6] Cohabitation is no longer a minority pastime, but has become the norm for a significant proportion of the population, although whether it is replacing or merely preceding marriage remains an open question.

One of the most significant recent legal innovations in the United Kingdom has been the enactment of a civil partnership law to provide a legal status, comparable to marriage, for same-sex couples to enter into through a registration process. But there are few estimates of the size of the lesbian, gay or bisexual population for whom this measure is intended. The government used a figure of 5% of the Great Britain population in seeking to determine the possible take-up of the registration procedure.[7] Alternatively, the General Household Survey found 2% of households to consist of two or more unrelated adults, and 8% cohabiting, of whom an unknown proportion may be same-sex couples, compared with 47% made up of married couples, 31% single people, 10% lone parents and 2% consisting of two or more families together.[8] These statistics suggest that although the overall numbers of different family types may be small, the 'norm' of the married couple, whilst still reflecting the majority of 'family' modes, no longer encompasses the majority

---

[2] The peak was in 1972, with nearly 500,000 marriages.

[3] Data are taken from *Population Trends 119* 'Report: Marriages in England and Wales, 2003' (Spring, 2005) 71.

[4] For the legal and social policy issues arising, see the articles in (2001) IJLPF 'Special Issue: Unmarried Cohabitation in Europe' and (2004) Law and Policy Issue 1 on Cohabitation.

[5] ONS, *Social Trends* 36 (2006) p 27.

[6] J Haskey, 'Cohabitation in Great Britain: past, present and future trends—and attitudes' *Population Trends* 103, Spring, (2001) 4–25. For a comparison of the position in Britain and Europe, see K Kiernan, 'Unmarried Cohabitation and Parenthood in Britain and Europe' (2004) Law and Policy 33–55.

[7] DTI, Women and Equality Unit, *Civil Partnership: A framework for the recognition of same-sex couples* (2003) Annex A(1) p 76.

[8] ONS, *Living in Britain: General Household Survey 2002* (2004) Table 3.5.

of the population, and the law will increasingly have to cater for relationships which do not fit neatly within the traditional model of family building within marriage. Nonetheless, the law of marriage will remain important for a sizeable number of people for some time to come and, as we will see, it continues to provide the 'benchmark' against which other relationships are measured and (to a greater or lesser extent) accommodated in the law.

1 THE RIGHT TO MARRY

The right to marry is enshrined in human rights law, and may be seen as a fundamental part of the freedom of the individual to form personal relationships according to his or her own inclination. The focus of the European Convention on Human Rights was on the risk of totalitarian state control and the aim was to carve out an area of personal liberty beyond the interference of the state. Modern concerns may now extend to how far the state should *enable* the formation and recognition of relationships, either where these may be opposed by other family members (such as in the case of some cultures where the tradition of arranged marriages may tip over into the abuse of forced marriage) or by sections of the community (such as opposition to same-sex or polygamous marriages).

Article 12 of the European Convention provides that:

'Men and women of marriageable age have the right to marry and to found a family according to the national laws governing the exercise of this right.'

This Article has been interpreted by the European Court of Human Rights as being 'mainly concerned to protect marriage as the basis of the family' and thus establishing only one right—the right to marry and found a family.[9] In other words, there is no right, as so far understood, to found a family *outside* marriage. By contrast, Art 9 of the Charter of Fundamental Rights of the European Union asserts 'The right to marry *and* the right to found a family shall be guaranteed',[10] implying the recognition of two separate rights.

The European Court has yet to rule on whether the right to marry is limited to those entering a heterosexual union. It has not yet recognised same-sex relationships as an aspect of the Art 8 right to respect for family life, holding only that homosexual conduct is an aspect of one's *private* life.[11] However, notwithstanding its linkage of the right to marry with that of founding a family, the Court *has* held in *Goodwin v United Kingdom*[12] that marriage no longer implies a procreative purpose which would restrict those eligible to enter it to persons of the opposite sex:

'Article 12 secures the fundamental right of a man and woman to marry and to found a family. The second aspect is not however a condition of the first and the inability of any couple to conceive or parent a child cannot be regarded as *per se* removing their right to enjoy the first limb of this provision.'

It went on to assert that whilst the right is 'subject to the national laws of the Contracting States . . . the limitations thereby introduced must not restrict or reduce the right in such

---

[9] *Sheffield and Horsham v United Kingdom* (1999) 27 EHRR 163.   [10] Emphasis added.

[11] *Kerkhoven v Netherlands*, Application 15666/89 (1992, unreported). In *Salgueiro da Silva Mouta v Portugal* (2001) 31 EHRR 47 it did recognise a homosexual father as having a 'family life' with his child but did not rule on the nature and quality of his relationships with other men.

[12] [2002] 2 FLR 487 at paras 98–9.

a way or to such an extent that the very essence of the right is impaired.' It added that the margin of appreciation left to states in translating the rights in the Convention into national law cannot be so broad as to amount to an effective bar on the individual's right to marry. In *Goodwin* the issue was whether a transsexual could be prevented from marrying a person of her choice because her legal gender, fixed at birth, no longer reflected her identity. The Court found:

'that it is artificial to assert that post-operative transsexuals have not been deprived of the right to marry as, according to law, they remain able to marry a person of their former opposite sex. The applicant in this case lives as a woman, is in a relationship with a man and would only wish to marry a man. She has no possibility of doing so. In the Court's view, she may therefore claim that the very essence of her right to marry has been infringed.'

By the same reasoning, it would not be a valid argument to assert that a homosexual could still marry a person of the opposite sex, if the only person he or she would ever contemplate marrying was of the same sex—the very right to marry would be rendered nugatory. It is therefore certainly possible that we will see, at some point in the future—although how soon that might be is open to question—a successful challenge to a bar on same-sex marriage.[13]

B THE NATURE OF MARRIAGE

Quite apart from its abstract meaning as the social institution of marriage, 'marriage' has two distinct meanings: the ceremony by which a man and woman become husband and wife, or the *act of marrying*; and the relationship existing between a husband and his wife, or the *state of being married*.[14] This distinction largely corresponds with its dual aspect of contract and status.

1 MARRIAGE AS A CONTRACT

'Marriage, whether civil or religious, is a contract, formally entered into. It confers on the parties the status of husband and wife, the essence of the contract being an agreement between a man and a woman to live together, and to love one another as husband and wife, to the exclusion of all others. It creates a relationship of mutual and reciprocal obligations, typically involving the sharing of a common home and a common domestic life and the right to enjoy each other's society, comfort and assistance.'[15]

In English law, marriage is an agreement by which a man and a woman enter into a certain legal relationship with each other and which creates and imposes mutual rights and duties. Looked at from this point of view, marriage is clearly a contract. It presents similar problems to other contracts—for example, of form and capacity; and like other contracts

---

[13] See J Murphy, 'Same-sex marriage in England: a role for human rights?' [2004] CFLQ 245; A Morris and S Nott, 'Marriage Rites and Wrongs: Challenges to Orthodoxy' (2005) 27 JSWFL 43.

[14] R Graveson *Status in the Common Law* (1982) pp 80–1.

[15] Per Munby J in *Re E (An Alleged Patient); Re Sheffield City Council v E and S* [2004] EWHC 2808 (Fam); [2005] 1 FLR 965.

it may be void or voidable. But it is, of course, quite unlike any commercial contract, and consequently it is sui generis in many respects. In particular we may note the following distinctive characteristics:

(1) The law relating to the capacity to marry is different from that of any other contract.

(2) A marriage may only be contracted if special formalities are observed.

(3) The grounds on which a marriage may be void or voidable are for the most part completely different from those on which other contracts may be void or voidable.

(4) Unlike other voidable contracts, a voidable marriage cannot be declared void ab initio by rescission by one of the parties, but may be set aside only by a decree of nullity pronounced by a court of competent jurisdiction.

(5) A contract of marriage cannot be discharged by agreement, frustration or breach. Apart from death, it can be terminated only by a formal legal act, pronounced by a court of competent jurisdiction.

2 MARRIAGE AS CREATING STATUS

This second aspect of marriage is much more important than the first. It creates a status, that is, 'the condition of belonging to a particular class of persons [ie married persons] to whom the law assigns certain peculiar legal capacities or incapacities.'[16]

In the first place, whereas the parties to a commercial agreement may make such terms as they think fit (provided that they do not offend against rules of public policy or statutory prohibition), the spouses' mutual rights and duties[17] are very largely fixed by law and not by agreement. An increasing number of these may be varied by consent: for example, the spouses may release each other from the duty to cohabit. But many may still not be altered: thus neither may contract out of his or her power to apply to the court for financial relief in the event of divorce.[18]

Secondly, unlike a commercial contract, which cannot affect the legal position of anyone who is not a party to it, marriage may also affect the rights and duties of third persons and the relationship of the individual with government bodies. So, for example, private or state pensions may be payable to a person by virtue of their status as a surviving spouse.

3 DEFINITION OF MARRIAGE

The classic definition of marriage in English law is that of Lord Penzance in *Hyde v Hyde*:[19]

'I conceive that marriage, as understood in Christendom, may ... be defined as the voluntary union for life of one man and one woman to the exclusion of all others.'

It will be seen that this definition involves four conditions.

---

[16] C Allen 'Status and Capacity' (1930) 46 LQR 277, 288. In this article the author critically discusses a number of other definitions of status and analyses this elusive legal concept. See also Graveson, op cit.

[17] For the view that there are virtually no duties attached to marriage any more, see R Deech 'Divorce Law and Empirical Studies' (1990) 106 LQR 229 at pp 243–4.

[18] Matrimonial Causes Act 1973, s 34. See below p 954.   [19] (1866) LR 1 P & D 130, 133.

First, the marriage must be *voluntary*. Thus, as we shall see,[20] it can be annulled if there was no true consent on the part of one of the parties.

Secondly, it must be *for life*. If by marriage 'as understood in Christendom' Lord Penzance was referring to the view traditionally taken in Western Europe by the Roman Catholic Church and some other denominations, his statement is of course unexceptional. But it does not mean that by English law marriage is indissoluble: divorce by judicial process had been possible in England for over eight years when *Hyde v Hyde* was decided. The gloss put on the dictum by the Court of Appeal in *Nachimson v Nachimson*[21]—that it must be the parties' intention when they enter into the marriage that it should last for life—is unsatisfactory. This may well be the intention of the vast majority, but, if, say, two people enter into a marriage for the sole purpose of enabling a child to be born within marriage, intending never to live together but to obtain a divorce by consent at the earliest opportunity, it cannot be doubted that their union is a marriage by English law.[22] The only interpretation that can be put on Lord Penzance's statement is that the marriage must last for life unless it is previously determined by a decree or some other act of dissolution.[23]

Thirdly, the union must be *heterosexual*.

Fourthly, it must be *monogamous*. Neither spouse may contract another marriage so long as the original union subsists.

4 CIVIL PARTNERSHIP [24]

In 2004, Parliament enacted the Civil Partnership Act, and established a mechanism to enable those in same-sex relationships to achieve a status functionally equivalent to marriage, and thus give recognition to their partnership. Section 1 of the Act provides that

'(1) A civil partnership is a relationship between two people of the same sex ("civil partners")—

(a) which is formed when they register as civil partners of each other - . . . or

(b) which they are treated . . . as having formed . . . by virtue of having registered an overseas relationship[25]. . . .

(3) A civil partnership ends only on death, dissolution or annulment.'

The model of creating a broadly equivalent but separate legal status, rather than extending marriage to same-sex couples, originated in Denmark[26] and was rapidly adopted in

[20] Below, pp 82 et seq.   [21] [1930] P 217, CA.
[22] See below, p 88. The updated definition of marriage proposed at a symposium held in 1994 and reported in [1994] Fam Law 341, has a similar flaw: 'marriage is the voluntary union of a man and a woman, solemnised in public according to law, and is based upon mutual commitment and intended to last for life, to the exclusion of all others'.
[23] *Nachimson v Nachimson* (above) at 225, 227 (per Lord Hanworth MR), 235 (per Lawrence LJ), 243–4 (per Romer LJ).
[24] See M Harper et al, *Civil Partnership: The New Law* (2005) Chaps 1–3 for background, and DTI Women and Equality Unit, *Civil Partnership: A framework for the recognition of same-sex couples* (2003).
[25] In accordance with Part 5 Ch 2 of the Act. Note the unsuccessful challenge to this provision in *Wilkinson v Kitzinger and Attorney-General (Lord Chancellor intervening)* [2006] EWHC 835 (Fam).
[26] See L Nielsen, 'Family rights and the "registered partnership" in Denmark' (1990) IJLF 297; M Dupuis 'The Impact of Culture, Society and History on the Legal Process: An Analysis of the Legal Status of Same-Sex

many other, mainly European, jurisdictions.[27] It enables governments to avoid the charge that they are 'weakening' the institution of marriage and allows them to present the measure as an anti-discrimination device and even as a 'pro-family' policy. Thus, the UK government summarised the advantages of civil partnership registration as:

'an important equality measure for same-sex couples ... who are unable to marry each other. It would provide for the legal recognition of same-sex partners and give legitimacy to those in, or wishing to enter into, interdependent, same-sex couple relationships that are intended to be permanent. Registration would provide a framework whereby same-sex couples could acknowledge their mutual responsibilities, manage their financial arrangements and achieve recognition as each other's partner. Committed same-sex relationships would be recognised and registered partners would gain rights and responsibilities which would reflect the significance of the roles they play in each other's lives. This in turn would encourage more stable family life.

It is a matter of public record that the Government has no plans to introduce same-sex marriage.'[28]

We explore throughout this book how far civil partners in fact have the same rights and obligations as spouses under the 2004 Act. It may suffice here to note that the approach of the legislation is almost entirely to equate both institutions, and one can thus apply the same view of civil partnership as being both a special kind of contract, and as providing a separate legal status, as applied to marriage above.

In states which have enacted civil partnership laws, the extent to which the registered partnership resembles marriage in its legal consequences varies according to national preference; so too does the question whether it is a status open to heterosexual as well as same-sex couples.[29] A variant on the model is to view it primarily as registration of a *contract* between the parties, rather than as registration of their *relationship,* as in France, where the *pacte civil de solidarité (PACS)* leaves it primarily to the parties to shape the terms and conditions of their union, although certain additional rights and obligations are attached. The French *pacte* may be entered into by both hetero- and homosexual parties, and is avowedly intended to be different and not equivalent to marriage.[30] It may thereby have some attraction for those couples, be they heterosexual or same-sex, who reject the traditional values attached to marriage.

By contrast, some same-sex lobbies seek the opening up of marriage to same-sex couples, arguing that only this approach is compatible with constitutional or human rights requirements. Only a few jurisdictions have so far adopted this view; the Netherlands introduced same-sex marriage in 2001, with Belgium, Spain and Argentina enacting similar laws subsequently. Constitutional challenges to a bar on same-sex marriage have

---

Relationships in the United States and Denmark' (1995) 9 Int J of Law and the Family 86; M Broberg, 'The registered partnership for same-sex couples in Denmark' (1996) CFLQ 149.

[27] See DTI op cit Tables 1, 2.   [28] Ibid paras 1.2, 1.3.

[29] As in the Netherlands, for example. See A Barlow, 'Regulation of Cohabitation, Changing Family Policies and Social Attitudes: A Discussion of Britain Within Europe' (2004) *Law and Policy* 57 especially pp 61–7.

[30] But see E Steiner, 'The spirit of the new French registered partnership law—promoting autonomy and pluralism or weakening marriage?' [2000] CFLQ 1, who describes it as 'ersatz marriage' at p 8. See also R Probert, 'From lack of status to contract: assessing the French *Pacte Civil de Solidarité* (2001) 23, 3, JSWFL 257

been brought across Canada and the USA, and have succeeded in the former but not the latter.[31] As we have noted above, a successful challenge based on Art 12 of the European Convention on Human Rights cannot be ruled out in the future.

The Civil Partnership Act was introduced by the government in response to two private member's bills which had earlier been presented to Parliament.[32] It was enacted against a backdrop of developing judicial activism concerning the rights of homosexuals, in particular based on the view that continuing discrimination could no longer be upheld since the Human Rights Act 1998 had incorporated the European Convention into domestic law.[33] Although attempts were made to wreck the Bill by extending its ambit to, for example, two elderly sisters living together, a general party political consensus ensured its successful passage and it entered into force on 5 December 2005, enabling the first registrations to take place on 21 December 2005.

C AGREEMENTS TO MARRY OR FORM A CIVIL PARTNERSHIP

A marriage is commonly preceded by an agreement to marry, or 'engagement'. At common law such agreements amounted to contracts provided that there was an intention to enter into legal relations (as there probably would not be in the case of an 'unofficial engagement'). Their highly personal and non-commercial nature gave them certain peculiar characteristics, but as a general rule they were governed by the general principles of the law of contract. Consequently, if either party withdrew from the engagement without lawful justification, the other could sue for breach of contract. Such actions became rare after the Second World War (and were seldom, if ever, brought by men), partly no doubt because of the difficulty of proving damage, but probably largely as a result of a change in social views.[34]

The fact that actions for breach of promise of marriage were still occasionally brought raised the question of their utility. If either party to an engagement was convinced that he (or she) ought not to marry the other, it was highly doubtful whether public policy was served by letting the threat of an action push him into a potentially unstable marriage or by penalising him in damages if he resiled. The Law Commission therefore recommended the abolition of these actions[35] and this recommendation was implemented by the Law

---

[31] See L Glennon, 'Displacing the "conjugal family" in legal policy—a progressive move?' [2005] CFLQ 141; S Katz, *Family Law in America* (2003) pp 53–8. For the view that the goal of those seeking equality for homosexuals should not be assimilation with marriage, see K Norrie, 'Marriage is for heterosexuals—may the rest of us be saved from it' [2000] CFLQ 363.

[32] See the Relationships (Civil Registration) Bill 2001, presented to the House of Commons by Jane Griffith MP, which would simply have extended the rights of marriage to any couple (hetero- or homosexual) who registered their relationship, and the Civil Partnerships Bill 2002, presented to the House of Lords by Lord Lester of Herne Hill, also open to both hetero and homosexual couples, but which was a much more ambitious scheme which sought to move the law forward from that applicable to existing marriages.

[33] See *Fitzpatrick v Sterling Housing Association Ltd* [2001] 1 AC 27, HL; *Ghaidan v Godin-Mendoza* [2004] UKHL 30, [2004] 2 AC 557, discussed above at p 8 and below at pp 101–2.

[34] The civil judicial statistics do not disclose how many actions were brought. Nor do we know how far the existence of the action led to settlements out of court.

[35] Law Com No 26 *Breach of Promise of Marriage* (1969).

Reform (Miscellaneous Provisions) Act 1970 s 1. This provides that no agreement to marry shall take effect as a legally enforceable contract and that no action shall lie in this country for breach of such an agreement, wherever it was made.

1 CONTINUING SIGNIFICANCE OF ENGAGEMENTS

However, the fact that a couple have agreed to marry each other is not without all legal significance. There may still be advantages to being able to show an engagement having taken place, in relation to certain types of property disputes.[36] Problems can therefore arise in establishing what constitutes a legally recognisable agreement to marry, and in proving that it was ever made.

(a) The meaning of an agreement to marry

It could be argued that an engagement should only be recognised if it would have amounted to a legally enforceable contract at common law. In *Shaw v Fitzgerald*,[37] however, Scott Baker J held that an agreement to marry was capable of recognition under the Law Reform (Miscellaneous Provisions) Act 1970 s 2 (discussed below) even though at common law the contract would have been regarded as contrary to public policy because one of the parties was married to a third person. The test must therefore be whether there was an unconditional agreement to marry.

(b) Proof of an engagement

The difficulty of proving an engagement actually took place has been recognised in the Family Law Act 1996 s 44. This provides that where an engagement is relied upon as the basis for seeking orders under Part IV of that Act,[38] there must be produced to the court evidence in writing of the existence of the agreement to marry, or evidence by the gift of an engagement ring by one party to the agreement to the other, in contemplation of their marriage, or evidence of a 'ceremony entered into by the parties in the presence of one or more other persons assembled for the purpose of witnessing the ceremony'.[39] The aim of these requirements is to avoid lengthy enquiries into whether an engagement had, or had not been entered into.[40] But the section seems to leave room for dispute as to its interpretation. For example, does an engagement party constitute a 'ceremony', since the choice of this word might more naturally imply some kind of formal betrothal procedure?

In other contexts, no statutory test is laid down for proving that an engagement existed, but the court is likely to seek evidence of a similar kind as is required under s 44.

2 CIVIL PARTNERSHIP AGREEMENTS

These are the equivalent to an engagement in the case of prospective civil partners. Section 73 of the Civil Partnership Act 2004 mirrors s 1 of the Law Reform (Miscellaneous Provisions) Act 1970 in providing that an agreement to register as civil partners[41] does not

---

[36] See below at pp 132–3, 146.   [37] [1992] 1 FLR 357.

[38] Non-molestation or occupation orders, discussed below, at pp 224–5.   [39] Section 44(2)(b).

[40] Law Com No 207 *Domestic Violence and Occupation of the Family Home* (1992) para 3.24.

[41] Including entering into an overseas relationship in accordance with Part 5, Chapter 2 of the Act.

have effect as a contract giving rise to legal rights and is not actionable for breach. Oddly, the section borrows the language of s 1(2) to provide that it does not affect any action commenced before it came into force, but unlike engagements to marry, an agreement to register as a civil partner would have had no prior legal validity anyway.[42]

D ENTRY INTO MARRIAGE

In order that a man and woman may become husband and wife, two conditions must be satisfied: first, they must both possess the capacity to contract a marriage, and secondly, they must observe the necessary formalities.[43]

1 CAPACITY TO MARRY

In order that a person domiciled in England and Wales should have capacity to contract a valid marriage, the following conditions must be satisfied:

   (a) one party must be male and the other female;

   (b) neither party must be already married or in a civil partnership;

   (c) both parties must be over the age of 16; and

   (d) the parties must not be related within the prohibited degrees of consanguinity or affinity.[44]

(a) Sex

'Transsexual people[45] are born with the anatomy of a person of one sex but with an unshakeable belief or feeling that they are persons of the opposite sex. They experience themselves as being of the opposite sex ... The aetiology of this condition remains

---

[42] Section 44 of the Family Law Act 1996 also applies to proof of a civil partnership agreement for the purposes of the domestic violence provisions of that Act. It is hard to imagine what sort of 'ceremony' could be contemplated in this context.

[43] Where a couple come from different countries, or are married abroad, the question may arise as to which law is to be applied to determining these two matters. As regards the formalities for marriage, these are determined by the law of the place where the marriage is celebrated (the lex loci celebrationis). The position regarding capacity is more difficult, but is broadly based on the law of the parties' domicile (lex domicilii), though whether this depends exclusively upon each party's ante-nuptial domicile, or upon the intended matrimonial domicile, is problematic. For discussion, see the 8th edition of this work at pp 26–33.

[44] A further prohibition is to be found in the Royal Marriages Act 1772, which was passed to prevent the contracting of highly undesirable marriages by the younger brothers of King George III. It provides that no descendant of King George II (other than the issue of princesses who have married into foreign families) may marry without the previous consent of the Sovereign formally granted under the great seal and declared in Council. Any marriage coming within the Act, consent to which has not been obtained, will be void; but if the descendant in question is over the age of 25 and gives 12 months' notice of the intended marriage to the Privy Council, it may be validly contracted unless both Houses of Parliament have in the meantime expressly declared their disapprobation of it. For discussion of the Act see S Cretney 'The Royal Marriages Act 1772: A Footnote' (1995) 16 Statute Law Review 195. For the complications arising from the Act, as revealed by the marriage of the Prince of Wales to Camilla Parker Bowles in 2005, see S Cretney, 'Royal Marriages: The Law in a Nutshell' [2005] Fam Law 317; and his letter at [2005] Fam Law 507; R Probert, 'The wedding of the Prince of Wales: royal privileges and human rights' [2005] CFLQ 363.

[45] See S Edwards Sex and Gender in the Legal Process (1996) ch 1.

uncertain. It is now generally recognised as a psychiatric disorder, often known as gender dysphoria or gender identity disorder. It can result in acute psychological distress.'[46]

The treatment for this condition is often to provide the person with the outward physical characteristics of his or her preferred gender, through both hormone treatment and gender-reassignment surgery—operations to effect a 'sex-change'. The condition was first considered by an English court in *Corbett v Corbett*.[47] The petitioner in this case was born a man; before the marriage the respondent had undergone a surgical operation for the removal of 'her' male genital organs and the provision of artificial female organs. After dealing at length with the medical evidence Ormrod J (who was also a qualified medical practitioner) concluded that a person's biological sex is fixed at birth (at the latest) and cannot subsequently be changed by artificial means. That being so, the respondent, who was male at birth, was not a woman and the marriage was therefore void.

In this case the respondent was to be regarded as male by three independent biological criteria: chromosomal, gonadal and genital. There are persons, however, who are male by one test and female by another (known as 'inter-sex'). Ormrod J deliberately left open the question of capacity to marry in such cases, but he was inclined to give greater weight to the appearance of the genital organs. However, in *W v W (Nullity)*[48] Charles J held that, in the case of an inter-sex, the decision as to whether the person is male or female for the purpose of marriage should be made having regard also to psychological and hormonal factors, and secondary sexual characteristics. There, the respondent had been born of indeterminate sex but her parents had registered her as a male. As she grew up, she regarded herself as female and developed a female body shape, although her chromosomal and gonadal sex was male. She underwent surgery to enable her to have penetrative sex as a woman. It was held that she was a female for the purposes of marriage and thus her marriage to a man was valid.

It has been suggested that from a social and domestic point of view the psychological gender of a transsexual (that is the sex to which the individual feels that he or she belongs) is of greater importance than biological sex.[49] Accordingly, as the parties to such a union regard themselves as belonging to opposite sexes (a view presumably shared by others), a marriage between them should be valid, at least provided that the transsexual party has undergone surgery of the type described. This, coupled with other arguments based on human rights and, more recently, further medical evidence concerning differences in brain structure of transsexuals, was argued in a number of cases taken to the European Court of Human Rights following *Corbett v Corbett*. In a number of decisions, the European Court

---

[46] Per Lord Nicholls of Birkenhead in *Bellinger v Bellinger* [2003] UKHL 21, [2003] 2 AC 467 at para 7.
[47] [1971] P 83.
[48] [2001] Fam 110. See also P-L Chau and J Herring, 'Defining, Assigning and Designing Sex' (2002) 16 Int Jo Law, Policy and the Family 327.
[49] See I Kennedy 'Transsexual and Single Sex Marriage' 2 (1973) Anglo-American Law Review 112; J Taitz 'A Transsexual's Nightmare: The Determination of Sexual Identity in English Law' (1988) 2 Int J of Law and Fam 139. See also the Australian courts' rejection of the *Corbett* approach discussed in J McConvill and E Mills, '*Re Kevin* and the Right of Transsexual Persons to Marry in Australia' (2003) 17 Int Jo Law, Policy and the Family 251. But for the view that this, while providing a solution for individual transsexuals, ignores an underlying problem of social construction of stereotyped gender roles, see K O'Donovan 'Transsexual Troubles: The Discrepancy between Legal and Social Categories' in S Edwards (ed) *Gender, Sex and the Law*.

upheld the approach taken in *Corbett v Corbett* but recognised the hardship which transsexuals might suffer from an inflexible law and noted that social attitudes in Europe have
been changing. It stressed the need to keep the law under review[50] and the government
established an inter-departmental working group to examine the issue, which did not,
however, result in proposals for change. Finally, in *Goodwin v United Kingdom*[51] and *I v
United Kingdom*[52] the Court ran out of patience with the United Kingdom and found that
the lack of any means of a transsexual altering his or her birth registration as being of a
particular sex amounted to a breach of Arts 8 (in respect of the right to respect for *private*
life) and 12. In essence, the Court considered that English law did not respect the dignity
of the transsexual individual, because of the embarrassment and intrusion such people
may suffer when called upon to reveal their birth registration, and their inability to live
fully under the law as persons of their chosen gender.

This ruling placed the United Kingdom government under an obligation to bring the
law into line with the Convention. This obligation was strengthened when the House of
Lords found that s 11(c) of the Matrimonial Causes Act 1973 was incompatible with the
Convention and made a declaration of incompatibility. In *Bellinger v Bellinger*[53] a male to
female transsexual sought a declaration that the marriage she had entered into in 1981 was
valid. Her application was dismissed and the House of Lords dismissed her final appeal.
Although it was potentially open to the House to read the provision as referring to gender,
rather than biological sex,[54] it rejected this argument, holding that it would 'necessitate
giving the expressions "male" and "female" in that Act a novel, extended meaning: that a
person may be born with one sex but later become, or become regarded as, a person of the
opposite sex.'[55] Instead, recognising the complexity of amending the law, the House
concluded that the matter must be left to Parliament.

With commendable speed, once it was finally galvanised into action, the government
duly brought forward and Parliament enacted the Gender Recognition Act 2004.[56]
This does not alter the law on capacity to marry,[57] but provides a means whereby a
transsexual may be given legal recognition of his or her acquired gender through the grant
of a 'gender recognition certificate'. The transsexual must apply under s 1 of the Act to a
Gender Recognition Panel which will determine the application.[58] The basis for grant of a

---

[50] *Rees v United Kingdom* (1986) 9 EHRR 56; *Cossey v United Kingdom* [1991] 2 FLR 492; *X, Y and Z v
United Kingdom* [1997] 2 FLR 892; *Sheffield and Horsham v United Kingdom* [1998] 2 FLR 928.

[51] [2002] 2 FLR 487. See C Bessant, 'Transsexuals and Marriage after *Goodwin v United Kingdom*' [2003]
Fam Law 111, R Sandland, 'Crossing and Not Crossing: Gender, Sexuality and Melancholy in the European
Court of Human Rights' (2003) 11 Fem LS 191.

[52] [2002] 2 FLR 518.

[53] [2003] UKHL 21, [2003] 2 AC 467. See S Gilmore, '*Bellinger v Bellinger*—Not quite between the ears and
between the legs—Transsexualism and marriage in the Lords' [2003] CFLQ 295; A Bradney, 'Developing
Human Rights? The Lords and Transsexual Marriages' [2003] Fam Law 585, S Cowan, ' "That Woman Is a
Woman!" The Case of *Bellinger v Bellinger* and the Mysterious (Dis)appearance of Sex' (2004) 12 Fem LS 79.

[54] See S Poulter 'The Definition of Marriage in English Law' (1979) 42 MLR 409 at 421–5. Section 11 of
the Matrimonial Causes Act 1973 re-enacted s 1 of the Nullity of Marriage Act 1971, which received the royal
assent 17 months after judgment was delivered in *Corbett v Corbett*.

[55] Per Lord Nicholls of Birkenhead at para 36.

[56] See S Gilmore, 'The Gender Recognition Act 2004' [2004] Fam Law 741, R Sandland, 'Feminism and the
Gender Recognition Act 2004' (2005) 13 Fem LS 43.

[57] Although it does make some changes to marriage law, see below p 90.

[58] Sch 1(1). Those eligible to sit on such a panel must be legally or medically qualified.

certificate is that the applicant is living in the other gender, or has changed gender under the law of another country or territory outside the United Kingdom. One of the reasons for the reluctance of the House of Lords simply to re-interpret the existing law was concern regarding the point at which a person may be said to have 'acquired' their new gender and be recognised as such—must he or she have had full surgery, for example? Section 2 of the Act requires that the panel must be satisfied that the applicant has, or had, gender dysphoria, that he or she has lived in the acquired gender throughout the period of two years ending with the date on which the application is made, intends to continue to live in the acquired gender until death, and complies with the requirements imposed by and under s 3. These requirements include evidence as to the treatment he or she is having or has undergone.

A 'full' certificate will be granted unless the applicant is already married, in which case an 'interim' certificate will be issued.[59] Where a full certificate is granted, the Secretary of State must send a copy to the Registrar General, who will maintain a gender recognition register, not open to the public. The Registrar enters the person's details in the gender recognition register and annotates the original birth register to enable a confidential trace between the two to be made. The effect is that[60]

'the person's gender becomes for all purposes[61] the acquired gender (so that, if the acquired gender is the male gender, the person's sex becomes that of a man and, if it is the female gender, the person's sex becomes that of a woman).'

Thus, someone like Mrs Bellinger may, having acquired such a certificate, then enter into a valid marriage with a person of the opposite sex to her acquired gender.[62]

(b) Age

Both by canon law and at common law a valid marriage could be contracted only if both parties had reached the legal age of puberty, viz 14 in the case of a boy and 12 in the case of a girl. If either party was under this age when the marriage was contracted, it could be avoided by either of them when that party reached the age of puberty; but if the marriage was ratified (as it would impliedly be by continued cohabitation), it became irrevocably binding.[63]

It is perhaps surprising that this remained the law until well into the twentieth century. In the words of Pearce J:[64]

'According to modern thought it is considered socially and morally wrong that persons of an age, at which we now believe them to be immature and provide for their education, should have the stresses, responsibilities and sexual freedom of marriage and the physical strain of

---

[59] For the effect of this, and its conversion to a full certificate, see below p 90.   [60] Section 9(1).

[61] But not in respect of things done, or events occurring, before the certificate is issued: s 9(2), and the fact that a person's gender has been altered does not affect his or her status as the father or mother of a child: s 11. Thus, a male to female transsexual who had fathered a child outside marriage and had not acquired parental responsibility would not automatically acquire it on becoming a female. See below p 409.

[62] So long as the spouse is aware that she has changed gender: see below p 93. For equivalent provision for civil partners, see below p 99.

[63] Co Litt 79; Blackstone *Commentaries*, i, 436.

[64] *Pugh v Pugh* [1951] P 482 at 492. See further Law Com No 33 *Nullity of Marriage* (1970), paras 16–20; Report of the Latey Committee on the Age of Majority 1967, Cmnd 3342, paras 166–177.

childbirth. Child marriages by common consent are believed to be bad for the participants and bad for the institution of marriage.'

This change of thought led to the passing of the Age of Marriage Act in 1929. Section 1 (now re-enacted in the Marriage Act 1949 s 2) effected two changes in the law. First, it was enacted that a valid marriage could not be contracted unless both parties had reached the age of 16, and secondly any marriage in which either party was under this age was made *void* and not voidable as before.[65] However, the problems identified by Pearce J do not seem to be affected by marriage age—the number of people marrying at a young age has steeply declined, while sexual experience among young people has increased in recent years.[66]

(c) Prohibited degrees

Most, if not all, states prohibit certain marriages as incestuous. The prohibited relationship may arise from consanguinity (ie blood relationship) or from affinity (ie relationship by marriage). Before the Reformation, English law adopted the canon law of consanguinity and affinity,[67] but one of the results of the break with the Roman Catholic Church was the adoption of a modified table of prohibited degrees. Since 1949 the prohibitions have been statutory and are contained in the First Schedule to the Marriage Act, as amended:[68]

PART 1
Adoptive child
Adoptive parent
Child
Former adoptive child
Former adoptive parent
Grandparent
Grandchild
Parent
Parent's sibling[69]
Sibling
Sibling's child

PART 2
Child of former civil partner
Child of former spouse

[65] In Australia, a court may authorise the marriage of a person aged up to two years under the minimum age (18) in 'exceptional and unusual' circumstances: Marriage Act 1961 s 12 (as amended). For discussion of this provision meeting the needs of ethnic minorities, see P Parkinson 'Multiculturalism and the Regulation of Marital Status in Australia' in NV Lowe and G Douglas (eds) *Families across Frontiers* (1996) 309.

[66] The number of women aged 16 to 19 who married in 2003 was 6860, only slightly more than a third of the number (17,738) in 1991. Only 1800 men aged under 20 married in 2003: *Population Trends* 119 (2005) Table 5. 'Almost all' women and men in this age group have their first sexual intercourse outside marriage: Wellings et al *Sexual Behaviour in Britain* (1994) pp 74–5.

[67] See Pollock and Maitland *History of English Law*, ii, 383–7. The rules that emerged lacked theological or sociological justification and 'are the idle ingenuities of men who are amusing themselves by inventing a game of skill which is to be played with neatly drawn tables of affinity and doggerel hexameters': ibid, 387.

[68] Most recently by the Civil Partnership Act 2004 Sch 27 para 17.

[69] Sibling means a brother, sister, half-brother or half-sister: Sch 1, para 1(2), as amended.

Former civil partner of grandparent
Former civil partner of parent
Former spouse of grandparent
Former spouse of parent
Grandchild of former civil partner
Grandchild of former spouse

PART 3
Parent of former spouse
Parent of former civil partner
Former spouse of child
Former civil partner of child

Consanguinity

In the case of consanguinity, prohibition is based on moral and eugenic grounds. Most people view the idea of sexual intercourse (and therefore marriage) between, say, father and daughter or brother and sister with abhorrence; furthermore, the more closely the parties are related, the greater will be the risk of their children inheriting undesirable genetic characteristics. The degrees of relationship based on consanguinity are set out in Part I of the Schedule to the Marriage Act; marriage within these degrees is completely prohibited.[70] Because of the eugenic basis of the prohibition it includes not only relationships traced through the whole blood but also those traced through the half blood,[71] and it is immaterial that the parents of either of the parties (or of any person through whom the relationship is traced) have not been married to each other.[72]

Affinity

In the case of affinity, prohibition was originally based on the theological concept that husband and wife were one flesh, so that marriage with one's sister-in-law was as incestuous as marriage with one's own sister.[73] Today, the justification must be sought on social and moral grounds. (Some will also have religious objections to certain marriages,[74] but in a pluralist society this must be a matter for the individual's conscience.) Marriage with a near relation of a former spouse is liable to create tensions within the family, particularly if the spouse is still alive, and the possibility of marriage to a stepchild could in some cases lead to sexual exploitation. Even if this were not so, difficulties could well arise if, say, a man were to become the brother-in-law of his other stepchildren and the stepbrother-in-law of his own children. There is a stronger reason for forbidding marriage with a stepchild to whom the other party has been in loco parentis, for this can readily be seen as an abuse of the relationship. In circumstances of this sort prohibition could be justified on the ground that the function of the marriage laws is to support the family and the relationships that uphold it. On the other hand, it must be remembered that degrees of

---

[70] Marriage Act 1949 s 1(1). The list relating to relatives between whom sexual intercourse is a criminal offence is now congruent with this Schedule: see Sexual Offences Act 2003 s 64.

[71] See the definitions of 'brother' and 'sister' in the Marriage Act 1949 s 78(1).

[72] *Hains v Jeffell* (1696) 1 Ld Raym 68; *R v Brighton Inhabitants* (1861) 1 B & S 447.

[73] For the same reason in the Middle Ages extra-marital sexual intercourse created prohibited degrees.

[74] See Archbishop of Canterbury's Group, *No Just Cause, The Law of Affinity in England and Wales* (1984) pp 30–2.

affinity can be created only by marriage: there is nothing to prevent a man from cohabiting with his stepdaughter outside marriage or marrying the daughter (by another man) of a woman with whom he has himself been living.[75]

Wide dissatisfaction with the rules relating to affinity resulted in a gradual relaxation of the restrictions, most recently in 1986 by the Marriage (Prohibited Degrees of Relationship) Act, passed after the publication of *No Just Cause*, the report of a group set up by the Archbishop of Canterbury to consider the problem following four private Acts to permit marriage within the prohibited degrees.

The present law represents a compromise between the conflicting principles mentioned above. The remaining prohibited degrees of affinity are divided into two groups, but in neither case is the prohibition absolute. The first group (set out in Part II of the Schedule to the Marriage Act) is retained in order to protect stepchildren against possible exploitation. A person may not marry his or her stepchild or stepgrandchild unless both parties have attained the age of 21 and the latter was not at any time before reaching the age of 18 a 'child of the family' in relation to the other.[76] 'Child of the family' is defined as a child who has lived in the same household as the other and been treated by the latter as a child of his or her family.[77] It will thus be seen that there is nothing to prevent a man from marrying his stepdaughter if, say, she was brought up by her grandparents so that he was never in loco parentis to her. The inclusion of the second group (set out in Part III of the Schedule) is the result of a compromise between those who, like the majority of the Archbishop's group, saw no reason for prohibiting marriage with a son-in-law or daughter-in-law and those who feared that the possibility of such a union might give rise to sexual rivalry between parent and child and thus undermine family relationships. Consequently, a man may not marry his son's wife unless both his son and the son's mother are dead; similarly a woman may not marry her daughter's husband unless both the daughter and the daughter's father are dead. In addition, in either case both parties must be over the age of 21.[78] However, the European Court of Human Rights has held that this restriction is a breach of the right to marry under art 12 of the European Convention on Human Rights, on the basis that, since parties could obtain a private Act of Parliament to circumvent the ban, the ostensible objective of protecting the integrity of the family is not sustainable. The law is therefore currently under review.[79]

(d) Monogamy

As a result of the English view of marriage as a monogamous union, neither party may contract a valid marriage whilst he or she is already married to someone else, or in a civil partnership. If a person has already contracted one marriage, he cannot contract another

---

[75] For an example, see *Smith v Clerical Medical and General Life Assurance Society* [1993] 1 FLR 47.

[76] Marriage (Prohibited Degrees of Relationship) Act 1986 s 1(1); Marriage Act 1949 s 1(2), (3) and Sch 1, Pt II, as amended by Sch 1 to the Act of 1986.

[77] Marriage (Prohibited Degrees of Relationship) Act 1986 s 1(5); Marriage Act 1949 s 78 (as amended). The phrase 'treated as a child of the family' also appears in the definition of 'child of the family' in the Matrimonial Causes Act 1973 and is presumably intended to be interpreted in the same way: see below, pp 288–90.

[78] Marriage (Prohibited Degrees of Relationship) Act 1986 s 1(3), (4); Marriage Act 1949 s 1(4), (5) and Sch 1, Pt III (as amended).

[79] *B and L v United Kingdom (Application No 36546/02)* [2006] 1 FLR 35. See draft Marriage Act 1949 (Remedial) Order 2006.

until the first spouse dies or the first marriage is annulled or dissolved.[80] It follows that a mistaken belief that the first marriage has been terminated, for example, by the death of the spouse,[81] is immaterial: what is relevant is whether it has in fact been terminated. Consequently, the second marriage may be void even though no prosecution for bigamy will lie in respect of it.[82]

2 FORMALITIES OF MARRIAGE

(a) Historical introduction

The history of the English law relating to the formalities of marriage—even the state of the law immediately before the passing of Lord Hardwicke's Act in 1753—is still a matter of considerable doubt.[83] Canon law emphasised the consensual aspect of the contract and before the Council of Trent in 1563 no religious ceremony had to be performed: all that was necessary was a declaration by the parties that they took each other as husband and wife, either by a promise expressed in the present tense—'per verba de praesenti'—(eg 'I take you as my wife [or husband]'), in which case the marriage was binding immediately, or by a promise for the future—'per verba de futuro'—(eg 'I shall take you as my wife [or husband]'), in which case it became binding as soon as it was consummated. But it became customary for the marriage to be solemnised in church after the publishing of banns (unless this was dispensed with by papal or episcopal licence) and with the consent of the parents of either party who was under the age of 21. The marriage would then be contracted at the church door in the presence of the priest, after which the parties would go into the church itself for the celebration of the nuptial mass.

The common law favoured such open ceremony, for upon the existence of the union might depend many property rights and the identity of the heir at law. But in the course of time the reason for the common law's preference for such a marriage was forgotten, and neither the publishing of banns nor the presence of any other witness was any longer considered necessary; the emphasis shifted to the presence of the priest (or, after the Reformation, a clerk in holy orders), so that eventually the rule was laid down that a valid marriage at common law could be contracted only per verba de praesenti exchanged in his presence.[84] The 'clandestine marriage' carried out in secret was thus as binding as if it had been solemnised in church. And even where the couple exchanged vows without the

---

[80] But this does not apply if the first marriage was void: below, p 70.

[81] Or by the grant of a divorce decree which is void, eg Butler v Butler (Queen's Proctor Intervening) [1990] 1 FLR 114; Manchanda v Manchanda [1995] 2 FLR 590, CA.

[82] For the position regarding polygamous marriages celebrated abroad, see below p 75.

[83] See the conflicting opinions expressed in R v Millis (1844) 10 Cl & Fin 534, HL. See Swinburne Spousals; Pollock and Maitland History of English Law ii 362 et seq; the judgment of Sir W Scott in Dalrymple v Dalrymple (1811) 2 Hag Con 54; the opinion of the judges in Beamish v Beamish (1861) 9 HL Cas 274, HL.

[84] R v Millis (1844) 10 Cl & Fin 534, HL. There is little doubt that the decision was based on a misunderstanding of the medieval law: Pollock and Maitland, loc cit. See further Hall 'Common Law Marriage' [1987] CLJ 106 at pp 112 et seq; Lucas 'Common Law Marriage' [1990] CLJ 117. During the Commonwealth, marriages could be celebrated before Justices of the Peace. For the view that the case is authority for the proposition that exchange of vows creates a binding marriage but does not produce the legal consequences of a valid marriage celebrated by a priest, see R Probert, 'The Impact of the Marriage Act of 1753: Was it Really "A Most Cruel Law for the Fair Sex"?' (2005) 38(2) Eighteenth-Century Studies 247, cited by that author in 'Royal privileges and human rights' [2005] CFLQ 000 at n 109.

presence of an ordained priest or deacon, either per verba de praesenti or per verba de futuro with subsequent sexual intercourse, the marriage, whilst not producing all the legal effects of marriage at common law, was still valid for many purposes. Such a union was indissoluble, so that, if either party to it subsequently married another, the later marriage could be annulled.[85]

Reform of the common law

It needs little imagination to picture the problems which resulted from such a state of law. A person who had for years believed himself to be validly married would suddenly find that his marriage was a nullity because of a previous clandestine or irregular union, the existence of which he had never before suspected. Children could marry without their parents' consent, and if the minor was a girl with a large fortune, the common law rule that a wife's property vested in her husband on marriage made her a particularly attractive catch. The 'Fleet' parsons thrived—profligate clergy who traded in clandestine marriages. By the middle of the eighteenth century matters had come to such a pass that there was a danger in certain sections of society that such marriages would become the rule rather than the exception.[86]

It was to stop these abuses that Lord Hardwicke's Act was passed in 1753.[87] The principle underlying this Act was to secure publicity by enacting that no marriage[88] should be valid unless it was solemnised according to the rites of the Church of England in the parish church of the parish in which one of the parties resided, in the presence of a clergyman and two other witnesses. Unless a licence had been obtained, banns had to be published in the parish church of the parish in which each party resided for three Sundays. If either party was under the age of 21, parental consent had to be obtained as well, unless this was impossible to obtain or was unreasonably withheld, in which case the consent of the Lord Chancellor had to be obtained. If these stringent provisions were not observed, the marriage would in the vast majority of cases be void.

Whilst Lord Hardwicke's Act effectively put a stop to clandestine marriages in England, it caused an almost greater social evil. For the new law was so stringent that many couples deliberately evaded it by getting married in Scotland. This was particularly the case when one of the parties was a minor and parental consent was withheld; so that the 70 years following the passing of the Act saw an increasing number of 'Gretna Green' marriages. It was in an attempt to prevent this that the Marriage Act 1823 was passed to replace Lord Hardwicke's Act. A marriage was now to be void only if both parties *knowingly and wilfully* intermarried in any other place than the church wherein the banns might be published, or without the due publication of banns or the obtaining of a licence, or if they *knowingly and wilfully* consented to the solemnisation of the marriage by a person not in holy orders. In all other cases the marriage was to be valid notwithstanding any breach in the prescribed formalities.

This Act remained the principal Act governing the formalities of marriage in England

---

85 *Bunting v Lepingwell* (1585) 4 Co Rep 29a. See Probert op cit.
86 See L Stone *Uncertain Unions: Marriage in England 1660–1753* (1992).
87 S Parker 'The Marriage Act 1753: A Case Study of Family Law-Making' (1987) 1 Int J Law and Fam 133.
88 Marriages according to the usages of the Society of Friends (Quakers) and according to Jewish rites were exempt from the provisions of the Act.

for over 125 years, although it was substantially amended during that time.[89] In particular, the Marriage Act 1836, reflecting the growth of religious toleration in the early years of the nineteenth century, was enacted to deal with the criticism that the law forced Roman Catholics and Protestant dissenters to go through a religious form of marriage which might well be repugnant to them. This Act, together with the Births and Deaths Registration Act 1836, accordingly created superintendent registrars of births, deaths and marriages, who were empowered to issue certificates to marry as an alternative to the publication of banns or the obtaining of a licence. But the real importance of the Act lay in the fact that it permitted marriages to be solemnised in other ways than according to the rites of the Church of England and it enabled places of worship of members of other denominations to be registered for the solemnisation of marriages. It now became lawful for marriages to be celebrated in these 'registered buildings' in accordance with whatever religious ceremony the members wished to adopt, provided that at some stage the parties took each other as husband and wife per verba de praesenti.

Marriage Acts 1949–1994

By 1949 the law relating to the formalities of marriage could be found only by reference to more than 40 statutes, quite apart from the case law which had grown up as the result of their judicial interpretation. The purpose of the Marriage Act 1949 was to consolidate these enactments in one Act.

The 1949 Act has since been amended by a series of Acts.[90] Notably, restrictions governing the place in which the marriage ceremony may be performed have been liberalised,[91] and the reduction of the age of majority to 18 by the Family Law Reform Act 1969 meant that anyone aged 18 or over may now marry without the consent of any other person.[92] Further amendments, such as to permit marriages to take place in one's own home, have been planned,[93] but are yet to be implemented, and these are discussed further below. There are also additional requirements imposed on couples where one is subject to immigration control. Such requirements are intended to restrict the use of marriage (or civil partnership) as a device to facilitate entry into, or remaining in, the United Kingdom.[94]

In addition to laying down the legal requirements relating to the preliminaries to

---

[89] For example, jurisdiction to make an order dispensing with parental consent was extended to county courts and magistrates' courts by the Guardianship of Infants Act 1925 s 9.

[90] The Marriage Act 1949 (Amendment) Act 1954; Marriage Acts Amendment Act 1958; Marriage (Enabling) Act 1960; Marriage (Wales and Monmouthshire) Act 1962; Marriage (Registrar General's Licence) Act 1970; Marriage Act 1983; Marriage (Wales) Act 1986; Marriage (Prohibited Degrees of Relationship) Act 1986; Marriage Act 1994, Marriage Ceremony (Prescribed Words) Act 1996, Immigration and Asylum Act 1999.

[91] The Marriage (Registrar General's Licence) Act 1970 permits a licence to be issued to authorise a marriage anywhere when one of the parties is suffering from a serious illness and cannot be moved; the Marriage Act 1983 permits a certificate to be issued to authorise a marriage of a house-bound or detained person in the place where he or she is confined or detained; and the Marriage Act 1994 permits the solemnisation of civil marriages in premises approved by local authorities.

[92] Section 2(1) implementing the recommendations of the Latey Committee on the Age of Majority 1967, Cmnd 3342.

[93] See General Register Office, *Civil Registration: Vital Change* Cm 5355 (2002); *Civil Registration: Delivering Vital Change* (2003). The government envisaged using the provisions of the Regulatory Reform Act 2001 to amend the law, but decided against this in 2004.

[94] See eg Asylum and Immigration (Treatment of Claimants, etc) Act 2004 ss 19 et seq held in breach of Arts 12, 14 ECHR in *R (Baiai and others) v Secretary of State for the Home Department* [2006] EWHC 823 (Admin), [2006] 2 FCR 131.

marriage and the place and method of solemnisation, the Marriage Acts also regulate the registration of marriages.[95] Proper registration is of extreme importance not only to the parties themselves but also to others (including government departments) who may wish to have evidence of the marriage.

(b) Preliminaries

Marriages of persons under the age of 18

If either party to the marriage is over the age of 16 but under the age of 18, certain persons are normally required to give their express consent to the marriage or are given a power to dissent from it. The purpose of this provision is, of course, to prevent children contracting unwise marriages. Doubtless in 1753 Parliament was primarily concerned to see that property did not get into the hands of undesirable suitors; today the object is to cut down the number of potentially unstable unions.[96]

The law relating to those whose consent is required was extensively changed by the Children Act 1989. Normally it will be that of each parent with parental responsibility and each guardian (if any). Hence an unmarried father cannot withhold consent unless he has acquired parental responsibility by means of being registered as the child's father, a parental responsibility agreement or order.[97] But if a residence or special guardianship order is in force with respect to the child, the consent required is that of the person or persons with whom the child is living or is to live under the order, or each of the special guardians, and not that of parents or guardians.[98] If a care order is in force, the local authority designated in the order must consent *in addition to* parents, guardians or special guardians.[99]

If consent cannot be obtained by reason of absence or inaccessibility, the Registrar General may dispense with it. Alternatively, if the consent is withheld, the consent of the court may be obtained instead. The 'court' for this purpose is the High Court, a county court or a magistrates' court sitting as a 'family proceedings court'.[100]

The Law Commission recommended that the consent requirement be repealed, considering it 'illogical, easily circumvented or surmounted, and of doubtful benefit to the very children whom it is trying to help.'[101] It noted that there has never been a consent requirement in Scotland, yet the divorce rate for teenage marriages there was better than in England and Wales. Given the declining number of teenage marriages, this issue may well wither away.

[95] See Pt IV of the Marriage Act 1949 (as amended) and the Marriage (Registrar General's Licence) Act 1970 s 15. See Law Com No 53 *Report on Solemnisation of Marriage* (1973), Annex, para 104–118 for a critical review of the present law and for suggestions for reform, discussed further below at p 63.

[96] Report of the Latey Committee (above) paras 135–177; J Priest 'Buttressing Marriage' [1982] Fam Law 40 pp 43–5.

[97] See below, pp 409–22. Registration bestows parental responsibility only in respect of registrations after 1 December 2003.

[98] If a residence order was in force immediately before the child reached the age of 16 but is no longer in force, the consent required is that of the person or persons with whom he lived or was to live.

[99] Marriage Act 1949 s 3(1), (1A), and (1B), as amended and added by the Children Act 1989, Schs 12 and 15 and Adoption and Children Act 2002, Sch 3. If the child is a ward of court, the court's consent must be obtained: ibid, s 3(6). No consent is required at all if the child is a widow or widower: s 3(1), (3).

[100] Ibid, s 3(1)(b), (5), as amended. For the meaning of 'family proceedings court', see above, p 16. There is no statutory right of appeal from an order of the court giving or withholding consent: *Re Queskey* [1946] Ch 250.

[101] *Review of Child Law: Guardianship and Custody* (Law Com No 172 (1988) para 7.11).

Giving notice and obtaining authorisation to marry

The rules differentiate between marriages to be performed according to the rites of the Church of England and the rest, be they religious or civil. Civil weddings made up over two-thirds (68%) of weddings in 2003.[102]

Marriages according to the rites of the Church of England

A marriage may be solemnised according to the rites of the Church of England (which includes the Church in Wales)[103] only after the publication of banns or on the authority of a common licence, a special licence or a superintendent registrar's certificate.[104]

Publication of banns. Publishing banns is intended to publicise the proposed marriage (so that, for example, a parent of a person under 18 could declare his dissent and thus render publication of the banns void). They must normally be published in the parish church of the parish in which the parties reside, or if they reside in different parishes, in the parish church of each of the two parishes.[105] If the parties wish to be married in another church or authorised chapel which is the normal place of worship of either of them, banns must be published there as well as in their parish churches.[106]

Banns must be published on three Sundays normally during morning service by a clergyman of the Church of England.[107] The form of words is prescribed by the rubric in the Book of Common Prayer.[108]

Since the purpose of publishing banns would be defeated if the parties could not be identified, they must be referred to by the names by which they are generally known. This will usually be their original Christian names and surname, or in the case of a woman who has been previously married, her married surname;[109] but if a person has assumed some other name by which he is generally known, the banns should be published in that name.[110]

Common licences. Licences dispensing with the necessity of the publication of banns have been granted since the fourteenth century. They are now known as common licences (to distinguish them from special licences granted only by the Archbishop of Canterbury) and may be granted by the bishop of a diocese acting through his chancellor or one of the latter's surrogates.

Unlike the publication of banns, for which no statutory declaration need be made, before a licence may be granted, one of the parties must swear:

(i)   that he or she believes that there is no impediment to the marriage;

---

[102] ONS, *Population Trends 119* (Spring 2005) Table 1.   [103] Marriage Act 1949 s 78(2).
[104] Ibid, s 5.   [105] Ibid, s 6(1).   [106] Ibid, s 6(4), s 72.
[107] Ibid, s 7 and s 9. A clergyman is entitled to a week's notice in writing before he publishes banns: s 8.
[108] Ibid, s 7(2).
[109] Per Sir R Phillimore in *Fendall v Goldsmid* (1877) 2 PD 263, 264. But see *Chipchase v Chipchase* [1942] P 37 for an example of a long-deserted wife going by a name other than her married surname, with a consequent holding that there had been undue publication.
[110] For an example of due publication under an assumed name, see *Dancer v Dancer* [1949] P 147. See also *R v Billinghurst Inhabitants* (1814) 3 M & S 250. For the converse case of an undue publication under the original surname, see *Tooth v Barrow* (1854) 1 Ecc & Ad 371. For undue publication where a false name has been used to conceal a party's identity, see *Small v Small* (1923) 67 Sol Jo 277; *Gompertz v Kensit* (1872) LR 13 Eq 369. But if banns are published in a name by which the party is not known at all, there cannot be a due publication even though there is no intention to deceive.

(ii) that either party has resided for 15 days in the parish or district, or that the church in which the marriage is to take place is the regular place of worship of one of them; and

(iii) if either of them is a minor, that all consents required by the Act have been obtained or dispensed with, or that the court has consented to the marriage, or that there is no person whose consent is required.[111]

Any person seeking to prevent the granting of a licence may enter a caveat stating the ground of his objection. In such a case the licence may not be granted until the caveat is withdrawn or the ecclesiastical judge with jurisdiction has decided that it ought not to obstruct the grant.[112] Such caveats are nowadays rarely entered.

Special licences. A special licence may be granted only by the Archbishop of Canterbury acting through the Master of the Faculties.[113] A special licence differs from any other authorisation to marry according to the rites of the Church of England, in that it may permit the parties to marry at any time and in any place.[114]

Superintendent registrar's certificates. As an alternative to banns, or where a person is house-bound or detained, a marriage may be solemnised on the authority of a super-intendent registrar's certificate.[115]

Marriages to be solemnised otherwise than according to the rites of the Church of England

All marriages other than those celebrated according to the rites of the Church of England may be solemnised only on the authority of a superintendent registrar's certificate or the Registrar General's licence.[116] The certificate corresponds roughly to banns or a common licence, and the Registrar General's licence to a special licence. A third option, the certifi-cate 'with licence', which permitted the parties, on payment of an enhanced fee, to marry after only one clear day's notice, was abolished in 1999, following the government's view that couples needed 'more time to reflect on the nature of the commitment they are entering into and to take up marriage preparation, if they wished to do so.'[117] A more cogent objection to the procedure was that it negated the possibility of publicising the intended marriage and thus prevented any effective challenge to its taking place.

Superintendent registrar's certificate. Written notice of the proposed marriage must be given to the superintendent registrar of the registration district in which the parties have

---

[111] Marriage Act 1949 s 16(1).   [112] Marriage Act 1949 s 16(2).

[113] The office of the Master of the Faculties is performed by the Dean of the Arches.

[114] Marriage Act 1949 s 79(6). The criteria that the Faculty applies include the following: one of the parties can show a genuine and long-standing connection with the church or chapel in which they wish to marry; the parties' families approve of the marriage; the incumbent or minister in charge of the parish in which the parties would be entitled to marry has been consulted; the minister in charge of the church where the service is to be held must have consented. Where, as if often the case, the parties seek a special licence in order to marry in a school or college chapel, one of the parties must have a connection with the institution, either as a member (or former member) of staff or as a pupil or student.

[115] Marriage Act 1949 s 17, s 26(2). See further below.

[116] The Marriage Act 1949 does not expressly so enact, but this is its obvious intention and must be its effect. For arguments to the contrary, see C Barton 'Irregular Marriages' (1973) 89 LQR 181 and J Hall 'Common Law Marriage' [1987] CLJ 106. See also J Thompson 'Irregular Marriages' (1974) 90 LQR 28.

[117] Home Office, *Supporting Families* (1998) para 4.27. Immigration and Asylum Act 1999 s 160.

resided for at least seven days immediately beforehand, or, if they have resided in different districts, then to the superintendent registrar of each district.[118] Each party[119] must give notice and at the same time make a solemn declaration in similar terms to that required for a common licence.[120] The superintendent registrar must then enter the details of the notice in his marriage notice book and display the notice or a copy of it in a conspicuous place in his office for 15 successive days.[121]

As with the granting of a common licence, anyone may enter a caveat against the issue of a certificate. The certificate may not then be issued until either the caveat has been withdrawn or the superintendent registrar or the Registrar General has satisfied himself that it ought not to obstruct the issue of the certificate.[122] If no impediment has been shown and the issue of the certificate has not been forbidden, the superintendent registrar must issue it at the end of the 15 days.[123] The waiting period may be shortened if the Registrar General is satisfied that there are compelling reasons for reducing it because of the exceptional circumstances of the case.[124]

Registrar General's licence. Until 1970 the only way in which a person could be married elsewhere than in a church or authorised chapel, a registered building or a register office was on the authority of a special licence, according to the rites of the Church of England. To overcome this difficulty the Marriage (Registrar General's Licence) Act 1970 was passed to enable the Registrar General to issue a licence authorising the solemnisation of a marriage elsewhere than in a register office, registered building or now, approved premises. But whereas a special licence can serve one of two purposes—to enable a person to marry even though he or she is too ill or infirm to be moved and to permit a wedding to take place for purely social reasons in a church or private chapel where the parties' banns could not be published—the Registrar General's licence is intended to serve only the first. Consequently, its issue is subject to two important limitations. First, the Registrar General must be satisfied that one of the parties is seriously ill and not expected to recover and that he cannot be moved to a place where the marriage could be solemnised under the provisions of the 1949 Act. Secondly, no such marriage may be solemnised according to the rites of the Church of England, for which a special licence may be obtained.[125]

---

[118] Marriage Act 1949 s 27(1). For the matters which the notice must contain, see s 27(3), s 27A, s 27B, and s 27C (as amended). The marriage need not be solemnised in that district, however: Marriage Act 1949 ss 35–6 (as amended by the Marriage Act 1994 s 2).

[119] The requirement that each party give notice in person was introduced by the Immigration and Asylum Act 1999 s 161 and had been proposed by the government in *Supporting Families* (above) loc cit.

[120] Ibid, s 28. The superintendent registrar is entitled to demand written evidence that the consents required have been given if either party is a minor: Family Law Reform Act 1969 s 2(3).

[121] Ibid, s 27(4), s 31(1) as amended by Immigration and Asylum Act 1999 s 160.

[122] Ibid, s 29. A number of caveats were entered to the civil wedding of the Prince of Wales in 2005, on the basis that members of the Royal Family may not marry by a civil ceremony, but were all dismissed by the Registrar General. See R Probert, 'The wedding of the Prince of Wales: royal privileges and human rights' [2005] CFLQ 363. Where the objection is that a consent to the marriage of a child has not been obtained, any person whose consent is required may effectively prevent the marriage by the much simpler means of writing 'forbidden' against the entry in the marriage notice book, in which case the certificate may not be issued unless the consent of the court has been obtained: s 30.

[123] Ibid, s 31(2). Quaere whether he can revoke the certificate before the marriage is solemnised if he discovers some impediment (eg that one party is a minor and parental consent has not been given).

[124] s 31(5A).   [125] Marriage (Registrar General's Licence) Act 1970 s 1.

These provisions were made largely redundant by the Marriage Act 1983 which enables a house-bound person to be married at home or in hospital,[126] but there are still occasions when the Registrar General's licence will be required and about 220 such marriages are performed annually:[127] for example, Quaker and Jewish marriages cannot be solemnised under the 1983 Act, but they can be on the Registrar General's licence. Secondly, the Registrar General's licence may be sought if there is a danger that the party will die within the 15 days before the superintendent registrar's certificate could be issued (although presumably this would constitute a compelling reason for reducing the waiting period). Thirdly, the wording of the statement under the 1983 Act, which the house-bound person's medical practitioner is required to sign before a certificate can be issued, implies that the house-bound person is likely to survive for three months.[128] If this strict interpretation is correct, a person cannot be 'house-bound' if he is expected to die within that period. It seems unfortunate that the 1983 Act was not drafted so as to cover these cases and thus eliminate the need for the Registrar General's licence.

(c) Solemnisation of the marriage

According to the rites of the Church of England

All marriages according to the rites of the Church of England must be solemnised by a clerk in holy orders of that Church in the presence of at least two other witnesses.[129] Except where the marriage is solemnised on the authority of a special licence, it must also be solemnised between 8 am and 6 pm.[130] The marriage must be solemnised within three months of the completion of the publication of the banns, the grant of the licence or twelve months from the entry of notice in the superintendent registrar's marriage notice book, as the case may be.[131]

No clergyman is obliged to solemnise the marriage of a divorced person whose former spouse is still alive; a marriage which would have been void before the passing of the Marriage (Prohibited Degrees of Relationship) Act 1986 because of the relationship of the parties; or a marriage of a person whose gender has become the acquired gender under the Gender Recognition Act 2004. Nor can he be forced to permit such a marriage to be solemnised in the church or chapel of which he is the minister.[132]

---

[126] See below p 62.

[127] General Register Office, *Civil Registration: Delivering Vital Change* (2003) para 3.6.1.

[128] 'It is likely that it will be the case for at least . . . three months . . . that . . . he ought not to move or be moved from [the place where he is].'

[129] Ibid, s 22, s 25. The precise words of the ceremony need not be spoken by the parties and consent may be given by signs, eg in the case of a mute person: *Harrod v Harrod* (1854) 1 K & J 4. The marriage is probably contracted as soon as the parties have taken each other as husband and wife: *Quick v Quick* [1953] VLR 224 (Australia).

[130] Ibid, s 4, s 75(1)(a). The wedding may take place only in one of the churches or chapels in which banns were published, or in the church or chapel specified in the common licence or certificate: s 12(1), s 15 and s 25(a), (d).

[131] Ibid, s 12(2), s 16(3), s 33. In the case of a superintendent registrar's certificate, the period is three months if one of the parties is house-bound or detained, or resident in Scotland or N Ireland: ss 26(1)(dd), 37, 38.

[132] Matrimonial Causes Act 1965 s 8(2); Marriage Act 1949 s 5A (added by the Marriage (Prohibited Degrees of Relationship) Act 1986 s 3 and Gender Recognition Act 2004 Sch 4 para 3).

According to other religious rites

A marriage on the authority of a superintendent registrar's certificate may be solemnised in a registered building; according to the usages of the Society of Friends or of the Jews; or the place where a house-bound or detained person is.[133] In any case the marriage must be solemnised within 12 months of the entry being made in the marriage notice book;[134] and, unless it is a Quaker or Jewish marriage, it must also be solemnised between 8 am and 6 pm, with open doors and in the presence of at least two witnesses in addition to the superintendent registrar and registrar or, alternatively, the registrar or authorised person.[135]

Marriage in a registered building

Any building which is certified as a place of religious worship[136] may be registered by the Registrar General for the solemnisation of marriages.[137] Bradney has suggested that relatively few buildings used by non-Christian faiths are registered, owing, in his view, to the stringent requirements for such registration.[138]

A marriage in a registered building may take place only if there is present a registrar of marriages or an 'authorised person'[139] who will normally be a minister of the particular faith or denomination. The functions of the registrar (or authorised person) are to ensure that certificates have been issued, that the provisions of the Marriage Act relating to the solemnisation are complied with, and to register the marriage. The marriage may be in any form, provided that, at some stage in the ceremony, a declaration is made similar to that required when the marriage is in a register office, and the parties contract the union per verba de praesenti.[140]

Quaker and Jewish marriages

The 1949 Act preserves the right of the Society of Friends to solemnise marriages according to their own usages. Provided that the rules of the Society permit it, a marriage may be contracted in this way even though one or both parties are not members of the Society.[141] The privilege of the Jewish community to celebrate marriages according to their own rites is also preserved. In this case, however, both parties must profess the Jewish religion.[142]

Marriage in naval, military and air force chapels

Part V of the Marriage Act enables certain persons to marry in naval, military and air force chapels certified as such by the Secretary of State for Defence. The purpose of this is to

---

[133] Ibid, s 26(1) (as amended by the Marriage Act 1983 Sch 1 and the Marriage Act 1994 s 1(1)).

[134] Unless one of the parties is house-bound or detained, or resident in Scotland or N Ireland: s 33.

[135] Ibid, s 4, s 44(2), s 45(1), s 45A(2), (3) and s 75(1)(a) (as amended and added by the Marriage Act 1983 Sch 1). The requirement that the marriage must be solemnised with open doors does not apply to the marriage of a house-bound or detained person.

[136] Under the Places of Worship Registration Act 1855.

[137] See the Marriage Act 1949 s 41 and s 42, as amended by the Marriage Acts Amendment Act 1958 s 1(1), and the Marriage (Registration of Buildings) Act 1990 s 1(1). The marriage must normally be solemnised in the registration district in which one of the parties resides: s 34, s 36; but see s 35 for exceptions.

[138] A Bradney 'How not to marry people' [1989] Fam Law 408.

[139] Ibid, s 44(2). A marriage conducted in breach of these requirements is void: *Gereis v Yagoub* [1997] 1 FLR 854; see below, p 73.

[140] Marriage Act 1949 s 44(1), (3).

[141] Ibid, s 47. This privilege was first granted by the Marriage (Society of Friends) Act 1860.

[142] Marriage Act 1949 s 26(1)(d).

enable members of the Forces and their daughters to marry in garrison churches etc. Consequently, before a marriage may be solemnised in such a chapel, at least one of the parties must be a serving or former member of one of the regular armed forces or a child or step-child of such a person.[143]

Civil marriages

Marriage in a register office. The parties may marry in a register office[144] in the presence of the superintendent registrar and also of a registrar of marriages. They must declare that they know of no impediment why they should not be joined in matrimony and then contract the marriage per verba de praesenti.[145] No religious service may be used in a superintendent registrar's office, but, if the parties so wish, the marriage there may be followed by a religious ceremony in a church or chapel.[146] In this case the marriage which is *legally* binding for all purposes is that in the register office.[147] This provision is useful if the parties wish to be married in a private chapel in which banns may not be published (eg the chapel of an Oxford or Cambridge college) without being put to the expense of obtaining a special licence, or in a non-conformist place of worship which is not a registered building.[148]

Marriage in approved premises. The Marriage Act 1994[149] gave effect to some of the proposals the government put forward in a White Paper in 1990, *Registration: proposals for change.*[150] The main reform was to permit local authorities to give approval for certain premises to be used for weddings,[151] so that couples who do not want a religious ceremony may marry in more pleasant surroundings than those at many register offices. Guidance from the Registrar General explains that the Act is intended:

'. . . to allow civil marriages to take place regularly in hotels, stately homes, civil halls and similar premises without compromising the fundamental principle of English marriage law and Parliament's intention to maintain the solemnity of the occasion.'[152]

'Premises' is defined in r 2(1) of the Marriages (Approved Premises) Regulations 1995 as 'a permanently immovable structure comprising at least a room, or any boat or other vessel which is permanently moored.' Marriages may not take place in the open air or on a moving vehicle, nor in a building with a recent or continuing religious connection. Thus, while a wedding could take place in the Brighton Pavilion, it could not be celebrated under

---

[143] Marriage Act 1949 s 68, as amended by the Armed Forces Act 2001, Sch 6.

[144] Which may be in a district other than that where the certificate or licence was issued: Marriage Act 1949 s 35, s 36 (as amended).

[145] Marriage Act 1949, s 45(1), s 44(3). The form of words to be used is: 'I call upon these persons here present to witness that I, *AB*, do take thee, *CD*, to be my lawful wedded wife [or husband].' A Welsh form may be used: s 52. As to marriages of mute persons, see *Harrod v Harrod* (1854) 1 K & J 4.

[146] This may be a religious marriage rite, or, as was the case for the Prince of Wales in 2005, a blessing.

[147] Ibid, s 45(2), s 46.

[148] The addition of 'approved premises' for the performance of weddings does not render this redundant, since such premises may not be used for religious services: Marriage Act 1949 s 46A(4).

[149] See C Barton 'Weddings to Go—the Marriage Act 1994' [1995] Fam Law 153.

[150] Cm 939, following a Green Paper, Cm 531 (1988). On the latter, see A Bradney, 'How not to marry people' [1989] Fam Law 408.

[151] Inserting s 46A into the Marriage Act 1949.

[152] *Guidance in pursuance of s 26(1)(bb) of the Marriage Act 1949*, para 3.

the posts at the Cardiff Millennium Stadium; 'an old ironclad battleship'[153] would be suitable, but the Mersey ferry would not. Perhaps disappointingly, a marriage could not take place in a chapel in a stately home, even if the room is no longer used as such. Weddings at home are not permitted, and the provision of Las Vegas-style wedding chapels is unlikely to satisfy the requirement that the solemnity of the occasion be maintained. Weddings in approved premises accounted for 27% of all weddings in 2003.[154]

Only civil weddings may be performed in approved premises; the marriage must be solemnised in the presence of two witnesses and the superintendent registrar and a registrar of the registration district in which the premises are situated. There must be access to the general public, and each of the parties must make the same declaration and use the same form of words as are used in weddings in registered buildings in the presence of a registrar.[155]

Marriages of house-bound and detained persons

The requirement that the marriage must be solemnised in a register office or a registered building (or now on approved premises) meant that a person could not marry on a superintendent registrar's certificate at all if he was incapable of leaving home or any other building (for example, a hospital or prison) where he happened to be.[156] As we have seen, the position was partly ameliorated by the provisions of the Marriage (Registrar General's Licence) Act 1970, but these apply only to those who are fatally ill. A complaint to the European Commission of Human Rights was made by a prisoner that Art 12 of the European Convention on Human Rights—the right to marry—had been infringed when he was refused permission to leave the prison to get married, and there was no mechanism to enable him to marry inside the prison.[157] As part of a friendly settlement of the case, the government introduced a wider relaxation in the Marriage Act 1983, which enables a house-bound or detained person to be married in the place where he is for the time being.

A house-bound person is defined as one who, owing to illness or disability, ought not to be moved from the place where he is and who is likely to remain in this condition for three months. A detained person is one who is detained in a mental hospital (otherwise than for short periods of assessment) or prison.[158]

The marriage may take place only in the building where the house-bound or detained person is. It may take the form of a civil ceremony or a religious ceremony (including a ceremony according to the rites of the Church of England) but Quaker and Jewish marriages are not covered by the Act.[159] Unless the marriage is solemnised according to the rites of the Church of England (when the service must be taken by a clerk in holy orders), a registrar must be present and, if the ceremony is a purely civil one, the superintendent

---

[153] ONS *First data for marriages at 'approved premises'* ONS (98) 62 (1998).

[154] ONS, *Population Trends* 119 (Spring 2005) Fig 1.

[155] Marriage Act 1949 s 46B inserted by the 1994 Act.

[156] Although it was not uncommon for a prisoner to be released for a short period to enable him to marry.

[157] *Hamer v UK* (1982) 24 D & R 5; see also *Draper v UK* (1980) 24 D & R 72 (European Commission on Human Rights).

[158] Marriage Act 1983 s 1 and Sch 1 (amending the Marriage Act 1949 s 78). If a doctor in charge of a mental patient believes that the patient could not give a valid consent to marry (see below, pp 86–7, 89), he may enter a caveat with the Superintendent Registrar: LAC (84) 9, para 9.

[159] They require a Registrar General's licence: see above p 59.

registrar must be present as well.[160] About 100 such marriages are performed each year.[161]

(d) Proposals for reform of formalities

The present law relating to the formalities of marriage is still in principle based upon the provisions of Lord Hardwicke's Act and the Marriage Act 1836. It thus reflects the desire to prevent the clandestine marriages which were the disgrace of eighteenth-century England. In this respect the law is now hopelessly out of date. Clandestine marriages are no longer the social evil that they were at that time; nor does the modern law effectively prevent them. Provided that both parties are over the age of 18, a marriage can usually be solemnised on a common licence or a superintendent registrar's certificate without the knowledge of the parties' friends or relations. The ease with which people can travel round the country and acquire a new residence makes it virtually impossible for the parents of a determined minor to forbid his marriage before it takes place.

The law has been reviewed several times. A Working Party was set up by the Law Commission and the Registrar General in 1973[162] and the Conservative government produced a White Paper of 1990.[163] The Labour government then produced its proposals in 2002.[164] It originally planned to implement these by means of a 'Regulatory Reform Order'[165] which would have avoided primary legislation but, having been advised by the relevant Parliamentary committees that this was inappropriate, it abandoned this attempt[166] and thorough reform is still awaited, although some of the changes proposed earlier were made by the Immigration and Asylum Act 1999.

The government's major objective was the modernisation of the registration system. It described the effect of the existing system as placing 'severe limitations on the ability of the system of marriage in England and Wales to meet the needs of modern society.' It considered that 'radical change is necessary to remove the current restrictions, together with many of the anomalies that exist between civil and religious marriages, and to provide a more flexible and responsive system of marriage that is better able to meet the needs and expectations of those wishing to marry.'[167]

It therefore proposed a 'celebrant based' system for marriage, with the place and time of the marriage a matter for the parties (and the celebrant). In England, there would be a common system of preliminaries for all couples, regardless of the type of eventual ceremony, thus resulting in the abolition of banns and the common licence (although the

---

[160] Marriage Act 1949 s 17 and s 45A (as amended and added); Marriage Act 1983 s 1(6).

[161] General Register Office, *Civil Registration: Delivering Vital Change* (2003) para 3.5.1.

[162] See Law Com No 53 (*Solemnisation of Marriage*), 1973.

[163] *Registration: proposals for change*, Cm 939, following a Green Paper *Registration: a modern service*, Cm 531 (1988).

[164] ONS, *Civil Registration: Vital Change* Cm 5355 (2002), see C Barton, 'White Paper Weddings—The Beginnings, Muddles and Ends of Wedlock' [2002] Fam Law 431.

[165] General Register Office, *Civil Registration: Delivering Vital Change* (2003). See R Probert, 'Lord Hardwicke's Marriage Act—Vital Change 250 Years On?' [2004] Fam Law 585.

[166] Ministerial Statement, 1 March 2005.

[167] General Register Office, *Civil Registration: Delivering Vital Change* (2003) para 3.1.2. The General Synod of the Church of England conducted a parallel review: *Just Cause or Impediment? A Report from the Review of Aspects of Marriage Law Working Party* (2001) and *The Challenge to Change* (2002). The Church in Wales also reviewed the law. The government's proposals incorporate those of the Anglican churches.

Special Licence would remain). In Wales, however, these would be retained.[168] Couples would be able to give notice of their intention to marry at any register office (or to their local priest in England, in the case of Anglican adherents) rather than, as at present, only at their local office. On giving notice, they would be provided with information about marriage preparation and support services. The information given would be entered on a database which would enable checks on identity, multiple notices being given, etc to be easily made. After the 15-day waiting period, a 'schedule' would be issued to the couple, confirming that the marriage ceremony may proceed.[169] This would be signed by the couple, the celebrant and their witnesses immediately after the ceremony, and returned to the registration service for updating the database. Buildings would no longer need to be approved or registered for the purpose of conducting marriages, so that it would be possible to marry in a private house (or Windsor Castle, for example). Couples having religious ceremonies would no longer be required to marry in their district of residence. The aim would be to extend the current flexibility regarding venue and timing, enjoyed only by Quakers and Jews, to all intending to marry.

While civil ceremonies would remain purely civil and would be celebrated in places with no religious connotation, it would be possible to hold a religious ceremony in some other places, such as hotels. The words of the ceremony would be for the parties (or their religious authorities) to determine, although it would still be necessary at some point to make a declaration (albeit in non-prescribed form) that the parties take each other as husband and wife.

E PRESUMPTION OF MARRIAGE [170]

It has long been established that, if a man and woman cohabit and hold themselves out as husband and wife,[171] this in itself raises a presumption that they are legally married. It is important, however, not to fall into the trap of regarding such a situation as a 'common law marriage'. The presumption of marriage asserts that the parties *are* validly married, albeit that there is a lack of evidence conclusively to show this. By contrast, the phrase 'common law marriage' is frequently used, completely erroneously, to suggest that a couple who plainly never did enter into a marriage (or even intend to marry), have *acquired* the status of marriage through mere cohabitation.[172]

Under the presumption, if the marriage is challenged, the burden lies upon those challenging it to prove that there was in fact no marriage, and not upon those alleging it to prove that it has been solemnised. It might be thought that, in an age where cohabitation is so readily socially accepted, a wish to establish that a marriage had taken place would no longer

---

[168] See para 3.7.71.

[169] In the case of couples marrying in the Church in Wales, the clergy would hold and complete the schedule: para 3.7.116.

[170] See the excellent article by A Borkowski, 'The presumption of marriage' [2002] CFLQ 251.

[171] Borkowski notes that some of the authorities appear to require both cohabitation and 'repute' whilst others focus on cohabitation, but he concludes that, even in such cases, the element of repute was present: ibid p 253. Cf the rule of Scottish common law which recognised 'marriage by cohabitation with habit and repute', abolished by s 3 of the Family Law (Scotland) Act 2006.

[172] See A Barlow et al, 'Just a piece of paper? Marriage and cohabitation' in A Park et al (eds), *British Social Attitudes* (2001) pp 45–6, found 59% of cohabitants believed such status exists.

be of much concern, but on the contrary, it may be important to establish the position where, for example, the parties have been married abroad and have no written or other evidence of the solemnisation, and if the validity of the marriage is called into question where entitlement to immigration, benefits or property depends upon the answer.[173]

Borkowski identifies two forms of the presumption—the first where there is insufficient proof that the parties went through a ceremony of marriage[174] and the second where the parties are proved to have gone through a ceremony but there are doubts as to its validity.[175] Three modern cases have arisen where the presumption has been relied upon, all relating to scenarios of the second type. In *Chief Adjudication Officer v Bath*[176] the respondent had undergone a Sikh marriage ceremony in a temple in London in 1956 and then lived with her 'husband' for 37 years and had two children. On his death, she claimed a widow's pension but the Department for Social Security dismissed her claim on the basis that she had not gone through a ceremony in accordance with the Marriage Act 1949, there being no evidence that the temple had been registered for marriages.[177] The Benefits Agency appealed against the ruling of the Social Security Commissioner that she could rely on the common law presumption of marriage. The Court of Appeal rejected their appeal, confirming the existence of the presumption based on cohabitation for a significant period of time.[178] As Evans LJ put it,[179]

'when the man and woman have cohabited as man and wife for a significant period there is a strong presumption that they have agreed to do so, in proper form. . . . When there is, as there is in England, a legal requirement that the marriage ceremony shall take a certain form, then the presumption operates to show that the proper form was observed, and it can only be displaced by what I would call positive, not merely "clear" evidence. . . . How positive, and how clear, must depend among other things upon the strength of the evidence which gives rise to the presumption—primarily, the length of cohabitation and evidence that the parties regarded themselves and were treated by others as man and wife.'

Here, although the tribunal had found that the temple was not a registered building, this did not, of itself, render the marriage void.[180] As Evans LJ pointed out, to hold that a failure to comply with all the formal requirements of a ceremony prevents reliance on the presumption, yet to permit such reliance in the absence of evidence of the parties having gone through any ceremony at all would be a remarkable and unjust conclusion to draw.[181]

The two other cases both concerned divorce petitions, where the respondent cast doubt on the validity of the marriage in order to seek to frustrate the petitioner's claims. In *Pazpena de Vire v Pazpena de Vire*[182] the petitioner claimed that the parties were married, by proxy, in Uruguay. The respondent claimed that the marriage certificate he had brought back from there was a forgery. But the couple lived together for 35 years, their child's birth certificate showed the petitioner as the respondent's 'wife' and she was granted an Argentine passport on that basis. It was held that the length of cohabitation and the public

---

173 For examples, see *Mahadervan v Mahadervan* [1964] P 233; *Re Spence* [1990] 2 FLR 278.

174 Op cit p 252. He cites eg *Lyle v Ellwood* (1874) LR 19 Eq 98.

175 Eg *Wilkinson v Payne* (1791) 4 Term Rep 468.

176 [2000] 1 FLR 8, CA.   177 See above p 60.

178 Thirty-seven years is obviously a significant length of time, but in *Mahadervan v Mahadervan* [1964] P 233 a six-month period sufficed.

179 [2000] 1 FLR 8, at para 31, CA.   180 See below p 78.   181 At para 32.

182 [2001] 1 FLR 460.

and official recognition of the marriage raised the presumption of marriage which the opposing evidence, including flaws in the drafting of the marriage certificate, was inadequate to rebut. Finally, in *A-M v A-M (Divorce: Jurisdiction: Validity of Marriage)*[183] the parties, both Muslims, went through an Islamic ceremony in a flat in London and were advised that the wedding would not be recognised in English law. In order to regularise the position, they went to Sharjah where the husband attempted to divorce his wife by talaq so that he could then re-marry her in accordance with local law, which would have been recognised as effective in England and Wales. However, the local judge advised him that it was immoral to divorce the wife simply to protect her position in English law and the talaq was revoked. The wife was not told of this. The parties continued to live together for a number of years. It was held that the husband *might* have subsequently organised a second, valid marriage ceremony in the Middle East without telling the wife, and that she could rely on the presumption that a valid marriage existed, raised by the parties' cohabitation and their public reputation of being husband and wife, which could be rebutted only by strong and weighty evidence to the contrary.

The purpose of the presumption seems clearly protective: in former times, and still for members of minority ethnic communities, upholding the validity of a marriage avoids the stigma that would otherwise be attached to mere cohabitation. There are still significant legal advantages, as we shall see,[184] to being married, not the least of which is the availability of the courts' powers on divorce, and where a couple have held themselves out as married,[185] it is desirable to give the benefit of the doubt and the legal protection that follows, to the party, usually economically weaker than the other, who asserts the existence of the marriage.

F ESTABLISHING THE VALIDITY OF THE MARRIAGE

As we have noted above, certain consequences flow from marital status and it may be necessary to establish whether a valid marriage exists in order to take advantage of them. There are two mechanisms, in particular, that may be used to obtain a ruling on this point—the grant of a declaration or of a decree of nullity.

1 DECLARATION AS TO MARITAL STATUS

Section 55 of the Family Law Act 1986 confers a power to make a declaratory order regarding marital status on the High Court and county courts.[186]

---

[183] [2001] 2 FLR 6.   [184] See below Chapters 3 et seq.

[185] Note, however, that in *Pazpena de Vire v Pazpena de Vire* (above) at para 68, the judge considered that a party could not be estopped by his conduct from seeking to rebut the presumption. As regards estoppel per rem judicatam, see the discussion in the 9th edition to this work at pp 102–104.

[186] See also s 63 (meaning of 'court'). These provisions implemented the Law Commission's recommendations in Law Com No 132 (*Report on Declarations in Family Matters*). Previously the power had derived partly from statute (going back to the Legitimacy Declaration Act 1858) and partly from the inherent jurisdiction of the High Court (which was abolished in this respect by s 58(4)). There was also a decree of jactitation of marriage which restrained the respondent from wrongfully boasting or asserting that he or she was

An application may be made for one or more of the following declarations:

(a) that a marriage was at its inception a valid marriage;

(b) that a marriage subsisted, or did not subsist, on a given date;

(c) that a divorce, annulment or legal separation obtained outside England and Wales is, or is not, entitled to recognition in this country.

It will be observed that there is no power to apply for a declaration that a marriage was void ab initio: in this case the correct procedure is to petition for a decree of nullity, when the court may make ancillary orders relating to children and financial relief.[187]

Although a declaration will normally be sought by one of the parties to the marriage, others may be legitimately interested in its validity. For example, the trustees of a pension fund may wish to establish whether a woman is the widow of a former employee. Applications for a declaration may therefore be brought by anyone, but the court must refuse to hear a case if it considers that the applicant does not have a sufficient interest in the outcome of the proceedings.[188] In any event it may refuse to make a declaration if to do so would be manifestly contrary to public policy.[189]

A declaration is a judgment in rem and binds everyone including the Crown (which may be important if, for example, the applicant is seeking British citizenship or claiming the right to live in this country).[190] Consequently, the Attorney-General is to be given notice of an application and may intervene in any proceedings.[191]

The court has jurisdiction only if one of the parties to the marriage is domiciled in England and Wales at the time of the application or has been habitually resident in this country for one year before that date or, alternatively, if one of them is dead and he or she satisfied either of these conditions at the time of his or her death.[192]

2 DECREE OF NULLITY

Whilst a declaration is perhaps more likely to be obtained where it is sought to establish that a valid marriage does subsist, a decree of nullity may be sought in order clearly to establish that the requirements for a valid marriage have *not* been satisfied. This may result in the marriage being held to be either 'void' or 'voidable'. It is necessary to examine the historical background governing the development of this distinction in order to understand its significance.

(a) Historical background

The view of the Roman Catholic church that marriage is a sacrament meant that the law relating to marriage became a part of the canon law, over which the ecclesiastical courts claimed exclusive jurisdiction.[193] This had a profound effect on subsequent legal

---

married to the petitioner. Proceedings for jactitation (which were virtually obsolete) were abolished by s 61 of the 1986 Act. See further, S Cretney, *Family Law in the Twentieth Century: A History* (2003) at 143 n 6.

[187] Family Law Act 1986 s 58(5)(a), (b). See below, Chapters 17 and 18.

[188] Ibid, s 55(3).   [189] Ibid, s 58(1).

[190] Ibid, s 58(2). But no declaration is to affect any judgment or decree already made: s 60(3).

[191] Ibid, s 59 and s 60(2)(c); Family Proceedings Rules 1991 r 3.16(4). Other interested persons may also be required to be made parties: s 60(2)(b).

[192] Ibid, s 55(2).   [193] Pollock and Maitland *History of English Law*, ii, 364–6.

developments. Not only were these courts the only tribunals competent to declare whether the parties were validly married, but the Roman Catholic doctrine of the indissolubility of marriage became a tenet of English law.

Whilst this doctrine precluded the courts from granting decrees of divorce, it did not stop them from declaring that, although the parties had gone through a ceremony of marriage, some impediment prevented their acquiring the status of husband and wife. The same principles were applied by the English ecclesiastical courts after the breach with Rome in the sixteenth century. Such marriages were said to be *void* for, although the parties by going through a ceremony had apparently contracted a marriage, the result of the impediment was that there was never a marriage either in fact or in law. Consequently, the marriage could be formally annulled by a decree of an ecclesiastical court and, even without such a decree, either party was free to contract another union (unless he or she was already married to somebody else). As the marriage was a complete nullity, its validity could also be put in issue by any other person with an interest in so doing, even after the death of one or both of the parties to it. So, for example, after his death, a man's brother might claim his estate on the ground that his marriage had been void, with the result that his children, being illegitimate, could not inherit and his 'widow', never having been married, could not claim dower.[194]

By the beginning of the seventeenth century, however, the royal courts were becoming concerned at the ease with which marriages could be set aside and the issue bastardised. This was more likely to work injustice after the parties' death, when relevant evidence might no longer be available. Accordingly, they cut down the ecclesiastical courts' jurisdiction by forbidding them to annul marriages in certain cases after the death of either party.[195] This had the result of dividing impediments into two kinds: civil and canonical. If the impediment was civil—for example, the fact that one of the parties was married to a third person at the time of the ceremony—the marriage was still void ab initio and its validity could be put in issue by anyone at any time, whether or not the parties were still alive. If the impediment was canonical—for example, the fact that one of the parties was impotent—the validity of the marriage could not be questioned after either party had died. The rule thus developed that such a marriage must be regarded as valid unless it was annulled during the lifetime of both parties. Until that time it had the capacity to be turned into a void marriage: in other words, it was *voidable*. Once a decree of nullity had been pronounced, however, it acted retrospectively and the marriage was then regarded as having been void from the beginning. Consequently, the parties reverted to their pre-marital status and their children were automatically bastardised. The distinction between void and voidable marriages was described by Lord Greene MR:[196]

'A void marriage is one that will be regarded by every court in any case in which the existence of the marriage is in issue as never having taken place and can be so treated by both parties to it without the necessity of any decree annulling it: a voidable marriage is one that will be regarded by every court as a valid subsisting marriage until a decree annulling it has been pronounced by a court of competent jurisdiction.'

---

[194] See p 128 below.
[195] See Jackson *Formation and Annulment of Marriage* (2nd edn, 1969) pp 54–5.
[196] *De Reneville v De Reneville* [1948] P 100 at 111, CA.

After the introduction of judicial divorce in 1857, the voidable marriage came to occupy a position midway between the void marriage and the valid marriage. The annulment of a voidable marriage, like divorce, changes the parties' status by a judicial act, and whatever the theoretical differences between them are, both are means of terminating a marriage that has broken down. Divorce,[197] however, does not act retrospectively; the parties are still regarded as having been husband and wife up to the time when the decree was made absolute. Some of the inconveniences of the retrospective operation of the decree of nullity of a voidable marriage were removed by statute or avoided by the courts: for example, children of the marriage remain legitimate[198] and it has never been possible to set aside transactions carried out on the assumption (valid at the time) that the parties to a voidable marriage were husband and wife.[199] Nevertheless, many anomalies remained and the retrospective effect of the decree was artificial and confusing and 'in truth perpetuated a canonical fiction'.[200]

The law of nullity was reviewed by the Law Commission in 1970.[201] In view of the criticisms that had been levelled against the anomalous nature of the voidable marriage, the Law Commission examined the question whether the concept should be abolished altogether and the grounds for annulling a voidable marriage included amongst the facts from which irretrievable breakdown of the marriage might be inferred as the ground for divorce. They rejected the proposal for three reasons. First, certain Christian denominations and their members draw a clear distinction between the annulment and the dissolution of marriage and would be offended if the distinction were blurred. Secondly, some people, associating divorce with stigma, preferred to keep matters involving no moral blame such as impotence and mental disorder as grounds for nullity.[202] Thirdly, the bar which then applied to divorce within the first three years of marriage was clearly inappropriate to the grounds for nullity.[203] The Law Commission, however, made extensive recommendations with the object of resolving uncertainties and removing anomalies. Effect was given to these by the Nullity of Marriage Act 1971, which to a large extent codified the law of nullity. This Act was in turn repealed and its provisions re-enacted in the Matrimonial Causes Act 1973.

(b) The current distinction between void and voidable marriages

Grounds for annulment

Essentially, a marriage will be *void* if either party lacks capacity to contract it or if the ceremony is formally defective. It was once doubtful whether lack of consent made a

---

[197] See Chapter 6 below.

[198] Originally, Law Reform (Miscellaneous Provisions) Act 1949 s 4 (1), but see now the Matrimonial Causes Act 1973 s 16, discussed below, p 94.

[199] See *Re Eaves* [1940] Ch 109, CA.

[200] Per Lord Goddard CJ in *R v Algar* [1954] 1 QB 279 at 288, CCA.

[201] Law Com No 33, *Nullity of Marriage* (1970).

[202] But this overlooks the fact that moral blame attaches to some of the grounds for nullity (eg pregnancy by another man).

[203] During the ten years 1976–84 there were on average just over 1,000 petitions a year. In the years 1985–90 the average was 567 and in the years 1991–96 the average was 699. It is significant that the large drop in 1985 occurred in the first full year in which it became possible to petition for divorce after one year of marriage. In 2004, there were 492 petitions and 244 decrees absolute. No breakdown is now provided of the grounds relied upon: *Judicial Statistics 2004* (2005) Table 5.5.

marriage void or voidable, but in the case of marriages contracted after 31 July 1971, the 1973 Act specifically provides that this will make them voidable.

With the doubtful exception of lack of consent, the only ground on which a marriage could be voidable after 1929[204] was that one of the parties was impotent. The Matrimonial Causes Act 1937 added four new grounds: the respondent's wilful refusal to consummate the marriage, either party's mental disorder, the respondent's venereal disease, and the respondent wife's pregnancy by another man. Under the 1973 Act, impotence, the four statutory grounds (with some modifications) and lack of consent are grounds on which a marriage is *voidable* and the Gender Recognition Act 2004[205] adds two further grounds relating to cases where one of the parties has undergone gender re-assignment.

Necessity for decree

The vital distinction between a void and a voidable marriage is that the former, being void ab initio, needs no decree to annul it, whilst the latter is in all respects a valid marriage until a decree absolute of nullity is pronounced. Hence, if either party dies before a decree is granted, a voidable marriage must be treated as valid for all purposes and for all time.[206] On the other hand, either party to a *void* marriage may lawfully contract a valid marriage with someone else without having the first marriage formally annulled.

Even though, in respect of a void marriage, a decree of nullity can only be declaratory and cannot effect any change in the parties' status, there may be good reason for obtaining such a decree. First, there may be some doubt whether on the facts or the law applicable the marriage is void: whether, for example, one party was already married or there was a due publication of banns. Secondly, a decree of nullity is a judgment in rem, so that no one may subsequently allege that the marriage is in fact valid. But the most important reason for bringing proceedings is that the court has power on granting a decree to make certain ancillary orders, and a party may therefore present a petition in order, for example, to obtain a property adjustment order or financial provision for herself[207] and any children of the family.[208] As the parties are not married, this is in fact the only way in which the 'wife' may obtain maintenance purely for herself.

Third parties' rights

From what has been said, it follows that third parties must treat a voidable marriage as valid unless a decree has been pronounced. On the other hand, if it is alleged that a marriage is void, any person with an interest in so doing may prove as a question of fact that there has never been a marriage at all. Suppose that property is settled on trust for A for life with remainder to his widow or, if he leaves no widow, to B absolutely. A goes through a ceremony of marriage with W who survives him. Even though the marriage between W and A was voidable, B cannot dispute its validity to prove that W is not A's

---

[204] When the Age of Marriage Act 1929 rendered a marriage void if either party was under the age of 16: see above p 49.

[205] See below p 90.

[206] *Re Roberts* [1978] 3 All ER 225, CA (revocation of will executed before marriage).

[207] See eg *J v S-T (Formerly J) (Transsexual: Ancillary Relief)* [1997] 1 FLR 402, CA, explaining *Whiston v Whiston* [1995] Fam 198, CA.

[208] The powers to order financial provision for children are subject to the restrictions under the Child Support Act 1991, discussed below, pp 947ff. The meaning of 'children of the family' is discussed below, pp 338–40.

widow: but he can show, even after A's death, that the marriage between them was void and that consequently the remainder over to him takes effect, for W, never having been A's wife, cannot now be his widow. But if a decree of nullity had been pronounced before A's death, then, whether the marriage was void or voidable, everyone is bound by it and W may not now assert that she is A's widow. It is easy to imagine other cases in which the validity of a marriage might be impeached: for example, others interested in property might wish to prove that the alleged marriage had not revoked the will of one of the parties to it.[209]

Conversely, it might be in the interest of one of the parties to prove that the marriage was void. Suppose that a testator devises property to W so long as she remains his widow and, if she remarry, to X. W subsequently goes through a ceremony of marriage with K. In the event of a dispute between W and X over the beneficial interest in the property after the ceremony, W clearly succeeds if she can show that the marriage between herself and K is void.[210]

Effect of the decree

If the marriage is void ab initio, the decree does not affect the parties' status at all. In the case of a voidable marriage, effect has been given to the Law Commission's recommendation that to remove the difficulties caused by the retrospective effect of the decree, it should operate to annul the marriage only as respects any time after it had been made absolute and that the marriage should continue to be treated as having existed up to that time.[211]

(c) Petitions

Jurisdiction to grant decrees of nullity (whether the marriage was alleged to be void or voidable) was transferred from the ecclesiastical courts to the new Divorce Court set up by the Matrimonial Causes Act 1857, and was vested in the High Court by the Judicature Act 1873. Divorce county courts now have jurisdiction to hear all petitions.[212]

It was an established practice in the ecclesiastical courts to permit a petition to be presented not only by one of the parties to the marriage but also, in certain circumstances, by third persons as well and it would appear that this is still good law.[213] However, it seems that a third person can no longer petition if the marriage is voidable.[214] So far as void marriages are concerned, there seems to be a confusion between two principles: first, that anyone can show that a marriage is (or was) void in any proceedings in which this is relevant and, secondly, that it is open to the parties to obtain a decree of nullity which, as a

---

[209] See Harrod v Harrod (1854) 1 K & J 4; Re Peete [1952] 2 All ER 599; Re Park's Estate [1954] P 89, and Re Spence [1990] Ch 652, CA.

[210] Allen v Wood (1834) 1 Bing NC 8.

[211] Matrimonial Causes Act 1973 s 16, discussed below, p 94.

[212] Matrimonial and Family Proceedings Act 1984 s 33. See further, above, pp 13ff.

[213] See the Matrimonial Causes Act 1857 s 22, which provided that the Divorce Court should apply the same principles as the ecclesiastical courts had applied. The rule was regarded as good law by Collingwood J in J v J [1953] P 186, by Ormrod J in Kassim v Kassim [1962] P 224 at 234, and by the Law Commission in Law Com No 33 para 87, and Law Com No 48 (Jurisdiction in Matrimonial Causes, 1972), para 50. Its existence is confirmed by implication by the Domicile and Matrimonial Proceedings Act 1973 s 5(3)(c), dealing with the court's jurisdiction after the death of one or both parties.

[214] See Re Roberts [1978] 3 All ER 225 at 227 (per Walton J). This view is supported by the fact that it is now expressly provided by statute that the respondent may raise the petitioner's own conduct as a bar in all such cases: see below, pp 90–2. This scarcely makes sense if the petitioner is not the other spouse.

judgment in rem, binds all the world. There is, however, a fundamental difference between, on the one hand, permitting a third person to prove that a marriage was void in order to establish a claim to one party's estate after his death and, on the other, permitting him to seek a judgment in rem to this effect before or after the death of the two persons involved. Petitions are now rarely, if ever, brought by strangers and it is urged that the power to do so should be abolished.[215]

The rules governing jurisdiction as between the courts of different States are set out in s 5 of the Domicile and Matrimonial Proceedings Act 1973, as amended. This distinguishes between countries governed by the revised Brussels II[216] EC Council Regulation of 27 November 2003, and other States. Under Art 3 of this Regulation, jurisdiction shall lie with the courts of the State:

'(a) in whose territory:
    the spouses are habitually resident, or
    the spouses were last habitually resident, insofar as one of them still resides there, or
    the respondent is habitually resident, or
    in the event of a joint application, either of the spouses is habitually resident, or
    the applicant is habitually resident if he or she resided there for at least a year immediately before the application was made, or
    the applicant is habitually resident if he or she resided there for at least six months immediately before the application was made and is either a national of the Member State in question or, in the case of the United Kingdom and Ireland, has his or her "domicile" there;

(b) of the nationality of both spouses or, in the case of the United Kingdom and Ireland, of the "domicile" of both spouses.

A spouse who is habitually resident in the territory of a Member State or is a national of a Member State, or, in the case of the United Kingdom and Ireland, has his or her "domicile" in the territory of one of the latter Member States, may be sued in another Member State only in accordance with this article.'[217]

Under Art 7, where no court of a Member State has jurisdiction under this article, jurisdiction is determined by the laws of the relevant State. Where a respondent is not habitually resident in, nor a national of a Member State or, in the case of the United Kingdom and Ireland, is not domiciled there, but is a national of a Member State and is habitually resident within the territory of another Member State, he or she may, like the nationals of that State, avail him or herself of the rules of jurisdiction applicable in that State. It is therefore necessary to consider the rules governing jurisdiction as laid down by our domestic law, for those cases not covered by this Regulation.

In such circumstances, the court has jurisdiction if either party is domiciled in England and Wales on the date when proceedings are begun, or either party died before that date, and was domiciled here or had been habitually resident throughout the period of one year

[215] See the Law Commission's view, Law Com No 132 (*Declarations in Family Matters*, 1984), paras 3.29–3.32.
[216] Council Regulation (EC) 2201/2003 concerning jurisdiction and the recognition and enforcement of judgments in matrimonial matters and matters of parental responsibility.
[217] And Arts 4 and 5 (which are derivative of Art 3): see Art 6.

ending with the date of the death. The same rules apply whether the marriage is alleged to be void or voidable and it is immaterial whether the party domiciled or resident here is the petitioner or the respondent.

(d) Decrees

A decree of nullity is made in two stages: the decree nisi followed by the decree absolute.[218] The rules relating to the application for a decree nisi to be made absolute (including the restrictions imposed where children of the family are involved) are exactly the same as they in divorce.[219] The marriage is finally annulled when the decree is made absolute and a party to a voidable marriage may not remarry until then.

3 GROUNDS ON WHICH A MARRIAGE WILL BE VOID

Section 11 of the Matrimonial Causes Act 1973 expressly provides that a marriage celebrated after 31 July 1971 (when the Nullity of Marriage Act 1971 came into force) shall be void only on the grounds there set out.[220] The present grounds can be divided into two: those relating to capacity and those relating to formal requirements, but it is first necessary to consider the question of when the parties' defective actions give rise to a marriage capable of being classed even as 'void'.

(a) A void marriage—or no marriage at all?[221]

A void marriage is strictly speaking a contradiction in terms: to speak of a void marriage is merely a compendious way of saying that, although the parties have been through a ceremony of marriage, they have never acquired the status of husband and wife owing to the presence of some impediment. And if they have never been through a ceremony at all, their union cannot even be termed a void marriage. However, this in turn raises the difficult problem of what form of ceremony will be sufficient to enable the court to grant a decree of nullity. The matter may be of considerable practical importance, because only if the court pronounces a decree does it have power to make orders relating to financial provision for the spouses and the adjustment of their rights in property.[222]

This first reported case where this precise issue was raised is *Gereis v Yagoub*.[223] The parties went through a purported ceremony of marriage at a Coptic Orthodox Church not registered for marriages,[224] the ceremony being conducted by a priest who was not authorised to conduct marriages and without notice of the marriage having been given to the superintendent registrar. In fact the parties had been advised by the priest to go through a

---

[218] Matrimonial Causes Act 1973 s 15.   [219] See below, pp 278, 280–1.

[220] These are all grounds on which a marriage celebrated before that date would be void. In addition, it is probable that lack of consent on the part of one of the parties formerly made a marriage void, in which case a marriage celebrated before 1 August 1971, affected by lack of consent, will remain void. It is also possible that a marriage celebrated before 1 August 1971 was void if one of the parties was divorced and the time for appealing against the decree absolute had not expired: see *Dryden v Dryden* [1973] Fam 217 at 239.

[221] See R Probert, 'When are we married? Void, non-existent and presumed marriages' (2002) 22 Legal Studies 398.

[222] Though it by no means follows that the court will grant ancillary relief following the granting of a nullity decree: see *J v S-T (Formerly J) (Transsexual: Ancillary Relief)* [1997] 1 FLR 402, CA and *Whiston v Whiston* [1995] Fam 198, CA.

[223] [1997] 1 FLR 854.   [224] See above, p 60.

civil ceremony of marriage first, but no civil ceremony was performed. After the church ceremony the parties lived together for nearly a year, but after the breakdown of their relationship the petitioner sought a decree of nullity, which the respondent opposed on the basis that there had not even been a void marriage.

In granting the decree the judge, relying on earlier statements[225] that the ceremony 'must be at least one which will prima facie confer the status of husband and wife', considered that the ceremony in this case 'bore the hallmarks of an ordinary Christian marriage and . . . both parties treated it as such, at least to the extent that they cohabited after it, whereas they had not before, that they had sexual intercourse, which they had not before, and that the respondent had claimed married man's tax allowance, which he had not before'.[226] Moreover, he was satisfied that those who attended the ceremony clearly assumed that they were attending an ordinary Christian marriage. Having found as a fact that both parties were aware of the need to go through some form of ceremony at the civil register office, the judge held that the marriage was void in that both had knowingly and wilfully intermarried in disregard of the formalities required by the Marriage Act 1949.[227]

In reaching this decision the judge accepted that proceedings which were a sham or a charade, such as where the ceremony takes place in a play, could not be regarded as creating any marriage at all, not even a void marriage. Similarly, in these cases where what had happened could not possibly amount to a marriage as, for example, a ceremony of engagement, there could be no marriage at all. The judge also referred to the decision in *R v Bham*[228] in which a prosecution had been brought against the accused for performing a ceremony of marriage contrary to s 75(2)(a) of the Marriage Act 1949. In that case a ceremony of *Nishan* (a potentially polygamous marriage in accordance with Islamic form) was performed in a private house in England between a Muslim man and a 16-year-old English girl who had adopted the Muslim faith. Quashing a conviction for knowingly and wilfully solemnising a marriage, the Court of Criminal Appeal said:[229]

'What, in our judgment, was contemplated by [the Marriage Act] . . . in dealing with marriage and its solemnisation, and that to which alone it applies, was the performing in England of a ceremony in a form known to and recognised by our law as capable of producing, when there performed, a void marriage.'

If this is the correct test, then, as has been pointed out elsewhere,[230] a union between two homosexuals would not qualify even as a void marriage, notwithstanding that s 11(d) of the 1973 Act makes a marriage void on the grounds that the parties are not respectively male and female.[231] Presumably, that provision should be regarded as operating only where there is some genuine doubt as to the gender identity of a party.[232]

Another problem with this approach is that it could lead to injustice in the case of those, particularly members of ethnic minorities, who may go through religious ceremonies even

---

[225] Such as that of Humphreys J in *R v Mohamed (Ali)* (1943) [1964] 2 QB 350n, cited by Thompson J in *R v Bham* [1966] 1 QB 159 at 169B, CCA.

[226] [1997] 1 FLR 854, at 858.

[227] And therefore within the Matrimonial Causes Act 1973 s 11(a)(iii): see below at pp 76–8.

[228] [1966] 1 QB 159.   [229] At 169.

[230] See R Bailey-Harris [1997] Fam Law at 476.   [231] Discussed above, pp 45–8.

[232] In the classic case of transsexuals. See *J v S-T (Formerly J) (Transsexual: Ancillary Relief)* [1997] 1 FLR 402, CA and its subsequent litigation: *J v C (Void Marriage: Status of Children)* [2006] EWCA Civ 551— 'marriage' of two persons of same sex no marriage at all.

in private houses[233] under the misapprehension that they are thereby contracting a legally recognised marriage. It is submitted that in deciding whether to grant a decree, some regard should be paid to the parties' belief that they were contracting a legally valid marriage: only if both knew that the ceremony could not make them husband and wife by English law should they be in the same position as a couple who cohabit without going through any ceremony at all.[234]

(b) Lack of capacity

Obviously lack of capacity to marry, which was discussed above,[235] will ipso facto make the marriage void. If the relevant law is English, the marriage will be void on the following grounds:

(a) That the parties are related within the prohibited degrees of consanguinity or, if the conditions set out in the Marriage Act 1949 are not observed, within the prohibited degrees of affinity.[236]

(b) That either of them is under the age of 16.[237]

(c) That either of them is already married or a civil partner.[238]

(d) That they are not respectively male and female.[239]

(e) That either party to a polygamous marriage celebrated abroad was at the time of the ceremony domiciled in England and Wales.[240] This is subject to the overriding principle that a foreign rule of law must be applied instead of the English rule when the conflict of laws so requires.[241] Consequently, if the proper law to apply is that of the proposed matrimonial home, the marriage may still be valid notwithstanding that one of the parties is domiciled in this country.[242]

(c) Formal defects

Whether failure to comply with the formal requirements relating to the marriage ceremony will make the marriage void must be determined by reference to the lex loci celebrationis.[243]

If the marriage is solemnised in England and Wales, not every defect in the formalities set out in the Marriage Act will render the ceremony a nullity. Whilst public policy requires that these formalities should be strictly observed, the consequences of avoiding any marriage where there was some technical defect, however slight, would be socially even more undesirable. English law has reached a compromise between these conflicting demands of public policy in that some formal defects will not render the marriage void at

---

[233] See eg *A-M v A-M (Divorce: Jurisdiction: Validity of Marriage)* [2001] 2 FLR 6 discussed above at p 66. This will become particularly important if the government's proposals to permit weddings in private houses are enacted.

[234] And even there, as we have seen, the presumption of marriage may give protection. See above pp 64–6.

[235] At pp 45–52.

[236] Matrimonial Causes Act 1973 s 11(a)(i),(iii).   [237] Section 11(a)(ii).

[238] Section 11(b) as amended by Civil Partnership Act 2004 Sch 27 para 40. See, for example, *Whiston v Whiston* [1995] Fam 198, CA.

[239] Section 11(c). See above p 48 for the effects of the Gender Recognition Act 2004.

[240] Section 11(d).   [241] Matrimonial Causes Act 1973 s 14 (1).

[242] See *Radwan v Radwan (No 2)* [1973] Fam 35.   [243] See above, p 45 n 43.

all, whilst in the case of the rest the marriage will be void only if *both* parties contracted it with knowledge of the defect. In other words, it is impossible for a person in England and Wales innocently to contract a marriage which is void because of a formal defect. The real sanction is afforded by the criminal law, for if a party knowingly fails to comply with the Marriage Act, he or she will frequently have to make a false oath or declaration and thus commit perjury.[244] This should adequately safeguard the marriage law without prejudicing the position of the innocent spouse.

Defects which will never invalidate a marriage

The Marriage Act 1949 specifically enacts that a marriage shall *not* be rendered void on any of the following grounds:[245]

(a) that any of the statutory residence requirements was not fulfilled (whether for the purpose of the publication of banns or of obtaining a common licence or super-intendent registrar's certificate);

(b) that the necessary consents had not been given in the case of the marriage of a minor by common licence or a superintendent registrar's certificate;[246]

(c) that the registered building in which the parties were married had not been certified as a place of religious worship or was not the usual place or worship of either of them; or

(d) that an incorrect declaration had been made in order to obtain permission to marry in a registered building in a registration district in which neither party resided on the ground that there was not there a building in which marriages were solemnised according to the rites of the religious belief which one of them professed.

Although these are the only formal defects specifically stated not to invalidate a marriage, it is a general rule that, if the irregularity is not one which the Act expressly states may invalidate it, the defect will never make the ceremony a nullity.[247] Hence, for example, even though the parties are aware that two witnesses are not present at the ceremony, the marriage will still be perfectly valid.[248]

Defects which may invalidate a marriage

Only in the following cases will a failure to comply with the provisions of the Marriage Act

---

[244] See the Perjury Act 1911 s 3, and the discussion in *J v S-T (Formerly J) (Transsexual: Ancillary Relief)* [1997] 1 FLR 402 at 425–6, per Ward LJ. If a material alteration is made to any document (eg the date on a superintendent registrar's certificate), this will be punishable under the Forgery Act 1913. See also the Marriage Act 1949 s 75, and the Marriage (Registrar General's Licence) Act 1970 s 16 (punishment of offences relating to the solemnisation of marriages).

[245] Section 24 and s 48. See also s 47(3) (authorisation of marriage according to the usages of the Society of Friends), s 71 (evidence of marriages in naval, military and air force chapels) and s 72 (usual place of worship), and the Marriage (Registrar General's Licence) Act 1970 s 12 (marriages solemnised on the Registrar General's licence).

[246] The Act refers to consents only where the parties are married on the authority of a superintendent registrar's certificate, but the same is true where they are married by common licence: *R v Birmingham Inhabitants* (1828) 8 B & C 29.

[247] *Campbell v Corley* (1856) 28 LTOS 109.

[248] *Campbell v Corley* (above); *Wing v Taylor* (1861) 2 Sw & Tr 278.

make the marriage void, and then only if *both* parties were aware of the irregularity at the time of the ceremony.[249]

Marriage according to the rites of the Church of England. In the case of a marriage according to the rites of the Church of England (otherwise than by special licence), the following come within the rule:[250]

(a) That (except in the case of the marriage of a house-bound or detained person) the marriage was solemnised in a place other than a church or chapel in which banns may be published.

(b) That banns had not been duly published, a common licence obtained or a superintendent registrar's certificate duly issued.

(c) That, in the case of the marriage of a child by banns, a person entitled to do so had publicly dissented from the marriage at the time of the publication of the banns.[251]

(d) That more than three months had elapsed from the completion of the publication of the banns, the grant of a common licence or more than 12 months[252] since the entry of the notice of marriage in the superintendent registrar's marriage notice book, as the case may be.

(e) That, in the case of a marriage by superintendent registrar's certificate, the ceremony was performed in a place other than the church, chapel or other building specified in the notice of marriage and certificate.

(f) That the marriage was solemnised by a person who was not in Holy Orders.

Other marriages. In the case of other marriages, the following come within the rule:[253]

(a) That due notice of marriage had not been given to the superintendent registrar.[254]

(b) That a certificate had not been duly issued.

(c) That more than 12 months[255] had elapsed since the entry of the notice in the superintendent registrar's marriage notice book.

---

[249] The Act speaks of 'knowingly and wilfully' intermarrying, and it is not clear whether it is sufficient that both parties should know as a question of fact that the formality is not complied with or whether in addition they must know as a question of law that the defect will invalidate the marriage. The point was left open by Lord Penzance in *Greaves v Greaves* (1872) LR 2 P & D 423 at 424–5. The former construction seems the more natural, even though its adoption would have the effect of invalidating more marriages. The issue was not adverted to in *Gereis v Yagoub* [1997] 1 FLR 854, discussed above, p 73.

[250] Marriage Act 1949 s 25 (as amended by the Marriage Act 1983 Sch 1).

[251] Contrast the position where the marriage of a child is by common licence or a superintendent registrar's certificate: see above.

[252] Three months if one of the parties is house-bound or detained, or resident in Scotland or N Ireland: Marriage Act 1949 ss 26(1)(dd), 37, 38.

[253] Marriage Act 1949 s 49 (as amended). The same rules apply if the marriage is solemnised on the authority of the Registrar General's licence: Marriage (Registrar General's Licence) Act 1970 s 13. In particular, such a marriage will be void if the parties knowingly and wilfully intermarry more than one month after the entry of notice.

[254] In the due form. Lack of notice to the superintendent register was relied upon in *Gereis v Yagoub* [1997] 1 FLR 854. Notice in a false name does not invalidate the notice or the marriage: see above.

[255] Three months if one of the parties is house-bound or detained, or resident in Scotland or N Ireland: Marriage Act 1949 ss 26(1)(dd), 37, 38.

   (d) That the marriage was not solemnised in the building specified in the notice and certificate.

   (e) That in the case of a marriage on approved premises the marriage was solemnised on premises that were not approved.

   (f) That the marriage was solemnised in the absence of a superintendent registrar or registrar or (if it was solemnised in a registered building or on approved premises) in the absence of a registrar or authorised person or (in the case of the marriage of a house-bound or detained person) in the absence of a superintendent registrar or registrar whose presence was required.

(d) Proposals for reform

The present rule that a marriage will not be void on the ground of a formal defect unless both parties were aware of it has the advantage that it is impossible for a party mistakenly to contract such a marriage. It also produces uncertainty, however. If there has been some irregularity which could invalidate the marriage, dishonest parties may have the option of deciding whether it is to be regarded as valid or void, for it may be extremely difficult to disprove whatever evidence they give about their knowledge or lack of knowledge of the defect at the time of the ceremony. Similar uncertainty could surround the validity of the marriage of the scrupulous 'for most people have no difficulty in sincerely convincing themselves that what they would like to have occurred is what in fact occurred'.[256] Consequently, the Law Commission concluded that the test of whether a marriage is void on the ground of formal irregularity should be objective and not depend on the parties' knowledge or complicity.[257]

4 VOIDABLE MARRIAGES

The six grounds on which a marriage celebrated after 31 July 1971 will be voidable are set out in s 12 of the Matrimonial Causes Act 1973.[258] Five of these grounds are, with two slight modifications, the same as those which existed before 1 August 1971. The remaining ground—lack of consent—probably made the marriage void before that date.[259] If this was the effect of lack of consent, marriages affected by it and celebrated before 1 August 1971 will still be void.

(a) The unconsummated marriage

Even in canon law a marriage was not always finally and irrevocably indissoluble if it had not been consummated by the sexual act. If at the time of the ceremony either spouse was incapable of consummating it, he or she was regarded as lacking the physical capacity (as distinct from the legal capacity) to contract a valid marriage, and the union could therefore be annulled. If, on the other hand, the marriage remained unconsummated because of one party's refusal to have sexual intercourse, canon law

---

[256] Law Com No 53 *Report on Solemnisation of Marriage in England and Wales* (1973), Annex, para 121.
[257] See further, ibid, paras 121–133.
[258] Re-enacting the Nullity of Marriage Act 1971 s 2, which came into force on 1 August 1971.
[259] For a full discussion of the problem, see the 4th edition of this book, at pp 79–83.

offered no relief, because the ground of complaint was conduct following the ceremony.[260] Despite this, decrees were probably in fact given in some cases in reliance on the presumption that, if the marriage had not been consummated after three years' cohabitation through no fault of the petitioner, the respondent must be impotent.[261] The law was put on a more rational footing by the Matrimonial Causes Act 1937, which enacted that a marriage should be voidable if it had not been consummated owing to the respondent's wilful refusal to do so. This was frequently criticised because it offended against the principle that an impediment avoiding a marriage should exist at the time of the ceremony. The Law Commission, however, recommended that it should remain a ground for nullity; the most cogent reason they advanced was that the petitioner is often uncertain whether failure to consummate is due to the respondent's impotence or wilful refusal, and in practice will then plead both grounds in the alternative. Notwithstanding this practical justification, the whole concept seems artificial. The petitioner's real complaint is that he (or she) is being deprived of normal sexual relations because of the respondent's impotence or conduct.[262] If intercourse takes place once (perhaps after great delay and difficulty), the petitioner's power to petition for nullity disappears and his or her sole remedy lies in divorce if the respondent is unable or unwilling to have further sexual relations.

It must be emphasised that non-consummation as such does not make a marriage voidable. There are two separate grounds on which a party may petition: that the marriage has not been consummated owing to the incapacity of either party to consummate it, or that it has not been consummated owing to the respondent's wilful refusal to do so.[263]

Meaning of consummation

A marriage is said to be consummated as soon as the parties have sexual intercourse after the solemnisation.[264] The distinction between the act of intercourse and the possibility of that act resulting in the birth of a child must be kept clear: once the parties have had intercourse the marriage is consummated even though one or both are infertile.[265] If this were not so, the marriage could never be consummated if, for example, the wife were beyond the age of child-bearing. Conversely, if the spouses have not had intercourse, the birth of a child as the result of fecundation ab extra or artificial insemination or other methods of assisted reproduction will not amount to consummation.[266]

To amount to consummation, the intercourse must, in the words of Dr Lushington in *D-E v A-G*[267] be 'ordinary and complete, and not partial and imperfect'. Hence, as in *D-E v A-G*, there will be no consummation if the husband does not achieve full penetration in

[260] *Napier v Napier* [1915] P 184, CA.

[261] *G v M* (1885) 10 App Cas 171, HL, at 189–90; cf *SY v SY (otherwise W)* [1963] P 162 at 171, CA. The petitioner did not have to rely on this presumption and could always allege impotence during the first three years of marriage.

[262] For discussion of the significance of sexual conduct within family relationships, see C Barton, 'Sex and the Family' [2005] Fam Law 628.

[263] Matrimonial Causes Act 1973 s 12(a), (b).

[264] Not before the solemnisation. Hence the marriage is not consummated by reason of the fact that the parties have had pre-marital intercourse: see *Dredge v Dredge* [1947] 1 All ER 29.

[265] *D-E v A-G* (1845) 1 Rob Eccl 279; *Baxter v Baxter* [1948] AC 274, HL.

[266] See *Clarke v Clarke* [1943] 2 All ER 540; *L v L* [1949] P 211.   [267] Above at n 265.

the normal sense. The necessity of complete intercourse has raised difficulties where the spouses use some form of contraception. In *Baxter v Baxter*,[268] however, the House of Lords held that the marriage had been consummated notwithstanding the husband's use of a condom. As Lord Jowitt LC pointed out, the possibility of conception is irrelevant to the question of consummation, and when Parliament passed the Matrimonial Causes Act in 1937 (the statute on which the petition was based) it was common knowledge that many people, especially young married couples, used contraceptives and that in common parlance this would amount to consummation.[269] The House of Lords deliberately left open the question whether coitus interruptus would amount to consummation,[270] but it has since been held at first instance that it does.[271] It has also been held that a marriage is consummated even though the husband is physically incapable of ejaculation after penetration,[272] but not if he is incapable of sustaining an erection for more than a very short period of time after penetration.[273]

Inability to consummate

A marriage is voidable if it has not been consummated owing to the incapacity of either party to consummate it.[274] Inability to consummate may be due to physiological or psychological causes and may be either general or merely as regards the particular spouse.[275] As s 12(a) enacts the common law rule that a petitioner may show that the marriage has not been consummated because of *either* spouse's incapacity, petitions can be based on the petitioner's own impotence.[276] This follows from the premise that one of the objects in giving relief when the marriage cannot be consummated is to prevent the formation of an adulterous union[277] and the recognition of the fact that a spouse may be impotent as regards the other spouse, but be perfectly capable of having normal sexual intercourse with others.[278]

At common law it was said that relief would be granted only if the impotence was incurable, and the term 'incapacity' presumably still imports this element. In this context, however, 'incurable' has received an extended meaning and impotence will be considered incurable not only if it is wholly incapable of any remedy, but also if it can be cured only by an operation attended by danger or, in any event, if it is improbable that the operation will be successful or the party refuses to undergo it.[279] But where petitioners rely upon

---

[268] [1948] AC 274, HL, overruling in this respect *Cowen v Cowen* [1946] P 36, CA.   [269] At 286.

[270] At 283.

[271] *White v White* [1948] P 330; *Cackett v Cackett* [1950] P 253. But the contrary was held in *Grimes v Grimes* [1948] P 323.

[272] *R v R* [1952] 1 All ER 1194.

[273] *W (otherwise K) v W* [1967] 3 All ER 178n. Note also that there can be consummation even though the wife's vagina has been artificially extended: *SY v SY (otherwise W)* [1963] P 37, CA (or, presumably, now that change of gender can be legally recognised, where it has been wholly constructed).

[274] Matrimonial Causes Act 1973 s 12(a).

[275] Impotence from psychological causes must amount to invincible repugnance and not merely unwillingness or reluctance: *Singh v Singh* [1971] P 226, CA.

[276] This rule was finally established in *Harthan v Harthan* [1949] P 115, CA.

[277] See *D-E v A-G*, above, at 299.

[278] See *C v C* [1921] P 399. Hence, if each is impotent as regards the other, either may petition: *G v G* [1912] P 173.

[279] *S v S (otherwise C)* [1956] P 1 at 11; *M v M* [1957] P 139; cf *L v L* (1882) 7 PD 16; *G v G* (1908) 25 TLR 328.

their own impotence, it is submitted that the court might well take the view that they should not be allowed to complain of the situation if the impediment could be removed without danger.[280]

The petitioner's knowledge of the respondent's impotence before marriage is not necessarily a bar to the petition,[281] although if he or she knew that impotence was a ground for nullity, marrying the respondent in the circumstances might amount to such conduct as would entitle the latter to invoke the statutory bar under s 13 of the 1973 Act.[282]

At common law impotence was a ground for avoiding the marriage only if it existed at the time of the solemnisation and there was still no practical possibility of the marriage being consummated at the date of the hearing.[283] Consequently, if a party was capable of having sexual intercourse at the time of the ceremony but became impotent before the marriage was consummated (for example, as the result of an injury), it is doubtful whether a petition for nullity could have succeeded. The Act, however, makes no reference to incapacity at the time of the marriage, and it therefore seems that a petition could succeed in these circumstances.

Wilful refusal to consummate

A marriage will be voidable if it has not been consummated owing to the *respondent's* wilful refusal to do so.[284] As the petitioner is complaining of marital misconduct, he or she may not of course rely on his or her own refusal. Wilful refusal connotes 'a settled and definite decision come to without just excuse', and the whole history of the marriage must be looked at.[285] In *Kaur v Singh*[286] where the parties, who were both Sikhs, married in a register office on the understanding that they should not cohabit until they had gone through a religious ceremony of marriage in a Sikh temple, it was held that in the circumstances the husband's refusal without excuse to make arrangements for such a ceremony amounted to wilful refusal to consummate the marriage.

Refusal to have intercourse in any form will clearly come within the statute, and so may wilful refusal to take treatment (attended by no danger) to remove a physical or psychological impediment to consummation.[287] If there has been no opportunity to consummate

---

[280] A wilful refusal to take treatment in such a case might amount to wilful refusal to consummate the marriage: *S v S (otherwise C)* above at 15–16.

[281] *Nash v Nash* [1940] P 60 at 64–5; *J v J* [1947] P 158 at 163, CA at 44 (overruled on another point by *Baxter v Baxter*, above).

[282] See below, p 93.

[283] *Napier v Napier* [1915] P 184, CA; *S v S (otherwise W)* [1963] P 162, [1962] 2 All ER 816, CA, approving *S v S (otherwise C)* [1956] P 1, [1954] 3 All ER 736. For if the party is cured or curable at the time of the hearing, he or she could not have been incurably incapable at the time of the solemnisation. In Scotland, it has been held that the party must have been incurable at all times since the solemnisation: *M v W* 1966 SLT 25. This is a logical extension of the rule.

[284] Matrimonial Causes Act 1973 s 12(b).

[285] Per Lord Jowitt LC in *Horton v Horton* [1947] 2 All ER 871, HL at 874. He left open the question whether the petitioner could succeed if he had originally refused to consummate but then changed his mind, by which time the respondent had changed her mind and refused to let the petitioner have intercourse; cf *Potter v Potter* (1975) 5 Fam Law 161, CA (husband's refusal due to loss of sexual ardour for wife in similar circumstances not wilful).

[286] [1972] 1 All ER 292, CA, following *Jodla v Jodla* [1960] 1 All ER 625. See also *A v J* [1989] 1 FLR 110 (wife's decision to postpone indefinitely a religious ceremony was found to be 'adamant and uncompromising').

[287] *S v S (otherwise C)* [1956] P 1 at 15–16.

the marriage (for example, because one party is in prison), an indication by one of them that he will not consummate it at any time in the future has been held to entitle the other to petition forthwith: the latter is not bound to wait to see whether the respondent changes his mind when the opportunity arises.[288] It cannot be a wilful refusal to consummate for one spouse to insist upon the use of contraceptives or, probably, of coitus interruptus.

Once the marriage has been consummated, it will not be voidable if one spouse subsequently refuses to continue to have intercourse. In these circumstances, as in the case of the use of contraceptives or the practice of coitus interruptus against the other spouse's will, the latter's only remedy lies in divorce.

(b) Lack of consent

Section 12(c) of the Matrimonial Causes Act 1973 provides that a marriage shall be voidable if either party did not validly consent to it, whether in consequence of duress, mistake, unsoundness of mind or otherwise. As has already been pointed out,[289] lack of consent probably made the marriage void at common law. The reason for making such a marriage voidable is that the parties themselves may wish to ratify it when true consent can be given and consequently third parties should not be able to impeach it.[290]

It will be seen that the petitioner may rely on the fact that the respondent did not consent to the marriage even though the petitioner himself was responsible for this state of affairs, for example by inducing a mistake or uttering threats. Whilst this logically followed when lack of consent made the marriage void, it may leave a respondent who wishes to adopt the marriage with a legitimate sense of grievance in such circumstances. Nevertheless, he or she will have no defence to the petition unless he or she can plead one of the statutory bars.[291]

We must now consider what facts will be regarded in law as vitiating consent.

Duress

If, owing to fear or threats, one of the parties is induced to enter into a marriage which, in the absence of compulsion, he or she would never have contracted, the marriage will be voidable.

The fear may be due to a number of causes. In *Buckland v Buckland*,[292] for example, the petitioner, a youth aged 20 resident in Malta, was groundlessly charged with defiling the respondent, a girl of 15. Although he protested his innocence, he was twice advised that he

---

[288] *Ford v Ford* [1987] Fam Law 232. The result is socially desirable, but it is difficult to see how the respondent's conduct comes within the wording of the Act (the marriage *has not been* consummated, not *will not* be consummated).

[289] See above, p 78.

[290] See Law Com No 33, paras 11–15. Cf. Marriage (Scotland) Act 1977 s 20A (inserted by s 2 Family Law (Scotland) Act 2006) codifies the Scots common law rule that the marriage is void where a party gave consent by duress or error, or was incapable of understanding the nature of marriage.

[291] See below, pp 90ff.

[292] [1968] P 296. See also *Scott v Sebright* (1886) 12 PD 21 (threats to make petitioner bankrupt, to denounce her and finally to shoot her); *Griffith v Griffith* [1944] IR 35 (fear of prosecution for unlawful carnal knowledge); S Poulter 'The Definition of Marriage in English Law' (1979) 42 MLR 409 at 410–18. All the earlier cases are collected and exhaustively discussed by A Manchester 'Marriage or Prison: the Case of the Reluctant Bridegroom' (1966) 29 MLR 622.

stood no chance of an acquittal but would probably be sent to prison for a period of up to two years unless he married her. He did so and it was held that he was entitled to a decree of nullity. Nor is it necessary that the fear should have been inspired by any acts on the other party's part. A striking example is to be seen in *Szechter v Szechter*.[293] The petitioner was a Polish national who had been arrested by the security police in Warsaw. After 14 months' interrogation and detention in appalling conditions she was sentenced to three years' imprisonment for 'anti-state activities'. Her health, which had always been poor, deteriorated rapidly and she came to the conclusion that she would not survive the sentence; if she did come out of prison alive, she believed that she was likely to be re-arrested and in any case would be unable to get any job other than one of a menial nature. The respondent was a distinguished Polish historian of Jewish origin whose presence in Poland was something of an embarrassment to the authorities and whom they were prepared to allow to emigrate. In order to effect the petitioner's release he divorced his wife and went through a ceremony of marriage with the petitioner in prison. The scheme was successful, and eventually all the parties reached England, where the petitioner brought proceedings for nullity so that the respondent and his first wife could remarry. A decree was granted. In so doing Simon P applied the following test:[294]

'It is, in my view, insufficient to invalidate an otherwise good marriage that a party has entered into it in order to escape from a disagreeable situation, such as penury or social degradation. In order for the impediment of duress to vitiate an otherwise valid marriage, it must, in my judgment, be proved that the will of one of the parties thereto has been overborne by genuine and reasonably held fear caused by threat of immediate danger (for which the party is not himself responsible), to life, limb or liberty, so that the constraint destroys the reality of consent to ordinary wedlock.'

There may be rare cases where the party is so terrified that he (or she) does not know what he is doing at all: a marriage contracted in such circumstances must be voidable as there is no consent whatever. In other cases the reference to the party's will being overborne has been criticised on the ground that she does in fact consciously choose to enter into marriage rather than accept the alternative presented to her.[295] The court must then decide whether the circumstances were such that it would be socially more objectionable to tie the party to the union than to permit her to repudiate it: the need to uphold the institution of marriage must be balanced against the need to do justice to the individual. This must depend on what she perceived to be the probable consequences of refusing to enter into the marriage and her capacity to resist the pressure brought to bear on her. If she is more susceptible to this pressure than another might be, the marriage should still be annulled, even though a person of ordinary courage and resilience would not have yielded to it.[296]

Applying this test, it may be doubted whether the three limitations which Simon P placed upon the operation of duress as a ground for nullity are desirable or supported by earlier authorities. First, if the condition that the fear must be reasonably held means that

---

[293] [1971] P 286. See also *H v H* [1954] P 258 (marriage contracted in Budapest to enable woman to escape from Hungary where she was likely to be sent to prison or concentration camp); *Parojcic v Parojcic* [1959] 1 All ER 1 (fear imposed by petitioner's father).

[294] At 297–8.   [295] Ingman and Grant 'Duress in the Law of Nullity' [1984] Fam Law 92.

[296] *Scott v Sebright* (1886) 12 PD 21 at 24; *Cooper v Crane* [1891] P 369 at 376.

the marriage will be voidable only if a reasonable person, placed in the position of the petitioner, would have concluded that the threats would have been implemented if the marriage had not taken place, it is directly contrary to the view stated earlier by Butt J in *Scott v Sebright*[297] and it is submitted that the latter is to be preferred. If a person is in a mental state in which he is no longer capable of offering resistance to threats, it seems immaterial that it would be obvious to a reasonable person, similarly placed, that the other has no intention of carrying them out at all.[298]

Secondly, although Scarman J's decision in *Buckland v Buckland* is clear authority for the proposition that the fear must arise from some external circumstances for which the party is not himself responsible, it is doubtful whether this rule is correctly expressed. In that case the petitioner succeeded because his fear arose from the false charge preferred against him; presumably he would have failed had he actually been guilty of the offence. Originally it was said that the fear must be unjustly imposed;[299] and whilst it could not be justly imposed if the party was not responsible for the events which had given rise to the threat, it does not follow that it will be justly imposed if he was responsible.

Moreover, it seems that Simon P's third condition, namely that the fear must be caused by 'threat of immediate danger to life, limb or liberty', should no longer be regarded as correct. The Court of Appeal applied it in *Singh v Singh*[300] and *Singh v Kaur*,[301] but only a year after the latter case Ormrod LJ, delivering the leading judgment of the court in *Hirani v Hirani*,[302] denied the need for such threats. The petitioner was a 19-year-old woman of Hindu Indian origin. She formed a relationship with a Muslim man and within a fortnight of discovering this her parents arranged for her to marry a man from their own community, telling her that if she refused, they would throw her out of the home. Having nowhere to go and no financial means, she went through with the ceremony at a register office, but the marriage was not consummated and she left after six weeks. She petitioned for nullity and on appeal, Ormrod LJ stated that the relevant question is 'whether the pressure . . . is such as to destroy the reality of consent and overbears the will of the individual'.[303]

Hirani was followed in *P v R (Forced Marriage: Annulment: Procedure)*[304] where the petitioner was compelled to enter into a marriage with her cousin while she was staying in Pakistan. Although, in that case, there was evidence of the threat and use of

---

[297] (1886) 12 PD 21 at 24. But Simon P's views are supported by *Buckland v Buckland* [1968] P 296 at 301 (per Scarman J) and *H v H* [1954] P 258 at 269 (per Karminski J).

[298] This was the view of the Law Commission in Law Com No 33, at p 27. Davies 'Duress and Nullity of Marriage' (1972) 88 LQR 549 suggests that the rule that the fear must be reasonably entertained applies only when it is imposed by someone other than the respondent or his agent. This is ingenious but it is not the basis of any reported case and could work injustice. In *Parojcic v Parojcic* (above), for example, the petitioner entered into the marriage because her father threatened to send her back to Yugoslavia if she did not do so; why should she be tied to the marriage if a reasonable woman in her position would have realised that he had no intention of implementing his threat?

[299] *Griffith v Griffith* [1944] IR 35 at 43–4.   [300] [1971] P 226, CA.

[301] (1981) 11 Fam Law 152, CA.

[302] (1983) 4 FLR 232, CA. Ormrod LJ had also given the leading judgment in *Singh v Kaur*.

[303] In Scotland the '*Hirani* test' rather than the '*Szechter* test' was followed in two cases in which the petitioning Pakistani woman was forced to go through with an arranged marriage due to family pressure: see *Mahmood v Mahmood* 1993 SLT 589 and *Mahmud v Mahmud* 1994 SLT 599. For an interesting analysis of these cases see A Bradney 'Duress, Family Law and the Coherent Legal System' (1994) 57 MLR 963.

[304] [2003] 1 FLR 661. See also *NS v MI* [2006] EWHC 1646 (Fam).

force, and of detaining her against her will, the problem of 'forced marriages'[305] being imposed on some children from minority ethnic communities has resulted in an awareness of the need for greater understanding of the pressures faced by such young people and for sensitivity in laying down an appropriate test of duress. Indeed, such awareness has resulted in the establishment of a Forced Marriage Unit by the Home Office and Foreign Office to provide guidance,[306] advice and practical aid concerning the issue. It describes a forced marriage as:

'one where one or both parties are coerced into a marriage against their will and under duress. Duress includes both physical and emotional pressure. Forced marriage is an abuse of human rights and cannot be justified on any religious or cultural basis. It is, of course, very different from arranged marriage, where both parties give their full and free consent to the marriage. The tradition of arranged marriages has operated successfully within many communities and many countries for a very long time. . . . It is a form of domestic violence and an abuse of the human rights. Victims can suffer many forms of physical and emotional damage including being held unlawfully captive, assaulted and repeatedly raped.'[307]

The Unit can help arrange for minors to be made wards of court and their passports confiscated to prevent them being taken and married overseas and, if they are already abroad, can liaise with consular officials to work with the local police and judiciary to try to prevent the marriage, and, 'in extreme cases, can mount a "rescue mission" to rescue and repatriate victims.'[308] The question of whether to make forcing a person into marriage a specific criminal offence, however, has been rejected as likely to drive the practice underground.[309]

It is submitted that such initiatives reflect an understanding that non-physical threats can be just as stressful and over-powering as the threat of physical violence,[310] and there should be no question of preventing a victim of such abuse from receiving redress. Moreover, as Coleridge J noted in *P v R (Forced Marriage: Annulment: Procedure)*,[311] it is important that a decree of nullity, rather than of divorce, is made available, to avoid the stigma that would otherwise attach to the petitioner within her community.

Mistake

A mistake will affect the marriage in two cases only. First, a mistake as to the identity (but not as to the attributes) of the other contracting party will make the marriage voidable if this results in one party's failing to marry the individual whom he or she intends to marry.

---

[305] See Home Office, *A Choice by Right* (2000).

[306] See Joint FCO/Home Office Action Plan *Forced Marriage—The Overseas Dimension* (2000); Home Office/FCO/ACPO, *Dealing with Cases of Forced Marriage: Guidance for Police Officers* (2nd ed, 2005); see also The Law Society, *Family Law News* (April 2004) special issue.

[307] http://www.homeoffice.gov.uk/comrace/race/forcedmarriage/.

[308] Ibid. See too, in the case of an *adult, Re SK (Proposed Plaintiff)(An Adult by way of her Litigation Friend)* [2004] EWHC 3202 (Fam) [2005] 2 FLR 230—High Court may exercise its inherent jurisdiction to make orders to ensure young adult woman believed to be detained by family in Bangladesh was able to exercise free will regarding her marital status.

[309] See FCO/Home Office, *Forced Marriage: A Wrong not a Right* (2005) and Statement by Baroness Scotland, 8 June 2006.

[310] See *Scott v Sebright* (1886) 12 PD 21, where the respondent's threats to see that bankruptcy proceedings were taken against the petitioner and to 'accuse her to her mother and in every drawing-room in London of having been seduced by him' were apparently regarded as grounds (along with a threat to shoot her) for annulling the marriage.

[311] [2003] 1 FLR 661.

In the New Zealand case *C v C*,[312] the woman married the man in the erroneous belief that he was a well-known boxer called Miller. It was held that the marriage was not invalidated by the mistake because she married the very individual she meant to marry. Secondly, the marriage will be voidable if one of the parties is mistaken as to the nature of the ceremony and does not appreciate that he is contracting a marriage. In *Valier v Valier*[313] the husband, who was an Italian and whose knowledge of the English language was poor, was taken to a register office by the wife and there went through the usual form of marriage. He did not understand what was happening at the time, the parties never cohabited and the marriage was never consummated. It was held that he was entitled to a decree of nullity. But if each party appreciates that he or she is going through a form of marriage with the other, no other type of mistake apparently can affect the contract.[314] Thus, it has been held that the marriage will not be invalidated by a mistake as to the monogamous or polygamous nature of the union,[315] the other party's fortune,[316] the woman's chastity,[317] or the recognition of the union by the religious denomination of the parties.[318]

Unlike a commercial contract, neither a fraudulent nor an innocent misrepresentation will of itself affect the validity of a marriage.[319] But if the misrepresentation induces an operative mistake (eg as to the nature of the ceremony), the marriage will be made voidable by the latter.[320]

Unsoundness of mind

This will affect a marriage only if, as a consequence, *at the time of the ceremony* either party was unable to understand the nature of the contract he was entering into. There is a presumption that he was capable of doing so, and the burden of proof therefore lies upon the party impeaching the validity of the marriage.[321] In *Re E (An Alleged Patient); Sheffield City Council v E and S*[322] E, who was aged 21, had hydrocephalus and spina bifida and was said to function at the level of a 13-year-old. She moved in with a man, S, aged 37, who had a history of sexual violence. The local authority discovered that they were planning to marry and sought an order under the inherent jurisdiction of the High Court to stop them

---

[312] [1942] NZLR 356. But if A becomes engaged to B, whom she has never seen before, by correspondence, and C successfully personates B at the wedding, the marriage would be voidable because A intends to marry B and nobody else: ibid, p 359. It would be void if the personation invalidated the publication of banns: see above, p 56.

[313] (1925) 133 LT 830. See also *Ford v Stier* [1896] P 1, and *Kelly v Kelly* (1932) 49 TLR 99 (mistaken belief that ceremony was formal betrothal); *Mehta v Mehta* [1945] 2 All ER 690 (mistaken belief that Hindu marriage ceremony was ceremony of religious conversion); *Alfonso-Brown v Milwood* [2006] EWHC 642 (Fam) (Ghanaian engagement ceremony).

[314] *Moss v Moss* [1897] P 263 at 271–3; *Kenward v Kenward* [1950] P 71 at 79 (per Hodson J); revsd [1951] P 124 at 133–4, (per Evershed MR).

[315] *Kassim v Kassim* [1962] P 224.   [316] *Wakefield v Mackay* (1807) 1 Hag Con 394 at 398.

[317] Even though she is pregnant by another man: *Moss v Moss* (above).

[318] *Ussher v Ussher* [1912] 2 IR 445.

[319] *Swift v Kelly* (1835) 3 Knapp 257 at 293; *Moss v Moss* (above) at 266.

[320] *Moss v Moss* (above), at 268–9.

[321] *Harrod v Harrod* (1854) 1 K & J 4, 9. But if the person is proved to have been generally insane, there will be a presumption that he was insane at the time of the marriage, and the burden of proof will consequently shift onto the party seeking to uphold its validity: *Turner v Meyers* (1808) 1 Hag Con 414 at 417.

[322] [2004] EWHC 2808 (Fam) [2005] Fam 326. For a recent Australian decision, see *AK v NC* (2004) FLC 93, and the discussion by F Bates, 'Capacity to Enter into Marriage: A New Australian Perspective' [2005] IFL 28.

from marrying or associating, asserting that it was in E's best interests neither to marry, nor to associate with, S and that she lacked the capacity to make decisions about where she should live, whether she should have contact with S and whether she should marry him. In determining a preliminary issue concerning what questions E should be asked by experts appointed to advise on her capacity to marry, Munby J followed the test formulated by Singleton LJ in *In the Estate of Park:*[323]

'Was the [person] . . . capable of understanding the nature of the contract into which he was entering, or was his mental condition such that he was incapable of understanding it? To ascertain the nature of the contract of marriage a man must be mentally capable of appreciating that it involves the responsibilities normally attaching to marriage. Without that degree of mentality, it cannot be said that he understands the nature of the contract.'

He held that the court had no jurisdiction to consider whether it was in E's best interests to marry, or to marry S. Its task in cases of this type is to determine whether a person has capacity to marry, pure and simple. This involves determining whether he or she can understand the nature of the marriage contract, ie that he or she is mentally capable of understanding the duties and responsibilities that normally attach to marriage. It is not enough that someone appreciates that he or she is taking part in a marriage ceremony or understands its words. 'That said, the contract of marriage is in essence a simple one, which does not require a high degree of intelligence to comprehend. The contract of marriage can readily be understood by anyone of normal intelligence.'[324] He was also at pains to stress that:

'There are many people in our society who may be of limited or borderline capacity but whose lives are immensely enriched by marriage. We must be careful not to set the test of capacity to marry too high, lest it operate as an unfair, unnecessary and indeed discriminatory bar against the mentally disabled. . . . Equally, we must be careful not to impose so stringent a test of capacity to marry that it becomes too easy to challenge the validity of what appear on the surface to be regular and seemingly valid marriages.'[325]

It is worth noting also that the Mental Capacity Act 2005, s 1(4) provides that a person 'is not to be treated as unable to make a decision merely because he makes an unwise decision' and s 27(1)(a) of the 2005 Act provides that no decision under the Act can be taken on behalf of a person in relation to consent to marry.

In the absence of any binding English authority, it is submitted that the effect of drunkenness and drugs will be the same as that of unsoundness of mind. Consequently, the marriage will be voidable if, as a result of either, one of the parties was incapable of understanding the nature of the contract into which he was entering.[326]

---

[323] [1954] P 112 at 127, CA; cf Karminski J (in the Div Court) [1954] P 89 at 99; Birkett LJ at 134–5; Hodson LJ at 137; *Hunter v Edney* (1881) 10 PD 93 at 95; *Durham v Durham* (1885) 10 PD 80 at 82.

[324] [2004] EWHC 2808 (Fam) [2005] 2 FLR 965 at para 68.

[325] Ibid paras 144, 145. Note, however, that an injunction may be granted to restrain those responsible for an adult lacking capacity from taking steps to arrange a marriage for her: *M v B, A, S (By her Litigation Friend, the Official Solicitor)* [2005] EWHC 1681 (Fam) [2006] 1 FLR 117; *Re SA* [2005] EWHC 2942 (Fam) [2006] IFLR 867. Query whether such an injunction could be issued against the intending spouse?

[326] See *Legey v O'Brien* (1834) Milw 325; *Sullivan v Sullivan* (1818) 2 Hag Con 238 at 246 (per Sir W Scott).

'Sham marriages'

Cases like *Szechter v Szechter*[327] raise a further question: is a 'sham marriage'—that is, where the parties go through the form of marriage purely for the purpose of representing themselves as married to the outside world with no intention of cohabiting—to be regarded in law as a nullity?

Since the House of Lords' decision in *Vervaeke v Smith*[328] there can be no doubt that such marriages are perfectly valid provided the parties freely consented to contracting them. In that case a Belgian prostitute went through a ceremony of marriage with a British subject so that she could apply for British citizenship and thus escape deportation. The parties had no intention of living together and saw each other again on only one or two occasions. The majority of the House considered it indisputable that the marriage was valid.

This problem is most likely to arise in the context of the United Kingdom's restrictive immigration laws. For these purposes, s 24(5) of the Immigration and Asylum Act 1999 defines a sham marriage as:

'a marriage (whether or not void)—

(a) entered into between a person ("A") who is neither a British citizen nor a national of an EEA State other than the United Kingdom and another person (whether or not such a citizen or such a national); and

(b) entered into by A for the purpose of avoiding the effect of one or more provisions of United Kingdom immigration law or the immigration rules.'

Under the same section, if a superintendent registrar to whom a notice of marriage has been given, or any other person who has attested a declaration accompanying such a notice, has reasonable grounds for suspecting that the marriage will be a sham marriage, or a marriage is solemnised in the presence of a registrar of marriages and before, during or immediately after the solemnisation the registrar has reasonable grounds for suspecting that the marriage will be, or is, a sham marriage, he or she must report their suspicion to the Immigration and Nationality Directorate of the Home Office without delay.[329]

Such cases may come to light in contexts some way removed from suspicions raised at the time of the marriage, or through a party seeking a nullity decree. For example, in *Bhaiji v Chauhan (Queen's Proctor Intervening)*[330] they emerged at the divorce stage. Five divorce petitions, all involving couples of Indian ethnicity, one party having British and the other Indian citizenship, were found to be strikingly similar and appeared to involve marriages entered into so as to enable the Indian spouse to obtain indefinite leave to remain. All the petitions were dismissed. In *R (K) v London Borough of Lambeth*[331] the

---

[327] [1971] P 286.

[328] [1983] 1 AC 145, per Lord Hailsham LC at 151–2, and Lord Simon at 162. Lord Brandon agreed with both speeches. See also *Silver v Silver* [1955] 2 All ER 614; *Puttick v A-G* [1980] Fam 1; Rogers 'Sham Marriages' (1974) 4 Fam Law 4; Wade 'Limited Purpose Marriages' (1982) 45 MLR 159, particularly at 169–70.

[329] Reporting of Suspicious Marriages and Registration of Marriages (Miscellaneous Amendments) Regulations SI 2000/3164. There is no duty to report suspicions if the wedding is to be by an Anglican ceremony, apparently because there is no evidence of abuse of the relevant preliminaries. Query whether this is discriminatory within Art 14 of the ECHR? c.f. *R (Baiai and Others) v Secretary of State for the Home Department* [2006] EWHC 823 (Admin). See D Stevens, 'The Immigration and Asylum Act 1999: A Missed Opportunity?' (2001) 64 MLR 413 at 420–421.

[330] [2003] 2 FLR 485.   [331] [2003] EWHC 871 (Admin) [2003] 2 FLR 439.

claimant was a Kenyan national whose claim for asylum was rejected. She married an Irish national but the marriage was regarded as a sham and instructions for her removal from the country were issued. Meanwhile, she was refused benefits on the basis that she was a dependant of an EEA national (the Irish husband). She appealed on the basis that she was not his dependant, the marriage being one of convenience only. It was held that the motive for her entering into the marriage was irrelevant, as was the fact that she and her husband might have separated. She was a 'spouse'—a lawfully married person—within the meaning of the relevant regulations and therefore ineligible for support, even though, simultaneously, she was not regarded as a 'spouse' for the purpose of remaining in the jurisdiction.[332]

(c) Mental disorder

A marriage is voidable if, at the time of the ceremony, *either party*, though capable of giving a valid consent, was suffering (whether continuously or intermittently) from mental disorder within the meaning of the Mental Health Act 1983 of such a kind or to such an extent as to be unfitted for marriage.[333] 'Unfitted for marriage' in this context has been defined as 'incapable of carrying out the ordinary duties and obligations of marriage'.[334]

This ground must be distinguished from that already considered, namely, unsoundness of mind producing lack of consent. In the case of mental disorder it is presumed that the party was capable of giving a valid consent to the marriage but that the general state of his or her mental health at the time of the ceremony was such that it is right that the marriage should be annulled. It will be observed that the petitioner does not have to rely on the respondent's mental disorder, but may rely on his or her own. This is necessary to enable a party to withdraw from a marriage entered into in ignorance of the existence or extent of his or her illness or the effect which it would have upon his or her married life.

(d) Venereal disease and pregnancy by another

A marriage is voidable if at the time of the ceremony *the respondent* was suffering from venereal disease in a communicable form.[335] 'Venereal disease' is not defined in the Act.[336]

A husband may petition for nullity if at the time of the marriage *the respondent wife* was pregnant by someone other than himself.[337]

Both these grounds, which were introduced by the Matrimonial Causes Act 1937, were thought necessary because there was otherwise no matrimonial relief for fraud or misrepresentation, and it was thought unjust to bind a person to marriage in these circumstances.[338]

---

[332] Equally, of course, she was seeking to argue simultaneously that she should be regarded as a spouse for the purpose of remaining in the jurisdiction, but that she should not be so regarded for the purpose of claiming support.

[333] Matrimonial Causes Act 1973 s 12 (d). 'Mental disorder' means mental illness, arrested or incomplete development of mind, psychopathic disorder and any other disorder or disability of mind: Mental Health Act 1983 s 1(2).

[334] *Bennett v Bennett* [1969] 1 All ER 539.   [335] Matrimonial Causes Act 1973 s 12(e).

[336] In the 8th edition of this work (at p 96) we discussed whether venereal disease includes AIDS, but we do not think that that point is arguable given the various ways in which the HIV infection can be transmitted.

[337] Ibid, s 12(f).

[338] Query whether the case for their continued retention as grounds for nullity is now so compelling?

(e) Gender re-assignment

The Gender Recognition Act 2004 introduced two new grounds into s 12, to provide for situations where one of the parties has undergone gender re-assignment. Section 12(g)[339] provides that a decree may be granted where an interim gender recognition certificate has been issued to either party to the marriage, provided that proceedings are brought within six months of the date of issue of that certificate.[340] Once the decree absolute of nullity has been granted, a full certificate must then be issued by the court, enabling the relevant party to acquire his or her new legal gender. The aim of this provision is presumably to prevent the parties to the marriage from effectively, and legally, becoming same-sex spouses.[341] However, it will be possible for them to become civil partners instead, with an abridgment of the procedural requirements for registering their partnership.[342]

Section 12(h)[343] provides that a decree may be granted where the respondent is a person who has changed gender within the terms of the 2004 Act before the marriage. This provision appears intended to provide the same protection for a petitioner against fraud or misrepresentation on the part of the other party, as those above concerning venereal disease or pregnancy, but the analogy is questionable. It must be at least arguable that a person's gender is a fundamental aspect of his or her identity—this certainly seems to have been the view taken by the European Court of Human Rights in *Goodwin v United Kingdom*[344]—and not merely an 'attribute'. On this basis, a mistake as to the partner's gender would be covered by s 12(c) and this provision is unnecessary.

(f) Bars to relief

Like any other voidable contract, at common law a party to a voidable marriage might effectively put it out of his own power to obtain a decree of nullity by his own conduct. There are currently three statutory bars to the grant of a decree.[345]

Petitioner's conduct

Section 13(1) of the Matrimonial Causes Act 1973 provides:

'The court shall not . . . grant a decree of nullity on the ground that the marriage is voidable if the respondent satisfies the court—

(a) that the petitioner, with knowledge that it was open to him to have the marriage avoided, so conducted himself in relation to the respondent as to lead the respondent reasonably to believe that he would not seek to do so; and

(b) that it would be unjust to the respondent to grant the decree.'

The principle underlying the forerunner to this bar was summarised by Lord Watson:[346]

'In a suit for nullity of marriage there may be facts and circumstances proved which so

---

[339] Inserted by Gender Recognition Act 2004 Sch 2 para 2.
[340] Matrimonial Causes Act 1973 s 13(2A) inserted by Gender Recognition Act 2004 Sch 2 para 3.
[341] But S Gilmore, 'The Gender Recognition Act 2004' [2004] Fam Law 741 at 743 notes that the Parliamentary Joint Committee on Human Rights considered it to be a disproportionate measure and recommended its reconsideration.
[342] Civil Partnership Act 2004 Sch 3. See below pp 96.
[343] Inserted by the Gender Recognition Act 2004 Sch 4 para 5.   [344] [2002] 2 FLR 487.
[345] See Law Com No 33, paras 36–45 and 76–86.   [346] *G v M* (1885) 10 App Cas 171, HL at 197–8.

plainly imply, on the part of the complaining spouse, a recognition of the existence and validity of the marriage, as to render it most inequitable and contrary to public policy that he or she should be permitted to go on to challenge it with effect.'

The same principle underlies the statutory bar. Before we examine the question of the petitioner's conduct in more detail, however, three preliminary points must be made. First, the court will be bound to apply the bar only if the respondent satisfies it that the statutory conditions are fulfilled. Not only does this mean that the burden of proof is on the respondent, but if he or she chooses not to raise the bar at all, the court must grant a decree if a ground has been made out even if it is clear from the facts that these conditions are satisfied:[347] the bar no longer rests on public policy.[348] Secondly, no conduct on the petitioner's part can raise the bar unless he (or she) knew at the time that it was open to him to have the marriage avoided. This means that he must have been aware not only of the facts upon which the petition is based (for example, that he is not the father of the child that the respondent was carrying at the time of the marriage), but also that these facts would entitle him to petition for a decree of nullity.[349] Any act or omission when he was ignorant of either of these matters must be disregarded.[350] Thirdly, only conduct in relation to the petitioner can act as a bar.

Positive acts

Any positive act by the petitioner may raise the bar if a reasonable person in the respondent's position would have concluded that the petitioner intended to treat the marriage as valid and the respondent in fact drew this conclusion. In *D v D*[351] the parties adopted two children at a time when the husband knew that he could have the marriage annulled because of his wife's refusal to consummate it. He later brought nullity proceedings. It was held that by agreeing to the adoption he had so conducted himself in relation to the wife as to lead her to believe that he would not seek to do so.

In some circumstances the mere fact that the petitioner has married the respondent at all may reasonably lead the latter to believe that the former will not subsequently petition for nullity. If a man marries a woman knowing that one of them is impotent or suffering from mental disorder and knowing also that this is a ground for nullity, the woman may reasonably conclude that he intends to treat the marriage as valid and thus raise the marriage itself as a bar if he does petition. For the same reason a party who has deprived the other of the power of consenting freely to the marriage by inducing a mistake or uttering threats may not be able to petition. A similar case arises if the parties entered into an agreement before marriage that they would not have sexual intercourse. Although this is regarded as contrary to public policy and is therefore not binding on them,[352] it may preclude either of them from obtaining a decree of nullity if the marriage is in fact never

---

[347] This point was not taken in *D v D* [1979] Fam 70, where the wife, having raised the defence, then elected not to pursue it. Dunn J, however, held that in such circumstances it could not be said to be unjust to grant the decree.

[348] *D v D* (above).

[349] The respondent is presumed to know the law and the burden is on him to prove that he did not: *W v W* [1952] P 152 at 162, CA.

[350] This re-enacts the common law rule: see *G v M* (above), at 186.   [351] [1979] Fam 70.

[352] See *Brodie v Brodie* [1917] P 271.

consummated and the agreement led the respondent to believe that the petitioner would not bring proceedings.[353] If one of the parties is old, infirm or seriously crippled, the marriage may well have been on this understanding, express or implied. A fortiori, an agreement between the spouses that the petitioner will not institute proceedings for nullity will be a good defence to a petition.[354]

Delay

Just as some active step on the petitioner's part may bar him from bringing proceedings for nullity, delay in bringing them may equally bar him if he knows that it is open to him to have the marriage avoided and the delay has led the respondent reasonably to believe that he does not intend to do so. The question must be one of fact: did the petitioner's delay lull the respondent into a false sense of security or a false belief that he would not petition?

Injustice of decree

In addition to proving that the petitioner has led the respondent to believe that he will not seek to have the marriage avoided, the latter must also show that it would be unjust to him (or her) to grant the decree. As in the case of divorce, justice will rarely be served by refusing to set aside a marriage that is already dead, but there will undoubtedly be some cases when it would be manifestly unjust to grant a decree against an unwilling respondent. For example, a respondent in a position of the wife in *D v D*[355] might satisfy the court that it would be unjust to her to annul the marriage because she would be left with two adopted children. The defence is perhaps most likely to succeed if the petitioner relies on his own impotence (or mental disorder), for consideration must necessarily be given to the respondent's attitude and reaction to a situation for which she is in no way responsible.[356] Among the matters which the court should take into account in deciding whether to grant a decree are the length of time the marriage has lasted, the existence of any children of the family, any religious or other personal objections that the respondent has to the decree, and the financial loss that he (or she) might suffer as a result of nullity (for example, the loss of pension rights).

Lapse of time

In all cases, except those based on impotence or wilful refusal to consummate or where an interim gender recognition certificate has been issued, a decree of nullity must normally be refused if the proceedings were not instituted within three years of the date of the marriage.[357]

---

[353] See *Morgan v Morgan* [1959] P 92; *Scott v Scott* [1959] P 103n.

[354] See *Aldridge v Aldridge* (1888) 13 PD 210.

[355] For the facts see above, p 91. In this case it was held not to be unjust to grant the decree because the respondent did not pursue the defence.

[356] See *Pettit v Pettit* [1963] P 177 CA. The husband did not discover that he could petition on the ground of his own impotence for more than 20 years after the marriage and after the birth of a child as the result of fecundatio ab extra. Under the old law of approbation the court refused to grant the decree because it would have been inequitable to do so. If the husband had known all along that he could petition, it is submitted that the decision would be the same today.

[357] Matrimonial Causes Act 1973 s 13(2). This is independent of the bar last considered, and even if the petition is brought within three years, the respondent may still raise the petitioner's delay or other conduct as a bar if it reasonably led him to conclude that the petitioner would not seek to have the marriage annulled.

The reason for this bar is to ensure that the parties' status is not left in doubt for too long: consequently there is no power to extend the period, even though the petitioner was unaware of the facts or that they made the marriage voidable. This may well work injustice, however. The Law Commission concluded that hardship was most likely to arise if the complaining party was mentally disordered. They had in mind two problems in particular: old and lonely people not fully in possession of their faculties may well become the object of attention of fortune hunters, and a petition may have to be presented by the party's litigation friend who may not become aware of all the facts during the first three years of the marriage.[358] Following the Commission's recommendation, the court is thus empowered[359] to grant leave for the presentation of a petition based on any ground, notwithstanding that more than three years have elapsed since the date of the marriage, provided that the petitioner has suffered from mental disorder within the meaning of the Mental Health Act 1983 at any time during the first three years of the marriage and that the court considers that it would be just to do so.

Lapse of time is not a bar in the case of inability or wilful refusal to consummate the marriage, because the petitioner may properly try to overcome the impediment or aversion for a longer period than three years.[360]

A six-month period is allowed for a petition to be brought under s 12(g). If that is not done, it would still be open to a party to petition on another ground (or to seek a divorce). The person with the acquired gender could then apply (or apply again) for a full certificate to be granted by the gender recognition panel, rather than the court.[361]

Petitioner's knowledge

If the petition is based on the respondent's venereal disease, pregnancy by another man, or acquired gender, the decree must be refused unless the court was satisfied that the petitioner was ignorant of the facts alleged at the time of the marriage.[362]

5 EFFECT OF DECREE

Although a decree has always been necessary to annul a voidable marriage, at common law (as in the case of a void marriage) it pronounced the marriage 'to have been and to be absolutely null and void to all intents and purposes in the law whatsoever'. Consequently, before the decree the parties were regarded as husband and wife both in law and in fact but after the decree absolute they were deemed in law never to have been married at all. The logical application of this anomalous doctrine produced some startling results. Children of a voidable marriage were automatically bastardised by the decree; the trusts under a marriage settlement all failed and the interest of the person entitled before the solemnisation of the marriage revived. Some of these anomalies were swept away by statute—for example, children of a voidable marriage retained their legitimacy—and after the Second World War there was an increasing tendency for the judges to regard decrees of nullity in

---

[358] See Law Com No 116 (*Time Restrictions on Presentation of Divorce and Nullity Petitions*, 1982), Pt III.

[359] Matrimonial Causes Act 1973 s 13(2) and (4) as amended by the Matrimonial and Family Proceedings Act 1984 s 2. Note that the petition does not have to be based on the petitioner's mental disorder.

[360] See Law Com No 33, paras 79–85.

[361] Gender Recognition Act 2004 s 5. The application must be made within six months of the decree.

[362] Matrimonial Causes Act 1973 s 13(3) as amended.

respect of voidable marriages more like decrees of divorce.[363] This doctrine was never consistently applied, however, and by 1971 it was becoming increasingly difficult to predict in any given case what approach the court would adopt.

With the purpose of sweeping away the remaining anomalies and clarifying the law it is now provided:[364]

'A decree of nullity granted after 31st July 1971 in respect of a voidable marriage shall operate to annul the marriage only as respects any time after the decree has been made absolute, and the marriage shall, notwithstanding the decree, be treated as if it had existed up to that time.'

This leaves no doubt that the parties must now be regarded as having been married throughout the whole period between the celebration of a voidable marriage and the decree absolute. What is not clear is the effect of the decree on the parties' status after it has been made absolute. The Act expressly states that it shall operate to annul the marriage, not to terminate it. This implies that the effect is different from that of a decree of dissolution. However, it is submitted that the consequences of the annulment of a voidable marriage must be the same as those of the dissolution of a valid one.

The section has effect only if the decree absolute was granted on or after 1 August 1971 (when the Nullity of Marriage Act came into operation). In the case of a decree pronounced before this date it may still be necessary to consider the law as it was before the Act was passed.[365]

6 IS THERE A CONTINUING NEED FOR NULLITY?

In practical terms the law of nullity has little current relevance. The number of orders is small[366] and for the most part those that want to end the marriage tie can do so by divorcing. Moreover, since annulments only affect voidable marriages after the decree, it has now become conceptually hard to distinguish voidable marriages ended by an annulment and marriages ended by divorce. Whether the law of nullity in its current form should be retained, and if not, how it should relate to the law of divorce, are questions that need to be addressed.

Although the inevitable corollary of having criteria governing the validity of marriage is to have a concept of a void marriage, it does seem questionable to retain the concept of a voidable marriage. It seems particularly hard to justify having wilful refusal to consummate as a ground of voidability since that arises purely from a post-marital decision and is surely properly regarded as a reason for divorce.[367] The same could now be said regarding a

[363] *R v Algar* [1954] 1 QB 279, [1953] 2 All ER 1381, CCA (wife remained incompetent to give evidence against husband); *Wiggins v Wiggins* [1958] 2 All ER 555 (second marriage contracted during subsistence of voidable marriage remained void notwithstanding annulment of the first).

[364] Matrimonial Causes Act 1973 s 16, re-enacting the Nullity of Marriage Act 1971 s 5, and implementing the recommendations of the Law Commission: Law Com No 33, paras 21–22 and 25.

[365] See the 4th edition of this book, pp 69–71.

[366] In 2004, for example, only 492 petitions were filed and only 308 decrees nisi and 244 decrees absolute were granted: *Judicial Statistics 2004* (2005) Table 5.5.

[367] Compare the Law Commission's view (Law Com No 33, *Nullity of Marriage*, 1970), discussed above, p 79. The government's White Paper on Divorce *Looking to the Future* (1995) Cm 2799, para 4.52 stated that 'consultees did not view the law of nullity as relevant to a revision of the divorce law' and that the 'possibility

spouse's change of gender after the marriage. The concept of the voidable marriage has been abolished in Australia,[368] and it is submitted that this example should be followed. Whether in consequence the law of divorce should be amended so as to provide a 'fast track' for the other s 12 grounds is debatable. There may be a case for not operating the 12-month time bar on starting proceedings, but this could equally be argued for in other cases, for example, domestic violence, where no such abridgement has been deemed suitable.[369]

G ENTRY INTO A CIVIL PARTNERSHIP

As we have seen, the Civil Partnership Act 2004 creates an institution for same-sex couples which is effectively the same as marriage. However, a major difference is that civil partnership is a legal, not a religious, status. No provision is made in the Act to enable it to be brought into existence via any religious ceremony, even if the parties might be adherents of a religion which would, for example, bless their union.

We explain the rules governing the creation of a civil partnership in the same way as we have discussed those governing marriage. The parties must satisfy the requirements both as to capacity and formalities.

1 CAPACITY

Section 3(1) of the 2004 Act provides that

'Two people are not eligible to register as civil partners of each other if—

  (a) they are not of the same sex,

  (b) either of them is already a civil partner or lawfully married,

  (c) either of them is under 16, or

  (d) they are within prohibited degrees of relationship.'

This negative formulation of eligibility provides that, apart from the requirement that the parties to a civil partnership *must* be of the same sex, the rules of capacity are otherwise the same as for a marriage. The question whether those *within* family relationships, who fall, of course, within the prohibited degrees, should be permitted to register was debated in Parliament, the argument being that the advantages of civil partnership (in particular, exemption from say, inheritance tax liability) should be extended to eg elderly siblings. The House of Lords did in fact pass such a clause, deliberately intended as a wrecking amendment by those opposed to legal recognition of same sex relationships, but it was overturned in the House of Commons and eventually defeated.[370]

---

that the ground for nullity of wilful refusal to consummate the marriage should be removed because of the need to prove fault was not supported'.

[368] By the Family Law Act 1975 (Cth).   [369] See below, p 266.

[370] See the discussion by M Harper et al, *Civil Partnership: The New Law* (2005) paras 4.8–4.11.

2 FORMALITIES

Since there is no provision for a religious ceremony as a means of creating a civil partner-ship, the formalities that must be satisfied are all variants of those that apply to civil marriages.

(a) Preliminaries

Civil partner under 18

Section 4 provides that consent must be given by the appropriate persons where a child aged 16 or 17 wishes to enter into a civil partnership. These are the same as for a mar-riage.[371] However, if a person whose consent is required objects, he or she may forbid the issue of a civil partnership document[372] by giving written notice to that effect.

Registration procedure

The Act provides for four different registration procedures—the standard procedure; the procedure for house-bound persons; that for detained persons; and the special procedure for cases where a person is seriously ill and not expected to recover.[373] It will be seen that these reflect the provisions for marriage by Superintendent Registrar's certificate, marriage of house-bound or detained persons; and the Registrar General's licence.

The standard procedure.[374] Under the standard procedure, each party must give notice to a registration authority[375] of the proposed civil partnership and must have resided in England and Wales[376] for at least seven days immediately before giving the notice. The notice must be accompanied by a declaration regarding eligibility to enter into the part-nership. The notice must be publicised and the parties must wait 15 days before they can register.[377] At the end of the waiting period, provided no objection has been made to the registration authority, they will be issued with a civil partnership schedule (akin to that which has been proposed for marriages).[378] They then have 12 months from the date that the first notice (if they did not give notice together) was recorded, in which to register.

Procedures for house-bound and detained persons.[379] Where a party is unable to attend to register the civil partnership because of illness or disability, or because he or she is detained then, as for marriage, arrangements can be made for the registration to take place at the place where he or she is confined. In such cases, the notice must be accompanied by a medical statement or supporting statement (depending upon whether the person is house-bound or detained) and the period in which they must register is three months rather than 12.

The special procedure.[380] Where one of the proposed civil partners is seriously ill and not

---

[371] See above p 55 and Civil Partnership Act 2004 Sch 2.   [372] See below p 97.

[373] Section 5(1).

[374] Sections 8–17. Note that where one of a couple has obtained an interim gender recognition certificate and his or her marriage has accordingly been annulled, then the couple may then register as civil partners without having to wait for 15 days from giving notice. They must register within one month: Sch 3 paras 1–4.

[375] Which need not be the one where they intend the registration to take place: s 8(1).

[376] See s 20 for the position where one party is a non-resident.

[377] The Registrar General may shorten the period where he is satisfied that there are compelling reasons because of the exceptional circumstances of the case to do so: s 12(1).

[378] See above p 64.   [379] Sections 18–20.   [380] Sections 21–27.

expected to recover, the partnership may be registered under the special procedure. This provides that one of them (not both) must give notice of the proposed partnership, to the registration authority for the area in which it is proposed that the registration take place (rather than, as under the standard procedure, to any registration authority), and providing evidence of the partner's illness and that he or she understands the nature and purport of signing a Registrar General's licence. The authority must inform the Registrar General of such notice, and he may give his authority to them to issue a Registrar General's licence if he is satisfied that the conditions as to illness and eligibility are met. Once the licence is issued, the parties have one month in which to register.

(b) Registration

Registration must take place in England and Wales.[381] It may not be in religious premises and the place must be specified in the notice of proposed civil partnership. If registering under the standard procedure, the place must be one open to the public and will have to have been agreed with the registration authority in whose area it is located. That authority may itself provide a place in its area for registrations to be held, but is not required to do so.[382] Pending the enactment of the Government's proposals regarding the liberalisation of marriage ceremonials, one assumes that premises will be 'approved' as they currently are for weddings.[383]

Unlike a wedding, where the marriage comes into existence on the parties' exchange of the requisite words, a civil partnership is created when each partner has signed, in the presence of the civil partnership registrar and their two witnesses,[384] the civil partnership document—the schedule or licence that has been issued to them.[385] No religious service may be used while the civil partnership registrar is officiating at the signing of the document.[386]

H ESTABLISHING THE VALIDITY OF A CIVIL PARTNERSHIP

1 DECLARATION

As with a marriage, a person may apply to the High Court or county court for a declaration regarding the validity of a civil partnership.[387] The provisions are similar to those applying to marriage and are not discussed further here.[388]

---

[381] Note that s 210 allows for an Order in Council to be made to permit partners to register at a British consulate in an overseas territory if, inter alia, one of them is a United Kingdom national and there are insufficient facilities for them to enter into the equivalent of a civil partnership under the law of that territory. Section 211 makes similar provision for armed forces personnel.

[382] Section 6.

[383] Section 35 provides that the Chancellor of the Exchequer may by order make amendments to the Act and to subordinate legislation to assimilate its provisions with those regarding the formation of civil marriages.

[384] A person so designated by a registration authority for its area: s 29(1).

[385] Sections 2(1) and 7(1).   [386] Section 2(5).   [387] Civil Partnership Act 2004 s 58.

[388] See above p 66. For the provisions governing recognition of civil partnerships (or the equivalent) entered into overseas, see ss 212–17 and the discussion by M Harper et al *Civil Partnership—The New Law* (2005) paras 4.38–4.42. A Canadian same-sex marriage was recognised only as a civil partnership in

2 ANNULMENT OF A CIVIL PARTNERSHIP

As with a marriage, provision is made for the annulment of a civil partnership and the same distinction is drawn between partnerships that are void and those that are voidable. A nullity *order*, rather than decree, is granted by the court, although it is given in two stages, a conditional and final order, akin to a decree nisi and absolute.[389]

The following are the grounds for annulment.

(a) Void civil partnerships

A civil partnership is void if, at the time when they do so, the couple are not eligible to register under s 3, discussed above.[390] It is also void[391] if both parties know, at the time of registering, that due notice of the proposed civil partnership has not been given; that the civil partnership document has not been duly issued; that the applicable period for registration has expired; that the place where they are registering is not that which was specified in the notice they have given; that a civil partnership registrar is not present; or that, in the case of a minor, a person whose consent is required has forbidden the issue of the civil partnership document.[392] It may be noted that this last instance is different to the position in relation to marriage. There, unless a relevant person has objected to the calling of banns, a marriage contracted in the absence of a necessary consent is *not* void.[393] The reason for the distinction may be that the drafters of the Civil Partnership Act wished to make a process equivalent to objecting to banns available to parents etc. Alternatively, though less likely, perhaps, it may have been thought that parents may be more likely to seek to prevent an adolescent child from entering into a same sex union than from getting married. But it is hard to see how making the partnership *void* would support such parents' concerns. Given that the legal position is different with most marriages, the provision is arguably both disproportionate and discriminatory.

(b) Voidable civil partnerships

Section 50 sets out the grounds on which a civil partnership is voidable. These are the same as for marriage, except for two omissions. First, there is no provision for an inability or wilful refusal to consummate to constitute a ground for annulment. This is because the concept of consummation, which is inherently heterosexual (if not hetero-sexist) does not apply to a same-sex relationship. Secondly, the fact that the respondent was suffering from venereal disease at the time of the registration is not a ground for nullity. It is unclear why this ground has been omitted. Interestingly, and perhaps paradoxically, the respondent's being pregnant by someone other than the applicant *is* included as a ground. Since same-sex partners cannot conceive together, whenever a respondent is pregnant, she will always have become so by means of a person other than the applicant. Quite possibly in this context, a sperm donor will be the father. Moreover, whilst the original motivation for including this ground as a basis for annulling a marriage was to prevent a man having spurious children foisted upon him, under the 2004 Act, this ground will only ever be available to female civil partners, the reason for whose

Wilkinson v Kitzinger and Attorney-General (Lord Chancellor intervening), 30 July 2006, Polter P rejecting the argument that this was discriminatory.

[389] Section 37.   [390] At p 95.   [391] Civil Partnership Act 2004 s 49(b).
[392] Under Sch 2 para 6 or 12. See above p 96.   [393] See above pp 57 and 77.

objection to the partner being pregnant will presumably be rather different from that of a heterosexual man.

The same bars to relief apply to voidable civil partnerships as to voidable marriages.[394] The same objections to the concept of voidable civil partnerships may also be made and indeed, the grounds are arguably even more anomalous, as noted above. It is understandable that the Civil Partnership Act includes them as currently drafted, since the approach of the legislation was to import, as far as possible, the provisions relating to marriage, into the legal concept of civil partnership. Should the opportunity ever be taken to re-think the law on marriage, however, there would be scope to evaluate whether all such provisions are in fact necessary and desirable, both in the context of hetero and same-sex relationships.

I RECOGNITION OF COHABITATION

1 INTRODUCTION

As we noted in Chapter 1[395] and at the beginning of this chapter, one of the most significant developments in recent decades has been the growth in the number of couples, both heterosexual and same-sex, living together outside marriage. There is a continuing and long-standing debate concerning how far such couples should be given a recognised legal status, akin, if not equal, to marriage and this debate has prompted a variety of policy responses in different parts of the developed world.[396] In England and Wales, the pattern has been to give ad hoc recognition as a response to particular needs in particular contexts, and we discuss these as they arise in the following chapters of this book. The concern here is to focus upon how, in these varying contexts, cohabitation has been defined and recognised, and to consider how far cohabitation is required to mimic marriage in order to be given such recognition.

Whilst extra-marital cohabitation might be assumed to be a modern phenomenon, it is clear that what has changed in the past half-century, in contrast to before, has been a decline in the social stigma that attaches to it, and hence its degree of visibility and acceptability. But there have always been some couples who have lived together without benefit of marriage,[397] and Probert[398] has shown how legislation (albeit subordinate legislation) passed as early as 1914 recognised the 'unmarried wives' of soldiers as being eligible to receive separation allowances whilst their 'husbands' were serving at the front. As she points out, the fact that such allowances were made did not imply a liberal attitude to such relationships. The motivation was to encourage military recruitment and keep up morale in war time. Later recognition of cohabitation may similarly be seen as having complex motives. It has often been a response to what has become seen as a pressing social problem, as, for example, in the extension of remedies for domestic violence to those who

---

[394] Section 51, and see above pp 90–3.   [395] See above p 2.

[396] See Baroness Hale of Richmond, 'Unmarried Couples in Family Law' [2004] Fam Law 419; and the valuable discussion in the various essays collected in the special issue of (2004) 26 *Law and Policy* edited by A Barlow and R Probert.

[397] See S Parker, *Informal Marriage, Cohabitation and the Law 1753–1989* (1990); R Probert, 'Cohabitation in Twentieth Century England and Wales: Law and Policy' (2004) 26 *Law and Policy* 13.

[398] R Probert, ' "Unmarried wives" in war and peace' [2005] CFLQ 1.

cohabit and not just those who marry.[399] The purpose of such extension was to ensure that victims could be protected, regardless of the structure of their family arrangements. Perhaps it has also reflected a (sometimes rather resigned) acceptance of changing social mores, rather than a whole-hearted embrace of diversity in family form, as, for example, in the context of the rules on eligibility for welfare benefits and tax credits, which treat unmarried couples living in the same household as if they were married. The purpose here is not protective, but limiting. The state seeks to confine its exposure to having to give financial support to families, by assuming that those who live together are mutually dependent, even though there is no legal obligation on one cohabitant to support the other.[400]

Although case law has inevitably developed to interpret the meaning of statutory language used to define cohabitation, it has not been possible for the courts themselves to develop a concept of cohabitation which might attract legal rights and obligations. In the property sphere, for example, which we discuss in Chapters 3 and 4, the focus of attention has been on property and financial ties arising because of the parties' conduct towards each other, usually regardless of the nature of the personal relationship between the parties. It has been for Parliament to enact provisions expressly identifying cohabitants as included within their scope. We therefore turn to consider the varying definitions utilised by Parliament and consider how the courts have interpreted them.

2 DEFINING COHABITATION

The 1970s saw the first real recognition of cohabitants as a class for whom legal provision should be made. The Domestic Violence and Matrimonial Proceedings Act 1976, for example, which enabled an applicant to obtain an injunction to control a spouse's behaviour or even to exclude him or her from the matrimonial home, also applied to 'a man and a woman who are living with each other in the same household as husband and wife'.[401] The subsequent case law illustrates the difficulties that can arise in interpretation of this kind of definition.

(a) 'Are living with each other'

First, taken literally, it could imply that, once a partner had left the home because of the other's violence, he or she was no longer 'living with' the other so as to come within the statute and claim its protection. The courts therefore interpreted it to mean that the parties must have been living together at the time of the incident which led the applicant to leave the home.[402] But if the applicant failed to take action until some time after he or she had left, the court might conclude that it could no longer be said that the couple were living together.[403]

(b) 'In the same household'

Secondly, it will be noted that the provision required the couple to be living 'in the same household'. This too could cause problems if the couple's relationship had deteriorated

---

[399] See below pp 208–11.
[400] See below Chapters 3 and 16.   [401] Section 1(2).   [402] *O'Neill v Williams* [1984] FLR 1, CA.
[403] See eg *Harrison v Lewis* [1988] 2 FLR 339, CA where there was a nine-month delay in taking proceedings and the court held it had no jurisdiction.

but they were still living under the same roof. In *Adeoso v Adeoso*[404] the couple lived in a two-bedroomed flat. They slept in separate rooms and communicated only by notes. They continued to share the living expenses. Ormrod LJ described their situation as

'exactly comparable to a marriage which is in the last stages of break-up. . . . In practical terms you cannot live in a two-room flat with another person without living in the same household. You have to share the lavatory, share the kitchen, share the bathroom and take great care not to fall over one another in most of these cases; and it would be quite artificial to suggest that two people living at arm's length in such a situation, from which they cannot escape by reason of the housing difficulties, are to be said to be living in two separate households.'[405]

Difficulty may arise at the start of a relationship too. Many couples 'drift' into living together, gradually spending more time under the same roof, with one partner gradually moving his or her belongings into the other's property. At what point can it be said that the couple are now living in the same household with each other? This may be relevant both to provisions of the type included within the domestic violence legislation, where it is sufficient that the parties are currently (albeit expansively defined) living together, and to those where they must have been living together for a certain period of time before they come within their scope. For example, the Inheritance (Provision for Family and Dependants) Act 1975 and the Fatal Accidents Act 1976 both include a cohabitant who had lived with the deceased for at least two years within the list of those who may make a claim. In *Kotke v Saffarini*[406] the partners each had their own home. The deceased had worked away from both during the week, but kept a change of clothes and spent most weekends at the claimant's house. He used his own home as his postal address, and when their child was born, he gave it as his address on the birth certificate. Later, he began to use his partner's address as his for official purposes. The Court of Appeal upheld the trial judge in distinguishing between wanting to live in the same household, planning to do so, and actually doing so, and agreed with his conclusion that the deceased's 'centre of gravity' had not shifted until after the couple discovered that the claimant was pregnant. She thus failed to satisfy the two-year threshold for making a claim under the Act.

(c) 'A man and a woman'

Thirdly, the Domestic Violence and Matrimonial Proceedings Act referred to 'a man and a woman' living with each other. Its successor section, contained in the Family Law Act 1996 s 62(1), also defined cohabitants as 'a man and a woman who, although not married to each other, are living together as husband and wife'. It has been convincingly argued that such a definition could not be interpreted so as to include same-sex partners because the language is too clear and unambiguous.[407] By contrast, the House of Lords were able to rule that a similar provision in the Rent Act 1977 *could* be re-interpreted so as to be Convention-compliant. Schedule 1 para 2(2) to that Act provided that '*a person*[408] who was living with the original tenant as his or her wife or husband shall be treated as the

---

[404] [1980] 1 WLR 1535, CA.   [405] At 1537D–E, 1539A–B.

[406] [2005] EWCA Civ 221, [2005] 2 FLR 517.

[407] R Bailey-Harris and J Wilson, '*Mendoza v Ghaidan* and the Rights of De Facto Spouses' [2003] Fam Law 575.

[408] Emphasis added.

spouse of the original tenant' so as to be able to take over a protected tenancy on the tenant's death. In *Fitzpatrick v Sterling Housing Association Ltd*,[409] before the Human Rights Act 1998 came into force, the House had considered that these words were gender-specific and could not be extended to cover couples of the same sex. However, the issue arose before them again in *Ghaidan v Godin-Mendoza*.[410] This time, they ruled that restricting the ambit of the provision to heterosexual couples was discriminatory towards those of the same sex, and that such discrimination infringed Art 14 of the European Convention on Human Rights taken with the right to respect for one's home under Art 8. Finding no objective or reasonable justification for such discrimination,[411] the House held that the provision should be interpreted so as to give effect to the surviving partner's Convention rights. They thus held, agreeing with the Court of Appeal, that the words 'as his or her wife or husband' should be read as stating 'as *if they were* his or her wife or husband'.

It is most unlikely that the different wording used in the two Acts was anything other than accidental, yet it would have deprived same-sex partners of a remedy in what is certainly no less serious a situation—domestic violence—than being required to leave one's home because the landlord will not accept a person as their tenant. Clearly, also, same-sex partners may require the same protection from domestic violence as heterosexuals, just as it was recognised in the 1970s that cohabitants might deserve the same protection as spouses. This provision would therefore probably be regarded as incompatible with the European Convention on Human Rights. To prevent such a ruling, it was first amended to:

'two persons who, although not married to each other, are living together as husband and wife or (if of the same sex) in an equivalent relationship'.[412]

This definition was further amended by the Civil Partnership Act 2004[413] and now reads:

'two persons who are neither married to each other nor civil partners of each other but are living together as husband and wife or as if they were civil partners'.

(d) 'As husband and wife'[414]

These changing definitions identify another potential problem for those seeking to apply them to different factual situations. To live together 'as husband and wife' implies some *quality* in the arrangement which differs from, say, that of landlord and lodger, or flat-sharing friends, or even family members of different generations. It goes to the essence of the relationship, but what does it entail? The various authorities[415] on this point were fully

---

[409] [2001] 1 AC 27, HL. See A Diduck, 'A Family by any other Name . . . Or Starbucks™ Comes to England' (2001) 28 *Journal of Law and Society* 290. See further below pp 1101–4.

[410] [2004] UKHL 30, [2004] 2 AC 557. Lord Millett dissented. See R Probert, 'Same-Sex Couples and the Marriage Model' (2005) 13 Fem LS 135.

[411] See also the same conclusion reached by the European Court of Human Rights in *Karner v Austria* [2003] 2 FLR 623 in relation to the phrase 'life companion' used in the equivalent Austrian legislation.

[412] By the Domestic Violence, Crime and Victims Act 2004 s 3.   [413] Sch 9 para 13.

[414] Cf the criterion used in the Immigration Rules (HC 395) para 295A: a 'relationship akin to marriage'. See below p 126.

[415] See *Atkinson v Atkinson* [1988] 2 FLR 353; *Crake v Supplementary Benefits Commission; Butterworth v Supplementary Benefits Commission* (1981) FLR 264; *Re J (Income Support: Cohabitation)* [1995] 1 FLR 660; *Re Watson (Deceased)* [1999] 1 FLR 878.

reviewed in *Kimber v Kimber*.[416] There, the ex-husband was required to pay maintenance to his former wife until she remarried or cohabited. He claimed that her fiancé was cohabiting with her, and stopped payments. She then sued for the arrears. The fiancé had been a lodger in the ex-wife's bed and breakfast establishment, but he moved out and rented a flat elsewhere. However, he spent much of his time with her, often staying the night, and he helped her run the business. In concluding that the couple were cohabiting, the judge considered the following factors, or 'signposts', as material:

'(1) Living together in the same household

Generally this means that the parties live under the same roof, illness, holidays, work and other periodical absences apart. . . .

(2) A sharing of daily life

Living together seems to me to inevitably involve a mutuality in the daily round: a sharing of tasks and duties. . . .

(3) Stability and a degree of permanence in the relationship; that it is not a temporary infatuation or passing relationship such as a holiday romance. . . .

(4) Finances

Is the way in which financial matters are being handled an indication of the relationship? . . .

(5) A sexual relationship

It is enough for me to state that this is admitted and is ongoing. . . .

(6) Children

(7) Intention and motivation

(8) The opinion of the reasonable person with normal perceptions.'[417]

By contrast, in *Butterworth v Supplementary Benefits Commission*,[418] the female applicant was refused welfare benefits on the basis that she was cohabiting. In fact, she was being cared for in her own home after a serious accident by her former partner. The court on appeal found that he was doing this out of loyalty and friendship. He had his own bedroom and they did not have a sexual relationship. He did cook and perform household tasks that she was unable to carry out because of her injuries. Both regarded the arrangement as temporary until the applicant had recovered. The court concluded that the couple were not living together as husband and wife, because it was not their intention to do so.

Hitherto, and as such cases indicate, the courts have tended to focus on the degree to which the parties' lives are intertwined. But in *Nutting v Southern Housing Group Ltd*[419] the court looked instead at the degree of permanent commitment in the relationship. The claimant had had a tempestuous same-sex relationship with his partner, at one time being ordered from the flat (of which the partner was sole tenant) and imprisoned for breach of a non-molestation order. The partner had now died. The claimant sought to succeed

---

[416] [2000] 1 FLR 383.

[417] At pp 391–3. Compare the Family Law (Scotland) Act 2006 s 25(2), which provides: 'In determining whether a person is a cohabitant of another person the court shall have regard to—(a) the length of the period during which A and B have been living together (or lived together); (b) the nature of their relationship during that period; and (c) the nature and extent of any financial arrangements subsisting, or which subsisted, during that period.'

[418] (1981) FLR 264.   [419] [2004] EWHC 2982 (Ch) [2005] 1 FLR 1066.

him as tenant under the Housing Act 1988 (a provision equivalent to that in issue in the *Fitzpatrick* and *Ghaidan* cases above). The court accepted that the ruling in *Ghaidan* meant that the provision should be interpreted as extending to same-sex couples but rejected the claim. On appeal it was held that the couple had not been living together as if they were husband and wife. Evans-Lombe J upheld the first instance judge, who had emphasised the need to establish that the relationship was an emotional one of 'mutual lifetime commitment rather than simply one of convenience, friendship, companionship or the living together of lovers'.[420] Further, he considered that the relationship must also be one which has been presented to the outside world 'openly and unequivocally so that society considers it to be of permanent intent—the words "till death us do part" being apposite'.[421]

In emphasising these criteria, the court confronted the question of what is meant by the expression, living 'as husband and wife', as distinct from 'as lovers'. It demonstrated that the statutory language in such provisions does indeed apply marriage-likeness, or marriage-equivalence, as the key criterion for eligibility, and as we saw above, one of the fundamental features of marriage is that it is intended to last for life. Circumstances may well arise where a couple who 'cohabit' would find it difficult honestly to say that they intended or even hoped to do so for the rest of their lives.[422] Yet, in some statutory contexts, despite the requirement of the relationship having to be 'marriage-like', such a strict test should not be imposed. For example, under the Family Law Act 1996, a court deciding whether to make an occupation order in favour of a cohabitant must in any event have regard to the 'level of commitment' in the couple's relationship[423] and this test replaces a former requirement to 'have regard to the fact that they have not given each other the commitment involved in marriage.'[424] The latter formulation was regarded as pejorative, but either test recognises that one may be 'living as husband and wife', without making exactly the same kind of commitment to each other as spouses do.

It will be noted that Evans-Lombe J also appeared to regard it as essential that the parties' relationship was 'openly and unequivocally' presented to the outside world. But here again, he may have gone too far. In reaching this view, he referred in particular to the speech of Lord Millett in *Ghaidan v Godin-Mendoza*.[425] His Lordship (who actually dissented in that case) certainly emphasised the importance of 'outward appearances'[426] but with respect, both he and the court in *Nutting* may have been confusing the requirement to satisfy an objective test of whether a couple can be said to be living as husband and wife, with a necessity to *present* themselves as so living. The two are different things. One might

---

[420] At para 9.   [421] Ibid.

[422] See the conflicting findings on the nature of cohabitants' commitment to each other, in C Smart and P Stevens, *Cohabitation breakdown*, 2000; C Lewis et al, *Cohabitation, separation and fatherhood*, 2002; J Lewis, *The End of Marriage? Individualism and Intimate Relationships*, 2001; A Barlow and G James, 'Regulating Marriage and Cohabitation in 21st Century Britain' (2004) 67 MLR 143; M Maclean and J Eekelaar, 'The Obligations and Expectations of Couples within Families: Three Modes of Interaction' (2004) 26 JSWFL 117; J Eekelaar and M Maclean, 'Marriage and the Moral Bases of Relationships' (2004) 31 JLS 510. It appears that many cohabitants assume their relationship carries the same legal consequences as marriage, often because they believe it to be a 'common law marriage': see A Barlow and S Duncan, 'Supporting families? New Labour's communitarianism and the "rationality mistake" Parts I and 2' (2000) 22, JSWFL 23 and 129.

[423] Section 36(6)(e) as amended by Domestic Violence, Crime and Victims Act 2004 s 2(2).

[424] Family Law Act 1996 s 41 until repealed by Domestic Violence, Crime and Victims Act 2004 s 2(1).

[425] [2004] UKHL 30, [2004] 2 AC 557.   [426] Para 92.

imagine that some couples, especially same-sex couples, would seek to keep the nature of their relationship private from their neighbours, employers and family. It should not follow that the life they share together cannot be classed as 'marriage-like'. Indeed, it would be ironic if, just because it used to be more common for cohabiting women to take their partner's name and refer to themselves as 'Mrs', in order to avoid the stigma of being known to 'live in sin', a couple who now choose not to demonstrate the intimacy of their relationship to the outside world should be regarded as not cohabiting. Moreover, the original 'cohabitation rule', from which the criteria in *Kimber v Kimber*[427] were drawn, was developed precisely because benefit claimants hid the fact that they were cohabiting from the outside world in general and the authorities in particular.

We saw above that the Civil Partnership Act has amended the law to import into the relevant legislation a new definition of cohabitation for same-sex partners of 'living as if civil partners'. It remains to be seen how the courts will attempt to define this, given the problems inherent in determining what 'living as husband and wife' entails.

3 A GENERAL DEFINITION?

Such issues demonstrate some of the sensitivities and difficulties in arriving at a workable general definition of cohabitation for which a legal status might be arrived at. They indicate why the extension of legal protections has been ad hoc, and why the definitions have not been uniform. Context is of paramount importance in this area of the law. For example, we noted above that a claimant must demonstrate having lived for two years with the deceased when claiming under the Fatal Accidents Act 1976 or Inheritance (Provision for Family and Dependants) Act 1975. Other jurisdictions adopt different qualifying periods, such as, in New Zealand, where a three-year qualifying period, or the birth of a child, is required for a claim under the Property (Relationships) Act 1976.[428] Any such periods are bound to be arbitrary and can work injustice: a woman who has been living with a man for 18 months may be as much in need of compensation if he is killed as if she had been living with him for two years.

Whether it would be possible or desirable to produce a uniform definition and status to apply to all contexts is a debatable point and not one which either the Government or Parliament seem keen to tackle in the near future.

---

[427] [2000] 1 FLR 383.
[428] See B Atkin, 'The rights of married and unmarried couples in New Zealand—radical new laws on property and succession' [2003] CFLQ 173.

3

THE PERSONAL AND PROPERTY CONSEQUENCES OF MARRIAGE, CIVIL PARTNERSHIP AND COHABITATION

A INTRODUCTION

This chapter explores the personal legal consequences of adult intimate relationships. and then considers the property consequences. Since marriage was, and probably still remains, the officially preferred form of adult union as far as the state is concerned,[1] it is helpful to view it as the benchmark against which other intimate relationships can be measured. We thus consider the different consequences of marriage and then examine how far civil partnership mirrors these. Finally, where appropriate, we discuss the position of those who cohabit.

In examining the legal effects of an adult relationship, two issues need to be considered. First, how does their marriage (or other relationship) affect the parties' legal relationship vis-à-vis each other? Here, the common law doctrine of unity of the spouses, explained below, is important historically, but now has little continuing significance in the wake of the political and social movement towards sexual equality between men and women.[2] Secondly, how far is the parties' relationship legally privileged over other domestic relationships? Here, one can see, in the face of a declining marriage rate and an increase in cohabitation and other family forms, a trend towards providing uniform rules to deal with people's relationships, regardless of their legal form. This is most apparent and most developed in the case of civil partnerships, which were, as we saw in Chapter 2, overtly intended to put same-sex partners in as similar a legal position as spouses as possible, without actually allowing them to 'marry' each other. But, as will be seen, it is premature to argue that marital status is irrelevant to determining a person's legal rights and obligations.

---

[1] See eg Home Office, *Supporting Families* (1998) Introduction, para 8: 'marriage is still the surest foundation for raising children and remains the choice of the majority of people in Britain. We want to strengthen the institution of marriage to help more marriages to succeed'; para 4.3: 'we do share the belief of the majority of people that marriage provides the most reliable framework for raising children.'

[2] For a fascinating global historical comparison of marriage laws, see A Gautier, 'Legal Regulation of Marital Relations: An Historical and Comparative Approach' (2005) 19 Int Jo of Law, Policy and the Family 47.

1 THE DOCTRINE OF UNITY

At common law the principal effect of marriage was that for many purposes it fused the legal personalities of husband and wife into one. According to Blackstone:[3]

'By marriage, the husband and wife are one person in law; that is, the very being or legal existence of the woman is suspended during the marriage, or at least is incorporated and consolidated into that of the husband; under whose wing, protection, and *cover*, she performs everything; and is therefore called in our law-French a *feme-covert* . . . Upon this principle of a union of person in husband and wife, depend almost all the legal rights, duties, and disabilities, that either of them acquire by the marriage.'

The principle was enunciated in the *Dialogus de Scaccario* in the twelfth century and repeated by every leading common law writer since.[4] But it may be doubted whether this doctrine was ever a firmly established rule of the common law. For example, while it operated to prevent any action at common law between the spouses, if a tort was committed either by or against a married woman, both she and her husband were joined as co-defendants or co-plaintiffs to the action. In another context, a woman on marriage ipso facto acquired her husband's domicile but not his nationality.

Neither equity nor the ecclesiastical law accepted the doctrine of unity of personality, and both gave married women access to their courts and even permitted actions between spouses. But it was not until the Married Women's Property Act 1870 that a wife was given an extremely limited right to maintain an action in her own name in the courts of common law. Whilst a series of statutes culminating in the Law Reform (Married Women and Tortfeasors) Act 1935 substantially put a married woman in the same legal position as a single woman, they were typical of so much English legislative reform in that they created extensive exceptions to the old rules without abolishing outright the fundamental principle on which the anomalies were based.

The doctrine of unity was doubtless biblical in origin[5] but in time, it became the legal justification for subordinating the wife's will and acts to those of her husband, and the embodiment of patriarchy. It is doubtful whether the view that marriage as such creates a legal unity of personalities, irrespective of the social implications, survived the decision of the Court of Appeal in *Midland Bank Trust Co Ltd v Green (No 3)*.[6] A husband and wife were sued for conspiracy; it was argued that they could not be liable on the ground that they were one person in law and therefore could not conspire with each other. This defence failed. At first instance Oliver J concluded:[7]

'Unless I am compelled by authority to do so—and I do not conceive that I am—I decline to apply, as a policy of law, a mediaeval axiom which was never wholly accurate and which appears to me now to be as ill-adapted to the society in which we live as it is repugnant to common sense.'

The same sentiments were expressed in the Court of Appeal, where Oliver J's judgment was affirmed. Lord Denning MR expressed himself in these words:[8]

---

[3] *Commentaries*, i, 442.

[4] See G Williams 'The Legal Unity of Husband and Wife' (1947) 10 MLR 16 at pp 16–18, and the exhaustive judgment of Oliver J in *Midland Bank Trust Co Ltd v Green (No 3)* [1979] Ch 496.

[5] Genesis 2, 24; Genesis 3, 16.   [6] [1982] Ch 529, CA.   [7] [1979] Ch 496 at 527.

[8] At 538–9.

'Nowadays, both in law and in fact, husband and wife are two persons, not one ... The severance in all respects is so complete that I would say that the doctrine of unity and its ramifications should be discarded altogether, except in so far as it is retained by judicial decision or by Act of Parliament.'

In more picturesque language Sir George Baker P said that to hold that a husband and wife could not be liable in the tort of conspiracy because they were one person:

'... would ... be akin to basing a judgment on the proposition that the Earth is flat, because many believed that centuries ago. We now know that the Earth is not flat. We now know that husband and wife in the eyes of the law and in fact are equal.'[9]

The concept of civil partnership is a purely statutory creation and the Civil Partnership Act 2004 creating it contains no overt extension to it of any common law vestiges of the doctrine of unity. However, a residual notion of married couples as forming one unit may still be found in the—statutory—taxation system, and is applicable to eligible civil partners.[10] For example, both spouses and civil partners are exempt from tax on lifetime gifts and inheritance tax in relation to transfers between each other.[11] Moreover, there is still a tax allowance payable to married people (and now civil partners) aged over 70.[12] This was previously available to all married couples. It may be payable to either spouse or civil partner, or apportioned between them. It might once have been justified as reflecting the economic reality that in many instances the husband was the main breadwinner in the family and the head of the household. Its continued limited existence could be justified as reflecting the fact that, in the case of older couples, who have had that traditional division of labour during their marriage, the wife is less likely to have significant pension entitlements and is more likely to be dependent upon the husband's pension and other resources built up over his career. However, it is more difficult to make the same justification in the case of civil partners. The more likely reason for its retention is that it is politically expedient to provide certain tax benefits to the married, but that the cost of such an allowance is restricted by limiting it to the smaller number of couples who are elderly. Having committed itself to equality of treatment between spouses and civil partners, the government had to grant the same tax advantages to the latter regardless of logic.

2 CONSORTIUM

The slow movement toward equality of the spouses was reflected by changes in the common law concept of consortium, an abstract notion which appears to mean living together as husband and wife with all the incidents (insofar as these can be defined) that flow from that relationship.[13] At one time it would have been said that the husband had the right to

---

[9] At 542.

[10] See too the Married Women's Property Act 1882, s 11 and the Life Assurance Act 1774: spouse (or civil partner—Civil Partnership Act 2004 s 70) may insure own life for benefit of spouse or children and may insure the other's life and recover without showing financial loss—*Reed v Royal Exchange Assurance Co* (1795) Peake Add Cas 70; *Griffiths v Fleming* [1909] 1 KB 805, CA.

[11] Inheritance Taxes Act 1984 s 18, as amended by Tax and Civil Partnership Regulations 2005 SI 2005/3229 reg 7.

[12] Income and Corporation Taxes Act 1988 s 257A and s 257AB (inserted by Tax and Civil Partnership Regulations 2005 SI 2005/3229 reg 52).

[13] Per Lord Campbell in *Lynch v Knight* (1861) 9 HL Cas 577 at 589.

his wife's consortium whilst the latter had not so much a reciprocal right to her husband's consortium as a correlative duty to give him her society and her services—a view which was not entirely obsolete in the middle of the nineteenth century. A clear illustration of the wife's legal subjection to her husband can be seen in the old common law rule that a woman who murdered her husband was guilty of petit treason, like the vassal who slew his lord or the servant who slew his master.[14] The wife's basic duty was to submit to the husband, in return for which the husband would protect and support her. As one judge described marriage:

'It is an engagement between a man and woman to live together, and love one another as husband and wife, to the exclusion of all others. This is expanded in the promises of the marriage ceremony by words having reference to the natural relations which spring from that engagement, such as protection on the part of the man, and submission on the part of the woman.'[15]

The husband was also accepted at one time as having the right physically to restrain or confine his wife to the house,[16] and it was only in 1891 that this view was finally rejected. In R v Jackson[17] the wife had gone to live with relations whilst her husband was absent in New Zealand. After his return she refused to live with him again. Consequently he arranged with two men that they should seize her as she came out of church one Sunday afternoon. She was then put into a carriage and taken to her husband's residence, where she was allowed complete freedom of the house but was not permitted to leave the building. She then applied for a writ of habeas corpus and it was unanimously held by the Court of Appeal that it was no defence that the husband was merely confining her in order to enforce his right to her consortium. This principle was reinforced subsequently by the Court of Appeal in R v Reid,[18] where it was held that a husband who steals, carries away or secretes his wife against her will is guilty of the common law offence of kidnapping her. As Cairns LJ said:[19]

'The notion that a husband can, without incurring punishment, treat his wife, whether she be a separated wife or otherwise, with any kind of hostile force is obsolete.'

A further aspect of the husband's right to consortium was the action at common law to obtain damages against anyone who interfered with his right. This could take the form of enticement (a tort also available to a wife),[20] harbouring the wife, or adultery. The last began as the common law action for criminal conversation[21] by which the husband could obtain compensation for the loss of his wife's comfort and society as the result of the adulterer's wrongful act. This action was abolished by the Matrimonial Causes Act 1857 and replaced by a statutory claim for damages in the divorce court which was almost always made on a petition for divorce. In addition, if the husband lost his wife's services as the result of a tort committed against her, he could maintain a separate and independent

---

14 The distinction between petit treason and murder was abolished in 1828 by 9 Geo 4, c 31 s 2.

15 Durham v Durham (1885) 10 PD 80 at p 82 per Sir James Hannen P.

16 And thus also physically to punish her. See R v Lister (1721) 1 Stra 478, Re Cochrane (1840) 8 Dowl 630.

17 [1891] 1 QB 671, CA.   18 [1973] QB 299, CA.   19 At 303.

20 Gray v Gee (1923) 39 TLR 429. This replaced an earlier writ of ravishment or trespass vi et armis de uxore rapta et abducta available only to the husband.

21 See L Stone Road to Divorce (1990) Part IX.

action against the tortfeasor. This served a useful purpose: if, for example, the wife was seriously injured as the result of the defendant's negligence, it provided a means by which the husband could recover the expenses to which he had been put, such as for medical and nursing care, the provision of help to look after himself and the children, and visiting her whilst she was in hospital. But although a wife might be put to similar expenses if her husband was injured, the action was not available to her.[22] Actions of this kind came to be regarded as out-moded and patriarchal, and by 1982, had all been abolished.[23] However, more general provisions to compensate family members where a relative is *killed* as a result of wrongdoing were introduced by statute as early as 1846 by the Fatal Accidents Act (commonly called Lord Campbell's Act). This permitted certain dependants of a person killed as the result of the defendant's wrongful act, neglect or default to recover the financial loss suffered as a result of the death. The Act was amended extensively by further legislation in the course of the next 100 years, and eventually consolidated in the Fatal Accidents Act 1976.[24]

This movement for the equality of the rights of the sexes also gradually extended into other fields of private law. In 1923 Parliament equated the rights of the spouses to petition for divorce;[25] in 1925 it established the principle that they have equal rights with respect to their children;[26] in 1967 it gave each of them the power to apply for an order regulating their rights to occupy the matrimonial home;[27] and in 1978 it gave them reciprocal rights to seek maintenance from each other.[28] All these changes reflect the modern view that the wife is no longer the weaker partner subservient to the stronger, but that both spouses are the joint, co-equal heads of the family. It seems to be clear that, insofar as consortium still exists, 'a husband has a right to the consortium of his wife, and the wife to the consortium of her husband',[29] and these rights must now be regarded as exactly reciprocal.[30]

But the question arises whether it makes sense to talk of consortium as continuing to exist at all. There are, of course, still areas of law which depend upon case law rather than statute for development. We will see below, for example, that the law on 'breach of confidence' has been invigorated by the advent of the Human Rights Act 1998, with significant case developments leading towards the recognition of a right to privacy which may have particular importance regarding intimate relationships. On this basis, one might argue

---

[22] *Best v Samuel Fox & Co Ltd* [1952] AC 716, HL.

[23] It is, however, possible to obtain compensation in tort for losses incurred where a relative gives up work or incurs expenses to care for a family member injured by the defendant's negligence, but in such a situation the nature of the relationship is immaterial, and damages would be payable whether it is a cohabitant, spouse, parents or other who gives up work to look after the injured claimant: *Cunningham v Harrison* [1973] QB 942, CA; *Donnelly v Joyce* [1974] QB 454, CA.

[24] This in turn was amended by s 3 of the Administration of Justice Act 1982. These provisions are discussed below, at pp 1124–8.

[25] Matrimonial Causes Act 1923.

[26] Guardianship of Infants Act 1925; see S Cretney 'What will the women want next?' (1996) 112 LQR 110. In point of fact, their position was not exactly equal until implementation of the Children Act 1989. See below, p 355.

[27] Matrimonial Homes Act 1967.   [28] Domestic Proceedings and Magistrates' Courts Act 1978.

[29] Per Scrutton LJ in *Place v Searle* [1932] 2 KB 497 at 512, CA.

[30] See also *Re E (An Alleged Patient); Sheffield City Council v E and S* [2004] EWHC 2808 (Fam) [2005] 1 FLR 965 paras 109–132.

that there may still be a residual, common law area of the concept of consortium.[31] Moreover, the Civil Partnership Act 2004 does not contain any provisions referring to the extension of consortium to civil partnerships and this may indicate, as the government were at pains to insist, that it is *not* the same as marriage and also underscore a continuing role for 'consortium' as conveying some message about the unique quality of marriage.

However, the fact that it is so difficult to identify any such residual area which has not, in practice, been superseded by statute, together with the trend towards greater equalisation of the position of married and unmarried partners makes this an unconvincing argument. Indeed, as we show below, where the common law provides the basis for legal protection, it is increasingly likely to apply to any and all couples who are at least in 'marriage-like' relationships. This suggests that it is now more sensible to consider what the 'consequences of marriage' (and other intimate relationships) may be rather than to attempt to pigeon-hole some of these into 'aspects of consortium'.

B PERSONAL CONSEQUENCES

(a) Use of surname

Adults may use any surname they choose provided that there is no intention to perpetrate a fraud.[32] Many wives still take their husband's surnames on marriage, although they may continue to be known by their former names for professional or business purposes.[33] Likewise a woman may retain her former husband's name after the marriage has been terminated either by death or by divorce, and a man has no such property in his name as to entitle him to sue for an injunction to prevent his divorced wife from using it unless, at any rate, she is doing so for the purpose of defrauding him or some other right of his is being invaded.[34] Similarly, an unmarried woman may use the surname of the man with whom she is living if she wishes (and vice versa), although she may be civilly or criminally liable if she does so for the purpose of defrauding another.

There seems no reason why civil partners should not be able to adopt a common surname in accordance with these rules should they wish. Clearly, there is no norm as to which partner's name is more likely to be used: perhaps a combined surname may prove popular.

---

[31] See the discussion by S Cretney, J Masson and R Bailey-Harris, *Principles of Family Law* (7th ed, 2002) at paras 3–001–3–007.

[32] The execution and enrolment of a deed poll merely provide evidence of the executant's intention to be known by a different name and have no other legal significance.

[33] Other countries take a much stricter approach and lay down firm rules to determine whose surname may be used, but this may amount to a breach of Arts 8 and 14 of the European Convention on Human Rights: see *Burghardz v Switzerland* [1995] Fam Law 71 (ECHR).

[34] *Cowley v Cowley* [1900] P 305, CA; affd [1901] AC 450, HL; cf *Du Boulay v Du Boulay* (1869) LR 2 PC 430, PC at 441. Thus, if she holds herself out as his wife after he has remarried, she may be guilty of libel or slander if the reasonable inference is that he is not legally married to his second wife.

(b) Sexual intercourse

As we have seen, the incapacity of either spouse or the wilful refusal of the respondent to consummate the marriage will entitle the petitioner to a decree of nullity.[35] As regards sexual intercourse *after* consummation, Hale wrote in the eighteenth century:[36]

'But the husband cannot be guilty of a rape committed by himself upon his lawful wife, for by their mutual matrimonial consent and contract the wife hath given up herself in this kind unto her husband which she cannot retract.'

Although Hale cited no authority for this view, it was generally regarded as a correct statement of the common law.[37] But the change in attitude towards the relationship of the spouses during the present century led the courts to seek ways of limiting the scope of the husband's immunity,[38] and the issue was ultimately reviewed by the House of Lords in *R v R*[39] in 1991.

The wife left the husband and told him that she intended to petition for divorce. Some three weeks later he broke into her parents' house, where she was living, and attempted to have sexual intercourse with her against her will. The trial judge ruled that the husband's immunity had been lost, whereupon he pleaded guilty to attempted rape. He then appealed to the Court of Appeal and, when his appeal was dismissed, to the House of Lords. Lord Keith, with whose speech the other members of the House agreed, maintained that the common law is capable of evolving in the light of changing social, economic and cultural developments. Marriage, he pointed out, 'is in modern times regarded as a partnership of equals and no longer one in which the wife must be the subservient chattel of the husband'. Consequently any reasonable person must now regard Hale's proposition as unacceptable.[40] The only obstacle to declaring that a husband had no immunity was the Sexual Offences (Amendment) Act 1976 s 1 which, for the first time, laid down a statutory definition of rape including the words '*unlawful* sexual intercourse'. This phrase usually connotes extra-marital intercourse[41] and consequently it could be argued that the Act had reintroduced the old common law rule by making it impossible for a husband to rape his wife in any circumstances. Lord Keith rejected this argument on the grounds that it was inconceivable that Parliament had this intention and that 'unlawful' in this context could not reasonably import the existing common law exceptions. The House therefore

---

[35] Above pp 78–82.

[36] 1 Hale PC 629. But he could be guilty of aiding and abetting another to rape her: *Lord Audley's Case* (1631) 3 State Tr 401, HL; *R v Leak* [1976] QB 217, CA.

[37] It was not until *R v Clarence* (1888) 22 QBD 23 that judicial doubts were expressed about its correctness.

[38] A number of cases held that consent could be retracted following a court order or by the parties' agreement: *R v Clarke* [1949] 2 All ER 448 (consent withdrawn after decree of judicial separation); *R v O'Brien* [1974] 3 All ER 663 (decree nisi of divorce); *R v Steele* (1976) 65 Cr App Rep 22, CA (non-molestation injunction); *R v Roberts* [1986] Crim LR 188, CA (separation deed). In *R v Miller* [1954] 2 QB 282 it was also held that a husband could not insist on his right to have intercourse by force, and thus would be guilty of assault on his wife. See also *R v Kowalski* [1988] 1 FLR 447, CA (husband guilty of indecent assault by forcing wife to submit to fellatio before sexual intercourse).

[39] [1992] 1 AC 599, HL.   [40] At 616D–E.   [41] See *R v Chapman* [1959] 1 QB 100, CCA.

concluded that the word was mere surplusage and that 'in modern times the supposed marital exception in rape forms no part of the law of England'.[42]

The European Court of Human Rights subsequently rejected a complaint by R that the House of Lords' ruling was in breach of Art 7 of the European Convention because it had retrospectively criminalised his act, the court holding that the line of cases which had already eroded the marital immunity had rendered their Lordships' ultimate ruling reasonably foreseeable, and further that:

'... the abandonment of the unacceptable idea of a husband being immune against prosecution for rape of his wife was in conformity not only with a civilised concept of marriage but also, and above all, with the fundamental objectives of the Convention, the very essence of which is respect for human dignity and human freedom.'[43]

It may still be argued that there remains a mutual right to, or perhaps legitimate expectation of, sexual intercourse after the marriage had been consummated, and that a refusal to have intercourse, or perhaps an unreasonable rationing of its frequency, might ground a petition for divorce based upon behaviour such that one spouse could not reasonably be expected to live with the other.[44]

It is less certain what the position is in relation to a civil partnership. We have seen[45] that consummation is not a requirement of the partnership. How far the partnership was nonetheless intended or expected to have a sexual dimension to it in the minds of the legislators is unclear. After all, Parliament finally rejected an attempt to open up partnerships to couples who are clearly not engaged in a sexual relationship, such as two elderly sisters. A reluctance to contemplate the details of sexual behaviour in same-sex relationships and to attempt to prescribe what these should entail no doubt influenced its approach. It might therefore be left to the parties themselves, in the context of dissolution of the partnership, to determine how important the sexual aspect was to them and thus whether a 'failure' of it could lead to an application based on 'behaviour' as above.

(c) 'Marital confidences'

If a marriage breaks down, bitterness and vindictiveness may lead one spouse to break marital confidences and to broadcast information imparted and received on the shared understanding that it would go no further. Does the law offer the other any remedy in such circumstances?

The 'not altogether comfortable'[46] label of breach of confidence provides the appropriate

---

[42] At p 489. Section 1 was subsequently amended by the Criminal Justice and Public Order Act 1994 s 142 to delete the reference to 'unlawful' sexual intercourse. See also Law Com Report No 205 (*Rape within Marriage*). The offence of rape is now contained in s 1 of the Sexual Offences Act 2003.

[43] *CR v United Kingdom; SW v United Kingdom* [1996] 1 FLR 434 para 42 (at 448–9). See S Palmer 'Rape in Marriage and the European Convention on Human Rights' (1997) 5 Fem LS 91; P Ghandhi and J James 'Marital rape and retrospectivity—the human rights dimensions at Strasbourg' (1997) 9 CFLQ 17.

[44] *P(D) v P(J)* [1965] 2 All ER 456 (wife guilty of cruelty in refusing intercourse, although due to invincible fear of conception and childbirth) but cf *Mason v Mason* (1980) 11 Fam Law 143 (wife's refusal to have intercourse more than once a week was not behaviour such that the husband could not be expected to live with her). See further below pp 267–9.

[45] At pp 98–9.

[46] Per Lord Nicholls of Birkenhead in *Campbell v MGN Ltd* [2004] UKHL 22, [2004] 2 AC 457 at para 14.

cause of action for what is now better described as 'misuse of private information'.[47] In the face of the developing jurisprudence of the European Court of Human Rights[48] and the cultural phenomenon of increased interest in (and exposure of) celebrity, the English courts have been constrained to develop this action[49] to balance out the rights protected under Arts 8 (right to respect for private life) and 10 (freedom of expression) of the European Convention on Human Rights.[50] There are three elements which must be satisfied. First, the information must be confidential: ie 'available to one person (or a group of people) and not generally available to others, provided that the person (or group) who possesses the information does not intend that it should become available to others.'[51] The second requirement at one time was understood to be that the information must have been communicated by the confider to the confidant in circumstances of confidence. It is clear that the relationship of husband and wife would satisfy this condition. As Ungoed-Thomas J said in *Argyll v Argyll*:[52]

'There could hardly be anything more intimate or confidential than is involved in that relationship, or than in the mutual trust and confidences which are shared between husband and wife. The confidential nature of the relationship is of its very essence and so obviously and necessarily implicit in it that there is no need for it to be expressed.'

But in any case, it has since been held that an obligation of confidence may arise even where the information in question has not been confided by a confider to a confidant.[53] For example, in *Venables and Thompson v News Group Newspapers Ltd and others*[54] an injunction to prevent the reporting of information which might identify the newly released killers of the toddler, James Bulger, was granted against the whole world, the duty of confidence arising from the nature of the information itself, regardless of the circumstances in which the information might come to the knowledge of a person who might wish to publish it. The knowledge, actual or imputed, that information is private will normally impose on anyone publishing that information the duty to justify what, in the absence of justification, will be a wrongful invasion of privacy.

Thirdly, there must be an unauthorised use of that information to the detriment of the party communicating it.[55]

The courts have recognised that people are now likely to enter into a greater range of

---

[47] Per Lord Nicholls of Birkenhead in *Campbell v MGN Ltd* [2004] UKHL 22, [2004] 2 AC 457 at para 14.

[48] In particular, *von Hannover v Germany* (2005) 40 EHRR 1.

[49] 'We cannot pretend that we find it satisfactory to be required to shoe-horn within the cause of action of breach of confidence claims for publication of unauthorised photographs of a private occasion.' Per Lord Phillips of Worth Matravers MR in *Douglas and Others v Hello! Ltd and Others (No 2)* [2005] EWCA CIV 595 [2005] 2 FCR 487 at para 53.

[50] See G Phillipson, 'Transforming Breach of Confidence? Towards a Common Law Right of Privacy under the Human Rights Act' (2003) 66 MLR 726.

[51] Ibid para 55.

[52] [1967] Ch 302 at 322. The case concerned an action by the Duchess of Argyll to restrain her former husband, the Duke, from publishing stories about her (and her matrimonial misconduct) in *The People* Sunday newspaper.

[53] *Attorney-General v Guardian Newspapers Limited (No 2)* [1990] 1 AC 109 per Lord Goff of Chieveley at 281.

[54] [2001] Fam 430.

[55] See *Coco v A N Clark (Engineers) Ltd* [1969] RPC 41 at 47, applying *Saltman Engineering Co, Ltd v Campbell Engineering Co Ltd* (1948) [1963] 3 All ER 413n, CA, and followed in *Stephens v Avery* [1988] Ch 449.

intimate relationships than hitherto, and the question has arisen whether marriage is still sufficiently different and special—perhaps privileged—as to require that information about sexual relationships and behaviour *outside* marriage should be treated differently, with less protection against disclosure being offered. In *Stephens v Avery*[56] Sir Nicholas Browne-Wilkinson V-C held that an injunction could be granted to prevent the defendant from disclosing to a newspaper details of the plaintiff's lesbian relationship with a third person which had been communicated and received expressly in confidence. He left open the question whether the relationship of unmarried sexual partners in itself creates a duty of confidentiality or whether an earlier case, in which it had been held that a homosexual relationship did not raise such a duty,[57] was correctly decided. The issue was considered further in two cases, *Theakston v MGN Ltd*[58] and *A v B plc and another*.[59] Both concerned people in the public eye; the first a TV presenter and the second a footballer. In each case, the sexual exploits of the claimants were to be revealed in 'kiss and tell' stories in national newspapers unless restrained by injunction. In *Theakston*, Ouseley J noted that

'There is a whole range of relationships in human life in which sexual activity may occur, from marital relationships to unmarried but long term partnerships, to extra marital relationships long and short term, from one night stands to yet more fleeting encounters with prostitutes. Indeed it may well be that the very concept of a relationship for the purpose of confidentiality is simply inapplicable to such transitory or commercial sexual relationships. Sexual activities which can be intimate, private and personal and which might attract confidentiality can fall far short of full sexual intercourse; a passionate embrace could have all those qualities. Intimate physical relations can occur in a range of places from a private house to a hotel bedroom, to a car in a secluded spot, to a nightclub or indeed to a brothel.'[60]

He disagreed with Jack J who, at first instance in *A v B plc and another*[61] had continued an injunction restraining publication of the revelations of two women who had had sex with the (married) footballer. Jack J had considered[62] that no distinction should be drawn between relationships within and outside marriage. The Court of Appeal rejected this view, on the basis that it made no allowance for the variety of relationships noted by Ouseley J and the rather transient nature of the footballer's relations with the two women. It thus seems that the court will look to the nature of the relationship. Where it is as intimate and confidential as that of a married couple—which presumably, may be assumed in the case of a civil partnership—it is submitted that confidences exchanged between them are entitled to the same protection as similar confidences between spouses.[63]

(d) Evidence in legal proceedings

When one considers the question of testimony in legal proceedings, two principles of public policy may come into conflict. The first is the need to protect a person from having

---

[56] Ibid.

[57] *M and N v Kelvin MacKenzie and News Groups Newspapers Ltd* (1988) (unreported) cited in *Stephens v Avery* (above) at 456 and 482–3 respectively.

[58] [2002] EWHC 137 (QB), [2002] EMLR 398.   [59] [2002] EWCA Civ 337, [2003] QB 195.

[60] [2002] EWHC 137 (QB), [2002] EMLR 398 at para 57.   [61] [2001] 1 WLR 2341.

[62] Ibid at 2354, para 56.

[63] See also the guidelines given by the Court of Appeal in *A v B plc and another* [2001] 1 WLR 2341 at para 11(xi): 'Obviously, the more stable the relationship the greater will be the significance which is attached to it.'

to give evidence against his or her spouse or civil partner. The second is that in any proceedings, civil or criminal, no evidence should be excluded if it will help the court or the jury to arrive at the truth.

Competence

At common law neither the parties nor their spouses were competent witnesses in civil proceedings or (with very few exceptions) in criminal proceedings. A spouse's evidence was excluded for a number of reasons: the fact that it might be untrustworthy, the wish to preserve marital harmony and to protect marital confidences, and the undesirability of having a witness giving evidence against his or her spouse and the consequent unfairness of permitting evidence to be given for the spouse. In civil proceedings this rule was abolished by the Evidence Amendment Act 1853 and spouses became competent to give evidence for any party. In criminal proceedings, the Criminal Evidence Act 1898, which also for the first time made the accused generally competent to give evidence on his or her own behalf, enabled a spouse to give evidence for the defence subject to some qualifications. Various statutes also made the spouse a competent witness for the prosecution in the case of certain crimes, mainly of a sexual nature or against children.

The Police and Criminal Evidence Act 1984 s 80 made the accused's spouse a competent witness for the prosecution, the accused and any co-accused in all cases unless the couple were charged jointly. The Youth Justice and Criminal Evidence Act 1999 amended the general competence rules and s 53 of that Act now provides that all persons are competent at every stage in criminal proceedings to give evidence. Where they are witnesses for the prosecution, they are competent unless charged and liable to conviction in the proceedings. A spouse, civil partner (or cohabitant) is therefore a competent witness for the prosecution where he or she has pleaded guilty or the charges against him or her have been dropped.

Compellability

Once spouses became competent in civil proceedings, the main reason for their not being compelled to give evidence disappeared. The Evidence Amendment Act 1853 accordingly made them compellable as well as competent. The Civil Partnership Act 2004 s 84 extends this (as an enactment or rule of law concerning a spouse giving evidence) to civil partners.

The arguments against forcing a person to give evidence against his or her spouse or partner in *criminal* proceedings are, however, more cogent.[64] The Police and Criminal Evidence Act struck a compromise.[65] For the first time the spouse was made a compellable witness for the *accused* in all cases unless the spouses are charged jointly. But he or she (and now a civil partner)[66] may be compelled to give evidence for the *prosecution* or a person jointly charged with the accused in only three cases. These are:

(a) if the offence charged involves an assault on, or injury or a threat of injury to, the spouse or civil partner or a person under the age of 16;

(b) if the offence charged is a sexual offence[67] against a person under the age of 16; and

(c) if the offence charged consists of attempting or conspiring to commit any of

---

[64] See *Hoskyn v Metropolitan Police Comr* [1979] AC 474, HL, and the critique by S Edwards *Sex and Gender in the Legal Process* pp 202–5.

[65] Section 80. See Creighton 'Spouse Competence and Compellability' [1990] Crim LR 34.

[66] Section 80 as amended by Civil Partnership Act 2004 Sch 27 para 97.   [67] As defined in s 80(7).

the above offences or of aiding, abetting, counselling, procuring or inciting their commission.

However repugnant it may seem to force a person to give evidence against his or her spouse or partner facing a criminal charge, in these cases the principle is outweighed by the need to enable the prosecution to produce evidence without which it would often be impossible to prove the offence. This will be effective, however, only if the witness is prepared to give evidence, and there is no doubt that a number of prosecutions, particularly of offences involving assault, are not brought because of the victim's unwillingness to testify, whether from fear or some other cause.[68]

The arguments for and against the compellability of spouses apply equally to unmarried couples and to other family relationships. Although the policy decision was taken to align civil partnerships as far as possible with marriages and thus extend this provision to civil partners, in view of the current trend to bring spouses more into line with other witnesses, it is highly unlikely that these rules would be extended to other relationships.

(e) Contracts[69]

Between spouses or partners

The fact that a couple have an intimate relationship has played a significant part in the court's determination of whether any agreement they have reached between them should be regarded as a binding contract. An agreement between spouses will clearly be enforceable if it represents a business arrangement, but the courts have traditionally refused to interfere in the running of the home by giving legal effect to the sort of arrangements that spouses living together make every day in order to regularise their domestic affairs. The leading case is still *Balfour v Balfour*[70] where the Court of Appeal held that an agreement, under which the husband, who was about to go abroad, promised to pay the wife £30 a month in consideration of her not looking to him for further maintenance, was unenforceable because there was no intention to enter into legal relations. If the spouses are cohabiting when they enter into the agreement, there is a presumption that they do not intend to be legally bound.[71]

---

[68] See Edwards, loc cit. Where not compellable, the failure of the spouse or civil partner of a person charged in any proceedings to give evidence in the proceedings shall not be made the subject of any comment by the prosecution: Police and Criminal Evidence Act 1984 s 80A.

[69] For discussion of the role and limitations of contract in regulating agreements between intimate partners, see J Wightman, 'Intimate Relationships, Relational Contract Theory, and the Reach of Contract' (2000) 8 Fem LS 93.

[70] [1919] 2 KB 571, CA. See also *Spellman v Spellman* [1961] 2 All ER 498, CA (agreement as to ownership of car unenforceable).

[71] This appears to be the view of the majority of the Court of Appeal in *Gould v Gould* [1970] 1 QB 275. The presumption does not operate if the parties have separated or are at arm's length and about to separate: in these circumstances their intention becomes a question of fact to be inferred from all the evidence. In most cases of this kind, where the agreement relates to financial arrangements, it will be almost impossible to conclude that they did not intend to be legally bound by the terms. However, it should be noted that spouses or civil partners cannot oust the jurisdiction of the courts to determine with finality their financial and property relations, because the courts assert a public interest in ensuring both that a party is financially protected as far as possible and that the state's burden in covering any shortfall in such protection is limited: *Hyman v Hyman* [1929] AC 601, *Sutton v Sutton* [1984] Ch 184. For further discussion of this issue, and for the separate question of pre-nuptial agreements, see below pp 953ff and 1012–14.

A refusal to find an intention to enter into legal relations has also been demonstrated in cases concerning unmarried partners. In *Horrocks v Forray*[72] the executors of a man's will sought possession of a house in his name, occupied by the defendant and her two children. She had been the man's mistress for some 17 years and claimed that she had a contractual licence[73] to remain in the house. But the Court of Appeal held that although the man may have intended to make some provision for her financial security, this did not amount to an intention to enter into a binding agreement to do so, still less to relate specifically to her being permitted to occupy the house. As Scarman LJ put it,

'whatever relationship did exist between these two, it could as well be referable to the continuance of natural love and affection as to an intention to enter into an agreement which they intended to have legal effect.'[74]

In the absence of the agreement being made by deed, it may be equally difficult to establish that there was any consideration for it. In the context of occupation of the family home, it has been held that if one partner has given up some existing right or suffered some other detriment to go and live with the other, it may be possible to regard this as consideration and thus give rise to a contractual licence. In *Tanner v Tanner*,[75] for example, the plaintiff bought a house for the defendant and their twin daughters and the defendant surrendered a rent-controlled tenancy to move into it. When the plaintiff later claimed possession of the house, it was held that, as the defendant had furnished consideration by giving up the security of her flat, the licence was a contractual one. But in *Horrocks v Forray*, Megaw LJ, whilst not basing his decision on the point, was satisfied that the woman had made no equivalent sacrifice sufficient to found consideration for the man's alleged offer to look after her.[76]

A complicating factor in establishing consideration in the case of agreements between unmarried partners has been the role of public policy. At one time, an agreement between cohabitants might have been struck down as based on 'immoral consideration' because of its promoting a sexual relationship outside marriage. As Lord Wright stated in *Fender v St John Mildmay*,

'The law will not enforce an immoral promise, such as a promise between a man and a woman to live together without being married or to pay a sum of money or to give some other consideration in return for an immoral association.'[77]

But such a view was refined in *Sutton v Mishcon De Reya and Gawor and Co*,[78] at least in relation to the question of whether partners may contract with each other as regards their financial and property rights. The claimant formed a sado-masochistic relationship with a wealthy businessman, in which the claimant was the 'master' and the businessman his 'slave'. They jointly instructed the first defendants to draft a deed designed to 'create

---

[72] [1976] 1 All ER 737, CA.
[73] Relying on the decision of the Court of Appeal in *Tanner v Tanner* [1975] 3 All ER 776, CA discussed further below.
[74] At 547; See, to like effect, *Layton v Martin* [1986] 2 FLR 227.
[75] [1975] 3 All ER 776, CA, discussed further below at p 189.   [76] 745a.   [77] [1938] AC 1 at 42.
[78] [2003] EWHC 3166 (Ch), [2004] 1 FLR 837. See M Pawlowski, 'Cohabitation Contracts: The *Sutton* Case' [2004] Fam Law 199, R Probert, '*Sutton v Mischon de Reya and Gawor & Co*—Cohabitation contracts and Swedish sex slaves' [2004] CFLQ 453.

legally binding arrangements as to financial and other matters'[79] and which documented that the slave would give all his financial assets to the master. The couple were advised that the agreement might be regarded as unenforceable. The relationship broke down, and the claimant sued the solicitors and another firm which had advised him about the terms of a separation for negligence. Hart J, striking out the claim, held that whilst a property contract between two people who were cohabiting *could* be valid, the agreement in issue was primarily a contract for sexual relations outside marriage[80] and therefore unlawful. He considered that the agreement sprang directly from and was intended to give meaning to the sexual master/slave fantasy that the couple were enacting.[81] The distinction between an agreement concerning sexual relations on the one hand, and property rights arising from a relationship which involves sexual relations on the other, thus appears still to exist in English law, but at least it is clear that the latter should not now be struck down, without more, simply because the parties are in a sexual relationship.[82]

Precedents for the drafting of 'cohabitation contracts',[83] as they are commonly known, have been available for some time, although the extent of their use is unknown. It seems wise, as Wilson suggests,[84] to separate the financial terms from any non-financial ones, so that a court can 'blue pencil' any objectionable clauses without rendering the whole agreement unenforceable. Both parties should also have independent legal advice, to guard against any later question of undue influence.

Contracts with third parties

At common law a married woman had no contractual capacity and neither she nor her husband could sue or be sued on any contract made by her except as his agent. Equity did not take the same strict view, and if a wife had separate property, she could bind this by contract although she could not render herself *personally* liable on any agreement. To enable wives to carry on dealings with tradesmen for household goods, clothes etc, the law recognised them as agents for their husbands, and would enforce, against the husband, the pledging of his credit for the purchase of such articles. The agency device was particularly important for deserted wives with no means of support, who had what was called an 'agency of necessity', finally abolished only in 1970, which permitted them to incur debts against the husband's liability.[85]

---

[79] At para 11.

[80] It has been argued that categorising non-marital sexual relations as 'unlawful' is contrary to Art 8 of the ECHR and that marital status is irrelevant—the court will not, even within a marriage, enforce sexual relations: see G Wilson, '*Sutton* in Practice' [2004] Fam Law 202.

[81] At para 23.

[82] His Lordship considered that the agreement would in any case have been unenforceable either because of actual undue influence by the claimant over his partner, or because there was no intent to enter into legal relations, but the latter ground appears dubious given the care taken by both parties to have the agreement drawn up by solicitors in the first place. See the comment by R Bailey-Harris at [2004] Fam Law 247. The Committee of Ministers of the Council of Europe adopted a recommendation (R (88) 3, adopted on 7 March 1988) that property contracts between unmarried couples should not be considered invalid solely because of the fact of their unmarried status.

[83] See C Barton, *Cohabitation Contracts* (1985), A Barlow, *Cohabitants and the Law* (2001, 3rd edn), E Kingdom, 'Cohabitation Contracts and the Democratization of Personal Relations' (2000) 8 Fem LS 5.

[84] Op cit at 204.

[85] This agency was distinct from that pertaining while the spouses lived together, and was lost if the wife were herself guilty of a matrimonial offence.

Legislation gradually recognised the contractual capacity of married women. The Married Women's Property Act 1882 (which provided that all property acquired by a wife after 1882 should remain her separate property) gave a wife full contractual capacity and enacted that every contract entered into by her otherwise than as an agent should be deemed to be a contract with respect to her separate property and should bind it. Section 1 of the Law Reform (Married Women and Tortfeasors) Act 1935 provided that a married woman is capable of rendering herself and being rendered liable in respect of any contract, debt or obligation, and of suing and being sued in contract, and also that she is subject to the law relating to bankruptcy and the enforcement of judgments and orders as if she were a feme sole.

(f) Torts

The fiction of legal unity produced two separate rules in tort. First, if a tort was committed by or against a married woman, her husband had to be joined as a party to the action and failure to do so could be pleaded in abatement. Secondly, no liability in tort could arise between spouses and no action in tort could be brought by either of them against the other.

A married woman was given the power to maintain an action in her own name to recover her separate property by the Married Women's Property Act 1870[86] and a full power to sue in respect of any tort committed against her by the Married Women's Property Act 1882.[87] But it was not until the Law Reform (Married Women and Tortfeasors) Act 1935 that husbands *qua husbands* finally ceased to be liable for their wives' torts in all circumstances. And it was only by the Law Reform (Husband and Wife) Act 1962 s 1 that each spouse was given the same right of action against the other in tort as though they were not married. This applies equally to an action brought after the marriage has been dissolved (or presumably annulled) in respect of a tort committed during matrimony,[88] but in one respect the law here is different, for if the action is brought during the subsistence of the marriage, the court has a discretion to stay the action in two cases. First, it may do so if it appears that no substantial benefit would accrue to either party from the continuation of the proceedings. This is designed to prevent trivial actions brought to air matrimonial grievances;[89] consequently, it is not contemplated that the power would be exercised if the parties were no longer living together as an economic unit and the damage was real, or if the spouse was a purely nominal defendant and the real purpose of the action was to recover damages from a source outside the family. Such would be the case, for example, if the driver of a car wished to claim an indemnity from his insurance company. Secondly, the court may stay the action if it relates to property and the questions in issue could more conveniently be disposed of by an application under s 17 of the Married Women's Property Act 1882. Equivalent provision has been made for civil partnerships.[90]

(g) Criminal law

The doctrine of unity never applied generally in the criminal law so as to make a husband vicariously liable for his wife's crimes or to prevent either of them from being liable

---

[86] Section 11.   [87] See now the Law Reform (Married Women and Tortfeasors) Act 1935 s 1(c).
[88] Section 3(3).
[89] See Ninth Report of the Law Reform Committee 1961, Cmnd 1268, paras 10–13.
[90] Civil Partnership Act 2004 s 69.

in most cases for a crime committed against the other, but it does still have certain consequences which should be considered.

Marital coercion

There was a rule of common law that if a married woman committed certain offences in the presence of her husband, this raised a rebuttable presumption[91] that she had committed the crime under his coercion and consequently he and not she was prima facie liable to be convicted. Both the origin and the extent of this rule are uncertain, and it had become anomalous by the twentieth century. It was abolished by the Criminal Justice Act 1925 s 47, which replaced it with the following statutory defence:

'On a charge against a wife for any offence other than treason or murder it shall be a good defence to prove that the offence was committed in the presence of, and under the coercion of, the husband.'

In other words, this section changed the law by placing the burden of proof upon the wife to prove the coercion.[92] Coercion means something other than a threat of physical violence, which is a defence available to anyone charged with a criminal offence except murder and, perhaps, treason. It is apparently sufficient for the wife to show that her will was overborne by the wishes of her husband so that she is forced against her will to commit the offence.[93]

This defence must be strictly construed. Hence it is not available to a woman cohabiting with a man outside marriage[94] or to a woman who mistakenly believes that she is married to the man applying coercion.[95] Nor has it been extended to civil partners, thus reflecting perhaps one of the very few differences between marriage and civil partnership. It is clearly discriminatory and hence potentially challengeable under the European Convention on Human Rights and it is surely time it was abolished.

Conspiracy

It is now provided by statute that a husband and wife may not be convicted of conspiring together,[96] and it is generally believed that this was the position at common law. But this does not prevent them from being convicted of conspiring with the other and a third person.[97]

Theft

Under the doctrine of unity husband and wife were deemed to have unity of possession, so that neither could be guilty of stealing the other's property. But once the concept of separate property had been extended by the Married Women's Property Act 1882, it was obvious that the fiction once more worked an anomaly. Under the current law, for the purposes of the Theft Acts, a husband and wife are to be regarded as separate persons and each can now be convicted of theft of the other's property, obtaining it by deception and

---

[91] *R v Smith* (1916) 12 Cr App Rep 42, CCA; *R v Torpey* (1871) 12 Cox CC 45.

[92] On the balance of probabilities: *R v Shortland* [1995] Crim LR 893. [93] Ibid.

[94] *R v Court* (1912) 7 Cr App Rep 127, CCA.

[95] *R v Ditta, Hussain and Kara* [1988] Crim LR 42, CA. The court also queried, obiter, whether a wife could raise the defence if the marriage were polygamous.

[96] Criminal Law Act 1977 s 2(2)(a), now extended to civil partners: Civil Partnership Act 2004 Sch 27 para 56. Either may be convicted of inciting the other to commit a crime.

[97] *R v Chrastny* [1992] 1 All ER 189, CA.

so forth.[98] But the consent of the Director of Public Prosecutions is required for prosecution for any offence of stealing or doing unlawful damage to property which at the time belongs to the accused's spouse (or now civil partner), or for any attempt, incitement or conspiracy to commit such an offence.[99] The purpose of this provision is to reduce the risk of a prosecution which might prejudice a continuation of the parties' relationship, though one must question how stable that relationship could be in such circumstances.

(h) Citizenship and the right to live in the United Kingdom [100]

Although at first sight the question of citizenship might appear to have little to do with family law, in fact it has close connections with it for a number of reasons. In the first place, a person's right of abode in the United Kingdom may be valueless to him or her if other members of the family do not share it. In turn the acquisition of British citizenship depends in most cases upon the possession of such citizenship by at least one parent.[101] Finally, the rules relating to the naturalisation of the spouse or civil partner of a British citizen are less stringent than those relating to the naturalisation of other persons.

British citizenship

The doctrine of unity had no application at common law with respect to nationality. A foreign woman did not acquire British nationality by marrying a British subject, and a woman who was a British subject did not lose her status by marrying a foreigner. This rule was reversed by legislation during the nineteenth century,[102] but a series of statutes passed since 1914 reflected the change in status of married women by reverting to the common law principles.[103] This meant that a woman who was not a citizen of the United Kingdom and Colonies did not become such a citizen by marrying a man who possessed citizenship; however, she was entitled to acquire it by registration.

The British Nationality Act 1981 removed this entitlement and placed both husbands and wives of citizens on the same footing. The Civil Partnership Act 2004 amended these provisions to cater for civil partners. Now, if a woman (or man), who is not a British citizen, marries or forms a civil partnership with a citizen and wishes to acquire citizenship herself, she must apply for naturalisation unless she qualifies to be registered as a citizen in her own right.[104] However the applicant need have been in the United Kingdom

---

[98] Theft Act 1968 s 30(1); Theft Act 1978 s 5(2). Either of them may also be guilty of the theft of property belonging to them both jointly.

[99] Ibid s 30(4).   [100] See generally, *Butterworths Immigration Law Service.*

[101] We discuss the acquisition of British citizenship by children below at pp 335 and 870.

[102] Aliens Act 1844 s 16; Naturalisation Act 1870 s 10(1).

[103] Status of Aliens Act 1914 s 10; British Nationality and Status of Aliens Act 1918 s 2(5); British Nationality and Status of Aliens Act 1933 s 1(1). These Acts provided that a British woman marrying a foreigner should not lose her British nationality if she did not acquire that of her husband, that the status of the wife of a man who acquired or lost British nationality after the marriage should not automatically follow that of her husband but that she should be given the option of doing likewise, and that a woman who was a British subject at birth should be entitled to resume British nationality if the state of which her husband was a subject was at war with this country. The same principles were applied to citizenship of the United Kingdom and Colonies under the British Nationality Act 1948.

[104] The basic requirements are that the person is a British Dependent Territories or Overseas citizen, a British subject (but not citizen) or a British protected person under the Act; has lived here for five years and is not in breach of the immigration laws or subject to immigration restrictions under those laws: British Nationality Act 1981 s 4.

for only three years (and not five years as is usually the case). She must be of good character, have sufficient knowledge of English, Welsh or Scots Gaelic, and sufficient knowledge about life in the United Kingdom,[105] and not subject to any restriction under the immigration laws on the period for which she may remain here.[106]

A woman who is a British citizen no longer loses her citizenship on marrying an alien although, if she acquires her husband's nationality, she may divest herself of British citizenship by registering a declaration of renunciation like anyone else possessing dual nationality.[107] The position is the same for a person who forms a civil partnership with a foreign citizen and acquires that partner's nationality.

Right of abode and freedom of movement

'All those who . . . have the right of abode in the United Kingdom shall be free to live in, and to come and go into and from, the United Kingdom without let or hindrance' except for the need to establish their right.[108] It is possessed by all British citizens and those Commonwealth citizens who had the right before 1 January 1983, when the British Nationality Act 1981 came into force. Persons coming from the Channel Islands, the Isle of Man and the Republic of Ireland are generally exempt from immigration control.[109] Nationals of countries within the European Economic Area Agreement[110] are entitled to enter and reside in a territory in order to exercise a Community right (ie to take up employment or self-employment). Except for these and one or two other special cases,[111] all other persons, whatever their citizenship or nationality, may enter this country and stay here only if they are permitted to do so under the Immigration Rules made by the Home Secretary.[112] Permission may be unconditional or, if the individual is here for a particular purpose (for example, as a student or to take up employment), it may be given for a limited period of time and made subject to other conditions such as registration with the police.[113]

A person with the right of abode has no right to be accompanied by members of his family: they must obtain entry clearance or leave to enter or remain.[114] Anyone refused

---

[105] A spouse was not formerly required to have knowledge of the language. This extension and the provision regarding knowledge of life in the United Kingdom were added by the Nationality, Immigration and Asylum Act 2002 s 1.

[106] Section 6(2) and Sch 1, paras 3 and 4. Absences may be disregarded if they total no more than 270 days of which no more than 90 days may have been in the last 12 months. The applicant must not have been in breach of the immigration laws at any time during the three years.

[107] British Nationality Act 1981 s 12.   [108] Immigration Act 1971 s 1(1).

[109] Ibid s 1(3), s 9 and Sch 4, as amended.

[110] Immigration Act 1988 s 7. European Economic Area Agreement, signed at Oporto, 1993 and amended by Protocol at Brussels, 1993, incorporated into English law by the European Economic Area Act 1993 and Immigration (European Economic Area) Regulations 2000 SI 2000/2326.

[111] Immigration Act 1971 s 8.

[112] HC 395 (1994 and extensively amended subsequently). It has been suggested that since the Rules are now drafted similarly to a statute or statutory instrument, they should be interpreted in the same way and that the approach taken in *Alexander v Immigration Appeal Tribunal* [1982] 1 WLR 1076, 1080 G, HL: 'They are not to be construed with all the strictness applicable to the construction of a statute or statutory instrument. They must be construed sensibly according to the natural meaning of the language which is employed': per Lord Roskill is no longer good law. See *Butterworths Immigration Law Service* Division B, 'Immigration Rules' Introduction.

[113] Immigration Act 1971 s 1(2), (4) and s 3, as amended.

[114] *R v Secretary of State for the Home Department, ex p Rofathullah* [1989] QB 219, CA. Rules which made it harder for husbands to join their wives in this country were ruled contrary to Arts 8, 13 and 14 of the

such leave may seek to complain under Art 8 of the European Convention on Human Rights,[115] which protects a person's right to respect for his family life, but the proviso, Art 8(2), which permits a state to interfere with the right where this is in accordance with the law and necessary 'in the interests of national security, public safety or the economic well-being of the country . . .' must be borne in mind. The European Court of Human Rights has been wary of allowing complainants to circumvent immigration controls by reliance upon the Convention, but is more likely to support the argument where the person is liable to deportation which would mean separation from a family he has established in the country from which he is to be deported, than where a person is complaining that a family member is being refused entry so that a family life can be developed.[116] The Immigration Rules and guidance to immigration officers have been amended in the light of Convention jurisprudence to try to ensure that decisions taken are not in breach of its terms.

Spouses and civil partners. A person who wishes to marry[117] or form a civil partnership here and requires leave to enter or remain in the United Kingdom must satisfy the 'qualifying condition'.[118] This is that he has an entry clearance granted expressly for the purpose of enabling him to marry or form a civil partnership in the United Kingdom; the written permission of the Secretary of State to marry or form a civil partnership here; or is settled here.[119]

Under the Immigration Rules no one is to be granted entry clearance, leave to enter or leave to remain as a spouse[120] of another if either the applicant or the sponsor will be aged under 18 on the date of arrival in the United Kingdom or (as the case may be) on the date on which the leave to remain or variation of leave would be granted, be regarded as the husband or wife of another if he or she is under the age of 18.[121] Formerly, the age limit was 16. It has been raised to deter early (possibly forced) marriages as a means of gaining entry to the United Kingdom. Secondly, because problems were apparently being caused by men entering the country with two or more wives, a woman, W, will not be given permission to enter or stay here as the wife of a man, H, if (a) her marriage is de facto polygamous (even though the husband had no other wife when she married him) and (b) another wife of H has been in the United Kingdom since her marriage or has been granted entry clearance to enter this country as H's wife, unless W has been lawfully in this

European Convention on Human Rights in *Abdulaziz, Cabales and Balkandali v UK* (1985) 7 EHRR 471. The rules were accordingly amended (HC 503) to make it equally hard for wives to join their husbands.

[115] Note that Protocol 4 to the Convention guarantees the right to freedom of movement, but has not been ratified by the United Kingdom. For discussion of Art 8 and its application to immigration issues, see H Storey 'The Right to Family Life and Immigration Case Law at Strasbourg' (1990) 39 ICLQ 328.

[116] Storey, op cit.

[117] On the authority of a superintendent-registrar's certificate: Asylum and Immigration (Treatment of Claimants, etc) Act 2004, s 19. It has been held that the Act is contrary to Arts 12 and 14 of the ECHR because it does not impose this restriction on those seeking to marry according to Anglican rites: *R (Baiai and others) v Secretary of State for the Home Department* [2006] EWHC 823 (Admin), [2006] 2 FCR 131.

[118] Civil Partnership Act 2004 Sch 23 para 2.

[119] Immigration (Procedure for Marriage) Regulations 2005, SI 2005/15, reg. 6.

[120] For civil partners, see *Statement of Changes in Immigration Rules* (October 2005) HC 582.

[121] HC 395 para 277.

country otherwise than as a visitor at a time when there was no such wife satisfying condition (b).[122]

If a person of either sex is present and settled[123] in the United Kingdom or is admitted for settlement, his or her spouse[124] will be granted entry clearance provided that they show that their marriage is genuine, ie that the parties have met and intend to live together permanently as husband and wife. They must also demonstrate that they can maintain and accommodate themselves and any dependants without recourse to public funds.[125] Before 1997, there was an additional requirement to show that the 'primary purpose' of the marriage was *not* to obtain entry into the United Kingdom. The restriction was imposed because of the belief that in the past some men (particularly from the Indian subcontinent) were obtaining entry into this country by contracting arranged marriages, sometimes by proxy, to women (or possibly young girls) whom they had never met.[126] The rule was abolished because, in the words of the Home Secretary, it was 'arbitrary, unfair and ineffective and has penalised genuine marriages, divided families and unnecessarily increased the administrative burden on the immigration system'.[127] He could also have added that the rule was racially discriminatory and placed the applicants in the frequently hopeless position of having to prove a negative.

If an EEA national[128] exercises a Community right to enter and remain in the United Kingdom, permission to enter must be given to his spouse (regardless of the nationality of the spouse).[129] Thus, a non-EEA national who marries a British citizen with the right of abode may avoid the requirements for entry set out above if the British citizen exercises a Community right abroad and the couple then return to this country again to exercise a Community right. For example, suppose W, a British citizen, goes to work in France, where she meets and marries H, a non-EEA citizen. If they then come to the United Kingdom so that W can take up a job here, H must be permitted to enter and remain by virtue of European law.[130]

---

[122] Ibid, paras 278–280. This restriction does not apply if W has been in the United Kingdom before 1 August 1988 and she came for settlement as H's wife. See also the Immigration Act 1988 s 2, which applies to women who had the right of abode under s 2(2) of the Immigration Act 1971 as originally enacted.

[123] If he is here lawfully, is ordinarily resident here and is free from any restriction on the period for which he may remain: ibid, para 6.

[124] The same requirements apply to fiancé(e)s: para 290.   [125] Para 281, as amended.

[126] For the problem of sham marriages, see above p 88 and *Bhaiji v Chauhan (Queen's Proctor Intervening)* [2003] 2 FLR 485. In *R (Kimani) v Lambeth London Borough Council* [2003] EWCA Civ 1150 [2004] 1 WLR 272 the appellant, a Kenyan national, married an Irish citizen and sought entry to the UK as a spouse of a EEA national (see below). The Secretary of State considered the marriage one of convenience and she appealed. Meanwhile, the local authority declined to support her on the basis that she was the spouse and thus dependant of an EEA national of a state other than the UK. Her argument that, for this purpose, 'spouse' should mean someone not in a marriage of convenience was, perhaps unsurprisingly, rejected.

[127] HC, Hansard Written Answers, 5 June 1997 col 219. The rule was abolished with effect from that date in respect of both pending and future applications. But for the view that the rule has simply been replaced by other provisions intended to detect 'sham' marriages, see D Stevens, 'The Immigration and Asylum Act 1999: A Missed Opportunity?' (2001) 64 MLR 413 at 420–421 and discussion above at p 88.

[128] That is, a national of a member state of the European Union, Iceland, Liechtenstein or Norway.

[129] Regulation EEC 1612/68 Art 10, extended to EEA nationals by the EEA Agreement (above, p 123 n 110). Cohabitants of EEA nationals are not within Art 10: *Reed v Staatsecretariat van Justitie* [1987] 2 CMLR 164, but must be considered for entry subject to the same exercise of discretion as would apply to any others.

[130] *R v Immigration Appeal Tribunal and Surinder Singh, ex p Secretary of State for the Home Department*: C-370/90 [1992] Imm AR 565. However, such a person may be refused entry on grounds of public policy,

Cohabitants. A person may be permitted entry if he or she has been living with a partner in a 'relationship akin to marriage' for two years.[131] Any previous marriage (or similar relationship) by either partner must have permanently broken down, and the parties must not be involved in a consanguineous relationship with one another. The same requirements regarding accommodation and maintenance apply as for spouses etc.

Deportation

Where a person who is not a British citizen is liable to deportation (eg because he has overstayed the limit on his permission to remain in the country, or has been convicted of a criminal offence and the court has recommended his deportation), the immigration officer must consider all the known relevant factors before making a decision and, in particular, the length of residence in this country, the strength of connections with this country, domestic or compassionate circumstances and any representations made on their behalf.[132]

The European Court of Human Rights laid down similar guiding principles concerning this issue in *Boultif v Switzerland:*[133]

'[in the case of someone who has been convicted of an offence] the nature and seriousness of the offence; the length of the applicant's stay in the country from which he is going to be expelled; the time elapsed since the offence was committed as well as the applicant's conduct in that period; the nationalities of the various persons concerned; the applicant's family situation, such as the length of the marriage; and other factors expressing the effectiveness of a couple's family life; whether the spouse knew about the offence at the time when he or she entered into a family relationship; and whether there are children in the marriage, and if so, their age. Not least, the Court will also consider the seriousness of the difficulties which the spouse is likely to encounter in the country of origin, though the mere fact that a person might face certain difficulties in accompanying her or his spouse cannot in itself exclude an expulsion.'[134]

Deportation may be ordered against the spouse or civil partner of a deportee where he or she has no right of abode.[135] The Home Secretary will not normally order the deportation

---

public security or public health: EC Directive 64/221; see *Van Duyn v Home Office.* 41/74 [1975] Ch 358, (action can only be taken based upon the personal conduct of the individual, and criminal convictions are relevant only so far as they provide evidence of a present threat to public policy or security). The same applies to a person liable to be deported, but the removal must be proportionate to the threat: *Machado v Secretary of State for the Home Department* [2005] EWCA Civ 597 [2005] 2 CMLR 43.

[131] Para 295A.

[132] Para 364. See also Home Office Circular on Deportation, DP/3/96 para 5. The circular has been held compatible with Art 8 of the European Convention on Human Rights: *R v Secretary of State for the Home Department ex parte Isiko* [2001] 1 FLR 930, CA.

[133] [2001] 2 FLR 1228 at para 48.

[134] Compare *Gul v Switzerland* (1996) 22 EHRR 93—no breach of Art 8 to refuse entry to Turkish couple's two sons when mother too ill to leave Switzerland to go back to Turkey, because the boys had never lived in Switzerland and the father had kept up contact with them in Turkey; *Boughaneni v France* (1996) 22 EHRR 228—no breach of Art 8 to deport a Tunisian national from France where he had cohabited with a woman and formally acknowledged their child, because he had sufficient links with Tunisia and the criminal offences which had resulted in his deportation were serious.

[135] Immigration Act 1971 s 3(5) and s 5, as amended by Civil Partnership Act 2004 Sch 27 para 37 See HC 395 Part 13.

of a spouse who has qualified for settlement in his or her own right or who has been living apart from the other spouse.[136]

The Immigration Rules apply equally to civil partners. It may be noted that the European Commission of Human Rights held inadmissible, in *ZB v United Kingdom*[137] a complaint that the decision to deport the applicant would disrupt the same-sex relationship he had established here and so was a breach of his Art 8 right to respect for his private life. The Commission considered that 'it cannot in principle be regarded as an interference with the right to respect for private life given the state's right to impose immigration controls and limits.' However, it must be doubted whether such a view would be taken now, either at the Strasbourg or domestic level, and it is submitted that the position of unmarried partners, be they heterosexual or in same-sex relationships, should be considered in line with the *Boultif* criteria, giving due attention to the 'nature and quality' of the partnership.

C PROPERTY CONSEQUENCES OF RELATIONSHIPS

(a) Historical introduction

Reflecting the previous pre-eminent importance that society attached to marriage, the law of 'family' property was, until the 1970s and 1980s, virtually exclusively concerned with the effects of marriage. In this regard, however, the development of the law clearly reflects the development of the status of the wife from being a subservient member of the family to becoming its co-equal head. In contrast, the impact of cohabitation outside marriage upon the concept and development of property ownership has, until recently, been negligible. This is so even though, as we have seen,[138] the incidence of cohabitation has steadily increased and can certainly no longer be regarded as being unusual. Pending thoroughgoing reform, we can observe that one of the key contemporary roles of so-called strict property law is the determination of disputes between cohabitants, although that law was essentially conceived and developed for married couples.

We begin our discussion of ownership with a brief historical résumé of the effects of marriage upon rights in property.

Common law[139]

Interests in land. At common law the husband gained control over all freehold lands which his wife held at the time of marriage or which she subsequently acquired during marriage. The wife had no power to dispose of her real property during marriage, although the spouses could dispose of the whole estate together. The wife's leasehold property belonged absolutely to her husband. If the husband died before the wife, she immediately resumed

---

[136] Para 365. A deported spouse may seek re-admission if the marriage comes to an end: para 389.

[137] Application No. 16106/90.   [138] See above p 37.

[139] For further details and authorities, reference must be made to the editions of standard works on real and personal property and equity published during the nineteenth and early twentieth centuries. The classic exposition of the common law position is to be found in Blackstone's *Commentaries*, vol ii. See also Dicey *Law and Opinion* (2nd edn) pp 371–95.

the right to all her freeholds; if she predeceased him, her estates of inheritance descended to her heir, subject to the husband's right, as 'tenant by the courtesy of England', to an estate for his life in all her freeholds in possession.

Not surprisingly, during marriage the wife took no interest in her husband's real property but, if she survived him, she became entitled by virtue of her 'dower' to an estate for life in a third of all her husband's freeholds of which he had been seized in possession at any time during marriage, provided that she *could* have borne a child capable of inheriting, whether such a child was ever born or not.

If land were granted to a husband and wife together, they were said to take *by entireties* and received an interest which could not be turned into a tenancy in common by sever-ance. Hence, unless they disposed of the estate during marriage, the survivor was bound to take the whole. If land were granted to a husband, his wife and a third person, then by virtue of the doctrine of unity, the spouses were regarded as one person and consequently they were entitled to only one-half of the rent and profits and the third person was entitled to the other half.

Interests in personal property. All personalty in possession belonging to the wife at the time of the marriage, or acquired by her during the marriage, vested absolutely in the husband, who therefore had the power to dispose of them inter vivos or by will. Even if he died intestate during the wife's life, they did not revert to her. The only exception to this rule applied to those articles of apparel and personal ornament (known as the wife's *parapher-nalia*) which were suitable to her rank and degree. Whilst the husband could dispose of these during his lifetime, he could not deprive her of them by bequest, and on his death they became her property and did not form a part of his estate.[140]

Equity

The wife's separate estate. The most important contribution of equity to the law relating to a married woman's property was the development of the concept of the separate estate. By the end of the sixteenth century[141] it was established that if property (both realty and personalty) was conveyed to trustees *to the separate use* of a married woman, she retained in equity the same right of holding and disposing of it as if she were a 'feme sole'.[142] She could therefore dispose of it inter vivos or by will and, like any other beneficiary of full age who was absolutely entitled, she could call upon her trustees to convey the legal estate. Only if she died intestate in respect of her separate estate did the husband obtain the same interest that he would have had in her equitable property had it not been settled to her separate use. Moreover, even if property were conveyed, devised or bequeathed to a mar-ried woman to her separate use with the legal estate vested in the husband, he was deemed in equity to hold it on trust for her and he acquired no greater interest in it than he would have done if it had been conveyed to trustees on similar terms.

---

[140] Unless the husband's estate was insolvent, in which case his creditors could take the wife's paraphernalia in satisfaction but not her necessary clothing.

[141] See Holdsworth *History of English Law*, v, pp 310–15.

[142] In other words, an unmarried woman. If property were settled on an unmarried woman to her separate use, it also remained her separate estate after marriage. Hence, if an engaged woman settled her property on herself to her separate use without her fiancé's concurrence, he could have the settlement set aside as a fraud on his marital rights.

The restraint upon anticipation. Whilst the separate estate in equity did much to mitigate the harshness of the common law rule, there remained one situation which it did not meet. There was nothing to prevent a married woman from assigning her beneficial interest to her husband, thereby vesting in him the interest which the separate use had sought to keep out of his hands. To circumvent this, equity developed about 1800 the concept known as the restraint upon anticipation.[143] This could be imposed only if property was conveyed, devised or bequeathed to a woman's separate use, and, once it attached, it prevented her from anticipating and dealing with any income until it actually fell due.

The restraint on anticipation was designed to protect not only the wife but also the members of her family who would be entitled to the property on her death.[144] Whilst it effectively kept the property out of the hands of her husband and his creditors, it had one obvious drawback in that even where it was in the wife's interest to deal with property subject to a restraint, nothing short of a private Act of Parliament could remove it. To overcome this difficulty the Conveyancing Act 1881 gave the court power to bind her interest in such property provided that this was for her benefit.[145] But the court could only render a specific disposition binding. It had no general power to remove the restraint altogether.

Statutory reform[146]

By the middle of the nineteenth century it was clear that the old rules would have to be reformed. More middle-class women were earning incomes of their own, either in trade, or on the stage or by writing, and there were a number of scandalous cases of husbands impounding their wives' earnings for the benefit of their own creditors, or even mistresses. No relief could be obtained by the woman whose husband deserted her and took all her property with him. The separate use and restraint upon anticipation were clumsy devices which in practice only affected the property of the daughters of the rich, who would have carefully drawn marriage settlements and would be the beneficiaries under complicated wills. Agitation for reform eventually produced a series of Acts of ever wider scope.[147]

Married Women's Property Acts. The most important of these was the Married Women's Property Act 1882.[148] It provided that any woman marrying after 1882 should be entitled to retain all property owned by her at the time of the marriage as her separate property and that, whenever she was married, any property acquired by a married woman after 1882 should be held by her in the same way.[149] Section 1(1) stated:

'A married woman shall ... be capable of acquiring, holding and disposing, by will or

---

[143] See WG Hart 'The Origin of the Restraint upon Anticipation' (1924) 40 LQR 221.

[144] O Kahn-Freund in *Matrimonial Property Law* (ed Friedmann) p 274. For the position in equity generally, see Dicey *Law and Opinion* (2nd edn) pp 375–82.

[145] Section 39, subsequently replaced by the Conveyancing Act 1911 s 7, and the Law of Property Act 1925 s 169.

[146] See D Stetson *A Woman's Issue: the politics of family law reform in England* (1982).

[147] See Dicey, op cit, pp 382–95.

[148] In fact many of the 1882 Act's wider provisions had been anticipated in an earlier Bill which, in its cut-down form, became the Married Women's Property Act 1870. That Act, which was repealed by the 1882 Act, remains of historical importance in that it gave a statutory extension to the existing equitable concept of the separate estate, the device that was later to be used in the Act of 1882.

[149] Sections 2 and 5.

otherwise, of any real or personal property as her separate property, in the same manner as if she were a feme sole, without the intervention of any trustee.'

The sweeping nature of these changes should be appreciated. It became impossible for a married man to acquire any further interest in his wife's property by operation of law. No further tenancies by entireties could be created. A widower could claim an interest in his deceased's wife's property acquired after 1882 only if she died intestate with respect to it. But in one sense the changes were even more fundamental than these, for whilst the statute adopted the equitable concept of separate property,[150] it went further by vesting in the wife the *legal* interest in her property. Indeed, subject to the restraint on anticipation, which was left unaffected, a married woman's capacity to hold and dispose of property was very nearly the same as that of a feme sole.

The 1925 property legislation changed the rules of succession on intestacy;[151] in particular dower was abolished. Any remaining tenancies by entireties were abolished, and a grant to a husband, his wife and a third person will now give each of them a third interest in the property.[152]

By 1935 to speak of 'separate property' was becoming something of an anomaly, since married women in almost all cases had the same capacity to hold and dispose of it as a man or a feme sole. This was eventually recognised in the Law Reform (Married Women and Tortfeasors) Act 1935, which abolished the concept of the separate estate and gave to the wife the same rights and powers as were already possessed by other adults of full capacity. Although the Act did not affect any existing restraint on anticipation, it rendered void any attempted imposition of a restraint in any instrument executed after 1935 and in the will of any person dying after 1945.

Although after 1945 restraint upon anticipation was bound to disappear in the course of time, the 1935 Act did not affect the validity of restraints already imposed. Whilst the court could sanction individual dispositions if these were for the wife's benefit,[153] the only way in which a restraint could be wholly removed was by a private Act of Parliament. It was the presentation of a Bill for this purpose that ultimately led to the passing of the Married Women (Restraint upon Anticipation) Act 1949, which removed all restraints whenever imposed, and thus rendered the property to which they were attached freely alienable.

By extending the equitable principle of the separate estate, the Married Women's Property Acts replaced the total incapacity of a married woman to hold property at common law with a rigid doctrine of separate property. In Dicey's words,[154] 'the rules of equity, framed for the daughters of the rich, have at last been extended to the daughters of the poor'. But, as Kahn-Freund pointed out,[155] the effects of the Acts were much wider than this. Spouses' property may be broadly divided into that intended for common use

[150] Hence, for example, a married woman still could not be made bankrupt unless she came within the express provisions of s 1(5) by carrying on a trade separately from her husband.

[151] See below, pp 1095ff.

[152] Law of Property Act 1925 s 37. After 1882 the spouses could sever their half-share because *between themselves* they took as ordinary joint tenants.

[153] See above p 129. If the restraint were attached to land, the woman could sell the land under the provisions of the Settled Land Act 1925, but the restraint continued to attach to the capital.

[154] *Law and Opinion* (2nd edn) p 395.

[155] In Friedmann (ed) *Matrimonial Property Law*, pp 267 et seq. See also his article, 'Recent Legislation on Matrimonial Property' (1970) 33 MLR 601.

and consumption in the matrimonial home and that intended for personal use and enjoyment. The latter may be in the form of savings or investments or derived from the interest on these, and it is obvious that, whilst in a poor family almost the whole of the property will fall into the first category, the richer the spouses the greater the fraction of their property which will fall into the second. Before 1883 the matrimonial home and its contents would almost invariably be vested in the husband to the exclusion of the wife, and the latter's separate property did little more than protect her investments. But, impelled by a movement which was ultimately to secure the almost complete legal equality of the sexes, Parliament extended the doctrine of separation to property forming the matrimonial home as well—a situation which the equitable concept was never intended to cover and with which it was ill adapted to deal.

This was inevitably bound to produce difficulties. During the Second World War many married women were wage earners as well, and what before then had been something of an exception has now become the usual situation in most families. To apply the strict doctrine of separate property to matrimonial assets in such circumstances was manifestly absurd. As a result, judges sought to adapt the principle by regarding both spouses as having an interest in the matrimonial home in many cases, even though the legal estate is vested solely in the husband,[156] and a similar approach was later employed in relation to unmarried cohabitants.[157]

Impact of divorce reform in 1969 and 1970. Although property ownership can be in issue both during and after the spouses' cohabitation, in practice most problems arise following marital breakdown. Until the reforms governing divorce which came into operation in 1971,[158] spouses, like anyone else, had to resolve their disputes under the strict law, and for the most part they would do so by applying under s 17 of the Married Woman's Property Act 1882.[159] In the early 1970s, however, this picture changed dramatically, for under what was originally s 4 of the Matrimonial Proceedings and Property Act 1970 and later re-enacted as s 24 of the Matrimonial Causes Act 1973, the court was given wide powers for the transfer and settlement of property on divorce, nullity and judicial separation.[160] In *Williams v Williams*[161] the Court of Appeal made it clear that whenever possible spouses should rely on the court's wide powers to adjust property rights. Consequently, the need to make an enquiry into the precise interest that each spouse has in the matrimonial home or other assets has in this context been largely removed. Civil partnerships have a similar adjustive regime and the same point therefore applies to them.[162]

(b) The modern law

It should not be thought, however, that even between spouses (or civil partners) the question of ownership is now merely academic.[163] Strict property rights are still of the greatest importance on the death or insolvency of one spouse, because they alone will have to be applied to resolve any dispute between the other spouse and the personal representatives or creditors. Furthermore, a spouse may not wish to take matrimonial proceedings,

---

[156] See below p 151.   [157] See below pp 155ff.   [158] See below Chapter 18.
[159] Discussed below at p 144.   [160] Discussed below pp 1003ff.   [161] [1976] Ch 278, CA.
[162] Civil Partnership Act 2004 s 72 and Sch 5.
[163] See *Kowalczuk v Kowalczuk* [1973] 2 All ER 1042 at 1045, CA; *Griffiths v Griffiths* [1974] 1 All ER 932 at 941, CA.

or may not be able to apply for a property adjustment order because she (or he) has remarried or formed a civil partnership.

In any event, since the court's adjustive powers are confined to divorce, dissolution, nullity and separation proceedings, the strict law remains the governing law to determine property rights between cohabitants. The discussion below accordingly considers the law as it relates both to married (including civil partners) and unmarried partners.

(c) Property acquired by the partners

Property owned by the partners on entering the relationship

Presumptively, marriage, civil partnership, engagement or cohabitation will not affect the ownership of property vested in either of the partners at the time. This will also be true of property which is used by them jointly in the family home (for example, furniture), in the absence of an express gift of a joint interest in law or in equity.

Gifts between engaged couples[164]

At common law a gift made by one party to an engagement to the other in contemplation of marriage could not be recovered by the donor if he was in breach of contract. This meant, for example, that if the man broke off the engagement without legal justification, he could not recover the engagement ring, but he could do so if the woman was in breach of contract.[165]

In conformity with the principle[166] that the parties' rights with respect to property should not depend upon their responsibility for the termination of the agreement, s 3(1) of the Law Reform (Miscellaneous Provisions) Act 1970 provides:

'A party to an agreement to marry who makes a gift of property to the other party on the condition (express or implied) that it shall be returned if the agreement is terminated shall not be prevented from recovering the property by reason only of his having terminated the agreement.'[167]

Whether a particular gift was made subject to an implied condition that it should be returned if the marriage did not take place must necessarily be a question of fact to be decided in each case. Normally, birthday and Christmas presents will vest in the donee absolutely, whilst property intended to become a part of the family home (for example, furniture) will be conditional. It is suggested that the general test to be applied should be: was the gift made to the donee as an individual or solely as the donor's future spouse (or partner)? If it is in the latter class, it will be regarded as conditional, whereas if it is in the former, it will be regarded as absolute and recoverable only in the same circumstances as any other gift—for example, on the ground that it was induced by fraud or undue influence.

The engagement ring is specifically dealt with by the 1970 Act.[168] The gift is presumed to

---

[164] Including couples who have agreed to register as civil partners: s 73(3) of the Civil Partnership Act 2004.

[165] *Cohen v Sellar* [1926] 1 KB 536; *Jacobs v Davis* [1917] 2 KB 532. There is no direct authority for the position if the agreement was terminated otherwise than by breach, eg by agreement or death. It was generally assumed that the donor (or his personal representatives) could recover conditional gifts: see *Cohen v Sellar*.

[166] See above p 43.

[167] The equivalent provision for those agreeing to register may be found in s 74(5), Civil Partnership Act 2004.

[168] There is no equivalent provision for those agreeing to register, presumably because a tradition of giving a ring on such an occasion has not yet been established.

be absolute, but this presumption may be rebutted by proving that the ring was given on the condition (express or implied) that it should be returned if the marriage did not take place for any reason.[169] One would have thought that by current social convention an engagement ring was still regarded as a pledge and that the presumption ought to have been the other way. As it is, the ring is likely to be recoverable only in the most exceptional circumstances, for example if it can be shown that it was an heirloom in the man's family.

If a gift in contemplation of marriage is made to one or both of the engaged couple by a third person (as in the case of wedding presents), it is, in the absence of any contrary intention, conditional upon the celebration of the marriage and must therefore be returned if the marriage does not take place for any reason at all. A contrary intention will clearly be shown if the gift is for immediate use before the marriage.[170]

Income and investments

So far as income is concerned, spouses, civil partners, cohabitants and former engaged couples are in the same legal position. Case law, however, tends only to relate to spouses.

The income of either partner, whether from earnings or from investments, will prima facie remain his or her own property.[171] But where the partners pool their incomes and place them into a common fund, it seems that they both acquire a joint interest in the whole fund. Further, it seems clear that the principle of a joint interest in a common fund rests not upon the relationship between the contributors, but upon the purpose for which the fund was founded and the use to which it is put.[172]

In *Jones v Maynard*[173] the husband, who was about to go abroad with the RAF, authorised his wife to draw on his bank account, which was thereafter treated as a joint account. Into this account were paid dividends on both the husband's and the wife's investments, the husband's pay and allowances, and rent from the matrimonial home which was their joint property and which had been let during the War. The husband's contributions were greater than the wife's; the spouses had never agreed on what their rights in this fund were to be, but they regarded it as their joint savings to be invested from time to time. The husband withdrew money on a number of occasions and invested it in his own name, and finally, after the spouses had separated, he closed the account altogether. The marriage was later dissolved and the plaintiff sued her former husband for a half share in the account as it stood on the day it was closed and in the investments which he had previously purchased out of it. Vaisey J held that the claim must succeed. He said:[174]

'In my judgment, when there is a joint account between husband and wife, a common pool into which they put all their resources, it is not consistent with that conception that the account should thereafter ... be picked apart, and divided up proportionately to the respective contributions of husband and wife, the husband being credited with the whole of his earnings and the wife with the whole of her dividends ... In my view a husband's

---

169 Law Reform (Miscellaneous Provisions) Act 1970 s 3(2). For an illustration of the evidential difficulties in establishing such a condition, see *Cox v Jones* [2004] EWHC 1486 (Ch) [2004] 2 FLR 1010.

170 See *Jeffreys v Luck* (1922) 153 LT Jo 139. One would expect the same principle to apply to civil partnerships.

171 See *Dixon v Dixon* (1878) 9 Ch D 587 (stock settled to the wife's separate use); *Barrack v M'Culloch* (1856) 3 K & J 110 (rents from houses settled to the wife's separate use); *Heseltine v Heseltine* [1971] 1 All ER 952 (income from wife's investments).

172 *Paul v Constance* [1977] 1 All ER 195, CA.   173 [1951] Ch 572.   174 At 575.

earnings or salary, when the spouses have a common purse and pool their resources, are earnings made on behalf of both; and the idea that years afterwards the contents of the pool can be dissected by taking an elaborate account as to how much was paid in by the husband or the wife is quite inconsistent with the original fundamental idea of a joint purse or common pool.

In my view the money which goes into the pool becomes joint property. The husband, if he wants a suit of clothes, draws a cheque to pay for it. The wife, if she wants any housekeeping money, draws a cheque, and there is no disagreement about it.'

What, then, constitutes a 'common purse'? It would seem on principle to be essential that there must be a fund intended for the use of both partners from which either may withdraw money, and this will normally take the form of a joint bank account. Where they both contribute to this fund, as in *Jones v Maynard*, this intention will be imputed to the parties in the absence of any other agreement; where, however, the fund is derived from the income of one partner alone, it is a question of fact whether this is to remain his or her exclusive property, or whether there is an intention to establish a common fund.

In this instance, as between spouses and, possibly, engaged couples, the equitable doctrine of the 'presumption of advancement' could at one time have come into play. This held that a transfer of property from husband to wife was prima facie to be regarded as an outright gift rather than, as would otherwise be presumed the case, giving rise to a resulting trust under which the recipient holds the property on trust for the transferor. The reason for the presumption was the recognition that wives were financially dependent upon their husbands, who had a duty to maintain them. Hence, if the wife (or fiancée) were the sole contributor to the joint account she would take the whole beneficial interest,[175] whilst if the husband (or fiancé) were the sole contributor, the presumption could operate so as prima facie to give her an interest.[176] But this would be rebutted if, for example, it could be shown that the power to draw on the account was given for the husband's convenience by enabling the wife to draw cheques for the payment of housekeeping expenses.[177] Moreover, even though the beneficial interest in a joint account was initially vested in one spouse alone, his or her intention might change, and it might be converted into a joint interest.[178] The courts are unlikely to use the presumption of advancement today, given greater financial equality between the spouses, and in particular, it would seem inapposite in the case of civil partners, whose relationship and status must be predicated on an ideological assumption that they are equals.[179]

---

[175] *Heseltine v Heseltine* (above) (houses purchased by husband out of joint account provided by wife's money held to belong to her absolutely). Contrast *Boydell v Gillespie* (1970) 216 Estates Gazette 1505 (wife's directing that property bought with her money should be conveyed into names of both spouses jointly held to give both an interest in it).

[176] *Re Figgis* [1969] 1 Ch 123. Although the effect of these presumptions is considerably weaker today than it used to be.

[177] *Marshal v Crutwell* (1875) LR 20 Eq 328; *Hoddinott v Hoddinott* [1949] 2 KB 406, CA at 413; *Harrods Ltd v Tester* [1937] 2 All ER 236, CA (where the whole of the balance of a bank account opened by the husband in the wife's name was held to belong to the husband); *Simpson v Simpson* [1992] 1 FLR 601 at 617 (transfer of money by husband into joint account intended only to ensure that wife could pay expenses during his final illness).

[178] *Re Figgis* (above) at 145.

[179] Arguably, it could still operate in relation to spouses in a case like *Re Figgis*, where both parties are dead and there is virtually no direct evidence of the parties' intentions at all. But as Nourse LJ observed in

If either partner withdraws money from the common purse, property bought with it prima facie belongs solely to that person if it is for his or her personal use (for example, clothes), but to both jointly if it is for their joint use (for example, a car). Investments purchased by means of the common purse will similarly belong to the purchaser unless it is clear that they are intended to represent the original fund. In *Re Bishop*[180] large sums had been withdrawn by both spouses to purchase investments in their separate names. In many cases blocks of shares were bought and half put in one name and half in the other; other money was spent in taking up shares offered to the husband by virtue of rights which he possessed as an existing shareholder in the companies concerned. In these circumstances Stamp J held that the presumption could not be rebutted, so that the spouse in whose name the shares had been purchased was entitled to the whole beneficial interest in them. He distinguished *Jones v Maynard*, where Vaisey J held that the husband was to be regarded as trustee for them both of investments which he had purchased; for in that case the spouses had agreed that when there had been a sufficient accumulation the money should be invested and that that was to be their savings.

Like any other joint interest the balance of the fund will accrue to the survivor on the death of either partner, as it did in *Re Bishop*.

Allowances for housekeeping and maintenance—special provision for wives

Originally the same principles were applied to the question of ownership of a housekeeping allowance as to income and investments. Hence, it was consistently held that if a husband supplied his wife with a housekeeping allowance out of his own income, any balance and any property bought with the allowance prima facie remained his property.[181] This could work an injustice, for it took no account of the fact that any savings from the housekeeping money were as much due to the wife's skill and economy as to her husband's earning capacity.[182] It was to remedy this that the Married Women's Property Act 1964 was passed. Section 1 provides:

'If any question arises as to the right of a husband or wife to money derived from any allowance made by the husband for the expenses of the matrimonial home or for similar purposes, or to any property acquired out of such money, the money or property shall, in the absence of any agreement between them to the contrary, be treated as belonging to the husband and wife in equal shares.'

The Act applies only if the allowance is provided by the husband; it does not apply to the case where the wife goes out to work to support a husband who does the housekeeping.[183] In

---

McGrath v Wallis [1995] 2 FLR 114 at 115, even in these circumstances he was unable to recollect a case in which the presumption was applied in the last 30 years. The Family Law (Property and Maintenance) Bill 2005, which did not proceed, would have abolished the presumption.

[180] [1965] Ch 450.

[181] *Blackwell v Blackwell* [1943] 2 All ER 579, CA; *Hoddinott v Hoddinott* [1949] 2 KB 406, CA, in which the husband was held entitled to winnings from the football pools, the stake for which had been paid by the wife out of the housekeeping allowance.

[182] See the judgments of Denning LJ in *Hoddinott v Hoddinott*, above, at 416, and *Rimmer v Rimmer* [1953] 1 QB 63 at 74 CA.

[183] Cf the equivalent provision in Scotland: the Family Law (Scotland) Act 1985 s 26 applies to both husbands and wives.

such a case the allowance and any property bought with it presumably remain the wife's.[184] The Act does not apply at all to civil partners, cohabitants,[185] nor to engaged couples; consequently the common law rules are still relevant to these and any unspent balance or property or investments purchased with it will belong to the provider of the housekeeping allowance. It is nevertheless open to the courts to infer an intention that the unspent allowance should belong to the partners jointly.

So far as the application of the 1964 Act is concerned, it is not clear what the phrase 'expenses of the matrimonial home or similar purposes' covers. If, for example, a husband gives his wife money to pay off instalments of the mortgage on the matrimonial home, she may well be regarded as no more than his agent and thus acquire no interest in the house; but if he gives her a housekeeping allowance out of which it is intended that she should pay the instalments, it has been suggested that the effect of the section is to give her a half share in the fraction represented by each payment.[186] In the absence of any binding authority the words 'expenses of the matrimonial home' seem more apt to describe money spent in running it than in acquiring it.

If the allowance is made for this purpose, the rule applies not only to the money but also to any property bought with it. Hence, if the wife were to buy furniture with the house-keeping savings, it would presumptively belong to her and her husband equally. This can be rebutted by proof of an agreement between the spouses. Presumably, such agreements may be express or implied. It would be absurd, for example, where the wife uses part of the allowance to buy clothes for herself, that a half share of them should belong to the husband.[187]

The Act has a further weakness. The money or property is to be treated as belonging to the spouses in equal shares. Consequently, on the death of one, the whole beneficial interest will *not* automatically pass to the survivor (as it does in the case of the 'common purse'),[188] but half will go to the personal representatives of the other. It is highly doubtful whether this is what the spouses will want or expect.[189] Neither this rule nor its

---

[184] Earlier cases indicate that if the wife gives money to her husband for use in the home, she is deemed to give it to him as head of the family and the money therefore becomes his: see eg *Edward v Cheyne (No 2)* (1888) 13 App Cas 385, HL; *Re Young* (1913) 29 TLR 319 (where the presumption was rebutted on the facts). But it is unlikely that the courts would take such a view today. The Morton Commission recommended that the allowance should belong to both spouses equally, whichever of them provided it: Cmd 9678, para 701. See further Law Com Working Paper No 90 (*Transfer of Money between Spouses*) and Law Com No 175, *Matrimonial Property Law* (1989).

[185] The Scottish Law Commission (see Scot Law Com No 135, 1992, paras 16.12–16.13) did recommend extending the equivalent provision in Scotland to cohabitants and this was done by the Family Law (Scotland) Act 2006.

[186] See the conflicting views in *Tymoszczuk v Tymoszczuk* (1964) 108 Sol Jo 676, and *Re Johns' Assignment Trusts* [1970] 2 All ER 210n at 213.

[187] Perhaps a more difficult case would arise if the wife bought herself an expensive piece of jewellery. In the case of a 'common purse' contributed to by both, the property would belong to the wife exclusively: see above p 135.

[188] See above p 135.

[189] In their desire to remedy the injustice caused by earlier cases where the marriage had broken down, the promoters of the Bill apparently overlooked the obvious fact that most marriages survive and that, whilst a joint interest can always be severed by the unilateral act of one party, it requires the conscious act of both to turn a tenancy in common into a joint tenancy.

consequences will be known to the vast majority of spouses and it is not inconceivable that a half-share of furniture will inadvertently pass under a residuary bequest.

Given these difficulties, it is hardly surprising that little use seems to have been made of the Act. The Law Commission[190] recommended its repeal and that instead there should be a statutory presumption that property bought for the joint use or benefit of spouses should belong to them jointly. An attempt to render the Act gender-neutral, and to extend its scope to civil partners, was also made in 2005 in a private member's bill introduced into the House of Commons.[191]

Personal property

Any property purchased by one partner with his or her own money will presumptively belong exclusively to the purchaser. Property bought out of money coming from the 'common purse' will also presumptively belong to the purchaser if it is for his or her own use.[192] But this presumption is obviously rebuttable. Thus, property bought by one partner as a gift for the other will become the donee's. Hence, if a man buys clothes for his partner or gives her money to buy them for herself, they become her property,[193] and the same rule will prima facie apply in any other case where goods are bought for the other's personal use.[194] Property bought by one party but intended for both to enjoy may be subject to an express trust. For example, in *Rowe v Prance*[195] a man bought a boat from the proceeds of sale of his former matrimonial home, telling his mistress that they would live together on it and sale round the world. She accordingly gave up her rented house and put her furniture in storage. The man told her that the title to the boat was in his name because only he had an Ocean Master's certificate, but that the boat was 'ours'. When the relationship ended, it was held that an express trust existed, under which the couple held equal shares.[196]

Difficulties can arise if one partner's money is used to buy property which is conveyed into the other's name or into joint names or, alternatively, if both partners' money is used to buy property which is conveyed into the name of only one of them. In this respect a distinction needs to be drawn between spouses (and possibly engaged couples, but query civil partners?) and unmarried cohabitants. So far as the latter are concerned, property bought by one partner and put into the name of the other is presumptively held on a resulting trust by the latter for the purchaser. So far as spouses are concerned, the doctrines of resulting trust and presumption of advancement can come into conflict, as already

---

[190] Law Com No 175 (*Matrimonial Property*, 1985). Note that the Government considers the Act to be incompatible with Protocol 7 of the European Convention on Human Rights and has undertaken to reform it so that the UK can ratify this Protocol: Hansard, HL Written Answers, col 197, 21 April 1998.

[191] Family Law (Property and Maintenance) Bill (2 November 2005): the bill did not progress.

[192] See above p 135.

[193] *Masson, Templier & Co v De Fries* [1909] 2 KB 831, CA. Contrast *Rondeau, Le Grand & Co v Marks* [1918] 1 KB 75, CA, where it had been agreed that they should remain the husband's property.

[194] *Re Whittaker* (1882) 21 Ch D 657 (piano). But cf *Windeler v Whitehall* [1990] 2 FLR 505 at 517 (dressing table bought for unmarried cohabitant remained purchaser's property).

[195] [1999] 2 FLR 787.

[196] Note that no writing was required, nor was it necessary to establish an implied, resulting or constructive trust, because the boat constituted personal, not real, property. For the position regarding land, see below pp 153ff.

noted above.[197] These presumptions have always been rebuttable by contrary evidence, for example that the wife intended a gift or that the husband intended to keep the beneficial interest.[198] But, as the members of the House of Lords agreed in *Pettitt v Pettitt*,[199] they are much less strong today because some explanation of the parties' conduct will usually be available unless they are both dead. Lord Diplock went so far as to question whether they were still valid at all. As he observed, they are no more than a judicial inference of what the spouses' intention most probably was, drawn in cases relating to the propertied classes of the nineteenth and early twentieth century among whom marriage settlements were common and where the wife rarely contributed to the family income by her earnings.[200]

Gifts to partners from third parties

Whether a gift made by third parties belongs to one partner alone or to both of them is a question of the donor's intention. In the case of wedding presents it has been held that it is reasonable to assume in the absence of any evidence to the contrary that the husband's friends and relations intended to make the gift to him and the wife's to her,[201] but one might regard this approach as outmoded and consider that today it would be more reasonable to assume that a gift, at least where use of the item will be joint, should be regarded as made to both spouses or civil partners.[202]

(d) Transactions between partners

Undue influence

With the exceptions discussed below in the case of chattels, gifts between partners are subject to the general law. Indeed, it should be noted that even the relationship of marriage

---

[197] At p 134. See *Mercier v Mercier* [1903] 2 Ch 98, CA (presumption of resulting trust for wife); *Silver v Silver* [1958] 1 All ER 523, CA (presumption of advancement). Hence, if the husband had property conveyed to both spouses and a stranger, all three would hold on trust for the husband and wife jointly: *Re Eykyn's Trusts* (1877) 6 Ch D 115. There is a presumption of advancement even though the marriage is voidable: *Dunbar v Dunbar* [1909] 2 Ch 639; but not if the husband knows it to be void, for then there is to his knowledge no duty to maintain: *Soar v Foster* (1858) 4 K & J 152. Query if he does not know it is void. The presumption of advancement is also raised if a man has property conveyed into his fiancée's name: *Moate v Moate* [1948] 2 All ER 486, but the correctness of this decision is not beyond doubt: see Lowe 'The Advancement of an Intended Wife: A Reply' (1976) 120 Sol Jo 141.

[198] The husband may not rebut the presumption by adducing evidence of his own fraudulent or unlawful intention: *Re Emery's Investments' Trusts* [1959] Ch 410 (evasion of tax in the USA); *Tinker v Tinker* [1970] P 136, CA (defrauding creditors). Where the transferor is not obliged to rely on the illegality in order to establish his interest, the claim can succeed: see *Tribe v Tribe* [1995] 2 FLR 966, CA (father and son).

[199] [1970] AC 777 at 793 HL per Lord Reid; at 811 per Lord Hodson; at 814–15 per Lord Upjohn; at 824 per Lord Diplock.

[200] Nonetheless, the government considers that the presumption would need to be abolished before the UK could ratify Protocol 7 to the European Convention on Human Rights: see Hansard, HL Written Answers, col 197, 21 April 1998.

[201] *Samson v Samson* [1960] 1 All ER 653, CA. Spouses' subsequent conduct may turn a gift to one of them into joint property: *Samson v Samson*. Presumably, a similar approach is applicable to engagement presents, assuming that they are intended as an unconditional gift (ie they are not returnable if the marriage does not take place).

[202] See *Midland Bank plc v Cooke* [1995] 4 All ER 562, CA, discussed below, pp 161, 167 (a wedding cash present provided by the groom's parents held to be intended to be a gift to both spouses equally) and *Kelner v Kelner* [1939] P 411, (£1,000 deposited by the wife's father at the time of the marriage in a joint bank account in both spouses' names ordered to be divided equally between them).

(in contrast to the relationship between parent and child) does not ipso facto give rise to a presumption that either has exercised undue influence over the other.[203] Undue influence may be described as occurring

'whenever the consent thus procured ought not fairly to be treated as the expression of a person's free will. . . . Equity identified broadly two forms of unacceptable conduct. The first comprises overt acts of improper pressure or coercion such as unlawful threats. . . . The second form arises out of a relationship between two persons where one has acquired over another a measure of influence, or ascendancy, of which the ascendant person then takes unfair advantage.'[204]

Whilst the relationship between husband and wife,[205] fiancés,[206] or cohabitants or same-sex partners,[207] *can* be regarded as giving rise to circumstances in which the second form of undue influence may occur, this must be established on the individual facts. Thus, in *Glanville v Glanville*[208] where children disputed a deed of gift, made by their then terminally-ill father, leaving the matrimonial home outright to his second wife rather than a life interest as set out in an earlier will, the judge held that this was not a case where the facts presented 'spoke for themselves' so as to enable him to conclude that the wife *must* have put undue pressure on her husband. However, once the complainant brings forward evidence showing that he or she (or the vulnerable person such as, in *Glanville*, the husband) placed trust and confidence in the other party in relation to the management of his or her financial affairs, and that a transaction has taken place which is not readily explicable simply by virtue of the relationship of the parties,[209] the evidential burden will then shift to the other to produce evidence to counter the inference of undue influence which otherwise should be drawn.[210] The possibility of undue influence having occurred is

---

[203] *Howes v Bishop* [1909] 2 KB 390, CA; *Mackenzie v Royal Bank of Canada* [1934] AC 468, PC; *Bank of Credit and Commerce International SA v Aboody* [1990] 1 QB 923, CA; *Barclays Bank plc v O'Brien* [1994] 1 AC 180, HL Contrast *Bank of Montreal v Stuart* [1911] AC 120, PC, where undue influence was in fact exercised.

[204] *Royal Bank of Scotland plc v Etridge (No 2)* [2001] UKHL 44, [2002] 2 AC 773 *per* Lord Nicholls of Birkenhead at paras 7–8. See M Haley, '*Royal Bank of Scotland plc v Etridge (No 2)*: The O'Brien defence—a compromise reworked?' [2002] CFLQ 93.

[205] *Barclays Bank plc v Rivett* [1999] 1 FLR 730, CA (wife exercising undue influence over husband).

[206] *Zamet v Hyman* [1961] 3 All ER 933, CA.

[207] *Barclays Bank plc v O'Brien* [1994] 1 AC 180 at 188E per Lord Browne-Wilkinson. The parties to an intimate sexual relationship need not live together: *Midland Bank plc v Massey* [1994] 2 FLR 342, CA. But for the view that undue influence is much less likely to arise in same-sex relationships because of the absence of a gendered power dynamic, see R Auchmuty, 'When Equality is not Equity: Homosexual Inclusion in Undue Influence Law' (2003) 11 Fem LS 163.

[208] [2002] EWHC 1587 (Ch). To similar effect, see *Dailey v Dailey* [2003] 3 FCR 369, PC—while husband had entrepreneurial instinct, he was an unlettered man and the wife handled the paperwork in their business. She did not establish that he had exercised undue influence over her when she transferred her interest in a jointly owned parcel of land to him. Cf *Simpson v Simpson* [1992] 1 FLR 601: husband suffering from fatal brain tumour held to be under wife's undue influence when he transferred the bulk of his estate to her.

[209] Explaining the meaning of the requirement to show that the transaction was 'manifestly disadvantageous', as stated by Lord Scarman in *National Westminster Bank plc v Morgan* [1985] AC 686, 703–7.

[210] Thus it is unhelpful to present such relationships as forming a distinct presumptive category, as had been done previously (see *Barclays Bank plc v O'Brien* [1994] 1 AC 180 at 190 *per* Lord Browne-Wilkinson): *Royal Bank of Scotland plc v Etridge (No 2)* [2001] UKHL 44, [2002] 2 AC 773 *per* Lord Nicholls at para 17; Lord Hobhouse of Woodborough at para 107, Lord Scott of Foscote at para 161. Rather, the 'presumption' 'has the same function in undue influence cases as *res ipsa loquitur* has in negligence cases. It recognises an evidential state of affairs in which the onus has shifted': *Per* Lord Scott ibid. For an example of a defendant

of particular importance in the context of disputes with third parties regarding the fate of the matrimonial home, and is discussed further below.[211]

Chattels

To perfect a gift of a chattel there must be an intention on the part of the donor to pass property to the donee and, in addition, either a deed executed by the former or a delivery of the chattel to the latter. Gifts by deed will be rare between couples in intimate relationships but, when they do occur, will usually present no difficulties since the intention can be inferred from the execution of the deed.[212] But a partner[213] who alleges that the other has effected a gift by delivery has to surmount two obstacles. First, since partners frequently use each other's property, an intention to make a gift cannot readily be inferred from permission to use the chattel in question, and consequently the burden of proof upon a partner alleging a gift will probably be higher than upon a stranger.[214] Secondly, it may be well-nigh impossible in many cases to prove delivery. Where the goods are intended for the exclusive use of the donee (for example, clothes or jewellery), delivery will normally take place at the time the gift is made by a physical handing over and taking; but if the goods in question have already been used by both partners in the family home and will continue to be used in this way (for example, articles of furniture), there is not likely to be any apparent change of possession. There may indeed be an effective symbolic delivery of one chattel as representing the whole, but partners are hardly likely to carry out such an artificial act, the significance of which will not occur to them.[215]

English courts have been slow to infer a delivery of a chattel from one spouse to the other,[216] doubtless because of the danger that they may fraudulently allege a prior gift of the husband's goods to the wife in order to keep them out of the hands of the former's creditors. A good example of this reluctance is *Re Cole*,[217] in which the husband completely furnished a new house before his wife set foot in it. When she arrived, he put his hands over her eyes, took her into the first room, uncovered her eyes and said, 'Look'. She then went into all the other rooms and handled various articles; at the end the husband said to her, 'It's all yours'. The furniture nevertheless remained insured in his name. He

---

failing to discharge this evidential burden, see *Humphreys v Humphreys* [2004] EWHC 2201 (Ch), [2004] All ER (D) 136 (Oct): son influencing mother to enter into unfair arrangement whereby she would become sole legal owner of her home, a former secure tenancy bought with the aid of a 60% discount on the purchase price, but he would receive whole of beneficial interest on her death in return for meeting the mortgage payments on the remaining 40%.

[211] At pp 183ff.

[212] But for a dispute between former fiancés as to the true intention behind an apparent bill of sale transferring ownership of a car from one to the other, see *Cox v Jones* [2004] EWHC 1486 (Ch) [2004] 2 FLR 1010 (transfer found to be effective although no money changed hands).

[213] That is, a spouse, fiancé, civil partner or cohabitant.

[214] See *Bashall v Bashall* (1894) 11 TLR 152, CA.

[215] *Lock v Heath* (1892) 8 TLR 295 (husband held to have given all his furniture to wife by symbolic delivery of chair). For an effective constructive delivery by a father to his daughter, see *Kilpin v Ratley* [1892] 1 QB 582.

[216] Nor is there any reason to think that any different attitude would be taken in the case of alleged gifts between other partners.

[217] [1964] Ch 175, CA. Would the court have arrived at the same decision if, say, after the husband's death the question had arisen whether the goods belonged to the wife or to his personal representatives? See also *Bashall v Bashall* (above); *Valier v Wright & Bull Ltd* (1917) 33 TLR 366.

subsequently became bankrupt and the question arose whether the trustee or wife was entitled to the goods in question. It was held that the wife had failed to establish an effective delivery, and consequently the gift to her was never perfected. In the circumstances it would always seem wisest for a gift of goods used by both spouses to be made by means of a deed.

Voidable transactions

It is easy to see how transactions between partners might be used as a means of defrauding creditors. To a person who is on the verge of bankruptcy or who is about to engage in a hazardous business operation, there is a great temptation to settle the bulk of his property on trust for his partner and children and thus keep it out of the hands of his creditors and at the same time ensure that his family will be provided for. Parliament has sought to protect the creditors of the rogue who incidentally benefits his family, whilst not prejudicing the members of the family of a person who settles property in good faith and then runs into financial difficulties. If, for example, a husband, fearing insolvency, transfers property to his wife or children, his creditors or trustee in bankruptcy could seek to have the transfer set aside in the following circumstances.

Transactions defrauding creditors. Section 423 of the Insolvency Act 1986[218] is designed to protect the creditors of a person who has entered into a transaction at an undervalue with the intention of defeating their claims. This could take the form, for example, of disposing of property which would otherwise be available to satisfy a judgment debt, or of dealing with property that has been charged in such a way as to deprive the creditor of the value of his security. Unlike s 339 (discussed below), s 423 is neither time-limited nor confined to insolvencies.

A 'transaction' for this purpose includes any gift, agreement or arrangement.[219] A transaction is deemed to be at an undervalue if the party entering into it (whom we will call the debtor) received no consideration,[220] or the value he received was significantly less than the value he gave,[221] or if he entered into it in consideration of marriage.[222] The court must be satisfied that the debtor's purpose in entering into the transaction which is being attacked was to put assets beyond the reach of a person who is making (or may at some time make) a claim against him or, alternatively, to prejudice the interests of such a person in some other way.[223]

Proceedings may be brought by anyone prejudiced by the transaction or capable of being prejudiced by it (who is referred to as a 'victim of the transaction'). Presumably in the latter case he must establish that there is a very strong probability that he will be

---

[218] Replacing s 172 of the Law of Property Act 1925, which in turn replaced (with amendments) 13 Eliz 1, c 5.

[219] Insolvency Act 1986 s 436. Thus a tenancy for a farm or a lease may be set aside if a husband granted it to his wife with the intention of depriving the mortgagees of the land in question of the right to take vacant possession of it; see respectively *Agricultural Mortgage plc v Woodward* [1996] 1 FLR 226, CA and *Lloyd's Bank Ltd v Marcan* [1973] 3 All ER 754, CA.

[220] See eg *Midland Bank plc v Wyatt* [1995] 1 FLR 697 (transfer of interest to daughters).

[221] See *Reid v Ramlort Ltd* [2004] EWCA Civ 800 [2004] BPIR 985.

[222] Insolvency Act 1986 s 423(1).

[223] Ibid, s 423(3). See *Trowbridge v Trowbridge* [2003] 2 FLR 231—payments made by husband to second wife set aside as done in order to thwart enforcement of consent order in favour of first wife.

prejudiced in the future; it cannot have been Parliament's intention to permit anyone to apply to have a transaction set aside on the ground that he might possibly be prejudiced by it. Proceedings may also be brought by the debtor's trustee in bankruptcy or by the supervisor of a voluntary arrangement approved by his creditors.[224]

If the conditions set out above are satisfied, the court may make such order as it thinks fit to restore the position to what it would have been if the transaction had not been entered into and to protect victims' interests.[225] Its powers are extensive. In particular it may order a person (whether or not he was a party to the transaction) to transfer to another (either absolutely or for the benefit of all victims) any property in his hands transferred as part of the transaction (or any other property, including money,[226] representing the proceeds of sales of such property) and to account for any benefits received. It may also release or discharge the whole or part of any security given by the debtor.[227]

The transaction is voidable and not void: consequently no order can be made against anyone who was not a party to it if he acquired an interest in it in good faith, for value and without notice of the circumstances by virtue of which an order could be made under s 423.[228] Hence if, say, the debtor gave property to his wife with intent to defraud a creditor and she then sold it to X, she could be made to account for the value of the benefit she had received, but X could not if he was a bona fide purchaser without notice of the fraud.

Transactions at an undervalue entered into by a bankrupt. Section 339 of the Insolvency Act 1986[229] gives even wider protection to creditors. It is not necessary to prove any intent to defraud a creditor, but the debtor must have been made bankrupt. The trustee of his estate may apply to the court for an order if the bankrupt entered into a transaction at an undervalue. The terms 'transaction' and 'at an undervalue' bear the same meaning as they do under s 423.[230] The trustee may attack any transaction effected up to five years before the presentation of the petition on which the debtor was adjudged bankrupt, but if it was entered into more than two years before that date, no order may be made unless at the time of the transaction the bankrupt was insolvent or became insolvent in consequence of entering into it. There is a rebuttable presumption that this condition is satisfied if the transaction was entered into with 'an associate', including, among others, the bankrupt's spouse or former spouse, civil partner or former civil partner, reputed spouse, or relative.[231] The phrase 'reputed husband or wife' is unusual. It looks at first sight as though it is

[224] Insolvency Act 1986 s 423(5) (definition of 'victim') and s 424. Any application is to be treated as made on behalf of every victim of the transaction.

[225] Ibid, s 423(2). In *Re Maddever* (1884) 27 Ch D 523, CA, it was held (under earlier legislation) that a speciality creditor could have a conveyance set aside 10 years after it had been executed and that the doctrine of laches had no application.

[226] See the definition of 'property' in s 436 of the Insolvency Act 1986.   [227] Ibid, s 425(1).

[228] Ibid, s 425(2)–(3). Presumably constructive notice will deprive the transferee of protection: see (under s 172 of the Law of Property Act 1925) *Lloyds Bank Ltd v Marcan* [1973] 2 All ER 359 at 369.

[229] Replacing s 42 of the Bankruptcy Act 1914.

[230] Ibid, s 339(3) and s 436. In the absence of consideration, a benefit is not protected merely because it was conferred in pursuance of an order for financial provision made under s 24 of the Matrimonial Causes Act 1973 on divorce, nullity or separation: Matrimonial Causes Act 1973 s 39, as amended by the Insolvency Act 1985 Sch 8, and the Insolvency Act 1986 Sch 14. See for equivalent provision in the case of civil partnerships, Civil Partnership Act 2004 Sch 5 para 77.

[231] Insolvency Act 1986 s 339, s 341(1)(a), (2) and s 435. There is a special period in the case of a criminal bankruptcy: s 341(4)–(5). A person is insolvent if he is unable to pay his debts or his assets are less than his

intended to apply to transactions between parties living together as husband and wife but, if this is so, the draftsman may largely have failed in his purpose, because the word 'reputed' implies that they must also be regarded as married.[232]

The court may make such order as it thinks fit to restore the position to what it would have been had the bankrupt not entered into the transaction. It has much the same powers as it has under s 423, except that property has to be transferred to the trustee in bankruptcy. Similarly, property may be recovered from a third person into whose hands it has come unless he is, or acquired it through, a bona fide purchaser for value and without notice of the circumstances entitling the court to make an order.[233] In addition, the court may permit anyone adversely affected by the order to prove in the bankruptcy for the loss he has suffered.[234]

Money lent by one partner to the other

A loan by one partner to the other usually raises no presumption of a gift by way of advancement, so that the lender will be able to recover the sum lent in the absence of evidence that a gift was intended.[235]

If the borrower becomes bankrupt, his or her spouse or civil partner is not entitled to any payment out of his estate until all other creditors have been paid in full.[236]

(e) Disputes between partners [237]

So long as partners are living amicably together, the questions of who owns what and what rights short of ownership one partner may have in the property of the other rarely have to be answered, but they become vital if the relationship breaks down. This adds considerably to the difficulty, for the parties rarely contemplate the collapse of the relationship when they acquire property, and their respective rights in it are never discussed, let alone defined. Hence the courts are faced with the problem of having to infer an intention which the partners never formulated at all.[238]

As regards property apart from land (which is discussed in the following chapter), there are three different ways of solving disputes open to them.

---

liabilities (including contingent and prospective liabilities): s 341(3). 'Relative' means brother, sister, uncle, aunt, nephew, niece, lineal ancestor or lineal descendant, including relations of the half blood, and treating a person's illegitimate child, stepchild and adopted child as his own child. 'Associate' also includes the spouse, civil partner, former spouse or civil partner, and reputed spouse of a relative, and a relative of the bankrupt's spouse or former spouse, civil partner or former civil partner, or reputed spouse: s 435(1), (2) and (8) (as amended by the Civil Partnership Act Sch 27 para 121).

232 This also begs the question: by whom must they have been regarded as husband and wife? In the Scots law of presumption of marriage by cohabitation with habit and repute, the parties had to be generally regarded as married amongst the circle in which they moved: see E Clive *Law of Husband and Wife in Scotland* (2nd edn) pp 64–5. Note that the rule of law by which marriage could be constituted by cohabitation with habit and repute has been abolished by s 3 of the Family Law (Scotland) Act 2006.

233 Insolvency Act 1986 s 342(2), (4).   234 Ibid, s 342(1), (3).

235 *Hall v Hall* [1911] 1 Ch 487 (mortgage of the wife's property to secure a loan to the husband). Contrast *Paget v Paget* [1898] 1 Ch 470, CA, where the facts indicated that a gift was intended.

236 Insolvency Act 1986 s 329 as amended by Civil Partnership Act 2004 Sch 27 para 116. This applies if the lender was the bankrupt's spouse or civil partner at the commencement of the bankruptcy, whether or not they were married or had formed a civil partnership when the loan was made.

237 The term 'partner' is again used here as a generic term to refer to spouses, civil partners, engaged couples and cohabitants.

238 See *Re Rogers' Question* [1948] 1 All ER 328, CA; *Cobb v Cobb* [1955] 2 All ER 696 at 699, CA.

Action for damages in tort or contract

Either spouse or partner may protect his or her interests in property by suing the other in tort, for example in trespass or conversion.[239] Either may also bring an action against the other for the recovery of land. In this connection it should be remembered that, if the spouses are jointly in possession of property or are jointly entitled to possession, one may be liable in trespass if he or she completely ousts the other, or in conversion if he or she destroys the property or disposes of it.[240] As we have seen, there are difficulties in establishing legally binding contractual ties between intimate partners, but actions on the contract may certainly be attempted.

Proceedings for an injunction

Either partner may obtain an injunction to prevent the other from committing a continuing or threatened wrong against the plaintiff's property.[241] In practice this remedy is most frequently sought when one partner is trying to exclude the other from the family home, and the particular problems that arise in that context are dealt with in Chapter 5.[242]

Proceedings under s 17 of the Married Women's Property Act 1882[243]

Section 17[244] provides that 'in any question between husband and wife as to the title to or possession of property'[245] either of them may apply for an order to the High Court or a county court and the judge 'may make such order with respect to the property in dispute . . . as he thinks fit'.[246] These proceedings are usually invoked when the marriage has broken down. Disputes over rights in property may still be going on after the marriage has been legally terminated, and consequently s 17 was extended to enable former spouses to make an application for a period of three years after a decree absolute of divorce or nullity.[247]

It will be seen that under s 17 the court has jurisdiction to determine questions of title and possession. In order that it may do this, it had been held that there must be in existence specific property or a specific fund with respect to which the order might be made and that, if the property or fund had ceased to exist, there was no power to make what would be in effect an order for damages for trespass, conversion or debt.[248] This

---

[239] Above p 120.

[240] Torts (Interference with Goods) Act 1977 s 10. The court may stay the action if the questions in issue could be disposed of more conveniently by an application under s 17 of the Married Women's Property Act 1882: see below.

[241] This may be done by bringing an action in tort under the Law Reform (Husband and Wife) Act 1962, in proceedings under the Family Law Act 1996, or by way of ancillary relief in other matrimonial proceedings.

[242] See below pp 230ff.

[243] Equivalent provision is made for civil partners by s 66 of the Civil Partnership Act 2004. The provision does not extend to cohabitants.

[244] As amended. Replacing and extending the Married Women's Property Act 1870 s 9.

[245] Including choses in action (*Spellman v Spellman* [1961] 2 All ER 498, CA at 501) and property of which the claimant is a bare trustee and in which he has no beneficial interest at all (*Re Knight's Question* [1959] Ch 381, [1958] 1 All ER 812). If there is no question as to title or possession but one spouse is, eg, seeking to enforce what is now a trust for land (formerly a trust for sale: see below) against the other, proceedings under s 17 are inappropriate and the same proceedings should be taken as would be taken between strangers: *Rawlings v Rawlings* [1964] P 398, CA.

[246] Proceedings in the High Court are now assigned to the Family Division.

[247] Matrimonial Proceedings and Property Act 1970 s 39. The summary procedure under s 17 has also been made available to parties to an agreement to marry that has been terminated: see below p 146.

[248] *Tunstall v Tunstall* [1953] 2 All ER 310, CA.

clearly worked injustice if the defendant had already disposed of the property or fund in question: this was remedied by s 7 of the Matrimonial Causes (Property and Maintenance) Act 1958, which gives the court power in such a case either to order the defendant to pay to the plaintiff such sum of money as represents the latter's interest in the property or fund, or to make an order with respect to any other property which now represents the whole or part of the original.[249]

For some years there was considerable judicial controversy over the width of the powers which the wording of the section gave to the judges.[250] It was, however, finally settled by the House of Lords in *Pettitt v Pettitt*[251] that the court has no jurisdiction under this section to vary existing titles and no wider power to transfer or create interests in property than it would have in any other type of proceedings. At the most it has, in the words of Lord Diplock, 'a wide discretion as to the enforcement of the proprietary or possessory rights of one spouse in any property against the other'.[252] Furthermore, the fact that the marriage has broken down, the circumstances of the breakdown and the conduct of the parties cannot affect title in the absence of an agreement between the spouses, and are therefore all irrelevant to the outcome of proceedings brought under s 17.[253] But by using its powers to make different types of orders, the court may effectively control the way in which the property is used without departing from the principle that it cannot alter the title. Thus it may order a spouse to give up possession of a house, to deliver up chattels, to transfer shares and other choses in action, or to pay over a specific fund, and it may even forbid him to dispossess the other spouse or to deal with the property in any way inconsistent with the other's rights.[254] Similarly, the court may order the property to be sold and direct how the proceeds of sale are to be divided[255] or, if both spouses have an interest, it may order one of them to transfer his or her share to the other on the latter's paying the value of the property transferred.[256]

On the breakdown of a marriage or civil partnership, one of the spouses or partners will normally seek a divorce, nullity or separation and invoke the court's wider powers to make a property adjustment order under s 24 of the Matrimonial Causes Act 1973 or Sch 6 Part 2 of the Civil Partnership Bill. Consequently proceedings under s 17 are now likely to be invoked only if the person seeking relief is unable or unwilling to take other proceedings, or has remarried or repartnered before applying for a property adjustment order.[257]

Disputes between engaged couples and between unmarried cohabitants

The main distinction between the property rights of unmarried cohabitants on the one hand and spouses or civil partners on the other is that property adjustment orders are not available to the former. Similarly, property adjustment orders are not available to

---

[249] The equivalent provision for civil partners is contained in s 67 of the Civil Partnership Act 2004.

[250] See further below pp 151–2.   [251] [1970] AC 777, HL.

[252] At 820.   [253] *Pettitt v Pettitt* (above).

[254] As in *Lee v Lee* [1952] 2 QB 489n, CA. In *Re Bettinson's Question* [1956] Ch 67, it was held that an order could be made with respect to property which was subject to the doctrine of community of property under the law of the parties' domicile (California).

[255] Matrimonial Causes (Property and Maintenance) Act 1958 s 7(7); Civil Partnership Act 2004 s 66(2).

[256] *Bothe v Amos* [1976] Fam 46, CA.

[257] Even so, proceedings are sometimes still taken by spouses involved in marital breakdown: see eg *A v A (Costs Appeal)* [1996] 1 FLR 14.

engaged couples.[258] Consequently, disputes between cohabitants or former cohabitants and engaged or formerly engaged couples over the ownership, occupation or use of property must be resolved, generally speaking, by applying the ordinary legal rules applicable to strangers. There is, however, one distinction between former engaged couples and cohabitants in that s 2(1) of the Law Reform (Miscellaneous Provisions) Act 1970 provides that any rule of law relating to spouses' rights in relation to property in which either or both has or have a beneficial interest, shall apply in like manner to the former fiancés and they can apply for an order under the Married Women's Property Act 1882 s 17.[259] Engaged couples could well start to buy a house in contemplation of their marriage, and this may give them rights in property which are virtually indistinguishable from those acquired by married couples. However, it was the abolition of actions for damages for breach of promise of marriage, which deprived them of the means of recovering the expenses they had lost if the marriage did not take place, that prompted[260] making the summary procedure of s 17 available to the parties to an agreement to marry which has been terminated.[261] Where land is concerned, there seems little advantage in applying under s 17 rather than under s 14 of the Trusts of Land and Appointment of Trustees Act 1996, for while the powers under the latter are at least as extensive,[262] they are not fettered, as are those under s 17, by having to relate to property in which either or both had an interest while the agreement was in force or by the requirement to bring the action within three years of the termination of the agreement.[263] Furthermore, an action under s 14 avoids any problems of deciding whether there was an agreement to marry in the first place.[264]

(f) Disputes between one of the partners and a stranger

The question to be considered here is how far rights in property created or affected by marriage, civil partnership, engagement or cohabitation can be enforced by one of the partners against a third person. The latter may claim in one of a number of capacities, for example, as a purchaser for value from the other partner, as the other's creditor or trustee in bankruptcy, or as a beneficiary entitled to a deceased partner's estate. It is essential to decide first what rights the claiming partner has against the other partner and then how far these rights are enforceable against the third person. This will depend upon the application of general principles of the law of property, and in particular the nature of the latter's title. If he is, say, the man's donee, the woman may enforce against him all those rights (other than purely personal rights) which she would have against her partner; if he is a purchaser of a legal estate or interest for value, he will take the property subject to the

---

[258] See *Mossop v Mossop* [1989] Fam 77.

[259] For couples who had agreed to register their partnership see Civil Partnership Act 2004 ss 68, 74.

[260] See Law Com No 26, *Breach of Promise of Marriage*, paras 35–42. For the abolition of actions for breach of promise, see above, p 43.

[261] By the Law Reform (Miscellaneous Provisions) Act 1970 s 2(2). For an example, see *Marsh v Von Sternberg* [1986] 1 FLR 526. For civil partners, see Civil Partnership Act 2004 s 66.

[262] But note s 14 has no application in respect of pure personalty and is thus discussed below, pp 173–6.

[263] These requirements for an application under s 17 are set out in s 2(2) of the Law Reform (Miscellaneous Provisions) Act 1970 and, for civil partners, under s 74(4) of the Civil Partnership Act 2004.

[264] See, for example, *Shaw v Fitzgerald* [1992] 1 FLR 357, discussed above at p 44.

woman's legal rights, but will not be bound by her equitable interests if he purchased in good faith and without notice of them.[265]

(g) Reform proposals

There needs to be a complete overhaul of the whole field of family property law, which, as can be seen, is complex and often outmoded in its approach. Leaving aside the question of how those who have not married or registered their partnership should be dealt with,[266] there is still a need to clarify and update the law as it should apply to those who do acquire the status of spouse or civil partner. Solutions adopted by other legal systems include community of property (under which the property belonging to both spouses or partners is administered by the husband or both and divided between them or their personal representatives when the marriage/partnership comes to an end), community of gains (which limits community to property acquired during the marriage/partnership otherwise than by gift or inheritance), and deferred community (under which each remains free to acquire and dispose of his or her own property, but at the end of the marriage/partnership any net gain or surplus is divided equally between them). English courts already have a wide discretion to adjust rights by ordering the transfer and settlement of property follow-ing divorce, dissolution of partnership, nullity and separation. There are also extensive powers to order provision for members of the family and other dependants out of the estate of a deceased person. Bearing these points in mind, the Law Commission, consider-ing the position of spouses in 1978, concluded that it was not necessary to introduce any form of community of property in this country: most remaining hardship would be avoided if the spouses were co-owners of the matrimonial home, which is the most substantial asset in the majority of families. Even at that time well over a half of all married couples who owned their homes did so jointly,[267] and the Commission recommended that the principle of co-ownership should be extended by statute to all spouses.[268]

What they envisaged was that spouses should be statutory co-owners of any property, freehold or leasehold, used as their matrimonial home unless they otherwise agreed or, in the case of a gift, the donor, settlor or testator otherwise stipulated.[269] Once the statutory trust attached to the land, neither would be able to dispose of it unless the other consented or the court dispensed with his or her consent.[270] The Commission rejected the possibility of introducing compulsory co-ownership of goods, partly because the value of used goods is so much less than half that of new goods that compensation in the form of half their actual value would not enable the loser to replace them. Instead they proposed that either spouse should be able to apply for an order concerning the use and enjoyment of 'house-hold goods'.[271] In deciding whether to make such an order, the court should be guided

---

[265] See further below p 182.   [266] See above p 105 and below pp 171ff.

[267] See Todd and Jones *Matrimonial Property* (HMSO).

[268] Law Com No 86 (Third Report on *Family Property*). See also Law Commission Working Paper No 42 and Law Com No 52 (First Report on *Family Property*); report of the Morton Commission, Cmd 9678, Pt IX.

[269] The Commission contemplated other exceptions. The most important was the ability of a spouse to exclude the house from co-ownership if he owned it at the time of the marriage.

[270] If one spouse's name did not appear on the title, she (or he) would be able to protect her interest by registering it as a land charge.

[271] That is, 'any goods, including a vehicle, which are or were available for use and enjoyment in or in connection with any home which the parties to the marriage have at any time during the marriage

particularly by the extent to which the applicant needed them to meet the normal requirements of his or her daily life and family responsibilities. If the other spouse contravened an order, the court could order him to pay the applicant such sum (which could be the replacement value) as it thought fair and reasonable by way of compensation.[272]

These proposals represented a compromise between the present English system of separate property and a comprehensive adoption of a system of community. They did not, however, command universal support and were not implemented. The Law Commission re-examined the issue of ownership of the family home some years later, and its arguments and conclusions are discussed in the next chapter.

Meanwhile, in 1985, the Law Commission considered the problem again insofar as it concerns pure personalty.[273] They highlighted a number of anomalies and inequalities in the law, including the rules relating to the acquisition of property out of a housekeeping allowance and the operation of the presumption of advancement.[274] They also pointed out that the law can work arbitrarily: for example, if the wife pays all the housekeeping bills out of her own earnings and the husband uses his to buy a car for the parties' joint use, the car will belong to him, whilst if they pool their earnings in a joint account, it will belong to them both. The Commission went back on their earlier recommendation and proposed that, if one spouse acquires property intended wholly or mainly for the use or benefit of both, beneficial ownership should vest in both jointly. This would be subject to a contrary intention on the part of the purchaser or transferor, provided that it was made known to the other at the time, and would not apply to property acquired by way of gift or inheritance or purchased or transferred wholly or mainly for the purpose of business.[275] The reason for proposing that the property should be held jointly and not in equal shares was the belief that this is what the parties themselves would wish and intend.[276]

The implementation of this proposal would obviously lead to a considerable increase in the number of chattels jointly owned and there is the risk that a purchaser from one party only would not acquire a good title. This risk, however, exists already: the buyer of a family car assumes that the seller is the absolute owner and does not enquire about the source of the funds with which it was originally bought. The Commission believed that the proposed change would introduce a fair rule and provide much greater certainty in this area of the law. It is certainly less complex than their earlier recommendations, but at present it seems no more likely to be implemented.

---

occupied as their matrimonial home'. Goods would be excepted if third parties had an interest in them, eg goods subject to hire, hire-purchase and conditional sale agreements.

[272] This would be in addition to the usual penalties for disobeying an order of the court. A person receiving the goods could also be ordered to pay compensation if he was aware of the order. In appropriate cases the party disposing of the goods could be ordered to pay compensation even though no order was in force.

[273] Law Com No 175 (*Matrimonial Property*, 1985). Land was excluded from the Commission's recommendations because of its peculiar nature.

[274] See Law Com Working Paper No 90 (Transfer of Money between Spouses).

[275] The Commission would also exclude policies of life assurance, which could mature many years after the termination of the parties' relationship.

[276] Cf s 25 of the Family Law (Scotland) Act 1985, under which there is a presumption that each spouse has an equal share in any household goods (excluding money or securities; cars, caravans or other road vehicles; or domestic animals) obtained in prospect of or during the marriage other than by gift or succession from a third party.

4

THE FAMILY HOME

A INTRODUCTION

The right to respect for one's home, enshrined in Art 8(1) of the European Convention on Human Rights, has been described as an aspect of the broader right to privacy contained in that article,[1] and one's home as

'the place where [a person] and his family are entitled to be left in peace free from interference by the state or agents of the state. It is an important aspect of his dignity as a human being, and it is protected as such and not as an item of property.'[2]

The word 'home' in Art 8 is an autonomous concept which does not depend on its meaning under domestic law. Whether or not a particular habitation constitutes a 'home' will depend on the facts—it is the place where a person lives (or intends to live)[3] on a settled basis, but it is not necessary to show that one has the legal right to occupy the property.[4] The right to respect for one's home (not, it should be noted, a right *to a home*)[5] has been prayed in aid primarily in support of claims to occupy public-sector rented property, but arguably it may have significance in litigation between private individuals where the court has to determine whether to order possession or sale, and this is discussed below.

The family home[6] may have two functions. Its primary purpose, reflected in this interpretation of the European Convention, is to provide shelter for the parties and their family. At the same time, if it is held in freehold or on a long lease, it will constitute the most significant asset that most couples own and is thus an extremely valuable investment.[7] If the relationship breaks down, these two aspects may come into conflict. Both parties may

---

[1] By Lord Hope of Craighead in *Harrow v London Borough Council v Qazi* [2003] UKHL 43 [2004] 1 AC 983 at para 50. For criticism of the linkage of the right to respect for one's home with the right to privacy, rather than as importing a clear right to 'occupancy', see I Loveland, 'The Impact of the Human Rights Act on Security of Tenure in Public Housing' [2004] Public Law 594 at 601–3.

[2] *Per* Lord Millett ibid at para 89.

[3] As in *Gillow v United Kingdom* (1986) Series A, No 109; 11 EHRR 335.

[4] *Wiggins v United Kingdom* (1978) 13 DR 40; *Harrow London Borough Council v Qazi* (above).

[5] *Chapman v United Kingdom* (2001) 33 EHRR 399.

[6] For an interesting critique of the concept of the 'family home' see L Fox, 'Creditors and the concept of "family home": a functional analysis' (2005) Legal Studies 201, who argues (at p 227) that focusing on the individual's relationship with the property, rather than family status, would enable the 'legal concept of home to reflect more accurately the values associated with occupiers' attachments to their homes.'

[7] Its proprietary nature may be protected by Protocol 1, Art 1 to the Convention—the right to peaceful enjoyment of possessions.

wish to continue in exclusive occupation (with or without children); alternatively, one may wish to do so while the other may wish to realise his or her investment. A party deprived of both the value of the home and the right to occupy it will often find it impossible to purchase other accommodation, and if the house is sold and the proceeds divided between them, both may face the same predicament. The problem may also arise if one party is insolvent, for a mortgagee may wish to realise his security or a trustee in bankruptcy may wish to sell the home to enlarge the assets available to the creditors. It will therefore be seen that the interests of the creditors may come into direct conflict with those of the rest of the family who still need a roof over their heads.

There are thus two distinct but interrelated problems: ownership and occupation. The first is concerned with the question, in whom are the legal and beneficial interests in the property vested? The second is concerned with the question, what rights of occupation does each party have in the home irrespective of ownership? After discussing the current law governing ownership, we consider the proposals that have been suggested for reform, and compare the English approach with that taken in other jurisdictions. We then consider occupation rights. We then move on to discuss the problems that arise if one of the parties is insolvent. Finally, we examine the additional security a party may enjoy if the property is leasehold and subject to statutory control.

B OWNERSHIP

1 THE BACKGROUND TO THE CURRENT LAW

Unlike continental European systems, English law has never developed a special regime for dealing with matrimonial or family property. Consequently, whenever ownership of family assets is in issue recourse must be had to the ordinary rules governing property law.[8]

Before the Second World War the potential injustice of applying ordinary property rules to the ownership of family assets was barely an issue. At that stage few working class families owned their own homes, and cohabitation outside marriage was almost non-existent. In the vast majority of middle class families the husband was the sole earner and, if the home was purchased, it was conveyed into his name, with the result that the whole beneficial interest would vest in the husband to the exclusion of the wife.[9] With low divorce rates and stable home prices, litigation was uncommon.

After the War the social and economic climate changed. It became common for wives to work during marriage. Property ownership increased,[10] with purchases being made with the aid of mortgages. Property prices began to rise and divorce rates spiralled upwards. The combination of these factors resulted in much more litigation being brought in

---

[8] See below, pp 153–71 for the circumstances in which issues of ownership will need to be settled in the family context.

[9] *Re Sims* [1946] 2 All ER 138. Hence rent received from a lodger was held to belong exclusively to the husband: *Montgomery v Blows* [1916] 1 KB 899, CA.

[10] Just under half of all households were in owner-occupied property in 1971, increasing to 70% by 2003–4: ONS, http://www.statistics.gov.uk/ (2005).

respect of what for most was the key asset, the family home. This in turn brought into sharp relief the starkness of the application of strict rules of property ownership and the doctrine of separation of ownership as between the spouses. It thus became crucial to determine which spouse paid what bills and expenses, since only payments related to the purchase of the property could give rise to ownership. The iniquities of this approach were only too plain to see for, as Lord Denning MR pointed out, it may be purely a matter of convenience which spouse pays off the mortgage and which pays the other household expenses: they give no thought to the legal consequences of their acts (of which they are probably ignorant) and it is unjust to give the wife an interest in the house if she happens to pay the mortgage but not if she pays the household bills instead.[11]

True to form Lord Denning MR was not content to allow what he considered to be an injustice. Seizing on the wording of s 17 of the Married Women's Property Act 1882:

'In any question between husband and wife as to the title to or possession of property, either party . . . may apply by summons or otherwise in a summary way to any judge of the High Court of Justice . . . and the judge . . . may make such order with respect to the property in dispute . . . as he thinks fit',

he held that the court had a discretionary power over family assets. As he put it in *Hine v Hine*:[12]

'. . . the jurisdiction of the court over family assets under section 17 is entirely discretionary. Its discretion transcends all rights, legal or equitable, and enables the court to make such order as it thinks fit. This means, as I understand it, that the court is entitled to make such order as appears to be fair and just in all the circumstances of the case.'

In his view, therefore, provided the spouse (normally the wife at that time) had made a substantial contribution to the overall household expenses she would be held to have a beneficial share of the property, regardless of whether the money was put towards the deposit or mortgage, even though the property was in the husband's name alone.

Lord Denning MR's approach was controversial, and eventually the issue came before the House of Lords, first in *Pettitt v Pettitt*[13] and then in *Gissing v Gissing*,[14] where it was delivered a death blow. As we saw in the previous chapter, it was held that properly interpreted, s 17 is purely a procedural provision designed to facilitate the speedy disposal of property disputes between the spouses, whereby the court could make a declaration of ownership. As Lord Morris put it in *Pettitt v Pettitt*,[15] under s 17 the question for the court was ' "Whose is this?" and not—"To whom shall this be given?" '. Following this unanimous ruling, two fundamental rules emerged. First, it is clear from *Pettitt v Pettitt* that English law knows of no doctrine of community of property or any separate rules of law applicable to family assets.[16] Consequently, if one spouse buys property intended for common use with the other—whether it is a house, furniture or a car—this cannot per se give the latter any proprietary interest. From this follows the second principle, stated in

---

[11] See eg *Fribance v Fribance* [1957] 1 All ER 357 at 360, CA, and *Falconer v Falconer* [1970] 3 All ER 449 at 360, CA.

[12] [1962] 1 WLR 1124 at 1127–8, CA.   [13] [1970] AC 777, HL.

[14] [1971] AC 886, HL.   [15] [1970] AC 777 at 798E–F.

[16] At 800–1 (per Lord Morris), 810 (per Lord Hodson), and 817 (per Lord Upjohn).

Gissing v Gissing,[17] that if either of them seeks to establish a beneficial interest in property, the legal title to which is vested in the other, he or she can do so only by establishing that the legal owner holds the property on trust for the claimant. This latter principle, however, masks considerable difficulties which, as we discuss shortly, continue to arise today.

The injustice which Lord Denning in particular sought to avoid was largely removed by the Matrimonial Proceedings and Property Act 1970, which gave the court a power to make property adjustment orders on pronouncing a decree of divorce, nullity or judicial separation and expressly required it to take into account inter alia 'the contributions which each of the parties has made . . . to the welfare of the family'.[18] We saw in Chapter 3 that this jurisdiction makes it unnecessary to resort to other means to compensate a spouse, and that proceedings to establish property rights should not be taken when an application could be made for an order in matrimonial proceedings (or the equivalent jurisdiction applicable to civil partners). But as we noted, it may still be necessary to determine what interest in property a spouse or civil partner has where:

(1) she (or he) is unable or unwilling to take matrimonial or equivalent proceedings;

(2) she has remarried or repartnered without applying for a property adjustment order in proceedings for dissolution or nullity (when her power to do so will be barred);[19]

(3) it has to be decided, on the death of one of the spouses or partners, whether an interest forms part of his or her estate or vests in the survivor;

(4) it has to be decided, on the insolvency of one of the spouses or partners, what property is available for his or her creditors.

Furthermore, as unmarried or unregistered cohabitants are unable to petition for divorce or other matrimonial relief, neither can apply for a property adjustment order in matrimonial or dissolution proceedings. Hence, unless they have children (when a property adjustment order can be made under the Children Act 1989),[20] any claims they may have must be resolved solely by reference to the law of property. With the growing incidence of cohabitation this particular use of property law has become of major concern. It is perhaps ironic that the law evolved to settle the property claims of spouses now derives much of its contemporary significance in relation to unmarried couples.

Former engaged couples are, like unmarried cohabitants, barred from using the court's adjustive powers under the Matrimonial Causes Act 1973.[21] However, in two other respects they are treated in the same way as spouses in that they can use s 17 of the Married Women's Property Act 1882 to seek judicial resolution of property disputes between them, and s 37 of the Matrimonial Proceedings and Property Act 1970 to claim a beneficial interest by means of improvements they have made to each other's property.[22] Although the former right is hardly significant now that it is broadly settled that the ordinary principles of the law of trusts apply to the property of married and unmarried couples

---

[17] [1971] AC 886 at 896 (per Lord Reid), 900 (per Lord Dilhorne), and 904–5 (per Lord Diplock).
[18] See now the Matrimonial Causes Act 1973 s 24 and s 25(2)(f) and below, pp 1003–5 and 1044–7.
[19] See below, p 985.   [20] See below, p 968.
[21] *Mossop v Mossop* [1989] Fam 77, CA.
[22] Section 17 and s 37 respectively were extended to former engaged couples by the Law Reform (Miscellaneous Provisions) Act 1970 s 2(1)–(2). It may also be that the presumption of advancement applies to engaged couples: see *Moate v Moate* [1948] 2 All ER 486, but note above p 134 n 179.

alike, and anyway summary relief in respect of land may be sought under s 14 of the Trusts of Land and Appointment of Trustees Act 1996, the latter right can be useful.[23]

2 THE CURRENT LAW

(a) The primary importance of the documents of title

As we have said, *Pettitt v Pettitt* and *Gissing v Gissing* established that no special rules apply to the ownership of family assets and that instead one must apply ordinary property principles. The application of these principles requires first having to establish legal ownership and then to determine equitable or beneficial ownership. To determine these issues one should first have recourse to the documents of title, for as Lord Upjohn said in *Pettitt v Pettitt*:[24]

'If the property in question is land there must be some lease or conveyance which shows how it was acquired.

. . .

If that document declares not merely in whom the legal title is to vest but in whom the beneficial title is to vest that necessarily concludes the question of title as between the spouses for all time, and in the absence of fraud or mistake at the time of the transaction the parties cannot go behind it any time thereafter even on death or break-up of the marriage.'

Hence, as the Court of Appeal held in *Goodman v Gallant*,[25] if the document of title expressly declares in whom not only the legal title but also the beneficial interests are to vest, it will be conclusive in the absence of fraud or mistake.[26] Accordingly, if, as is common in the case of spouses, the family home is conveyed to both partners on express trust for themselves as joint tenants in equity, this must give them a joint interest in the proceeds of sale, and if either of them severs the joint interest, they will become equitable tenants in common in equal shares.[27] If the conveyance declares they are to hold as tenants

---

[23] For a discussion of the application of s 37, see below p 169.

[24] [1970] AC 777 at 813 E.

[25] [1986] Fam 106, CA. Contrast *Re Gorman* [1990] 1 All ER 717, where the parties were not bound by the declaration because they had not signed the transfer. The transfer was nevertheless evidence (in the circumstances conclusive) of their common intention at the time the property was acquired.

[26] As in *Thames Guaranty Ltd v Campbell* [1985] QB 210, CA. The spouses had agreed that the property should belong beneficially to the wife but that it should be conveyed into their joint names. The solicitor, assuming that they wished to take a joint beneficial interest, drafted the transfer to them as joint tenants in law *and equity*. It was held that the transfer could be rectified by deleting the words italicised, thus leaving both spouses as trustees for the wife alone. A declaration in the transfer deed that the survivor is entitled to give a valid receipt for capital does not constitute an express trust of the beneficial interests: *Stack v Dowden* [2005] EWCA Civ 857 [2006] 1 FLR 254.

[27] *Goodman v Gallant* (above). The presentation of a divorce petition including a prayer for a property adjustment order does not effect a severance, so that if one spouse dies before the order is made, the whole interest will vest in the other by survivorship: *Harris v Goddard* [1983] 3 All ER 242, CA. Cf *Kinch v Bullard* [1999] 1 WLR 423: terminally ill wife initiated divorce proceedings and instructed solicitors to sever joint tenancy in matrimonial home so that her half share could form part of her estate. Husband then suffered heart attack and was taken to hospital and the wife, wishing to take the whole of the beneficial interest, destroyed the solicitor's letter, severing the tenancy, which had been addressed to the husband and posted to the house. Husband died before wife—held severance effective to prevent her from taking whole interest.

in common in equal shares or in some other proportion, they will be similarly bound by the wording. For this reason solicitors acting for parties buying their home should enquire what their intentions are and spell them out in the conveyance to prevent dispute in the future.[28]

If the document is silent as to the beneficial ownership, then it is open to the non-legal owner and even joint legal owners[29] to claim entitlement to a share of the property under a trust. To substantiate such a claim the claimant must establish that the legal owner holds the property in trust inter alia for the claimant. The establishment of such a trust is dependent upon the parties' common intention.

(b) Establishing a beneficial interest

Precisely how that intention can be established has proved problematic. It should be appreciated at the outset that the concept of 'intention' in this context is a notional one.[30] It does not necessarily reflect both parties' intentions, for, as Lord Diplock pointed out in *Gissing v Gissing*,[31] a party's intention in this context must mean that which his words and conduct led the other to believe that he holds. It is therefore no objection that the party making the representation actually intended to hold the property for himself.[32] Further, it was held in *Midland Bank plc v Cooke*[33] that even if both parties admit that neither had discussed nor intended any agreement as to the proportion of their interests, this did not preclude the court from inferring one. Another complicating factor is the requirement under the Law of Property Act 1925 s 53(1)(b) that a valid declaration of trust of a beneficial interest in land[34] needs to be in writing. This means that if, for example, one partner purchases the home entirely out of his own money and has it conveyed into his own name, an oral agreement between the partners that the other is to take a beneficial share will not per se give her an interest. It will amount to no more than an imperfect gift, which equity will not perfect, or to a declaration of trust, which is required to be evidenced in writing.

Section 53(2) of the 1925 Act, however, does not require 'the creation or operation of resulting, implied or constructive trusts' to be in writing. Accordingly, as Lord Diplock said in *Gissing v Gissing*,[35] in the absence of writing the claimant to a beneficial interest will

---

[28] Per Bagnall J in *Cowcher v Cowcher* [1972] 1 All ER 943 at 959. As Dillon LJ repeated in *Springette v Defoe* [1992] 2 FLR 388 at 390, 'it is very much to be deplored that solicitors should fail to take steps to find out and declare what the beneficial interests are to be, when the legal estate in a house is acquired by two persons in their joint names'. The Land Registration Rules 2003 rr 58, 206 and Sch 1 require that where land is to vest in joint proprietors they must state whether they hold on trust for themselves beneficially as joint tenants, tenants in common or on any other trusts (on Form TR1).

[29] See eg *Springette v Defoe*, above; *Huntingford v Hobbs* [1993] 1 FLR 736, CA; *Stack v Dowden* above.

[30] See the analyses of N Glover and P Todd, 'The myth of common intention' (1996) 16 Legal Studies 325 and S Gardner, 'Rethinking Family Property' (1993) 109 LQR 263 at 264–5.

[31] *Gissing v Gissing* [1971] AC 886 at 906. See also *Lightfoot v Lightfoot-Brown* [2005] EWCA Civ 201 [2005] 2 P&CR 377.

[32] As in *Eves v Eves* [1975] 3 All ER 768, CA and *Grant v Edwards* [1986] Ch 638, CA.

[33] [1995] 4 All ER 562 at 574–5, CA.

[34] Note, however, there is no requirement for writing to create express trusts in respect of chattels. *Paul v Constance* [1977] 1 All ER 195, CA (furniture); *Rowe v Prance* [1999] 2 FLR 787 (boat).

[35] Above, at 905.

need to establish an interest under a resulting, implied or constructive trust. Although his Lordship went on to say[36] that from this point of view it does not matter what type of trust it is, such a classification may be important when it comes to assessing the quantum of any interest established.[37] As we shall see, however, this classification issue is not without its problems.

A further complicating factor is that, while the creation of a beneficial interest depends upon the parties' common intention, all too frequently the parties themselves have given no thought to the question of ownership. According to the majority in *Pettitt v Pettitt* it was not open to the court to impute an agreement to the parties where the evidence adduced showed there was none. As Lord Morris put it:[38] 'The court does not devise or invent a legal result.' In *Gissing v Gissing* Lord Diplock (who had been in the minority in *Pettitt v Pettitt*) accepted that it was not open to the court to impute an agreement to the parties but held that it could nevertheless *infer* an intention from their conduct or words insofar as they would be reasonably understood by the other party. Hence, if one partner led the other to believe that she would share a joint beneficial interest in the house, such an intention will be imputed to him whatever his inward intention. In other words, the court may have to infer an intention the parties never articulated, but it cannot impute to them an agreement they clearly did not make.

Although *Pettitt* and *Gissing* were important decisions, settling once and for all that there was no power under s 17 of the Married Women's Property Act 1882 to vary property interests and that non-economic contributions to the purchase of the family home could never give rise to a beneficial interest, they nevertheless left a number of uncertainties. In particular, it was unclear precisely what type of conduct could properly be considered to give rise to an inference that the parties intended to share the property. There was also uncertainty as to whether their Lordships, particularly in *Gissing v Gissing*, were really considering the creation of resulting or constructive trusts.

(c) Resulting trust

Property bought by one party and put into the name of the other is presumptively held on a resulting trust by the latter for the purchaser.[39] For example, in *Carlton v Goodman*,[40] Mr Goodman, a sitting tenant, negotiated to buy the house he occupied from his landlord, but lacked sufficient income to finance the mortgage. Ms Carlton (with whom he had a relationship but who did not live with him), joined him in obtaining a mortgage based on their joint incomes and the house was conveyed into their joint names. The deposit and all the mortgage payments were met by Mr Goodman. He died intestate and a dispute arose as to whether the beneficial interest in the house was shared by Ms Carlton. It was held that the presumption that the joint owners held the property on trust absolutely for Mr Goodman, on the basis of his having made all the payments, was not rebutted. Although Ms Carlton argued that her assumption of liability under the mortgage should

---

[36] Ibid.   [37] See below p 164.   [38] Ibid at 804.

[39] The presumption of advancement could still apply in the case of property bought by the husband and put in the wife's name, but as noted above, that presumption is readily rebutted: *McGrath v Wallis* [1995] 2 FLR 114, CA.

[40] [2002] EWCA Civ 545, [2002] 2 FLR 259.

give rise to a presumption that she was to have some share, as had been held in previous cases,[41] the court took the view that on the facts, the parties had never intended her to receive a share.[42]

As it was put by Dillon LJ in *Walker v Hall*,[43] the proportions in which the parties hold the property in a resulting trust depend upon their contributions:

'. . . it has been consistently held that where the purchase money for property acquired by two or more persons in their joint names has been provided by those persons in unequal amounts, they will be beneficially entitled as between themselves in the proportions in which they provided the purchase money.'

This can be illustrated in *Huntingford v Hobbs*.[44] The appellant and the respondent lived together in the respondent's former matrimonial home which had been transferred to her in her divorce settlement. They decided to move to a property to be purchased for £63,250. The respondent provided £38,860 capital from the sale of her home and the parties took out a joint endowment mortgage for £25,000 for the remainder of the price. The respondent had no income and it was understood that the appellant would pay the instalments. The relationship broke down and the appellant left the property to marry another woman. He sought a sale of the property and a declaration as to the trusts on which the equitable interest was held. It was held that the respondent should be treated as having contributed her cash contribution, the appellant should be treated as having contributed the whole of the sum borrowed on mortgage, and the property should be owned by the two of them in shares proportionate to such contributions, resulting in 61% to the respondent and 39% to the appellant.

Where the property is put into the other's name for an improper purpose, such as to defeat creditors, or to perpetrate a fraud, a resulting trust can still be asserted provided that it can be established without having to rely on the illegal act. In *Tinsley v Milligan*,[45] for example, the lesbian partners purchased a house in which they lived together. The house was put in the sole name of the plaintiff, in order to enable them to claim benefits fraudulently from the Department of Social Security, but it was understood that they were joint beneficial owners of the property. The defendant disclosed the frauds to the DSS and was required to pay the money back. The parties' relationship ended and the plaintiff moved out, leaving the defendant in occupation. The plaintiff gave the defendant notice to quit and brought proceedings claiming possession and asserting sole ownership of the property. The defendant counterclaimed for an order for sale and for a declaration that the property was held by the plaintiff on trust for the parties in equal shares. By a majority, the House of Lords held that it was unnecessary to give the reason for the conveyance into the sole name of the plaintiff in order to establish the trust, as this could be done by showing that the defendant had contributed to the purchase price of the property, and that there was a common understanding between the parties that they owned the property equally. As there was no evidence to rebut the presumption of a

---

[41] See eg *Evans v Hayward* [1995] 2 FLR 511, CA; *Springette v Defoe* [1992] 2 FLR 388, CA; *Huntingford v Hobbs* [1993] 1 FLR 736, CA.

[42] Mummery LJ considered that this meant the presumption of resulting trust in her favour had never arisen; Ward LJ considered that it meant it was rebutted.

[43] [1984] FLR 126 at 133.   [44] [1993] 1 FLR 736, CA.   [45] [1995] 1 AC 340, HL

resulting trust having arisen, the defendant was therefore entitled to succeed on her counterclaim.[46]

(d) Constructive trust

Instead of evidence of their individual contributions to the purchase of the property giving rise to the presumption of a *resulting* trust, there may be evidence of what is known as a 'common intention' between the parties that they are to share in the ownership of the property, establishing a *constructive* trust.[47] Such common intention may be demonstrated in two ways, laid down definitively by the House of Lords in *Lloyds Bank plc v Rosset.*[48]

The Rosset tests

According to Lord Bridge a distinction needs to be made in cases where there has been an agreement between the parties to share the property and those where there has not. For convenience we will label these situations respectively *Rosset 1* and *Rosset 2*.

Rosset 1

According to Lord Bridge:[49]

'The first and fundamental question *which must always be resolved* is whether independently of any inference to be drawn from the conduct of the parties in the course of sharing the house as their home and managing their joint affairs, there has at any time prior to acquisition, or exceptionally at some later date, been any agreement, arrangement or understanding reached between them that the property is to be shared beneficially.'

Such a finding must be based upon evidence of express discussions between the parties 'however imperfectly remembered and however imprecise their terms must be have been'.

As Waite J subsequently observed in *Hammond v Mitchell*,[50] this first requirement means:

'. . . that the tenderest exchanges of a common law courtship may assume an unforeseen significance many years later when they are brought under equity's microscope and subjected to an analysis under which many thousands of pounds of value may be liable to turn on this fine question as to whether the relevant words were spoken in earnest or in dalliance and with or without representational intent.'

Yet it is clear that such discussions must be pleaded in the greatest detail both as to the language and to the circumstance.[51] In *Hammond* itself it was held sufficient that the man had said to the woman soon after completion:

'Don't worry about the future because when we are married [the house] will be half yours anyway and I'll always look after you and [their child]'.

---

[46] See also *Lowson v Coombes* [1999] 1 FLR 799, CA (man and mistress).

[47] Where the evidence does not establish a common intention, the court may fall back on the resulting trust: *Springette v Defoe* [1992] 2 FLR 388, CA.

[48] [1991] 1 AC 107, HL.   [49] Ibid at 132.   [50] [1992] 2 All ER 109 at 121.

[51] But in the absence of any contrary evidence the court may have no choice but to believe the case presented by the claimant: see *Re Lorraine Share* [2002] 2 FLR 88—claimant's case flatly contradicted earlier representations made by her when she was made bankrupt, but the trustee in bankruptcy declined to cross-examine her.

In contrast, in *Springette v Defoe*[52] it was held insufficient that the parties had a mutual but uncommunicated belief or intention to share the property for, as Steyn LJ said,[53] 'Our trust law does not allow property rights to be affected by telepathy.'

Other instances where the court has found sufficient evidence of an agreement to share include the owner telling his partner that, although her name would not go onto the deeds, her assumption of joint liability for a mortgage debt charged to his farm would be sufficient proof that she had a 'right' to it,[54] a man assuring his partner that if she would help run his business affairs for him while he was in prison he would share various of his assets with her, even though the precise extent of his promise was unclear,[55] and a man telling his partner that he would put her name on the title when he had time.[56]

Lord Bridge himself instanced two 'outstanding examples' of cases falling into this first category, namely *Eves v Eves*[57] and *Grant v Edwards*.[58] Both cases involved cohabiting couples, and in both the female partner had clearly been led by the male partner to believe that when they set up home together the property would belong to them jointly. In *Eves* the man told his female partner that the only reason the home was to be in his name alone was because she was under 21 and that but for her age he would have had the house put in joint names.[59] Subsequently the woman did a great deal of manual work including breaking up concrete, demolishing and rebuilding a shed, stripping wallpaper and painting the wood-work, to renovate the dirty and dilapidated house that the man had bought. In *Grant v Edwards* the defendant told the plaintiff that her name was not going on the title because that would prejudice her in matrimonial proceedings between her and her husband. The plaintiff made no contributions to the initial purchase price but, despite having four children, went out to work and applied her earnings to the household expenses without which, the Court of Appeal accepted, the mortgage could not have been paid whilst at the same time leaving the family enough money to live on.

Provided an agreement can be proved then, according to Lord Bridge:

'... it will only be necessary for the partner asserting a claim to a beneficial interest against the partner entitled to the legal estate to show that he or she has acted to his or her detriment or significantly altered his or her position in reliance on the agreement in order to give rise to a constructive trust.'[60]

In *Eves and Eves* and *Grant v Edwards* what seemed to characterise the contributions

---

[52] [1992] 2 FLR 388, CA.

[53] Ibid at 394. For the view that the court should have found a constructive trust based on 'Rosset 2' (see below), see *Oxley v Hiscock* [2004] EWCA Civ 546 [2005] Fam 211 *per* Chadwick LJ at para 46.

[54] *Hyett v Stanley* [2003] EWCA Civ 942 [2004] 1 FLR 394.

[55] *Chan Pui Chun v Leung Kam Ho* [2002] EWCA Civ 1075 [2003] 1 FLR 23.

[56] *Drake v Whipp* [1996] 1 FLR 826, CA.   [57] [1975] 3 All ER 768, CA.

[58] [1986] Ch 638, CA.

[59] He admitted in evidence that this was just an excuse.

[60] *Lloyd's Bank plc v Rosset* [1991] 1 AC 107, 132G. For detrimental reliance see generally A Lawson 'The things we do for love—detrimental reliance in the family home' (1996) 16 Legal Studies 218. Note *Wayling v Jones* [1995] 2 FLR 1029, CA, in which it was held that once conduct had been proved from which detrimental reliance could be inferred, the burden switches to the defendant to show that the claimant had not acted in reliance upon the promise. See *G v G (Matrimonial Property: Rights of Extended Family)* [2005] EWHC 1560 (Admin) [2006] 1 FLR 62 where the husband's claim that members of his extended family had beneficial interests in the large family home was rejected as there was no evidence of any having acted to their detriment in reliance of a share.

made by the women was that they comprised conduct on which, in Nourse LJ's words,[61] 'the woman could not reasonably have been expected to embark unless she was to have an interest in the house.' In other words, even where there has been a prior agreement to share, detrimental reliance requires more than living with the man, having a baby by him and looking after the family and home. Thus, in *Midland Bank plc v Dobson*[62] the wife's claim to a beneficial interest in the matrimonial home, which was in her husband's name alone, failed because it was held that the wife's using part of her income for household expenses, including the purchase of domestic equipment, and doing some ordinary decorating, did not amount to detrimental reliance. By contrast, in *Cox v Jones*,[63] the couple were both barristers whose relationship ended in acrimony and dispute over several items of property including a flat and a house. It was held that, in relation to the flat, which was intended as an investment property, the woman had given up the chance to purchase it in her own name by agreeing to her partner, who could more easily raise the money, doing so and that this represented detrimental reliance by her on the understanding that he would hold the property as her nominee. In relation to the house, which had been intended as a joint home, the woman had put her legal career on hold to oversee the renovations to the property and had significantly lost earnings as a result.

Whether detrimental reliance can be established otherwise than by contributions of money or money's worth seems doubtful. There are some hints, however, in *Hammond v Mitchell*[64] that non-financial contributions can be relevant. In that case the main evidence of detrimental reliance lay in the claimant agreeing to postponing her interest in the property to that of the bank's charge (executed to secure a loan for the defendant's business ventures, which, had they had been unsuccessful, might have involved the whole property having to be sold), but Waite J also took account, at any rate when considering the quantum of the claimant's interest,[65] of the claimant's contribution as 'mother/helper/unpaid assistant and at times financial supporter to the family prosperity.'

Hammond v Mitchell is important for another point, namely, that where there is more than one property involved it is essential to establish whether the agreement to share applies to all properties or just one. In *Hammond* itself the arrangement was only held to extend to the matrimonial home in England and not to another property in Spain.

Notwithstanding that conduct considered sufficient to establish detrimental reliance may be limited to contributions in money or money's worth, it is clear that the test of such reliance is less onerous than having to establish an interest where there is no prior agreement to share. As Lord Bridge observed in *Lloyds Bank plc v Rosset*,[66] the contributions made in both *Eves v Eves* and *Grant v Edwards*, 'fell far short of such conduct as would by itself have supported the claim in the absence of an express representation by the male partner that she was to have such an interest.'

Rosset 2

According to Lord Bridge in *Rosset*:[67]

'In sharp contrast with this situation [ie *Rosset 1*] is the very different one where there is no evidence to support a finding of an agreement or arrangement to share, however reasonable

---

[61] [1986] Ch 638 at 648.   [62] [1986] 1 FLR 171 at 177, CA.
[63] [2004] EWHC 1486 (Ch) [2004] 2 FLR 1010.   [64] [1992] 2 All ER 109.
[65] Discussed further below p 164.   [66] [1991] 1 AC 107 at 133.   [67] Ibid at 132–3.

it might have been for the parties to reach such an arrangement if they had applied their minds to the question, and where the court must rely entirely on the conduct of the parties both as the basis from which to infer a common intention to share the property beneficially and as the conduct relied on to give rise to a constructive trust. In this situation direct contributions to the purchase price by the partner who is not the legal owner, whether initially or by payment of mortgage instalments, will readily justify the inference necessary to the creation of a constructive trust. But, as I read the authorities, it is at least extremely doubtful whether anything less will do.'

In *Rosset* itself, where there was found to be no prior agreement or arrangement to share the property, it was held that neither a common intention that the house was to be renovated as a joint venture nor a common intention that it was to be shared as the family home was sufficient to indicate that both parties were to take an interest; nor could such an inference be drawn from the wife's own renovations to the property and her supervision of the building works over a period of some six weeks before completion and for another six weeks after that. Echoing earlier sentiments as to what type of work a woman could normally be expected to do, Lord Bridge commented:[68]

'... it would seem the most natural thing in the world for any wife, in the absence of her husband abroad, to spend all the time she could spare and to employ any skills she might have, such as the ability to decorate a room, in doing all she could to accelerate progress of the work quite irrespective of any expectation she might have of enjoying a beneficial interest in the property.'

Lord Bridge instanced both *Pettitt v Pettitt*[69] and *Gissing v Gissing*[70] as falling into this second category and in neither did the claim for a beneficial interest succeed. In the former, where the house was bought in the wife's name, the husband failed to establish an interest by reason of the 'ephemeral' improvements he effected to the property by his internal decoration, the laying of a lawn and his construction of a well and a garden side wall.[71] Similarly, Mrs Gissing failed since, rather than paying for the deposit or mortgage on the home, she paid for her own and the son's clothes and supplemented the housekeeping allowance.

But perhaps the most infamous example of a second category case where the claim failed is *Burns v Burns*.[72] In that case Mrs Burns (as she was known), who had lived with her partner for 19 years, failed to establish a beneficial interest in the family home, having given up her job to have the couple's two children and then, when she did begin to earn money, had spent it on the household's expenses, fixtures and fittings in the house and the family's clothing.

In none of these cases was there a contribution either to the initial deposit or legal charges or to subsequent mortgage repayments. Where there is such a direct financial

---

[68] [1991] 1 AC 107 at 131.
[69] [1970] AC 777, HL. But note that substantial improvements can be sufficient for a spouse to obtain an interest under s 37 of the Matrimonial Proceedings and Property Act 1970, discussed below p 169.
[70] [1971] AC 886, HL.
[71] See also *Midland Bank plc v Cooke* [1995] 4 All ER 562, CA, in which it was held that the wife's contribution to the maintenance and improvement of the property was not itself sufficient to raise an inference that the property was to be shared. See further below.
[72] [1984] Ch 317, CA.

contribution, then even if it is relatively small (see below), it seems that the court will readily infer a common intention to share the property. This is implicit in all the speeches in *Gissing v Gissing* and was spelled out by Viscount Dilhorne and Lord Diplock,[73] as well as by Lord Bridge in *Rosset*. This contribution may come directly out of the claimant's own earnings or resources, or out of a common fund to which both parties contributed.[74]

A most extreme example of a finding of a direct contribution of this nature is *Midland Bank plc v Cooke*,[75] in which it was held that a wedding present of just over £1,000 cash provided by the groom's parents was intended to be a gift to both spouses equally, so that the wife could be credited with half of it. Since it was used towards the payment of the initial deposit on the house, it was held there could properly be inferred a common intention to share the property.

Whether anything less than direct contributions to the deposit, legal charges or mort-gage will give rise to an inference that the parties intended to share the property is uncertain. Lord Bridge was clearly of the view that indirect contributions by way of payments to the household expenses could never give rise to such an inference, even if it could be shown that without these contributions the legal owner could not have paid the mortgage instalments. This is evident from his Lordship's comment that the woman's contribution in *Grant v Edwards*, without which, as the Court of Appeal accepted, the payments could not have been paid and the household expenses met, would not have been sufficient in the absence of an express agreement to share. However, Lord Bridge's com-ments are obiter and seem at variance with those of Lord Diplock in particular in *Gissing v Gissing*. In that case Lord Diplock pointed out that if the wife had made an initial contri-bution to the deposit or legal charges which indicated that she was to take some interest in the property, the court should also take account of her contribution to the mortgage instalments, even though these were indirect, because this would be consistent with a common intention that the payment of other household expenses would release the hus-band's money to pay off the mortgage and would thus be her contribution to the purchase of the home. But, he added, if the wife had made no initial contribution to the purchase, no direct contribution to the repayment of the mortgage, and 'no adjustment to her contribution to other expenses of the household which it can be inferred was referable to the acquisition of the house', she cannot claim an interest in it 'merely because she continued to contribute out of her own earnings or private income to other expenses of the household'.[76] Lord Pearson similarly considered that there could be a contribution 'if

---

[73] [1971] AC 886 at 900 and 907.

[74] See eg *Gordon v Douce* [1983] 2 All ER 228 (woman contributed through past savings of the deposit and then contributed towards the housekeeping expenses and repairs and improvements, and outgoings); *Risch v McFee* [1991] 1 FLR 105, CA (woman initially made a loan to her partner so as to buy out his wife's interest in the house in divorce proceedings and later paid a sum to the man to pay off some of the outstanding mortgage; no interest was paid on the loan nor was repayment sought: it was held that the plaintiff succeeded in establishing a beneficial interest). A direct contribution may also give rise to a larger share: *The Mortgage Corporation v Silkin and Another; The Mortgage Corporation v Shaire* [2001] 4 All ER 364 (where the parties raised a second mortgage in order to buy out the woman's first husband's share in the home and in so doing the woman gave up all claims to further ancillary relief from her husband: held that the husband's half share in the home was held 50/50 by the woman and her partner and hence the woman was entitled to 75% of the value of the home).

[75] [1995] 4 All ER 562, CA, discussed further below.   [76] [1971] AC 886 at 907–10, HL.

by arrangement between the spouses one of them by payment of the household expenses enables the other to pay the mortgage instalments'.[77]

Griffiths LJ indicated the way the court should approach the problem in *Bernard v Josephs:*[78]

'... the fact that one party paid the mortgage may indicate that it was recognised by the couple that that party was solely responsible for providing the purchase price and therefore to be regarded as the sole beneficial owner. But often where a couple are living together and both are working and pooling their resources, which one of them pays the mortgage may be no more than a matter of internal accounting between them. In such a case the judge must look at the contributions of each to the "family" finances and determine as best he may what contribution each was making towards the purchase of the house. This is not to be carried out as a strictly mathematical exercise; for instance, if the man was ill for a time and out of work so that the woman temporarily contributed more, that temporary state of affairs should not increase her share, nor should her share be decreased if she was temporarily unable to work whilst having a baby. The contributions must be viewed broadly by the judge to guide him to the parties' unexpressed and probably unconsidered intentions as to the beneficial ownership of the house.'

Notwithstanding Lord Bridge's comment to the contrary, it was held at first instance in *Le Foe v Le Foe and Woolwich plc*[79] that an inference that the property is to be shared can be drawn where the claimant makes only indirect contributions to the mortgage, thus enabling the family economy to function. As the trial judge noted, echoing the view of Griffiths LJ above, to hold that only an initial direct contribution could give rise to a share would be to decide such cases 'by reference to mere accidents of fortune, being the arbitrary allocation of financial responsibility as between the parties.'[80]

(e) Proprietary estoppel

According to Lord Bridge in *Lloyds Bank plc v Rosset,*[81] once an agreement to share property has been found the claimant must show:

'... that he or she has acted to his or her detriment or significantly altered his or her position in reliance on the agreement in order to give rise to a constructive trust or proprietary estoppel.'

In so commenting his Lordship seemed therefore to equate constructive trusts with proprietary estoppel. This in turn has led to much academic speculation[82] as to whether the two concepts have been assimilated. There can be little doubt that the two have been increasingly drawn together. This is evident from Browne-Wilkinson V-C's comments in *Grant v Edwards* that:[83]

---

[77] At 903.   [78] [1982] Ch 391 at 403–4, CA.   [79] [2001] 2 FLR 970.

[80] At para 49. See also *Gissing v Gissing* (above) at 903 (per Lord Pearson) and 980 (per Lord Diplock); *Burns v Burns* [1984] Ch 317 at 329 (per Fox LJ) and 344 (per May LJ). For the view that shared parental responsibility should found the basis for an equitable share in the family home, see C Sawyer, 'Equity's children—constructive trusts for the new generation' [2004] CFLQ 31.

[81] [1991] 1 AC 107 at 132.

[82] See D Hayton 'Equitable Rights of Cohabitees' (1990) 54 Conv 370; S Gardner 'Rethinking Family Property' (1993) 109 LQR 263; S Nield, 'Constructive trusts and estoppel' (2003) 23 Legal Studies 311.

[83] [1986] Ch 638 at 656.

'... useful guidance may in the future be obtained from the principles underlying the law of proprietary estoppel which in my judgment are closely akin to those laid down in *Gissing v Gissing*. In both, the claimant must to the knowledge of the legal owner have acted in the belief that the claimant has or will obtain an interest in the property. In both, the claimant must have acted to his or her detriment in reliance on such belief. In both, equity acts on the conscience of the legal owner to prevent him from acting in an unconscionable manner by defeating the common intention. The two principles have been developed separately without cross-fertilisation between them: but they rest on the same foundation and have on all other matters reached the same conclusions.'

Similar views have been expressed in subsequent cases.[84] However, it is premature to say that the two are one and the same.[85] As Nourse LJ observed in *Stokes v Anderson*,[86] while it is possible that the House of Lords will, at some future point, assimilate the two, 'they have not yet been assimilated'. One plausible distinction is that recourse to constructive trusts needs to be had in cases where the claim is that the property in issue has been jointly acquired, whereas estoppel becomes relevant where the property has unquestionably already been acquired by one person who, by his or her *subsequent* conduct, has led the claimant to think that he or she will share it. It remains now to consider those cases where recourse has been had to proprietary estoppel.

The essence of proprietary estoppel was described by Edward Nugee QC (sitting as a deputy High Court judge) in *Re Basham*:[87]

'Where one person, A, has acted to his detriment on the faith of a belief, which was known to and encouraged by another person, B, that he either has [been] or is going to be given a right in or over B's property, B cannot insist on his strict legal rights if to do so would be inconsistent with A's belief.'

To this should be added the requirement that B must know of the existence of his own right which is inconsistent with that claimed by A, for otherwise he is in the same position as A, who will therefore acquire no prior equity.[88] If these conditions are established, B is bound to make good, as far as he can, the expectation he has encouraged.

The similarity to a constructive trust is immediately apparent in that in each case the person claiming the interest in property must have acted to his or her detriment, but one distinction is that the claimant under a constructive trust must prove that she (or he) acted in reliance on a common intention that she should take an interest in the property,

---

[84] See eg Chadwick LJ in *Oxley v Hiscock* [2004] EWCA Civ 546 [2005] Fam 211 at para 66; Robert Walker LJ in *Yaxley v Gotts* [2000] Ch 162 at 176 and 180.

[85] However, it has been held that the exception provided for resulting, implied or constructive trusts by s 2(5) of the Law of Property (Miscellaneous Provisions) Act 1989 to the requirement that a contract for the sale or other disposition of an interest in land must be in writing, applies also to proprietary estoppel: *Yaxley v Gotts and Gotts* [2000] Ch 162, CA.

[86] [1991] 1 FLR 391 at 399, CA.

[87] [1986] 1 WLR 1489 at 1504–1505 cited with approval by Balcombe LJ in *Wayling v Jones* [1995] 2 FLR 1029 at 1031.

[88] *Coombes v Smith* [1986] 1 WLR 808. A promise to ensure someone 'financial security' without some specification of which property, or range of property (such as their whole estate) will be given or shared, will not suffice: *Layton v Martin* [1986] 2 FLR 227 at 239; *Lissimore v Downing* [2003] 2 FLR 308. Cf *Re Basham (decd)* [1986] 1 WLR 1489 at 1503H; *Jennings v Rice* [2002] EWCA Civ 159, [2003] 1 FCR 501, para [46] per Robert Walker LJ.

whereas an estoppel will arise if her acts result from her being misled by the other's conduct. A further distinction lies in the fact that, if the claimant adopts a detrimental course of conduct, there is a rebuttable presumption that she has done so in reliance on the assurances given to her.[89]

As with constructive trusts, the claimant must have acted to his or her detriment, but such detriment need not consist of the expenditure of money or other quantifiable financial detriment, so long as it is something substantial. In *Gillett v Holt*,[90] for example, the appellant left school without obtaining any qualifications at the urging of a wealthy farmer who became his 'patron'. On the strength of assurances that he would be left his estate, the appellant worked as the farm manager for many years, and, as Robert Walker LJ put it, he and his wife 'deprived themselves of the opportunity of trying to better themselves in other ways'.

The claimant's acts must have been induced by his or her mistaken belief.[91] So in *Lissimore v Downing* the claimant failed to establish estoppel after she moved in with a founder member of the rock band, 'Judas Priest', on his lavish country estate, because this 'represented an exciting opportunity . . . which lifted her out of a humdrum life' and not because she expected a share of his assets.[92] The owner of the property must also know of the claimant's mistake: he cannot encourage a belief of which he was ignorant.[93] On the other hand, as the Court of Appeal held in *Wayling v Jones*,[94] once it is established that the promise has been made and that there has been conduct by the claimant of such a nature that an inducement could be inferred, the burden of proof shifts to the defendant to establish that the plaintiff had not relied on the promise.

A good example of the operation of proprietary estoppel is *Pascoe v Turner*,[95] in which the plaintiff and defendant, who was his housekeeper, began to live together as husband and wife. After the relationship broke down, the plaintiff, who had moved out, told the defendant, 'The house is yours and everything in it'. Relying on his statement, she spent money on redecoration, improvements and repairs. On his claim to possession of the house, the Court of Appeal held that, by encouraging or acquiescing in the defendant's belief that the house was hers, he was estopped from denying this and that the only way in which the equity thus arising could be satisfied was by compelling him to transfer the house to her.

(f) Quantification of shares

Up to now we have been discussing the circumstances in which a spouse or partner may take a beneficial interest in the family home. We must now consider a second question: what is the size of the interest that each acquires? This in turn will depend upon the nature of interest established. So far as trusts are concerned the interest may be created by means

---

[89] *Greasley v Cooke* [1980] 3 All ER 710, CA; *Coombes v Smith* (above) at 821. It is also to be noted that, according to *Wayling v Jones*, above, the promises relied upon do not have to be the *sole* inducement for the conduct.

[90] [2001] Ch 210, CA.

[91] Hence there can be no estoppel if the claimant knew that the other reserved his right to change his mind or to revert to the original position: see *A-G of Hong Kong v Humphreys Estate (Queen's Gardens) Ltd* [1987] AC 114, PC.

[92] [2003] 2 FLR 308 *per* HH Judge Norris QC at para 55. See to similar effect, *Coombes v Smith* [1986] 1 WLR 808; cf the same principle applied to constructive trusts: above p 158.

[93] *Brinnand v Ewens* (1987) 19 HLR 415, CA.   [94] Above.

[95] [1979] 2 All ER 945, CA. See Sufrin (1979) 42 MLR 574.

of an express trust (if in writing), a resulting trust, or a constructive trust. In the first two instances there is little difficulty in quantifying the parties' shares. Thus, if the conveyance spells out the beneficial interests, the court must give effect to it.[96] If the property is vested in the parties jointly on an express trust for themselves as joint tenants, they will become equitable tenants in common in equal shares if either of them severs the joint interest.[97] Similarly, if they take as tenants in common, the court must give effect to the trust thereby created and divide the proceeds in the proportions stated.

Quantification in cases of resulting trust

If the circumstances in which the property was bought are held to give rise to a resulting trust, the beneficial interests will be proportionate to the parties' contributions.[98] It is evident, however, that the courts are increasingly reluctant to rely on resulting trusts, at any rate in cases involving family homes.[99] Indeed, in *Drake v Whipp*[100] counsel for the claimant was rebuked for conceding, notwithstanding the evidence, both from conversations and direct contributions to the acquisition of the property, of a common understanding to share, that this was a case where the share should be assessed only on the basis of a resulting trust.

Just occasionally however, it is proper to rely on a resulting trust where, for example, a constructive trust would be held void under the insolvency rules.[101] Thus in *Re Densham*,[102] although the Court of Appeal was prepared to accept that the parties' pooling of resources was clear evidence of an intention to share the property equally, since such an interest would have been void as against the trustee in bankruptcy on the basis that it was a 'voluntary' gift by the legal owner, reliance had instead to be placed on a resulting trust based upon the claimant's financial contribution to the initial deposit.

Quantification in cases of constructive trust

Quantifying the interests held under a constructive trust is not straightforward.[103] As Chadwick LJ pointed out in *Oxley v Hiscock*, 'in many such cases, the answer will be provided by evidence of what [the couple] said and did at the time of the acquisition. But, in a case where there is no evidence of any discussion between them as to the amount of the share which each was to have—and even in a case where the evidence is that there was no discussion on that point—the question still requires an answer.'[104] The answer given to

---

[96] Unless the conveyance can be rectified as a result of fraud or mistake: see above p 153.

[97] *Goodman v Gallant* [1986] Fam 106, CA.

[98] This is not to say that it is always easy to quantify the contributions. For some examples of the application of resulting trusts see eg *Huntingford v Hobbs* [1993] 1 FLR 736, CA; *Springette v Defoe* [1992] 2 FLR 388, CA; *Cowcher v Cowcher* [1972] 1 All ER 943; and *Marsh v Von Sternberg* [1986] 1 FLR 526.

[99] See eg *Midland Bank plc v Cooke* [1995] 4 All ER 562, CA; see G Battersby 'How not to judge the quantum (and priority) of a share in the family home' (1996) 8 CFLQ 261; P Wylie 'Computing Shares in the Family Home' [1995] Fam Law 633; M Pawlowski '*Midland Bank v Cooke*—A New Heresy?' [1996] Fam Law 484.

[100] [1996] 1 FLR 826, CA.   [101] Discussed further, below, pp 192ff.

[102] [1975] 3 All ER 726, CA, which is therefore authority for saying that a resulting trust can lie alongside a constructive trust. See also *McHardy & Sons (A Firm) v Warren and Hutton* [1994] 2 FLR 338, CA (resulting trust relied upon because of a third party claim).

[103] The same problems could equally well arise if the claimant establishes an estoppel—see below.

[104] [2004] EWCA Civ 546 [2004] 3 All ER 703 at para [68]. See S Gardner, 'Quantum in *Gissing v Gissing* Constructive Trusts' [2004] LQR 541, M Thompson, 'Constructive Trusts, Estoppel and the Family Home' [2004] Conv 496, S Edwards, 'Property Rights in the Family Home—Clarity at Last' [2004] Fam Law 524.

the question in that case may now be taken to have provided the definitive approach to be adopted by the courts.

The couple cohabited in a property originally rented by the woman as a secure tenant. She exercised her right to buy, the money for the purchase being provided by the man. This property was put in her sole name, subject to a charge in the man's favour, but when the couple moved, their new home was vested in the man alone with no charge or declaration of trust in favour of the woman, despite advice from her solicitor to the contrary. The man contributed £60,700 and the woman £36,300 to the purchase price, the remaining £30,000 being acquired by way of mortgage, and the payments met by both of them. When their relationship ended, the home was sold, the woman receiving £33,000 from the proceeds of some £232,000. She then sought a declaration that the proceeds were held by the man in equal shares, succeeding at first instance. The man appealed. The Court of Appeal rejected the view that, in a *Rosset I* case, the parties' agreement, arrangement or understanding must extend to defining the extent of their respective shares. Nor did it consider, in a *Rosset II* case, that the shares must necessarily be proportionate to the amount of the claimant's direct contributions to the purchase.[105] Rather, Chadwick LJ concluded that:

'each is entitled to that share which the court considers fair having regard to the whole course of dealing between them in relation to the property.'[106]

On this basis, he decided that the man's contribution, being larger than the woman's, should result in his receiving 60% of the proceeds of sale—a proportion, in fact, very close to that which could have been arrived at by applying a resulting trust approach. A clearer instance of the exercise of a broad discretion operating may perhaps be seen in *Cox v Jones*, discussed above.[107] In the absence of evidence of any express arrangement as to the woman's share in the house bought in the man's name, where the man funded the purchase and the woman's contribution lay in her forgoing income in order to devote herself to managing the renovations to the property, a 25% share was deemed fair.

In reaching his conclusion, Chadwick LJ recognised that such a discretionary approach might sit ill with the traditional, property-based approach based, ostensibly, on fixed entitlements.[108] In particular, it goes against the view that the parties' interests should be fixed at the outset of the purchase.[109] He noted three different judicial attempts to get round this problem.[110] The first was that suggested in *Gissing v Gissing*:[111]

'the parties are taken to have agreed at the time of the acquisition of the property that their respective shares are not to be quantified then, but are left to be determined when their relationship comes to an end or the property is sold on the basis of what is then fair having regard to the whole course of dealing between them. The court steps in to determine what is fair because, when the time came for that determination, the parties were unable to agree.'

The second was the suggestion by Waite LJ in *Midland Bank plc v Cooke*:[112]

'The court undertakes a survey of the whole course of dealing between the parties "relevant

---

[105] At para [40].   [106] At para [69].   [107] [2004] EWHC 1486 (Ch) [2004] 2 FLR 1010.
[108] See, in particular, its rejection by Dillon LJ in *Springette v Defoe* [1992] 2 FLR 388.
[109] See *Marsh v Von Sternberg* [1986] 1 FLR 526 at 533.
[110] [2004] EWCA Civ 546 [2004] 3 All ER 703 at para [70].
[111] [1971] AC 886 at 909, followed by Nourse LJ in *Stokes v Anderson* [1991] 1 FLR 391.
[112] [1995] 4 All ER 562 at 574.

to their ownership and occupation of the property and their sharing of its burdens and advantages" in order to determine "what proportions the parties must be assumed to have intended [from the outset] for their beneficial ownership". On that basis the court treats what has taken place while the parties have been living together in the property as evidence of what they intended at the time of the acquisition.'

The third was that suggested by Browne-Wilkinson V-C, in *Grant v Edwards*:[113]

'The court makes such order as the circumstances require in order to give effect to the beneficial interest in the property of the one party, the existence of which the other party (having the legal title) is estopped from denying.'

In concluding that this last was the most satisfactory explanation, Chadwick LJ rejected the reasoning in approaches one and two as artificial in attributing to the parties a common intention that the extent of their respective beneficial interests in the property should be fixed as from the time of the acquisition, when all the evidence pointed to the conclusion that, at the time of the acquisition, they had given no thought to the matter. In his view, 'the time has come to accept that there is no difference in outcome, in cases of this nature, whether the true analysis lies in constructive trust or in proprietary estoppel.'[114]

However, the court did accept the view of Waite LJ in *Cooke* that the survey undertaken by the court will go beyond acts of direct contribution of the sort that are needed to found a beneficial interest in the first place, but will take into consideration all conduct which throws light on the question of what shares were intended. The whole course of dealing between the parties in relation to the property will include 'the arrangements which they make from time to time in order to meet the outgoings (for example, mortgage contributions, council tax and utilities, repairs, insurance and housekeeping) which have to be met if they are to live in the property as their home.'[115]

This may lead to striking results, as in *Cooke* itself. There, Mrs Cooke worked throughout the marriage, notwithstanding that she had three children. The matrimonial home, costing £8,500 was purchased in the husband's sole name, by means of a mortgage of £6,450, with the balance met from the husband's savings and a wedding present from his parents of £1,100. As noted above, this present was regarded as being made to each of the spouses jointly. At first instance, she was held to have a share of 6.47% of the value of the property, reflecting the £550 contribution (half the cash wedding gift) she made to the total purchase price of £8,500. She made no direct contributions to the mortgage repayments but instead used her earnings to pay for the other household outgoings including paying contractors' bills in connection with improvements to the house and garden. She also undertook joint and several liability for certain legal charges taken out by her husband. The Court of Appeal, looking at this history, concluded that the 'inescapable' inference from the parties' joint conduct was their presumed intention to share the property equally. Accordingly, they awarded Mrs Cooke a half interest in the house.

But as can be seen by the results in *Oxley v Hiscock* and *Cox v Jones*, it does not follow from the Court of Appeal's clear affirmation that the court is concerned with arriving at the fair outcome, that there is a presumption that there should be equal shares, and however generous one might now view the constructive trust doctrine, it still falls far short

---

[113] [1986] Ch 638 at 656, 657, approved by Robert Walker LJ in *Yaxley v Gotts* [2000] Ch 162 at 177.
[114] At para [71].   [115] At para [69].

of the recognition given in the divorce jurisdiction to the contributions made by spouses to their relationship, which will give rise to a starting point of equal shares.[116] Reliance on 'fairness' as the criterion also means that it remains difficult to predict the outcome of any given case, since so much will turn on the individual judge's assessment of the evidence presented.[117] What does seem clear is that it should make no difference whether the home is in joint or sole names.[118] Although Chadwick LJ in *Oxley v Hiscock* specifically confined his judgment to cases where the property is purchased in the sole name of one of the couple, consideration of the whole course of dealing was also given in *The Mortgage Corporation v Shaire*,[119] with the woman receiving a 75% share based on her original half interest in the former matrimonial home and her acquiring half of the ex-husband's other half interest when she and her new partner bought him out.

Quantification in cases of proprietary estoppel

The remedy granted where a proprietary estoppel is made out is whatever is necessary to satisfy the equity which has arisen in consequence of the misrepresentation. This has resulted in the extremely generous outcome, in *Pascoe v Turner*, of the complete transfer of the property to the claimant.[120] With the further blurring of the doctrines of constructive trust and proprietary estoppel, especially in relation to quantum, as espoused by Chadwick LJ in *Oxley v Hiscock*, one might expect the courts to adopt much the same approach as they would take in a constructive trust case, whilst bearing in mind that the latter can only result in a sharing of the beneficial interest, whereas an estoppel may be remedied by means of other devices such as, in *Greasley v Cooke*,[121] a right of occupation. A useful criterion which could equally apply to constructive trust cases was the reminder in *Gillett v Holt*[122] that:

'The court's aim is, having identified the maximum, to form a view as to what is the minimum required to satisfy it and do justice between the parties. The court must look at all the circumstances, including the need to achieve a "clean break" so far as possible and avoid or minimise future friction.'[123]

This test of proportionality was also applied in *Jennings v Rice*.[124] There, the appellant had been a part-time gardener and odd-job man for an elderly lady since 1970. By the late 1980s, she had stopped paying him for his work but gave him £2,000 to put towards acquiring a property. She reassured him that she would 'see him right' in her will. During the 1990s,

---

[116] See p 1020 below.

[117] Query if being a spouse still gives the claimant an advantage? As well as *Midland Bank plc v Cooke* (above), the wife was also credited with a half share in *Le Foe v Le Foe and Woolwich plc* [2001] 2 FLR 970. See too, *Supperstone v Hurst* [2005] EWHC 1309 (Ch), [2005] BPIR 1231: statement made at earlier date that spouses owned in equal shares a compelling factor in so finding, taking account of what the court considered fair, having regard to the whole course of dealing. Michael Biggs QC, the judge, noted that 'joint tenancy is not obviously either unjust or inappropriate as between husband and wife in relation to their matrimonial home'. Cf *Drake v Whipp* [1996] 1 FLR 826—one-third share to woman; *Eves v Eves* [1975] 3 All ER 768, CA—one quarter share.

[118] See *Pettitt v Pettitt* [1970] AC 777 at 813 *per* Lord Upjohn.

[119] [2001] 4 All ER 364. See also *Stack v Dowden* [2005] EWCA Civ 857 [2006] 1 FLR 254: although property in joint names, woman entitled to 65% share based on whole course of dealing.

[120] See also *Wayling v Jones*, where the plaintiff was awarded the proceeds of sale of the deceased's hotel that he had promised the plaintiff.

[121] Above.   [122] [2000] 2 FLR 266 at 292B.

[123] See *Pascoe v Turner* [1979] 1 WLR 431, 438–9.   [124] [2002] EWCA Civ 159, [2003] 1 FCR 501

he provided her with personal care as she became more infirm, and slept at her house so that she could feel secure. On being left nothing when she died, he claimed her entire estate, valued at over £1.2 million. The Court of Appeal upheld the trial judge's decision to award the appellant a sum of £200,000, considering him to have been correct to consider the likely cost of providing the lady with the kind of personal care that the appellant had provided at around £200,000, as the appropriate sum to award him. As Aldous LJ put it,

'The value of that equity will depend upon all the circumstances including the expectation and the detriment. The task of the court is to do justice. The most essential requirement is that there must be proportionality between the expectation and the detriment.'[125]

Agreement to vary beneficial interests

It is possible for the parties to agree to vary the size of their beneficial interests after the property has been bought. The variation is required to be in writing;[126] if it is not, it will be enforceable as a parole agreement of which equity will grant specific performance only if it is supported by valuable consideration.[127] Even if the parties did not enter into an express agreement, it might be possible to infer one from their conduct, for example by the use of a legacy to pay off the mortgage or by a permanent or substantial change in the contributions which they originally agreed or intended to make.[128]

(g) Improvements to the family home

It may be argued that the parties' interests in the home have been varied if, after purchase, one of them has been solely responsible for enhancing its value by extension or improvement (either by cash payments or by doing the work himself). Unlike a contribution to the purchase price, the mere fact that A does work on B's property does not of itself give A any interest in it. To establish such an interest, A must show that the expenditure was incurred or the work done in pursuance of an agreement or common intention that it should do so or, alternatively, that B has led A to believe that the improvement would confer an interest on him so as to give rise to a proprietary estoppel.[129]

The position of spouses, civil partners and former engaged couples

The injustice that this could cause led to the passing of s 37 of the Matrimonial Proceedings and Property Act 1970.[130] This provides:

'... where a husband or wife contributes in money or money's worth to the improvement of real or personal property in which or in the proceeds of sale of which either or both of them has or have a beneficial interest, the husband or wife so contributing shall, if the contribution is of a substantial nature and subject to any agreement to the contrary express or implied, be treated as having then acquired by virtue of his or her contribution a share or an enlarged share, as the case may be, in that beneficial interest . . .'

---

[125] At para [36]. [126] Law of Property Act 1925 s 53.

[127] *Cowcher v Cowcher* [1972] 1 All ER 943 at 950.

[128] See *Gissing v Gissing*, above, at 908; *Burns v Burns* [1984] Ch 317, 344–5.

[129] *Pettitt v Pettitt* (above), particularly at 818 (per Lord Upjohn). See also *Thomas v Fuller-Brown* [1988] 1 FLR 237, CA; *Harwood v Harwood* [1991] 2 FLR 274 at 294, CA.

[130] Enacted on the recommendation of the Law Commission: see Law Com No 25, paras 56–8 and pp 102–5. It applies to engaged couples by virtue of s 2(1) of the Law Reform (Miscellaneous Provisions) Act 1970. A similar provision applies to civil partners under s 65 of the Civil Partnership Act 2004.

Section 37 (which refers to the improvement of any property and not merely to that of the home) applies whether the contribution is in money or money's worth: in other words, it does not matter whether the claimant does the job himself or pays a contractor to do it. In the latter case, however, he must show that his contribution is identifiable with the improvement in question: a general contribution to the family's finances (like an indirect contribution to the price) will give him an interest in the home only if it is referable to the improvement.[131]

There are two limitations on the operation of the section. First, it will apply only if the contribution is of a substantial nature. Whether any particular improvement is sufficiently substantial to bring it within the ambit of the section is a question of fact: in *Re Nicholson*[132] the installation of central heating for £189 in premises worth £6,000 was regarded as a substantial contribution, but the purchase of a gas fire worth less than £23 was not. Secondly, the section applies 'subject to any agreement between the spouses to the contrary express or implied', so that if they agreed that the improvements should confer no interest on the party making them, this will be conclusive.

Section 37 applies in any proceedings including, for example, litigation between one spouse and a stranger claiming through the other. If the parties agreed on the size of the interest which the improvements were to confer on the spouse making them, the court must give effect to the agreement; in other cases it has power to make such order as appears just in all the circumstances. Normally this should reflect the amount by which the value of the property was increased at the time: if, for example, the wife puts the value of the husband's house up from £80,000 to £100,000, she should obtain one-fifth of the price when it is sold.[133] The section also applies if both spouses have a beneficial interest in the property before the improvements are made: hence, if in the above example the spouses were tenants in common of the house in equal shares when the wife made the improvements, she should now obtain three-fifths of the price.[134] In practice, the provision is rarely used, being superseded by the courts' wider powers of ancillary relief on divorce, although it might conceivably be relied on by a spouse in cases involving third party claims to the family home, such as on insolvency.

The position of cohabitants

As s 37 does not apply to unmarried couples unless they are engaged to be married, one of them may claim an interest or enhanced interest in the home as a consequence of improvement only by reference to the general law. The claimant may be able to prove or spell out an agreement between the parties that the work should have this effect; alternatively, it may be possible to infer from their conduct that this was their common intention. As in other cases of constructive trusts, however, the court will not be justified in drawing this conclusion unless the work is such that the party in question could be expected to carry it

---

[131] *Harnett v Harnett* [1973] Fam 156 at 167, per Bagnall J. (The question did not arise on appeal: [1974] 1 All ER 764, CA.)

[132] [1974] 2 All ER 386.

[133] Query the position if the 'improvement', although substantial in money terms, does not actually increase the value of the property in the market, eg the installation of double glazing? It is submitted that it should give rise to a share pro rata with the current value of the property; thus, if £10,000 is expended on a house worth £100,000, it should result in a 10% share.

[134] *Re Nicholson* (above).

out only if he or she were to acquire an interest in the property as a result. In *Pettitt v Pettitt*[135] (where the parties were married) the husband alleged that as the result of doing work on the matrimonial home (which had been purchased by the wife out of her own money) he had increased its value by over £1,000. Most of the work consisted of redecorating the bungalow in question, but he had also made a garden, built a wall and patio, and done other jobs outside. The House of Lords unanimously held that he could claim nothing on the ground that, in the absence of an express agreement, he could acquire no interest by doing work of an ephemeral nature or 'do-it-yourself' jobs which any husband could be expected to do in his leisure hours.

3 REFORM[136]

The law concerning ownership of the family home was referred to the Law Commission for review in 1995. The Commission published a Discussion Paper on the issue in 2002.[137] They identified the following key problems with the current law:[138]

(i) the search for the parties' common intention can be an unrealistic exercise yet much depends upon the court's conclusion as to what that common intention was;

(ii) the line between which types of contributions will, and will not, count towards the acquisition of an interest in the property is not clear;

(iii) extensive work in and around the home, which may include looking after the children of a relationship, appears not to 'count' in giving rise to an interest;

(iv) quantifying the share may be extremely difficult and has led to decisions which are inconsistent and difficult to reconcile;[139]

(v) the uncertainty of the law can lead to lengthy and costly litigation.

The Law Commission sought to produce a scheme which a) would not depend upon the nature of the relationship between the claimant and the owner—thus, they sought to include not only cohabiting partners, but also relatives such as an adult child living with parents or two siblings sharing a home, or indeed any combination of 'home sharers'; and b) would be based on contributions to the shared home, and not on the parties' intentions (save in the case of express declaration of trust). They considered that a contribution-based scheme would have the advantages of certainty and predictability as it

---

[135] [1970] AC 777, HL. The husband had to rely on the general law because the case was decided before the passing of the Matrimonial Proceedings and Property Act 1970.

[136] See eg Lord Browne-Wilkinson 'Constructive Trusts and Unjust Enrichment' (1991 Holdsworth Club Lecture); S Gardner 'Rethinking Family Property' (1993) 109 LQR 263; R Bailey-Harris 'Financial rights in Relationships Outside Marriage: A Decade of Reform in Australia' (1995) 9 Int J of Law and Family 233 and 'Dividing the Assets on Breakdown of Relationships Outside Marriage: Challenges for Reformers' (1998) SPTL Address; A Barlow and C Lind, 'A matter of trust: the allocation of rights in the family home' (1999) 19 LS 468.

[137] Law Commission, *Sharing Homes: A Discussion Paper* (2002). For valuable comment, see J Mee, 'Property rights and personal relationships: reflections on reform' (2004) 24 LS 414, J Miles, 'Property law v family law: resolving the problems of family property' (2003) 23 Legal Studies 624, S Wong, 'Trusting in Trust(s): The Family Home and Human Rights' (2003) 11 Fem LS 119.

[138] Ibid Executive Summary para 7 and Report paras 2.105–2.112.

[139] It may be that the decision in *Oxley v Hiscock* [2004] EWCA Civ 546 [2004] 3 All ER 703 has reduced this difficulty, although lack of predictability would still seem to be a major problem.

would be possible to value contributions objectively and there would be no need to rely on vaguely remembered, or imputed, agreements. Ignoring the nature of the parties' relationship was intended to ensure that the scheme could operate without discrimination between different classes of relationship.

However, they found themselves unable to arrive at a workable set of proposals. In particular, they could not produce a scheme which would result in a fair outcome based on contributions alone, without taking account of the different nature of the relationships between different sorts of parties, but they considered that the policy implications of a scheme which would only apply, say, to cohabitants, would take the project beyond the remit of a law reform body and lay properly with government instead. They therefore confined themselves to urging legal advisers to encourage parties to make express written arrangements setting out what they intend their rights to be, most often by means of a declaration of trust; of course, this does not assist the situation where one party joins another in a home that has already been acquired and where it is most unlikely that the parties will think that they need to consult a lawyer. The Law Commission accordingly urged the courts to adopt greater flexibility in recognising an indirect contribution to the mortgage (by means of paying the household bills and thereby enabling the other party to pay the mortgage instalments) but they stopped short of recommending that the courts take account of non-financial contributions such as caring for the home and family. They also endorsed the broad approach to quantification of shares evinced in decisions such as *Le Foe v Le Foe*[140] and *Midland Bank plc v Cooke*[141] and would no doubt approve of the approach based on fairness adopted in *Oxley v Hiscock*.[142]

Deeper policy questions, such as whether the courts should be given a general adjustive power akin to that under the Matrimonial Causes Act 1973, and whether, if so, any distinction should be made between spouses and those who have chosen to live together without marrying[143] in applying such a power, remain to be answered. Other questions include whether the presence of children should make any difference, whether special consideration should be given only to marriage-like relationships and how third party interests are to be fairly balanced. Other jurisdictions,[144] such as Australia[145] and New Zealand[146] have introduced legislative schemes dealing with these points and the Law Society has advocated allowing cohabitants who have lived together for at least two years, or who have had a child, to seek property adjustment or lump sum orders on separation, in order to remedy any economic disadvantage they might have suffered as a result of the relationship.[147] In Scotland, the Family Law (Scotland) Act 2006 s 28 [CL 21] introduces

---

[140] [2001] 2 FLR 970, 982.   [141] [1995] 2 FLR 915, 926.

[142] [2004] EWCA Civ 546 [2004] 3 All ER 703.

[143] On which see R Bailey-Harris 'Law and the Unmarried Couple: Oppression or Liberation?' (1996) 8 CFLQ 137.

[144] See *Sharing Homes* Part IV; L Fox, 'Reforming property law—comparisons, compromises and common dimensions' [2003] CFLQ 1.

[145] See M Pawlowski, 'Property rights of home-sharers: recent legislation in Australia and New Zealand' (2001) 10 Nottingham LJ 20.

[146] See B Atkin, 'The rights of married and unmarried couples in New Zealand—radical new laws on property and succession' [2003] CFLQ 173.

[147] The Law Society, *Cohabitation: The case for clear law* (2002) paras 94–105. The Society also makes suggestions concerning other aspects of cohabitants' relationships and these are dealt with in Chapters 17–19 below.

an adjustive regime similar to that suggested by the Law Society,[148] The Northern Ireland Law Reform Advisory Committee has also recommended that a home acquired by cohabitants during their relationship should be held jointly.[149] Meanwhile, the Law Commission issued a consultation paper in May 2006 provisionally recommending a scheme akin to that proposed by the Law Society, and limited to the situation 'where the applicant can establish that the economic effects of the relationship, positive and negative, are not fairly shared between the parties on separation'.[150] Pending the final recommendations of the Law Commission, the government instituted a publicity campaign to bring the lack of legal rights pertaining to cohabiting partners to a wider public attention in the hope of encouraging such partners to take specific legal advice to protect themselves.[151]

4   ENFORCING THE TRUST

(a) The court's powers under s 14 of the Trusts of Land and Appointment of Trustees Act 1996 [152]

Before implementation of the Trusts of Land and Appointment of Trustees Act 1996, a trust for sale arose whenever land was conveyed to two or more people either as beneficial joint tenants or as tenants in common. As its name implied, the creation of such trusts imposed an ultimate obligation upon the trustees to sell the property,[153] and, if the trustees refused to sell the trust property, s 30 of the Law of Property Act 1925 enabled any person interested to apply to the court for an order directing them to give effect to the trust, whereupon the court could make such order as it thought fit. Section 30 could be used to force the sale of a matrimonial home, because, if both spouses had a beneficial interest in it either as joint tenants or as tenants in common, a trust for sale was automatically created. Following the Law Commission's recommendations,[154] trusts for sale were replaced by trusts of land. Under the 1996 Act all existing trusts for sale, whether express or implied, became trusts of land, and in situations where formerly an implied trust for sale would have arisen there now arises a trust of land. One of the crucial differences between trusts of

---

[148] Indeed, the Scots proposals pre-dated the Law Society: see Scot Law Com No 135 *Report on Famiily Law* (1992) Part XVI, para 16.23 and Scottish Executive, *Family Matters: Improving Family Law in Scotland* (2004) Section 4.

[149] Matrimonial Property (2000) LRAC No 8 cited by Law Commission, *Sharing Homes* at p 78.

[150] Law Commission, *Cohabitation: The Financial Consequences of Relationship Breakdown*, Consultation Paper No. 179 (2006) at para 6.50.

[151] See http://wwwadvicenow.org.uk/go/livingtogether/ For the view that modern social conditions may not be so adverse to the average cohabiting woman as might be thought from 'hard cases' such as *Burns v Burns* [1984] 2 WLR 582, see R Probert, 'Trusts and the Modern Woman—Establishing an Interest in the Family Home' [2001] CFLQ 275.

[152] See generally S Baughen 'Trusts of Land and Family Practice' [1996] Fam Law 736; M Harwood 'A Home for Life—The New Trusts of Land Act' [1997] Fam Law 182; Hopkins 'The Trusts of Land and Appointment of Trustees Act 1996' (1996) 60 Conv 411, G Ferris and G Battersby, 'The Impact of the Trusts of Land and Appointment of Trustees Act 1996 on Purchasers of Registered Land' (1998) 62 *Conveyancer* 168.

[153] Though the Law Commission have said (Law Com No 181, *Transfer of Land, Trusts of Land* para [3.4]) even under the old definition set out by the LPA 1925 s 205(1)(xxix) (this section has now been amended) the courts considered that it meant something other than the trustees being under a duty to sell: see eg *Re Parker's Settled Estates* [1928] 1 Ch 247; *Re Ryder and Steadman's Contract* [1927] 2 Ch 62; *Re Norton* [1929] 1 Ch 84; *Re Beaumont Settled Estates* [1937] 2 All ER 353; and *Re Sharpe's Deed of Release* [1939] Ch 51.

[154] See Law Com No 181, *Transfer of Land, Trusts of Land* (1989).

land and trusts for sale is that *implied* trusts of land no longer carry an obligation to sell, and even in *express* trusts there is an implied power to postpone a sale indefinitely.[155]

While the parties are living together, they are likely to agree on the disposal of their home, but if their relationship breaks down and they separate, one may well wish to remain in the former home and the other to have it sold so as to realise the capital. If the parties are married, the courts prefer to use their wide powers to make property adjustment orders under the Matrimonial Causes Act 1973, because they can then make a fair order after taking all relevant facts into account.[156] But this can be done only if one of them seeks a divorce, a decree of nullity, or judicial separation; consequently, if no such proceedings are taken and, a fortiori, if they are unmarried or unregistered partners, this course is not open to them, and they will be compelled to invoke the court's powers under s 14 of the Act 1996, which replaced s 30 of the 1925 Act.

This provision enables any person who is a trustee of land or who has an interest in property subject to a trust of land[157] to seek a court order either relating to the exercise by the trustees of any of their functions or to 'declare the nature or extent of a person's interest in property subject to the trust'.[158] In each case the court may make such order as it thinks fit.[159] Although s 14 allows a court to order a sale, its powers are not limited to this. It also includes the power to declare the nature and extent of a person's interest in the land in question, which is the same power as under s 17 of the Married Women's Property Act 1882 and s 66 of the Civil Partnership Act 2004. The provisions are sufficiently wide, it is thought,[160] to enable the court both to order the trustees not to exercise their powers and to make intermediate orders, such as ordering an occupying beneficiary to pay an occupation rent to another beneficiary not in occupation.

Section 15 of the 1996 Act provides a set of guidelines on matters to be taken into account when exercising the powers under s 14. The aim of the guidelines is, in the Law Commission's words,[161] to 'consolidate and rationalise' the former approach adopted by the courts under s 30 of the Law of Property Act 1925, without, however, restricting the exercise of judicial discretion.[162]

Under s 15(1) the matters to which the court is to have regard include:

'(a) the intentions of the person or persons (if any) who created the trust,

(b) the purpose for which the property subject to the trust is held,

---

[155] See s 5 and s 4 respectively.

[156] *Tee v Tee and Hillman* [1999] 2 FLR 613, CA. Civil partners will also be able to take advantage of the equivalent jurisdiction: Civil Partnership Act 2004 s 72 and Sch 5.

[157] This is narrower than that recommended by the Law Commission, in that it does not permit *any* interested person to apply. See also *Re Ng (A Bankrupt), Trustee of the Estate of Ng v Ng* [1998] 2 FLR 386.

[158] In the case of unmarried partners, where there are children, and both parties have an interest in the property, there should usually be an application under s 15 and Sch 1 to the Children Act 1989 made at the same time and dealt with by the court simultaneously: *W v W (Joinder of Trusts of Land Act and Children Act Applications)* [2003] EWCA Civ 924 [2004] 2 FLR 321.

[159] Section 15 sets out matters to which the court must have regard when exercising these powers: see below.

[160] See Baughen, op cit, at 737. It has also been held that there is power to order one party to buy out the interest of the other in return for transfer of title in the property: *Lawrence v Bertram (Judgment on Preliminary Issue)* [2004] Fam Law 323 (Croydon County Court).

[161] Law Com No 181 (*Transfer of Land, Trusts of Land,* 1989) para 12.9.

[162] Ibid at 12.10. See also *TSB Bank plc v Marshall, Marshall and Rodgers* [1998] 2 FLR 769.

(c) the welfare of any minor who occupies or might reasonably be expected to occupy any land subject to the trust as his home, and

(d) the interests of any secured creditor or any beneficiary.'

Section 15(3) also requires the court to have regard to the circumstances and wishes of any beneficiaries of full age and entitled to an interest in possession in property subject to the trust. The matters in s 15 are not listed in order of priority, and, in the view of Arden LJ,[163] are not exhaustive in structuring the court's discretion under s 14. Thus, a judge was entitled under s 15(3) to have regard to the mother's wishes and circumstances in seeking a sale of the former family home when the father wished to postpone sale to enable him to remain there bringing up the children. It should be noted that these guidelines do not apply where a trustee in bankruptcy is seeking an order;[164] in such a case different guidelines apply.[165]

Although in general terms these guidelines may be said[166] to 'mirror' the factors formerly considered by the court when determining the 'collateral purpose' of a trust under the 1925 Act, the approach of the courts to balancing the competing interests of the parties, especially in a case of bankruptcy, has changed and the old authorities relating to s 30 should be treated with caution.[167] For example, one important change is the guideline relating to children's welfare. By making such welfare an independent consideration, the Act has implemented the Law Commission's recommendations[168] aimed at ensuring that a case such as *Re Evers' Trust*,[169] in which the mother's need for a home with her three children was fully taken into account, is likely to be preferred to those such as *Re Holliday (a bankrupt)*,[170] in which the court dismissed the notion that it was a collateral object of the trust to preserve the house as a home for the children. This will be especially likely now that the court can clearly order the occupying beneficiaries to pay an occupation rent.[171]

On the other hand, there is no reason to suppose that the new powers will have altered the court's basic stance, that if two people (whether married or not) buy property as a home for themselves (together with any children they may have), the underlying purpose of the trust is to provide a home and not an investment.[172] Consequently, so long as that purpose subsists, the trust should not be executed and the property should not be sold.[173]

---

[163] *W v W (Joinder of Trusts of Land and Children Act Applications)* [2003] EWCA Civ 924, [2004] 2 FLR 321 at para [26].

[164] Section 15(4).   [165] Viz those under the Insolvency Act 1996 s 335A, discussed below, p 195.

[166] Baughen, op cit, 737.

[167] *The Mortgage Corporation v Shaire* [2001] 4 All ER 364. See further below at p 195.

[168] Law Com No 181 at para 12.9.   [169] [1980] 3 All ER 399, CA.

[170] [1980] 3 All ER 385, CA. See also *Chhokar v Chhokar* [1984] FLR 313 and *Dennis v McDonald* [1982] Fam 63, CA.

[171] Compare *Bernard v Josephs* [1982] Ch 391, CA, in which the court ordered the property to be sold, but attached a condition that the order should not be enforced if the one paid the other the value of his share within a stated period.

[172] But the precise scope of such purpose may be difficult to identify: see *Laird v Laird* [1999] 1 FLR 791, where the district judge and circuit judge on appeal differed in their assessment of what the parties had intended.

[173] *Re Buchanan-Wollaston's Conveyance* [1939] Ch 738, [1939] 2 All ER 302, CA; *Williams v Williams* [1976] Ch 278, [1977] 1 All ER 28, CA; *Re Evers' Trust* [1980] 3 All ER 399, CA; *Bernard v Josephs*, CA, above; *Chhokar v Chhokar*, above; *Abbey National plc v Moss* [1994] 1 FLR 307, CA.

Relevant to the question of whether the purpose still subsists is s 12(1) of the 1996 Act, which provides that a person who is beneficially entitled to an interest in possession in land subject to a trust of land is entitled, by reason of his interest, to occupy the land at any time if at that time (a) the purposes of the trust include making the land available for his occupation, or (b) the land is held by the trustees so as to be so available. Subsection (1) does not, however, confer on a beneficiary a right to occupy land if it is either 'unavailable or unsuitable for occupation by him'.[174] In *Chan Pui Chun v Leung Kam Ho*,[175] the Court of Appeal held that, in determining whether a property continued to be suitable for the unmarried partner to occupy after the couple's relationship had ended, the court must consider not only 'the general nature and physical characteristics of the particular property but also a consideration of the personal characteristics, circumstances and requirements of the particular beneficiary'. It concluded that since the respondent only wished to remain in the property until she had completed a course of studies, it remained 'suitable' for her to occupy for that limited length of time. Moreover, Jonathan Parker LJ added that he 'would have taken some persuading that a property which was on any footing suitable for occupation by Miss Chan and Mr Leung whilst they lived together should be regarded as unsuitable for occupation by her alone once Mr Leung had left.'[176]

However, once the purpose for which the property was acquired has been discharged, the court is likely to order a sale.[177] It has been suggested that the 'intentions of the persons or persons who created the trust' must be an intention which they had in common, such that the original intention as to the purpose of the trust may only be changed by agreement of all those concerned. If, then, the original intention in acquiring the property is found to be to provide a home for the adult partners, there must be evidence that they have *agreed* to change the purpose to make it a home for themselves and their children subsequently if one partner wishes to rely on this as a reason for postponing sale.[178]

Two further points should be noted. First, on the death of one of the parties the other's share will become a part of his estate (unless the parties were joint tenants) and may not pass to the survivor. In this situation the court should take the same facts into account as it does when the parties separate during their joint lives and should not order a sale unless the property no longer serves the purpose of providing a family home for the survivor.[179] Secondly, if one party becomes insolvent, there may be a dispute between his creditors and the other party. The particular problems that this gives rise to will be considered later in this chapter.[180]

---

[174] Section 12(2).   [175] [2003] 1 FLR 23, para [101] per Jonathan Parker LJ, CA.
[176] At para [102].
[177] *Jones v Challenger* [1961] 1 QB 176CA. Cf *Bedson v Bedson* [1965] 2 QB 666, CA, where the wife had deserted her husband, and the property in question (a draper's shop with a flat over it) had been bought out of the husband's savings and was his sole livelihood, the sale was refused.
[178] According to Arden LJ in *W v W (Joinder of Trusts of Land and Children Act Applications)* [2003] EWCA Civ 924, [2004] 2 FLR 321 at paras [22]–[24]. For an example of the purpose of a trust changing to encompass the provision of a home for the wife and children, and hence requiring the postponement of sale for 10 years until the home was no longer needed for the children, see *F v F (S Intervening)(Financial Provision: Bankruptcy: Reviewable Disposition)* [2002] EWHC 2814 (Fam) [2003] 1 FLR 911.
[179] *Stott v Ratcliffe* (1982) 126 Sol Jo 310, CA.   [180] Below, p 192ff.

(b) Distribution of assets after sale: equitable accounting

Even though the primary purpose of the trust may have come to an end on the separation of the parties, the trust for land nevertheless remains and the property in effect becomes an investment. This cannot affect the size of the beneficial interests, however: hence, as the Court of Appeal held in *Turton v Turton*,[181] if the parties hold as tenants in common in equal shares, each will be entitled to half the proceeds when the property is sold or, if one of them buys the other out, to half the value at the time of the transfer.[182]

Further accounting between the parties, however, may be necessary. If one of them spends money on the property after they have separated, he will usually be entitled to call on the other to contribute to the expenditure if this preserves or enhances the value of the asset, because both will derive the benefit of the increased value when the investment is realised. In *Bernard v Josephs*,[183] for example, the proceeds of sale were divided between the parties only after the plaintiff had paid to the defendant the sum of £2,650 which the latter had spent on decorating the house and so increased the price obtained.

The position regarding the payment of mortgage instalments is less clear. In *Cracknell v Cracknell*,[184] where the matrimonial home was owned jointly, the wife left to live with another man. The husband continued to pay the instalments and the Court of Appeal held that she should compensate him for half the total payments he had made after their separation. In *Suttill v Graham*,[185] on the other hand, on virtually identical facts the Court of Appeal concluded that the wife should be required to compensate the husband only for the capital sum he had repaid, apparently on the ground that that alone increased the value of the equity. As we shall see below, the position may be complicated by the need to pay an occupation rent. Leaving this question aside, in the face of conflicting decisions of the Court of Appeal, *Cracknell v Cracknell* is to be preferred because, as was pointed out in *Re Gorman*,[186] the mortgagee will have a charge on the property for both unpaid interest and capital, so that the value of the equity is increased by the payment of both.

A similar question that arises after separation is whether the party who remains in the home must pay an occupation rent to the other (or to the trustee in bankruptcy). In

[181] [1988] Ch 542, CA, following *Walker v Hall* [1984] FLR 126, CA, and disapproving *Hall v Hall* (1981) 3 FLR 379, CA, where it had been held that in the case of unmarried cohabitants the home should be valued at the time of separation.

[182] If the property is subject to a mortgage which, as between the parties, one alone is responsible for repaying, the unpaid debt should be debited to his share. Suppose that H and W buy a house for £50,000, of which W provides £25,000 in cash and H provides £25,000 borrowed from X. Each will get half the proceeds of sale, but H will have to repay the loan out of his half. The same result should follow if the lender is a building society which takes a mortgage on the property. This principle was applied in *Cowcher v Cowcher* [1972] 1 All ER 943 at 959, and *Re Densham* [1975] 3 All ER 726. See P Sparkes 'The Quantification of Beneficial Interests' (1991) 11 OJLS 39 at 46–52.

[183] [1982] Ch 391. See also *Byford v Butler* [2003] EWHC 1267 (Ch) [2004] 1 FLR 56. Query whether the plaintiff should have had to pay only half of the expenditure, which is the extent to which the value of her half share had been increased. It was accepted that the wife should recover only half her expenditure in similar circumstances in *Re Gorman* [1990] 1 All ER 717. See also *Clarke v Harlow* (12 August 2005), [2005] NLJ 1486: before there can be a duty to account there must be a breach or failure to comply with some obligation owed by one party to the other.

[184] [1971] P 356, CA. See also *Wilson v Wilson* [1963] 2 All ER 447, CA; *Davis v Vale* [1971] 2 All ER 1021, CA.

[185] [1977] 3 All ER 1117, CA. The Court of Appeal purported to follow *Leake v Bruzzi* [1974] 2 All ER 1196, CA, but see below.

[186] [1990] 1 All ER 717. The court followed *Bernard v Josephs* (above) where, however, *Suttill v Graham* was not cited.

Dennis v McDonald[187] the Court of Appeal held that if the parties are co-owners, whether in law or equity, each is entitled to possession: consequently, if one leaves voluntarily, he or she is not entitled to any rent. If, however, one forces the other to leave, justice demands that he should pay rent to compensate the latter for the right she has lost and the need to pay for accommodation elsewhere: in *Dennis v McDonald* the sum ordered to be paid was one-half of what would be a fair rent under the Rent Act.[188] It has been subsequently held in the High Court that it is not necessary to establish that one party has been excluded from the property before the party remaining can be required to pay an occupation rent. The purpose of determining whether such a rent is payable is to enable the court to do justice between the parties. For example, in *Byford v Butler*,[189] the husband was made bankrupt but he and the wife continued to live in the matrimonial home, the wife meeting the mortgage payments. The trustee in bankruptcy made no effort to realise his interest in the property until after the husband's death some nine years after the bankruptcy.[190] The wife argued that she should not be obliged to pay an occupation rent but it was held that the fact that there has not been an ouster or forcible exclusion from the property is not conclusive. As Lawrence Collins J pointed out, the trustee cannot reside in the property nor can he derive any financial enjoyment from the property while the bankrupt's spouse resides in it, and the bankrupt spouse's creditors can derive no benefit from it until he exercises his remedies.[191] Since the wife had had the benefit of continuing to live in the property, it was just to require her to pay an occupation rent.

If the party in occupation is bound to pay rent and is also paying mortgage instalments, it may be simpler (as was in fact agreed by the parties in *Byford v Butler*) to regard the payment of interest as equivalent to the payment of rent and thus avoid a double computation. In such circumstances it would be proper to order the party who has left to account for his or her proportionate part of the repayment of capital only. This occurred in *Leake v Bruzzi*,[192] where the wife left the husband and obtained a divorce based on the fact that her husband's behaviour had been such that she could not reasonably be expected to live with him.

5 PROTECTION OF BENEFICIAL INTERESTS

(a) Overriding interests

Although the Trusts of Land and Appointment of Trustees Act 1996 in some ways strengthens the beneficiary's right to be consulted before trustees can exercise any of their powers,[193] it does not obviate the problem that if the house is sold or mortgaged, the beneficiaries' equitable interests are overreached and a purchaser of a legal estate (including a legal mortgagee or chargee) is not bound by them even though he has notice of them, provided that he pays the proceeds of sale or other capital money to two or more trustees

---

[187] [1982] Fam 63, CA.   [188] Rent Act 1977 s 70(1)–(2), and disregarding s 70(3).

[189] [2003] EWHC 1267 (Ch) [2004] 1 FLR 56, following *Re Pavlou (A Bankrupt)* [1993] 1 WLR 1046.

[190] The Insolvency Act 1986 s 283A (inserted by the Enterprise Act 2002 s 261) provides that, as regards bankruptcies occurring from 1 April 2004, the trustee must effectively deal with the property within three years, or it will re-vest in the bankrupt.

[191] At para [40].

[192] [1974] 2 All ER 1196, CA. The wife was urged to adopt this solution in *Re Gorman*, above. But this may not be the proper approach if little remains to be paid on the mortgage so that the interest element is low.

[193] Viz by s 11 of the 1996 Act.

(or a trust corporation).[194] Hence, once the property is sold and the beneficial interests overreached, the beneficiaries cannot enforce any right of occupation or possession even though they were not parties to the conveyance. Similarly, if the property is mortgaged by two or more trustees, the beneficiaries' interest shifts onto the equity of redemption, and whilst they will be able to remain in possession so long as the mortgage remains in existence, they cannot enforce any right to do so if the mortgagee exercises his statutory right of sale. In *City of London Building Society v Flegg*[195] a husband, wife and the wife's parents agreed to buy a house in which all four could live. The property was conveyed to the husband and wife alone but the wife's parents, who had provided part of the purchase money, also had a beneficial interest. The husband and wife later mortgaged the property to the plaintiffs, who sought possession of the premises when the spouses became insolvent. It was held that, although the wife's parents had a right to occupy the premises against their son-in-law and daughter, they had none whatever against the building society which was protected by having paid the sum borrowed to the two trustees.

The same conclusion would be reached if the husband and another were joint legal tenants of the matrimonial home in which the wife had a beneficial interest either under an express trust or by virtue of a resulting or constructive trust. If the owners of the legal estate sold or mortgaged it, the wife's interest would be overreached and so unenforceable against the purchaser or mortgagee.[196] A similar result would obtain in the case of cohabitants. In practice difficulty arises if the legal estate is vested in one partner only (say, the man) and the woman has a beneficial interest under a resulting or constructive trust. The man should appoint another trustee (who would normally be his partner) but in many cases this will not be done, and if the man sells or mortgages the house, the purchaser or mortgagee will deal with him alone. If the man acts without the knowledge or consent of the woman, can she enforce her rights against the new legal owner if he seeks possession of the premises or takes steps to realise his security?

If the legal title is registered under the Land Registration Act 2002, she may enter a restriction against the property.[197] In practice this may be of little use unless the wife or cohabitant seeks legal advice on the breakdown of her relationship before the man deals with the land. The woman is much more likely to be helped by the fact that her undivided share gives her an 'overriding interest'. In *Williams and Glyn's Bank Ltd v Boland*[198] the husband was registered as the sole proprietor of the legal estate of the matrimonial home, but the wife had contributed a substantial sum towards the purchase and was admittedly an equitable tenant in common to the extent of her contribution. The husband later

---

[194] Law of Property Act 1925 s 27(1) as amended by the Trusts of Land and Appointment of Trustees Act 1996 Sch 3, para 4(8).

[195] [1988] AC 54, HL. Some caution must be exercised when reading Lord Oliver's judgment, since some of his reasoning is based on the doctrine of conversion, which has since been abolished by the Trusts of Land and Appointment of Trustees Act 1996. Nevertheless, it seems clear that the decision survives the 1996 Act.

[196] If the wife could raise a proprietary estoppel against the husband, it is not clear whether this would still be good against the purchaser or mortgagee: see Thompson (1988) 52 Conv 108 at 120. It would be anomalous if an estoppel gave her greater protection than an express trust.

[197] Land Registration Act 2002 s 42. For the value of seeking a restriction order under s 46 of the Act, see S Carrigan, 'Land Registration Act 2002, s 46: A Guided Missile' [2005] Fam Law 722. A spouse or civil partner with no beneficial interest could register her home rights by a notice against the property: Family Law Act 1996 s 31(10).

[198] [1981] AC 487, HL.

executed a legal mortgage to the appellant bank, which made no enquiries of the wife.
When the husband failed to pay the sum secured, the bank started proceedings for possession of the house with a view to selling it under their powers as mortgagees. The wife
resisted the action on the ground that her interest took priority over the bank's by virtue
of what was then s 20(1) of the Land Registration Act 1925. The House of Lords held that
the wife's physical presence in the house coupled with the right to exclude others without a
right to occupy clearly gave her actual occupation, and the fact that the husband (the
owner of the legal estate) was also in actual occupation could not affect this. Furthermore,
although the land was held on (what was then a) trust for sale, pending sale the wife had
an interest subsisting in reference to the land itself. Her claim must therefore succeed.

   Williams and Glyn's Bank Ltd v Boland created a number of difficulties for prospective
purchasers (and particularly prospective mortgagees).[199] In particular, what if a person
moved into a property, thus taking up 'actual occupation', between the creation of a charge
(such as a mortgage) and its registration? This situation arose in *Abbey National Building
Society v Cann*[200] where the mortgage charge was not registered until a month after the
completion of the purchase. The House of Lords held that the claimant (there, the
respondent's mother) must be in occupation at the date of completion. Schedule 3 para 2
to the Land Registration Act 2002 now refers to an overriding interest belonging to the
person in actual occupation 'at the time of the disposition', thus ensuring that the chargee
will take priority.

   A further problem arose concerning the meaning of 'actual occupation'. It should be
given its ordinary meaning of possession or presence on the land: 'actual' indicates physical possession as distinct from legal possession by receipt of rents and profits.[201] The term
is apparently not synonymous with 'reside':[202] a person can obviously occupy one property and reside in another, and he can occupy premises by an agent, eg a caretaker.[203] The
facts of *Lloyds Bank plc v Rosset*[204] illustrate the difficulties that can arise. The husband
purchased a semi-derelict house, partly with the aid of a charge in favour of the appellant
bank. The vendor let the husband and his wife into possession some six weeks before
completion and the creation of the charge, and during this time the wife spent almost
every day on the premises directing building work and doing some decorating herself, and
she occasionally slept there. The majority of the Court of Appeal held that the presence of
the builders (who were agents of both parties) coupled with that of the wife amounted to
actual occupation by her because 'there was . . . physical presence on the property by the
wife and her agent of the nature that one would expect of an occupier having regard to the
then state of the property'.[205] Mustill LJ, dissenting on this point, thought that the tradesmen's presence would not indicate to an enquirer that a person with a claim adverse to the
owner's was in occupation: they were working on the site rather than in occupation of it,

---

[199] See Law Com No 115 (*Implications of Williams and Glyn's Bank Ltd v Boland*) 1982; Law Com 188
(*Overreaching: Beneficiaries in Occupation*) 1989.
   [200] [1991] 1 AC 56, HL.
   [201] Per Lord Wilberforce in *Williams and Glyn's Bank Ltd v Boland* [1981] AC 487 at 505.
   [202] See *Lloyds Bank plc v Rosset* [1989] Ch 350, CA.
   [203] *Lloyds Bank plc v Rosset*, above; *Abbey National Building Society v Cann*, above, at 93 (per Lord Oliver).
   [204] [1989] Ch 350, CA. Having held that the wife acquired no beneficial interest (see above, p 160), the
House of Lords found it unnecessary to consider whether she was in actual occupation when the charge was
created: [1991] 1 AC 107, HL.
   [205] Per Nicholls LJ at 379.

and the wife's activities were more in keeping with preparing the house for occupation than with occupation itself.[206] This view certainly accords with that of the House of Lords in *Abbey National Building Society v Cann*,[207] where they held that the activities of the workmen laying carpets and carrying in furniture were no more than preparatory steps leading to the assumption of actual residential occupation later, and that consequently the respondent's mother could not be said to be in actual occupation of the house when the charge was created. Like possession, 'occupation' connotes some form of continuity rather than periodic visits and, it is submitted, should be unambiguous.

Schedule 3 para 2 to the 2002 Act now provides that a relevant interest will override unless it is

'(b) an interest of a person of whom inquiry was made before the disposition and who failed to disclose the right when he could reasonably have been expected to do so;' or

(c) an interest—

(i) which belongs to a person whose occupation would not have been obvious on a reasonably careful inspection of the land at the time of the disposition, and

(ii) of which the person to whom the disposition is made does not have actual knowledge at that time.'

Sub-paragraph (b) replaces the old law which referred to enquiry being made of the person in occupation and their rights not being disclosed. Sub-paragraph (c), however, is intended to lessen the burden on those enquiring about title. It is not the person's interest that has to be obvious, but the occupation. This should mean that the result in *Kingsnorth Finance Ltd v Tizard*[208] should not recur. There, the husband slept in the matrimonial home with the two children of the marriage; because the marriage was in difficulty, the wife slept elsewhere but came to the house each day to feed the children. When the husband was away (as happened frequently), she slept there. The husband then applied for a loan from the plaintiffs to be secured by a mortgage on the house. It was held that the wife was in occupation, even though she was not there when the plaintiff's agent made his enquiries, and the husband had temporarily removed all signs of her periodic visits. The test in para 2(c) is not one of constructive notice but the less demanding one of being obvious on a reasonably careful inspection of the land. However, even if the occupation is not apparent, the exception does not apply where the buyer has actual knowledge of the occupation.[209]

(b) Unregistered land

If the land is unregistered, the position is more complex. A partner cannot register her interest under the Land Charges Act 1972.[210] The basic principle was summarised by Lord Oliver in *City of London Building Society v Flegg*:[211]

[206] At 398–9.   [207] [1991] 1 AC 56, HL. For the facts, see above, p 180.
[208] [1986] 2 All ER 54. The case dealt with unregistered land, but this can make no difference to this point.
[209] Law Com No 271, *Land Registration for the Twenty-First Century: A Conveyancing Revolution* (2001) para 8.61.
[210] Interests arising under a trust of land are expressly excluded from the definition of a general equitable charge: Land Charges Act 1972 s 2(4) (as amended). A spouse or civil partner with no beneficial interest could register home rights as a Class F land charge under s 2(7).
[211] [1988] AC 54 at 83, HL.

'The reason why a purchaser of the legal estate (whether by way of outright sale or by way of mortgage) from a single proprietor takes subject to the rights of the occupying spouse is . . . because, having constructive notice of the trust as a result of the beneficiary's occupation, he steps into the shoes of the vendor or mortgagor and takes the estate subject to the same equities as those to which it was subject in the latter's hands, those equities and their accompanying incidents not having been overreached by the sale . . .'

This implies that anyone dealing with the land will be protected only by the general equitable doctrine that a bona fide purchaser of a legal estate for value will take it free of any equitable interest of which he does not have actual or constructive notice. Hence, if he takes an equitable interest (for example, if a bank takes an equitable charge from the husband), the partner must have priority. A purchaser of a legal estate will normally have constructive notice of the rights of any person in occupation of the land: this raises the question whether the fact that the spouse or cohabitant is residing in the house will itself be sufficient notice of their interest to give priority over the purchaser. In *Caunce v Caunce*[212] Stamp J held that it will not do so, because her presence is not inconsistent with the husband's being the sole beneficial owner, but this case was doubted, although not expressly overruled, in *Williams and Glyn's Bank Ltd v Boland*.[213] One of the principal objections to holding that the wife's occupation (and a fortiori a female cohabitant's) gives the purchaser constructive notice of her rights is that this compels him to make distasteful and embarrassing enquiries. In an earlier case dealing with the so-called 'deserted wife's equity', Upjohn J, refusing to cast upon a prospective purchaser or mortgagee the duty to enquire whether the owner of the property in question had deserted his wife, said:[214]

'If the law were otherwise it would mean that every intending purchaser or lender must inquire into the relationship of husband and wife and inquire into matters which are no concern of his and will bring thousands of business transactions into the area of domestic life and ties. That cannot be right.'

This applies with equal force to the problem we are considering here. It is doubtful, however, whether these cases can still be regarded as good law since the decisions in *Williams and Glyn's Bank Ltd v Boland* and *Abbey National Building Society v Cann*. Clearly nothing said in either case is binding in this context because both were concerned with registered land. But in *Boland*'s case the House of Lords was obviously more concerned to protect the wife than the purchaser. In the words of Lord Wilberforce:[215]

'The extension of the risk area follows necessarily from the extension, beyond the pater-familias, of rights of ownership, itself following from the diffusion of property and earning capacity. What is involved is a departure from an easy-going practice of dispensing with enquiries as to occupation beyond that of the vendor and accepting the risks of doing so. To

---

[212] [1969] 1 All ER 722.

[213] [1981] AC 487 at 505, (per Lord Wilberforce, with whom three other members of the House agreed); ibid at 511 (per Lord Scarman). But it has been held that minor children (who might have a beneficial interest in the property) cannot rely on actual occupation to protect that interest: they are there because their parent is there. They have no right of occupation of their own. No inquiry can be made of minor children or consent obtained from them in the manner contemplated by the legislation, especially when they are of tender years at the material date: *Hypo-Mortgage Services Ltd v Robinson (Note)* [1997] 2 FLR 71.

[214] *Westminster Bank Ltd v Lee* [1956] Ch 7 at 22.

[215] *Williams and Glyn's Bank Ltd v Boland*, above, at 508–9.

substitute for this a practice of more careful enquiry as to the fact of occupation and, if necessary, as to the rights of occupiers cannot, in my view of the matter, be considered as unacceptable except at the price of overlooking the widespread development of shared interests in ownership.'

(c) Consent to transaction by spouse or partner

If the wife or partner consents to the transaction—and a fortiori if she is a party to the conveyance of mortgage—she cannot argue that any interest she may have in the property takes priority over the purchaser's or mortgagee's. Furthermore, if she knows that the house can be bought only with the help of a loan and supports the husband's proposal that this would be secured by a mortgage, then, as the Court of Appeal held in *Bristol and West Building Society v Henning*,[216] it must have been the parties' common intention that the charge should take priority over both their beneficial interests. To secure his position the mortgagee may insist on the wife's being party to the charge, and this will in any event be necessary if the legal estate is vested in both spouses jointly. He runs an obvious risk, however, if he leaves the husband to procure the wife's signature to the instrument. In practice, this is most likely to occur if the husband seeks a secured loan or overdraft to finance a business venture and the only security he can offer is that of the matrimonial home.[217] If the husband knows that the wife may be unwilling to agree, he may resort to undue influence or misrepresentation to obtain her consent. The House of Lords laid down definitive guidance to lenders to deal with this situation and to avoid being bound by the wife's interest in *Royal Bank of Scotland v Etridge (No 2)*.[218] First, they held that a lender will be put on inquiry whenever one party to a personal relationship of which the lender is aware offers to stand surety for another's debts. The lender should insist on the prospective surety attending a private meeting with its representative, at which she will be told of the extent of her liability and risk, and urged to take independent legal advice. The lender is not obliged, itself, to provide such advice. The independent legal adviser must explain to the surety the purpose of her involvement and obtain her confirmation that she wishes him to act and advise her on the legal and practical implications of the proposed transaction. In advising the surety, the solicitor does not act as agent for the lender, which is entitled to proceed on the basis that the solicitor has given her proper advice. Where such steps are taken, the lender will be protected from any attempt to resist enforcement of the charge by the surety based on misrepresentation or undue influence.

If the purchaser or mortgagee takes a legal estate subject to the wife's beneficial interest, the transaction will still have the effect of granting him whatever beneficial interest the

---

216   [1985] 2 All ER 606, CA (unregistered land). See also *Paddington Building Society v Mendelsohn* (1985) 50 P & CR 244, CA (registered land); *Equity and Law Home Loans Ltd v Prestidge* [1992] 1 All ER 909, CA (replacement mortgage). Had the House of Lords found in *Abbey National Building Society v Cann*, above, that the respondent's mother had an overriding interest, they would have held that it would not have prevailed over the appellant's interest for the same reason.

217   For an empirical study of this phenomenon, see B Fehlberg 'Money and Marriage: Sexually Transmitted Debt in England' (1997) 11 Int Jo of Law and Family 320.

218   [2001] UKHL 44, [2002] 2 AC 773, discussed above at p 139. See M Haley, '*Royal Bank of Scotland plc v Etridge (No 2)*: The *O'Brien* defence—a compromise reworked?' [2002] CFLQ 93; R Bigwood, 'Undue Influence in the House of Lords: Principles and Proof' (2002) 65 MLR 435; D Morris, 'Surety Wives in the House of Lords: Time for Solicitors to "Get Real"?' (2003) 11 Fem LS 57.

husband has.[219] But even if he finds himself saddled with the wife's interest, it does not follow that she will be able to stay in occupation indefinitely. The purchaser will be entitled to take proceedings for an order for sale: in deciding whether to order the property to be sold, the court must take into account the same facts as it would if the proceedings had been brought by the husband, in whose shoes the purchaser now stands. If the husband is insolvent, the court may enforce a sale in bankruptcy proceedings and leave the wife to claim her share of the proceeds.[220]

C OCCUPATION

Legal and beneficial ownership of land carries with it a prima facie right of occupation. Furthermore, at common law a wife had a right to occupy the matrimonial home by virtue of her right to her husband's consortium. This latter right has now become a statutory right for both spouses and civil partners, as provided for by the Family Law Act 1996.[221]

1 'HOME RIGHTS'

It was at one time accepted as the duty of the spouses to live together as far as their circumstances would permit, and remedies are still available to a spouse who has been deserted.[222] In accordance with the view that the husband was the head of the household, the earlier opinion was that he had the right to determine where the matrimonial home was to be, and a judicial dictum to this effect is to be found as late as 1940.[223] Today, however, this, like other domestic matters of common concern, is something in which both spouses have a right to be heard and which they must settle by agreement,[224] or, failing that, ultimately by separation and divorce.

It is uncertain whether a duty to cohabit is imposed upon civil partners. Whereas a decree of judicial separation lifts the obligation from spouses[225] a separation order has no such stated effect in relation to civil partners.[226] Yet desertion and separation form bases for petitions for divorce and for applications for financial support.[227] Given that there is no means of enforcing the obligation in a marriage there would seem to be no difference in practice in either case. The important dimension of the status of marriage or civil partnership is the right to occupy the family home which it brings with it.

---

[219] *Ahmed v Kendrick* [1988] 2 FLR 22, CA. In this case the husband and wife were joint tenants in law and equity. The husband sold the house to the defendant and forged the wife's signature on the transfer. It was held that, whilst this could not convey the legal estate, it severed the husband's joint tenancy in equity so that the spouses now held the property on trust for the wife and the defendant in equal shares. The court held that the decision to the contrary in *Cedar Holdings Ltd v Green* [1981] Ch 129, CA, could not be regarded as authority since *Williams and Glyn's Bank Ltd v Boland* (above).

[220] See below p 192ff.

[221] As amended by s 82 and Sch 9 para 1 to the Civil Partnership Act 2004.

[222] See below pp 269–71 and 958.

[223] *Mansey v Mansey* [1940] P 139 at 140. See also *King v King* [1942] P 1 at 8.

[224] *Dunn v Dunn* [1949] P 98 at 103 at 823, CA. See also *McGowan v McGowan* [1948] 2 All ER 1032 at 1035; *Walter v Walter* (1949) 65 TLR 680; *Hosegood v Hosegood* (1950) 66 (pt 1) TLR 735 at 739, CA.

[225] Matrimonial Causes Act 1973 s 18(1), discussed below at pp 302–4.

[226] Civil Partnership Act 2004 ss 56, 57.   [227] Ibid Sch 6.

(a) Background

If spouses are joint tenants in law or if both of them have a beneficial interest in the matrimonial home, each will prima facie be entitled to occupy it as owner, and have equal rights to stay in the property or seek to dispose of it. If the legal and equitable title is vested in the husband alone, the wife could claim a common law right of occupation by virtue of her right to her husband's consortium and her right to be maintained by him, which right would be primarily discharged by his providing her with a home.[228] However, in *National Provincial Bank Ltd v Ainsworth*[229] the House of Lords rejected a series of cases decided between 1952 and 1965 which had created the so-called 'deserted wives' equity' under which it had been held that a deserted wife could assert her common law right to remain in the matrimonial home not only against her husband, but also against third parties. They ruled that, where the husband had left the wife and children in the matrimonial home, and then conveyed it to a company in which he had a controlling interest, which in turn charged the home to the appellant bank as security for a loan, the wife's interest in remaining in the home could not prevail against the creditors' interest in realising their security in the property.[230]

The Matrimonial Homes Act 1967 was enacted to improve the position of such 'deserted wives' by clarifying what rights to occupy the home arise on marriage, and by providing a mechanism whereby third parties could be bound by spousal rights. The legislation, which laid down 'rights of occupation' was amended and consolidated,[231] and is now contained in Part IV of the Family Law Act 1996. This has in turn been amended by the Civil Partnership Act 2004 so that civil partners are treated in the same way as spouses. The amended provisions adopt slightly different terminology, now referring simply to 'home rights'.[232]

(b) The definition of 'home rights'

By s 30(1) and (2) of the 1996 Act, if

'(a) one spouse or civil partner ("A") is entitled to occupy a dwelling-house by virtue
of—

    (i)   a beneficial estate or interest or contract; or

    (ii) any enactment giving A the right to remain in occupation; and

  (b) the other spouse[233] or civil partner ("B") is not so entitled,

...

---

[228] See *Price v Price* [1951] P 413 at 420–1, CA; *W v W (No 2)* [1954] P 486 at 515–16. Husbands had the same right where the wife was sole legal and equitable owner, arising from the wife's duty to cohabit with the husband: *Shipman v Shipman* [1924] 2 Ch 140, CA.

[229] [1965] AC 1175, HL.

[230] In many cases, the wife could have the sale set aside as a transaction intended to defeat her claim for financial relief in divorce proceedings (see below, p 1072) but the argument failed in *Ainsworth* as against the Bank, because the Bank was a bona fide purchaser for value without notice of the husband's intention.

[231] Matrimonial Homes Act 1983.

[232] See Civil Partnership Act 2004 s 82 and Sch 9, amending Family Law Act 1996 s 30 et seq.

[233] It may be necessary first to determine whether the parties are validly married (or registered in a civil partnership): *Ramsamy v Babar* [2003] EWCA Civ 1253 [2005] 1 FLR 113 (husband separated from first wife who was holding the home on trust for him claimed the second marriage was void and thus the second wife was not entitled to occupy the home under s 30. County court should have investigated the validity of the marriage to decide whether s 30 was applicable).

B has the following rights ("home rights")—

   (a) if in occupation, a right not to be evicted or excluded from the dwelling-house or any part of it by A except with the leave of the court given by an order under s 33;[234]

   (b) if not in occupation, a right with the leave of the court so given to enter into and occupy the dwelling-house.'

One spouse or civil partner entitled to occupy

Home rights only arise where one of the parties is entitled to occupy the dwelling-house. Such entitlement may be by virtue of a beneficial estate or interest, contractual right or a statutory right. Where entitlement depends upon an estate or interest, any right to possession conferred on a mortgagee under or by virtue of the mortgage, is disregarded.[235] A party who lives in a house because he is a lodger or domestic servant will have a contractual right to occupy, while a statutory tenant under the Rent Acts[236] will have a statutory right.

Other spouse or civil partner not entitled

Where the other party in fact has an equitable interest in the dwelling-house, he or she is to be treated as *not* having such an interest for the purpose of establishing home rights.[237] This enables him or her to take advantage of the protection offered by s 30 and s 31 in the event of a sale of the property by the entitled party.

Dwelling-house

Section 63 provides that 'dwelling-house' includes

   '(a) any building, or part of a building which is occupied as a dwelling,[238]

   (b) any caravan, house-boat or structure occupied as a dwelling,
      and any yard, garden, garage or outhouse belonging to it and occupied with it.'[239]

The dwelling-house must have been, or been intended by the spouses to be, a matrimonial home of theirs (or, in the case of civil partners, a 'civil partnership home of theirs').[240] This means that where, for example, a property has been bought by one spouse, with the intention that it will be the matrimonial home, but the parties separate before they move into it, the non-entitled spouse may claim home rights in respect of it. Similarly, if one party has rented a property and then leaves, the other has the right to occupy even if the party's continuing entitlement stems from a newly-granted tenancy.[241]

   If the couple live in a town house and have a country cottage, each property may be a dwelling-house in respect of which home rights may arise.[242] On the other hand, if the couple live in one home, and rent out another, never intending to live in it, home rights do

---

[234] See below pp 231–2.   [235] Section 54(1)(2).   [236] See below, pp 197–9.
[237] Section 30(9).
[238] In *Kinzler v Kinzler* [1985] Fam Law 26, CA, it was held that the whole of a hotel owned by the parties, and not just their living quarters, was the matrimonial home, because there was only one front door and one kitchen.
[239] Para (b) does not apply where home rights are being asserted against third parties under s 31: s 63(4).
[240] Section 30(7) as amended by Civil Partnership Act 2004 Sch 9 para 8.
[241] *Moore v Moore* [2004] EWCA Civ 1243 [2005] 1 FLR 666.
[242] But a party may only register rights against one home at a time: see below, p 187.

not exist in respect of the rented-out property,[243] nor do they arise in respect of property acquired by one party for him- or herself to live in subsequent to their separation.

(c) The effect of having home rights

Where a spouse or civil partner has rights under s 30, he or she cannot be excluded from the dwelling-house by the other except by a court order[244] and, where not currently in occupation, may be given the right to enter by order. In either case, the order to be sought is an occupation order under s 33 of the Act, and the spouse or civil partner is an 'entitled applicant' for the purposes of that section.[245]

Where the party who is the owner or tenant etc leaves home and stops paying the mortgage, rent or other outgoings, the party with home rights has the right to keep up the payments in order to preserve his or her occupation and prevent the mortgagee or landlord from seeking possession.[246]

(d) Registration of home rights

The main aim in enacting the original Matrimonial Homes Act 1967 was to strike a balance between protecting a non-entitled spouse from eviction and ensuring that those who *bona fide* acquired rights in the dwelling-house from her husband should not be prevented from enjoying those rights. The mechanism chosen to achieve this balance was by enabling, and requiring, the non-entitled spouse to register her rights as a charge on the dwelling-house where that was held by virtue of an estate or interest.

Section 31 of the 1996 Act[247] provides that a spouse's or civil partner's home rights are a charge on the estate or interest, with the same priority as if it were an equitable interest created at whichever is the latest of the following dates—the date on which the entitled spouse acquired the estate or interest, the date of the marriage or formation of the civil partnership, or 1 January 1968.[248] To bind a third party, the charge *must* be registered.[249] In the case of registered land, this is done by means of a notice under the Land Registration Act 2002.[250] Where the title is unregistered, registration is achieved by means of a Class F land charge under the Land Charges Act 1972.[251] The charge will bind any person deriving title under the other spouse or civil partner, except that it will be void against any purchaser of the land or any interest in it for value if it is not registered before

---

[243] See *Collins v Collins* (1973) 4 Fam Law 133, CA, for an example.

[244] '[T]he right is in essence a personal and non-assignable statutory right not to be evicted from the matrimonial home in question during marriage or until the court otherwise orders' per Megarry J in *Wroth v Tyler* [1974] Ch 30 at 46G.

[245] See below, p 231.   [246] Section 30(3)–(6).

[247] As amended by Civil Partnership Act 2004 Sch 9 para 2.

[248] Section 31(2), (3) as amended. The last of these is the date the Matrimonial Homes Act 1967 came into force. Where the matrimonial home rights are a charge on the interest of the other party under a trust, and there is or could be no other beneficiary under the trust, they are a charge also on the estate or interests of the trustees: s 31(5).

[249] But for discussion of the development of the doctrine of undue influence as a mechanism to protect a spouse's (or other intimate partner's) continuing occupation of the home against attempts by purchasers and creditors to obtain possession, see above, p 138ff.

[250] Section 31(10) as amended. Home rights are not capable of amounting to an overriding interest within para 2 of Schs 1 or 3 to the 2002 Act: s 31(10)(b).

[251] Section 2(7).

completion.[252] As a party out of occupation may need even greater protection than one physically in the house, her charge may be registered even though she has not yet been given leave by the court to enter and occupy.[253]

A spouse or civil partner is entitled to have only one charge registered at a time. Consequently, if the couple have two homes, she must decide against which one she will register her charge. If, after registering one, she registers another, the first registration must be cancelled.[254]

(e) Duration of home rights

Home rights will usually come to an end on the death of the other spouse or civil partner or on the dissolution or annulment of the marriage or civil partnership, unless the court has ordered that they should continue after the termination of the relationship (whether by death or a court order).[255] Rights will also come to an end if the owning party disposes of his estate or interest in the home, unless they have been registered and hence are binding upon the purchaser.[256] It may be advisable to seek an order extending rights beyond the termination of the marriage, as this may be the only way of protecting the spouse if the home cannot be made the subject of a property adjustment order.[257] However, where the object of registration is purely to freeze assets with a view to an ancillary relief claim, the court may set the registration aside.[258] A court has also awarded damages to a purchaser where a wife registered her charge without informing her husband before he could complete a sale, thus preventing him from giving the purchaser vacant possession.[259]

A prospective purchaser will not usually remain ignorant of a charge having been registered before completion of the purchase, and a failure to detect such registration may well give rise to an action against the purchaser's solicitor for negligence. However, should a purchaser be placed in such circumstances, the easiest remedy will be to seek an occupation order to terminate the party's home rights.[260] This was done in the pre-1996 Act decision, *Kashmir Kaur v Gill*.[261] There, the wife left home because of the husband's violence and registered her charge. The husband sold the property to a blind respondent, whose solicitors failed to discover the registration. The Court of Appeal, by a majority, upheld the trial judge's rejection of the wife's claim for an order declaring her right to occupy the house and prohibiting the respondent from entering, because the respondent's need to occupy outweighed that of the wife. Under s 34(2) of the 1996 Act, the court may make an occupation order in proceedings between a party with home rights and a person deriving

---

[252] Land Charges Act 1972 s 4(8); 'purchaser' includes a mortgagee, but in the usual situation where a property is purchased with the aid of a mortgage, the matrimonial home rights charge is not protected by registration until after the mortgage is created, and hence the mortgagee takes priority.

[253] *Watts v Waller* [1973] QB 153, CA. If the party subsequently makes an unsuccessful application for such leave, the registration will be cancelled.

[254] Family Law Act 1996 Sch 4, para 2 as amended by Civil Partnership Act 2004 Sch 9 para 15.

[255] Section 33(5) as amended.

[256] See above. But see *Moore v Moore* [2004] EWCA Civ 1243, [2005] 1 FLR 666: entitlement to occupy continued during the notice period, and should the entitled spouse have entered into a new lease on the property, the other spouse would have continued to be able to exercise her rights.

[257] See below, p 1003.   [258] *Barnett v Hassett* [1981] 1 WLR 1385.

[259] *Wroth v Tyler* [1974] Ch 30.   [260] Family Law Act 1996 s 33(3)(e) and s 34.

[261] [1988] Fam 110, CA.

title from the other spouse (or civil partner) 'if it considers that in all the circumstances it is just and reasonable to do so.' While Sir Denys Buckley dissented in *Kashmir Kaur v Gill* on the basis that the respondent could have no better claim to occupy than the husband from whom he had derived title, and that the court should therefore have considered the *husband's* circumstances when weighed against the wife's rather than the respondent's, the broad test set out in s 34(2) would appear to leave it open to a court to find in the purchaser's favour in a similar case in the future.

2 OTHER FORMS OF PROTECTED OCCUPATION

What we are now concerned to discuss are other means by which rights of occupation may be acquired. This issue is of principal relevance to unmarried heterosexual and unregistered same-sex couples, since if ownership is vested in one of them alone the other's right of occupation must be found by reference to the general law of property. In the following discussion we assume for the purpose of illustration that the couple are heterosexual and that the property is vested in the man.

(a) Contractual licence

If the woman has given up some existing right or suffered some other detriment to go and live with the man, it may be possible to regard this as consideration and thus give the woman a contractual licence. In *Tanner v Tanner*,[262] for example, the plaintiff bought a house for the defendant and their twin daughters and the defendant surrendered a rent-controlled tenancy to move into it. When the plaintiff later claimed possession of the house, it was held that, as the defendant had furnished consideration by giving up the security of her flat, the licence was a contractual one.

The facts of *Tanner* were unusual in that the parties never lived in the house together. The problem more likely to arise is that facing a woman who, having set up home with a man in property belonging to him, is ordered to leave when their relationship breaks down. Even if she suffered a detriment, for example by giving up a secure tenancy like the defendant in *Tanner*, it would usually be impossible to spell out any promise by the man that she could continue to reside in the house if he no longer wished to live with her. Any such undertaking is more likely to be given at the point of breakdown if the man leaves, but unless the woman suffers some fresh detriment (such as a reciprocal undertaking to pay rent or other outgoings), any consideration would be past and therefore ineffective to establish a contract.

Even if it is possible to spell out a contractual licence, it may well be difficult to infer the period for which the parties intended that the woman should be entitled to stay in the premises. In *Tanner v Tanner* the Court of Appeal took the view that the defendant had a licence to remain in the house so long as the parties' children were of school age and it was reasonably required as a home for them and their mother. There was necessarily something arbitrary about terminating the licence when the children reached the age of 16 because they might continue in full-time education after that, but it was reasonable to imply that it should cease, say, if their mother married. The woman is likely to be less favourably treated if the children of the owner of the property are not living with her. In

---

[262] [1975] 3 All ER 776, CA. Contrast *Horrocks v Forray* [1976] 1 All ER 737, CA.

Chandler v Kerley[263] the defendant and her husband had sold their former matrimonial home to the plaintiff on the understanding that the defendant (who proposed to marry the plaintiff after her divorce) would continue to live there with him and the two children of her marriage. The relationship between the parties broke down very shortly afterwards and the plaintiff sought possession of the house. The Court of Appeal held that he could not have intended to assume the burden of housing the defendant and another man's children indefinitely, and that the licence was terminable on her being given 12 months' notice, which would enable her to find other accommodation.

(b) Licence by estoppel

By analogy with proprietary estoppel, one party may claim a licence if the other has led her to believe (or has acquiesced in her belief) that she has, or will be given, permission to remain in the house and she acts to her detriment in reliance on this belief. A classic example is *Greasley v Cook*.[264] The defendant had entered the service of a family as a maid. Later she and one of the sons cohabited in the family house for nearly 30 years; she looked after the family as a whole and in particular cared for the daughter who was mentally ill. She received no payment and asked for none because the members of the family had led her to believe that she would be entitled to remain in the house as long as she wished. In those circumstances, it was held that she should be able to do so and the plaintiffs' action for possession failed. As in other cases of proprietary estoppel, it must be shown that the woman acted in reliance on the belief that she was to have a licence; the fact that she goes to live with the owner of the property and permits herself to become pregnant will not of itself give her any right to remain there.[265]

As the cases cited above show, the extent of the resulting equity is to make good the expectations which the owner has encouraged, insofar as fairness between the parties permits this to be done.[266]

(c) Constructive trust

In one case, *Ungurian v Lesnoff*,[267] it was held that the facts established a trust rather than a licence. The defendant had left Poland and abandoned her career there in reliance on the parties' common intention that the plaintiff would buy a house where she could live with her children. In these circumstances Vinelott J held that full effect would not be given to this intention by inferring an irrevocable licence to occupy the house, but that the plaintiff held it on trust to permit her to live there for the rest of her life.[268] While this must turn on the inference that the court drew from the parties' conduct, it is not immediately obvious why the judge reached this conclusion, for which he gave no reason.[269]

---

[263] [1978] 2 All ER 942, CA. It is not clear what the consideration for the licence was: presumably it was the defendant's taking less than half the proceeds of sale because she was to continue to live in the house.

[264] [1980] 3 All ER 710, CA. See also *Maharaj v Chand* [1986] AC 898, PC.

[265] *Coombes v Smith* [1986] 1 WLR 808.

[266] See *Re Basham* [1987] 1 All ER 405 at 417; Moriarty 'Licences and Land Law' (1984) 100 LQR 376.

[267] [1990] Ch 206.

[268] In other words, a strict settlement had been created. The plaintiff could sell the property with the defendant's consent and buy another residence for her in substitution for it.

[269] It can have important consequences if the owner sells the property without the occupant's consent. But note the analysis in *Ungurian v Lesnoff* has now been superseded by the Trusts of Land and Appointment of Trustees Act 1996 which prevents any more strict settlements of land being created. Cf *H v M (Property*

(d) Bare licence

In other cases the woman will find herself no more than a bare licensee and the owner may recover possession of the premises after giving her reasonable notice to quit. The period given must be sufficient to enable her to find accommodation for herself and any children living with her.

(e) Rights against third persons

Even where the owner of the parties' home or former home cannot evict the other party, the latter's position may become precarious if the former dies or disposes of the property.

If the occupant holds under a trust, a purchaser will be bound by her right of occupation in the same circumstances as he would be bound by a beneficial interest in the property itself, and her presence there may give him notice of her rights.[270] In particular, a volunteer (for example, a devisee of the home) will take subject to them. A contractual licence, on the other hand, confers only a personal right on the licensee.[271] Consequently, a cohabitant who has such a licence could enforce it against the other party's personal representatives, who are bound by his contractual obligations,[272] but not against a purchaser (even though he took with notice of it) unless the circumstances of the purchase make him a constructive trustee. A constructive trust will not be imposed in reliance on slender material:[273] the purchaser must have behaved in such a way as to make it unconscionable to permit him to deny the occupant's rights, for example by giving an express assurance that they would be respected,[274] or paying a lower price because the land was subject to them.[275] The threat of litigation may be sufficient to deter a prospective purchaser, but a vendor anxious to dispose of the property at the highest price is unlikely to impose terms which would create a trust.

A licence by estoppel may put the occupant in a stronger position, because an equity by estoppel is capable of binding successors in title.[276] The position, however, is not clear. At the most, it is submitted, the requirement that the owner should satisfy the expectations raised by his conduct makes him in effect a constructive trustee; on the other hand, the same facts could give rise to a contractual obligation or an estoppel, and it would be anomalous if a person relying on the latter were in a stronger position than one given an express promise that she would remain in occupation.

Occupied by Wife's Parents) [2004] EWHC 625 (Fam) [2004] 2 FLR 16: husband and wife purchased wife's parents' farm when it had gone into receivership. Held, parents had no proprietary interest by means of constructive trust or estoppel, as they had not acted to their detriment, but, by agreement with the husband and wife, they were entitled to live in the farm for as long as they wished; query what kind of licence they had?

[270] See above p 180ff.   [271] *Ashburn Anstalt v Arnold* [1989] Ch 1, CA.

[272] This was apparently assumed in *Horrocks v Forray* [1976] 1 All ER 737, CA, although the executor's claim for possession succeeded because it was held that the defendant did not have a contractual licence.

[273] *Ashburn Anstalt v Arnold*, above, at 26.

[274] As in *Lyus v Prowsa Developments Ltd* [1982] 2 All ER 953. The fact that the land is transferred expressly subject to the occupant's rights does not of itself create a constructive trust, because this merely gives the transferee notice of their existence.

[275] As in *Binions v Evans* [1972] Ch 359, CA.   [276] Land Registration Act 2002 s 116.

D INSOLVENCY AND THE FAMILY HOME

1 MORTGAGES AND CHARGES

If the sole legal owner of the family home mortgages it and later fails to pay the mortgage instalments, the mortgagee may wish to obtain vacant possession in order to realise his security. Even though the mortgagor has no defence to the claim, his or her spouse or partner may be protected if she or he did not concur in the mortgage, in which case of course the mortgagor will be able to remain in occupation as well. For the purpose of illustration it will be assumed that legal ownership is vested in the husband or male cohabitant.

We have already considered the circumstances in which a mortgagee will take subject to any beneficial interest which the wife or partner has in the property.[277] Even if she has no such interest, a wife (or civil partner) will be able to enforce her rights of occupation under the Family Law Act 1996 provided that she registered them before the mortgage was taken.[278] In most cases this will be valueless, because she will not have registered her rights if the home was mortgaged before the parties went into possession, and in practice she is unlikely to have done so even if she was in occupation when the husband (or civil partner) charged the property. An unmarried cohabitant's position will similarly depend on whether a purchaser is bound by such right of occupation as she has.[279]

If a wife's or partner's beneficial interest takes priority over a mortgage, the mortgagee, as a person interested, may bring proceedings to enforce the trust of land under the Trusts of Land and Appointment of Trustees Act 1996 s 14. On principle, the mortgagee should have no greater right than the husband or partner Hence, it could be argued that if the wife (or partner) and children are occupying the house as the family home, the primary object of the trust will still be in existence and the court should not order a sale. But in *Bank of Ireland Home Mortgages Ltd v Bell and Bell*,[280] it was held that a powerful consideration for the court to take into account is whether the creditor is receiving proper recompense for being kept out of his money, for which repayment is overdue. Thus, where the husband left the wife soon after executing a charge on the matrimonial home, and where no payments of capital or interest were received by the lender for several years and the debt was now some £300,000, the first instance judge had been wrong to refuse to order a sale because he considered that the wife and her son were still fulfilling the purpose of the trust in living there. Moreover, the wife's ill health, according to the Court of Appeal, was a factor relevant to determining *when* the sale should take place, but not *whether* it should do so.

A similar problem arises if the parties are living together in the property without children. Although the house will still be the family home, the right of the mortgagee to enforce his security cannot be entirely ignored, and there seems little justification for permitting the wife or partner to remain when the other has no defence against a claim for possession, particularly if the mortgagee could take bankruptcy proceedings, when the court would almost certainly order the house to be sold after postponing sale for one year.[281]

---

[277] See above p 178ff.   [278] See above p 187.   [279] See above pp 189–91.
[280] [2001] 2 FLR 809, CA.   [281] See below pp 194–6.

Similar considerations would apply if the mortgagee brought proceedings to terminate the wife's or partner's right of occupation.[282]

If the mortgagee is aware of the spouse's or partner's rights, he will insist on her agreeing that the charge should take priority over them, and it would be prudent for him to give himself the maximum protection by insisting on her concurring in the mortgage in any event. Even if she does so, a wife or civil partner (as distinct from an unmarried cohabitant) is still given a degree of protection by the Family Law Act 1996. This provides that, if a spouse or civil partner entitled under the Act to occupy the whole or part of the home makes any payment or tender in respect of rent, mortgage payments or other outgoings affecting the home, this shall be as effective as though it were made by the owner.[283] If the mortgagee brings proceedings to enforce his security, the court may stay or suspend the execution of any order made, if the mortgagor is likely to be able to pay all sums due within a reasonable time.[284] The wife or civil partner is given further protection by the requirement that the mortgagee must serve her with notice of proceedings if her right of occupation is registered; in any event she is generally entitled to be made a party if the court is satisfied that she may be expected to make such payments (or do anything else in satisfaction of the mortgagor's obligations) as might affect the outcome of the proceedings.[285] The difficulty is that the mortgagee is not bound to give her notice of the husband's default. As a result, such massive arrears may have accumulated before she gets to hear of them that she will find it impossible to pay them off within a reasonable time, even though she might have been able to pay each instalment as it fell due.

The provisions mentioned in the last paragraph do not apply to an unmarried cohabitant, whose only hope of preserving her right would be to seek an agreement with the mortgagee that she should pay off the arrears.

2 BANKRUPTCY

If the family home forms part of the assets of a bankrupt, his interest in it will vest in the trustee in bankruptcy immediately his appointment takes effect.[286] Hence, if the bankrupt and his (or her) spouse or partner are tenants in common,[287] the latter will retain her equitable share which will not be available for the other's creditors. Consequently, in bankruptcy the parties' interests in property will be of paramount importance.

---

[282] See above, pp 188–9 and 191.   [283] Section 30(3).

[284] Administration of Justice Act 1973 s 8; *Halifax Building Society v Clark* [1973] 2 All ER 33, CA; *Governor & Co of the Bank of Scotland v Grimes* [1985] 2 All ER 254, CA.

[285] Family Law Act 1996 ss 55–6. A similar right to resist possession proceedings is given where the dwelling-house is held under a secure or assured tenancy: Housing Act 1985 s 85(5) as amended by Civil Partnership Act 2004 Sch 9 para 18; Housing Act 1988 s 9(5) as amended by Civil Partnership Act 2004 Sch 9 para 23. The right extends to those other than spouses or civil partners, who have an occupation order in their favour: Family Law Act 1996 Sch 8, paras 53, 59.

[286] Some tenancies protected by statute will not vest in the trustee unless he serves a notice on the bankrupt (as he might do, for example, if the tenancy had a saleable value): Insolvency Act 1986 s 283(3A) and s 308A (added by the Housing Act 1988 s 117).

[287] If they are equitable joint tenants, the joint tenancy will be severed when the property vests in the trustee, and the trustee and the other party will become equitable tenants in common in equal shares.

(a) Voidable transactions

The trustee may wish to have the spouse's or cohabitant's interest set aside under s 339 or s 423 of the Insolvency Act, the details of which have already been discussed.[288] Homes recently purchased may well be caught by s 339. If within the period of two years preceding the presentation of the bankruptcy petition the man had bought the family home with his own money and had it conveyed into the partners' joint names as equitable beneficial owners, the trustee may claim the spouse's or cohabitant's beneficial interest as one obtained in a transaction at an undervalue. The same result would follow if the partner had contributed significantly less than the value of her equitable share or, in similar circumstances, if the house had been purchased more than two years but less than five years before the petition and the purchaser was then insolvent.

(b) Protection of members of the bankrupt's family[289]

Whether the bankrupt (who, for the sake of example, will be assumed to be the husband) is the sole beneficial owner of the matrimonial home or has a limited beneficial interest, the trustee in bankruptcy will normally wish to sell it to increase the assets available for the creditors. This will bring their interests into direct conflict with those of the members of the bankrupt's family who wish to retain the property as a family home.

Section 336 of the Insolvency Act protects the occupation rights of the bankrupt's spouse. No home right under Part IV of the Family Law Act 1996 may be acquired in the period between the presentation of the petition and vesting of the bankrupt's property in the trustee, so that if the bankrupt marries during that period his wife will have no statutory rights. But existing rights of occupation under the Act will continue in force and bind the trustee, whether or not they are registered. The trustee has the same power to apply to the court to have these rights terminated, suspended or restricted as the husband would have had.[290] It will be observed that these provisions do not apply to an unmarried cohabitant.

Children (whether or not they are related to the bankrupt) are given protection by s 337, which applies when the bankrupt is entitled to occupy a dwelling house[291] by virtue of any estate or interest. If any person under the age of 18, who had his home with the bankrupt when the bankruptcy petition was presented and when the bankruptcy order was made, had at any time occupied that house with the bankrupt, the bankrupt has the same right of occupation against the trustee as a spouse under the Family Law Act 1996 and cannot be evicted from the house without the leave of the court.[292] This protection is additional to that given by s 336 and is of importance if the children are living with the bankrupt but not with his wife (e.g. because she is dead or the spouses are divorced), or if the mother is living with the bankrupt but is not married to him.

If the bankrupt and his spouse or former spouse are trustees of land or the beneficial owners of a dwelling house, the trustee in bankruptcy may apply to the court for an order to sell the property under s 14 of the Trusts of Land and Appointment of Trustees Act 1996.

---

[288] See above p 141ff.

[289] See generally M Davey 'Creditors and the family home' in C Bridge (ed) *Family Law Towards the Millennium: Essays for P M Bromley* (1997) 331 at 347–52; B Soni, 'Insolvency and the Matrimonial Home' [2004] Fam Law 596.

[290] Insolvency Act 1986 s 336(1)–(2), as amended.

[291] This is defined as in the Family Law Act 1996: see above p 186; ibid, s 385(1).

[292] Ibid, s 337(1)–(4). Note that the children need not be the bankrupt's own children.

Alternatively, he may apply to have the occupation rights of the bankrupt's spouse or former spouse terminated. In either case, the court must make such order as it thinks just and reasonable, having regard to the interests of the creditors, to the conduct of the spouse or former spouse so far as contributing to the bankruptcy, to the needs and financial resources of [that person], to the needs of any children and to all the circumstances of the case other than the needs of the bankrupt.[293] The court may make any order that it could make under Part IV of the Family Law Act 1996 and so could permit the bankrupt to remain in occupation if he paid an occupation rent or other outgoing.[294] In either case, if the application is made more than a year after the property vested in the trustee, it is to be assumed that the creditors' interests outweigh all other considerations, unless the circumstances are exceptional.[295]

Insolvency practitioners will generally delay making any application under either section for a year so as to be able to take advantage of the presumption in favour of making an order after that time. This will effectively give the bankrupt and his spouse or partner a year in which to find other accommodation. After this period the Act gives statutory effect to the position under the old law, when the creditors would always prevail unless the circumstances were exceptional.[296] The fact that the family will be rendered homeless is an inevitable consequence of the sale and is not exceptional;[297] although the bankrupt or his wife would not usually be ordered to surrender possession until they had had reasonable time to make other arrangements.[298] Examples of the court finding exceptional circumstances include cases of ill-health, such as *Judd v Brown*,[299] in which the bankrupt's wife had had recent major surgery for cancer and was about to undergo extensive chemotherapy treatment. There, a sale was refused. It is more common to find the court *postponing* sale for an appropriate period of time.[300] Sale may also be postponed to enable the

[293] S 335A and s 336(4), added by the Trusts of Land and Appointment of Trustees Act 1996 Sch 3, para 23. The addition of s 335A implements the Law Commission's recommendation (Law Com No 181), at para 12.12 to provide similar guidelines even where the bankrupt spouse is a beneficial owner. If the application is made to terminate the bankrupt's own rights of occupation given by s 337, regard must similarly be had to 'the interests of the creditors, the bankrupt's financial resources, the needs of the children and all the circumstances of the case other than the needs of the bankrupt': s 337(5). The welfare of children is irrelevant if the claim is brought under the Charging Orders Act 1979 instead: *Pickering v Wells* [2002] 2 FLR 797.

[294] The payment of outgoings will not give him any proprietary interest in the property: ibid, s 338.

[295] Ibid, s 335A(3), s 336(5) and s 337(6). It has been doubted at first instance whether the requirement to show that the circumstances are exceptional is compatible with the ECHR, but the matter did not fall for resolution on the facts: *Barca v Mears* [2004] EWHC 2170 (Ch) [2005] 2 FLR 1.

[296] *Zandfarid v Bank of Credit and Commerce International SA (in liquidation)* [1997] 1 FLR 274; *Barclays Bank plc v Hendricks* [1996] 1 FLR 259; *Lloyds Bank plc v Byrne and Byrne* [1993] 1 FLR 369, CA; *Re Lowrie* [1981] 3 All ER 353, CA; *Re Citro* [1991] Ch 142, CA; *Re Gorman* [1990] 1 All ER 717.

[297] *Re Lowrie* (above) at 356.

[298] *Barclays Bank plc v Hendricks*, above; *Re Turner* [1975] 1 All ER 5; *Re McCarthy* [1975] 2 All ER 857. But immediate possession might be given to the trustee eg if the spouse was being obstructive: *Re McCarthy* at 859.

[299] *Judd v Brown, Bankrupts (Nos 9587 and 9588 of 1994)* [1998] 2 FLR 360. This decision was not affected by a successful appeal in respect of other properties involved: *Judd v Brown* [1999] 1 FLR 1191, CA.

[300] See eg *Re Bremner (A Bankrupt)* [1999] 1 FLR 912—home not to be put up for sale until three months after the death of the bankrupt (aged 79 and in poor health; sale postponed to enable his wife to care for him); *Claughton v Charalambous* [1999] 1 FLR 740—sale suspended so long as the wife, who was aged 60 and had reduced life expectancy due to renal failure, continued to live in the property, which had been fitted with a chair-lift.

spouse to take negligence proceedings against her legal advisers in respect of their advice to her regarding the property.[301] It has, by contrast, been held not to amount to exceptional circumstances that the value of the bankrupt's share of the property will be exceeded by the debt owed, or the expenses incurred in the bankruptcy proceedings.[302] It is suggested that the circumstances pertaining in a case under the earlier law, *Re Holliday*[303] should still be classed as failing within the 'exceptional' category. The husband and wife were beneficial joint tenants of the matrimonial home. The husband presented a petition in his own bankruptcy to frustrate the wife's application for a property transfer order in divorce proceedings, and there was no evidence that any of his creditors would have petitioned. If an immediate sale had been ordered, the wife was unlikely to have been able to find alternative accommodation for herself and her three children in the neighbourhood, so that their education would have been upset, and in the particular circumstances of the case a postponement would not have worked undue hardship on the creditors. The Court of Appeal held that in these exceptional circumstances 'the voice of the wife seeking to preserve a home for herself and the children ought in equity to prevail' and ordered that the house should not be sold for five years.

However, in the more usual type of case, it will be rare for creditors not to be prejudiced by a delay in the sale of more than a few months; consequently, if the trustee applies for an order after the first year, the court is likely to order an immediate sale unless the welfare of the children makes it imperative that they should stay in the matrimonial home, eg because they have reached a critical stage in their education.[304]

E STATUTORY PROTECTION OF LEASEHOLD PROPERTY [305]

Almost a third of the population rent their homes,[306] and we must now consider their position in the light of the relevant statutory provisions. It should be noted at the outset that the law governing the rented sector is currently the subject of a thorough review by the Law Commission, which has set out radical ideas for its reform. Since these have yet to be finalised, they are not discussed here.[307]

---

[301] *Re Gorman (A Bankrupt) ex part the Truste of the Bankrupt v The Bankrupt and Another* [1990] 2 FLR 284; cf *Trustee of the Estate of Eric Bowe (A Bankrupt) v Bowe* [1998] 2 FLR 439.

[302] *Re Ng (A Bankrupt), Trustee of the Estate of Ng v Ng* [1998] 2 FLR 386; *Trustee of the Estate of Eric Bowe (A Bankrupt) v Bowe* (above).

[303] [1981] Ch 405, CA.   [304] See *Re Lowrie* [1981] 3 All ER 353 at 356, CA.

[305] Agricultural tenancies are not dealt with in the text and the reader should consult specialist works for details of these.

[306] Law Com No 284, *Renting Homes* (2003) para 2.1.

[307] See Law Com Consultation Paper No 162, *Renting Homes: 1, Status and Security* (2002), Law Com Consultation Paper No 168, *Renting Homes: 2, Co-occupation, Transfer and Succession* (2002) and Law Com No 284, *Renting Homes* (above). There is a valuable history of the legal control of the rented sector in Law Com Consultation Paper No 162 'Part II: The Evolution of Housing Law'.

1 THE PRIVATE SECTOR

Rent control is the outcome of a chronic shortage of rented property and began in this country in 1915 as the result of the shortage in the First World War. Until 1988 it was coupled with security of tenure, on the ground that limiting the rent a landlord could charge gave no protection if he could evict the tenant, and security of tenure was valueless if the landlord could charge a rent which the tenant could not afford to pay. Rent control, however, itself produces a shortage of accommodation since landlords may be prevented from charging the market rent. Consequently, when houses became vacant, many landlords preferred to sell rather than re-let and there was no incentive for developers to build new property for letting. During the 1980s the Conservative Government introduced legislation in an attempt to bring more rented accommodation onto the market. The result was to leave a bewildering array of types of tenancy offering differing levels of protection to the tenant.

(a) Regulated tenancies under the Rent Act 1977

These are a diminishing proportion of private tenants, since it has not been possible to create a new tenancy according to the Rent Act's terms since 15 January 1989 when the Housing Act 1988 Part I came into force. However, tenants still falling within the 1977 Act have significant protection both as regards the rent they can be charged, and their security of tenure.

A tenancy governed by the Rent Act is known as a regulated tenancy. A tenant in occupation under a contractual lease is known as a 'protected tenant' and is protected from arbitrary eviction by the terms of the contract. The Act also gives the tenant a wide measure of protection *after* the lease ends. If he remains in possession after his contractual lease has been determined—for example, if his term has expired or he has been given notice to quit in accordance with the provisions of the lease—his tenancy becomes a 'statutory tenancy'.[308] In certain circumstances a deceased tenant's spouse or partner also becomes a statutory tenant.[309] A statutory tenant is generally speaking bound by all the terms and conditions in the original lease and entitled to the benefit of them.[310]

Fair rent

In the absence of agreement between them, either the landlord or the protected tenant may apply, during the contractual period of the tenancy, for a 'fair rent' to be determined and registered by a Rent Officer. Once this is registered, it becomes the maximum rent that the landlord can charge under that, or any subsequent regulated tenancy, for the next two years.[311]

---

[308] Rent Act 1977 ss 1–2; if there were two or more joint contractual tenants, but not all are in possession at the end of the contractual tenancy, those remaining become statutory tenants: *Lloyd v Sadler* [1978] QB 774, CA. A husband's permitting his wife to remain in possession of the matrimonial home as a condition of paying a reduced sum under a maintenance order does not create the relationship of landlord and tenant so as to give the wife the protection of the Rent Act: *Bramwell v Bramwell* [1942] 1 KB 370, CA; cf *Marcroft Wagons Ltd v Smith* [1951] 2 KB 496, CA (daughter permitted to remain in possession after her mother's death for a short time not protected by the Act).

[309] See below, pp 1101–4 succession chapter   [310] Rent Act 1977 s 3.   [311] Section 67.

Protection from eviction

In order to claim the protection given by the Act against eviction, the statutory tenant must occupy the premises as his residence, for the policy of the Act is to protect the home and not to give the tenant any wider privileges.[312] A person may be in occupation of more than one home for this purpose simultaneously, as where he works in two places and has a home in each of them which he occupies when he is at that particular place: whether he can be said to occupy one as his second home is a question of fact and degree.[313] Likewise, a temporary absence will not suffice to bring his statutory tenancy to an end. Thus it was held that a wife who had gone away because of illness, leaving her furniture in the house in which her husband occasionally slept and to which she hoped to return as soon as her health improved, was still in occupation and was entitled to the protection of the Act.[314] But a mere intention to occupy will not be sufficient, and consequently it was held that a man who left his house deserted whilst serving a sentence of imprisonment ceased to be a statutory tenant.[315] He could have averted this result only 'by coupling and clothing his inward intention with some formal, outward, and visible sign of it', for example by installing a caretaker or relative to preserve the premises for his homecoming.[316] Conversely, if the tenant leaves the premises with no intention of ever returning, he loses the status of a statutory tenant, even though he leaves his furniture there with a caretaker or relative.[317]

But there is one important exception to this rule, designed to protect the tenant's spouse. If one spouse or civil partner[318] is a protected or statutory tenant but the other is in occupation of the premises by virtue of his or her home rights under the Family Law Act 1996, s 30(4)(a) of that Act provides that this is to be regarded as occupation by the tenant himself.[319] This is so even though the person in occupation is there against the tenant's will. This exception was originally grafted onto earlier Acts by the Court of Appeal and was based on the husband's common law obligation to maintain his wife and to provide her with accommodation.[320] So long as the tenant's spouse or civil partner is occupying the premises as her (or his) residence, the protected or statutory tenancy will continue

---

[312] *Kavanagh v Lyroudias* [1985] 1 All ER 560, CA (tenant sleeping in one house but spending rest of time in another not in occupation of first house as his residence). See Brierley 'The Rent Act 1977 and the Absent Tenant' (1991) 54 Conv 345.

[313] See *Hampstead Way Investments Ltd v Lewis-Weare* [1985] 1 All ER 564, HL.

[314] *Wigley v Leigh* [1950] 2 KB 305, CA. See also *Camden London Borough Council v Goldenberg* [1997] 1 FLR 556, CA (McCowan LJ dissenting)—a grandson who moved out of his grandmother's flat on marriage, but failed to find permanent alternative accommodation with his wife and moved back in after a few months, retained continuity of residence for purpose of being assigned a *secure* tenancy (see below, p 200) because the flat remained his postal address and he left his possessions there.

[315] *Brown v Brash* [1948] 2 KB 247, CA.   [316] Per Asquith LJ, ibid, at 254–5.

[317] *Skinner v Geary* [1931] 2 KB 546, CA (sister); *Robson v Headland* (1948) 64 TLR 596, CA (divorced wife and son); *Beck v Scholz* [1953] 1 QB 570, CA (caretakers); *Colin Smith Music Ltd v Ridge* [1975] 1 All ER 290, CA (deserted cohabitant and their children); *Duke v Porter* (1986) 19 HLR 1, CA (nobody resident).

[318] Family Law Act 1996 s 30(4)(a) as amended by the Civil Partnership Act 2004 Sch 9 para 1(5).

[319] Hence the tenancy will not have the protection of the Rent Act if it has never been the matrimonial home, because neither the Family Law Act 1996 (see above, p 66) nor the case law carried forward from the earlier Acts will apply: *Hall v King* [1988] 1 FLR 376, CA. No order need have been made under the Act. A spouse (like a tenant) who is temporarily absent will remain in occupation for the purpose of the Act if he retains the corpus of possession and the intention to return: *Hoggett v Hoggett* (1979) 39 P & CR 121, CA.

[320] *Brown v Draper* [1944] KB 309, CA.

notwithstanding that the tenant is residing elsewhere.[321] No such protection exists for a cohabitant.

Recovery of possession

If a statutory tenant and his or her spouse or partner both leave the premises, this automatically brings the tenancy to an end, and the landlord may retake possession or, if necessary, recover it by suing any trespasser on the property.[322] But so long as a protected or statutory tenancy is in existence, the landlord may obtain an order for possession only if the conditions laid down by the Rent Act are fulfilled. These are of two kinds. First, where suitable alternative accommodation is available to the tenant or one or more of the 'discretionary grounds' for possession (such as non-payment of rent) exist,[323] the court may make an order unless it thinks this unreasonable. Secondly, if the landlord establishes one or more 'mandatory grounds' (for example, the landlord is an 'owner-occupier', ie had previously himself occupied the property, and requires it again for his own residence), then the court must make the order and has no overriding discretion to refuse.[324]

(b) Tenancies under the Housing Act 1988

The Housing Act 1988 Part I created two new forms of tenancy for the private rented sector: 'assured' and 'assured shorthold' tenancies.

Assured tenancies

An assured tenancy enables the landlord to charge the market rent for the property,[325] although the tenant may still only be evicted if the landlord can prove one or more of a range of statutory grounds for possession against him, not including the expiry of the contractual period. An assured tenancy becomes a 'statutory' periodic assured tenancy at the end of that period.

Assured shorthold tenancies

An assured shorthold tenancy, in addition to enabling the landlord to charge the market rent,[326] also provides for possession to be obtained simply by virtue of the tenancy coming to the end of the contractual period, by proceedings following the serving of a possession notice.[327] As originally enacted, the shorthold had to be granted for a term certain of not less than six months. This is no longer a requirement, although the landlord cannot ask for an order for possession until six months after the beginning of the tenancy.[328] The shorthold tenant, unlike an assured tenant, may not terminate a fixed-term shorthold before the expiry of the term.

---

[321] See *Hall v King* (above) and the judgment of Kerr LJ (with which Ewbank J agreed) in *Griffiths v Renfree* [1989] 2 FLR 167 at 172–3. Once the landlord has obtained an order for possession and this has taken effect, the tenant is no longer entitled to remain in possession by virtue of the Rent Act, and consequently the spouse loses his or her home rights and becomes a trespasser, but she (or he) can still apply for the order to be suspended: Rent Act 1977 s 100, as amended by the Housing Act 1980 s 75(3).

[322] *Brown v Draper* [1944] KB 309, CA; *Middleton v Baldock* [1950] 1 KB 657 at 661–2, CA.

[323] Rent Act 1977 s 98(1) and Sch 15 Part I.   [324] Sch 15 Part II.

[325] Although, if the landlord proposes an increase in the rent, the tenant may refer the increase to a rent assessment committee, which must determine the appropriate market rent: Housing Act 1988 ss 13–14.

[326] Again, subject to the possibility of a review of any increase.   [327] Ibid, s 21.

[328] Section 21, as amended by Housing Act 1996 s 99.

Because it became clear that there was little advantage to landlords in granting assured, as opposed to shorthold, tenancies, and that accordingly most tenancies being granted were of the latter type, the Housing Act 1996 s 96 provides that, from 28 February 1997, a tenancy satisfying the criteria is presumed to be an assured shorthold tenancy, subject to certain exceptions.[329] In practice, assured tenancies are granted primarily by housing associations.

Like a regulated tenancy, either type of assured tenancy must be of a dwelling house let as a separate dwelling. The tenant (or each of joint tenants) must be an individual (and not a corporation) and the tenant, or at least one of joint tenants, must occupy the dwelling house as his only or principal home.[330] A tenant who leaves the premises temporarily will presumably continue to occupy them so long as he retains the corpus of possession and the intention of returning, but if during his absence his principal residence is elsewhere, the tenancy will cease to be assured even though he leaves someone else (other than his spouse or civil partner) in occupation. During his absence neither he nor the occupant can claim the benefit of security of tenure given by the Act (although if the tenancy is a contractual one, the landlord will be able to determine it only in accordance with the terms of the lease). Occupation by a spouse or civil partner with home rights is to be treated as that of the other.[331] The tenancy presumably remains assured if a sole tenant moves out leaving his or her spouse or civil partner in occupation, at least so long as the dwelling house remains the latter's only or principal home.

2 PUBLIC SECTOR TENANCIES

Tenants of premises let by various public authorities formerly lacked security from eviction, but the gap was largely closed by the provisions of the Housing Act 1980, now consolidated in the Housing Act 1985, which created a new concept, that of the 'secure tenancy', under which the landlord may only gain possession by order of the court on proof of various statutory grounds.

(a) Secure tenancies under the Housing Act 1985

A secure tenancy arises (subject to the grant of an introductory tenancy, discussed below) whenever the landlord is a local authority or one of certain other public bodies[332] and the tenant is an individual occupying the dwelling house as his only or principal home (or, in the case of joint tenants, each of them is an individual and at least one of them satisfies this condition).[333] Where the secure tenancy is for a fixed-term, on expiry of the term a 'periodic secure tenancy' will automatically arise unless the landlord grants a fresh fixed term or

---

[329] Housing Act 1988 s 19A and Sch 2A. The most notable are where there is express provision in the tenancy to the contrary, and where local authority tenancies (which had 'secure tenancy' status, discussed below) have been transferred to the private sector, in which case the tenants are assured tenants of the new landlord.

[330] Housing Act 1988 s 1 and Sch 1. For accommodation partly shared with persons other than the landlord and the effect of subletting part of the premises, see ss 3–4.

[331] Family Law Act 1996 s 30(4)(b) as amended.

[332] But not housing associations, which may only grant assured tenancies: Housing Act 1985 s 80(1) as amended.

[333] Ibid, s 81 as amended.

other periodic tenancy.[334] Thus, the tenant has the same kind of protection from eviction as a protected or assured tenant in the private sector.

Since public authority housing policies could be frustrated if the tenant could assign the tenancy to anyone he chose, there are restrictions on such assignment. Any purported assignment of a secure tenancy will be ineffective unless it is made:

(a) by way of exchange with another secure or an assured tenant;[335]

(b) in pursuance of a property adjustment order made under s 24 of the Matrimonial Causes Act 1973, s 17 of the Matrimonial and Family Proceedings Act 1984 (property adjustment order after overseas divorce) or Sched 1 para 1 to the Children Act 1989;[336] or

(c) to a person who could have been a qualified successor had the tenant died immediately before the assignment.[337]

The tenancy will cease to be a secure tenancy if the tenant parts with possession of the dwelling house or sublets the whole of it or if it is vested or disposed of in the course of the administration of a deceased tenant's estate. Unless the tenancy passes to a qualified successor, once it has ceased to be a secure tenancy, it cannot become one again.[338] The provisions of the Act apply equally to a person occupying a dwelling house as a licensee if he would have had a secure tenancy had his licence been a lease.[339]

Recovery of possession

The landlord can bring a secure tenancy to an end only by obtaining an order for possession, and the court cannot make such an order unless certain conditions are fulfilled. There are 18 grounds on which an order can be made. The first eight of these, including non-payment of rent or other breach of covenant, and domestic violence by the tenant or the tenant's partner,[340] are 'discretionary' grounds, in that the court must find it reasonable to make the order for possession in addition to being satisfied that the ground has been proved. Grounds 9 to 11, which include overcrowding and the need of the landlord to redevelop the property, are 'mandatory' grounds where, if the landlord also proves that suitable alternative accommodation will be available to the tenant and his family, possession must be ordered once the ground has been established. The remaining grounds, which apply, for example, where the property was let to the tenant in consequence of his employment, require the court to be satisfied as to *both* the reasonableness of making the order, *and* the availability of alternative accommodation.[341] The House of Lords has held that courts determining a possession claim may assume that domestic law on the issue is compatible with Art 8 of the European Convention on Human Rights and that the

---

[334] Ibid, s 86(1).   [335] Ibid, s 91(3)(a).

[336] Section 91(3)(b). The court may consider the authority's housing policy when deciding whether to make the order: *Jones v Jones* [1997] 1 FLR 27, CA. It is unclear why no reference is made to the possibility of transfer being ordered under the Family Law Act 1996 Sch 7.

[337] Section 91(3)(c); *Camden London Borough Council v Goldenberg* [1997] 1 FLR 556, CA; see below p 1104.

[338] Housing Act 1985 ss 90–93 as amended.   [339] Section 79(3).

[340] Added (as Ground 2A) by the Housing Act 1996 s 147(1).

[341] Housing Act 1985 s 84(2) and Sch 2.

landlord has acted compatibly with the Convention rights of the occupier in deciding to enforce possession. It is then up to the occupier to claim and establish that enforcing possession would be incompatible with his Convention rights, and the majority of the House considered that this could not be done by reference to the occupier's personal circumstances alone.[342]

As with a protected or assured tenant, the secure tenant may terminate the tenancy by notice to quit or surrender.[343]

Right to buy

As valuable as his security of tenure is the secure tenant's 'right to buy' his property from the landlord. This right was granted to 'council tenants' by the Thatcher government of the 1980s as one of its most significant pieces of social engineering, with the aim of bringing about a full 'property-owning democracy'. Not only can the tenant buy the property and thus deplete the local authority's housing stock, but he may do so at a highly preferential price. The Housing Act 1985 Part V provides that the right is to buy the freehold in the case of a house, and a long lease in respect of a flat. The secure tenant (or his or her spouse) must have resided in the property for two years.[344] The price at which the property is bought is fixed according to the open market value (not including inter alia the fact that the tenant is in occupation, and the value of any improvements he may have made), subject to a discount ranging, according to the length of time the tenant has resided in the property, from 32 to 60% (in the case of a house) or from 44 to 70% (in the case of a flat).[345]

If the tenant sells the property within three years, he is required to repay a proportion or all of the discount, depending upon the period elapsed since he acquired the property.[346] This caused problems in the past in the event of a divorce. In *R v Rushmoor Borough Council, ex p Barrett*,[347] it was held that an order for sale made under s 24A of the Matrimonial Causes Act 1973[348] attracted the operation of this penalty, whereas a property adjustment order made under s 24 was exempt within s 160 of the Housing Act. This was obviously anomalous, and s 24A was added to the list of exempt disposals by the Housing Act 1996.[349]

Introductory tenancies

To enable local authorities to deal more easily with antisocial tenants, Part V of the Housing Act 1996 also permits such authorities to grant new tenants (or licensees) a special introductory tenancy to operate as a 'trial run' for one year. The landlord may seek possession within the year without proof of grounds (although a court order is still necessary), although notice of the reasons for such possession must be given to the tenant, who may seek a review.[350] If the tenant survives the trial period, the tenancy is automatically converted into a secure tenancy.

---

[342] See *Lambeth London Borough Council and another v Kay and others; Price and others v Leeds City Council* [2006] UKHL 10, [2006] 2 FCR 20, in which the House considered that its earlier judgment in *Harrow London Borough Council v Qazi* [2003] UKHL 43 [2004] 1 AC 983, where the majority held that possession proceedings could not be defended by reference to Art 8, was irreconcilable with the later ECtHR judgment in *Connors v United Kingdom* (2004) 40 EHRR 189 and required modification.

[343] Section 79 and s 81.   [344] Section 119.

[345] Sections 126–9.   [346] Section 155.   [347] [1988] 2 All ER 268, CA.

[348] See below.   [349] Section 222, Sch 18 para 15(3).   [350] Housing Act 1996 s 129.

F THE POSITION OF THE SEPARATED SPOUSE OR PARTNER [351]

If the spouse or civil partner of a tenant remains in the family home after the couple separate and continues to pay the rent herself, a number of legal consequences follow. The payment of rent by the person in occupation who has home rights under the Family Law Act 1996 is as good as if made by the tenant.[352] If the landlord is unaware of the separation and assumes that the tenant is still in personal occupation of the premises, he will regard the spouse or partner as the tenant's agent and the lease will still be vested in the tenant. If the landlord is aware that the tenant has left but continues to take the rent from the spouse or partner, it is a question of fact whether he treats her as the tenant's agent (in which case he will remain the legal tenant) or whether he has accepted her as a new tenant (in which case she will become a new contractual tenant).[353] The fact that the landlord accepts rent from the person remaining, with full knowledge of the facts, is not per se evidence of his having granted her a new lease, for he cannot automatically evict her and consequently has no alternative to taking the rent from her.[354] But if no new tenancy is brought into existence, the original tenant continues to hold under the old tenancy.

Where the property is held on a joint tenancy, any one of the tenants may serve a notice to quit in order to bring the contractual tenancy to an end before the term expires, but the consent of all is required to continue a periodic tenancy. Consequently if the couple are joint tenants and one of them indicates to the landlord that he or she does not intend to renew the tenancy at the end of the current period, the other will lose her or his protection on expiry of the tenancy.[355] The same position applies where the spouse or civil partner is a sole tenant who surrenders the lease.[356] However, pending actual termination, the spouse or partner retains her home rights as against the other partner, which may give her some short-term relief.[357]

---

[351] See C Hunter and S Blandy, 'Relationship breakdown, women and tenants' rights—choice or paternalism' [2004] CFLQ 165; M Davis and D Hughes, 'An End of the Affair—Social Housing, Relationship Breakdown, and the Human Rights Act 1998' [2004] Conv 19.

[352] Family Law Act 1996 s 30(3).

[353] Social landlords (local authorities and housing associations, etc) are guided by DETR, *Relationship Breakdown: A Guide for Social Landlords* (1999). See also *R (Bibi) v Camden London Borough Council* 2004] EWHC 2527 (Admin), [2005] 1 FLR 413: local authority, in considering whether to allocate a new tenancy to a separated parent, should take into account (though is not bound by) any shared residence order that has been made and not assume that children are to have their main residence with one parent only. Cf ODPM, *Homelessness Code of Guidance for Local Authorities* (2002) para 8.10 which seems to assume that shared residence is 'very exceptional'.

[354] See *Morrison v Jacobs* [1945] KB 577, CA. A public sector landlord is under no obligation to offer the remaining partner a tenancy under human rights law: *Royal Borough of Kensington and Chelsea v O'Sullivan* [2003] EWCA Civ 371, [2003] 2 FLR 459.

[355] *Hammersmith and Fulham London Borough Council v Monk* [1992] 1 AC 478, HL. For the view that such an outcome may infringe the occupant's human rights, see I Loveland, 'Rethinking the rule in *Hammersmith and Fulham London Borough Council v Monk*: A Human Rights Perspective' (2002) 3 EHRLR 327, but this argument was rejected by the House of Lords in *Harrow v London Borough Council v Qazi* [2003] UKHL 43 [2004] 1 AC 983. An alternative device may be to convert the tenancy into a sole one via a deed of release: *Burton v Camden London Borough Council* [1998] 1 FLR 681, CA.

[356] *Sanctuary Housing Assocation v Campbell* [1999] 2 FLR 383, CA.

[357] *Moore v Moore* [2004] EWCA Civ 1243 [2005] 1 FLR 666.

(a) Transfer of tenancies on divorce, dissolution, nullity and separation

If the marriage or civil partnership ends, the tenant's spouse or civil partner will lose his or her home rights given by the Family Law Act 1996 and consequently could be evicted.[358] To meet this difficulty, the court granting a decree of divorce, nullity or judicial separation, in the case of marriage, or an order for separation, nullity or dissolution, in the case of a civil partnership, may make an order transferring the tenancy to the tenant's spouse or civil partner.[359] The transfer order may not take effect before the decree of nullity or divorce is made absolute.[360] An application may not be made if the applicant has remarried or formed a(nother) civil partnership.[361]

The tenancy must still be in existence when the application for a transfer is made. Consequently, if the tenant (who we will assume is the husband) leaves the premises and gives notice to quit after a divorce decree has been made absolute, the wife cannot apply for a transfer, since her occupation is no longer attributed to her former husband and he has effectively terminated the tenancy.[362]

The Family Law Act 1996 sets out guidelines to which the court must have regard when deciding whether to order a transfer.[363] The court must consider the circumstances in which the tenancy was granted to either or both parties, or the circumstances in which either or both became a tenant under the tenancy. It must also take into account the respective housing needs and resources of the parties and any relevant child,[364] the parties' financial resources, the likely effect of transferring or not transferring the tenancy on the health, safety or well-being of the parties and any relevant child, and the suitability of the parties as tenants.[365] The Law Commission, on whose recommendations these provisions are based,[366] drew an analogy with the case law governing orders for sale of property under what is now the Trusts of Land and Appointment of Trustees Act 1996 ss 14–15[367] and it has been suggested that where the purpose of acquiring the tenancy was to provide a home for the parties and their children, the court might be disposed to transfer the tenancy to the spouse looking after the children.[368]

---

[358] While an occupation order under s 33(5)(b) or s 33(10) may provide for these rights to continue after termination of the marriage, it would seem, by analogy with *Harrow v London Borough Council v Johnstone* [1997] 1 WLR 459, HL (discussed below p 255) that this does not prevent the tenant from giving a lawful and effective notice to quit, thus bringing the tenancy to an end. See Law Com Consultation Paper No 168, *Renting Homes 2: Co-occupation, Transfer and Succession* (2002) paras 3.65–3.68.

[359] Family Law Act s 53 and Sch 7 as amended by the Civil Partnership Act 2004 Sch 9. The landlord must be given an opportunity of being heard: 1996 Act Sch 7, para 14(1). Orders for transfer of tenancies other than *statutory* tenancies may be made under s 24 of the Matrimonial Causes Act 1973 (see eg *Jones v Jones* [1997] 1 FLR 27, CA and the discussion below p 1003) and under Sch 1 to the Children Act 1989, discussed below p 971; for the advantages of using Sch 7 rather than these alternatives, see M Horton, *Family Homes and Domestic Violence: The New Legislation* (1996) pp 219–220.

[360] Or the order is made final, in the case of nullity or dissolution of a civil partnership: Family Law Act 1996 Sch 7 para 12(a)(b) as amended by the Civil Partnership Act 2004 Sch 9 para 17.

[361] Sch 7, para 13 as amended by the 2004 Act Sch 9 para 18.

[362] *Lewis v Lewis* [1985] AC 828, HL.   [363] Sch 7, para 5.

[364] Defined by s 63(2) as a child who is living with, or who might reasonably be expected to live with either party to the proceedings; or whose welfare is in question in Children Act or Adoption Act proceedings, or whose interests the court considers relevant.

[365] Section 33(6)(a)–(c) and Sch 7, para 5(c). Conduct may also be considered: *Re H (A Child)*, 20 July 2006 (unreported), CA.

[366] Law Com No 207, *Domestic Violence and Occupation of the Family Home* (1992) paras 6.3–6.9.

[367] Discussed above p 173.   [368] Horton, op cit, p 221.

A transfer takes effect as a compulsory assignment, and the transferee takes subject to all the benefits and burdens of the covenants and the transferor ceases to be liable under them,[369] in the absence of a court order directing otherwise.[370] In the case of a statutory tenancy the transferee becomes the statutory tenant in place of the transferor. If the spouses are joint tenants, the court has a similar power to extinguish the interest of one of them and vest the tenancy exclusively in the other.[371]

The Family Law Act gave an additional power to the court to order the applicant to pay either immediate, or deferred, compensation to the transferor of the tenancy, by lump sum or instalments. This is a potentially far-reaching provision, although the Law Commission did not consider such orders to be very likely.[372] In deciding whether to exercise the power to make an order for compensation, the court must have regard to all the circumstances, including the financial loss that would otherwise be suffered by the transferor, the financial needs and resources of the parties, and their present and future financial obligations to each other and any relevant child.[373] The matters which might be relevant could range from the payment of removal expenses, to the transferor's loss of his right to buy in respect of a secure tenancy.

(b) Unmarried cohabitants

Until the enactment of Sch 7 to the Family Law Act 1996, the special position of the spouse (and now civil partner) under the legislation we have been considering was not shared by the tenant's unmarried partner. If unmarried cohabitants are joint tenants, obviously each will be able to claim the benefits of security afforded to the tenant, but, as we have seen, if the tenancy is a periodic one, a notice to quit by one tenant determines the tenancy of both at the end of the current period,[374] although a deed of release may convert the tenancy into a sole one.[375] If one of them (say, the man) is the sole tenant and he temporarily leaves the premises with the intention of returning, the occupation of the other will enable the tenant to continue to enjoy the protection given by the various Acts (just as the occupation of a relative would) provided that, if he is an assured or secure tenant, he does not in the meantime establish his principal home elsewhere. If, on the other hand, he leaves perman-ently, his partner's occupation will not be attributed to him, so she will not have security of tenure: the landlord can terminate the lease, as the premises will no longer be the tenant's home.

If the tenancy is secure, a cohabitant's position is stronger in one respect than if it were in the private sector: as she could be a qualified successor on the tenant's death, the latter can assign his tenancy to her so as to make her a secure tenant, provided that he does so while they are still living together.[376] Otherwise, if she wishes to remain on the premises,

---

369 Family Law Act 1996 Sch 7, para 7(1)–(2).   370 Family Law Act 1996 Sch 7, para 11.
371 Family Law Act 1996 Sch 7, para 8(1)–(2).   372 Law Com, op cit, paras 6.10–6.11.
373 Sch 7, para 10(4).
374 *Hammersmith and Fulham London Borough Council v Monk* [1992] 1 AC 478, HL.
375 *Burton v Camden London Borough Council* [1998] 1 FLR 681, CA.
376 Section 91(3)(c), s 87 and s 113(1). Same-sex cohabitants could be included within this protection, either by application of the ruling of the House of Lords in *Ghaidan v Godin-Mendoza* [2004] UKHL 30 [2004] 2 AC 557 (reading the reference in s 113(1) to persons living together as husband and wife to include same-sex partners) or, under the Civil Partnership Act 2004 Sch 8 para 27, which amends s 113(1) so as to refer to persons living together as if they were civil partners.

she must try to persuade the landlord to terminate the lease and grant her a fresh tenancy, or, if a joint tenant, obtain a deed of release to convert the tenancy into a sole one. Alternatively, she can try to take advantage of the provisions of Sch 7 to the Family Law Act 1996.

Transfer of tenancies under Family Law Act 1996 Sch 7

Notwithstanding concerns in Parliament that the extension of protection to cohabitants under Part IV of the Family Law Act 1996[377] might undermine the institution of marriage, it appears to have been happy with, or to have failed to take notice of, a highly significant step on the way towards equalising the position of married and unmarried couples. The power under Sch 7 to transfer tenancies, which we discussed above, applies to cohabitants (and former cohabitants)[378] as well as to spouses and former spouses, civil partners and former civil partners.

Cohabitants are defined, by s 62(1),[379] as

'two persons who are neither married to each other nor civil partners of each other but are living together as husband and wife or as if they were civil partners'.

The court may make an order to transfer the tenancy of the dwelling-house in which the couple cohabited, when they have ceased living together.[380] When deciding whether to make an order, the court must have regard, where only one of the cohabitants was entitled to occupy the property,[381] in addition to the matters noted in respect of spouses or civil partners,[382] to the following factors:

— the nature of the parties' relationship, and in particular the level of commitment involved in it;

— the length of time they cohabited;

— whether they have had any children together, or have had parental responsibility for any children; and

— the length of time since they ceased to cohabit.[383]

The court may also exercise its powers, noted above, to adjust the parties' liabilities in respect of the tenancy and to order the transferee to compensate the transferring tenant. Unlike former spouses, a former cohabitant may apply even after he or she has married or begun to cohabit with someone else, although this will clearly be a factor the court will take into account when determining whether to make the order.

How far the courts are prepared to make these orders in respect of cohabitants is not known. If they do in fact show a willingness to do so in appropriate cases (presumably where the couple lived together for a long time, and perhaps more likely where they were

---

[377] See below, pp 234–8.   [378] Sch 7, para 1.

[379] As amended by Civil Partnership Act 2004 Sch 9 para 13. Prior to that Act entering into force, the relevant definition was 'two persons who, although not married to each other, are living together as husband and wife or (if of the same sex) in an equivalent relationship;' as inserted by s 3 of the Domestic Violence, Crime and Victims Act 2004.

[380] Sch 7, paras 3(2), 4(b). A transfer cannot be made where the tenancy is held jointly by the entitled cohabitant and a third party: *Gay v Sheeran* [1999] 2 FLR 519, CA.

[381] See below p 234.   [382] Above p 204.

[383] Section 36(6)(e)–(h), as amended, discussed below p 236.

joint tenants), it may well be asked why there is no equivalent power to make a transfer order in respect of owner-occupied property.[384] Of course, as the discussion throughout this chapter will have demonstrated, should that development be enacted, the whole law of family property will have been fundamentally realigned.

---

[384] See the comment by M Hayes in her written evidence to the House of Lords Special Public Bill Committee, Session 1994–95 HL 55, p 37.

5

DOMESTIC VIOLENCE

A INTRODUCTION

This chapter deals with the legal responses to a variety of forms of personal behaviour within the domestic sphere which may amount to physical or emotional abuse. 'Domestic violence' is a term that can be criticised, as it appears to signify a concern purely with violent behaviour.[1] However, the law has gradually widened its recognition of the range of behaviour encompassed within the term, and of the range of relationships which ought to be classed as 'domestic'. The Home Office defines domestic violence as:

'Any violence between current and former partners in an intimate relationship, wherever and whenever the violence occurs. The violence may include physical, sexual, emotional and financial abuse.'[2]

It is now understood that infliction of violence is not restricted to spousal relationships but may involve cohabitants and others;[3] while unacceptable behaviour may include not just acts of violence but also acts of harassment, or pestering and unwanted attentions (now sometimes referred to, in extreme cases, as 'stalking'), or sometimes even simply the unpleasantness associated with the breakdown of a close relationship.[4] At the same time, there has also been a growing recognition that violence is not to be excused, just because it takes place between family members, and that it may amount to criminal offences ranging from the minor to the most serious.

It is difficult to estimate the scale of domestic violence or abuse with any confidence. The British Crime Survey found that around four per cent of men and women reported that they had been physically assaulted by a current or former partner in the previous year; women were twice as likely as men to have been injured, and three times as likely to have suffered frightening threats. They were also more likely to have been assaulted three or

---

[1] For discussion of the difficulties with this terminology, see L Smith *Domestic Violence: an overview of the literature* Home Office Research Study No 107 (1989) ch 1.

[2] Home Office, *Safety and Justice: The Government's Proposals on Domestic Violence* (2003) Cm 5487 at para 7. Yet even within government, there are different working definitions: see the discussion by HM Inspectorate of Constabularies and HM Inspectorate of the Crown Prosecution Service, *Violence at Home* (2004) paras 1.9–1.14, who recommend a common definition be adopted.

[3] Children may also be the victims, and indeed, there is a strong correlation between abuse of an adult and abuse of the child (see H Davidson 'Child Abuse and Domestic Violence: Legal Connections and Controversies' (1995) 29 Fam LQ 357), but this chapter is confined to consideration of adult relationships. Mechanisms expressly designed to deal with violence against children are discussed in Chapter 14.

[4] For the range of behaviour and criminal offences which may be involved, see Crown Prosecution Service, *Policy on Domestic Violence* (2001) Annex A.

more times. When asked if they had *ever* been physically assaulted by a current or former partner, 23% of women, and 15% of men aged 16 to 59 reported that they had been. 30% of domestic violence is estimated to start during a woman's pregnancy, and existing violence often escalates during it.[5] The period after a couple have separated is a particularly vulnerable time for women, with 22% of separated women reporting having been assaulted in the previous year.[6] Around two women per week are killed by their partners or ex-partners in the UK, and around 42% of the total number of murdered women, are killed by a partner or ex-partner.[7] Yet non-reporting of domestic violence is a particular problem: it has been estimated that the average victim will undergo 35 or more assaults, over a seven-year period, before approaching the police or another domestic violence agency, for help.[8]

The range of legal mechanisms used to control the perpetrator's behaviour and provide effective protection for the victim may go well beyond the traditional criminal responses normally associated with the terms 'violence' or 'abuse'. In particular, the use of the civil law, to control personal behaviour or the occupation of the family home, or the use of public law through the provision of alternative accommodation for the family or individual family members, have been seen as being potentially more helpful to the victims than reliance on penal sanctions. However, this approach has been challenged in recent years, with a renewed emphasis in government policy on the issue on viewing domestic abuse as a criminal matter.[9] In this chapter, we begin with a brief summary of the legal history, then consider the remedies offered by the criminal law, the civil law, and housing law.

1 HISTORICAL DEVELOPMENTS

Violence in the home is a phenomenon long recognised by legal commentators. Although Hale had denied that a husband had a legal power to administer corporal punishment to his wife,[10] it was stated in Bacon's *Abridgment* in 1736 that a husband might beat his wife (but not in a violent or cruel manner) and confine her.[11] Blackstone, writing some 30 years later, maintained that, whilst the practice had become obsolete in polite society, 'the lower rank of people, who were always fond of the old common law, still claim and exert their ancient privilege'.[12] Little was heard of the problem for another century until Parliament

---

[5] Home Office, op cit para 23.

[6] C Mirrlees-Black and C Byron, *Domestic Violence: Findings from the BCS Self-Completion Questionnaire: Research Findings No 86* (1999) Home Office Research, Development and Statistics Directorate. See also C Humphreys and R Thiara, 'Neither justice nor protection: women's experiences of post-separation violence' (2003) 25, 3, JSWFL 195.

[7] C Flood-Page and J Taylor (eds), *Crime in England and Wales 2001/2002: Supplementary Volume* (2003) Home Office p 12.

[8] T Hall and S Wright, *Making it count: A practical guide to collecting and managing domestic violence data* (2003) NACRO.

[9] For the view that human rights law should be used as a means of compelling state action to protect those harmed by domestic violence, see S Choudhry and J Herring, 'Righting Domestic Violence' (2006) 29 Int Jo of Law, Policy and the Family 95.

[10] *Lord Leigh's Case* (1674) 3 Keb 433, where he said that *castigatio* meant no more than admonition and confinement.

[11] Tit Baron and Feme (B).   [12] *Commentaries* i 455.

intervened in 1878 following a campaign drawing attention to the brutal treatment of many working-class women.[13] The Matrimonial Causes Act 1878 gave a criminal court, before which a man was convicted of aggravated assault on his wife, the power to make a separation and maintenance order in her favour and to vest in her the legal custody of the children of the marriage under the age of 10 years if it felt that her future safety was in peril.[14]

Almost another 100 years passed before the question again became one of public concern. Publicity was generated by the setting up of women's aid refuges[15] to which women and their children could flee from violence, and the feminist movement lobbied for action. A Select Committee of the House of Commons heavily criticised the effectiveness of the existing remedies open to women who were the victims of violence at the hands of their husbands or the men with whom they were cohabiting.[16] At that time, remedies were limited to taking criminal proceedings or to pursuing civil actions (eg for damages in tort for a battery, or to assert a property right in the home), and seeking to have an injunction attached, under which the respondent was enjoined from 'molesting, assaulting or otherwise interfering with' the applicant and/or any children. It was also possible during the course of divorce or other matrimonial or family proceedings between the parties, to apply for an injunction to require a party to leave the matrimonial home or let the applicant back in. However, it was considered that it was unduly burdensome to require an applicant to take substantive proceedings when she really only wanted the injunction, and accordingly it was provided in the Domestic Violence and Matrimonial Proceedings Act 1976 that a spouse or cohabitant could seek a non-molestation or ouster injunction from the county court without having to take any other proceedings. Magistrates were subsequently given similar powers by the Domestic Proceedings and Magistrates' Courts Act 1978 to make 'personal protection' and 'exclusion orders', although only in respect of physical violence inflicted by a spouse.[17]

Notwithstanding these express statutory provisions, it continued to be common for a party to seek an injunction, especially to exclude the other party from the home, during divorce or other proceedings relating to the children. However, in 1983, Lord Brandon, delivering the leading speech in the House of Lords in *Richards v Richards*,[18] pointed out

[13] See Frances Power Cobbe *Wife Torture in England* (1878); and for modern examinations of the Victorian response, see A James Hammerton *Cruelty and Companionship: Conflict in Nineteenth-Century Married Life* (1992), M Doggett *Marriage, Wife-Beating and the Law in Victorian England* (1992). See also S Cretney, *Family Law in the Twentieth Century: A History* (2003) pp 752–6.

[14] Section 4.

[15] Particularly by Erin Pizzey in Chiswick. See her *Scream Quietly or the Neighbours will Hear* (1974). See also M Borkowski, M Murch and V Walker *Marital Violence* (1983). It has been argued that from 1948 to 1966, 'an unrecognised and hidden refuge for women and children from violent men' was provided by the power of local authorities to provide emergency accommodation to homeless families under Part III of the National Assistance Act 1948. When government policy was widened in 1966 (after the famous 'Cathy Come Home' television drama had highlighted the break-up of families due to the lack of accommodation) to include husbands within the category of those eligible for assistance, this refuge was lost: R Morley and G Pascall 'Women and homelessness: proposals from the Department of the Environment Part II, Domestic Violence' (1996) 18 JSWFL 327 at 328.

[16] See the *Report of the Select Committee on Violence in Marriage* HC 553 (1974–75) and on *Violence in the Family* HC 329 (1976–77).

[17] Sections 16–18, following the recommendations of the Law Commission in Law Com No 77, *Report on Matrimonial Proceedings in Magistrates' Courts.*

[18] [1984] AC 174, HL.

that a spouse with statutory rights of occupation of the matrimonial home given under the Matrimonial Homes Act 1967 (later consolidated in the 1983 Act of the same name)[19] could not be evicted or excluded from the matrimonial home by the other except with the leave of the court *given by an order under that Act.* He added that it must follow that the owner of the property could be evicted only under a like order, and presumably the same argument would apply if both had a legal estate in the land. Consequently, if the parties were married, an ouster injunction could be granted only in proceedings taken under that Act or under the Domestic Violence and Matrimonial Proceedings Act 1976. After this decision, it could be said that the civil law relating to protection and control of occupation of the home was contained in three statutory jurisdictions, each governed by different rules and criteria—the Domestic Violence and Matrimonial Proceedings Act 1976 which applied to both married and cohabiting couples, the Domestic Proceedings and Magistrates' Courts Act 1978 and the Matrimonial Homes Act 1983, which each applied only to spouses—and a residual jurisdiction, through the Supreme Court Act 1981 s 37 and the County Courts Act 1984 s 38 or under the court's inherent powers, to grant an injunction to any applicant as an adjunct to substantive proceedings.

2 PROPOSALS FOR REFORM

In *Richards v Richards* Lord Scarman observed:[20]

'The statutory provision is a hotchpotch of enactments of limited scope passed into law to meet specific situations or to strengthen the powers of specified courts. The sooner the range, scope and effect of these powers are rationalised into a coherent and comprehensive body of statute law, the better.'

The invitation to review the law was taken up by a number of bodies, who also took the opportunity to review services and policy. 'Victim Support' convened an inter-agency working party to review the type and extent of service provision available to the victims of domestic violence. It reported in 1992, and regarded the provision of refuges, and a greater emphasis upon tackling violence through the criminal justice system as the keys to improved protection.[21] The Home Affairs Committee of the House of Commons also conducted an inquiry into the scale of the problem of domestic violence, and the responses to it. They produced no radically new proposals, concentrating upon the promotion of greater public awareness of the problem, and, as had Victim Support, upon heightening official commitment to existing remedies such as the provision of refuges and initiatives in the criminal justice system.[22]

(a) The Law Commission proposals

The Law Commission examined the civil law.[23] They identified a number of inconsistencies and anomalies: the scope of the remedies offered by the various courts differed; the criteria they applied in exercising their discretion when deciding whether to make an

---

[19] See above p 185.   [20] [1984] AC 174 at 206–7, HL.

[21] Victim Support, *Domestic Violence: Report of a National Inter-Agency Working Party* (1992).

[22] Home Affairs Committee, *Third Report Domestic Violence* HC 245 (1993).

[23] *Report on Domestic Violence and Occupation of the Family Home*, Law Com No 207, 1992, following Law Com Working Paper No 113 *Domestic Violence and Occupation of the Matrimonial Home.*

ouster order were outdated and failed to take account of the different situations with which the courts have to deal; no protection was given to former cohabitants and others falling outside specific categories of applicant, except for the often inadequate remedies offered by the law of torts; and the courts had no means of adjusting cohabitants' rights of occupation apart from their limited powers under the Domestic Violence and Matrimonial Proceedings Act. The aim of the Law Commission's proposals for reform was threefold. First, to remove these gaps, anomalies and inconsistencies from the law; secondly, to provide at least as much protection to victims as was currently available; and thirdly, to seek to minimise hostilities between the adults.[24] The Commission proposed revising the existing law to give all courts the same powers to make orders, and in respect of a wider range of applicants who could be broadly described as associated with the respondent by virtue of a family or similar relationship. They also proposed altering the criteria upon which orders were to be granted. There was a particular problem concerning the grant of

ouster injunctions, because, since *Richards v Richards*, courts considering whether to issue such an injunction had been required to apply the criteria laid down in s 1(3) of the Matrimonial Homes Act 1983, under which the court had to have regard to:

'. . . the conduct of the spouses in relation to each other and otherwise, to their respective needs and financial resources, to the needs of any children and to all the circumstances of the case.'

This focused the court's attention as much upon the reasonableness of the respondent's conduct as upon the needs of the applicant and children, and led courts to regard ousters as 'Draconian' orders,[25] not to be made lightly. The effect was to place the dominant emphasis upon the parties' conduct, and to reduce the significance of the effects felt by the victims.[26] The Commission considered that courts should be encouraged to make ouster orders more readily.

The Conservative Government, intending to implement most of the Law Commission's proposals, duly introduced these, in the Family Homes and Domestic Violence Bill, into the House of Lords, under a procedure intended to speed up the legislative process in respect of 'uncontroversial' law reform measures based on the recommendations of the Law Commission.[27] However, although the Bill proceeded successfully through the upper Chamber, when it moved to the House of Commons, it was lost when a number of Conservative MPs opposed it, fearing that its provisions would undermine marriage by offering protection from violence and the ability to remain in the family home to unmarried couples.[28] With shortage of Parliamentary time, and a wish to avoid trouble with his own back benches, the Lord Chancellor withdrew the Bill 'to look again at the details'. The

---

[24] At para 1.2.

[25] *Summers v Summers* [1986] 1 FLR 343, CA; *Wiseman v Simpson* [1988] 1 All ER 245, CA.

[26] Some courts, however, were prepared to grant an order even though violence could not be proved: *Scott v Scott* [1992] 1 FLR 529, CA, *Khan v Khan* [1995] 2 FLR 221, CA.

[27] See *Family Homes and Domestic Violence Bill Proceedings of the Special Public Committee* (1994–95) HL Paper 55.

[28] While one might not be surprised at the ignorance of the editor and columnists of the Daily Mail who appear to have been unaware that cohabitants had been protected by the law for nearly twenty years under the Domestic Violence and Matrimonial Proceedings Act 1976, the equal ignorance of this fact by MPs might appear to be less excusable.

following session, it emerged as part of the Family Law Bill, and, with some changes, now forms Part IV of the Family Law Act 1996, which is discussed below.

(b) Stalking and harassment

Alongside these careful reviews of the existing law and practice, a concern to produce speedy legislation to deal with an apparently new problem, that of 'stalking', also produced more hurried reforms. 'Stalking' has been defined as:

'... a campaign of harassment or molestation of another, usually with an undertone of sexual attraction or infatuation.'[29]

During 1995 and 1996, a number of cases appeared in the media, from which it seemed that the criminal law[30] could not be used successfully to cope with such conduct, and calls were made to introduce new legislation to plug the gap. Eventually, after an unsuccessful attempt by a private member to introduce legislation, proposals were brought forward by the government,[31] resulting in the Protection from Harassment Act 1997, containing both civil and criminal powers.[32] The breadth of the provisions in this Act, and the vagueness of its language, are a stark contrast to the careful and detailed, not to say complex, provisions in Part IV of the Family Law Act 1996.

(c) 'Safety and Justice'

Further measures to tackle domestic violence were incorporated in a White Paper published in 2003, setting out the government's strategy on the issue. This strategy is based on 'prevention, protection and justice, and support.'[33] The first of these approaches—prevention—is aimed at changing public attitudes through information and education campaigns, so that domestic violence becomes unacceptable, providing help for victims as early as possible, ensuring that they have adequate advice and information on how to get access to support and legal protection,[34] and reducing re-offending. The second—protection and justice—seeks to build on initiatives taken by the police and Crown Prosecution Service (CPS) during the 1990s to tackle problems in the processing of domestic violence cases in the criminal justice system and to strengthen further the civil remedies available to victims. The final approach—support—is geared to improving access to safe accommodation and financial support on leaving a violent partner and on providing necessary support to children and young people affected by domestic violence.

Delivery of this strategy requires a multi-agency approach, utilising a range of services in both the statutory and voluntary sectors, including, of course, the police and CPS, health, housing and social services authorities, and organisations such as Victim Support and Women's Aid.[35] Work on creating such an approach had already begun with the

---

29 C Wells 'Stalking: The Criminal Law Response' [1997] Crim LR 463.

30 The civil law was also inadequate, due to the limitations noted at pp 211–12 above.

31 Home Office and Lord Chancellor's Department, Consultation Paper, *Stalking—The Solutions* (1996).

32 See T Lawson-Cruttenden and N Addison *Guide to the Protection from Harassment Act 1997* (1997).

33 Home Office, op cit para 19.

34 In a survey of 200 lone parents, R Moorhead et al found that domestic violence victims struggled to find appropriate advice and had to resort to numerous different services before getting help: *The Advice Needs of Lone Parents* pp 44–5.

35 See N Harwin, G Hague and E Malos (eds) *The Multi-Agency Approach to Domestic Violence: New Opportunities, Old Challenges* (1999).

establishment of local 'domestic violence fora' designed to co-ordinate the development of services, improve practice via training, support new projects to aid victims, raise awareness of domestic violence amongst the general public and set up preventative programmes in schools and for perpetrators. The Crime and Disorder Act 1998 also requires local author-ities and the police to form local crime and disorder reduction partnerships, which must address, inter alia, domestic violence in conducting local audits and developing strategies for tackling crime and disorder. Such partnerships may work with domestic violence fora where these have been established. All such bodies should have regard to guidance issued by the Home Office on responding to domestic violence.[36] As a further measure intended to promote and utilise multi-agency working, s 9 of the Domestic Violence, Crime and Victims Act 2004 provides for 'domestic homicide reviews'. These are to be held into the circumstances in which the death of a person aged 16 or over has, or appears to have, resulted from violence, abuse or neglect by a person to whom he was related or with whom he was or had been in an intimate personal relationship, or a member of the same household as himself, in order to identify the lessons to be learnt from the death. Those participating include police, local authorities, probation boards and health authorities and trusts. Such reviews mirror those carried out after the deaths of children in suspected child abuse and neglect cases.[37]

We discuss and evaluate the legal dimensions of this strategy below.

B PROTECTION AFFORDED BY THE CRIMINAL LAW [38]

1 PROBLEMS WITH THE CRIMINAL JUSTICE SYSTEM

A family member is in a similar legal position to any other person who may be prosecuted for assaulting another (whether for common assault or an assault occasioning actual bodily harm) or for committing one of the more serious offences of wounding, causing grievous bodily harm, rape (within or outside marriage)[39] or even attempted murder. In practice, however, the criminal law was little used by victims of domestic violence until recently. The reasons are numerous. First, there was a traditional reluctance by the police to become involved in a 'domestic' incident, partly because of a perception that the complainant would decline to press charges and so waste police time, and partly because of the strongly male, and sexist, 'canteen culture' which pervaded the police service.[40] Recognition of the seriousness of violence within the family led to an attempt by

---

[36] Home Office, *Domestic Violence: Breaking the Chain: Multi-Agency Guidance for Addressing Domestic Violence* (2003).

[37] See Chapter 14 below.

[38] See S Edwards, *Policing 'Domestic' Violence* (1989) ch 2 and *Sex and Gender in the Legal Process* (1996) ch 5; HM Inspectorate of Constabularies and HM Inspectorate of the Crown Prosecution Service, *Violence at Home* (2004).

[39] See above, p 112, and for consideration of the legality of the retrospective declaration that rape within marriage is a criminal offence, see P Gandhi and J James 'Marital rape and retrospectivity—the human rights dimensions at Strasbourg' (1997) 9 CFLQ 17.

[40] See S Edwards *Sex and Gender in the Legal Process* pp 196–8.

government to change this attitude by issuing a Home Office Circular in 1990 reminding police officers 'of their responsibility to respond as law enforcement officers to requests from victims for help, and of their powers to take action in cases of violence'.[41] A number of police services revised their policies in respect of domestic violence as a result of this circular, and several established Domestic Violence Units to provide a specialist service offering liaison between police and victims, advice to investigating officers, training in how to handle domestic violence incidents, and co-operation with other agencies in tackling the problem.[42] Continuing evidence that the police were still sometimes failing to arrest an attacker at the scene of the crime, or of failing to record a domestic incident as a crime, resulted in a revised Circular, issued in 2000, which, inter alia, created a presumption of arrest, requiring an officer to justify in writing any decision not to arrest.[43] The government also identified complexity in the grounds on which police officers may arrest for common assault, and uncertainty on their part as to whether they could arrest for this offence where they have not themselves witnessed it. The Police and Criminal Evidence Act 1984 was accordingly amended to add common assault to the list of offences arrestable without a warrant[44] but subsequently, the distinction between arrestable and non-arrestable offences was abolished anyway.[45]

Where police action is taken, the criminal justice system may still operate to deter or discourage victims from making a complaint. The Crown Prosecution Service, which must decide on whether to proceed with a charge, and on what offence to prosecute, has been accused of frequently discontinuing, or 'down criming' a charge,[46] thus reinforcing the perception that 'domestic' violence is regarded as less serious than other crime, and deterring victims from making complaints. Its policy was in turn revised in 2001, with an emphasis on seeking to overturn this perception, and domestic violence co-ordinators were appointed to handle domestic violence cases, identify and take forward strategic issues such as training, and work closely with domestic violence fora in their areas.

Yet a joint inspection[47] of current police and CPS practice in relation to domestic violence cases found that, in a study of 463 domestic violence incidents in six police forces, only 25% resulted in a crime being recorded. The basis for not recording incidents as

[41] Home Office Circular 60/1990, quoted in Home Affairs Committee Third Report, *Domestic Violence* HC 245 para 14.

[42] Ibid, paras 23–32, and see S Edwards *Sex and Gender in the Legal Process* pp 193–5.

[43] Home Office Circular 19/2000.

[44] Police and Criminal Evidence Act 1984 Sch 1A para 14A inserted by the Domestic Violence, Crime and Victims Act 2004 s 10. The police may also be confused as to their powers to arrest for a threatened breach of the peace: see *Foulkes v Chief Constable of Merseyside Police* [1999] 2 FLR 789 where the Court of Appeal found that a husband, excluded from his home after his wife changed the locks, was unlawfully arrested and detained when police arrived at the property and sought to remove him to prevent an altercation. Thorpe LJ, with whom Schiemann LJ agreed, considered that the breach of the peace regime is inappropriate to deal with domestic disputes and rights of occupation in the home, but this leaves the remaining occupant, who might fear what will happen if the police do not remove the excluded party, with no remedy other than to seek a civil order (see below) which may take some time.

[45] Serious Organised Crime and Police Act 2005 s 110.

[46] S Edwards *Sex and Gender in the Legal Process*, p 200–1; A Cretney and G Davis 'Prosecuting "Domestic" Assault' [1996] Crim LR 162.

[47] See HM Inspectorate of Constabularies and HM Inspectorate of the Crown Prosecution Service, *Violence at Home* (2004) Ch 6.

crimes was mainly because the victim withdrew the allegation or declined to provide a statement. In all, charges were made in 21% of recorded incidents but a number of cases were dropped by the CPS, either because of insufficient evidence or, more rarely, because it was not in the public interest to proceed. In a similar sample of 418 cases dealt with by the CPS, the prosecution dropped the case in 28% of cases, compared with a national discontinuance average of around 13%. Where cases proceeded to court, over three-quarters of defendants pleaded guilty, but those contesting charges were more likely to be acquitted than for other offences. Summing up the situation, at each stage in the criminal justice process, the Inspectorates found around a 50% drop out rate, with only 11% of domestic violence matters recorded as crimes resulting in a conviction.

It can be seen that the key factor influencing whether a case will proceed through the criminal justice process is the attitude of the victim.[48] Reluctance to give evidence against the perpetrator is hardly surprising. Where a prosecution is brought, the complainant may be placed under considerable emotional strain and may have good reason to fear reprisals if the accused is released on bail pending his trial or, in any case, after his ultimate release. Although an accused's spouse is a compellable witness for the prosecution in cases of assault and unmarried partners have always been compellable,[49] there were instances in the past of insensitive handling of victims who are too scared to testify. Attempts to support victims and witnesses have been enacted alongside attempts to promote greater sensitivity in both the police and CPS to handling witnesses' concerns.[50] Complainants may not always have to give oral testimony, since under s 23 of the Criminal Justice Act 1988 a statement made in a document by a person to a police officer may be admissible as evidence of any fact of which direct oral evidence by that person would be admissible, where the witness does not give oral evidence through fear. The court has a discretion whether to admit the statement, and must take account of the risk of unfairness to the accused in the lack of an opportunity to cross-examine the witness. This could provide a means of protecting a victim from some of the stress of giving evidence, but appears to have been rarely invoked by the prosecution in domestic violence cases.[51] Of greater significance, Part II, Chapter I of the Youth Justice and Criminal Evidence Act 1999 sets out 'special measures' that can be taken where the court is satisfied that the quality of evidence given by a witness is 'likely to be diminished by reason of fear or distress on the part of the witness in connection with testifying in the proceedings.' The measures that can be taken include enabling the witness to give evidence from behind a screen so that she cannot see the accused,[52] providing a live video link to give evidence from outside the court,[53] excluding persons (other than the accused and his representatives) from the court where it appears to the court that there are reasonable grounds for believing that the person will seek to intimidate the witness,[54] video-recording the witness's evidence in chief,[55] and enabling cross-examination also to take place by video-recording.[56] How

---

[48] See M Burton, 'Prosecution decisions in cases of domestic violence involving children' (2000) 22, 2, JSWFL 175 and L Ellison, 'Prosecuting Domestic Violence without Victim Participation' (2002) 65 MLR 834.

[49] Police and Criminal Evidence Act 1984 s 80, see above p 116.

[50] See CPS, *Policy on Prosecuting Cases of Domestic Violence* (2005).

[51] See S Edwards, *Reducing Domestic Violence . . . What Works? Use of the Criminal Law* (2000) Home Office Policing and Reducing Crime Unit.

[52] Section 23.   [53] Section 24.   [54] Section 25(4)(b).   [55] Section 27.

[56] Section 28 (not yet in force).

much use is made of these measures has yet to be made known but they could go a significant way in easing the stress on the witness of the court process. However, they do not address a victim's fear of the longer-term implications of prosecution for domestic violence—what will happen after the trial?

Even where a prosecution is successful, there remains the question of the appropriate sentence. In the past, it appeared that leniency was frequently shown to 'domestic' violence perpetrators. However, the Court of Appeal has reiterated that any such leniency is misplaced. For example, in *R v McNaughten*,[57] it stated that:

'. . . we must firmly emphasise that the seriousness of an incident of violence is not diminished merely because it takes place in a "domestic environment". Whenever and wherever it happens an offence of violence is an offence of violence.'

Yet there is research evidence to show that such cases are more likely to result in a non-custodial sentence or lighter sentence.[58] The matter is complex. Whilst a non-custodial sentence may leave the victim vulnerable to further abuse, imprisonment may be equally damaging, curtailing the perpetrator's income which may have supported the family, and, unless some form of treatment is available during his sentence, leaving him no better able to manage his behaviour than before. Final recommendations on the issue are currently awaited from the Sentencing Guidelines Panel.[59]

2 PROTECTION FROM HARASSMENT

During the 1990s, public recognition of 'harassment' as behaviour deserving of criminal sanction led to a number of initiatives to widen the ambit of existing offences,[60] and to create new offences designed expressly to deal with the problem.

(a) Extending the ambit of existing offences

A series of unwanted telephone calls during which the caller simply remained silent, but which put the recipients in immediate fear for their safety and caused them psychological injury, was held capable of amounting to assault occasioning actual bodily harm in *R v Ireland, R v Burstow*.[61] Such pestering by phone-calling is well-documented in the law reports as a form of harassment when a relationship has broken down,[62] and the precedent could therefore be used in an appropriate 'domestic' case. However, it should be noted that

---

[57] [2003] 2 Cr App R (S) 142.

[58] A Cretney and G Davis, 'Prosecuting Domestic Assault: Victims Failing Courts, or Courts Failing Victims?' (1997) 36 *The Howard Journal* 146; E Gilchrist and J Blissett, 'Magistrates' Attitudes to Domestic Violence and Sentencing Options', (2002) 41 *The Howard Journal* 348. But there may be good reasons for some disparity in approach, such as taking a wish by the victim and perpetrator to continue their relationship into account: see Sentencing Guidelines Panel, *Overarching Principles: Domestic Violence Consultation Guideline* (2006) Section D.

[59] Ibid.

[60] See the discussion by C Wells 'Stalking: The Criminal Law Response' [1997] Crim LR 463 at pp 465–9; T Lawson-Cruttenden 'Psychological assault and harassment' (1996) 146 NLJ 1326.

[61] [1998] AC 147, HL. See Gardner 'Stalking' (1998) 114 LQR 33.

[62] See, for example, *Khorasandjian v Bush* [1993] QB 727, CA (overruled as to the law by *Hunter and Others v Canary Wharf Ltd* [1997] AC 655, HL), *Johnson v Walton* [1990] 1 FLR 350, CA, *Smith v Smith* [1988] 1 FLR 179, CA.

the appellant had pleaded guilty, and it may be difficult to establish the apprehension of immediate personal violence required for the offence of assault.[63]

There are other, statutory, offences which might be relevant.[64] Section 4A of the Public Order Act 1986[65] makes it an offence if a person, with intent to cause harassment, alarm or distress, uses threatening, abusive or insulting words or behaviour thereby causing the victim harassment, alarm or distress. Section 1 of the Malicious Communications Act 1988[66] provides that it is an offence to send a letter, electronic communication or any article which conveys, inter alia, a threat, with the purpose of causing distress or anxiety to the recipient or to any other person to whom he intends that it or its contents or nature should be communicated. The sender has a defence if he can show that the threat was used to reinforce a demand made by him on reasonable grounds and that he believed, and had reasonable grounds for believing, that the use of the threat was a proper means of reinforcing the demand.[67] The difficulty of convicting under these provisions lies primarily in proving the appropriate mens rea on the part of the accused.

(b) The Protection from Harassment Act 1997

The Protection from Harassment Act 1997 is intended to overcome these problems. It is intended to apply primarily to 'stalkers',[68] who may often be strangers to the victim, but it is drafted in broad terms, and may be invoked by a spouse or partner, or by someone who falls outside the range of those covered by the Family Law Act 1996 Part IV, discussed below. The Act contains both criminal and civil law provisions. The former are dealt with here, and the latter below.[69]

Harassment

Section 1 of the Act provides that:

'(1) A person must not pursue a course of conduct—

    (a) which amounts to harassment of another; and

    (b) which he knows or ought to know amounts to harassment of the other.

(2) For the purposes of this section, the person whose course of conduct is in question ought to know that it amounts to harassment of another if a reasonable person in possession of the same information would think the course of conduct amounted to harassment of the other.'

Although the Act does not define harassment, s 7(2) provides that 'references to harassing a person include alarming the person or causing the person distress'. It also provides that

---

[63] Where psychiatric illness is the injury complained of as a result of an assault, psychiatric evidence must be produced to establish the causal link: *R v Morris* [1998] 1 Cr App Rep 386, CA.

[64] For a full survey of 'threats' offences, some of which would be applicable to the domestic sphere, see P Alldridge 'Threats Offences—A Case for Reform' [1994] Crim LR 176.

[65] Inserted by Criminal Justice and Public Order Act 1994 s 154. The offence is punishable by up to six months' imprisonment and/or a fine not exceeding level 5 of the standard scale.

[66] As amended by the Criminal Justice and Police Act 2001, s 43.

[67] The penalty is imprisonment for a term not exceeding six months and/or to a fine not exceeding level 5 on the standard scale.

[68] The term probably derives from the United States, where the first 'anti-stalking' law was enacted by California; see D Morville 'Stalking Laws: Are They Solutions for More Problems?' (1993) 71 Wash ULQ 921.

[69] At p 247.

a ' "course of conduct" must involve conduct on at least two occasions'.[70] Under s 2, a person who pursues a course of conduct in breach of s 1 is guilty of the offence of harassment, and liable on summary conviction to imprisonment for up to six months or a fine not exceeding level 5 on the standard scale or both.[71] It is clear that the objective test of mens rea utilised in s 1(1)(a) is designed to overcome the problems of the other statutory offences discussed above, and it has been held that a person suffering from schizophrenia, who made threats in letters to his local MP, was rightly convicted of the offence.[72] The provision that harassment includes causing alarm or distress also obviates the need to prove psychological injury as is required for a charge of assault.

It is necessary, however, to show that the conduct complained of has occurred on at least two occasions, so that a single incident (for example, bursting in on the estranged spouse while he or she is at work, and shouting and swearing at her in front of colleagues, or sending photographs of the victim in a semi-nude state to a national newspaper[73]) would not be an offence under this Act, though the former activity might be under the Public Order Act 1986 s 4A, and the latter might be covered by the 1997 Act if, as appears to occur frequently, the perpetrator gave the 'exclusive' prints to a number of different tabloid newspapers.[74] The requirement to show a course of conduct appears to differentiate the kind of harassment intended to be covered from, eg sexual harassment in the workplace, where a single incident would suffice.[75] It is not always easy to establish that a course of conduct has occurred. There must be a nexus or link between the incidents complained of, and each incident must be proved. Thus, in *Lau v DPP*[76] the appellant was found by the stipendiary magistrate to have slapped his girlfriend on one occasion and then, some months after that incident, and after she had ended the relationship, to have threatened her new boyfriend with violence. The Divisional Court held that although a mere two incidents may amount to a course of conduct, one has to examine the context in which they occur.[77] Here, there was insufficient evidence (on the facts as proved) to justify linking the two incidents together. It has been suggested that it may therefore be sensible to base a prosecution on individual counts of assault where there is doubt whether the incidents can be sufficiently linked to each other.[78] It appears that the police will tend to wait before

---

[70] Section 7(3).   [71] Section 2(2).

[72] *R v Colohan* [2001] EWCA Crim 1251 [2001] 2 FLR 757.

[73] *Johnson v Walton* [1990] 1 FLR 350, CA.

[74] But cf *C v C (Non-Molestation Order: Jurisdiction)* [1998] Fam 70, where a former husband was refused a non-molestation order under Part IV of the Family Law Act 1996 to restrain his ex-wife from making revelations to a tabloid newspaper, because, inter alia, the aim was to seek to impose a gagging order which would threaten the freedom of the press. It is arguable that a court would apply similar reasoning to refuse to find the offence under s 1 made out.

[75] *Porcelli v Strathclyde Regional Council* [1986] ICR 564, Court of Session; *Scott v Combined Property Services Ltd* (1996) EAT/757/96.

[76] [2000] 1 FLR 799. See also *R v Patel* [2004] EWCA Crim 3284, [2005] 1 FLR 803.

[77] See *Hipgrave and Hipgrave v Jones* [2004] EWHC 2901 (QB), [2005] 2 FLR 174 where the Divisional Court stressed that whether two acts eight months apart amounted to a course of conduct was a factual question for the judge (who held that they did).

[78] See the comment by R Bailey-Harris at [2001] Fam Law 185 on *R v Hills* [2001] 1 FLR 580, CA, a decision relating to the more serious offence under s 4 (see below).

arresting a suspect until at least three complaints have been made by the victim in order to ensure that a course of conduct can be proved.[79]

Putting in fear of violence

The Act also creates a more serious offence under s 4, which provides that:

'A person whose course of conduct causes another to fear, on at least two occasions, that violence will be used against him is guilty of an offence if he knows or ought to know that his course of conduct will cause the other so to fear on each of those occasions.'

It has been suggested, by Lord Steyn in *R v Ireland*, that it will be difficult to prove that a victim has cause to fear that violence *will*, rather than *may* be used against her, and that therefore this provision is not well-suited to dealing with the problem of menacing phone calls.[80] However, the mens rea is to be judged objectively, which should make the burden of proof somewhat easier for the prosecution. For this offence, the maximum sentence, if the accused is convicted on indictment, is five years' imprisonment, a fine, or both, or, on summary conviction, to imprisonment for six months, the statutory maximum fine, or both.[81] Where a person is tried on indictment, the jury may return a verdict under s 2 where they find him not guilty under s 4.[82]

Restraining orders

An important feature of the 1997 Act is the power, contained in s 5, to enable a court sentencing a person for any offence[83] to make an order, similar to a civil injunction, called a 'restraining order', which prohibits the defendant from doing anything which amounts to further harassment or will cause a fear of violence on the part of the victim of the offence or any other person mentioned in the order. Thus, a criminal court, sentencing the defendant for an offence of harassment or assault of his wife, could make a restraining order against him in respect of their children as well. Conditions may be attached to the order, such as requiring the defendant not to contact the victim or her family, to keep away from the victim's home or workplace. The order may be of fixed or indefinite duration.[84] Both the prosecution and the defence may lead, as further evidence, any evidence that would be admissible in proceedings for an injunction under s 3 of the Act.[85] In other words, the court will decide whether to make a restraining order applying the civil standard of proof, and the civil rules on admissibility of evidence. Yet breach of the terms of an order without reasonable excuse is itself an offence punishable by imprisonment of up to five years and/or a fine.[86] Such an order is intended to deal with the problem, noted above,

---

[79] J Harris, *The Protection from Harassment Act 1997—An Evaluation of its Use and Effectiveness, Research Findings No 130* (2000) Home Office Research, Development and Statistics Directorate.

[80] [1998] AC 147 at 153C.   [81] Section 4(4).

[82] Section 4(5). Though it is preferable to add a count to the indictment to allow for this: *R v Patel* [2004] EWCA Crim 3284 [2005] 1 FLR 803.

[83] As originally enacted, this power applied only to convictions under the 1997 Act. Section 12 of the Domestic Violence, Crime and Victims Act 2004 extended the power to conviction for any offence.

[84] Section 5(3)(b). The prosecutor, defendant or any person mentioned in the order may apply to the court for it to be varied or discharged: s 5(4).

[85] See below at p 247.

[86] Where convicted on indictment; on summary conviction, the penalty is imprisonment for up to six months and/or the maximum statutory fine: s 5(5).

that criminal penalties may be inadequate to protect the victim from further offences. But putting a person at risk of a criminal sanction for breach of a civil order is controversial as an erosion of civil liberties.

The potential interference with the freedom of the individual has also been made much more significant by s 5A[87] of the Act. This now provides for a restraining order to be made even where the defendant has been acquitted,[88] if the court considers it necessary to do so to protect a person from harassment by the defendant. This is an even more controversial innovation since it means that a person who has been found not guilty of the substantive offence may still be made subject to penal consequences.

Sentencing for offences under the Act

Guidance was given by the Court of Appeal (Criminal Division) in *R v Liddle; R v Hayes*[89] concerning the approach to be taken by a court sentencing under either s 2 or s 4 and for breach of a restraining order. The court must first consider whether the offence in issue is the lesser or grave one. It must then consider whether there is a history of disobedience to court orders, be they civil or criminal, by the defendant; the seriousness of the defendant's conduct (which could, of course, range from violence to expressions of unwanted affection); whether there has been persistent misconduct; the physical and psychological effect upon the victim, whether the victim requires protection, and the level of risk the defendant poses to the victim or the victim's children or family; the defendant's mental health, and whether he is ready to undergo treatment; and the defendant's reaction to the court proceedings, including whether he has pleaded guilty, whether he has shown remorse and whether he has shown recognition that he needs help. Taking these factors into account, the court considered that, for a first offence, 'a short, sharp sentence' may be appropriate, depending on the degree of repetition, prior breach of orders and the nature of the misconduct. For a second offence, a sentence of 15 months on a plea of guilty is an appropriate starting point. In fact, the first appellant was sentenced to a total of 15 months for his three separate offences, and the second appellant for 11 months for his two. Clearly, it is acceptable to go down as well as up from the court's 'starting point'.

Use of the 1997 Act

The government had predicted that there would be no more than around 200 prosecutions per annum,[90] but the 1997 Act proved more popular with prosecutors than it had expected and there were nearly 6000 prosecutions in the Act's first full year of operation.[91] This is probably because relatively few cases of 'stalking' actually occur. Instead, the Act has been used overwhelmingly where the perpetrator and victim know each other, either

[87] Inserted by s 12(5) of the Domestic Violence, Crime and Victims Act 2004.

[88] Or where an appeal has been allowed, in which case, the matter may be remitted to the Crown Court: s 5A(3).

[89] [1999] 3 All ER 816.

[90] Figure cited by T Lawson-Cruttenden and N Addison 'The Protection from Harassment Act' (1997) 147 NLJ 983.

[91] J Harris, *The Protection from Harassment Act 1997—An Evaluation of its Use and Effectiveness, Research Findings No 130* (2000) Home Office Research, Development and Statistics Directorate.

as neighbours or having had an intimate relationship which has ended badly and the Act has proved a useful alternative to civil remedies or to other criminal offences. Indeed, it has been said that where a case of breach of a non-molestation order under the Family Law Act 1996[92] requires a sentence near the top of the range, proceedings may be better brought under the 1997 Act than the former.[93] However, the proportion of harassment cases dropped by the CPS—39%—is much higher than the average for all offences of 14%. The majority of cases were dropped because of inadequate evidence, but a third were terminated because the victim did not wish to proceed,[94] suggesting that the Act is not a panacea for the problems discussed above with using other substantive criminal offences in domestic violence cases. Around half of all convictions have resulted in a restraining order being made, but the most frequent sentence given for the offence itself, contrary to the impression given by *R v Liddle, R v Hayes*, has been a conditional discharge, in 46% of one sample of cases.[95] This lenient attitude to the offences under the Act may explain why it has been felt necessary to strengthen the courts' powers to make restraining orders, but a rate of breach of these orders at around 40%[96] suggests that offenders may not take them too seriously. Moreover, only around a third of those in breach receive a custodial sentence,[97] suggesting that the courts are wary of treating these offenders in a harsh way. This may reflect attitudes to sentencing for harassment in courts used to dealing with offences that they consider much more serious and deserving of longer sentences. But the result is that victims may continue to worry that offenders are not being robustly dealt with despite the array of measures apparently available to the courts.

3 CRIMINAL INJURIES COMPENSATION

While it is likely that a domestic violence victim's main concern will be to obtain protection from the abuser, either in the form of penal measures which remove him from the scene or deter him from repetition, or in the form of the provision of safe housing (discussed below), the winning of compensation may also be valuable, both in the financial redress it may give, and also as public recognition that the victim was not to blame for the violence.[98] In many instances, the perpetrator may not have sufficient assets to make him worth suing in tort, but the Criminal Injuries Compensation Scheme[99] provides a state-funded avenue of redress. Under the scheme as it currently operates,[100] compensation may be paid to an applicant who has sustained a criminal injury directly attributable

---

[92] Discussed below at p 243.   [93] *Robinson v Murray* [2005] EWCA Civ 935[2005] 3 FCR 504.

[94] Harris op cit.   [95] Ibid. Binding over was equally common.

[96] See Sentencing Advisory Panel, *Sentencing Guidelines on Domestic Violence Cases: Consultation Paper* (2004) para 53. In 2002, the average sentence length for those given custody was 2.8 months at the magistrates court and 11.1 months at the Crown Court.

[97] Ibid.   [98] C Cobley 'Financial Compensation for Victims of Child Abuse' (1998) 20 JSWFL 221.

[99] The scheme, which had been a non-statutory ex gratia scheme since its inception in 1964, was placed on a statutory footing by the Criminal Injuries Compensation Act 1995, and the current rules came into force on 1 April 2001.

[100] The funding of the Scheme, and its place within a broader governmental strategy for assisting victims of crime, is the subject of ongoing review: see Home Office, *Compensation and Support for Victims of Crime* (2004) and *Rebuilding Lives—supporting victims of crime* (2005) Ch 2. As part of this review, s 57 of the Domestic Violence, Crime and Victims Act 2004 makes provision to enable all or part of a compensation award to be recovered from offenders.

to a crime of violence (including arson or an act of poisoning). It seems that a threat of violence, such as an assault without physical contact, or possibly a threat amounting to harassment under the 1997 Act, would suffice.[101] Mental injury, in the form of a medically recognised psychiatric or psychological illness, is included within the scheme. An application must normally be brought within two years of the incident giving rise to the injury.[102] It is not necessary for the perpetrator to have been convicted for an award to be made. Any award will be made up of a standard amount of compensation according to a tariff of amounts for differing injuries (ranging from £1,000 to £250,000)[103] together with a sum for loss of earnings.

Originally, the scheme excluded virtually all cases of domestic violence. There were a number of reasons for this: it was feared that it would be difficult to establish the facts; there would be a large number of claims, many of them trivial; if the parties were subsequently reconciled, any compensation awarded would increase the family assets as a whole and consequently the offender would benefit from his own wrong.[104] It was obvious, however, that many seriously injured women were being prevented from making genuine claims. Consequently the scheme was modified in 1979 to permit domestic violence claims,[105] although some account is still taken of these fears.

Under the scheme, a claims officer employed by the Criminal Injuries Compensation Authority must be satisfied that there is no likelihood that an assailant would benefit if an award were made, or, if the victim is a minor, that it would not be against his interest to make an award. If, at the time of the injury, the victim and assailant were living in the same household as members of the same family, compensation can be claimed only if the following conditions are satisfied:[106]

'(a) the assailant has been prosecuted in connection with the offence, except where a claims officer considers that there are practical, technical or other good reasons why a prosecution has not been brought; and

(b) in the case of violence between adults in the family, a claims officer is satisfied that the applicant and the assailant stopped living in the same household before the application was made and are unlikely to share the same household again.'[107]

Domestic violence victims are particularly likely to have suffered a series of incidents before finally complaining to the police. The scheme provides that, in such a case, the victim may qualify for compensation only for the single most recent incident, if in relation to the earlier incidents she failed to report them to the police without delay and/or failed to co-operate with the police in bringing the assailant to justice. Where the applicant is entitled to compensation for the series of assaults, however, she will qualify for an award as the victim of a pattern of abuse, rather than for a separate award for each incident.[108]

---

[101] Criminal Injuries Compensation Authority, *Guide to the 2001 Compensation Scheme* (2001) para 14.

[102] Home Office, *The Criminal Injuries Compensation Scheme* TS1 (2001) para 18.

[103] Home Office, op cit, p 25.   [104] M Freeman *Violence in the Family* p 182.

[105] Claims based on domestic violence before that date cannot be brought: *R v CICB, ex p P* [1993] 2 FLR 600.

[106] Home Office, *The Criminal Injuries Compensation Scheme* (2001) para 17.

[107] A man and woman living together as husband and wife will be treated as members of the same family: query two persons in a same-sex relationship?

[108] Home Office, *The Criminal Injuries Compensation Scheme* (2001) at p 29.

The claims officer may withhold or reduce compensation if all reasonable steps have not been taken promptly to inform the police; the applicant has failed to co-operate with the police or other authority in attempting to bring the assailant to justice, or has failed to co-operate with the authority in connection with the compensation application; the applicant's conduct before, during or after the incident giving rise to the application makes it inappropriate to make a full, or any award at all;[109] or the applicant's character, as shown by his criminal convictions, makes it inappropriate to make a full (or any) award.[110]

It will be seen that these requirements impose some burdens upon the victims of domestic violence. We have seen that victims may be reluctant to prosecute, for a variety of reasons, which are not usually 'practical' or 'technical' but have more to do with fear of the repercussions of taking action. Are such reasons 'good' ones in the eyes of claims officers? If the victim, having initiated police action, then withdraws her complaint, will her conduct make it inappropriate to make an award? And, most importantly, only where the parties' relationship has broken down and appears to be over, will an award be made. Clearly, relationships where, despite violence or other abusive behaviour having occurred, there is still some scope for reconciliation, are outside the scope of this scheme.

It is not surprising, with all the shortcomings surrounding the criminal justice system, that victims may prefer to turn to the civil law for a remedy.

C CIVIL LAW REMEDIES [111]

As noted above, the law relating to the grant of orders intended to enjoin the respondent from attacking or pestering the victim, or to exclude him from the family home, had become a confused and complicated jumble of jurisdictions. Part IV of the Family Law Act 1996 was intended to simplify and improve the protection given by the civil courts, largely by bringing jurisdictions together, but there remains a residual power in the courts to issue injunctions ancillary to substantive proceedings, and there is also power to bring a claim in civil proceedings for breach of s 1 of the Protection from Harassment Act 1997, backed up by an injunction.[112] We discuss these in turn.

1 THE FAMILY LAW ACT 1996 PART IV [113]

(a) The scheme of Part IV

Part IV sets out the rights of spouses to occupy the matrimonial home where they lack a proprietary right to do so.[114] It provides for two categories of orders to be made, occupation orders[115] and non-molestation orders.[116] The High Court, county courts and

---

[109] Including where excessive consumption of alcohol or use of illicit drugs by the victim contributed to the circumstances which gave rise to the injury suffered: ibid para 14.

[110] Ibid, para 13.   [111] See R Bird and N Fricker (eds) *Emergency Remedies in the Family Courts*.

[112] There is also power, available to courts dealing with both spouses and cohabitants whose home is held on a tenancy, to provide a long-term solution to their problem by transferring the home between them, and this was discussed above at pp 204–7.

[113] See R Bird *Domestic Violence: Law and Practice* (2006, 5th ed).

[114] These are called 'home rights' and are discussed in detail above at pp 184–9.

[115] Sections 33–41.   [116] Section 42.

magistrates' courts all have jurisdiction to make such orders, subject to the Lord Chancellor's power to specify that certain types of proceedings be commenced in, or transferred to, a specified level of court,[117] and to a restriction in s 59(1) preventing magistrates from hearing cases where there is a disputed question as to a party's entitlement to occupy any property, unless it is unnecessary to determine that question in order to deal with the case. The Law Commission's aim of creating a unified jurisdiction has therefore not quite been achieved, although all courts will at least be applying the same rules in the same types of case. Part IV also continues, and enhances, former powers to grant orders ex parte,[118] to accept undertakings in lieu of making orders,[119] to enforce orders,[120] and to deal with abuse against children.[121]

(b) Non-molestation orders

Although the Act deals with non-molestation orders after occupation orders, we discuss them first, because they are the more likely and common order to be granted: over twice as many non-molestation orders as occupation orders were granted by county courts in 2003.[122]

Section 42(1) provides that a non-molestation order:

'... means an order containing either or both of the following provisions—

(a) provision prohibiting ... the respondent from molesting another person who is associated with the respondent;

(b) provision prohibiting the respondent from molesting a relevant child.'[123]

What is molestation?

Reflecting the response to the Law Commission's proposals that any attempt at a definition might reduce the level of protection afforded by the former law, 'molestation' is

---

[117] Section 57. The Family Law Act 1996 (Part IV) (Allocation of Proceedings) Order 1997 SI 1997/1896 provides that proceedings will generally be commenced in either the family proceedings court or county court. Applications by children must be made to the High Court.

[118] Section 45.   [119] Section 46 as amended.   [120] Section 47 as amended, ss 50–1.

[121] Section 52 and Sch 6, discussed at p 726. It also contains power, never brought into force, in s 60, to provide for rules of court setting out when prescribed persons may act on behalf of another to bring proceedings under this Part of the Act. This stemmed from a Law Commission recommendation (Law Com No 207 paras 5.18, 5.20) that the police be given the power, as in certain Australian states, to seek civil remedies on the victim's behalf. This was said, inter alia, to remove the burden of stress upon the victim to take action, This recommendation was not accepted by the government, on the basis that introducing a power to seek a civil remedy would represent too radical a departure from the core criminal justice functions of the police. However, the opposition pressed an amendment to the Family Law Bill to introduce a paving provision, which became s 60 of the Act, to enable some form of representative action to be introduced through rules of court. No further action has been taken on implementing this provision. For consideration of how it might be implemented, see M Burton, 'Third party applications for protection orders in England and Wales: service providers' views on implementing Section 60 of the Family Law Act 1996' (2003) 25 JSWFL 137.

[122] In 2004, 23357 non-molestation orders and 9075 occupation orders were granted: *Judicial Statistics 2004* (2005) Table 5.9.

[123] A 'relevant child' is defined by s 62(2) (as amended) as any child who is living with, or might reasonably be expected to live with either party to the proceedings, any child in relation to whom an order under the Adoption Act 1976, the Adoption and Children Act 2002 or the Children Act 1989 is in question in the proceedings, or any other child whose interests the court considers relevant.

deliberately not defined in the Act.[124] Instead, its meaning is left to case law under the
previous legislation, where it had been regarded as meaning 'deliberate conduct which
substantially interferes with the applicant or child, whether by violence, intimidation,
harassment, pestering or interference sufficiently serious to warrant intervention by a
court.'[125] This clearly overlaps with, though is wider in terms than, the concept of harassment under the Protection from Harassment Act 1997, since there is no requirement to
prove a 'course of conduct', meaning conduct on at least two occasions. On the other
hand, the 1997 provision may be broader in scope, since it provides that harassment
includes causing alarm or distress, whereas molestation must pass a 'seriousness' hurdle,
and it is open to a court to consider that the conduct complained of is not sufficiently
serious to warrant its intervention.[126]

Who may apply for an order?

Under the former law, problems arose because only spouses or cohabitants could seek an
injunction or order without also having to take civil proceedings, usually in tort. The Law
Commission were concerned to extend the range of applicants for non-molestation
orders, but were against providing a remedy open to anyone, regardless of their relationship with the respondent.[127] They reasoned that a domestic or family relationship justifies
special remedies and procedures because the proximity of the parties gives rise to heightened emotions in situations of stress, and because of the likelihood that the relationship
will continue. They considered that extending equal protection to neighbours, tenants and
victims of sexual harassment would be going too far.[128] However, the Protection from
Harassment Act 1997, as we shall see, opens up the possibility of obtaining an injunction
to restrain harassment to any person who can prove that the respondent has acted in
breach of s 1.

Instead, the Law Commission proposed basing eligibility upon a person's 'association'
with another, and suggested a range of such associations. Not all of these were accepted by
the government at first but the list was subsequently widened by the Domestic Violence,
Crime and Victims Act 2004.[129] Those eligible are set out in s 62(3) as follows:

'a person is "associated with" another person if—

(a) they are, or have been married to each other;[130]

---

[124] Law Com No 207 at para 3.1.
[125] His Honour Judge Fricker 'Molestation and Harassment after *Patel v Patel*' [1988] Fam Law 395 at 399.
[126] In *C v C (Non-Molestation Order: Jurisdiction)* [1998] Fam 70, Sir Stephen Brown P held that a non-
molestation order should only be granted where there was some conduct which clearly harassed and affected
the applicant to such a degree that the court's intervention was called for, and refused an order to prevent a
former wife passing details about her ex-husband and their marriage to a tabloid newspaper. See also
Spindlow v Spindlow [1979] Fam 52, CA, where, although the respondent father was excluded from the home
(on grounds which were later disapproved by the House of Lords in *Richards v Richards* [1984] AC 174), a
non-molestation order was lifted because the only conduct complained of was one incident where he pushed
the mother onto a settee, shouting at her, and threatening to smack her daughter.
[127] As is possible in New South Wales, South Australia, Western Australia and Tasmania: see the discussion
by the Law Commission in Report No 207 para 3.9. Similar concern at the problems of opening up the
jurisdiction too far were expressed, in a related context, by Lord Goff of Chievely in *Hunter v Canary Wharf
Ltd* [1997] AC 655 at 693F, discussed further below at p 248.
[128] Ibid paras 3.17, 3.19.   [129] Sections 3 and 4.
[130] The provisions of Part IV apply to polygamous as well as monogamous marriages: s 63(5).

(aa) they are or have been civil partners of each other;[131]

(b) they are cohabitants[132] or former cohabitants;[133]

(c) they live or have lived in the same household, otherwise than merely by reason of one of them being the other's employee, tenant, lodger or boarder;

(d) they are relatives;[134]

(e) they have agreed to marry one another (whether or not that agreement has been terminated);[135]

(eza) they have entered into a civil partnership agreement (as defined by section 73 of the Civil Partnership Act 2004) (whether or not that agreement has been terminated);[136]

(ea) they have or have had an intimate personal relationship with each other which is or was of significant duration;[137]

(f) in relation to any child, they are both persons falling within subsection (4); or

(g) they are parties to the same family proceedings'.[138]

Section 62(4) provides that:

'a person falls within this subsection in relation to a child if—

(a) he is a parent of the child; or

(b) he has or has had parental responsibility for the child.'[139]

Under s 43, a child under the age of 16 may seek an order, with leave of the court, which may only be granted if the court is satisfied that the child has sufficient understanding to

---

[131] Amended by Sch 9 para 13 to the Civil Partnership Act 2004.

[132] Defined by s 62(1)(a), as amended by Sch 9 para 13 to the Civil Partnership Act 2004, as meaning 'two persons who are neither married to each other nor civil partners of each other but are living together as husband and wife or as if they were civil partners'.

[133] This phrase does not include a couple who subsequently marry or become civil partners of each other: s 62(1)(b) as amended.

[134] Defined in s 63(1) (as amended) as '(a) the father, mother, stepfather, stepmother, son, daughter, stepson, stepdaughter, grandmother, grandfather, grandson or granddaughter of that person or that person's spouse, former spouse, civil partner or former civil partner or (b) the brother, sister, uncle, aunt, niece, nephew or first cousin (whether of the full blood or the half blood or by marriage or civil partnership) of that person or of that person's spouse, former spouse, civil partner or former civil partner and includes, in relation to a person who is cohabiting or has cohabited with another person, any person who would fall within paragraph (a) or (b) if the parties were married to each other or were civil partners of each other'.

[135] Section 44 provides that such an agreement must be evidenced in writing, or by the gift of an engagement ring, or by a ceremony entered into by the parties in the presence of witnesses—which looks like the definition for an old-fashioned betrothal ceremony, but quaere whether it would be satisfied by an engagement party? See above, p 44. No application for a non-molestation order may be brought in reliance on a former engagement more than three years after the date on which it was terminated: s 42(4).

[136] Amended by Sch 9 para 13 to the Civil Partnership Act 2004. Similar provision for proof of having entered into the agreement as applies to engagements is set out in s 44 as amended.

[137] Added by s 4 of the Domestic Violence, Crime and Victims Act 2004.

[138] These are defined in s 63(1) and (2) as amended.

[139] Additionally, s 62(5), as amended, provides that, if a child has been adopted or freed for adoption, or an adoption agency has power to place him for adoption or he has become the subject of a placement order, two persons are also associated with each other if one is the natural parent, or parent of such a natural parent, and the other is the child, or any person who is an adoptive parent of the child, or has had the child placed with him for adoption. The aim of this provision is presumably to enable adopters to utilise the Act to obtain orders to prevent birth relatives from 'pestering' the adoptive family.

make the application. The test is the same as applies in relation to a child seeking leave to seek a s 8 order under the Children Act 1989, and the case law relating to that test is equally applicable.[140]

This list covers the main groups who are regarded as needing protection by virtue of an order, although it is not unproblematic. Couples whose marriage or cohabitation relationship has ended were excluded from the ambit of the former law, yet it appears that a significant number of cases of domestic violence may involve such couples,[141] and hence they are now included.[142] But the difficulty of establishing whether a relationship involved cohabitation may still occur. For example, in *G v G (Non-molestation Order: Jurisdiction)*[143] the applicant had maintained to the Department of Social Security that she and the respondent did *not* live together, but then sought an order from the magistrates asserting that they spent about five nights a week together. On appeal against the magistrates' refusal to make an order, the court held that three of the 'signposts' which may establish a cohabiting relationship were present[144] and the court was clear that the 1996 Act should be given a purposive interpretation in order to bring someone within, rather that outside, its protection unless this was clearly impossible. A similar purposive approach was taken in *Chechi v Bashier*.[145] Here, a man engaged in a land dispute with his relatives in Pakistan sought non-molestation orders against his brother and nephews. The trial judge discharged the ex parte orders that had been made, considering that the dispute was better dealt with as a civil matter and that the family relationship between the parties was incidental. The Court of Appeal, whilst upholding the judge's exercise of his discretion, nonetheless affirmed that the 1996 Act is intended to extend protection to a wide class of 'family' relationships and that suitable cases should certainly be within its ambit.[146]

Once it is accepted that those in a relationship which does not *presently* involve cohabitation ought to be able to seek an order, yet not to open up the jurisdiction to all-comers, it then becomes necessary to determine where to draw the boundaries and thereby define what apparently amounts to a domestic or family relationship. This list gives us a picture of modern thinking on this issue, and it is interesting how rapidly such thinking has changed. As originally provided in the 1996 Act, for example, same-sex couples were not expressly included, although if they lived together, they would fit within category (c). Nor were intimate relationships which did not involve cohabitation included, although the Law Commission had recommended that they should be.[147] The experience of working with the limitations of the original provisions, the human rights-led inclusion of same-sex relationships within the definition of 'family' and recognition that personal relationships are taking a more diverse range of forms than hitherto,[148] led to the further broadening of the definitions in s 62.

---

[140] Children Act 1989 s 10(8), discussed below at pp 545–9.   [141] See Law Com No 207 para 3.18.

[142] But note that former spouses, partners or cohabitants of a person's current spouse, partner or cohabitant are not 'associated' with that person.

[143] [2000] 2 FLR 532.

[144] See *Crake v Supplementary Benefits Commission* [1982] 1 All ER 498, noted above at p 102.

[145] [1999] 2 FLR 489, CA.

[146] For the Court's consideration of the power of arrest which may be attached to an order, see below at p 242 n 241.

[147] Ibid, para 3.26.   [148] See above p 6.

When may an order be made?

The court may make an order on a free-standing application, or where an application is made in other family proceedings.[149] It may also make an order of its own motion in any family proceedings to which the respondent is a party, if it considers that the order should be made for the benefit of any other party, or of any relevant child,[150] and, when the court is considering whether to make an occupation order, it must also consider whether to make a non-molestation order of its own motion.[151] This is to enable breach of the order to be dealt with more effectively by the police, who may arrest without warrant for breach of a non-molestation, but not an occupation, order.[152] These provisions give flexibility both to parties and the court. Clearly, an applicant should be able to obtain an order without having to take other proceedings, but it is equally useful to enable an application to be attached to proceedings already under way, and to give the court a reserve power to make an order even where no application has been made. Indeed, such a power might prove helpful where a party is reluctant to be seen to be seeking an order for fear of antagonising the respondent.

Criteria for the grant of an order

In deciding whether to make the order, and if so, in what manner:

'... the court shall have regard to all the circumstances, including the need to secure the health, safety and well-being—

(a) of the applicant; and

(b) of any relevant child.'[153]

The purpose of this test is to focus the court's attention upon the victim's need for protection, rather than to scrutinise the nature and quality of the perpetrator's conduct,[154] and to give guidance, especially to magistrates, in exercising the powers under the section.

Terms of a non-molestation order

Under s 42(6), a non-molestation order may be worded to refer to molestation in general, to particular acts of molestation, or to both, which gives the court flexibility to outline certain kinds of prohibited conduct or to leave the prohibition in general terms.[155] For example, a court could prohibit the respondent from telephoning the victim, or from

---

[149] Section 42(2)(a). Family proceedings are defined in s 63(1), (2) and, by virtue of s 42(3), include proceedings where the court has made an emergency protection order under s 44 of the Children Act 1989 which includes an exclusion requirement: see below p 726.

[150] Section 42(2)(b). A relevant child is any child who is living with or might reasonably be expected to live with either party to the proceedings; any child in relation to whom an order under the Adoption and Children Act 2002 or the Children Act 1989 is in question in the proceedings; and any other child whose interests the court considers relevant: s 62(2).

[151] S 42(4A) and (4B), inserted by Sch 10, para 36 to the Domestic Violence, Crime and Victims Act 2004.

[152] See further below at p 241.   [153] Section 42(5) as amended.

[154] Although it has been held that, where the respondent could not help her conduct, which was due to dementia, a non-molestation order should not be made: *Banks v Banks* [1999] 1 FLR 726 (county court); cf *P v P (Contempt of Court: Mental Capacity)* [1999] 2 FLR 897, CA: as long as the respondent understands that an order has been made forbidding him from doing certain things, and that he will be punished if he does them, he has sufficient understanding for an order and for a finding of contempt to be made.

[155] Law Com No 207 para 3.2.

loitering outside her place of work, or from coming within a certain distance of her home.[156]

The order may be for a fixed period or until further order. The Court of Appeal has held that the purpose of a non-molestation order is not, as was the understanding under the former law, simply to give a breathing space to the parties for the tensions to die down between them. There may be cases where it may be appropriate for the order to last for a much longer period, and the courts are not obliged to consider whether such cases are 'exceptional' or 'unusual' before making an order of indefinite duration.[157]

An order made in other family proceedings will cease to have effect if those proceedings are withdrawn or dismissed.[158] This is regrettable: the withdrawal or dismissal of a party's application for, say, a contact order in children proceedings does not necessarily mean that a non-molestation order, which the court considered appropriate in the light of those proceedings, is no longer required. Presumably, the onus is on the victim to apply for a free-standing order in such circumstances.

The order may be varied or discharged on application by the respondent or applicant, and, where it was made on the court's own motion, may be varied or discharged by the court, even though no application has been made.[159]

(c) Occupation orders

The second type of order which can be made under the 1996 Act is far more complicated. An occupation order may declare or regulate the right to occupy the family home, but the detailed terms of the order will vary according to the eligibility of the applicant, as will the criteria determining whether the order should be granted. Declaratory orders may 'declare, confer or extend occupation rights', while regulatory orders 'just control the exercise of existing rights'.[160]

Who may apply?

Applications may be free-standing or made in other family proceedings, but the court has no power to make an order of its own motion.[161] The range of permitted applicants is much narrower than in the case of non-molestation orders, because the Law Commission were concerned that the interference with the enjoyment of property rights when requiring a respondent to leave his own home or let the applicant into it is harder to justify where the applicant has no such property rights herself.[162] They also considered that, for non-entitled applicants, the purpose of seeking an order is to obtain short-term protection until they can find an alternative home, whereas entitled applicants might be seeking medium- or long-term regulation of the property.[163] The Act accordingly does not employ the concept of the 'associated person' used in relation to non-molestation orders, but instead distinguishes between two categories of applicant: those deemed 'entitled', and those who are 'non-entitled' applicants, in property law terms. We deal with the position of entitled applicants first, and then with non-entitled applicants.

---

[156] As in *Burris v Azadani* [1995] 1 WLR 1372, CA.
[157] *Re B-J (Power of Arrest)* [2000] 2 FLR 443, CA.   [158] Section 42(7) and (8).
[159] Section 49(1) and (2).   [160] Law Com No 207 para 4.1.
[161] Section 39(2).   [162] Law Com No 207 para 4.7.   [163] Ibid.

Entitled applicants

Under s 33(1)(a), an entitled applicant is a person who:

'(i) is entitled to occupy a dwelling-house by virtue of a beneficial estate or interest or contract or by virtue of any enactment giving him the right to remain in occupation, or

(ii) has home rights[164] in relation to a dwelling-house'.

Such an applicant may seek an order where the dwelling-house[165] is or at any time has been the home of the applicant and a person with whom he is associated,[166] or was intended by them to be their home.[167]

Types of occupation orders in favour of entitled applicants

Under s 33, the applicant may seek an order containing any of a list of provisions specified. Declaratory orders may simply declare that the applicant is entitled to occupy the home by virtue of property law or home rights,[168] or may provide that the applicant's home rights are to continue beyond the death of the other spouse or civil partner, or the termination of the marriage or civil partnership.[169] Such orders per se seem to have limited utility, except in situations where, perhaps, the applicant is contesting a property claim by a third party with whom he or she is associated, such as, for example, her brother-in-law who is a joint owner of the family home,[170] or where there is a need to safeguard the applicant's position after divorce or death of the other party, perhaps pending resolution of any ancillary relief or family provision claim which might be made.

Of greater utility are regulatory orders. These may:[171]

'(a) enforce the applicant's entitlement to remain in occupation as against the ... respondent . . .;

(b) require the respondent to permit the applicant to enter and remain in the dwelling-house or part of the dwelling-house;

(c) regulate the occupation of the dwelling-house by either or both parties;

(d) if the respondent is entitled [as mentioned in s 33(1)(a)(i)], prohibit, suspend or restrict the exercise by him of his right to occupy the dwelling-house;

---

[164] As amended by the Civil Partnership Act 2004 Sch 9 para 4. Home rights are granted by s 30(2) and discussed above at pp 185–9.

[165] Section 62(1) defines a dwelling house, for the purposes of an occupation order, as including (a) any building, or part of a building which is occupied as a dwelling, (b) any caravan, house-boat or structure which is occupied as a dwelling, and any yard, garden, garage or outhouse belonging to it and occupied with it.

[166] As defined by s 62(3). No application may be brought based on a former agreement to marry or form a civil partnership after the period of three years beginning with the date the engagement or agreement was terminated: s 33(2) as amended.

[167] Section 33(1)(b). See *Moore v Moore* [2004] EWCA Civ 1243, [2005] 1 FLR 666 noted above at p 186.

[168] Section 33(4) as amended.

[169] Section 33(5) (as amended) but an order may not be made after the death of either of the former parties: s 33(9)(a).

[170] But cf *Kalsi v Kalsi* [1992] 1 FLR 511, CA: a wife was not entitled to declaration of her rights of occupation in the matrimonial home as against her husband's three brothers who were legal owners, with her husband, of the property.

[171] Section 33(3).

(e) if the respondent has home rights in relation to the dwelling-house and the applicant is the other spouse or civil partner,[172] restrict or terminate those rights;

(f) require the respondent to leave the dwelling-house or part of the dwelling-house; or

(g) exclude the respondent from a defined area in which the dwelling-house is included.'

These provisions can be used flexibly to meet the circumstances of the particular case. For example, an order could prevent the respondent from changing the locks of the home to keep the applicant out, or require him to let her back in; require either party to quit the home at certain times, for example, at weekends; require the respondent to leave the home, or prohibit him from entering certain parts of it, eg a bedroom; or, as in *Burris v Azadani*,[173] prohibit him from entering within a certain distance of the home.

Criteria for an order in favour of entitled applicants

No test is laid down for the court to apply when deciding whether to make a simple declaratory order that the applicant is a person entitled, since the issue will depend purely on whether the court finds that the applicant has the property or home rights contended for. Where the court is considering whether to extend home rights beyond the death of the other spouse or civil partner, or after the termination of the marriage or civil partnership, it may do so whenever it considers that, in all the circumstances, it is just and reasonable.[174]

The balance of harm test

In relation to making a regulatory order, the Law Commission were concerned to provide a test which would meet the varied circumstances which might arise in individual cases, such as the degree of danger being faced by the applicant, the ability to find alternative accommodation at short notice, and any need for a longer-term solution to the problem. They were also keen to deal with the perceived shortcomings of the test under the old law which, as we have seen, placed emphasis upon the misconduct of the respondent rather than upon the needs of the applicant and any children, effectively reintroducing the concept of fault into the law when the trend has been to promote settlement of problems without recrimination.[175] Accordingly, they proposed a 'balance of harm' test, which would enable the court to strike a balance between being fair to respondents on the one hand, and ensuring the protection of the victims on the other, and which would elevate the court's *power* to make an order into a *duty* to do so, where the effects upon the victims are sufficiently grave.

Section 33(7) accordingly provides that if it appears to the court that the applicant or a relevant child is likely to suffer significant harm attributable to the conduct of the respondent if an order is not made, the court *must* make an order unless it appears that the respondent or a relevant child is likely to suffer greater harm in consequence of the order being made. 'Significant harm' is a term taken from the Children Act 1989.[176] 'Harm' is defined in s 63(3) to mean, in relation to a person aged 18 or over, ill-treatment or the impairment of health, and, in relation to a *child*, ill-treatment or the impairment of health or development. Interestingly, the section provides that ill-treatment includes sexual abuse only in relation to a child. The reason for this limitation is unclear.

---

[172] As amended by the Civil Partnership Act 2004 Sch 9 para 4(4).
[173] [1995] 1 WLR 1372, CA; 250 yards from the home.   [174] Section 33(8).
[175] Law Com No 207 paras 4.20, 4.23.   [176] See s 31, discussed below, p 737.

The working of s 33(7) is usefully illustrated by *B v B (Occupation Order)*.[177] The wife left the husband after suffering serious violence, and took their two-year-old daughter with her. She was housed temporarily by the local authority in bed and breakfast accommodation. Meanwhile, the husband remained in the matrimonial home, with his six-year-old son by a former partner. The husband appealed against the making of an occupation order requiring him (and his son) to leave. The Court of Appeal held that, weighing the respective likelihood of harm, the husband's son would suffer more harm if an occupation order were made than the wife and daughter would if it were not, because the husband would be regarded by the local authority as having made himself intentionally homeless and therefore entitled only to temporary accommodation. His child might then have to be taken into care. By contrast, the mother would eventually be rehoused by the authority in suitable permanent accommodation. Thus, even though the Court was at pains to condemn the husband's conduct, it did not consider it appropriate to make the order sought.

It should be noted that the Law Commission's formulation of this presumption did not require a causal connection between the harm and the respondent's conduct.[178] This was inserted by Parliament. However, the Court of Appeal has stressed that it is the effect of the conduct, rather than the intention of the doer, on which the court must concentrate. Thus, a judge was wrong to consider that harm suffered by the two sons of the marriage was not attributable to the husband's conduct because he had not intentionally contributed to the strained atmosphere in the home pending resolution of the spouses' divorce.[179]

The discretionary test

Where the balance of harm test is not established, it does not follow that an order will not be made. The court must then go on to consider whether, as a question of discretion, it should make an order, taking into account the factors listed in s 33(6).[180]

Under s 33(6), the court is required to have regard to all the circumstances, including:

'(a) the housing needs and resources of each of the parties and of any relevant child;

(b) the financial resources of each of the parties;

(c) the likely effect of any order, or of any decision by the court not to exercise its powers under subsection (3), on the health, safety or well-being of the parties and of any relevant child; and

(d) the conduct of the parties in relation to each other and otherwise.'

In exercising its discretion whether to make an order, the court must bear in mind, according to the Court of Appeal, that occupation orders continue to be regarded as Draconian measures to be confined to exceptional cases, as they were under the former law.[181] It probably remains the case that, in the absence of actual violence beyond the

---

[177] [1999] 1 FLR 715, CA. See F Kaganas, '*B v B (Occupation Order)* and *Chalmers v Johns*: Occupation Orders under the Family Law Act 1996' [1999] CFLQ 193.

[178] Ibid.

[179] *G v G (Occupation Order: Conduct)* [2000] 2 FLR 36, CA. Nonetheless, they upheld his refusal of an order because it would have been Draconian in the circumstances: see further below. Cf *Banks v Banks* [1999] 1 FLR 726 (county court), where the judge refused to make the order, inter alia, because the wife, who suffered from dementia, could not help her conduct.

[180] Per Thorpe LJ in *Chalmers v Johns* [1999] 1 FLR 392, at p 396D, CA; *G v G (Occupation Order: Conduct)* [2000] 2 FLR 36, CA.

[181] Ibid. For criticism of this view, see M Humphries, 'Occupation Orders Revisited' [2001] Fam Law 542.

merely trivial, it will be very difficult to persuade a court to exclude the respondent. However, the statistics on the number of orders made suggest that, as the Law Commission had hoped, courts have become more willing to focus on the needs of the victim and to make occupation orders more readily where these are required. Whereas, under the old law, in the last year of operation, nearly seven times as many non-molestation injunctions were granted as ouster injunctions, by 2003, the ratio of non-molestation orders to occupation orders was two to one.[182]

Duration of orders in favour of entitled applicants

By s 33(10), orders may be made for a specified period, until the occurrence of a specified event, or until further order. Under the former law, orders were generally limited to three months' duration with the possibility of renewal,[183] but this was felt to be inadequate in many instances to achieve a resolution of the parties' problems, and 'not obviously appropriate to the regulation of occupation between those who have equal rights to occupy'.[184] As with non-molestation orders, either party may apply for a variation or discharge of the order.[185]

Non-entitled applicants

The Law Commission considered that, where a person has no property right in the home, the possibility of obtaining an occupation order should be limited to cohabitants (who were protected under the Domestic Violence and Matrimonial Proceedings Act 1976 anyway), former cohabitants, and former spouses, as these were the classes of relationship most in need of protection.[186] Accordingly, the Act provided that these may seek an occupation order where the respondent is entitled under property law to occupy the dwelling-house but the applicant is not, as 'non-entitled applicants'.[187] The Civil Partnership Act 2004 extends this protection to former civil partners.[188] The order must be in respect of a dwelling-house which is the home they are living in, or have at any time lived in or intended to live in together (if formerly married, as their matrimonial home; if former civil partners, as their civil partnership home).[189] Additionally, spouses, former

---

[182] In 1996, 19,707 non-molestation injunctions and 2,945 ouster injunctions were granted: *Judicial Statistics 1996* (1997) Table 5.9. In 2003, 21818 non-molestation orders and 9317 occupation orders were granted: *Judicial Statistics 2003* (2004) Table 5.9. Note, the statistics do not distinguish between occupation orders in favour of entitled, and non-entitled, applicants and the figures quoted cover both types.

[183] *Practice Note* [1978] 1 WLR 1123. Orders were also made of indefinite duration in some cases: see *Spencer v Camacho* (1983) 4 FLR 662, CA and *Galan v Galan* [1985] FLR 905, CA.

[184] Law Com No 207 para 4.35, 4.36.

[185] Section 49. Where an applicant's home rights are a charge on the estate or interest of the other spouse or civil partner, or of trustees for that other, an order under s 33 against the other may be varied or discharged on the application of any person deriving title under the other or trustees and affected by the charge: s 49(3) as amended.

[186] See Law Com No 207 para 4.8.

[187] Under the former law, it was clearly established by the House of Lords in *Davis v Johnson* [1979] AC 264, HL that non-entitled cohabitants could obtain ouster injunctions under the Domestic Violence and Matrimonial Proceedings Act 1976, but the jurisdiction did not extend to those whose cohabitation had ceased a significant time before proceedings were brought: *Harrison v Lewis* [1988] 2 FLR 339, CA, *McLean v Nugent* (1980) 1 FLR 26, CA. Former spouses were outside the ambit of the 1976 Act.

[188] Civil Partnership Act 2004 Sch 9, para 6 amending s 35 of the Family Law Act 1996.

[189] Section 35(1)(c) as amended—former spouses or former civil partners; s 36 (as amended by the Domestic Violence, Crime and Victims Act 2004 Sch 10 para 34)—cohabitants or former cohabitants.

spouses, civil partners or former civil partners, cohabitants and former cohabitants may seek an order where *neither* party is entitled to occupy the dwelling-house, in respect of the home they are currently living in.[190] This category is intended to deal with the, perhaps relatively uncommon, situation where the couple are occupying a property either as squatters or, more likely, as bare licensees.

Non-entitled applicants where the respondent has property rights

In respect of applications brought by non-entitled applicants where the respondent has property rights, it is necessary to consider three separate issues. First, what provisions may be included in an order? Secondly, what criteria apply to the grant of an order, and to the provisions included within it? Thirdly, how long may an order last? On these last two issues the Act distinguishes between former spouses and former civil partners on the one hand, and current or former cohabitants on the other.

Provisions in the order

Declaratory provisions. If the applicant is currently in occupation in the dwelling-house an order must contain the following provisions:

'(a) giving the applicant the right not to be evicted or excluded from the dwelling-house or any part of it by the respondent for the period specified in the order; and

(b) prohibiting the respondent from evicting or excluding the applicant during that period.'[191]

Where the applicant is not in occupation, the order must include provision:

'(a) giving the applicant the right to enter into and occupy the dwelling-house for the period specified in the order; and

(b) requiring the respondent to permit the exercise of that right.'[192]

These provisions were termed by the Law Commission as 'occupation rights orders', granting a right to occupy the home to applicants who do not already possess such a right.[193]

Regulatory provisions. Additionally, it is provided that a court may also include provisions in the order to:

'(a) regulate the occupation of the dwelling-house by either or both of the parties;

(b) prohibit, suspend or restrict the exercise by the respondent of his right to occupy the dwelling-house;

(c) require the respondent to leave the dwelling-house or part of the dwelling-house; or

(d) exclude the respondent from a defined area in which the dwelling-house is included.[194]

---

[190] Section 37(1)—spouses and former spouses, s 37(1A)—civil partners and former civil partners; and s 38(1) (as amended)—cohabitants and former cohabitants.

[191] Section 35(3) as amended—former spouses and former civil partners; and s 36(3)—cohabitants and former cohabitants.

[192] Section 35(4)—former spouses and former civil partners; and s 36(4)—cohabitants and former cohabitants.

[193] Law Com No 207 para 4.3.

[194] Section 35(5)—former spouses and former civil partners; and s 36(5)—cohabitants and former cohabitants.

Taken together, these two types of provisions provide the same protection in practice to a non-entitled applicant as to an entitled applicant.[195]

Criteria for an order

Former spouses and former civil partners. In respect of the declaratory provisions in an order, s 35(6) provides that the court must have regard to all the circumstances, including:

'(a) the housing needs and housing resources of each of the parties and of any relevant child;

(b) the financial resources of each of the parties;

(c) the likely effect of any order, or of any decision by the court not to [grant an order], on the health, safety or well-being of the parties and of any relevant child;

(d) the conduct of the parties in relation to each other and otherwise;

(e) the length of time that has elapsed since the parties ceased to live together;

(f) the length of time that has elapsed since the marriage or civil partnership[196] was dissolved or annulled; and

(g) the existence of any pending proceedings between them [relating to ancillary relief or property].'[197]

The first four of these factors are the same as apply to applications by entitled applicants. The last three factors are intended to focus attention upon the 'qualification' of the applicant for an order. By this, the Law Commission appear to have meant that, where an applicant is not on an equal footing in property rights terms with the respondent, she needs to show some justification for obtaining a declaratory order giving rights she would not otherwise have, separate from the basic need for protection which is catered for in the regulatory parts of the order.[198]

As far as determining which regulatory provisions might be included, the court is directed to consider the factors in paragraphs (a) to (e)—which may perhaps be viewed as the 'practical' issues, as distinct from ones concerning legal status and proceedings—and then apply the same 'balance of harm' presumption as applies to entitled applicants.[199]

Cohabitants and former cohabitants. Clearly, some of the factors relevant to former spouses or civil partners, such as the length of time which has elapsed since their marriage or partnership ended, cannot be applicable to cohabitants. Equally, the length and nature of a cohabiting relationship can vary enormously, and may be highly relevant to the question whether it would be just to make an order against a respondent. Accordingly, the Law Commission recommended that courts consider certain specific factors pertaining to the cohabitants' relationship when determining whether to make a declaratory order.[200]

---

[195] But the permitted duration of an order is different: see below, p 237.

[196] Inserted by Sch 9 para 5 to the Civil Partnership Act 2004.

[197] The proceedings specified are those for a property adjustment order under the Matrimonial Causes Act 1973 (in relation to former spouses), a property adjustment order under Part 2 of Sch 5 to the Civil Partnership Act 2004 (in relation to former civil partners), for a property order against a parent under the Children Act 1989 Sch 1, or relating to the legal or beneficial ownership of the dwelling-house: s 35(6)(g) as amended.

[198] See Law Com No 207 para 4.10.   [199] Section 35(7)–(8); see the discussion above, p 232.

[200] Law Com No 207 paras 4.10–4.13.

Parliament chose to emphasise the distinction in the 'quality' of the relationship of those who have made a public commitment to each other by being married or having formed a civil partnership as compared with cohabitants, and added to the relevant criteria. Thus, by s 36(6), as amended, the court is obliged to consider, in addition to the factors common to entitled applicants and former spouses and former civil partners:

'(e) the nature of the parties' relationship and in particular the level of commitment involved in it;[201]

(f) the length of time during which they have cohabited;[202]

(g) whether there are or have been any children who are children of both parties or for whom both parties have or have had parental responsibility;

(h) the length of time that has elapsed since the parties ceased to live together; and

(i) the existence of any pending proceedings between them over property.'[203]

It will be seen that in assessing the nature of the parties' relationship, the court must have regard in particular to the level of commitment involved in it. This replaces a more pejorative formulation, originally included as s 41 of the 1996 Act, which required the court 'to have regard to the fact that they have not given each other the commitment involved in marriage.' This provision was inserted by Parliament to stress the symbolic significance of marriage and to penalise cohabitation, but it is doubtful whether it added very much to the other factors which are specified. It is unlikely that a court, hearing an application by a woman who had lived with her partner for twenty years, raised their children and run a business together, was going to reject her application because they 'did not get round to the paperwork'. By the same token, a court is, under the revised wording, just as unlikely as before to show much sympathy to a financially independent applicant with no children who moves into her boyfriend's house for a month and then, having given up her own rented property, attempts to exclude him from his home.

When determining whether to include any regulatory provisions in the order, the court is required to consider the same common factors as before, and the balance of harm test.[204] However, for cohabitants and former cohabitants, this test does not operate as a *presumption* in favour of making an order but only as a further consideration. This differentiation was inserted by Parliament as a further attempt to differentiate marriage (and presumably, now, civil partnership) from cohabitation, and out of concern that courts should not be constrained to make orders where the applicant could point neither to property entitlement nor to recognised relationship status as a qualification for an order.

Duration of an order

The Law Commission considered that the purpose of occupation orders for non-entitled applicants is to provide relatively short-term protection to enable the applicant to find alternative accommodation, await the outcome of any legal proceedings over the property, or, one might add, to reconcile with the respondent.[205] Whereas entitled applicants are

---

[201] Amended by s 2(2) of the Domestic Violence, Crime and Victims Act 2004.

[202] Amended by Sch 10 para 34(3) to the Domestic Violence, Crime and Victims Act 2004.

[203] The proceedings specified are those for a property order under the Children Act 1989 Sch 1 or those relating to the legal or beneficial ownership of the dwelling-house.

[204] Section 36(7)–(8).   [205] Law Com No 207 paras 4.7 and 4.19.

able to obtain orders of unlimited duration, the Act restricts this for non-entitled applicants, once again distinguishing between those who have been married (or in a civil partnership) and those who have not.[206]

Former spouses and former civil partners. Section 35(10) limits the length of an order in favour of a non-entitled former spouse or former civil partner to a specified period not exceeding six months, although the order may be extended on one or more occasions.

Cohabitants and former cohabitants. Section 36(10) similarly limits the duration of an order to a *maximum* period of six months, but, in line with Parliament's concern to restrict protection for this group of applicants, additionally provides that only one extension may be given, for a further maximum period of six months.

The consequence of these provisions, especially for cohabitants, is to provide a clear advantage, not simply to those who are married or in a civil partnership, as opposed to those who cohabit, but to those who can establish property rights compared with those who cannot. If Parliament had really wished to stress the value it attached to the formal legal commitment demonstrated by entry into marriage or civil partnership, it could have discriminated against even those cohabitants who have property rights, for example, by requiring the court to consider the nature of their relationship with the respondent, or by imposing a limit on the duration of any order, but it chose to do so only against those applicants who are the most vulnerable—those who have not acquired a proprietary right or interest in their home.

Applicants are likely wherever possible to attempt to bring themselves within the entitled category by seeking to establish a property right. However, this is not straightforward. It is open to a person to apply for an order as a non-entitled applicant, whilst preserving the right to claim a legal or equitable interest in any property in other proceedings,[207] but the crucial question under s 33, where no *legal* title can be established, is not whether a person has a beneficial interest, but whether such an interest gives him the right to occupy the dwelling-house. Sections 35(11) and 36(11) provide that a person who has an equitable interest in the house, or in the proceeds of sale of the house, but no legal title, is to be treated as a non-entitled applicant, so that the application is governed by s 35 or s 36, whilst still having the option of establishing such right to occupy and hence the right to apply under s 33.[208] Bearing in mind that most applicants are likely to be seeking an order as a matter of some urgency, and considering that magistrates' courts may not determine disputed questions of entitlement to occupy,[209] applicants may have to cut their losses by relying on the non-entitled provisions, in the hope that they will satisfy the criteria for the grant of an order. There is, at least, a back-stop provision, since a court may grant an order under the appropriate qualifying section, even though the application has been brought under another.[210]

Neither party entitled to remain in occupation of the home

Where neither spouse nor civil partner has a property right in respect of the family home, then neither can have home rights, and therefore cannot be classed as an entitled applicant.[211] Similarly, former spouses, civil partners or cohabitants may be living in a property

---

[206] The order may be varied or discharged on the application of either party: s 49.
[207] Section 39(4).   [208] Sections 35(12) and 36(12).   [209] Section 59.
[210] Section 39(3).   [211] See s 30(1)(a).

in which neither has the right to remain, for example, as bare licensees or squatters. Since the former law permitted spouses and cohabitants to obtain ouster injunctions in such circumstances, the Law Commission recommended that the protection continue, and be extended to the other classes of non-entitled applicants.[212] Sections 37[213] and 38 duly permit applicants to obtain regulatory orders[214] to control occupation of the property by the applicant and respondent. In respect of spouses and civil partners, and former spouses and former civil partners, the criteria for making such an order are the same as apply to entitled applicants, including the balance of harm presumption.[215] No consideration of the applicant's qualification to seek an order is required, since she has no lesser entitlement to occupy the property than the respondent. However, any order made is subject to a maximum duration of six months, although it may be extended on more than one occasion.[216] A court considering whether to make an order in favour of a cohabitant or former cohabitant must have regard to the factors common to all applications,[217] and then consider the balance of harm test, although not as a presumption.[218] The order may have effect for up to six months, and may be renewed once.[219]

(d) Additional provisions

Where the court makes an order under s 33, s 35 or s 36, it may, at the same time, or at any time afterwards, include additional provisions.[220] It may impose on either party an obligation as to the repair and maintenance of the property or the payment of rent, mortgage or other outgoings. This may be important to preserve the long-term security of the property. For example, it would clearly be regrettable to control the parties' occupation but leave it open to the occupant to neglect the property, or for the party in a position to pay, but now excluded, to fall behind with payments, resulting in repossession. It may also require the occupying party to make periodical payments to the other, as compensation for that person's loss of occupation. Further, it may grant either party the possession or use of furniture or other contents of the home; order either party to take reasonable care of these, and order either party to take reasonable steps to keep the dwelling-house and contents secure. Such provisions may be important, as it is not unknown for a party, before letting an applicant back into the property, to strip the home of its contents, or to damage it.[221] Unfortunately, however, they are unenforceable. In *Nwogbe v Nwogbe*[222] the Court of Appeal upheld the trial judge's view that, since the provisions in s 40 are not expressly mentioned in any of the legislation concerning the enforcement of debts and judgments,[223] there was no power to commit the husband, who had failed to pay the monthly

212 See Law Com No 207 para 4.8.
213 As amended by Sch 9 para 8 to the Civil Partnership Act 2004.
214 Declaratory orders cannot be made, since, by definition, the parties have no right to occupy the property. The provisions which may be included in the order are set out in s 37(3)—spouses and former spouses—and s 38(3)—cohabitants and former cohabitants.
215 Section 37(4).   216 Section 37(5).
217 Section 38(4). Viz: housing needs, financial resources, likely effect of any order on the health, safety or well-being of the parties or a relevant child and the parties' conduct.
218 Section 38(5).   219 Section 38(6).   220 Section 40.
221 See *Davis v Johnson* [1979] AC 264, HL.   222 [2000] 2 FLR 744, CA.
223 Debtors Act 1869, ss 4 and 5, Administration of Justice Act 1970, s 28 and Sch 8, Attachment of Earnings Act 1971, Sch 1.

rent on the matrimonial home, to prison for contempt of court.[224] Despite the court's opinion that this required urgent attention, the lacuna has not yet been closed.

(e) Enforcing orders

Introduction of power of arrest

Breach of the terms of a court order may be a civil contempt of court, but contempt procedures normally take a number of days and in the meantime the victim may be at risk. Consequently, the Domestic Violence and Matrimonial Proceedings Act 1976 and the Domestic Proceedings and Magistrates' Courts Act 1978 both empowered the court, on making an order restraining the respondent from using violence (but not just molest-ation), or excluding a respondent from the home, to attach a power of arrest to the order. This enabled the police to arrest a respondent without a warrant, and to detain him for up to 24 hours before bringing him before a judge. Such a power could only be included where there was proof that the respondent had caused physical (or in the case of the 1976 Act, psychological) harm to the applicant or a child, and was likely to do so again. Coupled with this limitation, courts also considered that the civil liberties implications of empowering summary arrest and detention for breach of a civil order were such that the power should only be used 'where men or women persistently disobey injunctions and make a nuisance of themselves to the other party and to others concerned'.[225] Thus, the power was attached in only a minority of cases.[226]

The Law Commission were impressed by the weight of opinion supporting a presump-tion in favour of attaching a power of arrest in any case where there had been violence or threatened violence, viewing the power as 'a simple, immediate and inexpensive means of enforcement which underlines the seriousness of the breach to the offending party',[227] and they recommended accordingly. Section 47 of the Family Law Act 1996 therefore originally provided that if a court made an occupation or non-molestation order and it appeared to the court that the respondent had used or threatened violence against the applicant or a relevant child:

'. . . it shall attach a power of arrest to one or more provisions of the order unless satisfied that in all the circumstances of the case the applicant or child will be adequately protected without such a power of arrest.'[228]

Although there was still a need to show violence, rather than 'mere' pestering etc, before a power could be attached, the addition of evidence of the threat of violence made the provision much wider than under the former law. Moreover, the incorporation of a pre-sumption in favour of attachment tilted the balance towards a focus upon protection of

---

[224] The Court appears to have thought that none of the provisions in s 40 are enforceable, but query those which do not relate to the payment of money? Where money is still sought, a spouse or civil partner could seek a periodical payments order instead but, as M Humphries points out, 'Occupation Orders Revisited' [2001] Fam Law 542, such an order would then impinge on any income-related welfare benefits being received by the applicant.

[225] Per Ormrod LJ in *Lewis v Lewis* [1978] Fam 60 at 63, CA. A similar approach was taken under the magistrates' jurisdiction: *Widdowson v Widdowson* (1982) 4 FLR 121.

[226] In 1996, of 22,652 injunctions granted under the 1976 Act, 10,049 (44%) had powers of arrest attached: *Judicial Statistics 1996* Table 5.9.

[227] Law Com No 207 para 5.13.   [228] Section 47(2).

the victim from further harm, resulting in a much higher proportion of orders being made with the power attached: in 2004, 20,890 non-molestation orders (89%) out of 23,357 included the power of arrest, as did 7,640 (84%) out of 9,075 occupation orders.[229]

Breach of a non-molestation order made a criminal offence[230]

However, the Government considered that police officers were often unclear about whether they could arrest a respondent under the attached power or not, especially where it was attached only to particular provisions in the order. They noted that information on orders and powers of arrest is not recorded centrally, with inconsistent arrangements for exchanging information between police forces.[231] They were also concerned that, where the victim had to apply for an arrest warrant because no power had been attached, she was at risk of further violence pending its issue.[232] The Domestic Violence, Crime and Victims Act 2004 therefore inserted s 42A into the 1996 Act, to provide that:

'(1) A person who without reasonable excuse does anything that he is prohibited from doing by a non-molestation order is guilty of an offence.'

Those seeking to enforce the non-molestation order will have to choose whether to charge the offence or proceed via contempt proceedings, as the defendant cannot be punished twice over.[233] One would expect the criminal route to be preferred, both because it clarifies the powers of the police and because the maximum sentence on conviction on indictment is a term of imprisonment of five years plus a fine,[234] compared with two years imprisonment for contempt.[235] The objective test imposed for liability for the offence appears in line with the mental element required for the offence of harassment under the Protection from Harassment Act 1997.[236]

Unlike the original power of arrest under s 47, which was limited to cases where it appeared to the court that the respondent had used or threatened violence, the criminal offence may apply to a breach in respect of non-violent incidents of 'molestation', although these, presumably, will be dealt with summarily.

Power of arrest for breach of occupation order

It will be noted that breach of an occupation order has *not* been made a criminal offence, but that when a court is deciding whether to make an occupation order, it must consider whether to make a non-molestation order of its own motion.[237] Doing so will, of course,

---

[229] *Judicial Statistics 2004* (2005) Table 5.9.

[230] For a useful discussion, see DJ R Hill, 'The Domestic Violence, Crime and Victims Act 2004' [2005] Fam Law 281.

[231] Home Office, *Safety and Justice* (2003) para 46. The Government were 'minded' to introduce a register of civil orders to enable the police and prosecutors to check a suspect's history (see para 59), but have not yet done so. However, they did create an information sharing protocol for crime reduction agencies, including those working in the domestic violence field: see www.crimereduction.gov.uk/informationsharing.

[232] Home para 46.

[233] Section 42A(3)(4). Cf conviction for other offences is not precluded by an earlier punishment for contempt, although the court should take this into account: *DPP v Tweddell* [2001] EWCA Admin 188 [2002] 2 FLR 400. See also *Hale v Tanner* [2000] 1 WLR 2377 CA, *Lomas v Parle* [2003] EWCA Civ 1804 [2004] 1 WLR 1643 discussed below at p 244. See C Bessant, 'Enforcing Non-Molestation Orders in the Civil and Criminal Courts' [2005] Fam Law 640.

[234] Section 42A(5)(a). The maximum for summary conviction is imprisonment for 12 months plus a fine not exceeding the statutory maximum.

[235] Contempt of Court Act 1981 s 14(1).   [236] See above p 219.   [237] Above at p 229.

bring in the criminal sanction for breach of the latter order which, one might assume, will usually encompass acts in breach of the occupation order as well. However, the court might decide that it is inappropriate to make the respondent subject to a non-molestation order, or that breach of the occupation order requires separate enforcement. Section 47 therefore now provides that, while it is no longer possible to attach a power of arrest to a non-molestation order, the court may continue to do so, in the same circumstances as hitherto, when making an occupation order.[238] Where such a power is attached, a police constable may arrest without warrant a person whom he has reasonable cause for suspecting to be in breach of any provision in the occupation order to which the arrest power is attached.[239]

In *Re B-J (Power of Arrest)* the Court of Appeal held that the duration of the power of arrest may be shorter than that of the order to which it is attached.[240] This may seem illogical, since the point of attaching the power is to enable enforcement of the order. However, the court considered that while it may be appropriate to make the substantive order of indefinite or long duration because of the circumstances between the parties, it would put the cart before the horse to limit the order because the court feels that it is unnecessary that the power of arrest last so long.[241] Equally, it is unjust to the respondent to hold him at risk of arrest for a period longer than is necessary to ensure his compliance.

Warrant for arrest

Where the court has made a non-molestation order, or a power of arrest has not been attached to an occupation order (or only to certain provisions of it), the applicant may apply for the issue of a warrant for the respondent's arrest if she considers that he has failed to comply with the order.[242] This enables the applicant to utilise the more effective powers under s 47 to get the respondent before the court than relying on civil contempt powers alone, but it is hard to see when such a warrant would be needed in respect of breach of a non-molestation order since this is arrestable anyway. Use of such warrants is low, with 135 issued in 2004:[243] in practice, the power of arrest attached to the original order is much more important.

Dealing with the respondent after arrest

If the respondent is arrested for breach of the non-molestation order under s 42A, he will be subject to the usual criminal justice processes regarding detention, charge and remand. Where, however, the arrest is made under s 47, its purpose is to bring the respondent before the relevant judicial authority for punishment for contempt. This must be done

---

[238] As amended by the Domestic Violence, Crime and Victims Act 2004 Sch 10 para 38. See DJ R Hill, 'Abolition of the Power of Arrest' [2005] Fam Law 474.

[239] Section 47(6).   [240] [2000] 2 FLR 443, CA.

[241] Cf the Court of Appeal's view, in *Chechi v Bashier* [1999] 2 FLR 489, that the trial judge had correctly declined to make a non-molestation order where the power of arrest that would have been attached to it would have given the applicant too much power over his relatives, in the particular family dynamics in that case: see above at p 228.

[242] Section 47(8) as amended. The application must be substantiated on oath and the relevant judicial authority must have reasonable grounds for believing that the respondent has failed to comply with the order. For 'relevant judicial authority' see s 63(1).

[243] *Judicial Statistics 2004* (2005) Table 5.9.

within 24 hours from the time of the arrest,[244] and he may then be remanded, on bail or in custody,[245] or dealt with for the breach.[246] But it may be noted that a minor cannot be committed for contempt, although a power of arrest may still be attached to the order made against him which may be useful in removing him from the scene.[247] The respondent need not understand the nature of the contempt jurisdiction or the concept of contempt; it is enough that he understands that an order has been made against him and that he will be punished if he breaks its terms. It was therefore appropriate for a judge to continue an injunction with a power of arrest attached against a deaf and dumb man with limited vision, but who had an average IQ, in response to his breach, on 29 occasions, of the original order not to go back to the former matrimonial home.[248]

In determining how to punish a breach of a non-molestation or occupation order, the courts have laid down what can sometimes appear rather conflicting guidelines. In *Neil v Ryan*[249] the Court of Appeal held that an immediate sentence of imprisonment was justified where the respondent committed a serious assault on the victim in plain disregard of the non-molestation order. They considered that unless such an attack was met with immediate committal, the wrong message would be sent to the perpetrator. Nonetheless, in *Hale v Tanner*,[250] they considered that a suspension of imprisonment should usually be the first compliance strategy to be considered by a court dealing with contempt, and indeed reduced a suspended sentence from six months to 28 days where the perpetrator had continued to bombard her ex-boyfriend with phone calls after a non-molestation order had been made. The Court made allowance for the fact that no immediate threat of violence had been made, that the perpetrator had admitted the allegations, that she was the mother of a young child and that she had not been present or represented in court when the original order was made. It also took account of the fact that the perpetrator was facing separate criminal charges. However, in *H v O (Contempt of Court: Sentencing)*[251] the Court of Appeal stressed the importance of passing comparable sentences to those that a criminal court would hand down, whilst paying due regard to the two-year maximum sentence available under s 14 of the Contempt of Court Act 1981. It upheld an immediate sentence of imprisonment, although it cut the length from 12 to nine months.

244 Excluding Christmas Day, Good Friday or any Sunday: s 47(7). Where the arrest is pursuant to a warrant, the respondent must be brought before the court immediately.

245 The remand may be for the purpose of enabling a medical examination of the respondent to be carried out. Should it be suspected that the respondent is suffering from mental illness or mental impairment, he may be remanded under the Mental Health Act 1983 s 35 for a report: s 48.

246 The possible sanctions range from making no order but warning the respondent as to his future conduct, to sequestration of assets, (immediate or suspended) committal to prison or committal to a hospital under the Mental Health Act 1983: s 51; see Horton, op cit para 9.5.2.

247 *Re H (Respondent under 18: Power of Arrest)* [2001] 1 FLR 641, CA.

248 See above p 229 n 154 and, for contempt, see *P v P (Contempt of Court: Mental Capacity)* [1999] 2 FLR 897, CA.

249 [1998] 2 FLR 1068, CA. See also *A-A v B-B* [2001] 2 FLR 1, CA (Moroccan husband and wife; husband sentenced to 12 months' imprisonment for raping wife soon after non-molestation and occupation orders made: wife too ashamed to go to the police or tell her family).

250 [2000] 1 WLR 2377, CA.

251 [2004] EWCA Civ 1691 [2005] 2 FLR 329. Where a case warrants a sentence at the top of the range, consideration should be give to using the Protection from Harassment Act 1997 instead: *Robinson v Murray* [2005] EWCA Civ 935 [2005] 3 FCR 504 and *Carabott v Huxley* [2005] All ER(D) 80 (Aug). See also *Loughran v Pandya* [2005] EWCA Civ 1720: two years' suspended sentence cut to eight months because breaches not the most serious contempts of court.

In *Hale v Tanner*, the Court upheld the trial judge's order that the period of suspension be until the underlying non-molestation order expired. In *Griffin v Griffin*[252] the Court of Appeal agreed with the first instance judge that it is permissible to impose a suspended sentence of imprisonment to last as long as the substantive orders remain in effect, even though, in that case these were of indefinite duration. However, it is not possible for the court, where a contemnor wishes to purge his contempt, to order that the remainder of a sentence of imprisonment be suspended so long as the respondent obeys the terms of the underlying orders, where this would extend beyond the probable date of his release having served the full sentence.[253]

Sometimes, as noted in *Hale v Tanner*, concurrent proceedings may be taken against the perpetrator in both the civil and criminal jurisdictions, in respect of the same, or connected, incidents. In *Lomas v Parle*,[254] the husband made threats to kill his wife and was charged with common assault. He was given bail and continued his threats. The wife obtained non-molestation orders, and he was sentenced to 56 days in prison for breach of these. On his release, he continued to threaten the wife and was charged under the Protection from Harassment Act 1997. He received a community sentence for the assault charges, and a restraining order and conditional discharge for the harassment offence. Further breaches of the non-molestation order led to another sentence of four months' imprisonment. On release, his campaign against the wife continued, and he was due to be sentenced for breach of the restraining order. The wife appealed against a further term of four months imprisonment for breach of the non-molestation order.[255] The Court of Appeal agreed that the sentence was unduly lenient and would have raised it to ten months. However, they noted that there is a risk of double jeopardy where the perpetrator is facing separate proceedings, which is compounded by the possibility that he will be represented by different lawyers and that the courts may not know what each is doing. They therefore held that an eight-month sentence was appropriate, and laid down guidelines for coping with such concurrent proceedings. Whilst an important objective for the judge in contempt proceedings is to uphold the authority of the court by demonstrating that its orders may not be flouted with impunity, there is a shared deterrent objective with the criminal courts in the punishment of domestic violence by imprisonment. The first court to sentence the perpetrator should do so on the basis of the case before it and not anticipate or allow for a likely future sentence by the other court. It will be for that court to reflect the prior sentence in its judgment, in order to ensure that the defendant is not punished twice for the same offence. The second court must be fully informed of the factors and circumstances reflected in the first sentence; it will need information on the basis of the first sentence and a transcript of the first court's judgment. Since committal proceedings may be heard more quickly than criminal proceedings, the application to commit should be issued promptly after the alleged breach and listed without delay. This will ensure that, if proved, the contempt will have been punished before any sentence in the parallel criminal proceedings.

---

[252] [2000] 2 FLR 44, CA.   [253] *Harris v Harris* [2001] EWCA Civ 1645, [2002] 1 FLR 248.
[254] [2003] EWCA Civ 1804 [2004] 1 WLR 1643. See M Burton, '*Lomas v Parle*—Coherent and effective remedies for victims of domestic violence: time for an integrated domestic violence court?' [2004] CFLQ 317.
[255] The power to increase a sentence of committal clearly exists but must be exercised sparingly: *Wilson v Webster* [1998] 1 FLR 1097, *Linnett v Coles* [1987] QB 555.

Clearly, courts dealing with committal are constrained by the two-year maximum sentence which may be imposed,[256] but the Court considered that they should seek, where possible, to ensure that the sentences passed are not manifestly discrepant with sentences for harassment under the 1997 Act.[257] Where other criminal offences have been charged, with higher maxima, it will be more difficult to achieve this consistency, however. Interestingly, the Court was advised that sentences for harassment are significantly higher than those imposed for breach of non-molestation orders, but this hardly seems borne out by the facts in this particular case, nor by the analysis of sentencing practice noted above.[258] Indeed, one might observe that the failure of the criminal courts to punish the perpetrator effectively—or even to remand him in custody—contributed to his seizing 'any leniency as little more than an opportunity to resume his campaign against the wife.'[259] But the Court of Appeal also considered that measures other than imprisonment might, in the long run, be more effective than custody and, given the emotional state of perpetrators, this seems an important consideration.[260] At present, however, the sanctions for contempt are limited.[261]

(f) Ex parte orders

It was possible under the former legislation to obtain an order ex parte (without notice), although this was rare, especially in respect of what were then called ouster orders. The courts considered that orders should only be made where it was necessary to act quickly to avert a real and immediate danger of serious injury or irreparable damage,[262] and that, where possible, substituted service or abridgement of the period of notice should be used instead. The Law Commission recognised the drawbacks of ex parte orders: they might be based on misconceived or malicious allegations with no opportunity for the court to test these out. There is, moreover, no opportunity to try to resolve the parties' differences by agreed undertakings,[263] nor is there scope for bringing home to the respondent the seriousness of the situation and the importance of compliance with the order.[264] However, the need to provide a protective remedy as a matter of urgency, or to provide a breathing-space to enable an applicant to pursue her remedy, led them to recommend a test which would balance these competing considerations.

Section 45 now provides that a court may make either a non-molestation or occupation

---

[256] For the superior courts, and one month for inferior court: s 14(1) Contempt of Court Act 1981.

[257] See above at p 221. See also *H v O (Contempt of Court: Sentencing)* [2004] EWCA Civ 1691, [2005] 2 FLR 329 where the court noted that societal attitudes to domestic and other violence associated with harassment and molestation as demanding rather more condign punishment than had been the case in the past.

[258] At p 222.   [259] Per Thorpe LJ at para 41.

[260] See also *Aquilina v Aquilina* [2004] EWCA Civ 504, sentence for breach of non-molestation orders reduced from six months to three months, the court urging both parties, who were in dispute over their children, to 'take a deep breath and to review where they are and to start making positive arrangements that will enable them to separate with dignity' per Ward LJ at para 13.

[261] See s 14 of the Contempt of Court Act 1981. There are no community penalties or commitment to anger management programmes available, for example.

[262] *Ansah v Ansah* [1977] Fam 138, CA; *G v G (Ouster: Ex Parte Application)* [1990] 1 FLR 395, CA; *Practice Note* [1978] 2 All ER 919.

[263] Discussed below.   [264] Law Com No 207, para 5.6.

order ex parte where 'it considers it just and convenient to do so', but must have regard to all the circumstances, including:

'(a) any risk of significant harm to the applicant or a relevant child, attributable to conduct of the respondent, if the order is not made immediately;

(b) whether it is likely that the applicant will be deterred or prevented from pursuing the application if an order is not made immediately; and

(c) whether there is reason to believe that the respondent is aware of the proceedings but is deliberately evading service and that an applicant or a relevant child will be seriously prejudiced by the delay involved [in effecting service].'[265]

The court making an order must afford the respondent the opportunity of a full hearing as soon as is just and convenient, and the duration of any occupation order made at the full hearing must be calculated taking into account the date when the ex parte order was made.[266] The court may attach a power of arrest to an ex parte occupation order[267] if it appears that the respondent has used or threatened violence against the applicant or a relevant child, and there is a risk of significant harm to them, attributable to the respondent's conduct, if the power of arrest is not attached to the order immediately. In such a case, the court may provide that the power of arrest is to last for a shorter period than the other provisions in the order, which reflects the concern that the respondent's civil liberties are doubly jeopardised in a case where, first, he is at risk of arrest for a civil matter, and secondly, he has had no opportunity to contest the making of the order.[268]

(g) Undertakings

An undertaking whereby the respondent gives a promise to the court in the terms of the proposed order, for example, that he will not molest the applicant, and will leave the home within seven days, became a common[269] and popular alternative mechanism to the making of an order under the former law. It was to the respondent's advantage, since no finding of fact would be made on the applicant's allegations against him. It was to the court's advantage, because it obviated the need for a full hearing and thus saved time. And it was to the applicant's advantage, inter alia because she did not need to give evidence against the respondent in court, and because an undertaking has the effect of an order of the court and is therefore enforceable through contempt proceedings. It was also said to reduce confrontation and defuse explosive situations.[270] The Association of District Judges

---

[265] Section 45(2).   [266] Section 45(3), (4).

[267] Section 47(3) as amended by Sch 10 para 38(4) to the Domestic Violence, Crime and Victims Act 2004.

[268] See President's Direction: Family Law Act 1996 Part IV [1998] 1 FLR 496.

[269] Jones et al, 'Domestic violence applications: an empirical study of one court' (1995) 17 JSWFL 67, Tables 15 and 16 found nearly half of non-molestation applications were resolved by means of an undertaking in the court they studied, and District Judge Bird put the proportion at 80% in his memorandum to the House of Lords Special Public Committee, Written Evidence p 7. Magistrates did not have the power to accept undertakings.

[270] DJ S Gerlis 'The Family Homes and Domestic Violence Bill—Undermining the Undertaking' [1994] Fam Law 700. The problems of utilising mediation to deal with domestic violence are discussed by F Kaganas and C Piper 'Domestic Violence and Divorce Mediation' (1994) 16 JSWFL 265 and F Raitt 'Domestic Violence and divorce mediation: A rejoinder' (1996) 18 JSWFL 11.

submitted to the House of Lords Special Public Bill Committee that the practice of giving undertakings should be covered by legislation and not simply by rules,[271] and s 46 (as amended) accordingly deals with the issue by empowering all courts, including the magistrates, to accept an undertaking from any party to the proceedings.

It was formerly well-established[272] that a police power of arrest could not be attached to an undertaking, and this was put into statutory form in s 46(2). The applicant who agrees to an undertaking rather than proceeding with her application therefore runs the risk of facing difficulty if she needs practical enforcement measures to be taken in the future.[273] However, s 46(3) now provides that a court shall not accept an undertaking 'instead of making an occupation order in any case where, apart from this section a power of arrest would be attached to the order.'[274] Section 46(3A)[275] also directs a court not to accept an undertaking instead of making a non-molestation order where it appears that the respondent has used or threatened violence against the applicant or a relevant child (the same test as for attaching a power of arrest) and, for their protection, it is necessary to make a non-molestation order so that any breach may be punishable under s 42A. Accordingly, a court ought not to accept an undertaking where it would otherwise make an order which could be enforceable by a power of arrest. This approach was criticised on the basis that it would prevent courts, and deter applicants, from accepting undertakings, even though these may otherwise be appropriate solutions to the family crisis.[276] But the proportion of cases where an undertaking is accepted still appears to be quite high. In 2004, undertakings were accepted in 3,319 cases, some 42%, compared with 8,091 on notice applications for both types of order.[277]

2 PROTECTION FROM HARASSMENT ACT 1997

Before the Protection from Harassment Act 1997, attempts were made to extend the existing law of tort to cover harassment. It was held in *Patel v Patel*[278] that harassment does not amount to a distinct tort. However, relying upon old cases,[279] where it had been held that conduct calculated to impair the plaintiff's health, and having that effect, was a tort, the Court of Appeal in *Burnett v George*[280] was able to hold that pestering having the like consequence could be restrained by injunction. An attempt to broaden tort law further by classifying harassment as a form of private nuisance was made in *Khorasandjian v Bush*.[281] There, it was held, in addition to applying *Burnett v George*, that persistent telephone calls made to the plaintiff at the home she shared with her parents, constituted an actionable interference with her ordinary and reasonable use and enjoyment of the property which amounted to nuisance, even though she was not the legal occupier of the property. However, in *Hunter v Canary Wharf Ltd*[282] the House

---

[271] House of Lords Special Public Committee, *Written Evidence* p 6.

[272] *Carpenter v Carpenter* [1988] 1 FLR 121, CA.

[273] See the concerns expressed by A Kewley 'Pragmatism before principle: the limitations of civil law remedies for the victims of domestic violence' [1996] JSWFL 1.

[274] As amended by Sch 10 para 37 to the Domestic Violence, Crime and Victims Act 2004. See above p 242.

[275] Ibid.   [276] S Gerlis, 'Undertakings Redeemed' [1996] Fam Law 233.

[277] *Judicial Statistics 2004* (2005) Table 5.9.   [278] [1988] 2 FLR 179, CA.

[279] *Wilkinson v Downton* [1897] 2 QB 57; *Janvier v Sweeney* [1919] 2 KB 316, CA.

[280] [1992] 1 FLR 525, CA.   [281] [1993] QB 727, CA.   [282] [1997] AC 655, HL.

of Lords overruled the decision on this point, although not on the view that there is a tort of carrying out conduct calculated to harm, and resulting in harm to, the victim.

The civil law was tidied up by the 1997 Act, which, as well as creating the new criminal offences of harassment and putting a person in fear of violence,[283] also created a statutory tort of harassment, based on a claim brought 'by the person who is or may be the victim of the course of conduct in question'.[284]

Section 3(2) provides for damages to be awarded for, inter alia, any anxiety caused by the harassment, and any financial loss which results. It has been said that the prospect of damages may be attractive in cases (perhaps few?) where the perpetrator has the means to satisfy the award, and it has been held that there is no bar on concurrent applications under both s 42 of the 1996 Act and this provision. Where that is done, the application should be issued in the same court, consolidated, and tried by a judge with jurisdiction in both civil and family cases.[285] The High Court or county court may also issue an injunction to prohibit further harassment, and the plaintiff may apply for a warrant for arrest to be issued where he or she considers that the defendant has broken the terms of such an injunction.[286] Breach of the injunction may be punishable either as a contempt of court or, where the defendant has no reasonable excuse, as an offence.[287] According to the Divisional Court in *Hipgrave and Hipgrave v Jones*[288] although breach is therefore potentially a criminal offence, the standard of proof for the issue of the injunction itself is the ordinary civil standard. It distinguished seeking an injunction under s 3 from say, an anti-social behaviour order sought by a public authority (where the criminal standard applies),[289] as the former is a private remedy sought by an individual.

3 INTEGRATED DOMESTIC VIOLENCE COURTS[290]

In *Lomas v Parle*, the Court of Appeal drew attention to the

'unsatisfactory nature of the present interface between the criminal and family courts in [domestic violence] cases. It is expensive, wasteful of resources and time-consuming. It is stressful for the victim to move from court to court in order to obtain redress and protection from the perpetrator.'[291]

They suggested that the passage of the Domestic Violence Crime and Victims Bill was an opportunity to explore the possibility of integrated courts to see if they might avoid the

---

[283] See the discussion above at p 218ff.

[284] Section 3(1). For procedural issues, see DJ R Hill, 'Protection from Harassment' [2005] Fam Law 364 at pp 366–367.

[285] *Lomas v Parle* [2003] EWCA Civ 1804 [2004] 1 WLR 1643 at para 44.

[286] But the court cannot attach a power of arrest at the time of issuing the injunction. As with an application for an arrest warrant under s 47(8) of the Family Law Act 1996, the application must be substantiated on oath, and the court must have reasonable grounds for believing that the defendant has broken the injunction: s 3(5).

[287] Section 3(6)–(8). The offence is punishable on indictment by imprisonment for a term not exceeding five years and/or a fine; or, on summary conviction, to imprisonment for a term not exceeding six months, and/or a fine: s 3(9).

[288] [2004] EWHC 2901 (QB), [2005] 2 FLR 174.   [289] *R v McCann* [2003] 1 AC 787.

[290] For a valuable description, see M Burton, 'Domestic Violence—From Consultation to Bill: Closer integration of the civil and criminal justice systems' [2004] Fam Law 128.

[291] At para [51].

problems they had identified. However, although the Government sought opinions on the creation of specialised courts,[292] no legislative measures have yet been taken to develop them. Instead, local initiatives have been taken to establish courts, operating only in the criminal jurisdiction, and only at the magistrates' level as yet, to focus on domestic violence cases. These courts list domestic violence cases for a single dedicated session, and promote multi-disciplinary working amongst the relevant agencies.[293] Evaluation suggests that they can speed up the processing of cases and help victims feel more able to proceed with cases, although they have not altered the types of charge, outcome, or sentence imposed. Such findings parallel those in the United States, which have also found greater use of plea-bargaining. The next step, of providing criminal and civil jurisdiction in the same court, has been taken in several states in the USA, in Canada and in Europe. But whilst judges and prosecutors apparently consider that these produce administrative efficiency and reduced recidivism, defendants' lawyers considered the courts to be biased. A chief advantage of the integrated court appears to be, as the Court of Appeal had hoped, that it can prevent the victim being shifted from pillar to post and ensure that there is full awareness of all the circumstances in the case, but concern has also been expressed that women can be pressurised into pursuing the criminal justice route against their will, or that they may even be deterred from using the court at all, for fear of having their children removed.[294]

In the remaining parts of this chapter, we discuss other means of obtaining prohibitive orders, and then turn to the law governing the provision of accommodation as a means of support to those who are escaping violence or an intolerable atmosphere at home.

4 INJUNCTIONS IN OTHER CIVIL PROCEEDINGS

The 1996 Act is intended to cater for a wide range of family relationships where some form of protective order is required, and the Protection from Harassment Act 1997 provides a jurisdiction dealing with harassment as statutorily defined, but there may remain a need to consider the general jurisdiction of the courts to provide injunctions, ancillary to substantive proceedings, in situations which might fall outside these two statutes.

There is considerable uncertainty in the case law regarding the basis of a general jurisdiction to grant injunctions. It is proposed to discuss first, the *statutory* basis to do so. The Supreme Court Act 1981 s 37 and the County Courts Act 1984 s 38 provide that the High Court and county courts may grant an interlocutory or final injunction 'in all cases in which it appears to the court to be just and convenient to do so.' In *Richards v Richards*,[295] the House of Lords held that an injunction may be granted under this jurisdiction only to support an existing legal or equitable right. Secondly, we discuss the existence of an

---

[292] Home Office, *Safety and Justice* (2003) paras 19, 20.

[293] For consideration of the use of social work support and mediation as an adjunct to the courts in such cases, see H Laufer, 'Managing Domestic Violence Cases in Family Court Social Services in Israel' (2004) 18 IJLPF 38.

[294] M Burton, 'Domestic Violence—from Consultation to Bill: Closer integration of the civil and criminal justice systems' [2004] Fam Law 128.

[295] [1984] AC 174, HL per Lord Hailsham LC at 200, Lord Scarman at 212 and Lord Brandon at 218. Lord Diplock and Lord Bridge concurred.

'*inherent jurisdiction*',[296] to grant injunctions. This has been relied upon to protect litigants in pending proceedings, and also, so far as the High Court is concerned, to protect children.

(a) Injunctions under the statutory jurisdiction

Injunctions to restrain a tort

The usual means of demonstrating interference with a right of the plaintiff is to establish that the defendant has committed a tort or other actionable wrong. An owner or tenant of property may rely upon the torts of trespass[297] or nuisance, although the former will not lie against a defendant who is also entitled to occupy the property.[298] A battery or assault by the defendant upon the plaintiff will clearly give rise to an action in damages and the possibility of an injunction to restrain repetition of the behaviour, and we have seen that harassment which is intended to cause, and results in, harm to the victim, may be actionable. However, this is narrower in scope than the statutory tort of harassment and there would appear to be little point in seeking to rely upon it. Furthermore, Lord Hailsham LC, in *Richards v Richards* considered that, where Parliament had laid down a statutory regime to govern a particular issue—ouster from the family home—it was not open to the courts to determine the matter without applying that regime.[299] The same reasoning may be held to apply to attempts to invoke the common law torts where statute, either under the Family Law Act or the Protection from Harassment Act, has laid down alternative criteria.[300]

Injunctions to support rights in relation to children

There appears to be no difficulty in granting a *non-molestation* injunction under the jurisdiction conferred by the Supreme Court Act or County Courts Act, ancillary to a s 8 order under the Children Act 1989 to protect a person's exercise of parental responsibility,[301] but there are conflicting decisions as to whether an *ouster* injunction can be ordered.[302] In *Ainsbury v Millington*[303] the Court of Appeal held that such an order could not be granted against a father who was the joint tenant of the home in which he and the mother had formerly cohabited, allied to a claim for custody, care and control by the

---

[296] In *Richards v Richards* [1984] AC 174, HL, it was asserted that the 'inherent jurisdiction' to grant injunctions is either absorbed by statute (Lord Hailsham at 199G), or its exercise is governed by statute (Lord Scarman at 212E, Lord Brandon at 218F,). However, the 'inherent jurisdiction' has continued to be referred to and relied upon, as is discussed below at p 252.

[297] *Lucas v Lucas* [1992] 2 FLR 53, CA.   [298] *Ainsbury v Millington* [1986] 1 All ER 73, CA.

[299] [1984] AC 174 at 199–200. Concurred in by Lord Diplock.

[300] On this basis, old cases suggesting that a non-molestation injunction may be granted to a spouse simply qua spouse may be open to doubt: *Robinson v Robinson* [1965] P 39; *Montgomery v Montgomery* [1965] P 46, although these decisions may be explicable as examples of protecting a litigant during pending proceedings, see below, p 251.

[301] *M v M (Residence Order: Ancillary Injunction)* [1994] Fam Law 441. See also *C v K (Inherent Powers; Exclusion Order)* [1996] 2 FLR 506; *Re P (Care Orders; Injunctive Relief)* [2000] 2 FLR 385; *Tameside Metropolitan Borough Council v M (Injunctive Relief: County Courts: Jurisdiction)* [2001] Fam Law 873 (county court).

[302] See the discussion by HH Judge Fricker 'Inherent Jurisdiction, Ouster and Exclusion' [1994] Fam Law 629, and by HH Judge Barnett, 'Inherent Jurisdiction, Ouster Orders and Children' [1997] Fam Law 96.

[303] [1986] 1 All ER 73, CA.

mother.[304] The mother could not assert a superior property right to his, and there was no power to grant the order ancillary to the child proceedings, as this would run counter to the House of Lords' reasoning in *Richards v Richards* to the effect that an ouster application was not a proceeding in which the custody or upbringing of a minor was in question. The decision was followed in *M v M*,[305] a case involving former spouses, where the father was the sole owner of the property. However, in *Wilde v Wilde*,[306] again involving former spouses, the court, considering itself bound by an earlier decision,[307] but without referring to *Ainsbury v Millington*, held that there was either an inherent jurisdiction to make an ouster order where this was desirable in the interests of the child, or a power under the statutory jurisdiction to grant injunctions to enforce the mother's right of care and control.[308] The main thrust of the court's reasoning in *Wilde v Wilde* related to the existence of an inherent jurisdiction, which is discussed further below, but the court's view that an injunction could be used to enforce a parental right was adopted by Wall J in *C v K (Inherent Powers: Exclusion Order)*,[309] where he held, preferring *Wilde v Wilde* to *Ainsbury v Millington*, that a joint tenant could be excluded from the former family home in order to ensure the free exercise by the other tenant of a residence order in respect of her granddaughter. The factual situations arising in all of these cases would now be within the ambit of the Family Law Act 1996, but the question of their impact on the surviving jurisdiction to issue injunctions remains unclear.

Injunctions to support right to pursue litigation free from intimidation

It has long been established that a court may grant an injunction to protect a litigant from intimidation from another party to pending proceedings,[310] and it has been argued that such cases are explicable as supporting a right to pursue remedies before the courts free from any pressure or influence from another party to the litigation.[311] However, they may also be viewed as illustrations of the exercise of the court's inherent jurisdiction, discussed below.

Link between cause of action and injunction

Even where the plaintiff can point to an actionable wrong, an injunction may only be granted to protect the right being asserted. Thus, it must 'bear some sensible relationship to the cause of action'.[312] An injunction ordering a person out of the house is clearly related to an action based on trespass to the property, but would not be if allied to a claim for financial provision, for example.[313] Defining an 'exclusion zone' around a property

---

304 An order may be granted in favour of a *sole* tenant allied to such proceedings: *Re W (a minor)* [1981] 3 All ER 401, CA.

305 [1988] 1 FLR 225, CA.   306 [1988] 2 FLR 83, CA.

307 *Quinn v Quinn* (1983) 4 FLR 394, CA.

308 An attempt to rationalise these cases was made by Thorpe J in *Pearson v Franklin (Parental Home: Ouster)* [1994] 2 All ER 137, CA on the basis that they must be distinguished according to the marital status of the parties. However, given that the Family Law Act 1996 caters for both married and formerly married, and cohabiting and formerly cohabiting couples, his explanation has been superseded and no longer helps in determining the continuing rationale for the exercise of the jurisdiction.

309 [1996] 2 FLR 506.

310 *Silverstone v Silverstone* [1953] 1 All ER 556; *Montgomery v Montgomery* [1965] P 46.

311 See HH Judge Barnett, 'Inherent Jurisdiction, Ouster Orders and Children' [1997] Fam Law 96.

312 Per Finer J in *McGibbon v McGibbon* [1973] Fam 170 at 173.

313 *Des Salles d'Epinoix v Des Salles d'Epinoix* [1967] 2 All ER 539, CA (non-molestation order).

within which the defendant must not go may be permitted where it is necessary to protect the applicant.[314]

(b) A remaining inherent jurisdiction?

Notwithstanding the views of Lords Hailsham and Scarman in the House of Lords in *Richards v Richards* to the effect that the 'inherent jurisdiction' is contained within the statutory power in the Supreme Court Act 1981 and County Courts Act, courts have continued to assert the existence of such a jurisdiction not subsumed within the statute.[315]

It is clear that the High Court exercising its parens patriae jurisdiction may make orders to protect children where necessary, and the old decisions asserting an 'inherent jurisdiction' may be examples of the exercise of that power. For example, in *Stewart v Stewart*[316] Sir George Baker P held that he had power to grant an ouster injunction 'because there are two young children who have to have a roof over their heads', and in *Wilde v Wilde*[317] Purchas LJ traced the origins of this view back to the exercise of the wardship jurisdiction, in *Re Spence*.[318] What is unclear is whether more recent decisions are similarly explicable. The difficulty is that they appear to assert that this inherent jurisdiction exists in the county court, yet such a view is in clear conflict with decisions of the Court of Appeal that the county court has no inherent power to grant injunctions to protect children at all.[319]

It is also unclear whether there is a further 'inherent' jurisdiction to protect litigants during proceedings, or whether this has been subsumed within the statutory provisions. It is submitted that it should be so regarded, as more in keeping with the thrust of the reasoning in *Richards v Richards*, and compatible with the view that the county court is a statutory jurisdiction which enjoys no inherent powers at all.

As far as the High Court's parens patriae jurisdiction is concerned, it is now understood that wardship is an aspect of this jurisdiction.[320] On this basis, it has been held that the inherent jurisdiction may be invoked by a local authority to obtain an injunction preventing a suspected sexual abuser from visiting the home and children of his woman friend.[321] More controversially, in *Re S (Minors)(Inherent Jurisdiction: Ouster)*,[322] the same approach was taken by Connell J in response to a local authority's application to have the children's father excluded from the home. The father conceded that the court had power to make the order, but his Lordship's view that the inherent jurisdiction was applicable and appropriate took no account of the statutory regime governing exclusion from the matrimonial home, and on that account appears to be in conflict with the House of Lords' approach in *Richards v Richards*.[323]

It is regrettable that, as Wall J put it, there remains 'a substantial degree of confusion, both about the nature of the inherent jurisdiction and the extent of the powers exercisable

[314] *Burris v Azadani* [1995]1 WLR 1372, CA (but note that the injunction was interlocutory in that case).
[315] *Wilde v Wilde* [1988] 2 FLR 83,CA; *Re S (Minors) (Inherent Jurisdiction: Ouster)* [1994] 1 FLR 623; *C v K (Inherent Powers; Exclusion Order)* [1996] 2 FLR 506 (obiter).
[316] [1973] Fam 21.   [317] [1988] 2 FLR 83, CA.   [318] (1847) 2 Ph 247.
[319] *D v D (County Court Jurisdiction: Injunctions)* [1993] 2 FLR 802, CA; *Devon County Council v B* [1997] 1 FLR 591, CA.
[320] See below p 883.   [321] *Devon County Council v S* [1994] Fam 169.   [322] [1994] 1 FLR 623.
[323] It would probably now be regarded as also conflicting with the power of a court to include an exclusion requirement in the terms of an emergency protection or interim care order, under Sch 6 to the Family Law Act 1996, discussed at p 726.

under it.'[324] Indeed, there appears to be confusion as to whether there is one inherent jurisdiction, or two, and whether, assuming there are two, that one at least of these extends to the county court. It is also discomforting to find that there is so much uncertainty surrounding the question of when a party can be ousted from property. However, the statutory jurisdictions providing civil remedies appear to have proved sufficient, in most cases, to render these questions largely academic.

D REMEDIES THROUGH HOUSING LAW

Even if a victim of violence obtains an order under the jurisdictions discussed above, this may provide only an interim solution to the problem. Moreover, many victims will seek to leave the home and put themselves and their children out of harm's way rather than rely on the uncertain compliance of the perpetrator with any court order. Some victims will have to flee the home at short notice. All will require some form of alternative accommodation, be it temporary or permanent. The third facet of the government's strategy for tackling domestic violence, support, is manifested, in part, by its response to this particular need. The provision of temporary refuges is one means by which urgent accommodation needs may be met, and indeed, as noted at the beginning of this chapter, the establishment of the first women's refuge in the 1970s refocused policy-makers' attention on the problem of domestic violence. But although the number of refuge places has grown,[325] many victims must find alternatives, such as staying with friends and relatives, being placed in hostels, or in temporary accommodation such as bed and breakfast hotels. The duties of local authorities to respond to the problem of homelessness caused by domestic violence are outlined below, after first considering what remedies are available under landlord and tenant law.

1 ACTIONS IN RELATION TO TENANCIES [326]

(a) Transfer of tenancy

One long-term solution to the housing dilemma of a victim of violence, which is available to a spouse, civil partner or cohabitant whose home is rented, is to seek a transfer of the

---

[324] In *C v K (Inherent Powers; Exclusion Order)* [1996] 2 FLR 506 at 511.

[325] With 3,073 places in 2002 and with plans to expand provision by 273 units of accommodation throughout England: *Safety and Justice* (2003) p 42.

[326] Query whether ss 153A–153E of the Housing Act 1996 (as inserted by the Anti-Social Behaviour Act 2003 s 13) could be used by a social landlord to seek an injunction from the High Court or county court to protect a domestic violence victim? These replace s 152, which clearly seemed to be applicable, but the requirement for the injunction is now to show conduct 'which is capable of causing nuisance or annoyance to any person, and . . . which directly or indirectly relates to or affects the housing management functions of a relevant landlord.' The injunction may be made without notice; and a power of arrest may be attached. If such use were possible, it would enable a social landlord (most likely a local authority) to take action under these provisions on behalf of a victim of domestic violence too frightened to act herself. Such a course side-steps the concern expressed during the passage of Part IV of the Family Law Act 1996 at the idea of the police doing so. The objection of involving a criminal justice agency in civil proceedings does not apply to a housing authority. Whether such an authority would be prepared to act in this way is another matter. The object of the provisions is to deal with 'anti-social behaviour', epitomised by gangs of youths terrorising estates, and the authority will naturally be reluctant to spend its money on obtaining a remedy for a victim which she could obtain for herself.

tenancy by court order. We note this option here and discuss it in detail elsewhere. The courts have the power to effect such a transfer in respect of couples whose marriage or partnership has been terminated, under the Matrimonial Causes Act 1973 s 24,[327] Civil Partnership Act 2004 s 72 and Sch 5,[328] and the Family Law Act 1996 s 53 and Sch 7.[329] There is also power to make such a disposition for the benefit of children, under Sch 1 to the Children Act 1989.[330] Sch 7 extended the court's power to apply to cohabitants who have ceased to cohabit.[331] The Law Commission recommended this latter extension (which already existed in Scotland), to ensure that a tenancy, probably granted by a local authority or housing association on the assumption that it would provide a home for the cohabiting couple and their children, should continue to provide a secure home for the children even though their parents' relationship has broken down,[332] and also to do justice between the couple.

If the victim could therefore obtain some short- to medium-term protection, possibly under Part IV of the 1996 Act, she might then be able to seek an order under these powers for a permanent solution to her housing problem.

(b) Eviction

Where a dwelling-house held on a secure or assured tenancy was occupied by a married couple, civil partners or a cohabiting couple, and one partner has left because of violence or threats of violence against him or her or a member of his or her family, the landlord may seek an order for possession.[333] It might be thought that this could be a useful device to justify the landlord terminating the violent partner's right to occupy, and then granting the victim a new tenancy for herself. However, the court must be satisfied that the partner who has left is unlikely to return.[334]

(c) Victim terminating tenancy [335]

A more effective device is for a victim who is herself a joint tenant of the property to give notice of termination to the landlord, on the understanding that the landlord will then grant her a fresh tenancy in her sole name. It was held by the House of Lords in *Hammersmith and Fulham London Borough Council v Monk*[336] that the appropriate notice, as required under the tenancy, given unilaterally by one joint tenant is effective to bring the tenancy to an end, notwithstanding the other tenant's lack of agreement, or even knowledge.[337] Since such a device avoids the usual requirement of notice before eviction,

---

[327] See below, p 1003.   [328] See below, p 1085.   [329] See above, p 204.
[330] See below, p 971.
[331] Defined, as under Part IV of the Act, in s 62(1) as amended, and now applying to same-sex couples. See S Bridge 'Transferring Tenancies of the Family Home' [1998] Fam Law 26.
[332] Law Com No 207 para 6.3.
[333] Housing Act 1985 Sch 2 Part 1, Ground 2A (secure tenancy), as amended by the Civil Partnership Act 2004 Sch 8 para 33; Housing Act 1988 Sch 2 Part 2, Ground 14A (assured tenancy), as amended by the Civil Partnership Act 2004 Sch 8 para 43(3).
[334] Ibid.
[335] For a valuable discussion, see M Davis and D Hughes, 'An End of the Affair—Social Housing, Relationship Breakdown, and the Human Rights Act 1998' [2004] Conv 19.
[336] [1992] 1 AC 478, HL.
[337] A joint tenant who gives notice without the other's knowledge does not act in breach of trust: *Crawley Borough Council v Ure* [1996] QB 13, CA.

and enables the victim effectively to obtain a transfer of the tenancy which could normally only be done by order under Sch 7 to the Family Law Act 1996,[338] it is perhaps not surprising that in *Hounslow London Borough Council v Pilling*[339] the Court of Appeal attempted to curtail the ambit of the decision, by holding that the notice given to the landlord must be 'appropriate', ie given at the end of the tenancy period, and not in the middle of it. Nor must the notice be in breach of the Protection from Eviction Act 1977, under which at least four weeks' notice in writing must be given.[340]

However, in *Harrow London Borough Council v Johnstone*,[341] the House of Lords continued its robust approach, holding that where a husband had obtained an injunction prohibiting his wife from excluding him from the matrimonial home, it was still open to the wife to give notice to the landlord terminating the tenancy on the understanding that they would grant her a new tenancy once her husband was evicted. The House considered that the narrow terms of the injunction did not extend to prohibiting the wife from giving notice to quit, and hence the wife and landlord had not acted in contempt of the court's order in seeking to bring the husband's right to occupy the house to an end, but were entitled to do what they had. Their Lordships also accepted that the local authority's action was in accordance with their housing allocation policy, whereby they would not grant a new tenancy to a family already in possession of another, unless that was surrendered first.[342] In the light of this decision, it seems unlikely that obtaining an occupation order declaring that the applicant is entitled to occupy the house would prevent the quitting tenant from giving, or the landlord from acting on, a notice to quit.[343] Nor, according to the House of Lords in *London Borough of Harrow v Qazi*,[344] is taking possession proceedings a breach of the remaining partner's Art 8 right to respect for his home under the European Convention on Human Rights.

There is an undoubted difficulty in balancing the interest of the victim of violence to be rehoused safely, against that of the remaining partner who might have had security of tenure until the joint tenancy was unilaterally terminated, and whose interest must in turn be weighed against that of the landlord in controlling and allocating limited housing stock. The Law Commission have provisionally recommended that a joint occupier should be able to withdraw from a joint tenancy by giving notice to the landlord, without at the same time destroying the whole occupation agreement (as they would term it). But they also ask whether the landlord should be able to seek possession where the property is unsuitable for the remaining occupier, subject to reasonableness and the provision of suitable alternative accommodation.[345]

---

[338] Above.   [339] [1994] 1 All ER 432, CA.   [340] Section 5(1) as amended.

[341] [1997] 1 WLR 459, HL.

[342] Nor is a notice to quit a 'disposition' of property which may be set aside under the Matrimonial Causes Act 1973 s 37 in divorce proceedings: *Newlon Housing Trust v Al-Sulaimen* [1999] 1 AC 313, HL. See below p 1072. It has similarly been held that the remaining spouse of a sole tenant who surrenders her lease cannot resist possession proceedings unless he has registered his home rights under s 31 of the Family Law Act 1996: *Sanctuary Housing Association v Campbell* [1999] 2 FLR 383, CA.

[343] See the discussion by Davis and Hughes, op cit.

[344] [2003] UKHL 43, [2004] 1 AC 983 (joint tenancy). See also *London Borough of Newham v Kibata* [2003] EWCA Civ 1785, [2004] 1 FLR 690 (sole tenancy).

[345] Law Com Consultation Paper No 168, *Renting Homes 2: Co-occupation, Transfer and Succession* (2002) paras 3.65–3.68.

2 SEEKING HELP UNDER THE HOMELESSNESS LEGISLATION [346]

A victim of domestic violence or other intolerable behaviour may seek help from the local authority in finding alternative accommodation, on the basis that she is homeless, as defined by statute. Relationship breakdown is the second highest cause of homelessness, resulting in just over 27,000 households being accepted as unintentionally homeless and in priority need (20% of all such acceptances) in England in 2003–04. Of these, 65% of cases involved domestic violence.[347]

Part VII of the Housing Act 1996, as amended by the Homelessness Act 2002,[348] imposes a duty on all local housing authorities[349] to secure that advice and information about homelessness and its prevention, are available free of charge to any person in their district;[350] where they have reason to believe that a person may be homeless or threatened with homelessness, to enquire into the circumstances to determine whether he is eligible for assistance, and if so, whether any duty is owed to him under the Act;[351] and to secure that suitable accommodation is made available to a person[352] who is homeless, in priority need of accommodation, and who did not become homeless intentionally (subject to the requirements of Part VI of the 1996 Act concerning allocation of their own accommodation).[353]

(a) Definition of homeless

A person is homeless for the purpose of the Act if he has no accommodation available for his occupation in the United Kingdom or elsewhere, which he (together with any other person who normally resides with him as a member of his family or any other person who might reasonably be expected to reside with him):[354]

'(a) is entitled to occupy by virtue of an interest in it or by virtue of an order of a court, or

(b) has an express or implied licence to occupy, or

(c) occupies as a residence by virtue of any enactment or rule of law giving him the right to remain in occupation or restricting the right of another person to recover possession.'[355]

---

[346] See A Arden and C Hunter, *Homelessness and Allocations* (2003, revised 6th ed).

[347] ODPM, *Homelessness Statistics: September 2004 and Delivering on the Positive Outcomes: Policy Briefing 10* (2004) p 14. See also ODPM, *Homelessness Statistics: September 2002 and Domestic Violence* (2002).

[348] For an evaluation, see G Pascall et al 'Changing housing policy: women escaping domestic violence' (2001) 23 JSWFL 293.

[349] Viz, a district council, a London borough council, the Common Council of the City of London, a Welsh county council or county borough council or the Council of the Isles of Scilly: Housing Act 1985 s 1 as amended.

[350] Housing Act 1996 s 179.   [351] Section 184.

[352] Excluding persons from abroad and asylum seekers: Housing Act 1996 ss 185, 186, as amended. Note that s 185(4) has been declared incompatible with the European Convention on Human Rights: *R (Morris) v Westminster City Council* [2004] EWHC 2191 (Admin) [2005] 1 WLR 865.

[353] Section 193. There is an interim duty to accommodate where the authority have reason to believe that the person would be eligible, pending their decision: s 188.

[354] Section 176; an unborn child is not such a person—*R v London Borough of Newham, ex p Dada* [1996] QB 507, CA.

[355] Section 175(1). Paragraph (c) covers a spouse with home rights.

He is also homeless if he has such accommodation but he cannot secure entry to it.[356]

Section 175(3) provides that a person shall not be treated as having accommodation unless it is accommodation which it would be reasonable for him to continue to occupy, and in so determining, under s 177, domestic violence is expressly to be taken into account:

'(1) It is not reasonable for a person to continue to occupy accommodation if it is probable that this will lead to domestic violence or other violence[357] against him, or against—

    (a) a person who normally resides with him as a member of his family, or

    (b) any other person who might reasonably be expected to reside with him.

(1A) For this purpose "violence" means

    (a) violence from another person; or

    (b) threats of violence from another person which are likely to be carried out; and violence is "domestic violence" if it is from a person associated with the victim.'[358]

An authority should not take into account whether the victim could have taken action against the perpetrator to restrain his violence: the relevant question is whether domestic violence will probably follow if the person remains in occupation, and the availability of other remedies does not answer the probability question.[359]

Interestingly, while the Act incorporates the same definition of 'associated person' in relation to the person who is inflicting the violence as is to be found in Part IV of the Family Law Act 1996 (as amended), it does not define what is meant by 'family'. Although the term 'associated person' is intended to convey some form of domestic relationship, it is wider than what is conveyed by the word 'family'. The Code of Guidance, to which housing authorities are to have regard in discharging their functions under the Act, suggests that it would include cohabiting couples, foster children, housekeepers and companions, and carers of the elderly or disabled.[360]

A person is to be regarded as threatened with homelessness if it is likely that he will become homeless within 28 days.[361]

'Accommodation' means a place which can fairly be described as accommodation and which it would be reasonable, having regard to the general housing conditions in the district, for the person to continue to occupy, and in R v Brent London Borough Council, ex p Awua[362] the House of Lords held, contrary to earlier case law, that there is no

---

[356] Section 175(2)(a). Thus, a spouse who cannot gain entry because the locks have been changed may be regarded as homeless.

[357] Other violence added by s 10(1)(a) Homelessness Act 2002. Such violence could include racial harassment, or intimidation.

[358] Authorities vary in the extent of proof they require to be satisfied that a person is at risk of violence. Malos and Hague found that while some accept the victim's own word, others require corroboration from doctors, police, solicitors etc: E Malos and G Hague Domestic Violence and Housing: Local authority responses to women and children escaping from violence in the home (1993).

[359] Bond v Leicester City Council [2001] EWCA Civ 1544, [2002] 1 FCR 566 per Hale LJ at para 27.

[360] ODPM, Homelessness Code of Guidance for Local Authorities (2002) para 6.3. The Code is not binding upon housing authorities, although they are obliged to have regard to it under s 182: De Falco v Crawley Borough Council [1980] QB 460, CA.

[361] Section 175(4).

[362] [1996] AC 55. It was held that temporary accommodation is not, ipso facto, unsuitable, although accommodation likely to be available for under 28 days would not be sufficient, as the applicant would then be threatened with homelessness within the statutory definition.

requirement that it be settled or permanent. The question arises whether a woman who has fled with her children to a refuge may be regarded as homeless notwithstanding that she has a roof over her head. In *R v Ealing London Borough Council, ex p Sidhu*[363] it was held that she should be so regarded, otherwise she could not call on the housing authority for assistance unless the refuge gave her 28 days' notice to leave, in which case she would be 'threatened with homelessness': a procedure which would merely pile stress on stress unnecessarily. Lord Hoffmann in *Awua* agreed that a person whose only accommodation was a night shelter or hostel which he had to leave during each day and could only return to at night would not be regarded as 'having accommodation'[364] and the Code of Guidance advises that it should not be regarded as reasonable to expect a person to remain in a refuge in the medium or longer term.[365]

(b) Priority need

Persons with a priority need include inter alia:

'(a) a pregnant woman or a person with whom she resides or might reasonably be expected to reside;

(b) a person with whom dependent children reside or might reasonably be expected to reside;

(c) a person who is vulnerable as a result of old age, mental illness or handicap or physical disability or other special reason,[366] or with whom such a person resides or might reasonably be expected to reside . . .'[367]

In addition, under the relevant regulations, in England, if an applicant has had to cease to occupy accommodation because of violence or threats of violence which are likely to be carried out, she will be in priority need if she is vulnerable as a result.[368] A person is 'vulnerable' where he is 'less able to fend for oneself so that injury or detriment will result where a less vulnerable man will be able to cope without harmful effects.'[369] This may well exclude many applicants from eligibility. A more generous approach is taken in Wales, where applicants who have been subject to domestic (but not other) violence or are at risk of such violence, or would be if they returned home, are also included.[370]

The applicant's dependent child need not be wholly and exclusively dependent on or reside solely with her.[371] Nor is it necessary to have a residence order in the applicant's favour to demonstrate that she has a child residing, or reasonably expected to reside, with her.[372] Where a shared residence order has been made, a local authority may not decline to

---

[363] (1982) 3 FLR 438.   [364] At 67A.   [365] At para 6.26.

[366] This could include a young person or an adult with no children who has left home to escape abuse or violence: *Kelly v Monklands District Council* 1986 SLT 169, Ct of Sess (young person); *R v Kensington and Chelsea London Borough Council, ex p Kihara* (1996) 29 HLR 147, CA.

[367] Section 189(1).

[368] Homelessness (Priority Need for Accommodation) (England) Order 2002 (SI No 2051).

[369] *R v Waveney DC ex p Bowers* [1983] QB 238 at 244H–245A.

[370] Homeless Persons (Priority Need)(Wales) Order 2001 (SI No 607).

[371] *R v London Borough of Lambeth, ex p Vagliviello* (1990) 22 HLR 392, CA (applicant could have priority need although child residing with him only 312 days a year).

[372] *R v Ealing London Borough Council, ex p Sidhu* (above n 363).

rehouse a parent in a dwelling large enough to accommodate her children, simply because the other parent has already been so housed. However, it is entitled to consider other factors including shortage of housing in its stock, and the fact that the property will be under-occupied for part of the time when the children are not there.[373] Presumably, the authority should not, without more, decline to help where the parents have agreed to share residence rather than obtained an order.

A dependent child may not apply for accommodation in his own right as being in priority need, as his accommodation is provided for him by his family, and the housing authority owes no separate duty to the child. Thus, it was held not to be open to parents to put forward an application for help in the name of their four-year-old son, because they had become homeless intentionally and were hence not eligible for assistance.[374]

(c) Intentional homelessness

The extent of the authority's duty to a homeless person in priority need depends upon whether or not they are satisfied that he became homeless (or threatened with homelessness) intentionally. If they are not so satisfied, they must secure that accommodation is available for his occupation.[375] In the case of a person threatened with homelessness, they must take reasonable steps to secure that his accommodation does not cease to be available.[376] If they are so satisfied, they are bound only to secure accommodation for his occupation for such period as they consider will give him a reasonable opportunity of securing accommodation for himself, and provide him with advice and appropriate assistance to help him find accommodation.[377] The question of whether a person is or is not intentionally homeless is therefore a crucial one.

A person is to be regarded as becoming homeless intentionally if he deliberately does or fails to do something as a result of which he ceases to occupy accommodation which is available for his occupation and which it would have been reasonable for him to continue to occupy.[378] Thus a tenant will become homeless intentionally if he loses possession of premises as a result of *wilfully* failing to pay rent or breaking some other covenant in his lease: there is no need to prove that he intended to become homeless. If another member of the family encourages or acquiesces in conduct which results in the tenant's becoming homeless intentionally (for example, a wife who turns a blind eye or does nothing to prevent her husband from dissipating his earnings instead of paying the rent), that person will be regarded as intentionally homeless as well. The housing authority are entitled to assume acquiescence unless the evidence indicates the contrary;[379] but they

---

[373] *R (on the application of Bibi) v Camden London Borough Council* [2004] All ER (D) 123 (Oct). See also *R v Oxford CC ex p Doyle* (1997) 30 HLR 506. C.f. ODPM, *Homelessness Code of Guidance for Local Authorities* (2002) para 8.10 which seems to assume that shared residence is 'very exceptional'.

[374] *R v Oldham Metropolitan Borough Council, ex p Garlick* [1993] AC 509, HL; it was also held in that case that an application may not be made in the name of an adult dependent who is mentally incapacitated, since any offer of accommodation must be considered and evaluated by the applicant. Where the applicant is intentionally homeless, a housing authority is not obliged to comply with a request under s 27 of the Children Act 1989 from the social services department, seeking to fulfil its duties under Part III of that Act, to help find accommodation in order to keep a family together: *R v Northavon District Council, ex p Smith* [1994] 2 AC 402, HL.

[375] Section 193(2).   [376] Section 195(2).   [377] Section 190.   [378] Section 191(1).

[379] *Lewis v North Devon District Council* [1981] 1 All ER 27. If the spouse acts in good faith in ignorance of a relevant fact, she will not be regarded as having acquiesced and therefore will not be intentionally homeless: *R v Mole Valley District Council, ex p Burton* (1988) 20 HLR 479.

are bound to give separate consideration to the position of each resident and in the absence of acquiescence they will be obliged to secure accommodation for the person at fault if he resides with one who has not become homeless intentionally.[380]

It will be observed that the question is whether the tenant became homeless intentionally, not whether he is now homeless intentionally. Consequently if, as in *Din v Wandsworth London Borough Council*[381] the applicant deliberately left available accommodation, he will be considered to have become homeless intentionally even though he would probably have been evicted later and thus have become homeless unintentionally. Conversely, if, as in *Gloucester City Council v Miles*,[382] the applicant became homeless because her husband had vandalised her home to such an extent that it became uninhabitable, she will not be homeless intentionally even though, had she stayed there, she would probably have become so through non-payment of rent.

The same test is to be applied mutatis mutandis to determine whether a person is *threatened* with becoming homeless intentionally.

(d) Local connection

Where a victim of violence leaves not simply her home, but also the area where it is situated, the housing authority to whom she applies for help may argue that she has no close connection with their area, and should be housed by the authority for the area from which she came. They may seek to refer her case to that other authority under s 198 of the Act. However, they cannot do this where the applicant or any person who might reasonably be expected to reside with the applicant will run the risk of domestic violence from a person with whom they are associated, or of threats of violence from such a person which are likely to be carried out.[383]

E   A CRIMINAL OR CIVIL MATTER?

Whether the legal response to domestic violence should see it primarily as a criminal matter, with the focus on punishment and deterrence, or as a civil issue where the primary object is to secure the safety of the victims, is a continuing question for policy makers. The complexities show that there is no easy way forward. The much greater focus in recent policy making on the criminal justice route as the response to domestic violence may admirably reflect an increased awareness of the criminal nature of such behaviour and a determination to leave behind patriarchal value judgments about its seriousness. On the other hand, there is a danger that the views of the victim can be lost in a willingness to

---

[380] *R v Mole Valley District Council, ex p Burton* (above); *R v London Borough of Ealing, ex p Salmons* (1990) 23 HLR 272.

[381] [1983] 1 AC 657, HL.   [382] [1985] FLR 1043, CA.

[383] Section 198(2), (3). The housing authority have a duty to ascertain if an applicant would suffer violence if she returned or stayed at home: *R v Greenwich London Borough Council, ex p Patterson* [1993] 2 FLR 886, CA. However, if the applicant has previously been secured accommodation by another authority within the previous five years, that authority retains the duty to assist, even where domestic violence is proved: s 198(4) and Homelessness Regulations 2000 SI 2000/701 reg 6 (also applicable to Wales). This hardly addresses the problem found by Malos and Hague that women may often be pressured to return to the authority for the area they have left to seek help there: E Malos and G Hague *Domestic Violence and Housing: Local Authority Responses to Women and Children escaping from Violence in the Home* (1993).

react 'toughly' and to ignore her longer-term needs. Moreover, there is still a need for greater recognition of the emotional dimension, especially when set in the context of a failed or terminated relationship. It was noted above that women who have separated from their partners are at increased risk of violence.[384] It is also clear that disputes between parents over their children, especially concerning contact, may often take place in a setting in which violence, or fear of violence, is alleged by a resident parent as a reason for refusing contact and where violence is indeed inflicted by the non-resident parent as a means of exerting power over the other.[385] It is also increasingly accepted that violence against an adult partner is associated with violence against a child[386] and indeed, s 31(9) of the Children Act 1989 now provides that 'harm' includes 'impairment suffered from seeing or hearing the ill-treatment of another'.[387] The 'family' context of such violence cannot be ignored when determining how best to respond to it in the search to protect those at risk.

The most recent government attempt to 'join up' its thinking and strategy through a three-pronged approach which utilises education and prevention, protection and legal processes, and support through housing and other services such as information and advice, would appear to be the correct way forward. However, translating principles into practice is a formidable task, in the face of limited resources, especially for alternative accommodation for victims, and a legal system (in both its criminal and civil forms) which remains complex and fragmented.

---

[384] Above at p 209.

[385] See Lord Chancellor's Advisory Board on Family Law, Children Act Sub-Committee, *A Report to the Lord Chancellor on the Question of Parental Contact in Cases where there is Domestic Violence* (2000).

[386] See the literature cited by C Humphreys and C Harrison, 'Focusing on safety—domestic violence and the role of child contact centres' [2003] CFLQ 237.

[387] As amended by s 120 of the Adoption and Children Act 2002.

6

DIVORCE AND DISSOLUTION

A INTRODUCTION[1]

Divorce law has always been one of the most contentious subjects in family law. Marriage and its place in modern society are seen as significant political and cultural issues, with the 'health' of society somehow bound up with the extent to which marriages appear to be stable or 'failing'. Since the English law of marriage derives from the Canon law, religious sensibilities have also been engaged and the Church of England has wielded considerable influence in the shape and rate of reform. Making divorce 'too easy' has been seen by some as a means of undermining traditional family life and hence the stability of society whilst others have sought to liberalise divorce precisely in order to assist the emancipation of women from the traditional role of housewife. Confusion between the rate of marriage breakdown and the rate of divorce has often marked the debates over whether and how the law should be reformed. It is true to say that the number of divorces granted each year has increased substantially over the past century and particularly in the post-war period. For example, just before the Second World War, in 1938, the number of divorce decrees granted was 6,092. By 1968, the number had increased to 45,036. The law then underwent a major reform, which made it easier to obtain a divorce against the other spouse's will, and the number of divorces began a steep climb, with the occasional year or two when the figures plateaued, to the most recent figures of 153,689 in 2004.[2] But all that these figures show is the number of divorces granted in any given year, not the number of marriages which broke down. We cannot say for certain what the marriage breakdown rate is, nor whether it is higher than in previous times when divorce was harder to obtain, although it is likely that this is the case because of changing social attitudes to personal relationships. A bar or restriction on divorce does not, of itself, prevent marriage breakdown, although it is a continuing matter of debate as to how far a restrictive divorce law would restrain breakdowns or encourage couples to reconcile.[3]

The enactment of the Civil Partnership Act 2004 has introduced a new form of legal status[4] with its own rules for termination. Rather than refer to civil partners as obtaining a 'divorce', the Act instead uses the term 'dissolution'; however, the provisions are very

---

[1] See the *Finer Report on One-Parent Families* (1974) Cmnd 5629, Pt 4, s 2 and s 3; L Stone *Road to Divorce: England 1530–1987* (1990) and *Broken Lives: Separation and Divorce in England 1660–1857* (1993); SM Cretney, *Family Law in the Twentieth Century: A History* (2003) Part II.

[2] *Judicial Statistics 2004* (2005) Table 5.5.

[3] Compare R Deech 'Divorce Law and Empirical Studies' (1990) 106 LQR 229 with J Eekelaar and M Maclean 'Divorce Law and Empirical Studies—A Reply' (1990) 106 LQR 621.

[4] See Chapter 2 above pp 95–9.

similar to those pertaining on divorce, and are therefore discussed after we have examined the development and detail of the current divorce law.[5]

Divorce before 1857

The doctrine of the indissolubility of marriage was accepted by the English ecclesiastical courts after the Reformation, so that these courts had no power to pronounce a decree of divorce (as opposed to nullity) which would permit the parties to remarry.[6] The only way in which an aggrieved party could obtain a full divorce ('divorce a vinculo matrimonii') was by Act of Parliament, the expense of which was beyond the reach of most.[7]

The Matrimonial Causes Act 1857

The possibility of obtaining a divorce without having to petition Parliament was eventually introduced by this Act. In addition to vesting the existing jurisdiction of the ecclesiastical courts in a new statutory Divorce Court (from which it was transferred to the High Court in 1875)[8] the Act for the first time in English law permitted full divorce by judicial process. But the law retained a distinction between the position of the husband and that of the wife which had applied to parliamentary divorce. A husband could petition for divorce on the ground of adultery alone, whilst a wife had to prove either adultery coupled with incest, bigamy, cruelty or two years' desertion, or, alternatively, rape or an unnatural offence.[9]

The purpose of the Act was primarily to change the process by which divorce was obtained from a legislative one to a judicial one: the principle that divorce was a remedy for a matrimonial wrong remained, and adultery was regarded as the only matrimonial offence which would justify the dissolution of the marriage bond. Here one sees reflected the mid-Victorian attitude to sexual morality: whilst one act of adultery by a wife was considered unforgivable and gave the husband the power to petition for divorce without more, she could not even rely on a series of associations by him unless the adultery was 'aggravated'.

Extension of the grounds for divorce

The law remained in this state until the Matrimonial Causes Act 1923 put the husband and wife in the same position by permitting the latter to petition on the ground of adultery alone.[10] A P Herbert's Matrimonial Causes Act 1937 further extended the grounds for divorce by permitting either spouse to base a petition on the other's cruelty, desertion for three years, or (subject to certain other conditions) supervening incurable insanity.[11] This

[5] See pp 301-2.

[6] Although they could pronounce decrees of restitution of conjugal rights (which called upon a deserting spouse to resume cohabitation), and of divorce 'a mensa et thoro', which was a decree of separation relieving the petitioner from the duty of cohabiting with the respondent.

[7] There were on average fewer than two divorces by statute a year on the husband's petition, while in total only four were granted on the wife's petition. See Stone, op cit.

[8] By the Judicature Acts 1873–75.   [9] Matrimonial Causes Act 1857 s 27.

[10] Matrimonial Causes Act 1923 s 1. It did not strictly equate the spouses' rights, for the wife could still petition on the grounds of the husband's rape or unnatural offence, while there was no corresponding basis for the husband's petition.

[11] The Act largely gave effect to the recommendations of the majority of members of a Royal Commission appointed in 1909 (the Gorrell Commission, Cd 6478). For a lively account of the history of the passage of this bill through Parliament, see Sir Alan Herbert's The Ayes have it (1937), and for a more recent discussion of it, see S Redmayne 'The Matrimonial Causes Act 1937: A Lesson in the Art of Compromise' (1993) 13 OJLS 183.

last provision introduced, for the first time, the possibility of obtaining a divorce even though the respondent was in no way at fault.

The Divorce Reform Act 1969

In the decades following the Second World War there was a vast increase in the number of divorces, and although this must in some measure reflect an increase in the number of marriages that had broken down, other factors came into play. Legal aid enabled many to obtain a divorce who could not previously have afforded it; the attitude of society towards divorced spouses (particularly 'guilty' spouses) had changed; and many religious bodies were taking a far less rigid attitude. More than 90% of all petitions were undefended, and some of these undoubtedly amounted to divorce by consent.

Consequently, the idea that the purpose of divorce was to provide a remedy available only to the 'innocent' spouse for a matrimonial wrong committed by the other seemed to many to be an outdated concept. It was argued that divorce should be available to either spouse when the marriage has irretrievably broken down: to insist on the commission of a matrimonial offence lays stress upon the symptoms of breakdown rather than on the breakdown itself. The introduction of this principle would, it was argued, reduce the number of stable illicit unions where there was no foreseeable chance of the parties being able to marry or of their children being legitimated because the spouse of one of them refused to release his or her partner on account of religious or moral scruple, financial advantage or vindictiveness. On the other hand, some regarded the idea as fundamentally unjust in that it would enable a party to take advantage of his own wrong and obtain a divorce against the will of an innocent spouse, who might have a conscientious objection to divorce, and because an 'innocent' wife in particular might suffer serious financial hardship as a consequence of the decree.

Against this background, a Royal Commission (the Morton Commission) was appointed to enquire into the law of England and Scotland concerning marriage and divorce, and published its report in 1956.[12] The Commission were divided on how far the concept of the matrimonial offence should remain the exclusive basis for divorce, and could not reach a clear consensus on reform. Consequently nothing significant happened until two major publications appeared in 1966. In the first, Putting Asunder, a group appointed by the Archbishop of Canterbury to consider the law of divorce in contemporary society came down in favour of the breakdown theory. Logically they argued that this must be the sole ground of divorce and that possible abuse must be guarded against by a judicial inquest in each case. Putting Asunder was referred to the Law Commission, who in turn produced a report, 'Reform of the Grounds of Divorce: the Field of Choice'.[13] They concluded that the Archbishop's group's proposals for a full judicial enquiry in every case were impracticable, and put forward a number of possible alternatives based on the fundamental assumption that the aims of a good divorce law are:

'. . . to buttress, rather than undermine, the stability of marriage, and when, regrettably, a marriage has irretrievably broken down, to enable the empty legal shell to be destroyed with the maximum fairness and the minimum bitterness, distress and humiliation.'

Their own preference was for introducing as an additional ground for divorce the break-

[12] Cmd 9678. [13] Cmnd 3123.

down of the marriage as evidenced by a period of separation, which should be shorter if the respondent consented than if he did not.

The consequence was the passing of the Divorce Reform Act 1969. It represented a compromise between the views put forward by the Archbishop's group and the Law Commission. All the old grounds for divorce were abolished and replaced by one ground—that the marriage had irretrievably broken down. This, however, could only be established by proof of one or more of five facts set out in the Act. Various safeguards for the financial protection of the respondent, who was now potentially at risk of being divorced against his or her will, and after having committed no matrimonial wrong, were introduced.

B THE MATRIMONIAL CAUSES ACT 1973

This Act consolidated the Divorce Reform Act together with reforms relating to the financial and property consequences of divorce.[14]

1 JURISDICTION

The current rules on jurisdiction set out in s 5 of the Domicile and Matrimonial Proceedings Act 1973 distinguish between cases covered by EC Regulation EC No 2201/2003 of 27 November 2003 (Brussels IIR)[15] and others. It will be recalled that the Regulation largely attaches jurisdiction to habitual residence. Where no court has jurisdiction as a result of the Regulation, s 5(2)(b) provides that the English court also has jurisdiction to entertain proceedings for divorce (or judicial separation) if, and only if, either of the spouses is domiciled[16] in England and Wales on the date when proceedings are begun. Brussels IIR determines which court will have jurisdiction and which must stay any proceedings[17] where it is applicable, but otherwise, Sch 1 para 9 to the Act provides that:

'(1) where before the beginning of the trial or first trial in any matrimonial proceedings . . . which are continuing in the court it appears to the court—

   (a) that any proceedings in respect of the marriage in question, or capable of affecting its validity or subsistence, are continuing in another jurisdiction; and

   (b) that the balance of fairness (including convenience) as between the parties to the marriage is such that it is appropriate for the proceedings in that jurisdiction to be disposed of before further steps are taken in the proceedings in the court or in those proceedings so far as they consist of a particular kind of matrimonial proceedings,

---

[14] Matrimonial Proceedings and Property Act 1970.   [15] Discussed at p 34.

[16] Or habitually resident for one year. Presence leading to the establishment of domicile or habitual residence need not be lawful: *Mark v Mark* [2005] UKHL 42 [2006] 1 AC 98. A question of jurisdiction based on the application of law cannot be compromised and the failure by a party to assert a sustainable jurisdictional base does not deprive the court of jurisdiction if such a base exists: *R v R (Divorce: Jurisdiction: Domicile)* [2006] 1 FLR 389.

[17] See also FPR 1991 SI 1991/1247 r 2.27A(2) and *Chorley v Chorley* [2005] EWCA Civ 68 [2005] 2 FLR 38 where it was held that the English court should stay proceedings pending a decision by the French court to determine whether divorce proceedings in that state were begun by a 'requête initiale' (conciliation hearing)—which it held they were.

the court may then, if it thinks fit, order that the proceedings in the court be stayed or, as the case may be, that those proceedings be stayed so far as they consist of proceedings of that kind.'

The question whether to direct a stay turns, according to the House of Lords in *de Dampierre v de Dampierre*[18] on whether the facts connect the suit more closely with another forum; if so, the court should not be deterred from remitting the case to that forum simply because that would deprive one party of a juridical advantage provided that substantial justice will still be done.[19]

To prevent a possible conflict of jurisdictions within the United Kingdom, here is also provision in Sch 1 para 8 for a *mandatory* stay of proceedings in England and Wales where proceedings are pending in Scotland, Northern Ireland, Jersey, Guernsey and the Isle of Man. A stay will be ordered (i) if the parties have resided together since the marriage was celebrated, (ii) the place where they have resided together (or where they resided when the English proceedings were begun) is in the other jurisdiction, and (iii) one of them has been habitually resident in that jurisdiction throughout the year ending with the date when they last resided together.

2 THE SUBSTANTIVE LAW

(a) Irretrievable breakdown the sole ground for divorce

By s 1(1) of the Matrimonial Causes Act 1973 there is only one ground for divorce: that the marriage has broken down irretrievably. Irretrievable breakdown, however, may be established only by proving one or more of the five facts set out in s 1(2). If none of these is established, the court may not pronounce a decree even though it is satisfied that the marriage is at an end.[20] Although it is the duty of the court 'to inquire, so far as it reasonably can, into the facts alleged' by both parties,[21] in practical terms the burden on the petitioner is solely to establish one of the facts and it is for the respondent in a defended suit to show, if he wishes, that the marriage has not broken down irretrievably. No petition may be brought during the first year of the marriage, in order to discourage couples from 'giving up' too easily should their marriage fall into difficulties early on.[22]

(b) The five facts for proving irretrievable breakdown

The respondent's adultery

The first fact on which the petitioner may rely is that the respondent has committed adultery and that the petitioner finds it intolerable to live with him.[23] It will be seen that there are two limbs. Adultery by itself is not sufficient: Parliament accepted that infidelity may be a symptom of breakdown rather than a cause of it and that an isolated act of adultery may not even be a symptom.

---

[18] [1988] AC 92.

[19] See *Breuning v Breuning* [2002] EWHC 236 (Fam) [2002] 1 FLR 888, *Bloch v Bloch* [2002] EWHC 1711 (Fam), [2003] 1 FLR 1 (both South Africa), *Otobo v Otobo* [2002] EWCA Civ 949, [2003] 1 FLR 192 (Nigeria)

[20] As in *Richards v Richards* [1972] 3 All ER 695.   [21] Matrimonial Causes Act 1973 s 1(3).

[22] Matrimonial Causes Act 1973 s 3 as amended by the Matrimonial and Family Proceedings Act 1984.

[23] Ibid, s 1(2)(a).

Adultery may be defined as voluntary sexual intercourse between two persons of the opposite sex, of whom one or both are married but who are not married to each other.[24] Receiving donor insemination does not constitute adultery[25] and nor do anal intercourse or non-penetrative sex. The adultery must be voluntary, so if a married woman is raped, she does not commit adultery.[26]

Whether or not the petitioner finds it intolerable to live with the respondent is clearly a question of fact and the test is subjective: did this petitioner find it intolerable to live with this respondent?[27]

The Act does not require any causal connection between the two limbs. After some initial doubts, when it was suggested that the petitioner should be able to allege that he found it intolerable to live with the respondent only if this was in consequence of the adultery, the Court of Appeal held in *Cleary v Cleary*[28] that the statute must be interpreted literally and that the petitioner may therefore rely not only on the adultery but also on any other matter to show that further cohabitation would be intolerable to him. In that case, the husband took the wife back after the adultery but she continued to correspond with the man in question, went out at night and finally left the husband to live with her mother. The court held that the husband had established irretrievable breakdown even though he found life with the wife intolerable not on account of her adultery but because of her subsequent conduct.[29] This approach is open to criticism: it is difficult to reconcile it with the provision, intended to encourage the parties to attempt a reconciliation, that cohabitation for a period not exceeding six months after the petitioner discovers the respondent's adultery shall be disregarded in determining whether he finds it intolerable to live with the respondent,[30] which implies that it must be the discovery of the adultery that makes cohabitation intolerable.

The respondent's behaviour

The petitioner may establish that the marriage has irretrievably broken down by showing that the respondent has behaved in such a way that the petitioner cannot reasonably be expected to live with him.[31] This provision is frequently, but erroneously, abbreviated to 'unreasonable behaviour',[32] thereby suggesting that all one has to look at is the quality of the respondent's behaviour, whereas in fact what is important is the effect of that conduct upon the petitioner.[33]

---

[24] *Dennis v Dennis* [1955] P 153.

[25] So held in Scotland in *Maclennan v Maclennan* 1958 SLT 12. Nor would a husband commit adultery by acting as a sperm donor so long as insemination was the treatment method used. So acting without the spouse's knowledge or consent could well be sufficient for a petition based on behaviour, however, see below.

[26] *Clarkson v Clarkson* (1930) 143 LT 775.

[27] *Goodrich v Goodrich* [1971] 2 All ER 1340, 1342; *Pheasant v Pheasant* [1972] Fam 202, 207.

[28] [1974] 1 All ER 498, CA.

[29] See also *Carr v Carr* [1974] 1 WLR 1534, CA, where, although the Court of Appeal doubted whether *Cleary v Cleary* was correct, it regarded itself as bound to apply it—petitioner found life intolerable because of respondent's treatment of their children.

[30] Matrimonial Causes Act 1973, s 2(2). Cohabitation for more than six months prevents the petitioner from relying on the previous acts of adultery in any subsequent petition: s 2(1).

[31] Ibid, s 1(2)(b).

[32] Described as a 'linguistic trap' by Ormrod LJ in *Bannister v Bannister* (1980) 10 Fam Law 240, CA.

[33] *Ash v Ash* [1972] Fam 135; *Pheasant v Pheasant* [1972] Fam 202, *Livingstone-Stallard v Livingstone-Stallard* [1974] Fam 47, *O'Neill v O'Neill* [1975] 1 WLR 1118, CA.

Whether the respondent's behaviour has been such that the petitioner can no longer reasonably be expected to live with him is essentially a question of fact. In contrast to the test of intolerability under s 1(2)(a), however, the question is whether the petitioner can reasonably be expected to live with the respondent, and it is for the court, and not the petitioner, to answer it.[34] The test is thus objective, but this is not the same as asking whether a hypothetical reasonable spouse in the petitioner's position would continue to live with the respondent. The court must have regard to the personalities of the individuals before it, however far these may be removed from some hypothetical norm, and it must assess the impact of the respondent's conduct on the particular petitioner in the light of the whole history of the marriage and their relationship. The test generally accepted is that formulated by Dunn J in *Livingstone-Stallard v Livingstone-Stallard* [35]and adopted by the majority of the Court of Appeal in *O'Neill v O'Neill*:[36]

'Would any right-thinking person come to the conclusion that this husband has behaved in such a way that this wife cannot reasonably be expected to live with him, taking into account the whole of the circumstances and the characters and personalities of the parties?'

The question is one of fact. Thus a wife has obtained a decree against a husband who has treated her with violence;[37] whose domineering manner led him to belittle her and level abuse and unwarranted criticism at her;[38] who made the matrimonial home virtually uninhabitable for months by carrying out building operations (which he was not qualified to do) as well as quite unjustifiably alleging that the two children of the marriage were not his;[39] and whose controlling and undermining behaviour carried on during the divorce proceedings in which he alleged that she had committed adultery and that she had improper financial motives for both marrying and then divorcing him so that 'the husband had pulled away every foundation and cornerstone of the matrimonial relationship.'[40] Similarly, a husband has successfully relied on his wife's association with another man stopping short of adultery,[41] from which it appears to follow that a petitioner could complain of the respondent's adultery under this head without having to show that he found life with the other intolerable.

However, the petition must amount to more than a complaint that the parties are incompatible, that they no longer have anything in common and cannot communicate,[42] or that one of them is bored with the marriage.[43] In *Pheasant v Pheasant*,[44] Ormrod J dismissed the petition of a husband whose sole charge against the wife was that she was unable to give him the demonstrative affection for which he craved whereas, as the judge found, she had given him all the affection she could and nothing in her behaviour could be regarded as a breach of any of the obligations of a marriage.

Behaviour implies some form of conduct and not just a state of mind. As Baker P put it in *Katz v Katz*:[45]

'Behaviour is something more than a mere state of affairs or a state of mind, such as for

[34] See *Ash v Ash* [1972] Fam 135, 139–140.   [35] [1974] Fam 47, 54.
[36] [1975] 1 WLR 1118, CA.   [37] *Ash v Ash* (above).
[38] *Livingstone-Stallard v Livingstone-Stallard* (above).   [39] *O'Neill v O'Neill* (above).
[40] *Hadjimilitis (Tsavliris) v Tsavliris (Divorce: Irretrievable Breakdown)* [2003] FLR 81.
[41] *Wachtel v Wachtel (No 1)* Times, 1 August 1972.
[42] As in *Buffery v Buffery* [1988] 2 FLR 365, CA.   [43] As in *Kisala v Kisala* (1973) 117 Sol Jo 664.
[44] [1972] Fam 202.   [45] [1972] 3 All ER 219, 223.

example a repugnance to sexual intercourse, or a feeling that the wife is not reciprocating the husband's love, or not being as demonstrative as he thinks she should be. Behaviour in this context is action or conduct by one which affects the other. Such conduct may either take the form of acts or omissions or may be a course of conduct, and, in my view, it must have some reference to the marriage.'

The whole history of the marriage must be looked at: the cumulative effect of a series of acts might well amount to behaviour which the petitioner cannot reasonably be expected to put up with, even though each of them taken separately might be too trivial.[46]

How far can one regard as 'behaviour' conduct over which the respondent has no control? In *Thurlow v Thurlow*,[47] as a result of severe epilepsy, the wife became progressively less able to function. She threw things at her mother-in-law (with whom the parties lived), burnt articles on the electric heater and wandered into the street. Eventually, she became bedridden and incontinent and was admitted to hospital when her husband could no longer cope with the situation. There was no reasonable hope that her condition would improve and the husband petitioned for divorce on the basis of her behaviour. Rees J granted him a decree. He stated explicitly that, if the behaviour in question stems from misfortune, such as mental or physical illness or an accident, the court must take full account of all the obligations of the married state including the normal duty to accept and share the burdens imposed by the respondent's ill-health. But it must also consider the length of time the petitioner has had to bear them, the effect upon his health and his capacity to bear the stresses imposed, and in the end must decide whether he can fairly be required to live with the respondent.[48]

As with adultery, if the parties have lived with each other in the same household for a period or periods not exceeding six months after the last act or incident relied on by the petitioner, this is to be disregarded in determining whether he can reasonably be expected to live with the respondent.[49] But where the parties have continued to live together in excess of six months, the statute gives no guidance on whether the petitioner can continue to rely on the acts complained of. Since there is no express bar on doing so, as there is with adultery, it would seem that it is left to the court to consider whether continuing cohabitation nullifies the petitioner's assertion that he or she cannot reasonably be expected to live with the respondent. There may be good reasons, such as a lack of anywhere else to go, which prevent the petitioner from leaving.[50]

The respondent's desertion

The petitioner may show that the marriage has irretrievably broken down by proving that the respondent has deserted the petitioner for a continuous period of at least two years immediately preceding the presentation of the petition.[51] Desertion consists of the

---

[46] *Stevens v Stevens* [1979] 1 WLR 885.   [47] [1976] Fam 32.   [48] Ibid at 44.
[49] Matrimonial Causes Act 1973, s 2(3).   [50] See eg *Bradley v Bradley* [1973] 3 All ER 750, CA.
[51] Matrimonial Causes Act 1973 s 1(2)(c). For the computation of the period of two years, see *Warr v Warr* [1975] Fam 25. Where the spouses attempt a reconciliation, which fails, the court must disregard any period or periods not exceeding six months in which the parties have lived together in the same household. But the periods of cohabitation must be ignored in calculating the length of time the parties have been apart: Matrimonial Causes Act 1973 s 2(5), so that a trial reconciliation of say, three months will require the petitioner to wait until two years and three months have elapsed from the initial point of desertion before he or she can present a petition based on this fact.

unjustifiable withdrawal from cohabitation without the consent of the other spouse and with the intention of remaining separated permanently.

There can be no desertion unless there is a de facto separation between the spouses. Usually, this will occur when one spouse leaves the matrimonial home. But it may be impossible for the spouse wishing to leave to find accommodation elsewhere and the situation may arise where the spouses continue to live under the same roof but where one shuts himself off from the other so that they are living as two units rather than one. The correct test to be applied in such a case is: Are the spouses living as two households or as one?[52] This is strictly construed. Cohabitation must have entirely ceased: it cannot be desertion if any matrimonial services are performed even though these are isolated and intermittent.[53]

Even though there is a de facto separation, there will be no desertion unless the guilty spouse has the intention of remaining permanently separated from the other. There is no question of desertion if one spouse is temporarily absent on holiday or business, or for reasons of health.[54] Nor will there be desertion if the absence is involuntary, for example owing to service in the armed forces or imprisonment. But in such cases there will be desertion if the intention can be specifically proved, for example, if the respondent makes it clear that he wishes to have nothing more to do with the petitioner.[55]

Historically, desertion is a matrimonial offence; consequently there can be no desertion if the separation is by consent.[56] Whether consent has been given is a question of fact. It may be expressly given as a simple licence to go, or be embodied in a separation agreement, or it may be implied by the party's conduct. For example, in *Joseph v Joseph*[57] the wife persuaded the husband to grant her a get which by Jewish law effects a divorce.[58] Although this would not dissolve the marriage by English law it was held by the Court of Appeal that the wife had thereby shown her consent to living apart from her husband and could therefore no longer assert that he was in desertion.

If one spouse has a reasonable cause or excuse for leaving the other, then there will be no unjustifiable separation and consequently he will not be in desertion. For example, in *Quoraishi v Quoraishi*[59] where the couple were Muslims and the husband took a second wife in Bangladesh against the will of the first wife, the latter was held not to be in desertion when she left him. Such conduct on his part would also found a petition based on his behaviour.

Finally, it should be noted that it need not be the spouse who takes the physical step of leaving the matrimonial home who will be in desertion. Where one spouse behaves in such a way that the other is virtually compelled to leave, the former may be in law the deserter, and is said to be in constructive desertion.[60]

This fact has come to be relied upon only rarely, because the petition will usually be based on two years' separation if the respondent consents. A petitioner might wish to use

---

[52] *Hopes v Hopes* [1949] P 227, at 231, 236.

[53] Cf *Naylor v Naylor* [1962] P 253—desertion established where parties lived separately under same roof; with *Hopes v Hopes* (above)—no desertion where husband joined in certain activities with rest of family and an outsider would not have seen anything abnormal in the situation.

[54] *G v G* [1964] P 133.   [55] *Beeken v Beeken* [1948] P 302, CA.   [56] *Pardy v Pardy* [1939] P 288.

[57] [1953] 2 All ER 710, CA.   [58] See further below, p 277.   [59] [1985] FLR 780, CA.

[60] *Graves v Graves* (1864) 3 Sw & Tr 350; *Hall v Hall* [1962] 3 All ER 518, CA; *Saunders v Saunders* [1965] P 499.

it, however, if the respondent is in desertion and refuses to consent to a decree; and even after five years' separation (when the respondent's consent was not required) it avoids the possibility that the respondent will use s 5 or s 10 of the Matrimonial Causes Act to oppose or delay the granting of the decree absolute.[61]

Two years' separation and the respondent's consent to the decree

The petitioner may establish that the marriage has broken down irretrievably by showing that the spouses have lived apart for a continuous period of at least two years immediately preceding the presentation of the petition and that the respondent consents to the decree being granted.[62] This was one of the most controversial provisions of the Divorce Reform Act, because it introduced, albeit to a limited extent, divorce by consent.

The 1973 Act provides that spouses are to be treated as living apart unless they are living with each other in the same household.[63] On this basis, the courts have built up two principles. First, if the spouses are living under the same roof, they can be regarded as living apart only if they are living in two households: in other words there must be the same degree of separation as is necessary to constitute desertion.[64] Hence they will not be living apart if they share their meals and living accommodation, even though they sleep in separate rooms, no longer have sexual intercourse and largely live their own lives.[65] Conversely, they will be treated as still living apart if the wife, having left her husband for another man, subsequently takes him in as a lodger because he is ill and has nowhere else to go.[66]

But even if the spouses are physically separated, it does not follow that they are living apart for the purpose of the Act. The second principle, formulated by the Court of Appeal in *Santos v Santos*[67] is that they will not be so treated unless consortium has come to an end. So long as both spouses intend to share a home when circumstances permit them to do so, consortium is regarded as continuing.[68] Consequently, before they can be said to be living apart, one of them at least must regard the marriage as finished. If they agree to separate or one deserts the other, it will be obvious to both that consortium is at an end; if the separation is temporary or enforced (for example, because of a business trip or treatment in hospital), consortium will usually continue, but it will come to an end if either spouse decides not to return to the other. In the latter case the Court of Appeal in *Santos* further held that it is not necessary for that spouse to communicate his or her decision to the other and the statutory period can begin to run immediately. Suppose, for example, that a husband is serving a long term of imprisonment and his wife stands by him and regularly visits him; one of them resolves not to live with the other again but says nothing and the visits continue as before. Two years after making this decision he or she may petition for divorce with the other's consent. At first sight this seems surprising, but it accords with the policy of the Act. The period of separation is designed to provide evidence that the marriage has broken down irretrievably and this of itself justifies a

---

[61] See below, pp 273–7.

[62] Section 1(2)(d). As with computing the period for desertion, periods not exceeding six months' cohabitation since separation began do not prevent the period from running, but must be added on to ensure that a full two years' separation has elapsed before a petition can be presented: s 2(5).

[63] Matrimonial Causes Act 1973 s 2(6), see *Santos v Santos* [1972] Fam 247, CA.

[64] *Mouncer v Mouncer* [1972] 1 All ER 289.   [65] Ibid. Cf *Hopes v Hopes* [1949] P 227.

[66] *Fuller v Fuller* [1973] 2 All ER 650, CA.   [67] [1972] Fam 247, CA.   [68] See above p 108.

restrictive interpretation of the words 'living apart' by requiring evidence that consortium was at an end during the whole of the period. But equally, the fact that one spouse has regarded the marriage as dead for at least two years must normally be pretty clear evidence that it has broken down irretrievably whether or not the other knew of this. As we will see below, the procedural mechanisms for satisfying the court that the marriage has broken down irretrievably make it easy for a spouse to indicate that he or she did indeed regard the marriage as over for the requisite length of time prior to issuing the petition.

The respondent must affirmatively consent to the decree; it is not sufficient that he does not oppose it.[69] It follows that a petitioner cannot seek a decree relying on this fact if the respondent cannot be found or cannot give a valid consent because of mental illness. The mental capacity required to give consent to dissolution of a marriage is the same as that required for its formation: did the respondent understand the nature and consequences of what he was doing?[70] He must be given such information as will enable him to understand the effect of the decree being granted.[71] He may withdraw his consent at any time before a decree nisi is pronounced, and if he does so (or does not give his consent in the first place) and two years' separation is the only fact alleged by the petitioner, the proceedings must be stayed.

After decree nisi[72] the respondent has only a qualified power to withdraw his consent and to attempt to prevent the decree from being made absolute. If the court grants a decree solely on the fact of two years separation coupled with the respondent's consent, the respondent may apply to have the decree nisi rescinded on the ground that the petitioner misled him (whether intentionally or unintentionally) about any matter which he took into account in deciding to give his consent.[73] The court is not bound to rescind the decree; presumably it will do so only if the respondent has been seriously misled. A change of mind after the decree has been made absolute[74] will be too late.

Five years' separation

The fifth fact on which a petitioner may rely is that the spouses have lived apart for a continuous period of at least five years immediately preceding the presentation of the petition.[75] This fact is identical with the last except that the period of separation is five years and the respondent's consent to the divorce is not required. This provision was even more controversial than that based on two years' separation with consent, because it enables the marriage to be dissolved against the will of a spouse who has committed no matrimonial offence and who has not been responsible for the breakdown of the marriage. On the one hand it was hailed as a measure that would bring relief to hundreds of couples who would otherwise live in stable illicit unions unable to marry because one or both of them could not secure release from another union; on the other hand it was castigated as a 'Casanova's charter', permitting middle-aged men to put away their first wives in

---

[69] *McG v R* [1972] 1 All ER 362. The usual way of proving consent is by producing the completed acknowledgement of service stating that the respondent consents to the decree, which must be signed by him personally: See FPR 1991 r 2.10 and Form M6.

[70] *Mason v Mason* [1972] Fam 302.   [71] Matrimonial Causes Act 1973 s 2(7).

[72] See below p 280.

[73] Matrimonial Causes Act 1973 s 10(1). The matters on which a respondent is most likely to be misled are those relating to financial provision.

[74] See below p 281.

[75] Matrimonial Causes Act 1973 s 1(2)(e). Section 2(5) applies to the computation of the five-year period.

preference for new, younger spouses. If five years' separation is established, a decree can still be refused if it would cause the respondent grave financial or other hardship.[76]

(c) Protection of the respondent and children

There are various provisions designed to give protection to the respondent to the petition, and to the parties' children. These are intended to try to ensure that those most directly affected by the petitioner's decision to seek a divorce are not *unduly* adversely affected by the ending of the marriage (no one could claim that a divorce could very easily be made painless for all concerned). In the case of the respondent, it is for him or her to raise the relevant provision as part of the case, either to prevent or to delay the divorce going through. In the case of children, there is automatic consideration of the arrangements proposed for their future care and upbringing in every case (see below).

(d) Protection of the respondent

One way of ensuring that the court properly considers the respondent's perspective could be for him or her simply to defend the divorce and argue that the petitioner has not proved one of the five facts establishing that the marriage has irretrievably broken down. However, in practice, very few petitions are defended. The courts, and hence lawyers advising their clients, have taken the view that, if one party adamantly asserts that the marriage is over, there is usually little to be gained from allowing the other to try to contest the assertion, and it is difficult to obtain legal aid to defend the divorce. Where a spouse nonetheless insists on resisting the petition, it can be seen from cases like *Hadjimilitis (Tsavliris) v Tsavliris (Divorce: Irretrievable Breakdown)*,[77] noted above, that the very act of defending may persuade the court that the marriage is indeed over. There, the husband's attacks on the wife's marital 'failings' and motives somewhat undermined his claims that he wanted a reconciliation with her, and the court concluded that the wife had made out her case.

So instead of a general attempt to defend the petition, the respondent may, in appropriate cases, be advised to ask the court to utilise either of two mechanisms: the refusal of the divorce entirely, or the postponement of the decree absolute.

Refusal of the decree

If the petitioner relies on five years' separation, s 5 of the Act permits the respondent to oppose the grant of a decree nisi on the ground that the dissolution of the marriage would result in grave financial or other hardship to him and that it would be wrong in all the circumstances to dissolve the marriage. This provision was introduced in response to those concerns noted above that the five-year separation fact could be used to divorce an 'innocent' spouse against his or her will. In the vast majority of cases, the wife is much more likely to suffer hardship, particularly financial hardship, from the granting of a decree than the husband and so the following discussion is based on the assumption that it is the wife who is resisting the husband's petition, but it must be remembered that precisely the same principles apply if the respondent is the husband.

The hardship must result from the dissolution of the marriage: it is not enough for the respondent to show that hardship would result if the divorce were based on five years' separation, as distinct from some other fact. In *Grenfell v Grenfell*[78] the wife presented a

---

[76] See below.   [77] [2003] 1 FLR 81.   [78] [1978] Fam 128, CA.

petition based on her husband's behaviour. He cross-petitioned on the basis of five years' separation, and in her reply the wife pleaded that, as she was a practising member of the Greek Orthodox Church, her conscience would be affronted if the marriage were to be dissolved 'otherwise than on grounds of substance'. It was held that, as she was seeking a divorce herself, she could not argue that she would suffer hardship if the marriage were to be dissolved and so her reply was struck out.

Additionally, the hardship must be the result of the dissolution and not of the break-down of the marriage.[79] Hence, the fact that the husband will be supporting two families and have less money with which to support his wife and first family will be irrelevant if he is already living with the woman he wishes to marry and has children by her. Moreover, the hardship must be 'grave'. Whether or not there would be grave hardship must be considered 'subjectively in relation to the particular marriage and the circum-stances in which the parties lived while it subsisted',[80] but what matters is not whether the respondent feels that she would suffer (which she would in most cases) but whether sensible people knowing all the facts would think so.[81] It has been said that one must look at the situation through the eyes of the respondent and then judge objectively the reality of the apprehension.[82]

Hardship includes the loss of the chance of acquiring any benefit which the respondent might acquire if the marriage were not dissolved.[83] The potential loss of rights on the husband's intestacy will usually be immaterial because he will usually be advised to make a will in favour of other beneficiaries; and whether the marriage is dissolved or not, the wife will have a claim under the Inheritance (Provision for Family and Dependants) Act 1975.[84] In practice, grave financial hardship will be due to one (or both) of two causes. First, the wife will no longer be able to claim certain social security benefits (such as bereavement allowance[85] or retirement pension) by virtue of her husband's contributions. This may not apply in respect of retirement pension if the divorce takes place after she reaches pension-able age or it is granted before then but she does not remarry until after that date.[86] In any case, the Court of Appeal in *Reiterbund v Reiterbund*[87] laid down the principle that the court must not ignore the claims the wife has to means-tested benefits such as income support. There is no stigma attached to the receipt of such benefits and it can make no difference to the wife which public fund the money comes from. If, therefore, the amount she would receive from such benefits is not substantially less than what she would receive from the contribution-based benefit, she will suffer no hardship as a result of the divorce. If, on the other hand, she is likely to be earning a wage after her husband's death or retirement, she might receive considerably more from the contributory benefit because

---

[79] *Talbot v Talbot* (1971) 115 Sol Jo 870.

[80] Per Dunn LJ in *Talbot v Talbot* (above) approved in *Mathias v Mathias* [1972] Fam 287, 299.

[81] Per Lawton LJ in *Rukat v Rukat* [1975] Fam 63, 73. To quote his example, 'The rich gourmet who because of financial stringency has to drink vin ordinaire with his grouse may well think he is suffering hardship, but sensible people would say he was not.'

[82] *Balraj v Balraj* (1980) 11 Fam Law 110, CA. See also *Rukat v Rukat* (above) at 72.

[83] Matrimonial Causes Act 1973 s 5(3).   [84] See below, pp 1107.

[85] Which replaced widow's pension in 2001 (Social Security Contributions and Benefits Act 1992 s 39B, inserted by Welfare Reform and Pensions Act 1999 s 55).

[86] Social Security (Widow's Benefit and Retirement Pensions) Regulations, SI 1979/642 (as amended), reg 8.

[87] [1975] Fam 99, CA.

her earnings will not reduce it as they would reduce the sum received by way of income support. Each case must turn on its own facts: in *Reiterbund v Reiterbund* the wife could not rely on the potential loss of a widow's pension as grave financial hardship because she was likely to remain incapable of earning her own living and would therefore still be partially dependent on income support whether she received the pension or not.

The other likely cause of grave financial hardship will be the potential loss of pension rights, other than those payable under the state retirement pension scheme, accruing to an employee's widow. This is much less significant a problem than hitherto, because provisions were introduced into the law in 1995 and 1999 to enable a court to allocate either pension payments, or pension rights, to the divorced spouse, as part of the overall financial settlement reached in the suit.[88] Even before these provisions came into effect, the courts were wary about refusing a divorce on this ground and petitioners were usually able to persuade the court that the offer of some alternative form of financial provision would adequately compensate for the wife's loss or that her overall financial situation would cushion her sufficiently. For example, in *Le Marchant v Le Marchant*,[89] the husband was able to offset the loss of the widow's pension by means of a transfer to the wife of the matrimonial home, a delayed lump sum payable on his retirement and the benefit of a life assurance policy payable to her on his death. In *Archer v Archer*,[90] the husband was a consultant surgeon with high earnings, but whose capital assets were modest. His wife had assets of her own worth some £500,000 producing an income of around £12,000 per annum, and she received periodical payments from him of a further £18,000 per annum. The husband accepted that he should continue to maintain her during their joint lives but not that he should compensate her for loss of pension if he predeceased her. The wife argued that she would suffer grave hardship by not being able to claim the widow's pension of £11,000 per annum under the husband's pension scheme, but the Court of Appeal upheld the judge's decision that although this would be a substantial loss and cause her some hardship, given the capital available to her, it could not be said to be grave. But where the court is not satisfied that the wife's loss has been offset, it is likely to adjourn the proceedings, to enable (or persuade) the husband to find some better means of meeting the wife's needs.[91] It is extremely rare for a court to refuse the decree, one reported case being *Julian v Julian*[92] where the court dismissed the husband's petition when he could not improve on his offer to take out an annuity for the wife of some £215 per annum compared with the potential widow's pension she could receive of £790 per annum.

The position of the children may also be relevant in determining whether the respondent would suffer financial hardship. In *Lee v Lee*[93] the wife needed accommodation to look after her son, who needed constant nursing and care. The husband's proposal to sell the matrimonial home and give the wife half the proceeds of sale would not have enabled her to buy a flat for this purpose, and his petition was dismissed.[94]

---

[88] The Pensions Act 1995, s 166, which came into force in 1996, amended the Matrimonial Causes Act 1973 by inserting ss 25B-D to enable the 'earmarking' of pension payments to the divorced spouse. The Welfare Reform and Pensions Act 1999 Sch 3, which came into force in 2000, inserted s 21A and ss 24B-D into the 1973 Act to enable the making of a pension sharing order in respect of pension rights. See below at pp 999ff.

[89] [1977] 3 All ER 610, CA.   [90] [1999] 1 FLR 327, CA.

[91] *K v K (Financial Relief: Widow's Pension)* [1997] 1 FLR 35.   [92] (1972) 116 Sol Jo 763.

[93] (1973) 117 Sol Jo 616.

[94] On appeal, the divorce was granted because the son had died in the meantime: (1975) 5 Fam Law 48.

There is no clear judicial definition of what hardship other than financial hardship might mean, but the reported cases involve respondents alleging that divorce is anathema to them on religious grounds or that it would result in social ostracism. For example, in *Banik v Banik*[95] the wife was a Hindu still living in India. It was held by the Court of Appeal that it was not sufficient that the divorce would cause her distress and unhappiness or that she personally would regard it as immoral or contrary to the rules of her community; she must establish that shame, disgrace or degradation would fall on her. Whether this would amount to grave hardship if it were established is a question of fact and degree: the defence has not been successful in any reported case.[96]

Even if the respondent does prove that the decree would cause her grave hardship, the court must still pronounce a decree unless it also considers that it would be wrong to do so. The use of 'wrong' in this context is unusual and its meaning is ambiguous and obscure; in *Brickell v Brickell*[97] Davies LJ thought that it meant 'unjust or not right in all the circumstances of the case'. The court has to take into account specifically the conduct and interests of the parties and the interests of any children[98] and other persons concerned (for example, the person whom the petitioner wishes to marry), and in the end will have to balance those interests against the hardship that the divorce would cause the respondent.[99] Age, earning capacity and intention to remarry and the length of time that the parties have cohabited will be relevant, and in practice the courts are unlikely to refuse a divorce if the wife is young, healthy and capable of earning her own living, or if the marriage has lasted for only a short time, or has been effectively over for many years.[100] The respondent's conduct may likewise be a vital fact, and in *Brickell v Brickell* a decree was pronounced against a wife who had deserted her husband and broken up his business by her conduct even though the potential loss of a pension caused her grave financial hardship. Although the children's interests must be considered, the Court of Appeal in *Mathias v Mathias*[101] apparently paid no regard to the wife's argument that the husband's remarriage (which would be possible only if he were granted a divorce) could cause financial hardship to their child. The husband's father had left half his residuary estate (which was worth £20,000) to the husband's legitimate children in equal shares, and by remarrying the husband might have further legitimate children and thus reduce the existing child's interest.[102]

Even though reliance on s 5 is rarely, if ever, successful, it has been regarded as 'an important protection for a small group of people who may still face serious hardship which the law is unable at present to redress in other ways' and its retention in the law has been recommended.[103] The government has agreed, noting that the bar might well provide

[95] [1973] 3 All ER 45, CA. The court remitted the case for rehearing and a decree was later pronounced because the wife's statement that she would become a social outcast could be discounted and it would not be wrong to dissolve the marriage: see 117 Sol Jo 874.

[96] See also, *Parghi v Parghi* (1973) 117 Sol Jo 582 (Hindu wife resident in Bombay); *Rukat v Rukat* [1975] Fam 63 (Roman Catholic wife with family in Sicily); *Balraj v Balraj* (1980) 11 Fam Law 110, CA (wife resident in Kshatriya community in India; divorce would also reduce daughter's marriage prospects).

[97] [1974] Fam 31, CA.

[98] Who include children over the age of 18: *Allan v Allan* (1973) 4 Fam Law 83.

[99] See *Rukat v Rukat* (above) at 75, *Mathias v Mathias* [1972] Fam 287, 299 CA.

[100] *Mathias v Mathias* (above) at 301–2; *Rukat v Rukat* (above) at 76.   [101] Above.

[102] Note that, unless expressly provided to the contrary, both children born inside and outside marriage are entitled to take an inheritance: Family Law Reform Act 1969, s 15.

[103] Law Com No 190 para 5.75.

a useful 'bargaining chip' to a weaker spouse during negotiations[104] although how often it plays a part in the small number of divorces brought under the five years' separation fact is unknown.

Postponement of decree absolute[105]

In cases based on two and five years' separation. If a decree nisi is granted on the basis of two or five years' separation, the respondent may apply for it not to be made absolute unless the court is satisfied: (a) that the petitioner should not be required to make financial provision for the respondent; or (b) that the financial provision made by the petitioner for the respondent is reasonable and fair or the best that can be made in the circumstances.[106] This is another weapon given to the respondent to use against the petitioner. The threat to delay the petitioner's remarriage, for example, by holding up the decree absolute, may be regarded as a legitimate tactic if the petitioner is deliberately evading his financial responsibilities. The court may withhold the decree absolute until the petitioner has remedied his failure to make payments for a child of the family under an existing separation agreement, even though there is no continuing obligation, if non-payment in the past leaves the respondent at a financial disadvantage and there is no other ready way of enforcing the petitioner's obligation.[107] But in order to prevent a respondent from abusing the provision, the court may, even if it finds that the petitioner has not made such reasonable financial provision as he should have made, nonetheless make the decree absolute if it appears that there are circumstances making it desirable that this should not be delayed *and* the court has obtained a satisfactory undertaking from the petitioner that he will make such financial provision as the court may approve.[108] In practice, it should rarely be necessary for a respondent to a petition based on two years' separation to rely on s 10 since she could simply decline to give her consent to the decree if she were unhappy with the petitioner's financial proposals. In the case of a petition based on five years' separation, the potential of s 10 as another bargaining chip for the respondent should not be underestimated, and a failure to explore the possibility of using it may result in a finding of professional negligence against the wife's legal adviser.[109]

In cases of religious marriage. In recent years, Orthodox Jewish women seeking a divorce have publicised the problem of the '*agunah*', or 'anchored woman'.[110] Under Jewish law, only the husband can divorce his wife. Where he refuses to do so, then, although she may have obtained a divorce under English law, she remains married in the eyes of her religion and is unable to remarry according to Jewish rites. A husband could exploit this rule by only agreeing to divorce the wife under Jewish law (referred to as giving her a *get*) upon her acceptance of a smaller financial settlement. Section 10A of the Matrimonial Causes Act 1973,[111] seeks to redress this unfairness. It provides that if the parties were married to each other in accordance with usages of the Jews, or any other prescribed religious usages,

---

104 Green Paper para 6.62; White Paper para 4.47.; cf *Wickler v Wickler* [1998] 2 FLR 326, where the husband's application for a decree absolute was refused because there was a risk that he would wash his hands of any further involvement in the financial proceedings if it were granted.

105 The court's general power to withhold a decree absolute is discussed below at p 281.

106 Matrimonial Causes Act 1973 s 10(2),(3).   107 *Garcia v Garcia* [1991] 3 All ER 451, CA.

108 Section 10(4).   109 *Griffiths v Dawson & Co* [1993] 2 FLR 315.

110 See M Freeman 'The Jewish Law of Divorce' [2000] IFL 58.

111 Added by the Divorce (Religious Marriages) Act 2002.

and are required to co-operate if the marriage is to be dissolved in accordance with those usages, the court may, on the application of either party, order that a decree of divorce is not to be made absolute until a declaration made by both parties that they have taken such steps as are required to dissolve the marriage in accordance with those usages is produced to the court. The order may only be made if the court is satisfied that in all the circumstances of the case it is just and reasonable to do so, and it may be revoked (presumably on the application of either party) by the court at any time.[112] Thus, if a Jewish husband sought a civil divorce from his wife, she could apply to the court for an order, in effect, that he give her a *get*. However, where the wife seeks the divorce and the husband either opposes or does not care if the marriage is terminated, it would seem that he could still frustrate her, since he could simply ignore the order or delay his compliance, again potentially exploiting the wife's financial vulnerability by forcing her to agree to an inferior settlement.

(e) Protection of children

In every case where there are children of the family under the age of 16, or whom the court expressly directs should be included,[113] it has to consider the arrangements proposed for the children's future after their parents' divorce. At one time, the court had to be positively satisfied with these arrangements, or consider that they were the best that could be devised in the circumstances, before it could grant the decree absolute. However, research showed that this was an ineffective means of checking that arrangements were suitable,[114] and the Law Commission considered that the court's supervisory stance did not sit well alongside its preferred approach of non-intervention and of trusting most parents to fulfil their parental responsibility to their children.[115] The provision was therefore amended by the Children Act 1989, so that all the court has to do is to consider the arrangements, as set out on a detailed 'statement of arrangements form', and decide whether it should exercise any of its powers under the Children Act 1989 with respect to them. In exceptional circumstances the court may still direct that the decree is not to be made absolute until further order, if it is of the opinion that it is likely to have to exercise its powers under the Children Act with respect to certain children of the family and it needs to give further consideration to the case.[116] The district judge may, if not satisfied, also direct that further evidence be filed, that a welfare report be ordered, or that the parties attend before him. In practice, however, it is rare for any of these measures to be taken. The information provided in answer to the questions on the form may tell the district judge relatively little about the children's real welfare needs in order to put him or her on enquiry, and since the statement is filed with the petition at the start of the proceedings, it may be out of date by the time the district judge scrutinises it.[117] In practice, as the Law Commission intended, the court trusts the parents, and the lawyers trust their clients, to make suitable arrangements for their children, and expect a respondent to raise any concerns he or she may have when

---

[112] Section 10A(3).   [113] For example, because a child is disabled.

[114] See G Davis, A Macleod and M Murch, 'Undefended divorce: Should s 41 of the Matrimonial Causes Act 1973 be Repealed?' (1983) 46 MLR 121.

[115] Law Com No 172 para 3.6.

[116] Matrimonial Causes Act 1973 s 41 (as amended).

[117] For an assessment of the working of this provision, see G Douglas et al, 'Safeguarding children's welfare in non-contentious divorce: towards a new conception of the divorce process' (2000) 63 MLR 177.

acknowledging service of the petition or by issuing an application for an order under the Children Act 1989, which will take the case out of the s 41 process and enable a court to hold a full Children Act hearing to determine the outcome.

3 THE PROCEDURE FOR OBTAINING THE DIVORCE[118]

(a) The special procedure

Consideration of the substantive law governing the grant of a divorce provides only a partial and inaccurate picture of what the experience of obtaining a divorce is like for those involved. This is because, as noted, virtually all divorce petitions are undefended: in other words, the respondent does not attempt (either from the start, or once he or she has taken advice or realised that the marriage is indeed over) to resist the grant of the divorce. This is not to say that most couples experience an amicable divorce; there may be much to argue over when it comes to determining how the financial and property consequences are to be dealt with, and what pattern of arrangements is to be made for the future care of the couple's children. But as far as the decree itself is concerned, there is no effective contest between the parties, and this state of affairs long pre-dated the advent of the Matrimonial Causes Act.

Yet notwithstanding the fact that the suit was uncontested, before 1973, the petitioner's evidence was heard in open court together with that of any other witness necessary to support his case. Appearance in court often led to considerable anxiety for the petitioner and to costs which, whether borne by the parties or the legal aid fund, were significant and growing rapidly. It also involved a great deal of judicial time.[119] Consequently, in 1973 a 'special procedure' was introduced to dispense with the need to give evidence in court if the case was not defended.[120] Originally it applied only to petitions based on two years' separation, but from 1977 all undefended petitions for divorce were dealt with under this procedure. At the same time, legal aid for the divorce itself was withdrawn.[121] This change in procedure may in some ways be seen as the most fundamental, yet relatively unremarked-upon change in divorce since the introduction of judicial divorce in 1857, since it seems to have marked the end of attempts to provide any effective scrutiny of a party's case for obtaining a divorce and has rendered the substantive law outlined above no more than a template to which the spouse or the lawyer must fit the facts on which the petitioner chooses to rely in establishing irretrievable breakdown.

---

[118] Family Proceedings Rules 1991 r 2.

[119] E Elston, J Fuller and M Murch 'Judicial Hearings of Undefended Divorce Petitions' (1975) 38 MLR 609.

[120] Where the petition is defended, the respondent must file an answer to the petition within 21 days after the expiration of the time limit for giving notice of intention to defend: FPR 1991 r 2.12. The case is then heard in open court in the usual way. In *N v N* [1992] 1 FLR 266, the wife presented a petition based on the husband's behaviour. They agreed to try a reconciliation during which the wife would not proceed with her suit and that, if the reconciliation attempt failed, the husband would not defend the petition. Five months later, the wife decided the reconciliation attempt had failed and she renewed her petition. The husband applied to file an answer out of time, but it was held that the agreement not to defend was perfectly proper.

[121] Although it may still be obtained to make or oppose an application for an order for non-molestation or occupation, financial relief or in relation to children, but not to make an application in relation to children if there is no reason to believe that it would be opposed. Many petitioners find themselves having to draft their own divorce petition, the pitfalls of which exercise were demonstrated in *Young v Purdy* [1996] 2 FLR 795, CA.

Under the special procedure, the petitioner commences proceedings by issuing a petition to the divorce county court, accompanied by an affidavit verifying the contents of the petition and a statement of the arrangements proposed for the children of the family, together with certain other information and any corroborative evidence on which the petitioner intends to rely. The district judge then enters the cause in the special procedure list. If he is satisfied that the petitioner has proved his case and is entitled to a decree, he makes and files a certificate to this effect and a day is fixed on which a judge or district judge pronounces the decree nisi in open court. Neither party needs to be present when this is done. While scrutiny of the documentation might reveal technical errors, it is unlikely to reveal defects of substance.[122]

The effect of the introduction of this procedure was inevitably to ensure that there can be no real investigation of the truth of the allegations made in the divorce petition if the respondent chooses not to challenge them,[123] or is not in a position to do so.[124] However, there is still an outside chance that an abuse may come to light. In *Bhaiji v Chauhan, Queen's Proctor Intervening (Divorce: Marriages Used for Immigration Purposes)*[125] for example, court staff became suspicious when they found strong similarities between five petitions presented by litigants acting in person. All the parties were of Indian ethnicity and in each case one spouse was a UK citizen and resident and the other a recent entrant to the UK who had relied on the marriage to obtain indefinite leave to remain. In four of the cases, the period of time between obtaining such leave and the alleged breakdown of the marriage was very short. The cases were transferred for full hearing in the High Court which dismissed all but one (which was withdrawn), on the basis that the allegations made in the petitions were false.

Parties seeking a quick divorce have little to lose by bringing the petition on the basis of one of the fault facts—adultery or behaviour—rather than waiting the two years for a no fault decree. Around 70% of petitions are based on the 'fault' facts and around the same proportion are sought by wives rather than husbands.[126]

(b) Decrees

The divorce decree is made in two stages: the decree nisi, followed by the decree absolute.[127] The petitioner may apply for the decree to be made absolute at any time after the expiration of six weeks from the granting of the decree nisi unless the court fixes a shorter time in the particular case;[128] if the petitioner fails to apply for a decree absolute, the respondent may apply at any time after the expiration of three months from the earliest date on which the petitioner could have applied.[129] Should the respondent apply before this period

---

[122] Law Com No 192 *The Ground for Divorce* (1990) para 2.2.

[123] See *Callaghan v Hanson-Fox* [1992] Fam 1; *Moynihan v Moynihan (Nos 1 and 2)* [1997] 1 FLR 59.

[124] *Akhtar v Rafiq* [2006] 1 FLR 27: wife had returned to Pakistan, husband forged wife's thumbprint on acknowledgement of service form and decree was granted in 1992. Husband 'remarried' and had five children. Wife sued for divorce in 2003 and the forgery came to light. Held decree must be set aside where there had been no proper service and the irregularity was only discovered after the event.

[125] [2003] 2 FLR 485.   [126] ONS (2004), *Population Trends 121* Fig 2.

[127] Subject to the provisions of s 10 and s 41 of the 1973 Act discussed above. For the reasons for the two-stage process, see Cretney, *Family Law in the Twentieth Century: A History* (2003) 178.

[128] Matrimonial Causes Act 1973 s 1(5) and *Practice Direction* [1977] 2 All ER 714.

[129] Matrimonial Causes Act 1973 s 9(2).

has expired, and the court wrongly grants the decree absolute, it is void.[130] There is a discretion whether to permit the respondent's application, and it may be refused where financial matters are outstanding and the petitioner will be prejudiced if the respondent is permitted to obtain the freedom to remarry before these are resolved.[131]

The delay is intended to provide an opportunity for an unsuccessful respondent to appeal against the granting of the decree nisi, or for the Queen's Proctor[132] or any other person to intervene to show cause why the decree should not be made absolute. The parties themselves may have reasons for wishing to have the decree rescinded. For example, in *S v S (Rescission of Decree Nisi: Pension Sharing Provision)*[133] the court rescinded a decree nisi granted in 1999, on the wife's application with the husband's consent, so that they could take advantage of the power, only granted to courts in respect of petitions presented after 1 December 2000, to make a pension sharing order.[134] Upholding public policy may also be in issue. In the old days of the matrimonial offence, the Queen's Proctor investigated allegations of collusion or other abuse of the divorce process by the spouses (primarily in order to prevent them obtaining a divorce 'by consent'). The office still exists to enable the court to call on the Queen's Proctor's services either to investigate modern day abuses,[135] or to act as amicus curiae (as was done in *S v S*).

The marriage ceases as soon as the decree is made absolute, and either spouse is then free to remarry. The decree nisi does not have this effect, and if either party remarries before it has been made absolute, the second marriage is void.[136]

4 RECONCILIATION

The emphasis of the law is on *irretrievable* breakdown and certain provisions in the Matrimonial Causes Act are designed to promote reconciliation between the parties. For example, if the petitioner instructs a solicitor to act for him, the latter is required to certify whether or not he has discussed with the petitioner the possibility of reconciliation and given him the names and addresses of persons qualified to help effect a reconciliation between estranged spouses.[137] However, not all petitioners instruct a solicitor, and the provision is generally regarded as serving little purpose.[138] The disregard of periods of cohabitation following instances of 'fault' or during separation is also intended to encourage the parties to try to repair the marriage without feeling that they would thereby 'lose' the basis of their petition.

---

[130] *Manchanda v Manchanda* [1995] 2 FLR 590, CA; *Dennis v Dennis* [2000] 2 FLR 231.

[131] *Smith v Smith* [1990] 1 FLR 438; *Wickler v Wickler* [1998] 2 FLR 326. Cf *Re G (Decree Absolute: Prejudice)* [2002] EWHC 2834 (Fam) [2003] 1 FLR 870—no prejudice to wife to grant husband's application for decree absolute where husband not proved likely to obstruct financial proceedings.

[132] See SM Cretney, *Family Law in the Twentieth Century: A History* (2003) pp 178–181.

[133] [2002] 1 FLR 457.

[134] Cf *H v H (Pension Sharing: Rescission of Decree Nisi)* [2002] EWHC 767 (Fam) [2002] 2 FLR 116: application refused because of husband's lack of consent and unfairness to him in such circumstances to permit wife to circumvent the commencement date set by Parliament. To similar effect, see *Rye v Rye* [2002] EWHC 956 (Fam) [2002] 2 FLR 981.

[135] As in *Bhaiji v Chauhan, Queen's Proctor Intervening (Divorce: Marriages Used for Immigration Purposes)* [2003] 2 FLR 485, noted above.

[136] As happened in both *Manchanda v Manchanda* and *Dennis v Dennis* above.

[137] Ibid, s 6(1); Family Proceedings Rules 1991 r 2.6(3) and Form M3.

[138] *Report of the Matrimonial Causes Procedure Committee* (the Booth Committee) (1985) paras 4.42–4.43.

There is little empirical evidence on the extent to which those contemplating divorce may attempt reconciliation nor how successful such attempts may be. Davis and Murch have suggested that there is potential for reconciliation in a significant number of cases, based on their findings that some couples may feel swept along the divorce track without adequate time to stop and reflect on whether this is what they really want. But they also note that it does not follow that such couples' marriages could have been 'saved' by the legal process seeking to facilitate their reconciliation.[139] One study,[140] following up 1,491 people who had taken part in a pilot scheme intended to test out certain provisions aimed at reforming the Matrimonial Causes Act (and which are discussed below), found that 19% of those contacted, who had been contemplating divorce at the time of the pilot, were still living with their spouse two years later. The researchers commented, however, that while some respondents felt their marriages had been strengthened, the interview data left an impression of marriages 'continuing largely because spouses have learnt to make the best of imperfect circumstances . . . There is no doubt that the continuation of co-residence is not necessarily an indicator that the marriage has been "saved".' The results offer a cautionary message to those who might seek to promote reconciliation as the right way forward when a marriage gets into difficulties and confirm that the fact that a marriage does not find its way into the divorce statistics does not mean that the relationship itself is healthy.

5 MEDIATION [141]

Dissatisfaction with the procedural aspects of the law and the ineffectiveness of the provisions intended to encourage reconciliation led individual courts and practitioners to introduce an alternative mechanism for helping couples to deal with the consequences of their divorce—mediation, or, as it was originally known, conciliation.[142] A clear lead was given by the *Finer Report on One-Parent Families*, which defined conciliation as:

'. . . assisting the parties to deal with the consequences of the established breakdown of their marriage, whether resulting in a divorce or a separation, by reaching agreements or giving assents or reducing the area of conflict upon custody, support, access to and education of the children, financial provision, disposition of the matrimonial home, lawyers' fees, and every other matter arising from the breakdown which calls for a decision on future arrangements'.[143]

Family mediation has been said to have the following objects:

[139] G Davis and M Murch, *Grounds for Divorce* (1988) Ch 4.

[140] J Walker and P McCarthy, 'Picking Up the Pieces' [2004] Fam Law 580.

[141] There is a vast literature. See, in particular, G Davis *Partisans and Mediators* (1988); L Parkinson *Conciliation in Separation and Divorce* (1986); J Haynes *Alternative Dispute Resolution: The Fundamentals of Family Mediation* (1993); J Walker et al *Mediation: The Making and Re-Making of Co-operative Relationships* (1994).

[142] Mediation has become the preferred term in recent years, although some practitioners distinguish between in-court 'conciliation' appointments which tend to be very time-limited and which are part of the court process and so effectively compulsory, and out of court 'mediation' which is more open-ended and depends upon the parties' motivations and rate of progress. See further below.

[143] Cmnd 5629, para 4.288 (1974).

'to help separating and divorcing couples to reach their own agreed joint decisions about future arrangements; to improve communications between them; and to help couples work together on the practical consequences of divorce with particular emphasis on their joint responsibilities to co-operate as parents in bringing up their children.'[144]

The mediator must be—and must be seen to be—neutral: he may clarify issues and propose possible solutions, but he must not seek to impose any of them on the parties.[145]

The growth of interest in mediation reflects the changed attitude towards divorce generally, and the shift of emphasis from the fact of dissolution to its consequences and especially its effect on the children of the marriage. Research suggests that children find emotional adjustment more difficult if the parents' relationship is hostile and conflict between them continues after divorce or separation, particularly if contact with one parent is not maintained.[146] One of the strongest arguments in favour of mediation is that the possibility of bitterness will be reduced and the prospects of both spouses continuing to play an active role as parents will be enhanced if they can reach agreement. The adversarial procedure of the courts, on the other hand, may well exacerbate antagonism,[147] although this can be exaggerated: the vast majority of spouses reach agreement either by themselves or with the assistance of their lawyers, who will adhere to mandatory and voluntary professional codes of conduct[148] requiring them to adopt a non-confrontational approach to the case anyway.[149]

However, whether mediation is appropriate in situations where one party may have subjected the other to domestic violence, or has threatened such violence, is debatable.[150] It may be that, where the threatened party feels protected by the mediator, she (usually) can then feel able to participate. A further dilemma concerns the involvement of children in mediation. While mediators regard children's interests as central to most mediation work, the question of how far they should be involved in the mediation process itself is an open one, with mediators themselves divided on its appropriateness and feasibility.[151]

Two types of mediation developed alongside the statutory divorce procedure: 'in-court'—which may still be referred to as 'conciliation'—and 'out-of-court', usually described as 'mediation'.

---

[144] Lord Chancellor's Department, (1995) *Looking to the Future: Mediation and the Ground for Divorce* para 6.17.

[145] This distinguishes a mediator from an adjudicator (who has the power to impose a solution), an arbitrator (by whose decision the parties have agreed to be bound), and a negotiator (who acts on behalf of one party only).

[146] J Pryor and B Rodgers, (2001) *Children in Changing Families: Life after Parental Separation.*

[147] See eg the *Report of the Inter-departmental Committee on Conciliation* (1983), para 1.13; Parkinson, op cit p 69; M Murch *Justice and Welfare in Divorce* (1980) 210.

[148] See the Law Society, *Family Law Protocol* (2002) and the Resolution (Solicitors Family Law Association) Code of Practice: http://www.sfla.org.uk/code_practice.php.

[149] For a detailed study of how family lawyers work, see J Eekelaar, M Maclean and S Beinart, *Family Lawyers: The Divorce Work of Solicitors* (2000).

[150] Compare M Roberts 'Family Mediation and the Interests of Women—Facts and Fears' [1996] Fam Law 239, who suggests that domestic violence may make mediation inappropriate (although she also argues that research evidence finds few other situations where women are disadvantaged by mediation), and M Black and D Price 'Mediation and the Shadow of the Past' [1996] Fam Law 693, who report positively on the use of mediation in cases of violence.

[151] See M Murch et al, *Safeguarding Children's Welfare in Uncontentious Divorce: A Study of s 41 of the Matrimonial Causes Act 1973* Lord Chancellor's Department Research Series 7/99, (1999) Ch 7.

(a) In-court schemes

In 1971, courts were encouraged to refer a case to the court welfare officer when it was considered that conciliation might be helpful.[152] In 1977, a scheme to incorporate this approach into the normal divorce process was launched in the Bristol county court, and similar schemes were subsequently introduced in many others.[153] The parties, sometimes with their solicitors, attend an appointment for directions before the district judge; if the issues are essentially issues of law or fact, the district judge can assist by pointing the way towards a possible resolution, but if they are emotional or involve children, the parties talk to a CAFCASS officer who seeks to help them reach an agreement. If agreement is reached, the district judge can make the necessary consent orders. In some schemes, the parties may be required to bring their children, usually over the age of about nine, where it is thought appropriate for them to be seen by the CAFCASS officer.[154] If the parties cannot reach an agreement, the welfare officer acting as mediator may subsequently be asked to make a report to the court, but it is accepted that these two roles cannot be combined and that the same officer should not carry out both functions.[155] A similar scheme relating to financial and property issues in the divorce was introduced on a nationwide basis in 2000.[156] Similar in approach to the Civil Procedure Rules 1998 (although the procedure pertaining in family courts was piloted from 1996 and hence pre-dated these), the 'ancillary relief procedure' as it is known, imposes judicial case management on the conduct of proceedings, and in particular requires that a 'financial dispute resolution' appointment be held at which the district judge encourages the parties to reach agreement, including by giving them a neutral evaluation of the likely outcome if the case proceeds to a trial. Should the mediation appointment fail to produce a settlement, the case will be heard by a different district judge.

There is some evidence that parties may feel under pressure to reach a decision in as short a time as possible in these kinds of appointment, and some complain of crude arm-twisting and a search for a compromise regardless of the justice of the case.[157] But although official enthusiasm for mediation has lessened since the 1990s, when it was apparently seen by some, as we discuss below, as a panacea for all the problems of the divorce process, it remains regarded as a crucial measure of encouragement to parties in family disputes to reach agreement themselves rather than to take up court time and public expense by persisting to a final hearing, and new mechanisms are being introduced to try to deal with particularly protracted and bitter disputes over children involve further attempts at mediation.[158]

---

[152] *Practice Direction* [1971] 1 All ER 894.

[153] For a history of the launch of mediation in Bristol, both within the court and outside, see J Westcott (ed) *Family Mediation: Past, Present and Future* (2004). For a full evaluation of schemes run by CAFCASS, see HMCSI, *Seeking Agreement: CAFCASS: A Thematic Review by MCSI of the operation of schemes involving CAFCASS at an early stage in private law proceedings* (2003).

[154] See, for example, *District Judge's Direction: Children: Conciliation* [2004] 1 FLR 974 in respect of applications for orders relating to children at the Principal Registry in London. For an account of the scheme and an evaluation of its success, see DJ Glenn Brasse, 'Conciliation is Working' [2004] Fam Law 722.

[155] *Scott v Scott* [1986] 2 FLR 320, CA; *Re H (Conciliation: Welfare Reports)* [1986] 1 FLR 476; *Practice Direction* [1986] 2 FLR 171. See also Booth Committee Report below paras 4.61–4.63.

[156] FPR 1991 (as amended) rr 2.51B–2.70. See E Da Costa, 'Ancillary Relief—The New Procedure' [2000] Fam Law 248. The scheme is discussed in more detail in Chapter 18.

[157] G Davis and K Bader [1985] Fam Law 42, 82; C Piper *The Responsible Parent* (1993).

[158] See below.

(b) Out-of-court mediation

Out-of-court mediation is independent of the court, in the sense that parties are not referred to it by the court, and a mediator's services are available to them before they embark on litigation. The chances of success of out-of-court mediation are said to be greater because the parties are more likely to resort to it before they take up entrenched positions. It began in 1978, also in Bristol, as a result of the initiative of a group committed to taking action following the publication of the *Report of the Committee on One-Parent Families*. A number of other independent services have since been set up in other parts of the country.[159] Most couples are referred by solicitors or refer themselves.

(c) Communications made in the course of mediation

Mediation is unlikely to be successful if there is a danger that a statement made by one party in the course of negotiations may later be put in evidence by the other if they fail to arrive at an agreement. In *Re D (Minors) (Conciliation: Disclosure of Information)*[160] the Court of Appeal held that evidence of statements or communications made in conciliation relating to proceedings under the Children Act is inadmissible in the proceedings except where it clearly indicates that the maker has caused, or is likely to cause, serious harm to the well-being of the child.[161] In relation to financial matters, a similar privilege applies to the financial dispute resolution appointment.[162]

(d) Binding nature of agreements

No agreement between the parties can oust the jurisdiction of the court,[163] so that any terms on which they agree in the course of mediation will be binding only when approved by the court. The court may take the view that it should give effect to a clause in an agreement relating to financial provision freely entered into between the parties, even though it would have made a more generous award.[164] Although a party could resile from an agreement if he or she had been misled, it would obviously be imprudent to accept an offer in ignorance of the other's income and assets. Mediators therefore advise clients that they should consult lawyers before they seek to have their agreement formalised.

(e) Public funding for mediation

The government attempted in the 1990s to boost the use of out of court mediation in family cases by making it a condition of receiving publicly funded legal help (legal aid) that the applicant first undergo an 'intake assessment' by a mediator to determine whether mediation is suitable to their dispute.[165] If mediation is deemed suitable, then the applicant will be denied legal help if they refuse to attempt mediation. But research suggests that only a minority of cases will go down the mediation track even where 'encouraged' to

159 See http://www.ukcfm.co.uk/findingaMediator.htm for details of members of the UK College of Family Mediators.
160 [1993] Fam 231, CA.
161 But many CAFCASS-run schemes appear to be non-privileged: see HMCSI op cit para 2.10.
162 FPR 1991 (as amended) r 2.61E (1), (4).   163 See below, p 954.
164 *Edgar v Edgar* [1980] 3 All ER 887, CA: see below, p 1010.
165 This provision was first introduced by Part III of the Family Law Act 1996, and is now, in revised form, contained in the Legal Services Commission Funding Code, made under s 8 of the Access to Justice Act 1999.

do so by the legal aid system. Davis and his colleagues[166] monitored publicly funded mediation for the Legal Services Commission in the 1990s, in another pilot scheme aimed at reform of the divorce law. They found that while mediation was deemed suitable for two-thirds of those attending an intake assessment in their sample, this proportion dropped to 41% of those attending whose primary reason for attendance was to get legal aid. Where mediation was deemed unsuitable, in 71% of cases the reason given was the partner's reluctance or failure to attend. Since the Funding Code now exempts an applicant for legal aid from undergoing an intake assessment if the other party is contacted by the mediator and is found to be unwilling to attend, it seems that the Legal Services Commission has accepted that its ability to restrict public funding for legal representation in family cases—and more positively to encourage the use of mediation—is inevitably limited by the degree to which the other party is prepared to attempt mediation himself. Only by incorporating mediation as a mandatory step in the formal legal process could significantly higher rates of use probably be achieved. Compulsion has been regarded as contrary to the ethos of mediation, with its focus on party control and autonomy of decision-making, yet it has been successfully introduced into the ancillary relief jurisdiction through the financial dispute resolution appointments noted above, and is frequently compulsory in other jurisdictions. Indeed, in-court conciliation appointments are arguably close to compulsory already.[167]

6 'COLLABORATIVE LAW' [168]

Although not a form of mediation, it is convenient to mention here an initiative imported from the United States in recent years, known as 'collaborative law'. This is a process in which the parties each instruct their own lawyer to advise, negotiate and assist them in resolving their dispute, as normal. However, the clients and lawyers sign a binding written agreement, known as a participation agreement, whereby they undertake not to issue or pursue proceedings at court where there is a dispute. Should the client wish to pursue court action, they will have to instruct a different lawyer. The parties with their lawyers hold settlement meetings at which they all work to achieve settlement of the issues in dispute between them. Recourse may be had to other advisers, such as accountants and therapists and child counsellors, during the process. Whilst similar to the conciliatory approach practised by many family lawyers in their negotiations already, and to mediation in its use of face to face meetings, the distinguishing feature of collaborative law is the commitment not to litigate, which is said to focus the attention of both lawyers and clients on the search for a settlement. It has been eagerly endorsed by a number of legal

---

[166] G Davis et al, *Monitoring Publicly Funded Mediation* (2000), Ch 4, Part 4. For other aspects of their findings, see in addition to the full report, G Davis et al, 'Mediation and Legal Services—The Client Speaks' [2001] Fam Law 110, G Bevan et al, 'Can Mediation Reduce Expenditure on Lawyers?' [2001] Fam Law 186, G Davis et al, 'Family Mediation—Where Do We Go From Here?' [2001] Fam Law 265 and R Dingwall and D Greatbatch, 'Family Mediators—What Are They Doing?' [2001] Fam Law 378.

[167] Davis et al suggest that it would not be unduly oppressive to make mediation—or at least, an exploration with both parties of the scope for mediation—compulsory at the first appointment stage: 'Family Mediation—Where Do We Go From Here?' [2001] Fam Law 265 at 267. The House of Commons Constitutional Affairs Select Committee has made the same recommendation: see *Family Justice: The Operation of the Family Courts* (2004–5) HC 116–1 para 94.

[168] See K Fretwell, 'How to get a good divorce' (2003) NLJ 1877, J Pirrie, 'Collaborative Family Law—Perspectives from Training' [2004] Fam Law 216.

practitioners in this country, perhaps because they found that training as mediators, which many lawyers undertook in the 1990s and offering mediation did not prove attractive to clients and they hope that this may prove more palatable, as being closer to what clients 'expect' legal assistance to look like. It is too early to speculate on the success of this approach in England and Wales, although it is said to be successful in the USA.[169]

C PROPOSALS FOR REFORM

During the 1980s and 1990s, criticisms of the substantive and procedural law governing divorce resulted in several reform proposals being advocated. Legislation eventually followed in the shape of the Family Law Act 1996, but uncertainty about the viability and desirability of the new legislative process eventually led to a decision not to bring the relevant provisions of the Act into force. We trace below the sequence of events, to identify what the criticisms of the law were, how it was suggested they be dealt with, and why, in the end, no changes were implemented.

1 THE BOOTH COMMITTEE ON MATRIMONIAL CAUSES PROCEDURE

In 1982 a committee chaired by Booth J was established to examine divorce procedure. The main thrust of their Report, published in 1985, was that bitterness between the parties might be reduced if unnecessary acrimonious allegations were eliminated and defended suits kept to a minimum; furthermore, parties should be encouraged and helped to settle financial matters and questions relating to children themselves with the benefit of legal advice and, if necessary, the assistance of mediators.

They also proposed that there should be an initial hearing within about 10 weeks of filing the application in every case involving children to whom s 41 of the 1973 Act applied[170] and also in cases where the respondent had stated an intention to oppose the grant of the decree. The purpose of the hearing would be to make orders in respect of agreed matters, to refer the parties to mediation where appropriate, to define the issues remaining between them, and to give directions.[171]

The Committee recommended that the terms 'decree nisi' and 'decree absolute' be replaced by 'provisional decree' and 'final decree', and that the latter should normally issue automatically four weeks after the grant of the former. To protect a party where this would work hardship (for example, because no order had been made for financial relief) the court would be given a power to delay the final decree in appropriate cases.

Although no action was taken on most of their recommendations, a number were later developed by the Law Commission in their own proposals for more thorough-going reform of the law.

---

[169] Fretwell, op cit.   [170] See above, p 278.   [171] Report para 3.5.

2 THE LAW COMMISSION'S PROPOSALS

Research showed that the objectives of the law, as laid down by the Law Commission in their 1966 Report, were not being met,[172] and the Law Commission looked again at the problem, issuing a Discussion Paper in 1988[173] and a report in 1990.[174]

(a) The Law Commission's criticisms of the 1973 Act

'It is confusing and misleading'

The sole ground for divorce is stated to be the irretrievable breakdown of the marriage, suggesting that fault is not the basis for granting a divorce, but such breakdown, no matter how profound, will not lead to a divorce decree unless a spouse can point to one of the five facts, three of which do involve fault. Further, the real reason for the breakdown might have nothing to do with the fact presented in the petition, the allegations becoming a peg on which to hang the petition, regardless of their significance (or insignificance) for the parties. No real scrutiny can be conducted into the truth of the allegations, and a petitioner might be encouraged to bolster the petition with trivial or exaggerated allegations.[175]

'It is discriminatory and unjust'

The two years' separation with consent fact is relied upon more often by those in the higher socio-economic groups, while the poorer have to rely on the less satisfactory fault facts in order to obtain a speedier divorce and hence resolution of their financial and property problems.[176] It is discriminatory and unjust to provide a civilised no fault basis for divorce which is, in practice, unavailable to a large part of the population because many couples cannot afford to part and live in separate households for two years before the divorce. The fault facts themselves do not result in a clear allocation of 'blame' for the breakdown of the marriage, since the petitioner might have been equally to blame although his conduct is not raised because the respondent does not defend the case. Even where respondents wish to dispute the allegations made in the petition by defending the suit, they are usually told that it would be a waste of time and money because the divorce will be granted anyway.

'It distorts parties' bargaining positions'

Given the difficulty facing a spouse in challenging allegations in the divorce suit itself, the scope for dispute is usually displaced from the divorce petition itself to the ancillary matters. One party who is more anxious or reluctant for the divorce to occur might be placed in a correspondingly weaker or stronger position in bargaining over matters relating to money and the children.

'It provokes unnecessary hostility and bitterness'

A fundamental objective of the Divorce Reform Act 1969 was to minimise the bitterness, distress and humiliation experienced by the parties in obtaining their divorce. But the

---

[172] See, in particular, Davis and Murch, *Grounds for Divorce* (1988).

[173] *Facing the Future—A Discussion Paper on the Ground for Divorce* Law Com No 170.

[174] *The Ground for Divorce* Law Com No 192.   [175] Law Com No 192 paras 2.8–2.12.

[176] Examination of 477 cases begun in the years 1980 to 1984 revealed that 36% of those in social group I relied upon the two years' separation fact, compared with 17% in social group V: Law Com No 192 Appendix C, Table 2.

system encourages each to make allegations against the other and to portray the other in as bad a light as possible to support the petition. This provokes resentment, hostility and distress in the other spouse at a time when the couple are experiencing severe stress and unhappiness in coming to terms with the ending of their marriage. Their emotional misery is simply compounded by the legal process.

'It does nothing to save the marriage'

Despite the provisions intended to promote reconciliation which, as we saw,[177] have had little effect, the law in fact thrusts the parties further apart by encouraging the making of allegations of misconduct against each other or by requiring them to separate. Attention is placed upon how to prove irretrievable breakdown rather than on how to try to mend the marriage.

'It can make things worse for the children'

Children whose parents divorce may suffer more subsequently if the parents remain in conflict.[178] The law does nothing to reduce such conflict: indeed, it frequently exacerbates it.

(b) The options for reform

These criticisms convinced the Law Commission that the law required further reform. In deciding how to achieve this, the Law Commission drew up a new set of objectives for the law, which show interesting differences from their 1966 formulation.[179] It was 'generally agreed' that the law should:

'... try to support those marriages which are capable of being saved ... enable those which cannot be saved to be dissolved with the minimum of avoidable distress, bitterness and hostility ... encourage, so far as possible, the amicable resolution of practical issues relating to the couple's home, finances and children and the proper discharge of their responsibilities to one another and to their children ...'

and

'... seek to minimise the harm that the children of the family may suffer, both at the time and in the future, and to promote so far as possible the continued sharing of parental responsibility for them.'[180]

These objectives reflect both an emphasis on mediation, in response to the developments in the provision of mediation pioneered during the 1970s and 1980s, and also the shift of attention towards the children of the marriage and the fundamental ideology of parental responsibility which underpins the Children Act 1989 (enacted shortly before this report was published).

The Commission rejected a return to a fault-based system on the basis that, first, the law is capable of assessing fault only in the crudest way, and secondly, that denying divorce except on grounds of fault is an illogical and ineffective way of promoting good marital conduct. Equally, divorce by immediate unilateral demand was rejected as providing no means of protecting the respondent, and divorce by mutual consent would not cater for

---

[177] See above, p 281.
[178] J Pryor and B Rodgers, (2001) *Children in Changing Families: Life after Parental Separation.*
[179] Above, p 264.   [180] Law Com No 192 para 3.1.

cases where one spouse steadfastly refuses to consent. In many other jurisdictions which reformed their law after the Divorce Reform Act, the preferred model was a simple period of separation, but the Law Commission criticised it for its discriminatory effects against those who are poor. Instead, they recommended that divorce should no longer be seen as a single event but should be granted only after a process continuing for a period of time. This would demonstrate that the breakdown is irretrievable, give the parties the opportunity of facing up to the consequences of divorce and enable the practical problems to be resolved.

(c) The Law Commission's proposed scheme

The process they contemplated would begin by either (or preferably both) of the parties lodging at a court a sworn statement that he or she (or both) believes that the marriage has broken down. Each party would then be given a comprehensive information pack explaining inter alia the purpose of the period of consideration and reflection, the effects of divorce and separation, the powers of the court, and the nature and purpose of counselling, reconciliation and mediation. No later than 12 weeks after the making of the statement, the court would hold a preliminary assessment to review progress, make directions and consider whether mediation might be appropriate in helping the parties reach agreements.[181] After 11 months either or both of them would be able to apply for an order for divorce on making a declaration that the maker (or makers) believed that the breakdown of their marriage is irretrievable. In the intervening period the parties could be offered counselling or mediation, and the court could make orders relating to children, financial provision and property adjustment. This would reflect the principle that the practical consequences of divorce should ideally be settled before the marriage is dissolved. The court would normally make an order for divorce a month after the application (giving a minimum period of 12 months from the lodging of the initial statement). As under the 1973 Act, however, it should be able to postpone the order in exceptional circumstances, if this were necessary to enable it to consider whether it should exercise any of its powers under the Children Act in respect of any children of the family or to make any proper financial arrangements. The court would also be able to refuse an order for divorce if this would result in grave financial or other hardship to one of the parties and it would be wrong in the circumstances to dissolve the marriage.

3 THE GOVERNMENT'S RESPONSE [182]

Notwithstanding the government's unhappy experience in enacting the Child Support Act 1991,[183] and the fact that hitherto divorce legislation had been regarded as too controversial to be handled as a government measure, the Lord Chancellor decided to introduce plans to reform the divorce law, issuing a consultation paper in 1993,[184] followed by a

---

[181] The assessment would be roughly equivalent to the initial hearing recommended earlier by the Booth Committee: above, p 287.

[182] For assessments of the government's proposals, see A Bainham 'Divorce and the Lord Chancellor: Looking to the Future or Getting Back to Basics?' (1994) 35 Cambridge LJ 253; SM Cretney 'Divorce Reform in England: Humbug and Hypocrisy or a Smooth Transition?' in M Freeman (ed) *Divorce, Where Next?* (1996).

[183] See below p 929.

[184] *Looking to the Future: Mediation and the Ground for Divorce* Cm 2424 (hereafter, 'Green Paper').

White Paper in 1995.[185] The key to this insistence on taking control of divorce reform would appear to lie, at least in part, in the government's further refinement of the objectives of divorce law. Now, these were stated as being:

— to support the institution of marriage;

— to provide practicable steps to prevent the irretrievable breakdown of marriages;

— to ensure that couples understand the practical consequences of divorce before making any irreversible decision;

— where divorce is unavoidable, to minimise the bitterness and hostility between the parties and to reduce the trauma for the children; and

— to keep costs to the minimum.[186]

The government accepted the Law Commission's recommended scheme of a period of consideration and reflection having to elapse as evidence of the irretrievable breakdown of the marriage. It also seized upon mediation as a mechanism which would, it said, be better able than the legal process to identify marriages capable of being saved, and would thus enhance the opportunities for reconciliation. Where reconciliation was not achievable, the couple would be encouraged to resolve their differences and co-operate in sorting out the arrangements necessary for their, and their children's, future lives more amicably. The government regarded mediation as cheaper than litigation and estimated that the average cost of comprehensive mediation (in which both financial and child issues are dealt with) was about £550 per case, while the average cost of a matrimonial bill paid by the Legal Aid Fund in 1992/93 was £1,565.[187] Faced with such potential savings, the government proposed that legal aid would be channelled to pay for mediation as well as legal assistance and representation, and indeed, as we have noted above, it was duly enacted that a party would have to justify why he or she should have legal assistance as opposed to mediation.[188]

The government's proposals differed from those of the Law Commission in significant respects. First, they placed much greater emphasis upon the role of mediation and sought to minimise the input of lawyers, whom they regarded as adding to the costs and adversarial nature of the proceedings. In what was largely a caricature of the prevailing system, the White Paper postulated two basic models of the divorce process. In the traditional model, the parties would, at the instigation of their lawyers, take up opposing stances and exploit, at considerable financial cost to themselves and the Legal Aid Fund, the adversarial nature of the legal system to battle to a standstill, either through prolonged negotiation or, at last, through resort to the court, and emerge at the end, embittered and hostile, to the detriment, most significantly, of their children's emotional well-being.[189] As the White Paper put it:

'Marriage breakdown and divorce are . . . intimate processes, and negotiating at arm's length through lawyers can result in misunderstandings and reduction in communication between

---

185 Cm 2799 (hereafter, 'White Paper'). The White Paper had the same title as the earlier Consultation Paper.

186 Ibid, para 3.5. For a sceptical view of the feasibility of realising these objectives, see G Davis, 'Divorce Reform—Peering Anxiously into the Future' [1995] Fam Law 564.

187 Green Paper paras 9.28, 9.30.   188 Legal Aid—Targeting Need Cm 2854 (1995). See above p 285.

189 For research findings which illuminate, to some extent, the validity of this model, see G Davis and M Murch Grounds for Divorce (1988); G Davis, SM Cretney and J Collins Simple Quarrels (1994).

the spouses. Lawyers have to translate what their clients say and pass it on to the other side. The other side's lawyer then translates again and passes information on to his or her client. There can thus be a good deal of misunderstanding and a good deal of anger about what is said and how it is said.'[190]

By contrast, in their alternative model, couples would engage constructively, through mediation, to arrive at an agreement worked out by themselves, face to face, with an enhanced ability to communicate with each other, in an atmosphere of greater co-operation:

'... bitterness and hostility are reduced through the mediation process and couples are helped to manage conflict to the benefit of their children and themselves. Communication is improved, making it more likely that arrangements for the children will last, or if they need to be changed by force of circumstances, making it more likely that the couple can negotiate new arrangements in a constructive manner, and in the best interests of each child.'[191]

The aim was to encourage parties away from reliance upon lawyers as the main source of help during their divorce. The lawyer might, the government recognised, be a useful resource if legal advice is needed during the mediation process, and at the end to translate the parties' agreement into a legal arrangement, usually perhaps a draft consent order to be laid before the court. But beyond this, the intention was to limit assistance except where it is clear that mediation is unsuitable because of the parties' particular circumstances.

Secondly, instead of having a preliminary assessment during the period for consideration and reflection, they proposed that the initial appointment become a purely information-giving service which would be compulsory for anyone initiating the divorce process.[192]

A third important change related to the settling of ancillary arrangements before the divorce would be granted. The Law Commission argued that, while one of the strengths of the period for consideration and reflection would be that it would enable the parties to decide upon the financial and other arrangements consequent upon the divorce, and while there should be power for the courts to make final orders relating to these before the dissolution of the marriage, it would be wrong to require the parties to have resolved all issues concerning children, property and finance before a divorce order could be made. They reasoned that this would 'create a formidable bargaining chip for the more powerful or determined party', who could thereby delay the grant of the divorce.[193] Instead, they proposed that the court should have the power to postpone the divorce where granting it without any delay would cause hardship to the spouse or children.[194] The government, however, reversed this position. They were influenced by the argument that 'people who marry should discharge their obligations undertaken when they contracted their earlier marriage, and also their responsibilities which they undertook when they became parents, before they became free to remarry.'[195] Accordingly, there should be no divorce until arrangements have been finalised, unless delay would cause hardship to a spouse or child.

[190] White Paper, para 5.19.   [191] Ibid, para 5.24.
[192] Green Paper para 8.12; White Paper para 6.15.
[193] Law Com No 192 para 5.56.   [194] Ibid, para 5.58.
[195] White Paper para 4.26 and Hansard HL Debs, 30 November 1995, col 703.

4 DIVORCE UNDER THE FAMILY LAW ACT 1996[196]

The government's Family Law Bill had a difficult passage through Parliament, and several further changes were made to the legislation before it received the Royal Assent in 1996. Part I, which contains 'general principles' in s 1, and Part III, which concerned legal aid,[197] were implemented. Part II, which set out the new divorce law, was not, for reasons explained once an outline of the proposed law has been given below.

(a) The 'general principles'

Section 1 of the Act[198] requires the court, and any person exercising functions under Parts II and III of the Act, to have regard to the following general principles:

'(a) that the institution of marriage is to be supported;

(b) that the parties to a marriage which may have broken down are to be encouraged to take all practicable steps, whether by marriage counselling or otherwise, to save the marriage;

(c) that a marriage which has irretrievably broken down and is being brought to an end should be brought to an end—

   (i)   with minimum distress to the parties and to the children affected;

   (ii) with questions dealt with in a manner designed to promote as good a continuing relationship between the parties and any children affected as is possible in the circumstances; and

   (iii) without costs being unreasonably incurred in connection with the procedures to be followed in bringing the marriage to an end; and

(d) that any risk to one of the parties to a marriage, and to any children, of violence from the other party should, so far as reasonably practicable, be removed or diminished.'

These principles, which closely reflect the objectives set out in the Government's White Paper noted above (with the addition, at the opposition's insistence, of the reference to the need to minimise the risk of domestic violence), were intended to guide courts and others in their application of the relevant provisions. But since Part II has not been implemented, and Part III has been superseded, s 1 would appear to be redundant, although the principles serve as a legislative statement of the goals of a 'good' divorce law.

(b) Divorce procedure under Part II

In line with the Law Commission's proposed scheme, Part II would have required the person seeking a divorce to go through a series of steps, over a period of time, designed to ensure that the marriage could not be saved, that the applicant understood the implications of the divorce, and that sufficient attention had been paid to the consequences both for the spouses and their children, before the marriage was finally legally terminated.

---

[196] For a critical analysis of the ideology and philosophy of the Act, see H Reece, *Divorcing Responsibly* (2003) and 'Divorcing Responsibly' (2000) 8 Fem LS 65.

[197] Subsequently replaced by the Access to Justice Act 1999 and the LSC Funding Code.

[198] Which came into force on 21 March 1997.

The information meeting

The Act provided that a spouse (or both spouses) initiating the divorce, or contesting it, or seeking an order to be made in connection with the divorce, must have attended an information meeting first.[199] The purpose of the meeting was to communicate a range of information relating to divorce, the process and its consequences, and also to 'mark the seriousness of the step being taken'.[200] The government had wanted meetings to be organised for groups of intending divorcees, as is done in Australia and parts of the USA, but this was rejected by Parliament as demeaning and embarrassing.[201]

The information to be given in the meeting would include that relating to marriage counselling and other marriage support services; the importance to be attached to the welfare, wishes and feelings of children; how the parties might acquire a better understanding of the ways in which children can be helped to cope with the breakdown of a marriage; the nature of the financial questions that may arise on divorce or separation, and services which are available to help the parties; the protection available against domestic violence, and how to obtain support and assistance; mediation; the availability of independent legal advice and representation; where the parties could get advice about obtaining legal aid; and the divorce and separation process.

These items reflected the greater attention which is now paid to the needs of the children of divorced couples and the desire to ensure that couples understood the implications of starting the divorce process.[202] It was also hoped that it would give them an opportunity to consider the value of attending marriage counselling and of an attempt at reconciliation.

Statement of marital breakdown

Once three months had elapsed since the applicant had attended an information meeting, he or she (or both spouses together) would have been permitted to file with the court a statement of marital breakdown.[203] The object of this delay was to provide a 'cooling-off period' during which the parties could explore the scope for reconciliation. The statement would declare that the maker or makers believed that the marriage had broken down, although *not* that they believed it had broken down irretrievably, since it was the purpose of the period for reflection and consideration (see below) to establish this. As with the current law one year time bar on presenting a petition, a spouse would not have been permitted to file a statement before the first anniversary of the marriage.[204]

Period for reflection and consideration

The irretrievable breakdown of the marriage would have been established by the passing of a period for reflection and consideration, lasting for a basic period of nine months.[205] This period could be extended in certain circumstances, such as where the parties wished

[199] Family Law Act 1996 s 8(2).
[200] Hansard HL Debs, 30 November 1995, col 702 (Lord Mackay LC).
[201] See the White Paper: Cm 2799, paras 7.14–7.16 and for withering criticism of such an innovation, see SM Cretney 'Divorce Reform in England: Humbug and Hypocrisy or a Smooth Transition?' in Freeman (ed) *Divorce, Where Next?* p 48, G Davis 'Divorce Reform—Peering Anxiously into the Future' [1995] Fam Law 564.
[202] Compare the findings of G Davis and M Murch *Grounds for Divorce* (1988) pp 57–67 and the government's findings that there is widespread ignorance of the possibilities open to couples whose marriage is in difficulty but who have not yet decided on a divorce: See White Paper para 7.1.
[203] Ibid, s 6.   [204] Ibid, s 7(6).
[205] The time would begin to run 14 days after the day the statement was received by the court: s 7(3).

to attempt a reconciliation, or one party did not accept that the marriage was over and applied to the court for an extension of time. The period would also be automatically extended for six months where there was a child of the family under the age of sixteen. This was a significant change from previous thinking. The argument that divorce should be harder—or, at least, take longer—where children are involved had been resisted by the Law Commission on the basis that it could cause the parties to feel bitter and resentful towards their children,[206] but parliamentarians considered that parents should be required to take more time to ensure that the marriage was truly over for the sake of their children and voted through the amendment to require the extension (except where there was a non-molestation or occupation order in force or the court was satisfied that delaying the divorce would be significantly detrimental to the welfare of any child of the family).[207]

The aim of the period was for the parties to use it to explore further the scope for reconciliation, with the help of marriage counselling if desired, or to seek to come to terms with the ending of the marriage and settle their post-divorce arrangements, preferably via mediation.[208]

The divorce order

At the end of the requisite period, either or both of the parties would have been able to apply for the divorce order (not 'decree'). Under a provision akin to s 5 of the Matrimonial Causes Act 1973, a court could have refused to grant the divorce order on the application of a spouse claiming that dissolution of the marriage would result in substantial financial or other hardship to him or her or to a child of the family; and that it would be wrong, in all the circumstances (including the conduct of the parties and the interests of any child of the family), for the marriage to be dissolved.

It will be recalled that the government decided that no divorce order should usually be made unless the parties' future arrangements had been finalised first. These 'arrangements' concerned the parties' finances and property,[209] any religious divorce requirements,[210] and the welfare of any dependent children. It was noted above[211] that s 41 of the 1973 Act provides that the court has to consider the arrangements proposed for the children's future after their parents' divorce, and whether it should exercise any of its Children Act 1989 powers with respect to them. Section 11 of the 1996 Act repeated this provision, but also set out a 'checklist' of factors to which the court must have particular regard, including the wishes and feelings of the child considered in the light of his age and understanding and the circumstances in which those wishes were expressed; the conduct of the parties in relation to the upbringing of the child; the general principle that it is desirable for a child to have regular contact with his non-resident parent and other relatives, and any risk to the child.

The aim behind this checklist was to ensure that the court addressed the issues

---

[206] Law Com No 192 para 5.28; White Paper para 4.18.

[207] Section 7(12)(b). Lord Irvine of Lairg considered that there would be 'very many cases' where concern that delaying the divorce would be detrimental to a child's interests would be justified: Hansard HL Debs, 27 June 1996, col 1071.

[208] White Paper paras 6.17–6.21.   [209] See Ch 18 below.

[210] As in what is now s 10A of the Matrimonial Causes Act 1973, discussed above at p 277.

[211] See p 278.

considered by Parliament to be most relevant to the child's welfare at the point of the parents' divorce and would arguably have required a more probing document than is currently provided by the statement of arrangements form filed by the petitioner under s 41 of the Matrimonial Causes Act.[212] In particular, its explicit reference to the child's wishes and feelings would have required the applicant, somehow, to demonstrate that he or she had taken those into account (at least in respect of older children) and hence had tried to consult the child about what was happening in the family, which current research suggests is far from the norm.[213]

The divorce order would have dissolved the marriage, coming into force on its being made and thus doing away with the two-stage process of decree nisi and absolute.

5 THE PILOT SCHEMES AND THEIR OUTCOMES

The complexity of the proposed system, and experience of introducing the child support scheme in 1993 without first having tested it out, to disastrous political effect,[214] led the incoming Labour government in 1997 to tread carefully when it came to deciding how to implement Part II. Two major pilot projects were set up to determine this, designed and monitored by independent researchers, one project relating to the provision of the information meeting, and the other to publicly funded mediation.

The researchers monitoring the information meetings developed a variety of formats for delivery of the requisite information in order to see which might be most effective. These included group meetings (even though the legislation required individual meetings, it was felt, given the successful experience in other jurisdictions, that group meetings could be offered as an additional facility to users), postal packs, videos and CD roms as well as more traditional talks. Since the legislation was not in force, the researchers had to rely on volunteers who were invited to participate in the study and this, inevitably, meant that the pilot could not completely mimic the effect that a compulsory scheme might have had. Even so, the researchers recruited nearly 8,000 people to attend meetings and nearly 1,500 who received postal packs of information. These were sufficiently large numbers to enable some reliable findings to be reached. Whilst 90% of those attending meetings were glad they had gone and valued the information they received, unfortunately for the government, the findings revealed more problems than successes with the shape of the legislative scheme. First, the scheme required the delivery of standard form 'information' to all those participating, but this took no account of the individual circumstances and stages in the marriage breakdown that different participants might have experienced. Whilst some, whose marital problems were relatively new, simply wanted advice on what they should do next, others were much clearer about what they were going to do and wanted information on specific issues such as the financial implications. A 'one size fits all' package of information meant that many participants would find parts of the meeting of no use to them and for those who had determined on a divorce, receiving information about attempting marriage counselling and reconciliation was a waste of time. Moreover, participants

---

[212] Ibid.

[213] See eg I Butler et al, *Divorcing Children* (2003), C Smart et al, *The Changing Experience of Childhood: Families and Divorce* (2001).

[214] See below p 931.

wanted *advice* tailored to their individual needs, but those providing the meetings were not empowered to give this. The headline statistics that most disappointed the government, however, were that only 7% of those attending marriage-support focused meetings indicated that their attendance meant that a divorce was now less likely; indeed the information meeting 'tended to tip those who were uncertain about their marriage into divorce mode'. Only 23% of participants went to marriage counselling in the two years following their attendance at a meeting and only 10% of participants went to mediation over the two year period, of whom 37% reached agreement on the matters in dispute with their spouse. By contrast, 73% of participants went to a solicitor in the two year period, demonstrating that, contrary to the government's hope, people still saw solicitors as a legitimate and authoritative source of information and advice and viewed counselling and mediation as less relevant to them.[215]

Given these findings, and the cost implications of providing one-to-one meetings (which the pilot found were the most popular format) with at least 150,000 prospective divorcees per annum[216] it is not surprising that the government decided not to go ahead with this particular experiment. But what of the mediation pilot scheme? Was this any more successful?

Unlike the information pilots, the researchers monitoring mediation had a semi-captive sample to investigate, because, as explained above, the provision of legal aid for family matters was, under Part III of the Family Law Act, made dependent on a prior exploration of whether the case was suitable for mediation. The researchers thus were able to monitor the use of mediation in conditions more or less akin to those that would pertain if the legislation were brought fully into force. They were able to scrutinise over 4,500 monitoring forms compiled by mediation providers on individual clients and to interview over 1,000 of these clients. But they found that the number of mediations undertaken as a result of the new legal provisions was lower than expected, so that although many clients underwent an assessment to determine if mediation was suitable for them, this did not translate into a major increase in the resort to mediation proper; in other words, for various reasons (most often the unwillingness of the other spouse to attempt it) mediation was not regarded as 'suitable' for this particular legal aid client. Of those who did go to mediation, the response was generally favourable, with around 70% of those using mediation to resolve disputes finding it fairly helpful or very helpful. The researchers urged caution in assessing 'success rates' for mediation, since the lack of a complete agreement does not mean that the parties did not make progress in improving their communication with each other or in getting closer to some sort of settlement. Nonetheless, they found that 45% of those experiencing mediation about children issues, and 34% using mediation for financial disputes, had reached agreement.

Overall, these figures look encouraging, suggesting that mediation can provide a useful service for a number of divorcing spouses. But when the researchers also asked clients about their attitudes to solicitors, they found that these scored even higher in terms of

---

[215] All data are taken from J Walker et al, *Information Meetings and Associated Provisions within the Family Law Act 1996: Final Evaluation Report* (2001). For Walker's reflections on the research, see J Walker, 'Information Meetings Revisited' [2000] Fam Law 330 and 'The Information Meeting Pilots—Using and Abusing Evidence?' [2001] Fam Law 817.

[216] A rough average of the number of divorce petitions filed each year: had respondents wished to attend as well, 300,000 or more individual meetings might have to be arranged each year.

client satisfaction. Moreover, they could not find that use of mediation had a significant impact on legal costs incurred, although they did find that, as might be expected, those mediation services operating in the not-for-profit sector, as compared with solicitor-mediators, were cheaper.[217] The conclusion drawn by the government was thus once again a negative one—mediation was unlikely to be taken up in the numbers required to have a major impact on legal aid expenditure, and it could not be regarded as the corner-stone, or panacea, that some policy-makers had originally hoped at the time the Act was drafted.

D THE AFTERMATH OF THE 1996 ACT AND THE FUTURE OF DIVORCE REFORM

The government's decision not to implement Part II of the Family Law Act was both welcomed and attacked by commentators. One of the 'presentational' problems which had faced the Law Commission and the government when issuing their original proposals was how to avoid the trap of being accused of making divorce 'harder' or 'easier'. On the one hand, by requiring parties to wait at least a year from start to finish of the divorce process, it could be said that the new law would make divorce harder than under the Matrimonial Causes Act where, when the 'fault' facts are relied on, it is possible to go from angry break-up to final decree within the space of three or four months. The waiting stage under the 1996 Act was a deliberate attempt to answer those critics of the current law that it does not sufficiently help couples to explore the scope for reconciliation or to give them time to come to terms with the implications of ending their marriage. A period of careful 'reflection and consideration' could be a challenging and sobering experience requiring spouses to face up to the consequences of their actions, both for themselves and for their children. The new divorce law, on this view, would be 'harder', but better. Equally, it was argued by some that removing any reference to 'fault' as a basis for divorce would make divorce much easier, and potentially quicker, than now. No longer would a spouse have to justify their petition to end their marriage by asserting one of the five facts proving irretrievable breakdown, but simply wait things out for the appropriate length of time. Marriage obligations would be rendered nugatory since nothing would turn on a spouse's fulfilment or abandonment of the marriage oath—an entirely 'blameless' spouse could now be divorced in not much more than a year, instead of being able to hold the other to their marital commitments for five years.

Those commentators who rejected both of these arguments, and who, by and large, welcomed the abolition of the doctrine of fault as completing the job which should have been achieved in the 1960s, still found flaws in the proposed divorce regime. The requirement to go through a series of procedural steps in the right order appears based on an

---

[217] All data are taken from G Davis et al, *Monitoring Publicly Funded Mediation* (2001). See also G Davis et al, 'Mediation and :Legal Services—The Client Speaks' [2001] Fam Law 110, G Bevan et al, 'Can Mediation Reduce Expenditure on Lawyers?' [2001] Fam Law 187, G Davis et al, 'Family Mediation—Where Do We Go from Here?' [2001] Fam Law 265 and R Dingwall and D Greatbatch, 'Family Mediators—What Are They Doing?' [2001] Fam Law 378. For the view that access to legal aid for mediation should be determined by the district judge as 'gate-keeper', see G Davis and G Bevan, 'The future public funding of family dispute resolution services' (2002) 24, 2, JSWFL 175.

assumption that nearly all couples have similar needs and have similar powers of rational behaviour and can thus divorce in a 'civilised' fashion, but the information meeting pilots demonstrated that people have different agendas and different capacities to make use of counselling and mediation. The mediation pilots also showed that mediation cannot (at least in current circumstances) replace the more familiar mechanisms of lawyer support and negotiation and that most people still regard divorce as a primarily 'legal' issue on which they want an expert's advice and assistance.

Nor would the new regime have done away with all the criticisms levelled at the current law by the Law Commission, and noted above.[218] Although it would not have been necessary for the spouses to separate in order to establish irretrievable breakdown, the prospect of remaining under the same roof whilst the period of reflection and considera- tion elapsed (for 15 months where there were children, plus the three months initial 'cooling off' time) would not be an easy one to contemplate. Those financially better off would be able to separate and negotiate at a distance; those not able to do so would be forced to live in what might be an extremely difficult atmosphere for many months, which could hardly be conducive to the well being of any children of the family. There would still be opportunities to exploit one spouse's stronger bargaining position, by seeking to spin things out through extensions, or attempts to block the divorce order, at the cost of the other party's compromising on the financial or other consequences to their detriment.[219]

But there were valuable features of the new law, which it would be a shame to forget. Opportunities to receive well-devised information about the process and the implications of divorce, and to meet a marriage counsellor, were important innovations which could be very helpful, if delivered at a time and manner suited to those involved. The greater emphasis on the children's welfare, wishes and feelings chimed very closely with current thinking on the importance of these issues and would have encouraged parents to pay greater attention to these than they are currently required to do. And the abolition of fault would have finally brought English law up to date with majority views about the limits of the law in seeking to impose moral judgments on intimate conduct.

The possibility of further reform cannot be ruled out, given that the defects of the Matrimonial Causes Act have been authoritatively laid out by the Law Commission and Parliament clearly agreed that some sort of reform is required. But the political difficulties of enacting the Law Commission's scheme, which resulted in a much less coherent, and more complicated, regime than had been planned, demonstrated that divorce reform remains a very controversial matter and one which governments should undertake only where they are sure of their ground. In the 1960s, once the Church of England came on side, the 'liberals' advocating the introduction of irretrievable breakdown could claim a broad social consensus for reform. No such political consensus existed in the 1990s; nor was there a large group of constituents pressing for reform in order to be able to remarry. Indeed, whilst research showed that couples did not exactly enjoy going through their

---

[218] See pp 288–9.

[219] It has also been argued that the law was hijacked by a lobby more concerned to uphold traditional notions of marriage and morality than to grapple with the realities of family life: see E Hasson, 'Setting a Standard or Reflecting Reality? The "Role" of Divorce Law, and the Case of the Family Law Act 1996' (2003) 17, 3, IJLPF 338, E Hasson, 'The Street-Level Response to Relationship Breakdown: A Lesson for National Policy?' [2004] JSWFL 35.

divorce, few wanted to see change which would make *their own* situation 'harder' or require them personally to wait any longer for their decrees.

Since the government announced in 2001 that it would not implement Part II,[220] policy-makers' attention has therefore shifted, perhaps wisely, to seeing how the surrounding aspects of divorce procedure can be improved rather than to focus on the substantive requirements. (More cynically, perhaps, one might also suggest that the experience of the impact of the special procedure on how divorces are obtained provided an object lesson in how to achieve profound change without signalling it too publicly.) Information leaflets about separation and divorce, redesigned from those originally developed for the information meeting pilots, have been made available from the Department for Constitutional Affairs in versions aimed at both adults and children of different ages.[221] These are intended to provide a combination of helpful information about what happens when relationships break down and brief advice 'bullet points' on how to deal with this. Secondly, in their conclusions on the information meeting pilots,[222] Walker and her colleagues had suggested that a network of local services providing advice, marriage support, counselling, mediation, and legal services, should be established to enable clients to obtain access to the particular kind of help they required, when needed, and regardless of the position they have reached within the legal process. The Family Advice and Information Service, known as FAInS,[223] was accordingly introduced on a trial basis by the Legal Services Commission in 2002 whereby solicitors (in the first instance) could be used as initial points of contact who could then refer clients on to the appropriate service for their specific requirements, especially for non-legal, more emotional and practical help.[224] Mediation providers were to be added as further first points of referral for FAInS clients, which is important since although the majority of those facing family break-up do consult a solicitor,[225] these are not always their first port of call. Indeed, one could argue that other, more general advice providers, such as CABx, should also be regarded as gatekeepers to more specialist services,[226] since they may see clients who are reluctant to use solicitors either because of cost, or uncertainty about what is to happen with their marriage.

At the same time as greater access to information and non-legal services is being promoted as a means of helping couples deal with the practical and non-legal aspects of divorce, further restrictions on access to legal aid have been introduced to attempt to pin back the costs of legal assistance. No legal aid of any kind will be forthcoming for the drafting of a divorce petition (such help had in any case been limited, under the special procedure, to basic legal help for those dependent on social security benefits). The logic of such a development is to move to an overtly administrative system of divorce, at least for 'straightforward' cases, as is done in some other jurisdictions, such as Russia. Just as one

---

[220] Announcement by Lord Chancellor, 16 January 2001.

[221] They may be downloaded from http://www.dca.gov.uk/family/divleaf.htm.

[222] J Walker et al, *Information Meetings and Associated Provisions within the Family Law Act 1996: Final Evaluation Report* (2001).

[223] The scheme was originally entitled 'Family Advice and Information Networks' or FAINS. The title was changed, apparently due to 'confusion' amongst providers about what the networks might consist of: see LSC, *Family Mediation Bulletin, Issue No 1*, April 2003.

[224] See J Walker, 'FAInS—A New Approach for Family Lawyers?' [2004] Fam Law 436.

[225] See H Genn, *Paths to Justice: what people do and think about going to law* (1999) p 115.

[226] See R Moorhead et al, *The Advice Needs of Lone Parents* (2004) p 41.

does not need to visit a lawyer (although the rise of pre-nuptial agreements may render such a visit increasingly useful), still less a court, to get married so we might one day conclude that there is no need to send papers to a court and have the skilled eye of a highly-paid judge cast over them to sanction the ending of that marriage. Increasing attempts to harmonise law across Europe may provide a way forward in order both to simplify and unify divorce laws for an ever more mobile population.[227]

E DISSOLUTION OF CIVIL PARTNERSHIP[228]

The basic approach of the Civil Partnership Act 2004 was to assimilate as closely as possible the rules governing such partnerships with those already applicable to marriage, without actually referring to the former as a type of 'marriage'. The rules on terminating a valid civil partnership are therefore similar to those applying to divorce.

First, s 219 of the Act enables the Lord Chancellor to make regulations, in particular corresponding to the provisions contained in Council Regulation (EC) No. 2201/2003 (Brussels IIR), in respect of jurisdiction for the dissolution of a civil partnership where one of the partners is or has been habitually resident in or a national of another member state, or is domiciled in a part of the United Kingdom or the Republic of Ireland. Laws creating civil partnerships, although spreading, are not by any means yet general even in Europe, so that there may be situations where a couple have registered a partnership here, but are then unable to dissolve it in a state where they now live. Thus, s 221 gives jurisdiction if it is provided under the regulations made under s 219, no other court has it and either civil partner is domiciled in England and Wales on the date when proceedings are begun, or the parties registered as civil partners in England and Wales and it appears to the court to be in the interests of justice to assume jurisdiction in the case.[229]

No application (not 'petition') to dissolve a civil partnership may be brought within one year of its formation, although the application may be based on matters which occurred during this period.[230] Secondly, the ground for dissolution is the irretrievable breakdown of the civil partnership, to be established by proof of one or more of *four* facts.[231] These are the same as for divorce, with the omission of adultery and intolerability, it being accepted that adultery is defined as sexual intercourse between parties of the opposite sex, one of whom is married.[232] As Harper et al comment, one party's infidelity is as likely to be the cause of (or perhaps one should say, contribute to) the irretrievable breakdown of a civil partnership as it is in a marriage, but the difficulties (political if not legal) of providing an equivalent provision could have been substantial. As they go

---

[227] For a distillation of common European principles and a resulting suggested common divorce law, see N Lowe, K Boele-Woelki, F Ferrand, C Gonzales Beilfuss, M Jantera-Jareborg, D Martiny and W Pintens, *Principles of European Family Law Regarding Divorce and Maintenance Between Former Spouses*, (2004). For consideration of divorce in the most restrictive European country to permit it, Ireland, see J Burley and F Regan, 'Divorce in Ireland: The Fear, the Floodgates and the Reality' (2002) 2, Int Jo Law, Policy and the Family 202.

[228] See Civil Partnership Act 2004 Part 2, Ch 2; M Harper et al, *Civil Partnership: The New Law* (2005) paras 4.43—4.50.

[229] See M Harper and K Landells, 'The Civil Partnership Act 2004 in Force' [2006] Fam Law 963 at 968.

[230] Civil Partnership Act 2004 s 41.   [231] Section 44.   [232] *Dennis v Dennis* [1955] P 153.

on to suggest, such unfaithfulness may be embraced within the concept of 'behaviour' in any case.[233]

The Act includes the same provisions designed to facilitate reconciliation as appear in the Matrimonial Causes Act, that is, providing for rules to court to require the solicitor to certify whether he or she has discussed the possibility with the applicant,[234] and disregarding periods of living together for up to six months,[235] The court is required, as in divorce, to scrutinise the arrangements proposed for any children of the family and may postpone grant of the final order if it considers that there are exceptional circumstances which make this desirable.[236] The Act also applies the same protection concerning financial provision for respondents in cases based on separation by enabling the court to refuse an order based on five years' separation,[237] rescind a conditional order if satisfied that the respondent was misled by the applicant into giving his or her consent to the dissolution, or postpone the finalising of the dissolution until satisfied as to the financial settlement proposed.[238] However, since same-sex marriage is not permitted in religious law and a civil partnership is a non-religious union, there is no equivalent to s 10A (postponement of decree absolute to encourage dissolution according to religious rites) of the Matrimonial Causes Act 1973.

The special procedure, being a creature of secondary legislation, is not mentioned in the Act, but one would expect dissolution proceedings to be governed by it (or its equivalent) in the same way as divorce. A dissolution 'order'[239] (not 'decree') will be pronounced in two stages, as with divorce, referred to as a 'conditional' and 'final' order[240] with the same usual minimum interval of six weeks between the two, with the possibility of the court shortening the period, as for divorce.[241] The Queen's Proctor may investigate issues arising during the proceedings.[242]

F JUDICIAL SEPARATION AND SEPARATION ORDERS

(a) Judicial separation in marriage

Before the introduction of judicial divorce in 1857, a spouse could obtain an order from the ecclesiastical courts, called a divorce a mensa et thoro,[243] relieving the petitioner of the duty to cohabit with the respondent, so that neither spouse could be held in desertion while it was in force. But the parties remained husband and wife, so that neither of them was free to remarry. An equivalent power was given to the civil courts in 1857, through the grant of a decree of 'judicial separation', under which the petitioner had to prove exactly the same grounds as for a divorce.

The advantage of the decree lay mainly in the fact that it gave the court jurisdiction to order financial provision for the wife; consequently, as long as the grounds for divorce were limited, she could obtain a degree of both financial and physical protection. But

---

[233] See Harper et al op cit para 4.48 and *Wachtel v Wachtel (No 1) The Times*, 1 August 1972.
[234] Section 42.   [235] Section 45.   [236] Section 63.   [237] Section 47.
[238] Section 48.   [239] Section 37(1)(a).   [240] Section 37(2).
[241] Section 38.   [242] Section 39.   [243] Meaning 'from bed and board'.

alternative ways of obtaining maintenance, the ease with which divorce can now be obtained, and the possibility of obtaining remedies for domestic violence, have long tended to provide more appropriate mechanisms for spouses than judicial separation per se. Nonetheless, an order denoting a legal separation rather than a divorce may still be useful. First, a spouse may have a conscientious or religious objection to divorce (although the religion itself may not recognise the civil divorce anyway); secondly, an elderly spouse whose marriage has broken down will remain entitled to a widow's or widower's pension on the death of the other, which may be of substantial financial importance.

Research in the early 1980s found that many petitions for separation were at that time brought within the first three years of marriage, when, until the law was changed by the Matrimonial and Family Proceedings Act 1984, no petition for divorce could be presented unless the petitioner established that he or she would suffer exceptional hardship or that the respondent had behaved with exceptional depravity.[244] The separation would be converted into a divorce once the three year time bar was passed. The Law Commission noted[245] a decline in the number of petitions and decrees granted for judicial separation after the 1984 change, no doubt reflecting the ability to obtain an earlier divorce. The annual number has declined since then, with 742 petitions, and 419 decrees granted in 2004.[246]

When divorce law was reformed by the Divorce Reform Act 1969, the basis for obtaining a judicial separation was also amended to keep the law in line.[247] However, since the marriage is not terminated by the decree, it is not necessary to establish its 'irretrievable breakdown' but simply one or more of the five 'facts' which, for this purpose, constitute the 'grounds' for the decree.[248] Moreover, a petition may be presented during the first year of the marriage.

As for a divorce, the petitioner must file a statement of arrangements if there are children of the family, under s 41 of the Matrimonial Causes Act, but ss 5 and 10 of the Act do not apply because the decree does not alter the parties' marital status. For the same reason, the decree is not pronounced in two stages, but takes effect immediately it is pronounced.

The principal effect of the decree is that it relieves the petitioner from the duty to cohabit with the respondent.[249] The court has power to make a number of orders relating

---

[244] See Law Com No 116 (Time Restrictions on Presentation of Divorce and Nullity Petitions); H Garlick 'Judicial Separation: A Research Study' (1983) 46 MLR 719; S Maidment *Judicial Separation—A Research Study* (1982).

[245] Law Com No 192 para 4.8.   [246] *Judicial Statistics 2004* (2005) Table 5.5.

[247] See s 17, Matrimonial Causes Act 1973. When considering divorce reform in 1990, the Law Commission accepted that the possibility of obtaining a 'separation' as distinct from a divorce should be retained: Law Com No 192 para 4.8. so that when the Family Law Act 1996 was enacted, new provisions for 'separation orders' were included. Unless the arguments change, one would expect any further reform of divorce to require similar provision to be made for those objecting to divorce on conscientious or other grounds.

[248] A spouse who later seeks a divorce may (subject to the provisions of s 2 regarding resumed cohabitation) rely on the facts presented for the judicial separation decree, and the decree is to be treated as sufficient proof of any fact by reference to which it was granted: s 4 (1)(2) Matrimonial Causes Act 1973.

[249] Matrimonial Causes Act 1973 s 18(1).

to the children of the family and to financial relief.[250] The decree will also affect the devolution of a spouse's property if he or she dies intestate.[251] But it must be remembered that for all other purposes the spouses remain husband and wife; neither of them is at liberty to remarry, for example, and such of the common law disabilities arising from marriage as remain will continue in force.[252]

(b) Separation in civil partnership

Equivalent provisions apply to separation orders, as they are known,[253] in cases of civil partnership. The basis of the order is proof of one of the four facts which may be relied on in dissolution, without the need to establish irretrievable breakdown.[254] The same provisions governing reconciliation and the interests of children of the family apply as on dissolution.[255] However, the effect of a separation order does not include the lifting of an obligation to cohabit with each other, as is the case in judicial separation. It is uncertain whether such an obligation exists in a civil partnership[256] but of course, the same restriction on entering into a new civil partnership (or marriage) applies as on judicial separation.

---

[250] See below p 18 and Chapter 18.   [251] See below p 1095.
[252] Eg as to compellability as a witness: see above p 116.   [253] Civil Partnership Act 2004 s 37(1)(d).
[254] Section 56.   [255] Sections 42, 45, 63.   [256] See above p 111.

7

PARENTS AND CHILDREN

A INTRODUCTION

The parent–child relationship is one of the key relationships in family law and, as we shall see, the nature and focus of that legal relationship has undergone profound change. However, before we discuss this relationship we must first consider the equally fundamental questions of who in law is a parent and who a child.

With regard to parentage it will be seen that the acquisition of the legal status can be achieved in three ways: it can be assigned automatically, or it can be acquired through the making of a parental order under the Human Fertilisation and Embryology Act 1990 or through adoption. It has been observed[1] that this multiplicity of mechanisms operates on a continuum of state regulation, from minimal, if any, control in the case of the mother who happens to be unmarried, to lengthy state investigation with the applicant's suitability to be a parent in the case of adoption.

We begin this chapter by discussing the first two of these mechanisms of ascribing parenthood. We discuss adoption in Chapter 15.

B WHO ARE THE PARENTS OF A CHILD?[2]

1 INTRODUCTION

At one time it would have gone without saying that the person who gave birth to the child was the mother and the person by whom she conceived was the father. Indeed, traditionally the law has taken the blood tie or genetic link as the test of parenthood.[3] However, with the advance of medical science, and in particular with the advent of human assisted reproduction, the position has now become more complicated.

Reflecting these advances and following detailed inquiry into the whole subject by

---

[1] G Douglas and N Lowe 'Becoming a Parent in English Law' (1992) 108 LQR 414.

[2] For interesting discussion of this issue see A Bainham 'Parentage, Parenthood and Parental Responsibility: Subtle, Elusive, Yet Important Distinctions' in *What is a Parent?* (eds A Bainham, S Day Sclater and M Richards) ch 2, J Herring 'Parents and Child' in *Family Law, Issues, Debates, Policy* (ed Herring) ch 4 and R Probert 'Families, assisted reproduction and the law' [2004] CFLQ 273.

[3] Hence the use of blood tests (now known as 'scientific tests') to determine parentage: see below, p 325. For the legal significance of parentage see below, p 334.

the Warnock Committee on Human Fertilisation and Embryology,[4] there is now comprehensive legislation in the form of the Human Fertilisation and Embryology Act 1990 governing issues arising from assisted reproduction, including, inter alia, the question of who is to be regarded as a parent.

Before discussing who in law are regarded as parents of a child it is helpful to say a little about the different techniques of assisted reproduction.

2 TECHNIQUES OF HUMAN ASSISTED REPRODUCTION[5]

(a) Artificial insemination

Artificial insemination refers to the placing of semen into a woman's vagina, cervix or uterus (ie womb) by means other than sexual intercourse. If the woman's husband's sperm is used, the process is referred to as artificial insemination by husband or AIH. If someone else's sperm is used, it is known as artificial insemination by donor, or DI—donor insemination. There are between 800 and 1,000 births by DI each year.[6]

(b) In vitro fertilisation (IVF)

The technique of in vitro fertilisation is to take a ripe egg from the woman's ovary just before ovulation (ie when the egg would have been released naturally). It is then mixed with sperm in a dish (in vitro) so that fertilisation can occur. If the egg is fertilised, it is returned to the uterus, where it may implant, and then develop as normal. In 2001 there were 465 live births by this method.[7]

(c) Egg and embryo donation

Egg collection technology coupled with IVF makes it possible to obtain an egg from a donor for transfer to another woman having been fertilised with either the husband's or a donor's sperm in vitro. It will be appreciated that IVF treatment has therefore created the possibility that the woman who gives birth to a child may not be the genetic mother. In the case of embryo transfer neither the woman nor her partner (unless his sperm is used) will be genetically related to the child.

(d) Surrogacy

Surrogacy[8] involves one woman carrying a child for another with the intention that the child be handed over. It is not to be confused with the techniques for human assisted

---

[4] Report on the Committee of Inquiry into Human Fertilisation and Embryology (1984) Cmnd 9314 whose recommendations were essentially accepted in the government's White Paper *Human Fertilisation and Embryology: A Framework for Legislation* (1987) Cm 259.

[5] See generally G Douglas *Law, Fertility and Reproduction* (1991) ch 6, E Jackson, *Regulating Reproduction: law, technology and autonomy* (2001) and the Warnock Report, above, chs 3–7. New techniques are being continually developed and refined, and the text refers only to the main types used, which have particular significance for family law. For a historical perspective on artificial insemination and other techniques of human assisted reproduction, see S Cretney *Family Law in the Twentieth Century* (2003) 540–4. For valuable overviews see R Deech 'The Legal Regulation of Infertility Treatment in Britain' in *Cross-Currents—Family Law Policy in the US and England* (eds S Katz, J Eekelaar and M Maclean) ch 8 and S Sheldon 'Fragmenting Fatherhood: The Regulation of Reproductive Technologies' (2005) 68 MLR 523.

[6] See Cretney, above, and Probert above at 279.   [7] See Probert, above at 275.

[8] See the definition in the Surrogacy Arrangements Act 1985 s 1(2).

reproduction just described, though the surrogate may well have conceived by one of those methods. We discuss the effect and regulation of surrogacy agreements later in this chapter.[9]

3 WHO IS THE LEGAL MOTHER? [10]

Until the advent of in vitro fertilisation, provided the fact of the birth could be proved, there could be no doubt that the woman giving birth must in law be the child's mother. As Lord Simon was able to say as late as 1976 in *The Ampthill Peerage* case,[11] 'Motherhood, although also a legal relationship, is based on a fact, being proved demonstrably by parturition.'

There is no doubt that, where the woman has conceived by artificial insemination or by in vitro fertilisation of her ovum, she is the legal mother. The difficulty arises where the person giving birth is not the child's genetic mother but is the carrying mother as a result of egg or embryo donation. As Scott Baker J said in *Re W (Minors) (Surrogacy)*,[12] 'The advent of IVF presented the law with a dilemma: whom should the law regard as the mother?' Arguments can be led either way. On the one hand, given the biological connection, it could be argued that the genetic mother should be regarded as the child's legal mother. On the other hand, because of the bizarre consequences that would follow if the genetic mother is unknown (for example, the child's birth would have to be registered with the name of the mother unknown),[13] there would seem a strong case for considering the carrying mother the legal mother.[14] An alternative approach altogether is to hold the *intending* parent the legal parent.

This approach was adopted in the Californian decision *Johnson v Calvert*.[15] In that case, in pursuance of a surrogacy agreement, one of the commissioning mother's eggs was fertilised in vitro with her husband's sperm and transferred to the surrogate, who successfully carried it to term. During the pregnancy the surrogate and the commissioning couple fell out, and each sought a declaration of parentage of the child. It was accepted that blood tests showed the commissioning parents to be the genetic parents of the child. In holding that it was the commissioning parents who were the child's legal parents, Panelli J commented that it was they who 'affirmatively intended the birth of the child, and took the steps necessary to effect in vitro fertilisation. But for their acted-on intention the child would not exist' and the commissioning mother, 'who intended to procreate the

---

[9] Below, p 318.   [10] See Probert, above, at 275–9.   [11] [1977] AC 547 at 577, HL.

[12] [1991] 1 FLR 385 at 386.

[13] But note the practice in France to permit mothers to give birth anonymously—a practice which was controversially held not to be in breach of Art 8 of the European Convention on Human Rights see *Odièvre v France* [2003] 1 FCR 621 on which see E Steiner, 'Odièvre v France—Desperately seeking mother—anonymous births in the European Court of Human Rights' [2003] CFLQ 425.

[14] See P Bromley 'Aided Conception—the Alternative to Adoption' in Bean (ed) *Adoption, Essays in Social Policy, Law and Sociology* ch 11 at pp 189–90.

[15] 5 Cal 4th 84 (1993), noted by G Douglas (1994) 57 MLR 636. But cf *Moschetta v Moschetta* (1994) 25 Cal App 4th 1218, in which the Californian Court of Appeal held that the surrogate was the only mother of the child and refused to enforce the surrogacy agreement and on which see S Bridge 'Assisted Reproduction and Parentage in Law' in *What is a Parent?* (eds A Bainham, S Day Schlater and M Richards) 73 at 86–7. For the view that a person's intention or desire to be regarded as a parent and to fulfil the functions of parent is in fact the primary test of legal parentage in English law, see C Barton and G Douglas *Law and Parenthood* (1995) 50ff.

child—that is she who intended to bring about the birth of a child that she intended to raise as her own—is the natural mother under California law'.

Although the application of this notion of intending to be a parent is a rational way of solving the so-called 'womb leasing' problems as in *Johnson v Calvert*, one important problem in using it as a *general* test of determining parenthood is that it would involve accepting the corollary that lack of intention is a means of avoiding parenthood. As one commentator[16] has pointed out:

'Hitherto, the law in the United Kingdom has generally refused to permit someone to avoid liability (if not responsibility) for a child on the ground that he or she had not *intended* the child's conception or birth. It is no answer to the Child Support Agency for the absent parent to say that he thought the child's mother was on the pill, or even that his condom split during intercourse.'

But she adds:

'. . . it is possible for a sperm or egg donor to waive their parental status and responsibility in respect of any resulting child under the terms of the Human Fertilisation and Embryology Act 1990. Parents may also give their child up for adoption. So our law does recognise the intention *not* to be a social parent in certain circumstances.'

So far as English law is concerned, the position at common law has still to be determined. The matter was raised in *Re W (Minors) (Surrogacy)*[17] (which, like *Johnson v Calvert*, was a womb leasing case), but left open upon an undertaking by the commissioning genetic parents[18] that they would apply for a 'parental order' under s 30 of the Human Fertilisation and Embryology Act 1990[19] as soon as the provision was implemented. However, adopting the Warnock Committee's recommendation,[20] s 27(1) of the Human Fertilisation and Embryology Act 1990 provides:

'The woman who is carrying or has carried a child as a result of the placing in her of an embryo or of sperm and eggs, and no other woman, is to be treated as the mother of the child.'

Where this provision applies, then in all cases the woman giving birth and no other woman will, unless the child is subsequently adopted[21] or a parental order[22] is subsequently made, be treated as the legal mother regardless of genetic connection. Section 27, however, does *not* have retrospective effect[23] and only applies in relation to children carried by women as a result of the placing in them of embryos or of sperm and eggs, or of their artificial insemination on or after 1 August 1991.[24] For this reason it may still be

---

[16] Douglas, above, at 640.   [17] Above.

[18] The genetic mother had no womb but was able to produce the eggs, which were taken from her medically and fertilised in vitro by her husband's sperm. Two resultant embryos were implanted in the surrogate host mother, who gave birth to the twins who, having been handed over by the surrogate, had lived with the 'commissioning couple' ever since. The local authority argued that the couple should register themselves as private foster parents, which prompted them to seek a declaration of parentage.

[19] Discussed below, pp 315ff.   [20] Above, at para 6.8.   [21] Section 28(2).

[22] Parental orders are discussed below, pp 315ff.

[23] Section 49(3) See also *Re M (Child Support Act: Parentage)* [1997] 2 FLR 90, discussed further below at p 312 n 54.

[24] The date on which s 27 came into force, by SI 1991/1400.

necessary to resolve the position at common law. On the other hand, the section applies regardless of whether the woman was in the United Kingdom or elsewhere at the time of the placing in her of the embryo or the sperm and eggs.[25]

4 WHO IS THE LEGAL FATHER?[26]

The position regarding who is the legal father is more complicated than that of the mother, for while in general the genetic father (ie the man whose sperm fertilised the egg)[27] is regarded as the legal father, this is not a universal rule. Conversely, there are occasions when, notwithstanding the absence of any genetic link, a man will be treated as the legal father.

(a) When genetic fathers are not legal fathers

Two exceptions to the general rule that the genetic father is the legal father are provided by s 28(6) of the Human Fertilisation and Embryology Act 1990.[28] These are:

    (a) where he is a donor whose sperm is used for 'licensed treatment'[29] and whose consent to the use of his sperm has been obtained in accordance with the requirements of Sch 3 to the 1990 Act (ie sperm donors whose sperm is used for assisted reproduction treatment); and

    (b) where, subject to certain exceptions, his sperm is used after his death.

One incidental but important effect of these exceptions is that there will be occasions when a child has no legal father.[30]

Licensed sperm donors

This exception only applies to licensed sperm donors. So-called unlicensed donors are regarded as fathers.[31] But even where the donation is licensed s 28(6) will not always operate to prevent a man being regarded as the legal father of a resulting child. In *Leeds Teaching Hospitals NHS Trust v A*[32] a man consented to his sperm being used for his wife but the clinic mistakenly injected the sperm into another woman's eggs. It was held[33] that notwithstanding s 28(6) he was the legal father of the resulting twins, because the use of

---

[25] Section 27(3). But there is no domicile requirement, nor is there a requirement that the child be born in England and Wales, but the provisions can only apply where, by the conflict of law rules, English law is held to be the applicable law.

[26] See Sheldon, above, at 540ff and Probert, above, 279–81.

[27] As Bracewell J pointed out in *Re B (Parentage)* [1996] 2 FLR 15 at 21, it is irrelevant *how* the sperm fertilises the egg; sexual intercourse is *not* a prerequisite to fatherhood.

[28] Which only applies to children carried by women as a result of the placing in them of embryos or of sperm and eggs, or of their artificial insemination on or after 1 August 1991: s 49(3).

[29] Ie treatment which requires those who offer it to have been licensed under the 1990 Act Sch 2. See generally G Douglas *Law, Fertility and Reproduction*, above, p 110ff.

[30] Such as in those cases where such children are born to a woman who has no husband or partner deemed to be the legal father under s 28(2) and (3), discussed below.

[31] See *Re M (Sperm Donor Father)* [2003] Fam Law 94 where the man concerned responded to an advertisement by a lesbian couple.

[32] [2003] EWHC 259 (QB), [2003] 1 FLR 1091.

[33] This was an incidental decision, the main suit being the (unsuccessful) seeking of a declaration of parentage by the husband of the woman giving birth. See further below at p 312.

his sperm was not in conformity with the terms of his consent as the provision requires.[34] This seems a harsh decision and surely not what Parliament intended. As one commentator has observed[35] it means that donors must trust clinics not to make mistakes.

Formerly, the absence of parenthood was coupled with anonymity for the licensed donor but in an important policy change this right was ended with respect to children conceived as a result of sperm donated on or after 1 April 2005. Such children will, upon attaining the age of 18 (ie from April 2023 at the earliest), have the right to be given identifying information provided by donors to the relevant clinic.[36] While this change is designed to promote children's right to identity[37] it seems likely that it will also operate as a powerful disincentive to would-be sperm donors.[38]

Posthumous use of sperm

Formerly, the rule was both simple and strict, namely, in no circumstances could a man be regarded as the father where his sperm was used after his death. This was so regardless of whether he consented to such use before his death.[39] However, this strict rule has now been amended by the Human Fertilisation and Embryology (Deceased Fathers) Act 2003 which was passed in part as a response to a ruling by Sullivan J in February 2003 in a case brought by the children born to Diane Blood in which he declared that the right to deny the children the right to name Mr Blood as their father was incompatible with their Art 8 rights under the Human Rights Convention.[40]

According to the 2003 Act a man whose sperm was used after his death will, if he was (a) married to the mother before death; or (b) not married to the mother but where he and the woman had been provided with treatment services together[41] before his death, be treated as the father provided he: (1) consented in writing (and did not withdraw that consent) (a) to that use and (b) to being treated as the father; (2) the mother elected in writing within 42 days from the child's birth[42] to enable the man's particulars to be entered on the birth register, and (3) no other person is to be treated as the father.[43] A

[34] See Sch 3, para 5.   [35] Herring *Family Law* (2nd edn) 291.

[36] Human Fertilisation and Embryology Authority (Disclosure of Donor Information) Regulations 2004 (SI 2004/1511) reg 2(3). For some background discussion of events leading to this change see S Sheldon 'Fragmenting Fatherhood: The Regulation of Reproductive Techniques' (2005) 68 MLR 523 at 547.

[37] See *Donor Information Consultation* (Dept of Health 2002) and *Response to the Department of Health's consultation on donor information* (HFEA, 2002). But note the criticism eg by J Wallbank 'Reconstructing the HFEA 1990: is blood really thicker than water?' [2004] CFLQ 387 at 393, who points out that even with these changes there is no obligation upon parents to tell their children of their mode of conception.

[38] This has already been the experience in the United Kingdom, particularly Scotland, see eg the BBC News website, 10 June 2006.

[39] Before sperm can be used or stored the donor must have consented in writing: 1990 Act Sch 3 para 1; cf *R v Human Fertilisation and Embryology Authority, ex p Blood* [1999] Fam 151, CA, in which, following the Court of Appeal ruling that the Human Fertilisation and Embryology Authority had failed to pay sufficient regard to the effect of the EC Treaty whereby a citizen was entitled to receive services in another member state, the applicant was allowed to take her dead husband's sperm to Belgium for treatment. This was notwithstanding that written consent to the obtaining of his sperm had not been given by the husband before his death. Mrs Blood subsequently had two children by such treatment.

[40] *Blood and Tarbuck v Secretary of State for Health* (unreported 28 February 2003) cited in the Appendix to Lord Steyn's judgment in *Ghaidan v Godin Mendoza* [2004] UKHL 30, [2004] 2 AC 519.

[41] For the meaning of 'treatment together', see the discussion below at p 313.

[42] This period can be extended, upon application, by the Registrar General provided he is satisfied that there is a compelling reason: Human Fertilisation and Embryology Act 1991, s 28 (5F), (5G).

[43] Section 28(5A) and (5B).

similar position obtains where the creation of the embryo was brought about using the man's sperm before his death but the embryo was placed in the woman after his death.[44] Although the Act came into force in December 2003 it has retrospective effect to the implementation date of the original 1990 Act (viz. 1 August 1991).[45]

The effect of being acknowledged as the father in these circumstances is largely symbolic. It has no effect on succession rights.[46]

(b) Where non-genetic 'fathers' are treated as legal fathers

The position at common law

At common law only genetic fathers could be regarded as legal fathers. The strictness of this position, however, made no allowance for the use of the various techniques of assisted reproduction, the object of which is for childless couples to have children that they can regard as their own. A good example is the DI child conceived by a wife because her husband was infertile or because he was the possible carrier of an inheritable disease, but whom (as usually will be the case) the couple wished to treat as though he or she were the husband's child.[47] The absence of legal fatherhood made little difference to the legal relationship between him and the child, because his treating the child as his own made the latter a child of the family[48] and, since the sperm donor's identity would not normally be divulged, there was virtually no risk of legal claims arising between the donor and the child.[49] Nevertheless, there were potentially a number of longer-term problems. For example, the child had no entitlement to the husband's estate, if the latter died intestate,[50] nor any claim if any of his mother's relatives died intestate, nor if property was held on trust for the husband's children or the wife's legitimate children. If the child made such a claim and the spouses knew that the husband was not the father, they had either to connive at the deception or be forced to disclose facts which they had wished to keep secret.

The position under the Family Law Reform Act 1987

Following pressure to change the law[51] the Family Law Reform Act 1987 s 27 provided that a child born in England and Wales after implementation of its provisions (viz 4 April 1988) as the result of the artificial insemination of a woman, who at the time of the insemination was a party to a marriage[52] and was artificially inseminated with the semen

---

[44] Section 28(5A) and (5B).

[45] Special provision is made to dispense with the need for consent where the man died before implementation of the 2003 Act. This enabled Diane Blood to register her late husband as the father of her two children.

[46] See s 29 (3A), (3B).

[47] They might even register the husband as the father. If the husband is known not to be the father, the person registering the birth will commit an offence under the Perjury Act 1911 s 4.

[48] Unless the spouses separated before the child's birth. See below, p 340.

[49] Before the 1990 Act good clinical practice required the doctor carrying out the insemination not to divulge the donor's identity.

[50] Although he would have a claim to provision under the Inheritance (Provision for Family and Dependants) Act 1975 as a 'child of the family': see below, p 1110.

[51] Both the Law Commission (Law Com No 118 paras 12.9 and 12.11) and the Warnock Committee (at para 4.17) had recommended change.

[52] Being a marriage not at the time annulled or dissolved, but including a void marriage if, at the time of the insemination, both or either of the parties reasonably believed that the marriage was valid. It is presumed,

of someone other than the other party to the marriage, 'shall not be treated as the child of any person other than the parties to that marriage', unless it is proved to the court's satisfaction that the other party to the marriage did not consent to the insemination. In other words, under this provision, a DI child born to a married couple is presumptively the child of both parties, and the presumption can be rebutted only by showing[53] that the husband did not consent to the artificial insemination of his wife.

The position under the Human Fertilisation and Embryology Act 1990

Section 27 only applied to DI children and not to those born as a result of using other forms of assisted reproduction. Section 28 of the Human Fertilisation and Embryology Act 1990, however, makes provision for other forms of assisted reproduction, as well as artificial insemination.[54] Specifically, s 28(2) provides that where a married woman[55] is carrying or has carried a child as the result of the placing in her of an embryo, or sperm and eggs, or of her insemination, then notwithstanding that the sperm was not that of her husband, he and no other person[56] is treated as the father of the child,[57] unless it is shown that he did not consent to his wife's treatment. This provision is, however, subject to s 28(5)(a), by which the common law presumption of legitimacy based on marriage[58] takes priority over the requirement of the husband's consent. What this seems to mean[59] is that the husband will be regarded as the father unless the issue is raised, when, if he did not consent, the presumption will have to be rebutted, usually by means of scientific tests.

As between spouses the issue of consent rarely arises not least because a clinic is unlikely to provide services to a married woman without her husband's consent,[60] but one case where it did—albeit by accident—was *Leeds Teaching Hospital NHS Trust v A*.[61] In that case two couples, Mr and Mrs A, a white couple, and Mr and Mrs B, a black couple, were undergoing sperm injection treatment (the mixing of the husband's sperm with his wife's eggs) at the same clinic. Due to a mix-up by the clinic Mr B's sperm was used to impregnate Mrs A, who later gave birth to twins. It was held that Mr A was not the father under the terms of s 28(2) since, because of the fundamental mistake by the clinic,[62] he could not

---

unless the contrary is shown, that one of the parties did so believe: s 27(2). It will be noted that the problem about whether a mistake of law can support a reasonable belief (discussed below at p 343) would appear to be relevant in this context.

[53] Presumably, upon the balance of probabilities.

[54] Note that this provision is not retrospective: s 49(3). This means that s 27 of the Family Law Reform Act 1987 will continue to apply to DI children born on or after 4 April 1988 but before the commencement of s 28 (viz 1 August 1991): s 49(4). Neither Act applies to children born *before* 4 April 1988: see *Re M (Child Support Act: Parentage)* [1997] 2 FLR 90.

[55] For these purposes, marriage includes (subject to what is said below) a void marriage if, as is presumed until the contrary is shown, at the time of the treatment resulting in the child's birth, one of the parties reasonably believed that the marriage was valid: s 28(7)(b); but it does not include the case where a judicial separation was in force: s 28(7)(a). According to *J v C (Void Marriage: Status of Children)* [2006] EWCA Civ 537, (2006) *Times* 1 June, s 28 does *not* apply where the parties to the 'marriage' are both female.

[56] Section 28(4).   [57] See, for example, *Re CH (Contact: Parentage)* [1996] 1 FLR 569.

[58] See below, pp 341ff.   [59] See Douglas, op cit, at p 129.

[60] See the Human Fertilisation and Embryology Authority Code of Practice, para 5.7.

[61] [2003] EWHC 259 (QB), [2003] 1 FLR 1091.

[62] At para [29] Butler-Sloss P accepted that non-fundamental mistakes may not vitiate consent.

be taken to have consented to the actual treatment of his wife, viz., being impregnated by someone else's sperm.[63]

The 1990 Act goes further by enacting in s 28(3) that, where donated sperm is used for a woman in the course of licensed 'treatment services'[64] provided for her and a man together, then that man, and no other person, shall be treated as the father of the child if s 28(2) does not apply (for example, where the woman is not married or where there is a judicial separation order in force). As Hale LJ has observed,[65] s 28(3)

'is an unusual provision, conferring the relationship of parent and child on people who are related neither by blood nor by marriage. Conferring such relationships is a serious matter, involving as it does not only the relationship between father and child but also between the whole of the father's family and the child. The rule should only apply to those cases which clearly fall within the footprint of the statutory language'.

Although Parliament clearly had unmarried couples in mind when passing this provision[66] (it is established that the provision has no application to married couples)[67], there is no necessity to prove cohabitation, nor, conversely, does it follow that 'simply because a man is living with a treated woman he is being provided with treatment services'.[68] The key test is whether the man and woman had 'treatment together'. This concept, however, has proved troublesome with various different approaches being suggested.[69] But one approach that has gained general favour is that of Bracewell J in *Re B (Parentage)*,[70] namely to consider on all the facts whether the man and woman could be said to have embarked on a 'joint enterprise' the object of which is for the woman to conceive and give birth, rather than to concentrate on what happens to the individual partner. Bracewell J's approach was later approved by the Court of Appeal in *R v Human Fertilisation and Embryology Authority, ex p Blood*,[71] though in that case itself it was held that the posthumous use of sperm taken from the husband while in a coma was not capable of constituting 'treatment . . . together'. In *Re R (IVF: Paternity of Child)*[72] Lord Walker said

'where there is IVF treatment using embryos created with donor sperm, the infertile male

---

[63] Neither could he rely on the common law presumption of paternity (discussed below at p 321) since that was overridden by DNA tests showing Mr B to be the father. It was precisely because the treatment fell outside that to which Mr B had consented that he was to be regarded as the father ie s 28(6) did not apply, see above p 309.

[64] See s 2(1).

[65] *Re R (A Child)(IVF: Paternity of Child)* [2003] EWCA Civ 182, [2003] Fam 129 at [20] cited, with apparent approval, by Lords Hope and Walker on appeal to the HL, see [2005] UK HL 33, [2005] 2 FLR 843 at [6] and [39] respectively.

[66] See Lord Mackay, Hansard, HL Debs 20 March 1990, cols 209–10.

[67] See *Leeds Teaching Hospital NHS Trust v A*, above.

[68] Per Johnson J in *Re Q (Parental Order)* [1996] 1 FLR 369 at 372.

[69] According to Johnson J in *Re Q (Parental Order)*, above, the provision envisages a situation in which the man involved receives medical treatment. But this was clearly too restrictive and as Johnson J himself observed, above at 371, begs the question as to what 'treatment' is envisaged. Another approach was to equate 'treatment together' with treatment 'as a couple', see *U v W (A-G Intervening)* [1998] Fam 29, per Wilson J, but that was regarded by Hale LJ in *Re R (A Child)(IVF: Paternity of Child)*, above at [23] as an 'unnecessary gloss' on the wording of the statute.

[70] [1996] 2 FLR 15.

[71] [1999] Fam 151 at 179, per Lord Woolf MR. See also *Evans v Amicus Healthcare Ltd* [2004] EWCA Civ 727, [2005] Fam 1 at [93], per Arden LJ.

[72] [2005] UK HL 33, [2005] 2 FLR 843 at [26].

partner cannot easily be described as participating in the treatment. If he is to be regarded as participating he must do more than simply consent to his partner's treatment. His conduct must be such as to make his partner's treatment something of a joint enterprise (an expression used by Bracewell J in *Re B (Parentage)* . . .'.

Whether there is a joint enterprise is a question of fact to be determined in each case taking into account the parties' conduct and, where relevant, the clinic's perspective as demonstrated by the records that are required to be kept.[73] Examples of 'treatment together' are *Re B (Parentage)*[74] where the couple attended the hospital together and, knowing that the sperm which the man donated[75] was not to be used for impregnation that day, had waited a short time to ensure that the donation was satisfactory[76] and *U v W (A-G Intervening)*,[77] in which an unmarried couple voluntarily attended a fertility clinic even after they knew that donor sperm as well as the man's own sperm was to be used.

In *Re B* Bracewell J held in effect that once it had been established that a joint enterprise existed the parties' consent to the treatment continued until it was withdrawn. Hence in that case it did not matter that the man and woman had separated by the time of insemination. But this approach is now established to be wrong. According to *Re R (IVF: Paternity of Child)*[78] the correct test is to judge the issue at the time of the treatment leading to the birth. In *Re R* itself both the woman and man signed a consent form for in vitro fertilisation and the man acknowledged that they were being treated together even though his sperm would not be used. The initial embryo placement was unsuccessful and before the second placement, which was successful, the couple had separated. The woman, however, did not reveal this separation to the clinic and on the contrary led them to believe that they were still a couple. It was held that the second embryo placement leading to the birth of child could not be considered to be the result of 'treatment together' and that therefore the man could not be regarded as the father, within the terms of s 28(3).

It is established[79] that where the wrong sperm is used due to a mix-up by the clinic the child's birth cannot be regarded as the result of 'treatment together'. A fortiori an express withdrawal of consent will negate the idea of treatment together.[80]

There is no requirement that the resulting child be born in England and Wales, but s 28 can only apply where, by the conflict of laws rules, English law is the applicable law, which means that at least one of the parties must either be domiciled or habitually resident here at the time of the treatment or insemination. On the other hand, s 28(8) expressly states that the provisions apply 'whether the woman was in the United Kingdom or elsewhere at the time of placing in her of the embryo or the sperm and eggs or her artificial

---

[73] See Lord Hope in *Re R (IVF: Paternity of Child)*, above, at [19].   [74] Above.

[75] Bracewell J rejected the man's argument that his donation of sperm had been a casual favour and there had been no joint enterprise to conceive a child.

[76] It did not matter for these purposes that the father had not been counselled, for as Bracewell J (above at 21) pointed out, s 2(1) which defines treatment services as 'medical, surgical or obstetric services', makes no mention of counselling.

[77] [1998] Fam 29, per Wilson J.   [78] [2005] UK HL 33, [2005] 2 FLR 843.

[79] *Leeds Teaching Hospital NHS Trust v A*, above.

[80] See *Evans v Amicus Healthcare Ltd*, above. Note: the applicant subsequently failed in her action before the European Court of Human Rights, see *Evans v United Kingdom* [2006] 1 FCR 588, European Court of Human Rights.

insemination.' However, this provision is effectively limited to children born to married women since, as Wilson J pointed out in *U v W*,[81] in the case of an unmarried mother, for the man to be regarded as the father under s 28(3), the 'treatment services' must be provided by a 'licensed person'. Accordingly, treatment abroad will fall outside the provision, even though that could be said to be restrictive of the freedom to provide services for all nationals of member states within the European Union.[82]

5 PARENTAL ORDERS [83]

Under s 30(1) of the Human Fertilisation and Embryology Act 1990 the court[84] is empowered to make what is known as a 'parental order' providing for a child to be treated in law as the child of the parties to a marriage in circumstances where the child has been carried by a woman other than the wife, as a result of the placing in her of an embryo or sperm and eggs, or her artificial insemination following the use of gametes of one or both of the spouses.[85] This power is subject to a number of conditions.

Applications can only be made by a husband and wife (note the 1990 Act has *not* been amended by the Civil Partnership Act 2004 and does not therefore apply to civil partners, though why this should be so is not clear) both of whom must be at least 18 and at least one of whom must be domiciled in part of the United Kingdom or the Channel Islands or Isle of Man.[86] The application must be made within six months of the child's birth.[87] At the time of the application the child's home must be with the husband and wife.[88] Before any order can be made, the court must be satisfied that the carrying woman and the father (including a person who is a father by virtue of s 28(2) or s 28(3))[89] have freely and with full understanding of what is involved, agreed unconditionally to the making of an *order* (ie not to the application).[90] In this regard the surrogate mother's agreement is ineffective

---

[81] Above at 37.   [82] Viz under Art 59 of the Treaty of Rome: see *U v W*, above at 40ff.

[83] See generally G Douglas *Law Fertility and Reproduction* pp 158–61; C Barton and G Douglas *Law and Parenthood* pp 69–72; D Morgan and R Lee *Human Fertilisation and Embryology Act 1990* pp 153–4. This section was a late addition to the legislation prompted by the much publicised 'Cumbria' case, subsequently reported as *Re W (Minors) (Surrogacy)* [1991] 1 FLR 385. It was brought into force on 1 November 1994: SI 1994/1776.

[84] The High Court, county court or magistrates' court: HFEA 1990 s 30(8)(a).

[85] Section 30 does not apply if the child was conceived as the result of normal intercourse between the husband and the surrogate mother, as occurred in *Re Adoption Application (Payment for Adoption)* [1987] Fam 81.

[86] HFEA 1990 s 30(2), (3)(a) and (4).

[87] Section 30(2). Special retrospective provision was made for children born before the Act, permitting application to be made within six months of the coming into force of the Act.

[88] Section 30(3)(a).

[89] See *Re Q (Parental Order)* [1996] 1 FLR 369. But cf in Scotland *C and C (Petitioners and Respondents to Adopt X)* [1997] Fam Law 9 and 226.

[90] Section 30(5). Evidence of the agreement is governed by the Adoption Act 1976 s 61 as applied to parental orders by the Parental Orders (Human Fertilisation and Embryology) Regulations 1994. Note: the application of the 1976 Act has been expressly preserved for the purposes of the 1994 Regulations, see the Adoption and Children Act 2002 (Commencement No 10 Transitional and Savings Provisions) Order 2005 2005 SI/2897, Art 14.

if given less than six weeks after the child's birth.[91] No agreement is required if a person cannot be found or is incapable of giving an agreement.[92]

The wisdom of requiring the surrogate's (and, where appropriate, the father's) consent to the making of the order rather than to the making of the application is surely questionable, since a late withdrawal of consent after the child has been placed with the applicants will bar the court from making a s 30 order (though not an adoption order[93] nor a s 8 order under the Children Act 1989)[94] regardless of the child's welfare.

The court must also be satisfied that no money or other benefit has been given, paid or received by the spouses in connection with the making of the order, the giving of agreement, the handing over of the child, or the making of any arrangements with a view to the making of the order.[95] This prohibition does not apply to payment of reasonable 'expenses reasonably incurred', which presumably will cover such things as the surrogate's expenses for maternity clothes, travel for the assisted reproduction treatment and for ante-natal check ups, and possibly for her loss of earnings consequent on giving up work to have the baby.[96] Further payments or benefits may be authorised by the court. Although the point had been made[97] that, since the court will only become apprised of the matter when the application is made, to be effective, authorisation will have to be retrospective, it has been held that the court does indeed have such a power.[98] In *Re C; Application By Mr And Mrs X Under S 30 Of The Human Fertilisation and Embryology Act 1990*[99] a couple who had been advised by the organisation[100] that introduced them to the surrogate that the usual amount allowed for expenses was £10,000 nevertheless agreed to pay £12,000. This sum expressly included compensation for loss of earnings. However, as the couple discovered after the pregnancy, the surrogate was in fact on income support. It was held in these circumstances that the payment could not be considered to be for 'expenses reasonably incurred' but that nevertheless it should be authorised retrospectively upon the basis that the couple had acted honestly and in good faith throughout, the sum of £12,000 was not an unreasonable sum for expenses if it included compensation for loss of earnings and it was manifestly in the child's interests that she should be treated in law as the child of the couple.

While an application is pending, no parent or guardian can remove the child from the applicant's home against the applicant's will without leave of the court.[101]

In deciding whether or not to make a parental order the court is bound by s 6 of the

---

[91] Section 30(6). A similar provision is made in adoption: see below, p 852.

[92] Section 30(6). 'Cannot be found' and 'incapable of giving agreement' presumably have the same meaning as in adoption: see below, pp 855–6.

[93] See eg in Scotland *C v C (Petitioners and Respondents to Adopt X)*, above.

[94] Discussed below, pp 514ff.

[95] Section 30(7). Nor can the court hear the application if a previous application in respect of the same child by the same applicants has been dismissed, unless the court dismissing the application directed that the provision was not to apply, or there has been a significant change of circumstances: Adoption Act 1976 s 24 as applied to parental orders by the 1994 Regulations (for the continued application of the 1976 Act see n 90 above).

[96] In *Re C; Application By Mr and Mrs X under s 30 of the Human Fertilisation and Embryology Act 1990* [2002] EWHC 157 (Fam), [2002] 1 FLR 909, expenses included loss of actual earnings, potential loss of earnings, maternity clothes, food, cravings, housework/home help, telephone calls, life insurance and wills.

[97] By Douglas, above, at pp 159–60.   [98] Per Johnson J in *Re Q (Parental Orders)*, above at 373.

[99] [2002] EWHC 157 (Fam), [2002] 1 FLR 909.

[100] Viz. Childlessness Overcome Through Surrogacy ('COTS').

[101] Adoption Act 1976 s 27(1) as applied to parental orders by the 1994 Regulations.

Adoption Act 1976, rather than s 1(1) of the Children Act 1989, and must therefore give first (but not paramount) consideration 'to the need to safeguard and promote the welfare of the child throughout his childhood'.[102] Interestingly, this has not been changed notwithstanding that under the Adoption and Children Act 2002 s 1(2) the child's welfare is now the paramount consideration when deciding whether to make adoption orders.[103]

As s 30(8) makes clear, parental order proceedings are to be regarded as 'family proceedings' for the purpose of the Children Act 1989, which means that, as well as making or refusing a parental order, the court is also empowered to make a s 8 order,[104] or to give a s 37 direction inviting the local authority to investigate the circumstances of the case,[105] whether or not such an application is made.[106]

The effect of parental orders is governed not by the primary legislation but instead by the Parental Orders (Human Fertilisation and Embryology) Regulations 1994,[107] which specifically apply (suitably amended) certain provisions of the Adoption Act 1976.[108] It is thus clear that, like an adoption order, a parental order vests parental responsibility for the child *exclusively* in the applicants, and extinguishes the parental responsibility any person had before the order. It also extinguishes any prior order under the Children Act 1989 and any previous duty to make maintenance payments.[109] The child who is the subject of a parental order shall be treated in law 'as if he had been born as the child of the marriage of the husband and wife (whether or not he was in fact born after the marriage was solemnised).[110] Such a child shall be treated in law as if he were not the child of any other person.[111] The status prevents the child being illegitimate.[112] Notwithstanding the making of a parental order, the child stays within the prohibited degrees with his birth family for the purpose of marriage and incest.[113] For the purpose of disposition of property, while the 's 30 child' is not to be treated as the child of any person other than the new parents, this does not prejudice any interest or expectant interest vested in possession before the making of the parental order.[114]

All parental orders are registered in a Parental Order Register maintained by the Registrar General in the General Register Officer.[115] Provision is made for the person who is the subject of a parental order and who has attained the age of 18 to be supplied with information enabling him to obtain a copy of his birth certificate, having first been advised of the counselling services available to him.[116]

---

[102] Adoption Act 1976 s 6 as applied to parental orders by the 1994 Regulations.

[103] For the continued application of the 1976 Act see n 90 above.

[104] Discussed below, pp 514ff.   [105] Section 37 is discussed at p 580.

[106] See s 10(1)(b) of the 1989 Act.   [107] SI 1994/2767.

[108] The power to do this is provided by s 30(9)(a) of the 1990 Act. For the preservation of the 1976 Act for these purposes see n 90, above.

[109] Adoption Act 1976 s 12(1)–(3) as applied by the 1994 Regulations.

[110] Ibid, s 39(1) as applied by the 1994 Regulations.

[111] Ibid, s 39(2) as applied by the 1994 Regulations.

[112] Ibid, s 39(4) as applied by the 1994 Regulations.

[113] Ibid, s 47(1) as applied by the 1994 Regulations.

[114] Ibid, s 42, ss 44–46 as applied by the 1994 Regulations.

[115] Ibid, s 50 as applied by the 1994 Regulations: see also the Forms of Entry to Parental Orders Regulations 1994, SI 1994/2981.

[116] Ibid, s 51 as applied by the 1994 Regulations.

6 SURROGACY AGREEMENTS[117]

Although the precise arrangements may differ, a surrogacy agreement is basically one by which a woman ('the carrying mother') agrees to bear a child for someone else ('the commissioning parents'). For the purposes of the Surrogacy Arrangements Act 1985, a 'surrogacy arrangement' is one made before the woman began to carry the child 'with a view to any child carried in pursuance of it being handed over to, and parental responsibility being met (so far as practicable) by another person or persons'.[118] It is the essence of such agreements that the carrying mother agrees to hand over the baby at birth to the commissioning parents and not to exercise any parental responsibility that she may have in respect of the child. Such agreements came into prominence as a result of the much publicised 'Baby Cotton' case,[119] which is believed to be the first case in the United Kingdom of a commercially arranged surrogacy agreement.[120]

The 'Baby Cotton' case aroused public debate about the desirability of such agreements in general and of commercial surrogacy in particular. Notwithstanding that the weight of public opinion seemed to be against the practice of surrogacy,[121] the Warnock Committee nevertheless did not recommend imposing a complete ban. Instead they recommended that it be a criminal offence for a person to be involved in negotiating or making a surrogacy arrangement on a commercial basis.[122] Adopting this recommendation, s 2(1) of the Surrogacy Arrangements Act 1985 provides:

'No person shall on a commercial basis do any of the following acts in the United Kingdom, that is—

(a) initiate or take part in any negotiations with a view to the making of a surrogacy arrangement,

(b) offer or agree to negotiate the making of a surrogacy arrangement, or

(c) compile any information with a view to its use in making, or negotiating the making, of surrogacy arrangements,

and no person shall in the United Kingdom knowingly cause another to do any of those acts on a commercial basis.'

Section 3 also makes it an offence for *anyone* to advertise that a woman is willing to enter into or to facilitate the making of a surrogacy arrangement or that any person is looking for a woman to become a surrogate mother.[123]

---

[117] See generally *Surrogacy: Review for Health Ministers* (Chair: Professor Margaret Brazier, 1998) Cm 4068, G Douglas *Law, Fertility and Reproduction* ch 7; P Bromley 'The Legal Aspects of Surrogacy Agreements' in *Children and The Law* (ed D Freestone) p 1; and the Report of the Committee of Inquiry into Human Fertilisation and Embryology (the Warnock Report) Cmnd 9314, ch 8. See also M Hibbs 'Surrogacy Legislation—Time for Change' [1997] Fam Law 564 and L Harding 'The Debate on Surrogate Motherhood' [1987] JSWL 37. For a succinct statement of the law see the summary by Hale LJ in *Briody v St Helen's and Knowsley Area Health Authority* [2001] EWCA Civ 1010, [2001] 2 FLR 1094 at [10].

[118] Section 1(2) as amended by the Children Act 1989 Sch 13 para 56.

[119] Reported as *Re C (A Minor) (Wardship: Surrogacy)* [1985] FLR 846.

[120] But it was not the first surrogacy agreement to come before the court: see *A v C* [1985] FLR 445, CA (decided in 1978).

[121] Cmnd 9314 at para 8.10.   [122] At para 8.18.

[123] The penalty for involvement in a surrogacy arrangement is imprisonment for up to three months and a fine not exceeding level five, and for unlawful advertising, a fine not exceeding that level. The consent of the

To constitute an offence the arrangement must be made before the surrogate mother begins to carry the child, and it must be made with a view to the child being handed over to, and the parental responsibility being exercised (so far as practicable) by another person or persons. It is to be noted that the surrogate mother and the 'commissioning' parents are excluded from liability for their participation in the arrangements (though they can be liable for the advertising offence). It is also to be noted that it is only an offence knowingly to assist in the negotiations for a commercial surrogacy arrangement.[124]

Although the participating individuals might not commit an offence under the 1985 Act, in cases where the arrangement was expressly made with a view to the child's adoption by the commissioning parents, where money is paid or agreed to be paid, the contracting parties prima facie commit an offence under the adoption legislation.[125] Now, however, as we have seen, s 30 of the Human Fertilisation and Embryology Act 1990 permits a court to order that a child born as a result of a surrogacy arrangement be treated as that of the commissioning parents, if a number of conditions are met. Hence, provided arrangements do not infringe the Surrogacy Arrangements Act 1985, those made in contemplation of a parental order cannot be held illegal.

The availability of a parental order does not however solve all problems about enforceability. What, for example, is the position if the surrogate mother refuses to hand over the child, or if the commissioning parents refuse to accept the child? In its original form, notwithstanding the recommendation of the Warnock Committee,[126] the 1985 Act was silent on whether surrogacy arrangements were enforceable, although the generally accepted view was that they were not. The matter has now been put beyond doubt by s 1A of the Surrogacy Arrangements Act 1985,[127] which unequivocally states that 'No surrogacy arrangement is enforceable by or against any of the persons making it'.

Given that such arrangements are unenforceable, what then happens to the child? If there is no dispute between the parties, there is no compulsion to go to court. However, given that the surrogate mother will be treated as the child's legal mother even if she is not the genetic mother,[128] it would seem advisable for the commissioning parents to seek a parental order. If they are unable to do this because, for example, the surrogate mother has withdrawn her consent or has refused to hand over the child, the commissioning parents can still seek a s 8 order[129] under the Children Act 1989. In this event it is clear that in resolving any disputes the court is bound to treat the child's welfare as its paramount consideration and is not

Director of Prosecutions is necessary for prosecution. The offences are triable summarily and an information can be laid up to two years after the commission of the offence instead of the usual period of six months.

[124] It is not an offence to help in carrying out the arrangement after it has been made. An unsuccessful attempt was made to change this in the Surrogacy Arrangements (Amendment) Bill 1986.

[125] Viz Adoption Act 1976 s 57, though the court could subsequently authorise payment: see eg *Re An Adoption Application* [1992] 1 FLR 341; and *Re Adoption Application (Payment for Adoption)* [1987] Fam 81, (discussed below, p 881); and in Scotland see *C and C (Petitioners and Respondents to Adopt X)* [1997] Fam Law 9 and 226. See also, in relation to parental orders, *Re Q (Parental Order)* [1996] 1 FLR 369.

[126] Cmnd 9314 at para 8.19.

[127] Introduced by s 36(1) of the Human Fertilisation and Embryology Act 1990.

[128] Under s 27 of the Human Fertilisation and Embryology Act 1990, discussed above at p 308. Furthermore, if she is married and conception has resulted from assisted reproduction methods (commonly surrogacy agreements take the form of the woman agreeing to be artificially inseminated with the commissioning man's semen), her husband may be treated as the legal father pursuant to s 28 of the 1990 Act (discussed above, p 312).

[129] Discussed in Ch 12.

bound by the terms of the agreement.[130] Another possibility, provided the child is handed over, is for the commissioning parents to apply to adopt the child.[131]

Whether the current law adequately balances all the relevant interests can be debated. Some additional protection is afforded to the child, or potential child, in that local authorities have been reminded of their responsibilities to ensure that the child is not at risk as a result of a surrogacy agreement, whether or not it is for money.[132] However, the difficulty of the English position of not banning such arrangements even where money changes hands,[133] yet not allowing such arrangements to be enforceable, was highlighted in the much publicised Karen Roche case. It seems[134] that this woman, having made an arrangement with a Dutch couple, falsely claimed that she had terminated the pregnancy, and then entered into a second arrangement. Following the disquiet raised by this case, the government commissioned a review which was conducted under the Chairmanship of Professor Margaret Brazier.[135] That review recommended inter alia that payments to surrogate mothers should only cover genuine expenses associated with the pregnancy and that additional expenses should be prohibited to prevent surrogacy arrangements being entered into for financial benefit and that legislation should define expenses in broad terms of principle and empower Ministers to issue directions on what constitutes reasonable expenses and the methods by which expenses shall be proven. It also recommended that agencies should be required to be registered by UK Health Departments and operate in accordance with a Code of Practice to be drawn by the Department of Health in consultation with the other UK Health Departments. In the event, however, no action has been taken.

C PROOF OF PARENTAGE[136]

1 MOTHERS

Normally, proving who the mother is presents no difficulties, because the fact of birth and identity can be established by the evidence of the doctor or other persons present at the birth and, as Lord Simon said in the *Ampthill Peerage* case,[137] motherhood is proved demonstrably by parturition: mater est quam gestatio demonstrat. However, it is not

---

[130] Section 1(1) of the Children Act 1989. Nevertheless, it seems likely that if the carrying mother wishes to keep the child and is in a position to give the child a loving and caring home, she will be allowed to do so—cf *A v C* [1985] FLR 445, CA and *Re P (Minors) (Wardship: Surrogacy)* [1987] 2 FLR 421; cf in the USA the notorious decision *Re Baby M* 537 A 2d 1227 (1988) in which the terms of the agreement were applied.

[131] As happened in *C and C (Petitioners and Respondents to Adopt X)*, above.

[132] See DHSS Circular LAC 85 (12).

[133] Under British Medical Association guidelines, surrogate mothers can be paid 'reasonable expenses' of up to £10,000. See Hibbs, op cit n 117, at 565.

[134] See Hibbs, above.

[135] *Surrogacy: Review for Health Ministers of Current Arrangements for Payments and Regulation* (1998) Cm 4068.

[136] For a fascinating historical discussion of the law in this respect see S Cretney *Family Law in the Twentieth Century* 529–36. See also N Lowe 'The Establishment of Paternity under English Law' ICCS Colloquy (Strasbourg, 1999) 80–96. For a discussion of the position in certain European decisions see R Blauwhoff ' "Motherless" Paternity Tests and Minors in Europe' [2005] IFL 146.

[137] [1977] AC 547.

unknown for mothers to be given the wrong children in maternity hospitals and there have been cases where parents have attempted to pass off a suppositious child as their own, usually in order to defraud others who would be entitled to property in default of children of the marriage.[138] Difficult problems of proof may also arise in the context of immigration where first-hand evidence of the birth may be absent.[139]

2 FATHERS

(a) Use of presumptions

Presumption that the mother's husband is the father[140]

Before the advent of blood tests and more recently DNA testing, paternity could normally be inferred only from the fact that the alleged father had sexual intercourse with the mother about the time when the child must have been conceived. Consequently, if two men had intercourse with her during the relevant period, it would be impossible to prove affirmatively which was the father. Moreover, the fact that intercourse took place can in most cases be proved only by the evidence of the parties themselves or circumstantially from their conduct and the opportunities which were presented to them.

The impossibility of proving affirmatively the paternity of the child led at least as early as the twelfth century to the adoption of the civil law maxim: Pater est quem nuptiae demonstrant—that is, if a child is born to a married woman, her husband is presumed to be his father until the contrary is proved.[141] This means that, if it is alleged that the husband is not the father, the burden of rebutting the presumption is cast on the asserter. This presumption applies even though the child is born so soon after the marriage that he must have been conceived beforehand[142] and, in the case of a posthumous child, if he was born within the normal period of gestation after the husband's death.[143] Difficulty arises, however, if the birth takes place an abnormally long time afterwards. In *Preston-Jones v Preston-Jones*[144] the House of Lords agreed that judicial notice could be taken of the fact that there is a normal period of gestation (although the period is variously given as 270 to 280 days or as nine months),[145] but Lord MacDermott added that judicial notice must also be taken of the fact that the normal period is not always followed. Although the longer the period deviates from the normal, the more easily will the presumption be rebutted until there comes a time when it is not raised at all, it is difficult to say where the line is to be drawn.[146]

---

[138] See eg *Slingsby v A-G* (1916) 33 TLR 120, HL, where the wife deceived her own husband; cf the popular belief, current at the time, that the son born to James II's consort was smuggled into the queen's room in a warming pan in order to prevent the descent of the Crown to James's Protestant daughters.

[139] See eg the case of Mrs Sabah referred to in [1986] Fam Law 66.

[140] See C Barton and G Douglas, *Law and Parenthood*, 54ff.

[141] Glanvil, book 7, ch 12. See also Bracton, col 6, Co Litt 373; Blackstone's *Commentaries*, 457; Nicolas *Adulterine Bastardy*; and Lord Simon who said in the *Ampthill Peerage* case [1977] AC 547 at 577: ' "Fatherhood" . . . is a presumption'.

[142] See *Gardner v Gardner* (1877) 2 App Cas 723, HL; *R v Luffe* (1807) 8 East 193; *Anon v Anon* (1856) 23 Beav 273; *Turnock v Turnock* (1867) 36 LJP & M 85.

[143] *Re Heath* [1945] Ch 417 at 421–2 per Cohen J.

[144] [1951] AC 391. See further, below, p 324 n 172.

[145] Per Lord Simonds at 401, Lord Morton at 413, Lord MacDermott at 419.

[146] See above, at 402, 403, 407, 413–14.

The presumption applies equally in the case of a child born after a decree of divorce. In *Knowles v Knowles*[147] the child could have been conceived before or after the decree absolute. Wrangham J held that the presumption of legitimacy operated in favour of presuming that conception took place whilst the marriage was still subsisting and that the husband was the father, although, as he pointed out, in such circumstances the presumption may be rebutted much more easily.

Conflicting presumptions arise if the child must have been conceived during the subsistence of a marriage since terminated by the husband's death or divorce and the mother has remarried before the birth. It is submitted, however, that in the absence of evidence to the contrary the first husband should be presumed to be the father, since it ought to be presumed that the mother had not committed adultery.[148] If, however, the child must have been conceived when the husband and wife were living apart under a decree of judicial separation, there is no presumption that the husband is the father, since it is presumed that the spouses observed the decree and did not have intercourse.[149]

A Lord Chancellor's Consultation Paper[150] raised the question whether the presumption of paternity should be put on a statutory footing in line with Scotland,[151] but in the event no action was taken.

The position where the child is born to an unmarried mother

At common law, since the presumption of paternity was based on the presumption of legitimacy, there could be no presumption of fatherhood outside marriage. This meant and still means that the birth of a child to a cohabiting couple does not in itself raise any presumption and that consequently the man must prove his paternity if he wishes to assert fatherhood. However, it has long been accepted that entry of a man's name as that of the father on the registration of the child's birth is prima facie evidence of his paternity,[152] a point that can only be strengthened by the fact that such registration now confers parental responsibility on the man.[153] In such cases, given the relative weakness for the presumption of a married man's paternity,[154] it is hard to distinguish the legal position of the married man and the unmarried man named as the father. In both cases the onus in any court proceedings lies on those wishing to prove that the man is not the father. Although it

---

[147] [1962] P 161; cf *Re Leman's Will Trusts* (1945) 115 LJ Ch 89. It is submitted that the dictum to the contrary in *Re Bromage* [1935] ch 605 at 609 cannot be supported.

[148] See *Re Overbury* [1955] ch 122, where Harman J found in favour of the first husband's paternity on the facts.

[149] *Hetherington v Hetherington* (1887) 12 PD 112; *Ettenfield v Ettenfield* [1940] P 96 at 110. The reason is hardly satisfactory, because the decree relieves the petitioner from the duty of cohabiting with the respondent: it does not forbid cohabitation, let alone sexual intercourse. The same rule applied to magistrates' separation orders when they had power to make them, but the presumption would not be displaced if there was in force a maintenance order but no separation order: *Bowen v Norman* [1938] 1 KB 689. In any event, the reasoning has no application to voluntary separation; cf *Ettenfield v Ettenfield* (above), but the presumption may be rebutted more easily: *Knowles v Knowles* [1962] P 161 at 168.

[150] *1. Court Procedures for the Determination of Paternity* (1998) paras 31ff.

[151] Viz Law Reform (Parent and Child) (Scotland) Act 1986 s 5.

[152] *Brierley v Brierley* [1918] P 257; Births and Deaths Registration Act 1953, s 34(2). See also the Lord Chancellor's Consultation Paper, above, at para. 26 which observes that a certified copy of registration is accepted as prima facie evidence of paternity in most matters of inheritance nationality and citizenship.

[153] See below at p 410.   [154] See below at p 330.

has still not been authoritatively resolved, the better view is that the making of a parental responsibility agreement also provides prima facie evidence of paternity.[155]

Whether there should be a presumption of paternity in the case of cohabiting couples, as there is in some Commonwealth jurisdictions,[156] was considered but rejected by the Law Commission[157] on the basis that, unlike marriage, which requires no further evidence, cohabitation is not so easy to prove. It is submitted, however, that there is no reason why there should not be a *presumption* of paternity in cases where a couple have made a parental responsibility agreement.

Findings of parentage in previous court proceedings

Former proceedings may also raise an estoppel as to paternity. For example, if the issue of the child's parentage has been determined in divorce proceedings, the finding will bind the spouses as between themselves, but it cannot bind either of them as against a third person, nor can it bind the child or any other person who was not a party to the proceedings.[158] On the other hand, under the Civil Evidence Act 1968,[159] where a person has been found to be the father (including, presumably, any case in which a parental responsibility order has been made in favour of an unmarried father since it is implicit in all such orders that the man in question has been found or adjudged to be the father of the child in question)[160] in any relevant proceedings[161] before any court in the United Kingdom, that is prima facie evidence[162] of paternity in any subsequent proceedings.

Rebutting the presumption

Standard of proof. At common law the generally accepted view was that the presumption could only be rebutted by evidence establishing beyond reasonable doubt that the husband could not be the father. However, the Family Law Reform Act 1969 s 26 states that the presumption may be rebutted upon the balance of probabilities.[163] In *S v S, W v Official Solicitor (or W)*[164] Lord Reid thought that this meant that even weak evidence must prevail

---

[155] See the Lord Chancellor's Consultation Paper, above at para 28. Parental responsibility agreements are discussed below at pp 411ff.

[156] Such as Tasmania, New South Wales and Ontario; see Law Com No 118 at para 10.53, n 120.

[157] Above, at para 10.54.

[158] *B v A-G* [1965] P 278. But the husband's failure to deny that a child is a child of the family in undefended proceedings will not raise an estoppel, because to permit it to do so might invite unnecessary litigation: *Rowe v Rowe* [1980] Fam 47, CA.

[159] Section 12, as amended by the Family Law Reform Act 1987 s 29 and SI 1995/756.

[160] Per Johnson J in *R v Secretary of State for Social Security ex p W* [1999] 2 FLR 604.

[161] Defined to mean National Assistance Act 1948 s 42, Social Security Act 1986 s 26, proceedings under the Children Act 1989, and proceedings which would have been relevant proceedings for the purposes of s 12 of the Civil Evidence Act 1968 in the form in which it was in force before the passing of the Children Act 1989 (viz Family Law Reform Act 1969 s 6, Guardianship of Minors Act 1971, Children Act 1975 s 34(1)(a), (b) or (c), Child Care Act 1980 s 47, Family Law Reform Act 1987 s 4, and proceedings for revocation of a custodianship order under the Children Act 1975 s 35) and the Child Support Act 1991 s 27: Civil Evidence Act 1968 s 12(5), as amended by the Courts and Legal Services Act 1990 s 116, Sch 16, para 2, Child Support Act 1991 s 27(5) and SI 1995/756, Art 6.

[162] It is not, however, binding.

[163] This implements the recommendations of the Law Commission: see Law Com No 16, *Blood Tests and the Proof of Paternity in Civil Proceedings* (1968), para 15.

[164] [1972] AC 24 at 41, HL.

if there is no other evidence to counterbalance it. On the other hand, in *Serio v Serio* [165] it was held that the standard of proof required was not simply that needed in an ordinary civil action but that commensurate with the seriousness of the matter at issue. However, this latter decision has since been discredited for, as Lord Lloyd pointed out in *Re H (Minors) (Sexual Abuse: Standard of Proof)*,[166] requiring that the standard of proof should be 'commensurate with the seriousness of the issue involved' implies that it might be more than a mere balance of probabilities, which 'seems to read words into the statute which are not there'. *Re H* establishes that there is but one civil standard of proof, namely the balance of probabilities.[167] Perhaps, surprisingly in view of *Re H*, the House of Lords (Committee of Privileges) in *Re Moynihan*[168] once again applied the standard set out in *Serio v Serio*. But this seems wrong in principle and in any event, per incuriam. It is submitted that *Serio* cannot be considered good law and that, as Lord Reid said in *S v S*, even weak evidence will be sufficient to rebut the presumption if there is nothing to counterbalance it. It has been held that the inference of paternity drawn from an unjustified refusal to undertake a DNA test[169] is sufficient to rebut the presumption of legitimacy.[170]

What has to be rebutted. Although as will be seen,[171] disputed issues of paternity are normally settled by DNA tests, the presumption of paternity can be rebutted by showing the husband and wife did not have intercourse at the relevant time.[172] Where such marital intercourse cannot be excluded the husband must show that the child is not the issue of that intercourse to rebut the presumption of paternity. This normally implies that the wife has committed adultery. It is established, however, that the fact that the wife has committed adultery does not per se[173] rebut the presumption, because this evidence merely shows that the husband or the adulterer could be the father.[174] In these circumstances, although it is possible to seek to rebut the presumption by the admission of evidence of facial resemblance,[175] racial[176] or genetic characteristics (sometimes referred to as 'anthropological tests'),[177] as we have said, the practice in England and Wales is to determine disputes with the aid of DNA tests.

---

[165] (1983) 4 FLR 756 at 763, CA per Sir David Cairns. See also *Re JS (A Minor) (Declaration of Paternity)* [1981] Fam 22, CA and *W v K (Proof of Paternity)* [1988] 1 FLR 86.

[166] [1996] AC 563 at 577, HL: Lord Lloyd dissented, but not specifically on this issue.

[167] *Re H* was concerned with the application of s 31 of the Children Act: see below, pp 744ff.

[168] [2000] 1 FLR 113, 119–20 (Lord Jauncey) and 123 (Lord Slynn).   [169] Discussed below at p 330.

[170] *Secretary of State for Work and Pensions v Jones* [2003] EWHC 2163 (Fam), [2004] 1 FLR 282.

[171] See below p 325.

[172] Indeed before the advent of blood tests this was the ground on which a husband was most likely to succeed. See eg *Preston-Jones v Preston-Jones* [1951] AC 391, HL, husband's absence from wife; the *Banbury Peerage Case* (1811) 1 Sim & St 153, HL, husband's impotence and the *Aylesford Peerage Case* (1885) 11 App Cas 1, HL, and *Morris v Davies* (1837) 5 Cl & Fin 163, HL, intrinsic unlikelihood of sexual intercourse between the spouses. Note also *Smith v May* (1969) 113 Sol Jo 1000 in which the presumption was rebutted even though the parties admitted sharing the same bed.

[173] Aliter if the husband can be shown to be infertile.

[174] *Francis v Francis* [1960] P 17 and *Gardner v Gardner* (1877) 2 App Cas 723, HL.

[175] See *C v C and C (legitimacy: photographic evidence)* [1972] 3 All ER 577.

[176] See *Slingsby v A-G* (1916) 33 TLR 120 at 122, HL.

[177] The Law Commission (Law Com No 16 *Blood Tests and the Proof of Paternity in Civil Proceedings*, para 16) did not recommend the introduction of such tests in England because of doubts about their medical validity.

(b) The use of blood and DNA tests to establish parentage[178]

The nature of the tests

In cases where parentage (usually paternity) is in issue the most cogent evidence is likely to be obtained by DNA tests. Such tests may be used either to rebut the presumption or allegation of paternity or to establish parentage.

Until DNA tests became publicly available[179] reliance was placed on blood tests. Based on the fact that certain characteristics of a person's blood are inherited and that if the mother's blood does not possess a characteristic possessed by the child, he must have inherited it from the father, blood tests could go some way in resolving issues of paternity. The great drawback of such tests, however, is that, although they can definitely show that a man *cannot* be the father, they can only show with varying degrees of probability that he *is* the father.[180] In contrast, DNA tests (or genetic fingerprinting as it is sometimes known) can, by matching the alleged father's DNA bands with those of the child's (having excluded those bands that match the mother's) make positive findings of paternity with virtual certainty.[181] Furthermore, such tests can be carried out on a variety of bodily tissue (including hair, for example) or bodily fluids (for example, saliva which can be tested by taking mouth swabs)[182] and not simply on blood.

At one time directions could only be made for the use of blood tests but now[183] courts can make directions for the use of 'scientific tests' which permits, subject to necessary consents,[184] tests to be carried on bodily samples taken from the relevant persons.

Although much of the jurisprudence about to be discussed concerned the use of 'blood' rather than 'scientific' tests no legal significance is attached to this. In other words case law developed on blood tests applies without qualification to scientific tests.

The power to give directions for the use of scientific tests

The power to give directions for the use of scientific tests is governed by s 20 of the Family Law Reform Act 1969.[185] This provides that any court may, of its own motion or upon application by any party to the proceedings, direct scientific tests to be used in any *civil* proceedings[186] in which the parentage of any person is to be determined. The power under

---

[178] See generally S Cretney *Family Law in the Twentieth Century* 536–540 and A Grubb and D Pearl *Blood Testing, Aids and DNA Profiling* (1990) ch 6.

[179] 1 June 1987—see *Re J (A Minor) (Wardship)* [1988] 1 FLR 65.

[180] Though, as these tests were being perfected, the degree of probability could be very high, in some cases over 99.8%: see the scales referred to in *Armitage v Nanchen* (1983) 4 FLR 293. See also *Serio v Serio* (1983) 4 FLR 756, CA.

[181] See Barton and Douglas, op cit at 59–60. See R Yaxley 'Genetic Fingerprinting' [1988] Fam Law 403; Grubb and Pearl, op cit, p 161 et seq; and A Bradney 'Blood Tests, Paternity and the Double Helix' [1986] Fam Law 378.

[182] This is the most common way in which DNA tests are conducted.

[183] Ie April 2001, when the amendments provided by the Family Law Reform Act 1987 were brought into force: see Family Law Reform Act 1987 (Commencement No. 3) Order 2001, SI 2001/777.

[184] Discussed below at p 329.

[185] For the common law position see *S v S; W v Official Solicitor* [1972] AC 24, [1970] 3 All ER 107, HL discussed in the 7th edition of this work at p 248 and Law Com No 16, *Blood Tests and the Proof of Paternity in Civil Proceedings* (1968).

[186] 'Civil proceedings' includes proceedings under the Child Support Act 1991, s 27 (discussed below, p 936): *Re E (A Minor) (Child Support Act: Blood Test)* [1994] 2 FLR 548.

s 20 is sometimes loosely referred to as a power to *order* scientific tests, but as Ward LJ pointed out in *Re H (A Minor) (Blood Tests: Parental Rights)*:[187]

'... section 20 does not empower the court to order blood tests, still less to take blood from an unwilling party: all it does is permit a direction for the use of blood tests to ascertain paternity'.

Accordingly, the appropriate wording of the direction is not to direct the parties to provide bodily samples but to direct that scientific tests be used to show that a party to the proceedings is or is not the father or mother of the child in question.

Notwithstanding Ward LJ's clear statement, a distinction should be drawn between adults and children. As Hale J pointed out in *Re R (A Minor) (Blood Tests: Constraint)*,[188] while there is an absolute embargo against forcing an adult to supply a sample against his will, there is no such bar against ordering a sample from a child even to the extent of ordering physical restraint against him or her.

Where no issue of parentage falls to be directed then there is no power to make a direction under s 20. Hence, in *Hodgkiss v Hodgkiss*,[189] for example, the judge was held wrong to have made a direction in divorce proceedings to settle the paternity of two children since no issue of paternity had been raised in the proceedings, the husband having conceded that the children were 'children of the family'. Similarly, if there are no 'civil proceedings' in existence there is no freestanding power to direct tests to be taken.[190]

It is important to appreciate that s 20 does not inhibit the giving of evidence. If all the parties agree, they do not have to obtain the court's consent before having a test carried out.[191] What the Act does is to give the court a discretion to direct a test if they do not agree. Section 20 is silent as to when such a direction should be made, but in *S v S, W v Official Solicitor (or W)*[192] Lord Reid expressed the view that the provision could not have possibly been intended to confer an unfettered discretion on county courts and magistrates' courts and that instead it must be left to the superior courts to settle the principles.

S v S establishes the important point that, when considering whether to make a direction, the court was not exercising its so-called custodial jurisdiction, but was instead exercising its protective jurisdiction.[193] This meant that the correct test was not to make a direction where it is in the child's best interests to do so, but only to refuse to make a direction where it would be against the child's interests to do otherwise,[194] for example, where, 'having regard to the facts and circumstances of a particular case, his interests are such that their protection necessitates the withholding from a court of evidence which may be very material',[195] or if 'it would be unjust to order a test for a collateral reason to

---

[187] [1996] 4 All ER 28 at 36, CA. For the human rights implications of the inability to enforce a direction, see below p 331.

[188] [1998] Fam 66.   [189] [1984] FLR 563, CA. But see the comment at [1985] Fam Law 87.

[190] Per Balcombe LJ in *Re E (Parental Responsibility: Blood Tests)* [1995] 1 FLR 392 at 400–1, CA.

[191] See for example the practice under the Child Support Act, discussed below, p 936.

[192] [1972] AC 24, [1970] 3 All ER 107, HL. See M Hayes 'The Use of Blood Tests in the Pursuit of Truth' (1971) 87 LQR 86.

[193] The distinction between the two jurisdictions is explored further below at p 458.

[194] Per Lord Reid at 45.   [195] Per Lord Morris at 53.

assist a litigant in his or her claim'.[196] The House of Lords refused to accept that the mere fact that a test could establish conclusively that the child was illegitimate was sufficiently against his interest to withhold consent, even though, as in *W v Official Solicitor*, this would leave him with no known father at all. This danger is far outweighed by the demands of public policy that all relevant evidence should be made available. Furthermore, the suppression of evidence would not encourage the mother's husband, whose suspicions would be unallayed, to accept the child as his, whereas he might be prepared to do so if a test did not exclude his paternity; and the child himself in later life might resent the fact that a full investigation was not conducted at the time. It will usually be in the child's interest—as well as in the public interest—that the truth should out.[197]

As Balcombe LJ later put it in *Re F (A Minor) (Blood Tests: Parental Rights)*,[198] *S v S* established inter alia that:

'Public policy no longer requires that special protection should be given by the law to the status of legitimacy . . . The interests of justice will normally require that available evidence be not suppressed and that the truth be ascertained whenever possible . . . In many cases the interests of the child are also best served if the truth is ascertained . . . However, the interests of justice may conflict with the interests of the child. In general the court ought to permit a blood test of a young child to be taken unless satisfied that that would be against the child's interests; it does not first need to be satisfied that the outcome of the test will be for the benefit of the child . . . It is not really protecting the child to ban a blood test on some vague or shadowy conjecture that it may turn out to be for its advantage or at least to do it no harm.'

Notwithstanding general agreement as to what the test is, there has been some difficulty and inconsistency in applying it.[199] In *Re F* itself, the Court of Appeal upheld a refusal to make a direction upon the application of a man claiming to be the father (and who had never seen the child) and opposed by the mother, in a case where the child had been conceived and brought up in an existing marriage, albeit that at the time of conception the mother had been having sexual relations with her husband and the applicant. The court held that the child's welfare depended upon her relationship with the mother and on the stability of the family unit, which included the mother's husband. Anything which might disturb that stability was likely to be detrimental to the child's welfare and therefore, unless this could be counter-balanced by other advantages to her of ordering a test, it would be wrong to do it.

In *Re F* the Court of Appeal seemed to be saying that, if the child is being brought up in an intact family and the test is opposed by the parent, then it is likely to be thought contrary to the child's interests for a direction to be made. But if that was what was meant it cannot stand with subsequent case law. For example, in *Re H (A Minor) (Blood Tests: Parental Rights)*,[200] soon after a married woman began a sexual relationship with another man she became pregnant. However, notwithstanding this affair she continued to have

[196] Per Lord Hodson at 58.

[197] *S v S* (above), at 45 (per Lord Reid) 55–6 (per Lord Morris), 59 (per Lord Hodson).

[198] [1993] Fam 314 at 318, CA, on which see J Fortin 'Re F: The Gooseberry Bush Approach' (1996) 57 MLR 296 and Barton and Douglas, above, at 61.

[199] See generally J Fortin *Children's Rights and the Developing Law* (2nd edn, 2003) 394–8.

[200] [1997] Fam 89, CA.

sexual relations with her husband, who five years previously had had a vasectomy (though he had never checked on the success of that operation). At first the mother intended to leave her husband and set up home with her lover, but she ended the affair before the child was born. When the child was born, his birth was registered in her husband's name. As in *Re F*, the mother opposed the making of a blood test direction upon an application by the lover, who was seeking contact. She argued that pursuing contact would destabilise her own marriage which had only recently been put together again, and that that would be to the child's disadvantage.

In making the direction the Court of Appeal emphasised that the mother's refusal to undergo a test herself was *not* determinative of whether the court should direct such a test,[201] though it remained a factor to be taken into account.[202] But a more important factor was, according to Ward LJ, the right of every child to know the truth about their parentage unless their welfare clearly justifies the 'cover up'. As he pointed out, this right to know is underlined by Article 7 of the UN Convention on the Rights of the Child. Among other factors to be considered, his Lordship considered that[203] any gain to the child from preventing any disturbance to his security had to be balanced against the loss to him of the certainty of knowing who he was. Accordingly, while the risk of disruption to the child's life both by the continuance of the paternity issue as well as the pursuit of the s 8 order were obviously factors which impinged on the child's welfare, they were not, in his judgment, determinative of whether to make a direction. Although Ward LJ himself did not accept that the two cases were indistinguishable,[204] it is hard to reconcile *Re F* and *Re H*, though the latter seems more in tune with the House of Lords' approach in *S v S*. The normality of making directions was again emphasised in *Re H and A (Paternity: Blood Tests)*[205] and in which Thorpe LJ stressed the application of two key principles, namely (1) that the interests of justice are best served by the ascertainment of truth; and (2) the court should be furnished with the best available science and not to have to rely upon presumptions and inferences. However, in that case, notwithstanding the 'profoundest misgivings' about the first instance refusal to make a direction on the basis that it would damage the twins' family (the husband intimated that he would very likely leave home if tests established that he was not the father)[206] the case was remitted for a re-trial.

Notwithstanding their normality, directions are not always made. One profitable line of argument has been to persuade the court that there is no need to determine paternity to settle an issue at all. As the Court of Appeal stressed in *Re JS (A Minor)*,[207] a paternity issue should be pursued only if it has a material bearing on some other issue which has to be tried, and a scientific test should be directed only when this condition is satisfied.

Re JS was followed in *K v M (Paternity: Contact)*,[208] in which it was held unnecessary

---

[201] Wall J's conclusion to the contrary in *Re CB (A Minor) (Blood Tests)* [1994] 2 FLR 762 at 773H was therefore disapproved.

[202] In the case of a haemophiliac father, for example, it may be a very powerful argument: per Ward LJ, above at 101.

[203] Above at 105.   [204] Above at 106.

[205] [2002] EWCA Civ 383, [2002] 1 FLR 1145. Note also *Re T (Paternity: Ordering Blood Tests)* [2001] 2 FLR 1190 in which a direction was made notwithstanding the mother's opposition on the basis it would create a serious risk of destabilising the present arrangements viz a husband and wife bringing up a seven-year-old boy. Note also that six years previously a magistrates' court had refused to make a direction.

[206] Thorpe LJ was not convinced that the marriage was as stable as alleged.

[207] [1981] Fam 22, CA.   [208] [1996] 1 FLR 312.

to consider the paternity of the child to determine the only live issue, namely contact. Similarly, in *O v L (Blood Tests)*,[209] in which the mother asserted that the husband was not the father of the child after they separated nearly three years after the child's birth and, in response to her husband's application for contact, only sought a blood test in an effort to forestall this, it was held unnecessary to define the precise nature of the relationship between the husband and the child in order for contact between them to be fostered. What these cases seem to demonstrate at any rate in this context is that the child's welfare in having contact is more important than establishing so-called father's rights.

The need for consent

In the case of adults (and those aged 16 or 17) there is no compulsion attached to the direction. This is made clear by s 21 which expressly provides that, except in the case of a person suffering from mental disorder,[210] bodily samples may not be taken from a person aged 16 or over unless he or she consents. In the case of those under the age of 16, s 21(3), as originally enacted, simply provided that a sample could be taken for such a person 'if the person who has care and control agrees'. This led to a conflict of view as to whether this provision meant that those with care and control had a right of veto.[211] To resolve that conflict s 21(3) has been amended to provide that in the absence of the requisite consent a sample may be taken 'if the court considers that it would be in [the child's] best interests for the sample to be taken'.[212] This enjoinder to consider the child's best interests seems, however, to lie at odds with the general test established by *S v S, W v Official Solicitor*[213] as to when to make a direction in which the House of Lords expressly rejected the 'best interests of the child' approach. In *Re T (Paternity: Ordering Blood Tests)*[214] Bodey J solved this potential dilemma by ruling that while the child's welfare is not paramount when considering whether to make a direction instead 'one has to apply the test of his best interests, weighing those best interests against the competing interests of the adults who would be affected one way or another, according to whether the applications were granted or refused'. He further pointed out that under Art 8 of the European Convention on Human Rights while all the parties had the right to respect for their private and family life if those rights pulled in different directions, then the child's right to know his true identity was the weightiest consideration. On the facts of the case Bodey J had little difficulty in making a direction on the basis that the seven-year-old child's interests in knowing his true identity (which issue was in the public domain following the mother's husband's proclamation of his paternity on citizen's band radio) outweighed the interests of both the mother and her husband.

Although there can be few quibbles with the overall outcome, one might nevertheless

---

[209] [1995] 2 FLR 930, CA. See also *M (D) v M (S) and G (M (DA) Intervening)* [1969] 1 WLR 843—direction refused where sole reason for application was to prove the wife's adultery.

[210] See further below.

[211] See *Re R (A Minor) (Blood Tests: Constraint)* [1988] Fam 266 in which Hale J held that to get round the lack of parental consent the child could be ordered to be delivered into the care and control of the Official Solicitor, who could then consent on the child's behalf. Cf *Re O (A Minor) (Blood Tests: Constraint)* [2000] Fam 139 in which Wall J considered that Hale J's stratagem was wrong because it was a device to circumvent the plain provision of the Act. He nevertheless thought that the resulting right of veto was not human rights compliant.

[212] Section 21(3)(b) added by the Child Support, Pensions and Social Security Act 2000, s 82.

[213] [1972] AC 24, HL, discussed above at p 326.   [214] [2001] 2 FLR 1190.

question whether Bodey J's approach was strictly correct. His interpretation of the test to be applied in making a direction is dubious (the House of Lords in *S v S* held that a direction should only be refused where it could be shown to be against the child's interests) and in any event seems to conflate the question of whether to make a direction with whether to override a person with care and control's refusal to allow a sample to be taken from a child. The correct approach, it is submitted, is first to decide according to the principles set out in *S v S* whether to make a direction and then to apply s 21(3) to determine whether or not a sample should be taken from the child. Although the tests are not the same it has, however, to be admitted that once it has been shown not to be harmful to the child for a direction to be made, it will almost inevitably follow that it will be in the child's best interests to have a sample taken from him or her to establish parentage.

In the case of a person (including those under the age of 16) suffering from a mental disorder and who does not understand the nature of the test, consent must be obtained from the person who has care and control and in addition the medical practitioner responsible for the person's care must certify that the taking of a sample will not be prejudicial to his welfare.[215]

The inferences from a refusal to consent

Although there is a power of refusal under s 21, s 23(1) permits the court to draw such inferences as appear proper from a person's failure to give consent or to take steps to give effect to the direction.

It has been held that these powers of inference are wholly at large and are wide enough to extend to an inference drawn as to the child's actual paternity. Indeed, in *Re A (A Minor) (Paternity: Refusal of Blood Test)*[216] Waite LJ went so far as to say that given the background of scientific advance:

'. . . if a mother makes a claim against one of the possible fathers,[217] and he chooses his right not to submit to be tested, the inference that he is the father of the child should be virtually inescapable. He would certainly have to advance very clear and cogent reasons for his refusal to be tested—reasons which it would be just and fair and reasonable for him to be allowed to maintain.'

It is well established that the inference from a refusal to provide a sample for a scientific test is stronger than the presumption of legitimacy. In *Secretary of State For Work and Pensions v Jones*,[218] for example, it was held that the justices had erred in giving greater weight to the presumption of legitimacy than to the inference of paternity drawn from the respondent's failure to provide a sample for a DNA test. In this case the mother, although married to someone else, had been exclusively living with the respondent for nine months around the time of conception. She named him as the father in her application for child support, but the respondent whilst indicating his possible paternity, nevertheless failed to provide a sample to enable a test to be carried out. Butler-Sloss P, setting aside the

---

[215] Section 21(4).

[216] [1994] 2 FLR 463 at 473, CA. For an earlier example of a husband reasonably refusing to submit to a blood test, see *B v B and E (B intervening)* [1969] 3 All ER 1106, CA.

[217] At the time of conception the mother was having sexual relationships with three different men.

[218] [2003] EWHC 2163 (Fam), [2004] 1 FLR 282. See also *F v Child Support Agency* [1999] 2 FLR 244.

magistrates' decision, declared the respondent to be the father. In *Re G (Parentage: Blood Sample)*[219] Ward LJ said:

'. . . the forensic process is advanced by presenting the truth to the court. He who obstructs the truth will have the inference drawn against him.'

In that case the trial judge was held to have misdirected himself when failing to draw the inference from a man's his refusal to submit to a test.[220]

Under s 23(2), if a party makes a claim relying on the presumption of legitimacy, the court may dismiss the claim even though there is no evidence to rebut the presumption. The last provision would apply, for example, to a wife claiming maintenance for a child whom she alleges is that of her husband and who refuses to have herself and the child tested.[221] To bar the claimant from relief in such circumstances appears on the face of it to be reasonable: the difficulty is that an adverse inference drawn against an adult party might also be adverse to the child. It is questionable whether Parliament was right to give a court power to refuse to make an order for example for maintenance, because the mother declines to submit to a blood test, when it could have made submission compulsory; what one must guard against is drawing the wholly illogical conclusion that the child cannot be that of the husband.

In *Re O (A Minor) (Blood Tests: Constraint)*[222] Wall J suggested that notwithstanding the power to draw inferences from a refusal to comply with a direction, the inability simply to enforce a direction may mean that Part III of the 1969 Act will need to be reformed to become human rights compliant. But whether this is right remains to be seen for although the establishment of parentage engages both Article 6 and 8,[223] given that inferences can be drawn from a refusal to comply with a direction thereby leading to a finding, it is not at all clear that a breach of Article 8 would be established.[224]

3 DECLARATIONS OF PARENTAGE

Following the amendments made by the Child Support, Pensions and Social Security Act 2000[225] there are just two ways[226] in which the issue of parentage may be determined by the court, namely, by a finding in the course of existing proceedings, or by a formal declaration of parentage. The drawback of the former is that any judicial decision is a judgment in personam and consequently only binds the parties to it and their privies, ie persons claiming through them. Formal declarations, on the other hand, are binding for all purposes.

---

219 [1997] 1 FLR 360 at 366, CA.
220 Though in fact in the appeal he was given a further opportunity to change his mind.
221 See *Re H (A Minor) (Blood Tests: Parental Rights)* [1997] Fam 89.
222 [2000] Fam 139 at 155. 223 See eg *Ramussen v Denmark* (1985) 7 EHRR 371, ECtHR.
224 Cf *Mikulic v Croatia* [2002] 1 FCR 720, ECtHR where a breach was found only because under Croatian law there was no alternative means of establishing paternity other than a DNA test. See also *Odièvre v France* [2003] 1 FCR 621, ECtHR, in which the French law permitting a mother to give birth anonymously was held not to violate the child's Art 8 rights.
225 These reforms came into force on 1 April 2001. For the background leading to the reform, see the Lord Chancellor's Consultation Paper *Court Procedures for the Determination of Paternity* (1998).
226 Formerly, a declaration could be obtained under the Child Support Act 1991, s 27 but that was only effective for child support and maintenance purposes. This method was abolished by the 2000 Act reforms.

Under s 55A of the Family Law Act 1986[227] any person may apply to the High Court, county court or magistrates' court for a declaration as to whether or not a person named in the application is or was the parent of another person so named. This is wider than the former powers under s 56 in three key respects. First, declarations may be sought from magistrates' courts as well as county courts and the High Court. Secondly, applicants are not confined to the child and thirdly, declarations may be sought that the person is or was *not* the parent of the named person (as well of course that he is or was the parent).

Jurisdiction to entertain an application is based on either person's[228] domicile or habitual residence for one year in England and Wales either the date of application, or if dead, at the time of death.[229] To guard against vexatious applications (typically from third parties) courts have, (except where the declaration sought is as to whether or not the applicant is the parent of the named person; the named person is the parent of the applicant, or the named person is the other parent of a named child of the applicant),[230] a discretion not to hear an application if it considers that the applicant does not have a sufficient personal interest.[231] Furthermore, where one of the named persons in the application is a child the court may refuse to hear it 'if they consider that the determination of the application would not be in the child's best interests'.[232] Where a court refuses to hear an application it may order that the applicant should not apply for the same declaration without leave of the court.[233]

Where the truth of the proposition sought to be declared is proved to the court's satisfaction the court must make a declaration of parentage unless to do so would be manifestly contrary to public policy.[234] If a declaration is made, it is binding upon the Crown and all other persons,[235] and the Registrar-General will be informed.[236] If the declaration is refused, the court cannot grant a declaration for which an application was not made.[237]

4 REGISTRATION OF BIRTHS

As we have seen,[238] inclusion of the father's name in the register of births is prima facie evidence of his paternity. Under the Births and Deaths Registration Act 1953 s 2 the

---

[227] This section was inserted by s 83 of the Child Support, Pensions and Social Security Act 2000 and provides a common procedure for obtaining declarations of parentage formerly provided by s 56 of the Family Law Act 1986 and s 27 of the Child Support Act 1991. The procedure for making such application is governed by the Family Proceedings Rules 1991 r 3.13 (High Court and county court and the Family Proceedings Courts (Matrimonial Proceedings etc) Rules 1991, r 3B (magistrates' courts)).

[228] Ie the applicant or the person named in the application. Formerly, jurisdiction was founded only upon the applicant's domicile or habitual residence.

[229] Section 55A(2).   [230] Section 55A(4).

[231] Section 55A(3). Note that for these purposes where an application for a declaration of parentage is made by the Secretary of State in connection with a maintenance calculation under the Child Support Act 1991 the person with care is deemed to have a sufficient interest if she is the applicant for a maintenance calculation: s 27 of the Child Support Act 1991, to which s 55A(3) is expressly made subject.

[232] Section 55A(5). This provision might be thought to raise similar issues to those under s 21(3) of the Family Law Act 1969, discussed above at p 329.

[233] Section 55A(6).   [234] Section 58(1).   [235] Section 58(2).

[236] Section 55A(7).   [237] Section 58(3).

[238] Above p 322. Registration also vests parental responsibility if the man is not married to the mother, see below p 410.

child's married parents are obliged to register the birth within 42 days.[239] However, the unmarried father has no obligation to register himself as the father and indeed, has no general right to do so, in striking contrast to many continental European legal systems which permit a man to make a binding voluntary recognition of his paternity,. The unmarried father's name may, however, be entered on the register in the following circumstances:[240]

(i)   at the joint request of the mother and the father, in which case both must sign the register;

(ii) at the mother's request upon production of a declaration[241] by her and the father to the effect that he is the father;

(iii) at the father's request upon production of a declaration by him and the mother to the effect that he is the father; or

(iv) at the written request of either the mother or the father upon the production of a copy of a parental responsibility agreement, a parental responsibility order or a court order requiring him to make financial provision for the child.

If the child's birth has been registered with no father named, it may be re-registered showing the father's name if one of the above conditions is satisfied.[242] Re-registrations can also be made by the Registrar-General upon receiving satisfactory evidence that the child has become a legitimated person[243] or upon being notified of a declaration of parentage being made either under s 55A or s 56 of the Family Law Act 1986.[244] Notwithstanding that declarations of parentage offer the only means by which unmarried fathers can have their paternity registered without the mother's consent, such re-registrations have no effect on the allocation of parental responsibility.[245]

5 DISCOVERING GENETIC PARENTAGE [246]

Children may of course consult the birth register to discover who their registered parents are. Moreover, as we discuss in Chapter 15, when they reach 18, adopted children are

[239] For registering posthumous fathers of children conceived after their death, see s 10ZA of the 1953 Act, added by the Human Fertilisation and Embryology (Deceased Fathers) Act 2003, s 2(1), Sch, para 3.
[240] Births and Deaths Registration Act 1953 s 10 as substituted by the Family Law Reform Act 1987 s 24 and amended by the Children Act 1989 Sch 12, para 6.
[241] Namely a duly signed and witnessed declaration on a prescribed from—viz Form 2 under Sch 1 to the Registration of Births and Deaths Regulations 1987.
[242] Births and Deaths Registration Act 1953 s 10A, as substituted by the Family Law Reform Act 1987 s 25 and amended by the Children Act 1980 Sch 12, para 6. Special arrangements are made for the registration of parental orders under s 30 of the Human Fertilisation and Embryology Act 1990 by Sch 1 to the Parental Orders (Human Fertilisation and Embryology) Regulations 1994 and for adoptions under the Adoption and Children Act 2002, Sch 1.
[243] Births and Deaths Registration Act 1953, s 14.
[244] Section 14A, added by the Family Law Reform Act 1987, s 27 and amended by the Child Support, Pensions and Social Security Act 2000, s 83(5). Declarations are discussed above at p 332 and below at p 345.
[245] Responsibility is only conferred when the man is registered as the unmarried father under s 10(1) and 10A(1) of the 1953 Act and not, therefore, under s 14A, see Children Act 1989 s 4(1A), discussed below at p 410.
[246] See generally J Masson and C Harrison 'Identity: Mapping the Frontiers' in N Lowe and G Douglas (eds) *Families Across Frontiers* (1996) 277–94, and Barton and Douglas, above, 83–9.

generally entitled to see their original birth certificate, thus enabling them to trace their birth parents. In addition, following the recommendations of the Warnock Committee[247] that a child should have a right, when 18, to basic information about his ethnic and genetic origins, s 31(4) of the Human Fertilisation and Embryology Act 1990 provides that an adult,[248] having been given a suitable opportunity to receive proper counselling,[249] may apply to the Human Fertilisation and Embryology Authority to give him notice stating whether or not the information contained in the Authority's register shows that, but for ss 27–29 of the 1990 Act, some other person would or might be his parent. If it does, the Authority must give the applicant such information as is permitted by the regulations about the person concerned or about whether a person specified in the request as a person whom the applicant proposes to marry would or might be related. However, in many cases such information could only be of a non-identifying nature, since s 31(5) and the accompanying Regulation specifically prohibited identifying the licensed donor of eggs or sperm. It was thought that permitting children to discover the donor's identity would deter people from acting as donors, and there was a sharp division of opinion as to whether it would be in the child's interest to learn of the fact of donation.[250] However, as previously discussed,[251] the right to anonymity for a licensed sperm donor has been ended with respect to children conceived as a result of sperm donated on or after 1 April 2005. Consequently such children will, upon attaining the age of 18 (ie as from April 2023 at the earliest), be able to obtain identifying information from the Human Fertilisation and Embryology Authority.[252]

D THE LEGAL SIGNIFICANCE OF PARENTAGE

Like a number of other legal systems, English common law refused to accept that the mere fact of parenthood gave rise to a legally recognised relationship between parent and child. Instead it chose to recognise only the legal relationship between parent and *legitimate* child. We discuss the concept and significance of legitimacy when considering the child's position (see below). Suffice to say here that, although the significance of status has declined, English law continues to distinguish parents, and in particular fathers, whose children have been born in lawful wedlock from those whose children have not. Hence,

---

[247] Report of the Committee of Inquiry into Human Fertilisation and Embryology (1984) Cmnd 9314, para 4.21.

[248] A person under the age of 18 has a more limited right to request information about a person he proposes to marry: s 31(6)(b) and (7).

[249] Section 31(3) of the Human Fertilisation and Embryology Act 1990.

[250] See G Douglas *Law Fertility and Reproduction*, 132–6. But see the criticisms of S Maclean and M Maclean 'Keeping secrets in assisted reproduction: the tension between donor anonymity and the need of the child for information' (1996) 8 CFLQ 243; and K O'Donovan 'What shall we tell the children?' in R Lee and D Morgan (eds) *Birthrights* (1994) 105–8.

[251] See above p 310.

[252] Human Fertilisation and Embryology Authority (Disclosure of Donor Information) Regulations 2004 (SI 2004/1511) reg 2(3). For the background to this change, see *Donor information consultation* (Department of Health 2002) and *Response to the Department of Health's consultation on donor information* (HFEA, 2002).

while all mothers automatically have parental responsibility, only fathers whose children are legitimate automatically have such responsibility.[253]

That, however, is not to say that parenthood per se has no legal significance. For example, each parent is liable to maintain his child, and an application for child support may be brought under the Child Support Act 1991 against non-resident parents. Rights of succession automatically flow from the parent–child relationship,[254] as do the rules on prohibited degrees of marriage[255] and incest. All parents have a right to apply without leave for a s 8 order under the Children Act 1989[256] and there is a presumption that a child in local authority care should have reasonable contact with each parent.[257] We consider these issues elsewhere, but another issue which we will now discuss is that of citizenship and the right to remain and settle in the United Kingdom.

1 ACQUISITION OF BRITISH CITIZENSHIP

(a) By birth

At common law, birth in this country automatically conferred British nationality. However, under the British Nationality Act 1981[258] a child is a British citizen by virtue of birth here or in a qualifying territory under the British Overseas Territories Act 2002, only if one of his parents[259] is at the time a British citizen or settled in this country (ie ordinarily resident in the United Kingdom or in a qualifying territory without being in breach of the immigration laws or subject to any restriction on the period for which he or she may remain).[260-1]

Where a child born here is not a British citizen at birth, he is entitled to be registered as one during his minority if either of his parents becomes a British citizen or settles in this country.[262]

A child born in this country is also entitled to be registered as a British citizen if, during each of the first ten years of his life he was not absent from the United Kingdom for more than 90 days.[263] This provision is aimed at enabling children who can be said to have a real link with this country and who have not spent a substantial part of their early childhood in, for example, their parents' homeland, to acquire citizenship.

---

[253] Children Act 1989 s 2(1) and (2), discussed below, p 409.   [254] See Chapter 19.

[255] See above, p 49.   [256] See below, p 543.

[257] Children Act 1989 s 34, discussed below, pp 791ff.   [258] Section 1(1), as amended.

[259] British Nationality Act 1981, s 50(9), amended by the Nationality, Immigration and Asylum Act 2002, s 9(1) to include a person treated as the child's father by virtue of Human Fertilisation and Embryology Act 1990, s 28 or a person who satisfies prescribed requirements as to paternity.

[260-1] Section 1(1) and s 50(2)–(5). The parent will not be regarded as settled, however, if he has been specially exempt from the immigration laws or his exemption flows from being a member of a Commonwealth or foreign force or, generally speaking, of a diplomatic mission. A newly born infant found abandoned in this country will be presumed to be a British citizen unless the contrary is shown: s 1(2). A posthumous child's nationality will depend upon the citizenship status of the parent in question at the time of the parent's death: s 48.

[262] Section 1(3).

[263] Section 1(4). In special circumstances the Secretary of State may permit registration even though the applicant has been absent for more than 90 days in any one or more years: s 1(7).

(b) By descent

At common law, children not born within British territory acquired British nationality only in very limited circumstances (for example, if they were the children of a British ambassador). Legislation later widened the rules, but the British Nationality Act 1948 reimposed limitations and these were extended by the 1981 Act. Under this Act a person born outside the United Kingdom and the qualifying territories is a British citizen only if, at the time of his birth, either of his parents is a British citizen otherwise than by descent, or is a British citizen in service under the Crown or a European Community institution or in some similar designated service.[264] This has had the effect of considerably reducing the number of children to whom citizenship by descent can be transmitted.

The severity of the Act is partly mitigated by two provisions granting an *entitlement*[265] to be registered as a British citizen, which are designed to protect a child of a citizen by descent with a substantial connection with this country. First, if the parent was in the United Kingdom or a qualifying territory during some period of three years preceding the child's birth and one of that parent's own parents was a British citizen otherwise than by descent, the child is entitled to be registered as a British citizen within twelve months of his birth, even though this event occurred abroad[266] (it will be seen that this limits transmission by this means to the second generation). Secondly, if either parent is a citizen by descent and the child and both his parents have been in the United Kingdom for three years since his birth, he may be registered as a British citizen provided that he is still a minor and both his parents consent.[267]

2 LEAVE TO REMAIN AND SETTLE IN THE UNITED KINGDOM [268]

Where indefinite leave[269] to enter the United Kingdom is sought for a child, entry clearance from abroad will first be required, unless he or she was born here.[270] The child must be under 18 years of age, unmarried, not leading an independent life nor having formed an independent family unit, and must be able to be maintained without recourse to public funds in suitable accommodation.[271] The child must be seeking to enter in order to

---

[264] Section 2.

[265] The Secretary of State also has a *discretion* to register a minor on application, if he thinks fit: s 3(1).

[266] Section 3(2)–(3). Absences totalling no more than 270 days during the period of three years are to be disregarded. In special circumstances the Secretary of State may accept an application for registration up to six years after the child's birth: s 3(4).

[267] Section 3(5)–(6). Absences totalling not more than 270 days are to be disregarded in each case. Only one parent need satisfy these conditions if the other has died or their marriage or civil partnership has been terminated or they are legally separated.

[268] See J Rosenblatt and I Lewis *Children and Immigration* (1997).

[269] Similar requirements apply where limited leave is sought, but the child must be accompanying or joining a parent: HC 395 paras 301 and 302. For children of students or other special categories, see Rosenblatt and Lewis, above, ch 3. Children who are EEA nationals are admitted to accompany or join the EEA national exercising their right to freedom of movement: paras 255–62. Where the child is not himself an EEA national, an EEA family permit can be issued: paras 258–61.

[270] Ibid, para 299 as amended.   [271] Para 297, as amended.

accompany or join either or both parents[272] who are settled, or entering to settle, here, or a relative who is settled here if there are serious and compelling family or other considerations making exclusion of the child undesirable and suitable arrangements have been made for the child's care.

Where the child is seeking to live with only one parent when the other is still alive, it must be shown that the parent has sole responsibility for the child's upbringing.[273] The fact that other relatives have had day-to-day care of the child will not prevent such sole responsibility being established[274] (indeed, how could it, since by definition in many cases the child will be seeking to *join* a parent from whom he or she has been separated), but sharing responsibility between parents will prevent leave being given.[275] Such an approach is hardly compatible with the emphasis upon shared parental responsibility under the Children Act 1989. However, it is clear that 'responsibility' in this context is not intended to convey any legal significance, and the role of all relevant members of the child's family must be taken into account.[276]

Where the child was born in the United Kingdom, but does not have British citizenship, no prior entry clearance is required, provided that the child has not been absent from the United Kingdom for more than two years. The same requirements as above must be satisfied, except those concerning maintenance and accommodation.[277] The definition of 'parent' is also widened to include 'a person to whom there has been a genuine transfer of parental responsibility on the ground of the original parent(s)' inability to care for the child'.[278]

A child of a polygamous marriage cannot be given leave to enter or remain, where the mother would not be granted such leave.[279]

3 DEPORTATION [280]

Immigration decisions will often raise human rights claims, since a refusal of entry to join a family relative is likely to interfere with the person's right to respect for family life under Art 8 of the European Convention on Human Rights. Particularly serious problems may arise where the question of deportation has to be considered. A child may find him or herself liable to deportation from the country where he or she has been born, or grown up, because of a parent's failure to persuade the authorities to let him or her stay here.

The general approach of the European Court of Human Rights is to bow to the judgment of the national authorities, in the recognition that there are strong policy, and indeed, political, issues at stake.[281] Equally, however, the authorities are alive to the

---

[272] Defined to include a step-parent where the birth parent is dead, adoptive parent provided the adoption order is recognised by the United Kingdom, and an unmarried father whose paternity has been proved: para 6.

[273] Para 297(i)(e). It will depend upon the facts as to how long a parent will have had to have such sole responsibility for the purpose of the Rules: *Nmaju and Others v Entry Clearance Officer*, 6 September 2000, CA.

[274] *R v Immigration Appeal Tribunal, ex p Uddin* [1986] Imm AR 203.

[275] *Williams v ECO Bridgetown Barbados* [1975] Imm AR 111.

[276] *Martin v Secretary of State for the Home Department* [1972] Imm AR 71.   [277] Para 305.

[278] Para 6.   [279] Para 296.   [280] See Home Office Circulars on Deportation DP/4/96 et seq.

[281] *Berrehab v Netherlands* (1988) 11 EHRR 322. See Storey 'The Right to Family Life and Immigration Case Law at Strasbourg' (1990) 30 ICLQ 328; K O'Donnell 'Parent–Child Relationships within the European Convention' in N Lowe and G Douglas (eds) *Families Across Frontiers* (1996) 135–50.

human rights implications and have evolved certain rules of discretion in determining how rigorously to enforce their deportation decisions.

Where a parent is liable to deportation, and his child has lived with him or her in the United Kingdom for seven years or more, the authorities will not normally carry out the deportation, although each case is considered on its merits.[282] For example a child will not normally be deported if he and his mother are living apart from the deportee, he has spent some years in the United Kingdom and is nearly 18, he has left home and is financially independent, or he married before deportation came into prospect. If a child is still at school, the Home Secretary will take into account the effect deportation would have on his education as well as plans for his care and maintenance if he stays here.[283]

Where family proceedings are taken in order to enable either a parent or the child to evade immigration control, the Treasury Solicitor may be instructed to intervene in the proceedings as a respondent, filing an affidavit setting out the child's immigration history and the Secretary of State's objections.[284]

E THE MEANING OF 'CHILD'

At common law a child attained his majority at the age of 21 but, following the Latey Committee's recommendation,[285] the age of majority, as enacted by s 1(1) of the Family Law Reform Act 1969, is now 18. A 'child' may therefore be said to be a person under the age of 18.[286] This definition is also in line with Article 1 of the UN Convention on the Rights of the Child 1989 which states:

'For the purposes of the present Convention a child means every human being below the age of 18 years unless, under the law applicable to the child, majority is attained earlier.'

Although for some purposes an unborn child may be regarded as a 'child', whenever the term is used in a statute it is presumed, unless the contrary intention can be shown, only to refer to a live child, ie after the child has been born.[287]

F THE MEANING OF 'CHILD OF THE FAMILY'

It is convenient to discuss here a recurring concept employed in family legislation, namely that of 'child of the family'. Broadly speaking, this concept is intended to embrace those children who have been brought up as if they were members of the spouses' or civil partners' family, it being felt reasonable to fix on those spouses or partners duties of

[282] Home Office Policy Statement, 24 February 1999, and Explanatory Memorandum 69/99.
[283] Para 367: see R v Immigration Appeal Tribunal, ex p Bakhtaur Singh [1986] Imm AR 352.
[284] Home Office Circular on Deportation DP/4/96 paras 10 and 11.
[285] Committee on the Age of Majority 1967, Cmnd 3342, para 134.
[286] This is the definition of 'child' under s 105(1) of the Children Act 1989. It is to be noted that not all laws relating to children are linked to the age of majority. In fact there is little consistency in the age below which legislation concerning children applies.
[287] See Elliot v Joicey [1935] AC 209, HL; D (A Minor) v Berkshire County Council [1987] AC 317; and R v Newham London Borough Council, ex p Dada [1996] QB 507, CA.

maintenance and protection whether or not they are the biological parents. At one stage, the definition differed according to which legislation was involved but, although the concept is employed in a number of different statutes,[288] happily the core definition is now the same. It is to be noted that a child may only be a 'child of the family' where he has been brought up by parties to a marriage or civil partnership, and not therefore by cohabitants. The common definition is that a child of the family is:

(a) a child of both spouses or partners; and

(b) any other child, not being a child who is placed with those parties as foster parents by a local authority or voluntary organisation,[289] who has been treated by both of those parties as a child of the family.

In the case of spouses category (a) refers to any child, including an adopted child, who is treated in law as being a child of the spouses. In the case of civil partnerships only an adopted child can be a child of both partners.[290] Subject to the exceptions mentioned above, category (b) includes any child whom both parties to a marriage or civil partnership have treated as a member of the family. There is no requirement that either spouse or partner be the natural parent of the child. Hence, relatives (or even foster parents, provided the child is not in the care of a local authority or voluntary organisation) caring for the child on a long-term basis may be held to be treating the child as one of the family. In the case of grandparents it has been said[291] that the court should always give due weight to the pre-existing relationship between the grandparent and the child and in particular investigate whether the grandparents were simply providing everyday or secondary cover, or whether the parents had left them to assume primary responsibility for their child in the foreseeable future. Whether a child has been so treated is a question of fact. Common sense excludes some children, for example, young lodgers, and relatives who are being looked after during their parents' temporary absence. In all cases, however, the test is an objective one, namely to consider as an independent outside observer whether the evidence shows that the child was treated as a member of the family.[292] It has been held, for instance, that a child can be a 'child of the family' even though a maintenance order against the natural father in respect of the child remains in force,[293] and the fact that the

---

[288] See Matrimonial Causes Act 1973 s 52, as amended by the Children Act 1989 Sch 12, para 33; Domestic Proceedings and Magistrates Court Act 1978 s 38, as amended by the Children Act 1989 Sch 12, para 43; and the Children Act 1989 s 105(1), as amended by the Civil Partnership Act 2004, s 25(3). Note also the Marriage Act 1949, s 1(3) and the truncated definition in s 78(1), discussed above at p 51.

[289] This is in line with the general policy of limiting the right of foster parents to apply for orders vesting some control over the child so as not to discourage parents from allowing their child to be fostered. See below p 544.

[290] Adoption by registered partners is permitted under the Adoption and Children Act 2002, see ss 49 and 144(4)(aa).

[291] Per Thorpe LJ in Re A (Child of the Family) [1998] 1 FLR 347 at 350.

[292] See Teeling v Teeling [1984] FLR 808 at 809, CA, per Ormrod LJ, and D v D (Child of the Family) (1981) 2 FLR 93, CA.

[293] See Carron v Carron [1984] FLR 805, CA, where, following their marriage, the mother and stepfather took the mother's two children into their household and lived together for four years. That, according to Ormrod LJ, made it inevitable that there should be a finding that the two children were children of the family. In the case of private foster parents, the fact that a child is still being maintained by the natural parents could well indicate that the child was not a child of the foster parents' family, but it will not be decisive: see Law Com No 25, Report on Financial Provision in Matrimonial Proceedings, paras 23–32.

husband mistakenly believed the child to be his will not prevent the child from being a child of the family if the husband treated him as such.[294] A similar position applies to partners to a civil partnership.

There are two sets of circumstances in which it may be legally impossible for a child to be treated as a child of the family. First, there must be a family of which the child may be treated as a member: consequently a child may not become a child of the family if the unit never existed in the first place,[295] or if it has ceased to exist. In the latter regard, if, for instance, the wife has a child by another man after her husband has left her, but the husband agrees to treat the child as his own even though they continue to live apart, such a child cannot be a child of the family.[296] Once a family has been shown to exist, however, a child can be a child of the family even if the spouses have lived together for an extremely short period.[297] A similar position applies to partners to a civil partnership. Secondly, a child cannot be treated as a child of the family before he is born. In *A v A (Family: Unborn Child)*[298] the husband had married the wife knowing her to be pregnant and believing himself to be the father. Six days after the marriage the wife left him. When the child was born five months later, she was obviously not the husband's child but the daughter of a Pakistani man with whom the mother had also had intercourse before the marriage. The only evidence that the husband had treated the child as his own was the fact that he had married the mother, but Bagnall J held that 'treatment' involved behaviour towards a child who must be in existence. This seems a narrow and technical interpretation which is capable of working injustice[299] and it is urged that it ought not to be followed.[300]

It is submitted that a child of the parties who has subsequently been adopted by someone else cannot normally be a 'child of the family'. An adopted child ceases in law to be a child of the birth parents and therefore falls outside the first part of the definition, and the provisions about treating a child cannot refer to conduct before the adoption. A husband's failure to deny that a child is a child of the family in undefended divorce proceedings does not stop him from asserting otherwise in subsequent proceedings.[301] A similar position applies to a partner involved in dissolution proceedings to end the partnership.

---

[294] See *W (RJ) v W(SJ)* [1972] Fam 152.   [295] See *W v W (Child of the Family)* [1984] FLR 796, CA.

[296] *M v M (Child of the Family)* (1980) 2 FLR 39, CA. Aliter if the parties resume living together: see *Teeling v Teeling*, above.

[297] See *W v W (Child of the Family)*, above, where the man spent barely a fortnight with his wife and the child.

[298] [1974] Fam 6.

[299] This may be particularly harsh with regard to family provision after death, where the same definition is used under the Inheritance (Provision for Family and Dependants) Act 1975 s 1(1)(d). See below, p 1110.

[300] However, the decision has since been approved by Sheldon J, sitting in the Court of Appeal, in *W v W (Child of the Family)*, above. See also *Re Leach* [1986] Ch 226 at 223, CA, per Slade LJ.

[301] *Rowe v Rowe* [1980] Fam 47, CA. See also *Healey v Healey* [1984] Fam 111.

G THE CHILD'S STATUS

1 INTRODUCTION

Most systems of jurisprudence have drawn a distinction between the legal position of a child born of a legally recognised union and that of a child born of an illicit union or as a result of a casual act of intercourse. Children born in the latter circumstances are commonly accorded an inferior legal status and have markedly fewer rights than those born to formal unions. This was certainly true of the common law, which, like Roman law and the modern systems based on it,[302] adhered rigidly to the rule that no child could be legitimate unless he was born or conceived in wedlock.[303] At common law an illegitimate child had no legal relationship with his father or, initially, with his mother. However, as a result of successive Acts of Parliament, the harshness of this position has been significantly mitigated and the concept of legitimacy has been widened: children born illegitimate may now be legitimated if their parents subsequently intermarry and, most importantly, the legal disadvantages attached to illegitimacy have nearly all been removed.[304] As a result of these changes the question whether a child is legitimate or illegitimate has become markedly less important. Nevertheless, unlike some systems such as that in New Zealand,[305] and despite a suggestion by the Law Commission that the concept should be abolished here,[306] the basic status of legitimacy and illegitimacy remains and is to some extent still relevant in determining the legal relationship between a child and his parents.

2 THE CONCEPT OF LEGITIMACY [307]

(a) The position at common law

At common law a child is legitimate if his parents were married at the time of his concep-

---

[302] But this was not the only criterion accepted in Western Europe. See, further, Woolf *Private International Law* (2nd edn) p 385, and the *American Restatement of the Conflict of Laws* s 137 and *Comment*, where it is pointed out that in some legal systems a person may be the legitimate child of one parent but not of the other.

[303] Though it has always been possible for the legislature to legitimate a person who is illegitimate at common law.

[304] For the drawing of an interesting parallel between the decline in importance of legitimacy and the decline of the great landed families for whom the protection of patrilineal descent was crucial, see J Eekelaar *Family Security and Family Breakdown* 13–15.

[305] Where as a result of the Status of Children Act 1969 s 3(1) (since amended by the Care of Children Act 2004, Part 4) no distinction is drawn between the status of children born to married parents and those born to unmarried parents: see *Butterworth's (NZ) Family Law in New Zealand* (11th edn, 2003) 6.502, and Bromley and Webb *Family Law* pp 429–39. The New Zealand enactment has served as a model for other legislation in parts of Australia and Canada: see J Eekelaar *Family Law and Social Policy* (2nd edn) p 139. Note also that in Scotland, s 21 of the Family Law (Scotland) Act 'abolishes' illegitimacy.

[306] Law Com Working Paper No 74, *Illegitimacy*. But note the Lord Chancellor's Consultation Paper (1998) on *The Law on Parental Responsibility for Unmarried Fathers* canvassed views on whether all fathers should have parental responsibility.

[307] For the historical development of the law see generally, S Cretney *Family Law in the Twentieth Century*, ch 15.

tion or at the time of his birth.[308] Commonly, legitimate children are both conceived and born in wedlock, but a similar status is accorded to other classes of children:

(a) those whose parents were married when they were born even though they must have been conceived before the marriage;[309] and

(b) those whose parents were married at the time of their conception, even though the marriage was terminated before their birth.

Consequently, a posthumous child may be legitimate, as will be the child whose parents' marriage was terminated by divorce between the time of his conception and his birth.[310]

In the absence of authority, it is thought that a child conceived as a result of pre-marital intercourse, whose parents then marry but whose father dies before his birth, is legitimate. Had the father survived, the child would certainly have been legitimate[311] and, as we have seen, the common law does not bastardise a child merely because he is born posthumously.

It seems beyond argument that a child conceived during the marriage as a result of artificial insemination with the husband's own semen (AIH) is legitimate and, conversely, at common law, the child conceived as a result of artificial insemination by the semen of a donor other than the husband (DI) is illegitimate. What, however, is the child's status if the wife conceives by AIH after her husband's death? At common law, such a child must surely be illegitimate, for were the position otherwise children *conceived* by the parties *after* their divorce would also have to be regarded as legitimate.[312] The common law has still to determine the status of a child born to a host mother but genetically of commissioning parents.[313]

(b) Statutory changes

Legitimacy of children of void marriages

Since a void marriage is a marriage neither in fact nor in law, children of such a marriage were necessarily illegitimate at common law. However, following the recommendation of the Morton Commission on Marriage and Divorce,[314] the law was changed by the Legitimacy Act 1959, now replaced by the Legitimacy Act 1976. Section 1(1) provides:[315]

---

[308] Blackstone's *Commentaries* 446 and 454–7. For a full account of the common law relating to legitimacy and a detailed examination of the cases before 1836, see Nicolas *Adulterine Bastardy*.

[309] Co Litt 244 a; Blackstone's *Commentaries* i 454. See also Nicolas, above, and the cases cited above, p 321 n 142.

[310] *Knowles v Knowles* [1962] P 161.

[311] Similarly, if the child was born to a mother who is 'brain dead' but kept alive on a life support machine until the child's birth.

[312] See P Bromley 'Aided Conception: The Alternative to Adoption' in Bean (ed) *Adoption, Essays in Social Policy, Law and Sociology* (1984) 174 at 175. It seems doubtful that this position will have changed following the Human Fertilisation and Embryology (Deceased Fathers) Act 2003, discussed above at p 301.

[313] Query the effect of the Human Fertilisation and Embryology Act 1990, in relation to in vitro fertilisation taking place on or after 1 August 1991 (before that date, the matter is solely governed by the common law—see above p 308).

[314] Cmnd 9768, paras 1184–6. This recommendation was intended to reflect the position in Scottish common law and many other jurisdictions which recognised the harshness of declaring as illegitimate children of parents whose marriage turned out to be void, at least where one, if not both, of the parents was ignorant of the invalidity.

[315] As amended by the Family Law Reform Act 1987 s 28(1).

'The child of a void marriage, whenever born, shall . . . be treated as the legitimate child of his parents if at the time of the insemination resulting in the birth or, where there is no such insemination, the child's conception (or the time of the celebration of marriage if later) both or either of the parties reasonably believed that the marriage was valid.'

In common with other provisions relating to status, s 1(2) provides that the section applies only if the child's father was domiciled in England and Wales at the time of the child's birth or, if he died before the birth, immediately before his death.[316]

In *Re Spence*[317] it was held that s 1(1) does not apply to a child *born*[318] before his parents entered into a void marriage.

As originally worded, the Act seemed to lay the burden of proof upon the person asserting the legitimacy, a burden which might be difficult to discharge, particularly if the issue is raised many years after 'the marriage'. However, s 1(4) now provides[319] that, in relation to any child born on or after 4 April 1988,[320] it is to be presumed, unless the contrary is shown, that one of the parties reasonably believed, at the relevant time, that the marriage was valid. Another problem with the provision is the meaning of 'reasonably believed'. It seems to be established that this imports an objective test, ie the belief must be one that a reasonable person would have held in the circumstances.[321] This test led to doubt whether a mistake of law would support a reasonable belief. However, following the Law Commission's recommendations,[322] s 1(3)[323] now provides that such a mistake can support a reasonable belief.

Legitimacy of children of voidable marriages

At common law a decree of nullity, where the marriage was voidable, had retrospective effect and automatically bastardised the issue of the marriage.[324] When the grounds for nullity were extended by the Matrimonial Causes Act 1937, it was appreciated that this rule might work hardship in those cases where the marriage was annulled because the respondent was of unsound mind, or epileptic, or was suffering from a venereal disease in a communicable form, since the wife might conceive before the petitioner discovered the existence of the impediment. Consequently the 1937 Act provided that in these cases any child born of the marriage should be legitimate notwithstanding the annulment of the marriage.[325] Where the respondent was pregnant by a man other than the petitioner,

---

[316] See the provisions relating to legitimatio per subsequens matrimonium, below, p 344.

[317] [1990] Ch 652, CA. See G Douglas (1990) 2 Journal of Child Law 56 (comment on the first instance decision subsequently upheld by the Court of Appeal). It would similarly appear that a child conceived by artificial insemination by donor whose mother's marriage is void by reason of having 'married' another female, must also be regarded as illegitimate if the ruling in *J v C (Void Marriage: Status of Children)* [2006] EWCA Civ 537, 2006 *Times* 1 June is followed through to its logical conclusion.

[318] Aliter if conceived before but born after the putative ceremony.

[319] Added by s 28(2) of the Family Law Reform Act 1987 following the Law Commission's recommendation in Law Com No 118 *Illegitimacy* at para 10.51.

[320] The date on which the amendment came into force.

[321] *Hawkins v A-G* [1966] 1 All ER 392 at 397. Note the criticisms of this test by Bevan *Child Law* (1989) 247.

[322] Law Com No 118, para 10.52.   [323] Added by the Family Law Reform Act 1987 s 28(2).

[324] See above at p 93.   [325] Section 7(2).

the question of the legitimacy of the child did not arise, and apparently the legislature did not foresee that any child would be born if the marriage had not been consummated. Since then, however, cases concerning children born as a result of pre-marital intercourse,[326] or fecundatio ab extra,[327] and of artificial insemination have come before the courts.[328]

This anomaly was first removed by the Law Reform (Miscellaneous Provisions) Act 1949 s 4(1) which provided that any child who would have been the legitimate child of the parties to a voidable marriage had it not been annulled should be deemed to be their legitimate child.[329] The same result is now reached by s 16 of the Matrimonial Causes Act 1973 which, by enacting that a voidable marriage shall be treated as if it had existed up to the date of the decree absolute, must necessarily preserve the legitimacy of any child born or conceived between the date of the marriage and the date of the decree, as well as that of any child legitimated by the marriage.[330]

Legitimation[331]

Canon law adopted the Roman law rule that a bastard would become legitimate if his parents subsequently intermarried, provided that they had been free to marry each other at the time of the child's birth. But the importance of establishing the identity of the heir at law, to whom descended the valuable private rights and important public duties of the ownership of an inheritable estate of freehold land in the Middle Ages, led the common law to reject this doctrine of legitimatio per subsequens matrimonium, and an attempt to introduce it by the Statute of Merton in 1235 was successfully resisted by the temporal peers. Consequently, no form of legitimation was recognised by English law until the passing of the Legitimacy Act 1926, by which time the property legislation of 1925 had rendered it almost wholly unnecessary to establish the identity of the heir save in the case of the descent of an unbarred entailed interest.

The Legitimacy Act 1926 provided that a child should be legitimated by the subsequent marriage of his parents. But it also adopted the canon law rule that legitimation was impossible if either parent was married to any other person at the time of the child's birth.[332] However, a child conceived whilst one of his parents was married could still be legitimated if this marriage was terminated before his birth, and in many cases decrees of divorce were expedited for this reason. The Legitimacy Act 1959 extended those provisions to children born when either or both of their parents were married.[333] These Acts have now been repealed and their provisions re-enacted in the Legitimacy Act 1976. Section 2 provides:

'. . . where the parents of an illegitimate person marry one another, the marriage shall, if the

[326] As in *Dredge v Dredge* [1947] 1 All ER 29.
[327] As in *Clarke v Clarke* [1943] 2 All ER 540.　　[328] As in *REL v EL* [1949] P 211.
[329] This provision, however, did not have retrospective effect. Consequently, except in those cases provided for in s 7(2) of the Matrimonial Causes Act 1937, the children of voidable marriages annulled before 16 December 1949 remain illegitimate: *Re Adams* [1951] Ch 716.
[330] For s 16, see above, p 94. The section will not legitimate a child who never was legitimate (eg because the husband was not the father): *Re Adams*, above.
[331] For a fascinating account of the historical development of the law on legitimation, see S Cretney *Family Law in the Twentieth Century* 547–54.
[332] Section 1(2).　　[333] Section 1.

father of the illegitimate person is at the date of the marriage domiciled in England and Wales, render that person, if living, legitimate from the date of the marriage.'

A person will be legitimated by this section only if his father was domiciled in England and Wales at the time of the marriage. Legitimation does not have retrospective effect, so that no one can be legitimated unless he is still alive when his parents marry.[334] The fact that an adopted child is to be regarded as the child of the adoptive parent and of no other person does not prevent an illegitimate child from being legitimated if he has been adopted solely by one of his parents who then marries the other parent.[335]

3 DECLARATIONS OF STATUS [336]

As we have seen,[337] the question of a child's status may be put in issue in a number of ways. Normally, however, any judicial decision will be a judgment in personam and consequently will bind only the parties to it and their privies, ie persons claiming through them. The desirability of a procedure to enable a disputed question of legitimacy to be settled once and for all led to the passing of the Legitimacy Declaration Act 1858, which was repealed and substantially re-enacted in the Matrimonial Causes Act 1973 s 45. Under s 45 any person could petition for a decree that he was legitimate or that he or his parents or grandparents were validly married. But a petitioner could not obtain a declaration of legitimacy of anyone other than himself,[338] nor was there any power to declare anyone illegitimate,[339] or to make a declaration of paternity of any illegitimate child.[340]

Following a review by the Law Commission,[341] s 45 was repealed and replaced by s 56 of the Family Law Act 1986 and rewritten by the Family Law Reform Act 1987, s 22.[342] Under s 56 the 'child' but no one else can seek a declaration that he or she is the legitimate child of his or her parents; and that the applicant has become or has not become a legitimated person. Such applications may be made either in the High Court or county court.[343]

These provisions are subject to a number of safeguards, reflecting the Law Commission's concern that bare declarations could be abused. Hence, no application can be made unless the applicant is domiciled or has been habitually resident for one year in England and Wales at the date of the application.[344] There is power, at any stage of the proceedings,

[334] Or, if they were married before the date on which the Act by virtue of which he was legitimated came into force, on that date. Legitimacy Act 1926 s 1(1); Legitimacy Act 1959 s 1(2); Legitimacy Act 1976 Sch 1 para 1. But if the parents had married before the relevant Act came into force, the children could be legitimated on that date, even though one or both parents had already died: Re Lowe [1929] 2 Ch 210.

[335] Legitimacy Act 1976 s 4. Indeed in such circumstances the adoption can be revoked upon application of any of the interested parties: Adoption and Children Act 2002, ss 55(1), see below, p 868.

[336] For declarations in other family matters, see above, pp 66 and 97, and 331ff.   [337] Above, p 331.

[338] Aldrich v A-G [1968] P 281.   [339] B v A-G [1966] 2 All ER 145n.

[340] Re JS (A Minor) (Declaration of Paternity) [1981] Fam 22, CA.

[341] See Law Com No 118, paras 10.1–10.27 and Law Com No 132, Declarations in Family Matters, paras 3.9–3.14.

[342] Note also the amendments by the Child Support, Pensions and Social Security Act 2000, which removed the power to make a declaration of parentage under s 56 of the 1986 Act.

[343] Family Law Act 1986 s 63. The procedure is governed by the Family Proceedings Rules 1991 r 3.1.4 for declarations of parentage and r 3.14 for declarations of legitimacy and legitimation.

[344] Family Law Act 1986 s 59(1).

to send the papers to the Attorney General and, whether or not such papers are sent, the Attorney General can intervene in the proceedings.[345]

Where the truth of the proposition to be declared has been proved to the court's satisfaction, the court shall make that declaration 'unless to do so would be manifestly contrary to public policy'.[346] If a declaration is made, it is binding upon the Crown and all other persons,[347] and the Registrar General will be informed.[348] If the declaration is refused, the court cannot grant a declaration for which an application has not been made.[349]

4 THE SIGNIFICANCE OF THE CHILD'S STATUS

At common law the illegitimate child, being filius nullius, had no legal relationship with either of his parents and consequently had no rights, for example, to receive maintenance,[350] to succeed to their property, or to other benefits normally accruing from the relationship of parent and child. Many of these disabilities subsisted until well after the Second World War, but have since been whittled away. For example, following the reforms of the Family Law Reform Acts of 1969 and 1987, children whose parents are not married now have full rights of intestate succession.[351] They can also succeed as an heir to an entailed estate.[352] Such children can now make claims as dependants both under the Inheritance (Provision for Family and Dependants) Act 1975 and the Fatal Accidents legislation.[353] Substantial improvements have been made to the right of support. Indeed, under the Children Act 1989 Sch 1 either parent can be ordered to pay to the other or to the child secured or unsecured periodic payments, lump sum payments, or make property transfers.[354]

Despite these important changes it cannot yet be said that children whose parents are unmarried are in exactly the same legal position as those whose parents are married (though as one commentator has put it,[355] the fact that the child's parents are unmarried no longer stamps the child as legally fundamentally different from the child whose parents are married).

One important difference is that, whereas parties seeking a divorce must necessarily have their plans for their child's future scrutinised by the court,[356] there is no similar scrutiny in cases where unmarried parents separate.[357-60]

There remains one further area of discrimination, namely with regard to succession to a title of honour.

[345] Section 59(2).
[346] Section 58(1). This proviso seems to put into statutory form the power exercised in *Puttick v A-G* [1980] Fam 1: see also above, p 67.
[347] Section 58(2).   [348] Section 56(4).   [349] Section 58(3).
[350] But see S Cretney *Principles of Family Law* (4th edn) 1984, p 594.
[351] See below, p 1099.   [352] Family Law Reform Act 1987 s 19(2).
[353] Fatal Accidents Act 1976 as substituted by the Administration of Justice Act 1982: discussed below, pp 1124ff.
[354] Discussed below at pp 968ff.   [355] S Cretney *Family Law in the Twentieth Century* 565.
[356] Under s 41 of the Matrimonial Causes Act 1973, discussed above, p 278.
[357-60] Though, note, there is a similar scrutinising process when dissolving a civil partnership, see s 63 of the Civil Partnership Act 2004.

(a) Titles of honour

With regard to titles of honour, s 19(4) of the 1987 Act makes it clear that, despite the new construction of the term 'heir', children of unmarried parents will not be able to succeed to property which is limited to devolve along with a dignity or title of honour. However, this should not be read as meaning that such children will never be able to succeed, since that will depend upon the terms of the letters patent issued under the Great Seal. At the moment they are in a form[361] which limits succession to the 'heirs ... of his body lawfully begotten', which is enough to show a contrary intention against devolvement to children whose parents are unmarried. However, if in the future the form 'to X and the heirs of his body' were used, then any child could succeed under the terms of s 19(2).

(b) The position of legitimated children

With regard to a *legitimated* child, it is expressly provided that such a person shall have the same rights and obligations in respect of the maintenance and support of himself and other persons as if he had been born legitimate, and any legal claim for damages, compensation, allowances etc, by or in respect of a legitimate child shall apply in the case of one legitimated.[362] Similarly, for the purpose of determining whether he is a British citizen he is to be treated as being born legitimate as from the date of his parents' marriage.[363] Subject to what is said later with respect to rights in property,[364] a legitimated person is in the same position as if he had been born legitimate. On the other hand, a legitimated person is not entitled to succeed to a title of honour.[365]

5 SHOULD REFERENCE NOW BE MADE TO LEGITIMACY AND ILLEGITIMACY?

(a) Background to the Family Law Reform Act 1987

At one time the Law Commission favoured what at the time was thought to be the radical plan that the status of illegitimacy should be abolished altogether.[366] They argued that since the label was itself discriminatory, true equality demanded not simply the removal of the remaining areas of legal discrimination but the abolition of the very status. Indeed, so strongly were they committed to this view that they were prepared to countenance the necessary corollary of their recommendations: that all fathers should be treated equally. The overwhelming response, however, was against giving all fathers automatic rights,[367]

---

[361] See the discussion in Law Com No 118 at para 8.26.   [362] Legitimacy Act 1976 s 8.
[363] British Nationality Act 1981 s 47(1).   [364] See below.
[365] Legitimacy Act 1976 Sch 1, para 4(2). A similar disability attaches to children who are treated in law as the child of the mother and her husband in cases where the child has been carried by a woman as a result of her artificial insemination, or the placing in her of an embryo or of sperm and eggs: Human Fertilisation and Embryology Act 1990, s 29(4)(b).
[366] For an influential argument against giving all fathers automatic rights, see M Hayes (1980) 43 MLR 299, though J Eekelaar 'Second Thoughts on Illegitimacy Reform' [1985] Fam Law 261 argued that the status could have been abolished without giving all fathers equal rights. But for the current debate as to whether all fathers should have automatic parental responsibility see below, pp 409ff.
[367] See their Working Party No 74 on *Illegitimacy* (1979).

and accordingly, in their full report on *Illegitimacy*,[368] the Law Commission did not advocate abolition of that status, but recommended instead a change in terminology, with the terms 'marital' and 'non marital' replacing so far as possible 'legitimate' and 'illegitimate'.

Before these recommendations were acted upon, the issue was examined by the Scottish Law Commission.[369] They observed[370] that:

'... so long as marriage exists and children are born there will be children born out of marriage. In some cases of children born out of marriage, the parents will marry each other after the birth: in others they will not. These are facts and, short of abolishing marriage, there is nothing the law can do about them.'

Like the English Law Commission they did not recommend abolishing the status of illegitimacy, but unlike that body the Scots could see no merit in introducing the new terms 'marital' and 'non-marital'. As they said,[371] that 'was just another way of labelling children, and experience in other areas, such as mental illness, suggests that new labels can rapidly take on old connotations'. They concluded that they did not wish to see 'a discriminatory concept of "non-maritality" gradually replace a discriminatory concept of "illegitimacy" '. Accordingly, they recommended that the terms 'legitimate' and 'illegitimate' as applied to people, should wherever possible cease to be used in legislation. To achieve this they recommended that, where distinctions based on marriage were necessary, future legislation should distinguish between fathers rather than children. Where it was thought necessary to distinguish people on the basis of whether or not their parents were married to each other at any relevant time (which they hoped would be a 'very rare exception') it should be done expressly in those terms. The Scottish Law Commission's proposals were enacted in the Law Reform (Parent and Child) (Scotland) Act 1986.

Following these developments, the English Law Commission reconsidered its proposals and in a second report, published in October 1986,[372] advocated reform along the Scottish lines. Their recommendations were enacted by the Family Law Reform Act 1987.

(b) The Family Law Reform Act 1987

Apart from making important changes to the status of some children born as a result of donor insemination and amending the provision dealing with children of void marriages, the 1987 Act has left untouched the basic concept of legitimacy. However, implementing the strategy of reducing the need to refer to the concept, in cases where it is still necessary to distinguish between children born within marriage and those born without, the Act introduced the important change that reference be made to the parents, rather than to the children, and whether or not they are married to each other. This general approach is set out by s 1 of the 1987 Act.

Section 1(1) provides that references in the 1987 Act and any succeeding Act or statutory instrument to 'mothers' or 'fathers' or 'parents' refers, unless the contrary intention appears, to all such persons regardless of whether they have or had been married to each other at any time. The clarity of this opening provision is immediately obscured by

---

[368] Law Com No 118 (1982), particularly at Part IV.

[369] Scot Law Com No 82 (1984). It was also examined by the Irish Law Reform Commission: see W Duncan 'Abolishing Illegitimacy—A Discussion of the Law Reform Commission's Proposals' (1983) 5 Dublin University Law Journal 29–41.

[370] Above, at para 9.1.   [371] Above, at para 9.2.   [372] Law Com No 157.

definitional provisions designed to distinguish (in simple terms) parents (primarily fathers) of legitimate from those of illegitimate children. To avoid using the words 'legitimate' or 'illegitimate', s 1(2) refers instead to a person whose parents were not married to each other at the time of the child's birth. However, it was recognised that this shorthand definition was insufficient by itself, because a child can be legitimate even though his parents were not married at the time of his birth. Accordingly s 1(2) is made subject to s 1(3), so that references to 'a person whose father and mother were not married to each other at the time of the child's birth'[373] do not include (and correspondingly, references to a person whose parents were married to each other at the time of his birth *do* include) cases where the child is:

(a) rendered legitimate by s 1 of the Legitimacy Act 1976 even though his parents' marriage is void;

(b) legitimated by reason of his parents' subsequent marriage;

(c) adopted; and

(d) 'otherwise treated in law as legitimate'.[374]

The resulting law can be confusing. For example, as will be seen,[375] s 2(1) of the Children Act 1989 states that: 'where a child's father and mother were married to each other at the time of his birth, they shall each have parental responsibility for the child', whereas according to s 2(2) if they were not so married then only the mother has such responsibility. The unsuspecting reader might think that these provisions mean what they say and conclude that parental responsibility is only automatically vested in a father if he is married to the mother at the time of the child's birth. In fact, however, he will also have responsibility if he had divorced his wife at the time of the child's birth, and he will acquire it automatically if he subsequently marries the mother.

Whether the law needed to have been so complex is debatable.[376] Despite its resulting complexity, in deference to the clear spirit of the 1987 Act, we shall avoid where possible labelling children and, as a matter of shorthand convenience, will refer to mothers or fathers as 'unmarried' when referring to parents of a child whose mother and father are not and have not been married to each other.

---

[373] By s 1(4) a child's birth is to be taken to include the period beginning with insemination resulting in his birth or, where there was no such insemination, his conception, and ends with his birth.

[374] This covers the case, for example, where the child is conceived through the placing in the woman of an embryo or sperm and eggs or of her artificial insemination and is born to a married woman and who therefore, by virtue of ss 27–29 of the Human Fertilisation and Embryology Act 1990, is treated as being the child of the woman and her husband.

[375] Below, p 408.

[376] See eg N Lowe 'The Family Reform Act 1987—Useful Reform but an Unhappy Compromise?' (1988) Denning LJ 77.

H THE CHANGING NATURE OF THE PARENT–CHILD RELATIONSHIP [377]

1 INTRODUCTION

Like society's views about the role of the family and of the individual members within the unit, the legal attitude towards the parent–child relationship has not remained static. The principal catalyst for legal change in the past has been the rise of individualism, first with respect to women and then, perhaps even more important, with respect to children.[378] With regard to the former, the growing calls for women's rights during the nineteenth century led in the end to the fundamental change that, whereas formerly parental rights were vested in the father (at any rate in respect of legitimate children), they are now shared between the father and the mother. The growing acceptance that a child is a person in his own right[379] led first to concern about his welfare and protection and, more recently, to the recognition that in certain circumstances at least he might have rights of his own. This in turn has led to a fundamental change in the nature of parental authority. In the past it was accurate to think of the parental position in terms of rights and duties, for at common law fathers had almost complete autonomy over their legitimate children, and their interest was akin to a proprietorial one;[380] by the 1980s, however, the emphasis had clearly shifted towards parental responsibility,[381] which position is now firmly entrenched in the Children Act 1989.

Although the overall effect of these developments has been to weaken the parents' position, it would be a mistake to infer that the issue of parental responsibility is no longer important. On the contrary, the position of parents remains of key importance in English law. Indeed, it is through the medium of parental responsibility that the law in effect recognises the general *right* of parents both to bring up their own children and to a large extent to do so in their own way.[382] We discuss in detail the concept of parental responsibility in Chapter 8, but we conclude this chapter by examining the changing nature of the parent–child relationship.

---

[377] See generally S Cretney, *Family Law in the Twentieth Century* ch 16 and N Lowe 'The Legal Position of Parents and Children in English Law' [1994] Singapore Journal of Legal Studies 332.

[378] The legal and social background to these developments is well summarised by S Maidment *Child Custody and Divorce* (1985) chs 4 and 5.

[379] There are those who maintain that until the seventeenth century the concept of childhood did not exist: see eg Ariès *Centuries of Childhood*, though this view has not escaped criticism. See the references in Maidment, above, at 91–2.

[380] See further below. Ironically, the common law has not been entirely immutable: see, for instance, *R v D* [1984] AC 778, HL, where in holding that even a father could be guilty of the common law offence of kidnapping his own child, Lord Brandon said (at 805), 'The common law, however, while generally immutable in its principles . . . is not immutable in the way it adapts those principles in a radically changing world and against the background of radically changed social conventions and conditions.'

[381] See eg Woolf J in *Gillick v West Norfolk and Wisbech Area Health Authority* [1984] QB 581 at 596, who said that the interests of parents are more accurately described as responsibilities and duties.

[382] Note that in Scotland the Children (Scotland) Act 1995, s 2(1) expressly provides for parents to have 'the rights' inter alia 'to control, direct or guide, in a manner appropriate to the stage of development of the child, the child's upbringing'. See further below at p 374.

2 THE INITIAL STRENGTH OF THE FATHER'S POSITION

(a) Legitimate children

The position at common law

Common law recognised the natural duties of protecting and maintaining one's legitimate minor children, and although the machinery for enforcing these duties was almost wholly ineffective, nevertheless they could properly be regarded as unenforceable legal obligations.[383] Moreover, it is obvious that, at any rate in early law, these duties could be performed only if the parent actually had the custody of the child, and in many cases the father would be the only member of the family who would be physically capable of carrying them out. Consequently, it is not surprising to discover that his duty to protect carried with it the correlative right to the custody of all minor children and that this right was absolute even against the mother, except in the rare cases where the father's conduct was such as gravely to imperil the children's life, health or morals. Custody carried with it many rights and powers in addition to care and control. A father was entitled to the services of his children in his custody and to correct them by administering reasonable corporal punishment. He alone might determine the form of their religious and secular education. Whilst his powers were never as wide as those of the paterfamilias in Roman law, the same fundamental approach is apparent. Physical control represented the kernel of this right; without it the others could not be enforced, and the procedural machinery of the common law was such that only his right could be specifically enforced by the writ of habeas corpus.

At common law, therefore, the father was entitled to the legal custody of his legitimate children until they reached the age of 21,[384] but his rights could be lost if to enforce them would probably lead to the physical or moral harm of the child,[385] or if his claim was not made bona fide.[386] After his death, the mother was entitled to the legal custody of her minor children for nurture,[387] but even this right was superseded after 1660 if the father appointed a testamentary guardian under the provisions of the Tenures Abolition Act.[388] Common law accorded no other right to the mother as such, and so absolute against her were the father's rights that he could lawfully claim from her possession even a child at the breast.[389]

The intervention of equity

The common law position was tempered by the intervention of equity. The jurisdiction of equity to intervene between parent and child is derived from the prerogative power of the

---

383 For a more detailed account see P Pettit 'Parental Control and Guardianship' in Graveson and Crane (eds) A Century of Family Law (1957) ch 4.

384 Thomasset v Thomasset [1894] P 295, CA; Re Agar-Ellis (1883) 24 Ch D 317, CA.

385 Such as apprehension of cruelty or grossly immoral or profligate conduct: Re Andrews (1873) LR 8 QB 153 at 158.

386 If his purpose was to hand the child over to another, for example: Re Turner (1872) 41 LJQB 142.

387 R v Clarke (1857) 7 E & B 186 at 200.   388 See the 7th edition of this work at p 350.

389 R v De Manneville (1804) 5 East 221—a father who had separated from his wife forcibly removed an eight-month child while it was actually at the breast and carried it away almost naked in an open carriage in inclement weather. The court, in upholding his right to custody, said it would draw no inferences to the disadvantage of the father. See also R v Greenhill (1836) 4 Ad & El 624—a father's right to custody of his three daughters aged five and under was upheld notwithstanding he was living with an adulteress and nothing could be said against the mother. The children went to live with their paternal grandmother.

Crown as parens patriae to interfere to protect any person within the jurisdiction not fully sui juris. This power was exercised by the Lord Chancellor, and although it fell into abeyance when the Court of Wards was set up in 1540, successive Chancellors began to use their powers more and more extensively when this court was abolished in 1660.[390] From the Court of Chancery the jurisdiction passed to the High Court under the Judicature Acts of 1873 and 1875.

One advantage that equity had over the common law was that its procedure was much better adapted to deal with disputes concerning children. Common law, limited as it was to the issue of a writ of habeas corpus, could only enforce the right to physical control; equity, on the other hand, acts in personam, so that it could not only make orders concerning, for example, the child's education, but also effectively ensure that they were carried out. A further step that could be taken was to have the child made a ward of court.[391] This procedure had a number of advantages. Not only could the person to whom care and control was given always turn to the court for advice, but the ward remained under the permanent control of the court during minority, so that any dereliction of duty on the part of the carer and any interference with the ward were punishable as a contempt of court. Furthermore, the court could give care and control of the child to his own parent, which meant that the child would remain in the latter's possession whilst the court could ensure that the parental powers were exercised in the child's best interests.

The increasing influence of equity[392]

At first the intervention of equity scarcely had any impact upon the father's position. It left untouched the common law duties of a parent and indeed gave prima facie effect to the father's right to custody of his legitimate children, unless he had forfeited it by his immoral or cruel conduct, or was seeking to enforce it capriciously or arbitrarily. As Cotton LJ said in Re Agar-Ellis:[393]

'This court holds this principle—that when, by birth, a child is subject to a father, it is for the general interest of families, and for the general interest of children, and really for the interest of the particular infant, that the Court should not, except in very extreme cases, interfere with the discretion of the father, but leave to him the responsibility of exercising that power which nature has given him by the birth of the child.'

On the other hand there was a growing view,[394] which ultimately prevailed, that the welfare of the child was the first consideration and equity would not hesitate to deprive a

[390] Holdsworth History of English Law, vi 648. The Court of Wards was set up by the 32 Hen 8, c 45, and abolished by the Tenures Abolition Act 1660.

[391] For the history and development of wardship see N Lowe and R White Wards of Court (2nd edn, 1986), ch 1 and J Seymour 'Parens Patriae and Wardship Powers: Their Nature and Origins' (1994) 14 Ox J of Legal Studies 159. Wardship is discussed further in Chapter 16.

[392] See N Lowe 'The House of Lords and the Welfare Principle' in C Bridge (ed) Family Law Towards the Millennium—Essays for P M Bromley (1997) 125 and 127–34.

[393] (1883) 24 Ch D 317, at 334, CA in which the father's right to custody was upheld and communication with her mother prevented on the grounds that his daughter's affection for him might thereby be alienated.

[394] Arguably the 'germ' of the welfare principle was sown in two early House of Lords' decisions, Johnstone v Beattie (1843) 10 Cl & Fin 42 and Stuart v Marquis of Bute (1861) 9 HL Cas 440, both of which concerned guardians rather than parents.

father of his rights if it would clearly be contrary to the child's interests to give effect to them. In the words of Lord Esher MR in *R v Gyngall*:[395]

'The court is placed in a position by reason of the prerogative of the Crown to act as supreme parent of the child, and must exercise that jurisdiction in the manner in which a wise, affectionate, and careful parent would act for the welfare of the child. The natural parent in the particular case may be affectionate, and may be intending to act for the child's good, but may be unwise, and may not be doing what a wise, affectionate, and careful parent would do. The Court may say in such a case that, although they can find no misconduct on the part of the parent, they will not permit that to be done with the child which a wise, affectionate, and careful parent would not do. The court must, of course, be very cautious in regard to the circumstances under which they will interfere with the parental right ... The court must exercise this jurisdiction with great care, and can only act when it is shown that either the conduct of the parent, or the description of the person he is, or the position in which he is placed, is such as to render it not merely better, but—I will not say "essential", but—clearly right for the welfare of the child in some very serious and important respect that the parent's rights should be suspended or superseded; but ... where it is so shown, the Court will exercise its jurisdiction accordingly.'

Hence, although originally equity interfered with the father's rights hardly less readily than the common law, by the end of the nineteenth century it would do so if there was any threat of physical or moral harm to the child; and if a father once abandoned or abdicated his right, he would not be allowed to reassert it arbitrarily if this would be contrary to the child's interests.[396]

As in other fields, equity ensured that, where its own rules were in conflict with those of common law, the former should prevail. It would not only grant an injunction to restrain a person from applying for a writ of habeas corpus to obtain the custody of a child,[397] but would also prevent a person who had already obtained the writ from interfering with the child if this was not in his interests.[398] As in the case of other conflicts between law and equity, the Judicature Act 1873 expressly provided that the rules of equity relating to the custody and education of minors should prevail over those of common law.[399] Notwithstanding this enjoinder, it seems evident that on occasion at least the courts continued to apply common law principles at the expense of equity even into the twentieth century.[400] Moreover, it seems fair to say that at the end of the nineteenth century, notwithstanding the growing influence of equity, the courts remained essentially 'parent focused', though

---

[395] [1893] 2 QB 232 at 241–2, CA. See also *Re O'Hara* [1900] 2 IR 232, CA; *Official Solicitor v K* [1965] AC 201, HL.

[396] See *Re O'Hara*, above, at 240–1; *Re Fynn* (1848) 2 De G & Sm 457 at 474–5.

[397] Per Lindley LJ in *R v Barnardo, Jones's Case* [1891] 1 QB 194 at 210, CA.

[398] *Andrews v Salt* (1873) 8 Ch App 622.

[399] Section 25(10) (now the Supreme Court Act 1981 s 49). But even before this the common law courts recognised the superiority of the jurisdiction of the Court of Chancery to the extent that, if proceedings were pending in the latter court, an application for habeas corpus would be stayed until the decision of Chancery was known: *Wellesley v Duke of Beaufort* (1827) 2 Russ 1 at 25–6, *R v Isley* (1836) 5 Ad & El 441.

[400] See eg *Re Agar-Ellis*, above, and *R v New* (1904) 20 TLR 583; see further, n 404 below.

undoubtedly the seeds had been sown for the development of the welfare principle which would eventually take precedence over parents' rights.

(b) The position with regard to illegitimate children

At common law a child born outside marriage was filius nullius and consequently none of the legal powers or duties which flowed from the relationship of parent and legitimate child was accorded him or his parents.[401] This meant, inter alia, that the father could not claim custody.[402] Eventually it became accepted that the right of control vested in the mother,[403] who indeed as against third parties was in as strong a position as the father in respect of his legitimate children.[404]

Although, as we have seen,[405] most of the legal disabilities attached to illegitimacy have now been removed by statute, it remains the case that unless he subsequently acquires it by being formally registered as the father, by court order or by agreement, parental responsibility is vested in the mother to the exclusion of the father, even where the latter's paternity is not in doubt.[406]

3 THE STRENGTHENING OF THE MOTHER'S POSITION

The inevitable corollary of the strength of the father's position was the weakness of the mother's in respect of legitimate children. However, during the nineteenth century Parliament intervened in a series of statutes, the effect of which was to whittle down the father's rights further and also to give the mother positive rights to custody which even equity did not accord to her. The history of this change in attitude can best be seen by a brief examination of the principal provisions of each statute.

(a) Talfourd's Act 1839

This Act marks a decisive point in the history of family law, for it empowered the Court of Chancery to give the mother custody of her children until they reached the age of seven and access to them until they came of age. But the Act specifically provided that no order was to be made if the mother had been guilty of adultery.

(b) Custody of Infants Act 1873

This extended the principle of Talfourd's Act by empowering the court to give the mother custody until the child reached the age of 16. It did not, however, repeat the proviso relating to her adultery. The Act provided that arrangements as to custody or control in separation deeds (which had formerly been held void as contrary to public policy) were to be enforceable so long as they were for the child's interests.

---

[401] Blackstone *Commentaries* i, 458–9.   [402] See eg *R v Soper* (1793) 5 Term Rep 278.

[403] See eg *Barnardo v McHugh* [1891] AC 388, HL, in which an unmarried mother successfully invoked habeas corpus proceedings following Dr Barnardo's failure to deliver her illegitimate son to a person named by her.

[404] See eg *R v New*, above, in which the Court of Appeal upheld a mother's right of custody to her illegitimate daughter, as against foster parents with whom the child had been living for 10 years, to the extent of removing the child and placing her in a Church of England Home where no one would be allowed to visit her until she had been there for two years.

[405] Above, p 346.   [406] See now the Children Act 1989 s 2 (1)–(2), discussed below, p 409.

(c) Guardianship of Infants Act 1886

Neither of these two earlier Acts gave mothers rights as such, but were concerned to extend the court's discretion to grant orders in the mother's favour. However, a third Act, the Guardianship of Infants Act 1886, not only extended judicial discretion by empowering the court to give the mother custody of her children until they reached the age of 21, but also stopped the father from defeating the mother's right after his death by appointing a testamentary guardian and enacted that the mother was to act jointly with any guardian so appointed. Furthermore, for the first time it gave limited powers to a mother to appoint testamentary guardians.

(d) Twentieth century developments

Although, as we shall see, the move to establish maternal rights proved to be of passing significance, with attention becoming more focused on the child's welfare, the process of equalising parental rights continued in the twentieth century. The Guardianship of Infants Act 1925 provided that in any proceedings before any court[407] neither the father nor the mother should be regarded as having a claim superior to the other in respect of the custody or upbringing of the child.[408] It also gave the mother the same right to appoint testamentary guardians as the father. The Guardianship Act 1973 gave each parent (of a legitimate child) equal and separately exercisable rights. Finally, with the abolition by s 2(4) of the Children Act 1989 of the archaic rule that during his lifetime the father was the sole guardian of his legitimate child, it can now be said that the legal position of married parents with respect to their children is equal.[409]

4 THE INCREASING RECOGNITION OF THE CHILD'S POSITION

(a) The evolution and development of the welfare principle[410]

The position before 1925

A striking feature of the early law was its apparent lack of concern for the child. By the end of the last century, however, there seemed to be a growing awareness of the child's welfare, possibly triggered by the development starting in the mid-nineteenth century that children should have a right to basic education and the general rise of individualism.[411] For example, under the Custody of Infants Act 1873 a parental agreement about custody could

---

[407] Jurisdiction to make orders relating to custody etc, which had formerly been exercisable only by the High Court and (since 1886) by county courts, was extended (subject to certain exceptions) to magistrates' courts. See above p 13.

[408] This direction was repeated in s 1 of the Guardianship of Minors Act 1971, but as Baroness Hale observed in *Re J (A Child)(Custody Rights: Jurisdiction)* [2005] UK HL 40, [2005] 3 WLR 14 at [18], the proposition that the court should disregard whether the claim of the father was superior to that of the mother and vice versa was regarded as 'too obvious' to require repetition in s 1(1) of the Children Act 1989.

[409] Note, however, that in relation to unborn children fathers have no rights: see *Paton v British Pregnancy Advisory Service Trustees* [1979] QB 276, and *C v S* [1988] QB 135, CA, discussed below, p 429.

[410] See generally N Lowe 'The House of Lords and the Welfare Principle', above, n 392, 127ff; Maidment *Child Custody and Divorce* ch 4. See also J Hall 'The Waning of Parental Rights' [1972B] CLJ 248.

[411] See further I Pinchbeck and M Hewitt *Children in English Society* Vol 1 (1969) and Vol 2 (1973).

not be enforced if the court did not think that it was for the child's benefit. Further, the Guardianship of Infants Act 1886 directed the court to have regard to the child's welfare as well as to the conduct and wishes of the parents when deciding custody applications. The most obviously child-centred statute was the Custody of Children Act 1891, which was passed as the direct result of a number of cases in which parents had succeeded in recovering from Dr Barnardo children whom they had placed in his now famous 'homes', or whom they had abandoned and he had taken in. It provided that if a parent had abandoned or deserted his child or allowed him to be brought up by, and at the expense of, another person, school, institution or local authority, in such circumstances as to show that he was unmindful of his parental duties, he had to prove that he was fit to have custody of the child claimed.

The more enduring development, however, was judicially inspired. We have already noted[412] equity's changing attitude during the nineteenth century, beginning with a marked reluctance to interfere with a father's right to custody and ending with its increasing readiness to interfere if it was in the child's interests to do so.[413] It is evident that during the early part of the twentieth century still more weight was being placed upon the child's welfare.[414]

A key case in this respect is *Ward v Laverty*,[415] in which a paternal great-aunt of three orphaned children applied for a writ of habeas corpus with a view to the children being placed in the custody of their paternal relatives and being brought up, according to their deceased father's wishes as set out in his will, as Roman Catholics. At the time of the application the children were living with their maternal grandparents and being brought up as Presbyterians. They had been brought there nearly four years previously by their mother when she left their father before his death. Immediately after leaving her husband she removed her eldest daughter from the Catholic school she had been attending and sent her instead to a Protestant school. After his death the mother herself reverted to being a Presbyterian and died a member of that church nearly three years later. Viscount Cave LC, with whom the other Law Lords agreed, considered the law to be well settled:[416]

'On the question of religion in which a young child is to be brought up, the wishes of the father of the child are to be considered; and if there is no other matter to be taken into account, then according to the practice of our Courts, the wishes of the father prevail. But that rule is subject to the condition, that the wishes of the father only prevail if they are not displaced by considerations relating to the welfare of the children themselves. *It is the welfare of the children, which according to rules which are now well accepted, forms the paramount consideration in these cases.* Some of the earlier judgments contain sentences in which perhaps greater stress is laid upon the father's wishes than would be placed upon them now, but in the more recent decisions and especially since the passing of the Guardianship of

---

[412] Above, p 352.

[413] Maidment, above, at pp 99–100 argues that this readiness was promoted by the provisions of the Guardianship of Infants Act 1886.

[414] In fact the first recorded judicial use of the word 'paramount' in this context seems to be in *Re A and B (Infants)* [1897] 1 Ch 786 at 792, per Lopes LJ; see Lord Upjohn in *J v C* [1970] AC 668 at 722C. Note also the reference to the paramountcy of the child's welfare in *Scott v Scott* [1913] AC 417, HL at 437 per Viscount Haldane.

[415] [1925] AC 101.   [416] At 108.

Infants Act, 1886, s 5 of which Act shows the modern feeling in these matters, the greater stress is laid upon the welfare and happiness of the children' (emphasis added).

Viscount Cave observed that before the mother's death the father's family had shown little interest in the children and even in their evidence before the courts did not profess any affection for them. In contrast, the children were happy where they were and the grand-parents were fond of them and ready and willing to care for them. The eldest child was found to be bright and intelligent and had strong convictions in favour of the Presbyterian faith. Moreover, she was happy where she was. The court had no doubt that her welfare was best served by leaving her with her maternal grandparents. With regard to the two younger children the court considered that they were too young to have religious convictions, but it was accepted that it was not for their welfare to be separated from their elder sister nor from their loving grandparents. Accordingly, these considerations were held to 'prevail over the wishes of the father'.

Ward v Laverty has generally been overlooked by academic writers,[417] yet by applying a child-centred approach to a habeas corpus application, what it seemed to establish was that, no matter what jurisdiction was being invoked, the court was bound to apply the paramountcy of the child's welfare test to resolving the dispute. Whether Viscount Cave was right to say that it was 'settled law' that the child's welfare was 'paramount' is debatable[418] but, given that this was a House of Lords decision, it was surely authoritative in its own right.

Perhaps one reason why Ward v Laverty has never really been regarded as a leading decision was that it was an appeal from Northern Ireland.[419] Alternatively, it may have been thought to have been limited to the resolution of disputes concerning the religious upbringing of children. More likely, however, it may have been thought to have been overtaken by s 1 of the Guardianship of Infants Act 1925,[420] which provided that in—

'. . . any proceedings before any court [in which] . . . the custody or upbringing of an infant or the administration of any property belonging to or held on trust for an infant, or the application of the income thereof, is in question, the court, in deciding that question, shall regard the welfare of the infant as the first and paramount consideration.'

Whatever the true position was before 1925, the striking difference between this Act and that of 1886 with regard to the weight to be placed on the child's welfare is evidence of quite a remarkable change of thought. Whether the 1925 Act was intended to do anything more than further the process of equalising parental rights, whilst at the same time extending the courts' discretionary power to override the absolute rights of the father in custody cases, seems debatable.[421] Furthermore, it now seems clear that at that time

---

[417] See the analysis by Lowe, above, at 132.

[418] See P Pettit 'Parental Control and Guardianship' in Graveson and Crane (eds) A Century of Family Law ch 4 at 76.

[419] Though this should surely be irrelevant, as a decision of the House of Lords from Northern Ireland is as binding as an appeal from England.

[420] Which ironically, as Lord Upjohn observed in J v C [1970] AC 668 at 723, was destined never to apply to Northern Ireland.

[421] See below, p 359 n 427.

Parliament was certainly not intending the child's welfare to be the court's *sole* consideration.[422]

J v C [423]

Notwithstanding *Ward v Laverty*, the courts began to interpret s 1 of the 1925 Act narrowly and indeed, prior to the House of Lords' decision in *J v C*, there remained Court of Appeal authority[424] for saying that the Act only applied to disputes between fathers and mothers over their legitimate children, and apparent authority[425] for saying that the wishes of an unimpeachable parent were to be preferred to the welfare of the child. Both propositions, however, were firmly laid to rest by the House of Lords in *J v C*. In that case a Spanish couple came to England looking for work. Whilst here the mother gave birth to a boy, but because she was ill the baby went to live with English foster parents. When the couple later returned to Spain they took the boy with them, but whilst they were in Spain the boy's health deteriorated and at the parents' request he was returned to the foster parents in England. The parents meanwhile went to West Germany to look for work and, having successfully improved their economic position, returned to Spain some two years later. Whilst in West Germany the parents made no attempt to contact their son and were only prompted to seek his return after receiving a somewhat tactless letter from the foster parents describing how 'English' the boy had become. The ensuing proceedings proved protracted and in any event the parents were poorly advised and only belatedly formally applied for the return of the child. Consequently, it took a further five years before the case was heard by the House of Lords. By that time the boy, who had spent all but 18 months of his 10½ years with the foster parents in England, had become well integrated into the family. Moreover, he had been brought up as an English boy, spoke little Spanish and scarcely knew his parents. On the other hand, the Spanish parents now lived in 'an entirely suitable' modern three-bedroomed flat in Madrid. The father had a good steady job and the mother's health was completely restored.[426]

At first instance Ungoed-Thomas J awarded care and control to the English foster parents, and this decision was unanimously upheld by the Court of Appeal. On appeal to the Lords it was accepted that the decision was only challengeable if it could be shown that the trial judge had exercised his discretion upon some wrong principle. Accordingly, it was submitted that united parents were prima facie entitled to the custody of their infant children and the court should only deprive them of care and control if they were unfitted by character, conduct or position in life to have this control. Thus in the case of

---

[422] See the scholarly analysis of the history of the 1925 legislation by S Cretney ' "What will the Women Want Next?" The Struggle for Power within the Family 1925–1975' (1996) 112 LQR 110 at 129–31, who convincingly shows that it was definitely intended not to be the sole consideration, since, ironically, it was Viscount Cave who had the word 'sole' removed from the Bill and replaced by the words 'first and paramount'.

[423] [1970] AC 668.

[424] *Re Carroll* [1931] 1 KB 317 in which the Court of Appeal upheld the mother's wish to remove her illegitimate daughter from a Protestant Adoption Society so as to place her with another Society where she would be brought up as a Catholic, notwithstanding the lower court's finding that the child's welfare would be best served by leaving her where she was.

[425] *Re Thain* [1926] Ch 676, although in *J v C* [1970] AC 668 at 711, Lord MacDermott considered the headnote misleading.

[426] All this was in stark contrast to the position when the parents first returned to Spain after leaving England, when the father was a lowly paid worker and the family lived in what were virtually slum conditions.

unimpeachable parents (which for the purposes of argument the appellants were assumed to be) the court should, save in very exceptional cases, give care and control to those parents. It was consequentially argued that, notwithstanding s 1 of the Guardianship of Infants Act 1925 which, it was contended, only applied to disputes between parents and not between parents and non-parents, the child's welfare was not the first and paramount consideration. The House of Lords unanimously rejected these submissions.

All their Lordships were agreed that s 1 of the 1925 Act was not confined, as the preamble seemed to imply,[427] to disputes between parents, but was of 'universal application', and insofar as *Re Carroll*[428] held otherwise, it was overruled. As Lord MacDermott (with whom Lord Pearson expressly agreed) pointed out, the wording of s 1 seemed to be deliberately wide and general, relating to *any* proceedings before any court and, so worded,[429] 'would apply to cases, such as the present, between parents and strangers'.

The significance of *J v C* cannot be over-emphasised. First, it established that s 1 of the 1925 Act applied as much to disputes over a child's upbringing between parents and third parties as it did to disputes between parents.[430] Indeed, it is clear that the decision was meant to have a general application to proceedings concerning the upbringing of children. As Lord Guest put it, s 1 had 'universal application'. Secondly, it unequivocally established that the child's welfare is so overwhelmingly important that it can outweigh the interests of even so-called unimpeachable parents in seeking to look after their own child against a third party. A fortiori it is the dominant consideration in disputes between parents.

Subsequent applications of J v C

Shortly after the decision in *J v C*, s 1 of the 1925 Act was repealed and re-enacted in s 1 of the Guardianship of Minors Act 1971. The influence of *J v C* became more apparent. For

---

427 The preamble stated: 'Whereas Parliament by the Sex Disqualification (Removal) Act 1919, and various other enactments has sought to establish equality in law between the sexes, and it is expedient that this principle should obtain with respect to the guardianship of infants and the rights and responsibilities conferred thereby'. However, as their Lordships pointed out, relying on *A-G v Prince Ernest Augustus of Hanover* [1957] AC 436, preambles cannot control the ambit of sections of an Act. Interestingly, notwithstanding this unanimous view, in the later House of Lords decision, *A v Liverpool City Council* [1982] AC 363 at 371, Lord Wilberforce described the provision as a 'sex equality' enactment. See also in similar vein *Richards v Richards* [1984] AC 174 at 203, per Lord Hailsham LC. See also S Cretney ' "What will the Women Want Next?" The Struggle for Power within the Family 1925–1975', above, 128–33 who examines the Parliamentary history of s 1 and concludes 'It seems inconceivable that legislation which would have resulted in a child being kept from his family by an outsider able to offer a better upbringing would have been well received in 1925; and this outcome was certainly unforeseen by anyone involved in drafting the 1925 Act.'

428 Above.   429 [1970] AC 668 at 710.

430 Nevertheless, the House of Lords overturned a decision of the lower courts to award primary residence to the former same-sex partner of the biological mother's two children after the mother had flouted the terms of a shared residence order. The House emphasised that the fact that a person is the natural parent (ie in this case, both the biological and psychological parent) of the children 'while raising no presumption in her favour, is undoubtedly an important and significant factor in determining what will be best for them now and in the future.' Per Baroness Hale of Richmond in *Re G (children) (residence; same-sex partner)* [2006] UKHL 43 at 44. Lord Nicholls of Birkenhead went further at para 2: 'in the ordinary way the rearing of a child by his or her biological parent can be expected to be in the child's best interests, both in the short term and also, importantly, in the longer term. I decry any tendency to diminish the significance of this factor. A child should not be removed from the primary care of his or her biolgoical parents without compelling reason.'

example, the Court of Appeal in *S (BD) v S(DJ) (Children: Care and Control)*[431] finally quashed the notion that the so-called 'unimpeachable parent' stood in a more favourable position as against the other who was guilty of matrimonial misconduct, and established in effect that the interests of justice as between the parents do not outweigh the welfare principle. In other words, if the welfare of the child so demands, he or she should be looked after by the so-called 'guilty' parent, however unjust the other will believe the decision to be. Hence, matrimonial misconduct is relevant only insofar as it reflects on that person as a parent. Furthermore, in *S (BD) v S (DJ)* Ormrod LJ (who was a great champion of children's welfare) deprecated the use of the term 'unimpeachable' parent in this context. As he said:[432]

'I have never known and still do not know what it means. It cannot mean a parent who is above criticism because there is no such thing. It might mean a parent against whom no matrimonial offence has been proved. If so it adds nothing to the record which is before the court and in any event is now outmoded. I think in truth it is really an advocate's phrase.'

In *Re B (A Minor) (Wardship: Sterilisation)*[433] the application of the welfare principle can be seen in another context. In that case an application was made to sanction the sterilisation of a 17-year-old girl who inter alia had a severely limited intellectual capability. Evidence was adduced that, while she had already been shown to be vulnerable to sexual approaches, she could not be placed on any contraceptive regime and was incapable of knowing the causal connection between intercourse and childbirth. It was further shown that she could not understand the nature of pregnancy nor what was involved in delivery. In sanctioning the operation notwithstanding its irreversible nature, the Law Lords unanimously rejected the argument based on the Canadian Supreme Court decision in *Re Eve*[434] and an earlier English High Court decision in *Re D (A Minor) (Wardship: Sterilisation)*[435] that, because what was in issue was 'non-therapeutic' treatment, the court had no power to act. As Lord Bridge put it:[436]

'To say that the court can never authorise sterilisation of a ward as being in her best interests would be patently wrong. To say that it can only do so if the operation is "therapeutic" as opposed to "non therapeutic" is to divert attention from the true issue, which is whether the operation is in the ward's best interest, and remove it to an area of arid semantic debate as to where the line is to be drawn between "therapeutic" and "non therapeutic" treatment.'

Similarly, Lord Oliver observed[437] that if—

'. . . the expression "non-therapeutic" was intended to exclude measures taken for the neces-sary protection from future harm of the person over whom the jurisdiction is exercisable, then I respectfully dissent from it for it seems to me to contradict what is the sole and paramount criterion for the exercise of the jurisdiction, viz the welfare and benefit of the ward.'

---

[431] [1977] Fam 109. See also *Re K (Minors) (Children Care and Control)* [1977] Fam 179, CA. See Hall [1977] CLJ 252.

[432] At 115–16. In *Re R (Minors) (Wardship: Jurisdiction)* (1981) 2 FLR 416 at 425, Ormrod LJ referred to the 'unimpeachable parent' as being in 'forensic limbo'.

[433] [1988] AC 199, HL.   [434] (1986) 31 DLR (4th) 1.

[435] [1976] Fam 185. See also N Lowe and R White *Wards of Court* (2nd edn) paras 7–6, note 6, and 7–11.

[436] [1988] AC at 205.   [437] At 212.

Further important reaffirmation of *J v C* was made by the House of Lords in *Re KD (A Minor) (Ward: Termination of Access)*,[438] in which a local authority sought the termination of a mother's already limited contact with her son, who for the previous four of his four-and-three-quarter years of life had been living with foster parents. It was argued for the mother that the right to see her son was a parental right which would only be displaced where the court was satisfied that the exercise of the right would be positively inimical to the interest of the child. It was further contended that this right had been affirmed as a fundamental human right under the European Convention on Human Rights. Both contentions were rejected. As Lord Oliver put it:[439]

'. . . the contention that a parent has a right of access was out of line with an approach which has been universally acted upon ever since the decision of your Lordships' House in *J v C*.'

In Lord Oliver's view, the law recognised the parent's position by taking it to be a normal assumption that a child benefits from having continued contact with both parents. Nevertheless that position must always be qualified by considerations of what is best for the welfare of the particular child in question. So understood, his Lordship could find nothing in the European Court of Human Rights' decision *R v UK*[440] which 'contradicts or casts any doubt upon that decision [ie in *J v C*] or which calls now for any re-appraisal of it by your Lordships'.

By the end of the 1980s it was clear that when called upon to determine a child's upbringing the courts were effectively treating the child's welfare as the sole consideration in the sense that all the circumstances of the case were weighed in the balance to determine what was in the best interests of the child concerned. Nevertheless the fact remained that under the 1971 Act the child's welfare was still expressed to be '*the first* and paramount interest'.

However, reflecting the fact that the words 'first and' had become redundant, the Children Act 1989 s 1(1) now simply states that:

'When a court determines any question with respect to—

(a) the upbringing of a child; or

(b) the administration of a child's property or the application of any income arising from it,

the child's welfare shall be the court's paramount consideration.'

We shall consider in more detail the history and application of s 1 in Chapter 10. Suffice to say here that the new formulation was neither intended nor has it in fact altered the pre–1989 Act position, though that is not to say that there have been no problems concerning its application, not least of which has been its compatibility with Human Rights following the implementation of the Human Rights Act 1998.[441]

---

[438] [1988] AC 806.   [439] Above at 827.

[440] (1988) 10 EHRR 74, [1988] 2 FLR 445 in which the United Kingdom was found to be in breach of Article 8 of the Convention (right of respect for family life) because under the law at the time parents had no means of challenging access decisions in relation to a child in local authority care. In fact, this and other European Court of Human Rights' decisions did cause the government to provide under s 34 of the Children Act 1989 a presumption of reasonable contact between a child in care and his family. See R White, P Carr and N Lowe *The Children Act in Practice* (3rd edn) para 1.7.

[441] See below p 451.

(b) Children's ability to make decisions for themselves [442]

Although the application of the welfare principle obviously dilutes parental authority it does not in itself give a child rights as such. Indeed, until the issue comes before the court, parents still generally have considerable authority over their children. There has, however, been a discernible trend towards the greater empowerment of children, though, as will be seen, English law has (so far) generally stopped short of giving children what are sometimes referred to as autonomy rights.

R v D [443]

In *R v D* the question was raised as to whether at common law a father could be guilty of kidnapping his own child. In his defence the father had sought to rely on the alleged paramountcy of his position at common law. In rejecting this defence the House of Lords, whilst acknowledging that it might well have succeeded in the nineteenth century, were not prepared to apply it in the case before them. As Lord Brandon put it:[444]

'The common law . . . while generally immutable in its principles, unless different principles are laid down by Statute, is not immutable in the way in which it adapts, develops and applies those principles in a radically changing world and against the background of radically changed social conventions.'

As his Lordship pointed out:

'. . . the paramountcy of a father's position in the family home [has] been progressively whittled away, until now, in the second half of the 20th century, [it] can be regarded as having disappeared altogether.'

Having rejected this defence, the House of Lords further considered whether the child's consent to removal would be a defence. In ruling that it could, Lord Brandon said:[445]

'I see no good reason why, in relation to the kidnapping of a child, it should not in all cases be the absence of the child's consent which is material, whatever its age may be. In the case of a very young child, it would not have the understanding or intelligence to give its consent, so that absence of consent would be a necessary inference from its age. In the case of an older child, however, it must, I think be a question of fact for a jury whether the child concerned has sufficient understanding and intelligence to give its consent . . . While the matter will always be for the jury alone to decide, I should not expect a jury to find at all frequently that a child under 14 had sufficient understanding and intelligence to give its consent.'

The significance of *R v D* is twofold. First, it puts the final nail in the coffin of the father's supremacy within the family even under the common law. Secondly, it accepts the proposition that children even as young as 14 might be competent to make some decisions for themselves. It is this latter point that became developed further in the next House of Lords decision, *Gillick v West Norfolk and Wisbech Area Health Authority*.

---

[442] See generally M Freeman *The Rights and Wrongs of Children* (1983), particularly ch 2; and J Fortin *Children's Rights and the Developing Law* (2nd edn, 2003), particularly ch 1.

[443] [1984] AC 778, HL, on which see N Lowe (1984) 134 NLJ 995.

[444] Above at 805.   [445] Above at 806.

Gillick v West Norfolk and Wisbech Area Health Authority[446]

Gillick concerned a government circular in which doctors were advised that in 'most unusual circumstances' it would be proper for them to give contraceptive advice and treatment to a girl under the age of 16 without her parents' knowledge or consent. The applicant, a mother of four daughters under the age of 16, sought a declaration that this was unlawful, because it infringed her parental right to be informed and to veto any medical treatment of her children, at any rate until they were 16.[447] The action failed and her contention about parental rights was rejected, because it was held that the law does not recognise any rule of absolute parental authority until a fixed age and that even with regard to contraceptive treatment a girl of sufficient maturity and understanding could give a valid consent. On this basis the circular could not be said to be unlawful, since girls of sufficient maturity, even if under the age of 16, could themselves consent to the contraceptive treatment. Indeed, the majority view seemed to be that as parental authority exists for the benefit of the child and not for the parent, it lasts only as long as a child needs protection, and will consequently end when the child is sufficiently mature to make the decision for himself. As Lord Scarman put it:[448]

'The underlying principle of the law ... is that parental right yields to the child's right to make his own decisions when he reaches a sufficient understanding and intelligence to be capable of making up his own mind on the matter requiring decisions.'

Of course, even under this analysis a crucial question is, when will a child be considered to have sufficient understanding to be considered what has since become known as '*Gillick* competent'? In part this will depend upon the nature of the issue involved. In the context of consenting to medical treatment, for example, it would not require much intelligence to appreciate that a broken leg needs mending whereas, as *Gillick* itself shows, considerable understanding is required in the case of consenting to the prescription of contraceptive treatment. In that context Lord Scarman said:[449]

'It is not enough that she should understand the advice which is being given: she must also have sufficient maturity to understand what is involved. There are moral and family questions, especially her relationship with her parents, long-term problems associated with the emotional impact of pregnancy and its termination; and there are risks to health of sexual intercourse at her age, risks which contraception may diminish but cannot eliminate.'

With respect to Lord Scarman this looks suspiciously like importing into this area of law the doctrine of informed consent, which in the context of the tort of negligence at least the House of Lords has rejected.[450] It may indeed be doubted whether many adults—let alone a child under the age of 16—could validly consent to contraceptive treatment under Lord Scarman's test. In practice it seems likely that consideration will only be given to whether

---

[446] [1986] AC 112, HL, for an extended analysis of which see Barton and Douglas, above, 118ff; Fortin *Children's Rights and the Developing Law*, above, chs 3 and 5; J Eekelaar (1986) 102 LQR 4; A Bainham 'The Balance of Power in Family Decisions' [1986] CLJ 262; and also J Eekelaar 'The Emergence of Children's Rights' [1986] 6 OJLS 161.

[447] When by reason of s 8 of the Family Law Reform Act 1969 children can give a valid consent.

[448] [1986] AC 112 at 184A.   [449] Above at 189.

[450] In *Sidaway v Board of Governors of the Bethlem Royal Hospital and the Maudsley Hospital* [1985] AC 871, HL. See also S Cretney *All ER Annual Review 1985* at 175.

the child has sufficient maturity to understand the advice.[451] Even this, however, will not be easy for a practitioner to judge.

It might have been supposed that once it is established that a *Gillick* competent child has consented to the proposed treatment, no further inquiry need be made and the continued involvement of the parent may be ignored. In fact, however, the *Gillick* decision does not go that far. It does not give doctors a carte blanche to prescribe contraceptives to girls under the age of 16. According to Lord Fraser,[452] as well as being satisfied that the girl understands his advice, the doctor must also be satisfied that he cannot persuade her to allow him to inform her parents, that she is very likely to begin or continue to have sexual intercourse with or without contraceptive treatment, that without the advice or treatment her health is likely to suffer and that her best interests require him to give the advice, treatment or both without parental consent. Even with respect to simpler treatment Lord Fraser seemed to contemplate some parental involvement. Hence, while he did not doubt the capacity of a 15-year-old to consent to having a broken arm set, he added that 'of course the consent of the parents should normally be asked.'[453]

Gillick was subsequently applied in *R (on the application of Axon) v Secretary of State for Health and another*[454] in which a parent unsuccessfully sought judicial review of a 2004 Department of Health document[455] advising that a medical professional can provide advice and treatment on sexual matters for young people under the age of 16 without the knowledge and consent of their parents. Interestingly, in so ruling, Silber J held, following Lord Scarman's judgment in *Gillick*, that where the young person understood the advice provided by the medical professional and its implication (ie had satisfied the '*Gillick* competence' test) the parent ceased to retain an Art 8 Convention right in relation to that decision.

Gillick—a false dawn?

Although *Gillick* may simply be seen as a further (albeit important) example of the diminution of parental authority in the eyes of English law, potentially it was of much greater significance, for it seemed to acknowledge that children themselves have the power to make their own decisions. Had this been how the decision was interpreted, then it might fairly have been described as a landmark of children's rights. However, as we shall now see, it has been subsequently restrictively interpreted, and for those who saw *Gillick* as establishing autonomy rights for mature children it has so far[456] proved a false dawn. The two leading cases are *Re R (A Minor) (Wardship: Medical Treatment)*[457] and *Re W (A Minor) (Medical Treatment: Court's Jurisdiction)*,[458] both decided by the Court of Appeal.

---

[451] Which is all Lord Fraser seemed to require: see *Gillick v West Norfolk and Wisbech Area Health Authority*, above, at 174.

[452] Above at 174. It must be a matter of doubt whether in practice a medical practitioner will always be so thorough as Lord Fraser's test demands.

[453] Ibid at 169 and 409 respectively.   [454] [2006] EWHC 37 (Admin), [2006] 1 FCR 175.

[455] 'Best Practice Guidance for Doctors and other Health Professionals on the Provision of Advice and Treatment to Young People under Sixteen on Contraception, Sexual and Reproductive Health'.

[456] See the interesting comments of Munby J in *Re Roddy (A Child)(Identification: Restriction on Publication)* [2003] EWHC 2927 (Fam), [2004] 2 FLR 949 at [57] and in *E (By Her Litigation Friend The Official Solicitor) v Channel Four and St Helens Borough Council* [2005] EWHC 1144 (Fam), [2005] 2 FLR 913 at [56].

[457] [1992] Fam 11, CA; G Douglas 'The Retreat from *Gillick*' (1992) 55 MLR 569.

[458] [1993] Fam 64, [1992] 4 All ER 627, CA; N Lowe and S Juss 'Medical Treatment—Pragmatism and the

Re R concerned a 15-year-old girl who had suffered emotional abuse and had become suicidal. Fears for her mental state led the local authority to intervene and a place was found for her at an adolescent psychiatric unit. Her condition was felt to warrant the use of sedatives and drugs. However, during a lucid period the girl indicated that she would refuse any such treatment. Despite the unit's insistence on the necessity of the treatment the local authority declined to consent and instead took the issue to court. Perhaps controversially, the court unanimously held that R lacked the necessary maturity to decide whether to take the medication on the basis that *'Gillick* competence' could not fluctuate on a day-to-day basis, so that the child is one day regarded as competent, while on another day she is not. Accordingly, the unanimous decision was to sanction the treatment. Lord Donaldson MR, however, went further. He held (obiter) that all *Gillick* had decided was that a competent child could consent to medical treatment but that it did not decide that such a child could veto medical treatment. In his view, both parents (and presumably anyone with parental responsibility) and the court retain the power to consent to treatment even of a *'Gillick* competent child', notwithstanding that the child has refused treatment. He considered that there are concurrent powers to consent (which he described as being 'keys which unlock the door') and only if *all* the 'key holders' fail or refuse to consent will a veto be treated as binding.

This important limitation on the effect of *Gillick* has since been confirmed in the second Court of Appeal case, *Re W*. This concerned a 16-year-old girl who suffered anorexia and who refused treatment. Her condition was such that without treatment she would shortly die. Because the child was 16 she had a statutory right (under Family Law Reform Act 1969 s 8)[459] to give a valid consent to treatment. The question was, however, did s 8 or *Gillick* give her an absolute power of veto? Again the Court of Appeal, though this time unanimously, held that neither s 8 nor *Gillick* could be considered to vest in the child a power of veto. Instead they held that the High Court could (and in this case, should) overrule the child's wishes. They rejected the argument that implicit in a right to consent must also be a power of veto. In so concluding, Lord Donaldson MR and Balcombe LJ acknowledged that Lord Scarman's reference to the termination of parental authority upon the child's reaching competence could be taken to suggest that the refusal of a child below the age of 16 to accept medical treatment was determinative. Both, however, doubted whether Lord Scarman meant anything more than that the child's parents lose their exclusive rights to consent upon the child becoming *'Gillick* competent.' Even if he had meant that such children have a right of veto, then both their Lordships thought he was wrong.[460] Rejecting

Search for Principle' (1993) 56 MLR 865; J Eekelaar 'White Coats and Flak Jackets—Doctors, Children and the Courts Again' (1993) 109 LQR 182; and J Masson '*Re W*: Appealing from a golden cage' (1993) 5 Jo of Child Law 37. See also *Re P (Medical Treatment: Best Interests)* [2005] EWHC 2327 (Fam), [2004] 2 FLR 1117 (in which Johnson J, though accepting that a refusal of medical treatment by a child can be determinative, nevertheless overrode a 16 year old Jehovah's Witnesses objections by permitting the hospital to administer blood or blood treatments provided there was no other form of treatment available); *Re M (Medical Treatment: Consent)* [1999] 2 FLR 1097 (in which Johnson J overrode an intelligent 15 year old girl's refusal to have a heart transplant because she did not want someone else's heart). Note also *Re L (Medical Treatment: Gillick Competence* [1998] 2 FLR 810 at 813E per Sir Stephen Brown B (14-year-old Jehovah's Witness found not to be competent but even if she had been the court would have overridden her wishes) and *Re C (Detention: Medical Treatment)* [1997] 2 FLR 180.

[459] Discussed in detail at p 306 of the 8th edition of this work.

[460] But note the contrary view taken by Silber J in *R (on the application of Axon) v Secretary of State for Health* [2006] EWHC 37 (Admin), [2006] 1 FCR 175.

the notion that the child's views were determinative did not mean that the court would pay no regard to the child's wishes. On the contrary, as Lord Donaldson MR said, 'good parenting involves giving minors as much rope as they can handle without an unacceptable risk that they will hang themselves'. Yet, as Balcombe LJ said, 'if the court's powers are to be meaningful there must come a point at which the courts, whilst not disregarding the child's wishes, can override them in the child's own best interest, objectively considered'. In his view, such a point comes when the child, in refusing treatment, is threatened with death or severe permanent injury. He cited in support Ward J's trenchant comment in *Re E (A Minor)*[461] that the court, 'in exercising its prerogative of protection, should be very slow to allow an infant to martyr himself'.

Not surprisingly, these decisions have generated considerable comment, for they bring into sharp relief the issue of allowing competent children to make decisions for themselves (ie whether they have autonomy rights) as against the paternalistic approach of protecting them from doing (at any rate, irreparable) harm to themselves. As can be seen, the Court of Appeal favour the latter approach, though one of the intrinsic difficulties of doing so is being able to accept that a child can be competent to give a valid consent yet not be competent to exercise a power of veto.[462] One suggestion, however,[463] is that based on the premise that, since a doctor will act in the best interests of his patient, it is perfectly rational for the law to facilitate this and hence allow a *Gillick* competent' child to give a valid consent, and also to protect the child against parents opposed to what is professionally considered to be in his or her best medical interests. In contrast, it is surely right for the law to be reluctant to allow a *child* to be able to veto treatment designed for his or her benefit, particularly if a refusal would lead to the child's death or permanent damage. In other words, the clear and consistent policy of the law is to protect children against wrong-headed parents and against themselves with the final safeguard, as *Re W* unequivocally establishes, of giving the court the last word in cases of dispute.

(c) The international dimension [464]

Discussion of the legal relationship between parent and child can no longer focus solely on the domestic position. Regard must also be had to international instruments and in particular to the UN Convention on the Rights of the Child 1989, to which the UK is a party, and to the initiative of the Council of Europe, which are beginning to have increasing influence.

So far as the UN Convention is concerned, two Articles in particular may be noted. First, Art 3(1) provides:

[461] (1990) 9 BMLR 1.

[462] With respect to Lord Donaldson MR, it is difficult to follow his distinction between consenting to and determining treatment.

[463] See Lowe and Juss, above, 871–2.

[464] See inter alia Barton and Douglas, above, 34–43; Fortin, above, ch 2; G Van Bueren *The International Law on the Rights of the Child* (1993); S Detrich 'Family Rights Under the United Nations Convention on the Rights of the Child' and K O'Donnell 'Parent-Child Relationships Within the European Convention', both in N Lowe and G Douglas (eds) *Families Across Frontiers* (1996) at 95–114, and 135–50 respectively.

'In all actions concerning children, whether undertaken by public or private social welfare institutions, courts of law, administrative authorities or legislative bodies, the best interests of the child shall be a primary consideration.'

As can be seen, this Article provides an international obligation to apply the best interests of the child test and as such is clearly similar to the paramountcy test under s 1(1) of the Children Act 1989. It may be observed, however, that in one sense Art 3 is narrower than the domestic provision, in that the enjoinder to regard the best interests as *a primary* consideration is not as strong as to regard the child's welfare as the *paramount* consideration. On the other hand, Art 3, by applying to administrative authorities and legislative bodies, is wider than s 1(1) which only applies to court proceedings.[465]

The second important Article is Art 12 which provides:

'1. States parties should assure to the child who is capable of forming his or her own views the right to express those view freely in all matters affecting the child, *the view of the child being given due weight in accordance with the age and maturity of the child* [emphasis added].

2. For this purpose the child shall in particular be provided the opportunity to be heard in any judicial and administrative proceedings affecting the child, either directly, or through a representative or an appropriate body, in a manner consistent with the procedural rules of national law.'

It will be seen that Art 12(1) stops short of giving even mature children autonomy rights. Although the precise meaning of the phrase 'the views of the child being given due weight in accordance with the age and maturity of the child' is unclear, it is submitted that the English position of reserving the power of the court to override the wishes of a *Gillick* competent child does not breach Art 12(1). Neither *Re R* nor *Re W* establishes that the views of such competent children are ignored; far from it: considerable stress was placed on the need to have the greatest regard to such views. Further, as we shall see,[466] s 1(3)(a) of the Children Act 1989 specifically directs the court, at any rate in contested private law proceedings for s 8 orders, to have regard to the ascertainable wishes and feelings of the child. The Act also provides a mechanism for children of sufficient understanding to initiate proceedings in their own right.[467] Although these provisions go a long way to satisfying the requirements of Art 12, it can be argued[468] that a possible breach could be occasioned in cases where the parents are agreed and the views of children are consequently overlooked.[469]

The European Convention on Human Rights has not proved a particularly effective vehicle for the promotion of children's rights as such.[470] Nevertheless, there have been some important initiatives by the Council of Europe, as for example, through its 1990

---

[465] Though local authorities have a general duty to safeguard and promote the welfare of children in need in their area and of those they are 'looking after' under s 17 and s 22 of the Children Act 1989 (discussed below at pp 699 and 796).

[466] Below, p 584.   [467] Children Act 1989 s 10(2)(b), discussed below, pp 503ff.

[468] See N Lowe 'The Legal Position of Parents and Children in English Law' [1994] Singapore Journal of Legal Studies 332 and 346.

[469] See further below, p 478.

[470] See the interesting discussion by Fortin, above pp 52–63.

Recommendation[471] inter alia to appoint a special ombudsman for children and its 1996 Recommendation[472] to encourage governments to adopt co-ordinated and child-focused policies at national and local levels. One result of these initiatives has been the drafting of the European Convention on the Exercise of Children's Rights 1996, which is aimed at supplementing the UN Convention by assisting children to exercise their substantive rights set out in the Convention. At the time of writing, however, the UK has not signed that Convention, nor has it followed all the Recommendations.

[471] Recommendation No 1121 on the *Rights of Children.*
[472] Recommendation No 1286 on a *European Strategy for Children.*

8

PARENTAL RESPONSIBILITY

A INTRODUCTION

Before the Children Act 1989 statutes still referred to 'parental rights and duties' or 'parental powers and duties' or the 'rights and authority' of a parent. Not only were these terms inconsistent with one another but, as the Law Commission had earlier commented:[1] 'It can be cogently argued that to talk of "parental rights" is not only inaccurate as a matter of juristic analysis but also a misleading use of ordinary language.' In their Report on Guardianship and Custody[2] the Commission were concerned that because of the continued use of such terms the law did not adequately promote the view that parenthood is a matter of responsibility rather than of rights. Accordingly they recommended the introduction of the concept of 'parental responsibility' to replace all the ambiguous and misleading terms previously employed in statutes. In the Commission's view, this concept 'would reflect the everyday reality of being a parent and emphasise the responsibility of all who are in that position'.[3] They also noted that such a change would bring English Law into line with the Recommendation on Parental Responsibilities adopted in 1984 by the Committee of Ministers of the Council of Europe.[4]

The government accepted the Commission's recommendation, and 'parental responsibility' has now become a pivotal concept of the 1989 Act.

1 INTERNATIONAL ACCEPTANCE OF THE CONCEPT OF PARENTAL RESPONSIBILITY

The shift away from parental power as reflected by such expressions as 'parental rights and duties' or 'parental power and duties' to that of parental care as encapsulated by the concept of 'parental responsibility' was by no means peculiar to English law. Such a change was effected, for instance, in what was then West Germany, when the term 'parental power' (elter Gewalt) was replaced by 'parental care' (elterliche Sorge) in 1970.[5] In Norway, the term 'parental responsibility' was introduced in their Children Act 1981, replacing such

---

[1] Law Com No 118 *Illegitimacy* (1982) para 4.18.   [2] Law Com No 172 (1988).
[3] Ibid at para 2.4.   [4] Recommendation No R(84)4, for further details of which see below.
[5] See R Frank 'Family Law and the Federal Republic of Germany's Basic Law' (1990) 4 Int Jo of Law, Policy and the Family 214. See also N Dethloff and D Martiny, German Report, particularly the response to Q5 in *European Family Law in Action, Vol III Parental Responsibilities* (eds. K Boele-Woelki, B Bratt and I Curry-Sumner, 2005). This useful volume contains the responses to a detailed questionnaire on parental responsibilities written by experts from 22 different European jurisdictions. For the position in several jurisdictions world-wide see 'The Symposium on Comparative Custody Law' in (2005) 39 FLQ 247.

terms as 'parental authority' and 'parental power'.[6] A similar reform was introduced in Austria in 1989.[7] More recently the term has been adopted in the domestic legislation of, for example, Australia,[8] the Isle of Man,[9] Northern Ireland[10] and Scotland.[11]

International impetus for change was first given by the already mentioned Council of Europe 1984 Recommendation on Parental Responsibilities, the Council agreeing that:[12]

'The term "parental responsibilities" described better the modern concept according to which parents are, on a . . . basis of equality between parents and in consultation with their children, given the task to educate, legally represent, maintain, etc their children. In order to do so they exercise powers to carry out duties in the interests of the child and not because of an authority which is conferred on them in their own interests.'

World wide recognition of the concept of parental responsibility has been given by its use in the UN Convention on the Rights of the Child[13] and the term is now regularly used in international instruments concerning children.[14]

2 CONTEXTS IN WHICH PARENTAL RESPONSIBILITY IS RELEVANT

To have a better understanding of the concept of parental responsibility it is important to appreciate that it is concerned with a number of different relationships. In his leading analysis, Eekelaar[15] argues that the concept can represent two ideas: one, that parents must behave dutifully towards their children; the other, that responsibility for bringing up a child belongs to parents, not the State. Both these ideas are important and both are embodied in the Act. The former idea is well summed up by Lord Mackay LC, who said[16] when introducing the Bill, that the concept of 'parental responsibility':

---

[6] See Smith and P Lødrup *Children and Parents—The relationship between children and parents according to Norwegian Law*, ch 5. See also T Sverdrup and P Lødrup, Norwegian Report, particularly the response to Q5 in *European Family Law in Action, Vol III Parental Responsibilities*, above.

[7] See M Roth, Austrian Report, particularly the response to Q5 in *European Family Law in Action, Vol III Parental Responsibilities*, above.

[8] Under the Family Law Reform Act 1995 (Cth).   [9] Under the Manx Family Law Act 1991.

[10] Under the Children (Northern Ireland) Order 1995. Note also the amendment to the definition of guardianship in New Zealand in the Care of Children Act 2004, Part 2, to include reference to 'responsibilities'.

[11] Under the Children (Scotland) Act 1995, which came into force in November 1996.

[12] See para 6 of the Explanatory Memorandum to the Recommendation. Note also the Council of Europe's 'White Paper' of 15 January 2002 on principles concerning the establishment and legal consequences of parentage (CJ-FA (2001) 16 rev.

[13] See in particular Art 18(1) which states: 'States Parties shall use their best efforts to ensure recognition of the principle that both parents have common responsibilities for the upbringing and development of the child. Parents or, as the case may be, legal guardians, have the primary responsibility for the upbringing and development of the child. The best interests of the child will be their basic concern.' See also Arts 5 and 9.

[14] See, for example, the 1993 Hague Convention on the Protection of Children and Co-operation in Respect of Intercountry Adoption, Art 21(1)(b), the 1996 Hague Convention on Jurisdiction, Applicable Law, Recognition, Enforcement and Co-operation in respect of Parental Responsibility and Measures for the Protection of Children, Art 16(1) and Council Regulation (EC) No. 2201/2003 of 27 November 2003 concerning jurisdiction and the recognition and enforcement of judgments in matrimonial matters and the matters of parental responsibility, repealing Regulation (EC) No. 1347/2000 (the revised Brussels II Regulation).

[15] J Eekelaar, 'Parental responsibility: State of Nature or Nature of the State?' [1991] JSWFL 37.

[16] 502 HL Official Report (5th series) col 490.

'. . . emphasises that the days when a child should be regarded as a possession of his parents, indeed when in the past they had a right to his services and to sue on their loss, are now buried forever. The overwhelming purpose of parenthood is the responsibility for caring and raising the child to be a properly developed adult both physically and morally.'

This comment is echoed by the Department of Health's introductory guide to the Children Act[17] which states that parental responsibility:

'. . . emphasises that the duty to care for the child and to raise him to moral, physical and emotional health is the fundamental task of parenthood and the only justification for the authority that it confers.'

Both these comments reflect in turn the earlier landmark decision of *Gillick v West Norfolk and Wisbech Area Health Authority*,[18] in which Lords Fraser and Scarman emphasised that parental power to control a child exists not for the benefit of the parent but for the benefit of the child.

Although the Law Commission themselves considered[19] that the change of terminology from rights and duties to responsibility would make little change in substance to the law, symbolically saying a parent has responsibilities rather than rights in itself conveys a quite different message. Ironically, however, following the implementation of the Human Rights Act 1998, this framework has to operate in a much more 'rights' orientated context. Indeed it can be at least as important to determine whether a parent has a Convention right as it is to determine whether he or she has parental responsibility, since public authorities must respect that right.[20]

It is the enduring nature of responsibility, particularly when allied with the so-called principle of non-intervention under s 1(5),[21] that embodies the second idea referred to by Eekelaar, namely that responsibility for child care belongs to parents rather than the State. As another commentator has put it,[22] by providing that responsibility should continue despite, for example, a court order that the child should live with one of them, parents 'are to understand that the state will not relieve them of their responsibilities'. This is further underscored by the fact that responsibility cannot be voluntarily surrendered to a public body[23] and that, even where a care order is made compulsorily placing the child in local authority care, the parents still retain their responsibility.[24] In short, the 1989 Act through the concept of parental responsibility emphasises the idea that 'once a parent always a parent', and that prima facie the primary responsibility for deciding what should happen to their children even upon their separation should rest with the parents themselves.

Apart from the parent-child and the parent-state relationships, there is another

---

[17] *Introduction to the Children Act 1989* (HMSO, 1989) para 1.4.
[18] [1986] AC 112, HL, discussed above at pp 363ff.   [19] Law Com No 172 at para 2.4.
[20] See further below at p 376. Note also that having parental responsibility also means that, for the purposes of the Hague Convention on Civil Aspects of International Child Abduction 1980, the individual has 'rights of custody'. See further p 639.
[21] Discussed below at pp 475ff.
[22] S M Cretney 'Defining the Limits of State Intervention: The Child and the Courts' in *Children and the Law* (ed D Freestone, 1990) 58 at p 67.
[23] When the child is 'accommodated' by a local authority under s 20, discussed in Chapter 14, parental responsibility is not acquired by the authority: see the discussion by Eekelaar, above at pp 40–2.
[24] The effect of care orders is discussed below, pp 771ff.

relationship in which the concept of parental responsibility is relevant, namely, as between parents and other individuals. It can be as important to parents that they can look after their children without interference by other individuals as by the State. On the other hand, de facto carers (whether short-term or long-term) need some authority to take normal 'day-to-day' decisions whilst looking after the child. These potentially conflicting stand-points are accommodated by the 1989 Act since, although in the first instance only those with parental responsibility are entitled to make decisions in relation to the child, such persons are nevertheless permitted to 'arrange for some or all [of their responsibility] to be met by one or more persons acting on his behalf.'[25] Furthermore, those without par-ental responsibility but who have care of the child can 'do what is reasonable in all the circumstances of the case for the propose of safeguarding or promoting the child's welfare.'[26] In other words, while those with parental responsibility are, as against other individuals, primarily in control of the child's upbringing, other persons can take decisions about the child either on the basis of parental delegation or, in the case of de facto carers, on the basis of (short-term) necessity.

As s 2 makes clear, not only can more than one person have parental responsibility at the same time but, perhaps more importantly, a person does not cease to have responsibi-lity just because someone else acquires it.[27] Furthermore, each holder of responsibility can in theory[28] continue to exercise it by himself or herself without the need to consult any other holder, subject only to the overriding condition that he or she must not act incompatibly with any existing court order.[29]

It remains now to consider the meaning and scope of parental responsibility; who has parental responsibility; in respect of whom there is responsibility; the duration of responsibility; the position of those sharing responsibility; and the position of those caring for children without parental responsibility.

B THE MEANING AND FUNCTION OF 'PARENTAL RESPONSIBILITY'[30]

1 THE NEED TO DEFINE PARENTAL RESPONSIBILITY

Parental responsibility needs to be definable by some means, so that parents can know what they can or cannot do in relation to their child and, as importantly, so that others can know what the parents' position is. For example, do they need to obtain parental

---

[25] Section 2(9), discussed below, p 434.   [26] Section 3(5)(b), discussed below, p 435.

[27] Section 2(5) and (6) discussed below at pp 434ff.

[28] But note Re C (Welfare of Child: Immunisation) [2003] EWCA Civ 1148, [2003] 2 FLR 1095, Re PC (Change of Surname) [1997] 2 FLR 730, and Re G (Parental Responsibility: Education) [1994] 2 FLR 964, CA, discussed below at p 432.

[29] Section 2(7) and (8) discussed below at p 432.

[30] See N Lowe 'The Meaning and Allocation of Parental Responsibility—A Common Lawyer's Perspective' (1997) 11 Int Jo of Law, Policy and the Family 192 at 193–7. For a survey of the position in 22 different European jurisdictions see European Family Law in Action, Vol III Parental Responsibilities, above. See also for a wider global view, the 'Symposium on Comparative Custody Law' in (2005) 39 FLQ 247.

permission to take a child on an educational outing? Do doctors need parental consent before medically treating the child and is that consent binding on the child?

Quite apart from the individual's point of view, the courts' powers can sometimes be dependent upon the scope of parental responsibility. They can only make a 'prohibited steps order' to prevent any 'step which could be taken by a parent in meeting his parental responsibility for a child' and a 'specific issue order' to determine 'a specific question which has arisen, or which may arise in connection with any aspect of parental responsibility for a child.'[31]

Notwithstanding the demonstrable need to be able to define what parental responsibility comprises, the question remains as to whether this should be done by means of a general statutory provision or simply left to case law and statutory provisions dealing with specific points. The Scottish Law Commission considered that there are advantages in having a general statutory statement of parental responsibilities, namely:[32]

'(a) that it would make explicit what is already implicit in the law;

(b) that it would counteract any impression that a parent has rights but no responsibilities; and

(c) that it would enable the law to make it clear that parental rights are not absolute or unqualified, but are conferred in order to enable parents to meet their responsibilities.'

These arguments seem convincing. It is surely right that as a matter of principle some attempt be made to give general statutory guidance on the meaning of what is after all a pivotal concept of child law.

2 CAN THERE BE A MEANINGFUL GENERAL DEFINITION?

In contrast to the Scottish Law Commission, the earlier inquiry of the English Law Commission concentrated on whether there could be a comprehensive definition of parental responsibility. They concluded[33] that although there was a superficial attraction in providing a comprehensive list of the incidents of responsibility, it was impracticable to do so. They pointed out that such a list would have to change from time to time to meet differing needs and circumstances, and would have to vary with the age and maturity of the child and circumstances of the case.

While there is some validity in this view, particularly if it is sought to provide a comprehensive definition, it by no means follows that *some* useful guidance cannot be given, but this more limited approach was not apparently considered by the Commission. In the event the Children Act implements the strategy recommended by the Law Commission, and s 3(1) simply provides that:

---

[31] Under s 8(1) of the Children Act, discussed below, pp 526ff. Jurisdiction may also depend upon its scope since within Member States of the EU (other than Denmark) matters relating to parental responsibility are governed by the revised Brussels II Regulation, discussed below at p 560ff. In this respect, however, regard must be had to its international meaning under the Regulation, the final arbiter upon which, is the European Court of Justice at Luxembourg.

[32] See Scot Law Com, Discussion Paper No 88 *Parental Responsibilities and Rights, Guardianship and the Administration of Children's Property* (1990) para 2.3.

[33] Law Com No 172 para 2.6.

'. . . "parental responsibility" means all the rights, duties, powers, responsibility and authority which by law a parent of a child has in relation to the child and his property.'

This provision seems a poor one, for not only might it rightly be said to be 'a non-definition',[34] but it also immediately throws one back to the rights and duties model which 'responsibility' was supposed to replace.[35]

In contrast to the English position, the Children (Scotland) Act 1995, implementing the recommendation of the Scottish Law Commission,[36] provides first by s 1(1):

'A parent has in relation to his child the responsibility—

(a) to safeguard and promote the child's health, development and welfare;

(b) to provide, in a manner appropriate to the stage of development of the child—

    (i) direction;

    (ii) guidance,

    to the child;

(c) if the child is not living with the parent, to maintain personal relations and direct contact with the child on a regular basis; and

(d) to act as the child's legal representative,

but only in so far as compliance with this section is practicable and in the interests of the child.'

To enable a parent to fulfil those parental responsibilities, s 2(1) provides that a parent:

'has the right—

(a) to have the child living with him or otherwise to regulate the child's residence;

(b) to control, direct or guide, in a manner appropriate to the stage of development of the child, the child's upbringing;

(c) if the child is not living with him, to maintain personal relations and contact with the child on a regular basis; and

(d) to act as the child's legal representative.'

---

[34] So described by Lord Meston in the debate on the Bill: HL Debs Vol 502, col 1172.

[35] Note Ward LJ's criticisms in *Re S (Parental Responsibility)* [1995] 2 FLR 648 at 657. A not dissimilar 'definition' is provided in the Australian legislation: see Family Law Act 1975 (Cth) s 61B, save that there is no mention of 'rights'. Note also Council Regulation (EC) No. 2201/2003 of 27 November 2003 (the revised Brussels II Regulation) under which parental responsibility is defined (see Art 2(7)) as meaning 'all rights and duties relating to the person or the property of a child which are given to a natural or legal person by judgment, by operation of law or by agreement having legal effect. The term shall include rights of custody and rights of access'. Article 1(2) and (3) respectively set out what is and what is not included in the concept. The Council of Europe's 'White Paper' on *Principles Concerning the Establishment and Legal Consequences of Parentage* defines in Principle 18 parental responsibilities as 'a collection of duties and powers, which aims at ensuring the moral and material welfare of children, in particular

- Care and protection
- Maintenance of personal relationship
- Provision of education
- Legal presentation
- Determination of residence and
- Administration of property'.

[36] Scot Law Com No 125 *Report on Family Law* (1992) paras 2.1 ff.

The Scottish legislation shows that it is possible to provide helpful general guidance as to the meaning of parental responsibility. It neatly handles the problem of dealing with children of different ages and maturity by the simple expedient of stating that the responsibility to give direction and guidance should be 'in a manner appropriate to the stage of development of the child.' By making separate provisions for responsibilities and rights, it grapples with the problem of having to deal not only with the parent-child relationship (in which context the expression 'responsibility' seems absolutely right, because parents ought to act on their children's behalf rather than on their own)[37] but also with the relationship both between the parents themselves and between parents and the State and other individuals (in which context the expression 'rights' still seems appropriate, since, as against others, parents can still be regarded as having the power and authority to bring up their children as they see fit).[38] It also avoids the problem of being too specific and instead leaves the courts free to determine particular issues on a case by case basis.

However, although the Scottish approach seems preferable to the English on this point, English law seems to have worked reasonably well so far and it is probably not now worth amending the 1989 Act.[39]

The above discussion presupposes that the function of parental responsibility is to confer the ability to make decisions about a child's upbringing and indeed this does seem the underlying purpose of the concept as is discussed in the Department of Health's *Introduction to the Children Act 1989* which observes:[40]

'... the effect of having parental responsibility is to empower a person to take most decisions in the child's life.'

It is evident, however, that the judiciary do not always share this view for in some cases[41] they have stressed that the attribution of parental responsibility confers a type of status[42] rather than real rights. However, as has been observed,[43] they are not always consistent about this and there is therefore a 'tension about whether parental responsibility is about real decision-making power, or whether it is of more symbolic value, recognising the [parents'] commitment to the child'.

---

[37] See C Barton and G Douglas *Law and Parenthood*, 18–28.

[38] Using Hohfeld's analysis (Hohfeld *Fundamental Legal Conceptions as Applied in Judicial Reasoning*, 1919), it might be more accurate to say that, at any rate as against third parties, parents have a 'privilege' to bring up children as they see fit in the sense that others have 'no right' to interfere. As against the State, however, this privilege is more limited, since the State can interfere with parental upbringing once it falls below the accepted threshold as set out in s 31 of the Children Act 1989, discussed below, pp 736ff.

[39] But note the call for reform along the Scottish lines in *People Like Us* (Report of the Review of the Standards for Children Living Away from Home—the Utting Report) (Department of Health and Welsh Office, 1997) para 6.2 and recommendation 9.

[40] Para 2.4.

[41] See in particular *Re S (Parental Responsibility)* [1995] 2 FLR 648, *Re S (A Minor)(Parental Responsibility)* [1995] 3 FCR 564, and *Re C and V (Contact and Parental Responsibility)* [1998] 1 FLR 392, discussed below at p 417.

[42] According to J Eekelaar 'Parental Responsibility—A New Legal Status?' (1996) 112 LQR 233, this status is best understood as the legal recognition of the exercise of social parenthood.

[43] J Herring *Family Law* (2nd edn) 358–359.

3 FURTHER PRELIMINARY OBSERVATIONS

Before examining some of the more important aspects of parental responsibility, some preliminary observations may be made. First, although the broad definition under s 3(1) necessarily refers to the pre-1989 Act position,[44] it must do so subject to the change of emphasis from rights to responsibilities. One problem in particular is deciding whether a former 'right' attaches only to a parent or guardian or to anyone with parental responsibility.[45] As the Law Commission commented,[46] the incidents of parenthood with which they were concerned were those that related to the care and upbringing of a child and not specifically incidents that attached to parents qua parents.

Secondly, the exercise of parental responsibility may be qualified by agreement of the parties (for example, the father agreeing that the child is to live with the mother) or by order of the court. In the latter instance the extent to which responsibility can be asserted is effectively limited by the paramountcy of the child's welfare, which principle the court is bound to apply in any proceedings concerning his upbringing or the administration of his property.[47]

Thirdly, the older the child the less extensive and important parental responsibility may become. As Lord Denning MR eloquently put it in respect of custody:[48]

'. . . it is a dwindling right which the court will hesitate to enforce against the wishes of the child, the older he is. It starts with the right of control and ends with little more than advice.'

Fourthly, the ambit of responsibility varies. It is widest when enjoyed by parents or guardians, but less extensive when vested in others by means of a residence order, or in local authorities by reason of a care order.[49] It is narrowest when vested in those who have obtained an emergency protection order.[50]

Fifthly, the absence of responsibility does not necessarily mean that a person has no obligation towards the child. For example, unmarried fathers have a statutory duty to maintain their children regardless of whether they also have parental responsibility.[51] Conversely, the absence of responsibility does not automatically mean that an individual has no 'rights', for if a person has a relationship with the child which amounts to 'family life' within the meaning of Art 8 of the European Convention on Human Rights then that right must be respected by public authorities.[52]

---

[44] For which see J Eekelaar 'What are Parental Rights?' (1973) 89 LQR 210; J Hall 'The Waning of Parental Rights' [1972B] CLJ 248; S Maidment 'The Fragmentation of Parental Rights' [1981] CLJ 135 and Law Com Working Paper No 91 *Guardianship* paras 2.25 et seq.

[45] For example, the right to confer a child's name (discussed below at p 396) or to dispose of a child's corpse (discussed below at p 400).

[46] Law Com No 172 para 2.7.   [47] Children Act 1989, s 1(1), discussed in Chapter 10.

[48] *Hewer v Bryant* [1970] 1 QB 357, CA at 369. Even so, parents do not lose all their responsibility even where their child is '*Gillick* competent': see above, pp 363ff.

[49] See below at pp 550 and 771 respectively.   [50] See below, p 725.   [51] See below, p 419.

[52] See eg *Sahin v Germany, Sommerfield v Germany* [2003] 2 FLR 671, ECtHR and *Elsholz v Germany* [2000] 2 FLR 486, ECtHR in which failing to respect an unmarried father's position with regard to contact was held to be in breach of Art 8.

4 WHAT PARENTAL RESPONSIBILITY COMPRISES[53]

In the absence of an agreed list it is suggested that parental responsibility comprises at least the following:[54]

— Bringing up the child.

— Having contact with the child.

— Protecting and maintaining the child.

— Disciplining the child.

— Determining and providing for the child's education.

— Determining the child's religion.

— Consenting to the child's medical treatment.

— Consenting to the child's marriage.

— Consenting to the child's adoption.

— Vetoing the issue of a child's passport.

— Taking the child outside the United Kingdom and consenting to the child's emigration.

— Administering the child's property.

— Naming the child.

— Representing the child in legal proceedings.

— Disposing of the child's corpse.

— Appointing a guardian for the child.

Whether parental responsibility can also be said to comprise the right to receive information about the child and the power to control publicity about the child can be debated and will be discussed later in this chapter.[55] It can also be debated whether sharing liability for criminal offences should now also be added to the list.[56]

Consenting to a child's marriage was considered in Chapter 2. Appointment of a testamentary guardian, consenting to a child being adopted and maintenance are discussed respectively in Chapters 9, 15 and 17.

(a) Bringing up the child

A key aspect of parental responsibility is that of looking after and bringing up the child. How best this responsibility should be expressed is a matter of debate. At common law parents (originally fathers of legitimate children) were said to have a right to possession of the child.[57] But as we said in the last edition,[58] in the modern context, it seems better to say that those with responsibility have a prima facie right to bring up their own children and

---

[53] See also Barton and Douglas, above, 114 ff; Clarke Hall and Morrison on *Children* (10th edn) 1 [197]ff; Butterworths *Family Law Service* 3A [751] ff (Ch 3); and D Hershman and A McFarlane *Children Law and Practice*, Division A.

[54] Some commentaries include children's services, but as will be seen (see below, p 401) parental responsibility cannot now be said to include a right to domestic services.

[55] See below, pp 402ff   [56] Ie in cases of breach of parenting orders—see below p 406.

[57] See eg *Re Agar-Ellis* (1883) 24 Ch D 317.   [58] At p 351.

the power to determine where they should live. To speak of possessory rights, particularly in the context of the parent–child relationship, harps back to a concept from which that of parental responsibility was seeking to escape[59] and in any event to speak of possession only makes real sense in the case of babies. However, both in the context of the parent-State relationship and that between parents and other individuals, it makes more sense to dwell on rights and indeed it has been forcibly argued[60] that the 'possessory right is now justified, not as an archaic relic of patriarchal domination over other family members, but as reflecting the liberal view that the family and the members who comprise it should be free from arbitrary state inference'. Nevertheless 'possession' seems too strong a concept even in this context. What is really at stake is the power to control. In the final analysis, however, this debate may be nothing more than semantic for it is common ground that parental responsibility embodies the right to bring up a child free both from arbitrary interference by the State (which right is protected by Art 8 of the European Convention on Human Rights)[61] and from the interference by other individuals. In this latter context it will be noted that the right to bring up the child is protected by the criminal law to the extent that persons without responsibility commit the crime of child abduction if they remove the child without lawful authority.[62] As between individuals with parental responsibility the right is qualified to the extent that removal of a child outside the United Kingdom without the consent of other individuals with parental responsibility can amount to a crime.[63]

Associated with bringing up the child is the power physically to control a child's movements, at any rate until the years of discretion,[64] and it is established that responsibility includes the power to control the child's movements whilst in someone else's care.[65] On the other hand, it is also established that a parent, and therefore presumably any other person with parental responsibility, can commit the common law crime of kidnapping[66] or unlawful imprisonment[67] if a child (old enough to make up his own mind) is forcibly taken or detained against his will.

Associated with the prima facie responsibility to bring up the child are questions about the child's domicile and habitual residence. Under the Domicile and Matrimonial Proceedings Act 1973 s 3 a child cannot have an independent domicile until he attains the age of 16. Until then the child born within marriage takes the father's domicile, unless he has his home with his mother and has no home with his father.[68] The child born outside marriage takes the mother's domicile.

---

[59] See the speech of Lord Mackay LC when introducing the Children Bill to Parliament, see above p 370, n 16.

[60] See G Douglas *An Introduction to Family Law* (2nd edn) p. 85.

[61] See eg *TP and KM v United Kingdom* (2002) 34 EHRR 2, [2001] 2 FLR 549 in which the failure of a local authority properly to investigate an allegation of child abuse resulting in a mother and child being wrongly separated for a year was held to violate Art 8. For further discussion of this case see below p 813.

[62] Child Abduction Act 1984 s 2: discussed below, p 407.

[63] Under the Child Abduction Act 1984 s 1 (as amended by the Children Act 1989). Note the defences, however, under s 1(5).

[64] *R v Rahman* (1985) 81 Cr App Rep 349, CA at 353, per Lord Lane CJ. See also *Hewer v Bryant* [1970] 1 QB 357 at 373, CA, per Sachs LJ.

[65] *Fleming v Pratt* (1823) 1 LJOS 194.

[66] *R v D* [1984] AC 778, HL: see N Lowe (1984) 134 NLJ 995.

[67] *R v Rahman* (above). See Khan [1986] Fam Law 69.

[68] Domicile and Matrimonial Proceedings Act 1973 s 4.

Normally, while the parents live together the child is regarded as having the same habitual residence as the parents.[69] Although in cases where the parents separate the child's habitual residence will in due course follow that of the principal carer, neither parent with parental responsibility has a unilateral right to change their child's residence without the other's consent.[70] In principle there seems no reason why a child of sufficient maturity cannot establish his own residence.[71]

(b) Contact with the child

Prima facie parental responsibility encompasses seeing or otherwise having contact with the child (though it is commonly said that contact is a right of the child rather a right of the parent).[72] While not an absolute right, since in any litigation it will be contingent upon the child's welfare, nevertheless as Lord Oliver said in *Re KD (A Minor) (Ward: Termination of Access)*:[73]

'As a general proposition a natural parent has a claim to [contact with] his or her child to which the court will pay regard and it would not I think, be inappropriate to describe such a claim as a "right".'

This 'right' is protected to the extent that there is a statutory presumption of reasonable contact between a child in local authority care or under emergency protection and, amongst others, those with parental responsibility.[74] These latter provisions were enacted following the European Court of Human Rights ruling[75] that the absence of any right to challenge a termination of contact by a local authority amounted to a breach of Arts 8 and 13 of the Convention. It should also be noted that Art 9(3) of the UN Convention on the Rights of the Child 1989 provides:

'States Parties shall respect the right of the child who is separated from one or both parents to maintain personal relations and direct contact with both parents on a regular basis, except if it is contrary to the child's best interests.'

It has been argued[76] that since it is a normal assumption that a child will benefit from

---

[69] See eg *Re M (Minors) (Residence Order: Jurisdiction)* [1993] 1 FLR 495 at 500, per Balcombe LJ. NB it is not, however, a proposition of law that a child's habitual residence is that of the parents: *Re M (Abduction: Habitual Residence)* [1996] 1 FLR 887 at 895, per Sir John Balcombe.

[70] See eg *Re S (Minors) (Abduction: Wrongful Retention)* [1994] Fam 70.

[71] See *Re A (Wardship: Jurisdiction)* [1995] 1 FLR 767 per Hale J.

[72] See eg *M v M (Child: Access)* [1973] 2 All ER 81, per Wrangham J, and see Art 9(3) of the UN Convention on the Rights of the Child 1989, set out below.

[73] [1988] AC 806 at 827, HL.

[74] Children Act 1989, s 34(1) and s 44(13) discussed at pp 791 and 725 respectively. As S Cretney and J Masson observe in *Principles of Family Law* (6th edn, 1997) at 622: 'although parental responsibility does not give an absolute right to contact with a child those with such power . . . do have a right to a court adjudication of restriction of contact'.

[75] See *R v UK, O v UK, W v UK* [1988] 2 FLR 445. See also *Kosmopoulou v Greece* [2004] 1 FLR 800, ECtHR and *Hokkanen v Finland* (1995) 14 EHRR 139, [1996] 1 FLR 289, ECtHR, in which the failure by the State to enforce a parent's right of access was held to be a breach of Art 8, and *Ciliz v The Netherlands* [2000] 2 FLR 469, ECtHR, deportation of a divorced father before the conclusion of a contact hearing held to violate Art 8.

[76] See Clarke Hall and Morrison, above, at para 1[207].

continued contact with both parents,[77] it may be that parental responsibility properly encompasses the prima facie duty to allow the child to have contact with either or both parents. Whether such responsibility extends to a parent having an obligation him or herself to maintain contact with the child can, in the absence of any ruling by a domestic court or the European Court of Human Rights, be debated.[78]

If parental responsibility encompasses the power to control the child's movements, it would seem to follow that it includes the power to restrict those with whom the child may have contact. In *Nottingham County Council v P*,[79] in which it was sought to exclude the father from the matrimonial home and to restrict his contact with his children (on the basis of his sexual abuse), Ward J saw 'the force of the submission' that steps taken by a parent in meeting his parental responsibility are necessarily wide steps and could extend to controlling contact with the other parent. In *Re M (Care: Leave to Interview Child)*[80] Hale J was more forthright, commenting: 'Until the child is old enough to decide for himself, a parent undoubtedly has some control over whom he may see and who may see him'. Accordingly, it seems that parental responsibility embraces controlling those with whom the child may have contact.[81]

(c) Protection

Physical and moral protection

Although it is undoubtedly an aspect of parental responsibility to afford physical protection to the child, at common law a duty is owed by anyone who willingly undertakes to look after another who is incapable of looking after himself. Hence this duty can be owed to a step-child or foster child[82] and can continue after the child reaches his majority, if he is unable to look after himself owing to some physical or mental disability.[83] Whether the duty exists in any given case depends inter alia upon the necessity of protection. A disabled mother, for example, would not be under any duty to protect a healthy son aged 17. In *R v Shepherd*,[84] where a girl aged 18, who normally lived away in service but returned home from time to time, died there in childbirth, it was held that her mother was under no duty to send for a midwife because the girl was beyond the age of childhood and was entirely emancipated.

As will be seen, breach of the duty can lead both to criminal and civil liability.

Criminal liability

A person will be criminally liable for assault if he inflicts physical injury on a child or puts

[77] See eg Lord Oliver in *Re KD*, above, at 827 and *M v M (Child: Access)* [1973] 2 All ER 81, per Wrangham J at 85 and per Latey J at p 88.
[78] In Scotland the Children (Scotland) Act 1995 s 1(1)(d) (set out at p 374 above) clearly states that a parent has a responsibility to maintain personal relations and direct contact with the child. But even supposing that there is a theoretical duty to see the child, it would be difficult to impose this order on an unwilling parent. See further below, pp 521–2.
[79] [1994] Fam 18, 23.
[80] [1995] 1 FLR 825. See also *Re F (Specific Issue: Child Interview)* [1995] 1 FLR 819, CA.
[81] This point is not without significance when determining the ambit of specific issue and prohibited steps orders under s 8: see below, pp 526ff.
[82] *R v Bubb* (1850) 4 Cox CC 455; *R v Gibbins and Proctor* (1918) 13 Cr App Rep 134, CCA.
[83] *R v Chattaway* (1922) 17 Cr App Rep 7, CCA (starvation of a helpless daughter aged 25).
[84] (1862) Le & Ca 147. (The age of majority was then 21.)

him in fear that he will do so. However, where breach of the duty to protect the child takes the form of neglect, abandonment or some other omission, the common law criminal sanctions are wholly inadequate to ensure the child's protection, not least because no offence is committed unless the child's health actually suffers as a result. In practice, so far as the criminal law is concerned, the common law duty has been superseded by the statutory duty contained in the Children and Young Persons Acts 1933 to 1969.[85]

Section 1(1) of the 1933 Act provides:

'If any person[86] who has attained the age of sixteen years and has responsibility for any child or young person under that age, wilfully assaults, ill-treats, neglects, abandons, or exposes him, or causes or procures him to be assaulted, ill-treated, neglected, abandoned, or exposed, in a manner likely[87] to cause him unnecessary suffering or injury to health (including injury to or loss of sight, or hearing, or limb, or organ of the body, and any mental derangement), that person shall be guilty of [an offence] . . .'[88]

By s 17 of the Act the following are liable under s 1:[89]

'(a) any person who—

    (i) has parental responsibility for him (within the meaning of the Children Act 1989); or

    (ii) is otherwise legally liable to maintain him; and

(b) any person who has care of him.'

This wording is extremely wide and would cover, for example, a schoolteacher and anyone over the age of 16 acting as a baby-sitter.

The object of the Act is to make criminal any wilful course of conduct likely to cause physical or mental injury to the child. The Act itself specifies that neglect shall include failure to provide adequate food, clothing, medical aid[90] or lodging or, if the parent or guardian is unable to provide any of these, failing to take steps to procure them through the State.[91] But clearly many other types of cruelty and neglect are covered, such as beating a child, locking him up alone, leaving him in an otherwise deserted house or shutting him out in inclement weather, if such acts are likely to cause the child concerned suffering

---

85 Viz the Children and Young Persons Act 1933; Children and Young Persons (Amendment) Act 1952; Children and Young Persons Act 1963; Children and Young Persons Act 1969 as amended by the Children Act 1989 Schs 12 and 13.

86 There can be joint liability: see *R v Gibson and Gibson* [1984] Crim LR 615, CA.

87 It has been held that 'likely' should be understood as excluding only what would fairly be described as highly unlikely: *R v Willis* [1990] Crim LR 714, applying remarks of Lord Diplock in *R v Sheppard* [1981] AC 394 at 405.

88 The phrase 'in a manner likely to cause . . . injury to health' governs the whole of the preceding phrase 'wilfully assaults . . . abandoned, or exposed': *R v Hatton* [1925] 2 KB 322, CCA. The section has virtually superseded the Offences against the Person Act 1861 s 27, which relates to the abandonment and exposure of children under two years of age. The former defence under s 1(7) permitting parents, teachers and those having lawful charge of the child to administer punishment was repealed by the Children Act 2004, s 58, discussed below at p 387.

89 The Act says 'presumed to be liable', but the presumption is apparently irrefutable: *Brooks v Blount* [1923] 1 KB 257.

90 Unreasonable refusal to permit a surgical operation may amount to wilful neglect: *Oakey v Jackson* [1914] 1 KB 216.

91 Children and Young Persons Act 1933 s 1(2)(a).

or ill-health. A person will be liable, however, only if his act is wilful: hence he must either know that his conduct might cause suffering or injury to health, or not care whether this results or not.[92] A parent who does not know that the child's health is at risk will not be guilty of an offence if he fails to summon medical aid even though a reasonable person would be aware of this fact: if he does know this, however, he will presumably be guilty even though he has some religious or other reason for refusing to provide assistance.[93]

Under s 5 of the Domestic Violence, Crime and Victims Act 2004 a person is guilty of an offence if a child dies, as a result of an unlawful act (which includes a course of conduct or omission) of a person who was a member of the same household or had frequent contact with the child. Parents (and others having responsibility for children) may also be criminally liable for causing the death of a child under the age of three by overlying it in bed whilst drunk,[94] for allowing a child under the age of 12 to be in a room containing an unguarded fire or other heating appliance with the result that the child is killed or seriously injured,[95] or for permitting children under the age of 16 (subject to certain exceptions) to take part in or train for dangerous performances.[96] Similarly it is an offence to allow a child under the age of 16 to beg,[97] and penalties are imposed upon parents who permit children to take part in entertainments or to go abroad for the purpose of performing for profit except under stringent conditions.[98]

Civil liability

There are two possible civil actions arising from a breach of the duty to protect: an action for assault and a common law action for damages in negligence. So far as the former is concerned, parents or others having responsibility or care of the child stand in no special position. Like anyone else they can be liable in damages for such assaults and, though such actions are rare, an example can be found in *Pereira v Keleman*[99] in which a father was held liable in damages to each of his three daughters in respect of his physical and indecent assaults.

So far as negligence claims are concerned, the child must prove that he has been injured as a result of the other's breach of duty to take care to avoid such acts or omissions as are foreseeably likely to injure him. Where a duty of care exists independently so that, had the injured person been a stranger, he could have recovered from the tortfeasor, the relationship of parent and child should not ipso facto bar the action. An obvious example would occur if a child, who is a passenger in his father's car, is injured as a result of the latter's negligent driving. The father's duty of care similarly extends to an unborn child, whereas the mother's duty to an unborn child arises only when she is driving a motor vehicle.[100]

---

[92] *R v Sheppard* [1981] AC 394, HL.

[93] As in *R v Senior* [1899] 1 QB 283 (religious objection to calling in medical aid), which appears to have been approved on its facts in *R v Sheppard*, above. Cf the new offence of causing or allowing the death of a child under s 5 of the Domestic Violence, Crime and Victims Act 2004, outlined below.

[94] Children and Young Persons Act 1933 s 1(2)(b).

[95] Section 11 as amended by the Children and Young Persons (Amendment) Act 1952 s 8.

[96] Sections 23–4; Children and Young Persons Act 1963 s 41 and Schs 3 and 5.

[97] Children and Young Persons Act 1933 s 4.

[98] Section 25; Children and Young Persons Act 1963 ss 37–40 and 42.   [99] [1995] 1 FLR 428.

[100] The Congenital Disabilities (Civil Liability) Act 1976 s 2. Liability can only accrue provided the child is born alive: s 4(2)(a).

Where there is no independent duty, so that the child has to rely solely on the common law duty to protect owed to him by his parent or other person having parental responsibility or of those simply looking after him, the position is less clear. In *Surtees v Kingston-upon-Thames Borough Council*[101] the plaintiff, then aged two, had, whilst in foster care, an accident in which she sustained serious injuries to her foot. The injuries were caused by immersion in water hot enough to cause third degree burns. Although the precise circumstances were disputed, the court accepted the foster parents' explanation that whilst the foster mother was out of the bathroom the plaintiff somehow placed her foot in the wash basin and switched on the hot water tap. The foster mother took the plaintiff immediately to a doctor, who treated her daily. It was held that on these facts the action for negligence should fail.[102] With respect to the foster parents it was held that, in the domestic circumstances in which the foster mother was performing her normal household duties, the kind of injury sustained by the plaintiff was not foreseeable. In reaching this decision both Stocker LJ and Browne-Wilkinson V-C were mindful of the danger of imposing an impossibly high standard of care in domestic situations. It was expressly accepted that for this purpose the duty owed by foster parents was exactly the same as that owed by a parent. Browne-Wilkinson V-C further observed:[103]

'There are very real public policy considerations to be taken into account if the conflicts inherent in legal proceedings are to be brought into family relationships . . . The studied realm of the Royal Courts of Justice . . . is light years away from the circumstances prevailing in the average home. The mother is looking after a fast-moving toddler at the same time as cooking the meal, doing the housework, answering the telephone, looking after the other children and doing all the other things that the average mother has to cope with simultaneously, or in quick succession, in the normal household. We should be slow to characterise as negligent the care which ordinary loving and careful mothers are able to give to individual children, given the rough-and-tumble of home life.'

The reluctance to impose too high a standard of care upon those looking after children should not be taken to imply that such carers will never be held to be negligent. An instructive decision is that of the New Zealand Court of Appeal in *McCallion v Dodd*.[104] In that case parents alighted from a bus at night with their two children and started to walk along the road in the dark. The mother, who was deaf and, as the father knew, was not wearing her hearing aid, took the plaintiff, aged four, by the hand and the father carried the baby in his arms. A car driven by the defendant hit the mother and the plaintiff, killing

---

[101] [1991] 2 FLR 559, CA. But note also *X (Minors) v Bedfordshire County Council* [1995] 2 AC 633, HL *Barrett v Enfield London Borough Council* [2001] 2 AC 550, HL, *W v Essex County Council* [2001] 2 AC 592, HL and *D v East Berkshire Community Health NHS Trust* [2005] UK HL 23, [2005] 2 AC 373 on the possible liability of local authorities, discussed below p 810. For the position in Australia see N Mullany 'Civil Actions for Childhood Abuse in Australia' (1999) 115 LQR 565 and the authorities there cited.

[102] It was conceded that the authority could not be liable if the foster parents were exonerated from blame, though in any event Stocker LJ considered obiter that as a matter of causation the claim against the authority was bound to fail unless the injuries were deliberately inflicted. For a criticism of this observation see G Douglas [1991] Fam Law 426–7. It is established that foster parents are not agents of the local authority: *S v Walsall Metropolitan Borough Council* [1986] 1 FLR 397, CA.

[103] [1991] 2 FLR at 583–4; but cf Beldam LJ, who dissented.

[104] [1966] NZLR 710. See D Mathieson 'Can a Child Sue his Parents in Tort?' (1967) 30 MLR 96. See also *S v Walsall Metropolitan Borough Council,* above, where damages were awarded against foster parents in respect of injuries suffered by a child whilst in their care.

the mother and severely injuring the boy. The plaintiff sued the defendant in negligence, and the defendant claimed contribution from the father on the ground that he had also broken a duty of care owed to the plaintiff. The jury found that the defendant had been negligent and that the father had been negligent in permitting the boy to walk in the road on the wrong side and in the path of oncoming traffic. On appeal it was unanimously held that, even though the boy was under the immediate control of his mother, the father continued to be under a special duty because of her deafness. Turner and McCarthy JJ thought that no duty of care was created purely by the relationship of parent and child, but that it arose from the fact that the father had taken the boy onto the road,[105] although admittedly the relationship is evidence of the fact that the parent has undertaken the duty to supervise and control the child's conduct.[106] North P, however, thought that, although a stranger would be liable in negligence only if he had assumed or accepted the care of the child, parents 'at all times while present are under a legal duty to exercise reasonable care to protect their children from foreseeable dangers' and that duty cannot be shed by a parent who is present.[107] In most cases it will make little difference which view is correct, but the wider rule formulated by North P is to be preferred. Indeed, it is submitted that it should be even more broadly based. If a parent leaves a child in the care of one known to be unreliable and the child comes to harm as the result of the latter's irresponsibility, the parent should be civilly liable.

It was unanimously held that there was no question of the plaintiff's damages being reduced as the result of the father's negligence. The court followed *Oliver v Birmingham and Midland Omnibus Co Ltd.*[108] in which the plaintiff, aged four, was crossing a road with his grandfather, who was holding his hand, when an omnibus bore down on them. The grandfather let go of the plaintiff's hand and jumped to safety; the plaintiff was struck by the omnibus owing to the driver's negligence and was injured. It was held that his action for damages against the omnibus company was not affected by his grandfather's contributory negligence.

(d) Discipline [109]

The common law position

A necessary part of bringing up a child is the power to exercise discipline over the child. Discipline can take different forms, for example, it has been held[110] that restraint of a child's movement is usually well within the realms of reasonable discipline. But analyses have tended to concentrate on the more controversial aspect of discipline, namely, the power to inflict corporal punishment. At common law a person with parental responsibility could lawfully chastise and inflict moderate and reasonable corporal punishment for the purpose of correcting a child or punishing an offence.[111] Moreover, it was established that these powers could be delegated either expressly[112] or impliedly but they could only be

---

[105] At 725 and 728.   [106] Per McCarthy J at 729.   [107] At 721.   [108] [1933] 1 KB 35.

[109] See generally J Fortin *Children's Rights and the Developing Law* (2nd edn, 2003) pp 276–85 and R Smith ' "Hands-off parenting?" towards a reform of the defence of reasonable chastisement in the UK' [2004] CFLQ 261.

[110] Per Lord Lane CJ in *R v Rahman* (1985) 81 Cr App Rep 349 at 353, CA.

[111] *R v Hopley* (1860) 2 F & F 202; *R v Woods* (1921) 85 JP 272.

[112] See *Sutton London Borough Council v Davis* [1994] 1 FLR 737 in which a local authority's decision to refuse to register a child minder who would not comply with their 'no smacking policy' (the child minder had

exercised by those in loco parentis to the child.[113] It was in this way that teachers were empowered to administer corporal punishment.[114] This power was given statutory form by s 1(7) of the Children and Young Persons Act 1933 which provided:

'Nothing in this section shall be construed as affecting the right of any parent, teacher, or other person having the lawful control or charge of a child or young person to administer punishment to him.'

Even at common law the power to administer punishment only extended to inflicting *reasonable* corporal punishment.[115] If it went beyond that it was unlawful and would render the individual criminally liable for assault or, depending on the gravity, for more serious offences.[116] It was also established that disciplinary acts amounting to degrading punishment[117] or inflicted without parental consent, are in breach of the European Convention on Human Rights.[118]

Calls for reform

Pressure to reform this position had been mounting for some time with advocates for change arguing that it is morally wrong to permit physical punishment of children and symbolically important that the State should respect the physical integrity of all its citizens, and because of the danger that punishment can quickly degenerate into abuse. The principal argument for maintaining the status quo is that many parents think that some punishment is justified and that a complete ban would be unenforceable.

An important catalyst for change has been the European Court of Human Rights and a series of decisions, notably *Tyrer v United Kingdom*,[119] *Campbell and Cosans v*

had the parent's permission to smack her daughter) was overturned by the court. Note the comments on this decision by J Dewar at [1994] Fam Law 493–4. This has now been reversed: see the Day Care and Child Minding (National Standards) (England) Regulations 2003 (SI 2003/1996) reg 5.

[113] See eg *R v Woods*, above, in which it was held to be unlawful for an elder brother to administer corporal punishment on his younger sibling where both were living with their father.

[114] See the review of Elias J in *R (On the Application of Williamson) v Secretary of State for Education and Employment* [2001] EWHC Admin 960, [2002] 1 FLR 493 at [19] et seq (judgment upheld on appeal at [2005] UK HL 15, [2005] 2 FLR 374) citing *Cleary v Booth* [1893] 1 QB 465 and *Ryan v Fildes and Others* [1938] 3 All ER 517.

[115] Note *R v H (Assault of Child: Reasonable Chastisement)* [2001] EWCA Crim 1024, [2001] 2 FLR 431 in which it was held that where reasonable chastisement was raised as a defence to criminal charges, a judge should direct the jury to consider the following: '(i) the nature and context of the defendant's behaviour; (ii) the duration of that behaviour; (iii) the physical and mental consequences in respect of the child; (iv) the age and personal characteristics of the child; [and] (v) the reasons given by the defendant for administering the punishment'.

[116] Children and Young Person Act 1933 s 1; *R v Derriviere* (1969) 53 Cr App Rep 637, CA—West Indian father convicted of occasioning actual bodily harm to his 13-year-old son. If the child dies, the parent could be guilty of manslaughter or even murder. An unreasonable restraint of a child's movement can render a parent guilty of unlawful imprisonment: *R v Rahman*, above.

[117] See *Costello-Roberts v UK* (1996) 19 EHRR 293, [1994] ELR 1, in which slippering a seven-year-old was held not to be degrading.

[118] Corporal punishment without parental consent was held to be in breach of the European Convention on Human Rights: see *Campbell and Cosans v UK* (1982) 4 EHRR 293, E Ct HR (albeit in the context of a parent's right to determine the child's education), discussed by G Douglas (1988) 2 Int J Law and Fam 76. Note also Art 37 of the UN Convention on the Rights of the Child, which inter alia states that no child shall be subject to degrading treatment.

[119] (1979–80) 2 EHRR 1, E Ct HR—which concerned judicial corporal punishment (birching) in the Isle of Man—held to have violated Art 3.

UK^{120} and *Costello-Roberts v United Kingdom*,[121] led directly or indirectly to ending the power to inflict corporal punishment on children in all schools,[122] children's homes,[123] foster placements[124] and nurseries.[125] These embargos do not outlaw forms of discipline falling short of corporal punishment.[126]

Notwithstanding the above-mentioned changes, there was continued resistance to curbing parents' power to administer corporal punishment. This remained so in spite of a Council of Europe Recommendation that legislation on corporal punishment of children be reviewed;[127] that it had been banned in a growing number of European countries;[128] that Art 19 of the United Nations Convention on the Rights of the Child enjoins States to take appropriate measures to protect children from violence inter alia whilst in care of their parents;[129] and despite a recommendation by the Scottish Law Commission[130] that striking a child with an implement should be banned. However, once again the catalyst for eventual reform was a European Court of Human Rights' ruling, namely, *A v United Kingdom (Human Rights: Punishment of Child)*.[131] In that case a step-father of a

---

[120] Above—which involved a Scottish school's use of the 'tawse' (a split leather belt).   [121] Above.

[122] Education Act 1996, s 548 (as substituted by s 131 of the School Standards and Framework Act 1998) which, as Elias J pointed out in *R (On the Application of Williamson) v Secretary of State for Education and Employment*, above at [16], removes the defence of justification, which is necessary if the intentional infliction of physical harm is not to be considered unlawful, rather than prohibiting corporal punishment as such. In *Williamson* the House of Lords (at [2005] UKHL 15, [2005] 2 FLR 374) rejected a claim by head teachers, teachers and parents of four independent schools that this statutory prohibition breached their right to freedom of religion under Art 9 or Art 2 of Protocol 1.

[123] Children's Homes Regulations 2001 (SI 2001/ 3967), reg 17(5)(a), which simply prohibits the use of any form of corporal punishment.

[124] Fostering Services Regulations 2002 (SI 2002/57), reg 28(5)(b), Sch 5, point 8 which requires foster parents in England to make a written agreement not to administer corporal punishment.

[125] The Day Care and Child Minding (National Standards) (England) Regulations 2003 (SI 2003/1996) reg 5. This follows the earlier ban imposed in Wales, see Smith, above, at 263.

[126] It should be noted that under the Education Act 1996 s 550A, school staff are empowered to use 'such force as is reasonable in the circumstances' to prevent a pupil committing an offence. The distinction between this so-called restraining power and corporal punishment can be a fine one. See the discussion by C Hamilton 'Rights of the child—a right to and a right in education' in C Bridge (ed) *Family Law Towards the Millennium, Essays for P M Bromley* ch 6.

[127] Recommendation No R85(4) on Violence in the Family (1985), para 12. As the explanatory memorandum notes: 'It is the very assumption that corporal punishment of children is legitimate that opens the way to all kinds of excesses and makes the traces or symptoms of such punishment acceptable to third parties'.

[128] Eg in Sweden (1979), Finland (1984), Denmark (1986), Norway (1987), Austria (1989) and Italy (1996). For the position in 22 European jurisdictions see *European Family Law in Action Vol III Parental Responsibilities*, above, answer to Q8(d) and see Fortin, above, at 284, n 74.

[129] Indeed in 2002 the UN Committee on the Rights of the Child recommended that the UK should as a matter of urgency prohibit all corporal punishment in the family: *Concluding Observations of the Committee on the Rights of the Child: United Kingdom of Great Britain and Northern Ireland* UN Doc E/C. 12/1/Add 79, para 36.

[130] See Scot Law Com Discussion Paper No 88 *Parental Responsibilities and Rights, Guardianship and Administration of Children's Property* (1980) paras 2.44ff and Scot Law Com No 135 *Report on Family Law* (1992) paras 2.67ff. Notwithstanding public support for their recommendation that striking a child with an implement should be banned, no such provision was included in what became the Children (Scotland) Act 1995. However, under s 51 of the Criminal Justice (Scotland) Act 2003, blows to the head, shaking, or the use of an implement are banned.

[131] [1998] 2 FLR 959 on which see A Bainham 'Corporal Punishment of Children: A Caning for the United Kingdom' [1999] CLJ 29 and C Barton 'The Thirty Thousand Pound Caning—an "English Vice" in Europe' [1999] CFLQ 63.

nine-year-old boy repeatedly hit him with a garden cane, causing bruises which lasted up to a week. He was tried but acquitted for assault causing actual bodily harm. The European Court ruled that the UK had failed to provide the child with sufficient protection against a punishment that amounted to degrading treatment and had accordingly violated Art 3. In response to this decision the Government issued a Consultation Paper[132] and seemed prepared to accept that domestic law needed amending in the light of *A v United Kingdom*. However, after analysing the responses to the Consultation Paper,[133] the Government concluded that there was no need for change as s 3 of the then implemented Human Rights Act 1998 obliged the courts to take account of the European Court of Human Rights' ruling. This conclusion did not dampen calls for reform. The House of Commons Health Committee,[134] for instance, when considering the report of the Victoria Climbié inquiry,[135] urged the Government to 'remove the increasingly anomalous reasonable chastisement defence'. Eventually, some reform was achieved when Lord Lester's amendment to what is now the Children Act 2004 was accepted in the House of Lords.[136]

The Children Act 2004 s 58

Section 58(1) of the Children Act 2004, introduced with effect from 15 January 2005,[137] provides that in relation to charges[138] of wounding and causing grievous bodily harm, assault occasioning actual bodily harm and cruelty to persons under the age of 16, 'battery of a child cannot be justified on the ground that it constituted reasonable punishment'. Section 58(3) additionally provides that 'Battery of a child causing actual bodily harm to the child cannot be justified in any civil proceedings on the ground that it constituted reasonable punishment'.

Although the general defence under s 1(7) of the Children and Young Persons Act 1933 is also repealed,[139] it is to be noted that these reforms do not ipso facto remove the right to smack children. The defence of reasonable chastisement can continue to be pleaded in proceedings for common assault before magistrates[140] while batteries *not* occasioning actual bodily harm (popularly translated as hitting without leaving a mark) are still permitted. In other words, s 58 stops short of imposing an outright ban on corporal punishment. Even whilst going through Parliament the provisions were criticised for not going far enough[141] and no doubt there will be further calls for reform.

---

[132] *Protecting Children, Supporting Parents: A Consultation Document on the physical punishment of children* (2000).

[133] *Analysis of Responses to the Protecting Children, Supporting Parents Consultation Document* (2001).

[134] *Sixth Report of the House of Commons Health Committee—The Victoria Climbié Inquiry Report* HC 270 (TSO, 2003).

[135] Lord Laming, *The Victoria Climbie Inquiry*, Cm 5730 (2003).

[136] On which see Smith, above, at pp 271–2.

[137] See s 67(7)(f) of the 2004 Act.

[138] Respectively under ss 18 or 20 of the Offences Against the Person Act 1861, s 47 of the 1861 Act and s 1 of the Children and Young Persons Act 1933.

[139] By s 58(5) of the 2004 Act.

[140] See the Explanatory Notes to the 2004 Act at para 236.

[141] See the Joint Committee on Human Rights HL 161/HC 537 discussed by Smith, above, at 272.

(e) Education [142]

As Ward LJ observed in *Re Z (A Minor) (Identification: Restrictions on Publication)*[143] 'arranging for education commensurate with the child's intellectual needs and abilities is [an] . . . incident of the parental responsibility which arises from the duty of the parent to secure the child's education'. This responsibility is long established and derives from the common law right of a parent to determine what education the child should receive.[144] Parents' rights to determine their children's education are also protected by the European Convention on Human Rights to the extent of respecting their religious and philosophical convictions.[145]

At common law, because the duty was unenforceable,[146] parents could formerly choose not to have their children educated. This right, however, has long since been overturned. Now parents of every child between the ages of five and 16 have to ensure that the child receives 'efficient full-time education suitable (a) to his age, ability and aptitude and (b) to any special educational needs he may have, either by regular attendance at school or otherwise'.[147]

'Parent' for these purposes includes any person who is not a parent but who has parental responsibility for the child or who has care of the child.[148]

Those with parental responsibility or who have care of children can discharge their duty by ensuring that they attend independent[149] rather than state schools or even by educating them at home, provided in this latter instance that the local education authority is satisfied that the child is receiving efficient and full-time education suitable to his age etc. Where state education is relied upon, except where the child has been permanently excluded from two or more schools, education authorities and governing bodies of maintained schools are required to comply with 'parental' wishes as to choice of school, save, importantly, where compliance would 'prejudice the provision of efficient education or the efficient use of resources' or, if the admission arrangements to the preferred school are based on pupils with high ability or with aptitude and compliance would be incompatible with those criteria.[150]

---

[142] See generally N Harris *Law and Education, Regulation, Consumerism and the Education System* (1993); C Piper 'Parental Responsibility and the Education Act' [1994] Fam Law 146 (but note both publications pre-date the 1996 Education Act).

[143] [1997] Fam 1 at 26.

[144] For a striking example see *Tremain's Case* (1719) 1 Stra 167, discussed by S Cretney, J Masson and R Bailey-Harris, *Principles of Family Law* (7th edn) at 18–013. See also *Andrews v Salt* (1873) 8 Ch App 622—father's wishes to be respected after his death.

[145] Protocol No 1, Art 2.   [146] See *Hodges v Hodges* (1796) Peake Add Cas 79.

[147] Education Act 1996 ss 7–8. If the child is living with both parents, the statutory duty is cast on both of them: *Plunkett v Alker* [1954] 1 QB 420. For a useful discussion of the 1996 Act see Clarke Hall and Morrison, Division 6.

[148] Education Act 1996 s 576(1). This definition can cover a local authority foster parent: *Fairpo v Humberside County Council* [1997] 1 FLR 339.

[149] Disputes between the parents about appropriate schooling may be resolved by means of a specific issue or prohibited steps order under s 8 of the Children Act 1989: see eg *Re P (Parental Dispute: Judicial Determination)* [2002] EWCA Civ 1627, [2003] 1 FLR 286, *Re W (children)(education: choice of school)* [2002] EWCA Civ 1411, [2002] 3 FCR 473, *Re A (Specific Issue Order: Parental Dispute)* [2001] 1 FLR 121 and *Re P (A Minor) (Education)* [1992] 1 FLR 316, CA.

[150] Education Act 1996 s 9 and the School Standards of Framework Act 1998, s 86; it will be noted therefore that education authorities are not under an absolute duty to comply with parental wishes. See further Clarke Hall and Morrison at 6 [522]. For the position of children with special educational needs, see Clarke Hall and Morrison at 6 [901]ff.

To enable a reasoned choice to be made 'parents' must be given information about the primary and secondary education available[151] and inter alia the curriculum and subject choice.[152]

The obligation to ensure that a child is receiving education suitable to his or her needs is enforceable in different ways. For example, it remains possible for a local authority social services department to institute care proceedings in cases of persistent non school attendance.[153] However, action is more likely to be taken by the local education authority. If it appears to an education authority that a child is not receiving suitable education, they may serve a notice requiring a parent to satisfy the authority that the child is receiving such education.[154] If a parent on whom a notice has been served fails to satisfy the authority that the child is receiving suitable education or in the authority's opinion it is expedient for the child to attend school, the authority must then serve on the parent a school attendance order.[155] Failure to comply with the order is an offence.[156] However, before instituting proceedings for the offence, the education authority must consider whether it would be appropriate to apply instead, or in addition, for an education supervision order under s 36 of the Children Act 1989.[157]

Before instituting proceedings for an education supervision order, the education authority must consult the appropriate social services authority.[158] The latter may decide to provide support for the child and family under Part III[159] or to institute care proceedings.[160]

An education authority may apply for an education supervision order on the ground that the child concerned is of compulsory school age and is not receiving full-time education suitable to his age, ability and aptitude and any special education needs he may have.[161] Unless proved to the contrary, the ground is deemed to be satisfied if a school attendance order is not complied with or the child is not regularly attending the school at which he is a registered pupil.[162]

Under an education supervision order, the supervisor has the duty to advise, assist and befriend and give directions to the child and the parents so as to secure that the child is properly educated.[163]

The supervisor must also consider what further steps to take if his directions are not complied with.[164] He may seek new directions or apply for a discharge of the order. A

---

[151] School Standards and Framework Act 1998, s 92.   [152] Education Act 1996, s 408.

[153] Formerly, truancy was a specific ground for making a care order, but now under the Children Act application has to be made under s 31 (discussed below at pp 732ff). But for a case where such an application succeeded see Re O (A Minor) (Care Proceedings: Education) [1992] 1 WLR 912, discussed below at p 755.

[154] Education Act 1996 s 437(1).   [155] Section 437(3).

[156] Section 443. There is also a separate offence under s 444 if a child of compulsory school age and who is a registered pupil fails to attend school regularly. Formerly, parents could be fined but not imprisoned for such offences. However, under s 444(8A) parents can be imprisoned for up to three months. An alternative sanction is for the court to make a parenting order if the court is satisfied that such an order would prevent further offences: Crime and Disorder Act 1998, ss 8 and 9. See further Clarke Hall and Morrison at 6 [611].

[157] Section 447. Where prosecutions are brought, the court trying the case may direct the education authority to apply for an education supervision order, but the latter has a discretion not to apply if, after consulting the local authority, it is thought that the child's welfare will be satisfactorily safeguarded without an order: s 447(2).

[158] Children Act 1989 s 36(8)–(9).   [159] Discussed below, p 698.   [160] See note 153 above

[161] Section 36(3)–(4).   [162] Section 36(5).   [163] Sch 3, para 12(1)(a).

[164] Sch 3, para 12(1)(b).

parent who persistently fails to comply with a direction is guilty of an offence.[165] Where a child persistently fails to comply with a direction, the education authority must notify the social services authority, which is obliged to investigate the child's circumstances.[166]

An education supervision order may last up to one year but may be extended for up to a further three years at a time.[167] It ceases to have effect when the child reaches the compulsory school leaving age or when he becomes subject to a care order.[168] The order may be discharged upon the application of the child, parent or education authority.[169]

(f) Religious upbringing[170]

A person with parental responsibility has a right to determine the child's religious education, though there is no duty to give a child a religious upbringing. As Wall J said in *Re J (Specific Issue Orders: Muslim Upbringing and Circumcision)*[171] 'Parental responsibility . . . clearly includes the right to bring up children in a particular religious faith, or in none'. Based on the common law,[172] this right to determine the child's religious education is protected to the extent that a local authority cannot cause a child in their care 'to be brought up in any religious persuasion other than that in which he would have been brought up if the order had not been made'.[173] Parents with parental responsibility and those caring for the child can require a child's exclusion from religious studies lessons and school assembly.[174] Although the courts will seek to pay 'serious heed to the religious wishes of a parent'[175] (and indeed to prevent a parent bringing up his child *simply* on the basis of his religious belief is contrary to the European Convention on Human Rights),[176] in the event of a dispute the court must treat the child's welfare as the paramount consideration.[177]

---

[165] Sch 3, para 18.   [166] Sch 3, para 19.   [167] Sch 3, para 15(1)–(5).

[168] Sch 3, para 15(6).   [169] Sch 3, para 17.

[170] See generally C Hamilton *Family Law and Religion* (1995) and A Mumford 'The Judicial Resolution of Disputes Involving Children and Religion' (1998) 47 ICLQ 117.

[171] [1999] 2 FLR 678 at 685—decision upheld by the Court of Appeal at [2001] 1 FLR 571.

[172] See *Andrews v Salt* (1873) 8 Ch App 622 The rule, see eg *Hawksworth v Hawksworth* (1871) LR Ch App 539, that unless there were exceptional circumstances children had to be brought up in the religion of their father was abolished by the Guardianship of Infants Act 1925, s 1. See generally H Bevan *Child Law* (1989) paras 11.02–11.16.

[173] Children Act 1989 s 33(6)(a). Formerly, under the Adoption Act 1976, s 7 adoption agencies were required, when placing a child for adoption, to have regard, so far as practical, to any wishes of the child's parent or guardian as to the child's religious upbringing. But under the Adoption and Children Act 2002, s 1(5) there is the more general requirement that agencies 'must give due consideration' to the child's religious persuasion when placing for adoption, rather than specifically having to have regard to parental wishes.

[174] Schools Standards and Framework Act 1998, s 71, discussed in Clarke Hall and Morrison at 6 [407].

[175] *J v C* [1969] 1 All ER 788 at 801, per Ungoed-Thomas J.

[176] See *Hoffmann v Austria* (1993) 17 EHRR 293, E Ct HR (note the comment at [1994] Fam Law 673 and *Palau-Martinez v France* [2004] 2 FLR 810, E Ct HR). But a parent's right to manifest his religion has to be balanced against the welfare of the child and the rights of the other parent—see Thorpe LJ in *Re J (Specific Issue Orders: Muslim Upbringing and Circumcision)* [2000] 1 FLR 571 at 575, CA, discussed further below at p 392.

[177] See eg *Re S (Minors) (Access: Religious Upbringing)* [1992] 2 FLR 313, CA, *Re P (A Minor)(Residence Order: Child's Welfare)* [2000] Fam 15 and *Re J (Specific Issue Orders: Muslim Upbringing and Circumcision)* above.

(g) Medical treatment[178]

Any person over the age of 16 who has responsibility (in the sense of having de facto control) for a child under the age of 16 has a duty to obtain essential medical assistance for that child.[179] However, in most cases, before any treatment can be given, medical practitioners need a valid consent, for without it they may be open to a prosecution for battery upon the child or for one of the graver forms of assault, or be subject to a claim in tort for trespass for which the practitioner may be liable regardless of fault.[180] Such consent is not always required: practitioners have long been advised that in an emergency treatment may be given if the well-being of the child could suffer by delay caused in obtaining consent.[181] There is also some authority[182] for saying that consent is not required if those with parental responsibility have abandoned or, possibly, neglected the child. In cases of doubt, however, a ruling can be sought from the court because it is well established (see below) that the High Court can override either the giving or the refusal to give consent. Conversely, consent might not always exonerate a medical practitioner, as for example where the treatment is clearly against the child's interests, though even then there might be some situations where leave can properly be given. For example, the transplant of a child's kidney to a twin may not be in the donor's medical interests, but if, having been properly guided by medical advice, a reasonable person with parental responsibility, weighing the risks to the donor against the advantage to the other, would give his consent, all concerned should be given legal protection.[183] Although this absence of any consent may lay the practitioner open to an action *by or on behalf of the child*, apart from seeking an injunction to prevent the proposed treatment, it is difficult to see what other legal action a person with parental responsibility could bring in his own right.[184]

Prima facie anyone with parental responsibility (including a local authority)[185] can give a valid consent to the child's surgical, medical or dental treatment. However, this power of consent does not necessarily extend to all forms of treatment and, furthermore, is without prejudice to the ability of a 16-to-17-year-old or a '*Gillick* competent' child under the age of 16 to give a valid consent;[186] nor does it preclude the court from

---

[178] For consent to medical treatment see generally E Jackson *Medical Law: Text, Cases and Materials*, Ch 4; I Kennedy and A Grubb *Medical Law: Text and Materials* (3rd edn, 2000) Chs 5 and 6, and J Mason and A McCall Smith *Law and Medical Ethics* (7th edn by J Mason and G Laurie, 2006) Ch 10. See also J Munby 'Consent and Treatment: Children and the Incompetent Patient' in *Principles of Medical Law* (2nd edn edited by A Grubb, assisted by J Laing, 2004) 205.

[179] Children and Young Persons Act 1933 s 1. Note especially s 1(2)(a) under which parents, guardians and other persons legally liable to maintain the child are deemed to have neglected the child in a manner likely to cause injury to the child's health by failing to provide, or to take steps to procure the provision of, inter alia, medical aid.

[180] See eg *Re R (A Minor) (Wardship: Medical Treatment)* [1992] Fam 11 at 22, per Lord Donaldson MR.

[181] Upon the basis of the common law defence of necessity: cf Ministry of Health Circular F/19/113 1967 and Home Office Circular 63/1968. See also *Re F (Mental Patient: Sterilisation)* [1990] 2 AC 1 at 52, per Lord Bridge and *Re A (Children)(Conjoined Twins: Surgical Separation)* [2001] Fam 47, CA. per Brooke LJ.

[182] *Gillick v West Norfolk and Wisbech Area Health Authority* [1986] AC 112, HL per Lord Scarman at 189 and Lord Templeman at 204.

[183] For a discussion of this problem see Kennedy and Grubb *Medical Law: Text and Materials* above at 778ff.

[184] Parents no longer have the right to sue for the loss of their child's services: see below, p 401. However, practitioners could be subject to disciplinary action by their professional body.

[185] See *R v Kirklees Metropolitan Borough Council, ex p C (A Minor)* [1992] 2 FLR 117 and *A Metropolitan Borough Council v DB* [1997] 1 FLR 767.

[186] See the discussion above at pp 363ff.

subsequently overriding an otherwise valid consent or from sanctioning treatment otherwise opposed. In any event, no practitioner can be forced to give treatment contrary to his clinical judgment.[187] Hence, as Lord Donaldson MR observed in *Re W (A Minor) (Medical Treatment: Court's Jurisdiction),*[188] no question of consenting or refusing consent arises unless and until a medical or dental practitioner advises such treatment and is willing to undertake it.

The position of those with parental responsibility

Although as a general rule anyone with parental responsibility can give a valid consent to the child's medical treatment, the power is subject to a number of qualifications. First, not all those with parental responsibility are in the same position. In particular, those having responsibility by virtue of an emergency protection order only have authority to take such action 'as is reasonably required to safeguard or promote the welfare of the child'.[189] Hence, while such persons may be able to give a valid consent to day-to-day treatment, they cannot agree to major elective surgery.

Secondly, even parents with parental responsibility are not empowered to consent to all forms of treatment. According to Lord Templeman in *Re B (A Minor) (Wardship: Sterilisation)*[190] sterilisation of a girl under the age of 18 can only be lawfully carried out with leave of a High Court judge. Notwithstanding that Lord Templeman was the only Law Lord to say this and that the precise legal basis for his assertion remains uncertain, it has since been accepted as the basic position,[191] though whether a similar requirement extends to other forms of treatment has yet to be decided.[192] However, High Court leave is not required to perform an operation for therapeutic reasons even though a side effect (but not its main purpose) will be to sterilise the child. Furthermore, notwithstanding that a decision as to sterilisation is a matter for the judge, not all responsibility is thus removed from parents (or others with parental responsibility), since they retain the responsibility to bring the issue before the High Court.[193]

Apart from these qualifications, the power of consent vested in those with parental responsibility extends to most forms of surgical, medical or dental treatment including treatment by drugs or for drug abuse and, by analogy with s 8(2) of the Family Law Reform Act 1969, diagnostic procedures such as HIV testing and, by reason of s 21(3) of that Act (as amended), the taking of bodily samples from the child to be used in tests to determine parentage,[194] and ritual circumcision.[195]

---

[187] *Re J (A Minor) (Child In Care: Medical Treatment)* [1993] Fam 15, CA. See also *Portsmouth NHS Trust v Wyatt* [2005] EWHC 2293 (Fam), [2006] 1 FLR 652.

[188] [1993] Fam 64 at 83.

[189] Children Act 1989 s 44(5)(b).

[190] [1988] AC 199 at 205, HL, discussed by A Grubb and D Pearl 'Sterilisation and the Courts' [1987] CLJ 439. A similar conclusion was reached by the Australian High Court in *Department of Health v JWB and SMB* (1992) 66 ALJR 300.

[191] At any rate, as Lord Donaldson MR put it in *Re W (A Minor) (Medical Treatment)* [1993] Fam 64 at 79: 'parties might well be advised to apply to the court for assistance'.

[192] It might conceivably cover all irreversible treatment for non-therapeutic reasons.

[193] *Re HG (Specific Issue Order: Sterilisation)* [1993] 1 FLR 587. See also *Practice Note* [1993] 3 All ER 222. Discussed further below at p 549.

[194] Though in this case the power can be overridden by the court: see above, p 329.

[195] *Re J (Specific Issue Orders: Child's Religious Upbringing)* [2000] 1 FLR 571, CA.

The third qualification on the power of consent vested in those with parental responsibility is the age of the child. Although the matter is not entirely free from doubt, following *Re W (A Minor) (Medical Treatment: Court's Jurisdiction)*,[196] it seems that those with parental responsibility retain their power to give a valid consent throughout the child's minority.[197] This, however, is subject to three important qualifications namely:

(1) that a child aged 16 or 17 or who is '*Gillick* competent' if under the age of 16 can give a valid consent—which cannot be countermanded by an adult;[198]

(2) although in theory a valid consent may be given by an adult with parental responsibility notwithstanding the opposition of the '*Gillick* competent' or 16- or 17-year-old child, in practice no treatment should be given without prior court sanction;[199] and

(3) any decision by a parent can subsequently be overridden by the High Court.

The court's powers

It has long been established that the High Court can override a decision by a parent to consent or refuse consent to the child's medical treatment. For example, in *Re D (A Minor) (Wardship: Sterilisation)*[200] a gynaecologist intended to sterilise a mentally handicapped girl aged 11 (with her parent's consent) to prevent the possibility of her having children in the future. An educational psychologist concerned with the case then made the child a ward of court. Heilbron J concluded that there was no foreseeable risk of an unwanted pregnancy and that, as the girl would have sufficient understanding to be able to make up her own mind on the matter when she was older, the operation should not take place. Conversely, in *Re A (Children: Conjoined Twins: Surgical Separation)*[201] the court sanctioned, contrary to the parents' wishes, the separation of conjoined twins notwithstanding that the inevitable result would be to kill the weaker twin but preserve the life of the stronger twin. In *Re C (HIV Test)*[202] the court ordered, contrary to the parents' wishes, an HIV test to be carried out on a baby, and in *Re C (Welfare of Child: Immunisation)*[203] the court ordered, contrary to the wishes of the one-parent carer, that the children concerned

---

[196] [1993] Fam 64, CA, discussed further below.

[197] This view was most clearly expressed by Lord Donaldson MR, but it seemed also to be accepted by Balcombe LJ, both of whom expressly rejected the contention that Lord Scarman should have been taken to be saying in *Gillick v West Norfolk and Wisbech Area Health Authority* [1986] AC 112, HL that parents of a '*Gillick* competent' child had no right at all to consent to medical treatment of the child. But note to the contrary *R (on the Application of Axon) v Secretary of State for Health and another* [2006] EWHC 37 (Admin), [2006] 1 FCR 175 per Silber J.

[198] See Lord Donaldson MR in *Re W* [1993] Fam at 83–4.

[199] This, at any rate, was Nolan LJ's view in *Re W* [1993] Fam at 94. Even Lord Donaldson MR, at 84, thought that a child's refusal was a very important consideration for parents deciding whether themselves to give consent.

[200] [1976] Fam 185, [1976] 1 All ER 326.   [201] [2001] Fam 147.

[202] [1999] 2 FLR 1004. But note at first instance Wilson J declined to order the mother to stop breast feeding her baby. After detailed consideration the Court of Appeal refused permission to appeal against this judgment, see [1999] 2 FLR at 1017. For a comment on this decision, see A Downie '*Re C (HIV Test)* The Limits of parental autonomy' [2000] CFLQ 197.

[203] [2003] EWCA Civ 1148, [2003] 2 FLR 1095, on which see K O'Donnell '*Re C (Welfare of Child: Immunisation)*—Room to Refuse? Immunisation, welfare and the role of parental decision making' [2004] CFLQ 213.

I

I'll

I

I

should have the MMR vaccination. Other examples include *Re B (A Minor) (Wardship: Medical Treatment)*[204] in which the court sanctioned, contrary to the parents' wishes, a life-saving operation for a newly born Down's Syndrome child; *Re B (Wardship: Abortion)*[205] in which the court, overruling the mother's objections, gave permission for a 12-year-old to have an abortion, and *Re R (A Minor)(Blood Transfusion)*[206] in which the court overrode opposition to a blood transfusion by parents who were Jehovah's Witnesses.

It is also accepted that the High Court's powers of consent are wider than those of a parent and can extend, for example, to sanctioning a child's sterilisation.[207] It has been held in relation to a terminally ill child that a court can authorise treatment to relieve the child's suffering even if this means shortening the child's life.[208] In deciding what order to make it is established that the court's paramount duty is to decide what is in the best interests of the child,[209] not the reasonableness of the parents' refusal of consent.[210] There is therefore no proposition of law that the court cannot order non-essential invasive medical treatment in the face of rooted opposition by the child's primary carer.[211] This approach does not, however, mean that the parents' standpoint can be ignored. A good, if controversial, example is *Re T (a minor) (wardship: medical treatment)*.[212] In that case a child aged 18 months was suffering from a life-threatening liver defect. The medical advice was that the child should have a liver transplant as the prospects of success were good, whereas without the transplant the child's life expectancy was just over two years. The parents refused to consent. The child had already undergone surgery which had caused much pain and distress, and the mother, who had a deep-seated concern as to the benefits of major invasive surgery and post-operative treatment and about the dangers of failure long-term as well as short-term, refused to consent, taking the view that it was better for her child to spend the rest of his short life without the pain, stress and upset of intrusive surgery. No one doubted the sincerity of

[204] [1981] 1 WLR 1421, CA.   [205] [1991] 2 FLR 426.   [206] [1993] 2 FLR 757.

[207] See *Re B (A Minor) (Wardship: Sterilisation)* [1988] AC 199 at 205, per Lord Templeman. See also *Re R (A Minor) (Wardship: Consent To Medical Treatment)* [1992] Fam 11 at 25B and 28C–F.

[208] *Re C (A Minor) (Wardship: Medical Treatment)* [1990] Fam 26, CA. Note also *Re C (A Baby)* [1996] 2 FLR 43 in which the court authorised the discontinuation of artificial ventilation of a brain-damaged child. See also *Re C (Medical Treatment)* [1998] 1 FLR 384 in which the court approved a hospital's proposal—opposed by the child's parents who, being Orthodox Jews, could not contemplate a course of action which would indirectly shorten life—to withdraw ventilation and thereafter not to reinstate it in the case of a 16-month-child suffering from a fatal disease, since life-sustaining treatment would simply delay death without significantly alleviating suffering. For a similar type of decision see *A National Health Service Trust v D* [2000] 2 FLR 677 in which Cazalet J observed that allowing a child to die with dignity fell within Art 3 of the European Convention on Human Rights (as established by *D v United Kingdom*) (1997) 24 EHRR 423) and could not therefore be considered to be in breach of the right to life under Art 2.

[209] For a discussion of whether the test is different when considering whether to overrule a competent child's decision, see Lowe 'The House of Lords and the welfare principle' in Bridge (ed) *Family Law Towards the Millennium, Essays for P M Bromley* (1997) 125 at 170.

[210] Per Butler-Sloss LJ in *Re T (a minor) (wardship: medical treatment)* [1997] 1 All ER 906 at 913, applying inter alia *Re B (A Minor) (Wardship: Sterilisation)* [1988] AC 199, HL.

[211] Per Thorpe LJ in *Re C (Welfare of Child: Immunisation)* [2003] EWCA Civ 1148, [2003] 2 FLR 1095 at [22].

[212] Above. For a criticism of this decision see C Bridge 'Parental power and the medical treatment of children' in *Family Law Towards the Millennium, Essays for P M Bromley*, above, 295 at 325–8, who considers the decision to be too parent-centred. It is instructive to compare this decision with that of Heilbron J in *Re D (A Minor) (Wardship: Sterilisation)*, above, discussed above.

the mother's views and both parents were described as caring and devoted to the child. An added complication of the case was that at the time of the action the family were living abroad, so that it was not certain that an order authorising the treatment would be implemented.

The court was acutely aware of the difficulties that the case presented—was it in the best interests of the child to have a peaceful if short life with devoted parents, or should the court give its consent to the liver transplant and order the child's return to this country with all the distress and uncertainties that that would entail? In the exceptional circumstances of the case it was held that the child's best interests required that his future treatment should be left in the hands of his devoted parents.

(h) Vetoing the issue of a passport

Since 5 October 1998 it has no longer been possible to apply to put children's names on adults' passports. Instead applications have to be made for children to be issued with their own passports though passports already issued to parents with their children's names upon them remain valid.[213] As the guidance issued by the UK Passport Agency explains,[214] in the absence of any objection being lodged at the Agency's passport office, standard passport facilities are normally granted to children with the consent of either parent or a person acting in loco parentis. Where the child's parents are not married to each other, the mother's consent is required if the father does not have parental responsibility.[215] Where it is known that the child is a ward of court,[216] the court's consent is required.

In the absence of any court order, objections to the issue of a passport will usually only be considered in limited circumstances, namely from an unmarried mother, or from the police where they have notified the Agency of an intention to exercise their power of arrest under the Child Abduction Act 1984.[217] However, objections will also be considered inter alia where the court has ordered that the child is not to be removed from the jurisdiction and, as is expressly stated on the face of a contact or residence order: '*Any* person with parental responsibility may ask the United Kingdom Passport Agency . . . not to issue a passport allowing the child to go abroad without the knowledge of that person'.[218]

(i) Taking the child abroad and arranging for the child's emigration

Subject to the obtaining of the necessary passports, parents with parental responsibility acting in unison have the power to take their child outside the United Kingdom and can therefore arrange for his emigration. Neither parent has the *unilateral* right, if the other parent has parental responsibility, to take or remove the child, under the age of 16 from the United Kingdom without the other's consent,[219] since to do so is an offence under the

---

[213] Home Office News Release 142/98. It is to be noted that arrangements for obtaining a one-year British Visitor's Passport having ended, these controls govern *all* applications for British passports for children.

[214] Reproduced at [1994] Fam Law 651. See also *Practice Direction* [1986] 1 All ER 983.

[215] For the position of unmarried fathers with respect to parental responsibility see below, p 409.

[216] Wardship is discussed in Chapter 16.   [217] Discussed further below, p 616.

[218] Form C43. Emphasis added.

[219] 'United Kingdom' means England and Wales, Scotland and Northern Ireland: Interpretation Act 1978 Sch 1. For the purposes of this Act the 'consent' required does not have to be in writing. It is a defence under s 1(5) of the Child Abduction Act 1984 if the child is removed: (a) in the belief that the other person has consented or would have done had he been aware of all the relevant circumstances; (b) after taking all

Child Abduction Act 1984 s 1(1). Guardians and special guardians are empowered to remove the child from the United Kingdom unless there are other persons with parental responsibility, in which case their consent is also required.[220]

The powers of removal are further fettered in the event of the making of a residence or care order. A person in whose favour a residence order is made is thereby entitled to remove the child from the United Kingdom for a period of less than one month without anyone's permission,[221] but can only remove the child for a period in excess of one month with the *written* consent of every person having parental responsibility or with leave of the court.[222] The making of a care order prevents any person from removing the child from the United Kingdom without the written consent of every person with parental responsibility[223] or leave of the court, though the local authority themselves can arrange for the child's removal for a period of less than one month without anyone's permission[224] and, with approval of the court, may make arrangements for the child in their care to live outside England and Wales.[225] The net result of these provisions is that where the child is to be removed from the United Kingdom for more than one month the consent all those who have parental responsibility or leave of the court must be obtained.

(j) Naming the child [226]

Although it can simply be said that naming a child is an aspect of parental responsibility the law on this issue is surprisingly complicated. There are two aspects: the initial conferring of the name and the subsequent changing of it. A distinction can also be made between first or given names and surnames.

Conferring names

The power to confer the name is vested in those who can register the child's birth, which in turn is governed by the Births and Deaths Registration Act 1953, as amended. As Butler-Sloss LJ explained in *Re W (A Child)(Illegitimate Child: Change of Surname)*,[227] the 1953 Act[228]

'requires registration of the birth of a child within 42 days of birth. The Registration of Births and Deaths Regulations 1987, as amended by the Registration of Births and Deaths

---

reasonable steps to communicate with the other person the accused had been unable to do so; or (c) the other person has unreasonably refused to consent. Section 1(5)(c) does not apply if the person who refused consent had a residence order or custody order in his favour: s 1(5A), added by the Children Act 1989 Sch 12, para 37(3). In cases where there is sufficient evidence to raise the application of s 1(5) the burden is on the prosecution to show that s 1(5) does not apply: s 1(6).

[220] Special guardians only require consent to take the child out of the United kingdom for more than three months: Child Abduction Act 1984, s 1(4)(b, as amended by the Adoption and Children Act 2002. For further discussion of special guardianship, see below pp 604ff.

[221] Children Act 1989 s 13(2).

[222] Ibid, s 13(1). Cf. the position of special guardians, see n 220 above.   [223] Ibid, s 33(7)(b).

[224] Ibid, s 33(8)(a).   [225] Ibid, s 33(8)(b) and Sch 2, para 19.

[226] See generally A Bond 'Reconstructing families—changing children's surnames' (1998) 10 CFLQ 17.

[227] [2001] Fam 1 at [2].

[228] Sections 2 and 10. This compulsory method of registration conforms with the requirement under Art 7 of the United Nations Convention on the Rights of the Child that children be registered immediately after birth and from birth, have the right to a name and nationality. For the background to Art 7 see J Fortin *Children's Rights and the Developing Law* (2nd edn) 399.

(Amendment) Regulations 1994, set out the requirements for registration. These include the name and surname of the child. Regulation 9(3)(b) provides

"... the surname to be entered shall be the surname by which at the date of the registration of the birth it is intended that the child shall be known".

When the parents are married the duty to provide the relevant information lies on both parents. When the parents are not married at the time of his birth the mother alone has the duty to register the birth.'

To this may be added that in the case of abandoned children the person having charge of the child can apply to the Registrar General to have the birth registered.[229]

The 1953 Act, therefore, effectively confines the power to confer a name on the child (other than an abandoned child) to each of the married parents or the unmarried mother, i.e. parents who have parental responsibility for the child immediately he or she is born.

Although the 1953 Act places an obligation on married parents and unmarried mothers to register the child's birth and name it does not dictate what surname to register. Hence, although by convention a child born to married parents takes his father's surname, the father cannot insist upon this.[230] Conversely, while a child whose parents are not married normally takes the mother's surname, he may be known by his father's,[231] although the father has no right to insist upon this.[232]

While it is mandatory to register a surname there is no similar obligation to register first names,[233] and even where they are registered, as Thorpe LJ pointed out in Re H (Child's Name: First Name)[234] it is 'commonplace for a child to receive statutory registration with one or more given names and, subsequently, to receive different given names, maybe at baptism or, maybe, by custom or adoption'. In short, as Thorpe LJ said, given names 'have a much less concrete character'.

Notwithstanding their significance inter alia with regard to names, registrations are essentially a matter of record. Hence, as Thorpe LJ has pointed out,[235] '[O]nce a child has received official registration, then that registration stands indefinitely, save perhaps in quite exceptional circumstances.' The finality of registrations is well illustrated by Re H (Child's Name: First Name).[236] In that case a father, without informing his wife, registered

[229] Section 3A.
[230] There is nothing in the Registration of Births, Deaths and Marriages Regulations 1987 requiring the father's name to be given priority and it seems that the mother is entitled to register the child in her name: D v B (Surname: Birth Registration) [1979] Fam 38, sub nom D v B (Otherwise D) (Child: Surname) [1979] 1 All ER 92, CA.
[231] See eg Re P (Parental Responsibility) [1997] 2 FLR 722, CA.
[232] See eg Dawson v Wearmouth [1999] 2 AC 308, HL, on which see M Hayes 'Dawson v Wearmouth What's in a name? A child by any other name is surely just as sweet?' [1999] CFLQ 423.
[233] See reg 9(3)(a) of the 1987 Regulations which directs the registrar, if a first name is not given to 'enter only the surname, preceded by a horizontal line'.
[234] [2002] EWCA Civ 190, [2002] 1 FLR 973 at [14]. But note Re D, L and LA (Care: Change of Forename) [2003] 1 FLR 339, discussed below.
[235] In Re H (Child's Name: First Name), above, at [12].
[236] Above. The couple had separated when the wife was 6 weeks' pregnant. The father had no further contact until the day of the birth when he visited the hospital to discuss the names which the child should be given.

the child with his own choice of given names. The wife subsequently registered the child with a different given name. It was accepted that the father's registration, being the first in time, prevailed and the mother's registration was cancelled. The Court of Appeal, however, ruled that the mother was free to use her chosen given name.[237]

Changing names

Notwithstanding the finality of registrations it is perfectly possible to change the child's name either formally by court order[238] or by deed poll or informally. In point of fact to effect a change there is no requirement to execute a formal deed for a change of surname since a person may call himself what he likes. However, the execution and enrolment of a need may be useful for evidential purposes.[239] There is no formal provision for changing a child's first or given name.

As we discuss in Chapter 12[240] disputes over name changes are not infrequent, but here we are concerned with who has the legal right to make or agree to such changes.

Where only one person has parental responsibility (as, for example, where a married parent survives the other or in the case of unmarried parents where only the mother has parental responsibility) then, as Holman J said in *Re PC (Change of Surname)*,[241] 'that person has the right and power lawfully to cause a change of surname without any other permission or consent'. However, once the child's name has been registered then, again in the words of Holman J,[242] '[w]here two or more people have parental responsibility for a child then one of those people can only cause a change of surname if all other people having parental responsibility consent or agree' or he or she obtains an appropriate court order. This is clearly the position where a residence order is in force since s 13(1)(a) of the Children Act 1989 expressly states that no person may cause the child to be known by a new surname without either the written consent of every person who has parental responsibility for the child or leave of the court. A similar position obtains upon the making of a special guardianship order,[243] a care order[244] and a placement order for adoption.[245] The position where there are no court orders is perhaps not so clear cut. Indeed in *Re PC*[246] it was specifically argued that in such cases there was no restriction on any person unilaterally changing a child's name. Holman J, however, ruled otherwise pointing out[247] the bizarre consequences of the argument, namely that where

'parents have not agreed about their child or not been able to trust each other so that a residence order had to be made; or where (putting it loosely) they have caused or risked significant harm to their child so that a care order has had to be made, the "rights" of both

---

[237] See further below at p 399.

[238] An adoption order entitles the adopters to change the child's name which is entered on Adopted Children Register (see below p 866). The court can also sanction a change of surname when making a special guardianship order: Children Act 1989, s 14B(2)(a) (see further below at p 607) or by making a specific issue order under s 8 or when granting leave under s 13(1)(a) of the 1989 Act (see further below at p 550).

[239] See the Enrolment of Deeds (Change of Name) Regulations 1994, SI 1994/604.

[240] See below p 550.   [241] [1997] 2 FLR 730 at 739.

[242] In *Re PC (Change of Surname)*, above at 739. Holman J left open whether in the case of older children, particularly those over the age of 16, the child's own consent was also required.

[243] Children Act 1989, s 14C(3), discussed below p 608.

[244] Section 33(7), discussed below at p 774.

[245] Adoption and Children Act 2002, s 28(2), (3)(a), discussed below p 842.   [246] Above.

[247] Above at 736.

parents in relation to a change of name are carefully preserved; whereas where parents have been able to agree and have not caused or risked harm to their child the "rights" of either parent can be literally overborne by the other.'

He also rejected the argument, based on s 2(7) of the Children Act 1989 (which allows any one holder of parental responsibility to act alone without the other),[248] that one spouse can now unilaterally change a child's surname. In his Lordship's view, in the absence of a residence order being made, the 1989 Act cannot be taken to have altered the former law[249] under which it was clear that one married parent could not change his child's name without his spouse's consent.[250]

Although Holman J's arguments seem convincing his decision has yet to be approved by the appellate courts.

One interesting result of the current position is that whereas the conferring of names is exercisable only by parents with parental responsibility, the power to agree or refuse to agree to its change is exercisable by *any* person with parental responsibility.

It will be noted that the statutory provisions already referred to and the decision in *Re PC* are concerned with changing surnames. However, it cannot be assumed that there is unlimited freedom to change given names. In *Re D, L and LA (Care: Change of Forename)*,[251] for example, it was held that foster carers (who do not have parental responsibility) had no power to change the child's given names. There is perhaps less concern about parental carers changing forenames but even this issue has been litigated.[252]

(k) Representation

In general a child can only bring or defend legal proceedings, at any rate in the High Court and county court, by his 'litigation friend'.[253] Similarly, if civil proceedings are brought against him he must be represented by a guardian.[254] Parents have long been regarded as having the prima facie[255] entitlement to act in each of those capacities, and presumably anyone with parental responsibility is in the same position.[256] It should be noted that with

---

[248] See below, p 432.

[249] His Lordship relied upon *Y v Y (Child: Surname)* [1973] Fam 147, [1973] 2 All ER 574, but for an earlier authority to the same effect see *Re T (otherwise H) (An Infant)* [1963] Ch 238, [1962] 3 All ER 970.

[250] *Practice Direction* [1995] 1 All ER 832.

[251] [2003] 1 FLR 339. Butler-Sloss P held, the correct course where foster carers think a change of name is desirable is to inform the social worker in charge of the case. In foster placements the parents should always be consulted and if a change cannot be achieved by consent, it might be necessary to involve the High Court's inherent jurisdiction (query why a specific issue order could not be sought instead?).

[252] See *Re H (Child's Name: First Name)* [2002] EWCA Civ 190, [2002] 1 FLR 973, discussed above at p 397.

[253] CPR 1998, r 21.2(2).

[254] It should be noted that r 21.2 only applies to proceedings before the High Court and county court. The better view is that in the absence of any express restrictions children are entitled to conduct their own proceedings before magistrates' courts.

[255] *Woolf v Pemberton* (1877) 6 Ch D 19. Note there is a power of removal if a proper case is made out: *Re Taylor's Application* [1972] 2 QB 369, (successful application to remove a parent who refused to accept compromise of thalidomide application, though decision to remove the particular parent was reversed on appeal).

[256] In Scotland the matter is put beyond doubt by s 2(1)(d) of the Children (Scotland) Act 1995: see above, p 374.

respect to proceedings under the Children Act 1989 and under the High Court's inherent jurisdiction special rules apply, so that children of sufficient age and understanding do not need to act through a next friend or guardian.[257]

(l) Disposing of the child's corpse

It is established that a parent who has the means to do so is bound to provide for the burial of his deceased child.[258] Such a duty, which presumably may also be discharged by cremating the child, may therefore properly be considered to be an aspect of parental responsibility. However, in *R v Gwynedd County Council*[259] it was held that, as the local authority's responsibility towards a child in care ceased upon the child's death, the right to bury the child vested in the parent rather than the foster parent. Put into the language of the 1989 Act it can be said that, as the local authority's responsibility ended upon the child's death, the right to bury the child vested exclusively in the parents with parental responsibility.[260] Similarly, those who have parental responsibility by means of a residence order will lose it upon the child's death. Accordingly, the right to dispose of a child's corpse seems exclusively to be vested in parents with parental responsibility and guardians.

This aspect of parental responsibility falls outside the scope of the Children Act 1989, since that Act is properly be considered to be confined to dealing with live children.[261] In *Fessi v Whitmore*[262] which concerned a dispute as to the disposal of a dead child's ashes, it was accepted that the 1989 Act was not the appropriate statutory vehicle to decide the matter, but neither did the judge think it was, properly considered, a matter of administering the child's estate. In the judge's view the issue was more in the nature of a dispute between two equally entitled trustees (ie the mother and father) and decided the issue on the basis of an evaluation of the arguments advanced by each parent. Whether this approach will be accepted by the appellate courts remains to be seen, but it is submitted that the appropriate procedure for resolving disputes of this kind is to invoke the High Court's inherent jurisdiction.[263] In *Buchanan v Milton*,[264] which involved a dispute between the birth mother and adoptive mother over the disposal of an adult child's remains, the case was determined with reference to s 116(1) of the Supreme Court Act 1981 under which applications can be made to be appointed as administrator of the deceased's estate.

---

[257] Family Proceedings Rules 1991 r 9.2A, added by the Family Proceedings (Amendment) Rules 1992 r 6, for the operation of which see *Re T (A Minor)(Child: Representation)* [1994] Fam 49, CA, discussed below at p 504. For an overview see C Sawyer 'The competence of children to participate in family proceedings' (1995) 7 CFLQ 180.

[258] *R v Vann* (1851) 2 Den 325, 15 JP 802, approved by Lord Alverstone LJ in *Clark v London General Omnibus Co Ltd* [1906] 2 KB 648, CA at 659 and followed in *R v Gwynedd County Council, ex p B* [1992] 3 All ER 317, CA.

[259] Above.

[260] It should be noted, however, that local authorities have permissive powers to arrange for the child's burial or cremation should the parents not wish or be able to exercise their rights: Children Act 1989 Sch 2, para 20.

[261] Section 105(1) defines child as 'a person under the age of eighteen' and following the normal rules of construction 'person' presumptively refers to a live person: see eg *Elliot v Joicey* [1935] AC 209, HL, and *R v Newham London Borough Council, ex p Dada* [1996] QB 507, CA. For a similar interpretation of 'child' under the Children and Young Persons Act 1969 s 70(1) see *Re D (A Minor)* [1987] AC 317, HL.

[262] [1999] 1 FLR 167.   [263] The inherent jurisdiction is discussed in Ch 16.

[264] [1999] 2 FLR 844.

(m) Child's services

Formerly, at common law, persons with parental rights were entitled to the domestic services of their unmarried children under the age of 18 actually living with them as part of the family. The significance of this lay in the fact that it provided the parent with his only common law remedy against a stranger for interference with parental rights.[265] However, insofar as the loss of service is due to a tort committed against the child, the parents' cause of action has been abolished by the Administration of Justice Act 1982 s 2(b). Furthermore, it has been held[266] that there is no cause of action against a stranger for interference with parental rights in respect of the relationship with their children. For practical purposes, therefore, parental responsibility cannot be said to include a right to domestic services.[267]

(n) Administration of property

Parental responsibility includes the rights, powers and duties which a guardian of the estate (appointed before the Children Act 1989 came into force)[268] would have had in relation to the child and his property.[269] Such rights include the right 'to receive or recover in his own name, for the benefit of the child, property of whatever description and wherever situated which the child is entitled to receive or recover.'[270]

Parental responsibility does *not* include rights of succession to the child's property.[271] Indeed, it seems that a parent has no rights as such in the property of a child of any age and therefore, in the absence of any agreement, has no claim, for instance, on the child's wages.[272] The ownership of gifts to a child is more problematic and would in the first place depend on the value of the gift and the age of child. In the case of gifts to young children the legal interest probably vests in the parents (or other persons having parental responsibility for the child), but as a result of s 3(3) of the 1989 Act such goods would then be held on trust for the child. In the case of gifts to older children,[273] it is thought that the property belongs to the child. In practice, if a minor is entitled to property of any value, he will normally derive it under a settlement or will or on an intestacy, and the legal ownership will therefore usually vest in trustees.[274]

Notwithstanding that parental responsibility does not include a right of succession, since children cannot generally[275] make a valid will, in practice parents (but not others with parental responsibility) have a right to inherit their children's property.[276]

---

[265] Discussed in extenso in the 6th edition of this work at pp 329 et seq.

[266] *F v Wirral Metropolitan Borough Council* [1991] Fam 69, CA and *Re S (A Minor) (Parental Rights)* [1993] Fam Law 572, discussed further below at p 408.

[267] See below, p 408.   [268] Before 14 October 1991.   [269] Children Act 1989 s 3(2).

[270] Section 3(3).   [271] Section 3(4)(b).   [272] See *Williams v Doulton* [1948] 1 All ER 603.

[273] At what stage a child makes the transition from younger to older for these purposes is uncertain and will be a question of fact to be determined in each case.

[274] If a child is absolutely entitled to property under a will or on an intestacy, the personal representatives may appoint trustees of the gift for the beneficiary and vest the property in them: Administration of Estates Act 1925 s 42(1). Depending upon the terms of the instrument creating the interest, parents (or others with parental responsibility) may be able to make a claim on the fund for the child's maintenance and education.

[275] Aliter if they are on actual military service: Wills (Soldiers and Sailors) Act 1918 s 1 (as amended by the Family Law Reform Act 1969 s 3(1)(b)).

[276] Administration of Estates Act 1925 Pt IV and the Family Law Reform Act 1987 s 18(2), discussed further below at p 1100.

(o) Information about the child

There is a growing jurisprudence both as to the right to obtain information about a child and as to whether parental responsibility carries with it the power to control publicity about a child. Nevertheless, as will be seen, it remains unclear both as to whether parental responsibility confers a right per se to the obtaining of information about the child and, insofar as it confers the power to control publicity, whether this can be said be a separate incident of responsibility or simply another aspect of the power to protect the child. It is for these reasons that rights in respect of information about a child were not included in the 'list' of what parental responsibility comprises.[277] Nevertheless it is convenient to discuss the foregoing issues under the one umbrella heading. We begin by considering the power to obtain information about the child.

Obtaining information about the child

The common law is largely silent on a parent's position with regard to having access to information about the child. Case law has been concerned with the issue of disclosure of evidence in court proceedings, but in those cases the parents claimed a right to see the evidence on the basis of their alleged rights as parties to the litigation rather than as parents per se.[278] In *Re C (Disclosure)*,[279] however, a guardian successfully sought leave to withhold information gained in care proceedings and which the 16-year-old child concerned did not want to be revealed, from the mother who was party to the proceedings, Johnson J commented[280] that quite apart from her entitlement as a party to the proceedings to know all the evidence 'her very status as . . . mother must give her some strong entitlement to information about her daughter.' On the facts, however, he held that, because he was satisfied that there was a high degree of probability that disclosure would be harmful to the child, the information should be withheld.

Access to information about a child is now governed by the Data Protection Act 1998. In general terms, parents, or those with parental responsibility, can request disclosure of information held about the child.[281] However, one commentary advises[282] that if the data controller has any doubts as to the entitlement of the person making the request to do so, 'it will be prudent to refuse access and leave the issue to be decided by a competent court which can weigh what is in the best interests of the child'.

In relation to information relating to the child's health, a person with parental responsibility can make a request for information but over and above other restrictions[283] health data are exempt from disclosure if the information was:

'(a) provided by the data subject in the expectation that it would not be disclosed to the person making the request;

---

[277] See above, p 377.

[278] See, for example, *Official Solicitor v K* [1965] AC 201, HL.

[279] [1996] 1 FLR 797.   [280] Above at 803.

[281] Formerly there were disparate provisions as, for example, under the Access to Health Records Act 1990, the Access to Personal Files Act 1987, and the Access to Personal Files (Social Services) Regulations 1989.

[282] R Jay and A Hamilton *Data Protection, Law and Practice* (2nd edn, 2003) at 10.06.

[283] There is a general exemption on having to reveal information that is likely to cause serious harm to the physical or mental health or condition of the data subject or any other person: Data Protection (Subject to Access Modification) (Health) Order 2000 (SI 2000/413) reg 5(1).

(b) obtained as a result of any examination or investigation to which the data subject consented in the expectation that the information would not be disclosed; or

(c) which the data subject has expressly indicated should not be so disclosed.'

But it is expressly provided that the child (data subject) can change his mind and allow access which had been previously vetoed.[284]

So far as education is concerned, the data controller is exempt from the need to comply with a request in circumstances where the data consists of information as to actual or potential child abuse, and compliance would not be in the interests of the data subject.[285]

So far as social work information is concerned, there is no entitlement in respect of information:

'(a) provided by the data subject in the expectation that it would not be disclosed to the person making the request;

(b) obtained as a result of any examination or investigation to which the data subject consented in the expectation that the information would not be disclosed; or

(c) which the data subject has expressly indicated should not be so disclosed.'[286]

Controlling publicity about the child

At one time it was thought that questions concerning publicity about a child fell outside the ambit of parental responsibility.[287] It has become evident through case law, however, that the position is not so straightforward. There is, as Ward LJ pointed out in *Re Z (A Minor) (Identification: Restrictions of Publicity)*,[288] a number of different situations in which the issue of publicity can be involved. At one end of the spectrum is the situation where some third party, such as the media, publishes without parental involvement information about the child and/or his family. It seems clear that in this type of instance the issue of publicity cannot be regarded as an aspect of parental responsibility.[289] At the other end of the spectrum is the publication of information that is properly regarded as being confidential to the child. That, according to *Re Z*, clearly involves an aspect of parental responsibility. In *Re Z* a mother sought the discharge of an injunction restraining publicity about her child so that a film could be broadcast publicising treatment of the child (who would have been clearly identified in the film) at a unit specialising in the treatment of children with special educational needs. In holding that the restraint of publicity in these circumstances was an aspect of parental responsibility, Ward LJ held that:[290]

'Placing this particular child at this institute is a proper discharge by this mother of her responsibility to secure her [ie the child's] medical and educational advancement. It then

---

[284] Reg 5(3).

[285] Data Protection (Subject to Access Modification) (Education) Order 2000 (SI/414) reg 5.

[286] Ibid.

[287] See, for example, the Department of Health's *Guidance and Regulations*, vol 1 *Court Orders* (1991) at para 2.31 which is repeated in the Guidance to the Northern Ireland Order, vol 1, *Court Orders and Other Legal Issues* (1995), para 5.17.

[288] [1997] Fam 1, CA, discussed also above at p 460. See the comments on this case by H Fenwick 'Clashing Rights, the Welfare of the Child and the Human Rights Act' (2004) 67 MLR 889.

[289] See eg *Re M and N (Minors) (Wardship: Publication of Information)* [1990] Fam 211, CA and *R v Central Independent Television plc* [1994] Fam 192, CA, discussed above, p 460.

[290] Above at 26.

becomes her duty to respect the confidence of her treatment and/or education at the institute. *It is an incident of her parental responsibility to decide whether to preserve or to publish matters relating thereto which are confidential to the child.*' [Emphasis added.]

In between these two extremes is the type of situation that arose in *Re W (Wardship: Publicity)*[291] in which a father stood by and acquiesced in his teenage sons taking their story to the press.[292] The majority view[293] in that case was that it was at least 'arguable' that publishing information about a child was a 'non-parental activity' and, as such, was not an aspect of parental responsibility. However, Hobhouse LJ disagreed, commenting:[294]

'Whether or not an immature child should become involved with the media is something which clearly can affect the welfare of the child and falls within the scope of the proper discharge of parental duties . . . An immature child will often be unable to judge when it is truly to his advantage to invite the media into his life; he may not appreciate the distress and harm it may cause him and not be able to cope with it when it occurs. There is a risk of harm to the child which requires the exercise of parental responsibility in the interests of the child's welfare. A parent has the responsibility and the authority and power as part of his upbringing of the child to control, if needs be, his child's contact with the media.'

Although it must be stressed that it was a dissenting judgment, Hobhouse LJ's view seems a powerful one, and moreover is in line with the cases that establish[295] that giving leave to interview a child by solicitors acting for the father in criminal proceedings is an aspect of parental responsibility. It remains to be seen whether the law will be developed along these lines. In this respect note might be taken of *Re S (A Child)(Identification: Restrictions on Publication)*[296] in which the House of Lords ruled that in the light of the Human Rights Act 1998 the foundation of the jurisdiction to restrain publicity now derives from the European Convention on Human Rights. Consequently there was no need to consider the scope of the inherent jurisdiction. Whether this line of reasoning extends to Ward LJ's analysis by which the court has power to restrain publicity under s 8 of the Children Act 1989[297] is by no means clear. But even if Ward LJ's analysis does stand the test of time it is by no means easy to predict into which category a particular situation might fall. What information, for example, will be thought to be confidential to the child and what freedom does the parent or those with parental responsibility have to publicise their own story?[298]

---

[291] [1995] 2 FLR 466, CA.

[292] An article was published in the *Independent* newspaper entitled 'Our fight to stay with Dad', together with a picture of the boys in silhouette from which they could nevertheless be identified.

[293] Per Balcombe LJ, ibid at 472, with whom Waite LJ agreed.   [294] Ibid at 476–7.

[295] See *Re M (Care: Leave to Interview Child)* [1995] 1 FLR 825 and *Re F (Specific Issue: Child Interview)* [1995] 1 FLR 819, CA, discussed above, p 463 n 102. It also seems to be favoured by Ward LJ in *Re Z*, above at 27, who also pointed out that in any case the majority's views were obiter.

[296] [2004] UK HL 47, [2005] 1 AC 593.   [297] Discussed below at p 460.

[298] In *Re H-S (Minors) (Protection of Identity)* [1994] 3 All ER 390 in which a transsexual father, with whom the children were now living, wanted to publicise the family story, Ward J seemed to think that the issue of publicity did not involve an aspect of parental responsibility, yet might not the children's care and upbringing be thought to be confidential? See now *Clayton v Clayton* [2006] EWCA Civ 878: father free to publicise his case (but not details of proceedings) after final order made, provided welfare of child does not require continuing anonymity.

5 LIABILITY FOR CHILDREN'S ACTS

Hitherto we have been concerned with what responsibility comprises, but another related issue is the potential liability of those having parental responsibility.

(a) Contracts

It is established that a parent (and therefore any person with parental responsibility) will never be liable as such for any contract made by the child.[299] Such persons may, however, be liable on the ordinary principles of agency if they have authorised the child to make the contract or, in the case of unauthorised contracts, by estoppel or ratification.[300]

(b) Torts

As in the case of contracts, neither parents nor others with parental responsibility will be liable as such for a child's tort unless they have authorised its commission.

A parent or someone with parental responsibility[301] may also be personally liable if he himself has been negligent by affording the child an opportunity of injuring another. This is a particular application of the tort of negligence, and the test is therefore: did the parent by his act or omission cause or permit his child to do an act which was foreseeably likely to harm the person injured and against which a reasonably prudent parent would have guarded? If so, he will be liable. In *Newton v Edgerley*[302] the defendant permitted his son aged 12 to have possession of a shotgun but did not instruct him how to handle it when others were present. Although the defendant had forbidden his son to use the gun when other children were near, he was nonetheless held personally liable in negligence for the injury to a child who was accidentally shot by his son, because he ought to have foreseen that his son would succumb to temptation and consequently should either have forbidden him to use the gun at all or have instructed him how to handle it in the presence of others. On the other hand, in *Donaldson v McNiven*[303] the defendant had let his son aged 13 buy an airgun. He forbade him to fire it outside the house (he was only permitted to fire it in the cellar) and the boy gave his word that he would not do so. One day, however, he took it outside, fired it and put out the plaintiff's eye. The father was held not to be liable, for he had taken all reasonable precautions to ensure that the gun was fired in a safe place and no damage would have resulted but for the son's disobedience and folly, which the defendant could not reasonably have foreseen.

Although these cases both deal with liability for permitting a child to have a dangerous toy or weapon, there is no reason why it should be restricted to this field. Thus, if an adult in charge of a young child on a busy road negligently lets him run into the traffic with the

---

299 *Mortimore v Wright* (1840) 6 M & W 482.

300 See generally works on the law of contract and agency.

301 Note the difficulty of establishing negligence by a local authority in respect of a child in their care discussed below, p 810.

302 [1959] 3 All ER 337. See also *Bebee v Sales* (1916) 32 TLR 413.

303 [1952] 2 All ER 691, CA. See also *Jauffir v Akhbar*, *The Times*, 10 February 1984; *Gorely v Codd* [1966] 3 All ER 891.

result that the driver of a car, in swerving to avoid the child, injures himself or another, that adult must on principle be liable for the damage.[304]

(c) Crimes

At common law a parent was not liable for his child's crimes unless he himself was guilty of aiding and abetting. But the fact that a child's criminal propensities may be due to bad home influence or a lack of parental supervision has now been recognised by statute. The court before which a child has been found guilty of an offence can, with the consent of the offender's parent or guardian, order the parent or guardian to enter into a recognizance to take proper care of him and exercise proper control over him (failure unreasonably to consent is punishable by a fine not exceeding £1,000).[305] Where the offending child is aged between 10 and 15 the court has a duty to exercise the above mentioned powers if it is satisfied in all the circumstances that their exercise would be desirable in the interests of preventing the child committing further offences.[306] Alternatively, if a court imposes a fine or costs or makes a compensation order for the commission of an offence by a child under the age of 17, it may order that these be paid by the child's parent or guardian (but not other persons even if they have parental responsibility) unless the latter cannot be found or the court is satisfied that he has not conduced to the commission of the offence by neglecting to exercise due care or control of the child.[307] Under the Crime and Disorder Act 1998, as amended, where a court makes a child safety order or an anti-social behaviour order in respect of a child or the child has committed an offence or the parent has failed to comply with a school attendance order or to secure the regular attendance of a registered pupil, the court may make a parenting order.[308] In the case of a child under the age of 16 who has been convicted of an offence where the court is satisfied that a 'parenting order' would help prevent a re-occurrence of the offending behaviour, it is obliged to make such an order.[309] The parenting order requires a parent to comply for up to 12 months with

---

[304] See *Carmarthenshire County Council v Lewis* [1955] AC 549, HL, where a school authority was liable in similar circumstances for negligently letting a child run out of the school premises onto a road with the result that a lorry driver was killed. See further Waller 'Visiting the Sins of the Children' (1963–65) 4 Melbourne ULR 17.

[305] Powers of Criminal Courts (Sentencing) Act 2000, s 150(1),(2).

[306] Section 150(1)(a). If the court decides not to exercise these powers it must state in open court why it is not so satisfied: s 150(1)(b).

[307] Children and Young Persons Act 1933 s 55; Children and Young Persons Act 1969 s 3(6) and Schs 5 and 6; Administration of Justice Act 1970 Sch 11; Criminal Justice 1972 Sch 5. The court must exercise this power if the child is under 14. A local authority having parental responsibility for a child or young person who is in their care or who is being provided with accommodation by them is regarded as a parent or guardian for these purposes: Children and Young Persons Act 1933 s 55(5) (added by the Criminal Justice Act 1991 s 57(2)), reversing *Leeds City Council v West Yorkshire Metropolitan Police* [1983] 1 AC 29, HL. See also *D (a minor)v DPP* [1995] 2 FLR 502 in which it was held to be a defence for the local authority (as for a parent) that they have done everything that could reasonably and properly be done to protect the public from the offender. Where a local authority allows a child to be under the charge or control of a parent or guardian, that person can be liable, though it is a question of fact whether the arrangements made between the parties constitute a transfer of control: *Leeds City Council v West Yorkshire Metropolitan Police*, above. See G Samuel 'Legal Reasoning and Liability for People' (1982) 98 LQR 358. See also the Criminal Law Act 1977 s 36 (liability of parent or guardian for unpaid fine).

[308] Crime and Disorder Act 1998, s 8. For a full discussion of parenting orders see eg A Bainham *Children—The Modern Law* (3rd edn) 638 and the references there cited.

[309] Section 9. If it is not so satisfied the court should state in open court the reasons why: s 9(1)(b).

such requirements as are specified in the order and in particular may require the parent to attend a counselling or guidance programme for up to three months. A parent can subsequently be fined up to a maximum of £1,000 for failing to comply with the parenting order. As an alternative to being made subject to parenting orders, under the scheme introduced by the Anti-Social Behaviour Act 2003 parents may voluntarily enter into parenting contracts, inter alia with schools, local education authorities or youth offending teams as appropriate. Under these contracts parents, on the one hand agree to comply with the requirements set out in the contract for a specified period while on the other hand the school, local education authority or youth offending team provides or arranges support to the parent to help with compliance.[310]

6 LIABILITY FOR INTERFERENCE WITH PARENTS' AND CHILDREN'S RIGHTS

(a) Criminal liability

Although the contrary view was once held,[311] there is apparently no common law offence of taking a child against his parents' will.[312] However, under the Child Abduction Act 1984 s 2, it is an offence for a person 'unconnected'[313] with the child to take or detain, without lawful authority or reasonable excuse, a child under the age of 16 so as to remove him from or to keep him out of the lawful control[314] of any person having or entitled to lawful control of him.[315] The offence may be committed in respect of a child of either sex, and regardless of whether the interference is permanent or temporary. There is no need to prove force or fraud, so it can be an offence to persuade a child to leave his parents. Under this Act a person is regarded as 'taking' a child if he causes or induces the child to accompany him or any other person or causes the child to be taken.[316] It is a defence if the accused can show that he reasonably believed that the child was 16[317] or, in the case of an unmarried father, that he was or reasonably believed himself to be the child's father.[318]

---

[310] Anti-Social Behaviour Act 2003, s 25.   [311] East Pleas of the Crown, 429–30.

[312] The removal must be against the child's will: R v Hale [1974] QB 819. It is, however, established that a parent can be guilty of the common law offence of kidnapping his own child: R v D [1984] AC 778, HL, and see N Lowe 'Child Abduction and Child Kidnapping—II: The Common Law Position and its Relationship with the Child Abduction Act 1984' (1984) 134 NLJ 995; and of unlawfully imprisoning his own child: R v Rahman (1985) 81 Cr App Rep 349; CA; see A Khan 'False Imprisonment of a Child by a Parent' [1986] Fam Law 69. For a discussion of the statutory offence under s 1 of the Child Abduction Act 1984, see below, p 616.

[313] One who is not a parent, guardian or special guardian and has no residence or custody order in his favour: s 1(2) of the Child Abduction Act 1984.

[314] Lawful control is a question of fact and the concept of control may vary according to the person having the control, whether it be a parent, a schoolmaster or a nanny: R v Mousir [1987] Crim LR 561, CA. 'Control' does not have a spatial element and 'taking' does not involve detaining: R v Leather [1993] 2 FLR 770, CA—the accused was held rightly convicted for asking two children to help him look for a stolen bicycle since the children were deflected from what they would have otherwise been doing.

[315] This provision implements with some modification the recommendations of the Criminal Law Revision Committee in their 14th Report, Offences Against the Person, 1980 Cmnd 7844, paras 239–49. The offence carries a maximum penalty of seven years' imprisonment: Child Abduction Act 1984 s 4.

[316] Child Abduction Act 1984 s 3(a). There is a similar definition of 'detain' under s 3(c).

[317] Section 2(3)(b).

[318] Section 2(3)(a). But note there can be no such defence where a man abducts the wrong child by mistake: R v Berry [1996] 2 Cr App R 226, CA.

(b) Civil liability

Damages for loss of services

The former tort of wrongfully depriving a parent of his child's services was abolished by the Administration of Justice Act 1982.[319]

Damages for interference with parental responsibility

There is no known tort of interference with parental rights nor therefore with parental responsibility.[320] The leading case is *F v Wirral Metropolitan Borough Council*,[321] which involved a complaint by the parents that what was originally understood by them to be a short-term placement with foster parents, to which arrangement they had agreed, became a long-term arrangement, to which they had not agreed, and that this therefore constituted a wrongful interference with their rights. In support of this argument they prayed in aid Art 8 of the European Convention of Human Rights and the European Court's decision in *R v United Kingdom*[322] as recognising a right of consortium between parent and child as one of the 'fundamental elements of family life'. After an exhaustive review of the law the Court of Appeal unanimously concluded, in Purchas LJ's words that 'neither under the old common law, apart from the action per quod servitium amisit, nor under modern authority is there a parental right necessary to found a cause of action against a stranger upon which the common law would grant a remedy in damages.'

The Fatal Accidents Act 1976

Parents and children come within the category of dependants for the purposes of the Fatal Accidents Act 1976,[323] so that either may sue any person who has unlawfully caused the death of the other for compensation for pecuniary loss resulting from the death.[324]

C WHO HAS PARENTAL RESPONSIBILITY [325]

1 THE POSITION AT THE CHILD'S BIRTH

(a) Married parents

Section 2(1) of the 1989 Act provides that where the father and mother of the child were married to each other at the time of the child's birth, they each have parental responsibility.

---

[319] Section 2(b). But cf *Donnelly v Joyce* [1974] QB 454, CA on the question of damages in an action brought by the child. See also *Hunt v Severs* [1994] 2 AC 350, HL.

[320] Note, however, *C v K (Inherent Powers: Exclusion Order)* [1996] 2 FLR 506, in which Wall J pointed out that persons can be restrained from interfering with the exercise of parental responsibility and that the courts could use their powers to exclude a third party from the family home to protect the exercise of parental responsibility. For the court's power generally to exclude persons from the family home, see Chapter 5.

[321] [1991] Fam 69, CA, on which see A Bainham 'Interfering with Parental Responsibility. A New Challenge for the Law of Torts?' (1990) 3 Jo of Child Law 3. See also *Re S (A Minor) (Parental Rights)* [1993] Fam Law 572.

[322] [1988] 2 FLR 445, E Ct HR.

[323] Section 1, as substituted by the Administration of Justice Act 1982 s 3(1).   [324] See Chapter 19.

[325] See generally N Lowe 'The Meaning and Allocation of Parental Responsibility—A Common Lawyer's Perspective' (1996) 11 Int Jo of Law, Policy and the Family 192 at 197ff.

The phrase 'married to each other at the time of the child's birth' has to be interpreted in accordance with s 1 of the Family Law Reform Act 1987.[326] Read with s 1(2)–(4) of the 1987 Act,[327] s 2(1) refers to a child whose parents were married to each other at any time during the period beginning with insemination or (where there was no insemination) conception and ending with birth, but also includes a child who:

   (a) is treated as legitimate by virtue of the Legitimacy Act 1976, s 1;[328]

   (b) is a legitimated person within the meaning of s 10 of the 1976 Act;[329]

   (c) is an adopted child;[330] or

   (d) is otherwise treated in law as legitimate.[331]

Stated simply, this means that both the father and the mother automatically each have parental responsibility in respect of their legitimate children.[332]

(b) Unmarried parents

Where the father and mother of the child were not married to each other at the time of the child's birth (effectively meaning where the child is illegitimate) then s 2(2) of the Children Act 1989 provides that the mother but not the father has parental responsibility for the child.[333]

(c) Non-parents

Since only parents have automatic parental responsibility for a child, then no other person has such responsibility at the time of the child's birth.

2 ACQUISITION OF PARENTAL RESPONSIBILITY SUBSEQUENT TO THE CHILD'S BIRTH

Although parental responsibility is automatically assigned either to each of the married parents or to the unmarried mother at the time of the child's birth, the Act makes clear provision for others to acquire responsibility after the child's birth.

(a) Acquisition of parental responsibility by the unmarried father

The unmarried father does not automatically have parental responsibility but, as s 2(2)(b) states, he can subsequently acquire it in accordance with the provisions of the 1989 Act. He can acquire responsibility in the following ways:

   (a) by subsequently marrying the child's mother;

   (b) by being registered as the father on the child's birth certificate;

---

[326] Section 2(3) of the Children Act 1989.

[327] Discussed above, p 349. For a discussion of the legal position of the man whose wife makes a parental responsibility agreement with another man, see below, p 419.

[328] See above, p 342.   [329] See above, p 344.   [330] See below, p 869.

[331] See above, pp 341ff.

[332] Which expression should also be taken to include children in respect of whom a parental order has been obtained under the Human Fertilisation and Embryology Act 1990 s 30, discussed above at p 315.

[333] This position has been ruled Human Rights compatible, see *B v UK* [2000] 1 FLR 1, ECtHR discussed below at p 428.

   (c) upon taking office as a formally appointed guardian of the child;

   (d) by making a parental responsibility agreement with the mother;

   (e) by obtaining a parental responsibility order;

   (f) by obtaining a residence order, in which case a separate parental responsibility
order *must* be made.

Subsequent marriage

By subsequently marrying the mother, the father brings himself within s 2(1) of the 1989
Act and, provided the child is under the age of 18 at the time,[334] will therefore automatically have parental responsibility. Because conferment of responsibility is an *automatic*
consequence, although the Act does not expressly say so, the parents' subsequent marriage
must be regarded as superseding the effect of registration and overriding any prior parental responsibility order or agreement which means that responsibility cannot then be
ended by a court order other than adoption or a parental order.[335]

Registration as the father

Based on a suggestion canvassed in a Lord Chancellor's Consultation Paper,[336] the Children Act 1989 has been amended[337] to provide for the unmarried father's acquisition of
parental responsibility following his registration as the child's father. For these purposes
the registration must be under either s 10(1)(a)–(c) or s 10A(1)(a)–(c) of the Births and
Deaths Registration Act 1953[338] (or their Scottish or Northern Irish equivalents).[339]
Although re-registrations can confer parental responsibility they will do so only providing
they fall within the terms of s 10A(1) of the 1953 Act, namely, where no father has
previously been named and the re-registration is with the mother's consent. Re-
registrations following a declaration of parentage[340] (which is the only means that an
unmarried man has of registering his fatherhood without the mother's consent) do not
confer parental responsibility since they fall under s 14A of the 1953 Act.[341] Although, at
first sight, this might seem anomalous, this will prevent men who have not been registered
as fathers circumventing the requirement when seeking parental responsibility orders,
effectively against the mother's wishes, of having to show that the making of such an order

---

[334] It is therefore possible for a child to be legitimated by his parents' subsequent marriage, yet for the
father not to have or to have had parental responsibility.

[335] Viz under s 30 of the Human Fertilisation and Embryology Act 1990. For the court's power to end
agreements see below, p 421.

[336] *(1) Court Proceedings for the Determination of Paternity; (2) The Law on Parental Responsibility for
Unmarried Fathers* (1998) paras 39 et seq.

[337] By the Adoption and Children Act 2002, s 111. A similar change has been made in Scotland; see the
Family Law (Scotland) Act 2006, s 23.

[338] Discussed above at p 333.

[339] Viz the Registration of Births, Deaths and Marriages (Scotland) Act 1965, ss 18(1)(a)–(c), 2(6) and
20(1)(a) and the Births and Deaths Registration (Northern Ireland) Order 1976, Art 14(3)(a)–(c). As the law
now stands, registrations in the Channel Islands and Isle of Man or in any foreign jurisdiction will not confer
parental responsibility, though under s 4(1B) of the Children Act 1989 the Lord Chancellor has the power to
add to the list of enactments under which registration confers parental responsibility.

[340] Ie under the Family Law Act 1986, s 55A(7) or s 56(4), see above at pp 331 and 345.

[341] Discussed above at p 333.

is in the child's best interests.[342] Because the legislation is *not* retrospective[343] only relevant registrations made on or after 1 December 2003[344] confer parental responsibility.

Although the acquisition of parental responsibility is an automatic consequence of a relevant registration it does not put unmarried fathers in exactly the same position as the married father since, unlike the latter, the court can, upon application by any person with parental responsibility or, with court leave, the child, order that the father shall cease to have that responsibility.[345] Moreover, parental responsibility dates from the registration, not the child's birth.[346]

Allowing unmarried fathers to acquire parental responsibility from registration is the latest step in improving such men's legal position with respect to their children,[347] and it is likely to have a significant impact. According to the Office for National Statistics[348] about 80% of births outside marriage are registered by both parents[349] and, assuming this trend continues,[350] it means that the vast majority of unmarried fathers of children now being born have parental responsibility without taking any further action. In turn registration will virtually eliminate the need to make agreements and over time should significantly reduce the need to make parental responsibility orders.[351]

Guardianship

To become a guardian, the father must formally have been appointed as such by the child's mother, or by the court in accordance with the terms set out in s 5 of the 1989 Act (discussed in Chapter 9). Such an appointment can only take effect after the mother's death.

Parental responsibility agreements

Pursuant to s 4(1)(b) the father and mother may by a parental responsibility agreement provide for the father to have parental responsibility for the child. Such agreements, however, only have effect if they are made in prescribed form and recorded in the prescribed manner.[352] Both the prescribed form and manner of recording are provided for by the Parental Responsibility Agreement Regulations 1991.[353]

There are no prescribed age limits on those making agreements and there is no reason

---

[342] Discussed below at p 414.   [343] See s 111(7) of the Adoption and Children Act 2002.

[344] Ie when s 111 was brought into force, see Adoption and Children Act 2002 (Commencement No. 4) Order 2003 (SI 2003/3079).

[345] Children Act 1989, s 4(2A), (3).

[346] If the mother dies before registration, since he cannot register himself as the father, the unmarried father can only acquire parental responsibility by court order or on being appointed a guardian.

[347] See further below.   [348] ONS 2001, *Social Trends 31.*

[349] Of these about 75% of parents live at the same address.

[350] One fear canvassed by the Lord Chancellor's Consultation Paper is that the change in the law might have the perverse effect of discouraging unmarried fathers from identifying themselves at registration or even lead to a general reduction of birth registrations.

[351] This impact has not, however, been immediate. Indeed more orders (10,522) were made in 2004 than in any other previous year. In 2003, for example, 9,524 orders were made, in 2002, 8,240 and in 2001, 8,151. See Table 5.3 in *Judicial Statistics* for each year.

[352] Section 4(2). However, as J Masson and M Morris *Children Act Manual* point out at 24, an informal agreement could still operate as a delegation of responsibility under s 2(9): discussed below at p 434.

[353] SI 1991/1478, as amended by SI 1994/3157, discussed below. Note these Regulations were again amended in 2005 (see SI 2005/2088) to apply to agreements with step-parents, discussed below at p 422.

to suppose that valid agreements cannot be made by parents under the age of 18.[354] On the other hand, it seems unlikely that valid agreements can be made with respect to an unborn child.[355] Although it is clear from the prescribed formalities (discussed below) that binding agreements can only be made in England and Wales there is uncertainty as to the required connection of the parties to this jurisdiction. According to *Re S (A Minor)(Parental Responsibility)*[356] jurisdiction to make parental responsibility *orders* is not dependent upon the child's habitual residence or even presence in England and Wales. So by analogy no such connection is required to make a valid agreement. However, *Re S* pre-dates the revised Brussels II Regulation[357] which clearly applies both to the making of parental responsibility agreements and orders,[358] and which requires jurisdiction to be based on the child's habitual residence or, failing that, presence.[359] This Regulation applies in matters of recognition and enforcement within Member States of the European Union (other than Denmark) and therefore does not directly affect the decision in *Re S* which involved a child reputedly in India, though whether that decision will now be revisited remains to be seen. In cases falling outside the Regulation and, assuming *Re S* continues to apply, presumably at least one of the parents must have a real connection with this jurisdiction.

It is established that a local authority in whose care the child is, cannot prevent the mother from making a parental responsibility agreement with the father.[360]

This power to make parental responsibility agreements implements the recommendation of the Law Commission. As the Commission pointed out,[361] although the father could apply for what was then a parental rights and duties order under s 4 of the Family Law Reform Act 1987, the need to resort to judicial proceedings to obtain parental responsibility seemed 'unduly elaborate, expensive and unnecessary unless the child's mother object[ed]'. On the other hand, in recommending this power, the Commission was also aware of the dangers of undue pressure being exerted upon mothers to make such agreements.[362] Accordingly, they recommended a relatively formal procedure whereby, in order to be binding, the agreement would have to be in a prescribed form and checked by the county court, to ensure that the parents were fully aware of the importance and effect of what they were doing.[363] This recommendation was not initially implemented. Instead, all

---

[354] An analogy should *not* be drawn with capacity to make contracts: parental responsibility agreements are probably best regarded as being agreements sui generis and not strict contracts, since it is difficult to see what consideration is given by the father when making the agreement.

[355] Agreements may only be made in respect of a 'child' as defined by s 105(1). There is a presumption against interpreting such definitions as including children en ventre sa mere: see *Elliot v Joicey* [1935] AC 209, HL, and *R v Newham London Borough Council, ex p Dada* [1996] QB 507, CA.

[356] [1998] 1 WLR 1701, CA.

[357] Viz. Council Regulation (EC) No. 2201/2003 of 27 November 2003, discussed at pp 34ff.

[358] The Regulation applies inter alia to *all* civil matters relating to the *attribution* of parental responsibility (see Art 1(b) and Recital 5(b)) and applies to agreements as well as court orders (see Art 46).

[359] See Arts 8 and 13 respectively.

[360] *Re X (Minors)(Care Proceedings: Parental Responsibility)* [2000] Fam 156 in which Wilson J held that the 'facility' under s 4(1)(b) is self-contained and does not depend upon the exercise of parental responsibility. Compare *Re W (minors)(removal from jurisdiction)* [1994] 1 FCR 842 in which the High Court accepted an undertaking not to make a parental responsibility agreement.

[361] Law Com No 172 para 2.18.

[362] Indeed, it was because of the potential pressure, that the Law Commission did not originally recommend the power to make binding agreements—see Law Com No 118 *Illegitimacy* (1982) para 4.39.

[363] Which was argued to be unworkable anyway by S Cretney: see 'Defining the Limits of State Intervention: The Child and the Courts' in *Children and the Law* (ed D Freestone) at pp 65–6.

that was formally required was that the agreement in prescribed form should be signed by both parents and witnesses and subsequently filed in the Principal Registry of the Family Division. However, as the Children Act Advisory Committee observed,[364] this highly informal scheme was not without its difficulties. In some cases agreements were apparently filed with the mother's signature forged. Accordingly, a new procedure was introduced in 1995[365] under which applicants must take their completed form to a local family proceedings court or county court or to the Principal Registry, where a justice of the peace, a justices' clerk or court officer authorised by a judge to administer oaths will witness the parents' signature and sign the certificate of the witness. As before, the duly completed form, together with two copies, should then be taken or posted to the Principal Registry.[366] Sealed copies will be returned to the mother and father,[367] while the record is open to public inspection. No fee is charged to the parents for the formal recording of their agreement, though a charge is payable by those wishing to inspect the record.[368]

Notwithstanding the 1994 changes, the formalities for making binding parental responsibility agreements remain perfunctory. In particular, there is no investigation of whether the agreement is in the child's best interests nor of why the parents are entering into it. Indeed there is no effective check on whether, for example, the man is the father of the child concerned. Notes attached to the Agreement Form explain that the agreement will not take effect until the form has been received and recorded at the Principal Registry but that, once it has, it can only be brought to an end by a court order or upon the child reaching 18. It also warns: 'The making of this agreement will affect the legal position of mother and father. You should both seek legal advice before you make the Agreement.'

Whether such warnings, together with the need to take the agreement to court, are sufficient to allay the fears, expressed both by the Law Commission and during the passage of the Bill,[369] that mothers may be bullied into conferring rights upon the fathers at a time when they are particularly vulnerable to pressure, is hard to say.[370] Perhaps not surprisingly, following the 1994 reform, after a steady rise between 1992 and 1994, the number of agreements fell sharply in 1995 but rose again in 1996.[371] Since 1996 no national statistics have been published. However, it must be assumed that now that unmarried fathers acquire parental responsibility by reason of their registration on the child's birth certificate few agreements will be made between parents in the future.

---

[364] In their Report 1992/93, p 13.

[365] See the Parental Responsibility Agreement (Amendment) Regulations 1994, SI 1994/3157.

[366] Art 3(1).   [367] Art 3(2).   [368] Art 3(3).

[369] See particularly Lord Banks, 502 HL Official Report (5th series) cols 1180–82 and 503 HL Official Report col 1319.

[370] In *Re W (A Minor) (Residence Order)* [1992] 2 FLR 332, CA, a mother did assert that she had signed an agreement under pressure, though this was under the old procedure.

[371] According to the CAAC Report 1993–94 (Appendix 1) 2,941 agreements were registered in 1992, 4,411 in 1993 and 'around' 5,280 in 1994. In 1995, the numbers fell 36% to an 'estimated' 3,455 (CAAC Report 1994/1995 Appendix 1). In 1996 the number of agreements rose 4% to an estimated 3,590 (CAAC Final Report, 1997, Appendix 2). Many have commented on the low number of agreements (a phenomenon also noted in Scotland where in 2003 there were 20,542 joint registrations by unmarried parents but only 502 formal agreements: Registers of Scotland, Scottish Executive). However, as G Douglas *Introduction to Family Law* (2nd edn) 59, has said (relying on research by R Pickford *Fathers, Marriage and the Law* (1999)) while the main reason for the low take-up is ignorance of the procedure, in addition 'inertia and a diffidence about raising the issue with the child's mother may also play a part'.

Parental responsibility orders

Under s 4(1)(a) of the 1989 Act the court may, upon the application of an unmarried father (ie not upon its own motion), order that he shall have parental responsibility for the child. Applications may be made to the High Court, county court or the family proceedings court.[372] If the applicant's paternity is in doubt and a fortiori if it is disputed, it will have to be proved before the action may proceed.[373] In any event, it is implicit in every order made under s 4 that the man in question has been found or adjudged to be the father of the child in question.[374] An application may be made only in respect of a 'child', that is a person under the age of 18.[375] According to the Court of Appeal in *Re S (Parental Responsibility: Jurisdiction)*[376] it is not necessary for the child to be habitually resident, present or even born in England and Wales to found jurisdiction to make a s 4 order. But this decision predates the revised Brussels Regulation[377] which clearly applies to such orders[378] and which requires for recognition and enforcement purposes within Member States of the European Union (other than Denmark) that jurisdiction be founded on the child's habitual residence or, failing that, presence in the Member State.[379] Whether the passing of the Regulation will provide a reason for revisiting *Re S* remains to be seen but even were it to be applied in cases not caught by the Regulation then presumably the applicant (or mother) must have some real connection with England and Wales.

Applications under s 4 are sometimes referred to as free-standing applications to distinguish them from residence order applications by unmarried fathers, in which s 4 orders are made as an ancillary but automatic consequence of making the residence order.[380] As Waite J commented in *Re CB (A Minor) (Parental Responsibility Order)*[380a], '. . . there is an unusual duality in the character of a parental responsibility order: it is on the one hand sufficiently ancillary by nature to pass automatically to a natural father without inquiry of any kind when a residence order is made in his favour; and, on the other hand, sufficiently independent, when severed from the context of a residence order, to require detailed consideration upon its merits as a free-standing remedy in its own right.'

It is accepted that in deciding whether or not to make a parental responsibility order the court must, in line with the general principles of the Act, treat the child's welfare as its paramount consideration[381] and be satisfied that making the order would be better for the

---

[372] Section 92(7). In practice the majority of applications are made to the family proceedings courts; nearly 70% of the 3,332 orders made in 1992/93 were made by magistrates—CAAC Report 1992/93, Appendix 1, p 93.

[373] See *Re F (A Minor) (Blood Tests: Parental Rights)* [1993] Fam 314, CA.

[374] See *R v Secretary of State for Social Security, ex p W* [1999] 2 FLR 604, per Johnson J.

[375] Section 105(1). For the reasons discussed above at p 412 n 355 it is not thought orders can be made in respect of unborn children.

[376] [1998] 2 FLR 921, CA, per Butler-Sloss LJ who pointed out that the jurisdictional rules contained in the Family Law Act 1986 do not expressly apply to s 4 orders and should not therefore be used to curb jurisdiction make such orders.

[377] Viz. Council Regulation (EC) No. 2201/2003 of 27 November 2003, discussed at p 34.

[378] The Regulation applies to *all* civil matters relating to the *attribution* of parental responsibility, see Art 1(b) and Recital 5.

[379] See Arts 8 and 13 respectively.   [380] Section 12(1), see further below at p 550.

[380a] [1993] 1 FLR 920 at 929.

[381] Pursuant to s 1(1), discussed above at pp 455ff; *Re H (Parental Responsibility)* [1998] 1 FLR 855, CA at 859 per Butler-Sloss LJ. But note *Re G (A Minor) (Parental Responsibility Order)* [1994] 1 FLR 504 at 508 in which Balcombe LJ seemed not to have regarded as beyond argument that an application for a parental

child than making no order at all.[382] There is no enjoinder to have regard to the check-list set out by s 1(3),[383] though there is nothing to prevent the court from considering it if it so wishes. This means that the court is not obliged to have regard to older children's wishes: yet, as has been pointed out,[384] given that, if the father applies instead for a residence order which is opposed by the mother, the court must have regard to the child's wishes, it is difficult to see why the check-list should not apply at the very least to contested s 4 applications. Furthermore, since a child with sufficient understanding may, with leave, apply to have the order ended[385] it is logical to assume that such a child's view may be relevant to deciding whether to make the order in the first place.[386]

The restriction under s 9(6) which prevents the court from making a s 8 order in respect of a child aged 16 or over save in 'exceptional circumstances'[387] does not apply to the making of s 4 orders.

According to *Re H (Minors) (Local Authority: Parental Rights) (No 3)*[388] in deciding whether or not to make an order the following factors will undoubtedly be material, namely:

'(1) the degree of commitment which the father has shown towards the child; (2) the degree of attachment which exists between the father and the child; (3) the reasons of the father for applying for the order.'[389]

In *Re C (Minors)*[390] Mustill LJ stated the basic test to be:

'... was the association between the parties sufficiently enduring; and has the father by his conduct during and since the application shown sufficient commitment to the children, to justify giving the father a legal status equivalent to that which he would have enjoyed if the parties had married?'

For some time *Re H* was considered to be the leading case and it became established, for instance, that the so-called '*Re H*' considerations should be expressly considered in all free-standing s 4 applications[391] and furthermore, provided a concerned though absent father fulfils the '*Re H* test', then 'prima facie it would be for the welfare of the child that such an

responsibility order is not a question relating to the child's upbringing and is therefore not governed by s 1(1). But for convincing arguments that such an order does relate to the child's upbringing, see Hershman at [1994] Fam Law 650.

[382] Pursuant to s 1(5), discussed below at p 581. However, in R White, P Carr and N Lowe *The Children Act in Practice* (3rd edn) at para 3.57, n 2 it is pointed out that it could be argued that s 1(5) does not apply, since a parental responsibility order relates to the parent and not the child. The authors considered, however, that such an argument was likely to be rejected.

[383] Discussed above, pp 468ff.

[384] By M Doggett, 'Unmarried fathers and section 4 before and after the Children Act 1989' (1992) JCL 39 at 41. See also White, Carr and Lowe, above at para 3.57 and Clarke Hall and Morrison on *Children* Vol 1, para 1[294].

[385] Section 4(3)(b) and (4), discussed below, p 421.

[386] In practice it is not unusual to ask for a welfare report, when no doubt the child's view can be brought to the court's notice.

[387] Discussed below, p 539.   [388] [1991] Fam 151 at 158, CA.

[389] The basic application form for a parental responsibility order specifically asks the applicant to state his reasons for making the application: Family Proceedings Rules 1991, Form C 1.

[390] [1992] 2 All ER 86 at 93.

[391] *S v R (Parental Responsibility)* [1993] 1 FCR 331, per Thorpe J.

order is made.[392] However, in *Re H (Parental Responsibility)*[393]. Butler-Sloss LJ, in particular, disapproved of the notion that case law had created a presumption that a devoted father will ordinarily be granted an order. As she put it, the '*Re H* requirements' are an important starting point in the making of a responsibility order, but they are not the only factors, and even if they are satisfied the court has an overarching duty to apply the paramountcy test and determine whether the making of an order is for the child's welfare. The point is well put in *Re M (handicapped child: parental responsibility)*:[394]

'parental responsibility is not a reward for the father for his commitment to and involvement with [the child] but an order which would only be made in [the child's] best interests'.

It is evident that the courts are still disposed to grant orders to committed fathers. As Ward LJ put it in *Re C and V (Contact and Parental Responsibility)*,[395] because it is desirable for the sake of a child's self-esteem to grow up, wherever possible, having a favourable and positive image of an absent parent, then applying the paramountcy test: 'wherever possible, the law should confer on a concerned father that stamp of approval because he has shown himself willing and anxious to pick up the responsibility of fatherhood and not to deny or avoid it'. This standpoint echoes that taken in *Re S (Parental Responsibility)*.[396] In that case, after the breakdown of his relationship with the mother, an unmarried father was convicted of possession of obscene literature (comprising indecent photographs of children). Because of this the mother severed contact between the father and his daughter but resumed it when the child's resulting distress and deterioration of her behaviour became apparent. That contact later developed into unsupervised staying contact. The father then applied for a parental responsibility order, which the mother vigorously opposed upon the basis of the father's conviction and his unreliability about money. At first instance the father's application was rejected primarily because it would 'give him scope to interfere in many different ways with the present arrangements for the child'. This decision was, however, reversed on appeal, Ward LJ stressing[397] that objecting to the order because of the rights and power that it would confer demonstrated 'a most unfortunate failure to appreciate the significant change that the Act has brought about where the emphasis is to move away from rights and to concentrate on responsibilities' His Lordship continued:

'It is wrong to place undue and therefore false emphasis on the rights and duties and the powers comprised in "parental responsibility" and not to concentrate on the fact that what is at issue is conferring upon a committed father the status of parenthood for which nature has already ordained that he must bear responsibility.'

[392] Per Balcombe LJ in *Re G (A Minor) (Parental Responsibility Order)* [1994] 1 FLR 504 at 508. See also his similar comments in *Re E (Parental Responsibility: Blood Tests)* [1995] 1 FLR 392 at 398.
[393] [1998] 1 FLR 855, CA.   [394] [2001] 3 FCR 454.
[395] [1998] FLR 392 at 397, CA in which an order was made notwithstanding that the father had been convicted of possessing obscene literature (comprising indecent photographs of children) and was not paying maintenance for the children.
[396] [1995] 2 FLR 648, CA, on which see J Eekelaar 'Parental Responsibility—A New Legal Status?' (1996) 112 LQR 233.
[397] Above at 657.

He added that it seemed to him to be important to ensure that wherever possible:

'. . . the law confers upon a committed father that stamp of approval, lest the child grow up with some belief that he is in some way disqualified from fulfilling his role and that the reason for the disqualification is something inherent which will be inherited by the child, making her struggle to find her own identity all the more fraught.'

In the subsequent decision, *Re S (Parental Responsibility)*[398] Sir Stephen Brown P again emphasised that a s 4 order does not affect the day-to-day care of children,[399] but does provide status for the father. Given that unmarried fathers now automatically gain parental responsibility upon being registered the father it remains to be seen whether a *pre*-December 2003 registration will be regarded as a factor in deciding whether or not to make a s 4 order.[400]

Consistent with the emphasis upon the consequent status conferred by a s 4 order it has been held that orders can be made notwithstanding that the child is in local authority care or is about to be freed for adoption,[401] nor is the question of enforcement necessarily decisive.[402] In *Re H (A Minor) (Contact and Parental Responsibility)*,[403] an order was made even though the father had been denied a contact order. Indeed in *Re C and V (Contact and Parental Responsibility)*[404] the Court of Appeal stressed that applications for contact and parental responsibility were to be treated as wholly separate applications, so that the dismissal of the former did not necessarily mean that the latter should also be dismissed. It has also been held[405] that the court should not use its power to make a parental responsibility order as a weapon to force a father to make maintenance payments for the upkeep of his child. In all cases, however, the test remains whether it is for the child's welfare that an order be made. Lack of insight into a daughter's needs and an inability to get on with social workers is not reason in itself to refuse an order,[406] nor similarly is it justifiable to base a refusal solely on the acrimony between the parents,[407] nor because of transsexuality.[408]

Although failure to satisfy the so-called '*Re H*' criteria is likely to lead to a refusal to make a parental responsibility order it may be that where the commitment and attachment criteria cannot presently be met because, for example, the father has never seen the

---

[398] [1995] 2 FLR 648, CA.

[399] For the effects of a s 4 order see below at p 419.

[400] For a possible hint that it might be relevant, see *Re J-S (Contact: Parental Responsibility)* [2002] EWCA Civ 1028, [2003] 1 FLR 399 at [54], per Ward LJ.

[401] See respectively *D v Hereford and Worcester County Council* [1991] Fam 14, and *Re H (Minors) (Local Authority: Parental Rights) (No 3)* above; freeing for adoption (which is now replaced by placement orders) is discussed below at p 837. But cf *W v Ealing London Borough Council* [1993] 2 FLR 788, CA, in which the application was dismissed because the children were being prepared for a termination of contact with their parents pending their introduction to prospective adopters, and to change that would have left them in limbo and confused.

[402] *Re C (Minors)*, above.   [403] [1993] 1 FLR 484, CA.   [404] Above.

[405] *Re H (Parental Responsibility: Maintenance)* [1996] 1 FLR 867, CA.

[406] *Re G (A Minor) Parental Responsibility Order)*, [1994] 1 FLR 504.

[407] *Re P (A Minor) (Parental Responsibility Order)* [1994] 1 FLR 578.

[408] *Re L (Contact: Transsexual Application)* [1995] 2 FLR 438, in which a 'father' who to outward appearances was a woman was granted a s 4 order.

child, it will be appropriate to adjourn the application to see whether the criteria can be established in the future.[409]

Although in practice parental responsibility orders are commonly granted,[410] not all applications succeed. One telling factor against granting an order is violence. In *Re H (Parental Responsibility)*,[411] for instance the order was refused because the father had been found to have injured his son in circumstances indicating deliberate cruelty and possibly sadism. In *Re T (A Minor) (Parental Responsibility)*[412] an order was refused where the father had treated the mother with hatred and violence, showing no regard for the child's welfare. Improper motive is another relevant factor. In *Re P (Parental Responsibility)*,[413] for instance, an order was refused because it was found that the father intended to use the order for improper or inappropriate ends to try to interfere with and possibly undermine the mother's care. Other examples of refusal include *Re J (Parental Responsibility)*[414] in which the child (then aged 12) and who was born after the parents' separation, had infrequent contact with her father and did not want contact. Moreover the raison d'être for the father's application, namely his concern about the mother's involvement with drugs, no longer existed. In *M v M (Parental Responsibility)*[415] an order was refused because the father was found to be mentally incapable of discharging the functions embraced within the concept of parental responsibility. In *Re P (Parental Responsibility)*[416] the Court of Appeal declined to interfere with a refusal to make an order based in part on the father's criminal conduct, holding that a court was entitled to take into account, as relevant but not conclusive, factors such as that the father was in prison and the circumstances of the criminal conduct for which the sentence was imposed.

Once it is found to be in the child's interests that both parents should have parental responsibility, this should be reflected by the making of a s 4 order and not by making 'no order' pursuant to s 1(5).[417]

[409] See *Re D (Parental Responsibility)* [2001] EWCA Civ 230, [2001] 1 FLR 971 and *Re M (Sperm Donor Father)* [2003] Fam Law 94. In the latter case a parental responsibility order was made subject to the father's undertaking not to visit the child's school nor to contact any health professional connected with the child's care: *Re D (contact and parental responsibility: lesbian mothers and known father)* [2006] EWHC 2 (Fam), [2006] 1 FCR 556.

[410] In 2004 214 (2% of all disposals) applications were refused: *Judicial Statistics* 2004, Table 5.3. This is a drop from 374 (4%) in 2001 and 511 (6%) in 2000, see Table 5.3 for each year's statistics.

[411] [1998] 1 FLR 855, CA. See also *Re G (a child)(domestic violence: direct contact)* [2001] 2 FCR 134, CA—order refused because of the child's fear and anxiety about the father and *Re L (A Child)(Contact: Domestic Violence)* [2001] Fam 260, CA—order refused because of the father's violence and desire to control the child.

[412] [1993] 2 FLR 450, CA.

[413] [1998] 2 FLR 96, CA. The father was deeply confused over sexual boundaries (he was in possession of a number of photographs of pre-pubescent children) and had little appreciation of the difference between abusive and appropriate behaviour. See also *Re M (handicapped child: parental responsibility)* [2001] 3 FCR 454—order refused because the father was likely to misuse it to interfere with the mother's care thus causing her stress and potentially undermining her ability to care properly for the child.

[414] [1999] 1 FLR 784.   [415] [1999] 2 FLR 737.

[416] [1997] 2 FLR 722, CA. But cf *Re S (Parental Responsibility)* [1995] 2 FLR 648, discussed above at p 417.

[417] Per Wilson J in *Re P (A Minor) (Parental Responsibility Order)* [1994] 1 FLR 578. For discussion of the application of s 1(5), see below, p 581. In view of this ruling the number of 'no orders' seems high, 472 (4%) out of 12,160 court disposals in 2004: Table 5.3, *Judicial Statistics* 2004.

Residence orders

If a court grants an unmarried father who does not otherwise have parental responsibility[418] a residence order (but not any other s 8 order),[419] then by s 12(1) it is also bound to make a *separate* s 4 order. The importance of the s 4 order being made separately is that it will not automatically come to an end if the residence order is ended, but will require an express order ending it, if the child is still a minor.

The effect of parental responsibility orders and agreements

The effect of a court order or a properly recorded agreement is the same, namely it confers parental responsibility upon the unmarried father. In most cases he will share responsibility jointly with the mother or, if the mother is dead, with any formally appointed guardian. He could also share responsibility with a special guardian or some other person in whose favour a residence order has been made. The legal position of a husband whose wife makes a parental responsibility agreement with another man is not clear. Prima facie that agreement confers responsibility on that other man, yet because of the presumption of paternity[420] the woman's husband could also be regarded as having responsibility. Of course, once the issue is before the court the conundrum can be solved by a finding of paternity, but what is the position before that? There is no objection in principle to two men having parental responsibility in relation to a child, but because in this situation only one man can actually be the child's father, only one of them can be regarded as having responsibility. Although the making of an agreement is some evidence that the husband might not be the father, it seems unlikely that the court would regard an agreement alone as sufficient to rebut the presumption of the husband's paternity. One cannot shut one's eyes to the possibility that both the mother and the other man might know that the husband is or could be the father, but want to exclude him if the other man is prepared to accept the child is his. In many cases, however, there is likely to be other evidence, for example that before the birth the woman had left her husband to live with the other man.[421]

Although in general terms it is correct to say[422] that an unmarried father with parental responsibility is in the same legal position with regard to the child as if he had married the mother, the effect should be neither overestimated nor under-estimated. Even without responsibility the father is regarded as a 'parent' for most purposes of the Children Act 1989.[423] He has, for example, the right to apply to the court for a s 8 order[424] and is entitled to reasonable contact with a child in local authority care.[425] Furthermore, the lack of parental responsibility does not mean that such fathers have no statutory duty to maintain their children.[426] On the other hand, conferring parental responsibility upon unmarried fathers does not alter the status of the child. Hence the child will still not be able to succeed

---

[418] Where he has previously made a parental responsibility agreement, for example.

[419] Section 8 orders are discussed in Chapter 12.   [420] Discussed above, pp 321ff.

[421] It is also relevant to know who is registered as the father.

[422] See eg Department of Health's *Guidance and Regulations*, Vol 1, 'Court Orders', para 2.5.

[423] See above, p 346.   [424] Under s 10(4), discussed below, p 543.

[425] Under s 34, discussed below, p 790.

[426] On the contrary, unmarried fathers can be 'non-resident parents' for the purposes of the Child Support Act 1991: see below, p 932. For this reason Waite J must be regarded as being mistaken when he commented in *Re C (Minors) (Parental Rights)* [1992] 1 FLR 1 at 9 that *upon* being vested with parental responsibility the father assumes 'an immediately enforceable burden' to maintain the child.

to a title of honour through his parents.[427] Furthermore, as the courts have stressed,[428] the granting of a s 4 order does not per se entitle the father to interfere with the day-to-day running of affairs affecting the child, at any rate whilst the child is living with another carer.[429]

Notwithstanding the courts' entreaties not to concentrate on the rights conferred by a s 4 order, it is nevertheless instructive to enquire how the legal position of an unmarried father changes upon being vested with parental responsibility. The principal effects are:

(1) he becomes a 'parent' for the purposes of the adoption legislation and can therefore withhold his agreement to a proposed adoption or placement order;[430]

(2) he becomes entitled to remove his child (under the age of 16) from local authority accommodation,[431] and, if he is willing and able to provide accommodation or to arrange for accommodation to be provided for his child, may object to his child being accommodated in the first place;[432]

(3) he can appoint a guardian;[433]

(4) he can give a valid consent to his child's medical treatment[434] and require full medical details from the child's medical practitioner;[435]

(5) he has the power to consent to his child's marriage;[436]

(6) he is empowered to express a preference as to the school at which he wishes his child's education to be provided; to initiate and be involved in the procedure for statementing of a child with special needs; to withdraw his child from sex education in local education authority schools and to receive full comprehensive reports from his child's school;[437]

(7) the mother will need to obtain his consent to take the child (under the age of 16) outside the United Kingdom;[438]

(8) he will be entitled to sign passport applications and to oppose the granting of a passport for his child;[439]

(9) he will be considered to have 'rights of custody' for the purposes of the Hague Convention on International Child Abduction.[440]

---

[427] Above at p 347.

[428] Re S (A Minor) (Parental Responsibility) [1995] 3 FCR 564; Re A (A Minor) (Parental Responsibility) [1996] 1 FCR 562; Re P (A Minor) (Parental Responsibility Order) [1994] 1 FLR 578.

[429] And note eg Re P (Parental Responsibility) [1998] 2 FLR 96, CA, where the motivation to undermine the mother's care was held to justify refusing to make an order in favour of a devoted father.

[430] Adoption and Children Act 2002, ss 21, 47(2) and 52(6), see below at pp 850 and 839.

[431] Children Act 1989 s 20(8), discussed below at p 706.

[432] Section, s 20(7); discussed below at p 706.   [433] Section 5(3).   [434] See above, p 391.

[435] For instance, under the Access to Health Records Act 1990: see above, p 402. See also Re H (A Minor) (Shared Residence) [1994] 1 FLR 717, CA.

[436] Marriage Act 1949 s 3(1A)(a)(i): see above, p 55.

[437] Under the School Standards and Framework Act 1998, ss 71 and 86 and Education Act 1996 Part IV: see above, p 388.

[438] Child Abduction Act 1984 s 1(3)(a)(ii): see above, p 395.

[439] See the Guidance issued by the UK Passport Agency reproduced at [1994] Fam Law 651, discussed above at p 395.

[440] He will have locus standi to seek the child's return under the Hague Convention: see the discussion below, pp 639ff.

Notwithstanding that a s 4 order undoubtedly strengthens the unmarried father's legal position in relation to his child, it is important to stress that the mother loses relatively little by the making of the order. She is under no general obligation (but see below) to consult the father about the child's upbringing[441] and, so long as the child is living with her, the father has no right to interfere with the day-to-day management of the child's life, and indeed any attempt or threat to do so can be controlled by a s 8 order.[442] What the mother undoubtedly loses is the *unilateral* right to remove the child from the UK[443] and, more controversially, it may be that she needs to consult the father about a change of school,[444] or surname.[445] She also loses the ability to appoint a guardian to take effect upon her death, unless she has a residence order in her favour.[446]

The fact that a s 4 order does not entitle an unmarried father to intermeddle in the day-to-day management of the child prompts the question as to why applications are made. Indeed the judiciary themselves have sometimes commented that the growing number of applications is based on a fundamental misunderstanding of the nature of the order.[447] For some, however, the judicial recognition of what has been described[448] as the exercise of their 'social parenthood' will undoubtedly be important. Whatever the reasons, the numbers of such orders have steadily increased, from 2,762 in 1992, 5,587 in 1996, 7,786 in 2000 to 10,522 in 2004.[449] It is anticipated, however, that in time the number will drop, given that unmarried fathers registered as such on or after 1 December 2003 automatically have parental responsibility.

Ending parental responsibility acquired by registration, court orders or agreements

Parental responsibility orders and agreements remain effective notwithstanding that the couple live together or subsequently separate. They will, however, automatically end once the child attains his majority.[450] Parental responsibility acquired by registration similarly ends upon the child attaining his majority. Apart from these instances parental responsibility may be brought to an end only upon a court order to that effect.[451] Such an order may be made upon the application (ie *not* of the court's own motion) of:

(1) any person who has parental responsibility for the child (this will include the father himself) or,

(2) with leave of the court, the child himself.[452]

---

[441] By reason of s 2(7), discussed further below at p 432.

[442] See eg Ward LJ's comments in *Re S (Parental Responsibility)* [1995] 2 FLR 648 at 657.

[443] Under s 1 of the Child Abduction Act 1984 she will require the father's consent to leave the country.

[444] See *Re G (A Minor) (Parental Responsibility: Education)* [1994] 2 FLR 964, CA, discussed below at pp 433–4.

[445] See *Re PC (Change of Surname)* [1997] 2 FLR 730, discussed above, p 398.

[446] Children Act 1989 s 5(7), discussed below, p 441.

[447] See eg *Re S (Parental Responsibility)*, above, per Ward LJ who said that s 4 applications 'have become one of those little growth areas born of misunderstanding', see also *Re S (A Minor) (Parental Responsibility)* [1995] 3 FCR 564.

[448] J Eekelaar 'Parental Responsibility—A New Legal Status' (1996) 112 LQR 233 at 235.

[449] See Table 5.3 of Judicial Statistics of the relevant year. But as I Butler, G Douglas, N Lowe, L Noakes and A Pithouse 'The Children Act 1989 and the unmarried father' (1993) 5 *Journal of Child Law* 157, pointed out such figures only represented a tiny proportion of the overall number of unmarried fathers.

[450] Children Act 1989 s 91(7) and (8).   [451] Section 4(2A).   [452] Section 4(3).

In the latter case, the court may grant leave only if it is satisfied that the child has sufficient understanding to make the proposed application.[453] The court may not end a s 4 order while a residence order in favour of the unmarried father remains in force.[454]

In deciding whether to order the cessation of parental responsibility acquired by registration, court order or agreement, the court must regard the child's welfare as its paramount consideration and be satisfied that making such an order is better than making no order at all.[455] Nevertheless, it is submitted that the court should be slow to make such an order, particularly when it made a s 4 order in the first place. The position might be different following an agreement where, for example, it could be shown that the mother had been subjected to undue pressure to sign. Given that parental responsibility vested in the married father may be ended only upon the child's adoption, the ending of a residence order in the unmarried father's favour should not automatically mean that parental responsibility should also come to an end. In any event, a separate order expressly ending the s 4 order will be required to end the father's parental responsibility. In *Re P (Terminating Parental Responsibility)*,[456] Singer J emphasised that the ability to apply to terminate parental responsibility should not be used as a weapon by the dissatisfied mother of a non-marital child. Nevertheless, on the facts responsibility was terminated, the father having been responsible for inflicting appalling injuries on the child.

3 ACQUISITION OF PARENTAL RESPONSIBILITY BY STEP-PARENTS

As originally enacted the Children Act 1989 made no special provision for step-parents to acquire parental responsibility. Instead they were treated like any other individual non-parent (for which, see below). However, following reform introduced by the Adoption and Children Act 2002[457] provision is now made for a step-parent who is married[458] to or is a civil partner[459] of the parent who has parental responsibility for the child,[460] to obtain parental responsibility either by agreement or court order. Section 4A(1) of the 1989 Act provides:

'Where a child's parent ("parent A") who has parental responsibility for the child is married to or is a civil partner of a person who is not the child's parent ("the step-parent") —

---

[453] Section 4(4). For a similar requirement when seeking leave to apply for a s 8 order, see s 10(8), discussed below at p 548.

[454] Section 11(4).

[455] Pursuant to s 1(1) and (5); and see *Re P (Terminating Parental Responsibility)* [1995] 1 FLR 1048.

[456] Above; cf *Re G (Child Case: Parental Involvement)* [1996] 1 FLR 857, CA in which an appeal against a revocation of a parental responsibility agreement was successful.

[457] Section 112 inserting s 4A into the Children Act 1989 with effect from 30 December 2005 (see Adoption and Children Act 2002 (Commencement No 9) Order 2005, SI 2005/2213). This in turn has been amended by the Civil Partnership Act 2004, s 75(2).

[458] Ie cohabitation is not sufficient.

[459] Ie a party to a formally registered civil partnership under the Civil Partnership Act 2004.

[460] Accordingly the provisions only apply to a step-mother if she is married to a father with parental responsibility. Presumably, however, s 41A will be triggered if the father acquires parental responsibility *after* his marriage to the step-mother, as for example, by becoming the child's guardian.

(a) parent A or, if the other parent also has parental responsibility for the child, both parents may by agreement with the step-parent provide for the step-parent to have parental responsibility for the child; or

(b) the court may, on the application of the step-parent, order that the step-parent shall have parental responsibility for the child.'

Although there have been calls to improve the status of step-parents,[461] the motivation for the reform is to provide an alternative to adoption. As the Explanatory Notes to the 2002 Act[462] say, the intention of the provision is 'to provide an alternative to adoption where a step-parent wishes to acquire parental responsibility for his or her step-child. It has the advantage of not removing parental responsibility from the other birth parent and does not legally separate the child from membership of the family of the other birth parent'. Given this background and given that the 2002 Act permits joint adoption by couples whether or not they are married to each other[463] it is perhaps ironic that it is not open to a cohabiting partner of the parent to seek parental responsibility by agreement or order.[464]

So far as parental responsibility agreements are concerned it will be noted that if both birth parents have parental responsibility (ie because they were married or, if not, the unmarried father was registered as the father or had responsibility by reason of an order or agreement) then the agreement must be made between the step-parent and *both* the child's mother and father.[465] The non-resident parent's involvement in this regard can be questioned for, as has been pointed out,[466] while on the one hand it could be seen as giving the non resident parent a bargaining chip, on the other the non resident parent essentially loses nothing by the step-parent gaining parental responsibility.[467] The non-resident parent's involvement, however, is in line with the judicially imposed requirement that important decisions in a child's life should not be unilaterally taken by one parent.[468] But whatever the merits of doing so, the mandatory involvement of the non-resident parent in

[461] See eg J Masson 'Old families into new: a status for step-parents' in M Freeman (ed) *State, Law and the Family* (1984) ch 14 pp 237 et seq and see p 391 of the previous edition of this work.
[462] Para 268. This reform implements a long standing proposal first made in *Adoption: The Future* Cm 2288 (1993) paras 5.20–5.22 and cl 85 of the Draft Bill attached to *Adoption—A Service for Children* (Department of Health and Welsh Office, 1996). Interestingly, the Law Commission had much earlier (see Working Paper No. 91 *Guardianship* (1985) paras 4.15–4.19) canvassed views about the possibility of step-parents acquiring responsibility by administrative rather than judicial means, but did not pursue the point because it attracted little support at the time: Law Com No. 172 *Guardianship and Custody* (1988) para 2.22. It might also be noted that no such reform has been introduced in Scotland despite the reform of the unmarried father's position made in the Family Law (Scotland) Act 2006.
[463] See Adoption and Children Act 2002, ss 50 and 144(a)(b), discussed below at p 844.
[464] But such a couple can apply for a joint residence order the effect of which is to vest parental responsibility in the parent's partner, see p 516.
[465] Of course, where only the mother has parental responsibility an agreement only needs to be with her ie the father need not be involved but A Bainham *Children—The Modern Law* (3rd edn) at 236 questions whether this is human rights compliant.
[466] See S Cretney, J Masson and R Bailey-Harris *Principles of Family Law* (7th edn) at 18–042.
[467] Bainham, above at p 236 takes issue with the diminution argument arguing that the enhanced status for step-parents 'could be seen as shutting out, or at least diluting, the parental contribution of the non-resident parent'. The counter to this is surely that the de facto position will already be seen as diluting the non-resident parents position and, in any event, as Cretney et al point out, there is nothing to prevent the resident parent delegating responsibility to the step-parent.
[468] See eg *Re G (Parental Responsibility: Education)* [1994] 2 FCR 964, CA and *Re C (Welfare of Child: Immunisation)* [2003] EWCA Civ 1148, [2003] 2 FLR 1095, discussed below at p 433.

making agreements, is likely to lead to conflict and one must doubt whether many such tri-partite agreements will be made.

Given that the same formalities are required for making the agreement with step-parents as for making one between the parents,[469] there is no scrutiny of whether the agreement is in the child's interests nor is there any requirement to involve the child him or herself. Although this means that the child cannot veto the making of the agreement, as will be seen, the child can apply to a court to end the agreement. Whether this is human rights compliant remains to be seen. As with unmarried fathers no specific provision is made regarding age requirements for those making an agreement; on whether the agreement can be made in respect of an unborn child or one that is married, or on any jurisdictional rules. However, the position must be the same as for unmarried parents.[470]

The court's power to make a parental responsibility order is exercisable only upon the application of the step-parent[471] which is the same position as for orders for unmarried fathers.[472] This means, for instance, that upon an adoption application there is no power to make a parental responsibility order instead. Unlike for the unmarried father, no provision is made for the automatic making of a parental responsibility order following the making of a residence order in a step-parent's favour.[473] Consequently in such cases unless the step-parent has responsibility by way of a separate order or agreement, responsibility will cease upon the ending of the residence order.[474]

No specific provision is made regarding jurisdiction to make orders but the position must be the same as for making orders in favour of unmarried fathers.[475] Similarly, by analogy with unmarried fathers,[476] and in line with the general principles of the Children Act 1989 in deciding whether or not to make an order, the court must treat the child's welfare as its paramount consideration and be satisfied that making the order is better than making no order at all. On the other hand, there is no obligation to apply the welfare checklist under s 1(3) and thus no necessity to have regard even to an older children's wishes, though whether it would be human rights compliant to ignore those wishes can be debated. No doubt the jurisprudence on whether to make a parental responsibility order in favour of the unmarried father[477] will be relevant to step-parent applications but the analogy is not exact since in most cases the application will be made with the mother's consent and the opposition will come from the non-resident father.

Parental responsibility agreements and orders remain effective notwithstanding the couple's subsequent separation or even divorce. They will, however, automatically end once the child attains his majority.[478] As with unmarried fathers, agreements and orders in favour of step-parents can be brought to an end by a subsequent court order. Such orders

---

[469] Children Act 1989, s 4A(2) and the Parental Responsibility Agreement Regulations 1991 as amended by the Parental Responsibility Agreement (Amendment) Regulations 2005, SI 2005/2808.

[470] See the discussion above at p 411.   [471] See s 4A(1)(b).   [472] See above at p 414.

[473] Ie s 12(1) of the Children Act 1989 only applies to unmarried fathers.

[474] For this reason step-parents might well be advised when applying for a residence order also to seek a parental responsibility order.

[475] For a discussion of which see above p 414.   [476] See above ibid.

[477] See above ibid.

[478] Children Act 1989, s 91(7), 8 as amended by the Adoption and Children Act 2002, Sch 3, para 68(b) and (c).

can be sought by *any* person with parental responsibility (including, therefore, the non-resident parent) or with leave of the court, by the child himself.[479] In this latter case, leave can only be granted if the court is satisfied that the child has sufficient understanding to make the application.[480] As we have seen, seeking the ending of an agreement is the only way a child can be directly involved and the only guaranteed way of being involved in respect of court orders. By analogy with unmarried fathers, in deciding whether to end an order the court must apply the welfare principle.[481]

4 ACQUISITION OF PARENTAL RESPONSIBILITY BY OTHER INDIVIDUALS

Those who are not parents do not have parental responsibility automatically, but they can acquire it. For example, any person taking office as a guardian has parental responsibility for the child concerned.[482] Similarly any person (who is not a parent or guardian) in whose favour a residence order has been made has parental responsibility for the duration of the order,[483] though this will not entitle him to agree or refuse to agree to the making of an adoption order, nor may he appoint a guardian.[484] Individuals who are appointed as special guardians[485] have parental responsibility for the child which they can exercise to the exclusion of anyone else apart from another special guardian.[486] Unlike those with residence orders in their favour special guardians can appoint a guardian[487] and can consent or withhold consent to the child's adoption (though not to the exclusion of the parent's right to do so).[488] An individual also acquires parental responsibility upon being granted an emergency protection order, though this will only entitle him to take 'such action in meeting his responsibility for the child as is reasonably required to safeguard or promote the welfare of the child (having regard in particular to the duration of the order)'.[489]

Local authorities can also acquire parental responsibility. They will do so on the making of a care order,[490] when they will share responsibility with any parent, special guardian or step-parent who has parental responsibility by virtue of a s 4A agreement or order. If they are satisfied that it is necessary to do so to safeguard or promote the child's welfare, however, they may determine the extent to which a parent, guardian, or special guardian of the child may meet his parental responsibility for him.[491] In no event, however, will a local authority be empowered to change the child's religion, to agree to his adoption, or to appoint a guardian.[492] Local authorities also acquire parental responsibility to the same limited extent as individuals upon being granted an emergency protection order.

---

[479] Children Act 1989, s 4A(3).   [480] Section 4A(4).

[481] See *Re P (Terminating Parental Responsibility)* [1995] 1 FLR 1048, discussed above at p 422.

[482] Section 5(6).   [483] Section 12(2).   [484] Section 12(3)(b) and (c).

[485] Special guardianship is discussed below at p 604ff.   [486] Children Act 1989, s 14C(1).

[487] Section 5(4), as amended by s 115(4)(b) of the Adoption and Children Act 2002.

[488] The power of the court is vested in parents and guardians, see s 47(2) of the 2002 Act and for these purpose 'guardians' include 'special guardians' see s 144(1). However, s 14C(2)(b) of the Children Act 1989 preserves the parents' right to consent.

[489] Children Act 1989 s 44(4)(c) and s 44(5)(b). Emergency protection orders are discussed below at pp 721ff.

[490] Section 33(3)(a). The effect of care orders is discussed below, pp 771ff.

[491] Section 33(3)(b) and (4), as amended by the Adoption and Children Act 2002, Sch 3, para 63.

[492] Section 33(6), as amended by the Adoption and Children Act 2002, Sch 3 para 63.

5 SHOULD THE ALLOCATION OF PARENTAL RESPONSIBILITY BE FURTHER MODIFIED?

(a) Unmarried fathers[493]

The legal position of unmarried fathers has progressed a long way from the common law position of having no legal relationship at all with his child (nor little possibility of establishing one)[494] to the current position of being able to acquire parental responsibility upon being registered as the father, or by court order or by agreement. The law nevertheless stops short of giving *all* fathers automatic parental responsibility and thus equating the position of unmarried fathers with that of married fathers and all mothers. Should all fathers be treated equally?

A comprehensive discussion of this issue has been conducted by the Scottish Law Commission.[495]

Addressing the common arguments against giving automatic parental responsibility to unmarried fathers, the Commission observed:[496]

1. It was not self evident that where a child is born as a result of a casual liaison the unmarried father should not have parental responsibility. As they put it: 'some fathers . . . will be uninterested but that is no reason for the law to encourage and reinforce an irresponsible attitude'.

2. The argument that conferring automatic parental responsibility on the unmarried father would cause offence to mothers struggling to bring up their children without support from the fathers was not thought to be a weighty argument for denying responsibility to all unmarried fathers for, as they observed: 'the important point in all these cases is that it is not the feelings of one parent in a certain type of situation that should determine the content of the law but the general interests of children and responsible parents.'

3. The Commission dismissed the argument that there might be a risk of interference

---

[493] See generally N Lowe 'The Meaning and Allocation of Parental Responsibility—A Common Lawyer's Perspective' (1997) 11 Int Jo of Law, Policy and the Family 192 at 198ff and the Lord Chancellor's Consultation Paper (1998) on *The Law on Parental Responsibility for Unmarried Fathers*. For the position in other European jurisdictions, see *European Family Law in Action Vol 1, 111: Parental Responsibilities* (eds K Boele-Woelke, B Braat and I Curry-Sumner)—Answers to Q20.

[494] Unmarried fathers only acquired the right to apply for custody under the Legitimacy Act 1959, s 3 (subsequently re-enacted by the Guardianship of Minors Act 1971, s 14). Prior to that the only legal means for an unmarried father to acquire care and control was by instituting wardship proceedings.

[495] See Scot Law Com Discussion Paper No 88 *Parental Responsibilities and Rights, Guardianship and Administration of Children's Property* (1990) and Scot Law Com No 135 *Report on Family Law* (1992). Earlier discussion in England and Wales had first been prompted by the English Law Commission's proposal in their Working Paper No 74 *Illegitimacy* (1979) to abolish the status of illegitimacy with the consequence that all fathers would be in the same legal position. That suggestion met with little favour (for a summary of the criticisms see Law Com No 118 (1st Report on *Illegitimacy*, 1982) para 4.26 on which see M Hayes (1980) 43 MLR 299) and in their later review of the Law Com No 172, *Guardianship and Custody*, 1988, the Commission considered that the issue of giving unmarried fathers automatic status had been fully canvassed and rejected.

[496] See Discussion Paper No 88 paras 2.4ff and Scot Law Com No 135 paras 2.38ff and discussed inter alia by A Bainham 'Reforming Scottish Children Law—sense from North of the border' (1993) 5 Jo of Child Law 3 at 5–7.

and harassment by the father if he had automatic responsibility,[497] essentially because this was a parent-centred rather than a child-centred argument. In the Commission's view it 'seems unjustifiable to have what is in effect a presumption that any involvement by an unmarried father is going to be contrary to the child's best interests.' In any event the Commission did not believe that the risk of harassment would be increased by the proposed change of law.

4. The argument that it is undesirable to involve all unmarried fathers in care and adoption proceedings was countered by pointing out that it could equally be said to be a grave defect that a man who has been the social father to the child should have no legal position in such matters merely because he and the child's mother have not married each other.

The Commission additionally observed that, provided each holder of parental responsibility can exercise that responsibility independently of the other,[498] the completely absent parent (whether married or not) is not a problem, since the care-giving parent can make any decision about the child's upbringing without consulting the other. Finally, the Commission considered that under the UN Convention on the Rights of the Child 1989 there is an obligation to treat all fathers equally. Specifically, the Commission pointed[499] to Art 9(3), under which States Parties are obliged to respect the child's right to contact with both parents, and Art 18(1), which obliges States Parties to: 'Use their best efforts to ensure recognition of the principle that both parents have common responsibilities for the upbringing and development of the child.'[500]

Having set out the arguments, the question of giving unmarried fathers automatic responsibility was put out for public consultation.[501] In contrast to the earlier English experience, more agreed than disagreed with the idea. Furthermore, support came from a wide variety of sources including, significantly, several women's groups. The Commission accordingly recommended that:[502] 'In the absence of any court order regulating the position, both parents of the child should have parental responsibilities and rights whether or not they are or have been married to each other.' As the Commission powerfully observed:[503]

'The question is whether the starting position should be that the father has, or has not, the normal parental responsibilities and rights. Given that about 25% of all children born in

---

[497] This was an argument which weighed heavily with the English Law Commission: see above.

[498] As they generally can under English law under s 2(7): discussed below at p 432. For the equivalent provision in Scotland, see the Children (Scotland) Act 1995 s 2(2).

[499] Scot Law Com No 135 para 2.49.

[500] This interpretation of Art 18 has not gone unchallenged, for it has been suggested that the provision was simply intended 'to focus upon responsibility in the strict sense of duty, rather than the expanded English and Scottish definitions which embrace rights as well.' In other words, imposing a duty to support a child on *all* parents regardless of marital status could be said to satisfy any obligation under the Article: G Douglas 'The significance of international law for the development of family law in England and Wales' in C Bridge (ed) *Family Law Towards the Millennium—Essays for P M Bromley* 85 at 106, n 19. The Commission did not consider whether the law was compatible with the European Convention on Human Rights, on which see further below.

[501] By the Scottish Law Commission's Discussion Paper No 88: see para 2.31.

[502] Scot Law Com No 135 *Report on Family Law* (1992) para 2.50.   [503] Ibid at para 2.48.

Scotland in recent years have been born out of wedlock,[504] and that the number of couples cohabiting outside marriage is now substantial, it seems to us that the balance has now swung in favour of the view that parents are parents, whether married to each other or not. If in any particular case it is in the best interest of a child that a parent should be deprived of some or all of his or her parental responsibilities and rights, that can be achieved by means of a court order.'

Despite what would appear to be a carefully argued case, the government rejected the Commission's recommendation, so that under the Children (Scotland) Act 1995, as under the English Children Act 1989, the unmarried father does not automatically have parental responsibility.[505]

At that stage it seemed unlikely that the government would reconsider the position of the unmarried father under English law, but in 1998 the Lord Chancellor issued a Consultation Paper[506] inviting views on the then current position. The Paper sought views inter alia on whether parental responsibility should be conferred automatically on all unmarried fathers and, if so, whether it should be revocable or whether there should be any circumstances in which the mother can override the assumption that the father had parental responsibility. Evidently, the response did not encourage the Department to recommend the equal treatment of all fathers though, as we have seen,[507] it did recommend giving parental responsibility to unmarried fathers who are registered as such on the child's birth certificate. In any event, the Department's view[508] that even the then law did not breach human rights has since been vindicated by the decision of the European Court of Human Rights in *B v UK*[509] in which an unmarried father complained that by only according to married fathers automatic parental responsibility English law has discriminated against unmarried fathers in the protection given to their relationships with their children as compared with the protection given to married fathers and was therefore in breach of Art 14 taken in conjunction with Art 8 of the European Convention of Human Rights. The European Court of Human Rights ruled the complaint inadmissible since, given the range of possible relationships between unmarried children and their children, there exists 'an objective and reasonable justification for the difference in treatment between married and unmarried fathers with regard to the automatic acquisition of parental rights'.

(b) Giving the courts a general power to make parental responsibility orders

Unlike both Scottish and Australian law,[510] English law does not vest in the courts a *general* power to make parental responsibility orders. Experience suggests that such a power

---

[504] The percentage of such children is even higher in England and Wales. According to the figures from the Office for National Statistics, in 2004 42.2% of children were born out of wedlock.

[505] Such fathers will have parental responsibility upon registration as the father on the birth certificate, see Family Law (Scotland) Act 2006, s 23. Like English law, this provision is *not* retrospective.

[506] *1. Court Proceedings for the Determination of Paternity; 2. The Law on Parental Responsibility for Unmarried Fathers*, paras 39 ff.

[507] Ibid.   [508] At para 67.

[509] [2000] 1 FLR 1, ECtHR. *Note* this decision pre-dated the change in the law giving parental responsibility to men registered as the father.

[510] The powers to make respectively a parental responsibility or a parenting order are conferred by s 11(2) of the Children (Scotland) Act 1995 and s 61D of the Australian Family Law Act 1975.

would be useful in this jurisdiction. A good example is *Re WB (Residence Orders)*[511] where a man, who thought he was the child's father and only discovered he was not as a result of a paternity test, found that because the child was to live with the mother there was no means by which he could be given parental responsibility.[512] The power could also be useful in the case of orphans.[513]

D IN RESPECT OF WHOM IS THERE RESPONSIBILITY?

Parental responsibility exists in respect of a 'child', that is, a person under the age of 18.[514] It is a moot point as to whether responsibility exists for a married child.[515]

1 THE POSITION WITH REGARD TO UNBORN CHILDREN[516]

The 1989 Act is silent on when parental responsibility begins but, in the absence of any indication to the contrary, references to 'child' in the Act must be taken to mean a live child.[517] Accordingly, no one has parental responsibility until the child is born.

It would appear that fathers have no rights over foetuses. At any rate, this was the reasoning of Sir George Baker P in *Paton v British Pregnancy Advisory Service Trustees*[518] when he refused a husband's application for an injunction to prevent his wife from having an abortion. An unmarried father was similarly refused an injunction in *C v S*.[519] In *Paton*'s case strong obiter doubts were also expressed as to whether the court should interfere even if the medical practitioners involved had not acted in good faith in issuing the certificate required by the Abortion Act 1967 and there was an obvious attempt to commit a crime: it is not for the civil courts to interfere with the exercise of doctors' discretion under the Act. This view may appear to have been weakened by the fact that both Heilbron J and the Court of Appeal in *C v S* were prepared to hear argument that the

---

[511] [1995] 2 FLR 1023. For a different type of example see *Re W (Arrangements to Place for Adoption)* [1995] 1 FLR 163

[512] The court refused to grant him a shared residence order for the 'artificial' purpose of allocation of responsibility; cf *Re H (Shared Responsibility: Parental Responsibility)* [1995] 2 FLR 883, where such an order was made to alleviate confusion in the child's mind, and *Re G (Residence: Same-Sex Partner)* [2005] EWCA Civ 462, [2005] 2 FLR 957, where a shared residence order was made in the case of same sex partners whose relationship ended specifically to give the non-parent partner parental responsibility to prevent her being marginalised by the respondent. See also the discussion below at p 516.

[513] For the position of taking orphans into local authority care, see below, p 749.

[514] Children Act 1989 s 105 (1).   [515] See below, p 431.

[516] See generally G Douglas *Law, Fertility and Reproduction* pp 82–3 and 187–9.

[517] See *Elliot v Joicey* [1935] AC 209, HL. For a similar interpretation of the meaning of 'child' under the Children and Young Persons Act 1969 s 70(1) see *Re D (A Minor)* [1987] AC 317, HL. Note also *R v Newham London Borough Council, ex p Dada* [1996] QB 507, CA interpreting the Housing Act 1985 s 75.

[518] [1979] QB 276. See further I Kennedy (1979) 42 MLR 324; Phillips (1979) 95 LQR 332; N Lowe (1980) 96 LQR 29 and N Lowe and R White *Wards of Court* (2nd edn, 1986) paras 2–3. The husband also failed before the European Commission of Human Rights, which ruled that although he had locus standi to bring the complaint, there had been no breach of the Convention since the abortion was certified as being necessary for the wife's health: *Paton v UK* (1980) 3 EHRR 408.

[519] [1988] QB 135, CA.

proposed abortion was contrary to the provisions of the Infant Life (Preservation) Act 1929 s 1. However, Sir John Donaldson MR commented that even if a breach of the 1929 Act could have been proved, 'strong consideration' would still have been paid to Sir George Baker P's comment that the matter would be better left to the Director of Public Prosecutions, who could then consider whether prosecutions should be brought. It is submitted that even if the abortion were ex facie illegal the father still could not obtain an injunction to prevent the commission of the proposed criminal act once it is accepted that he has no right which would be affected.[520]

Re F (In Utero)[521] unequivocally establishes that there is no power to ward an unborn child, though interestingly the principal reason for so holding was the unacceptable clash between the unborn child's interests and those of the mother that the exercise of wardship would inevitably entail, rather than the foetus's having no rights of its own to protect.

2 THE POSITION WITH REGARD TO EMBRYOS[522]

As one commentator has said:[523] 'The advent of assisted reproduction and the ability to fertilise an ovum in vitro and to maintain the resulting embryo for a number of days has required the law to work out whether, and how, to protect such an embryo'. The legal framework is now provided for by the Human Fertilisation and Embryology Act 1990, which in turn is based upon the recommendations of the Warnock Report.[524] Detailed consideration of this Act lies outside the scope of this work;[525] nevertheless, it is worth noting that in contradistinction to his position with regard to a foetus, the father (as well as the mother) does have rights with respect to an embryo in vitro whilst outside the womb. Whilst stopping short of providing for ownership, the 1990 Act nevertheless provides that embryos can only be used, stored or disposed of with the consent of the persons whose gametes were used to create the embryo in vitro.[526]

E DURATION OF PARENTAL RESPONSIBILITY

An important aspect of parental responsibility under the Children Act 1989 is its enduring nature, and in particular that it is not lost merely because someone else acquires it. Nevertheless, responsibility does not have an unlimited duration. As it can only exist in respect of a 'child', parental responsibility ends upon the child attaining his majority. It

---

[520] See *Gouriet v Union of Post Office Workers* [1978] AC 435, HL. But see Kennedy, above.

[521] [1988] Fam 122, CA. N Lowe 'The Limits of Wardship Jurisdiction' (1988) 1 Journal of Child Law 6 and J Fortin 'Can You Ward a Foetus?' (1988) 51 MLR 768. For a further discussion of this case see Chapter 16.

[522] See Douglas, above, ch 3 and I Kennedy and A Grubb *Medical Law: Text and Materials* (3rd edn) 1283ff.

[523] Douglas, above at p 33.

[524] Report of the Committee of Inquiry into Human Fertilisation and Embryology (1984) Cmnd 9314.

[525] For more detailed reading, see eg D Morgan and R Lee *The Human Fertilisation and Embryology Act 1990* and G Douglas 'The Human Fertilisation and Embryology Act 1990' [1991] Fam Law 110.

[526] Sch 3. Either parent has an unconditional right to withdraw their consent and following that withdrawal the embryo(s) must be destroyed: *Evans v Amicus Healthcare Ltd* [2004] EWCA Civ 727, [2005] Fam 1, which position has since been ruled human rights law compliant, see *Evans v United Kingdom* (Application No 6339/05), *The Times*, 17 March 2006, ECtHR.

will clearly end upon the child's death.[527] Upon the making of a parental order[528] or an adoption order,[529] parental responsibility is transferred to the person or persons in whose favour the order is made.[530] Non-parents who have responsibility by reason of a residence order, local authorities which have responsibility by reason of a care order, and anyone who has responsibility by reason of an emergency protection order, only does so for the duration of the order.[531]

Apart from the above-mentioned circumstances there is uncertainty as to whether other events can end parental responsibility. Before the Children Act 1989 there was authority for saying that the right of custody ended upon the child's marriage[532] and that it was suspended whilst the child was serving in the armed forces,[533] but it remains to be decided whether a similar position will be taken with regard to parental responsibility. There is also conflicting opinion as to whether responsibility ceases in respect of any aspect of a child's upbringing about which the child himself is sufficiently mature to make his own decisions.[534] Perhaps the better view in each of these situations is that parental responsibility does not end, but that the scope for its exercise is limited.

Unlike under Scottish Law[535] there is no general power under English law to divest a parent[536] of parental responsibility. Whether there should be a general divesting power can be debated. On the one hand, such a possibility would deal with the point made by others[537] that, just as it may be wrong to deny automatic parental responsibility to 'meritorious' unmarried fathers, so it is questionable to vest it in 'unmeritorious' *married* fathers, as for example where conception took place as a result of rape within marriage. Furthermore, there are cases where a parent has behaved so appallingly, either towards the child or other members of the family, that one could argue that that person should no longer have responsibility. On the other hand, a general divesting power cuts across the

---

[527] It is established, however, that even if the child had been in care the parent retains the right to bury (or, presumably, cremate) the child: *R v Gwynedd County Council, ex p B* [1992] 3 All ER 317, CA, discussed above, p 400.

[528] Viz an order made under the Human Fertilisation and Embryology Act 1990, s 30, discussed above at pp 315ff.

[529] Adoption and Children Act 2002, s 46 discussed below at p 867.

[530] Apart from these orders there is no other means of depriving parents of their *automatic* parental responsibility during the child's minority. However, if such power exists in a foreign jurisdiction then the English courts may be forced to recognise it, see *Re AMR (Adoption: Procedure)* [1999] 2 FLR 807—Polish order depriving parents of their parental authority held to deprive them of parental responsibility under English law.

[531] See respectively s 12(2), s 33(3) and s 44(4)(c).

[532] See eg *Hewer v Bryant* [1970] 1 QB 357 at 373, CA per Sachs LJ; *R v Wilmington Inhabitants* (1822) 5 B & Ald 525 at 526 and *Lough v Ward* [1945] 2 All ER 338 at 348.

[533] *R v Rotherfield Greys Inhabitants* (1823) 1 B & C 345 at 349–50.

[534] See the comment of Lord Scarman in *Gillick v West Norfolk and Wisbech Area Health Authority* [1986] AC 112 at 186, which suggests it does, but which was specifically rejected by Lord Donaldson MR in *Re R (A Minor) (Wardship: Medical Treatment)* [1992] Fam 11 at 23, and both by Lord Donaldson MR and Balcombe LJ in *Re W (A Minor) (Medical Treatment) (Court's Jurisdiction)* [1993] Fam 64 at 75–6 and 87, discussed above at pp 363–6.

[535] See s 11(2)(a) of the Children (Scotland) Act 1995.

[536] A mother or married father. Parental responsibility orders and agreements can be ended by the court under s 4(3): see above. Those who acquire responsibility via a residence order only have it for the duration of the order.

[537] Such as the Scottish Law Commission: see Scot Law Com No 88 para 2.47 and C Barton and G Douglas *Law and Parenthood* 93–4.

principle that responsibility should be enduring.[538] On balance, however, provided any divesting power is subject to the overarching principle of the paramountcy of the child's welfare, there does seem a case for amending English Law.

F SHARING PARENTAL RESPONSIBILITY FOR A CHILD

Although self-evident, given the position of married parents under s 2(1) of the Children Act 1989, s 2(5) nevertheless expressly provides that more than one person may have parental responsibility for the same child at the same time. Section 2(6) further provides that a person with parental responsibility does not cease to have it solely because some other person subsequently acquires it. This latter provision which, in the words of one commentator,[539] 'encapsulates the ethos of continuing parental responsibility' means, for example, that a parent will not lose responsibility because someone else such as a step-parent, grandparent, foster parent or, even, a local authority acquires it. Section 2(6) should not, however, be read as meaning that a court order can never end a parent's responsibility. An adoption order clearly does, because the statute expressly says so.[540]

Where parental responsibility is shared, then, by s 2(7), each person in whom it is vested 'may act alone and without the other (or others) in meeting that responsibility' except where a statute expressly requires the consent of more than one person in a matter affecting the child.[541] This power to act independently, however, is subject to the important limitation under s 2(8), namely, that a person with parental responsibility is not entitled to act in any way that could be incompatible with a court order.[542]

The ability to act independently was intended to mean, not simply that neither parent has a right of veto, but also that there is no legal duty upon parents to consult each other[543]

---

[538] The enduring nature of responsibility is emphasised, in the case of an unmarried father acquiring responsibility by virtue of a residence order made in his favour, by the requirement under s 12(1) to make a separate parental responsibility order, so that the subsequent ending of the residence order will not ipso facto end the responsibility.

[539] A Bainham *Children, The New Law, The Children Act 1989* para 2.18.

[540] Adoption and Children Act 2002 s 46(2)(a). As Lord Mackay LC said, during the Debates on the Children Bill (588 HL Official Report (5th series) col 1175), the word 'solely' is used advisedly in s 2(6), ie an adoption order deprives a parent of responsibility not solely because adoptive parents acquire it but because the 2002 Act expressly extinguishes it.

[541] This latter qualification preserves, for example, the embargo imposed by the Child Abduction Act 1984 s 1 against one parent taking the child (under the age of 16) outside the United Kingdom without the other's consent (in this regard it will be noted that neither parent can unilaterally change the child's habitual residence: *Re S (Minors) (Child Abduction: Wrongful Retention)* [1994] 1 FLR 82 per Wall J and *Re A (Wardship: Jurisdiction)* [1995] 1 FLR 767 per Hale J) and maintains the need to obtain *each* parent's agreement to an adoption order as laid down by s 47(2) of the Adoption and Children Act 2002.

[542] The absence of a court order does not necessarily mean that parental responsibility may be exercised without qualification. For example, since ultimate responsibility for a ward of court rests with the court (see below, p 886), the warding of a child must immediately operate at least to limit freedom of action.

[543] This resolved the uncertainty of the former law, which seemed to impose no duty to consult but did confer a power of veto: see Law Com Working Paper No 96 *Custody* para 2.34 et seq.

since, in the Law Commission's view,[544] such a duty was both unworkable and undesirable. It was expressly contemplated that even where a residence order had been granted in one parent's favour, subject to not acting incompatibly with a court order, each parent could still exercise that responsibility without having to consult the other and with neither having a right of veto over the other's action. Referring to the example of a child living with one parent and going to a school nearby, the Commission considered that while it would be incompatible for the other parent to arrange for the child to have his hair done in a way which would exclude him from the school, it would be permissible for that parent to take the child to a sporting occasion over the weekend, no matter how much the parent with whom the child lived might disapprove. According to the Commission the intended independence of each parent was to be seen as part of the general aim of encouraging both parents to feel concerned and responsible for the welfare of the children.[545]

The intended scheme of the Act had been criticised on the basis that it was difficult to see how failing to provide for consultation, at any rate with respect to serious or long-term decisions affecting the child, could promote joint parenting following breakdown.[546] Evidently the courts have sympathy for that point of view for, despite the apparently clear wording of s 2(7), the Court of Appeal in *Re G (A Minor) (Parental Responsibility: Education)*[547] seemed to have assumed that there remains[548] a duty to consult, at any rate over long-term decisions. In that case a father who had custody, care and control under a court order arranged for his son to attend a local education authority boarding school without informing the mother. In Glidewell LJ's view the '. . . mother, having parental responsibility, was entitled to and indeed ought to have been consulted about the important step of taking her child away from the day school that he had been attending and sending him to boarding school. It is an important step in any child's life and she ought to have been consulted.'

Since *Re G* it has been held that s 2(7) does not entitle one spouse to change the child's surname without consent of the other;[549] nor to permit the circumcision of a child against the wishes of the other.[550] It has also been held[551] that hotly contested issues of immunisation belong to that small group of important decisions that ought not to be carried out or arranged by the one-parent carer in the absence of agreement of those with parental responsibility.

---

[544] Law Com No 172 para 2.07.   [545] At para 2.10.

[546] See A Bainham [1990] Fam Law 192 at 193. But for a strong counter view see J Eekelaar 'Rethinking Parental Responsibility' [2001] Fam Law 426 at 429 and by the same author 'Do parents have a duty to consult?' (1998) 114 LQR 337. See also the thoughtful analysis, including the notion that a right of veto is not synonymous with the 'right to be consulted', by S Maidment, 'Parental Responsibility—Is There A Duty To Consult? [2001] Fam Law 518. For an interesting empirical survey of the general public's view as to who should be in control over decision making see G Potter and C Williams 'Parental responsibility and the duty to consult—the public's view' [2005] CFLQ 207.

[547] [1994] 2 FLR 964, CA.

[548] This seems a throw-back to the pre-1989 Act law and in particular to *Dipper v Dipper* [1981] Fam 31, CA, discussed in the 7th edition of this work at pp 295 and 302.

[549] *Re PC (Change of Surname)* [1997] 2 FLR 730 per Holman J.

[550] *Re J (Specific Issue Orders)(Muslim Upbringing and Circumcision)* [2000] 1 FLR 571, CA. In that case Butler-Sloss P also included sterilisation among the group of important decisions needing more than just the one-parent carer's consent.

[551] *Re C (Welfare of Child: Immunisation)* [2003] EWCA Civ 1148, [2003] 2 FLR 1095 at [16]–[17], per Thorpe LJ.

What other examples will fall into this group of important decisions is a matter of speculation but in one sense, it makes no difference whether or not there is a duty to consult, for in either case in the event of a disagreement the burden will be on the complaining parent to take the issue to court. Even so, the court's approach to s 2(7) is questionable.[552]

G EFFECT OF THIRD PARTIES ACQUIRING PARENTAL RESPONSIBILITY

As s 2(6) makes clear, neither parent loses parental responsibility solely because someone else has acquired it through a court order. This means, for example, that upon divorce a father does not lose responsibility even if a step-father also acquires it under a court order or agreement.[553] In this situation the mother, step-father and father all share responsibility for the child and, subject to not acting incompatibly with a court order and, subject to the case-law just discussed, each can exercise their responsibility independently of the others. A similar situation arises if grandparents or other relations or foster parents have residence orders or even special guardianship orders[554] made in their favour. Another effect of s 2(6) is that parents do not lose parental responsibility when a local authority obtains a care order, nor where an emergency protection order is made.[555]

H DELEGATION OF PARENTAL RESPONSIBILITY

Whilst preserving the previous position that a person with parental responsibility may not surrender or transfer any part of that responsibility to another, s 2(9), permits those with responsibility to 'arrange for some or all of it to be met by one or more persons acting on his behalf'. Such delegation can be made to another person who already has parental responsibility[556] or to those who have not, such as schools or holiday camps. The aim of this provision is to encourage parents (regardless of whether or not they are separated) to agree among themselves on what they believe to be the best arrangements for their children. Section 2(9) does not, however, make such arrangements legally binding. Consequently, they can be revoked or changed at will. Furthermore, as s 2(11) provides, delegations will not absolve a person with parental responsibility from any liability for failure on his part to discharge his responsibilities to the child.[557]

---

[552] A similar view is taken by R White, P Carr and N Lowe *Children Act in Practice* (3rd edn) at 3.92.

[553] It will be noted that step-parents may acquire parental responsibility only through an order or agreement or upon being appointed a guardian. They do not acquire responsibility simply by marrying the child's parent. This 'disconnection' between responsibility and divorce is a trend noted in other jurisdictions, see the observations by D Blair and M Weiner 'Resolving Parental Custody Disputes—A Comparative Explanation' (2005) 39 (2) FLQ 247 at 255.

[554] This is stated more forcibly by s 14C(1)(b), discussed below at p 608.

[555] Discussed below at pp 773 and 725 respectively.　　　　[556] Section 2(10).

[557] For example, not to neglect, abandon, expose or cause or procure a child under the age of 16 to be assaulted or ill-treated etc under s 1 and s 17 of the Children and Young Persons Act 1933: see above, pp 381–2.

I CARING FOR A CHILD WITHOUT HAVING PARENTAL RESPONSIBILITY

Resolving the confusion of the pre-1989 Act law[558] the Children Act clarifies the legal position of those who are caring for a child but who do not have parental responsibility, by providing that they 'may (subject to the provisions of this Act) do what is reasonable in all the circumstances for the purpose of safeguarding or promoting the child's welfare'. As in the Department of Health's *Guidance and Regulations* observes,[559] what is reasonable 'will depend upon the urgency and gravity of what is required and the extent to which it is practicable to consult a person with parental responsibility'. In other words all that s 3(5) does is to clothe the de facto carers with the *minimum* power necessary to provide for the day-to-day care of the child. So, for example, while a carer may be able to consent to the child's medical treatment in the event of an accident, he will not be able to consent to major elective surgery. Indeed, it may be difficult for the carer to convince a doctor that he has sufficient authority to consent to medical treatment which may be desirable but not essential.[560] Whether a significantly greater latitude for action should be given to those caring for orphans remains an interesting point.

It is on the basis of s 3(5) that it is thought that a foster parent of a child being accommodated by a local authority could properly refuse immediately to hand over the child to a parent who is drunk or who turns up in the middle of the night. On the other hand, it is clear that s 3(5) does not empower a de facto carer to change a child's habitual residence merely by taking the child out of the jurisdiction[561] nor to obtain a passport for the child,[562] or to change the child's surname.[563] It has also been held[564] that because they do not have parental responsibility local authorities have no power to transfer an 'accommodated' child from residential care to foster care without the parents' permission.[565] Anyone who cares for a child is obliged not to assault, ill-treat, neglect, abandon or expose the child in a manner likely to cause unnecessary suffering or injury to health.[566]

---

[558] See Law Com No 172 para 2.16.   [559] Vol 1, *Court Orders*, para 2.11.

[560] See, for example, Johnson J's comments in *B v B (A Minor) (Residence Order)* [1992] 2 FLR 327 at 330. His Lordship also observed that notwithstanding s 3(5) a maternal grandmother, who was the de facto carer, found in practice that the education authorities were reluctant to accept her authority to give consent, for example, to the child going on a school trip, and insisted upon having the mother's written authority.

[561] See *Re S (A Minor) (Custody: Habitual Residence)* [1998] AC 750, HL, per Lord Slynn.

[562] Per Butler-Sloss LJ in *Re S (Abduction: Hague and European Convention)* [1997] 1 FLR 958 at 962.

[563] *Re D, L and LA (Care: Change of Surname)* [2003] 1 FLR 339.

[564] *R v Tameside Metropolitan Borough Council, ex p J* [2000] 1 FLR 492.

[565] Accommodation is discussed below at pp 703ff.

[566] Children and Young Persons Act 1933 s 1.

9

GUARDIANSHIP

A INTRODUCTION

The term 'guardian' has a variety of meanings,[1] but the specific concern of this chapter is the institution of legal guardianship over children during their minority. Formerly, the concept of guardianship was a complex one and it was well described[2] as a formula used to attribute powers over a child's upbringing to a particular individual or individuals. However, following its reform by the Children Act 1989 guardianship can now be said to be the legal status under which a person has parental responsibility for a child following the death of one or both of the child's parents. In short, a 'guardian' is someone who has been formally appointed to take the place of the child's deceased parent.

1 THE POSITION OF GUARDIANS BEFORE THE CHILDREN ACT 1989

Before its reform by the Children Act 1989, guardianship had become a complicated product of common law, equity and statute.[3] Its early history was succinctly described by the Law Commission as follows:[4]

'The institution of guardianship was originally of concern only to those who had property. It began as a lucrative incident of feudal tenure and developed as a means of safeguarding a family's property and securing its transmission from one generation to another. Subsequently it became the instrument for maintaining the authority of the father over the upbringing of his children.'

The pre-1989 Act law recognised both parental and non-parental guardianship. With regard to the former, notwithstanding the general equalisation of spouses' rights,[5] it

---

[1] See, for example, the use of 'guardianship' under the Mental Health Act 1983 s 10(1), under which a guardian may be appointed for a person who has attained the age of 16 and who is, or appears to be, suffering from a mental disorder. The term 'guardian' is not to be confused with a 'children's guardian' or guardian ad litem, who is a person appointed to represent a child in legal proceedings: see below, pp 492ff, nor with 'special guardianship' introduced by the Adoption and Children Act 2002 under which non parents can be appointed as special guardians during the parents' lifetime, see below pp 604ff. But note the definition of 'guardian' in s 144(1) of the 2002 Act which is said to include special guardians.

[2] S Cretney Principles of Family Law (4th edn, 1984) p 296.

[3] For an excellent summary of the history see the Law Commission Working Paper No 91 on Guardianship (1985), Part 11. For a detailed history see eg Holdsworth History of English Law (7th edn, 1966) Vol 111. See also H Bevan Child Law (1989) ch 4, and ch 10 of the 7th edition of this work.

[4] In their Working Paper No 91 at para 3.1.   [5] See above, pp 354ff.

remained the case that during his lifetime the father was the sole guardian of his legitimate children. It was only upon his death that the mother became a guardian either alone or jointly with any other guardians appointed by the father. The common law made no provision for guardianship of illegitimate children and, even though the mother was eventually recognised[6] as having exclusive parental rights and duties, she was not formally regarded as a guardian.[7] With regard to non-parental guardianship, statute eventually conferred[8] equal rights on mothers and fathers to appoint a testamentary guardian in respect of legitimate children, with the mother having the exclusive right to do so with respect to her illegitimate children. Testamentary appointments took effect upon the death of the appointing parent even if the other parent was still alive. However, if the latter objected, he or she could apply to the court to prevent the appointee from acting. A guardian could also apply to court if he considered the parent unfit to have custody, and the court had various powers to resolve such disputes.[9]

The courts also had power to appoint guardians. Under the Guardianship of Minors Acts 1971 and 1973 a magistrates' court, county court or High Court each had power to make appointments following the death of either or both parents. In addition it was generally thought that the High Court retained an inherent jurisdiction to appoint guardians.[10]

Historically, the law recognised two separate functions of guardians: the protection of the person and the protection of the property of the ward. These functions could be split between guardians of the person, with no right to control the ward's property, and guardians of the estate, with no right to control the ward's person.[11] Although the 1925 property legislation virtually rendered guardianship of the estate obsolete, it remained useful to appoint the Official Solicitor, for example, to administer an award made to the child by the Criminal Injuries Compensation Board in respect of injuries caused by the parents.[12]

Guardians (unless of the estate only) had broadly similar rights and duties with respect to the child as a parent,[13] but they were not in exactly the same position.[14] For example, unlike parents, guardians could not be made liable to maintain their wards, nor could they appoint a guardian themselves. On the other hand, they probably had wider powers than

---

[6] Children Act 1975 s 85(1).

[7] Though in *Re A* (1940) 164 LT 230 it was held that the Guardianship of Infants Act 1925 had given the mother the right to appoint a testamentary guardian for her illegitimate child.

[8] Restricted rights were first conferred by the Guardianship of Infants Act 1886 and equal rights by the Guardianship of Infants Act 1925, which was then consolidated by the Guardianship of Minors Act 1971.

[9] See pp 352–3 of the 7th edition of this work.

[10] Though this had been doubted by *Re C (Minors) (Adoption by Relatives)* [1989] 1 All ER 395, CA. In fact the Guardianship Act 1973 s 7(2) expressly preserved the High Court's inherent power to appoint a guardian of the estate.

[11] If there was no separate guardian of a minor's estate, a guardian appointed by a deceased parent or by the court under the Guardianship of Minors Act 1971 had all the rights, powers and duties of a guardian of the estate in addition to being guardian of the person: Guardianship Act 1973 s 7.

[12] See Law Commission Working Paper No 91, note 95.

[13] For example, both had a statutory right to consent to the marriage of a child under the age of 18 and to agree to the child's adoption.

[14] For a detailed analysis of the former position see Law Commission Working Paper No 91, paras 2.24–2.35, and pp 355–60 of the 7th edition of this work.

parents in respect of the child's property.[15] There was uncertainty as to whether a guardian had a right of access to the child and, indeed, as to who had the right to care and control of the child where the parent was still alive. As the Law Commission concluded,[16] the inter-relationship between the legal status of parent and guardian was obscure, particularly where the parent was also described as a guardian.

2 THE NEED FOR REFORM

The notion of parental guardianship confused the separate legal concepts of parenthood and guardianship and in the Law Commission's view it was both sensible and practical to regard parenthood as the primary concept and to distinguish it from the role of a guardian who acts in loco parentis.[17] Accordingly they recommended abolishing the rule under which parents, who for all practical purposes had the same rights and authority, were sometimes guardians and sometimes not.[18] On the other hand, although little was known about the frequency of guardianship appointments,[19] the Commission considered[20] that the law should provide some means of supplying a person or persons who could step into the shoes of a parent or parents who have died. Following consultation the Commission found unanimous support for the power both of the parents and courts to appoint guardians.[21] The Commission also canvassed opinion as to whether there should be some form of public control of guardians appointed by parents, for example, by subjecting non-related guardians to the same provisions as private foster parents.[22] In the event, however, these suggestions were not pursued,[23] nor were the suggestions for extending guardianship to permit inter vivos appointments.[24] A number of other suggestions for reform[25] were, however, recommended, namely vesting full parental responsibility in guardians, simplify-ing the method by which parents can appoint a guardian, providing in general that parental appointments come into force only upon the death of the surviving parent, and changing and clarifying the courts' powers both to appoint and remove guardians. Save for the abolition of guardians of the estate,[26] the Law Commission's recommendations on guardianship were enacted by the Children Act 1989.

---

[15] For example, a guardian but not a parent could give a valid receipt on the child's behalf for a legacy: see Law Com Working Paper No 91, para 2.33.

[16] Working Paper No 91, para 2.35.   [17] Ibid, para 3.2.

[18] Law Com Report No 172 on *Guardianship and Custody* (1988) para 2.2.

[19] Though they did commission a small study undertaken by Priest in the North East of England—see Appendix B of Working Paper No 91.

[20] Working Paper No 91 para 3.17.   [21] Law Com No 172 para 2.2.

[22] Law Com Working Paper No 91, paras 3.23 et seq.

[23] Law Com No 172 para 2.32.

[24] Discussed in Working Paper No 91 paras 4.19 et seq. Note, however, the subsequent proposal (in the Consultative Document on Adoption Law, para 6.5) that courts be empowered to appoint so-called 'inter vivos' guardians. This was later developed into the special guardianship provisions added to the Children Act 1989 and discussed below at pp 604 et seq.

[25] See Law Com No 172 paras 2.23–2.31.

[26] Law Com No 172 para 2.24—see further below at p 439.

B THE CURRENT LAW

The law of guardianship is exclusively controlled by s 5 and s 6 of the Children Act 1989.[27] The concept of parental guardianship has been abolished[28] and, save for the exceptional case where the unmarried father becomes a guardian,[29] the status is now confined to those non-parents formally appointed to take the place of a deceased parent or parents.

With one exception it is no longer possible to appoint different types of guardians. This exception is the High Court's inherent power to appoint a guardian of a child's estate, which has been preserved by s 5(11) and (12).[30] This power, however, is limited in that only the Official Solicitor can be so appointed, and even then only when the consent of the persons with parental responsibility has been signified to the court or when, in the court's opinion, such consent cannot be obtained or may be dispensed with.[31] In practice such appointments are likely to be confined to cases where the parents are dead or where it is unsuitable for them to be involved (for example, where they had caused injuries to the child in respect of which compensation has been paid).

Guardians of the estate apart, all guardians have parental responsibility for the child,[32] which effectively places them in the same legal position as parents, at least so far as the care and upbringing of the child is concerned. The conferment of full parental responsibility was central to the role of guardians as envisaged by the Law Commission. As they put it:[33]

'The power to control a child's upbringing should go hand in hand with the responsibility to look after him or at least to see that he is properly looked after. Consultation confirmed our impression that it is now generally expected that guardians will take over any responsibility for the care and upbringing of a child if the parents die. If so, it is right that full legal responsibility should also be placed upon them.'

One consequence of having parental responsibility is that guardians can themselves appoint guardians. Appointments can also be made by a parent with parental responsibility or court.

---

[27] This is not to say that an English court will not recognise a guardianship appointment made abroad but note the controversy as to the meaning of 'guardian' for the purposes of adoption, see below, p 851 n 265.

[28] Following the express abolition of the rule of law that a father is the natural guardian of his legitimate children by s 2(4) of the Children Act 1989, and the repeal (by Sch 15) of s 3 of the Guardianship of Minors Act 1971 which provided that upon the death of one parent the other became the guardian of any legitimate child.

[29] Such as upon the mother's death following an appointment by her or the court.

[30] Implemented 1 February 1992: SI 1991/828. The Law Commission (see Law Com No 172 para 2.24) recommended the abolition of this power, arguing that trusteeship would adequately and more appropriately fill any gap.

[31] CPR 1998, r 22.12(2). Appointments may be made only in certain defined circumstances, for example, when the Criminal Injuries Compensation Authority has made or intends to make an award to the child, when payment to the child has been ordered by a foreign court or tribunal, or when the child is entitled to the proceeds of a pension fund, and in any other case where, in the court's view, such an appointment seems desirable: CPR 1998, r 22.12(1).

[32] Children Act 1989 s 5(6).   [33] Law Com No 172 para 2.23.

1 APPOINTMENT OF GUARDIANS

(a) Private appointment of guardians

Any parent with parental responsibility (ie not an unmarried father without such responsibility), any guardian and any special guardian may appoint an individual to be the child's guardian.[34] Although reference is made to 'an individual', more than one person may be appointed as a guardian.[35] Furthermore, an additional guardian or guardians can be appointed at a later date.[36] There is nothing to prevent an appointment being made by two or more persons jointly.[37]

There is no restriction or control upon who may be appointed (even another child, it seems, could be appointed),[38] nor are there any means of scrutinising an appointment unless a dispute or issue is subsequently brought before the court.[39] Appointments can be made only in respect of children under the age of 18.[40]

Whereas formerly the appointment had to be by deed or will, under s 5(5) it is sufficient that the appointment is made in writing, dated and signed by the person making it. This simpler method of appointment is intended to encourage parents (particularly young parents who are notoriously reluctant to make wills) to appoint guardians.[41] Section 5(5) does not preclude appointments being made in a will since such means will satisfy the minimum requirements.[42] An appointment made by will but not signed by the testator will be valid if it is signed at the direction of the testator in accordance with the Wills Act 1837 s 9.[43] An appointment will also be valid in any other case provided it is signed at the direction of the person making the appointment, in his presence and in the presence of two witnesses who each attest the signature.[44] These latter provisions cater for the blind or physically disabled persons who cannot write.[45]

Revoking an appointment

Section 6 of the Children Act 1989 deals with the formerly complex question of revocation

---

[34] Section 5(3)–(4) as amended by the Adoption and Children Act 2002, s 114 (s14G(4)). Special guardianship is discussed below at pp 604ff.

[35] This is implicit in s 6(1) which refers to 'an additional guardian'. In any event, under the Interpretation Act 1978 s 6(c), unless there is a contrary intention, words in the singular in a statute presumptively include the plural. But 'individual' does not include a 'body': see below, p 443.

[36] Section 6(1).

[37] Section 5(10). Such an appointment only takes effect on the death of all the appointers: see further below at p 441.

[38] Though, as Hershman and McFarlane *Children—Law and Practice* at J [9] comment, it seems questionable that one child should have parental responsibility over another. Nevertheless, the power can occasionally be useful: see *Re A, J and J (minors) (Residence and Guardianship Orders)* [1993] Fam Law 568; and see below, p 444 n 71.

[39] See below, p 448 for discussion of the courts' powers to remove a guardian. The complete absence of regulation is commented upon by Douglas and Lowe 'Becoming a Parent in English Law' (1992) 108 LQR 414 at 428.

[40] Section 105(1). Quaere whether (a) an appointment would take effect once the child is married, or (b) a valid appointment may be made before the child is born: see below, p 449.

[41] See Law Com No 172 para 2.29.

[42] See Lord Mackay LC's comments at 502 HL Official Report (5th Series), col 1199.

[43] Section 5(5)(a).   [44] Section 5(5)(b).

[45] But not those who are mentally incapacitated: cf Department of Health's *Children Act 1989: Guidance and Regulations*, Vol 1 *Court Orders*, para 2.18.

of appointments. Under s 6(1) a later appointment revokes an earlier appointment (including one made in an unrevoked will or codicil) made by the same person in respect of the same child, unless it is clear that the purpose of the later appointment is to appoint an additional guardian. Under s 6(2) the person who made the appointment (including one made in an unrevoked will or codicil) can expressly revoke it in a signed written and dated instrument. Under s 6(3A) a dissolution or annulment of marriage on or after 1 January 1996 revokes an appointment of the former spouse as a guardian unless a contrary intention appears from the appointment.[46] Similarly, under s 6(3B), in the case of a registered civil partnership the dissolution or annulment of the partnership by a court order revokes an appointment by the former partner unless a contrary intention appears by the appointment.[47] Section 6(4) further provides that an appointment made in a will or codicil is revoked if the will or codicil is revoked. An appointment, *other than* one made by will or codicil, will also be revoked if the person making it destroys the document with the intention of revoking the appointment.[48]

When the appointment takes effect

Unlike under the previous law, an appointment no longer automatically takes effect upon the death of the appointing parent. Instead, the appointment normally takes effect upon the death of the sole remaining parent with parental responsibility.[49] If the appointing person is already the sole parent with parental responsibility, then the appointment will take effect immediately upon his death.[50] Under s 5(7)(b), as amended by the Adoption and Children Act 2002 however, an appointment takes effect immediately upon the death of the appointing person if there was a sole[51] residence order in his favour at the time of his death or upon the death of the only or last surviving special guardian. In these latter instances, the surviving parent has no right to object, but he can apply to the court for an order ending the appointment.[52] The rationale for delaying the operation of a guardianship appointment is to avoid unnecessary conflict between a surviving parent and a guardian appointed by the deceased parent. As the Law Commission said,[53] there seems little reason why the surviving parent should have to share parental responsibility with a guardian who almost invariably will not be living in the same household. In effect the law protects the surviving parent from interference by an outsider; though, of course, if that parent wishes informally to seek the help of the appointee, he can do so without jeopardising his parental status. In such circumstances, however, the surviving parent cannot object

---

[46] This provision was added by the Law Reform (Succession) Act 1995 (on which see Barton and Wells 'A Matter of Life and Death—The Law Reform (Succession) Act 1995' [1996] Fam Law 172 at 174, who make the point that an appointment of a cohabitant would *not* be revoked by the couple's subsequent estrangement). For the purposes of this provision the dissolution or annulment includes both those made by a court of civil jurisdiction in England and Wales and those recognised in England and Wales by virtue of Part II of the Family Law Act 1986.

[47] This provision was added by the Civil Partnership Act 2004, s 76. For these purposes the dissolution or annulment includes both those made by a court in England and Wales and those recognised in England and Wales by virtue of the Civil Partnership Act 2004, Part 5, Ch 3: s 6(3B)(b) of the 1989 Act.

[48] Section 6(3).   [49] Section 5(8).   [50] Section 5(7)(a).

[51] Aliter, if a residence order had also been made in favour of a surviving parent: s 5(9). Quaere the position where a joint appointment has been made? Hershman and McFarlane, op cit at J [37] consider that the appointment will not take effect until the death of the surviving parent, relying on s 5(10), but the position is perhaps not beyond doubt.

[52] Section 6(7), discussed further below at p 448.   [53] Law Com No 172 para 2.28.

to the appointment, although under s 6(7) he can seek a court order to end it. On the other hand, if the *appointee* wishes to challenge this position, he will need to seek the court's leave to obtain a s 8 order.

While this basic standpoint seems right (and furthermore, brings English law into line with the Council of Europe recommendation on guardianship)[54] where the child was living with both parents in a united family before the death of one of them, different considerations apply where the parents are divorced or separated. Endorsing the Law Commission's view,[55] the law takes the position that, if there was a court order that the child should live with the parent who had died, that parent should be able to provide for the child's upbringing in the event of his death. However, this standpoint has been called into question by one commentator, who said:[56]

'The survivor will, of course, have joint parental responsibility with the guardian but will have the onus of bringing the child's position before the court in the event of a disagreement between them.[57] This is not very easy to reconcile with the ethos of continuing parental responsibility following divorce. It casts the non-residential parent in the role of an outsider who is liable to interfere with the child rather than that of a concerned parent who is anxious to step into the breach left by the deceased.'

In any event, this position creates uncertainty about who is entitled to take over the physical care of the child, since prima facie both the guardian and the surviving parent have equal claims.[58] This standpoint has also been criticised for *not* making provision for cases where the spouses are separated, or even divorced, but where there is no residence order.[59] The father, for example, may simply have abandoned his family. As the Scottish Law Commission said:[60]

'In many of these cases it might well be desirable for an appointment of a guardian to be capable of coming into operation, even though there is a surviving parent somewhere.'

Disclaiming the appointment

Section 6(5) of the Children Act 1989 provides a formal right for a guardian to disclaim an appointment. This right, which applies only to appointments made by a parent or a guardian (ie not to court appointments), must be exercised 'within a reasonable time of

---

[54] Recommendation R84(4) *Parental Responsibilities*, Principle 9. Indeed, as the Law Commission pointed out (ibid at para 2.27), before the Children Act amendments the UK was the only member country of the Council of Europe that permitted guardianship to operate during the lifetime of a surviving parent.

[55] Above at para 2.28.   [56] Bainham *Children: The New Law* (1990), para 2.40.

[57] Under s 6(7), for example, he can seek a court order to end the appointment: see further below.

[58] In *Children: The Modern Law*, (3rd edn, 2004) Bainham concludes, at 230 'The rather unsatisfactory outcome . . . is that the onus to commence proceedings will be on the person wishing to change the existing arrangements.'

[59] Such a scenario is now more likely to arise, since it will be by no means uncommon, because of the so-called non-intervention principle under s 1(5), for no orders to have been made.

[60] Scot Law Com No 135 *Report on Family Law* (1992), para 3–11, repeating what was said in Discussion Paper No 88 *Parental Responsibilities and Rights, Guardianship and the Administration of Children's Property* (1990) para 3.11. Accordingly, no change was recommended, so that in Scotland (see the Children (Scotland) Act 1995 s 7) it remains the case that a guardianship appointment made by the deceased parent comes into effect notwithstanding the survival of the other parent. For an example of where the Scottish position could be advantageous see *Re A, J and J (Minors) (Residence and Guardianship Orders)* [1993] Fam Law 568: see below, p 444 n 71.

his first knowing that the appointment has taken effect'.[61] Furthermore, it must be disclaimed by an instrument in writing, signed by the appointee. There is provision to make regulations for the recording of such disclaimers (which would then be ineffective unless recorded)[62] but at the time of writing no regulations have been made.

As White, Carr and Lowe comment:[63]

'Welcome as this new power is, it does make it all the more important for parents to discuss their proposed appointment with the person concerned. It seems desirable for some official guidance to be published reminding parents of the desirability of prior consultation.'

(b) The court's power to appoint guardians

When the power may be exercised

Under s 5(1) of the 1989 Act the High Court, a county court or a magistrates' court[64] may appoint an 'individual' to be a child's guardian if:

'(a) the child has no parent with parental responsibility for him; or

(b) a residence order has been made with respect to the child in favour of a parent, guardian or special guardian of his who has died while the order was in force or;

(c) paragraph (b) does not apply, and the child's only or last surviving special guardian dies'.

Although by reason of the Interpretation Act 1978 s 6(c),[65] the court is not prevented from appointing more than one guardian, nevertheless by confining the power to the appointment of an 'individual', a court cannot appoint a *body* such as a local authority to be a guardian.[66] This latter restriction is contrary to the recommendations made in the Government White Paper, *The Law on Child Care and Family Services*,[67] and has already proved inconvenient.[68] It is suggested that this restriction could usefully be removed.

In line with the general restriction against appointing guardians during the lifetime of a parent with parental responsibility, the court's power arises only:

(1) where the child has no parent with parental responsibility; or

(2) upon the death of a parent, guardian or special guardian in whose favour a residence order was in force, or[69]

(3) point (2) does not apply and the child's only or surviving special guardian dies.[70]

---

[61] See by way of example *Re SH (Care Order; Orphan)* [1995] 1 FLR 746 in which it was said that local authority foster parents intended to revoke a guardianship appointment by the mother.

[62] Under s 6(6).   [63] *The Children Act in Practice* (3rd edn, 2002) para 3.118.

[64] See s 92(7).   [65] See above, p 440 n 35.

[66] Nor can this embargo be overcome by seeking the appointment of what was described as an 'artificial individual', namely the director of social services: per Hollis J in *Re SH (Care Order: Orphan)* [1995] 1 FLR 746 at 749.

[67] Cm 62, 1987.

[68] See *Birmingham City Council v D, Birmingham City Council v M* [1994] 2 FLR 502, in which the local authority unsuccessfully sought care orders in respect of orphans accommodated by them, essentially in order to obtain parental responsibility; cf *Re SH (Care Order: Orphans)* [1995] 1 FLR 746 and *Re M (Care Order: Parental Responsibility)* [1996] 2 FLR 84, in which, in rather different circumstances, care orders *were* made in respect of orphans. See further below, p 750.

[69] Except where a residence order was also made in favour of the surviving parent: s 5(9).

[70] The references to special guardianship were added by the Adoption and Children Act 2002, s 115(4).

Although the first embargo is strict,[71] it nevertheless only applies where the child has no *parent* with parental responsibility. The court can therefore make an appointment even though the child already has a guardian (other than the child's unmarried father)[72] and it can also make an appointment notwithstanding that the child's unmarried father is still alive, provided he has not obtained parental responsibility.[73]

Who may apply?

The Act is silent as to who can apply to become a guardian, but it is generally thought that *any* individual[74] (including, in theory, a child) may apply to be appointed. There is no requirement that leave of the court must first be obtained. On the other hand, an application can only be made under s 5 by an individual himself wishing to be a guardian. However, since under s 5(2) the court has power in any family proceedings to make an appointment of its own motion, once proceedings are in train there would seem to be nothing to stop any other interested person, including the child himself, from seeking the appointment of another individual to be a guardian.[75]

In respect of whom may applications be made?

An application may be made only in respect of a 'child', that is, a person under the age of 18.[76] There is no express embargo against making an appointment in respect of a married child, although it remains to be seen whether in practice the courts would be prepared to make an appointment in such a case.[77] On normal principles of construction there would appear to be no power to appoint a guardian of a child until it is born.[78]

Exercising the power

In accordance with the general principles under s 1, when deciding whether to make an appointment, the court is enjoined to regard the child's welfare as the paramount consideration and to be satisfied that making an order is better than making no order at all. It is not, however, obliged to have specific regard to the circumstances set out in s 1(3), though the court is free to do so if it so wishes. There is no restriction comparable to that under s 9(6) appertaining to s 8 orders that appointments with respect to 16- or 17-year-olds should only be made in 'exceptional circumstances'. In deciding whether to make an appointment the court can, pursuant to a s 7,[79] call for a welfare report.

Since s 5 proceedings rank as 'family proceedings' the court can make, either upon

---

[71] See eg *Re A, J and J (Minors) (Residence and Guardianship Orders)* [1993] Fam Law 568—no power to appoint an elder sibling to be a guardian because father was still alive, notwithstanding that he was living out of the jurisdiction and was believed to be suffering from mental illness.

[72] Since a guardian has parental responsibility (s 5(6)), presumably an unmarried father who is a guardian will be regarded as a 'parent' with parental responsibility for these purposes.

[73] By agreement with the mother or by a court order in accordance with s 4, discussed above at pp 409ff.

[74] But not a 'body' such as a local authority.

[75] Such a possibility was canvassed by the Law Commission in their Working Paper No 91 at para 3.49.

[76] Section 105(1).

[77] A similar problem obtained in respect of the former law, but the Law Commission (see Working Paper No 91 para 3.64) was inclined to leave the question open.

[78] See *Elliot v Joicey* [1935] AC 209, HL and *R v Newham London Borough Council, ex p Dada* [1996] QB 507, CA.

[79] Discussed below at p 487.

application or upon its own motion, any s 8 order in addition to or instead of appointing a guardian.[80]

Although, the court is empowered to appoint more than one guardian at one time or indeed on different occasions, as one commentary has pointed out,[81] it seems unlikely that a court would appoint a subsequent guardian knowing that the two or more guardians would be in conflict. It has also been said[82] that it would be unusual, though not an absolute bar, to appoint persons as guardians who have never actually seen the children.

2 EFFECT OF BEING APPOINTED A GUARDIAN

Apart from where the Official Solicitor is appointed guardian for a child's estate,[83] all persons appointed as guardians, whether by private appointment or by the court, have parental responsibility for the child.[84]

(a) Distinguishing guardians from parents

Following the Children Act 1989 reforms, the *concepts* of parenthood and guardianship are now legally distinct: parents are no longer regarded as guardians and, apart from exceptional cases in which an unmarried father is appointed a guardian, no guardians will be parents. Guardians are nevertheless in a similar legal position to parents with parental responsibility. The key difference is that, unlike a parent, a guardian cannot be a 'liable relative' under the Social Security Administration Act 1992,[85] nor a 'non-resident parent' under the Child Support Act 1991,[86] and no court may order a guardian to make financial provision for, or a transfer of property to a child, under the Children Act 1989.[87] This means that, although guardians are under a duty to see that the child is provided with adequate food, clothing, medical aid and lodging[88] and to educate the child properly,[89] no financial orders can be made against them nor are they liable to contribute to the maintenance of a child who is being looked after by a local authority.[90] The absence of any general legal liability on guardians to maintain children might seem at odds with the general policy of awarding them full parental responsibility. The Law Commission, however, considered[91] that, apart from representing a major change of policy, the imposition of financial liability upon guardians might 'act as a serious deterrent to

---

[80] Section 10(1).

[81] Hershman and McFarlane, at J [30] relying on *Re H (An Infant)* [1959] 1 WLR 1163.

[82] Per Purchas LJ in *Re C (minors) (adoption by relatives)* [1989] 1 All ER 395, CA.

[83] For an account of the legal position of a guardian of the estate, see Law Com Working Paper No 91 para 2.23.

[84] Section 5(6).   [85] Section 78(6) and s 105(3), discussed below at p 925.

[86] Section 3, discussed below at p 932.

[87] Viz s 15 and Sch 1, discussed below at p 968. However, in divorce, nullity and separation proceedings between a guardian and his or her spouse or the equivalent proceedings between a guardian and his or her civil partner, there is power under the Matrimonial Causes Act 1973 and the Civil Partnership Act 2004 to make financial provision for the child, provided he or she is a 'child of the family'.

[88] Pursuant to the Children and Young Persons Act 1933 s 1(2)(a): see above, p 381.

[89] Pursuant to the Education Act 1996 s 7, s 8 and s 576(1): see above, p 388.

[90] Only parents are so liable, see Children Act 1989, Sch 2, para 21(3). Similarly guardians cannot be liable to contribute to the costs of services provided by a local authority for a child and his family, see 29(4) of the 1989 Act.

[91] Law Com No 172 at para 2.25.

appointments being made or accepted'. It should also be added that guardians have no rights of succession upon the child's death, nor can a child take British citizenship from his guardian.

(b) Distinguishing guardians from 'non-parents' with residence orders in their favour

Guardianship, like a residence order made in favour of a non-parent, vests parental responsibility for the duration of the order but, unlike the latter,[92] it also gives a guardian the right to consent to or withhold consent to the child's placement for adoption and to the making of an adoption order and to appoint a guardian. Furthermore, although the process of granting residence orders to third parties bears some resemblance to the court process of appointing guardians, the resulting orders are conceptually different, in that the guardian replaces the deceased parent or parents, whereas a person will normally be granted a residence order whilst the child's parents are alive and will therefore share parental responsibility with them.

(c) Distinguishing guardians from de facto carers

The key difference between guardians and de facto carers is that the latter, even though they have the de facto control, have no parental responsibility for the child. If a parent is dead or is unfit to exercise his responsibilities, it is clearly essential for someone to stand in loco parentis to a child; but by English law parental responsibility will not vest in a person unless he has been formally appointed as a guardian either by a deceased parent or by a court order. In a large number of cases, of course, this never happens; and if both parents die, a child's grandparents or other near relations will assume de facto control of the child without taking steps to have themselves appointed legal guardians. Although such persons do not have parental responsibility, nevertheless, as we have seen,[93] under s 3(5) of the 1989 Act they 'may (subject to the provisions of this Act) do what is reasonable in all the circumstances for the purpose of safeguarding or promoting the children's welfare'. There is also, both at common law and under the Children and Young Persons Act 1933, a duty to afford protection.[94] Furthermore, anyone who cares for a child will be criminally liable under the 1933 Act[95] if they wilfully fail to provide the child with adequate food, clothing, medical aid or lodging. Similarly, the Education Act 1996 places such persons under a duty to see that the child receives full-time education.[96]

(d) Distinguishing guardians from private foster parents

An important difference between a privately appointed guardian and a private foster parent is that, unlike the former, the latter, despite the absence of any formal legal status, is nevertheless still subject to public scrutiny and regulation. If a child is deemed to be privately fostered, then the carers will be subject to the provisions of Part IX of the Children Act 1989, the purpose of which is to ensure that the child is visited periodically by local authority officers, who must satisfy themselves that the child's welfare is

---

[92] See s 12(3), discussed above, p 550.   [93] Above at p 435.   [94] See above at pp 380ff.
[95] Section 1 and s 17.   [96] Sections 7–8 and s 576(1).

being satisfactorily safeguarded and who must give any necessary advice to the foster parents.[97]

A privately fostered child is a child, under the age of 16, who is cared for and accommodated (whether for reward or not) by someone *other than* his parent,[98] a person having parental responsibility for the child or a relative[99] for a period or intended period of 28 days or more.[100] However, to ensure that normal domestic arrangements are not within the scope of these provisions, they do not apply if the child lives in the same premises as a parent or a person having parental responsibility for the child, or a relative who has assumed responsibility for him. The provisions are also excluded where the child is being looked after by a local authority,[101] or lives in accommodation provided by a voluntary organisation, or in a school in which he is receiving full-time education,[102] a hospital, a nursing or mental nursing home, or is subject to a supervision order.[103]

(e) Disputes between guardians

In those cases where more than one guardian has been appointed and they are in dispute with each other over the child's upbringing they are free to apply to the court for a s 8 order under the Children Act 1989 or alternatively under s 6(7) to terminate theirs or the other's appointment (see below).

3 TERMINATION OF GUARDIANSHIP

(a) Automatic termination

The guardian's duties clearly cease if the child dies,[104] and automatically end when he attains the age of 18.[105] Whether the guardian's powers cease upon the child's marriage is perhaps debatable for, while s 5 imposes no such express limitation, it may well be held that there is no scope for the operation of guardianship, save perhaps in respect of the child's property. In any event, it seems unlikely that a guardian would be permitted to interfere with the activities of a married child even if the guardianship continues.

---

[97] Children Act 1989 s 67(1) and the Children (Private Arrangements for Fostering) Regulations 1991 (SI 1991/2050). For a discussion of private fostering under the Children Act see Vol 8 of the Department of Health's *Guidance and Regulations* and Clarke Hall and Morrison on *Children* 1 [1736]ff.

[98] Including the unmarried father.

[99] Defined by s 105(1) of the 1989 Act as 'grandparent, brother, sister, uncle or aunt (whether of the full blood or half blood or by affinity) or a step-parent'.

[100] Children Act 1989 s 66. An intention to look after a child for more than 28 days may be inferred from the facts: cf *Surrey County Council v Battersby* [1965] 2 QB 194.

[101] The selection and supervision of *local authority* foster parents is highly regulated under the Foster Placement (Children) Regulations 1991 (SI 1991/910).

[102] Note that children under 16 who are pupils at a school which is not maintained by a local education authority are treated as privately fostered if they live at the school during school holidays for more than two weeks: Sch 8, para 9.

[103] As these provisions are complementary to those relating to protected children under the Adoption Act 1976, they do not apply to such children either: Sch 8, para 5.

[104] Though quaere whether a guardian has a duty to bury or cremate the child?—cf *R v Gwynedd County Council, ex p B* [1992] 3 All ER 317, CA, discussed above at p 400.

[105] Section 91(7)–(8). Butterworths *Family Law Service* at 3A [1536] points out that there is nothing in the 1989 Act to prevent a guardian being appointed conditionally or until the child reaches a specified age below 18, in which cases the appointment will end in accordance with its terms.

Guardianship also ends upon the death of a sole guardian, unless, pursuant to the powers vested by s 5(4), the guardian has appointed another individual to be the child's guardian in his place. If a guardian dies leaving others in office, the survivors continue to be guardians.

(b) Removal by the court

Under s 6(7) of the Children Act 1989 a court[106] can make an order bringing any appointment made under s 5 to an end. Such an order can be made at any time upon the application of:

(1) any person who has parental responsibility including the guardian; or

(2) the child himself, with leave of the court; or

(3) upon the court's own motion in any family proceedings, if the court considers that the appointment should be brought to an end.

In deciding whether to end the guardianship, the court must be guided by the welfare principle, pursuant to s 1(1) of the 1989 Act.[107] If, for example, the guardian expresses an unwillingness to continue, the court is unlikely to consider it to be for the child's welfare that the appointment should continue. But the power to end the appointment is not confined to cases where the guardian wishes to be released. In the past appointments have been brought to an end because of actual or threatened misconduct of the guardian (for the court will attempt to avert a possible danger to the ward rather than wait for it to happen),[108] the abandonment of his rights for such a length of time that it would not be in the child's interests to permit him to reassert them,[109] or merely because of a change of circumstances which rendered it for some reason better for the child to have a new guardian.[110] If it decides to end the guardianship, the court may appoint another individual to take the former guardian's place. It is also open to the court to make a s 8 order. Indeed, it has been pointed out,[111] where the court orders a guardian's removal it may have to consider the appointment of a new guardian to prevent a hiatus in parental responsibility for the child.

4 EVALUATING THE CURRENT LAW

Under the Children Act 1989 guardianship has the clearly defined role of facilitating the replacement of a deceased parent by another person in whom is vested parental responsibility. Furthermore, by simplifying the procedure for making private appointments, the law has arguably done all that it can to encourage the making of such appointments. However, the complete absence of control on private appointments is striking and is in

---

[106] The High Court, county court or a magistrates' court: s 92(7).

[107] It is not, however, *bound* to apply the checklist in s 1(3)—see s 1(4)—but it should only, pursuant to s 1(5), make an order upon being satisfied that to do so is better than making no order at all.

[108] *Beaufort v Berty* (1721) 1 P Wms 703 at 704–5; *Re X* [1899] 1 Ch 526, at 531, CA.

[109] *Andrews v Salt* (1873) 8 Ch App 622.

[110] *Re X* (above) at 535–6; *F v F* [1902] 1 Ch 688, where a guardian who had become a Roman Catholic was removed although she had made no attempt to influence her ward, a Protestant.

[111] Bainham *Children—The Modern Law* (3rd edn) 232.

marked contrast, for example, to the plethora of controls on adoption and even private fostering.[112] The closest analogy is with making parental responsibility agreements, but such agreements can only be made between unmarried parents and between parents and step-parents, and even these have to be witnessed in court and centrally recorded.[113]

This absence of control could be justified on the basis that parents are in a better position than either the courts or local authorities to decide who is best able to care for their children after their death. In any event, there remains the safeguard of the local authority's investigative powers to protect children in need or at risk. In practice, little is known about the operation of private guardianship.[114] Research is needed, for example, to discover how common such appointments are; how many are made without even the appointee's knowledge or consent; how many such appointments are disclaimed; and most important, whether there is any evidence to suggest that children may be at risk of abuse by guardians. Similarly, little is known about the use made of the court's powers to make guardianship appointments. There are, for example, no national statistics of the numbers of applications and orders made under s 5. However, judging from the paucity of case law, little use seems to be made of the courts' powers. Again, further research is needed.

---

[112] See Douglas and Lowe 'Becoming a Parent in English Law' (1992) 108 LQR 414, at 428 and 432.

[113] See above, pp 446ff.

[114] Apart from the valuable but small scale study by Priest appended to Law Com Working Paper No 91. See also Scot Law Com, Discussion Paper No 88 para 3.2.

10

THE WELFARE PRINCIPLE

A THE PARAMOUNTCY OF THE CHILD'S WELFARE

Section 1(1) of the Children Act 1989 lays down the cardinal principle that:

'When any court determines any question with respect to:

(a) the upbringing of a child; or

(b) the administration of a child's property or the application of any income arising from it,

the child's welfare shall be the court's paramount consideration.'

1 THE BACKGROUND TO SECTION 1(1)

As we discussed in Chapter 7[1] notwithstanding that before the Children Act 1989 courts were directed[2] to treat the child's welfare as their '*first and* paramount consideration', judicial decisions, in particular that of the House of Lords in *J v C*,[3] had effectively rendered the words 'first and' redundant. The 1989 Act's paramountcy formulation therefore simply reflects that previously well established position and, as such, was not intended to alter the law or practice. Indeed, in *Re O and another (Minors) (Care: Preliminary Hearing); Re B*[4] Lord Nicholls said that the approach adopted by Lord MacDermott in *J v C* when applying the welfare principle under what was then the Guardianship of Infants Act 1925 was 'equally applicable' to that under the 1989 Act. In this regard Lord MacDermott had classically stated that the principle connotes:[5]

'a process whereby when all the relevant facts, relationships, claims and wishes of parents, risks, choices and other circumstances are taken into account and weighed, the course to be followed will be that which is most in the interests of the child's welfare as that term has now to be understood'.

What *J v C* was commonly taken to have established[6] and therefore confirmed by s 1(1) of the 1989 Act, was that the child's welfare was in effect the court's sole concern and that

---

[1] See above pp 356–62.

[2] Viz by s 1 of the Guardianship of Minors Act 1971 which in turn re-enacted s 1 of the Guardianship of Infants Act 1925.

[3] [1970] AC 668, discussed above at pp 358–60.   [4] [2003] UKHL 18, [2004] 1 AC 523 at [24].

[5] [1970] AC 668 at 710–11.   [6] See pp 311 and 316 of the 9th edition of this work.

other factors were relevant only to the extent that they would assist the court in ascertaining the best solution for children. However, the problem with that interpretation, as we discuss below, is that it is difficult to see how it complies with the requirement under the European Convention on Human Rights[7] to respect the rights of the parents as well as the child. As will be seen,[8] however, the domestic courts have modified their stance on the application of the paramountcy principle, while at the same time the European Court of Human Rights has increasingly recognised the predominant position of the child.

In choosing the paramountcy formulation, the government rejected the Law Commission's recommendation,[9] that 'when determining any question under the Act the welfare of *any child likely to be affected* shall be the court's *only* concern.' The Commission were unhappy with a pure paramountcy formulation, being concerned inter alia[10] that litigants might still be tempted to introduce evidence that had no relevance to the child in the hope of persuading the court to balance one against the other. Even if this fear had been justified,[11] the Law Commission's own formulation carried the equally undesirable risk of courts refusing to hear evidence unless it directly addressed the question of what is best for the child.

The Law Commission's proposal to consider the welfare of *any* child was also open to the objection that it could lead to wide and speculative enquiries, which ultimately could blur the court's view and duty towards the welfare of the child before it,[12] and force it to compromise between the interests of two or more children.[13] In any event, once the enjoinder to consider the welfare of the particular child before the court is departed from, there seems no reason to stop at the welfare of other children. A plausible case could be made out to include the welfare of others, eg an adult but disabled sibling who is still living with the family or an infirm parent or grandparent, each of whom could be argued to have a claim for equal consideration. However, any such broadening might have had the effect of weakening the protection of children, which the Law Commission itself was not prepared to contemplate.[14]

2 IS THE PARAMOUNTCY PRINCIPLE HUMAN RIGHTS COMPLIANT?

As mentioned in Chapter 7,[15] a decade before the Human Rights Act 1998 it had been unsuccessfully argued before the House of Lords in *Re KD (A Minor)(Ward: Termination of Access)*[16] that the paramountcy principle was incompatible with the European Convention on Human Rights. In Lord Templeman's view[17] there was 'no inconsistency of

---

[7] Ie in particular the right to respect for private and family life under Art 8.   [8] See below.

[9] Clause 1(2) of the Draft Bill published in Law Com No 172, *Review of Child Law, Guardianship and Custody*, 1988.

[10] See ibid, para 3.14.

[11] Which was doubtful given that the paramountcy formulation had been well tested before the Act and seemed to produce the right balance both in terms of the evidence submitted and the weight put on it.

[12] It will be noted, however, that the largely redundant s 2 of the Child Support Act 1991 does enjoin the Secretary of State or any child support officer to 'have regard to the welfare of any child likely to be affected by his decision'. See below, p 932.

[13] For the application of s 1(1) to more than one child, see below, p 465.

[14] Law Com No 172 at para 3.12.   [15] Above at p 361.   [16] [1998] AC 806.

[17] Above at 812.

principle or application between the English rule and the Convention rule'. While Lord Oliver concluded[18]

'such conflict as exists is, I think, semantic only and lies only in differing ways of giving expression to the single common concept that the natural bond and relationship between parent and child gives rise to universally recognised norms which ought not to be gratuitously interfered with and which, if interfered with at all, ought to be so only if the welfare of the child dictates it'.

Although this analysis has not gone unchallenged in academic circles[19] the House of Lords' ruling might have been taken as definitive but for the fact that the 1998 Act provided an opportunity for a general re-appraisal.[20] However, the judiciary were quick to confirm the paramountcy principle's compatibility with human rights. In *Re L (A Child)(Contact: Domestic Violence)*,[21] Butler-Sloss P considered that the prevailing preference for children's interests was entirely compatible with Art 8(2) of the European Convention on Human Rights. As she pointed out, in *Hendricks v Netherlands*[22] it was held that where there was a serious conflict between the interests of a child and one of his or her parents which could only be resolved to the disadvantage of one of them it was the child's interests that had to prevail under Art 8(2). As Butler Sloss P put it:

'The principle of the crucial importance of the best interests of the child has been upheld in all subsequent decisions of the European Court of Human Rights.'

She pointed in particular to *Johansen v Norway*[23] in which the Court commented that 'the parent cannot be entitled under Article 8 of the Convention to have such measures taken as would harm the child's health and development'.

In *Payne v Payne*[24] Thorpe LJ similarly had no doubts as to the compatibility of the paramountcy principle with Convention. He observed:

'The acknowledgement of child welfare as paramount must be common to most if not all judicial systems within the Council of Europe. It is of course enshrined in Art 3(1) of the United Nations Convention on the Rights of the Child 1989. Accordingly the jurisprudence of the European Court of Human Rights inevitably recognises the paramountcy principle, albeit not expressed in the language of our domestic statute.'

---

[18] Above at 825.

[19] See in particular the analysis of J Herring 'The Human Rights Act and the welfare principle in family law—conflicting or complementary?' [1999] CFLQ 223, discussed below at p 454.

[20] Academic speculation about the impact of the 1998 Act on the paramountcy principle was extensive. J Fortin 'The HRA's impact on litigation involving children and their families' [1999] CFLQ 237, for example, was concerned that the Convention would dilute the paramountcy principle. See also the analyses of H Swindells 'Crossing The Rubicon—Family Law Post The Human Rights Act 1998' in *Family Law—Essays For The new Millennium* (ed S Cretney) 55 at 62–6. A Bainham 'Children Law At The Millennium' in *Family Law Essays for the new Millennium,* 113 at 125–6 and F Kaganas and C Piper 'Grandparents and contact: "rights or welfare" revisited' (2001) 15 Int Jo of Law Policy and the Family 250. Herring's analysis will be discussed separately below.

[21] *Re L (A Child)(Contact: Domestic Violence); Re V (A Child)(Contact: Domestic Violence); Re M (A Child)(Contact: Domestic Violence); Re H (Children)(Contact: Domestic Violence)* [2001] Fam 260 at 277.

[22] (1982) 5 EHRR 223. In fact this case was decided by the Commission and not the European Court of Human Rights as suggested by Butler-Sloss P.

[23] (1996) 23 EHRR 33, ECtHR.   [24] [2001] EWCA Civ 166, [2001] 1 FLR 1051 at [38] and [57].

Accordingly, Thorpe LJ concluded:

'whilst the advent of the 1998 Act requires some revision of the judicial approach to conclusion, as a safeguard to an inadequate perception and application for a father's rights under arts 6 and 8, it requires no re-evaluation of the judge's primary task to evaluate and uphold the welfare of the child as the paramount consideration, despite its inevitable conflict with adult rights'.

It is noticeable that by analysing the paramountcy principle in terms of prioritising children's welfare where it conflicts with parents' interests, both Butler-Sloss P and Thorpe LJ have apparently moved away from the traditional view that children's welfare should be the court's only concern which, as we have said, would seem to be incompatible with human rights law. However, as Thorpe LJ clearly said, this shift is only a semantic one and there seems little doubt that neither he nor Butler-Sloss P thought that the 1998 Act would cause an English court to reach a different decision than it would otherwise have done.[25]

As a matter of fact since these two decisions the European Court of Human Rights has seemingly moved closer to the English position, by commenting in *Yousef v Netherlands*[26]

'that in judicial decisions where the rights under art 8 of parents and those of the child are at stake, the child's rights must be the paramount consideration. If any balancing of interests is necessary, the interests of the child must prevail . . .'.

This is the first time that the Court of Human Rights has expressly referred to the *paramountcy* of the child's rights and its decision confirms a trend towards greater emphasis on the predominance of children's rights under the Convention.[27]

Notwithstanding the apparent converging of European human rights jurisprudence with English domestic case law, it can still be argued that there is a real difference between them. Put succinctly and to adopt the words of one commentator,[28] while the scales might apparently start even in the sense that both parents and children have rights under the European Convention, under English domestic law the scales heavily are weighted in favour of children. This difference of approach has been highlighted particularly by Herring.[29]

---

[25] For a similar conclusion see A Bainham 'Protecting Children and their Rights' [2002] Fam Law 279 at 288.

[26] (2003) 36 EHRR 20, [2003] 1 FLR 210 at [73]. In *CF v Secretary of State for the Home Department* [2004] EWHC 111 (Fam), [2004] 2 FLR 517 at [103] Munby J referred to *Yousef* (above) as establishing that the welfare principle was a 'core principle' of human rights law. It might be noted, however, that the European Court conflated 'rights' and 'interests'.

[27] Compare the statement in *Yousef* with the earlier ones, eg in *W v Federal Republic of Germany* (1985) 50 D & R 219 where the European Commission held that national courts should take into consideration the interests of children; *Hendricks v Netherlands*, above, where the Commission referred to the interests of children predominating and *Hoppe v Germany* [2003] 1 FLR 384 at para [49] where the court referred to the interests of children being of 'particular importance'. For an analysis of other European Court decisions see A Vine 'Is the Paramountcy Principle Compatible with Article 8?' [2000] Fam Law 826 at 828–30. In Fortin's view, see *Children's Rights and the Developing Law* (2nd edn) 57, the Convention jurisprudence suggests that some of the fears about the impact of the 1998 Act on the paramountcy principle 'were exaggerated'.

[28] A Bainham 'Family Rights in the Next Millennium' in (2000) 53 Current Legal Problems 473 at 489. In fact this comment was made in the context of a possible conflict between the Convention and the United Nations Convention on the Rights of the Child 1989, discussed below.

[29] See 'The Human Rights Act and the welfare principle in family law—conflicting or complementary' [1999] CFLQ 223 at 230ff and further developed in *Family Law* (2nd edn) at 377–99.

Taking the example of seeking to deny a parent contact with his or her child, he argues that whereas under the Convention the starting point is the parent's right to contact and to justify its breach there must be clear and convincing evidence that the contact would infringe the rights of the child to such an extent as to make the infringement of the parent's right necessary and proportionate; under English domestic law the starting point is that contact is in the child's interests which can be rebutted by evidence that his or her welfare is not enhanced in the particular case. He argues that as a result less evidence is required to deny contact under domestic law than under Convention law and furthermore while it is a factual issue under the domestic law it is a legal issue under the Convention.

Although Herring's arguments are perfectly tenable one suspects nevertheless that a properly arrived at domestic law outcome based on the paramountcy principle as it is now understood is unlikely to be held in breach of the Convention.[30] In any event, as Bainham has pointed out,[31] the Human Rights Convention is not the only relevant international instrument for there is also the United Nations Convention on the Rights of the Child 1989 (to which the UK is a party) and that, as is discussed below, directs national courts to treat the best interests of the child as the primary concern. In other words if there is a real difference between domestic law and human rights law then there is also a clash of international Conventions.

It is submitted that the only practical solution is that which both English domestic law and Human Rights Convention law have arrived at, namely, that while parents' interests cannot be ignored, in cases of conflict it is the child's interests that take priority. Whether this means that the welfare principle itself is beyond criticism will be discussed later.[32]

3 COMPARISON WITH UN CONVENTION

Section 1(1) of the 1989 Act might be compared with Art 3(1) of the UN Convention on the Rights of the child 1989 (to which the UK is a party) which states:

'In all actions concerning children, whether undertaken by public or private social welfare institutions, courts of law, administrative authorities or legislative bodies, the best interests of the child shall be the primary consideration.'

This Article provides an international obligation[33] to apply the 'best interests of the child' test and as such is clearly similar to the paramountcy test under s 1(1) of the 1989

---

[30] Vine, above, at 830, considers it significant that in *Scott v UK* [2000] 1 FLR 958 (in which inter alia a complaint was made under Art 8 about the dismissal of a mother's application for increased contact under the Children Act 1989, s 34 (discussed below at pp 791ff)), the European Court not only made no criticism of the paramountcy principle but concluded on the facts of the case that a decision based on the welfare of the child fell well within the domestic court's margin of appreciation.

[31] 'Family Rights in the Next Millennium', above, at 489.   [32] See below pp 471–2.

[33] As a matter of strict law since the UN Convention has not been incorporated by statute into English domestic law, courts are not bound to apply it: see *British Airways v Laker Airways* [1985] AC 58, HL and see more specifically *Re P (Children Act: Diplomatic Immunity)* [1998] 1 FLR 624 at 628 per Stuart-White J and *R v Central Criminal Court, ex p S* [1999] 1 FLR 480 at 487, per Sullivan J. Nevertheless as Ward LJ said in *Re P (A Minor)(Residence Order: Child's Welfare)* [2000] Fam 15 at 42 although the Convention may not have the force of law it commands and receives respect. It might be noted that under the Children's Commissioner for Wales Appointment Regulations 2001 (SI 2001/3121) the Children's Commissioner for Wales has to 'have regard' to the UN Convention in the discharge of his duties. This is the first reference to the UN Convention in UK legislation. It is not referred to in connection with the other UK Commissioners.

Act.[34] However, the enjoinder to regard the child's best interests as a *primary* consideration is not as strong (though possibly more Human Rights compliant) as to treat the child's welfare as the *paramount* consideration. On the other hand, by applying to public and private social welfare institutions, administrative authorities and legislative bodies, Art 3(1) has a wider application than s 1(1) which, as we discuss below, only applies in court proceedings.

B WHEN THE PARAMOUNTCY PRINCIPLE APPLIES[35]

As s 1(1) states, the paramountcy principle applies whenever a court is called upon to determine any question about the child's upbringing or the administration of his property. Section 1(1) is therefore of general application and is not restricted to Children Act proceedings. It is established, for example that the provision is applicable to wardship proceedings,[36] including non-Convention[37] child abduction cases,[38] and is similarly applicable to the exercise of the High Court's inherent jurisdiction.[39]

As we discussed in Chapter 7,[40] *J v C* establishes that the principle applies equally to disputes between parents and other individuals, as well as to disputes between parents.[41] So far as Children Act proceedings are concerned, as the Department of Health's Guidance on the 1989 Act states,[42] it applies *whenever* a court is considering whether to make a s 8 order (ie regardless of who the parties[43] are, what the issue is[44] or in which proceedings the issue is raised).[45] It has been held that it applies when considering whether to make a parental responsibility order under s 4[46] and when considering whether to give leave

---

[34] Indeed in *Payne v Payne* [2001] EWCA Civ 168, [2001] 1 FLR 1052 at (38) Thorpe LJ went as far as to say that the paramountcy principle was 'enshrined' by Art 3(1).

[35] See generally, White Carr and Lowe *The Children Act in Practice* (3rd edn, 1995) paras 2.8ff; and Clarke Hall and Morrison on *Children* 1[83]ff.

[36] *J v C* [1970] AC 668, HL, discussed above, p 358. Wardship is discussed in Chapter 16.

[37] That is, cases not governed by either the 1980 European Custody Convention or the 1980 Hague Abduction Convention: see Chapter 13.

[38] See *Re J (A Child)(Custody Rights: Jurisdiction)* [2005] UK HL 40, [2005] 3 WLR 14, discussed below at p 623.

[39] See *Re A (Children)(Conjoined Twins: Surgical Separation)* [2001] Fam 147, *Re T (A Minor) (Wardship: Medical Treatment)* [1997] 1 All ER 906, CA and *Re W (A Minor) (Medical Treatment: Court's Jurisdiction)* [1993] Fam 64, CA.

[40] Above, p 359.

[41] Though this is not to say that parents and non-parents stand on exactly the same footing: see below, pp 543ff.

[42] *Guidance and Regulations*, Vol 1, *Court Orders*, para 2.57.

[43] See eg *Re S (Contact: Grandparents)* [1996] 1 FLR 158 at 164 per Wall J, which involved an application for contact by a grandparent.

[44] Including, for example, the child's religious upbringing and determining whether a boy should be ritually circumcised: *Re J (Specific Issue Orders: Muslim Upbringing and Circumcision)* [1999] 2 FLR 678, decision upheld on appeal: [2000] 1 FLR 571.

[45] See *Re RJ (Fostering: Person Disqualified)* [1999] 1 FLR 605, CA, order made in wardship proceedings, see further below at p 900.

[46] Per Butler Sloss LJ in *Re H (Parental Responsibility)* [1998] 1 FLR 855 at 659. This issue, however, may not be beyond argument: see Balcombe LJ in *Re G (A Minor) (Parental Responsibility Order)* [1994] 1 FLR 504 at 507–8 and *Re E (Parental Responsibility)* [1994] 2 FLR 709 at 715 who pointed out that it was arguable that such applications do not concern the upbringing of the child.

under s 13 either to change a child's surname[47] or to remove a child from the United Kingdom.[48]

With regard to public law proceedings under the Children Act, it is clear that the paramountcy principle applies at the welfare stage of care proceedings,[49] ie after deciding whether or not the statutory threshold under s 31[50] has been crossed. It also applies to deciding whether to make contact orders under s 34[51] and to applications to discharge care orders under s 39.[52] It has also been held[53] that the paramountcy principle applies to deciding whether leave should be given to a local authority to withdraw their application for a care order.

C WHEN THE PARAMOUNTCY PRINCIPLE DOES NOT APPLY [54]

The paramountcy principle is not of unlimited application. It does not directly apply outside the context of court litigation, and even where an issue is before a court it will only apply provided the child's upbringing or the administration of his property is *directly* in question, and even then only if the principle has not been expressly or impliedly excluded either by the 1989 Act itself or by some other statute.

1 THE PARAMOUNTCY PRINCIPLE DOES NOT APPLY OUTSIDE THE CONTEXT OF LITIGATION

The paramountcy principle only applies, if at all, in the course of litigation. Unlike Art 3(1) of the UN Convention on the Rights of the Child[55] it has no *direct* application to institutions (such as prison authorities),[56] administrative authorities (such as local authorities)[57] or legislative bodies. Furthermore it does not apply to parents or other individuals with respect to their day-to-day or even long-term decisions affecting the child. As one commentator has put it:[58]

---

[47] Per Wilson J in *Re B (Change of Surname)* [1996] 1 FLR 791 at 793, CA. The paramountcy principle equally applies to applications to change names under s 33(7), see *Re S (Change of Surname)* [1999] 1 FLR 672 at 674, per Thorpe LJ.

[48] *Payne v Payne* [2001] EWCA Civ 166, [2001] 1 FLR 1052, per Thorpe LJ.

[49] See eg *Re O and another (Minors)(Care: Preliminary Hearing); Re B (A Minor)* [2003] UKHL 18, [2004] 1 AC 523 at [23] per Lord Nicholls. See further below, pp 755–6.

[50] Discussed below, pp 736ff.

[51] *Re T (Minors) (Termination of Contact: discharge of order)* [1997] 1 All ER 65, CA and *Re B (Minors) (Termination of Care: Paramount Consideration)* [1993] Fam 301, CA.

[52] See eg *Re T and E (Proceedings: Conflicting Interests)* [1995] 1 FLR 581.

[53] *Southwark London Borough v B* [1993] 2 FLR 559, CA. The paramountcy principle equally applies to determining whether to stay an order: *Re M (application for stay of order)* [1996] 3 FCR 185, CA.

[54] See N Lowe 'The House of Lords and the welfare principle' in C Bridge (ed) *Family Law towards the Millennium—Essays for P M Bromley* (1997) 125 at 150ff.

[55] Set out above at p 454.

[56] See eg *R (P) v Secretary of State for the Home Department, R (Q) v Secretary of State for Home Department* [2001] EWCA Civ 1151, [2001] 1 WLR 2002 at [89] per Lord Phillips MR.

[57] See eg *R (Howard League for Penal Reform) v Secretary of State For The Home Department)* [2002] EWHC 2497 (Admin), [2003] 1 FLR 484 at [35], per Munby J.

[58] A Bainham *Children: The Modern Law* (3rd edn, 2005) 48.

'It can hardly be argued that parents, in taking family decisions affecting a child, are bound to ignore completely their own interests, the interests of other members of the family and, possibly, outsiders. This would be a wholly undesirable, as well as an unrealistic objective.'

Accordingly, parents are not bound to consider their children's welfare in deciding, for example, whether to make a career move, to move house or whether to separate or divorce.[59]

It is also established that the paramountcy principle does not govern the application of Part III of the 1989 Act.[60] As Butler-Sloss LJ said in *Re M (A Minor) (Secure Accommodation Order)*:[61]

'The framework of Part III of the Act is structured to cast upon the local authority duties and responsibilities for children in its area and being looked after. The general duty[62] of a local authority to safeguard and promote the child's welfare is not the same as that imposed upon the court in s 1 (1) placing welfare as the paramount consideration.'

In Butler-Sloss LJ's view[63] s 1 was not designed to be applied to Part III of the Act. Accordingly, in deciding pursuant to s 17(1) what level of services to provide for children in need in their area, local authorities are not obliged to treat the welfare of individual children as their paramount consideration,[64] nor, similarly, when deciding pursuant to s 22 how best to discharge their duties in relation to children looked after by them,[65] though in this latter instance the welfare of the child remains an important consideration.[66]

2 THE PARAMOUNTCY PRINCIPLE DOES NOT APPLY TO ISSUES ONLY INDIRECTLY CONCERNING THE CHILD'S UPBRINGING

An important limitation on the application of the paramountcy principle established by the House of Lords in *S v S, W v Official Solicitor*[67] is that it only applies where the child's upbringing or the administration of his property etc is *directly* in issue. In *S v S* the court was asked to make what was then a blood test direction for the purpose of determining paternity. It had been submitted that no direction should be made unless it could be shown to be in the child's interest that there should be such a test. In other words, the court was bound to apply the paramountcy principle. Rejecting that submission, the House of Lords unanimously held that the correct approach was for the court to make a blood test direction unless it could be shown to be against the child's interests to do so.

---

[59] See B Dickens 'The Modern Function and Limits of Parental Rights' (1981) 97 LQR 462 at 471, who asserts (correctly, it is submitted) that parental responsibility is not to do positive good but to avoid harm.

[60] Discussed below, pp 698ff.   [61] [1995] Fam 108 at 115.

[62] Pursuant to the Children Act 1989 s 17(1) and s 22(3).

[63] Above, expressly disagreeing with comments to the contrary in Vols 1 and 4 of the Department of Health, *Guidance and Regulations* on the 1989 Act.

[64] It is generally thought that s 17 is so phrased as to avoid the duty being applied to individual children: see below, p 699 n 46.

[65] Section 22(6) expressly states that the need to protect members of the public from serious injury overrides any duty even to promote and safeguard the interests of any individual child, let alone treating that child's welfare as the paramount consideration.

[66] Per Charles J in *Re P (Children Act 1989, ss 22 and 26: Local Authority Compliance)* [2000] 2 FLR 910 at 923.

[67] [1972] AC 24. See also above, p 326.

In Lord MacDermott's view what the court was being asked to do was to exercise its protective rather than its custodial jurisdiction, because the question raised:[68]

'... is quite distinct from the question of custody and other questions mentioned in s 1 of the Guardianship of Infants Act. It is true that in deciding as to the custody of a child its welfare may depend on the weighing and assessment of various factors including the rights and wishes of the parents and that the question of paternity may therefore not only arise but be very relevant. But that is not to make the question of paternity a question of custody. It is only part of the process in deciding the ultimate and paramount question, namely, what is best for the welfare of the child.'

This distinction between issues directly and indirectly concerning the child's upbringing was later adopted by the majority in *Richards v Richards*,[69] in which an application made in divorce proceedings by a mother to exclude her husband from the matrimonial home was held not to be governed by the paramountcy principle. Lord Hailsham LC said:[70]

'In my view the Guardianship of Minors Act criterion is to be applied only in proceedings of the type specified in the section, ie proceedings in which custody, upbringing, or the proprietary jurisdiction implied by s 1(b) fall to be decided as a matter *directly* in issue ...' [Emphasis added.]

Richards can also be taken to vindicate Sir John Pennycuick's view in *Re X (A Minor) (Wardship): Jurisdiction)*[71] that an application to restrain the publication of a book containing salacious details of a child's dead father, on the grounds that it would be harmful to the child, was not governed by the paramountcy principle because the subject-matter only indirectly concerned the child's upbringing.

In summary, what *S v S* established and *Richards v Richards* confirmed was that:

(i) the paramountcy principle only applies when the child's upbringing etc is directly in issue;

(ii) even where the paramountcy principle does not apply, the court retains a protective jurisdiction to prevent a child from suffering harm; but

(iii) in exercising the latter jurisdiction, the child's welfare is not the only or necessarily the most important consideration to be taken into account.

Not surprisingly, given the weight of judicial authority, it is clear that s 1(1) of the 1989 Act similarly only applies where the child's upbringing is directly in issue. It was on this basis that it was held in *R (P) v Secretary of State for the Home Department*[72] that the paramountcy principle had no application to the lawfulness of prison policy to separate children once they reached 18 months from their imprisoned mothers and partly on this basis that it was held in *Re A (Minors) (Residence Orders: Leave to Apply)*[73] that s 1(1) does

---

[68] At 50G. See also Lord Hodson at 58C–D and G–H.

[69] [1984] AC 174, HL, discussed above, p 250.   [70] At 203H. See also Lord Brandon at 223F.

[71] [1975] Fam 47, CA.

[72] *R (P) v Secretary of State for the Home Department, R (Q) v Secretary of State for the Home Department* [2001] EWCA Civ 1151, [2001] 1 WLR 2002.

[73] [1992] Fam 182 at 191G–H. It has been similarly held that the paramountcy principle does not apply to applications for leave under s 91(17): *Re T (Minor) (Termination of Contact: discharge of order)* [1997] 1 All ER 65, CA.

not apply when determining whether to grant adults[74] leave to apply for a s 8 order, since, in Balcombe LJ's words, 'in granting or refusing an application for leave to apply for a section 8 order the court is not determining a question with respect to the upbringing of the child concerned'. That question only arises when the court hears the substantive application. In *Re H (A Minor) (Blood Tests: Parental Rights)*[75] it was held that the child's welfare is not the paramount consideration when determining whether to give directions for blood (now scientific) testing to determine parentage.

It has been held that the paramountcy principle does not apply to determining whether an unmarried father should be served with notice of care proceedings,[76] nor to resolving a mother's application that the father cease to be party to the discharge of care proceedings,[77] nor importantly, when considering whether a parent be committed to prison for a flagrant breach of a court order concerning a child,[78] nor to determining whether to issue a witness summons against a child,[79] nor to the issue of making directions for interim assessments under s 38(6) of the Children Act 1989;[80] nor to resolving a dispute between a birth mother and an adoptive mother over the disposal of their deceased adult child's remains;[81] nor in determining whether costs should be given in family proceedings.[82]

Notwithstanding that this basic distinction is firmly established, it can still be a matter of fine judgment as to what amounts to 'direct' and 'indirect' for these purposes. There are two areas in particular in which the application of the paramountcy principle has proved problematic, namely with regard to publicity and to procedural issues.

(a) Publicity

In *Re S (A Child)(Identification: Restrictions on Publication)*,[83] the House of Lords held that since the coming into force of the Human Rights Act 1998 the foundation of the jurisdiction to protect children from publicity now derives from the European Convention on Human Rights and involves the balancing of the right to respect for private and family life under Art 8 and the right to freedom of expression under Art 10. Consequently in the case before them and any similar case it was no longer necessary to consider the preceding

---

74 According to Charles J in *Re S (Contact: Application By Sibling)* [1998] 2 FLR 897, Stuart-White J in *Re C (Residence: Child's Application for Leave)* [1995] 1 FLR 927 and Booth J in *Re SC(A Minor) (Leave to Seek Residence Order)* [1994] 1 FLR 96 a similar position obtains in respect of children seeking leave; cf *Re C (A Minor) (Leave to Seek Section 8 Orders)* [1994] 1 FLR 26, per Johnson J, who thought the paramountcy principle did apply.

75 [1997] Fam 89, CA.   76 *Re X (Care: Notice of Proceedings)* [1996] 1 FLR 186, per Stuart-White J.

77 *Re W (Discharge of Party to Proceedings)* [1997] 1 FLR 128.

78 *A v N (Committal: Refusal of Contact)* [1997] 1 FLR 533, CA. It is similarly inapplicable when considering whether to make enforcement orders and order for financial compensation for breaches of contact orders: see respectively ss 11L(7) and 11O(14) of the Children Act 1989, inserted by the Children and Adoption Act 2006.

79 *Re P (Witness Summons)* [1997] 2 FLR 447, CA. See also *R v Highbury Corner Magistrates Court, ex p Deering* [1997] 1 FLR 683.

80 Per Holman J in *Re M (Residential Assessment Directions)* [1998] 2 FLR 371 at 381–2 and per Charles J in *Re P (Children Act 1989, ss 22 and 26: Local Authority Compliance)* [2000] 2 FLR 910 at 923. See further below, p 781.

81 Per Hale J in *Buchanan v Milton* [1999] 2 FLR 844 at 857.

82 Per Wilson J in *Q v Q (Costs: Summary Assessment)* [2002] 2 FLR 668 at [14].

83 [2004] UK HL 47, [2005] 1 AC 593.

case law about the existence and scope of the inherent jurisdiction of the High Court[84] to restrict publicity to protect children. However, such case-law was thought not to be wholly irrelevant to the ultimate balancing exercise to be carried out under the Human Rights Convention. This requirement to balance Art 8 rights with Art 10 rights means that the child's welfare cannot be the paramount consideration and indeed in *Re S*, itself the House of Lords upheld the decision not to grant an injunction prohibiting the identification of the defendant in a criminal trial charged with the murder of her elder son in order to protect her younger son from harm. In other words the younger child's welfare was *not* paramount (ie s 1(1) of the Children Act 1989 did not apply). Having to balance the child's Art 8 rights with those of freedom of expression under Art 10 does not inevitably mean that publicity will never be restrained.[85] Indeed in the first post-*Re S* decision, *A Local Authority v W, L, W, T and R (By the Children's Guardian)*[86] an injunction was granted. In that case a mother of two children was awaiting sentence having pleaded guilty to a charge that she had knowingly infected the father of one of the children with HIV. Both children were in foster care and the elder (who was not HIV positive) attended a nursery away from the immediate area where her mother's identity was not known. The applicant local authority, fearing that if publicity was given to the identity and HIV status of the mother that could give rise to a general outcry at the nursery and also make it more difficult to find alternative carers for the children, successfully sought an injunction restraining the publication of the parents' identity in connection with the criminal proceedings and of the details of the nursery placements.

Having to balance Art 8 and Art 10 rights in fact reflects the line generally taken previously, namely, that since the curbing of publicity (even that directly concerning the child) only indirectly concerns the child's upbringing, the child's welfare was not paramount but had instead to be weighed in the balance with the freedom of the press.[87] The *Re S* analysis, however, does call into question the line taken in at least two earlier decisions, namely, *R v Central Independent Television plc*[88] and *Re Z (A Minor)(Identity: Restrictions on Publication)*.[89] In the former it was held that, if the allegedly harmful publication does not relate to the care and upbringing of children over whose welfare the court is exercising a supervisory role, then not only is the child's welfare not paramount but it is not relevant at all. This approach could presumably be justified in post *Re S* terms by saying that in such cases the child's Art 8 rights are not engaged at all and therefore only Art 10 has to be considered. More problematic, however, is *Re Z* which was a case in which the mother wanted her child, as Ward LJ put it, 'to perform for the making of the film' about her treatment at the unit dealing with special educational needs. It was held that because, unlike the other cases, the issue was concerned with a parent's exercise of parental responsibility in waiving the child's right to confidentiality with respect to her education the child's welfare was paramount and that therefore the

---

[84] The High Court's inherent jurisdiction is discussed in Ch 16.

[85] In this regard note might be taken of cl 6 of the Press Complaints Commission's Code of Practice for Journalists which is designed to protect the welfare of children.

[86] [2005] EWHC 1564 (Fam), [2006] 1 FLR 1, per Potter P.

[87] See p 329 of the previous edition of this work relying inter alia upon *Re H (Minors)(Injunction: Public Interest)* [1994] 1 FLR 519, CA.

[88] [1994] Fam 192, CA.   [89] [1997] Fam 1, CA.

film should not be broadcast. Whether this analysis can survive *Re S* remains to be seen.[90]

(b) Procedural issues

Although, on one view it may be said that the paramountcy principle can also apply to procedural issues (it is certainly arguable that in deciding that a parent did not have a right to see the Official Solicitor's report compiled in connection with an application to look after the child, and that the court had the power to withhold it from the parties, the House of Lords in *Official Solicitor v K*[91] was applying such a principle)[92] an alternative analysis[93] is that in certain instances the courts, motivated by their concern to protect children generally will not rigidly apply all procedural rules designed to provide overall justice to parties to litigation but will nevertheless only refrain from applying them in a particular case where they are satisfied that to do so would be harmful to the individual child concerned. Such an analysis can be justified by saying that disclosure only indirectly concerned the child's upbringing and is arguably supported by another House of Lords decision, *Re L (A Minor) (Police Investigation: Privilege)*.[94] In that case, to assist an investigation as to whether a criminal offence had been committed, the police sought leave to have sight of a medical report written by an expert engaged by the mother in the course of care proceedings and filed with the court.

Ordering the disclosure Lord Jauncey (giving the majority judgment) drew a distinction between privilege attaching to communications between solicitor and client and that attaching to reports by third parties prepared on the instructions of a client for the purposes of litigation. Whilst the former, perhaps properly referred to as 'legal professional privilege', was absolute,[95] the latter, better described as 'litigation privilege', was a creature of adversarial procedure and as such had no place in proceedings under the Children Act 1989. In drawing this conclusion Lord Jauncey had in mind the approach of *Official Solicitor v K*, namely that the court should not disable itself from being able to safeguard and promote the interests of children involved in Children Act proceedings by rigidly applying procedural rules. As he put it:[96]

'... if litigation privilege were to apply ... it would have the effect of subordinating the welfare of the child to the interests of the mother in preserving its confidentiality. This would appear to frustrate the primary object of the Act.'

Having ruled that the court had a discretion to order disclosure even to non-parties, the

---

[90] In *A Local Authority v W, L, T and R*, above, at [24] Potter P referred specifically to *Re Z* as having limited value but this was in respect of its analysis of the protective powers of the court under its inherent jurisdiction.

[91] [1965] AC 201, HL.

[92] See the headnote statement at [1965] AC 202, 'that the paramount consideration of the Chancery Division in exercising its jurisdiction over wards of court was the welfare of the infants'. The headnote to the All England report is in similar terms: see [1963] 3 All ER 191.

[93] See N Lowe, 'The House of Lords and the welfare principle', above at 153–8.

[94] [1997] AC 16. See also *Re D (Minors)(Adoption Reports: Confidentiality)* [1996] AC 593, HL, which establishes that non-disclosure of reports should be the exception not the norm and should be ordered only when the case for doing so is compelling.

[95] Following the House of Lords ruling in *R v Derby Magistrates' Court, ex p B* [1996] AC 487.

[96] [1997] AC at 27F.

majority could not fault the trial judge's exercise of discretion. In this respect it should be noted that Bracewell J expressly said:[97]

'The application before me does not relate to the upbringing of the child and, therefore, is not governed by s 1 of the Children Act 1989. Welfare must be weighed, but it can be displaced in some circumstances. The interests of the child or children must always be very important factors, since it is the essence of the proceedings to protect those interests and the reason why the courts have imposed the curtains of privacy. There is the competing claim of public interest in the due administration of justice which requires police forces to make informed decisions before deciding whether to prosecute. The potential charge of administering a noxious substance to a child is a very serious criminal offence with life threatening implications, not only for E [the child in question], but for any other child which the mother may have.'

Balancing these interests, Bracewell J came down in favour of disclosure and her approach, endorsed by the House of Lords, is a classic exposition of the exercise of the protective jurisdiction which, as the learned judge pointed out, was relevant here because disclosure did not directly concern the child's upbringing.

The minority (Lords Nicholls and Mustill) did not accept the separate distinction of litigation privilege nor that there was no element of an adversarial character in Children Act proceedings. Lord Nicholls considered that parents and other parties should be entitled to a fair hearing notwithstanding any special role of judges in family proceedings. As he strikingly put it,[98] 'The paramountcy principle must not be permitted to become a loose cannon destroying all else around it.' With respect, this seems to be going too far: the reason for relaxing the procedural rule was not because of the paramountcy principle but rather so as not to prevent courts in general from being able to safeguard and promote children's interests as set out in the Children Act. In making this decision the child's interests have to be weighed against other interests. Such a process can hardly be described as a loose cannon.

It is implicit in *Re L* that not all procedural rules can be changed even to protect children—so for example, legal professional privilege attaching to solicitor–client communications is absolute. The same is true for the rules of appeal, as was established in *G v G (Minors: Custody Appeal)*,[99] in which the House of Lords rejected the argument based on the paramountcy principle that special rules of appeal apply in (what were then) custody cases. Instead the Lords specifically endorsed the principles set out by Lord Scarman in *B v W (Wardship: Appeal)*,[100] that an appellate court cannot intervene:

'. . . unless it is satisfied either that the judge exercised his discretion on a wrong principle or that, the judge's decision being so plainly wrong, he must have exercised his discretion wrongly.'

Perhaps the most convincing reason for reaching this conclusion, which after all in practice still leaves a wide area of discretion to the appellate court, is the point made by Lord Fraser that:[101]

---

[97] [1995] 1 FLR 999 at 1007.   [98] [1997] AC at 13B.   [99] [1985] 1 WLR 647, HL.
[100] [1979] 1 WLR 1041 at 1055F.
[101] [1985] 1 WLR 647 at 652A. But for an excellent critique of this case see J Eekelaar (1985) 48 MLR 704.

'. . . the desirability of putting an end to litigation, which applies to all classes of cases, is particularly strong because the longer legal proceedings last, the more are the children, whose welfare is at stake, likely to be disturbed by the uncertainty.'

Put in theoretical terms, the issue of when an appellate court should intervene does not directly concern a child's upbringing and hence the paramountcy principle does not apply. Furthermore, as the normal rules of appeal do not inhibit the courts from performing their proper role of safeguarding the child's interests, there is no need to provide special rules.

(c) Other areas of uncertainty

There is uncertainty as to whether the paramountcy principle applies to determining whether to give leave to interview children involved in court proceedings with a view to preparing an adult's defence in criminal proceedings.[102] There is also uncertainty concerning the applicability of the paramountcy principle to the determination of forum conveniens, though the predominant view now is that it does not.[103]

3 THE PARAMOUNTCY PRINCIPLE DOES NOT APPLY IF EXCLUDED BY OTHER STATUTORY PROVISIONS

Even where a child's upbringing is directly in issue the court is not always bound by the paramountcy principle. It clearly will not be if statute expressly provides an alternative test or expressly excludes its operation. Applications for parental orders under s 30 of the Human Fertilisation and Embryology Act 1990, for example, directly concern the child's upbringing, but in determining them the court is expressly bound[104] to treat the child's welfare as its first (but not paramount) consideration. The child's welfare is also expressed to be the first consideration in proceedings relating to the adjustment of property and financial matters on divorce,[105] while s 105(1) of the Children Act 1989 expressly excludes

---

[102] In *Re F (Specific Issue: Child Interview)* [1995] 1 FLR 819, CA, Waite LJ was prepared to assume that s 1(1) of the 1989 Act applied whereas in *Re M (Care: Leave to Interview Child)* [1995] 1 FLR 825 Hale J held that the child's welfare was not the overriding consideration. Relying on the cases concerning the issue of witness summons, White, Carr and Lowe, above, at 2.23 consider that Hale J's view is to be preferred.

[103] See the review by Munby J in *Re V (Forum Conveniens)* [2004] EWHC 2663 (Fam) [2005] 1 FLR 718 at [18]-[19], preferring the views of Thorpe J in *Re S (Residence Order: Forum Conveniens)* [1995] 1 FLR 314 at 325 and Bracewell J in *Re D (Stay of Children Act Proceedings)* [2003] EWHC 565 (Fam), [2003] 2 FLR 1159 at [21] to those of Waite J in *H v H (Minors)(Forum Conveniens)* [1995] 1 FLR 314 at 324–5. In Scotland, Lord Maclean also preferred Thorpe J's analysis, see *B v B* 1998 SLT 1245 at 1246. *Re S* was also followed by Wilson J in *M v M (Stay of Proceedings: Return of Children)* [2005] EWHC 1159 (Fam), [2006] 1 FLR 138.

[104] By the Adoption Act 1976, s 6 as applied to parental orders by the Parental Orders (Human Fertilisation and Embryology) Regulations 1994. Note the 1976 Act has been expressly preserved for the purposes of these Regulations by the Adoption and Children Act (Commencement No 10 Transitional and Savings Provisions Order) 2005, Art 14.

[105] By the Matrimonial Causes Act 1973 s 25(1), for the application of which see *N v N (Consent Orders: Variation)* [1993] 2 FLR 868, CA and *Suter v Suter and Jones* [1987] Fam 111, CA, discussed below, p 1021. Before the Adoption and Children Act 2002 the child's welfare was only treated as the first consideration in adoption proceedings: Adoption Act 1976, s 6.

maintenance from the definition of child's upbringing and so disapplies the paramountcy principle.[106]

It is also clear that the paramountcy principle can be *impliedly* excluded by statute. For example, it has been held that the paramountcy principle is inconsistent with the duties of local authorities under s 25(1)(b) of the Children Act 1989 and therefore has no application to the question of making secure accommodation orders.[107] Similarly, the criteria set out in s 10(9) for determining whether to grant adults leave to apply for s 8 orders have been held to be inconsistent with the application of the paramountcy principle.[108] It is also clear that while the paramountcy principle applies in proceedings under Parts IV and V of the 1989 Act, it will only come into play provided the applicant can satisfy the court that the preconditions for a care order or for an emergency protection order have been made out.[109] As Bainham has pointed out:[110]

'. . . the more limited application of the welfare principle in care proceedings reflects the need to set limits to the power of the state to intervene in the family by defining more specifically the circumstances in which this is permissible while in other areas the differing weighting of the child's welfare is the mechanism whereby Parliament stipulates the relative importance to be attached to the often conflicting interests of children and adults.'

It has been said that the question of whether the future of children should be decided in one part of the United Kingdom rather than another is determined by statute[111] and that their welfare is not the paramount consideration in reaching that decision.[112]

In other cases, it may not be a specific provision that impliedly excludes the paramountcy principle but rather the whole scheme of legislation. The courts have refused, for example, to apply the paramountcy principle so as to interfere with discretionary powers clearly vested by Parliament in another body or court. Hence it is clearly established that the principle cannot be invoked to interfere with the discretionary powers vouchsafed to local authorities to look after and manage children in their care,[113] nor to interfere with the discretionary power vested in the immigration service.[114]

---

[106] This means that s 1(1) has no application to court applications for maintenance (insofar as they are still permitted under the Child Support Act 1991: see below, p 966) and probably has no application to proceedings for lump sums or property orders for the child under Sch 1 to the 1989 Act; cf *K v H (Child Maintenance)* [1993] 2 FLR 61.

[107] *Re M (A Minor) (Secure Accommodation Order)* [1995] Fam 108, CA. Secure accommodation is discussed below at pp 709ff.

[108] *Re A (Minors) (Residence Orders: Leave to Apply)* [1992] Fam 182, CA.

[109] See *Humberside County Council v B* [1993] 1 FLR 257.   [110] *Children, The New Law*, at p 11.

[111] Ie the Domicile and Matrimonial Proceedings Act 1973, Sch 1, para 8(1).

[112] See *M v M (Abduction: England and Wales)* [1997] 2 FLR 263 at 275F, per Millett LJ. The child's welfare is similarly not paramount when deciding whether to make a return order under the 1980 Hague Abduction Convention, see below p 631. The paramountcy principle is ousted by a successful claim to diplomatic immunity under the terms of the Diplomatic Privileges Act 1964, see *Re P (Children Act: Immunity)* [1998] 1 FLR 624.

[113] *A v Liverpool City Council* [1982] AC 363, HL, which remains good law. See also *Re B (Minors) (Termination of Contact: Paramount Consideration)* [1993] Fam 301 at 309, per Butler-Sloss LJ. See further below, pp 795–7.

[114] *Re Mohamed Arif (An Infant)* [1968] Ch 643, CA. Note also *R v Secretary of State for the Home Department, ex p Gangadeen, R v Secretary of State for the Home Department, ex p Khan* [1998] 1 FLR 762, CA in which it was held that the treating of the child's welfare as an important but not paramount consideration was not contrary to Art 8 of the European Convention on Human Rights, having regard to such decisions as *Abdulaziz v UK* (1985) 7 EHRR 471.

4 APPLYING THE PARAMOUNTCY PRINCIPLE TO MORE THAN ONE CHILD

One of the inherent difficulties in applying the paramountcy principle is with respect to cases involving two or more children with conflicting interests. This issue can arise either where the applicant is a child or where the application concerns siblings.

(a) Child-parents and babies

The leading case is *Birmingham City Council v H (A Minor)*[115] which concerned a 15-year-old child and her baby who had both been made the subjects of interim care orders. The mother was disturbed and aggressive and made attempts to harm herself, as a result of which the baby was removed to foster parents. At the subsequent full care hearing the mother sought contact with her child. The evidence suggested that it was not in the baby's interests for contact to continue but it was in the mother's interests that it should. The question was, therefore, squarely raised as to whose welfare was paramount, the baby's or the mother's?

The House of Lords ruled that the baby's welfare was paramount. According to Lord Slynn (who gave the main judgment), s 34 (which governs contact with a child in care) makes it clear that the subject-matter of the application is the child in care in respect of whom an order is sought (ie in this case, the baby) and that, accordingly:[116]

'[the] question to be determined relates to that child's upbringing and it is that child's welfare which must be the court's paramount consideration. The fact that the parent is also a child does not mean that both parent's and child's welfare is paramount and that each has to be balanced against the other.'

Lord Slynn said that the same analysis would be applicable if the child was the applicant, because it would still be—

'. . . that child's welfare which is directly involved and which is paramount even if the other named person is also a child. The welfare of any other named person, even if a child, is not also paramount so as to require a balancing exercise to be carried out.'

The *Birmingham* decision has been criticised[117] both for being confined to s 34 and for its application of the 'subject-matter-of-the-application' approach even when interpreting s 34. However, with regard to the former it now seems evident from the subsequent Court of Appeal decision in *F v Leeds City Council*[118] that such an approach is of broad application. In that case the court rejected a 17-year-old mother's argument that in deciding whether to make a care order in respect of her baby (who had been removed from her within hours of the birth) the baby's welfare alone should not be treated as the paramount consideration since she herself was a child whose upbringing was in question. The Court of Appeal held, following *Birmingham*, that, since the baby and not the mother was the subject matter of the application and the only child to be named in the order, no question relating to the mother's upbringing arose and hence there was no requirement to treat her welfare as paramount.

---

[115] [1994] 2 AC 212, HL (discussed further below, p 793) and see G Douglas 'In Whose Best Interests?' (1994) 110 LQR 379.
[116] At 222.   [117] By Douglas, above.   [118] [1994] 2 FLR 60, CA.

With regard to the House of Lords' interpretation of s 34, it has been pointed out that, while it 'breaks the tie' as between a parent who is a child and her baby, it will not do so where one sibling in care applies for contact with another sibling in care, for it will not be possible to say which child is the subject-matter of the application unless this is to be determined simply by the accident of who brought the application.[119] As against this, however, it seems right to treat a baby's welfare as superior to the mother's for, as was argued in the *Birmingham* case,[120] 'vulnerable infants ought not to be deprived of the protection of the welfare principle because they have a teenage mother'. Accordingly it is submitted that, instead of leaving it open,[121] the Lords should have adopted the wider argument that an application by a parent (who is still a child) for contact with his or her own child falls outside the scope of s 1(1), since it only relates to the child's position as a parent and not to the child parent's own upbringing. Such an approach would have been well in line with the well developed jurisprudence of confining the paramountcy principle to issues *directly* concerning the child's upbringing and would have provided a simpler test.

(b) Balancing the interests of siblings

As has been suggested, the *Birmingham* decision is not easy to apply, if at all, in cases involving siblings. In *Re F (Contact: Child in Care)*,[122] in which a child in care wanted contact with his four siblings who were not in care, Wilson J observed that where an application was properly made under s 34 (viz where the parents or siblings were content to have contact but the resistance emanated from the local authority) the child in care's welfare would be the paramount consideration, since that child would be the 'named person'. On the other hand, if that child were to apply for a s 8 contact order with his siblings, it would be the latter's welfare that would be paramount. Whether it is sensible for the issue of paramountcy to depend on which application is brought can surely be questioned, but even accepting this analysis it will still not solve the problem of competing interests between sibling children each of whom is in care, in the case of applications by each of them for contact with the other.

In such a situation the Court of Appeal's approach in the *Birmingham* case seems more apposite, ie to balance the children's interests and find a preponderance in favour of one or the other.[123] A similar approach also seems inevitable in resolving private law applications concerning sibling children where their interests conflict. This was Wall J's view in *Re T and E (Proceedings: Conflicting Interests)*,[124] in which he commented, obiter:

'... where a number of children are all the subject of an application or cross-application to the court in the same set of proceedings, and where it was impossible to achieve what was in the paramount interests of each child, the balancing exercise described in the Court of Appeal (in the *Birmingham* case) had to be undertaken and the situation of least detriment to all the children achieved.'

This approach has now been authoritatively endorsed by the Court of Appeal in *Re A*

[119] See the detailed analysis by Douglas, above at 382, and see *Re F (Contact: Child in Care)* [1995] 1 FLR 510, discussed below.
[120] [1994] 2 AC at 215G.   [121] [1994] 2 AC at 223H.   [122] Above.
[123] See Douglas, above, at 382.   [124] [1995] 1 FLR 581 at 587.

(Children)(Conjoined Twins: Surgical Operation)[125] which concerned the issue of whether the conjoined twins should be surgically separated when to do so would preserve the life of one (Jodie) but inevitably kill the other (Mary). In sanctioning the operation Ward LJ said,[126] applying the Court of Appeal approach taken in the *Birmingham* case:

'If the duty of the court is to make a decision which puts Jodie's interests paramount and that decision would be contrary to the paramount interests of Mary, then, for my part, I do not see the court can reconcile the impossibility of fulfilling each duty by simply declining to decide the very matter before it. That would be a total abdication of the duty which is imposed on us. Given the conflict of duty, I can see no other way of dealing with it than by choosing the lesser of the two evils and so finding the least detrimental alternative. A balance has to be struck somehow and I cannot flinch from undertaking that evaluation, horrendously difficult though it is'.

A less dramatic example of the balancing approach is the pre-Children Act decision in *Clarke-Hunt v Newcombe*,[127] in which the Court of Appeal upheld a decision not to separate two brothers but to place them together with their mother even though it was against the elder boy's wishes and possibly slightly detrimental to his interests.

D THE MEANING OF WELFARE

The term 'welfare' as such is not defined in the 1989 Act and, although the welfare principle had been the cornerstone of child law for some considerable time before the new legislation, it is surprisingly difficult to find judicial articulation of its meaning. One of the few statements is that of Lindley LJ who in 1893 said:[128]

'. . . the welfare of the child is not to be measured by money alone nor by physical comfort only. The word welfare must be taken in its widest sense. The moral and religious welfare must be considered as well as its physical well-being. Nor can the ties of affection be disregarded.'

Rather more recently Butler-Sloss P has commented[129] that 'best interests encompasses medical, emotional and all other welfare issues'. But perhaps the best modern statement of the meaning of 'welfare' is that made in a New Zealand case by Hardy Boys J who said:[130]

' "Welfare" is an all-encompassing word. It includes material welfare, both in the sense of an adequacy of resources to provide a pleasant home and a comfortable standard of living and in the sense of an adequacy of care to ensure that good health and due personal pride are maintained. However, while material considerations have their place, they are secondary matters. More important are the stability and the security, the loving and understanding care and guidance, the warm and compassionate relationships, that are essential for the full development of the child's own character, personality and talents.'

---

[125] [2001] Fam 147.   [126] Above at 192.   [127] (1982) 4 FLR 482, CA.

[128] *Re McGrath (Infants)* [1893] 1 Ch 143 at 148.

[129] In *Re A (Medical Treatment: Male Sterilisation)* [2000] 1 FLR 549 at 555, referred to by Ward LJ in *Re A (Children)(Conjoined Twins: Surgical Separation)* [2001] Fam 147 at 180.

[130] In *Walker v Walker and Harrison*, noted in [1981] NZ Recent Law 257 and cited by the Law Commission Working Paper No 96, *Custody* (1985), para 6. 10.

Ideally, the court should be concerned to promote the child's long-term future.[131] However, while there are cases where the court has clearly anticipated future contingencies such as parental acquisition of employment and remarriage,[132] or where regard has been had to furthering the child's education and general prospects,[133] inevitably the court will tend to concentrate on the immediate ties and environment of the child.

It is sometimes said that in applying the welfare principle the court must act in the child's best interests and, indeed, that is the phrase used by Art 3(1) of the UN Convention on the Rights of the Child.[134] However, this may put an unduly sanguine gloss on the court's functions: it should be appreciated that a judge is not dealing with what is ideal for the child but simply with what is the best that can be done in the circumstances. Perhaps not untypical of the dilemmas faced by the court is that described by Cumming-Bruce LJ as being before the trial judge in *Clarke-Hunt v Newcombe*:[135]

'There was not really a right solution; there were two alternative wrong solutions. The problem for the judge was to appreciate the factors in each direction and to decide which of the two bad solutions was the least dangerous, having regard to the long-term interests of the children . . .'

1 THE CHECKLIST

Although the 1989 Act does not define 'welfare', it introduced a checklist of relevant factors to which in certain circumstances (discussed below) the court must have regard when deciding what, if any, order to make. The introduction of a checklist had been recommended by the Law Commission,[136] both as 'a means of providing greater consistency and clarity in the law' and 'as a major step towards a more systematic approach to decisions concerning children'.

In other words, the object is not to redefine what is meant by 'welfare' but to provide a means by which greater homogeneity can be achieved in exercising the court's undoubtedly wide discretion in determining what is best for the child. The inestimable advantage of a list is that it enables everyone from the judge to the litigant, the advocate to the CAFCASS officer, to focus on the same issues at the same time.

2 THE CONTENTS OF THE 'LIST'

The checklist, which is contained in s 1(3) is as follows:

'(a) the ascertainable wishes and feelings of the child concerned (considered in the light of his age and understanding);

---

[131] Unless perhaps where the short-term disadvantages are so overwhelming as to rule out the long-term option: see eg *Thompson v Thompson* [1987] Fam Law 89, CA.

[132] See respectively *Re DW (A Minor) (Custody)* [1984] Fam Law 17, CA and *S (BD) v S(DJ)* [1977] Fam 109, CA.

[133] See *May v May* [1986] 1 FLR 325, CA (order made in favour of father who was more academic than the mother); and cf *Re DW*, above, and *Re O (Infants)* [1962] 2 All ER 10, CA (boy's long-term future better in Sudan, girl's in England).

[134] Discussed above, p 367.   [135] (1982) 4 FLR 482, CA.

[136] Law Com No 172, paras 3.17 et seq.

(b) his physical, emotional and educational needs;

(c) the likely effect on him of any change in his circumstances;

(d) his age, sex, background and any characteristics of his which the court considers relevant;

(e) any harm which he has suffered or is at risk of suffering;

(f) how capable each of his parents, and any other person in relation to whom the court considers the question to be relevant, is of meeting his needs;

(g) the range of powers available to the court under this Act in the proceedings in question.'

We shall consider later[137] in more detail how the checklist applies in particular cases, but at this stage it is relevant to make the following observations.

First, the checklist is not exhaustive and indeed might properly be regarded as the minimum that will be considered by the court. It has been held, for instance, that it is quite proper to take into account financial considerations as well.[138] To be consistent with human rights law it has been suggested by one commentator[139] that the rights of parents should now be included in the list. During the discussions preceding the Children and Adoption Act 2006 there was much discussion as to whether the checklist should be amended to ensure that the courts have regard to the importance of sustaining a relationship between the child and the non-resident parent. The Government view was that the checklist was not the place to include it.[140] It is always open to the court to specify other matters which it would like to see included in a welfare report.[141]

Secondly, the content of the checklist follows that recommended by the Law Commission save for the addition of s 1(3)(g), the purpose of which is to emphasise the court's duty to consider not only whether the order being sought is the best for the child but also the alternatives that the Act makes available. This, as we shall see,[142] has particular application in care proceedings, in which it is incumbent upon the court to consider not just whether or not to make the care order but whether, for example, a residence order under s 8 would better serve the child's interests. This duty also reflects the general policy of vesting in the courts at all levels greater responsibility for the management and conduct of children cases.

Thirdly, although the statutory checklist was new to the Children Act, with the exception of s 1(3)(g), the factors themselves were drawn from previous practice. Nevertheless, it is to be noted that s 1(3)(a) provided the first mandatory direction to the courts to have regard[143] to the child's own wishes both in the context of private disputes over children

---

[137] See below, pp 584 et seq.   [138] *Re R (Residence Order: Finance)* [1995] 2 FLR 612, CA.

[139] A Bainham 'Family Rights in the Next Millennium' (2000) 53 Current Legal Problems 473 at 490.

[140] See the *Government Reply to the Report from the Joint Committee on the Draft Children (Contact) and Adoption Bill* Cm 6583 (June 2005) para 121. Ironically, the now abandoned s 11(4) of the Family Law Act 1996 which was to have directed the courts admittedly only in divorce and separation cases to have particular regard to

'the general principle that, in the absence of evidence to the contrary, the welfare of the child will be best served by

   (i) his having regular contact with those who have parental responsibility for him and with other members of his family . . .'

might have served as a statutory model. Note also Art 4 of the Council of Europe Convention on Contact Concerning Children 2003.

[141] See below, p 487.   [142] Below, p 763.

[143] Though note: the child's wishes are *not* expressed to be determinative. See further below, p 585.

following their parents' separation or divorce and in care proceedings.[144] Whether the child's wishes should have been part of the checklist can be debated. It could be argued that such wishes are independent of their welfare.[145] Moreover, making it a separate requirement to listen to children would have given greater recognition to children being treated as individuals in their own right.

3 WHEN THE CHECKLIST APPLIES

Section 1(4) directs the courts to have regard to the checklist in contested s 8 applications and in *all* proceedings under Part IV of the 1989 Act including therefore all applications for care and supervision orders. There is, however, nothing to prevent the courts from considering the factors in other proceedings if they so choose,[146] and indeed, particularly in contested applications under s 4 and s 5,[147] it would seem prudent to do so. In *Re B (Change of Surname)*,[148] Wilson J commented that, notwithstanding that he did not have to apply the checklist to determine an application for leave to change a child's surname, the list remained 'a most useful aide memoire of the factors that may impinge on the child's welfare'. In *Payne v Payne*,[149] in which an application for leave to remove a child from the jurisdiction was made under s 13, Thorpe LJ went further, commenting:

'Although technically an application brought under s 13(1) is not subject to the welfare checklist the trial judge should nevertheless take the precaution of regarding the checklist factors when carrying out his welfare appraisal.'

The reason for restricting the application of s 1(3) to contested s 8 cases is that in many family proceedings such as divorce there is often no choice as to where and with whom the child should live. If s 1(3) applied to all s 8 cases, courts might feel compelled to investigate even these cases in depth.[150] Such an investigation would not only be a waste of resources but also, arguably, an unwarranted intrusion into family autonomy.

Although s 1(3) specifically directs *the court* to have regard to the checklist, it is clearly useful to legal advisers and their clients both in preparing and in arguing their case. Furthermore, as Holman J pointed out in *Re B (Care Proceedings: Notification of Father Without Parental Responsibility)*,[151] the rules[152] require CAFCASS officers to have regard to the checklist. The Law Commission envisaged[153] that the list would enable parties to prepare relevant evidence and that focusing clients' minds on the real issues might help to promote settlements.

Where it is mandatory to apply the checklist it is clearly preferable that express reference

---

[144] Compare adoption, where it has always been incumbent upon the court to give due consideration to the child's wishes having regard to his age and understanding, see the Adoption Act 1926, s 3(b) re-enacted in the Adoption Acts of 1950, s 5(1)(b), 1958, s 7(2), 1976, s 6. See now s 1(4)(a) of the Adoption and Children 2002, discussed below at p 833.

[145] For the importance of listening to children and the impact of the Children Act 1989 in this respect see *The Children Act Now—Messages from Research* (Dept of Health, 2001), ch 5.

[146] *Southwark London Borough v B* [1993] 2 FLR 559, CA; *Re W (A Minor) (Medical Treatment: Court's Jurisdiction)* [1993] Fam 64, CA, per Thorpe J.

[147] Discussed above at pp 414 and 443 respectively.   [148] [1996] 1 FLR 791 at 793, CA.

[149] [2001] EWCA Civ 166, [2001] 1 FLR 1052 at (30).   [150] See Law Com No 172 at para 3.19.

[151] [1999] 2 FLR 408 at 415.   [152] Viz FPR 1991, r 4.11(1), FPCA 1999, r 11.

[153] Law Com 172 at para 3.18.

is made to it. However, it seems to be accepted that higher court judges (ie not magistrates) are entitled to have it assumed in their favour that the checklist was in their mind without subjecting them to the laborious necessity of relating their findings to the specific item in the list 'one by one'.[154] Nevertheless, as the Court of Appeal has observed,[155] the checklist does represent an extremely useful and important discipline and ensures that all relevant matters are considered and balanced.

E CRITICISMS OF THE WELFARE PRINCIPLE

Although, as we discussed earlier,[156] the paramountcy principle is best regarded as being human rights compliant and is consistent with Art 3(1) of the United Nations Convention on the Rights of the Child, both its paramountcy and indeed the very notion of welfare have been criticised.

The paramountcy principle has been criticised on the grounds that it pays too little attention to the interests of parents and other members of the family and generally ignores the reality of family life, namely, that children are not brought up in a vacuum but live in a relationship or series of relationships with other family members. In short, the court's understanding of the welfare principle has been said to be unduly individualistic with the child wrongly being seen simply in isolation. This has led at least one critic[157] to suggest that the paramountcy rule be abandoned and replaced within a framework which recognises that the child is merely one participant in a process in which the interest of all the participants count. Another[158] has sought to categorise parents' and children's interests as either primary or secondary and to suggest that a child's secondary interests give way to a parent's primary interests. A third suggestion[159] is that the concept of welfare be broadened to comprise what is described as a 'relationship-based welfare approach', whereby instead of conceiving the problem as a clash between (usually) children and parents in terms of weighing two conflicting interests, the issue should be regarded as deciding what is a proper parent-child relationship which in turn is grounded upon the premise that it is beneficial for a child to be brought up in a family that is based on relationships which are fair and just (but which may involve the child having to make some sacrifices).

While each of these approaches, and particularly the latter two, arguably bring to the fore a better articulation of a fair balance of family interests, none of the proposals are

---

[154] See eg *Oldham Metropolitan Borough Council v E* [1994] 1 FLR 568 at 576, per Waite LJ and *Re V (Residence: Review)* [1995] 2 FLR 1010 at 1018, per Russell LJ.

[155] *B v B (Residence Order: Reasons for Decision)* [1997] 2 FLR 602, CA—residence order made by a recorder without reference to the checklist because neither party had made complaints against the other, remitted for a re-hearing.

[156] See above at pp 451–4.

[157] H Reece 'The Paramountcy Principle: Consensus or Construct?' (1996) 49 Current Legal Problems 267.

[158] A Bainham 'Non-Intervention and Judicial Paternalism' in *Frontiers of Liability* (ed P Birks) 161 and developed in ' "Honour Thy Father and Mother": Children's Rights and Children's Duties' in *Children's Rights and Traditional Values* (eds Douglas and Sebba) 93.

[159] See J Herring 'The Welfare Principle and the Rights of Parents' in *What is a Parent?* (eds A Bainham, S Day Sclater and M Richards) 89 and developed in 'The Human Rights Act and the welfare principle in family law—conflicting or complementary?' [1999] CFLQ at 233. But see also by the same author—'Farewell Welfare?' (2005) 27 Jo of Social Welfare and Family Law 159 for a 'defence' of the welfare principle.

problem-free. Abandoning the paramountcy principle is open to the objection that it would leave the child too unprotected and would, in any event, run counter to the UN Convention on the Rights of the Child. Thinking of welfare as protecting primary interests and balancing secondary ones will not solve the problem of resolving clashes between primary interests and in any event is too complicated. Complexity of approach is also a criticism that may be thrown at the relationship-based welfare suggestion. Moreover, as Herring himself admitted,[160] the courts may already be thought to have accommodated the approach 'even if in an unarticulated way'. However, the very chameleon qualities of the welfare principle as applied by the courts have led to charges that the concept is too uncertain and value laden, and ironically, 'might fail to provide sufficient protection to children's interest because its use conceals the fact that the interests of others, or, perhaps, untested assumptions about what is good for children, actually drive the decision'. This latter charge has led Eekelaar to speculate[161] about abandoning the welfare principle as it is currently understood in favour of a concept of 'well-being' (which he defines as being indicated by the degree of success achieved in realising the person's significant goals in life) which he argues would offer a more nuanced approach.[162] He concludes:[163]

'Of course, children must be seen to have rights ... They must be seen to have the right to begin writing the script of the way their life is to unfold. But the claims of other parties to procedural justice and to the protection of their well-being must not be overlooked. Children's rights should be seen as a species of people's rights: in this case, people on their way to becoming adults. In themselves, these rights are no different from adults' rights. Due allowance being made for issues of competence and children's special vulnerability, they should be respected just as adults' rights should be; certainly no less, but also no more.'

F   DELAY PRIMA FACIE PREJUDICIAL TO THE CHILD'S WELFARE [164]

Section 1(2) enjoins the court, in any proceedings in which any question with respect to a child's upbringing arises, 'to have regard to the general principle that any delay in determining the question is likely to prejudice the welfare of the child'. Since this principle applies to all proceedings concerning a child's upbringing[165] it is not confined to proceedings under the 1989 Act, but applies equally, for example, proceedings under the High Court's inherent jurisdiction (separate provision is now made for adoption proceedings).[166] However, the accompanying timetabling provisions (discussed below) are confined to

---

[160] See [1999] CFLQ at 233.   [161] J Eekelaar 'Beyond the welfare principle' [2002] CFLQ 237.
[162] Above at 243.   [163] Above at 249.
[164] See generally *Scoping Study on Delay in Children Act Cases* (Lord Chancellor's Department, 2002), on which draft Report see A Finlay 'Delay and the Challenges of the Children Act' in *Delight and Dole* (eds Thorpe and Cowton) 5 at 10ff. A McFarlane 'Delay: A Cause of Significant Harm' [2003] Fam Law 453 and M Booth *Avoiding Delay in Children Act Cases* (1996), summarised at [1996] Fam Law 598–601, 643–5.
[165] Note, however, the exclusion of maintenance from the definition of 'upbringing' under s 105(1).
[166] Viz by s 1(3) of the Adoption and Children Act 2002, discussed below at p 834.

Children Act proceedings (though in practice they are applied to proceedings under the inherent jurisdiction).[167]

The case for making some provision about the deleterious effect of delay was cogently argued by the Law Commission.[168] They pointed out that 'prolonged litigation about their future is deeply damaging to children, not only because of the uncertainty it brings for them, but also because of the harm it does to the relationship between the parents and their capacity to co-operate with one another in the future'. Despite its importance, however, neither the Law Commission's draft Bill nor the Bill originally presented to Parliament made the avoidance of delay a general principle. Indeed, it was only at the final House of Lords stages that this provision was promoted to the opening section, Lord Mackay commenting[169]

'After the welfare principle, the need to avoid delay is one of the most important policies underlying the Bill. It is therefore proper that it should appear in clause 1.'

The need for speed is also underscored by Art 6 of the European Convention on Human Rights under which everyone is entitled to a fair and public hearing in the determination of his civil rights and obligations *within a reasonable time.*[170]

Notwithstanding s 1(2) it should not be thought that delay[171] is always detrimental to the child's welfare. As Ward J observed in *C v Solihull Metropolitan Borough Council,*[172] while delay is ordinarily inimical to the welfare of the child, planned and purposeful delay may well be beneficial. Hence, the delay of a final decision for the purpose of ascertaining the result of an assessment is obviously for rather than against the child's interests. In *Re B (A Minor) (Contact) (Interim Order),*[173] for example, magistrates were held to be 'plainly wrong' in refusing to make an interim contact order during which arrangements for the reintroduction of contact were to be assessed, because it infringed the principle of the avoidance of delay as set out in s 1(2). It may be similarly beneficial to a child to make a temporary order to allow 'a volatile family situation' involving children to settle down.[174] On the other hand, what s 1 (2) aims to prevent is unnecessary and unplanned delay for

---

[167] See R White, P Carr and N Lowe *Children Act in Practice* (3rd edn) 2.58. Separate timetabling provisions apply to adoption proceedings, see s 109 of the Adoption and Children Act 2002, discussed below at p 834.

[168] Law Com No 172, para 4.55.   [169] See 512 HL Official Report (5th Series) Vol 720.

[170] For an example where undue delay has been held to be in breach of Art 6 see eg *Süss v Germany* [2006] 1 FLR 522, ECtHR, protracted access dispute for over a decade only ending when the child became 18 and similarly *EO and VP v Slovakia* [2004] 2 FCR 242, ECtHR—protracted dispute over the education of a 14-year-old which had to be discontinued when child became 18.

[171] See I Butler et al 'The Children Act and the Issue of Delay' [1993] Fam Law 412, who point out that 'delay is a relative phenomenon and needs to be distinguished from "duration". A complex case may, quite appropriately and expeditiously, remain in the courts for several weeks while a relatively simple matter that ought to be dealt with within days might take three weeks and hence be subject to significant delay, yet still be of moderate duration.'

[172] [1993] 1 FLR 290 at 304.   [173] [1994] 2 FLR 269.

[174] As in the pre-Children Act decision *Re S (Minors) (Custody)* [1992] 1 FCR 158, CA. See also *Re K (Non-Accidental Injuries: Perpetrator: New Evidence)* [2004] EWCA Civ 1181, [2005] 1 FCR 285 in which while the delay principle was acknowledged, there were thought to be 'powerful' considerations on the other side, namely, the public interest in the identification of the perpetrator of the non-accidental injuries on the children and the possibility, dependent on that finding, of the children being reconciled with their mother.

reasons that have nothing to do with the child's welfare.[175] It has been said, for example, that to delay a harsh decision is to delay for 'no purpose'.[176] As the criterion to be applied is the welfare of the *child*, detriment to the *family* is not of itself a relevant factor. It was on this basis that in *Re T-B (Care Proceedings: Criminal Trial)*[177] it was held that the fact there was a pending criminal trial was not enough to justify delaying the hearing of the care proceedings.

The principal effect of s 1(2) is to place the onus upon the courts[178] to ensure that all proceedings concerning children are conducted as expeditiously as possible. As Wall J put it:[179]

'The non-adversarial approach in children's litigation means . . . that whatever the forensic stance of the litigant, delay in the prosecution of applications relating to children should not be permitted even where it is perceived to be in the interests of one of the adult parties. Furthermore . . . the courts have a duty to be proactive in ensuring that applications once launched are not allowed to moulder.'

To this end the courts are directed[180] both in applications for s 8 orders and for orders under Part IV to draw up a timetable and to give appropriate directions for adhering to that timetable. The procedure for the timetabling of proceedings is governed by the Rules,[181] the general strategy of which is that, until the application is finally disposed of, a definite return date must be fixed before the end of any directions appointment or other hearing of the case.[182] Once the time has been fixed, it cannot be extended save by leave of the court.[183] The court may be robust in insisting that any timetable is met. In *Re B and T (Care Proceedings: Legal Representation)*,[184] for example, parents who had failed to comply with directions were effectively precluded from legal representation by the refusal of an

---

[175] For examples of cases in which delay was thought to have prejudiced the children's welfare, see *B v B (Minors) (Interviews and Listing Arrangements)* [1994] 2 FLR 489, CA and, most strikingly, *Re A and B (Minors) (No 2)* [1995] 1 FLR 351.

[176] Per Ward LJ in *Re M (Child's Upbringing)* [1996] 2 FLR 441 at 460, CA.

[177] [1995] 2 FLR 801, CA. Note also *Re B and T (Care Proceedings: Legal Representation)* [2001] 1 FLR 485, CA, discussed below.

[178] But note that, according to Wall J in *B v B (Child Abuse: Contact)* [1994] 2 FLR 713 at 736, practitioners too have a duty to ensure that cases do not drift. But s 1(2) does not of itself mean that CAFCASS must make an officer available for appointment as a guardian in care proceedings on receiving a request from the court: *R v Children and Family Court Advisory and Support Service* [2003] EWHC 235 Admin, [2005] 1 FLR 953.

[179] In *B v B (Minor) (Interviews and Listing Arrangements)* [1994] 2 FLR 489 at 492, CA. See also *Re A and B (No 2)*, above.

[180] By s 11(1) and s 32(1). Similar but separate timetabling powers are conferred by s 109 of the Adoption and Children Act 2002, in relation to adoption proceedings.

[181] The Family Proceedings Rules 1991 (FPR), which govern proceedings in the High Court and county court, and the Family Proceedings Courts (Children Act 1989) Rules 1991 (FPCA), which govern proceedings in the magistrates' courts.

[182] FPR 1991 r 4.4(2), FPCA 1991 r 4(2), for details of which see eg Clarke Hall and Morrison on *Children* 1[163].

[183] FPR 1991 r 4.15(1), FPCA 1991 r 15(4).

[184] [2001] 1 FLR 485. See also *Blunkett v Quinn* [2004] EWHC 2816 (Fam), [2005] 1 FLR 648—application to adjourn proceedings for parental responsibility and contact because of the mother's ill-health was refused, inter alia, because delay would be damaging to the father-child relationship; and *Re C (Section 8 Order: Court Welfare Officer)* [1995] 1 FLR 617, CA in which it was held that in view of s 1(2) a court can, in appropriate cases, depart from the recommendation in a welfare report even though the reporter did not attend court to give oral evidence.

adjournment application made by solicitors who had just been instructed on the first day of a five day hearing. In so ruling the Court of Appeal considered that having regard to the overall fairness of the proceedings and the need to balance the parents' rights against those of the children to an early determination of their future, the parents' Art 6 rights to a fair trial were not violated by the refusal to adjourn. Among the possible sanctions against practitioners for failing to comply with the timetable are being personally penalised in costs, being held guilty of professional misconduct,[185] or ultimately being held guilty of contempt of court.

At the time of implementation of the Children Act 1989 there were expectations that private law cases would be generally disposed of within 16 weeks and public law cases within 12 weeks.[186] Both expectations have proved to be wildly optimistic and there have been a number of investigations into the causes of delay.[187] One result of these reports has been to introduce with effect from November 2003 in the case of public law proceedings a *Protocol for Judicial Case Management in Public Law Children Act Cases*[188] the object of which is to prescribe a 40-week target for the general completion of such proceedings. We discuss the protocol in more detail in Chapter 14.[189]

G ORDERS TO BE MADE ONLY WHERE BETTER THAN NO ORDER

1 INTRODUCTION AND BACKGROUND

An important and innovative principle is provided by s 1(5), namely, that whenever a court is considering whether to make one or more orders under the 1989 Act with respect to a child, it 'shall not make the order or any of the orders unless it considers that doing so would be better for the child than making no order at all'. Section 1(5) is intended to focus attention as to whether any court order is necessary.[190] It can also be seen as part of the underlying philosophy of the 1989 Act to respect the integrity and independence of the family save where court orders have some positive contribution to make towards the child's welfare.

According to the Department of Health's *Guidance and Regulations*,[191] s 1(5) has two main aims:

---

[185] See *Re M* (1989) *The Times*, 29 December, CA.

[186] See respectively Law Com No. 172 at para 4.54 and the *Scoping Study*, op cit, at para 24, referred to by Baroness Hale in *Re G (A Minor)(Interim Care Order: Residential Assessment)* [2005] UKHL 68, [2005] 3 WLR 1166 at [58].

[187] Eg the *Scoping Study*, see above, and the Booth Report, above. See also R Bailey-Harris, G Davies, J Barron and J Pearce *Monitoring Private Law Applications Under the Children Act: A Research Report to the Nuffield Foundation* (1998).

[188] [2003] 2 FLR 719.   [189] See p 758.

[190] This implements that Law Commission's recommendations with regard to private law proceedings, see Law Com No 172, paras 3.2–3.4, and those of the Child Care Review (DHSS 1985) paras 15.24–15.25 and the government's White Paper *The Law on Child Care and Family Services* Cm 62, 1987, para 59, with respect to public law proceedings.

[191] Vol 1, *Court Orders*, para 1.12.

'. . . the first is to discourage unnecessary court orders being made, for example as part of a standard package of orders. If orders are restricted to those cases where they are necessary to resolve a specific problem this should reduce conflict and promote parental agreement and co-operation. The second aim is to ensure that the order is granted only where it will positively improve the child's welfare and not simply because the grounds for making the order are made out as, for example, in care proceedings where the court may decide that it would be better for a particular child not to be in local authority care.'

We consider in later chapters[192] what impact s 1(5) has had in particular proceedings, but here we confine our discussion to technical questions of when the provision applies and whether it creates a burden of proof to show that a proposed order is for the child's benefit and to its interrelationship with the paramountcy principle.

2 WHEN SECTION 1(5) APPLIES

As s 1(5) itself states, it applies where a court is considering whether or not to make one or more orders *under the 1989 Act*. Accordingly, it has no direct application in proceedings in which courts are considering whether or not to make orders relating to children outside the Act.[193] In this respect, s 1(5) has a narrower ambit than either s 1(1) or s 1(2).

In *K v H (Child Maintenance)*[194] Sir Stephen Brown P held that s 1(5) does not apply to applications for financial provision[195] for a child under Sch 1 to the Act. The principal reason for so holding was that like s 1(1), which his Lordship took to be the general controlling provision for the overall application of s 1, s 1(5) 'is principally directed to orders relating to the upbringing of a child, the administration of a child's property or the application of any income arising from it'. Accordingly, since an application for financial provision neither concerns the child's upbringing nor the administration of his property, s 1(5) does not apply. The alternative reason for holding s 1(5) inapplicable was that, given it is clearly in a child's interests that proper provision be made for his financial needs, a court order is preferable to relying on the parties' oral agreement,[196] since that proves a better means of safeguarding the future both in the sense of providing for future variations and of being able to deal with any subsequent enforcement issues.

Whether his Lordship was right to say that s 1(1) was intended to provide the overall criterion for the operation of s 1 may be debated, but in practice it is likely to be the case that s 1(5) will not apply if s 1(1) does not. For example, in *Re M (Secure Accommodation Order)*,[197] which established that s 1(1) does not apply to the question of whether to make

---

[192] Viz Chapter 12 (private law proceedings, pp 581ff) and Chapter 14 (public law proceedings, pp 764ff).

[193] Such as orders under the wardship or inherent jurisdiction (though presumably, however, there is nothing to prevent the court from taking a similar approach, if they so choose). However, a similar enjoinder now applies in adoption proceedings, see s 1(6) of the Adoption and Children Act 2002, discussed below at p 834.

[194] [1993] 2 FLR 61.

[195] That is, periodical payments, which was what *K v H* concerned, or lump sums or property orders.

[196] Aliter for *written* agreements which can, subject to the Child Support Act 1991, be varied by the court, eg under Sch 1, paras 10 and 11 to the 1989 Act.

[197] [1995] 1 FLR 418, CA.

a secure accommodation order under s 25,[198] Butler-Sloss LJ expressly held that, because of the need to protect the public as well as the child, s 1(5) does not apply either. Again, in deciding whether to grant leave to apply for a s 8 order where it is established that the paramountcy principle does not apply,[199] it seems right to say that s 1(5) is also subsumed by the criteria set out in s 10(9).[200]

3 DOES SECTION 1(5) CREATE A BURDEN OF PROOF TO SHOW THAT A PROPOSED ORDER IS FOR THE CHILD'S BENEFIT?

The application of s 1(5) has proved problematic. It quickly became referred to as establishing a 'non-intervention principle' or no order principle' and was said to reflect a basic philosophy of the 1989 Act, memorably described as 'privatising the family',[201] though perhaps more accurately by others as a policy of deregulation[202] or non-intervention, which in turn rests 'on the belief that children are generally best looked after within the family with both parents playing a full part and without resort to legal proceedings'.[203] However, insofar as these epithets suggest that orders are presumed to be unnecessary, their use has been deprecated in some quarters. As one commentator has pointed out[204] neither the Law Commission nor the statute says that court orders are presumed to be unnecessary and 'most certainly' neither suggested that in public care proceedings there was a legal presumption against the making of care or supervision orders. In his view if epithets are required he suggests a more accurate one could be the 'no *unnecessary* order principle'.

This debate is allied to an important issue as to whether s 1(5) is properly considered as creating a formal burden of proof on those seeking an order to show that its making is for the child's benefit. In *Re X and Y (Leave To Remove From Jurisdiction: No Order Principle)*[205] Munby J held that it did, for as he put it, relying on principles said to be distilled from the House of Lords' decision in *Dawson v Wearmouth*:[206]

'The burden is on the party applying for an order to make out a positive case that on a balance of probabilities it is in the interests of the child that that order should be made. If he fails to make out that positive case the application will fail.'

However, this analysis was disapproved by the Court of Appeal in *Re H (Children)(Residence Order: Condition)*,[207] Thorpe LJ commenting that he did not think that the dicta

---

[198] Secure accommodation is discussed below at pp 709–17.

[199] See *Re A (Minors) (Residence Orders: Leave to Apply)* [1992] Fam 182, CA, discussed below, p 546.

[200] In particular s 10(9)(c), which directs the court to consider the risk of harm to the child that the proposed application might cause. See further below at p 545.

[201] Inter alia by S Cretney 'Privatising the Family: The Reform of Child Law', (1989), Denning LJ 15 and A Bainham 'The Privatisation of the Public Interest in Children' (1990) 53 MLR 206.

[202] See eg G Douglas 'Family Law under the Thatcher Government' (1990) 17 JLS 411 at 425, n 17.

[203] *Introduction to the Children Act 1989* (HMSO 1989) para 1.3.

[204] A Bainham 'Changing families and changing concepts—reforming the language of family law' (1998) 10 CFLQ at 2–4.

[205] [2001] 2 FLR 118.

[206] [1999] 2 AC 308 relying in particular upon comments made by Lord Mackay at 321A and Lord Hobhouse at 325H–326E. According to Munby J there was no difference in substance between what was said by the House of Lords in *Dawson* and what they said in *S v M (Access Order)* [1997] 1 FLR 980 (on appeal from Scotland).

[207] [2001] EWCA Civ 1338, [2001] 2 FLR 1277.

drawn from the House of Lords' cases bear 'the weight of the edifice that Munby J sought to build on them'.

Although Munby J clearly considered the burden of proof to be of general application, it was not absolutely clear whether the rejection of it in Re H was a total objection or merely confined to relocation cases[208] in which there is acute dissension among the parties such that, in Thorpe LJ words 'No order is simply not an option. The court has to impose one order or the other in the application of the paramount principle of welfare.' A more telling comment indicative of a total rejection of Munby J's ruling was Thorpe LJ's earlier observation made in *Payne v Payne*[209] where he said that he 'did not think that such concepts of presumption and burden of proof have any place in Children Act 1989 litigation where the judge exercises a function that is partly inquisitorial'. Any doubts that Munby J was wrong have since been dispelled by *Re G (Children)(Residence: Making of Order)*[210] in which Ward LJ firmly rejected the notion that s 1(5) raises a presumption against making an order. As his Lordship said,[211] s 1(5):

'is perfectly clear. It does not . . . create a presumption one way or another. All it demands is that before the court makes any order it must ask the question: Will it be better for the child to make the order than making no order at all?'

4 FORM OF ORDER

If the court decides to make no order because it feels that it is in the best interests of the child that no order be made, then a formal order to that effect must be made.[212] A decision not to make an order still ranks as a 'decision', and reasons for making it should therefore be given.[213]

5 THE INTERRELATIONSHIP OF THE PARAMOUNTCY PRINCIPLE AND SECTION 1(5)

Although s 1(5) can be seen as complementing the welfare principle, since it cannot be in the best interest of a child to be the subject of unnecessary court orders, it has been argued[214] that in reality the welfare principle has been 'hijacked by non-interventionism' on the basis that the non-interventionist stance taken in the 1989 Act means that parental wishes, especially where both are in agreement, will determine an increasing number of issues affecting children.

Although there is some tension between s 1(1) and 1(5) it is surely going too far to suggest that the paramountcy principle has been 'hijacked' by the operation of s 1(5). As will be seen,[215] even in the private law context, the proportion of 'no orders' made under s 1(5) is relatively small (though of course it is unknown how many applications are

---

[208] Relocation cases are discussed below at pp 556–9.

[209] [2001] EWCA Civ 166, [2001] 1 FLR 1052—another relocation case.

[210] [2005] EWCA Civ 1283, *The Times* 14 September 2005.   [211] At para [10].

[212] FPR 1991 r 4.21(4), FPCA 1991 r 21(6).   [213] *S v R (Parental Responsibility)* [1993] 1 FCR 331.

[214] A Bainham 'The Privatisation of the Public Interest in Children' (1990) 53 MLR 206 at 221. See also A Bainham 'The Children Act 1989, Welfare and Non-Interventionism' [1990] Fam Law 143 at 145.

[215] Below, p 583.

simply not being pursued).[216] Furthermore, most agreements are likely to provide the best arrangements that can be made for the children in the circumstances. In any case it may be questioned whether the pre-1989 Act law was so very different.[217] Under the former law the courts were generally reluctant to interfere with arrangements agreed between the parents. Under the 1989 Act the difference may simply be that the court may make no order at all rather than make an order reflecting the parents' agreement. Nevertheless there is a danger that by making no order in the light of parental agreement the court could overlook the child's wishes.[218] If they do so in the case of older children, there could be a breach of Art 12 of the UN Convention on the Rights of the Child.[219] Accordingly, courts should be alive to this possibility and seek some assurance that the child in question does not object to the arrangements agreed between the parents.

[216] Nor should the number of withdrawn applications be overlooked, since a proportion of these withdrawals may have been motivated by a desire to avoid a 'no order'. The number of withdrawals generally exceeds that of 'no orders'. For example, in 2004, 380 care order applications were withdrawn compared with 306 'no orders'; 140 contact applications were withdrawn compared with 38 'no orders'. So far as 'private law proceedings' are concerned, it is estimated that only about 10% of parents experiencing relationship breakdown go to resolve contact issues with the majority of parents reaching satisfactory arrangements by themselves: see DFES/DCA *Children's Needs, Parents' Responsibilities: Supporting Evidence for the Consultation Paper* (2003) paras 11,19. This finding may be borne in mind in evaluating the official statistics which record 2751 applications for contact as being withdrawn compared with 3002 'no orders' and 1480 applications for residence being withdrawn compared with 1246 'no orders' and: *Judicial Statistics*, Annual Report 2004, Tables 5.2 and 5.3. It may be noted that the number of 'no orders' rose significantly in 2004 and were virtually double that of 2003 when there were 652 residence and 1522 contact 'no orders'. See 2003 Judicial Statistics Table 5.3.

[217] In any event, it may be questioned whether the welfare principle itself is truly child-centred. See eg Maidment *Child Custody and Divorce*, p 149, who argues that decisions in the past were 'made for adults by adults about adults'.

[218] This is evidence that this is indeed the case in the context of divorce see, G Douglas et al 'Safeguarding Children's Welfare in Non-Contentious Divorce: Towards a Non Conception of the Legal Process?' (2000) 63 MLR 177 at 190–1.

[219] Under which there is an international obligation for courts to give due weight to a child's views: see below, p 482.

11

THE VOICE OF THE CHILD

A INTRODUCTION

As we discussed in Chapter 7, historically the great shift in English law governing parent and child was the move from the position where children were of no concern at all to one where their welfare is the court's paramount concern. But this has not been the only change for a more recent and no less significant development has been the shift away from treating children as passive victims of family breakdown towards regarding them as participants and actors in the family justice system.[1] One consequence of this shift is that in various family proceedings it has become incumbent upon the court to ascertain and duly to take into account children's own wishes and views. Research, too, has increasingly investigated children's experiences of and views on the family justice system.[2]

In this chapter we begin by discussing what obligation there is to take the child's views into account then we discuss how those views are investigated. Thirdly, we consider the law and practice governing the child's direct participation in legal proceedings concerning them and finally, we consider the role of the newly created Commissioners for Children to look after children's interests.

B THE OBLIGATION TO HAVE REGARD TO THE CHILD'S VIEWS

1 DOMESTIC LAW

(a) Adoption

Ever since it was introduced into English law it has been incumbent upon the courts to give due consideration to the wishes of the children concerned having regard to his or her

---

[1] See N Lowe and M Murch 'Children's participation in the family justice system—translating principles into practice' [2001] 13 CFLQ 137.

[2] See, for example, the studies in the ESRC programme: *Children 5–16: growing into the twenty-first century*, referred by Lowe and Murch, op cit, 145, n 61; B Neale and C Smart 'Agents or Dependents? Struggling to listen to Children in Family Law and Family Research' Working Paper No 3 (1999); C Thomas, V Beckford, N Lowe, M Murch, *Adopted Children Speaking* (1999), I Butler, L Scanlan, M Robinson, G Douglas, M Murch *Divorcing Children—children's experience of their parents' divorce* (2003) and G Douglas, M Murch, C Miles and L Scanlan *Research into the Operation of Rule 9.5 of the Family Proceedings Rules 1991* (DCA, 2006).

age and understanding.[3] Currently, the obligation, which lies on both courts *and* adoption agencies, is to have regard, whenever they are coming to decisions relating to the adoption of a child, to the child's ascertainable wishes and feelings considered in the light of the child's age and understanding.[4]

(b) Private law proceedings under the Children Act 1989

For a long time adoption was unique in requiring courts to have regard to children's wishes. In private law proceedings concerning children such an obligation was not formally imposed until the Children Act 1989 was implemented.[5] Now as part of the welfare checklist the court must, as in adoption, have regard to the 'ascertainable wishes and feelings of the child concerned (considered in the light of his age and understanding)'.[6] However, as we discussed in Chapter 10 the *obligation* to apply the checklist in private law proceedings only arises in *contested* applications for s 8 orders.[7] This means that even where private law orders are sought under the Act, if the *adults* are agreed, there is no compulsion to consult the children. Indeed one of the reasons for limiting the application of the checklist to contested cases is to protect family autonomy. This has a particular impact in the context of divorce since under the revised s 41 of the Matrimonial Causes Act 1973,[8] divorce courts are only required to consider whether they should exercise any of their powers under the Children Act 1989 in relation to any children of the family and only in exceptional cases delay the granting of the divorce decree. This direction has, according to some,[9] shifted the focus of the court's attention 'away from having to be satisfied that the divorce may proceed in the interests of the children, to finding some exceptional reason why the divorce should not go ahead. The assumption which lies behind this approach is that parents may be trusted in most cases, to plan what is best for their children's futures, and that, where they are in agreement on this, it is unnecessary and potentially damaging for the state, in the guise of the court, to intervene'.

It is evident that Parliament itself had cause to rethink the wisdom of this non-interventionalist strategy and s 11 of the Family Law Act 1996 would have amended s 41 so as to have obliged a divorce court, when deciding whether it should exercise its powers under the Children Act, (a) to treat the child's welfare as the paramount consideration and (b) to have particular regard to a checklist of factors including 'the wishes and feelings of the child considered in the light of his age and understanding and the circumstances in which those wishes were expressed'.

---

[3] See the Adoption of Children Act 1926, s 3(b).

[4] Adoption and Children Act 2002, s 1(1) and (4)(a).

[5] Though as Butler-Sloss LJ said in the pre-Children Act decision, *Re P (A Minor)(Education)* [1992] 1 FLR 316 at 321: 'The courts over the last few years have become increasingly aware of the importance of listening to the views of older children and taking into account what children say, not necessarily agreeing with what they want nor, indeed, doing what they want, but paying proper respect to older children who are of an age and maturity to make up their minds as to what they think is best for them.'

[6] Children Act 1989, s 1(3)(a).

[7] Section 1(4)(a). The s 8 orders, namely, residence, contact, specific issue and prohibited steps orders, are discussed in Ch 12.

[8] See above p 278.

[9] G Douglas, M Murch, L Scanlan and A Perry 'Safeguarding Children's Welfare in Non-Contentious Divorce: Towards a New Conception of Legal Process?' (2000) 63 MLR 177 at 183–4. As the authors point out, contrary to the Law Commission's recommendation, under r 2.39 of the Family Proceedings Rules 1991, this scrutiny is not carried out until after the district judge has determined that the petition is made out.

Commenting on this provision, the Lord Chancellor (Lord Irvine) said[10] it:

'is fully in tune with the new and increasing contemporary awareness that a child is a person in his or her own right . . . the divorce process must now have regard to the interests and views of the children. They will now have a right to be consulted about the proposals which parents are making for the future in which they have a vital interest.'

In the event, however, together with the rest of the divorce reform contained in Part II, s 11 has not been implemented—and there are no plans to do so.

(c) Public law proceedings

In contrast to private law proceedings it is incumbent upon the court to have regard to the child's ascertainable wishes and feelings in *all* proceedings (whether or not contested) under Part IV of the Children Act.[11] Furthermore, as we discuss shortly, in such proceedings the child will be represented by a children's guardian.[12]

(d) Is the domestic law human rights compliant?

It is perhaps debatable whether the absence of an obligation to ascertain and consider children's views in uncontested s 8 order applications is in breach of the European Convention on Human Rights. Attention has tended to focus[13] upon the human rights implications of the absence of a right to separate representation in private law proceedings (discussed below).[14] There is clearly a case for arguing that the absence of a duty to consider the child's views violates Art 6 which guarantees *everyone* a right to a fair trial and because the outcome of the case affects the child's family life, it could be said also to infringe procedural rights under Art 8. But this has been by no means established by Human Rights jurisprudence[15] and in relation to Art 6 it could be argued that the absence of an obligation to consider the child's views is a matter of substantive rather than procedural law to which the Article therefore has no relevance.[16]

2 INTERNATIONAL LAW

As one commentary has said,[17] internationally the impetus for promoting a new focus on children's participation in the legal process was given by the United Nations Convention on the Rights of the Child 1989. Article 12 in particular states:

---

[10] Hansard, HL Debs Vol 573, Col 1076 (June 1996).

[11] Children Act 1989, s 1(3)(a) and (4)(b). Part IV proceedings basically refer to care proceedings, see Ch 14. Although this obligation is confined to Part IV hearings and not therefore emergency proceedings under Part V, the court can appoint a guardian for the child for these, as well, see below.

[12] Under s 41 of the 1989 Act, discussed below at p 492.

[13] See e.g. Mr Justice Munby 'Making Sure the Child is Heard? Part 2 Representation' [2004] Fam Law 427, J Fortin 'The HRA's impact on litigation and their families' [1999] CFLQ 237 and C Lyon 'Children's Participation in Private Law Proceedings' in *No Fault or Flaw: The Future of the Family Law Act 1996* (eds M Thorpe and E Clarke) 70.

[14] At p 499.

[15] Indeed the decision of the European Court of Human Rights in *Sahin v Germany, Sommerfeld v Germany* [2003] 2 FLR 671 (discussed below at p 502) might be thought to point to the contrary.

[16] Cf *TP and KM v United Kingdom* [2001] 2 FLR 549.

[17] Lowe and Murch, op cit, at 138. See also the analysis by Douglas, et al 'Research into the Operation of Rule 9.5 of the Family Proceedings Rules 1991', op cit, at 2.5ff.

'States Parties shall assure to the child who is capable of forming his or her own views the right to express those views freely in all matters affecting the child, the views of the child being given due weight in accordance with the age and maturity of the child. . . . The child shall in particular be provided the opportunity to be heard in any judicial and administrative proceedings affecting the child, either directly, or through a representative or appropriate body, in a manner consistent with procedural rules of national law.'

Also, not to be overlooked, is Art 9(2) which provides that in any proceedings concerning the separation of a child from his or her parents 'all interested parties shall be given the opportunity to participate in the proceedings and make their views known' [emphasis added]. The reference to all interested parties must include the child.[18]

As Fortin has said[19] the import of Art 12 is that 'it requires *any* child who is capable of forming his or her own views to have the right to express their views, due weight thus being given to those views, in accordance with the child's age and maturity'.

However, symbolically important as Arts 9 and 12 may be, they lack detail and it was to address this that the Council of Europe devised its 1996 Convention on the Exercise of Children's Rights.[20]

The 1996 Convention aims to supplement the UN Convention, inter alia, by providing procedural mechanisms by which the voice of the child can be heard in legal proceedings concerning them. In particular Art 3 provides that a child 'considered by internal law as having sufficient understanding' shall, in the case of judicial proceedings affecting him or her, be granted and entitled to request the following rights:

'a. to receive all relevant information;

b. to be consulted and express his or her views;

c. to be informed of the possible consequences of compliance with these views and the possible consequences of any decision.'

While Art 4 further provides for children to have the right:[21]

'to apply, in person or through other persons or bodies, for a special representative in proceedings before a judicial authority affecting the child where internal law precludes the holders of parental responsibilities from representing the child as a result of a conflict of interest with the latter.'

As one commentator has said[22] the Convention has not had an enthusiastic reception, with another[23] going as far as to say that it is 'weak' and 'toothless' especially when compared with the European Convention on Human Rights.

---

[18] See A Moylan 'Children's Participation in Proceedings—The View from Europe' in *Hearing the Child* (eds M Thorpe an J Cadbury) 175.

[19] *Children's Rights and the Developing Law* (2nd edn) 199.

[20] The Convention came into force in 2000 following ratification by Greece, Poland and Slovenia. At the time of writing there are 10 Contracting States to this Convention.

[21] This is subject to Art 9 which empowers the judicial authority to appoint a special representative for children (irrespective of their capacity or understanding) in cases of a conflict of interest between a child and the holders of parental responsibility. See further the Explanatory Report on the Convention published in 1997 by the Council of Europe.

[22] A Bainham *Children The Modern Law* (3rd edn) 579.

[23] M Freeman *The Moral Status of Children* at 39.

The United Kingdom has not signed this Convention and has given no indication of doing so.

C HOW CHILDREN'S VIEWS ARE INVESTIGATED

Even where their views and wishes and feelings have to be taken into account, children are not normally made parties to private law proceedings (and will not therefore be separately represented)[24] though there is power to do so, at any rate, in proceedings before the High Court and county court.[25] In these proceedings the normal process through which the court will learn of the child's views, wishes and feelings, is by a court welfare report which can be ordered under s 7 of the Children Act 1989. These reports are provided by officers who are now called Children and Family Reporters. Reporters, as we discuss below, are independent of the parties and are appointed by the court to investigate and report on the child's circumstances.

In public law proceedings the position is different. There, the child is a party to the proceedings though rarely appearing in person before the court, and is commonly represented by what is now called the children's guardian who in turn can instruct a solicitor. The creation of a system for separate representation of children by guardians in fact pre-dates both the Children Act 1989 and the UN Convention on the Rights of the Child, being first introduced in 1984 (before that the child's interests were assumed to be represented by the parents).[26]

Before examining the differing roles of children and family court reporters and guardians, it is necessary to say something about the service that administers them.

1 CAFCASS

(a) The previous position

Before the reforms introduced in 2001 by the Criminal Justice and Court Services Act 2000 there were three separate services concerned with making reports about and/or representing children in family proceedings, namely the Guardian ad Litem and Reporting Officer (GALRO) Service, the Family Court Welfare Service and the Children's Branch of the Official Solicitor's Department.

The GALRO service was administered and financed by local authorities each of which had to set up a panel. The guardians ad litem themselves had to be qualified in social work and be a member of a panel. However, to ensure that the guardian was independent of all the parties, particularly the local authority involved in the particular case, the individual appointed could not (a) be a member or officer or servant of the local authority or authorised person bringing the proceedings, or (b) have been at any time in the past an officer of the authority or voluntary organisation who has been directly

---

[24] But note the power to appoint a child's guardian under s 41(6A) of the 1989 Act, inserted by the Adoption and Children Act 2002 s 122(1)(b), discussed below.

[25] FPR 1991, r 9.5, discussed below at p 499.

[26] The need to give the child a separate voice in care proceedings was first highlighted in 1974 by the Field-Fisher Committee of Inquiry into the death of Maria Colwell (HMSO, 1974).

concerned in that capacity in arrangements relating to the care or accommodation and welfare of the child, or (c) be a serving probation officer. Although the courts jealously protected guardians' independence, quashing, for example, in one case,[27] an attempt by one authority to lay down in advance the normal maximum time that should be spent on any particular case, the system was open to obvious doubts about the true independence of guardians. A clear conflict arose if, for example, the local authority made a complaint about the conduct of a case by a guardian since it was still involved in considering whether that guardian should continue to serve on the panel. In short, as we said in the last edition,[28] if guardians were to be seen as being truly independent, it was necessary to have some independent body which could both oversee and supervise their work.

The Family Court Welfare Service was formerly a branch of the Probation Service and what were then called court welfare officers were qualified probation officers.[29]

At one time the Official Solicitor played a large role in representing children especially in wardship proceedings[30] but even before the creation of CAFCASS had gradually retreated from the role, save in the most difficult cases and particularly those involving medical treatment.[31]

(b) The decision to change the system

There seemed an obvious case for rationalisation of these separate schemes and in the autumn of 1997 a joint review by interested Government departments and bodies concluded that each of the above services could provide an improved service to the courts, better safeguard the interests of children and reduce wasteful overlaps and increase efficiency.[32] Following this review, the Lord Chancellor announced in 2000 the decision to set up the Children and Family Court Advisory and Support Service (CAFCASS).[33] This was achieved by the Criminal Justice and Court Services Act 2000 which came into force in April 2001.

(c) The current position

CAFCASS is a non-departmental public body sponsored by the Department for Education and Skills, with ministerial responsibility resting with the Minister for Children, Young People and Families. Its key aim is 'putting children first' by supporting children and their families in Family Courts and other settings ensuring that their voices are heard, so decisions can be reached that are in the best interests of children.[34] The service replaces and combines the services of the former GALRO service, the Family Court Welfare Service and the Children's Division of the Official Solicitor's Office. Former employees of the

---

[27] *R v Cornwall County Council, ex p Cornwall and Isles of Scilly Guardians ad Litem and Reporting Officers Panel* [1992] 2 All ER 471.

[28] At 556.

[29] For a brief discussion of the history of the service see e.g. S Cretney *Family Law in the Twentieth Century—A History* at 770, N Lowe and R White *Wards of Court* (1st edn, 1979) ch 9 and the references there cited.

[30] See eg N Lowe and R White *Wards of Court* (2nd edn, 1986) ch 9.

[31] See eg R White, P Carr and N Lowe *Children Act in Practice* (2nd edn, 1995) 10.22–10.25.

[32] *Support Services in Family Proceedings—Future Organisation of Court Welfare Services* (1998).

[33] *Setting up a unified Children and Family Court Advisory and Support Service (CAFCASS) "Children First"* (2000).

[34] CAFCASS *Annual Report and Accounts 2001–2002* at p 8.

latter two services are now CAFCASS employees while former members of the GALRO panels can either be CAFCASS employees or self employed.

A further development has been the Children Act 2004, s 35 under which the functions of CAFCASS relating to family proceedings[35] involving the welfare of children ordinarily resident in Wales was transferred to the National Assembly for Wales. Consequent upon this transfer the work of CAFCASS officers in Wales is performed by 'Welsh family proceedings officers'.

Following the creation of CAFCASS changes were made to the names of its various officers. In particular, court welfare officers became known as 'children and family court reporters'[36] and guardians ad litem have become known as 'children's guardians'. The former responsibilities of the Official Solicitor to represent children who are the subject of family proceedings have been taken over by the 'CAFCASS High Court team'[37] (formerly known as 'CAFCASS Legal', which term is now used to describe the CAFCASS in-house lawyers). All CAFCASS employees and contractors are expected to work in accordance with the *CAFCASS Service Principles and Standards*.[38] Inspectors of the magistrates' court service are responsible for inspecting and reporting to the Lord Chancellor on the performance of CAFCASS and its officers.[39] Any individual wishing to complain about any aspect of the work of CAFCASS may do so according to the terms of its complaints process.[40]

The principal functions of CAFCASS are set out by s 12(1) of the 2000 Act, namely, to

'(a) safeguard and promote the welfare of children,

(b) give advice to any court about any application made to it in any such [family] proceedings,

(c) make provision for the children to be represented in such proceedings, and

(d) provide information, advice and other support for the children and their families.'

The point has been made[41] that under s 12(1)(a) the duty to safeguard and promote children's welfare (which is comparable to local authority functions under Part III of the Children Act 1989)[42] falls short of treating children's welfare as paramount. This is in contrast to the *Service Standards* though the two can be reconciled by remembering that whereas s 12(1)(a) is referring to children in general, *Service Standards* relates to working with a particular child.

(d) Criticisms of CAFCASS

Despite the obvious sense in amalgamating the disparate schemes for safeguarding children's interests, CAFCASS has been the subject of considerable criticism. It certainly

---

[35] Which has the same meaning as in the Criminal Justice and Court Services Act 2000, s 12, see Children Act 2004, s 35(3).

[36] Rather confusingly, however, a local authority officer appointed under s 7 of the Children Act 1989 (discussed below) is known as a 'welfare officer'.

[37] For the types of cases that should be handled by the team, see *CAFCASS Practice Note* [2004] 1 FLR 1190.

[38] Published in March 2003 (CAFCASS).   [39] See s 17 of the 2000 Act.

[40] See Butterworths *Family Law Service* at 3A [5027] ff.

[41] See Butterworths *Family Law Service* at 3A [5002.2].   [42] Discussed below at p 698.

had, as one commentary puts it,[43] a troubled introduction including the quashing of its decision to use only employed contacts and not to proceed with the option of self-employment for former guardians ad litem.[44] One consequence of this early dispute was the haemorrhaging away from the service of experienced guardians who decided to retire rather than work for CAFCASS.[45] As highlighted in a report by the House of Commons Select Committee on CAFCASS[46] a major cause of the initial problems was the unrealistically short timetable for the establishment of the service which, in the Committee's view was a serious misjudgment. Other problems identified by the Committee included unacceptable delays, shortage of qualified staff and confused lines of accountability.

In response to the criticisms, CAFCASS introduced national standards which, as we have discussed, are measured by HM Magistrates' Courts Services Inspectorate. It also introduced a complaints procedure. But while the service may well have improved its performance after a poor beginning,[47] as one commentator has pertinently said,[48] the key question is whether the service will be able to cope adequately both with the expansion of separate representation in private law proceedings[49] and the already onerous provision of representation in public law proceedings.

2 WELFARE REPORTS

(a) The power under section 7

As we have said, the principal means of ascertaining the child's view in private law proceedings is through a welfare report.[50] Section 7(1) of the 1989 Act empowers any court, when considering *any* question with respect to a child under the 1989 Act, to ask an officer of the Service (ie CAFCASS) or a Welsh family proceedings officer or a local authority to report to the court 'on such matters relating to the welfare of that child as are required to be dealt with in the report'. Insofar as this role is taken on by a CAFCASS officer it will be discharged by a children and family reporter. The power to ask for a report in relation to *any* issue under the 1989 Act means that welfare reports may be ordered in care proceedings. However, as we discuss shortly, this independent role is usually undertaken by guardians who, unlike children and family reporters, represent the child in the proceedings. Nevertheless, on occasion it might be necessary for a reporter to act in care cases to save time and resources. Indeed, in some cases such a reporter may have already done so,

---

[43] Butterworths *Family Law Service* at 3A [5001.2].

[44] *Re (on the application of the National Association of Guardians ad Litem and Reporting Officers) v Children and Family Court Advisory and Support Service* [2001] EWHC 693 (Admin), [2002] 1 FLR 255.

[45] But note the rejection of this allegation by J Tross (the then CAFCASS Chief Executive) in 'CAFCASS—Moving Forward' [2002] Fam Law 829, at 830.

[46] Published in July 2003 and summarised in [2003] Fam Law 626. Note also the government reply: *The Response of the Government and the Children and Family Court Advisory and Support Service to the Constitutional Affairs Committee's Report on Children and Family Court Advisory and Support Service* (CAFCASS) (2003) Cm 6004.

[47] See J Tross 'CAFCASS Present and Future' [2004] Fam Law 731.

[48] A Bainham *Children The Modern Law* (3rd edn) 587.

[49] From 2003–4 to 2004–5 there was a 108% rise in requests to the service for one of its officers to assume the role as guardian ad litem under FPR 1991, r 9.5. See below pp 499ff.

[50] For a consumer view of the Service see A Buchanan, J Hunt, H Bretherton and V Bream *Families in Conflict: Perspectives of Children and Parents in the Family and Court Welfare Service* (2003).

for example, in family proceedings where the court decides, after hearing the evidence, that it should exercise its powers under s 37 and invite the local authority to investigate the case with a view to the authority applying for a care or supervision order.[51]

Section 7 empowers the courts in private law proceedings to ask a local authority to report rather than a children and family reporter. However, this is not intended to result in local authorities being asked as a matter of routine, but only in those cases where they have an obvious connection with the case.[52] If a local authority is already involved, applications may properly be made to the court hearing the private law proceedings for them to provide a report under s 7.[53] Where there are both private law proceedings and investigations being carried out by the police and social services, then s 7 can and should be used to require the local authority to report to the court on the nature, progress and outcome of the investigation. In this way the court can ensure the co-ordination of the private law proceedings with the statutory local authority child abuse investigations.[54]

Under s 7(5) it is the duty of the local authority or reporter to comply with any court request for a welfare report. However, where the court decides to ask the local authority to report, it can ask them to arrange for this to be done either by one of their officers or 'such other person (other than an officer of the Service or a Welsh family proceedings officer) as the authority consider appropriate'.[55] There is no power under s 7 to order a local authority to instruct a child psychiatrist to prepare a report for the court,[56] nor more generally to order any form of residential assessment.[57] It should be appreciated that both a children and family reporter and a local authority welfare officer have an independent role, being neither the child's representative nor a witness for either party. In relation to the reporter (CFR) it has been said[58] that manifestly he:

'acts independently and exercises an independent discretion as to the nature and extent of his investigations and inquiries an no less in the manner in which he approaches them . . . It is through the CFR that the judge most evidently executes that part of his function which is inquisitorial. The CFR in turn depends upon the judge to give due weight in the scales of justice to the outcome of his investigations. Both judge and CFR are united sharing the same ultimate objective, namely, the protection of children and the advancement of their welfare. In pursuit of that overriding objective each must be free to operate independently as well as collaboratively and independent operation includes the exercise of an independent discretion'.

---

[51] Discussed below at p 580.

[52] See Law Com No 172, para 6.17. For examples of a welfare report being prepared by a local authority in private law proceedings, see *Re M (Intractable Contact Dispute: Interim Care Order)* [2003] EWHC 1024 (Fam), [2003] 2 FLR 636, report ordered in a father's application to enforce a contact order against the mother who had made allegations of sexual abuse by the father; and *Re H (Abduction: Grave Risk)* [2003] EWCA Civ 355, [2003] 2 FLR 141, an international child abduction case.

[53] Per Wall J in *W v Wakefield City Council* [1995] 1 FLR 170.

[54] Per Wall J in *Re A and B (Minors) (No 2)* [1995] 1 FLR 351 at 368–9.

[55] Section 7(1)(b). This is intended to cover the situation where, as a result of close co-operation, the NSPCC, for example, acting on behalf of the local authority, is seen to be the key worker for the particular child: see R White, P Carr and N Lowe *A Guide to the Children Act 1989* (1990), para 8.6.

[56] *Re K (Contact: Psychiatric Report)* [1995] 2 FLR 432, CA.

[57] *R v R (Private Law Proceedings: Residential Assessment)* [2002] 2 FLR 953.

[58] Per Thorpe LJ in *Re M (Disclosure: Children and Family Reporter)* [2002] EWCA Civ 1199, [2002] 2 FLR 893 at [26].

Before the creation of CAFCASS, welfare officers were thought to be officers of the court but now it has since been said[59] that the Children and Family Reporters are not officers of the court but officers of the service, though nothing seems to turn on this distinction.

(b) When reports should be ordered

As explained by the 'Best practice note' drafted by the Children Act Advisory Committee (hereinafter referred to as *Best Practice*),[60] the ordering of a welfare officer's report is a judicial act requiring inquiry into the circumstances of the child. A report should not be ordered unless there is a live issue under the Children Act, and before a report is ordered consideration should be given to the power to refer the parties (with their consent) to mediation. According to the *Private Law Programme*[61] wherever possible a CAFCASS officer should be available at the First Hearing Dispute Resolution appointment both to the court and the family, to facilitate early dispute resolution rather than the provision of a formal report. Commonly, the decision to order a report will be taken at the preliminary stages of the proceedings, though there is power to order a report at any stage. The court has an unappealable discretion to decide whether or not to ask for a report.[62] Apart from appreciating that welfare officers' time is limited and must be spent on cases where it will be most valuable,[63] and, mindful of the general duty under s 1(2) to be aware of the likelihood of delay prejudicing the child's welfare, the court might have to balance the advantages to be gained from a report against the disadvantage of the time it takes to obtain it.[64] Nevertheless, the expectation is that some sort of report will be required in most contested cases.

If a report is ordered, then, as *Best Practice* explains:

'. . . the judge, district judge or justices' clerk should explain briefly to the parties what will be involved and should emphasise the need to co-operate with the welfare officer and specifically to keep any appointments. In particular when the principle of contact is in dispute the parties should be told that the welfare officer will probably wish to see the applicant parent alone with the child. It should also be emphasised that the report, when received, is a confidential document and must not be shown to anyone who is not a named party to the application'.

It has long been established[65] that the reporting and mediation roles are quite distinct and to some extent incompatible and that accordingly, as CAFCASS *Service Principles and Standards* now states:[66]

---

[59] Per Wall J in *Re M*, above, at [96].

[60] See *Handbook of Best Practice in Children Act Cases* (CAAC 1997) Appendix A. Although this was drafted before the creation of CAFCASS, as Clarke Hall and Morrison says at 1 [1243], it still appears to remain best practice with appropriate amendments to terminology.

[61] Issued by the then President, Dame Elizabeth Butler-Sloss in November 2004 (published in January 2005), discussed above at p 20.

[62] *Re W (Welfare Reports)* [1995] 2 FLR 142, CA.

[63] As the Law Commission observed (Law Com No 172, para 6.15), the court has to be moderate when exercising its powers. Note also *Re B (Minors), B v B* (1973) 3 Fam Law 43, in which the court expressed its disapproval of ordering more than one report in any case.

[64] See eg *Re H (Minors) (Welfare Reports)* [1990] 2 FLR 172, CA.

[65] See *Scott v Scott* [1986] 2 FLR 320, CA, and *Re H (Conciliation: Welfare Reports)* [1986] 1 FLR 476. The Booth Committee (Report of the Matrimonial Causes Procedure Committee, 1985) at para 4.63 had already recommended that the same officer should not both conciliate and later report in the same case.

[66] Ibid at 3.29.

'If CAFCASS is subsequently ordered to prepare a report by the Court, another Practitioner should be assigned to the case and should not be given access to any information or statements made during the course of the mediation process.'

It also expected that such appointees should carry out their investigative task and not subsequently assume a mediation role.[67]

It has been held that, once the report is ordered, the desirable practice is to ascertain when it can be expected and to fix a specific date in the light of that information.[68]

(c) The form, content and disclosure of reports

Once appointed, reporters or welfare officers are generally expected to investigate the circumstances of the child or children concerned and the important figures in their lives with a view to providing the court with factual information on which to make a decision.[69] There is a duty upon children and family reporters and welfare officers to see the child whenever possible with each of the parties to a residence or contact application, for as Johnson J commented in *Re P (A Minor) (Inadequate Welfare Report)*,[70]

'The whole point of the . . . system is that, because in the nature of things the court cannot itself observe the relationship between the children and the parents, the [reporter or welfare officer] acts as the eyes and ears of the court and provides the court with an independent and objective assessment of the relationships involved. Here the report was inadequate. The inquiry was conducted in such a way as to make it impossible for her to form any views about the relationships involved.'

A *fortiori* all children should be seen by the court welfare officer unless there are strong reasons for not doing so. If a child is not seen the reasons for this should be given in the report.[71]

The report may be made in writing or orally as the court requires.[72] In practice it is usually made in writing in accordance with CAFCASS format and guidelines.[73] According to those guidelines, reports will:

'3.11.1 set out all relevant information which the Practitioner has acquired through his/her enquiries, making clear from what service the information has been obtained and distinguishing between matters of fact and matters of opinion;

3.11.2 make clear recommendations (or explain why recommendations cannot be made) which draw on relevant aspects of the Welfare Checklist;

3.11.3 explain the basis upon which those recommendations have been made, including reasons both for and against those recommendations.'

It is inevitable that to some extent a reporter or welfare officer will rely on hearsay evidence. Indeed, it has been said that in the nature of things such reporters or officers

---

[67] *Scott v Scott*, above. See also *National Standards*.

[68] *B v B (Minors) (Interviews and Listing Arrangements)* [1994] 2 FLR 489.

[69] Per Dillon LJ in *Scott v Scott*, above, at 322.

[70] [1996] 2 FCR 285 at 291. See also *Re W (A Minor) (Custody)* (1983) 4 FLR 492, at 501, CA, per Cumming-Bruce LJ.

[71] But cf the findings of Buchanan et al, op cit.

[72] Section 7(3). The normal expectation is that the report will be written.

[73] See para 3.10 of the CAFCASS *Services, Principles and Standards*.

could not do what is required of them and comply with the hearsay rule.[74] However, although s 7(4) provides that, regardless of any rule of law which would otherwise prevent it from doing so, the court may take into account any statement contained in (or evidence given in respect of matters referred to in) the report, regard should still be had to *Thompson v Thompson*.[75] In that case it was said that on controversial issues, eg making adverse findings against a party, if a reporter or officer is constrained to pass on second-hand evidence, he should endeavour to make this explicit and indicate his source of information and his reasons, if he has any, for agreeing with such an opinion.

The children and family court reporter or welfare officer must file his report either as directed by the court or, in the absence of a direction, at least 14 days before the hearing at which it will be given or considered, and as soon as practicable the court must serve a copy of the report on the parties and any guardians.[76] The report is a confidential document and should not be disclosed to anyone other than a party, his legal representative, the CAFCASS officer and the Legal Services Commission without the leave of the court.[77] In exceptional cases the court can order that the report should not be disclosed to the parties.[78] Accordingly, reporters or welfare officers should give no undertaking that what they are told will be kept confidential and not disclosed in the report.[79] It is established that the divorce county court has jurisdiction to grant leave for information contained in a welfare report in a previous case to be used in the case before it.[80] Notwithstanding the confidentiality of the report it has been held[81] that a children and family reporter does *not* require court leave to report concerns about possible child abuse to the relevant statutory authorities.

The previous requirement that the children and family reporter or welfare officer had to attend the hearing unless excused by the court has been changed. It is now provided[82] that upon the filing of a report the court *may* direct that the welfare officer attend. As *Best Practice* states, when such a direction is given, the court should 'ensure that the officer gives evidence as soon as possible after the case has opened (and in any event on the first day) and is released after the evidence has been completed'. This change of rules and practice represents another attempt to ensure that calls on welfare officers' time are kept to a minimum. Nevertheless, these developments are not intended to prejudice the right of any party to question the reporter or welfare officer about his

---

[74] Per O'Connor LJ in *Webb v Webb* [1986] 1 FLR 462 at 463, CA.

[75] [1986] 1 FLR 212n at 216–17, CA. See also *Edwards v Edwards* [1986] 1 FLR 187, and *H v H (A Minor), K v K (minors)* [1990] Fam 86, CA.

[76] Family Proceedings Rules 1991 r 4.13(1), as amended; Family Proceedings Courts (Children Act 1989) Rules 1991 r 13(1), as amended.

[77] Family Proceedings Rules 1991 r 4.23(1); Family Proceedings Courts (Children Act 1989) Rules 1991 r 23(1).

[78] *Re M (Minors) (Disclosure of Evidence)* [1994] 1 FLR 760, CA and *Re B (Minor) (Disclosure of Evidence)* [1993] Fam 142, CA, but note that the appropriate test is probably now that laid down in *Re D (Minors) (Adoption Reports: Confidentiality)* [1996] AC 593, HL.

[79] *Re G (Minors) (Welfare Report: Disclosure)* [1993] 2 FLR 293, CA.

[80] *Brown v Matthews* [1990] Ch 662, CA.

[81] *Re M (Disclosure: Children and Family Reporter)* [2002] EWCA Civ 1199, [2002] 2 FLR 893—during preparation of the report the mother and sister alleged that the father had behaved inappropriately in front of the children.

[82] Family Proceedings Rules 1991 r 4.13(3), as amended; Family Proceedings Courts (Children Act 1989) Rules 1991 r 13(3), as amended.

report.[83] However, it is important not to draw the reporter or welfare officer into the adversarial battle between the parties. As Thorpe LJ said in *Re B (Residence Order: Status Quo)*,[84] the function of the reporter or officer

'is essentially to submit for the guidance of the judge very carefully considered reports. I cannot imagine a case in which it would be necessary for the [children and family reporter] to be exposed to a whole day of what was effectively cross-examination by one side or the other. It is wasteful of the [reporter's] precious time and, in the end, it does not help the judge who wants to see the wood and is invariably helped by being spared the trees.'

Recommendations contained in a s 7 report are not binding upon the court but if a court departs from a recommendation it should state the reasons for so doing.[85] Although there are several reported examples of the court not following a recommendation,[86] in practice the children and family reporter's view commands great respect and it should be appreciated that in most cases he is the most influential figure in the decision-making process.[87]

Normally, clear-cut recommendations should only be rejected after hearing the welfare officer's oral evidence.[88] However, bearing in mind the principle of delay set out in s 1(2), it is within the court's power to depart from a recommendation even where the officer does not attend the hearing.[89]

3 THE ROLE OF THE CHILDREN'S GUARDIAN

(a) Distinguishing guardians and children and family court reporters [90]

As discussed earlier in this chapter, the crucial role of giving children a voice in public law proceedings in particular is provided by the 'children's guardian'.

Unlike children and family court reporters, guardians represent children in the proceedings and are therefore parties to them. They also have the duty to instruct legal representation for the child.[91]

Notwithstanding these differences guardians and children and family court reporters have many functions in common. Both have a duty to report to the court and be examined on their report and both are under a duty to consider the welfare or interests of the child

---

[83] Family Proceedings Rules 1991 r 4.13(3)(b) and r 13(3)(b) and see *Re I and H (Contact: Evidence)* [1998] 1 FLR 876, CA.

[84] [1998] 1 FLR 368 at 371.

[85] See eg *Re V (Residence: Review)* [1995] 2 FLR 1010, CA and *Re L (Residence: Justices Reasons)* [1995] 2 FLR 445; *Re P (A Minor) (Contact)* [1994] 1 FCR 285 and *M v C (Children Orders: Reasons)* [1993] 2 FLR 584.

[86] See eg *Re P (A Minor) (Inadequate Welfare Report)* [1996] 2 FCR 285; *Re W (A Minor) (Custody)* (1983) 4 FLR 492, 13 Fam Law 47, CA; *Leete v Leete and Stevens* [1984] Fam Law 21; and *H v H* [1984] Fam Law 112, CA.

[87] See eg M Murch *Justice and Welfare in Divorce* (1980) ch 8.

[88] *Re W (Residence)* [1999] 2 FLR 390, CA. *Re CB (Access: Court Welfare Reports)* [1995] 1 FLR 622, CA. See also *Re F (Minors) (Contact: Appeal)* [1997] 1 FCR 523, CA.

[89] *Re C (Section 8 Order: Court Welfare Officer)* [1995] 1 FLR 617, CA.

[90] For interesting research on this issue see A James, A James and S McNamee 'Constructing Children's Welfare in Family Proceedings' [2003] Fam Law 889.

[91] These differences were highlighted by Butler-Sloss LJ in *Re S (A Minor) (Guardian Ad Litem/Welfare Officer)* [1993] 1 FLR 110 at 114–15, CA.

and thus to advise the court independently of the other parties as to what is best for the child. These similarities prompted Butler-Sloss LJ to say that one would not normally expect to have both a guardian and welfare officer appointed in the same case.[92] A further blurring of the distinction between the two officers is with respect to training. CAFCASS officers are now recruited as 'convergence trained' officers which means that they are trained in the functions of both children's guardians and children and family reporters.[93]

There are certain restrictions on who can be appointed as a guardian. For example, a serving probation officer who in that capacity has previously been concerned with the child or his family cannot be appointed nor should an individual who is a member, officer or servant of the local authority that is party to the proceedings.[94] These restrictions emphasise and preserve the independence of the children's guardian.

(b) When guardians should be appointed

Under s 41 of the Children Act 1989 courts are required in 'specified proceedings' to appoint a children's guardian for the child 'unless satisfied that it is not necessary to do so in order to safeguard his interests'. When first introduced 'specified proceedings' essentially meant public law proceedings[95] and was intended to lead to appointments being the norm in care proceedings.[96] Notwithstanding this expectation, it was held in *R v CAFCASS*[97] that the Service is not under a duty to make provision to enable it, immediately on request by the court to make available an officer of the Service for appointment as guardian. The general target, however, has been stated to have appointments made in two working days[98] (though the Protocol for Judicial Case Management in Public Law Children Act Cases[99] requires the appointment to be made on the day proceedings commence).

The difference between representation in public and private law proceedings is striking and is a vivid illustration that (prior to the amendments mentioned below) the dichotomy between private and public law proceedings has not been harmonised by the 1989 Act.[100]

In the context of adoption, the Adoption and Children Act 2002, s 122(1)(a) amended s 41(6) of the 1989 Act to extend 'specified proceedings' to include applications for the making or revoking of an adoption placement order made under s 21 of the 2002 Act.[101]

---

92 In *Re S (A Minor) (Guardian Ad Litem/Welfare Officer)*, above at 116. But for a case where this was done see *L v L (Minors) (Separate Representation)* [1994] 1 FLR 156, CA. Note also *Re T and E (Proceedings: Conflict of Interests)* [1995] 1 FLR 581 in which Wall J observed that it was not necessary to appoint more than one guardian to represent children involved in the same proceedings even if their interests conflict.

93 See Clarke Hall and Morrison at 1[1229].   94 FPCA 1991 r 10(7); FPR 1991 r 4.10(7).

95 'Specified proceedings' are defined by s 41(6) and include care and supervision proceedings, cases where a s 37 direction has been made, discharge applications, applications under Part V of the Children Act and contact in care proceedings under s 34.

96 During the debates on the Bill, David Mellor MP said on behalf of the government that guardians should be appointed in over 90% of cases: HC Official Report, SC B, 23 May 1989, col 255.

97 [2003] EWHC 235 (Admin), [2005] 1 FLR 953.

98 Per Wall J in *Re J (Care Proceedings: Disclosure)* [2003] EWHC 796 (Fam), [2003] 2 FLR 522—a delay of 6 weeks in that case was said to be 'unacceptable'. In the context of emergency protection proceedings, a delay of 10 days was thought to be 'wholly unacceptable', per Munby J in *X Council v B (Emergency Protection Orders)* [2005] 1 FLR 341.

99 [2003] 2 FLR 719, discussed further below at p 758.

100 See *W v Wakefield City Council* [1995] 1 FLR 170.   101 Discussed below at p 840.

But more radically s 122(1)(b) of the 2002 Act extends the definition of 'specified proceedings' by adding s 41(6A) which provides that Rules of Court may bring within the definition proceedings for the making, varying or discharging of a s 8 order.[102] It remains to be seen how wide or narrow the Rules will be.

(c) The guardian's duties

The guardian's general duty is to safeguard the interests of the child,[103] and more specifically to advise on the following:

'(a) whether the child is of sufficient understanding for any purpose including the child's refusal to submit to a medical or psychiatric examination or other assessment that the court has power to require direct or order;

(b) the wishes of the child in respect of any matter relevant to the proceedings, including his attendance at court;

(c) the appropriate forum for the proceedings;

(d) the appropriate timing of the proceedings or any part of them;

(e) the options available to the court in respect of the child and the suitability of each such option including what order should be made in determining the application;

(f) any other matter on which the court seeks his advice or about which he considers that the court should be informed.'[104]

In addition, since they should normally be appointed at an early stage in the proceedings,[105] guardians should also be able to advise the court about the discharge of an emergency protection order, the making or extending of interim care or supervision orders and about directions in interim orders.

Unless one has already been appointed (which in many areas has become frequently the case in view of CAFCASS's inability to appoint a guardian at the beginning of proceedings),[106] the guardian (save where he is an Officer of the Service authorised to conduct litigation and intends to conduct the proceedings on the child's behalf)[107] is required to appoint a solicitor to act for the child.[108] However, notwithstanding this duty

---

[102] On which see M Millin 'Speaking for Children' [2003] Fam Law 217. Note also s 122(2) of the 2002 Act which inserts s 93(2)(bb) into the 1989 Act under which Rules of Court may make provision for children to be separately represented in proceedings, see below p 500.

[103] Section 41(2)(b).

[104] Family Proceedings Courts (Children Act 1989) Rules 1991 (FPCA 1991) r 11(4); FPR 1991 r 4.11(4).

[105] Ibid, r 10(1) and r 4.10(1) respectively. Though the court has power to make an appointment at any stage of the proceedings.

[106] As pointed out by Clarke Hall and Morrison at 1[1272] and note *Appointment of Solicitors for Children: Recommended Good Practice for court appointment of solicitors for children in specified proceedings in absence of children's guardian* (a good practice statement prepared by a sub-committee of the Advisory Committee on Judicial Case Management in Public Law Children Act Cases).

[107] See FPR 1991, r 4.11A(2) [not reproduced in FPCA 1991]. Aliter if the child wishes to instruct a solicitor direct and the child's guardian or court considers that he is of sufficient understanding to do so. As Clarke Hall and Morrison at 1[1272.1], n 2 point out, this provision seems odd for why should a guardian instruct a solicitor for the child given that he wishes to instruct one himself?

[108] Ibid, r 11(2) and 4.11(2) respectively. Under s 41(3), (4) the court may appoint a solicitor for the child if there is no guardian or if the child, having sufficient understanding to instruct a solicitor, wishes to do so, or if the court thinks that it is in the child's interests to be represented. But this power is confined to 'specified proceedings': *Re W (A Minor) (Contact)* [1994] 1 FLR 843.

to instruct a solicitor the Legal Services Commission may decide that the merits of a case do not warrant legal representation and refuse legal aid.[109]

Once both a guardian and a solicitor have been appointed, it is for the former to consider how the case should be presented in court on the child's behalf and to give instructions to the solicitor.[110] However, where the child wishes and is able to give instructions on his own behalf[111] which conflict with those of the guardian, the solicitor must take his instructions from the child.[112] In that event the guardian continues with his or her duties save for instructing the solicitor.[113]

(d) Discharging the duties

To carry out his duties, a guardian must investigate all the circumstances, including interviewing such persons as he thinks appropriate or as the court directs, inspect local authority records (see below), and bring to the court's attention such records and documents which in his opinion may be of assistance to the case. He may also obtain such professional assistance as he thinks appropriate or which the court directs him to obtain.[114] According to the CAFCASS Service Principles and Standards[115] guardians should work in a manner and at a pace which are appropriate to the child's age and understanding and the seriousness of the child's situation. He should develop a comprehensive understanding of the child's needs in the light of the child's age and understanding.

The guardian's investigations are confidential,[116] but it is for the court and not the guardian to waive that confidentiality.[117] Consequently, all information relevant to the enquiry should be disclosed in the report. It is not within the guardian's power to promise a child to withhold information from the court.[118] On the other hand, information revealed to the guardian in the course of the investigations should not be disclosed to third parties without prior court leave. This latter proposition is not, however, entirely straightforward, for on the basis of Oxfordshire County Council v P[119] and Re G (a minor) (social worker: disclosure),[120] both of which involved the disclosure of parental admissions about the responsibility for non-accidental injuries to their children, it seems that while guardians should not disclose the information direct to the police without court leave, they can properly disclose the information to the social worker involved in the case and in turn that

---

[109] W and Others v Legal Services Commission [2000] 2 FLR 821.

[110] See the Protocol for Working Relationship between Children Panel solicitors and Guardians ad Litem (Law Society, 2000).

[111] In cases of doubt, expert opinion might be required: Re H (A Minor) (Care Proceedings: Child's Wishes) [1993] 1 FLR 440.

[112] See FPCA 1991 r 12(1) and FPR 1991 r 4.12(1). See C Sawyer 'The competence of children to participate in family proceedings' (1995) 7 CFLQ 180.

[113] He may, with leave, have legal representation: ibid, r 11(3) and 4.11(3) respectively.

[114] See r 11(9) and r 4.11(9) respectively. But note r 18(1) and r 4.18(1) under which no medical or psychiatric examination of the child for the purpose of adducing evidence should be carried out without leave of the court.

[115] See para 2.5.

[116] Per Ward J in Oxfordshire County Council v P [1995] Fam 161 and per Hale J in Cleveland County Council v F [1995] 2 All ER 236.

[117] See Re G (Minors) (Welfare Report) [1993] 2 FLR 293, CA.

[118] Compare Re D (Minors) (Adoption Reports: Confidentiality) [1996] AC 593, HL.

[119] Followed by Cleveland County Council v F, above.   [120] [1996] 2 All ER 65, CA.

information can be revealed to the police at a subsequent child protection conference without court leave.[121]

The 1989 Act gives the guardian extensive rights to examine and take copies of any records of or held by a local authority or the NSPCC in relation to a child and compiled in connection with any function of the social services committee.[122] These include child protection conference minutes[123] and files prepared in the exercise of the authority's function as an adoption agency.[124] The guardian does not, however, have a right to see Crown Prosecution Service files, although the court may order such disclosure.[125]

At the end of these investigations the guardian produces a written report advising on the interests of the child.[126] Like a children and family reporter's report, the guardian's report should set out all the relevant information which the guardian has acquired through his enquiries, making clear the source and distinguishing matters of fact and opinion. It should make clear recommendations or explain what recommendations cannot be made.[127]

As with other court documents, the report is confidential and should not be disclosed to those other than the parties, their legal representatives and the Legal Services Commission without leave of the court.[128] Furthermore, it is clear that this confidentiality continues after the conclusion of the hearing. It has been held,[129] for example, that court leave was required to disclose the report to a family centre which was connected with the social services department and which offered therapeutic treatment to the children concerned.

Guardians are, unless specifically excused, required to attend court hearings[130] and can be questioned about their reports. However, as Ward LJ observed in Re N (Child Abuse: Evidence),[131] guardians should be careful not to confuse their roles. They cannot and should not attempt to be experts in all matters about which they have to report, though as experienced social workers they may well have expertise in a particular area. Ward LJ also observed that the guardians have to decide in the exercise of their duty to safeguard the child's interests, whether or not they believe what the child says. It is therefore reasonable for that belief to be stated in the report as a basis for reaching a conclusion and giving the advice advanced. There is no entitlement to sideline the guardian on the ground that his recommendation has been adverse to that party in an earlier part of the case.[132]

As with court welfare reports, the evidence and recommendations of guardians are not binding on the court,[133] but they are very influential and in any event the court should give its reasons for departing from them.[134]

---

[121] See N Lowe 'Guardians Ad Litem and Disclosure' [1996] Fam Law 618.

[122] But not therefore of the housing or education committees.

[123] Children Act 1989 s 42(1) as amended by the Courts and Legal Services Act 1990 Sch 16, para 18.

[124] Re T (A Minor) (Guardian ad Litem: Case Record) [1994] 1 FLR 632, CA.

[125] Nottingham County Council v H [1995] 1 FLR 115.

[126] Unless the court otherwise directs, this should be filed with the court seven days before the date fixed for the hearing. Copies are served by the court on the parties as soon as practicable thereafter: FPCA 1991 r 11(7) and FPR 1991 r 4.11(7).

[127] See CAFCASS Service Principles and Standards para 3.

[128] FPCA 1991 r 23(1); FPR 1991 r 4.23(1).

[129] Re C (Guardian ad Litem: Disclosure of Report) [1996] 1 FLR 61.

[130] FPCA 1991 r 11(4); FPR 1991 r 4.11(4).   [131] [1996] 2 FLR 214 at 223, CA.

[132] Re U (Re-Opening of Appeal) [2005] EWCA 52, [2005] 2 FLR 444 at [99], per Butler-Sloss P.

[133] See eg Buckinghamshire County Council v M [1994] 2 FLR 506, CA.

[134] See eg Re W (Minor) (Secure Accommodation Order) [1993] 1 FLR 692.

Normally the guardian's appointment ceases at the conclusion of the proceedings and it has been held,[135] for example, that a court cannot order that a guardian should have contact with a child after a care order has been made. It is now clear that the appointment will end upon the making of a supervision order.[136] Nevertheless it seems that the conclusion of proceedings may not ipso facto mean that the guardian becomes functus officio. At any rate this was the view of Stuart-White J in *Oxfordshire County Council v L and F*[137] in which he held that the guardian should continue to be involved in proceedings brought after a care order had been made for the disclosure of documents of those proceedings to the police and for a variation of injunctions controlling publicity.

(e) Commentary

One effect of the introduction of guardians in public law proceedings has been to give such persons greater authority in the eyes of the court though it may be questioned why greater weight should be given to the guardian's opinion than to that of any other witness of similar expertise. As has been observed,[138] the guardian is likely to have more experience than the average social worker, but is working alone, with limited supervision. There is no evidence that guardians are appointed for their expertise in a particular type of case. If the local authority put forward a cogent case supported by expert evidence based on the considered opinion of experienced staff, surely the court should express with equal clarity its reasons for departing from their recommendations? But this quibble apart, what is now generally referred to as the 'tandem model' of representation of children (whereby, as Thorpe LJ put it in *Mabon v Mabon*[139] 'the court appoints a guardian . . . , who will almost invariably have a social work qualification and a very wide experience of family proceedings. He then instructs a specialist solicitor who, in turn, usually instructs a specialist family barrister') works well particularly in public law proceedings. Thorpe LJ referred to the model as a 'Rolls-Royce' model which is the envy of many other jurisdictions. In Wall LJ's view[140]

'the "tandem model" of representation serves the interests of . . . children very well. The child has the input of expertise from the different disciplines of lawyer and guardian, who are able, with the court's permission, to call on additional expertise and advice where necessary. In public law proceedings s 42 of the Children Act 1989 gives the court sweeping powers of investigation on the child's behalf. At the same time, the child concerned is protected from the corroding consequences of adversarial litigation. Children are not required to give evidence and be cross-examined: they do not have access to the sensitive documentation generated by the case. The system is, of course, paternalistic

---

[135] *Kent County Council v C* [1993] Fam 57. For the position in cases where a s 37 direction has been made see *Re CE (Section 37 Direction)* [1995] 1 FLR 26 and *Re S (Contact: Grandparents)* [1996] 1 FLR 158, CA; guardian's appointment should be ended by a judicial rather than an administrative act.

[136] Following the repeal by Sch 4 to the Adoption and Children Act 2002 of s 12(5)(b) of the Criminal Justice and Court Service Act 2000, thus reversing *Re MH (A Child) and Re SB and MB (Children)* [2004] 2 FLR 1334.

[137] [1997] 1 FLR 235. But cf Butler-Sloss LJ in *Re G (Minor) (Social Worker: Disclosure)* [1996] 2 All ER 65 at 71 who commented: 'The guardian has no function outside the proceedings to which he has been appointed. *When these proceedings are completed his function is ended*' [emphasis added].

[138] R White, P Carr and N Lowe, *Children Act in Practice* (2nd edn) at 10.45.

[139] [2005] EWCA Civ 634, [2005] Fam 366 at [25].   [140] In *Mabon v Mabon*, ibid at [40].

in approach, but it usually works well, in my experience, even in cases where the child has sufficient understanding to participate in the proceedings concerned without a guardian.'

Whether this Rolls-Royce model will be retained, however, is subject to review[141] and at the time of writing seems to be under threat, inasmuch as it is being questioned whether guardians should be legally represented.

D THE CHILD'S DIRECT PARTICIPATION IN PROCEEDINGS

1 PRIVATE LAW PROCEEDINGS

As has been said, children's involvement, if at all, in private law proceedings is limited. They are not normally parties to the proceedings and their view will either be conveyed to the court through a welfare report or via the parents. However, it is not always the case that children do not have a direct involvement in even a private law case. First, even where they are not parties, it is open to a judge to interview children in private. Secondly, there are occasions when children can be made parties to proceedings brought by the parents. Finally, it is open to children, at least those of sufficient age and understanding, to initiate proceedings themselves.

(a) Judicial interviews with children in private

Practice varies widely with regard to judges seeing children in private. Although there was pre-Children Act authority that only the High Court and county court had power to do so,[142] it has since been held[143] that in exceptional circumstances magistrates can also see a child in private.

The Rules are silent as to when it is appropriate to conduct an interview in private, though the general view seems to be that it is a practice that should not readily be undertaken. In any event, the decision whether or not to interview a child in private is entirely a matter for the judge (ie it is unappealable). As Ormrod LJ put it in *D v D*:[144]

'If ever a matter was a personal matter for a judge it is the question of seeing or not seeing the children. It is a highly sensitive decision both for a judge himself and a judge, in my judgment, is fully entitled to make up his own mind ... about whether or not to see children. It is a very delicate situation indeed in my experience and it can be extremely

---

[141] See *A Fairer Deal for Legal Aid* Cm 6591 (HMSO, 2005). See also the *Stakeholder Update: Key Issues* paper (issued by the DCA and Dfes in October 2005) summarised by 'Child Care Review Update' [2005] Fam Law 844, which referred to research showing that child clients sometimes felt alienated by poor quality representation, ill informed of their rights and unclear as to the roles of their representatives. It was also commented that some court time was being spent on administrative tasks which could potentially be performed in other forums.

[142] See *Re T (An Infant)* (1974) 4 Fam Law 48; *Re T (A Minor)(Welfare Report Recommendation)* (1977) 1 FLR 59; and *Re W (Minors)* (1980) 10 Fam Law 120.

[143] Per Booth J in *Re M (A Minor) (Justices' Discretion)* [1993] 2 FLR 706. See also *Re W (Child: Contact)* [1994] 1 FLR 843 and *Re K (A Minor) (Contact)* [1993] Fam Law 552.

[144] (1979) 2 FLR 74. See also *Clarke-Hunt v Newcombe* (1982) 4 FLR 482, CA at 485, per Butler-Sloss J.

embarrassing to a judge when he can see already the likelihood that he will come to a decision which is adverse to the wishes of the child.'

Balcombe LJ made a similar point in the post-Children Act decision, *Re R (A Minor) (Residence: Religion)*,[145] when he said: 'a judge's decision whether or not personally to interview a child must above all be a question for the exercise of judicial discretion'.

As Wall LJ commented in *Mabon v Mabon*,[146] the reluctance of the English judge to talk to children in private

'has several origins, but one of them is undoubtedly rooted in the rules of evidence and the adversarial mode of trial. What is said in private by the child to the judge cannot be tested in evidence or in cross examination. As a consequence a judge in England and Wales cannot promise a child that any conversation with the child will be entirely confidential. That fact may inhibit children from expressing their true wishes and feeling to the judge . . .'.

The fact that if a judge does interview a child in private he cannot promise confidentiality also means that he should be cautious in agreeing to see the child in such circumstances.[147]

Although there is old authority[148] to the effect that reliance ought not to be placed on an interview unless the child is more than eight years old, it is doubtful whether judges would consider themselves bound to rigid rules in that regard.

(b) Children as parties[149]

Children are not automatically parties to private law proceedings. Indeed as we discussed in Chapter 8,[150] the power to conduct litigation on their child's behalf is generally thought to be an aspect of parental responsibility. Nevertheless it is within the High Court's and county courts' (but not magistrates' courts') power to order that a child be made a party to proceedings and consequently be separately represented.[151] The primary means of doing this is under r 9.5 of the Family Proceedings Rules.[152] However, as we discussed

[145] [1993] 2 FLR 163, CA. For a case where it was held appropriate to see a child in private, see *Re F (Minors) (Denial of Contact)* [1993] 2 FLR 677, CA (the judge saw two boys aged 12 and nine in connection with a contact application by a transsexual father).
[146] [2005] EWCA Civ 634, [2005] Fam 366 at [38].
[147] Per Wall J in *B v B (Minors) (Interviews and Listing Arrangements)* [1994] 2 FLR 489, CA at 496. See also *Elder v Elder* [1986] 1 FLR 610, CA; *Dickinson v Dickinson* (1982) 13 Fam Law 174; and *H v H (Child: Judicial Interview)* [1974] 1 All ER 1145, CA.
[148] *Ingham v Ingham* [1976] LS Gaz R 486, CA.
[149] See generally G Douglas, M Murch, C Miles and L Scanlan *Research into the operation of Rule 9.5 of the Family Proceedings Rules 1991* (DCA, March 2006), J Fortin *Children's Rights and the Developing Law* (2nd edn) ch 7 and M Murch 'The Voice of the Child in Private Law Proceedings in England and Wales' [2005] IFL 8.
[150] Above at p 399.
[151] As Douglas et al, above at 2.1, n 8 point out strictly speaking being separately represented and being joined as a party are two separate things but in *L v L (Minors)(Separate Representation)* [1994] 1 FLR 156 it was held that where a child is separately represented he or she should also be joined as a party, though note this is not always appropriately done, see C Blackburn 'Rule 9.5 Demystified' (2005) 15 *Seen and Heard* 19.
[152] This rule replaced earlier powers to make a child a party, namely RSC Ord 90, r 1(1) and 3(22) County Court Rules 1981, Ord 15, r 1 and the Matrimonial Causes Rules 1977, r 115(1),(2). For a long time the most developed use of separate representation powers was in wardship in which the child's interests were represented by the Official Solicitor, see N Lowe and R White, *Wards of Court* (2nd edn) ch 9, (see also 3.8 for discussion of making a ward a defendant to the proceedings). For the current position of when a child can and should be made a party to wardship proceedings see below p 892.

earlier,[153] through an amendment by s 122 of the Adoption and Children Act 2002, provision is made to add proceedings for the making, varying or discharging of s 8 orders to 'specified proceedings'. Under these powers children would be represented by a children's guardian as under public law proceedings. The 2002 Act also makes provision[154] for amending the rules (ie r 9.5) for a child to be separately represented by a guardian ad litem.

Rule 9.5 provides:

'if in any proceedings it appears to the court that it is in the best interests of any child to be made a party to the proceedings, the court may appoint

(a) an officer of the Service or a Welsh family proceedings officer;

(b) (if he consents) the Official Solicitor, or

(c) (if he consents) some other proper person

to be the guardian ad litem of the child with authority to take part in the proceedings on the child's behalf.'

It will be noted that the Rule 9.5 appointee is still described as the 'guardian *ad litem*' and is therefore distinguishable from the children's guardian appointed in 'specified proceedings'. According to the *President's Direction*[155] where separate representation is ordered consideration should first be given to appointing a CAFCASS officer. The decision about which particular officer to allocate is a matter for CAFCASS but where it is an officer from CAFCASS Legal there is normally no need to appoint a solicitor as the litigation will usually be conducted in-house.[156] Where that would cause delay or if there is some other reason for not doing so, the court may appoint someone else such as a solicitor known to the court[157] or the National Youth Advocacy Service (NYAS).[158]

As the *President's Direction*[159] makes clear, notwithstanding that the court must treat the child's welfare as its 'primary consideration', the decision to make a child a party should only be taken in cases of 'significant difficulty'. The criteria are as follows:

'3.1 Where a CAFCASS officer has notified the court that in his opinion the child should be made a party (see FPR 4.11B(6)).

3.2 Where the child has a standpoint or interests which are inconsistent with or incapable of being represented by any of the adult parties.

3.3 Where there is an intractable dispute over residence or contact, including where all contact has ceased, or where there is irrational but implacable hostility to contact or where the child may be suffering harm associated with the contact dispute.

3.4 Where the views and wishes of the child cannot be adequately met by a report to the court.

---

[153] See above at p 493.

[154] Adding s 93(2)(bb) to the Children Act 1989. Effectively, the 2002 Act amendments replace the regulatory making powers for children's separate representation provided for by s 64 of the Family Law Act 1996 which has not and will not be implemented.

[155] *President's Direction: Representation of Children in Family Proceedings Pursuant to the Family Proceedings Rules 1991, r 9.5* [2005] 1 FLR 1188.

[156] See *CAFCASS Practice Note (Representation of Children in Family Proceedings Pursuant to Family Proceedings Rules 1991. Rule 9.5* [2004] 1 FLR 1190.

[157] See eg *Re K (Replacement of Guardian ad Litem)* [2001] 1 FLR 663.

[158] See eg *Re C (a child)* [2005] EWCA Civ 300.   [159] Above, at para 4.

3.5 Where an older child is opposing a proposed course of action.

3.6 Where there are complex medical or mental health issues to be determined or there are other unusually complex issues that necessitate separate representation of the child.

3.7 Where there are particular complications outside child abduction, in particular where it may be necessary for there to be discussions with overseas authorities or a foreign court.

3.8 Where there are serious allegations of physical, sexual or other abuse in relation to the child or there are allegations of domestic violence not capable of being resolved with the help of a CAFCASS officer.

3.9 Where the proceedings concern more than one child and the welfare of the children is in conflict or one child is in a particularly disadvantaged position.

3.10 Where there is a contested issue about blood testing.'

As Douglas et al observe,[160] paras 3.2, 3.4 and 3.5 all make reference to the child having a position or views contrary to those proposed by adults which is, as they say, reflective of a 'voice'-based approach and is evidence of a greater sensitivity to the need to hear the child's wishes and feelings. The other examples either concern the complexity of the case or the welfare of the child and reflects the more traditional approach of the courts. According to Thorpe LJ in *Mabon v Mabon*[161] the Rule 9.5 system of representation is

'essentially paternalistic. The guardian's first priority is to advocate the welfare of the child he represents. His second priority is to put before the court the child's wishes and feelings'.

Case law generally reflects the view[162] that welfare is the primary rationale for making separate representation appointments and in particular 'a desire to ensure that a conflict of interests of the parents does not obscure the real needs of the child'. In Douglas et al's view the courts' overall concern when ordering separate representation 'is to obtain a complete picture of the situation, where necessary presented by someone who is independent of the parents' positions. And this will often be motivated less by a concern to hear the child than to explore conflicts of evidence or to hear arguments that neither adult party wishes to put forward'.

Although no national statistics are kept on the overall proportion of cases in which appointments under r 9.5 are made, various studies suggest that it ranges from 2% in some areas up to 10% in others.[163] It does seem, however, that overall the number of

---

160 Op cit at 2.33.   161 [2005] EWCA Civ 634, [2005] Fam 366 at [26].

162 See Douglas et al, op cit at 2.38, relying inter alia upon *Re H (Contact Order)(No 2)* [2002] 1 FLR 22—contact dispute after father threatened to kill himself and the children; *Re A (Contact: Separate Representation)* [2000] 1 FLR 663, contact dispute in which the parents were so antagonistic to each other neither could be regarded as able to put their child's interests first; *Re F (Contact Restraint Order)* [1995] 1 FLR 956, CA—fears about accepting children's, especially young children's, views at face value—in this case children aged seven and six stated that they did not want contact with their father. See also *Re W (Contact: Joining Child as Party)* [2001] EWCA Civ 1830, [2003] 1 FLR 681—a seven-year-old child reluctant to have contact with his father. Note also *Re L (Minors)(Separate Representation)* [1994] 1 FLR 156 in which (what was then) the court welfare officer felt she could not adequately present the children's (aged 14, 12 and nine) views to the court and *Re C (Prohibition on Further Applications)* [2002] EWCA Civ 292, [2002] 1 FLR 1136—a case of alleged 'parental alienation syndrome'.

163 See Douglas et al, op cit, at 2.48. In a separate study at Leeds combined court centre, it was found that in a 12-month period from 2001 to 2002, separate representation was ordered in 7.3% of cases: C Bellamy and G Lord 'Reflections on Family Proceedings Rule 9.5' [2003] Fam Law 265.

appointments has risen sharply. According to CAFCASS, requests for its officers to assume the role of guardians ad litem rose from 549 in 2002–4 to 1,141 in 2004–5.[164] This dramatic rise prompted the President of the Family Division to issue a *Practice Direction* restricting appointments to circuit judges save where the district judge considers the case to be exceptional because there is no resident circuit judge and the matter is urgent. Where a guardian is appointed, consideration must be given to transferring the case to the High Court.

As Wall LJ put it in *Mabon v Mabon*[165] the rules 'sensibly' make provision for where the guardian and children fall out:

'In these circumstances, r 9.2(A)(4) gives children the right to apply to the court for permission to prosecute or defend the remaining stages of the proceedings without the guardian, and r 9.2A(6) makes it clear that the court must grant that permission and remove the guardian if it considers that the children concerned have sufficient understanding to participate in the proceedings concerned without a guardian.'

This test for removing a guardian has been described[166] as a 'one-stage test' and is solely dependent upon the child's competence. This is the same as where children seek to initiate proceedings on their own behalf and it is in that context that the issue will be discussed.

(c) Is the lack of automatic party status human rights compliant?

There has been much speculation as to whether the child's lack of automatic party status in private law proceedings is human rights compliant. The most obvious Article in point is Art 6 which guarantees that in the determination of his civil rights and obligations '*everyone* is entitled to a fair and public hearing within a reasonable time by an independent and impartial tribunal established by law'. And there are those who have argued[167] that Art 6 could be thought to vest a right in a child to have separate representation in proceedings concerning him or her. Some[168] have gone further and suggested that 'the way in which children are currently treated by the private family proceedings process might arguably been in breach of Art 14 which prohibits discrimination on any ground and that a child's or young person's age could certainly be included within this'.

To date, however, there is no European Court of Human Rights decision that supports this speculation. Indeed to the contrary the Grand Chamber of the European Court of Human Rights' ruled in *Sahin v Germany; Sommerfeld v Germany*[169] that Germany

---

[164] CAFCASS Annual Report and Accounts 2004–2005 (HC 109 TSO) at 29.

[165] [2005] EWCA 634, [2005] Fam 366 at [41].

[166] Per Coleridge J in *Re N (Contact: Minor Seeking Leave to Defend and Removal of Guardian)* [2003] 1 FLR 652.

[167] See J Fortin 'The HRA's impact on litigation involving children and their families [1999] CFLQ 237 at 244. See also her arguments in *Children's Rights and the Developing Law* (2nd edn) at 213, where she also speculated whether lack of party status could be in breach of procedural rights under Art 8.

[168] C Lyon 'Children's Participation in Private Law Proceedings' in *No Fault or Flaw: The Future of the Family Law Act 1996* (eds M Thorpe and E Clarke, 2000) 70. Query whether this argument would be accepted since the courts might well say that there are good reasons for differentiating between children and adults in the matter of participating in legal proceedings, with the former needing more protection from, for example, the rigours of cross-examination, than the latter.

[169] [2003] 2 FLR 671.

had not violated the Convention in *Sahin*'s case, by the German court's reliance on the findings of experts concerning a five-year-old's view. As the court pointed out, contrary to its earlier Chamber decision[170] it is going too far to say that domestic courts should always hear evidence from a child in court. Of course that ruling might not apply to older more mature children but in that respect it is important to take into account that a specific duty of a children and family reporter is to consider whether the child should be given party status and to advise the court accordingly.[171] Moreover, it is open to a child of sufficient understanding, to acquire party status according to the procedure set out in the Family Proceedings Rules 1991, r 9.2A (discussed below). In short, even for older children the lack of automatic party status might not, particularly when these other safeguards and mechanisms for requiring party status are taken into account, be in breach of Art 6.

2 PUBLIC LAW PROCEEDINGS

As previously discussed, the child is a party to public law proceedings and will be represented by the children's guardian. Nevertheless notwithstanding that party status, the Rules[172] give the court a discretion to hear the case in the child's absence if it considers it in the interests of the child, having regard to the matters to be discussed or the evidence likely to be given, and the child is represented by a guardian or solicitor. In other words, the child does not have an absolute right to attend the hearing and indeed there is a general view that it is commonly not in his or her interests to do so.[173]

Notwithstanding the foregoing, the child's evidence may be heard by the court if it is of the opinion that the child understands the duty to speak the truth and has sufficient understanding to justify his evidence being heard.[174] More commonly, however, the child will have been interviewed beforehand and the evidence will be presented in court on the child's behalf by the interviewer.[175]

E CHILDREN AS LITIGANTS

1 THE SUBSTANTIVE LAW

Historically, before the Children Act 1989, one of the few ways that a child could initiate his or her own proceedings was by making him or herself a ward of court.[176] Even after implementation of the 1989 Act this remains a possible option. However, in most cases the preferable course is to seek leave to apply for a s 8 order under the Children Act. The ability for children to seek s 8 orders was one of the innovations of the 1989 legislation. We

---

[170] *Sahin v Germany; Sommerfeld v Germany; Hoffman v Germany* [2002] 1 FLR 119.

[171] FPR 1991, r 4.11B(5) and (6), FPCA 1991 R 11B(5) and (6).

[172] FPCA 1991 r 16(2), (7); FPR 1991 r 4.16(2).

[173] See eg *Re C (A Minor) (Care: Child's Wishes)* [1993] 1 FLR 832 in which it was held that guardians ad litem should think carefully about the arrangements for children who are to be present in court.

[174] Children Act 1989 s 96(2).

[175] This hearsay evidence is admissible under the Children (Admissibility Hearsay of Evidence) Order 1993.

[176] See N Lowe and R White *Wards of Court* (2nd edn, 1986) at 3–4. Wardship is discussed in Ch 16.

discuss this course of action in Chapter 12.[177] Suffice to say here, that court leave (which can only be granted where the court is satisfied that the child has sufficient understanding to make the application)[178] is a necessary prerequisite to seeking a s 8 order[179] and such leave applications have to be made in the High Court.[180]

Apart from the right, subject to leave, to apply for s 8 orders, the 1989 Act confers on a child of sufficient understanding a number of other rights. He can, for example, again subject to court leave, apply to (a) have a parental responsibility order made under s 4 or s 4A brought to an end;[181] (b) to have a guardianship appointment made under s 5 brought to an end;[182] and (c) have a special guardianship order varied or discharged.[183] So far as public law orders are concerned, a child can apply for the discharge or variation of a care or supervision order[184] and for the discharge of an emergency protection or child assessment order.[185] It will be noted, however, that the child has no right to apply for the review or discharge of a secure accommodation order.[186]

2 THE PROCEDURE

Under rule 9.2 of the Family Proceedings Rules 1991 the general principle is that a child may bring family proceedings in the High Court or county court by his next friend and defend any such proceedings by his guardian ad litem.[187] This provision is in line with the general inability of children to conduct legal proceedings without what is more generally referred to as a litigation friend.[188] However, as an exception to this general principle, rule 9.2A enables a child who is entitled to begin, prosecute or defend proceedings under the Children Act 1989 and under the High Court's inherent jurisdiction to do so without a next friend or guardian ad litem. According to rule 9.2A a child may do so either where the court has given leave or where a solicitor considers that the child is able, having regard to his age and understanding, to give instructions and has accepted instructions from the child to act for him in the proceedings.[189]

The leading decision in *Re T (A Minor) (Child: Representation)*[190] establishes that where the court considers that the child does not have sufficient understanding, though the solicitor's assessment of the child's capacity to instruct him is otherwise, the court is the final arbiter and can appoint a next friend or guardian ad litem. It also established, however, that once it is found that the child has sufficient understanding to instruct a solicitor the court has no power to interfere.

Precisely what level of understanding a child must have to pass the r 9.2A test has been

---

[177] At pp 548ff.   [178] See s 10(8).   [179] Section 10(1)(a)(ii).

[180] *Practice Direction (Application by Children: Leave)* [1993] 1 FLR 313.

[181] Section 4(3)(b) and s 4A(3)(b), discussed above at p 421.

[182] Section 6(7)(b), discussed above at p 448.

[183] Section 14D(1)(e), (3) and (4), discussed below at p 609.

[184] Section 39, discussed below at p 787.

[185] Section 45(8) and 43(12), discussed below at p 727 and p 729.

[186] Secure accommodation orders are discussed below at pp 713ff.

[187] It has been said that children are entitled to conduct their own proceedings before magistrates' courts. But see R White (1992) 142 NLJ 64.

[188] Civil Procedure Rules 1998, Part 21. Family proceedings are the only context in which reference is still made to a 'Next Friend'. In all other proceedings the term 'litigation friend' is used instead.

[189] Rule 9.2A(1)(b).   [190] [1994] Fam 49.

the subject of much thought[191] and litigation. According to Thorpe J *Re H (A Minor)(Care Proceedings: Child's Wishes)*[192] the level of understanding required to enable a child to instruct a solicitor is not as high as that required to make an informed decision to refuse psychiatric or medical treatment. The leading case is *Mabon v Mabon*[193] in which the Court of Appeal overturned a refusal to grant three brothers, aged 17, 15 and 13, separate representation. In reaching this conclusion, Thorpe LJ recognised that there is now 'a keener appreciation of the autonomy of the child and the child's consequential right to participate in decision-making processes that fundamentally affect his family life'. Consequently courts must accept that in the case of articulate teenagers 'the right to freedom of expression and participation outweighs the paternalistic judgment of welfare'. However, his Lordship added:

'In testing the sufficiency of a child's understanding, I would not say that welfare has no place. If direct participation would pose an obvious risk of harm to the child, arising out of the nature of the continuing proceedings and, if the child is incapable of comprehending that risk, then the judge is entitled to find that sufficient understanding has not been demonstrated. But judges have to be equally alive to the risk of emotional harm that might arise from denying the child knowledge and participation in the continuing proceedings.'

On the facts of *Mabon* Thorpe LJ agreed with the submission that it would be unthinkable to exclude the young men from knowledge of and participation in legal proceedings that affected them so fundamentally.

It is nevertheless his duty to assess the child's understanding throughout the case. In this regard the solicitor will be guided by the SFLA's *Guide to Good Practice for Solicitors for Children*.[194] Any leave which has been granted by the court under r 9.2A can subsequently be revoked by the court if it considers that the child does not have sufficient understanding.[195]

Although the gradual move towards child autonomy and away from a welfare based approach will be welcomed by many, the child litigant nevertheless does pose some difficult problems for the family justice system. It may be questioned, for example, whether it is necessary for the child to participate fully in the proceedings as if he were an adult. Should he be subject to the full rigours of cross-examination or be entitled to examine all the papers?[196]

---

[191] For early discussion see eg Mr Justice Thorpe 'Applications by children under the Children Act' [1994] Fam Law 20, D Burrows 'A child's understanding' [1994] Fam Law 579, E Walsh 'Applications by Children: Paternalism v Autonomy' [1994] Fam Law 663. See also the valuable study by C Sawyer *The Rise and Fall of the Third Party: Solicitors' Assessment of the Competence of Children to Participate in Family Proceedings* (1995).
[192] [1993] 1 FLR 440.   [193] [2005] EWCA Civ 634, [2005] Fam 366.
[194] 6th edn, 2002.   [195] FPR 1991, r 9.2A (8).
[196] See the discussion in R White, P Carr and N Lowe: *Children Act in Practice* (2nd edn, 1995) 10.16ff.

F THE CHILDREN'S VIEWS AND EXPERIENCES OF THE FAMILY JUSTICE SYSTEM

There is a growing body of research[197] to suggest that most practitioners in the family justice system lack the necessary skills and understanding for effective face to face work with children. These studies highlight three areas of concern:[198]

(1) Historically in our culture children are not used to being listened to. For example, as Schofield and Thoburn have commented:[199] 'Children in our society are not accustomed to having their views taken into account in their everyday lives at home or at school. We do not live in a culture which supports participation by children'.

(2) Many adults seem to have difficulties in listening to children. A number of reasons has been advanced for this. For example, Neale has commented:[200] 'Adults view children as essentially other. They are seen as less important and they are dependent and less powerful. Language is a tool used communally or on the basis of shared understandings. Adults interpret what children say. Welfare professionals do so on the basis of their understanding of what is in the child's best interest.' Smith[201] postulates that adults fear they will upset children by talking about difficult experiences such as separation and divorce. Hunt and Lawson[202] comment that many professionals are aware of their lack of training and experience in talking to and listening to children. Even more challengingly, Day Sclater and Piper assert[203] that adults protect themselves from their own vulnerabilities by projecting them (*unconsciously*) on to the children. They suggest that in order to keep that anxiety contained adults rationalise that it is vital *not* to listen to children's own constructions of their needs but instead to act as if they know children's best interests better than they do. Finally, Murch et al believe[204] that many adults (including welfare professionals, solicitors and judges) confuse 'participation' with decision making. They are reluctant even to speak or to listen to children because they see this as inappropriately asking the child to decide.

---

[197] Much of which is summarised by A O'Quigley *Listening to children's views and representing their best interests—a summary of current research* (1999).

[198] See N Lowe and M Murch 'Children's participation in the family justice system—translating principles into practice' [2001] CFLQ 137 at 143 et seq.

[199] G Schofield and J Thoburn *Child Protection: the voice of the child in decision making* (1996) at p 62. Note also the comment by A L James and A James 'Pump up the Volume' (1999) 6(2) *Listening to Children in Separation and Divorce in Childhood* 206 : 'Ours is a culture that does not particularly like children. The adage that "children should be seen and not heard" has an authentically English ring about it.'

[200] B Neale 'Dialogues with children in participation and choice in family decision making' (unpublished paper) (1999).

[201] Smith *All Change* UK Youth (Spring 1999) at 12.

[202] J Hunt and J Lawson *Crossing the boundaries—the views of practitioners of Family Court Welfare and Guardian ad Litem work on the proposal to create a unified court welfare service* (1999) at p 38.

[203] S Day Sclater and C Piper *Undercurrents of Divorce* (1999) Dartmouth, 8.

[204] M Murch, G Douglas, L Scanlan, A Perry, C Lisles, K Bader, M Borkowski *Safeguarding children's welfare in uncontentious divorce; a study of section 41 of the Matrimonial Causes Act 1973*, pp178–85, Lord Chancellor's Department, Research Series No 7/99.

(3) Children can have disturbing experiences when talking to professionals. In this respect the Review by O'Quigley[205] makes five important and troubling points:

    (a) Children were generally reluctant to talk to outsiders about family issues as this was seen as disloyal and liable to lead to an escalation of problems.

    (b) Professionals were seen as having been interventionist rather than supportive.

    (c) The discussions that children had with professionals often felt like interrogations.

    (d) Adults were frequently experienced as judgmental and intrusive in their approach.

    (e) Discussions were often not treated as confidential.

Neale and Smart concluded their study thus:[206] 'Professionals may be perceived as inflexible, intrusive, condescending, deceitful, untrustworthy, disrespectful and reinforcing in a myriad of ways their superiority to the child.'

Drawing on the findings of two child focussed research projects conducted by Cardiff University,[207] Lowe and Murch[208] identified some common experiences, namely (1) children had misconceptions about the court and the legal process—many associated courts with criminal wrongdoing and many were afraid having to go to court; others were just ignorant of legal process and were often left to 'suss it out' for themselves, (2) children felt isolated and ignorant of what was happening and felt the need for reliable information, and (3) children needed support particularly through the shock and worry experienced by them on hearing of their parents' separation and, in the adoption context particularly during the move to the adoptive home. Lowe and Murch concluded from these findings that the ability of both professionals and parents to communicate with children and be sensitive to their needs were 'the absolute minimum requirements of putting into practice legal obligations to ascertain and have regard to children's wishes and feelings'. They also considered that 'there is a crying need to develop ways and means to explain the court process and to familiarise children with the court room and judge before any hearing'.

The findings of a subsequent study of children's experience of separate representation under Rule 9.5[209] reinforces the above messages. This study found that while most of the children liked the idea of someone appointed by the court to help them have their say in the proceedings, a number were ignorant and confused about the legal process and imagined courts to be ' "scary places" with judges who have the capacity to "punish" their parents'. They felt that the court and the judge should be 'child friendly' and that they needed someone accessible to them, apart from their parents, to support them through the litigation process. A number wanted to be kept informed about the progress of the case. In their eyes a 'good' guardian was someone who gave them enough time to get to know them (hasty interrogations were disliked), who could be trusted and who would communicate at their level and who would give clear explanations as to the role of both the guardian and of the legal process.

---

[205] Op cit n 197.   [206] Op cit at 33.

[207] Ie I Butler et al *Divorcing Children—children's experience of their parents' divorce* (2003), and C Thomas et al *Adopted Children Speaking* (1999).

[208] Op cit n 198.

[209] G Douglas et al *Research into the operation of Rule 9.5 of the Family Proceedings Rules 1991* (2006).

G LOOKING AFTER CHILDREN'S WIDER INTERESTS—THE COMMISSIONERS FOR CHILDREN [210]

1 BACKGROUND

As one commentary has put it,[211] the use of a 'children's Commissioner' or ombudsman has come to be regarded as one of the most effective means of ensuring that the separate and special interests of children promoted by the United Nations Convention on the Rights of the Children 1989 are protected. Many states have accordingly established such an office as part of their response to meeting their obligations under the Convention with Norway being the first to do so in 1981.[212] Calls for an office in the United Kingdom began at least in 1991 with a report promoted by the Gulbenkian Foundation,[213] but it was the criticism by the United Nations Committee on the Rights of the Child (to whom the United Kingdom had submitted its first compliance report) and the recommendation that a children's ombudsman should[214] be appointed that ultimately led to the creation of the Commissioners in the United Kingdom. That proposal was taken up by the House of Commons Select Committee on Health in 1998 which formally recommended the creation of a UK Commissioner. However, at first the Government resisted these calls and instead the initiative was taken up first in Wales[215] where the Children's Commissioner for Wales took up his appointment in 2001, then in Northern Ireland,[216] with the post being taken up in 2004 and then in Scotland[217] where the post was taken up in 2004. Finally, the government agreed to create a comparable post for England which it did via Part 1 of the Children Act 2004 which came into force in November 2004. The first Commissioner for Children in England was appointed in March 2005.

---

[210] See J Williams, 'Effective government structures for children?: The UK's four Children's Commissioners' [2005] CFLQ 37.

[211] K Hollingsworth and G Douglas 'Creating a children's champion for Wales? The Care Standards Act 2000 (Part V) and the Children's Commissioner for Wales Act 2001' (2002) 65 MLR 58.

[212] There are also well-established comparable offices in Australia, Canada, Germany, New Zealand and Switzerland. According to an article (published in 2000) in the *Guardian* newspaper cited by Hollingsworth and Douglas, above, there are at least 18 such offices. Ireland created a Children's Ombudsman in 2002. See also M Seneviratne 'Ombudsman for Children' (2001) 23 JSWFL 217.

[213] M Rosenbaum and P Newell *Taking Children Seriously: a Proposal for a Children's Rights Commissioner.*

[214] Children's Rights Office, *Proposal for an Office of Children's Rights Commissioner* (1997). As Clarke Hall and Morrison comment, at 9[3], the appointment of an independent office had been strongly promoted by the Council of Europe through its 'European Strategy for Children' Recommendation 1286 (1996).

[215] The impetus was the Waterhouse report *Lost in care: Report on the Tribunal of Inquiry into the abuse of children in care in the former county council areas of Gwynedd and Clwyd since 1974*, HC, 201 (2000). See generally Hollingsworth and Douglas, op cit.

[216] The Commissioner for Children and Young People (Northern Ireland) Order 2003, SI 2003/439 (NI 11).

[217] The Commissioner for Children and Young People (Scotland) Act 2003.

2 OVERVIEW OF THE ENGLISH COMMISSIONER'S ROLE[218]

The Children's Commissioner for England has the dual role of being both the Commissioner for England and also for Wales in non-devolved matters, Scotland in reserved matters, and Northern Ireland in excepted matters.

By s 2(1) of the 2004 Act the Children's Commissioner has a general mandate to promote awareness of the views and interests of children in England Wales, and by s 2(2):

'may in particular . . .

(a) encourage persons exercising functions or engaged in activities affecting children, to take account of their views and interests;

(b) advise the Secretary of State on the views and interests of children;

(c) consider or research the operation of complaints procedures so far as relating to children;

(d) consider or research any other matter relating to the interests of children: publish a report on any matter research by him under this section'.

There are two means by which the English Commissioner may launch an investigation, namely, on his own initiative as provided for by s 3 but subject to prior consultation with the Secretary of State;[219] or pursuant to s 4, on direction by the Secretary of State. Although in each case the trigger for the inquiry is the case of an individual child, its purpose is confined to investigating and making recommendations of issues of public policy of relevance to other children. The Commissioner is specifically barred from conducting an investigation of the issue of an individual child.[220]

The power vested by s 3 to permit the Commissioner to conduct an inquiry on his own initiative was an amendment to the original Bill which would have only provided for inquiries upon the Secretary of State's direction. Even so, there must still be concerns about the Commissioner's independence. Implicit in the requirement to consult is that the Commissioner will need the Secretary of State's consent to go ahead or is at least subject to a ministerial veto. Furthermore, the power to 'direct' an inquiry under s 4 rather than to 'request' one has, as one commentary put it,[221] 'an odd flavour in comparison with the UK Commissioners', who are clearly independent of the relevant devolved governing powers'.

Another major criticism of the 2004 Act is that in contrast to the other Commissioners in the United Kingdom who are required by law to promote and safeguard the 'rights' of children, the Commissioner's general function in England under s 2(1) is only to promote 'awareness of the views and *interests* of children in England' which is arguably more restrictive. However, in this regard note might be taken of s 2(11) which directs the Commissioner, when considering what constitutes the interest of children, to have regard to the United Nations Convention on the Rights of the Child.

One further problem is the interelationship with the other UK Commissioners since, as has been said, the English Commissioner has powers over non-devolved matters yet those

---

[218] See generally B Clucas 'The Children's Commissioner For England: The Way Forward?' [2005] Fam Law 290.

[219] See s 3(3).

[220] Section 2(7). As is the Scottish Commissioner. Compare the Welsh and N Ireland Commissioner's powers: see Williams, op cit, at pp 41, 43, 48–50.

[221] Clucas, op cit at 292.

other Commissioners have generally much stronger powers. As one commentary put it[222] 'this is seen as potentially insensitive to the needs and rights of children in those countries and insulting to the other Commissioners.'

In summary, the provisions governing the functions of the English Commissioner for Children are disappointingly weak and as one commentary has concluded[223] what ought to have been

'a cause for celebratory fireworks ... more nearly resembles a damp squib. The existing legislation represents an opportunity lost rather than seized, and the post will require a very strong candidate indeed, in addition to changes in the law, to become a true children's champion'.

---

222 Clarke Hall and Morrison 9[4].   223 Clucas, op cit, at 293.

12

THE COURT'S POWERS TO MAKE ORDERS UNDER PART II OF THE CHILDREN ACT 1989

A INTRODUCTION

This chapter considers the courts' powers under Part II of the Children Act 1989 to make orders, other than financial orders,[1] in what are termed 'family proceedings'.

Part II is based on the Law Commission's recommendations contained in its *Report on Guardianship and Custody*.[2] The Commission commented[3] that, while the main principles of the pre–1989 Act law were reasonably clear and well accepted, the details were complicated and confusing, with the result that it was 'undoubtedly unintelligible to ordinary people, including the families involved' and on occasion may have prevented families or the courts from 'finding' the best solution for their children.

The Commission were also concerned that the former law made the stakes too high. As they pointed out,[4] all the research evidence[5] shows that children who fare best after their parents' separation are those who are able to maintain a good relationship with both parents. While recognising the obvious limitation that law cannot make people co-operate, the Commission argued that at least it should not stand in their way. Hence, if the parties can co-operate with each other, the law should intervene as little as possible, but if they cannot, the law should at least try to 'lower the stakes' and avoid the impression that the 'loser loses all'.

With the above considerations in mind and with the general aim of making the law simpler, clearer and fairer for children and their families the Law Commission recommended[6]

---

[1] The powers to make financial orders are governed by s 15 and Sch 1, for discussion of which, see Ch 17.

[2] Law Com No 172, 1988.

[3] At para 1.1. See also the supplemental study by Priest and Whybrow *Custody Law And Practice In Divorce and Domestic Courts* (1986) (Supplement to Law Com Working Paper No 96).

[4] Law Com No 172, para 4.5.

[5] Notably that of Wallerstein and Kelly *Surviving the Breakup* (1980). See also Wallerstein and Blakeslee *Second Chances: Men, Women and Children a Decade After Divorce* (1990); Richards and Dyson *Separation, Divorce and the Development of Children: A Review* (1982); and J Pryor and B Rodgers *Children in Changing Families: Life After Parental Separation* (2001).

[6] Law Com No 172, para 8.2.

that the differing powers of the various courts should be replaced by a new set of powers common to all courts and which are designed to be less emotive and more flexible.

Under the Children Act 1989, the courts are empowered to make a range of orders, collectively known as 's 8 orders', ie residence orders, contact orders, prohibited steps orders and specific issue orders. Although s 8 orders are closely associated with private law disputes they can be made in *any* family proceedings[7] including, therefore, in public law proceedings.[8] In other words the s 8 powers provide what has been described[9] as a 'basic menu' of orders available under the Act.

As well as providing this range of powers, Part II also makes clear provision for determining who can apply for an order. The basic scheme (under s 10) is that some people, for example parents, guardians or special guardians, are entitled to apply for any s 8 order, while others, eg relatives, are required to seek the court's leave either to intervene in existing family proceedings or to initiate their own proceedings to seek a s 8 order.

An important change under the 1989 Act was the removal of the court's power in matrimonial and other private law proceedings concerning children to make committal to care or supervision orders.[10] Instead, under s 37 courts can direct the local authority to investigate the circumstances but it is for authority and not the court to decide whether an application for a care or supervision order should be made. However, in place of these former powers is the power under s 16 to make 'family assistance' orders, the object of which is to provide short-term help for the family.

After operating for many years virtually unamended there has been a number of changes to Part II. A raft of new powers both to promote contact (for example, to make contact activity directions or conditions) and to enforce contact orders (including the power to impose an unpaid work requirement and to order compensation to another for a financial loss caused by a breach) has been introduced by the Children and Adoption Act 2006. These powers are respectively discussed in the context of contact orders and enforcement powers. A further power to make special guardianship orders has been added by the Adoption and Children Act 2002. These orders, together with so-called 'enhanced residence orders' also introduced by the 2002 Act, are intended to provide alternative orders to adoption for non parents. These powers are discussed at the end of this chapter.

That it was felt necessary to introduce new powers over contact is indicative of the fact that these have proved to be the least successful of the s 8 powers.[11] They are also a

---

[7] For the full meaning of which, see p 564 below.

[8] To put into context these powers to make s 8 orders in both private and public law it might be noted that whereas in 2004, 31,878 residence orders were made in private law proceedings, 2,976 orders were made in public law proceedings, while the respective figures for contact were 70,169 as against 2,045, for prohibited steps orders 9,556 as against 235 and for specific issue orders there were 3,893 as against 162: Tables 5.2 and 5.3 of the 2004 Judicial Statistics. For the number of orders made annually 1992–2000, see the summary in R White, P Carr and N Lowe: *The Children Act in Practice* (3rd edn) 137.

[9] See S Cretney *Family Law* (4th edn) 242.

[10] For details see pp 297–8, 306, 308 and 369 of the 7th edition of this work.

[11] Statistically, they are also the order most frequently sought. In 2004, for example, of the 125,794 applications made for s 8 orders in private law proceedings, 76,426 (61%) were for contact and of these, 70,169 (92%) were granted. By way of comparison there were 34,782 applications for residence (28% of the total number of private law applications) of which 31,878 (92%) were granted. The number of contact orders made annually has risen spectacularly from 17,589 in 1992 to 46,070 in 2000 to 70,169 in 2004—an overall rise of 390%. In contrast, residence orders rose from 16,515 in 1992 to 25,809 in 2000 to 31,878 in 2004—an

response in part to an influential report *Making Contact Work*[12] and in part to a high profile campaign by pressure groups such as Families need Fathers and Fathers 4 Justice which have brought alleged gender bias in the judicial resolution of residence and, particularly, contact disputes very much to the fore.[13]

The 2006 Act is also interesting for pursuing the twin track policy of, on the one hand, offering aid to facilitate self help and resolution but on the other, if that does not work, of imposing orders with punitive sanctions. However, note must also be taken of the new general powers under section 16A inserted into the Children Act 1989 by the 2006 Act requiring CAFCASS officers to carry out a risk assessment and provide it to the court, if in the course of carrying out any function in private family law proceedings under the 1989 Act (including monitoring of contact orders or even working on alternative dispute resolution) the officer is given cause to suspect that the child concerned is at risk of harm. While this power might be an important safeguard for children's safety, it marks an important shift in State intrusion into private family life and might operate as a disincentive to seek court orders.

One final point before discussing the Part II powers in detail is that, as the Children Act Sub Committee's Report *Making Contact Work*, put it:[14]

'Whilst there is plainly a role for the court in resolving contact disputes, there is a widespread perception that such disputes are better addressed outside the court system. There is a widespread feeling that an application to the court should be the last resort.'

Although this comment is specifically aimed at contact disputes it is clearly apposite to all private law disputes over children. Indeed English law has long recognised the importance of alternative dispute resolution mechanisms in helping to solve family problems.[15]

In 1997 the Children Act Advisory Committee published a *Handbook of Best Practice in Children Act Cases* on which they advised[16] that consideration should first be given to 'whether the dispute between the parties could be resolved in any way other than litigation. Most areas have a mediation service which would be able to attempt to deal with disputes by way of negotiation and agreement. *There is rarely anything to be lost, and normally much to be gained, by mediation.*' [Emphasis added.]

Building on a scheme first introduced in the Principal Registry in London, there has been since March 2004 a nationwide scheme[17] under which *all* applications for a s 8 order (including variations) under the Children Act have to be listed in a conciliation list unless specifically removed by the district judge concerned. As stated in para 4.2 of the *Direction*:

'It is essential that both parties and any legal advisers having conduct of the case attend the

---

overall rise of 193%. Cf the study by C Smart et al *Residence and Contact Disputes in Court* Vol 1 DCA Research Series 6/03 in which over half (60%) of their sample began with an application for a residence order.

[12] A Report to the Lord Chancellor by the Advisory Board on Family Law; Children Act Sub-Committee, 2002.

[13] On which see R. Collier 'Fathers 4 Justice, the law and the new politics of Fatherhood' [2005] CFLQ 511.

[14] Ibid.   [15] See the discussion in Ch 6.

[16] Children Act Advisory Committee, June 1997, para 38.

[17] *District Judge's Direction—Children: Conciliation* [2004] 1 FLR 974. For further details see Brasse G 'Conciliation is Working' [2004] Fam Law 722. Note that this Direction applies even where there are allegations of domestic violence. Note the research by Trinder et al *Making Contact Happen or Making Contact Work? The Process and Outcomes of In-Court Conciliation* (DCA Research Series 3(06)).

appointment. The nature of the application and matters in dispute will be outlined to the district judge and the CAFCASS officer. The conciliation appointment will be conducted with a view to the parties reaching an agreement, and if appropriate, discussion away from the court room will be facilitated. Conciliation is a legally privileged occasion. All the discussions will be privileged and will not be disclosed on any subsequent hearing (other than at a further conciliation appointment) or upon any later application.'

'The Private Law Programme'[18] which comprises guidance issued by the then President of the Family Division, Dame Elizabeth Butler-Sloss, supersedes the 2004 scheme. According to the programme in all private law proceedings under Part II of the Children Act 1989 there should be 'first hearing dispute resolution appointments'. These should be listed within a 'target window' of four to six working weeks from the issue of application. Children aged nine or over are also generally expected to attend the appointment hearing. Where agreement is reached, the district judge will make such orders, if any, as they are appropriate. If no agreement is reached then directions are given for an early hearing and disposal of the application. Neither the district judge nor the CAFCASS officer involved in the appointment can be involved in any subsequent substantive hearing of the dispute.

It has been stressed[19] that mediation/conciliation is vital at all stages of the court process including an appeal. There have been proposals to place even more emphasis on mediation in children cases, including referrals to information meetings,[20] though the Government have stopped short of planning to make mediation compulsory.[21] It is planned to publish best practice guidance for conciliation schemes.

B SECTION 8 ORDERS

1 THE POWERS

The expression 'a section 8 order' means any of the orders mentioned in s 8(1), ie a contact order, a prohibited steps order, a residence order and a specific issue order. It also includes any order varying or discharging a s 8 order.[22] In making any s 8 order the court has further supplemental powers (designed to ensure maximum flexibility) under s 11(7) inter alia to make directions or impose conditions.[23]

(a) Residence orders

A residence order—

---

[18] Issued in November 2004 and published in 2005.

[19] See *Al-Khatib v Masry and others* [2004] EWCA Civ 1353, [2005] 1 FLR 381.

[20] See eg the Government Green Paper *Parental Separation: Children's Needs and Parental Responsibilities* Cm 6273 (July 2004). This has been incorporated into the contact activity direction and was introduced by the Children and Adoption Act 2006, see below p 524. But note the Parliamentary Joint Committee on the Draft Children (Contact) and Adoption Bill: First Report HL Paper 100–1/HC 400–1's recommendation that the 2006 legislation should give the courts a discretion to refer parties to mediation. As they put it, exploring the prospects for mediation was not and should not be confused with compulsory mediation.

[21] See the Government's response to the 2004 Green Paper: *Parental Separation: Children's Needs and Parents' Responsibilities Next Steps* Cm 6452 (January 2005).

[22] Section 8(2).   [23] Discussed below at pp 531ff.

'. . . means an order settling the arrangements to be made as to the person with whom the child is to live'.

Residence orders determine with whom the child is to live. Although by determining with whom the child will live the order effectively determines *where* the child will live, in the absence of a prohibited steps order[24] or, unless the court adds a direction or condition,[25] the person in whose favour the residence order has been made is free to live in or subsequently move to any location within the UK.[26]

Residence orders should not be regarded primarily as a means of reallocating parental responsibility. This is more obviously so as between married parents since, based on the fundamental principle that 'changes in the child's residence should interfere as little as possible in his relationship with both his parents',[27] each parent retains full parental responsibility and with it the power to act independently, unless this is incompatible with a court order, regardless of who has a residence order.[28] But even where the making of a residence order does have the effect of conferring parental responsibility, as it does when made in favour of those who do not already have it,[29] it is normally inappropriate to make such an order *solely* for that purpose. That, at any rate was Thorpe J's view in *Re WB (Residence Orders)*.[30] In that case the applicant (who was the mother's cohabitant) having discovered just before the hearing that he was not the child's father, failed in his attempt to obtain a shared residence order.[31] Although it was acknowledged that this was the only means by which he could acquire parental responsibility, Thorpe J nevertheless refused to interfere with the justices' decision to grant a residence order to the mother and defined contact to the applicant, holding that it would be inappropriate and 'quite artificial' to make a shared residence order solely for that purpose. However, in a much later decision, *Re G (Residence: Same-Sex Partners)*,[32] the Court of Appeal granted a joint residence order, in respect of two children conceived by AID, to both partners to a same-sex relationship specifically to give the non-parent partner parental responsibility to prevent her being marginalised by the mother. Furthermore, *Re WB* had earlier been distinguished in *Re H (Shared Residence: Parental Responsibility)*,[33] in which the Court of Appeal upheld the making of a shared residence order so as to vest the stepfather with parental responsibility for his step-son, since on the facts it would alleviate the confusion in the child's mind to

---

[24] See eg *Re H (Children)(Residence Order: Condition)* [2001] EWCA Civ 1338, [2001] 2 FLR 1279, discussed below at p 535.

[25] Viz under s 11(7) (discussed below, pp 531ff). In practice the courts are reluctant to restrain the residence holder's freedom of movement: see below, pp 533–6.

[26] But not *outside* the UK without either court leave or the consent of everyone with parental responsibility: s 13(1)(b), discussed below, p 555.

[27] See Law Com No 172, para 4.16.

[28] See paras 3.62 et seq. But note *Re G (A Minor) (Parental Responsibility: Education)* [1994] 2 FLR 964, CA, and *Re PC (Change of Surname)* [1997] 2 FLR 730 and *Re J (Specific Issue Orders)(Muslim Upbringing and Circumcision)* [2001] 1 FLR 571, CA, discussed above, p 433.

[29] Under s 12(2)–(3), discussed below, p 550.   [30] [1995] 2 FLR 1023 (decided in 1992).

[31] 'Shared' residence orders are discussed below.   [32] [2005] EWCA Civ 642, [2005] 2 FLR 957.

[33] [1995] 2 FLR 883, CA. Note also *Re AB (Adoption: Joint Residence)* [1996] 1 FLR 27 in which an adoption order was made in favour of one partner and a joint residence order was made in favour of the unmarried couple, in part to ensure that both had parental responsibility. This, of course, was a perfectly legitimate use of residence orders since the child was living with both partners. Nonetheless the need to make such orders has been removed by the Adoption and Children Act 2002 under which (see below p 844) same-sex couples can jointly adopt.

have the comfort and security of knowing not only that his stepfather (whom he had only just discovered was not his natural father) wished to treat him as his child but that the law would give some stamp of approval to that de facto position. In Ward LJ's view[34] unlike *Re WB*, where, as he put it, a shared residence order would be likely to foment disputes which would ill serve the children's welfare, this was a case where a shared residence order was 'not artificial but of important practical therapeutic importance' and where its making reflected 'the reality of the father's involvement and . . . the need for him to be given some status with the school to continue to play his part as both parties wish to do.' In *G v F (Contact and Shared Residence: Applications for Leave)*[35] Bracewell J considered that *Re H* had made it clear that a shared residence order may be appropriate for the purposes of conferring parental responsibility on a non-parent provided it was not simply a device or the sole reason for the application.

Although *Re WB* reflected the original intention behind the 1989 Act it is apparent that the courts have found it inconvenient to apply the ruling strictly, (though it is worth pointing out that the amendments introduced by the Adoption and Children Act 2002 and the Civil Partnership Act 2004 permitting step-parents (i.e. spouses or civil partners of parents) to seek parental responsibility orders,[36] have reduced the need to use residence orders to allocate parental responsibility). But regardless of the correctness or otherwise of *Re G* and *Re H* the better solution, as we have argued earlier in this book,[37] is to vest the court, as in Scotland,[38] with a general power to make parental responsibility orders in favour of anyone. Were this to be done the courts could then confine residence orders to what they are essentially designed for, namely, to determine with whom the child is to live.

Where as a result of a residence order 'the child lives, or is to live, with one of two parents who each have parental responsibility for him', that order will cease to have effect if the parents live together for a continuous period of more than six months.[39]

Joint and shared residence orders

Although residence orders are said to settle the arrangements to be made as to *the person* with whom the child is to live, they can, both because of the general presumption under the Interpretation Act 1978 s 6(c) that words appearing in a statute in the singular include the plural, and the implication of s 11(4)[40] be made in favour of more than one person.[41] A court can therefore make an order in favour of a parent and step-parent,[42] a cohabiting couple,[43] grandparents,[44] or foster parents.[45] In these cases, what may be conveniently

---

[34] Above at 889.   [35] [1998] 2 FLR 799.
[36] Under s 4A (as amended) of the Children Act 1989, discussed above at p 422.
[37] See above p 431.   [38] Discussed below.
[39] Section 11(5). For an example of where such an order did come to such an end see *Re P (Abduction: Declaration)* [1995] 1 FLR 831, at 834, CA.
[40] See the Children (Scotland) Act 1995, s 11(2).
[41] In theory there is nothing to stop the court making an order in favour of more than two people, although in practice it is rarely likely to do so.
[42] See *Re H (Shared Residence: Parental Responsibility)*, [1995] 2 FLR 883, CA.
[43] See eg *Re AB (Adoption: Joint Residence)*, above and *Re C (A Minor) (Residence Order: Lesbian Co-parents)* [1994] Fam Law 468 (joint residence order made to the mother and her female cohabitant).
[44] See eg *Re W (A Minor) (Residence Order)* [1993] 2 FLR 625, CA.
[45] See eg *Re M (Adoption or Residence Order)* [1998] 1 FLR 570, CA.

described as 'joint residence orders' are being made in favour of couples living together, but the power is not so restricted, for under s 11(4) residence orders may also be made in favour of two or more persons who do not live together. These latter type of orders are sometimes known as 'shared residence' orders and will be so called in this Chapter though the courts themselves do not always do so. In theory it is within the court's powers to make both a joint and shared residence order in favour of both parents and their respective new partners, though as yet there is no reported example of such an order.

Shared care arrangements vary: at one end of the spectrum is the case of the child spending half their time with each parent,[46] at the other end is the more common situation of the child spending weekdays with one parent and weekends with the other, or term time with one parent and school holidays with the other. Rather than having to reflect these arrangements by making a residence order in favour of one parent and contact in favour of the other, the Law Commission believed[47] that it would be 'a far more realistic description of the responsibilities involved . . . to make a residence order covering both parents'. In so recommending the Commission were not advocating that children *should* share their time between their parents (an arrangement which they thought would rarely be practical or for the child's benefit)[48] but they were recommending the reversal of a pre-Children Act decision, *Riley v Riley*,[49] which held that courts could not as a matter of principle make what would now be a shared residence order. As the Department of Health's *Guidance and Regulations* admirably put it at the time of the Act's implementation:[50]

'. . . it is not expected that it will become a common form of order because most children will still need the stability of a single home, and partly because in the cases where shared care is appropriate there is less likely to be a need for the court to make any order at all. However, a shared care order has the advantage of being more realistic in those cases where the child is to spend considerable amounts of time with both parents, [and] brings with it certain other benefits (including the right to remove the child from accommodation provided by a local authority under section 20), and removes any impression that one parent is good and responsible whereas the other parent is not.'

The court's approach to making shared residence orders has been an evolving one. Early post-Children Act authority[51] suggested that such orders should only be made in exceptional circumstances but this was resiled from in *A v A (Minors)(Shared Residence Order)*.[52] In upholding an order dividing equally the time the children were to live with each parent outside school term time, Butler-Sloss commented[53] that whilst it was a matter

---

[46] So-called '50/50 shared residence orders' are relatively rare, see eg the comments of Davis J in *R (Bibi) v Camden London Borough Council* [2004] EWHC 2527 (Admin), [2005] 1 FLR 413 at [42(3)].

[47] Law Com No 172, para 4.12.

[48] For some empirical evidence as to the children's experience of shared residence orders, see B. Neale, J. Flowerdew and C. Smart 'Drifting Towards Shared Residence?' [2003] Fam Law 904. Note also the attempts in Australia to promote shared residence briefly referred to by L McCallum 'Shared Residence: Just a Label?' [2004] Fam Law 528. See also F Kaganas and C Piper 'Shared parenting—a 70% solution?' [2002] CFLQ 365.

[49] [1986] 2 FLR 429, CA. But note that in *J v J (Joint Care and Control)* [1991] 2 FLR 385 the Court of Appeal sanctioned a joint (or 'shared') caring arrangement.

[50] Vol 1 *Court Orders*, para 2.28.

[51] *Re H (A Minor)(Shared Residence)* [1994] 1 FLR 717 at 728, per Purchas LJ.

[52] [1994] 1 FLR 669 at 678, CA.   [53] Above at 677.

for individual discretion, in general terms it had to be demonstrated that there was a positive benefit in making what she termed the unusual order of shared residence. However, in what is now the leading case, *D v D (Shared Residence Order)*,[54] the Court of Appeal distanced itself both from the requirement of exceptional circumstances and of the need to show a positive benefit. Hale LJ said that she:[55]

'would not add any gloss on the legislative provisions, which are always subject to the paramount consideration of what is best for the children concerned'.

Butler-Sloss P agreed and, having pointed to the Court of Appeal's developing application of the new concept, said:[56]

'Now nine years later with far greater experience of the workings of the Act it is necessary to underline the importance of the flexibility of the Children Act 1989 in s 8 orders and, consequentially, that the Court of Appeal should not impose restrictions upon the working of the statute not actually found within the words of the section.'

In *D v D* itself the Court of Appeal upheld a decision to make a shared residence order where the children were in effect living with both parents, having homes with each of them and were coping well with the arrangements. The parents, on the other hand, were at loggerheads over the arrangements and had frequently resorted to court proceedings. The hope was that the order would reduce the conflict between the parents.

A shared residence order was also made in not dissimilar circumstances to *D v D* in *A v A (Shared Residence)*[57] in which the children were happily spending 50% of their time with each parent while the adults themselves were incapable of working in harmony. In Wall J's view this was a prime case for a shared residence order since it not only reflected the reality that the children were dividing their time equally between their parents but it also reflected the fact that the parents were equal in the eyes of the law having equal duties and responsibilities towards their children. Moreover it avoided the risk that a sole residence order could have been misinterpreted as enabling control by one parent when what the family needed was co-operation as recognised by the shared residence order.[58]

Both *D v D* and *A v A* scotch the notion that a harmonious relationship between the parents is a prerequisite for making a shared residence order.[59] In *A v A* Wall J commented[60]

'*D v D* makes it clear that a shared residence order is an order that the children live with both parents. It must therefore reflect the reality of the children's lives. Where children are living with one parent and are either not seeing the other parent or the amount of time to be spent with the other parent is limited or undecided, there cannot be a shared residence order. However, where children are spending a substantial amount of time with both their parents,

---

[54] [2001] 1 FLR 495, CA.   [55] Above at para (32).   [56] At para (39).

[57] [2004] EWHC 142 (Fam), [2004] 1 FLR 1195.

[58] Note the attempt to avoid future disputes by the attachment to the order of a Schedule of items relating to the exercise of parental responsibility.

[59] See the comments to that effect by Thorpe LJ in *Re R (Children)* [2005] EWCA Civ 542 at [11]. See also *Re P (children) (shared residence order)* [2005] EWCA Civ 1639, [2006] 1 FCR 309, in which the trial judge was held wrong to refuse to make a shared residence order on the basis that it would affect the issue of control and power between the parents.

[60] Above at para [119].

a shared residence order reflects the reality of the children's lives. It is not necessarily to be considered an exceptional order and should be made if it is in the best interests of the children concerned.'

Illustrative of these two themes are *Re A (Children)(Shared Residence)*[61] and *Re F (Shared Residence Order).*[62] The former case concerned three children, two girls who lived with their mother and a boy who lived with his father. The boy was unwilling to see his mother and was not doing so and there was also some uncertainty about one of the girls' contact with her father. In setting aside the shared residence orders[63] Hale LJ emphasised that since a residence order was about where a child is to live it was difficult to make a shared residence order 'about a child who is not only not living with one of the parents but is for the foreseeable future, unlikely even to visit with that parent'.

In *Re F*, on the other hand, a shared residence order (with the children spending school terms with the mother and holidays with the father) was made in respect of two young children notwithstanding the fact that the mother lived in Edinburgh which was a considerable distance and in another jurisdiction from the father's home in Hampshire, England. Thorpe LJ repeated the view that a shared residence order had to reflect the underlying reality of where the children lived their lives and not deal with parental status. He specifically rejected the notion that a shared residence order was only apt where the children alternated their two homes evenly. As Wall J later commented in *A v A*[64] in relation to *Re F* 'If the home offered by each parent was of equal status and importance to the children an order for shared residence would be valuable.'

Where a residence order is made in favour of two persons who do not live together, then under s 11(4), the order may specify the periods during which the child is to live in the different households concerned. Such directions may be general rather than specific and in some cases may not be needed at all. Since a residence order only settles the arrangements as to the person with whom the child is to live, any other conditions that are needed must be specified separately by the court either acting under the powers vested by s 11(7)[65] or possibly at large.[66] Indeed, given that under a shared residence order neither carer is obliged to consult the other unless this is specified in the order, it is important that the order is clear on points which are fundamental to the success of the arrangement.[67]

'Interim' residence orders

The combination of s 11(3) which permits the court to make, inter alia, a residence order 'even though it is not in a position to dispose finally of those proceedings' and s 11(7)(c) under which orders can be made for a specified period enables courts to make interim provision by way of a residence order for a limited period.[68] The Act, however, makes no distinction between a final residence order and one made as an interim measure. Indeed,

---

[61] [2001] EWCA Civ 1795, [2002] 1 FCR 177.   [62] [2003] EWCA Civ 592, [2003] 2 FLR 397.

[63] These orders were originally coupled with orders for care and control respectively to the mother in respect of the girls and the father in respect of the boy, which was clearly outside the 1989 Act powers.

[64] Above at para [121].   [65] Discussed below, pp 531ff.

[66] See *A v A (Shared Residence)* [2004] EWHC 142 (Fam), [2004] 1 FLR 1195 in which a Schedule was attached.

[67] For an attempt to do this see the Schedule attached to the shared care order made in *A v A* above.

[68] It is apparently possible to make an interim residence order run alongside the main order: see *Re M (Minors) (Interim Residence Order)* [1997] 2 FCR 28, CA.

as Bracewell J has observed in *S v S (Custody: Jurisdiction)*:[69] 'It has become common parlance to speak of "interim residence orders", but in fact there is no such creature within the Children Act 1989.' Hence *all* such orders, even those expressed to last for a matter of days, have the same effect and will, for example, discharge any existing care order,[70] confer, for the duration of the order, parental responsibility on those who do not already have it,[71] and empower the residence holder to remove the child from the UK for a period of less than one month.[72]

Ex parte applications and orders

Although applications for residence orders can be made ex parte[73] (that is, where no notice is given to the respondent), they should only be granted exceptionally.[74] It is accepted, for instance, that they are appropriate in cases of child abduction,[75] while in *Re Y (a minor) (ex parte residence orders)*[76] an ex parte order in favour of a grandmother was thought justified in a case where the mother, who had a history of mental instability, had phoned her threatening to commit suicide. It is evident, however, that the circumstances need to be compelling. In *Re G (Minors) (Ex Parte Interim Residence Order)*,[77] for instance, an allegation that the mother had been taking cannabis was not thought to justify making an ex parte order in favour of the father. In *Re P (A Minor) (Ex Parte Interim Residence Order)*[78] an ex parte order was held to have been wrongly granted where the child was in no immediate danger, since she was already under the scrutiny of the local authority.

Even where it is appropriate to make an ex parte order, that order should normally only be for a short duration.[79] In most cases those wishing to challenge such orders should await the full hearing rather than appeal.[80]

---

[69] [1995] 1 FLR 155 at 157.

[70] Under s 91(1): see below, pp 787–8. Where an 'interim' order is thought justified, careful thought needs to be given to its length and, mindful of the general enjoinder under s 1(2) to treat 'delay' as prima facie detrimental to the child's interest, courts should ensure that it is no longer than absolutely necessary: see eg *Re O (Minors) (Leave To Seek Residence Order)* [1994] 1 FLR 172, where, on the facts, five weeks' duration was thought too long. See also *Re Y (A Minor) (Ex Parte Interim Orders)* [1993] 2 FCR 422, discussed below.

[71] Under s 12(2): see below, p 550.

[72] Under s 13(2) (below, p 555). Presumably this power of removal is subject to the length of the order— an order expressed to last only a few days cannot be taken to vest a power of removal in excess of that. 'Interim' orders are recognised and enforceable under the European Convention on Recognition and Enforcement of Decisions Concerning Children 1980: see *Re S (A Minor) (Custody: Habitual Residence)* [1998] AC 750, HL, discussed below, p 679, and no doubt they are similarly recognised and enforceable under Brussels II, discussed below at p 672. They also take effect as a 'superseding' order for the purpose of the Family Law Act 1986, see further below at p 689.

[73] Family Proceedings Rules 1991 r 4.4(4) as amended by SI 1992/2067, and Family Proceedings Courts (Children Act 1989) Rules 1991 r 4(4) as amended by SI 1992/2068. Originally no such provision had been made, see the discussion at p 416 of the previous edition of this work.

[74] See *Re G (Minors)(Ex Parte Interim Residence Order)* [1993] 1 FLR 910 at 912, per Butler-Sloss LJ and Note: *Re J (Children: Ex Parte Orders)* [1997] 1 FLR 606 at 609, per Hale J.

[75] See *Re B (Minors)(Residence Order)* [1992] Fam 162, per Butler-Sloss LJ.   [76] [1993] 2 FCR 422.

[77] Above.

[78] [1993] 1 FLR 915, CA. See also Note: *Re J (Children: Ex Parte Orders)* above—an ex parte order requiring the handing over of a young child [aged three] to a parent with whom he had not lived for 20 months was only likely to be justified in exceptional circumstances.

[79] See *Re Y*, above, in which Johnson J held that 12 weeks was too long and that the norm should be seven days.

[80] Per Purchas LJ in *Re P*, above at 917–18.

(b) Contact orders

A contact order requires:

'... the person with whom the child lives, or is to live, to allow the child to visit or stay with the person named in the order, or for that person and the child otherwise to have contact with each other'.

By providing for the child to visit or stay with the person named in the order, the emphasis is clearly on the child rather than the parent.[81] As the words 'otherwise to have contact with each other' make clear, contact orders embrace both physical and non-physical contact and may therefore range from long or short visits to contact by letter or telephone.[82] Whether a contact order is *necessarily* directed against the person with whom the child lives or is to live, as the opening part of the definition suggests, or whether the closing words 'or for the person and the child otherwise to have contact with each other' can properly be regarded as empowering a court to make an independent order simply providing for the child to have contact with a person named in the order, has not expressly been addressed by the courts. However, in *Re H (Minors) (Prohibited Steps Order)*[83] the underlying assumption was that such orders are directed against the person with whom the child is living etc. As will be seen, the distinction is not without importance when determining the court's power to prohibit contact[84] and to enforce the order.[85]

Orders may provide for the child to have contact with any person (including, where appropriate, a sibling) and more than one contact order may be made in respect of a child. In theory, it is within the court's powers to provide for the child to have contact with an unwilling parent but given that such orders are 'against' the person with whom the child lives, they would be unenforceable. The question whether or not the court should have power to compel an unwilling parent to have contact with a child was debated in the discussions leading to the Children and Adoption Act 2006. The Joint Committee on the Draft Children (Contact) and Adoption Bill were in favour of the introduction of such a power[86] but the Government dismissed the suggestion saying:[87]

'We would be concerned about the implications that would arise if contact orders were to be used to force someone, against their wishes, to have contact with a child. The child's welfare must be the paramount consideration in making decisions about their upbringing and there are serious issues raised about the potential distress, or even harm, such contact could cause to the child or children involved.'

A contact order can be the sole order made even between parents and may be

---

[81] This is more in keeping with the views expressed by Wrangham J in *M v M (Child: Access)* [1973] 2 All ER 81 that access is properly to be regarded as a right of the child rather than a right of the parent.

[82] For examples of contact by post see eg *A v L (Contact)* [1998] 1 FLR 361 and *Re M (A Minor) (Contact: Conditions)* [1994] 1 FLR 272—both involving letter contact with a father in prison, and *Re L (Contact: Transsexual Applicant)* [1995] 2 FLR 438 (indirect contact with transsexual father). *Re D (Parental Responsibility: IVF Baby)* [2001] 1 FLR 972, CA—indirect contact with a man deemed to be the father under the Human Fertilisation and Embryology Act 1990. For examples of indirect contact with violent or abusive parents being ordered, see eg *Re S (Violent Parent: Indirect Contact)* [2000] 1 FLR 481, *Re H (Contact: Domestic Violence)* [1998] 2 FLR 42, CA and *Re M (Sexual Abuse Allegations: Interviewing Techniques)* [1999] 2 FLR 92.

[83] [1995] 1 WLR 667, CA, discussed further below at p 523.   [84] See below, ibid.

[85] See below, p 572.   [86] See their First Report HL Paper 100–1/HC 400–1.

[87] See the *Government Reply to the Report from the Joint Committee* CM 6583 (June 2005).

appropriate where there is no dispute as to the person with whom the child is to live. Orders can provide for contact to take place at Contact Centres. The role of these Centres has been said[88] to be 'one of the most important developments in the last ten years'. They are a useful means of providing a temporary venue for supported contact in cases where the child's parents are unable to provide an alternative. They are not, however, intended to be places for contact over the long-term, nor are they the equivalent of professionally supervised contact. Orders can also provide for contact to take place abroad.[89]

Although courts can make orders for 'reasonable contact',[90] if that is the sole order between parents, then, having regard to s 1(5),[91] one may question the need to make the order at all. Such an order might, however, be justified where the applicant is not a parent, eg a grandparent, since without an order such a person has no locus standi in relation to the child[92] and it might be valuable if the person with whom the child lives is hostile to the absent parent having contact and might therefore seek to prevent it. Where restricted or supervised contact is thought appropriate the court may attach any directions or conditions under s 11(7).

Like residence orders, contact orders requiring one parent to allow the child to visit the other parent[93] automatically lapse if the parents subsequently live together for a continuous period of more than six months.[94] Under the general provisions of s 11(3) a court can make an 'interim contact order' in cases where it is not in a position finally to dispose of proceedings. However, it has been held[95] that courts should be cautious about making such interim orders where the principle of contact is in dispute and substantial factual issues are unresolved. Where sexual abuse is alleged against a parent and the child is showing behavioural problems then, even if on the available evidence abuse is not likely to be established but further investigation is necessary, while it might be appropriate to allow contact to continue, it is not appropriate to make an order for staying contact.[96]

While the child is with a parent on a contact visit that parent may exercise parental responsibility, at any rate with respect to short term matters,[97] without consulting the other, provided he does nothing which is incompatible with any existing court order.[98]

---

[88] See *Making Contact Work*, op cit, ch 8.

[89] *Re F (A Minor)(Access Out of Jurisdiction)* [1973] Fam 198.

[90] Before the 1989 Act orders for 'reasonable' access were very common and the Department of Health's *Guidance and Regulations*, Vol 1, *Court Orders* at para 2.29 anticipated that orders for reasonable contact would be the 'usual order'. Interestingly a similar comment is made in the Department of Health and Social Services' *Guidance and Regulations to the Children (Northern Ireland) Order 1995*, Vol 1, *Court Orders and Other Issues*, para 5.11 (published in 1996).

[91] Discussed above at p 475 and below, p 581.   [92] See below, pp 544–8.

[93] Aliter if the order is directed against someone other than a parent or if the child is permitted contact with a third party.

[94] Section 11(6).

[95] Per Wall J in *Re D (Contact: Interim Orders)* [1995] 1 FLR 495. An example of where such an order might be justified is where previously satisfactory contact has been arbitrarily terminated by the 'residential parent'.

[96] *Re W (Staying Contact)* [1998] 2 FLR 450, CA. It may not, however, be possible, particularly in domestic violence cases, to make an interim order without hearing oral evidence or the advice of a children and family reporter: see *Re M (Interim Contact: Domestic Violence)* [2000] 2 FLR 377, CA.

[97] But, possibly, not to take important steps that have long term consequences for the child: see eg *Re G (Parental Responsibility: Education)* [1994] 2 FLR 964, CA discussed above at pp 432–4.

[98] See above, p 432.

Prohibiting contact

When the 1989 Act was first implemented it was thought that orders denying contact required a prohibited steps order. As the Department of Health's *Guidance and Regulations* stated:[99]

'. . . a s 8 order is a positive order in the sense that it requires contact to be allowed between an individual and a child and *cannot be used to deny contact*' [emphasis added].

However, this reasoning was rejected by the Court of Appeal in *Nottingham County Council v P*.[100] Sir Stephen Brown P commented:

'Submissions were made to the court to the effect that a contact order in any event necessarily implied a positive order and that an order which merely provided for "no contact" could not be construed as a contact order. There are certain passages in editorial comment which seem to support that view. We do not share it. We agree with the judge that the sensible and appropriate construction of the term contact order includes a situation where a court is required to consider whether any contact should be provided for. An order that there shall be "no contact" falls within the general concept and common sense requires that it should be considered to fall within the definition of "contact order" in section 8(1).'

However, in the subsequent decision, *Re H (Minors) (Prohibited Steps Order)*,[101] the Court of Appeal made a prohibited steps order against a mother's former cohabitant preventing him from having or seeking contact with her children, to whom it was considered he posed a risk. It was held that it was only by this means that the order could be directed (and thus enforced) against the man. Butler-Sloss LJ commented that had a 'no contact' order been made it would have been directed against the mother, who would thus have been obliged to prevent contact. That would have been inappropriate in this case, since she neither wanted the children to have such contact nor had she the power to control it.[102]

In the light of these decisions it would seem that the appropriate order for prohibiting contact is determined by considering against whom it should be directed.[103] If it is against the person with whom the child is living or is to live, then an order for 'no contact' should be made. If, as seems more likely to be the case, it is against some other person, then a prohibited steps order is appropriate.[104] It has to be said that the current position is unnecessarily complicated. The better view is, surely, as was originally envisaged, that a complete denial of contact should be made by a prohibited steps order.[105] Accordingly, it is submitted that in this respect the ruling in *Nottingham* was wrong.

[99] Vol 1, *Court Orders*, para 2.30.
[100] [1994] Fam 18 at 38–9, CA, discussed further below at pp 529 and 530.
[101] [1995] 1 WLR 667, CA.
[102] The children were of school age and, as Butler-Sloss LJ said, 'With the best will in the world the mother could not protect her children going to and from school or at play . . .'
[103] Though, as was observed earlier (above, p 521), it is not beyond argument that a contact order is not necessarily directed against anyone.
[104] Presumably, on this analysis, where it is thought necessary and appropriate to direct an order against both persons, both a 'no contact' and a prohibited steps order should be made.
[105] Interestingly, the *Guidance* to the Northern Ireland Order, above, states at para 5.15 that, although it will be a matter for judicial interpretation whether a contact order can be used to deny contact, in the light of the *Nottingham* and *Re H* decisions 'it would seem appropriate to use a prohibited steps order to deny contact.'

Warning notices

As part of the package of measures introduced by the Children and Adoption Act 2006 to improve the enforcement of contact orders, it is provided by s 11L of the Children Act 1989 (as inserted by the 2006 Act) that *whenever* a court makes or varies a contact order, it must attach a notice warning of the consequences for failing to comply. As we discuss later in the chapter,[106] as well as being able to impose sanctions for contempt of court, courts can also make enforcement and financial compensation orders.

(c) Contact activity directions and conditions

As part of the strategy to facilitate contact, powers to make contact activity directions and conditions have been introduced by the Children and Adoption Act 2006 via the insertions of ss 11A to 11G into the Children Act 1989.[107] Directions can only be made where a court is *considering* whether to make (or to vary or discharge) a contact order. They cannot be given on a final contact order.[108] Conversely, conditions can only be made upon the making (or variation) of a contact order. The latter are part of a formal order and are therefore enforceable on pain of contempt, by an enforcement order or by a financial compensation order.[109] Although there are no formal sanctions for non compliance with directions, due account can be taken of any breaches[110] in the final disposal of the contact issue.

Contact activity directions

A direction is defined in s 11A as one 'requiring a party to the proceedings to take part in an activity that promotes contact with the child concerned'.

It must specify both the activity and the person providing the activity. The activities that may be so required include (a) programmes, classes and counselling or guidance sessions of a kind that may assist a person as regards establishing, maintaining or improving contact with a child and, may, by addressing a person's violent behaviour, enable or facilitate contact; (b) sessions in which information or advice is given as regards making or operating arrangements for contact with a child including making arrangements by means of mediation.[111] On the other hand, a direction cannot be used to require medical or psychiatric examinations or mediation.[112]

Somewhat questionably, directions can only be made where there is some dispute over contact[113] and children can only be made to take part in an activity if they are the parent

---

[106] See below pp 572ff.

[107] For the background to these measures see the Government Green Paper's *Parental Separation: Children's Needs and Parents' Responsibilities* Cm 6273 (July 2004), *Parental Separation: Children's Needs and Parent's Responsibilities: Next Steps* Cm 6452 (January, 2005); the Draft Children (Contact) and Adoption Bill Cm 6462 (February 2005); the Joint Committee on the Draft Children (Contact) and Adoption Bill: First Report HL Paper 100–1/HL (the so-called 'Scrutiny Committee') and *The Government Reply to the Report from the Joint Committee* Cm 6583 (June 2005). For comments on the proposals see J Masson and C Humphreys 'Facilitating and Enforcing Contact: The Bill and the Ten Per Cent' [2005] Fam Law 548.

[108] Section 11A(7).   [109] Discussed below at pp 567, 572 and 573 respectively.

[110] A CAFCASS officer can be asked to monitor compliance with a direction and to report to the court any failure to comply, s 11G.

[111] Financial assistance to help individual pay providers for their services might be available from the State: s 11F.

[112] Section 11A(6).

[113] This provision has been criticised as unnecessarily limiting the court's powers. Furthermore there is no requirement that contact must be disputed when imposing *conditions*, see below.

of the child concerned. Directions cannot be made in contact applications in adoption proceedings.[114]

In deciding whether to make a direction, 'the welfare of the child concerned is to be the court's paramount consideration'.[115] The court must also be satisfied that the activity is appropriate in the circumstances of the case; that the provider of the activity concerned is suitable to provide it and the activity is available in a place to which it is reasonable to expect the person in question to travel.[116]

Contact activity conditions

Like a direction, under s 11C a contact activity condition 'requires an individual to take part in an activity that promotes contact with the child concerned'.

It must similarly specify both the activity and the person providing the activity and the activity conditions are the same as those that can be specified in a direction and are subject to the same prohibitions.[117] Under s 11D conditions can only be imposed upon a child if he or she is a parent of the child concerned. Conditions cannot be added to contact orders made in adoption proceedings and conditions can only be imposed on individuals who are habitually resident in England and Wales. Like directions, in deciding whether to make a condition the court must be satisfied that the activity is appropriate in the circumstances of the case; that the provider of the activity concerned is suitable to provide it and the activity is available in a place to which it is reasonable to expect the person in question to travel.[118] However, unlike when making directions, there is *no* express requirement to treat the child's welfare as the paramount consideration when making conditions.[119]

There are other differences between condition and directions. As has been said, conditions can only be made upon the making (or variation) of a contact order.[120] There is therefore no stated requirement that there needs to have been a dispute over contact. Unlike directions, which can be imposed upon parties, the individuals upon whom conditions can be imposed are limited to the person with whom the child concerned lives or is to live; a person whose contact with the child is provided for by the contact order; and a person upon whom the contact order imposes a condition under s 11(7)(b) of the Children Act 1989. A final but crucial difference between directions and conditions is that the latter but not the former are enforceable.[121]

(d) Monitoring contact

In addition to asking CAFCASS officers to monitor compliance with contact activity directions and conditions, under s 11H a court can also ask a CAFCASS officer to monitor

---

[114] Section 11B. The section also provides that the individual must be habitually resident in England and Wales.

[115] Section 11B(9).   [116] Section 11E.

[117] Section 11C(5). Note in particular that conditions cannot require medical or psychiatric examinations or mediation.

[118] Section 11E.

[119] This seems a curious omission but on general principles, applying s 1(1), courts will have to treat the child's welfare as the paramount consideration in determining whether to add conditions.

[120] Contact orders can be varied so as to impose a condition: s 11C(2).

[121] Though for both directions and conditions, CAFCASS officers can be asked to monitor the compliance and report to the court any failure to comply: s 11G.

compliance with a contact order (other than those made in adoption proceedings) and to report to the court on such matters relating to compliance as the court may specify. Such monitoring roles can last up to one year. Those who can be subject to monitoring are a person who is required to allow contact with the child; a person whose contact with the child is provided for; and a person who is subject to a condition under s 11(7)(b) of the Children Act 1989.

(e) Prohibited steps orders

A prohibited steps order—

'. . . means an order that no step which could be taken by a parent in meeting his parental responsibility for a child, and which is of a kind specified in the order, shall be taken by any person without the consent of the court'.

This is one of two orders under the 1989 Act (the other being a specific issue order), which are modelled on the wardship jurisdiction, and intended to broaden all the courts' powers when dealing with children.

It empowers a court to place a *specific* embargo upon the exercise of any aspect of parental responsibility. This is in contrast to the vague requirement in wardship that 'no important step' in the child's life be taken without the court's prior consent.[122] This order can be put to a variety of uses. It can, for example, be used to prohibit contact with a parent or someone else,[123] to restrain a particular medical operation, including the ritual circumcision of a boy without the consent of the other parent or the court,[124] restrain changing the child's surname,[125] the child's schooling or religion, and preventing the child's removal from his home before the court has had time to decide what order, if any, should be made.[126] Another example, instanced by the Law Commission,[127] is to impose an embargo that the child should not be removed from the United Kingdom, which they said might be useful in cases where no residence order has been made so that the automatic restriction against removal under s 13 does not apply.[128] Even where the s 13 restrictions do apply it might still be possible to obtain a prohibited steps order to prevent repeated removal of children outside the United Kingdom for periods of less than one month by the residential parent. Furthermore since s 13 only prevents a child's removal

---

[122] Wardship is discussed in Ch 16. It is assumed that an order as vague as prohibiting any important step could not be made as a prohibited steps order.

[123] *Re H (A Minor) (Prohibited Steps Order)* [1995] 1 WLR 667, CA, discussed above at p 523.

[124] *Re J (Specific Issue Orders: Muslim Upbringing and Circumcision)* [1999] 2 FLR 678, per Wall J upheld on appeal: [2000] 1 FLR 571, CA. See also *Re S (Specific Issue Order: Religion: Circumcision)* [2004] EWHC 1282 (Fam), [2005] 1 FLR 236.

[125] At any rate in the absence of a residence order: see *Dawson v Wearmouth* [1999] 2 AC 308, HL. Where there is a residence order, applications concerning a change of name should be made under s 13: see *Re B (Change of Surname)* [1996] 1 FLR 791, CA, discussed below, p 550.

[126] See *Guidance and Regulations*, Vol 1, *Court Orders* at para 2.31.

[127] The embargo under s 13(1)(b) and (2) is discussed below, p 555. In the absence of a residence order, the Child Abduction Act 1984 (see above, p 395) operates to prevent unilateral removal. However, a prohibited steps order could be made to prevent a child's removal outside England and Wales rather than the United Kingdom as a whole.

[128] Law Com No 172, para 4.20. This comment is repeated by the Department of Health's *Guidance and Regulations*, Vol 1, *Court Orders*, at para 2.31.

outside the United Kingdom, a prohibited steps order is a possible option[129] to prevent relocation *within* the United Kingdom.[130]

Although the order itself must relate to parental responsibility, it is clear that it can be made against anyone regardless of whether he has parental responsibility. Hence orders can be made against an unmarried father whether or not he has responsibility and similarly against a third party, for example to restrain a former cohabitant (notwithstanding that he was not even a party) from contacting or seeking to have contact with the child,[131] or to restrain an individual or group from associating with the child.

Provided the order is of some value to the applicant it can be made even though the child is abroad.[132] Applications for prohibited steps orders can be made ex parte, and an order may be made either in conjunction with another s 8[133] order or on its own.

(f) Specific issue order[134]

A specific issue order—

'... means an order giving directions for the purpose of determining a specific question which has arisen, or which may arise, in connection with any aspect of parental responsibility for a child'.

These orders enable a specific question relating to the child to be brought before the court, the aim of which is not to give one parent or the other a general 'right' to make decisions in a particular respect, but to enable a particular dispute to be resolved.[135] It was held in *Re HG (Specific Issue Order: Sterilisation)*[136] that there is no necessity for there to be a dispute between the parties before the power arises to make a specific issue order; it is sufficient that there is a question to be answered. In that case an unopposed application[137] for a specific issue order was granted giving High Court sanction for the sterilisation of a 17-year-old mentally subnormal child. Like prohibited steps orders, applications for specific issue orders may be made ex parte[138] and orders may be made either in conjunction with another s 8 order or on their own. Examples of specific issue

---

[129] Another is to seek a condition to be imposed on a residence order, see below p 531.

[130] See *Re H (Children)(Residence Order: Condition)* [2001] EWCA Civ 1338, [2001] 2 FLR 1277, discussed below at p 535.

[131] *Re H* above. In the case of non-parties, orders cannot be enforced until they have been served on the respondent: see Clarke Hall and Morrison on *Children* Vol 1 at 1[666].

[132] See *Re D (a minor)* [1992] 1 All ER 892, CA—a mother, in breach of an undertaking given to the English court, failed to return the child from Turkey: an order for the child's return was thought helpful to the father in bringing proceedings in Turkey.

[133] FPR 1991 r 4.4(4); FPC (CA 1989) R 1991 r 4.4. Such orders are sometimes made in the context of international child abduction, often at the request of the abducting parent, to prevent removal by the other. See *Re S (Minors) (Abduction)* [1994] 1 FLR 297, CA.

[134] See generally S Gilmore 'The nature, scope and use of the specific issue order' [2004] CFLQ 367.

[135] Department of Health's *Guidance and Regulations,* Vol 1, *Court Orders,* para 2.32.

[136] [1993] 1 FLR 587.

[137] The application was thought necessary in view of Lord Templeman's lone dictum in *Re B (A Minor) (Wardship: Sterilisation)* [1988] AC 199 at 205, (discussed above at p 392) that High Court sanction is always required for a child's sterilisation. See also *Practice Note* [1993] 3 All ER 222.

[138] Family Proceedings Rules 1991 r 4.4(4); Family Proceedings Courts (Children Act 1989) Rules 1991 r 4(4). For an example of an *order* being made ex parte see *Re D (A Minor)(Child: Removal From Jurisdiction)* [1992] 1 WLR 667, CA.

orders include *Re C (Welfare of Child: Immunisation)*,[139] in which the court orderd, contrary to the mother's wishes, the child's immunisation; *Re R (A Minor) (Blood Trans-fusion)*,[140] in which the court ordered inter alia that, in an imminently life-threatening situation, the child in question be given a blood transfusion without the consent of her parents, who were Jehovah's Witnesses; *Re F (Specific Issue: Child Interview)*,[141] in which an order was made permitting a defence solicitor to interview children for the purpose of providing evidence in criminal proceedings against their father; *Re D (A Minor)*,[142] in which a mother was ordered to return the child to the jurisdiction; and *Re A (Child-ren)(Specific Issue Order: Parental Dispute)*[143] in which the court ordered, at the French father's request, that the two children should attend the Lycée Français in London even though since their parents' separation they were living with their English mother in England. Specific issue orders can also be sought to resolve disputes over children's religious upbringing;[144] to inform children about their father's identity and even very existence;[145] to return the children to their home jurisdiction;[146] and, provided no resi-dence order is in force, to obtain court leave to change a child's name[147] or to take the child out of the UK.[148]

(g) Limits on the courts' powers to make specific issue and prohibited steps orders [149]

Orders must concern 'an aspect of parental responsibility'

An important limitation both on prohibited and specific issue orders is that they must concern an aspect of parental responsibility. Courts cannot, therefore, make a prohibited steps order forbidding contact between the parents,[150] or protecting one parent from being

---

[139] [2003] EWHC 1376 (Fam), [2003] 2 FLR 1054, upheld on appeal: [2003] EWCA Civ 1148, [2003] 2 FLR 1095. See also *Re C (HIV Test)* [1999] 2 FLR 1004, CA—in which a specific issue order was granted that a baby be tested for HIV.

[140] [1993] 2 FLR 757.

[141] [1995] 1 FLR 819, CA. See also *Re M (Care: Leave To Interview Child)* [1995] 1 FLR 825, discussed above at p 463 n 102.

[142] Above.

[143] [2001] 1 FLR 121, CA. See also *Re W (children)(education: choice of school)* [2002] EWCA Civ 1411, [2002] 3 FCR 473.

[144] See *Re S (Specific Issue Order: Religion: Circumcision)* [2004] EWHC 1282 (Fam), [2005] 1 FLR 236 in which a Muslim mother separated from the Hindu father unsuccessfully sought a specific issue order for both children to become practising members of the Islamic faith and for the boy to be circumcised. A similar application was refused in *Re J (Specific Issue Orders: Muslim Upbringing and Circumcision)* [1999] 2 FLR 678, upheld on appeal at [2000] 1 FLR 571.

[145] *Re K (Specific Issue Order)* [1999] 2 FLR 280—application rejected.

[146] See eg *Re J (A Child)(Custody Rights: Jurisdiction)* [2005] UK HL 40, [2005] 3 WLR 14, discussed below at p 623.

[147] See *Dawson v Wearmouth* [1999] 2 AC 308, HL and *Re W (A Child)(Illegitimate Child: Change of Surname)* [2001] Fam 1, CA discussed below at p 552.

[148] *Re D (A Minor)(Child: Removal From Jurisdiction)* [1992] 1 WLR 667, CA.

[149] See also below, p 539 for a discussion of the general restrictions on making s 8 orders and, in particular, pp 540–2 in relation to the fetters on local authority use.

[150] *Croydon London Borough Council v A* [1992] Fam 169; cf *F v R (Contact)* [1995] 1 FLR 227 in which Wall J accepted that such an embargo could be incorporated as a condition to a residence or contact order under s 11(7), though this decision is now difficult to square with *D v N (Contact Orders: Conditions)* [1997] 2 FLR 797, CA discussed below, p 532.

assaulted by the other,[151] nor may it make a specific issue order compelling a local authority to provide support services,[152] since neither contact between adults nor the provision of support services has anything to do with parental responsibility. It has been doubted whether there is power to dictate to a parent what is said to the child about his or her origins.[153]

No power to order a parent's removal from the family home

In *Nottingham County Council v P*[154] Sir Stephen Brown commented that 'it is very doubtful indeed whether a prohibited steps order could in any circumstances be used to "oust" a father from a matrimonial home.' Similarly, in *Pearson v Franklin*[155] Nourse LJ commented that Parliament could not have intended that ouster orders are capable of being made under the guise of specific issue orders. It was therefore held that a specific issue order (and by implication a prohibited steps order) could not be used to interfere with rights of occupation. In *Re M (Minors) (Disclosure of Evidence)*[156] the Court of Appeal took *Nottingham* to have established that there is no jurisdiction under the Children Act to exclude a parent from the home for the protection of the child, and in *Re D (Prohibited Steps Order)*[157] Ward LJ clearly stated that there is no jurisdiction to make an ouster order under the Children Act.[158]

Aside from justifying this position as a matter of policy (ie that because of their drastic effect Parliament should be taken to confer the power to make ouster orders only where a statute clearly so provides) a possible theoretical justification for this lack of power is that ouster orders relate to matters of occupation rather than parental responsibility.[159]

No power to make disguised residence or contact orders

Section 9(5)(a) prevents the court from making a prohibited steps or a specific issue order 'with a view to achieving a result which could be achieved by a residence or contact order'. This provision was made to guard against the slight risk, particularly in uncontested cases, that the orders might be used to achieve the same practical results as residence or contact orders but without the same legal effects.[160] A clear example of the

---

[151] *M v M (Residence Order: Ancillary Jurisdiction)* [1994] Fam Law 440 in which Johnson J also held that an injunction could nevertheless be sought under the appropriate domestic violence legislation, as an ancillary action to the Children Act application.

[152] *Re J (Specific Issue Order: Leave To Apply)* [1995] 1 FLR 669, per Wall J.

[153] See *J v C and E (A Child)* [2006] EWCA Civ 551 at [14], per Wall LJ.

[154] [1994] Fam 18 at 39E–F, CA.   [155] [1994] 2 All ER 137 at 141d–e, per Nourse LJ, CA.

[156] [1994] 1 FLR 760.

[157] [1996] 2 FLR 273. See also *Re D (Residence: Imposition of Conditions)* [1996] 2 FLR 281, CA. Both these cases also establish that the inability to make an ouster order by way of a prohibited steps or specific issue order cannot be overcome by using s 11(7). See also *D v N (Contact Order: Conditions)* [1997] 2 FLR 797, CA, discussed below, p 532.

[158] Though probably an application for an occupation order under Part IV of the Family Law Act 1996 (discussed above at pp 230ff) can be brought as an ancillary action to the Children Act application; cf *M v M (Residence Order: Ancillary Injunction)*, above n 151. For the court's power to make ouster orders under the High Court's inherent jurisdiction and upon making an emergency protection or interim care order, see below, pp 726, 784 and 906 respectively.

[159] This line of argument was hinted at by Nourse LJ in *Pearson v Franklin*, above, but it is not beyond question, since ouster orders are viewed as being primarily about protection and only incidentally about occupation. See the discussion above at p 252.

[160] Law Com No 172, para 4.19. Department of Health's *Guidance and Regulations*, Vol 1, *Court Orders*, para 2.34.

type of order forbidden by s 9(5)(a) is *M v C (Children Orders: Reasons)*[161] in which justices purported to make a specific issue order returning the children to their mother which could and should have been achieved by a residence order. But other examples are less obvious. For instance, in *Re B (Minors) (Residence Order)*[162] it was held that s 9(5)(a) operates to prevent the making of a specific issue order to return a child to a parent in the case of a snatch, since such an order could be made by means of a residence order with appropriate conditions attached under s 11(7).[163] In *Nottingham County Council v P*[164] it was held to be contrary to s 9(5)(a) to order, upon a local authority application under s 8, that a father vacate the household and that the child should have no further contact with him save under local authority supervision since the application patently sought to determine the residence of the children (that is, by regulating who could live in the household) and the degree of contact which the children might have with the father. In this latter regard the Court of Appeal, as we discussed earlier,[165] rejected the argument that an order for 'no contact' could not be made as a contact order under s 8. However, in the subsequent Court of Appeal case, *Re H (Minors) (Prohibited Steps Orders)*,[166] it was held that a prohibited steps order restricting a former cohabitant from contacting or seeking contact with the children did not contravene s 9(5), since unlike an order for no contact under s 8 it could properly be directed and enforced against the man rather than the mother.

No power to make orders that are denied to the High Court acting under its inherent jurisdiction

Section 9(5)(b) prevents the court from exercising its power to make a specific issue or prohibited steps order 'in any way which is denied to the High Court (by s 100(2)) in the exercise of its inherent jurisdiction.'[167] According to the Department of Health's *Guidance and Regulations*,[168] s 9(5)(b) prevents local authorities applying for a prohibited steps or specific issue order as a way of obtaining (a) the care or supervision of a child; (b) an order that the child be accommodated by them, and (c) any aspect of parental responsibility.[169] In *Re S and D (Children: Powers of Court)*[170] it was held by reason of s 9(5)(b) and s 100(2)(b) there was no power to restrain a parent from removing the child from local authority accommodation[171] pursuant to the rights conferred by s 20(7). It must also follow that there is similarly no power to restrain a parent from objecting to his child being accommodated in the first place pursuant to the right conferred by s 20(7).[172]

---

[161] [1993] 2 FLR 584.

[162] [1992] Fam 162, CA; cf *Re D (A Minor)(Child: Removal From Jurisdiction)* [1992] 1 WLR 667, CA, in which a specific issue order *was* made ordering a parent abroad to return the child to the jurisdiction.

[163] The power to add conditions etc under s 11(7) is discussed below.　　[164] [1994] Fam 18, CA.

[165] See above, p 523.　　　[166] [1995] 1 WLR 667, CA.

[167] The High Court's inherent jurisdiction is discussed in Ch 16.

[168] Vol 1, *Court Orders*, at para 2.33.

[169] For further discussion of local authority use of prohibited steps and specific issue orders see below pp 541–2.

[170] [1995] 2 FLR 456, CA.　　　[171] Local authority accommodation is discussed below at pp 703ff.

[172] Discussed below, p 706. Query whether it is possible for a prohibited steps order to be made upon the parent's application to prevent the other parent from objecting to the child's accommodation?

(h) Additional directions and conditions

The power to make interim orders, to delay implementation of orders, or to attach other special conditions is conferred by s 11(7)[173] which provides that a s 8 order may:

(a) contain directions as to how the order is to be carried out;

(b) impose conditions to be complied with by any person in whose favour the order has been made or any parent or any non-parent who has parental responsibility, or any parent with whom the child is living;

(c) specify the period for which the order or any provision in it is to have effect; and

(d) make such incidental, supplemental or consequential provision as the court thinks fit.

These powers are exercisable by *any* court making a s 8 order.

Directions and limited duration orders

The power under s 11(7)(a) to give directions as to how an order is to be put into effect is designed[174] to enable the court to smooth the transition in cases, for example, where the child's residence is changed or to define more precisely what contact is to take place under a contact order. It also provides a means by which a first instance court can stay an order, for example by directing that any transfer of residence be delayed pending an appeal.[175]

The power under s 11(7)(c) to specify the period for which a s 8 order, or any provision in it, is to have effect is intended[176] to empower the court inter alia to make what are effectively interim orders. Accordingly, the court can make an order for a limited duration coupled with a direction that the matter be brought back to court at a later specific date. This type of order could be useful in cases where more information is required,[177] or to allow time to monitor the effectiveness of, for example, the contact arrangements.[178] Another use of a limited duration order might be to make a holding order pending an appeal.

Conditions and other supplemental orders

At first sight the power under s 11(7)(b) and (d) to add conditions and to make 'such incidental, supplemental or consequential provision as the court thinks fit' seems to give the court considerable scope for making a wide range of supporting provisions to s 8 orders. However, in recommending what were described as 'supplemental provisions' the Law Commission specifically said[179] that they did 'not expect these supplemental powers to be used at all frequently, as most cases will not require them and all are subject to the general rule that orders should only be made where they are the most effective means of

---

[173] Occasionally, however, courts accept undertakings rather than imposing conditions. See eg *Re R (A Minor) (Residence; Religion)* [1993] 2 FLR 163, CA (aunt granted contact on the undertaking that she would not speak or communicate with the child in any way in relation to religious or spiritual matters).

[174] See Law Com No 172, para 4.22.

[175] See *Re J (A Minor) (Residence)* [1994] 1 FLR 369 at 375, per Singer J.

[176] Law Com No 172, para 4.24.

[177] Under s 11(3) courts can make a s 8 order even though they are not in a position finally to dispose of proceedings.

[178] As in *Re B (A Minor) (Contact: Interim Order)* [1994] 2 FLR 269.

[179] See Law Com No 172 at para 4.21. All that the *Guidance and Regulations*, Vol 1, *Court Orders* at para 2.22 states is that the supplemental etc powers 'enable the new orders [ie s 8 orders] to be as flexible as possible and so reduce or remove the need to resort to wardship'.

safeguarding or promoting the child's welfare'. The Commission instanced[180] three examples of when they could be useful:

(1) in the case of a dispute about which school the child should attend, making it a condition of a residence order that the child attend a particular school;

(2) where there is a real fear that on a contact visit the parent will remove the child from the country and not return him, making it a condition of the contact order that any such removal is prohibited;[181] and

(3) where there is real concern that the person with whom the child will live will not agree to a blood transfusion, making it a condition of the residence order to require the parent to inform the other parent so that the latter can agree to it.[182]

Notwithstanding the intention that they should have a limited role, these provisions have generated considerable case law and even now their full ambit cannot be stated with certainty. Indeed, in *D v N (Contact Order: Conditions)*[183] Sir Stephen Brown P commented (in the context of imposing conditions on a contact order) that he considered 'that it may be necessary for a court in the future to give further consideration to the true nature, meaning and effect of conditions imposed under s 11(7)'. Nevertheless certain things are clear. First, s 11(7) only vests ancillary or supportive powers to those under s 8. Accordingly, it cannot be regarded as giving the courts completely novel and independent powers to make, for example, conditions about the parties' finances or property ownership. It is on this basis, for instance, that it is established that s 11(7) cannot be used to interfere with rights of occupation. As Ward LJ said in *Re D (Prohibited Steps Order)*:[184]

'Section 11(7), in my judgment, is ancillary to the making of a s 8 order. It is governed by the provisions for the making of a s 8 order and does not allow the importation by the back door of the matters laid down in the Matrimonial Homes Act[185] or proper adjustment of rights of occupation.'

What is properly regarded as supportive or supplemental can be problematic. In *Re M (A Minor) (Contact: Conditions)*[186] Wall J considered that since the powers were only supportive there was no jurisdiction under s 11(7) to direct one parent to write to the other about the child's progress. In *Re O (Contact: Imposition of Conditions)*,[187] however, the Court of Appeal overruled this proposition, holding instead that s 11(7) empowered the courts to compel one parent to send to the other such information about the child's

---

[180] Above at para 4.23.

[181] Lord Mackay LC at 505 HL Official Report (5th Series) col 345 envisaged conditions being imposed forbidding a parent from moving the child to another town. For examples of where this was done, see *B v B (Residence: Condition Limiting Geographic Area)* [2004] 2 FLR 979 and *Re S (a child)(residence order: condition)(No 2)* [2002] EWCA Civ 1795, [2003] 1 FCR 138. But cf *Re S (a child)(residence order: condition)* [2001] EWCA Civ 847, [2001] 3 FCR 154 and *Re E (Residence: Imposition of Conditions)* [1997] 2 FLR 638, CA, discussed below, pp 534–6.

[182] See the pre-Children Act decision, *Jane v Jane* (1983) 4 FLR 712, CA, in which effectively the father was given the power to consent to medical treatment but the mother (a Jehovah's Witness) looked after the child.

[183] [1997] 2 FLR 797 at 802, CA.

[184] [1996] 2 FLR at 279. Note also *D v N (Contact Order: Conditions)*, above, discussed below p 536.

[185] Now repealed and replaced by Part IV of the Family Law Act 1996: see Ch 5.

[186] [1994] 1 FLR 272 at 281.   [187] [1995] 1 FLR 124 at 132–3 per Sir Thomas Bingham MR.

progress as would promote meaningful contact between the child and the non-residential parent. In the subsequent decision, *F v R (Contact: Justices' Reasons)*[188] Wall J approved an agreed condition to an indirect contact order that the father was not to contact or enter a day centre or school at which the child was a pupil without either the mother's or the court's prior permission. It might also be possible to make an order for supervised contact provided the supervisor is one of the persons listed in s 11(7)(b).[189]

Secondly, as s 11(7)(b) itself expressly states, conditions may only be imposed on the persons there listed and, according to Booth J in *Leeds City Council v C*,[190] the power to make incidental etc orders under s 11(7)(d) is similarly confined.[191] This means that, as local authorities are not listed, there is no power under s 11(7) to order contact to be supervised by a local authority.[192] However, notwithstanding the aforementioned inability, it is to be noted that the list itself is quite wide, enabling the court to impose obligations not only upon the person in whose favour the s 8 order is made, but also upon any parent,[193] any other person who has parental responsibility, or any other person with whom the child is living. Furthermore, provided the person is included in the list it is no objection that he is not a party.[194]

Thirdly, it is well established that restraints on making s 8 orders in the public law context apply equally to the exercise of the supplemental powers under s 11(7). As Balcombe LJ observed in *D v D (County Court Jurisdiction: Injunctions)*:[195]

'... s 11, just as much as s 8, falls within Part II (the private law part) of the 1989 Act and those words cannot be construed as giving the court a power to interfere with the exercise by other bodies[196] of their statutory or common law power, whether derived from other parts of the 1989 Act or elsewhere.'

Similarly, as *Nottingham County Council v P*[197] shows, courts should not use their s 11(7) powers effectively to allow local authorities to intervene in family life under the Act's private law provisions.

Thirdly, as with all Part II powers, s 11(7) is governed by the paramountcy principle and should only be invoked where the child's welfare requires.[198]

As already indicated, beyond the foregoing three points, the overall application of s 11(7)(b) and (d) is still a little uncertain, but to complete the discussion consideration will now be given to the application of the supplemental powers specifically in relation to residence orders.

With regard to residence orders it seemed at first that the courts were prepared to interpret s 11(7) widely, for in *Re B (A Minor) (Residence Order)*,[199] Butler-Sloss LJ, having referred to the powers under s 11(7)(a) to add directions, commented:

---

[188] [1995] 1 FLR 227.   [189] See below.   [190] [1993] 1 FLR 269.

[191] As Booth J pointed out, at 273, if it were not, then s 11(7)(b) would be unnecessary. See also *Re DH (A Minor) (Child Abuse)* [1994] 1 FLR 679 at 700–1, per Wall J.

[192] In Booth J's view the appropriate remedy is a family assistance order, discussed below, pp 577ff.

[193] Including, therefore, the unmarried father who does not have parental responsibility for the child.

[194] See *Re H and Others (Minors) (Prohibited Steps Order)* [1995] 1 WLR 667, discussed above, p 523, in which it was held that when making a prohibited steps order against a non-party there was power under s 11(7)(d) to give that person liberty to apply on notice to vary or discharge the order.

[195] [1993] 2 FLR 802, at 813, CA.   [196] In this case, the local authority and the police.

[197] [1994] Fam 18, CA, discussed below at pp 541–2.   [198] See Law Com No 172 at para 4.21.

[199] [1992] Fam 162 at 165, CA.

'Speaking for myself, I read that very broadly as giving the judge who makes a residence order the jurisdiction to attach conditions or directions which I think are very much the same thing, as to how the children should be cared for and where they should be once the residence order has been made.'

She accordingly held that s 11(7) empowered a court, when making a residence order, to require a child to be returned; to direct the return of the child to the former matrimonial home and to the interim care of one parent; and to direct that the child remain with that parent pending the full inter partes hearing. It has become apparent, however, that a significant restriction on the application of s 11(7) is that the condition must not be incompatible with the residence order itself. In *Birmingham City Council v H*,[200] Ward J refused to make a residence order with the conditions that the mother was to live at a particular unit and comply with all reasonable instructions from the unit's staff, perhaps even to hand over the child to the care of the staff. As he pointed out, this latter condition was tantamount to saying that some other person could assume parental responsibility, which was clearly inconsistent with the residence order to which the condition would have been attached.

The point has since been developed in three Court of Appeal decisions. In the first, *Re D (Residence: Imposition of Conditions)*,[201] a consent order was made under which two children were returned to live with their mother (they had previously been living with their paternal grandmother) on condition that she did not in the interim bring the children into contact with a former partner, nor allow him to reside at her current address or such other address as she may reside with the children. Subsequently, the mother applied to the court to allow her former partner to reside at her home. At first instance, the application was refused, but on appeal the Court of Appeal considered the judge had failed to look at the matter as a contested residence application and remitted the case for a full consideration of the competing claims of the mother and the father and grandmother. In so concluding Ward LJ commented that the:[202]

'. . . case concerned a mother seeking, as she was entitled to, to allow this man back into her life because that is the way she wished to live it. *The court was not in a position so to override her right to live her life as she chose.* What was before the court was whether, if she chose to have him back, the proper person with whom the children should reside was herself or whether it would be better for the children that they lived with their father or with the grandmother' [emphasis added].

This restrictive view was followed in *Re E (Minors)(Residence: Condition)*[203] in which the Court of Appeal held that s 11(7) did not empower a court to impose upon the carer of a child the condition that he or she should reside at a particular address, since such a restriction 'sits uneasily with the general understanding of what is meant by a residence order.' As Butler-Sloss LJ explained:[204]

'A general imposition of conditions on residence orders was clearly not contemplated by

---

[200] [1992] 2 FLR 323; cf *C v Solihull Metropolitan Borough Council* [1993] 1 FLR 290 in which Ward J made a residence order conditional upon the parents undertaking a programme of assessment, and co-operating with all reasonable requests by the local authority to participate in that programme.
[201] [1996] 2 FLR 281.   [202] Above at 284.   [203] [1997] 2 FLR 638.
[204] [1997] 2 FLR 638 at 642.

Parliament and where the parent is entirely suitable and the court intends to make a residence order in favour of that parent, a condition of residence is in my view an unwarranted imposition upon the right of the parent to choose where he/she will live within the UK or with whom. There may be exceptional cases, for instance, where the court, in the private law context, has concerns about the ability of the parent to be granted a residence order to be a satisfactory carer but there is no better solution than to place the child with that parent. The court might consider it necessary to keep some control over the parent by way of conditions which include a condition of residence. Again, in public law cases involving local authorities, where a residence order may be made by the court in preference to a care order, s 11(7) conditions might be applied in somewhat different circumstances.'

In the third decision, *Re S (a child)(residence order: condition)*[205] Thorpe LJ considered that:

'in defining the possibility of exception [in *Re E*] Butler-Sloss LJ was guarding against the danger of never saying never in family litigation. The whole tenor of her judgment is plain to me, in that she was giving the clearest guide to courts of trial that, whereas it was not safe to say never in cases in which the imposition of such a condition would be justified, it would be highly exceptional and probably restricted to a case, as yet unforeseen and may be difficult to foresee, in which the ability of the primary carer to perform to a satisfactory level required the buttress of a s 11(7) order.'

In Thorpe LJ's view Butler-Sloss LJ's judgment in *Re E* was not to be interpreted as giving the trial judges a 'general latitude to strive for some sort of ideal over and above the rival proposals of the available primary carers'. It was accordingly held that the judge had been wrong to grant the mother a residence order in respect of a Down's Syndrome child with a serious heart condition coupled with a condition that she should reside in Croydon (she wanted to live in Cornwall) although the matter was remitted to the first instance court for further investigation. However, at that remitted hearing the trial judge, bearing in mind the evidence that loss of contact with her father would be harmful to the child, still considered the case 'highly exceptional' and imposed the same condition as before. On appeal,[206] the Court of Appeal held that it could not interfere with the trial judge's finding that the case was exceptional. *Re S (No 2)* is not the only example of restrictions being imposed. In *Re H (Children)(Residence Order: Condition)*[207] it was considered justifiable to couple a residence order with a prohibited steps order to prevent the father taking the children to Northern Ireland, inter alia, because their sense of loss of their mother as a close and regular contact would be akin to a bereavement. In *B v B (Residence: Condition Limiting Geographic Area)*[208] a condition that the mother should reside within an area 'bounded by the A4 to the north, the M25 to the West and the A3 to the south and east', was temporarily imposed inter alia in the context of the mother making two applications to go to Australia with the prime motive of getting away from the father.

Notwithstanding these examples it is clear that such conditions will rarely be justified though perhaps establishing an exceptional case is not quite as hard as Thorpe LJ imagined in *Re S*. It might also be, as Butler-Sloss LJ indicated in *Re E*, that tighter restrictions are justified in the public law context in which, given the choice between local

[205] [2001] EWCA Civ 847, [2001] 3 FCR 154.
[206] *Re S (a child)(residence order: condition)(No.2)* [2002] EWCA Civ 1795, [2003] 1 FCR 138.
[207] [2001] EWCA Civ 1338, [2001] 2 FLR 1277.   [208] [2004] 2 FLR 979.

authority care and a residence order, it might be right to opt for the latter, provided the court is given some degree of control. In this context note might also be taken of *Re T (A Minor) (Care Order: Conditions)*,[209] in which rather than make a care order the court made both a supervision order and a residence order, coupling the latter with a condition that the father was not to share a bed with the child in any circumstances. In adding the latter condition the court was aware of the practicalities of enforcing any such order, but given the rigorous scrutiny which the court was confident that the local authority would exercise, it felt that any breach was likely to come to the authority's attention and as such the condition was 'a useful addition to the child protection measures already in force'.[210]

In contrast to residence orders there seems to be a greater latitude to attach conditions to contact orders. In *Re O (Imposition of Conditions)*[211] Sir Thomas Bingham MR considered that ss 8 and 11(7) give the court a wide and comprehensive power to make orders and set conditions which effectively ensure and facilitate contact between the child and the non residential parent. Disagreeing with an earlier decision, *Re M (a Minor)(Contact: Conditions)*,[212] his Lordship held that whilst judges should not impose duties which parents could not realistically be expected to perform, they could compel the person with a residence order and who is hostile to contact to read the other parent's communications with the child without censorship. It was also held to be wrong to place unnecessary limits on the number of letters the absent parent could send.[213] Subsequently in *F v R (Contact: Justices' Reasons)*[214] Wall J approved an agreed condition to an indirect contact order that the father was not to contact or enter a day centre or school at which the child was a pupil without either the mother's or the court's prior permission. It might also be possible to make an order for supervised contact provided the supervisor is one of the persons listed in s 11(7)(b).[215] There are, however, limits to what can be imposed. In *D v N (Contact Order: Conditions)*[216] it was held that when making an order for defined contact it was wholly inappropriate to use s 11(7) to make orders (inter alia forbidding the father to molest the mother or her relatives, from entering or damaging certain premises belonging to those relatives, or from corresponding with the mother's employers) which related more to the protection of the mother from perceived harassment than to the management of contact.

The restraints on making s 8 orders in the public law context apply equally to the exercise of the supplemental powers under s 11(7). As Balcombe LJ observed in *D v D (County Court: Jurisdiction: Powers of Court)*:[217]

'... s 11, just as much as s 8, falls within Pt II (the private law part) of the CA 1989 and those words cannot be construed as giving the court a power to interfere with the exercise by other

---

[209] [1994] 2 FLR 423, CA at 440, per Nourse LJ.

[210] However, there surely does come a point when conditions simply become unrealistic, as the court recognised in the pre-Children Act decision in *B v B (Custody: Conditions)*, in which it struck out as impracticable a condition that the custodial parent put the children to bed by 6.30pm.

[211] [1995] 2 FLR 124, CA.   [212] [1994] 1 FLR 272.

[213] Ie disagreeing with Wall J's ruling in *Re M*, above, that orders permitting absent parents to write to or telephone a child should be carefully defined and usually expressed by reference to a maximum 'not more than' formula.

[214] [1995] 1 FLR 227.   [215] See above p 533.   [216] [1997] 2 FLR 797, CA.

[217] [1993] 2 FLR 802 at 813, CA.

bodies[218] of their statutory or common law powers, whether derived from other parts of the CA 1989 or elsewhere.'

Similarly, as *Nottingham County Council v P*[219] shows, courts should not use their s 11(7) power, even when acting on their own motion, effectively allowing local authorities to intervene in family life under the Act's private law provisions.

(i) Restricting further applications under s 91(14)

Section 91(4) allows the court on 'disposing of any application for an order' under the Children Act 1989 to restrain future applications without the leave of the court. Although perhaps more associated with private law orders, this power can be exercised both in respect of private *and* public law proceedings.[220] These orders represent a substantial interference with a citizen's right of unrestricted access to the courts and how this should be balanced against the child's welfare was carefully considered in *Re P (A Minor)(Residence Order: Child's Welfare).*[221] Butler-Sloss LJ commented:

'A number of guidelines might be drawn from the cases . . . It is, however, important to remember that these are only guidelines intended to assist and not to replace the wording of the section . . .

(1) Section 91(14) should be read in conjunction with section 1(1) of the Children Act 1989 which makes the welfare of the child the paramount consideration.

(2) The power to restrict applications to the court is discretionary and in the exercise of its discretion the court must weigh in the balance all the relevant circumstances.

(3) An important consideration is that to impose a restriction is a statutory intrusion into the right of a party to bring proceedings before the court and to be heard in matters affecting his/her child.

(4) The power is therefore to be used with great care and sparingly: the exception and not the rule.

(5) It is generally to be seen as a useful weapon of last resort in cases of repeated unreasonable applications.

(6) In suitable circumstances (and on clear evidence) a court might impose the leave restriction in cases where the welfare of the child requires it, although there was no past history of making unreasonable applications.

(7) In cases under paragraph 6 above, the court will need to be satisfied: first, that the facts go beyond the commonly encountered need for a time to settle to a regime ordered by the court and the all too common situation where there is animosity between the adults in dispute or between the local authority and the family and; second, that there is a serious risk that, without the imposition of the restriction, the child or the primary carers will be subject to unacceptable strain.

---

[218] Ie in this case the local authority and the police.

[219] [1994] Fam 18, CA, discussed below at p 541.

[220] See *Re P (Children Act 1989, ss 22 and 26: Local Authority Compliance)* [2000] 2 FLR 910. But note s 91(15) imposes an automatic bar on making further applications without court have within six months of a previous application to discharge a care, supervision or education supervision order or for the substitution of a supervision order for a care order or a child assessment order and similarly s 91(17) does so following the refusal of a contact application under s 34.

[221] [2000] Fam 15 at 37–8.

(8)   A court may impose the restriction on making applications in the absence of a request from any of the parties, subject, of course, to the rules of natural justice such as an opportunity for the parties to be heard.

(9)   A restriction may be imposed with or without limitation of time.

(10) The degree of restriction should be proportionate to the harm it is intended to avoid. Therefore the court imposing the restriction should carefully consider the extent of the restriction to be imposed and specify, where appropriate, the type of application to be restrained and the duration of the order.

(11) It would be undesirable in other than the most exceptional cases to make the order ex parte'.

Her Ladyship continued:

'It was suggested to us that s 91(4) may infringe the Human Rights Act 1998 and European Convention for the Protection of Human Rights and Fundamental Freedoms 1950, Art 6(1), by depriving a litigant of the right to a fair trial. I do not consider that submission to be correct. The applicant is not denied access to the court. It is a partial restriction[222] in that it does not allow him the right to an immediate inter partes hearing. It thereby protects the other parties and the child from being drawn into the proposed proceedings unless or until a court had ruled that the application should be allowed to proceed'.

Clearly another relevant factor is the length of the order: the longer the prohibition the greater the justification needs to be. Another factor is whether the order is by consent or not. Although a court may make a s 91(4) order of its own motion, the parties should be warned so as to allow a proper opportunity for representations.[223]

Where a s 91(14) order has been made, leave to make a further application should not be granted lightly and generally only inter partes.[224] Such applications are not governed by the criteria set out in s 10(9),[225] rather the test is simply whether the applicant has demonstrated any need for renewed judicial investigations.[226]

As Wall J has said[227] the s 91(14) power is very flexible and the scope of circumstances in which it can be used is extremely wide.

---

[222] It is, however, possible to impose an absolute prohibition under the inherent jurisdiction, see *Re R (Residence: Contact: Restricting Applications)* [1998] 1 FLR 749.

[223] *Re S (Contact: Prohibition of Applications)* [1994] 2 FLR 1057, where it was also doubted whether the court could impose a condition eg for psychiatric support for any further application. See also *Re C (Prohibition on Further Applications)* [2002] EWCA Civ 292, [2002] 1 FLR 1136, *Re G (Contempt: Committal)* [2003] EWCA Civ 489, [2003] 2 FLR 58 and *Re F (Restrictions on Applications)* [2005] EWCA C499, [2005] 2 FLR 950.

[224] *Re N (S91(14) Order)* [1996] 1 FLR 356.   [225] Discussed below at pp 545ff.

[226] *Re A (Application for Leave)* [1998] 1 FLR 1, CA, per Thorpe LJ, doubting *Re G (Child Case: Parental Involvement)* [1996] 1 FLR 857 in which the test was said to be whether there was an arguable case, and not whether there was a reasonable likelihood that the substantive action would succeed.

[227] In *A v A (Shared Residence)* [2004] EWHC 142 (Fam), [2004] 1 FLR 1195 at [27]—for details of the order see below p 539. Cf *Re B (Section 91 (14) Order: Direction)* [2003] EWCA Civ 1966, [2004] 1 FLR 871.

2 GENERAL RESTRICTIONS ON MAKING SECTION 8 ORDERS

(a) Children aged 16 or over

Section 9(7) and (6) respectively provide that a s 8 order (other than a variation or discharge) should not be made in respect of a child who has attained the age of 16, nor should any order be expressed to have effect beyond a child's sixteenth birthday, unless the court is satisfied that the 'circumstances of the case are exceptional'.[228] Orders not expressed to extend beyond the child's 16th birthday automatically end when he reaches 16.[229] Where a direction is made, the order will cease to have effect when the child reaches the age of 18.[230] These provisions may be contrasted with s 12(5), added by the Adoption and Children Act 2002, under which courts are empowered to make a so-called 'enhanced residence order' which continues until the child's 18th birthday and is not subject to the requirement that there be 'exceptional circumstances', and which we discuss later in this chapter.[231]

There is no definition of and little judicial guidance on what is meant by 'exceptional circumstances' for the purposes of s 9(6). Moreover the position is further complicated by the availability of enhanced residence and special guardianship orders[232] which are more likely to be used where the child is to live with non-parents or guardians.[233] In other words, s 9(6) is only likely to be relevant when an extended residence order is sought in favour of parents or guardians, or whether other types of s 8 orders are at issue. In the former context the example given by the Department of Health's *Guidance and Regulations*[234] of a case where the child concerned is mentally handicapped remains a good one. The requirement was held to be satisfied in *A v A (Shared Residence)*[235] in which a shared residence order was made until each child reached their majority and coupled with a s 91(14) order as a package designed to put an end to the parents' litigation over the children and to encourage them to exercise their parental responsibility.

So far as contact orders are concerned it has been held[236] that there was nothing unusual about a mother and child being unable to come to a happy arrangement as to their future relationship and consequently s 9(6) was not satisfied.

---

[228] According to Butler-Sloss LJ in *Re B (Minors)(Application for Contact)* [1994] 2 FLR 1 at 6, though not directly applicable a similar regime applies to s 34 contact orders.

[229] Children Act 1989 s 91(10).   [230] Section 91(11).   [231] See below at p 603.

[232] Special guardianship is discussed below at p 604. It has only been possible to make these and enhanced residence orders since 30 December 2005.

[233] Note that before the availability of enhanced residence orders and special guardianship Hale LJ had commented in *Re B (Adoption By One Natural Parent To Exclusion Of Other)* [2001] 1 FLR 589 at 594–5 that extending an order until 18 was most likely to be appropriate where a child was living with a person such as a relative or foster parent who did not otherwise have parental responsibility and it was contemplated that the child would stay with that person for the rest of their childhood. See also *Re M (A Minor)(Immigration: Residence Order)* [1993] 2 FLR 858 where s 9(6) was held satisfied in the case of a child who had no relatives in this country and who needed protection until adulthood, and an extended order was made in favour of the foster mother. This case would now probably be better brought as a special guardianship application.

[234] Vol 1, *Court Orders*, para 2.49. Note also the Law Commission, (Law Com No 172 at para 3.25) which, whilst holding to the view that circumstances where it is right to make an order will be rare, instanced the case in which it is necessary to protect an older child from the consequences of immaturity, citing *Re SW (A Minor) (Wardship: Jurisdiction)* [1986] 1 FLR 24 where a 17-year-old girl was made a ward for the few remaining months of her minority in an attempt to control her behaviour.

[235] [2004] EWHC 142 (Fam), [2004] 1 FLR 1195.

[236] *Re N (Minors)* (1999, unreported, Lexis Nexis).

(b) Children in local authority care

Section 9(1) prevents the court from making a s 8 order, other than a residence order, with respect to a child who is already the subject of a local authority care order.[237] This embargo is based on the well established principle,[238] endorsed both by the *Review of Child Care Law*[239] and the Law Commission[240] that in general the court's 'private law' powers should not be used to interfere with local authorities' exercise of their statutory parental responsibility.

However, residence orders are different from the other s 8 orders, since their whole purpose is to determine with whom the child is to live. Hence, such orders may be made even though the child is in care. Obviously, if the court thinks the child ought to be living with someone else (who will also have parental responsibility), this is inconsistent with the continuation of the care order. The Law Commission[241] thought that, in principle, just as care orders may supersede whatever previous arrangements for the child's upbringing have been made, so should residence orders. Accordingly, s 91(1) provides that the making of a residence order discharges any existing care order.

Applications for residence orders in respect of a child in care operate, therefore, as applications to discharge care orders. For those with parental responsibility this remedy provides an alternative to seeking a discharge under s 39.[242] For others, eg fathers who do not have parental responsibility or relatives, an application for a residence order is the only means open to them to seek a discharge of a care order.

One effect of the embargo under s 9(1) is that the court cannot make a care order *and* a s 8 order.[243] However, because the embargo only applies where a child is subject to a care order there is nothing to prevent a court making a supervision order and a s 8 order,[244] nor will s 9(1) apply where the child is being 'accommodated' by a local authority under s 20.[245] Furthermore, even if the child is initially the subject of a care order, once a residence order has been made, since that discharges the care order, any other s 8 order can *then* be made.[246]

(c) Restrictions in the case of local authorities

Section 9(2) prevents local authorities from applying for and the courts from granting them a residence or contact order.[247] The embargo is intended to prevent local authorities

---

[237] But there is no embargo against a s 8 contact order being made at the behest of a child in care for contact with siblings who are not in care: see *Re F (Contact: Child in Care)* [1995] 1 FLR 510, discussed below, p 793, and *Re W (Application for Leave: Whether Necessary)* [1996] 3 FCR 337n.

[238] See *A v Liverpool City Council* [1982] AC 363, HL, discussed below at p 803.

[239] DHSS, 1985, paras 8.2–8.10.   [240] Law Com No 172, para 4.52.   [241] Above at 4.53.

[242] Discussed below at p 787.

[243] But where there are competing care and residence order applications the judge is not bound to make a positive finding on the residence order application before considering whether there is jurisdiction to grant a care order: *Oldham Metropolitan Borough Council v E* [1994] 1 FLR 568, CA. On the other hand, a court should not make a final care order if a parent's residence order application is pending and a final assessment is needed: *Hounslow London Borough Council v A* [1993] 1 WLR 291.

[244] See eg *Re M and J (Wardship: Supervision and Residence Orders)* [2003] EWHC 1585 (Fam), [2003] 2 FLR 541 and *Re T (A Minor) (Care Order: Conditions)* [1994] 2 FLR 423, CA.

[245] Discussed below at pp 703ff.

[246] At least in favour of the individual. The position with regard to local authorities is more complicated as explained below.

[247] The embargo also extends to variations of residence or contact orders: see *Re C (Contact: Jurisdiction)* [1995] 1 FLR 777, CA. Query whether an authority could apply for a residence order in favour of someone else? See below, p 550.

from obtaining parental responsibility other than by a care order under s 31.[248] If local authorities wish to restrict contact to a child accommodated by them, they must seek a care order and have the matter dealt with in those proceedings. The combined effect of s 9(1) and (2) is that where a child is in care, a local authority cannot apply for *any* s 8 order. On the other hand, authorities may seek leave of the court to obtain a prohibited steps or specific issue order in respect of a child *accommodated* by them, though this provision may not be used as a disguised route to seeking a residence or contact order.[249]

Notwithstanding their entitlement to seek leave to apply for a prohibited steps or specific issue order in respect of a child not in their care, it is established by *Nottingham County Council v P*[250] that, where intervention is thought necessary to protect children from significant harm, authorities must take direct action under Part IV of the 1989 Act (ie by initiating care proceedings) rather than seeking to invoke the court's powers under Part II. In that case, following allegations of sexual abuse made against her father by the eldest daughter, the local authority obtained emergency protection orders in respect of two younger children. The father voluntarily left the family home leaving the two girls residing with their mother. The local authority, resisting judicial encouragement to bring care proceedings,[251] persisted in their application for a prohibited steps order[252] requiring the father neither to reside in the same household as the girls nor to have any contact with them unless they wished it. In rejecting their application, Sir Stephen Brown P commented:[253]

'We consider that this court should make it clear that the route chosen by the local authority in this case was wholly inappropriate. In cases where children are found to be at risk of suffering significant harm within the meaning of section 31 of the Children Act 1989 a clear duty arises on the part of local authorities to take steps to protect them. In such circumstances a local authority is required to assume responsibility and to intervene in the family arrangements in order to protect the child. A prohibited steps order would not afford the local authority any authority as to how it might deal with the children. There may be situations, for example, where a child is accommodated by a local authority, where it would be appropriate to seek a prohibited steps order for some particular purpose. However, it could not in any circumstances be regarded as providing a substitute for an order under Part IV of the 1989 Act.'

This comment was ringingly endorsed in *Langley v Liverpool City Council.*[254] Indeed, having observed[255] that a prohibited steps order was 'a private law remedy required to prevent threatened or repeated misconduct, generally in a warring family', Thorpe LJ went as far as to say that he had 'yet to encounter a case in which a local authority has decided

---

[248] Discussed below, pp 733ff.   [249] Section 9(5), discussed above at pp 529–30.

[250] [1994] Fam 18, CA—see above at pp 530 and 533.

[251] Both Judge Heald, at first instance, and Ward J had made s 37 directions. These directions are discussed below, p 580.

[252] For which they had been granted leave to apply.

[253] [1994] Fam at 39. In any event, it was doubted whether there was any power to make an ouster order under s 8. For a critique of this decision see inter alia C Cobley and N Lowe 'Ousting Abusers—Public or Private Law Solution?' (1994) 110 LQR 38.

[254] [2005] EWCA Civ 1173, [2006] 1 FLR 342 at [78].

[255] Ibid at [77]. But note the examples to the contrary outlined below.

that it can achieve the end that its child protection duties require by applying for a prohibited steps order'.

Nottingham was subsequently applied in *F v Cambridge County Council*[256] to prevent a local authority being granted leave to intervene in private law proceedings. In that case the father, a Schedule 1 offender, sought limited contact with his children who were living with their mother. The local authority were opposed to the father having contact, but did not themselves seek a care order since they accepted that the mother was able to look after the children properly. Stuart-White J held, following *Nottingham*, that unless and until the s 31 threshold had been met, the local authority could not intervene in family life, and hence leave to join as a party to private law proceedings should be refused.

Although these decisions severely limit local authority use of prohibited steps and specific issue orders, they do not mean that the powers can never be used. They could properly be invoked, for example, to protect a child accommodated by a local authority from a threat posed by a non-family member[257] or to resolve specific problems concerning an orphan.[258] It may also be a proper use of s 8 for local authorities to obtain court sanction (or restraint) of medical treatment.[259] In other words, provided the local authority is not seeking to be vested with parental responsibility, nor directly to interfere with the exercise of responsibility by others, then it continues to be open to them to seek leave to apply for a prohibited steps or specific issue order.

(d) Other restrictions

It has been said that residence orders cannot be made in favour of a child applicant, at any rate, where the child is seeking to live with someone else.[260] However, it is submitted that it cannot be said that a residence order can *never* be made in favour of a child. It must surely be open to the court to make a residence order in favour of a mother who herself is a child in respect of her own child, and there seems no objection in principle[261] to granting such an order in appropriate cases in favour of a child applicant in respect of a sibling.

---

[256] [1995] 1 FLR 516. It might, however, be possible to overcome this embargo by invoking wardship proceedings, see eg *Re RJ (Wardship)* [1999] 1 FLR 618 and *Re W and X (Wardship: Relatives Rejected As Foster Carers)* [2003] 2206 (Fam), [2004] 1 FLR 415, discussed below at pp 900–1. See also *Re K (Contact: Psychiatric Report)* [1995] 2 FLR 432, CA. See also the comments of Wall J 'The courts and child protection—the challenge of hybrid cases' [1997] CFLQ 354 at 355–6.

[257] To prevent abduction by a friend, for example, or possibly by a relative.

[258] See *Birmingham City Council v D, Birmingham City Council v M* [1994] 2 FLR 502, discussed below, p 750.

[259] See *Re C (HIV Test)* [1999] 2 FLR 1004, CA, in which a local authority successfully applied for a specific issue order that a baby born to an HIV positive mother be tested for HIV and *Re R (A Minor) (Blood Transfusion)* [1993] 2 FLR 757 in which Booth J held that the proper remedy for a local authority wishing to obtain sanction for a blood transfusion for a child not being looked after by them, contrary to his parents' (who were Jehovah's Witnesses) wishes was a specific issue order.

[260] Per Booth J in *Re SC (A Minor) (Leave To Seek Residence Order)* [1994] 1 FLR 96 at 100.

[261] It cannot be objected that because the making of a residence order confers parental responsibility on those who do not already have it an order cannot be made in favour of a child, since of course mothers (and fathers named on the birth certificate or who are married to the mother) have parental responsibility even if they are minors.

3 WHO MAY APPLY FOR SECTION 8 ORDERS?

The Act adopts a so-called 'open door' policy whereby some persons are entitled to apply, while others can, with leave of the court, apply for s 8 orders either by intervening in existing 'family proceedings' or by initiating their own proceedings.

The detailed scheme, set out by s 10 (which governs both initiating and intervening in family proceedings) is as follows.

(a) Persons entitled to apply without leave

Parents, guardians, special guardians, step-parents who have parental responsibility by virtue of a s 4A agreement or order,[262] and those with a residence order in their favour are entitled to apply for any s 8 order.[263] As Bainham points out,[264] this group of people have such a close connection with the child that it would be inappropriate to present them with the additional hurdle of applying for leave to obtain a court hearing.

In the light of the Family Law Reform Act 1987 the expression 'parent' clearly includes the unmarried father.[265] It does not, however, include birth parents whose child has been adopted.[266]

In addition to the above, certain other persons are entitled to apply for a residence order or contact order without leave:[267]

(a) Any party to a marriage (whether or not subsisting) or any civil partner in a civil partnership (whether or not subsisting) in relation to whom the child is a 'child of the family';[268]

(b) Any person with whom the child has lived for a period of at least three years (this period need not be continuous but must not have begun more than five years before, or ended more than three months before the making of the application);[269]

(c) Any person having the consent of:

(i) each of the persons in whose favour a residence order is in force;

(ii) the local authority, if the child is subject to a care order; or

(iii) in any other case, each of the persons who have parental responsibility for the child.

A person not otherwise included in the above mentioned categories will nevertheless be entitled, pursuant to s 10(6), to apply for a variation or discharge of a s 8 order if either the order in question was made on his application or, in the case of a contact order, he is named in that order. This means, for instance, that a child named in a contact order

---

[262] Discussed above at pp 422–5.   [263] Section 10(4), as amended.

[264] *Children, The New Law*, para 3.36.

[265] Cf *Re C (Minors) (Adoption: Residence Order)* [1994] Fam 1. For discussion of the 1987 Act, see above, pp 349–50.

[266] *Re C*, above.   [267] See s 10(5) and s 10(5)(aa) added by the Civil Partnership Act 2004, s 77.

[268] This provision primarily refers to step-parents but can include any married person or registered partner, including grandparents, see *Re A (Child of the Family)* [1998] 1 FLR 347, CA, who has treated the child as a child of the family (the meaning of which is discussed above at p 338).

[269] Section 10(10).

will not need leave to apply to vary it.[270] Section 10(7) reserves the power of rules of court to prescribe additional categories of people who may make applications without prior leave. These powers have not yet been exercised.

(b) Persons entitled to apply with leave

The general scheme is that anyone, including the child himself (which is reflective of the obligation under Art 12(1) of the UN Convention on the Rights of the Child)[271] and any body, authority or organisation professionally concerned with children, who is not otherwise entitled to apply, can seek leave of the court to apply for any s 8 order.[272] The only exception to this scheme is any person 'who is, or was at any time during the last six months, a local authority foster parent'[273] who must have the consent of the local authority to apply for the court's leave, unless he is a relative of the child or the child has been living with him for at one year preceding the application.[274]

The purpose of imposing this additional restriction on local authority foster parent applications is to prevent applications unduly interfering with the local authority's plans for the child and so undermining their efforts to bring stability to the child's life.[275] It is also intended to guard against the risk of deterring parents from voluntarily using the fostering services provided by local authorities which, it is argued, could easily happen if the restrictions were relaxed.

Ironically, in the one case to consider s 9(3), *C v Salford City Council*,[276] parents sought to challenge the propriety of the consent given by the local authority. In that case a child suffering from Down's Syndrome had been accommodated by the local authority and placed with foster parents. Subsequently, the foster parents expressed their wish to adopt, but as Roman Catholics they were unacceptable as prospective adopters to the parents, who were Jewish. The foster parents accordingly, and with the consent of the local authority, sought leave to apply for a residence order. The parents argued that, because of their dual function as an adoption agency and as an accommodating local social services authority, the local authority should not or could not have consented to the foster parents' application. Rejecting this argument, it was held that for the purposes of s 9(3) it was the consent of the social services authority accommodating the child that was required, and therefore the authority's role as an adoption agency was not part of that consent. It was further held that the difficult balance of the welfare factors in the case was justification in itself for having the issues resolved by the court. Accordingly, leave to apply for a residence order was granted.

---

[270] Per Wilson J in *Re W (Application For Leave: Whether Necessary)* [1996] 3 FCR 337n, [1996] Fam Law 665. For this purpose no distinction is to be made between direct and indirect contact.

[271] See further above, p 482.

[272] Section 10(1)(a)(ii). Local authorities are subject to the restrictions in s 9, discussed above, pp 540–2. Note that it is within the court's power to give a person leave to intervene but not to become a party: see *Re S (Care: Residence: Intervener)* [1997] 1 FLR 497, CA.

[273] Ie any person with whom any child is 'looked after' by a local authority within the meaning of s 22(3), discussed below at p 796.

[274] Section 9(3), as amended by s 113 of the Adoption and Children Act 2002 which reduced the period from an anomalous three years (see the discussion at p 434 of the last edition of this work).

[275] See Lord Mackay LC in 502 HL Official Report (5th series), cols 1221–2. This provision had not been recommended by the Law Commission.

[276] [1994] 2 FLR 926, per Hale J. But note this restriction does not bar the court from making an order on its own motion: *Gloucestershire County Council v P* [2000] Fam 1, CA, discussed below p 566.

(c) The leave criteria

The leave criteria are set out in s 10(8) and (9). Section 10(8) states

'Where the person applying for leave to make an application for a section 8 order is the child concerned, the court may only grant leave if it is satisfied that he has sufficient understanding to make the proposed application for a section 8 order.'

Section 10(9) states

'Where the person applying for leave to make an application for a section 8 order is not the child concerned, the court shall, in deciding whether or not to grant leave, have particular regard [to certain criteria set out below].'

At one time it was commonly thought that the former applied to children seeking leave and the latter to adults seeking leave. However, in *Re S (A Minor)(Adopted Child: Contact)*[277] Charles J considered that approach too simplistic. He pointed out that the application of these provisions is not dependent upon whether or not the applicant is a child but upon whether or not the applicant is 'the child concerned'. He considered that for these purposes the phrase 'the child concerned' means the child who is the subject of the application.[278] If he is not, then s 10(9) applies rather than s 10(8). In *Re S* itself the child (who was adopted) was seeking contact with another sibling and could not therefore be the subject-matter of the action and hence was not 'the child concerned'. Accordingly, s 10(9) was held to apply.

On Charles J's analysis s 10(9) can apply to both adults *and* children seeking leave, while s 10(8), though confined to child applicants, will apply where the child is regarded as the subject of the action, as for example where a residence or contact order with another adult is being sought. This analysis has not escaped criticism.[279] One problem, it is pointed out, of applying s 10(9) to child applicants is that it might appear that the child's age and understanding (referred to in s 10(8)) are not relevant. However, according to Charles J that factor *can* be taken into account since the criteria in s 10(9) are not meant to be exclusive. But even if this solution is accepted there remains the difficulty that s 10(9)(b) directs the court to consider 'the applicant's connection with the child' which does not sit easily with the interpretation that s 10(9) can apply to child applicants.

One thing that is clear is that whether leave is sought by a child under s 10(8) or (9), applications need to be made to the High Court.[280]

The application of s 10(9)

Section 10(9) states:

'Where the person applying for leave to make an application for a section 8 order is not the child concerned, the court shall, in deciding whether or not to grant leave, have particular regard to—

   (a) the nature of the proposed application for the section 8 order;

   (b) the applicant's connection with the child;

---

[277] [1999] Fam 283.
[278] Which interpretation reflects the House of Lords' decision in *Birmingham City Council v H (A Minor)* [1994] 2 AC 212 on the application of the paramountcy principle under s 34, see above p 465.
[279] See R White, P Carr and N Lowe: *The Children Act in Practice* (3rd edn) at 5.116.
[280] See *Practice Direction (Application by Children: Leave)* [1993] 1 FLR 313, where merely refers to the requirement for leave under s 10.

(c) any risk there might be of that proposed application disrupting the child's life to such an extent that he would be harmed by it; and

(d) where the child is being looked after by a local authority—
   (i) the authority's plans for the child's future, and
   (ii) the wishes and feelings of the child's parents.'[281]

It was held in *Re A (Minors) (Residence Order: Leave to Apply)*[282] that when deciding whether to grant leave the paramountcy principle under s 1(1) has no application. There were three reasons for reaching this conclusion. First, in granting or refusing a leave application the court is not determining a question with respect to the child's upbringing. That question only arises when the court hears the substantive application. Secondly, some of the guidelines, for example s 10(9)(a), (c) and (d)(i), would be otiose if the child's welfare was paramount. Thirdly, in any event there 'would have been little point in Parliament providing that the court was to have particular regard to the wishes and feelings of the child's parents, if the whole decision were to be subject to the overriding (paramount) consideration of the child's welfare'. Notwithstanding this ruling, s 10(9) is not to be regarded as providing the *exclusive* guidelines, nor as preventing the court from considering the checklist under s 1(3). It is therefore quite proper to consider the child's own views.[283]

At one time it had been held[284] that in deciding whether or not to grant leave, the court should assess whether the substantive application would have a reasonable prospect of success, but in *Re M (Care: Contact: Grandmother's Application for Leave)*[285] it was held that that test was too rigid and that instead the proper approach should be to enquire whether there is a 'good arguable case'. But in turn *Re M* has been called into question by the Court of Appeal in *Re J (Leave to Issue Application for Residence Order)*[286] in which Thorpe LJ expressed concern that the courts had been substituting the 'good-arguable case' test for that laid down by Parliament which anxiety was heightened 'where applicants manifestly enjoy Art 6 rights to a fair trial and, in the nature of things, are also likely to enjoy Art 8 rights'.

Where leave has been given there is no consequent presumption that such an order be made.[287] The requirement of leave is intended to act as a filter to protect the child and his family against unwarranted interference with their comfort and security, whilst ensuring that the child's interests are properly respected.[288] In general terms the more

---

[281] Though not, as Bainham points out, ibid at para 3.43, the wishes and feelings of the child. But see below.

[282] [1992] Fam 182, CA.

[283] *Re A (A Minor) (Residence Order: Leave To Apply)* [1993] 1 FLR 425, per Hollings J.

[284] See *G v Kirklees Metropolitan Borough Council* [1993] 1 FLR 805, per Booth J.

[285] [1995] 2 FLR 86 at 98, CA.

[286] [2002] EWCA Civ 1364, [2003] 1 FLR 114. See also *Re W (Care Proceedings: Leave to Apply)* [2004] EWHC 3342 (Fam), [2005] 2 FLR 468.

[287] See eg *Re A (Section 8 Order: Grandparents' Application)* [1995] 2 FLR 153, CA and *Re W (Contact: Application by Grandparent)* [1997] 1 FLR 793. The refusal to give leave is a serious issue and failure to give reasons for the decision constitutes a fundamental defect: per Connell J in *T v W (Contact: Reasons for Refusing Leave)* [1996] 2 FLR 473. See also *Re W (Contact Application: Procedure)* [2000] 1 FLR 263.

[288] As Lord Mackay LC eloquently put it (502 HL Official Report (5th Series), col 1227):

'There is clearly a danger both in limiting and expanding the categories of person who may apply for orders in respect of children. On the one hand, a too wide and uncontrolled gateway can expose children and families to the stress and harm of unwarranted interference and the harassment of actual or threatened proceedings. If too narrow or overcontrolled the gateway may prevent applications which would benefit or safeguard a child from harm.'

tenuous the applicant's connection with the child the harder it will be to obtain leave.[289] Conversely, the closer the connection the more readily leave should be given. As the Law Commission put it,[290] the requirement of leave will 'scarcely be a hurdle at all to close relatives such as grandparents . . . who wish to care for or visit the child'. On the other hand, as Lord Mackay LC commented[291] in his response to the many attempts during the passage of the Bill to give grandparents an entitlement to apply for a residence or contact order:

'. . . [t]here is often a close bond . . . between a grandparent and a grandchild . . . and in such cases leave, if needed, will no doubt be granted. Indeed, in many cases it will be a formality; but we would be naive if we did not accept that not all interest shown by a grandparent in a child's life is necessarily benign, even if well intentioned. Arguably, at least until we have some experience of wider rights of application, the law should provide some protection to children and their parents against unwarranted applications by grandparents when they occur'.

Since implementation, another concern voiced by the court is the consequential delay in having too many parties to the proceedings, and Butler-Sloss LJ has said specifically that it is undesirable that grandparents whose interests are identical with those of the mother should be separately represented.[292] In contrast in *Re J (Leave to Issue Application for Residence Order)*[293] Thorpe LJ commented

'it is important that trial judges should recognise the greater appreciation that has developed of the value of what grandparents have to offer, particularly to children of disabled parents. Judges should be careful not to dismiss such opportunities without full enquiry'.

[289] Any person seeking leave must file a written request setting out the reasons for the application and a draft of the application for making of which leave is sought: Family Proceedings Rules 1991 r 4.3(1); Family Proceedings Courts (Children Act 1989) Rules 1991 r 3(1). Leave can be granted with or without a hearing: ibid, r 4.3(2) and r 3(2) respectively. In practice such applications are 'almost always an application on the papers' and there will rarely be a welfare report available: *Re A (Section 8 Order: Grandparents' Application)* [1995] 2 FLR 153 at 157, per Butler-Sloss LJ. According to Wilson J in *Re W (Contact Application: Procedure)*, above, it should be exceptional to grant leave ex parte. For further discussion, see White, Carr and Lowe *Children Act in Practice*, op cit, at 5.125.
[290] Law Com No 172, para 4.41.
[291] 503 HL Official Report (5th series), col 1342. For a discussion of the legal position of grandparents under the 1989 Act see generally *The Children Act—What's in it for Grandparents?* (3rd edn, Grandparents' Federation, 1996) and N Ferguson with G Douglas, N Lowe, M Murch and M Robinson *Grandparenting in Divorced Families* (2004) pp 72–4. For a defence of the leave requirement for grandparents see G Douglas '*Re J (Leave to Issue Application for Residence Order)* Recognising grandparents' concern or controlling their interference?' [2003] CFLQ 103, and G Douglas and N Ferguson 'Grandparents After Divorce' [2003] Fam Law 653.
[292] *Re M (Minors) (Sexual Abuse: Evidence)* [1993] 1 FLR 822 at 825. The difficulty in practice is that the parties themselves will not always consider their interests identical.
[293] [2002] EWCA Civ 1364, [2003] 1 FLR 114 at [19], on which see G Douglas '*Re J (Leave to Issue Application for Residence Order)* Recognising Grandparents' concern or controlling their interference?' [2003] CFLQ 103. Cf *L v Finland* [2000] 2 FLR 118 in which the European Court of Human Rights assumed that the grandparent-grandchild relationship was not as significant as the parent-child relationship. Even so Wilson J suggested in *Re W (Contact Application: Procedure)*, above, that the absence of a presumption that it is in the interests of a grandchild to have contact with a grandparent, may not be Human Rights compliant.

Nevertheless it is in the nature of the requirement that even grandparents are not always granted leave.[294]

Careful consideration also needs to be given to applications for leave by individuals in respect of children in care. In *Re A (Minors) (Residence Order: Leave to Apply)*[295] the Court of Appeal refused an application for leave to apply for a residence order in respect of four children originally placed with the applicant for long-term fostering but who had been removed from her by the local authority nearly six months earlier.[296] Section 10(9)(d)(i) expressly provides that the court is to have particular regard to the authority's plans for the child. Furthermore, in view of the authority's statutory duty under s 22(3) to safeguard and promote the welfare of any child in its care, it was held that the court should approach the application for leave on the basis that 'the authority's plans for the child's future are designed to safeguard and promote the child's welfare and that any departure from those plans might well disrupt the child's life to such an extent that he would be harmed by it'.[297] In other words the court should not allow such applications to become a back door means of reviewing local authority decisions.[298]

The application of s 10(8)

Where the applicant for leave is the 'child concerned', s 10(8) provides that leave can only be granted provided the court is satisfied that the child has sufficient understanding to make the proposed application. There is no hard and fast rule for determining whether the child is of sufficient age and understanding. As Sir Thomas Bingham MR said in *Re S (A Minor) (Independent Representation)*:[299]

'. . . the rules eschew any arbitrary line of demarcation based on age and wisely so. Different children have differing levels of understanding at the same age. And understanding is not absolute. It has to be assessed relatively to the issues in the proceedings. Where any sound judgment on these issues calls for insight and imagination which only maturity and experience can bring, both the court and the solicitor will be slow to conclude that the child's understanding is sufficient.'

Even if the child is found to be competent, leave might not necessarily be granted. *In Re H (Residence Order: Child's Application For Leave)*,[300] for example, a competent child was refused leave because his father could adequately represent his views to the court.

Apart from requiring the court to be satisfied about the child's understanding, the Act itself gives no further guidance, particularly as it is accepted that the guidelines under

---

[294] See eg *Re (A Minor) (Contact: Leave to Apply)* [1995] 3 FCR 543 in which Douglas Brown J upheld a magistrate's refusal to give a grandmother leave since, given the total opposition by the parents and the serious disharmony between them, the application had no prospect of success. Though note this decision was applying the new discredited test laid down by *G v Kirklees Metropolitan Borough Council* [1993] 1 FLR 805, see the discussion above at p 546.

[295] [1992] Fam 182.

[296] In fact the application was made one week before the expiry of six months from the removal, but it was agreed between the parties that the local authority would not object to the application as they could have done under s 9(3), and that the mother would not pursue her action for judicial review.

[297] Per Balcombe LJ [1992] Fam at 189.

[298] See also *Re M (Prohibited Steps Order: Application for Leave)* [1993] 1 FLR 275 in which a former guardian sought leave to challenge a local authority's decision not to take care proceedings—application remitted to justices for a re-hearing.

[299] [1993] Fam 263 at 276.   [300] [2000] 1 FLR 780.

s 10(9) do not apply where a child is seeking leave.[301] According to Charles J in *Re S (A Minor)(Adopted Child: Contact)*[302] this lack of guidance is indicative that the court is to have regard to the interests of the child. It is, however, generally accepted that in determining whether to grant leave the child's welfare is *not* the paramount consideration. As Booth J held in *Re SC (a Minor)(Leave to Seek Residence Order)*,[303] applying in turn *Re A (Minors)(Residence Orders: Leave to Apply)*,[304] when determining an application for leave under s 10 (whether it be under s 10(8) or (9)) the court is *not* determining a question in respect of the upbringing of the child concerned (that question only arises if leave is granted and the court determines the substantive application) and that therefore s 1(1) does *not* apply.[305] To this might be added, that not regarding the child's welfare as paramount has the merit of according a child of sufficient understanding to make the application some degree of independence which seems more in keeping with the spirit of the Act.

According to *Re HG (Specific Issue Order: Sterilisation)*[306] parents, at any rate when applying for leave that their child be sterilised, can apply for leave on that child's behalf in cases where the child lacks the necessary understanding to apply on his own behalf. The advantage of this ruling is that in these cases legal aid can be sought on behalf of the child rather than the parents.[307]

(d) Applying for orders in favour of someone else

The Act is silent on whether applications may be made for a s 8 order in favour of someone else. However, implicit in the ability of a child to obtain leave for such orders is that they, at least, can seek a residence order in favour of another person.[308] As Booth J said in *Re SC (A Minor) (Leave to Seek Residence Order)*:[309]

'In my judgment the court should not fetter the statutory ability of the child to seek any s 8 order, including a residence order, if it is appropriate for such an application to be made. Although the court will undoubtedly consider why it is that the person in whose favour a proposed residence order would be made is not applying, it would in my opinion be wrong to import into the Act any requirement that only he or she should make the application.'

Whether the courts would be disposed to permit applications other than by children for

---

[301] The wording of s 10(9) itself makes this quite clear, as was accepted both in *Re C (A Minor) (Leave To Seek Section 8 Orders)* [1994] 1 FLR 26 and *Re SC (A Minor) (Leave To Seek Residence Order)* [1994] 1 FLR 96 both of which were predicated upon the view that s 10(8) applied to children seeking leave, while s 10(9) applied to adults seeking leave. But it was also implicitly accepted by Charles J in *Re S (A Minor)(Adopted Child: Contact)* [1999] Fam 283, [1999] 1 All ER 648, who, as discussed at p 545, considered the application of s 10(8) and (9) to be dependent upon whether or not the applicant was the child concerned.

[302] Above.

[303] [1994] 1 FLR 96 at 99. See also in *Re C (Residence: Child's Application for Leave)* [1995] 1 FLR 927, per Stuart White J, *North Yorkshire County Council v G*, [1993] 2 FLR 732, per Douglas Brown J, and *Re S (a Minor)(Adopted Child: Contact)*, above, per Charles J.

[304] [1992] Fam 182, discussed above at p 458.   [305] See the discussion at pp 457ff above.

[306] [1993] 1 FLR 587, per Peter Singer QC (as he then was).

[307] In *Re HG* the parents did not qualify for legal aid.

[308] As Booth J pointed out in *Re SC (A Minor) (Leave to Seek Residence Order)* [1994] 1 FLR 96 at 100, residence orders cannot be made in favour of the child applicant himself, since that would vest parental responsibility in him by reason of s 12(2).

[309] Ibid, at 100 E–F.

residence or contact orders in favour of someone else remains to be seen. However, it seems unlikely that local authorities would be permitted to do so,[310] for, even supposing that s 9(2) (which provides: 'No application may be made by a local authority for a residence order or contact order and no court shall make such an order in favour of a local authority') is interpreted as not barring residence or contact applications in favour of someone else,[311] there is still the objection that, contrary to the ruling in *Nottingham County Council v P*,[312] local authorities would thereby be permitted to intervene in family life via Part II rather than Part IV of the 1989 Act.

4 EFFECT OF RESIDENCE ORDERS

(a) Parental responsibility

Whilst in force, residence orders confer parental responsibility on those in whose favour they are made such as grandparents or other relatives, or foster parents, who would not otherwise have that responsibility.[313] In the case of 'unmarried fathers' however, upon making a residence order in their favour, the court is *bound* to make a *separate* parental responsibility order under s 4.[314]

(b) Change of child's surname [315]

Under s 13(1)(a), it is an automatic condition of residence orders[316] that no person may cause the child to be known by a new surname without either the written consent of every person who has parental responsibility or leave of the court.[317] Although it is not a *statutory* requirement to have the *child's* consent,[318] in *Re PC (Change of Surname)*[319] Holman J expressly left open whether the consent of an older child, particularly if over the age of 16, was both necessary and sufficient. In any event, if the child objects he may seek leave to apply for a prohibited steps order to prevent the change.[320] Furthermore, as

---

[310] They might plausibly wish to apply, for example, for a residence order in favour of grandparents who, though capable, are reluctant to apply for themselves.

[311] If the word 'and' is read conjunctively rather than disjunctively it could be argued that all that s 9(2) prevents is local authorities applying for residence or contact orders on their own behalf.

[312] [1994] Fam 18, CA, discussed above, pp 541–2.

[313] Section 12(2). Note the restrictions on that responsibility under s 12(3), discussed above at p 425.

[314] Section 12(1), discussed above at p 419. Note that this power does not extend to step-parents notwithstanding that they are now able to apply for parental responsibility orders, see above p 424.

[315] For the position of *conferring* a name see above p 396.

[316] For similar rules where the child is subject to a care order, see s 33(7)–(8) discussed below, p 774.

[317] It is perhaps a moot point as to whether leave is necessary to use a hyphenated name: see *P v N (Child: Surname)* [1997] 2 FCR 65 (Dorchester county court) which suggested it is not. Sed quaere? Note in *Re R (Surname: Using Both Parents')* [2001] EWCA Civ 1344, [2001] 2 FLR 1358 in which the parents were urged to use both their names, there was a suggestion that in the absence of the parties' agreement, court leave was not required to sanction the change. For the difficulties of enforcing an embargo against a name-change see below p 569.

[318] Attempts were in fact made to amend s 13 so as to require the child's consent: see 502 HL Official Reports (5th series) col 1262, by Lord Meston, and 503 HL Official Reports, col 1347 by Lord Elwyn Jones.

[319] [1997] 2 FLR 730 at 739. Nonetheless the support inter alia of a 16-year-old for a name change did not inhibit the court from refusing the change in *Re B (Change of Surname)* [1996] 1 FLR 791, CA, discussed below.

[320] See Lord Mackay LC, 502 HL Official Report (5th series), col 1264.

Wilson J observed in *Re B (Change of Surname)*,[321] 13(1)(a) can only operate as an inhibition on the adult residence holder not to cause the children to be known by a different surname. As he put it:

'It does not, because in effect it cannot, proscribe the surname which the children ask teachers, friends and relatives to attribute to them.'

According to *Practice Direction (minor: change of surname: deed poll)*[322] applications for formal change of surname should be made to the Central Office (Filing Department), and must be supported by the production of the consent in writing of every person having parental responsibility. In the absence of such consent the application will be adjourned until court leave is given.

It has been held[323] that, wherever there is a pre-existing residence order, applications to change names are properly made under s 13(1)(a) rather than as a specific issue order under s 8.[324] Conversely, where there is no pre-existing order application must be made for a s 9 order).[325] Although technically this means that there is no *obligation* to apply the welfare checklist,[326] it is accepted that it remains a useful aide mémoire.[327] A more serious consequence of requiring applications to be made under s 13 is that the consequential directions are probably not enforceable.[328] As with all applications directly concerning children's upbringing, in resolving disputes over children's names, the child's welfare is the court's paramount consideration.

Section 13(1)(a) implements the recommendation of the Law Commission[329] which, like the Court of Appeal in the pre-Children Act decision, *W v A (Minor: Surname)*,[330] considered a child's surname to be an important symbol of his identity and relationship with his parents and that, while it may be in his interests for it to be changed, it was not a matter on which a parent with whom the child lives should be able to take unilateral action.

Case law since the Act very much reflects this attitude. Indeed in *Dawson v Wearmouth*[331] Lord Jauncey commented:

'The surname is . . . a biological label which tells the world at large that the blood of the name flows in its veins. To suggest that a surname is unimportant because it may be changed at any time by deed poll when the child has obtained more mature years ignores the importance of initially applying an appropriate label to that child.'

[321] [1996] 1 FLR 791 at 795, CA.   [322] [1995] 1 All ER 832.
[323] By *Re B (Change of Surname)* [1996] 1 FLR 791, CA. But note the query raised by Hale J in *Re M (Leave To Remove Child From Jurisdiction)* [1999] 2 FLR 334, discussed below at p 556.
[324] This in any event is implicit in r 4.1(2)(a) and (c) of the Family Proceedings Rules 1991 and by the different form for the order under s 13, viz Form C 44 as opposed to C 43, which is required by r 4.21(5).
[325] *Dawson v Wearmouth* [1999] 2 AC 308 at 325 per Lord Hobhouse, *Re W (A Child)(Illegitimate Child: Change of Surname)* [2001] Fam 1 at [9], per Butler-Sloss LJ.
[326] Viz that provided by s 1(3), discussed below, pp 584ff.
[327] Per Wilson J in *Re B*, above at 793. In *Re C*, above, Butler-Sloss LJ assumed that the checklist applies regardless of whether the application was under s 8 or s 13.
[328] See *Re P (Minors) (Custody order: Penal Notice)* [1990] 1 WLR 613, CA, discussed below, p 568.
[329] Law Com No 172, para 4.14.
[330] [1981] Fam 14, CA, which in turn decisively rejected such cases as *R (BM) v R (DN)* [1978] 2 All ER 33, CA and *D v B* [1979] Fam 38, CA, which had held that the issue was relatively unimportant and that fathers were tending to lay too much emphasis on it when the purpose was to avoid embarrassment and there was no intention of destroying their links with their children.
[331] [1999] 2 AC 308 at 323.

But this comment, which went much further than any of the other Law Lords, has been criticised as being too emotive and overblowing the importance of names and thus encouraging litigation.[332] Moreover, it is clear that not all judges hold to this view. Indeed in *Re R (Surname: Using Both Parents)*[333] Hale LJ suggested that Lord Jauncey was effectively dissenting from the other Law Lords and that his views were not consistent with the modern law. She added[334] that it was a 'matter of great sadness' that

'it is so often assumed, and even sometimes argued, that fathers need that outward and visible link in order to retain their relationship with, and commitment to, their child. That should not be the case. It is a poor sort of parent whose interest in and commitment to his child depends upon the child bearing his name. After all, that is a privilege which is not enjoyed by many mothers, even if they are not living with the child. They have to depend upon other more substantial things.'

Whatever the status of Lord Jauncey's comments, what *Dawson v Wearmouth* undoubtedly establishes is that a court should not sanction a change of the child's surname unless there is some evidence that it will lead to an improvement in his or her welfare. Indeed it was precisely because the issue is governed by the paramountcy principle that the Lords in *Dawson* were able to dismiss the father's arguments based on Art 8 of the European Convention on Human Rights since, as Lord Hobhouse put it,[335] the issue of name changes is concerned with children's welfare, not fathers' rights.[336]

The most comprehensive guidance on the relevant considerations in determining name disputes is to be found in *Re W (A Child)(Illegitimate Child: Change of Surname)*,[337] in which Butler-Sloss LJ said:

'(e) On any application the welfare of the child is paramount, and the judge must have regard to the section 1(3) criteria.

(f) Among the factors to which the court should have regard is the registered surname of the child and the reasons for the registration, for instance recognition of the biological link with the child's father. Registration is always a relevant and important consideration but it is not in itself decisive. The weight to be given to it by the court will depend upon the other relevant factors or valid countervailing reasons which may tip the balance the other way.

(g) The relevant considerations should include factors which may arise in the future as well as the present situation.

(h) Reasons given for changing or seeking to change a child's name based on the fact that

---

[332] See in particular the analysis by M Hayes '*Dawson v Wearmouth:* "What's in a name? A Child by any other name is surely just as sweet?" ' [1999] CFLQ 423. For other comments on *Dawson* see J Herring 'Name This Child' [1998] CLJ 266 and A Bainham 'In the Name of the Father?' [1999] CLJ 492.
[333] [2001] EWCA Civ 1344, [2001] 2 FLR 1358 at [13].   [334] Above at [18].
[335] [1999] 2 AC 308 at 329.
[336] It might be thought that the strictness of English law on name changes is consistent with Arts 7 and 8 of the UN Convention on the Rights of the Child, which respectively provide for a right to name and a right to preserve that name. But as G Douglas, *An Introduction to Family Law* (2nd edn) 88 and J Fortin *Children's Rights and the Developing Law* (2nd edn) 399 point out, neither Article was designed with parental disputes in mind; rather they were concerned with the problem of stateless children and those abducted from their families by dictatorial military regimes.
[337] [2001] Fam 1 at 7–8.

the child's name is or he is not the same as the parent making the application do not generally carry much weight.

(i) The reasons for an earlier unilateral decision to change a child's name may be relevant.

(j) Any changes of circumstances of the child since the original registration may be relevant.

(k) In the case of a child whose parents were married to each other, the fact of the marriage is important and I would suggest that there would have to be strong reasons to change the name from the father's surname if the child was so registered.

(l) Where the child's parents were not married to each other, the mother has control over registration. Consequently on an application to change the surname of the child, the degree of commitment of the father to the child, the quality of contact, if it occurs, between father and child, the existence or absence of parental responsibility are all relevant factors to take into account.'

Of course the above observations are only guidance and each case has to be decided upon its own facts on the basis of the paramountcy principle. Nevertheless court leave for a change of name has generally proved hard to obtain. As Ward LJ has put it in *Re C (Change of Surname)*:[338]

'... there is a heavy responsibility on those who seek to effect a change ... good reasons have to be shown.'

Examples of judicial refusal to sanction name changes include *Re F (Child: Surname)*,[339] in which it was held that there was no reason to suppose that a young girl at school was going to be embarrassed or particularly unusual in being registered at a school under a different name from the current surname of her mother. In other words, there was no case for saying that it was in the child's interests to change her name.

Leave was also refused in *Re B (Change of Surname)*,[340] in which the Court of Appeal rejected the argument that a first instance judge had erred when refusing to give leave for a change of name because he had not taken notice of the children's views. Whilst agreeing that 'orders which ran flatly contrary to the wishes of normal adolescent children were virtually unknown to family law', that principle did not extend to the formal change of surname from that of the father to the stepfather.[341] In Wilson J's view that would only serve to injure the link between the father and the children, which was not in the latter's best interests. In so ruling Wilson J rejected the argument that it was embarrassing for the children to be known by a surname other than that of the adult care givers, commenting

---

[338] [1998] 2 FLR 656 at 667, CA.

[339] [1993] 2 FLR 837n. See also *Re T (Change of Name)* [1998] 2 FLR 620, CA and *G v A (Children: Surname)* [1995] 2 FCR 223n, in which an unmarried father obtained a prohibited steps order restraining the mother from changing the children's surnames. For a striking pre-Children Act example, see *W v A (Minor: Surname)* [1981] Fam 14, in which the Court of Appeal refused to reverse a decision declining to permit a change of name even though the child was emigrating to Australia with his mother and stepfather. Query whether it would be sufficient if the father had disappeared from the scene entirely or if his name had notorious associations because of his conduct?

[340] [1996] 1 FLR 791, CA.

[341] This was because the inhibition against a change of name lay against the mother rather than against the child. As Wilson J pointed out, at 795, the child himself is free to ask others to address him in whatever name he chooses regardless of any s 13 directions.

that 'there is . . . no opprobrium nowadays for a child to have a different surname from that of adults in the household'.

In *A v Y (Child's Surname)*,[342] a name change was refused because the child would be confused by the change, while in both *Dawson v Wearmouth*,[343] in which an unmarried father wanted his one month old child's name being changed to his (the child had been registered by the mother in her ex-husband's name), and *Re R (Surname: Using Both Parents)*,[344] in which a mother wanted to change the child's surname upon taking up residence in Spain, leave was refused because no benefit to the child could be demonstrated.

In contrast to the above cases, leave was granted in *Re S (Change of Names: Cultural Factors)*[345] in which a Muslim mother, divorced from the Sikh father and now living in a Muslim community, was permitted to use Muslim names, including her current Muslim nickname for the child in daily life and at school. She was not, however, given leave to change the name formally as that would contribute to an undesirable elimination of the child's Sikh identity. In *Re W (Child)(Illegitimate Child: Change of Surname)*[346] one mother[347] was permitted to change her son's name to avoid having the same as his father who was a notorious criminal so as to protect him from what she genuinely feared was a real risk of harm if his identity was revealed in the new locality where they were living. Another mother[348] was similarly allowed to do so following the father's convictions for indecent assaults upon a 17-year-old girl and his 11-year-old niece. Finally, reference might also be had to *Re H (Child's Name: First Name)*[349] in which a mother whose non-registration of name was cancelled because it was made after the father's registration, was permitted to use her given name for the child, though no order to that effect was necessary. In so ruling Thorpe LJ commented that given names 'have a much less concrete character.'

Where the name has already been changed (whether lawfully or not), the issue as to what the child should continue to be called is still governed by the welfare principle. However, it may be too stark to concentrate simply on whether it is in the child's interests for the name to be changed back, since attention also needs to be paid to whether it was in the child's interests to change the name in the first place.[350] Nevertheless, it seems on the case law easier to persuade the court to sanction a change of name that has already occurred than to permit a prospective change. In *Re P (Parental Responsibility)*[351] the court rejected an application by an unmarried father that his name be restored to his two children. The court noted that the names had been changed some time ago, following the father's long-term imprisonment, when the mother decided to make a fresh start both for herself and her children. It was not thought to be in their interest for the name to be changed back. Even in *Re C (Change of Surname)*,[352] where it was held that the unmarried

---

[342] [1999] 2 FLR 5.   [343] [1999] 2 AC 308.   [344] [2001] EWCA Civ 1344, [2001] 2 FLR 1358.
[345] [2001] 2 FLR 1005.   [346] [2001] Fam 1, CA. This case comprised three separate appeals.
[347] Viz in the *A* case.   [348] Viz in the *B* case.
[349] [2002] EWCA Civ 190, [2002] 1 FLR 973, CA. See also the discussion at p 397 above.
[350] See eg *Re T (Change of Name)* [1998] 2 FLR 620, CA.   [351] [1997] 2 FLR 722, CA.
[352] [1998] 2 FLR 656, CA. See also another *Re C (Change of Surname)* [1998] 1 FLR 549, CA where the children concerned were living with their unmarried father and had already assumed his name. The court rejected the mother's application that they should be known by her maiden name since she herself no longer used it as she had married someone else.

mother's original decision to change her child's surname following the breakdown of her relationship with the father was not justified, the Court of Appeal resolved nevertheless that a further change now was not in the child's interests.

(c) Removal of child from the United Kingdom [353]

Under s 13(1)(b), where a residence order is in force, no person may remove the child from the United Kingdom without either the *written* consent of every person who has parental responsibility or leave of the court. In *Re H (Children)(Residence Order: Condition)*[354] the Court of Appeal rejected the argument[355] that s 13(1)(b) requires court leave to remove the child from the jurisdiction (and therefore in this case to remove the child to Northern Ireland) rather than from the United Kingdom (i.e. England and Wales, Scotland and Northern Ireland).[356] Accordingly, there is no obligation on a residence order holder to obtain permission to relocate anywhere *within* the United Kingdom, though, as has been previously discussed,[357] such internal relocations can be prevented by means of a prohibited steps order or by the imposition of s 11(7) condition but to justify such restriction the circumstances need to be exceptional.[358]

Temporary removals for less than one month

Under s 13(2) a person in whose favour a residence order has been made can remove the child for a period of less than one month without anyone's permission. This latter provision places those with a residence order in a special position. It is normally an offence under the Child Abduction Act 1984[359] to remove a child under the age of 16 without the consent[360] either of those having parental responsibility or leave of the court.

Permitting unrestricted temporary removals is intended[361] to allow a person in whose favour a residence order has been made to make arrangements for holidays without having to seek the permission of the non-resident parent or parents, and without even having to give notice. This principle presumably extends to each person in whose favour a joint or shared residence order is made. Although there is no limit on the number of temporary removals permitted, in cases of dispute parents are entitled to seek a prohibited steps order

[353] For a fuller discussion of this issue see N Lowe, M Everall and M Nicholls *International Movement of Children Law Practice and Procedure* chs 6 and 7 (domestic law) and 8 (the position in some other jurisdictions). For discussion of the Canadian position see eg C Davies 'The Effect of Social Change on Family Structure: Mobility Issues in the Canadian Context' in *The Changing Family, Family Forms and Family Law* (eds J Eekelaar and T Nhlapo) 601, and C. Barton 'When did you next see your father?' [1997] 9 CFLQ 73.

[354] [2001] EWCA Civ 1338, [2001] 2 FLR 1277.

[355] Relying on inter alia the side-note to s 13 which refers to 'removal from jurisdiction' rather than jurisdictions; s 108(12) which applies particular provisions of the 1989 Act, but not s 13, to Northern Ireland [s108(11) does a similar thing in relation to Scotland] and to the exercise of power under s 101 to make delegated legislation in making the Children (Prescribed Orders—Northern Ireland, Guernsey and Isle of Man) Regulations 1991.

[356] Interpretation Act 1978, s 5, Sch 1. Note the Isle of Man and the Channel Islands are *not* part of the United Kingdom.

[357] Above at pp 526 and 534.

[358] See *Re S (a child)(residence order: condition)* [2001] EWCA Civ 847, [2001] 3 FCR 154 and *Re H* above, discussed above at p 535 and below at p 556.

[359] Discussed above at p 396.

[360] Though, unlike the requirement under the 1989 Act, the consent does not have to be in writing.

[361] Law Com No 172, para 4.15.

to curtail the right or to apply for a restriction of the right to be added to the residence order, pursuant to the court's powers to add conditions under s 11(7).[362]

Removals for more than one month

Where permission is sought to take the child out of the United Kingdom for more than one month specific application for leave must be made to the court.[363] Where leave is sought under s 13 then under s 13(3), the court may grant leave either generally or for specified purposes. However, it is not entirely settled whether leave should be sought under s 13 rather than by way of a specific issue order. Applying the approach to names[364] it seems that it should, but this has been queried by Hale J in *Re M (Leave To Remove Child From Jurisdiction)*.[365] As she pointed out, in the absence of a residence order an application must be made for a s 8 order, but 'if a person can apply [for a s 8 order] when there is no residence order in force, it is odd that they should have to use a different route when there is a residence order. The Family Proceedings Rules[366] may provide for a different route but it does not follow that it is the exclusive or only route.'

No matter by what route or by whom (it is equally open to the non-resident parent, for example, to seek leave to remove the child) the matter is raised, the court's general approach should be the same,[367] namely, in deciding whether to grant leave the court must apply the principle of the paramountcy of the child's welfare under s 1(1). But the application of the paramountcy principle in this context is by no means straightforward. As Thorpe LJ observed in the leading case, *Payne v Payne*,[368] the applicant in a relocation case is invariably the mother and primary carer, her motivation for moving generally arises from her remarriage or urge to return home and the father's opposition is commonly founded on a resultant reduction in his contact with, and influence on the child. As Thorpe LJ recognised, before *Payne* two propositions had been consistently applied: the paramountcy of the child's welfare and the view that refusing the primary carer's reasonable proposals for relocation is likely to impact detrimentally on the welfare of the dependent children. Consequently, a reasonable application to relocate will be granted unless the court concludes that it is incompatible with the children's welfare.[369] *Payne* affirmed both that the Children Act 1989 had not altered this approach and that the 'internal application' of the European Convention on Human Rights following the

---

[362] See eg Department of Health's *Guidance and Regulations*, Vol 1, *Court Orders*, para 2.27 and Lord Mackay LC, 503 HL Official Report (5th series), col 1354.

[363] According to Thorpe J in *MH v GP (Child: Emigration)* [1995] 2 FLR 106 such cases should be heard either in the High Court or county court depending on the complexity of the decision; cf his earlier comment in *Re L (A Minor) (Removal from Jurisdiction)* [1993] 1 FCR 325 that such applications should be made to the High Court. In *Re K (Removal From Jurisdiction: Practice)* [1999] 2 FLR 1084 at 1086–7 Thorpe LJ also said that where applications involve considerations of foreign legal systems and which may require the putting in place of mirror orders, they should normally be dealt with by a Family Division judge.

[364] See eg *Re B (Change of Surname)* [1996] 1 FLR 791, discussed above at p 553.

[365] [1999] 2 FLR 334 at 340.   [366] Viz FPR 1991, rr 4.1(2)(a) and (c) and 4.21(5).

[367] See *Re S (a child)(residence order: condition)*, above. Technically whereas it is mandatory to apply the welfare checklist in contested s 8 applications, it is only discretionary to do so under s 13, though even then Thorpe LJ has said in *Payne v Payne* [2001] EWCA Civ 166, [2001] Fam 473 at [33] that courts should nevertheless take the precaution of doing so.

[368] At [27]. For a comment on this case see A Perry '*Payne v Payne*: leave to remove children from the jurisdiction' [2001] CFLQ 455.

[369] In this respect the principles were set out in *Poel v Poel* [1970] 1 WLR 1469, to which, as Thorpe LJ said in *Re H (Application To Remove From Jurisdiction)* [1998] 1 FLR 848, later cases have added little.

implementation of the Human Rights Act 1998 did not 'necessitate a revision of the fundamental approach to relocation applications formulated by this court and consistently applied over so many years'. Nevertheless to guard against a risk of 'too perfunctory an investigation resulting from too ready an assumption that the [primary carer]'s proposals are necessarily compatible with the child's welfare', Thorpe LJ suggested that the courts should adopt the following discipline[370]

'[40] (a) Pose the question: is the mother's application genuine in the sense that it is not motivated by some selfish desire to exclude the father from the child's life? Then ask is the mother's application realistic, by which I mean founded on practical proposals both well researched and investigated? If the application fails either of these tests refusal will inevitably follow.

(b) If however the application passes these tests then there must be a careful appraisal of the father's opposition: is it motivated by genuine concern for the future of the child's welfare or is it driven by some ulterior motive? What would be the extent of the detriment to him and his future relationship with the child were the application granted? To what extent would that be offset by extension of the child's relationship with the maternal family and homeland?

(c) What would be the impact on the mother, either as the single parent or as a new wife, or a refusal of her realistic proposal?

(d) The outcome of the second and third appraisals must then be brought into an overriding review of the child's welfare as the paramount consideration directed by the statutory checklist insofar as appropriate.

[41] In suggesting such a discipline I would not wish to be thought to have diminished the importance that this court has consistently attached to the emotional and psychological well-being of the primary carer. In any evaluation of the welfare of the child as the paramount consideration great weight must be given to this factor.'

Although Thorpe LJ has since said[371] that trial judges should direct themselves only by reference to *Payne* he has also acknowledged[372] that his guidance is unhelpful in its layout inasmuch as it is easy to assume that para [40] contains the totality of the discipline whereas it is important to understand that para [41] (stressing the importance of the primary carer's well-being) is as much a part of the discipline as if it had been expressed in para [40] (c). Indeed a number of post-*Payne* refusals of leave at first instance have either been overturned on appeal or remitted for retrial on the basis that too little regard was paid to the primary carer's well being.[373]

In *Re B (Leave To Remove: Impact Of Refusal)*[374] the Court of Appeal rejected the argument that there was a difference in principle between so-called 'lifestyle cases', that is, where the desire to relocate was inspired by a desire to improve general living conditions and those more familiar cases of the carer wishing to return to her native country or where a specific employment opportunity has arisen for a member of the family. As Thorpe LJ

---

[370] At [40] and [41].

[371] In *Re H (Children)(Residence Order: Condition)* [2001] EWCA Civ 1332, [2001] 2 FLR 1277 at [17].

[372] In *Re B (Leave To Remove: Impact Of Refusal)* [2004] EWCA Civ 956, [2005] 2 FLR 239.

[373] See eg *Re B*, above, *Re G (Removal From Jurisdiction)* [2005] EWCA Civ 170, [2005] 2 FLR 166 and *Re B (Removal From Jurisdiction)*; *Re S (Removal From Jurisdiction)* [2003] EWCA Civ 1149, [2003] 1 FLR 1043.

[374] Above.

said[375] there is but one standard to be applied to all cases. The applicant's explanation for relocating is the core of the case and the judge must assess that explanation and weigh it in the balance with the other considerations outlined in *Payne*. In *Re A (Temporary Removal From Jurisdiction),*[376] however, it was accepted that a distinction should be made between applications for permanent removal and those for a temporary removal. As Thorpe LJ put it[377] 'The more temporary the removal, the less regard should be paid to the principles stated in *Payne v Payne*'. In that case the trial judge was held to have underestimated the impact on the mother's career plans of his refusal to grant her leave to go to South Africa for two years to carry out her research and complete her PhD. Leave was accordingly granted.

As previously intimated, *Payne v Payne* is predicated upon the premise that the application for leave is being made by the primary carer but that will not always be the case. In *Re Y (Leave To Remove From Jurisdiction)*[378] a five-year-old child was effectively sharing his home equally with each parent and on the facts he was found to be well settled, bilingual and bicultural. In those circumstances Hedley J concluded that the cost to the child of a move from Wales to Texas was too high and leave to remove him by the mother was refused. It should also be added that in *Payne* itself Butler-Sloss P expressly said[379] that the observations were made upon the premise that residence is not a live issue. If there is a real dispute as to which parent the child should live with and the decision is finely balanced, then the future plans of each parent are clearly relevant, but if the decision as to residence is clear then the plans for removal from the jurisdiction are not likely to be significant in the decision about evidence. The corollary of this is that it by no means automatically follows that because an application for leave to remove has been refused, the applicant should lose residence of the child.[380]

In *Re C (Permission To Remove From Jurisdiction)*[381] Charles J considered that the most important point of *Payne* was that the existence of a reasonable application for leave to remove (and to be reasonable the application has to be genuine, not motivated by an inappropriate selfish desire, and practical) does not create a presumption in favour of leave being given. Nevertheless a reasonable application will only be refused if it is incompatible with the child's welfare and in that regard where the court concludes that a refusal would have a detrimental impact upon the care that the primary carer would give then that harm will usually outweigh the likelihood of harm likely to flow from the reduction of contact with the non residential parent. In short the best chance of opposing a leave application is to show that the application should fail at the first hurdle.

Some examples of applications failing at this first hurdle include *Tyler v Tyler*[382] in which a father, who had enjoyed frequent contact with his two boys now aged nine and six, successfully opposed the mother's request for leave to emigrate to Australia to join her family. It was found in that case, however, that the mother's dominant motive was bitterness towards her husband and that furthermore she would be able to cope with the

---

[375] At [17].
[376] [2004] EWCA Civ 1587, [2005] 1 FLR 639.   [377] At [13].   [378] [2004] 2 FLR 330.
[379] Above at [86].   [380] *Re T (Removal From Jurisdiction)* [1996] 2 FLR 352, CA.
[381] [2003] EWHC 596, [2003] 1 FLR 1066. Leave granted to a Singaporean mother to take two boys aged seven and five to Singapore.
[382] [1989] 2 FLR 158, CA.

disappointment if permission were refused. Leave was also refused in *M v A (Wardship: Removal From Jurisdiction)*[383] where the mother's plans to move to Canada were ill thought-out, little researched and did not accommodate the needs of the children who loved both homes and did not want the status quo changed. Another example is *R v R (Leave To Remove)*[384] in which a mother was refused leave to take her children to France on the basis that she did not have the emotional stability to establish a new life in another country and her plans to do so were insufficiently thought out.

Two earlier and different type of examples are *M v M (Minors) (Jurisdiction)*,[385] in which, leave was refused because the first instance judge had given insufficient weight to the children's (aged 12 and 10) own views and *MH v GP (Child: Emigration)*[386] in which leave was refused because of the overriding importance of maintaining and developing the relationship between the child (a boy aged four) and his father. The court may, in granting leave, impose conditions, for example requiring the deposit of a sum of money until the parent with leave obtains 'authentication' of the contact order in the foreign court and complies with an order relating to the child's education; upon evidence of compliance, the deposit would be released,[387] or requiring the swearing of a solemn oath on the Quran.[388]

Comparison with internal relocations

As previously discussed,[389] there are no formal restrictions on relocating within the United Kingdom though a court prohibition can be sought. Furthermore whereas a principal carer will ordinarily be granted leave to remove a child outside the United Kingdom unless the court concludes that it is incompatible with the child's welfare, no condition restricting the area of residence within the United Kingdom will be imposed on the principal carer save in exceptional circumstances. The rationale for this less stringent approach is that, in Thorpe LJ's words in *Re H (Children)(Residence Order, Condition)*,[390] within 'the same sovereignty there will be the same system of laws, with the same rights of the citizen, rights for instance to education, health care and statutory benefits'. He added 'Equally, it can be said that within Europe, while perhaps the burden on the applicant may be greater, it is equally mitigated by the fact that within the Community there is the same fundamental approach to social issues and a real endeavour to achieve harmonisation, obviously in social policy but also in family justice.'

---

[383] [1993] 2 FLR 715. See also for similar examples *H v F (Refusal of leave to remove a child from the jurisdiction)* [2005] EWHC 2705 (Fam), [2006] 1 FLR 776 and *Re T (Removal From Jurisdiction)* [1996] 2 FLR 352, CA in which leave was refused because of the applicant's poorly considered plans; cf *Re W (Minors) (Removal From Jurisdiction)* [1994] 1 FCR 842 where the allegation of ill-thought plans failed on the facts, Thorpe J holding that the applicant was not required to guarantee the precise details of the future life but merely had to establish the interest, capacity and capability to pursue the plans.

[384] [2004] EWHC 2572 (Fam), [2005] 1 FLR 687.   [385] [1993] 1 FCR 5, CA.

[386] [1995] 2 FLR 106.

[387] *Re S (Removal From Jurisdiction)* [1999] 1 FLR 850, CA. In *Re L (Removal From Jurisdiction: Holiday)* [2001] 1 FLR 241 the mother was required to deposit a bond which was to be released upon the child's return.

[388] *Re A (Security For Return To Jurisdiction)(Note)* [1999] 2 FLR 1.   [389] See above p 535.

[390] [2001] EWCA Civ 1338, [2001] 2 FLR 1277 at [20].

5 WHEN SECTION 8 ORDERS CAN BE MADE

(a) General jurisdictional rules

Jurisdiction to make, but not to vary or discharge,[391] s 8 orders is governed by Part I of the Family Law Act 1986 which has been amended[392] to take account of the revised Brussels II Regulation.[393] For the purposes of this Act s 8 orders are known generally as 'Part I orders' but more specifically as 's 1(1)(a) orders'. According to s 2(1) of the 1986 Act a court shall not make a s 1(1)(a) order unless

'(a) it has jurisdiction under the Council Regulation [i.e. Brussels II], or

(b) the Council Regulation does not apply but

    (i) the question of making the order arises in or in connection with matrimonial proceedings and the condition in section 2A . . . is satisfied, or

    (ii) the condition in section 3 . . . is satisfied.'

On the face of it this seems simple enough: jurisdiction should be based on Brussels II unless that Regulation does not apply, in which case jurisdiction is based on ss 2A or 3 of the 1986 Act. In turn the Regulation on its face only applies to issues arising between Member States (other than Denmark) and therefore has no application to issues arising between a Member State and a 'non-Brussels II State', nor to matters arising *within* a Member State. So far as England and Wales is concerned, on this orthodox view, jurisdiction as between Brussels II states is governed by the Regulation, but as between other parts of the United Kingdom and Isle of Man and with non-Brussels II states, it is governed by the rules set out in the 1986 Act. As will be discussed, however, whether the wording of the Regulation and the 1986 Act achieves this simple scheme is far from clear. However, to put the debate in context it is first necessary to consider the jurisdictional rules as set out both by the Regulation and the 1986 Act.

The application of the revised Brussels II Regulation[394]

The Regulation provides rules for the determination of jurisdiction over matters of parental responsibility as between *all* Member States of the European Union[395] except Denmark.[396] In outline the jurisdictional rules are as follows:

---

[391] Family Law Act 1986, s 1(1)(a). See *Re S (Residence Order: Forum Conveniens)* [1995] 1 FLR 314 in which jurisdiction to vary a contact order was exercised notwithstanding that the child was living in Holland with his mother. But note that this case would now be governed by the Brussels II Regulation. Although it makes sense to exclude variations and discharges of orders within a purely intra-United Kingdom context since courts keep jurisdiction over continuing orders (see below) it is a mistake to exclude them, as s 1(1)(a) apparently does, from the operation of the Regulation.

[392] By the European Communities (Jurisdiction and Judgments in Matrimonial and Parental Responsibility Matters) Regulations 2005, SI 2005/265.

[393] Viz Council Regulation (EC) No 2201/2003 of 27 November 2003 concerning jurisdiction and the recognition and enforcement of judgments in matrimonial matters and the matters of parental responsibility, repealing Regulation (EC) No 1347/2000. For the background to this revised Regulation see above pp 32–5.

[394] See generally N Lowe, M Everall and M Nicholls *The New Brussels II Regulation* (Family Law 2005) ch 5.

[395] Ie including the 10 states acceding to the Union in May 2004.   [396] See Art 2(3).

(a) Primary jurisdiction is given to the State in which the child is habitually resident at the time the court is seised[397] (Art 8);

(b) If habitual residence cannot be established and Art 12 (see below) does not apply, jurisdiction is based on the child's presence (Art 13);

(c) Where no Member State has jurisdiction under Arts 8–13 then a Member State can assume jurisdiction according to its own domestic rules (Art 14).

This scheme is subject to the following exceptions:

(i) in the case of a child's *lawful* movement to another Member State, the court that made an access order retains jurisdiction to modify it for three months (Art 9);[398]

(ii) special rules apply in cases of a child's *wrongful* removal or retention (Art 10);[399]

(iii) courts having jurisdiction to deal with divorce, legal separation or annulment have jurisdiction 'in any matter relating to parental responsibility connected with that application' provided at least one of the spouses has parental responsibility for the child and *any* other holder of responsibility accepts the jurisdiction *and* that is in the child's best interests[400] to exercise it (Art 12(1));

(iv) jurisdiction is also conferred on a Member State if the child has a 'substantial connection' with that State in particular by virtue of one of the holders of parental responsibility being habitually resident there or that the child is a national of that State *and* jurisdiction of the court has been accepted by all the parties to the proceedings at the time the court is seised *and* that it is in the child's best interests (Art 12(3)).

None of the foregoing rules prevents courts of a Member State 'from taking such provisional, including protective measures in respect of persons or assets in that State' according to domestic law (Art 20). Provision is also made by Art 15 to allow a transfer of a case in whole or in part from a court with jurisdiction to a court of another Member State.

The application of the Family Law Act 1986[401]

Apart from incorporating the Brussels II Regulation the general aim of the Family Law Act 1986 is to avoid conflicts of jurisdiction arising within the United Kingdom[402] and specified

---

[397] 'Seised' is defined in Art 16 as lodging the document that institutes the proceedings 'provided that the applicant has not subsequently failed to take the steps he was required to take to have service effected on the respondent'.

[398] Jurisdiction is lost if the holder of access rights accepts jurisdiction of the new court by participating in proceedings there.

[399] Discussed below at p 674.

[400] Art 12(1)(b) actually refers to the 'superior' interests of the child but this is a mistake which is not made in other language versions nor elsewhere in the Regulation.

[401] This Part implements the recommendations of the English and Scottish Law Commissions in their Report, *Custody of Children—Jurisdiction and Enforcement within the United Kingdom* (Law Com No 138, Scot Law Com No 91, 1985). For a full discussion and critique of the Act, see N Lowe 'The Family Law Act 1986—A Critique' [2002] Fam Law 39, and N Lowe, M Everall and M Nicholls *International Movement of Children, Law Practice and Procedure* ch 3.

[402] Meaning England and Wales, Scotland and Northern Ireland: s 42.

dependent territories (that is, at the moment, the Isle of Man).[403] To this end the Act provides for uniform jurisdictional rules when making 's 1(1)(a) orders', the scheme of which is:

(a) jurisdiction is prima facie vested in the UK court in which divorce, nullity or separation proceedings are continuing; but

(b) if there are no such proceedings, jurisdiction is vested in the UK court of the jurisdiction in which the child is habitually resident; and

(c) where neither (a) or (b) applies, jurisdiction is vested in the UK court of the place where the child is physically present.

As under the Regulation notwithstanding that a court properly has jurisdiction on one of the above bases there is a discretion to refuse or stay applications.[404] It is to be noted, however, that unlike the Regulation there is *no* emergency jurisdiction to make a s 1(1)(a) order.[405] There is no jurisdiction to make orders under the Children Act 1989 in relation to children who are members of the household of a parent claiming diplomatic immunity.[406] Save where the person enjoying immunity initiates proceedings, that immunity can only be waived by the sending state and not the individual concerned.[407]

So far as (a) is concerned, while divorce or nullity proceedings under the Matrimonial Causes Act 1973, (where jurisdiction is based on a *spouse's* domicile or habitual residence for one year)[408] are continuing, the court can make a s 8 order in relation to children of the family.[409] Proceedings are 'continuing' for this purpose from the time the petition is filed until the child reaches 18 in Northern Ireland or the Isle of Man or 16 in Scotland, unless those proceedings have been dismissed.[410] Even if the proceedings have been dismissed, there is still jurisdiction to make a s 8 order if it is made forthwith or where an application had been made on or before the dismissal.[411] A similar position obtains in respect of judicial separation (and separation order) proceedings save that there is no jurisdiction to make a s 8 order if divorce or nullity proceedings are 'continuing' in Scotland, Northern Ireland or the Isle of Man.[412]

---

[403] Section 43 and the Family Law Act 1986 (Dependent Territories) Order 1991, SI 1991/1723. References to the UK court also include the Isle of Man court.

[404] Section 2A(4), which is confined to matrimonial proceedings and s 5, which is of general application.

[405] The emergency jurisdiction, based on the child's presence, is confined to the High Court's inherent power (discussed in Ch 16) to make s 1(1)(d) orders: s 2(3)(b)(ii).

[406] *Re P (Children Act: Diplomatic Immunity)* [1998] 1 FLR 624, per Stuart-White J (on which see C Barker 'Re P (Minors) Child abduction and international immunities—balancing competing policies' [1998] CFLQ 211) applying the Vienna Convention on Diplomatic Relations 1961 as incorporated into English law by the Diplomatic Privileges Act 1964 Sch 1. Query whether this is human rights compliant? At the time of the decision the Human Rights Act 1998 was not in force. For a similar position in wardship see *Re C (An Infant)* [1959] Ch 363, discussed below at p 889.

[407] *Re P (Children Act: Diplomatic Immunity)*, above, applying Art 32 of the Vienna Convention.

[408] See the Domicile and Matrimonial Proceedings Act 1973, (discussed above at p 265) which also provides a not dissimilar scheme of priority within the UK, for the application of which see *M v M (Abduction: England and Scotland)* [1997] 2 FLR 263, CA.

[409] Defined by s 42(4)(a) in line with the definition in s 105(1) of the Children Act 1989, discussed above at pp 338–40.

[410] Section 42(2)–(3). See eg *B v B (Scottish Contact Order: Jurisdiction to Vary)* [1996] 1 WLR 231, and note *Re B (Court's Jurisdiction)* [2004] EWCA Civ 681, [2004] 2 FLR 741—stayed proceedings cease to be 'continuing'. English orders also 'continue' until the child reaches 18.

[411] Section 2A(1)(c).   [412] Section 2A(2).

Although on its face the 1986 Act provides a simple overall scheme the legislation is bedevilled by complexity and inadequate drafting which have been commented upon on more than one occasion by the judiciary. Thorpe J, for example, commented[413] that 'Part I of the Family Law Act 1986 is not easy to understand either in its layout or its language', and Wall J referred[414] to it as 'a complex, much amended and thoroughly unsatisfactory statute'. More damning still, the 1986 Act has failed to prevent conflicts of jurisdiction arising between the UK courts, the very raison d'étre of its original enactment. Space forbids a full discussion of the complexities;[415] it suffices to highlight two main defects.

First, the apparent simplicity of the prioritising scheme of the 1986 Act is flawed to the extent that matrimonial proceedings take precedence *whenever* they are instituted. Consequently while in the absence of matrimonial proceedings jurisdiction can properly be taken on the basis of the child's habitual residence, such proceedings are liable to be overtaken or 'trumped' by subsequent matrimonial proceedings.[416] Similarly, proceedings based on the child's presence can be trumped by those subsequently based on the child's habitual residence.

The second complication concerns so-called superseding orders, that is, Part I orders made during the subsistence of another Part I order.[417] Provided the second order is competently made,[418] it will supersede the earlier order. Even interim or holding orders have that effect even if it is unintended.[419]

The inter-relationship between the Regulation and the 1986 Act

The key differences between the jurisdictional rules provided for by the revised Brussels II Regulation and those under the 1986 Act are that (a) whereas under the Regulation the primary rule of jurisdiction is the child's habitual residence with the matrimonial court only having jurisdiction if at the very least all holders of parental responsibility agree, under the 1986 Act jurisdiction is primarily vested in the court hearing the matrimonial proceedings and (b) under the 1986 Act the court that validly made a s 8 order keeps jurisdiction throughout the lifetime of that order, whereas there is no equivalent retention of jurisdiction under the Regulation.

Because of these two differences the application of the two instruments can produce opposing results. Take the simple scenario of the child being habitually resident in Scotland but divorce proceedings being instituted in England. Under the Regulation Scotland should have jurisdiction whereas according to the 1986 Act England would have it. This therefore brings into sharp relief the question as to which instrument applies. A different conundrum arises if the child is habitually resident in a non-Brussels II State and divorce proceedings have been instituted in England. The question then is whether the English court can take jurisdiction according to the 1986 Act. The first scenario raises an interpretation issue of the Regulation; the second an issue of interpretation of the 1986 Act.

---

[413] *Re S (Residence Order: Forum Conveniens)* [1995] 1 FLR 314 at 320.

[414] *Re G (Adoption: Ordinary Residence)* [2002] EWHC 2447 (Fam), [2003] 2 FLR 944 at 951.

[415] For a full discussion, see Lowe at n 401 above.

[416] See, for example, *A v A (Forum Conveniens)* [1999] 1 FLR 1.

[417] See Family Law Act 1986 ss 6(1) (England and Wales), 15(1) (Scotland) and 23(1) (Northern Ireland).

[418] This is made expressly clear in s 15(1) and has been held to be implicit in ss 6(1) and 23(1): *D v D (Custody: Jurisdiction)* [1996] 1 FLR 574 at 582, per Hale J.

[419] *S v S (Custody: Jurisdiction)* [1995] 1 FLR 155. See also *T v T (Custody: Jurisdiction)* [1992] 1 FLR 43. For a critical analysis of these cases see Lowe, above, at 47–8.

So far as the former scenario is concerned the orthodox view is that as the Regulation only regulates matters *between* Member States it does not affect jurisdictional issues arising *within* a Member State. Hence, the 1986 Act applies and therefore the English court has overriding jurisdiction. This view might be thought to be supported by the *Practice Guide*[420] to the Regulation which states that 'The Regulation determines merely the Member State whose courts have jurisdiction, but not the court which is competent within that Member State', though whether this simply means that the Regulation leaves to each State to determine what *level* of court should hear a particular case, can be debated. Beevers and McClean[421] argue that Art 66(c) (which provides that 'any reference to the authority of a Member State shall refer to the authority of a territorial unit within that State which is concerned') could be interpreted as meaning that any reference to a court of a Member State must also be read as referring to the court of a territorial unit within that State. Hence the Regulation applies to our scenario and the Scottish courts have jurisdiction.[422] Still others argue[423] that even if the orthodox view prevails, as a matter of desirable practice no court in the United Kingdom or the Isle of Man should take jurisdiction if another court within that State has jurisdiction under the Regulation, since that will be the only way that an order will be recognisable and enforceable throughout Member States.

So far as the second scenario is concerned, the orthodox view is that since (assuming Art 12 does not apply) no Member State has jurisdiction under the Regulation, then by Art 14, England is free to apply its own rules and hence by the terms of the 1986 Act has jurisdiction.[424] But again this orthodoxy has been challenged by Beevers and McClean who point out[425] that as currently worded the 1986 Act only applies its own provisions if and when the Regulation does not apply. In other words Art 14 cannot be relied upon. One possible reply to this is that one applies ss 2A and 3 by reason of Art 14 and thus comes within s 2(1)(a). In other words, reliance may not need to be placed on s 2(1)(b).

However, contentions such as these only add weight to the general plea that the whole of the 1986 Act should be reconsidered. There is much to be said for simply applying the Regulation rules to all scenarios.[426]

(b) Family proceedings

Under s 10(1) the court[427] is empowered to make a s 8 order 'in any family proceedings in which a question arises with respect to the welfare of any child'. The term 'family

---

[420] *Parental Responsibility in the European Union—Practice Guide for the Application of the New Brussels II Regulation* (European Commission) p 20.

[421] 'Intra-UK Jurisdiction in Parental Responsibility Cases: has Europe Intervened?' [2005] IFL 129 at 130.

[422] This view is supported by N Lowe 'Negotiating The Revised Brussels II Regulation' [2004] IFL 205 at 209.

[423] Lowe, Everall and Nicholls *The New Brussels II Regulation*, op cit, at 5.21.

[424] Although it is evident that the 1986 Act has been treated as applying to cases where the child is connected with jurisdictions outside the UK and Isle of Man there is some debate about what was intended, see Thorpe J in *Re S (Residence Order: Forum Conveniens)* above at 521 and note Singer J's observation in *Re P (A Child: Mirror Orders)* [2000] 1 FLR 435 at 437 that the Preamble to the Act does not, on its face, contemplate this legislation having effect outside the confines of the UK.

[425] Above at 131–2.   [426] Lowe, Everall and Nicholls, above, 5.22–5.23.

[427] The High Court, county court or magistrates' court: s 92(7).

proceedings' is defined by s 8(3)[428] as meaning any proceedings 'under the inherent jurisdiction of the High Court in relation to children' or under the enactments listed in s 8(4). With regard to the former, which refers both to wardship and to proceedings under the general inherent jurisdiction of the High Court,[429] s 8(3) states that local authority applications to invoke the High Court's inherent jurisdiction fall outside the definition.

The enactments listed in s 8(4), as amended, are as follows:

— Parts I, II and IV of the 1989 Act;

— Matrimonial Causes Act 1973;

— Domestic Proceedings and Magistrates' Courts Act 1978;

— Matrimonial and Family Proceedings Act 1984, Part III;

— Family Law Act 1996;

— Adoption and Children Act 2002;

— Crime and Disorder Act 1998, ss 11 and 12

— Civil Partnership Act 2004, Schs 5 and 6

Applications under s 30 of the Human Fertilisation and Embryology Act 1990 also rank as 'family proceedings'.[430]

Based on the Law Commission's recommendation[431] and intended to rationalise, harmonise[432] and, in some cases, expand the courts' powers, the wide ambit of the definition of 'family proceedings' should be noted. For example, the inclusion of Part IV of the 1989 Act means that the court can make s 8 orders in care proceedings. Similarly, the court can now make s 8 orders in adoption, in family protection proceedings under the Family Law Act 1996 and in financial relief proceedings. The reason for including these proceedings is that by extending the range of options the court will be better able to meet the child's needs.[433]

The inclusion of wardship proceedings under 'family proceedings' furthers the policy of reducing the need to resort to the jurisdiction,[434] because there will be less incentive to use it if the outcome is likely to be the same as in other proceedings. Furthermore, where an application is made the expectation is that, where appropriate, the court will make a s 8 order and discharge the wardship.[435]

---

[428] Note s 8(3) only provides the exclusive definition of 'family proceedings' for the purpose of making s 8 orders. For other purposes, eg the admission of hearsay evidence, recourse might also be had to the definition in s 92(2): *R v Oxfordshire County Council (Secure Accommodation Order)* [1992] Fam 150.

[429] Discussed in Ch 16.

[430] Human Fertilisation and Embryology Act 1990 s 30(8). For a discussion of s 30, see above, pp 315ff.

[431] Law Com No 172, para 4.37.

[432] Note, however, that, whereas the court is obliged to consider the children in applications for financial relief under the Domestic Proceedings and Magistrates' Courts Act 1978, there is no such duty in an application under s 27 of the Matrimonial Causes Act 1973.

[433] In the case of family protection proceedings, as the Law Commission observed (above at para 4.25), the needs of the children are frequently an important factor in determining the relief sought and it was 'highly artificial' for the court to be able to exclude one person from the matrimonial home, at least in part for the children's sake, yet not to be able to order that the child should live with the parent remaining in the home. It might be noted, however, that in these proceedings the court is not *obliged* to consider children and that in many cases the matter will be too urgent for it to do so.

[434] Law Com No 172, para 4.25. Wardship is discussed in Ch 16.

[435] As was done in *Re T (Minor) (Child: Representation)* [1994] Fam 49, CA and *C v Salford City Council* [1994] 2 FLR 926, discussed below, pp 898–9.

Wide though the definition is, however, it does not include all proceedings concerning children. In particular it does not include those under Part V of the 1989 Act. This means that in applications for emergency protection orders and child assessment orders the court cannot make a s 8 order. There is similarly no power to make s 8 orders in international child abduction proceedings under the Child Abduction and Custody Act 1985,[436] nor in proceedings brought under the Family Law Act 1986.[437]

(c) Any child

Section 10(1) allows an order to be made in respect of 'any child'. In other words, the court's powers are not limited to 'children of the family',[438] or to the biological children of the parties, though, as we have discussed, the powers are restricted when the child reaches the age of 16.[439] By the normal rules of interpretation[440] 'child' only refers to live persons. There is therefore no power to make s 8 orders in respect of unborn or deceased children.

(d) Upon application or upon the court's own motion

Section 10(1) provides that s 8 orders can be made either upon application or, once proceedings have begun, by the court itself whenever it 'considers that the order should be made *even though no such application has been made*' [emphasis added]. Although the Law Commission expected[441] that orders would normally be made upon application, the significance of the courts' ability to make s 8 orders on their own motion should not be overlooked, since in theory once family proceedings are on foot there is at least a risk that the court might choose to make a s 8 order in respect of the child regardless of the parties' wishes. If, however, a court is minded to make an order that has not been argued for, it should inform the parties of that intention and give them the opportunity to make submissions on the desirability of the proposed option.[442] It has also been said[443] that it could only be in wholly exceptional circumstances that a residence order should be imposed on unwilling recipients.

In *Gloucestershire County Council v P*[444] it was held that the flexibility given to a judge by s 10(1)(b) to make a residence order upon his own initiative is not limited by the restrictions imposed by ss 9 and 10(3).[445] It was thus held to be no bar on the court granting a residence order in favour of foster parents that the parties themselves were

---

[436] Discussed in Ch 13.

[437] The 1986 Act deals inter alia with abduction within the UK (see Ch 13), and declarations of status, discussed above at pp 331 and 345.

[438] The meaning of which is discussed above, pp 338–40.

[439] Pursuant to s 9(6): see above, p 539.

[440] See *Elliot v Joicey* [1935] AC 209, HL; *D (A Minor) v Berkshire County Council* [1987] 1 All ER 20, HL; and *R v Newham London Borough Council, ex p Dada* [1996] QB 507, CA.

[441] Law Com No 172, para 4.38.

[442] See eg *Croydon London Borough Council v A* [1992] Fam 169, and *Devon County Council v S* [1992] Fam 176. In both these cases the observations were made in respect of magistrates' court decisions, but the principle ought to be of general application. Query the position on appeal: see eg *Re F (Minors) (Denial of Contact)* [1993] 2 FLR 677 in which the Court of Appeal refused to make a family assistance order inter alia because the point had not been argued at first instance.

[443] Per Stuart-White J in *Re K (Care Order or Residence Order)* [1995] 1 FLR 675 at 683, in which devoted grandparents did not wish to have legal responsibility in respect of two grandsons (who were suffering from a muscle-wasting disease) they were looking after.

[444] [2000] Fam 1, CA, Thorpe LJ dissenting.	[445] Discussed above p 540.

prohibited from seeking court leave to apply for such an order though as Butler-Sloss LJ observed it would only be in 'a most exceptional' case that it would be right to make an order in favour of foster-parents who could not themselves apply. A similarly purposive interpretation was applied in *Re G (Leave to Appeal: Jurisdiction)*[446] when upholding a decision to make an 'interim' residence order upon an application for leave to allow a child in care to go to Scotland, even though this evaded the difficulties of Sch 2 to the Children Act 1989 Butler-Sloss LJ said:[447]

'Judges cannot dispense with the Children Act. What they can dispense with are unnecessary procedural difficulties within the general powers of the Children Act to arrive at what the judge thinks under s 1 of the Children Act to be the interests of the child, with the child's welfare being the paramount consideration.'

6 ENFORCING SECTION 8 ORDERS[448]

Enforcing s 8 orders can be a difficult and protracted matter which in any event needs to be handled sensitively. The imposition of penal sanctions for breaking court orders (discussed below) should not be thought of as being the norm in children cases. On the contrary, they should be sought only where all other alternatives are seen to be ineffective. Even then, careful thought needs to be given to the provocative and emotional effect that applications for enforcement can have in themselves. Above all it is important not to lose sight of the *child's* welfare in these disputes though, as we shall see, in deciding whether to impose a penal sanction the child's welfare has been held *not* to be the paramount consideration.[449]

(a) Family Law Act 1986 s 34

Under s 34 of the Family Law Act 1986,[450] where a person is required by a s 8 order to give up a child to another person and the court that made the order is satisfied that the child has not been given up, it may make an order authorising an officer of the court or a constable to take charge of the child and deliver him to that other person.[451] Since this power, which is available to *any* court, enables such orders to be enforced without recourse to penal procedures, it should normally be preferred to those latter powers. However, because an order under s 34 cannot be granted unless or until the order to give up the child has been disobeyed,[452] it might be preferable in emergencies to obtain an ex parte

---

[446] [1999] 1 FLR 771.   [447] At 773.

[448] See generally N Lowe 'Enforcing orders relating to children' (1992) 4 Journal of Child Law 26 and, especially in relation to enforcing contact orders, see *Making Contact Work*, ch 14 and, inter alia, the Government Green Papers *Parental Separation: Children's Needs and Parents' Responsibilities* CM 6273 (July 2004) and *Parental Separation: Children's Needs and Parents' Responsibilities: Next Steps)* CM 6452 (January 2005).

[449] *A v N (Committal: Refusal of Contact)* [1997] 1 FLR 533, CA, discussed below at p 571.

[450] See generally N Fricker and P Bean *Enforcement of Injunctions and Undertakings* p 80 et seq, N Fricker et al: *Emergency Remedies and Procedures* (2nd edn) 158 et seq and Lowe, Everall and Nicholls *International Movement of Children—Law Practice and Procedure*, ch 10.

[451] Note that the police generally have a duty to assist in the handing over of a child where there is a threat of danger or a breach of the peace: *R v Chief Constable of Cheshire ex p K* [1990] 1 FLR 70. There is also power under s 33 of the 1986 Act for a court to order any person whom it has reason to believe may have relevant information as to the child's whereabouts to disclose it to the court.

[452] Though it can be applied to a suitably worded contact order, viz one that formally requires the handing over of the child for contact purposes.

order under the High Court's inherent jurisdiction[453] authorising the tipstaff to find and recover the child.[454]

(b) The courts' general enforcement powers for contempt of court

More general powers of enforcement are, in the case of the High Court and county court, provided by the law of contempt of court, and in the case of magistrates' courts, by s 63(3) of the Magistrates' Courts Act 1980.

The High Court and county court powers

As far as the two higher courts are concerned (in this respect the powers of the High Court are no greater than those of the county court),[455] the breaking of a court order or an undertaking incorporated in an order constitutes a contempt of court for which the contemnor may be fined, imprisoned or have his property sequestered.[456] The first remedy is unusual.[457] The latter remedy (under which the contemnor's assets are frozen)[458] is useful in cases where the offender is abroad but has assets in this country.[459] The major sanction for breaking a s 8 order is by committal, by which means the offender can be imprisoned for a maximum period of two years.[460]

Before any committal order may be made the court has to be satisfied beyond reasonable doubt[461] that the defendant knowingly broke the order. Furthermore, it is a requirement[462] that a penal notice (that is, a notice formally warning the person against whom the order is made that failure to obey it constitutes a contempt of court for which the offender may be sent to prison) must have been attached to the order in question. Penal notices, however, can only be attached to orders that are injunctions or injunctive in form.[463] In other words, to be enforceable at all the order must, as the Children Act Advisory Committee states:[464] 'set out in explicit terms precisely what it is that the person in question must do, or must refrain from doing' and in the former case it must also specify the time within which the act is to be done.

The requirement that the order be in injunctive form means that not all s 8 orders and

---

[453] Discussed in Ch 16.

[454] See Fricker, op cit, at p 248 and N Fricker 'Injunctive Orders Relating to Children' [1993] Fam Law 226 at 229–30.

[455] *Re F (Contact: Enforcement: Representation of Child)* [1998] 1 FLR 691, CA.

[456] These powers are briefly referred to in the Children Act Advisory Committee (CAAC) Report 1992/93 ch 5, but for detailed discussion reference should be made to Arlidge, Eady and Smith on *Contempt* (2nd edn), ch 12, Borrie and Lowe's *The Law of Contempt* (3rd edn) ch 14 and Miller *Contempt of Court* (3rd edn) ch 14.

[457] See Butler-Sloss P in *Re S (Contact: Promoting Relationship With Absent Parent)* [2004] EWCA Civ 18, [2004] 1 FLR 1219 at [28] in the context of enforcing contact orders. See generally, Borrie and Lowe, op cit, 635–9 and Miller, op cit, at 2.16.

[458] There is also power both to order the sale of sequestered assets and to direct that money raised by the sequestrators be used to pay for the costs of tracing the child and instituting proceedings abroad: see respectively *Mir v Mir* [1992] Fam 79, and *Richardson v Richardson* [1989] Fam 95.

[459] It is therefore particularly useful in cases of child abduction—see below, p 619.

[460] Contempt of Court 1981, s 14(1).

[461] See eg *Dean v Dean* [1987] 1 FLR 517, CA, and *Re Bramblevale Ltd* [1970] Ch 128, CA.

[462] CPR 1998, Sch 1, RSC Ord 45 r 7(4) and see *Supreme Court Practice* 45/1/7 for forms (High Court); CCR Ord 29 r 1(3) (county court).

[463] *Re P (Minors) (Custody Order: Penal Notice)* [1990] 1 WLR 613, CA, and *D v D (Access: Contempt: Committal)* [1991] 2 FLR 34, CA.

[464] CAAC Report 1992/93 at 44. For the procedure of adding a penal notice, see Family Proceedings Rules 1991 r 4.21A.

associated directions can be enforced by committal. It is clear, for example, that the embargoes against changing the child's surname and removing him from the UK, as provided for by s 13[465] and clearly stated on the face of a residence order,[466] are not *per se* enforceable by committal orders.[467] If therefore sanctions for contempt are being sought, it will be necessary to obtain a prohibited steps order[468] clearly setting out what action must be refrained from and backed by a penal notice.

Since residence orders are said only to settle 'the arrangements to be made as to the person with whom the child is to live', they are clearly not injunctive in form and are not therefore enforceable in themselves in the two higher courts.[469] To make such orders prima facie enforceable courts must attach precise directions or conditions, for example that the child be returned to a specific place at a specific time,[470] pursuant to their powers under s 11(7).

Although in their statutory form contact orders *are* injunctive in terms and are therefore prima facie enforceable, as *D v D (Access: Contempt: Committal)*[471] shows, an order which is declaratory in terms, eg providing for reasonable contact, cannot have a penal notice attached to it and cannot therefore be enforced by committal. As the Children Act Advisory Committee has said:[472] 'To be enforceable by committal, an order for contact ... [has] ... to specify when and probably where, the child [is] to be allowed contact as well as with whom'. It is similarly necessary to spell out in a prohibited steps or specific issue order precisely what is prohibited or required, and in the latter case by when the act in question is required to be completed.

Orders are normally only enforceable against parties to the proceedings, but it can also be a contempt for someone else knowingly to frustrate a court order.[473]

Magistrates' courts' general enforcement powers

Magistrates' enforcement powers are governed by the Magistrates' Courts Act 1980 s 63(3) which provides:

'Where any person disobeys an order of a magistrates' court ... to do anything other than the payment of money or to abstain from doing anything the court may —

(a) order him to pay a sum not exceeding £50 for every day during which he is in default or a sum not exceeding £5,000; or

(b) commit him to custody until he has remedied his default for a period not exceeding 2 months;

but a person who is ordered to pay a sum for every day during which he is in default or who is committed to custody until he has remedied his default shall not by virtue of this section

---

465 Discussed above, pp 550ff.   466 Viz Form C 43.   467 See *Re P* above.

468 But note the decision in *Re B (Change of Surname)* [1996] 1 FLR 791, CA (discussed above at pp 553–4), in which it was held that where there is an existing residence order an application to change name had to be made under s 13 rather than s 8.

469 See the arguments of Lowe, op cit, at p 27. This would seem to be the raison d'être for s 14 in relation to enforcing orders in the magistrates' court. See below.

470 For an example of this type of order see *Re B (Minors) (Residence Order)* [1992] Fam 162, CA.

471 [1994] 1 FLR 34.   472 CAAC Report 1992/93, p 44.

473 See *Re K (Minors) (Incitement to Breach Contact Order)* [1992] 2 FLR 108 (solicitor held guilty of contempt for advising a client mother to break an access order); *Re S (Abduction: Sequestration)* [1995] 1 FLR 858 (contempt for a friend to assist mother in abducting child).

be ordered to pay more than [£5,000][474] or be committed for more than 2 months in all for doing or abstaining from doing the same thing contrary to the order (without prejudice to the operation of this section in relation to any subsequent default).'

Section 14 of the 1989 Act makes express provision for the enforcement of residence orders under s 63(3) of the Magistrates' Courts Act 1980. At first sight this special provision might be thought to mean that the other s 8 orders are not enforceable in the magistrates' court. However, the reason for making such provision for residence orders is that they might otherwise be thought declaratory only and therefore not enforceable.[475] No such difficulty attends the other s 8 orders (at any rate, in their statutory form), which accordingly are enforceable under s 63(3).

Unlike in the higher courts there is no provision for adding a penal notice to a magistrates' courts order. According to the Family Proceedings Courts (Children Act 1989) Rules 1991 r 24 a person (in whose favour a residence order has been made) wishing to enforce it must:

'. . . file a written statement describing the alleged breach of the arrangements settled by the order, whereupon the justices' clerk shall fix a date, time and place for a hearing of the proceedings and give notice as soon as practicable, to the person whom it is alleged is in breach of the arrangements settled by that order, of the date fixed'.

No specific rule is laid down for the enforcement of s 8 orders other than residence orders, but it seems sensible to assume that a similar procedure is applicable to them. It is at any rate clear that to be enforceable under s 63(3) an order must specify exactly what is to be done. In *Re H (Contact: Enforcement)*[476] it was held that the failure to specify in a contact order where the handover was to take place was fatal to the complaint.

Section 63(3) of the 1980 Act is not happily worded and seems more apt to deal with continuing breaches. Nevertheless the provision can be interpreted[477] as empowering magistrates to punish past breaches, though this point has still to be authoritatively resolved.

Determining whether to impose a penalty

Even if the court is satisfied that an order has been knowingly broken by the defendant, it should regard the enforcement powers both for contempt and under the 1980 Act to imprison or fine as remedies of the last resort. As Ormrod LJ commented in *Ansah v Ansah*,[478] 'Committal orders are remedies of the last resort; in family cases they should be the very last.' Further, as Hale LJ observed in *Hale v Tanner*:[479]

---

[474] The provision in fact still mentions £1,000, but it clearly should be changed in line with the maximum fine provided by subsection (a).

[475] Following *Webster v Southwark London Borough Council* [1983] QB 698. Query why the opportunity was not taken to make s 14 applicable to residence orders made in the High Court and county court?

[476] [1996] 1 FLR 614.

[477] See *P v W (Access Order: Breach)* [1984] Fam 32 at 40 per Wood J.

[478] [1977] Fam 138 at 143, CA. Note also Bennett J's comment in *Re H*, above, that magistrates should 'take the greatest possible caution before proceeding with a hearing under s 63—they should only proceed with the greatest possible caution to use a weapon of last resort'.

[479] [2000] 1 WLR 2377 at [25], CA, discussed above at p 243. See the comments thereon by R Kay 'Guidelines on Sanctions for Breach: *Hale v Tanner*' (2001) 64 MLR 595, particularly 598–601.

'Family cases, it has long been recognised, raise quite different considerations from those elsewhere in the civil law. The two most obvious are the heightened emotional tensions that arise between family members and often the need for those family members to continue to be in contact with one another because they have children together or the like . . .'

Nevertheless, it would be wrong to extract any general principle from Ormrod LJ's dictum in *Ansah v Ansah*, and in appropriate cases it may well be right to imprison an offender.[480] Indeed, following the Court of Appeal decision in *A v N (Committal: Refusal of Contact)*,[481] in which it was held that, in considering whether to commit a mother for her persistent and flagrant breach of a contact order with the father, the child's welfare was a material but not the paramount consideration, imprisonment might be more likely than in the past,[482] though as far as breach of contact orders are concerned, regard will now have to be had to the power to make enforcement orders under the provisions introduced by the Children and Adoption Act 2006, which are discussed below. Although in principle similar caution should be exercised when considering the imposition of penal sanctions upon the non-residential parent there may nevertheless be less concern for the child's welfare in so doing.[483]

Limitations of the contempt powers

Though they have their place in the coercive armoury both to ensure compliance with court orders and to deter breaches, the contempt remedies are limited and increasing criticism has been voiced at the apparent ease with which contact orders in particular could be frustrated or simply ignored. As Bracewell J observed in *V v V (Contact: Implacable Hostility)*[484] the option of committing the contemnor to prison or to suspend the prison term, always at best a blunt remedy,

'may well not achieve the object of reinstating contact; the child may blame the parent who applied to commit the carer to prison; the child's life may be disrupted if there is no-one capable of or willing to care for the child when the parent is in prison; it cannot be anything other than emotionally damaging for a child to be suddenly removed into foster care by social services from a parent, usually a mother, who in all respects except contact is a good parent'.

---

[480] See eg *Jones v Jones* [1993] 2 FLR 377, CA.

[481] [1997] 1 FLR 533, CA in which a mother was committed to prison for 42 days for her persistent and repeated breaches of a contact order. See also *Re S (Contact Dispute: Committal)* [2004] EWCA Civ 1790, [2005] 1 FLR 812—mother's committal for seven days (with an interim residence order to father) for repeated breaches, upheld on appeal; *F v F (Contact: Committal)* [1998] 2 FLR 237, CA (mother's appeal against a suspended committal for seven days was dismissed); *C v C (Access Order: Enforcement)* [1990] 1 FLR 462, CA (mother imprisoned for seven days). Cf *Re K (Contact: Committal Order)* [2002] EWCA Civ 1559, [2003] 1 FLR 377 wrong to impose a committal on a mother without legal representation, notwithstanding her numerous breaches.

[482] Though this is not to say that the penal remedy should be frequently resorted to, cf *Re F (Contact: Enforcement: Representation of Child)* [1998] 1 FLR 691, CA.

[483] See eg *G v C (Residence Order: Committal)* [1998] 1 FLR 43, CA (father imprisoned for eight months for repeated breaches of order not to threaten or abuse the mother).

[484] [2004] EWHC 1215 (Fam), [2004] 2 FLR 851 at [10]. See also *Re S (Contact: Promoting Relationship With Absent Parent)* [2004] EWCA Civ 18, [2004] 1 FLR 1279 at [28] per Butler-Sloss P and Lord Justice Wall 'Enforcement of Contact Orders' [2005] Fam Law 26 at 30–1.

Nor is a fine any better, for as Bracewell J said: 'This option is rarely possible because it is not consistent with the welfare of the child to deprive a parent on a limited budget'.

It was in response to criticisms such as these that new measures were introduced by the Children and Adoption Act 2006 to increase the options of the court when dealing with breaches of contact orders.[485] It is to these remedies that we now turn.

(c) Contact enforcement orders

A new sanction for failing to comply with contact orders, the enforcement order, has been introduced by the Children and Adoption Act 2006, via the insertion of ss 11J-N into the Children Act 1989. Under s 11J where the court[486] it satisfied beyond all reasonable doubt that a person has failed to comply with a contact order it may make an enforcement order which is an order imposing an unpaid work requirement up a maximum of 200 hours[487] on the person who has broken the order. According to the Explanatory Notes to the Bill, in addition to a breach of a contact order, a breach of a contact activity condition[488] or of a condition attached to contact order under s 11(7), constitutes a breach of a contact order for these purposes though the Act does not expressly say so.

No enforcement order may be made if the court is satisfied that the person in breach had a reasonable excuse for failing to comply though the burden is on the person in breach to prove on the balance of probabilities that he had a reasonable excuse; nor can an order be made against someone who was under 18 at the time of the breach.

Orders can only be made on the application of:

'(a) the person who is, for the purposes of the contact order; the person with whom the child concerned lives or is to live;

(b) the person whose contact with the child concerned is provided for in the contact order;

(c) any individual subject to a condition under section 11(7)(b) or a contact activity condition imposed by the contact order; or

(d) the child concerned.'

In the latter case the child must obtain the leave of the court and leave may only be given if the court is satisfied that the child has sufficient understanding to make the proposed application. It will be noted that the inclusion of (a) above means that in theory a resident parent can seek an enforcement order against a non-resident parent. However, it is by no means clear that a contact order can be made against such a person under s 8[489] and still less

---

[485] For the background to these measures see the Government Green Papers *Parental Separation: Children's Needs and Parents' Responsibilities* Cm 6273 (July 2004), *Parental Separation: Children's Needs and Parents' Responsibilities: Next Steps* Cm 6452 (January 2005); the Draft Children (Contact) and Adoption Bill Cm 6462 (February 2005); the Joint Committee on the Draft Children (Contact) and Adoption Bill: First Report HL Paper 100–1/HC 400–1 (the so-called 'Scrutiny Committee') and *The Government Reply to the Report from the Joint Committee* Cm 6583 (June 2005). For comments on the proposals see J Masson and C Humphreys 'Facilitating and Enforcing Contact: The Bill and the Ten Per Cent' [2005] Fam Law 548. Note that the more draconian of the suggested sanctions, namely, curfews and tagging, were not included in the 2006 Act.

[486] Ie High Court, county court or magistrates' court: s 92(7) of the Children Act 1989.

[487] Sch A1, para 4 to the Children Act 1989 as added by Sch 1 to the 2006 Act. An enforcement order can be suspended for such period as th court thinks fit: s 11J(a).

[488] But note, not a contact activity *direction*. These conditions and directions are discussed above at p 524.

[489] See the discussion above at p 521 and note the similar criticism made by Masson and Humphreys, op cit, at 552.

against an unwilling parent[490] though it is true that the non-resident parent could be in breach of conditions attached to an order under s 11(7), for example, for failing to return the child at a certain time and place or for breach of a contact activity condition.

By s 11L in deciding whether to make an enforcement order the court must be satisfied that its making is necessary to secure compliance and that 'the likely effect on the person of the enforcement order proposed to be made is proportionate to the seriousness of the breach . . .'. The court is also required, before making the order, to obtain and consider information about the person upon whom the order would be imposed. The unpaid work must be local and information must be obtained about the effect of the order on the individual. Importantly, in making an enforcement order the child's welfare is *not* the paramount consideration though the court must take it into account.[491] Whether this is adequate protection for the child can be debated.

On making an enforcement order 'the court is to ask' a CAFCASS officer or a Welsh family proceedings officer to monitor compliance and to report to the court.[492]

More than one enforcement order may be made in relation to the same person on the same occasion and such an order is said to be 'without prejudice' to s 63(3) of the Magistrates' Courts Act 1980 as it applies in relation to contact orders.[493] An enforcement order can subsequently be revoked or amended, and, if it is itself broken, the court may amend it or make it more onerous, or impose another enforcement order.[494] When making the enforcement order the court *must* attach to that order a notice warning of the consequences of non-compliance.[495]

It is hard to say how useful enforcement orders will be, although it seems likely that they will generally be looked to ahead of imposing any contempt sanction. It has to be said, however, that many of the limitations and difficulties attendant on the contempt sanctions[496] apply equally to enforcement orders.

(d) Compensation for financial loss

A second type of order which may be imposed upon breach of a contact order, introduced by the Children and Adoption 2006 (by inserting ss 11O and 11P into the Children Act 1989), is to order financial compensation for financial loss occasioned by the breach. The example always cited is the cost of a holiday that has been lost because of the breach but it would also include wasted travel costs though presumably these will have to be substantial enough to justify court time being spent on the issue.

Under s 11O where a court is satisfied[497] that an individual has failed to comply with a

---

[490] Ironically, the Government itself rejected the proposal that the court should have the power to compel an unwilling parent to have contact with the child, see above p 521.

[491] This is the implication of s 11L(7) which provides that when making an enforcement order, the court 'must take into account the welfare of the child who is the subject of the contact order'.

[492] Section 11M(1).

[493] Section 11J(10) and (13) respectively. Query why the higher courts' contempt powers are also not expressly preserved.

[494] Sch A1, Part 2.

[495] Section 11N. This is the equivalent of a penal notice having to be attached to an order before contempt sanctions may be imposed, but in this instance, *all* courts are under the same obligation.

[496] Discussed above at p 570.

[497] The Act is silent on the standard of proof but presumably the breach must be proved beyond all reasonable doubt though it is a more open question upon what standard the court needs to be satisfied that the loss has been occasioned by the breach.

contact order[498] and a relevant party[499] has suffered financial loss because of the breach, it can order the person in breach to pay compensation up to the amount of the loss. There is a defence of 'reasonable excuse' for which the burden[500] is on the person claiming to have a reasonable excuse.

Only the person suffering loss can apply and in any event claimants are limited to the resident parent, the person with whom contact was ordered, an individual subject to a condition under s 11(7)(b) or a contact activity condition or, with court leave, the child.[501]

In deciding what compensation to order, the court must take into account the financial circumstances of the individual in breach and the child's welfare (which, as for enforcement orders, is not the paramount consideration). An amount ordered to be paid as compensation may be recovered as a 'civil debt'.

It remains to be seen how useful compensation orders will be.

7 VARYING AND DISCHARGING ORDERS

All s 8 orders may subsequently be varied or discharged. Indeed, this is one of the important distinguishing features between these orders and adoption.[502]

All the substantive and procedural requirements for the making of a s 8 order apply to their subsequent variation or discharge.[503]

8 APPEALS

(a) Routes of appeal and procedure[504]

There is a right of appeal against the making or the refusal to make any s 8 order under the Children Act, including s 8 orders. Appeals from magistrates' decisions lie to the High Court;[505] those from county courts and the High Court lie to the Court of Appeal.[506] While there is no automatic embargo against a party appealing against a consent order, it seems that leave of the court that made the order will be required.[507] Where no leave is granted, the proper procedure is to apply to the first instance court to vary the order.[508]

Apart from the case of consent orders leave is not required to appeal from a magistrates' decision. However, as from May 2000, leave has been required to appeal to the Court of

---

[498] According to the Explanatory Notes to the Act, breaching a contact order includes breaching a condition attached to a contact order.

[499] Ie a person who is entitled to apply for an order under s 11O(6), see below.

[500] Presumably upon the balance of probabilities, but unlike enforcement orders the Act is silent on this.

[501] Leave can only be given if the court is satisfied that the child has sufficient understanding to make the proposed application.

[502] Adoption is discussed in Chapter 15.

[503] Section 8(2), which provides that 'a section 8 order means inter alia, any order varying or discharging such an order'.

[504] See generally White, Carr and Lowe: *Children Act in Practice* (3rd edn), op cit, 13.1ff and Clarke Hall and Morrison on *Children* 1[1491]ff.

[505] Children Act 1989 s 94.   [506] County Courts Act 1984 s 77(1); Supreme Court Act 1981 s 16.

[507] See *Re R (Contact: Consent Order)* [1995] 1 FLR 123, CA.

[508] *Re F (A Minor) (Custody: Consent Order: Procedure)* [1992] 1 FLR 561, CA.

Appeal.[509] In this latter respect a distinction is made between first appeals and second appeals (that is, appeals from decisions that themselves were the determination of an appeal). In the case of first appeals permission should normally be sought from the trial court first[510] but if that application is refused or if no application was made at the first instance hearing, permission can then be sought from the Court of Appeal.[511] In the case of second appeals permission *must* be sought from the Court of Appeal.[512] In either case if the appeal court refuses permission without a hearing the applicant has the right to ask for an oral hearing.[513] There is, however, no appeal from a decision of the appeal court made at an oral hearing either to allow or to refuse permission to appeal to that court.[514] The test for determining whether to grant permission is predictably less stringent for first appeals than for second appeals. In the former the court must consider that the appeal would have a real prospect of success or there is some other compelling reason why the appeal should be heard.[515] In the latter leave cannot be given unless the case raises an important principle or practice or there is some other compelling reason for the Court of Appeal to hear it.[516]

Appeals from the Court of Appeal lie to the House of Lords.[517] Leave to appeal must be granted either by the Court of Appeal or, more commonly, by the Appeals Committee of the House of Lords.[518]

(b) The position pending appeal

Under the general powers to impose directions and conditions under s 11(7) of the Children Act 1989[519] the operation of any s 8 order can be postponed pending an appeal, or other interim arrangements can be made.[520]

(c) The powers of appellate courts

An appellate court may grant or dismiss the appeal. Alternatively, if it is satisfied that the original order was wrong but is unsure upon the evidence what orders should be made, it can remit the case for a rehearing and in the meantime give appropriate directions.

---

[509] This is when the procedure introduced by the Civil Procedure Rules 1998, Pt 52 came into operation. The only exceptions to the leave requirement are in respect of committal orders, refusals to grant habeas corpus and secure accommodation orders: CPR 1998, r 52.3(1).

[510] *Practice Direction* 52, para 4.6 the rationale being that the first instance court is usually in the best position to determine whether leave to appeal should be given.

[511] CPR 1998, r 52.3(2), (3) and *Practice Direction* 52, para 4.7.

[512] CPR 1998, r 52.13 and *Practice Direction* 52, para 4.9.　　[513] CPR 1998, r 52.3(4).

[514] *Practice Direction* 52, para 4.8 referring to a s 54(4) of the Access to Justice Act 1999.

[515] CPR 1998, r 52.3(6).　　[516] CPR 1998, 5 52.13(2).

[517] Administration of Justice Act 1977, s 9. In exceptional cases 'leap frog' appeals may be directly to the House of Lords from the High Court in accordance with the Administration of Justice Act 1969, ss 12 and 15. *A v Liverpool City Council* [1982] AC 363 (discussed below at p 803) is a notable example of a leapfrog appeal.

[518] For the procedure set eg Rayden and Jackson on *Divorce and Family Matters* (17th edn) 50–88ff.

[519] Discussed above, pp 531ff.

[520] Magistrates apparently have no powers to order a stay pending an appeal and an application needs to made to the High Court (Children Act Advisory Committee: *Handbook of Best Practice in Children Act Cases*, (1997) para 92). Stays should not normally be granted for more than 14 days: cf *Hereford and Worcester County Council v EH* [1985] FLR 975 at 977, per Wood J.

Exceptionally, the appellate court can hear fresh evidence to resolve its doubts about the original decision.[521]

In deciding whether to allow an appeal there are no special rules governing appeals in cases involving children. The leading case is *G v G (Custody: Appeal)*,[522] in which the House of Lords held that an appellate court[523] cannot overturn a first instance decision merely upon the basis that it disagrees with it. An appellate court has no power simply to substitute its own view. Instead it has to be satisfied that either the judge has erred as a matter of law (ie he applied the wrong principle) or that he relied upon evidence that he should have ignored or ignored evidence that he should have taken into account or that the decision was so 'plainly wrong' that the only legitimate conclusion was that the judge had erred in the exercise of his discretion. Although this latter ground gives scope for argument in any particular case,[524] it is to be emphasised that the test is difficult to satisfy.[525] Applying *G v G*, Lord Nicholls has forcefully observed[526]

'The Court of Appeal is not intended to be a forum in which unsuccessful litigants, where no error occurred at first instance, may have a second trial of the same issue by different judges under the guise of an appeal. The mere fact that appellate judges might have reached a different conclusion had they been carrying out the evaluation and balancing exercise does not mean that the first instance judge fell into error.'

Whether the law should be so restrictive on appeal is debatable.[527] In *G v G* the House of Lords took the view that there is desirability in putting an end to litigation, particularly as in many cases there is no obviously right answer.[528] They also endorsed the view

---

[521] Per Lord Scarman in *B v W (Wardship: Appeal)* [1979] 3 All ER 83 at 95–6, HL. The admission of fresh evidence is at the court's discretion: see *A v A (Custody Appeal: Role of Appellate Court)* [1988] 1 FLR 193, CA; *M v M (Minor: Custody Appeal)* [1987] 1 WLR 404, CA; *Re C (A Minor) (Wardship Proceedings)* [1984] FLR 419, CA; and *Ladd v Marshall* [1954] 3 All ER 745. The admission of fresh evidence may justify upholding the original decision even though it has been held plainly wrong: *M v M (Minor: Custody Appeal)*, above. Appeals concerning children do not, however, automatically call for an up-to-date welfare report: *M v M (Welfare Report)* [1989] 2 FLR 354, CA.

[522] [1985] 1 WLR 647, HL. See J Eekelaar (1985) 48 MLR 704 and J Robinson [1985] Fam Law 330.

[523] A similar rule applies to appeals to the High Court from magistrates' courts, to a circuit judge from a district judge and to the Court of Appeal from a High Court judge (see *Re W (A Child)(Illegitimate Child: Change of Surname)* [2001] Fam 1 at [23], per Butler-Sloss LJ, CA.

[524] Though it might be argued that the use of the phrase 'plainly wrong' is too inhibiting, at any rate where the trial judge is a High Court judge, since erstwhile colleagues in the Court of Appeal might be reluctant to arrive at such an apparently damning conclusion.

[525] See eg *May v May* [1986] 1 FLR 325, CA. In *Re T (A Minor)* [1986] Fam Law 189, CA, it was stated that legal aid should not be granted for hopeless appeals, while in *Re G (A Minor) (Role of the Appellate Court)* [1987] 1 FLR 164, CA, it was said that where appeals which were unarguable in the light of *G v G* were brought by legally aided parties, the court might have to consider whether appropriate orders for costs ought to be made to ensure that public money was not wasted. Note also *Re O (Costs: Liability of Legal Aid Board)* [1997] 1 FLR 465, CA.

[526] *Re B (A Minor)(Adoption: Natural Parent)* [2001] UKHL 70,[2002] 1 WLR 258, at [17].

[527] See the excellent critique by Eekelaar, above. However, in terms of the non-application of the paramountcy principle, the decision can be justified on the basis that the appeal rules do not *directly* concern the child's upbringing and since those rules do not inhibit the appellate courts from being able to safeguard the child's interests, there is no need for special rules: see N Lowe 'The House of Lords and the welfare principle' in C Bridge (ed) *Family Law Towards the Millennium—Essays for P M Bromley* 125 at 158.

[528] See Lord Fraser [1985] 1 WLR at 651 referring to *Clarke-Hunt v Newcombe* (1982) 4 FLR 482 at 488, CA, per Cumming-Bruce LJ.

that an appellate court should be chary of overruling a decision, particularly in cases concerning the upbringing of children where it is so important to have seen the parties and witnesses.[529]

It is desirable in all cases concerning children that appeals should be heard as speedily as possible, but it is particularly important in cases where a transfer of residence has been ordered. In *Practice Note (Minors: Listing of Appeals)*[530] it was stated that in such cases appeals should be heard within 28 days of the decision.[531]

C OTHER POWERS

1 FAMILY ASSISTANCE ORDERS

Section 16 of the 1989 Act empowers the court to make a 'family assistance order'. Such an order requires either a CAFCASS officer to be made available or the local authority[532] to make an officer of the authority available 'to advise, assist and (where appropriate) befriend any person named in the order'.[533] Those who may be named are: any parent (which includes the unmarried father), guardian or special guardian of the child, any person with whom the child is living or in whose favour a contact order is in force with respect to the child, and the child himself.[534]

This power replaced the former power to make supervision orders in private law proceedings and must in turn be distinguished from supervision orders made under s 31.[535] As the Department of Health's *Guidance and Regulations* puts it:[536]

'A supervision order is designed for the more serious cases, in which there is an element of child protection involved. By contrast, a family assistance order aims simply to provide short-term help to a family, to overcome the problems and conflicts associated with their separation or divorce. Help may well be focused more on the adult than the child.'

These powers have since been amended by the Children and Adoption Act 2006.

(a) When orders may be made[537]

Family assistance orders may be made in any 'family proceedings', whether or not any other order has been made.[538] The power may be exercised only by the court acting upon its own motion, though there is nothing to stop parties requesting the court to make such

---

[529] See eg *Re F (A Minor) (Wardship: Appeal)* [1976] Fam 238, CA.

[530] [1984] 1 WLR 1125, CA. See also *Ridgway v Ridgway* [1986] Fam Law 363, CA, which stressed the need for legal aid to be granted quickly.

[531] Failure by barristers (or solicitors) to exercise the greatest possible diligence in complying with the time limits imposed by the courts for the preparation of appeals may be regarded as professional misconduct: *Re M (A Minor)* (1989) *The Times*, 29 December, CA.

[532] Subject to s 16(7); see below.   [533] Section 16(1).   [534] Section 16(2), as amended.

[535] Discussed below, pp 766ff.

[536] Vol 1, *Court Orders*, para 2.50 and cited by Wall J in *Re DH (A Minor) (Child Abuse)* [1994] 1 FLR 679 at 704. See also Law Com No 172, para 5.19.

[537] For an examination of the pre-2006 Act practice see A James and L Sturgeon-Adams *Helping families after divorce. Assistance by order?* (1999)

[538] Section 16(1).

an order during the course of family proceedings.[539] However, the lack of the right to apply for such an order would seem to prevent parties from applying to the court *solely* for a family assistance order.

As originally enacted, before any order can be made, the court had to be satisfied that 'the circumstances of the case are exceptional'.[540] The Act did not however define what is meant by 'exceptional circumstances', but in general it was clear that the order could not be made as a matter of routine. However, under the Children and Adoption Act 2006, the requirement that there be exceptional circumstances has been removed as part of a policy to enable such orders to be used more often particularly to facilitate contact. Nevertheless the Department of Health's *Guidance* comment that[541] 'it will be particularly important in all orders for the court to make plain at the outset why family assistance is needed and what it is hoped to achieve by it' remains good advice.

Before any order can be made the court must be satisfied that the consent of every person named in the order, *other than the child*, has been obtained.[542] There is, therefore, no formal requirement that the child himself should consent, nor is there a statutory requirement to ascertain the child's own wishes and feelings about such an order, since the enjoinder to do so under s 1(3) does not apply to making s 16 orders.[543] Nevertheless, there is nothing to prevent the court from discovering the child's view (nor from applying the whole s 1(3) checklist) and where the child is mature enough to make his own decisions, it would seem prudent to do so.

A family assistance order may not be made requiring a local authority to make one of its officers available unless the authority agrees or the child concerned lives or will live in its area.[544] It is not a proper use of a family assistance order to require a local authority to provide someone for escort duty where no family member is prepared to take the children to visit their father in prison.[545]

(b) Effect and duration of order

Section 16 gives no guidance as to which officer should be appointed nor is it clear whether the court is empowered to appoint a particular CAFCASS officer or Welsh family proceedings officer or a particular type of local authority officer (for example, a housing officer rather than one from social services).[546] In the private law context the most

---

[539] Though note *Re F (Minors) (Denial of Contact)* [1993] 2 FLR 677 in which the Court of Appeal refused to consider making a family assistance order, since the point had not been argued at first instance and, in the absence of being able to show that the original order was wrong, the court had no power to make such an order or remit the case back.

[540] Section 16(3)(a).   [541] Ibid at para 2.52.   [542] Section 16(3)(b).

[543] See above, pp 470–1. The government rejected the recommendation of the Joint Committee on the Draft Children (Contact) and Adoption Bill HL Paper 100–1/HL 400–1, that this requirement of consent be removed on the basis that would not be constructive to 'advise, assist and befriend' an unwilling or even hostile party. This rejection has not convinced everyone. Indeed the President's Interdisciplinary Conference urged the Government to reconsider their opposition to the recommendation.

[544] Section 16(7). But see *Re C (Family Assistance Order)* [1996] 1 FLR 424 where, having made an assistance order directing the local authority to make an officer available, the local authority subsequently returned to the court to say that it did not have the resources to carry the order out. Johnson J declined to take further action.

[545] *S v P (Contact Application: Family Assistance Order)* [1997] 2 FLR 277. Cf *Re E (Family Assistance Order)* [1999] 2 FLR 212, discussed below at p 580.

[546] See L Coubrough 'Family Assistance Orders' [1993] Fam Law 598.

appropriate appointee is likely to be the children and family reporter who has compiled the welfare report for the court, while in care proceedings, the obvious candidate is the social worker attached to the particular case.

Under s 16(4) a family assistance order may direct specified persons named in the order to keep the address of any person named in the order so that he can visit them. As originally enacted, if a s 8 order was also in force, the officer was empowered to refer to the court the question of whether a s 8 order should be varied or discharged.[547] However, under the Children and Adoption Act 2006 this provision has been strengthened and now provides that where a s 8 order is also in force the family assistance order 'may direct the officer concerned to report to the court on such matters relating to the section 8 order as the court may require (including the question whether the section 8 order ought to be varied or discharged)'.[548] In addition the 2006 Act also provides that where a contact order is in force the family assistance order 'may direct the officer concerned to give advice and assistance as regards establishing, improving and maintaining contact to such of the persons named in the order as may be specified in the order'.[549]

A family assistance order is intended to be only a short-term remedy. Hence, s 16(5) originally provided that unless a shorter period is specified the order will have effect only for six months from the day on which it is made. But under the Children and Adoption Act 2006 this period has been extended to 12 months. There is no restriction on making any further order.[550]

(c) Family assistance orders in practice [551]

Before implementation of the 1989 Act it was uncertain how many family assistance orders would be made,[552] but according to the *Children Act Report 1995–1999*[553] the number ranged between 'about 600 to around 1000 annually'. It remains to be seen what effect the changes made by the Children and Adoption Act 2006 will have but the intention is to increase their use.

The few reported cases show that a major role of family assistance orders is in facilitating contact and this will clearly be expanded by the reforms made by the Children and Adoption Act 2006. In *Re M (Contact Family Assistance Order)*[554] for example, the Court

---

[547] Section 16(6).   [548] Section 16(6) as inserted by s 6(5) of the 2006 Act.

[549] Section 16(4A) added by s 6(3) of the 2006 Act.

[550] See Department of Health's *Guidance and Regulations*, op cit, at para 2.52, and the implicit acceptance of that proposition by Booth J in *Leeds County Council v C* [1993] 1 FLR 269 at 272.

[551] See *Making Contact Work* (A Report to the Lord Chancellor by the Advisory Board on Family Law: Children Act Sub Committee, 2002) Ch 11, L Trinder and N Stone 'Family assistance order—professional aspiration and party frustration' [1998] CFLQ 291 and J Seden 'Family Assistance Orders and the Children Act: Ambivalence About Intervention or a Means of Safeguarding and Promoting Children's Welfare?' (2001) 15 Int Jo of Law, Policy and the Family 226.

[552] Some thought that, because of the requirement of 'exceptional circumstances' (criticised for being 'unduly restrictive' by A Bainham *Children: The Modern Law* (1st edn) at p 37) coupled with the need to obtain the consent of the adults it is sought to assist, orders would be made infrequently. Others mooted whether such orders would be made relatively frequently as a 'half way house' means of making 'no orders' pursuant to s 1(5).

[553] Cm 4579, January 2000.

[554] [1999] 1 FLR 75, CA. A s 91(14) order was also added to prevent the father making an application to the court without leave before the expiration of the family assistance order.

of Appeal proposed (subject to obtaining the mother's consent)[555] making a family assistance order to facilitate indirect contact between the children and their father in respect of whom the mother had a genuine fear. In *Leeds City Council v C*,[556] in Booth J held that the only appropriate way in which a court could make provision for supervision of contact by a local authority was by an order under s 16 and not by attaching a condition under s 11(7). However, in *Re DH (A Minor)(Child Abuse)*[557] Wall J observed that while:

'... in the conventional case a supervision order under s 31 will not be appropriate where the object is simply to achieve contact supervised by a local authority ... where the threshold criteria under s 31 are met in relation to the necessity for contact to be supervised, it may be appropriate to make a supervision order rather than an order under s 16.'

Despite this comment it is evident that family assistance orders have a useful role to play in providing local authority assistance to supervise contact.[558] In *Re E (Family Assistance Order)*[559] a family assistance order was made against the wishes of a local authority (into whose area the family had moved) in order to supervise contact between a child and her mother who was in a psychiatric unit. A family assistance order was also made in *Re U (Application to Free for Adoption)*,[560] where, having rejected a local authority application to free a child for adoption and granting instead a residence order to grandparents, the Court of Appeal felt that a s 16 order was a useful way of monitoring the child's placement with them.

2 SECTION 37 DIRECTIONS

Before the Children Act 1989 courts could, in exceptional circumstances, commit children upon their own motion into local authority care or make supervision orders in private law proceedings.[561] This power, however, ran counter to the policy under the 1989 Act to have just one route into care. Accordingly, it was abolished. Under s 37, however, if in *any* family proceedings, 'it appears to the court that it may be appropriate for a care or supervision order to be made ... the court may direct the appropriate authority to undertake an investigation of the child's circumstances'.

Section 37 empowers a court to direct that an investigation is undertaken but it has no power to direct a local authority to bring care proceedings.[562] All that an authority is bound to do under the direction is undertake the investigation but if after doing so they decide not to apply for a care or supervision order they must inform the court of their reasons for so deciding.[563]

---

[555] This part of the order was directed to life on the file for 14 days to give the mother (who was not at the appellate hearing) through her solicitors the opportunity to consent to the order being made.
[556] [1993] 1 FLR 269.   [557] [1994] 1 FLR 679 at 702.
[558] *B v B (Child Abuse: Contact)* [1994] 2 FLR 713 at 738, ironically also per Wall J. See also *Re R (A Minor) (Residence: Religion)* [1993] 2 FLR 163, CA—a case involving a father who was a member of the Exclusive Brethren.
[559] [1999] 2 FLR 512.   [560] [1993] 2 FLR 992, CA.
[561] See the 7th edition of this work at pp 297–8, 306 and 308.
[562] The absence of any such power to direct local authorities to take steps to protect children was criticised in *Nottingham County Council v P* [1994] Fam 18, by Sir Stephen Brown P. See also Mr Justice Wall 'The courts and child protection—the challenge of hybrid cases' [1997] 9 CFLQ 345 at 348–50.
[563] Section 37(3). Unless the court directs otherwise, the local authority must inform the court within eight weeks of the direction: s 37(4).

Although courts are not empowered to commit a child into care they can, when making a direction, make an interim care order (provided the relevant criteria are satisfied).[564] As the section itself says and the courts have subsequently emphasised, s 37 directions should only be made where it appears that it might be appropriate to make a public law order. It is therefore generally inappropriate in a purely private law dispute, but while not a panacea it can on occasion be useful in intractable contact disputes provided there is a coherent care plan of which temporary or permanent removal of the children from the parents is an integral part.[565]

D DECIDING WHAT ORDERS, IF ANY, TO MAKE

1 APPLYING THE PRINCIPLE UNDER SECTION 1(5) [566]

As already discussed, the controlling principle in deciding whether or not to make an order under Part II of the 1989 Act is the paramountcy of the child's welfare.[567] In applying this principle the court's first task is to decide whether to make an order at all, since under s 1(5) the court is directed not to make an order under the 1989 Act 'unless it considers that doing so would be better for the child than making no order at all'.

(a) The substantive law

While there may be no formal burden of proof[568] it remains the case that the court must be satisfied than an order is for the benefit of the particular child. This requirement is clearly easier to satisfy in contested applications. Indeed it has been said that making 'no order' is inappropriate if the court is clearly charged with the responsibility for settling a dispute. In *Re W (A Minor) (Contact)*,[569] upon a father's application for defined contact following the mother's refusal to comply with a previous order for reasonable contact and her declared intention not to obey any further order, the first instance decision to make a 'no order' was held to be an abdication of responsibility. The point has also been made that there is a clear distinction between dismissing an application and making a 'no order'. If the making

---

[564] Section 38(1)(b). Interim care orders are discussed below at pp 778ff.

[565] See eg *Re M (Intractable Contact Dispute: Interim Care Order)* [2003] EWHC 1024 (Fam), [2003] 2 FLR 636. But cf *A v A (Shared Residence)* [2004] EWHC 142 (Fam), [2004] 1 FLR 1195 where a direction was held inappropriate because of the substantial delay that it would engender when the children were in urgent need of respite and crucially because foster care was inappropriate; and *Re L (Section 37 Direction)* [1999] 1 FLR 984 CA where the case was nowhere near the public law threshold. For other cases on the application of s 37 see eg *Re CE (Section 37 Direction)* [1995] 1 FLR 26, on the consequential role of the guardian; *Re M (Official Solicitor's Role)* [1998] 2 FLR 815, CA—inappropriate to use s 37 if the Official Solicitor is invited to investigate, and *Re H (A Minor)(Section 37 Direction)* [1993] 2 FLR 541—where direction is given 'child's circumstances' should be widely construed. There is some evidence that FPR 1991 r 9.5 is being used to appoint a guardian ad litem (see Ch 11) instead of giving a s 37 direction because of local authorities' lack of resources.

[566] See A Bainham 'Changing families and changing concepts—reforming the language of family law' [1998] 10 CFLQ 1 at 2–4.

[567] As laid down by s 1(1) of the Children Act 1989, discussed above at pp 450ff.

[568] See the discussion above at p 477.

[569] [1994] 2 FLR 441, CA. Note Thorpe LJ's similar comments in *Re H (Children)(Residence Order: Condition)* [2001] EWCA Civ 1338, [2001] 2 FCR 1277 at [19] referred to above at p 535. See also *Re P (A Minor)(Parental Responsibility Order)* [1994] 1 FLR 578.

of the latter is tantamount to dismissing a parent's application for contact, as opposed to holding that an order was not necessary, then, according to Wall J in *D v D (Application for Contact)*,[570] the court should at least take a proactive role and consider whether any further application should be made and, if so, when and in what circumstances.

Although it might be easier to persuade the court to make an order in contested cases it by no means follows that no order can be granted if the parties are agreed. In this respect reference can still be usefully made to the Department of Health's *Guidance* on the 1989 Act:[571]

'There are several situations where the court is likely to consider it better for the child to make an order than not. If the court has had to resolve a dispute between the parents, it is likely to be better for the child to make an order about it. Even if there is no dispute, the child's need for stability and security may be better served by making an order. There may also be specific legal advantages in doing so. One example is where abduction of the child is a possibility, since a court order is necessary for enforcement proceedings in other parts of the United Kingdom under the Family Law Act 1986, and under the European Convention and under the Hague Convention an order will be necessary if the aggrieved party is, for example, an unmarried father or a relative who would not otherwise have "rights of custody". An advantage of having a residence order is that the child may be taken out of the country for periods of less than one month without the permission of other persons with parental responsibility or the court, whereas without an order this could amount to an offence under the Child Abduction Act 1984. Also if a person has a sole residence order in his favour and appoints a [testamentary] guardian for the child, the appointment will take effect immediately on that person's death, even where there is a surviving parent. Depending on the circumstances of the case, the court might therefore be persuaded that an order would be in the child's interest.'

The *Guidance*'s reference to the need for stability and security needs to be read with caution. It is all too easy to advance this argument, but if s 1(5) is to have any meaning the court cannot, as a matter of routine, make orders for this reason. Indeed, in the past, the Children Act Advisory Committee expressed concern[572] that applications were still being made (and presumably granted) so as to provide the parent with care with the security of an order even though there is no dispute about the child's residence or contact.

Similarly, since it can be argued in *every* case that the holder of a residence order can remove the child from the United Kingdom for periods of less than one month and that any guardianship appointment comes into force on the residence holder's death, the court will surely require some especial justification for making an order on that basis.

One circumstance not mentioned in the *Guidance* but which could justify the making of a residence or contact order is where the applicant, eg an unmarried father or relative, has no parental responsibility, since it can always be argued that unless an order is made he or she will not otherwise have locus standi in relation to the child.[573] In *B v B (A Minor) (Residence Order)*[574] Johnson J accepted this argument when he granted in what he described as 'the

---

[570] [1994] 1 FCR 694.

[571] Vol 1, *Court Orders*, para 2.56. Repeated verbatim in the Northern Ireland *Guidance* at para 5.48.

[572] CAAC Report 1992/93, p 25.   [573] See s 10(4) and (6).

[574] [1992] 2 FLR 327. Another circumstance that might justify the making of a consent order is where it can be shown that without an order the person looking after the child will not be accorded priority on a local

unusual circumstances of the case' an unopposed application for a residence order by a grandparent with whom the child had been living for over 10 years. In *Re S (Contact: Grandparents)*[575] a grandparent sought a contact order. By the time the matter came to court the judge was persuaded that the mother would permit contact and he therefore made no order relying on s 1(5). On appeal it was held that, having decided it was in the child's welfare to have contact with the grandparent, and given the history of antagonism between the parties, a contact order should have been made even though the parties were in agreement at the time of the court hearing. The making of the order would ensure that contact did take place and avoid the need to return to court in the event of a disagreement.

(b) The application of s 1(5) in practice

Before implementation of the 1989 Act there was considerable speculation as to how s 1(5) would apply in practice. It will be recalled[576] that the provision was intended to have most impact in private law proceedings and in particular in divorce and separation proceedings, the concern being that orders relating to children should cease to be seen as merely 'part of the divorce package'. How far such orders have ceased to be part of the package has yet to be fully researched.[577] The indicators, however, are that the impact of s 1(5) has not been as great as might have been expected. A study conducted in the late 90s by Bristol University found that 'no orders' were made in about 5% of cases.[578] National statistics point to a declining proportion of 'no orders'. Early indicators were that about 9% of all private law orders were 'no orders'[579] a proportion which was still reflected for example in 1996.[580] However, in 2000 this proportion dropped to about 4% of orders and there was a similar proportion in 2004.[581] What of course cannot be known is how many applications were deterred in the first place by s 1(5).

2 APPLYING THE WELFARE PRINCIPLE

(a) General considerations

As previously discussed,[582] pursuant to s 1(4) it is mandatory for the court, in contested applications for s 8 orders, to have regard to the statutory checklist. However, before

---

authority housing list. Although this practice was deprecated by the Children Act Advisory Committee (see CAAC Report 1992–93, p 25), if local authorities are still operating this policy (for the position when the Act was first implemented see Yell (1992) 89 Law Soc Gaz (August Issue) p 20), it would seem to be in the child's interest that a residence order be made.

[575] [1996] 1 FLR 158, CA.   [576] See the discussion above at p 475.

[577] According to one early piece of research conducted in two major divorce courts in East Anglia the number of 'no orders' was high: A Bainham *Children—The Modern Law* p 130, fn 96.

[578] See R Bailey-Harris, J Barron and J Pearce 'Settlement culture and the use of the "no order" principle under the Children Act 1989' [1999] CFLQ 53. They also found that at county court level practitioners and district judges took a variety of approaches to s 1(5).

[579] See the analysis in R White, C Parr and N Lowe, *The Children Act in Practice* (2nd edn) at 2.49 based upon the analysis of the CAAC Reports 1991/92 and 1992/3.

[580] See p 464 of the previous edition of this work based on Table 5.3 of the Judicial Statistics Annual Report 1996.

[581] Based respectively on an analysis of Table 5.3 of the Judicial Statistics Annual Report 2000 and Table 5.3 of the Judicial Statistics Annual Report 2004.

[582] See above, pp 470–1.

discussing the application of the checklist, it is important to stress that its role is to aid the court to determine what is best for the child, not to provide *rules* for so determining. It remains the case that beyond saying that the child's welfare is the paramount consideration there are no *rules* for determining disputes over children. As Dunn LJ put it in *Pountney v Morris*:[583]

'There is only one rule; that rule is that in a consideration of the future of the child the interests and welfare of the child are the . . . paramount consideration. But within that rule, the circumstances of each individual case are so infinitely varied that it is unwise to rely upon any rule of thumb, or any formula to try to resolve the difficult problem which arises on the facts of each individual case.'

Among the most agonising cases are those where the court has to decide which of two capable, loving and caring parents should look after the child. It is in these cases where the checklist that we are about to discuss comes most prominently into play. Of course, it is in the nature of a finely balanced case that some factors will weigh heavily on the side of one claimant while others will favour the other, but it is clear that in reaching its conclusion the court should consider all the circumstances of the case, and in the light of the evidence adduced, make the best decision it can. As Megarry J pointed out in *Re F (An Infant)*,[584] the problem cannot be solved arithmetically or quantitatively by using some sort of 'points system'.

(b) The statutory checklist

The ascertainable wishes and feelings of the child concerned (considered in the light of his age and understanding).[585]

This enjoinder to consider the child's wishes and feelings is reflective of the international obligation under the UN Convention on the Rights of the Child 1989, Art 12(1).[586] However, by referring to the child's 'wishes and feelings' s 1(3)(a) is wider than Art 12, which is confined to 'views'. Very young children have discernible 'feelings', even if they cannot yet express their views. In any event, the wishes and feelings need not be conveyed directly but can be obtained by third parties, commonly the children and family reporter.

Although it was only since the 1989 Act that the courts became formally obliged in private law cases other than adoption[587] to consider the child's wishes and feelings, in practice the courts had long done so. As Butler-Sloss LJ said in *Re P (A Minor) (Education)*,[588] shortly before implementation of the 1989 Act:

'The courts, over the last few years, have become increasingly aware of the importance of listening to the views of older children and taking into account what children say, not

---

[583] [1984] FLR 381 at 384, CA.   [584] [1969] 2 Ch 238 at 241.

[585] For the background to this provision see Law Com No 172, paras 3.22 et seq. See also J Eekelaar 'The Interests of the Child and the Child's Wishes—The Role of Dynamic Self-Determinism' (1994) 8 Int Jo of Law and the Family 42.

[586] See above, p 482.

[587] In adoption proceedings it has always been incumbent upon the court to give due consideration to the wishes of the child concerned having regard to their age and understanding, see the Adoption of Children Act 1926, s 3(b) which was re-enacted in the Adoption Acts of 1950, s 5(1)(b), 1958, s 7(2) and 1976, s 6. It is now part of the adoption checklist in the Adoption and Children Act 2002, s 1(4).

[588] [1992] 1 FLR 316 at 321, CA.

necessarily agreeing with what they want nor, indeed, doing what they want, but paying proper respect to older children who are of an age and maturity to make their minds up as to what they think is best for them, bearing in mind that older children very often have an appreciation of their own situation which is worthy of consideration by, and the respect of, the adults, and particularly including the courts.'

Despite being placed first in the welfare checklist, the child's view is not expressed to be determinative.[589] As Butler-Sloss LJ put it in *Re P (Minors) (Wardship: Care and Control)*:[590]

'How far the wishes of children should be the determinative factor in their future placement must of course vary on the particular facts of each case. Those views must be considered and may, but not necessarily must, carry more weight as the children grow older'.

On the other hand, it has also been said that where all other factors are evenly balanced it is appropriate to recognise the extra significance of an older child's views.[591] Nevertheless, the court's obligation is to *consider* the child's wishes and feelings but not necessarily to give effect to them. It must be remembered that the child may have been coached or brainwashed[592] by one parent or have become enmeshed in the parents' problems and have learned to say what they think is expected of them,[593] and that sometimes even an older child's own wishes are so contrary to his or her long-term welfare that the court may feel justified in overriding them. In *Re M (Family Proceedings: Affidavits)*,[594] for example, which a father applied for a residence order based largely on his 12-year-old daughter's wishes. Although the welfare report indicated that either parent was suitable as a carer, given that the child had hitherto lived with her mother and had not had the opportunity to have any clear idea of what living with her father would really be like (the contact visits to her father had always taken place at the paternal grandparents' home), the judge upheld the welfare officer's 'instinct' that her long-term welfare would be better governed by her remaining with her mother. On appeal, the Court of Appeal rejected the argument that, given either parent was suitable, the child's views should have tipped the balance, and

---

[589] *Re W (Minors) (Residence Order)* [1992] 2 FCR 461, CA; *Re W (A Minor) (Residence Order)* [1993] 2 FLR 625, CA.

[590] [1992] 2 FCR 681 at 687. See also *M v M (Minor: Custody Appeal)* [1987] 1 WLR 404, CA at 411, per May LJ.

[591] *Re F (Minors) (Denial of Contact)* [1993] 2 FLR 677, CA. See also *Re P (Minors) (Wardship: Care and Control)* [1992] 2 FCR 681 at 689H per Butler-Sloss LJ, cited by Cazalet J in *Re H (A Minor) (Shared Residence)* [1994] 1 FLR 717 at 724E. Note Wilson J's comment in *Re B (Change of Surname)* [1996] 1 FLR 791, CA, that it was virtually unknown to make residence or contact orders that run contrary to the wishes of normal adolescent children. However, this comment should perhaps be treated with some caution. It certainly should not be regarded as a statement of principle—see below.

[592] See eg *Re R (A Minor) (Residence: Religion)* [1993] 2 FLR 163, CA, in which the wishes of a nine-year-old boy to remain with a member of the Exclusive Brethren were overridden.

[593] See *V v V (Contact: Implacable Hostility)* [2004] EWHC 1215 (Fam), [2004] 2 FLR 851 at [44] where Bracewell J also commented that the children in that case had become skilled in reiterating the view of their principal carer.

[594] [1995] 2 FLR 100, CA; cf *Re M (Child's Upbringing)* ('the Zulu boy case') [1996] 2 FLR 441, where the 10-year-old's wishes did seem to be ignored—see the editorial at (1996) 146 NLJ 669. See also cases such as *Re P (Medical Treatment: Best Interests)* [2003] EWHC 2327 (Fam), [2004] 2 FLR 1117; *Re W (A Minor) (Medical Treatment: Court's Jurisdiction)* [1993] Fam 64, CA; *Re E (an infant)* (1990) 9 BMLR 1 and *Re M (Child: Refusal of Medical Treatment)* [1999] 2 FLR 1097 (discussed above, p 365), where respectively a 17, a 16 and two 15-year-olds' refusal to have medical treatment was overridden.

upheld the first instance decision. The court accepted that the judge had properly taken the child's wishes into account but was not obliged to follow them, if, as here, it was not felt to be in the child's interests to do so.

The child's physical, emotional and educational needs

Although some have argued that to speak of needs may be simply a way of expressing adult preferences in an apparently child-centred way,[595] it is nevertheless clear that in practice the child's needs together with the parents' capabilities are the major concern in most cases.

Physical needs. Physical needs can include the need for adequate accommodation but, as Wood J said in *Stephenson v Stephenson*,[596] in most cases 'disadvantages of a material sort must be of little weight'. The court's major concern is for the child's security and happiness, not his material prospects. Any other approach would automatically put a poor parent (and mothers in particular) at a disadvantage. Nevertheless, a party's financial position cannot be entirely ignored: for example, if he is so poor that he cannot even provide a home, this in itself might be sufficient to refuse him a residence order.[597] Even in a less extreme case a parent who can offer a child good accommodation must, other things being equal, have the edge over the one who cannot.[598] But again the quality of the home life that the child will have must not be measured in purely material terms: the amount of time and energy that a parent can devote to his care and upbringing is of considerable importance. This may mean that a mother who can spend the whole of her time with her children will have an advantage over a father who is out at work all day, whatever alternative arrangements he can make to have them looked after.[599] However, in *B v B (Custody of Children)*,[600] where an unemployed father was successfully looking after his child, it was held that the judge had erred in law in putting into the balance as a determining factor the man's moral duty to find work and not to rely upon the benefits provided by the welfare state.[601]

Emotional needs. The child's emotional needs will often be a crucial element in the case. Chief among these needs is that of attachment perhaps to a particular parent or to a sibling or even to a family. It is also considered to be a fundamental emotional need of every child to have an enduring relationship with both parents.

With regard to attachment to a particular parent one influential notion, at any rate in

---

[595] See eg S Maidment *Child Custody and Divorce*, (1985) p 149, who comments, 'when a court makes a . . . decision it may attempt to heed the child's needs but it is essentially making a decision as to which available adult . . . is to care for the child . . .'

[596] [1985] FLR 1140 at 1148, CA.

[597] Though note that for the purposes of the Housing Act 1996 a person caring for a child and who is unintentionally homeless has a priority need. See further above at p 258.

[598] *Re F (An Infant)* [1969] 2 Ch 238.

[599] See *Re K (Minors)(Children: Care and Control)* [1977] Fam 179, CA; *S (BD) v S (DJ)* [1977] Fam 109, CA.

[600] [1985] FLR 166, CA.

[601] Nevertheless, there seems to be some lingering judicial suspicion about a man giving up work to look after his children: see eg *Re S (Children)* [2002] EWCA Civ 583 in which a residence order was granted to the mother notwithstanding that she was the 'bread winner' and the father had taken on a 'house husband' role in which Thorpe LJ, perhaps tellingly, referred to the 'very different role and functions of men and women'. See also *B v B (Custody of Child)* [1985] FLR 462, CA.

the past, has been that young children need their mothers.[602] Indeed, Lord Donaldson MR went so far as to say in *Re W (A Minor) (Residence Order)*[603] that:

'. . . there is a rebuttable presumption of fact that the best interests of a baby are served by being with its mother, and I stress the word "baby". When we are moving on to whatever age it may be appropriate to describe the baby as having become a child, different considerations may well apply. But, as far as babies are concerned, the starting-point is, I think, that it should be with its mother'.

Babies apart, however, it is well established[604] that there is no *principle, rule* or *presumption* that even a young child should live with his mother, nor is there a principle or presumption that an older boy should be with his father.[605] Indeed, as Butler-Sloss LJ made clear,[606] as a matter of law 'there is no presumption that one parent should be preferred to another parent at a particular age [of the child]'. However, this is not to say that a 'maternal preference' can be ignored for, notwithstanding that there seems to be no scientific basis for thinking eg that young children benefit most from a maternal upbringing,[607] or indeed that the child's well-being is affected by the sex of the parent with whom he is living,[608] it is a consideration at any rate inasmuch as courts are prepared to acknowledge that certain arrangements are more often consistent with good child raising than others. As Lord Jauncey put it in *Brixey v Lynas*:[609]

'. . . the advantage to a very young child of being with its mother is a consideration which must be taken into account in deciding where lie its best interests in custody proceedings in which the mother is involved. It is neither a presumption nor a principle but rather recognition of a widely held belief based on practical experience and the workings of nature. Its importance will vary according to the age of the child and to the other circumstances of each individual case such as whether the child has been living with or apart from the mother and

---

[602] This maternal preference was undoubtedly influenced by Bowlby's and others' theories of maternal deprivation: see the discussion in S Maidment *Child Custody and Divorce* at pp 182–4. See further the discussion in the 7th edition of this work pp 323–6.

[603] [1992] 2 FLR 332 at 336, CA. In this case the baby was less than four weeks old.

[604] See, for example, *Aldous v Aldous* (1974) 5 Fam Law 152, CA, per Megaw LJ. See also *Re A (Children: 1959 UN Declaration)* [1998] 1 FLR 354, CA in which the first instance judge, apparently relying on Principle 6 of the UN Declaration of the Rights of the Child (1959) did appear to accept it as a principle that children of tender years are better off with their mother. He was overruled on appeal and the relevance of the 1959 Declaration was doubted, especially as it was not reflected in the 1989 UN Convention on the Rights of the Child.

[605] See *Re C (A) (an infant), C v C* [1970] 1 All ER 309, CA.

[606] In *Re S (A Minor) (Custody)* [1991] 2 FLR 388, CA at 390.

[607] See the summary of various research findings in Maidment *Child Custody and Divorce*, op cit, pp 182–6. See also M King 'Maternal Love, Fact or Myth?' (1974) 4 Fam Law 61.

[608] This is not to say that divorce does not affect children differently according to their age, on which see eg G Harold and M Murch 'Inter-parental conflict and children's adaptation to separation and divorce: theory, research and implications for family life, practice and policy' [2005] CFLQ 185 and the research there cited and reviewed; Wallerstein and Kelly *Surviving the Breakup* (1980) and J Pryor and B Rodgers *Children in Changing Families: Life After Parental Separation* (2001).

[609] 1996 SLT 908 at 9111, [1996] 2 FLR 499 at 505, on which see E Sutherland 'The unequal struggle— Fathers and children in Scots Law' [1997] CFLQ 191. For previous expressions of the common advantages of motherhood, see for example, *Re W (A Minor)(Custody)* (1982) 4 FLR 492 at 504, per Cumming-Bruce LJ and *Re S (A Minor)(Custody)* [1991] 2 FLR 388 at 390, CA and *Re A (A Minor)(Custody)* [1991] 2 FLR 394 at 400, CA, per Butler-Sloss LJ.

whether she is or is not capable of providing proper care. Circumstances may be such that it has no importance at all. Furthermore it will always yield to other competing advantages which more effectively promote the welfare of the child. However, where a very young child has been with its mother since birth and there is no criticism of her ability to care for the child only the strongest competing advantages are likely to prevail'.

In that case, on an appeal from Scotland, the House of Lords were asked to consider what weight, if any, should be attached to the natural ability of mothers to care for very young children. At first instance, despite the fact that the 15-month-old girl was happy and well cared for by her mother, custody was granted to the father on the basis of the latter's more advantageous social background. This decision was overruled on appeal because it had overlooked the advantages both of maternal care of very young children and of maintaining the status quo. In dismissing the father's further appeal the Lords rejected the argument that the court had erred in allegedly accepting the principle of maternal preference.

Another 'emotional need' is that of sibling support. In general the courts dislike separating children. As Purchas LJ said in *C v C (Minors: Custody)*:[610]

'It is really beyond argument that unless there are strong features indicating a contrary arrangement . . . brothers and sisters should wherever possible, be brought up together, so that they are an emotional support to each other in the stormy waters of the destruction of their family.'

Occasionally this consideration can be decisive. In *Adams v Adams*,[611] for example, the mother sought an order to look after her daughter but not her son, but her application failed because it was held preferable to keep the two children together. In *Clarke-Hunt v Newcombe*[612] it was held that, as it was in the younger boy's interests to be with his mother and it was inappropriate to separate the brothers, both boys should live with her, even though it was against the elder boy's wishes and possibly slightly detrimental to his interests. However influential this consideration may be, it is of course not a rule and there will be cases when separation of siblings is appropriate or unavoidable. In *B v B (Residence Order: Restricting Applications)*,[613] for example the trial judge had ordered two brothers to live with their mother, but the older boy then 'voted with his feet' by going to live with his father. The judge subsequently and reluctantly concluded that the younger child should remain with the mother because she met his needs and that the older child should continue to live with the father. His decision was upheld by the Court of Appeal.

Another aspect of emotional need is that of attachment to the family. Clearly this will

---

[610] [1988] 2 FLR 291 at 302, CA. See also *Adams v Adams* [1984] FLR 768 at 772, CA, where Dunn LJ said: 'All these cases depend upon their own facts, but it is undesirable, other things being equal, that children should be split when they are close together in age and obviously fond of one another . . . Children do . . . support one another and give themselves mutual comfort, perhaps more than they can derive from either of their parents.' But the disapproval of splitting siblings is not new: see *Re Besant* (1879) 11 Ch D 508 at 512, CA, per Jessel MR.

[611] Above.   [612] (1982) 4 FLR 482, CA.

[613] [1997] 1 FLR 139, CA. See also *Re D (Care: Natural Parent Presumption)* [1999] 1 FLR 134, CA in which it was held that too much importance had been attached in that case to the need to keep the siblings together; *Re B (T) (A Minor) (Residence Order)* [1995] 2 FCR 240, CA, in which on the facts, maintaining the status quo was held to be more important to the child than being with his siblings; and *Re O (Infants)* [1962] 2 All ER 10, CA (boy's long-term future thought to be better served by being with his father in the Sudan, whereas the girl's was with her mother in England).

come into play where the dispute is between parents and third parties. Although, as was made clear in *J v C*,[614] the paramountcy of the child's welfare principle applies equally to disputes between parents and other individuals as well as to disputes between parents, nevertheless the courts have also recognised the prima facie strength of the parents' position based on their view that children have a basic interest in being brought up by their own family. As Balcombe LJ put it in *Re W (A Minor) (Residence Order)*:[615]

'It is the welfare of the child which is the test, but of course there is a strong presumption that, other things being equal, it is in the interests of the child that it shall remain with its natural parents but that has to give way to particular needs in particular situations.'

But it is important not to go too far in this respect[616] for as the Court of Appeal subsequently pointed out,[617] the guiding star remained the paramountcy-of-the-child's-welfare test. There is no presumption in favour of the natural parent to be found anywhere in the 1989 Act and consequently any judicial overlay of the words of the statute had to be treated with caution. In any event, as was pointed out, the biological parents might not always be the natural parent in the eyes of the child and in cases where the child had been in the long-term care of a non-parent it will be the latter person who is the child's psychological parent. However, in *Re G (children) (residence: same-sex partner)*[618] the House of Lords reinstated an order giving primary residence to the birth mother of two children conceived by donor insemination, because the fact that she was their natural parent had been given insufficient weight by the lower courts.

A controversial application of the view that a child is better off being brought up in his own family is *Re M (Child's Upbringing)*.[619] In that case the Court of Appeal ordered the immediate return of a 10-year-old Zulu boy to his natural parents (who had previously been retained by the applicant whilst in South Africa as household employees) in South Africa, notwithstanding that he had been brought up for the last four years exclusively by the white applicant in England, and apparently ignoring both the child's own wishes and strong medical advice that an immediate return would be harmful. As Neill LJ put it:[620]

'Of course there will be cases where the welfare of the child requires that the child's right to be with his natural parents has to give way in his own interest to other considerations. But I am satisfied that in this case, as in other cases, one starts with the strong supposition that it is in the [child's] interests . . . that he should be brought up with his natural parents'.

---

[614] [1970] AC 668, HL, discussed above, pp 358ff.

[615] [1993] 2 FLR 625 at 633 expressly approving similar comments made by Lord Donaldson MR in *Re H (A Minor) (Custody: Interim Care and Control)* [1991] 2 FLR 109 at 113, CA, who in turn was explaining earlier dicta (per Fox LJ) in *Re K (A Minor) (Ward: Care and Control)* [1990] 1 WLR 431, CA.

[616] Decisions such as *Re D (Care: Natural Parent Presumption)* [1999] 1 FLR 134 went as far as to say that positive reasons were required before residence orders would be made in favour of non-parents.

[617] *Re H (A Child: Residence)* [2002] 3 FCR 277, CA in which the child had lived most of her life with the maternal grandparent.

[618] [2006] UKHL 43.

[619] [1996] 2 FLR 441, CA. For a critique of this case see Lowe 'The House of Lords and the Welfare Principle' in Bridge (ed) *Family Law Towards the Millennium—Essays for P M Bromley* 125 at 164–5, and as Thorpe LJ subsequently said in *Note: Re O (Family Appeals: Management)* [1998] 1 FLR 431 that 'with the advantage of hindsight' it might be said that the court fell into error in placing the weight that it did on the biological attachment.

[620] At 453. In fact, the boy later returned to England with the mother's consent to resume living with the applicant.

Another not unrelated emotional need is that of every child to have an enduring relationship with both parents.[621] This, as we discuss shortly, has important ramifications for contact applications.

Educational needs. Education is an important aspect of a child's upbringing and the question of which school is to be attended is a relevant factor in deciding who should look after the child. Occasionally, parental attitude to education can be significant. In *May v May*[622] care and control was granted to the father inter alia because he laid greater emphasis on academic achievements in contrast to the freer and easier attitude of the mother and her cohabitant to the time the children (aged eight and six!) should be doing homework.

Other needs. Needs have also been held to include medical needs and hence, provided it is for the child's benefit, it is within the court's power to make an order for the taking of a blood sample to ascertain whether the child is HIV positive.[623]

The likely effect on the child of any change in his circumstances

Section 1(3)(c) is the statutory enactment of the 'status quo' or continuity factor, which in practice is particularly important in resolving private law disputes,[624] the courts being well aware of the dangers of removing a child from a well-established home.[625] As Ormrod LJ said in *D v M (A Minor: Custody Appeal)*:[626]

'. . . it is generally accepted by those who are professionally concerned with children that, particularly in the early years, continuity of care is a most important part of a child's sense of security and that disruption of established bonds is to be avoided whenever it is possible to do so.'

Good reasons will have to be adduced to justify moving a child from a well established home,[627] the courts being understandably reluctant to move a child even as an interim measure in the absence of a full investigation of the facts, particularly if there is a doubt about the capability of the person with whom the child is to live.[628] Nevertheless, there will be occasions, albeit exceptional, where such a course is necessary to protect the child in the

---

[621] Per Wilson J in *Re M (Contact: Welfare Test)* [1995] 1 FLR 274 at 278, CA.

[622] [1986] 1 FLR 325, CA.

[623] See *Re C (HIV Test)* [1997] 2 FLR 1004, FD and CA and *Re W (A Minor) (HIV Test)* [1995] 2 FCR 184, per Kirkwood J.

[624] Empirical evidence showed that before the Children Act 1989 the courts normally made orders confirming the current situation and only rarely (in less than 1% of the cases studied by Eekelaar, Clive, Raikes and Clarke *Custody in Divorce* (1977) paras 13.14 and 13.29) ordered that the child be moved.

[625] Compare *Re Thain* [1926] Ch 676 in which the traumas of being moved were dismissed as being transitory.

[626] [1983] Fam 33 at 41.

[627] See eg *Re B (Residence Order: Status Quo)* [1998] 1 FLR 368, CA in which the first instance judge was held wrongly to have placed speculative improvements in contact over and above the consideration of continuity of care. See also *Re B (T) (A Minor) (Residence Order)* [1995] 2 FCR 240, CA in which, on the facts, maintaining the status quo was thought to be more important to the child than being with her siblings, and *Re L (Residence: Justices' Reasons)* [1995] 2 FLR 445 (inadequate reasons given by magistrates for upsetting the status quo).

[628] See eg *Re J (Children: Ex Parte Order)* [1997] 1 FLR 606 in which Hale J observed (at 609) that ex parte orders handing over a young child to a parent with whom she has not lived for 20 months should surely be exceptional. See also *Elder v Elder* [1986] 1 FLR 610, CA and *Re W; Re L (Minors) (Interim Custody)* [1987] Fam Law 130, CA, where the mother had a drink and anxiety problem.

short term. An example is *Re G (Minors) (Ex Parte Interim Residence order)*,[629] in which the mother admitted that she and her partner had taken drugs (though she maintained that she had now stopped and would not continue in the future) and that the children aged 10, eight, seven and five had known about it.

The status quo is, however, only a factor and the court may well think that the child's welfare in any particular case might be better served by being moved. As Ormrod LJ pointed out in *S v W*:[630]

'. . . the status quo argument depends for its strength wholly and entirely on whether the status quo is satisfactory or not. The more satisfactory the status quo, the stronger the argument for not interfering. The less satisfactory the status quo, the less one requires before deciding to change.'

The maintenance of the status quo becomes a stronger argument the longer the child has been with one party,[631] and is especially powerful if the other has lost contact with the child. On the other hand, if, as in *Allington v Allington*,[632] the parties have only been separated for a few weeks and the absent parent has maintained regular contact with the child, there can effectively be no status quo argument at all. In assessing what the status quo is the court should examine the whole history of the case and not simply the position immediately before the hearing. Hence, where a parent has 'snatched' a child from the other, the court may properly regard the status quo as being the position before the snatch.[633] There is however, no rule that the child should be returned in snatching cases. The only principle is that the child's welfare is the paramount consideration.[634]

The child's age, sex, background and any characteristics of which the court considers relevant

Consideration of the child's age is obviously linked to other matters such as the child's wishes and when combined with sex can be relevant to the choice of parents, which we have already discussed.

Religious considerations. The child's background can include his religious upbringing. In the past this was of crucial significance, but today this consideration is of much less importance.[635] It is inconceivable, for instance, that a parent would be refused a residence order on the ground of atheism.[636] In the case of a very young child (and probably any child of no fixed religious beliefs) the question of religious upbringing will have little bearing on the outcome of the case.[637] In *Re J (Specific Issue Orders: Muslim Upbringing*

---

[629] [1993] 1 FLR 910, CA.   [630] (1980) 11 Fam Law 81 at 82, CA.

[631] It also needs to be borne in mind that the younger the child the greater the effect of the passage of time on the child's attachment and adjustment: see Goldstein, Freud and Solnit *Beyond the Best Interests of the Child* (1973).

[632] [1985] FLR 586, CA.

[633] As in *Edwards v Edwards* [1986] 1 FLR 187; affd [1986] 1 FLR 205, CA.

[634] *Re J (A Minor) (Interim Custody: Appeal)* [1989] 2 FLR 304, CA. But see Ch 13 for the position of international child abduction under the Hague and European Conventions and Brussels II Regulation.

[635] For a full discussion of religious issues see C Hamilton *Family, Law and Religion* (1995) chs 4 and 5 and A Mumford 'The Judicial Resolution of Disputes Involving Children and Religion' (1998) 47 ICLQ 117. See also the discussion above at p 390.

[636] Compare *Shelley v Westbrooke* (1817) Jac 266n in which the poet Shelley was denied custody on this ground.

[637] See *Re C (MA) (An Infant)* [1966] 1 All ER 838 at 856 and 864–5, CA.

and Circumcision)[638] the child concerned (aged 5) was being brought up as a non-practising Christian in accordance with the beliefs of his mother with whom he lived and as a non-practising Muslim when staying with his father. He could therefore be said to have no settled religious faith. Wall J declined to make a specific issue order that the child be brought up in the Muslim religion. A similar decision was made in *Re S (Specific Issue Order: Religion: Circumcision)*[639] where the two children born to a Muslim mother and Hindu father had been brought up as Hindus, with Islamic influences but with neither being strict adherents to their respective faiths.

On the other hand, where religious upbringing is clearly part of the child's upbringing, the court may well consider that continuation of religious observance is vital if the evidence suggests that otherwise the child could suffer emotional disturbance.[640] Nevertheless, even in these circumstances there is no rule that it can never be right to force a child to abandon his religious beliefs, since ultimately such beliefs are subservient to what is perceived as being overall in a child's best interests.[641] This is well illustrated in *Re R (A Minor) (Residence: Religion)*,[642] in which the court was faced with the stark choice of either granting a father a residence order in respect of his nine-and-a-half year old son, in which case the child would effectively be excluded from the Exclusive Brethren within which society he had hitherto grown up, or granting a residence order to members of the sect, in which case, because of the strict rules of the fellowship, his son would no longer even see his father. In upholding the first instance decision to grant the father a residence order, the Court of Appeal made it clear that their decision was not based on a value judgment as to the tenets of the particular religion, but rather that it was thought to be in the boy's long-term interests to continue to be brought up by his father. In reaching this decision the court followed *Re T (Minors) (Custody: Religious Upbringing)*,[643] in which Scarman LJ commented that:

'. . . it was not for the court to pass any judgment on the beliefs of parents where they are socially acceptable and consistent with a decent and respectable life . . .'

In other words, being a Jehovah's Witness, for example, does not ipso facto mean that that parent should not be granted a residence order,[644] but membership of an extreme sect could have this consequence. In *Re B and G (Minors) (Custody)*[645] the decisive factor in denying a father and stepmother an order to look after the children which they had been doing for five years was that they were scientologists and so held views which were found to be 'immoral and obnoxious'. In appropriate cases, eg where the care-giver has a different religion from that of the child, it would be open to the court to make a residence

---

[638] [1999] 2 FLR 678—decision upheld by the Court of Appeal at [2000] 1 FLR 571.

[639] [2004] EWHC 1282 (Fam), [2005] 1 FLR 236.

[640] This certainly influenced Willmer LJ in *Re M (Infants)* [1967] 3 All ER 1071, CA at 1074.

[641] See Balcombe LJ in *Re R (A Minor) (Residence: Religion)* [1993] 2 FLR 163 at 180, CA.

[642] Ibid.   [643] (1975) 2 FLR 239, CA.

[644] Although parties are sometimes asked to undertake not to involve their children, for example, in the house-to-house visiting conducted by Jehovah's Witnesses: see eg *Re C (Minors) (Wardship: Jurisdiction)* [1978] Fam 105, CA. It is a violation of the European Convention on Human Rights to discriminate on the grounds of religion, see *Palau-Martinez v France* [2004] 1 FLR 810, E Ct HR and *Hoffman v Austria* [1994] 1 FCR 193, E Ct HR.

[645] [1985] FLR 493, CA. The court felt that it could not rely on the father's undertaking to remove the children from 'the evil forces of scientology'.

order on condition that the child's religious upbringing will be continued.[646] On the other hand, it could be a condition of an order that the adult does not involve a child in his religion.[647]

Racial, cultural and linguistic background. Racial origin, cultural background and linguistic background[648] are issues that should be considered under this head and are likely on occasion to prove difficult.

The preservation of links with the child's culture and heritage are important issues that should not be overlooked.[649] Such considerations were clearly a key motivating force in *Re M (Child's Upbringing)*,[650] in which the Court of Appeal ordered the return of a Zulu boy to his mother in South Africa, while in *Re M (Section 94 Appeals)*[651] the failure to address the question of race when denying contact of a mixed race girl (who was confused about her racial origin) to her black father, was held to justify the Court of Appeal reversing the decision. Nevertheless important though culture and heritage may be, the rule remains that it is the child's welfare that is the paramount consideration. In *Re P (A Minor)(Residence Order: Child's Welfare)*[652] in which Jewish Orthodox parents sought to have their child (born with Downs Syndrome) returned to them, notwithstanding that for the previous four years she had been living with a non-practising Catholic couple under a residence order, the Court of Appeal upheld the first instance decision that on the evidence of the child's limited ability to understand and appreciate the Jewish religion, her religious and cultural heritage was *not* an overwhelming factor.

Any harm which the child has suffered or is at risk of suffering

The 'harm' referred to in s 1(3)(e) has the same meaning as it does for the purposes of care proceedings,[653] and accordingly means both ill-treatment and the impairment of health or development. It clearly covers both physical and psychological trauma. It also covers sexual abuse which, if proved, is obviously likely to be a significant consideration but even so may not inevitably mean that the abuser should not, for example, be allowed contact.[654] Following the amendment by the Adoption and Children Act 2002[655] the definition of 'harm' has been extended to include 'impairment suffered from seeing or hearing the

---

[646] In the past, however, the court has been content to accept undertakings to this effect: see eg *Re E (An Infant)* [1963] 3 All ER 874, where a Jewish couple were required to bring up a ward of court as a Roman Catholic; and *J v C* [1970] AC 668, HL, where Protestants gave a similar undertaking to bring up the child as a Roman Catholic. Contrast *Roughley v Roughley* (1973) 4 Fam Law 91, CA.

[647] See eg *Re R (A Minor) (Residence: Religion)*, [1993] 2 FLR 163, CA, where an aunt was granted contact upon her undertaking not to speak or communicate with the child in any way in relation to religious or spiritual matters or make any reference to the Exclusive Brethren as a religious group; cf *Re C (Minors) (Wardship: Jurisdiction)*, above.

[648] Considerations to which local authorities must have specific regard under s 22(5)(c): see below, p 796.

[649] These issues are particularly relevant in so-called non-Convention abduction cases (discussed in Ch 13), see *Re J (A Child)(Custody Rights—Jurisdiction)* [2005] UKHL 40, [2005] 3 WLR 14.

[650] [1996] 2 FLR 441, CA, discussed above.   [651] [1995] 1 FLR 546, CA.

[652] [2000] Fam 15, CA.

[653] Section 105(1) provides that 'harm' has the same meaning as in s 31(9), discussed further below, p 737.

[654] See *H v H (Child Abuse: Access)* [1989] 1 FLR 212, CA; *L v L (Child Abuse: Access)* [1989] 2 FLR 16, CA; and *C v C (A Minor) (Child Abuse: Evidence)* [1988] 1 FLR 462; cf *Re R (A Minor) (Access)* [1988] 1 FLR 206, CA.

[655] Section 120, which was brought into force on 31 January 2005 by the Adoption and Children Act 2002 (Commencement No 7) Order 2004.

ill-treatment of another'. This amendment is intended to emphasise the potential harm caused to a child, for example, by witnessing violence perpetrated by one parent on another.

It will be noted that apart from actual harm, s 1(3)(e) also encompasses 'risk' of harm. Such a risk could for example, emanate from the parents' past alcoholism,[656] or sexual abuse. It is, however, established that s 1(3)(e) deals with actual harm or risk of harm and not with possibilities. As Butler-Sloss LJ said in *Re M and R (Child Abuse: Evidence)*:[657]

'The court must reach a conclusion based on facts, not on suspicion or mere doubts. If, as in the present case, the court concludes that the evidence is insufficient to prove sexual abuse in the past, and if the fact of sexual abuse in the past is the only basis for asserting a risk of sexual abuse in the future, then it follows that there is nothing (except suspicion or mere doubts) to show a risk of future sexual abuse.'

Re M and R also establishes that the appropriate standard of proof is the preponderance of probabilities.[658] However, the undoubted difficulties of proving primary allegations in some cases do not justify not investigating them at all.[659] The proper approach is to consider first whether the primary allegation on which the risk of harm is said to be based can be proved and then, assuming it can, to decide whether or not that is a risk of harm to satisfy s 1(3)(e).

Although *Re M and R* has not escaped criticism,[660] Lord Nicholls has subsequently commented in *Re O (Minors)(Care: Preliminary Hearing)*[661] that, without hearing full arguments on the matter, he found the conclusions of the Court of Appeal in *Re M and R* 'attractive' and added:

'It would be odd if, on this point, the approach in proceedings for section 8 orders were different from the approach in care proceedings.'

How capable each of the child's parents, and any other person in relation to whom the court considers the question to be relevant, is of meeting his needs

A wide variety of circumstances can be brought under this heading, ranging from the parents' medical condition to their lifestyle.

It is to be noted that as well as parents the capability of any other person in relation to whom the court considers the question to be relevant must also be examined. This will clearly include any new partner (formal or informal) of the parent.[662]

---

[656] See eg *Re L (Residence: Justices' Reasons)* [1995] 2 FLR 445.

[657] [1996] 2 FLR 195 at 203, applying the same test as applies to s 31 following the House of Lords' ruling in *Re H (Minors) (Sexual Abuse: Standard of Proof)* [1996] AC 563, discussed below at pp 744ff. See also *Re P (Sexual Abuse: Standard of Proof)* [1996] 2 FLR 333, CA. See also *Re W (Residence Order)* [1999] 1 FLR 869, CA (judge not entitled to assume that an uninhibited attitude to nudity posed a risk of harm to the children).

[658] Ibid at 203, expressly rejecting the contention that because the child's welfare was paramount the standard of proof for establishing harm should be less than the preponderance of probabilities.

[659] See eg *Re L (Residence: Justices' Reasons)*, [1995] 2 FLR 445, in which magistrates were held wrong not to deal expressly with the father's contention that the mother's former alcohol problems had resumed.

[660] See eg I Hemingway and C Williams '*Re M and R: Re H and R*' [1997] Fam Law 740.

[661] [2003] UK HL 18, [2004] 1 AC at [45].

[662] See eg *Scott v Scott* [1986] 2 FLR 320, CA (mother's cohabitant found to have committed acts of indecency against the child), and *M v Birmingham City Council* [1994] 2 FLR 141 at 147, per Stuart-White J.

3 CONSIDERATIONS WHEN MAKING CONTACT ORDERS

(a) Overview of difficulties

As noted elsewhere in this chapter[663] more applications (61% in 2004) are made for contact orders than any other s 8 order. They also pose some of the greatest problems.[664] As Wall J commented:[665]

'Disputes between separated parents over contact to their children are amongst the most difficult and sensitive cases which judges and magistrates have to hear. Nobody should pretend that they are easy, or that there is any one-size-fits-all solution'.

One of the great scourges of the system is the protracted contact dispute. As Butler-Sloss P has said:[666]

'There are many reasons for these long, drawn-out parental disputes over contact. In many such cases, the parents may not be able to agree because they have allowed their feelings of hurt and guilt at the separation together with anger post-separation to poison their perception of the other parent. Such feelings lay the foundations of continued hostility to the other parent and an unwillingness or even an inability to agree even to discuss anything with him/her. This continuing animosity over the failed relationship and inability to communicate with the other parent creates a serious impediment to any kind of fruitful relationship between the child and the non-resident parent. There are other impediments to contact such as a desire to exclude the other partner in the failed relationship from the new life, the influence of new partners or spouses or of grandparents, excessive use of drink or drugs, the mental or physical ill-health of one or both parents, a parent who has been violent, intimidating, or harassing of the other parent and/or the child, or allegations of physical, sexual or emotional abuse.'

Although it is important, as Butler-Sloss P went on to say, citing Sir Thomas Bingham in *Re O (Contact: Imposition of Conditions)*,[667] that the parents 'should not be encouraged or permitted to think that the more intransigent . . . and the more unco-operative they are, the more likely they are to get their own way', there are, sadly, many cases where the person seeking contact has, in the face of such obduracy and the apparent impotence of the legal system, simply given up. A particularly depressing example is *Re D (Intractable Contact Dispute: Publicity)*[668] in which the mother continually sabotaged contact arrangements over a period of five years resulting in court orders, penal notices, suspended prison sentences and finally a period of imprisonment. There were 43 hearings conducted by 16 different judges after numerous adjournments. The parents' and experts' evidence totalled 950 pages. Eventually, the father gave up. He had, in the words of Munby J, been let down by the system. There had been appalling delays in the court system, the courts had

---

[663] See above p 512 n 11.

[664] See generally Lord Justice Wall 'Enforcement of Contact Orders' [2005] Fam Law 26. For an overview of the position in other jurisdictions see J Hunt and C Roberts *Intervening in litigated contact: ideas from other jurisdictions* (Family Policy Briefing No 4, 2005).

[665] *Re O (Contact: Withdrawal of Application)* [2003] EWHC 3031 (Fam), [2004] 1 FLR 1259 at [6](1).

[666] *Re S (Contact: Promoting Relationship With Absent Parent)* [2004] EWCA Civ 18, [2004] 1 FLR 1279 at [23].

[667] [1995] 2 FLR 124 at 129.

[668] [2004] EWHC 727 (Fam), [2004] 1 FLR 1226. The father similarly gave up in *Re O*, above.

failed to get to grips with the mother's groundless allegations, and her defiance of its orders and had failed to enforce them.

It was to meet cases like *Re D* that new measures designed both to facilitate contact in the first place (that is the ability to make contact activity directions or conditions and more easily to make family assistance orders) and to enforce orders that are made (through enforcement and financial compensation orders) were introduced by the Children and Adoption Act 2006.[669] There are other strategies open to the courts such as providing for contact to take place at contact centres[670] or to refer parties for therapy.[671] But although these will undoubtedly help it would be idle to assume that the obdurate parent will go away or that protracted contact disputes will suddenly become a past phenomenon. Moreover parents must take their share of responsibility for the state of affairs that they have created. Given the difficulties of these types of cases, they should be heard by the High Court.[672]

Although many of the of obdurate parents frustrating contact in the reported cases are mothers, they are by no means exclusively so.[673] Nevertheless, as Butler-Sloss P observed in *Re S (Contact: Promoting Relationship With Absent Parent)*,[674] in practice after separation the majority of children remain with the mother so that it is the father that is the more likely parent to seek a contact order. This means that it is all too easy to make the accusation of gender bias if contact is denied. However, the courts are adamant about their gender neutrality. As Wall J has put it:[675]

'The courts are not anti-father and pro-mother or vice versa. The court's task, imposed by Parliament in s 1 of the Children Act 1989, in every case is to treat the welfare of the child or children concerned as paramount, and to safeguard and promote the welfare of every child to the best of its ability.'

Another issue that is sometimes raised before the courts is that of parental alienation, that is, an allegation that the children's hostility towards one parent (normally the non-resident parent) has been deliberately fostered by the other (normally the resident parent). There is little doubt about the existence of this phenomenon but one debate (particularly prevalent in the United States of America) is whether there is such a thing as 'Parental Alienation Syndrome'.[676] The English court's attitude is that it is inappropriate to call it a syndrome[677] but at the same time it should not be assumed that a child's hostility to contact has been deliberately fostered by the residential

---

[669] These new measures are discussed above at pp 524ff and 572ff.   [670] See above p 522.

[671] There is no formal power to do so and the recommendation that it be included in the Children and Adoption Act 2006 fell on deaf ears. Nevertheless courts can refer parents to therapy and draw inferences from their refusal to comply: *Re S (Unco-operative Mother)* [2004] EWCA Civ 597, [2004] 2 FLR 710.

[672] See eg *Re S (Unco-operative Mother)*, ibid and *Re M (Children)* [2005] EWCA Civ 1090.

[673] See eg *Re M (Children)*, ibid, in which the court believed that the children's implacable hostility to their mother had been encouraged by the father.

[674] Above at [19].

[675] *Re O (Contact: Withdrawal of Application)*, [2003] EWHC 3031 (Fam), [2004] 1 FLR 1259 at [6](3).

[676] See the discussion by C Bruch 'Parental Alienation Syndrome and Alienated Children—getting it wrong in child custody cases' [2002] CFLQ 381.

[677] See in particular the paper prepared by Drs Sturge and Glaser for the Court of Appeal in *Re L; V, M and H (Contact: Domestic Violence)* [2001] Fam 260 published under the title 'Contact and Domestic Violence—The Experts' Court Report' [2000] Fam Law 615 at 622–3 and Lord Justice Wall 'Enforcement of Contact Orders' [2005] Fam Law at 29.

parent.[678] As with all issues, the allegation of hostility requires careful investigation and evaluation.[679]

One final point that might be made in this brief overview and a return to the theme mentioned at the beginning of the chapter is that contact works best when it is voluntarily agreed between the parents. In other words recourse to the court should be the last resort. As Wall J observed in *Re O (Contact: Withdrawal of Application)*:[680]

'Fortunately, most separating parents are able to negotiate contact without the need to go to court. Contact disputes are best resolved outside the court system . . . Contact in my experience works best when parents respect each other and are able to co-operate; where the children's loyalties are not torn, and where they can move between their parents without tension, unhappiness or fear of offending one parent or the other. Such cases rarely come to court. The courts, therefore, have to deal with the cases in which there is no agreement'.

(b) Predisposition to maintain contact with both parents

As with all issues directly concerning the child's upbringing, the controlling principle in deciding whether or not to make a contact order is the paramountcy of the child's welfare.[681] Furthermore, the principle applies regardless of whether the child's parents are married to each other,[682] and whether it is sought to end or reintroduce contact.[683] Bearing this principle in mind, it would be wrong to say that *as a matter of law* there is a presumption that a parent should be permitted contact.[684] Nevertheless, the de facto position is that the courts are predisposed to maintaining contact with both parents[685] it being repeatedly said that the court should be slow to deny contact between a child and his or her parent. As Butler-Sloss put it in *Re S (Contact: Promoting Relationship With Absent Parent)*:[686]

---

[678] See eg *Re O (Contact: Withdrawal of Application)* above, in which the father's assertion of alienation by the mother was rejected, the children's hostility being found to be due to the father's own behaviour.

[679] See *T (Contact: Parental Alienation: Permission to Appeal)* [2002] EWCA Civ 1736, [2003] 1 FLR 531, where the alienation was held not to have been adequately investigated.

[680] Above at [6](8)–(9).

[681] See generally *Re KD (A Minor) (Ward: Termination of Access)* [1988] AC 806, [1988] 1 All ER 577, HL, which expressly rejected the argument based on Art 8 of the European Convention for the Protection of Human Rights following the decision in *R v United Kingdom* (1987) 10 EHRR 74, [1988] 2 FLR 445, that what is now contact was a parental right which should only be displaced where the court was satisfied that the exercise of the right would be positively inimical to the child's interests.

[682] See eg *Re M (Contact: Supervision)* [1998] 1 FLR 727, CA in which an unmarried father was granted supervised contact notwithstanding his problems concerning drug and alcohol abuse, occasional lack of control over his temper and the lack of a permanent home. Step-parents and grandparents are not in such a strong position: see respectively *Re H (A Minor) (Contact)* [1994] 2 FLR 776, *Re W (Contact: Application by Grandparent)* [1997] 1 FLR 793 and *Re A (Section 8 Order: Grandparent Application)* [1995] 2 FLR 153, CA.

[683] See eg *Re R (A Minor) (Contact)* [1993] 2 FLR 762, CA, in which the court stressed the need for a five-year-old to be told who her father was and to be reintroduced to him despite not having seen him for three years. See also *A v L (Contact)* [1998] 1 FLR 361 (discussed further below) and *Re H (Minors) (Access)* [1992] 1 FLR 148, CA.

[684] It is on this basis that the decision by the House of Lords on appeal from Scotland in *S v M (Access Order)* [1997] 1 FLR 980, sub nom *Sanderson v McManus* 1997 SLT 629, that technically the onus of proof is on the parent (in this case an unmarried father) to show that continued contact is for the child's welfare, could be justified. However, as Lord Clyde observed 'true questions of the burden of proof will almost invariably fade into insignificance after any inquiry'. See E Sutherland 'The unequal struggle—Fathers and children in Scots Law' [1997] 9 CFLQ 191.

[685] But there is no similar predisposition in the case of step-parents, see n 682 above.

[686] [2004] EWCA Civ 18, [2004] 1 FLR 1279 at [32].

'No parent is perfect but "good-enough parents" should have a relationship with their children for their own benefit and even more in the best interests of the children. It is, therefore, most important that the attempt to promote contact between a child and the non-residential parent should not be abandoned until it is clear that the child will not benefit from continuing the attempt.'

Butler-Sloss LJ has also pointed out in *Re R (A Minor) (Contact)*,[687] that the principle of continuing contact is underlined by the UN Convention on the Rights of the Child 1989, Art 9(3) of which states:

'States Parties shall respect the right of the child who is separated from one or both parents to maintain personal relations and direct contact with both parents on a regular basis, except if it is contrary to the child's best interests'.

Furthermore as the European Court of Human Rights held in *Glaser v UK*,[688] Art 8 of the European Convention on Human Rights 'includes a right for a parent to have measures taken with a view to his or her being reunited with the child and an obligation of national authorities to take measures' both in public and private law proceedings. However, the court also acknowledged that the obligation of national authorities to take measures to facilitate contact by a non-custodial parent after divorce was not absolute and that where it might appear to threaten the child's interests or interfere with his or her Art 8 rights, it was for those authorities 'to strike a fair balance between them'.

According to Balcombe LJ in *Re H (Minors) (Access)*[689] the correct test in these types of cases is to ask whether there are cogent reasons why a child should be denied contact with his parent, rather than to ask whether any positive advantages are to be gained by continuing or resuming contact. However, although this approach has been followed on subsequent occasions,[690] arguably the more principled short-hand approach is that suggested by Wilson J in *Re M (Contact: Welfare Test)*,[691] namely that the court should consider whether the fundamental need of every child to have an enduring relationship with both parents is outweighed by the depth of harm to the particular child that might thereby be caused by the contact order. In *Re P (Contact: Supervision)*,[692] Wall J summarised the principles as follows:

---

[687] [1993] 2 FLR 762 at 767, CA.

[688] [2001] 1 FLR 148 at (65)–(66). See also *Haase v Germany* [2004] 2 FLR 39, ECtHR and *Kosmopoulou v Greece* [2004] 1 FLR 900, ECtHR and, with respect to unmarried father's rights, see *Sahin v Germany, Sommerfeld v Germany* [2003] 2 FLR 671, ECtHR.

[689] [1992] 1 FLR 148 at 152. In that case the court ordered visiting contact for an introductory period pending a full welfare report, notwithstanding that the father had not seen his children for over three years. See also *Re B (Minors) (Access)* [1992] 1 FLR 140, CA in which a father's eccentric and bizarre but not violent behaviour was held not to justify refusing contact.

[690] See, for example, Wall J's comments in *Re O (Contact: Withdrawal of Application)* [2003] EWHC 3031 (Fam), [2004] 1 FLR 1258 at [6](3)–(4): 'The courts recognise the critical importance of the role of both parents in the lives of their children ... Unless there are cogent reasons against it, the children of separated parents are entitled to know and have the love and society of both their parents. In particular, the courts recognise the vital importance of the role of non-resident fathers in the lives of their children, and only make orders terminating contact when there is no alternative.' See also *Re R (A Minor) (Contact)* [1993] 2 FLR 762, CA; *Re D (A Minor) (Contact: Mother's Hostility)* [1993] 2 FLR 1, CA; *Re H (Contact: Principles)* [1994] 2 FLR 969, CA. and *Re W (A Minor) (Contact)* [1994] 2 FLR 441, CA.

[691] [1995] 1 FLR 274 at 278–9, CA.

[692] [1996] 2 FLR 314 at 328, CA, relying on *Re O (Contact: Imposition of Conditions)* [1995] 2 FLR 124 at 128–30 per Sir Thomas Bingham MR.

'(1) Overriding all else, as provided by s 1(1) of the 1989 Act, the welfare of the child is the paramount consideration, and the court is concerned with the interests of the mother and the father only in so far as they bear on the welfare of the child.

(2) It is almost always in the interests of the child whose parents are separated that he or she should have contact with the parent with whom the child is not living.

(3) The court has powers to enforce orders for contact, which it should not hesitate to exercise where it judges that it will overall promote the welfare of the child to do so.

(4) Cases do, unhappily and infrequently but occasionally, arise, in which a court is compelled to conclude that in existing circumstances an order for immediate direct contact should not be ordered, because so to order would injure the welfare of the child . . .

(5) In cases, in which, for whatever reason, direct contact cannot for the time being be ordered, it is ordinarily highly desirable that there should be indirect contact so that the child grows up knowing of the love and interest of the absent parent with whom, in due course, direct contact should be established.'

This last point is to be noted, namely that, even where direct contact might be inappropriate, the court should still consider indirect contact as a means of preserving some kind of relationship with the absent parent. In *A v L (Contact)*,[693] for example, the father was serving a long-term prison sentence and, notwithstanding the unwillingness of any relative to facilitate any form of contact, the court thought it right to make an order for indirect contact (using the good offices of the mother's solicitors), Holman J stressing the child's fundamental right to have some knowledge of and some contact with his natural father. In many other cases the court has been concerned that every effort is made to preserve contact or the possibility of contact to the extent of referring the parents to therapy or other professional help.[694] In these cases it is likely that contact activity directions or conditions would now be made.[695]

Notwithstanding the predisposition to preserve contact with both parents wherever possible, there are obviously occasions when it is not in the child's interests to do so. Examples include cases where the parent has sexually abused his child[696] and where continued contact was shown to be directly harmful to the child either physically[697] or emotionally in the sense of undermining the child's security.[698] In *Re F (Minors) (Denial of*

[693] [1998] 1 FLR 361. Holman J was anxious that the boy (a three-year-old) should know who his father was, and he therefore held that it was wrong for the justices to have accepted the mother's view (even though this was also accepted by the father) that the child should not be told about his parentage until he grew older. See also the similar concern and approach in *Re R (A Minor) (Contact)* [1993] 2 FLR 762, CA.

[694] See eg *Re M (Children)* [2005] EWCA Civ 1090, *Re S (Unco-operative Mother)* [2004] EWCA Civ 597, [2004] 2 FLR 710 and *Re S (Contact: Promoting Relationship With Absent Parent)* [2004] Civ 18, [2004] 1 FLR 1279.

[695] See above pp 524ff.

[696] See eg *S v S* [1988] Fam Law 128, CA and *Re R (A Minor) (Child Abuse)* [1988] Fam Law 129. Though note proof of sexual abuse does not ipso facto mean that contact should be denied: see *H v H (Child Abuse: Access)* [1989] 1 FLR 212, CA and *C v C (Child Abuse: Evidence)* [1988] 1 FLR 462.

[697] See eg *Re C (Contact: No Order for Contact)* [2000] 2 FLR 723, in which indirect contact was refused with a father who had been absent for three years and against whom the child had an extreme adverse reaction; and *Geapin v Geapin* (1974) 4 Fam Law 188, CA where a boy suffered serious asthmatic attacks when in contact with his father.

[698] See eg *Re C (Minors) (Access)* [1985] FLR 804, CA; *Williams v Williams* [1985] FLR 509, CA (though the children were being indoctrinated against their father); and *Wright v Wright* (1980) 2 FLR 276, CA.

Contact),[699] in which contact with a transsexual father was refused primarily because of the children's (boys aged 12 and nine) own wishes; *Re T (A Minor) (Parental Responsibility: Contact)*,[700] an unmarried father was denied contact because of his violence towards the mother and his blatant disregard for the child's welfare; *Re C and V (Contact and Parental Responsibility)*,[701] in which the child had severe medical problems requiring constant and informed medical attention which the mother, but not the father, was able to give; and *Re D (A Minor) (Contact: Mother's Hostility)*[702] and *Re H (A Minor) (Parental Responsibility)*,[703] in which respectively the mother's and stepfather's implacable hostility towards contact with an unmarried father was held to justify prohibiting contact. Nevertheless, despite these latter two decisions, as Balcombe LJ said in *Re J (A Minor) (Contact)*,[704] judges should be very reluctant to allow one parent's implacable hostility[705] to deter them from making a contact order where they believe the child's welfare requires it. Where one parent makes contact difficult or impossible for the other, the court could transfer residence.[706] However, this remedy should not be adopted to solve a relatively straightforward contact problem.[707]

Contact may also be refused on the ground of indirect harm as, for example, where the effect on the care-giving parent is so adverse as to impair that parent's care of the child.[708] Normally this factor is only likely to justify prohibiting contact where the non-care-giving parent's conduct causes genuine and justified anxiety about the child's well-being.[709] In addition to refusing to make a contact order, the court can also make an order under s 91(4) restraining future applications without its leave. But, as we discussed earlier,[710] this is a draconian measure which should not be made lightly.

(c) Should the predisposition to preserve contact be put in statutory form?

Although there has been some debate as to whether there ought to be a *statutory* presumption of contact with both parents, or at any rate to amend the welfare checklist

---

[699] [1993] 2 FLR 677, CA. See also *Re L (Contact: Transsexual Applicant)* [1995] 2 FLR 438. For pre-1989 Act cases following the children's wishes, see eg *Re N (A Minor) (Access: Penal Notices)* [1991] FCR 1000, [1992] 1 FLR 134, CA and *Churchard v Churchard* [1984] FLR 635.

[700] [1993] 2 FLR 450, CA. See also *Re A (Contact)* [1998] 2 FLR 171, and *Re D (Contact: Reasons for Refusal)* [1997] 2 FLR 48, CA (mother found to be genuinely fearful for herself and her child). Other examples might include sexual abuse, or physical abuse. But note violence does not *per se* justify a refusal of contact: see further below.

[701] [1998] 1 FLR 392, CA.   [702] [1993] 2 FLR 1, CA.

[703] [1993] 1 FLR 484. See also *Re B (Contact: Stepfather's Opposition)* [1997] 2 FLR 579, CA in which the dismissal of the father's contact application was held to be justified because of the threat of the child's stepfather to reject the child and the mother.

[704] [1994] 1 FLR 729 at 736. See also *Re S (Contact: Grandparents)* [1996] 1 FLR 158 and *Re P (Contact: Supervision)* [1996] 2 FLR 314, CA.

[705] But note *Re D (Contact: Reasons for Refusal)* [1997] 2 FLR 48, CA, in which Hale J observed that the term 'implacable hostility' usually refers to the type of case where no good reason could be discerned for a parent's opposition to contact.

[706] This was done in *V v V (Contact: Implacable Hostility)* [2004] EWHC 1215 (Fam), [2004] 851.

[707] Per Thorpe LJ in *Re B (Residence Order: Status Quo)* [1998] 1 FLR 368, CA.

[708] Such an argument failed on the facts in *Re P (Contact: Supervision)* [1996] 2 FLR 314, CA, but succeeded in *Re H (children)(contact order)(No 2)* [2000] 3 FCR 385.

[709] See *Re BC (A Minor) (Access)* [1985] FLR 639, CA and *M v J (Illegitimate Child: Access)* (1982) 3 FLR 19. See also *Wright v Wright* (1980) 2 FLR 276, CA, where the mother feared that her husband, a Jehovah's Witness, would 'indoctrinate' her children.

[710] See above p 537.

to ensure that courts have regard to the importance of sustaining a relationship between the child and the non-resident parent, the government did not agree to putting
it in the Children and Adoption Act 2006.[711] Ironically, had the Government not
abandoned plans to implement Part II of the Family Law Act 1996 there would effectively
have been a statutory presumption of contact at any rate in the context of divorce or
separation cases since, by s 11(4) the courts were to have been directed

'to have particular regard to—

"... the general principle that, in the absence of evidence to the contrary, the welfare of the
child will be best served by—

(i)   his having regular contact with those who have parental responsibility for him and
       with other members of his family . . .".'

But given that the courts have made it crystal clear that they recognise the importance of
maintaining the child's relationship with both parents there is no need for such reform
and indeed there are dangers of so-called satellite litigation were some poorly drafted
statutory provision to be introduced. A fortiori it would be wrong to legislate, as some
have argued, for a presumption of equality of time spent by a child with each parent. As
Butler-Sloss P has convincingly said[712]

'This approach to contact would not be in the best interests of many children whose welfare
is the issue before the courts. The court is not and should not be tied to a certain number of
days which would be automatically ordered to be spent by the absent parent with the child.
Children of all ages and circumstances may be the subject of contact orders and one blanket
type of order may inhibit the court arriving at the decision which reflects the best interests
of each individual child.'

(d) Contact and domestic violence [713]

Another issue frequently encountered particularly in contact cases is an allegation of
domestic violence. In this regard it will be noted that violence does not per se justify a
refusal of contact;[714] it is a matter of discretion, not principle. But in Re M (Contact:
Violent Parent)[715] Wall J commented that too little weight was sometimes given to the need
of a violent parent to change behaviour so as to demonstrate fitness to have contact. In
Re H (Contact: Domestic Violence)[716] the Court of Appeal refused to interfere with a
decision that despite the judge's misgivings about the father, including his violence, there
was not enough evidence to outweigh the normal principle that contact was in the children's interests. By contrast in Re A (minors)(domestic violence)[717] resumption of contact
with a previously violent father was denied. Interim contact orders in cases of domestic

---

[711] See the Government Reply to The Report from the Joint Committee on the Draft Children (Contact) and
Adoption Bill Cm 6583 (June 2005) para 121, also discussed above at p 521.

[712] In Re S (Contact: Promoting Relationship With Absent Parent) [2004] EWCA Civ 18, [2004] 1 FLR 1279
at [26].

[713] See A Perry 'Safety first? Contact and family violence in New Zealand: an evaluation of the presumption
against unsupervised contact' [2006] CFLQ 1.

[714] Re F (A Child)(Contact Order) [2001] 1 FCR 422 and Re H (Contact: Domestic Violence) [1998] 2 FLR
42, CA.

[715] [1999] 2 FLR 321.   [716] Above.   [717] [1999] 1 FCR 729.

violence raise particularly difficult issues. The court may allow indirect contact in cases where direct contact is not considered appropriate.[718]

In the leading case, *Re L (A Child), Re V (A Child), Re H (A Child)(Contact: Domestic Violence)*,[719] the Court of Appeal dismissed four appeals by fathers against orders allowing them indirect contact, but refusing them direct contact in cases of a background of domestic violence between the spouses and partners. It was held that there were no presumptions for or against contact with a violent parent, and the only principle applicable was the paramountcy of the child's welfare. Drawing both on *A Report to the Lord Chancellor on the Question of Parental Contact in Cases Where There is Domestic Violence*[720] which was presented by the Children Act sub-committee to the Lord Chancellor on 29 February 2000, and on an expert report (since published)[721] prepared by Dr Claire Sturge and Dr Danya Glaser on contact from a child and adolescent psychiatry perspective, Butler-Sloss LJ commented:[722]

'The family judges and magistrates need to have a heightened awareness of the existence of and consequences (some long-term) on children of exposure to domestic violence between their parents other partners. There has, perhaps been a tendency in the past for courts not to tackle allegations of violence and to leave them in the background on the premise that they were matters affecting the adults and not relevant to issues regarding the children. The general principle that contact with the non-residence parent is in the interests of the child may sometimes have discouraged sufficient attention being paid to the adverse effects on children living in the household where violence has occurred. It may not necessarily be widely appreciated that violence to a partner involves a significant failure in parenting— failure to protect the child's carer and failure to protect the child emotionally. In a contact or other s 8 application, where allegations of domestic violence are made which might have an effect on the outcome, those allegations must be adjudicated upon and found proved or not proved. It will be necessary to scrutinise such allegations which may not always be true or may be grossly exaggerated. If however there is a firm basis for finding that violence has occurred, the psychiatric advice becomes very important. There is not, however, nor should there be, any presumption that, on proof of domestic violence, the offending parent has to surmount a prima facie barrier of no contact. As a matter of principle, domestic violence of itself cannot constitute a bar to contact. It is one factor in the difficult and delicate balancing exercise of discretion. The court deals with the facts of a specific case in which the degree of violence and the seriousness of the impact on the child and on the resident parent have to be taken into account. In cases of proved domestic violence, as in cases of other proved harm or risk of harm to the child, the court has the task of weighing in the balance the seriousness of the domestic violence, the risks involved and the impact on the child against the positive factors, if any, of contact between the parent found to have been violent and the child. In this context, the ability of the offending parent to recognise his past conduct, be aware of the need to change and make genuine efforts to do so, will be likely to be an important consideration.'

Re L is an important decision to which judges should now have regard.[723]

---

[718] *Re S (Contact: Indirect Contact)* [2000] 1 FLR 481.   [719] [2001] Fam 260, CA.
[720] See now the fully published Report *Making Contact Work*.   [721] [2000] Fam Law 615.
[722] Ibid at 272–3.
[723] In *Re H (A Child)(Contact: Domestic Violence)* [2005] EWCA Civ 1404, *The Times*, 28 December 2005, the trial judge was severely criticised for having had no regard to the decision in *Re L*, the Sturge/Glaser report and the guidelines set out in *Making Contact Work* and approved in *Re L*.

Subsequent to *Re L* etc Butler-Sloss P refused direct contact to a violent father who had killed his wife.[724] All contact was also refused in a case[725] where there had been 'unusually high levels of domestic violence', because of the harm to the living child with the mother suffering from psychological and emotional conditions induced by that contact. It has been said that a refusal of contact in cases of domestic violence where there is a risk of emotional destabilisation to the child promotes the child's right to family life with its primary carer pursuant to Art 8 of the European Convention on Human Rights.[726]

E ENHANCED RESIDENCE ORDERS

As part of the strategy to offer alternatives to adoption the Adoption and Children Act 2002[727] amended s 12 of the Children Act 1989 so as to provide for so-called 'enhanced residence orders'. By the inserted s 12(5) the court is empowered when making a residence order in favour of any person *who is not a parent or guardian of the child* 'to direct, at the request of that person, that the order continue in force until the child reaches the age of eighteen . . .'. Furthermore and, importantly, by s 12(6) where a residence order includes such a direction, an application to vary or discharge the order may only be made with the leave of the court. Although even without these provisions it was possible to make a similar order, namely, to extend a residence order until the child is 18 under s 9(6) and to couple that order with a s 91(4) direction, the circumstances needed to be exceptional.[728] Under s 12(5) and (6) the circumstances do not have to be exceptional. Indeed to the contrary, they are likely to become routine orders for non-parents.

As the Explanatory Notes to the 2002 Act explains, the intention behind this reform is 'to provide a further means of delivering enhanced security where the holder of the residence order who is not the child's parent is caring for the child on a long term basis'.[729] The hope is that these changes will provide greater legal security for such persons as grandparents or other relatives, step-parents or foster parents while retaining the legal relationship between the birth family and the child which would be lost on adoption.

While it remains to be seen how much use will be made of this order it is worth pointing out that while it offers would-be applicants slightly less protection than a special guardianship order (discussed below), unlike the latter it does offer non-parents a purely private law remedy without involving local authorities. However, another factor that may become relevant is financial support. Although it is possible to obtain a residence order allowance[730] it might well be easier to obtain financial assistance with a special

---

[724] *Re G (Direct Contact: Domestic Violence)* [2000] 2 FLR 865.

[725] *Re M and B (Children)(Contact: Domestic Violence)* [2001] 1 FCR 116, CA.

[726] *Re Q (Contact: Natural Father)* (2001, unreported).

[727] Section 114, brought into force on 30 December 2005 by Adoption and Children Act 2002 (Commencement No 9) Order 2005, SI 2005/2213.

[728] For a discussion of ss 9(6) and 91(4) see above pp 539 and 537 respectively.

[729] According to the *Review of Adoption Law* (HMSO, 1992) para 6.4 residence orders per se were 'not perceived as being likely to offer a sufficient sense of permanence for a child and his carers'.

[730] Under Sch 1, para 15 to the Children Act 1989 as amended by s 78(3) of the Civil Partnership Act 2004, local authorities have a non-enforceable discretion (compare *Re K and A (Local Authority: Child Maintenance)* [1995] 1 FLR 688) to pay to persons *other* than parents or their spouses or civil partners with a residence order in their favour a contribution towards the cost of the accommodation and maintenance of the

guardianship order while adoption also offers the possibility of obtaining an adoption allowance.[731]

F SPECIAL GUARDIANSHIP

1 INTRODUCTION

A key part of the strategy to offer alternative legal options to adoption introduced by the Adoption and Children Act 2002 is the creation of the status, special guardianship. The proposal to have a new form of guardianship was first made in the Consultative Document on Adoption Law in 1992.[732] At that stage it was proposed that there should be a power to appoint what was to be called 'the child's inter vivos guardian' (hardly an attractive title). Such guardians were to have all the rights, duties and powers of a guardian under s 5 of the 1989 Act[733] save for the power to agree to the child's adoption. This proposal was not, however, included in the draft Adoption Bill 1996[734] but eventually re-emerged in its current form[735] in the 2002 Act.

The provisions governing special guardianship are provided by ss 14A-G of the Children Act 1989 (as inserted by s 115 of the 2002 Act) and came into force on 30 December 2005.[736]

Special guardianship orders are intended to provide a more permanent status for non-parents than that provided by a residence order but unlike adoption[737] they do not extinguish the legal relationship between the child and his or her birth family. In other words these new orders are intended to meet the needs of children for whom adoption is not appropriate (e.g. older children who do not wish to be adopted) but who cannot return to their birth parents and who 'would benefit from the permanence provided by a legally secure family placement'.[738] Special guardians are distinguishable from guardians since unlike the latter, who replace the deceased parents, they take office during the parents' lifetime.[739] Furthermore unlike guardians, special guardians have to be appointed by a court, ie there is no power to make private appointments. Special guardians are in a similar position to non-parent residence holders, particularly those in whose favour an enhanced

child. This power is, however, apparently exercised haphazardly: see the *Residence Order Allowance Surveys* (England and Wales) published by the Grandparents' Association (1998).

[731] For discussion of financial support for special guardians see below p 610 and for adoption allowances see below p 836.

[732] Department of Health 1992, para 6.5.   [733] Section 5 is discussed above at pp 439–45.

[734] Attached to the Government White Paper 'Adoption—A Service for Children' (1996).

[735] In fact its current form is similar to custodianship orders which had been introduced in 1985 by the Children Act 1975, Part II and abolished by the Children Act 1989 and which ironically also began with a proposal to amend guardianship see the Report of the Departmental Committee on Adoption of Children (the 'Stockdale/Houghton' Report) 1972 Cmnd 5107, ch 6. Custodianship was extensively discussed in ch 11 of the 7th edition of this work.

[736] Adoption and Children Act 2002 (Commencement No 9) Order 2005, SI 2005/2213.

[737] See Adoption and Children Act 2002 s 46(2), discussed below at p 867.

[738] See the Explanatory Notes to the 2002 Act, para 18 and the Explanatory Memorandum to the Special Guardianship Regulations 2005, (SI 2005/1109) para 7.2.

[739] See above p 441.

residence order has been made, inasmuch as they have parental responsibility for the child for the duration of the order which they share with the parents (though in this respect the power to act without consulting parents is expressed in rather more clear terms).[740] However, as we discuss below, special guardians are in a stronger position than residence holders in that they are entitled to appoint a guardian, to remove a child from the United Kingdom for up to three months and are more likely to obtain court leave to change the child's surname. Another crucial difference, and importantly from the point of view of security, it is more difficult for parents to apply to vary or discharge a special guardianship order than even to vary or discharge an enhanced residence order.[741] A further difference and evidence of the hybrid nature of the order is that unlike residence holders, special guardians are entitled to local authority support services.

2 THE POWER TO MAKE SPECIAL GUARDIANSHIP ORDERS

(a) Who can be appointed

A special guardianship order is an order appointing one or more individuals to be a child's special guardian, or special guardians.[742] By confining the power to appoint 'individuals' it is clear that the court cannot appoint a body such as a local authority nor what has been described as an 'artificial individual' such as a director of social services.[743] On the other hand, orders may be granted to a single individual or a couple, whether married or not. Only non-parents can be appointed.[744] Individuals must be aged 18 or over.[745]

(b) Applying for an order

The court (i.e. the High Court, county court or magistrates' court)[746] may make a special guardianship order either upon application or upon its own motion in any 'family proceedings'.[747] Guardians, those with a residence order in their favour, those with whom the child has lived for a period of at least three years[748] and any person having the consent of (i) each of the persons in whose favour a residence order is in force (ii) the local authority if the child is subject to a care order; or (iii) in any other case, each of the persons who have parental responsibility for the child, are *entitled* to apply for a special guardianship

---

[740] Compare s 14C(1)(b), which states that a special guardian 'is entitled to exercise parental responsibility to the exclusion of any other person with parental responsibility for the child (apart from another special guardian)', with s 2(7) which permits, in the case of multi holders of parental responsibility, that each 'may act alone without the other (or others) in meeting that responsibility'.

[741] Compare s 14D(3) and (5) which provides that inter alia parents require court leave to apply to vary or discharge a special guardianship order which cannot be given 'unless there has been a significant change in circumstances since the making of the . . . order', with s 12(6) which simply requires court leave to apply to vary or discharge an enhanced residence order.

[742] Section 14A(1).

[743] See the similar restriction in appointing guardians under s 5 of the 1989 Act and applied in *Re SH (Care Order: Orphan)* [1995] 1 FLR 746, discussed above at p 443.

[744] Section 14A(2)(b).   [745] Section 14A(2)(a).   [746] Section 92(7).

[747] Section 14A(6)(b). 'Family proceedings' are defined by s 8(3),(4) above, see p 564. Inter alia this means that the court has power to make special guardianship orders in adoption proceedings. Conversely, the court can make a s 8 order in a special guardianship application.

[748] The period of three years need not be continuous but must not have begun more than five years before nor ended three months before the making of the application: s 14A(5)(c) applying s 10(10).

order.[749] Anyone else, for example, grandparents who have not provided a home for the child for the requisite period and the child himself, must obtain court leave.[750] In deciding whether to grant leave the court must have regard to the same criteria as for deciding whether to grant leave to apply for a s 8 order.[751] Local authority foster parents (unless relatives) will additionally need the consent of the local authority, if the child has not lived with them for one year.[752]

(c) Jurisdiction

For jurisdiction purposes special guardianship orders rank as 'Part 1 orders',[753] and are therefore subject to the same domestic rules under the Family Law Act 1986 as s 8 orders.[754] However, although it is not so stated in the 1986 Act jurisdiction to make special guardianship orders must also be subject to the revised Brussels II Regulation[755] under which the primary basis of jurisdiction is the child's habitual residence and the potential conflicts between the two instruments that we discussed in relation to s 8 orders[756] also apply to special guardianship.

(d) Local authority involvement in making applications

A prerequisite of applying is the need for applicants to give three months' written notice to the local authority of their intention to apply for such an order.[757] The local authority[758] must then investigate the matter and prepare a report for the court about the suitability of the applicant and any other relevant matters.[759] The court, too, has power to direct a local authority to make such an investigation and report[760] and indeed must do so if it wishes to make such an order.[761] In other words in no circumstances can a special guardianship order be made without a local authority report.

3 PRINCIPLES UPON WHICH ORDERS ARE MADE

In deciding whether or not to make a special guardianship order the court must regard the child's welfare as the paramount consideration and be satisfied that making an order is

---

[749] Section 14A(5).   [750] Section 14A(3)(b).

[751] Section 14A(12) applying s 10(8) and (9) discussed above at pp 545.

[752] Section 14A(4) applying s 9(3)(as amended).

[753] See Family Law Act 1986, ss 1(1)(aa) and 2(2A) inserted by the Adoption and Children Act 2002, Sch 3, paras 47 and 48.

[754] For which see above p 561.   [755] See above p 560.   [756] At p 560.

[757] Section 14A(7). But note this three month period does not apply where a person has leave to make a competing application for a special guardianship order at a final adoption hearing: Adoption and Children Act 2002, s 29(6). As C Bridge and H Swindells *Adoption The Modern Law* point out at 7.118, this prevents the competing application delaying the adoption hearing.

[758] But they can arrange for someone else to carry out the investigation: s14A(10).

[759] Section 14A(8). The matters to be dealt with in the report are specified in the Schedule to the Special Guardianship Regulations 2005 (SI 2005/1109) (note that separate Regulations, viz the Special Guardianship (Wales) Regulations 2005 (SI 2005/1513) apply to Wales). They include a detailed assessment of the child and the child's family (including in each case their wishes and feelings), of the prospective special guardian(s) and finally details of the local authority including details of any past involvement with the applicant, a summary of support services available and where the authority has decided not to provide any, the reasons why, their overall recommendations on whether or not a special guardianship order should be made and what arrangements there should be for contact between the child and his relatives.

[760] Section 14A(9).   [761] Section 14A(11).

better than making no order at all.[762] It must also apply the welfare checklist under s 1(3).[763] It is also obliged to be mindful of the general principle[764] that delay is likely to prejudice the child's welfare and to that end courts are empowered to set timescales for proceedings involving special guardianship applications.[765]

4 POWERS WHEN MAKING A SPECIAL GUARDIANSHIP ORDER

Before making an order the court must consider whether a contact order (for example, to enable continued contact with the parents or other members of the family) should be made at the same time.[766] This latter power signals that unlike adoption orders, special guardianship with contact is not to be regarded as unusual. The court must also consider whether any existing s 8 order (such as a residence or contact order) should be varied or discharged.[767] While it is easy to contemplate an existing contact order (whether or not modified) running alongside a special guardianship order, the making of a special guardianship order is surely normally incompatible with the continuation of an existing residence order.[768] It is therefore surprising that a special guardianship order does not automatically discharge a residence order.[769] However, given that it does not, courts need to be aware of the need to make an express discharge order. There is no restriction comparable to that under s 9(6) with respect to s 8 orders, that orders relating to 16 or 17-year-olds should only be made in exceptional circumstances.[770]

On making a special guardianship order the court may also give leave for the child to be known by a new surname.[771] This express power will no doubt encourage such applications and signals a difference between these orders and adoption, where a new surname is automatic, and a residence order where a change of name is not encouraged.[772] This is not to say, however, that such orders should always be made. It would not be appropriate to do so, for example, in the face of opposition from a child anxious to preserve his or her identity. The court can also give permission for the child to be taken outside the United Kingdom for more than three months.[773] As with s 8 orders the court is empowered to add

[762] Section 1(1) and (5) of the 1989 Act discussed above at pp 450ff and 581 respectively. These provisions apply by reason of the fact that the special guardianship provisions are inserted into Part II of the 1989 Act.

[763] See the specific amendment by the Adoption and Children Act 2002, s 115(3) to s 1(4)(b) of the Children Act 1989. The checklist provisions apply by reason of the fact that the special guardianship provisions are inserted into Part II of the 1989 Act.

[764] Under s 1(2), discussed above at pp 472ff.   [765] See s 14E.

[766] Section 14B(1)(a). The local authority report should contain a recommendation on suitable contact arrangements, see Sch, para 10 to the Special Guardianship Regulations 2005.

[767] Section 14B(1)(b).

[768] Perhaps one exception is where the residence holder is the spouse or civil partner living with the applicant for a special guardianship order though even in this circumstance one would expect the couple to make a joint application for special guardianship.

[769] Likewise the *subsequent* making of a residence order does not automatically discharge a special guardianship order but that residence holder can then apply for a discharge: s 14D(1)(c).

[770] However, no special guardianship order may be made, where an adoption placement order (discussed below at p 840) is in force unless an application for a final adoption order has been made *and* the applicant has obtained leave to make the application.

[771] Section 14B(2)(a).   [772] See above pp 550ff.   [773] Section 14B(2)(b). See further below.

directions and conditions to any special guardianship order,[774] and to make provisions which have effect for a specified period.[775]

5 THE EFFECTS OF SPECIAL GUARDIANSHIP ORDERS

Special guardians have, for the duration of the order, parental responsibility for the child which, for the most part, they can exercise to the exclusion of anyone else, apart from another special guardian.[776] As intimated earlier, the power to act to the *exclusion* of anyone else is stronger than under s 2(7) which generally permits co-holders of parental responsibility to 'act alone and without the other (or others)'. Put in other terms[777] whereas a residence order is based upon the concurrent exercise of parental responsibility, special guardianship is based upon its exclusive exercise. However, whether this makes any real difference seems doubtful since even a residence holder is in a stronger position than others with parental responsibility. Moreover, like a residence holder, a special guardian is not empowered to exercise responsibility independently in circumstances where the law requires the consent of *all* parties with parental responsibility,[778] for example, sterilisation,[779] ritual circumcision,[780] immunisation,[781] and changes in the child's education.[782] It will be noted that special guardians are not said to be able to act to the 'exclusion' of another special guardian but presumably the normal rule under s 2(7) that a co-holder of responsibility can act alone applies to joint special guardians.

Special guardians are empowered to consent to the child's adoption[783] but not to the prejudice of the parents' right to consent or withhold consent.[784] On the other hand, neither they nor anyone else can (a) cause the child to be known by a new surname or (b) remove a child from the United Kingdom for a period of more than three months, while a special guardianship order is in force.[785]

If a care order is subsequently made, the local authority has the power to determine the extent to which a special guardian may meet his parental responsibility.[786] Similarly, if an adoption placement order is in force the special guardian's exercise of parental responsibility may be restricted by the adoption agency.[787]

Special guardians have the power to appoint a guardian to take their place upon their death.[788] Conversely, they will have an obligation to take reasonable steps to inform

---

[774] Section 14E(4).

[775] Section 14E(5), applying s 11(7) (see above pp 531ff), save s 11(7)(c) under which there is a general power to make an order for a specified time.

[776] Section 14C(1).　　[777] See Butterworths *Family Law Service* 3A [4485].

[778] Section 14C(2)(a).　　[779] This example is given in the Explanatory Notes to the Act at para 277.

[780] *Re J (Specific Issue Orders)(Muslim Upbringing and Circumcision)* [2000] 1 FLR 571, CA, discussed above at p 591.

[781] *Re C (Welfare of Child: Immunisation* [2003] EWCA Civ 1148, [2003] 2 FLR 1095, discussed above at p 528.

[782] Cf *Re G (A Minor)(Parental Responsibility: Education)* [1994] 2 FLR 964, CA, discussed above at p 433.

[783] This is because by s 144(1) of the Adoption and Children Act 2002 'guardians' include 'special guardians' and by s 47(2) guardians can consent or withhold consent to adoption.

[784] Section 14C(2)(b).　　[785] Section 14C(3).

[786] Section 33(3)(b), as amended by the Adoption and Children Act 2002, Sch 3, para 63(a)(i).

[787] Adoption and Children Act 2002, s 29(7)(a) applying s 25(4).

[788] Section 5(4) of the Children Act 1989 as amended by the Adoption and Children Act 2002, s 115(4)(b).

parents with parental responsibility and guardians that the child has died.[789] They are also entitled to remove the child from the United Kingdom for a period of *less* than three months.[790] A special guardianship order automatically discharges any existing care order and related s 34 contact order[791] but, as we have seen does not automatically discharge any existing s 8 order. Nor does an order prevent a subsequent application being made for a residence order though leave of the court will be required.[792] A subsequent residence order does not automatically discharge a special guardianship order but the residence holder can apply for its discharge.[793]

As the Explanatory Notes to the Act explain:[794]

'The intention is that the special guardian has a clear responsibility for all the day to day decisions about caring for the child or young person and for taking decisions about his upbringing. But the order retains the basic link with the birth parents, unlike adoption. They remain legally the child's parents, though their ability to exercise their parental responsibility is limited. They retain the right to consent or not to the child's adoption or placement for adoption.'

6 VARIATION AND DISCHARGE

Unlike adoption orders, special guardianship orders may be varied or discharged either upon application or upon the court's own motion.[795] The scheme as to who can apply with or without leave, as provided by s 14D, is complicated. Section 14D(1) sets who can apply:

'(a) the special guardian (or any of them, if there are more than one);

(b) any parent or guardian of the child concerned;

(c) any individual in whose favour a residence order is in force with respect to the child;

(d) any individual not falling within any of paragraphs (a) to (c) who has, or immediately before the making of the special guardianship order had, parental responsibility for the child;

(e) the child himself; or

(f) a local authority designated in a care order with respect to the child.'

But s 14D(3) then provides that the following require court leave to apply, namely:

'(a) the child;

(b) any parent or guardian of his;

(c) any step-parent of his who has acquired, and has not lost, parental responsibility for him by virtue of section 4A;

(d) any individual falling within subsection (1)(d) who immediately before the making of the special guardianship order had, but no longer has parental responsibility for him.'

---

[789] Section 14C(5).
[790] Section 14C(4). Cf residence orders which may entitle the residence holder to remove a child from the United Kingdom for a period of less than *one* month, see above p 555. Note the entitlement to remove does not apply if an adoption placement order is in force: Adoption and Children Act 2002, s 29(7)(b).
[791] Section 91(5A) added by Sch 3 to the 2002 Act. Section 34 orders are discussed below at pp 792ff.
[792] Section 10(7A) added by Sch 3, para 56(d) to the 2002 Act.   [793] Section 14D(1)(c).
[794] See para 278.   [795] Section 14D(1) and (2) respectively.

The difficulty is determining to whom s 14D(3)(d) can refer, given, in view of s 14D(3)(c),[796] that it does not refer to step-parents. The only individual who could come within the provision is one in whose favour an emergency protection order had been granted.

This complication apart the overall scheme is that those who can apply without leave are: the special guardian(s), an individual (*other* than a parent or guardian) with a residence order in their favour and, if a care order is subsequently made, the designated local authority. Those that can apply with leave are: any parent or guardian, anyone else other than a special guardian, parent or guardian or a residence order holder who had parental responsibility immediately before the making of the special guardianship order, and the child him or herself.

So far as the child is concerned, leave may only be granted if the court is satisfied that the child has sufficient understanding to make the application.[797] In the case of parents, guardians and step-parents who have parental responsibility by virtue of a s 4A parental responsibility order or agreement, leave may be granted provided the court 'is satisfied that there has been a significant change in circumstances since the making of the special guardianship order'.[798] This latter restriction is important and is designed to provide additional security for special guardians.

Although the Act is silent on this, presumably when considering whether to grant a variation or discharge the court must apply the paramountcy of the child's welfare principle.

7 DURATION OF ORDER

No specific provision is made for the duration of a special guardianship order but in accordance with general principles it must come to an end upon the child attaining 18[799] or upon the death of the child or special guardian (or surviving special guardian in the case of a joint appointment).[800] It remains a moot point whether it ends upon the child's marriage.

8 SPECIAL GUARDIANSHIP SUPPORT SERVICES

Section 14F makes important provision requiring local authorities to make arrangements within their area of special guardianship support services, namely, to provide counselling, advice and information and any other services, including financial support, as prescribed by regulation.[801] The intention[802] is to ensure that local authorities put in place a range of support services, including financial support, to be available where appropriate for special

---

[796] This reference to step-parents is confusing since they are not specifically named in s 14D(1) though must fall within s 14D(1)(d).

[797] Section 14D(4).   [798] Section 14D(5).

[799] References to a 'child' in the Children Act 1989 generally refer to a child under 18, see 105(1). It is also the underlying assumption in the provision of financial support, see reg 9 of the Special Guardianship Regulations 2005.

[800] This would be in line with the position in guardianship, see above p 447.

[801] Viz the Special Guardianship Regulations 2005. For an interesting discussion of the policy behind the introduction of these Regulations, see the Explanatory Memorandum to the Special Guardianship Regulations 2005.

[802] See the Explanatory Notes, para 282.

guardians and their children. To this end the local authority is obliged upon the request of a relevant child[803] looked after by them (or previously looked after before the making of a special guardianship order), a special guardian or prospective special guardian or a parent of such a child, to carry out an assessment of that person's needs (including the need for financial support) for special guardianship support services.[804] In other cases the local authority may carry out such an assessment upon the written request inter alia of the child or a special guardian or any person whom the local authority consider to have a significant and ongoing relationship with a relevant child[805] but if they are minded not to, they must give the person 'notice of the proposed decision (including the reasons for it) and must allow the applicant a reasonable opportunity to make representations in relation to that decision'.[806] Where the local authority do decide to provide support services (other than advice or information) on more than one occasion they must provide a plan[807] and keep that plan under review.[808] These provisions are given additional teeth by the obligation under s 14G for local authorities to establish a procedure for considering representations (including complaints) made to them in respect of these support services by either special guardians or their children.

Under the Special Guardianship Regulations the prescribed services (in addition to counselling advice and information) comprise those to enable relevant children, the special guardians or prospective special guardians and the parents of relevant children to discuss matters relating to special guardianship; assistance, including mediation services in relation to contact arrangements; services in relation to a relevant child's therapeutic needs and assistance to ensure the continuance of the relationship between a relevant child and a special guardian, or prospective special guardian.[809] In each of these cases the services may include giving assistance in cash.[810]

A key part of the special guardianship support services is financial support. Such support is only payable in the circumstances provided for under reg 6 of the 2005 Special Guardianship Regulations and is only payable to the special guardian or prospective special guardian where the local authority consider it is necessary to ensure that the special guardian or prospective special guardian can look after the child; that the child needs special care which requires a greater expenditure of resources than would otherwise be the case because of his illness, disability, emotional or behavioural difficulties or the consequences of his past abuse or neglect; it is appropriate to contribute to any legal costs; it is appropriate to contribute to the expenditure necessary for the purposes of accommodating and maintaining the child, including the provision of furniture and domestic equipment, alternations to and adaptations of the home, provision of meals, of transport and of clothing and toys and other items necessary for the purpose of looking after the child.

Support may also include a remuneration element in cases where it was paid to the former local authority foster parent of a child who has now become the special guardian

---

[803] Viz a child subject to a special guardianship order, or to an application for such an order or in respect of whom the court is considering such an order and has asked the local authority to investigate and report: Special Guardianship Regulations 2005, reg 2(1).

[804] Section 14F(4) and reg 11(1) of the 2005 Regulations.

[805] Section 14F(3) and reg 11(2) of the 2005 Regulations.   [806] Reg 11(3) of the 2005 Regulations.

[807] Section 14F(6) and reg 14 of the 2005 Regulations.   [808] Ch 4 of the 2005 Regulations.

[809] Reg 3(1)(b)(d) of the 2005 Regulations.   [810] Reg 3(2) of the 2005 Regulations.

or prospective special guardian.[811] Payments may be paid periodically or as a single sum.[812] Support ceases to be payable if the child ceases to have a home with the special guardian or prospective special guardian; ceases full-time education or training and commences employment; qualifies for income support or jobseekers allowance in his own right; or attains the age of 18 unless he continues in full-time education or training, when it may continue until the end of the course of training he is then undertaking.[813]

Financial support is reviewable upon any relevant change of circumstances and, in any event, annually.[814]

9 COMMENTARY

Although these provisions are reminiscent of the former custodianship provisions,[815] which did not prove immediately successful, there is every reason to believe that they will prove to be more useful. Certainly the name is better, while the provisions themselves are much more straightforward. Moreover, special guardianship clearly offers more security than residence orders while the provisions governing support are likely to be a further inducement to potential applicants. Prima facie one would expect the main users to be relatives, particularly grandparents,[816] foster parents, particularly of older children, who feel they can take over parental responsibility from the local authority, and sibling groups where the older child is the carer and the sibling relationship is more important to a younger child than the need for adoption. It may also be appropriate where the cultural demands are such that adoption is not appropriate to those involved.[817] One issue, however, that might detract from their widespread use by relatives is the requirement to notify and be investigated by local authority. For such would-be applicants the purely private law provisions for a so-called enhanced residence order[818] might be more attractive.

One other factor that must be borne in mind is whether the courts will take the view that there is a hierarchy of orders such that because of human rights considerations adoptions may not be regarded as a proportionate remedy in any case where special guardianship is thought to provide an adequate response.

---

[811] Reg 7.

[812] Reg 8. Note also no support is payable until the conditions set in reg 10 have been complied with.

[813] Reg 9.   [814] Reg 18.   [815] See n 735 above.

[816] In their study for the Department of Health, E Bullard, E Malos and R Parker found that more than half of custodianship applications were by grandparents: *Custodianship: Caring for other people's children* (HMSO, 1991) Tables 24–8.

[817] See the Explanatory Memorandum to the Special Guardianship Regulations 2005, p 11.

[818] Discussed above at p 603.

13

INTERNATIONAL PARENTAL CHILD ABDUCTION

A INTRODUCTION

The subject of this chapter is parental child abduction, that is, the unilateral removal of children across jurisdictional boundaries or the unilateral retention of children in another jurisdiction by one parent without the other's consent. The factual background of abductions can vary enormously: at one end of the scale is the situation where one parent, usually the mother, decides unilaterally to return with her children to her home country following a break-down of the relationship with her husband or partner or where one parent takes the children on holiday with the other's consent but then decides not to return; at the other end of the scale is where the abduction itself is violent, as for example in the infamous *Tiemann*[1] case (a German case) where a French mother (who had herself abducted the children from Germany in the first place) was ambushed in country woods by men acting for her estranged husband, dragged from her car, and watched helplessly as the men drove away with her two terrified children (a boy aged seven and a girl aged three) screaming in the back of the car. Somewhere in between perhaps is where the abduction is a deliberate attempt to frustrate an unfavourable residence or custody order. Nor should post-abduction conduct be overlooked for while some will live relatively settled lives, others will be constantly covering their tracks hiding from the authorities.

No matter how the abduction is perpetrated, its effects on the children can be devastating. It is likely to be traumatic in the short term and potentially permanently damaging in the long term. As the International Forum on Parental Child Abduction[2] put it:

'Children who are abducted will have already suffered from their parents' separation but, in addition, they will experience the trauma of being suddenly cut off from their familiar environment—a parent, grandparents, school and friends. This experience is devastating enough, but many children do not understand what is happening or why the abducting parent is hiding from the police or taking precautions against re-abduction. Such a "state of war" between parents catches the children in a horrible cross-fire.'

The effects on the parents are also traumatic. Again as the Forum put it:

'victim parents are suddenly plunged into a bewildering world where helplessness, despair and disorientation compete. The emotional trauma is compounded by the daunting

---

[1] BVerfGE 99, 145 (FRG).   [2] 1999, National Center for Missing and Exploited Children, USA.

practical obstacles to retrieving children or even to gaining access to them. Simply finding out where to get help can be difficult. Parents often face unfamiliar legal, cultural, and linguistic barriers. Their emotional and financial resources can be stretched to the limit. In the meantime, the abducted children are often led to believe that the victim parent has abandoned them. Then the children, in anger and hurt, assert that they do not want contact with the victim parent. As the years pass, the chances of recovering the children diminish. Many victim parents feel it would be easier to come to terms with the shock of bereavement than with a situation marked by prolonged uncertainty and anxiety.'

Statistical surveys of the 1980 Hague Abduction Convention[3] estimate that up to 1,280 applications either for return of or access to children abducted across international borders were made under that Convention in 1999 worldwide rising to 1,540 in 2003. However, it is rather harder to give firm statistics on the number of children abducted to and from England and Wales. According to official statistics[4] the English Child Abduction Unit (discussed below) made 232 applications and received 180 applications under the 1980 Hague Abduction Convention and the 1980 European Custody Convention in the year ending 31 March 2004. According to the 2003 Statistical Survey of applications made under the 1980 Hague Abduction Convention, the English Central Authority made 191 applications involving 241 children and received 159 applications involving 297 children. None of the above statistics include abductions to and from countries that are not parties to the Conventions dealing with abduction but according to statistics provided by the Foreign and Commonwealth Office, between 2003 and the first quarter of 2006 the office handled up to 345 cases.[5] In addition to the above mentioned cases there are also those in which the children have been wrongfully taken or retained in other parts of the United Kingdom. In that respect it has been estimated[6] that as many as four children per week are abducted by their parents to other parts of the United Kingdom.

Until the 1980s there was little international co-operation on parental child abduction and custody or residence orders made in one jurisdiction were generally neither recognised nor enforceable in another. This state of international 'anarchy' operated as an encouragement to would-be abductors who, by appropriate forum shopping, could hope to take their children from one jurisdiction to another and there obtain judgment in their favour. However, during the 1970s negotiations began which eventually led to

---

[3] See respectively N Lowe, S Armstrong and A Mathias 'A Statistical Analysis of Applications made in 1999 under the Hague Convention of 25 October 1980 on the Civil Aspects of International Child Abduction', Prel. Doc. No. 3 (Revised Version, November 2001) available on the Hague website (hereinafter referred to as 'the 1999 Statistical Survey'), and N Lowe, E Atkinson and K Horosova 'A Statistical Analysis of Applications made in 2003 under the Hague Convention of 25 October 1980 on the Civil Aspects of International Child Abduction', presented to the 5th meeting of the Special Commission in September/October 2006 (hereinafter 'the 2003 Statistical Survey').

[4] See the Official Solicitor for England and Wales' Annual Report for 2003–2004, reported at [2004] IFL 203, Table 1.

[5] In 2005 Reunite, the leading UK charity dealing with abductions, dealt with 307 abductions comprising 193 under the Hague and 113 non-Hague involving a total of 454 children. In addition they dealt with 72 (68 Hague and four non-Hague) contact cases, involving 108 children.

[6] See (1986) 130 Sol Jo 325.

two quite different international conventions being agreed. The first in time was the European Convention on the Recognition and Enforcement of Custody of Children and on Restoration of Custody of Children (hereafter 'the 1980 European Custody Convention') which was signed in Luxembourg by 15 member states on 20 May 1980. The second was the Hague Convention on the Civil Aspects of International Child Abduction (hereafter 'the 1980 Hague Abduction Convention') which was formally adopted on 24 October 1980 but which was formally signed by four States, Canada, France, Greece and Switzerland on October 25—which is why the Convention bears the latter date. The United Kingdom ratified both these Conventions in August 1986. For some time these were the only international instruments dealing with child abduction but now there is a third important instrument, this time devised by the European Union, namely, Council Regulation (EC) No. 2201/2003 of 27 November 2003[7] (which replaced the earlier Regulation No 1347/2000 of 28 May 2000).[8] These are usually referred to as the Brussels II Regulations. There are yet more international instruments in the wings. Together with the other Member States of European Union, the United Kingdom has signed but not yet ratified the 1996 Hague Protection of Children Convention.[9] The United Kingdom has also indicated its readiness to ratify the 2003 Council of Europe Convention on Contact Concerning Children.[10] Both these latter instruments have useful contributions to make to resolving cross-border problems concerning access.

As if these instruments are not enough there is, in addition, the Family Law Act 1986 under which certain orders relating to children made in one part of the United Kingdom or the Isle of Man can be enforced in another part of the United Kingdom or the Isle of Man. As a result of these developments there are different laws dealing with abduction depending on the country to or from which the child has been taken or brought. Thus, while the chances of foiling an attempted abduction and of recovering a child wrongfully taken have improved, the resulting law is complex.

B PREVENTING CHILDREN FROM BEING ABDUCTED OUT OF THE UNITED KINGDOM[11]

The best chance of recovering the child is to prevent him from leaving the jurisdiction in the first place. To this end the innocent party may invoke both the criminal and the civil law.

---

[7] Concerning jurisdiction and the recognition and enforcement of judgments in matrimonial matters and the matters of parental responsibility, repealing Regulation (EC) No. 1347/2000, OJ 2003 L338/1

[8] OJ 2000 L160.

[9] The 1996 Hague Convention on Jurisdiction, Applicable Law, Recognition, Enforcement and Co-operation in Respect of Parental Responsibility and Measures for the Protection of Children.

[10] ETS 192.

[11] See generally N Lowe, M Everall and M Nicholls *International Movement of Children, Law Practice and Procedure*, (2004) ch 9. Note also the Guide to Good Practice under the Hague Convention of 25 October 1980 on the Civil Aspects of International Child Abduction—*Part III—Preventive Measures*.

1 CRIMINAL SANCTIONS

(a) Child Abduction Act 1984[12]

Under the Child Abduction Act 1984 s 1(1)[13] it is an offence for a parent to take his own child (under the age of 16) out of the United Kingdom[14] without the requisite consents,[15] ie of the other parent, anyone else[16] with parental responsibility or leave of the court.[17] The only exception to this is where a person has a residence order in his or her favour or is a special guardian, in which case he or she is permitted to remove the child outside the United Kingdom for a period respectively of less than one month or three months without anyone's consent, unless this is in breach of a prohibited steps order.[18] Where a parent has sole parental responsibility, as for example the unmarried mother where the father has not acquired parental responsibility by registration as the father or by a court order or agreement,[19] or where the married parent is the sole living parent, then no consent for the child's removal from the jurisdiction is required.

Although the principal object of the Act is to deter parents from abducting their children out of the country, it also provides the means by which innocent parents can seek to stop the abduction. Because it is an offence to *attempt* to take a child out of the United Kingdom, the police can arrest anyone they reasonably suspect of attempting to take a child out of the county contrary to the provisions of the 1984 Act.[20] Furthermore, if the police decide to act they can, through their 'All Ports Warning System', effect a port stop, or port alert as it is sometimes known.

(b) The All Ports Warning System[21]

Under this system, details of the child at risk of abduction are circulated by way of the police national computer broadcast facility to immigration officers at ports and airports throughout the country, who will then assist the police in trying to prevent that child from leaving the country. As this is the only means of effecting a port alert,[22] any

---

[12] See generally Lowe, Everall and Nicholls, op cit, 9.4ff. N Lowe 'Child Abduction and Child Kidnapping—The New Laws' (1984) 134 NLJ 960 and Scot Law Memorandum No 67.

[13] Discussed above at pp 395–6. Exceptionally the common law offences of child kidnapping (see *R v D* [1984] AC 778, HL), discussed above, p 362, or unlawful imprisonment (see *R v Rahman* [1985] Crim LR 596) might be relevant, but these should not be prosecuted where the alleged offence is covered by the 1984 Act: *R v C (Kidnapping: Abduction)* [1991] 2 FLR 252, CA.

[14] Viz England and Wales, Scotland and Northern Ireland. But *not* including the Channel Islands or the Isle of Man. It is *not* therefore an offence under this Act to remove a child to another part of the United Kingdom.

[15] The consent does *not* have to be in writing.

[16] Ie guardians, special guardians and those with a residence order (but not an emergency protection order) in their favour.

[17] Child Abduction Act 1984 s 1(3). But note that where the child is a ward of court, court leave will always be required.

[18] Section 1(4) and (4A).

[19] As emphasised by Hale J in *Re W; Re B (Abduction: Father's Rights)* [1999] Fam 1 at 6.

[20] For a successful prosecution for an attempted abduction, see *R v Griffin* [1993] Crim LR 515, CA.

[21] See generally *The Child Abduction Act 1984: 'Port Stop' Procedures* Home Office Circular No 21/1986 and Lowe, Everall and Nicholls, op cit at 9.55ff.

[22] Formerly, there was a 'stop list' procedure operated by the Home Office which could only be activated if the child was a ward of court or if an injunction restraining the child's removal from the jurisdiction had been obtained.

parent fearing that his child might be taken out of the country and wishing to take advantage of this facility must inform the police, who maintain a 24-hour service in this regard.[23]

Before instituting a port alert the police must be convinced that the complaint is bona fide and the danger of removal real and imminent.[24] Although it is not necessary to have obtained a court order beforehand,[25] the existence of an order will be good evidence of the seriousness of the request for action from the police. Parties seeking police assistance should furnish as much information as possible, and in particular furnish the following details:[26]

(a) name, sex, date of birth, description and passport number of child;

(b) name, sex, description, nationality and passport number of abductor;

(c) their relationship;

(d) whether the child will assist in the removal;

(e) name, relationship, nationality and telephone number of applicant;

(f) solicitor's name and telephone number;

(g) likely time of travel, port of embarkation and port of arrival.

Where the threat of removal may not easily be apparent but is nevertheless real and imminent it is possible for an applicant to ask the court to include in an order a request by the court for a Port Alert. On rare occasions where no one else is able to institute an Alert the court itself may direct the National Ports Office to institute a port alert.[27] Once the alert is activated, the child's name will remain on the stop list for four weeks.[28] In the past a port alert was reasonably effective, if invoked in time and the ending of the system of placing a child on a parents' passport, in October 1998, would have increased its effectiveness. However, this latter development was more than countered by the ending, also in October 1998, of routine embarkation controls. The effectiveness of the alert is dependent on liaison between the police at individual air and sea ports and the security staff at those ports. It has been recommended[29] that there should be improved awareness training for airport security staff in handling the child warning list.

2 COURT PROHIBITIONS AGAINST REMOVAL

(a) The need for court orders

Although, as has been said, in view of the Child Abduction Act 1984 there is no requirement to obtain a court order to obtain a port alert, there are nevertheless still advantages in having such an order:

[23] *Practice Direction (Child: Removal from Jurisdiction)* [1986] 1 All ER 983.

[24] Within 24–48 hours: *Practice Direction*, above.

[25] Though note in the case of children aged 16 or 17 a court order *is* required, since the Child Abduction Act 1984 does not apply. In practice abduction of such older children is unusual.

[26] *Practice Direction*, above.   [27] See Lowe, Everall and Nicholls, op cit, at 9.57.

[28] Query whether this is long enough?

[29] See the Embarkation Control Review which reported to the Home Office in 1999.

1. It establishes the applicant's bona fides, which may help to convince the police of the need for action.[30]

2. A specific order prohibiting the child's removal can act as a deterrent in itself.

3. It will enable the applicant to enlist the aid of government agencies to trace the child.[31]

4. The High Court can specifically order publicity to trace the child.[32]

5. In cases where there is inadequate information as to the child's whereabouts the court can order any person who is believed to have that information to disclose it to the courts.[33]

6. Upon obtaining a prohibition against removal, steps can be taken to prevent the issue of a UK passport,[34] or, if one has already been issued, to ask the court to order its surrender.[35] To prevent the reissue of a passport the court will notify the Passport Agency in every case in which a surrender of a passport has been ordered.[36] It has been held[37] that the High Court's inherent jurisdiction extends to ordering the surrender of a *foreign* national's passport where to do so is in the child's best interests.

7. An order will be required if it becomes necessary to invoke the 1980 European Custody Convention or to recover the child from another part of the United Kingdom or the Isle of Man.[38]

8. It will enable outstanding disputes to be resolved upon the child's return, or sanctions to be imposed if the child is not returned.[39]

---

[30] It may be possible that some forces have still not heard of the 1984 Act, but great efforts have been made to ensure that the police are aware both of the 1984 Act and the Port Alert system.

[31] *Practice Direction (Disclosure of Addresses)* [1989] 1 All ER 765 as amended by *Practice Direction* [1995] 2 FLR 813. The agencies mentioned are the Department of Social Security (now Work and Pensions), Office of Population Census and Surveys (now Office for National Statistics), National Health Service (more specifically the National Health Service Agency Central Register), Passport Office (now Agency) and the Ministry of Defence. In *Re C (A Minor) (Child Support Agency: Disclosure)* [1995] 1 FLR 201 it was held that notwithstanding that it is not mentioned by the *Direction* the court can request disclosure from the Child Support Agency. Other bodies, such as the Driver and Vehicle Licensing Agency, the Home Office Immigration and Nationality Directorate and the local education authority may also be able to offer assistance. Similarly, the assistance of telephone companies can also be useful in tracing children: see C Atkinson and M Nicholls 'Tracing and Recording Telephone Calls' [1996] Fam Law 104, C Atkinson [1996] Fam Law 491 and Lowe, Everall and Nicholls, op cit, at 10.22.

[32] *Practice Direction* [1980] 2 All ER 806.

[33] Family Law Act 1986 s 33. For the case of wardship see FPR 1991 r 5.1(7)–(8).

[34] See the guidance issued by the Passport Agency at [1994] Fam Law 651.

[35] Family Law Act 1986 s 37.

[36] *Practice Direction (Minor: Passport)* [1983] 2 All ER 253. For the procedure see further *Protocol from the President's Office (Communicating with the Passport Office)* [2004] 1 FLR 640. A prohibition may not be indefinite and in certain circumstances solicitors may be under a duty of care to their clients to renew the application to the Service: *Hamilton Jones v David Snape (A Firm)* [2003] EWHC 3147 (Ch), [2004] 1 FLR 774.

[37] *Re A-K (Foreign Passport: Jurisdiction)* [1997] 2 FLR 569, CA. Note also that if a solicitor agrees to hold a foreign passport he owes a duty of care to the other parent not to let it out of his possession: *Al-Kandari v JR Brown & Co* [1988] QB 665, CA.

[38] See below, pp 679–85 and 689 respectively.   [39] See below at p 619.

(b) Orders that may be obtained

An applicant may obtain a prohibited steps order forbidding a child's removal from the United Kingdom or any specified part of the United Kingdom under s 8 of the Children Act 1989.[40] Furthermore, as we have seen, an embargo against removal from the United Kingdom for any period in excess of one month is automatically included in any residence order.[41]

An embargo against the child's removal from the jurisdiction can also be obtained by making the child a ward of court.[42] The unique advantage of wardship is that the embargo automatically arises immediately the child is warded,[43] and no other relief need be sought. It is this immediate effect that makes it advantageous to invoke wardship if no other proceedings are already on foot. Furthermore, unlike the automatic embargo against removal on a residence order,[44] a removal of a ward without court leave is punishable as a contempt.[45] In practice wardship remains the pre-eminent jurisdiction for dealing with abducted children.[46]

Whatever means are used, speed is of the essence if an attempted abduction is to be foiled, but even if all preventive measures have been taken in good time there is no guarantee that the child's removal will be stopped.

In cases where the court is prepared to give leave for the child's removal from the jurisdiction measures can be taken to secure the child's return. One option is to obtain an order in the foreign country to a similar effect to that made by the English court. These are known as 'mirror orders'.[47] There is also power in wardship proceedings and presumably in the High Court generally to require the person given leave to enter into a bond to ensure that the child will be duly returned.[48] Subsequently, if the order is broken the court can order the bond to be forfeited and assigned to the aggrieved party. Other actions that can be taken following the breaking of a court order are fining or committing the contemnor (ie the person breaking the order) to prison or, more potently in some cases, sequestering

---

[40] See, for example, Re D (A Minor)(Child Removal From Jurisdiction) [1992] 1 WLR 315, CA, according to which such orders can be applied for ex parte and, in appropriate cases, can be enforced without notice. NB, however, even if a prohibited steps or specific issue order is obtained, the port alert procedure must still be activated by the applicant.

[41] Section 13(1)(b) and s 13(2) discussed above, pp 555–9. But note the difficulties of enforcing the direction: see n 44 below.

[42] Wardship is discussed in Chapter 16. NB the embargo normally prohibits the ward's removal from England and Wales without the court's leave. However, under the Family Law Act 1986 s 38, unless the court has directed otherwise, leave is not required to take the child to another part of the United Kingdom or the Isle of Man if matrimonial proceedings are continuing, or if the child is habitually resident there.

[43] See below, p 885.

[44] Re P (Minors) (Custody Order: Penal Notice) [1990] 1 WLR 613, CA, discussed by Lowe 'Enforcing Orders Relating to Children' (1992) 4 Jo of Child Law 26.

[45] Indeed, at common law it is a contempt to remove a ward, irrespective of the defendant's knowledge of the wardship: Re J (An Infant) (1913) 108 LT 554, but cf Re F (Otherwise A) (Publication of Information) [1977] Fam 58 at 88 per Lord Denning MR.

[46] See N Lowe and M Nicholls 'Child Abduction—The Wardship Jurisdiction and the Hague Convention' [1994] Fam Law 191. But note the comment in Lowe, Everall and Nicholls, op cit, at 9.31 that the disadvantage is that few foreign jurisdictions will be familiar with the concept.

[47] See Lowe, Everall and Nicholls, op cit at 9.38.

[48] For details of which see Clarke Hall and Morrison on Children 2[4]. It is the normal practice for there to be consent to the giving of the bond and it is not appropriate to impose it on a party who was not responsible for the child's removal: see Re H (Minors) (Wardship: Surety) [1991] 1 FLR 40, CA.

the contemnor's assets.[49] This latter remedy can be a useful lever against the abducting parent who has left property in this country, particularly as it is now established that the court has power to order the sale of sequestered assets and can direct that the money raised by the sequestrators be used to pay the costs of tracing the child and instituting proceedings abroad for the return of the child etc.[50]

C DEALING WITH CHILDREN ABDUCTED TO OR BROUGHT FROM A 'NON-CONVENTION COUNTRY' OUTSIDE THE UNITED KINGDOM

1 DEALING WITH CHILDREN ABDUCTED TO A 'NON-CONVENTION COUNTRY'[51]

Once a child is removed outside the United Kingdom or the Isle of Man to a country that is not party to an international instrument[52] dealing with abduction to which the United Kingdom is also a party (which, for convenience, we will call 'non-convention countries'), the chances of recovering the child may be slim. Unless the abducting spouse returns voluntarily, the only legal means[53] is to institute appropriate civil proceedings in the country to which the child has been taken, if that is known, or, if the country in question has an extradition treaty with the United Kingdom, to try to have the abductor extradited for abduction and return the child.[54] The Foreign and Commonwealth Office (FCO) Consular Department can offer practical (but not legal) advice to individuals[55] while the domestic courts exercising family jurisdiction can seek diplomatic assistance from the FCO in London and from the relevant British Embassies and High Commissions abroad.[56]

2 DEALING WITH CHILDREN ABDUCTED FROM A 'NON-CONVENTION COUNTRY'

Children brought to England and Wales from a non-convention country remain subject to the common law. Such cases are commonly litigated under the wardship jurisdiction[57]

---

[49] The effect of a sequestration order is to freeze the contemnor's assets: see above, p 568.

[50] See respectively *Mir v Mir* [1992] Fam 79, and *Richardson v Richardson* [1989] Fam 95.

[51] See generally Lowe, Everall and Nicholls, op cit, 457ff, Clarke Hall and Morrison on *Children* 2[23] and A Hutchinson, R Roberts and H Setright *International Parental Child Abduction*.

[52] Ie the 1980 Hague Abduction Convention, the 1980 European Custody Convention, Brussels II or the Anglo-Pakistan Protocol.

[53] As opposed to re-abducting the child.

[54] Apart from the length of time involved in obtaining extradition, an important drawback of the procedure is that only the 'wrongdoer' is extradited, so that there is no guarantee that the child will be returned.

[55] *Practice Note (Minor: Removal from Jurisdiction)* [1984] 1 WLR 1216. Help can also usefully be sought from REUNITE.

[56] Liaison Between Courts in England and Wales and British Embassies and High Commissions Abroad [2004] Fam Law 68. Assistance can include: locating the child, conducting interviews and facilitating travel arrangements but *not* to retaining passports or to paying for the child's repatriation.

[57] Wardship is discussed in Chapter 16.

but they can be the subject of s 8 proceedings under the Children Act 1989.[58] Provided the jurisdictional rules are satisfied,[59] a child may be made a ward of court after he has been brought to this country even if the removal from another jurisdiction was unauthorised.[60] Regardless of which proceedings are brought the substantive law to be applied is the same.

(a) The basic issue and dilemma[61]

Although it was not always the case[62] it has long been settled that the English courts are not bound by foreign custody orders[63] and instead must, applying the principle of the paramountcy of the child's welfare, make their own independent judgment of the appropriate course of action.[64] A fortiori they must make their own assessment where there is no foreign court judgment. The judgment that has to be made is whether to order the child's return to the place whence he or she was taken or to allow him or her to remain in England and Wales. In making this choice, however, the court must first decide whether it should investigate the full merits of the case or simply make a summary order for the child's return. This choice is further complicated by the question of how far, if at all, the foreign law in question should be investigated, in order for the court to be satisfied that if returned the child's welfare will continue to be treated as the paramount consideration.

Deciding whether or not to make a return order presents the court with a dilemma. If it refuses to make a return order that will be seen as giving an advantage to the wrongdoer (ie the abducting parent, who may, though not necessarily, have deliberately flouted a foreign court order), yet while a court can hardly condone abduction both in the interests of justice and comity, a refusal may well be justified in the interests of the child, which interests the court is statutorily enjoined to secure. In other words in these types of dispute the court has to balance the individual child's welfare and the twin needs of policy of (a) not encouraging abduction and (b) not antagonising foreign regimes lest they adopt a policy of non-return of children habitually resident in England and Wales.

As will be seen, in *Re J (A Child)(Custody Rights: Jurisdiction)*,[65] the House of Lords settled the principles to be applied in non-convention cases, explained how these principles are to be applied in such cases and discussed the relevance of human rights law. However, to put this decision into context it will be useful to consider briefly the development of the law leading up to it.

---

[58] In the leading case, *Re J (A Child)(Custody Rights: Jurisdiction)* [2005] UK HL 40, [2005] 3 WLR 14, for example, an application was made for a specific issue order for the child's return.

[59] Viz those under ss 1–3 of the Family Law Act 1986, set out below, p 689.

[60] In fact a child who has been taken from a *convention* country may also be warded, but the wardship is liable to be overridden by a subsequent convention application. Should the convention application fail, however, then any earlier wardship proceedings are revived and may be determined upon their merits: see *Re M (A Minor) (Abduction: Child's Objections)* [1994] 2 FLR 126. A similar position applies to s 8 proceedings.

[61] For a detailed examination of the pre-*Re J* law see Lowe, Everall and Nicholls, op cit, 20.2ff.

[62] Historically, a distinction was made between children who were British subjects and those that were not. In the former case a foreign court order was not regarded as binding: *Dawson v Jay* (1854) 3 De G, M & G 764; in the latter the foreign order was binding save in exceptional cases: *Nugent v Vetzera* (1866) LR 2 Eq 704.

[63] Not even (before the implementation of the Family Law Act 1986) an order made in Scotland. For a notorious example see *Babington v Babington* 1955 SC 115, discussed below at p 689.

[64] *Re B's Settlement* [1940] Ch 54, and *McKee v McKee* [1951] AC 352, PC.

[65] [2005] UKHL 40, [2005] 3 WLR 14.

(b) The developing response to child abduction

At one time, the practice of the court was to make a 'summary' order for the child's return (ie there would be no full investigation into the merits of the case) unless a return could be shown to be harmful to the child.[66] In this way it was felt that the child's welfare was reasonably protected whilst the abduction was discouraged. That approach, described by some[67] as parent-centred and designed to ensure that the kidnapper (as they were then referred to) did not gain advantage by his wrongdoing, was held to be inconsistent with the welfare principle as applied by the House of Lords in *J v C*,[68] and it became firmly established that the decision whether to make a summary order or to hear the full merits of the application must be determined according to the child's welfare.[69] But in turn, this welfare approach became diluted when the courts began to treat non-convention cases as quasi Hague Abduction Convention cases. For example, in *Re F (A Minor) (Abduction: Jurisdiction)*[70] the Court of Appeal, emphasising that it was normally in the child's interests not to be abducted and that any decision about his upbringing was best decided by the court in the state in which he had hitherto been habitually resident, held that a return should be ordered provided the English court was satisfied that (a) the foreign court in question would apply principles acceptable to the English court and (b) there were no contra-indications such as those referred to in Art 13 of the Hague Convention.[71]

The problem with applying the Hague Abduction Convention even by analogy was, as Ward LJ pointed out in *Re JA (Child Abduction: Non Convention Country)*,[72] that when applying the Convention, the *individual* child's welfare is *not* the paramount consideration whereas it is in non-convention cases. Moreover, whereas in non-convention cases evidence has to be adduced to justify the return, in Hague cases evidence needs to be adduced to prevent a return. However, even before *Re JA* the courts had resiled from any idea of applying the Hague principles other than in a general way.[73]

The other proposition espoused by *Re F*, that a return should not be ordered unless the foreign court in question would apply principles acceptable to English law, proved far from straightforward.[74] It raised two issues:

(1) to what extent does evidence have to be led as to the principles and procedure the foreign court will apply; and

(2) how tolerant should the English court be to legal systems that have different notions of child welfare.

[66] See *Re H (Infants)* [1966] 1 All ER 886, CA, and *Re E (D) (An Infant)* [1967] Ch 287, CA.
[67] See Lowe, Everall and Nicholls, op cit, at 20.63.
[68] [1970] AC 668, HL, discussed above, pp 358ff.
[69] *Re L (Minors) (Wardship: Jurisdiction)* [1974] 1 WLR 250, CA (the House of Lords declined to hear an appeal against this ruling: see [1974] 1 WLR 266) and *Re R (Minors) (Wardship: Jurisdiction)* (1981) 2 FLR 416, CA.
[70] [1991] Fam 25, CA. See also *G v G (Minors) (Abduction)* [1991] 2 FLR 506, CA (decided in 1989) upon which the court relied in *Re F*. For a thoughtful review of this and other decisions, see D McClean and K Beevers 'International child abduction—back to common law principles' [1995] CFLQ 128.
[71] Art 13 of the Hague Convention is discussed below at pp 649ff.   [72] [1998] 1 FLR 231 at 234.
[73] See *D v D (Child Abduction: Non-Convention Country)* [1994] 1 FLR 137, *Re P (A Minor)(Child Abduction: Non-Convention Country)* [1997] Fam 45 and *Re Z (A Minor)(Abduction: Non-Convention Country)* [1999] 1 FLR 1270.
[74] See generally the analysis by U Khaliq and J Young 'Cultural diversity, human rights and inconsistency in the English courts' (2001) 21 LS 192.

With regard to the former there was a dispute as to whether any evidence needed to be led at all. In a trilogy of decisions by Waite LJ culminating in *Re M (Minors)(Abduction: Peremptory Return)*[75] and supported by Thorpe and Pill LJJ in *Osman v Elasha*,[76] it was held that unless evidence is led to the contrary it should be presumed that judges in other countries will apply principles acceptable to English law. However, in *Re JA (Abduction: Non-Convention Country)*[77]. Ward LJ (with whom Lord Woolf and Mummery LJ agreed) castigated this approach on the basis that not to make enquiries was an abdication of the court's duty to the child.

The second issue concerning the English courts' tolerance of other systems that do not espouse similar notions of child welfare similarly did not admit of simple solutions but there was a very definite trend, based upon notions of comity, 'do as you would be done by',[78] to order a return. This trend was evidenced by three decisions in particular, *Osman v Elasha*,[79] *Al Habtoor v Fotheringham*[80] and *Re S (Child Abduction: Asylum Appeal)*.[81] The effect of these decisions has been summarised[82] as holding, at any rate where the parents have a close connection with the foreign State in question, that to justify a refusal to return, strong evidence was required that the foreign law's principles was repugnant in the sense of persecution of ethnic, sex or other discrimination and not merely different to the English notion of welfare principles. The problem with this approach was that it was questionable whether the individual child's welfare was really being treated as the paramount consideration.

It was this rather uncertain unsatisfactory state of the law that the House of Lords was called upon to resolve in *Re J (A Child)(Custody Rights: Jurisdiction)*.[83]

(c) The law as settled by *Re J*

At issue in *Re J* was whether a young boy (who himself had US, UK and Saudi Arabian citizenship) who had been retained in England by his mother (who had dual UK and Saudi citizenship) without his father's (who was Saudi Arabian) consent should be summarily returned to Saudi Arabia. The House of Lords upheld the first instance decision not to make the summary return order sought by the father. In so ruling the House of Lords settled the principles to be applied in non-convention cases, explained how those principles are to be applied in such cases, and discussed the relevance of human rights. The leading judgment was given by Baroness Hale.

The principles

Agreeing with Hughes J at first instance the House of Lords held that in non-convention cases the child's welfare is paramount and that the specialist rules and concepts contained

---

[75] [1996] 1 FLR 478. See also *Re M (Abduction: Non-Convention Country)* [1995] 1 FLR 89, and *Re M (Jurisdiction: Forum Conveniens)* [1995] 1 FLR 224.

[76] [2000] Fam 62.

[77] Ibid. In that case the court refused to order a child's return to the United Arab Emirates, the evidence being that that State's court powers were limited and that the child's welfare was not the test.

[78] But for a convincing critique on this reliance on comity see Khaliq and Young, op cit.

[79] Ibid. In that case three children born of Sudanese parents were returned to Sudan notwithstanding that under Sudanese law the mother, having remarried, was not permitted to obtain custody. For a criticism of this decision see J Young 'The Constitutional Limits of Judicial Activism: Judicial Conduct of International Relations and Child Abduction' (2003) 66 MLR 823.

[80] [2001] EWCA Civ 186, [2001] 1 FLR 951.   [81] [2002] EWHC 816 (Fam), [2002] 2 FLR 437.

[82] By Lowe, Everall and Nicholls, op cit, at 20.70.   [83] [2005] UKHL 40, [2005] 3 WLR 14.

in the 1980 Hague Abduction Convention are not applicable. Baroness Hale pointed out[84] that like its statutory predecessors,[85] s 1 of the Children Act 1989 is of general application and there is 'no warrant, either in statute or authority, for the principles of the Hague Convention to be extended to countries which are not parties to it'. Furthermore there was ample authority[86] for the application of the paramountcy principle even in a case where a friendly foreign State has made orders about the child's future. However, notwithstanding its general application it was consistent with the welfare principle to order the child's return to a foreign jurisdiction without conducting a full investigation of the merits if that was in the child's best interests. In that respect Baroness Hale approvingly referred to[87] the locus classicus, namely Buckley LJ's comments in *Re L (Minors)(Wardship: Jurisdiction)*:[88]

'To take a child from his native land, to remove him to another country where, maybe, his native tongue is not spoken, to divorce him from the social customs and contacts to which he has been accustomed, to interrupt his education in his native land and subject him to a foreign system of education, are all acts (offered here as examples and of course not as a complete catalogue of possible relevant factors) which are likely to be psychologically disturbing to the child, particularly at a time when his family life is also interrupted. If such a case is promptly brought to the attention of a court in this country, the judge may feel that it is in the best interests of the infant that these disturbing factors should be eliminated from his life as speedily as possible. A full investigation of the merits of the case in an English court may be incompatible with achieving this. The judge may well be persuaded that it would be better for the child that those merits should be investigated in a court in his native country.'

Baroness Hale concluded[89] the application of the above mentioned principles means:

'that there is always a choice to be made. Summary return should not be the automatic reaction to any and every unauthorised taking or keeping a child from his home country. On the other hand, summary return may very well be in the best interests of the individual child.'

Deciding whether or not to make a summary return order

As Baroness Hale pointed out,[90] the focus must be on the individual child in the particular circumstances of the case. She therefore rejected the contention that there should be 'a strong presumption' that it is 'highly likely' to be in the best interests of a child subject to unauthorised removal or retention to be returned to the country of habitual residence so that any issues which remain can be decided there. As Baroness Hale said, such an approach would come so close to applying Hague Convention principles by analogy that it would be indistinguishable from it in practice. Furthermore such a presumption is incapable of taking into account the huge variety of circumstances which can arise in these cases. In her Ladyship's view,[91] the most one can say is:

---

[84] [2005] UKHL 40, [2005] 3 WLR 14 at [22].
[85] Viz Guardianship of Infants Act 1925, s 1 and the Guardianship of Minors Act 1971, s 1.
[86] Viz *Re B's Settlement* [1940] ch 54, *McKee v McKee* [1951] AC 352 expressly approved by the House of Lords in *J v C* [1970] AC 668.
[87] Ibid at [26].   [88] [1974] 1 WLR 250 at 264.   [89] Ibid at [28].   [90] Ibid at [29].
[91] Ibid at [32].

'that the judge may find it convenient to start from the proposition that it is better for a child to return to his home country for any disputes about his future to be decided there. A case against his doing so has to be made. But the weight to be given to that proposition will vary enormously from case to case. What may be best for him in the short run may be different from what will be best for him in the long run. It should not be assumed . . . that allowing a child to remain here while his future is decided here inevitably means that he will remain here forever.'

Baroness Hale identified a number of factors that are important in determining what decision should be made:[92]

(a) *The degree of the child's connection with each country*, ie with which country does the child have the closer connection; what is his 'home' country? In this respect factors such as nationality, where the child has mostly lived, first language, race or ethnicity, religion, culture and education are all relevant.

(b) *The length of time the child has spent in each country*—uprooting a child from one environment and bringing him to a completely unfamiliar one, especially if done clandestinely, may well not be in his best interests, but if he is already familiar with this country and has been here for some time without objection, it may be less disruptive to remain a little longer while his medium and longer term future is decided than it would be to return.

(c) *The difference of approach of the other foreign legal system*—the extent to which the difference of approach of the legal system of the country to which it is sought to return the child is relevant depends on the particular facts. English law does not start from any prior assumptions about what is best for any individual child and it would be wrong to say that the future of every child within the jurisdiction of the English courts must be decided according to the English conception of child welfare. Nevertheless differences between the legal systems are relevant and, depending upon the facts may be decisive. For example, where there is a genuine issue between the parents as to which country it is best for the child to live, it must be relevant whether that issue is capable of being tried in the courts of the country to which the return is being sought. If those courts have no choice but to do as the father wishes so that the mother cannot ask them to decide with an open mind which country is best for the child then the English court must ask itself whether it is in the child's best interests to enable that dispute to be heard.[93] The absence of a relocation jurisdiction may be a decisive factor[94] but not if the mother could not in any event make a good case for relocation. It may also be that the connection of the child and all the family with the other country is so strong that any difference between the legal systems should carry little weight.

---

[92] Ibid at [33]–[40], of which the following is a summary.

[93] In *Re J* itself Hughes J refused to make a return order on the basis that were the father to make allegations about the mother's association with another man (an allegation he made but withdrew in the proceedings before Hughes J) in any subsequent hearing before the Sharia Court in Saudi Arabia, the latter court was bound to find in favour of the father.

[94] Baroness Hale, considered that Hughes J had underplayed the importance of this factor and had been wrong to leave it out of account, see ibid [46].

(d) *The effect of the decision upon the child's primary carer* is relevant but not decisive. A child cared for by nannies or sent away to boarding school may move between countries much more readily than a child who has been looked after by a single primary carer. On the other hand, there is an understandable reluctance to allow a primary carer to profit from her own wrongdoing by refusing to return with the child if the child is ordered to return. Consequently it is often entirely reasonable to expect the carer to return with the child. Equally, however, there are occasions where it is necessary to consider whether it is indeed reasonable to expect the carer to return, the sincerity of the declared refusal to do so and what is to happen to the child if the carer does not also return.

One other circumstance not mentioned in *Re J* is the significance of the family being involved in asylum proceedings. In that respect it should be noted that when exercising its jurisdiction the court is *not* precluded from ordering the child's return (if that is in the child's best interests) merely because of the family's involvement in such proceedings.[95]

The relevance of human rights

Deciding whether or not to return a child abroad necessarily engages human rights and in particular those conferred by Art 6 (right to a fair trial), Art 8 (right to respect for private and family life) and Art 14 (prohibition against discrimination taken in conjunction with, for these purposes, Arts 6 and 8) of the European Convention on Human Rights. In *Re J*[96] the Court of Appeal considered that those rights had limited territorial effect and that therefore the fact that the mother might experience in Saudi Arabia what in England would be breaches of those rights did not render the English court in breach if it returned the child there. However, on appeal, Baroness Hale pointed out[97] that the House of Lords have since held[98] that 'our obligations may be engaged where there is a real risk of particularly flagrant breaches . . . in the foreign country'. In *Re J* itself there was no such risk. She also pointed out that in relation to Art 8 there is a distinction between 'domestic' cases where family life here may be disrupted by a forced return to another country and 'foreign' cases where the only breach would take place abroad. However, in her Ladyship's view, this distinction adds nothing to the welfare inquiry since the strength of the child's connection with this country and the effect upon his parent here are in any event relevant to whether a summary return is in the child's best interests. However, Baroness Hale appeared to consider[99] that human rights considerations might be relevant if, akin to Art 20 of the Hague Abduction Convention,[100] the return 'would not be permitted by the

---

[95] See *Re S (Child Abduction: Asylum Appeal)* [2002] EWCA Civ 843, [2002] 2 FLR 465, in which it was held that s 15 of the Immigration and Asylum Act 1999 was not intended to circumscribe the duty and discretion of a judge exercising the wardship jurisdiction, but was instead directed to the immigration authorities. See also *Re H (Child Abduction: Mother's Asylum)* [2003] EWHC 1820 (Fam), [2003] 2 FLR 1105 in which it was held to be in the child's best interests to be returned to his habitual residence in Pakistan notwithstanding that the mother (who had lawfully kept her son in the UK) had been granted asylum on the basis of a well-founded fear of persecution.

[96] Reported as *Re J (Child Returned Abroad: Human Rights)* [2004] 2 FLR 85.　　　[97] Ibid at [42].

[98] See *R (Ullah) v Special Adjudicator; Do v Immigration Appeal Tribunal* [2004] UKHL 26, [2004] 2 AC 323.

[99] Ibid at [43]–[45].

[100] In fact Art 20 of the 1980 Hague Abduction Convention has not been incorporated by UK, see further below at p 647.

fundamental principles of the requested State relating to the protection of human rights and fundamental freedoms'. In other words any discrimination in the foreign country which was contrary to Art 14 of the European Convention on Human Rights would permit, but not require, the court to refuse to return the child.

The need to act urgently

Notwithstanding *Re J* it remains of the essence in these cases that the judge should act urgently.[101] This means, as Waite LJ observed in *Re M (Abduction: Non-Convention Country)*:[102] that 'the court has no time to go into matters of detail. The case has to be viewed from the perspective of a quick appraisal of its essential features.' The need for speed also includes the appellate process, it being held by the Court of Appeal in *Re J* (but not commented upon in the House of Lords) that where expedition is directed in international child cases the court's expectation is that the appeal will be listed within approximately six weeks of the direction.

Commentary

Re J brings both welcome clarity and a return to principle which was in danger of being lost in the pre *Re J* case law. However, there will remain difficult cases to solve though even in this respect there is now useful guidance.

(d) The special case of Pakistan [103]

In January 2003, the President of the Family Division and the Honourable Chief Justice of Pakistan, in consultation with senior members of the family judiciary of the United Kingdom and the Islamic Republic of Pakistan, signed a record of 'consensus' which has since become known as the Anglo-Pakistani Protocol. The kernel of the Protocol lies in paragraphs 1 and 2[104] which state:

'1. In normal circumstances the welfare of a child is best determined by the courts of the country of the child's habitual/ordinary residence.

2. If a child is removed from the UK to Pakistan, or from Pakistan to the UK, without the consent of the parent and with a custody/residence order or a restraint/interdict order from the court of the child's habitual/ordinary residence, the judge of the court of the country to which the child has been removed shall not ordinarily exercise jurisdiction over the child, save insofar as it is necessary for the court to order the return of the child to the country of the child's habitual/ordinary residence.'

In other words, under the terms of the Protocol each state is normally expected to respect each other's custody or residence orders. Whilst this Protocol can only operate as

---

[101] As Baroness Hale commented at [41] the considerations to be taken into account in determining what order to make 'should not stand in the way of a swift and unsentimental decision to return the child to his home country' if that is what his interests require.

[102] [1995] 1 FLR 89, at 90, CA.

[103] A rather less formal arrangement has been negotiated with Egypt and there are active negotiations with Bangladesh.

[104] The full text of the Protocol is set out in Lowe, Everall and Nicholls, op cit, at 23.6. See also Clarke Hall and Morrison, on *Children* at 2 [34.1] and 2 [52.11]. Further guidance on the operation of the Protocol has been issued by the President: see 'Implementation of the UK-Pakistan Judicial Protocol on Child Contact and Abduction: Guidance from the President's Office' [2004] IFL 191.

guidance, it is intended nevertheless to have a strong influence on the way judges exercise their discretion in Anglo-Pakistan cases and it has since been held that English judges should have regard to it even in cases (commonly those where there is no existing order or in so-called holiday cases) falling outside the Protocol.[105]

Although it seems more helpful than not in promoting the interests of children in having this mutual understanding, and indeed the Protocol seems to be working well[106] the propriety of having a Protocol negotiated by the judiciary has been questioned.[107] It may be similarly argued that, in any event, the Protocol is incompatible with the House of Lords' ruling in *Re J (A Child)(Custody Rights: Jurisdiction).*[108]

D DEALING WITH CHILDREN ABDUCTED TO OR BROUGHT FROM A 'CONVENTION COUNTRY'

1 THE RELEVANT INTERNATIONAL INSTRUMENTS

The United Kingdom is party to three international instruments dealing with international parental child abduction, namely, the 1980 Hague Convention on Civil Aspects of International Child Abduction (hereafter 'the 1980 Hague Abduction Convention'); the 1980 European (or Luxembourg) Convention on the Recognition and Enforcement of Custody of Children and on Restoration of Custody of Children (hereafter 'the 1980 European Custody Convention') and Council Regulation (EC) No 2201/2003 of 27 November 2003 concerning jurisdiction and the recognition and enforcement of judgments in matrimonial matters and the matters of parental responsibility, repealing Regulation (EC) No 1347/2000 (hereafter 'the revised Brussels II Regulation').

The United Kingdom implemented the two 1980 Conventions through the Child Abduction and Custody Act 1985.[109] Both Conventions apply to children (under the age of 16) taken from the United Kingdom to another country that has implemented that convention (known as a 'Contracting State') and vice versa. At the time of writing there are 76 Contacting States to the 1980 Hague Abduction Convention and 34 to the 1980

---

[105] See *Re H (Child Abduction: Mother's Asylum)* [2003] EWHC 1820 (Fam), [2003] 2 FLR 1105—child ordered to be returned notwithstanding the fact that the mother had been granted asylum in the UK on the grounds of her husband's violence. The return was subject to undertakings by the husband inter alia to divorce his wife, to allow her to continue to care for the child until the court ordered otherwise, non-molestation and not to seek disclosure of her address in Pakistan until the court directed otherwise.

[106] As of January 2006 there have been at least eight applications (of which five return orders were made) that have been dealt with by the English courts under the strict terms of the Protocol, with 24 (of which 13 return orders were made) under the spirit of the Convention and 25 holiday cases (with 24 return orders being made) in which the Protocol has been cited. Note also the experience of one barrister, see D Binns 'The UK-Pakistan Protocol' [2004] Fam Law 359.

[107] See J Young 'The Constitutional Limits of Judicial Activism' (2003) 66 MLR 823.

[108] Discussed above at p 623.

[109] For a helpful explanation of the objectives of this Act see Lord Hailsham LC in 460 HL Official Report (5th series) cols 1248 et seq, 1985. The 1985 Act contains in its Schedules the texts of the two conventions as implemented by the UK. The full text together with explanation can be found in 1981 Cmnd 8155 (the European Convention) and in 1981 Cmnd 8281 (the Hague Convention). For general contemporary discussion of the Hague Convention see the Explanatory report by E Pérez-Vera (1982) and A E Anton (1981) 30 ICLQ 537, and of the European Convention see R L Jones (1981) 30 ICLQ 467.

European Convention.[110] Unlike the European Custody Convention, which is confined to Europe, the Contracting States to the 1980 Hague Convention include countries from the Americas, parts of Africa, Asia and Australasia as well as from Europe. Indeed, apart from the UN Convention on the Rights of the Child 1989, the Hague Abduction Convention has the most contracting states of any international convention dealing with family law and was the first international instrument governing family matters which the USA has ratified.

The revised Brussels II Regulation, came into force on 1 March 2005, having replaced the original Regulation which had been in force since March 2001.[111] Being an EU Regulation the instrument is directly binding on the United Kingdom. Consequently there is no implementing legislation but Regulations have been made under s 2(2) of the European Communities Act 1972 to make domestic law consistent with the revised Regulation.[112] The revised Regulation binds all Member States of the European Union except Denmark.[113]

2 THE STRATEGY AND AIMS OF THE INTERNATIONAL INSTRUMENTS

A key difference between the two 1980 conventions is that whereas the Hague Abduction Convention is concerned with the return of children wrongfully removed in breach of rights of custody or in breach of rights of access, the European Custody Convention is concerned with the recognition and enforcement of custody orders and decisions relating to access. In other words, whereas it is a prerequisite for applicants to have a court order in their favour to invoke the European Convention, it is not necessary to have such orders to invoke the Hague Abduction Convention. Nevertheless, although their strategy is different, both conventions have the same basic aims, namely to trace abducted children, to secure their prompt return and to organise or secure effective rights of access. Insofar as it applies to child abduction[114] the revised Brussels II Regulation governs jurisdiction and, akin to that of the European Custody Convention, provides for a system of recognition and enforcement of custody and access orders. However, unlike the European Convention the Regulation also applies to legally binding agreements.[115] In addition it makes provision for how the courts should apply the 1980 Hague Abduction Convention when considering return applications made by one Member State to another and governs what is to happen if a court refuses to return a child under that Convention. Although not without its complications, in broad terms as between Member States of the European Union the primary instrument is the revised Brussels II Regulation which takes precedence over both

---

[110] A full list of Contracting States can be found in Clarke Hall and Morrison on *Children*, Div 2. Liechtenstein is the only State to have ratified the European Custody Convention but not the Hague Abduction Convention.

[111] A useful guide to the Regulation has been produced by the European Commission, see 'Parental Responsibility in the European Union—Practice Guide for to the Application of the Brussels II Regulation' (2005).

[112] See (for England and Wales) The European Communities (Jurisdiction and Judgments in Matrimonial and Parental Responsibility) Regulations 2005, SI 2005/265.

[113] See Art 2(3) of the revised Regulation.

[114] The Regulation has a wider ambit than governing abduction, see above p 32.

[115] See Art 46 discussed below at p 676.

the 1980 Conventions.[116] Where the Regulation does not apply then so far as the United Kingdom is concerned the 1980 Hague Abduction Convention takes precedence over the 1980 European Custody Convention.[117]

Under each of the 1980 Conventions contracting states are bound to set up an administrative body known as the 'Central Authority' which has the duty of tracing the child and taking steps, if necessary by court proceedings, to secure the child's return or to secure access. These tasks are carried out mainly at the expense of each authority. To secure the prompt return of children and to achieve the other obligations under the conventions[118] Central Authorities are expected to co-operate with each other. In practice this administrative system has proved highly successful and, cemented by triennial reviews of the working of the Hague Convention and through meetings organised by the Council of Europe in the case of the European Convention, there has developed a close liaison and understanding between the various Central Authorities.[119]

Under Art 53 of the revised Brussels II Regulation Member States also have to set up a Central Authority. It was envisaged that the same bodies that exercise that function under the 1980 Conventions would also operate the Regulation. Inter alia, Authorities must provide information and assistance to holders of parental responsibility seeking recognition and enforcement of decisions on their territory, in particular concerning rights of access and the return of the child.[120] Central authorities must bear their own costs in discharging their duties and offer their services free of charge.[121]

In England and Wales the Central Authority for all three instruments is the Lord Chancellor.[122] In turn these functions are exercised on the Lord Chancellor's behalf by the Official Solicitor through the Child Abduction Unit. In the case of children taken from England and Wales the transmission of applications overseas will normally be handled by the Child Abduction Unit. In the case of children wrongfully brought to this country the practice is that, upon receiving an application in correct form, the Child Abduction Unit instructs a firm of solicitors on the client's behalf.[123] The firm must then immediately apply for public funding, which in the case of applications made under the 1980 Convention (but not the Regulation) will be granted regardless of the applicant's means and which will not be subject to a merits test.[124] In other words, an important advantage for a foreign citizen in using a convention rather than a domestic jurisdiction such as wardship is that they will be able to obtain free legal representation.[125] Once legal aid is granted, the solicitor has sole responsibility for the conduct of the case.

A second technique used by each instrument is to curb the power of the domestic courts in each contracting state to make an independent judgment of what is in the interests of a particular child, so that a return will normally be ordered.

---

[116] See Art 60(a) and (e) of the revised Regulation.

[117] See s 16(4)(c) of the Child Abduction and Custody Act 1985.

[118] Viz those set out in Art 7 of the Hague Convention and Art 5 of the European Convention.

[119] See C Bruch 'The Central Authority's role under the Hague Abduction conventions—A friend indeed' (1994) 28 Family LQ 34.

[120] See Art 55.   [121] See Art 57.   [122] Child Abduction and Custody Act 1985 ss 3 and 14.

[123] They are not instructed on the Unit's behalf.

[124] Community Legal Service (Financial) Regulations 2000, reg 3(1)(f).

[125] Such arrangements, however, are not reciprocated in every other convention country, notably the USA.

3 THE 1980 HAGUE ABDUCTION CONVENTION [126]

(a) What the Convention is trying to do

Securing prompt returns and respect for rights of access

One of the beauties of the 1980 Hague Abduction Convention is the simplicity of its obligations which are set out in Art 1:

'(a) to secure the prompt return of children wrongfully removed to or retained in any Contracting State; and

(b) to ensure that rights of custody and access under the law of one Contracting State are respected in other Contracting States.'

These objectives are based, as the Preamble explains, upon the firm conviction 'that the interests of children are of paramount importance in matters relating to their custody' and upon the desire 'to protect children internationally from the harmful effects of their wrongful removal or retention and to establish procedures to ensure their prompt return to the State of their habitual residence, as well as to secure protection for rights of access'.

Different remedies are given for the breach of rights of custody and for breach of rights of access. The former are protected by Art 12 by the remedy of the child's speedy return; the latter by Art 21 by remedies to organise and secure the effective exercise of access.

Although there is no formal hierarchy of objectives under this Convention,[127] the vast majority of applications (84% according to the 2003 Statistical Survey) are for return.

The relevance of the child's welfare

Although the Preamble refers to the 'paramount' importance of the interests of the children in matters relating to their custody this should not be taken to mean that an *individual* child's welfare is paramount in a Hague return application. As the Canadian Supreme Court pointed out,[128] the Preamble 'speaks of the "interests of children" generally, not the

---

[126] See generally N Lowe, M Everall and M Nicholls *International Movement of Children, Law Practice and Procedure*, P Beaumont and P McEleavy *The Hague Convention on International Child Abduction*, C Bruch 'Child Abduction and the English Courts' in A Bainham and D Pearl (eds) *Frontiers of Family Law* (1993) ch 4; C Bruch 'How to Draft a Successful Family Law Convention' in J Doek, H van Loon and P Vlaardingerbroek (eds) *Children on the Move*; A Dyer 'Case-law and Co-operation as the Building blocks for Protection of International Families' in N Lowe and G Douglas (eds) *Families Across Frontiers* 27–40; A Dyer 'the Hague Convention on the Civil Aspects of International Child Abduction towards global co-operation' (1993) 1 Int Jo of Children's Rights 273–92; P Nygh 'The International Abduction Convention' in *Children on the Move* 29–45; M Savolainen 'The Hague Convention on Child Abduction of 1980 and Its Implementation in Finland' (1997) 66 Nordic Jo of International Law 101; R Schuz 'The Hague Child Abduction Convention and the United Nations Convention on the Rights of the Child' in *Family Life and Human Rights* (eds P Lødrup and E Modvar) 721; and L Silberman 'Hague International Child Abduction Convention: A Progress Report' (1994) 57 Law and Contemporary Problems 210.

[127] See the Perez-Vera Report at para 18 but cf *Thomson v Thomson* [1994] 3 SCR 551, Can Sup Ct, in which La Forest J commented that it was clear 'that the primary object of the Convention is the enforcement of custody rights'.

[128] Per La Forest J in *Thomson v Thomson*, above. See also eg *Re M (A Minor)(Child Abduction)* [1994] 1 FCR 390 at 392–3, per Butler-Sloss LJ (England); *De Lewinski v Director General, NSW Department of Community Services* (1996) 70 ALJR 932 at 941 (Australia), *Clarkson v Carson* [1996] I NZLR 349 (New Zealand) and *Currier v Currier* 845F. Supp 916 at 920 (1996) (USA). Note that the English courts take the view that even where an exception to the obligation to return has been established the child's welfare is still not

interest of the particular child before the court'. Furthermore, Art 16 expressly forbids the court of the requested State from deciding on the merits of the rights of custody until it has been determined that the child is not to be returned under the Convention.[129] In summary, the Convention is predicated upon the premise that children's interests are generally best served in cases of wrongful removal or retention by promptly returning them to the State of their habitual residence.

The fact that an individual child's interests are not the paramount consideration when determining a return application prompts the question as to the 1980 Convention's compatibility with the requirement under Art 3 of the UN Convention on the Rights of the Child 1989 that in all actions concerning children 'whether undertaken by public or private social welfare institutions, courts of law, administrative authorities or legislative bodies, *the best interests of the child shall be a primary consideration*'.

This issue has been expressly litigated in Australia[130] where the charge of incompatibility was rejected inter alia on the ground that Art 11 of the UN Convention entreats States 'to take measures to combat the illicit transfer and non-return of children abroad'. It may also be pointed out that Art 35 of the UN Convention requires States to 'take all appropriate national, bilateral and multilateral measures to prevent the abduction of children for any purpose or in any form'. In any event, surely the most persuasive argument is that by providing admittedly limited exceptions to the obligation to return,[131] the Hague Convention does, in principle, pay sufficient regard to the interests of each individual child especially as it is not determining the merits of any custody dispute but rather the forum in which that dispute must be determined. At any rate, it was this line of argument that led the German Constitutional Court in *G and G v Decision of OLG Hamm*[132] to rule that the 1980 Convention was compatible with the UN Convention.

Prompt returns are also entirely compatible with the European Convention on Human Rights. The English courts, for example, take the view that a return order under the 1980 Convention is unlikely to be thought to be in breach of Art 8 of the European Human Rights Convention as interfering with the right to respect for family life particularly as the abduction will have disrupted the child's living arrangements in the first place.[133] Furthermore, the European Court of Human Rights has held that the failure *expeditiously* to enforce a return order under the Hague Convention can be a breach of Art 8 on the basis of a failure to meet the positive obligation on States to ensure effective respect for family life by taking measures to enforce a parent's right to be reunited with his or her child.[134]

---

paramount in deciding whether to order a return. This has been questioned by P Nygh 'The international abduction of children' op cit at 36.

[129] See also Art 19 which provides that a decision to return the child under the Convention 'shall not be taken to be a determination on the merits of any custody issue'.

[130] *In the Marriage of Murray and Tam* (1993) 16 Fam LR 982, discussed by Nygh, op cit, at pp. 40–41. See also *McCall and the State of the Central Authority* (1994) 18 Fam LR 307.

[131] Viz those under Arts 12(2), 13 and 20.   [132] January 18 1995, 35 ILM 529 (1996).

[133] See *Re F (Abduction: Child's Right to Family Life)* [1999] Fam Law 806 in which custody of two girls had been shared between the unmarried Portuguese parents. However, the mother, who had subsequently come to England with one daughter and wrongfully detained the other, unsuccessfully argued that by splitting the two siblings a return order would be in breach of Art 8 ECHR. As Cazalet J pointed out, the mother's own actions had disrupted the previous settled arrangements sanctioned by the Portuguese court.

[134] See *Ignaccolo-Zenide v Romania* (Application No. 31679/96), (2001) 31 EHRR 7, ECtHR *Sylvester v Austria* (Application Nos 36812/97 and 40104/98) [2003] 2 FLR 211, ECtHR on which see W Duncan *The*

Whether the Hague Convention strikes the right balance can be legitimately debated. There are those who argue that generally too little attention is paid to the interests of the children,[135] while, on the other, there are those who will say too great a latitude is given, principally though the exceptions provided by Art 13, to courts to refuse a return. Nevertheless, it is to be observed that not only is the 1980 Convention thought to be basically compatible with the two major so-called Rights Conventions, but also that its fundamental premise that the court of the State of the child's habitual resident is best able to hear the merits of a custody case, forms the basis of the 1996 Hague Convention on the Protection of Children[136] and very much underpins the recently agreed revision of the Brussels II Regulation, under which, as between Member States of the European Union, even if the Requested State refuses to make a return order under the Hague Convention, the child's home court still retains jurisdiction to hear the merits of a custody dispute.[137]

(b) When the Convention applies

Under Art 4 this Convention applies to any child, under the age of 16 and habitually resident in one contracting state, who has wrongfully been removed or retained in another contracting state.[138] To appreciate the scope of this Article it is necessary to explore first the meaning of 'habitual residence' and then of 'wrongful removal or retention'.

Habitual residence[139]

The general meaning. According to Bracewell J in *Re D (Abduction: Habitual Residence)*[140] the question of habitual residence is determined by the court of a requested State applying its own domestic law (i.e. in the case of application to England and Wales, English law). Whether this is strictly true may be open to doubt since it would be more in keeping with the approach to such concepts as 'rights of custody'[141] to treat it as a 'Convention concept'.

Habitual residence is not defined either by the Convention or the statute and, although it has become the standard international connecting factor, it is in truth a difficult

---

Judges' Newsletter Vol VI, Autumn 2003, 53–54 and *Maire v Portugal* (Application No. 48206/99) [2004] 2 FLR 653, ECtHR. See also the excellent analysis by A Schulz 'The 1980 Hague Child Abduction Convention and the European Convention on Human Rights' in (2002) 12 *Transnational Law and Contemporary Problems* 355.

[135] For a critical examination of the application of the welfare principle under the Convention, see R. Schuz 'The Hague Child Abduction Convention: Family Law and Private International Law' (1995) 44 ICLQ 771.

[136] Discussed below at p 687.   [137] See below pp 668ff.

[138] But for the purposes of access it has been held sufficient for the child to be habitually resident in *a* Contracting State at the time of breach: *Re G (A Minor)(Enforcement of Access Abroad)* [1993] Fam 216, discussed further below at p 670. In the case of a re-abduction, the court may refuse to hear the case: *Re O (Child Abduction: Re-Abduction)* [1997] 2 FLR 712 (child abducted to Sweden and then to England). See also *Best v Hesketh* [2005] EWCA Civ 1380, [2006] 1 FLR 593. Cf in Germany in which the Constitutional Court in the *Tiemann* case BVerfGE 99, 145 (FRG) ruled in effect that because in cases of re-abduction both parents had disqualified themselves as agents of the child's best interests, the child had to be represented by a third person and be heard by the court.

[139] See generally Lowe, Everall and Nicholls, op cit, 4.24 et seq and Clarke Hall and Morrison, 2[44]ff.

[140] [2005] EWCA 518 (Fam), [2005] 2 FLR 403 at [2].   [141] Discussed below at p 639ff.

concept to pin down.[142] According to Balcombe LJ in *Re M (Minors) (Residence Order: Jurisdiction)*[143] four basic propositions may be deduced from the authorities:

'(1) "Habitual" or "ordinary residence" refers to a person's abode in a particular place or country which he has adopted voluntarily and for settled purposes as part of the regular order of his life for the time being whether of short or of long duration . . .[144]

(2) Habitual residence is primarily a question of fact to be decided by reference to all the circumstances of any particular case . . .

(3) There is a significant difference between a person ceasing to be habitually resident in country A, and his subsequently becoming habitually resident in country B. A person may cease to be habitually resident in country A in a single day if he or she leaves it with a settled intention not to return to it but to take up long-term residence in Country B instead. Such a person cannot, however, become habitually resident in Country B in a single day. An appreciable period of time and a settled intention will be necessary to enable him or her to become so. During that appreciable period of time the person will have ceased to be habitually resident in country A but not yet have become habitually resident in country B . . .

(4) Where the habitual residence of a young child is in question, the element of volition will usually be that of the person or persons who has or have the parental responsibility for that child.'

None of the aforementioned four propositions is easy to apply. Take the second proposition, for example, that a child's habitual residence is primarily a question of fact. While it is undoubtedly true that there must be a factum of residence (though even here there is a problem of new born babies),[145] there are undoubtedly a number of *legal* issues associated with the concept. For example, so far as the English courts are concerned, it is the residence immediately before the wrongful removal or retention that is relevant,[146] while both the third and fourth propositions mentioned above are in themselves legal propositions.

With the possible exception of new born babies it is clear that the minimum requirement is that there must be a factum of residence—a person who has never lived here

---

[142] Ironically, one of the reasons for using it is to avoid the concept of 'domicile', which is even more difficult to apply, since it depends upon the party's intention where he or she is *permanently* to reside. Habitual residence is also thought less artificial than 'nationality'. For discussion of the merits of the various connecting factors see H Thue 'Connecting Factors in International Law' in N Lowe and Douglas (eds) *Families Across Frontiers* 53.

[143] [1993] 1 FLR 495 at 499–500 and repeated by him in *Re M (Abduction: Habitual Residence)* [1996] 1 FLR 887 at 890. For a not dissimilar summary see also *Al Habtoor v Fotheringham* [2001] EWCA Civ 186, [2001] 1 FLR 951 at [23]–[25], per Thorpe LJ.

[144] Per Lord Scarman in *Shah v Barnet London Borough Council* [1983] 2 AC 309 at 343; *Kapur v Kapur* [1984] FLR 920 at 926. Note also *Gateshead Metropolitan Borough Council v L* [1996] 3 All ER 264 at 267, [1996] 3 WLR 426 at 429 in which Wilson J said that since *Shah* 'ordinary residence and habitual residence have been synonymous'. A similar view was expressed by Butler-Sloss LJ in *M v M (Abduction: England and Scotland)* [1997] 2 FLR 263 at 267 and in *Armstrong v Armstrong* [2003] EWHC 777 (Fam), [2003] 2 FLR 375 at [31]. However, in another context (viz claiming income support) Lord Slynn said in *Nessa v Chief Adjudication Officer* [1999] 1 WLR 1937, HL that although it was unnecessary to decide the issue he was not satisfied 'that they were always synonymous'. See also *Re G (Adoption: Ordinary Residence)* [2002] EWHC 2427 (Fam), [2003] 2 FLR 944, 951–2 per Wall J in relation to s 105(6) of the Children Act 1989.

[145] Discussed below at p 637.   [146] See eg *Re S (A Minor)(Abduction)* [1991] 2 FLR 1, CA.

cannot possibly be habitually resident here. However, it is equally true that a mere visit will not be sufficient. In considering what factors may make the factum of residence 'habitual', Waite J has helpfully observed:[147]

'Habitual residence is a term referring, when it is applied in the context of married parents living together, to their abode in a particular place or country which they have adopted voluntarily and for settled purposes as part of the regular order of their life for the time being, whether of short or of long duration.

All that the law requires for a "settled purpose" is that the parents' shared intentions in living where they do should have a sufficient degree of continuity about them to be properly described as settled.'

His Lordship added, however, that because of the summary nature of Convention proceedings, detailed enquiries into the parties' intentions are not required. As he put it:[148]

'A settled purpose is not something to be searched for under a microscope. If it is there at all it will stand out clearly as a matter of general impression.'

It is now clear[149] that provided it is 'settled' the purpose may be of long or short-term duration and can be associated with education,[150] business, employment[151] (including a military posting)[152] or joining a family. As Lord Slynn put it in *Nessa v Chief Adjudication Officer*[153] 'the requisite period is not a fixed period. It may be longer where there are doubts'. It follows from this comment that where there are no doubts, residence can become 'habitual' in a relatively short time. Evidence of the required intention can be satisfied by a relatively short period of residence. In *Re F (A Minor) (Child Abduction)*,[154] for example, the Court of Appeal approved a judicial finding that a family had acquired a fresh habitual residence only one month after arrival in a new country. In that case Butler-Sloss LJ observed[155] that a court 'should not strain to find a lack of habitual residence where, on a broad canvas, the child has settled in a particular country' since without such an habitual residence the child cannot be protected under the Convention.

In *Re V (Abduction: Habitual Residence)*[156] it was held that because the family had two established homes, one in London where they spent the winter and the other in Corfu

[147] *Re B (Minors) (Abduction) (No 2)* [1993] 1 FLR 993 at 995. See also *A v A (Child Abduction)* [1993] 2 FLR 225 in which Rattee J commented that habitual residence is not to be equated with an intention to stay in a place permanently but that it is sufficient if the intention is to take up long-term residence there.

[148] Ibid at 998.

[149] See *Al Habtoor v Fotheringham* [2001] EWCA Civ 186, [2001] 1 FLR 951 at [37] and *Re R (Abduction: Habitual Residence)* [2003] EWHC 1968 (Fam), [2004] 1 FLR 216 at [41], per Munby J.

[150] *Shah v Barnet London Borough Council* [1983] 2 AC 309. This means that *Re H (Abduction: Habitual Residence: Consent)* [2000] 2 FLR 294 in which a Swedish mother who was in England for a period of study was nevertheless still habitually resident in Sweden, was probably wrong.

[151] See *R v R (Abduction: Habitual Residence)*, above.

[152] *Re A (Abduction: Habitual Residence)* [1996] 1 FLR 1: children of a US serviceman posted to Iceland and who had lived there with the requisite degree of continuing and settled purpose were habitually resident there.

[153] [1999] 1 WLR 1937 at 1943, HL.   [154] [1992] 1 FLR 548, CA.

[155] Ibid at 555–6; cf *Re A (Abduction: Habitual Residence)* [1998] 1 FLR 497 in which a stay of three weeks of an intended six-week visit was held not to establish an habitual residence.

[156] [1995] 2 FLR 992, per Douglas Brown J. But cf *Ikimi v Ikimi* [2001] EWCA Civ 873, [2002] Fam 72, in which the Court of Appeal rejected the proposition that for the purposes of the Domicile and Matrimonial Proceedings Act 1973, s 5(2), it was not possible to have two habitual residences simultaneously. See also *Armstrong v Armstrong* [2003] EWHC 777 (Fam), [2003] 2 FLR 375.

where they spent the summer, they could be regarded as being habitually resident in both places. However, because concurrent habitual residence is not a concept that fits in with the aims of the Convention it was held that their habitual residences should be regarded as sequential, that is, whilst in London they were habitually resident in England and when in Corfu they were habitually resident in Greece. A further complication is that each parent may have a different purpose as to where they are living. Accordingly, it is quite possible for parents living together to have a different habitual residence.[157]

The leading authority for the third proposition is the House of Lords' decision in *Re J (A Minor) (Abduction: Custody Rights)*.[158] In that case an unmarried mother, a UK national, without the father's knowledge or consent left him in Western Australia and flew to England with her child, intending to live permanently in England. It was held that in these circumstances, on leaving Australia, she had abandoned her habitual residence there but had not, at the relevant date (viz in this case within the first three weeks of arrival here),[159] yet acquired an habitual residence in this country.

With regard to the fourth proposition, as Waite J put it in *Re B (Minors) (Abduction) (No 2)*:[160]

'The habitual residence of the young children of parents who are living together is the same as the habitual residence of the parents themselves and neither parent can change it without the express or tacit consent of the other or an order of the court.'

There is no authority directly concerning an older child, but in such cases the basic position might well be different[161] in that it might be possible for a '*Gillick* competent' child to establish his or her own habitual residence.

The habitual residence of children. Although it will normally be the case that while the parents are living together their young child will be regarded as having the same habitual residence as the parents, it is not an invariable rule. Indeed, in *Re M (Abduction: Habitual Residence)*[162] the Court of Appeal rejected the suggestion that it was a proposition of law that a 'child's habitual residence is that of the parents unless they agree that it shall have some other habitual residence and so long as that agreement continues'. Accordingly, while parents can agree either expressly or impliedly that their child should live apart from them and thus either retain[163] or acquire[164] an habitual residence different from their own, it by no means automatically follows that upon the ending of that agreement the child's

---

[157] See *Re N (Abduction: Habitual Residence)* [2000] 2 FLR 899.

[158] [1990] 2 AC 562 at 578, per Lord Brandon; cf *Re B (Child Abduction: Habitual Residence)* [1994] 2 FLR 915 in which it was held that where a child had acquired an habitual residence in England it was not lost by the child returning to Canada for a short period of under four months, while his parents attempted (unsuccessfully) a reconciliation.

[159] See further below at p 640.

[160] [1993] 1 FLR 993 at 995. See also *Re F (A Minor) (Child Abduction)* [1992] 1 FLR 548 at 556.

[161] See Hale J in *Re A (Wardship: Jurisdiction)* [1995] 1 FLR 767.   [162] [1996] 1 FLR 887 at 895.

[163] See the hypothetical example given in *Re M (Abduction: Habitual Residence)* ibid at 894 of a child born in India and who had spent the whole of his or her life there with grandparents, while the parents came to this country and acquired a habitual residence in England.

[164] As, for example, where parents agree to send their child to live with relatives abroad, as in *Re M (Abduction: Habitual Residence)*.

habitual residence reverts to that of the parents.[165] An agreement to send a child abroad for some temporary purpose will not be sufficient to change that child's habitual residence. For this purpose sending a child abroad to a boarding school is in itself unlikely to be regarded as being more than for the 'temporary purpose of education'.[166]

Of course, the foregoing problems only arise where the child is living apart from the parents. Where the child is living with both his parents it would seem hard to resist the proposition that he or she shares the same habitual residence as that of the parents. But even this proposition is not without its difficulties as, for example, where notwithstanding their living together the parents have different habitual residences. This occurred in Re N (Abduction: Habitual Residence)[167] and it was held that because a child's habitual residence cannot be changed simply by one parent acting unilaterally,[168] the acquisition by one parent but not the other of a new habitual residence could not be said to have changed the children's habitual residence. Another difficulty raised in B v H (Habitual Residence: Wardship)[169] is the position of a baby who is born in one jurisdiction but whose parents are habitually resident in another. In that case Charles J held that 'generally a baby born of a married couple (who are habitually resident in England at the time of the birth of the child) will also be habitually resident in England, notwithstanding that he (or she) is born abroad'. In reaching this conclusion he rejected the contention that it is established that no-one, including therefore a new-born baby, can have an habitual residence in a jurisdiction in which he or she has never been physically present, since that would amount to a proposition of law rather than fact. He was careful not to make his own position a proposition of law recognising that the issue was one of fact. In that regard he instanced the example of where the parents intend the child to live with grandparents abroad. Whether Charles J's decision will stand future scrutiny remains to be seen.[170]

Further problems are caused where the parents separate. In such cases the child's habitual residence may change and will, in due course, follow that of the principal carer with whom he resides. However, where both parents have equal rights of custody, such a change cannot be immediately effected simply by one parent unilaterally removing the child[171] (particularly if that parent is under a duty to return the child pursuant to a court order),[172] although it could occur, for example, by order of the court or by agreement of the parties.[173] If, on the other hand, only one parent has parental responsibility, then a change can be

---

[165] Re M (Abduction: Habitual Residence), where, pursuant to parental agreement, the child was sent to and remained living with his grandparents in India and in which it was held that, upon the mother's withdrawal from that agreement, the child's habitual residence could not revert to that of his mother in England, since there was no current factum of residence there. Indeed, without finally deciding the point Sir John Balcombe commented that 'in all probability' the child was still habitually resident in India.

[166] See Re A (Wardship: Jurisdiction), above, approved on this point by the Court of Appeal in Re M (Abduction: Habitual Residence), above. See also P (GE) (An Infant) [1965] Ch 568 at 585, per Lord Denning MR.

[167] [2000] 2 FLR 899.   [168] Discussed below.   [169] [2002] 1 FLR 388.

[170] In the subsequent decision Re W and B (Child Abduction: Surrogacy) [2002] 1 FLR 1008, 1016, Hedley J certainly seemed to have doubts. Charles J's alternative tentative suggestion that account might be taken of the circumstances while the child is still a foetus is highly controversial and must surely be wrong.

[171] Re S (Minors) (Abduction: Wrongful Retention) [1994] Fam 70.

[172] Re R (Wardship: Child Abduction) (No 2) [1993] 1 FLR 249, CA.

[173] See eg Re F (Minors) [1992] FCR 595 (agreement); Re O (A Minor) (Child Abduction: Habitual Residence) [1993] 2 FLR 594 (court order).

effected unilaterally.[174] For example, in *Re M (Minors) (Residence Order: Jurisdiction)*[175] an unmarried mother unilaterally changed her children's habitual residence when she moved them from the care of the grandparents. But, where the sole holder of parental responsibility dies, the child's habitual residence cannot change simply upon his removal from the jurisdiction by a person who has his care but not parental responsibility. Thus in *Re S (A Minor) (Custody: Habitual Residence)*[176] it was held that a child, whose Irish unmarried mother (and the sole holder of parental responsibility) was habitually resident in England before her death, remained habitually resident in England notwithstanding his removal to Ireland by his maternal grandparents.

Since it is a requirement to be habitually resident in a contracting state, it follows that the Convention is not retrospective in the sense that the wrongful act must have taken place after the contracting state has implemented the Convention.[177]

'Wrongful' removal or retention[178]

Although it is not necessary for the applicant to have a court order in his favour, nevertheless to invoke the Hague Convention he must show[179] that the removal or retention is 'wrongful' within the meaning of Art 3. For these purposes the act is 'wrongful' if (a) it is in breach of rights of custody accorded to a person or institution or other body, either jointly or alone, by the law of the contracting state in which the child is habitually resident, and (b) if at the time of removal or retention those rights were actually exercised either jointly or alone, or would have been so exercised but for the removal or retention.

It will be noted that Art 3 refers both to wrongful *removal* and wrongful *retention*. It has been held by the House of Lords in *Re H, Re S*[180] that these are separate and mutually exclusive events, both of which occur once and for all on a specific occasion. *Removal* occurs 'when a child, which has previously been in the state of its habitual residence, is taken away across the frontier of that state, whereas *retention* occurs where a child, which has previously been for a limited period of time outside the state of its habitual residence, is not returned on the expiry of such limited period'.[181]

Alternatively, a retention can subsequently become 'wrongful' if, following the removal, the court of the child's habitual residence makes a valid order giving interim care and control to the applicant and for the return of the child which is not obeyed.[182] In *Re B*

---

[174] But note *Re B (A Minor) (Abduction)* [1994] 2 FLR 249, CA, in which a removal was held 'wrongful' for the purpose of the Hague Convention notwithstanding that the father had neither official custodial status nor a court order in his favour but was looking after the child at the time of abduction (discussed further below at p 640).

[175] [1993] 1 FLR 495, CA.　　　[176] *Re S (A Minor) (Custody: Habitual Residence)* [1998] AC 750, HL.

[177] *Re H (Minors) (Abduction: Custody Rights), Re S (Minors) (Abduction: Custody Rights)* [1991] 2 AC 476, HL. A similar conclusion had been reached in Scotland *Kilgour v Kilgour* 1987 SLT 568. For this reason the implementation dates (for which see Clarke Hall and Morrison) are important.

[178] See generally Lowe, Everall and Nicholls, op cit, at 14.4 et seq.

[179] Failure to discharge this burden is fatal to the application: see *Re M (A Minor) (Abduction)* [1996] 1 FLR 315, where experts disagreed on whether under Greek law an interim custody order vested exclusive rights to determine the child's place of residence. Accordingly, the application failed.

[180] *Re H (Minors) (Abduction: Custody Rights), Re S (Minors) (Abduction: Custody Rights)*, above.

[181] Per Lord Brandon ibid at 500.

[182] *Re S (A Minor) (Custody: Habitual Residence)* [1998] AC 750, HL.

(Minors) (Abduction) (No 2)[183] Waite J held that because the Convention should be construed purposively rather than semantically, proper effect could only be given to the term 'retention' if it was construed as being wide enough to comprise not only acts of physical restraint on the part of the retaining parent, but also judicial orders obtained on his initiative. However, as Wall J has pointed out in *Re S (Minors) (Abduction: Wrongful Retention)*,[184] it is only where such applications provide clear evidence of a party's intention to break the agreement that such acts can be considered wrongful. It would not, for example, be wrongful to seek court orders solely to protect the child's presence within the jurisdiction in accordance with the agreement.

Since 'wrongful removal' is not a continuing state of affairs, it follows that a subsequent removal after a temporary return of the child to the state of habitual residence constitutes a new 'wrongful removal' within the meaning of Art 3.[185] Accordingly, the time limits under the Convention[186] run from the date of the second removal.

In each case removal or retention refers to removal or retention out of the jurisdiction of the courts of the state of the child's habitual residence. Wrongful removal or retention within the borders of the state of the child's habitual residence falls outside the scope of the Convention.[187]

Rights of custody

Central to the notion of wrongful removal or retention under Art 3 is that the act must be in breach of rights of custody. The general approach in determining this issue has been well summarised by Dyson LJ in *Hunter v Murrow (Abduction: Rights of Custody)*.[188] The first task, the so-called 'domestic law question', is to establish what rights, if any, the applicant had under the law of the state in which the child was habitually resident immediately before his or her removal or retention. This question is determined in accordance with the domestic law of that State[189] and involves deciding what rights are recognised by that law and how these rights are characterised.[190] The second task, the so-called 'Convention question', is to determine whether those rights are properly to be categorised as 'rights of custody'. This is a matter of international law and depends upon the application of the autonomous meaning of the phrase 'rights of custody' as understood by the English courts.

As Art 5(a) states, ' "rights of custody" includes rights relating to the care of the person

---

[183] [1993] 1 FLR 993. See also *Re AZ (A Minor) (Abduction: Acquiescence)* [1993] 1 FLR 682 at 689 per Sir Michael Kerr.

[184] [1994] Fam 70.

[185] See *Re S (Child Abduction: Delay)* [1998] 1 FLR 651, per Wall J but he left open whether mere physical presence, however transient, can form the basis of a fresh wrongful removal under Art 3.

[186] Viz 12 months under Art 12: see further below.

[187] See *Re H, Re S* above at 498, per Lord Brandon, and *Re V (Abduction: Habitual Residence)* [1995] 2 FLR 992.

[188] [2005] EWCA Civ 976, [2005] 2 FLR 1119 at [46]–[47].

[189] Including, according to Munby J in *Re JB (Child Abduction)(Rights of Custody: Spain)* [2003] EWHC 2130 (Fam), [2004] 1 FLR 796 its private international law. In that case it was found that notwithstanding their habitual residence in Spain, because all the parties were British nationals, their personal law (in that case English law) would be applied.

[190] In *Hunter v Murrow* itself, it was held that the English court was not bound by a New Zealand Court's declaration (under Art 15, discussed below) that a father's rights of access were sufficient to amount to rights of custody).

of the child, and, in particular the right to determine the child's place of residence'. Such rights, as Art 3 says, may arise by 'operation of law or by reason of a judicial or administrative decision, or by reason of an agreement having legal effect under the law of that State'. These rights may be vested in an individual, institution or a body, including (see below) the court.

Rights of custody vested in individuals. In broad terms, so far as English law is concerned, 'rights of custody' should be understood in the context of the Children Act 1989, ie to refer to parental responsibility. All those vested with parental responsibility have 'rights of custody' for the purpose of the Convention, whether that responsibility is vested automatically, as in the case of married parents and unmarried mothers, or, in the case of unmarried fathers, by virtue of being registered as the father, a parental responsibility agreement or order.[191] It has been held[192] that an unmarried father who had been granted interim care and control in wardship proceedings after the child's removal (but while the child still remained habitually resident in the jurisdiction from where he was taken) did have 'rights of custody' notwithstanding that they were on an interim basis and that he shared them with the High Court.

Similarly, again in broad terms, so far as foreign jurisdictions are concerned, those who have automatic parental rights or have custody orders in their favour will generally be regarded as having rights of custody. In this latter respect it has been held[193] that it is inappropriate for an English court to go behind a decision of a competent court of another Contracting State dealing with custody.

As previously intimated, it is now well established that the concept of 'rights of custody' is not confined to any national law meaning. However, although this had been hinted at by the Court of Appeal in *Re C (A Minor)(Abduction)* [194] a restrictive approach was adopted by the House of Lords in *Re J (A Minor)(Abduction: Custody Rights)* [195] only a year later. In that case it was held that the Convention only protected established legal rights and not de facto custody. Accordingly, notwithstanding that the child in question was living with both the unmarried parents at the time of removal, it was held that the father (who, under the then Western Australian Law, had no formal rights) had no 'rights of custody'.

Re J, however, was decided before the second meeting of the Special Commission held in 1993 to review the operation of the Convention at which it was concluded that 'rights of custody' should have an autonomous convention meaning. Reflecting this, *Practice Note: Hague Convention: (Application for Return Orders by Unmarried Fathers)* pointed out,[196] that the key concept of 'rights of custody' was not dependent for its meaning on any single legal system but instead 'draws its meaning from the definition, structure and purposes of the Convention'. In turn Waite LJ said in *Re B (A Minor) (Abduction)*:[197]

'. . . the Convention is to be construed broadly as an international agreement according to its general tenor and purpose, without attributing to any of its terms a specialist meaning which the word or words in question may have acquired under the domestic "law of England" and that "rights of custody" is a term which, when so construed, enlarges upon, and is not

---

[191] Child Abduction and Custody Act 1985 Sch 3.
[192] *Re S (A Minor) (Custody: Habitual Residence)* [1997] 4 All ER 251, HL.
[193] See *Re E (Abduction: Rights of Custody)* [2005] EWHC 848 (Fam), [2005] 2 FLR 759, per Potter P.
[194] [1989] 1 FLR 403.   [195] [1990] 2 AC 562.   [196] [1998] 1 FLR 491.
[197] [1994] 2 FLR 249, CA. See also *Re F (A Minor) (Abduction; Custody Rights Abroad)* [1995] Fam 224, CA.

necessarily synonymous with the simple connotations of "custody" when that word is used alone . . .'

In his view,[198] provided the aggrieved parent was, at the time of the wrongful removal or retention, exercising functions in the requesting state of a parental or custodial nature, he could be regarded as having 'rights of custody' without the benefit of any court order or official custodial status. *Re B* was relied upon by Cazalet J in *Re O (Abduction: Custody Rights)*[199] to hold that German grandparents who had been exclusively looking after the child in question for over 12 months before the mother took the child to England had 'rights of custody' for the purposes of Art 3.

However, as Hale J observed in *Re W; Re B (Child Abduction: Unmarried Father)*,[200] the recognition of these so-called 'inchoate rights' as being within Arts 3 and 5 is hard to reconcile with the House of Lords' decision in *Re J (A Minor) (Abduction: Custody Rights)*.[201] A distinguishing factor of *Re B* and *Re O* was that, unlike *Re J*, the applicant was exercising responsibility either alone or with someone who did not have custodial rights. At any rate, the Central Authority takes the view that on the basis of *Re J* 'de facto joint custody is not enough'.[202] This is also the view of Munby J who, in *Re C (Child Abduction)(Unmarried Father: Rights of Custody)*,[203] concluded that the authorities show that there can be circumstances in which an unmarried father will acquire rights of custody even if he is not the sole primary carer of the child and even if he is sharing care with another person *other* than the mother. But that is as far as the authorities go and to go any further would be inconsistent with *Re J*. In *Re G (Abduction: Rights of Custody)*[204] a paternal grandmother was held to have acquired rights of custody by virtue of a long-term placement (which had subsisted for over a year before the child's removal) coupled with a right to make decisions for the child. In the same case the unmarried father was held to share those rights by virtue of living with his mother (the grandmother) and the child for four months. However, it can be a matter of fine judgment as whether even de factor sole carer of a child will be sufficient to vest rights of custody. In *Re J (Abduction: Acquiring Custody Rights By Caring For Child)*,[205] for example, it was held that a father's short-term care of a child in Greece while the mother was working in England in an effort to rescue the family's financial position did not give him rights of custody, since on the facts the mother had neither abandoned her child nor delegated her role while she was of necessity abroad solely to sort out the family's finances.

Although it seems inevitable that in the light of the development of inchoate rights *Re J* will at some point have to be revisited not least to make it child centred rather than adult centred, there is in fact no consistent international view on the meaning of rights of custody. Thus while the inchoate rights concept has been accepted in New Zealand[206] it has not, for example, been accepted in Ireland.[207]

---

[198] Peter Gibson LJ dissented on this point, while Staughton LJ appeared to hold that the applicant's 'right of custody' arose out of an agreement made with the mother.

[199] [1997] 2 FLR 702.   [200] [1998] 2 FLR 146 at 155. See also *Practice Note*, above.

[201] Above.   [202] *Practice Note*, above.

[203] [2002] EWHC 2219 (Fam), [2003] 1 FLR 252. See also *Re F (Abduction: Unmarried Father: Sole Carer)* [2002] EWHC 2896 (Fam), [2003] 1 FLR 839, and *Re H (Child Abduction)(Unmarried Father: Rights of Custody)* [2003] EWHC 492 (Fam), [2003] 2 FLR 153.

[204] [2002] 2 FLR 703.   [205] [2005] 2 FLR 791.   [206] *Anderson v Paterson* [2003] NZFLR 641.

[207] *HI v MG (Child Abduction: Wrongful Removal)* [2000] IR 110.

It is one thing to argue that de facto care amounts to rights of custody but quite another to suggest that rights of access do so. As Hale J observed in *S v H (Abduction: Access Rights)*,[208] the Convention draws a distinction between 'rights of custody' and 'rights of access' and the court should be reluctant to allow the latter to metamorphose into the former. In that case an unmarried mother with sole custody of her son who came lawfully to England was held not to have acted in breach of the father's 'rights of custody', since he had no parental authority and the access order in his favour did not entitle him to prevent the mother taking the child out of the jurisdiction. A similar result obtained in *Re V-B (Abduction: Custody Rights)*[209] in which it was held that an access order coupled with a right to be consulted on where the child should reside but without a power of veto was insufficient to vest the father with rights of custody. In contrast, in *Re P (A Child)(Abduction: Custody Rights)*[210] it was held that a ne exeat clause (i.e. a clause forbidding removal from the jurisdiction) in a New York order was sufficient to give the father (who otherwise only had visitation rights) a 'right to custody' regardless of whether the New York State or Federal Law so regarded it.[211]

Rights of custody vested in a court. Since it was first mooted by Lord Donaldson MR in *Re C (A Minor)(Abduction)*,[212] it has been accepted in a number of jurisdictions[213] that pending proceedings can give rise to a right of custody in the court seised of them. The leading English case is *Re H (A Minor)(Abduction: Rights of Custody)*[214] which involved a child's removal from Ireland to England by her mother during her father's application to be appointed as the child's guardian and for defined access. That application was adjourned by consent with access to the father being agreed but the mother subsequently took the child to England without the father's consent. The House of Lords, agreeing with the Court of Appeal, held that on the facts of this case the removal was in breach of rights of custody vested in the court, since the application for guardianship raised the issue of custody within the meaning of the Convention. What *Re H* establishes, at any rate in general terms, is that before a court can have rights of custody for these purposes the application before it must itself raise a question of custody within the meaning of the Convention. Conversely, an application that in substance only seeks the determination of contact is not sufficient to vest 'rights of custody'.[215] Even then, the mere issue of proceedings is insufficient; they must

---

[208] [1998] Fam 49, [1997] 3 WLR 1086.

[209] [1999] 2 FLR 192, CA. Note also *Hunter v Murrow (Abduction: Rights of Custody)* [2005] EWCA Civ 976, [2005] 2 FLR 1119 in which regular access constituting substantial intermittent possession and care, was not enough to constitute 'rights of custody'.

[210] [2004] EWCA Civ 971, [2005] Fam 293.

[211] It is a matter of some controversy as to whether a ne exeat clause attached to an access order ipso facto confers rights of custody. The American view, see *Croll v Croll* 239 F3d 133 (2d Cir 2000) and *Gonzalez v Gutierrez* 9th Cir No 02–55079 is that it does not but there seems no universal view on this. For a discussion of this issue see L Silberman 'Patching Up the Abduction Convention', op cit at 45 and M Weiner 'Navigating the Road Between Uniformity and Progress: The Need for Purposive Analysis of The Hague Convention on the Civil Aspects of International Child Abduction' (2002) 33 Colum Hum Rts L Rev 275.

[212] [1989] 1 FLR 403.

[213] See eg *Secretary, AG's Department v TS* [2000] Fam CA 1692 (Australia); *Thomson v Thomson* [1994] 3 SCR 551 (Canada); *HI v MG (Child Abduction: Wrongful Removal)* [2000] IR 110 (Ireland); *Re Olson v Olson* 1994 FP 37/94 (New Zealand) and *Seroka v Bellah* 1995 SLT 204 (Scotland)—all cited by Lowe, Everall and Nicholls, op cit at 14.67.

[214] [2000] 2 AC 291, HL.   [215] See *Re V-B (Abduction: Custody Rights)*, above.

at least be served (this is perhaps open to argument in the case of wardship proceedings)[216] and possibly be actively pursued.

Actual exercise of rights of custody

Article 3(b) requires that at the time of the removal or retention, the rights of custody 'were actually exercised either jointly or alone or would have been but for the removal or retention'. In *Re H; Re S (Abduction: Custody Rights)*[217] Lord Brandon considered that the provision should be construed widely meaning that the custodial parent in maintaining the stance and attitude of such a parent. Consequently a parent who consents to his child travelling or living abroad for a period is not only exercising rights of custody when giving that permission but is still doing so while the child is away.[218]

A similarly wide and purposive approach is evident from the decisions that imprisonment or hospitalisation does not in itself suspend rights of custody or their actual exercise.[219]

A potential problem is the relationship between Art 3(b) and Art 13(a) under which a return may be refused if the applicant 'is not actually exercising custody rights at the time of removal or retention'.[220] As we discuss below,[221] there is a similar problem about whether to deal with consent under Art 3 or Art 13(a) and in that context it is now settled that it should generally be dealt with under Art 13. It is suggested that a similar resolution be applied to the Art 3(b)/Art 13(a) conundrum.

When removals or retentions are wrongful

Normally, a wrongful removal or retention will be in breach of someone else's rights, but it has been accepted by the English courts that a removal or retention is 'wrongful' if it is in breach of custody rights vested in a court,[222] or even of the defendant's own rights.[223]

While it is clearly 'wrongful' if the removal is contrary to an express court order,[224] it is also 'wrongful' if the removal is prohibited according to the general law of the jurisdiction from where the child was taken.[225] Similarly, it is 'wrongful' to retain a child beyond the time allowed by a court or beyond the period agreed by the parties. In *Re S (Minors) (Abduction: Wrongful Retention)*[226] it was held that retention of a child *before* the expiry of

---

[216] It is long established jurisprudence (see Ch 16) that once a child becomes a ward of court no important step can be taken in the child's life, including taking the child out of the jurisdiction, without the court's consent, which would on the face of it seem to vest rights of custody in the court. But in the Court of Appeal in *Re H* (see [2000] 1 FLR 201 at 211) Thorpe LJ clearly signalled that mere issue of wardship proceedings was insufficient and Lord Mackay in the House of Lords seemed to agree.

[217] [1991] 2 AC 476 at 500–501.

[218] See eg *W v W (Child Abduction: Acquiescence)* [1993] 2 FLR 211 and in New Zealand, see *Ryan v Phelps* NZFLR 865.

[219] *Re L (A Child)* [2005] EWHC 1237 (Fam), [2006] 1 FLR 892, *Re A (Abduction: Rights of Custody Imprisonment)* [2004] 1 FLR 1, (imprisonment) and in Scotland, *S v S* 2003 SLT 344 (hospitalisation).

[220] Discussed below at p 650.   [221] See p 644.   [222] See above.

[223] *Re H (A Minor) (Abduction)* [1990] 2 FLR 439 ('wrongful' for a parent with interim custody in her favour to remove the child from the jurisdiction).

[224] *Re C (A Minor) (Abduction)* [1989] 1 FLR 403, CA.

[225] *C v C (Minors) (Child Abduction)* [1992] 1 FLR 163.

[226] [1994] Fam 70, per Wall J. See also *H v H (Child Abduction: Stay of Domestic Proceedings)* [1994] 1 FLR 530 in which Thorpe J held that a similar position obtained from the unilateral abandonment of an agreement to be in England for an unspecified period.

the agreed period was wrongful when the mother had announced her intention never to return the child. According to Wall J in *Re S*, a retention becomes wrongful from the time the parent abandons the intention to honour the agreement.[227]

The Central Authority takes the view[228] that disobedience to a chasing order (ie an order requiring a child's return) made after an otherwise lawful removal can only constitute a 'wrongful retention' for the purposes of the Convention provided the child is still habitually resident in England and Wales when the chasing order was made.

'Wrongful' removal and state immunity. It has been held[229] that the return of a government diplomat and his family in compliance with a direct order of his employing government was 'an act of a governmental nature and therefore subject to state immunity from legal process'. Accordingly, such a removal could not be considered 'wrongful' for the purposes of the Hague Convention.

'Wrongful' removal and the issue of consent. As Holman J pointed out in *Re C (Abduction Consent)*,[230] it can plausibly be said that a removal or retention cannot be 'wrongful' if done with the consent of the other party. In his view, however, such an argument cannot be made under the Hague Convention, since the issue of consent is specifically dealt with under Art 13(a) (discussed below) as providing an exception to the obligation to order the child's return. In *Re O (Abduction: Consent and Acquiescence)*[231] Bennett J disagreed with Holman J insofar as he was implying that the issue of consent must always be dealt with under Art 13(a). In his view, whether consent comes within Art 3 or Art 13(a) depends on the facts. As he put it:[232]

'If the "non-removing" parent asserts or effectively has to concede that on the face of it he gave his consent, but asserts that it is vitiated by deceit or threats or some other vitiating factor, which he must raise in order to establish that his consent was no true consent, then the matter falls to be dealt with under Art 3. If, on the other hand, the very fact of consent is in issue, as it was in *Re C*, then the matter comes within Art 13(a) and the burden falls upon the person who asserts consent to prove it.'

In *Re P (A Child)(Abduction: Custody Rights)*[233] however, the Court of Appeal upheld Holman J's view. As Ward LJ put it.

'If the giving of consent prior to the removal had the effect that the removal could never be classified as wrongful or in breach of the right of custody then there would be no need for Art 13 at all ... The Policy of the Convention is to protect children internationally from the harmful effects of their wrongful removal or retention. If a child is removed in prima facie breach of a right of custody, then it makes better sense to require the removing parent to justify the removal and establish that the removal was with consent rather than require

---

[227] Contrast the view of Sir Michael Kerr in *Re AZ (A Minor) (Abduction: Acquiescence)* [1993] 1 FLR 682 at 689D who doubted whether an uncommunicated decision to abandon an agreement could constitute a wrongful retention.

[228] *Practice Note*, above.   [229] *Re P (Diplomatic Immunity: Jurisdiction)* [1998] 1 FLR 1026.

[230] [1996] 1 FLR 414 at 417.   [231] [1997] 1 FLR 924.

[232] Ibid at 940. In *T v T (Child Abduction: Consent)* [1999] 2 FLR 912, Charles J disagreed with Bennett's 'ingenious reasoning' and preferred Holman J's analysis.

[233] [2004] EWCA Civ 971, [2005] 293 at [33]. For the implications of this ruling with regard to the application of Art 11 of the revised Brussels II Regulation, see below p 665.

the claimant, asserting the wrongfulness of the removal, to prove that he or she did not consent.'

(c) Declarations [234]

Article 15 permits the judicial or administrative authorities of a Contracting State to request from the authorities of the State of the child's habitual residence a declaration that the removal or retention was 'wrongful' within the meaning of Art 3. Although Art 15 can apparently also be used to obtain a ruling as to what domestic law rights were enjoyed by the applicant before the removal or retention, in *Hunter v Murrow (Abduction: Rights of Custody)*,[235] the Court of Appeal cautioned against making such requests particularly if they are solely for determinations of so-called Convention questions, namely, whether removals or retentions are 'wrongful'.

Applicants in England and Wales seeking a declaration must do so under the Child Abduction and Custody Act 1985, s 8. Applications must be made to the High Court. The section is drafted in wide terms and a declaration can properly be made at the request of any person appearing to the court to have an interest in the matter and notwithstanding the pendency of other proceedings in another Contracting State determining the child's habitual residence, provided it would serve some useful purpose and not simply delay proceedings.[236] It is no objection that the person seeking the declaration is no longer living in England and Wales.[237]

Declarations are discretionary remedies and may be refused if they can make no contribution towards, or might delay or otherwise impede, the application for a return order.[238] Since of necessity, when considering applications for a declaration the requesting State will have to consider matters which may be contested in the proceedings in the requesting State,[239] they can be no more than persuasive and cannot bind the parties or the authorities of the requested State, who can accept as much or as little of the judgment as they choose.[240]

(d) Who can invoke the Convention

Article 8 provides that '*any* person, institution or other body claiming that a child has been removed or retained in breach of custody rights' (emphasis added) may apply for the child's return. Hence, although commonly applicants are individuals having 'rights of custody' or 'rights of access', it would seem that *any* person (including possibly the child himself, if old enough), institution or body (eg local authorities or courts) may seek assistance provided it can be shown that the child's removal or retention is 'wrongful' within the meaning of Art 3.[241]

---

[234] See generally Lowe, Everall and Nicholls, op cit, ch 15.

[235] [2005] EWCA Civ 976, [2005] 2 FLR 1119.

[236] *Re P (Abduction: Declaration)* [1995] 1 FLR 831.

[237] *Re L (Children)(Abduction: Declaration)* [2001] 2 FCR 1.

[238] See eg *Re P (Diplomatic Immunity: Jurisdiction)* [1998] 1 FLR 1026—declaration refused when it could make no contribution to proceedings in the USA in which the issue was whether the children should live with their American father or in Germany with their German mother.

[239] See eg *Re P (Abduction: Declaration)* above, where habitual residence was in issue.

[240] See *Hunter v Murrow* above, at [27], per Thorpe LJ.

[241] According to the 2003 Statistical Survey, op cit, about 4% of applications are made by non-parents.

(e) Seeking a child's return

The general procedure

A person claiming that a child has been taken to or detained in another contracting state, and who wishes to secure the child's return, can seek assistance from the Central Authority of the child's habitual residence or from the authority of the state to which the child has been taken. Direct application may be made to the judicial or administrative authorities of a contracting state. Applicants would normally be best advised to apply via their own Central Authority.

Under Art 8 applications should contain:

(a) information concerning the identity of the applicant, of the child and of the person alleged to have removed or retained the child;

(b) where available, the date of birth of the child;

(c) the grounds on which the applicant's claim for return of the child is based;

(d) all available information relating to the whereabouts of the child and the identity of the person with whom the child is presumed to be.

An application may be supplemented inter alia by an authenticated copy of any relevant decision or agreement. In the case of wardship it is helpful to supply evidence of the court's permission to apply under the Convention.

Upon receiving the relevant documents the Central Authority will transmit the application to the appropriate Central Authority (Art 9) in another Contracting State which must then take steps to discover the child's whereabouts and seek the child's return. The authorities must act expeditiously. If no decision has been reached within six weeks of the commencement of proceedings, the requesting Central Authority or the applicant has the right to request a statement of the reasons for delay (Art 11).[242] The Central Authority may refuse an application where it is manifest that the requirements of the Convention are not fulfilled or that the application is not well founded (Art 27).[243]

The court's role

To facilitate the child's return, application may be made to a judicial or administrative authority of the requested state. However, if the issue goes to a court, that court is forbidden by Art 16 from investigating the merits of the rights to custody until it has been determined that the child is not to be returned under the Convention or unless the application has not been lodged within a reasonable time following receipt of the notice.[244] Equally, a decision to return the child is not to be taken to be a determination on the merits of any custody

---

[242] It will be noted that this provision stops short of directing States to resolve return applications within six weeks. However, there *is* a six week *obligation* imposed by Art 11(3) of the revised Brussels II Regulations, see further below p 667.

[243] According to the 2003 Statistical Survey, op cit, the English child abduction unit rejected 6% of applications as against a global average of 6%.

[244] Effectively this freezes any prior applications, including, in England and Wales, any residence order or wardship applications: s 9 and s 27 of the Child Abduction and Custody Act 1985.

issue (Art 19). So far as England and Wales is concerned all Convention applications are dealt with by the High Court.[245]

Under the Child Abduction and Custody Act 1985, s 5, once an application has been made to the court, such interim directions may be given as the court thinks fit 'for the purpose of securing the welfare of the child concerned or of preventing changes in the circumstances relevant to the determination of the application'. Exercising this power, it has been held appropriate to authorise the Tipstaff to collect the child and return him to the applicant, even before the child's arrival in the jurisdiction[246] and, in circumstances when all other alternative arrangements have been considered and found wanting, and notwithstanding the statutory scheme under the Children Act 1989, to make arrangements to place the child with a local authority.[247] Interim directions may also include orders for electronic tagging[248] and for direct or indirect contact.

By Art 12 the court is directed, if the application is brought within one year of the removal, to 'order the return of the child forthwith'. If more than a year has elapsed, the child should still be returned 'unless it is demonstrated that the child is now settled in its new environment'. Article 12, however, is subject to Art 13, which provides for exceptional circumstances (outlined below) in which a return may be refused. The burden of establishing these exceptions lies on the defendant. The Convention provides, via Art 20, an additional ground for refusing a return where to do so 'would not be permitted by the fundamental principles of the requested State relating to the protection of human rights and fundamental freedoms'. However, the United Kingdom has not implemented Art 20 in part because its meaning and scope 'would at least be uncertain, in part because it could not "be easily accommodated in a UK legal text' and in part because in any event situations triggering Art 20 would probably be covered by Arts 12 and 13.[249] In fact, global use of this exception is extremely limited.[250]

The normal expectation is that the court will order the child's return. Accordingly it is hard to establish an exception. It has been held, for example, to be no defence that legal representation may not be available in the state to which the child is to be returned nor that such an order would mean the separation of the child and her care-giving mother.[251]

---

[245] Child Abduction and Custody Act 1985 s 4; by contrast, in a number of other jurisdictions (eg Germany and USA) jurisdiction is vested in courts at the lowest level. Some, like Germany and France, have changed their system to reduce the number of courts competent to hear Hague cases, see respectively N Lowe, S Armstrong and A Mathias *Country Report: Germany* (NCMEC 2002) and N Lowe, S Armstrong, A Mathias and M Navarro *Country Report: France* (NCMEC 2002).

[246] *Re N (Child Abduction: Jurisdiction)* [1995] Fam 95.

[247] *Re C (Abduction: Interim Directions: Accommodation by Local Authority)* [2003] EWHC 3065 (Fam), [2004] 1 FLR 653.

[248] In which case representatives of the parties should contact the Office of the President to assist in making enquiries and arrangements: *Re C,* above.

[249] See Lord Hailsham LC in the debate on the Child Abduction and Custody Bill in Hansard HL Deb Vol 461 at col 1175. But had the 1985 Act followed rather than preceded the Human Rights Act 1998, there would have been no reason not to incorporate Art 20, see *Re J (A Child)(Custody Rights: Jurisdiction)* [2005] UKHL 40, [2005] 3 WLR 14 at [44] per Baroness Hale. For a detailed discussion of Art 20 see Lowe, Everall and Nicholls, op cit, at 17.86 et seq.

[250] According to the 1999 statistical survey no application was refused on this ground and according to the 2003 survey there were four such refusals, all in Chile. For an argument that it should be used more often see M Weiner 'Strengthening Article 20' (2004) 38 Univ of San Francisco Law Review 701, summarised at [2005] IFL 209.

[251] *Re K (Abduction: Psychological Harm)* [1995] 2 FLR 550, CA.

Even if an exception is established, the court still has a discretion to order a return under Art 18.[252] It is conceivable that a child's return might be successfully opposed on grounds *outside* the terms of Art 12 or Art 13, but the court is likely to be reluctant to undermine the spirit of the Convention.[253]

Although there is understandably voluminous case law on the application of the exceptions, it is to be emphasised that globally, judicial refusals are comparatively unusual. According to the 1999 and 2003 Statistical Surveys,[254] only 11% and 12% respectively of return applications ended in a judicial refusal to return.

If a return is ordered,[255] then any other custody order ceases to have effect, but if a return is refused then, unless the revised Brussels II Regulation applies, the court can hear any other application upon its merits.[256]

It remains now to consider the application of the exceptions under Art 12 and Art 13 as interpreted by the English courts.

The application of Article 12 where the commencement of proceedings is more than 12 months after the wrongful removal or retention

Where the commencement of proceedings is more than 12 months after the wrongful removal or retention, Art 12 provides that a return should still be ordered 'unless it is demonstrated that the child is now settled in its new environment'. The deliberate concealment of a child does not stop the year's time running. As Thorpe LJ said in *Cannon v Cannon*[257]

'I would not support a tolling rule that the period gained by concealment should be disregarded and therefore subtracted from the total period of delay in order to ascertain whether or not the 12-month mark has been exceeded. That seems to me to be too crude an approach which risks to produce results that offend what is still the pursuit of a realistic Hague Convention outcome.'

If the child returns to the state of habitual residence only to be removed again then, for the purposes of Art 12, time begins to run from the date of the second removal.[258]

In *Re N (Minors) (Abduction)*[259] Bracewell J held that 'now' refers to the date of the commencement of proceedings and not the date of the hearing; that 'settled' involves both a physical element in the sense of relating to or being established in a community and an emotional constituent denoting security; and that 'new environment' encompasses place, home, school, people, friends, activities and opportunities but not, per se, the relationship with the parent. With regard to the meaning of 'settled' Thorpe J said in *Re M (A Minor)*

---

[252] See below p 662.

[253] *In Re B (Minors) (Abduction)* [1993] 1 FLR 988, for example, the court rejected an application to have proceedings stayed or dismissed because of the applicant's active participation in the respondent's English family proceedings.

[254] Op cit.

[255] The practice of the English courts is to return the child to the state of his habitual residence and not to the person: *B v K (Child Abduction)* [1993] 1 FCR 382, per Johnson J and *Re A (A Minor) (Abduction)* [1988] 1 FLR 365 at 373 per Nourse J.

[256] Child Abduction and Custody Act 1985 s 25 and Art 16. 'Custody orders' include s 8 orders under the Children Act 1989: Child Abduction and Custody Act 1985 Sch 3. The revised Brussels II Regulation is discussed below at p 664.

[257] [2004] EWCA CIV 1330, [2005] 1 WLR 32 at [51].

[258] *Re S (Child Abduction: Delay)* [1998] 1 FLR 651.   [259] [1991] 1 FLR 413.

(Abduction: Acquiescence)[260] that 'any survey of the degree of settlement of the child must give weight to emotional and psychological, as well as to physical settlement'. On the facts he considered that a four-year-old who had been brought to this country 15 months previously was now settled in his new environment. This approach has now been firmly endorsed by the Court of Appeal in *Cannon v Cannon*[261] in which Thorpe LJ concluded, after a thorough review of both domestic and international authority, that 'it is not enough to regard only the physical characteristics of settlement. Equal regard must be paid to the emotional and psychological elements'.

Although deliberate concealment and subterfuge by the abductor cannot, ipso facto, prevent there being 'settlement', as Thorpe LJ has put it in *Cannon v Cannon*:[262] 'the burden of demonstrating the necessary elements of emotional and psychological settlement is much increased. The judges of the Family Division . . . should look critically at any alleged settlement that is built on concealment and deceit especially if the defendant is a fugitive from criminal justice.' Indeed in Thorpe LJ's view 'it will be very difficult indeed for a parent who has hidden the child away to demonstrate that it is settled in its new environment'. However, at the remitted hearing[263] Kirkwood J did find the girl in question to be 'settled'.

Cannon, overruling Singer J at first instance,[264] also establishes that even if 'settlement' is established the court retains a discretion nevertheless to order the child's return.[265] However, at the remitted hearing, Kirkwood J, having accepted that the greater the degree of turpitude the more unwilling the court should be to decline to order a return, nevertheless in the light of evidence painting 'a clear and compelling picture' of a happy, successful, stable, settled and flourishing child who was settled in every sense, declined to order her return.

Failure to conduct Convention proceedings with proper diligence and speed may entitle the court to strike the application out.[266]

The application of Article 13(a)[267]

Under Art 13(a) the authority may refuse to order the child's return if it is shown that the person, institution or other body having the care of the person of the child was not actually exercising the custody rights at the time of removal or retention, or has consented to or subsequently acquiesced in the removal or retention. Refusals based on the non-exercise of custody rights are relatively unusual.[268] Indeed, there is no reported English example of a

---

260 [1996] 1 FLR 315 at 321.

261 Ibid at [61]. For a review of some Commonwealth jurisdictions' discussions see J Caldwell 'Child welfare defences in child abduction cases—some recent developments' [2001] CLFQ 121 at 133–4.

262 Ibid at [61].

263 Reported as *Re C (Abduction: Settlement)(No 2)* [2005] 1 FLR 938.

264 Reported as *Re C (Abduction: Settlement)* [2004] EWHC 1245 (Fam), [2005] 1 FLR 127.

265 See the discussion below at p 662.

266 See eg *Re G (Abduction: Striking Out Application)* [1995] 2 FLR 410, per Connell J. Alternatively, the court can exercise its discretion not to return the child provided, at any rate, an exception under Art 13 (see below) can first be established: *Re S*, above.

267 See Lowe, Everall and Nicholls, op cit, at 17.36 et seq.

268 According to the 1999 and 2003 statistical surveys, op cit, globally, there were only three cases in each year of refusals being solely resting on this ground, but with respectively a further one and six relying on this ground in conjunction with another.

refusal being so based. It has been held that being imprisoned[269] or hospitalised[270] does not mean that for these purposes the left behind parent is not exercising rights of custody.

In practice the two most common applications of Art 13(a) are in relation to consent and acquiescence. Even so, according to the 1999 and 2003 surveys[271] globally, there were only four refusals in each year *solely* based on consent (although a further eight and 10 refusals respectively relying upon this ground in conjunction with another) and only four refusals in 1999 and two in 2003 relying solely on acquiescence (with respectively a further two and three relying on this ground in conjunction with another).[272]

Although often pleaded in the alternative, consent and acquiescence are mutually exclusive. As Lord Donaldson MR put it in *Re A (Minors)(Abduction: Custody Rights)*,[273] the difference between the two 'is simply one of timing. Consent, if it occurs, precedes the wrongful taking or retention. Acquiescence, if it occurs, follows it.'

As with all defences the burden of proof lies on the person seeking to invoke it.[274] With regard to consent, as Waite LJ put it in *Re B (A Minor) (Abduction)*:[275]

'. . . the only starting-point that can be stated with reasonable certainty is that the courts of the requested State are unlikely to regard as valid a consent that has been obtained through a calculated and deliberate fraud on the part of the absconding parent'.

In *Re W (Abduction: Procedure)*,[276] Wall J considered that to establish consent the evidence needs to be clear and compelling, which in his Lordship's view means that the evidence normally needs to be in writing or evidenced by documentary material. Accordingly, a parent must establish the defence 'on the face of the documentation' since, if he cannot do so, 'oral evidence is unlikely to affect the issue and will not be entertained'. However, in *Re C (Abduction: Consent)*[277] Holman J, while agreeing that the evidence needs to be clear and cogent, took issue with Wall J over the need for writing. As he pointed out, 'Article 13 does not use the words "in writing", and parents do not necessarily expect to reduce their agreements and understandings about their children to writing, even at the time of marital breakdown'. In his view it is sufficient that the defence is clearly established. He also disagreed with Wall J that consent had to be 'positive' if that meant 'express'. In Holman J's view it is possible in an appropriate case to infer consent from conduct. In *Re K (Abduction: Consent)*[278] Hale J, preferring Holman J's views on both counts to those of Wall J, said that while it was obvious that consent must be real, positive and unequivocal, it

---

[269] See *Re A (Abduction: Rights of Custody: Imprisonment)* [2004] 1 FLR 1 and *Re L (A Child)* [2005] EWHC 1237 (Fam), [2005] Fam Law 90.

[270] See the Scottish decision, *S v S*, 2003 SLT 344.   [271] Op cit.

[272] In England and Wales one application made in 2003 was refused on the basis of consent and one on acquiescence.

[273] [1992] Fam 106 at 123.

[274] The standard of proof is on the balance of probabilities, though the evidence needs to be 'cogent' (as understood in the light of Lord Nicholls' judgment in *Re H (Minors)(Sexual Abuse: Standard of Proof)* [1986] AC 563 (discussed below at p 744): see *Re H (Abduction: Habitual Residence: Consent)* [2000] 2 FLR 294 at 301, per Holman J.

[275] [1994] 2 FLR 249 at 261, CA.   [276] [1995] 1 FLR 878.

[277] [1996] 1 FLR 414 at 418 and 419. For other examples of consent see *Re K (Abduction: Consent: Forum Conveniens)* [1995] 2 FLR 211, CA and *Re D (Abduction: Acquiescence)* [1998] 2 FLR 335, CA; cf *Re R (Minors) (Abduction)* [1994] 1 FLR 190.

[278] [1997] 2 FLR 212. See also Hale J in *P v P (Abduction: Acquiescence)* [1998] 1 FLR 630 at 633, not commented upon on appeal (see [1998] Fam Law 512, CA).

did not necessarily have to be in writing. She further held that once given (and acted upon) it cannot subsequently be withdrawn by the parent who gave it subsequently thinking better of it. Wall J has now reconsidered his view and accepts Holman J's analysis.[279]

The leading case on the meaning of 'acquiescence' under Art 13 is *Re H (Minors) (Abduction: Acquiescence)*,[280] in which the House of Lords abandoned previous attempts to distinguish between active and passive acquiescence,[281] holding that instead a common approach was to be applied in all cases. That approach was summarised by Lord Browne-Wilkinson to be as follows:[282]

'(1) For the purposes of Article 13 of the convention, the question whether the wronged parent has "acquiesced" in the removal or retention of the child depends upon his actual state of mind. As Neill LJ said in *Re S (Minors) (Abduction: Acquiescence)* [1994] 1 FLR 819 at 838: "... the court is primarily concerned, not with the question of the other parent's perception of the applicant's conduct, but with the question whether the applicant acquiesced in fact."

(2) The subjective intention of the wronged parent is a question of fact for the trial judge to determine in all the circumstances of the case, the burden of proof being on the abducting parent.

(3) The trial judge, in reaching his decision on that question of fact, will no doubt be inclined to attach more weight to the contemporaneous words and actions of the wronged parent than to the bare assertions in evidence of his intention. But that is a question of the weight to be attached to evidence and is not a question of law.

(4) There is only one exception. Where the words or actions of the wronged parent clearly and unequivocally show and have led the other parent to believe that the wronged parent is not asserting or going to assert his right to the summary return of the child and are inconsistent with such return, justice requires that the wronged parent be held to have acquiesced.'

In other words, unless the defendant can prove to the court's satisfaction that the applicant clearly acquiesced, the defence can succeed only if it can be brought within the 'exceptional' category.

Following *Re H* the first question a court must settle is whether looking at the subjective mind of the wrongful person after the child's removal he or she had in fact acquiesced or 'gone along' with that removal. A good example is *Re M (Abduction)(Consent: Acquiescence)*[283] in which a father, knowing his wife intended a permanent removal, took the line that she would do as she wished (he assumed that she would not manage on her own in England and would therefore return to Greece) and did not change his attitude after the removal in July until the following February. He was held to have acquiesced. Similarly, in *Re D (Abduction: Acquiescence)*[284] the court had no difficulty in finding acquiescence where

---

[279] See *Re M (Abduction)(Consent: Acquiescence)* [1999] 1 FLR 171.

[280] [1998] AC 72, HL. See R Bailey Harris (1997) 113 LQR 529 and D McClean 'International child abduction—some recent trends' (1997) 9 CFLQ 387 at 395–8.

[281] First established in *Re A (Minors) (Abduction: Custody Rights)* [1992] Fam 106, CA and inter alia in *Re AZ (A Minor) (Abduction: Acquiescence)* [1993] 1 FLR 682, CA and *Re S (Minors) (Abduction: Acquiescence)* [1994] 1 FLR 819.

[282] Ibid at 90.   [283] [1999] 1 FLR 171

[284] [1998] 2 FLR 335, CA. Cf *Re B (Minors)(Acquiescence)* [1993] 1 FLR 988—merely entering an appearance in the abductor's court application is not in itself acquiescence.

the applicant had genuinely agreed to the making of a residence order in favour of the abducting parent and intended to return (in this case to Wales) to live near the children.

Re D was notable in that the father was found to have acquiesced even though he mistakenly thought that the Hague Convention did not apply to his case. This case raises the general issue of the extent to which knowledge of the wrongfulness of the act is relevant to the issue of acquiescence. According to Butler-Sloss LJ in *Re S (Abduction: Acquiescence)*[285] while knowledge of the facts and that the act of removal or retention is wrongful will normally be necessary, to expect the applicant necessarily to have knowledge of the rights which can be enforced under the Convention is to set too high a standard. In that case, seeking contact and not a summary return of the child after being given adequate and realistic advice, but not being fully informed of his rights under the Convention, was held to amount to acquiescence.

Each case has to be assessed on its own facts but absence of court action does not necessarily indicate acquiescence,[286] though delay in taking any action can be so indicative.[287] In *Re H* itself, it was held that the father, who was an Orthodox Jew, had not acquiesced in the children's removal from Israel to England merely by obeying the instruction of his local Beth Din to ignore English proceedings brought by the mother.

The fact that the applicant has applied for custody in the State of the child's habitual residence is a strong indication that there has been no acquiescence,[288] though there is nothing necessarily inconsistent with acquiescing in a current state of affairs and applying for the child's care and control at a later date.[289]

Although in principle acquiescence can be evidenced by written statements, it is well established that they must be written in clear and unambiguous terms.[290] Extracting a single and ambiguous sentence from a four page letter, for example, will not be enough to establish acquiescence.[291] Furthermore, in Lord Browne-Wilkinson's view, the clear and unequivocal conduct that brings the case within the exception is not normally to be found in passing remarks or letters written by a parent who has recently suffered the trauma of the removal of his children.

Clearly, the most difficult part of *Re H* is that which relates to the 'exception'. According to Lord Browne-Wilkinson, one example is *Re AZ (A Minor) (Abduction: Acquiescence)*,[292] in which a mother, with the father's consent, took their child from Germany (where the father was stationed with the US Air Force) to England to stay with her family. Once there the mother decided not to return. She left her son with her sister and the father asked her to look after him until he could come to England a little later. However, before his arrival

---

[285] [1998] 2 FLR 115 at 122, CA.

[286] *Re F (A Minor) (Child Abduction)* [1992] 1 FLR 548, CA. See also *Re R (Minors) (Abduction)* [1994] 1 FLR 190 (delay inter alia because of legal advice to await the outcome of domestic proceedings in France and because of the subsequent 'deplorable' delay in the French Central Authority's communication with the English Central Authority) and *Re S (Minors) (Abduction: Acquiescence)* [1994] 1 FLR 819, CA (delay due to erroneous legal advice).

[287] See eg *W v W (Child Abduction: Acquiescence)* [1993] 2 FLR 211 (father's inactivity for some 10 months after learning of his wife's decision not to return held to amount to acquiescence).

[288] *Re A (Minors) Abduction* [1991] 2 FLR 241, CA.

[289] *Re A Z (A Minor)(Abduction: Acquiescence)* [1993] 1 FLR 682.

[290] See eg *Re A (Minors) (Abduction: Custody Rights)*, above. Indeed, such clear statements can come within Lord Browne-Wilkinson's 'exceptional category'.

[291] Per Millett LJ in *Re R (Child Abduction: Acquiescence)* [1995] 1 FLR 716 at 733.   [292] Above.

the aunt applied for a residence and prohibited steps order. The father was served with the papers after his arrival in England but he indicated that he would not contest the application. However, some three months later he told the family for the first time that he intended to take the boy back to Germany, though it was not for another six weeks that he finally initiated Convention proceedings. The Court of Appeal held that the father had 'acquiesced'. In Lord Browne-Wilkinson's view[293] Re AZ was what he expected to be a rare example of a case falling into the exceptional category where the wronged parent's conduct is so clear as not to require proof of his subjective intention, ie it was a case 'in which the wronged parent, knowing of his rights, has so conducted himself vis-à-vis the other parent and the children that he cannot be heard to go back on what he has done and seek to persuade the judge that all along he has secretly intended to claim the summary return of the children'. Other examples falling into this exceptional category mentioned by Lord Browne-Wilkinson were[294] the signing of a formal agreement that the child is to remain in the country to which he has been abducted and the active participation in proceedings in the country to which the child has been abducted to determine the child's long-term future. Another example is Re B (Abduction: Acquiescence)[295] where, following his wife's removal of their child to England, the father at first negotiated with her suggesting that he would not oppose her move if the reconciliation he was proposing failed and subsequently deciding to settle in England and seek contact in the English court. It was held notwithstanding his ignorance of the Convention (neither his American nor English lawyers apparently mentioned it to him) that his conduct overall amounted to acquiescence.

On the other hand, as the Court of Appeal held in P v P (Abduction: Acquiescence),[296] merely seeking to compromise a situation by allowing the abducting parent to remain in the country to which he or she has gone, provided that the wronged parent is satisfied as to other matters in issue between them, will not, in the absence of any concluded agreement, be regarded as falling into the 'exceptional category'.

In this case, after the mother had left the father in Cyprus and taken the child to England, the father sought through his lawyer in Cyprus to negotiate a settlement under which the child would reside with his mother in England but have extensive staying contact with him in Cyprus. When these negotiations failed, the father issued Hague Convention proceedings. It was held that in the absence of a concluded agreement the father could not be said to have 'acquiesced' within the meaning of Lord Browne-Wilkinson's 'clear and unequivocal' conduct category. Indeed Ward LJ agreed with Hale J's observation at first instance that:

'... it would be most unfortunate if parents were deterred from seeking to make sensible arrangements, in consequence of what is usually an acknowledged breakdown in the relationship between them, for fear that the mere fact that they are able to contemplate that the child should remain where he has been taken will count against them in these proceedings. Such negotiations are, if anything, to be encouraged'.[297]

It is established that an acquiescence cannot subsequently be withdrawn.[298]

---

[293] [1998] AC 72 at 89F.   [294] Ibid at 89D–E.   [295] [1999] 2 FLR 818.
[296] [1998] 2 FLR 835, CA.   [297] Ibid.
[298] Re A (Minors) (Abduction: Custody Rights) [1992] Fam 106, CA, not commented upon on this point by the House of Lords in Re H, above, and followed in Re S (Abduction: Acquiescence) [1998] 2 FLR 115 at 122, CA per Butler-Sloss LJ.

The application of Article 13(b)

Under Art 13(b) the court may refuse to order the child's return if it is shown that 'there is a grave risk that his or her return would expose the child to physical or psychological harm or otherwise place the child in an intolerable situation'. As the Perez-Vera Report comments,[299] whereas the Art 13(a) exceptions are based on the wronged parent's conduct, Art 13(b) clearly derives from the consideration of the child's interests inasmuch as 'the interest of the child in not being removed from its habitual residence . . . gives way before the primary interest of any person in not being exposed to physical or psychological danger or being placed in an intolerable position'.

Perhaps not surprisingly, Art 13(b) is the most litigated of all the exceptions and, notwithstanding a generally strict interpretation adopted in most jurisdictions (see below) it is the one most often successfully invoked. According to the 1999 and 2003 statistical surveys,[300] globally a fifth of all judicial refusals were based on this ground.

The burden of establishing one of these exceptions is difficult to discharge. As Ward L said in *Re C (Abduction: Grave Risk of Psychological Harm)*,[301] so far as the English courts are concerned there is:

'. . . an established line of authority that the court should require clear and compelling evidence of the grave risk of harm or other intolerability which must be measured as substantial, not trivial, and of a severity which is much more than is inherent in the inevitable disruption, uncertainty and anxiety which follows an unwelcome return to the jurisdiction of the court of habitual residence'.

It has, for example, been held that the risk of physical or psychological harm must be more than an ordinary one, ie weighty, substantial and not trivial.[302] While the epithet 'grave' is and was intended to be an 'intensive qualifier',[303] it is important to appreciate, however, that 'grave' qualifies the risk and not the ensuing harm. As Balcombe LJ observed in *Re E (A Minor)(Abduction)*,[304] the defendant 'does not have to prove that the return of the child would place him in an intolerable situation [nor *mutatis mutandi* "exposing the child to physical or psychological harm"], but that there is a grave risk that his return would place him in an intolerable situation'.

Not only is the burden strict but also in general terms it is wrong to allow the abducting parent to rely upon adverse conditions brought about by a situation which he or she has created by his or her own conduct for as was famously said[305] that would 'drive a coach and four through the Convention . . .'. But as Potter P has pointed out[306] that 'is not a principle articulated in the Convention or the [Child Abduction and Custody Act 1985] and should not be applied to the effective exclusion of the very defence itself which is in terms directed to the questions of risk of harm to the child and not the wrongful conduct of the abducting parent'.

Case law abounds with examples of failed Art 13(b) pleas. In *N v N (Abduction: Article*

---

[299] Op cit at para 29 and see also para 116.

[300] Op cit. No refusal based on Art 13b was made in England and Wales in the 2003 survey, compared with four in the 1999 survey.

[301] [1999] 1 FLR 1145 at 1154, CA.   [302] *Re A (A Minor) (Abduction)* [1988] 1 FLR 365, CA.

[303] See the discussion in the Perez-Vera Report, op cit, at para 116.   [304] [1989] 1 FLR 135 at 143.

[305] Per Butler-Sloss LJ in *C v C (Minor: Abduction: Rights of Custody Abroad)* [1989] 1 WLR 645.

[306] Per Potter P in *S v B (Abduction: Human Rights)* [2005] EWHC 733 (Fam), [2005] 2 FLR 878 at [49].

13 Defence),[307] for example, an allegation of sexual abuse by the applicant was not held sufficient to justify a refusal to return. Similarly in *Re S (Abduction: Return into Care)*[308] the defence failed notwithstanding that there were serious allegations of sexual abuse against the mother's cohabitant because the court accepted that the matter would be adequately dealt with and the child protected by the Swedish authorities upon the child's return. In *Re M (Abduction: Intolerable Situation)*[309] the defence again failed, notwithstanding the mother's genuine fear of physical harm by her husband who, having been imprisoned for murdering someone whom he believed to be having an affair with the mother, was due to be released, since the court again believed that the mother would be adequately protected by the Norwegian authorities to whom mirror undertakings had been given. In *Re K (Abduction: Psychological Harm)*[310] a mother, who contended that as she had no immigration status she would be unable to support herself and would not therefore exercise any possession rights as defined by a Texan court, failed to convince the court that the child would be placed in an intolerable position if ordered to be returned to the USA. In *Re L (Abduction: Pending Criminal Proceedings)*[311] it was held that neither the possibility of criminal proceedings being brought nor even the possibility of the mother being arrested at the airport on her return was enough to establish a grave risk of harm to the children.

In *Re S (Abduction: Intolerable Situation: Beth Din)*[312] Connell J rejected a mother's defence that it was not possible for her to get justice from the religious court in Israel, the Beth Din, and that as a woman she would be discriminated against in Israel since she would be unable to obtain a 'get' without the positive assistance and consent of the father. It has also been held[313] to be wrong to place too much weight on the interests of a child who was not the subject of the Convention.

A harsh example of a court not allowing a defendant to rely upon her own wrongdoing is *Re C (Abduction: Grave Risk of Physical or Psychological Harm)*[314] in which a mother wrongfully removed her six-year-old son together with his 16-year-old half-sister (who was not the subject of the proceedings) from Cyprus. The evidence was that the girl had not been happy in Cyprus, was well settled in England and would refuse to return. The mother pleaded that returning the boy to Cyprus would mean splitting the family, forcing her to choose whether to stay in England with her daughter or to go to Cyprus with her son. Notwithstanding this terrible dilemma, the mother's pleas fell on deaf ears.

Another issue of major concern[315] is the operation of Art 13(b) in the context of domestic violence. The English courts have been reluctant to base refusals to return on allegations of violence. A leading example is *TB v JB (Abduction: Grave Risk of*

---

[307] [1995] 1 FLR 107.   [308] [1999] 1 FLR 843.   [309] [2000] 1 FLR 930.

[310] [1995] 2 FLR 550, CA.

[311] [1999] 1 FLR 433 (but note that the US rules have since been eased through the use of 'Significant Public Benefit Parole'). See also *Re C (Abduction: Grave Risk of Psychological Harm)* [1999] 1 FLR 1145, CA.

[312] [2000] 1 FLR 454.   [313] *Re C (Abduction: Grave Risk of Psychological Harm)*, above.

[314] [1999] 2 FLR 478, CA. For a case involving not a dissimilar dilemma and in which the Art 13(b) plea failed see *S v B (Abduction: Human Rights)* [2005] EWHC 753 (Fam), [2005] 2 FLR 878.

[315] See M Weiner 'International Child Abduction and the Escape from Domestic Violence' (2000) 69 Fordham Law Review 593, M Kaye 'The Hague Convention and the Flight from Domestic Violence: How Women and Children are being Returned by a Coach and Four' (1999) 13 Int Jo of Law, Policy and the Family 191 and C Bruch 'The Unmet Needs of Domestic Violence and Their Children in Hague Abduction Cases' (2004) 38 Fam LQ 529.

Harm).[316] This case was unusual in that the source of the alleged risk to the children in question was not their father, the mother's first husband, but the mother's second husband, the father of her youngest child who was not the subject of the proceedings. The mother, who indisputably had wrongfully removed the three children by her first husband (plus her child by her second husband) from New Zealand to England, claimed that her primary motivation for leaving was to get away from her second husband (against whom there were allegations of maltreatment both of the mother and of the children and of bizarre behaviour) and that she was too frightened to return. The first husband applied for the return of the three elder children but at first instance this was refused under Art 13(b) on the basis of expert evidence that the mother was seriously vulnerable to the anxieties created by the second husband and that she was suffering from mild to moderate depression which would be exacerbated by a return. Accordingly, the children (who were each found to be troubled and upset) would be exposed to harm because the mother would face the same risks as previously and might cease to cope with the pressure that could be placed on her. On appeal, however, by a majority this decision was overruled. In Laws LJ's view, Art 13(b) could only be satisfied in truly exceptional cases of which this was not one. Arden LJ accepted that deterioration of the mother's condition and consequently in her ability to care for her children could be sufficient to satisfy Art 13(b) but she considered that in evaluating such a risk the court was entitled to expect that the mother would make all appropriate use of orders of the New Zealand courts for her and her children's protection. In her Ladyship's view, given the New Zealand court's powers to protect the mother and her children, a 'grave risk' could not be said to have been made out. Dissenting, Hale LJ recognised the vulnerability of victims of domestic abuse and did not believe that on these facts the New Zealand courts could protect the mother and therefore the children and thus an Art 13(b) defence had been made out.[317] Many might agree with this latter standpoint. Furthermore, as we discuss shortly, there have been refusals based on violence.

One final example of the difficulty of succeeding under Art 13(b) is *Re S (Abduction: Custody Rights)*[318] in which a mother claimed that because of the worsening situation in Israel (which was for all intents and purposes at war) she was paralysed with fear at the very thought of returning there and that therefore because she would be unable to provide day-to-day care her child would suffer grave harm. The Court of Appeal, however, refused to interfere with a decision to return the child. Whilst acknowledging that there was a *risk* of harm because of the worsening situation it was not felt to be so great as to amount to a grave risk within the contemplation of Art 13(b), nor did they accept the argument that because of her anxieties and concern (which were considerable) the child was at grave risk from the breakdown of the mother's health. The court accepted that the *mother* would find a return to Israel 'intolerable' but that was not the test under Art 13(b).

Despite the difficulty of discharging the burden there are examples of where the defence

---

[316] [2001] 2 FLR 515, CA. See also *Re H (Abduction: Grave Risk)* [2003] 2 FLR 41 in which the Court of Appeal did not consider that in that case the Belgian authorities' previous failure to protect children from their dominating and violent father, per se, justified a refusal to make a return order.

[317] Subsequent to this decision the mother sought to set the order aside on the twin basis of fresh evidence as to her emotional state and the impracticality of enforcing the order, but this attempt failed: *Re B (Children)(Abduction: New Evidence)* [2001] EWCA Civ 625, [2001] 2 FCR 531. However, the children strongly resisted being taken to the airport and a stay was placed on the return order.

[318] [2002] EWCA Civ 908, [2002] 2 FLR 815.

has succeeded. In *Re F (A Minor) (Abduction: Custody Rights Abroad)*[319] a return order was refused because, accepting the defendant's uncontroverted affidavit evidence, the applicant had been shown to be violent towards the child and had been engaged in a campaign of intimidation and harassment against the mother, which had adversely affected the child. Another example of an Art 13(b) refusal based on violence is *Re D (Article 13B: Non-Return)*[320] in which a mother was shot in the head and shoulder allegedly at the behest of her husband with whom she was involved in an acrimonious and protracted custody dispute over their two children aged seven and five. The children were anxious for their own safety and in the exceptional circumstances of the case, it was accepted that their psychological welfare was put at 'grave risk beyond the normal disruption of an enforced return'.

However, it must not be supposed that Art 13(b) refusals can only be based on violence or abuse. Indeed, in *Re W (Abduction: Domestic Violence)*[321] Wall LJ rejected the suggestion made at first instance in that case[322] that there is no realistic chance of an Art 13(b) defence ever being established unless there has been violence or other specific abuse to the child, him or herself. As he put it: 'It is well recognised that in the context of domestic violence the position of the child is vitally affected by the position of the mother'. In this respect reference may be made to *Re G (Abduction: Psychological Harm.)*[323] A return was refused on the basis that if the mother were to return with the children, as she would have done had the order been made, there was a grave risk that the children would have been exposed to psychological harm because their mother's mental health would seriously deteriorate. This seems an extreme decision and some caution needs to be exercised when applying it. It is to be noted that the court was satisfied that the mother was not someone who was seeking to manipulate the court in order to get her own way. Ewbank J also observed that, notwithstanding the children's habitual residence was in Texas, all the parties were English. The defence might also be established if it can be shown in relation to the law of the requesting state that there is some fixed embargo on allowing the removal of children or precluding the removal of children by a parent who had once wrongly removed them, or where the length of time that the requesting state might take to decide issues concerning the children is excessive.[324]

Another example is *B v K (Child Abduction)*,[325] in which, having held that two older siblings should not be returned because of their objections (see further below), Johnson J ruled that a return order should also be refused in respect of a third child since, if he were returned and his two siblings were not, he would be exposed to psychological harm and placed in an intolerable position within the meaning of Art 13(b).

---

[319] [1995] Fam 224. This was the first time the Court of Appeal had refused a return on this ground. See also *Re M (Minors) (Abduction: Psychological Harm)* [1998] 2 FCR 488, CA.

[320] [2006] EWCA Civ 146.

[321] [2004] EWCA Civ 1366, [2005] 1 FLR 727 at [49].

[322] See *Re W (Abduction: Domestic Violence)* [2004] EWHC 1247 (Fam), [2004] 2 FLR 499, per Baron J.

[323] [1995] 1 FLR 64, per Ewbank J.

[324] Per Singer J in *Re O (Child Abduction: Undertakings)* [1994] 2 FLR 349, above, though in that case the defence was not made out.

[325] [1993] 1 FCR 382. Note also *Ontario Court v M and M (Abduction: Children's Objections)* [1997] 1 FLR 475 (child's fears that she would have to live with her grandmother and lose her father held to amount to placing her in an 'intolerable position').

This strict approach to the application of Art 13(b) is taken by most major jurisdictions[326] save Australia, where the Australian High Court in *DP v Commonwealth Central Authority*[327] has taken a markedly different line, with the majority going so far as to say that there is no warrant for:

'[the] conclusion that reg 16(3) [which implements Art 13b of the Convention] is to be given a "narrow" rather than a "broad" construction. There is, in these circumstances, no evidence choice to be made between a "narrow" and "broad" construction of the regulation. If that is what is meant by saying that it is to be given a "narrow construction" it must be rejected. The exception is to be given the meaning its words require'.

They did, however, add:

'That is not to say, however, that reg 16(3)(b) will find frequent application. It is well nigh inevitable that a child, taken from one country to another without the agreement of one parent, will suffer disruption, uncertainty and anxiety. That disruption, uncertainty and anxiety will recur, and may well be magnified, by having to return to the country of habitual residence. Regulation 16(3)(b) and Art 13(b) of the Convention intend to refer to more than this kind of result when they speak of a grave risk to the child of exposure to physical or psychological harm on return'.

Whether this in itself signals a broader approach to Art 13(b) (which, if so, is difficult to square with what was intended) remains to be seen. However, as already intimated, even within those jurisdictions where an undoubtedly restrictive interpretation operates, there is some evidence to suggest that courts may be becoming more ready to consider that the defence is made out,[328] although in the light of *TB v JB (Abduction: Grave Risk of Harm)*,[329] it is evident that, before the English courts at any rate, it remains an extremely difficult exception to establish, and indeed in *Re S (Abduction: Custody Rights)*,[330] the Court of Appeal expressly distanced itself from the Australian decision in this regard.

The generally strict interpretation of Art 13(b) has not escaped criticism. One argument is that the courts too readily assume that children will be adequately protected on their return. Cases like *TB v JB (Abduction: Grave Risk of Harm)*[331] highlight this issue. One solution is that Central Authorities should accept a wider responsibility to protect children

---

[326] See notably *Friedrich v Friedrich* 78 F 3d 1060 (6th Civ 1996) in the USA, *AS v PS* [1998] 2 IR in Ireland, *Thomson v Thomson* [1994] 3 SCR 551 (Canada), *Re Q Petitioner* 2001 SLT 243 (Scotland). The article is also restrictively interpreted in Germany, France, Switzerland. See the authorities cited by Lowe, Everall and Nicholls, op cit, at 17.92.

[327] (2001) 180 ALR 402.

[328] See the arguments by J Caldwell, 'Child welfare defences in child abduction cases—some recent developments' [2001] CFLQ 121 at 25 et seq. See also, in the United States, *Blondin v Dubois* 238 F 3d 153 Cir 2001), discussed by M Weiner, 'Navigating the Road Between Uniformity and Progress: The Need for Purposive Analysis of the Hague Convention on the Civil Aspects of International Child Abduction' (2002) 33 Columbia HRLR 276 at 339 et seq. Although both the 1999 and 2003 Statistical Surveys found that Art 13(b) was the most frequently relied upon to justify a refusal to return, in fact the number and proportion of such refusals was virtually the same.

[329] [2001] 2 FLR 515.   [330] [2002] EWCA 908, [2002] 2 FLR 815 at [45], per Ward LJ.

[331] Above.

upon their return.[332] A second more fundamental criticism[333] is that whereas the Convention was predicated upon abductors being non-carers it is now clear that the majority are in fact the primary carers[334] and that in turn begs the question whether it is in children's interests generally to be returned to their home jurisdiction. In reply it has been said[335] that this alleged shift in the pattern of abduction does not necessarily mean that the Convention has become increasingly flawed for there remains the argument that it is basically wrong for children to be uprooted from their home by unilateral act of either parent and taken to a foreign jurisdiction and thus to be separated from the other parent. However, whether Art 13(b), as it currently operates, properly draws the balance can and, no doubt, will continue to be debated.

An additional reason for the difficulty of establishing a defence under Art 13(b) is the English court practice of accepting undertakings, since they can alleviate what might otherwise be regarded as an intolerable situation.[336] As Butler-Sloss LJ explained in the leading case, *Re M (Minors) (Abduction: Undertakings)*,[337] undertakings are accepted to make the return of children easier and to provide for their necessities such as a roof over their heads and adequate maintenance. They are intended, however, to have a short life, ie until the court of the child's habitual residence becomes seized of the proceedings. Accordingly, the court should be careful not in any way to usurp or be thought to usurp the functions of the court of habitual residence. Furthermore, undertakings must not be so elaborate that their implementation might become bogged down in protracted hearings and investigations.

The child's objections[338]

Article 13 also permits a refusal to make a return order if the judicial or administrative authority 'finds that the child objects to being returned and has attained an age and degree of maturity at which it is appropriate to take account of its views'. According to the 1999 statistical survey,[339] globally, the child's objections were relied upon in whole or in part in 22 of the 107 refusals, and according to the 2003 survey[340] in 23 of the 149 refusals.

The English courts do not make automatic enquiries of the child's position. As Butler-Sloss LJ has observed,[341] 'There is nothing in Art 13 or the Child Abduction and Custody Act 1985 (which enacts the Convention), which provides for automatic inquiry into the views of older children . . .'. Furthermore as Waite J held in *P v P (Minors) (Child*

---

[332] This was discussed extensively at the third and fourth meeting of the Special Commission to review the Convention, see Lowe, Everall and Nicholls, op cit, 17.137–138.

[333] See in particular M Freeman 'In the Best Interests of Internationally Abducted Children?—Plural, Singular, Neither or Both?' [2002] IFL 77 and R Schuz 'The Hague Child Abduction Convention: Family Law and Private International Law' (1995) 44 ICLQ 771.

[334] According to the 2003 Statistical Survey, op cit, where 69% of abductors were either the primary or joint primary carer.

[335] Lowe, Everall and Nicholls, op cit, at 17.140.

[336] Per Singer J in *Re O (Child Abduction: Undertakings)*, above. Note also *Re K (Abduction: Child's Objections)* [1995] 1 FLR 977 (court entitled to have regard to whether any risk of harm can be reduced or extinguished by undertakings). For the practice on undertakings, so called safe harbour orders and mirror orders see Lowe, Everall and Nicholls, op cit, at 17.123 et seq and D McClean 'International child abduction—some recent trends' (1997) 9 CFLQ 387 at 392–5.

[337] [1995] 1 FLR 1021, CA.   [338] See generally, Lowe, Everall and Nicholls, op cit, at 17.41, et seq.

[339] Op cit. In England and Wales there were two refusals based on the child's objections in the 2003 survey.

[340] Op cit.   [341] In *Re M (A Minor)(Child Abduction)* [1994] 1 FLR 390 at 394.

Abduction),[342] the court is not bound to adjourn the case to inquire into the nature of the child's objection and degree of maturity, merely because the issue has been raised. It is therefore incumbent upon the defendant to provide sufficient evidence at the outset for the court to take cognisance of the child's objections, and it is then in the court's discretion to decide by what means and to what extent such views should be investigated.[343] Exceptionally, however, the court may be put on enquiry (as, for example, where the child refuses to board the flight to take him back to the requesting State in compliance with a return order)[344] that the child's objection is a real issue.

To bring the case within this exception requires the judge to make findings of fact both as to whether the child objects and whether the child has attained an age and degree of maturity at which it is appropriate to take account of the child's views. These findings are sometimes referred to as the 'gateway findings'.[345] According to the leading case, *Re S (Minors) (Abduction: Custody Rights)*,[346] this part of Art 13 is independent of the rest of it. Accordingly, there is no additional requirement to establish that there is a grave risk that a return order would expose the child to psychological harm etc. *Re S* also establishes that for these purposes the return to which the child objects is that which would otherwise be ordered under Art 12. The court is not required to consider whether the child objects to returning in any circumstances, eg to see the other parent on an access visit. On the other hand, it is established by *Re M (A Minor) (Child Abduction)*[347] that under Art 13 the court is entitled to take into account the child's objection to returning to the person and not simply to the country.

There is no chronological threshold below which a child's view will not be taken into account, though in general the younger the child the less likely that he will have the maturity to make it appropriate to take his views into account.[348] Practice varies between contracting states. So far as England and Wales is concerned the objections of children as young as a girl aged eight and a boy aged seven have been held to justify a refusal to return,[349] and there have been two reported cases where the objection of nine-year-olds have been relied upon.[350] These, however, are relatively unusual cases, and children below the age of 10 or 11 are not normally considered sufficiently mature. Indeed Hale J has said[351]

---

[342] [1992] 1 FLR 155.   [343] *Re M (A Minor) (Child Abduction)*, above.

[344] As in *Re HB (Abduction: Children's Objections)* [1998] 1 FLR 422, CA and *Re M*, above.

[345] Per Waite LJ in *Re S (Minors) (Abduction: Acquiescence)* [1994] 1 FLR 819 at 826.

[346] [1993] Fam 242, sub nom *Re S (A Minor) (Abduction)* [1993] 2 All ER 683, CA.

[347] [1994] 1 FLR 390, CA.

[348] Per Balcombe LJ in *Re R (Child Abduction)* [1995] 1 FLR 717 at 730.

[349] *B v K (Child Abduction)* [1993] 1 FCR 382. See also *Re M (Minors) (Abduction: Psychological Harm)*, above—views of brothers aged nine and eight taken into account with some hesitancy. Compare *Re K (Abduction: Child's Objections)* [1995] 1 FLR 977 in which a child aged just under eight was held on the facts not to be of an age and maturity in which it was appropriate to take account of her views. In one German case the objections of a four-year-old were relied upon—see Lowe and Perry 'The Operation of the Hague and European Conventions on International Child Abduction between England and Germany, Part II' [1998] International Family Law 52 at 55.

[350] *Re S (A Minor) (Abduction: Custody Rights)* [1993] Fam 242, sub nom *Re S (A Minor) (Abduction)* [1993] 2 All ER 683, CA; and *Ontario Court v M v M (Abduction: Child's Objections)* [1997] 1 FLR 475. Other cases include *Re S (Child Abduction: Delay)* [1998] 1 FLR 651 (10-year-old); *Re R (Abduction: Hague and European Conventions)* [1997] 1 FLR 663 (10-year-old); *Re HB (Children's Objections) (No 2)* [1998] 1 FLR 564 (12-year-old); and *Re R (A Minor) (Abduction)* [1992] 1 FLR 105 (14-year-old).

[351] In *Re R (Abduction: Hague and European Conventions)* [1997] 1 FLR 663 at 667.

that she would regard the chronological age of 10½ as normally being on the borderline. Conversely, the same judge also remarked[352] that it would be difficult to suggest that a 13-year-old of normal intelligence and maturity should not have his or her views taken into account. Most convention countries, however, do not apparently generally consider the views of children under the age of 10. In the 1999 Statistical Survey,[353] there were two cases in which the objections of children under the age of seven being relied upon with a further six where the children were aged between eight and ten. The 2003 Survey[354] found one case of the objection of a child under the age of seven being relied upon, and a further four where the children were aged between eight and ten.

According to Ward LJ in *Re T (Abduction: Child's Objections to Return)*[355] to establish a defence under Art 13 based on the child's objections the proper approach is first to establish whether the child objects to being returned to the country of habitual residence 'bearing in mind that there may be cases where this is inevitably and inextricably linked with an objection to living with the other parent that the two factors cannot be separated'. It is then necessary to ascertain the age and degree of maturity in order to establish whether it is appropriate to take account of the child's views.

In *Re S* the Court of Appeal refused to lay down general guidance to be adopted in ascertaining the child's view and degree of maturity. Instead, each issue was thought to be a question of fact 'peculiarly within the province of the trial judge'. Similarly in *Re T* Ward LJ commented[356] that he 'would not wish to venture any definition of maturity. Clearly the child has to know what has happened to her and to understand that there is a range of choice. A child may be mature enough for it to be appropriate for her views to be taken into account even though she may not have gained the level of maturity that she is fully emancipated from parental dependence and can claim autonomy of decision-making'.

In his view, however, in determining the strength and validity of the child's views it is necessary to examine the child's own perspective of what is in his or her own short, medium or long term interests; the extent to which the reasons for objection are rooted in reality or might reasonably appear to the child to be so grounded; the extent to which those views have been 'shaped or even coloured' by undue parental pressure direct or indirect, and the extent to which the objections would be mollified on return and, where this is the case, upon removal from any pernicious influence from the abducting parent.

To help the court evaluate the child's views it is permissible for a child to be questioned by a suitably skilled independent person (eg a CAFCASS officer) with a view to discovering how far the child is capable of understanding, and does actually understand, the implications of objecting to being returned.[357] In exceptional cases the child can be made a party to the proceedings.[358] Even where it is appropriate to take account of the child's views, as Wilson J put it in *Re J and K (Abduction: Objections of Child)*[359] that does not relieve the court of the task of deciding, in the discretionary analysis, what weight should

---

[352] In *Re HB (Abduction: Children's Objections)* [1997] 1 FLR 392.   [353] Ibid.   [354] Ibid.

[355] [2000] 2 FLR 192, CA. See also *Re J (Abduction: Child's Objections To Return)* [2004] EWCA Civ 428, [2004] 2 FLR 64.

[356] [2000] 2 FLR 192 at 203.

[357] Per Waite LJ in *Re S (Minors) (Abduction: Acquiescence)* [1994] 1 FLR 819 at 827.

[358] See *Re M (A Minor) (Abduction: Child's Objections)* [1994] 2 FLR 126, CA and *Re HB (Abduction: Children's Objections)* [1998] 1 FLR 422, CA.

[359] [2004] EWHC 1985 (Fam), [2005] 1 FLR 273, discussed further below.

be afforded to the objection. Furthermore, according to an important ruling in *Zaffino v Zaffino (Abduction: Children's Views)*,[360] while in the case of siblings it is right to consider each child separately in deciding whether or not that child objected to being returned and had attained an age and maturity at which it was appropriate to take account of his or her views, at the discretionary stage of deciding what order to make, each child cannot be considered in isolation: the child's place within the family and the consequences of the exercise on that child must also be considered.

Among the reported cases of where a return has been refused on the basis of the child's objections are *Re R (A Minor: Abduction)*[361] in which a 14-year-old was threatening suicide if returned; *Re J (Abduction: Child's Objections To Return)*[362] in which the 11-year-old girl's objections related to her mother's alcoholism, and *Re B (abduction: views of children)*,[363] in which the refusal was based on the objections of children aged 12 and seven who had become well and truly settled after being in England for more than two years.

The residual discretion to return

Although there never has been a doubt as to whether there is a discretion to order the child's return notwithstanding the establishment of an Art 13 exception as the provision is clearly written in permissive form, there has been an argument as to whether a similar discretion exists once an exception under Art 12 has been established. Article 12 is not in permissive form and so on the face of it attention must be focused on Art 18 which provides:

'The provisions of this Chapter do not limit the power of a judicial or administrative authority to order the return of the child at any time'.

The meaning of Art 18 is obscure but it could either be interpreted as vesting a general discretion to order a return or alternatively as simply preserving the application of any domestic powers outside the Convention to order a return.[364] So far as the English approach is concerned it has been authoritatively resolved by the Court of Appeal in *Cannon v Cannon*,[365] following a thorough review of the international jurisprudence, that Art 18 vests a general discretion to return, though Thorpe LJ considered that Art 12 itself could be interpreted as vesting a discretion to return notwithstanding the establishment of the exception.

So far as the exercise of the discretion is concerned the leading case is *Re A (Minors)*

---

[360] [2005] EWCA Civ 1012, [2006] 1 FLR 410.   [361] [1992] 1 FLR 105.

[362] [2004] EWCA Civ 428, [2004] 2 FLR 64. See also *Re L (Abduction: Child's Objections To Return)* [2002] EWHC 1864 (Fam), [2002] 2 FLR 1042—objections of a 14-year-old based on his anxiety and distress caused by his poor relationship with his father and the effects of being exposed to the disharmony between his parents.

[363] [1998] 3 FCR 260. For other examples see *Re (Minors)(Abduction: Custody Rights)* [1993] Fam 242— (nine-year-old's views respected); *B v K (Child Abduction)* (objections of a girl aged eight and boy aged seven held to justify a refusal to return); *Re M (A Minor)(Abduction: Child's Objections)* [1994] 2 FLR 416 (objection of a boy aged 13 held to justify a refusal to return); *Ontario Court v M and M (Abduction: Child's Objections)* [1997] 1 FLR 457 (a nine-year-old girl's objections to being returned to her grandmother taken into account); *Re S (Child Abduction: Delay)* [1998] 1 FLR 651 (refusal to return based upon a 10-year-old girl's objections to being returned to her father in Germany).

[364] For a discussion of this conundrum, see Lowe, Everall and Nicholls op cit at 17.1–4 and 17.30–17.35.

[365] [2004] EWCA Civ 1330, [2005] 1 FCR 169 overruling Singer J at first instance, reported as *Re C (Abduction: Settlement)* [2004] EWHC 1245 (Fam), [2005] 1 FLR 147.

(Abduction Acquiescence) (No 2),[366] which establishes that, while the court is entitled to take the child's interests into account, it is not bound to treat those interests as the paramount consideration, but must instead balance them against the fundamental purpose of the Convention, namely to order the child's return.

In *H v H (Abduction: Acquiescence)*[367] Waite LJ suggested that the following factors should govern the exercise of the discretion:

'(a) the comparative suitability of the forum in the competing jurisdictions to determine the child's future in the substantive proceedings;

(b) the likely outcome (in whichever forum they be heard) of the substantive proceedings;

(c) the consequences of the acquiescence, with particular reference to the extent to which a child may have become settled in the requested state;

(d) the situation which would await the absconding parent and the child if compelled to return to the requesting jurisdiction;

(e) the anticipated emotional effect upon the child of an immediate return order (a factor which is to be treated as significant but not as paramount);

(f) the extent to which the purpose and underlying philosophy of the Hague Convention would be at risk of frustration if a return order were to be refused'.

In *H v H* it was held that the first instance judge had wrongly been swayed by his sympathy for the father, and had failed to consider important issues such as which was the more appropriate forum and what was the likely outcome of the substantive proceedings. The Court of Appeal refused to return the child. In *Re S (Child Abduction: Delay)*[368] Wall J held that once an exception under Art 13 had been established it was proper to take into account, in deciding whether to return the child or not, the applicant's delay in pursuing his or her Convention remedy.

It is an interesting point as to whether this discretion should be exercised differently according to which exception has been established. In *Re D (Abduction: Discretionary Return)*,[369] it was argued that where consent is proved so that in effect the abduction is not wrongful, 'the spirit of the Convention [is] less potent a factor in favour of return than in other cases under Art 13'.

However, be that as it may, it by no means follows that once consent has been established that there is no room for the exercise of the discretion to return under art 18. On the contrary, in *Re D* itself, Wilson J ordered the children's return to France notwithstanding that the father had established that the mother had consented to the children living with him in England, principally on the basis that were he to do otherwise the children might never have been able to visit France to see their mother because of the father's fear that the French custody order to the mother would then be enforced.

There has been some dispute about the nature of the discretion to return a mature child notwithstanding his or her objection. On the one hand in *Re R (Child Abduction:*

---

366 [1993] Fam 1, CA.

367 [1996] 2 FLR 570 at 574–5, CA (not overruled on this point by the House of Lords).

368 [1998] 1 FLR 651.

369 [2000] 1 FLR 24 at 36. Cf Hale J's comment in *Re K (Abduction: Consent)* [1997] 2 FLR 212 at 220 that where consent is established, frustrating the purposes of the Convention 'scarcely comes into the question'.

Acquiescence)[370] Balcombe LJ (with whom Sir Ralph Gibson agreed) was of the view that the establishment of the child's objections simply triggered a discretion not to return and in exercising that discretion the court must very much bear in mind the policy of the Convention. On the other hand in the same case, Millett LJ considered that if the child 'is of sufficient age and maturity for his views to be taken into account, the Convention clearly envisages that he will not be returned against his wishes to be overridden'. However, it is now accepted[371] that Balcombe LJ's approach is correct and that of Millett LJ too restrictive.

(f) Handling international child abduction within the Brussels II States[372]

Introduction and background

The original Brussels II Regulation[373] did not affect the operation of the 1980 Hague Abduction Convention, since Art 4 provided:

'The courts with jurisdiction within the meaning of Article 3 shall exercise their jurisdiction in conformity with the Hague Convention of 25 October 1980 on the Civil Aspects of International Child Abduction, and in particular Articles 3 and 16 thereof'.

However, quite a different stance is taken by the revised Regulation[374] with Art 60(e) providing that in relations between Member States of the European Union[375] the Regulation takes precedence over the 1980 Convention insofar as they concern matters governed by this Regulation.

The background to this radical change of policy is interesting.[376] It began with a French proposal aimed at facilitating the exercise of cross-border rights of access[377] which was followed by the European Commission's own proposal[378] aimed at improving the original Regulation but which controversially addressed the problem of child abduction through provisions on jurisdiction and on the return of the child. After discussion, the two proposals were amalgamated into a new Commission proposal made in May 2002.[379] This proposal would have effectively disapplied the 1980 Convention within the Community in favour of allowing courts of the State to which the child had been abducted at best only to

---

[370] [1995] 1 FLR 716.

[371] See *Zaffino v Zaffino (Abduction: Children's Views)* [2005] EWCA Civ 1012, [2006] 1 FLR 410 at [19], per Thorpe LJ.

[372] See generally Lowe, Everall and Nicholls *The New Brussels II Regulation* ch 6, N Lowe 'Regulating International Child Abduction—Brussels Style' (2002/3) 6 Contemporary Issues in Law 315 and 'Negotiating the Revised Brussels II Regulation' [2004] IFL 205.

[373] Council Regulation (EC) No 1347/2000 of 28 May 2000.

[374] Council Regulation (EC) No 2201/2003 of 27 November 2003.

[375] Except Denmark, see Art 2(3).

[376] See eg N Lowe 'The Growing Influence of the European Union on International Family Law—A View from the Boundary' (2003) 56 Current Legal Problems 439 at 470 et seq.

[377] Initiative of the French Republic with a view to adopting a Council Regulation on the mutual enforcement of judgments on rights of access to children, OJ 2000 C234/7.

[378] Proposal for a Council Regulation on jurisdiction and the recognition and enforcement of judgments in matters of parental responsibility OJ No C332 of 27.11.2001, 269.

[379] Proposal for a Council Regulation concerning jurisdiction and the recognition and enforcement of judgments in matrimonial matters and in matters of parental responsibility repealing Regulation (EC) No 1347/2000 and amending Regulation (EC) No 44/2001 in matters relating to maintenance, Brussels 3.5.2002 Com (2002) 222 Final.

make provisional holding orders and even then only provided the exceptions akin to those set out in Art 13 of the Abduction Convention applied, with the courts of the child's habitual residence free to make custody orders according to the merits. The proposal attracted passionate and protracted debate[380] with relevant Member States being split down the middle. Negotiations continued on this point throughout the rest of 2002 and just when the Commission appeared to be giving up on getting agreement the Danes brokered a compromise. That compromise was broadly that applications for return of children wrongfully removed or retained would continue to be dealt with under the 1980 Hague Convention but in the event of a refusal to return the court then had to notify the court of the requesting State which in turn had to notify the parties giving them the opportunity to pursue the custody claim which would be decided upon the merits. If that court then required the child's return, that order would be enforceable without further question.

This compromise seemed to satisfy all parties and negotiations were eventually completed in November 2003. In fact, however, the impact of the Regulation on the operation of the 1980 Hague Abduction Convention is, as we shall now see, rather more intrusive than might have been contemplated at the time of the compromise.

The impact of the Regulation on the 1980 Hague Abduction Convention

The basic scheme of the revised Regulation, which became fully operative from 1 March 2005, is:

(a) to preserve the pre-eminence of the 1980 Convention for dealing with applications for the return of abducted children but nevertheless to give some direction on how that Convention should be applied as between Member States; and

(b) to govern the position in cases where a court refuses to make a return order under the Convention.

The crucial provision is Art 11.

Article 11(1) enjoins the authorities of Member States when dealing with applications for the return of a child 'wrongfully removed in a Member State other than the Member State where the child was habitually resident immediately before the wrongful removal or retention' to apply paragraphs 2 to 8. Paragraphs 2–5 comprise directions on how return applications should be handled under the 1980 Hague Convention; paragraphs 6–8 govern what is to happen if a return order is refused.

According to the Guide[381] the judge must first determine whether a 'wrongful removal or retention' has taken place *in the sense of the Regulation*. It points out that the definition in Art 2(11)(b) is similar but not identical to that under Art 3 of the 1980 Hague Abduction Convention. If this advice is right, it means that a new set of jurisprudence on the meaning of wrongful removal or retention will be required and upon which the European Court of Justice will be the final arbiter.

---

[380] See the debate between N Lowe 'Article 5(3) of the Draft EU Regulation on Parental Responsibility—Dealing with Child Abduction' [2002] IFL 36 and I Karsten 'Article 5(3) of the Draft EU Regulation on Parental Responsibility—A Reply' [2002] IFL 42.

[381] Viz 'Parental Responsibility in the European Union—Practice Guide for the Application of the New Brussels Regulation' drawn up by the European Commission (2005).

Applying Articles 12 and 13 of the Hague Convention in compliance with the Regulation
Article 11(2) of the Regulation provides:

'When applying Articles 12 and 13 of the 1980 Hague Convention,[382] it shall be ensured that
the child is given the opportunity to be heard during the proceedings unless this appears
inappropriate having regard to his or her age or degree of maturity'.

Recital (19) states that while the hearing of the child plays an important role in the
application of the Regulation the instrument 'is not intended to modify national procedures'. Furthermore the *Guide* points out that it is not necessary for the child's view
to be heard at the actual court hearing. With these points in mind it was generally felt that
the system operating before the Regulation in England and Wales was essentially compliant inasmuch as the child's views are adequately investigated by a CAFCASS officer
and notwithstanding that the child is not normally made a party to the proceedings.
Nevertheless it has been argued that to be totally compliant more attention needs to be
paid to the child's views. As one commentary has put it,[383] 'There have been very distressing cases where the first time that the strength of the child's feelings have become clear is
when he or she refuses to leave their room or to board the plane to be taken to the
requesting state'.

As well as requiring the child to be heard, Art 11(5) also provides that:

'A court cannot refuse to return a child unless the person who requested the return of the
child has been given an opportunity to be heard'.

Given the general practice (designed to facilitate speedy disposals) not to hear oral
evidence when determining Hague applications, Art 11(5) is potentially problematic.
Its impact has been slightly mitigated by the ability to conduct the hearing using the
arrangements set out in Regulation (EC) No 1206/2001 on co-operation between courts of
the Member States in taking of evidence in civil and commercial matters. By this Regulation
a party can be heard in their home State and, as the *Guide* says, the use of video and 'conference call' proposed by the Regulation could be useful. However, helpful though this latter
Regulation is, the requirement to hear the applicant is bound to slow down the proceedings
nor is it clear how much will normally be gained over and above written submissions.

According to Art 11(4):

'A court cannot refuse to return a child on the basis of Article 13b of the 1980 Hague
Convention if it is established that adequate arrangements have been made to secure the
protection of the child after his or her return'.

The idea behind Art 11(4) is to reinforce the principle of immediate return by restricting the exceptions allowed for under Art 13 of the Hague Abduction Convention to a strict
minimum.[384] Article 11(4) of the revised Regulation goes further than Art 13(b) of the
Hague Convention by, as the *Guide* explains it, extending the obligation to return even if
the requisite Art 13(b) harm can be proved if it is established that the authorities in the
Member State of origin have made arrangements to secure the child's protection after the

---

[382] Discussed above at pp 646ff.   [383] Lowe, Everall and Nicholls, op cit at 6.14.
[384] But note that Art 11(4) only applies to refusal to return under Art 13(b) and does not, for example,
apply to refusals based on the child's objections: *Re M (A Child)* [2006] EWCA Civ 630.

return. According to the *Guide* it is not enough just to establish that procedures exist but instead it must be shown that the authorities in the Member State of origin have taken concrete measures to protect the child in question. To establish that it is envisaged that the assistance of the Central Authority in the State of origin will be vital. However, what is not clear, is who has the burden of proof. If Art 13(b) is established, is it for the applicant to show adequate means of protection are in place or is it to be presumed unless proved otherwise? It may be noted, however, that in return applications made in England and Wales the originating summons must identify 'any details of measures taken by courts or authorities to ensure the protection of the child after its return to the Member State of habitual residence of which the applicant is aware'.[385]

Depending upon its interpretation Art 11(4) might require some change of approach by the English courts but it is not anticipated to make a great difference given that the Art 13(b) exception is so rarely established.[386]

According to Art 11(3):

'A court to which an application for return of a child is made as mentioned in paragraph 1 shall act expeditiously in proceedings on the application, using the most expeditious procedures available in national law.

Without prejudice to the first subparagraph, the court shall, except where exceptional circumstances make this impossible, issue its judgment no later than six weeks after the application is lodged'.

Although the need for speedy disposal is written all over the 1980 Hague Abduction Convention it stops short of directing Contracting States to resolve applications within six weeks, though, arguably at least, it provides such a target time frame. Article 11(3) prima facie at least translates this target into an obligation. However, although it is clearly the spirit of the revised Regulation that Member States should at least have in place procedures that ensure that court hearings will normally be completed (according to the *Guide* this *includes* both enforcement and appeals) within six weeks, in fact this obligation is expressed to be 'without prejudice' to the obligation to use 'the most expeditious procedures available in national law'. On a strict interpretation, therefore, Art 11(3) only requires courts to use the most expeditious procedure available regardless of whether that would normally meet the six week target. In other words, Art 11(3) does not oblige Member States to introduce *new* procedures so as to meet the six week deadline. No changes have been made in England and Wales though there has long been the expectation that Hague applications will normally be disposed of within six weeks. As Thorpe LJ put it in *Re C (Abduction: Grave Risk of Physical or Psychological Harm)*,[387] Hague Convention applications are 'intended to be a hot pursuit remedy and if courts permit [them] to linger into anything else they aid the creation of unnecessary litigation issues'. Accordingly, 'The Goal for which we should strive is jurisdiction, both at first instance and on appeal, should be six weeks from initiation to a decision'. On the other hand, where States already have speedy procedures in place they will be expected to comply with them. The *Guide*,

[385] FPR 1991, r 6.4(3).
[386] See in particular *Re H (Abduction: Grave Risk)* [2003] EWCA Civ 355, [2004] 1 FLR 141 and *TB v JB (Abduction: Grave Risk of Harm)* [2001] 2 FLR 595 which turned on the issue of whether, respectively the Belgian and New Zealand authorities could adequately protect the children concerned, see above p 655.
[387] [1999] Fam 478 at 488.

however, is clearly committed to the view that Member States are obliged to meet the six week deadline.[388] In its first ruling on the application of the revised Regulation, the Court of Appeal[389] made it clear that it expects Art 11(3) to be complied with. As Wall LJ put it,[390] 'Failure to adhere to the timetables proposed will not only result in the English court being in breach of its international obligations, it will represent an unacceptable abnegation of the court's responsibility to address cases of international child abduction—a matter in which, in the past, we have taken legitimate pride.'

Although in principle Art 11(4) is to be welcomed, it remains to be seen to what extent this six-week deadline will in fact be met, but on the basis of the findings of the 1999 Statistical Survey most Member States will struggle to comply.[391] In *Re M (A Child)*,[392] Thorpe LJ commented, 'If the six-week target is proving generally unpracticable, it may have to be reconsidered.'

The position following a refusal to return

The area where the revised Regulation breaks entirely new ground is with respect to the position following a refusal to return. According to Art 11(6) once a court has refused to order a return under Art 13 of the Hague Convention (but note *not* under the other provisions),[393] it:

'must immediately either directly or through its central authority transmit a copy of the court order on non-return and of the relevant documents, in particular a transcript of the hearings before the court, to the court with jurisdiction or central authority in the Member State where the child was habitually resident immediately before the wrongful removal or retention, as determined by national law. The court shall receive all the mentioned documents within one month of the date of the non-return order.'

Unless the court of habitual residence is already seised by one of the parties, then, according to Art 11(7):

'the court or central authority that receives the information mentioned in paragraph 6 must notify it to the parties and invite them to make submissions to the court, in accordance with

---

[388] Under EC law there are sanctions against States for failing to meet their Community obligations: By Art 10 of the EC Treaty Member States must take all appropriate measures to ensure the fulfilment of their Treaty obligations (including obligations resulting from actions taken by the Community institutions, such as this Regulation). In the event of a Member State's failure to do so the Commission may take the defaulting State before the ECJ pursuant to the procedure laid down in Art 226 EC. The obligation imposed on Member States by Art 10 extends to national courts in respect of matters within their jurisdiction (Case 14/83 *Vol Colson v Kamann v Land Nordrhein-Westfalen* [1984] ECR 1891, [1986] 4 CMLR 430) although hitherto the Commission has not taken a Member State before the ECJ under Art 226 because of the actions (or failure to act) of its judiciary. Furthermore, individuals who suffer damage as a consequence of a Member State's failure to fulfil its Community obligations may sue that State for damages in the national court (Cases C–46, 48/93 *Brasserie du Pécheur SA v Germany, R v Secretary of State for Transport ex parte Factortame Ltd and others* [1996] ECR I-I1029, [1996] 1 CMLR 889).

[389] In *Re M (A Child)* [2006] EWCA Civ 360.   [390] At [88].

[391] See the detailed analysis by N Lowe 'In the Best Interests of Abducted Children? Securing Their Immediate Return under the 1980 Hague Abduction Convention' in *Les Enlèvements D'Enfants Á Travers Les Frontiéres* (ed H Fulchiron) 245.

[392] Above at [47].

[393] Eg Arts 12(2) or 20. Nor does it apply to rejections of an application under the 1980 Convention because the case does not comply with the requirements under Art 3, discussed above at p 633.

national law, within three months of the date of notification so that the court can examine the question of custody of the child'.

If no submissions are received by the court within this three-months time limit, the case must be closed.

These provisions aim:

(a) to prevent the court of the requested State from assuming jurisdiction following a refusal to return the child; and

(b) give the parties the opportunity of having determined a 'custody application' on its merits in the child's 'home court'.

If, following that adjudication (for which no time limit is prescribed), the court order requires the child to be returned, then by Arts 11(8), 40(1)(b) and 42, such an order is automatically enforceable, that is, 'without the need for a declaration of enforceability and without any possibility of opposing its recognition' simply upon the issue of a certificate by the judge of origin.[394]

Although some have said that this scheme enables the court of habitual residence to 'trump' a no return order, it seems a reasonable compromise in itself. The 1980 Hague Abduction Convention does not deal with jurisdiction after a refusal to return and it is not unreasonable to vest that jurisdiction in the court of the child's habitual residence. The clear problems of doing so, though, are that the child and the abductor will not be present in that jurisdiction (though as Recital (20) and the *Guide* point out, it is possible to hear both the child and abducting parent in the state in which they are staying by using the arrangements laid down in Regulation (EC) No 1206/2001 on cooperation between the courts of the Member States in taking evidence in civil or commercial matters) and that there is a danger of delay in disposing of the custody application. In this latter respect it might have been better if provision had also been made for the expeditious disposal of the merits hearing.

It remains to be seen how satisfactorily these provisions will operate in practice though at the same time it needs also to be remembered that refusals to return under the 1980 Hague Abduction Convention are relatively unusual.[395] It has, however, been speculated[396] that there could be more refusals, particularly in cases of domestic violence, since the court of the requested State might prefer to allow the abductor and child at least to remain in a relatively safe environment pending an adjudication upon the merits of the child's home court.

(g) Securing rights of access [397]

The two key provisions are Arts 7 and 21. Under Art 7 Central Authorities are generally enjoined to co-operate with each other and to promote co-operation amongst the

---

[394] For details of this so-called 'fast track' enforcement procedure, see below p 678.

[395] According to the 1999 Statistical Survey of the 251 return applications made between Member States in 1999 only 33 were refused.

[396] See N Lowe, 'Negotiating the Revised Brussels II Regulation' [2004] IFL 205.

[397] See generally N Lowe 'Regulating Cross-Border Access to Children' in *Perspektivan Des Familienrechts— Festschrift Für Dieter Schwab* (eds S Hofer, D Klippel and U Walter, 2005) 1153 at 1159–65; L Silberman 'Patching Up the Abduction Convention: A Call for a New International Protocol and a suggestion for

competent authorities in their respective States to achieve the Convention's obligations including, therefore, to ensure that rights of access are 'effectively respected' in compliance with Art 1(b). They are particularly enjoined 'either directly or through any intermediary' to take all appropriate measures; '(f) to initiate or facilitate the institution of judicial or administrative proceedings with a view . . . in a proper case, to make arrangements for organising or securing the effective exercise of rights of access'.

Under Art 21 applications for organising or securing the effective exercise of rights of access can be presented to a Central Authority in the same way as an application for the child's return. For the purposes of English law a decision relating to access means a decision as to the contact which a child may or may not have with any person.[398] Article 21 also requires the Authority to promote the peaceful enjoyment of access rights and to take steps to remove, as far as possible, all obstacles to their exercise, including taking proceedings to organise or protect access.

According to the leading decision, *Re G (A Minor) (Enforcement of Access Abroad)*,[399] Art 21 continues to apply even where the child is habitually resident in England and Wales at the time of the application.[400] However, this case also establishes that whilst it may impose duties upon the Central Authority, unlike Art 12 which confers a right in public law which is directly enforceable in an English court, Art 21 imposes no duties whatever upon judicial authorities. Indeed Hoffmann LJ queried whether Art 21 was so vague or permissive as to create no rights at all, but insofar as it might, those rights were in public law and enforceable only against the Central Authority. Accordingly, applicants who are seeking contact rather than a return of the child should apply for a contact order under the Children Act 1989 s 8, which will be heard on the merits. It was further held in *Re T (Minors) (Hague Convention: Access)*[401] that upon receiving an application under Art 21 the Central Authority's only duty is to make appropriate arrangements for providing English solicitors to act on the applicant's behalf to institute proceedings under the Children Act 1989. It is not incumbent upon the Central Authority to issue a summons under the Child Abduction and Custody Act 1985 but for the applicant to apply for an order under the Children Act 1989. Furthermore, the advantageous provision for what is now legal representation does not apply to applications under the Children Act nor may a legal representation certificate issued under the Convention be extended to these proceedings. Since Convention proceedings are regarded as being exhausted upon presentation to court, no stay operates against the contact proceedings under the 1989 Act.[402]

In view of these restrictions, as Hoffmann LJ pointed out in *Re G*, in appropriate cases

---

Amendments to ICARA' (2003) 38 Texas Int LJ 41; 'Transfrontier Access/Contact and the Hague Convention of 25 October 1980 on the Civil Aspects of International Child Abduction'—Final Report, Preliminary Document No 5 of July 2002 for Special Commission of September/October 2002 (hereafter the 'Duncan Report'); Lowe, Everall and Nicholls, op cit, ch 25 at 25.2 et seq and N Lowe 'Problems Relating to Access Disputes under the Hague Convention on International Child Abduction' (1994) 8 Int Jo of Law and the Family 374.

[398] Child Abduction and Custody Act 1985 s 27(4).

[399] [1993] Fam 216, CA. See also *Practice Note* [1993] 1 FLR 804.

[400] It is sufficient for the application of Art 21 that the child is habitually resident in *a* contracting state before any breach of a right of access: Art 4.

[401] [1993] 2 FLR 617. For a shorter report of this case see *Re T (Minors) (International Child Abduction: Access)* [1993] 3 All ER 127n.

[402] See Bracewell J in *Re T* [1993] 2 FLR 617 at 621.

applicants might be better advised to apply to enforce access under the 1980 European Custody Convention.[403] However, it will often not be possible to use this Convention to enforce access orders since actions instead must be brought under what is now the revised Brussels II Regulation[404] wherever that applies (ie in actions involving Member States of the European Union, other than Denmark).[405]

It is an interesting point as to whether the English courts will continue to construe Art 21 so restrictively since in *Hunter v Murrow (Abduction Rights of Custody)*[406] Thorpe LJ signalled that the decision in *Re G* may have to be revisited. His reasoning was that the Convention is a living instrument but as revisions of the text are 'simply impracticable . . . evolutions necessary to keep pace with social and other trends must be achieved by evolutions in interpretation and construction'. He maintains that this is permissible by reason of Art 31(3)(b) of the Vienna Convention on the Law of Treaties 1969, which allows a construction that reflects 'any subsequent practice in the application of the treaty which establishes agreement of the parties regarding its interpretation'. According to Thorpe LJ in the 12 years since *Re G* 'the majority of the common law contracting states have adopted a more positive position and thus one that extends the utility of the Convention. Plainly in my judgment, when the point returns for consideration to this court, it is open to the court to reconsider the issue in the light of international jurisprudence. Since the question is to be decided according to the Hague Convention law this court is not eternally bound by the decision properly taken over 12 years ago reflecting international jurisprudence as it then was.'

Quite apart from the question of whether a common law court can, when interpreting Conventions, abandon previous decisions, Thorpe LJ's assertion that the majority of common law jurisdictions interpret Art 21 as imposing duties on the court is questionable. Importantly, for example, the *Re G* approach is taken in the USA with decisions such as *Bromley v Bromley*[407] and *Tejeiro Fernandez v Yeagar*[408] establishing that Art 21 does not give the courts any independent authority to enforce rights of access in respect of children. Ireland, too, deals with access under its domestic legislation.[409] Admittedly, other common law jurisdictions take a less rigid line. In New Zealand, for example, it has been held[410] that while the relevant legislation implementing the Hague Convention[411] did not of itself specify a right to apply to court it had clearly to remove the right before it could be inferred that there is no right of application for access to a court. In Australia courts deal

---

[403] Discussed below at p 679.   [404] Discussed below at pp 672ff.

[405] See *Re G (Foreign Contact Order: Enforcement)* [2003] EWCA Civ 1607, [2004] 1 WLR 521, applying the original Regulation. The consequence of this is that the European Convention can only be invoked to enforce access orders made in Bulgaria, Denmark, Iceland, Liechtenstein, Norway, Romania, Serbia and Montenegro, Switzerland, the former Yugoslav Republic of Macedonia and Turkey.

[406] [2005] EWCA Civ 976, [2005] 2 FLR 1119 at [30]–[31].

[407] 30 F Supp 2d 857 (ED Pa 1998), US District Ct for the Eastern District of Pennsylvania.

[408] 121 F Supp 2d 1118 (WD Mich 2000), US District Ct for the Western District of Michigan. See also *Janzik v Shand* No. 99C 6515, 2000 WL 1745203 (DN111. Nov. 27, 2000).

[409] See N Lowe and S Armstrong *Country Report: Ireland* (NCMEC 2002) 4.2. For the more complicated position in Canada see eg N Lowe, S Armstrong and A Mathias: *Country Report: Canada* (NCMEC 2002) 4.1–4.2.

[410] See *Secretary for Justice v Sigg* (1992) 10 FRNZ 164 and *Gumbrell v Jones* [2001] NZFLR 593.

[411] New Zealand has chosen not simply to directly incorporate the Convention into its domestic law but also to re-enact it in its own terms. See now the Care of Children Act 2004 Part 2, sub-part 4 on which see N Lowe and K Hollingsworth *Country Report: New Zealand* (NCMEC 2005).

with access under the implementing Regulations[412] rather than under domestic legislation. In Scotland, following *Donofrio v Burrell*[413] and the amended Rule 70.5(2) of the Rules of the Court of Session applications to enforce 'rights of access granted by any court of a Contracting party to the Hague Convention' can be made to the court 'under the Convention'.[414] But like England and Wales it is accepted that Art 21 does not confer upon individuals private rights or remedies attributable to the Convention nor does it place any obligation on the judicial authorities of the requested State.

The position in civil law jurisdictions is similarly varied with some such as Italy, Spain and Mexico regarding Art 21 as binding on the courts while others such as Sweden and France do not. Other States, for example, the Netherlands interpret Art 21 as empowering the Central Authority to bring a court action with the application being determined upon domestic law principles. Yet a further variation is that applying in Slovakia which regards Art 21 as binding upon the courts where a court order is sought to be enforced but applying domestic law to the enforcement of 'rights of access' falling short of a court order.[415]

In short, even if *Re G* is revisited, it is not at all certain how Art 21 should be interpreted We will discuss later,[416] whether in the light of the varied interpretation, Art 21 should be reformed.

4 THE REVISED BRUSSELS II REGULATION[417]

As previously discussed,[418] since March 2001 a new international instrument has come into play when considering abductions within Member States of the European Union (other than Denmark), namely, the so-called Brussels II Regulation. The original Regulation[419] was relatively limited in its scope applying only to matters of parental responsibility for children of both spouses involved in matrimonial proceedings; provided complex and inappropriate rules of jurisdiction and made no provision for an administrative body to help litigants.[420] Most, if not all, these shortcomings have been addressed by the revised Brussels II Regulation (still sometimes referred to as Brussels IIA but now commonly abbreviated to BIIR),[421] which came into force in March 2005 and which repealed the original Regulation. It is on this revised instrument that we now concentrate.

---

[412] Like New Zealand, Australia has re-enacted the Convention in its own terms under the Family Law (Child Abduction Conventions) Regulations 1986, as amended.

[413] 2000 SLT 1051, extensively discussed by Lowe, Everall and Nicholls, op cit 25.27 et seq.

[414] Consequently applicants will have the benefit of free Legal Aid. A not dissimilar position operates in Israel, see N Lowe and R Schuz: *Country Report: Israel* (NCMEC, 2005), 4.1/4.2.

[415] For a review of the different positions, see the Duncan Report, n 397.   [416] See below p 686.

[417] See generally Lowe, Everall and Nicholls *The New Brussels II Regulation A Supplement to International Movement of Children* (2005) and N Lowe 'Negotiating the Revised Brussels II Regulation' [2004] IFL 205.

[418] See above p 664.

[419] Council Regulation (EC) No 1347/2000 of 29 May 2000 on jurisdiction and the recognition and enforcement of judgments in matrimonial matters and in matters of parental responsibility for children of both spouses.

[420] For a critique of the limitations of the original Regulation, see eg Lowe 'New International Conventions Affecting the Law Relating to Children—a Cause for Concern?' [2001] IFL 171 and 'The Growing Influence of the European Union on International Family Law—A View From The Boundary' [2003] 56 *Current Legal Problems* 440, 457–64 and the authorities there cited.

[421] Council Regulation (EC) No 2201/2003 of 27 November 2003 concerning jurisdiction and the recognition and enforcement of judgments in matrimonial matters and the matters of parental responsibility, repealing Regulation (EC) No 1347/2000.

(a) The general scope of the revised Regulation

Unlike the 1980 Hague Abduction Convention or the 1980 European Custody Convention, no specific acts of improper or wrongful removals or retentions are needed to trigger the general application of the Regulation, rather it applies more generally to the recognition and enforcement of orders or enforceable agreements[422] in 'civil matters relating to . . . the attribution, exercise, delegation, restriction or termination of parental responsibility'.[423] Parental responsibility for these purposes specifically includes rights of custody and rights of access and also encompasses guardianship and the placement of a child in a foster family or in institutional care.[424] The holder of parental responsibility may be a natural person or a legal person.[425]

'Child' is not defined and as the *Practice Guide* says,[426] the Regulation does not therefore prescribe a maximum age. That is left to national law. This therefore preserves the Scottish practice of dealing with children up to the age of 16 rather than 18 as in England and Wales and Northern Ireland. In this latter respect it will be noted that the Regulation has a wider scope than either the Hague or European Convention which only applies to children under the age of 16. What the *Guide* does not deal with is whether the Regulation can have any application to unborn children.[427]

The Regulation binds all Member States of the European Union except Denmark[428] and, for recognition and enforcement purposes, applies as between Member States and not *within* a Member State. Accordingly, the Regulation does not govern the recognition and enforcement of orders within the United Kingdom.[429]

(b) Application of the Regulation to child abduction

The Regulation makes specific provision to deal with child abduction in a number of different ways. First, special rules of jurisdiction apply in the case of wrongful removals or retention. Secondly, as already discussed,[430] it regulates how courts should operate return applications made under the 1980 Hague Abduction Convention and governs what happens following a refusal to return under that Convention. Thirdly, it makes special provision for access orders involving cross border issues both in terms of jurisdiction and enforcement. All these measures are without prejudice to the general provision for recognition and enforcement.

---

[422] See Art 46.

[423] Art 1(1)(b). By Art 1(1)(a) the Regulation also applies to civil proceedings relating to divorce, legal separation and annulment, referred to above at p 32.

[424] Arts 1(2) and 2(7). Art 1(3) excludes from the Regulation establishing or contesting the parent-child relationship, adoption, names, emancipation, maintenance obligations, trusts and succession and measures taken as a result of criminal offences committed by children.

[425] Art 2(7).

[426] 'Parental Responsibility in the European Union—Practice Guide for the Application of the new Brussels II Regulation' (discussed at p 665 above) para 2.1.

[427] Compare *B v H (Habitual Residence: Wardship)* [2002] 1 FLR 388 (discussed above at p 637) in which it was tentatively suggested that it might be possible for a father who does not have parental responsibility to issue proceedings to give him rights of custody in respect of his unborn child. Although, as a matter of English law (see eg *C v S* [1998] QB 135, discussed above at p 429) such a suggestion seems untenable, it might have been better had the Regulation specifically dealt with the matter.

[428] See Art 2(3) and above at p 664.

[429] These issues are governed by the Family Law Act 1986, discussed below at p 689ff.

[430] Above at p 664.

Special rules of jurisdiction in cases of wrongful removal or retention

In the case of *wrongful* removals or retentions,[431] Art 10 provides that the courts of the child's former habitual residence retain jurisdiction until the child acquires a new habitual residence in another Member State *and* either:

(a) *each* person, institution or other body having rights of custody has acquiesced in the removal or retention; or

(b) the child has resided in the second Member State for at least one year after the holders of rights of custody have or should have had knowledge of the child's whereabouts *and* the child is settled in his or her new environment *and* either no request for a return has been lodged (or has been withdrawn) in that period, or the case has been closed pursuant to Article 11(7) (discussed below) or a custody judgment not entailing the child's return has been made in the State of the former habitual residence.

This provision is aimed at preventing jurisdiction being changed by abduction. Terms such as 'acquiescence' and 'settled in his or her new environment' are not defined. Although domestic courts will naturally have regard to the jurisprudence developed respectively under Arts 13(a) and 12(2) of the 1980 Hague Abduction Convention,[432] under the Regulation the ultimate arbiter of their meaning will be the European Court of Justice.

Special provisions for dealing with cross-border access

Article 9 provides that in the case of a child's *lawful* movement from one Member State to another *and* acquisition of an habitual residence there then by way of exception to the basic rule vesting jurisdiction in the State of habitual residence, the court that made the access order retains jurisdiction to modify it for three months following the removal (unless the holder of the access rights accepts jurisdiction of the new court by participating in proceedings there) provided the holder of access rights by the judgment continues to be habitually resident in the State of Origin.

This is a useful provision to review the access rights, or other contact arrangements and to adapt them to the new circumstances. But it is a limited provision. It only comes into play upon the acquisition of the new habitual residence. Furthermore, as the *Guide* points out, there must be a pre-existing court decision;[433] the provision only applies to lawful moves; it only applies for the three month period dating from the child's physical move; the holder of access rights must still be habitually resident in the State of Origin and must not have accepted the jurisdiction shifts, and it does not prevent the new court from

---

[431] Ie, pursuant to Art 2(11), a removal or retention which is:

'(a) . . . in breach of custody acquired by judgment or by operation of law or by an agreement having legal effect under the law of the Member State where the child was habitually resident immediately before the removal or retention; and

(b) provided that, at the time of removal or retention, the rights of custody were actually exercised, either jointly or alone, or would have been so exercised but for the removal or retention. Custody shall be considered to be exercised jointly when, pursuant to a decision or by operation of law, one holder of parental responsibility cannot decide on the child's place of residence without the consent of another holder of parental responsibility.'

[432] From which Convention they are ultimately borrowed, though the Article itself is modelled on Art 7 of the 1996 Hague Protection Convention.

[433] Note there is no modifying power over access *agreements*. Art 46 is confined to recognition and enforcement.

dealing with other issues. It should also be noted that the State of Origin only has jurisdiction to 'modify' the order which presumably does not include the power to end contact. The time period is particularly short and if Art 9 is to be interpreted strictly in the sense that even if seised of the case jurisdiction to modify ends immediately three months have elapsed from the child's move (as the *Guide* suggests it must be), then domestic courts will need a fast track procedure to deal with such applications.

So far as recognition and enforcement are concerned the revised Regulation makes the fundamental change that a judgment on rights of access issued in one Member State is *directly* and immediately recognisable and enforceable in another Member State if it is accompanied by a certificate. Furthermore it will be possible to oppose recognition of the judgment.[434] This procedure is discussed further below.

Although the court of enforcement cannot review an access judgment or agreement nor change its substance, it may, by Art 48, 'make practical arrangements for organising the exercise of rights of access, if the necessary arrangements have or have not sufficiently been made in the judgment delivered by the courts of the Member State having jurisdiction as to the substance of the matter *and provided the essential elements of this judgment are respected*' [emphasis added].

In other words, akin to the powers under the 1980 European Custody Convention, courts have some modifying powers. While this is a welcome provision it is not as clearly worded as Art 11(2) of the 1980 Convention. Much will turn on how the phrase 'the essential elements of the judgment' is construed. Will it preclude, for example, altering the place and frequency of access?[435] As the *Guide* points out, Art 48 is *not* a jurisdictional rule and does not confer jurisdiction as to the substance on the court of enforcement.

In addition to these substantive provisions, applicants can also invoke the aid of Central Authorities, not just to channel their applications but also for information and assistance and, importantly, to facilitate agreements through mediation or other means. As the *Guide* says,

'It is generally considered that mediation can play an important role in eg child abduction cases to ensure that the child can continue to see the non-abducting parent after the abduction and to see the abducting parent after the child has returned to the Member State of Origin.'

(c) Recognition and enforcement

The Regulation adopts the same type of method of recognition and enforcement as under the 1980 European Custody Convention. Apart from the crucial change of introducing what may be termed the 'fast track' procedure of enforcement, the revised Regulation makes no changes to the original Regulation with regard to the recognition and enforcement of judgments relating to parental responsibility. But what was new to the revised instrument was the creation of Central Authorities to which holders of parental responsibility are able to submit requests for assistance.[436] 'Assistance' includes, pursuant to Art 55,

---

[434] But holders of parental responsibility are nevertheless still free to seek recognition and enforcement of a judgment by applying for *exequatur*, see Art 40(2).

[435] The interpretation of Art 11(2) of the 1980 European Custody Convention is discussed below at p 684. If the approach of Thorpe LJ in *Re G (Foreign Contact Order: Enforcement)* [2003] EWCA Civ 1607, [2004] 1 FLR 378 is followed, there would be a wide latitude to modify orders.

[436] Article 57(1).

the collection and exchange of information inter alia on the child's situation, facilitating communication between the courts, and facilitating agreements between the parties through mediation (the importance of which is stressed by the *Guide*) or other means. Central Authorities must also 'provide information and assistance to holders of parental responsibility seeking recognition and enforcement of decisions on their territory, in particular concerning rights of access and the return of the child'. All these duties may be discharged either directly or through public authorities or other bodies. Importantly, Central Authorities must bear their own costs in discharging their duties and offer their services free of charge.[437]

Recognition

Orders and agreements (if they are enforceable in the Member State of Origin)[438] relating to parental responsibility made under the revised Regulation are automatically recognised by all other Member States to the Regulation without the need to invoke any special procedure.[439] Nevertheless any interested party[440] can apply for a judgment or agreement to be or not to be recognised.[441] *Limited* grounds for non-recognition are provided for by Art 23,[442] namely:

'that the judgment is manifestly contrary to the public policy of the Member State in which recognition is sought;[443]
taking into account the best interests of the child, it was given (except in the case of urgency) without the child being given an opportunity to be heard, in violation of the fundamental principles of procedure in that Member State;[444]
it is irreconcilable with a later judgment given in that state or another Member State, or the state of the child's habitual residence;
it was given in default of appearance and the person in default was not served;
or without giving an opportunity for a holder of parental responsibility to be heard.

These are the *only* grounds for refusing recognition. Moreover, Arts 26 and 24 respectively forbid the courts to review either the jurisdiction of the court of origin or a judgment as to its substance.

Potentially the widest of these exceptions is the first but following *Re S (Brussels II:*

---

[437] Article 57(4) and (3). Query whether these provisions extend to the costs of taking legal proceedings? See Lowe, Everall and Nichols, op cit at 3.3, who think that they do not.

[438] See Art 46.   [439] Art 21(1).

[440] According to the Borras Report (the Explanatory Report on what was then the Brussels II Convention) [1988] OJ C221/27, paras 65 and 80 the concept of an 'interested party' should be broadly interpreted so it may include not only the parents and children but also 'the public prosecutor or other similar bodies' where permitted in the State addressed.

[441] Art 21(3). Recognition proceedings may be stayed if the judgment is under appeal: Art 27.

[442] These grounds replicate those provided for by Art 15(2) of the original Regulation. According to Recital (21) 'the grounds for non-recognition should be kept to the minimum required'.

[443] Under the analogous provision in the Brussels I Regulation (viz Council Regulation (EC) No 44/2001 on Jurisdiction and the Recognition of Judgments in Civil and Commercial Matters) the public policy defence has been narrowly construed by the ECJ, according to which even fraud is insufficient: *Societé d'Information Service Realisation v Amperstand Software BV*, *The Times*, 29 July 1993, CA.

[444] As the Borras Report, above, at para 73, points out, while this exception is confined to the relevant rules of the Member State in question, nevertheless those rules must take account of Art 12 of the UN Convention on the Rights of the Child (see p 482 above).

Recognition: Best Interests of the Child)(No 1)[445] it is evident that it will be hard to establish. In *Re S* it was argued that the exception should have prevented recognition of a Belgian access order because (a) the father had untruthfully represented to the Antwerp first instance court that the mother had brought the child concerned to England without his consent and (b) were the order to be enforced there would be the danger that the father would unlawfully keep the child in Belgium. The argument was rejected, for as Holman J said:

'To say something is contrary to public policy is a high hurdle, to which the Article adds the word "manifestly".'

Neither of the arguments were thought to come close to crossing the hurdle.

Enforcement

As Lowe, Everall and Nicholls put it,[446] there are two routes to enforcement under the Regulation, the ordinary route and the 'fast track' for enforcing access orders for the return of a child under Art 11(8). Under the ordinary procedure it is necessary to obtain a declaration of enforceability (which means, in the United Kingdom, having to register the judgment) before enforcement. In contrast under the 'fast track' procedure the order can be enforced directly, provided that the appropriate certificate has been issued by the court of origin.

The ordinary procedure. According to Art 28(1), in general an enforceable judgment on the exercise of parental responsibility made in one Member State can be declared enforceable in another Member State upon the application of any interested party.[447] However, under Art 28(2) judgments only become enforceable within the UK when, upon application of any interested party, they have been registered for enforcement.[448] The national law of the enforcing State governs both the procedure for applying to enforce[449] (though applicants who are holders of parental responsibility are entitled to information and assistance from the Central Authority)[450] and the enforcement procedure itself.[451] Nevertheless as the *Practice Guide* says,[452] 'it is of the essence that national authorities apply rules which secure efficient and speedy enforcement of decisions issued under the Regulation so as not to undermine its objectives'. In any event, Art 3(1) states that the court applied to 'shall give its decision without delay'.

---

[445] [2003] EWHC 2115 (Fam), [2004] 1 FLR 571.   [446] *The New Brussels II Regulation* at 7.9.

[447] For the meaning of which, see n 440 above.

[448] Query the advantage of having this registration requirement?

[449] Art 30. For the procedure in England and Wales, see FPR 1991, ch 5, under which applications have to be made to the High Court (Family Division) and filed at the Principal Registry. For details see Lowe, Everall and Nicholls, above, at 7.12 et seq. Where it is sought to enforce an order *made* in England and Wales in another Member State application for a certified copy of the judgement sought to be enforced should be made to the court that made the order: FPR 1991, r. 7.49, FPC 1991, r 21M.

[450] Art 55(b). But note unlike the 1980 Hague Abduction and European Custody Convention applicants do not qualify for legal representation at public expense save to the extent that applicants who benefited from complete or partial legal aid are entitled 'to benefit from the most favourable legal aid . . . provided by the law of the Member State addressed'. Art 50.

[451] Art 47(1).

[452] *Practice Guide for the application of the new Brussels II Regulation* (drawn up by the European Commission 2005) p. 43.

Although in no event at any stage of the enforcement process can a judgment be reviewed as to its substance,[453] Art 31(2) does permit a refusal to enforce upon the same limited grounds upon which a refusal to recognise a judgment can be based.[454] Indeed according to *Re S (Brussels II: Recognition: Best Interests of Child)(No 2)*,[455] while there is an overriding duty to enforce an order previously 'recognised', what is now Art 31(2) nevertheless permits a refusal even in these circumstances.

Under Art 36 provision is made for partial enforcement, with Art 36(1) permitting the court not to enforce the whole order and Art 36(2) permitting the applicant only to request a partial enforcement. In the latter case, as Holman J observed in *Re S*,[456] the court need not enforce an order save in those respects requested but in the former case the power is strictly limited, namely, to relieve a court from seeking to enforce that which is impossible, it being incumbent upon the court to enforce the rest. No provision is made to *vary* an order but according to *Re S* there is a power to 'phase in' an order.[457]

Re S also establishes that in determining an enforcement application the court is *not* bound to treat the child's welfare as its paramount consideration.[458] Any decision made on an enforcement application may be appealed.[459]

The fast-track procedure. Access orders and orders made under Art 11(8)[460] are *directly* enforceable (that is, without the need for declaration of enforceability nor with the possibility of opposing recognition) in another Member State provided the appropriate certificate has been issued by the court of the Member State of Origin.[461] In the case of an Art 11(8) order the certificate is issued by the judge of origin[462] of his or her own motion using the standard form in Annex 4 to the Regulation. In access cases, where the rights of access involve a cross border situation at the time that the judgment is given, the certificate must be issued ex officio when the judgment becomes enforceable, even if only provisionally, or a certificate may be issued subsequently.[463] The certificate itself must be issued in standard form provided for in Annex III.[464] The party seeking enforcement must produce both a coy of the judgement and the certificate.[465] No appeal lies against the issuing of the certificate (though in cases of error it is possible to seek ratification before the judge of origin).[466] The actual enforcement procedure is a matter for the domestic law of each Member State.[467]

---

[453] Art 31(3).   [454] See in particular Art 23, discussed above at p 676.
[455] [2003] EWHC 2974 (Fam), [2004] 1 FLR 582, per Holman J.   [456] Above at [11].
[457] Above at [14].   [458] See [14].   [459] Art 33.
[460] Viz orders requiring the child's return made in proceedings in the requesting state following a refusal to return under the 1980 Hague Abduction Convention by the requested State—discussed above at p 668.
[461] See respectively Arts 11(8) and 41(1).   [462] Ie a judge in the court that made the original order.
[463] Art 41(3).   [464] Art 41(2).   [465] Art 45.   [466] Art 43.   [467] Art 47.

5 THE EUROPEAN CUSTODY CONVENTION [468]

(a) When the Convention applies

This Convention applies to the 'improper removal' of any person of any nationality who is under the age of 16 and who does not have the right to decide his own place of residence.[469] Under Art 1(d), 'improper removal' means:

'the removal of a child across an international frontier in breach of a decision relating to his custody which has been given in a Contracting State and which is enforceable in such a State; "improper removal" also includes:

(i) the failure to return a child across an international frontier at the end of a period of the exercise of the right of access to this child or at the end of any other temporary stay in a territory other than that where the custody is exercised;

(ii) a removal which is subsequently declared unlawful within the meaning of Article 12.'

The requirement that the improper removal be across 'an international frontier' means that the Convention has no application to abductions within the British Isles. In other words, it is not sufficient in itself that a child is removed from one legal system to another. It a prerequisite under this Convention that an applicant has an order in his favour, although under Art 12, if there is no enforceable decision at the time of the removal, an application may subsequently be made by any interested person for a declaration that the removal is 'improper'.[470]

This power has been widely interpreted by the English courts. In *Re S (A Minor) (Custody: Habitual Residence)*[471] the House of Lords held that Art 12 and s 23(2) of the 1985 Act effectively empower courts to make orders which can *subsequently* make the child's continuing retention in another country an 'improper removal' within the meaning of Art 1(d). In that case it was held that an unmarried father, habitually resident in England at the time of his child's removal, had 'an interest in the matter' for the purposes of s 23(2) notwithstanding that he did not have parental responsibility, and that following the granting of interim care and control to the father, the retention thereafter by the aunt became improper, so that the court was entitled to make the declaration of 'improper removal' within the meaning of Art 1(d). More questionably, in *Re S (Abduction) (European Convention)*,[472] following the child's removal to Denmark by the mother, the unmarried father (who had already instituted Children Act proceedings before the removal) obtained ex parte an interim residence order and then successfully sought a declaration. Hollis J held that in these circumstances he was entitled to make the declaration notwithstanding

---

[468] See generally R Jones 'Council of Europe Convention on Recognition and Enforcement of Decisions Relating to the Custody of Children' (1981) 30 ICLQ 46,7 Lowe, Everall and Nicholls, op cit, ch 19 and Clark Hall and Morrison on *Children* 2[74]ff.

[469] By parity of reasoning with *Re H (Abduction: Child of 16)* [2000] 2 FLR 51 the Convention will cease to apply to a child upon his attaining the age of 16 even if the application was made before he was 16. There is, however, still the power to deal with the child whilst a minor under the High Court's inherent jurisdiction.

[470] In England and Wales such a declaration can be made in any 'custody proceedings': Child Abduction and Custody Act 1985 s 23(2). 'Custody proceedings' are defined in Sch 3 and refer principally to residence orders.

[471] [1998] AC 750, HL.   [472] [1996] 1 FLR 660.

that when the abduction took place the father had no right to determine the child's place of residence.

Under Art 1(c) 'a decision relating to custody' means a decision of a judicial or administrative authority insofar as it relates to the care of the person of the child including the right to decide on the place of his residence, or to the right of access to him. It is clear that a residence or contact order under s 8 of the Children Act 1989 will satisfy this requirement. Whether it includes a foreign court making a return order under the 1980 Hague Abduction Convention has yet to be determined, though sensible arguments can be raised either way.[473]

Unlike the 1980 Hague Abduction Convention it has been held, at any rate in England, that the European Custody Convention has retrospective effect.[474] Hence, orders made before a State implemented the Convention can be enforced in this country.

(b) Recognition and enforcement

Under Art 7 decisions relating to custody made and enforceable in one Contracting State are recognised and enforceable in every other contracting state. But to secure that recognition and enforcement, an application has to be made for those purposes in the other Contracting State. Although this scheme applies equally to custody and to access orders, the latter raises a number of separate issue which will be discussed later.

(c) Applying for the child's return

To secure the child's return, an application may be made through a Central Authority together with the appropriate documents.[475] Upon receiving the application the Central Authority in the state addressed must, without delay, take appropriate steps, inter alia, to secure the recognition and enforcement of the custody order.[476] Recognition and enforcement are achieved by registering the court order in a court of the Contracting State to which the child has been taken. In England and Wales applications to register must be made in the High Court.[477] Once the order is registered the court has the same powers of enforcement as if it had made the original order,[478] and in this way the child's return can be ordered.

Although registration and enforcement normally go hand in hand, it was established by *Re H (A Minor) (Foreign Custody Order: Enforcement)*[479] that whilst registration is a sine qua non condition of enforcement, enforcement does not automatically follow recognition, since there is a discretion to apply the exceptions (under Arts 9 and 10, discussed below) to the issue of enforcement notwithstanding a previous registration.

(d) Refusing recognition or enforcement

Where an application has been made promptly after an improper removal, recognition and enforcement of the order and restoration of the child must normally follow but there are exceptions, namely, those provided by Arts 9 and 10. The burden of proving one of

[473] See *Re L (Abduction: Pending Criminal Proceedings)* [1999] 1 FLR 433 at 442, per Wilson J.
[474] *Re L (A Minor) (Child Abduction)* [1992] 2 FLR 178, per Booth J.
[475] Art 4(2). The requisite documents are listed in Art 13.   [476] Art 5.
[477] Child Abduction and Custody Act 1985 s 16. For the procedure see FPR 1991, Part VI.
[478] Ibid, s 18, and Art 7.   [479] [1994] Fam 105, CA.

the exceptions lies on the person opposing the recognition or enforcement and the court is expected to recognise and register the order unless it *expressly* finds one of the exceptions proved.[480] In no event is the court entitled to review a foreign decision as to its substance.[481]

The precise latitude for refusal depends upon whether the Contracting State has implemented Art 8. If it has, then, provided the application is made within six months of the child's removal, registration is virtually mandatory, since only the narrow exceptions under Art 9 may be raised. However, most Contracting States, including the United Kingdom,[482] pursuant to the right under Art 17 to take a reservation on Art 8, have not implemented that Article.[483] In these states, registration may, in all cases, be refused within the terms of Art 9 or Art 10.[484]

As just intimated, the exceptions provided by Art 9 are narrow and may best be thought of as comprising procedural defects in the making of the order sought to be enforced. Accordingly, under this Article registration or enforcement may be refused where:

(a) through no fault of the defendant, he or she was not served with notice of the relevant proceedings in the state of origin;

(b) the court of origin lacked competence to make the order in question since it was not founded on the habitual residence of any of the parties; or

(c) there was already a prior decision in the state addressed which became enforceable before the improper removal.

The exceptions provided by Art 10 are considerably wider, particularly that under Art 10(1)(b),[485] which permits refusal—

'where it is found that by reason of a change of circumstances, including the passage of time but not including a mere change in the residence of the child after an improper removal, the effects of the original decision are manifestly no longer in accordance with the welfare of the child.'

---

[480] *Re A (Foreign Access Order: Enforcement)* [1996] 1 FLR 561, CA.   [481] Art 9(3).

[482] The UK did not implement Art 8 because it was felt to be too draconian and contrary to the provisions of the Hague Convention: see Lord Hailsham LC in 460 HL Official Report (5th series) col 1253, 1985. For the list of other states making a similar reservation, see Lowe, Everall and Nicholls, op cit, at 19.14, n 21.

[483] Permitting a reservation to be taken on Art 8 was the compromise arrived at to accommodate two opposing views, namely that the return of recently abducted children should be virtually automatic as against the view that the requested State should retain an ultimate discretion to refuse a return where this would be manifestly contrary to the child's view. See Jones, op cit, at 472–473, where he fully articulates the debate.

[484] Note: under Art 17(2) where a child is removed from a State that has made a reservation on Art 8, to a State that has not, the latter State can nevertheless apply Art 10. In other words, in the spirit of reciprocity no advantage can be taken of the one State entering and the other not entering a reservation.

[485] Art 10(1)(a) refers to the effect of the decision being 'manifestly incompatible with the fundamental principles' of the law in the state addressed (on which note the failed applications in *Re G (A Minor)(Child Abduction: Enforcement)* [1990] 2 FLR 325 and *T v R (Abduction: Forum Conveniens)* [2002] 2 FLR 544, discussed by Lowe, Everall and Nicholls op cit, at 19.110); Art 10(1)(c) refers to children who are nationals or habitual residents in the state addressed and who have no such connection with the state of origin; and Art 10(1)(d) refers to the incompatibility of the decision with a decision given in the state addressed or enforceable in that state after being given in a third state. For a refusal on this ground see *Re M (Child Abduction: European Convention)* [1994] 1 FLR 551 where enforcement proceedings began after an English court had made an interim residence order and it was not thought to be in the children's welfare to be returned pending the outcome of the English decision since they had lived in England for the last 18 months.

Before making any decision under Art 10(1)(b) the court is required by Art 15 to ascertain the child's views 'unless this is impracticable having regard in particular to his age and understanding'. It will be noted, however, that unlike the Hague Convention a refusal is not permitted because of the child's objections per se.

In line with the spirit of the Convention, Art 10(1)(b) has been interpreted strictly by the English courts. It has been emphasised that for the exception to operate at all there must be a change of circumstances,[486] and that there is a heavy burden to discharge to show that the original order is 'manifestly no longer in accordance with the child's welfare'. It has been held,[487] for instance, that it is not enough to show that the child has settled well and is happy. Notwithstanding this heavy burden there have been cases where registration and enforcement have been refused. For example, in *F v F (Minors) (Custody: Custody Order)*[488] it was held that a foreign order for custody should not be enforced where the children had been in England for 21 months, and 12 months had elapsed between the enforcement hearing and the making of the foreign order. Similarly, in *Re R (Abduction: European and Hague Conventions)*[489] recognition and enforcement of a Swiss order in favour of grandparents were refused on the basis that the mother had since remarried and the emotional and financial support that her new spouse provided had transformed the situation, with the child in question now thriving and happy and emphatically not wishing to return to Switzerland. The Court of Appeal upheld Hale J's conclusion that the order was manifestly no longer in accordance with the child's welfare. Article 10(1)(b) was also found to be satisfied in *T v R (Abduction: Forum Conveniens)*[490] in which a return to a father in Sweden after living for four years with the mother in England, was held to be manifestly not in the child's short-term interests.

(e) Adjourning recognition and enforcement

Article 10(2) permit the court to postpone recognition and/or enforcement:

'(a) if an ordinary form of review of the original decision has been commenced;

(b) if proceedings relating to the custody of the child, commenced before the proceedings in the State or origin were instituted, are pending in the State addressed;

(c) if another decision concerning the custody of the child is the subject of proceedings for enforcement or of any other proceedings concerning the recognition of the decision'.

It will noted that unlike the grounds for refusing recognition or enforcement, the pending of other proceedings relating to the child is a ground for adjournment. In *T v R (Abduction: Forum Conveniens)*[491] it was held that if the court refuses to recognise the original order under Art 10(1), it can nevertheless adjourn the application rather than dismiss it. In that case, having found Art 10(1)(b) satisfied, Charles J, exercising his inherent jurisdiction, and upon the father undertaking not to take any steps to remove the

---

[486] Per Leggatt LJ in *Re A (Foreign Access Order: Enforcement)*, above at 564.

[487] Per Booth J in *Re G (A Minor) (Abduction: Enforcement)* [1990] 2 FLR 325. See also *Re L (Child Abduction: European Conventions)* [1992] 2 FLR 178 and *Re K (A Minor) (Abduction)* [1990] 1 FLR 387.

[488] [1989] Fam 1.

[489] [1997] 1 FLR 663, CA. Enforcement was also refused in *Re H (A Minor) (Foreign Custody Order)* [1994] Fam 105, in which a 13-year-old girl, who had been in the UK for about five years, was adamant that she did not wish to have any further contact with her father.

[490] [2002] 2 FLR 544. But note this application was adjourned, see below.   [491] Ibid.

child from the mother's care, ordered the child's return to Sweden but staying the order so as to allow the mother to institute custody proceedings in Sweden. In that way he felt able to promote the child's long term interests.

(f) Interim powers

As under the 1980 Hague Abduction Convention, the court has wide powers to make interim orders pending the determination of the application for registration and enforcement.[492]

(g) Effect on other domestic proceedings

As under the 1980 Hague Abduction Convention, the domestic courts' powers to hear the merits of other custody proceedings are restricted during the pendency of an application for registration.[493] Upon registration all other custody orders cease to have effect,[494] but if registration is refused other applications can be heard on their merits.[495]

(h) Applying for access [496]

Under Art 11(1) decisions on rights of access are recognised and enforceable in the same way as decisions relating to custody. According to *Re A (Foreign Access Order: Enforcement)*[497] the scheme of the Convention is plain and the task of the judge is clear, namely to recognise and register the foreign access order unless an exception under Art 9 or 10 is established. The burden for establishing a defence lies on the party opposing registration.

It is as hard to invoke the exception when resisting the enforcement of an access order as it is when opposing the enforcement of custody. Thus in *Re A* itself, in which a father was seeking to enforce a French access order under which there was to be staying access in France every August, it was held that the 'hardening' of the children's objections to going to France came nowhere near the change of circumstances rendering the original decision 'manifestly no longer in accordance with the child's welfare', as envisaged by the Convention. In not dissimilar circumstances in *Re G (Foreign Contact Order: Enforcement)*[498] Thorpe LJ commented:

'The European Convention would be rendered impotent and its policy frustrated were primary carers able to avoid enforcement by asserting circumstances and developments that cry out for profound investigation by the courts of the jurisdiction primarily seised.'

In *Re L (Abduction: European Convention: Access)*,[499] however, the enforcement of an access order made in France in favour of grandparents was refused because it was predicated on the basis that the children were living in France close to the grandparents in circumstances in which there were no practical difficulties in the way of contact, whereas the children were now living in England with their parents. It was held that in these

---

[492] See s 19 of the Child Abduction and Custody Act.
[493] Ibid, s 20(1). For the exceptions see s 20(2).   [494] Ibid, s 25(1).   [495] Ibid, s 20(1).
[496] For a detailed analysis see Lowe, Everall and Nicholls, op cit, at 25.42ff and N Lowe 'Regulating Cross Border Access to Children' in *Perspektivan Des Familienrechts Festschrift für Dieter Schwab* (eds S Hofer, D Klippel and U Walter) 1153, 1154–8.
[497] [1996] 1 FLR 561, CA.   [498] [2003] EWCA Civ 1607, [2004] 1 FLR 378 at [24].
[499] [1999] 2 FLR 1089.

circumstances, given that the French order would have required the children (aged seven and three) to travel to France twice a month for contact, it was neither practical nor in the children's interest to enforce it and that therefore the defence under Art 10(1)(b) that enforcement was 'manifestly no longer in accordance with the welfare of the [children]' was made out.

Notwithstanding the general scheme to register or to refuse to register access order, Art 11(2) empowers the competent authority addressed to 'fix the conditions for implementation and exercise of the right of access taking into account, in particular, undertakings given by the parties on this matter'. In the words of one leading commentator on the Convention:[500]

'The wording of Art 11(2) represents the outcome of extensive discussion in the Committee of Experts. It reflects the difficulty frequently encountered in practice in establishing how access is to be given where the parents fail to agree on times and places. The court or other competent authority in the State where the child is living will ordinarily be in the best position to decide such details in default of agreement, since it will have better facilities than the court in the State of origin to make the necessary enquiries and a greater knowledge of local circumstances (such as, for example, when school holidays begin and end).'

In effect, Art 11(2) enables the state addressed to modify decisions of other contracting states to make them consistent with local practice. However, as the Court of Appeal emphasised in *Re A (Foreign Access Order: Enforcement)*,[501] this modifying power is still subject to the embargo under Art 9(3) against reviewing orders as to their substance. In their view Bracewell J had, at first instance, transgressed this provision when, purportedly exercising her powers under Art 11(2), she modified a French order that the father have annual contact in France by granting him staying access in England instead even though it was known that the father could only afford staying access in France. As Waite LJ put it:[502]

'The radical change made by the judge to the French court order by giving the father access in England which he cannot afford to take up, instead of staying access in France which is what the French judge had directed, could not possibly have been brought within the implementation provisions of Art 11. Such a change would have amounted, as Leggatt LJ has said, to a review of the foreign decision as to its substance, a step which is specifically prohibited by Art 9(3).'

Although the decision in *Re A* was understandable, given the father's inability to afford access abroad, it amounted to a restrictive interpretation of Art 11(2) but a more liberal approach has since been signalled by Thorpe LJ when he commented in *Re G (Foreign Contact Order: Enforcement)*[503]

'Conventions for international enforcement of contact orders are prone to overreach themselves in their ambitions. Access orders can seldom be written on stone tablets. The orders are peculiarly vulnerable to change of circumstance, the maturation of children, and the dynamics within sometimes the old family and sometimes a newly constituted family. In consequence enforcement, not only after lapse of time but after relocation and in a foreign

---

[500] R Jones (1981) 30 ICLQ 467 at 472.   [501] [1996] 1 FLR 561.   [502] Above at 568.
[503] [2003] EWCA Civ 1607, [2004] 1 FLR 378 at [27].

court, is always likely to be problematic. *These realities, in my judgment, demand a liberal construction of Art 11(2) in order to achieve the overriding objectives of the European Convention, one of which is to ensure that the act of relocation does not avoid the orders for contact made by the court that granted permission.*' [Emphasis added.]

One can only agree. Unless it is thought right to limit Art 11(2) to being a purely supplementary power (for example, to give some definition to open ended orders such as defining school holidays or 'reasonable' access) then some flexibility has surely to be permitted. Even so where the line is to be drawn in a particular case will still be problematic.

Although relatively unsophisticated, the 1980 European Custody Convention at least provides a direct international mechanism by which an access order made in the Contracting State can be enforced in another. Indeed for many countries prior to Brussels II Regulations this Convention provided the only means of doing so.[504] Furthermore, by squarely making it a Convention obligation upon the court to do so, this Convention is superior to the 1980 Hague Abduction Convention and one crucial consequence of this is that applicants are entitled to free legal representation regardless of means or merits. Hence, where applicants have a choice, they would be well advised to seek to invoke the European Convention rather than the Hague in seeking to enforce access decisions.[505]

The extra flexibility provided for by Art 11(2) particularly as interpreted by Thorpe LJ in *Re G* also makes these provisions superior to those of the 1980 Hague Abduction Convention. Yet despite these positive points, it has nevertheless to be acknowledged that this part of the Convention has not proved an outstanding success. This is due in part to the fact that (a) it is confined to enforcing existing orders; (b) in any event Contracting States are limited to those within the Council of Europe; and (c) it has been superseded within Member States of the European Union (other than Denmark) by the revised Brussels II Regulation.

6 EVALUATING THE USE AND EFFECT OF THE INSTRUMENTS

Although both the 1980 Conventions have attracted growing numbers of Contracting States, it is evident that the Hague Abduction Convention has proved far more useful than the European Custody Convention. In practice even before the coming into force of the Brussels II Regulation, the European Custody Convention was little used. In part this is because the need for a custody or access order limits its scope, but it seems its restricted use also stems from its alleged complexity.[506] In contrast there is general agreement that the Hague Convention is generally working well. However, whether this view is oversanguine can be debated. Both the 1999 and 2003 Statistical Surveys found that overall 50% of return applications ended either in the child's voluntary return or in a return order

---

[504] Though action to enforce access orders is provided for by the 1961 Hague Child Protection Convention to which Austria, France, Germany, Italy, Luxembourg, the Netherlands, Poland, Portugal, Spain, Switzerland and Turkey are contracting States.

[505] Empirical evidence did suggest that before the coming into force of the Brussels II Regulations the European Convention was more commonly used for access disputes than the Hague. Lowe and Perry 'International Child Abduction—the English Experience', (1998) 47 ICLQ 127, found that in 1996, whereas only 6% of incoming Hague applications were for access, 25% of European applications were. The figures for outgoing applications were 17% and 42% respectively, though in each case the actual numbers were small.

[506] See Lowe and Perry 'International Child Abduction—the English Experience', op cit.

made by the court. While this might seem a relatively low proportion it needs to be appreciated that a relatively high proportion (15% in 2003, 14% in 1999) of applications were withdrawn[507] and a further proportion (6% in 2003, 11% in 1999) were rejected.[508] Furthermore, in both surveys a further 9% of applications were still pending at the end of the research period.[509] In fact a relatively small percentage (12% in 2003, 11% in 1999) ended in a judicial refusal to return. Put another way, of the applications that went to court only 28% of applications were refused in 2003 and 26% in 1999. In that sense the Convention is generally working as it was intended to.

So far as speed is concerned the Hague Abduction Convention sets a six week target for return (a target which has been made an obligation by the revised Brussels II Regulation). It is evident, however, that return applications are disposed of rather more slowly than this (though still, one suspects, considerably quicker than domestic applications would generally be determined). Both the 2003 and 1999 surveys found that voluntary returns were effected in an overall average of about 12 weeks, with judicial returns taking an average of being 14 to 15 weeks and judicial refusals between 21 and 25 weeks. It is generally acknowledged that England and Wales stands out as a model Convention country. Applications for return are generally completed within seven-and-a-half weeks and the proportion of judicial refusals (9%) is low.[510] Of course, some Contracting States perform worse than others, but even here international pressure can be brought to bear on countries which are thought to be falling below the accepted Convention standards. In this regard the periodic reviews conducted by the Permanent Bureau at the Hague are enormously helpful and influential. It remains to be seen what impact the revised Brussels II Regulation will have but the hope is that as between EU Member States return applications will generally be disposed more quickly (though in this respect the fear has been expressed that States will simply prioritise Brussels II applications) and it may be that there will be even fewer refusals.[511]

One area where even the Hague Convention is acknowledged not to be working well, is in relation to access.[512] Not only do they form a minority of applications but in terms of outcome and speed they are markedly less successful than return applications. According to the 1999 Statistical survey, 43% of access applications ended in access being gained as a result of a voluntary agreement or court order but this rate declined to only 34% in the 2003 survey. In the latter survey, 65% of applications resolved judicially and 62% resolved voluntarily took over six months to do so.

There has been much discussion in the Special Meetings of the Commissions reviewing the Hague Convention as to what, if anything, to do about access. At the 2002 Meeting it was agreed that the Bureau draw up a Good Practice Guide. While this might help it will not solve all the problems. However, in this respect note might be taken of other international instruments that might make a contribution in this area. One such instrument is

---

[507] The 1999 survey found a variety of reasons for withdrawals including lack of finance, on the one hand, and parties reaching a private agreement on the other.

[508] This would be because the child was too old or could not be found or was found in another State.

[509] In each study the period ended 18 months after the last application could have been received in 30 June 2001 and 2005 respectively.

[510] See the 2003 and 1999 Statistical Studies, op cit.   [511] But note the comment above at p 669.

[512] The issue was acknowledged and extensively discussed at the Second Special Commission Meeting of the Review of the Hague Convention held in 1993.

the 1996 Hague Convention on the Protection of Children which does have useful provisions on access. As we mentioned in Chapter 1,[513] this Convention seeks to (a) provide common jurisdictional rules (b) provide for the recognition and enforcement of orders and (c) establish co-operation between Contracting States to achieve the Convention's purposes. It is this last respect that is most pertinent to access issues. For example, under Art 31(b) Central Authorities must directly or through public authorities or other bodies 'facilitate, by mediation, conciliation or other means, agreed solutions for the protection of the person or property of the child in situations to which the Convention applies'.

This has obvious application to access disputes.

In addition to the duties expressly imposed upon Central Authorities, further provisions designed to promote co-operation are provided by Art 35. Article 35(1) in particular provides:

'The competent authorities of a Contracting State may request the authorities of another Contracting State to assist in the implementation of measures of protection taken under this Convention, especially in securing the effective exercise of rights of access as well as of the right to maintain direct contacts on a regular basis.'

Another useful provision is Art 35(2) which permits a parent who is seeking to obtain or maintain access but who is living in one Contracting State while the child is habitually resident in another Contracting State to request the competent authorities of the State in which the child is residing to 'gather information or evidence and may make a finding on the suitability of that parent to exercise access and on the conditions under which access is to be exercised'. This information is then admissible evidence in proceedings in the child's habitual residence and indeed, under Art 35(3), the court may adjourn proceedings pending the outcome of such a request.

At the time of writing, although all EU Member States have signed the 1996 Convention, because of political wrangles principally between the United Kingdom and Spain, it has not been ratified.

Yet another international instrument of potential relevance is the Council of Europe's 2003 Convention on Contact Concerning Children which is not yet in force.[514] The Convention usefully sets out general principles which domestic courts should observe when dealing with contact issues and contains some provisions directly concerned with the recognition and enforcement of transfrontier contact cases including the novel provision of providing a procedure for advance recognition and enforcement of contact orders and provision for the prompt return of children at the end of a period of transfrontier contact.

While these latter two Conventions could be useful they undoubtedly make the legal landscape more complicated and indeed there is a real danger that the proliferation of international instruments will in themselves defeat the very object of improving the law regulating the cross border movement of children.

Access is not the only issue of concern. Other debates concern the lack of legal aid (particularly in the USA) and whether there should be concentrated jurisdiction when dealing inter alia with Hague cases. But perhaps the acid test of success is whether the

---

[513] Above at p 28. For a detailed discussion of the 1996 Convention see eg Lowe, Everall and Nicholls, *International Movement of Children* ch 24 and 25.60 et seq.

[514] For a detailed discussion of the 2003 Convention see Lowe, Everall and Nicholls, op cit, 25.83 et seq.

Conventions deter would-be abductors. This is much harder to assess. However, there does seem to have been a discernible trend away from abductions by the non-primary carer to those by the primary carer.[515] In their analysis of 1996 cases handled by the Child Abduction Unit, Lowe and Perry found[516] that 70 per cent of abductions were by mothers and commonly in all cases abductors tended to be returning to their jurisdiction of nationality (ie 'going home'). This finding has been replicated in both the 1999 and 2003 Statistical Surveys.[517] The latter, in particular, found that in the cases where information was available, 69% of abductors were either the primary or joint primary carer and just over half were returning to their home country. In other words, the abductions were generally not aimed, as another study[518] termed it, at 'throwing off pursuers by escaping abroad', but instead abductors were 'returning to a culturally familiar country where family and legal support may be available'.

One theory about the changing pattern of abduction is that the Conventions deter would-be abductors in the popular sense of the word, ie men (or non-primary carers) 'kidnapping' their children. On the other hand, the deterrent effect of the Convention has not been so strong among women because, it is argued, their motivation is likely to be to escape violent or abusive relationships.[519] Whether this is so has yet to be definitely established but there is undoubted concern that there is no real mechanism under the Conventions for ensuring the child's safety after being returned, nor indeed for ensuring that any steps are subsequently taken. This in turn led to the suggestion at the third review of the Hague Convention[520] that Central Authorities ought to be obliged to take responsibility for children returned under the Convention. Although this suggestion drew substantial support, no formal action has yet been taken because of the extra commitment and costs involved. In practice, however, there is considerable liaison both between the judiciary and the Central Authorities, and in cases of real concern it is possible to make informal arrangements.

One further challenge is in respect of Islamic countries which have so far not acceded to the Convention. The dilemma here is that while it is desirable to have as many nations as possible within the 'Convention fold', not all nations hold to the same basic values and, in particular, they may not treat all parents equally, having different concepts of what is in children's interests.

E DEALING WITH CHILDREN TAKEN TO OR BROUGHT FROM ANOTHER PART OF THE UNITED KINGDOM AND ISLE OF MAN

1 INTRODUCTION

Before implementation of the Family Law Act 1986, orders made in another part of the United Kingdom were treated no differently from an order made in any other part of the world: they were neither recognised nor enforceable. Moreover, as different parts of the

---

[515] See D McClean 'International child abduction—some recent trends' (1997) 9 CFLQ 387 at 388.
[516] Op cit.   [517] Op cit.   [518] G Greif and R Hager *When Parents Kidnap* (1993).
[519] See the discussion by Lowe and Perry, op cit.   [520] By the Australian delegation.

United Kingdom had different jurisdictional rules there could be, and were, cases where competing orders were made in respect of the same child. No case illustrates this better than *Babington v Babington*.[521] In that case the wife, a Scottish domiciliary, left the matrimonial home in Scotland to live in England. She made her 11-year-old daughter, who attended a boarding school in England but who hitherto had spent her holidays with the parents in Scotland, a ward of court.[522] The effect of wardship was to prevent the child going to Scotland without the court's consent.[523] Meanwhile the husband, also a Scottish domiciliary, petitioned the Scottish Court of Session for what was then custody and access. Taking the view that as the court of domicile it had pre-eminent jurisdiction, it granted access to the husband. The husband then applied to the English court for leave to take the child out of the jurisdiction. The wife opposed the application and sought leave herself to take the child to Switzerland for a holiday. Notwithstanding the Scottish order the English court refused the husband's application and granted the wife's instead. As the English and Scottish Law Commissions subsequently commented:[524]

'The English court disregarded the order of the Scottish court and the Scottish court disregarded the fact that the child was an English ward of court. The English court's order prevailed merely because it could be enforced, although the child had stronger connections with Scotland where she was domiciled, had her home, and normally spent her holidays.'

Clearly, this state of affairs was unsatisfactory,[525] and after protracted discussions[526] between the English and Scottish Law Commissions, recommendations[527] were made upon which the Family Law Act 1986 is based. This Act, which applies to England and Wales, Scotland and Northern Ireland,[528] has since been extended to apply to the Isle of Man.[529]

2 THE FAMILY LAW ACT 1986

The 1986 Act essentially does two things. First it provides for common rules of jurisdiction throughout the United Kingdom and the Isle of Man (hereinafter simply referred to as the UK). Secondly, it provides a system for the recognition and enforcement throughout the UK of orders made in any one part of the kingdom or dependent territory.

(a) Common jurisdictional rules

The aim of the 1986 Act is to ensure that only one court in the UK has jurisdiction to make a 'Part 1 order' over a child, except in emergencies. 'Part 1 orders' are defined by

---

[521] 1955 SC 115.

[522] Jurisdiction being taken on the basis of the child's presence in England and Wales.

[523] The full effects of wardship are discussed in Chapter 16.

[524] Law Com Working Paper No 68 and Scot Law Com Memorandum No 23, *Custody of Children—Jurisdiction and Enforcement within the United Kingdom* (1976) para 3.12.

[525] Although *Babington* caused deep resentment in Scotland, where it was dubbed 'legal kidnapping', the Scottish courts could be equally unco-operative: see eg *Hoy v Hoy* 1968 SLT 413 discussed in N Lowe and R White *Wards of Court* (1st edn, 1979) at 29.

[526] It took nine years to produce the final report following the working paper.

[527] Viz *Custody of Children: Jurisdiction and Enforcement within the United Kingdom*, Law Com No 138 and Scot Law Com No 91, 1985. For further discussion, see Lowe and White *Wards of Court* (2nd edn, 1986) paras 17.29 to 17.31.

[528] See s 42 of the 1986 Act.

[529] Family Law Act 1986 (Dependent Territories) Order 1991 (SI 1991/1773), Sch 3.

s 1(1)(a) and (d) to mean, so far as England and Wales is concerned, s 8 orders under the Children Act 1989 (excluding variations or discharges) and orders made under the High Court's inherent jurisdiction giving care of the child to any individual or providing for contact with or the education of the child, but excluding variations or discharges of such orders.

As we have discussed the rules in Chapter 12,[530] it suffices here simply to outline the basic scheme, which is:[531]

(1) to vest primary jurisdiction in the UK court in which divorce, nullity or separation proceedings and the equivalent proceedings in connection with civil partnerships are continuing;

(2) where there are no such proceedings continuing, primary jurisdiction vests in the UK court in which the child is habitually resident;

(3) where the child is not habitually resident in any part of the UK, jurisdiction vests in the UK court in which the child is physically present.

With regard to point (2) above reference also needs to be made to s 41, which provides that a child under the age of 16 who has been wrongfully removed or retained outside a part of the UK in which he has been habitually resident will be deemed to continue to be habitually resident in that part for one year after the removal.[532] 'Wrongfully' is defined by s 41(2) as being a removal to or a retention in another jurisdiction either without the consent of all persons having the right to determine where the child is to reside or in contravention of a court order.[533] By s 41(3) such deemed habitual residence ceases if the child becomes 16 or habitually resident in another part of the UK with the consent[534] of all those having the right to determine where the child is to reside and not in contravention of a court order. In any event once the year has elapsed then jurisdiction passes to the part of the UK in which the child has become habitually resident.[535]

Section 41 is clearly designed to prevent any jurisdictional advantage being gained by abducting a child from one part of the UK to another (the provision has no extra territorial effect and does not therefore apply to children wrongfully removed to or from a jurisdiction outside the UK).[536] However, while it has the merit of clearly setting out when the child will be deemed to be habitually resident in a part of the UK despite no longer being there, it has been questioned whether the period of one year is too long for those purposes.[537]

---

[530] See above, pp 561–3.   [531] Family Law Act 1986 s 2, s 2A and s 3.

[532] Section 41(1). For a case where this was applied, see D v D (Custody: Jurisdiction) [1996] 1 FLR 574.

[533] But such an order must still be in force: see Re M (Minors) (Residence Order: Jurisdiction) [1993] 1 FLR 495, CA.

[534] But it seems that it must be proved that the consent is to the child becoming 'habitually' resident, ie it is not enough to show consent to a temporary removal: see D v D (Custody: Jurisdiction), above at 580.

[535] Re B (Court's Jurisdiction) [2004] EWCA Civ 681, [2004] 2 FLR 741.

[536] Re S (A Child: Abduction) [2002] EWCA Civ 1941, [2003] 1 FLR 1008—no application of s 41 in respect of a child brought from Germany and retained in Wales.

[537] See N Lowe and R White Wards of Court (2nd edn) at 17–59.

(b) Recognition and enforcement [538]

Under s 25 of the 1986 Act any Part I order[539] made by a court in any part of the UK and in force in respect of a child under the age of 16 is to be recognised in any other part of the UK. This means, for example, that a prohibition against the child's removal from any part of the UK will be effective throughout the UK.[540]

Recognition does not itself mean that the order will be enforced.[541] Instead, application must be made to the court that made the original order for it to be registered in another part of the UK. Under s 27(1) any person on whom rights have been conferred by a Part 1 order may apply for that order to be registered in another part of the UK. Such applications must be made in the prescribed manner containing the prescribed information and be accompanied by the prescribed documents.[542] Upon receiving the application the court must, unless it appears that the order is no longer in force, forward to the appropriate court (that is the Supreme Court of the relevant jurisdiction, ie the English High Court, the Northern Ireland High Court, the Scottish Court of Session or the Manx High Court):

(a) a certified copy of the order,

(b) prescribed particulars of any amending order, and

(c) a copy of the application and accompanying documents.[543]

Upon receipt of the said copies, the appropriate officer must then cause the order to be registered.[544]

It will be noted that under this system there is no scrutiny as to why it is sought to register the order, ie there is no need to show that a removal is imminent. It can therefore be invoked as an insurance, for example, where the parties come from different jurisdictions and it is felt that the one might be tempted to return home.

Once the order is registered, the registering court has the same enforcement powers as it would have had, had it made the original order which is the subject of the application for enforcement.[545] Even so, an application to enforce the order is still required.[546] At the enforcement hearing, objections may be made by any interested party, for example upon the grounds that the original order was made without jurisdiction or because of changed circumstances, that the original order should be varied. The court has power either to enforce the order or to stay or to dismiss the application.[547]

Pending the outcome of the application the court may give such interim directions as it sees fit.[548] It has been held[549] that when considering an enforcement application the

---

[538] See generally Lowe, Everall and Nicholls *International Movement of Children—Law, Practice and Procedure*, 11.3 et seq.

[539] Except those in relation to a child in local authority care. It might be noted that the courts can only enforce Part I orders and not, for example, injunctions: see *Re K (Wardship: Jurisdiction: Interim Order)* [1991] 2 FLR 104, CA.

[540] Section 36.   [541] Section 25(3).

[542] Section 27(2) and see FPR 1991, Part VI (High Court and county court) and Magistrates' Courts (Family Law Act 1986) Rules 1988 (magistrates' courts).

[543] Section 27(3).   [544] Section 27(4).   [545] Section 29(1).   [546] Ibid.

[547] Sections 30–31. The power to order a stay may be appropriate, for example, where the original order was made without jurisdiction: see Law Com 138 and Scot Law Com No 91 at para 5.33.

[548] Section 29(2).

[549] Per Stephen Brown P in *Re M (Minors) (Custody: Jurisdiction)* [1992] 2 FLR 382 at 386–7. A similar position obtains in Scotland: see *Cook v Blackley* 1997 SLT 853.

English court must not purport to act as a court of appeal from the court having jurisdiction in another part of the UK. Consequently, the judge should not question the correctness of the procedures and orders of the other UK court.

It will be noted that, as under the 1980 European Custody Convention,[550] a prior court order is an essential prerequisite for action under the 1986 Act, but unlike that Convention there is no administrative body to help with the application. Furthermore, the costs of enforcement fall upon the parties themselves, The enforcement system itself seems elaborate and can at times be seriously slow.[551] Not surprisingly, they are infrequently invoked.[552] It has been suggested[553] that the whole enforcement process under the 1986 Act needs to be rethought. In particular it has been questioned whether it is sensible to have a two stage process, namely, registration and then enforcement. Why not, instead, have a straightforward mandatory scheme of automatic mutual recognition and enforcement?

---

[550] Discussed above at p 679.

[551] See eg *Glaser v United Kingdom* [2001] 1 FLR 153, ECtHR, in which proceedings to enforce an English contact order in Scotland took three years although, given the complexity of the case, it was held, perhaps surprisingly, not to be a breach of Art 6 of the European Convention on Human Rights.

[552] In 2001, for example, there were just 27 registrations throughout the UK (the majority being of English orders registered in Scotland).

[553] By Lowe, Everall and Nicholls, op cit, at 11.32–11.35.

14

CHILDREN AND LOCAL AUTHORITIES

A INTRODUCTION

There is a variety of reasons why parents cannot or should not be allowed to look after their own children. They may be prevented from doing so by illness or the child may be beyond their control. Alternatively, a parent may be unwilling or unfit to bring up his own child: he may have abandoned the child, for example, or physically or sexually abused him, or he may have neglected him. The task of handling these difficult problems is entrusted to local authorities (more specifically, after the Children Act 2004, children's services authorities). For this purpose, local authorities in England are non-metropolitan counties, metropolitan districts and London Boroughs,[1] and, prior to the Children Act 2004, they were required to set up a single social services committee responsible for all the relevant services with the day-to-day running of the authority's social services under the control of the Director of Social Services.[2] Following the Victoria Climbié inquiry (the Laming Report) recommendations,[3] and the government's review published in its Green Paper *Every Child Matters*,[4] Part 2 of the Children Act 2004 inter alia makes provision to ensure clear accountability for children's services.[5] To this end the Act requires local authorities in England[6] to create a director of children's services[7] who is accountable for the local authority's education and social services functions insofar as they relate to children. Directors of children's services are also expected to steer local co-operation arrangements in relation to children's services. Part 2 also requires the designation of a lead member for children's services to mirror the director's responsibilities at a local political level.[8] The 2004 Act also requires[9] children's services authorities to prepare and publish a children and young people's plan which sets out their strategy for services for children and relevant young people.

---

[1] Children Act 1989 s 105(1). In Wales, local authorities are counties or county boroughs.
[2] Local Authority Social Services Act 1970 s 6.   [3] Cm 5730 (2003).
[4] Published in September 2003.
[5] See the Explanatory Notes to the 2004 Act summarised at [2005] Fam Law 74, and *Every Child Matters: Next Steps* (2004). This Act is to be further amended by the Childcare Act 2006.
[6] Separate provisions are made for Wales by Part 3 of the 2004 Act.
[7] Section 18, which came into force in April 2005 to the extent of empowering such appointments. There are to be separate directors of adult social services.
[8] Section 19.   [9] Section 17.

1 THE DEVELOPMENT OF LOCAL AUTHORITY POWERS [10]

The powers and duties of local authorities to protect and care for children derive from the Children Act 1989. In striking contrast to the previous law, which had developed piecemeal, the 1989 Act provides a comprehensive and unified scheme for dealing with children in need.

To put the 1989 Act in its context it is worth briefly adverting to the earlier law. That law was based on two Acts, namely the Child Care Act 1980 and the Children and Young Persons Act 1969. The former Act consolidated earlier Acts, principally the Children Act 1948, parts of the Children and Young Persons Act 1963, and the Children Act 1975. The Children Act 1948 resulted from a report of the Curtis Committee,[11] which was set up to inquire into existing methods of providing for children deprived of a normal home life and to consider what steps should be taken to ensure that they were brought up under conditions best calculated to compensate for their lack of parental care. Reflecting the concerns of the Committee the 1948 Act imposed on a local authority a duty to receive a deprived child into care in certain circumstances and then to bring him up according to his best interests. Wherever possible the authority had to secure his discharge from care to parents, relatives or friends as soon as may be.

During the 1950s there was an increasing awareness of the need to prevent families breaking up and children being received into care. Social and economic factors were seen to be important in family difficulties. Juvenile delinquency began to be attributed in many instances to 'deprivation' rather than 'depravity'. It was thought that intensive preventative work with families could help to solve the problems of offenders and non-offenders.

The Ingleby Committee,[12] set up in 1956, investigated these matters and subsequently the Children and Young Persons Act 1963 was enacted, under which all local authorities had as their first duty to give advice, guidance and assistance to diminish the need to receive children into care.

Prevention and rehabilitation became the keynote of much of the subsequent work of local authorities, and it was expected that this would lead to an improvement in the prevention of delinquency.

These principles were further emphasised in the Children and Young Persons Act 1969. Both offenders and non-offenders were to be dealt with in the same system, and the provisions were designed to discourage either coming before the courts. For both, the powers of the court were directed towards treatment. In fact, the objective of reducing the relevance of criminal law by raising the age of criminal responsibility was never implemented.

In the 1970s questions were again raised about the nature and efficiency of child care services. Difficulties were experienced as a result of changes in the structure of local

---

[10] For a masterly historical survey see S Cretney *Family Law in the Twentieth Century* chs 18 and 19 and L Fox Harding *Perspectives in Child Care Policy* (1997) and N Parton *Governing the Family: Child Care, Child Protection and the State* (1991).

[11] Cmd 6922. For a full and fascinating discussion both of the circumstances before the setting up of the Committee and of the Report itself see S Cretney *Family Law in the Twentieth Century* pp 671–85 and 'The State as a Parent: The Children Act 1948 in Retrospect' (1998) 114 LQR 419 and for a shorter version see 'The Children Act 1948—Lessons for today?' [1997] CFLQ 359.

[12] Cmnd 1191.

authorities.[13] Children's departments, previously responsible for services to children and their families, were replaced by larger social services departments with responsibilities for the old, handicapped and mentally ill, as well as for children. The creation of a profession to manage all these inevitably lowered the level of child care expertise and raised the pressure of workloads. All this in a bureaucratic structure made it impossible in many instances for local authorities to provide the personalised services for children envisaged in the 1948 Act.

Lack of constructive long-term planning caused increasing concern. In spite of the apparent emphasis on returning children to their parents, it was considered that substantial numbers of children in care were unlikely ever to go back to their families and could not benefit from waiting in vain hope.[14]

There was a rising body of opinion that it was not necessarily in a child's interest to return to his natural parents. This was given philosophical expression in the book *Beyond the Best Interests of the Child*,[15] where the importance of the 'psychological' parent (that is, the primary carer) was emphasised. The issue came into the public eye, however, in 1973 when Maria Colwell was killed by her stepfather after she had been removed from foster parents.[16] Inevitably, there was a demand for a curtailment of parental rights, so that children could be better protected from parental rejection, and plans could be made for their long-term welfare. However, there were contrary arguments, for example, that it was often bad social work practice rather than parental failure which led to children languishing in care. Strengthening the powers of local authorities and third parties might serve to reinforce bad practice and lack of planning, and encourage foster parents, for example, to sabotage a parent's efforts to recover a child.

The trend towards greater recognition of children as individuals could not be ignored. The resulting legislation, the Children Act 1975, accordingly required a local authority to give first consideration to the need to safeguard and promote the welfare of the child throughout his childhood.

Still different concerns were being voiced in the 1980s. Studies had raised awareness of the damage that local authority care (however well-meaning) could do to family links,[17] but this in turn 'encouraged local authorities to operate strong gate-keeping techniques to prevent children entering the system' with the result that care was denied to those who needed it. 'Social work thus became something which was done to clients rather than a way of helping families to help themselves'.[18] Yet another concern highlighted by the 'Cleveland crisis'[19] was whether local authorities had become too powerful at the expense of family autonomy.

---

[13] Under the Local Authority Social Services Act 1970.

[14] See J Rowe and L Lambert *Children Who Wait* (1973).

[15] J Goldstein, A Freud and A Solnit (1973).

[16] See the Report of the Committee of Inquiry into the Care and Supervision provided in relation to Maria Colwell (1974) HMSO.

[17] See eg S Millham, R Bullock, K Hosie and J Haak *Lost in Care* (1986) and *Social Work Decisions in Child Care* (1985).

[18] S Cretney, J Masson and R Bailey-Harris *Principles of Family Law* (7th edn, 2003) p 697.

[19] Which was concerned with the scope of removal of scores of children because of alleged sexual abuse; and on which see the highly influential Report of the Inquiry into Child Abuse in Cleveland, 1987 (the 'Butler-Sloss Report'), 1988 Cm 412.

The Children Act 1989 attempted to take on board the lessons and experience of the past and to draw anew the balance between family autonomy and local authority powers to protect children.[20]

A further period of activity began in the late 1990s with the 'Quality Protects' programme in England[21] and 'Children First' in Wales[22] and continued with publication in 2002 of the Joint Chief Inspector's report *Safeguarding Children*[23] and in 2003 of the *Victoria Climbié Inquiry Report*[24] and the Government's response to the latter two reports in its paper *Keeping Children Safe*.[25] One result of these enquiries and reports has been to shift the emphasis from child protection to the safeguarding of children. As *Keeping Children Safe* put it,[26] the Reports 'show us how to move towards a better children's safeguards system, where child protection services are not separate from support for families, but are part of the spectrum of services provided to help and support children and families'.

The legislative response to the above mentioned reports together with the Government's Green Paper *Every Child Matters*,[27] was the Children Act 2004. That Act did a number of things, including strengthening the support services for children and their families, ensuring clear accountability for children's services which has involved, as referred to at the beginning of this Chapter, making fundamental changes to local authority organisational structure, and ensuring a voice for children and young people at national level through the establishment in England of a Children's Commissioner.[28]

The 2004 Act has already been amended by the Childcare Act 2006.[29] The 2006 legislation introduces a new legal framework for the integrated regulation and inspection of early education and childcare services, places duties on local authorities to improve the outcomes for young children, securing sufficient childcare and providing information to children.

One further development has been the publication in 2006 of the Review of the Child Care Proceedings System in England and Wales, the major concern of which was the spiralling costs of care proceedings (which rose 42% in the five years running up to the review).[30] Overall, the Review's recommendations aim to avoid court proceedings where possible or desirable (to this end it recommends more consistent use of pre-proceedings initiatives such as Family Group Conferences); improve the consistency and quality of care applications (to this end it recommends that (a) the local authority case and proposed care plan are clearly set out in short documents written in simple language and (b) there should be a pre-proceedings guidance and a best practice checklist); improve case management during proceedings (here the main recommendation is for a revised first hearing); to positively engage families and children and to improve professional relationships and inter-agency working.

---

[20] For the genesis of the Act, see above pp 369–72, 511–14.
[21] See *Quality Protects Circular: Transforming Children's Services* LAC (98) 28.
[22] *The Children First Programme in Wales: Transforming Children's Services*, Welsh Office Circular 20/97.
[23] Department of Health, 2002.   [24] Cm 5730 (2003).   [25] Cm 5861 (2003).
[26] Above at para 4.   [27] Cm 5860 (2003).   [28] Discussed in Chapter 11.   [29] Viz by s 16.
[30] Other concerns were the complexity of cases and the unnecessarily adversarial nature of proceedings.

2 THE CURRENT LAW: SOME KEY UNDERLYING PRINCIPLES

(a) Non-intervention

One of the great achievements of the Children Act 1989 was to provide a single comprehensive code governing both private and public law. As we have seen in previous chapters, one of the underlying philosophies of the Act is that of non-intervention, and this basic standpoint is one of the key changes in the public law arena. As Lord Mackay said in his Joseph Jackson Memorial Lecture:[31]

'. . . the integrity and independence of the family is the basic building block of a free and democratic society and the need to defend it should be clearly perceivable in the law. Accordingly, unless there is evidence that a child is being or is likely to be positively harmed because of a failure in the family, the state, whether in the guise of a local authority or a court, should not interfere.'

This basic non-interventionist standpoint is emphasised by the fact that compulsory measures can only be taken following a court order and that no order may be made unless the basic threshold of 'significant harm' can be proved. Moreover, the presumption under s 1(5)[32] that no order should be made at all unless it is for the child's welfare applies equally to proceedings involving local authorities. Even where an order is thought justified, the court may still not make a care order if it thinks that an alternative s 8 order would be better.

(b) Working in partnership

A second key principle, allied both to the non-intervention principle and to the enduring nature of parental responsibility, is that local authorities must work in partnership with the parents. There is a strong enjoinder on authorities to make voluntary agreements with parents for the benefit of their children. As the Department of Health's *Guidance* puts it:[33]

'One of the key principles of the Children Act is that responsible authorities should work in partnership with the parents of a child who is being looked after and also with the child himself, where he is of sufficient understanding, provided that this approach will not jeopardise his welfare. A second, closely related principle is that parents and children should participate actively in the decision-making process. Partnership will only be achieved if parents are advised about and given explanations of the local authority's powers and duties and of the actions the local authority may need to take, for example, exchanges of information between relevant agencies . . . This new approach reflects the fact that parents always retain their parental responsibility. A local authority may limit parents' exercise of that responsibility when a child is looked after by a local authority as a result of a court order, but only if it is necessary to do so to safeguard and promote the child's welfare . . .

The development of a successful working partnership between the responsible authorities and the parents and the child, where he is of sufficient understanding, should enable the placement to proceed positively so that the child's welfare is safeguarded and promoted.'

The encouragement to work in partnership should not, however, be misconstrued: it does

---

[31] (1989) 139 NLJ 505 at 507.   [32] Discussed in detail at pp 475–9.
[33] Vol 3, *Family Placements*, paras 2.10 and 2.11.

not mean that compulsory measures to remove children from their families cannot be taken until voluntary efforts have failed. If the child's welfare demands it, compulsory measures should immediately be taken.[34]

Not unrelated to the partnership ideal is the vision that the services which, under Part III of the Act, local authorities are obliged to provide should be seen as a positive response to the needs of children and not as a mark of failure by the family or the professionals.

(c) Maintenance of links between the child and his family

In cases where it is necessary for children to live away from home either as a result of voluntary agreement or compulsory intervention, stress is repeatedly placed on the importance of children maintaining links with their family. As *The Care of Children: Principles and Practice in Regulations and Guidance* puts it:[35]

'There are unique advantages for children in experiencing normal family life in their own birth family and every effort should be made to preserve the child's home and family links.'

To this end local authorities are under a general duty when safeguarding the welfare of children in need to promote the upbringing of children by their families[36] and, if they are looking after[37] the child, to endeavour to promote contact between the child and his parents.[38] Even when in care or subject to an emergency protection order there is a presumption that the child will have reasonable contact with his family. Local authorities wishing to restrict this must obtain the prior sanction of the court.[39]

B LOCAL AUTHORITY SUPPORT FOR CHILDREN AND FAMILIES[40]

Part III of the 1989 Act contains provisions relating to the services that a local authority must or may provide for children and their families. For the first time services for children in need and disabled children are brought together under one statute. The provisions are intended to enable authorities to support family life, although they may in certain circumstances charge for the service. The Children Act 2004 requires local authorities (that is, the children's services authorities) to make arrangements to promote co-operation between themselves and key partner agencies and other relevant bodies, including the voluntary and community sector, to improve the well-being of children in the area.[41] For these purposes 'well-being' refers to physical and mental health and emotional well-being; protection from harm and neglect; education, training and recreation; the contribution made by

---

[34] See *Children Act Report 1992*, para 2.21, discussed below, p 732.   [35] (HMSO, 1989) p 8.
[36] Children Act 1989 s 17(1)(b).   [37] For the meaning of this see below, p 795.
[38] Children Act 1989 Sch 2, para 15.   [39] Ibid, s 34, discussed below, pp 790ff.
[40] See generally Department of Health's *Guidance and Regulations*, Vol 2, *Family Support, Day Care and Educational Provision for Young Children*. Part III is based on recommendations of the *Review of Child Care Law* (DHSS, 1985) and the government's White Paper *The Law on Child Care and Family Services* (Cm 62, 1987).
[41] Sections 10 (England), 25 (Wales). For a short explanation of the aims and background to the 2004 Act, see the Explanatory Notes to the Act. The key partner agencies are defined in ss 10(4) and 25(4) respectively.

them to society and social and economic well-being.[42] Furthermore, in making such arrangements authorities must have regard to the importance of parents and other persons caring for children in improving the well-being of children.[43]

It is tempting for lawyers to overlook this part of the Act, especially as it does not deal with 'court-based' law. Nevertheless, it is not without relevance to the practising lawyer since such services, both in the sense of past support to a particular family and what future support might be given, are important factors in deciding whether or not to make a care order. Furthermore as one commentary[44] points out, there is 'an inextricable link between the provision of support and minimal intervention, which shapes the functions of both local authorities and the courts. Research[45] has shown that this link is 'frequently under-emphasised by professionals'.

1 GENERAL DUTY TO CHILDREN IN NEED

Under s 17(1) every local authority has a general[46] duty:

'(a) to safeguard and promote the welfare of children in their area who are in need; and

(b) so far as is consistent with that duty to promote the upbringing of such children by their families,

by providing a range and level of services appropriate to those needs.'

A child[47] is defined as being 'in need' if:[48]

'(a) he is unlikely to achieve or maintain, or to have the opportunity of achieving or maintaining a reasonable standard of health or development without the provision for him of services by a local authority under this Part;

(b) his health or development is likely to be significantly impaired or further impaired, without the provision for him of such services; or

(c) he is disabled.'

For these purposes 'health' means physical or mental health and 'development' means physical, intellectual, emotional, social or behavioural development.[49]

---

[42] Ss 10(2), 25(2).

[43] These duties will be further widened by the Childcare Act 2006, which inter alia will mean that local authorities will need to improve the outcomes of the most disadvantaged children at a faster rate.

[44] *Butterworths Family Law Service* at 3A [2201.4].

[45] *Child Protection Messages from Research* (Dept of Health, 2003) 23.

[46] *R (G) v Barnet London Borough Council; R (W) v Lambeth London Borough Council* [2003] UKHL 57, [2004] 2 AC 208, on which see D Cowan 'On need and gate keeping' [2004] CFLQ 331. The inclusion of the word 'general' was intended to reverse *A-G (ex rel Tilley) v London Borough of Wandsworth* [1981] 1 All ER 1162, which had held under the former law that the welfare duty applied to individual children.

[47] A person under the age of 18: Children Act 1989 s 105(1). Under normal canons of interpretation 'child' means a 'live' child and therefore has no application to unborn children: see *Elliot v Joicey* [1935] AC 209, HL and *R v Newham London Borough Council, ex p Dada* [1996] QB 507, CA. The local authority must assess the age of a person claiming to be under the age of 18 and give adequate reasons for deciding that he is not: *R (B) v Merton London Borough Council* [2003] EWHC 1689 (Admin), [2003] 2 FLR 888.

[48] Section 17(10).

[49] Section 17(11). This is the same definition as in s 31(9) in care proceedings: see below, p 737.

It will be appreciated that this definition is wide. Furthermore, as the Department of Health's *Guidance* observes:[50]

'Sometimes the needs will be found to be intrinsic to the child, at other times however it may be that parenting skills and resources are depleted or under-developed and thus threaten the child's well-being.'

Furthermore the duties owed to a child in need do not cease merely because the child is in a Young Offenders Institution or other prison establishment.[51]

In discharging this general duty towards children in need, s 17(3) states that the services may be provided for the family of a particular child in need or for any member of his family, if they are provided with a view to safeguarding or promoting the child's welfare. For these purposes, 'family' includes any person who has parental responsibility for the child and any other person with whom he had been living.[52] It is thus not limited to relatives. The object of s 17(3) is to promote the upbringing of children by their families. Hence, parents' own circumstances may be such as to require the service provision so as to safeguard or promote their child's welfare within the family. Nevertheless local authorities have no *duty* to provide accommodation for a child's *parent* to enable the child to live with that parent.[53] Nevertheless the House of Lords in the *Lambeth* case[54] have also held that an authority has the power to provide accommodation for a child in need and his family. Section 17(6) has been specifically amended[55] to include the provision of accommodation. A child so accommodated, however, is not being 'looked after' by a local authority for the purposes of s 22.[56]

A child 'in need' also includes a disabled child, who, for the purposes of the Act, is a child who is—

'blind, deaf or dumb or suffers from mental disorder of any kind or is substantially and permanently handicapped by illness, injury or congenital deformity or such other disability as may be prescribed'.[57]

As a child in need, a disabled child is able to benefit from the same services as other children. Accordingly local authorities are obliged to provide such children with services so as to minimise the effect of their disabilities and to give them the opportunity to lead lives that are as normal as possible.[58]

Following an amendment introduced by s 53 of the Children Act 2004, before determining what, if any, services to provide for a child, the local authority is required, so far as is

---

[50] Vol 2, para 2.5.

[51] *R (Howard League for Penal Reform) v Secretary of State for the Home Department* [2002] EWHC 2497 (Admin), [2003] 1 FLR 484 and *R (D) v Secretary of State for the Home Department* [2003] EWHC 155 (Admin), [2003] 1 FLR 979.

[52] Section 17(10).

[53] *R (G) v Barnet London Borough Council; R (W) v Lambeth London Borough Council* [2003] UKHL 57, [2004] 2 AC 208.

[54] Above.

[55] By s 116 of the Adoption and Children Act 2002, which came into force in November 2002.

[56] Discussed further below at p 795.   [57] Section 17(11).

[58] Sch 2, para 6, on which see inter alia *R (BG) v Medway Council* [2005] EWHC 1932 (Admin), [2006] 1 FLR 663. See also the Department of Health's *Guidance*, Vol 2 at para 2.18. Local authorities must keep a register of children with disabilities in their area: Sch 2 para 2.

reasonably practical and consistent with the child's welfare to ascertain the child's wishes and feelings regarding the provision of those services and having regard to his age and understanding give due consideration to such wishes and feelings as they have been able to ascertain.[59]

The services provided under Part III may include giving assistance in kind or in exceptional circumstances in cash, unconditionally or conditionally as to repayment.[60] Direct payments may be made to a person with parental responsibility for a disabled child of 16 or 17, the purpose of which is to enable the recipient(s) to purchase a service which would otherwise have been provided by the authority itself.[61] Authorities are required to have regard to the means of the child and each of his parents, although no person is liable for repayment at any time when he is in receipt of income support or income-based jobseeker's allowance.[62] An authority may also contribute to the cost of looking after a child who is living with a person under a residence order, such as a relative or foster parent, except where that person is a parent or step-parent.[63]

Authorities are required to facilitate the provision of Part III services by other, in particular, voluntary organisations, and may make such arrangements as they see fit for others to provide such services (eg day care or fostering services).[64] An authority or organisation must comply with such a request if it is compatible with their own statutory or other duties and obligations and does not unduly prejudice the discharge of any of their functions.[65]

2 SPECIFIC DUTIES AND POWERS

In pursuance of the general duty, authorities have specific duties and powers which are set out in Sch 2, Pt I, among which are the following.

(a) Identification of children in need

Every local authority must take reasonable steps to identify the extent to which there are children in need in their area.[66] They must also publish information about the services they provide and, where appropriate, that other organisations or bodies provide.[67] They must also take such steps as are reasonably practicable to ensure that those who might benefit from the services receive the information relevant to them.[68]

---

[59] Children Act 1989, s 17(4A) which gives statutory backing to guidance issued under s 7 of the Local Authority Social Services Act 1970 in relation to s 17, see the Explanatory Notes to the 2004 Act.

[60] Section 17(6), (7). For an example of a potentially re-payable loan see *R (BG) v Medway Council*, above.

[61] Section 17A inserted by the Carers and Disabled Children Act 2000, s 17(1).

[62] Section 17(8), (9) as amended by the Jobseekers Act 1995 Sch 2, para 19(2).

[63] Schedule 1, para 15. In their study *Residence Order Allowance Survey* (1996) the Grandparents' Federation found that the practice among local authorities with regard to residence order allowances varied enormously both as to whether the allowance was paid at all and, where it was, as to its duration. Whilst acknowledging that the provision of allowances is one of the most difficult parts of a residence order policy, the Department of Health has nevertheless recommended that all authorities should have a policy addressing inter alia when they should be considered, whether they should be capped, and how the rates and periods should be set: *Children Act 1989, Residence Orders Study* (Social Services Inspectorate, 1995) 6.2.

[64] Section 17(5) and see further Department of Health's *Guidance and Regulations*, Vol 2, para 2.11.

[65] Children Act 1989 s 27.   [66] Sch 2, para 1.   [67] Sch 2, para 1(2)(a).

[68] Sch 2, para 1(2)(b).

(b) Promoting the upbringing of children by their families

Local authorities should make provision for advice, guidance, counselling and home help. This could include family aids or perhaps therapists who might advise on improving family dynamics. Occupational, social, cultural or recreational activities or assistance with holidays may be provided.[69] Where a child is being looked after by a local authority, the authority shall, unless it is not reasonably practicable or consistent with his welfare, endeavour to promote contact between the child and his family and shall ensure that they are kept informed of where he is being accommodated. However, the authority is not required to disclose the whereabouts of the child if he is in care and the authority has reasonable cause to believe that disclosure would prejudice the child's welfare.[70] Expenses may be paid for visits to or by children.[71]

Every local authority must provide such family centres (ie a centre at which a child, his parents, a person with parental responsibility or any person looking after the child may attend) for (a) occupational, cultural, social or recreational activities, or (b) advice, guidance or counselling, or (c) be provided with accommodation whilst receiving these) as they consider appropriate in relation to children within their area.[72]

(c) Prevention of abuse and neglect

Every authority shall take reasonable steps through the provision of Part III services to prevent children in their area suffering ill-treatment or neglect. There is a duty to inform another authority, if a child who the authority believe is likely to suffer harm lives or proposes to live in the area of that authority.[73] There is a connected duty to take reasonable steps, through the provision of Part III services, to reduce the need to bring proceedings for care or supervision orders, or to bring criminal proceedings in respect of children.[74]

(d) Provision of accommodation by third party to protect children

Where it appears to an authority that a child is suffering or is likely to suffer ill-treatment at the hands of another person living at the same premises and that other person proposes to move from those premises, the authority may assist that other person to obtain accommodation, including giving assistance in kind.[75] This provision is a response to concern expressed in the Cleveland Report[76] that children, who were allegedly sexually abused, were removed from the family home, when it might have been in their interests for the alleged abuser to have left, if he could have been provided with alternative accommodation. Under this provision local authorities can assist those who are willing to leave voluntarily, but they have no power to order removal of a person from a child's household. However, the Children Act 1989 was amended by the Family Law Act 1996 so that a court may now also make an order requiring the alleged abuser to leave the family home, when making emergency protection orders and interim care orders.[77]

---

[69] Sch 2, para 8.   [70] Sch 2, para 15.   [71] Sch 2, para 16.   [72] Sch 2, para 9.
[73] Sch 2, para 4.   [74] Sch 2, para 6.   [75] Sch 2, para 5.   [76] Cm 412, 1988.
[77] Viz s 38A and s 44A, discussed below, pp 726 and 784.

(e) Day care

Every local authority is required to provide such day care as is appropriate for children in need within their area who are five or under and not yet attending school.[78] Day care is defined as any form of care or supervised activity provided for children during the day, whether or not on a regular basis.[79] The authority may provide day care for such children even though they are not in need.[80] They may also provide facilities including training, advice, guidance and counselling for those who are caring for children in day care or who accompany children in day care. The provision of day care by others, in particular voluntary organisations should be facilitated by local authorities.[81]

Under s 19 authorities are required to review their day care provision and, according to the Department of Health's *Guidance*,[82] authorities should have an agreed policy for discharging their general duty to provide day care for children in need. However, past research suggests[83] that there has been little progress on co-ordinated action, identification of levels of need or increase in provision. Rather, lack of resources has made it generally difficult to develop or expand day care facilities. This rather patchy provision became the subject of greater government concern as part of its broader initiatives concerning employment policy.[84]

(f) Duty to consider racial groups

In making any arrangements either for the provision of day care under s 18 or to encourage persons to act as local authority foster parents, the authority shall have regard to the different racial groups to which children in need in their area belong.[85]

3 ACCOMMODATING CHILDREN IN NEED

A key service under Part III of the 1989 Act is accommodation, under which local authorities may arrange, *without court intervention*, for the child to live away from home either with foster parents, relatives or in a community, voluntary or registered children's home.[86]

Accommodation replaced what was formerly known as 'voluntary care' but, reflecting the change of philosophy under the Act, whereas voluntary care was perceived to be a mark of failure either on the part of the family or those professionals and others working to support them, accommodation is intended to be seen, in the words of the government's White Paper.[87]

'. . . as part of the range of services a local authority can offer to parents and families in need of help with the care of their children. Such a service should, in appropriate circumstances, be seen as a positive response to the needs of families.'

A typical example of where help might be needed is where the mother falls ill and the rest of the family cannot cope.

---

[78] Section 18(1). See generally Department of Health's *Guidance and Regulations*, Vol 2, paras 3.3 et seq.
[79] Section 18(4).   [80] Section 18(2).   [81] Section 17(5).   [82] Viz Vol 2 at ch 9.
[83] Thomas Coram Research Unit *Implementing the Children Act for Children under 8* (1994).
[84] See DSS *New ambitions for our country: A new contract for welfare* 1998, Cm 3805.
[85] Sch 2, para 11.   [86] Section 23(2).
[87] *The Law on Child Care and Family Services* (Cm 62, 1987) para 21. The government rejected the recommendation of the *Review of Child Care Law* that there should be a dual system of 'shared care' and 'respite care'.

An essential characteristic of this service is that it should be voluntary, ie it should (save where the parents are dead or have abandoned the child) be based clearly on continuing parental agreement, and operate as far as possible on a basis of partnership and co-operation between the local authority and parents.

Consistent with this philosophy, the authority do not acquire parental responsibility while they are 'accommodating children',[88] nor are there any formal restrictions on parents with parental responsibility removing their children under the age of 16 out of accommodation.[89] Another important innovation of the 1989 Act is to require written accommodation agreements (discussed below)[90] between local authorities and the parents.

The adult basis of the scheme is to be noted.[91] It means that children under the age of 16 cannot insist on being accommodated against their parents' wishes even if they are 'Gillick-competent'.[92]

(a) The duty and discretion to accommodate

Under s 20 local authorities have both an obligation and a discretion to provide accommodation. The obligation is imposed by s 20(1) whereby local authorities must provide accommodation where a child in need appears to require it as a result of:

'(a) there being no person who has parental responsibility for him;

(b) his being lost or abandoned; or

(c) the person who has been caring for him being prevented (whether or not permanently, and for whatever reason) from providing him with suitable accommodation or care.'

In *R(G) v Barnet London Borough Council*[93] it was accepted that the words 'for whatever reason', in s 20(1)(c) should be given the widest possible scope and that 'it makes no difference whether the reason is one which the carer has brought about by her own act or is one which she was resisting to the best of her ability'.[94] As Lord Nicholls succinctly put it[95] 'A child is not to be visited with the shortcomings of his parents'. It is accordingly clear that accommodation may be provided because of the disability of the child as well as the disability of the parent.[96] Although technically this duty is owed to children under the age of 18,[97] in relation to those aged 16 or 17 the duty to accommodate only arises where the local

---

[88] But see below, p 708 for liability for the criminal acts of a child whilst being accommodated by a local authority.

[89] See s 20(8), discussed below at p 706 (aliter where the child is 16 or 17: see s 20(11), discussed below ibid).

[90] At p 707.

[91] But note the duty under s 20(6) to ascertain and take account of the child's wishes—see further below at p 705.

[92] Section 20(7) (discussed below at p 706) seems conclusive on this point, but see the discussion in J Herring *Family Law* (2nd edn) 517–18.

[93] *R (G) v Barnet London Borough Council; R (W) v Lambeth London Borough Council; R (A) v Lambeth London Borough Council* [2003] UKHL 57, [2004] 1 FLR 454. For further discussion of this case see p 709.

[94] Per Lord Hope, above at para [100].

[95] Above at para [24]. Note Lord Nicholls dissented in this case.

[96] See R White, P Carr and N Lowe *Children Act in Practice* (3rd edn) 6.26 and Clarke Hall and Morrison on *Children*, para 1[1637].

[97] Formerly the duty applied to children under the age of 17.

authority consider that their welfare 'is likely to be seriously prejudiced' if they do not provide them with accommodation.[98]

How these criteria should be interpreted is largely a matter for the local authority since, being the basis of voluntary agreement, they are unlikely to come before the courts.[99] Hence, although 'abandoned' has been interpreted under the adoption legislation as 'leaving the child to its fate',[100] it is unclear whether this is how it should be interpreted in this context. It is also a matter for judgment whether in some cases the child's welfare requires a care order[101] rather than an agreement for accommodation.

Whether accommodation is best regarded as a short-term remedy or as an appropriate means of solving long term problems has been debated in relation to orphans and those children whose parents cannot be found.[102] In this context it now seems to be accepted that, although in theory local authorities can adequately look after such children without having parental responsibility,[103] it is nevertheless preferable, where possible,[104] for local authorities to obtain a care order, since the consequential acquisition of parental responsibility will avoid any possible difficulties or delays that might ensue in authorising decisions, for example, as to the child's medical treatment.[105]

In addition to the obligation to provide accommodation, s 20 vests in local authorities a *discretion* to provide accommodation in two instances. First, under s 20(4) in the case of *any* child (ie not simply a child in need) within their area, even though a person who has parental responsibility for him is able to provide him with accommodation, a local authority may provide accommodation 'if they consider that to do so would safeguard or promote the child's welfare'. It is under this provision that so-called respite care may be given. Secondly, under s 20(5) a local authority may provide accommodation for any person aged 16–21 if they consider that to do so would safeguard or promote the child's welfare.

In all cases, before providing accommodation the authority must, as far as is reasonably practicable and consistent with the child's welfare, ascertain the child's wishes and feelings regarding the provision of accommodation and give due consideration to them, having regard to his age and understanding.[106]

---

[98] Children Act 1989 s 20(3).

[99] Save in the context of an action for judicial review (discussed below, p 805) on the basis that a local authority was refusing a service they were bound to provide. See further below at pp 707–8.

[100] *Watson v Nikolaisen* [1955] 2 QB 286.   [101] See below pp 732ff.

[102] Such situations are not so uncommon: in the year ending 31 March 1996, for example, 430 children started to be 'looked after' because they had no parents and another 950 because they were abandoned or lost: *Children Looked After by Local Authorities* Dept of Health, Personal Social Services, Local Authority Statistics A/F 96/12, Table J.

[103] Since under s 3(5) a local authority may do all that is reasonable to safeguard or promote the child's welfare, while a prohibited steps or specific issue order could solve any particular dispute.

[104] See *Birmingham City Council v D, Birmingham City Council v M* [1994] 2 FLR 502, discussed further, below, p 750.

[105] See *Re SH (Care: Order Orphan)* [1995] 1 FLR 746 at 749 per Hollis J, and *Re M (Care Order: Parental Responsibility)* [1996] 2 FLR 84, discussed further, below, p 750.

[106] Children Act 1989 s 20(6), as amended by s 53(2) of the Children Act 2004.

(b) Limits on providing accommodation

It is of the essence of the service that it is voluntary.[107] Hence the authority cannot provide accommodation if any person with parental responsibility for the child, who is willing and able to provide or arrange for accommodation,[108] objects to the authority so doing.[109] Furthermore, any person with parental responsibility may remove the child from accommodation at any time.[110] These powers of objection and removal do not apply:

(a) where a child of 16 or over agrees to being provided with accommodation;[111] or

(b) where the person agreeing has a residence order in his favour, is a special guardian, or has the care of the child by virtue of an order made under the High Court's inherent jurisdiction.[112]

The statutory right to remove a child from accommodation without notice was one of the more controversial provisions of the 1989 Act.[113] Formerly, there had been a requirement to give 28 days' written notice of an intended removal once the child had been looked after for six months or more. Such a period of notice was, it was argued, necessary to allow the child to prepare himself for his return home and to protect the child from any rash decision on the part of the parents.[114] The government's view, however, was that any period of notice 'would blur the distinction between compulsory and voluntary' care.[115] In their view nothing should undermine the voluntary nature of the service. In line with this philosophy it has been held[116] that in the absence of a court order the local authority is powerless to prevent a mother from removing her children from accommodation. In particular the authority could not rely either on its general duty under s 22(3) to safeguard and promote the child's welfare, nor on the power under s 3(5) to do what is reasonable to promote the child's welfare. Precisely what court order Ward J had in mind may be speculated upon, since it is clear that the court cannot make a specific issue or prohibited steps order requiring a local authority to provide accommodation against the wishes of a parent.[117] It may, however, be possible for one parent to obtain a prohibited steps order

[107] Parental consent is not, however, necessarily required, since accommodation may be provided where the parents are dead or where they have abandoned the child.
[108] These words were added at a later stage of the Bill to prevent a person simply objecting while having no intention of looking after the child. J Masson and M Morris *Children Act Manual* (1992) at p 62 suggest that the words 'able and willing' could be interpreted to invalidate the objection of a homeless or inadequately housed parent.
[109] Children Act 1989 s 20(7). For an example of an objection, see *Re B (A Minor) (Care Order: Criteria)* [1993] 1 FLR 815.
[110] Section 20(8). [111] Section 20(11).
[112] Section 20(9), as amended. The inherent jurisdiction is discussed in Chapter 16.
[113] See eg HC Deb, 18 May 1989, Standing Committee B, cols 137–54.
[114] See above at col 142 per R Sims.
[115] See above at col 149 per D Mellor. Formerly, local authorities not infrequently used the period of notice to decide to take compulsory measures to keep the child, the House of Lords having ruled in *Lewisham London Borough v Lewisham Juvenile Court Justice* [1980] AC 273, that there was no compulsion to return a child immediately upon receiving the request.
[116] *Nottinghamshire County Council v J* (26 November 1993, unreported), per Ward J, cited by D Hershman and A McFarlane *Children Law and Practice* at G[195].
[117] This would seem to be the result of s 9(5)(b); and see *Re S and D (Children) (Powers of the Court)* [1995] 2 FLR 456 at 462, per Balcombe LJ. But note *Re G (Minors) (Interim Care Order)* [1993] 2 FLR 839 at 843, CA, in which a mother's undertaking not to withdraw her agreement to the continuing accommodation of her children was accepted by the court.

preventing the other from objecting. Similarly, it remains a moot point as to whether s 3(5) would justify foster parents refusing to hand over a child to an inebriated parent.[118]

Notwithstanding the clear recognition of the right of removal, there has been no reported evidence of any great difficulties in this regard. In practice the period of removal is one of the matters that should be covered in any accommodation agreement, though it is to be emphasised that an agreement can be of no more than persuasive effect. In particular it cannot in itself prevent the parent exercising the right of removal though this is not to say that the local authority cannot then institute care proceedings in appropriate cases.[119]

(c) Accommodation agreements[120]

It is central to the philosophy of the Act that an authority should seek to reach agreement with the parent or other person with parental responsibility on such matters as the purpose of accommodating the child, the period for which accommodation might be provided, schooling and contact with the child.

Provision for making agreements is governed by the Arrangements for Placement of Children Regulations 1991 which, as the Department of Health's *Guidance* explains:[121]

'. . . place a statutory duty on responsible authorities to draw up a plan in writing for a child whom they are proposing to look after or accommodate in consultation with the child, his parents and other important individuals and agencies in the child's life (regulation 3). Planning for the child should begin prior to placement. After placement, the plan should be scrutinised and adjusted (if necessary) at the first review four weeks after the date the child was first looked after and at subsequent reviews.'

(d) Challenging a refusal to accommodate

A refusal to accommodate cannot be challenged by means of a specific issue order under s 8. In *Re J (Specific Issue Order: Leave to Apply)*[122] it was held that a specific issue order could not be used to challenge a local authority decision that a particular child was not 'in need', nor therefore to require the authority to provide appropriate support under Part III (which could of course include accommodation). In Wall J's view:[123]

'the question as to whether or not a child is in need does not raise a specific question which arises in connection with any aspect of parental responsibility for the child. A s 8 order is inapplicable to the exercise of a local authority's powers and duties under Part III of the Act.'

However, Wall J did consider that such a decision was amenable to judicial review.[124] Such actions, however, are in practice difficult to win, especially since much of s 20(1) is itself a

---

[118] As argued by White, Carr and Lowe, above at 6.55 and Clarke Hall and Morrison on *Children* at 1[1645], but cf *Nottinghamshire County Council v J*, above.

[119] See *R v Tameside Metropolitan Borough Council, ex p J* [2000] 1 FLR 942 at 949 per Scott Baker J. Clarke Hall and Morrison, above at 1[1647], have long argued that breach of an agreement might provide evidence for an application for an emergency protection order or a care order.

[120] See generally Department of Health's *Guidance and Regulations*, Vol 3, *Family Placements*, paras 2.13 et seq, which is repeated in Vol 4, *Residential Care*, paras 2.13 et seq.

[121] See generally Department of Health's *Guidance and Regulations*, Vol 3, paras 2.17–2.74 and Vol 4, paras 2.17–2.74.

[122] [1995] 1 FLR 669.   [123] Above at 673.

[124] Above at 673–4. Judicial review is discussed more generally below at p 805.

matter of discretion. The better first recourse is to use the local authority's complaints procedure under s 26.[125]

In *R v Royal Borough of Kingston-upon-Thames, ex p T*[126] an action for judicial review failed, inter alia, because the local authority's offer of accommodation different from that sought by the mother and the child in question (ie a project home offering support and accommodation for Vietnamese families), was held not to be perverse or unreasonable (notwithstanding that the child's elder sister was already accommodated at the project) so as to be amenable to judicial review, but to be well within the parameters of reasonableness, particularly taking into account the cost of the sought-after placement. It might be similarly difficult to challenge a local authority decision that a particular child is not a child in need.[127] This is not to say that an action can never succeed. In *Re T (Accommodation by Local Authority)*[128] the court quashed the Director of Social Services' decision not to ratify the decision of a complaints panel that the 17-year-old child should be accommodated under s 20(3), on the basis that her welfare would otherwise be seriously prejudiced. In that case the Director was held to have erred when he decided that past provision of support given to her under s 17 made it unlikely that the child's future welfare would be seriously prejudiced if she were not provided with accommodation.

(e) The effect of being accommodated

Accommodated children are not in local authority care nor does the authority thereby acquire parental responsibility. Consequently a local authority cannot transfer an accommodated child from residential care to foster care without the parents' permission[129] nor can foster parents unilaterally change the child's name.[130] However, this is not to say that accommodation has no legal effect. Accommodated children are among those who are 'looked after' by the local authority, upon which certain consequential duties are imposed.[131] Furthermore, it has been held in *McL v Security of State for Social Security*[132] that because an accommodated child was in the de facto care of the local authority the mother could not claim child benefit. Equally, however, the fact of accommodation cannot be ignored when determining liability under s 55 of the Children and Young Persons Act 1933 for a child's criminal act. Accordingly, where a child is in the de facto care of the local authority and the parent has no control over the child at the time, that parent cannot be said to be responsible for the child's actions.[133]

(f) Accommodation in practice

In practice the overwhelming proportion of children 'looked after' by local authorities are those accommodated by them. According to the Department of Health's statistics *Children*

---

[125] See *R v Royal Borough of Kingston-upon-Thames, ex p T* [1994] 1 FLR 798 and *R v Birmingham City Council, ex p A* [1997] 2 FLR 841. The complaints procedure is discussed below at p 798.

[126] Above.   [127] See *Re J (Specific Issue Order: Leave to Apply)*, above.   [128] [1995] 1 FLR 159.

[129] See *R v Tameside Metropolitan Borough Council ex parte J* [2000] 1 FLR 942.

[130] *Re D, L and LA (Care: Change of Forename)* [2003] 1 FLR 339.

[131] See below at p 795. Note also *R (Berhe) v Hillingdon London Borough Council* [2003] EWHC 2075 (Admin), [2004] 1 FLR 439.

[132] [1996] 2 FLR 748, giving a wide definition of the words 'in the care of the local authority' contained in Sch 9 to the Social Security Contributions and Benefits Act 1992.

[133] *TA v DPP* [1997] 2 FLR 887, CA, per Sir Ian Glidewell. Local authorities may be liable under s 55(5) of the 1933 Act added by the Criminal Justice Act 1991 s 57(2).

Looked After by Local Authorities,[134] 67% of children who began to be looked after during the year ending 31 March 2004 were accommodated under s 20. For the most part the period of accommodation is short, generally less than eight weeks.[135]

Soon after the implementation of the Children Act some local authorities seemed to think that unless or until accommodation agreements had broken down there was no scope for taking compulsory care proceedings. To counteract this apparent belief the Department of Health published guidance[136] stressing that local authorities should not feel inhibited from seeking compulsory measures and where an authority 'determines that control of the child's circumstances is necessary to promote his welfare then compulsory intervention . . . will always be the appropriate remedy'. Since then the number of care orders has steadily increased.[137]

Another problem of accommodation is how the s 20 duty relates to the duties to homeless persons under the Housing legislation.[138] In *R v Northavon District Council, ex p Smith*[139] the House of Lords held that the nature and scope of the functions of the housing and social services departments were not intended to change as a result of the duty to co-operate imposed under the 1989 Act. Broadly, this means that the burden of accommodating intentionally homeless children falls on social services whereas the burden of rehousing homeless families falls on the housing authorities. This approach was followed in a second House of Lords' decision, *R (G) v Barnet London Borough Council*[140] in which it was accepted that a local authority providing a child with accommodation was not under a duty to accommodate the child's family as well. As Lord Hope commented[141] 'the provision of residential accommodation to rehouse a child in need so that he can live with his family is not the principal or primary purpose of [the Children Act 1989]'.

4 SECURE ACCOMMODATION [142]

(a) Introduction

Secure accommodation is not to be confused with s 20 accommodation. Children who are subject to secure accommodation lose their right to leave the secure unit (be it a room or building) of their own free will, though they should at the same time have the benefit of

---

[134] The 2004 Report, Table 14. Note, however, that as a proportion of those being looked after as on 31 March 2004, only 31 per cent were accommodated.

[135] Ibid, Table 16.

[136] *Children Act Report 1992*, para 2.21.

[137] See the discussion in R White, P Carr and N Lowe *Children Act in Practice* (3rd edn, 2002) paras 8.7ff.

[138] See also the discussion of this broad issue in relation to s 17 above at p 704.

[139] [1994] 2 AC 402.

[140] *R (G) v Barnet London Borough Council; R (W) v Lambeth London Borough Council; R (A) v Lambeth London Borough Council* [2003] UKHL 57, [2004] 1 FLR 454, on which see D Cowan 'On need and gatekeeping' [2004] CFLQ 331. For further discussion of this case in relation to s 17, see above p 704.

[141] Above at para [92].

[142] For wider discussion see D Harris and J Timms *Between Hospital and Prison or thereabouts* (1993) and R Bullock *Secure treatment outcomes—the care careers of very difficult adolescents* (1998). Note that the ensuing discussion is confined to *civil* proceedings for secure accommodation. There are separate provisions dealing with *criminal* proceedings for which, see Clarke Hall and Morrison on *Children* 7[202] ff.

specialist services to promote and safeguard their welfare. Though clearly draconian, secure accommodation may be the only means of dealing with adolescent children who have a history of aggressive behaviour. As the Department of Health's *Guidance* comments[143]

'Secure accommodation has an important role to play amongst the range of residential services and facilities provided by local authorities. Both in terms of the safety and security of the premises, the skills and enhanced levels of staff available, and the specialist programmes which can be provided, a secure placement may be the most appropriate, and only, way of responding to the likelihood of a child suffering significant harm or injuring himself or others.'

Yet, as the *Guidance* stresses,[144] because the restriction of a child's liberty is a serious step it should only be taken as a ' "last resort" in the sense that all else must have been comprehensively considered and rejected' and 'never because no other placement was available at the relevant time, because of inadequacies of staffing, because the child is simply being a nuisance or runs away from his accommodation and is not likely to suffer significant harm in doing so, and never as a form of punishment'.

Secure accommodation was not new to the Children Act 1989. It was first developed[145] in response to disturbances in open approved schools following which three special units were built, the first one opening in 1964. These buildings were later transferred to the control of local authorities following the implementation of the Children and Young Persons Act 1969. Under that Act, where a care order had been made,[146] the local authority had the power, without court control, to restrict a child's liberty to the extent they considered appropriate. But concern over (a) the extensive use of secure accommodation in community homes[147] and (b) the need to comply with the European Convention on Human Rights[148] led to the introduction in 1983 of new safeguards. Under this scheme, provided for by the Child Care Act 1980, local authorities were precluded from placing children in their care in secure accommodation unless statutory criteria applied and needed to obtain a court order if they wished to keep a child in secure accommodation for more than 72 hours in any period of 28 days.[149] Though not identical either in its application or in its wording, the scheme introduced by the 1980 Act has essentially been adopted by the Children Act 1989.

---

[143] Vol 4 *Residential Care* at 8.5.   [144] Both in Vol 1 *Court Orders* at 5.1 and in Vol 4, at 8.5.

[145] See the summary by M Parry 'Secure accommodation—the Cinderella of family law' [2000] CFLQ 101.

[146] But not otherwise, ie there was no comparable statutory power to restrict the liberty of a child in so-called 'voluntary' care.

[147] See eg a Report of a DHSS Working Party *Legal and Professional Aspects of the Use of Secure Accommodation for Children in Care* (HMSO, 1981), a Report of the Parliamentary Penal Affairs Group (1981) referred to by M Parry, above, at 102 and H Bevan *Child Law* (Butterworths 1989) 728.

[148] Viz Art 5(4) under which 'Everyone who is deprived of his liberty by arrest or detention shall be entitled to take proceedings by which the lawfulness of his detention shall be decided speedily by a court and his release ordered if the detention is not lawful'. In *X v United Kingdom* (1981) 4 EHRR 181 the European Court of Human Rights held that it was unlawful to deprive mentally ill patients of their liberty by executive decision.

[149] Section 21A. Unlike the 1969 Act, the 1980 Act applied inter alia both to children in voluntary care and those subject to a care order.

(b) Secure accommodation under the Children Act 1989

The basic scheme

It is fundamental to the scheme under the Children Act 1989 that local authorities[150] should not use secure accommodation unless the criteria set out in s 25(1) are met. Even then, all other options should have been considered and rejected. Indeed, local authorities have an express duty under Sch 2, para 7(c) to the 1989 Act 'to avoid the need for children within their area to be placed in secure accommodation'.

Provided they are satisfied that the s 25(1) criteria are met, local authorities can keep a child looked after[151] by them in secure accommodation for up to 72 hours in aggregate in any period of 28 days without a court order,[152] but beyond this court sanction is required. Before that sanction can be given, the court must be satisfied that 'any relevant criteria' for keeping a child in secure accommodation are met.[153]

The meaning of secure accommodation

Section 25(1) defines accommodation as that 'provided for the purposes of restricting liberty'. This is potentially a wide definition for as the Department of Health's *Guidance* points out,[154] 'any practice or measure which prevents a child from leaving a room or building of his own free will may be deemed by the court to constitute "restriction of liberty" '. It is established that secure accommodation is *not* limited to accommodation provided with the approval of the Secretary of State;[155] rather the key element is the restriction of liberty. On this basis, a unit for the treatment of mentally disturbed children was held[156] to be secure accommodation since its purpose was to restrict the liberty of children there with a view to modifying their behaviour. Similarly, in *A Metropolitan Borough Council v DB*,[157] it was held that a maternity ward at a hospital was secure accommodation since staff had been instructed to confine the child in question to the ward and could utilise a key/pass system to that end. In contrast, in *Re C (Detention: Medical Treatment)*[158] Wall J, whilst agreeing 'that premises which are not designed as secure accommodation may become secure accommodation because of the use to which they are put in the particular circumstances of individual cases', nevertheless considered that the more natural meaning of the phrase 'provided for the purpose of restricting liberty' is ' "designed for, or having as its primary purpose" the restriction of liberty'. He accordingly held that a private hospital clinic designed primarily to provide treatment for eating disorders and which was not equipped with devices to restrict entry or exit (there

---

[150] A similar regime applies to certain other bodies providing residential accommodation, namely, health authorities, Primary Care Trusts, National Health Service Trusts, local education authorities, care homes and independent hospitals, see Children (Secure Accommodation Regulations 1991 (SI 1991/1505)). A separate scheme applies to children detained under the Mental Health Act 1983 and the Powers of Criminal Courts (Sentencing) Act 2000, ss 90–91.

[151] Ie children both accommodated by the local authority or subject to a care order, see further below.

[152] Children (Secure Accommodation) Regulations 1991, reg 10(1).

[153] Children Act 1989, s 25(3).   [154] Vol 4, at 8.10.

[155] Secure accommodation in a children's home must have the prior approval of the Secretary of State: Children (Secure Accommodation) Regulations 1991, reg 3.

[156] *R v Northampton Juvenile Court, ex p London Borough of Hammersmith and Fulham* [1985] 1 FLR 193—applying s 21A of the Child Care Act 1980.

[157] [1997] 1 FLR 767.   [158] [1997] 2 FLR 180.

were no locks on the individual bedroom doors and the main doors were only locked at night), was not secure accommodation.[159]

Who can be subjected to secure accommodation?

So far as the powers under s 25 are concerned only children being 'looked after' by a local authority may be placed in secure accommodation. As discussed later[160] 'looked after' children refer both to those who are subject to a care order and those accommodated by the local authority for a continuous period of more than 24 hours.[161] This means that children who have been accommodated for 24 hours or less cannot be placed in secure accommodation by a local authority. Further restrictions, imposed by Regulations,[162] prohibit the use of secure accommodation for children over 16 who are accommodated under s 20(5)[163] and those kept away from home under a child assessment order.[164] The Regulations also provide[165] that a child under the age of 13 cannot be placed in secure accommodation in a children's home without the Secretary of State's specific approval.

The criteria for restricting liberty by secure accommodation

Section 25(1) specifies the criteria which must apply before a child being looked after by a local authority can be placed, and, if placed, kept in secure accommodation,[166] namely,

'(a) that—

    (i) he has a history of absconding and is likely to abscond from any other description of accommodation; *and*

    (ii) if he absconds, he is likely to suffer significant harm; *or*

(b) that if he is kept in any other description of accommodation he is likely to injury himself or other persons.'

(Emphasis added.)

To fall within s 25(1)(a) the criteria set out in *both* sub paras (i) and (ii) must be satisfied.

---

[159] Accordingly, in Wall J's view, this left him free to exercise his inherent jurisdiction to direct the clinic to detain the 12 year old anorexic child as an inpatient using reasonable force if necessary. Had the clinic been secure accommodation s 25 would have operated to oust the inherent jurisdiction. For a critique of Wall J's approach, see A Downie 'Extra-Statutory Confinement—Detention and Treatment under the Inherent Jurisdiction' [1998] CFLQ 101 at 102.

[160] See below p 795.   [161] Children Act 1989, s 22(2).

[162] Viz Children (Secure Accommodation) Regulations 1991, regs 5(2)(a) and (b).

[163] Discussed above at p 705. Note: this restriction does not prevent a court, when making a secure accommodation order in respect of a child under 16, from specifying a length that goes beyond the child's sixteenth birthday, see *Re G (Secure Accommodation)* [2000] 2 FLR 259, CA.

[164] For a discussion of which, see below pp 728–30.

[165] Reg 4 of the 1991 Regulation, as amended. Before this Regulation the minimum age was 10.

[166] Although the above text reflects the Department of Health's *Guidance* (Vol 4 at para 8.26), s 25(1) actually states that a child may *not* be placed or kept in secure accommodation *unless* the criteria are satisfied which, according to Hoffmann LJ in *Re M (A Minor)(Secure Accommodation Order)* [1995] Fam 108 at 117, means that rather than being expressed as a grant of power, sub s (1) amounts to restriction on a power which is presumed to exist. In his Lordship's view that power to restrict liberty 'is an ordinary incident of parental responsibility conferred by the Art on the local authority with respect of children in its care'. Whether this is a fair interpretation of s 25(1) may be questioned. It certainly is questionable whether parental responsibility to restrict liberty goes nearly as far as that permitted under the Act, see *Re K (A Child)(Secure Accommodation Order: Right To Liberty)* [2001] Fam 377, discussed below at p 716, and the analysis of Parry, above, at 104–5.

It is not therefore sufficient just to prove absconding[167] but it must also be shown that if the child absconds he is likely to suffer significant harm.[168] On the other hand, the criteria in s 25(1)(a) and (b) are disjunctive and it is accordingly unnecessary to satisfy both limbs.[169] So far as s 25(1)(a) is concerned it has been held[170] that the word 'likely' has the same meaning in both sub paras (i) and (ii) and as under s 31 should be construed as meaning 'a real possibility or a possibility that cannot sensibly be ignored'.

The application of the s 25 criteria is crucial. As the Department of Health's *Guidance* says[171] 'it is unlawful for the liberty of a child to be restricted [either by a local authority or the court] unless one of these criteria is met, no matter how short the period in security'.

Seeking court authorisation

If a local authority wishes to keep a child in secure accommodation for more than 72 hours they need a court order. Applications should be made by the authority looking after the child to the family proceedings court, unless proceedings are pending in a higher court in respect of the same child in which case an application should be made to that court.[172]

As proceedings under s 25 are 'specified proceedings' for the purpose of s 41,[173] the court must appoint a children's guardian for the child unless it is considered unnecessary.[174] Although the court has a discretion not to appoint a guardian it cannot make a secure accommodation order in respect of a child who is not legally represented unless he has been informed of his right to apply for publicly funded representation and, having had the opportunity to do so, has refused, or failed to apply.[175]

The court's function under s 25

According to s 25(3) of the 1989 Act it is the court's duty, on hearing an application, 'to determine whether any relevant criteria for keeping the child in secure accommodation are satisfied'. If they are, then by s 25(4), the court 'shall make an order authorising the

---

[167] But note that *one* previous absconding will amount to a 'history' of absconding for the purposes of s 25(1)(a)(i): *R v Calder Justices, ex p C* (4 May 1993, unreported) cited by Clarke Hall and Morrison on *Children* at 7 [176]. 'Absconding' has been interpreted to mean 'to hide oneself; to go away hurriedly and secretly: see *R C (Secure Accommodation Order: Representation)* [2001] EWCA Civ 458, [2001] 2 FLR 169, CA.

[168] The phrase 'likely to suffer significant harm' has the same meaning as for care proceedings (discussed below at pp 744ff), see *Re G (Secure Accommodation Order)* [2001] 1 FLR 884, 896 per Munby J and see further below.

[169] *Re D (Secure Accommodation Order)(No. 1)* [1997] 1 FLR 197—justices held wrong to have refused to make an order in the case of a 14-year-old child who was clearly at risk of self harm but who could not be found to have absconded.

[170] See *S v Knowsley Borough Council* [2004] EWHC 491 (Fam), [2004] 2 FLR 716 at [36] ff, per Charles J.

[171] Vol 4 at 8.27.   [172] See Child (Allocation of Proceedings) Order 1991, art 3(1), (3).

[173] FPR 1991, r 4.2; FPC (CA 1989) R 1991, r 2(2).

[174] FPR 1991, r 4.10(1); FPC (CA 1989) R 1991, r 10(1). According to Bracewell J in *Re AS (Secure Accommodation Order)* [1999] 1 FLR 103 it is only in the most exceptional case that it will not be appropriate to appoint a guardian. Note: children capable of doing so may instruct their own solicitor, see eg *Re C (Secure Accommodation Order: Representation)* [2001] EWCA Civ 458, [2001] 2 FLR 169, discussed below at p 716. As to the right of the child to attend proceedings, see eg *Re W (A Minor)(Secure Accommodation Order: Attendance At Court)* [1994] 2 FLR 759, a child should only be allowed to attend where it is thought to be in his or her interest, but according to J Fortin *Children's Rights and the Developing Law* (2nd edn) children are routinely allowed to attend proceedings. But note also *Re D (Secure Accommodation Order)* [1997] 1 FLR 197 in which Singer J thought it unusual for a 14 year old to give evidence and that if it could be avoided this should be.

[175] Children Act 1989, s 25(6).

child to be kept in secure accommodation and specifying the maximum period for which he may be kept'.[176]

According to Hoffmann LJ in *Re M (A Minor)(Secure Accommodation)*[177] the court's function under s 25 is 'to control the exercise of power by the local authority rather than to exercise an independent jurisdiction in the best interests of the child'. In the same case, however, Butler-Sloss LJ commented that whether it was a reviewing power or a general duty to consider the welfare of the child was 'a matter of words'. They both agreed, however, that though important, the child's welfare is *not* the paramount consideration (that is, s 1(1) has no application to s 25 proceedings).[178] Instead the court's duty is similar to that of the local authority. Consequently, as Hoffmann LJ put it, 'the duty of the court is to put itself in the position of a reasonable local authority and to ask, first, whether the conditions in sub s (1) are satisfied and secondly, whether it would be in accordance with the authority's duty[179] to safeguard and promote the welfare of the child (but subject to the qualification in s 22(6))[180] for the child to be kept in secure accommodation and, if so, for how long'.

Re M is also authority to saying that s 1(5)[181] has no application to s 25 proceedings. As Butler-Sloss LJ said, the mandatory requirement of s 25(4) means that it must prevail over s 1(5).

The decision that s 1 has no application to s 25 proceedings resolved previous conflicting case-law and overrides the Department of Health's *Guidance.*[182] Although *Re M* has not escaped academic criticism,[183] Butler-Sloss LJ was surely right to say that the application of the paramountcy principle does not lie easily with the enjoinder to protect others. In any event, the 'compromise' of requiring the court to consider the child's welfare as part of the 'relevant criteria' to the extent of having to safeguard and promote that welfare effectively means that, at any rate with respect to absconding and self-harm, there should be little difference in outcome than if those interests were of paramount importance.

Once the relevant criteria have been found to be satisfied the court must, pursuant to s 25(4), specify the maximum length of the order. Initially, the maximum length that can be specified is three months[184] but orders may subsequently be renewed upon application for periods of up to six months at a time.[185] In determining the length the court must consider carefully the purpose to be achieved and, consistent with the need to be human

---

[176] If the court is not in a position to decide whether any of the relevant criteria are met and adjourns the hearing it can make an interim secure accommodation order: s 25(5).

[177] [1995] Fam 108. This reflects the view of Ward J at first instance. For a not dissimilar view see *Re K (A Child)(Secure Accommodation Order: Right To Liberty)* [2001] Fam 377 at [60].

[178] For a general discussion as to the application of s 1(1), see above pp 455–64.   [179] See s 22(3).

[180] This provision permits the local authority to exercise their powers where necessary to do so to protect members of the public from serious injury.

[181] By which courts should not make orders unless in doing so it is better than making no order, see above pp 475–9.

[182] See Vol 1 at 5.1 and Vol 4 at 8.47 which assumes the application of s 1(1) and 1(5).

[183] See P Bates 'Secure accommodation orders—in whose interests?' [1995] CFLQ 70 and Parry, above, at 110–11.

[184] Children (Secure Accommodation) Regulations 1991, reg 11. This will *include* the period of a prior interim order, see *C v Humberside County Council* [1994] 2 FLR 759. Time runs from the date of the order and not from when a child is subsequently placed in secure accommodation: *Re B (A Minor) (Secure Accommodation)* [1995] 1 WLR 232.

[185] Reg 12 of the 1991 Regulation.

rights compliant, the order should be proportionate to the harm found,[186] and only be for so long as is necessary and unavoidable.[187]

The effect of an order

A secure accommodation order is permissive inasmuch as it authorises but does not require the local authority to use it.[188] If, during the order, the local authority is satisfied that the criteria cease to apply, then the child must be discharged from the secure accommodation.[189] It is incumbent upon local authorities to keep secure placements under review.[190] Notwithstanding a court order, children who are accommodated by the authority may be removed from secure accommodation at any time by those with parental responsibility.[191] To prevent this the local authority must, where they can, obtain a care order.[192]

Appeals etc

An appeal both against the making of or refusal to make an order by the family proceedings court lies to the High Court.[193] Where the appeal is against the making of an order, the child may be kept in secure accommodation but not if it is against a refusal.[194] Appeals in respect of secure accommodation orders remain one of the few cases where leave is *not* required to appeal to the Court of Appeal.[195]

No provision is made for the discharge of a secure accommodation order. Consequently, if an order has been validly made but it is subsequently alleged that the criteria no longer apply, the local authority's continuing retention of the child in a secure unit must be challenged either by judicial review or habeas corpus proceedings or, possibly under ss 6 and 7 of the Human Rights Act 1998.[196] According to Charles J in *S v Knowsley Borough Council*,[197] judicial review is likely in most cases to be the most appropriate remedy and can be combined with points made under the Human Rights Act 1998.

Is s 25 human rights compliant?

It will be recalled[198] that the scheme on which s 25 is based, was drafted with the European Convention on Human Rights in mind but the worries then concerned the absence of any court involvement. Despite addressing that issue there was, at the time of the

---

[186] Cf *Re O (Supervision Order)* [2001] EWCA Civ 16, [2001] 1 FLR 923, discussed below at p 770.

[187] See the Department of Health's *Guidance* Vol 1, 5.1 approved in *R v Oxfordshire County Council (Secure Accommodation Order)* [1992] Fam 150.

[188] See *Re W (A Minor)(Secure Accommodation Order)* [1993] 1 FLR 692 at 695. Note also Charles J's observation in *S v Knowsley Borough Council* [2004] EWHC 491 (Fam), [2004] 2 FLR 716 at [46] that a court is not entitled to dictate how a local authority should exercise their duties.

[189] See *LM v Essex County Council* [1999] 1 FLR 988 in which Holman J left open the question of whether the discharge should be immediate. See also *Re K (A Child)(Secure Accommodation: Right to Liberty)* [2001] Fam 377 at [30] per Butler-Sloss P and [97] per Judge LJ.

[190] See regs 16 and 17 of the 1991 Regulation, for the application of which, see Parry, op cit, at 113.

[191] See s 25(9).   [192] See eg *M v Birmingham City Council* [1994] 1 FLR 141.

[193] See Section 94(1) of the Children Act 1989.

[194] See the Department of Health's *Guidance*, Vol 4, 8.49.

[195] See the Civil Procedure Rules 1998, r 52.3(1).

[196] See *LM v Essex County Council* [1999] 1 FLR 988 in which Holman J 'provisionally' considered that after making the secure accommodation order the court becomes functus officio and hence, some fresh action is required.

[197] [2004] EWHC 491 (Fam), [2004] 2 FLR 716 at [63]ff.   [198] See above at p 710.

implementation of the Human Rights Act 1998, intense speculation as to whether s 25 was compatible with the Convention.[199] This was soon tested in *Re K (A Child)(Secure Accommodation Order: Right To Liberty)*[200] in which a declaration of incompatibility was sought[201] in respect of s 25. It was argued that secure accommodation amounted to a deprivation of liberty within the meaning of Art 5(1) of the Human Rights Convention[202] and could not be justified by any of the exceptions provided for in that Article.

The application was rejected by the Court of Appeal. While in the majority's view[203] secure accommodation did amount to a deprivation of liberty so as to engage Art 5(1) rights, it was held to be justified by reason of Art 5(1)(d) which allows the detention of a minor by lawful order for the purpose of educational supervision. In reaching this latter conclusion the majority relied upon *Koniarska v UK*[204] in which the European Commission on Human Rights declared inadmissible a challenge to the use of secure accommodation and highlighted that 'educational supervision' should not be rigidly equated with classroom education and can include the giving of instruction to a minor to correct dysfunctional behaviour. Although it was accepted that it could be a breach to use such an order without providing any educational supervision, it was observed that the complaint would be about the action of the local authority and not about the statutory provision. In any event s 25 was not to be considered incompatible with the Convention merely because it did not itself mention educational supervision.

Although *Re K* authoritatively settled the compatibility of s 25 with human rights its justification on the basis of educational supervision is not without controversy[205] while Thorpe LJ's approach that secure accommodation is within the normal parental powers seems surely unsustainable.[206]

A different human rights point was raised in *Re C (Secure Accommodation Order: Representation)*.[207] In that case, the child being dissatisfied with the guardian's approach, instructed another solicitor to represent her. Through an oversight that solicitor was not served with notice of the proceedings. Consequently the child in question only had two hours to instruct her on how to respond to a 15 page statement prepared by the local authority. Although the Court of Appeal accepted not only that the child's rights to a fair trial under Art 6 of the Human Rights Convention were particularly important in secure accommodation proceedings where the child's very liberty is at stake, but also that those

---

[199] See eg Parry, above, at 105.   [200] [2001] Fam 377, CA.

[201] Such actions are brought under s 4 of the Human Rights Act 1998.

[202] By which 'Everyone has the right to liberty and security of person'.

[203] Butler-Sloss P and Judge LJ. Thorpe LJ dissented on this, holding that 'the deprivation of liberty was a necessary consequence of an exercise of parental responsibility for the protection and promotion of his welfare'. For this he relied upon the European Court of Human Rights' decision in *Nielsen v Denmark* (1989) 11 EHRR 175.

[204] Application No. 33670/96 (12 October 2000).

[205] For a critical analysis see J Masson: '*Re K (A Child)(Secure Accommodation Order: Right to Liberty)* and '*Re C (Secure Accommodation Order: Representation)* securing human rights for children and young people in secure accommodation' [2002] CFLQ 77. As Masson points out, the court seems not to have appreciated that the Education Act 1996, s 562 disapplies the educational duties to those detained under a court order.

[206] This seems to be Butler-Sloss P's view see *Re K* above, at [29]. Note also the point made by Judge LJ at [101] that under an order far more supervision and attention is provided than any normal parent could reasonably be expected to provide.

[207] [2001] EWCA Civ 458, [2001] 2 FLR 169.

rights should be the same as those charged with a criminal offence, it nevertheless upheld the propriety of the secure accommodation order.

Re C has surely rightly been criticised[208] both for making no reference to the requirement under Art 6(3)(c) that the accused should have adequate time and facilities to prepare their defence and for ignoring whether there was a breach of the Art 6(1) right to 'equality of arms'.

(c) Commentary

While secure accommodation may be the only viable means for dealing with highly disturbed adolescents (nor can it be denied that some children undoubtedly benefit from the regime)[209] yet, as one commentator has said,[210] 'the power to restrict a child's liberty strikes at the core of a law relating to the upbringing of children, which purports to place a premium on the welfare of the child and which is of central and increasing importance within family law'. Consequently, if for no other reason, there is an understandable anxiety as to whether secure accommodation is only being used, as the *Guidance* clearly states[211] that it should be, as a last resort. Some say[212] that in fact far too many orders are obtained unnecessarily, for example, simply to cure the 'absconding habit' of children or as a means of obtaining medical treatment rather than by using the mental health legislation. Nor is it thought that court scrutiny, at any rate at the magistrates' level, is always sufficiently rigorous.[213]

In Parry's view[214] all this argues for the need to make clear that 'it is the restrictive purpose for which any accommodation is used, rather than the primary purpose of the accommodation, which is the determining factor'. He also questions whether it is right not to treat each child's welfare as the paramount consideration[215] subject to being alive to the need to protect members of the public from serious injury. In his view both the court and a guardian ought to be required to pay particular regard to a 'secure accommodation welfare checklist'.

C INVESTIGATION OF CHILD ABUSE[216]

Local authorities have a statutory duty both to investigate (either themselves or via another agency) the child's circumstances and to determine what action, if any, should be taken. This duty is imposed by s 47(1), under which local authorities are obliged, upon being informed that a child in their area is the subject of an emergency protection order, is in police protection, has contravened a curfew order made under the Crime and Disorder

---

[208] See J Masson [2002] CFLQ 77, 90 and J Fortin *Children's Rights and the Developing Law* (2nd edn) 239.
[209] See Bullock et al, above at n 17.   [210] Parry, above, 115.   [211] Vol 1, *Court Orders* at 5.1.
[212] See Fortin, above, at 501.
[213] Fortin, above, for example cites (at 501) *Re W (A Minor)(Secure Accommodation Order)* [1993] 1 FLR 692 in which magistrates were criticised for making an order to last for three months rather than five weeks as recommended by the guardian.
[214] Above, at 115.
[215] As established by *Re M (A Minor)(Secure Accommodation)* [1995] Fam 108, discussed above at p 714.
[216] See generally R White, P Carr and N Lowe *Children Act in Practice* (3rd edn) 7.8 ff and M Hayes 'Child Protection from Principles and Polices to Practice' [1998] CFLQ 119.

Act 1998, or where they have reasonable cause to suspect that a child who lives or is found in their area is suffering or is likely to suffer significant harm, to 'make or cause to be made, such enquiries as they consider necessary to enable them to decide whether they should take any action to safeguard or promote the child's welfare'.[217]

Having reasonable cause to *suspect* that the child is suffering or is likely to suffer significant harm is, as Scott Baker J pointed out in *Re S (Sexual Abuse Allegations: Local Authority Response)*,[218] a low threshold for the understandable reason that the obligation is to make enquiries 'with a view to deciding whether to take any action to safeguard or promote the child's welfare'. As Lord Nicholls later put it:[219] 'local authorities would be prevented from carrying out effective and timely risk assessments if they could only act on the basis of proven facts'. In *Re S* itself an action for judicial review against a local authority for acting upon a s 47 investigation[220] was dismissed despite the claimant's previous acquittal on indecent assault charges. Notwithstanding *Re S* there must still be objectively reasonable grounds for embarking upon a s 47 investigation.[221]

Section 47 is principally directed towards the investigation of the circumstances of children living at home or who have been removed from home in an emergency.[222] Where enquiries substantiate concerns about the child's safety the Social Services Department must arrange a so-called strategy discussion which may comprise a telephone discussion or a meeting involving different professionals. The prime tasks of such a discussion are to share information, decide whether s 47 enquiries should be initiated or continued; agree on what action is immediately needed to protect the child and/or to provide interim services and support and to decide what information should be shared with the family save where that might place a child at risk or jeopardise a police investigation of an offence.[223]

In discharging their child protection duties local authorities do not work alone. As the Department of Health's *Guidance* puts it:[224]

'The authority cannot expect to be the sole repository of knowledge and wisdom about particular cases. Full inter-agency co-operation including sharing information and participating in decision-making is essential whenever a possible care or supervision case is identified.'

Facilitating inter-agency co-operation are two important bodies: at the planning and

[217] Local authorities are also obliged to investigate the child's circumstances following a court decision made under s 37 in other family proceedings (discussed above at p 580) or upon being notified by a local education authority that a child has persistently failed to comply with a direction given in an education supervision order (Children Act 1989 Sch 3, para 17).

[218] [2001] EWHC Admin 334, [2001] 2 FLR 776 at [36].

[219] *Re O and Another (Minors)(Care: Preliminary Hearing); Re B (A Minor)* [2003] UKHL 18, [2004] 1 AC 523 at [18].

[220] The local authority, believing that the claimant presented a risk, resolved to share this information with the claimant's new partner who had children of her own.

[221] See *Gogay v Hertfordshire County Council* [2001] 1 FLR 280.

[222] Though as Hale LJ pointed out in *Gogay v Hertfordshire County Council*, above, at (27) the section can be adapted to cases where children are already subject to a care order. In *Gogay* itself there was some confusion as whether the case involved a s 47 investigation or a disciplinary action against one of the local authority staff.

[223] See *Working Together to Safeguard Children—A guide to inter-agency working to safeguard and promote the welfare of children* (HMSO, 1999) (hereafter *Working Together*) para 5.28. *Working Together* is a revised version of *Working Together Under the Children Act 1989* (HMSO, 1991).

[224] Vol 1, para 3.10.

policy level, Local Safeguarding Children Boards (formerly Area Child Protection Committees) and, at the local level, Child Protection Conferences.[225] The principal tasks of the former[226] include advice on, and the review of, local practice and procedure for inter-agency co-operation including training. The task of the latter is to decide what action, if any, should be taken in individual cases.

Membership of both the Local Safeguarding Children Boards and the Child Protection Conferences comprises representatives from the various professions and agencies concerned with children, in particular from the social services, the NSPCC, the police, education, the health authority, general medical practice, the health visiting service, the probation service and appropriate voluntary organisations. In the case of the Local Safeguarding Children Boards membership is drawn from senior representatives of each of these agencies.

As the 1991 *Working Together* emphasised:[227]

'The child protection conference is central to child protection procedures. It is not a forum for a formal decision that a person has abused a child. That is a matter for the courts. It brings together the family and the professionals concerned with child protection and provides them with the opportunity to exchange information and plan together. The conference symbolises the inter-agency nature of assessment, treatment and the management of child protection.'

There are two kinds of Child Protection Conference, the initial child protection conference and the child protection review. The purpose of the former, which should only be called after investigation has been made under s 47, is first to decide whether the child should be placed on the Child Protection Register,[228] and secondly, to recommend a future plan for the child. As Lord Browne-Wilkinson put it in *X (Minors) v Bedfordshire County Council*[229]

'The child protection conference is an essential step in each individual case. It brings together the professionals involved in that case and the family. It decides whether a child should be put on the Child Protection Register and makes recommendations for action'.

If it is decided to place the child on the Register, the conference must appoint a named 'key worker' whose prime task is to fulfil the statutory obligations of his agency to protect the child and to co-ordinate inter-agency co-operation.[230] The child and his family will therefore be placed under close scrutiny, but the key worker must ensure that they are fully engaged in the child protection plan.[231]

The purpose of the child protection review is generally to review the child protection plan, examine the current level of risk and ensure that the child continues to be adequately protected. The review must also consider whether inter-agency co-ordination is

---

[225] See generally *Working Together*. Area Child Protection Committees were formerly known as Area Review Committees, and Child Protection Conferences as Case Conferences: see p 450 of the 7th edition of this work.

[226] See *Working Together*, paras 4.1 ff.   [227] See n 225f above at para 6.1.

[228] For a discussion of Protection Registers see *Working Together*, paras 5.99 et seq.

[229] [1995] 2 AC 633 at 747. It may be noted that statements made at child protection conferences attract qualified but not absolute privilege: *W v Westminster City Council* [2004] EWHC 2866 (QB), [2005] 1 FLR 816.

[230] See *Working Together*, paras 5.75 et seq.   [231] Above, para 5.76.

functioning effectively and consider whether the child's name should continue to be on the Register.[232]

Although there is no right for parents to attend the Child Protection Conference,[233] *Working Together* makes it that clear their exclusion must be justified, as, for example, where one parent is the alleged abuser or if there is a high level of conflict between family members. If they are excluded other means of communicating their views to the Conference should be found.[234] According to *Working Together*,[235] children who have sufficient understanding and are able to express their wishes and feelings and to participate in the process of investigation should also be encouraged to attend conferences.

The Child Protection Conference's dual function of promoting the dissemination of information about a child among various agencies and of co-ordinating the work of these services is crucial to the management of child protection. All too often in the past tragedies have resulted in cases where vital information about a child's circumstances has not been communicated to the local authority. With properly co-ordinated services there is a better chance of spotting warning signs of abuse or neglect and of constructive action being taken before crisis points have been reached. As against this, however, there is the danger of excessive investigation which in itself may be damaging to the child and family, and of having too many children under investigation. These at any rate were two of the concerns voiced in *Messages from Research*.[236] Other concerns were that too much focus was placed on specific incidents rather than on examination of the child's needs and that in cases where the test of 'significant harm'[237] is not thought to be satisfied there tends to be a failure to provide any Part III services, regardless of the child's needs.

After publication of this research, many authorities amended their policies to reduce the number and impact of investigations, though whether this has always been a carefully thought out strategy or simply a knee-jerk reaction to the research remains to be seen.[238] The key message is that the proper discharge of the investigative duties under s 47 requires them to be in proportion to the circumstances. Clearly, the nature of that investigation must depend on the seriousness and possible cause of any harm, whether the child (and other children) is in a safe place, and on what is already known about the family. If the child has already suffered significant harm then there will need to be an investigation of some kind so as to establish cause. If the harm is serious enough to give rise to the possibility that a criminal offence has been committed, or its cause is not adequately explained, the case ought then to be referred to a Police Child Protection Team.

[232] Above, para 5.91.
[233] See *R v Harrow London Borough Council, ex p D* [1990] Fam 133,CA. See generally D Savas 'Parental participation in case conferences' [1996] CFLQ 57.
[234] Above, para 5.58.   [235] Above, para 5.57.
[236] *Child Protection Messages from Research* (Department of Health, 1995), which makes the point that of the 160,000 annual referrals to the child protection system, 40,000 (25%) are closed after only limited investigation.
[237] This concept is the linchpin of s 31: see below, pp 737ff.
[238] Note the *Victoria Climbié Inquiry Report* Cm 5730, 2003, 17.102–103 considered that there remains a misunderstanding regarding the use of ss 17 and 47 which in Victoria's case led to a fatal failure of the authorities to protect her.

D SHORT-TERM PROTECTION

1 INTRODUCTION

As the Department of Health's *Guidance* points out,[239] action under s 47 'should be seen as the usual first step when a question of child protection arises . . .'[240] It may be that, the matters having been investigated, the problems can be solved with the co-operation of the family and no further formal action is necessary. On the other hand, further action may be thought imperative to protect the child. Short-term protection is governed by Part V of the Act, which, as the *Guidance* puts it, is designed:

'. . . to ensure that effective protective action can be taken when this is necessary within a framework of proper safeguards and reasonable opportunity for parents and others connected with the child to challenge such actions before a court. The measures are short-term and time-limited, and may or may not lead to further action . . .'

The two principal court orders under Part V are emergency protection orders and child assessment orders. In addition, powers are given to the police to take a child into police protection. We discuss each of these powers in turn.

2 EMERGENCY PROTECTION ORDERS[241]

(a) Introduction

The purpose of an emergency protection order is to provide for the immediate removal or retention of a child in a genuine emergency. As the Department of Health's *Guidance* stresses[242] it is an 'extremely serious step' and should not be regarded 'as a routine response to allegations of child abuse or as a routine first step in initiating care proceedings'. Orders necessarily engage Art 8 human rights (ie to respect for private and family life) and intervention has to be proportionate to the risk involved.[243] As Munby J has advised in *X Council v B (Emergency Protection Orders)*[244]

'(i) An EPO, summarily removing a child from his parents, is a "draconian" and "extremely harsh" measure, requiring "exceptional justification" and "extraordinarily compelling reasons". Such an order should not be made unless the FPC [ie. family

---

[239] Vol, *Court Orders*, para 4.78.

[240] Without such intervention the local authority is unlikely to succeed on any application for an emergency protection order or child assessment order.

[241] See generally, J Masson 'Emergency Intervention to Protect Children: Using and Avoiding Legal Controls' [2005] CFLQ 75. the Department of Health's *Guidance and Regulations*, Vol 1, *Court Orders*, paras 4.28 et seq. The provisions are based on the recommendations of the *Review of Child Care Law* (DHSS, 1985, ch 13) following widespread criticism (see eg T Norris and N Parton 'Administration of Place of Safety Orders' [1987] JSWL 1) of place of safety orders which emergency protection orders replaced.

[242] Vol 1, *Court Orders* para 4.30.

[243] Removal of babies will be particularly hard to justify in the light of the decision of the European Court of Human Rights in *P, C and S v United Kingdom* (2002) 35 EHRR 546, [2002] 2 FLR 631. See also *K and T v Finland* [2001] 2 FLR 707. Compare, however, *Re M (Care Proceedings: Judicial Review)* [2003] EWHC 850 (Admin) [2003] 2 FLR 171.

[244] [2004] EWHC 2005 (Fam), [2005] 1 FLR 341 at para [57].

proceedings court] is satisfied that it is both necessary and proportionate and that no other less radical form of order will achieve the essential end of promoting the welfare of the child. Separation is only to be contemplated if immediate separation is essential to secure the child's safety: "imminent" danger must be "actually established".

(ii) Both the local authority which seeks and the FPC which makes an EPO assume a heavy burden of responsibility. It is important that both the local authority and the FPC approach every application for an EPO with an anxious awareness of the extreme gravity of the relief being sought and a scrupulous regard for the European Convention rights of both the child and the parents'.

Even if intervention is thought necessary, it should always be done sensitively with a view to promoting the child's interests and, so far as it is consistent to do so, without overlooking the interests of the other members of the family. So-called 'dawn raids' (ie. where children are removed from their families during the night), for example, should rarely be necessary.[245] In any event, thought should always be given to whether the alleged abuser, rather than the child, should be removed from the family.[246]

(b) The grounds for an emergency protection order

Likely to suffer harm

Section 44(1) provides the first of three grounds upon which an emergency protection order may be made, namely that on the application of any person the court is satisfied that there is reasonable cause to believe that the child is likely to suffer significant harm if he:

(i)   is not removed to accommodation provided by or on behalf of the applicant; or

(ii) does not remain in the place in which he is then being accommodated.

Although commonly the applicant will be the local authority or NSPCC, *any* person may apply under this provision, including even a parent or relative.[247] Where the applicant is not the relevant local authority, provision has been made for the authority, if they think it is in the child's best interests, to take over the order and therefore the powers and responsibilities for the child that go with it.[248] The court (and not the applicant) must be satisfied about likelihood of significant harm.[249] The ground itself is prospective, so that evidence of past or even current harm is not sufficient unless it indicates that harm is likely to recur in the future. Moreover, the risk of harm contemplated should be that which is

---

[245] Such removals, for example in Orkney's and Rochdale's satanic child abuse cases (see respectively R Brett 'Orkney: aberration or system?' (1991) 3 Journal of Child Law 143 and *Rochdale Borough Council v A* [1991] 2 FLR 192), caused considerable public disquiet. In *Re A (Minors)(Child Abuse: Guidelines)* [1992] 1 All ER 153 it was held that they should only be effected when there are clear grounds for believing significant harm would otherwise be caused to the children or vital evidence is only obtainable by such means.

[246] Viz by an exclusion order, discussed below at p 726, or by other means, on which see C Cobley 'Child abuse, child protection and the criminal law' (1992) 4 Journal of Child Law 78.

[247] In such cases the local authority will also have to become involved, because under s 47(1) they have a duty to investigate upon being informed of the existence of such an order. For the difficulties of individuals obtaining an extension, see below, p 726.

[248] See the Emergency Protection Order (Transfer of Responsibilities) Regulations 1991, discussed by the Department of Health's *Guidance and Regulations*, Vol 1 at paras 4.32 et seq.

[249] For discussion of the meaning of 'significant harm' and 'likelihood' see below, p 737.

anticipated during the period of the order.[250] On the other hand, this prospective test can be satisfied even though the harm to the particular child has not yet occurred, eg where a convicted sexual offender moves in with the mother.

Denial of access to the child

Under s 44(1)(b) an order can be made upon application of a local authority where they are making enquiries under s 47(1)(b) because they (ie the local authority) have reasonable cause to suspect that a child is suffering, or is likely to suffer, significant harm,[251] and 'those enquiries are being frustrated by access to the child being unreasonably refused to a person authorised to seek access and that the applicant has reasonable cause to believe that access to the child is required as a matter of urgency'. Similar provision is made[252] for an application in the same circumstances by an authorised person (ie the NSPCC).[253]

Section 44(1)(b) and (c) were intended[254] to be used in emergencies where enquiries cannot be completed because the child cannot be seen but there is enough cause to suspect the child is suffering or is likely to suffer significant harm. In cases where there is a need for further investigation of a child's health and development but he is thought to be safe from immediate danger, the proper order, if any, is a child assessment order.[255] The Department of Health's *Guidance and Regulations* puts the point well, commenting:[256]

'The hypothesis of the grounds at section 44(1)(b) and (c) is that this combination of factors is evidence of an emergency or the likelihood of an emergency.'

It also makes the further point:

'The court will have to decide whether the refusal of access to the child was unreasonable in the circumstances. It might consider a refusal unreasonable if the person refusing had had explained to him the reason for the enquiries and the request for access, the request itself was reasonable, and he had failed to respond positively in some other suitable way—by arranging for the child to be seen immediately by his GP, for example. Refusal of a request to see a sleeping child in the middle of the night may not be unreasonable,[257] but refusal to allow access at a reasonable time without good reason could well be.'

Section 44(1) provides the minimum conditions that must be satisfied before an order can be made. However, it is not intended that upon being satisfied of the condition under s 44(1) the court should automatically make an order. The court must still consider both the welfare principle, pursuant to s 1(1) and whether or not to make an order, pursuant to

---

[250] See *Re C and B (Care Order: Future Harm)* [2001] 1 FLR 611 at (19), per Hale LJ.

[251] The duties under s 47 are discussed above at pp 717ff.   [252] Section 44(1)(c).

[253] Children Act 1989 s 31(9).

[254] The provision was introduced following a recommendation in the Kimberley Carlile inquiry (*A Child in Mind*, para 7.24). It was a late amendment to the legislation and was little debated.

[255] See points (iii) and (iv) forcibly made by Munby J in *X Council v B (Emergency Protection Orders)* [2004] EWHC 2015 (Fam), [2005] 1 FLR 341 at [57], and re-emphasised by McFarlane J in *Re X: Emergency Protection Orders* [2006] EWHC 510 (Fam), who made the point that (a) mere lack of information or a need for assessment can never of themselves establish the existence of a genuine emergency and (b) cases of emotional abuse will rarely, if ever, warrant an emergency protection order. See further below at p 724. Child assessment orders are discussed below, pp 728ff.

[256] Vol 1, para 4.39.

[257] Indeed, removals in the middle of the night will require special justification: cf *Re A (Minors) (Child Abuse: Guidelines)* [1992] 1 All ER 153, per Hollings J.

s 1(5). Since these proceedings are not 'family proceedings'[258] the court cannot make a s 8 order. On the other hand, it can give directions about contact and medical or psychiatric examination or other assessment of the child.[259] It has been said[260] that where the removal of a baby is thought justified 'one would normally expect arrangements to be made by the local authority to facilitate contact on a regular and generous basis'.

(c) Procedure

Unless arising from a s 37 direction to investigate,[261] or there are proceedings pending in a higher court, an application for an emergency protection order must be made in the magistrates' family proceedings court and cannot be transferred to a higher court.[262] Application may, with leave of the clerk, be made ex parte,[263] though hearings can be inter partes and indeed the court has the power to direct that the application be made inter partes.[264] According to Munby J in *X Council v B (Emergency Protection Orders)*[265] an ex parte application is normally only appropriate where the case is of genuine emergency or other great urgency (and even then in most cases some informal notice ought to be able to be given to the parents) and where an application is so made the evidential burden is even heavier with applicants (normally the local authority) being duty bound to make 'the fullest and most candid and fresh disclosure of all the circumstances known to them'. An order can be made by a single justice.[266] However, wherever possible applications, even those made ex parte, should be made to a court.[267] A court hearing the application may take account of any statement contained in any report made to the court in the course of or in connection with the hearing or any evidence given during the hearing, which is in the opinion of the court relevant to the application.[268] This enables the court to give proper weight to hearsay, opinions, health visiting or social work records and to medical reports. Save in wholly exceptional circumstances, parents must be given adequate prior notice of the application and of the evidence the local authority is relying upon.[269]

---

[258] As defined by s 8(3), (4), discussed above, p 564.
[259] Children Act 1989 s 44(6), discussed below.
[260] Per Munby J in *Re M (Care Proceedings: Judicial Review)* [2003] EWHC 850 (Admin), [2003] 2 FLR 171 at [44] point (iv).
[261] Discussed above, p 580.
[262] The Children (Allocation of Proceedings) Order 1991 Arts 3 and 7(2).
[263] Family Proceedings Courts (Children Act 1989) Rules 1991 r 4(4). There has been some reluctance on the part of the courts to hear ex parte applications: see *The Children Act Report 1992* (1993) Cm 2144). But see the findings by J Masson 'Emergency Intervention to Protect Children: Using and Avoiding Legal Controls' [2005] CFLQ 75 at 89.
[264] Rule 4(5).
[265] [2004] EWHC 2015 (Fam), [2005] 1 FLR 341 at [57] points (viii) and (ix). See also *Re X: Emergency Protection Orders* [2006] EWHC 510 (Fam) at [101].
[266] Rule 2(5)(a).
[267] See the Department of Health's *Guidance and Regulations*, Vol 1, para 4.46 and following the recommendations of the *Report of the Inquiry into Child Abuse in Cleveland in 1987* (Cm 412, 1968) p 252.
[268] Children Act 1989 s 45(7).
[269] Per Munby J in *X Council v B (Emergency Protection Orders)* [2004] EWHC 2015 (Fam), [2005] 1 FLR 341 at [57] point (vii) repeating what he said in *Re M* above at [44] point (iii).

(d) The effects of an order

An emergency protection order authorises, but does not direct,[270] either the removal to or prevention of removal from accommodation provided by or on behalf of the applicant.[271] In the former instance the order operates as a direction to any person who is in a position to do so to comply with any request to produce the child to the applicant.[272] The court may also authorise an applicant to enter specified premises and search for a child and may include another child in the order if it believes there might be another child on the premises.[273]

The order gives the applicant parental responsibility for the child,[274] but this is limited: the power to remove or to prevent removal can only be exercised to safeguard and promote the child's welfare.[275] Hence, for example, if the applicant gains access and finds that the child is neither harmed nor likely to be harmed, he may not remove the child.[276] In any event, an applicant can exercise responsibility only insofar as it is reasonably required to safeguard or promote the child's welfare, having regard in particular to the duration of the order.[277] It would not therefore be appropriate to make any changes in the child's life which would have a long-lasting effect.

(e) The power to add directions

In the absence of a court direction the applicant must, during the subsistence of the order, allow the child reasonable contact with his parents, any other person with parental responsibility, any person with whom he was living immediately before the order, any person in whose favour there is a contact order in relation to him and any person acting on behalf of those persons.[278] The court, however, may give such directions as it considers appropriate about contact and may impose conditions.[279] Nevertheless, where the local authority is the applicant, the court will generally leave contact to the authority's discretion or at any rate order that reasonable contact be negotiated.[280] If therefore the local authority wishes to restrict contact, it should seek a court direction to that effect.

Medical evidence is likely to be of importance in any future care proceedings, so that early decisions or directions about examinations are crucial. For this reason, although the parental responsibility acquired on the making of the order would permit the applicant to consent to the child's examination or assessment, it might be preferable to seek directions

---

[270] According to Munby J in *X Council v B* above at [57] point (xii) even after it has obtained an order the local authority is still under an obligation to consider less drastic alternatives to emergency removal.

[271] Section 44(4)(b).   [272] Section 44(4)(a).

[273] Section 48(3), (4). This does not give the power to make a forced entry. If the applicant is refused or likely to be refused entry, the court may issue a warrant authorising a constable to assist in the execution of the order using reasonable force if necessary: s 48(9).

[274] Section 44(4)(c).

[275] Section 44(5)(a). Removals should normally be at an agreed time following consultation with appropriate professionals. A proper explanation must be given to the child: Department of Health's *Guidance and Regulations*, Vol 1, para 4.58.

[276] Similarly, if a return appears safe, the child should be returned: s 44(10). In each case this might occur where the alleged abuser vacates the home.

[277] Section 44(5)(b).

[278] Section 44(13). This presumption of reasonable contact is in line with the general policy of the Act: see the discussion below, p 582.

[279] Section 44(6) and (8).

[280] See the Department of Health's *Guidance and Regulations*, Vol 1, at para 4.62.

on the issue. Section 44(6)(b) empowers the court to make directions as to a medical or psychiatric examination or other assessment of the child, and under s 44(8) the court may direct that there be no such examination or assessment. Although s 44(7) expressly provides that, notwithstanding a court order, the child can, if of sufficient understanding to make an informed decision, refuse to submit to an examination or other assessment, as we discuss in relation to the equivalent provision in relation to interim care,[281] it has been controversially held[282] that the High Court has an inherent power to override that refusal.

(f) The power to add an exclusion requirement[283]

Following amendments introduced by the Family Law Act 1996 courts can add an exclusion requirement to any emergency protection order.[284] Such an order requires the person named in the order to leave the child's home or defined area where the home is situated and prohibits him from re-entering the home or defined area.[285] This power, conferred by s 44A of the 1989 Act, is subject to the court being satisfied of three conditions:

(1) there is reasonable cause to believe that the child will consequently not be likely to suffer significant harm or that the enquiries will cease to be frustrated;

(2) there is someone (whether a parent or some other person) living in the home who is able and willing 'to give to the child the care which it would be reasonable to expect a parent to give to him'; and

(3) that that other person consents[286] to the exclusion requirement.

The exclusion requirement may last no longer than the emergency protection order, though it can be made for a shorter period.[287] In any event, the exclusion ceases to be enforceable if the applicant removes the child for more than 24 hours.[288] A power of arrest may be attached to the requirement.[289]

Instead of making the exclusion requirement, the court is empowered to accept undertakings in similar terms.[290] However, although such undertakings are enforceable through contempt proceedings, no power of arrest can be attached.[291]

(g) Duration of the order

In the first instance an emergency protection order may be granted for up to eight days.[292] Save where the applicant is an individual,[293] the court can, upon application, grant one

---

[281] Viz s 38(6), discussed below, p 781.

[282] Per Douglas Brown J in *South Glamorgan County Council v W and B* [1993] 1 FLR 574.

[283] See generally the Law Commission report Law Com No 207, *Domestic Violence and the Occupation of the Family Home* (1992) paras 6.15ff.

[284] Separate statements of evidence in support of exclusions which must be served personally on the relevant person, are required: FPR 1991 r 4.25A, FPCA 1991, r 25A and *Re W (Exclusion: Statement of Evidence)* [2000] 2 FLR 666.

[285] Section 44A(3).

[286] The consent must either be written or given orally to the court: FPR 1991 r 4.24; FPCA 1991 r 25.

[287] Section 44A(4).   [288] Section 44A(10).   [289] Section 44A(5).   [290] Section 44B.

[291] Section 44B(2).

[292] Section 45(1); cf the former place of safety orders which could be granted for up to 28 days.

[293] Section 45(4) only permits application by those entitled to apply for a care order, viz a local authority or 'authorised person'.

period of extension[294] for a further seven days.[295] It has been said[296] that no order should be made for 'any longer than is absolutely necessary to protect the child' and that where an application is made ex parte very careful consideration should be given to making the order for the 'shortest possible period commensurate with the preservation of the child's immediate safety'.

There is no appeal against the making or refusal to make an emergency protection order.[297] However, an application to discharge the order may be made by the child, parent, any other person with parental responsibility or any person with whom the child was living before the order was made,[298] except where the person was given notice of and present at the original hearing.[299] No application for discharge can be heard before the expiry of 72 hours after the making of the order.[300]

The inability to appeal a *refusal*[301] to make or extend an order has been criticised on more than one occasion. A striking example was *Re P (Emergency Protection Order)*,[302] in which justices refused to extend an order notwithstanding firm medical evidence pointing to a risk of life-threatening abuse (the mother having being diagnosed as suffering from fabricated illness syndrome by proxy). The inability to challenge that refusal prompted Johnson J to comment[303] that consideration should be given to providing a mechanism for review, though he added that such a mechanism would have to be one which could operate very quickly.

(h) The use of emergency protection orders

Compared with the annual numbers of place of safety orders made before the 1989 Act (about 5,000) the number of emergency protection orders since the Act has been dramatically low. Indeed, under half that number, 2,300 were made in 1993 and, although this rose to 3,100 in 1994, they had dropped back again to about 2,565 by 1996.[304] Since then they dropped back further to 1,728 in 2002, but rose to 2,061 in 2003 and to 2,390 in 2004.[305] Given that the new powers were not intended to be used as a routine way of starting care proceedings, some reduction in numbers was to be expected. However, given the subsequent sharp fall in the number of emergency protection orders (as against a general rise in care orders) it is clear some other explanation needs to be sought. It has been suggested[306] that against a general background of local authorities being less interventionist, they are in fact more prepared to make alternative arrangements, and in particular to accommodate a child without prejudicing the possibility of later seeking a care order after a further investigation.

---

[294] Section 45(6).   [295] Section 45(5).

[296] Per Munby J in *X Council v B (Emergency Protection Orders)* [2004] EWHC 2015 (Fam), [2005] 1 FLR 341 at [57] point (v).

[297] Section 45(10).   [298] Section 45(8).   [299] Section 45(11).   [300] Section 45(9).

[301] Technically it might be possible to challenge an unreasonable refusal by judicial review.

[302] [1996] 1 FLR 482. See also *Essex County Council v F* [1993] 1 FLR 847, per Douglas Brown J.

[303] Ibid at 484–5.

[304] These at times inexact statistics can be found in the CAAC Reports of 1997, 1994/5 and 1993/4. See in particular Table 2C of the 1997 Report (note that the graph is based on a six-month period). See J Masson 'Emergency Intervention to Protect Children: Using and Avoiding Legal Controls' [2005] CFLQ 75.

[305] See *Judicial Statistics* for 2002–2004, Table 5.2.

[306] R White, P Carr and N Lowe *Children Act in Practice* (3rd edn) 7.51.

3 CHILD ASSESSMENT ORDERS [307]

Described as 'a multi-disciplinary assessment in non-emergency situations',[308] a child assessment order had no parallel in the pre-1989 Act law. It was first proposed in the Kimberley Carlile Report,[309] but the order was only included in the 1989 Act as a late amendment in response to a demand for a power to be able to see, examine and assess a child where there is concern as to his welfare, in the face of lack of co-operation from those responsible for him.

(a) Application and criteria

As with applications for care and supervision orders,[310] only the local authority and the NSPCC (as the only authorised person)[311] may apply for a child assessment order.

Under s 43(1) the court may make an order if it is satisfied that:

'(a) the applicant has reasonable cause to suspect that the child is suffering or is likely to suffer significant harm;

(b) an assessment of the state of the child's health or development, or of the way in which he has been treated, is required to enable the applicant to determine whether or not the child is suffering, or is likely to suffer, significant harm; and

(c) it is unlikely that such an assessment will be made, or be satisfactory, in the absence of a child assessment order.'

It has been said[312] that if the real purpose of an application is to have the child assessed then consideration should be given as to whether that objective 'cannot equally effectively, and more proportionately' be achieved by a child assessment order rather than emergency protection order. Nevertheless it is to be emphasised that this order is not intended to be in any sense a substitute for an emergency protection order. Indeed s 43(4) specifically enjoins the court *not* to make an assessment order if there are grounds for making an emergency protection order and the court thinks it ought to make such an order. The court is empowered to treat an application for an assessment order as an application for an emergency protection order.[313] The fact that applications are made on notice[314] and the hearing is inter partes further emphasises that these orders are not designed to deal with emergencies.

As the Department of Health's *Guidance* says:[315]

'The principal conditions are very specific. The order is for cases where there are suspicions, but no firm evidence, of actual or likely significant harm in circumstances which do not constitute an emergency; the applicant considers that a decisive step to obtain an assessment

---

[307] See generally R Lavery 'The Child Assessment Order—A Re-Assessment' [1996] CFLQ 41 and J Dickens 'Assessment and the Control of Social Work: An Analysis of Reasons for the Non-Use of the Child Assessment Order' [1993] JSWFL 88.

[308] By David Mellor 158 HC Official Report, col 596.

[309] *A Child in Mind—The Report of an Inquiry into the Death of Kimberley Carlile* (1987).

[310] But cf emergency protection orders, discussed above, p 722.

[311] Children Act 1989 s 31(9) and s 43(13).

[312] Per Munby J in *X Council v B (Emergency Protection Orders)* [2004] EWHC 2015 (Fam), [2005] 1 FLR 341 at [49] and [57] point (iv). See also *Re X: Emergency Protection Orders* [2006] EWHC 510 (Fam).

[313] Section 43(3).   [314] Section 43(11).   [315] Vol 1, para 4.8.

is needed to show whether the concern is well founded or further action is not required and that informal arrangements to have such an assessment carried out have failed.'

Accordingly, the *Guidance* suggests that such an order:

'. . . will usually be most appropriate where the harm to the child is long-term and cumulative rather than sudden and severe. The circumstances may be nagging concern about a child who appears to be failing to thrive; or the parents are ignorant or unwilling to face up to possible harm to their child because of the state of his health or development; or it appears that the child may be subject to wilful neglect or abuse but not to such an extent as to place him at serious immediate risk.'[316]

Even if the court is satisfied as to the existence of the conditions, it is not bound to make the order. As with other orders under the 1989 Act, the court must, pursuant to s 1(1) and (5), have regard to the paramountcy of the child's welfare and be satisfied that making the order would be better for the child than making no order at all. However, because these proceedings do *not* rank as 'family proceedings',[317] the court *cannot* make a s 8 order.

A child assessment order cannot be made where an emergency protection or care order is made, but in principle there is no reason why it cannot be made in respect of an accommodated child, and it can co-exist with a s 8 order.

(b) Effect, commencement and duration of the order

A child assessment order has the twofold effect of placing a duty on any person, who is in a position to do so, to produce the child to the person named in the order and to comply with such directions relating to his assessment as may be specified,[318] and of authorising any person carrying out the assessment, or any part of it, to do so in accordance with the order.[319]

The maximum period of the order is seven days, but this period runs from the date specified in the order and not from the date on which the order was made.[320]

Section 43(6) empowers the court to make directions on any matter relating to the assessment, including directions as to the kind of assessment which is to take place and with what aim, by whom and where it will be carried out, and whether it will be subject to conditions, such as that the assessment should be a joint one involving experts appointed by the child's parents or the children's guardian as well as by the local authority. If an intrusive examination is to take place, such as a biopsy or genital examination, specific direction should be given. The order should include a direction as to whom the result of the assessment should be given.

Directions may also be made about whether and, if so, for how long, a child may be kept away from home.[321] Indeed, since an assessment order does not confer parental responsibility, the child may only be kept away from home in accordance with court directions. If

---

[316] Above at para 4.9.

[317] See s 8(3), (4), discussed above, p 564. Nor need the checklist under s 1(3) be applied: *Re R (Recovery Orders)* [1998] 2 FLR 401.

[318] Section 43(6).   [319] Section 43(7).

[320] Section 43(5). It is thought that the period must run continuously rather than eg one day a week for seven weeks: see Clarke Hall and Morrison, on *Children*, para 1[1133].

[321] Section 43(9).

the child is to be kept away from home, the order must contain such directions as the courts thinks fit as to the contact the child is to be allowed to have with other persons.[322]

Notwithstanding any court directions, if the child is of sufficient understanding to make an informed decision he may refuse to submit to a medical or psychiatric examination or other assessment.[323]

(c) The use of child assessment orders

The expectation that child assessment orders would not be made frequently[324] has been borne out by experience. For example, in the year ending 30 September 1992 only 105 applications were made, as opposed to 2,215 emergency protection orders.[325] In the following 12 months, only 94 applications were made, of which 26 were withdrawn, and only 55 orders granted.[326] The relatively high level of withdrawals supports the supposition that in many cases the threat of the order may be sufficient to persuade parents to agree to an assessment, in which case there will be no need for an order. One reason for the lack of use of assessment orders is the seven-day time limit; indeed one researcher found[327] this to be one of the key reasons for not seeking to use the powers. Clearly, given the limited length of the order, any assessment of the child will be little more than an initial one (for this reason arrangements for the assessment need to be carefully planned). Although it has been suggested[328] that it was misconceived to apply any time limit to the order, it is important to bear in mind that the whole purpose of the order is to obtain sufficient evidence either to allay fears about the child's well-being or to justify further action. Seven days should therefore give enough time to achieve this limited purpose.

Among other reasons suggested[329] for its lack of use are the length of time before an order can be obtained and, given the requirement of an inter partes hearing combined with lack of resources, local authorities 'are not likely to spend time and money on taking proceedings to coerce unco-operative parents in marginal cases'. Whether more use might be made following Munby J's comments in *X Council v B (Emergency Protection Orders)*[330] that the 1989 Act provides a 'carefully calibrated hierarchy of means' to respond to a child's needs and that any order 'must provide for the least interventionist solution consistent with the preservation of the child's immediate safety', remains to be seen.

The s 43 powers will remain of some use, particularly where parents are ignorant or resistant to thinking about the possible harm to their child because of the state of his health or development.

---

[322] Section 43(10).

[323] Section 43(8). There is a similar provision (s 44(7)) in relation to emergency protection orders, upon which note *South Glamorgan County Council v W and B* [1993] 1 FLR 574, discussed below, p 784.

[324] As the Department of Health's *Guidance*, Vol 1, para 4.23 says 'The child assessment order should be used sparingly'.

[325] Children Act Report 1992 (HMSO).

[326] Children Act Report 1993 (HMSO). As Lavery, above, at 42 points out, consideration of such orders is conspicuously absent from the later Children Act Advisory Committee Reports and they have never been included in *Judicial Statistics*.

[327] Dickens, above at 97.   [328] Lavery, above at 55.

[329] R White, P Carr and N Lowe *Children Act in Practice* (2nd edn, 1995) para 7.31.

[330] [2004] EWHC 2015 (Fam), [2005] 1 FLR 341 at [49].

4 POLICE PROTECTION [331]

As under the former law,[332] the police have limited but important powers to protect children. Indeed, in some areas out of hours protection is arranged through the use of police protection.[333] Section 46(1) of the 1989 Act enables a constable who has reasonable cause to believe that a child would otherwise be likely to suffer significant harm either to remove him to suitable accommodation and keep him there, or to 'take such steps as are reasonable to ensure that the child's removal from any hospital, or other place, in which he is then being accommodated, is prevented'. No child may be kept in police protection for more than 72 hours.[334]

As there is no power of search attached to this provision,[335] a child can only be taken into police protection once the officer has found the child.[336] Commonly the power has been used to hold children such as runaways or glue sniffers or those whose parents have abandoned them. It may also be used where an officer attends a domestic dispute and finds a child living in unhygienic conditions. *Langley v Liverpool City Council*[337] establishes that although the s 46 power to remove a child can be exercised even where an emergency protection order is in force, a police officer who knows that such an order is in force should not exercise the s 46 power unless there are compelling reasons to do so. In other words, removal of children should usually be effected pursuant to an emergency protection order and s 46 invoked only where it was not practical to do so.

Section 46(4) requires a constable taking a child into police protection to inform, as soon as is reasonably practicable, relevant local authorities, the child, his parents and other specified persons about the steps that have been taken in relation to the child.

He must secure that the case is inquired into by a 'designated officer'. That officer on completing his enquiries must release the child, unless he considers that there is still reasonable cause for believing that the child would be likely to suffer significant harm if released.[338] Where the child remains at risk the designated officer may seek an emergency protection order on behalf of the local authority,[339] if necessary, without consultation.[340]

The police do not acquire parental responsibility, but must do what is reasonable in all the circumstances of the case for the purpose of safeguarding or promoting the child's welfare, having regard in particular to the length of the period during which the child will be in police protection.[341]

---

[331] See generally the Department of Health's *Guidance and Regulations*, Vol 1, paras 4.71 et seq; C Cobley *Child Abuse and The Law* (1995) pp 51ff; C Cobley 'Child Abuse, Child Protection and the Criminal Law' (1992) 4 Journal of Child Law 78; and A Borkowski 'Police Protection and Section 46' [1995] Fam Law 204.

[332] Viz the Children and Young Persons Act 1969 s 28(2).

[333] See M Booth *Delay in Public Children Act Cases Second Report* (1996) para 8.15.

[334] Children Act 1989 s 46(6).

[335] See the Department of Health's *Guidance and Regulations*, op cit, para 4.71.

[336] Compare the powers to enter and search premises to save life or limb: s 17(1)(e) of the Police and Criminal Evidence Act 1984.

[337] [2005] EWCA Civ 1173, [2006] 1 WLR 375.   [338] Section 46(5).   [339] Section 46(7).

[340] Section 46(8). It is normally expected that there will be consultation: see *Working Together*, above para 5.24 and Borkowski, above, at 205.

[341] Section 46(9).

E CARE AND SUPERVISION PROCEEDINGS

1 INTRODUCTION

The Children Act 1989 places considerable importance on local authorities working in partnership with families and the avoidance wherever possible of court proceedings. Furthermore, as Lord Clyde observed in *Lancashire County Council v B*,[342] even the making of a care application is a step not lightly to be embarked upon since the

'stress which care proceedings may well impose on the parents may . . . . itself be damaging to the child. If the parents are themselves in fact innocent of any harm to the child the proceedings may simply be defeating the basic purpose and the policy of the Act. The initiating of proceedings may in some cases be readily and immediately a matter of obvious necessity. But in other cases it may be something not to be embarked upon without careful deliberation and a professional objectivity'.

As Lord Clyde said,[343] the need for caution and restraint is underlined by Art 8 of the European Convention on Human Rights. The expectation[344] is that voluntary arrangements through the provision of services to the child and his family should always be fully explored (though this should not be taken to mean that they must always be entered into first)[345] before compulsory powers are sought from the courts. Nevertheless, restraint is not always justified and voluntary arrangements will not solve all problems and the Children Act 1989 makes provision, in the form of care and supervision orders, for compulsory measures to be taken to safeguard and promote children's welfare. Even so, as the Department of Health's *Guidance* emphasises,[346] where a care or supervision order is thought to be the appropriate remedy because control of the child's circumstances is necessary to promote his welfare, 'applications in such proceedings should be part of a carefully planned process'.[347]

No child may be taken into care without a court order. There is only one route into care,[348] ie as a result of a care order being made under s 31. Courts cannot make care or supervision orders on their own motion nor can they require a local authority to take proceedings.[349] Instead such orders can only be made upon an application by a local authority or authorised person.[350] On the other hand, once proceedings have been started

---

[342] [2000] 2 AC 147 at 170.   [343] Above at 170.

[344] See the Department of Health's *Guidance and Regulations*, Vol 1, *Court Orders*, para 3.2.

[345] See the *Children Act Report 1992*, para 2.21, discussed above at p 698.

[346] Vol 1 at para 3.2.

[347] Furthermore, an application should proceed only after the child protection conference (discussed above, pp 719–20) has concluded, having taken legal advice, that no other course is open: see *Court Orders*, paras 3.10 and 3.12.

[348] Under the former law there were at least 12 different routes into compulsory care: see eg the *Review of Child Care Law*, Discussion Paper No 3, and the 7th edition of this work at pp 440 et seq. Furthermore, local authorities can no longer look to wardship as an alternative means of obtaining care orders. For a discussion of how local authorities formerly used wardship, see pp 466–8 of the 7th edition of this work.

[349] See *Nottingham County Council v P* [1994] Fam 18, CA.

[350] The only 'authorised person' is the NSPCC: see below.

they can only be withdrawn with leave of the court which means that the court[351] is thereafter in final control of the ultimate disposal of the application.[352]

2 INITIATING PROCEEDINGS

(a) Applicants

Under s 31(1) of the Children Act 1989 only a local authority or authorised person may apply for a care or supervision order. An 'authorised person' is defined by s 31(9) as the National Society for the Prevention of Cruelty to Children (NSPCC) and any of its officers or any other person authorised by the Secretary of State, of which there are none as yet. Where an authorised person proposes to make an application, he must, if it is reasonably practicable to do so and before making the application, consult the authority where the child is ordinarily resident.[353]

The police and local education authorities cannot apply for care or supervision orders, though the latter may apply for an education supervision order.[354] Parents or guardians have no right to initiate proceedings themselves and the 1989 Act has no procedure equivalent to that under the former law[355] which enabled parents to force a local authority to take action in relation to a child beyond their control.[356]

(b) In respect of whom applications may be made

No care or supervision orders may be made with respect to a child who has reached the age of 17 (or 16 if he is married).[357] This means, unlike the former law, that compulsory measures cannot be taken in respect of such adolescents,[358] although such persons may themselves approach the authority with a view to being provided with accommodation.[359]

---

[351] Accordingly, a care order can be made even though a local authority no longer wishes to pursue its application. For an example, see Re M (A Minor) (Care Order: Threshold Conditions) [1994] 2 AC 424, HL, discussed below at pp 740ff.

[352] Family Proceedings Rules (FPR) 1991 r 4.5, Family Proceedings Courts (Children Act 1989) Rules (FPCA) 1991 r 5. In deciding whether to grant leave the child's welfare is the paramount consideration: London Borough of Southwark v B [1993] 2 FLR 559, CA (in which leave was granted). It is a decision that needs to be considered as carefully as any other decision and opportunity should be given to the guardian to express his or her views: Re F (A Minor)(Care Order: Withdrawal of Application) [1993] 2 FLR 9 (leave refused). See also Re N (Leave to Withdraw Care Proceedings) [2000] 1 FLR 134 (leave refused) and X Council v B (Emergency Protection Orders) [2004] EWHC 2015 Fam, [2005] 1 FLR 341 (leave granted).

[353] Section 31(6). Note also the restrictions under s 31(7).

[354] Under s 36, discussed above, pp 389–90.

[355] Under the Children and Young Persons Act 1963 s 3 (as amended).

[356] As J Masson and M Morris Children Act Manual say (at p 97) 'A parent who is unable to control his child can only request assistance from the local authority and make a complaint under s 26(3)(b) [discussed below, pp 798ff] if it is refused.'

[357] Children Act 1989 s 31(3). Orders can still be made if the child is under 16 and validly married according to the laws of another country: cf Alhaji Mohamed v Knott [1969] 1 QB 1.

[358] See Re SW (A Minor) (Wardship: Jurisdiction) [1986] 1 FLR 24 where the High Court acting under its inherent jurisdiction committed a 17-year-old into care (which power is specifically abolished by s 100(2)(a)). For a criticism of this change see N Lowe (1989) 139 NLJ 87, but cf J Eekelaar and R Dingwall (1989) 138 NLJ 217 and A Bainham Children: The New Law (1990), at para 5.7.

[359] Above, p 705.

(c) Parties

The child and any person with parental responsibility are all automatically parties in care proceedings.[360] It is open to any other person to apply to be joined as a party and within the court's powers to direct that they be joined.[361] Although fathers without parental responsibility are not automatically parties they should nevertheless be served with notice of the proceedings and as a general rule, unless there is some justifiable reason for not doing so, they should be permitted to participate in the proceedings as a party where they wish to do so.[362]

(d) To which court applications should be made

Before the Children Act 1989 care proceedings could only be brought in the magistrates' courts, although in practice more difficult cases could be brought under the High Court's wardship jurisdiction.[363] County courts had no jurisdiction to hear public law cases.[364] The 1989 Act, however, vests original jurisdiction to hear care proceedings in all three tiers of court.[365] However, under the scheme introduced by the Children (Allocation of Proceedings) Order 1991, applications must normally[366] be commenced in the magistrates' family proceedings court,[367] but with a power to transfer proceedings to the county court or from there to the High Court (i.e. there is no power to transfer proceedings directly from the magistrates' court to the High Court). There is also power to transfer laterally, ie from one magistrates' or county court to another.

The scheme under the 1991 Allocation Order is that upon receipt of the application, the magistrates' clerk has to consider whether the proceedings should be transferred to a higher court or laterally to another magistrates' court. With regard to lateral transfers the main criteria are accelerating the determination of the proceedings and to consolidate proceedings with other pending family proceedings,[368] but another justification can be the general convenience of the parties. Lateral transfers are not often made.[369]

Under Art 7 cases can be transferred to a county court either upon a party's application or upon the court's own motion. The three main criteria justifying a transfer are that:

    (a) the proceedings are exceptionally grave, important or complex;[370]

---

[360] FPR 1991 r 4.7(1); FPCA 1991 r 7(1).

[361] For the procedure see r 4.7(2), (3) and r 7(2), (3), respectively.

[362] See *Re B (Care Proceedings: Notification of Father Without Parental Responsibility)* [1999] 2 FLR 408. Cf *Re P (Care Proceedings: Father's Application To Be Joined As Party)* [2001] 1 FLR 781, where because of delay, leave was refused, the father having previously chosen not to participate in the proceedings. Art 6 of the Human Rights Convention was held not to be thereby breached.

[363] Wardship is discussed in Ch 16.

[364] Though in private law proceedings concerning children they did have the power to commit children into care. This power was abolished by the 1989 Act.

[365] See ss 31(1) and 92(7) (definition of 'court').

[366] The exception is where a higher court makes a s 37 direction, discussed above at p 580.

[367] Children (Allocation of Proceedings) Order 1991 Art 3(1). See above p 17.

[368] The Children (Allocation of Proceedings) Order 1991 Art 6.

[369] See R White, P Carr and N Lowe *Children Act in Practice* (3rd edn, 2002) para 4.29.

[370] Ie (see Art 7(1)(a)) on account of:

    (i)   the complicated or conflicting evidence about the risks involved to the child's physical or moral well-being or about other matters relating to the welfare of the child;

    (ii) the number of parties;

(b) it is appropriate for the proceedings to be heard together with other pending family proceedings; and

(c) it would significantly accelerate the determination of the proceedings.

The object of this scheme is to have a flexible system under which all care proceedings can be expeditiously dealt with at an appropriate level of court. It was envisaged[371] that the majority of cases (ie the so-called straightforward applications) would be resolved at the magistrates' level, with the minority (ie the longer and more complex or difficult cases) of between 15 and 20% being disposed of by the higher levels of court. Generally speaking this expectation has been borne out by experience. In 1996, for example, the Children Act Advisory Committee[372] reported that between 22 and 26% of public law cases were transferred to care centres.[373] The *Scoping Study on Delay in Children Act Cases*[374] later found that the family proceedings courts dealt with about two thirds of public law cases but that this picture varied considerably with between 6% and 50% (and in one case more than 50%) of applications being transferred upwards. According to the 2004 Judicial Statistics, 14,485 (66%) of the 22,051 public law applications were dealt with by the magistrates' courts.

It is important that transfers are made as efficiently and promptly as possible. Indeed it is a key object of the *Protocol for Judicial Case Management in Public Law Children Act Cases*[375] that cases requiring a 'transfer up' are identified at the earliest opportunity. According to the Protocol transfers should be considered at the first hearing in the family proceedings court (ie by day 6) and by day 11 there should be an allocation hearing to consider in which court the application should be heard.

Whether it is right to vest jurisdiction in the bottom court at all (making a care order is after all one of the most drastic of civil law orders) can be debated but although recommendations have been made to review the criteria for transfer[376] there is little evidence of disputes or dissatisfaction with the level of court. Research does, however, suggest[377] that local authority solicitors are more likely to endorse a transfer than guardians.

(iii) conflict with the law of another jurisdiction;
(iv) some novel or difficult point of law; or
(v) some question of general public interest.

Note: it is neither necessary nor desirable to transfer proceedings to a superior level of court merely because a breach of human rights is alleged since such complaints should be dealt with by the court dealing with the care proceedings, per Wall LJ in *Re V (Care Proceedings: Human Rights)* [2004] EWCA Civ 54, [2004] 1 WLR 1435 and per Potter P in *Westminster City Council v RA, B and S* [2005] EWHC 970 (Fam), [2005] 2 FLR 1309.

[371] See CAAC Report 1992/93 p 46.   [372] CAAC Final Report June 1997, p 76.   [373] Table 5.1.
[374] Lord Chancellor's Department, 2002, para 80.
[375] June 2003, LCD, reproduced together with the *Practice Direction* at [2003] FLR 719. The Protocol is discussed in more detail below at p 758.
[376] See eg para 118 of the *Scoping Study* and *A Review of Care Administration in Family Proceedings* (HMMCSI, May 2001) para 2.13.
[377] J Plotnikoff and R Woolfson *Timetabling of Interim Care Orders Study* (Social Services Inspectorate, 1994).

3 THE THRESHOLD CRITERIA [378]

(a) Some preliminary observations

No care or supervision order may be made unless the conditions set out by s 31(2) have been satisfied.[379] These conditions have come to be known as the 'threshold criteria' to emphasise the point that they are not in themselves grounds or reasons for making a care or supervision order, but rather the minimum preconditions for obtaining such orders. As Lord Mackay LC said in his Joseph Jackson Memorial Lecture:[380]

'Those conditions are the minimum circumstances which the government considers should always be found to exist before it can ever be justified for a court even to begin to contemplate whether the State should be enabled to intervene compulsorily in family life.'

Echoing this comment Lord Nicholls said in *Re O and another (Minors)(Care: Preliminary Hearing); Re B (A Minor)*[381]

'The purpose of this threshold requirement is to protect families, both adults and children, from inappropriate interference in their lives by public authorities through the making of care and supervision orders.'

By requiring the State to justify its interference beyond purely welfare considerations[382] the threshold conditions helps to ensure that domestic law is human rights compliant.[383]

Satisfaction of the threshold criteria permits the court to proceed to the second stage, commonly referred to as the 'welfare stage', in which the court must decide what, if any, order to make.[384] At this stage, but not before, the child's welfare is paramount, and the court must have regard to the welfare checklist set out in s 1(3) including any harm the child has suffered or is at risk of suffering and how capable each of his parents is of meeting his needs and, having regard to s 1(5), whether making any order is better for the child than making no order.

(b) The criteria

Section 31(2) provides that a court may only make a care or supervision order if it is satisfied:[385]

---

[378] See generally Department of Health's *Guidance and Regulations*, Vol 1, *Court Orders*, paras 3.15 et seq; M Freeman 'Care After 1991'; S Cretney 'Defining the Limits of State Intervention: The Child and the Courts', both in D Freestone (ed) *Children and the Law* (1990) pp 130 et seq and pp 58 at 68–71 respectively. For a collection of multi-disciplinary papers see M Adcock and R White (eds) *Significant Harm* (2nd edn, 1998).

[379] But note: failure to satisfy the conditions does not necessarily mean that the child will be returned to his or her parents since the court can still make a s 8 order, see below p 765.

[380] (1989) 139 NLJ 505 at 506.   [381] [2003] UK HL 18, [2004] 1 AC 523 at para [14].

[382] The *Review of Child Care* (DHSS, 1985) para 15.10 expressly rejected compulsory State intervention being based on the welfare principle.

[383] The European Court of Human Rights has repeatedly stressed the gravity of removing children from their families particularly where this results in terminating contact, see eg *P, C and S v United Kingdom* (2002) 35 EHRR 31, [2002] 2 FLR 631 (removal of a child at birth held not to be justifiable in the particular circumstances). Human rights considerations remain equally relevant at the 'welfare stage', see *Re B (Care: Interference With Family Life)* [2003] EWCA Civ 876, [2003] 2 FLR 813.

[384] The 'welfare stage' is discussed below at p 755.

[385] Because the *court* must be satisfied that the criteria exist, it is not relieved of that duty because the parties agree: see *Re G (A Minor) (Care Proceedings)* [1995] Fam 16.

'(a) the child concerned is suffering significant harm, or is likely to suffer significant harm; and

(b) the harm or likelihood of harm is attributable to—

    (i) the care given to the child, or likely to be given to him if the order were not made, not being what it would be reasonable to expect a parent to give to him; or

    (ii) the child's being beyond parental control.'

This wording reflects the recommendations of the Child Care Review.[386] The criteria comprise two separate limbs, each of which has to be satisfied. The first, sometimes referred to as the 'significant harm' condition, focuses on present or anticipated harm. The second, sometimes referred to as the 'attributable' condition, is that the harm or likelihood of harm is attributable to the lack of reasonable parenting of the child or to the child's being beyond parental control. In determining whether the threshold criteria are satisfied the child's welfare is *not* the court's paramount consideration.[387]

Soon after implementation, in *Newham London Borough v AG*,[388] Sir Stephen Brown P commented:

'I very much hope that in approaching cases under the Children Act 1989 the court will not be invited to perform in every case a strict legalistic analysis of s 31. Of course, the words of the statute must be considered, but I do not believe that Parliament intended them to be unduly restrictive when the evidence clearly indicates that a certain course should be taken in order to protect the child.'

One can readily sympathise with the notion that legalistic arguments should not be allowed to obscure the purpose of the provisions, namely to protect the welfare of children. Nevertheless, given that s 31 is the benchmark against which State intervention into the family is or is not justified, it seems perfectly proper that its meaning should be fully tested in court. In the event, s 31 has generated considerable case law including a number of House of Lords' decisions.

(c) The significant harm condition

Harm

'Harm' is defined by s 31(9)[389] to mean 'ill-treatment or the impairment of health or development including, for example, impairment suffered from seeing or hearing the ill-treatment of another'. Ill-treatment and impairment are to be regarded as alternatives, so that satisfaction of either is sufficient.[390] According to the Department of Health's *Guidance and Regulations*[391] ill-treatment is sufficient proof of harm in itself and it is not necessary to show that impairment of health or development has resulted or even is likely to result (though that will be relevant to the welfare stage).

'Ill-treatment' is defined by s 31(9) as including 'sexual abuse and forms of ill-treatment

---

[386] *Review of Child Care Law* (DHSS, 1985), paras 15.12–15.27, though during its progress through Parliament a number of changes were made to the wording: see below.

[387] See *Humberside County Council v B* [1993] 1 FLR 257.   [388] [1993] 1 FLR 281 at 289, CA.

[389] As amended by the Adoption and Children Act 2002, s 120.

[390] See the Department of Health's *Guidance and Regulations*, Vol 1, *Court Orders*, para 3.19.

[391] Vol 1, *Court Orders*, para 3.19. Consequently a child who is injured but who has made a complete recovery can still be demonstrated to have suffered 'harm' for the purposes of s 31.

which are not physical'. The inclusion of sexual abuse gives statutory recognition to the view that such abuse is by definition ill-treatment, though the Act neither defines the term nor indicates what comes within it.[392] Physical abuse is obviously ill-treatment (though even here there is a fine line between what may be regarded as reasonable corporal punishment by a parent and ill-treatment)[393] while emotional abuse,[394] neglect and, possibly, failure to obtain medical treatment constitute 'forms of ill-treatment which are not physical'.[395] The last instances could also amount to the 'impairment of health or development'. In *Re M (A Minor) (Care Order: Threshold Conditions)*[396] Bracewell J, perhaps controversially, held that the child suffered ill-treatment by being permanently deprived of the love and care of his mother when she was murdered in his presence. It has been said[397] that the amendment to the meaning of 'harm' introduced by the Adoption and Children Act 2002, namely including 'impairment suffered by seeing or hearing the ill-treatment of another', shows that abusive actions do not have to be aimed at the child, thus vindicating Bracewell J's decision. However, while in *Re M* few would quibble with the notion that the child was 'harmed' by the murder of the mother, it may be doubted whether this could really be said to constitute 'ill-treatment'.[398]

Section 31(9) defines development as 'physical, intellectual, emotional, social or behavioural development' and health as 'physical or mental health'. This seems, as one commentary has said,[399] 'wide enough to cover any case of neglect—poor nutrition, low standards of hygiene, poor emotional care or . . . failure to seek treatment for an illness or condition'. It has been held that truancy (formerly a specific ground for a care order) can cause a child 'harm' by the consequential impairment of intellectual or social development.[400] 'Harm' is also wide enough to embrace 'moral danger', which was formerly a specific ground for making a care order.[401] The extension of the meaning of 'harm' to

[392] Whether or not certain behaviour amounts to 'sexual abuse' can sometimes be problematic: cf, for example, *Re W (Minors) (Residence Order)* [1998] 1 FCR 75, CA which involved an uninhibited attitude towards nudity which in itself was not thought to be abusive. On this whole issue see the discussion by M Freeman, 'Care After 1991' in D Freestone (ed) *Children and the Law* (1990) pp 140–2.

[393] See Freeman, at pp 142–6. However, this line is now perhaps clearer with the removal, by s 58(1) of the Children Act 2004, of the defence of reasonable chastisement to charges of wounding or causing actual bodily harm etc (see the discussion above at p 387).

[394] See eg *Re M and R (Child Abuse: Evidence)* [1996] 2 FLR 195. Lord Mackay adverted to 'verbal abuse or unfairness' being encompassed by the definition: 503 HL Official Report col 342.

[395] See Freeman, above, at p 141.

[396] See [1994] Fam 95 at 103–4. This decision was upheld by the House of Lords [1994] 2 AC 424, discussed below.

[397] A Bainham, *Children—The Modern Law* (3rd edn), at 495.

[398] As J Whybrow at [1994] Jo of Child Law 88 at 89 points out, the ill-treatment was of the mother rather than the child. Cf R White, P Carr and N Lowe *Children Act in Practice* (3rd ed) at para 8.72, who support Bracewell J's view.

[399] J Masson and M Morris, *Children Act Manual*, p 99.

[400] *Re O (A Minor) (Care Proceedings: Education)* [1992] 1 WLR 912 per Ewbank J. See also *Re V (Care or Supervision Order)* [1996] 1 FLR 776, CA—a mother's resistance to allowing her 17-year-old son, who suffered from cerebral palsy, to attend a special school by keeping him at home instead was held likely to cause the boy 'significant harm'. Though in most cases an education supervision order under s 36 (discussed above at p 389) is more likely to be sought.

[401] See eg Freeman above, pp 154–5 and 161, who, referring to a pre-Children Act decision, *Alhaji Mohamed v Knott* [1969] 1 QB 1, involving a 13-year-old Nigerian child who was validly married under her country's law, thought that the child would now be considered to be suffering or likely to suffer significant harm by having intercourse with her husband, a man twice her age and who had venereal disease.

include 'impairment suffered from seeing or hearing the ill-treatment of another' is intended to emphasise the potential harm that a child can suffer having witnessed violence perpetuated by one parent on another.

Is the harm 'significant'?[402]

Whatever the nature of the harm, the court has to consider whether it is 'significant'. Vital though this is to the application of the condition, 'significant' is not defined in the Act. A dictionary definition adopted by case law[403] is that it should be 'considerable, noteworthy or important' and, reflecting the common-sense view, the Department of Health's *Guidance and Regulations* comments:[404]

'Minor shortcomings in health or minor deficits in physical, psychological or social development should not require compulsory intervention unless cumulatively they are having, or are likely to have, serious and lasting effects upon the child.'

Whether 'harm' is 'significant' is an issue of fact to be decided in each case, but it must be remembered that it is the harm that must be significant, not the incident that caused it. So, for example, while a broken leg is a serious injury, the implications of a small cigarette burn might be more significant. Similarly, behaviour such as shaking that might be innocuous to an older child might be very significant for a baby. In *Re O (A Minor) (Care Proceedings: Education)*[405] Ewbank J took the view that lack of suitable education leading to the impairment of the child's intellectual development was of itself 'significant harm'.

Comparison with 'similar child'

Where the harm is due to ill-treatment, no further guidance is given, but in the case of impairment of health or development, reference must be made to s 31(10), which provides:

'Where the question of whether harm suffered by a child is significant turns on the child's health or development, his health or development shall be compared with that which could reasonably be expected of a similar child.'

Although the general drift of this provision is understandable, (as one commentary says[406] the provision 'enables the intellectual development of a Down's Syndrome child, for example, to be compared with that of another such child, rather than imposing a "norm" which would be unfair') precisely what is meant by a 'similar child' in this context is hard to say. For example, is a deaf child of deaf parents a 'similar child' to a deaf child of hearing parents?[407] There is also the further question of how far one should have regard to the child's background and whether the courts should apply different standards to children from different ethnic backgrounds.[408] The Department of Health's *Guidance* comments:[409]

---

[402] See generally M Adcock and R White (eds) *Significant Harm*, above.

[403] See eg *Humberside County Council v B* [1993] 1 FLR 257 and *Chambers v Johns* [1999] 1 FLR 392, 398, per Otton LJ.

[404] Vol 1, *Court Orders*, para 3.2.   [405] [1992] 1 WLR 912.

[406] G Douglas, *An Introduction to Family Law* (2nd edn) p 147.

[407] This is one of a number of examples that Freeman uses (above, pp 147–9) to highlight the difficulties of this test.

[408] During the debates on the Bill (see 503, HL Official Report, col 354) Lord Mackay suggested that comparisons should be confined to physical (and presumably intellectual) attributes rather than background.

[409] Vol 1, para 3.20.

'The meaning of "similar" in this context will require judicial interpretation, but may need to take account of environmental, social and cultural characteristics of the child. The need to use a standard appropriate for the child arises because some children have characteristics or handicaps which mean that they cannot be expected to be as healthy or well-developed as others. Equally if the child needs special care or attention (because, for example, he is unusually difficult to control) then this is to be expected for him. The standard should only be that which it is reasonable to expect for the particular child, rather than the best that could possibly be achieved; applying a "best" standard could open up the risk that a child might be removed from home simply because some other arrangement could cater better for his needs than care by his parents.'

There has been remarkably little case-law on the meaning of s 31(10). In one case, Re D (Care: Threshold Criteria: Significant Harm),[410] it was suggested that what amounts to significant harm should not depend upon the child's cultural or ethnic background.

In Re O (A Minor) (Care Proceedings: Education)[411] Ewbank J held that in the case of a 15-year-old truant of average intelligence:

'... "similar child" meant a child of equivalent intellectual and social development, who has gone to school and not merely an average child who may or may not be at school.'

In other words, his Lordship was not prepared to compare the child with someone who was not properly attending school.

Is the child suffering significant harm?

The original Bill contained the words 'has suffered' rather than 'is suffering' but was changed to prevent an order being made 'on the basis of significant harm suffered several years previously and which is not likely to be repeated'.[412] Thus past harm is not in itself sufficient to satisfy the criteria, though it might be relevant to establishing future likelihood of harm. On the other hand, while the present tense implies an existing condition, it is now clear that that does not necessarily mean that the condition should exist at the date of the hearing. The leading decision is Re M (A Minor) (Care Order: Threshold Conditions).[413] In that case, after the father had murdered the mother in the children's presence, a four-month-old baby together with his half-siblings were accommodated by the local authority. Subsequently, the siblings went to live with a cousin of the mother, but she felt unable to look after the baby as well and he was accordingly fostered. Whilst in his foster placement the boy thrived and had regular contact with the mother's cousin and his siblings. However, because he could not remain with his foster mother indefinitely, seven

---

[410] [1998] Fam Law 656. For cases that have raised this issue under the old law see eg Alhaji Mohamed v Knott, above, and Re H (Minors) (Wardship: Cultural Background) [1987] 2 FLR 12.

[411] Above. For valuable comments on Re O see J Fortin 'Significant harm revisited' (1993) 5 Jo of Child Law 151.

[412] Per David Mellor MP, HC Official Report, Standing Committee B 23 May 1989, col 221. See also Re G (Care Proceedings: Threshold Conditions) [2001] EWCA Civ 968, [2001] 2 FLR 1111 at [16]—father found guilty of actual bodily harm for inflicting a cigarette burn on a child. No care proceedings brought as father and mother had separated (father subsequently died) and she was not implicated. This incident was properly ruled irrelevant in care proceedings subsequently brought in respect of the mother's upbringing of the child.

[413] [1994] 2 AC 424, HL. Note also Re G (Care Proceedings: Threshold Conditions) [2001] EWCA Civ 968, [2001] 2 FLR 1111 in which it was held that a local authority is entitled to rely upon information acquired after its intervention and even upon later events provided those later events are capable of proving the state of affairs at the time of the intervention.

months later the local authority brought care proceedings. By that time the cousin had changed her mind and sought a residence order in respect of the boy. The care proceedings were heard some 16 months after the murder, at a time when the father had received a life sentence. The local authority supported the cousin and were no longer actively seeking a care order. However, both the father and the guardian[414] supported the making of a care order with a view to the boy being adopted outside the birth family.

At first instance Bracewell J held that the threshold criteria were satisfied. In her view the relevant date for determining 'is suffering' was 'the period immediately before the process of protecting the child is first put into motion'. The Court of Appeal disagreed,[415] holding that the threshold criteria had to be satisfied at the date of the hearing. While this was not regarded as requiring the court to be satisfied that the child is suffering significant harm at the precise moment when the court is considering the application—it being sufficient if there is a continuum in existence at that time—nevertheless, as Balcombe LJ said:

'. . . it is not enough that something happened in the past which caused the child to suffer harm of the relevant kind if before the hearing the child has ceased to suffer such harm'.

Since the boy was thriving in foster care, it was held that, as at the date of the hearing, he could not be said to be suffering harm. Furthermore, since the cousin was willing to look after him and his father, being in prison, could not interfere, in the court's view there was no likelihood of future harm either.[416] Accordingly, the local authority failed to establish the threshold criteria.

The Court of Appeal decision caused considerable consternation. As one commentator said:[417]

'It seems to follow from Re M that the test of present harm cannot be satisfied if the child no longer exhibits symptoms of harm, for example, because good substitute care has been provided by a foster parent. This may mean that if a child is living away from home at the time of the hearing, the placement could only continue on a voluntary basis, which may be an insecure position for the child. If a risk arose of the parents removing the child, then an application for a care or supervision order would have to be made based on the harm which was likely to occur if the child returned home. Such an application might have to be made suddenly, whereas if the local authority already had an order it would be able to exert sufficient control to prevent such an emergency arising.'

The House of Lords, however, reversed the Court of Appeal, holding that, provided it can be shown that there was significant harm at the time of the local authority intervention, and so long as protective arrangements have thereafter been continuously kept in place, the fact that the child had been removed from harm at the date of the hearing will not defeat the plea that the child 'is suffering significant harm'. As Lord Mackay LC pointed out, the problem with the Court of Appeal approach is that it substantially deprives the first limb of s 31(2)(a) of effect. Moreover, in his view:[418]

'There is nothing in s 31(2) which . . . requires that the conditions to be satisfied are disassociated from the time of the making of the application by the local authority. I would

---

[414] Guardians are discussed in Ch 11.   [415] [1994] Fam 95.
[416] This aspect of the case will be discussed further: see below p 744.
[417] J Whybrow 'Re M—past, present and future significant harm' (1994) 6 Jo of Child Law 88 at 90.
[418] [1994] 2 AC 424 at 433.

conclude that the natural construction of the conditions in s 31(2) is that where, at the time the application is to be disposed of, there are in place arrangements for the protection of the child by the local authority on an interim basis which protection has been continuously in place for some time, the relevant date with respect to which the court must be satisfied is the date at which the local authority initiated the procedure for protection under the Act from which these arrangements followed.'

Lord Nolan agreeing, said:[419]

'Parliament cannot have intended that temporary measures taken to protect the child from immediate harm should prevent the court from regarding the child as one who is suffering, or who is likely to suffer significant harm within the meaning of s 31(2)(a), and should thus disqualify the court from making a more permanent order under the section. The focal point of the inquiry must be the situation which resulted in the temporary measures taken, and which has led to the application for a care or supervision order.'

Having ruled that the s 31 threshold was satisfied, the House of Lords made a care order notwithstanding that it was accepted that the mother's cousin, with whom the boy had by now spent seven months, had perfectly satisfactorily looked after him.[420] Although, their Lordships made it clear that they expected the boy to continue to live with her, they nevertheless held that 'having regard to the history and circumstances it was highly desirable that the local authority should exercise a watching brief on his behalf'.[421]

Although the final disposal is questionable and looks suspiciously like a conditional care order, which, is not permitted under the 1989 Act, it is submitted that the House of Lords were right to overrule the Court of Appeal on the meaning of 'is suffering'.[422] Notwithstanding the criticism that Re M weakens the position of the family,[423] the decision preserves flexibility which is crucial to child protection. In any event it is surely right to focus on the local authority's initial intervention. If that intervention is justified then it seems right that the subsequent application for a care order should be determined according to the broader considerations at the welfare stage and not simply judged according to the more technical requirements of the threshold condition. This, however, is not to say that Re M eliminates all consequential problems. Two in particular arise, namely, what constitutes 'protective arrangements' and when will 'harm' cease to be present following justifiable intervention by local authorities?

What are protective arrangements? An important element in Lord Mackay LC's judgment in Re M is that, although the court is permitted to examine the position at the point of intervention in determining whether the child is suffering the requisite harm, it can only do so where 'there are in place arrangements for the protection of the child by the local authority on an interim basis which protection has been continuously in place for some time'. Precisely what these 'arrangements' are is open to interpretation. While there was never any doubt that they include court-sanctioned arrangements such as interim care

[419] Above at 441.
[420] This is one of the ironies of the case, since at first instance Bracewell J had hesitantly concluded that the cousin might not be able to give the boy the quality of emotional care that he was likely to require. See the comments on this by S Cretney [1994] Fam Law at 503.
[421] [1994] 2 AC 424 at 440, per Lord Templeman.   [422] See above at p 741.
[423] See J Masson 'Social Engineering in the House of Lords—Re M' [1994] Jo of Child Law 170.

orders and emergency protection orders, there was initial speculation as to whether they also embrace accommodation. However, by expressly approving[424] *Northamptonshire County Council v S*[425] in which Ewbank J stated that in judging the criterion of 'is suffering' the court—

'. . . had to consider the position immediately before an emergency protection order, if there was one, or an interim care order, if that was the initiation of protection, or *as in this case, when the child went into voluntary care.*'[426]

Lord Mackay himself seemed to envisage accommodation as coming within the concept of protective arrangements. Subsequently, this interpretation of *Re M* commended itself to Charles J in *Southwark London Borough Council v B*[427] and in any event was applied in *Re SH (Care Order: Orphan)*[428] and *Re M (Care Order: Parental Responsibility)*.[429] Accordingly, there seems little doubt that accommodation is regarded as being within the concept of protective arrangements though whether there are any limits regarding the length of time that the child has been accommodated has yet to be decided (see below).

Whether other types of 'interventions', for example, where there is an ongoing investigation following an adjournment of a case conference,[430] can also be classified as 'protective arrangements' also remains to be decided but it seems unlikely that the term extends to such less formal arrangements.

When does harm cease after a justifiable intervention? Although local authority intervention cannot be justified upon purely past harm there remains the unresolved question of when harm ceases after justifiable intervention. In this respect there are two issues, namely, a temporal one and what may be described as a causative one. With regard to the former, does there come a point where intervention was so far in the past that it cannot really be said that the child 'is' suffering harm? The issue arises particularly in connection with accommodation which can itself be in place for years. It remains to be seen how far into the past the courts will be prepared to enquire, though it may be noted that in the *Northamptonshire* case the children had been in (what would now be called) accommodation for six months before the care application and 10 months before the hearing.[431]

The so-called causative issue arises if the raison d'etre for intervention ceases before the making of a care order as, for example, in the situation posed by one commentary[432] where the child is removed from home because of suspected child abuse and the abuser subsequently dies. While no-one could doubt that provided the remaining carer is capable of looking after the child a care order should not be made is that because the 'harm' has ceased or because it is not in the child's interests to make the order? In other words in such a situation does the application fail at the threshold or at the welfare stage? A pointer that it fails at the threshold stage is Lord Mackay's comment in *Re M*:[433]

---

[424] Above at 437.   [425] [1993] Fam 136 at 140.

[426] 'Voluntary care' was the forerunner of what is now local authority accommodation: see above, p 703.

[427] [1998] 2 FLR 1095 at 1109.   [428] [1995] 1 FLR 746, discussed below at p 750.

[429] [1996] 2 FLR 84, discussed below at p 750.

[430] This is one of the questions posed by J Masson [1994] Jo of Child Law 170.

[431] In *Re SH (Care Order: Orphan)* [1995] 1 FLR 746 the child had been accommodated for seven months before the care application and for 13 months by the time of the hearing.

[432] G Douglas: *An Introduction to Family Law* (2nd edn) 148.   [433] [1994] 2 AC 424 at 433–4.

'If after a local authority had initiated protective arrangements the need for these had terminated, because the child's welfare had been satisfactorily provided for otherwise, in any subsequent proceedings, it would not be possible to found jurisdiction on the situation at the time of initiation of these arrangements.'

Is the child likely to suffer significant harm?

The inclusion of the future element was an important innovation of the 1989 Act and was introduced to provide a remedy where harm had not occurred but there were considerable future risks for the child, eg where the child is in danger from birth,[434] where the parents are mentally ill or drug addicted,[435] where an abuser returns to the household, or where a previous child has died in suspicious circumstances in the household.

Perhaps not surprisingly, given its speculative nature, the prospective test has been the subject of intense argument not least about the meaning of 'is likely'. But other issues have also arisen, namely, about the relevance of potential carers and the time at which likelihood of significant harm is to be judged.

The meaning of 'is likely'— Re H. The leading case is *Re H (Minors) (Sexual Abuse: Standard of Proof)*.[436] In that case a mother had four daughters, two by her husband and two by her subsequent partner. Her eldest daughter made an allegation to the police that she had been sexually abused by the partner. She was subsequently accommodated by the local authority and the partner was charged but acquitted of rape. Notwithstanding this acquittal the local authority sought care orders in respect of the three younger children. They argued that, because of the lower standard of proof in civil cases, the court could still be satisfied that the partner had sexually abused the eldest daughter or at least find that there was a substantial likelihood of his having done so and from this hold that the other three girls were likely to suffer significant harm.

At first instance, the judge, though more than a little suspicious that the partner had abused the eldest daughter as she alleged, nevertheless held that he could not be sure 'to the requisite high standard of proof' that the girl's allegations were true. He accordingly dismissed the care order applications. His decision was subsequently upheld by a majority in the Court of Appeal and by a bare majority in the House of Lords. The closeness of the result bears testimony to the difficulties and anxieties raised by the case.

As the House of Lords saw it, the case raised the following questions: what was the meaning of 'likely' in this context; who had the burden of proof; what was the standard of proof and how was the assessment of future harm in s 31(2) to be conducted?

On the first of these issues it was unanimously held that 'likely' did not require the court to find that the harm was more likely than not: it was enough that the occurrence of

---

[434] Though to be human rights compliant removal of a child at birth will require especial justification, see *P, C and S v United Kingdom* (2002) 35 EHRR 31, [2002] 2 FLR 631, ECtHR (insufficient per se that mother had previously been convicted of deliberately causing injury to an elder child).

[435] See *Re D (A Minor)* [1987] AC 317, HL in which the Lords upheld the making of a care order under the former law in respect of a baby born with foetal drug syndrome derived from an addicted mother and whose parents continued to be drug dependent after the birth.

[436] [1996] AC 563, HL, on which see the thoughtful analyses by M Hayes 'Reconciling protection of children with justice for parents in cases of alleged child abuse' [1997] Legal Studies 1, and C Keating 'Shifting standards in the House of Lords—*Re H and Others (Minors) (Sexual Abuse: Standard of Proof)*' [1996] CFLQ 157.

such harm was a real possibility—'a possibility that cannot sensibly be ignored.' As Lord Nicholls said in a later case,[437] this is a comparatively low level of risk. There was similar unanimity over the burden of proof, namely that it was for the local authority as applicant to prove its case. There was broad agreement too that the standard of proof is the ordinary civil standard (the balance of probabilities).[438] In reaching this conclusion, their Lordships rejected the contention that to prove an allegation of sexual abuse required a standard between the civil and criminal standard. However, whereas Lord Nicholls (who delivered the majority judgment) accepted that, as one judge had put it:[439]

'The more serious the allegation the more cogent is the evidence required to overcome the unlikelihood of what is alleged and thus to prove it.'[440]

Lord Lloyd (who dissented) preferred a simple balance of probabilities test. As he pointed out, the test accepted by Lord Nicholls leads to the 'bizarre' result that the more serious the anticipated injury the more difficult it becomes for the local authority to satisfy the standard of proof and 'thereby ultimately if the welfare test is satisfied, [to] secure protection for the child'.

However, it was on the fourth issue, namely upon what evidence a risk of harm can be based, that there was major disagreement. The majority view was that s 31(2)(a) obliged the court to apply a two-stage test: first, to make a finding on the primary facts giving rise to the application and secondly, based on that finding, to assess whether a risk of future harm was a real possibility. In this case, given the trial judge's finding that sexual abuse had not been proved, there was nothing from which a risk of harm could be inferred. It was certainly not enough in the majority view to base a finding of a risk of harm on mere suspicions. Were it otherwise, as Lord Nicholls said,[441] it—

'. . . would mean that once apparently credible evidence of misconduct has been given, those against whom the allegations are made must disprove them. Otherwise it would be open to a court to hold that, although the misconduct has not been proved, it has not been disproved and there is a real possibility that the misconduct did occur. Accordingly, there is a real possibility that the child will suffer harm in the future, and, hence, the threshold criteria are met.'

His Lordship added that, although unproved allegations of maltreatment cannot form the basis of a finding by the court that either limb of s 31(2)(a) is established:[442]

'There will be cases where, although the alleged maltreatment itself is not proved, the evidence does establish a combination of profoundly worrying features affecting the care of the child within the family. In such cases it would be open to a court in appropriate circumstances to find that, although not satisfied the child is yet suffering significant harm,

---

[437] *Re O and Another (Minors)(Care: Preliminary Hearing); Re B (A Minor)* [2003] UKHL 18, [2004] 1 AC 523, at para [16].

[438] Accordingly, the first instance judge had erred on this issue. For an interesting discussion of this standard of proof and a comparison with the criminal law approach, see C Cobley 'The Quest for Truth: Substantiating Allegations of Physical Abuse in Criminal Prosecutions and Care Proceedings' (2006) 20 Int Jo of Law, Policy and the Family—forthcoming.

[439] Per Ungoed-Thomas J in *Re Dellow's Will Trusts, Lloyd's Bank v Institute of Cancer Research* [1964] 1 All ER 771 at 733.

[440] [1996] AC 563 at 586.   [441] Above at 591.   [442] Above at 591–2.

on the basis of such facts as are proved there is a likelihood that he will do so in the future'
[emphasis added].

Lord Nicholls emphasised, however, that this was not the case in *Re H*, since the only
allegation was that the cohabitant had sexually abused the eldest child and the cohabitant
himself otherwise had no history of abuse. Accordingly, when the allegation could not be
proved there was nothing from which it could be inferred that the younger girls were at
risk of harm.

The minority view was that the two-stage approach was wrong and over-complicated.
As Lord Lloyd put it:[443]

'Parliament has asked a simple question: Is the court satisfied that there is a serious risk of
significant harm in the future? The question should be capable of being answered without
too much over-analysis.'

Further, as Lord Browne-Wilkinson put it:

'To be satisfied of the existence of risk does not require proof of the occurrence of past
historical events but proof of facts which are relevant to the making of a prognosis.'[444]

In the minority view there were sufficient worrying findings (the so-called micro facts
such as the consistency of the eldest child's story, the wrongful denial of the cohabitant
that he had even been alone with the child, the mother's suspicion that something had
been going on and her attempt to dissuade one of the other children from speaking to
social workers) to justify the finding of a likelihood of harm.

The relevance of potential carers. According to Waite LJ in *Oldham Metropolitan Borough
v E*[445]

'... it is not enough to demonstrate that the person with parental responsibility for the child
cannot provide the required degree of care and safety: if, at the hearing date, there is
available some suitable carer within the family[446] willing and able to give the child care to a
reasonable parental standard, it is impossible to say that the criteria for a public law order
are satisfied.'

He justified this position by pointing out that it was the clear policy of the 1989 Act to
preserve, wherever possible, a child's link with his birth family. In other words, according
to *Oldham*[447] the likely care by potential carers (at any rate, where there are family members) is to be regarded as being relevant to the threshold test rather than to the welfare
stage. This was a questionable approach, since conflating the threshold and 'welfare' stages
unnecessarily restricts the court's powers. *Oldham* has since been overruled by the House
of Lords in *Re M (A Minor)(Care Order: Threshold Conditions)*[448] and the correct

---

[443] Above at 581.   [444] Above at 572.   [445] [1994] 1 FLR 568 at 572, CA.
[446] But note he left open whether a similar approach was appropriate where the carer or potential carer
was not a relative: see above at 572–3.
[447] A similar approach had been taken by the Court of Appeal in *Re M (A Minor)(Care Order: Threshold
Conditions)* [1994] Fam 95.
[448] [1994] 2 AC 424.

approach, it is submitted, is that stated by Ewbank J in *Northamptonshire County Council v S*:[449]

'The threshold test relates to the parent or other carer whose lack of care has caused the harm referred to in s 31(2)(a). The care which other carers might give to the child only becomes relevant if the threshold test is met.'

The time at which likelihood of significant harm is to be judged. It has been held[450] that the House of Lords' decision in *Re M (A Minor)(Care Order: Threshold Criteria)*[451] on the time when significant harm should be judged applies to both limbs of the threshold criteria under s 31(2)(a). Consequently, likelihood of harm should be assessed at the date of the care order application or, if temporary protective arrangements have been continuously in force from an earlier date, the date when the proceedings were initiated. However, where it is unclear whether there are relevant arrangements (for example, voluntary arrangements which were in place and which prevented significant harm or likelihood of such harm, have broken down) then there might be room for considering existing harm at the date of the initiation of protective arrangements but for the purpose of establishing likelihood of harm, the date when these arrangements broke down.[452]

Summary and critique. What *Re H* establishes is that to satisfy the likelihood of harm test under s 31(2)(a) where the application depends upon historical facts which are the subject of dispute the court must first be satisfied as to the existence of those facts. Once the factual foundation has been proved on the balance of probabilities the court can then exercise its discretion on whether those facts make it likely that the child will suffer significant harm. 'Likely' in this context means no more than a possibility that cannot sensibly be ignored. *Re H* has attracted considerable comment. As Hayes has eloquently written, the decision raises in an acute form the question:[453]

'. . . how can the law and the court strike the correct balance before dispensing dispassionate justice to parents and safeguarding children from actual or likely significant harm? Parents should not be at risk of having children taken from them on the basis of false allegations of child abuse. This is unjust, it is a violation of the rights of the parents, and it is a violation of the rights and interests of children. Yet if local authorities are required to produce very powerful evidence that children are being abused, or are at risk of abuse, before courts can intervene, this may lead to some vulnerable children being subjected to horrific forms of undetected ill-treatment within the privacy of the family home. This outcome too is unjust, and it is a violation of the rights of children to be protected by the civil law. The dilemma to be resolved is how the legal framework, and the legal process, can best reconcile safeguarding children from suffering significant harm with the obligation to respect parental autonomy and family privacy.'

---

449 [1993] Fam 136 at 141, cited, with apparent approval, by Lord Nicholls in *Lancashire County Council v B* [2000] 2 AC 147 at 167. See also Butterworths *Family Law Service* at 3A [3079], and *H v Trafford Borough Council* [1997] 3 FCR 113, per Wall J.

450 *Southwark London Borough Council v B* [1998] 2 FLR 1095 applying *Re M (Care Order: Parental Responsibility)* [1996] 2 FLR 84.

451 [1994] 2 AC 424, discussed above at pp 740–4.

452 Per Charles J in *Southwark London Borough Council v B*, below at p 1109.

453 'Reconciling Protection of Children with Justice for Parents in Cases of Alleged Abuse' (1997) 17 Legal Studies 1 at 1–2.

In Hayes's view *Re H* swings the law too heavily in favour of the rights of the parents and she wonders whether in the light of this Parliament should either lower the threshold generally or lower it for the purpose of obtaining supervision orders.

Without gainsaying some of the difficulties that undoubtedly flow from *Re H*, it is nevertheless submitted that *on the facts as found* the majority decision was right, for it does seem in principle to be wrong to justify local authority intervention into family life because of a risk of harm based on a mere suspicion. However, the propriety of the initial finding seems doubtful. Lord Lloyd was surely right when he said that the first instance judge was in fact applying the now discredited higher than ordinary standard of proof. Many will also agree with his Lordship's plea for a simple balance of probabilities test. Indeed, the so-called cogency requirement has met with a chorus of academic criticism. Not only does it carry the danger (as the minority in *Re H* pointed out) that the worse the danger the child is in the less likely the courts are to remove him or her from it[454] but also, at any rate in cases founded on a child's allegation (as in *Re H* itself), it is based on a questionable premise that there is a positive correlation between the severity of the abuse alleged and the probability that the child has lied.[455] More generally it has been pointed out that the probability of a possible event cannot help to determine whether it has in fact occurred in a particular instance.[456] Another problem of the cogency requirement is the practical one of distinguishing the evidence needed to satisfy it from that needed to satisfy the criminal standard. However, the suggestion made in *Re ET (Serious Injuries: Standard of Proof)*[457] that in very serious cases the difference between the civil and criminal standards of proof is 'largely illusory' was firmly rejected by the Court of Appeal in *Re U (A Child)(Department for Education and Skills Intervening)*.[458] Giving the judgment of the court, Butler-Sloss P reaffirmed that the 'standard of proof to be applied in Children Act cases is the balance of probabilities and the approach to these difficult cases was laid down by Lord Nicholls. . . . in *Re H*.' Justifying this position, Butler-Sloss P commented:

'The strict rules of evidence applicable in a criminal trial which is adversarial in nature is to be contrasted with the partly inquisitorial approach of the court dealing with children cases in which the rules of evidence are considerably relaxed.'

Another feature of *Re H* that should not be overlooked is that the application was based on a single issue whereas in most cases there will be a number of issues on which a likelihood of harm could be founded. In these latter cases, as Lord Nicholls acknowledged in *Re H*,[459] even if an allegation of maltreatment cannot be proved the evidence may establish a

---

[454] See eg J Spencer (1994) 6 JCL 160 and G Douglas *An Introduction to Family Law* (2nd edn) 150.

[455] See J Fortin *Children's Rights and the Developing Law* (2nd edn) 474 and J Herring *Family Law* (2nd edn) 537.

[456] S Cretney, J Masson and R Bailey-Harris *Principles of Family Law* (7th edn), para 22–032 (at p 734).

[457] [2003] 2 FLR 1205 at 1207, per Bodey J.

[458] [2004] EWCA Civ 567, [2005] Fam 134. See also *Re T (Abuse: Standard of Proof)* [2004] EWCA Civ 558, [2004] 2 FLR 838 in which Butler-Sloss P made the same points. *Re U* is also important for ending any speculation that the standard of proof had been changed by the acquittal of Angela Cannings (*R v Cannings* [2004] EWCA Crim 1, [2004] 1 All ER 725), her original guilt having been based on the now questionable evidence of Professor Sir Roy Meadow. See also C Cobley 'The Quest for Truth: Substantiating Allegations of Physical Abuse in Criminal Prosecutions and Care Proceedings' (2006) 20 Int Jo of Law, Policy and the Family—forthcoming.

[459] [1996] AC 563 at 591–2, cited above at p 745.

combination of profoundly worrying features from which a likelihood of harm *can* be inferred. Accordingly, local authorities would be well advised to avoid wherever possible relying on just the one allegation.[460]

One area where it was feared[461] that *Re H* would lead to difficulties, namely, where harm can be proved but not who caused it, has been diminished by another House of Lords' decision, *Lancashire County Council v B*[462] which as will be seen,[463] establishes that the threshold can be crossed even though the perpetrator of the harm cannot be identified. Nevertheless, notwithstanding *Lancashire*, the decision in *Re H* does mean that in certain situations the court could be powerless to intervene in profoundly worrying situations, such as where an older child had died in suspicious circumstances but non-accidental injury cannot be proved.[464] Whether these dangers are the inevitable price that one pays for respecting family autonomy or whether the balance in favour of child protection should be struck anew is hard to say. In the last edition,[465] we said that in part the answer would depend on just how many cases there were in which it is felt that children cannot be protected when they should have been. In that regard, although *Re H* has caused difficulties, it cannot be said to have led to many reported examples of worrying failures to establish the threshold.

The application of the threshold criteria to orphans and abandoned children

One of Balcombe LJ's concerns in *Re M* was that if the prospective harm test could be satisfied without regard to potential carers that would mean that where a child's parents had both been killed in an accident then, even if—

'. . . there was an aunt or uncle willing to take him into his or her family and bring him up with his siblings and cousins, it would nevertheless be open to the court to say that the second threshold condition was satisfied and make a care order. This would amount to a form of social engineering which we are satisfied is wholly outside the intention of the 1989 Act.'[466]

---

[460] This is not to say that reliance on a number of allegations does not raise its own difficulties, see *Re R (Care: Disclosure: Nature of Proceedings)* [2002] 1 FLR 755 (in which guidance is given as to how to conduct proceedings in cases of multiple allegations).

[461] See p 547 of the 9th edition of this work.

[462] [2002] 2 AC 147. See also *Re CB and JB (Care Proceedings: Guidelines)* [1998] 2 FLR 211 in which Wall J held that a finding of fact that one child was non-accidentally injured by one or both parents whilst in their joint care was sufficient to satisfy the threshold criteria not only to that child but also to a sibling who was not injured even though the court could not decide which parent was responsible, since the risk of harm to each child from either parent was substantial.

[463] See below pp 751–4.

[464] As in *Re P (A Minor) (Care: Evidence)* [1994] 2 FLR 751 (though note in that case a higher standard of proof was applied) and note also *Lancashire County Council v B* [2002] 2 WLR 346, CA, in which a care order application in respect of a child-minder's child was dismissed upon the failure to establish whether the childminder was responsible for the injuries to another child she was employed to look after. See further below p 753 n 484; cf *Re B (Non Accidental Injury)* [2002] EWCA Civ 752, [2002] 2 FLR 1133 in which the Court of Appeal upheld a first instance ruling that the threshold had been established even though the medical evidence did not positively establish but was consistent with non-accidental injury and that there was no more probable explanation (the judge had concluded that the child's subdural haemorrhages had been caused by shaking by one or other of the parents); and *Re P (Emergency Protection Order)* [1996] 1 FLR 482 in which Johnson J was satisfied that, because medical evidence had eliminated any medical cause for the child nearly suffocating, the mother must have been responsible.

[465] At p 547.   [466] [1994] Fam 95 at 105.

In line with this approach Thorpe J held in *Birmingham City Council v D, Birmingham City Council v M*[467] that it would be a plain distortion of the threshold test to find some theoretical risk of significant harm in the case of orphans who, at the time of the application for a care order, were being accommodated by the local authority and leading well-settled lives. In his Lordship's view the local authority had adequate powers to look after and safeguard and promote the children's interests.[468] The *Birmingham* decision, however, predated the House of Lords' decisions in *Re M* and *Re H*. Furthermore, arguments were solely directed towards the issue of prospective harm. In contrast, *Re SH (Care Order: Orphan)*,[469] attention was focused on the first limb of s 31(2)(a) for, as Hollis J put it, the House of Lords in *Re M* had held:

'that the word "is" in fact means "was" in the sense that the child was suffering significant harm when the rescue operation was instigated, provided the care of the child concerned was continued until the final hearing.'

In *Re SH* the child was already being accommodated at the time of his parents' death, the father having being suspected of perpetrating, and the mother of being implicated in, the sexual abuse of the boy. Hollis J held that, as the boy had been continuously accommodated since then, he could properly be considered at the date of the initial intervention to be suffering significant harm, thereby satisfying the first limb of s 31(2)(a). In other words, the passing of the threshold was due to the alleged sexual abuse rather than the death of the parents. However, in subsequently making the care order, Hollis J, in contrast to Thorpe J,[470] held that without having parental responsibility the local authority would have difficulties in convincing whoever was concerned that they had authority to decide what to do with the boy. Accordingly, he held that it was in the child's interests for the care order to be made.

The second post-House of Lords' decision, *Re M (Care Order: Parental Responsibility)*,[471] involved a baby found abandoned on the steps of a health centre who was discovered to have a number of medical problems likely to require medical intervention. In Cazalet J's view, the very fact of abandonment was enough to satisfy the existing harm limb of s 31(2)(a), since it amounted to a complete dereliction of parental responsibility and as such constituted 'ill-treatment'. His Lordship further held that as a result of the abandonment the baby was also likely to suffer significant harm, thus satisfying the second limb of s 31(2)(a). Like Hollis J, Cazalet J thought that, quite apart from the baby's particular problems, it was essential that some proper person or body have parental responsibility for the baby and that in this case it was vital for the local authority to have full powers of decision-making. He therefore made a care order.

Although this latter decision is authority for saying abandonment per se satisfies the threshold test, it is not yet beyond argument whether the death of both parents ipso facto

---

[467] [1994] 2 FLR 502.   [468] Viz under s 22(3), s 23(1) and s 24 of the 1989 Act.
[469] [1995] 1 FLR 746.

[470] This apparent difference of view can be explained on the basis that each judge was considering different questions: Thorpe J deciding whether the absence of responsibility ipso facto satisfied the prospective harm test—Hollis J determining whether it was in the child's interests, *the threshold test having been satisfied*, to vest parental responsibility via a care order in the local authority.

[471] [1996] 2 FLR 84.

satisfies the criteria. It is submitted, however, that now it is established[472] that the first limb of s 31(2)(a) can be satisfied as at the date of intervention, the *Birmingham* decision cannot be relied upon and indeed should have been decided the other way. In other words, the death of the parents ought to be regarded as falling within the existing harm criterion if at the time of local authority intervention (be it through accommodation or emergency protection) there is no other family member able and willing to look after the child.[473] On this basis there is no need to enquire whether the prospective harm test would also be satisfied, though it may well be thought that if potential carers are ignored at this stage, then that test too might be satisfied. Satisfaction of the threshold criteria, however, does not necessarily mean that a care order should be made. That issue, which is governed by the welfare principle,[474] must depend on all the circumstances, though (unless there are other individuals in whose favour a residence order should be made) the court will, as *Re SH* and *Re M* illustrate, be predisposed to make a care order to ensure that some person or body has parental responsibility for the child. However, if subsequent to the local authority intervention another family member does emerge as able and willing to look after the child, then no doubt the courts will, mindful of the general policy under the Children Act to maintain a child's links with his birth family, generally require cogent evidence why a residence order should not be made in that person's favour.[475] In this way it is submitted that Balcombe LJ's fears about social engineering were exaggerated, though this is not to say that the preferable solution to this problem would not have been, as the government White Paper originally proposed,[476] to allow local authorities to apply to become guardians.

(d) The attributable condition

Having satisfied itself that the harm is significant, the court is required by s 31(2)(b) also to be satisfied that this is attributable to the care given, or likely to be given, to the child and is not what a reasonable parent would give to the child (or, as we discuss below, is attributable to the child's being beyond parental control). This is now commonly known as 'the attributable condition'.

Is the harm attributable to the care given or likely to be given?

As the Department of Health's *Guidance*[477] says, harm caused solely by a third party is insufficient to satisfy the attributable condition unless the parent has unreasonably failed to prevent it. But what is the position, where it cannot be proved who is responsible for the child's injuries as, for example, where the parents blame each other or a third person? The leading case is *Lancashire County Council v B*.[478] There, a young child sustained serious

---

472 Viz by the House of Lords in *Re M (A Minor) (Care Order: Threshold Conditions)*, above.

473 If, following the parents' deaths, the child is being looked after by a relative, then to justify intervention the local authority would have to prove that the child is suffering or likely to suffer significant harm notwithstanding that relative's care of the child.

474 See below at pp 755ff.

475 Viz along the lines suggested by Balcombe LJ himself in *Re W (A Minor) (Residence Order)* [1993] 2 FLR 625 at 633, discussed above at p 589.

476 *The Law on Child Care and Family Services* (Cm 62, 1987) at para 25.

477 Vol 1, *Court Orders* at para 3.23.

478 [2000] 2 AC 147, HL, on which see A Bainham 'Attributing Harm: Child Abuse and the Unknown Perpetrator' (2000) 59 CLJ 458, J Herring 'The Suffering Children of Blameless Parents' (2000) 116 LQR 116 and A Perry '*Lancashire County Council v B* Section 31—Threshold or Barrier?' [2000] CFLQ 301. Note also *Re CB and JB (Care Proceedings: Guidelines)* [1998] 2 FLR 211, referred to at n 462 above.

non-accidental injuries but the unresolved question was who was responsible? There were three possible perpetrators, namely, either of the parents or the paid child-minder. The House of Lords ruled that where actual harm or risk of harm can be proved then in the case of so-called 'shared care arrangements' provided the harm can be shown to have been inflicted by one of the carers there is no need to identify the actual perpetrator of the harm to satisfy s 31(2)(b)(i). As Lord Clyde said, 'What the subsection requires is the identification of the incidence of harm, not the hand which caused, or may be likely to cause it.' In Lord Nicholls' view, the phrase 'the care given to the child' is not confined to the care given to the child by parents or other primary carers but in the case of shared care arrangements extends to the care given by any of the carers. Further, although he accepted that 'attributable to' connotes a causal connection between the harm and the care, in his view, that 'connection need not be that of a sole or dominant or direct cause and effect; a contributory causal connection suffices'. According to Lord Nicholls a more restrictive interpretation would mean that notwithstanding that a child has repeatedly sustained non-accidental injuries, the court would be powerless to intervene to protect the child unless it could be shown who was responsible. That, in his view, could not have been Parliament's intention and given that Parliament seems not to have foreseen this particular problem, the court must 'apply the statutory language to the unforeseen situation in the manner which best gives effect to the purposes the legislation was enacted to achieve'. In reaching this conclusion Lord Nicholls rejected the argument that the continuation of the care proceedings resulting in the child remaining in foster care infringed both the child's and her parents' right to respect for family life under Art 8 of the European Convention on Human Rights. In his view the steps taken were 'no more than those reasonably necessary to pursue the legitimate aim of protecting [the child] from further injury'.

The House of Lords were only concerned with the injured child of the parents but in fact care proceedings were originally also brought with respect to the child-minder's own child. The Court of Appeal,[479] however, dismissed that application upon the basis that in the absence of any injury to that child no existing harm could be shown and given that the perpetrator of the harm could not be identified, neither could any risk of harm be established.

What are shared care arrangements? One important limitation of the *Lancashire* decision is that it only applies where there are shared care arrangements. Precisely what amounts to such arrangements for these purposes has yet to be explored. In broad terms, however, it seems clear that it embraces all forms of multi-care arrangements and this includes those that both look after the child while the parents are at work and those such as babysitters who look after the child while the parents are out socially. But this is not to imply that the concept only extends to those exclusively caring for the child. There seems no reason to suppose that it does not include those such as grandparents who help look after the child with the parent. Whether it also extends to, for example, a peripatetic teacher who comes to the home to give a child private tuition perhaps can be debated. It might be noted that in a subsequent case[480] Butler-Sloss P seemed to imply that those who merely have 'fleeting contact' will not rank as 'carers' for these purposes.

---

[479] [2002] 2 WLR 346. There was no appeal against this decision.
[480] *North Yorkshire County Council v SA* [2003] EWCA Civ 839, [2003] 2 FLR 849 at [25].

It has been argued[481] that it is illogical to exclude non-carers, for example, a bully at school, '[i]f in the name of child protection, we are to permit children to be taken into care even if the parents may well be blameless, surely this should be so whoever else may have caused the harm?' But the key difference is that whereas the parents have to take responsibility for choosing other carers, they do not for non-carers.

The meaning of 'care'. The Act is surprisingly silent on precisely what is meant by 'care' in this context. Although 'care' could simply be interpreted as referring to the physical day-to-day care given to the child by the person with whom the child is living, it seems clear that it means more than this, connoting in addition the emotional care and the love and affection that one would expect of reasonable parents. Hence, in a case of a child being accommodated by a local authority but living with foster parents, the threshold criteria might still be satisfied notwithstanding that the parents are now able to look after their child, if in the past they have not been visiting or keeping in touch.[482] On the other hand, if the parent has shown all the care and concern that a reasonable parent would show to a child living away from home for a time, then on either interpretation the criteria would not be satisfied. In such cases, however, the court would have to consider whether it would be preferable to make a residence order in favour of the foster parents.[483]

Commentary. As Lord Nicholls himself recognised, the *Lancashire* decision means that the attributable condition may be satisfied when there is no more than a possibility that the parents were responsible for inflicting the injuries and that consequently parents who may be wholly innocent and whose care may not have fallen below that of a reasonable parent will face the possibility of losing their child with all the pain and distress that that involves.[484] What persuaded him to adopt this stance was 'the prospect that an unidentified, and unidentifiable, carer may inflict further injury on a child he or she has already severely damaged'. Without gainsaying the difficulties, it is submitted that *Lancashire* was right and goes some way to mitigating the consequences of the earlier ruling in *Re H*.[485] Were it to be necessary to prove who the actual perpetrator of harm is in every case it would, as one judge has observed,[486] render the statutory provisions ineffective to deal with a commonplace aspect of child protection. As Lord Nicholls said in the later decision, *Re O and another (Minors)(Care: Preliminary Hearing; Re B (A Minor))*,[487] the interpretation adopted by *Lancashire* 'is necessary to avoid the unacceptable consequence that, otherwise, if the court cannot identify which of the child's carers is responsible for inflicting the injuries the child will remain wholly unprotected'.

It is important to appreciate that *Lancashire* did not decide that a care order should be made but only that the threshold had been satisfied thus permitting the court then to

481 See J Herring *Family Law* (2nd edn) 540.
482 Hence, in a case like *M v Wigan Metropolitan Borough Council* [1979] Fam 36, where children were repeatedly looked after by the authority during the mother's difficult pregnancies but where the parents were reluctant to take responsibility for them, the criteria would be satisfied.
483 See post, p 765.
484 The dilemma in *Lancashire* was even greater since if the child-minder was responsible for the injuries not only was the child removed from innocent parents, but the child-minder's own child was left unprotected.
485 See the discussion above at p 747.
486 Wall J in *Re B (Minors)(Care Proceedings: Practice)* [1999] 1 WLR 238 at 248.
487 [2003] UKHL 18, [2004] 1 AC 523 at [19].

consider at the so-called welfare stage what, if any, order it should make.[488] But again, as Lord Nicholls acknowledged, the decision in *Lancashire* does pose considerable problems for determining what, if any, should be made inasmuch as it will not be known which individual was responsible for inflicting the injuries. We will discuss these problems further when considering the welfare stage[489] but another issue that has since arisen is what test should be applied when determining who the possible perpetrators are. This was an issue in *North Yorkshire County Council v SA*[490] where the trial judge considered that he should only *exclude* a carer as a possible perpetrator if there was 'no possibility' that he or she could have inflicted the injuries upon the child. The Court of Appeal held this to be the wrong test since it was 'patently too wide and might encompass anyone who had even a fleeting contact with the child in circumstances in which there was an opportunity to cause injuries'.[491] The correct test was held to be whether there is 'a likelihood or real possibility' that a particular person or persons was the perpetrator or a perpetrator of the inflicted injuries.[492] But whether the Court of Appeal was right to adopt this test is debatable since that is the established test for determining whether a child is 'likely' to suffer significant harm, the primary facts having been established on the basis of the balance of probabilities. Surely excluding possible perpetrators is part of the establishment of primary facts and accordingly the proper test should be whether on the balance of probability a particular person can be excluded as a possible perpetrator?

Not being what it would be reasonable to expect a parent to give to him

This rather inelegant phrase imports an objective test. It is therefore no answer to say that the care given was to the best of the parents' limited abilities.[493] Parents cannot argue that they have particular problems, that they are feckless, unintelligent, irresponsible, alcoholic, drug abusers, poor or otherwise disadvantaged, and are thus justified in providing a lower standard of care. It is no answer either that the care given was no different from that given by others in the same street or neighbourhood.[494] The Department of Health's *Guidance* suggests[495] that the court will wish to seek professional evidence on the standard of care which reasonable parents could be expected to provide, with support from community-wide services as appropriate, where the child's needs are complex or demanding.

The focus of attention is on the care given or likely to be given to the child in question, not to an average child. If, for example, the child has particular difficulties in relation to his behaviour or handicap, the court will have to consider what a reasonable parent would provide for him. In *Re V (Care or Supervision)*,[496] for example, a mother who was protective of her son who suffered from cerebral palsy sought to keep him at home rather than sending him to a specialist school. It was held that whilst the mother's care was beyond

---

[488] Indeed, it was for this very reason that Lord Clyde considered it justifiable to allow a degree of latitude in the scope of the threshold.

[489] See below at p 755.   [490] [2003] EWCA Civ 839, [2003] 2 FLR 849.

[491] Per Butler-Sloss P at [25].

[492] Per Butler-Sloss P at para [26], purportedly following *Re O and Another (Minors) (Care: Preliminary Hearing); Re B (A Minor)*, above.

[493] Contrast the pre-1989 Act decision *O'Dare v South Glamorgan County Council* (1980) 3 FLR 1, CA in which, but for the availability of wardship, the argument would have succeeded under the previous legislation.

[494] These matters may, however, be relevant to the question whether an order should be made.

[495] Vol 1 at para 3.23.   [496] [1996] 1 FLR 776, CA. Discussed below at p 768.

criticism on the grounds of devotion and affection it nevertheless fell short of the standard of care which it would be reasonably expected of her in the circumstances.

The child's being beyond parental control

As the Department of Health's *Guidance* states,[497] this alternative causal condition was provided for in the previous legislation but was not linked with harm to the child:

'It provides for cases where, whatever the standard of care available to the child, he is not benefiting from it because of lack of parental control. It is immaterial whether this is the fault of the parents or the child'.

In *Re O (A Minor) (Care Order: Education: Procedure)*,[498] Ewbank J commented that in respect of a 15-year-old truant:

'... where a child is suffering harm in not going to school and is living at home it will follow that either the child is beyond her parents' control or that they are not giving the child the care that it would be reasonable to expect a parent to give.'

According to *M v Birmingham City Council*,[499] the phrase 'being beyond parental control' imports no time element and is therefore 'plainly a substantial expression capable of describing a state of affairs in the past, in the present or in the future according to the context in which it falls to be applied'. It was also held that while 'parental control' refers to the parent of the child in question and not to parents, or reasonable parents, in general, regard can properly be had to the control exercised by that parent in conjunction with a partner even if that partner is not the parent of the child.

4 THE WELFARE STAGE

Crossing the threshold is not a reason for making a care order[500] but merely opens the way to the possibility that such an order may be made.[501] This is because, having considered the threshold criteria, it is incumbent upon the court in deciding what order, if any, to make to apply the general principles under s 1. This is known as the 'welfare stage'.[502] As Booth J made clear in *Humberside County Council v B*,[503] the two stages, namely the threshold and welfare stages, should be regarded as being quite separate, with only the latter governed by s 1.

At the welfare stage the court must, pursuant to s 1(1), regard the welfare of the child as the paramount consideration.[504] It is also *bound*[505] to have regard to the statutory check list contained in s 1(3),[506] and, pursuant to s 1(5), consider whether it is better for the child to make any order than to make no order at all. Another important consideration in

---

[497] Above at para 3.25. [498] [1992] 1 WLR 912 at 917–18. [499] [1994] 2 FLR 141 at 147.

[500] Per Lord Nicholls in *Re O and Another (Minors)(Care: Preliminary Hearing); Re B (A Minor)* [2003] UKHL 18, [2004] 1 AC 523 at [23].

[501] Per Lord Clyde in *Lancashire County Council v B* [2000] 2 AC 147 at 170.

[502] See Butler Sloss LJ in *Re M and R (Child Abuse: Evidence)* [1996] 2 FLR 195, at 202 CA.

[503] [1993] 1 FLR 257 at 261. Although this analysis was subsequently accepted as being correct by the Court of Appeal in *F v Leeds City Council* [1994] 2 FLR 60, as Ward J pointed out (at 67), it is not always easy clearly to demarcate the two-stage process.

[504] Discussed above, pp 450ff. [505] See s 1(4)(b). [506] Discussed above, pp 468ff.

determining what order to make is that of human rights, it being recognised[507] that the level of intervention must be proportionate to the nature and gravity of the harm established or feared.

As Lord Nicholls has observed,[508] applying the welfare principle involves both looking at the past and also looking into the future. In considering which course is in the child's best interests the court will have regard to all the circumstances of the case. It also has been said[509] that it is at the welfare stage that the non-adversarial or inquisitorial nature of the proceedings comes to the fore.

(a) Having regard to past events

Uncertain perpetrators

The leading case on this aspect of the welfare stage is *Re O and another (Minors)(Care: Preliminary Hearing); Re B (A Minor)*,[510] in which the House of Lords heard appeals in respect of two conflicting decisions of the Court of Appeal. In both cases the problem was that it could not be established which of the parents had injured the child or whether both had been responsible. In *Re B* the Court of Appeal held that since it had not been proved that the mother had been responsible for any of the child's injuries, the court should proceed at the welfare stage on the footing that she did *not* pose a risk to the child. In *Re O*, however, where again it could not be proved whether the mother or her partner had caused the injuries (from which the child died), it was held that the mother should *not* be disregarded as a risk to the elder sibling in the future. The House of Lords ruled that in these so-called 'uncertain perpetrator' cases the court should proceed at the welfare stage 'on the footing that each of the possible perpetrators is indeed, just that: a possible perpetrator'.[511] As Lord Nicholls said,[512] it would be grotesque that because neither parent considered individually has been proved to be the perpetrator the court should proceed at the welfare stage on the footing that neither represents a risk. Accordingly, the correct approach is to 'have regard, to whatever extent is appropriate', to the facts found by the judge at the preliminary hearing'.[513]

Although it is difficult to see what other solution the House of Lords could have reached, it does put a premium on the precise findings at the preliminary stage.[514] Moreover the effect of the decision, namely, as the mothers would see it in *Re O* etc, that their children would be removed from them on the basis of suspicions,[515] stands in contrast to the

---

[507] See in particular *Re C and B (Care Order: Future Harm)* [2001] 1 FLR 611, CA and *Re O (Supervision Order)* [2001] EWCA Civ 16, [2001] 1 FLR 923, discussed below at p 770.

[508] *Re O*, above, at [23].

[509] Per Charles J in *Re R (Care: Disclosure: Nature of Proceedings)* [2002] 1 FLR 755 at 772.

[510] Above, on which see M Hayes '*Re O and R; Re B*—Uncertain Evidence and Risk Taking in Child Protection Cases' [2004] CFLQ 63.

[511] Above at [28].   [512] Above at [26].   [513] Above at [31].

[514] As Lord Nicholls said (see [35]) the views and indications of the judge at the preliminary hearing can be of great assistance at the welfare stage and for these reasons judges should be astute to express such views as they can at the earlier hearing.

[515] See the discussion by J Herring *Family Law* (2nd edn) 543, who supports the view expressed by A Bainham 'Children Law at the Millennium' in *Essays for the new Millennium* (ed S Cretney) 113 at 124 that suspicions should be relevant to the making of supervision but not care orders. But this suggestion would surely be too restrictive to protect children adequately.

raison d'etre of Lord Nicholls' approach in *Re H.*[516] However, the crucial difference is that harm to the children concerned had been proved in *Re O* whereas it had not in *Re H.* In any event, the subsequent ruling in *North Yorkshire County Council v SA*[517] that possible perpetrators can be excluded if there is no real possibility that they are involved, does at least reduce the potential number of possible perpetrators in any particular case.

Unproved allegations of harm

Although not directly relevant to *Re O* Lord Nicholls made some observations[518] about 'the type of case where the threshold criteria are satisfied on one ground, such as neglect or failure to protect, but not on another ground, such as physical harm'. In such a case the question arises as to what extent the court can, at the welfare stage, 'take into account the possibility that the non-proven allegation might, after all, be true'. Since having regard at the welfare stage to allegations of harm rejected at the threshold stage would effectively deprive both the child and family of the protection intended to afford by the threshold conditions, Lord Nicholls concluded that at the welfare stage 'the court should proceed on the footing that the unproven allegations are no more than that'.[519]

This conclusion was said to be in accord with *Re M and R (Child Abuse: Evidence),*[520] in which the threshold criteria were met on the basis of emotional harm but allegations of sexual abuse were not found proved. The Court of Appeal rejected the argument based on the paramountcy test, that at the welfare stage the court could when assessing the risk of harm under s 1(3)(e) act on possibilities rather than proof on the preponderance of probabilities. As Butler-Sloss LJ said, 'It would be extraordinary if Parliament intended that evidence which is insufficient to establish that a child is likely to suffer significant harm for the purposes of s 31 should nevertheless be treated as sufficient to establish that a child is at risk of suffering harm for the purposes for s 1.' The trial judge's decision to ignore the allegations of sexual abuse at the welfare stage was thus upheld.[521]

(b) Having regard to the future—care plans

In deciding what order, if any, it should make at the welfare stage, regard must be had to s 1(5) which, as we have seen,[522] requires the court to consider whether it is better for the child to make any order than to make no order at all. To answer this question in the context of care proceedings the court will have to consider the plans which the authority is proposing for the child. These plans are known as 'care plans'.

The requirement to submit a care plan was only put on a statutory footing by amendments introduced by the Adoption and Children Act 2002[523] though in fact it had

---

[516] *Re H (Minors)(Sexual Abuse: Standard of Proof)* [1996] AC 563, discussed above at p 745.

[517] [2003] EWCA Civ 839, [2003] 2 FLR 849, discussed above at p 754.

[518] [2003] UKHL 18, [2004] 1 AC 523 at [37].

[519] A similar position obtains where unproved allegations are abandoned, see *Re R (Care: Disclosure: Nature of Proceedings* [2002] 1 FLR 755, approved by Lord Nicholls at [41].

[520] [1996] 2 FLR 195.

[521] Note the argument by J Herring *Family Law* (2nd edn) at 543 that there is a difference between ignoring unproven allegations as in *Re M and R* and treating them as unproven allegations as per Lord Nicholls in *Re O.*

[522] Above at p 475.

[523] Section 121 implemented on 30 December 2005: Adoption and Children Act 2002 (Commencement No. 9) Order 2005, SI 2005/2213.

long been the established practice.[524] Now s 31(3A) of the 1989 Act expressly states that no care order[525] can be made until the court has considered what is referred to as 'a s 31A plan'. Section 31A requires the appropriate local authority[526] in an application where a care order might be made[527] to prepare a care plan within a timescale set by the court. Furthermore, while such an application is pending the authority must keep the plan under review and 'if they are of the opinion some change is required, revise the plan, or make a new plan, accordingly'.[528]

When scrutinising care plans the court should consider whether they are the best available plans for the child and, if so, why an order is necessary to implement them. Although there are limits to this scrutiny process—it does not mean, for example, that there should be an over-zealous investigation into matters that are properly within administrative discretion[529]—nevertheless, even where a care order is the inevitable eventual outcome, the court should not be deflected from using the litigation process to maximum effect.[530]

If the court is not satisfied that the plan is in the child's interests it can suggest[531] changes and, if these are not accepted, it can refuse to make an order.[532] However, as we discuss later,[533] what the court cannot do is to keep the local authority plans under review inter alia by making a conditional care order although there is now a mechanism[534] in appropriate cases for getting the plan back before the court.

5 SOME PROCEDURAL AND EVIDENTIAL ISSUES

(a) The Protocol[535]

When the Children Act 1989 was first implemented it was expected that public law cases would be disposed of within 12 weeks. This expectation proved wildly optimistic and by

---

[524] Indeed the application form (Form C13) for a care or supervision order has always required the applicant to state the plans for the child. Note also *Manchester City Council v F* [1993] 1 FLR 419n and *Re J (Minors)(Care: Plan)* [1994] 1 FLR 253 in which Eastham and Wall JJ respectively said that the care plan should accord, if possible, with the format set out by the Department of Health's *Guidance and Regulations*, Vol 3, *Family Placements*, ch 2, para 2.62. See also Appendix F to the Protocol For Judicial Management In Public Law Children Cases [2003] 2 FLR 319.

[525] But note no care plan is required before an interim care order may be made: s 31A(5) and see *Westminster City Council v RA, B and S* [2005] EWHC 970 (Fam), [2005] 2 FLR 1309.

[526] Where more than one authority is involved, the care plan needs to be prepared in co-operation between them: *L v London Borough of Bexley* [1996] 2 FLR 595.

[527] But not an interim care order: s 31A(5).   [528] Section 31A(2).

[529] See Wall J in *Re J*, above, at 262.

[530] Per Thorpe LJ in *Re CH (Care or Interim Care Order)* [1998] 1 FLR 402, CA—the judge was wrong to refuse to hear evidence at the behest of the guardian ad litem, having reached a consensus which was acceptable to all the parties save for the guardian. Note also *Re H (Care: Change in Care Plan)* [1998] 1 FLR 193, CA—a parent was entitled to have an order based on a flawed care plan reconsidered, even if that order remained in force.

[531] But it cannot force changes. Note also that, while the court can make non-binding observations upon what it had in mind about the order, even these can cause difficulties: see *L v London Borough of Bromley* [1998] 1 FLR 709.

[532] Though in Nourse LJ's view, at any rate, such circumstances where a refusal will be justified will be rare: *Re T (A Minor) (Care Order: Conditions)* [1994] 2 FLR 423 at 429.

[533] See below, p 775.   [534] See below, p 778.

[535] See E Saunders, 'The New Care Protocol' [2003] Fam Law 774 Mr Justice Coleridge 'Another Big Bang' [2003] Fam Law 799 and D Hershman *Working with the Child Care Protocol* (2004). See also above at

2003 the average care case lasted for almost a year.[536] In a major attempt to combat what was seen as unacceptable delay in public law cases, a *Protocol for Judicial Case Management in Public Law Children Act Cases*[537] has been devised. Its overall object is 'to improve the completion of all cases within an overall timetable of not more than 40 weeks, save in exceptional and unforeseen circumstances.[538] To this end the Protocol provides detailed guidance on the management of applications at all the vital stages (viz the issue of the application; the first hearing in the Family Proceedings Court; the Allocation hearing and directions; the case management conference; the pre-hearing review and the final hearing) via what is described as a 'route map' and provides a target timetable for each stage. Designed to be as simple and user friendly as possible it is addressed to *all* the participants (including judges) in the process and sets out what action is to be taken by whom. One of the key principles is that there should be active case management by the court with a view to furthering the overall objective of speedy disposals. It applies to every public law case at every level.

Described[539] as 'a collation and distillation of best practice' rather than a fresh start, the Protocol was devised after widespread consultation. Whether it will be successful in achieving its overall 40 week disposal target remains to be seen. What is clear is that it is ultimately only guidance so, for example, it does not mean that cases that can be, should not be decided quicker. Its purpose has always to be kept in mind and, as was emphasised in *Re G (Protocol For Judicial Case Management In Public Law Children Act Cases: Application To Become Partly In Family Proceedings)*,[540] if the pursuit of that purpose requires a departure from the terms of the Protocol, then that has to be done with proper reasons being given.

(b) Admission of evidence

Before the 1989 Act all evidence in care proceedings was oral: now at all court levels, including therefore in the magistrates' court, written statements of the substance of the oral evidence which the party intends to adduce have to be submitted in advance of the hearing.[541] Similarly, copies of any documents, including expert's reports, on which a party intends to rely, have to be submitted in advance.[542]

Indeed, it is within the court's power to order disclosure of reports not being relied upon because, for example, they are not favourable to the commissioning parent.[543] Whether there is a *duty* to disclose such documents to the other parties has yet to be authoritatively resolved.[544] Further evidence or documents can only be brought in with the

---

p 20. Note also the proposals in the *Review of the Child Care Proceedings System in England and Wales* (2006) to revise the First Hearing in Care Proceedings to incorporate steps 1–3 of the Protocol.

[536] See the Foreword to the Protocol.

[537] [2003] 2 FLR 719. The Protocol came into force on 1 November 2003.

[538] *Court Business* Family Special Edition, October 2003. [539] The Foreword to the Protocol.

[540] [2004] EWHC 116 (Fam), [2004] 1 FLR 1119.

[541] FPCA 1991 r 17(1)(a); FPR 1991 r 4.17(1)(a). [542] Ibid, r 17(1)(b); r 4.17(1)(b).

[543] See *Re L (Minors) (Police Investigation: Privilege)* [1997] AC 16, HL.

[544] In *Essex County Council v R (Legal Professional Privilege)* [1994] Fam 167, Thorpe J thought there was a duty to disclose, but in *Barking and Dagenham London Borough Council v O* [1993] Fam 295 Douglas Brown J thought that the parties could only be required to disclose reports on which they intended to rely. In *Oxfordshire County Council v M* [1994] Fam 151, the Court of Appeal said it preferred the *Essex* decision, but see the analysis in Clarke Hall and Morrison, on *Children* at 1[1387]. Note that in *Re L*, above, Lord Jauncey refrained from expressing a conclusion on this issue. See C Tapper 'Evidential Privilege in Cases Involving Children' [1997] CFLQ 1 at 14ff.

court's leave.[545] Subject to the court's directions, copies of the written evidence are served on the other parties, also in advance of the hearing. Magistrates are expected to have read the written evidence ahead of the hearing.[546]

The submission of written evidence does not preclude the admission of oral evidence— indeed it is normal to hear such evidence.[547] The parties, however, do not have a *right* to insist on giving oral evidence. In *Re N (Contested Care Application)*,[548] for example, in which all the experts, including the psychiatrist instructed by the parents (whose experts were before the court at the pre-trial review) recommended care orders, Thorpe J considered that the full trial process should not continue at public expense. It is clear, however, that this power should be exercised with caution and in such a way that, unless the child's interests make it necessary, the rules of natural justice and the rights of the parents are fully and properly observed.[549]

Under the Children (Admissibility of Hearsay Evidence) Order 1993 hearsay evidence is admissible in care and supervision proceedings before any court. This means, for example, that videos of child interviews are admissible in the magistrates' courts as well as in the higher courts.

(c) Expert evidence[550]

No child can be medically or psychiatrically examined or otherwise assessed for the purpose of the preparation of expert evidence without leave of the court.[551] It is well established that the court should take a proactive role in the granting of leave. It should determine whether the evidence is required in the first place and, where it is, it should limit expert evidence to given categories of expertise and specify the numbers of experts to be called. It should also be proactive in laying down a timetable for the filing of the evidence, in making arrangements for the dissemination of the reports and in giving directions for experts to confer.[552]

Although expert evidence may be crucial in care proceedings, there has been some concern about its excessive or inappropriate use in care proceedings under the Children Act 1989 and the consequential delay in the conduct of proceedings.[553] The Children Act

---

[545] FPCA 1991 r 17(3); FPR 1991 r 4.17(3).

[546] FPCA 1991 r 21(1). The Family Proceedings Rules 1991 do not make such express provision for the higher courts, since advance reading of the documents is done as a matter of course.

[547] Though, given the advance submission of written evidence, there is no need for a witness to recite his statement, but he may confirm that it is true, amplifying and updating the contents where necessary and answering questions from the other parties and the court. See generally Children Act Advisory Committee Report 1993/94 p 24 and see *Practice Note: Case Management* [1995] 1 All ER 586.

[548] [1994] 2 FLR 992. See also *Re B (Interim Care Orders: Renewal)* [2001] 2 FLR 1217.

[549] *Re G (A Minor) (Care: Evidence)* [1994] 2 FLR 785. See also *Re I and H (Contact: Right To Give Evidence)* [1998] 1 FLR 876, CA.

[550] See generally the *Protocol for Judicial Case Management in Public Law Children Act Cases*, Appendix C, Sir N Wall and Judge I Hamilton *A Handbook for Expert Witnesses in Children Act Cases* (2000) and The Hon Mr Justice Wall (ed) *Rooted Sorrows* (1997).

[551] FPCA 1991 r 18; FPR 1991 r 4.18.

[552] *Re G (Minors) (Expert Witnesses)* [1994] 2 FLR 291. It is evident that these guidelines have not always been followed: see eg *Re CB and JB (Care Proceedings: Guidelines)* [1998] 2 FLR 211 where 13 expert witnesses submitted reports.

[553] One of the causes identified as leading to greater delay is the instruction of experts: see J Plotnikoff and R Woolfson *Timetabling of Interim Care Orders Study* (1994). See also Booth *Avoiding Delay in Children Act Cases* (1996).

Advisory Committee[554] advised that all experts should have certain basic skills which are set out in a core curriculum vitae. It is further established that:[555]

'(1) Expert evidence presented to the court should be, and should be seen to be the independent product of the expert uninfluenced as to form or content by the exigencies of litigation.

(2) An expert witness should provide independent assistance to the court by way of object-ive unbiased opinion in relation to matters within his expertise. An expert witness in the High Court should never assume the role of advocate.

(3) An expert witness should state the facts or assumptions on which his opinion is based. He should not omit to consider material facts which detract from his concluded opinion.

(4) An expert witness should make it clear when a particular question falls outside his expertise.

(5) If an expert's opinion is not properly researched because he considers that insufficient data is available then this must be stated with an indication that the opinion is no more than a provisional one.

(6) If, after exchange of reports, an expert witness changes his view on a material matter, such change of view should be communicated . . . to the other side without delay and when appropriate to the court.'

The role of experts came very much into the public domain by a line of controversial appeals in both criminal and civil matters where their evidence resulted or may have resulted in the wrongful conviction of parents accused of killing or seriously injuring their children. The most well known of these cases was *R v Cannings*.[556] Following this decision the Attorney General established a review of both current and past cases involving the prosecution of a parent or carer for killing an infant under the age of two, while local authorities were asked to review cases where victims and/or siblings had been taken into care on the basis of disputed medical evidence.[557] In the event only two parents had their convictions for killing their children quashed while five cases raised 'serious doubt' about the reliability of evidence that led to a care order being made.[558] Notwithstanding the relatively few cases ultimately affected by *Cannings* the salutary lesson is that experts should not attempt nor be permitted to go beyond their expertise.

Letters of instruction should identify relevant issues of fact, list the documents to be sent to the expert, include an agreed chronology and background history and should be disclosed to the other parties.[559] It has been held[560] that it should be a condition of appointment of any expert that he be required to hold discussions with other experts

[554] CAAC Report 1993/94, p 24.
[555] See *Re AB (Child Abuse: Expert Witnesses)* [1995] 1 FLR 181 at 194 per Wall J citing *National Justice Cia Naviera SA v Prudential Assurance Co Ltd* [1993] 2 Lloyd's Rep 68.
[556] [2004] EWCA Crim 1, [2004] 1 All ER 725.   [557] LAC (2004) 5.
[558] Only one of these cases was changed: see C Cobley 'The Quest for Truth: Substantiating Allegations of Physical Abuse in Criminal Proceedings and Care Proceedings' (2006) Int Jo of Family Law and Policy, forthcoming—relying inter alia on a press report in the *Independent* 17 November 2004.
[559] See *Re M (Minors)(Care Proceedings: Child's Wishes)* [1994] 1 FLR 749 and *Re T and E (Proceedings: Conflicting Interests)* [1995] 1 FLR 581.
[560] *Re C (Expert Evidence: Disclosure: Practice)* [1995] 1 FLR 204.

instructed in the same field of expertise in advance of the hearing to identify areas of agreement and dispute. Such discussion should be chaired by a co-ordinator such as the children's guardian, if there is consent to so act.[561] In *Re CB and JB (Care Proceedings: Guidelines)*,[562] however, Wall J held that there was no need to hold a meeting where there was agreement, and where there was disagreement a telephone conference, if properly chaired, might suffice.

As well as giving opinion as to the child's health, likely cause of injuries etc, an expert's evidence as to witness credibility is admissible.[563]

The purpose of expert evidence is obviously to assist the judge to reach the right decision, but the judicial task is make a decision in the light of all the evidence and the judge may therefore depart from an expert's opinion provided proper reasons are given.[564] Where there is a conflict between experts the court must resolve that conflict insofar as it is relevant to the issues before the court. Provided proper reasons are given the court is entitled to give greater weight to the opinion of one expert as against the other.[565]

(d) Split hearings [566]

So far as the conduct of proceedings is concerned, a practice that has developed is to have 'split hearings' so as first to determine contested issues of fact and then to consider what order should be made.[567] In this way allegations of physical or sexual abuse can be determined at an early stage, which then enables the substantive hearing to proceed more speedily and to focus on the child's welfare with greater clarity.

Split hearings are allowed for under the Protocol. Indeed according to the case-management checklist[568] consideration should be given at the first hearing/allocation stage or the later case-management stage as to whether a 'finding of fact hearing is necessary and, if so, what is the discrete issue of fact that is to be determined, by whom and when?'

Although not appropriate in every case, nor problem-free when they are used[569] split hearings can be a useful way of handling contested care cases. Furthermore, one potential area of difficulty has been removed by the Court of Appeal decision in *Re B (Split Hearing: Jurisdiction)*[570] that appeals can be heard against findings of fact.[571]

---

[561] See *Re Uddin (A Child)* [2005] EWCA Civ 52, [2005] 1 WLR 2398.   [562] [1998] 2 FLR 211.

[563] *Re M and R (Child Abuse: Evidence)* [1996] 2 FLR 195, CA.

[564] See *Re B (Care: Expert Witness)* [1996] 1 FLR 667. For a comprehensive review of the many issues involved see *A County Council v K, D and L* [2005] EWHC 144 (Fam), [2005] 1 FLR 851, per Charles J.

[565] See *Re J (Expert Evidence: Hearsay)* [1999] 2 FLR 661.

[566] See J Geddes 'Split Hearings—Are They Compatible with the Protocol?' [2004] Fam Law 43.

[567] See *Re S (Care Order: Split Hearing)* [1996] 2 FLR 773, per Bracewell J.

[568] See no. 55 on the checklist at Appendix A13 of the Protocol though as Geddes, above, at 45, points out, it remains unclear when such a hearing should or can be accommodated into the timetable.

[569] See Geddes, above, who says that in the past split hearings have themselves led to delay and muddle, not least when one judge hears the facts hearing and another the disposal. Hopefully, these problems will be addressed by the Protocol.

[570] [2000] 1 FLR 334.

[571] The argument that appeals can only lie against the making of an *order* were rejected by the Court of Appeal.

(e) Confidentiality of proceedings and the issue of disclosure[572]

Care proceedings are not open to the public and any reports or other evidence that is adduced are confidential and should not be disclosed to third parties without court leave, even after the proceedings have concluded.[573]

It has been held[574] that statements made to a guardian during her investigation (a mother admitting her responsibility for causing non-accidental injuries to her baby) require court leave to be disclosed but, on the other hand, oral statements made to social workers have been held to attract no such protection.[575]

In deciding whether to order disclosure regard must clearly be had to the circumstances, including to whom and why disclosure is sought. Commonly, disclosure will be sought by the police to enable them to pursue their criminal investigations. In such cases it is established[576] that consideration needs to be given to the interests of the child concerned (but note those interests are *not* the court's paramount consideration), the public interest in ensuring frankness in proceedings by preserving confidentiality, and another public interest in upholding the law by providing evidence for other court proceedings.

Another consideration in deciding whether to order disclosure is the problem of self-incrimination. In *Re L (Minors) (Police Investigation: Privilege)*[577] the House of Lords said that a court should not order disclosure compliance with which was likely to involve the danger of self-incrimination. In part this standpoint is supported by s 98(2) of the Children Act 1989, which provides that a statement or admission made in public law proceedings under the 1989 Act 'shall not be admissible in evidence against the person making it or his spouse in proceedings for an offence other than perjury'. The application of s 98(2) has not proved straightforward, but in an important decision, *Re EC (Disclosure of Material)*[578] the Court of Appeal held it only applies to evidence given in criminal proceedings and does not therefore prevent disclosure to the police to assist their investigations. This decision effectively renders the protection a hollow one and is not calculated to encourage frank disclosure in care proceedings.

6 COURT ORDERS

(a) Introduction

At the welfare stage of care proceedings the court must, pursuant to s 1(1) regard the welfare of the child as the paramount consideration; have regard to the statutory checklist contained in s 1(3) and in particular to s 1(3)(g) which directs the court to consider all its

---

572 See S Edwards 'Sealing One's Own Fate: Disclosure of Documents in Care Proceedings—On the Trail to the Abrogation of a Fair Trial?' [2005] CFLQ 13.

573 FPCA 1991 r 23(1); FPR 1991 r 4.23(1). Note this embargo is applied strictly: see eg *Re C (Guardian ad Litem: Disclosure of Report)* [1996] 1 FLR 61 in which it was held that court leave was required to disclose a guardian's report to a family centre which was connected with the social services department and which offered therapeutic treatment to the children concerned.

574 *Oxfordshire County Council v P* [1995] Fam 161, discussed above at p 495.

575 *Re G (a minor) (social worker: disclosure)* [1996] 2 All ER 65, CA, discussed above at p 495.

576 See eg *Oxfordshire County Council v L and F* [1997] 1 FLR 235, per Stuart-White J and the cases there cited.

577 [1997] AC 16, HL.   578 [1996] 2 FLR 725, CA.

options before deciding which order to make; and pursuant to s 1(5) only make orders where that is considered better for the child than making no order. The import of s 1(3)(g) is that since Part IV proceedings rank as 'family proceedings' for the purposes of s 8,[579] the court must, even if the threshold criteria are satisfied, consider whether it should make a s 8 order. This power to make a s 8 order can be exercised whether or not an application has been made for it.[580] Further, as s 31(5) makes clear, supervision orders can be made upon applications for care orders and care orders upon applications for supervision orders. It is also clear that care or supervision orders can be made even though the local authority no longer wish to pursue that option.[581] However, as Hale J observed in *Oxfordshire County Council v L (Care or Supervision Order)*,[582] 'there must in general be urgent and strong reasons to force upon the local authority a more draconian order than that for which they have asked'. Furthermore, if the court is minded to make an order which has not been sought, it must give the parties an opportunity to address the court on the desirability of making that order.[583]

In summary, at the welfare stage the court, guided by the welfare principle but not necessarily constrained by what the parties have themselves sought, has, if the threshold criteria have been satisfied, a wide range of powers to make no order at all, a s 8 order (with or without a supervision order), a supervision order, or a care order. Where the threshold criteria have not been satisfied, the court still retains its powers to make s 8 orders and is not bound to return the child to his or her parents.

Even where the threshold criteria have been satisfied, as Hale J has pointed out,[584] the court should not overlook the local authorities' preventive duties to children in need under Part III of the Act[585] and 'should begin with a preference for the less interventionist rather than the more interventionist approach'.[586] This latter point is now further under-scored by human rights considerations, it being well established[587] that whatever action is to be taken must be a proportionate response to the nature and gravity of the feared harm.

The key consideration in determining what, if any, order should be made is how much public control (as exercised by the local authority) is thought to be needed to protect the child in question. Where most control is needed, a care order will be appropriate. Where least control is required, then a s 8 order might be sufficient. Supervision orders come somewhere between those two options and may be appropriate where there is a concern about the parental care but not sufficient to warrant the removal of the child and the making of a full care order.[588]

---

[579] Section 8(3), (4).

[580] Viz pursuant to its powers under s 10(1)(b), discussed above at pp 566–7.

[581] See eg *Re M (A Minor) (Care Order: Threshold Conditions)* [1994] 2 AC 424, HL, discussed above at pp 740ff, in which a care order was made notwithstanding that the local authority wanted to withdraw their application; and *Re K (Care Order or Residence Order)* [1995] 1 FLR 675, discussed below, p 772, where a care order was made contrary to the authority's wishes.

[582] [1998] 1 FLR 70 at 73.   [583] *Croydon London Borough Council v A* [1992] Fam 169.

[584] See *Re O (Care or Supervision Order)* [1996] 2 FLR 755 at 759 and *Oxfordshire County Council v L (Care or Supervision Order)* [1998] 1 FLR 70 at 74.

[585] Discussed above at pp 699ff.   [586] In *Re O*, above, at 760.

[587] See *Re C and B (Care Orders: Future Harm)* [2001] 1 FLR 611 at (33) and (34), per Hale LJ, discussed further below at p 770, and *Re O (Supervision Order)* [2001] 1 FLR 923 at (27) and (28) also per Hale LJ, discussed further below at p 770.

[588] On rare occasions it might be appropriate to grant care and control to individuals under a wardship regime with legal control vested in the court, see eg *Re RJ (Wardship)* [1999] 1 FLR 618 or to make a

If the court is not in a position to make a final order it can make interim orders, ie an interim care or supervision order, or an interim s 8 order. It is to be observed that at the interim stage the court retains significantly more control over the child than when it makes a final order. The philosophy of the Act is that those in whom parental responsibility is vested should be able so far as possible to exercise that responsibility without interference by the court. This is equally true whether responsibility vests in individuals or in the local authority.

It remains to consider these options in more detail.

(b) Section 8 orders[589]

Where the threshold criteria are satisfied

Applying the proposition that the courts should begin with a preference for the least interventionist approach, in those cases where the threshold criteria have been satisfied and some order is thought necessary, consideration should first be given to the appropriateness of a s 8 order.

One example may be where it is felt that, though parental care had been inadequate in the past, given sufficient support in the future a parent could cope. A court could for instance grant a residence order to a parent on condition that she live at a mother and baby unit for some specified time.[590] In this type of case, although it is outside the court's power to make a specific issue order forcing the local authority to provide a particular service,[591] it is a legitimate expectation that a service will be provided, since notwithstanding the residence order the child may still qualify for services as a child in need.[592]

Another example where a care order might not be thought appropriate is where abuse has been proved but the perpetrator has since left, or is prepared to leave the home.[593] In such a case a residence order might be made in favour of the remaining parent, perhaps with a prohibited steps order forbidding the perpetrator from contacting the child.[594]

---

combination of s 8 orders and a supervision order under the overall umbrella of wardship, see *Re M and J (Wardship, Supervision and Residence Orders)* [2003] EWHC 1585 (Fam), [2003] 2 FLR 541 and *Re W and X (Wardship: Relatives Rejected As Foster Parents)* [2003] EWHC 2206 (Fam), [2004] 1 FLR 415, discussed further below at p 900.

[589] See generally N Lowe 'The Application of Section 8 Orders to Care Proceedings' in M Adcock, R White and A Holloway (eds) *Child Protection* (1992), pp 43–52.

[590] But note that further conditions, such as having to hand over the child to the care of staff if so requested, cannot be added, as that would be inconsistent with a residence order: see *Birmingham City Council v H* [1992] 2 FLR 323, discussed above at p 534; cf *C v Solihull Metropolitan Borough Council* [1993] 1 FLR 290 in which Ward J made a residence order conditional upon the parents undertaking a programme of assessment and co-operating with all reasonable requests by the local authority to participate in that programme.

[591] See *Re J (Specific Issue Order: Leave to Apply)* [1995] 1 FLR 669.

[592] Accordingly the local authority will be obliged to continue so to treat the child pursuant to the duties under s 17(1) and (10): see above, pp 699ff.

[593] For the powers to include an 'exclusion requirement' in interim care and emergency protection orders see below, p 784 and above, p 726. For the powers to make longer term exclusion orders under the Family Law Act 1996 Part IV see above, pp 230ff. Note also that under Sch 2, para 5 to the Children Act 1989, the local authority may give assistance, including cash, to enable that other person to obtain alternative accommodation.

[594] But it seems that what cannot be done is to make it a condition of the residence order that the parent does not invite the other parent, or named person, back into the home: see *Re D (Residence: Imposition of Conditions)* [1996] 2 FLR 281, CA, discussed above, p 534.

A further example is where a parent has been proved inadequate, for example through alcohol or drug dependence, but there is a relative who is already looking after or who could look after the child. In these circumstances a residence order in favour of the relative might be thought preferable to a care order.[595]

Provided the threshold criteria have been satisfied, it is open to the court to make both a s 8 and a supervision order.[596] The advantage of coupling a s 8 order with a supervision order is that the child's upbringing can be closely supervised, and it may be that where it is thought right to make conditional residence orders it will generally also be appropriate to make a supervision order.[597]

It is to be emphasised that the court cannot make both a s 8 order and a care order. The two are inconsistent.[598]

Where the threshold criteria cannot be satisfied

If the threshold criteria under s 31 cannot be satisfied then, although the court cannot make a care or supervision order, it can still make a s 8 order.[599] One example might be where a child accommodated by a local authority has been happily fostered for some time, and the parent wishes to resume care.[600]

The ability to make a residence order in favour of third parties, even though the threshold provisions cannot be satisfied, means that under the 1989 Act children can be removed or kept away from the care of their parents simply based upon the welfare principle. However, as already discussed, children will only be removed from their parental carers where welfare considerations positively demand it.[601]

(c) Supervision orders

Supervision orders can only be made provided the threshold criteria under s 31(2) have been satisfied. However, they can be and frequently are made where the application is for a care order.[602]

The nature and purpose of supervision orders[603]

A supervision order puts the child under the supervision of a designated local authority or a probation officer.[604] It does *not* vest parental responsibility in the local authority, nor does it fix them with the duty under s 22 to safeguard or promote the child's welfare.[605]

---

[595] See eg *Re H (A Minor) (Care or Residence Order)* [1994] 2 FLR 80, but cf *Re M (A Minor) (Care Order: Threshold Conditions)* [1994] 2 AC 424, HL (discussed above, p 740), in which a care order was made notwithstanding that the child was happily living with his mother's cousin, and *Re K (Care Order or Residence Order)* [1995] 1 FLR 675 (discussed below, p 772), in which the grandparents did not want the responsibility of a residence order. Furthermore, it seems unlikely that a court would wish to make an order in favour of the relative without first seeing that person.

[596] For an example, see *Re S (Parenting Skills: Personality Tests)* [2004] EWCA Civ 1029, [2005] 2 FLR 658.

[597] Compare the position on making an interim order under s 38(3) discussed below, p 786.

[598] Sections 9 and 91.

[599] It can also make a family assistance order under s 16, discussed above, pp 577–80.

[600] Cf *Re P (A Minor)(Residence Order: Child's Welfare)* [2000] Fam 15, CA in which in private law proceedings a residence order was made in favour of the applicant foster parents.

[601] See above p 764.   [602] Section 31(5)(a).

[603] See generally the Department of Health's *Guidance and Regulations*, Vol 1, *Court Orders*, paras 3.87ff.

[604] Section 31(1)(b). See also Sch 3, para 9 with regard to the selection of a supervisor.

[605] Section 22 is discussed below, p 795.

The court cannot make both a care order and a supervision order, though it may make both a s 8 order and a supervision order.[606]

The person, under whose supervision the child is or is to be, is known as the supervisor,[607] and for the duration of the order it is his or her duty:

'(a) to advise, assist and befriend the supervised child;[608]

(b) to take such steps as are reasonably necessary to give effect to the order; and

(c) where—

(i) the order is not wholly complied with; or

(ii) the supervisor considers that the order may no longer be necessary,

to consider whether or not to apply to the court for its variation or discharge.'[609]

These basic duties are substantially expanded by Sch 3,[610] which also empowers the court to make orders inter alia for the child's psychiatric or medical examinations.[611]

Supervision orders are designed for cases where an element of child protection is involved.[612] On the other hand, they do not give local authorities the same degree of control over parents as do care orders, from which they are thus clearly distinguishable.[613]

Duration of a supervision order

A supervision order is a short-term order and initially lasts for one year,[614] though it can be made for a shorter period.[615] It can, however, be extended upon an application by the supervisor for up to a maximum of three years from the date when the order was made.[616] An application to extend the period of a supervision order is governed by the welfare principle, so that further proof of the threshold criteria is not required.[617] On the other hand, the court has no power to vary the order to a care order. Instead, if that is what is required, the local authority must make a fresh application under s 31.[618]

Requirements imposed under a supervision order

The essence of a supervision order is to subject the supervised child (regardless of whether he consents) to certain directions by the supervisor. Thus Sch 3, para 2 provides that an order may require the supervised child to comply with any directions given from time to time by the supervisor which require him to do all or any of the following:

'(a) live at a place or places specified in the directions for a specified period or periods;

(b) present himself to a specified person at a place and on a day specified;

(c) participate in specified activities, such as education or training.'[619]

---

[606] See eg *Re B (Care: Expert Witness)* [1996] 1 FLR 667, CA, and *Re DH (A Minor) (Child Abuse)* [1994] 1 FLR 679.

[607] Section 105(1).   [608] Note that there is no duty owed to the parent.

[609] Section 35(1).   [610] See further below.   [611] See further below.

[612] Per Wall J in *Re DH (A Minor) (Child Abuse)* [1994] 1 FLR 679 at 702 relying on the Department of Health's *Guidance*, Vol 1, at para 2.50.

[613] See further below at p 769.   [614] Sch 3, para 6(1).

[615] *M v Warwickshire County Council* [1994] 2 FLR 593.   [616] Sch 3, para 6(3), (4).

[617] *Re A (Supervision Order: Extension)* [1995] 1 FLR 335, CA.

[618] Consequently, the s 31 threshold will have to be re-established as at the date of the hearing: *Re A*, above.

[619] Note that the original provision that such directions may only last for 90 days under Sch 3, para 7(1) was repealed by the Courts and Legal Services Act 1990 Sch 16, para 27.

The precise directions are a matter for the supervisor and not the court,[620] though in no event is the supervisor empowered to give directions as to the child's medical or psychiatric treatment.[621]

As well as empowering supervisors to make directions, a supervision order may also include a requirement that, with his or her consent, a 'responsible person'[622] take all reasonable steps to ensure that the child complies with any direction given by the supervisor.[623]

The fact that the responsible person must consent to the requirement being imposed is crucial to the operation of a supervision order, since there are no direct means of enforcing any of the directions or requirements,[624] and it has been held that the court has no power either to make such agreement a condition of the order[625] or to accept an undertaking to agree.[626]

Although the supervisor is not empowered to give directions as to the child's medical or psychiatric examination or treatment, they can be made the subject of specific direction by the court.[627] In each case, however, the power is, in the case of a child of sufficient understanding to make an informed decision, subject to that child's consent.[628]

At one stage it looked as though Sch 3 might be interpreted as giving the courts powers to make wider directions. In *Croydon London Borough Council v A (No 3)*,[629] for example, it was held that a court could direct that the supervised child and the mother live at a rehabilitation centre, while in *C v Solihull Metropolitan Borough Council*[630] Ward J said that he could not see why an interim supervision order could not be made subject to conditions. It is now apparent that this approach is wrong, for, as Waite LJ put it in *Re V (Care or Supervision Order)*:[631]

'The concept of a supervision order subject to conditions simply cannot be fitted into the framework of the Children Act legislation.'

As his Lordship pointed out:[632]

'Any provisions incorporated into a supervision order, either by direction of the supervisor or by requirements directly stated by the judge, are incapable of being enforced directly

---

[620] Sch 3, para 2(2).   [621] Sch 3, paras 2(3) and 5: discussed further below.

[622] Any person who has parental responsibility for the child and any other person with whom the child is living: Sch 3, para 1.

[623] Sch 3, para 3.

[624] The only sanction is for the supervisor to return to court and ultimately for the local authority to make a fresh application for a care order. See *Re V (Care or Supervision Order)* [1996] 1 FLR 776 at 785 per Waite LJ (see below).

[625] *Re V*, above.   [626] *Re B (Supervision Order: Parental Undertaking)* [1996] 1 FLR 676, CA.

[627] See Sch 3, paras 4 and 5. In the case of examinations the court can either require the supervised child to submit to a medical or psychiatric examination or to submit to any such examination from time to time as directed by the supervisor: Sch 3 para 4(1).

[628] Sch 3, para 4(4)(a) and para 5(5)(a). This wording is stronger than the equivalent provisions in s 38(6) (interim orders), s 43(8) (child assessment orders) and s 44(7) (emergency protection orders), so that even if the decision in *South Glamorgan County Council v W and B* [1993] 1 FLR 574 (discussed below, p 784) that the High Court has inherent jurisdiction to override a child's refusal is thought right, it may nevertheless be thought inapplicable here, given the nature of the provisions.

[629] [1992] 2 FLR 350, per Hollings J.   [630] [1993] 1 FLR 290 at 303–4.

[631] [1996] 1 FLR 776 at 785. See also *Re S (Care or Supervision Order)* [1996] 1 FLR 753, CA.

[632] Ibid at 786.

through any of the ordinary processes by which courts of law enforce obedience to their directions. The only sanction, when any infringement of the terms of a supervision order, or of directions given under it, occurs is a return by the supervisor to court. There the ultimate sanction will be the making of a care order under which the local authority will be given the necessary legal powers to enforce its will.'

Accordingly, Sch 3 should be narrowly construed insofar as it controls the courts' powers.

Supervision and care orders compared

Notwithstanding that before either order may be made the threshold conditions under s 31 have first to be satisfied, care orders and supervision orders are fundamentally different in that the former but not the latter (a) vests parental responsibility in the local authority and (b) places the local authority under an obligation, pursuant to s 22, to look after and to safeguard and promote the child's welfare. As Judge Coningsby QC put it in *Re S (J) (A Minor) (Care or Supervision Order)*:[633]

'We tend to look at supervision orders and care orders under the same umbrella because the threshold criteria for the coming into operation of the two is the same. But when we actually look at the content of the two orders we find they are wholly and utterly different. This is because of s 22 and because of the passing of parental responsibility. *Supervision should not in any sense be seen as a sort of watered down version of care. It is wholly different*' [emphasis added].

The effect of these differences is, as Bracewell J observed in *Re T (A Minor) (Care or Supervision Order)*,[634] that whereas the nature of a supervision order is to help and assist a child whilst leaving full responsibility with the parents, a care order places a positive duty on the local authority to promote the child's welfare and to protect him or her from inadequate parenting. As against this, however, as Hale J pointed out in *Re O (Care or Supervision Order)*,[635] whereas under a care order, contact apart, the court cedes all control over what is to happen to the children to the local authority, under a supervision order the local authority has to return to the court either for an extension, or for a care order if things do not go well. In this limited sense the court retains a greater control under a supervision order than under a care order.

In summary the two orders are different and the temptation to regard supervision simply as a less invasive form of care order should be resisted.[636]

Supervision or 'no order'

Although more attention has been paid to comparing supervision orders with care orders, as Wall J said in *Re K (Supervision Orders)*,[637] it is also important to consider the choice between making a supervision order and no order at all. Indeed it is incumbent upon the court, pursuant to s 1(5), to be satisfied that is in the child's interests to make any order rather than none at all. In this regard the decisive issue is whether the children need more protection than can be given voluntarily. It would be an inappropriate, for example, to

[633] [1993] 2 FLR 919 at 950 and cited with approval by Dillon LJ in *Re V*, above, at 788.
[634] [1994] 1 FLR 103 at 106–7, CA. [635] [1996] 2 FLR 755 at 760. [636] See *Re V*, above.
[637] *Re V*, above.

make a supervision order simply to persuade a reluctant local authority to fulfil its duties to the child concerned under Part III. In *Re K* itself a supervision order was held appropriate since that was the best means of promoting co-operation between the mother and the local authority would allocate greater resources to monitoring the family.

The use of supervision orders

Supervision orders are made less frequently than care orders. In 2004, for example, 3,012 supervision orders were made as against 7,796 care orders.[638] As one commentary has observed[639] 'Local authorities may be reluctant to invest in proceedings to obtain an order which has no powers of enforcement, and where the case is less serious'. Courts may well, however, grant a supervision order as an alternative to what may be seen as a draconian care order. Indeed as Hale J pointed out in *Re O (Care or Supervision Order)*,[640] courts can properly begin with a preference for the less rather than the more interventionist approach. This is further underscored by human rights considerations, namely, that any intervention into family life must be proportionate to the risks to the children.[641] In *Re O (Supervision Order)*,[642] for example, it was evident that the local authority's care plan contemplated a high level of service delivery but without great interference in the family's life nor was there a high risk of matters deteriorating (the mother had mental health problems). In these circumstances it was 'absolutely right' to make a supervision order.

Typically, a supervision order is a realistic option where the plan is for the child to remain at home with the parents and those parents are likely to co-operate with the local authority if the order was made. Supervision orders are not appropriate if there is evidence of immediate harm and it is sought to remove the child from the family, nor should they be used to control an otherwise obdurate or inadequate parent.[643]

The general need for parents to be co-operative should not be taken to mean that a supervision order is without effect. Indeed, one judge[644] has described it as part of a strong package, given that it provides for instant access into the home by a social worker. The ability to direct a treatment programme for the child combined with a finding that the threshold criteria are satisfied has also been described as a 'powerful tool',[645] and there seems no doubt that, where parents are prepared to co-operate, a supervision order has a useful role to play. In *Re B (Care or Supervision Order)*[646] Holman J held that a supervision rather than a care order was more appropriate in a case where the pressing needs of the children were for them to be closely monitored within their home and to undertake work with professionals away from home to teach them how to protect themselves. A supervision rather than a care order was also made in *Oxfordshire County Council v L (Care or Supervision Order)*,[647] where, although there were concerns about the standards of

---

[638] Judicial Statistics 2004, Table 5.2.

[639] R White, P Carr and N Lowe *Children Act in Practice* (3rd edn) 8.179.   [640] Above at 759–60.

[641] See *Re O (Supervision Order)* [2001] EWCA Civ 16, [2001] 1 FLR 923 at (27) and (28) and *Re C and B (Care Orders: Future Harm)* [2001] 1 FLR 611 at (33)–(34).

[642] Above.

[643] See eg *Re T and Re S*, above. But note Hale J's point in *Re O (Care or Supervision Order)*, above at 761 that lack of co-operation by a parent ought not *automatically* to be regarded as removing the supervision option, since it must depend on what assessment is needed.

[644] Judge Coningsby in *Re S (J) (A Minor) (Care or Supervision)*, above at 947.

[645] See White, Carr and Lowe, above at 8.179.   [646] [1996] 2 FLR 693.   [647] [1998] 1 FLR 70.

parenting, the parents themselves had responded well to help in the past and there was no evidence to suggest that they would not continue to be responsive in the future.

(d) Care orders

The effects of a care order

A care order places the child in the care of the designated local authority.[648] The making of a care order discharges any s 8 order,[649] supervision order, and a school attendance order. It also brings wardship to an end.[650]

As far as the designated authority is concerned, care orders have the twofold effect of:

(i)   requiring them 'to receive the child into their care and to keep him in their care while the order remains in force';[651] and

(ii) vesting parental responsibility in the authority.[652]

Whilst in their care local authorities are charged with the duty of safeguarding and promoting the child's welfare.[653]

Placing the child 'in the care' of the designated authority. Although it might be supposed that the effect of a care order is to remove the child from his family home and to place him in institutional or foster care, in fact the phrase 'placing the child in the care of' the authority is properly understood as placing the child under the *control* of the authority. Accordingly, it is consistent with a care order to plan for the child to remain at home with his or her parents.[654] However, where this is the plan, the court should consider why a care order is preferable to the less draconian alternatives of a supervision order or even a residence order. As Hale J said in *Oxfordshire County Council v L (Care or Supervision Order)*,[655] there are three broad reasons why a care order might be preferred to a supervision order where the child is to stay at home. First, it allows the authority to remove the child in cases of emergency and to place him or her elsewhere on a long-term basis—in each case without judicial sanction. But this, in her view, would only be appropriate where the parents' behaviour merits serious criticism. Secondly, it enables the local authority to share responsibility with the parents, which is an appropriate consideration where the parents are or are likely to be unco-operative. Thirdly, it gives the local authority specific duties in relation to the child which may be thought to go beyond the general duties imposed by Part III of the 1989 Act, but this should not be used as an excuse to encourage the local authority to perform statutory duties which they already owe to a child in need under Part III.

---

[648] Section 31(1)(a).

[649] It also discharges any *applications* for a s 8 order, which application should therefore be considered before a care order is made: *Hounslow London Borough Council v A* [1993] 1 WLR 291.

[650] Section, s 91(2)–(5).   [651] Section, s 33(1).   [652] Section, s 33(3)(a).

[653] Under s 22, discussed below, p 795.

[654] As at 31 March 2004 there were 5,900 children 'looked after' who were placed with parents, representing 10% of all children looked after: *Children Looked After by Local Authorities* Table 9.

[655] [1998] 1 FLR 70—a care order was not made because, notwithstanding the parents' past lapses, they were not unco-operative and seemed to have the capacity to work with and learn from the local authority social worker. See also *Manchester City Council v B* [1996] 1 FLR 324; cf *Re T (A Minor) (Care or Supervision Order)* [1994] 1 FLR 103, CA, in which a care order was made, the parents' previous four children having been removed on the basis of 'massive neglect'. *Re C (Care or Supervision Order)* [1999] 2 FLR 621—care order made notwithstanding that the local authority, supported by the parents, sought a supervision order.

Care orders might also be appropriate notwithstanding that the child will continue to live with relatives, though again there needs to be good reason for vesting control in the local authority. In *Re K (Care Order or Residence Order)*[656] care proceedings were brought in respect of two children aged five and six following an unexplained injury to the younger child and the accompanying disturbed and bizarre behaviour of the mother (who was subsequently found to be suffering from schizophrenia). Immediately after the incident the children went to live with their grandparents. Subsequently, both children were diagnosed as suffering from a muscle-wasting disease which would confine them to wheelchairs from about the age of 10. There was general agreement that the grandparents had responded magnificently to their grandchildren's needs and there was no question of removing them from their care. Indeed, the local authority, given the level of care by the grandparents, no longer wanted a care order. On the other hand, the grandparents considered that a care order would give them the support that they needed, not least when approaching their old age. It was held that in these unusual circumstances a care order should be made notwithstanding both that the children would continue to live with their grandparents and the local authority's opposition. It was thought right to vest parental responsibility in the authority, and to impose upon them the duty to look after the children, not least when they were older and more difficult to manage. Another consideration was the consequential financial support that would be given by the local authority if a care order was made, namely, a weekly boarding out allowance and a capital allowance to modify the current or any future home of the grandparents to accommodate the children's growing disabilities. As Stuart-White J said, while it would be wholly inappropriate to make a care order *solely* for the purpose of conferring a financial benefit on the carers, such a factor could nevertheless be properly be taken into account and weighed in the balance with other factors.[657]

'Designated authority.' Under s 31(8) the local authority designated in a care order (including an interim care order) is either:

(a) the authority in whose area the child is ordinarily resident; or

(b) where the child does not reside in the area of a local authority, the authority in whose area any circumstances arose in consequence of which the order is being made.

When determining ordinary residence, s 105(6) directs the court, inter alia, to ignore any period during which the child lives at school or other institution or while he is being accommodated by or on behalf of a local authority. This latter provision has become known as 'the disregard provision'.

Applying these provisions proved difficult but their proper interpretation has now been settled by the Court of Appeal. Based upon the premise that the statutory mechanism is intended only to provide a relatively 'rough and ready' method of designating which of two or more possible local authorities should carry statutory responsibility for a particular child and thus to provide a simple test to enable the court to make a rapid designation of

---

[656] [1995] 1 FLR 675.

[657] Though in respect it might be noted that residence order allowances can be paid by the local authority to individuals, see above p 701.

the authority responsible for the care order, *Northamptonshire County Council v Islington London Borough Council*[658] establishes the following:

(1) section 31(8)(b) is to be interpreted as if it said 'where the child does not *ordinarily* reside in the area of a local authority' etc;

(2) ordinary residence is to be judged by reference to where the child was living immediately before the disregard period and, save in exceptional circumstances, events during the disregard period are to be ignored and

(3) the provisions do not vest the court with a broad discretion to designate any local authority area that might loosely be said to be in the frame.

Two subsequent Court of Appeal cases, *C (A Child) v Plymouth County Council*[659] and *Re H (Care Order: Appropriate Local Authority)*[660] show that departure from this simple approach will rarely be justified.

As Thorpe LJ put it,[661] the decision in *Northamptonshire* on point (2) above was not intended to give the judge 'some sort of discretionary exit from the plain application of the mechanism contained in ss 31 and 105'. In *Re H*, however, it was accepted that the disregard provisions in s 105 should be narrowly construed particularly with regard to the meaning of 'accommodation'. So, for example, placement with relatives under s 23(6)[662] does not rank as accommodation for this purpose.[663]

It has been held[664] that if a care order would designate an authority other than that which applied for the order, there should be early liaison between them and a care plan prepared in co-operation between them.

There is no mechanism for transferring a care order from one authority to another. Accordingly, once a care order has been made, the duty to safeguard and promote the child's interest remains in the designated authority regardless of where the child is living, unless and until the order is ended.[665] This inability to transfer a care order seems an unfortunate gap in the legislation and is the reason why there has been so much litigation as to which authority should be 'designated' in the first place.

Vesting parental responsibility in the designated authority. Notwithstanding the vesting of parental responsibility in the local authority, parents do not lose their responsibility upon the making of a care order.[666] However, important and innovative though this notion of shared responsibility is, control very much rests with the local authority, as is emphasised by s 33(3)(b) which provides that the authority has the power to determine the extent to

---

[658] [2001] Fam 364, CA.

[659] [2000] 1 FLR 875, CA.   [660] [2003] EWCA Civ 1629, [2004] 1 FLR 534.

[661] In *C (A Child) v Plymouth County Council*, above at 879.   [662] Discussed below at p 796.

[663] In this respect the Court of Appeal expressly approved Wall J's analysis in *Re C (Care Order: Appropriate Local Authority)* [1997] 1 FLR 544, that a local authority permitting children in care to live at home were not providing accommodation for the purposes of s 105. See also *Re P (Care Proceedings: Designated Authority)* [1998] 1 FLR 80.

[664] Per Holman J in *L v London Borough of Bexley* [1996] 2 FLR 595.

[665] But note that responsibility for providing advice and assistance to young persons who have formerly been in care but who have attained their majority passes under s 24 to the authority in whose area that person is living: *R v London Borough of Lambeth, ex p Caddell* [1998] 1 FLR 253.

[666] Section 2(6). It will be noted, however, that those who have parental responsibility by virtue of a residence order, will lose it because a care order discharges the s 8 order.

which a parent, guardian, special guardian or a step-parent who has parental responsibility by virtue of s 4A order or agreement may meet his parental responsibility insofar as it is necessary to do so to safeguard or promote the child's welfare.[667] Nevertheless, those mentioned in s 33(3)(b) who have care of the child are still entitled to do what is reasonable in all the circumstances of the case for the purpose of safeguarding or promoting the child's welfare[668] and still retain any right, duty, power, responsibility or authority in relation to the child and its property under any other enactment.[669] It is also established[670] that notwithstanding a care order there is nothing to prevent unmarried parents from making a parental responsibility agreement since that is a self contained facility which does not depend upon the exercise of parental responsibility.[671]

Limitations on the exercise of local authority responsibility. The parental responsibility acquired by a local authority has some specific limitations. They are not allowed to cause the child to be brought up in any religious persuasion other than that in which he would have been brought up if no order had been made. They do not have the right to agree, or to refuse to agree, to an adoption order or a proposed foreign adoption order, nor to appoint a guardian.[672] Furthermore, while a care order is in force no person may cause the child to be known by a new surname without the written consent of every person with parental responsibility or by leave of the court.[673] The same consents are required before a child may be removed from the United Kingdom.[674]

If the local authority wish to arrange for a child in care to live outside England and Wales then, pursuant Sch 2 para 19(1), the court's approval is required.[675] By para 19(3) that approval may only be given if the court is satisfied that:

(a) to live outside the jurisdiction would be in the child's best interests;

(b) suitable arrangements have been or will be made for the child to live abroad;

(c) the child consents (or does not have sufficient understanding to consent);[676] and

---

[667] See eg *Re P (Children Act 1989, ss 22 and 26: Local Authority Compliance)* [2000] 2 FLR 910—in appropriate circumstances s 33(3)(b) permits the local authority to exclude a parent (here an unmarried father without parental responsibility) from information concerning, or participation in, decision making in relation to the child. Note also *Re P (Care Orders: Injunctive Relief)* [2000] 2 FLR 385 in which an injunction requiring the parents to allow their child to attend college without interference and permitting the local authority to monitor the family, was granted ancillary to the care order to support the rights conferred by s 33(3)(b). According to Judge Batterbury in *Re B (A Minor) (Child in Care: Blood Test)* [1992] Fam Law 533, since it is an incident of parental responsibility to take reasonable steps to ascertain who else shares that responsibility, the local authority should pay for what are now scientific tests to determine paternity.

[668] Section 33(5).

[669] Section 33(9). As, for example, the right to consent to the child's marriage. See above, p 55.

[670] *Re X (Parental Responsibility Agreement: Children in Care)* [2000] 1 FLR 517.

[671] This ruling must also apply to married parents making a parental responsibility agreement with a step-parent.

[672] Section 33(6).

[673] Section 33(7). Exceptionally (eg where all contact has been lost) an order can be granted ex parte: *Re J (A Minor) (Change of Name)* [1993] 1 FLR 699.

[674] Section 33(7) and (8)(a).

[675] Compare the position where the child is being accommodated, when the approval of everyone with parental responsibility is required: Sch 2, para 19(2).

[676] Sch 2, para 19(4).

(d) every person with parental responsibility for the child consents to the child living abroad or, if not, that consent is unreasonably being withheld.[677]

With regard to (d) it was held in *Re G (Minors) (Care: Leave to Place Outside the Jurisdiction)*[678] that the proper approach to determining whether consent was being unreasonably withheld was, applying what was then the analogous test in adoption as established in *Re W (An Infant)*,[679] to look at the broad band within which a reasonable person might exercise a responsible choice, taking into account the sacrifice contemplated, but bearing in mind that, unlike in adoption, the parent would not lose parental responsibility. As Thorpe J observed in *Re W (Care: Leave to Place Outside Jurisdiction)*,[680] 'the more the parents are asked to concede, the more readily is their withholding likely to be recognised as reasonable. The less they are being asked to agree the more readily will their withholding be labelled unreasonable.' In that case, where the local authority sought approval for a placement in Scotland in deference to the parents' own wishes, the court had no hesitation in concluding, without a full hearing, that their subsequent withholding of consent was irrational and unreasonable.

Duration of a care order

A care order lasts until the child is 18[681] unless it is brought to an end earlier. An application to discharge the care order may be made by any person with parental responsibility, the child himself, or the designated authority.[682] A person who does not otherwise have parental responsibility can, with court leave, apply for a residence order, which, if granted, ends a care order.[683] The making of an adoption or placement for adoption order also ends any order made under the Children Act 1989.[684]

Controlling the local authority after a care order

It is fundamental to the structure of the 1989 Act that, once a care order has been made, responsibility for looking after the child is vested in the authority and that therefore the court has no general power to keep the case under review. As Lord Nicholls explained in *Re S (Minors)(Care Order: Implementation of Care Plan; Re W (Minors)(Care Order: Adequacy of Care Plan)*,[685] this was a deliberate departure from the previous position under the wardship jurisdiction of the High Court, where the court retained power to give directions to the local authority. In line with this philosophy, as the Court of Appeal confirmed in *Re T (A Minor) (Care Order: Conditions)*,[686] the court cannot fetter local authority control over a child in care by imposing any conditions on a care order. As Nourse LJ put it,[687] 'it is clear beyond peradventure that the court has no power under s 31

---

[677] Sch 2, para 19(5).   [678] [1994] 2 FLR 301, per Thorpe J.

[679] [1971] AC 682. Adoption law was changed in this respect by the Adoption and Children Act 2002, see Ch 15.

[680] [1994] 2 FLR 1087.   [681] Section 91(12).   [682] Section 39(1), discussed below, p 787.

[683] Section 91(1).   [684] Adoption and Children Act 2002, ss 29(2) and 46(2)(b).

[685] [2002] UKHL 10, [2002] 2 AC 291 at [27].

[686] [1994] 2 FLR 423 applying *Re B (Minors) (Termination of Contact: Paramount Consideration)* [1993] Fam 301, CA and approving *Kent County Council v C* [1993] Fam 57, in which Ewbank J held there was no power on a care order to direct that a guardian ad litem remain involved to oversee a rehabilitation programme. See also *Re B (A Minor) (Care Order: Review)* [1993] 1 FLR 421 and *Re S (A Minor) (Care: Contact Order)* [1994] 2 FLR 222, CA, discussed below, p 793.

[687] At 428–9.

to impose any conditions on a care order'. In so holding, the Court of Appeal rejected the argument[688] that 'if the welfare principle is truly paramount, the court must have the power, when initiating the placement into care, to make an order which reflected the full scope of its perception of the child's welfare'. In the court's view[689] the scheme of the Act is clear: the welfare test applies when considering whether to make a care order, but there are no provisions which allow the court to rely on the welfare principle to superimpose conditions on the care order.

Although the court is not divested of *all* powers of control over a child in care, since it retains jurisdiction to consider issues of contact[690] and the power to grant a discharge[691] and to decide whether or not to make an adoption placement order and, ultimately, an adoption order,[692] the making of a care order effectively gives the local authority control over most of the future arrangements for the child including, crucially, determining where and with whom the child is to live and whether or not he should be rehabilitated with his family. Of course, as we have discussed,[693] in deciding whether to make the care order in the first place the court will have regard to the local authority's care plan, but while it can suggest changes to the plan it cannot force the authority to alter its plan and is ultimately faced with the stark choice of whether to accept it or reject it. Once it has made the care order it has no control over whether that plan is implemented.

Notwithstanding this clear position, as Baroness Hale said in *Re G (Interim Care Order: Residential Assessment)*[694] the 1997 President's inter-disciplinary Conference revealed that the courts had concerns about the lack of control over the implementation of the care plan once a care order had been made. This issue was subsequently brought into sharp relief in two cases; one involving Bedfordshire *(Re W)* and the other, Torbay *(Re S)*.

In the former case, Bedfordshire instituted care proceedings in respect of two children the care plan being that they should be placed with the maternal grandparents with continuing contact with the parents. The grandparents, however, lived in the United States but agreed to move to England to care for the children. At first instance, the judge concluded that the children were unable in the immediate future to return safely to their parents. All the parties agreed that the grandparents would be suitable carers but the evidence that they would be able to come to England was 'exiguous in the extreme'. Although the judge described the care plan as inchoate because of all the uncertainties involved, he nonetheless made care orders.

In the second case, Torbay sought care orders for three children. The care plan for the eldest was that he should remain in foster carer which was agreed. But the plan for the two younger children was that an attempt should be made to rehabilitate them with their mother. Counsel for the mother argued that a care order should not be made because she was sceptical about whether Torbay would carry out the plan. She contended that interim

---

[688] Raised by counsel for the guardian, above, at 427.   [689] Per Nourse LJ above at 429.

[690] Under s 34, discussed below, pp 790ff. The boundary between controlling contact under s 34 and attempting to fetter the local authority powers by making a conditional care order can be difficult to draw: see eg *Kent County Council v C*, above, but cf *Re B (A Minor) (Care Order)*, above, and compare *Re S (A Minor) (Care: Contact Order)*, above, with *Re E (A Minor) (Care Order: Contact)* [1994] 1 FLR 146, CA, discussed below, p 794.

[691] Under s 39, discussed below at pp 787ff.

[692] Viz under the Adoption and Children Act 2002, discussed in Ch 15.   [693] Above, p 757.

[694] [2005] UKHL 68, [2005] 3 WLR 1166 at [53].

orders should be made instead. The judge made the care orders expressing confidence that Torbay would implement the care plan. In fact, however, the plan was not implemented in part because of the financial crisis within Torbay leading to substantial cuts in the social services budget.

The Court of Appeal heard appeals in both these unrelated cases together in a decision reported as *Re W and B; Re W (Care Plan)*.[695] They reversed the Bedfordshire decision on the basis that the plan was too uncertain but declined to disturb the decision in the Torbay case. However, in reaching these decisions, as Lord Nicholls summarised it on appeal to the House of Lords,[696] the Court of Appeal fashioned two innovations, namely, enunciating guidelines intended to give a wider discretion to make interim care orders (discussed further below) and more radically a new procedure

'by which at the trial the essential milestones of a care plan would be identified and elevated to a "starred status". If a starred milestone was not achieved within a reasonable time after the date set at trial, the local authority was obliged to "reactivate the interdisciplinary process that contributed to the creation of the care plan". At least the local authority must inform the child's guardian of the position. Either the guardian or the local authority would then have the right to apply to the court for further directions'.

Subsequent to the Court of Appeal decision, application was successfully made to the trial judge in the Torbay case to star various items in the care plan. This starred plan appeared to be working well.

The principal reason that the Court of Appeal, and Thorpe LJ in particular, felt able to make such a radical decision was that without such a system it was their belief that the 1989 Act was incompatible with human rights and that they were consequently mandated by s 3 of the Human Rights Act[697] to interpret the Act in a way to make it compatible.

The House of Lords comprehensively rejected the Court of Appeal's reasoning and decision. Lord Nicholls, who gave the leading judgment, reiterated that the[698]

'cardinal principal of the Children Act is that when the court makes a care order it becomes the duty of the local authority designated by the order to receive the child into its care while the order remains in force. So long as the care order is in force the authority has parental responsibility for the child. The authority also has power to decide the extent to which a parent of the child may meet his responsibility for him . . . The Children Act 1989 delineated the boundary with complete clarity. Where a care order is made the responsibility for the child's care is with the authority rather than the court. The court retains no supervisory role, monitoring the authority's discharge of its responsibilities. That was the intention of Parliament.'

In his view, this clear transgression of the cardinal principle by the Court of Appeal was not justified on human rights grounds. In his view the basic scheme of the Act was not incompatible with Art 8 for as he pointed out it is not the Act that is incompatible; it is the subsequent local authority action or inaction, if any. In any event, the judicial innovation of 'starred milestones' went well beyond the bounds of interpretation as required by s 3 of

---

[695] [2001] EWCA Civ 757, [2001] 2 FLR 582.

[696] Reported as *Re S (Minors)(Care Order: Implementation of Care Plan; Re W (Minors)(Care Order: Adequacy of Care Plan)* [2002] UKHL 10, [2002] 2 AC 291.

[697] Section 3 is discussed above at p 25.   [698] At [23] and [25].

the Human Rights Act 1998 and was tantamount to legislation. He did, however, recognise that while parents might have effective remedies via judicial review[699] or under s 7 of the 1998 Act, such remedies might not always in practice be available to a child without a parent to act for him but that in itself was a breach of Art 13 which was not enacted in the 1998 Act.[700] He similarly acknowledged that a local authority failure to provide proper access to court as required by Art 6 would be a breach in an individual case but that in itself did not make the Act incompatible, though it might signify a lacuna in the Act.

Notwithstanding this comprehensive rejection of the Court of Appeal approach, both Lords Nicholls and Mackay stressed[701] that the decision should 'not obscure the pressing need for the Government to attend to the serious and practical problems identified by the Court of Appeal . . .'. In the response to this plea, s 118 of the Adoption and Children Act 2002, amending s 26 of the Children Act 1989, requires local authorities to keep care plans under review or make a new one where necessary *and* to appoint a person whose task it is to participate in the review, monitor the authority's functions, and, where appropriate refer the care plan to a CAFCASS officer who then has the power to refer the matter back to the court.

Although this scheme is quite similar to that proposed by the Court of Appeal, it has been pointed out[702] that since it relies on the willingness of a person working within the local authority to refer the matter to CAFCASS and on the expeditious work on the part of CAFCASS, rather than on a *requirement* to bring the matter back before the court, it might not necessarily solve the problem.

Whether the law should go further and require court sanction for making *any* subsequent changes to a rehabilitation plan can be debated.

(e) Interim orders

The court's powers to make interim care or supervision orders

Power to make either an interim care or interim supervision order is conferred by s 38. Such orders may be made, either following a s 37 direction by the court to a local authority to investigate the child's circumstances, or on an adjournment in care proceedings.[703] Under s 38(2) such orders cannot be made unless the court 'is satisfied that there are reasonable grounds for believing that the circumstances with respect to the child are as mentioned in section 31(2).' In other words, the court only has to be satisfied that there are reasonable grounds for believing that the so-called threshold conditions exist, rather than having to be satisfied as to their existence. In *Re B (A Minor) (Care Order: Criteria)*,[704] there was evidence before the court to satisfy the test that a girl was likely to suffer

---

[699] Judicial review is discussed below at p 805.   [700] See further discussion below at p 814.

[701] At [106] and [112] respectively.

[702] By R White, P Carr, N Lowe *Children Act in Practice* (3rd edn) at 8.112.

[703] Children Act 1989 s 38(1). When considering adjourning the case the court should be mindful of the general principle that under s 1(2) delay is prima facie prejudicial to the child's welfare. Proceedings should not be adjourned because criminal proceedings are pending against the alleged abuser: *Re TB (Care Proceedings: Criminal Trial)* [1995] 2 FLR 801, CA, contradicting *Re S (Care Order: Criminal Proceedings)* [1995] 1 FLR 151, CA.

[704] [1993] 1 FLR 815. Cf *Re M (Interim Care Order: Removal)* [2005] EWCA Civ 1594, [2006] 1 FLR 1043 in which the evidence was too speculative to give grounds even for a reasonable belief that the threshold criteria were met.

significant harm (arising from allegations of sexual abuse), but difficulties arose over the attribution of that harm. However, as Douglas Brown J said, it was enough that he had reasonable grounds for believing that the s 31 threshold was satisfied. As he put it 'I have not got to be satisfied that they exist in fact.' In that case an assessment was crucial to attributing blame and an interim care order was made which ensured that an investigation could properly be carried out. Notwithstanding these decisions it is important to emphasise that interim orders are not routine matters and even where the application is unopposed it is important that the court is satisfied as to the existence of the criteria and that the removal of a child from the life-long parents even on a temporary basis is fully justified. Failure to do so may be in breach of the parents' human rights.[705]

The nature of interim orders

As Lord Nicholls emphasised in *Re S (Minors)(Care Order: Implementation of Care Plan); Re W (Minors)(Care Order: Adequacy of Care Plan)*,[706] the purpose of an interim care order

'is to enable the court to safeguard the welfare of a child until such time as the court is in a position to decide whether or not it is in the best interests of the child to make a care order. When that time arrives depends on the circumstances of the case and is a matter for the judgement of the trial judge. That is the general, guiding principle'.

They are, in short, temporary holding measures. Moreover, it is also important to appreciate, as Waite LJ emphasised in *Re G (Minors) (Interim Care Order)*,[707] that:

'The regime of interim care orders laid down by s 38 is designed to leave the court with the ability to maintain strict control of any steps taken or proposed by a local authority in the exercise of powers that are by their nature temporary and subject to continual review. *The making of an interim care order is an essentially impartial step, favouring neither one side nor the other, and affording no one, least of all the local authority in whose favour it is made, an opportunity for tactical or adventitious advantage*' [emphasis added].

Further, as Cazalet J observed in *Hampshire County Council v S*:[708]

'Justices should bear in mind that they are not, at an interim hearing, required to make a final conclusion; indeed it is because they are unable to reach a final conclusion that they are empowered to make an interim order. An interim order or decision will usually be required so as to establish a holding position, after weighing all the relevant risks, pending the final hearing. Nevertheless, justices must always ensure that the substantive issue is tried and determined at the earliest possible date. Any delay in determining the question before the court is likely to prejudice the welfare of the child [see s 1(2) of the Act].'

Deciding whether to make a final or interim care order

In principle a final care order should not be made if important evidence remains outstanding or unresolved, eg where assessments are still being made and their outcome awaited. In *Hounslow London Borough Council v A*[709] magistrates were held to be wrong to make a final care order at a time when the assessment of the father as a full-time carer had not been completed. Similarly, in *C v Solihull Metropolitan Borough Council*,[710] where children,

---

[705] See *Re H (A Child)(Interim Care Order)* [2002] EWCA Civ 1932, [2003] 1 FCR 350.
[706] [2002] UKHL 10, [2002] 2 AC 291 at [90].   [707] [1993] 2 FLR 839 at 845.
[708] [1993] Fam 158 at 165.   [709] [1993] 1 FLR 702.   [710] [1993] 1 FLR 290.

the younger of whom had suffered serious non-accidental injuries whilst with the parent, were placed with their grandparents who had a residence order, Ward J held that, pending the outcome of an assessment of the parents to see whether it was safe to return the children to them, the proper order was an interim care order. Such an order kept control of events in the court, which in these circumstances was preferable both to returning the children to the parents subject to a supervision order and to making a full care order which effectively would have abdicated the court's responsibility to the local authority.

However, merely because some issues remain uncertain does not necessarily mean that an interim care order has to be made. For example, in Re L (Sexual Abuse: Standard of Proof)[711] the judge found that two children had been sexually abused. He also found that there was some prospect of rehabilitation with the mother but little such prospect with the father. The authority's care plan was based on removing the children from the family and placing them permanently for adoption. Although the judge expressed the hope that the local authority would be sympathetic to his views regarding rehabilitation, he nevertheless made a full care order in respect of each child based on the belief that an interim order should not be used to control what the local authority was doing. The Court of Appeal refused to interfere. After pointing out that once a care order is made, then—other than by control over contact—the court has no further part to play in the future welfare of the child, Butler-Sloss LJ commented:

'The Children Act provides for many of the most important decisions, including whether to place a child for adoption, to be made by the local authority and therefore there is nothing untoward in the judge leaving the ultimate decision in the hands of the local authority with whom the child is placed.'

She continued by pointing out that interim care orders should not be used to provide continuing control over the activities of the local authority and quoted with approval Wall J's earlier comments in Re J (Minors) (Care: Care Plan):[712]

'. . . there are cases (of which this is one) in which the action which requires to be taken in the interest of children necessarily involves steps into the unknown and that provided the court is satisfied that the local authority is alert to the difficulties which may arise in the execution of the care plan, the function of the court is not to seek to oversee the plan but to entrust its execution to the local authority.'

It has been said[713] that, once all the facts are known, it can seldom if ever be right for the court to continue adjourning the case, and certainly not just to enable the court to monitor the situation.

An attempt to challenge this approach was made in Re W and B; Re W (Care Plan)[714] in which Thorpe LJ expressed the view that the trial judges should have a 'wider discretion' to make an interim care order 'where the care plans seem inchoate or where the passage of

---

[711] [1996] 1 FLR 116. See also Re R (Care Proceedings: Adjournment) [1998] 2 FLR 390, CA.

[712] [1994] 1 FLR 253.

[713] Re P (Minors) (Interim Care) [1993] 2 FLR 742, CA. In overruling Hollings J's decision to make a succession of interim care orders until the placement of two young girls with their mother and her cohabitant who were proposing to move to Northern Ireland was settled, Waite LJ said: 'It can never be right for the court, in granting an interim care order at one sitting, to attempt to lay down a policy which would or might fetter the discretion of any future sitting to grant or refuse a further interim order.'

[714] [2001] EWCA Civ 757, [2001] 2 FLR 582 at [29].

a relatively brief period seems bound to see the fulfilment of some event or process vital to planning and deciding the future'. However, this approach did not find favour with the House of Lords.[715] Lord Nicholls emphasised[716] that 'an interim care order is not intended to be used as a means by which the court may continue to exercise a supervisory role over the local authority in cases where it is in the best interests of a child that a care order should be made'. However, he also said[717] that when deciding whether to make a care order 'the court should normally have before it a care plan which is sufficiently firm and particularised for all concerned to have a reasonably clear picture of the likely way ahead for the child for the foreseeable future'. Furthermore, he seemed to hint that that might lead to some extra flexibility commenting[718] that it was 'a moot point' whether his comments represented a small shift in emphasis from the existing case-law. In the subsequent House of Lords' decision, *Re G (A Minor)(Interim Care Order: Residential Assessment)*,[719] however, it was again emphasised that the court should resist the temptation to postpone making its final decision until any uncertainties have been resolved.

Making directions on interim applications[720]

One of the key differences between a full and interim order is that in the latter case the court may give certain directions. This power is conferred by s 38(6), which states:

'Where the court makes an interim care order, or interim supervision order, it may give such direction (if any) as it considers appropriate with regard to the medical or psychiatric examination or other assessment of the child; but if the child is of sufficient understanding to make an informed decision he may refuse to submit to the examination or other assessment.'

Although clearly empowering courts to make directions as to medical or psychiatric examinations of children,[721] the precise ambit of this provision has been the subject of considerable litigation. *Re O (Minors) (Medical Examination)*[722] and *Berkshire County Council v C*,[723] establish that a s 38(6) direction is binding upon the local authority and therefore (a) amounts to an 'order' that can be appealed under s 94, but (b) has otherwise to be obeyed, the lack of resources being no excuse.[724]

In *Re O* Rattee J upheld a magistrates' direction that medical tests be carried out on two children inter alia to determine whether they were HIV positive.[725] He dismissed the argument that the direction was made ultra vires (since the results of the tests were not

---

[715] The appealed case is reported as *Re S (Minors)(Care Order: Implementation of Care Plan); Re W (Minors)(Care Order: Adequacy of Care Plan)* [2002] UKHL 10, [2002] 2 AC 291.

[716] At [90].   [717] At [99].   [718] At [102].

[719] [2005] UKHL 68, [2005] 3 WLR 1166 at [57], per Baroness Hale.

[720] For a review of the legislative history see the analysis by Baroness Hale in *Re G*, above at [63]–[64].

[721] But it is not confined to such directions, see *Re B (Interim Care Order: Directions)* [2002] EWCA Civ 25, [2002] 1 FLR 547 in which the court directed the mother and child to live at a particular home. But note the criticism of this decision by Lord Scott in *Re G (A Minor)(Interim Care Order: Residential Assessment)* [2005] UKHL 68, [2005] 3 WLR 1166 at [12] that the order strayed beyond an 'assessment'. See further below at p 783.

[722] [1993] 1 FLR 860.   [723] [1993] 1 FLR 569.

[724] But see *Re JN (Care: Assessment)* [1995] 2 FLR 203 in which Thorpe J took no action against a local authority for thwarting an assessment by refusing to finance it.

[725] It has since been held that applications seeking HIV tests should be heard by the High Court. Note *Re HIV Tests* [1994] 2 FLR 116, per Singer J.

relevant to the court's consideration of the threshold under s 31) on the ground that the results were bound to have a bearing on the children's long-term future, ie they were relevant to the 'welfare stage' of the care proceedings.

A s 38(6) direction that the child be assessed by a suitably qualified social worker was similarly upheld in the *Berkshire* case, where Johnson J rejected the argument that the direction was ultra vires on the ground that it imposed an obligation on the authority that could conflict with their own assessment of the priorities of competing demands upon their limited financial resources (which, they submitted, was a matter for the Director of Social Services who is accountable to the authority's elected representatives). Johnson J acknowledged that such directions could have substantial implications for the authority, but nevertheless ruled that, provided proper account was taken of the financial and resource implications, the court could properly make such a direction.

The ambit of s 38(6) was again brought into issue in relation to whether it empowered the court to direct a residential assessment. The matter was authoritatively resolved by the House of Lords in *Re C (A Minor) (Interim Care Order: Residential Assessment)*.[726] In that case the child suffered unexplained injuries while in the care of his parents. An expert considered the injuries to be non-accidental and the local authority social workers them-selves recommended (supported by the guardian and the clinical psychologist) an in-depth assessment involving both parents and the child at a residential unit. The local authority, however, resisted the recommendation inter alia because of the lack of explanation for the injuries by the parents and because of their unstable relationship. They considered that rehabilitation could expose the children to an unacceptable level of risk and accordingly were not prepared to pay the considerable sum of £18,000–£24,000 for the residential placement, which in any event, in their view, had little chance of success. Could they be ordered to carry out the assessment? The House of Lords ruled that both s 38(6) and s 38(7) (which empowers the court to direct there be no such examination or assessment) should be broadly construed to confer jurisdiction on the court to order or prohibit any assessment which involves the participation of the child and which is directed to providing the court with material which is necessary to enable it to reach a proper decision at the final hearing. They rejected the argument based on the ejusdem generis principle that (a) 'assessments' had to be of the same type as medical or psychiatric; and (b) the powers were confined to assessments 'of the child' and not of the parents. With regard to the latter, Lord Browne-Wilkinson pointed out that it was impossible to assess a young child divorced from his environment or his parents.[727]

The House also rejected the argument that the local authority are better qualified than the court to decide whether expenditure on such a scale is a sensible allocation of their limited resources. Lord Browne-Wilkinson pointed out that such an argument could not be made in respect of directed medical treatment under s 38(6), so why should it be for other assessments? In any event, to hold otherwise would be tantamount to allowing—

'... the local authority to decide what evidence is to go before the court at the final

---

[726] [1997] AC 489. See also *Re M (Residential Assessment Directions)* [1998] 2 FLR 371, in which it was held that the child's welfare was not the paramount consideration when deciding whether to make directions under s 38(6).

[727] Though note that there is apparently no power of the court to order *parents* to take part in any assessment against their wishes—see Lord Browne-Wilkinson in *Re C.*

hearing—to allow the local authority by administrative decision to pre-empt the court's judicial decision.'

In his Lordship's view that cannot be the law. As he said, the 1989 Act:

'. . . should be construed purposively so as to give effect to the underlying intentions of Parliament. As I have sought to demonstrate, the dividing-line between the functions of the court on the one hand and the local authority on the other is that a child in interim care is subject to control of the local authority, the court having no power to interfere with the local authority's decisions save in specified cases. The cases where, despite that overall control the court is to have power to intervene are set out, inter alia, in s 38(6) and (7). The purpose of s 38(6) is to enable the court to obtain the information necessary for its own decision, notwithstanding the control over the child which in all other respects rests with the local authority. I therefore approach the subsection on the basis that the court is to have such powers to override the views of the local authority as are necessary to enable the court to discharge properly its function of deciding whether or not to accede to the local authority's application to take the child away from its parents by obtaining a care order.'

The ambit of s 38(6) was further considered by the House of Lords in *Re G (A Minor)- (Interim Care Order: Residential Assessment).*[728] The child in question had become the subject of care proceedings almost immediately upon her birth because of concerns about the mother's ability to care for her following the death of her second child resulting from non-accidental injuries. (Her first child was placed in her father's care). The local authority agreed to a six to eight week residential placement for the parents and child at a hospital specialising in the assessment and treatment of severely disturbed adults and their families. This period was later extended for a further four weeks specifically to assess the risk that the mother posed to the child. At the end of this period the hospital and an expert instructed by the local authority agreed that there was a significant shift in the mother's ability to address her involvement in the second child's death, and further that with appropriate therapeutic intervention the mother was likely to respond sufficiently well so as to be able to safely parent her child. The local health authority were not, however, willing to fund this further treatment and what was in issue was whether the court had the power under s 38(6) to direct the local authority to fund this treatment. Upholding the first instance decision, and overruling the Court of Appeal, the House of Lords held there was no power to make the direction since in effect it amounted to treatment of the mother rather than an assessment of the child's position.

A succinct summary of the decision was given by Lord Mance who said:[729]

'any assessment order by s 38(6) . . . by a court when making an interim care order, is intended to take place and be completed over a relatively short period, focussing on the current position of the child in that period; . . . What is not permissible under s 38(6) is the giving of directions for a longer process aiming at bringing about long-term change. Secondly, . . . directions under s 38(6) can only be made if they can properly be described as being with regard to the medical or psychiatric examination or other assessment "of the

---

[728] [2005] UKHL 68, [2005] 3 WLR 1166, for comments on which, see J Cohen and C Hale 'Treatment or Therapy: The House of Lords Decision in *Re G (Interim Care Order: Residential Assessment*' [2006] Fam Law 294.

[729] At [73].

child", rather than if they involve, as here, a programme focussed in substance on the child's parent and the improvement of her parenting skills.'

Baroness Hale concluded her judgment by saying:[730]

'what is directed under s 38(6) must clearly be an examination or assessment of the child, including where appropriate her relationship with her parents, the risk that her parents may present to her, and the ways in which those risks may be avoided or managed, all with a view to enabling the court to make the decisions which it has to make under the 1989 Act with the minimum of delay. Any services which are provided for the child and the family must be ancillary to that end. They must not be an end in themselves.'

Arguments about the parents' Art 8 rights were dealt with robustly. As Lord Scott said,[731] 'There is no Art 8 right to be made a better parent at public expense.' Among other issues raised by this case was (a) the length of the interim hearing itself, Baroness Hale, indicating that courts should not be spending a full day as in this case, on the application for an assessment and (b) the funding position, in which the question of whether or not a local authority can be compelled to fund that part of an assessment that will not be paid for by the Legal Services Commission,[732] was left open by the Lords.

While no doubt there will remain cases where it is hard to distinguish assessment from treatment there can be few quibbles with the overall thrust of *Re G*. To have held otherwise would have, as Baroness Hale pointed out,[733] conflicted with the cardinal principle,[734] namely, that it is for the court to decide (without undue delay) whether or not to make a care order and for the local authority to decide how the child should be cared for once an order has been made.

Notwithstanding that s 38(6) expressly says that a child of sufficient understanding to make an informed decision may refuse to submit to an examination or assessment Douglas Brown J held in *South Glamorgan County Council v W and B*[735] that he had an inherent power to override a competent child's refusal to submit to an examination. In doing so he purported to follow *Re W (A Minor) (Medical Treatment)*,[736] in which the Court of Appeal overruled a 16-year-old anorexic child's refusal of treatment. However, with respect to Douglas Brown J, it is one thing to interpret a statute—in the case of *Re W*, s 8 of the Family Law Reform Act 1969, which permits 16- and 17-year-olds to give valid consent to medical treatment—restrictively, but quite another flatly to contradict it. It is suggested that the *South Glamorgan* decision is bad law and ought not to be followed.

Attaching an exclusion requirement to an interim care order

The Law Commission considered[737] that the courts should be able to exclude a suspected abuser from the family so as to be able to protect a child without having to remove him or

---

[730] At [69].   [731] At [24].

[732] As Cohen and Hale, above, point out (at 297), the Legal Services Commission will not provide funding for anything that can be considered therapy or treatment, citing Legal Services Commission, 'Public Law Children Act Proceedings the Costs of Treatment, Therapy or Training' in *Focus* Issue 49 (December 2005).

[733] At [57].

[734] Following Lord Nicholls in *Re S (Minors)(Care Order: Implementation of Care Plan); Re W (Minors: Care Order: Adequacy of Care Plan)* [2002] UKHL 10, [2002] 2 AC 291 at [28] and discussed above at p 775.

[735] [1993] 1 FLR 574.   [736] [1993] Fam 64, CA, discussed above at p 365.

[737] Law Com No 207, *Domestic Violence and the Occupation of the Family Home* (1992).

her from the home. Implementing their recommendation, the Children Act 1989 was amended by the Family Law Act 1996 to empower the courts to add, either upon application or its own motion, an exclusion requirement to an interim care order.[738] This power is conferred by s 38A.

Under s 38A(1) an exclusion requirement may only be added to an interim care order and not therefore to an interim supervision order; nor, in the former case, may it be added to an order based on the child being beyond parental control. In any event, before an exclusion requirement may be made the court must be satisfied of three conditions:[739]

(1) there is reasonable cause to believe that if a relevant person is excluded from the child's home the child will cease to suffer or cease to be likely to suffer significant harm;

(2) there is another person (whether a parent or someone else) living in the home who is able to give the child the care which it would be reasonable to expect a parent to give; and

(3) that other person consents[740] to the inclusion of the exclusion requirement.

The exclusion requirement requires[741] the relevant person to leave the dwelling house in which he is living with the child, and prohibits him from re-entering. It may also exclude him from a defined area in which the dwelling house is situated. The requirement cannot last longer than the interim order though it can be made for a shorter period.[742] When seeking an exclusion requirement applicants must prepare a separate statement of the evidence in support and that statement together with a copy of the order must be served on the relevant person.[743] Best practice requires the statement to be separate and self-standing setting out in concise form the factual material relied upon, to state the relevant statutory requirements and to make it clear that the particular person is required to leave the dwelling house.[744]

The court can attach a power of arrest to the exclusion requirement,[745] which entitles a police constable to arrest without a warrant any person whom he has reasonable cause to believe is in breach of the requirement.[746] Instead of formally making an exclusion requirement courts can accept undertakings in similar terms,[747] but in these cases no power of arrest can be attached.[748]

If, while the exclusion requirement is in force, the local authority remove the child from the dwelling house for more than 24 hours, then the requirement or undertaking ceases to have effect.[749]

---

[738] For a similar power to add an exclusion requirement to an emergency protection order see above at p 726. The Law Commission, above at para 6.17, found no support for long-term exclusion as an alternative to a care order.

[739] Section 38A(2).

[740] This consent must be in writing or given orally to the court: FPR 1991 r 4.24; FPCA 1991 r 25.

[741] Section 38A(3).   [742] Section 38A(4).   [743] FPR 1991, r 4.24A, FPCA 1991, r 25A.

[744] Re W (Exclusion: Statement of Evidence) [2000] 2 FLR 666.   [745] Section 38A(5).

[746] Section 38A(8).

[747] Section 38B and see Sch 2 para 5—power to assist suspected perpetrator to obtain alternative accommodation, discussed above, p 702.

[748] Section 38B(2).   [749] Section 38A(10), s 38B(2).

Duration and renewal of interim orders

The duration of interim orders is governed by s 38(4)–(5) which is surely among the most obscurely worded provisions in the whole Act. However, it was established by *Gateshead Metropolitan Borough Council v N*[750] that the court is empowered in principle to make any number of interim orders. Under s 38(4) an initial order may last a maximum of eight weeks and any subsequent order for a maximum of four weeks. One complication is if the initial order is made for a short period, say for two weeks. In that case a second order can use up the remainder of the eight weeks, ie in the cited example, six weeks.

Alternative orders under s 8

As an alternative to making an interim care order the court may make a residence order or other s 8 orders for a limited period. As the Department of Health's *Guidance* says,[751] the two main objectives of these powers are 'to enable the child to be suitably protected while proceedings are progressing where this is required, and to see that interim measures operate only for as long as necessary'.

The combination of s 11(3) and s 11(7) allows the court to make an order for a specified period and subject to conditions, even though it is not yet in a position finally to dispose of the case. For example, the court could make a residence order until the next hearing in favour of a relative and control the child's contact with a parent for the time being through a contact order or a prohibited steps order.[752] under s 38(3), if the court makes a residence order upon an application for care or supervision, it *must* make an interim supervision order unless it is satisfied that the child's welfare will be satisfactorily safeguarded without it. In other words, there is a rebuttable presumption that if a residence order is made, so should an interim supervision order be. The power to make s 8 orders the court is governed by the paramountcy of the child's welfare under s 1(1) and by the enjoinder under s 1(5) not to make any order unless it considers that doing so would be better for the child than making no order.

7 APPEALS[753]

Before the Children Act 1989 the law governing appeals in public law cases was complicated and anomalous. Some, but not all, parties could appeal against the making of a care or supervision order, but there was no general right of appeal against the refusal to make such orders. Where appeals did lie from magistrates' decisions, they lay before the Crown Court and were by way of a full rehearing.[754] Under the Children Act 1989 the law is straightforward: anyone who was a party in the original proceedings may appeal against the making of or refusal to make a care or supervision order (including an interim order).[755] This means that, like any other party, local authorities now have full rights of appeal.

---

[750] [1993] 1 FLR 811.   [751] Vol 1, *Court Orders*, para 3.35.

[752] The precise order may depend against whom the order is sought to be enforced: see *Re H (Prohibited Steps Order)* [1995] 1 FLR 638, CA and the discussion above at p 523.

[753] For a detailed discussion see R White, P Carr and N Lowe *Children Act in Practice* (3rd edn) 13.1ff.

[754] See generally, H Bevan *Child Law* (1989) paras 14.114–14.116.

[755] Including a direction made under s 38(6): see *Re O (Minors) (Medical Examination)* [1993] 1 FLR 860. Note, however, *Re S (Discharge of Care Order)* [1995] 2 FLR 639, CA, in which it was held that an application to discharge a care order should be made rather than applying for an extension to appeal out of time.

Appeals from magistrates' decisions lie to the High Court,[756] and from the county court and High Court to the Court of Appeal.[757] In the latter case, however, permission to appeal is required,[758] save where the appeal is against inter alia a secure accommodation order made under s 25.[759] In this respect a distinction is drawn between first and second appeals (i.e. where the appeal is from a decision which itself was a determination of an appeal). In the former case permission to appeal will only be granted where the court considers that the appeal 'would have a real prospect of success' or 'there is some other compelling reason why the appeal should be heard'.[760] In the case of second appeals a more stringent test applies, namely, that permission should not be granted unless the appeal raises an important point of principle or practice or there is some other compelling reason to hear it.[761]

It is equally established[762] that these appeals are governed by the general principles laid down in *G v G (Minors: Custody Appeal)*,[763] ie that before an appeal can succeed the first instance decision has to be shown to be wrong; it is not enough that the appellate court would have reached a different decision.

8 DISCHARGE OF CARE ORDERS AND DISCHARGE AND VARIATION OF SUPERVISION ORDERS [764]

Section 39 of the Children Act 1989 makes provision for the discharge (but not a variation, since that would interfere with the general principle that management of compulsory care is the local authority's responsibility)[765] of care orders and for the variation and discharge of supervision orders.[766]

(a) Discharge of a care order

Under s 39(1) application for discharge of a care order may be made by any person who has parental responsibility, the child himself or the local authority. The requirement to have parental responsibility means that, since the making of a care order discharges any residence order,[767] only mothers, married fathers, unmarried fathers having parental responsibility by virtue of registration, a s 4 order or agreement,[768] guardians, special guardians and step-parents with responsibility by virtue of an order or agreement under s 4A may apply under s 39. Unmarried fathers without parental responsibility, relatives and foster parents cannot therefore apply under s 39, but they can seek to apply for a residence order under s 8 which operates to discharge a care order.[769] Unmarried fathers can apply as

---

[756] Children Act 1989 s 94(1) and FPR 1991 r 4.22.

[757] County Courts Act 1984 s 77(1) and Supreme Court Act 1981 s 16.

[758] Ie since May 2000 when the Civil Procedure Rules (CPR) 1998 r 52.3 was brought into force.

[759] CPR 1998, r 52.3(1).   [760] CPR 1998, R 52.3(6).   [761] CPR 1991, r 52.3(7).

[762] See eg *Croydon London Borough Council v A* above, and *Re G (A Minor) (Care Evidence)* [1994] 2 FLR 785, CA. In the case of appeals to the Court of Appeal see CPR 1998 r 52.11(3).

[763] [1985] 1 WLR 647, HL, discussed above, p 576.

[764] See generally the Department of Health's *Guidance and Regulations*, Vol 1, *Court Orders*, paras 3.54 et seq.

[765] Department of Health's *Guidance and Regulations*, Vol 1, para 3.54.

[766] For the background to the provision, see the *Review of Child Care Law*, DHSS, 1985, ch 20.

[767] Children Act 1989 s 91(2).   [768] Discussed above, pp 409ff.

[769] Children Act 1989 s 91(1). See also above at p 520.

of right for a residence order, but others will need first to apply for leave.[770] There is nothing to prevent those with parental responsibility from applying for a residence order rather than for a discharge under s 39, though unless there is a dispute between the applicants there would be little advantage in doing so.[771]

So far as the child is concerned, s 39(1)(b) has been interpreted[772] as giving a right to apply, so that unlike the private law there is no requirement to obtain the leave of the court. In practice most applications for discharge of care orders are made by local authorities, who are required by the Review of Children's Cases Regulations 1991[773] to consider at least at every statutory review of a case of a child in their care whether to apply for a discharge.[774] Furthermore, as part of each review the child has to be informed, inter alia, of steps he may take himself for the discharge of the order.

Rather than grant the discharge simpliciter the court is empowered to substitute a supervision order.[775] In doing this there is no requirement that the threshold provisions under s 31(2) be proved again.[776] Indeed, the controlling principle in all such applications is the paramountcy of the child's welfare,[777] and in reaching its decision the court is required to have regard to the statutory checklist under s 1(3).[778] This means, as the Court of Appeal held in *Re S (Discharge of Care Order)*,[779] that the jurisdiction under s 39 is entirely discretionary; there is, for example, no obligation upon the applicant to satisfy the court that the threshold requirements under s 31 no longer apply. Instead, in deciding what, if any, order to make, the primary focus must be on the child's welfare as it appears to be at the date of the discharge hearing. In assessing the child's welfare, an important consideration is, as s 1(3)(e) directs the court to consider, any harm that the child has suffered or is at risk of suffering. In the vast majority of cases the court is only likely to be concerned with evidence of recent harm and appraisal of current risk. However, the Court of Appeal in *Re S* accepted that on very limited occasions the court might properly be concerned with the soundness of the original findings in the earlier care proceedings. In so ruling, however, the court emphasised that the family courts should be alert to see that this theoretical power should not be abused by allowing issues that have already been determined to be litigated afresh. It may be added, however, that absence of a risk of harm to a child returning home may not in itself be enough to justify discharging the care order.[780] Parents (or the child) may have difficulty in establishing that a discharge is in the child's interests, especially where there has been little contact.[781]

---

[770] See below, p 805 for discussion of foster parents' use of this provision.

[771] See above, p 540. Quaere whether s 40(4) operates to permit the court to substitute a supervision order and whether the automatic embargo against re-applying for six months without leave of the court under s 91(15) applies upon a s 8 application? In the latter case the court can use its powers under s 91(14) to provide that no further application may be made without leave.

[772] *Re A (Care: Discharge Application by Child)* [1995] 1 FLR 599, per Thorpe J.   [773] Sch 2, para 1.

[774] Sch 1, para 5 to the 1991 Regulations, in respect of which, note the Law Society's *Good Practice in Child Care Cases* (2004) para 2.4 which reminds local authority solicitors to be mindful of this obligation.

[775] Children Act 1989 s 39(4). But it has no power to substitute an interim care order: *NP v South Gloucestershire County Council* (2005) 7 November, CA, cited by Clarke Hall and Morrison at 1 [1011].

[776] Section 39(5).   [777] Section 1(1).   [778] Discussed above, pp 468ff.

[779] [1995] 2 FLR 639, CA.

[780] See the *Review of Child Care Law*, op cit, para 20.17 and A Bainham *Children: The New Law* (1990) para 5.76.

[781] See *Re S and P (Discharge of Care Order)* [1995] 2 FLR 782 in which Singer J upheld a magistrates' decision, that having heard the mother's oral evidence, they should proceed no further with the case since it

Contrary to the recommendation of the *Review of Child Care Law*,[782] the 1989 Act makes no express provision to postpone the discharge of a care order to allow for a gradual or phased return of the child to his family. How far this can be done by other means is debatable. The best option would seem to be for the court to control rehabilitation through its powers under s 34 to make care contact orders (see further, below), though technically such orders can only be made upon express application. The power under s 40(3) to postpone the effect of a discharge order or to subject a care order to conditions, and which is suggested by some commentators[783] to provide the appropriate power, only arises where an appeal is pending. The alternative of granting a residence order to the parents coupled with conditions under s 11(7)[784] and even a supervision order is limited in the sense that essentially the child must live with the residence holder;[785] it would therefore not be possible to grant a residence order to the parents but to provide under s 11(7) that the child remains with its foster parents with increasing contact to the parents. In view of these difficulties one wonders why provision for phased returns was not made.[786]

Once an application has been disposed of, no further application without leave can be made within six months.[787]

(b) Discharge and variation of supervision orders

Under s 39(2) applications for discharge or variation of a supervision order may be made by any person who has parental responsibility for the child, the child himself or the supervisor. In addition, under s 39(3), a person who is not entitled to apply for a discharge but is a person with whom the child is living, can apply to vary a requirement made upon him under the supervision order.[788]

As with applications for the discharge of care orders, in deciding what order to make the court must apply the principle of the paramountcy of the child's welfare. It cannot, however, make a care order unless the criteria under s 31(2) have been satisfied.[789]

No application may be made without leave of the court within six months of the disposal of a previous application.[790]

---

was clearly hopeless. But note FPR 1991 r 4.16(2)(b); FPCA 1991 r 16(2)(b) which require the court to give the guardian, the solicitor for the child and the child himself, if of sufficient understanding, the opportunity to make representations.

[782] Above, para 20.26.

[783] J Masson and M Morris *Children Act Manual* (1992) p 118.

[784] See eg *Re G and M (Child Orders: Restricting Applications)* [1995] 2 FLR 416, where residence orders were made on condition that the mothers did not bring their children into contact with their fathers who had been found guilty of sexual offences on young people.

[785] See *Birmingham City Council v H* [1992] 2 FLR 323, discussed above at p 534.

[786] This was thought to be such a serious defect of the old law that in *Re J (A Minor) (Wardship: Jurisdiction)* [1984] 1 All ER 29 the Court of Appeal allowed a child to be warded as a rare exception to the so-called '*Liverpool* principle': see below, p 804.

[787] Children Act 1989 s 91(15).

[788] A requirement made under Sch 3 to the 1989 Act: see above, p 767.

[789] There is no similar provision to that substituting a supervision order for a care order under s 39(5), discussed above.

[790] Section 91(15).

F CONTACT WITH CHILDREN IN CARE [791]

1 INTRODUCTION

The Children Act 1989 places considerable importance on the active promotion by local authorities of contact between children being looked after by them and their families, even to the extent of helping with the costs incurred in the visit.[792] This duty continues after a care order has been made and is underscored by the general provision under s 34(1) that there be reasonable contact between the child and inter alia his parents, which can only be departed from by agreement or by court order.

Before the Act, although emphasis was placed on the importance of maintaining contact between the child and his family,[793] the arrangements were mainly within the exclusive control of the local authorities. Only if contact was refused or terminated (but not if restricted) was it possible for parents, guardians or custodians to challenge the decision in court.[794] Even this was an inadequate remedy, since no application could be made until well after the termination or refusal,[795] so that by the time the issue got to court, magistrates often had little choice but to uphold the local authority's decision.[796] Moreover it had been held[797] that once the termination or refusal had been upheld by the court there could be no further challenges.

Implementing the recommendations of the *Review of Child Care Law*,[798] and anticipating that the continued inability to challenge restrictions would be contrary to the European Conventions on Human Rights,[799] s 34 effectively turned the previous law on its head by requiring the local authority to seek a court order *before* terminating or restricting reasonable contact. This fundamental change, arguably among the most significant changes introduced by the 1989 Act,[800] means that parents and others have a more realistic chance

---

[791] See generally the Department of Health's *Guidance and Regulations*, Vol 1, *Court Orders*, paras 3.75 et seq and Vol 3, *Family Placements*, ch 6.

[792] Children Act 1989 Sch 2, para 16.

[793] In particular by the Code of Practice: Access to Children in Care, discussed in the 7th edition of this work at pp 469–70. The Code was superseded by the 1989 Act: cf Department of Health's *Guidance and Regulations*, Vol 3, at para 6.5.

[794] Child Care Act 1980 ss 12A–F, discussed in the 7th edition of this work at pp 481 et seq. It had become established that access decisions could not be 'reviewed' by the court in wardship (see below, p 803), though in cases of impropriety recourse could have been had to judicial review (discussed below, p 805).

[795] This was because notice of refusal or termination had first to be served by the local authority: Child Care Act 1980 s 12B.

[796] In a study carried out by S Millham, R Bullock, K Hosie and M Little *Access Disputes in Child Care* (1989) p 53, of 309 terminations notice only nine parents (3%) re-established contact through legal proceedings.

[797] *R v West Glamorgan County Council, ex p T* [1990] 1 FLR 339.

[798] Ch 21; cf the Second Report of the House of Commons Social Services Committee 1983–1984 (the 'Short Report') HC 360, paras 73 and 324 which expressed concern that local authority power had already been eroded too far by the access provisions under the Child Care Act 1980.

[799] See eg *R v United Kingdom* [1988] 2 FLR 445, E Ct HR; *O v United Kingdom* (1987) 10 EHRR 82, ECtHR; *W v United Kingdom* (1987) 10 EHRR 29, E Ct HR; and *B v United Kingdom* (1987) 10 EHRR 87, ECtHR.

[800] According to research by H Cleaver (see *Fostering family contact* (2000)) four times as many children in foster care had weekly contact with their parents after implementation of the Act as before.

of opposing local authority contact plans. Furthermore according to Wall J in *Re F (care: termination of contact)*,[801] the scheme under s 34 is fully 'Human Rights compliant'.

2 THE SCHEME UNDER SECTION 34

(a) The presumption of reasonable contact

The basic position, set out by s 34(1), is that local authorities must normally allow the child reasonable contact with his parents (including the unmarried father regardless of whether he has parental responsibility) or guardians, special guardians, step-parents who have parental responsibility by virtue of s 4A,[802] a person in whose favour there was a residence order immediately before the making of the care order and a person who had the care of the child by virtue of an order under the High Court's inherent jurisdiction. The local authority, the child and any person concerned are expected, as far as possible, to agree upon reasonable arrangements before the care order is made.[803] In any event, local authorities are expected to provide details of their proposals for contact when applying for an interim or full care order.[804] Section 34(11) requires the court, before making a care order,[805] to consider any contact arrangements that the authority have made or propose to make and to invite the parties to the proceedings to comment on those arrangements. As Ewbank J observed,[806] 'reasonable contact' is not the same as contact at the discretion of the local authority: rather it implies either that which is agreed between the local authority and the parties, or, in the absence of such an agreement, contact which is objectively reasonable.

(b) Departing from the general presumption

As an exception to the presumption of reasonable contact, s 34(6) permits a local authority in matters of urgency to refuse contact for up to seven days provided 'they are satisfied that it is necessary to do so in order to safeguard or promote the child's welfare'. In such cases the local authority are required to give written notice explaining the decision to the child, if he is of sufficient understanding, and to any person with whom there is a presumption of reasonable contact.[807]

Apart from this limited power it is incumbent upon the local authority to seek a court order restricting or denying contact,[808] if they wish to depart from the general presumption.[809]

---

[801] [2000] 2 FCR 481.

[802] Ie by a parental responsibility order or agreement, pursuant to the changes made by the Adoption and Children Act 2002, discussed above at p 422.

[803] See the Department of Health's *Guidance and Regulations*, Vol 1, para 3.76 and Vol 3, para 6.2.

[804] Vol 3, para 6.2.

[805] Including an interim care order: see s 33(11).

[806] In *Re P (Minors) (Contact with Children in Care)* [1993] 2 FLR 156 at 161; cf *L v London Borough of Bromley* [1998] 1 FLR 709 in which Wilson J held that a magistrates' order that contact be at the local authority's discretion could not be interpreted as absolving them of their duty to afford reasonable contact.

[807] Contact with Children Regulations 1991 reg 2.

[808] As they are entitled to do respectively under s 34(2) and (4).

[809] Once an order has been made it can be departed from by agreement: see further below.

(c) The position of the child and other interested persons

A child in care has the right[810] to make an application both for defined contact to be allowed with a named person and for an order authorising the authority to refuse to allow contact with any named person.[811] No doubt in most cases the authority will take the proceedings, but where, for example, the authority are thought to be obstructive, the child may wish to take the initiative. It has been held,[812] however, that the court has no power to force the person named in the order, or, if that person was a minor, the person with whom he or she lived, to have or permit the contact provided for.

It is also open to a person to whom the Act's presumption of reasonable contact applies,[813] and any other person who has obtained leave of the court,[814] to apply for an order about contact at any time if he is dissatisfied with the arrangements made or proposed for contact between the child and himself.[815] The ability of anyone to seek leave means that relatives and former foster parents, for example, may take steps to seek orders. In deciding whether to grant leave[816] it has been held[817] that the court should take account of the criteria set out in s 10(9),[818] which means[819] that the court should have particular regard at least to:

(a) the nature of the contact being sought;

(b) the connection of the applicant to the child (the more meaningful and important the connection to the child, the greater is the weight to be given to this factor);

(c) any disruption to the child's stability or security; and

(d) the wishes of the parents and local authority, which are important but not determinative.

(d) The court's powers

The court is empowered both on making a care order and subsequently, either upon application or acting upon its own motion,[820] to make such order as it considers appropriate as to the contact to be allowed,[821] to refuse contact with a named person,[822] and in each case to impose such conditions (for example, to restrict contact to specific periods or places) as are considered appropriate.[823] The wording of these provisions is wide enough to permit the court to make interim orders, including an interim order for no contact.[824] Although not defined, it is thought that, like a s 8 contact order (from which a s 34 order

---

[810] Note, therefore, that unlike when seeking s 8 orders the child does not need leave of the court, nor, consequently, need such an application be heard in the High Court; cf *Re A (Care: Discharge: Application by Child)* [1995] 1 FLR 599, discussed above, p 788.

[811] Children Act 1989 s 34(2) and (4).

[812] Per Wilson J in *Re F (Contact: Child in Care)* [1995] 1 FLR 510.

[813] Viz those persons mentioned in s 34(1). See above, p 791.   [814] Section 34(3)(b).

[815] Section 34(3).   [816] Leave may be granted by a single justice; FPCA 1991 r 2(5).

[817] *Re M (Care: Contact: Grandmother's Application For Leave)* [1995] 2 FLR 86, CA.

[818] Discussed above at pp 545–8.

[819] Per Ward LJ in *Re M*, above at 95–9 but note that Ward LJ's suggestion that the applicant should also have a good arguable case has since been said to be inappropriate, per Thorpe LJ in *Re J (Leave to Issue Application for Residence Order)* [1993] 1 FLR 114 at [18]–[19], discussed above at p 546.

[820] Children Act 1989 s 34(5).   [821] Section 34(2).   [822] Section 34(4).

[823] Section 34(7).   [824] See *West Glamorgan County Council v P* [1992] 2 FLR 369.

must generally be distinguished),[825] 'contact' under s 34 includes visiting, staying or other contact, for example by letter or telephone.[826] Wide though the powers are, the court is not entitled to make a contact order with a direction that the matter be brought back before the judge at a later date to enable him 'to keep an eye on the case',[827] nor that a guardian should have contact with the child after the care order,[828] in each case because that was simply an attempt to keep the care order under review. It has also been said that in view of the statutory presumption of reasonable contact there should be no need to make such an order *imposing* it.[829] There is no power under s 34 for courts to prohibit local authorities from permitting contact with children in their care.[830]

In deciding what, if any, order to make the court must apply the general principles set out by s 1, ie to regard the child's welfare as the paramount consideration, to consider the statutory check list and to make an order only where it is in the child's interests to do so. The application of the welfare principle where more than one child is involved has proved problematic. In *Birmingham City Council v H*,[831] where both mother and child were in care, the mother (who was herself a 15-year-old child) sought contact with her baby. The House of Lords ruled that, as s 34(4) made it clear that the subject matter of the application is the child in care in respect of whom an order is sought, it was the baby's welfare and not the mother's that was paramount. Lord Slynn also said that[832] if a child in care sought contact with a named person, then that applicant's welfare would still be paramount even if contact was being sought with another child. It seems apparent, however, from the subsequent decision, *Re F (Contact: Child in Care)*,[833] that that analysis depends on the precise nature of the action. In *Re F* a child in care sought contact with her four younger siblings who were not in care. The parents were opposed to such contact and Wilson J held that the application under s 34(2) was misplaced because it could not oblige the parents to permit the contact, since the compulsory effect only runs against the local authority. It was accepted that the appropriate action would have been to have sought a s 8 contact order which, since it concerned the children not in care, was not caught by the embargo under s 9(1).[834] In fact it emerged during the hearing before Wilson J that none of the children wanted contact, so that the s 8 application was dismissed by consent.

Notwithstanding this dismissal Wilson J made the following observations about the application of the welfare principle,[835] namely, that where under s 34(2) an applicant child is seeking contact with other children who are not in care and who are willing to see him, then it is the interests of the applicant child that are paramount. However, if an order is sought under s 8, then it would be the interests of the other children that would be paramount. Where the other children are also in care, some commentators,[836] following the above analysis, have taken the view that it is the children in respect of whom the order

---

[825] A s 8 contact order cannot be made in respect of a child in care: s 9(1), and any such order is discharged upon making a care order: s 91(2). NB, however, a child in care can seek a s 8 contact order in respect of another child not in care: see *Re F (Contact: Child in Care)* [1995] 1 FLR 510, discussed below.

[826] See eg White, Carr and Lowe, above at 8.146.

[827] *Re S (A Minor) (Care: Contact Order)* [1994] 2 FLR 222, CA.

[828] *Kent County Council v C* [1993] Fam 57.   [829] *Re S*, above.

[830] *Re W (Section 34(2) Orders)* [2000] 1 FLR 502, CA.

[831] [1994] 2 AC 212, HL, discussed also at p 465.   [832] Above, at 222.   [833] [1995] 1 FLR 510.

[834] Section 9(1) is discussed in detail above at p 540.   [835] Above at 513–14.

[836] See White, Carr and Lowe, above, at 8.151.

is sought whose welfare is paramount. Assuming this analysis to be correct[837] it may be questioned whether it is right that the issue of paramountcy should be determined simply by the accident of who brought the action.[838]

As will be appreciated, these provisions give the court wide power to control the future direction of the case and, although the court must always be mindful of what the local authority considers practicable, it is not limited by what the authority thinks is reasonable. As Butler-Sloss LJ put it in *Re B (Minors) (Termination of Contact: Paramount Consideration):*[839]

'The presumption of contact, which has to be for the benefit of the child, has always to be balanced against the long-term welfare of the child and particularly, where he will live in the future. Contact must not be allowed to destabilise or endanger the arrangements for the child and in many cases the plans for the child will be decisive of the contact application . . . *The proposals of the local authority, based on their appreciation of the best interests of the child, must command the greatest respect and consideration from the court, but Parliament has given to the court, and not to the local authority, the duty to decide on contact between the child and those named in section 34(1).* Consequently, the court may have the task of requiring the local authority to justify their long term plans to the extent only that those plans exclude contact between parent and child' [emphasis added].

Agreeing with this Simon Brown LJ subsequently observed:[840]

'. . . if on a s 34(4) application the judge concludes that the benefits of contact outweigh the disadvantages of disrupting any of the local authority's long term plans which are inconsistent with such contact then . . . he must give effect to it by refusing the local authority's application to terminate this contact.'

It has been observed[841] that contact should not be refused under s 34(4) whilst there remains a realistic possibility of rehabilitation of the child with the person in question.

(e) Variation and discharge

Upon application by the local authority, child or any person named in the order, the court can vary or discharge any previous order made under s 34.[842] This means that, unlike under the former law,[843] a refusal of contact does not prevent a further application being made.

---

[837] Charles J agreed with Wilson J's analysis in *Re S (Contact: Application by Sibling)* [1998] 2 FLR 897 at 908.

[838] See the criticism of the *Birmingham* decision by G Douglas 'In Whose Best Interests?' (1994) 110 LQR 379, who argues that ultimately each child's welfare has to be balanced against the other's.

[839] [1993] Fam 301 at 311, CA, overruling *West Glamorgan County Council v P (No 2)* [1993] 1 FLR 407.

[840] *Re E (A Minor)(Care Order: Contact)* [1994] 1 FLR 146, CA. See also *Berkshire County Council v B* [1997] 1 FLR 171—since the child's welfare was paramount, contact should be ordered if it was in the child's interests, notwithstanding that the long-term plan of the local authority envisaged termination of parental contact; cf *Re D and H (Termination of Contact)* [1997] 1 FLR 841, CA where it was held on the facts to be wrong to phase out contact contrary to the local authority's recommendations.

[841] Per Simon Brown LJ in *Re T (Minors) (Termination of Contact: Discharge of Order)* [1997] 1 All ER 65, CA.

[842] Section 34(9). Although the Act is not specific on the point, the making of a residence order under s 8 must discharge a s 34 order, since this is dependent upon the existence of a care order, which is itself discharged by virtue of s 91(1).

[843] See *R v West Glamorgan County Council, ex p T*, above.

However, under s 91(17) where an applicant has been refused contact he may not make another such application within six months without leave of the court.

In deciding whether or not to discharge a s 34 order it is established[844] that the child's welfare is the paramount consideration.[845] Upon such an application it is not normally appropriate to reinvestigate whether the original order was made appropriately and the court should be astute to screen out disguised appeals. Instead the court should have two main interlocking considerations in mind, namely, the extent to which circumstances have changed since the making of the order and, in the light of such changes, whether it remains in the child's interests for the original order to stay in place.

It is not always incumbent upon local authorities to seek court sanction to depart from the terms of a s 34 order, since the Contact with Children Regulations 1991[846] allow this to be done by agreement between the authority and the person in relation to whom the order is made, subject inter alia to the agreement of the child if he is of sufficient understanding.[847] The idea behind this provision is to allow for flexibility and partnership in contact arrangements and to obviate the need to go back to court when all concerned agree to this arrangement.[848] The existence of this remarkable power effectively to override a court order by consent has led one judge to say[849] that in cases where the court takes the view that there should be no contact to a child in care it would normally be better to make no order at all rather than an order authorising refusal under s 34(4). The problem, however, with making no order is that the local authority would then continue to be under an obligation to afford reasonable contact.[850]

G LOCAL AUTHORITY DUTIES TOWARDS 'LOOKED AFTER CHILDREN'[851]

The 1989 Act places a number of duties on the local authority in respect of children 'looked after' by them. The phrase 'looked after' refers both to children who are provided with accommodation (which is defined as accommodation for a continuous period of

---

[844] Re T (Minors) (Termination of Contact: Discharge of Order), above.

[845] Aliter where an application is made under s 91(17) for leave to apply—see Re T, above, at 74, per Simon Brown LJ; cf the similar stance in relation to applications for leave under s 91(14) taken by Wilson J in Re R (Residence: Contact: Restricting Application) [1998] 1 FLR 749, CA. See above, p 537.

[846] Reg 3.

[847] It is also incumbent upon the authority to give written notification within seven days to the child's parents or guardian, a person who had a residence order before the care order was made, a person who had care under an order made under the High Court's inherent jurisdiction and any other person whose wishes and feelings the authority consider relevant.

[848] See the Department of Health's Guidance and Regulations, Vol 3, para 6.31. Note also Re W (Section 34(2) Orders) [2000] 1 FLR 502, CA which establishes that courts cannot prohibit local authorities from agreeing to contact to a child in care.

[849] Ewbank J in Kent County Council v C [1993] Fam 57.

[850] See the comment at [1993] Fam Law 134.

[851] See generally Department of Health's Guidance and Regulations, Vol 3, paras 2.17–2.74 and Vol 4, paras 2.17–2.74 and, for a detailed discussion, Butterworths Family Law Service 3A [2469] ff.

more than 24 hours)[852] and to those who are in care as a result of a care order.[853] Children may also be looked after by or on behalf of a voluntary organisation.[854]

In relation to such a child, the authority have the duties to:

(a) safeguard and promote his welfare and to make such use of services available for children cared for by their own parents as appears to the authority reasonable in the case of a particular child;[855]

(b) ascertain as far as practicable the wishes and feelings of the child, his parents, any other person who has parental responsibility and any other person the authority consider to be relevant, before making any decision with respect to a child they look after or propose to look after;[856]

(c) give due consideration, having regard to his age and understanding, to such wishes and feelings of the child as the authority have been able to ascertain, to his religious persuasion, racial origin and cultural and linguistic background and to the wishes and feelings of any person as mentioned in (b) above;[857]

(d) safeguard and promote the welfare of a child looked after by promoting the child's educational achievement.[858]

Underscoring the general duty to consider rehabilitation with the family, s 23(6) provides that, unless to do so would not be reasonably practicable or consistent with the child's welfare, the authority should make arrangements for the child to live with his family. In any event, under s 23(7) the local authority must, so far as is reasonably practicable and consistent with the child's welfare, secure that the accommodation is near his home and that siblings are accommodated together.

Where an authority are 'looking after' a child, they must provide him with accommodation while he is in their care and must maintain him. To this end they may place the child with a family, a relative of his or any other suitable person on such terms as to payment or otherwise as the authority determines.[859] Placement may also be made in a community home, a voluntary home or a registered children's home or by such other arrangements as seem appropriate to the authority.[860]

With regard to placements with the child's own family, a distinction needs to be made between accommodated children and those in care. In the former case, as there are no formal restrictions on removal, he may simply be returned home, in which case the child ceases to be accommodated.[861] In the latter, a child may only be placed with a parent, or other person who has parental responsibility for him, or a person who had a residence order in respect of the child immediately before the care order was made, if a number of requirements, including consultation with certain prescribed persons and supervision and medical examination of the child, have been satisfied.[862]

---

[852] Children Act 1989 s 22(2).   [853] Section 22(1).

[854] Section 22(2). For guidance see *Looking after Children* (Dept of Health, 1995).

[855] Section 22(3).   [856] Section 22(4).   [857] Section 22(5).

[858] Added by the Children Act 2004, s 52.   [859] Section 23(2)(a).   [860] Section 23(2)(b)–(d).

[861] Outside this circumstance, however, it is by no means clear when accommodation ceases, in particular with regard to placements with relatives or friends.

[862] As laid down by the Children Act 1989 s 23(5) and Sch 2, para 13 and the Placement of Children with Parents etc Regulations 1991.

A key duty owed to looked after children is both to make and review the care plan. As one commentary put it[863] 'The purpose of the review is to consider the plan for the welfare of the child and then to monitor the progress of the plan and make decisions to amend the plan as necessary in the light of changed knowledge and circumstances'. Each case of a looked after child must first be reviewed within four weeks of becoming looked after; the second within three months and thereafter at least every six months.[864]

Each responsible authority must appoint an independent reviewing officer to carry out the review.[865] Local authorities also have duties to make provision of advocacy services for children or young persons wishing to make complaints.[866]

H DISPUTING LOCAL AUTHORITY DECISIONS

1 INTRODUCTION

Although, as the Department of Health's *Guidance* says,[867] the Children Act 1989 'envisages a high degree of co-operation between parents and authorities in negotiating and agreeing what form of action will best meet a child's needs and promote his welfare', nevertheless the required co-operation will not always be achieved or will break down. In any event, other members of the family may also be in dispute with the local authority: grandparents, for instance, may feel that they should be able to take over the care of the child. Disputes can also arise between foster parents and the authority. The former, for example, may wish to resist the latter's decision to remove a child from their care.

In some cases the objection may be unfounded, while in others the complaint will be of a relatively minor nature. Many such disputes can be and are resolved informally, often by patient counselling by social workers. However, not all disputes will thereby be solved and, while no doubt every effort is made to promote each child's welfare, serious mistakes are sometimes made by local authorities in their management of the child. There is little doubt too that the interests of parents, of the wider family, or of foster parents are, on occasion, unjustly ignored. The question therefore arises to what extent, and to whom, local authorities are or should be accountable for their management of children in care.

Apart from applying for a discharge of a care order under s 39 or challenging a decision about contact under s 34, which we have already discussed,[868] there are a number of other ways in which a local authority decision may be challenged. Use can be made of local authorities' formal complaints or representation procedures. Alternatively, applications may be made to the Secretary of State to use his default powers. Actions can be brought under the High Court's inherent jurisdiction or for judicial review or by seeking leave to apply for a residence order. A complaint can also be made to the 'local ombudsman'. Furthermore, it may be possible to sue the local authority for negligence or for violating a human right under the European Convention on Human Rights.

---

[863] Clarke Hall and Morrison on *Children* at 1[1660.3].

[864] Review of Children's Cases Regulations 1991 (SI 1991/895), reg 7.   [865] Reg 2A.

[866] Children Act 1989, s 24D and the Advocacy Services and Representation Procedure (Children) (Amendment) Regulations 2004 (SI 2004/719). The complaints procedure is discussed below at pp 798ff.

[867] Vol 3, *Family Placements*, para 10.3.

[868] Above at p 787 (discharge) and p 792 (contact under s 34).

We discuss each of these options in turn, but in the ensuing discussion it should be borne in mind that the issue of reviewing local authorities' action is not simple. Although ideally one would wish to safeguard both the child's and the parents' (or other interested adults') interests it must be remembered that ultimately priority must be given to the child's welfare. A local authority may, for example, have acted improperly, yet a court may nevertheless be forced to uphold their decision, because it has become in the child's interests to do so. On the other hand, while court scrutiny might be more effective if action had to be sanctioned by the court before it is carried out by the authority, such control might so fetter local authority action that the inevitable consequential delay would be to the general prejudice of children in care.

2 THE COMPLAINTS PROCEDURE [869]

As has been said, it is often possible to resolve problems informally, and indeed some local authorities appoint an officer specifically to support children and their representatives in participation in decision-making and in voicing their concerns.[870] Under s 26(3) of the Children Act 1989, however, it is mandatory for all local authorities to have a formal representation or complaints procedure in relation to their Part III powers and functions.[871] Furthermore, to ensure that there is an independent element, s 26(4) provides that at least one person who is not a member or officer of the authority concerned must take part in the consideration of the complaint or representation and in any discussions held by the authority about the action to be taken. Equally importantly, under s 26(8) there is an obligation to publicise the complaints procedure.[872] Rules governing the scope and procedure of the complaints scheme are provided by the Representations Procedure (Children) Regulations 1991. The Department of Health and the Social Services Inspectorate have also issued practice guidance.[873]

(a) Who can complain?

Under s 26(3) complaints may be made by:

    (a) a child whom the local authority are looking after or who is not being looked after but is in need. This is intended both to ensure that children are consulted on decisions taken about them and to establish the system of complaints procedures

---

[869] See generally the Department of Health's *Guidance and Regulations*, Vol 3, *Family Placements*, ch 10; C Williams 'The practical operation of the Children Act complaints procedure' [2002] CFLQ 25; C Williams and H Jordan 'Factors relating to publicity surrounding the complaints procedure under the Children Act 1989' [1996] CFLQ 337; and C Williams and H Jordan *The Children Act 1989 Complaints Procedure: A Study of Six Local Authority Areas* (1996); and for the background, *Review of Child Care Law* (DHSS, 1985), paras 220 et seq and A Bainham *Children, The New Law*, paras 4.62 et seq.

[870] See the Department of Health's *Guidance and Regulations*, op cit at para 10.13.

[871] Failure to have a procedure or having one that fails to comply with the regulations (set out below) can be remedied by invoking the Secretary of State's default powers under s 84 (discussed below at p 801); per Auld LJ in *R v London Borough of Barnet, ex p B* [1994] 1 FLR 592 at 598.

[872] As Williams and Jordan, op cit at 33.8 observe, a complaints procedure is 'otiose, if those most in need of such a procedure are unaware of its existence and operation'. In fact they were of the view that publicity for such schemes is generally disappointing.

[873] *The Right to Complain—Practice Guidance on Complaints Procedures in Social Services Departments*, HMSO 1991. Note also the Inspectorate's reports of 1993, 1994 and 1996.

for children the authorities are looking after.[874] It may also assist a child who believes he should be accommodated where the authority are refusing to offer the service;[875]

(b) a parent;[876]

(c) any person (other than a parent) with parental responsibility;

(d) any local authority foster parent; or

(e) such other person as the authority considers has a sufficient interest in the child's welfare to warrant representations being considered by them.

In addition young people can complain if they consider that the local authority has not given them adequate preparation for leaving care or adequate after-care.[877]

Although s 26(3) permits a wide range of people, including foster parents, to use the procedure, those falling into the final category may only be heard at the local authority's discretion.[878] This has been criticised as being too restrictive in the case of representations being made by concerned members of the wider family,[879] and problematic in other cases.[880]

(b) What may be complained about?

As s 26(3) says, the statutory complaints procedure caters for complaints about local authority support for families and their children under Part III of the 1989 Act. This, as the Department of Health's *Guidance* says:[881]

'. . . will include complaints about day care, services to support children within their family home, accommodation of a child, after-care and decisions relating to the placement of a child or the handling of a child's case. The processes involved in decision making or the denial of a service must also be covered by the responsible authority's arrangements.'

Matters falling outside Part III,[882] including the placing of a child's name on the Child Protection Register and complaints by private foster parents on their own behalf, do not have to be included in the scheme. However, as the Department of Health's *Guidance* says, a responsible authority should consider what other matters might appropriately be covered by the procedures to meet the requirements of the Regulations.[883]

[874] According to the Department of Health's *Guidance and Regulations*, op cit at para 107, the responsible authority should always check with the child (subject to his understanding) that a complaint submitted on his behalf reflects his views and that he wishes the person submitting it to act on his behalf.

[875] See also Ward J in *R v Royal Borough of Kingston-upon-Thames, ex p T* [1994] 1 FLR 798 at 812.

[876] Including the unmarried father.

[877] Children Act 1989 s 24(14), added by the Courts and Legal Services Act 1990 Sch 16, para 13.

[878] The procedure in these cases is governed by reg 4(4) of the Representations Procedure (Children) Regulations 1991.

[879] By Bainham, op cit, at p 86. Their principal form of redress will therefore be judicial review: see below, p 604.

[880] For example, as to whether a teacher, who is concerned about a child, can complain: see Williams and Jordan, op cit, at 338.

[881] Op cit at para 10.8.

[882] Except decisions about the 'usual fostering limit' included under the Representations Procedure (Children) Regulations 1991 reg 12(2).

[883] Ibid at para 10.9. In fact, as Williams and Jordan found, coverage varies considerably.

(c) Procedure and outcome

This is a two-stage process for handling complaints (which can be made at any time): a relatively informal stage and, if that does not resolve matters, a formal stage before a panel. Upon receipt of a complaint from an eligible person, the responsible authority must acknowledge it and send a leaflet describing how the procedure works and giving the name of the officer responsible for co-ordinating the handling of complaints.[884] The authority and an independent person must consider the representation and formulate a response within 28 days.[885] Their written decision must be sent to the complainant, the child (if different) and to any other person whom the authority considers has a sufficient interest in the child. The letter must also remind the complainant of his right to have his complaint considered by a panel. If the claimant is dissatisfied with the responsible authority's response, he has 28 days to request in writing that the complaint be heard by the panel,[886] which in turn must meet within 28 days after the receipt by the local authority of such a request.[887] The complainant and authority can each make written and oral submissions to the panel.[888] The panel must make a recommendation within 24 hours of its meeting and record it in writing,[889] and give written notification of it to the responsible authority, the complainant, the independent person (if he is not a member of the panel) and any other interested person.[890] The responsible authority must consider what action, if any, should be taken in the light of the panel's findings[891] and, within 28 days of the panel's recommendation, notify among others the complainant and the child (if of sufficient understanding) of their decision and reasons for taking that decision.[892] It is to be noted that there is no time limit for making a complaint.

Although a panel decision is not strictly binding upon the local authority,[893] as Peter Gibson LJ said in *R v London Borough of Brent, ex p S,*[894] it would be 'an unusual case when a local authority acted otherwise than in accord with the panel's recommendations and the independent person's views'. Furthermore, simply to ignore or failing reasonably to consider the recommendations will lay the authority open to judicial review.[895]

It may also be observed that authorities are required to monitor the operation and effectiveness of the procedure. To this end records of each complaint received and the outcome must be kept and an annual report dealing with the procedure's operation must be completed and presented to the Social Services Committee.[896]

---

[884] Department of Health's *Guidance and Regulations,* op cit, para 10.37.

[885] Regulation 6 of the 1991 Regulations. The independent person can inter alia interview the child and, if different, the complainant: reg 8(1).

[886] Regulation 8(2). The panel, which must include at least one independent person, is appointed by the local authority for this purpose: reg 8(2)–(3). As the Department of Health's *Guidance and Regulations,* op cit, at para 10.22 comments, this second stage of the procedure does not affect the complainant's right to complain about maladministration to the local ombudsman (discussed below, p 802), since the panel is not a decision-making body.

[887] Regulation 8(4).   [888] Regulation 8(5).   [889] Regulation 9(1).   [890] Regulation 9(2).
[891] Regulation 9(3).   [892] Children Act 1989 s 26(7)(b).

[893] This is implicit in s 26(7) which requires the authority, having had due regard to the findings, to 'take such steps *as are reasonably practicable*' [emphasis added].

[894] [1994] 1 FLR 203 at 211.

[895] Per Ward J in *R v Royal Borough of Kingston-upon-Thames, ex p T* [1994] 1 FLR 798 at 814. For examples, of where judicial review was successfully invoked see *Re T (Accommodation by Local Authority)* [1995] 1 FLR 159, discussed above at p 708, and *R v Avon County Council, ex p M* [1994] 2 FCR 259.

[896] Regulation 10. Note also the Social Services Inspectorate's Reviews of the Complaints Procedure.

(d) Impact of the complaints procedure

One impact of the complaints procedure has been to reduce the need and indeed the ability successfully to invoke the court's powers under judicial review (discussed further below). In *R v Birmingham City Council, ex p A*[897] an attempt was made to use judicial review to challenge a local authority's apparent inability speedily to place a child with special needs with an appropriate specialist foster parent. Sir Stephen Brown P commented that, in cases such as those where neither fact nor law was in dispute but instead the ground of complaint was the way the authority was carrying out its duty, the appropriate remedy was a complaint under s 26. It has been similarly held[898] that the complaints procedure would in ordinary circumstances provide a suitable alternative remedy to judicial review to question a local authority decision not to apply for a care order. But in *R v Royal Borough of Kingston-upon-Thames, ex p T*[899] Ward J went further, holding that it was the clear broad legislative purpose that the complaints procedure should be invoked in preference to judicial review in respect of matters within the remit of s 26. He pointed out that the remedy was quicker[900] and more convenient and he specifically rejected both the argument that because the panel was dominated by local authority membership it was likely to be biased, and that it was ineffective. In relation to the first he was satisfied that professional integrity would ensure fairness and in relation to the second he pointed to the availability of judicial review should any recommendation simply be ignored.

The effectiveness of the system is an important issue, particularly as the existence of the complaints system was used as one of the justifications for not imposing a general duty of care in tort upon local authorities.[901] Relatively little is known about the actual use made of the procedure,[902] though there is evidence that children themselves are reluctant to complain because of fear of victimisation or retaliation.[903] Research in other contexts[904] has found that people are generally reluctant to complain, either because they are tired of battling the system or cannot see the point in doing so, the damage already having been done.

3 DEFAULT POWERS OF THE SECRETARY OF STATE

Section 84 of the Children Act 1989 enables the Secretary of State to declare a local authority in default where he is satisfied that they have, without reasonable cause, failed to comply with a duty[905] under the Act. Such a declaration may contain such directions as are

---

[897] [1997] 2 FLR 841.

[898] Per Scott Baker J in *R v East Sussex County Council, ex p W* [1998] 2 FLR 1082. See also *R (BG) v Medway Council* [2005] EWHC 1932 (Admin), [2006] 1 FLR 663.

[899] [1994] 1 FLR 798.

[900] But note *R (B) v Merton London Borough Council* [2003] EWHC 1689 (Admin), [2003] 2 FLR 888 in which it was held that the lack of immediate relief under the complaints scheme did justify the use of judicial review to determine the age of an asylum seeker who had no means of support in the United Kingdom.

[901] See *X v Bedfordshire County Council* [1995] 2 AC 633, HL (discussed below at p 810).

[902] Though see C Williams and H Jordan *The Children Act 1989 Complaints Procedure: A Study of Six Local Authority Areas.*

[903] See C Williams and H Jordan 'Factors relating to publicity surrounding the complaints procedure under the Children Act' (1996) 8 CFLQ 337.

[904] See eg M Murch, N Lowe, V Beckford, M Borkowski and A Weaver *Supporting Adoption—Reframing the Approach* (1999) 251–2.

[905] Ie not simply a power, see Peter Gibson LJ in *R v London Borough of Brent, ex p S* [1994] 1 FLR 592.

necessary to ensure compliance with the duty within a specified period. In the event of further default, these directions may be enforced by application to the High Court for judicial review.

Although in theory this provides another option for aggrieved individuals to pursue disputes against a local authority, it was never expected that these powers would be exercised at all often,[906] still less that they will assist individuals, as it is more likely that the Secretary of State will exercise his powers, if at all, where an authority's failure to discharge its statutory duties affects a class as opposed to individual children.[907] The existence of these default powers does not bar applications for judicial review.[908]

4 APPLYING TO THE 'LOCAL GOVERNMENT OMBUDSMAN'[909]

Another procedure for questioning local authority decisions over children is to complain to the commissioner for local administration ('the local government ombudsman'). Under this procedure a local commissioner may investigate written complaints of 'maladminis-tration'. Before a complaint is made, the local authority must first be given an opportunity to address it[910] but if this approach does not produce a satisfactory result, a complaint can be made. Complaints can be made directly to the commissioner or through a councillor. The commissioner cannot normally investigate complaints concerning proceedings or events that occurred more than 12 months previously.[911] To find the complaint justified the local commissioner must find that the authority has been guilty of 'maladministra-tion'. The Court of Appeal has ruled[912] that it is not necessary for the complainant to spell out the particular maladministration which led to the injustice complained of; it is suf-ficient if he specifies the action alleged to be wrong. This is generally taken to refer to the procedure by which the decision is made or put into action rather than to the merits of the particular decision itself.[913] At the conclusion of his investigation the commissioner issues a report and, if he has found maladministration and injustice, he may recommend an ex gratia payment.[914] Although the local authority must consider these recommendations it is

---

[906] The similar default power under the Education Act is rarely used. See J Logie 'Enforcing statutory duties: the courts and default powers' [1988] JSWL 185.

[907] See HC Official Report S C 13 June 1989, col 492 per the Solicitor General, and Bainham, op cit, para 7.78. But note *R v London Borough of Brent, ex p S*, above, in which it was suggested that the default powers could be used as a remedy for an inadequate complaints system; and *R v Barnet London Borough Council, ex p B* [1994] 1 FLR 592 where the default powers were mentioned in relation to inadequate day care provision. Note also Lord Nicholls' comment in *Re S (Minors)(Care Order: Implementation of Care Plan); Re W (Minors)(Care Order: Adequacy of Care Plan)* [2002] UKHL 10, [2002] 2 AC 291 at [58] that the default powers under s 84 are not sufficient in practice to provide an adequate and timely remedy in individual cases.

[908] Per Peter Gibson LJ in *R v London Borough of Brent, ex p S*, above at 214.

[909] See N Lowe and H Rawlings (1979) 42 MLR 447 and (1979) 2, Adoption and Fostering 38, and D Oliver 'Challenging local authority decisions in relation to children in care—Part 2' (1989) 1 Journal of Child Law 58 at 61.

[910] Local Government Act 1974 s 26(5).

[911] Section 26(4). A free booklet explaining the procedure is available from the Commissioner.

[912] In *R v Local Commissioner for Administration for the North and East Area of England, ex p Bradford Metropolitan City Council* [1979] QB 287, CA.

[913] See the *Bradford* case, above.

[914] Awards of £1,000 have been recommended where a local authority failed to follow a case conference's recommendation, and of £2,000 where children were inappropriately interviewed about allegations of sexual abuse. See respectively Complaint 91/A/1176 and 90/c2717.

not *bound* to follow them and indeed, given the passage of time, may not be able to do so if that would be inconsistent with the child's welfare.

As a general mechanism for scrutinising administrative action, the procedure obviously has its merits, but like judicial review it is of questionable use in the context of local authority decisions in respect of children in care.[915] The main drawbacks are that the central concern is with procedural propriety and not the child's welfare; the commissioner may have no expertise in child matters; the investigation is itself a long process[916] and will probably result in delaying implementation of plans for the child's long-term future;[917] and, even if 'maladministration' is established, there is no power to interfere with the decision taken by the authority.[918]

5 WARDSHIP AND THE INHERENT JURISDICTION

(a) The position before the Children Act 1989 [919]

Before the Children Act 1989, local authorities, encouraged by the courts, frequently turned to wardship as a means of committing children to their care.[920] In stark contrast, although it was accepted that the wardship jurisdiction had not been abrogated by the comprehensive statutory scheme governing local authority care,[921] the courts refused to allow their prerogative jurisdiction to be used as a means of challenging authorities' decisions over children in care. The basic rationale for what became known as the '*Liverpool* principle' was that as Parliament had vouchsafed a wide discretion to local authorities over the manage-ment of children in care, it was not for the courts to subvert that policy by allowing parents and others a right of challenge through wardship and therefore outside the statutory system. As Lord Wilberforce said in *A v Liverpool City Council*:[922]

'In my opinion the court has no . . . reviewing power. Parliament has by statute entrusted to the local authority the power and duty to make decisions as to the welfare of children without any reservation of a reviewing power to the court.'

---

[915] In practice very few of the complaints made relate to local authority social services' decisions about children. In 1988, for example, only 160 such complaints were made out of a total 7,055—see D Hershman and A McFarlane *Children Law and Practice* G[932].

[916] Though in this respect it is to be noted that in *Re A Subpoena (Adoption: Comr for Local Administration)* [1996] 2 FLR 629 it was held that the Commissioner was entitled to subpoena a local authority to produce adoption documents.

[917] In the *Bradford* case, for example, where the claim of maladministration failed, the children were eventually adopted: see *Re SMH and RAH* [1990] FCR 966n (decided in 1979), though their placement was delayed pending the outcome of the Commission's investigations; cf *Re BA (Wardship and Adoption)* [1985] FLR 1008.

[918] In *Z and others v United Kingdom* [2001] 2 FLR 612, ECtHR, the Government accepted (see [107]) that in the particular circumstances of the case complaining to the Local Government Ombudsman and/or under the complaints procedure was insufficient to satisfy the requirements of Art 13 of the European Convention on Human Rights. See further below at p 814.

[919] See generally D Oliver 'Challenging Local Authority Decisions in Relation to Children in Care—Part I' (1988) 1 Journal of Child Law 26.

[920] See below, pp 895–6.

[921] See eg *Re M (An Infant)* [1961] Ch 328 at 345, CA per Lord Evershed MR; *Re B (Infants)* [1962] Ch 201 at 223, CA per Pearson LJ; and *A v Liverpool City Council* [1982] AC 363 at 373, HL per Lord Wilberforce.

[922] Ibid at 372. See N Lowe (1982) 45 MLR 96 and M Freeman (1982) 145 JPN 333 and 146 JPN 188 at 202.

In *Liverpool* itself, the House of Lords refused to interfere with a local authority's decision to restrict a mother's contact with her child in care to a monthly supervised visit limited to one hour at a day nursery.[923]

The '*Liverpool* principle' was applied by the House of Lords in *Re W (A Minor) (Wardship: Jurisdiction)*,[924] in which relatives unsuccess-fully sought to use wardship to challenge a local authority's decision to place a child with a stranger (with a view to adoption) rather than with them,[925] and in *Re M and H (Minors) (Local Authorities: Parental Rights)*,[926] in which an unmarried father failed in his application for custody of his child in local authority care.

These decisions successively barred the use of wardship as a means of challenge from foster parents, natural parents, relatives and unmarried fathers and there was little doubt that the '*Liverpool* principle' would equally have applied to *any* potential applicant, including a '*Gillick* competent' child. Not only was it established that the principle applied regardless of the applicant, but it had also been held to apply both in relation to a child in care and where the local authority were actively contemplating taking proceedings.[927]

Furthermore, in *Re W (A Minor) (Wardship: Jurisdiction)*[928] the House of Lords denied the existence of a residual category for intervention even in 'exceptional circumstances', while in *Re DM (A Minor) (Wardship: Jurisdiction)*[929] the Court of Appeal ruled that, even if a local authority could be shown to have acted improperly, the proper action was judicial review and not wardship.

Effectively,[930] therefore, by the time the Children Act 1989 was implemented wardship could not be used as a means of challenging local authority decisions unless the authority itself chose to submit to the jurisdiction.[931]

(b) The position after the Children Act 1989

Under the Children Act 1989 wardship and local authority care are incompatible in the sense that a child cannot both be in care and a ward of court.[932] Accordingly, it is clear that individuals seeking to challenge a local authority's decision in respect of a child in care can

---

[923] Under the law as it then stood, local authorities had complete discretion over the amount of contact with a child in care.

[924] [1985] AC 791, HL. See A Bainham (1986) 49 MLR 113.

[925] The birth parents had concealed from the rest of the family that they had asked the authority to take the child into care (they had agreed to an order freeing the child for adoption) and persuaded the authority, contrary to their normal practice, not to consult members of the wider family.

[926] [1990] 1 AC 686, HL. See M Hayes (1989) 1 Jo of Child Law 53. See also *Re TD (A Minor) (Wardship: Jurisdiction)* [1985] FLR 1150.

[927] See *Re E (Minors) (Wardship: Jurisdiction)* [1984] 1 All ER 21, CA; *W v Shropshire County Council* [1986] 1 FLR 359, CA; and *W v Nottingham County Council* [1986] 1 FLR 565, CA, discussed in the 7th edition of this work at p 474.

[928] [1985] AC 791, see particularly Lord Scarman at 797.   [929] [1986] 2 FLR 122, CA.

[930] Strictly it was still open to argue that the relevant body or court had inadequate powers to deal with the particular issue, but that the court in wardship proceedings had the necessary powers which the child's welfare required to be used: see *Re J (A Minor) (Wardship: Jurisdiction)* [1984] 1 All ER 29, CA. However, this so-called 'lacuna' argument rarely succeeded because the courts generally denied that there was an unintended gap in the relevant court's or body's powers. See the discussion in the 7th edition of this work at p 475.

[931] See eg *A v B and Hereford and Worcester County Council* [1986] 1 FLR 289.

[932] Children Act 1989 s 100(2)(c) and s 91(4), discussed below, p 896.

no longer even attempt to do so by wardship and that consequently there can be no question of the local authority submitting to the jurisdiction. It is, however, possible for a challenge to be mounted under the High Court's inherent jurisdiction (which is discussed in Chapter 16). Although the point has yet to be directly tested, it is thought that the 'Liverpool principle' will operate in this situation.[933] A fortiori the 'Liverpool principle' will apply in cases where a wardship application can still properly be made, ie where the child is not subject to a care order. A foster parent looking after a child accommodated by a local authority can still in theory ward a child, but if it is intended to challenge the authority's decision, eg to remove the child, then the 'Liverpool principle' will surely be applied.[934]

6 SEEKING LEAVE TO APPLY FOR A RESIDENCE ORDER

Mention has previously been made of the ability of parents and guardians to apply for a residence order as an alternative means of seeking a discharge of a care order.[935] However, it is open to *any* interested party to seek the court's leave to apply for a residence order, pursuant to s 10 of the Children Act 1989. This possible means of challenging a local authority decision was explored in *Re A (Minors) (Residence Orders: Leave to Apply)*,[936] in which a foster mother sought to challenge a local authority's decision that she should no longer be permitted to foster four children in their care. In the course of an action for judicial review, the applicant applied for leave to apply for a residence order. In refusing leave the Court of Appeal accepted that the ability of the court, pursuant to s 9(1), to make a residence order notwithstanding that the child is in care, represents a fundamental change in the law and that to that extent the 'Liverpool principle' had no direct application. However, that did not mean that on the application for leave the court should give no weight to the local authority's views. On the contrary, s 10(9)(d)(i) expressly provides that the court is to have particular regard to the authority's plans for the future. Furthermore, given that under s 22(3) it is the authority's duty to safeguard and promote the welfare of any child in its care, it was held that the court should approach the application on the basis that the authority's plans for the child's future were designed for his welfare and that any departure from such plans might well be harmful to the child. In other words the court should, in these circumstances, be slow to grant leave.

7 JUDICIAL REVIEW [937]

(a) Nature of the remedy

Judicial review is the standard administrative law remedy for correcting decisions[938] taken by inferior courts, tribunals and other bodies including local authorities. Applications are made to the Administrative Court. As the Civil Procedure Rules 1998, r 54.1(2)(a) states:

---

[933] This was Balcombe LJ's view in *Re A (Minors) (Residence Orders: Leave to Apply)* [1992] Fam 182, CA, discussed further below.

[934] As extended inter alia by *Re E (Minors) (Wardship: Jurisdiction)*, above, and the other cases cited at n 927 above.

[935] Above at, p 787.   [936] [1992] Fam 182.

[937] See generally H Wade and C Forsyth *Administrative Law* (9th edn, 2004).

[938] For the meaning of which, see below.

'a "claim for judicial review" means a claim to review the lawfulness of

(i) an enactment; or

(ii) a decision, action or failure to act in relation to the exercise of a public function.'

No special rules apply in children cases.[939] The function of the court, as Scott Baker J neatly expressed it, is 'to consider in each case not whether the decision itself is right or fair but whether the manner in which the decision is made is fair'.[940]

There are the following remedies:

(1) *mandatory orders* (formerly mandamus), that is, where a body is ordered to comply with statutory duty, for example, that the local authority provide some specific support service as set out in Part III of Sch 2 to the Children Act,[941] or to set up a complaints procedure that complies with the regulations issued under s 26.[942]

(2) *quashing orders* (formerly certiorari), that is, that the original decision be quashed as, for example, a Director of Social Services' decision not to ratify a complaints panel decision that a 17-year-old be accommodated;[943]

(3) *prohibiting orders* (formerly prohibition), that is, restraining a body from acting unlawfully; and

(4) *declarations* that an action or policy is unlawful[944] and/or an *injunction* to prevent an unlawful act taking place or an unlawful policy from continuing.[945]

It is also possible to include in a claim for judicial review a claim for damages but not to seek damages alone.[946] The court may at any time during the course of judicial review proceedings grant interim relief.[947]

(b) The requirements for judicial review

A prerequisite for a claim for judicial review is that there must be a reviewable 'decision'. In *R v Devon County Council ex p L*,[948] for example, it was held that a social worker's letter informing the applicant's cohabitant that he was suspected of sexual abuse did not

---

[939] But this is not to say that in judging the reasonableness of a local authority's action in respect of children in their care attention should not be paid to the authority's duty to safeguard the child's interests; cf *R v Harrow London Borough Council, ex p D* [1990] Fam 133, CA, per Butler-Sloss LJ cited below, p 809.

[940] *R v Hereford and Worcester County Council, ex p D* [1992] 1 FLR 448 at 457. See also Munby J's comment in *Re M (Care Proceedings: Judicial Review)* [2003] EWHC 850 (Admin), [2003] 2 FLR 171 at [25] that in judicial review proceedings 'the focus of the court's investigation . . . is not with the *merits* of the local authority's case but rather with the more limited question of the *legality* of the local authority's decision-making process'.

[941] See eg *R (on the Application of S) v London Borough of Wandsworth, London Borough of Hammersmith and Fulham, London Borough of Lambeth* [2001] EWHC Admin 709, [2002] 1 FLR 469 in which Lambeth and Wandsworth were ordered to make an assessment of whether the children concerned were in 'need'.

[942] See *R v London Borough of Barnet, ex p B* [1994] 1 FLR 592, 598 per Auld LJ. See above p 798.

[943] *Re T (Accommodation by Local Authority)* [1995] 1 FLR 159. If a quashing order is made the court may remit the matter to the decision-maker and direct it to reconsider the matter, but if it feels there is no purpose in remitting the court can make the decision itself: CPR 1998, r 54.19.

[944] See eg *R (Howard League for Penal Reform) v Secretary of State for the Home Department* [2002] EWHC 2497 (Admin), [2003] 1 FLR 484 and *R v Cornwall County Council, ex p L* [2000] 1 FLR 236.

[945] When seeking declarations or injunctions it is not *mandatory* to use the judicial review procedure laid down in the CPR 1998, Pt 54, see r 54.3.

[946] CPR 1998, R 54.3(2)   [947] CPR 1998, Pt 25.   [948] [1991] 2 FLR 541.

amount to a 'decision' and was not therefore amenable to judicial review. Even if there is a reviewable 'decision', to guard against frivolous, vexatious, or merely hopeless actions, applicants must first obtain permission to proceed.[949] Claims must be filed promptly and in any event not later than three months after the grounds to make the claim first arose.[950] Claims must, inter alia, state any remedy (including any interim remedy) being sought, and provide a detailed statement of the grounds for bringing the claim and be accompanied by any written evidence in support.[951]

Leave is not a formality for, as Balcombe LJ said in *R v Lancashire County Council, ex p M*,[952] there must be a reasonable prospect of the court coming to the decision that the local authority's conclusion was so unreasonable that no reasonable local authority could ever have come to it. Bearing in mind that as far as individuals are concerned some information will be confidential,[953] having to establish even a prima facie case may be difficult. Yet it is only if the applicant can first negotiate this hurdle that the matter will then be heard. Furthermore, in some cases it is likely to be held that an alternative remedy is preferable. Indeed, as we discussed earlier,[954] where neither fact nor law is in dispute but rather the way the local authority has carried out their duty, it is established[955] that the proper remedy is under the complaints procedure rather than judicial review. Challenges to proposed local authority care plans should generally be made in care proceedings rather than by judicial review.[956] Nevertheless the availability of an alternative remedy cannot be said, as a matter of principle, to mean that there cannot be a judicial review.[957]

To substantiate a claim for judicial review, the applicant must be able to bring himself within the so-called *Wednesbury* principle[958] as interpreted by the House of Lords in *Council of Civil Service Unions v Minister for the Civil Service*.[959] According to Lord Diplock in that case,[960] there are three main heads under which court intervention may be justified:

'illegality' (where there was an error of law in reaching the relevant decision);

'procedural impropriety' (where the relevant rules have not been complied with);

---

[949] CPR 1998, r 54.4. Applications for permission are generally considered on the papers alone. A claimant does not have the right to have the permission determined at an oral hearing, though there is a right to request that a decision to refuse or limit the grant of permission be reconsidered at an oral hearing: CPR 1998, r 54.12(3) and *Practice Direction—Judicial Review*, para 8.4.

[950] CPR 1998, r 54.5. See *Re S (Application for Judicial Review)* [1998] 1 FLR 790, CA where permission was refused the application being made four months after the expiration of the time limit.

[951] CPR 1998, Pts 8.2 and 54.2 and the accompanying *Practice Direction—Judicial Review*, paras 5.1, 5.6 and 5.7.

[952] [1992] 1 FLR 109 at 113, CA.

[953] Such as records compiled in relation to foster carers, see the Fostering Services Regulations 2002, reg 32.

[954] Above at p 801.

[955] *R v Birmingham City Council, ex p A* [1997] 2 FLR 841, per Stephen Brown P. Note also *R (M) v London Borough of Bromley* [2002] EWCA Civ 1113, [2002] 2 FLR 802 in which it was held that the appropriate remedy to a local authority decision to place a local authority employee on an index of individuals considered unsuitable to work with children, was to appeal to the care standards tribunal.

[956] See eg *Re M (Care Proceedings: Judicial Review)* [2003] EWHC 850 (Admin), [2003] 2 FLR 171, in which it was sought to challenge a local authority decision to apply for an emergency protection order in respect of a baby as soon as it was born; and *Re C (Adoption: Religious Observance)* [2002] 1 FLR 1119 where a guardian sought to challenge a local authority care plan.

[957] *R v High Peak Magistrates' Court, ex p* [1995] 1 FLR 568, per Cazalet J.

[958] Following *Associated Provincial Picture Houses Ltd v Wednesday Corpn* [1948] 1 KB 223, CA.

[959] [1985] AC 374, HL.   [960] Above at 410.

and 'irrationality' (where a decision 'is so outrageous in its defiance of logic or of accepted moral standards that no sensible person who had applied his mind to the question to be decided could have arrived at it').

(c) Circumstances in which judicial review has been sought [961]

In the context of disputing local authority decisions,[962] claimants are commonly parents, foster parents, prospective adopters, the children themselves and guardians. Complaints have been made about a variety of decisions, including refusing to accommodate a child,[963] rejecting a recommendation for a specialist residential placement of an accommodated child;[964] the placing of a child on a Child Protection Register,[965] deciding not to place the child at home on trial with the parents,[966] removing a child from foster parents,[967] removing a person from the list of approved adopters,[968] placing a local authority employee on an index of individuals considered unsuitable to work with children,[969] and disclosing to others allegations of child abuse by a named person.[970] Challenges have also been made against local authority policy not to permit solicitors to attend child protection case conferences on behalf of parents nor to provide parents attending such conferences with a copy of the minutes,[971] and paying lower rates in respect of the child's maintenance to short-term foster carers who were friends or relatives of the child.[972]

By no means all of the above applications were successful, but of those that were, an important factor was the failure of the local authority to allow the claimant to put his side of the case or otherwise to explain their reasoning. In *R v Devon County Council, ex p O (Adoption)*,[973] for example, which involved the removal of a child placed for adoption with the applicants, judicial review succeeded because the local authority failed to consult or give the claimants an opportunity to be heard. Another striking example is *R v Norfolk*

---

[961] For a useful chart of a summary of reported judicial review decisions, see Clarke Hall and Morrison at 1[1541].

[962] Of course claims concerning children can be made against bodies other than local authorities, as for example, prison authorities, see eg *R (P) v Secretary of State for the Home Department; R (Q) v Secretary of State for the Home Department* [2001] EWCA Civ 1151, [2001] 1 WLR 2002.

[963] See above, p 707.

[964] *Re T (Judicial Review: Local Authority Decisions Concerning Child In Need)* [2003] EWHC 2515 (Admin), [2004] 1 FLR 601.

[965] *R v Norfolk County Council, ex p M* [1989] QB 619; *R v Harrow London Borough Council, ex p D* [1990] Fam 133, CA; and *R v East Sussex County Council, ex p R* [1991] 2 FLR 358.

[966] *R v Bedfordshire County Council, ex p C* [1987] 1 FLR 239; cf *R v Hertfordshire County Council, ex p B* [1987] 1 FLR 239 (child removed after being placed at home on trial).

[967] *R (CD) v Isle of Anglesey County Council* [2004] EWHC 1635, [2005] 1 FLR 59, *R v Hereford and Worcester County Council, ex p D* [1992] 1 FLR 448 and *R v Lancashire County Council, ex p M* [1992] 1 FLR 109, CA.

[968] *R v London Borough of Wandsworth, ex p P* [1989] 1 FLR 387.

[969] *R (M) v London Borough of Bromley* [2002] EWCA Civ 1113, [2002] 2 FLR 802. See also *Re S (Sexual Abuse Allegations: Local Authority Response)* [2001] EWHC Admin 334, [2001] 2 FLR 776.

[970] *R v Devon County Council, ex p L* [1991] 2 FLR 541 and *R v Lewisham London Borough Council, ex p P* [1991] 1 WLR 308.

[971] *R v Cornwall County Council, ex p L* [2000] 1 FLR 236.

[972] *R (on the Application of L) and Others v Manchester City Council; R (on the Application of R) v Manchester City Council* [2000] EWHC Admin 707, [2002] 1 FLR 43.

[973] [1997] 2 FLR 388. Cf *R v Avon County Council, ex p Crabtree* [1996] 1 FLR 502, CA where the de-registration of an approved foster carer was only made after careful consideration and consultation. Consequently the action failed.

County Council, ex p M,[974] which concerned a plumber working in a house where a teenage girl made allegations that she was sexually abused by him. She had twice previously been the victim of sexual abuse and a few days later made similar allegations against another man. After a case conference the plumber's name was entered on (what was then called) the Child Abuse Register as an abuser. His employers were informed and they suspended him pending a full enquiry. The plumber first learned of these allegations through a letter informing him of the decision to place his name on the register. Waite J held that, given the serious consequences of registration for the plumber, the local authority had a duty to act fairly, which they had manifestly failed to do by not giving him an opportunity to meet the allegations.

The *Norfolk* case was exceptional and, as Butler-Sloss LJ said in *R v Harrow London Borough Council, ex p D*,[975] recourse to judicial review in respect of placing a name on the Child Protection Register ought to be rare. She further held that the courts should not encourage applications to review case conference decisions or recommendations, because it was important for those involved in this difficult area to 'be allowed to perform their task without having to look over their shoulder all the time for the possible intervention of the court'. Furthermore, she pointed out that in 'balancing adequate protection for the child and the fairness to an adult, the interest of an adult may have to take second place to the needs of the child'.[976] Notwithstanding these observations, there may still be occasions when judicial review is appropriate even of a decision to place a child's name on the Protection Register.[977]

Although Butler-Sloss LJ's remarks specifically concerned case conference decisions and recommendations, her observations about the need to balance considerations have general application.[978] Indeed, it can be said that in general, given the local authority's duty to safeguard the interests of children, in the absence of procedural irregularity it is hard to impugn a local authority decision. It is certainly not enough to question the wisdom of a decision. The applicant must discharge the heavy onus of showing that no reasonable local authority could have reached the particular decision complained of. In *R v Hertfordshire County Council, ex p B*[979] a mother's action for judicial review failed. In that case a child in care was allowed home on trial with the mother, but after three months was removed on the ground that rehabilitation had failed. A neighbour had asserted that the mother had come home late one night and being drunk lay in the snow for some time with her child

---

[974] Above. See also *R v Bedfordshire County Council, ex p C*, above; *R v Hereford and Worcester City Council, ex p D*, above; and *R v London of Wandsworth, ex p P*, above.

[975] [1990] Fam 133, CA.

[976] Above at p 138. See also *R v London Borough of Wandsworth, ex p P*, above, at 308 in which Ewbank J said: 'Foster-parents have to accept that their interests may have to be subordinated to the children they care for. Accordingly, provided the rules of fairness are complied with, the decision as to whether there is a risk or not, is one that has to be taken by the local authority. In the ordinary way, provided the rules of natural justice are complied with the foster-parents have no redress.' See also *R v Birmingham City Council, ex p A* [1997] 2 FLR 841.

[977] See eg *R v Hampshire County Council, ex p H* [1999] 2 FLR 359, CA.

[978] See also *R v East Sussex County Council, ex p R*, above; *R v Devon County Council, ex p L*, above; and *R v Lewisham London Borough Council, ex p P*, above.

[979] [1987] 1 FLR 239. See also *R (W) v Leicestershire County Council* [2003] EWHC 704 (Admin), [2003] 2 FLR 185, *R v East Sussex County Council, ex p R*, above; *R v Devon County Council, ex p L*, above; and *R v Lewisham London Borough Council, ex p P*, above.

running about. In fact it was found that the authority had been concerned with wider considerations, including the child's weight loss, his disruptive behaviour and hyperactivity. In dismissing the application Ewbank J observed that there were many cases where children were allowed home on trial and where the local authority had later to decide that it was not a success. Such a decision was well within the local authority's parental power and was not amenable to judicial review.

8 HABEAS CORPUS

Re S (Habeas Corpus); S v Harringey London Borough Council[980] establishes that where care proceedings are in existence habeas corpus has no role to play; indeed recourse to such proceedings is to be deprecated.

9 SUING THE LOCAL AUTHORITY FOR NEGLIGENCE

(a) The *Bedfordshire* decision

At one time, English law set its face against superimposing a common law duty of care on local authorities in relation to performance of their duties to protect children. The key case was *X (Minors) v Bedfordshire County Council*,[981] which comprised five test cases, two of which concerned the way local authorities had dealt with child abuse. In the *Bedfordshire* case, five children claimed damages for personal injury based either on breach of statutory duty or common law negligence by the local authority. The claims alleged that the local authority had failed properly to investigate reports suggesting that the children had been abused and therefore adequately to protect them. In contrast, in *M v Newham London Borough Council*[982] a child and her mother claimed damages for personal injury against the local authority, area health authority, and a psychiatrist on the basis of the child wrongfully being taken into care following a mistaken diagnosis identifying the mother's cohabitant as the abuser.

In both instances the House of Lords held that the actions failed, since breach of a statutory duty did not, by itself, give rise to any private law cause of action. In Lord Browne-Wilkinson's view,[983] as a general principle a cause of action will only arise 'if it can be shown, as a matter of construction of the statute, that the statutory duty was imposed for the protection of a limited class of the public and that Parliament intended to confer on members of that class a private action for breach of that duty'. His Lordship held that the careless performance of a statutory duty did not give rise to any cause of action in the absence of either a right of action for breach of a statutory duty or for breach of a common law duty of care.

Lord Brown-Wilkinson said that a distinction had to be drawn between those alleged negligent acts or decisions which involved policy matters, which were not justiciable in tort at all, and those which did not. Where policy matters were not involved, then it had to

---

[980] [2003] EWHC 2734 (Admin), [2004] 1 FLR 590.
[981] [1995] 2 AC 633, HL, on which see C Cane 'Suing public authorities in tort' (1996) 112 LQR 13, K Oliphant 'Tort' (1996) 49 Current Legal Problems 29 and 31 and R Bailey-Harris and M Harris 'The Immunity of local authorities in child protection functions—Is the door now ajar?' [1998] CFLQ 227.
[982] Dealt with in the same judgment.   [983] Above at 731.

be shown that the local authority had exercised its jurisdiction so unreasonably that it had acted outside the discretion entrusted to it by Parliament. In this latter case the plaintiff would then have to bring him or herself within the tripartite test established by *Caparo Industries plc v Dickman*:[984]

— Was the damage to the plaintiff reasonably foreseeable?

— Was the relationship between the plaintiff and the defendant sufficiently proximate?

— Was it just and reasonable to impose a duty of care?

Although *Bedfordshire* did not establish a blanket immunity for any action taken by a local authority in respect of children, it certainly limited the possibilities of action. However, a number of subsequent decisions have widened the scope for actions for negligence. Moreover, the House of Lords' decision was itself ruled in breach of the European Convention on Human Rights, and as we discuss later, an alternative to suing a local authority for negligence is to sue for breach of human rights.

(b) The retreat from *Bedfordshire*

The first significant change of position after *Bedfordshire* was the decision of the House of Lords in *Barrett v Enfield London Borough Council*,[985] not to strike out a claim for negligence against the local authority for their alleged catalogue of errors during the 17 years that the claimant had been in their care and which resulted in him leaving care with deep-seated psychological and psychiatric problems. Their Lordships drew distinction between deciding to take a child into care pursuant to a statutory duty, which unless it was wholly unreasonable so as not to be a real exercise of the discretion, was not normally justiciable, and looking after a child in care, when it might be easier to establish a breach of duty. However, while their Lordships were not prepared to strike out the claim,[986] the decision by no means indicated that the claim would in fact succeed. Indeed Lord Slynn expressly said that many of the allegations would be difficult to establish and were likely to fail.

Barrett was subsequently applied in *S v Gloucester County Council, L v Tower Hamlets London Borough Council*[987] in which claims for negligence were brought against the local authorities by children who alleged that the foster-fathers with whom they had been placed had abused them sexually and as a result they had suffered long-term damage. In each case the foster-fathers had eventually been convicted of sexual offences with children. According to May LJ[988] the relevant law derived from *Barrett* can be summarised as follows:

'(a) depending upon the particular facts of the case, a claim in common-law negligence may be available to a person who claims to have been damaged by failings of a local authority which was responsible under statutory powers for his care and upbringing . . .

(b) the claim will not succeed if the failings alleged comprise actions or decisions by the local authority of a kind which are not justiciable. These may include, but will not necessarily be limited to, policy decisions and decisions about allocating public funds;

---

[984] [1990] 2 AC 605 at 616–17, HL.   [985] [1995] 2 AC 633.

[986] Their Lordships were mindful of the obligation under Art 6 of the European Convention on Human Rights to allow everyone to have a fair and public hearing and referred expressly to the decision to *Osman v UK* (1999) 29 EHRR 345, [1999] 1 FLR 193, E Ct HR, on which see J Miles 'Human Rights and Child Protection' [2001] CFLQ 431 and C Gearty '*Osman* unravels' (2002) 65 MLR 87.

[987] [2000] 1 FLR 825, CA.   [988] Above at 848–849.

(c) the border line between what is justiciable and what is not may in a particular case be unclear. Its demarcation may require a more extensive investigation than is capable of being made from material in traditional pleadings alone;

(d) there may be circumstances in which it will not be just and reasonable to impose a duty of care of the kind contended for. It may often be necessary to conduct a detailed investigation of the facts to determine this question; and

(e) in considering whether a discretionary decision was negligent, the court will not substitute its view for that of the local authority upon which the state has placed the power to exercise discretion, unless the discretionary decision was plainly wrong. But decisions of, for example, social workers, are capable of being held to have been negligent by analogy with decisions of other professional people. Here again, it may well be necessary to conduct a detailed factual enquiry.'

Applying these principles it was held that the allegation that Gloucestershire had failed to deal with the abuse by the foster carer after being informed of it was actionable. However, in the case of Tower Hamlets there was held to be no real prospect of establishing negligence in their approval of the foster parents nor in their subsequent placement of the child with them and the action was struck out.

In *W v Essex County Council*[989] a foster child, known by the social worker to be an active sexual abuser, sexually abused the birth children of the foster carers. The Court of Appeal held that while the foster parents' claim for negligence against the local authority should be struck out, the children's should not. The majority held that a social worker placing a child with foster parents had a duty of care to the foster parents' children to provide them, before and during the placement, with such information about the placed child as a reasonable social worker would provide in all circumstances, and a local authority was vicariously liable for the conduct of its social worker relating to that. Although appeals were lodged on both counts, that relating to the children was not pursued but in relation to the action by the parents, the House of Lords held that that too should not be struck out on the basis that it could not be said that such a claim was unarguable. Indeed in a separate action against Essex county council, adoptive parents succeeded in obtaining damages in respect of injury, loss and damage sustained during the placement (but not after the adoption) of two siblings, the local authority being liable in negligence for not disclosing the boy's serious behavioural problems, including severe violence on his sister, which required constant adult supervision.[990]

Although in *D v East Berkshire Community Health NHS Trust*[991] Lord Nicholls accepted[992] that the law has moved on since the *Bedfordshire* decision (the Court of Appeal had unequivocally said that that decision did not survive the Human Rights Act 1998),[993] the House of Lords nevertheless restrained the seemingly relentless widening of the duty

---

[989] [1999] Fam 90, CA, reversed in part by HL at [2001] 2 AC 592.

[990] See *A v Essex County Council* [2003] EWCA Civ 1848, [2004] 1 FLR 749, CA upholding the first instance decision, reported as *A and B v Essex County Council* [2002] EWHC 2707 (QB), [2003] 1 FLR 615. If negligence is established, the Court of Appeal in *C v Flintshire County Council* [2001] 2 FLR 33 doubted whether the Judicial Studies Board guidelines on damages for psychiatric harm applied to cases of abuse of children in care by their carers. See also *KR v Bryn Alyn Community (Holdings) Ltd* [2003] EWCA Civ 85, [2003] 1 FLR 1203.

[991] [2005] UKHL 23, [2005] 2 FLR 284.   [992] See para [82].

[993] [2003] EWCA Civ 1151, [2003] 2 FLR 1166 at [83]–[85], per Lord Phillips MR.

of care owed by professionals when dealing with a child. In that case the Lords upheld the dismissal of claims by parents that medical professionals had negligently misdiagnosed child abuse. In so ruling, the Lords upheld the Court of Appeal's ruling that a distinction had to be made between the children's position and the parents' position. While in the former there can now be said to be a duty of care towards the child in relation to the investigation of suspected child abuse and the institution and pursuit of care proceedings, the same cannot be said of the parents. All that is owed to the parent is that clinical and other investigations must be conducted in good faith.[994]

10 SUING THE LOCAL AUTHORITY FOR BREACH OF HUMAN RIGHTS

A local authority decision can be challenged as being in breach of the European Convention on Human Rights. To succeed, the applicant must show that his convention right(s) have been violated, the most relevant of which are, in this context Art 8, under which there is 'the right to respect for . . . private and family life' and Art 6, under which there is a right to determine one's civil rights and obligations in a fair trial. Until the implementation of the Human Rights Act 1998 the only way of mounting such a direct action was to take the case to the European Court of Human Rights at Strasbourg, which meant having exhausted domestic remedies. Notwithstanding this impediment there have been a number of successful challenges. For example, in respect of the former inability of parents to question local authority decisions concerning contact with children in care[995] and an authority's refusal to give access to the case records of a child in their care.[996] More recently the four children denied relief by the House of Lords[997] in the *Bedfordshire* case and both the mother and child involved in the *Newham* decision, subsequently took their claims before the European Court of Human Rights. In both cases, respectively reported as *Z v United Kingdom*[998] and *TP and KM v United Kingdom*,[999] the claim that the striking out of the negligence claims by the House of Lords amounted to a breach of Art 6 of the Convention was rejected on the basis that while that Article generally safeguarded a right of access to the courts in respect of complaints of unlawful interference with civil rights, it did not guarantee a particular content of these civil rights or obligations. In other words, States can properly restrict those rights provided they do so for legitimate reasons and 'there is a reasonable relationship of proportionality between the means employed and the aim sought to be achieved'. In the Court's view the UK had legitimately restricted the application of negligence. Nevertheless despite this ruling the Court found other reasons for holding the UK to be in breach of the Convention in each of the two cases.

---

[994] See Lord Nicholls at [2005] UKHL 23, [2005] 2 FLR 284, [90]. Lord Bingham dissented. This ruling was followed in *D v Bury Metropolitan Borough Council* [2006] EWCA Civ 1, [2006] 1 WLR 917, in which it was held that the local authority did not owe a duty of care to the parents of a child who was the subject of a child abuse investigation.

[995] See eg *R v United Kingdom* [1988] 2 FLR 445, ECtHR and *O v UK* (1987) 10 EHRR 82, ECtHR.

[996] *Gaskin v United Kingdom* (1990) 12 EHRR 36, ECtHR.

[997] [1995] 2 AC 633, discussed above at p 810.

[998] [2001] 2 FLR 612, ECtHR, on which see the excellent analysis by R Bailey-Harris [2001] 2 FLR 549, ECtHR.

[999] [2001] 2 FLR, 549, ECtHR.

In *Z v United Kingdom* the European Court upheld the children's claim that there had been a breach of Art 3. The local authority were found to be aware of the appalling treatment and neglect suffered over a period of years by the applicants at the hands of their parents (the UK Government did not contest the Commission's finding that the treatment suffered by the children had reached the level of severity prohibited by Art 3, ie that it amounted to inhuman and degrading treatment) but had failed, despite the powers available to them, to take effective measures to bring it to an end. Accordingly, the State too had failed in its positive obligation under Art 3 to provide the applicants with adequate protection against inhuman and degrading treatment. The Court further held that notwithstanding the propriety of striking out the negligence claim, the absence of an effective remedy for the breach itself amounted to a breach of Art 13 (under which everyone should have an effective remedy for a violation of a Convention right). The court awarded £32,000 compensation to each applicant.

Since Art 3 was found to have been broken the Court in *Z* found it unnecessary to consider whether Art 8 had also been breached in that case. In *TP and KM v United Kingdom*, however, the Court upheld the mother and daughter's complaint that because the child had unjustifiably been taken into care and separated from her mother, both claimant's Art 8 rights had been breached. What constituted the violation in the Court's view was the local authority's failure to disclosure to the mother a video of the child's disclosure interview which in turn deprived the mother of an effective opportunity to deal with allegations that the child could not be safely returned to her. As in *Z* the absence of an effective domestic remedy was found to be a breach of Art 13 and each applicant was awarded £10,000.

Following the 1998 Act such challenges have first to be made domestically, though if they fail it is still possible to take the case to Strasbourg.[1000] It remains to discuss the domestic remedy.

(a) Actions under ss 7 and 8 of the Human Rights Act 1998

Section 7 of the Human Rights Act 1998 enables victims to bring proceedings against public authorities (which includes both local authorities and the courts)[1001] in respect of acts claimed to be incompatible with a Convention right and if successful, s 8 empowers the court to grant 'such relief or remedy, or make such order, within its powers as it considers just and appropriate'. These latter powers include awarding damages. As Lord Nicholls observed in *Re S (Minors)(Care Order: Implementation of Care Plan); Re W (Minors)(Care Order: Adequacy of Care Plan)*,[1002] 'The object of these sections is to provide in English law the very remedy Art 13 declares is the entitlement of everyone whose rights are violated.'

Actions may either be brought directly against the public authority alleged to be at fault (sometimes referred to as 'free-standing action') or can be raised in existing proceedings.

[1000] For guidance on how to bring such actions see L Clements, N Mole and A Simmons *European Human Rights—Taking a Case under the Convention* (2nd edn, 1999).

[1001] See s 6(3), discussed above at p 26.

[1002] [2002] UKHL 10, [2002] 2 AC 291 at [61]. As Lord Nicholls said, unlike Art 13 which makes it a 'right' to have an effective remedy, ss 7 and 8 simply provide a remedy for enforcing a Convention right. Note: the United Kingdom has *not* incorporated Art 13 into domestic law.

Freestanding actions have to be brought in an 'appropriate court or tribunal',[1003] but, as Hale J said, in *Re W and B (Children: Care Plan), Re W (Children)(Care Plan)*[1004]

'There is no definition of the "appropriate court or tribunal" for purpose of s 7(1)(a). The amended *Practice Direction* to Pt 16 of the Civil Procedure Rules 1998 requires any party who seeks to rely on the Human Rights Act to state that and give particulars in his statement of case. A claim against a local authority under s 7(1)(a) might therefore be brought as an ordinary civil claim in the country or the High Court.'

However, her Ladyship also pointed out, that a parent or child can invoke existing procedures in the Children Act 1989 to get the matter back before the care court and then rely upon s 7(1)(b), though it might be preferable to get the matter before higher courts rather than the family proceedings court since only they can grant an injunction and award damages.[1005]

There are important limits on the ability to invoke ss 7 and 8. First, the claimant has to show that he or she is a 'victim', that is, a person who is directly affected by the act or omission.[1006] It is therefore insufficient to be a secondary victim, which would have meant, for example, that the foster carers in *W v Essex County Council* would have had no action.[1007] Secondly, the action must be brought within one year of the act complained of, although claims after that can be admitted at the court's discretion.[1008] Thirdly, there must be no other appropriate remedy. Indeed, in *Re S (Minors)(Care Order: Implementation of Care Plan)*[1009] Lord Nicholls considered actions generally under s 7 to be a 'longstop remedy'. He commented 'One would not expect proceedings to be launched under s 7 until any other appropriate remedial routes have first been explored'. His Lordship did not explain why s 7 actions should be of 'last resort'.

So far as the quantum of damages is concerned, s 8(4) of the 1998 Act directs the court to 'take into account the principles applied by the European Court of Human Rights in relation to the award of compensation under Art 41 of the Convention'. Furthermore, Lord Woolf has argued extra judicially that damages under the Act should be 'on the low side by comparison to tortious awards'.[1010] For this reason, it might still be worthwhile seeking a remedy in negligence, at any rate in the alternative to an action under ss 7 and 8.

Perhaps because of these restrictions and limitations, there have not been many actions

---

[1003] Section 7(1)(a). According to *C v Bury Metropolitan Borough Council* [2002] EWHC 1438 (Fam), [2002] 2 FLR 868, per Butler-Sloss P, human rights challenges to care plans and placement of children in care should be heard in the Family Division of the High Court and, if possible, by judges with experience of sitting in the administrative court. But in *Re L (Care Proceedings: Human Rights Claims)* [2003] EWHC 665 (Fam) [2003] 2 FLR 160, Munby J considered that Human Rights complaints made during care proceedings should normally be dealt with in the context of those proceedings by the court dealing with them. In his view there is no need for a transfer to a higher court.

[1004] [2001] EWCA Civ 757, [2001] 2 FLR 582 at [74], not commented upon on appeal.

[1005] Above at [75].   [1006] Section 7(7) applying Art 34 of the Convention.

[1007] Cf *A and B v United Kingdom* [1998] 1 EHRLR 82 in which the father of a son who was beaten by his stepfather was not considered to be a 'victim'.

[1008] Section 7(5).   [1009] [2002] UKHL 10, [2002] 2 AC 291 at [62].

[1010] See 'The Human Rights Act 1998 and Remedies' in *Judicial Review in International Perspective* (eds Andenas and Fairgrieve) at 432 and 434. See his subsequent judgment in *Anufrijeva v Southwark London Borough Council* [2003] EWCA Civ 1406, [2004] UKHRR 1.

under ss 7 and 8 but one example is *Re M (Care: Challenging Decisions By Local Authority)*[1011] in which, following a review of their care plan for a child in their care, the local authority finally ruled out any further prospect of the child returning to live with her mother or of ever going to live with her father. In reaching this decision, however, the authority was held to have acted unfairly and therefore in breach of Art 8 by not involving the parents to a degree sufficient to provide their interests with the requisite protection. Exercising his powers under s 8 of the 1998 Act upon an application by the parents under s 7, Holman J set the local authority decision aside. He also gave directions for a full hearing of the review issues and of applications for the discharge of the care orders. Holman J's decision was specifically endorsed by Lord Nicholls in *Re S (Care Order: Implementation of Care Plan)*.[1012] At the same time his Lordship emphasised that wide though the powers are under s 8 they are nevertheless confined to acts or proposed acts which the court finds are or would be unlawful. It does not confer a power to give relief in respect of acts by public authorities who have not and are not proposing to act in breach of a Convention right.

[1011] [2001] 2 FLR 1300.   [1012] Above at [46].

15

ADOPTION

A INTRODUCTION

1 THE NATURE OF ADOPTION AND BACKGROUND TO THE 2002 LEGISLATION[1]

In English law adoption refers to the process by which a child's legal parentage is entirely and irrevocably transferred from one set of adults, usually the birth parents, and vested in other adults, namely the adoptive parents.[2] As the Houghton Committee's report[3] put it, adoption involves: 'the complete severance of the legal relationship between parents and child and the establishment of a new one between the child and the adoptive parent'. Apart from parental orders under s 30 of the Human Fertilisation and Embryology Act 1990[4] adoption is the only child-related order under English law that lasts throughout adulthood (an adoption is truly for life) and it is the only means by which parents can lose their parental responsibility for their child whilst a minor.

Adoption can only be effected through a court process, and the jurisdiction is entirely statutory. This is because at common law parental rights and duties were held to be inalienable.[5] Hence, no change of status comparable to the adoptio or adrogatio of Roman law could be recognised. The absence of such a mechanism generated considerable dissatisfaction both from couples who were childless and anxious to bring up another's child as their own, but who hesitated to do so because of the lack of safeguards, and from those

---

[1] For general reference see C Bridge and H Swindells *Adoption The Modern Law* (2003) and its sister work H Swindells and C Heaton *Adoption The Modern Procedure* (2006).

[2] In lay terms 'adoption' can have a wider meaning. For example, it is sometimes said that a person, particularly a stranger in blood, who looks after a child in the event of parental death or abandonment, has 'adopted' him. This relationship is described as foster parenthood in this book, and its legal consequences are referred to above at p 544. For the meaning of 'adoption' for the purposes of the Immigration Rules see *R v Immigration Appeal Tribunal, ex p Tohur Ali* [1988] 2 FLR 523, CA. Unlike French law, for example, which makes provision for two types of adoption, ie 'full adoption' which involves the transfer of parentage, and 'simple adoption' which does not break all links with the birth family, English law has but the one form (see further below).

[3] Cmnd 5107, 1972, at para 14. See also *Review of Adoption Law*, 'The Nature and Effect of Adoption' (No 1, 1990) at para 2, which describes adoption as the process by which the legal relationship between a child and his or her birth parents is severed and an analogous relationship between the child and the adoptive parents is established.

[4] See above at p 315.

[5] *Vansittart v Vansittart* (1858) 2 De G & J 249; *Walrond v Walrond* (1858) John 18; *Humphrys v Polak* [1901] 2 KB 385, CA; and *Brooks v Blount* [1923] 1 KB 257.

who had effected a de facto adoption but who felt vulnerable to the very real risk of the parents later turning up and taking the child back.[6]

Although there were a variety of factors[7] that contributed to the increased pressures for reform, the main catalyst was the substantial increase in the number of orphans following the First World War, which in turn led to a large increase in de facto adoptions. The resulting demand for reform led eventually to the passing of the Adoption of Children Act 1926.[8]

The 1926 Act was extensively amended in the light of subsequent experience and criticisms,[9] and all earlier legislation was repealed and consolidated by the Adoption Act 1958.[10] Further dissatisfaction with various aspects of the law and procedure led to the appointment of a Departmental Committee, the 'Houghton Committee', whose report was published in 1972.[11] Most of their recommendations (some of them in modified form) were accepted and incorporated into the Children Act 1975 which was eventually consolidated by the Adoption Act 1976.

Adoption was the one area of child law not to be reviewed during the 1980s. However, after the enactment of the Children Act 1989[12] a full scale review of adoption law was instigated. This review, which was conducted by an Inter-Departmental Committee under the aegis of the Department of Health,[13] eventually led to publication in 1996 of a government White Paper 'Adoption—A Service for Children' which included a proposed Adoption Bill—A Consultative Document.[14] Apart from the passing of the Adoption (Intercountry Aspects) Act 1999 which paved the way for the United Kingdom's ratification in June 2003 of the 1993 Hague Convention on Intercountry Adoption,[15] no action was taken on the 1996 'Bill'. However, a new initiative was launched in 2000 to review in

---

[6] The Report of the Committee on Child Adoption ('The Hopkinson Report') (1921) Cmnd 1254, para 13 commented that it was not unknown for parents who had previously rejected the child to reclaim him once he had reached the age when he could work and earn wages.

[7] Neatly summarised by S Cretney *Principles of Family Law* (4th edn) p 420. See also the Discussion Paper No 1, op cit at para 2. For a detailed discussion of the early history of adoption reform, see N Lowe 'English Adoption Law: Past, Present and Future' in *Cross Currents—Family Law and Policy in the US and England* (eds S Katz, J Eekelaar and M Maclean) 307.

[8] Passed following the 'Hopkinson Report', above, and two Reports (the 'Tomlin Reports') of the Child Adoption Committee, Cmnd 2401 and 2469 (1925).

[9] Following eg the Horsburgh Committee's Report on Adoption Societies and Agencies (1937, Cmd 5499), by the Adoption of Children (Regulation) Act 1939 (discussed below at p 834) and by the Adoption of Children Act 1949 which for the first time treated the child as that of the adopters for the purpose of inheritance (see below, p 1100).

[10] Which was based on the Hurst Committee's Report on the Adoption of Children (1954, Cmd 9248).

[11] Cmnd 5107. In fact after Sir William Houghton's death the chair was taken by Judge Stockdale.

[12] Sch 10 to which did amend the 1976 Act inter alia to bring adoption into line with the changes of concepts, terminology and philosophy introduced by the 1989 Act. See generally the Department of Health's *Guidance and Regulations on the Children Act 1989*, Vol 9, *Adoption Issues* and R White, P Carr and N Lowe *A Guide to the Children Act 1989* (1st edn) ch 11.

[13] This review produced four Discussion Papers (*The Nature and Effect of Adoption* (No 1, 1990), *Agreement and Freeing* (No 2, 1991), *The Adoption Process* (No 3, 1991) and *Intercountry Adoption* (No 4, 1992)) and three Background Papers (*International Perspectives* (No 1, 1990), *Review of Research Relating to Adoption* (No 2, 1990) and *Intercountry Adoption* (No 3, 1992)), and culminated in the publication of 'Adoption Law Review: Consultation Document' in 1992. Following this document a government White Paper 'Adoption—the Future' (Cm 2288) was published in 1993. Separate consultation papers 'Placement for Adoption' and 'The Future of Adoption Panels' were published in 1994.

[14] Published by the Department of Health and Welsh Office.   [15] Discussed below, pp 873ff.

particular adoption of children being 'looked after' by local authorities.[16] This led quickly to the publication of the Prime Minister's Review of Adoption[17] and of another Government White Paper: *Adoption: a new approach*.[18] That in turn led to the Adoption and Children Act 2002. This Act, which repealed the 1976 Act, eventually came fully into force on 30 December 2005.[19]

2 A COMPARISON OF ADOPTION WITH OTHER LEGAL RELATIONSHIPS AND ORDERS

As already said, an adoption order completely severs the legal relationship between the child and his birth parents and vests full parental responsibility exclusively in the adopters.[20] The result in brief is that for all legal purposes the adopters step into the shoes of the child's natural parents: by 'parents', in other words, is now meant not the child's birth parents, but his adoptive parents.[21] Such a relationship is thus distinguishable from that of a married parent and child, unmarried father and child, and guardian and ward. It resembles most closely the first, for, although there need be no blood relationship between the parties, the legal consequences are almost the same. It differs most markedly from the second, for the law does not automatically vest parental responsibility by reason of the blood relationship: adoption in fact does exactly the reverse. It resembles the third in that the adoptive parents, like guardians, stand in loco parentis to the child to whom they are not necessarily related by blood, but differs from it in that the relationship of guardian and ward does not make the child a member of the guardian's family, eg for the purposes of the devolution and acquisition of property.

An adoption order is distinguishable both from a residence order under s 8 of the Children Act 1989 and a special guardianship order under s 14A because it severs the legal ties between the child and his birth parent, whereas the latter do not. Furthermore, whereas an adoption order is permanent (ie the child remains a member of the adoptive family even after he attains his majority) and not variable,[22] the latter can subsequently be varied and, in any event, ceases to have effect once the child reaches the age of 18.

It is perhaps permanence rather than severance that is the more significant feature of an adoption order. At any rate, the psychological importance of having the security of a permanent order has been stressed by the courts[23] and, as one leading expert put it,[24] 'Although no one can guarantee what the future will hold, a permanent placement is one that is *intended* to last and which is given the legal security to make this possible. A permanent home provides the child with the basis for his healthy emotional development.'

---

[16] Ie children accommodated by local authorities or subject to care orders. See Ch 14.

[17] A Performance and Innovation Unit Report (2000).   [18] (2000) Cm 5017.

[19] By the Adoption and Children Act 2002 (Commencement No 9) Order 2005, SI 2005/2213.

[20] See the Adoption and Children Act 2002, s 46.

[21] The effects of an adoption order are discussed more fully below, pp 867ff.

[22] But for a limited power to set an adoption order aside, see below, p 868.

[23] See eg *Re F (A Minor) (Adoption: Parental Agreement)* [1982] 1 All ER 321 at 326, CA, per Ormrod LJ agreeing with Bridge LJ in *Re SMH and RAH* [1990] FCR 996n (decided in 1979).

[24] M Adcock 'Alternatives to Adoption' (1984) Adoption and Fostering Vol 8, No 1 at 12; cf J Triseliotis 'Permanency Planning' (1991) Adoption and Fostering, Vol 15, No 4.

3 ADOPTION AND HUMAN RIGHTS

There are two aspects to human rights issues arising from adoption: the extent, if any, of a right to adopt and the extent to which the granting of adoptions can be regarded as an interference with the exercise of the right for family life contrary to Art 8.

With regard to the first issue it is established that the Convention does not guarantee the right to adopt as such.[25] Furthermore because the right to respect for family life presupposes the existence of a family and does not safeguard the mere desire to found a family,[26] it was held in *Fretté v France*[27] that the denial of an application by a single homosexual man of authorisation to adopt, did not in itself violate any Convention right. However, where domestic law gives a right to apply to adopt it is incumbent upon the authorities not to discriminate against an applicant on grounds inter alia of sexual orientation, unless such discrimination may be justified. In *Fretté* it was held that, given the lack of uniformity among Contracting States regarding the acceptability of adoption by homosexuals, and because the national authorities were legitimately and reasonably entitled to consider that the right to adopt was limited by the interests of children eligible to be adopted, the decision to deny the applicant authorisation to adopt on the basis of his homosexuality, fell within the State's margin of appreciation.[28]

So far as the second issue is concerned, as Hale LJ said in *Re B (Adoption By One Natural Parent to Exclusion Of Other)*:[29]

'an adoption order is undoubtedly an interference by a public authority, in the shape of the court that makes it, with the exercise of the right to respect for family life, whether by the child . . . or by anyone else with whom [the child] enjoys "family life". Indeed it is the most drastic interference with the right which is permitted by the law'.

Accordingly, to be compliant with Art 8 the interference must fall within Art 8(2) being in accordance with the law and necessary in a democratic society inter alia to protect the rights and freedom of others. Again, as Hale LJ put it in *Re B*, to be necessary in a democratic society the interference 'must meet a pressing social need and be proportionate to that need. The more drastic the interference, the greater must be the need to do it'. On the other side of the coin, as her Ladyship said, in the 'right circumstances' adoption 'is a most valuable way of supplying a child with the "family for life" to which everyone ought to be entitled and of which some children are so tragically deprived'.

The broad scheme of English adoption law satisfies these requirements since, as we will see, the court, having considered all other options, must always be satisfied that adoption is in the interests of the child. Moreover, the interests of parents with parental responsibility are safeguarded to the extent that their consent to the adoption is required[30] or has to

---

[25] See *Fretté v France* [2003] 2 FLR 9 at [32], E Ct HR relying inter alia upon *X v Belgium and Netherlands* (1975) D & R 75.

[26] See *Marckx v Belgium* (1979–80) 2 EHRR 330.   [27] Above.

[28] But note the Court did find a breach of Art 6 on the facts.

[29] [2001] 1 FLR 589 at [37], CA. For further discussion of this case, which went to the House of Lords, see below pp 845–6.

[30] As Lord Nicholls pointed out in *Re B (Adoption: Natural Parent)* [2001] UKHL 70, [2002] 1 WLR 258 at [29] a parent who unconditionally consents to the adoption cannot complain that his or her Art 8 rights have been violated.

be specifically dispensed by the court. Even the unmarried father without parental responsibility is not without protection in the adoption process.[31]

To a certain extent English adoption law came under scrutiny before the European Court of Human Rights in *Scott v UK*.[32] In that case an alcoholic mother whose drinking problem had not been effectively controlled, complained that her Art 8 rights had been violated by a local authority (in whose care the child was placed) decision not to pursue rehabilitation at a meeting to which she had not been invited and a subsequent court decision to dispense with her consent to adoption. Her action failed, the Court ruling that the interference with family life was justified in the child's interests.

What has yet to be tested is whether the adopted child and possibly other members of the birth family, particularly siblings and grandparents, can claim a breach of their Art 8 rights by the severance of the legal ties with the whole family resulting from the adoption. It is certainly not beyond argument that the complete severance of legal ties with the whole family is a disproportionate effect of adoption.[33]

4 THE CHANGING PATTERN OF ADOPTION[34]

Since the 1960s there has been a dramatic reduction in the number of adoptions: from a peak of 24,831 orders made in England and Wales in 1968 there were just 5,354 orders in 2003.[35] One of the main reasons for this decline is the evident reduction in the number of babies available for adoption. In 1970, for instance, out of a total of 22,373 adoptions 8,833 (or 39%) were of babies, that is of children under the age of 12 months. Figures since then show a continuous drop in the overall total of adoptions of babies, declining from eg 4,548 in 1975 and 1,115 in 1989 to just 213 (four per cent) in 2003.[36] The decline in the number of babies available for adoption was noted in 1972 by the Houghton Committee[37] and was then thought to be accounted for by the reduction in the number of unwanted babies because of the increased availability of contraception and abortion. Furthermore, more unmarried mothers tend to keep their children because of the changing attitude to illegitimacy and the availability of state benefits and reasonable employment prospects

---

[31] See further below at p 851. It was the absence of any means of challenging or adoption by the unmarried father that led to Ireland being found to be in breach of the Convention in *Keegan v Ireland* (1994) 18 EHRR 344, [1994] 3 FCR 165, ECtHR.

[32] [2000] 1 FLR 958, ECtHR.

[33] See N Lowe 'English Adoption Law: Past, Present and Future' op cit at n 7 at 337–8.

[34] See generally S Cretney 'From Status to Contract?' in Rose (ed) *Consensus Ad Idem* 251, N Lowe 'Adoption Law; Past, Present and Future' op cit, and N Lowe 'The Changing face of adoption—the gift/ donation model versus the contract/services model' [1997] CFLQ 371.

[35] Marriage, Divorce and Adoption Statistics 2002 ONS Series FM2 No 30 Table 6.16. That Table also provides statistics of adoption orders made between 1993 and 2003. NB separate Tables are kept for court orders and for adoptions entered on the Adopted Children Register. The figures cited here and below are for court orders. The annual statistics contained in *Judicial Statistics* are at considerable variance with the above-mentioned statistics (for example, according to Table 5.4 of the 2003 Report only 4,713 orders were made) and are not considered to be as reliable as those published by the ONS. A comprehensive table of statistics of orders made from 1927 to 1971 is included in Appendix B of the Houghton Report. An analysis of the adoption orders made in 1975–83 can be found in the Children Act 1975 Second Report to Parliament (HMSO 1984).

[36] Marriage, Divorce and Adoption Statistics, above, Table 6.26.   [37] Op cit at para 20.

and day care provision. Today one would add that an increasing number of children are born to unmarried couples living together in a stable union.

Although attention has perhaps understandably been focused on the reduction in the number of baby adoptions, in fact there have also been large reductions in the number of adoptions of children in most age groups.[38] A possible explanation for this overall reduction is that, as it became increasingly accepted that unmarried mothers would keep their babies, so there developed a more general culture of families being reluctant to give up their children. Eventually, however,[39] a further major reason for the decline in adoption numbers was a change in the law consequent upon the Houghton Committee's recommendation[40] aimed at discouraging joint adoptions by birth parents and step-parents.[41] In 1971, for instance, 10,751 step-parent adoption orders were made and even in the late 1970s there were still over 7,000 a year, representing 70% of all adoptions. However, by 1983 there were 2,872 such orders, which represented 31.8% of the total number of orders made, while in 2004 there were just 1,107 such orders representing 23% of the overall number of adoptions.[42]

The obvious corollary of the decline in baby adoption is the rising proportion of older child adoptions. In 1970, for example, 20% of the children adopted were aged between five and nine with a further 10% aged 10 or over. By 1995 these proportions had risen to 37% and 31% respectively but in 2003 the proportions had dropped to 31% and 18% respectively.[43] These figures, however, mask another important change: in 1970, for instance, whereas most adoptions by non-relatives were of babies or toddlers, most of the adoptions of older children—in fact 90% of the five to nine age group and 84% of those aged 10 or over—were by step-parents. Today, the profile is different. Over three quarters (77% in 2004) of all adoptions are by non-relatives and one study by the Social Services Inspectorate[44] found that 62.9% of the children placed for adoption by the agencies inspected were aged six or over and only 3% were under the age of 12 months. Another study[45] found that of a sample of 1,525 children placed for adoption by adoption agencies in 1993–94, 42% were aged five or over. In other words, so far as adoptions by non-relatives are concerned, baby adoptions have now become relatively unusual, while the adoption of older children, those aged five or over, has become quite common (albeit slightly declining).

---

[38] In 1975, for example, 5,523 children aged between one and four were adopted, 7,278 between five and nine, and 3,316 between 10 and 14, whereas in 2003 the comparable figures were 2,481, 1,695 and 749 respectively: Table 6.26 of the Marriage, Divorce and Adoption Statistics.

[39] But note that the significant drop of adoptions between 1975, when there were 21,299 adoptions, 1976 when there were 17,621 and 1977 when there were 12,748, cannot be attributed to a decline of step-parent adoptions.

[40] Op cit at para 115.   [41] See below, p 846.

[42] *Judicial Statistics 2004* Annual Report Table 5.4.

[43] See Table 6.2a of the Marriage, Divorce and Adoption Statistics.

[44] *For Children's Sake II* (Department of Health, 1997). According to the findings of M Murch, N Lowe, M Borkowski, R Copner and K Griew *Pathways to Adoption* (HMSO, 1993) 81% of step-parent adoptions were of children aged five or above.

[45] By M Murch, N Lowe, A Weaver, M Borkowski, V Beckford with C Thomas *Supporting Adoption—Reframing the Approach.*

(a) The practice of adoption

Adoption of 'looked after' children[46]

A key change in adoption practice occurred when local authorities came to see adoption as a means by which they could secure the long-term welfare not just of babies but also of older children (including those who were physically or mentally disabled) in their care. This change of practice in turn sprang from the childcare policy which, in the 1970s, began in the United Kingdom to be termed permanency planning.[47] It was undoubtedly stimulated by the seminal work of Goldstein, Freud and Solnit, *Beyond the Best Interests of the Child*, published in 1973, in which they challenged the prevailing traditional mode of thought that biological and legal parenthood should take precedence over psychological parenthood. Their thesis was intended to reinforce the security of the adoptive, psychological parent–child relationship. Many of their—at the time revolutionary—notions subsequently came to be accepted by social work and legal practitioners working in the child care and adoption fields. Certainly they strengthened the view[48] that children from neglectful, disrupted and severely disordered families might often do much better if placed permanently with loving, secure and more stable families. Other research, particularly Rowe and Lambert's *Children Who Wait*, also published in 1973,[49] which emphasised the need for long term planning for children in care, together with Report of the Inquiry into the Death of Maria Colwell[50] (who had been killed by her stepfather after having been removed from foster parents), reinforced the view that for certain abused or neglected children long term care away from their families was in their best interests and that adoption was a key means of achieving this even where the birth parents were opposed to it.

Although not everyone was swayed by this permanency movement (and in any event it was not infrequently bad social work practice rather than parental failure that had led to many children languishing in care) and indeed there was something of a backlash in the mid to late 1980s, there were nevertheless lasting significant changes in adoption practice. First, local authorities made and continue to make determined efforts to secure adoption placements for so-called hard to place children to the extent of having extensive publicity campaigns, one of the best known being the 'Be My Parent' scheme organised by the British Agencies for Adoption and Fostering (BAAF).[51] Second, there was a consequential increase in the number of adoptions in which parental consent was dispensed with.[52] Third, there was an overall rise in the age of children adopted out of care. For example, at a time when the overall numbers of adoptions were falling, the number of children adopted

---

[46] Ie children subject to a care order or who are being accommodated by a local authority. See Ch 14.

[47] See particularly R Parker *Planning for Deprived Children*. See also M Ryburn 'In whose best interests?— post adoption contact with the birth family' [1998] CFLQ 53 at 55–6.

[48] It might be pointed out that the Curtis Report, above, at para 448 had espoused similar views and even the Hopkinson Report, above, at para 11 was strongly of the view that adoption was preferable to institutional care.

[49] See also M Adcock, R White and O Rowlands *The Administrative Parent*.

[50] Report of the Committee of Inquiry into the Care and Supervision provided in relation to Maria Colwell (1974) HMSO.

[51] Under which written profiles with photographs, or video profiles of individual (but unidentified) children are widely circulated. There have also been television campaigns from time to time.

[52] This was noted first by the House of Commons' Second Report on the Children Act 1975, HMSO, 1984, see Table B when 11% of applications involved dispensing with agreement. A later study by M Murch, et al: *Pathways to Adoption* found, in a sample applications made between 1986 and 1988, 19% involved dispensing with agreement.

from care rose from 1,488 in 1979 to 2,605 in 1990.[53] In the late 1990s the Labour government took a strong line on the value of local authorities planning for the adoption of those children whose long term interests are that they should not be returned to their birth families. Following concerns about the variable quality of adoption services which emerged from Social Service Inspectorate reports in 1996 and 1997[54] a Local Authority Circular, *Adoption—Achieving The Right Balance*,[55] was issued in August 1998. The Circular focused 'attention on adoption as an important and beneficial option in the care of children' and was 'intended to bring adoption back into the mainstream of children's services'. It emphasised that where:

'children cannot live with their families, for whatever reason, society has a duty to provide them with a fresh start and where appropriate a permanent alternative home. Adoption is the means of giving children an opportunity to start again; for many children, adoption may be their only chance of experiencing family life'.

This positive message about adoption was further underscored by the Government's Quality Protects Programme, one of the aims of which is to 'maximise the contribution that adoption can make to provide permanent families for children in appropriate cases'.[56] Further pressure to increase adoptions has been placed on local authorities by making the number of adoptions a performance indicator of good practice.[57] The Government's declared intention when introducing the 2002 Act was to achieve a 40% and, if possible, a 50% increase in the number of looked-after children who are adopted.

Not surprisingly, these initiatives have had an impact on both the number and proportion of public law adoptions. In 2001, for example, there were 3,061 adoptions of 'looked after' children.[58] These constituted 69% of all adoptions.

In short, public law adoptions, which were almost unimaginable when adoption was first introduced in 1927, now form the majority of all adoptions.

Before leaving the issue of public law adoptions, attention also needs to be drawn to related developing practices in this sphere. Conscious of the need to keep the number of placements of the child to a minimum and at the same time come to speedier decisions concerning the child's long-term placement a number of different schemes have been developing. One is so-called 'concurrent planning', which has been defined as 'the process of working towards family reunification, while at the same time establishing an alternative permanent plan'.[59] In other words, it involves the social worker working both with the

---

[53] See Adoption Review, *Discussion Paper No 3*, op cit, para 9. Of children who left care in the year ending March 1985, 5.8% were adopted: (1988) Adoption and Fostering, Vol 12, No 2 at 55. This proportion for the year end March 1988 rose to 7.4%: see Adoption Law Review, *Discussion Paper No 1*, para 56.

[54] Viz *For Children's Sake: An SSI Inspection of Local Authority Adoption Services* (Department of Health, 1996) and *For Children's Sake—Part II: An Inspection of Local Authority Adoption Services* (Department of Health, 1997). One suspects that the Government was also influenced by P Morgan's thesis that all children who have been in local authority care for 12 months ought to be adopted, see *Adoption and the Care of Children* (IEA, 1998).

[55] LAC (98) 20. A national survey of implementation of this Circular was carried out in 1999.

[56] *The Government's Objectives for Children's Social Services* (Department of Health, 1999), para 1–3.

[57] See Performance Indicator C23, at para 1.3.   [58] Reference to be supplied.

[59] By L Katz, Programme Director of the Seattle Concurrent Planning Project, where the idea was pioneered. Pilot schemes have been running in England and Wales see L Katz and B Clatworthy 'Innovation in Care Planning for Children' [1999] Fam Law 108 and 'The Goodman Team—Concurrent Planning' [2001] Fam Law 301.

child's foster carers as potential adopters should rehabilitation fail, *and* with the birth parents to secure rehabilitation. Less dramatic is so-called 'twin tracking' in which the social worker works with the birth parents on rehabilitation while the child is in a foster placement but at the same time preparing the ground for a care order or a long-term fostering or adoptive placement elsewhere. Slightly different is so-called 'contingency planning' whereby a plan has been made and is being moved forward but at the same time a fall-back position has been thought about and decided upon should the first plan fail.[60]

Adoption and contact[61]

Traditionally, adoption had been a secretive process designed not simply to facilitate the irrevocable transfer of parentage, but to protect unmarried mothers and their children from excessive stigma and to enable childless couples to avoid the oppressive taint of infertility.[62] Hence, law and practice were designed so that the birth parents would have nothing to do with the process of selecting adopters: on the contrary they would generally have no knowledge of the adopters and of course they would have no further contact with their child. Similarly, adopters would not know the birth parents' identity. One result of this secrecy was that adopters were generally reluctant to tell their children that they were adopted. Today, however, it would be regarded as bad practice for adopters to hide the fact that their child had been adopted.[63] Indeed, studies in the 1960s and 1970s had demonstrated the deleterious effect upon adopted children of not knowing their own identities,[64] and the law was eventually[65] changed permitting adult adopted children to obtain their original birth certificate and to pursue the possibility of establishing contact with their birth family.[66] Since the introduction of this right, an Adoption Contact Register has been created[67] which provides 'a safe and confidential way for birth parents and other relatives to assure an adopted person that contact would be welcome and to give a contact address'.[68]

This change of law only enables adopted children to consider contacting their family after they have attained adulthood, but another important change in practice has been to permit on-going contact with the birth family throughout the adoption. Commonly

---

[60] N Lowe and M Murch, K Bader, M Borkowski, R Copner and J Shearman *The Plan for the Child, Adoption or Long-term Fostering* found that social workers were often confused by these different policies.

[61] See generally M Ryburn 'In whose best interests?—post adoption contact with the birth family' (1998) 10 CFLQ 53.

[62] See J Triseliotis 'Open adoption' in *Open Adoption—The Philosophy and the Practice*, p 19.

[63] This is not an enforceable obligation: see eg *Re S (A Minor) (Adoption by Step-parents)* [1988] 1 FLR 418, CA. Such an attitude would, however, if known, militate against that person's approval as an adopter in the first place: see Lowe 'The Changing Face of Adoption', op cit, at pp 375–6.

[64] See A McWhinnie *Adopted Children: How They Grow Up* (1967) and J Triseliotis *In Search of Origins* (1973).

[65] With effect from November 1975 (upon the recommendation of the Houghton Committee, ibid at 303) though controversially it was introduced with retrospective effect. In fact the Hurst Committee, op cit at para 150, had recommended in 1954 that all adopters should be required to give a formal undertaking to tell the child about his or her adoption.

[66] By 1990 it was estimated that 33,000 children had taken advantage of the facility: Adoption Law Review, Discussion Paper No 1, note 140. For details of the current law see below at p 866.

[67] Originally by s 51A of the Adoption Act 1976 (inserted by the Children Act 1989, Sch 10, para 21). See now s 80 of the Adoption and Children Act 2002, discussed further below at p 866.

[68] Department of Health *The Children Act 1989, Guidance and Regulations*, Vol 9 *Adoption Issues* para 3.2.

referred to as 'open adoption',[69] this change came about when it became realised that the automatic termination of contact between the child and his natural family was not necessarily in the child's interests.[70] In turn, following the ground-breaking decision in *Re J (A Minor)(Adoption Order: Conditions)*,[71] the courts began to accept that it is not inconsistent with adoption for the child to have continued contact with his family. In *Re J* Rees J said, 'the general rule which forbids contact between an adopted child and his natural parent may be disregarded in an exceptional case where a court is satisfied that by so doing the welfare of the child may be best promoted'.[72] The access (contact) order was made to avoid lengthy litigation which would otherwise have damaged the child. This decision was authoritatively confirmed by the House of Lords in *Re C (A Minor) (Adoption Order: Conditions)*,[73] in which contact was preserved between a child who was in long-term care and a sibling. Although, as we shall see,[74] the courts have been reluctant to *impose* a formal contact order on adopters, in practice some form of continuing contact (whether direct or indirect) is not uncommon in agency adoptions. Post-adoption contact can take many different forms, namely, for example the exchange of information, reports and photographs most likely through a confidential adoption agency 'letter box' service. It can also include face-to-face meetings or take the form of indirect contact via telephone calls, texting and emails.[75]

A further stage of 'open adoption' is to involve the birth parents in the process of selecting adopters and there are some agencies that actively encourage this.

In summary, the stereotypical image of adoption being, as Sir Roger Ormrod once put it:[76] 'the process of amputating a baby from the mother and grafting it into another family, all contact with the natural mother being cut off so that a child is a child of the new family' is no longer reflective of today's practice. The reality is that adoption, whether by a step-parent or a stranger, is much more likely to be of an older child, and not infrequently having some form of continuing contact with his birth family.

Post-adoption support

The conventional view of the adoption was that it was an end in itself and that, having effected a legal transfer of the child from one family to another, the adoptive family were thereafter left to their own devices and resources to bring up the child on their own. This model, which has been labelled the 'gift/donation' model, sits uneasily with the adoption of older children and the growing practice of open adoption.[77] It has become increasingly

---

[69] See generally: Ryburn, op cit; A Mullender (ed) *Open Adoption—The Philosophy and the Practice* (1991); 'Openness in Adoption' (1991) Adoption and Fostering, Vol 15, No 4 at 81–115; and the Adoption Law Review, Discussion Paper No 1, op cit, Part C and paras 98–109 and the Consultative Document (1992) pp 9–14.

[70] See eg J Triseliotis 'Adoption with Contact' (1985) Adoption and Fostering, Vol 9, No 4 at 19 and J Fratter *Family Placement and Access*.

[71] [1973] Fam 106.   [72] Ibid at 115.   [73] [1989] AC 1, HL.   [74] Below at p 864.

[75] For a detailed discussion of contact see M Murch et al *Supporting Adoption*, op cit, ch 15. But note difficulties are frequently encountered in recruiting would-be adopters to accept ongoing contact. Research has also found that ongoing contact with the birth family was one of the key factors in local authorities choosing to place a child for long-term fostering rather than adoption, see N Lowe and M Murch et al *The Plan for the Child*.

[76] 'Child Care Law: a personal perspective' (1983) Adoption and Fostering, Vol 7, No 4 at 10, 15.

[77] See N Lowe 'The Changing Face of Adoption—the gift/donation model versus the contract/services model' [1997] CFLQ 371.

recognised that adoption is not the end of the process but merely a part of an ongoing and often complex process of family development and that in many, if not most, cases the adoptive family will need ongoing support.[78]

During the 1990s the provision of post-adoption support became the subject of more attention and is now an express obligation of adoption agencies under the 2002 Act. It can take many forms, ranging from the provision of allowances, the organisation of post-adoption contact, payment for the provision of therapy for the child, ongoing counselling for the adoptive (and birth) family including the child, the provision of updating information and the organisation of support groups.[79]

So far as adoption allowances are concerned, their initial introduction was not without controversy. They were first recommended by the Houghton Committee[80] on the basis that more adoptive homes might be found for children in need if adopters were financially supported to adopt. The issue was hotly contested in Parliament and indeed in Standing Committee it was only the chairman's casting vote that saved the provision.[81] Nevertheless, a provision permitting adoption agencies to submit a scheme for the payment of an adoption allowance for approval by the Secretary of State was introduced in 1982.[82] In fact by the 1990s virtually all statutory agencies and some voluntary agencies had successfully applied for approval of a scheme.[83] Reflecting this development, the law was changed by the Children Act 1989[84] so as to empower *all* agencies to pay an adoption allowance, provided cash payments conformed to the requirements set out by Regulations 1991.[85] Nevertheless as the guidance then stated:[86] 'Adoption allowances continue to be the exception rather than the norm'.

It has been suggested there should be a national standardised system of eligibility and level of support.[87] But this plea has so far fallen on deaf ears; the scheme under the 2002 Act is similar to the pre-existing scheme.[88]

Transracial and intercountry adoptions

As the BAAF study *Focus on Adoption*[89] put it, many of the children who had previously been considered 'unsuitable for adoption' were from minority ethnic groups. The British

---

[78] Interestingly, wide though the Houghton Committee (ibid) envisaged a comprehensive adoption service should be, it made no mention of post-adoption support. For discussion about what a post-adoption service should provide see the Review of Adoption Law, Discussion Paper No 3 *The Adoption Process*, para 88, the Consultative Document 1992 (ibid) Part VII; the government White Paper *Adoption: The Future* (1993 Cm 2288) 4.25.

[79] For a detailed study of those services offered during the adoption process see M Murch et al *Supporting Adoption*, op cit.

[80] Ibid, Recommendation 17. But see the discussion by Lowe, 'The Changing Face of Adoption', op cit, at 379.

[81] Standing Committee A (Ninth Sitting), cols 447–80.

[82] Viz Children Act 1975 s 32, subsequently re-enacted by s 56(4)–(7) of the Adoption Act 1976.

[83] See Lambert and Seglow *Adoption Allowances in England and Wales: The Early Years* (1988).

[84] Substituting s 57A for s 56 (4)–(7) of the Adoption Act 1976.

[85] Viz the Adoption Allowances Regulations 1991.

[86] *The Children Act 1989, Guidance and Regulations*, Vol 9, *Adoption Issues* at para 22.

[87] This is one of the recommendations of Murch et al *Supporting Adoption*, op cit, and see Lowe, op cit, at 383–4.

[88] The obligation to provide support including financial support is provided by s 4 as supplemented by the Adoption Support Services Regulations 2005, discussed below at pp 835–6.

[89] *Focus on Adoption* (compiled by McCallum, 1997) 1.4.3.

Adoption Project in the late 1960s pioneered permanent family placement for a number of
these children, but most were placed transracially. During the 1980s in particular it began
to be seriously questioned whether it was desirable to have transracial adoptions at all.[90] It
was evident that many agencies were against placing minority ethnic children with white
adopters, though a rigid policy to this effect is almost certainly open to judicial review.[91]
Although it undoubtedly seems desirable, all things being equal, that children should be
matched with families of a similar background of race, culture,[92] language and religion,
where this cannot be achieved it becomes a matter of fine judgment as to whether it is
better for the child *not* to be placed permanently, rather than with potential adopters from
an entirely different background.[93] In those cases that came before the courts, at any rate,
where an application was to end a well-established placement, there was no predisposition
towards racial matching.[94]

Research in the 1990s found that the number of children from ethnic minority backgrounds formed a small minority of those placed for adoption.[95] Although a number were
placed transracially,[96] practice varied from agency to agency, but in general statutory
agencies (especially Shire counties)[97] were more likely than voluntary agencies to do so.

Related to the issue of transracial adoptions is another matter of growing concern and
importance, namely intercountry adoption, where applicants seek to adopt children from
overseas, commonly from developing countries such as those in Latin America, South East
Asia, or more recently from Eastern Europe, particularly Romania, Bosnia, the former
Soviet Union and China. As the White Paper, *Adoption: The Future* comments:[98]

'The interest in adopting children from Eastern European countries was stimulated by
harrowing reports of orphaned or abandoned children in institutions which emerged after
the collapse of their communist regimes. The general decline in the number of babies and

---

[90] See inter alia Gill and Jackson *Adoption and Race: black, Asian and mixed race children in white families* (1983).

[91] See eg *Re J K (Adoption: Transracial Placement)* [1991] 2 FLR 340; *Re P (A Minor) (Adoption)* [1990] 1 FLR 96, CA; and *Re N (Minors) (Adoption)* [1990] 1 FLR 58.

[92] Indeed s 1(5) of the 2002 Act expressly obliges agencies when placing a child to give due consideration to these factors.

[93] For most of the time this highly charged debate has been conducted in the absence of research evidence on the effects of transracial adoption. However, research by J Thoburn, Norford and Rashid *Permanent Family Placement for Children of Minority Ethnic Origins* (1998) suggests that transracial adoptions are commonly successful, and the government announced in August 1998 its intention to stop adoption being blocked on these grounds.

[94] See eg *Re O (Trans-racial Adoption: Contact)* [1995] 2 FLR 597 and the cases cited in note 91 above.

[95] In the *Supporting Adoption* study, op cit, only 13% of children placed by statutory agencies and 21% by voluntary agencies were from ethnic minority backgrounds. The later study *The Plan for the Child* by N Lowe and M Murch et al found that looked after children from minority ethnic backgrounds and for whom returning home was no longer an option, were more likely to end up in a long-term fostering placement than to be adopted, either by design or default.

[96] In fact almost a quarter (24%) of minority ethnic children were placed transracially in the BAAF sample of local authority adoptions in 1995: *Focus on Adoption*, op cit, at 5.2.3. According to the *Pathways Study*, op cit, 44% of statutory agencies and 31% of voluntary agencies reported that they had placed children transracially, but 24% of the former and 54% of the latter positively said that they do not place transracially: see N Lowe 'Some Perspectives from National Research' in James (ed) *Post Placement Services in Adoption and Fostering* (1997) 2.8.

[97] See *Focus on Adoption*, op cit, 5.2.3.   [98] 1993, Cm 2288, para 6.6.

very young children now available for adoption in this country also helped to stimulate a general interest in adoption from overseas.'

However, unlike many Western European countries (for example, France and Sweden) where such adoptions account for the majority of adoptions, and the USA, where a substantial number of such orders are made,[99] the number in England and Wales is remarkably low. Although there are no reliable statistics, before 1990 there were thought to be between 50 and 60 children brought annually to the UK for adoption through official procedures with a further 60–70 a year recorded as arriving without prior entry clearance.[100] In the early 1990s, there were a number of adoptions of Romanian orphans. Indeed, writing in 1992 the *Adoption Law Review* commented[101] that since March 1990 over 400 children from Romania alone had been brought to the UK for adoption.[102] In 1998, however, the total number of intercountry adoptions through official procedures was 258,[103] amounting to 6% of all adoptions for that year.

It has been speculated[104] that one reason for the low numbers is the absence of any specialist adoption agencies or adoption service for would-be adopters of children from overseas. This in turn has meant would-be adopters having to rely upon their own efforts and initiative—with all the expense and time that this entails. It might also be said that some adoption agencies have been either openly hostile to intercountry adoptions or reluctant to accord them priority, which will have also had a deterrent effect. Nevertheless, it has never been the case that no agency has been prepared to support an intercountry adoption application and indeed during the 1990s agencies were officially encouraged to provide assistance and support. Indeed, guidance issued in 1998[105] enjoined local authorities to reflect a positive view of intercountry adoption. Now, local authorities are statutorily bound to provide an intercountry adoption service.[106]

Intercountry adoption raises a number of fundamental issues such as the obvious dangers of exploiting vulnerable birth parents, the possible undesirability of transracial

---

[99] Annual numbers of intercountry adoptions in the USA are 8–10,000, which is between 40% and 50% of the estimated global number of intercountry adoptions.

[100] See Adoption Law Review, Discussion Paper No 4, para 27. In the *Pathways Study*, op cit at para 2.7, inter-country adoption amounted to 3% of the total sample, but 6% of the London Sample.

[101] Adoption Law Review, ibid, para 27. For a profile of inter-country adoptions in 1995, see *Focus on Adoption* (BAAF, 1997) Ch 6.

[102] Though note adoptions from this country were halted by the Romanian government. On which see A Bainham 'International adoption from Romania—why the moratorium should not be ended' [2003] CFLQ 223.

[103] Brennan et al, 'Intercountry Adoption—the recognition of foreign adoptions in the simple and full forms' in the *Report on the Cross Border Movement of Children* (1999, Society for Advanced Legal Studies) Annex C at pp 121–2, from which it will be seen that a substantial proportion (47%) of these children came from China. In addition, according to the Explanatory Notes to the Adoption (Intercountry Aspects) Act 1999, para 5, there were thought to be approximately another 100 cases each year where people avoid official adoption procedures.

[104] By the Adoption Law Review, Discussion Paper 4, ibid at para 28. The Review also commented that the *comparatively* low figures may, in part, be accounted for the relatively high number of domestic adoptions and of babies compared with other Western countries. However, with the virtual demise of baby adoptions that now appears a weaker argument. See *Adoption: The Future* (1993, Cm 2288) para 6.9, and Adoption Law Review, Discussion Paper 4, op cit, at para 31.

[105] Local Authority Circular LAC (98) 20, op cit, at para 52.

[106] See Adoption and Children Act 2002, s 2(8), discussed below at p 873.

adoptions and the difficulty of international control. Against these are the need of the adopters themselves, who are often desperate to have children but who are too old to be considered by adoption agencies, at any rate to adopt babies and, not least, the desperate plight of some of the children such as the Romanian orphans. It is by no means easy to balance these considerations, though practicality suggests that attempting to control inter-country adoption is probably better than attempting to outlaw it and, as we discuss at the end of this chapter, a bold attempt at global control is provided for by the 1993 Hague Convention on Intercountry Adoption to which the United Kingdom is a Contracting State. It has been speculated that with these changes intercountry adoptions could be one of the growth areas of adoption.[107]

5 RESPONSIBILITY FOR PLACING CHILDREN FOR ADOPTION

(a) Prohibition of private placements

When adoption was first introduced into England and Wales by the Adoption of Children Act 1926, it was remarkably unregulated. The 1926 Act essentially provided, as one commentator has put it, 'a process whereby, under minimal safeguards supervised by the court, a civil contract was registered and recognised'.[108] In particular, there were no provisions regulating who could arrange adoptions. Although, following the recommendations of the Horsburgh Committee, it became an offence for a body of persons other than a registered adoption society or a local authority to make any arrangements for the adoption of children,[109] until 1982 there was no restriction on individuals *placing* children for adoption. In fact it had been appreciated for some time just what a crucial stage the placement process is. As the Hurst Committee, reporting in 1954, put it:[110] 'Once the child is placed, much harm and unhappiness may result if a change has to be made.' It was the Committee's view that adoptions arranged by persons of special experience and training stood a much better chance of success. However, whilst it recommended that social workers employed by societies be fully trained, it stopped short of recommending the prohibition of private or third party placements. That particular bullet was bitten by the Houghton Committee. Although commonly such private arrangements were made through doctors or even solicitors, there was, as the Committee pointed out,[111] nothing to prevent a mother making a placement with a casual acquaintance she had met at the launderette. This lack of control had obvious dangers: if the potential adopters were unsuitable (a not unlikely consequence, given the inexperience of the placers) the placement could be disastrous for the child; it could also lead to improper pressure being brought upon the mother. Following the Houghton Committee's recommendation[112] it became unlawful for a person other than an adoption agency to place a child for adoption unless the proposed adopter was a relative of the child or was acting pursuant to a High Court order.[113] From that moment,

---

[107] See N Lowe: 'English Adoption Law: Past, Present and Future' op cit at 334.

[108] S Cretney 'From Status to Contract?', in *Consensus Ad Idem*, op cit, at p 252.

[109] Originally by the Adoption of Children (Regulation) Act 1939 s 1.

[110] Op cit at para 24. See also Goodacre *Adoption Policy and Practice*, (1966), who advocated that all adoptions by strangers be handled by local authorities.

[111] Op cit, at para 81.   [112] Op cit, at para 92.

[113] Originally by s 28 of the Children Act 1975. Private placements are now prohibited by s 92 of the Adoption and Children Act 2002, discussed below at p 880.

as one commentary put it,[114] the process of the 'professionalisation of adoption work' was completed. So far as individuals seeking to adopt non-relatives are concerned, adoption is fully regulated and they require agency approval before they can even begin the adoption process.

(b) Adoption agencies

The task of both selecting potential adopters and placing children for adoption outside their families rests with adoption agencies, ie registered adoption societies (otherwise known as voluntary agencies) and local authorities, (otherwise known as statutory agencies).[115] At the time of writing there are 30 voluntary organisations[116] so that together with statutory agencies there are in all in over 150 adoption agencies in England and Wales.[117]

Voluntary societies have long helped to facilitate adoptions. Indeed, at one time they dealt with the majority of agency adoptions. In 1966, for example, they arranged 73% of such adoptions, though this had dropped to 60% in 1971. Now, with the demise of baby adoptions, the majority of agency work is done by statutory agencies. According to one study, out of a national sample of 1,557 children placed for adoption in 1993–94, 84% were placed by statutory agencies.[118] Some societies, eg the Catholic Children's Society and Church of England Children's Society, aim primarily to serve particular denominational interests. Some, such as Barnardos, are national organisations; others are local.

An adoption society (which must be a body corporate)[119] is a body whose functions consist of or include making arrangements for the adoption of children. At one time voluntary adoption societies were subject to local control but that was changed under the 1976 Act which introduced a central system.[120] Now, under the 2002 Act, a registered adoption society is a voluntary organisation registered under Part 2 of the Care Standards Act 2000. Approval and registration are governed by Regulation,[121] under which societies are required inter alia to provide a statement of purpose, and to satisfy the Commission as to the fitness of the registered provider and conduct of the society. Inspections take place every three years and the Commission has the power to grant, refuse and cancel registration.

The functions and duties of adoption agencies are tightly controlled by the Adoption Agency Regulations 2005.[122] Under these Regulations the agency is obliged to set up an adoption panel,[123] whose function with regard to every child referred to it is, inter alia, to

---

[114] N Lowe 'English Adoption Law—Past, Present and Future', op cit, at 325.

[115] Adoption and Children Act 2002, s 2(1), (2).   [116] See Clarke Hall and Morrison at 3[23].

[117] According to M Murch, et al Supporting Adoption, op cit, there were 160 agencies actively operating in 1994. A full list and location of agencies is published annually in Adopting a Child by BAAF.

[118] See N Lowe 'The changing face of adoption—the gift/donation model versus the contract/services model' [1997] CFLQ 371 at 374.

[119] Adoption and Children Act 2002, s 2(4).

[120] For a short resumé of the history of such control see Lowe, op cit at 373, and p 622 of the previous edition of this work.

[121] Voluntary Adoption Agencies and the Adoption Agencies (Miscellaneous) Amendments Regulations 2003.

[122] These apply to England. Separate Regulations apply to Wales.   [123] Regulation 3.

consider and make recommendations as to whether the child should be placed for adoption[124] and whether the prospective adopter is a suitable person to adopt the child.[125] The agency itself has extensive duties whenever it is considering adoption to provide a counselling service for the child and to explain to the child in an appropriate manner the procedure and legal implications of adoption to the child.[126] A similar duty is owed to the parents, guardians or any other person the agency considers relevant,[127] and to the prospective adopters.[128] The agency also has a duty to collect and collate information about the child and his parents, to make arrangements for medical examinations, to provide background information about the child to the prospective adopters, to visit the child after placement, and generally to provide advice and assistance.[129]

It will be seen therefore that through these provisions, which have steadily become more extensive, children are only placed for adoption with applicants who have been carefully screened by professional and experienced bodies.

B GENERAL PRINCIPLES WHEN REACHING DECISIONS ABOUT ADOPTION

1 THE WEIGHTING OF THE CHILD'S WELFARE

(a) The former position

Although the courts have always had to be satisfied that an adoption order is for the child's benefit, until the implementation of the Children Act 1975 there was no specific guidance on the weighting to be accorded to the child's welfare during the various stages of the adoption process. However, when it was introduced, the guiding principle, eventually provided by the Adoption Act 1976 s 6, directed courts and adoption agencies to give 'first rather than paramount consideration to the need to safeguard and promote the welfare of the child throughout his childhood when reaching any decision relating to adoption'.

(b) The position under the 2002 Act

Although, given the irrevocable severance of family ties, there is some justification in not treating the child's welfare as the paramount consideration, there are powerful counter-arguments. First, even supposing it is right to protect the parents' interests, there is little justification in applying the lesser weighting to issues that do not involve the parents. Accordingly, it may be thought right to have the paramountcy principle govern all adoption issues save that of dispensing with parental consent. That indeed was the proposal made in the Consultative Document in 1992.[130] Secondly, one can argue that looked at from the child's point of view his welfare ought to be considered paramount in all cases, including adoption, where his future upbringing is directly in issue. It was this argument

---

[124] Regulation 18. In making this recommendation the panel must have regard inter alia to the child's permanence report that agencies must prepare about the child's background, health and wishes and feelings as set out in reg 17.
[125] Regulation 26.   [126] Regulation 13.   [127] Regulation 14.   [128] Regulation 21.
[129] For further details see Clarke Hall and Morrison 3[33]ff.   [130] Ibid at paras 7.1ff.

that ultimately prevailed since, by s 1(1) and (2) of the 2002 Act in coming to a decision relating to the adoption of a child, the 'paramount consideration of the court or adoption agency must be the child's welfare, throughout his life'. The requirement to consider the child's welfare 'throughout his life' is to be noted and marks a further distinction between adoption orders, which have life-long effects, and orders made under the Children Act 1989 which do not. It does not, however, break new ground but reflects the position established by pre-2002 Act case law.[131] At the same time, however, the court or adoption agency is also directed to have regard to a statutory checklist[132] modelled on that under the Children Act,[133] namely, to consider the child's wishes and feelings, needs, age, sex, background and any harm which the child has suffered or is likely to suffer, but with the important additional requirements to consider:

'(c) the relationship[134] which the child has with relatives,[135] and with any other person in relation to whom the court or agency considers the question to be relevant, including—

   (i) the likelihood of any such relationship continuing and value to the child of its doing so,

   (ii) the ability and willingness of any of the child's relatives, or of any such person, to provide the child with a secure environment in which the child can develop, and otherwise to meet the child's needs,

   (iii) the wishes and feelings of any of the child's relatives, or of any such person, about the child.'

Although much depends on how these specific factors are interpreted, there can be little doubt that making the child's welfare paramount represents a fundamental shift from the previous position and makes it harder for a parent to oppose the adoption, at any rate once the child has been placed. In the last edition we speculated whether this new weighting would lead to agencies making more adoptive placements but, as the Government has since made clear, it is one of the avowed objectives of the 2002 legislation to deliver at least a 40% increase in the number of 'looked-after' children who are adopted.

(c) Religious, racial, cultural and linguistic considerations

At one time consent to adoption could be conditional on the child being brought up in a particular religion but this was changed by the Adoption Act 1976, s 7 which required agencies only to have regard so far as practical to parental wishes about the child's religious upbringing. This has been modified and extended by s 1(5) of the 2002 Act which requires an agency when placing a child for adoption to 'give due consideration to the child's religious persuasion, racial origin and cultural and linguistic background'.

---

[131] See eg Re B (Adoption Order: Nationality) [1999] 2 AC 136, HL and Re D (A Minor)(Adoption Order: Validity) [1991] Fam 137, CA.

[132] Section 1(4).   [133] Children Act 1989 s 1 (3), discussed above, p 468.

[134] Relationships are not confined to legal relationships: s 1(8)(a).

[135] Which for these purposes would include the birth parents: see s 1(8)(b).

(d) Delay

Section 1(3) enjoins both the court and adoption agency at all times to 'bear in mind that, in general, any delay in coming to the decision [relating to adoption] is likely to prejudice the child's welfare'. As under the Children Act 1989, to reinforce this general principle s 109 obliges the court to draw up a timetable to determine the question of whether an adoption order or placement order should be made without delay and to give appropriate directions to ensure that the timetable is adhered to.

(e) Making an order only where it is better for the child than not doing so

Again, mirroring the Children Act principles, s 1(6) of the 2002 Act directs the court to consider the whole range of powers available to it either under the 2002 Act or the Children Act 1989 and in any event 'not to make any order under this Act unless it considers that making the order would be better for the child than not doing so'.

C ADOPTION SERVICE

The first attempt to regulate adoption practice was by the Adoption of Children (Regulation) Act 1939. That Act introduced a system of local registration of adoption societies and empowered the Secretary of State to make regulations, inter alia: (a) to ensure that parents wishing to place their children for adoption were given a written explanation of their legal position; (b) to prescribe the inquiries to be made and reports to be obtained to ensure the suitability of the child and adopter; and (c) to secure that no child would be delivered to an adopter until he had been interviewed by a case committee.

Although the 1939 Act could be said to have created the rudimentary foundations of what might now be called an adoption service, it was only concerned with the placement of children and only controlled the activities of registered adoption agencies. Some changes were subsequently made to this system, not least in clarifying the role of local authorities in arranging adoptions, but it was not until the reforms prompted by the Houghton Committee's report that an adoption *service* could truly be said to have been created.

The Houghton Committee noted that at the time of their report (1972) only 96 out of 172 local authorities in England and Wales acted as an adoption agency and, even where they did, not all of them had integrated their adoption work with their other services for children and families. Further, the geographical spread of 63 voluntary societies then existing was uneven and in any event they offered a range of child care and family services.[136]

Being concerned to see the establishment of a nationwide comprehensive adoption service which would therefore be available to 'all those needing it in any part of the country', the Committee recommended that *all* local authorities should have a statutory duty to provide an adoption service as part of their general child care and family casework provision.[137] Further, recognising that voluntary adoption societies still had a valuable role to play, not least in providing a choice of service, the Committee recommended[138] that

---

[136] Cmnd 5107, paras 32–33.   [137] Paras 42 and 44 and Recommendation 2.
[138] Para 41 and Recommendation 3.

local authorities have a statutory duty 'to ensure, in co-operation with voluntary societies, that a comprehensive adoption service is available throughout their area'.

By 'comprehensive' the Committee envisaged that an adoption service:[139]

'. . . should comprise a social work service to natural parents, whether married or unmarried, seeking placement for a child . . . skills and facilities for the assessment of the parents' emotional resources, and their personal and social situation; short-term placement facilities for children pending adoption placement; assessment facilities; adoption placement services; aftercare for natural parents who need it; counselling for adoptive families. In addition, it should have access to a range of specialised services, such as medical services (including genetic, psychological assessment services, arrangements for the examination of children and adoptive applications, and medical adviser) and legal advisory services.'

The Houghton Committee's recommendations were accepted and subsequently enacted by s 1 of the Adoption Act 1976 under which it became the duty of *every* local authority to establish and maintain an adoption service. This duty is now provided for and expanded upon by the Adoption and Children Act 2002. Section 3 provides:

'Each local authority must continue to maintain within their area a service designed to meet the needs, in relation to adoption, of—

(a) children who may be adopted, their parents and guardians,

(b) persons wishing to adopt a child,

(c) adopted persons, their parents, natural parents and former guardians;

and for that purpose must provide the requisite facilities.'

As one commentary has said,[140] this is a much wider group than that formerly covered.

'Requisite facilities' must include making and participating in arrangements both for the adoption of the child and, importantly, for the provision of adoption support services.[141] In other words this duty covers all aspects of a local authority's activities in relation to adoption and applies to all types of adoption (ie whether domestic, or intercountry, relative, step-parent, foster carer or stranger adoption). Local authorities may meet their obligations to provide these services by ensuring that they are provided by a registered adoption society or any other person as prescribed by regulation.[142] Each local authority is required to publish their plan of the services that they maintain.[143]

One of the key innovations of the 2002 Act is the *clear* imposition to provide adoption support both pre- *and* post-adoption.[144] Such support services are defined as 'counselling, advice and information, and any other services prescribed by regulations'.[145] Under s 4 a whole range of people affected by adoption or the prospective adoption (including not just the child, his or her parents and prospective and adoptive parents but also the child's natural sibling(s), other children of the adoptive parents and adopted adults, their parents,

---

[139] See para 38.   [140] Bridge and Swindells, op cit, at 13.14.   [141] Section 3(2).
[142] Section 3(4).   [143] Section 5.
[144] Post-adoption support was only implicitly required under the previous legislation, see the discussion at p 624 of the previous edition of this work.
[145] Section 2(6) and see the Adoption Support Services (Local Authorities) (England) Regulations 2005. There are separate Regulations for Wales.

natural parents and former guardians)[146] may request an assessment of their need for adoption support services. This right to an assessment does not mean that any such person has a right to receive services. That remains a matter for the local authority. In other words the obligation is to carry out the assessment, not necessarily to act upon it. Nevertheless it is incumbent upon authorities to act reasonably.[147] If the local authority decide to provide any adoption support service they must prepare a plan and keep that plan under review.[148]

An assessment of needs includes consideration of whether some form of financial support may be appropriate. Such support may be payable to help secure a suitable adoption where a child cannot be readily adopted because of a financial obstacle.[149] Local authorities may provide financial support to adoptive parents *regardless* of whether the adoption was the result of an agency placement. It can take the form of a single payment to meet a specific need, or as a periodical or regular payment to meet a need likely to give rise to recurring expenditure.[150]

In addition prospective adopters now have a right to statutory adoption pay and leave and statutory paternity pay and leave.[151]

Whether it is sensible or practical, given the other calls on their time, to impose a duty on every local authority to provide an adoption service has been questioned.[152] Indeed, given the large numbers of adoption agencies and the relatively low number of adoptions, there does seem an overwhelming case for rationalisation, for there must surely be some minimum number of adoptions which the agency handles below which they cease to be viable. However, how this rationalisation could be achieved is highly problematic. Among the range of options are the amalgamation of agencies, removing the function from local authorities altogether and placing it solely in the voluntary sector, and, most contentiously, creating a new national adoption service.

D PLACEMENT FOR ADOPTION [153]

1 INTRODUCTION

One of the key changes made by the 2002 Act was the introduction of a new regime for the placement of children for adoption. As John Hutton (the minister) said during the debates on the earlier Bill[154]

'The new system is intended to provide greater certainty and stability for children by dealing as far as possible with parental consent *before* they have been placed with the prospective new family; to reduce the uncertainty for the prospective adopters, who possibly face a

---

[146] Adoption Support Services Regulation 2005, reg 4.

[147] See Bridge and Swindells, op cit, at 13.24 and Clarke Hall at 3 [500.131].

[148] Section 4(5).   [149] Adoption Support Services Regulations 2005, reg 8.

[150] Regulation 10. Note: financial support cannot include remuneration except in the case of former foster parents: reg 9.

[151] See the Paternity and Adoption Leave Regulations 2002.

[152] See in particular P Morgan *Adoption and the Care of Children* (1998) and N Lowe et al *Supporting Adoption*.

[153] See generally Bridge and Swindells, op cit, ch 9 and Clarke Hall and Morrison at 3 [100]ff.

[154] HC Debs Vol 365, no 59, col 708 (26 March 2001).

contested hearing at the adoption order stage; and to reduce the extent to which birth families are faced with a fait accompli at the final adoption hearing, if the child has been placed with prospective adopters for some time.'

(a) Freeing the child for adoption

This is not the first attempt to deal with the parents' position ahead of adoption placements. Under the former law provision had been made for a procedure known as 'freeing the child for adoption'. This procedure was itself introduced to address what was perceived as a weakness in the previous law, namely, the absence of a procedure whereby parental consent to adoption could be bindingly made before the final adoption hearing. Freeing was deceptively simple.[155] It provided a procedure whereby adoption agencies could seek a formal court order freeing the child for adoption which could only be granted if the court was satisfied either that those whose consent was required (primarily parents) had unconditionally agreed to the making of the order or that their agreement should be dispensed with. It was an important prerequisite of the order being granted, that the court was satisfied that adoption was in the child's interests and that the agency's plans for placement were realistic. The effect of the freeing order was to transfer parental responsibility from the parent to the agency.[156] The agency would then be able to place the child for adoption secure in the knowledge that provided the placement was satisfactory the final adoption would be made. In starkly simple terms a freeing order amounted to a 'mini adoption' in favour of the adoption agency.

(b) The shortcomings of freeing

Despite its apparent simplicity freeing was judged to be a failure.[157] Some of its shortcomings were as follows. First, there was no compulsion upon agencies to use freeing. While most people envisaged, and the Houghton Committee certainly intended, that it would be commonly used not least because that is what the birth parents (particularly mothers) would wish,[158] in practice the frequency of use varied from agency to agency, with some not using it at all and others using it some of the time. Secondly, and one of the main reasons for its relatively infrequent use, instead of being the speedy process that it was intended to be, it was in practice a lengthy process riddled with delay. Thirdly, and in part a response to the length of the proceedings, agencies sometimes used the process to free children already placed with prospective adopters.[159] The agencies' motive for doing this was to shield the would-be adopters from the stress of taking on the contest with the birth parents. But not everyone agreed that this was a legitimate use of the jurisdiction and in any event it was possible for the court to join the prospective adopters as parties. Fourthly, there was the unsatisfactory result that upon a freeing order being made the

---

[155] For a detailed discussion of the procedure see pp 650ff of the previous edition of this work.

[156] There were provisions to revoke a freeing order if, upon the parent's application following notification that the child had not been placed for adoption within 12 months of the making of the freeing order.

[157] See the Adoption Law Review Discussion Paper No 2 at para 76, N Lowe and M Murch et al *Report of the Research into the Use and Practice of the Freeing for Adoption Provisions* (1993) and in Scotland, Lambert, Buist, Triseliotis and Hall *Freeing Children for Adoption* summarised in (1990) 14 Adoption and Fostering 36.

[158] See eg M Hayes and C Williams 'Adoption of Babies, Agreeing and Freeing' [1982] Fam Law 233 at 236.

[159] The *Pathways Study* found this to be the case in 21% of cases, with a further 9% so placed during the pendency of the application: ibid, Table 3.36.

child was placed in what had been memorably described as 'adoption limbo' and became a 'statutory orphan'.

(c) Earlier proposals for reform

The shortcomings of the freeing process led the Adoption Law Review[160] to conclude that the process should be replaced by an entirely new procedure that better safeguarded the interests of all parties. The problem, however, was to devise a suitable alternative. The Consultative Document on Adoption Law[161] proposed that *all* agency placements for adoption (save those for babies) should be preceded by what was to be called a 'placement order'. Such an order could only be made where a specific placement was planned, it being envisaged that an application would be made following an introductory meeting between the child and the prospective adoptive parents. If, after an investigation by a guardian, it was found that the proposed adoption was not opposed, then a placement order would be granted by the court without a hearing. If the adoption was contested, then the agency would not be allowed to proceed with the placement (apart from continued 'introductions' between the child and prospective adopters) until the court had formally resolved the dispute.

These proposals met with considerable criticism.[162] As the subsequent White Paper *Adoption: The Future* put it:[163]

'Many acknowledge that the problem [the proposal] is intended to address does exist and needs remedy but fear the new procedure might prove cumbersome and might in some cases unnecessarily and without clear benefit add to the length and complexity of the adoption process.'

In 1994 a revised system was proposed,[164] providing for a more flexible approach which it was felt more appropriately dealt with, on the one hand, babies whose birth parents had requested adoption and, on the other, older children removed or kept from their parents against the latter's wishes. It was these later proposals that were incorporated into the proposed 1996 Adoption Bill, and were essentially replicated in the 2002 Act.

2 THE PLACEMENT SCHEME UNDER THE 2002 ACT

(a) The general scheme

The general scheme for adoption placements is set out by s 18. There are only two routes: placements with consent and those authorised by court order. By s 18(1) an adoption agency (except in the case of a child who is less than six weeks old)[165] may only place a child for adoption with prospective adopters where each parent or guardian[166] has consented to the placement or, if a local authority, where it has obtained a placement order. 'Placement' in this context includes not just the initial placement but also leaving a child

---

[160] Adoption Law Review, Discussion Paper No 2, *Agreeing and Freeing*, (1991) para 180.

[161] 1992, Recommendations 16–18, discussed at para 15.1–15.5.

[162] See eg N Lowe 'Adoption placement orders—freeing by another name' (1993) 5 Jo of Child Law 62.

[163] Cm 2288 (1993) para 4.9.   [164] *Placement for Adoption—a consultation document* (1994).

[165] Discussed below.   [166] Including special guardian, see s 144(1).

in an existing placement with prospective adopters. This last point covers the situation where a child is initially fostered but the agency later plan for the child's adoption by those foster carers. This meets one criticism of the former law that there was no formal process of control over local authorities changing the care plan from rehabilitation to adoption.

Before any placement for adoption may be made the agency must be satisfied that the child ought to be placed for adoption.[167]

Where a child is placed or authorised to be placed for adoption by a local authority, the child is a 'looked after child'.[168]

Unlike freeing, the birth parent(s) retain parental responsibility notwithstanding a placement, an authorisation to place or a placement order until the final adoption order is made, though it is shared with the adoption agency and prospective adopters with whom the child is placed.[169]

(b) Placing children with parental consent

Section 19 allows[170] an adoption agency (ie both a local authority or a registered adoption society)[171] to place a child for adoption where it is satisfied that each parent[172] or guardian[173] has consented[174] to the child being placed for adoption and that that consent has not been withdrawn. The consent may be to placements with identified[175] prospective adopters or with any prospective adopters who may be chosen by the agency. Alternatively, a specific consent can be combined with a general one if the initial placement breaks down.[176] Consent may be withdrawn at any point before an application for an adoption order has been made.[177]

Where a child has been placed for adoption following consent by the mother, and the father later acquires parental responsibility, he will be deemed to have given consent in the same terms as the mother.[178]

Special provision is made for the consensual placement of babies under six weeks old. The mother's consent is ineffective if given less than six weeks after the child's birth (this is

---

[167] Section 18(2).

[168] Ibid, s18(3). For the consequences of being 'looked after', see above p 795.

[169] Section 25, see further below at p 841.

[170] Save where care proceedings are pending or a care order or placement order was made after the consent was given: s 19(3).

[171] Ibid, s 2(1), discussed above at p 831.   [172] Ie a parent with parental responsibility: s 52(6).

[173] Including any special guardian: s 144(1).

[174] For the meaning of 'consent' see s 52, discussed below at p 852.

[175] As Bridge and Swindells, op cit, at 9.16 point out, 'identified' was deliberately chosen to enable parents to consent to a placement with specific adopters whose name they did not know but with whose characteristics and details they might be familiar with through, for example, an anonymous profile passed on by the agency.

[176] Section 19(2). Presumably if the consent is to a specific placement only, fresh consent or a court order is required to place the child elsewhere.

[177] Ibid s 52(4). If consent is withdrawn before placement the child must be returned within one week: s 31. If withdrawn after placement but before an application for adoption is made, the child must be returned within 14 days: s 32. This is, however, subject to a local authority not having a duty to apply for a placement order under s 22(1), see below.

[178] Section 52(9), (10).

to allow her time to recover from the birth)[179] but placements are permitted with her informal consent.[180] However, her formal consent is required after that before an adoption order can be made.[181]

At the same time as consenting to the placement, by s 20, a parent may also consent to the making of a future adoption order. This consent may be to adoption by identified prospective adopters or any prospective adopters chosen by the agency. This so-called 'advance consent' can still be withdrawn before any application to adopt is made but such withdrawal must be by notice in writing to the agency or in the form prescribed.[182] In addition to giving advance consent the parent can give notice to the agency that he or she does not wish to be informed when an application for an adoption order is made, and to withdraw any such notice.[183] In this way provision is made for a parent to relinquish their child for adoption and have no further involvement in the proceedings.

We discuss the legal effects of children being placed by agreement or order shortly but suffice it to say here that it affects the allocation of parental responsibility, ends the ability to apply for a residence order, puts contact in issue and materially restricts the parent's ability to oppose the making of the final adoption order. In other words, consenting to a child's placement for adoption has serious legal consequences and, given that no court is involved at this stage, puts a premium on the agency truly being satisfied that there is real and genuine agreement. In this respect it will be noted that the signing of the consent to placement form must be witnessed by a CAFCASS officer (or in Wales, a Welsh family proceedings officer) who has the responsibility for deciding that consent is freely and unconditionally given with a full understanding of the consequences.[184]

(c) Placement orders

As s 21(1) explains, a placement order is one made by a court authorising a *local authority* to place a child with any prospective adopters who may be chosen by the authority. It will be noted that only local authorities (and not, therefore, registered adoption agencies) are able to apply for a placement order.[185]

By s 22 local authorities *must* apply for a placement order if

(a) the child is placed for adoption by them or is being provided with accommodation by them,

(b) no adoption agency is authorised to place the child for adoption (ie there is no formal parental consent),

---

[179] Section 52(3).   [180] Section 18(1).   [181] Section 47(4).

[182] Section 20(3), 52(4), (8), and the Family Procedure (Adoption) Rules 2005, rr 24 and 28.

[183] Section 20(4). Under the 1976 Act, this non-involvement could be achieved by making a s 18(6) declaration, but in practice such declarations were made only in minority of cases, see Lowe et al *Report of the Research into the Use and Practice of the Freeing for Adoption Provisions*, op cit, Table 3.45.

[184] See the Family Procedure (Adoption) Rules 2005 rr 20, 24, 27 and 28 and the Practice Direction: Forms.

[185] As Bridge and Swindells, op cit, at 9.27 point out, it was eventually considered inappropriate to permit voluntary agencies to have a child compulsorily placed for adoption against the parents' wishes.

(c) the child has no parent or guardian or the authority consider that the conditions in s 31(2) of the Children Act (the so-called threshold conditions)[186] are met, *and*

(d) the authority are satisfied that the child ought to be placed for adoption.

Local authorities *must* also apply if they are satisfied that the child ought to be placed for adoption and either care proceedings are pending or a care order has been made and the authority are not authorised to place the child for adoption. Local authorities *may* also apply for an order notwithstanding that the child is subject to a care order and the authority is authorised to place the child for adoption with parental consent.

The overall effect of this scheme is that wherever a local authority are seeking a care order with adoption as the care plan or where their existing placement or plan moves to adoption, they must have that plan or placement authorised by a court order.

The court[187] may only make a placement order if (a) the child is subject to a care order or (b) it is satisfied that the statutory threshold criteria for making a care order is satisfied, or (c) the child has no parent or guardian.[188] Section 21(3) further provides that a court may only make a placement order if it is satisfied that each parent or guardian has consented to the placement for the child with any prospective adopters chosen by the authority and have not withdrawn that consent, or that their consent should be dispensed with.

In determining the application the court is bound by the general principles set out in s 1 and in particular must, having regard to the welfare checklist, treat the child's welfare as the paramount consideration and be satisfied that making the placement order is better for the child than not doing so.

A placement order remains in force until an adoption order is made or until the child marries, forms a civil partnership or reaches 18 or until it is revoked.[189] Revocation is governed by s 24. It may be sought at any time by the child or local authority or by anyone else provided they have court leave (which can only be given if there has been a change in circumstances since the order was made) and the child has not yet been placed with prospective adopters. Unless or until it is revoked the parents or guardians have no right to have their child returned.[190]

(d) The legal effects of placement

Placements or authorisations to place under s 19 and placement orders, give parental responsibility to the agency concerned and, where placed, to the prospective adopters. Although parents do not thereby lose parental responsibility, at all times the agency may determine that the parents' parental responsibility or that of the prospective adopters be restricted.[191] This latter power, however, is fettered to the extent that without court leave or

---

[186] These are the conditions that must be satisfied before a care order may be made, see the discussion above at pp 736ff.

[187] Ie High Court, county court or magistrates' court.

[188] Section 21(2). The inclusion of s 21(2)(b) corrected an omission in the original March 2001 Bill which would have meant that a placement order depriving a parent of his or her child could have been made in circumstances where a care order could not. But note the threshold criteria do *not* have to be satisfied if the child has no parent or guardian (which presumably includes a special guardian). For a discussion of the threshold criteria see above, pp 736ff.

[189] Section 21(4).   [190] Section 34.   [191] Section 25.

the parents' or guardians' written consent, no-one can cause the child to be known by a new surname or remove the child from the United Kingdom for any period of a month or more.[192] Subject to these latter restrictions, though, the local authority is in overall control.[193]

Placements or authorisations to place under s 19 prevent the parent or guardian from applying for a residence order and a guardian from applying for a special guardianship order without court leave.[194] Upon the making of a placement order, an existing s 8 order under the Children Act 1989 and any supervision order ceases to have any effect and while in force no prohibited steps order, residence order or specific issue order or supervision order or child assessment order may be made.[195] Separate provision is made for contact by s 26, under which, while existing s 8 contact orders cease to have effect upon s 19 placements or authorisations to place and placement orders, applications can nevertheless be made for a new contact order. In this respect note should be taken of the requirement under the Adoption Agencies Regulations 2005, reg 46 that agencies consider when deciding that a child be placed for adoption what arrangements they should make for contact. However, the point has been well made[196] that before the 2002 Act contact was rarely imposed on adopters or prospective adopters so that it remains to be seen whether the position will be any different under the 2002 legislation. It may also be noted that even where a s 26 contact order is made an agency can nevertheless refuse contact in cases of urgency for up to seven days.[197]

A further important consequence of a s 19 placement or placement order is that the parent may only oppose the making of an adoption order with court leave which can only be given if the court is satisfied that there has been a change in circumstances since the consent was given or the placement order was made.[198]

(e) Commentary

The regime for the placement of children for adoption is a key innovation of the 2002 Act. It is vital that it works.

There seem some clear advantages of the 2002 Act scheme over the former law. Having to obtain sanction either by parental consent or by court order *before* a 'placement' for adoption may be made provides welcome certainty. In this regard it seems a much better idea to require local authorities to obtain a placement order whenever adoption becomes part of the care plan in relation to a child in care rather than, as formerly, allowing them to apply for a freeing order at their discretion. The 2002 Act also solves the former problems of the so-called 'legal limbo status' of the freed child and provides a clear and workable scheme for revocation and for the position following the breakdown of a placement. However, one consequential disadvantage is that because parents retain their parental

---

[192] Section 28(2)–(4).

[193] This is not dissimilar to the local authority's position upon the making of a care order, see s 33(3)(b) of the Children Act 1989, discussed above at p 771.

[194] Section 28(1).

[195] Section 29, though note that with court leave a residence order or special guardianship order may be sought in any subsequent adoption application: s 29(4), (5).

[196] Clarke Hall and Morrison, at 3 [180].   [197] Section 27(2).

[198] Section 47(4), (5) and (7). A similar restriction applies to advance consent give under s 20, see s 47 (2)(b), (3) and (7).

status until the final adoption order is made, an agency when placing a child even after a placement order, cannot guarantee to any potential adopter that the parents will not subsequently oppose the making of an order. On the other hand, given that in such circumstances parental opposition can only be made with court leave, which may only be given if it is satisfied that there has been a change of circumstances since the order, their chances of successfully opposing the application would appear to be slight.

The requirement that an order be sought immediately adoption becomes part of the care plan is an attempt to ensure that the court can consider the issue before the matter becomes a fait accompli. This in turn is designed to meet the argument that freeing was stacked against the birth parents. However, it is vital, if the system is to work, that applications are both brought and heard promptly. The Act does make it a duty for both court and adoption agency to 'bear in mind that any delay in coming to the decision is likely to prejudice the child's welfare'[199] and vests both the power and the duty in the court to draw up timetables with a view to avoiding delay.[200] But whether this is sufficient to guarantee the end of the delays that so bedevilled the freeing procedure remains to be seen. Unless the system can be significantly speeded up, it is likely to work no better than the old system.

E THE MAKING OF ADOPTION ORDERS

1 WHO MAY BE ADOPTED

Unlike some systems, which clearly provide for the adoption of adults, English law had, until the 2002 Act, been strictly confined to the adoption of children. However, while it remains the case that *applications* may only be made in respect of a person who is under the age of 18,[201] *orders* can be made until the person has reached the age of 19.[202] As before, the child must be single and never having been married or entered a civil partnership.[203] An adopted child may be readopted.[204]

2 WHO MAY APPLY FOR ADOPTION

(a) Age, health, and domicile of applicant

Although the law has always prescribed a minimum age for adoptive applicants it has had different policies as to what that age should be. For example, when it was first introduced the applicant had to be 25 or not less than 21 years older than the child to be adopted.[205] Twenty-five remained the minimum age for some time but it was eventually lowered to a

---

[199] Section 1(3).   [200] Section 109.   [201] Section 49(4).

[202] Section 47(9). Apparently this change was made to ensure that applications for adoption would not be thwarted immediately upon the child becoming 18.

[203] Section 47(8) and (8A) added by the Civil Partnership Act 2004, s 79(3). The child's domicile does not affect jurisdiction: *Re B (S) (Infant)* [1968] Ch 201, but see below p 863 n 345.

[204] Section 46(5).

[205] Adoption of Children Act 1926, s 2. At that time the age of majority was 21.

uniform requirement of 21.[206] Now, reflecting changes made by the Children Act 1989, applicants must be 21, save where the application is made by a couple[207] where it is sufficient if one is the mother or father of the child and aged at least 18 and the other is at least 21.[208] Although there is no prescribed maximum age, it should be appreciated that in practice adoption agencies are unlikely to consider applicants over 40 (and often over 35) at any rate as potential adopters for healthy babies.[209] Obviously age, for example in the case of grandparent applicants, can be a factor that the court may take into account when deciding whether an adoption order would be for the child's benefit. Whether upper age limits should be made more explicit either in legislation or guidance was raised by the Adoption Law Review,[210] but no action was taken.

Although there are no statutory requirements in respect of the health of adopters, as the Adoption Law Review points out,[211] adoption agencies are required by the regulations to obtain a report on the prospective adopters' health.[212]

A sole applicant, or, in the case of an application by a couple, one of the applicants, must be domiciled and habitually resident for at least one year in a part of the British Islands.[213]

(b) Adoptions by one person or a couple

An application for an adoption order may be made by a couple or by one person.[214] Before the 2002 Act the only persons allowed to make a joint adoption application were married couples[215] but in a major reversal of policy[216] joint applications are now permitted by spouses, civil partners and by 'two people (whether of different sexes or the same sex) living in an enduring family relationship'.[217] In other words, spouses, civil partners and unmarried couples (whether of different sexes or the same sex) may all apply for joint adoptions though, on the face of it, only the latter have to prove that they are living 'in an

[206] Adoption Act 1976, s 14(1) and s 15(1). Under the Adoption Act 1958, as originally enacted, a sole applicant and at least one of joint applicants had to be aged 25 unless he or she was a parent or relative of the child. The Houghton Committee (at paras 70–8) recommended the introduction of a uniform age, because there was some evidence that the minimum age of 25 was preventing some suitable couples from adopting and a minimum age of 21 would give an opportunity of testing the strength of a teenage marriage.

[207] As defined by s 144(4), discussed below.

[208] Adoption and Children Act 2002, ss 50 and 51.

[209] See the discussion in the Adoption Law Review, Discussion Paper No 3, at paras 40 et seq. These conditions may be relaxed where approval is sought to adopt older children or those with disabilities: see para 43.

[210] Ibid at para 44.   [211] Ibid at para 46.

[212] Adoption Agencies Regulations 2005 reg 25(3)(a). These matters include personal and family history and the current state of health, including consumption of tobacco and alcohol. See also *R v Secretary of State for Health, ex p Luff* [1992] 1 FLR 59, where the court refused to quash a Department of Health recommendation to the Home Office that the adoptive applicants in respect of two Romanian children were unsuitable, because of the male applicant's health following a heart by-pass operation.

[213] Section 49(2), (3). 'British Islands' means the United Kingdom (ie England and Wales, Scotland and Northern Ireland) Channel Islands and the Isle of Man.

[214] Adoption and Children Act 2002, s 49(1).

[215] According to pre-2002 Act law if it later emerged that the joint applicants were not married to each other, the order was voidable and not void: *Re F (Infants)(Adoption Order: Validity)* [1977] Fam 165, CA, cf *Re RA* (1974) 4 Fam Law 182.

[216] On which, see A Marshall 'Comedy of Adoption—When is Parent not a Parent?' [2003] Fam Law 840.

[217] See the definition of 'couple' in s 144(4) of the 2002 Act, as amended by the Civil Partnership Act 2004, s 79.

enduring family relationship'.[218] Given that under the former law one member of an unmarried couple had been allowed to adopt, the 2002 Act reform was long overdue.[219] In any event, as Dr Harris MP put it:[220]

'Children must grow up in the real world. They must grow up in the 21st century in which 40% of children are born outside marriage and in which many people who are committed to one another choose not to marry. That applies to 15% of households and the figure is expected to rise to 30%.'

But as one commentary has said,[221] undoubtedly, the key motivation for the fundamental change was the widening of the pool of potential applicants for adoption to meet the overall object of 'giving a child the chance to live in a stable living family rather than being left in care'.

Save in the case of a step-parent application (which we discuss below) an order may not be made on the sole application of a married person or civil partner unless his spouse or partner cannot be found or is by reason of ill health, whether physical or mental, incapable of making an application for an adoption order[222] or, alternatively, if the spouses or partners have separated and are living apart and the separation is likely to be permanent.[223] This is designed to avoid the situation of a child being adopted by one of two spouses or civil partners living together, the other of whom refuses to apply for an order. If the sole applicant is the mother or father of the child, no order may be made unless the court is satisfied that the other natural parent is dead or cannot be found or by virtue of s 28 of the Human Fertilisation and Embryology Act 1990[224] there is no other parent, or there is some other reason justifying the child being adopted by the applicant alone. The court must record where appropriate that it is satisfied as to either of the first two mentioned facts or, in the latter case, record its reason.[225]

The central problem of this provision is its potential for severing the ties with the other birth parent rather than to promote the child's welfare[226] and this concern lay at the heart of a House of Lords' decision, *Re B (Adoption: Natural Parent)*[227] on the pre-2002 Act provision. There, a baby had been put up for adoption by an unmarried mother who had neither informed the father of her pregnancy nor the birth. By chance the local authority

---

[218] Nevertheless, when approving adopters, adoption agencies must in the case of *any* couple have proper regard to the need for stability and permanence in their relationship: Suitability of Adopters Regulations 2005. But note the pre-2002 Act decision in *Re WM (Adoption: Non-Patrial)* [1997] 1 FLR 132 where an adoption order was made despite the married couple separating *after* the making of the application.

[219] See eg *Re AB (Adoption: Joint Residence)* [1996] 1 FLR 27 and *Re W (Adoption: Homosexual Partner)* [1997] 2 FLR 406. As A Bainham *Children: The Modern Law* (2nd edn) 212 put it, it was illogical to be allowed to achieve singly what the couple could not achieve together.

[220] HC Deb Vol 385, col 969 (16 May 2002).

[221] C Bridge and H Swindells *Adoption: The Modern Law* 10.12, citing Dr Harris MP in HL Deb vol 388, cols 970–1.

[222] What does this provision contemplate? It is easy to see that a person's mental health may be such that he is incapable of making an application but difficult to see how his physical health can have this effect.

[223] Adoption and Children Act 2002, s 51(3) and (3A) [added by the Civil Partnership Act 2004 s 79(4)].

[224] Discussed above at p 309.   [225] Adoption and Children Act 2002, s 51(4).

[226] This was precisely the concern of the Houghton Committee, op cit, paras 98–102 on whose recommendations the provision is originally based.

[227] [2001] UKHL 70, [2002] 1 WLR 258, on which see A Bainham 'Unintentional Parenthood: the Case of the Reluctant Mother' [2002] CLJ 288 and S Harris-Short 'Putting the Child at the Heart of Adoption' [2002] CFLQ 325.

discovered the father's whereabouts and he, when contacted, expressed the desire to care for the child himself. The child was placed with him, and the father gave up work to look after her. Notwithstanding that he had parental responsibility for the child by reason of a parental responsibility agreement, he nevertheless sought adoption. Though she had reservations, the mother did not oppose the adoption and always maintained that she had no desire to interfere in the child's life. The question raised was whether it was in the child's interest for the mother to be excluded. At first instance[228] Bracewell J thought that it was, on the basis (a) that the father's anxiety about the mother's continuing status as a parent with parental responsibility would perpetuate insecurity for him and potentially affect the child's stability and (b) that the mother had consented and had no general wish to interfere. The Court of Appeal[229] set the adoption aside and substituted a residence order with some safeguards, holding that because of the general importance of having two parents adoption was, within the terms of Art 8 of the European Convention on Human Rights, a disproportionate response. The House of Lords, however, while agreeing that the circumstances in which it was in the best interests of the child to be adopted by one parent to the exclusion of the other were likely to be exceptional, could not fault Bracewell J's decision which was accordingly reinstated.

Re B stands as authority for saying that the three conditions that are contained in what is now s 51(4) are not exhaustive. Since s 51(4)(c) in particular is phrased a little more widely than its predecessor (by referring to 'some other reason justifying the child's being adopted by the applicant alone' rather than justifying the exclusion of the other parent), the new provisions must also be given a broad interpretation.[230]

(c) Step-parent adoptions

One of the important changes introduced by the 2002 Act was that it ended the necessity of the birth parent and new partner (who, prior to the 2002 Act, had to be the birth parent's spouse) having jointly to adopt. This former requirement meant that to effect a step-parent adoption the birth parent had to adopt their own child which was described[231] during the debates on the Bill as a 'ridiculous anomaly'. This key change is not exactly highlighted in the Act. It results from s 51(2) which provides that 'an adoption order may be made on the application of one person who has attained the age of 21 if the court is satisfied that the person is the partner of a parent of the person to be adopted' and s 46(3)(b) which says that in such cases the adoption by the partner 'does not affect the parental responsibility of that parent . . .'. It will be noted that these provisions apply equally to the birth parent's spouse, civil partner or anyone else with whom he or she has an 'enduring relationship'.[232] The point has been well made[233] that it seems anomalous to allow 'partners' to adopt in this way yet to restrict the ability to make parental responsibility agreements or orders to spouses and civil partners.[234] One curious and largely overlooked effect of this change is that the child becomes 'half adopted', which poses

---

[228] See *B v P (Adoption by Unmarried Father)* [2000] 2 FLR 717.
[229] See *Re B (Adoption By One Natural Parent To Exclusion of Other)* [2001] 1 FLR 589.
[230] See Bridge and Swindells, op cit, at 10.18.
[231] By John Hutton MP, HC Debs Vol 365, Col 709 (26 March 2001).
[232] See s 144(4) on the definition of 'partner'.
[233] A Bainham *Children—The Modern Law* (3rd edn) 277.   [234] Discussed above at p 422.

interesting questions about access to birth records, for example, and the consequences for succession purposes.

Whether the law should permit step-parent adoptions and, if so, to what extent, has long exercised reformers and legislators. In fact until the Children Act 1975 there were no formal restrictions on any type of step-parent adoption applications. The Houghton Committee, however, was concerned[235] about the growing number of such adoptions which by 1970 exceeded 10,000. They were particularly concerned with 'post-divorce' step-parent adoptions which they felt were an inappropriate use of the jurisdiction and, given the consequential extinguishment of the legal links with half his family, potentially damaging to the child. The Committee felt that the preferable alternative was to extend the provisions enabling a step-parent to apply to become a guardian.

Although the reform that was put in place did not exactly follow the Houghton Committee recommendations, nevertheless the courts were directed to dismiss 'post-divorce' step-parent adoption applications if they considered the matter would be better dealt with by an application to the divorce court for what was then a custody order.[236] This direction, which came into force in 1976, was at first taken to be a clear expression of a policy to discourage adoptions by parents and step-parents.[237] However, in an apparent volte face, the Court of Appeal held in *Re D (Minors) (Adoption by Step-Parent)*[238] that the section required the dismissal of the application only if it could be shown that the matter could be *better* dealt with by a joint custody order. This approach, as the Adoption Law Review put it, was more in accord with the actual wording of the provision, but did not reflect the original intentions of the Houghton Committee.[239]

Recognising that these legislative attempts to restrict step-parent applications had essentially failed the Children Act 1989 formally repealed them.[240] Indeed, by specifically

---

[235] Op cit at paras 103–110. As N Lowe pointed out in 'English Adoption Law—Past, Present and Future' op cit, unlike adoptions overall, step-parent adoptions continued to rise after the overall peak of 1968. In the case of legitimate children the numbers more than doubled from 4,038 in 1968 to 9,262 in 1975, while in the case of 'illegitimate' children, numbers rose from 4,479 in 1968 to 5,691 in 1974.

[236] Adoption Act 1976 s 14(3), in cases where the application was made jointly by a parent and step-parent, and s 15(4) where the application was by the step-parent alone.

[237] See, for example, Local Authority Circular LAC (76) 22 at para 10(ii) which stated, inter alia, that a parent and step-parent of a child 'will not normally be able to get an adoption order if the parent has custody of the child . . . following . . . divorce proceedings', and was so interpreted by the appellate courts, see eg *Re S (Infants)(Adoption by Parent)* [1977] Fam 173, and for a striking dismissal of an application, see *Re W v W (A Minor) The Times*, 26 November 1976. The impact of these decisions on the lower courts was by no means consistent: see the research findings of J Masson, D Norbury and A Chatterton *Mine, Yours and Ours*, summarised in (1982) Adoption and Fostering, Vol 5, No 2 at 7. The overall effect of the legislative restriction was dramatic: from its peak figure in 1975 numbers halved to 4,547 by 1977 and virtually halved again to 2,872 in 1983: Review of Adoption Paper No 3, *The Adoption Process*, Table 4.

[238] (1980) 2 FLR 102, CA, on which see J Priest 'Step-parent Adoptions: What is the Law?' [1982] JSWL 285 and R Rawlings 'Law Reform with Tears' (1982) 45 MLR 637. See also the Adoption Law Review Discussion Paper No 1, paras 29–46 and 125–134 and Discussion Paper No 3, paras 26–33.

[239] A similar interpretation was also placed upon the tortuously worded s 37 of the Children Act 1975, which applied to 'post-death' and 'illegitimate' step-parent adoptions: see *Re S (A Minor) (Adoption or Custodianship)* [1987] Fam 98, CA.

[240] Adoption Act 1976 s 14(3) and s 15(4) and the Children Act 1975 were repealed by the Children Act 1989 Sch 15.

enacting that a parent aged at least 18 could jointly apply with a spouse aged at least 21 to adopt his or her child, the 1989 Act seemed to give tacit approval to such applications.[241]

The whole issue of step-parent adoption was again raised during the Adoption Law Review, but although concern was expressed that some applications 'appear to be made without full consideration of the needs of the child', it was nevertheless felt inappropriate to prohibit such adoptions.[242] It was thought desirable, however, to amend the law to help discourage inappropriate applications. To this end the Consultative Document recommended various changes aimed at discouraging step-parent adoption, including the idea that it should be revocable where the new marriage ends in divorce or death before the child is 18, and that it should be possible for step-parents to acquire parental responsibility either by agreement or a court order.[243] In the event, the proposal that a step-parent adoption could be revocable was dropped but the 2002 Act, as we discussed in Chapter 12,[244] introduced as an alternative to adoption, the possibility of those married to (or in a civil partnership with) the parent acquiring parental responsibility either by agreement or court order.

Although it is tempting to say that step-parent adoptions should be prohibited, it is submitted that it would not be right to do so for there are occasions where adoption is appropriate, though in case of the death of one of the birth parents, one wonders whether guardianship would be more appropriate. The extension of the power to make parental responsibility agreements and orders is a welcome step, however, as providing another alternative. In this respect, though, given that step-parent adoptions are made frequently of children aged 10 or over,[245] one wonders whether express provision should have been made to safeguard their interests, for example, by making it mandatory to obtain older children's views or even, as was at one time proposed for adoption[246] requiring the consent of children aged 12 or more.

(d) Adoption by relatives [247]

Although there are no formal restrictions against relatives applying to adopt, the courts have long had reservations about granting adoption to such applicants fearing, inter alia, that an order would distort the natural relationship, particularly in the case of adoption by grandparents.[248] It was also felt that the severance of legal ties with the birth parents fits uneasily with an adoption within the family. Another concern in the case of grandparent

---

[241] See above, p 844.   [242] Consultative Document 1992, para 19.

[243] See Recommendations 19 and 20, discussed at paras 19.4 and 19.8.   [244] See above pp 422ff.

[245] See eg M Murch, N Lowe, M Borkowski, R Copner and K Griew *Pathways to Adoption* Table 3.10, which found 38% of children involved in step-parent adoptions were aged 10 or over.

[246] See Cl 41(7) of the proposed Adoption Bill attached to the 1996 White Paper on Adoption. See further below, p 852.

[247] See generally the Consultative Document, op cit at para 20 and Adoption Law Review, Discussion Paper No 1, paras 47–9 and 135 and Discussion Paper No 3, paras 26–33.

[248] As Vaisey J said in *Re DX (An Infant)* [1949] Ch 320 at 321, 'The ostensible relationship of sisters between those who are in fact mother and child is unnatural and its creation might sow the seeds of grievous unhappiness for them both . . .'. However, courts now seem less concerned about this theoretical consequence, see eg *Re C (A Minor) (Adoption Order: Condition)* [1989] AC 1, where Lord Ackner dismissed the contention that an adoption order should be refused because the child would be devastated to learn that her natural brother would no longer be in law her brother as being 'quite unreal'.

applicants could be their age.[249] It is accepted, however, that there remain circumstances where an adoption order in such cases may be justified.[250]

The Houghton Committee reiterated concern about such adoptions, fearing the consequential dangers of hiding the real circumstances from the child.[251] They considered that an application for guardianship would normally be preferable. Following the Committee's recommendations a new order, custodianship, was created, by which applicants could seek orders vesting in them parental rights and duties but which did not extinguish the legal relationship between the child and his birth parents.[252] It was hoped and expected that relatives would use this option rather than adoption,[253] but in the event the take-up was thought to be disappointing and it was abolished by the Children Act 1989 (although in fact the evidence showed that grandparents were beginning to apply for custodianship).[254] However, as we discussed in Chapter 12,[255] the Adoption and Children Act 2002 introduced an order, not dissimilar to custodianship, namely special guardianship. It also made provision for enhanced residence orders. Both these orders can be made on application or by the court of its own motion in any family proceedings including, therefore, adoption proceedings.

Although these alternatives are likely to diminish further the desirability of an adoption by relatives,[256] they do not eliminate the need. Given that it has the advantage of permanence, it is likely that, even with the alternatives, an adoption order will still be thought appropriate in cases where, for example, relatives have been the sole care-givers for some time, especially if the parents are virtual strangers to the child.[257] The Adoption Law Review[258] saw no reason to rule out the possibility of adoption by relatives, which they envisaged to be appropriate where the child's parents are dead, or living in another country and unlikely ever to be able to make parental decisions in respect of the child's upbringing. It is difficult to disagree with this conclusion and indeed the case for prohibiting adoption by relatives seems weaker than that for step-parents.

[249] See eg Re W (A Minor) (Adoption by Grandparents) (1980) 2 FLR 161, CA.
[250] See eg Re DX above Re G (DM) (An Infant) [1962] 2 All ER 546, and Re B (MF) (An Infant) [1972] 1 All ER 898, CA. In the latter case an order was granted even though continued contact between the siblings (only one of whom was adopted) was envisaged.
[251] Ibid at para 111.   [252] Discussed in ch 11 of the 7th edition of this work.
[253] See pp 375–6 of the 7th edition of this work.
[254] In their study for the Department of Health, E Bullard, E Malos and R Parker found that more than half of custodianship applications were by grandparents: Custodianship: Caring for other people's children (HMSO, 1991) Tables 24–8. On the other hand the court's power to make a custodianship order upon an adoption application was rarely exercised. Only two such cases were found in the Pathways to Adoption study, op cit, Table 2.10 See also Re S (A Minor)(Adoption: Custodianship) [1987] Fam 98, CA; and Re W (A Minor)(Adoption: Custodianship) [1992] Fam Law 64, CA. For earlier examples of such orders see eg Re O (A Minor)(Adoption by Grandparents) [1985] FLR 546, where paternal grandparents had looked after the child for four years following abandonment by the mother; and Re M (A Minor)(Adoption: Parental Agreement) [1985] FLR 664, where the child had been with grandparents since he was 11 weeks old and had had virtually no contact with his mother.
[255] See above p 604.
[256] Query whether it should further be considered whether to extend the power to make parental responsibility agreements and orders to relatives?
[257] See Re W (A Minor) (Adoption by Grandparents) (1980) 2 FLR 161 where an adoption order was granted as the court considered that it would be in the child's interests for the grandparents to be able to appoint testamentary guardians in the event of their death.
[258] See the Consultative Document, op cit, at para 20.4.

3 CONSENT TO THE MAKING OF AN ORDER

By s 47(2) it is one of the fundamental conditions for the making of an adoption order that:

'in the case of each parent or guardian of the child, the court is satisfied—

(a) that the parent or guardian consents to the making of the adoption order,

(b) that the parent or guardian has consented under section 20 (and has not withdrawn the consent) and does not oppose the making of the adoption order, or

(c) that the parent's or guardian's consent should be dispensed with.'

It is by this means that the law recognises and seeks to protect the parental interest. Indeed, so important is the right to refuse to consent, that it is not lost even if others, including a local authority, acquire parental responsibility.[259]

It will be noted that s 47(2) refers to parental *consent*. This represents a formal reversal of policy introduced by the Children Act 1975 which replaced 'consent' with 'agreement' as a deliberate attempt to move away from the parents' rights being akin to possession of their child. In fact this policy never really worked, in part because the judges frequently referred to 'consent' rather than 'agreement' and in any event the form that the parents were required to complete was entitled the Consent Form. The 2002 Act therefore merely reflects this de facto position.

(a) Whose consent is required?

The Act requires the consent of each parent or guardian. By 'parent' is meant a parent with parental responsibility.[260] It does not therefore include the unmarried father,[261] unless he has parental responsibility through registration, court order or agreement. However, if the mother has already consented to the child's placement for adoption before the father acquires parental responsibility, he will be deemed to have given consent.[262] The idea of this is to prevent the father from frustrating or obstructing an arrangement which the mother has already entered into with an adoption agency, and indeed without this provision authority for the placement would lapse immediately. Nevertheless it has been queried[263] whether this provision is in breach of Art 8 in respect of the father's right to respect for family life. Parent does not include 'step-parent' even if they have parental responsibility. In the case of an adopted child, 'parent' refers to each adoptive parent.[264] 'Guardian' refers to any person formally appointed by an individual or

---

[259] See Children Act 1989 s 12(3) and s 33(6)(b). For the position where a special guardianship order is made, see below.

[260] Adoption and Children Act 2002 s 52(6).

[261] See *Re M (An Infant)* [1955] 2 QB 479, CA; and *Re C (Adoption: Parties)* [1995] 2 FLR 483, CA.

[262] Adoption and Children Act 2002, s 52(9), (10).

[263] See Clarke Hall and Morrison on *Children* at 3 [325].

[264] But if the adoption order in question is a foreign order which is not recognised by the English court, then the birth parents' consent will still be required: *Re C (Foreign Adoption: Natural Mother's Consent: Service)* [2006] Fam Law 8, *Re G (Foreign Adoption: Consent)* [1995] 2 FLR 534. But note Charles J's reservations in *Re A (Adoption of a Russian Child)* [2000] 1 FLR 539 at 543.

by a court[265] and, by s 144(4), a special guardian. This latter right of consent, however, is said not[266] to affect 'any rights which a parent of the child has in relation to the child's adoption or placement for adoption.' This presumably means that notwithstanding that s 52(6) requires the consent of each parent *or* (in this case) special guardian, in fact the consent of both is required.

The position of the unmarried father without parental responsibility

As under the previous law, an unmarried father without parental responsibility is not automatically a party to the proceedings[267] nor is his consent required. The court does, however, have a discretion to make him a party.[268] Furthermore, under s 1(4)(f) of the 2002 Act both the court and adoption agency have to consider the wishes and feelings of the child's relatives including both the mother and father.[269] In any event, it had been established by *Re H, Re G (Adoption: Consultation of Unmarried Fathers)*[270] that as a matter of general practice, judges or district judges giving directions in adoption or (what are now) placement order applications should inform birth fathers of the proceedings unless for good reason the court decides that it is not appropriate to do so. Mothers should therefore be warned that at some stage the court will have to decide whether to add the father as a respondent. In other words, a mother has no automatic right to insist that the adoption proceedings be kept secret from the father. Nevertheless, as Thorpe LJ accepted in *Re G (Adoption Order)*[271] there can be a wide spectrum of circumstances: 'There will be cases in which the father will have very little merit, and accordingly, very little entitlement to consideration. At the other end of the scale, there will be cases in which the natural father should be given what will be something akin to the statutory right [of consent].' *Re H, Re G* illustrates this spectrum. In *Re H* the parents had had a relationship, including cohabitation, that had lasted several years and the father had shown a continuing commitment to the elder child. He was therefore entitled to respect for his family life with the child under Art 8 of the European Convention on Human Rights and to place the child for adoption without notice to him would breach this right. In contrast, in *Re G* the parents had never cohabited and their relationship did not have the constancy to show de facto family ties. Consequently the father had no Art 8 right and it was not necessary for him to be notified of the proceedings.

The position of the child

In deciding whether an adoption order will be for the child's welfare, the court and adoption agency are bound[272] to have regard to 'the child's ascertainable wishes and feelings regarding the [adoption] decision (considered in the light of the child's understanding)'. The child's *consent* is not, however, required.[273]

---

[265] Under the pre-2002 Act law there was a dispute as to whether to qualify as a guardian for these purposes, the appointment had to be made under s 5 of the Children Act 1989 and not therefore under foreign legislation. This narrow construction was favoured by Holman J in *Re D (Adoption: Foreign Guardianship)* [1999] 2 FLR 865 but the predominant view since then is that that approach was too narrow, see eg *Re J (Adoption: Consent of Foreign Public Authority)* [2002] EWHC 766 (Fam), [2002] 2 FLR 618, per Charles J and *Re AGN (Adoption: Foreign Adoption)* [2000] 2 FLR 431, per Cazalet J.

[266] Children Act 1989, s 14C(2)(b).   [267] See the Family Procedure (Adoption) Rules 2005, r 23.

[268] Family Procedure (Adoption) Rules 2005, r 23(3)(a).

[269] Adoption and Children Act 2002, s 1(8).   [270] [2001] 1 FLR 646, per Butler-Sloss P.

[271] [1999] 1 FLR 400 at 403, CA.   [272] Adoption and Children Act 2002, s 1(4)(a).

[273] In some other jurisdictions such as Scotland, the older child's consent is required: see eg Adoption Law Review, *Background Paper No 1*, paras 116–20.

The 2002 Act did not take up the recommendation[274] that an adoption order should not be made in relation to a child aged 12 or over unless the court was satisfied either that the child had consented or that he was incapable of doing so. That recommendation was open to the objection that it seemed to place on the child the responsibility for making the decision[275] and that in any event 12 was a particularly young age to choose and out of line with other provisions,[276] notably the Family Law Reform Act 1969 s 8, under which those aged 16 or over can give a valid consent to medical treatment.[277] Notwithstanding that formal consent is not required, the importance of the older child's views should not be underestimated and it is surely questionable practice to plan for an older child's adoption against their wishes.[278]

(b) Form of consent

By s 52(5), 'consent' means:

'consent given unconditionally and with a full understanding of what is involved;[279] but a person may consent to adoption without knowing the identity of the person in whose favour the order will be made'.[280]

Although it has long ceased to be possible to make consent conditional on the child being brought up in a particular religion,[281] when placing a child for adoption, adoption agencies must give 'due consideration to the child's religious persuasion, racial origin and cultural and linguistic background'.[282]

The mother cannot give an effective agreement until the child is six weeks old.[283] Unlike the previous law under which agreement could be given orally or in a non-standard

---

[274] See the Consultative Document, op cit at 9.5 and cl 41(7) of the proposed Adoption Bill.

[275] Particularly if the child were required formally to sign a consent form.

[276] Ironically, according to some research (see Fratter, Rowe, Sapsford and Thoburn *Permanent Family Placement: a decade of experience* (1991)), adoption placements at 12 are most likely to break down.

[277] Discussed above at p 363. Though in this respect it must be acknowledged that the courts have effectively lowered this age by accepting the validity of consent by '*Gillick* competent children' under the age of 16.

[278] See *Re M (Adoption or Residence Order)* [1998] 1 FLR 570, discussed below, p 857 in which a residence order rather than an adoption order was made in view of the 11-year-old child's objection to being adopted.

[279] There is some support for saying that a parent must know all the material facts before his consent should be regarded as having been given: cf *Re M (Minors)(Adoption)* [1991] 1 FLR 458, CA (order set aside where father consented to adoption by mother and step-father in ignorance that his wife, who died three months later, was terminally ill), discussed further below, p 868, and *Re An Adoption Application* [1992] 1 FLR 341 (mother's consent, given in ignorance that male applicant was involved in criminal proceedings, not to be relied upon).

[280] Applicants can still opt for anonymity, in which case they should apply before commencing proceedings for a serial number to be assigned to them: the Family Procedure (Adoption) Rules 2005, r 20. Thereafter proceedings must be conducted with a view to securing that the applicant is not seen or made known to any party who is not already aware of that person's identity except with his consent: r 20(4)(b). The various suggestions made by the Adoption Law Review, Discussion Paper No 3 at para 221 that leave be required and by the Consultative Document, op cit, at para 40.2 and 40.3 that the court should be able to discontinue the use of the serial number if it would be in the child's interests to do so and that birth parents should also be able to make use of a serial number have not been acted upon.

[281] This right was ended by the Adoption Act 1976—discussed above p 833.

[282] Adoption and Children Act 2002, s 1(5).

[283] This condition is designed to prevent the mother from being persuaded to give her agreement before she has recovered from the child's birth.

written form,[284] under the 2002 Act it is mandatory to use the prescribed consent form or a form to the like effect when either consenting to a placement under s 19 or to the giving of advance consent under s 20.[285] For non-agency adoptions (for example step-parent or relative adoptions) the law is less strict with the rules stating that consent *may* be given on a prescribed form or a form to like effect.[286]

Research evidence shows that many adoption applications proceed on the basis that they will be contested because the parent(s) has not signed the agreement, yet in many cases there is no intention actively to oppose the adoption application.[287] One of the reasons for this is that parents are reluctant to 'sign away' their children. The Consultative Document[288] attempted to address this problem by suggesting that parents should be able to attach a statement explaining why they thought it was for the child's welfare to be adopted and in the subsequent White Paper—*Adoption: The Future*[289] the Government signalled its intention to amend the consent form. In the event, however, no changes have yet been made.[290]

Where the parent is prepared to consent to a placement under s 19 or give advance consent to adoption under s 20 the adoption agency must request the appointment of a CAFCASS officer or a Welsh family proceedings officer to witness the signing of the consent form.[291]

So far as court proceedings (both for a placement order and for adoption) are concerned, wherever it appears that a parent is willing to consent, the court will appoint a reporting officer. That officer has to witness the signing of consent, having ensured so far as reasonably practical that the parent is giving consent unconditionally and with full understanding of what is involved, and having investigated all the circumstances relevant to that consent. He must then submit a confidential report to the court.[292]

4 DISPENSING WITH CONSENT

The requirement that unless unconditionally given the court must formally dispense with consent before it may make a placement for adoption or an adoption order is the means by which the law attempts to balance the parental interest with the child's welfare. Although, as will be seen, the 2002 Act has substantially re-drawn the balance in favour of securing the child's welfare, it is worth remembering that even under the former law while

---

[284] See eg *Re D (Adoption: Freeing Order)* [2001] 1 FLR 403 and *Re T (A Minor)(Adoption: Parental Agreement)* [1986] Fam 160 and s 61 of the Adoption Act 1976.

[285] Family Procedure (Adoption) Rules 2005, rr 17(1) and 28(1). The actual form is prescribed by the *Practice Direction 'Forms'*. Similarly a withdrawal of consent must be made in a prescribed form; s 52(8) of the 2002 Act.

[286] Family Procedure (Adoption) Rules 2005, r 28(2).

[287] N Lowe with M Borkowski, R Copner, K Griew and M Murch *Report of the Research into the Use and Practice of the Freeing for Adoption Provisions* (1993) at para 3.2.4. A similar finding was made by M Murch et al *Supporting Adoption—Reframing the Approach.*

[288] Op cit, at paras 10.9–10.11.　　　[289] (1993) Cm 2288.

[290] Similarly, no action was taken on the suggestion that consideration might be given to altering the substantive law so that parents should be required to indicate whether or not they are opposed to the adoption as distinct from requiring their positive consent.

[291] Adoption Agencies Regulations 2005, reg 20.

[292] See Part V of the Family Procedure (Adoption) Rules 2005.

contested adoptions were not the rarity they once were[293] in fact applications were rarely refused.[294]

(a) The pre-2002 Act position

Before discussing dispensing with consent under the 2002 Act, something needs to be said about the law as it operated before that. Under the Adoption Act 1976, before parental 'agreement' to adoption could be dispensed with, the court had to be satisfied as to the existence of one of seven grounds. The first of these grounds was that the parent 'cannot be found or is incapable of giving agreement' which is preserved by the 2002 Act. The other grounds, which have all been swept away by the 2002 Act, were that the parent or guardian:

'(b) is withholding his agreement unreasonably;

(c) has persistently failed without reasonable cause to discharge his parental responsibility for the child;

(d) has abandoned or neglected the child;

(e) has persistently ill-treated the child;

(f) has seriously ill-treated the child . . .'

The hallmark of grounds (c) to (f) was parental culpability, that is, they were fault-based grounds. On the other hand, ground (b) was clearly the catch-all ground and potentially quite wide. It was established by the leading case, Re W (An Infant)[295] that under this ground:

'. . . the test is reasonableness and not anything else. It is not culpability. It is not indifference. It is not failure to discharge parental duties. It is reasonableness in the context of the totality of the circumstances. But, although welfare per se is not the test, the fact that a reasonable parent does pay regard to the welfare of his child must enter into the question of reasonableness as a relevant factor. It is relevant in all cases if and to the extent that a reasonable parent would take it into account. It is decisive in those cases where a reasonable parent must so regard it . . .'

But while Re W arguably struck the fairest balance between the interests of the child and those of the parents and the adoptive applicants that could have been achieved under the law at that time, the test was itself open-ended and generated considerable case law.[296]

It also needs to be remembered that these dispensing grounds operated in a framework in which, when deciding whether or not to make an adoption order, the child's welfare was the first and not the paramount consideration. It was therefore not the case that an adoption would be made simply because it was for the child's welfare. Indeed it became

[293] In 1978, for example, 773 orders (representing 6.3% of all orders) were made without parental agreement, while in 1983 the figure was 956, representing 11 per cent, see respectively Children Act 1975, First Report to Parliament, HC 266, Table D and the Second Report, HMSO 1984, Table B, whereas in a sample of cases decided between 1986 and 1988 the Pathways to Adoption study, op cit, Table 2.11 found that 19% of applications to adopt were made without the mother's consent.

[294] In the Pathways to Adoption Study, op cit, as para 2.1, less than 1% of the applications in the sample were refused.

[295] [1971] AC 682 at 700, per Lord Hailsham LC.

[296] See the discussion at pp 638–48 of the previous edition of this work.

established[297] that in cases where agreement was withheld the courts were required to apply a two-stage process, namely to determine first whether it was for the child's welfare to be adopted and then, if it was, to determine whether parental agreement should be dispensed with.

The Adoption Law Review considered the position to be 'clearly unsatisfactory'.[298] As the Consultative Paper pointed out,[299] the so-called fault-based grounds for dispensing with parental agreement were objectionable both because faults or shortcomings of parental care do not ipso facto justify adoption as a suitable option for the child nor, where adoption is thought right, should they imply that parents are necessarily at fault. Responses to the Review largely favoured the removal of the fault-based grounds. The Review also considered[300] the unreasonable withholding ground unsatisfactory, since it remained problematic as to how much weight a reasonable parent should place on the child's welfare; and in any event it seems wrong to fix a parent with the stigma of being an 'unreasonable parent'.

(b) The position under the 2002 Act

The 2002 Act has replaced the previous seven grounds with just two. The first, that 'the parent or guardian cannot be found or lacks capacity (within the meaning of the Mental Capacity Act 2005) to give consent' is, as has been said, a virtual replication of the previous law, but the second that 'the welfare of the child requires the consent to be dispensed with', is entirely new. In applying these grounds the court is bound by s 1(2) to treat the child's welfare, throughout his life, as the paramount consideration and in assessing this the court must have regard to the 'welfare' checklist in s 1(4). As will be seen, the checklist is especially important when applying the welfare ground to dispense with consent.

Although the court must in all cases be satisfied that it is for the child's welfare to be adopted, it seems no longer possible, at any rate when applying the welfare ground for dispensation, to apply in any strict sense the two-stage test, namely, determining first whether adoption is in the child's interests and then to consider the dispensation issue, for once it has been found to be in the child's interests to be adopted consent must inevitably be dispensed with on the paramountcy test.

Cannot be found or lacks capacity within the meaning of the Mental Capacity Act 2005 to give consent

As originally enacted the 2002 Act exactly mirrored the former law, but s 52(1)(a) has since been amended by the Mental Capacity Act 2005[301] in relation to the lack of capacity to consent.

So far as 'cannot be found' is concerned, it is well established that consent will not lightly be dispensed with on this ground. In *Re F (R) (An Infant)*,[302] for instance, it was

---

[297] *Re C (A Minor) (Adoption: Parental Agreement: Contact)* [1993] 2 FLR 260, CA; *Re D (A Minor) (Adoption: Freeing Order)* [1991] 1 FLR 48, CA and *Re R (A Minor) (Adoption: Parental Agreement)* [1987] 1 FLR 391, CA. Note that in *Re C* the Court of Appeal expressly approved the first instance court deciding first to resolve the birth parents' application for a residence order before deciding their application for a contact order, and only after that determining the adoption application.

[298] Discussion Paper No 2, op cit, para 85, on which see E Cooke 'Dispensing with parental consent to adoption—a choice of welfare tests' [1997] CFLQ 259, and B Lindley and N Wyld 'The Children Act and the draft Adoption Bill—diverging principles' [1996] CFLQ 327.

[299] See para 12.5.   [300] See para 12.4.   [301] See s 67 and Sch 6.

[302] [1970] 1 QB 385, CA.

held that before the court could be satisfied that the parent 'could not be found' it had to
be shown that all reasonable and proper steps had been taken. In that case it was held that
all such steps had not been taken since in their search for the birth mother the applicants
had failed to get in touch with the maternal grandfather with whom the mother was still in
contact.

For these purposes reasonable steps will include making enquiries at the last known
address, asking questions of relatives and seeking the assistance of government bodies such
as the Department of Work and Pensions, or Passport Agency or Council Tax Office.

Occasionally, where the parents live abroad, circumstances or even the law may mean that
there are no practical means of communicating with them and consent has consequently
been dispensed with on the basis that they cannot be found.[303]

To establish incapacity to consent within the meaning of the Mental Capacity Act 2005
it must be shown that the parent is unable at that time (ie incapacity does not have to be
permanent) inter alia to understand the information relevant to the decision; retain that
information; use or weigh that information as part of the process of making the decision
or communicating that decision. This lack of capacity may be because of an impairment
of, or disturbance in, the functioning of the mind or brain.[304] Although this definition is
wide enough to cover mental disability and physical disability as for example by being in a
coma,[305] it is not as wide as the former law which had been held to include incapacity due
to ignorance.[306]

As one commentary has said[307] if the parent has a disability but expressly withholds
consent, the court may have to consider whether to dispose with that consent either on the
basis of incapacity or the welfare ground. In any event if the parent is or may be under a
disability, the court will have to consider appointing a Litigation Friend.[308]

The welfare of the child requires the consent to be dispensed with

It is tempting to say that since, under the former law, it will have first been decided that it
was in the child's interests to be adopted, then *all* the previous case law in which consent
was not dispensed with would now be reversed when applying this new ground in conjunction with the general enjoinder to regard the child's welfare as the paramount consideration. A fortiori all cases where consent was dispensed with under the former law
would be dispensed with under the 2002 Act. However, the first proposition in particular
is too simplistic and overlooks the checklist, crucial within which is s 1(4)(c) which directs
the court to consider:

'the likely effect on the child (throughout his life) of having ceased to be a member of the
original family and become an adopted person'.

And s 1(4)(f) which directs the court to consider:

'the relationship which the child has with relatives, and with any other person in relation to
whom the court or agency considers the relationship to be relevant, including—

---

[303] See *Re R (Adoption)* [1966] 3 All ER 613 (dangerous to contact parents living under a totalitarian
regime) and *Re A (Adoption of a Russian Child)* [2000] 1 FLR 539—contrary to Russian law to make contact
with the mother.
[304] See ss 1 and 2.   [305] See Clarke Hall and Morrison at 3 [481].
[306] See *Re R (Adoption)*, above.   [307] Clarke Hall and Morrison, ibid.
[308] See Family Procedure (Adoption) Rules 2005, r 25.

(i) the likelihood of any such relationship continuing and the value to the child of its doing so,

(ii) the ability and willingness of any of the child's relatives, or of any such person, to provide the child with a secure environment in which the child can develop, and otherwise to meet the child's needs,

(iii) the wishes and feelings of any of the child's relatives, or of any such person, regarding the child.'

It was certainly the government's expectation that it was via the checklist that the balance between the parents' and the child's interests would be struck.[309] How far s 1(4)(c) and (f) will make up for what one commentary has described[310] as 'the loss of the parental right of reasonably withholding consent' remains to be seen. However, it is interesting to speculate how at least some of the former case law might be decided under the 2002 Act.

Concentrating on examples of where consent was *not* dispensed with, one might first refer to *Re M (Adoption or Residence Order)*,[311] the so-called 'Oxford dons case'. There the child (M) was placed with the adoptive applicants when she was nearly nine years old. At that stage the birth mother was addicted both to drugs and alcohol. Although, given M's age, it was made clear to the applicants at the outset that if she did not want to be adopted, the court might well make a residence order, everyone's expectation was that M would be adopted. Unfortunately, the local authority failed to prepare the child for the adoption and in particular had paid no heed to M's own wishes not to be adopted. Despite M's position the placement seemed settled and nearly two years later the applicants applied to adopt. It was at this stage that M's own views came to the fore and the local authority then belatedly withdrew their support for the adoption. In the meantime the mother's position had dramatically improved. She was no longer dependent on drugs or alcohol and was living in a stable relationship with a new partner. She sought a residence order. Shocked by the turn of events, the applicants maintained the position that if they were not granted adoption they would not be prepared to keep M. They therefore rejected the mother's offer to withdraw her application and to consent to a residence order being made in their favour and to agree to the making of a s 91(14) direction limiting her future right to apply for a residence order. The Court of Appeal held by a majority[312] that the adoption application should be refused and a residence order coupled with a s 91(14) direction should be granted instead. In reaching this conclusion they ruled that although the first instance judge had been wrong not to explore the alternatives when considering whether it was in the interests of the child to be adopted, nevertheless, given her need for stability and security and faced with the applicant's ultimatum that they would reject her if the adoption was not granted, it was in M's interests to be adopted. Accordingly the first stage test had been satisfied. However, in the extraordinary circumstances of the case, it could not be said that the mother's withholding of her agreement was unreasonable. She had taken and

---

[309] See eg J Paton 'Adoption' in *Delight and Dole* (eds Thorpe and Cowton) 55 and John Hutton MP in HC Deb Vol 365, col 703 (26 March 2001).

[310] Bridge and Swindells, op cit, at 8.43.   [311] [1998] 1 FLR 570.

[312] Ward and Judge LJJ. Simon Brown LJ dissented on the ground that the advantages of adoption for the child were sufficiently strong as to justify overriding the mother's objection.

was entitled inter alia[313] to take into account her daughter's wish not to be adopted and to respect her not totally unrealistic wish to return to live with her. As Ward LJ put it:[314]

'The chance of M returning at some stage to her mother's home is not discounted by any of the experts. If that happens, how does a mother answer her child's angry challenge, "Why did you give me away to be adopted? Why did you not listen to what I was saying?" In my judgment, it would require fortitude bordering on indifference for a mother to shut her ears to what her child has said for so long, with so little contact to preserve the feelings for her old family notwithstanding so much love and nurture being shown by her new family.'

She was also held entitled to take into account the wishes of her other children to maintain the family link with M and of M's own affection for and need for contact with her sisters.

Could it be said, in view of s 1(4)(c), that M's welfare would have *required* the mother's consent to be dispensed with?

Another decision worth speculating upon is *Re B (Adoption Order)*.[315] There, a one-year-old boy was accommodated at the mother's request and subsequently happily placed with a foster mother. Throughout the placement the child maintained regular contact and an excellent relationship with his father. Three years later the father applied for a residence order. By consent a residence order coupled with a s 91(14) order restraining the father from applying for a residence order without court leave was made in favour of the foster mother with a parental responsibility order being made in favour of the father coupled with an order for generous contact. The local authority, however, were unhappy with this arrangement and encouraged the foster mother to apply for adoption which she did three years later. The Court of Appeal held that in these circumstances where the child was in reality a member of both the foster family and the birth father's family, the father could not be said to have been unreasonably withholding his consent particularly as he was supported by the guardian and a distinguished forensic expert advising him. Moreover, it was held that the trial judge (whose decision to dispense with consent was overturned) had paid insufficient attention to whether the interference with the father's right to family life which would result from the making of the order was 'necessary and proportionate' within Art 8(2) of the European Convention of Human Rights, given the completely satisfactory arrangement already reached without the order.

Again could it be said that the child's welfare in this case *required* the father's consent to be dispensed with?

Perhaps less problematic are older cases such as *Re H; Re W (Adoption: Parental Agreement)*[316] in which the Court of Appeal deliberately tried to restrict the application of the child's welfare when judging reasonableness. Of the two appeals, *Re W* is the more striking. It concerned a boy who had been taken into care when he was just under two years old. The mother's marriage had broken down and she had become an alcoholic and suffered depression. Subsequently, however, her marriage was dissolved, she made a

---

[313] She was also entitled to take into account that the local authority did not consider the adoption to be in M's interest, that the guardian had changed her mind, and that she was entitled to differ from the opinion of an expert just as the local authority and guardian had done.

[314] Ibid at 599–600.   [315] [2001] EWCA Civ 347, [2001] 2 FLR 26.

[316] (1983) 4 FLR 614, CA. See also *Re E (Minors)(Adoption: Parental Agreement)* [1990] 2 FLR 397, discussed at 644 of the previous decision.

complete recovery, and following her remarriage she sought, some five years after she had last seen her son, to re-establish contact. The local authority began to make arrangements for the mother to see her son, but these were never implemented because the mother was sent to prison for fraud. At that point the authority decided to support the foster parents, with whom the child had been for the last nine years, in their adoption application. The Court of Appeal, however, upheld the decision that the mother's refusal to agree to the adoption was reasonable, based principally upon the belief that there was at least a chance of future successful contact with the child.

This decision was controversial under the former law and would almost certainly not be followed under the 2002 Act since the child's welfare, given that future contact with the mother was highly speculative, would surely have required the consent to be dispensed with.

(c) Commentary

There can be little quarrel with the first dispensation ground since it is clearly necessary to make provision for cases where the parents cannot be found or are incapable of giving consent. Furthermore, no-one would surely lament the passing of the unreasonably with-holding test, nor the ending of the fault-based grounds. Nevertheless the welfare ground is not problem-free. The courts will have to settle whether it amounts to more than just a simple welfare test for, as others have pointed out,[317] if a simple welfare test is considered inadequate to justify the compulsory removal of children into care, how could it be right to justify the complete and irrevocable transfer of parentage? As we have previously argued, however, the welfare checklist is intended to strike some sort of balance between the child's and the parents' interest. Even so, there remains the fear of social engineer-ing,[318] and while it might be anticipated that the courts will be alive to this danger, it may be questioned whether it is right to leave them with such a sweeping discretion.

Although there are no easy answers as to how best to reconcile the child's welfare with the parents' interests, it is suggested that the earlier Consultative Paper's recommenda-tion[319] that the 'test should require the court to be satisfied that the advantages to the child of becoming part of a new family are so significantly greater than the advantages of any alternative option as to justify overriding the wishes of a parent or guardian' comes as close as any to maintaining the right balance. Although the probability is that the courts would work to this tenet anyway, it is submitted that it would have been preferable for such a test to have been written into the legislation. However the legislation is interpreted there is a great responsibility both upon adoption agencies and the courts to ensure that all the options have been carefully considered *before* an adoption placement is made[320] and to implement any adoptive plans expeditiously lest such an option becomes inevitable simply by effluxion of time.

---

[317] See eg Cooke, op cit at 263.
[318] See eg C Barton 'The Adoption Bill—The Consultative Document' [1996] Fam Law 431.
[319] Ibid, R 13. [320] See above, p 840, for discussion about placement orders.

F PROCEDURE FOR THE MAKING OF ADOPTION ORDERS

1 THE CHILD MUST LIVE WITH THE APPLICANTS BEFORE THE MAKING OF AN ORDER

Before any adoption order may be made there has to have been a 'settling in' period so as to be able to assess whether such a placement would be in the child's interests.[321] The required period is governed by s 42. This provides that in the case of agency placements, placements made in pursuance of a High Court order or where the applicant is a parent of the child, no application may be made unless the child has had his home with the applicant or, in the case of an application by a couple, with one or both of them at all times during the period of 10 weeks before the application. In the case of step-parents the period is six months, in the case of a non-agency application by local authority foster parents the period is one year;[322] and in any other case[323] the period is 'not less than three years (whether continuous or not) during the period of five years preceding the application'.

The former Act[324] expressly provided that in determining with whom the child has his home, any absence at a hospital or boarding school and any other temporary absence, was to be disregarded. This was apparently felt to be too restrictive (for example, it made no allowance for temporary absences by other parties) and it was felt better to leave the whole issue to the court's discretion.[325] However, it is to be noted that the possibility that the whole period could be spent away from the applicants' home is guarded against by the further provision that the agency placing him, or the local authority in non-agency placements, must have sufficient opportunities to see the child with the applicant or, in the case of a joint application, both applicants together in the home environment.[326]

'Home' is not defined in the Act but pre-2002 Act case law[327] considered that, though difficult to define with precision, it must comprise some element of regular occupation (whether past, present, or intended for the future, even if intermittent) with some degree of permanency, based on some right of occupation whenever it is required: it is where you find the fixed comforts of a home; the fixed residence of a family or household. Though

---

[321] Note that under s 35(2) an agency may, having served due notice, end the placement by that agency. See further above, p 841.

[322] Applications can be made earlier with court leave: s 42(6).

[323] Eg private foster parents or relatives. As Bridge and Swindells, op cit at 10.54 point out, this cumulative probationary period of three years where relatives concerned has been extended from the former requirement of 13 weeks, but this is a deliberate policy to discourage such applications and to encourage the use of other options.

[324] Viz Adoption Act 1976, s 72(1A).

[325] See Jacquie Smith MP in HC Deb Vol 386, no 150, col 191 (20 May 2002).

[326] Adoption and Children Act 2002, s 42(6). The wording is regrettably vague. Presumably the agency or authority must have significant opportunity to see whether the proposed adoption is likely to be for the child's welfare, but cf *Re Y (Minors) (Adoption: Jurisdiction)* [1985] Fam 136, where Sheldon J in effect refused to lay down how many visits may be necessary. Note also *Re WM (Adoption: Non Patrial)* [1997] 1 FLR 132, in which Johnson J held that what is now s 42(6) did not prevent the making of an order in favour of applicants who had since separated, provided there was sufficient opportunity to see the child with both parents.

[327] *Re Y (Minors) (Adoption: Jurisdiction)*, above.

ultimately a question of fact to be decided in each case, a house that is merely visited by members of the family is unlikely to constitute a 'home' for these purposes.[328]

2 NOTICE TO LOCAL AUTHORITY MUST BE GIVEN IN NON-AGENCY PLACEMENTS

At one time, whenever the child was below the upper limit of compulsory school age, all applicants other than parents had to notify the local authority of their intention to apply for adoption. The purpose of such notice was to ensure the proper supervision of children placed for adoption, as it was the local authority's responsibility to visit the child and to satisfy themselves as to his wellbeing. The Houghton Committee,[329] however, felt that where the placement had been made by an adoption agency the child's welfare could best be supervised by that agency. Following their recommendations, it is now only necessary to notify the local authority in cases where the child has not been placed for adoption by an adoption agency. In such cases the applicant must, not more than two years or less than three months before the order, give written[330] notice to the local authority within whose area the child has his home of the intention to apply for an adoption order.[331]

Upon receipt of such notice the local authority must investigate the matter, in particular the suitability of the applicants, and any other matter relevant to the child's long-term welfare and submit a report to the court.[332]

G FUNCTIONS AND POWERS OF THE COURT

1 WHICH COURT?

All three levels of original jurisdiction, namely, the High Court, county court and magistrates court have power to make both adoption orders and placement orders.[333] Applications to the county court must be made to specially designated 'adoption centres'. In general, applicants are free to choose the level of court in which to proceed. Before the 2002 Act most applications were made to the county court. There are, however, some restrictions on where applications may be issued pursuant to the Children (Allocation of Proceedings) Order 1991, as amended.[334] For example, an application for a Convention adoption order (discussed below) or for an order to which s 83 of the 2002 Act applies (ie where a child is habitually resident outside the British Isles is brought to the United

---

[328] But note *Re KT (A Minor: Adoption)* [1993] Fam Law 567 where 'home' was held to have been established by weekend visits.

[329] At paras 237–9.

[330] See the definition of 'notice' in the Adoption and Children Act 2002, s 144(1).

[331] Adoption and Children Act 2002, s 44. Where a person needs court leave to make an application pursuant to 42(4) and (5), discussed above, notice to adopt may only be given if that leave has been given: s 44(4).

[332] Section 42(5)–(6). Adoption agencies are under a similar obligation in respect of agency placements: s 43.

[333] Adoption and Children Act 2002, s 144(1) (definition of 'court').

[334] In particular by the Children (Allocation of Proceedings) (Amendment) (No 2) Order 2005.

Kingdom for adoption)[335] must be made to the High Court or county court.[336] In the latter case it should be commenced at an 'intercountry adoption centre'. Where the child has been subject to pre-existing divorce proceedings it is generally desirable in the case of step-parent adoption applications to bring proceedings in that court. Proceedings to vary or revoke an order (except one to revoke a placement order, which has to be commenced in the magistrates' court) should be made to the court which made the order.[337] Seeking to revoke a placement order or while one is in force, seeking leave for a contact order or to change the child's name or to take the child out of the United Kingdom, should be brought in the court that made the placement order.[338] Proceedings can be transferred from one county court to another and from a county court to the High Court and vice versa.[339] Applications started in a magistrates' court are heard by the family proceedings court,[340] and under the Allocation Order[341] there is power to transfer cases to the county court.

2 FUNCTIONS OF THE COURT

The court must be satisfied:

— that the order, if made, will be for the child's welfare;
— that each parent or guardian of the child freely, and with full understanding of what is involved, consents unconditionally to the making of the order or has consented under s 20 and has not withdrawn that consent, or that the consent should be dispensed with.

We have already considered the second of these issues but the first requires further elaboration.

Before a court can be satisfied that it should make an adoption order, it is enjoined by s 1(6) to consider all the available options and must conclude that it is better for the child to make the order than not doing so. In considering this it must treat the child's welfare as the paramount consideration (under s 1(2)) and apply the checklist under s 1(4). It needs to be appreciated that adoption is more than just determining with whom the child is to live. As Sir Stephen Brown P put it in *Re B (Adoption Order: Nationality)*:[342]

'Adoption is a very serious matter indeed. It confers a new status on the person adopted. It takes that person into a new family.'

The principal benefit of adoption is the long-term security that it confers, thus satisfying the adopters' need to know that the child is a full member of the family and the child's need to know that he or she is fully the child of these parents and that nothing can happen to take him or her away.[343] But if the court finds, for instance, that a residence order would better secure the child's long-term future, as for example where the child opposes the

---

[335] Discussed below at p 878.   [336] See Art 3A of the Allocation Order.
[337] Art 4(1A), but note the criticism by Clarke Hall and Morrison at 3[302], n 1 that this rule overlooks the interests of the child.
[338] Art 3(c)(2).
[339] Arts 10 and 12. The High Court similarly has power to transfer cases to the county court: Art 13.
[340] Children Act 1989 s 92.   [341] Art 8.   [342] [1998] 1 FLR 965 at 969.
[343] See eg *Re B (MF)(Infant)* [1972] 1 WLR 102, CA.

adoption, or that an enhanced residence order or special guardianship order would better suit the child's needs, particularly where the applicant is a relative, then it should make that order instead.[344]

Although 'welfare' is a sufficiently wide term to include material benefits conferred by adoption, it is important not to confuse the purpose of adoption[345] with the benefits of rights of abode and citizenship of this country. There must be a genuine intention that the applicants should stand in loco parentis to the child. An order will be refused where it is clear, for example, that the real motive for the application is to enable the child (particularly, if he has nearly attained his majority) to acquire British citizenship rather than to promote his welfare.[346] Benefit accruing after majority[347] is a relevant factor to be taken into account when deciding whether to make an order.[348]

3 THE COURT'S POWERS

(a) No power to add terms and conditions

The former power under s 12(6) of the Adoption Act 1976 that an adoption order 'contain such terms and conditions as the court thinks fit' has been repealed. Before the Children Act 1989 this power was the only means by which a court could make any order additional to the adoption order and as such had some importance, particularly as it was the legal vehicle by which the courts came to accept that it was consistent with adoption to provide for some regime of continuing contact between the child and his or her birth family.[349] However, the role of s 12(6) became marginalised in part because under the Children Act 1989 the court could make s 8 orders and in part because of the reluctance to impose conditions upon unwilling adopters,[350] the view being that it was generally desirable for the child to become as nearly as possible the natural child of the adopting parents and that a condition that derogated from that should not therefore be imposed. It was thus already clear that the scope for invoking s 12(6) was severely limited. Consequently its demise under the 2002 Act will not make any real difference in practice.

(b) The power to orders under the Children Act 1989

Proceedings under the Adoption and Children Act 2002 are designated 'family proceedings' for the purposes of the Children Act 1989.[351] Consequently, courts are empowered,

---

[344] Discussed below at p 864.

[345] See eg *Re WM (Adoption: Non Patrial)* [1997] 1 FLR 132 where financial advantage to the child being adopted was taken into account. See also *Re A (An Infant)* [1963] 1 All ER 531 at 534. If the child has a substantial connection with a foreign country (eg if he is domiciled there or is a foreign national), one of the matters to be taken into account in deciding whether the order will be for his benefit is whether it will be recognised in that country: *Re B (S) (An Infant)* [1968] Ch 204.

[346] See eg *Re J (Adoption: Non Patrial)* [1998] 1 FLR 225, CA.

[347] For example, the benefit of having a secure home and status, which could be particularly important if, as in *Re D (A Minor) (Adoption Order: Validity)* [1991] Fam 137, CA, the child is mentally incapable.

[348] Section 1(2).

[349] S Maidment 'Access and Family Adoptions' (1977) 40 MLR 293 argued that imposing access under s 12(6) was wrong since the power to add conditions was *solely* designed to deal with questions of religion. Contact is discussed below at p 864.

[350] See in particular *Re S (A Minor)(Blood Transfusion: Adoption Order: Condition)* [1994] 2 FLR 416, CA.

[351] Children Act 1989 s 8(4)(d), as amended.

either upon application, or upon their own motion, to make s 8 orders.[352] They are
also empowered, either upon application, or upon their own motion, to make a special
guardianship order.[353]

Adoption or residence order or special guardianship

As has been said, s 1(6) obliges the court in an adoption application to consider the whole
range of its powers before making an order.[354] This means, that regardless of whether or
not the parents consent, consideration must be given to whether *alternative* orders such as
a residence order, particularly an enhanced residence order,[355] or a special guardianship
order[356] would better serve the child's interests. If the change of status with its consequential severance of legal ties with the birth family and permanence brought about by the
adoption is not thought appropriate, perhaps because (as in *Re M (Adoption or Residence
Order)*[357]) the child objects or where the applicants are relatives or step-parents, then one
of the alternative orders might be thought appropriate. It remains to be seen how readily
the courts will make adoption orders in favour of relatives or step-parents under the 2002
Act.

Post Adoption Contact[358]

By s 46(6), before making an adoption order:

'the court must consider whether there should be arrangements for allowing any person
contact with the child; and for that purpose the court must consider any existing or proposed
arrangements and obtain the views of the parties to the proceedings'.

Although, as discussed earlier,[359] it has long been accepted that the court may make an
order for post-adoption contact this is the first statutory recognition of such a power.[360]

In deciding whether to make a contact order regard might still be had to the House
of Lords' decision in *Re C (A Minor)(Adoption Order: Conditions)*[361] in which Lord
Ackner said:

'The cases rightly stress that in normal circumstances it is desirable that there should be a
complete break, but that each case has to be considered on its own particular facts. No doubt
the court will not, except in exceptional cases, impose terms or conditions as to access to
members of the child's natural family to which the adopting parents do not agree . . . Where
no agreement is forthcoming the court will, with very rare exceptions, have to choose
between making an adoption order without terms or conditions as to access, or to refuse to
make such an order and seek to safeguard access through some other machinery, such as
wardship. To do otherwise would be merely inviting future and almost immediate litigation.'

---

[352] Children Act 1989, s 10(1)(b), discussed above, p 566.   [353] Ibid, s 14A(6).

[354] Even before the 2002 Act it was implicit that the court had to consider alternatives: see p 668 of the
previous edition of this work.

[355] Discussed above at pp 603ff.   [356] Discussed above at pp 604ff.

[357] [1998] 1 FLR 570, CA, discussed above, p 857.

[358] The following discussion is only concerned with the court's powers. In practice, some types of informal
arrangements (eg so-called letter contact) are commonly made, see above p 826.

[359] See above at p 863.

[360] Although, as Bridge and Swindells op cit at p 232, n 9, point out, it was only in the latter stages of the
Bill that this provision was added.

[361] [1989] AC 1, at pp 17–18, HL. See also the comments of the Adoption Law Review. Discussion Paper
No 1, paras 71–2.

Lord Ackner further observed that a distinction may properly be drawn between contact with birth parents and contact with other relatives, the former being harder to justify than the latter, if an adoption order is to be made.

Following *Re C* it was evident that the courts were reluctant to *impose* a contact order against the wishes of the adopters and, where the adopters agreed that contact should continue, it had been held[362] that there was no need for an order.[363] Although, given the general difficulty of enforcing contact orders, it is understandable that the courts should be hesitant about imposing such orders on unwilling adopters, it was evident that the objection went deeper than that, for, as Butler-Sloss LJ said in *Re T (Adoption: Consent)*,[364] 'the finality of adoption and the importance of letting the new family find its feet ought not to be threatened in any way by an order [for contact] in this case'. Whether the courts will take a similar attitude under the 2002 Act remains to be seen. But note should also be taken of *Re T (Adoption Children: Contact)*,[365] in which Balcombe LJ held that adopters cannot agree to indirect contact and then simply resile from it without explanation. Where they do, the court might well be disposed to grant the former parents leave to apply for a s 8 contact order. In this case leave was given, the court being satisfied that the proposed application would not disrupt the children's lives, although all that was in issue was the adopters' promise to provide the birth parents with annual reports.[366]

As well as making a contact order at the same time as an adoption order it is possible for a free-standing application for contact to be sought subsequently. However, applications by birth parents (who, post-adoption are no longer the child's legal parents) or relatives, including a sibling will require court leave, which will not be easily granted.[367]

Prohibited steps and specific issue orders

In theory in addition to making an adoption order the court may make prohibited steps and/or specific issue orders, but they are likely to be treated in the same way as s 12(6) conditions were[368] and will therefore be rarely justified.

(c) Refusal to make an order

Even before the 2002 Act, adoption applications by non-relatives were rarely refused. In the *Pathways Study*[369] conducted in the late 1980s, 96% of applications were granted, none were refused, the remaining 4% being withdrawn or adjourned. The Study's sample also found that 81% of step-parent adoption applications were granted.

---

[362] *Re T (Adoption: Contact)* [1995] 2 FLR 251, CA.

[363] Though this is not to say that orders were never made: see eg *Re O (Transracial Adoption: Contact)* [1995] 2 FLR 597.

[364] [1995] 2 FLR 251 at 257.   [365] [1995] 2 FLR 792, CA.

[366] Compare *Re E (Adopted Child: Contact: Leave)* [1995] 1 FLR 57 where leave was refused to the former parents to apply for a s 8 order to enforce a promise made at the dispensing stage of an adoption hearing that photographs and news about the child's schooling would be forwarded to them. It was held that the proper course would have been to apply to cancel the order or to appeal it on the ground that it was flawed.

[367] See eg *Re C (A Minor)(Adopted Child: Contact)* [1993] Fam, 210. Cf *Re E (A Minor)(Adopted Child: Contact: Leave)* [1995] 1 FLR 57. Steps need also be taken so that adoptive parents are not unnecessarily disturbed by a leave application, see *Re T (Minors)(Adopted Children: Contact)* [1995] 2 FLR 792 and see the discussion in Clarke Hall and Morrison at 3 [500.24].

[368] See above p 863.   [369] See Murch et al, op cit n 73.

Where a previous application for adoption has been refused by any court, a second application may not be made by the same person 'unless it appears to the court that, because of a change in circumstances or for any other reason, it is proper to hear the application'.[370]

H REGISTRATION OF ADOPTION AND THE ADOPTION CONTACT REGISTER

The Registrar General is obliged to maintain a separate register of adoptions known as the Adopted Children Register.[371] This register is not open to public inspection or search.[372] The Registrar General is also obliged to maintain an index of the Adopted Children Register.[373] Although s 78(2) states that any person may search the index and have a certified copy of any entry in the Register, this is subject to the embargo[374] that a person is not entitled to a copy of an entry in the Register relating to an adopted person who is under 18, save where the applicant has provided the Registrar General with the full name and date of birth of the adopted person who is under 18, and the full name of the adoptive parent(s).[375] As one commentary[376] says, this is a security measure intended to prevent the tracing of children without recourse to the proper channels.

By s 79 the Registrar General is required to make traceable the connection between any entry in the registers of live births or other records which has been marked 'Adopted' and any corresponding entry in the Adoption Children Register. The disclosure of this information is subject to the conditions set out in s 79 and the Regulations and is also dependent upon when the adoption order was made.[377]

The pre–2002 Act 'right' of an adopted adult upon reaching the age of 18 to apply for and receive copies of their birth certificate and thus to be able to trace their parents is preserved by s 60 and Sch 2. The mechanisms for doing this, however, are different according to when the adoption order was made. For those adults adopted before 30 December 2005 (ie when the 2002 Act came into force) the information may be sought directly from the Registrar-General. Pre–2002 Act case law established that this is not an absolute right. In *R v Registrar-General, ex p Smith*[378] for example, the Registrar-General's refusal to give details was upheld upon the basis that there was a real fear for the mother's life if identifying information had been disclosed to the adopted adult applicant. For those adults adopted after 30 December 2005 the system is different inasmuch as applications will be made to the adoption agency rather than to the Registrar-General. Moreover, the right is expressly made subject, by s 60(2), to the High Court's power to order otherwise. Under either method, before information is given applicants should be informed that counselling services are available and where they may be obtained.[379]

[370] Adoption and Children Act 2002, s 48(1).   [371] Adoption and Children Act 2002, s 77(1).
[372] Section 77(2).   [373] Section 78(1).   [374] Section 78(3).
[375] Adopted Children and Adopted Contact Registers Regulations 2005, reg 10.
[376] Clarke Hall and Morrison at 3 [500.46].
[377] For detailed discussion see Bridge and Swindells, op cit, ch 12 and Clarke Hall and Morrison at 3 [500.49].
[378] [1991] 2 QB 393, CA.   [379] See s 63.

The ability to trace and make contact with birth parents is one thing but it is quite another as to whether that contact is welcome. In this regard the Adoption Contact Register is important. This was first created in the 1990s[380] and is now provided for by s 80 of the 2002 Act. The purpose of the register is 'to put adopted people and their birth parents or other relatives in touch with each other where this is what they both want. The register provides a safe and confidential way for birth parents and other relatives to assure an adopted person that contact would be welcome and give a contact address.'[381] The register comprises two Parts: Part I, in which are maintained the name and address of any adopted person who is over 18 and has a copy of his birth certificate and who wishes to contact a relative; and Part II, in which are entered, subject to certain prescribed conditions,[382] the current address and identifying details of a relative[383] who wishes to contact an adopted person. A fee is charged for making an entry on either Part.[384]

Surprisingly, there is no requirement for counselling, nor is there a facility for exchanging limited information, such as medical information, in using the register.

I THE EFFECTS OF AN ADOPTION ORDER

1 COMPLETE AND PERMANENT TRANSFER OF LEGAL PARENTAGE

The 2002 Act has made no change to the main effect of an adoption order, namely, that it makes a complete and permanent transfer of legal parentage. Thus by s 46(1) an adoption order gives parental responsibility for the child to the adopter(s), while s 46(2) provides that the making of such an order operates to 'extinguish' the parental responsibility which any person (other than the adopter(s) or the parent in the case of step-parent adoptions)[385] had for the child immediately before the making of the order, though it does not affect parental responsibility so far as it relates to any period before the making of an order.[386]

An adoption order also operates to 'extinguish' any previous order, including a care order, made under the Children Act 1989.[387]

(a) Revocation of adoption orders

Notwithstanding that adoption orders are generally irrevocable, there is one circumstance where express provision is made to revoke an order, ie in the case of a person adopted by

---

[380] See the Adoption Act 1976, s 51A (added by the Children Act 1989, Sch 10, para 21).

[381] Department of Health's Guidance and Regulation, Vol 9, para 32.

[382] Ie that the applicant is aged 18 or over that the Registrar General has either the record of the applicant's birth or that the applicant is a relative: s 80(5).

[383] Ie 'any person who (but for his adoption) would be related to [the adopted person] by blood (including half-blood) or marriage': s 80(2).

[384] £15 for entry on Part I or £30 on Part II. See the Adopted Children and Adopted Contact Registers Regulations 2005, reg 9.

[385] Adoption and Children Act 2002, s 46(3)(b). For one effect of extinguishment see *Secretary of State for Social Services v S* [1983] 3 All ER 173, CA (the mother who takes her natural son to live with her after his adoptive mother's death is not his 'parent' and is therefore entitled to a guardian's allowance).

[386] Section 46(3)(a).   [387] Section 46(2)(b).

the mother or father alone who has subsequently become legitimated by his parents' marriage. In such a case, s 55 permits 'any of the parties concerned' to apply for a revocation. Applications should be made to the court that made the original order.

(b) Setting adoptions aside

Apart from the statutory power of revocation, there is a right of appeal both against the making and the refusal to make an adoption order.[388] In truly exceptional cases leave to appeal may be granted out of time. In *Re M (A Minor) (Adoption)*,[389] for example, a father agreed to an adoption of his children by his former wife and her new husband in ignorance of the fact that she was terminally ill. It was held in this 'very exceptional case' that in the children's interests the time for appeal would be extended and the adoption orders set aside on the ground that the father's ignorance of his wife's condition vitiated his consent. Similarly, leave to appeal out of time was granted and the adoption set aside in *Re K (Adoption and Wardship)*,[390] which was an horrific case involving a Bosnian 'orphan' who originally had been found beneath the corpses of persons thought to be her parents. The child had been allowed to come to England for medical treatment, and an English couple began to foster her after she left hospital. This couple then applied to adopt her at a time when they knew that the child's grandfather and aunt had been traced and wanted the child back and that the Bosnian Government had stopped all adoptions from that country. In the original adoption proceedings the judge had not deemed it necessary to appoint a guardian, nor was any attempt made to contact the child's guardian in Bosnia. In these extraordinary circumstances, amounting to a fundamental breach of natural justice, the Court of Appeal set the order aside.[391]

Re M and *Re K* are best looked upon as truly exceptional cases and certainly not as precedents laying down a general power to set orders aside. To put these cases in context we must consider *Re B (Adoption: Jurisdiction To Set Aside)*,[392] in which the applicant, whose origins were Arabic, unsuccessfully applied some 35 years after the order was made to set aside his adoption by a Jewish couple. As the Court of Appeal made clear, there is no general inherent power to set an adoption aside and, in the absence of procedural irregularities or mistakes, no power exists to revoke an order. To hold otherwise would be, in Swinton Thomas LJ's words, to 'undermine the whole basis upon which adoption orders are made, namely that they are final and for life as regards the adopters, the natural parents and the child'.

The only other way the adoption status may be changed is by a second adoption,[393] but this is not to say that even former parents have no other remedies, since the making of an

---

[388] Appeals from magistrates' courts lie to the High Court: Adoption Act and Children Act 2002, s 100 (applying s 94 of the Children Act 1989 to adoptions); in other cases to the Court of Appeal. An order made by a magistrates' or county court can be questioned by judicial review. As a matter of practice, when appealing against an adoption order the applicant should immediately seek a stay and expedited hearing: *Re PJ (Adoption: Practice on Appeal)* [1998] 2 FLR 252, CA.

[389] [1991] 1 FLR 458, CA.   [390] [1997] 2 FLR 221, CA.

[391] In the subsequent re-hearing (see [1997] 1 FLR 230) Sir Stephen Brown P held that although the adoption application should be refused, nevertheless care and control should be granted to the foster parents together with substantial contact to the child's birth family, with the child herself remaining a ward of court.

[392] [1995] Fam 239, CA.   [393] Which is expressly permitted by s 46(5).

adoption order does not prevent the normal application of private and public law in relation to the adoptive family. Former parents, like anyone else, may with court leave, seek to apply for s 8 orders in respect of the adopted child. However, leave will not normally be given and in any event would require, in Thorpe J's words,[394] 'some fundamental change of circumstances' before permitting the re-opening of crucial issues such as contact and a fortiori, residence. Nevertheless there is at least one reported example of a birth parent subsequently obtaining an order that the adopted child should live with her.[395]

2 THE CHILD'S CHANGE OF STATUS

The corollary of transferring parental responsibility is that the child's status is also changed. This is governed by s 67 which declares that from the date of adoption:

'(1) An adopted person is to be treated as if born as the child of the adopters or adopter.

(2) An adopted person is the legitimate child of the adopters or adopter[396] and, if adopted by

    (a) a couple, or

    (b) one of a couple under section 51(2),

is to be treated as the child of the relationship of the couple in question.

(3) An adopted person—

    (a) if adopted by one of a couple under section 51(2), is to be treated in law as not being the child of any person other than the adopter and the other one of the couple, and

    (b) in any other case, is to be treated in law, subject to subsection (4), as not being the child of any person other than the adopters or adopter;

but this subsection does not affect any reference in this Act to a person's natural parent or to any other natural relationship.

(4) In the case of a person adopted by one of the person's natural parents as sole adoptive parent, subsection (3)(b) has no effect as respects entitlement to property depending on relationship to that parent, or as respects anything else depending on that relationship.'

3 CONSEQUENCES OF THE CHANGE OF STATUS AND TRANSFER OF PARENTAGE

(a) Citizenship

Consistent with the change of status, a child (of whatever nationality) adopted by an order made by a court in the United Kingdom will become a British citizen if one of the adopters

---

[394] *Re C (A Minor) (Adopted Child: Contact)* [1993] Fam 210.

[395] See *Re O (A Minor) (Wardship: Adopted Child)* [1978] 2 All ER 27, CA, where the application succeeded; cf *Re C (A Minor) (Wardship: Adopted Child)* [1985] FLR 1114, CA.

[396] But note that adoption of an illegitimate child by a birth parent as sole adoptive parent will not prevent his legitimation if the adopter later marries the other parent: Legitimacy Act 1976, s 4. See above p 345.

is a British citizen.[397] On the other hand, adoption cannot deprive a child of British citizenship if he or she already has it.[398]

(b) Peerages, dignities and titles

An adoption does *not* affect the descent of any peerage or dignity or title of honour.[399] Similarly, it does not, in the absence of any contrary indication, 'affect the declaration of any property (expressly or not) to devolve (as nearly as the law permits) along with any peerage, dignity or title of honour.'[400]

(c) Change of surname

Although normally the child's surname is changed to that of the adopters on the making of the adoption,[401] technically, the power to change the name becomes vested in the adopter(s) who can therefore choose not to do so. Once registered, however, an adopter cannot thereafter in the case of a joint adoption, unilaterally change the name.[402]

(d) Prohibited degrees and incest

The adoptive child and his adoptive parents are deemed to come within the prohibited degrees of consanguinity, so that they may not intermarry or enter into a civil partnership.[403] This continues to apply if a subsequent adoption order is made; hence the child may not marry a former adoptive parent.[404] Adoption, however, does not prevent a marriage or civil partnership between the child and his adoptive sibling or with any other adoptive relative. Conversely, as the modern law takes some account of genetics, the child may not marry nor enter a civil partnership with any person who would have come within the prohibited degrees if no adoption had been made[405] For the purpose of incest the crime continues to relate to the child's birth relationships but, curiously, not to adoptive relatives.[406]

(e) Maintenance

Any duty to make payments for the child's maintenance by virtue of an order or agreement ceases upon the making of an adoption order unless the agreement constitutes a trust or expressly provides to the contrary.[407] One consequence of this is that after the

---

[397] British Nationality Act 1981 s 1(5). In the case of a joint adoption the child will acquire British citizenship if one of the adopters possesses it. He will retain British citizenship even if the order ceases to have effect for any reason: ibid, s1(6). But note *Re K (A Minor) (Adoption Order: Nationality)* [1995] Fam 38, CA, in which it was held that s 1(6) does not apply to appeals: hence citizenship can be lost if an appeal against the making of an order succeeds.

[398] Adoption and Children Act 2002, s 74(2).   [399] Adoption and Children Act 2002, s 71(1).

[400] Section 71(2)(3).

[401] The application form expressly provides for the new names to be identified.

[402] Ie adoptive parents are subject to the same law on names as the birth parents, see the discussion above at p 396.

[403] Marriage Act 1949 Sch 1, Part I of the Civil Partnership Act 2004 Sch 1.

[404] Adoption and Children Act 2002, s 74(1).

[405] Section 74(1)(a), applying the Marriage Act 1949 Sch 1, Part 1 and the Civil Partnership Act 2004 Sch 1.

[406] Section 74(1)(b) and (c) applying the Sexual Offences Act 2003, ss 64 and 65.

[407] Section 46(2)(d) and (4). These provisions do not affect liability for arrears existing at the time of the adoption order.

adoption no application for maintenance may be made against the child's father even if the adoption is by the mother alone. Liability for maintenance of an adopted child lies exclusively upon the adoptive parents.[408]

(f) Claims under the Inheritance (Provision for Family and Dependants) Act 1975 and the Fatal Accidents Act 1976

Since an adopted child is regarded as the child of his adopter or adopters, he or she may claim under the Fatal Accidents Act 1976 as a dependant of his adoptive parent or other adoptive relative, but not of his birth parent.[409] Similarly adoption bars the child's inheritance claims against the birth parents' estate under the Inheritance (Provision for Family and Dependants) Act 1975.[410]

(g) Pensions

An adoption order does *not* affect entitlement to a pension which is payable to or for the child's benefit provided it is in payment at the time of the order.[411]

(h) Insurance

The rights and liabilities of an insurance policy taken out by the birth parents for payment of funeral expenses upon the child's death transfer to the adoptive parents.[412]

(i) Property

When first introduced by the Adoption of Children Act 1926 adoption did not affect the devolution of property; the child remained the child of his birth parents.

That position was changed by the Adoption of Children Act 1949. Ever since, as regards interests in property, the general principle is that from the date of the adoption order an adopted child is deemed to become the child of the adopter or adopters and ceases to be regarded as the child of his birth parents or, if he has been previously adopted, of his former adopters, and therefore is no longer considered as related to any other person through his birth or former adoptive parents.

In the case of instruments made on or after 1 January 1976 or wills of testators dying on or after that date and subject to any contrary indication, an adopted child may claim in such cases whether the disposition takes effect before or after the adoption. A disposition depending on the date of birth of a child of the adoptive parent or parents is to be construed as though the adopted child was born on the date of his adoption and two or more children adopted on the same day rank inter se in the order of their actual births. This provision, however, does not affect the operation of any condition depending on the child's reaching an actual age.[413] Thus, if there is a bequest to K's eldest child at 18 and K adopts a child A and subsequently has a natural child B, A can claim when he reaches the age of 18 whether his adoption preceded or followed the testator's death.

---

[408] Child Support Act 1991 ss 1 and 54 and Social Security Administration Act 1992, ss 78(6) and 105(3).
[409] See *Watson v Willmot* [1991] 1 QB 140.
[410] See *Re Collins* [1990] Fam 56. See below, p 1109 n 150.
[411] Adoption and Children Act 2002, s 75.   [412] Section 76.
[413] Adoption and Children 2002, s 69(2)(a). A disposition includes a power of appointment and any other disposition of an interest in or right over property: ibid, s 73(2).

Section 69(4) expressly provides that an adoption 'does not prejudice any interest vested in the adopted child before the adoption, or any interest expectant (whether vested or not) upon an interest so vested'. The ambit of the provision, however, has been open to speculation. Suppose, for example, that there is a gift to X with remainder to his eldest son and that X's eldest son is S. If S has been adopted by someone other than X before the instrument creating the settlement takes effect, he can obviously claim nothing because he is no longer regarded as X's son at all. If X has died before S's adoption, so that S's interest has vested in possession, it is expressly preserved by s 69(4) notwithstanding the adoption. But what is the position if S is adopted after the disposition takes effect but before the interest vests in possession? In *Staffordshire County Council v B*[414] it was held that in such circumstances the child was still entitled to the interest notwithstanding his adoption since, properly interpreted, what is now s 69(4) did not require the interest of the child to be vested in possession, it being sufficient that the child's contingent interest arose out of an interest vested in possession.

Notwithstanding the general rule there are various provisions designed to ensure that a child *adopted by one of his unmarried parents as the sole adoptive parent* is not thereby deprived of an interest he could otherwise have taken. In the first place, such an adoption does not affect the child's entitlement to any property depending on his relationship to the adoptive parent.[415] Secondly, if a disposition depends on the date of birth of an illegitimate child, neither his adoption by one of his parents as sole adopter nor his legitimation if he has been adopted will affect his entitlement.[416]

Trustees and personal representatives are not liable if they distribute property in ignorance of the making or revocation of an adoption order, but beneficiaries may trace property into the hands of anyone other than a purchaser.[417]

J ADOPTION WITH A FOREIGN ELEMENT[418]

1 INTRODUCTION

As we discussed in the introduction,[419] a developing area of adoption is so-called 'intercountry adoption'. That is a general term referring to the adoption of a child usually resident abroad by adopters usually resident in the United Kingdom. But it may also refer to the adoption of a child resident in the United Kingdom by adopters resident overseas.

Although compared with a number of other jurisdictions there are still relatively few intercountry adoptions in England and Wales, the issue came into prominence in the

---

[414] [1998] 1 FLR 261.   [415] Adoption and Children Act 2002, s 70.

[416] Ibid, s 70; Legitimacy Act 1976 s 6(2). Similarly, the revocation of an adoption order following the marriage of a child's parents will not affect any claim he could have made to property had the order remained in force: Legitimacy Act 1976 s 4(2). If the child has been adopted and dies before his parents' marriage, he is deemed to be legitimate on that date for the purpose of preserving interests to be taken by or in succession to his spouse, children and remoter issue: Legitimacy Act 1976 s 5(6). For the effect of an adoption by a woman over 55 and the operation of the presumption that she is incapable of bearing children, see Adoption and Children Act 2002, s 69(5).

[417] Ibid, s 45.

[418] See generally Bridge and Swindells, op cit, chs 14 and 15 and Clarke Hall and Morrison 3 [500.156] ff.

[419] Above at p 828.

1990s in the wake particularly of the sad plight of Romanian and later Bosnian orphans which in turn led to more general media coverage and public interest in the horrifying conditions suffered by children in South American countries. In point of fact, however, many of the British intercountry adoptions are of children from China or from countries of the former Soviet Union.

As we discuss shortly, after an earlier less successful attempt through the 1965 Hague Convention on Jurisdiction, Applicable Law and Recognition of Decrees relating to Adoptions to provide a uniform law and jurisdiction,[420] a much bolder attempt to provide international regulation of intercountry adoption was successfully introduced by the 1993 Hague Convention on Protection of Children and Co-operation in Respect of Intercountry Adoption (hereafter 'the 1999 Hague Convention on Intercountry adoption') which the United Kingdom ratified in June 2003.

Following the United Kingdom's ratification of the 1993 Convention, there may be said to be three basic 'types' of intercountry adoptions namely (1) Convention adoptions (2) Overseas adoptions falling outside the Convention and (3) Children whose carers or prospective carers wish to bring the child to the United Kingdom for adoption here. Each of these issues will be discussed in turn.

2 THE 1993 HAGUE CONVENTION ON INTERCOUNTRY ADOPTION[421]

The United Kingdom ratified the 1993 Hague Convention on Intercountry Adoption in June 2003 through the Adoption (Intercountry Aspects) Act 1999 and consequential Regulations. However, most of the legislation governing intercountry adoption as it operates in England and Wales is contained in the Adoption and Children Act 2002 and the Adoption with a Foreign Element Regulations 2005.

Local authorities have responsibility for providing services in relation to the Convention as part of the Adoption Service. In practice much of the work is delegated to a small number of adoption societies approved by the Secretary of State to provide Convention adoption services.

The 1993 Convention has three basic objects:

(1) to establish safeguards to ensure that intercountry adoptions only take place after the best interests of the child have been properly assessed and in circumstances which protect his or her fundamental rights;

---

[420] That Convention was only ratified by Austria, Switzerland and the United Kingdom all of which denounced it upon ratifying the 2003 Convention. For a brief discussion of that Convention see pp 679–80 of the previous edition of this work and the references there cited.

[421] See generally The Explanatory Report by G Parra-Aranguren and by the same author 'An Overview of the 1993 Hague Inter-Country Adoption Convention' in N Lowe and G Douglas (eds) *Families Across Frontiers* (1996) at 565; W Duncan 'Conflict and Co-operation. The Approach to Conflicts of Law in the 1993 Hague Convention on Intercountry Adoption' in *Families Across Frontiers* at 577; R Frank 'The Recognition of Intercountry Adoption in the Light of the 1993 Hague Convention on Intercountry Adoptions' in *Families Across Frontiers* at 591; and M Brennan et al 'Intercountry Adoption—the recognition of foreign adoptions in the simple and full terms' in the Report on the *Cross Border Movement of Children* (1999, Society for Advanced Legal Studies).

(2) to establish a system of co-operation amongst Contracting States to ensure that these safeguards are respected; and

(3) to secure the recognition in Contracting States of adoptions made in accordance with the Convention.[422]

To achieve these broad objectives the Convention first makes a distinction between 'States of Origin' from which children are sent for adoption and 'Receiving States' in which the adopted child will live. It is the responsibility of a State of Origin, via its 'competent authorities'[423] to establish that the child is adoptable and that intercountry adoption as opposed to placement within the country of origin is in the child's best interests.[424] States of Origin are also obliged to have ensured that the requisite consents to the child's adoption (it will be noted that the Convention makes no attempt to prescribe what the internal laws on consent should be) have, after due counselling, been freely given with a full understanding of what is involved and without financial inducement.[425] Such States are similarly expected to ensure that, 'having regard to the age and maturity of the child', such a child has been counselled and duly informed about the effects of adoption and, where required, freely consented to the adoption without financial inducement.[426]

In contrast, the responsibility of Receiving States is to determine that the prospective adoptive parents are eligible and suited to adopt and to ensure that they have been counselled as may be necessary and, importantly, to have determined that the child is or will be authorised to enter and reside permanently in that State.[427]

The administrative mechanism through which the Convention operates is primarily through the tried and tested system of Central Authorities. Each contracting state is obliged to set up a Central Authority.[428] Under the Adoption (Intercountry Aspects) Act 1999, s 2(1) the United Kingdom has set up separate Central Authorities for England, Scotland and Wales. This is the first time that Wales has had such a separate body. In each of the former jurisdictions the Central Authorities are to be discharged by the Secretary of State and in Wales by the National Assembly for Wales. There is also a separate Central Authority for Northern Ireland. Central Authorities are generally charged to co-operate with one another,[429] to take all appropriate measures to prevent improper financial or other gain in connection with an adoption and to deter all parties from acting contrary to the rights of the Convention.[430] Under Art 9 Central Authorities are under a duty to collate, preserve and exchange information about the situation of the child and the prospective adopters, to facilitate and expedite proceedings, to promote development of adoption counselling and post-adoption services, and to respond to requests from other Central Authorities for information about a particular adoption situation.

These Art 9 duties may be discharged either by the Central Authority itself or by or with 'accredited bodies'. Accredited bodies should be authorised bodies capable of preparing

---

[422] See Art 1 and see the explanation in the government White Paper *Adoption: The Future* (1994, Cm 2288) paras 6.19 ff.

[423] See further below.   [424] Article 4(a) and (b).   [425] Article 4(c).   [426] Article 4(d).

[427] Article 5.   [428] Article 6.

[429] Article 7(1). Under Art 7(2) they must also provide information about the law, keep one another informed about the operation of the Convention and, as far as possible, eliminate any obstacles to its application.

[430] Article 8.

and arranging adoptions.[431] In the United Kingdom a registered adoption society is an accredited body.[432]

The procedure for facilitating a Convention adoption is as follows. Persons who are habitually resident in one Contracting State, who wish to apply to adopt a child habitually resident in another Contracting State, should apply to their own Central Authority.[433] If the Central Authority of the Receiving State is satisfied as to the applicants' eligibility and suitability to adopt, it should prepare and transmit the request to the Central Authority of the State of Origin.[434] There is a reciprocal duty on the State of Origin to prepare and transmit a report on the child that is considered adoptable and in that connection to ensure that the requisite consents have been given.[435]

Under Art 17 any decision in the State of Origin that a child should be entrusted to prospective adopters may only be made if the Central Authorities of *both* states agree that the adoption may proceed, the Central Authority of the State of Origin having ensured that the prospective adopters agree and the Central Authority of the Receiving State has approved such a decision, having considered the prospective adopters suitable and having determined that the child is or will be authorised to enter and reside permanently in that State. The adoption order is then made in the Receiving State.

Chapter V of the Convention deals with the important issue of the recognition and effects of a Convention adoption. The basic provision is Art 23, which provides that an adoption certified by the competent authority of the state of the adoption as having been made in accordance with the Convention shall be recognised by operation of law in the other Contracting States. Under Art 24 recognition may, however, be refused in a Contracting State if the adoption 'is manifestly contrary to its public policy, taking into account the best interests of the child'. So far as England and Wales are concerned the High Court may annul a Convention adoption or a Convention adoption order on the ground that the adoption is contrary to public policy.[436] But subject to this, the validity of a Convention adoption or Convention adoption order cannot be challenged in any court in England and Wales.[437]

Article 26(1) provides that recognition includes recognition of:

'(a) the legal parent–child relationship between the child and his or her adoptive parents;

(b) parental responsibility of the adoptive parents for the child;

(c) the termination of a pre-existing legal relationship between the child and his or her mother and father, if the adoption has that effect in the Contracting State where it was made.'

This, as one commentator has pointed out,[438] is not a comprehensive enumeration of the effects of recognition, but rather a list of the minimal consequences of recognition. Article 26(2) further provides that where the adoption has the effect of terminating a pre-existing legal parent–child relationship (in other words a 'full' adoption), the child is to

---

[431] Articles 10 and 11.   [432] Adoption (Intercountry Aspects) Act 1999, s 2(2).

[433] Article 14.   [434] Article 15.   [435] Article 16.

[436] Adoption and Children Act 2002, s 89(1). A 'Convention adoption' is an order effected under the law of a Convention country outside the British Islands, s 66(1)(c); a 'Convention adoption order' is an order made under the Convention within the British Islands, s 144(1).

[437] Ibid s 89(4).   [438] Duncan, op cit, at 586.

enjoy in all states where the adoption is recognised as well as the Receiving State, rights equivalent to those resulting from full adoption in such states.[439] The recognition issue is further complicated by Art 27 which provides:

'Where an adoption granted in the State of Origin does not have the effect of terminating a pre-existing legal parent-child relationship, it may, in the receiving State which recognises the adoption under the Convention, be converted into an adoption having such an effect—

    (a) if the law of the receiving State so permits; and

    (b) if the consents referred to Article 4 paragraphs (c) and (d) have been or are given for the purpose of such an adoption.'

Section 88 of the Adoption and Children Act attempts to deal with the problem of handling simple adoptions.[440] It provides that where a child has been adopted under a Convention order and the High Court is satisfied:

'(a) that under the law of the country in which the adoption was effected the adoption was not a full adoption;

(b) that the consents referred to in Article 4(c) and (d) of the Convention have not been given for a full adoption, or that the United Kingdom is not the receiving State (within the meaning of Article 2 of the Convention); and

(c) that it would be more favourable to the adopted child for a direction to be given under this subsection . . .'

the court may direct that the order shall not be treated as a full adoption, or not to the extent as may be specified in the direction. This provides a mechanism for the High Court to give a direction whether and to what extent a child adopted under a simple adoption under the Convention should be treated as if he were not the child of any person other than the adopter or adopters. It will be available only if the adoption was not a full adoption, if the consents to a full adoption were not given or the United Kingdom is not the receiving State. It must be more favourable to the adopted child for the direction to be given.

An order made under the 1993 Convention, whether by a United Kingdom court or outside the British Islands automatically confers British citizenship upon a child if he does not already have it, provided the adopter(s) are habitually resident in the United Kingdom and at least one of the adoptive parents is a British citizen.[441] Convention orders must also be entered on the Adopted Children Register.[442]

Although the 1993 Convention is a bold attempt to provide global control of intercountry adoption it generally seems to be working. Certainly in terms of Contracting States the Convention is highly successful. At the time of writing there are 68 Contracting States (comprising 49 ratifications and 19 accessions). Crucially, the USA has signed the Convention but has not yet ratified it. It is important to the overall success of the Convention that

---

[439] There is considerable doubt as to how this should be interpreted: see eg Frank, op cit and Brennan et al, op cit. The *Explanatory Report*, para 439 emphasises that Art 26 was the result of compromise and that it reflects the minimum consensus that could be reached.

[440] Ie adoptions which do not sever the legal relationship of the child with his birth family.

[441] British Nationality Act 1981, s 1(5), as amended.

[442] See now the Adopted Children and Adopted Contact Register Regulations 2005, regs 3–5.

it does. Perhaps one of the reasons for the Convention's success is that it is noticeably non-prescriptive, providing only for minimum safeguards, and avoids extensive use of traditional conflicts of laws rules. Instead the Convention provides a framework based on trust and co-operation. However, one important test of the Convention's success is whether receiving States have confidence in the ability of the State of Origin to ensure that the adoption process has been properly carried out and that in particular, both the child's and the birth family's interests have been properly safeguarded. It is important, too, that the Central Authorities are able to work and co-operate with one another. In this regard note will be taken of s 9 of the Children and Adoption Act 2006 which allows the Secretary of State to suspend intercountry adoptions from countries (including Convention countries) where the Secretary determines that it would be contrary to public policy to further the bringing of children into the United Kingdom by British residents from that State.[443]

3 OVERSEAS ADOPTIONS

Convention adoptions are not the only foreign adoptions recognised by English law. Recognition is also accorded to 'overseas adoption', by which is meant a non-Convention adoption 'of a description specified in an order made by the Secretary of State, being a description of adoptions effected under the law of any country or territory outside the British Islands'.[444] In short this means an adoption order made in a country or territory on the 'designated list'.[445]

Since they are expressly included in the definition of adoption in s 66(1)(d), overseas adoptions are automatically recognised as an adoption order in England and Wales. Consequently, there is no need to re-adopt domestically nor does its status need to be established in court proceedings. Indeed, to the contrary, the validity of an overseas order cannot be impugned in proceedings in any court in England and Wales,[446] save where the High Court orders it to cease as being contrary to public policy or that the authority that purported to authorise it was not competent to do so.[447] Although children of an overseas adoption are treated as children of their adopted parents (as in any other adoption) they do not necessarily acquire British citizenship, and they may be subject to immigration rules. However, where an overseas order has been obtained by UK citizens, the child does have a right of entry and may apply for British citizenship.[448]

Where an adoption order is made outside the British Islands but is neither a Convention nor an overseas adoption it may still be recognised according to the common law

---

[443] The government has in the past imposed a temporary suspension on adoptions from Cambodia, see P Cordery 'Suspension by the UK of Intercountry Adoptions' [2005] Fam Law 925 and the note to *R (Charlton Thomson and Others) v Secretary of State for Education and Skills* [2005] EWHC 1378 (Admin) at [2005] Fam Law 861.

[444] Adoption and Children Act 2002, s 87.

[445] Currently contained in the Adoption (Designation of Overseas Adoptions) Order 1973. The list comprises 39 Commonwealth countries (excluding inter alia India and Bangladesh) and 22 other countries including China, USA, South Africa, and Western European countries. This list is currently under review. Anyone habitually resident in the United Kingdom wishing to adopt from a country on the designated list will still have to comply with entry requirements: see Adoption with a Foreign Element Regulations 2005.

[446] Adoption and Children Act 2002 s 89(4).   [447] Ibid, s 89(2).

[448] British Nationality Act 1981, s 3(1).

principles established by *Re Valentine's Settlement*.[449] That case established that as a minimum the applicants must have been domiciled in the country in which the order was made and the child must have been resident there.

4 DOMESTIC ADOPTIONS OF FOREIGN CHILDREN

Before the United Kingdom's ratification of the 1993 Hague Intercountry Adoption Convention, couples seeking to adopt a foreign child would commonly bring the child into this country to be adopted according to English law. Although restrictions and control have since been considerably tightened[450] it is still possible to do so lawfully, namely by obtaining formal Home Office clearance[451] and being approved as adopters following a home study.[452]

Even if the rules are broken and an offence committed, an English court is not barred from making an adoption order though obviously regard must be had to all the circumstances.[453] It is established[454] that in determining whether adoption is in the child's interests benefits accruing from a change of immigration status can be taken into account but an order will not be made where the adopters do not intend to exercise any parental responsibility in what are termed as 'accommodation' adoptions. Applications should be made to an intercountry adoption centre in the county court or to the High Court.

5 RESTRICTIONS ON BRINGING CHILDREN INTO THE UNITED KINGDOM FOR ADOPTION

An important part of the control on bringing children into the United Kingdom for adoption is provided by s 83 of the 2002 Act, which provides regulatory power to restrict entry. This section applies to any British resident[455] who, save where the child is intended to be adopted under a Convention adoption order,[456]

'(a) brings, or causes another to bring, a child who is habitually resident outside the British Islands into the United Kingdom for the purpose of adoption by the British resident, or

(b) at any time brings, or causes another to bring, into the United Kingdom a child adopted by the British resident under an external adoption effected within the period of twelve months ending with that time.'[457]

---

[449] [1965] Ch 831.   [450] See below.

[451] The requirements for which are strict. They include being satisfied about the child's position and that there is written permission both from the birth parents and the authorities responsible for the child's care in his or her country of origin. See Clarke Hall and Morrison at 3[500–200]ff for details. Note also the guidance given by Bracewell J in *Re R (Intercountry Adoptions: Practice)* [1999] 1 FLR 1042.

[452] See further below.

[453] See, for example, *Re WM (Adoption: Non-patrial)* [1997] 1 FLR 132: a child was adopted abroad, and notwithstanding concerns as to the adopters' suitability (having been rejected by an adoption agency in this country), there was no option other than to make an adoption order in the child's interests.

[454] *Re B (Adoption Order: Nationality)* [1999] 2 AC 136, HL.

[455] Ie those who are habitually resident in the British Islands: s 83(1).   [456] Section 83(2).

[457] Section 83(1). Note the period mentioned in s 83(1)(b) was extended from six months to 12 months by the Children and Adoption Act 2006, s 14.

An 'external adoption' means an adoption of a child, other than a Convention adoption, effected under the law of any country or territory outside the British Islands whether or not the adoption is an adoption within the meaning of Chapter 4 of the 2002 Act or a full adoption.[458]

Pursuant to Regulations (now the Adoption with a Foreign Element Regulations 2005)[459] issued under s 83(4) prospective adopters have in effect to be assessed and approved as suitable to adopt by an adoption agency and to have obtained a certificate of approval by the Secretary of State (for which services the Secretary of State can now charge).[460] Where these conditions are complied with the child must have lived with the applicant(s) for six months before an application to adopt can be made. Where they have not, the requisite period is three years.[461]

Non-compliance with these provisions is an offence punishable upon summary conviction to imprisonment for maximum, or, upon conviction or indictment, imprisonment for up to 12 months and/or a fine of unlimited amount.[462] There is no time limit in respect of this offence.

6 REMOVING A CHILD FROM THE BRITISH ISLANDS FOR ADOPTION

A child who is a Commonwealth citizen or is habitually resident in the United Kingdom must not be removed from the United Kingdom to a place outside the British Islands for the purpose of adoption unless with the authority of a High Court order under s 84.[463] Any person who does so is guilty of an offence,[464] for which the penalty on summary conviction is imprisonment for up to six months and/or a fine not exceeding the statutory maximum and on indication is imprisonment of up to 12 months and/or a fine not exceeding the statutory maximum.[465]

An order under s 84 confers parental responsibility on the applicant and extinguishes the parental responsibility of any other person. An application may only be made if the child has had his home with both applicant(s) at all times during the preceding 10 weeks. An order cannot be made unless the court is satisfied that the adoption agency has had sufficient opportunity to see the child and the applicant in the home environment and that the requirements prescribed by the Adoption with Foreign Element Regulations 2005 have been met.

---

[458] Section 83(3).
[459] Previously the Adoption of Children from Overseas Regulations 2001.
[460] Section 91A of the Adoption and Children Act 2002 (added by the Children and Adoption Act 2006, s 13).
[461] Adoption with a Foreign Element Regulations 2005, reg 9.   [462] Section 83(7)(8).
[463] Section 85(1).   [464] Section 85(4).   [465] Section 85(6).

K OFFENCES

1 ILLEGAL PLACEMENTS

As previously discussed, ever since 1982 it has been an offence for an individual, other than an adoption agency, to place or make arrangements for the child's adoption, unless the proposed adopter is a relative or he is acting in pursuance of a High Court order. This restriction has been strengthened by s 92 of the 2002 Act. Now any person who is not an adoption agency or acting in pursuance of a High Court order commits on offence by:

'(a) asking a person other than an adoption agency to provide a child for adoption;

(b) asking a person other than an adoption agency to provide prospective adopters for a child;

(c) offering to find a child for adoption;

(d) offering a child for adoption to a person other than an adoption agency;

(e) handing over a child to any person other than an adoption agency, with a view to the child's adoption by that or another person;

(f) receiving a child handed over to him in contravention of paragraph (a);

(g) entering into an agreement with any person for the adoption of a child or for the purpose of facilitating the adoption of a child, where no adoption agency is acting on behalf of the child in the adoption;

(h) initiating or taking part in negotiations of which the purpose is the conclusion of an agreement within paragraph (g);

(i) causing another person to take any of the steps mentioned in paragraphs (a) to (h).'

No offence is committed under paras (d), (e), (g), (h), or (i) if the prospective adopters are parents, relatives[466] or guardians or a partner of the parent of the child.[467]

The above offences are punishable on summary conviction by imprisonment of up to six months and/or a fine of £10,000.[468] Prosecutions may be brought up to six years after the commission of the offence.[469]

The widening of the scope of the offences and the introduction of tougher penalties provides a powerful deterrent to illicit adopters. Whether it is wide enough to cover all illicit arrangements remains to be seen. For example, while it is not confined, as the previous offence was, to domestic placements,[470] presumably, the principle of the non extra-territorial application of offences will mean that if *all* the arrangements take place abroad no offence will be committed. Moreover, it remains the case that s 92 does not

---

[466] Defined by s 144(1) as 'grandparent, brother, sister, uncle or aunt, whether of the full blood or half-blood or by marriage or civil partnership'. Pre–2002 Act cases, *Re S (Arrangements for Adoption)* [1985] FLR 579, CA and *Re C (Minors)(Wardship: Adoption)* [1989] 1 All ER 395, CA establish that great aunts and uncles are not 'relatives' for these purposes nor is a 'commissioning non-genetic partner' in a surrogacy arrangement: *Re MW (Adoption: Surrogacy)* [1995] 2 FLR 759.

[467] Section 92(3), (4). For other 'defences' see s 93(2)–(4).   [468] Section 93(5).

[469] Section 138. This is considerably longer than the usual time limit of six months for summary offences under s 127(1) of the Magistrates Courts Act 1980.

[470] See eg *Re Adoption Application 8605489/99 (1988)*.

prevent private *fostering* placements being made nor is there anything to prevent such foster parents from subsequently applying to adopt. However, if it is clear that the foster arrangement is a mere subterfuge, an offence will be committed.[471]

According to the pre–2002 Act decision, *Re G (Adoption: Illegal Placement)*,[472] while there is no power retrospectively to authorise an illegal placement, the High Court never-theless retained the power to grant the adoption. It remains to be seen whether this remains the case.[473]

2 ILLEGAL PAYMENTS

It has always been regarded as wrong for people to buy and sell children for adoption and the 2002 Act continues the policy of making it an offence to do so. However, unlike the 1976 Act under which courts were directed[474] not to make an adoption order where illegal payments had been made, there is no such express prohibition in the 2002 Act, nor conversely, is there power retrospectively to authorise payments.[475]

Illegal payments are governed by s 95 under which it is an offence for a person to make[476] or receive any payment or reward[477] (other than an 'excepted payment', discussed below) for the adoption of a child giving any consent for a child's adoption, removing from the United Kingdom a child who is a Commonwealth citizen or is habitually resident in the United Kingdom to a place outside the British Isles for the purpose of adoption; for making arrangements for making illegal placements for adoption[478] and for the commis-sioning or preparing of prohibited reports.[479] As with illegal placements, those guilty of an offence under s 95 are liable on summary conviction to imprisonment of up to six months and/or a fine of up to £10,000.[480]

'Excepted payments' are those for reasonable expenses such as legal and medical expenses in relation to adoption, payments to a local authority or registered adoption society for expenses incurred for arranging the adoption if a child whose country of origin is outside the United Kingdom and those for reasonably incurred travel and accommodation expenses where a child is being taken out of the United Kingdom.[481]

---

[471] As in *Gatehouse v Robinson* [1986] 1 WLR 18.

[472] [1995] 1 FLR 403, CA. See Sandland 'Problems in the Criminal Law of Adoption' [1995] JSWFL 149.

[473] Bridge and Swindells, op cit at 16.41, cautiously think the same position will be applied.

[474] Viz s 24(2) of the 1976 Act.

[475] This was formerly provided for by s 57(3) of the 1976 Act, which had been interpreted as permitting the court retrospectively to authorise payments and thus to make an adoption order, see *Re G (Adoption: Illegal Placement)*, ibid at 405, per Balcombe LJ (obiter), *Re Adoption Application (Payment for Adoption)* [1987] Fam 81 and *Re WM (Adoption: Non Partial)* [1997] 1 FLR 132.

[476] Including agreeing or offering to make such payments: s 95(3)(b).

[477] By s 97(b) 'payment' includes reward.

[478] Ie those made in contravention of s 92, discussed above.

[479] Ie those made in contravention of s 94 which prohibits reports being carried out by non-professionally qualified staff, see the Restriction on the Preparation of Adoption Reports Regulations 2005.

[480] Section 95(4).   [481] Section 96.

3 ADVERTISEMENTS

Under s 123 it is an offence to publish or distribute an advertisement or information or to cause such an advertisement or information to be published or distributed indicating that a parent or guardian wants the child to be adopted, that a person wants to adopt a child, that a person other than adoption agencies are willing to make arrangements for the adoption or that a person is willing to remove a child from the United Kingdom for the purposes of adoption. In the light of the so-called 'Internet twins case' involving a North Wales couple who had contacted American organisations via the internet,[482] the offence under s 123 includes advertisements or information being distributed via any electronic or electronic-magnetic means. The offence itself, however, is confined to the United Kingdom and the provisions do not apply to publications or distributions by or on behalf of an adoption agency.

The penalty for a s 123 offence is a term of imprisonment of up to three months and/or a fine not exceeding level 5 on the standard scale.[483]

---

[482] See BBC News website, 23 January 2001.
[483] Section 124(3). Note the requirement under s 124 to prove that the accused knew or had reason to suspect that s 123 applied to the advertisement or information.

16

THE HIGH COURT'S INHERENT POWERS IN RESPECT OF CHILDREN

A INTRODUCTION

No discussion of child law would be complete without having regard to the High Court's inherent powers in respect of children. It should be appreciated that the development of these powers, principally under the aegis of the wardship jurisdiction, was highly influential in the modern development of law and practice concerning children, and that the Children Act 1989 now incorporates many of its features. Even now, long after the implementation of the 1989 Act, the residual inherent powers remain useful, particularly when the statutory system offers no suitable remedy.

Before the Children Act, discussion of these inherent powers would have focused solely on the wardship jurisdiction which, as will be seen, is not based on any statute but is an ancient jurisdiction derived from the sovereign's obligation as parens patriae to protect the person and property of those of his subjects, such as children, who are unable to look after themselves. However, in the light of the changes made by the Children Act 1989[1] it is important to distinguish the well-established wardship jurisdiction from the separate inherent jurisdiction of the High Court referred to in the 1989 Act.

Although the existence of a parens patriae power to protect children independent of wardship had been expressly acknowledged by the court[2] before the 1989 Act, there had been little cause to develop it, given the wide-ranging nature of the wardship jurisdiction. However, in his Joseph Jackson Memorial Lecture,[3] Lord Mackay LC commented:

'... in the government's view wardship is only one use of the High Court's inherent parens patriae jurisdiction. We believe, therefore, that it is open to the High Court to make orders under its inherent jurisdiction in respect of children other than through wardship.'

The Children Act 1989 is predicated on this view. Indeed, as we shall see, if a local

---

[1] Discussed below, pp 896ff.

[2] See eg *Re N (Infants)* [1967] Ch 512, and *Re L (An Infant)* [1968] P 119, CA, and note also the suggestion by Ewbank J in *R v North Yorkshire County Council, ex p M (No 3)* [1989] 2 FLR 82 that the High Court had an inherent power in other proceedings to make a child a ward of court.

[3] (1989) 139 NLJ 505 at 507. See also the Department of Health's *Guidance and Regulations*, Vol 1, *Court Orders*, paras 3.98 et seq.

authority wishes to obtain a High Court order in respect of a child already in care, they must seek to invoke the inherent rather than the wardship jurisdiction.[4]

Although it has been said[5] that the High Court's inherent jurisdiction is equally exercisable whether the child is or is not a ward of court, there are important conceptual differences between the two jurisdictions. In particular, unlike wardship, the exercise of the inherent jurisdiction does not place the child under the ultimate responsibility of the court. This means that at no point will the child be subject to the rule obtaining in wardship that all important steps in the child's life have to be sanctioned by the court.[6] In other words, the inherent jurisdiction empowers the High Court to make orders dealing with particular aspects of the child's welfare, whereas wardship additionally vests in the court a continuing supervisory function over the child. Accordingly, notwithstanding the commonality of the powers and the 1989 Act's tendency to obscure the distinction by using the term 'inherent jurisdiction' to refer to both wardship and the residual jurisdiction,[7] it is probably best to regard wardship as one manifestation of the inherent jurisdiction.[8]

B WARDSHIP[9]

1 HISTORICAL DEVELOPMENT

Wardship has a fascinating history. Its origins[10] lie in feudal times, when it was an incident of tenure by which, upon a tenant's death, the lord became guardian of the surviving infant heir's land and body. Although there was a protective element in the guardianship in that the lord was supposed to look after his ward, maintaining and educating him

---

[4] See below, pp 896–8 and 904–5.

[5] Per Lord Donaldson MR in *Re W (A Minor) (Medical Treatment)* [1993] Fam 64, CA; *Re M and N (Minors) (Wardship: Publication of Information)* [1990] Fam 211, CA. See also *Re Z (A Minor) (Identification: Restrictions on Publicity)* [1997] Fam 1, CA.

[6] *Re W (A Minor) (Medical Treatment: Court's Jurisdiction)* [1993] Fam 64 at 73 F–G, per Lord Donaldson MR.

[7] M Parry 'The Children Act 1989: Local Authorities, Wardship and the Revival of the Inherent Jurisdiction' [1992] JSWFL 212 has observed, at 213: 'Section 100 has the marginal heading for guidance, "Restriction on use of wardship jurisdiction", whereas the substance of the section relates to the inherent jurisdiction as much as to wardship'. Note also that s 8(3) includes the 'inherent jurisdiction' in the definition of 'family proceedings', which is intended to cover both jurisdictions.

[8] Note Ward LJ's comment in *Re Z (A Minor) (Identification: Restrictions on Publication)* [1997] Fam 1 at 14, CA that 'For all practical purposes the jurisdiction in wardship and the inherent jurisdiction over children is one and the same . . .'.

[9] For a detailed analysis of the jurisdiction before the Children Act 1989 see N Lowe and R White *Wards of Court* (2nd edn, 1986); Custer 'The Origins of the Doctrine of *Parens Patriae*' (1978) 27 Emory LJ 195; J Seymour 'Parens Patriae and Wardship Powers: Their Nature and Origins' (1994) 14 Oxford Journal of Legal Studies 159; S Abramowicz 'English Child Custody Law 1660–1839: the Origins of Judicial Intervention in Parental Custody' (1999) 99 Columbia LR 1344; and Law Com Working Paper No 101 *Wards of Court*. For valuable accounts by (then) High Court judges, see Cross 'Wards of Court', (1967) 83 LQR 200 and Balcombe 'Wardship' (1981–2) Lit 223. For a post Children Act discussion see HHJ Mitchell 'Whatever Happened to Wardship?' [2001] Fam Law 130 and 212.

[10] For a more detailed historical account see Lowe and White *Wards of Court*, op cit, at paras 1.1 et seq and the references there cited. See also *Re Eve* (1986) 31 DLR (4th) 1, Canadian Supreme Court.

according to his station, the right was a valuable one since, inter alia, the lord was entitled to keep the profits of the land until the heir reached his majority. No one benefited more than the Crown (whose rights arose upon the death of a tenant-in-chief) and in 1540 the Court of Wards was created to enforce the sovereign's rights and the execution of his duties in connection with wardship. These rights, together with the Court of Wards, were abolished in 1660.[11] The wardship jurisdiction, however, survived in the hands of the Court of Chancery.

Jurisdiction was claimed upon the basis that the sovereign, as parens patriae, had a duty to protect his subjects, particularly those, such as infants,[12] who were unable to protect themselves, and that this duty had been delegated to the Lord Chancellor and through him to the Court of Chancery. Although there is some doubt about the historical validity of this claim, by the end of the nineteenth century (by which time jurisdiction had become vested in the Chancery Division of the High Court), it had become the authoritatively accepted basis of the jurisdiction.[13] Furthermore, it became established that the jurisdiction was not dependent upon the existence of property belonging to the infant.[14] At about the same time it had become established that decisions had to be based on what was best for the ward.

Although by the turn of the twentieth century wardship had acquired most of the characteristics of the modern jurisdiction,[15] it did not really begin to develop until the old procedural shackles were removed in 1949.[16] Further impetus to the use of wardship was given in 1971 when the jurisdiction was transferred to the newly created Family Division of the High Court[17] and thereby became available in the provinces (through the district registries) as well as in London (in the Principal Registry).

Until 1986 wardship had been an exclusively High Court jurisdiction, but since then it has been possible, at any rate after the main issues have been resolved, to transfer cases to the county court.[18]

2 CHARACTERISTICS OF THE WARDSHIP JURISDICTION

(a) Control vested in the court

A unique and fundamental characteristic of the jurisdiction is that throughout the wardship legal control over both the child's person and property is vested in the court. As Lord Scarman put it,[19] once a party persuades the court that it should make the child its ward

---

[11] By the Tenures Abolition Act 1660.

[12] And, originally, lunatics. However, it is now accepted that there is no longer a parens patriae jurisdiction with regard to mentally handicapped adults: *Re F (Mental Patient: Sterilisation)* [1990] 2 AC 1, HL.

[13] *Johnstone v Beattie* (1843) 10 Cl & Fin 42 at 120 per Lord Eldon LC, and *Hope v Hope* (1854) 4 De GM & G 328 at 344–5 per Lord Cranworth LC.

[14] See *Re Spence* (1847) 2 Ph 247 at 251 per Lord Cottenham LC. In fact, until 1949 it was common practice to begin wardship by making a nominal settlement upon the child and then commencing an action to administer the trusts of the settlement: see *Re D* [1943] Ch 305 at 306 and *Re X's Settlement* [1945] Ch 44 at 45.

[15] See eg *R v Gyngall* [1893] 2 QB 232 at 248, CA per Kay LJ.

[16] By the Law Reform (Miscellaneous Provisions) Act 1949.

[17] Under the Administration of Justice Act 1970 s 1(2) and Sch 1.

[18] Pursuant to s 38(2)(b) of the Matrimonial and Family Proceedings Act 1984.

[19] In *Re E (SA) (A Minor)* [1984] 1 All ER 289, HL at 290.

'the court takes over ultimate responsibility for the child'. Although, in the past at any rate, wardship was quite frequently referred to as a 'parental jurisdiction', the court is not in the same position as a parent or other persons with parental responsibility in any strict sense. As Lord Donaldson MR has said, it is clear that:

'... the practical jurisdiction of the court is wider than that of parents. ... It is also clear that this jurisdiction is not derivative from the parents' rights and responsibilities, but derives from, or is, the delegated performance of the duties of the Crown to protect its subjects ...'[20]

The effects of the court's control

Being under the court's protection does not mean that the ward is physically in the court's or judge's care, but rather that the child and those with parental responsibility or otherwise having de facto care and control are subject to the court's control. This control is both an immediate and automatic consequence of wardship.[21] As Cross J put it,[22] once the child has been made a ward, 'no important step in the child's life can be taken without the court's consent'. Failure to obtain the court's consent constitutes a contempt of court, for which the ultimate sanction is imprisonment and a fine.[23]

Extent of control

Despite the potential draconian sanction it is not easy to say precisely what constitutes an 'important step'.[24] It is well established that a ward may not marry[25] nor leave the jurisdiction without the court's consent. Formerly, the latter embargo meant that leave was required before a ward could travel outside England and Wales. However, under the Family Law Act 1986 s 38 the automatic[26] embargo no longer prevents the child's removal to another part of the United Kingdom in which divorce or other matrimonial proceedings (in respect of the ward's parents) are continuing or in which the child is habitually resident.

Other 'steps' requiring prior court consent include: applying to adopt[27] and, presumably now applying for an adoption placement order,[28] moving a ward to new care-givers, as for example, seeking compulsory admission to hospital of a mentally ill ward;[29] changing the ward's whereabouts;[30] making material changes in a ward's education;[31]

---

[20] In *Re R (A Minor) (Wardship: Medical Treatment)* [1992] Fam 11 at 24, CA. See also *Re W (A Minor) (Medical Treatment)* above.

[21] The control begins as soon as the originating summons has been issued and without any specific court order. It ends when the wardship ends. Whether such immediate and automatic wide-ranging protection can be justified has been questioned by the Law Commission: Law Com Working Paper No 101 paras 4.3 and 4.13.

[22] In *Re S (Infants)* [1967] 1 All ER 202 at 209.   [23] See Lowe and White, above, ch 8.

[24] For a detailed discussion see N Lowe and White, above, ch 5.

[25] See now the Marriage Act 1949 s 3(6).

[26] But the court can still make a specific order prohibiting the ward's removal from England and Wales.

[27] See *F v S (Adoption: Ward)* [1973] Fam 203, CA.

[28] Cf *Re F (Wardship: Adoption)* [1984] FLR 60, CA which held that applying to free a ward for adoption required court consent.

[29] Mental Health Act 1983 s 33. See also *Re CB (A Minor) (Wardship: Local Authority)* [1981] 1 All ER 16 at 24, CA per Ormrod LJ. But note there is no requirement to obtain leave to apply for an emergency protection order: *Re B (Wardship: Place of Safety Order)* (1979) 2 FLR 307.

[30] Family Proceedings Rules 1991 r 5.1(9). If this is a simple change of residence it is sufficient to inform the Registry.

[31] See the Notice of Wardship issued with the originating summons.

performing major medical treatment on a ward;[32] and even conducting psychiatric or psychological examinations.[33]

Warding a child does not *in itself* impose a complete ban on publicity about the child[34] but, because court proceedings are confidential (unless judgment is given in open court), it is a contempt to publish any information relating to those proceedings.[35] The interrelationship between wardship and the criminal law is not straightforward but in summary, while leave is not required for the police to interview a child who has been arrested merely because he happens to be a ward,[36] nor to call a ward as a witness in criminal proceedings, it is required to interview a ward on behalf of a defendant in a criminal trial[37] and for the Crown Prosecution Service to administer a caution to a ward.[38] Leave is also required to apply on a ward's behalf for compensation from the Criminal Injuries Compensation Authority.[39]

Leave to petition the European Commission on Human Rights to examine a court decision about a ward, though an important step, does *not* require court leave.[40]

(b) The special nature of the jurisdiction

Because legal control of the child vests in the court, wardship proceedings have always been regarded as special. In *Re E (SA) (A Minor) (Wardship)*[41] Lord Scarman commented that when exercising its wardship jurisdiction a court:

'. . . must never lose sight of a fundamental feature of the jurisdiction, namely, that it is exercising a wardship, not an adversarial jurisdiction. Its duty is not limited to the dispute between the parties: on the contrary, its duty is to act in the way best suited in its judgment to serve the true interest and welfare of the ward. In exercising wardship jurisdiction, the court is a true family court. Its paramount concern is the welfare of its ward.'

---

[32] *Re G-U (A Minor) (Wardship)* [1984] FLR 811 (abortion) and according to Lord Templeman in *Re B (A Minor) (Wardship: Sterilisation)* [1988] AC 199 at 205, (sterilisation); cf *Re E (A Minor) (Medical Treatment)* [1991] 2 FLR 585 in which it was held the court's consent was not required to perform an operation for therapeutic purposes even though a side effect was to sterilise the child. Leave is probably required to conduct blood tests to establish paternity: see Lowe and White, above, at para 5–24.

[33] *Practice Direction* [1985] 3 All ER 576.

[34] *Re L (A Minor: Freedom of Publication)* [1988] 1 All ER 418 and *Re W (Minors) (Wardship: Contempt)* [1989] 1 FLR 246. But note *Re S (A Child)(Identification: Restrictions on Publicity)* [2004] UKHL 47, 1 AC 593 which establishes that jurisdiction to restrain publicity is now properly to be regarded as being founded upon the European Convention on Human Rights rather than on any inherent powers.

[35] Administration of Justice Act 1960 s 12. The embargo covers not simply the actual proceedings but also any documents, for example, the Official Solicitor's report prepared for the case: see *Re F (Otherwise A) (A Minor)* [1977] Fam 58. This embargo extends to showing papers to an independent social worker: see *Practice Direction* [1983] 1 All ER 1097, and *Re C (Wardship: Independent Social Worker)* [1985] FLR 56; to medical officers: *Practice Direction* [1987] 3 All ER 640; and to prospective adopters and their legal advisers: *Practice Direction* [1989] 1 All ER 169.

[36] *Re R, Re G (Minors)* [1990] 2 All ER 633, though those having care and control should inform the wardship court at the earliest opportunity. See also *Re K (Minors) (Wardship: Criminal Proceedings)* [1988] Fam 1.

[37] *Re R (Minors) (Wardship: Criminal Proceedings)* [1991] Fam 56, CA.

[38] *Re A (A Minor) (Wardship: Police Caution)* [1989] Fam 103.

[39] *Practice Direction* [1988] 1 All ER 182, and *Re G (A Minor) (Ward: Criminal Injuries Compensation)* [1990] 3 All ER 102, CA.

[40] Per Johnson J in *Re M (Petition to European Commission of Human Rights)* [1997] 1 FLR 755.

[41] [1984] 1 All ER 289 at 290, HL. For similar comments see eg Viscount Haldane in *Scott v Scott* [1913] AC 417 at 437, HL and Cross J in *Re B (JA) (An Infant)* [1965] Ch 1112 at 1117.

Before the Children Act the uniqueness of wardship was both especially marked and useful, since it could often be invoked to overcome other statutory jurisdictions or gaps in the law.[42] However, it is the policy of the Children Act, in the words of Butler-Sloss LJ:[43]

'... to incorporate the best of the wardship jurisdiction within the statutory framework without any of the perceived disadvantages of judicial monitoring of administrative plans.'

Hence, wardship now shares many of its characteristics with other child law jurisdictions. For example, in all family proceedings hearsay evidence is admissible[44] and the court can make s 8 orders whether or not they have been applied for.[45] The paramountcy principle applies in all proceedings concerning a child's upbringing and, following the Children Act, there has been a general move away from an adversarial approach in all children cases. Nonetheless wardship remains unique in that control over the child is vested in the court. Furthermore, that control arises immediately the child becomes a ward and only ceases when the wardship itself ceases.[46]

3 WHO CAN BE WARDED[47]

(a) Child must be a minor

Only minors, that is persons under the age of 18,[48] may be warded. There is some doubt whether a married minor can be warded.[49] Although formerly a matter of speculation[50] it is settled that a foetus cannot be made a ward of court.[51]

(b) The child must be subject to the jurisdiction

Any minor who can be said to owe allegiance to the Crown may be warded,[52] which in theory means any minor who is a British subject regardless of his place of birth, domicile

---

[42] Particularly in the context of committing children into local authority care: see below, pp 895–6.

[43] In Re B (Minors) (Termination of Contact : Paramount Consideration) [1993] Fam 301 at 310, CA.

[44] See the Children (Admissibility of Hearsay Evidence) Order 1993. In wardship hearsay evidence has always been admissible: Re W (Minors) (Wardship: Evidence) [1990] 1 FLR 203, CA. See now Art 2 of the 1993 Order.

[45] Children Act 1989 s 10(1)(b), discussed above, pp 564–7; cf Re E (SA), above.

[46] For when wardship begins and ends see below, p 891.

[47] See generally N Lowe 'Who can be made a ward of court?' (1989) 1 Jo of Child Law 6.

[48] Family Law Reform Act 1969 s 1.

[49] Re Elwes (No 2), The Times, 30 July 1958 suggests there is jurisdiction, whereas cases on guardianship, eg Mendes v Mendes (1747) 1 Ves Sen 89 at 91 per Lord Hardwicke LC; R v Wilmington (1822) 5 B & Ald 525 at 526 per Abbot CJ and Hewer v Bryant [1970] 1 QB 357 at 373 per Sachs LJ, suggest there is not. See Lowe and White, above, at paras 2.1 and 2.2.

[50] See eg J Phillips 'Wardship and Abortion Prevention' (1979) 95 LQR 332 and C Lyon and G Bennett 'Abortion—Whose Decision?' (1979) 9 Fam Law 35 at 36 who argued that, despite an apparent ruling to the contrary in Paton v Trustee of British Pregnancy Advisory Service [1979] QB 276, per Sir George Baker P, it was possible; cf N Lowe (1980) 96 LQR 29 and (1980) 131 NLJ 561.

[51] Re F (In Utero) [1988] Fam 122, CA; J Fortin 'Legal Protection of the Unborn Child' (1988) 51 MLR 54; and A Grubb and D Pearl (1987) 103 LQR 340. For a similar position taken in Canada, see Winnipeg Child and Family Services (Northwest Area) v G (1997) 152 DLR (4th) 193, Can Sup Ct but for the contrary view in New Zealand see Re An Unborn Child High Court, Hamilton M171/02, 11 October 2002 discussed in Butterworths' Family Law in New Zealand (11th edn) Vol 1 at 6.302A.

[52] See Re P (GE) (An Infant) [1965] Ch 568 at 587 per Pearson LJ.

or residence.[53] In practice, however, jurisdiction will not be taken in respect of a child who is neither present nor resident in England and Wales.[54] With the exception of a child who is a member of the household of a parent entitled to diplomatic immunity,[55] there is also jurisdiction to ward an alien minor who is physically present in England and Wales (even aliens owe temporary allegiance whilst present in the jurisdiction)[56] and, as the House of Lords have confirmed,[57] an alien child[58] who, though not physically present, is habitually resident in England and Wales at the time of the application.

Limitations imposed by the Family Law Act 1986

Notwithstanding the width of power to make a child a ward, jurisdiction to make orders giving care of a child to any person or providing for contact with, or the education of, a child ('a s 1(1)(d) order')[59] is more limited. By s 2(3) and s 3 of the Family Law Act 1986, as amended, a court cannot make a s 1(1)(d) order unless it has jurisdiction under the revised Brussels II Regulation[60] or, where that Regulation does not apply, the child is, at the relevant date,[61] either habitually resident in England and Wales or is present here and not habitually resident in another part of the United Kingdom or Isle of Man.[62] However, jurisdiction on either of the latter bases is normally excluded if, at the relevant date,[63]

---

[53] See *Harben v Harben* [1957] 1 All ER 379 at 381 per Sachs LJ.

[54] See *Al Habtoor v Fotheringham* [2001] EWCA Civ 186, [2001] 1 FLR 951 (child born in England, now resident in Dubai—jurisdiction declined) in which Thorpe LJ commented at [42] that exorbitant jurisdictional claims founded on nationality could no longer be justified. But note *B v H (Habitual Residence: Wardship)* [2002] 1 FLR 388, in which a baby born abroad and who had never been to England was nevertheless held to be habitually resident in England and Wales, and in respect of whom wardship orders were made. But note the doubts about the decision raised by Hedley J in *W and B v H (Child Abduction: Surrogacy)* [2002] 1 FLR 1008 at [23]. See further Lowe and White, above, at paras 2.6–2.7.

[55] *Re C (An Infant)* [1959] Ch 363. See also *Re P (Children Act: Diplomatic Immunity)* [1998] 1 FLR 624. In *Re Mohammed Arif (An Infant), Re Nirbhai Singh (An Infant)* [1968] Ch 643, Cross J doubted whether there is jurisdiction to ward an alien minor still present in the jurisdiction but who has been refused entry by immigration officials, but on appeal the point was left open. Nevertheless, wardship cannot in practice be used to challenge immigration decisions: see below, p 908.

[56] See *Hope v Hope* (1854) 4 De GM & G 328 at 346 per Lord Cranworth LC. For an extreme example see *Re C (An Infant), The Times,* 14 December 1956—child temporarily in England whilst en route from USA to USSR. See also *Johnstone v Beattie* (1843) 10 Cl & Fin 42 and *Re D (An Infant)* [1943] Ch 305. But note *Re D (Abduction: Habitual Residence)* [2005] EWHC 518 (Fam), [2005] 2 FLR 403, where presence induced by deception, was held insufficient to justify the exercise of the (inherent) jurisdiction.

[57] *Re S (A Minor) (Custody: Habitual Residence)* [1998] AC 750 at 764, HL.

[58] Including a stateless child.

[59] But excluding an order varying or revoking such an order: Family Law Act 1986 s 1(1)(d) as amended by the Children Act 1989, Sch 13, para 63(b). According to *Re V (Jurisdiction: Habitual Residence)* [2001] 1 FLR 253 at 263–4, an order for the return of a child to the United Kingdom comes within the ambit of s 1(1)(d).

[60] Viz Council Regulation (EC) No 2201/2003 of 27 November 2003 concerning jurisdiction and the recognition and enforcement of judgments in matrimonial matters and the matters of parental responsibility, repealing Regulation (EC) No 1347/2000, discussed above, at pp 32ff. Under this Regulation, the main rules of jurisdiction are the child's habitual residence or, failing that, presence, with special rules applying to international child abduction.

[61] That is, where an application is made for a s 1(1)(d) order, the date of the application or, where no such application has been made, the date of the order: s 7. This prevents the court having jurisdiction merely because the child has been warded in the past: see Law Com No 138, Scot Law Com No 91 para 4.28.

[62] Section 2(3)(a) and s 3(1).   [63] See n 61, above.

divorce, nullity or separation proceedings are continuing[64] in another part of the United Kingdom or the Isle of Man. The latter rule does not apply where the High Court considers 'that the immediate exercise of its powers is necessary for [the child's] protection, in which case the child's physical presence will suffice'.[65] The initial burden of proof lies upon the person seeking to invoke wardship to satisfy the court that it has jurisdiction, but once this has been discharged the burden of proof shifts to the defendant to establish that the child was no longer habitually resident here at the time of application.[66]

Although originally enacted principally to prevent conflicts of jurisdiction arising within the United Kingdom or the Isle of Man, these provisions have nevertheless always applied even where there is no potential conflict with another domestic court and continue to do so provided the Brussels II Regulation does not apply (ie where there is no potential conflict with other Member States of the European Union, other than Denmark).[67] Consequently, it is not possible to make a s 1(1)(d) order in respect of a British subject who is neither present nor habitually resident in the jurisdiction. There is, however, a residual jurisdiction to make orders not caught by s 1(1)(d) and which fall outside the scope of the Brussels II Regulation.[68] In *F v S (Wardship: Jurisdiction)*[69] Ward J held that the absence of jurisdiction under the 1986 Act did not preclude him from having jurisdiction to make an order requiring disclosure of the child's whereabouts. He refused, however, to order a parent to produce the child, since that would have enabled the court then to have taken jurisdiction under s 2(3)(b) if that was necessary for the child's protection. As he pointed out,[70] such an order would have provided 'a devious entry to the court by the back door where Parliament have so firmly shut the front door to [s 1(1)(d)] orders being made'.

Limitations imposed by the Brussels II Regulation and the Child Abduction and Custody Act 1985

Wardship cannot be used to circumvent the application of the Brussels II Regulation[71] and proceedings must be stayed pending a determination under it.[72] Similarly the jurisdiction cannot be used to avoid the application of either the 1980 Hague Abduction Convention on the 1980 European Custody Convention and any such application is frozen during the pendency of an application under either of those Conventions.[73]

---

[64] Proceedings are treated as 'continuing' from the issue of the petition until (unless the proceedings have been dismissed) the child reaches 18 in Northern Ireland and the Isle of Man, or 16 in Scotland: s 42(2), as amended by the Family Law Act 1986 (Dependent Territories) Order 1991 s 42(3). See, for example, *B v B (Scottish: Contact Order Jurisdiction To Vary)* [1996] 1 WLR 231.

[65] Section 2(3)(b)(ii). Precisely what will trigger this 'emergency jurisdiction' is a matter of some doubt: see further Lowe and White, above, para 2–6.

[66] *F v S (Wardship: Jurisdiction)* [1993] 2 FLR 686, CA.

[67] For discussion of the application of this Regulation see above pp 32–4.

[68] The Regulation has a wider scope than s 1(1)(d) since it generally applies, subject to Art 3, to the attribution, exercise, delegation, restriction or termination of parental responsibility (see Art 1(b)), and not simply to care, contact or education of a child as under the 1986 Act.

[69] [1991] 2 FLR 349, not commented upon in this respect by the Court of Appeal.

[70] Above at p 356. See also the supporting views of Wilson J in *Re V (Jurisdiction: Habitual Residence)* [2001] 1 FLR 253 at 264.

[71] See above at p 889.   [72] See FPR 1991 r 6.11A.

[73] The Child Abduction and Custody Act 1985 s 9, s 20, s 27 and Sch 3 and FPR 1991 r 6.11(4). These Conventions are discussed in Chapter 13.

(c) The discretion to exercise jurisdiction

In cases where the court has jurisdiction, it is nevertheless not bound to exercise it. The court generally refuses to exercise jurisdiction to review the exercise of discretionary powers vested in other bodies or tribunals such as local authorities[74] or the immigration service,[75] or to interfere with the normal operation of criminal proceedings[76] or military law.[77] The court is naturally reluctant to exercise jurisdiction where the child's presence is merely a fleeting one, and in cases where the child has been abducted into this country it is established, in cases not governed by the abduction Conventions (see Chapter 13), that the court must decide whether it is in the child's best interests to be returned immediately or to have the full merits of the case heard by the English court.[78] The court has a statutory power[79] to refuse to make orders or to stay proceedings if the matter has been or is being dealt with in proceedings outside England and Wales.

4 INVOKING WARDSHIP

(a) Starting and ending wardship

Under the Supreme Court Act 1981 s 41(1) no minor can be made a ward of court except by an order to that effect made by the High Court.[80] Under s 41(2), however, a child (other than a child who is subject to a care order)[81] becomes a ward *immediately* an application for wardship is made (that is, as soon as the originating summons is issued),[82] but he ceases to be one unless an application for an appointment to hear the summons has been made within 21 days.[83] A child does not otherwise cease to be a ward until either the court makes a specific order to that effect[84] or a care order is made in respect of a ward,[85] or until the child attains his majority.

(b) The parties to the proceedings

Any person having a proper interest may make a child a ward. In *Re D (A Minor) (Wardship: Sterilisation)*,[86] for example, an educational psychologist attached to a local authority

---

[74] *A v Liverpool City Council* [1982] AC 363, HL, discussed above, p 803 and, for a more recent discussion, *E (By her Litigation Friend, PW) v London Borough of X* [2005] EWHC 2811 (Fam).

[75] *Re Mohammed Arif (An Infant), Re Nirbhai Singh (An Infant)* [1968] Ch 643, CA, *Re F (A Minor) (Immigration: Wardship)* [1990] Fam 125, and *R (Anton) v Secretary of State For The Home Department, Re Anton* [2004] EWHC 2730/2731 (Admin/Fam), [2005] 2 FLR 818, CA. See further below, p 908.

[76] *Re K (A Minor) (Wardship: Criminal Proceedings)* [1988] Fam 1.

[77] *Re JS (A Minor) (Wardship: Boy Soldier)* [1990] Fam 182.

[78] *Re J (A Child)(Custody Rights: Jurisdiction)* [2005] UKHL 40, [2005] 3 WLR 14, discussed above at p 623.

[79] Under the Family Law Act 1986 s 5.

[80] Once a child has been made a ward, proceedings can be transferred to the county court: Matrimonial and Family Proceedings Act 1984 s 38(2)(b), but note *Practice Direction* [1992] 3 All ER 151.

[81] Supreme Court Act 1981 s 41(2A), added by the Children Act 1989 Sch 13, para 45(2).

[82] An originating summons may be issued by the Principal Registry or a district registry.

[83] FPR 1991 r 5.3(1)(a).   [84] Discussed below, p 897.   [85] Children Act 1989 s 91(4).

[86] [1976] Fam 185. See also the case referred to in *The Times* on 21 May 1985 where the Brook Advisory Centre warded a child to authorise an abortion.

warded a child to prevent her being sterilised. Children can also effectively ward themselves by issuing an originating summons.[87]

Before the Children Act 1989 these relaxed rules governing who could apply[88] meant that for many applicants wardship offered the only possible recourse to the court. Although proceedings under the Children Act are now normally more appropriate, it is to be noted that unlike that Act no formal court leave is required even for those unrelated to the child, to make the child a ward. Instead applicants must[89] provide in the summons a brief description of their interest in, or relationship to, the minor, and the particulars are then sent for recording in the register of wards.[90] If it appears that the application is an abuse of process, the summons may be dismissed. It has been held,[91] perhaps questionably,[92] that the High Court has an inherent power to make a child a ward of court of its own motion. On the other hand, it appears that the Official Solicitor cannot ward on his own initiative,[93] nor can a guardian qua guardian.[94] Formerly, local authorities could ward children, but their ability to do so, at any rate where there is a care order, has been ended by s 100 of the Children Act 1989.[95]

The rules are equally flexible as to who can be made defendants. Primarily, the person against whom the order is sought is made the defendant, but any other interested party can apply to be made a party.[96] Surprisingly, perhaps, the child is not automatically a party, but is made one only in cases where it is thought appropriate.[97] Examples of cases in which it may be appropriate to make the child a party are:[98]

  (a) where a teenage ward is in dispute with his or her parents so that the Official Solicitor can express the ward's views to the court;

  (b) where the ward is old enough to express a view, usually aged eight or over, where that view is likely to be of particular importance, for example, if there are allegations of 'brain-washing';

---

[87] Unless he has leave of the court or where a solicitor considers the child is able, having regard to his understanding, to give instructions and the solicitor has accepted those instructions, he must issue the summons through a next friend: FPR 1991, rr 9.2, 9.2A. See Butterworths *Family Law Service* 3A [6340]–[6342].

[88] Indeed, until *Re Dunhill* (1967) 111 Sol Jo 113, in which a night club owner warded one of his striptease artists purely for publicity purposes, there were no rules at all.

[89] FPR 1991 r 5.1(6).   [90] FPR 1991 r 5.1(4).

[91] *R v North Yorkshire County Council, ex p M (No 3)* [1989] 2 FLR 82 per Ewbank J and *Re S (Leave To Remove From Jurisdiction: Securing Return From Holiday)* [2001] 2 FLR 507 at 514, in which, without discussion, Hogg J warded the children. The court similarly appeared to ward the children in *Re W and X (Wardship: Relatives Rejected As Foster Carers)* [2003] EWHC 2206 (Fam), [2004] 1 FLR 415. See also the Mental Health Act 1983 s 96(1)(i).

[92] See the assessment of the authorities by Bracewell J in *Re AW (Adoption: Application)* [1993] 1 FLR 62 at 78–9 who concluded there was no such power.

[93] *Re D (A Minor) (Wardship: Sterilisation)*, above, but see Lowe and White, above, at para 9.5.

[94] *Re T (Minors) (Wardship: Jurisdiction)* [1990] Fam 1, CA, and *A v Berkshire County Council* [1989] 1 FLR 273, CA. But there is nothing to prevent guardians acting in their personal capacity from warding a child, see Clarke Hall and Morrison on *Children* at 1 [787].

[95] Discussed below, pp 896–8.

[96] In an application to restrain an undesirable relationship, discussed below, p 896, the person alleged to be undesirable should not be made a party: *Practice Direction* [1983] 2 All ER 672.

[97] See FPR 1991, r 5.1(3).

[98] See *Practice Direction* [1993] 2 FLR 641, giving guidance on the appointment of the Official Solicitor in family proceedings generally.

(c) where a specific task has to be carried out by an independent party, such as the psychiatric examination of a ward;

(d) where there are difficult issues on law or facts, such as international problems or questions affecting the life or death of the ward, disputed medical evidence or where there are special or exceptional points of law.

5 THE COURT'S POWERS

(a) Confirming or discharging the wardship

At the initial hearing the judge must first decide whether or not to continue the wardship. It is at this stage that issues of jurisdiction should be taken.[99] The wardship may be discharged if the court declines to exercise its jurisdiction, for example, because it considers the application spurious, because it declines to interfere with a decision of another body or tribunal, or because it decides that wardship is of no further benefit to the child. It should be discharged where there is no significant evidence on which to exercise the jurisdiction.[100] It is established[101] that the wardship should not be continued unless it offers advantages to the child concerned which cannot be secured by the use of the orders available under the 1989 Act or, presumably, under the residual inherent jurisdiction.

(b) Orders that can be made

Before the Children Act 1989 the unique combination of statutory and inherent powers meant that the court had jurisdiction to make a wide range of orders to protect both the person and property of its wards.[102] Indeed, as one commentary put it,[103] 'the law knew no greater form of protection for a child than wardship'.

However, in accordance with the deliberate policy to reduce the need to invoke the jurisdiction[104] the 1989 Act significantly narrowed the ambit of wardship by removing all powers to commit a ward into local authority care or to make supervision orders in respect of such a child. We discuss these changes shortly.

Another important change was brought about by the availability of s 8 orders (it may be recalled[105] that prohibited steps and specific issue orders were in fact modelled on the wardship court's inherent powers to protect children). Since wardship proceedings rank as 'family proceedings',[106] the court is empowered in those proceedings to make any s 8 order whether or not they have been applied for. Although the interrelationship between s 8 orders and the wardship jurisdiction has yet to be definitively explored, the better view is that:

---

[99] Particularly where the issue is one of discretion: see eg *Re D (A Minor)* (1978) 76 LGR 653.

[100] *Re F (Minors) (Wardship: Jurisdiction)* [1988] 2 FLR 123, CA. See also *Re Z (Minors) (Child Abuse: Evidence)* [1989] 2 FLR 3.

[101] See *Re T (A Minor) (Wardship: Representation)* [1994] Fam 49, CA, *Re M and J (Wardship: Supervision and Residence Orders)* [2003] EWHC 1585 (Fam), [2003] 2 FLR 541 and *Re W (Wardship: Discharge: Publicity)* [1995] 2 FLR 466, CA.

[102] For a discussion of these powers see pp 693-4 of the previous edition of this work.

[103] Lowe and White, above at para 1.1.

[104] See Law Com No 172, *Guardianship and Custody* at para 4.35.

[105] See above, p 564.   [106] Children Act 1989 s 8(3), discussed above, p 565.

(a) while it is consistent with the continuation of wardship to make a residence order, wardship should only be kept in place where there is good reason to maintain the court's continuing supervision; and

(b) while s 8 powers do not oust the court's inherent powers, whenever there is a choice, the former powers should be exercised.

With regard to (a), since a residence order only determines the person with whom the child is to live,[107] it is not inconsistent with the court's control over its ward to make such an order.[108] However, unless the court believes that there is some benefit in continuing the wardship, it should, upon making a residence order, discharge the wardship.[109] Where the wardship is ordered to continue, the parents, or anyone else who has a residence order, will still have parental responsibility but will be subject to the general need to obtain the court's consent with regard to any important steps in the child's life.[110] An alternative option, where it is resolved to continue the wardship, is to grant care and control rather than make a residence order.[111] Such an order gives day to day control of the child to the carers while preserving the court's overall legal control. Unlike a residence order it does not confer parental responsibility on those who do not already have it.

With regard to (b), it has been held that, unless there is some real advantage to the child, the statutory scheme should be used in preference to the wardship or general inherent jurisdiction.[112] Accordingly, in any wardship proceedings the court's inherent powers should only be exercised where there is no statutory alternative. Hence, for example, rather than making restraining orders under their inherent powers to prevent the ward's association with or prospective marriage to a particular person, or to prevent a person associating or communicating with or harbouring the ward, the court should make a prohibited steps order instead. Even where it is appropriate to exercise the inherent powers, consideration will still have to be given as to whether to continue the wardship. We discuss the current ambit of the inherent powers in the context of the High Court's general inherent jurisdiction.[113]

The former statutory power to make maintenance orders has been repealed,[114] and

---

[107] See above, p 515.

[108] See, for example, Re M and J (Wardship: Supervision and Residence Orders) [2003] EWHC 1585 (Fam), [2003] 2 FLR 541 where inter alia a residence order was made coupled with wardship. See further below. Although it had been established before the 1989 Act that the court had power to determine a ward's place of residence (see Re J (A Minor) [1989] Fam 85), it was well established that it could not make old style custody orders (see Re CB (A Minor) (Wardship: Local Authority) [1981] 1 All ER 16, CA) nor guardianship orders (see Re C (Minors) (Wardship: Adoption) [1989] 1 All ER 395, CA) since that was inconsistent with the court's continuing control over its wards. The latter embargo still applies, but there would be nothing to prevent the court from making a guardianship appointment and de-warding the child. The court's powers to appoint guardians are governed by s 5 of the Children Act 1989, discussed above, pp 443ff.

[109] See Re T (A Minor) (Child: Representation) [1994] Fam 49, CA, discussed further below at pp 898–9. Note that in Re M (Child's Upbringing) [1996] 2 FLR 441, CA (the 'Zulu Boy' case, discussed above, p 589) the wardship was maintained notwithstanding the order that the boy be returned to South Africa.

[110] See above, p 884.

[111] See R J (Fostering: Person Disqualified) [1999] 1 WLR 581, CA, and Re R J (Wardship) [1999] 1 FLR 618. See further below. But note R v R (Private Law Proceedings: Residential Assessment) [2002] 2 FLR 953, at 960 in which Holman J doubted whether the concept of 'care and control' survived the 1989 Act.

[112] See Re T, above, Re M and J, above, and Re R (A Minor) (Blood Transfusion) [1993] 2 FLR 757.

[113] See below, pp 903ff.

[114] The Family Law Reform Act 1969 s 6 was repealed by the Courts and Legal Services Act 1990, Sch 20.

insofar as the court has any power (in view of the Child Support Act 1991) to make financial provision for its ward, its jurisdiction to do so is governed by Sch 1 to the Children Act 1989, which is discussed in Chapter 17.

6 THE PRINCIPLES ON WHICH THE COURT ACTS

In the past statements have been made which suggest that the welfare of a ward is always the paramount consideration.[115] It is clear, however, that the individual ward's interests are not always thought to be overriding.[116] The best explanation for this seems to be that the paramountcy of the ward's welfare only applies when the court is called upon to exercise what used to be termed its custodial jurisdiction, and not where it is exercising a purely protective jurisdiction. In short the ward's welfare will only be the paramount consideration when s 1(1) of the Children Act 1989 applies, namely where his upbringing or the administration of his property is directly in issue.[117]

Where the court is called upon to exercise a purely protective jurisdiction (ie where the issue falls outside the scope of s 1(1) of the 1989 Act and is not governed by other statutes), the ward's welfare is not accorded any specially weighted interest, though it will remain an important consideration. Whether the court will protect a ward will depend on how seriously and how directly the child's interests may be harmed and how important any competing interests are.[118]

7 THE MODERN USE OF THE JURISDICTION

(a) The position before the Children Act 1989[119]

Before the Children Act 1989 the many and often unique characteristics of wardship proved useful to disparate applicants, although the high costs[120] and lengthy delays in obtaining a court hearing militated against an even greater use. Nevertheless, there had been, particularly during the 20 years preceding the Children Act 1989, a phenomenal rise in the number of wardships from 74 in 1951, 622 in 1971 to a peak of 4,961 in 1991.[121]

A key reason for this growth was the use of wardship by local authorities, who for a variety of reasons found it advantageous to use the prerogative jurisdiction rather than the statutory scheme to get children into care or to keep them there.[122] Local authority use of

---

[115] In *Re D (A Minor) (Justices' Decision: Review)* [1977] Fam 158 at 163, Dunn J memorably referred to the 'golden thread' running through the wardship jurisdiction, namely the welfare of the child 'which is considered in this court first, last and all the time'.

[116] See, for example, *Re M and N (Minors) (Wardship: Publication of Information)* [1990] Fam 211 at 223, where Butler-Sloss LJ expressly said that in cases where restraint of publicity is sought 'the welfare of the ward is not the paramount consideration'.

[117] The scope of s 1(1) is discussed above at pp 450ff.   [118] See below, pp 899ff.

[119] See generally Law Com Working Paper No 101 (1987) *Wards of Court*, Part III.

[120] The DHSS Child Care Review Costings Working Party (1986, para 5.21) estimated the average cost of an order confirming wardship to have been £5,960 in an uncontested case and £7,970 in a contested case.

[121] The 1951 and 1971 figures can be found in S Cretney *Principles of Family Law* (1st edn, 1974) p 289. The 1991 figure was published in the 1991 *Judicial Statistics* (CM 1991), Table 5.8.

[122] See J Hunt *Local Authority Wardship before the Children Act: The Baby or the Bathwater* (1993); J Masson and S Morton 'The Use of Wardship by Local Authorities' (1989) 52 MLR 762; and N Lowe 'The Role of Wardship in Child Care Cases' [1989] Fam Law 38.

wardship increased considerably in the latter half of the 1980s, accounting for up to 40% of all applications in 1985, rising to a high of 66% in 1989.[123]

Another important use of wardship was by relatives who, until 1985,[124] had no other means of initiating court proceedings either to seek to look after the child or to have contact. In 1985 24% of wardships involved relatives.[125]

Parents too used to look to wardship, particularly in relation to international child abduction, where the immediacy of the prohibition against a ward's removal from the country together with the wide jurisdictional rules were an obvious advantage.[126] A more traditional use of the jurisdiction was in the so-called 'teenage wardship', where parents warded their children to prevent their marriage to or continued association with someone considered to be 'undesirable'.[127] Though occasionally useful, this declined when in 1971 the age of majority was reduced to 18. In contrast to 'teenage wardships' there was some evidence of wardship being used by children against their parents.[128]

A further important role of wardship was in respect to novel cases, where the availability of High Court expertise, as well as the jurisdiction's wide powers, was clearly an advantage. A good example of this was in relation to determining the future of Britain's first and much publicised commercially arranged surrogate child.[129]

(b) The position after the Children Act 1989 [130]

Restrictions in public law cases

The major direct impact of the 1989 Act on the application of wardship is with respect to local authority use. The Act makes wardship and local authority care incompatible.[131] If a care order is made under s 31 in respect of a ward of court, the wardship ceases[132] and while a child is in care he cannot be made a ward of court.[133] Furthermore, both the former statutory and inherent powers to commit wards of court into local authority care and to make supervision orders have been respectively expressly repealed and revoked by s 100(1) and (2)(a). On the other hand, if in wardship proceedings it appears to the court that a care or supervision order might be appropriate, then, like any other court in 'family proceedings',[134] it can, pursuant to the powers under s 37,[135] direct a local authority to

---

[123] By 1991 this had dropped back to 55.5%.

[124] Until the implementation of the custodianship provisions: see the 7th edition of this work, ch 11.

[125] See Law Com Working Paper No 101 (1987) *Wardship* para 3.3. Grandparents were a particularly significant user of the jurisdiction: see Law Com Working Paper No 96 (1986) *Custody* para 5.38, n 92.

[126] See further Ch 13.

[127] See Cross *Wards of Court* (1967) 83 LQR 200 at 209 et seq; Turner 'Wardship and the Official Solicitor' (1977) 2 Adoption and Fostering 30 at 33; and Lowe and White, above, paras 12–1 et seq.

[128] See the 7th edition of this work at p 434.

[129] *Re C (A Minor) (Wardship: Surrogacy)* [1985] FLR 846.

[130] See generally R White, P Carr and N Lowe *Children Act in Practice* (3rd edition, 2002) paras 12.4ff; HHJ Mitchell 'Whatever Happened To Wardship?' [2001] Fam Law 130 and 212. M Parry 'The Children Act 1989: Local Authorities, Wardship and the Revival of the Inherent Jurisdiction' [1992] JSWFL 212; and A Bainham 'The Children Act 1989—The Future of Wardship' [1990] Fam Law 270.

[131] See the Department of Health's *Guidance and Regulations*, Vol 1, *Court Orders*, para 3.99.

[132] Children Act 1989 s 91(4).

[133] Section, s 100(2)(c) and the Supreme Court Act 1981 s 41(2A), added by Sch 13, para 45(2), to the 1989 Act.

[134] Wardship proceedings are 'family proceedings' by reason of s 8(3)(a).

[135] Discussed above, p 580.

investigate the child's circumstances with a view to the authority making an application. In the event of such an application being made,[136] a care or supervision order can only be made provided the threshold criteria under s 31 are satisfied.

However, the restrictions imposed by the 1989 Act do *not* prevent the High Court from exercising its inherent jurisdiction to decide a specific question in relation to a child in local authority care.[137]

In view of these restrictions it is tempting to say that the use of wardship by and against local authorities, which, as we have seen, accounted for such a large proportion of pre-1989 Act cases, has effectively been ended.[138] In theory, however, wardship remains an option where the child is *not* in their care, including those being accommodated by them. Although wardship cannot be used to bring about such an arrangement,[139] unlike care, accommodation is not incompatible with wardship. However, to invoke wardship local authorities will need court leave,[140] which may only be given upon the court being satisfied that: (a) the remedy sought to be achieved cannot be achieved by the making of a s 8 order (it must be remembered that local authorities can with court leave apply to a prohibited steps or specific issue order); and (b) the child is likely to suffer significant harm if the jurisdiction is not exercised. Even if leave is given, s 100(2)(d)[141] prevents the courts from making orders the effect of which is to confer upon authorities aspects of parental responsibility that they do not already have.

Since s 8 orders do not cover every situation, in cases where the local authority are not themselves seeking care but are nevertheless concerned about a child's well-being, wardship might still be the right solution, at any rate, where there is thought to be a need for the court's continuing control.

In *Re R (A Minor) (Contempt)*,[142] for example, a local authority warded a 14-year-old child accommodated by them to protect her from a relationship with a 33-year-old man. A local authority has also been known to ward children to protect them from being identified in a television programme about alleged paedophiles.[143] Wardship might also offer the best and sometimes the only means open to a local authority to protect 17-year-olds when most of the public law options are unavailable.[144] Other possible examples are safeguarding the interests of orphans or abandoned children[145] and cases where a local authority are concerned about the child's welfare but are not themselves seeking care and control as, for example, supporting foster parents' applications for care and control[146] or agreeing to a

---

[136] But there is no power to force the local authority to apply: see eg *Nottingham County Council v P* [1994] Fam 18, discussed above, p 530 and below, p 912.

[137] Discussed below, p 910.

[138] See A Bainham, *Children: The Modern Law* (2nd edn) p 406, who submitted that wardship (as distinct from the inherent jurisdiction) is redundant in public law cases. He does not repeat that assertion in the third edition.

[139] See s 100(2)(b).   [140] Pursuant to s 100(3), discussed further below, p 909.

[141] Discussed below, pp 904–5.

[142] [1994] 2 FLR 185, CA. Quaere whether a prohibited steps order could have been made in this case?

[143] *Cornwall County Council v BBC* (1994) unreported.

[144] See eg *Re F (Mental Health Act: Guardianship)* [2000] 1 FLR 192, CA, discussed below at p 902 and *Re D (Evidence: Facilitated Communication)* [2001] 1 FLR 148, which concerned allegations made by a 17-year-old with a mental age of two and who had lived in a special care unit that he had been sexually abused by his father. In the event the allegations were not proved and the wardship was discharged.

[145] See eg *Re C (A Baby)* [1996] 2 FLR 43, discussed below at p 900.

[146] See eg *Re J (Wardship)* [1999] 1 FLR 618.

residence order being made in favour of a mother and stepfather coupled with a supervision order;[147] where a local authority, learning of a surrogacy arrangement, are concerned about the child's welfare[148] and where they are concerned about the refusal to authorise medical treatment for a child.[149] In this latter context one advantage of wardship is the immediacy of the effect such that the moment the child becomes a ward of court the leave is required to carry out the proposed treatment. Nevertheless, unless the continuing control of the court is desirable or useful,[150] it is unlikely that the wardship would be continued. In any event it is usually equally effective simply to seek a prohibited steps or specific issue order.[151]

Private law cases

Although no express restraint is placed on the use of wardship by individuals by the 1989 Act, as the Department of Health's *Guidance and Regulations* puts it, its impact is considerable:

'By incorporating many of the beneficial aspects of wardship, such as the "open door" policy, and a flexible range of orders, the Act will substantially reduce the need to have recourse to the High Court.'

As a result of these changes, relatives are now generally better advised to seek, albeit with leave, s 8 orders or special guardianship orders in the lower courts. Similarly in most cases it is difficult to see what advantages parents would gain from wardship, rather than pursuing remedies under the 1989 Act.

As expected the statistics, insofar as they are available, do bear evidence of the dramatic decline in the private use of wardship. In 1991, the final year running up to implementation, 2,209 (accounting for 44.5 % of the record number of wardship applications made in that year) originating summonses were taken out by individuals.[152] In contrast in 1992 the total number of summonses issued was 492,[153] and similar numbers have been issued since.[154]

The ruling in Re T

Although the decline in the de facto use of wardship was predictable, it was more difficult to anticipate how the courts would react to cases where it was sought to invoke the jurisdiction. The leading case is *Re T (A Minor) (Child: Representation)*[155] in which the

---

[147] *Re M and J (Wardship: Supervision and Residence Orders)* [2003] EWHC 1585 (Fam), [2003] 2 FLR 541, discussed below at p 899.

[148] See *Re C (A Minor) (Wardship: Surrogacy)* [1985] FLR 846, and Local Authority Circular (85) 12.

[149] See *Re B (A Minor) (Wardship: Medical Treatment)* [1981] 1 WLR 1421, CA.

[150] As in *Re C (A Baby)*, above, discussed below at p 900.

[151] See eg *Re C (HIV Test)* [1997] 2 FLR 1004 in which, following local authority intervention, a specific issue order was made, ordering a baby to be tested for HIV.

[152] *Judicial Statistics* for 1991 (Cm 1991), Table 5.8.

[153] CAAC Report 1992/93, p 25. According to that report, 141 originating summonses for wardship were issued between January and July 1993, but we understand from the Information Management Unit of the Lord Chancellor's Department that a total of 269 summonses were issued in 1993. It is unknown how many of these summonses were issued by individuals but, given the embargo on the public law use of wardship, it is reasonable to assume that the vast majority were issued in the private law context. The 1993/94 Report gives no updating statistics for wardship and, curiously, no such information has been included in the *Judicial Statistics* since implementation of the 1989 Act.

[154] According to figures quoted by HHJ Mitchell at [2001] Fam Law 130 and obtained from the Statistical Support Office of the Court Service, there were 431 summonses issued in 1998 and 418 in 1999.

[155] [1994] Fam 49, CA.

Court of Appeal held that, given that FPR 1991 r 9.2A[156] applied to all 'family proceedings', in wardship, as in any other family proceedings, provided the child has sufficient understanding to bring or defend proceedings on his or her own behalf, the court has no power to impose a guardian ad litem on such a child against his or her wishes. It was further held that, given that there were no advantages either to the child or to the defendants[157] that were not also available in ordinary family proceedings under Part II of the 1989 Act, there was nothing which, in the words of Waite LJ, would justify giving the child 'the status, an exceptional status under the modern law as it must now be applied, of a ward of court'.[158]

In concluding that the continuation of wardship was inappropriate, Waite LJ commented that while it survives as an independent jurisdiction, the:

'. . . courts' undoubted discretion to allow wardship to go forward in a suitable case is subject to their clear duty, in loyalty to the scheme and purpose of the Children Act legislation, to permit recourse to wardship only when it becomes apparent to the judge in any particular case that the question which the court is determining in regard to the minor's upbringing or property cannot be resolved under the statutory procedures in Part II of the Act in a way that secures the best interests of the child; or where the minor's person is in a state of jeopardy from which he can only be protected by giving him the status of a ward of court; or where the court's functions need to be secured from the effects potentially injurious to the child, of external influences (intrusive publicity for example) and it is decided that conferring on the child the status of a ward will prove a more efficient deterrent than the ordinary sanctions of a contempt of court which already protect all family proceedings'.[159]

Some possible remaining uses of wardship

Given that no material changes have been made to the rules governing the issue of an originating summons, it is submitted that Waite LJ's comments in *Re T* ought not to be taken as restricting an individual's ability to make a child a ward of court in the first instance, though clearly the courts will require special justification to continue the wardship once the case comes before them. It remains now to consider what advantages there may be in issuing an originating summons and when the court might consider continuing the wardship.

One important remaining advantage of the wardship jurisdiction is its immediacy: as soon as the originating summons is issued, the child becomes a ward and no important step may then be taken without prior court sanction.[160] In effect the issuing of the originating summons provides a unique quasi-administrative mechanism by which the child's legal position can be immediately frozen, which is useful when dealing with emergencies, such as threatened child abduction, particularly when an international element is involved.[161] Invoking wardship can also be an effective way of halting a proposed medical operation on the child and can provide a usefully speedy means by which non-parents

---

[156] Through which children of sufficient understanding can seek to apply for s 8 orders without a next friend, and for general discussion of which see above p 504.

[157] Who were adoptive parents. The girl in question aged 13 was an adopted child who was seeking to live with her natural paternal aunt.

[158] Above at 65D. See also *Re M and J (Wardship: Supervision and Residence Orders)* [2003] EWHC 1585 (Fam), [2003] 2 FLR 541 at [26] where Charles J referred to the continuation of wardship as an exceptional course (though justified in that case, see below) and compare *C v Salford City Council* [1994] 2 FLR 926 in which Hale J could see no advantage in continuing the wardship.

[159] At 60.   [160] Discussed above at pp 886ff.   [161] See above, pp 619ff.

who would otherwise have to seek leave to apply for a s 8 order can safeguard their position, for example, by preventing parents from removing the child from their care pending a court hearing.

The court's wardship powers are wider than those under s 8 and where advantage needs to be taken of this and of the court's continued control then it would be proper both to invoke and to continue the wardship. In *Re W (Wardship: Discharge: Publicity)*,[162] for example, a father, having been granted care and control of four sons aged between 10 and 15 in earlier wardship proceedings, had unilaterally changed their schooling and acquiesced in them talking to the press about their 'fight to stay with their Dad'. His request to discharge the wardship was refused. In the Court of Appeal's view the continuation of the wardship was justified because no comparable protection could be achieved under the Children Act 1989, since it was impossible to make a prohibited steps order which could anticipate how the father might act, and because a prohibited steps order might not be appropriate to prevent the publishing of information about the children.[163] Furthermore, the continuing nature of the wardship meant that the Official Solicitor could remain involved and act as a buffer between the parents. The case could also be reserved to the same judge.

The court's overall control of its wards could also be thought to be advantageous, for example, in the case of an abandoned child, where no one looking after him has parental responsibility or, as in *Re C (A Baby)*,[164] in which Sir Stephen Brown P said that the courts were ready to assist with taking responsibility in cases of grave anxiety. In that case the child developed meningitis which left her brain-damaged and unable to survive without artificial ventilation and she would suffer increasing pain and distress with no hope of recovery. Sir Stephen Brown commented:

'It appeared appropriate that the courts should take responsibility for this child and relieve the parents in some measure of the grave responsibility which they have borne since her birth.'

The jurisdiction could also provide an effective means of protecting and managing a child's property interests in the event of the parents' death.

There is a growing cluster of cases concerning the public/private law divide in which wardship has been found to be useful. For example, it was found advantageous both in the short and long term in *Re R J (Fostering: Person Disqualified)*[165] and *Re R J (Wardship)*.[166] These decisions concerned three children who though happily placed with foster carers could not remain there following the implementation of the Children (Protection From Offenders (Miscellaneous Amendments) Regulations 1997,[167] since the foster-father had previously been formally cautioned for actual bodily harm to another foster child who was now adopted by him and his wife. Following the foster parents' intervention in care

---

[162] [1995] 2 FLR 466. But note that the House of Lords' ruling in *Re S (A Child)(Identification: Restrictions on Publication)* [2004] UKHL 47, [2005] 1 AC 593 that the foundation of jurisdiction to restrain publicity now derives from the European Convention on Human Rights rather than the inherent jurisdiction, probably means that the continuation of wardship is less likely to be thought justified to protect children from publicity.

[163] But note Hobhouse LJ's dissenting judgment and the subsequent decision in *Re Z (A Minor) (Identification: Restrictions on Publication)* [1997] Fam 1, CA, discussed above at pp 460–1.

[164] [1996] 2 FLR 43.   [165] [1999] 1 WLR 581, CA.   [166] [1999] 1 FLR 618.

[167] SI 1997/2308. This Regulation was intended to prevent paedophiles from becoming foster parents.

proceedings in which the birth mother was still seeking her children's return, the Court of Appeal in the first mentioned decision, held that although the 1997 Regulations did not prevent the court from making a residence order, in this case the preferable course was to discharge the interim care orders, make the children wards of court and grant interim care and control to the foster parents. In this way the status quo could be preserved as nearly as possible pending the full hearing and, by not granting even interim residence orders (which would have conferred parental responsibility on the foster parents) any perception of prejudice by the mother could be avoided. At the subsequent full hearing (the second mentioned decision) it was held, given the exceptional circumstances, that the appropriate long-term solution was to continue the wardship and to grant care and control to the foster carers. The advantage of this solution was said to be: (1) giving ultimate control to the court would be reassuring to the foster carers (who would otherwise have shared parental responsibility with the mother had they been granted residence orders); (2) it placed the children in a neutral setting, removing them to some extent from the pressure of the more adversarial nature of Children Act proceedings;[168] (3) it was only by this means that the local authority could remain involved in what had become a private law case and would therefore enable the authority to apply for certain orders which might not have otherwise been available to them given the prohibition against local authorities applying for s 8 orders,[169] and (4) it would similarly allow the children's guardian to continue to be involved.

Wardship was also held to be the appropriate solution in *Re W and X (Wardship: Relatives Rejected As Foster Carers)*, which concerned proceedings brought in respect of four children the three eldest of whom had lived with their maternal grandparents after the death of a sibling. It was common ground that the threshold criteria[170] had been satisfied. In relation to the three older children[171] the local authority's preferred option was to leave them with the grandparents but subject to a care order. However, because the local authority had previously rejected the grandparents as foster parents, Regulations[172] meant that this option could not be adopted since the authority would be obliged to remove the children from the grandparents as soon as the care order was made. In Hedley J's opinion this inability to pursue what was perceived to be the best option was a lacuna in the legislation[173] which wardship could properly remedy since it neither infringed the letter nor the spirit of s 100 given that the court were not seeking to control the local authority. Moreover, the children's placement warranted long-term external control which could not be achieved by a care order. Hedley J accordingly warded the children as well as making a supervision and residence orders in favour of grandparents.

What these aforementioned cases demonstrate is the courts' willingness to use wardship

---

[168] Query whether this reason is justifiable given the less adversarial nature of Children Act proceedings?

[169] Cf in particular *F v Cambridgeshire County Council* [1995] 1 FLR 516.

[170] Viz that the children were or were likely to suffer significant harm within the meaning of s 31(2) of the Children Act, discussed above at pp 737ff.

[171] No argument was raised over the youngest child in respect of whom a care order was made.

[172] Viz the Fostering Services Regulations 2002, SI 2002/57 (which only apply in England—for the Welsh equivalent see Fostering Services (Wales) Regulations 2003 SI 2003/237). Inter alia these Regulations prevent placement of children with unapproved foster parents.

[173] Indeed Hedley J went as far as to suggest that it was worth considering whether the Regulations were ultra vires inasmuch as they thwarted the court's duty under s 1(1) of the 1989 Act to treat the child's welfare as its paramount consideration.

to overcome restrictions imposed by Regulation on local authorities' freedom to put children in foster placements which would otherwise operate to the unwarranted detriment of the particular children concerned. But a fourth case, *Re M and J (Wardship: Supervision and Residence Orders)*,[174] is illustrative of a potentially wider use. Here, in care proceedings a mother and stepfather conceded the threshold criteria and agreed to the psychologist's recommendation that one boy should live with his father and the other with his maternal grandmother. The local authority did not entirely agree with these recommendations but nevertheless did not seek alternative orders. Although he recognised it as being an 'exceptional course' Charles J made a residence order and a supervision order coupled with wardship orders in respect of each child, and an order for contact. The justification for the wardship order was to manage the inevitable future tensions that would arise within the family which he felt that by themselves local authority may not have been able to handle.

A final illustration of the continued use of wardship is *Re F (Mental Health Act: Guardianship)*[175] which concerned a 17-year-old, who had a mental age of between five and eight and who had been accommodated by a local authority because of chronic neglect. Her seven siblings had been taken into care for the same reason but this option could not be exercised and therefore fell outside the care legislation. Her parents sought her return and the local authority as an alternative to care obtained a guardianship order under the Mental Health Act 1983. The Court of Appeal held that wardship was the more appropriate remedy not least because the 1983 Act was not a child centred jurisdiction and the child lacked the benefit of independent representation. Furthermore, on the particular facts wardship would enable a single judge to consider the interests of both the child in question and her seven siblings.

Whether these cases should be regarded as a series of 'one-off' decisions or as a core of law defining or beginning to set out the parameters within which wardship can continue to operate in what may be considered to be quasi public law remains to be seen. But what they undoubtedly illustrate is that it is premature to think wardship has no role to play in cases involving local authorities.

C THE INHERENT JURISDICTION[176]

1 JURISDICTION AND PROCEDURE

The inherent jurisdiction can be invoked either upon specific application or by the High Court itself in cases where it is already seized of proceedings.[177] Only the High Court has

---

[174] [2003] EWHC 1585 (Fam), [2003] 2 FLR 541.   [175] [2000] 1 FLR 192, CA.

[176] See generally White, Carr and Lowe, above at paras 12.24ff.

[177] See, for example, *Re R (A Minor) (Blood Test: Constraint)* [1988] Fam 66, in which Hale J held there to be power under the inherent jurisdiction to order a child to provide a blood sample for the purposes of establishing paternity; and *Re X (A Minor) (Adoption Details: Disclosure)* [1994] Fam 174, in which it was held to be an appropriate use of the inherent jurisdiction by the High Court hearing an adoption application to order that during the minority of the child in question the Registrar General should not disclose to any person without leave of the court the details of the adoption entered in the Adopted Children Register.

inherent powers to protect children.[178] Applications for declarations may also be made under the inherent jurisdiction.[179]

Applications to invoke the inherent jurisdiction must be made to the High Court.[180] Local authorities wishing to invoke the jurisdiction must first obtain leave of the court.[181] Although no specific procedure is laid down by the Family Proceedings Rules 1991,[182] in practice, like wardship, application is made by originating summons[183-4] with the petitioner filing, unless otherwise directed, an affidavit in support of the application.

Jurisdiction to make orders giving the care of a child to any person or providing for contact, or the education of a child, is governed by the Family Law Act 1986 and is co-extensive with the wardship jurisdiction.[185] It seems probable that jurisdiction to make orders outside the ambit of s 1(1)(d) is the same as in wardship.[186]

2 THE EFFECT OF INVOKING THE INHERENT JURISDICTION

Unlike wardship, the exercise of the inherent jurisdiction does not place the child under the ultimate responsibility of the court. This means that at no point will the child be subject to the rule obtaining in wardship that all important steps in the child's life have to be sanctioned by the court.[187]

3 THE COURT'S POWERS

(a) The general extent of the inherent powers

Proceedings under the inherent jurisdiction rank as 'family proceedings' for the purposes of the Children Act 1989,[188] so that in general terms the court is empowered either upon application or its own motion to make any s 8 order.[189] Although these statutory powers should be used whenever possible,[190] there will be occasions when either the courts are

---

[178] *D v D (County Court Jurisdiction: Injunctions)* [1993] 2 FLR 802, CA, in which it was held that the county court had no inherent power to grant injunctions. See also *Devon County Council v B* [1997] 1 FLR 591, CA and *Re S and D (Children: Powers of the Court)* [1995] 2 FLR 456, CA. A fortiori magistrates' courts have no inherent jurisdiction. Note, however, that where proceedings relating to the exercise of the inherent jurisdiction has been transferred from the High Court to the county court, pursuant to s 38(2)(b) of the Matrimonial and Family Proceedings Act 1984, the court can, pursuant to s 38(5), exercise the same powers as the High Court.

[179] CPR 1998, r 40.20. It is now possible to obtain interim declarations: CPR 1998, r 25.1(9).

[180] Supreme Court Act 1981 Sch 1, para 3(b)(ii), as amended by the Children Act 1989 Sch 13, para 45(3).

[181] Children Act 1989 s 100(3), discussed below, p 909.

[182] Part V specifically applies to wardship.

[183-4] Applications are generally headed 'In the matter of the Supreme Court Act 1981'.

[185] See above, p 888.   [186] See above, p 888.

[187] *Re W (A Minor) (Medical Treatment: Court's Jurisdiction)* [1993] Fam 64 at 73F-G, per Lord Donaldson MR. Note that this accords with Lord Mackay LC's comments in his Joseph Jackson Memorial Lecture (1989) 139 NLJ 505 at 508 that it was not thought 'appropriate or practicable for the responsibility for a child in the care of a public authority which is statutorily charged with looking after him to be subject to the detailed directions of another public authority, namely the courts.'

[188] Children Act 1989 s 8(3)(a).   [189] See above, pp 514ff.

[190] See *Re T (A Minor) (Child: Representation)* [1994] Fam 49, CA; and *Re R (A Minor) (Blood Transfusion)* [1993] 2 FLR 757.

barred from using them, as where children are already in local authority care,[191] or where what is being sought lies outside their scope. On these occasions recourse can properly be had to the court's inherent powers.

Before implementation of the 1989 Act there had been some speculation[192] as to whether these inherent powers were the same as those under the wardship jurisdiction, but it is now clear, that they are. As Lord Donaldson MR put it in *Re W (A Minor) (Medical Treatment: Court's Jurisdiction)*:[193]

'Since there seems to be some doubt about the matter, it should be made clear that the High Court's inherent jurisdiction in relation to children—the parens patriae jurisdiction—is equally exercisable whether the child is or is not a ward of court . . .'

(b) Express limitations imposed by the Children Act 1989

The Children Act 1989 s 100(2) expressly limits the exercise of the High Court's inherent jurisdiction by preventing (a) a child being placed in the care or put under the supervision of a local authority and (b) a child from being accommodated by or on behalf of a local authority. These embargoes are in line with the general policy of the Act to prevent the courts from making care or supervision orders other than under s 31.[194] Section 100(2)(d) also prevents the High Court from exercising its inherent jurisdiction:

'. . . for the purpose of conferring on any local authority power to determine any question which has arisen, or which may arise, in connection with any aspect of parental responsibility for the child.'

In other words, while the High Court may make orders under its inherent jurisdiction in respect of a child, in doing so it may not confer on the local authority any degree of parental responsibility that it does not already have.[195] This is less likely to cause problems where the child is in care, since the local authority will already be vested with parental responsibility.[196] Hence, the determination of a particular question by the court, for example, obtaining a return order against abducting parents, will not be contrary to s 100(2)(d).[197] Similarly, the court is free to determine the scope and extent of parental responsibility and can, for instance, make orders giving leave for a child in care to be interviewed by the father's solicitor to prepare a defence to criminal charges.[198] If the local authority do not have parental responsibility for the child, the High Court may not under its inherent jurisdiction make orders which in any way confer parental responsibility upon the authority. Hence, for example, while the court can sanction named persons to look after the child[199] it could not authorise a local authority to place the child. It has, however,

---

[191] See s 9(1)–(2) of the Children Act 1989, discussed above, pp 540–2.

[192] See the 8th edition of this work at 480–1.

[193] [1993] Fam 64 at 73F. See also Balcombe LJ at 85.   [194] Discussed above, pp 736ff.

[195] As it is expressed by the Department of Health's *Guidance and Regulations*, Vol 1, *Court Orders*, at para 3.102.

[196] See above, p 771.

[197] See *Southwark London Borough v B* [1993] 2 FLR 559 at 571 per Waite LJ.

[198] Per Hale J in *Re M (Care: Leave to Interview Child)* [1995] 1 FLR 825.

[199] As in *Re RJ (Wardship)* [1999] 1 FLR 618, *Re M and J (Wardship: Supervision and Residence Orders)* [2003] EWHC 1585 (Fam), [2003] 2 FLR 541 and *Re W and X (Wardship: Relatives Rejected as Foster Carers)* [2003] EWHC 2206 (Fam), [2004] 1 FLR 415.

been held wrong that s 100 be restrictively interpreted and that it is perfectly proper for a local authority to invite the court to exercise its inherent jurisdiction to protect children even if the exercise of that power would be an invasion of a person's parental responsibility, for example, by restricting a non-family member from contacting or communicating with the children in question.[200]

(c) Other restrictions on the exercise of the inherent powers[201]

Courts have traditionally declined to define the limits of their inherent powers to protect children and they have been habitually described as theoretically unlimited.[202] Nevertheless, although it is accepted that the High Court's inherent power to protect children is wider than that of a parent,[203] it is equally well established that, whatever may be the theoretical position, there are 'far-reaching limitations in principle' on the exercise of that jurisdiction.[204] As Ward LJ put it in *Re Z (A Minor) (Identification: Restrictions on Publication)*:[205]

'The wardship or inherent jurisdiction of the court to cast its cloak of protection over minors whose interests are at risk of harm is unlimited in theory though in practice the judges who exercise the jurisdiction have created classes of cases in which the court will not exercise its powers.'

However, because of the court's tendency to approach the issue on a case-by-case basis rather than by laying down general guidance, the precise limits, even to the extent of determining whether there are, as Ward LJ suggests, necessarily de facto rather than de jure limits, are still far from clear.

The de jure limits

Notwithstanding that the established limits have developed more as a result of practice than of strict legal restraint, there are clearly some de jure as well as de facto limits to protecting the child in question. They cannot be used, for instance, to protect the parent qua parent.[206] Secondly, there is no inherent power to make orders that are prohibited by

---

[200] Per Thorpe J in *Devon County Council v S* [1994] Fam 169, accepting the argument that the local authority were not seeking leave to apply to the court to confer any power upon themselves, but were asking the court to exercise its own powers.

[201] See generally N Lowe 'The Limits of the Wardship Jurisdiction, Part 2: The extent of the court's powers over a ward' (1989) 1 Jo of Child Law 44.

[202] See eg *Re W (A Minor) (Medical Treatment: Court's Jurisdiction)* [1993] Fam 64, at 81 per Lord Donaldson MR; *Re R (A Minor) (Wardship: Restrictions on Publication)* [1994] Fam 254 at 271, per Millett LJ; and *Re B (Child Abduction: Wardship Power to Detain)* [1994] 2 FLR 479 at 483, per Butler-Sloss LJ and at 487, per Hobhouse LJ, CA.

[203] See *Re R (A Minor) (Wardship: Consent to Medical Treatment)* [1992] Fam 11 at 25B and 28G and *Re W (A Minor) (Medical Treatment: Court's Jurisdiction)*, above. Note also that a similar standpoint has been taken by the Australian High Court in *Department of Health and Community Services v JWB and SMB* (1992) 66 ALJR 300.

[204] Per Balcombe LJ in *Re W*, above, at 85, citing Sir John Pennycuick in *Re X (A Minor) (Wardship: Jurisdiction)* [1975] Fam 47 at 61, CA.

[205] [1997] Fam 1 at 23.

[206] See *Re V (A Minor) (Wardship)* (1979) 123 Sol Jo 201, where the court refused to hear a father's cross-application for an ouster order against his wife. Quaere whether this is how best to categorise *Re J S (A Minor)* [1981] Fam 22, CA, in which it was held that there is no inherent power to make declarations of paternity? On this point cf *T v Child Support Agency* [1997] 2 FLR 875.

statute. As we have seen, the inherent power to commit children into local authority care or to make supervision orders has been expressly revoked by s 100(2)(a) of the Children Act.[207] As a general proposition, however, it would seem that the courts should be slow to hold that an inherent power has been abrogated or restricted by Parliament, and they should only do so where it is clear that Parliament so intended.[208] Moreover, it can be a matter of fine judgment to determine what the legislative intention is.[209] A further complication is that it is accepted that the inherent powers can be used to fill unintended lacunae in legislative schemes.[210]

A third possible limitation is that there is no inherent power to make orders that are purely statutory in origin, as, for example, to attach a power of arrest to a non-molestation order.[211] Whether there is a purely inherent power to make so-called ouster orders[212] is problematic. Until the House of Lords ruling in *Richards v Richards*[213] there was authority for saying that ouster orders could be made broadly on the basis of what was best for the

[207] See above, p 904. See also *Re O (A Minor)(Blood Tests: Constraint)* [2000] Fam 137 in which Wall J refused to exercise the inherent jurisdiction to override the refusal of a parent with care and control to consent to a blood sample being taken from her child as she was then entitled to do under the Family Law Reform Act 1969, s 21 (since amended by the Child Support, Pensions and Social Security Act 2000, s 82, discussed above at p 329). It is on this ground that Douglas Brown J's decision in *South Glamorgan County Council v W and B* [1993] 1 FLR 574 (discussed above at p 906) that the High Court has an inherent power to override a child's refusal to submit to an examination when placed inter alia in interim care can be criticised, since there is clear statutory power (see eg s 38(6)) to do so.

[208] For a scholarly treatise on the whole topic of inherent powers see Jacob 'The Inherent Jurisdiction of the Court' (1970) 23 Current Legal Problems 23. Indeed, it was for this reason that it had been held before the Children Act that, despite the then statutory scheme dealing with children in local authority care, the wardship jurisdiction had not thereby been ousted or abrogated, since the prerogative jurisdiction was neither expressly not by necessary implication so restricted: see *Re M (An Infant)* [1961] Ch 328 at 345, CA, per Lord Evershed MR and accepted by the House of Lords in *A v Liverpool City Council* [1982] AC 363. Query whether Douglas Brown J's ruling in *South Glamorgan*, above, can be justified on the ground that ss 38(6), 43(8) and 44(7) are properly regarded as not having abrogated the inherent power to override those wishes?

[209] Compare, for example, *Re RJ (Foster Placement)* [1998] 2 FLR 110 in which Sir Stephen Brown P considered granting care and control to disqualified foster parents would subvert the policy behind the Children (Protection From Offenders) Miscellaneous Amendments Regulations 1997, with that of the Court of Appeal at [1999] 1 WLR 581 (discussed above at p 900) which was content to say that the Regulations were not directed at the courts.

[210] See eg *Re W and X (Wardship: Relatives Rejected as Foster Parents)* [2003] EWHC 2206 (Fam), [2004] 1 FLR 415, discussed above at p 901 and *Re C (A Minor)(Adoption: Freeing Orders)* [1999] Fam 43, in which, relying on *Re J (A Minor)(Wardship: Jurisdiction)* [1984] 1 WLR 81 (which in turn relied upon dicta by Lord Wilberforce in *A v Liverpool City Council* [1982] AC 363, at 372–3), Wall J held remedying a lacuna under the then adoption law, that he had inherent power to revoke a freeing order notwithstanding the mother's declaration that she no longer wished to be involved with her child. For further discussion of this case, see R White, P Carr and N Lowe *Children Act in Practice* (3rd edn) at 12.40.

[211] See *Re G (Wardship) (Jurisdiction: Power of Arrest)* (1982) 4 FLR 538, discussed by Lowe, above, at 45–6. An alternative explanation of this case is that a distinction needs to be made between the power to make orders and the power to *enforce* them, the latter not being specially developed under the inherent jurisdiction—see also *Re B (Child Abduction: Wardship: Power to Detain)* [1994] 2 FLR 479, CA (no power to detain a person under the inherent jurisdiction in the absence of a finding of contempt). It is a nice point whether the power to make maintenance orders is a purely statutory power; cf the Report of the Committee on the Age of Majority (the Latey Committee) 1967 Cmnd 2342, para 250, which thought there was no inherent power and *Calderdale Borough Council v H and P* [1991] 1 FLR 461 and *W v Avon County Council* (1979) 9 Fam Law 33 in which it was held that there was an inherent power to make maintenance orders.

[212] An ouster order excludes another person from a particular property.

[213] [1984] AC 174, HL.

child, and it was not unknown for such orders to be made in wardship proceedings.[214] The decision in *Richards* seemed to put an end to such a line of reasoning, and in particular seemed to doubt the existence of an independent jurisdiction (ie outside that provided by the domestic violence legislation) to protect children by means of ouster orders.[215] Since *Richards*, however, there have been a number of Court of Appeal decisions which have complicated the position. In attempting to reconcile these post-*Richards* decisions, the Court of Appeal in *Pearson v Franklin*[216] concluded that distinctions have to be drawn according to whether the adult parties were spouses, former spouses, cohabitants or former cohabitants. Only if the adult parties were former spouses whose marriage has been dissolved by decree absolute is there an inherent power to make ouster orders.[217] Since *Pearson*, however, there have been two first instance decisions suggesting that the inherent powers may be wider. In the first, *Re S (Minors) (Inherent Jurisdiction: Ouster)*[218] Connell J granted a local authority's request under s 100 for leave to pursue an application to exclude a father from the matrimonial home, while in the second, *C v K (Inherent Powers: Exclusion Order)*[219] Wall J also concluded that there remained an inherent power to protect children by means of an ouster order. Whether the appellate courts will be disposed to uphold either decision remains to be seen, but so far as the former is concerned the need to do has been undermined by the power to include exclusion requirements in interim care orders and emergency protection orders introduced by the Family Law Act 1996.[220]

It has been argued[221] that a further limit to the jurisdiction is that there is no power to restrain the activities of those who are not in a family or personal relationship with the child in question. This argument was based on *Re X (A Minor) (Wardship: Jurisdiction)*,[222] in which the applicant sought in wardship to prevent the publication of a book containing details about the ward's dead father's alleged sexual predilections, on the basis that its publication would be grossly damaging to his 'highly strung' 14-year-old stepdaughter. The application failed, not because it was held that there was no such power, but because in this instance it was felt that freedom of speech was more important than the ward's welfare, which was in any event only indirectly at risk. The implications of reaching a contrary decision would have been enormous, since it would have meant that any activity that could be considered even indirectly harmful to a child might have been restrained by way of the wardship jurisdiction. Nevertheless, *Re X* is not authority for saying that the independent activities of others can never be restrained to protect a ward, or even that freedom of speech can never be curbed. Indeed, in *X County Council v A*,[223] for example, it

[214] See *Re V (A Minor) (Wardship)* (1979) 123 Sol Jo 201; *Rennick v Rennick* [1978] 1 All ER 817 at 819; and *Spindlow v Spindlow* [1979] Fam 52 at 58, in which Ormrod LJ assumed there was such a power. The matter was not beyond doubt, however: see to the contrary *Re D (Minors)* (1982) 13 Fam Law 111.

[215] See eg Lowe and White *Wards of Court* (2nd edn) 6–51.

[216] [1994] 1 WLR 370, discussed above at pp 251–308.

[217] Following *Webb v Webb* [1986] 1 FLR 541, and *Wilde v Wilde* [1988] 2 FLR 83, CA, each in turn applying *Quinn v Quinn* (1983) 4 FLR 394, CA.

[218] [1994] 1 FLR 623.   [219] [1996] 2 FLR 506.

[220] Discussed above at pp 784 and 726.

[221] R Everton 'High Tide in Wardship' (1975) 125 NLJ 930.   [222] [1975] Fam 47, CA.

[223] [1985] 1 All ER 53. Note the House of Lords' subsequent ruling in *Re S (A Child)(Identification: Restrictions on Publication)* [2004] UKHL 47, [2005] 1 AC 593 that the foundation of jurisdiction to restrain publicity is now properly regarded as deriving from the European Convention on Human Rights rather than the inherent jurisdiction.

was held that the press ought to be restrained from publishing details that could lead to the identity and whereabouts of the ward, who was the child of a woman (Mary Bell) once convicted of manslaughter. In this latter case the restraint was on publicity directly referring to the ward and which would have been directly harmful.

Not all the cases seeking to control the activities of those unconnected with the ward have concerned publicity. In the extraordinary case of *Re C (A Minor) (Wardship: Jurisdiction)*[224] an independent day school run by a charity on orthodox Jewish principles admitted the son of Jewish parents on stringent conditions (including that the child should not live with his parents), but then indicated that the boy would be required to leave at the end of his first term. The local authority, concerned for the child's future, issued wardship proceedings seeking a mandatory injunction against the school requiring it to educate the boy. The Court of Appeal upheld the ruling that the application be refused. As Sir Stephen Brown P put it:

'If theoretically [the court] possesses such a power, I am clearly of the view that it is beyond the practical boundary of its wardship jurisdiction. This jurisdiction is not appropriate for use as an alternative to, or a cloak for, what appears, in fact, to be a claim for breach of contract by the parents against the school.'

What these cases in general, and *Re C* in particular, show is that, whilst the courts are reluctant to hold that there is no power to control the activities of those unconnected with a ward, they will only exercise that power where it is essential to do so to protect the ward from direct harm. In other words, such a limitation is de facto rather than de jure.

The de facto limits

As Ward LJ said in *Re Z (A Minor)(Identification: Restrictions on Publication)*[225] the most obvious and well established of the de facto limits of the exercise of the inherent powers is where Parliament has entrusted the exercise of a competing discretion to another body or court. It has thus been long established that the court will not use its inherent powers to interfere with the exercise of discretion by local authorities over the children in their care,[226] the immigration service,[227] the prison service,[228] or by another court of competent jurisdiction.[229] By analogy it is also well established that there is no inherent power to

---

[224] [1991] 2 FLR 168, CA.   [225] [1997] Fam 1 at 23.

[226] See *A v Liverpool City Council*, [1982] AC 363, HL and *E (By her Litigation Friend, PW) v London Borough of X* [2005] EWHC 2811 (Fam), discussed above at p 908.

[227] See *Re Mohammed Arif (An Infant), Re Nirbhai Singh (An Infant)* [1968] Ch 643, CA; *Re F (A Minor) (Immigration: Wardship)* [1990] Fam 125, CA; *Re A (A Minor) (Wardship: Immigration)* [1992] 1 FLR 427, CA and *R (Anton) v Secretary of State For The Home Department, Re Anton* [2004] EWHC 2730/2731 (Admin/Fam), [2005] 2 FLR 818. However, the wardship might be continued to safeguard the children where that would not interfere with the immigration service's functions: *Re F*, above and *Re K and S (Minors) (Wardship: Immigration)* [1992] 1 FLR 432.

[228] *CF v Secretary Of State For The Home Department* [2004] EWHC 111 (Fam), [2004] 2 FLR 517, *London Borough of Islington v TM* [2004] EWHC 2050 (Fam) and *R (Howard League for Penal Reform) v Secretary of State for the Home Department)* [2002] EWHC 2497 (Admin), [2004] 1 FLR 484.

[229] See eg *Re A-H (Infants)* [1963] Ch 232; *Re K (KJS) (An Infant)* [1966] 3 All ER 154; and *Re PJ (An Infant)* [1968] 1 WLR 1976. Note also *Re G (A Minor) (Witness Summons)* [1988] 2 FLR 396—no power to set aside a witness summons issued by the US authorities in connection with a Court Martial to be held in England since, under the terms of the Visiting Forces Act 1952, the court martial was a sovereign court vested with exclusive powers.

order a doctor directly or indirectly to treat a child contrary to his or her clinical judgment.[230]

Quite apart from those limits, the courts also seem to be moving to a position of saying that the inherent jurisdiction should not be exercised so as to exempt the child from the general law, or to obtain rights and privileges for a specific child that are not generally available to all children.[231] It is established that the inherent powers cannot be used to interfere with the normal criminal process,[232] nor with the normal operation of military law.[233] At one time the courts were greatly exercised by the extent of the inherent power to shield a child from adverse publicity.[234] However, in *Re S (A Child)(Identification: Restrictions on Publication)*[235] the House of Lords ruled that the foundation of jurisdiction to restrain publicity is now properly regarded as being derived from the European Convention on Human Rights (and therefore involves balancing the right to respect for private and family life under Art 8 and the right to freedom of expression under Art 10) and not upon the inherent jurisdiction.

4 LOCAL AUTHORITY USE OF THE JURISDICTION

(a) The need to obtain leave
Although local authorities cannot look to the inherent jurisdiction as a means of putting them in charge of the child's living arrangements,[236] they can nevertheless seek to use it to resolve specific questions about the child's future. Indeed, because of the unavailability of wardship[237] and of s 8 orders (by reason of the embargoes in s 9(1) and (2)),[238] they may have to do so if the child is in their care. Nevertheless, this avenue is fettered because under s 100(3) of the 1989 Act local authorities must first obtain the court's leave to apply for any exercise of the High Court's inherent jurisdiction.[239]

(b) Criteria for granting leave
Under s 100(4)(a) the court must be satisfied that the result being sought cannot be achieved under any statutory jurisdiction. This bar applies even where the statutory remedy is contingent upon the local authority having first to obtain leave before being able to seek an order.[240] This restriction makes it difficult for an authority to obtain leave for the

---

[230] *Re J (A Minor) (Child in Care: Medical Treatment)* [1993] Fam 15, CA, and *Re C (Medical Treatment)* [1998] 1 FLR 384.

[231] See eg *Re R (A Minor) (Wardship: Restriction on Publication)* [1994] Fam 254 at 271, per Millett LJ and *R v Central Independent Television plc* [1994] Fam 192, CA.

[232] See eg *Re K (A Minor) (Wardship: Criminal Proceedings)* [1988] Fam 1.

[233] See *Re JS (A Minor) (Wardship: Boy Soldier)* [1990] Fam 182.

[234] See the discussion at 708–9 of the previous edition of this work.

[235] [2004] UKHL 47, [2005] 1 AC 593. Query whether in drawing the balance between Arts 8 and 10 it is all relevant whether the child is under the court's protective wing as suggested in *Re Z (A Minor)(Identification: Restrictions on Publication)* [1997] Fam 1?

[236] Children Act 1989 s 100(2).   [237] See above, p 896.

[238] Discussed above, pp 540–2.

[239] See *Devon County Council v B* [1997] 1 FLR 591, CA. But note that according to Charles J in *Re P (Care Orders: Injunctive Relief)* [2002] 2 FLR 385 insofar as powers are sought under s 37 of the Supreme Court Act 1981 (viz injunctive relief to support rights conferred by the Children Act 1989) leave is not required.

[240] Section, s 100(5)(b).

exercise of the inherent jurisdiction in respect of a child not in their care, since in those circumstance they could seek to obtain a prohibited steps or specific issue order under s 8[241] or possibly injunctive relief under s 37 of the Supreme Court Act 1981.[242]

In *Re R (A Minor) (Blood Transfusion)*[243] a local authority, wishing to obtain sanction for a blood transfusion for a child contrary to his parents' (who were Jehovah's Witnesses) wishes, were refused leave because, as the child was not in care, an appropriate remedy could have been obtained under s 8.[244]

Even if there is no alternative statutory remedy, s 100(4)(b) also requires the court to be satisfied that: 'there is reasonable cause to believe that if the court's inherent jurisdiction is not exercised with respect to the child he is likely to suffer significant harm'. Although this provision is in line with the need to establish at least a likelihood of significant harm before the court is entitled to intervene to make a care or supervision order,[245] it may be questioned whether this ground for leave should be so narrow. It has been pointed out[246] that, given that the local authority's objective cannot be the acquisition of parental responsibility, a less stringent test, such as the court having to be satisfied that the exercise of its inherent jurisdiction is necessary to secure the child's welfare, would not have upset the general philosophy of the 1989 Act and might have better served children's interests.

(c) Circumstances in which the criteria for giving leave might be satisfied

Local authorities are not often justified in having recourse to the inherent jurisdiction. The expectation is that, since they have parental responsibility, local authorities should make decisions for themselves.[247] Nevertheless, there will be occasions when recourse to the High Court will be appropriate. Lord Mackay LC instanced[248] the exercise of the inherent power to sanction or forbid an abortion being carried out on a child in care, where there are no other statutory means of seeking a court order and the decision, if wrong, is clearly likely to cause significant harm. In *Re W (A Minor) (Medical Treatment: Court's Jurisdiction)*[249] it was thought right to invoke the inherent jurisdiction to override a refusal of

---

[241] See eg *Re C (HIV Test)* [1999] 2 FLR 1004 in which a local authority successfully applied for a specific issue order to have a baby tested for HIV. But note the difficulties of doing so, see *Langley v Liverpool City Council* [2005] EWCA Civ 1181, [2005] 3 FCR 303 at [73]-[78] per Thorpe LJ and *Nottingham County Council v P* [1994] Fam 18, discussed above at pp 541–2.

[242] See *Re P (Care Orders: Injunctive Relief)* above—injunction granted under the Children Act 1989 to require parents to allow the child (who was being fostered) to attend school without interference.

[243] [1993] 2 FLR 757, per Booth J. This point was apparently overlooked by Thorpe J in *Re S (A Minor) (Medical Treatment)* [1993] 1 FLR 376; cf *Re O (A Minor) (Medical Treatment)* [1993] 2 FLR 149.

[244] Though Booth J was doubtful about whether a specific issue order could be granted ex parte.

[245] Under s 31 of the 1989 Act, discussed above at pp 732ff. It has been accepted that cases determining the meaning of 'likely to suffer significant harm' for the purpose of s 31 are also relevant to its meaning under s 100(4)(b)—per Connell J in *Essex County Council v Mirror Group Newspapers Ltd* [1996] 1 FLR 585. Leave was refused in that case. But as A Bainham, *Children—The Modern Law* (3rd edn) 537 points out, unlike s 31, s 100 only requires the court to be 'reasonably satisfied' that significant harm might result if the jurisdiction is not exercised.

[246] By J Eekelaar and R Dingwall (1989) 139 NLJ 217. See also N Lowe (1989) 139 NLJ 87 and Bainham above.

[247] See the Department of Health's *Guidance and Regulations*, Vol 1, paras 3.100–3.101 and the *Guidance* to the Northern Ireland Children Order, Vol 1, ch 11.

[248] (1989) 139 NLJ 505 at 507.

[249] [1993] Fam 64, CA, discussed above at pp 365ff. See also *Re C (Detention: Medical Treatment)* [1997] 2 FLR 180.

a 16-year-old anorexic child in care to consent to medical treatment. Other examples of medical treatment where leave is likely to be given include sterilisation,[250] contested cases involving emergency medical treatment of a child in care,[251] or where life saving treatment is in issue.[252]

The above medical problems are extreme examples of situations when High Court intervention might be justified, but circumstances do not always have to be so extraordinary. In *Southwark London Borough v B*[253] leave was granted to a local authority first to seek a return order of a child in care and then to enforce that order. In other cases, for example, where a local authority seeks an injunction to prevent a violent father from discovering his child's whereabouts,[254] or from molesting the child[255] or a social worker connected with the child,[256] then the inherent jurisdiction is the *only* means of obtaining the remedy and it should not be too difficult to satisfy the criteria for granting leave.

In *Devon County Council v S*[257] it was held appropriate to exercise the inherent jurisdiction to prevent a family friend (a Sch 1 offender and a paedophile) from having contact with the children and to prevent the mother from allowing the children to have contact with him, since there was no other means of obtaining such a remedy. In *Re M (Care: Leave To Interview Child)*[258] the jurisdiction was successfully invoked to permit a child in care to be interviewed by the father's solicitor with a view to preparing evidence in the father's defence in furthering criminal proceedings against him.

Although in theory the granting of leave does not automatically mean that the court must exercise its jurisdiction, given that it must be satisfied that the child is likely to suffer significant harm if the jurisdiction is not exercised[259] it would be an unusual case where leave was given and the jurisdiction not subsequently exercised.[260]

5 INDIVIDUALS' USE OF THE JURISDICTION

Although in theory it is open to individuals to invoke the inherent jurisdiction, it is unlikely to be used at all often, save perhaps in the context of international child abduction, not least because of the continued availability of wardship. Even in the one area where wardship is unavailable to individuals, namely where children are in local authority care, as we have discussed in Chapter 14,[261] the well-established embargo against using wardship to challenge local authority decisions applies equally to that use of the inherent jurisdiction.

---

[250] *Practice Note: (Minors and Mental Health Patients: Sterilisation)* [1993] 3 All ER 222.

[251] See *Re O (A Minor) (Medical Treatment)* [1993] 2 FLR 149.

[252] See eg *Re C (Medical Treatment)* [1998] 1 FLR 384, *Re T (A Minor) (Wardship: Medical Treatment)* [1997] 1 All ER 906, CA, and *Re C (A Baby)* [1996] 2 FLR 43.

[253] [1993] 2 FLR 559, CA.

[254] See *Re JT (A Minor) (Wardship: Committal to Care)* [1986] 2 FLR 107.

[255] See *Re B (A Minor) (Wardship: Child in Care)* [1975] Fam 36.

[256] This is one example of the exercise of the inherent jurisdiction known to the authors.

[257] [1994] Fam 169, per Thorpe J.   [258] [1995] 1 FLR 825, per Connell J.

[259] It is submitted that this requirement distinguishes s 100 from granting leave under s 10 to apply for a s 8 order, where it is established that there is no presumption that an order be made following the granting of leave: see above, p 546.

[260] For an example where leave was refused see *Essex County Council v Mirror Group Newspapers Ltd* [1996] 1 FLR 585, in which on the facts Connell J held the potential harm had not been established.

[261] See above, p 804.

D COMMENTARY

The restriction on the use of wardship by local authorities was one of the surprises of the original Children Bill, since it had neither been recommended by the *Review of Child Care Law* nor by the Law Commission and, indeed, flew directly in the face of a recommendation to the contrary by the Cleveland Inquiry Report.[262] Admittedly, in their earlier Working Paper on *Wards of Court*[263] the Law Commission had canvassed abolishing the jurisdiction altogether, but their final report on *Guardianship and Custody Guardianship*[264] expressly postponed making any substantial recommendations for the reform of wardship. In short, what is now s 100 of the 1989 Act was introduced on the government's own initiative[265] and without the benefit of widespread consultation.

During the passage of the Bill anxieties were expressed about the wisdom of curtailing the use of wardship by local authorities.[266] In particular there was concern that it was potentially detrimental to the interests of the children:

(1) to deprive local authorities, through the removal of the wardship option, from having direct access to the High Court;

(2) to remove the wardship safety net underpinning the statutory scheme for obtaining care or supervision orders;

(3) to curtail the power formerly enjoyed inter alia under the wardship jurisdiction to commit children into care on the court's own motion;

(4) to deprive the court of being able to use its flexible powers under wardship when making care or supervision orders.

Not all the above-mentioned concerns have proved to be well-founded in practice. In particular, the lack of direct access to the High Court in care cases has not proved problematic. The Allocation Rules seem to have been working well enough and there is little or no evidence to suggest that cases that should be heard by the High Court are not in fact being heard at that level.[267] Similarly, the experience of the Act so far is that the threshold provisions under s 31 have not been found wanting,[268] though time will tell whether they will apply to all situations where it is clearly right for a care order to be made.

On the other hand, concern has been expressed about the court's inability even to direct that the local authority institute care proceedings.[269] Such concern was voiced in *Nottingham County Council v P*[270] by Sir Stephen Brown P who said:

---

[262] Cm 412, 1988, para 16.37.   [263] Working Paper No 101, 1987.

[264] Law Com No 172, 1988, para 1.4.

[265] Lord Mackay LC explained in his Joseph Jackson Memorial Lecture (189) 139 NLJ at 507 that the government's decision to restrict its use was taken late in the day.

[266] See inter alia N Lowe (1989) 139 NLJ 87, but note the reply by J Eekelaar and R Dingwell at (1989) NLJ 217.

[267] See above, p 17.

[268] Though no doubt some would argue that the decision in *Re H (Minors) (Sexual Abuse: Standard of Proof)* [1996] AC 563, HL (discussed above pp 744ff) does expose serious flaws which perhaps the old style wardship could have countered.

[269] All the court can do is to made a direction under s 37 (discussed above at p 580) that a local authority investigate the child's circumstances.

[270] [1994] Fam 18 at 43, CA.

'This court is deeply concerned at the absence of any power to direct the authority to take steps to protect the child. In the former wardship jurisdiction it might well have been able to do so. The operation of the Children Act 1989 is entirely dependent upon the full co-operation of all those involved. This includes the courts, local authorities, social workers, and all who have to deal with children. Unfortunately, as appears from this case, if a local authority doggedly resists taking steps which are appropriate to the case of children at risk of suffering significant harm it appears that the court is powerless.'

As we have seen, the loss of the wardship jurisdiction does not deprive local authorities of all access to the High Court's inherent powers. Although more needs to be known of the de facto use of this jurisdiction,[271] case law (particularly the Court of Appeal ruling in *Re W (A Minor) (Medical Treatment: Court's Jurisdiction)*[272] that the powers under the general or residual jurisdiction are co-extensive with those under wardship, and Thorpe J's decision in *Devon County Council v S*[273] that s 100 should not be restrictively interpreted) shows that the High Court is prepared to use its inherent powers flexibly. So interpreted, the continuing availability of the wider inherent jurisdiction must go some way to allaying fears about the wisdom of restricting the ambit of the wardship jurisdiction.

Although the continued existence of both wardship and the general or residual inherent jurisdiction is undoubtedly a peculiarity of the current legal system for dealing with children and does not easily stand with a comprehensive statutory scheme, it is urged that they be retained. In the past wardship has served the interests of children well and it is evident that the High Court's inherent powers still have a useful, if small, role to play. There is no evidence that the judiciary are using their inherent powers to subvert the statutory scheme. On the contrary, they have shown restraint and only used them where no other remedy is available.

---

[271] No statistics are apparently maintained as to the number of applications made under s 100.
[272] [1993] Fam 64, CA, discussed above, p 913.   [273] [1994] Fam 169, discussed above, p 911.

17

FINANCIAL SUPPORT FOR
MEMBERS OF THE FAMILY

A INTRODUCTION

A legal obligation to provide financial support for another member of the family may be
seen as the most tangible recognition of the moral ties created by family relationships.[1]
Where such an obligation is imposed, it also sheds light on social conceptions of the appropriate scope of those ties.[2] Different societies at different times may impose the obligation upon different degrees of relationship.[3] Under the Poor Law, there was an obligation
(albeit enforceable only by the Poor Law authorities) to provide financial support for
one's grandparents and grand-children.[4] Until the nineteenth century, a child born outside wedlock was not entitled to support from either parent,[5] and an unqualified liability
on the father of such a child has existed only since 1987.[6] There is still no direct liability to
support an unmarried partner, although, through support for the child, there may be an
indirect imposition of a requirement to do so.[7]

Obligations to support may be enforced either through actions under the private law,
through both legally-recognised agreements and court actions, or through social security
law. The last is numerically more important and a more immediate and potentially long-
term source of support for families, both those which are functioning and those which
have broken down. We begin with a brief résumé of the historical development of the law;
then we examine those aspects of taxation and social security which relate directly to
family support. We then consider mechanisms whereby family members can seek support
from each other, namely under the child support scheme, private agreements and finally
court orders. Recognition of the ties of affection, regardless of marriage bonds, has in
some respects been more readily granted where a party has died, and the general question

---

[1] J Finch *Family Obligations and Social Change* (1989). But for a thought-provoking consideration of
precisely how the imposition of a legal duty of support can be justified, see S Altman, 'A Theory of Child
Support' (2003) 17 IJLPF 173.

[2] There is a growing literature on the nature of commitment and obligation (not limited to the financial)
in personal relationships: see in particular, J Eekelaar and M Maclean *The Parental Obligation* (1997) and
'Marriage and the Moral Bases of Personal Relationships' (2004) 31 JLS 510; J Lewis, *Marriage, Cohabitation
and the Law: Individualism and Obligation* (1999) and *The End of Marriage: Individualism and Intimate
Relationships* (2001).

[3] See J Millar and A Warman *Family Obligations in Europe* (1996): southern European states are more
likely to impose obligations upon the wider family; some northern European states impose obligations
upwards from children to parents, as well as downwards; Scandinavian states are less likely to impose any
support obligations at all.

[4] C Barton and G Douglas *Law and Parenthood* (1995) p 196.   [5] See below, p 917.

[6] Family Law Reform Act 1987 s 17.   [7] See below, p 973.

of how the moral support obligations of a deceased person are legally recognised is dealt with in Chapter 19.

1 THE DUTY TO MAINTAIN A SPOUSE OR CIVIL PARTNER

(a) At common law

The common law rules relating to spousal maintenance were the inevitable consequence of the doctrine of unity of legal personality.[8] The wife, lacking the capacity to hold property and to contract, could neither own even the necessities of life nor enter into a binding contract to buy them. Two principles followed. First, one of the essential obligations imposed upon a married man was to provide his wife with at least necessities; and secondly, a married woman could in no circumstances be held liable to maintain her husband. The common law rule that neither spouse could sue the other precluded her from enforcing her right by action if her husband failed to fulfil his duty to maintain her: this difficulty was overcome by giving the wife a power to pledge her husband's credit for the purchase of necessities if he did not supply her with them himself.

Scope of the husband's duty

The husband's common law duty to provide his wife with the necessities of life was prima facie complied with if he provided a home for her.[9] She had no right to separate maintenance in a separate home unless she could justify living apart from him. The fact of marriage raised a presumption that the husband was under a duty to maintain his wife. But her right to maintenance, generally speaking, was co-extensive with her right to her husband's consortium, and if her conduct released him from the duty to cohabit with her, he automatically ceased to be under a duty to maintain her.[10] A single act of adultery could automatically deprive her of her right, and if she deserted him her right was suspended until her desertion came to an end.[11]

The agency of necessity[12]

The power to pledge the husband's credit, termed the wife's agency of necessity, extended to the purchase of necessaries both for herself and for the spouses' minor children. The term 'necessaries' in this context included not only necessary goods such as food and clothing, but also necessary services such as lodging, medical attention and education. Although the wife could divest herself of the right to be maintained by her own conduct, the husband could not revoke the authority by his unilateral act.

The agency of necessity was of great importance so long as the wife was generally incompetent to contract and own property at common law. Both these disabilities were removed by the Married Women's Property Act 1882, and by the end of the nineteenth century she could obtain maintenance from her husband not only in the High Court but also much more speedily in the magistrates' court. When it also became possible for the wife

---

[8] See above, p 107.

[9] See *Price v Price* [1951] P 413, at 420–1, CA; *W v W (No 2)* [1954] P 486 at 515–16.

[10] *Chilton v Chilton* [1952] P 196 at 202.

[11] *Jones v Newtown and Llanidloes Guardians* [1920] 3 KB 381.

[12] For examples of the tactical use of this power, see L Stone *Broken Lives: Separation and Divorce in England 1660–1857* (1993) passim.

to obtain immediate assistance through the social security system, and to claim the benefits of the National Health Service and the legal aid scheme, the doctrine became an anachronism and was eventually abolished by the Matrimonial Proceedings and Property Act 1970.[13]

(b) The current position

Although the common law duty on the husband to maintain his wife still remains,[14] the means by which maintenance can be claimed by a spouse are now governed entirely by statute. Unlike the common law it is open to either spouse to claim maintenance from the other, and since claims for maintenance no longer depend upon the duty to cohabit, the commission of adultery or desertion is no longer a bar. The two statutes governing maintenance between separated spouses are the Domestic Proceedings and Magistrates' Courts Act 1978 and the Matrimonial Causes Act 1973 s 27. For civil partners the equivalent provision is contained in the Civil Partnership Act 2004 Schs 5 (Part 9) and 6.

2 PARENTS' DUTY TO MAINTAIN CHILDREN OF SPOUSES OR CIVIL PARTNERS

At common law a father was under a duty to maintain only his legitimate minor children and to provide them with food, clothing, lodging and other necessities. But the duty was wholly unenforceable. A child has never had an agency of necessity[15] and a father was under no legal obligation to reimburse a person who has supplied his child with necessaries. Unless he constituted the child his agent, the only way in which he could be compelled to fulfil his obligation was through the wife's agency of necessity, which extended to the purchase of necessities for the children of the marriage as well as for herself.[16] With the abolition of the wife's agency of necessity, the common law position is now of purely historical interest.

As with maintaining spouses and civil partners, the means by which financial provision can be claimed for children is governed by statute. Where it is sought to obtain financial provision for children alone, recourse must usually now be had to the Child Support Act 1991. Where this Act does not apply,[17] Sch 1 to the Children Act 1989 provides an alternative (and more flexible) jurisdiction. The statutes referred to above also contain powers to award maintenance for children, provided, again, that the Child Support Act is inapplicable.

3 SUPPORT OBLIGATIONS OUTSIDE MARRIAGE OR CIVIL PARTNERSHIP

Reflecting the common law position, it remains the case that even between cohabiting adults there is no duty to maintain, although, as we shall see, in assessing the level of

---

[13] Section 41. This followed the recommendations of the Law Commission: see Law Com No 25, paras 108–109 and Appendix II, paras 41–52 and 108. Section 41 was repealed by the Matrimonial Causes Act 1973 Sch 3, and not re-enacted.

[14] At attempt to abolish the common law duty was made by a private member's bill, the Family Law (Property and Maintenance) Bill in 2005–6. The bill did not progress.

[15] *Mortimore v Wright* (1840) 6 M & W 482.   [16] *Bazeley v Forder* (1868) LR 3 QB 559.

[17] See below, p 947.

maintenance to be paid by an unmarried parent for any child, an element to cover the costs of the carer may be included.[18]

With regard to children born outside marriage, at common law neither the father nor the mother was liable for maintenance.[19] Although the Poor Law legislation cast upon the mother the obligation of maintaining her illegitimate child, she could still not recover the expenses of maintenance from the father in the absence of any contract to that effect between them.[20] A statute of 1576 empowered justices to make an order against the unmarried father for the maintenance of an illegitimate child charged on the parish,[21] but it was not until the Poor Law Amendment Act 1844 that the mother was given the power to apply for an order for maintenance to be paid to herself. The law was amended and consolidated in the Bastardy Laws Amendment Act 1872 and again in the Affiliation Proceedings Act 1957. Under this legislation the right of unmarried mothers to claim from alleged fathers was circumscribed. For example, applications could only be made to magistrates' courts, applicants had to be 'single' mothers, claims had to be brought within three years of the child's birth,[22] and the mother's evidence had to be corroborated. These limitations were removed by the Family Law Reform Act 1987, now contained in the Children Act 1989, and, as we shall discuss, the Child Support Act 1991 has gone still further in equalising the law governing the support of children born inside and outside marriage.

4 ENFORCEMENT OF THE DUTY TO MAINTAIN

(a) Maintenance agreements

Once it was accepted that separation agreements were not contrary to public policy,[23] it became possible for a husband to enter into an enforceable contract to pay maintenance for his wife and his children. Now either spouse or civil partner may covenant to pay maintenance to the other, and either parent can covenant to pay maintenance for their children. Their rights are basically governed by the general principles of contract law but, as we shall see, some special rules apply to maintenance agreements.[24]

(b) State support

Broadly speaking, anyone over the age of 18 whose income falls below the relevant sum laid down by the legislation is entitled to apply for tax credits if in work, or welfare benefits (income support or job-seeker's allowance) if not in work or, in respect of children, child tax credits.[25] A spouse or partner without support will frequently turn to the state before taking any other action. If support is given to a party to a marriage or civil partnership, it is

---

[18] See below, p 973.   [19] *Ruttinger v Temple* (1863) 4 B & S 491.
[20] As to agreements to pay maintenance, see below, pp 955 et seq.   [21] 18 Eliz 1 c 3.
[22] Unless the father was voluntarily paying money for the child.
[23] See eg *Merritt v Merritt* [1970] 2 All ER 760, CA; *Re Windle* [1975] 3 All ER 987.
[24] See below, p 952.
[25] Determination of which benefit or credit is appropriate in different circumstances, and at what level of payment, is dependent upon the relevant legislation, discussed fully in CPAG, *Welfare Benefits and Tax Credits Handbook* (7th ed, 2005). The text below deals only with the position concerning families.

recoverable from that person's spouse or civil partner, and if support is given to any child under the age of 16, it is recoverable from either or both parents.[26]

(c) Obtaining maintenance from the courts

Until 1878 only the ecclesiastical courts or their successors, the Divorce Court and the High Court, could make orders for maintenance. The Matrimonial Causes Act 1878 enabled a criminal court, before which a married man had been convicted of an aggravated assault upon his wife, to make an order that she should no longer be bound to cohabit with him if it felt that her future safety was in peril.[27] The court could also order a husband to pay maintenance to a wife in whose favour such a separation order was made, and vest in her the legal custody of any children of the marriage under the age of 10. The powers of the magistrates' courts were gradually extended, although limits on the amount of maintenance which could be ordered to be paid each week remained until 1968 (£7.50 for a spouse and £3.50 for a child). After the divorce law was reformed in 1971, removing the emphasis upon marital misconduct and extending the court's powers to deal with the spouses' finances and property, the jurisdiction to order maintenance was also reformed to bring it into line with that approach.[28]

The separate limits for spouse and child illustrate the earlier lack of recognition that their needs cannot be divorced from one another.[29] The current family jurisdiction, however, has learnt this lesson, in providing that in deciding what orders to make for a *spouse or civil partner*, magistrates must treat the welfare of any child of the family as the first consideration.[30]

(d) The child support scheme

So far as maintenance for children is concerned, dissatisfaction with the effectiveness of the court system to collect amounts of maintenance which would be sufficient to provide realistic levels of support for them, and concern at the dramatic increase in the number of single-parent families dependent upon state benefits,[31] led to the introduction of the Child Support Act 1991, which came into effect in 1993. This set up an entirely new system of assessing and collecting maintenance for children, through the medium of a government agency, the Child Support Agency. The Act deprives the courts of jurisdiction to order maintenance for children in many instances, and permits the Agency to pursue non-resident parents for child support, often regardless of any prior settlements made on a divorce. No

---

[26] See below, p 925.

[27] See AJ Hammerton *Cruelty and Companionship: Conflict in Nineteenth-Century Married Life* (1992) pp 52–67.

[28] See Law Com No 77, *Report on Matrimonial Proceedings in Magistrates' Courts* and the Domestic Proceedings and Magistrates' Courts Act 1978.

[29] See also the discussion by J Eekelaar and M Maclean *Maintenance After Divorce* (1986) pp 21–8.

[30] Domestic Proceedings and Magistrates' Courts Act 1978 s 3(1) (or Civil Partnership Act 2004 Sch 6 para 4); the corresponding power of the county court or High Court under s 27 of the Matrimonial Causes Act 1973 (or Civil Partnership Act 2004 Sch 5 para 43(3)) imposes that duty only where an order is sought for the *child*: s 27(3). The Child Support Act 1991, however, represents a retrograde step in seeking once again to attempt to deal with one aspect of family finances—child maintenance—in isolation from the rest. See below, p 937.

[31] White Paper *Children Come First* Cm 1264 (1990) Vol 2, p i.

distinction is drawn between children whose parents were married to each other and those whose were not, but the basis of liability under the Act is parenthood,[32] so that the maintenance of step-children remains a matter for the courts and private law.

B STATE SUPPORT [33]

1 INTRODUCTION

The state may provide financial support to individuals and families through two main mechanisms. On the one hand, it may provide tax allowances (or 'credits') so that the beneficiary pays less tax than would otherwise be the case, and hence retains more of his income for expenditure on his own and his family's wants.[34] Entitlement to the tax credit depends upon earning, or having, an income of a size at which tax is payable and upon meeting the particular criteria (such as marital or parental status) laid down. On the other hand, the state may establish a social security system, whereby 'benefits' are paid to eligible applicants as a cash sum to meet their particular needs. Entitlement to such benefits may depend upon past contributions (the 'national insurance' approach), or simply upon fulfilment of criteria based on the particular needs to be met, such as disability or poverty.

Tax credits have the psychological and political advantages of presenting state support of those in need as if it were a mechanism which costs the state nothing (because what is done is to leave the recipient with more take-home pay) rather than as a direct expense for the state (because, although the amount of benefit paid to the recipient may be calculated according to his wages, it comes directly from the state). In reality, the state 'pays' under either system. However, tax credits carry less stigma to recipients and 'reinforce the distinction between the rewards of work and remaining on welfare'.[35]

The present social security system derives in part from the Beveridge reforms enacted in the National Assistance Act 1948 which abolished the old Poor Law.[36] Since then, however, there have been substantial changes. The present structure of the benefits of particular relevance to families is laid down in the Social Security Contributions and Benefits Act 1992 and Social Security Administration Act 1992 but the election of a Labour Government in 1997 led to a further review of the social security system and the development of a strategy intended to encourage more people into work and out of dependence upon state benefits.[37] One of the key elements in this strategy was to provide tax credits, rather than social security payments, as the bridge between total dependence upon benefits and take-up of full-time employment.[38]

---

[32] Child Support Act 1991 s 54.

[33] See G Douglas, 'The Family, Gender, and Social Security' in N Harris (ed), *Social Security Law in Context* (2000).

[34] For a discussion of the use of the tax system to meet welfare needs, see J Kvist and A Sinfield 'Comparing Tax Welfare States' in M May, E Brunsdon and G Craig (eds) *Social Policy Review 9* (1997).

[35] HM Treasury, *Work Incentives* (1998) para 3.19.

[36] For a full discussion of the historical context, see N Harris (ed) *Social Security Law in Context* (2000) Chapters 3–7.

[37] Department of Social Security, *New Ambitions for Our Country: A New Contract for Welfare* Cm 3805 (1998).

[38] *Work Incentives* (above) ch 3.

2 SUPPORT THROUGH TAX CREDITS

(a) Tax allowances

The assumption, at one time well-founded, that a married man would be expected to meet the bulk, if not all, of the financial needs of his wife and family out of his own income, was reflected by the grant, in 1918, of a married man's tax allowance enabling him to start to pay tax at a higher threshold than a single person. In 1990, in a belated acknowledgement of women's financial contributions to the living standards of their families, all married women became separately taxed from their husbands, and the allowance became a 'married couple's' allowance, payable to either spouse (although it continues to be paid to the husband unless the couple request its transfer to the wife, or apportionment between both of them).[39] The allowance is now only payable where one of the couple[40] is over 70 and its value has been steadily eroded, being payable at only 10% compared with the basic rate of tax at 22%.

(b) Working tax credit

In 1999, the government introduced 'Working Families Tax Credit' to replace the main in-work benefit to lower income families ('Family Credit').[41] The aim was to encourage the jobless to take employment, even at low wages, by providing, in effect, a government subsidy or wage supplement through the tax collection system. The tax credit was also assumed to carry less stigma than receiving a separately paid social security benefit. It has since been superseded by working tax credit,[42] which is also available to single people with no dependents, and child tax credit which is payable where the claimant or partner have at least one dependent child or qualifying young person for whom they are responsible. Credits are administered by HM Revenue and Customs, and paid into the recipient's bank or building society account. Assessment and payment are made on a yearly basis. A couple (which includes those who are married, civil partners, or living together as spouses or civil partners)[43] must claim jointly. Where a married couple or civil partners are separated 'in circumstances in which the separation is likely to be permanent',[44] either may claim. A claim may be made if the claimant (or partner) is responsible for a child[45] and works at least 16 hours per week,[46] or has no child but works 30 hours per week and is aged 25 or over. The claimant's annual income is compared with the 'income threshold figure'[47]

---

[39] Finance Act 1988, which came into effect on 6 April 1990. See OP Wylie, *Taxation of the Family* (4th ed, 1998) ch 1.

[40] Including civil partners, as introduced by the 2005 Budget.

[41] HM Treasury, *The Modernisation of Britain's Tax and Benefit System: Number 3 The Working Families Tax Credit and work incentives* (1998).

[42] Tax Credits Act 2002 s 10. See OP Wylie, *Child Tax Credit and Working Tax Credit* (2nd ed, 2004).

[43] Ibid s 3(3)(5A) as amended by the Civil Partnership Act 2004 Sch 24, para 144. A 'polygamous unit' must claim jointly with all partners, but a person's entitlement ceases if he or she becomes a member of such a unit or there is any change in the people who are members of that unit: Tax Credits (Polygamous Marriages) Regulations SI 2003/742.

[44] Tax Credits Act 2002 s 3(5).

[45] Up to the age of 16, or 19 if in full-time non-advanced education: Tax Credits Act 2002 s 8(3). For the meaning of 'responsible for' see below at p 921.

[46] Working Tax Credit (Entitlement and Maximum Rate) Regulations SI 2002/2005 reg 4. There are other bases of claim.

[47] Tax Credits (Income Thresholds and Determination of Rates) Regulations SI 2002/2008.

(£5,220 in 2006–7) and, if below that level, the maximum amount of working tax credit will be payable on top. If the annual income exceeds the threshold, the maximum working tax credit is reduced by 37% of the excess until it disappears. No account is taken of any capital that the claimant has, but income from capital is counted.

The amount of the maximum working tax credit is made up of a number of 'elements'[48] —a 'basic element' (worth £1,665 in 2006–7) and others depending upon circumstances, such as a couple or lone parent element (£1,640), an element if the hours worked amount to 30 per week or more (£680) and, importantly, a child care element which covers 80% of the average weekly child care costs incurred by the claimant up to a maximum of £300 per week for two or more children (hence the actual maximum allowance is £240 per week). This child care element is paid directly to the person mainly responsible for caring for the child, in response to concerns that otherwise, the credit might simply make the wage earner better off, with no consequential benefit to the family.[49]

(c) Child tax credit

It will be noted that the elements in working tax credit do not include an amount for any children in the family. This is because there is a separate child tax credit to cater for these. As above, the child or qualifying young person must be under the age of 16 or 19 (if in non-advanced education). The claimant must be 'responsible' for the child,[50] ie the child must normally live with the claimant or the claimant has the main responsibility for him or her. There is no statutory definition of 'normally living with', but Inland Revenue guidance[51] suggests that it covers situations of temporary absence such as being away at school or on holiday. Where parents live apart but share the care of a child (eg through a shared residence arrangement),[52] each could argue that the child 'normally' lives with him or her. However, the regulations do not permit more than one payment of child tax credit for a child, nor the splitting of such payment. In these circumstances, if the parents cannot agree who should claim, the regulations use the 'main responsibility' test under which the Revenue will have regard to the existence of any court orders specifying the arrangements; how many days per week the child lives with the claimant as compared with the other carer; who pays for the child's food, clothes and pocket money; where the child's clothes and toys are kept; who is the main contact for school, etc; who does the child's laundry; and who looks after the child when he or she is ill.[53] In *Hockenjos v Secretary of State for Social Security*[54] the claimant of a social security benefit (Jobseeker's Allowance—'JSA') was denied the additions then payable for children (now claimable through child tax credit), because he shared care with the mother, who was the recipient of child benefit,

---

[48] Ibid, passim.

[49] Ibid, para 2.12; *Work Incentives* (1998) para 3.25. The child care element may also be paid as vouchers which can be handed over directly to the provider of the child care services.

[50] Child Tax Credit Regulations SI 2002/2007 reg 3(1).

[51] Inland Revenue, *Tax Credits Technical Manual*, quoted in CPAG *Welfare Benefits and Tax Credits Handbook* (7th edition 2005) pp 1318, 1319.

[52] See above p 516.

[53] Ibid. Cf the test for child benefit, below p 927. Where the child is being accommodated by the local authority (see above p 703), is in custody, or is awarded child tax credit (for a child of her own) or a welfare benefit in her own right, the claimant is ineligible.

[54] [2004] EWCA Civ 1749, [2005] 1 FCR 286, see especially paras [49], [50].

which determined the issue of eligibility for the child additions in JSA.[55] Statistical analysis had found that 92% of men who shared the care of their children for at least 104 nights a year could not obtain child additions to income-based JSA because they were not in receipt of child benefit and that 8% of women who similarly shared care could not obtain the additions for the same reason.[56] The Court of Appeal held that this outcome was contrary to the Equal Treatment Directive,[57] since it discriminated against fathers. It may be queried whether the more flexible approach to 'responsibility' taken in the child tax credit scheme avoids this conclusion.

As with working tax credit, the amount of credit payable is again calculated according to the elements applicable to the claimant. These include a family element (£545 in 2006–7) and a child element of £1,765 for each child, with additions if the child is disabled. The amount of child tax credit payable is calculated as above in comparison with the annual income threshold figure. Where the claimant is eligible only for child tax credit, this is £14,155. Where he or she is eligible for working tax credit as well, the threshold is again £5,220 and once more, the taper is applied to any excess of income over the threshold.[58] As with the child care element of working tax credit, child tax credit is paid to the main carer of the child.

3 SOCIAL SECURITY BENEFITS[59]

(a) Introduction

Social security benefits comprise: (a) contributory benefits dependent upon the National Insurance contributions paid by the beneficiary,[60] such as contribution-based Jobseeker's Allowance and retirement pension; (b) non-contributory income-related benefits dependent upon a means test, such as income support; and (c) non-contributory, non income-related benefits—'universal' benefits to which all who fit within the category are entitled, most notably child benefit.

Contributory benefits are not discussed in detail here, since they do not relate directly to support for families.[61] However, it should be noted that the requirement to have made contributions to be eligible for the benefit (or for the full benefit) means that those unable to build up contributions, in particular women who give up work to have children,[62] may be disadvantaged. They may be ineligible for a full retirement pension based on their own

---

[55] Jobseekers Allowance Regulations, SI 1996/207, reg 77. See further below p 923.

[56] [2004] EWCA Civ 1749, [2005] 1 FCR 286 at para 14.   [57] EEC 79/7 Art 4.

[58] Entitlement to income support, income-based job-seekers allowance or pension credit gives an eligible claimant automatic entitlement to the maximum child tax credit applicable to his or her circumstances. There is an upper income eligibility threshold of £50,000 pa although it may still be possible to continue to receive credit above that level due to family circumstances. See CPAG *Welfare Benefits and Tax Credits Handbook* (7th ed, 2005) p 1366.

[59] See N Wikeley and A Ogus, *Wikeley, Ogus and Barendt's The Law of Social Security* (5th edn, 2002); N Harris (ed), *Social Security Law in Context* (2000).

[60] The benefits may also be payable to a spouse or civil partner or dependant of the contributor.

[61] For a detailed account, see Wikeley and Ogus, op cit, Harris (ed) op cit.

[62] Interrupted contributions may be supplemented by counting years of 'home responsibility': see Social Security Contributions and Benefits Act 1992 s 60.

contributions, and be dependent upon their husband's contribution record, in which case a reduced pension is payable to them. Women's career breaks, lower average earnings and concentration in lower status employment all combine to mean that they are also less likely to have access to valuable occupational or personal pensions.[63] If their marriages are terminated by divorce, they were, until 1995, unable to take advantage of the former husband's pension unless nominated by him as a beneficiary.[64] They will accordingly be more likely to have recourse to the non-contributory income-related benefits, to which we now turn.

Income-related (or means-tested) benefits are intended to provide a safety net through which no person should fall into destitution. There are two main types of such benefits relevant to families where the claimant is not working:[65] Income Support and income-based Jobseekers' Allowance (JSA). JSA is the benefit paid to those who are required to be available for employment as a condition of receiving benefit.[66] In two-parent families where neither adult is working, JSA will be the main benefit relied upon. The partner of a recipient of benefits such as JSA may be required to attend a 'work-focused interview' if they are not themselves working and the claimant has been in receipt of the benefit for at least 26 weeks.[67] Failure to attend may result in a lower rate of benefit being paid. Lone parents are not required to be available for employment and hence do not receive JSA, but may instead be eligible for Income Support.[68] JSA is not discussed in detail here, since it applies to all those who are unemployed and required to seek work.[69]

Income support is frequently the first line of support for a parent who is on her own with a child and unable to work full-time when her partner has left her. If she is later able to obtain a job, but one which is low-paid, she may be eligible for working tax credit and child tax credit to boost her income. The government aims to reduce dependence upon JSA and Income Support by encouraging the take-up of paid work. Such a strategy is said to reflect what single parents themselves want, and to teach a more positive attitude to work and independence among children.[70]

(b) Income support[71]

Eligibility

Section 124 of the Social Security Contributions and Benefits Act 1992 (as amended) together with the Income Support (General) Regulations 1987 r 21(3) provide that, to be eligible for Income Support and other income-related benefits, a claimant must be present in Great Britain and habitually resident in the United Kingdom,[72] and at least 16 years old.

---

63 See M Maclean *Surviving Divorce* (1991), A Perry et al *How parents cope financially on separation and divorce* (1999), G Douglas, 'The Family, Gender, and Social Security' in N Harris (ed), *Social Security Law in Context* (2000).

64 See now pension sharing and pension attachment orders, discussed below, pp 1000 and 1001.

65 Full-time: the claimant may claim where working up to 16 hours per week.

66 Jobseekers Act 1995 ss 1, 6.

67 Social Security Administration Act 1992 s 2AA (inserted by Employment Act 2002 s 49).

68 Income Support (General) Regulations 1987 reg 4ZA and Sch 1B, para 1.

69 For detailed consideration, see CPAG, op cit Chapters 15, 16, 32.

70 White Paper, *Children Come First*, Vol 1, Cm 1264, para 6.1. Department of Social Security, *New Ambitions for Our Country: A New Contract for Welfare* Cm 3805 ch 3, para 13.

71 See Wikeley and Ogus, op cit ch 8.

72 Or the Republic of Ireland, Channel Islands or the Isle of Man; the habitual residence requirement was added by reg 21(3) as amended by SI 1994/1807.

The claimant claims not just for himself or herself but for the spouse, civil partner or partner living with the claimant. However, since 6 April 2004, new claimants with children must claim for them through child tax credit. The claimant must:

(a) have no income, or an income below the 'applicable amount';

(b) have no capital, or capital below a prescribed amount;

(c) not be engaged in remunerative work;

(d) not be entitled to a Jobseeker's Allowance; and

(e) not be receiving relevant education.

The applicable amount is set by regulations, and comprises (a) the 'personal allowance' for which the claimant would be eligible, for example, allowance for a single adult (£57.45 per week in 2006–7), or married couple or civil partners (£90.10); (b) appropriate 'premiums' (for example, an extra sum for disability),[73] and (c) assessable housing costs made up of mortgage interest repayments, so long as these are not regarded as 'excessive'.[74]

If the claimant's income is below the 'applicable amount', the benefit received is the difference between the two sums. Apart from the claimant's home and certain other assets, capital will be taken into account in assessing eligibility. Capital above £16,000 renders the claimant ineligible for Income Support, while that between £6,000[75] and £16,000 will be treated as generating income, which will then reduce the amount of benefit payable.[76]

Since the claim is for the family unit, the income and capital of the couple are 'aggregated'.[77] Spouses or civil partners no longer living together may claim separately, as they live in separate units. In contrast, a couple living together as husband and wife or as civil partners[78] will be treated as a couple and their resources aggregated. The investigation of whether a claimant is living with another adult *as husband and wife* (or civil partner) is a controversial and complicated exercise, involving, as it may, investigation of intimate relationships and sexual conduct.[79] The income to be taken into account includes net earnings (with the first £20 per week disregarded for those who are lone parents)[80] and

---

[73] The 'family premium' which used to be paid is not payable for new claimants with children after 6 April 2004: The Income Support (General) Regulations 1987 Sch 2, para 11 (as amended).

[74] Capital payments are not included. The maximum loan which may be covered is £100,000. Where a new claimant took out a mortgage after 2 October 1995, no payments on it will be made for the first 39 weeks of income support. If the new claimant took out the mortgage before that date, or is a lone parent and claims income support because her spouse or partner has left her, no payments will be made on it for the first eight weeks, and payments will be limited to half the interest instalments for the next 18 weeks. Interest is paid at a standard rate rather than that which may actually be charged by the mortgagee: Income Support (General) Regulations 1987 Sch 3, paras 1, 8 and 11.

[75] A higher limit applies to those living in residential care or nursing homes: Income Support (General) Regulations 1987 reg 2(1).

[76] Income Support (General) Regulations 1987 reg 53.

[77] Social Security Contributions and Benefits Act 1992 s 136.

[78] Social Security Contributions and Benefits Act 1992 s 137 as amended by Civil Partnership Act 2004 Sch 24 para 46.

[79] See Ogus, Barendt and Wikeley, op cit pp 389–93, and see *Re J (Income Support: Cohabitation)* [1995] 1 FLR 660, *Kimber v Kimber* [2000] 1 FLR 383. See above p 102.

[80] Income Support (General) Regulations 1987 Sch 8, para 5.

all other gross income. Maintenance payments for a spouse or civil partner are fully taken into account and reduce Income Support entitlement pound for pound.[81] The first £10 per week of maintenance payments for a child may be disregarded in certain circumstances.[82]

Claimants must not be engaged in remunerative work, which for these purposes normally means 'work in which a person is engaged ... for not less than 16 hours a week being work for which payment is made ...'[83] Limited part-time work can therefore be undertaken, although earnings received will affect the amount of Income Support payable.[84]

'Liable relatives'

Under s 78(6) and s 105(3) of the Social Security Administration Act 1992:[85]

'(a) a man shall be liable to maintain his wife or civil partner and any children of whom he is the father; and

(b) a woman shall be liable to maintain her husband or civil partner and any children of whom she is the mother.'

Although liability to support a *spouse or civil partner* terminates on divorce or dissolution, liability to support children continues, and may not be excluded by a consent order.[86] From April 1993, the Child Support Act 1991[87] in practice superseded this provision where children are concerned. Liability under both the Social Security Administration Act and under the Child Support Act exists only in relation to a person's own children; there is no concept of 'child of the family' as in family proceedings.[88]

The Social Security Administration Act remains relevant in respect of spouses or civil partners. A 'liable relative' may be traced by the authorities, and asked to meet the obligation to maintain. Failure to make a contribution may result in proceedings being taken against the liable person in the magistrates' court under s 105, or s 106 of the 1992 Act or s 23 of the Jobseekers Act 1995. The former is a criminal prosecution whereby a person who persistently refuses or neglects to maintain himself, or anyone he is liable to maintain,

---

[81] Income Support (General) Regulations 1987 reg 55.

[82] These are that the claimant receives child support under the 'new rules' (see below p 939), gets child maintenance by agreement or court order paid for the first time after 3 March 2003, or gets voluntary child maintenance for the first time on or after 16 February 2004: Social Security (Child Maintenance Premium) Amendment Regulations SI 2004/98 reg 1(3).

[83] Income Support (General) Regulations 1987 reg 5(1).

[84] Interestingly, and reinforcing stereotyped images of women's work, childminding in the claimant's own home is not treated as remunerative work, and only one-third of the net earnings from childminding are taken into account in assessing the claimant's income: ibid, reg 6(1)(b).

[85] As amended by the Civil Partnership Act 2004 Sch 24 paras 61, 62.

[86] *Hulley v Thompson* [1981] 1 All ER 1128. Such an order ought not to be made, given the courts' recognition of the continuing parental obligation to maintain, eg in *Minton v Minton* [1979] AC 593, HL. The Child Support Act 1991 s 9(4) provides that any provision in an agreement which purports to restrict the right of a person to apply for a maintenance calculation under that Act shall be void.

[87] Discussed below, p 932.   [88] See p 338.

is guilty of an offence. Proceedings are rarely taken.[89] The latter two are civil proceedings which result in an order to pay a sum, weekly or otherwise, to the Secretary of State to meet the benefit being claimed.

(c) The Social Fund[90]

Income Support and income-based JSA are intended to meet the weekly needs of those with no, or very low income. The 'applicable amounts' do not take into account the need for larger purchases, such as for furniture, or even substantial items of clothing such as a winter coat. Before the social security reforms in the mid-1980s, help to purchase such items could be obtained by seeking a 'single payment', eligibility for which was subject to highly complex rules. Refusals led to numerous appeals to social security appeal tribunals. The cost of meeting single payments grew rapidly and was 'demand-led'. The Social Fund operates quite differently. It has two parts. One is non-discretionary, based on regulations, and provides maternity, funeral, cold weather or winter fuel payments to those on Income Support, income-based JSA, child tax credit above a certain level or working tax credit which includes a disability element.[91] Such payments are in the form of grants. The other is a discretionary fund available to Income Support or income-based JSA[92] claimants for the provision (usually)[93] of repayable *loans* for 'important intermittent expenses' (for example, essential furniture, bedclothes, reconnection charges) or for expenses caused by an emergency or a disaster (in which case, the recipient need not have been in receipt of other benefits), or to meet short-term needs or living expenses for a period not exceeding 14 days. There is no right of appeal to an independent tribunal against decisions taken by Social Fund Officers in relation to the discretionary fund.[94]

4 CHILD BENEFIT[95]

Direct financial aid to assist families bringing up children was proposed as long ago as 1796 by William Pitt. However, it was not until the Family Allowance Act 1945 that such a

---

[89] To improve the recovery of maintenance from absent parents, s 107 (as amended by the Civil Partnership Act 2004 Sch 24 para 63) provides that, where a parent is claiming income support for herself and her children, the Department may seek recovery from the other parent of an amount to meet the claimant's income support personal allowance, *even though the parents have not entered into a marriage or civil partnership with each other so that there is no liability to support the claimant herself.* If the claimant ceases to claim benefit, the order may be transferred to her under s 107(3), but the element covering her allowance will not be included. This provision therefore enables the Department to recover more of the actual costs of supporting the lone parent. Furthermore, s 108 enables it to enforce a *private* maintenance order obtained by the claimant, even without her consent to such action being taken. There is usually little incentive for a benefits recipient to take or enforce private proceedings (as the maintenance recovered simply reduced the benefit she would receive), but s 108 sidesteps this difficulty, by enabling the Department to pursue the absent parent of its own volition. It is unclear if any use is made of these provisions.

[90] See T Buck *The Social Fund: Law and Practice* (2nd ed 2000); Wikeley and Ogus, op cit, ch 13; S Rahilly, 'Social Security, Money Management, and Debt' in N Harris (ed) *Social Security Law in Context* (2000) ch 14.

[91] Or pension credit.   [92] Or those receiving Pension Credit.

[93] Community care *grants* may be available, inter alia, to relieve 'exceptional pressures' on the claimant or his or her family, eg to enable the claimant to set up home after relationship breakdown.

[94] Although independent Social Fund Inspectors, answerable to the Social Fund Commissioner, can review decisions of Social Fund Officers: see *Annual Reports of the Social Fund Commissioner.*

[95] See Wikeley and Ogus, op cit, ch 18.

scheme was put into practice. Under that Act family allowance was paid to the mother, but only to families with at least two children. The amount hardly changed in 20 years. Tax allowances for all children were also available to set against income tax. Since married women were then less likely to be in paid employment than is now the case, such allowances generally enhanced the take-home pay of the father, and it was argued that the children did not always receive the benefit of them. Integration and reform of the two schemes were called for in the late 1960s, and finally achieved under the Child Benefit Act 1975, after which child tax allowances were phased out.

The basic scheme is that Child Benefit is paid as a flat-rate benefit regardless of need for each child (although a higher amount is paid for the first),[96] usually to the mother.

Section 141 of the Social Security Contributions and Benefits Act 1992[97] provides:

'A person who is responsible for one or more children or qualifying young persons in any week shall be entitled . . . to a benefit . . . for that week in respect of the child or qualifying young person, or each of the children or qualifying young person for whom he is responsible.'[98]

Under s 143 a person is treated as responsible for a child (or young person) if he has the child living with him or is contributing to the cost of providing for the child at a weekly rate not less than the Child Benefit payable for that child. Where care of a child is split between parents, for example where there is a shared residence order, or extensive staying contact, they may agree between themselves who is to receive the benefit, or, in default of agreement, the Secretary of State may decide.[99] The recipient need not be a parent of the child, or even a relative, and there may be many cases where there are competing claims. Schedule 10 sets out an order of priority, so that a person having the child living with him or her has priority over a person contributing to the cost of providing for the child; a wife has priority over her husband where they are residing together; a parent takes priority over a non-parent; and a mother takes priority over an unmarried father where they are residing together. It has been noted above that when these rules were applied to income-based JSA, they were found to be contrary to European law as they are discriminatory against fathers.[100] Although the Equal Treatment Directive does not apply to child benefit, since this is not a benefit providing protection against the risks covered in the Directive, the question whether they might infringe the European Convention on Human Rights also arises. In *R (Barber) v Secretary of State for Work and Pensions*[101] such an argument was rejected, on the basis that the claimant was not discriminated against directly because he was treated no worse than any other person seeking a re-assignment of child benefit, and that there was insufficient evidence to show indirect discrimination. However, the statistics

---

[96] Thus reversing the old family allowance rule excluding the first child altogether: Child Benefit and Social Security (Fixing and Adjustment of Rates) Regulations 1976 (as amended) reg 2(1).

[97] As amended by the Child Benefit Act 2005 s 1(1).

[98] A child is defined by s 142 as a person under the age of 16; and a qualifying young person includes people under the age of 20 and receiving full-time non-advanced education or approved training.

[99] Social Security Contributions and Benefits Act 1992 Sch 10, para 5.

[100] *Hockenjos v Secretary of State for Social Security* [2004] EWCA Civ 1749, [2005] 1 FCR 286, discussed above at p 921.

[101] [2002] EWHC 1915 (Admin) [2002] 2 FLR 1181.

presented in *Hockenjos* suggest that such evidence does exist, and could form the basis for a renewed challenge under art 8 of the ECHR taken with Art 14.

Child benefit is paid at the rate of £17.45 per week for the first child (in 2006–7) and £11.70 for each successive child. Until 1998, an additional amount was payable in respect of the first child of a lone parent, in recognition of the extra financial burden on lone parents, but the then Conservative government proposed phasing it out, so as not to advantage lone parents over two-parent families, and the Labour government adopted this proposal.[102]

Child Benefit is not taxable and is not taken into account when assessing eligibility for working tax credit or child tax credit or claims made from 6 April 2004, for Income Support or income-based JSA.

5 CHILD TRUST FUNDS [103]

A rather different approach to family support was introduced by the Child Trust Funds Act 2004. Rather than focusing on present need, the legislation was enacted to encourage families to establish a savings account for children when can be accessed on reaching adulthood. The Act provides for all children born after 31 August 2002[104] to receive a voucher worth £250, with children from low income families (those in receipt of maximum CTC) or who are in care receiving an additional £250.[105] A further sum may be paid by the government when the child reaches the age of seven, but the real aim of the scheme is to encourage families themselves to add to the child's account throughout the child's dependency, up to a maximum of £1,200 per year.[106] Interest and gains made during this time will be tax-free.[107] The money accrued will become the child's, to do with as he or she wishes, on reaching the age of 18. The voucher is sent to the person eligible to receive child benefit for the child[108] and it must be placed in an account offered by an approved financial institution. Anyone (other than a local authority, or a parent under 16) with parental responsibility (known as the 'responsible person')[109] may open the account for the child, although this cannot be done jointly, and it has been suggested that this may be a source of some dispute between separated parents.[110] Where there is no responsible person or that person fails to open an account within 12 months of being sent the voucher, HM Revenue and Customs may do so for the child.[111] Where the child's parent is herself

---

[102] 'We believe that additional support should be provided for children in poorer families on the basis of the identifiable needs of children, not on whether there happens to be one parent or two. So there is no case for a one-parent benefit, and the Government will not return to that approach' (DSS, *New Ambitions for Our Country: A New Contract for Welfare* Cm 3805, p 57). Lone parents who received the addition before 5 July 1998 may still be eligible. In 2006–7, the additional amount is worth 10p per week.

[103] See N Wikeley, 'Child Trust Funds—Asset-based Welfare or a Recipe for Increased Inequality?' [2004] 11 Journal of Social Security Law 189 and 'Child Trust Funds—What Will Yours Grow Into?' [2005] Fam Law 285.

[104] Child Trust Funds Act 2004 s 2(1).

[105] Section 9(2) and the Child Trust Funds Regulations SI 2004/1450 reg 7.

[106] Child Trust Funds Regulations 2004 reg 9.   [107] Ibid reg 24.

[108] See above p 927. Where the child is in care and the parents have no contact with her, the Official Solicitor may receive the voucher: Child Trust Fund Regulations 2004 reg 33A.

[109] Section 3(8).

[110] See N Wikeley, 'Child Trust Funds—What Will Yours Grow Into?' [2005] Fam Law 285 at 286.

[111] Section 6.

under 16, the Inland Revenue will also open the account; on the parent reaching the age of 16, it will pass responsibility for managing it to her.

The goal of this innovation was to enable all children reaching adulthood to have some kind of 'nest egg' available to them to use for education, training, housing costs or even a nice birthday party, in the same way that children from better-off families have been able to enjoy. However, low-income families may be unable to contribute additional funds to the account during the child's dependency so that the ultimate size of the fund available to the child will still vary enormously. Moreover, out of around 2 million vouchers sent out in the first year of operation of the scheme, some 600,000 vouchers remained uninvested at the end of 12 months,[112] suggesting that many parents were either unable or unwilling to take the decision on how to invest the money. The child trust fund may therefore represent more of a gesture towards equality of opportunity and a pious attempt at encouraging saving than a major step in reducing the disparity between the children of the rich and the poor. Nonetheless, it may reflect a more fundamental realignment of welfare provision, in accordance with the emphasis on 'welfare to work' which underpins the tax credits system, towards encouraging people to help themselves and break from the 'dependency culture' so reviled by both the major political parties.

C MAINTENANCE UNDER THE CHILD SUPPORT ACT 1991 [113]

1 BACKGROUND

During the 1980s increasing attention was paid to the question of whether the existing provision for the assessment and collection of child maintenance through private law mechanisms was satisfactory. The law was amended in 1984 to require that, in deciding what orders for financial provision should be made on divorce or matrimonial breakdown, the court should give first consideration to the welfare whilst a minor of any child of the family,[114] and attempts were made to increase the awareness of the courts as to the real costs of raising children, by circulating them with information on current Income Support rates, and the National Foster Care Association's recommended rate for paying foster-parents. Notwithstanding the availability of such information, the government found that the 'going rate' for maintenance for one child, of any age up to 18, was £18 per week in 1990,[115] at a time when the National Foster Care Association was recommending a payment of £34.02 per week for a child under the age of five. Such disparity is hardly surprising, given the finding by Eekelaar that, in his survey of 38 registrars (now district judges) handling financial provision, 14 rejected the National Foster Care Association rates as irrelevant because they were regarded as unrealistically high.[116] The government found

---

112 See http://news.bbc.co.uk/1/hi/programmes/moneybox/4635006.stm, 21 January 2006.

113 See E Jacobs *Child Support: The Legislation* (6th ed, 2004); CPAG, *Child Support Handbook 2005/6* (2005).

114 See below, p 982.   115 White Paper, *Children Come First*, Cm 1264, Vol 1, para 1.5.

116 J Eekelaar *Regulating Divorce* (1991) p 95.

that maintenance awards represented only about 11% of total net incomes of absent parents on above average incomes.[117] It further found wide variations in the amounts of maintenance being awarded, one example being of two fathers, each earning £150 per week net. One was required to pay £5 per week in maintenance, and the other £50 per week.[118]

Not only was there concern that the amounts of maintenance awarded might be too low, but also that awards were neither being complied with nor adequately enforced.[119] Where maintenance awards are low, there is little incentive to seek their enforcement, especially where the recipient is in any event dependent upon social security benefits. Yet even where what was then the Department of Social Security had the power to seek enforcement against liable relatives, in only 23% of cases was the full amount of arrears of maintenance recovered.[120]

While low levels of maintenance and high proportions of orders in arrears were not particularly new, a further element which led to a determination to alter the law was the impact of these factors on the social security budget. The government found that about 770,000 single parents, or around two-thirds of the total number at that time, were dependent upon Income Support in 1989, up from 330,000 such families in 1980.[121] Fewer than one-quarter of these were receiving any maintenance, while the cost to the Treasury of their benefits was £3.2 billion in 1988/89. The cost of supporting lone parent families appeared incompatible with the renewed emphasis upon asserting and strengthening parental responsibility for children under the Children Act 1989.

The desire to do something more fundamental about parental obligations to support children was translated into the government's White Paper, *Children Come First*, published in 1990, and followed by the Child Support Act 1991.[122] The scheme set up by the Act drew, to some extent, upon similar initiatives in both the United States of America and Australia.[123] Its introduction was highly controversial, and its initial workings lived down to the expectations of those who criticised it as a futile attempt to re-impose 'traditional family values' on a society which has moved increasingly away from the normative typical family of married parents living with their dependent children. Reception of the new ideology promoted by the legislation was not helped by unacceptably high levels of error and inefficiency in the Child Support Agency.[124] Many parents 'with care' found that they saw none of the maintenance collected, as it was offset against Income Support paid to the

[117] *Children Come First*, loc cit.   [118] Ibid.

[119] S Edwards, C Gould and A Halpern 'The Continuing Saga of Maintaining the Family after Divorce' [1990] Fam Law 31.

[120] White Paper Vol 2, para 5.1.2, and see C Gibson 'The Future for Maintenance' [1991] CJQ 330.

[121] White Paper Vol 2 p i.

[122] See J Eekelaar 'A Child Support Scheme for the United Kingdom' [1991] Fam Law 15; M Maclean 'The Making of the Child Support Act 1991: Policy Making at the Intersection of Law and Social Policy' (1994) 21 Journal of Law and Society 505.

[123] See L Weitzman and M Maclean (eds) *Economic Consequences of Divorce: The International Perspective* Part Four; S Parker 'Child Support in Australia: Children's Rights or Public Interest?' (1991) 5 International Journal of Law and the Family 24.

[124] The Agency remains in crisis. Compare earlier reports on its working, such as the House of Commons Social Security Committee report, *The Performance and Operation of the Child Support Agency*, Session 1995–96 with the successor House of Commons Work and Pensions Committee's report, *The Performance of the Child Support Agency* (2005, HC 44) which continued to find failing management, inefficient procedures and poor levels of compliance with calculations. See further below p 949.

carer,[125] and were concerned that the activity of the Child Support Agency had disrupted their relationship with the non-resident parent. Children too seem to have suffered from the deterioration in the parents' relationships.[126] But it was the unprecedented level of anger expressed by those, mainly fathers, who were required to meet their obligations under the new scheme[127] that forced Parliamentarians to press, and government to act, to change the system.[128] Throughout the 1990s, a number of changes were made both to the primary legislation and to the horrendously detailed regulations underpinning it in various attempts to ameliorate the system.[129] Eventually, the incoming Labour government in 1997 undertook a more thorough-going reform,[130] enacting the Child Support, Pensions and Social Security Act 2000, which substantially amended the 1991 Act. This introduced a fundamentally different way of approaching the calculation of child support (the 'new rules'), seeking greatly to simplify the formula on which this is based, and came into force for new applications on 3 March 2003. However, existing cases remained subject to the 'old rules' until computerisation would permit their transfer onto the new scheme. Three years after the new rules came into force, the Agency was still unable to announce a date for transfer of existing cases. The discussion below deals with the basic system and the new rules. For details of the old rules, the reader is referred to the previous edition of this work.[131]

2 THE SCHEME OF THE ACT

The two key characteristics of the child support scheme are first, that it lays down a *formula* to be applied to calculate the amount of maintenance needed by the child and to be met by the absent parent. The original aim of the formula was to ensure that adequate amounts of maintenance are awarded, and to achieve consistency, so that families in similar circumstances will be assessed for similar amounts of maintenance. However, as is explained below, the new rules pay less attention to the adequacy of the maintenance and more to achieving a rough and ready 'fairness' or balance between the needs of payer and child alike. Secondly, the assessment, collection and enforcement of maintenance are carried out, not by the courts, but by the Child Support Agency, which comes under the wing of the Department for Work and Pensions.

(a) The Child Support Agency

The term 'Child Support Agency' does not in fact appear in the legislation, which instead

---

[125] Nearly 80% of applicants were receiving Income Support, with a further 12% on Family Credit, in a statistical survey carried out by the Child Support Agency in November 1995: *Quarterly Summary of Statistics* May 1996.

[126] G Gillespie 'Child Support—The Hand that Rocks the Cradle' [1996] Fam Law 162.

[127] See R Collier 'The Campaign against the Child Support Act: "errant fathers" and "family men" ' [1994] Fam Law 384; J Wallbank 'The Campaign for Change of the Child Support Act 1991: Reconstructing the "Absent Father" ' (1997) 6 Social & Legal Studies 191.

[128] The most thorough-going study of the system was carried out by G Davis et al, *Child Support in Action* (1998).

[129] See White Paper *Improving Child Support* Cm 2745 (1995), the Child Support Act 1995 and the last edition of this work especially pp 737–42.

[130] Department of Social Security, *Children First: A New Approach to Child Support* Cm 3992 (1998), *A New Contract for Welfare: Children's Rights and Parents' Responsibilities* Cm 4349 (1999).

[131] 9th edition pp 734–46.

refers to the Secretary of State, whose actions and decisions, of course, must be carried out in practice by officers in the Agency, who are referred to below as child support officers.

Where the exercise of any discretionary power[132] conferred by the Act is to be considered, the Secretary of State shall, under s 2, 'have regard to the welfare of any child likely to be affected by his decision'. This requirement is both narrower and wider than similar conditions in other legislation. Since welfare is not made the first consideration, still less the paramount consideration, s 2 is narrower than s 25(1) of the Matrimonial Causes Act 1973, or s 1 of the Children Act 1989. On the other hand, the duty to consider welfare lies in respect of *any* child who may be affected by the decision, and not just the child directly in issue. The Act gives no guidance on how welfare is to be taken into account, nor on how a balance should be struck between different children who may be affected. The provision has been characterised by one judge as 'hollow indeed'.[133]

(b) The relevant parties

Qualifying child

Section 1(1) provides that 'each parent of a qualifying child is responsible for maintaining him'. A child is defined in s 55 as a person under the age of 16, or under the age of 19 and receiving full-time non-advanced education, who has not been married. Such a child is a 'qualifying child' within s 3(1) if:

'(a) one of his parents is, in relation to him, a non-resident[134] parent; or

(b) both of his parents are, in relation to him, non-resident parents.'

Non-resident parent

A parent is a non-resident parent under s 3(2) if:

'(a) that parent is not living in the same household with the child; and

(b) the child has his home with a person who is, in relation to him, a person with care.'

A parent is defined in s 54 as 'any person who is in law the mother or father of the child'. This definition covers birth parents, parents by virtue of adoption, and parents by virtue of the Human Fertilisation and Embryology Act 1990. There is no concept of 'child of the family' which underpins private maintenance obligations.[135] The approach of the Act is, like the Social Security Administration Act 1992, to attach liability only to those with the legal status of parents.

Person with care

A 'person with care' is defined in s 3(3) as a person:

'(a) with whom the child has his home;

(b) who usually provides day to day care for the child (whether exclusively or in conjunction with any other person); and

---

[132] This excludes the calculation of the assessment under the formula, since this is not discretionary.

[133] Per Thorpe J in *R v Secretary of State for Social Security ex p Biggin* [1995] 1 FLR 851 at 855E–F.

[134] The original term was 'absent' parent, but this was criticised by the House of Commons Social Security Committee as offensive: *The Performance and Operation of the Child Support Agency* 2nd report of the House of Commons Social Security Committee, Session 1995–96, para 54 and was duly changed.

[135] See above, p 338.

(c) who does not fall within a prescribed category of person.'[136]

More than one person may be a person with care in relation to the child under s 3(5).

Where parents share the care of a child, disputes may arise as to which of them is the 'parent with care' and which the 'non-resident parent'. 'Day to day care' is defined in the regulations as meaning overnight care, and a person will be treated as having day to day care only if he or she cares for the child at least two nights per week over a 12-month period.[137] Where the child spends on average at least one night a week with the non-resident parent, a deduction in the amount of child support will be made.[138] Special provision is made for where a child is absent from home for a time, eg while at boarding school, and in determining who should be regarded as having day to day care, the Agency should have regard to all the circumstances, including who would be caring for the child if he were not away from home. The terms of any residence or contact order are relevant although not decisive.[139]

Application for a maintenance calculation under s 4

The person with care or a non-resident parent may apply to the Child Support Agency, under s 4(1), for a maintenance calculation to be made with respect to the qualifying child.[140] Application may also be made for the Agency to arrange for the collection and enforcement of the 'child support maintenance' so calculated. The person with care may apply by phone or face-to-face interview, or by completing a form which can be downloaded from the internet. A non-resident parent who applies will either complete a form or be sent one to check the information that the Agency has recorded by phone.

Application for a maintenance calculation under s 6

If, however, the person with care is the child's parent, and she (or her partner) is claiming Income Support or income-based Jobseekers' Allowance, she *must* usually authorise the Agency, when asked by it to do so, to take action under the Act to recover child support maintenance from the non-resident parent.[141] Once such authorisation is given, then a calculation can be undertaken even though the parent with care may not yet have been awarded the benefit.[142] Furthermore, even if the parent ceases to claim benefits before the process of calculation is completed, there is jurisdiction to continue and enforce the eventual calculation.[143]

---

[136] The Secretary of State shall not so prescribe parents, guardians, persons with a residence order in their favour, under s 8 of the Children Act 1989: s 3(4).

[137] Child Support (Maintenance Calculation and Special Cases) Regulations SI 2001/155 reg 1(2).

[138] Child Support Act 1991 Sch 1 paras 7, 8 (as amended).

[139] Child Support (Maintenance Calculation and Special Cases) Regulations reg 12; *C v Secretary of State for Work and Pensions* [2002] EWCA Civ 1854 [2003] 1 FLR 829.

[140] No such application may be made where there is in force a written maintenance agreement made before 5 April 1993 or maintenance order in respect of the child which was either made before 3 March 2003, or made after that date and has been in force for less than one year: Child Support Act 1991 s 4(10) as amended (see below p 948).

[141] For the situation where the parent does not wish to do so, see below p 934.

[142] *Secretary of State for Social Security v Harmon; Carter; Cocks* [1998] 2 FLR 598, CA.

[143] *R v Secretary of State for Social Security ex parte Harris* [1999] 1 FLR 837.

(c) Providing information to make the assessment

Parents with care

A person applying under s 4, or under a duty to authorise action under s 6, must, so far as she reasonably can, supply information to the Agency to enable the non-resident parent to be traced (if necessary), and the maintenance calculation made. To accommodate the concern that a parent dependent upon benefits (and therefore obliged to authorise action under s 6), might not wish to reveal the identity of the absent parent to the Agency, because she fears violence from him, or wishes to put an unhappy relationship behind her, s 6(8) and s 46(3) provide that the requirements to give authorisation, or provide information, can be waived by the Agency for what they call 'good cause', but which the statute defines as where they consider that there are reasonable grounds for believing that compliance would lead to a risk of the claimant, or any child living with her, suffering harm or undue distress as a result. In deciding this, the requirement to consider the child's welfare under s 2 will be relevant.[144]

Reduced benefit decision. However, as a deterrent to claimants who might prefer to withhold information, s 46(5) provides that, where the Secretary of State considers that there are no reasonable grounds for non-compliance, he may give a 'reduced benefit decision', whereby the amount of benefit otherwise payable will be reduced. If the parent co-operates by providing the relevant information, the reduction is lifted. In 1996, the Child Support Agency found that increasing numbers of parents with care were apparently willing to accept the reduction in order to avoid compliance.[145] The House of Commons Social Security Committee were concerned that this might reflect either an increasing resort to violent threats against a parent with care in order to evade liability, in which case they recommended that the Agency should inform the police,[146] or that many parents are colluding to evade the Agency's grasp by agreeing that, in return for her refusal to give the Agency the information needed, the non-resident parent will compensate the parent with care by making up her loss of benefit and perhaps paying her a little extra, but still an amount which is less than would be owed by him under a calculation.[147] As a consequence, the government increased the penalty to be incurred for failure to co-operate. Originally, there was a deduction of 20% of the Income Support adult personal allowance for the first six months, followed by 10% for a further 12 months, after which the penalty was exhausted. In 1996, the deduction was raised to 40% of the allowance, to last for three years, the penalty to be renewed if the parent with care is still on benefit and refusing to co-operate.[148]

---

[144] But there is no obligation to consult the absent parent on whether he considers there would be a risk to the child's welfare if an assessment were required to be authorised: *R v Secretary of State for Social Security ex p Lloyd* [1995] 1 FLR 856.

[145] *Child Support: Good Cause and the Benefit Penalty*, House of Commons Social Security Committee Fourth Report, Session 1995–96, June 1996, para 6. Only 16% of claims of 'good cause' were accepted; *Child Support Agency Annual Report and Accounts 1996/97* (1997).

[146] House of Commons Social Security Committee Second Report, Session 1995–96, para 51. The government rejected this suggestion, fearing that the risk of violence might be increased by such action: *Child Support: Reply by the Government to the Second Report from the Select Committee on Social Security Session 1995–1996* (1996) Cm 3191.

[147] House of Commons Social Security Committee Second Report, Session 1995–96, para 50.

[148] Now contained in Child Support (Maintenance Calculation Procedure) Regulations SI 2001/157 reg 11.

Non-resident parents

Information will also be needed from the non-resident parent in order to discover his means and liabilities. Non-resident parents and their current or recent employers are required to provide information. The Agency may also obtain information from the Inland Revenue, and local authorities administering housing benefit, as to the income or housing costs of a non-resident parent or person with care.[149] Inspectors may be appointed to exercise powers of entry and enquiry with a view to obtaining information required under the Act,[150] although there is no evidence that in practice use has been made of this power. On the contrary, the Agency has been described as a 'toothless dragon' which is ill-equipped, and reluctant, to challenge assertions by absent parents about their financial circumstances, especially when they are self-employed, and hence is incapable of determining the true situation from which a reliable and fair assessment could be made.[151]

Default maintenance decision. Under s 12 the child support officer may make a default maintenance decision where it appears to him that he does not have sufficient information to form a final judgment. The original aim of this provision (then called an 'interim maintenance assessment') was to set a higher assessment than might otherwise have been expected, in order to prompt the non-resident parent to provide the additional information needed so that the final figure could be reduced. In 1997, the average interim maintenance assessment was around £89 per week.[152] But the current system provides that a default decision imposes a flat rate figure depending upon the number of qualifying children—£30 for one, £40 for two and £50 for three or more—resulting in a much less punitive outcome for the non co-operating parent.[153]

(d) Disputes about parentage

A question may arise whether the non-resident parent is in fact the father (or mother) of the qualifying child. Under s 26, if the alleged parent denies parentage, the child support officer shall not make a maintenance assessment unless the case falls within one of a number of categories. These are where:

Case A1:   the child is habitually resident in England and Wales; the Secretary of State is satisfied that the alleged parent was married to the child's mother at some time in the period beginning with the conception and ending with the birth of the child; and the child has not been adopted;

Case A2:   the child is habitually resident in England and Wales; the alleged parent has been registered as the child's father under the relevant legislation for England and Wales, Scotland or Northern Ireland; and the child has not subsequently been adopted;

Case A3:   the result of a scientific test (within the meaning of s 27A)[154] taken by the alleged parent would be relevant to determining the child's parentage; and the alleged parent (a) refuses to take the test; or (b) has submitted to such a

---

[149] Child Support Act 1991 s 14.   [150] Section 15.

[151] G Davis et al, *Child Support in Action* (1998) p 97.

[152] *Quarterly Summary of Statistics* (covering period to February 1997).

[153] Child Support (Maintenance Calculation Procedure) Regulations 2001 reg 7.

[154] Below at p 936.

test and it shows that there is no reasonable doubt that the alleged parent is a parent of the child;

Case A: the parent has adopted the child;[155]

Case B: the parent has a parental order under s 30 of the Human Fertilisation and Embryology Act 1990;[156]

Case B1:   the Secretary of State is satisfied that the alleged parent is a parent of the child by virtue of ss 27 or 28 of the Human Fertilisation and Embryology Act 1990;[157]

Case C: a declaration that the alleged parent is the parent is in force under ss 55A or 56 of the Family Law Act 1986[158] and the child has not subsequently been adopted;

Case D: a declaration is in force under s 27 of the Act[159] and the child has not subsequently been adopted;

Case F:[160] the alleged parent has been found or adjudged to be the father of the child in relevant proceedings[161] in England and Wales or in affiliation proceedings in the United Kingdom, the finding still subsists and the child has not subsequently been adopted.[162]

Interestingly, as originally enacted, the Act did not provide that the marital presumption or the prima facie evidence of registration as the child's father would justify an assumption of parentage, perhaps because it was not contemplated that men would dispute their paternity when they had been married to the parent with care or had their name on the birth register. The change was made by the Child Support, Pensions and Social Security Act 2000,[163] when the opportunity was also taken to treat a refusal to take a DNA test which would determine the matter one way or the other in the same way as the courts would so treat it—ie by regarding that as evidence of parentage in itself.[164]

Where the alleged parent denies parentage and falls outside these categories, then the Agency will ask the relevant parties to undergo a DNA test at a reduced cost to the alleged non-resident parent. If he is found not to be the parent, the fee is refunded.[165] Under s 27 of the Child Support Act, the Agency or the person with care may also apply to the court[166] for

---

[155] See above, Chapter 15.   [156] See above, p 315.   [157] See above pp 307–15.

[158] See above. Or under the equivalent legislation in Scotland or Northern Ireland.

[159] See below.   [160] Case E applies to Scotland only.

[161] Within s 12 of the Civil Evidence Act 1968, as amended.

[162] The making of a parental responsibility order under s 4 of the Children Act 1989 necessarily incorporates a 'finding' of paternity for the purposes of Case F, even if the s 4 order is subsequently discharged on its merits: *R v Secretary of State for Social Security ex parte West* [1999] 1 FLR 1233, CA and (on the substantive issue) *R v Secretary of State for Social Security ex parte W* [1999] 2 FLR 604.

[163] Section 15(1). See N Wikeley, 'Child Support, Paternity and Parentage' [2001] Fam Law 125.

[164] See above p 330.

[165] Where the test is carried out other than by direction, and shows that the alleged parent cannot be excluded from being one of the child's parents, the Agency can recover the costs of the test from the non-resident parent if he accepts parentage or has been declared a parent: s 27A of the Child Support Act 1991.

[166] Children (Allocation of Proceedings) Order 1991, art 3(5), added by the Children (Allocation of Proceedings) Amendment Order 1993, provides that proceedings commence in the family proceedings court but may be transferred up to the county court or Family Division of the High Court.

a declaration under s 55A of the Family Law Act 1986[167] that a person is, or is not, a parent of the child.[168] In such proceedings, the child should be made a party and represented.[169]

(e) Making the child support calculation

The formula for calculating the amount of child support maintenance which the non-resident parent must pay for the qualifying child is set out in Sch 1 to the Act. Details of the 'old rules' may be found in the previous edition to this work.[170] Discussion here relates to the new rules.

The rate of child support payable depends upon the income of the non-resident parent. The 'general rule' is that the 'basic rate' applies, but a reduced, flat or nil rate may be applicable instead,[171] as explained below.

The basic rate

The non-resident parent pays 15% of his net weekly income for one qualifying child, 20% for two, and 25% where there are three or more such children.[172] Where the parent has other 'relevant children' (that is, children for whom he or his partner receives child benefit—effectively, children in his current relationship, be they his own, or step-children),[173] the same percentage reduction is to be made to his net income *before* it is applied in favour of his qualifying children.[174] This means that the income available for child support is correspondingly reduced, thus benefiting the children of his second family. This is contrary to the original scheme, which sought to prioritise the financial needs of the first family rather than the second, and it appears to be an attempt to encourage non-resident parents to pay at least something by way of child support in the knowledge that at least their current family's needs are not being squeezed.[175] It should also be noted that, unlike the original formula, which linked the amount payable to the 'needs' of the qualifying child (as assessed according to the relevant income support benefit rates then payable for such a child), the new rules make no attempt to determine what the qualifying child's financial needs might actually be. The focus is on getting the non-resident parent to pay a proportion of his income in recognition of his liability, regardless of how far this may or may not actually relieve the child's needs. However, the vast majority of children for whom

---

[167] See above p 332.

[168] As originally enacted, s 27 provided separate jurisdiction for making the declaration, but there was no appeal from a declaration made under this section: *T v Child Support Agency* [1997] 2 FLR 875, where a man was found to be the father of the child, after he had been notified of, but failed to attend, the hearing before the magistrates. Subsequent DNA testing established he was not the father. A declaration was granted under RSC Ord 15 r 16 to the effect that he was not the father of the child, but the court drew attention to the lack of any statutory right of appeal against such a finding. The amended section now brings the procedure within s 55A from which there is an appeal under s 60(5) of the 1986 Act.

[169] *Re L (Family Proceedings Court)(Appeal: Jurisdiction)* [2003] EWHC 1682 (Fam) [2005] 1 FLR 210.

[170] At pp 734–7.

[171] Child Support Act 1991 Sch 1 para 1, as amended by Child Support, Pensions and Social Security Act 2000 s 1 and Sch 1.

[172] Ibid para 2(1).

[173] Ibid para 10C(2). The original formula made only residual allowance for the non-resident parent supporting his step-children.

[174] Ibid para 2(2).

[175] Non-resident parents may indeed be likely to put the children of their current relationship before their 'own' children, according to a survey commissioned by the DWP: A Atkinson and S McKay, *Investigating the compliance of Child Support Agency clients*, Research Report no 285 (2005).

child support is payable are in families where the carer is in receipt of means-tested benefits and has been required to authorise a calculation under s 6 of the Act. The major part of the child support paid by the non-resident parent will simply be set off against the benefit payable, and thus, the child's needs will continue to be met through the social security system.[176] It is only where the non-resident parent can afford to pay enough to lift the family off benefits that the child would see any real difference, and most such cases will probably be dealt with outside the child support scheme anyway.[177]

Reduced rate

If the non-resident parent's net income is above £100 per week, but below £200, he pays the 'reduced rate' or a minimum amount of £5 per week.[178] The reduced rate is calculated by reference to a percentage of the net income between £100 and £200, depending upon the number of qualifying and relevant other children, and adding this to the minimum £5. For example, if the non-resident parent has a net income of £150 per week, one qualifying child and no relevant children, he pays 25% of £50 (= £12.50) + £5 = £17.50 per week in child support. For two qualifying children, the percentage is 35% and for three or more, it is 45%. The percentage of net income taken in child support reduces where he has relevant children, so that, for example, if he had three such children, it would reduce from 25% to 17.5% for one qualifying child (so that he would pay 17.5% of £50 (= £8.75) + £5 = £13.75 per week).[179]

Flat rate

A flat rate of £5 per week is payable where the non-resident parent's net income is £100 per week or less, or he is in receipt of certain welfare benefits. The rate is halved if he or his partner is in receipt of income support or income-based JSA and the partner is also a non-resident parent for whom a child support application is in force.[180]

Nil rate

No child support is payable if the non-resident parent has net income of below £5 per week, or is of a prescribed description, such as a student, child, prisoner, or person living in a care home.[181]

Net income. It will be seen that the amount of child support payable depends upon the net income of the non-resident parent. Unlike the original formula, no account is now taken of the income of the parent with care, the government taking the view (which has been strongly criticised by some)[182] that since the child shares that parent's standard of living anyway, a contribution by the carer to the support of the child is already being made.[183] To avoid a wealthy non-resident parent from having income taken from him far in excess of his child's needs, a ceiling is placed on the amount of net income that can be

[176] See below p 939.   [177] See below p 948.   [178] Ibid para 3.

[179] The relevant percentages are specified in Child Support (Maintenance Calculations and Special Cases) Regulations 2001 reg 3.

[180] Child Support Act 1991 Sch 1 para 4 and Child Support (Maintenance Calculations and Special Cases) Regulations 2001 reg 4.

[181] Ibid para 5 and reg 5.

[182] See, eg N Mostyn, 'The Green Paper on Child Support—Children First: a new approach to child support' [1999] Fam Law 95.

[183] *Children First: a new approach to child support* Cm 3992 (1998) p 31.

included in the calculation, of £2000 per week.[184] This means that the maximum amount of child support that could be paid will be £500 per week. However, in this situation, were it felt appropriate, an application for 'top up maintenance' could be made to the courts.[185]

Much therefore hinges on determining how much net income the non-resident parent has, but determining this is not necessarily a straightforward exercise. It includes earned income, self-employed earnings, tax credits and pension payments etc,[186] less income tax, national insurance contributions, contributions to a pension scheme, and, in the case of the self-employed, deductions and business expenses.[187] Calculating the net income of a self-employed person can be particularly problematic, with many parents with care claiming that misleading accounts may be submitted to the Agency in order to present a picture of reduced income. Nor have the regulations always been clear enough on what is, or is not, taken into account. For example, in *Smith v Secretary of State for Work and Pensions*[188] the non-resident parent was a street trader. Depending upon whether he could deduct capital allowances for the relevant tax year, his net income was either £169,000 or £20,000 pa. The House of Lords ruled that no deduction should be made so that the non-resident parent would be regarded as having the higher income, and stressing the unfairness of allowing the non-resident parent to expand his business and pay little tax whilst the mother struggled to maintain their children.[189]

Child maintenance premium. A criticism of the child support scheme has been that the vast majority of parents with care, who are s 6 applicants in receipt of Income Support or income-based JSA, have gained no financial advantage from child support payments as these merely go to offset the amount of social security benefits they receive. The first response to this criticism was the introduction of a 'child maintenance bonus'[190] whereby the parent with care would accrue £5 per week from the maintenance[191] being paid by the non-resident parent, the total accrued sum, up to a maximum of £1,000, to be paid over to the parent with care as a lump sum when she ceased to claim benefit by taking up work of at least 16 hours per week.

This complicated scheme was replaced by a 'child maintenance premium', which is a disregard under which up to £10 per week of maintenance will be ignored in assessing the claimant's entitlement to IS or income-based JSA. The government regarded this as a clear incentive to lone parents to co-operate with the Child Support Agency and to discourage avoidance or collusion with the non-resident parent.[192]

---

[184] Child Support Act 1991 Sch 1 para 10(3).   [185] See below p 949.

[186] An increase in pension payable where the recipient, a fireman, had to retire because of injury suffered in the course of employment was taken into account as part of the parent's net income under the 'old rules' and would still appear relevant: *Wakefield v Secretary of State for Social Security* [2000] 1 FLR 510.

[187] It was held, in *Secretary of State for Work and Pensions v M* [2006] UKHL 11, [2006] 2 WLR 637 that the old rules for determining net income, which permitted housing costs to be deducted as legitimate living expenses, but which treated non-resident parents living in same-sex relationships less generously than those in heterosexual partnerships, did not engage Art 8 taken with Art 14 of the European Convention on Human Rights and hence were not in breach of the Convention.

[188] [2006] UKHL 35.   [189] See Lord Walker of Gestingthorpe at para 64.

[190] Child Support Act 1995 s 10 and Social Security (Child Maintenance Bonus) Regulations SI 1996/3195.

[191] Including maintenance paid under a court order or by agreement: reg 1(2).

[192] See Department of Social Security, *Children First: a new approach to child support* Cm 3992, (1998) p 16.

(f) Variations

A formula-based approach to calculating how much child support should be made will always lead to some decisions that do not fit individual circumstances. Fairness may be sacrificed for consistency. The original formula was criticised so heavily by both parents with care and non-resident parents that one might say that it led to virtually no fair outcomes.[193] Eventually, in response to lobbying, the government was forced to enact further primary legislation, the Child Support Act 1995, amending the 1991 Act, which fundamentally struck at the objective of ensuring consistency by introducing an element of discretion into the process. Again, the legislation drew on the Australian model. However, whereas in Australia, it is for the courts to determine whether to give a 'departure order' diverting from the formula, in the United Kingdom, the discretion is vested in the Child Support Agency.[194] The 'new rules' further amended the legislation, renaming the process a 'variation'. Under ss 28A(1)[195] of the 1991 Act, where an application for a maintenance calculation is made, or a calculation is in force, the person with care or the non-resident parent may apply for the rules by which the calculation is made to be varied in accordance with the terms of the Act.[196]

The Secretary of State may agree to a variation if he is satisfied that the case falls within one or more of the cases set out in Sch 4B to the Act, or the regulations thereto, and it is his opinion that, in all the circumstances of the case, it would be just and equitable to agree.[197] There are three classes of case. First, special expenses which ought to be added to the net income of the non-resident parent so as to reduce his liability; secondly, certain property or capital transfers which occurred before 5 April 1993; and thirdly, additional cases which basically relate to the lifestyle of the non-resident parent.

Special expenses

Many complaints about the original formula related to the narrow range of items allowed to the absent parent as part of the income which was 'exempt' from liability, and the new rules narrowed these still further by limiting net income basically to take-home pay. Yet a parent may have many financial commitments which are a part of everyday life and which people are required, or certainly encouraged, to take on. On the other hand, the fundamental philosophy of the legislation is to require parents to meet their obligations to their children before incurring further expenditure and to prevent them from claiming that, because of such expenditure, they are less able to support their children. Thus, the government sought to extend, but only to a limited degree, the types of expenditure which absent parents would be able to claim as having a higher priority on their resources than the cost of maintaining their first family.

---

[193] For American perspectives on the strengths and weaknesses of employing a formula, see M Takas 'Improving Child Support Guidelines: Can Simple Formulas Address Complex Families?' (1992) 26(3) Fam Law Q 171; B Bergmann and S Wetchler 'Child Support Awards: State Guidelines vs. Public Opinion' (1995) 29(3) Fam LQ 483.

[194] There is provision for an application to be referred direct to an Appeal Tribunal (see below, p 945) where it is particularly novel or contentious: s 28D(1)(b).

[195] As amended by the Child Support, Pensions and Social Security Act 2000 s 5. Or, where a calculation has already been made, s 28G(1).

[196] Pending the outcome of such an application, the Secretary of State may give an 'interim maintenance decision' under s 12 of the Child Support Act, applying the formula in Sch 1.

[197] Section 28F as amended.

The items which may be claimed as special expenses[198] are as follows. First, there are costs incurred in maintaining contact with the qualifying children (many non-resident parents having complained that it was nonsensical to require them to pay so much maintenance that they could no longer actually afford to see their children);[199] and costs attributable to the long-term illness or disability of a relevant child.

These items will have usually arisen after the breakdown of the relationship. The next group of items relates to financial obligations incurred before the breakdown which continue to have to be met. Thus, a variation may be given for certain debts incurred before the breakdown in the relationship, and which were incurred for the parties' joint benefit or for the benefit of the person with care (if the non-resident parent is liable for the payments), or for the child (or a child who lived with them during their relationship). Many types of debt are excluded from consideration, such as credit card debts, legal costs of the separation or divorce, and debts taken over as part of a financial settlement of the divorce or separation.[200] The types of expenditure which would be covered include the purchase by credit agreement or hire purchase of furniture, home improvements, private medical or dental treatment, or taking out a loan to help an older child through university. Express provision is also made for the payment of the qualifying child's boarding-school fees, although the regulations provide that only the maintenance element of these may be allowed.[201]

An important addition made by the 2000 Act reforms was to allow for payments being kept up by the non-resident parent, for a mortgage on the home that the parties had shared, if the non-resident parent no longer has an interest in it, and the parent with care and qualifying child still live there.[202]

Property or capital transfers made before 5 April 1993

Linked to this point, the strongest criticism of the original formula was probably its lack of any recognition of the effect of divorce settlements on the parties' expectations of their continuing financial obligations to each other and to their children. The trend in the past 25 years has been towards a clean break on divorce,[203] whereby the wife—who is usually the children's carer—forgoes any maintenance for herself in return for a share, or larger share, in the capital and, most often, the transfer to her of the former matrimonial home. Implicit, at least in part, in such an arrangement, is the idea that the home will provide a continuing secure base for the couple's children. Accordingly, despite the view of the courts that parents cannot divest themselves of the obligation to maintain their children,[204] prior to the Child Support Act, couples often agreed that the father would pay little or no maintenance for the children. After the Act was implemented, it was argued that such a transfer of property represents, at least in part, capitalised maintenance for the

[198] Child Support Act 1991 Sch 4B para 2, as amended. The expenses must be over £15 per week where net income is £200 or more, and £10 per week for income below £200, except in relation to costs due to the illness or disability of a relevant child: Child Support (Variations) Regulations SI 2001/156 reg 15.

[199] For example, *B v M (Child Support: Revocation of Order)* [1994] 1 FLR 342. The Secretary of State may decide to allow a sum lower than the cost claimed if he regards this as unreasonably high, but he cannot set a figure so low as to make it impossible, in his opinion, for contact to be maintained at the frequency specified in any court order, so long as the contact is taking place: reg 15(3).

[200] See Child Support (Variations) Regulations 2001 reg 12.   [201] Ibid reg 13.

[202] Child Support Act 1991 Sch 4B para 2(3)(e).   [203] See below, p 1023.

[204] *Minton v Minton* [1979] AC 593, HL.

children, and should therefore reduce the non-resident parent's child support liability. The courts were unable to respond to this argument. In *Crozier v Crozier*,[205] a father applied to the court to have his divorce settlement set aside, on the basis that, when he had transferred his share in the former matrimonial home to the wife, he had done so in the light of a child maintenance liability of £4 per week. Under the child support assessment, he was expecting to pay some £29 per week. Booth J refused his application, holding that the fact that Parliament had changed the system for the assessment of maintenance liability for children did not fundamentally undermine the assumptions of the parties' original clean break agreement. She pointed out that it had been held long before the Act that the state, through the social security system, may pursue a liable relative to support his children, regardless of what might have been agreed or ordered under matrimonial law.[206]

Clearly, since the Act, legal advisers and courts have been aware of the limited recognition given to such settlements, and no unfairness is done to parties who have subsequently entered into agreements in full knowledge of this. But in respect of settlements that pre-date the Act's implementation, an injustice may be done if no recognition is given to the assumptions on which the parties negotiated. A variation may therefore be given in respect of transfers of capital or property which occurred before 5 April 1993.[207]

Additional cases

Although the main clamour for reform of the system came from non-resident parents seeking reductions in their child support liability, as noted above, concern was also expressed at the limited efforts apparently made by the Child Support Agency to establish the true financial situation of many non-resident parents who are self-employed or who appear to have complicated business affairs. Since one of the original motives for introducing the scheme was to tackle the all too common situation of lone parents and their children living on subsistence benefits while the other parent enjoys a much more affluent standard of living,[208] it is hardly surprising if many parents with care might resent the apparent disparity in lifestyle and seek to argue that the non-resident parent can afford to pay far more than he ostensibly appears to do. Accordingly, there is provision to give a variation where the non-resident parent has assets over £65,000;[209] a lifestyle inconsistent with his income;[210] income which has not been taken into account in the calculation (eg because the non-resident parent is a student, but has a part-time job); or he has diverted income (eg paying a new partner a company director's salary in his own business and drawing a small salary himself).

---

[205] [1994] Fam 114.   [206] *Hulley v Thompson* [1981] 1 All ER 1128.

[207] The amount of variation is determined according to the Child Support (Variations) Regulations 2001 regs 16, 17 with the minimum value of an eligible transfer being £5,000.

[208] Lenore Weitzman's famous study of divorce in America has been broadly reflected in this country by J Eekelaar and M Maclean *Maintenance after Divorce* (1986) ch 5, although they thought the non-resident parent's enhanced position was likely to be short-lived, given he might well start a second family.

[209] Sch 4B para 4 and Child Support (Variations) Regulations 2001 reg 18. There are exceptions, such as where the asset is the parent's home.

[210] See *Phillips v Pearce* [1996] 2 FLR 230, where an absent parent lived in a house worth £2.6 million and owned cars worth £190,000, but was assessed by the Child Support Agency as having no income from his share-dealing business and was given a nil calculation.

Determining what is just and equitable

Once the application is found to come within one or more of the cases in Sch 4B, the Secretary of State must then determine whether it would be just and equitable[211] to give a variation. Section 28E and s 28F provide guidance on how this is to be determined. Section 28E sets out two 'general principles':

'(a) parents should be responsible for maintaining their children whenever they can afford to do so;

(b) where a parent has more than one child, his obligation to maintain any one of them should be no less of an obligation than his obligation to maintain any other of them.'

These provisions were apparently intended to remind parents of their obligation and also to reassert that duties to the first family should not be superseded by those taken on towards the second.[212] But they can equally be read the other way—that the children of the second family should not be subordinated to those of the first. On this basis, the needs of all of a parent's children ought to be ranked and met equally. Either way, they are inconsistent with the formula approach, which, as we have seen, in fact enables the non-resident parent to support his second family more generously than his first.

The Secretary of State is not to have regard to the fact that the person with care might be receiving benefits so that any child support maintenance goes to offset entitlement. This is to forestall the argument that children rarely see any of the maintenance money, since the bulk of it goes to reduce the social security budget instead.

Section 28F and the regulations[213] set out further matters to which the Secretary of State either is, or is not, to have regard. These include whether, in the opinion of the Secretary of State, agreeing to a variation would be likely to result in a relevant person ceasing paid employment; and whether the non-resident parent could meet his costs without a variation, perhaps by cutting back on 'non-essential everyday requirements'. He must also consider, where the applicant is a non-resident parent, the extent of any liability to pay maintenance under a prior court order or agreement. Persons with care, however, may be justifiably annoyed to find that, while the non-resident parent applicant may point to a low liability under the former law as part of his case for justifying a variation, the fact that he had not actually kept up the payments is not to be taken into account![214] Other facts to be ignored include that the child's conception was unplanned; that a party may have been responsible for the breakdown in the relationship; that a new relationship has been formed; and that contact arrangements have, or have not, been made and are, or are not, being adhered to.[215] In reaching a decision, the officer will have regard to the representations of the parties, and the welfare of any child likely to be affected must also be considered, but, as with the general requirement to have regard to welfare under s 2 of the Act, it is unlikely that this may have much impact.

---

[211] It is hard to see what is added to the word 'just' by the word 'equitable'. The phrase appears to have been borrowed from the Australian legislation: Child Support (Assessment) Act 1989 s 98C(1)(b)(ii) and s 117(1)(b)(ii).

[212] See also below, p 1036.   [213] Child Support (Variations) Regulations 2001 reg 21.

[214] Regulation 21(2)(f). A failure to pay under a child support assessment is also to be ignored in considering what is just and equitable: ibid.

[215] Regulation 21(2).

The effects of a decision[216]

The Secretary of State may agree or refuse the application and then revise, supersede, or make, a child support calculation in the light of his decision. The extent of the difference in the calculated figure will depend upon the type of case. Where special expenses are allowed, these reduce the applicant's net income. Where a direction is given based on a property or capital transfer, the quantified weekly value of the transfer is subtracted from the maintenance calculation otherwise arrived at. Where the direction is given on the basis of lifestyle, the quantified amount of extra income is added to the non-resident parent's net income.

(g) Termination and alteration of calculations

Under Sch 1 para 16 the calculation ceases to have effect on the death of the non-resident parent or person with care; on there no longer being a qualifying child with respect to whom it would have effect (for example, where the child leaves school, or the parents move back in together so that there is no longer a non-resident parent); or on the non-resident parent ceasing to be the child's parent (that is, if the child is adopted or made the subject of a parental order). Additionally, a calculation must be cancelled at the request of a person who applied for it under s 4, or who was an applicant under s 6.[217]

Calculations are subject to a *periodic case check* on average every two years, to see if circumstances have changed and a revision is needed.[218] Under s 16 the Agency can *revise* a decision on the application of either party or of its own motion, within one month of notification of the decision or outside that period if the decision was made in error. This is a necessary power, given the level of error which continues to dog the Agency's work, even under the new, simplified, formula.[219] Under s 17, either party may apply for a *supersession* of the decision due to a change of circumstances, for example, where the non-resident parent becomes unemployed, or has another child with a new partner and therefore seeks a downward revision of his maintenance calculation. Equally, the person with care might seek an increase if the non-resident parent was known to have obtained a higher paid employment.[220]

The problem of keeping up to date with the numerous changes of circumstance in people's lives has proved particularly difficult for the Child Support Agency. It would not be unusual in the course of a year for a non-resident parent to be joined by a new partner and her children, to become a father of a child of his new relationship, to change jobs or become unemployed, to cease earning overtime or to gain a profit-related bonus of pay. The parent with care could experience just as many changes. Each could be the subject of an application for a supersession.

---

[216] See the Child Support (Variations) Regulations 2001 regs 23–5, 27. A variation will not be given where the amount of maintenance will be reduced to less than £5, and the maximum amount of net income which may be taken into account remains the ceiling amount of £2,000.

[217] Child Support Act 1991 ss 4(5), 6(5). A reduced benefit decision may be given in the latter case.

[218] Child Support Act 1991 s 16.

[219] See *CSA Annual Report and Accounts 2003–04* HC 782 (2004) which reported that the Agency achieved 82% accuracy in calculating maintenance under the new formula against a target rate of 90%.

[220] The decision cannot be superseded if the change in net income is less than 5%: Social Security and Child Support (Decisions and Appeals) Regulations SI 1999/991 reg 6B.

(h) Appeals

Under s 20 a 'qualifying person', ie a person with care or non-resident parent, may appeal to an appeal tribunal against a decision of the Secretary of State regarding a child support calculation (including a decision regarding a revision or supersession) or a reduced benefit decision. Parentage issues must be appealed to a family proceedings court.[221] The tribunal usually consists of a legally qualified member of the appeal tribunals panel, sitting alone. If complicated financial matters arise, an accountant may also sit.

If the appeal succeeds, the tribunal must remit the case to be dealt with by the Agency, and may give such directions as it considers appropriate. Further appeals on questions of law may be made to a Commissioner,[222] and then to the Court of Appeal.[223]

(i) Collection and enforcement[224]

One of the main objectives of the Act was to improve the collection and enforcement of maintenance. The Agency may carry out the collection and enforcement of calculations where this is requested by those applying for a calculation under s 4, and in respect of all s 6 calculations.[225] Section 30 gives the Secretary of State power to make regulations to collect and enforce other types of maintenance, such as periodical payments,[226] and the original intention was that ultimately all forms of periodical payments would be so collected, at least where the recipient is claiming benefits or has a child. At present, this is beyond the capacity of the Agency.

Section 31 empowers the Secretary of State to make a 'deduction from earnings' order, akin to an attachment of earnings order, directed to the non-resident parent's employer, instructing him to make deductions from earnings and pay them to the Secretary of State. However, the order is made by the Secretary of State (or, in practice, the Agency) and not by a court, although there is provision for an appeal to be made to a magistrates' court by a liable person who is aggrieved by the making of the order, or by its terms.[227] Like attachment of earnings orders, the order can be made before any arrears of payments have accrued.[228] Such an order is only suitable for those in regular employment.

---

[221] Section 45 and the Child Support Appeals (Jurisdiction of Courts) Order 1993.

[222] Office created by s 22.   [223] Sections 24 and 25.

[224] See N Wikeley, 'Compliance, Enforcement and Child Support' [2000] Fam Law 888.

[225] Section 29. Unsurprisingly perhaps, 'Maintenance Direct', whereby the non-resident parent makes payments directly to the parent with care rather than using the CSA collection service, is more popular with the former than the latter, and depends upon the level of trust between the two parents: A Bell, A Kazimirski and I La Valle, *An Investigation of CSA Maintenance Direct Payments: Qualitative study* (2006).

[226] Child Support (Collection and Enforcement of Other Forms of Maintenance) Regulations 1992. The Child Support Act 1991 (Consequential Amendments) Order 1993 provides that, from 1994, magistrates (but not other courts) may order that qualifying maintenance orders be collected by the Child Support Agency where it is already collecting child support maintenance.

[227] Section 32(5) and the Child Support (Collection and Enforcement) Regulations SI 1992/1989 reg 22. The magistrates may not question the validity of the assessment in respect of which the order is made. The non-resident parent's remedy is to seek a review of the assessment: *Secretary of State for Social Security v Shotton* [1996] 2 FLR 241. Similarly, an alleged failure to consider the welfare of a child affected by the assessment is not a ground for granting an appeal against a deduction from earnings order: *R v Secretary of State for Social Security, ex p Biggin* [1995] 1 FLR 851.

[228] The 'effective date' of a maintenance calculation, from which arrears of child support maintenance begin to accrue, is usually the date the non-resident parent is first notified of the application. Thus, arrears will inevitably accrue in such cases: Child Support (Maintenance Calculation Procedure) Regulations

Where payment has been missed, the Secretary of State may apply to a magistrates' court for a liability order against the liable person under s 33. The court must proceed on the basis that the maintenance calculation was lawfully and properly made, but where an appeal is pending against the calculation, the court may adjourn the proceedings if it would be oppressive to continue.[229] The resort to action for a liability order is not an interference with the non-resident parent's rights under Art 8 or Protocol 1, Art 1 of the European Convention on Human Rights, or, if it is an interference, it is proportionate as a means of seeking to ensure that parents fulfil their responsibilities to support their children.[230] This enables the Secretary of State either to levy 'the appropriate amount' (the amount of maintenance unpaid together with charges connected with the distress) through seizure of goods,[231] or to apply to the county court for a garnishee or charging order as if the amount unpaid were payable under a county court order.[232] Where such means have proved unsuccessful, he may apply to the magistrates' court to disqualify the non-resident parent from driving for up to two years[233] or to commit him to prison for a maximum period of six weeks,[234] but only if the court is of the opinion that there has been wilful refusal or culpable neglect to pay. Such drastic action is rarely taken. Between April 2001 and January 2005, only four driving licences were removed and only 15 prison sentences served.[235]

This array of powers would suggest that, once a non-resident parent has been tracked down and assessed, there should be little scope for avoiding compliance, but this has not proved to be the case. As at 31 March 2004, the Child Support Agency reported outstanding debt of £720.16 million and a further £947.7 million as 'probably uncollectable from previous years'. Of the £720.16m, £140.22 million was from new scheme cases and nearly £49m of that was categorised as 'possibly uncollectable', a position described as an astonishing state of affairs by MPs.[236] The government has mooted the possibility

---

SI 2001/157 reg 25. The Agency will usually seek to negotiate an arrears agreement with the payer. Voluntary payments made before a calculation is finalised, but not notified to the Agency do not count as offsetting arrears: *R v Secretary of State for Social Security ex parte Newmarch Singh* [2000] 2 FLR 663. Failure to pay arrears may result in penalty payments being imposed, not exceeding 25% of the sum owed for the appropriate week: Child Support Act 1991 s 41A.

[229] *Farley v Secretary of State for Work and Pensions* [2006] UKHL 31: Father claimed he and mother had made written maintenance agreement which over-rode the jurisdiction of the Child Support Agency to make a calculation (see further below p 948).

[230] *R (Denson) v Child Support Agency* [2002] EWHC 154 (Admin) [2002] 1 FLR 938.

[231] Section 35.

[232] Section 36. The duty to pay is not expressed as a civil debt and cannot be directly enforced by action in any civil court or by any means other than as provided in the Act: *Department of Social Security v Butler* [1996] 1 FLR 65. The Child Support legislation, according to the Court of Appeal, provides a complete code for the collection of payments due under maintenance assessments and the enforcement of liability orders made on the application of the Secretary of State. (If, however, a liability order has already been made under s 33, then the county court has jurisdiction to grant a *Mareva* injunction under the County Court Remedies Regulations 1991 reg 3(3)(a), (c).)

[233] Child Support Act 1991 ss 39A and 40B, inserted by Child Support, Pensions and Social Security Act 2000 s 16.

[234] Child Support Act 1991 s 40.

[235] HC Select Committee on Work and Pensions, *The Performance of the Child Support Agency* (2005, HC 44) para 168.

[236] Ibid para 104.

of involving private debt collection firms in the task of collecting child maintenance. However, the proposal that such firms would be able to keep part of the arrears they collect has been described as morally wrong.[237] Yet it is clear that, so far, one of the main aims of the child support scheme, to improve the collection and enforcement of maintenance, has not been realised, and something drastic needs to be done. A survey of non-resident parents' attitudes to child support helps explain this situation. The researchers found that many such parents resented the Child Support Agency and regarded it as aimed at 'errant fathers', a label they did not apply to themselves. They were often unaware of the true cost of bringing up children, and regarded child support payments as an additional 'burden' on top of what were often high living costs (such as large mortgages) which they had incurred after separating from the parent with care.[238] In the light of such views, it is unsurprising that non-resident parents may seek to avoid paying up.

Yet the House of Lords has held that a parent with care has no right under Art 6 of the European Convention on Human Rights to challenge how the Child Support Agency chooses, or does not choose, to enforce a calculation, as the Act, in the Court's view, has replaced any pre-existing rights of either a child or a parent to periodical payments for the maintenance of that child.[239] One commentator has summed up the child support scheme thus:

'Where arrears are enforceable, the CSA will often accept arrears payments that can run until children are into their thirties and more. Its appeals structure could not have been imagined by someone who wanted to design the most inefficient system conceivable . . . Many parents have multiple appeals running before the Child Support Appeal Tribunals, the Commissioners and back again: *Jarndyce v Jarndyce* [in Charles Dickens' *Bleak House*] would be a model of prompt justice compared with some of these cases.'[240]

3 THE RESIDUAL ROLE OF THE COURTS

In the face of such a damning indictment, it is not surprising that family lawyers will seek to advise their clients on means of avoiding the scheme wherever possible. This will depend upon the jurisdictional rules of the Act.

(a) Where there is no jurisdiction under the Child Support Act

Section 8(1) and (3) of the Child Support Act provides that:

'. . . in any case where the Secretary of State would have jurisdiction to make a maintenance calculation with respect to a qualifying child and a non-resident parent of his on an application duly made (or treated as made) by a person entitled to apply for such a calculation with respect to that child . . . no court shall exercise any power which it would otherwise have to

---

[237] See 'Family lawyers oppose CSA bailiffs' (2006) NLJ 126.

[238] A Atkinson and S McKay, *Investigating the compliance of Child Support Agency clients* Research Report No 285 (DWP 2005).

[239] *R (Kehoe) v Secretary of State for Work and Pensions* [2005] UKHL 48 [2006] 1 AC 42. For a powerful critique of this decision, see N Wikeley, 'A Duty but Not a Right: Child Support after *R (Kehoe) v Secretary of State for Work and Pensions*' [2006] CFLQ 287.

[240] D Burrows, '*Kehoe*: The CSA and the Child's Right to Maintenance' [2004] Fam Law 453.

make, vary or revive any maintenance order in relation to the child and non-resident parent concerned.'[241]

Under s 44 the Child Support Agency only has jurisdiction if the person with care, the non-resident parent and the qualifying child are habitually resident in the United Kingdom.[242] Where any of these is not so resident, the jurisdiction of the Agency is therefore excluded and the court may make an order.

Secondly, a child support assessment may only be made against a non-resident parent who is the parent of the qualifying child. Where maintenance is sought for a step-child, the jurisdiction of the courts, which is based on the concept of the 'child of the family',[243] will be the only applicable jurisdiction and the Act will not apply.

Thirdly, where a child is over the age of 16, or is not a qualifying child within s 3(1), the court may still have jurisdiction (for example, if the child is not in full-time non-advanced education but still needs financial support).[244]

Fourthly, and in practice, most importantly, an application for child support will be barred in certain circumstances where there is already a prior maintenance agreement or maintenance order by consent in force.[245] This has enabled those better-off parents who are not subject to the provisions of s 6 of the Act, because the parent with care is not claiming income support or income-based JSA, effectively to opt out of the child support scheme, so long as they could agree with each other on the terms of any maintenance for their children.[246] The child support scheme has thus become a scheme used either by the

---

[241] Section 10 brings a court order to an end on the making of a child support calculation. In *Askew-Page v Page* [2001] Fam Law 794, the county court held that, where a child support calculation had been made under s 6, a prior court order for maintenance could not be revived even though the calculation was subsequently cancelled.

[242] There is jurisdiction where the non-resident parent is not habitually resident in the United Kingdom, but is employed in the civil service of the Crown or is a member of the armed forces, or employed by a company or body of a prescribed description: s 44(2A).

[243] See above, p 338.

[244] Since the scheme of the Act imposes liability to pay child support maintenance only on a non-resident parent, where maintenance is sought from the person with care instead, the courts may continue to be used: s 8(10).

[245] Section 8(5). Where a consent order provided for a reduction in the amount of payments to be made under it in respect of payments arising under a child support assessment, it was held that this applied also to any child support payments in arrears at the time the order was made: *Warring-Davies v Secretary of State for Work and Pensions* [2005] All ER (D) 372 (Nov).

[246] Once a consent order has been made, the courts have jurisdiction to vary it: s 8(3A). Courts dealing with applications to vary should be provided with information as to the amount of any child support assessment which would be payable if the Agency had jurisdiction: *E v C (Calculation of Child Maintenance)* [1996] 1 FLR 472—for criticism of this as a potential abdication of responsibility by the court, see J Pirrie, 'Time for the Courts to Stand Up to the Child Support Act?—An Address to District Judges' [2002] Fam Law 114. Courts have facilitated the avoidance of the child support scheme by upholding the following: first, where the parties do not agree on the quantum of maintenance, the court may make a nominal order at the start of proceedings, by consent, and then vary it to the amount the court sees fit: see *V v V (Child Mainte-nance)* [2001] 2 FLR 799; secondly, the court may make an order (known as a 'Segal order') for spousal maintenance pending suit (see below p 991) which includes an amount for the costs of the children, such amount to be reduced pro tanto by any sums payable under a child support calculation (when subsequently made): *Dorney-Kingdom v Dorney-Kingdom* [2000] 2 FLR 855, CA and explained by DJ M Segal at 'Segal Orders' [2002] Fam Law 923. Compare *B v M (Child Support: Revocation of Order)* [1994] 1 FLR 342: s 8(4) permits the court to revoke a maintenance order, but it was held that it is not appropriate to do so simply to bring the applicant within the jurisdiction of the child support scheme.

poor, who have no choice in the matter, or by those parents with care whose relationship with their ex-partner is particularly bad, and this in part helps explain the extremely adverse criticism it has suffered since its inception. The Act provides that if a written maintenance agreement, concerning periodical payments for the benefit of the child, was made between the parties before 5 April 1993, then a s 4 application may not be made.[247] A maintenance order made by a court before 3 March 2003 similarly prevents a s 4 application being brought. However, when the government amended the Act to bring in the 'new rules', it provided that any order made on or after that date only excludes the child support jurisdiction for a period of one year, in order to prevent a permanent opting out of the scheme where one party might wish to utilise its provisions.[248]

(b) Orders instead of or in addition to child support

In some situations, notwithstanding the fact that a maintenance calculation may be carried out, it will remain possible to utilise the courts' jurisdiction. First, where there is a maintenance calculation in force, which was set at the ceiling fixed by Sch 1, and 'the court is satisfied that the circumstances of the case make it appropriate for the non-resident parent to make or secure the making of periodical payments under a maintenance order in addition to the child support maintenance' the court may continue to exercise its powers to award maintenance.[249] In the case of a very wealthy non-resident parent it will therefore still be possible to increase the amount of maintenance to be paid by recourse to the court. Similar powers exist in s 8(7) and (8) to enable the court to make a maintenance order where this is solely to meet costs incurred in receiving education or training, or to cover expenses attributable to the child's disability. School fees, support for a student, and special expenses connected with a child's disability may therefore be met through the court system.[250]

The 1991 Act defines a maintenance order as 'an order which requires the making or securing of periodical payments' and so does not affect the court's powers to make an order for the payment of a lump sum or property adjustment.[251] Although traditionally the courts have not approved of such orders as being appropriate for children, the jurisdiction to make them is unaffected by the Act, and, as discussed below, there may be situations where they will be suitable.

4 EVALUATION OF THE CHILD SUPPORT SCHEME

The changes to the child support scheme introduced in 2003 were intended by the government to achieve:

'a simple and more deliverable system focused on the needs of children and good, responsible

---

[247] Child Support Act 1991 s 4(10)(a).

[248] Section 4(10)(aa) inserted by the Child Support, Pensions and Social Security Act 2000, s 2. See the discussion by N Wikeley, 'Private Cases and the Child Support Agency' [2001] Fam Law 35.

[249] Section 8(6) as amended by Child Support, Pensions and Social Security Act 2000, s 1.

[250] In *C v F (Disabled Child: Maintenance Order)* [1998] 2 FLR 1, the Court of Appeal held that the court may require that such an order continue in effect after the child reaches the age of 19, since its jurisdiction to do so derives inter alia from the Children Act and not from the Child Support Act, and Sch 1, para 3(2) permits an order to extend beyond the child's nineteenth birthday.

[251] Section 8(11).

parents. Parents who face up to their responsibilities will receive a better service. Irresponsible parents will face effective and speedy sanctions. We will put the need for regular and reliable payments of maintenance at the heart of the new system and we will introduce effective and prompt sanctions for those who try to avoid providing for their children.'[252]

A study conducted in 2000,[253] in which nearly 2,500 parents with care and non-resident parents were interviewed about their views on the 'old rules' system, concluded that non-resident parents' perceptions of the fairness of the system, and their willingness to comply with it, reflected the degree to which their lives remained intertwined with those of their children, and they saw their obligations to their children as negotiable, not subject to the rigid fixed rules of the state scheme. The authors concluded that whilst the new scheme might address some complaints, such as the complexity of the old system, its lack of transparency and the level of errors made in calculating payments, it would be unable to redress the emotional dimension of the parent-child relationship and in particular, the unfairness felt by those non-resident parents who do not have ongoing contact with the children for whom they are expected to pay.[254] This suggests that the government's focus, quoted above, on parental responsibility, without making the linkage between child support and contact, is unlikely to be successful in encouraging greater compliance with the system.

Some lawyers have argued that the Child Support Agency should be abolished and its work returned to the courts. However, the workload of the Agency is enormous and vastly outstrips the capacity of the civil courts. In October 2004, it was handling around 1.2 million cases involving 1.4 million children, and it expected to receive around 345,000 new applications. By contrast, the courts made a mere 15,612 orders for children in ancillary relief proceedings in 2004.[255] The gendered and fraught nature of child support is reflected by the fact that 95% of non-resident parents were male, of whom nearly a quarter had a new partner, whilst 86% of parents with care (mostly women) had not formed new relationships. The perception that the scheme exists to deal with the poor is further underscored by the finding that around two-thirds of new applications were made under s 6—that is, the parent with care was claiming income support or income-based JSA (around three-quarters of applications under the old rules were s 6 cases) and nearly half (45%) of non-resident parents had no earned income. Problems of delay in processing cases, inaccuracy in calculations and ineffective collection and enforcement continue to dog the Agency, even though the whole thrust of the simplification of the formula was intended to improve its performance on these issues. In 2005, it was reported that whilst it was intended to collect 78% of maintenance due under its calculations, it achieved only 43%.[256] This was characterised as 'nothing less than a severe breach of trust.'[257]

---

[252] Department for Social Security, *A New Contract for Welfare: Children's Rights and Parental Responsibilities* (1999 Cm 4349) para 9.

[253] N Wikely et al, *National Survey of Child Support Agency Clients* (2001, DWP Research Report No 152), summarised by G Davis and N Wikeley, 'National Survey of Child Support Agency Clients—The Relationship Dimension' [2002] Fam Law 522.

[254] See the similar view found by G Gillespie, 'Child Support—When the Bough Breaks' [2002] Fam Law 528.

[255] *Judicial Statistics 2004* Table 5.7.

[256] HC Select Committee on Work and Pensions, *The Performance of the Child Support Agency* (2005, HC 44) para 30.

[257] Ibid para 31.

It was noted above that the new rules focus solely upon the non-resident parent's net income and do not seek to link the amount of child support to the child's actual needs.[258] This means that amounts payable may often be token rather than substantively directed towards the support of the child. In 2005, it was reported that the average weekly amount assessed as payable for one qualifying child under the new rules was £24, compared to £40 under the old rules.[259] It had been expected, or hoped, that a reduction in the average amount payable might produce an improved level of compliance, but this is clearly not the case. Moreover, the child maintenance premium, which was intended to enable s 6 applicants to see some advantage from the non-resident parent paying child support, has had limited impact. This is due both to delay in migrating cases from the old to the new rules, but also to the fact that few non-resident parents where the parents with care are on income support are assessed to pay more than £10, with many themselves on benefits and thus paying only the minimum £5 or nil (eg because of being in prison).[260]

In 2006, the government commissioned an independent review of the child support scheme, by Sir David Henshaw.[261] He concluded that parents should be encouraged to reach private agreements or obtain consent orders for maintenance, with a state-provided service operating as a back-up rather than first port of call. Parents with care who are in receipt of benefits should no longer be required to authorise the making of a child support calculation and should be allowed to keep any maintenance without it affecting their benefits. He recommended abolishing the Child Support Agency, establishing instead a new body focused on enforcement in a smaller number of difficult cases.

The government accepted the thrust of these proposals and promised fresh legislation. Whether it is realistic to assume, as the Henshaw Report appears to do, that, if allowed to do so, parents are (more) likely to arrive at and stick to private arrangements which will deliver meaningful levels of contribution to children's financial support may be debated.

D PRIVATE AGREEMENTS

1 BETWEEN SPOUSES AND CIVIL PARTNERS

Courts were traditionally reluctant to enforce agreements between cohabiting spouses on the ground that it is presumed that they had no intention to enter into legal relations.[262] Pre-nuptial agreements seeking to determine what divorce settlement should be made in the event of the marriage breaking down were once regarded as either contrary to public policy or irrelevant to the considerations which a court must take into account under

---

[258] See above p 937.

[259] HC Select Committee on Work and Pensions, *The Performance of the Child Support Agency* (2005, HC 44) para 87.

[260] Ibid para 135.

[261] Sir David Henshaw, *Report to the Secretary of State for Work and Pensions: Recovering Child Support: Rates to Responsibility* (2006) Cm 6894 and Government response at (2006) Cm 6895.

[262] *Balfour v Balfour* [1919] 2 KB 571; *Gould v Gould* [1970] 1 QB 275; *Re Windle* [1975] 3 All ER 987. See the discussion above at p 117.

Part II of the Matrimonial Causes Act 1973.[263] But no such arguments apply once the couple have separated[264] and, indeed, the general trend in the law and practice relating to financial provision after the breakdown of a marriage has been to encourage the making of fair agreements so as to obviate the need to resort to litigation.[265] To be legally enforceable, an agreement, traditionally called a maintenance agreement, must constitute a contract between the parties. Consequently, if it is not by deed,[266] the party seeking to enforce a promise to pay maintenance must show that she (or he) has furnished consideration. This will normally not be difficult because the undertaking will be embodied in a separation agreement in which each party gives consideration by releasing the other from the duty to cohabit, or will be part of a much more complicated financial transaction involving the division of property and the compromising of other claims. If there is no consideration at all, however, a promise not made by deed will be unenforceable. Basically the parties' rights and duties are determined by the general law of contract,[267] but the law imposes certain extra requirements in the case of spouses or civil partners, as a protection to them and the state.

(a) Maintenance agreements

Where the parties have separated and wish to sort out their financial liabilities, or where proceedings are under way but there is a need to settle some of their finances in the meantime, or they do not wish to make use of a court order for the purpose of settling their financial affairs, they may negotiate a 'maintenance agreement' for the purpose of s 34 of the Matrimonial Causes Act 1973.[268] In such a case, two particular rules apply: certain provisions may be void by statute, and in certain circumstances either party may apply to have the agreement altered. The result is that in many cases the financially weaker party (usually the wife) will have the best of both worlds, because she can hold the other to his covenant and also take other proceedings to obtain maintenance.[269] For this reason, and also because parties who have separated will probably in due course divorce and seek a final resolution of their financial and property relationship through the courts, maintenance agreements per se have become relatively uncommon in recent years.[270]

---

[263] See pp 1012–14 below. But compare *F v F (Ancillary Relief: Substantial Assets)* [1995] 2 FLR 45, where Thorpe LJ regarded the agreement as basically irrelevant to his determination of what orders to make under the 1973 Act, with *N v N (Foreign Divorce: Financial Relief)* [1997] 1 FLR 900 and *S v S (Divorce: Staying Proceedings)* [1997] 2 FLR 100 which both concerned determining the appropriate venue to settle the divorce involving foreign parties, and where the existence of a pre-nuptial agreement which *would* be applied in the foreign venue was regarded as a highly relevant circumstance. In both *M v M (Prenuptial Agreement)* [2002] 1 FLR 654 and *K v K (Ancillary Relief: Prenuptial Agreement)* [2003] 1 FLR 120 the court had regard to the terms of the agreement, whilst not enforcing it directly.

[264] *Merritt v Merritt* [1970] 2 All ER 760, CA.   [265] See below pp 1008–12.

[266] For the meaning of which see the Law of Property (Miscellaneous Provisions) Act 1989 s 1.

[267] It may therefore be set aside on the basis of frustration or mistake etc; cf *Amey v Amey* [1992] 2 FLR 89, where the wife died before an agreement could be put before the divorce court to be made into a consent order. Since terms of the agreement were based on the parties' past contributions and not their future health, the agreement stood.

[268] Or Sch 5 paras 67, 68 to the Civil Partnership Act 2004.

[269] A similar situation exists in relation to liability under the Child Support Act 1991: see p 949.

[270] The public policy of encouraging agreement rather than litigation is achieved through the device of having the court embody the agreement in a 'consent order' which settles the rights and duties of the parties

To come within s 34 of the Matrimonial Causes Act 1973,[271] an agreement must be *in writing* and made between spouses or former spouses. It must also be:

'(a) an agreement containing financial arrangements, whether made during the continuance or after the dissolution or annulment of the marriage; or

(b) a separation agreement which contains no financial arrangements in a case where no other agreement in writing between the same parties contains such arrangements.'

From this it will be seen that an agreement entered into after a divorce or nullity decree absolute can come within the statute only if it contains financial arrangements. An agreement containing no such arrangements can come within the statute only if it is a separation agreement made whilst the parties are still married to (or in a civil partnership with) each other.

Financial arrangements are defined as:

'... provisions governing the rights and liabilities towards one another when living separately of the parties to a marriage (including a marriage which has been dissolved or annulled) in respect of the making or securing of payments or the disposition or use of any property, including such rights and liabilities with respect to the maintenance or education of any child, whether or not a child of the family.'[272]

(b) Void provisions in maintenance agreements

It was at one time fairly common in separation agreements for the husband to covenant to make periodical payments to the wife in exchange for her giving an undertaking not to take any other steps to obtain maintenance from him. An application for maintenance in other matrimonial proceedings might also be compromised by the wife's promising to withdraw it in consideration of the husband's paying her maintenance or transferring property to her. In *Hyman v Hyman*,[273] however, the House of Lords held that no arrangement of this sort can preclude her from applying for financial relief in divorce proceedings. The reason for this decision is that the court's power to order the husband to maintain his former wife after divorce is intended to protect not only her but also any person dealing with her and, indirectly, the state, in view of the possibility of her having to apply for social security benefits. Consequently, it would be contrary to public policy to permit the parties to oust the court's jurisdiction by agreement.[274] This does not mean

at the time of the divorce etc; such orders are very common: see below, p 1008. The order cannot usually take effect until the divorce is granted, but the court can give approval prospectively: *Pounds v Pounds* [1994] 1 FLR 775 (cf *Wicks v Wicks* [1998] 1 FLR 470, CA).

[271] Or para 67 of Sch 5 to the Civil Partnership Act 2004, substituting a reference to civil partners for that of spouses.

[272] Matrimonial Causes Act 1973 s 34(2). See to like effect, Sch 5 para 67(2) to the Civil Partnership Act 2004. It has been held that this does not include the making of a lump sum payment: *Furneaux v Furneaux* (1973) 118 Sol Jo 204. Sed quaere? A lump sum is a 'payment'. The point was left open in *Pace v Doe* [1977] Fam 18 at 23, but the decision in *Furneaux* is consistent with the approach taken to the court's powers on variation of a court order under s 31 of the Act: *Boylan v Boylan* [1988] 1 FLR 282.

[273] [1929] AC 601, HL.

[274] Ibid, at 608 and 629. For a more recent example of application of this principle in the context of determining whether a disposition to a wife was void for the purposes of bankruptcy proceedings, see *Re Kumar (a bankrupt), ex p Lewis v Kumar* [1993] 2 All ER 700.

that the court will ignore the agreement in subsequent proceedings, and the wife may well be held to it.[275] The uncertainty of not knowing whether the court will, or will not, uphold the terms of an agreement has been criticised. In *Pounds v Pounds*[276] Hoffmann LJ characterised the position as the worst of all worlds and noted that counsel for one of the spouses in that case had told the court that in Northampton an agreement had an 80% chance of being upheld but that attitudes varied from district judge to district judge.

'In our attempt to achieve finely ground justice by attributing weight but not too much weight to the agreement of the parties, we have created uncertainty and, in this case and no doubt others, added to the cost and pain of litigation.'[277]

It must also be stressed that, unless the wife's undertaking not to claim financial provision is the sole or main consideration, it does not make the whole agreement unlawful, so that she may still elect to sue the husband on his covenant rather than to apply for maintenance.[278]

Section 34 of the Matrimonial Causes Act 1973[279] provides that any term in a 'maintenance agreement' purporting to restrict any right to apply to a court for an order containing financial agreements shall be void. It also provides that any other financial arrangements in the agreement shall not *thereby* be rendered void or unenforceable but shall be binding on the parties unless void or unenforceable for any other reason. The precise effect of this section is uncertain. Clearly the inclusion of the offensive term does not make the whole agreement illegal: consequently, even if the wife's undertaking not to apply for an order is the sole consideration, the husband can be sued if his covenant to pay her maintenance is made by deed. If it is not made by deed, however, it seems that the husband's promise is still not actionable if the sole consideration is the wife's undertaking not to institute other proceedings for the further reason that, as her promise is void, his promise is supported by no valuable consideration at all.[280]

(c) Alteration of maintenance agreements

Although any sum agreed on by the parties by way of maintenance might well have been reasonable at the time the agreement was made, it is obvious that in some cases an adherence to this in the light of subsequent events could work serious hardship. The husband's earning capacity may be reduced, which will make reasonable a reduction in the sum he has undertaken to pay the wife; alternatively, the wife's illness or increases in the cost of living may well make the sum absurdly small, particularly if it was agreed on some years ago. To overcome difficulties such as these, s 35 and s 36 of the Matrimonial

[275] See *Edgar v Edgar* [1980] 3 All ER 887, below, p 1010.   [276] [1994] 1 FLR 775.
[277] At p 791G.
[278] *Goodinson v Goodinson* [1954] 2 QB 118, CA. But if this is the sole or main consideration for the husband's promise to pay her maintenance, the whole agreement is illegal and unenforceable even if it is by deed: *Bennett v Bennett* [1952] 1 KB 249, CA.
[279] Or Sch 5 para 68 to the Civil Partnership Act 2004.
[280] *Sutton v Sutton* [1984] Ch 184, where an oral agreement was held void, since there was no other consideration.

Causes Act 1973 empower the court to alter any agreement which is a maintenance agreement for the purpose of s 34.[281]

2 BETWEEN PARENTS

(a) Validity

As the foregoing discussion shows, binding agreements made between spouses or civil partners can include making provision for their children, but they can also make binding agreements solely for the benefit of their children. Indeed, as early as 1842 it was recognised that an agreement between the mother and father of an illegitimate child that the latter should pay the former maintenance for the child was actionable.[282] The consideration for the father's promise has been variously stated: it is usually recognised as a counter-promise on the mother's part either to maintain the child herself (notwithstanding her liability to do so under what is now the Social Security Administration Act 1992)[283] or to refrain from taking proceedings.[284] If there is no agreement as to the time for which the father is to remain bound, it would seem that either side may terminate the contract by giving the other reasonable notice.[285] The father's liability will automatically terminate on the mother's death unless the parties otherwise agree, for her personal representatives cannot claim the benefit of the agreement without at the same time accepting the burden of maintaining the child—an obligation which will not normally have been contemplated.[286] On the other hand, since the father's obligation is not personal but can be met out of his estate, there seems to be no reason why his personal representatives should not be bound.[287]

Section 9(2) of the Child Support Act 1991 provides that maintenance agreements to or for the benefit of a child are not restricted by the Act. However, s 9(3) and (4) state that (subject to s 4(10)(a))[288] the existence of such an agreement cannot prevent a party, or any other person, from seeking a maintenance calculation under the Act, and any provision in the agreement purporting to restrict the right of any person to apply for a calculation shall be void. In *Smith v McInerney*,[289] it was held that, where, as part of a separation agreement, the husband had transferred his share in the matrimonial home to the wife in return for release from any future obligation to maintain her or the children, and the wife could not guarantee that he would not in the future be pursued for maintenance for their children under the Child Support Act 1991 s 6,[290] he was entitled to an indemnity from her in respect of any substantial periodical payments the Agency might extract from him. With respect, it is arguable that this approach conflicts with the spirit of s 9(4), since inevitably it may serve to deter the wife from seeking the child support to which her children are entitled.

---

281 Or Sch 5 paras 69–73 to the Civil Partnership Act 2004.

282 *Jennings v Brown* (1842) 9 M & W 496; cf *Tanner v Tanner* [1975] 3 All ER 776, CA.

283 *Ward v Byham* [1956] 2 All ER 318, CA.

284 *Jennings v Brown* (above); *Linnegar v Hodd* (1848) 5 CB 437.

285 *Knowlman v Bluett* (1873) LR 9 Exch 1.   286 *James v Morgan* [1909] 1 KB 564.

287 This was apparently accepted in *Jennings v Brown* (above). In each case, of course, it will be a question of the construction of the particular contract.

288 Discussed above at p 949.   289 [1994] 2 FLR 1077.   290 See above, p 933.

(b) Alteration of agreements

Powers to alter agreements made between fathers and mothers (regardless of whether they are married to each other) first introduced by the Family Law Reform Act 1987,[291] are now contained in Sch 1 paras 10 and 11 to the Children Act 1989. As with court orders, agreements may be altered only where the Child Support Act 1991 does not restrict this;[292] only written agreements may be altered; and only where the court is satisfied either:[293]

'(a) that, by reason of a change in the circumstances in the light of which any financial arrangements contained in the agreement were made (including a change foreseen by the parties when making the agreement) the agreement should be altered so as to make different financial arrangements; or

(b) that the agreement does not contain proper financial arrangements with respect to the child.'

Provided it is satisfied, the court may vary or revoke any financial arrangements when it may appear just to do so.[294]

E THE COURTS' JURISDICTION TO MAKE ORDERS FOR FINANCIAL SUPPORT [295]

1 ORDERS FOR SPOUSES OR CIVIL PARTNERS

(a) Introduction

There are two statutes providing powers to the courts to order financial support outside of divorce in respect of spouses: the Domestic Proceedings and Magistrates' Courts Act 1978, which applies only to the magistrates, and the Matrimonial Causes Act 1973 s 27 which applies to the county or High Court. There is equivalent provision for civil partners made under s 72 and Sch 6, and Sch 5 Part 9, to the Civil Partnership Act 2004.

The courts' jurisdiction to make such orders has declined in popularity. This is probably due to four main reasons. First, the availability of social security means that women who are unable to work due to child care responsibilities may be supported by the state and need not seek maintenance from their husbands when the marriage breaks down. In many ways the job centre has become the 'marital casualty clearing station' which the Law Commission had considered the function of the magistrates' courts when reviewing their jurisdiction in 1976.[296] Indeed, it was this preference for state support, with the

---

[291] Sections 15 and 16, introduced following the recommendations of the Law Commission, Law Com No 118, paras 6.42–6.46.

[292] Section 9(5).   [293] Sch 1, para 10(3).

[294] Any altered periodical payment provision should not in the first instance extend beyond the child's seventeenth birthday, save where the child is or will be receiving instruction at an educational establishment or undergoing training for a trade or profession, or where there are special circumstances: Sch 1, para 10(5).

[295] We deal here only with domestic jurisdiction. Courts may also have jurisdiction to enforce orders made in other parts of the United Kingdom or abroad, or to make orders against a person resident abroad, to be enforced in the other country. For details, see the 8th edition to this work, pp 701–7.

[296] Law Com No 77, *Report on Matrimonial Proceedings in Magistrates' Courts* para 2.4.

consequent drain on public resources, which, as we have seen lay, in part, behind the enactment of the Child Support Act.[297] Secondly, with the liberalisation of divorce by the Divorce Reform Act 1969, couples found that their marriages could be dissolved relatively quickly and easily,[298] and there was a less pressing need to seek a maintenance order in the meantime. Where such maintenance was required, it could be sought, once a petition had been filed for a divorce, via provision under the Matrimonial Causes Act 1973[299] or by agreement. Thirdly, as more women have remained in or returned to the work place notwithstanding marriage and having children, they have become more likely to favour a clean break from their husbands, involving no on-going financial support for themselves and, provided that their children's needs are met, they may be reluctant to seek orders for their own benefit. Finally, a further reason for reluctance to resort to law may have been the unpopularity of the magistrates' court as a forum for hearing matrimonial disputes because of its association with criminal matters. It is unlikely that the extension of the courts' powers to civil partners will reverse this situation.

(b) Orders under the Domestic Proceedings and Magistrates' Courts Act 1978 [300]

The equivalent provisions for civil partners are contained in Sch 6 to the Civil Partnership Act 2004 and are not discussed in detail here unless there is any difference in their application.

Jurisdiction

A magistrates' court may make an order under the Domestic Proceedings and Magistrates' Courts Act 1978 if, at the date of the making of the application, either the applicant or the respondent ordinarily resides within the local justice area for which the court acts.[301]

Orders for financial provision

Application for financial provision may be made in one of three different sets of circumstances. First, there is what one might term the 'normal' application, when the applicant must establish one of the grounds set out in s 1 of the Act. Secondly, if the spouses have agreed what financial provision should be made, either may apply to have the terms of the agreement embodied in a court order. Thirdly, the court may make an order if the spouses are living apart by agreement and the respondent has been making periodical payments to the applicant.

Applications under s 1.[302] Either party to a marriage may apply to a magistrates' court[303]

---

[297] Above, p 930.

[298] But see G Davis et al *Simple Quarrels* (1994) who demonstrate that this speed and ease are only relative; negotiations concerning divorce settlements can still take a number of years to conclude. See Ch 18.

[299] Matrimonial Causes Act 1973 s 22, see below p 991.

[300] For the background to the legislation see generally O McGregor, L Blom-Cooper and C Gibson *Separated Spouses; Report of the Committee on One-Parent Families*, Cmnd 5629, passim; Law Com No 77, *Matrimonial Proceedings in Magistrates' Courts*, Pt II.

[301] Section 30(1). See Law Com No 77, paras 4.77–4.90.

[302] Or Civil Partnership Act 2004 Sch 6 para 1.

[303] The magistrates may refuse to deal with an application if they consider that it would be more conveniently dealt with by the High Court: Domestic Proceedings and Magistrates' Court Act 1978 s 27; Civil Partnership Act 2004 Sch 6 para 8.

for an order on the ground that the respondent spouse has failed to provide reasonable maintenance for the applicant,[304] or has behaved in such a way that the applicant cannot reasonably be expected to live with the respondent, or has deserted the applicant. The ground must exist when the application[305] is made and also at the time of adjudication. The last two grounds may appear to be unnecessary for, if the respondent is making reasonable provision for the applicant, there will be no occasion for making an order. However, the respondent's behaviour is included to cover the case of the wife who is anxious to leave her husband on account of his conduct but knows that, if she does so, she will receive no maintenance from him. Desertion is included to enable a deserted wife whose husband is providing her with reasonable maintenance to obtain an order immediately without having to wait for him to stop paying her.[306]

Failure to provide reasonable maintenance. Whether the respondent has provided reasonable maintenance for the applicant or any child of the family is clearly a question of fact. To answer it the bench must ask itself a hypothetical question: assuming that a ground for applying for an order existed, what order should we make? If the provision in fact being made by the respondent is lower—or at least significantly lower—than this, then he must be failing to provide reasonable maintenance. The word 'failure' implies culpability only insofar as it suggests that the respondent has the means to make the provision; and as his resources must be taken into account in deciding what sum to order, the court must ex hypothesi be satisfied that he has the capacity to make the payments.

The respondent's behaviour. The wording is the same as that used for divorce or dissolution of civil partnership and must be interpreted in the same way.[307] It is not necessary, of course, for the applicant to show that the marriage or partnership has irretrievably broken down. In common with other matters of summary jurisdiction, an application must be made within six months of the occurrence of the act complained of.[308] This means that the applicant must rely on at least one incident that has occurred during this period, although acts committed more than six months before may be relevant in putting the respondent's conduct in the correct setting.[309]

The respondent's desertion. Reference should be made to desertion in connection with the law of divorce.[310] It should be noted, however, that there are some points of difference in the magistrates' jurisdiction. First, the desertion does not have to run for any minimum period of time: all that is necessary is that it should be running at the time of the application and the hearing. Further, if the respondent becomes incapable of having the intention to desert, owing to mental illness, the magistrates may not treat desertion as continuing.

Reconciliation. When hearing an application under s 1, the court is required to consider whether there is any possibility of a reconciliation between the parties and if, either then

---

[304] There is also a ground relating to failure to provide reasonable maintenance for any child of the family: s 1(b) or para 1(1)(b). See further below, pp 966 et seq.

[305] For procedure, see the Family Proceedings Courts (Matrimonial Proceedings Etc) Rules 1991.

[306] Law Com No 77 paras 2.6–2.11.

[307] *Bergin v Bergin* [1983] 1 All ER 905. See above pp 267–9.

[308] Magistrates' Courts Act 1980 s 127(1).   [309] Cf *Buxton v Buxton* [1967] P 48.

[310] See above pp 269–71.

or later, it appears that there is a reasonable possibility, it may adjourn the proceedings and, if it sees fit, request a CAFCASS officer or other person to attempt to effect one.[311] In the past courts have claimed to have achieved a measure of success in this regard but, as in the case of divorce, it may be more practicable in most cases to concentrate on mediation rather than reconciliation.[312]

Orders that may be made.[313] The court may order the respondent to do one or more of the following:

(a) to make periodical payments to the applicant;[314]

(b) to pay a lump sum not exceeding £1,000 for the applicant.[315]

It may allow the respondent to pay a lump sum or may order him to pay it by instalments.[316] All orders for periodical payments may run from the date of the application and may be made for a limited period of time.[317] This may be useful where a wife is likely to need money for a comparatively short period whilst she adjusts to living alone, because the husband will not have to go back to the court at a later date to seek a variation or discharge. Similarly, magistrates may use this device as a means of encouraging the wife to obtain paid employment, if they consider this to be the proper course (though before doing this justices should be confident that the wife can reasonably obtain employment). If she will continue to need maintenance after the end of the period stipulated, she should take care to have the order varied before it runs out, because otherwise it will automatically lapse and she will have to start fresh proceedings. The court may also order that the payments should begin from a future date, and it may wish to use this power if, for example, the husband is unemployed but is to start work in a short time. The order will terminate on the remarriage or formation of a civil partnership (but not divorce),[318] or death of the recipient or on the death of the person liable to make the payments.[319]

Consent orders. Magistrates are able to make a consent order without the applicant having to establish any ground. Under s 6,[320] upon either party's application and provided the court is satisfied that either the applicant or the respondent has agreed to make the

[311] Domestic Proceedings and Magistrates' Courts Act 1978 s 26, as amended by Criminal Justice and Court Services Act 2000 Sch 7 para 57; Civil Partnership Act 2004 Sch 6 para 7.

[312] See above, pp 281 et seq.

[313] Domestic Proceedings and Magistrates' Courts Act 1978 s 2; : Civil Partnership Act 2004 Sch 6 para 2.

[314] Such orders may subsequently be varied or revoked on the application of either spouse: s 20; or civil partner: Civil Partnership Act 2004 Sch 6 Part 6.

[315] A lump sum order may not be varied, although if it is payable by instalments, the amount of these, and the dates of their payment, may be varied: s 22; Civil Partnership Act 2004 Sch 6 para 41. For orders for children of the family, see below, p 966.

[316] Magistrates' Courts Act 1980 s 75.

[317] Domestic Proceedings and Magistrates' Courts Act 1978 s 2(1)(a) and (c), s 4(1) and s 5(2); Civil Partnership Act 2004 Sch 6 paras 2(1)(a) and (c), 26 and 27. Interim orders may also be made pending a final order or dismissal of the application: s 19; Civil Partnership Act 2004 Sch 6 para 20.

[318] Section 4(2) as amended by Civil Partnership Act 2004 Sch 27 para 57; Civil Partnership Act Sch 6 para 26(2).

[319] Section 4(1); Civil Partnership Act Sch 6 para 26(1)(b). An order ceases to have effect if the parties continue, or resume, living together for a continuous period exceeding six months: s 25(1), s 88(2); Civil Partnership Act Sch 6 para 29(2).

[320] Or Civil Partnership Act 2004 Sch 6 Part 2.

financial provision[321] specified in the application, it may make an order giving effect to the agreement.[322] The order may contain precisely the same terms as an order made following an application under s 1 except that, as the respondent has agreed to it, a lump sum may be for *any amount* and is not limited to £1,000. The court may not make the order proposed if it considers that it would be contrary to the interests of justice to do so.[323] This seems most likely to occur if the amount specified in the application looks too low, or if it appears that undue pressure has been put on either party. In such cases, however, it is open to the parties to come forward with a fresh agreement. Alternatively, the court itself might take the initiative and suggest what order would be appropriate: if the parties both agree, this may be embodied in an order.[324]

Orders following separation. In cases where the parties have separated and one party is actually providing the other with reasonable maintenance, the recipient may be concerned that, without the security of an order, he may choose to stop at any time. To secure her position, she may apply to the court under s 7.[325] The parties must have lived apart, without either being in desertion, for a continuous period exceeding three months, and one must have been making periodical payments for the benefit of the other or a child of the family.[326] 'Living apart' is not defined, but it presumably bears the same meaning as under the law of divorce.[327]

If these conditions are satisfied, the court may make an order for periodical payments for the benefit of the applicant for such term as may be specified.[328] The purpose of s 7 is to enable legal effect to be given to the de facto situation. Consequently, no lump sum order may be made and the court may not require the respondent to make payments which exceed in aggregate during any period of three months the amount actually paid by him for the benefit of the applicant during the three months immediately preceding the making of the application. If this is greater than the sum which the court would have ordered on an application under s 1, the respondent is protected by the further provision that the order must not be for more than this smaller sum.[329] Conversely, if the court considers that the sums paid fail to provide reasonable maintenance for the applicant, the ground under s 1 must necessarily be made out; the court may therefore treat the application as though made under that section and will then have full powers to make such orders for periodical payments and lump sum payments as it thinks fit.[330] Perhaps unsurprisingly,

---

[321] Periodical payments or lump sum payments: s 6(2).

[322] If proceedings are begun for an order under s 2 and the respondent then agrees to the order, the applicant may apply for an order under s 6: s 6(4); Civil Partnership Act 2004 Sch 6 para 14.

[323] Section 6(1)(b); Civil Partnership Act 2004 Sch 6 para 9(2)(b).

[324] Section 6(5); Civil Partnership Act 2004 Sch 6 para 13.

[325] Or Civil Partnership Act 2004 Sch 6 Part 3.

[326] Section 7(1); Civil Partnership Act 2004 Sch 6 para 15(1). The payments need not have been made to the applicant. Hence, for example, the payment of rent could amount to periodical payments for this purpose.

[327] Under which spouses living under the same roof may be regarded as living apart provided that they are living in two separate households: *Mouncer v Mouncer* [1972] 1 All ER 289; see above p 271.

[328] If the parties resume living together, the order ceases to have effect immediately: s 25(3); Civil Partnership Act 2004 Sch 6 para 29(5). Cf orders made under s 1 or s 6, which may continue in force for up to six months.

[329] Section 7(3); Civil Partnership Act 2004 Sch 6 para 17.

[330] Section 7(4); Civil Partnership Act 2004 Sch 6 para 18.

given its convoluted nature, very few orders appear ever to have been made under this section.[331]

Payment of maintenance. Upon the making of a periodical payments order, magistrates' courts are required to specify the method of payment,[332] which must be one of the following: payments made directly by the debtor to the creditor; payments made to the designated officer for the court or any other magistrates' court; payment by standing order or direct debit; payments made to the Secretary of State under the collection provisions of the Child Support Act;[333] and payments by way of an attachment of earnings order.[334]

The power to order payment by standing order (or some similar method) was introduced by the Maintenance Enforcement Act 1991[335] and is intended to ensure prompt payments without the parties having to come face to face. The more traditional method of providing for this is for payment to be made to the magistrates' court on behalf of the recipient.

Assessment

The Act sets out a checklist of the matters which a magistrates' court is to take into account when making an order. The court must 'have regard to all the circumstances of the case, first consideration being given to the welfare while a minor of any child of the family who has not attained the age of 18'.[336] In addition, in determining whether the respondent is to be required to make periodical payments or to pay a lump sum to the applicant and, if so, how much he is to pay, the court is directed 'in particular' to have regard to:[337]

'(a) the income, earning capacity, property and other financial resources which each of the parties to the marriage has or is likely to have in the foreseeable future, including in the case of earning capacity any increase in that capacity which it would in the opinion of the court be reasonable to expect a party to the marriage to take steps to acquire;

(b) the financial needs, obligations and responsibilities which each of the parties to the marriage has or is likely to have in the foreseeable future;

(c) the standard of living enjoyed by the parties to the marriage before the occurrence of the conduct which is alleged as the ground of the application;

(d) the age of each party to the marriage and the duration of the marriage;

(e) any physical or mental disability of either of the parties to the marriage;

(f) the contributions which each of the parties has made or is likely in the foreseeable

---

[331] Only 20 in 1992: Home Office Statistical Bulletin *Domestic Proceedings England and Wales 1992* Table 2. (No subsequent statistics have been published.)

[332] Magistrates' Courts Act 1980 s 59(1). This requirement is contingent upon the 'debtor' (ie the person against whom the order is made) being ordinarily resident in England and Wales at the time that the order was made: ibid, s 59(2).

[333] Added by the Child Support Act 1991 (Consequential Amendments) Order 1993. It is doubtful if the Agency has the capability to handle the collection of spousal maintenance, given its difficulties in enforcing child support, discussed above, p 946.

[334] Ibid, s 59(3), (6). Attachment of earnings orders are discussed below, p 978.

[335] Where payment is so ordered, the court can require the debtor to open an account: ibid s 59(4).

[336] Section 3(1): Civil Partnership Act 2004 Sch 6 para 3.

[337] Section 3(2): Civil Partnership Act 2004 Sch 6 para 5 makes equivalent provision. In the case of applications made under s 7 (Civil Partnership Act 2004 Sch 6 para Part 3), para (c) is amended to read: 'the standard of living enjoyed by the parties to the marriage before they lived apart' (s 7(5): Civil Partnership Act 2004 Sch 6 para 19).

future to make to the welfare of the family, including any contribution by looking after the home or caring for the family;

(g) the conduct of each of the parties, if that conduct is such that it would in the opinion of the court be inequitable to disregard it.'

Comparison with the matters which the court must take into account in making an order for financial relief after divorce shows that, with minor exceptions,[338] the guidelines are identical. As the law has been much more fully worked out in connection with divorce, detailed examination of these matters will be deferred until Chapter 18, but some general principles and certain points of dissimilarity should be mentioned here.

Absence of power to adjust property rights. The main difference between the powers of the magistrates' courts and those of divorce courts is that magistrates cannot make property adjustment orders. This is because the making of property adjustment orders is inconsistent with the principle that magistrates should regulate the parties' financial position during a period of marital breakdown which is not necessarily permanent or irretrievable. It is to be assumed that whichever spouse or civil partner is in the family home will stay there for the time being: if either of them wishes to bring about a change, he or she must invoke the jurisdiction of the courts in some other way.

No requirement to consider 'self-sufficiency'. Another important difference between magistrates' powers and those of the divorce court is that the former are not directed to consider whether the parties could become self-sufficient. Magistrates have no powers to make a 'clean break' order settling financial liability in a once-and-for-all order. On the other hand, they are directed to have regard to whether it is reasonable to expect a party to take steps to increase his earning capacity. This could justify, for example, making a periodical payments order to last for a limited time in a case where the applicant could reasonably be expected to start work or to obtain higher paid work. Even if such a limited term order were to be made, the applicant could still return to the court to seek an extension to the order,[339] or, if the order had already expired, could bring fresh proceedings to seek a new order.

First consideration to be given to the welfare of a child under the age of 18. This requirement is the same as on divorce and we discuss it more fully in that context.[340] Suffice to say here that (a) children's welfare is a consideration, even where the application is for *spousal* support; (b) priority is only given to children of the spouses' family;[341] and (c) the court is only required to give first and not paramount consideration to the child's welfare.[342] This means that other considerations should be taken into account and in some circumstances could be overriding. The enjoinder means, for instance, that the husband's moral obligations towards his second family should not be ignored.[343]

---

[338] Para (c) of s 25(1) of the Matrimonial Causes Act 1973 refers to 'the standard of living enjoyed by the family before the breakdown of the marriage'. The divorce court is additionally required to consider the loss, inter alia, of pension rights. See below, p 1051.

[339] There being no equivalent of s 28(1A) of the Matrimonial Causes Act 1973, which enables the court to direct that the party not be entitled to seek an extension of the term specified in the order (see below, p 1026).

[340] See below, p 1021.   [341] Not those of the parent's second family.

[342] On which, see *Suter v Suter and Jones* [1987] Fam 111, CA.

[343] See *Blower v Blower* [1986] 1 FLR 292. The balancing of needs and responsibilities to first and second families is also attempted under the Child Support Act, although there the approach has changed and is now to favour the second family: above at p 937.

The parties' needs. According to Dunn LJ in *Vasey v Vasey*,[344] the proper approach for magistrates, when considering an application for financial provision, is to make findings upon each of the matters set out in what is now s 3(2) and to balance the factors against one another to arrive at an order which is just and reasonable. But, as Dunn LJ also pointed out, the most important function of magistrates is to balance the needs and responsibilities against the financial resources.

Only the family's reasonable needs should be taken into account. The parties require shelter and food, but over and above this there can be no hard and fast rules, since what amounts to 'reasonable' must inevitably be judged against the available resources.[345] Commonly in cases before magistrates, the parties' means will be so slight that all the court can do is to concentrate on their needs, and thus the strictures of the House of Lords[346] against the concept of 'reasonable requirements' in 'big money' cases are of limited relevance. The need to support two families will often mean that the husband will not be able to keep both above subsistence level; in that case any order made must not reduce his resources to such an extent that, were he unemployed, he would be entitled to jobseeker's allowance. Given that he can be ordered to pay something, however, magistrates should make a full assessment of the sum, notwithstanding that it will be so small that the wife will still have to look to the Department of Work and Pensions to make up the balance.[347] To this extent the court must know what the benefits payable to both parties would be.[348]

Where the payer is himself dependent upon social security, the courts at one time considered that he should still be required to pay something, to remind him of his obligations.[349] However, in *E v C (Child Maintenance)*[350] it was held that, where a father would have been exempt from paying the minimum amount of child maintenance under the Child Support Act, magistrates hearing his application to reduce the maintenance he paid under a court order should have discovered what his child support liability would have been, and should have appreciated that where a person 'is on, by way of government benefits, fair subsistence, any order which deducts from that is an order which puts him into difficulties.'[351] A nominal order of £1 per annum for each child was substituted. Since obligations to one's children appear to carry more weight with the courts than obligations to a spouse, the same approach to the ability of the husband to pay should apply a fortiori where a wife is seeking maintenance from her husband.

The parties' conduct. In some cases the parties' conduct, or the short duration of the

---

[344] [1985] FLR 596 at 603, CA.

[345] One problem is the need for a car. Whether this is a reasonable need depends in part upon whether it is genuinely needed to get to work: cf *Clarke v Clarke* (1979) 9 Fam Law 15, where a car was not thought to be needed, and *Slater v Slater* (1982) 3 FLR 364, where it was. In *Girvan v Girvan* (1983) 13 Fam Law 213, where a husband had just been made redundant, it was thought that a television was a reasonable need, but not a video recorder.

[346] In *White v White* [2001] 1 AC 596.

[347] *Ashley v Ashley* [1968] P 582; *Barnes v Barnes* [1972] 3 All ER 872, CA. Contrast the situation where the couple are divorced, where the courts are readier to end the parties' financial ties even though this means one of them will be totally dependent upon state benefits: *Delaney v Delaney* [1990] 2 FLR 457, CA.

[348] *Williams v Williams* [1974] Fam 55.

[349] *Freeman v Swatridge* [1984] FLR 762, CA. The Child Support Act similarly seeks to do this by exacting the reduced or flat rate of maintenance except where the non-resident parent is exempt: see above, p 938.

[350] [1996] 1 FLR 472.   [351] Per Douglas Brown J at 476E–F.

marriage, may be significant. Both these facts are relevant on divorce and will be discussed in detail in Chapter 18. Suffice it here to say that the generally held view is that conduct will rarely be relevant. As Dunn LJ said, in *Vasey v Vasey*,[352] conduct should only be taken into account in exceptional cases, because 'experience has shown that it is dangerous to make judgments about the cause of breakdown of a marriage without full inquiry, since the conduct of one spouse can only be measured against the conduct of the other, and marriages seldom break down without faults on both sides'.[353] Even if conduct is thought to be relevant, magistrates should still balance that fact against all the others laid down by statute, and in particular against each party's needs.[354]

In cases where the marriage has been short-lived, reduced orders may be justified.[355]

Remarriage and cohabitation. The payer's remarriage will not normally be relevant in magistrates' proceedings, but it may become so if the order continues in force after a later divorce. In this case it may be proper to reduce the order because of the payer's increased financial responsibilities; the same result will follow if he lives with another woman, particularly if they have children whom he has to support.[356] Likewise, the wife's living with another man may lead the court make a reduced order, or none at all, not because she is committing adultery, but because the man will be, or may be expected to be, supporting her.

Lump sum payments. The power conferred on magistrates to order lump sum payments was introduced by the 1978 Act. Although such a power, of course, is of no practical value unless the respondent has the necessary capital (or, possibly, income),[357] there are a number of situations in which relatively small orders may be made. The Act itself provides that a lump sum may be ordered to meet any liability or expenses already incurred in maintaining the applicant or any child of the family:[358] in other words, in appropriate cases it will be an alternative to backdating the order. It might also be used to enable a wife to take a course of training, or even to help provide the capital to set her up in business. If the spouses have low incomes but the respondent has some savings, a just solution might be to order part of the savings to be paid to the applicant.

(c) Orders for financial provision under s 27 of the Matrimonial Causes Act 1973

Section 27 of the Matrimonial Causes Act 1973 provides that either party to a marriage may apply to a divorce court for an order on the ground that the other has failed to provide reasonable maintenance for the applicant. There is equivalent provision for civil

---

[352] [1985] FLR 596 at 603, CA.

[353] But note that divorce law provides limited means for holding an inquiry into the cause of the breakdown of the marriage, although conduct is a relevant factor in assessing the financial arrangements for the spouses: Matrimonial Causes Act 1973 s 25(2)(g).

[354] *Vasey v Vasey* (above). The wife actually conceded that a reduced order should be made, since she had deserted her husband after only nine months of marriage.

[355] See eg *Khan v Khan* [1980] 1 All ER 497; *Graves v Graves* (1973) 4 Fam Law 124; *Brady v Brady* (1973) 3 Fam Law 78.

[356] See *Delaney v Delaney* [1990] 2 FLR 457, CA.

[357] See *Burridge v Burridge* [1983] Fam 9, where the court ordered an unemployed husband to pay a lump sum by instalments, expecting him to obtain employment within six weeks.

[358] Section 2(2); Civil Partnership Act 2004 Sch 6 para 3.

partners in Sch 5 Part 9 to the Civil Partnership Act 2004. The court has jurisdiction if either party is domiciled in England and Wales, if the applicant has been habitually resident here for one year, or if the respondent is resident here.[359] The proceedings must be commenced in a divorce county court,[360] but the court has the power, either upon its own motion or upon application by a party, to order the transfer of the whole or any part of the proceedings to the High Court.[361]

The ground upon which an application may be made is the same as the first on which a spouse may apply to a magistrates' court for an order under the Domestic Proceedings and Magistrates' Courts Act 1978 s 1, ie that the respondent has failed to provide reasonable maintenance for the applicant. However, in determining whether this ground is made out and, if so, what order to make, the court is also required to take into account the matters set out in s 25(2) of the Matrimonial Causes Act 1973.[362] The welfare of a child of the family is to be regarded as the court's first consideration only where an application is made in respect of such a child, and not where maintenance for the applicant alone is sought, but it is doubtful whether this change of emphasis makes any difference in practice.

The court may make an interim order for periodical payments to the applicant if it appears that the latter is in immediate need of financial assistance.[363] If the ground is made out, the court may make one or more financial provision orders[364] against the respondent.

The question of assessment of orders is essentially the same as that of orders made in magistrates' courts, except that periodical payments may be secured and there is an unlimited power to order lump sum payments. Both these matters will be dealt with more fully when we consider financial provision after divorce;[365] in the case of lump sum payments, however, it should be borne in mind that the court has no power to make property adjustment orders under s 27, and consequently a lump sum order should not be used as a means of circumventing this restriction. Section 27(7)[366] specifically provides that a lump sum may be ordered to enable the applicant to meet any liabilities or expenses already incurred in maintaining herself (or himself); in addition, it may properly be ordered (as on divorce) whenever a capital sum is more valuable to the applicant than periodical payments.[367] Orders are payable and enforceable in the same way as orders for periodical payments on divorce.[368]

---

[359] Section 27(2); Civil Partnership Act 2004 Sch 5 para 39(2). The right of action does not extend beyond the parties' joint lives, hence, when one spouse died whilst proceedings were pending, the claim was held to have abated: *Harb v King Fahd Bin Abdul Aziz* [2005] EWCA Civ 1324 [2006] 1 WLR 578.

[360] Matrimonial and Family Proceedings Act 1984 s 34(1)(a); in respect of civil partnerships, in a designated 'civil partnership proceedings county court: see Matrimonial and Family Proceedings Act 1984 s 36B, as inserted by Civil Partnership Act 2004 Sch 27 para 92.

[361] Ibid, s 39 as amended.

[362] Section 27(3); Civil Partnership Act 2004 Sch 5 para 21. See below, pp 1030–61. These matters, which apply also in relation to divorce and dissolution of civil partnerships, are to be read as if they referred to a failure to provide reasonable maintenance instead of the breakdown of the marriage or civil partnership: s 27(3B): Civil Partnership Act 2004 Sch 5 para 43(4).

[363] Section 27(5); Civil Partnership Act 2004 Sch 5 para 40.

[364] Section 27(6); Civil Partnership Act 2004 Sch 5 para 41. Financial provision orders are orders for periodical payments (secured or unsecured) or for lump sums. A lump sum may be made payable in instalments and the instalments may be secured.

[365] See below, p 994 (secured payments) and p 995 (lump sum payments).

[366] Civil Partnership Act 2004 Sch 5 para 42(1).   [367] See below, p 997.

[368] See below p 1069.

It would seem that few applications are made for orders under s 27. Statistics are not now recorded for proceedings under this section. Most spouses would probably prefer to take the cheaper and speedier proceedings available in magistrates' courts unless they are also seeking a divorce, in which case the court has powers to deal with their financial needs anyway.[369]

2　OBTAINING FINANCIAL RELIEF FOR CHILDREN

(a)　Matrimonial and civil partnership jurisdictions

Where the Child Support Act does not apply,[370] it will be possible to utilise any of the jurisdictions discussed above to obtain an order for a child, as orders under the Domestic Proceedings and Magistrates' Courts Act 1978, the Matrimonial Causes Act 1973 and the Civil Partnership Act 2004 may be made payable both to the applicant and to, or for the benefit of, any 'child of the family'. The court may make an order for financial provision for a child whether or not it makes any other order relating to the child.

Factors to be considered

In deciding what, if any, orders should be made in addition to those considerations applicable to orders for spouses, discussed above, the court must also have regard to:[371]

(a)　the financial needs of the child;

(b)　the income, earning capacity (if any), property and other financial resources of the child;

(c)　any physical or mental disability of the child;

(d)　the standard of living enjoyed by the family before the occurrence of the conduct which is alleged as the ground of the application (or before the parties to the marriage lived apart); and

(e)　the manner in which the child was being and in which the parties expected him to be educated or trained.[372]

We have already considered the meaning of 'child of the family',[373] but it should be emphasised that just because a child is found to be a child of the family does not ipso facto mean that the respondent will be ordered to make financial provision for him.[374] When deciding whether to make an order against a party to the marriage in favour of a child who is not his natural or adopted child and, if so, how much to award, the court must further have regard:[375]

---

[369]　See below p 991.　　[370]　See above, p 947.

[371]　Domestic Proceedings and Magistrates' Courts Act 1978 s 3(4), s 7(5); Civil Partnership Act 2004 Sch 6 para 6.

[372]　A court hearing an application under s 27 of the Matrimonial Causes Act must consider a similar list of factors: s 27(3A) and s 25(3), as must a court hearing an application under Sch 5 Part 9 to the Civil Partnership Act 2004: para 44.

[373]　Above, p 338.

[374]　Compare liability under the Child Support Act 1991 (discussed above, p 932), which depends upon legal parenthood.

[375]　Domestic Proceedings and Magistrates' Courts Act 1978 s 3(3), s 7(5); Matrimonial Causes Act 1973 ss 27(3A), s 25(4); Civil Partnership Act 2004 Sch 5 paras 22(3), 44(3)(b); Sch 6 para 6(3).

(a) to whether he has assumed any responsibility for the child's maintenance and, if he did, to the extent to which, and the basis on which, he assumed that responsibility and to the length of time during which he disregarded that responsibility

(b) to whether in assuming and discharging that responsibility he did so knowing that the child was not his own child; and

(c) to the liability of any other person to maintain the child.

Whether a party assumed responsibility for a child must be judged objectively, and, in the absence of a clear contrary indication, the payment of the expenses of a family unit including the child implies an assumption of responsibility, even though other resources may be available for his maintenance.[376] In para (a), the word 'extent' refers to the amount of the spouse's contribution in contradistinction to the length of time during which he made it.[377] The reference in para (c) to the liability of any other person to maintain the child covers any liability enforceable at law, and thus embraces the potential liability of a parent or of a party to another marriage who has treated the child as a child of the family.[378] It will be seen that the need to take all these matters into account means that the court might well conclude, for example, that no order should be made against a husband who had married the wife in the mistaken belief that he was the father of her child, or who had made it clear at the time of the marriage that he was undertaking no financial responsibility for her children by a previous marriage if their own father was quite capable of providing for them.[379]

In determining what is reasonable maintenance for a child, as Bagnall J said in a comment approved by the Court of Appeal in *Lilford v Glynn*:[380]

'In the vast majority of cases the financial position of a child of a subsisting marriage is simply to be afforded shelter, food and education, according to the means of his parents.'

As we have seen, courts are encouraged to have regard to the level of support which would be assessed under the Child Support Act in deciding on an appropriate amount of maintenance for the child, including a nil amount.[381] Lump sum orders may be useful to meet particular expenses for a child, for example, to buy a uniform or other clothes for a new school, or to pay for fees and other incidental expenses on starting a course of training.

Duration of orders

Since some children will start earning when they reach the upper limit of the compulsory school age, no order for periodical payments is to extend in the first instance beyond the date of the child's birthday next following his attaining 16, unless the court thinks it right to specify a later date (as it obviously must if he is already over that age). No order may be made at all, however, if the child is over the age of 18, and an existing order

---

[376] *Snow v Snow* [1972] Fam 74 at 111–12, CA.

[377] *Roberts v Roberts* [1962] P 212.   [378] *Snow v Snow* (above) at 112.

[379] See *Bowlas v Bowlas* [1965] P 450, CA. In the case of an application under s 7 of the Domestic Proceedings and Magistrates' Courts Act 1978 the court shall not require the respondent to make payments for the benefit of a child of the family who is not his child if it would not have made an order in the child's favour in proceedings brought under s 1: s 7(3)(c).

[380] [1979] 1 All ER 441 at 447. See also *Kiely v Kiely* [1988] 1 FLR 248.

[381] *E v C (Child Maintenance)* [1996] 1 FLR 472, discussed above at p 963.

may not continue after his eighteenth birthday. To both limbs of this rule there are two exceptions: there is no age limit on the making or continuation of orders so long as the child is (or, if an order were made, would be) receiving instruction at an educational establishment or undergoing training for a trade, profession or vocation (whether or not he is also gainfully employed) or, in any event, if there are special circumstances justifying this.[382] Periodical payments could therefore continue indefinitely, if, for example, the child were incapable of earning his own living owing to some physical or mental disability. The order terminates on the death of the child or of the person liable to make the payments.[383]

Variation on the child's application

The child himself may apply for a variation if he has attained the age of 16. He may also, once he has attained the age of 16 but before he reaches 18, apply for an order to be revived.[384] He may well wish to take advantage of this provision if he decides to undergo further education or training at some stage after leaving school and beginning to earn his own living.

In practice, it seems likely that very few such applications are brought under these jurisdictions, since arrangements for the child will either be made under the divorce (or dissolution of civil partnership) jurisdiction discussed in the next chapter, or the Child Support Act. Of greater practical importance is the following jurisdiction, Sch 1 to the Children Act 1989.

(b) Proceedings under Sch 1 to the Children Act 1989

The courts are empowered by the Children Act 1989 s 15 and Sch 1 to make financial provision solely for the benefit of children in circumstances where the Child Support Act does not apply. The 1989 Act also permits children over the age of 18 to seek financial orders against their parents in certain circumstances. Usually, this jurisdiction is invoked when the parents have not been married to each other, although it is in fact available to married parents (or civil partners). As just noted, parents who have been married to each other would usually use the divorce jurisdiction and/or Child Support Act. However, this is not invariably the case: for example, in *Re S (Child: Financial Provision)*[385] the parents divorced abroad and the mother remarried soon after, and was thus unable to seek an order under the divorce jurisdiction[386] but she was held entitled to apply for an order under Sch 1.

---

[382] Domestic Proceedings and Magistrates' Courts Act 1978 s 5(1)–(3), s 6(7) and s 7(7); Matrimonial Causes Act 1973 s 29; Civil Partnership Act 2004 Sch 5 para 49, Sch 6 para 27. *G v G (Periodical Payment: Jurisdiction)* [1997] 1 FLR 368, CA; *B v B (Adult Student: Liability to Support)* [1998] 1 FLR 373, CA.

[383] Domestic Proceedings and Magistrates' Courts Act 1978 s 5(4), s 6(7) and s 7(7); Matrimonial Causes Act 1973 s 29(4); Civil Partnership Act 2004 Sch 5 para 49(6); Sch 6 para 27(6). Under the former Act, where payments are ordered to be made *to the child himself,* neither the continuation nor the resumption of cohabitation by the spouses will have any effect on the order unless the court otherwise directs: s 25(2).

[384] Domestic Proceedings and Magistrates' Courts Act 1978 s 20(12)(b); Matrimonial Causes Act 1973 s 27(6B) Civil Partnership Act 2004 Sch 5 para 55; Sch 6 para 39(b).

[385] [2004] EWCA Civ 1685 [2005] 2 FLR 94. Discussed further below p 970. See also *B v B (Transfer of Tenancy)* [1994] Fam Law 250.

[386] See further pp 1076–81 below for jurisdiction to make financial orders particularly after an overseas divorce.

When orders may be made

The court may make financial provision for children either upon application[387] or upon its own motion when making, varying or discharging a residence order.[388] Unless the child is a ward of court,[389] the court cannot make a Sch 1 order upon its own motion if it has not made a residence order.

Who can apply

Applications may be made by parents, guardians, special guardians and any person in whose favour a residence order is in force.[390] For these purposes 'parents' includes both married and unmarried parents (including the unmarried father)[391] and any party to a marriage (whether or not subsisting), or any civil partner in a civil partnership (whether or not subsisting) in relation to whom the child concerned is a child of the family, eg a step-parent.[392]

Although guardians are entitled to apply, they are unlikely to do so very often, since they can only take office during the lifetime of the surviving spouse when the deceased appointing parent had a residence order in his favour at the time of death.[393]

Against whom orders can be made

Orders may be made against either or both parents of the child. As with applicants, 'parents' for these purposes includes unmarried fathers[394] and step-parents of 'children of the family'. However, only those who have been married to, or in a civil partnership with, a parent of the child are within the definition of step-parent in Sch 1 para 16(2).[395]

Although there is power to order step-parents of 'children of the family' to make financial provision, the Law Commission envisaged that applications are more likely to be made by them.[396] No orders may be made against a guardian or special guardian. This is in line with the general policy of not making such persons liable to make financial provision

---

[387] Children Act 1989 Sch 1, para 1(1).

[388] Sch 1, para 1(6). Note also the powers under para 8 when making a residence order to vary or revoke any existing financial relief order made under any enactment other than the Children Act 1989. A court is required, when minded to make an order which has not been asked for or canvassed during the hearing, to give the parties an opportunity to make representations and to reopen the evidence: *Re C (Financial Provision: Lump Sum Order)* [1995] 1 FLR 925.

[389] Sch 1, para 1(7). Wardship is discussed in Ch 16.

[390] Sch 1, para 1(1) as amended by Adoption and Children Act 2002 Sch 3 para 71. Although a residence order must be in force before a financial order may be made in favour of a person other than a parent, an *application* may be made together with an application for a residence order: cf Family Proceedings Rules 1991 r 4.3(4).

[391] Children Act s 2(3).

[392] Sch 1, para 16(2) as amended by the Civil Partnership Act 2004 s78(4). See also *Re A (Child of the Family)* [1998] 1 FLR 347 (grandfather who had brought up grandchild as part of his own family).

[393] See above, p 441.

[394] Before the implementation of the Children Act, it had been held in *Hager v Osborne* [1992] 2 All ER 494, in respect of unmarried fathers, that equivalent provisions under the Guardianship of Minors Act 1971 were retrospective in the sense that they applied to children born before they came into force, and that the dismissal of a previous application following inconclusive blood tests did not preclude a fresh application being made so that advantage could be taken of DNA testing.

[395] Hence, a non-married step-parent cannot apply for, or be required to meet, an order under the Schedule: *J v J (A Minor: Property Transfer)* [1993] 2 FLR 56.

[396] Law Com No 172, para 4.63.

or property transfers in the same way as a parent.[397] Similarly, no orders can be made against those, other than parents, who have residence orders in their favour.[398]

Powers

The High Court, county courts and magistrates' courts all have jurisdiction to make Sch 1 orders, though magistrates' powers are more restricted than those of the higher courts.

All courts may order the making of unsecured periodical payments either to the applicant for the benefit of the child or to the child himself, or partly to both, for such term as may be specified in the order.[399] Similarly, they can order lump sum payments,[400] although in the case of magistrates' orders there is a prescribed maximum limit of £1,000 or such larger amount as the Secretary of State shall fix.[401] Lump sum orders may provide for payment to be made by instalments.[402] An order for periodical payments or lump sums may be made, notwithstanding that the child is living outside England and Wales.[403] The benefit for the child need not be direct: in *Re S (Child: Financial Provision)*[404] it was held that payments to enable the mother to travel to the Sudan and take proceedings there to enforce an order already granted by the Sudan court for the return of the child to her care, were capable of being for the child's benefit (although the Court of Appeal remitted the mother's application for determination on the merits). However, where the payment was sought to enable a parent to pursue legal proceedings with limited chances of success in the context of already very high legal costs and extensive litigation between the parents, the application was refused as being of no benefit to the child.[405]

The High Court and county court may additionally order the making of secured periodical payments, settlements of property and property transfers.[406] The statutory legal aid charge and the postponement of the charge over orders for money, where it is to be used to purchase a new home, apply to orders made under Sch 1.[407] A similarly broad view of 'benefit' for the child to that taken in *Re S* was applied in relation to a transfer of property in *K v K (Minors: Property Transfer)*.[408] There, it was held that the words 'the

---

[397] Ibid, para 2.25.

[398] See *S v X and X (Interveners)* [1990] 2 FLR 187 (third party interveners who had been granted custody were held not liable to maintain the child). Sch 1, para 15 provides that a local authority may make contributions to a person (other than a parent or step-parent of the child) with a residence order, towards the cost of the accommodation and maintenance of the child, but it is unclear how this could be enforced: see *Re K and A (Local Authority: Child Maintenance)* [1995] 1 FLR 688.

[399] Sch 1, para 1(1)(a), (b) and 1(2)(a); *G v G (Periodical Payments: Jurisdiction)* [1997] 1 FLR 368, CA.

[400] Sch 1, para 1(1)(a), (b) and 1(2)(c). A lump sum order may be made notwithstanding the respondent's bankruptcy: *Re G (Children Act 1989: Sch 1)* [1996] 2 FLR 171.

[401] Sch 1, para 5(2).   [402] Sch 1, para 5(5).

[403] Sch 1, para 14. Note that this paragraph is not exhaustive: *Re S (Child: Financial Provision)* [2004] EWCA Civ 1685 [2005] 2 FLR 94.

[404] Ibid. See R Bird, 'Child Maintenance: Cui Bono Revisited' [2005] Fam Law 471.

[405] *W v J (Child: Variation of Financial Provision)* [2003] EWHC 2657 (Fam) [2004] 2 FLR 300.

[406] Sch 1, paras 1(1)(a) and respectively 1(2)(b), (d) and (e). See E Cooke 'Property adjustment orders for children' (1994) 6 Jo of Child Law 156. Settlements and transfers may only be made once: Sch 1 para 1(5)(b). A lump sum may not be ordered where it is intended as a device akin to a settlement order as a means of avoiding the effect of sub-para (5): *Phillips v Peace* [2004] EWHC 3180 (Fam) [2005] 1 WLR 3246.

[407] Community Legal Service (Financial) Regulations 2000 reg 44(1)(d) as amended. The charge is discussed below p 1015.

[408] [1992] 2 All ER 727, CA. This case was brought under the Guardianship of Minors Act 1971, but it was accepted (at 733 per Nourse LJ) that the provisions of the Children Act 1989 were not materially different in this respect.

benefit of the child' are not confined to *financial* benefit for the child, so that powers to order a transfer are not restricted to orders giving the child a beneficial interest in the property. Accordingly, it was held that there was power to order an unmarried father to transfer to the mother for the benefit of the children his interest in the family home, namely a joint council tenancy.

In recommending the power to order transfers of property, the Law Commission thought[409] that the provisions could be useful to enable the court to make a once-and-for-all settlement in cases where the father did not intend to have anything to do with the child (although it could be argued that such a stance sits ill with the importance now attached to joint parenting and the value to the child of having a meaningful relationship with the non-resident parent). They noted that few commentators thought it a valid objection that a transfer was tantamount to giving the unmarried mother a right to support for her own benefit.[410] However, they did not envisage the power being used at all frequently, relying on the practice of the divorce courts to lean against making such orders, and especially the reluctance to award a child provision beyond dependency.[411] That practice has indeed been followed by courts when considering their powers under this jurisdiction; they appear to prefer to make a limited transfer (not dissimilar to *Mesher* orders in the divorce context)[412] until the child has grown up.[413] But where the parents were joints owners of the property while they were cohabiting, an order may provide that the mother is to retain a share in the property after the child's minority. In *Re B (Child: Property Transfer)*[414] a consent order provided that the former jointly owned family home was to be used for the mother to bring up the child, with the mother meeting the mortgage instalments, and the father making only nominal periodical payments to the child's support. It was to be sold when the child completed full-time education, and the mother was to receive 'for the benefit of' the child, 70% of the net equity. The mother and child fell out and disputed which of them was entitled to the 70% share. It was held that the mother was entitled to it, as recompense for having assumed responsibility for maintaining the child.[415]

Although it is perhaps an arguable point, applications for financial relief under the 1989 Act would appear to rank as 'family proceedings' for the purposes of s 8.[416] Accordingly,

---

[409] Law Com No 118, para 6.6.   [410] Ibid, para 6.7.

[411] See *Chamberlain v Chamberlain* [1974] 1 All ER 33, CA at 38 per Scarman LJ and *Draskovic v Draskovic* (1980) 11 Fam Law 87.

[412] See below p 1053.

[413] See *T v S (Financial Provision for Children)* [1994] 2 FLR 883, *A v A (A Minor: Financial Provision)* [1994] 1 FLR 657, discussed below p 974; but cf *Pearson v Franklin (Parental Home: Ouster)* [1994] 1 FLR 246 at 250B–C per Nourse LJ.

[414] [1999] 2 FLR 418, CA.

[415] For consideration of the care that needs to be taken in drafting the appropriate order, see E Cooke, 'Children and Real Property—Trusts, Interests and Considerations' [1998] Fam Law 349, who notes also that it is appropriate in the case of jointly owned property to bring proceedings under both this Act and the Trusts of Land and Appointment of Trustees Act 1996. In *W v W (Joinder of Trusts of Land Act and Children Act Applications)* [2003] EWCA Civ 924 [2004] 2 FLR 321, the Court of Appeal held that such joint applications *should* be made, and must be heard together, the Sch 1 application having leading status since the powers under this jurisdiction are more extensive.

[416] The argument centres on whether technically applications are made under s 15, which is within Part II of the Act and clearly 'family proceedings', or under Sch 1, which falls outside the definition of 'family proceedings' in s 8(3), (4).

the court has power to make any s 8 order upon its own motion as well as being able to exercise its powers under s 37 to direct the local authority to undertake an investigation into the child's circumstances. If this is so, it ensures that this jurisdiction is in line with that under the Domestic Proceedings and Magistrates' Courts Act 1978, Matrimonial Causes Act 1973 and Civil Partnership Act 2004.

Exercising the powers

In assessing what, if any, order to make and what amount will be appropriate, the court is directed[417] to have regard to all the circumstances of the case including the following matters:

(a) The income, earning capacity, property and other financial resources which [any parent, the applicant and any other person in whose favour the court proposes to make the order][418] has or is likely to have in the foreseeable future.

(b) The financial needs, obligations and responsibilities which [any parent, the applicant and any other person in whose favour the court proposes to make the order] has or is likely to have in the foreseeable future.

(c) The financial needs of the child.

(d) The income, earning capacity (if any), property and other financial resources of the child.

(e) Any physical or mental disability of the child.

(f) The manner in which the child was being, or was expected to be, educated or trained.

These guidelines are virtually the same as under the other jurisdictions save that the court is not specifically enjoined to have regard to the family's standard of living, and no weighting of the child's welfare is specified.[419] The child's welfare is, however, one of the relevant circumstances to be taken into account[420] and has been said to be a constant influence on the discretionary outcome of any claim.[421] It has also been held that courts should have information as to the level of any child support assessment that might otherwise be made, so that they can take this into account when exercising their discretion.[422]

The absence of an express direction concerning standard of living leaves open the question of whose standard of living an order should judge. This is likely to be a particularly difficult issue where an unmarried couple have never lived together. Where, for example, the mother is a woman who is never likely to enjoy a high income and the father earns a high salary, it is tempting to say that the child (for whose benefit the order is being made) ought not to be prejudiced by his mother's position, and this is the view of the

---

[417] Sch 1, para 4(1).   [418] Sch 1, para 4(4).

[419] The child's welfare is not the paramount consideration, because s 105(1) expressly excludes maintenance from the definition of upbringing, and unlike the other Acts there is no direction in Sch 1 to treat the child's welfare as the first consideration. See also *K v H (Child Maintenance)* [1993] 2 FLR 61 at 64G.

[420] *J v C (Child: Financial Provision)* [1999] 1 FLR 152.

[421] *Re P (Child: Financial Provision)* [2003] EWCA Civ 837 [2003] 2 FLR 865.

[422] *E v C (Child Maintenance)* [1996] 1 FLR 472.

courts.[423] In *J v C (Child: Financial Provision)*,[424] for example, where the father won the lottery after the parents' relationship (which had not included cohabitation) had ended, Hale J held that since parents are responsible for the children throughout their dependency, the fact that the father had become wealthy after the break-up did not affect the child's entitlement to be brought up in circumstances bearing some relationship with his current resources and standard of living. She also noted that the nature and duration of the parents' relationship were not matters of great weight—a child should not suffer because the pregnancy might have been unplanned.

However, if a child is to be brought up in living conditions closer to the payer's standard of living than those of the carer, the latter will clearly benefit, yet if she was not married to the payer, she is owed no duty of support for herself. The courts have been prepared nonetheless to recognise that the child must be looked after and that the child's primary carer must therefore receive an allowance sufficient to enable her to do this at the level appropriate to the other aspects of the standard of living (such as housing, private schooling, private health insurance, etc) that the child is to enjoy. This is well-illustrated by *Re P (Child: Financial Provision)*,[425] the leading authority on this issue. There, the parents had an intermittent sexual relationship resulting in the birth of their child. The father was an immensely wealthy businessman; the mother came from an affluent family background, had no career and was dependent upon her parents for her own standard of living. The Court of Appeal held that in a case where 'one or both of the parents lie somewhere on the spectrum from affluent to fabulously rich'[426] the court should first decide the kind of home that the respondent should provide for the child. Secondly, the judge should assess the cost of furnishing and equipping the home, and the cost of a family car. Then, the court must determine what the carer would reasonably require to fund her expenditure in maintaining the home and its contents and meeting her other living costs, such as travel, holidays, outings, etc. Finally, the court must assess the allowance to be made for the mother's care of the child and in so doing, must:

'recognise the responsibility, and often the sacrifice, of the unmarried parent (generally the mother) who is to be the primary carer for the child, perhaps the exclusive carer if the absent parent disassociates from the child. In order to discharge this responsibility the carer must have control of a budget that reflects her position and the position of the father both social and financial.'[427]

Applying this approach, the father was ordered to pay a sum of £1 million to purchase a house, a further sum of £100,000 for furnishings etc and periodical payments[428] of £70,000 per annum.

[423] See also *H v P (Illegitimate Child: Capital Provision)* [1993] Fam Law 515; *A v A (A Minor: Financial Provision)* [1994] 1 FLR 657—*Haroutunian v Jennings* (1977) 1 FLR 62, followed.

[424] [1999] 1 FLR 152.

[425] [2003] EWCA Civ 837 [2003] 2 FLR 865 on which see S Gilmore, '*Re P (Child)(Financial Provision)*—Shoeboxes and comical shopping trips—child support from the affluent to the fabulously rich' [2004] CFLQ 103.

[426] Ibid per Thorpe LJ at para 45.

[427] Ibid per Thorpe LJ at paras 48, 49. Note that the fact that the mother will be working full-time does not mean she should receive a lower allowance as the child's primary carer since it is a matter for her whether she chooses to work: *F v G (Child: Financial Provision)* [2004] EWHC 1848 (Fam) [2005] 1 FLR 261.

[428] These were for 'top up' maintenance over and above a child support assessment.

However, as noted above, the courts regard their function under Sch 1 as being to seek to secure the child's financial position during dependency, and capital windfalls in adulthood are not to be made. Thorpe LJ in *Re P* considered that the appropriate legal mechanism to apply, where circumstances permit, to the question of providing the child with a home, is to make a settlement of property order, and '[s]ince the respondent is entitled to the reversion, which in certain circumstances may fall in before the child's majority, the respondent must have some right to veto an unsuitable investment.'[429] Thus, in *T v S (Financial Provision for Children)*,[430] it was ordered at first instance that a property be bought from the father's resources, to be held on trust with sale postponed until the youngest of the five children of the parents reached the age of 21 or all had ceased full-time education, the equity then to pass to the children in equal shares. On appeal, Johnson J held that the property should revert to the father.[431] Similarly, in *A v A*, a house was settled upon trust for A for a term expiring six months after she reached the age of 18 or ceased full-time education. In *J v C* the reversion was not to take effect until the child reached the age of 21 (or ended her full-time education), Hale J recognising that increasingly, children are not fully independent until at least that age.

Since, in most circumstances, the Child Support Act has removed the jurisdiction to order periodical payments for a child, it has been held that it is not right to award a lump sum to the child instead, as a form of capitalised maintenance. The purpose of a lump sum, according to Johnson J in *Phillips v Peace*[432] should be to meet the child's need with respect to a particular item of capital expenditure, such as to provide a home or, for instance, to modify a home for a child with disabilities. There, the mother, having failed to obtain child support from the apparently wealthy father because he was assessed by the Child Support Agency as having a nil net income, was successful in obtaining an order under Sch 1 to require him to settle property for the mother and child to live in, with reversion to him when the child reached adulthood, and a lump sum for the cost of furnishings for the home.[433] It was later held, in renewed ligitation between these parents,[434] that a court may not make more than one settlement or transfer or property order against a parent, and if an order of one type has been made, the court cannot later make an order of the other type. Thus, the mother could not come back to court seeking various orders so that she could now acquire a larger property for her and the child to live in. Nor could she seek an additional lump sum to achieve the same result, even though the legislation permits further lump sum orders to be made,[435] since this would be a device intended to circumvent the prohibition on further property orders.

Where an order against a step-parent of a child of the family is contemplated, then, as under the other jurisdictions, the court is directed[436] to have regard to:

'(a) Whether that person had assumed responsibility for the maintenance of the child and, if so, the extent to which and the basis on which he assumed that responsibility and the length of the period during which he met that responsibility.

---

[429] [2003] EWCA Civ 837 [2003] 2 FLR 865 at para 45.   [430] [1994] 2 FLR 883.   [431] At 888–9.
[432] [1996] 2 FLR 230.
[433] Lump sum orders may also be made to enable the applicant to meet any liabilities or expenses incurred in connection with the birth of the child or in maintaining the child or reasonably incurred before the making of the order: Sch 1, para 5.
[434] *Phillips v Peace* [2004] EWHC 3180 (Fam) [2005] 2 FLR 1212.   [435] Sch 1 para 1(5)(a).
[436] Sch 1, para 4(2).

(b) Whether he did so knowing that the child was not his child.

(c) The liability of any other person to maintain the child.'

If the court makes an order against a person who is not the father of the child, it must record in the order that it is made on that basis.[437]

Duration, variation and enforcement

Orders for periodical payments may begin with the date of the making of the application and shall not in the first instance extend beyond the child's seventeenth birthday, and in any event shall not extend beyond his eighteenth birthday, save where the child is receiving instruction at an educational institution or undergoing training for a trade, profession or vocation 'whether or not he also is, will be or would be in gainful employment' or where there are other special circumstances.[438] Such circumstances will usually relate to the child, rather than, for example, the unwillingness of the respondent to provide full details of his present and future finances.[439]

Periodical payment orders may be made notwithstanding that the parents are living together but, as under the 1978 Act, cease to have effect if they continue to live together or subsequently resume living together for a continuous period of more than six months.[440] Unsecured orders cease upon the death of the payer.[441]

There is a general power to vary, suspend, revive and revoke orders for periodical payments, and the court may order the payment of a lump sum on an application for a variation. The power of a child over the age of 16 to apply for a variation or to revive an order is similar to that under the other jurisdictions.[442]

(c) Independent right of a child over 18 to seek financial relief from his parents

Sch 1 para 2 to the Children Act 1989 preserves the independent right, first introduced by the Family Law Reform Act 1987, of a person who has attained 18 years of age to apply for an order requiring either or both of his parents to make periodical and/or lump sum payments to him. Applications may be made in the magistrates' court as well as the county court or the High Court. Before any order may be made, the court must be satisfied that the applicant is or will be (or would be if an order were made) receiving instruction at an educational institution, or undergoing training for a trade, profession or vocation, or that[443] there are other exceptional circumstances justifying an order. An order may not be made if, immediately before the applicant reached the age of 16, a periodical payments order was in force,[444] nor may an order be made if the applicant's parents are living together in the same household.[445] In deciding what order to make, the court is to have

---

[437] Sch 1, para 4(3).

[438] Sch 1, para 3(1), (2). The jurisdiction exists even though the Child Support Act 1991 provides that a child support calculation (which may also be in force in respect of the same child) cannot continue after the child's nineteenth birthday: *C v F (Disabled Child: Maintenance Order)* [1998] 2 FLR 1, CA.

[439] *T v S (Financial Provision for Children)* [1994] 2 FLR 883 at 889C.   [440] Sch 1, para 3(4).

[441] Sch 1, para 3(3).   [442] Sch 1, para 6(4).   [443] Children Act 1989 Sch 1, para 2(1).

[444] Sch 1, para 2(3). As with the matrimonial jurisdictions (above p 968), if such an order is in force, the child, once he has attained 16, may himself apply for a variation or, if the order has ceased to have effect, can apply for a revival of the order: para 6(4), (5).

[445] Sch 1, para 2(4).

regard to the same circumstances as it would have in the case of other applications for financial orders under the Children Act 1989.[446]

Both the child and the parent (or parents) ordered to pay may subsequently seek a variation or discharge of a periodical payments order.[447] There is no power to vary a lump sum payments order save, where the sum has been ordered to be paid in instalments, to vary the number or amount or date of those instalments.[448]

3 ENFORCEMENT OF ORDERS [449]

(a) Registration of orders in other courts

Orders made by a magistrates' court may be registered in the High Court, and orders made by the High Court or a divorce or civil partnership proceedings court under s 27 of the Matrimonial Causes Act or Sch 5 to the Civil Partnership Act may be registered in a magistrates' court. The order must then be paid and can be enforced as though it has been made by the court in which it is registered. The purpose and details of this procedure will be considered further in Chapter 18.[450]

(b) Methods of enforcement

Money due under magistrates' courts maintenance orders may be enforced by distress or committal to prison.[451] Orders may also be enforced by the attachment of earnings procedure.[452] In addition, the defaulting payer (the debtor) may be fined up to £1,000 for his default to make periodical payments.[453] There are no up to date figures on the number of applications brought to enforce orders in this way.

(c) Procedure and general considerations for recovering arrears

The procedure for enforcement of orders made by the magistrates is laid down by the Magistrates' Courts Act 1980. If payments are being made to the relevant designated officer of the court, or by standing order (or its equivalent), the officer himself may take proceedings, provided that he has the written consent of the person to whom the money is to be paid.[454] No order for enforcement may be made except by an order on complaint.[455] On hearing such complaint the court must first decide whether to enforce the arrears in toto or to remit the whole or any part of them; the answer to this question must obviously depend upon the parties' financial position, their conduct and all the circumstances of the case. Arrears over one year old are not generally enforced unless there are special circumstances, and the court's approach must be to decide how to exercise its discretion to enforce the arrears, rather than how it should exercise its discretion to remit them.[456]

---

[446] Sch 1, para 4.   [447] Sch 1, para 2(5).   [448] Sch 1, para 5(6).

[449] See *Children Come First* Vol 2 (1990, Cm 1264) ch 5; S Edwards, C Gould and A Halpern 'The Continuing Saga of Maintaining the Family after Divorce' [1990] Fam Law 31.

[450] See below, p 1074.   [451] Magistrates' Courts Act 1980 s 76.

[452] Attachment of Earnings Act 1971 ss 1–2.   [453] Magistrates' Courts Act 1980 s 59B.

[454] Magistrates' Courts Act 1980 s 59A(3).   [455] Magistrates' Courts Act 1980 s 93(1)–(2).

[456] *B v C (Enforcement: Arrears)* [1995] 1 FLR 467. For an example of a case where special circumstances were present, see *C v S (Maintenance Order: Enforcement)* [1997] 1 FLR 298. Appeal against a refusal to remit lies to the Divisional Court of the Family Division under s 29 of the 1978 Act and r 8.2 of the Family Proceedings Rules 1991: *P v P (Periodical Payments: Appeals)* [1995] 1 FLR 563; *E v C (Child Maintenance)* [1996] 1 FLR 472; following *Berry v Berry* [1987] Fam 1, CA.

Where the court is minded to remit arrears, it must give notice to the complainant, so that she has the opportunity to argue against this.[457] Appeals against decisions on enforcement are by case stated to the High Court.[458]

The court may issue a warrant of distress, a warrant committing the payer to prison, or make an attachment of earnings order.[459]

Distress

The warrant directs the police to distrain on the husband's goods and to sell them to raise the sum adjudged to be paid.[460]

Committal

A warrant of committal (which may also be issued if payment is insufficient to satisfy the debt) commits the debtor to prison for a period varying from five days to six weeks, the maximum period being graduated according to the sum owed.[461] But since committal proceedings are in effect designed to punish the debtor for failing to carry out the order, he may be imprisoned only if the default was due to his wilful refusal or culpable neglect and the court feels that it is inappropriate to make an attachment of earnings order.[462]

Two further powers that the court possesses are those of ordering the payment of arrears by instalments and of postponing the issue of a warrant of committal upon conditions.[463] Used together, these powers constitute a valuable weapon, particularly when it is financially impossible for the debtor to pay off all the arrears at once. For example, suppose that £200 is due under the order: the court may order the debtor to be imprisoned

---

[457] R v Bristol Magistrates' Court, ex p Hodge [1997] 1 FLR 88.

[458] Magistrates' Courts Act 1980 s 111; Berry v Berry [1987] 1 FLR 105; R v Bristol Magistrates' Court, ex p Hodge [1997] 1 FLR 88.

[459] Magistrates' Courts Act 1980 s 76(1); Attachment of Earnings Act 1971 s 1(3)(a).

[460] Magistrates' Courts Rules 1981 r 54. A civilian enforcement officer may act instead of the police. The clothing or bedding of any person or his family or the tools, books, vehicles or other equipment which he personally needs to use in his employment, business or vocation, are exempt. The court may order the husband to be searched and any money belonging to him and found on him to be applied towards the arrears: Magistrates' Courts Act 1980 s 80.

[461] Magistrates' Courts Act 1980 s 76(2), s 93(7), s 132 and Sch 4.

[462] Magistrates' Courts Act 1980 s 93(6). No order for committal may be made unless the debtor has appeared in court; he may be arrested if he fails to answer the summons. The debtor's conduct must amount to deliberate defiance or reckless disregard: improvidence or dilatoriness are insufficient: R v Luton Magistrates' Court, ex p Sullivan [1992] 2 FLR 196. The onus of proving that default was not wilful or reckless falls on the debtor: R v Cardiff Magistrates' Court ex parte Czech [1999] 1 FLR 95. Magistrates who consider that the debtor has wilfully refused or culpably neglected to pay must record that they have considered his ability and means to pay the current arrears, and have considered the most suitable method by which he should do so before committing him to prison: SN v ST (Maintenance Order: Enforcement) [1995] 1 FLR 868. They must also ensure that the debtor has been given a full opportunity to respond to argument that he should be imprisoned, if necessary ensuring that he is legally represented: R v Slough Magistrates' Court, ex p Lindsay [1997] 1 FLR 695.

[463] Magistrates' Courts Act 1980 s 75 and s 77; Maintenance Orders Act 1958 s 18. The debtor must be permitted to comply with the conditions as actually laid down by the court. In McLeod v United Kingdom [1998] 2 FLR 1048, the European Court of Human Rights upheld a complaint by a debtor that the police had acted disproportionately in assisting her husband to remove goods from the former matrimonial home in her absence, on the ostensible ground of fear of breach of the peace. The applicant still had three days in which to hand over the property.

for 14 days, but the issue of the warrant of committal to be postponed on condition, say, that he pays off the arrears at the rate of £10 per week.

If the debtor pays the arrears, the order of committal immediately ceases to have effect and, if he pays a part of the sum due, the period of imprisonment is proportionately reduced.[464] But serving the sentence does not wipe off the arrears,[465] although no further arrears accrue whilst the debtor is in custody unless the court orders otherwise.[466]

Attachment of earnings

The Attachment of Earnings Act 1971 allows the enforcement of any judgment debt by attaching the debtor's earnings. Payment of any order for maintenance may be secured in this way.[467] Originally, attachment of earnings orders could only be made when an existing maintenance order was in arrears, but now such orders can be made by the court itself when making a maintenance order in the first place.[468]

In cases where it is sought to recover arrears, application may be made by the person to whom payments are due under the maintenance order, by a designated officer of the magistrates' court if an order is in force directing payments to be made through him, or by the debtor himself.[469]

If an attachment of earnings order is made, it is directed to the debtor's employer, not to the debtor himself. It orders the employer to make periodical deductions from the debtor's earnings and to remit the amount deducted to the collecting officer of the court.[470] The officer must then pay the money received to the person to whom the money is due under the order.[471]

The order must specify two rates: the *normal deduction rate*, which is the amount which the court thinks is reasonable to secure the payment of sums falling due under the order in the future together with the arrears already accrued; and the *protected earnings rate*, that is, the rate below which the debtor's earnings shall not in any event be reduced by payments deducted under the order.[472] The purpose of the latter is to keep the debtor's remaining income above subsistence level; consequently, only in exceptional circumstances would it be reasonable to fix it below the figure which, if it represented the debtor's total resources, would entitle him to apply for income-related benefits.[473]

Once an attachment of earnings order has been made, no committal order may be made as a consequence of proceedings begun beforehand; similarly, if a committal order is made or a warrant is issued after an attachment of earnings order has been made, the latter will automatically be discharged.[474] A court before which proceedings for committal or distress are brought may always make an attachment of earnings order instead if it thinks that that would be a more efficacious means of securing payment.[475]

---

[464] Magistrates' Courts Act 1980 s 79.

[465] Ibid, s 93(8). But the debtor cannot be imprisoned more than once for failure to pay the same sum: Maintenance Orders Act 1958 s 17.

[466] Magistrates' Courts Act 1980 s 94, for the committal will probably deprive the debtor of the power of earning his living in the meantime.

[467] Attachment of Earnings Act 1971 Sch 1. Such orders may also be made by the High Court and a county court: ibid, s 1.

[468] Magistrates' Courts Act 1980 s 59(3)(d) as amended.

[469] Attachment of Earnings Act 1971 s 3(1).   [470] Ibid s 6(1).   [471] Ibid, s 13.

[472] Ibid, s 6(5)–(6).   [473] *Billington v Billington* [1974] Fam 24.

[474] Attachment of Earnings Act 1971 s 8(1), (3).   [475] Ibid, s 3(4).

If the debtor ceases to be employed by the person to whom the order has been directed, it lapses until the court directs it to a fresh employer.[476]

As with deduction from earnings orders under the child support legislation, in many cases it may be questioned whether the value of an order to the payee is worth the administrative trouble that it causes. The procedure will be most effective when the debtor is in steady employment, but when he is in casual employment, he may be able to escape the order by the simple expedient of changing jobs frequently, if they are available to him.

---

[476] Ibid, s 9(4).

18

FINANCIAL RELIEF ON DIVORCE, DISSOLUTION, NULLITY AND SEPARATION

A INTRODUCTION

The increase in the rate of divorce has inevitably led to much greater significance being attached to the financial consequences of marriage breakdown, both for the parties and their children, and for the state. Research studies in this country, the United States and Australia, all confirm that, for mothers with children to care for, divorce is likely to have a major detrimental effect on their standard of living, while divorced men are likely to see no major decline in theirs.[1] The reason for the differential is primarily that the earning capacity of divorced women is less than that of men—they are more likely to have interrupted their careers to have children and hence earn lower amounts than men, and they are less likely to be able to resume (or remain in) full-time employment to make up the shortfall when their marriage breaks down. Even after their children have grown up, they are likely to remain less well off because they are unable to build up sufficient funds for a decent pension for when they retire.[2] The policy dilemma for government is to decide whether, and to what extent, it should attempt to meet the resulting shortfall by either making the former husband maintain, or compensate, the wife, or by taking on the burden through the social security system. As we saw in the previous chapter, attempting to make absent *parents* support their children and thus relieve public expenditure, at least in part, has been a consistent policy objective, though with limited success. As regards the termination of marriage (most usually by divorce),[3] the law again seeks to regard the financial consequences as a matter to be dealt with as far as possible by adjusting the spouses' assets and earnings between them, with state support providing a safety net. But while there is a legal logic to attaching liability to a parent, or a spouse, in recognition of a *continuing* legal

---

[1] For research into the system and its effects in England and Wales, see J Eekelaar and M Maclean *Maintenance After Divorce* (1986), G Davis, S Cretney and J Collins *Simple Quarrels: Negotiating Money and Property Disputes on Divorce* (1994), M Maclean and J Eekelaar *The Parental Obligation* (1997) ch 7, A Perry et al *How Parents Cope Financially on Marriage Breakdown* (2000), J Eekelaar, M Maclean and S Beinart, *Family Lawyers: The Divorce Work of Solicitors* (2000), G Davis et al, 'Ancillary relief outcomes' [2000] CFLQ 43, S Arthur et al, *Settling Up: Making Financial Arrangements After Divorce or Separation* (2002). For international perspectives see L Weitzman and M Maclean (eds) *Economic Consequences of Divorce* (1992) and the collection of articles contained in (2005) 19, 2, Int J of Law, Pol and Fam.

[2] See J Ginn and D Price, 'Do divorced women catch up in pension building?' [2002] CFLQ 157.

[3] And now, civil partnership and dissolution.

relationship between payer and recipient, the argument is more complicated once the legal tie between husband and wife has been ended.

In this chapter, for convenience, we discuss the law in the context of a divorce (but refer to dissolution of a civil partnership, nullity and separation where relevant), and we refer to the husband as the payer and the wife as recipient, unless otherwise specified. However, it should be noted that the obligations of the spouses and civil partners are equal and reciprocal.

1 DEVELOPMENT OF THE COURT'S POWERS

The ecclesiastical courts were able to give financial protection to a wife by ordering the husband to pay her alimony[4] pending suit and permanent alimony after granting a decree of divorce a mensa et thoro.[5] After 1857 this power was vested in the Divorce Court, which was also empowered on granting a decree of divorce to order the husband to secure maintenance for the wife's life.[6] If the husband had no capital on which the payments of maintenance could be secured, hardship was likely to be caused to the wife; this was cured in 1866, when the court was given the power to order the husband to pay unsecured maintenance to the wife. As this would have to come out of his income, however, the maximum term for which it could be ordered was the spouses' joint lives.[7] After 1937 a wife petitioning for divorce or judicial separation on the ground of her husband's insanity could be ordered to pay him alimony pending suit and, if the decree was granted, maintenance (secured or unsecured) or permanent alimony.[8] In 1963 the courts were given a power, long overdue, to order the payment of a lump sum in addition to or instead of maintenance or alimony on divorce, nullity and judicial separation.[9]

Except when the husband was incurably of unsound mind, orders for alimony and maintenance could not be made against a wife. This reflected the fact that in the middle of the nineteenth century it was very unlikely that a wife would have an income. She might have property settled to her own use, however, and as early as 1857 the court was empowered to order this to be settled for the benefit of the husband or children if he obtained a divorce or judicial separation on the ground of her adultery. This power was later extended to the property of wives who were divorced for cruelty or desertion.[10] On divorce or nullity, either party could benefit from the exercise of the court's jurisdiction, going back to 1859,[11] to vary ante-nuptial and post-nuptial settlements.

(a) The Matrimonial Causes Act 1973

Piecemeal modifications of the law spread over more than a century produced confusing anomalies, and pressure for wholesale reform increased after the passing of the Divorce Reform Act 1969, when the fear was expressed that many innocent wives, divorced against their will, would be left with inadequate provision. The result was the passing of the Matrimonial Proceedings and Property Act 1970, which was based upon the recommendations

---

⁴ Periodical maintenance.   ⁵ See above p 302.   ⁶ Matrimonial Causes Act 1857 s 32.
⁷ Matrimonial Causes Act 1866 s 1.   ⁸ Matrimonial Causes Act 1937 s 10(2).
⁹ Matrimonial Causes Act 1963 s 5.
¹⁰ Matrimonial Causes Act 1857 s 45; Matrimonial Causes Act 1884 s 3; Matrimonial Causes Act 1937 s 10(3).
¹¹ Matrimonial Causes Act 1859 s 5.

of the Law Commission.[12] Most of its provisions were repealed and re-enacted in Part II of the Matrimonial Causes Act 1973, which, in its amended form, governs the award of financial relief in the High Court and divorce county courts. The Act abolished the confusing variations in types of order for maintenance, and described all as 'financial provision', which may take the form of periodical payments or a lump sum payment. The court was given equal powers to order either spouse to make financial provision for the other, regardless of who is seeking the divorce. The Act also widened the court's powers in two important respects. First, the court's redistributive powers extend to all the assets that either or both the spouses own, irrespective of when and from whom they acquired them. Secondly, in making orders in respect of the spouses' property, the court is not bound to enforce existing rights and can, for instance, order the transfer of ownership from one spouse to another. This latter power was vested in the court partly in response to the decisions in *Pettitt v Pettitt*[13] and *Gissing v Gissing*,[14] which, as we have seen,[15] established that the powers under the Married Women's Property Act 1882 s 17 are declaratory only and that therefore the courts had no power to transfer ownership of property between spouses. These wider redistributive powers represent one of the key remaining distinctions between the ending of a marriage by divorce or nullity and the ending of cohabitation.

(b) Subsequent legislative change

The 1973 Act was amended by the Matrimonial Homes and Property Act 1981, which gave the divorce courts the express statutory power to order the sale of any of the spouses' property.[16] More importantly, the Matrimonial and Family Proceedings Act 1984[17] both extended the court's powers by enabling it to *impose* a clean break (ie a once-and-for-all settlement between the spouses with no continuing financial ties) upon a spouse,[18] and altered the way that the powers are to be exercised. Two of the most important changes were: (1) to require the court, when deciding what orders should be made, to give first consideration to the welfare, whilst a minor, of any child of the family under 18;[19] and (2) to impose a duty upon the court to consider whether it is appropriate so to exercise its powers that the financial obligations of each party terminate immediately or as soon as possible.[20] The 1984 Act also ended the obligation of the court to attempt to place the parties in the position that they would have been had the marriage not broken down.

---

[12] Law Com No 25, *Report on Financial Provision in Matrimonial Proceedings* (1969); see S Cretney 'The Maintenance Quagmire' (1970) 33 MLR 662.

[13] [1970] AC 777, HL.   [14] [1971] AC 886, HL. See also Law Com No 25, paras 64–75.

[15] Above, p 145.

[16] By s 7 which added s 24A to the 1973 Act. See also Law Com No 99 (*Orders for the Sale of Property under the Matrimonial Causes Act 1973*).

[17] This Act is based on the Law Commission's recommendations: see Law Com No 112 *The Financial Consequences of Divorce* (1981). See also their earlier paper, Law Com No 103 *The Financial Consequences of Divorce: The Basic Policy* (1980). For an interesting account of the background and reasons for the Law Commission recommending changes, see S Cretney 'Money After Divorce—The Mistakes We Have Made?' in M Freeman (ed) *Essays in Family Law* (1985) pp 34 et seq, particularly at pp 36–42.

[18] Under the Matrimonial Causes Act 1973 s 25A(3), which was originally added by s 3(4) of the Matrimonial and Family Proceedings Act 1984, and amended by the Welfare Reform and Pensions Act 1999, s 19, Sch 3, paras 1, 6.

[19] Section 25(1) as substituted by s 3 of the 1984 Act. For 'child of the family', see above p 338.

[20] Section 25A(1), (2) as substituted by s 3(4) of the 1984 Act.

Subsequently, the Pensions Act 1995[21] extended the court's powers to enable it to make orders directing that all or part of any lump sum or pension arising on a spouse's retirement be paid to the other spouse, and the Welfare Reform and Pensions Act 1999 further enabled the court to order a spouse's pension *rights* to be shared.[22]

(c) Dissolution of civil partnerships

We saw in Chapter 6 that there are provisions based on those applicable to divorce for the dissolution of a civil partnership.[23] The Civil Partnership Act 2004 accordingly provides similar financial relief, in Sch 5, for civil partners who separate, or terminate their partnership, to that available to spouses.[24] The provisions are not discussed separately in the following text unless they raise different issues to those relevant to divorce, but the table at the end of this chapter sets out the equivalent provisions in the two Acts.

2 POWERS OF THE COURT

The court has statutory power[25] to make an order against *either spouse* with respect to any one or more of the following matters:[26]

(1) Unsecured periodical payments to the other spouse.

(2) Secured periodical payments to the other spouse.

(3) Lump sum payments to the other spouse.

(4) Unsecured periodical payments for any child of the family.

(5) Secured periodical payments for any child of the family.

(6) A lump sum payment for any child of the family.

(7) Transfer of property to the other spouse or for the benefit of any child of the family.

(8) Settlement of property for the benefit of the other spouse or any child of the family.

(9) Variation of any marriage settlement.

Orders coming within (1)–(6) are collectively known as financial provision orders and those coming within (7)–(9) as property adjustment orders.[27]

Where a court makes a secured periodical payments order, a lump sum order or a property transfer order, it can further order a sale of property belonging to either or both spouses.[28]

The court has power to make financial provision orders (periodical payments and lump sums) directing that a share of a spouse's pension be 'attached' or 'earmarked' and paid to the other on retirement.[29] Under ss 21A and 24B it may also make a 'pension sharing

---

[21] Pensions Act 1995 s 166(1) which inserted ss 25B–25D (subsequently amended by the Welfare Reform and Pensions Act 1999, s 21, Sch 4) into the Matrimonial Causes Act 1973.

[22] Welfare Reform and Pensions Act 1999 Schs 3 and 4, inserting ss 21A, 24B–D into the 1973 Act.

[23] See above p 301.   [24] See s 72 (1) and Sch 5.

[25] But the court can accept a party's undertaking to accept other obligations: see below p 1015.

[26] Under the Matrimonial Causes Act 1973 s 21, s 23 and s 24.   [27] Ibid.

[28] Matrimonial Causes Act 1973 s 24A as added by the Matrimonial Homes and Property Act 1981 s 7. Orders for the sale of property are neither classified as financial provision nor property adjustment: see *Omielan v Omielan* [1996] 2 FLR 306, CA; *Harper v O'Reilly and Harper* [1997] 2 FLR 816.

[29] Under the Matrimonial Causes Act 1973, ss 25B–25D as inserted by the Pensions Act 1995 s 166(1).

order' to reallocate part or all of a spouse's accrued pension rights to the other on nullity or divorce.[30]

Although, as we shall see, there are statutory guidelines on the matters to be taken into account when exercising these powers, it should be appreciated at the outset that considerable discretion is left to the judge in deciding what order should be made in any individual case.[31] This discretion applies equally to determining what order should be made with regard to the spouses' property and with regard to their income. This vesting of wide discretion in the courts is in contrast to the position taken even in some other common law jurisdictions.[32] In New Zealand, for instance, the matrimonial home and family chattels must generally be divided equally, although there is discretion to adjust these shares to compensate for economic disparity between the separated parties,[33] while in Scotland there is a statutory presumption in favour of equal division unless special circumstances exist which justify a departure from this principle.[34] In 1998, the Government accepted the view of the Lord Chancellor's Ancillary Relief Advisory Group which had opposed the introduction of a similar approach in England and Wales. The Group preferred to retain a broad discretion, albeit on balance favouring the codification of the principles evolved

[30] As inserted by the Welfare Reform and Pensions Act 1999 Sch 3. See Department of Social Security *Pension Sharing on Divorce: reforming pensions for a fairer future* Cm 3345 (1998), discussed further below pp 999ff.

[31] For judicial acknowledgement of this discretion and that it should be exercised with restraint, see Waite J in *Thomas v Thomas* [1995] 2 FLR 668 at 670, CA: 'The discretionary powers conferred on the court by the amended ss 23–25 of the Matrimonial Causes Act 1973 to redistribute the assets of the spouses are almost limitless. That represents an acknowledgement by Parliament that if justice is to be achieved between spouses at divorce the court must be equipped in a society where the forms of wealth-holding are diverse and often sophisticated, to penetrate outer forms and get to the heart of ownership. For their part, the judges who administer the jurisdiction have traditionally accepted the Shakespearean principle that "it is excellent to have a giant's strength but tyrannous to use it like a giant" [*Measure for Measure*, II, ii, 107]. The precise boundaries of that judicial self-restraint have never been rigidly defined—nor could they be if the jurisdiction is to retain its flexibility.' For criticism of the operation of the discretionary approach see Davis, Cretney and Collins op cit, especially at ch 11.

[32] In most continental legal systems there is some form of community of property which severely restricts or even precludes the court from being able to redistribute the parties' property or even income. For an account of various community of property regimes, see Law Com Working Paper No 42, Part 5 and Appendix C. In most States of the USA there is a principle of equal division of property between the spouses. For research into the effects of this, see eg L Weitzman, *The Divorce Revolution* (1985), summarised by her in 'The Divorce Revolution and Illusion of Equality: A View from the United States' in M Freeman (ed) *Essays in Family Law 1985* at 91 and by the same author 'Marital Property: Its Transformation and Division in the United States' in L Weitzman and M Maclean (eds) *Economic Consequences of Divorce—The International Perspective* at 85. Such a divergence of approach between different jurisdictions towards the division of matrimonial assets undoubtedly leads to 'forum shopping', especially amongst the very wealthy. In *Dart v Dart* [1996] 2 FLR 286, CA the parties were American, and the wife's counsel asserted she could have expected an award of £100 million, and possibly even £200 million from the husband's fortune (conservatively estimated at £400 million) from a Michigan court. Thorpe LJ observed at 288 'It is plain that Mrs Dart decided she would do better in Michigan whilst Mr Dart thought he would do better in London'. The wife's application for a stay of the husband's English proceedings was dismissed, and the Court of Appeal upheld an award of (just) £10 million in her favour. The jurisdictional rules laid down in 'Brussels II' in relation to divorce and hence ancillary relief (see above p 265) are intended to try to limit such forum shopping at least amongst EU residents, although they may arguably have the opposite effect.

[33] Under the Property (Relationships) Act 1976 (as amended), save in certain defined circumstances, eg where the marriage has been of short duration. See B Atkin, 'The rights of married and unmarried couples in New Zealand—radical new laws on property and succession' [2003] CFLQ 173.

[34] Family Law (Scotland) Act 1985 s 9(1) and s 10(1). See *Lightbody (or Jacques) v Jacques* 1997 SC (HL) 20.

through the case law so as to enable parties to negotiate settlements with greater certainty.[35] No such codification has yet been enacted.

3 APPLICATION FOR RELIEF

An order for financial provision, property adjustment or pension attachment may be made on or after the grant of decree of nullity, divorce or judicial separation, but shall not take effect unless (in the case of the former two) the decree has been made absolute.[36] A pension sharing order may only be made on or after a decree of nullity or divorce.[37]

There is thus clearly power to order financial relief after a decree of nullity, even though the marriage is void.[38] In *Whiston v Whiston*[39] the Court of Appeal appeared to hold that a person who, knowingly being married, has gone through a ceremony of marriage to another cannot pursue a claim for ancillary relief against the innocent party under the Matrimonial Causes Act 1973; as a matter of policy, the court will not assist a person who must found a claim on the serious criminal offence of bigamy. However, subsequently, in *Rampal v Rampal (No 2)*[40] the Court distinguished *Whiston* and held that it was not authority for barring a claim by every culpable bigamist, regardless of the circumstances. Rather, the spouse's bigamy should be taken into account as one of the factors relevant to the court's exercise of its discretion under Part II of the 1973 Act, rather than a bar in limine causing the application to be struck out.[41] This brings bigamy into line with how other fundamental flaws in a marriage are to be treated when assessing claim made on nullity and in particular, with the Court's earlier, majority decision, in *J v S-T (Formerly J) (Transsexual: Ancillary Relief)*.[42] Here, after a 17-year marriage, the plaintiff was granted a decree of nullity on the basis that the parties were not respectively male and female. The defendant, a female, who had undergone sexual reassignment surgery, applied for financial provision. The judge had found that the defendant had committed perjury in declaring, at the marriage ceremony, that there was no lawful hindrance to it taking place. Potter LJ and Sir Brian Neill[43] declined to follow *Whiston* but, as a matter of the court's discretion, and taking into account the factors in s 25 of the Matrimonial Causes Act 1973 including the defendant's conduct, the application was dismissed.

It is a general principle of the Matrimonial Causes Act 1973 that, if the former spouse remarries, she (or he) must look to the new partner for financial provision for herself, and not to the old one. Consequently, a party who has remarried cannot apply for an order at all, except for a child of the family,[44] although an application already made can be

35 See [1998] Fam Law 381, 576 and 654. For further discussion of reform proposals, see below p 1081.
36 Matrimonial Causes Act 1973 ss 23(1)(5), 24(1)(3), 24B(1)(2).   37 Ibid s 24B(1)(2).
38 A fortiori there is power to order financial relief if the marriage is voidable: see *Johnston v Johnston* (1976) 6 Fam Law 17, CA.
39 [1995] Fam 198, CA.   40 [2001] EWCA Civ 989 [2001] 2 FLR 1179.
41 For a powerful critique of the Court of Appeal's approach in *Rampal* see C Sharp, 'Bigamy and Financial Relief' [2003] Fam Law 414.
42 [1997] 1 FLR 402, CA.
43 Ward LJ followed *Whiston* in holding that the application failed in limine; the defendant had attempted to gain a benefit from wrongdoing, and such a claim was against public policy.
44 Matrimonial Causes Act 1973 s 28(3), as amended by the Matrimonial and Family Proceedings Act 1984 s 5(3). If the embargo applies and the former spouse wishes to dispute ownership of any matrimonial property, he or she can, within three years after the divorce, seek a declaration under the Married Women's

entertained notwithstanding the remarriage.[45] This rule applies even though the second marriage is void or voidable:[46] the party's remedy lies in seeking financial provision in the nullity proceedings. Furthermore, an ancillary relief claim is not a cause of action which survives against the other party's estate, so that no order can be made after the death of either of them.[47] Where the order was sought by the surviving spouse, the effect of this is mitigated by the extensive powers given to the court by the Inheritance (Provision for Family and Dependants) Act 1975[48] but in *McMinn v McMinn (Ancillary Relief: Death of Party to Proceedings)*[49] the husband killed the wife before the court had granted decree absolute. The ancillary relief order that the district judge had made after decree nisi had not, therefore, taken effect, and the wife's executors were not able to take over her claim.

4 ANCILLARY RELIEF PROCEDURE

A petitioner seeking financial relief should apply for it in the petition; a respondent who files an answer should apply in the answer. If a spouse does not apply for financial relief in the petition (or answer), he or she must obtain the leave of the court to do so unless the parties are agreed on the proposed order.[50] However, the respondent to an undefended petition who does not file an answer may apply for relief without leave.[51]

When determining an application for ancillary relief, the court is exercising not merely a paternal, but also, in appropriate instances, an inquisitorial jurisdiction.[52] Following concern at the spiralling costs and complexity of cases, Booth J, with the concurrence of the President of the Family Division, issued a series of guidelines designed to be followed by practitioners in the preparation of substantial ancillary relief cases.[53] But these, though helpful, did not go far enough—in *F v F (Ancillary Relief: Substantial Assets)*[54] the parties' costs amounted to almost £1.5 million (albeit that the husband's wealth was estimated at between £150 and £200 million), which Thorpe J found unacceptable. He concluded:

Property Act 1882 s 17, in which case ownership will be determined upon strict property principles: *Bothe v Amos* [1976] Fam 46, CA. The embargo applies whenever the applicant remarried, even if the marriage took place before the implementation of the Matrimonial Causes Act 1973, thereby reversing *Bonning v Dodsley* [1982] 1 All ER 612, CA.

[45] *Jackson v Jackson* [1973] Fam 99. This does not apply to an application for periodical payments for the spouse which will in any case cease on remarriage: see below p 993.

[46] Matrimonial Causes Act 1973 s 52(3).

[47] *Dipple v Dipple* [1942] P 65; *McMinn v McMinn (Ancillary Relief: Death of Party to Proceedings)* [2002] EWHC 1194 (Fam), [2003] 2 FLR 823. It should be noted that the court has jurisdiction to make lump sum or property adjustment orders after a spouse's bankruptcy, although the court should have a clear picture of the bankrupt's assets and liability, and the expenses of the bankruptcy, and should consider the effect of the bankruptcy on the debtor spouse's ability to pay—*Hellyer v Hellyer* [1996] 2 FLR 579, CA.

[48] See below pp 1105–24.   [49] [2002] EWHC 1194 (Fam), [2003] 2 FLR 823.

[50] Family Proceedings Rules 1991, r 2.53(1),(2).   [51] Ibid r 2.53(3).

[52] *Hildebrand v Hildebrand* [1992] 1 FLR 244, *F v F (Ancillary Relief: Substantial Assets)* [1995] 2 FLR 45, *Kimber v Brookman Solicitors* [2004] 2 FLR 221, *Currey v Currey* [2004] EWCA Civ 1799 [2005] 1 FLR 952.

[53] *Evans v Evans* [1990] 2 All ER 147, subsequently embodied in a *Practice Note* [1990] 1 WLR 575.

[54] [1995] 2 FLR 45. See too *Piglowska v Piglowski* [1999] 1 WLR 1360: Assets estimated to be worth £127,400: costs exceeded £128,000. As Lord Hoffmann put it: 'Something has obviously gone badly wrong. Their Lordships gave leave to bring an appeal not merely because it appeared likely that the Court of Appeal had erred in law but also in the hope that they might be able to reduce the chances of such disasters happening to other people in the future.'

'It seems to me that as a society it is incumbent upon us to develop systems for the determination of financial disputes at a much more realistic cost.'[55]

In response to such calls, a pilot scheme providing a more stream-lined procedure, developed by Thorpe J and several highly experienced practitioners, was tested in selected courts in the mid-1990s,[56] and was introduced on a nation-wide basis in 2000.[57] The present procedure has, as its stated 'overriding objective', 'enabling the court to deal with cases justly'. This includes, so far as practicable,

'(a) ensuring that the parties are on an equal footing;

(b) saving expense;

(c) dealing with the case in ways which are proportionate—

(i) to the amount of money involved;

(ii) to the importance of the case;

(iii) to the complexity of the issues; and

(iv) to the financial position of each party;

(d) ensuring that it is dealt with expeditiously and fairly; and

(e) allotting to it an appropriate share of the court's resources, while taking into account the need to allot resources to other cases.'[58]

(a) Form E

The goals of the procedure are to reduce delay, facilitate settlement, limit costs and give the court closer control of the conduct of proceedings. Central to achieving this are two innovations. First, both parties must complete a 'Form E' which is intended (together with prescribed documents which must be attached to it) to contain sufficient information about their circumstances to enable the case to be disposed of, without either overwhelming the parties (or the court) with a surfeit of documentation, or concealing matters relevant to achieving a fair outcome. Both spouses are under a duty to make full, frank and up-to-date disclosure of their assets and circumstances.[59] A former practice, known as the 'millionaire's defence',[60] whereby wealthy respondents (almost always men) could decline to disclose their assets (in detail at least) on the basis that these were sufficient to meet any

---

[55] Ibid at p 69.

[56] For the background to the establishment of the pilot scheme see Thorpe J 'Procedural Reform in Ancillary Relief' [1996] Fam Law 356. The scheme was formally incorporated into the Family Proceedings Rules by the Family Proceedings (Amendment No 2) Rules 1997 (SI 1997/1056). See also the *Practice Direction Ancillary Relief Procedure: Pilot Scheme* [1997] 2 FLR 304.

[57] By the Family Proceedings (Amendment No 2) Rules 1999, SI 1999/3491, which apply to all applications for ancillary relief filed after 5 June 2000.

[58] Ibid r 2.51B.

[59] *Livesey (formerly Jenkins) v Jenkins* [1985] AC 424, HL. *Clibbery v Allan and Another* [2002] EWCA Civ 45 [2002] Fam 261. Cf *Rose v Rose* [2003] EWHC 505 (Fam) [2003] 2 FLR 197—wife's alleged lack of frankness regarding relationship with partner had not affected the husband's decision to settle. Deliberate deception may result in conviction for perjury: see T Paskins, 'Family Relief Disclosure—Beware of Perjury' [2004] Fam Law 57. Complex cases where disclosure is often pivotal should be managed by an allocated High Court judge: *K v K (Financial Relief: Management of Difficult Cases)* [2005] EWHC 1070 (Fam) [2005] 2 FLR 1137.

[60] *Thyssen—Bornemisza v Thyssen—Bornemisza (No 2)* [1985] FLR 1069, CA.

order that the court might make against them, was firmly disapproved by the Court of Appeal in *McFarlane v McFarlane; Parlour v Parlour*.[61] The court pointed out that it was both discriminatory to wives to require them to document their needs and resources, whilst permitting their husbands to conceal theirs, and unfair in preventing the court from obtaining a true picture of what such husbands could in fact afford.[62] However, it may be preferable to compromise on precision and detail in order to reduce costs, particularly where complex corporate dealings are involved.[63]

(b) Financial dispute resolution appointment

The second innovation in the procedure is that the progress of the case is actively managed by the court, with a fixed timetable, which can be varied only by judicial order, and the holding of a financial dispute resolution appointment ('FDR'), a privileged meeting at which the district judge (who will not hear the case if it fails to settle) assists the parties, and their legal advisers, in exploring common ground and narrowing the issues in dispute with a view to reaching agreement. This can include giving the parties an 'indication' or 'early neutral evaluation' of what the judge thinks would be the likely outcome of the case if no settlement were reached. The importance of caution in proceeding on such a course was emphasised by Thorpe LJ in *Rose v Rose*:[64]

'It is also important that judges should recognise the extent to which the parties will have invested in the FDR hearing. In many cases they will regard the words of the judge as a decisive statement of outcome. It is thus important that the judicial evaluation at the FDR should never be superficial or ill-considered. In view of the impact of the opinion and its capacity to collapse a reasonably held target, careful preparation and proper reflection are necessary safeguards to any forecast. Furthermore in the typical case that I have instanced the impact of the oral evidence at a trial can be decisive. The FDR is an invaluable tool for dispelling unreal expectations but in the finely balanced case it is no substitute for trial and thus should not be used as a discouragement to either an applicant or a respondent to go to trial in a case that can only be properly resolved by full and fair trial. . . . No doubt in this case, as in many, the parties feel the tension of the negotiation and the agony of deciding whether to exit from an extremely disturbing and stressful situation by compromise or to soldier on down an increasingly stressful road to a contested trial. It is inevitable that the FDR hearing will intensify the tension and stress which is persistent until the parties have freed themselves financially and emotionally from their previous relationship. The whole purpose and effect of the FDR would be lost or compromised were parties free to analyse and re-evaluate a crucial decision of the previous day or the previous week and to decide on further reflection that they made the wrong choice.'

If the case settles, the court will make a consent order. The parties are warned about

---

[61] [2004] EWCA (Civ) 872, [2005] Fam 171 per Thorpe LJ at para 83.

[62] Ibid. See dicta by Thorpe LJ at paras 78, 82 and Latham LJ at para 117. A solicitor may be ordered to produce documentation that may assist a wife in quantifying or locating the husband's assets or indeed his whereabouts: *Kimber v Brookman Solicitors* [2004] 2 FLR 221.

[63] *J v V (Disclosure: Offshore Corporations)* [2003] EWHC 3110 (Fam) [2004] 1 FLR 1042: wife's costs £700,000.

[64] [2002] EWCA Civ 208, [2002] 1 FLR 978, at paras 32, 44. For doubts about the merits of 'indications', see D Burrows, 'Judicial Indications: How Far Can You Go?' [2005] Fam Law 58.

the costs and time implications of not settling. However, if the case does not settle,[65] the final hearing will normally be before a district judge who may, however, refer the application to a judge.[66] Cases are normally heard in the divorce county court, but there is power to transfer proceedings to the High Court in cases of complexity, difficulty or gravity.[67] A final hearing may require more information to be before the court than was assembled for the FDR.[68] The court possesses extensive powers to enable one party to obtain additional information from the other,[69] and may make orders for discovery where financial and other documents and records are required to be produced.[70] Those who attempt to deceive the court by failing to make full disclosure will forfeit its sympathy,[71] and it is open to the court to draw the adverse inference that beneath a false presentation there are undisclosed assets.[72] The court may, in its discretion, penalise a reluctance or refusal to make proper disclosure in its order for costs.[73]

(c) Disclosure

One major potential drawback to full and frank disclosure is the risk that the information revealed will be passed on to the authorities. Both the Inland Revenue and the police may be interested in discovering material which might reveal evidence of tax evasion or criminal activity. In *S v S (Inland Revenue: Tax Evasion)*[74] Wilson J had found that the husband had

---

[65] The parties are encouraged to try out of court mediation as well as the FDR process, no matter how conflicted their positions: see the views of the Court of Appeal in *Al-Khatib v Masry* [2004] EWCA Civ 1353 [2005] 1 FLR 381.

[66] Family Proceedings Rules 1991 r 2.65.

[67] Including where there are substantial allegations of fraud, deception, non-disclosure, or conduct. See Matrimonial and Family Proceedings Act 1984 s 39; *Practice Direction* [1992] 3 All ER 151.

[68] See *W v W (Ancillary Relief: Procedure)* [2000] Fam Law 473.

[69] This includes the use of detailed questionnaires, and oral discovery: see *OS v DS (Oral Disclosure: Preliminary Hearing)* [2004] EWHC 2376 (Fam) [2005] 1 FLR 675.

[70] See eg *B v B (Financial Provision)* [1989] 1 FLR 119; *P v P* [1989] 2 FLR 241; *Newton v Newton* [1990] 1 FLR 33, CA; *Re T (Divorce: Interim Maintenance: Discovery)* [1990] 1 FLR 1. A useful power available to the court is the production appointment, whereby a person is ordered to produce documents which he could be required to produce at the hearing—see N Mostyn and P Moor, 'The Production Appointment' [1991] Fam Law 506 and D Burrows 'Production Appointments and *Khanna* Hearings' [1995] Fam Law 199. This is an effective means of obtaining advance disclosure, particularly from a reluctant witness. The application for an appointment should normally be made inter partes: *B v B (Production Appointment: Procedure)* [1995] 1 FLR 913. In appropriate cases an order may be made against third parties: compare *Frary v Frary* [1993] 2 FLR 696 with *D v D (Production Appointment: Procedure)* [1995] 2 FLR 497. In the latter case it was said that, where there was manifest evidence of non-disclosure, the court's discretion as to the bounds of disclosure should be broad rather than narrow. However, the production appointment can only be used to bring forward the time when disclosure occurs—it does not extend the court's powers as to the scope of disclosure which may be ordered: see *Frary v Frary* (above). The court may also make *Anton Piller* and *Mareva* injunctions, although such orders are draconian, and even where a spouse is devious and deceitful and has shown no respect for other court orders, such orders will only be granted in exceptional circumstances: *Araghchinchi v Araghchinchi* [1997] 2 FLR 142, CA. See also *Burgess v Burgess* [1996] 2 FLR 34.

[71] See *C v C (Financial Relief: Short Marriage)* [1997] 2 FLR 26, CA.

[72] *Baker v Baker* [1995] 2 FLR 829, CA; *Al Khatib v Masry* [2002] EWHC 108 (Fam) [2002] 2 FCR 539; *Minwalla v Minwalla and DM Investments SA, Midfield Management SA and CI Law Trustees Ltd* [2004] EWHC 2823 (Fam), [2005] 1 FLR 771.

[73] For discussion of costs see below p 1056. For examples of cases where a spouse's failure to make full disclosure was reflected in the costs award made by the court see eg *P v P (Financial Relief: Non Disclosure)* [1994] 2 FLR 381 and *S v S (Financial Provision) (Post Divorce Cohabitation)* [1994] 2 FLR 228 (the latter where costs were awarded on a full indemnity basis).

[74] [1997] 2 FLR 774.

wrongfully evaded payment of capital and income taxes. A copy of his judgment was passed to the Inland Revenue who applied under the Family Proceedings Rules 1991[75] for a copy of the documentation in the case. Wilson J postulated three competing interests at stake in such proceedings. First, there is the public interest that all tax due should be paid and that tax evaders should be convicted and sentenced. Secondly, it is in the public interest that in proceedings for ancillary relief the parties should make full and frank disclosure of their resources and thus often of aspects of their financial history. Thirdly, there is a public interest that litigation should come to an end. On the facts of the case, his Lordship concluded that since his finding had been of a general and inferential nature, disclosure of the documents sought would not aid the Revenue and it should therefore be ordered to hand over the transcript it had obtained. By contrast, in *R v R (Inland Revenue: Tax Evasion)*[76] he ruled that the Revenue should be permitted to keep a copy of a judgment in which he had again made a finding of tax evasion since there, the finding was made on explicit evidence, which the Revenue had then acted upon, and the public interest in reducing tax evasion outweighed that of candour in the proceedings. The public interest in law enforcement was also predominant in the view of Charles J in *A v A; B v B*[77] who considered that the court should itself report relevant material to the appropriate authority where this comes to light in the proceedings.

(d) Proceeds of Crime Act 2002

Parties in such situations should be warned of their privilege against self-incrimination, but there is clearly a risk that material will then be concealed from their legal advisers (or mediators)[78] and hence the court.[79] There was a danger that this risk had been compounded by the enactment of the Proceeds of Crime Act 2002. This Act, intended to clamp down on money-laundering, imposes criminal liability on a person who becomes 'concerned in an arrangement which he knows or suspects facilitates the acquisition, retention, use or control of criminal property by or on behalf of another person'.[80] Such liability may be avoided if the person makes an 'authorised disclosure' to, usually, the National Criminal Intelligence Service (NCIS) and obtains their consent to continue with the transaction. Should the fact of this disclosure in turn be revealed so as to prejudice any investigation an offence of 'tipping off' may be committed.[81] Finally, however, a professional legal adviser does not commit the tipping off offence if the disclosure is to (or to a representative of) his client in connection with the giving by the adviser of legal advice to the client, or to any person in connection with the legal proceedings or contemplated legal proceedings, provided that such tipping off is not made with the intention of furthering a criminal purpose.[82] The question arose whether, in ancillary relief (or other proceedings), a lawyer (or mediator) was obliged by these provisions to inform NCIS of any suspicions he or she might have regarding the activities of the client, to withhold information about such disclosure from the other client and to await authorisation from NCIS before taking any further steps in

[75] Rules 10.15(6), 10.20(3). [76] [1998] 1 FLR 922. [77] [2000] 1 FLR 701.
[78] See R ap Cynan, 'Mediators Playing POCA' [2004] Fam Law 290, who advises mediators to decline to act for the client rather than disclose information to NCIS.
[79] See the discussion by B Molyneux 'The Privilege against Self-Incrimination in Ancillary Relief Proceedings' [2001] Fam Law 603.
[80] Proceeds of Crime Act 2002 s 328(1). [81] Section 333. [82] Sections 333(3), 342(4).

the litigation—often taking several weeks and thus delaying the progress of the case. In *P v P (Ancillary Relief: Proceeds of Crime)*[83] the President of the Family Division held that such was indeed the position. However, in *Bowman v Fels*[84] the Court of Appeal rejected this view, holding that s 328 is not intended to cover or affect the ordinary conduct of litigation by legal professionals, including any step taken by them in litigation from the issue of proceedings up to its final disposal by judgment. Relying on Art 6 of the European Convention on Human Rights, they noted that:

'legal proceedings are a state-provided mechanism for the resolution of issues according to law. . . . Parliament cannot have intended that proceedings or steps taken by lawyers in order to determine or secure legal rights and remedies for their clients should involve them in "becoming concerned in an arrangement which . . . facilitates the acquisition, retention, use or control of criminal property", even if they suspected that the outcome of such proceedings might have such an effect.'[85]

The court went on to hold that, even if s 328 were to be interpreted as including legal proceedings within its ambit, it could not be interpreted as overriding the defence of legal professional privilege or require a lawyer to breach his duty to the court by disclosing to a third party outside the litigation documents revealed to him through the disclosure processes. Finally, the court rejected the argument that facilitating a settlement in proceedings could be construed as 'an arrangement' within the terms of the Act: such an interpretation would undermine the need to encourage consensual settlement of legal disputes.

This judgment importantly reassured lawyers (and other professionals involved with separating couples) that they can safely advise and assist their clients without fear of, in the words of one commentator, presenting 'an image to the client that the solicitor is a fully paid-up member of the police'[86] and should assist in encouraging clients to make proper disclosure (whilst not obviating the solicitor's duty to avoid becoming embroiled in potentially criminal evasion).

B ORDERS THAT MAY BE MADE

1 MAINTENANCE PENDING SUIT

The power to order the husband to pay maintenance pending suit goes back to the ecclesiastical courts. It was based on the idea that a wife was entitled to be maintained by

---

[83] [2003] EWHC Fam 2260 [2004] 1 FLR 193. See P Wylie, '*P v P (Ancillary Relief: Proceeds of Crime)*—Disclosure under the Proceeds of Crime Act 2002 of suspicions of tax evasion gained during ancillary relief negotiations' [2004] CFLQ 203; P Moor and C Frazer, 'NCIS or "Ensnared"—How the Proceeds of Crime Act 2002 Affects Family Law' [2003] Fam Law 885; A Watters and J Levy, 'Divorce and Revenue Investigations' [2004] Fam Law 26; P Pavlou, 'Losing Trust—Privilege After POCA' [2004] Fam Law 53.

[84] [2005] EWCA CIV 226 [2005] 2 FLR 247. See A Chandler, 'POCA and NCIS: *Bowman v Fels*' [2005] Fam Law 359; D Burrows, '*Bowman v Fels*: Privilege Revived' [2005] Fam Law 386. See also guidance from the Law Society at www.lawsociety.org.uk/documents/downloads/BowmanvFelsGuidance0905.pdf and S Young, '*Bowman v Fels*: New Guidance' [2005] NLJ 1514.

[85] At para 84.   [86] Wylie op cit at 209.

her husband so long as the marriage remained in existence; the purpose of interim orders was to ensure that she and any children of the marriage living with her obtained a sufficient allowance until the outcome of the proceedings.

The Matrimonial Causes Act 1973 gives the courts power, on a petition for divorce, nullity or judicial separation, to order either spouse to make such periodical payments to the other pending suit as it thinks reasonable.[87] No guidelines are laid down governing the exercise of the court's discretion,[88] although, so far as possible, all the circumstances are to be taken into account, with the most attention being paid to the spouses' immediate financial position and the needs of the children of the family.[89] The parties' standard of living will be highly relevant to determining what will be a 'reasonable' order, but other factors may be relevant: thus, in *M v M (Maintenance Pending Suit)*[90] the fact that the husband's lifestyle had been funded by his father, who no longer wished to do so in light of the divorce proceedings, needed to be taken into account in determining what award to make to the wife pending the final order. In *F v F (Ancillary Relief: Substantial Assets)*[91] Thorpe J said that even in 'big money' cases disputes about the amount of interim awards were 'almost unknown'. His Lordship added that in an application for maintenance pending suit it would be superfluous to conduct an extensive investigation into the parties' reasonable needs; nor was the level of an interim award significant in terms of the final outcome. If necessary any underprovision or overprovision at the interim stage could be corrected at the final hearing.[92]

It has been held, in *A v A (Maintenance Pending Suit: Provision of Legal Fees)*[93] that 'maintenance', which is not statutorily defined, is not restricted to the costs of 'daily living' but can include the costs of the legal proceedings themselves, where these are a pressing need and expense. There, the wife had no income or capital, but had her legal aid for the matrimonial proceedings withdrawn because the wealthy husband had made payments to her of maintenance pending suit, taking her above the income limit. The proceedings were legally complicated, and the wife's costs exceeded £80,000. The husband was ordered to

---

[87] Matrimonial Causes Act 1973 s 22. An order under s 22 cannot be categorised as a protective or provisional measure within Art 12 of the Brussels II Convention (Council Regulation (EC) 1347/2000 on Jurisdiction and the Recognition and Enforcement of Judgments in Matrimonial Matters and in matters of Parental Responsibility for Children of Both Spouses (2000) OJ L 160/19) so as to give jurisdiction after a court elsewhere has been seized: *Wermuth v Wermuth (No 2)* [2002] EWCA Civ 50, [2003] 1 WLR 942. However, the court has jurisdiction to make an order under s 22 where there is a preliminary issue as to whether there is jurisdiction to hear the divorce suit: *Moses-Taiga v Taiga* [2005] EWCA Civ 1013, [2006] Fam Law 266.

[88] The guidelines laid down under Matrimonial Causes Act 1973 s 25 (see below pp 1018–51) do not apply to orders made under s 22.

[89] See eg *Peacock v Peacock* [1984] 1 All ER 1069. In *Re T (Divorce: Interim Maintenance: Discovery)* [1990] 1 FLR 1, the court ordered a wealthy husband to pay his wife £25,000 per annum by way of maintenance pending suit. The fact that the parties had previously agreed this figure was considered to be compelling evidence of the sum which it was reasonable to award. The old practice (long discontinued) had been to bring the wife's income (if any) up to one-fifth of the spouses' joint income.

[90] [2002] EWHC 317 (Fam), [2002] 2 FLR 123.   [91] [1995] 2 FLR 45.

[92] See too *TL v ML and Others (Ancillary Relief-Claim against Assets of Extended Family)* [2005] EWHC 2860 (Fam), [2006] 1 FCR 465.

[93] [2001] 1 FLR 377. See also *G v G (Maintenance Pending Suit: Costs)* [2002] EWHC 306 (Fam), [2003] 2 FLR 71; *Al-Khatib v Masry* [2002] EWHC 108 (Fam), [2002] 1 FLR 1053; *Minwalla v Minwalla and DM Investments SA, Midfield Management SA and CI Law Trustees Ltd* [2004] EWHC 2823 (Fam), [2005] 1 FLR 771; *TL v ML* (above).

pay the wife £4,000 per month towards her legal costs, backdated to the discharge of her legal aid certificate. Holman J ruled that such an order was also justified by Art 6 of the European Convention on Human Rights which requires the parties to legal proceedings to have 'equality of arms'—ie that each party must be afforded a reasonable opportunity to present his case under conditions that do not place him at a substantial disadvantage vis-à-vis his opponent.[94]

Under the 1973 Act the court has no power to deal with the parties' *capital assets* by way of interim order.[95] In *Wicks v Wicks*,[96] after the marriage broke down, the wife claimed income support but was told that she would have to sell the matrimonial home, which had been put into her name by the husband who was being pressed by creditors. When the husband refused to give possession of the property, the wife sought, and was granted, within the ancillary relief proceedings, an order that the property be sold and part of the proceeds paid to her to be used to purchase a new home for herself and the children. The Court of Appeal held, overruling earlier authority,[97] that there was no power to make such orders, although a sale of the home could have been ordered under s 17 of the Married Women's Property Act 1882.[98]

2 PERIODICAL PAYMENTS

(a) Orders in favour of spouses

Unsecured payments

The court may order either spouse to make unsecured periodical payments to the other or to secure periodical payments to the other.[99] Any order for periodical payments may be backdated to the date on which the application for the order was first made.[100]

As periodical payments are intended for the payee's maintenance, they must in any event terminate on her (or his) death. Unsecured periodical payments will normally come out of the payer's income, which will presumably come to an end on his death; consequently an order for their payment cannot extend beyond the payer's death.[101] There is, however, no reason why *secured* payments should not continue after the payer's death, as the capital will always have been charged; consequently in this case the order can last for the payee's life.[102] Furthermore, (whether the payments are secured or not) the order must also provide for their termination on the payee's marriage.[103] She (or he) must thereafter look to the new spouse for support.

Formerly, it seemed doubtful whether a claim for periodical payments could be dismissed without the applicant's consent, so as to preclude the latter from making further

---

[94] *Dombo Beheer BV v Netherlands* (1993) 18 EHRR 213; *Airey v Ireland* (1979) 2 EHRR 305.

[95] Provisions to permit the award of a lump sum, under the Family Law Act 1996, Sch 2 para 3, have not been implemented.

[96] [1998] 1 FLR 470, CA.   [97] *Barry v Barry* [1992] 2 FLR 233; *Green v Green* [1993] 1 FLR 326.

[98] See above, p 144. But the court would then have no power to adjust the parties' respective beneficial interests. See G Brasse 'Interim Lump Sums' [1998] Fam Law 415.

[99] Matrimonial Causes Act 1973 s 23(1)(a), (b).   [100] Ibid, s 28(1)(a)(b).

[101] Matrimonial Causes Act 1973 s 28(1)(a).   [102] Ibid s 28(1)(b).

[103] Matrimonial Causes Act 1973 s 28(1)(a)(b). It is immaterial that the second marriage is void or voidable: ibid s 52(3).

application.[104] This meant that the courts had no power to impose a 'clean break' order upon the parties, ie a once-and-for-all order whereby the husband (in practice), usually in return for transferring a share (or larger share) of the capital assets to the wife, would not be required to make any periodical payments to her. However, in line with the policy introduced by the Matrimonial and Family Proceedings Act 1984 of directing the courts to consider whether the parties could become self-sufficient either immediately after the divorce or nullity or within a reasonable time thereafter,[105] there is now express statutory power to impose a 'clean break'. Under s 25A(3) of the Matrimonial Causes Act 1973, if the court considers that no continuing obligation should be imposed on a party to a marriage, it may direct that the other party shall not be entitled to make any further application for periodical payments. The court is also under a duty to consider making a 'deferred clean break order' where periodical payments continue for a fixed period only, during which time the recipient will be able to adjust 'without undue hardship' to the termination of financial dependence on his or her former spouse.[106]

Secured payments

The very fact of security obviously makes secured payments more attractive to the payee, for there is no problem of enforcement. By tying up the payer's capital, it also prevents him from trying to frustrate the order by disposing of his assets, and the payee will be protected even though the payer becomes bankrupt. We have also seen that the payee can continue to benefit from a secured order after the other's death; moreover, although the survivor cannot *apply* for an order after the other party's death, an order made before his death may be implemented by his personal representatives, who may therefore be called upon to carry it out.[107] Because of these advantages, the court may order a smaller sum to be secured than it would have ordered by way of unsecured provision.[108]

Payments may be secured by ordering the spouse against whom the order is made to transfer specified assets to trustees. They hold them on trust to pay the sum ordered to the payee and the balance to the payer or, alternatively, to pay the income to the payer so long as he complies with the order but to use the income and, if necessary, the capital, if he defaults. The court may alternatively order specific property to be charged with the payment of the sum in question. When the order comes to an end, the capital must be returned to the payer (or his estate, if he has already died) and any charge must be cancelled.

If a party is not in need of immediate provision but may require it in the future, a nominal order may be made secured on assets yielding a substantial income. She (or he) can then apply for a suitable variation if necessary; in the meantime the income can be paid over to the other party.[109]

The court is naturally anxious to give the maximum protection, particularly to a wife whom the husband has maltreated and is likely to leave penniless.[110] Whether periodical payments can be secured, however, must depend on the capital or secured income which the other has available, and the number of spouses against whom such an order can be made is obviously small. Thorpe LJ has commented that secured orders 'have been virtually

---

[104] Following the decision in *Dipper v Dipper* [1981] Fam 31, CA.
[105] Discussed below p 1023.   [106] Matrimonial Causes Act 1973 s 25A(2) and s 28(1A).
[107] *Hyde v Hyde* [1948] P 198; *Mosey v Mosey* [1956] P 26.
[108] *Chichester v Chichester* [1936] P 129.
[109] *Foard v Foard* [1967] 2 All ER 660.   [110] See *Aggett v Aggett* [1962] 1 All ER 190, CA.

relegated to the legal history books',[111] being replaced in practice by a commuted capital payment.[112]

(b) Orders in favour of children of the family

As well as having power to make orders in favour of a spouse the court may, in proceedings for divorce, nullity and judicial separation, provided that the provisions of the Child Support Act 1991 are inapplicable,[113] make periodical payment orders (which may be secured or unsecured) in favour of a 'child of the family'.[114] The court's power to make an order for a child over the age of 18 and the term for which periodical payments may be ordered are the same as under the Domestic Proceedings and Magistrates' Courts Act 1978.[115] Normally the sums will be payable by one spouse (or former spouse) to the other, but either (or presumably both)[116] of them may be ordered to make payments to a third person, if the child is living with that person, or to the child himself.[117] Unlike orders in favour of spouses there is no power to dismiss an application for periodical payments to or in favour of the child.

3 LUMP SUM PAYMENTS

The court may order either party to pay a lump sum or lump sums to the other.[118] It can also order a lump sum to be paid to a specified person for the benefit of any child of the family or to the child himself.[119] In practice, lump sum orders in favour of children, and

[111] *AMS v Child Support Officer* [1998] 1 FLR 955 at 964A.

[112] Discussed below, p 1061.   [113] See above, pp 947–9.   [114] See above, p 338.

[115] Section 29; see *B v B (Adult Student: Liability to Support)* [1998] 1 FLR 373, CA. For the 1978 Act, s 5(3)(b), see above, p 966.

[116] The court had power under previous legislation to make an order against both spouses: *Freckleton v Freckleton* [1966] CLY 3938.

[117] An application for an order may be made by a parent, guardian, any person in whose favour a residence order has been made with respect to the child or any other person who is entitled to apply for a residence order with respect to the child, a local authority, the Official Solicitor as guardian ad litem, or the child himself, if given leave: Family Proceedings Rules 1991 r 2.54.

[118] Matrimonial Causes Act 1973 s 23(1)(c).

[119] Ibid, s 23(1)(d). The court may *in the same order* direct the payment of more than one lump sum. These may be payable at different dates (eg one payable immediately to enable a wife to put down a deposit on a home and another payable when the husband sells the matrimonial home); one may be payable by instalments and the other not. Where a lump sum is payable by instalments, the court has power to vary the amount of, or even suspend or discharge future instalments which are due: *Tilley v Tilley* (1979) 10 Fam Law 89. This jurisdiction, however, is to be exercised with caution: *Penrose v Penrose* [1994] 2 FLR 621 at 634, CA (per Balcombe LJ). The court also has power to extend the time for payment of a lump sum, at least where the payer is not at fault for the delay, the payee is not prejudiced by it, and time for payment is not of the essence of the payment: *Masefield v Alexander* [1995] 1 FLR 100, CA. Interest may be payable where an extension of time is given, but this may be offset (and hence not ordered) where the payer is also making interim periodical payments: *H v H (Lump Sum: Interest Payable)* [2005] EWHC 1513 (Fam), [2006] 1 FLR 327. There is no power to make a second or subsequent order for a lump sum in favour of a spouse: *Coleman v Coleman* [1973] Fam 10. In *Hill v Hill* [1998] 1 FLR 198, CA (a case of remarkable facts), the parties agreed an order at the time of their divorce in 1969, whereby (inter alia) the wife received a lump sum of £75. After the divorce the parties cohabited for 25 years. In 1995 they separated and the wife sought a lump sum order. The Court of Appeal held that the 1969 settlement was not a comprehensive one. The lump sum in 1969 ('extremely rare at the time') would have been regarded as settlement of the wife's claim under s 17 of the Married Woman's Property Act 1882. There had been no proper adjudication and disposal of the wife's claim for a lump sum, and the court still had jurisdiction to deal with it.

in particular children whose parents are of limited means, are rare.[120] However, they have been used where a father declined to consent to the court's fixing periodical payments for the children (the common means of avoiding the potential jurisdiction of the child support scheme)[121] above the amount which he was prepared to pay, and which the court deemed inadequate. In order to ensure that the children were left with adequate support during their dependency, Wilson J, having made the periodical payments orders at the agreed level, also made lump sum orders in their favour to meet the shortfall.[122]

It is provided by the Matrimonial Causes Act 1973 that a lump sum may be ordered to enable the payee to meet any liabilities or expenses already incurred in maintaining herself or himself or any child of the family before an application is made.[123]

However, the most important use of this statutory power is to adjust the parties' capital assets. If, for example, the husband owns shares, the court may wish the benefit of a proportion of these to be given to the wife. It may do this directly by ordering them to be transferred to her, but it may alternatively order him to make a lump sum payment to her. This makes no financial difference to the wife and it will leave the husband free to sell some of his shares or to raise the money in some other way if he prefers to do so.[124] When the matrimonial home is the only capital asset and it is sold or the wife leaves and the husband remains,[125] the court will commonly make an order for the payment of a lump sum representing the value of that part of the assets of which the other party is to be given the benefit.[126]

The award of a lump sum is not confined to these two situations, however. It is, of course, true that an order will not be made if the consequence would be to deprive the payer of his livelihood, eg if a partner would have to realise his share of the partnership.[127] Nor is a lump sum order appropriate where the payer's wealth is locked up in assets which

[120] Per Booth J in *Kiely v Kiely* [1988] 1 FLR 248 at 251, CA.   [121] See above at p 948.

[122] *V v V (Child Maintenance)* [2001] 2 FLR 799. He distinguished *Phillips v Peace* [1996] 2 FLR 230 (discussed above at p 974) because there, the mother had originally invoked the child support jurisdiction and her application for a lump sum was intended to side-step the Child Support Agency's arrival at a nil assessment against the father, whereas in *V v V*, the mother had not applied, and, in light of the court's having made the periodical payments order at the level the father was prepared to countenance, now could not do so, to the CSA.

[123] Matrimonial Causes Act 1973 s 23(3): see *Askew-Page v Page* [2001] Fam Law 794 (county court) for an example of a lump sum order made to meet debts referable to the children.

[124] But the tax implications may need to be considered carefully in case a capital gains tax liability arises. In *M v M (Sale of Property)* [1988] 1 FLR 389, CA the judge ordered the wife to transfer her interest in the home to the husband in return for a lump sum of £50,000 which, he assumed, would be free of capital gains tax. On an examination of the facts, the Court of Appeal doubted the availability of the 'principal private residence' tax exemption. It ordered the property to be sold, with a lump sum of £60,000 being paid to the wife from the net sale proceeds.

[125] See Lord Denning MR in *Wachtel v Wachtel* [1973] Fam 72 at 96.

[126] In making such orders the court must, however, be aware of the statutory charge, discussed below, p 1015.

[127] *P v P* [1978] 3 All ER 70, CA; *B v B (Financial Provision)* [1989] 1 FLR 119 (aliter if the partnership is breaking up: cf *Davies v Davies* [1986] 1 FLR 497, CA). An order should not be made if there is no prospect that the party will be able to comply with it: *Martin v Martin* [1976] Fam 335, CA; *W v W (Periodical Payments: Pensions)* [1996] 2 FLR 480.

cannot readily be sold to raise capital, eg in a shareholding in a private family company.[128] But given these restrictions a lump sum will be ordered whenever it is more valuable to the payee than periodical payments, and it is impossible to lay down any hard and fast rules.[129]

Normally a lump sum payment should not be regarded as the capitalisation of period- ical payments, but rather as a separate provision on its own.[130] In computing the sum regard is to be had to the paying spouse's means and the needs of the other spouse and child. In the case of lengthy marriages the view may commonly be taken that the recipient spouse has earned a share in the matrimonial property and that therefore the contingency of remarriage should normally be irrelevant.[131]

Lump sums will be commonly ordered where one party has substantial means, but such an order might also be the best solution if the husband has a little capital (for example, the proceeds of sale of the matrimonial home) but little or no income: the capital may be of real value to the wife, because it will give her some financial base, whilst the husband will be relieved of the obligation of finding continuing support for her out of meagre earnings. A lump sum payment with consequent reduction in periodical payments may also be ordered if the wife (or husband) has particular need of capital, eg to enable her to pur- chase a house, furniture,[132] or the goodwill of a business,[133] or to clear off a mortgage with which she is buying a new house so that she can make a fresh start.[134] A further use is to protect the payee against probable default on the other's part, eg if it appears that the party against whom financial provision is being sought is likely to remove his assets from the

[128] *P v P* [1989] 2 FLR 241. Even if there is a liquidity problem, however, a lump sum may be ordered if the payer does not produce evidence that he cannot raise the necessary capital by borrowing upon the security of his assets rather than by selling them: *Newton v Newton* [1990] 1 FLR 33, CA; cf *H v H (Financial Provision: Lump Sum)* [1994] 2 FLR 304 where, although the husband's income was high, and he was willing to borrow to achieve a clean break, the court considered it would be 'wrong' to impose too great a borrowing requirement on him.

[129] Per Davies LJ in *Jones v Jones* [1971] 3 All ER 1201 at 1206, CA.

[130] *Trippas v Trippas* [1973] Fam 134 at 139, CA per Lord Denning MR. But cf Thorpe LJ in *AMS v Child Support Officer* [1998] 1 FLR 955, CA, who noted (at 964B) that capitalised maintenance has taken the place of secured periodical payments. And compare *Van Den Boogaard v Laumen* [1997] 2 FLR 399. There, the European Court of Justice held that a lump sum order in English ancillary relief proceedings was 'mainten- ance', and thus enforceable in the Netherlands under the terms of the then Brussels Convention on Jurisdic- tion and the Enforcement of Judgments in Civil and Commercial Matters. In reaching its decision, the court concluded that the crucial question was not the form which the order took, but its aim. As this was to enable the recipient spouse to provide for herself, after a consideration of her needs and resources, the award was 'concerned with maintenance'.

[131] See eg *Duxbury v Duxbury* (1987) [1992] Fam 62n; cf periodical payments which automatically cease upon the recipient spouse's marriage. Occasionally a party's remarriage will be a relevant factor (provided there are very real prospects: see *H v H (Financial Provision: Remarriage)* [1975] Fam 9). For example, if the party's financial resources are limited and a decision to give the wife capital (eg the matrimonial home) rather than periodical payments is regarded as the most satisfactory way of meeting her needs, it will be material to know if those needs will change as a result of remarriage.

[132] *S v S* [1977] Fam 127, CA.

[133] *Von Mehren v Von Mehren* [1970] 1 All ER 153, CA (husband ordered to pay £4,000 to his former wife to enable her to purchase a house which she intended to run as a boarding house). *Gojkovic v Gojkovic* [1992] Fam 40 (lump sum order of £1 million to wife to buy hotel).

[134] *Harnett v Harnett* [1974] 1 All ER 764, CA; cf *Calderbank v Calderbank* [1976] Fam 93, CA (husband given lump sum to enable him to buy house in which to live and see children to whom he had been granted contact).

jurisdiction,[135] or to enable the payee to take bankruptcy proceedings against a contumacious party.[136] Further advantages of a lump sum are that, as the payment is final, there are no continuing problems of enforcement, which may be of particular importance if the parties' relationship is particularly bitter.[137]

Lump sum applications should ordinarily be disposed of once and for all, but there is jurisdiction to adjourn the application where there is a *real* possibility of capital from a specific source becoming available in the near future.[138]

The court can order the sum to be paid in instalments and may also require the payment of instalments to be secured[139] and to carry interest.[140] Such an approach differs from an order for periodical payments because the total sum will be fixed and cannot be varied, and the balance will still be payable even if one of the parties dies before the whole sum has been paid. A striking example can be seen in *R v R (Lump Sum Repayments)*.[141] The husband, who ran the family farm and who could not raise cash on the strength of his shares in it, was ordered to pay the wife a lump sum of £30,000 immediately followed by 240 monthly instalments thereafter in a sum equivalent to the wife's obligations under a 20-year repayment mortgage for £225,000, to enable her to buy her own home. The payments were to be secured by the wife having a charge over the husband's shares in the farm, to act as 'judicious encouragement' to the company to ensure that the husband was able to meet his obligations to the wife.

Unlike a periodical payments order, the rights under a lump sum payment have all the incidents of outright ownership; they cannot be varied or discharged,[142] and so may be

[135] *Brett v Brett* [1969] 1 All ER 1007, CA.

[136] *Curtis v Curtis* [1969] 2 All ER 207, CA (husband who had considerable means and was practising delaying tactics, ordered to pay wife £33,600, capitalising an annual sum of £2,400). In *Wheatley v Wheatley* [1999] 2 FLR 205, it was held that a persistent refusal to comply with court orders, especially if so serious as to result in committal for contempt, was to be taken into account in deciding whether, exceptionally, bankruptcy proceedings were the right way to seek recovery of a matrimonial debt. A lump sum order is now provable in bankruptcy proceedings: r 12.3 of the Insolvency Rules 1986 (SI 1986/1925) as amended by SI 2005/527, r 44; introduced in light of comments by Balcombe LJ in *Woodley v Woodley (No 2)* [1993] 2 FLR 477, CA where he called for lump sum orders to be both provable and not released on discharge. For discussion, see T Costley-White, 'Bankruptcy—Back to Basics' [2000] Fam Law 181. The court may make a lump sum order notwithstanding the payer spouse's bankruptcy, provided the court considers the effect of the bankruptcy on the payer's ability to pay, and has a clear picture of his assets and liabilities: see *Woodley v Woodley* [1992] 2 FLR 417; *Hellyer v Hellyer* [1996] 2 FLR 579. If a husband obtains a bankruptcy order on his own petition and, because of his failure to disclose his financial position the order is an abuse of the process of the court, the order may be set aside and the court may order a lump sum: *F v F (Divorce Insolvency: Annulment of Bankruptcy Order)* [1994] 1 FLR 359.

[137] See *Griffiths v Griffiths* [1974] 1 All ER 932 at 942, CA.

[138] *Davies v Davies* [1986] 1 FLR 497, CA; *D v D (Lump Sum Order: Adjournment of Application)* [2001] 1 FLR 633, where Connell J upheld the trial judge's decision to adjourn the wife's lump sum application until the size of the husband's cash bonus under his employer's incentive scheme was known; cf *Burgess v Burgess* [1996] 2 FLR 34, CA, where the husband's prospects of obtaining substantial assets from his business were not taken into account, since there was no real likelihood of a sale. In *Michael v Michael* [1986] 2 FLR 389, CA, *K v K (Financial Provision: Conduct)* [1990] 2 FLR 225 and *H v H (Financial Provision: Capital Assets)* [1993] 2 FLR 335, a spouse's inheritance expectancy was held too remote, while in *MT v MT (Financial Provision: Lump Sum)* [1992] 1 FLR 362 the wife's application was adjourned until the death of her 83-year-old German father-in-law. Under German law the husband would automatically inherit one-eighth of his father's estate.

[139] Matrimonial Causes Act 1973 s 23(3)(c).   [140] Ibid s 23(6).

[141] [2003] EWHC 3197 (Fam), [2004] 1 FLR 928.

[142] Under the Matrimonial Causes Act 1973 s 31 as amended (see below p 1059).

validly assigned.[143] It follows that a wife, who is ineligible for legal aid, may assign part of her entitlement to a future lump sum order to her solicitors to pay off her legal fees in relation to ancillary relief proceedings. Such an assignment may enable a 'significant constituency of wives'[144] to secure proper legal advice and representation to assert their rights against their husbands, who are economically more powerful, and may be seeking to exploit their position in their conduct of the proceedings.[145]

4 ORDERS IN RELATION TO PENSIONS [146]

The court has power to make two kinds of orders in relation to pensions—pension attachment (formerly known as earmarking) orders, which are forms of financial provision order made under s 23, and pension sharing orders which are a separate type of order made under s 24B.

The Pensions Act 1995 amended the Matrimonial Causes Act 1973 to introduce new provisions giving the court powers to re-allocate the pension rights of the spouses.[147] By s 25B(1) of the Matrimonial Causes Act 1973 the court is placed under a duty to have regard to the spouses' pension entitlements, being:

(a) any benefits under a pension arrangement which a party to the marriage has or is likely to have; and

(b) any benefits under a pension arrangement which, by reason of the dissolution or annulment of the marriage, a party will lose the chance of acquiring.[148]

For this purpose, a pension arrangement is defined as an occupational pension scheme or personal pension scheme, a retirement annuity contract, an annuity or insurance policy

---

[143] *Sears Tooth (a firm) v Payne Hicks Beach (a firm)* [1997] 2 FLR 116. Wilson J acknowledged that lump sum orders which are payable by instalments may be varied and, as such, may, like periodical payments, be incapable of assignment. He added (at 126) that lump sums payable by instalments 'might need to be revisited in another case'.

[144] Ibid at 133 (per Wilson J).

[145] In providing a way for a spouse of modest means to fund the legal and other professional costs of ancillary relief proceedings *Sears Tooth* may prove of considerable significance. Wilson J suggested two requirements which are necessary for the assignment to be valid: the spouse concerned should be independently legally advised before entering into the deed of assignment, and the deed itself should be disclosed to the court. (In appropriate cases it may well be of tactical advantage for the existence of the deed to be disclosed to the opposing side.) Note also that one possible use of maintenance pending suit is to pay the recipient's legal and other professional costs in relation to ongoing ancillary relief proceedings (see above, p 992).

[146] See generally R Ellison and M Rae, *Family Breakdown and Pensions* 2nd ed (2001); R Bird, *Pension Sharing: The New Law* (2000); D Salter, 'A Practitioners' Guide to Pension Sharing' (Parts I, II and III) [2000] Fam Law 489, 543, 914; J Hanlon, 'Till divorce do our pension plan part' [2001] CFLQ 51; D Salter, *Pension Sharing in Practice: A Special Bulletin* 2nd ed (2003); A Dnes *The Division of Marital Assets following Divorce with Particular Reference to Pensions*, Lord Chancellor's Department Research Series 7/97.

[147] Pensions Act 1995 s 166 inserted ss 25B–D into the Matrimonial Causes Act 1973 (further amended by the Welfare Reform and Pensions Act 1999 Sch 4. These powers were made available in relation to divorces where proceedings were commenced after 1 July 1996: Pensions Act (Commencement) (No 5) Order 1996 (SI 1996/1675).

[148] Including any 'PPF compensation', ie 'Pension Protection Fund' compensation payable under Chapter 3 of Part 2 of the Pensions Act 2004: Matrimonial Causes Act 1973 s 25E inserted by Sch 12 para 3 of the Pensions Act 2004. For discussion, see D Salter, 'Pensions Law Simplification and the Family Lawyer' [2004] Fam Law 795.

purchased, or transferred, for the purpose of giving effect to rights under an occupational or personal pension scheme, and an annuity purchased or entered into for the purpose of discharging liability in respect of a pension credit.[149]

(a) Pension attachment

The court has powers to order the person responsible for the pension arrangement[150] to make payments (including lump sums) for the benefit of a pensioner's spouse as and when such payments fall due on retirement.[151] The order must express the amount of the payment as a percentage of the payment due to the pensioner.[152] If a pensioner enjoys the appropriate rights under the terms of the arrangement, the court may also order him to commute the whole or any part of the payments due,[153] or to nominate his spouse as the beneficiary of any lump sum payment which he may receive.[154] These provisions enable a court to 'earmark' some or all of a spouse's future pension in favour of the other. It has been held,[155] however, that their enactment does not *require* the court to compensate a spouse for actual or potential loss of pension benefits. All that they do is to provide a further option available to the court, as a form of financial provision order under s 23, to deal with the parties' assets in a way best suited to the circumstances of the case—and it will not always be appropriate to make an order of this kind. In *Burrow v Burrow*[156] the husband's pension scheme provided that he would be entitled on retirement to commute one-quarter of the capital in his pension fund, with the remaining three-quarters available to provide an annuity for life. The trial judge was held to have been wrong to earmark 50% of the annuity fund, because the husband might not retire for another fifteen years and it was difficult to predict so far in advance what might be the appropriate level of periodical payments for the wife at that time in the future. Instead, either party could apply for a variation of the periodical payments order which the court had also made, at the relevant time when it would be possible to fix a more appropriate level.

In addition to the problem of uncertainty inherent in attempting to assess future income and capital provision from a pension, attachment orders have a further drawback, which is that they only take effect when the pension becomes payable. As Wilson J put it:

'It is relevant to the present claim for me to stress the limitations of an attachment order as a vehicle for making provision for a wife out of the husband's pension rights. It does not carve out of his rights pension rights for her, bespoke to her needs and in particular to the length of her life. It merely impresses upon whatever may be payable to the husband under a pension scheme a compulsory redirection to the wife in satisfaction of his obligations under court orders. Thus no part of his pension is payable to the wife, whatever her age and however great her need, until, within the limits open to him under the scheme, the husband chooses to retire. Even more significantly, no further payment falls to be made to her in the event that following his retirement he predeceases her. In a sentence, the problem is that,

---

[149] Matrimonial Causes Act 1973 s 25D(3).

[150] Meaning the trustees or managers of the pension scheme, the annuity provider or the insurer: s 25D(4).

[151] Ibid, s 25B(4) and s 25C(2)(a).   [152] Ibid, s 25B(5).   [153] Ibid, s 25B(7).

[154] Ibid, s 25C(2)(b).   [155] In *T v T (Financial Relief: Pensions)* [1998] 1 FLR 1072.

[156] [1999] 1 FLR 508.

notwithstanding divorce, the wife who has the benefit only of an attachment order remains hitched to the husband's wagon.'[157]

(b) Pension sharing

A better solution is to make a pension sharing order instead.[158] This re-adjusts the spouses' pension entitlements and enables each party to make future pension arrangements independently of the other. The spouse in whose favour the order is made can either become a member of the other's pension scheme in her own right, or she can transfer the value of the ordered share into her own pension arrangement. The advantage of this approach over that of attachment is that, by allocating the pension *rights* at the time of the divorce, the intended recipient knows that she can take the benefit of those rights regardless of whether the other spouse dies before retirement.

Initial provision for pension sharing was made in the Family Law Act 1996[159] but was not brought into force. Instead, following consultations,[160] the Welfare Reform and Pensions Act 1999 was passed, and amended Part II of the Matrimonial Causes Act 1973.[161] A pension sharing order is an order which:

'(a) provides that one party's—

shareable rights under a specified pension arrangement, or shareable state scheme rights, be subject to pension sharing for the benefit of the other party, and

(b) specifies the percentage value to be transferred.'[162]

Shareable rights are any rights other than those in an excepted public service pension scheme and those specified in the Pension Sharing (Valuation) Regulations 2000 (widows'

---

[157] *R (Smith) v Secretary of State for Defence and Secretary of State for Work and Pensions* [2004] EWHC 1797 (Admin) [2005] 1 FLR 97 at para 15.

[158] But such an order may only be made after divorce or annulment, not judicial separation: Matrimonial Causes Act 1973, s 24B(1). For advice on the matters that need to be dealt with by practitioners advising clients on pension sharing, see D Salter, 'The Pitfalls of Pension Sharing Parts I and II' [2002] Fam Law 598 and 666; H Smith, B Brindley and A Sanger, 'The Reality of Pension Sharing Parts One and Two' [2003] Fam Law 517 and 679.

[159] Section 16.

[160] Department of Social Security, *Pension Sharing on Divorce: reforming pensions for a fairer future* Cm 3345 (1998).

[161] There are also several regulations including: Pensions on Divorce etc (Provision of Information) Regulations 2000 (SI 2000/1048), Divorce etc (Pensions) Regulations 2000 (SI 2000/1123), Pensions on Divorce etc (Charging) Regulations 2000 (SI 2000/1049), Family Proceedings Rules 1991, r 2.70 (as amended).

[162] Matrimonial Causes Act 1973 s 21A(1). A pension sharing order may only be made in respect of petitions filed after 1 December 2000. In *S v S (Rescission of Decree Nisi: Pension Sharing Provision)* [2002] 1 FLR 457, it was held that a decree nisi of divorce could be rescinded on the wife's application and fresh proceedings brought to enable the parties to take advantage of the pension sharing provisions. In this case, the husband consented to what was proposed and there were no children, or outstanding issues regarding maintenance, to be considered. In *H v H (Pension Sharing: Rescission of Decree Nisi)* [2002] EWHC 767, [2002] 2 FLR 116, where the husband strongly opposed the wife's application, it was held that it would be unfair and prejudicial to him to permit fresh proceedings to take place to enable the wife to get round the commencement date (see to similar effect, *Rye v Rye* [2002] EWHC 956 (Fam), [2002] 2 FLR 981). A cross-petition issued after the commencement date does not prevent the divorce proceedings being viewed as having begun earlier and hence prevents the parties from taking advantage of the pension sharing provisions: *W v W (Divorce Proceedings: Withdrawal of Consent after Perfection of Order)* [2002] EWHC 1826 (Fam), [2002] 2 FLR 1225.

and dependants' rights).[163] The basic state pension cannot be shared (since it already enables a divorced spouse to substitute the contribution record of their former spouse for their own) but the state earnings-related pension (SERPS) and shared additional pension may be.[164] The court may make one or more such orders, but cannot do so where the arrangement is already the subject of such an order, or a pension attachment order, between the parties.[165]

To settle pension rights, the couple have to obtain a valuation of these from any pension arrangement to which either or both belongs or has belonged in the past. The valuation will be based on a cash equivalent transfer value (CETV)[166] of the accrued rights. This is the lump sum value, in current money terms, of the rights under the pension arrangement which have accrued so far to the pension member, as measured by the amount which would be available in the event of a transfer being made to another pension arrangement if the member were to leave service. It assumes that the member's pensionable service ceases at the date of valuation, and does not include death-in-service benefits, discretionary benefits and future expectations.[167] As Singer J noted, in *T v T (Financial Relief: Pensions)*:[168]

'I should perhaps emphasise that these values are at best a guide, and that their apparent precision (down to the nearest pound) is illusory, and the product of mathematical rather than predictive accuracy. For they necessarily incorporate various assumptions (as to the rate of future inflation before and after the pension commences in payment; an appropriate discount rate reflecting the tax-exempt environment (currently) enjoyed by the pension fund; and of course that ultimately unpredictable factor, mortality). . . . Thus (as has been said of a Duxbury fund) the only fact which can be predicted with absolute accuracy is that the prediction will turn out to be inaccurate. These figures are therefore, at best and when it is appropriate to have regard to them at all, a guide rather than a rule.'

Depending upon the type of pension arrangement in question, recipients of a pension sharing order are able to become members of the scheme, or transfer the accrued rights to another. The pension arrangement is notified by the court of the order which it has made, and has four months to implement it.[169] The order is in the form of a percentage share of the member's rights,[170] and the scheme will recover, from the parties, the reasonable administrative costs involved, either in cash, or by deduction from the pension rights.[171] The recipient of the order acquires 'pension credits' in the original pension arrangement or that to which the rights are transferred.[172] Her eventual pension will depend on the

---

[163] SI 2000/1052 reg 2.

[164] Welfare Reform and Pensions Act 1999, s 47(2). See T Costley-White, 'SERPS—The Forgotten Asset' [2002] Fam Law 222.

[165] Matrimonial Causes Act 1973 s 24B(3),(5).

[166] Welfare Reform and Pensions Act 1999 s 30. See also the Divorce etc (Pensions) Regulations 2000 reg 3 and the Pension Sharing (Valuation) Regulations 2000.

[167] See D Salter, 'A Practitioners' Guide to Pension Sharing, Part 2' [2000] Fam Law 543. For problems in using the CETV as the basis for allocating shares in the parties' total assets (and confusing future income and capital emanating from a pension arrangement) see *Maskell v Maskell* [2001] EWCA Civ 858 [2003] 1 FLR 1138, comment by E Da Costa, 'Pensions—The *Maskell* Approach' [2002] Fam Law 848 and B Brindley, 'Black and White in Pensions' [2001] Fam Law 462.

[168] [1998] 1 FLR 1072 at 1079.   [169] Ibid s 34(1).

[170] Matrimonial Causes Act 1973 s 21A(1)(b).   [171] Matrimonial Causes Act 1973 s 24D.

[172] Welfare Reform and Pensions Act 1999 s 29.

rules of that arrangement and her own circumstances when the pension becomes due, and not those of the former spouse from whom the rights have been transferred. In particular, this means that normally, the pension credit member cannot receive the pension under an occupational pension scheme until she reaches statutory retirement age, even if her ex-spouse is permitted to draw the pension early.[173]

5 TRANSFER AND SETTLEMENT OF PROPERTY

The court may order either party to the marriage to transfer such property as may be specified to the other party or to or for the benefit of a child of the family. The court may also order either of them to settle any property for the benefit of the other party or any child of the family.[174] The court's power to transfer (but not to settle) property on a child over the age of 18 is limited to where the child is receiving instruction at an educational establishment or is undergoing training for a trade, profession or vocation, or where there are other special circumstances (eg the child is suffering from some physical or mental disability).[175]

The transfer power is currently of particular importance to enable the court to make appropriate orders with respect to the matrimonial home and similar assets (eg furniture or the family car), but it may also be ordered as an alternative to the payment of a lump sum when it is more sensible to order one spouse to transfer investments than to compel him to sell them to raise the necessary capital, or to supplement or replace periodical payments when the party in question has a limited interest (eg a life interest under a family settlement) which can conveniently be used for this purpose.

(a) Property that may be the subject of an order

The Act empowers the court to make an order with respect to any property to which the spouse in question is entitled either in possession or in reversion.[176] This form of words follows that of earlier Acts dealing with settlements of the wife's property, under which it was held that 'property' included income as well as capital,[177] and 'reversionary interests' embraced those to which the wife was contingently entitled as well as those already vested in interest.[178] The established view is that there is no power to order a transfer or settlement that the party could not make voluntarily: eg of a protected life interest (which is determinable on the occurrence of any event which will deprive the beneficiary of the

<hr/>

[173] R (Smith) v Secretary of State for Defence and Secretary of State for Work and Pensions [2004] EWHC 1797 (Admin), [2005] 1 FLR 97. See ss 101c(1) and 101b of the Pension Schemes Act 1993. Ways round this limitation are either, where possible, to transfer her rights to a personal pension scheme or to order the pension member to make periodical payments to the ex-wife to meet the payment gap: see D Salter, 'Pensions Law Simplification and the Family Lawyer' [2004] Fam Law 795 at 804.

[174] Matrimonial Causes Act 1973 s 24(1)(a)(b). For an example of settlement of property on children, see H v H (Financial Provision: Conduct) [1998] 1 FLR 971 (lump sum settled on trusts for husband to enable him to buy suitable home in which children could have contact with him; reversion to the children).

[175] Section 29(1)–(3).

[176] For an illustration of the breadth of the courts' powers in this regard see Harwood v Harwood [1991] 2 FLR 274, CA (husband ordered to transfer to wife his interest in assets of a dissolved partnership with a third party).

[177] See Savary v Savary (1898) 79 LT 607 at 610, CA; Style v Style [1954] P 209, CA.

[178] Stedall v Stedall (1902) 86 LT 124; Savary v Savary (above).

right to receive any part of the income), or of a lease containing a covenant against assignment.[179] The latter limitation may be of particular importance when the court is dealing with rights in the matrimonial home. Similarly it was accepted that the party must be able to claim the property *as of right*; hence, if he is a beneficiary under a discretionary trust, the court apparently has no power to order the settlement of any income which the trustees *may* in their discretion pay him,[180] nor presumably could it order the settlement of any property which *might* come to him as the result of the exercise of a power of appointment vested in another. In *Thomas v Thomas*,[181] the Court of Appeal suggested that the court should look at the reality of the situation; it ought not to disregard the potential availability of wealth from sources owned or administered by others. In appropriate circumstances a judge may frame his order to afford 'judicious encouragement' to third parties to provide a spouse with the means to comply with the court's view of the justice of the case. However, in *TL v ML*[182] it was pointed out that this should only be done where the payer can truly control the availability of the potential assets. Where, as there, these were in fact controlled by his parents (the 'patriarch' and 'matriarch' of the family shipping business), it was held inappropriate to regard them as available for transfer to the wife.

An order may also be made in respect of property which is the subject of a separate application to enforce a criminal confiscation order under the Drug Trafficking Act 1994 or Criminal Justice Act 1988: these Acts do not take priority over the Matrimonial Causes Act so that where the court considers it appropriate, it may transfer the property (in this case the matrimonial home) to the ex-spouse even though this may prevent the authorities from realising the full amount of the confiscation order.[183]

---

[179] See *Hale v Hale* [1975] 2 All ER 1090, CA. The question was left open by Lord Penzance in *Milne v Milne* (1871) LR 2 P & D 295, but cf *Loraine v Loraine* [1912] P 222, CA.

[180] *Milne v Milne* (above). Nevertheless, the existence of the interest can be taken into account: cf *Browne v Browne* [1989] 1 FLR 291, CA.

[181] [1995] 2 FLR 668, CA where the court applied the principles to a private family company (rather than a discretionary trust) where the shareholders were the husband, his brother, his mother and a family trust; *Rye v Rye* [2002] EWHC 956 (Fam), [2002] 2 FLR 981; complex accounting arrangements masked husband's true wealth but did not prevent substantial orders being made in favour of wife and children. See also *T v T and Others (Joinder of Third Parties)* [1996] 2 FLR 357 where the husband had transferred in excess of £25 million to a Jersey Trust, in respect of which he claimed he had no overall control. Wilson J held that he would need to join the trustees as parties to the proceedings to determine the truth. But cf *Scheeres v Scheeres* [1999] 1 FLR 241, where the Court of Appeal held that an order should not be founded on speculative assessment as to the likelihood of a business recovering from difficult trading conditions; and *George v George* [2003] EWCA Civ 202, [2004] 1 FLR 421: court should have adjourned to await outcome of proceedings in Queen's Bench Division against husband for recovery of a debt and not assumed that the transactions between the husband and the debtor were a sham.

[182] *TL v ML and Others (Ancillary Relief: Claim against Assets of Extended Family* [2005] EWHC 2860 (Fam), [2006] 1 FCR 465.

[183] Neither Act has priority: see *Re MCA: HM Customs and Excise Commissioners and Long v A and A; A v A (Long Intervening)* [2002] EWCA Civ 1039, [2003] 1 FLR 164; *CPS v Grimes, Grimes Intervening and Grimes v Grimes* [2003] 2 FLR 510, discussed by G More O'Ferrall, 'Ancillary Relief, Equitable Interests and Criminal Confiscation Orders' [2005] Fam Law 227. Cf *R v Ahmed; R v Qureshi* [2004] EWCA Crim 2599, [2005] 1 All ER 128: no engagement of Art 8 right to respect for one's home where confiscation order made in respect of property including jointly owned matrimonial home, although enforcement action would require consideration of this right. In *X v X (Crown Prosecution Service Intervening)* [2005] EWHC 296 (Fam), [2005] 2 FLR 487 it was held that it would be wrong to effect an ancillary relief settlement in such as way as to reduce the husband's liability under a confiscation order.

No transfer or settlement will be ordered if the property is outside the jurisdiction and effective control of the court.[184] But the fact that the property is situated abroad will not prevent the order from being made provided that it can be effectively enforced; and so the court might order the settlement of income receivable in this country from capital invested elsewhere. But if such an order might prove to be difficult to enforce, the court will prefer to make an order with respect to property in England.[185]

(b) Orders that can be made

The court can apparently order an absolute transfer of the whole of the party's interest in the property specified or any part of it. It has equally wide powers when ordering a settlement and may either divest the spouse of his whole interest[186] or grant a limited interest to the other spouse or children, leaving the beneficial owner with the reversion.[187] Although the factors which the court should take into account when deciding what order (if any) to make will be considered later,[188] it might be said here that the courts rarely make substantial capital orders in favour of children.[189] The transfer order effects a disposition creating an equitable interest in favour of the transferee at the moment it is made and vesting beneficial ownership in the transferee.[190]

6 VARIATION OF MARRIAGE SETTLEMENTS[191]

The court may make an order varying any marriage settlement for the benefit of the parties to a marriage and the children of the family or either or any of them, other than one in the form of a pension arrangement[192] The court may also make an order extinguishing or reducing the interest of either of the parties under any marriage settlement (again, other than a pension arrangement).[193] For this purpose, a marriage settlement means an ante-nuptial or post-nuptial settlement made on the parties, including one made by will.[194]

These powers are complementary to those already discussed and are used less in view of the wider powers to order transfer and settlements of property. But there are

---

[184] *Hamlin v Hamlin* [1986] Fam 11, CA.   [185] See *Style v Style* [1954] P 209, CA.

[186] As in *Compton v Compton* [1960] P 201where property was settled on children for life with remainder to grandchildren. Quaere whether the remainder to the grandchildren was not ultra vires, as this does not benefit *children of the family*.

[187] *Style v Style* above (settlement on husband for life).   [188] See below pp 1030–51.

[189] See *Kiely v Kiely* [1988] 1 FLR 248, CA; *Chamberlain v Chamberlain* [1974] 1 All ER 33, CA; *Lilford v Glynn* [1979] 1 All ER 441, CA; and *Draskovic v Draskovic* (1980) 11 Fam Law 87. But cf *H v H (Financial Provision: Conduct)* (above) and *Tavoulareas v Tavoulareas* [1998] 2 FLR 418, CA.

[190] *Mountney v Treharne* [2002] EWCA Civ 1174, [2002] 2 FLR 930. However, although the beneficiary may seek to enforce the order, it may be set aside on the transferor's bankruptcy under s 39 of the 1973 Act or s 284 of the Insolvency Act 1986: *Treharne & Sand v Forrester* [2003] EWHC 2784 (Ch), [2004] 1 FLR 1173.

[191] Note that the equivalent provision for civil partners is contained in Sch 5 para 7(3) to the Civil Partnership Act 2004, which refers to a 'relevant settlement'.

[192] Matrimonial Causes Act 1973 s 24(1)(c), as amended by the Welfare Reform and Pensions Act 1999 Sch 3 para 3.

[193] Ibid, s 24(1)(d) as amended by the Welfare Reform and Pensions Act 1999 Sch 3 para 3.

[194] Ibid, s 24(1)(c).

still cases where the only power that can be exercised is that of varying a settlement, eg if one party has an interest that cannot be transferred (such as a protected life interest) or if it is desired to vary or destroy limitations in favour of children or other beneficiaries.

The parties cannot oust the court's jurisdiction by agreement, nor apparently is this jurisdiction in any way fettered by express provisions in the settlement as to how the property is to be held if the marriage is terminated[195] or as to the choice of law determining its construction.[196]

The terms 'ante-nuptial and post-nuptial settlements' are used in a sense much wider than that usually given to them by conveyancers, the essential condition being that the benefit must be conferred on either or both of the spouses *in the character of spouse or spouses*.[197] It was even taken to extend to a personal pension scheme established by a businessman under which he and his spouse were beneficiaries.[198] This construction was used as a means of making adequate pension provision for the ex-wife at a time before pension attachment and pension sharing had been enacted. It is no longer possible to use the power to deal with pensions in this way[199] but the House of Lords' view in *Brooks v Brooks*[200] that a wide interpretation should be given to the term 'nuptial settlement' remains good law. Presumably, the definition of a 'relevant settlement' in relation to civil partners—'a settlement made, during its subsistence or in anticipation of its formation, on the civil partners including one made by will or codicil, but not including one in the form of a pension arrangement . . .'[201] will be given the same broad interpretation. It is perhaps unfortunate that the opportunity was not taken to clarify the definition to ensure that what must, after all, be an entirely new species of 'settlement' is indeed regarded as being equivalent to the traditional 'nuptial' settlement it is intended to mirror.

It is immaterial whether the benefit comes from one of the spouses or from a third person.[202] It is possible that a transaction may be a settlement for this purpose if it confers a benefit upon the children of the marriage, even though it confers none upon either spouse, provided that the beneficiaries take *in the character of children of the family*.[203] Similarly, a transaction which would otherwise be a settlement will not cease to be one because the spouses are removed as beneficiaries, if they remain able to control the decisions made under the settlement.[204]

---

[195] See *Prinsep v Prinsep* [1930] P 35 at 49, CA; *Woodcock v Woodcock* (1914) 111 LT 924, CA; Denning LJ in *Egerton v Egerton* [1949] 2 All ER 238 at 242, CA. In nullity proceedings a settlement may be varied even though the marriage is void: *Radziej v Radziej* [1967] 1 All ER 944; affirmed [1968] 3 All ER 624, CA.

[196] *Charalambous v Charalambous* [2004] EWCA Civ 1030, [2004] 2 FLR 1093.

[197] Per Hill J in *Prinsep v Prinsep* [1929] P 225 at 232. See also *Bosworthick v Bosworthick* [1927] P 64, CA at 69; *Worsley v Worsley* (1869) LR 1 P & D 648 at 651.

[198] *Brooks v Brooks* [1986] AC 375, HL. See also *C v C (Variation of Post-Nuptial Settlement: Company Shares)* [2003] EWHC 1222 (Fam), [2003] 2 FLR 493, where the husband's shareholding in his company was transferred into a settlement in the Cayman Islands, with the wife as a beneficiary.

[199] See s 24(1)(c) as amended.   [200] Above.   [201] Sch 5 para 7(3).

[202] *Prinsep v Prinsep* (above).

[203] Apparently so held in *Compton v Compton* [1960] P 201, (where, however, the wife was trustee and had a power of appointment in favour of children).

[204] *Charalambous v Charalambous* [2004] EWCA Civ 1030, [2004] 2 FLR 1093.

Provided that the condition stated above is fulfilled, it is immaterial that one or both of the spouses are merely the objects of a discretionary trust and can therefore claim nothing as of right.[205] A separation agreement comes within the section even if it is not in writing.[206] Similarly a bond by which a wife undertakes to pay an annuity to her husband,[207] and a policy of life assurance taken out by a husband for the benefit of his wife[208] have been held to be post-nuptial settlements.[209] But there cannot be a settlement for this purpose if there has been an absolute and unqualified transfer of property unless payments of some sort still have to be made at the time that the court has to enquire into the existence of the settlement.[210]

The court may vary a settlement only if it was made on the footing that the marriage *which is the subject of the divorce* should continue.[211] Thus, if a husband marries successively W1 and W2, a settlement made by him on the eve of his marriage to W1 cannot be varied in divorce proceedings brought by W2.[212] Conversely, if an agreement was ostensibly entered into on the footing that the marriage would be dissolved, it cannot be a post-nuptial settlement.[213]

7 ORDERS FOR THE SALE OF PROPERTY

As originally enacted, the Matrimonial Causes Act 1973 conferred no *express* power to order a sale of spouses' property. However, following the Law Commission's recommendation,[214] it is now expressly provided by s 24A[215] that where the court makes a secured periodical payments order, a lump sum order, or a property adjustment order, then it may make:

'... a further order for the sale of such property as may be specified in the order, being property in which or in the proceeds of sale of which either or both of the parties to the marriage has or have a beneficial interest, either in possession or reversion.'

[205] *E v E (Financial Provision)* [1990] 2 FLR 233 (post-nuptial settlement constituted where, during the subsistence of a marriage, property purchased by the husband's father was settled on a discretionary trust whose beneficiaries were the husband, the wife, the husband's children and remoter issue by any subsequent wife). See also *T v T (Joinder of Third Parties)* [1996] 2 FLR 357. In *Howard v Howard* [1945] P 1, CA, MacKinnon LJ left open the question whether a discretionary trust can be a post-nuptial settlement merely because one of the spouses comes within the class of possible beneficiaries. The court may vary such a settlement even though it is in a foreign form because the parties were domiciled elsewhere at the time of the marriage: *Forsyth v Forsyth* [1891] P 363 (and see also *Charalambous v Charalambous* (above) which concerned a Jersey trust).
[206] *Tomkins v Tomkins* [1948] P 170, CA; *Jeffrey v Jeffrey (No 2)* [1952] P 122, CA. If it were in writing it could also be varied under s 35 of the Matrimonial Causes Act (above p 954).
[207] *Bosworthick v Bosworthick* [1927] P 64, CA; cf *Parrington v Parrington* [1951] 2 All ER 916.
[208] *Gunner v Gunner* [1949] P 77 followed in *Brown v Brown* [1949] P 91.
[209] See too *N v N and F Trust* [2005] EWHC 2908 (Fam), [2006] Fam Law 181, where the matrimonial home had been bought by a company owned by a family trust and was held to be a nuptial settlement capable of variation within the subsection.
[210] *Prescott v Fellowes* [1958] P 260, CA. In *Brooks v Brooks* [1996] AC 375, HL, Lord Nicholls considered (at 391–2) that in the case of gifts the appropriate order would be a property transfer or property settlement order.
[211] *Young v Young* [1962] P 27, CA.
[212] *Burnett v Burnett* [1936] P 1. See also *Hargreaves v Hargreaves* [1926] P 42.
[213] *Young v Young* (above).
[214] Law Com No 99, *Orders for Sale of Property under the Matrimonial Causes Act 1973*.
[215] Added by the Matrimonial Homes and Property Act 1981 s 7.

The power to order a sale is a consequential or ancillary power and not an independent one. In other words, it can only be made where an order relating to the parties' capital has already been made under s 23 and s 24; it does not confer a jurisdiction to order a sale 'in the air'. That s 24A does not extend the court's powers has been emphasised in *Omielan v Omielan*,[216] where it was held that the section was inserted into the Act to clarify or expand the court's power of enforcement, implementation and procedure, ancillary to the substantive orders which it can make.

In the case of property belonging to one spouse and a third party the court is directed that, before it decides whether to order a sale, the third party must be given the opportunity to make representations, and any such representations are then to be included in the circumstances to which the court must have regard under s 25 of the 1973 Act.[217]

8 CONSENT ORDERS

(a) Encouraging agreement

There is nothing to prevent the parties themselves from agreeing to the terms of the financial provision and property adjustment orders to be made: indeed, the whole trend in recent years has been to encourage them to do so.[218] We have already noted the emphasis placed by the Ancillary Relief Procedure on the promotion of settlements.[219] Negotiated settlements may work to reduce hostility and acrimony between the parties;[220] furthermore, it makes obvious sense for the parties to reach agreement to save the costs of a full court hearing, which can be extremely heavy.[221]

(b) The information before the court

When the parties have come to terms, it is commonly sought to have their agreement incorporated into a court order. The court may make an order on the agreed terms only on

---

[216] [1996] 2 FLR 306, CA. See also *Harper v O'Reilly and Harper* [1997] 2 FLR 816; *Burton v Burton* [1986] 2 FLR 419; *Thompson v Thompson* [1986] Fam 38, CA.

[217] Matrimonial Causes Act 1973 s 24A(6), added by the Matrimonial and Family Proceedings Act 1984 Sch 1, para 11.

[218] The development of the so-called 'settlement culture' is not without its critics: see generally G Davis, S Cretney and J Collins *Simple Quarrels: Negotiating Money and Property Disputes on Divorce* (1994) and especially at pp 260–3. For further consideration of how solicitors encourage settlement by their clients, see J Eekelaar, M Maclean and S Beinart, *Family Lawyers: The Divorce Work of Solicitors* (2000).

[219] See above p 986.

[220] See eg Lord Scarman in *Minton v Minton* [1979] AC 593 at 608, HL: 'The law now encourages spouses to avoid bitterness after family breakdown and to settle their money and property problems.'

[221] See eg *F v F (Ancillary Relief: Substantial Assets)* [1995] 2 FLR 45, where the parties' total costs approached £1.5 million. See also *Piglowska v Piglowski* [1999] 1 WLR 1360, where the costs of £128,000 exceeded the parties' assets of £127,400; and *H v H (Financial Relief: Costs)* [1997] 2 FLR 57, where the husband was 'horrified' to find costs spiralling up to £175,000. At the third day of the hearing, the gap between the parties had narrowed to just £30,000 on the substantive issues. As Holman J remarked (at 58): 'If costs had not been incurred, a fair resolution of this case would have been easy. As it is, it has become impossible because the burden of costs is likely to be penurious to one or other or both of them.' The husband was ordered to pay the wife's costs, even though the sum involved virtually wiped out his liquid assets and it was by no means certain he would be able to raise the additional sums required by borrowings. See further below p 1056.

the basis of prescribed information furnished with the application.[222] The court retains the power, and indeed the duty, to scrutinise the proposed arrangements: in particular it must still have regard to the considerations set out in s 25 of the 1973 Act.[223] The realities of life in the Principal Registry and the divorce county courts, however, mean that district judges have only limited time to examine the terms of proposed consent orders put up to them and '. . . whilst the court is no rubber stamp nor is it some kind of forensic ferret'.[224] The paternal function of the court when approving financial consent orders is confined to a broad appraisal of the parties' financial circumstances, without descent into the valley of detail.[225] The fact that the parties have arrived at a settlement will itself be prima facie evidence that its terms are reasonable, at least if they were at arms length and were both legally advised:

'The statutory duty [ie to consider the proposed arrangements in the context of s 25 of the 1973 Act] cannot be ducked, but the court is entitled to assume that parties who are sui juris and who are represented by solicitors know what they want.'[226]

Consequently, the court will normally approve the terms of the agreement which is proposed by the parties, provided it is not contrary to public policy, and will incorporate it in an order.[227]

In *Livesey (formerly Jenkins) v Jenkins*[228] the House of Lords held that, because the court cannot properly discharge its function under s 25 without complete and up-to-date information, the parties owe a duty to the court to make full and frank disclosure of material facts to each other, not simply up to the time of the agreement, but right up until the time of the court order. Failure to make such disclosure can lead to the order being set aside. In *Livesey v Jenkins* the wife agreed to relinquish all claims for maintenance in return for the husband's agreeing to transfer to her his half-share in the matrimonial home. After the agreement had been reached, but before it had been embodied in a court order, the wife became engaged to be married, but this was not disclosed to the husband or the court. It was held that this failure to disclose was so important[229] that the order should be set aside. Lord Brandon, however, emphasised[230] that not every failure of disclosure would justify setting a consent order aside. On the contrary, to justify setting an order aside the absence of disclosure must have led the court to make a substantially different order from that which it would have made had there been full

---

[222] Matrimonial Causes Act 1973 s 33A added by the Matrimonial and Family Proceedings Act 1984 s 7 as amended by Welfare Reform and Pensions Act 1999 Sch 3 paras 1, 8. For the prescribed information, see the Family Proceedings Rules 1991 r 2.61. For further detail on the procedure, see *Pounds v Pounds* [1994] 1 FLR 775, CA.

[223] Discussed below pp 1018–51.   [224] *Harris v Manahan* [1997] 1 FLR 205 at 213, CA per Ward LJ.

[225] *Pounds v Pounds* [1994] 1 FLR 775 at 779, CA per Waite LJ.

[226] *Harris v Manahan* (above) at 213 per Ward LJ.

[227] *Dean v Dean* [1978] Fam 161, following *Brockwell v Brockwell* (1975) 6 Fam Law 46, CA.

[228] [1985] AC 424, HL approving *de Lasala v de Lasala* [1980] AC 546, PC and disapproving on this point *Wales v Wadham* [1977] 2 All ER 125.

[229] It will be appreciated that once the wife had remarried she would no longer be entitled to receive periodic payments, so she was not relinquishing very much.

[230] Ibid at 445.

disclosure.[231] This test has been strictly applied, no doubt to prevent a flood of applications to set aside on the basis of material non-disclosure.[232] For the same reason the Court of Appeal has sought to restrict the development of an earlier judicial suggestion[233] that the poor quality of legal advice which a spouse receives prior to entering into an agreement may enable him (or her) subsequently to resile from it. This approach had been adopted in *B v B (Consent Order: Variation)*,[234] where the judge held that the 'manifestly bad legal advice' which a wife received in agreeing to a fixed term periodical payment order, when she needed the security of lifetime support, justified the court in re-opening the order and extending the duration of the periodical payments. In *Harris v Manahan*,[235] however, the Court of Appeal recognised that, while bad legal advice did have a part to play in deciding whether a spouse should be held to a bargain, the need for finality in litigation requires that 'only in the most exceptional case of cruellest injustice' should bad legal advice be a ground for the court interfering with a consent order. The remedy for a badly advised spouse lies in an action in negligence against his (or her) solicitors in the appropriate case.

(c) The weight attached to the parties' agreement

A further problem arises if one of the parties wishes to go back on an agreement before the court approves it and embodies it in an order. We have already seen that the agreement cannot preclude an application to the court[236] but, as the Court of Appeal held in *Edgar v Edgar*,[237] considerable attention will be paid to it if it was entered into with full knowledge

---

[231] See also *Rose v Rose* [2003] EWHC 505 (Fam), [2003] 2 FLR 197. A similar rule applies to contested orders and to justify appealing Out of time: see *P v P (Consent Order: Appeal Out of Time)* [2002] 1 FLR 743 and below p 1063ff. On the procedure for setting aside a consent order, see *B-T v B-T (Divorce Procedure)* [1990] 2 FLR 1; *Harris v Manahan* above.

[232] See eg *Cook v Cook* [1988] 1 FLR 521, CA: court refused to set aside consent order because, allegedly, the wife had not disclosed the depth of her relationship with a third party. Held that any change in the quality of the wife's relationship would not have substantially affected the terms of the original order. Compare *Vicary v Vicary* [1992] 2 FLR 271, CA, consent order set aside where husband had not disclosed that negotiations were taking place for the sale of his company (which took place shortly after the order was made), significantly increasing the husband's asset worth; *T v T (Consent Order: Procedure to Set Aside)* [1996] 2 FLR 640, husband had 'dishonestly and fraudulently' concealed the true value of his business until it was taken over shortly after the making of the consent order, which was therefore set aside; *Den Heyer v Newby* [2005] EWCA Civ 1311, husband who did not make full disclosure could not complain of wife's delay (for a year after originally hearing about his increased wealth through sale of his company) in applying to set aside consent order.

[233] *Camm v Camm* (1982) 4 FLR 577 at 580, CA per Ormrod LJ (referring to his earlier judgment: *Edgar v Edgar* [1980] 3 All ER 887, CA). His Lordship made it clear that it was not necessarily negligent legal advice which was required.

[234] [1995] 1 FLR 9; cf the views of Hoffmann LJ in *Pounds v Pounds* [1994] 1 FLR 775, CA who said (at 791) of the principle of examining the quality of legal advice given to a spouse: 'It is . . . understandably a matter of surprise and resentment on the part of the other party that one should be able to repudiate an agreement on account of the inadequacy of one's own legal advisers, over whom the other party had control, and of whose advice he had no knowledge. We have created uncertainty and . . . added to the cost and pain of litigation.'

[235] Above. While recognising that on the facts the wife had suffered injustice, Ward LJ accepted, with regret, that 'a wronged individual is to be sacrificed on the high altar of policy'. He added (at 224): 'To deny justice to the wife is hard—and to that extent justice is imperfect; but justice must be done to the husband; to do justice to children is paramount; to do justice to the system into which these disputes are fed is essential.'

[236] Above, p 954.   [237] [1980] 3 All ER 887, CA.

of all the relevant facts and on legal advice.[238] Obviously a party will not be bound if the agreement was made under duress or undue influence, but the fact that one of the parties was in a superior bargaining position will not justify the other in going back on it unless the former took an unfair advantage by exploiting the position. In *Edgar v Edgar* a multi-millionaire and his wife entered into a separation deed in which the husband made capital provision for her amounting to some £100,000 and undertook to make periodical payments to her of £16,000 a year together with periodical payments for the children. In return she covenanted not to seek financial relief in any divorce proceedings that might take place in the future. She executed the deed after being warned by her legal advisers that she would probably obtain a much better order from the court. When divorce proceedings were launched, she attempted to resile from the agreement and claimed a lump sum payment. Dismissing her application, the Court of Appeal held that, although the husband's financial position put him in a much stronger bargaining position, there was no evidence that he had exploited it, and consequently the wife must be held to her agreement. The court might be justified in ignoring an agreement if the wife found it impossible to maintain herself owing to unforeseen circumstances[239] or, possibly, if injustice would be done for some other reason, but the facts of *Edgar v Edgar* make it clear that a large disparity between the sum that a wife stipulated for and that which the court might have awarded her will not itself be a ground for releasing her from the contract she made.[240]

The legal basis underpinning the position was spelled out by the Court of Appeal in *Xydhias v Xydhias*.[241] There, the parties reached an agreement and draft consent orders were produced by counsel. The husband then sought to withdraw his consent and have the case fully tried. The wife applied for an order in the terms of the agreement that had been reached. In upholding her successful application, the Court nonetheless made clear that the normal rules of contract do not apply in the matrimonial jurisdiction, and until the terms of an agreement have been embodied in a court order, they are not binding in law.[242] The purpose of the parties' negotiations is only to reduce the length and complexity of the proceedings and if the parties dispute whether an agreement was reached, it is for the court to determine this: good practice will usually ensure that heads of agreement signed by the parties, or a clear exchange of solicitors' letters, will establish the necessary consensus.[243] If the court concludes that the parties did reach an agreement, it then has to

---

[238] A lack of legal advice does not mean the agreement will be ignored: it may still be the best starting point for determining the eventual outcome of the case: *G v G (Financial Provision: Separation Agreement)* [2004] 1 FLR 1011, CA.

[239] *Wright v Wright* [1970] 3 All ER 209 at 214, CA.

[240] For a case where a total change in the parties' financial circumstances justified the court in departing from the terms of a separation agreement, see *Beach v Beach* [1995] 2 FLR 160.

[241] [1999] 1 FLR 683.

[242] Cf *Amey v Amey* [1992] 2 FLR 89, where the wife died before the parties' agreement could be embodied in a consent order. Scott Baker J considered that the agreement was valid and binding at common law. Presumably this decision is no longer good law.

[243] In *X v X (Y and Z intervening)* [2002] 1 FLR 508 minutes of a consent order had been agreed and the wife was held to the agreement therein. In *Rose v Rose* [2002] EWCA Civ 208, [2002] 1 FLR 978 the order had been agreed before the judge at the FDR, with the wife's counsel undertaking to draw it up. The Court of Appeal held that an unperfected order had in fact been made by the judge at the FDR and, without deciding what test should apply to determine when it might be appropriate to permit a party to resile before the order is perfected, held that the husband had failed to establish sufficient reasons for such action in his case. For the practical consequences, see R Dyke, 'The Rose Trident—The Unperfected Order' [2002] Fam Law 908.

consider whether its terms are vitiated by a factor such a non-disclosure, and the broader question of whether they should be upheld in the light of the court's duty under s 25. Many may agree with Hoffmann LJ (as he then was) who, in *Pounds v Pounds*,[244] described the current law as 'the worst of both worlds' since 'the agreement may be held to be binding, but whether it will be can be determined only after litigation'.[245]

(d) Pre-nuptial agreements[246]

The view of Thorpe J, in *F v F (Ancillary Relief: Substantial Assets)*,[247] that pre-nuptial agreements 'must be of very limited significance' in this jurisdiction, now seems of doubtful validity, although a court has yet to hold such an agreement binding. Indeed, as *Xydhias v Xhydias*[248] establishes that only the court can finally dispose of the parties' claims against each other, all that a court can do is to take the terms of the agreement into account, either as part of all the circumstances of the case, or as 'conduct' under s 25(2)(g) of the Matrimonial Causes Act 1973[249] and then consider how far it wishes to hold the parties to their arrangement. Thus, in *N v N (Foreign Divorce: Financial Relief)*[250] where the parties were Swedish nationals, Cazalet J considered that, while their pre-nuptial agreement would not be conclusive in England (as it was in Sweden), it was nonetheless a material consideration, to which the court should have regard in applying the criteria in s 25 of the 1973 Act. In *S v S (Divorce: Staying Proceedings)*[251] Wilson J said that there was a danger that the words of Thorpe J in *F v F* might be taken out of context. Looking to the future, his Lordship added:

'There will come a case . . . where the circumstances surrounding the pre-nuptial agreement and the provision therein contained might, when viewed in the context of other circumstances of the case prove influential or even crucial . . . I can find nothing in s 25 to compel a conclusion . . . at odds with personal freedoms to make agreements for ourselves . . . carefully struck by informed adults. It all depends.'

It seems that an agreement entered into close to the date of the wedding, without full legal advice and without proper disclosure as to assets will carry little or no weight.[252] Conversely, an agreement reached after proper legal advice may carry some weight, even though its terms are unfair to the payee, and even though it was signed under pressure. In *M v M (Prenuptial Agreement)*[253] the parties were Canadian. The woman became pregnant; the man was opposed to her having an abortion. She refused to have the child unless they married. Having undergone an acrimonious and expensive divorce from his first wife, the man refused to marry her unless she signed the prenuptial agreement he had had drawn up by his lawyers, under which the wife would receive £275,000 in the event of divorce. The husband's wealth at the time of the divorce, some five years later, was around £7.5 million, of which the wife now claimed £1.3 million. Connell J, holding that the

---

[244] [1994] 1 FLR 775, CA.   [245] Ibid at 791.

[246] For a comparative perspective, see B Fehlberg and B Smyth, 'Binding Pre-Nuptial Agreements in Australia: The First Year' (2002) 16, 1, IJLPF 127, B Clark, 'Should greater prominence be given to pre-nuptial contracts in the law of ancillary relief?' [2004] CFLQ 399.

[247] [1995] 2 FLR 45 at 66.   [248] [1999] 1 FLR 683, CA.   [249] Discussed below at pp 1047–51.

[250] [1997] 1 FLR 900.

[251] [1997] 2 FLR 100 at 102. See further, J Harcus 'Pre-Nuptial Agreements' [1997] Fam Law 669.

[252] *J v V (Disclosure: Offshore Corporations)* [2003] EWHC 3110, [2004] 1 FLR 1042.

[253] [2002] 1 FLR 654.

agreement should be taken into account as a relevant circumstance (but awarding the wife £875,000), commented:

'The circumstances of this case illustrate vividly that the existence of a prenuptial agreement can do more to obscure rather than clarify the underlying justice of the case. On the one hand this husband would not have married the wife unless she signed the agreement. On the other hand this wife signed the agreement because she was pregnant and did not relish single parenthood either for herself or for her child and because she wanted to marry the husband. In my view it would be as unjust to the husband to ignore the existence of the agreement and its terms as it would be to the wife to hold her strictly to those terms. I do bear the agreement in mind as one of the more relevant circumstances of this case, but the court's overriding duty remains to attempt to arrive at a solution which is fair in all the circumstances, applying s 25 of the Matrimonial Causes Act 1973.'[254]

But greater weight was given the agreement in *K v K (Ancillary Relief: Prenuptial Agreement)*.[255] Usually, the husband will be the wealthier party, but it does not follow that it is always the wife who is therefore under pressure to enter into the prenuptial agreement. As in *M v M* an unplanned pregnancy may exert pressure on both parties. In *K v K*, the wife became pregnant and her mother pressured the husband into agreeing to marry. Both parties came from wealthy backgrounds, the husband having wealth of around £25 million and the wife being a beneficiary of trusts valued at some £1 million. According to the prenuptial agreement, signed after each took legal advice, but without the husband having made full disclosure, if the marriage ended within five years, the wife was to receive £100,000 from the husband (to be increased by 10% pa compound) and the husband was to make reasonable financial provision for any children. The agreement made no provision for periodical payments for the wife. The marriage ended after 14 months, and the wife sought a lump sum of £1.6 million and periodical payments of £57,000 pa for herself in addition to the agreed £15,000 pa maintenance for their child. The husband offered a £120,000 lump sum (plus £600,000 to provide a home in which she could bring up the child). It was held that the husband had agreed to marry the wife, under pressure, on the understanding that her capital claim in the event of an early termination of the marriage would be governed by their agreement. Entry into the agreement constituted conduct which it would be inequitable to disregard under s 25(2)(g) and the capital element of the agreement should accordingly be upheld. However, it would be wrong to confine provision for the wife to the husband's offer, since this failed to recognise her role as the child's mother. Periodical payments for the wife of £15,000 pa were also therefore awarded (and a lump sum of £1.2 million ordered to provide the wife and child with a home that bore some relationship to the husband's standard of living).

The existence of an agreement, properly drawn up, after appropriate disclosure, and signed after legal advice, may well influence the court to produce a more modest award to a wife than might otherwise have been the case.[256] Nonetheless, the courts' current

---

[254] Ibid at para 26.

[255] [2003] 1 FLR 120. See N Francis and S Philipps 'New Light on Prenuptial Agreements' [2003] Fam Law 164.

[256] See dictum by Connell J in *M v M (Prenuptial Agreement)* [2002] 1 FLR 654 at para 44: 'a prenuptial agreement in my view is relevant as tending to guide the court to a more modest award than might have been made without it'.

approach appears to produce the same degree of uncertainty for the parties as that noted by Hoffmann LJ in relation to separation agreements.[257] There is likely to be increasing pressure to uphold the substance of agreements as wealthier parties enter into agreements as a means of seeking as far as possible to avoid the consequences of the courts' move towards a more equal division of the parties' assets.[258]

The government has suggested that prenuptial agreements could usefully be made binding, but subject to safeguards.[259] The agreement would not be binding if there is a child of the family, whether or not the child was born at the time the agreement was made; where under the general law of contract, the agreement is unenforceable; where either or both parties had not had independent legal advice; where enforcing the agreement would cause significant injustice to one or both parties or a child of the marriage; where there had not been full disclosure; and where the agreement was made less than 21 days before the wedding. These safeguards would have ruled out all of the agreements discussed above, and probably leave only a small number of wealthy but childless couples to be bound. The proposal did not find favour, primarily because of concern that parties' circumstances could change as time passed after the agreement so that it would be unfair to keep them to its terms,[260] and was abandoned. However, the opposing view is that prior agreements aid certainty and predictability, encourage private ordering, respect party autonomy and lessen the level and number of disputes. The majority of the judges of the Family Division have proposed that the terms of any prenuptial agreement should be an additional factor for the court to take into account under s 25 of the Matrimonial Causes Act 1973, and a minority would have gone further and provided that both pre- and post-nuptial agreements should be presumptively binding.[261] Building on this opinion, Resolution (the Solicitors' Family Law Association) have proposed enacting an amendment to s 25 to provide that agreements should be considered binding 'unless to do so will cause significant injustice to either party or to any minor child of the family.'[262] The merits of binding prenuptial agreements as a means of enhancing predictability of outcome and encouraging private ordering are likely to return to the fore in the near future.

(e) The effects of a consent order

It should be appreciated that, once the parties' agreement is incorporated into a court order, it derives its authority from the order and not from the agreement.[263] This has two important consequences. First, the court is no more entitled to make orders outside the terms of the 1973 Act than it is in respect of contested orders.[264] Secondly, the rules against

---

[257] Above at p 954.   [258] Discussed below at pp 1018–12.

[259] Home Office, *Supporting Families* (1998) ch 4.

[260] See The Law Society, *Financial Provision on Divorce: Clarity and Fairness—Proposals for Reform* (2003) para 3.15.

[261] See Wilson J, 'Ancillary Relief Reform: Response of the Judges of the Family Division to Government proposals (made by way of submission to the Lord Chancellor's Ancillary Relief Advisory Group) [1999] Fam Law 159 at 162–3.

[262] Resolution, *A More Certain Future—recognition of pre-marital agreements in England and Wales* (2004) para 7.7. For criticism, see C Barton, 'The SFLA and Pre-marital Agreements: A More Lucrative Future?' [2005] Fam Law 47.

[263] *de Lasala v de Lasala* [1980] AC 546, HL; *Thwaite v Thwaite* (1981) 2 FLR 280, CA; *Masefield v Alexander* [1995] 1 FLR 100, CA.

[264] See Lord Brandon in *Livesey v Jenkins* [1985] AC 424 at 444, and see *Belcher v Belcher* [1995] 1 FLR 916.

reopening 'clean break' orders[265] and varying property adjustment orders[266] apply equally to consent orders as they do to a contested order.[267] The courts have warned of the need for legal representatives to be especially careful in drafting the terms of proposed consent orders and to advise their clients on precisely what impact their agreement will have.[268] The failure by a legal adviser to protect his client's interests in respect of a consent order may constitute professional negligence, for which substantial damages may be awarded.[269]

It will not infrequently be the case that the parties will have reached an agreement which is perfectly proper in itself but which is outside the terms of the Matrimonial Causes Act 1973, as in *Livesey v Jenkins*, where, after the transfer of the husband's share in the matrimonial home, the wife agreed to be solely responsible for the mortgage and all other outgoings on the house and to be solely responsible for certain specific bank overdrafts. As we have said, the court has no power to incorporate such agreements in a consent order. However, it is possible to make such agreements binding by, for example, including them in an undertaking to the court,[270] or the court could dismiss the application conditionally upon the parties' entering into the agreement in question, known as a 'Tomlin order'.

9 THE LEGAL SERVICES COMMISSION'S STATUTORY CHARGE

In cases where either or both parties have been granted legal aid, an important factor to be borne in mind in deciding what orders should be made or agreed to is the Legal Services Commission's charge. Under the Access to Justice Act 1999 s 10(7), in return for the responsibility for all the legally aided party's appropriately taxed legal costs, the Legal Services Commission has a charge, to the extent of those costs, over property 'recovered or

---

[265] Discussed below pp 1064–9. The most common form of consent order provides for a clean break.

[266] See below pp 1060 et seq.

[267] See *Minton v Minton* [1979] AC 593, HL. For a good example of the harsh realities of the binding nature of a consent order see *Dinch v Dinch* [1987] 1 All ER 818, HL, in which it was held that there was no power to interfere with an agreement to a delayed sale of the matrimonial home, even though the husband by accepting voluntary redundancy had been unable to meet his maintenance commitments under the agreement.

[268] See eg *Dinch v Dinch*, above, at 820 per Lord Oliver; *Sandford v Sandford* [1986] 1 FLR 412 at 425 per Oliver LJ; and *Pounds v Pounds* [1994] 1 FLR 775 at 790 per Waite LJ.

[269] *Dickinson v Jones Alexander & Co* [1993] 2 FLR 521 (decided in 1989). Advocates no longer have immunity from negligence claims: *Arthur J S Hall & Co (a firm) v Simons; Barratt v Ansell and others (trading as Woolf Seddon (a firm)); Harris v Scholfield Roberts & Hill (a firm) and Another* [2000] 3 WLR 543, HL. Cf *Moy v Pettmann Smith (a firm) and Another*, [2005] UKHL 7, [2005] 1 WLR 903: barrister not negligent in giving advice at door of court where it may be inappropriate to hedge advice with extensive reasoned qualifications.

[270] Per Lord Brandon in *Jenkins v Livesey*, ibid at 444. But an undertaking given neither by deed nor for valuable consideration (and therefore not a contract) creates an obligation only towards the court. Consequently it can be enforced, eg by committal but not by an action for arrears by the payee: *Re Hudson* [1966] Ch 209. This may leave the payee completely unprotected on the other party's death, as in *Re Hudson*. Certain financial undertakings have been held to be enforceable by judgment summons—see *Symmons v Symmons* [1993] 1 FLR 317 (to pay school fees and a monthly maintenance supplement) and *M v M (Enforcement: Judgment Summons)* [1993] Fam Law 469 (undertaking to pay capital gains tax in respect of shares transferred by one spouse to another pursuant to consent order). But the extent to which undertakings are enforceable is not free from doubt or controversy—see R Bird 'Problems in Ancillary Relief Orders' [1990] Fam Law 420, N Mostyn and P Moor 'Enforcing Financial Undertakings by Judgment Summons' [1992] Fam Law 233, D Burrows ' "Undertakings" and Consent Orders' [1998] Fam Law 158, R Spon-Smith, 'Ancillary Relief Undertakings—Worth the Paper They're Written on?' [2003] Fam Law 685.

preserved'.[271] Periodical payments are expressly exempted from this charge, but in 2005 the government removed an exemption in respect of the first £3,000 of any lump sum or property adjustment order.[272] In effect, therefore, the Legal Services Commission is entitled to recover its costs out of lump sums, property adjustment orders or proceeds of sale insofar as they can be regarded as property 'recovered or preserved'. Given the high costs of proceedings, this charge can be substantial. In *Hanlon v Hanlon*,[273] for example, where the matrimonial home with an equity worth £10,000 was transferred to the wife, the wife's legal aid costs amounted to £8,025. In cases where the money or property recovered or transferred is to be used either to fund the purchase of a new home or as the funded party's home, then enforcement of the charge may be deferred (with interest).[274] In *Scallon v Scallon*[275] it was held that a court may assume that the discretion will be exercised to defer enforcement of the charge, so as not to frustrate the purpose of the court order.

The ambit of the statutory charge is both wide and at times bizarre. It has been held to apply, for example, to a lump sum payment in commutation and in full and final settlement of a spouse's rights to claim and receive periodical payments,[276] and to the obtaining of possession of an amount representing the share of the matrimonial home, even though title had not been in issue and the final order was a consent order.[277] In another case,[278] where both parties were legally aided and an order was made dividing the proceeds of the matrimonial home equally, the charge only attached to the husband's share because he had successfully resisted his wife's claim for a larger share, whereas it did not attach to the wife's share since the husband had made no claim to it.

Although it is clear that the existence of the charge can materially alter the effect or even destroy the intention of orders, it seems established that the court is not allowed to compensate for this (even where the higher costs are attributable to one side's intransigence) by making a larger award than would be the case had the parties' needs been considered without reference to the charge.[279] On the other hand, it would seem proper to make a different *type* of order if that would be a more efficient use of the parties' resources, such as a property transfer order rather than a lump sum order.[280]

---

[271] See *Parkes v Legal Aid Board* [1997] 1 FLR 77, CA where the Court of Appeal held that the charge applied to property co-owned by two unmarried parents. A compromise was reached whereby the female cohabitant would remain in the house with her child until certain events occurred, whereupon it would be sold and the proceeds divided between the parties. The Court of Appeal upheld the decision of the lower court that the obtaining, by the female cohabitant, of an exclusive right of occupation against her former cohabitant amounted to a 'recovery', so that the charge attached to her interest in the property.

[272] Community Legal Service (Financial) (Amendment) Regulations 2005 SI 589/2005 reg 18. Note that, in relation to the court's power to attach or share pensions, the charge will operate in relation to lump sums payable on an attachment order but not otherwise: see D Salter, 'The Pitfalls of Pension Sharing—Part 1' [2002] Fam Law 598 at 602.

[273] [1978] 2 All ER 889, CA.   [274] Community Legal Service (Financial) Regulations 2000 reg 52.

[275] [1990] 1 FLR 194, CA.

[276] *Stewart v Law Society* [1987] 1 FLR 223; *Watkinson v Legal Aid Board* [1991] 2 All ER 953, CA.

[277] *Curling v Law Society* [1985] 1 All ER 705, CA.   [278] *Parry v Parry* [1986] 2 FLR 96, CA.

[279] *Parry v Parry* (above) and *Collins v Collins* [1987] 1 FLR 226, CA. The decision in *Collins v Collins* appears to have been overlooked by Anthony Lincoln J in *B v B (Real Property: Assessment of Interest)* [1988] 2 FLR 490, where he expressly enlarged the award of a lump sum to a wife 'to allow for the legal aid charge'. Query the effect of the changes to the costs rules (see below p 1056) on this issue?

[280] Or a periodical payments order instead of a lump sum order—see eg *Anthony v Anthony* [1986] 2 FLR 353, CA. Lawyers must not try and manipulate the destination of money payable to an assisted person so as to avoid the statutory charge: *Manley v Law Society* [1981] 1 All ER 401; *Clark v Clark* [1989] 1 FLR 174. A

10 THE LIMITS OF THE COURT'S POWERS

Although the powers to redistribute spouses' property upon divorce etc are extremely wide, they are not unlimited. One obvious limitation is that the court has no power over property that does not belong to either of the spouses. It cannot order the sale of the matrimonial home which is owned by someone else as, for example, where the parties live in tied accommodation.[281]

The court also has no power to make an order against a third party, so no order should be made which will effectively have to be paid out of a spouse's new partner's capital or income, though that partner's assets are relevant to the extent that they relieve the spouse's needs.[282] A further consequence of this is that the court will not make an order against a limited company in which one or both of the spouses hold shares,[283] although this will not be the case where the company may be regarded as the spouse's 'alter ego', where he owns or controls all its shares, or a majority of them in circumstances where minority shareholdings may be disregarded.[284]

A further limitation of the court's powers is that the relief granted must come within the terms of the Matrimonial Causes Act 1973. In *Milne v Milne*,[285] for instance, it was held that there was no power to order a husband to take out an insurance policy to make capital provision for his wife because the Act only empowers payments to be made to a spouse or child of the family and not to a third party. It has been similarly held that there is no power to order one party to pay out of the proceeds of sale of the matrimonial home the debts of either party which were unconnected to the interest in the property.[286]

At first sight these latter limitations may seem an unfortunate gap in the court's powers, particularly as in some cases, in order to do justice between the parties, a complete restructuring of their financial affairs may be required. However, as we have seen,[287]

---

solicitor owes a duty of care to the Fund, and the court has an inherent jurisdiction to order a solicitor personally to pay costs to the Fund where it has suffered loss as a result of the solicitor's serious dereliction of duty: *Clark v Clark (No 2)* [1991] 1 FLR 179, CA.

[281] Exceptionally, where one or both of the spouses own property together with a third party, the court will have to determine the parties' respective beneficial entitlements before it can exercise its adjustive powers: see *Harwood v Harwood* [1991] 2 FLR 274, CA. Compare *Lloyds Bank plc v Semmakie* [1993] 1 FLR 34, CA, where the question of the extent of a spouse's beneficial interest arose *after* ancillary relief proceedings where the court held the wife had a half-share beneficial interest in the former matrimonial home. The husband's bank later commenced possession proceedings and the Court of Appeal held the wife was not subsequently estopped from claiming more than a one-half share: there was no privity between the wife and the bank in terms of the earlier matrimonial proceedings.

[282] *Macey v Macey* (1981) 3 FLR 7, and *Brown v Brown* (1981) 3 FLR 161. See further below, p 1035.

[283] *Crittenden v Crittenden* [1990] 2 FLR 361, CA (no statutory power to order a company, whose issued shares were held by the spouses, to sell its assets and goodwill, or to require the husband to enter into a covenant not to compete with a proposed purchaser).

[284] *Green v Green* [1993] 1 FLR 326 following *Nicholas v Nicholas* [1984] FLR 285, CA.

[285] (1981) 2 FLR 286, CA.

[286] *Burton v Burton* [1986] 2 FLR 419, and *Mullard v Mullard* (1981) 3 FLR 330. See also *Livesey (formerly Jenkins) v Jenkins)* [1985] AC 424, HL (wife agreeing to be solely responsible for discharging a bank overdraft and for mortgage repayments—held to be outside the court's powers to order). There appears to be no power to order a spouse to use money or property for a *designated purpose*. Similarly, there is no express statutory power to require a spouse to execute a charge over the former matrimonial home, although such orders appear to be frequently made in practice. See eg *Barber v Barber* [1993] 1 FLR 476, CA and *M v M (Property Adjustment: Impaired Life Expectancy)* [1993] 2 FLR 723, CA.

[287] Above, p 1015.

in practice this type of restructuring can be achieved by the parties giving binding undertakings to the court or on a Tomlin order.

C ASSESSMENT OF FINANCIAL PROVISION

1 GENERAL PRINCIPLES

(a) Fairness

Following the reform of the law in 1971, the general principles to be applied when the court is making an order for financial provision or the adjustment of property rights on divorce, nullity or judicial separation were contained in s 5 of the Matrimonial Proceedings and Property Act 1970 and re-enacted in s 25 of the Matrimonial Causes Act 1973. This section was amended by the Matrimonial and Family Proceedings Act 1984 following recommendations by the Law Commission.[288] Subsequently, there was uncertainty and disagreement as to the correct direction of any further statutory reform[289] but the House of Lords gave an important judgment in 2000 which re-aligned the approach that the courts are obliged to take when deciding how to exercise their discretion under Part II. *White v White*[290] concerned a couple who had been married for over 30 years, and ran a farming business in which both were partners. At the time of the divorce, their combined assets were valued at some £4.6 million, of which £1.5 million was in the wife's name. The first instance judge awarded her an additional lump sum of £800,000, based on her 'reasonable requirements' for housing, continuing to run a business, and income.[291] On appeal, the Court of Appeal raised the award to £1.5 million[292] taking account of the farming partnership and her contribution to the family as wife and mother. This gave her a share of the combined assets of some 40%. Both parties appealed to the House of Lords, which upheld the Court of Appeal's award, but took the opportunity, in the words of Lord Nicholls of Birkenhead, to spell out what the courts should be seeking to achieve in the ancillary relief jurisdiction:

---

[288] Law Com No 103 (*The Financial Consequences of Divorce: the Basic Policy*); Law Com No 112 (*The Financial Consequences of Divorce, The Response to the Discussion Paper*). For an interesting account of the Law Commission's role in promoting reform, see S Cretney 'Money After Divorce—The Mistakes We Have Made?' in M Freeman (ed) *Essays In Family Law* (1985) pp 34–42. The Law Commission were concerned at the general absence of empirical information about the working of divorce law and recommended (Law Com No 112 at para 46) that provision be made for monitoring any amending legislation. This recommendation was not implemented. For empirical research on the financial consequences of divorce, see J Eekelaar and M Maclean *Maintenance after Divorce* (1986); M Maclean and J Eekelaar *The Parental Obligation* (1997) ch 7; A Perry et al *How Parents Cope Financially on Marriage Breakdown* (2000); G Davis et al, 'Ancillary relief outcomes' [2000] CFLQ 43; S Arthur et al, *Settling Up: Making Financial Arrangements After Divorce or Separation* (2002).

[289] Lord Chancellor's Advisory Group on Ancillary Relief Report 1998; Home Office, *Supporting Families* (1998) Ch 4. For a 'law and economics' perspective which argues that the current law may create perverse incentives to divorce, see A Dnes, 'The Division of Marital Assets Following Divorce' (1998) 25 *Journal of Law and Society* 336.

[290] [2001] 1 AC 596.

[291] The significance of 'reasonable requirements' is discussed below, at p 1038.

[292] See [1998] 2 FLR 310.

'Everyone would accept that the outcome on these matters, whether by agreement or court order, should be fair. More realistically, the outcome ought to be as fair as is possible in all the circumstances. But everyone's life is different. Features which are important when assessing fairness differ in each case. And, sometimes, different minds can reach different conclusions on what fairness requires. Then fairness, like beauty, lies in the eye of the beholder. . . . In consequence, the legislation does not state explicitly what is to be the aim of the courts when exercising these wide powers. Implicitly, the objective must be to achieve a fair outcome. . . . But there is one principle of universal application which can be stated with confidence. In seeking to achieve a fair outcome, there is no place for discrimination between husband and wife and their respective roles. . . . If, in their different spheres, each contributed equally to the family, then in principle it matters not which of them earned the money and built up the assets. There should be no bias in favour of the money-earner and against the home-maker and the child-carer.'[293]

He reiterated and refined this approach in the later House of Lords ruling in *Miller v Miller; McFarlane v McFarlane*[294] by distinguishing between meeting the parties' future *needs*, which will usually be all that can be done with the limited resources available to the parties; providing *compensation* for any economic disadvantage a party may suffer as a result of the relationship (such as giving up a career to raise children); and finally *sharing* which reflects the equality of the parties' relationship and commitment to each other during the marriage.[295]

The impact of this reasoning, which might appear to be stating the obvious, has been profound in producing a shift in the exercise of the courts' discretion, most importantly in requiring courts to 'value' what husbands and wives do in a marriage as of equal worth, and thus in emphasising a conception of marriage as an equal partnership.[296] This may (but need not—as the decision in *White v White* itself demonstrates) result in the parties receiving equal shares in the family assets; an outcome which, whilst possibly reflecting popular expectation of what spouses *should* receive on divorce, was almost never ordered by courts prior to this decision. But his Lordship went on to state:

'A practical consideration follows from this. Sometimes, having carried out the statutory exercise, the judge's conclusion involves a more or less equal division of the available assets. More often, this is not so. More often, having looked at all the circumstances, the judge's decision means that one party will receive a bigger share than the other. Before reaching a

---

[293] At p 599 et seq. Although *White v White* concerned a 'big money' case where the available assets exceeded the parties' needs, it has been held that the emphasis on avoiding discrimination is of general application: see *Elliott v Elliott* [2001] 1 FCR 477 per Thorpe J at para 5.

[294] [2006] UKHL 24, [2006] 3 All ER 1 paras 1–4.

[295] Ibid paras 10–16. See, to like effect, Baroness Hale of Richmond at paras 137–144.

[296] For discussion, including critical comment, on the reasoning of the House of Lords and the implications of the judgment, see R Bailey-Harris, 'Fairness in Financial Settlements on Divorce' [2001] LQR 199; E Cooke, '*White v White*: A new yardstick for the marriage partnership' [2001] CFLQ 81; See A Diduck, Fairness and Justice for All? The House of Lords in *White v White* (2001) 9 Fem LS 173; P Duckworth and D Hodson, '*White v White*: Bringing Section 25 Back to the People' [2001] Fam Law 24; J Eekelaar, 'Back to Basics and Forward into the Unknown' [2001] Fam Law 30; DJ G Brasse, '*White v White*—A Return to Orthodoxy?' [2001] Fam Law 191; R Hayward-Smith '*White v White*—Revisited' [2001] Fam Law 682. For an interesting perspective considering fairness in the context of the circumstances of minority ethnic families, see S Edwards, 'Division of Assets and Fairness—"Brick Lane"—Gender, Culture and Ancillary Relief on Divorce' [2004] Fam Law 809.

firm conclusion and making an order along these lines, a judge would always be well-advised to check his tentative views against the yardstick of equality of division. As a general guide, equality should be departed from only if, and to the extent that, there is good reason for doing so. The need to consider and articulate reasons for departing from equality would help the parties and the court to focus on the need to ensure the absence of discrimination.'[297]

Lord Nicholls stressed that the introduction of a 'yardstick of equality' is not meant to be the same as a 'presumption' of equality, or even a 'starting point'[298] since this would be to go beyond the permissible bounds of interpretation of s 25. Nonetheless, it has been extremely influential in persuading courts (and legal advisers assisting the parties to negotiate in the shadow of the law)[299] that equal shares in the available capital may be the appropriate outcome, thus bearing out the view of Lord Cooke of Thorndon who doubted 'whether the labels "yardstick" or "check" will produce any result different from "guidelines" or "starting point".'[300]

To understand the significance of this shift in approach, it is necessary to explain the changes made to the statute by the Matrimonial and Family Proceedings Act 1984, which can now be seen as having laid the groundwork for the House of Lords' ruling.

The 1984 Act made three changes in the ways that courts are directed to exercise their powers, namely:

(1) the removal of the status quo ideal or minimal loss principle;

(2) giving priority to the welfare of any child of the family; and

(3) placing greater emphasis on the parties becoming self-sufficient.

(b) The removal of the status quo ideal or minimal loss principle

Under s 25, as originally enacted, the court was directed, as its overall object, to have regard to all the circumstances of the case and so to exercise its powers 'as to place the parties, so far as it is practicable and, having regard to their conduct, just to do so, in the financial position in which they would have been if the marriage had not broken down and each had properly discharged his or her financial obligations and responsibilities towards the other'. In most cases this objective or target (variously referred to as the status quo ideal or the minimal loss principle) was impossible to achieve, since few, if any, can afford to support two households at the same standard as the former one. One judge[301] described it as 'an elusive concept based on a difficult hypothesis', while one commentator[302] criticised it as being 'the mandate of restitution . . . misconceived [and] . . . almost always incapable of fulfilment'.

It was implicit in the status quo principle that a spouse had a right to life-long support from the other spouse even after divorce, but in their Discussion Paper the Law Commission questioned whether such a principle could any longer be justified, given, inter alia, the change to irretrievable breakdown as the basis of divorce, the impossibility in most cases of attaining the objective, and the changed economic role of women. The responses received by the Law Commission were overwhelmingly of the view that the status quo

---

[297] [2001] 1 AC 596, 605F–G.   [298] Ibid at p 606E.   [299] See above p 10.
[300] At p 615D–E.   [301] Bagnall J in *Harnett v Harnett* [1973] Fam 156 at 161.
[302] K Gray, *Reallocation of Property on Divorce* (1977) at p 319.

directive was no longer appropriate. Accordingly, in their final report, the Commission felt able to recommend its removal.

Although at first sight it seems odd not to have statutory guidance on the basic objective for the redistribution of resources after divorce,[303] it may be pointed out that even before the removal of the basic objective, the courts regarded themselves as being vested with very flexible and wide-ranging powers and that therefore even Court of Appeal decisions should be regarded as guidelines rather than precedents.[304]

Another possible effect of the removal of the status quo objective is that it must in theory be harder for a spouse to claim a share in the other's future income or capital, at any rate where there is an unexpected increase in wealth after the divorce. Under the former law it could simply have been argued that had the marriage not broken down the spouse would have had a share in that newly acquired wealth.[305] Under the current law the theoretical basis for any such claim is uncertain.[306] This is not to say that future income or capital is irrelevant. On the contrary, as will be seen, it is a factor that the courts are expressly obliged to take into account, since it will obviously be relevant to determining the future needs of the parties and of their ability to meet those needs.

(c) Treating the welfare of any child of the family as the first consideration

As we have said, with the removal of the status quo objective the court no longer has an overall statutory target. Instead, under s 25(1) of the Matrimonial Causes Act 1973[307] the court is directed, when considering whether to exercise its powers and, if so, in what manner:

'. . . to have regard to all the circumstances of the case, first consideration being given to the welfare while a minor of any child of the family who has not attained the age of eighteen.'

It will be observed that the court is required to give first and not paramount consideration to the welfare of any child of the family. This means, as was emphasised in *Suter v Suter and Jones*,[308] that the child's welfare is not the overriding consideration, though of course it is an important one. Thus, in *B v B (Financial Provision: Financial Provision: Welfare of Child and Conduct)*[309] where the father had abducted the child from the mother, had failed to disclose assets and was unlikely to pay maintenance, it was fair to order that the whole of the proceeds of sale of the former matrimonial home should be transferred to the wife so that she could use them to re-house herself and the child. The child's need for security

---

[303] Contrast Scottish law: see the Family Law (Scotland) Act 1985 ss 9, 10. The question of whether further statutory guidance would be desirable is discussed below pp 1081–4.

[304] See *Chamberlain v Chamberlain* [1974] 1 All ER 33, CA at 38, per Scarman LJ; *Sharpe v Sharpe, The Times*, 17 February 1981, CA, per Ormrod LJ.

[305] Compare *Trippas v Trippas* [1973] Fam 134, CA, where after the divorce the husband sold his business and thereby freed his capital and was ordered to pay his wife a lump sum, inter alia because, had they remained married, the wife would have had a 'good chance of receiving financial benefit on the sale of the business.'

[306] See, for example, the issues raised as to the correct purpose of periodical payments in *McFarlane v McFarlane; Parlour v Parlour* [2004] EWCA Civ 872, [2005] Fam 171, discussed further below at p 1026.

[307] As amended by the Matrimonial and Family Proceedings Act 1984 s 3 and further by the Welfare Reform and Pensions Act 1999 Sch 3, para 5.

[308] [1987] Fam 111, CA; cf *Anthony v Anthony* [1986] 2 FLR 353, CA, where not all the children's interests were necessarily identical.

[309] [2002] 1 FLR 555.

for the future was regarded (in addition to other factors relevant under s 25(2)) as an important consideration.

Priority is only accorded to children of the family[310] and not, for example, to any children of the spouses' second families, though a spouse's obligation to the second family is a relevant consideration in deciding what order to make.[311] It might be added that not even all children of the family are necessarily accorded priority. Where, for example, the child is not that of the husband, then even if he has 'treated' the child as one of the family he is not ipso facto liable to maintain him. In determining this, the court is directed by s 25(4) of the Matrimonial Causes Act to have regard:

'(a) to whether that party assumed any responsibility for the child's maintenance, and, if so, to the extent to which, and the basis upon which, that party assumed such responsibility and to the length of time for which that party discharged such responsibility;

(b) to whether in assuming and discharging such responsibility that party did so knowing that the child was not his or her own;

(c) to the liability of any other person to maintain the child.'

If the court decides that the husband is not liable[312] to maintain the child at all, then of course that child's welfare ceases to be of any relevance in that case.

Priority is only to be given to the child's welfare during his or her minority. This reflects the previously well established principle that orders for children should be related to their dependency and should not, in the absence of special needs such as mental or physical handicap, provide for continuing support during adulthood.[313] In fact the cases show that the court is prepared to take a broader view, and (if not necessarily according priority) at least recognise that a child's needs, and the period of his dependency, do not necessarily come to an end on his eighteenth birthday, but may continue, for example, until he or she completes university education or professional training. In *Richardson v Richardson (No 2)*[314] the Court of Appeal upheld the decision of Thorpe J,[315] who had set aside a consent order, and extended a periodical payment order in favour of the wife, so she could complete her responsibility for bringing up her two daughters whilst they were at college. As Thorpe J added:[316]

'In my judgment, the fact the children of the family are no longer minors is not decisive. What is decisive is that they are still dependent.'[317]

---

[310] For a detailed discussion of the meaning of 'child of the family', see above, p 338.

[311] See eg *Fisher v Fisher* [1989] 1 FLR 423, CA where the wife's responsibility to a child born after the marriage was dissolved was taken into account to increase a periodical payments order.

[312] As in *W v W (Child of the Family)* [1984] FLR 796, CA, and *Leadbeater v Leadbeater* [1985] FLR 789.

[313] See eg *Lilford v Glynn* [1979] 1 All ER 441, CA. It is on this basis that capital orders for children are not common: see *Kiely v Kiely* [1988] 1 FLR 248, CA; *Chamberlain v Chamberlain* [1974] 1 All ER 33, CA; cf *Griffiths v Griffiths* [1984] Fam 70, CA; *A v A (A Minor: Financial Provision)* [1994] 1 FLR 657.

[314] [1996] 2 FLR 617, CA.   [315] [1994] 2 FLR 1051.   [316] Ibid at 1054.

[317] See also eg *Barber v Barber* [1993] 1 FLR 476, CA, where the Court of Appeal rejected the husband's submission that the court should only have regard to the children's welfare whilst they were minors, and *B v B (Adult Student: Liability to Support)* [1998] 1 FLR 373, CA, where the father's argument that he should not be expected to support his daughter since she was receiving a full student maintenance grant was rejected in the light of the clear statutory recognition that support could be ordered under s 29 (see above, p 995).

(d) Placing greater emphasis on the parties becoming self-sufficient

Inextricably bound up with the idea that it is no longer appropriate to have a right to life-long support from a former spouse is that of expecting the former spouses to become financially independent of each other wherever, and as soon as, possible after the divorce. The idea of a 'clean break' from each other after divorce first came to prominence in *Minton v Minton* where Lord Scarman said:[318]

'There are two principles which inform the modern legislation. One is the public interest that spouses, to the extent that their means permit, should provide for themselves and their children. But the other—of equal importance—is the principle of "the clean-break". The law now encourages spouses to avoid bitterness after family break-down and to settle their money and property problems. An object of the modern law is to encourage each to put the past behind them and to begin a new life which is not overshadowed by the relationship which has broken down.'

The Law Commission found that there was widespread support for this view and that the courts should be more clearly directed to the desirability of 'promoting the severance of financial obligations between the parties at the time of divorce' and to give greater weight to the view that periodical payments in favour of one spouse 'should be primarily directed to secure wherever possible a smooth transition from marriage to the status of independence'.[319]

Following the Law Commission's recommendations, the courts are now, pursuant to s 25A(1) of the Matrimonial Causes Act 1973,[320] under a *duty* in all cases (other than in relation to maintenance pending suit) to consider:

'. . . whether it would be appropriate so to exercise those powers that the financial obligations of each party towards the other will be terminated as soon after the grant of the decree as the court considers just and reasonable.'[321]

If a periodical payments order is thought appropriate, the court is directed by s 25A(2) to consider:

'. . . whether it would be appropriate to require those payments to be made or secured only for such term as would in the opinion of the court be sufficient to enable the party in whose favour the order is made to adjust without undue hardship to the termination of his or her financial dependence on the other party.'

In effect, under s 25A(1) the court is directed to consider whether it can make an immediate 'clean break' order, ie an order which will settle once and for all the parties' financial liability to each other. If this is not thought possible, then under s 25A(2) the court is directed to consider whether it can nevertheless make a periodical payments order for a limited term rather than for an indefinite period. In order to achieve these objectives the

---

[318] [1979] AC 593 at 608, HL.

[319] Law Com No 112, para 30. The House of Lords had endorsed this view in *Minton v Minton* [1979] AC 593.

[320] Added by the Matrimonial and Family Proceedings Act 1984 s 3, as further amended by Welfare Reform and Pensions Act 1999 Sch 3, para 6.

[321] It will be noted that the statutory duty does not apply to judicial separation, since the marriage is not terminated.

court has been given the power under s 25A(3) to impose a clean break order upon the parties, by which it is empowered to direct that, if the court considers that no continuing obligation should be imposed on either party to make or secure periodical payments in favour of the other, the court may dismiss the application with a direction that the applicant shall not be entitled to make any further application.[322] Under s 28(1A) the court may direct that a party is not entitled to apply for an extension of a fixed term periodical payments order.[323] Further, under ss 31(7A)–31(7G),[324] where the court discharges a periodical payments order, or varies it to a fixed term, it may also make a lump sum, property adjustment or pension sharing order and direct that the recipient is not entitled to make any further application for periodical payments, or further extension of their duration.[325] This gives the court the power, previously lacking, to make a clean break order on a variation application, against the payee's will.[326]

In its most extended form, either type of clean break order will also incorporate a declaration that neither party may make any further application for a lump sum or property adjustment order,[327] nor be entitled to apply for financial provision out of the other's estate under the Inheritance (Provision for Family and Dependants) Act 1975.[328]

Imposing an immediate clean break

Although the courts had previously been able to make clean break orders, until 1984 they could not do so against a spouse's will. It was not expected, however, that the new power would lead to a sudden increase in the number of clean break orders. For example, in his evidence to the Special Standing Committee on the 1984 Bill,[329] the President of the Family Division said that an immediate clean break would be:

'... entirely inappropriate in cases in which the wife has a continuing charge of young children, or where the marriage has been long and the wife has not worked during it or during the larger part of it and is middle aged at the time of the divorce.'

He added:

---

[322] It should be noted that there is no comparable power to dismiss an application for periodical payments to or for the benefit of any child of the family. There is no provision for a 'clean break' between parent and child: see *Crozier v Crozier* [1994] 1 FLR 126, discussed above at p 942.

[323] See also s 25(2)(a), discussed below, p 1031 et seq, under which the court is directed to consider whether there is any increase in earning capacity which it is reasonable to expect a party to take steps to acquire.

[324] Inserted by Family Law Act 1996 Sch 8 para 16 and amended by Welfare Reform and Pensions Act 1999 Sch 3 paras 1, 7.

[325] The power extends only to dissolution of the marriage, not nullity: s 31(7A).

[326] The payer could offer, but the payee was entitled to refuse, a clean break on variation: *S v S* [1986] Fam 189.

[327] The court may make such a declaration despite the absence of express statutory authority: *H v H (Financial Provision)* [1988] 2 FLR 114.

[328] Inheritance (Provision for Family and Dependants) Act 1975 s 15 as amended by Matrimonial and Family Proceedings Act 1984, discussed below at p 1123. The court will only make this order if it considers it just to do so. It must therefore have evidence as to the likely size of the spouse's estate and an indication of those who are likely to have claims upon it: *Whiting v Whiting* [1988] 2 All ER 275, CA. Note also *Cameron v Treasury Solicitor* [1997] 2 FLR 716, CA where it was suggested (in the context of a consent order) that a clean break order which did not bar claims under the 1975 Act would be so irregular as to suggest a fundamental drafting error.

[329] HC Official Report, col 78, 22 March 1984.

'... it would be equally inappropriate where the evidence suggests an impossibility in obtaining employment however well equipped for this purpose the spouse may be.'

Judicial dicta and practice since the enactment of s 25A have borne out the view that there will be cases where a clean break is inappropriate, but at the same time, empirical evidence shows that it has become the preferred outcome and spousal maintenance is increasingly unusual.[330] There is still no *presumption* in favour of a clean break,[331] and the court's overriding duty is to achieve fairness, as *White v White* makes clear.[332] This may require an ongoing financial tie (if only for a fixed term), where, for example, there is inadequate capital to achieve a fair split, or where fairness cannot be achieved at present because of illiquid assets.[333] But a clean break has advantages where the payer is unreliable so that periodical payments cannot be awarded with confidence. In *Fournier v Fournier*[334] for example, where the first instance judge had considered it in the wife's interests to receive periodical payments and adjourn her lump sum application, it transpired that the husband was failing to comply with the orders made, including the transfer of the matrimonial home. The Court of Appeal held that it was preferable to impose an immediate clean break to avoid uncertainty and likely heavy costs of enforcement. Similarly, where the parties are very bitter towards each other, a clean break may be desirable.[335]

On the other hand, it is still relatively unusual to see an immediate clean break imposed against a party's will and in one such case, *Seaton v Seaton*,[336] the Court of Appeal refused to lay down any general guidelines, in part because the facts of the case were so unusual. In that case the wife had borne the financial burden of the marriage after the husband lost his job and because of a drink problem could not subsequently obtain another. Eventually she left him and some time after the separation the husband suffered a stroke which left him with permanent disabilities. At the time of the divorce the husband was living with his parents

---

[330] See A Perry et al, op cit; S Arthur et al, op cit. See also *Harman v Glencross* [1986] 1 All ER 545, CA at 557 per Balcombe LJ: the modern practice is to 'favour the clean break wherever possible'; see also *B v B (Financial Provision)* [1990] 1 FLR 20 at 26 per Ward J—primary object of the law is to make the parties self-sufficient.

[331] *SRJ v DWJ (Financial Provision)* [1999] 2 FLR 176, CA: wife still caring for youngest child and had given up her place in the world of work during a long marriage—clean break inappropriate even though husband could not afford more than nominal periodical payments in present cicumstances; *Phippen v Palmers (a firm)* [2002] 2 FLR 415: elderly wife should not have been advised to accept clean break leaving her with a shortfall in meeting her income requirements. But cf *Suter v Suter and Jones* [1987] Fam 11, CA, where, although a nominal order was eventually made, the Court of Appeal held that the trial judge should have considered whether the wife could become financially independent, even though she was caring for dependent children. See also *Whiting v Whiting* [1988] 2 All ER 275, CA, where, although the majority refused to overrule the trial judge, they stressed that declining to make a clean break order because of concern for the future and a wish to preserve a 'backstop' of support for the wife, may be the easy, but is not always the right solution.

[332] *F v F (Clean Break: Balance of Fairness)* [2003] 1 FLR 847: it was not just to leave wife with only a quarter of the capital assets other than pension funds; periodical payments order to enable her to share in the results of the husband's company until such time as sufficient capital could be realised to achieve a clean break.

[333] See eg *F v F (Clean Break: Balance of Fairness)* above; *McFarlane v McFarlane; Parlour v Parlour* [2004] EWCA Civ 872 [2005] Fam 171 discussed further below at pp 1026–8; *R v R (Lump Sum Repayments)* [2003] EWHC 3197 (Fam) [2004] 1 FLR 928. For the problems of valuing business interests in order to achieve fairness, see P Marshall, 'Divorce and the Family Business' [2003] Fam Law 406 and J Nedas 'Valuation Issues After *White* and Other Cases' [2004] Fam Law 187.

[334] [1998] 2 FLR 990, CA.

[335] See eg *Clifton-Brown v Clifton-Brown (orse CB v CB)* [1988] Fam Law 471.

[336] [1986] 2 FLR 398, CA.

and because of his limited capacity to enjoy life, his income, derived from his disability pension, was sufficient to meet his needs. It was held that in the circumstances it would be wrong to impose upon the wife a continuing obligation to support her husband and accordingly the husband's application for periodical payments was dismissed under s 25A(3).

Making deferred clean break orders

Even before 1984 the courts had the power to order a limited term periodical payments order, but the *requirement* to consider whether such an order should be made was introduced in that year. Similarly, the power under s 28(1A) to direct that no application can be made to extend the term provided for in an original periodical payments order was also introduced in 1984. It should be understood, however, that unless the court expressly adds a s 28(1A) direction, there is nothing to stop a spouse from returning to the court prior to the expiry of the term to ask that the term be extended.[337]

The desirability of a deferred clean break was considered by the Court of Appeal in *McFarlane v McFarlane; Parlour v Parlour*.[338] However, it should be noted that the facts of these conjoined appeals were highly unusual. In each, the husband had extremely high earnings (in the former case, the accountant husband earned some £753,000 pa and in the latter, the husband was a Premier League footballer earning £1.19 million pa), but the available capital assets were insufficient to achieve an appropriately fair clean break between the spouses.[339] The dispute between the parties concerned what periodical payments order should accordingly be made in favour of the wife. In each case, a joint lives order was made, with no limit of time, but the wives both disputed the level at which the payments were set (in the former case, at £180,000 pa,[340] and in the latter at £212,500 pa), arguing that they should receive amounts significantly above what they 'needed' to maintain a comfortable lifestyle. Allowing the appeals, but substituting limited term orders (of five years and four years respectively),[341] the court focused on what it saw as the

---

[337] *Richardson v Richardson* [1994] 1 FLR 286. So long as the application to extend the term is made before its expiry, the court has jurisdiction so to order, even though that order is made after the term has expired: *Jones v Jones* [2000] 2 FLR 307. However, the objective of achieving financial independence between the parties where this can be done without undue hardship meant that a fixed-term order was not extended in *Fleming v Fleming* [2003] EWCA Civ 1841, [2004] 1 FLR 667 where the wife and her cohabiting partner had means sufficient to meet their expenses. See E Hamilton, 'Extending the Extendable Term' [2005] Fam Law 466. Query the strength of this authority in the light of *Miller v Miller; McFarlane v McFarlane* [2006] UKHL 24, [2006] 3 All ER 1 discussed below.

[338] [2004] EWCA Civ 872, [2005] Fam 171. See DJR Bird, 'New Deal for Wives or More of the Same?' [2004] Fam Law 654.; E Cooke, 'Playing Parlour Games: Income Provision After Divorce' [2004] Fam Law 906; K O'Donovan, 'Flirting with academic categorisations—*McFarlane v McFarlane and Parlour v Parlour*' [2005] CFLQ 415; N Francis, 'If it's Broken—Fix It' [2006] Fam Law 104.

[339] Of course, if there are substantial capital assets available, then any potential hardship can be offset by ordering payment of the appropriate sums. See eg *Attar v Attar (No 2)* [1985] FLR 653, where, after a marriage lasting six months, a millionaire husband was ordered to pay £30,000 lump sum to his wife who, during the marriage, had given up her job as an air hostess, to enable her to adjust over a period of two years. In *S v S* [1986] Fam 189, it was thought that £400,000 was the appropriate figure to compensate the divorced wife of a millionaire pop star for the loss of periodic payments estimated at £70,000 a year.

[340] Having been reduced on initial appeal from £250,000.

[341] Although without a s 28(1A) direction. In the *Parlour* case, the husband's high income was expected to reduce as his playing career wound down and then ended, making the current level of periodical payments impossible to sustain in the long term.

duty to seek where possible to achieve a clean break within a reasonable time.[342] It also increased the level of periodical payments that the husbands would have to make during the limited term of the orders (to £250,000 pa in *McFarlane* and to £444,000 pa in *Parlour*), rejecting the view that the level of periodical payments awarded should be confined to satisfying the recipient's 'needs' (however generously interpreted).

Mrs McFarlane appealed to the House of Lords for restoration of the joint lives order. The House took the opportunity to review the general approach to ancillary relief cases in the wake of *White v White* by conjoining her appeal to that in another case,[343] and upheld her claim. Their reasoning for doing so was two-fold. First, they considered that, having established 'compensation' as a basis for achieving *fairness* between the parties, it could not be right to limit the level of periodical payments to what would satisfy the wife's 'needs'. Thus far, they agreed with the Court of Appeal, Secondly, however, the House considered that a five-year term was 'most unlikely to be sufficient to achieve a fair outcome'.[344] The onus should be on the husband, rather than the wife, to seek a variation as future circumstances changed.[345] As Baroness Hale put it, 'A clean break is not to be achieved at the expense of a fair result.'[346]

In so deciding, the House recognised that, as women have advanced in the work-place and in forging careers, the loss that they incur if they give this up to raise a family 'comes at a price which in most cases is irrecoverable.'[347] When the clean break principle was first introduced in the 1980s, this was not appreciated. The realisation of the importance of non-discrimination between the spouses, elucidated in *White v White* has therefore prompted a reconsideration of the correct balance to be drawn between the desirability of a clean break, and ongoing support to redress the financial disadvantage created by the marriage—and usually suffered by the wife rather than the husband. It is arguable, more-over, that wives who had accepted periodical payments orders set at a 'needs' level, or for a fixed term only, now have a claim to higher payments or an extended term in order to recognise the 'compensation' element of a fair settlement.

In considering whether to make a limited term order,[348] the court is directed under s 25A(2) to consider whether the party in whose favour an order is made can adjust *without undue hardship* to the termination of financial dependence on the other party. As was stressed in *Morris v Morris*,[349] this is a mandatory requirement needing specific evidence. It is unclear precisely what is meant by 'undue hardship' (though it is implicit that a party can expect some hardship), but it is evident that a limited term order and, a fortiori, a s 28(1A) direction should not be made upon some vague expectation that the dependent spouse will be able to obtain a job, nor should that spouse's potential earning capacity be unrealistically viewed. As was recognised in *M v M (Financial Provision)*,[350] the prospects

---

[342] See Thorpe LJ at para 66 and Wall LJ at para 133.

[343] *Miller v Miller; McFarlane v McFarlane* [2006] UKHL 24, [2006] 3 All ER 1. The *Miller* case was an appeal from *Miller v Miller* [2005] EWCA Civ 984, [2006] 1 FLR 151.

[344] Per Lord Nicholls at para 26. Lord Hope of Craighead noted that Scots law does not permit recognition of 'compensation' through continuing periodical payments beyond three years, and may work injustice in consequence. He urged that the matter be re-examined.

[345] Lord Nicholls at para 97, Baroness Hale at para 155.   [346] At para 134.

[347] Lord Hope at para 118.

[348] See J Harcus, 'Periodical Payments—End of Term?' [1997] Fam Law 340.

[349] [1985] FLR 1176, CA.   [350] [1987] 2 FLR 1. See also the discussion of s 25(2)(a) below, p 1031.

of a middle-aged woman returning to the job market after several years' absence are far from good. As Ward LJ said in *Flavell v Flavell*:[351]

'There is, in my judgment, often a tendency for these [ie finite term] orders to be made more in hope than in serious expectation. Especially in judging the case of ladies in their middle years, the judicial looking into the crystal ball rarely finds enough of substance to justify a finding that adjustment can be made without undue hardship. All too often, these orders are made without evidence to support them.'

There is no presumption that periodical payments should be terminated as soon as possible[352] but until *McFarlane v McFarlane* it did seem that the influence of the shift towards 'fairness' as represented by 'equality' had produced a greater willingness than such older cases[353] suggest to take a risk and seek to bring the parties to an eventual clean break. In *D v D (Financial Provision: Periodical Payments)*[354] for example, Coleridge J allowed the husband's appeal against a joint lives order and limited its term to 10 years where he considered that otherwise, the attempt to achieve equality between the spouses in the capital award would be frustrated. He left the door open to the wife, should her circumstances deteriorate, however, by refusing to attach a s 28(1A) direction.[355] Ultimately, the facts supported by evidence, may justify a reasonable expectation that the wife can and will become self-sufficient within the fixed term which the court may direct.[356]

(e) The current approach

The above discussion seeks to explain how the courts have arrived at their current approach. The 1984 Act established that the desirable goal of the jurisdiction (albeit not expressed as a statutory aim) is to enable the parties to achieve financial independence after divorce, rather than to impose continuing liability to keep the dependent spouse as far as possible in the manner to which he or (more usually) she had become accustomed.

---

[351] [1997] 1 FLR 353, CA at 358.

[352] *Barrett v Barrett* [1988] 2 FLR 516, CA. See also *C v C (Financial Relief: Short Marriage)* [1997] 2 FLR 26, CA.

[353] See also *Fisher v Fisher* [1989] 1 FLR 423, CA where the court increased the periodical payments in favour of a wife and child and refused to impose a time limit on the order, notwithstanding the child was born after the divorce, and was not the husband's. It was 'quite insupportable' for the husband to argue that by becoming pregnant, the wife had released the husband from his obligation to support her. Nor could the court ignore the wife's responsibility for the child because it was not a 'child of the family'.

[354] [2004] EWHC 445 (Fam), [2004] 1 FLR 988.

[355] See also *Waterman v Waterman* [1989] 1 FLR 380, CA (five-year term upheld but s 28(1A) direction lifted); *Mawson v Mawson* [1994] 2 FLR 985 (young couple, both of whom had careers, separated after a three-year marriage; there was a six-year-old child. On the basis that the husband continued to pay the child support assessment in respect of the child, Thorpe J ordered a periodical payment order of nine months which would enable the wife 'to stand on her own feet and bring to an end her financial dependency').

[356] Compare *N v N (Consent Order: Variation)* [1993] 2 FLR 868, CA, where the parties, who had a son, divorced after a seven-year marriage. An agreement was reached whereby (against legal advice) the wife accepted periodical payments for a five-year term, and entered into a 'side letter' whereby she agreed not to apply for an extension except 'for the protection of the child in a case of quite unforeseen circumstances of serious illness or disability'. The wife realised that she would not be successful as an opera singer, and decided to train as a barrister. She applied for an extension of the specified term. The Court of Appeal rejected her application. While questioning the appropriateness of a side letter in child cases, and whilst itself unenforceable, it was nonetheless 'highly relevant'. On the principles of *Edgar v Edgar* [1980] 3 All ER 887, CA, the court considered it should uphold an agreement freely entered into after legal advice.

The implicit question that then arose was on what basis the parties' assets should be divided in order to achieve that independence? In the majority of divorces, which are not 'big money' cases of the type discussed in detail above, the court continues to have to seek to meet the parties' basic needs (and those of their children) as they adjust to living in two households rather than one.[357] The most important of these is for accommodation and the major task will be to deploy the available powers so as to provide a home, first for the children (if any) and whoever is their primary carer, and secondly, if possible and appropriate, for the other spouse.[358] The support needs of the children should then be met. If there is continuing need for support for a dependent spouse (ideally only until she can achieve self-sufficiency), this may then be met if possible, either from a capital transfer which the recipient could then invest[359] or used to boost her available income (such as by taking a smaller mortgage on a new home and thus reducing her outgoings), or, if the spouse can afford them, by means of periodical payments. If any surplus assets remain, they may be used to redress financial disadvantage or shared out as the fruits of the marriage,[360] and it is here above all that the 'yardstick of equality' may be applicable, although broad equality will be sought in the whole package of orders made, both as to capital and ongoing support, as demonstrated above in *D v D (Financial Provision: Periodical Payments)*.[361]

In bringing 'equality' into the court's calculations, *White v White* can be seen as bringing a 'contribution' *or* 'recognition/compensation' approach to the assessment of the spouses' claims rather than one based primarily on needs, at least where the parties' assets allow. A spouse's contributions—in *White v White* as a full business partner in the farming enterprise, as well as a 'wife and mother'—should be recognised as giving her a claim to her due share. As will be seen below, however,[362] the contribution approach can give rise to disputes and competitions as to how much of a contribution one spouse has made compared to the other. It may be seen as stemming from a 'partnership of equals' view of marriage under which each spouse is seen as capable of making a contribution to the success of the family and therefore entitled to whatever value is put on that contribution—an 'equality of opportunity' model, one might say.[363] By contrast, as *Miller v Miller; McFarlane v McFarlane* demonstrates, a recognition/compensation approach can give allowance to the fact that one spouse (currently usually the wife) may give up the

---

[357] The following is derived from the 'principles' for ancillary relief suggested by the Government in its Consultation Paper, Home Office, *Supporting Families* (1998) Ch 4, as based on, in particular, the views of the Association of District Judges, enunciating what they saw as the current practice in England and Wales, in their Memorandum to the Lord Chancellor's Ancillary Relief Advisory Group, *Possible Reforms to the Substantive Law on Ancillary Relief Reform* (1998). See also J Eekelaar, M Maclean and S Beinart, *Family Lawyers: The Divorce Work of Solicitors* (2000) pp 125–8.

[358] But, as in *B v B (Financial Provision: Financial Provision: Welfare of Child and Conduct)* [2002] 1 FLR 555, this may not be achievable or desirable in every case.

[359] See *Duxbury* calculations, etc below at p 1038.

[360] It is unclear from *Miller v Miller; McFarlane v McFarlane* [2006] UKHL 24, [2006] 3 All ER 1 as to whether one starts with needs, moves on to compensation and then reaches sharing—if the available assets so allow, or whether sharing on an equal basis should be the starting point, to be tempered by needs and compensation: see Lord Nicholls at paras 15, 16 and Baroness Hale at para 144.

[361] [2004] EWHC 445 (Fam) [2004] 1 FLR 988.   [362] See pp 1044–7.

[363] See R Bailey-Harris, 'Dividing the Assets on Family Breakdown: The Content of Fairness' (2001) *Current Legal Problems* 533. For a critique of a 'formal equality' outcome, see A Scully, '*Parra v Parra*—Big money cases, judicial discretion and equality of division' [2003] CFLQ 205.

opportunity to make a full *financial* contribution to the family through her career or employment, by concentrating on child care and home-making. Or a spouse may simply be unable to contribute as much financially as the other, because of lesser earning ability, pay differentials in the labour market, or a poorer family background so that she or he cannot bring an inheritance into the family. This does not mean that this spouse's contribution is 'worth' any less than that of the bread-winning or wealthier spouse. On this view, marriage is a 'joint enterprise' in which both spouses make equal, but different, contributions to the welfare of the family and 'equality of outcome' will require that the economic balance between the spouses may accordingly need to be redressed to ensure that one is not unfairly disadvantaged after the marriage ends.[364] Structural inequalities in the labour market and wider society may mean it is impossible to remove all of the disadvantages faced by the economically weaker spouse. The goal must be only to achieve *fairness* as between the two parties to the marriage. The trend of recent cases suggests that the courts are trying to move towards such an equality of outcome model.

An added impetus towards applying the yardstick of equality may be produced by the implementation of Sch 5 to the Civil Partnership Act 2004 in relation to the dissolution of civil partnerships.[365] The traditional bread-winner/house-wife model of the relationship may be even less applicable to such partnerships than it is to modern marriage. But it would seem strange, and surely politically unacceptable, if civil partners appeared to be obtaining more generous settlements from the courts than spouses. Valuing the 'contributions' of civil partners without the straightjacket of stereo-typed thinking about the nature of the roles played by each partner may prove liberating.[366]

The question to discuss next is how the courts exercise their discretion in order to try to achieve fair outcomes.

2 FACTORS TO BE TAKEN INTO ACCOUNT WHEN ASSESSING WHAT ORDERS SHOULD BE MADE FOR A SPOUSE

Reference has already been made to the fact that, whilst the court must have regard to all the circumstances of the case, it must also take into account certain specific factors. Some of these are relevant to calculating the parties' resources and needs; others will lead the court to make a greater or smaller award than it otherwise would have done. Although the list is not intended to be exhaustive, it covers almost all the matters to which the court had always had regard in the past. However, it is important to note that the factors are not ranked in any kind of hierarchy and the weight given to any of them depends upon the facts in the individual case.[367] It is proposed to consider the facts in the order in which they are set out in s 25(2) of the Matrimonial Causes Act.[368]

---

[364] For discussion of the 'partnership of equals' and 'joint enterprise' models of marriage, see G Douglas, *An Introduction to Family Law* (2nd ed, 2004) p 11 and passim. The Scottish law attempts to achieve this redress too: see Family Law (Scotland) Act 1985 ss 9, 10.

[365] As pointed out by M Harper et al, *Civil Partnership: The New Law* (2005) at para 5.19.

[366] For consideration of the difference between same-sex and heterosexual partnerships in terms of the power dynamics (albeit in another context), see R Auchmuty, 'When Equality is not Equity: Homosexual Inclusion in Undue Influence Law' (2003) 11 Fem LS 163.

[367] *Piglowska v Piglowski* [1999] 1 WLR 1360, HL.

[368] As amended by the Matrimonial and Family Proceedings Act 1984 and Welfare Reform and Pensions Act 1999.

(a) 'The income, earning capacity, property and other financial resources which each of the parties to the marriage has or is likely to have in the foreseeable future, including in the case of earning capacity any increase in that capacity which it would in the opinion of the court be reasonable to expect a party to the marriage to take steps to acquire'

The court must have regard to all the income and capital belonging to the spouses.[369] So far as capital is concerned, provided it belongs to one of the spouses, it had been assumed that it must be taken into account and it is irrelevant how the spouse came to own it. However, once the yardstick of equality laid down in *White v White* became an important measure of arriving at a fair settlement, the question arose whether assets brought into the marriage, or not generated by the parties' joint efforts, such as a gift or inheritance or wealth produced by one earner's efforts, should be subject to sharing.[370] In *Miller v Miller; McFarlane v McFarlane*[371] the judges who gave the two leading speeches, Lord Nicholls and Baroness Hale agreed that the source of an asset is a relevant issue in determining how it is to be allocated or shared, but differed in their view of what forms of asset might be distinguished.[372] The issue was important because Mr Miller, a highly successful fund manager, had come into the marriage earning £1m per annum, and had received some £13m in a business deal shortly before the wedding. During the marriage, which lasted less than three years, his wealth grew to £17m. He also bought shares in the new company— 'New Star'—which he joined after the wedding, which were valued at between £12m and £18m by the time of the divorce hearing. At first instance, upheld by the Court of Appeal, Singer J awarded the wife, who had been earning £85,000 per annum before she was married, and who had no children, capital of £5m, comprising the former matrimonial home and a lump sum and other assets.

Lord Nicholls distinguished between property acquired during the marriage, otherwise than by inheritance or gift—the 'marital acquest' or 'matrimonial property'—which is the financial product of the parties' common endeavour, and other property which is not. The former should be subject to sharing, regardless of the length of the marriage. But non-matrimonial property which the parties bring into the marriage, or receive by gift or inheritance may be treated differently. In a short marriage, fairness may require that this should not be shared, reflecting 'the instinctive feeling that parties generally have less call upon each other on the breakdown of a short marriage.'[373] In longer marriages, such property may, by contrast, represent a contribution made to the marriage by one of the parties. On his reasoning, the shares that Mr Miller owned were 'matrimonial property' because their value had grown during the marriage thanks in part to the husband's efforts in working for New Star. They were therefore relevant to determining the award to the wife, and he dismissed Mr Miller's appeal.

---

[369] Where the spouses live with their extended family, it may be difficult to determine who owns what, with scope to claim that other family members in fact have a beneficial interest: *G v G (Matrimonial Property: Rights of Extended Family)* [2005] EWHC 1560 (Admin) [2006] 1 FLR 62 (claim rejected).

[370] In *White v White* [2001] AC 596 itself, the House of Lords upheld an unequal share of the parties' property because some of it had been acquired with financial help from the husband's father.

[371] [2006] UKHL 24, [2006] 3 All ER 1.

[372] Lord Hoffmann agreed with Baroness Hale. Lord Hope agreed with both Lord Nicholls and Baroness Hale. Lord Mance appeared to agree with Baroness Hale.

[373] At para 24. See further below at p 1040.

Baroness Hale categorised assets rather differently. She identified, on the one hand, *family assets* of a 'capital nature' such as the family home and its contents and of a 'revenue nature' such as earning capacity, plus other assets acquired for the benefit of the family such as furniture, holiday homes, insurance policies and family savings, and family businesses or joint ventures in which both parties work.[374] On the other hand, there may be *'business or investment assets which have been generated solely or mainly by the efforts of one party'* and in respect of which it cannot be demonstrated that the spouse's domestic contribution has contributed to their acquisition. In a very small number of cases where there are such assets, of which *Miller* might be one, the short duration of the marriage may justify a departure from the yardstick of equality of division. On this basis, the husband's shares were business assets generated solely by him and this, coupled with the shortness of the marriage, justified the departure from equal sharing which would otherwise have left Mrs Miller with very substantially more capital than the £5m she was awarded. Baroness Hale therefore also upheld that award.

It will be seen that their Lordships accordingly differed in deciding whether wealth generated by one spouse, which no real contribution of a domestic nature could be regarded as helping to acquire (Mr Miller could have paid a housekeeper for the wife's home-making services, after all) is a form of matrimonial 'acquest' or not, Lord Nicholls regarding it as such and Baroness Hale excluding it. Whilst both recognised, and it is important to emphasise, that in the majority of cases, it will not matter because all of the parties' assets must be brought into account to achieve a fair outcome, there will be some where the difference of opinion could be crucial. We return to this issue below, in the context of considering the duration of the marriage.[375]

They did appear to agree, however, that non-matrimonial assets, such as inheritance[376] or gifts, may, if the parties' means allow (*but this will be rare*), be left out of account in reaching a fair settlement.

Even damages recovered for loss of earnings, damage to property or personal injuries form part of the recipient's assets.[377] However, Scarman LJ was careful to point out that it would not be a correct exercise of the court's discretion to make an order which would in effect deprive the spouse of all benefit of the compensation:[378] the court apparently must

---

[374] At para 149.   [375] See below p 1040.

[376] For earlier consideration of how to handle an inheritance, see *White v White* [2001] 1 AC 596 at 994E–F where Lord Nicholls suggested that the spouse to whom the property was given should, where possible, be allowed to keep it. By contrast, it was held in *Norris v Norris* [2002] EWHC 2996 [2003] 1 FLR 1142 that an inheritance should not 'count double', both as an asset to be 'quarantined' from the pool of family assets *and* as a contribution to welfare (see below p 1044) and there were a number of subsequent decisions (see the review by N Francis and M Fisher, 'Departure from Equality: Inherited Property' [2005] Fam Law 218) which diverged according to whether an attempt is made to echo Lord Nicholls' approach and regard the inheritance as separate from the available pool or to take it into account when measuring the proposed outcome against the yardstick of equality. See also *P v P (Inherited Property)* [2004] EWHC 1364 (Fam), [2005] 1 FLR 576—fairness may require a different approach where the legacy accrues during the marriage, compared to a landed estate passed down through the generations. For cases where an inheritance was, arguably wrongly, 'quarantined', see *M v M (Financial Provision: Valuation of Assets)* [2002] Fam Law 509 (High Court of N Ireland); *H v H (Financial Provision: Special Contribution)* [2002] 2 FLR 1021; *Currey v Currey* [2004] EWCA Civ 1799 [2005] 1 FLR 952.

[377] *Daubney v Daubney* [1976] Fam 267, CA, cf *Jones v Jones* [1976] Fam 8, CA; *Wagstaff v Wagstaff* [1992] 1 All ER 275, CA

[378] In *Daubney v Daubney* at 277.

decide in each case what would be a fair sum to bring into account. The fact that an injured spouse may have special needs, or an impaired future earning capacity would, of course, be considered by the court in the exercise of its discretion.[379] But, subject to this, damages for personal injury are properly to be regarded as part of the financial resources available to the parties.[380]

In appropriate cases regard must be had to the husband's ability to earn higher wages by working overtime,[381] to raise money by overdrafts,[382] or loans secured on his property[383] or, if he is unemployed, to obtain work if he wishes.[384] Increases in either spouse's income or capital after their separation must also be considered, as these are properly to be regarded as part of their resources.[385] In the case of a very rich man, who may well live largely on capital and capital profits, his capital assets will be of particular importance,[386] and such a person's standard of living may be the best guide to the level of his real income.[387]

The court must have regard not only to the resources which each party has at the time of the hearing, but also to those which they are likely to have in the foreseeable future.[388] If the benefit is one to which a party may be contingently entitled in the future, the court may take it into account by ordering him to pay an appropriate lump sum if and when he acquires the interest.[389] An alternative approach, used in *Parra v Parra*[390] was to award the wife a charge for joint lives, by way of a claw-back, on land retained by the husband, should planning permission for residential use of the land be granted in future. Here, the chance of obtaining such permission was not high, but if it did transpire, the increase in value of the land would be very great. Where the value of a future asset

---

[379] See *C v C (Financial Provision: Personal Damages)* [1995] 2 FLR 171, in which the husband received a structured settlement damages award after a car accident of about £950,000, but potentially worth up to £5m if he achieved his estimated life expectancy. The court declined to award the wife a lump sum which would frustrate the husband's reasonable expectation of obtaining a suitable house and long-term care.

[380] This seems also to include compensation payments made by the Criminal Injuries Compensation Board (now Authority): see *A v A (Financial Provision: Conduct)* [1995] 1 FLR 345.

[381] *Klucinski v Klucinski* [1953] 1 All ER 683.   [382] *J-PC v J-AF* [1955] P 215, CA.

[383] *Newton v Newton* [1990] 1 FLR 33, CA.

[384] *McEwan v McEwan* [1972] 2 All ER 708; cf *Bromilow v Bromilow* (1976) 7 Fam Law 16. If the husband is in receipt of income support (or Jobseekers' allowance) and the payments made to him have not been reduced or stopped, this indicates that the Benefits Agency's officers are satisfied after extensive enquiries that he is genuinely unable to find work and, whilst this does not bind any court, is a valuable piece of evidence which should be taken into account: *Williams v Williams* [1974] Fam 55.

[385] *Schuller v Schuller* [1990] 2 FLR 193: wife's property inheritance after a decree absolute was taken into account to reduce her lump sum.

[386] *Brett v Brett* [1969] 1 All ER 1007, CA.   [387] See *W v W (No 3)* [1962] P 124.

[388] See M Daniel 'Considering Future Capital Assets' [1993] Fam Law 265. One particular difficulty may concern whether assets can be realised in order to pay a lump sum or effect a transfer to the recipient spouse. In *N v N (Financial Provision: Sale of Company)* [2001] 2 FLR 69, the court justified a departure from equal division of the surplus assets because of the illiquidity of the husband's assets; the wife received only 39%. Cf *M v M (Financial Provision: Valuation of Assets)* [2002] Fam Law 509, where McLaughlin J, of the High Court of Northern Ireland, considered that illiquidity went to the issue of how a settlement should be achieved, but not as to the size of share. For the problems of valuing business interests in order to achieve fairness, see *R v R (Company Valuation and Liquidity)* [2005] 2 FLR 365; P Marshall, 'Divorce and the Family Business' [2003] Fam Law 406 and J Nedas, 'Valuation Issues After *White* and Other Cases' [2004] Fam Law 187.

[389] *Calder v Calder* (1975) 6 Fam Law 242, CA (interest contingent on husband's surviving his mother).

[390] [2002] EWCA Civ 1886 [2003] 1 FLR 942. See A Scully, '*Parra v Parra*—Big money cases, judicial discretion and equality of division' [2003] CFLQ 205.

will be known reasonably shortly, the application may be adjourned.[391] On the other hand, if the contingency is too uncertain or remote, it may be left out of account altogether.[392]

The specific requirement to consider whether a spouse could increase his or her earning capacity results from an amendment introduced by the Matrimonial and Family Proceedings Act 1984 s 3. In his evidence to the Special Standing Committee[393] the President of the Family Division instanced what he described as the 'obvious case' of a husband who had reached the point in his career at which he had the right or an opportunity to take some examination which would lead to a higher grade or a better remunerated appointment. While this is an example of how the provision could be relevant, it is much more likely that attention will be directed to the wife's potential earning capacity. The provision is clearly related to the general requirement to consider whether the spouses can become self-sufficient.

It is to be noted that the court should only pay regard to any increase in earning capacity that it is 'reasonable' to expect the spouse to take steps to acquire. Obviously, in deciding this, the court must take into account all the circumstances of the case, but particularly relevant will be any commitments to look after any children;[394] the age, health and qualifications of the spouse; and the length of time since the spouse last worked. The courts seem well aware of the difficulties that older women in particular may experience in obtaining suitable employment.[395] In *Leadbeater v Leadbeater*,[396] for example, it was held to be unreasonable to expect a 47-year-old woman with no particular skills (she was, at the time of the marriage, the secretary to her former husband) to adapt to new methods used in offices, namely word processors and so on. However, it was thought that she could increase the number of hours that she was currently working as a receptionist. Hence, her earnings were assessed at £2,500 per year as against her actual earnings of £1,680.[397] On the other hand, in *Mitchell v Mitchell*[398] it was held that a wife who was an experienced secretary but who had taken a part-time job in a canteen could, when the children had left school (the

[391] *MT v MT (Financial Provision)* [1992] 1 FLR 362: wife's application adjourned pending the death of her 83-year-old German father-in-law: under German law, husband entitled to a fixed portion of his father's substantial estate; *D v D (Lump Sum Order: Adjournment of Application)* [2001] 1 FLR 633: application postponed until two months after amount of husband's bonus, derived from share options, became known (noted by D Rossettenstein, '*D v D*—Equality, fairness, risk and the distribution of share options on divorce' [2002] CFLQ 207). For an example of dealing with an adjourned application, notwithstanding the wife's remarriage in the interim, see *Re G (Financial Provision: Liberty to Restore Application for Lump Sum)* [2004] EWHC 88 (Fam) [2004] 1 FLR 997.

[392] See eg *Michael v Michael* [1986] 2 FLR 389 where, because of the uncertainty whether and when the wife would receive an interest under her mother's will, it was left out of account. This was followed in *K v K* [1990] 2 FLR 225 and *H v H (Financial Provision: Capital Assets)* [1993] 2 FLR 335. See also *Priest v Priest* (1987) 1 FLR 189, CA where a gratuity that could arise 15 years after the hearing was thought to be too far in the future to be taken into account.

[393] HC Official Report, col 77, 22 March 1984.

[394] This may include a child who is *not* the husband's, and who was born after the breakdown of the marriage: see *Fisher v Fisher* [1989] 1 FLR 423, CA.

[395] See also the discussion above at p 1026 in relation to the deferred clean break.

[396] [1985] FLR 789.

[397] See also *M v M (Financial Provision)* [1987] 2 FLR 1 in which the difficulties of another 47-year-old wife were discussed. See also *Boylan v Boylan* [1988] 1 FLR 282; *Barrett v Barrett* [1988] 2 FLR 516, CA; and *C v C (Financial Relief: Short Marriage)* [1997] 2 FLR 26, CA.

[398] [1984] FLR 387, CA.

younger child was 13), reasonably be expected to increase her earning capacity, and the resulting lump sum awarded to her reflected this.

Another issue is the presence of a new partner.[399] The fact that the wife has remarried or is about to remarry or is living with another man who is supporting her clearly affects her financial position. Remarriage automatically terminates periodical payments[400] and although, for this purpose, cohabitation is not necessarily to be equated with remarriage,[401] it may nonetheless lead the court to conclude that the wife no longer needs the husband's support;[402] but leaving aside the question of the matrimonial home, all these facts should generally be disregarded in dividing capital assets unless a lump sum award represents the capitalisation of periodical payments.[403] The wife is withdrawing her part of the capital from the former family partnership, and the amount she receives should not depend on what she proposes to do with it.[404] The mere chance that the wife may remarry at some time in the future should be ignored when dividing capital assets.[405]

It is established that the financial means of the husband's second wife are relevant (though there can be difficulties in discovering them),[406] but only to the extent that they diminish the needs of the husband, thereby extending his resources to support his first family. An order cannot be made which has the effect of making the new partner pay out of her income or capital.[407]

(b) 'The financial needs, obligations and responsibilities which each of the parties to the marriage has or is likely to have in the foreseeable future'

The most obvious examples of factors to be considered under this head are the parties' need to maintain themselves and their responsibility to provide for their dependants. In a short marriage, where one party has greater needs than the other, it may be appropriate (subject to ensuring the outcome is fair) to regard the satisfaction of these needs as the court's major objective. In *A v T (Ancillary Relief: Cultural Factors)*[408] for example, the spouses had married in Iran according to Sharia law, under which, if the wife sought a divorce, the husband could keep the marriage portion (equivalent in value to £60,000) he would otherwise pay to her under the marriage contract. The parties separated after only a

---

[399] See D Hodson 'The New Partner After Divorce' [1990] Fam Law 77, CA. [400] See above, p 993.

[401] *Atkinson v Atkinson* [1988] Fam 93, CA.

[402] See *Atkinson v Atkinson* [1995] 2 FLR 356 where the court reduced the periodical payments made by a wealthy man to his former wife from £30,000 to £10,000 per year. The wife cohabited with a younger man, and had provided a comfortable home enabling the latter to develop a successful business. The wife's new partner's worth was relevant insofar as it impacted on an assessment of the wife's financial needs. See also *Fleming v Fleming* [2003] EWCA Civ 1841 [2004] 1 FLR 667: a fixed-term periodical payments order should not be extended where the means of the wife and her cohabiting partner sufficed to discharge their living expenses.

[403] See eg *Duxbury v Duxbury* [1992] Fam 62n, CA.

[404] Ibid (it was irrelevant that the wife would spend part of a lump sum award to benefit her cohabitant); *Gojkovic v Gojkovic* [1992] Fam 40, CA (the wife had earned her share of the family wealth and was entitled to use the lump sum to purchase a hotel to run as a business).

[405] *S v S* [1976] Fam 18n at 23.

[406] See *Wynne v Wynne and Jeffers* [1980] 3 All ER 659, CA; *W v W* (1981) 2 FLR 291. One method is the so called 'production appointment' which may, in appropriate cases, be ordered against a third party—compare *Frary v Frary* [1993] 2 FLR 696 with *D v D (Production Appointment: Procedure)* [1995] 2 FLR 497.

[407] *Macey v Macey* (1981) 3 FLR 7, and *Brown v Brown* (1981) 3 FLR 161.

[408] [2004] EWHC 471 (Fam) [2004] 1 FLR 97.

few weeks of married life together in England, and the wife began divorce proceedings. She accrued debts of some £37,000 in trying to support herself after leaving the husband, and had a poor standard of living. Her prospects were bleak should she be unable to secure a religious divorce. Baron J awarded her a lump sum of £35,000 out of the husband's assets of around £300,000, on condition that he grant the wife a talaq divorce within three months.[409]

Usually, it will be desirable to ensure that the need of both parties for a suitable home is met, especially if they have children who will be spending time with each parent.[410] However, there is no principle or presumption that the available assets must be split to enable each spouse to acquire accommodation. In *Piglowska v Piglowski*[411] the first instance judge ordered that the wife was to receive the former matrimonial home in return for transferring a flat in Spain to the husband, who had remarried in Poland but wished to return to England. This was not worth enough to enable him to rehouse himself and his second wife and step-children in England but the House of Lords upheld the order as within the trial judge's discretion.

In supporting dependants, the maintenance of children must come first but in addition one must take into account the needs of a second spouse,[412] infirm parents, brothers and sisters unable to work, and any other person whom it is reasonable to expect either party to look after in the circumstances. It will be seen that not all these obligations are legally enforceable: in this context a moral obligation and the voluntary assumption of a responsibility (provided that it is reasonable) may be as relevant as a legal obligation. For example, a father's moral duty to make voluntary payments for the upkeep of his stepchild is indistinguishable for this purpose from his legal liability to comply with a court order.[413] But if the liability has been assumed in a purely voluntary way, the court can obviously take it into account only if it is reasonable. Thus repayments of a mortgage entered into

---

[409] Applying *S v S* [1977] Fam 127. Should he fail to do so, he would be obliged to pay her the full portion. The religious and cultural background of the parties played an important part in the judge's ruling: the parties had only a secondary attachment to the English jurisdiction and culture and the court took into account what an Iranian court would have done. In other short marriage cases, a more equal outcome may be sought: see below at p 1040.

[410] *M v B (Ancillary Proceedings: Lump Sum)* [1998] 1 FLR 53; *Calderbank v Calderbank* [1976] Fam 93. Where property is to be sold and the proceeds shared in order to meet the parties' needs, it is wrong to permit the payee to receive any surplus if the sale price exceeds the valuation of the property. A proportionate share, rather than a fixed amount, should be ordered: *Warner v Warner* [2005] All ER (D) 314 (Dec).

[411] [1999] 1 WLR 1360.

[412] *Barnes v Barnes* [1972] 3 All ER 872, CA. But this does not justify postponing the interests of the first family (and a fortiori any child of the family) to those of the second family: *Roberts v Roberts* [1970] P 1. In *S v S (Financial Provision: Departing from Equality)* [2001] 2 FLR 246, the liability of the husband to support his second family was held to justify the wife receiving only 46% of the assets, but in *H-J v H-J (Financial Provision: Equality)* [2002] 1 FLR 415 and *Norris v Norris* [2002] EWHC 2996 (Fam) [2003] 1 FLR 1142 this was regarded as inappropriate in a case where there are surplus assets: the husband assumes the liability of a second family by his own choice.

[413] *Blower v Blower* [1986] 1 FLR 292; *Roberts v Roberts*, above. See also *Williams v Williams* [1965] P 125, CA, and *P (JR) v P (GL)* [1966] 1 All ER 439 (concerning liability to educate children of a previous marriage); cf *Fisher v Fisher* [1989] 1 FLR 423, CA, for a mother's responsibility towards a child born outside the marriage. Note also *Vicary v Vicary* [1992] 2 FLR 271, CA (where there are plentiful resources, the financial provision made for a wife may include prospective payments which she might make to adult daughters and grandchildren, if such payments had been made during the marriage, and the husband had contributed to them or, at least, had not objected to the payments having been made).

after the parties separated in order to enable one of them to buy an expensive house may be disregarded if their financial position does not justify the purchase.[414]

As in the case of the parties' resources, the court must have regard to the needs, obligations and liabilities that they are likely to have in the foreseeable future as well as those already incurred at the time of the order.[415] In all cases the spouses are entitled to have only their *reasonable* needs taken into account but, of course, what is 'reasonable' very much depends upon the circumstances of each case. At the poverty end of the spectrum, for example, it has been held that a video recorder is not a reasonable need,[416] and running a car can only be a justified expense if it is needed to get to work.[417] Even if there are ample resources the claims must still be reasonable. In *Leadbeater v Leadbeater*,[418] for example, where the husband's assets amounted to some £250,000, it was held that while the wife could reasonably justify the purchase of a two bedroom house, given that she would live in it by herself, she could not justify the need for a three bedroom property.

'Big money' cases

At the wealthiest end of the spectrum it has been said that it is impossible to lay down guidelines to help calculate the appropriate levels of lump sum payments,[419] though in *Preston v Preston*[420] Ormrod LJ considered that the word 'needs' in s 25(2)(b) was equivalent to 'reasonable requirements', and seemed to hint there might be some ceiling to awards that might be made where the parties' available resources are very large. On the facts, the husband, who had capital assets estimated at £2.3 million, was ordered to pay a lump sum of £600,000 to produce an annual income of £20,000 after tax. In a number of later 'big money' cases the 'reasonable requirements' approach, with its ceiling on the award made to the wife, was adopted and followed.[421]

One consequence of such an approach was that the courts were necessarily drawn into a close scrutiny of a claimant wife's estimated budgeted expenditure;[422] another was that,

---

[414] See *G v P* [1978] 1 All ER 1099, CA.

[415] In *Al-Khatib v Masry* [2002] 1 FLR 1053, where the husband was immensely wealthy and had abducted the children to Saudi Arabia, the wife's needs were taken to include a 'fighting fund' of £2.5 million to enable her to take proceedings to seek the return of the children. The parties later reached an agreed settlement and the Court of Appeal set this sum aside but did not dispute the legitimacy of so ordering in an appropriate case: see *Al-Khatib v Masry* [2004] EWCA Civ 1353, [2005] 1 FLR 381.

[416] *Girvan v Girvan* (1983) 13 Fam Law 213.

[417] See eg *Clarke v Clarke* (1979) 9 Fam Law 15; *Delaney v Delaney* [1990] 2 FLR 457, CA; cf *Slater v Slater* (1981) 3 FLR 58.

[418] [1985] FLR 789.   [419] *Gojkovic v Gojkovic* [1992] Fam 40 at 50, per Russell LJ.

[420] [1982] Fam 17.

[421] See eg *O'D v O'D* [1976] Fam 83; *Page v Page* (1981) 2 FLR 198; *Preston v Preston* [1982] Fam 17; *H v H (Financial Provision: Lump Sum)* [1994] 2 FLR 309; *R v R (Financial Provision: Reasonable Need)* [1994] 2 FLR 1044; *W v W (Judicial Separation: Ancillary Relief)* [1995] 2 FLR 259; *Dart v Dart* [1996] 2 FLR 286, CA. But compare *C v C (Financial Relief: Short Marriage)* [1997] 2 FLR 26, where the Court of Appeal rejected an approach based on needs, saying it was only one factor to be considered under s 25; in addition to the wife's personal requirements, the court also had to consider the needs of the child of the marriage, whose welfare should be considered first under Matrimonial Causes Act 1973 s 25(1).

[422] See eg *F v F (Ancillary Relief: Substantial Assets)* [1995] 2 FLR 45 where Thorpe J scrutinised the details of the wife's suggested budget which had been produced acknowledging: '... there is every incentive to put the figures as high as they can reasonably be put and perhaps some temptation to gild the lily'. Among the items his Lordship found 'unjustifiable even in a super-rich case' were £5,000 for knick-knacks for the home,

particularly where it was used to award a lump sum calculated by reference to a wife's projected future income requirements, awards might be lower than might otherwise be the case. In *Dart v Dart*,[423] where the wife had made no direct contribution to the husband's family wealth, she was awarded approximately £10 million, despite claiming £122 million.

Unease at the inequality of outcome which such an approach could produce led to some tentative attempts to escape the approach in some cases, where, at least, the facts enabled the court to focus on some factor other than 'needs' or requirements as of significance. Thus, in *Gojkovic v Gojkovic*[424] the husband and wife had, by dint of their efforts, built up a hotel and property business worth over £4 million. The Court of Appeal held that the wife's substantial contribution to the development of the family business should be recognised and upheld the award of a lump sum of £1 million to the wife, which she intended to use to acquire and run her own hotel. In the later case of *Conran v Conran*,[425] Wilson J described as 'in every sense outstanding' the wife's contributions over 30 years in helping to develop the husband's 'Habitat' furniture stores and restaurants, her work and reputation as a nationally recognised cookery writer and journalist and her other family contributions. The judge considered the correct approach would be to assess the wife's reasonable requirements without reference to her contributions, and then to bring the latter into the balance. From the husband's total wealth of some £85 million, the wife was awarded £8.4 million for her 'reasonable requirements' and a further £2.1 million for her 'contributions'.[426]

Butler-Sloss LJ acknowledged in *Dart v Dart*[427] that the courts may have given too much weight to an assessment of a spouse's 'reasonable requirements' over and above the other criteria set out in s 25 of the Matrimonial Causes Act 1973, with the result, in 'big money' cases, that awards may have been 'over-modest'. She suggested that any change should be a matter for the legislature, but the House of Lords took the initiative in *White v White*.[428] Noting that the term 'reasonable requirements' does not appear in the statute itself, the House firmly rejected this approach as discriminatory, since, by limiting the wife's share to her 'reasonable requirements' (however generously interpreted) it enabled the husband to keep all of the surplus assets, regardless of the contributions that the wife might have made during the marriage.[429] Since this decision, it has been accepted that an award should not be limited to the dependent spouse's reasonable requirements, if there are surplus assets available to be shared.

One common feature of 'big-money' cases first made its appearance in *Duxbury v Duxbury*,[430] where *Preston* was followed to the extent that a capital sum was ordered which would produce an annual income of £28,000 (a figure calculated on the basis of *Preston* suitably adjusted to take account of inflation) which was thought to be a reasonable sum to preserve a luxurious standard of living. The firm of accountants who acted for the wife devised a sophisticated computer program, designed to take account of a number of

---

£12,000 for telephone bills and £4,000 to keep a Labrador. In *C v C (Financial Relief: Short Marriage)* [1997] 2 FLR 26, CA Ward LJ suggested the court should adopt a 'broad brush' approach in the determination of at least certain items of budgeted expenditure which a claimant spouse produces.

[423] [1996] 2 FLR 286, CA.   [424] Above. See also *White v White* [1998] 2 FLR 310, CA.
[425] [1997] 2 FLR 615.   [426] See further below at p 1044.
[427] [1996] 2 FLR 286, CA at p 305F–G.   [428] [2001] 1 AC 596.
[429] Ibid at p 608F–G. See further below p 1044.   [430] [1992] Fam 62n, CA.

financial and other variables, including life expectancy, inflation, tax, investment return and capital growth to produce an estimate of the lump sum required to meet the recipient's needs for life.[431] This so-called '*Duxbury* calculation' has been used by the courts as a helpful guide to the assessment of the requirements of a wife whose husband is wealthy.[432] However, as Butler-Sloss LJ explained in *Gojkovic v Gojkovic*,[433] it ought not to be elevated to a rigid arithmetical calculation; each case must be decided upon its own facts, and in accordance with the principles set out in s 25 of the Matrimonial Causes Act. Moreover, it may produce the '*Duxbury* paradox', whereby 'the longer the marriage and hence the older the wife, the less the capital sum required for a *Duxbury* type fund'.[434] As Lord Nicholls noted in *White v White*,[435]

'financial needs are only one of the factors to be taken into account in arriving at the amount of an award. The amount of capital required to provide for an older wife's financial needs may well be less than the amount required to provide for a younger wife's financial needs. It by no means follows that, in a case where resources exceed the parties' financial needs, the older wife's award will be less than the younger wife's. Indeed, the older wife's award may be substantially larger.'[436]

And he added that although a wish to leave money to one's children is not a financial 'need' within s 25(2)(b), the judge is entitled to have it in mind when arriving at a final figure, should the parties' assets permit.

(c) 'The standard of living enjoyed by the family before the breakdown of the marriage'

This factor overlaps with consideration of the parties' needs, discussed above. It is particularly important when substantial assets are available and one of the spouses has been living at a much higher level than he or she did before the marriage.[437] In *Calderbank v Calderbank*[438] the wife, a relatively rich woman, was ordered to pay a lump sum to the husband (who had no capital and had remarried) so that he might buy a house suitable to the former spouses' ways of life in which he might see his children. But neither party's standard of living should be raised above what it otherwise would have been, for

---

[431] For a further explanation by the program's inventor, see Lawrence '*Duxbury* Disclosure and Other Matters' [1990] Fam Law 12.

[432] See eg *S v S (Financial Provision) (Post Divorce Cohabitation)* [1994] 2 FLR 228; *H v H (Financial Relief: Costs)* [1997] 2 FLR 57. A simplified version of the *Duxbury* tables is published in a booklet produced annually by the Family Law Bar Association entitled 'At a Glance'.

[433] [1992] Fam 40, CA at 48. A similar approach was taken by Ward J in *B v B (Financial Provision)* [1990] 1 FLR 20 who discusses the limitations and restrictions of the '*Duxbury* calculation' and the dangers of its 'unblinkered application'. See also *Newton v Newton* [1990] 1 FLR 33, CA.

[434] Per Holman J in *White v White* at first instance, cited by Lord Nicholls of Birkenhead at [2001] 1 AC 596 at p 609C.

[435] Ibid p 609.

[436] See also *A v A (Duxbury Calculations)* [1999] 3 FCR 433: husband's contribution to 40-year marriage should be recognised by more than a *Duxbury* award.

[437] See eg *Dart v Dart* [1996] 2 FLR 286; *F v F (Ancillary Relief: Substantial Assets)* [1995] 2 FLR 45; *R v R (Financial Provision: Reasonable Needs)* [1994] 2 FLR 1044; *McFarlane v McFarlane; Parlour v Parlour* [2004] EWCA Civ 872, [2005] Fam 171.

[438] [1976] Fam 93, CA. See also *H v H (Financial Provision: Conduct)* [1998] 1 FLR 971, in which the children's welfare required that the husband—the family's 'poor relation'—should have a home they could regard as belonging to him.

this would in effect mean that the order was being used as a means of punishing the other.[439]

(d) 'The age of each party and the duration of the marriage'

Short marriages

This must be looked at in conjunction with the contribution made by each of them to the welfare of the family (considered below). Before *White v White*,[440] a spouse seeking provision after a short marriage could generally expect much less favourable terms than one who was divorcing after years of married life: she would have made less of a contribution to the family than a wife of long-standing.[441] However, even then, the particular needs and circumstances of the spouses had, of course, to be taken into account. If the breakdown of the marriage had caused a spouse financial loss or other hardship, she could expect a substantial order in her favour.[442] In *C v C (Financial Relief: Short Marriage)*,[443] for example, the Court of Appeal upheld an award 'at the very top of the bracket' where a marriage had broken down after just nine months, but there was a small child and the wife's fragile health had been seriously impaired by the marriage breakdown, and her prospects of successful medical treatment and her future earning capacity were uncertain.

However, since the House of Lords' decision in *White v White*, with its emphasis on non-discrimination and the yardstick of equality, there has been some uncertainty in how to assess the significance of the length of the marriage. In *GW v RW (Financial Provision: Departure from Equality)*[444] the judge found it 'fundamentally unfair to be required to find that a party who has made domestic contributions during a marriage of 12 years should be awarded the same proportion of the assets as a party who has made the domestic contributions for a period in excess of 20 years.'[445] He accordingly awarded the wife 40% of the assets. The judge was influenced by John Eekelaaar's argument that the:

'length of the marriage is relevant, in and of itself . . . to the amount allocated because it is

---

[439] See *Attwood v Attwood* [1968] P 591 at 595. Compare *H v H (Clean Break: Non Disclosure: Costs)* [1994] 2 FLR 309 where the wife lived frugally during the early years of the marriage with a view to long-term security. The judge held that while it would be wrong to penalise the wife for her frugality, nonetheless the standard of living during the marriage had to be taken into account. He assessed the wife's income requirements at £35,000 per annum, rather than the £46,000 for which the wife had argued. But cf *A v A (Financial Provision)* [1998] 2 FLR 180, where the family's past relatively simple lifestyle was not regarded as determining entirely the wife's future standard of living, which should reflect the reality of the husband's substantial wealth.

[440] [2001] 1 AC 596.

[441] In *Browne v Pritchard* [1975] 3 All ER 721, CA, the wife's half-share in the matrimonial home (to the purchase of which she had contributed nothing) was reduced to a third after a marriage which lasted only three years. In *Hobhouse v Hobhouse* [1999] 1 FLR 961, the marriage lasted four years and was childless. Both parties had inherited the bulk of their wealth: the husband had assets of around £8.5 million and the wife £500,000 with the prospect of a further £1.5 million on her mother's death. The wife was awarded a lump sum of £175,000 to enable her to re-establish her financial independence and return to her home in Australia.

[442] *Whyte-Smith v Whyte-Smith* (1974) 5 Fam Law 20 (separation after three months; breakdown caused wife illness and loss of job); *Abdureman v Abdureman* (1978) 122 Sol Jo 663 (separation after 12 weeks; wife had given up job and lost pension on marriage).

[443] [1997] 2 FLR 26, CA.   [444] [2003] EWHC 611 (Fam), [2003] 2 FLR 108.

[445] Ibid at para 43. See also *Leadbeater v Leadbeater* [1985] FLR 789: 25% should be discounted from the sum that was thought appropriate to meet the wife's reasonable needs since the marriage had been short, lasting only four years.

defensible to hold that parties who share their lives together *earn a share in one another's assets relative to the length of time they have shared their lives.*'[446]

One of the difficulties with this approach is in determining at what point the claimant spouse has 'earned' a full share of the available assets. The American Law Institute has fixed on the 20-year point as appropriate[447] and this was accordingly also adopted by the judge in *GW v RW*. But it is unclear why 20 years is a better target figure than 10, or 25, or any other. Nor does it follow that an equal share is necessarily inappropriate after a short marriage. In *Foster v Foster*[448] the parties were married for four years, and both had contributed what they could from their incomes to buying up properties for development and resale. The wife earned twice as much as the husband and had put much more capital into acquiring the properties than he had. She argued that this should be reflected in her share of the assets on divorce. The Court of Appeal held that where the capital surplus had been generated by the parties' joint efforts, it should not matter whether it had taken them a short or long time to build this up, and its division should be based on what was fair.[449] The court stressed that spouses may earn unequal amounts, but that these should not be *valued* as of unequal worth, just as non-financial contributions to welfare, through home-making and child care, should not be valued as of less worth than financial contributions.[450] This is a crucial point. If the reason for not valuing domestic contributions as inherently of less value than those of a financial nature is to avoid gender discrimination, then giving weight to the durational element is arguably as discriminatory to women as the previous 'reasonable requirements' approach, since it will usually be the wife who is seeking a share of the assets generated or owned by the husband and who therefore has to prove she has 'earned' her share. Moreover, it would surely be wrong, given the clear lack of priorities in s 25(2), to regard duration of the marriage as of greater significance than other factors, just as it was wrong to focus on a party's 'reasonable requirements' as setting a ceiling on her fair share of the assets.

In *Miller v Miller*[451] as we have noted, the marriage had lasted less than three years. The House of Lords agreed with the Court of Appeal that older cases which had focused on arriving at awards that enabled the wife to 'get back on her feet'[452] after a short marriage should no longer be followed, and that the approach taken in *Foster* is correct. As Lord Nicholls put it, 'A short marriage is no less a partnership of equals than a long marriage.'[453] Nonetheless, as we have seen above,[454] both he and Baroness Hale recognised that there is an 'instinctive feeling'[455] or 'perception'[456] that the parties have less of a claim upon each other after a short marriage and one might therefore expect that equal shares may be less appropriate as the outcome.

A further problem with focusing on the duration of the marriage is that this ignores the

---

[446] J Eekelaar, 'Asset Distribution on Divorce—The Durational Element' (2001) 117 LQR 552 at 556. See also J Eekelaar 'Asset Distribution on Divorce—Time and Property' [2003] Fam Law 828.

[447] *Principles of the Law of Family Dissolution: Tentative Draft No 4* (2000).

[448] [2003] EWCA Civ 565, [2003] 2 FLR 299.   [449] Ibid at para 19.

[450] Ibid at para 18. See below p 1044. However, the Court did not in fact award the spouses equal shares, but reinstated the trial judge's division of 61% to the wife and 39% to the husband.

[451] Heard with *McFarlane v McFarlane* [2006] UKHL 24, [2006] All ER 1. Discussed above at p 1027.

[452] *Robertson v Robertson* (1982) 4 FLR 387 at 392 per Balcombe J.   [453] At para 17.

[454] At pp 1031–2.   [455] Per Lord Nicholls at para 24.   [456] Per Baroness Hale at para 147.

parties' future lives. In *B v B (Mesher Order)*,[457] Munby J upheld a lump sum payment of £175,000 to the wife and periodical payments of unlimited duration, after a marriage lasting just 10 months. The marriage had produced a child, whom the wife would have the burden of caring for in the future, and this would accordingly impede her ability to accumulate capital and income for years to come. The husband had argued that the wife's periodical payments should cease on the child's fifth birthday and that he should have a charge on the house to be realised when the child had ceased education[458] but the uncertainty of the wife's future circumstances led the judge to conclude that such limitations would result in a settlement unfair to the wife. One could also argue that the wife's *future* contribution to the welfare of the child created by the marriage would be of greater significance than the time she had spent with the husband during that marriage.[459]

Measuring duration

This leads to another issue—what *is* the duration of the marriage? The court will take notice of the de facto, rather than de jure, length of the marriage, ie the length of time the parties lived together up to the point of separation.[460] However, a question of increasing importance is whether, and if so how, the court is to pay regard to the length of any *pre-marital* cohabitation between the parties? Is not this also part of the 'de facto' length of the marriage? With pre-marital cohabitation becoming the norm, it can be argued that earlier case-law which rejected this view[461] has become outmoded.

It might be thought that it would not be possible for the court to include such a period under this factor, which states clearly that it refers to the length of the *marriage*. But in *GW v RW*[462] the judge considered that:

'where a relationship moves seamlessly from cohabitation to marriage without any major alteration in the way the couple live, it is unreal and artificial to treat the periods differently. On the other hand, if it is found that the pre-marital cohabitation was on the basis of a trial period to see if there is any basis for later marriage then I would be of the view that it would not be right to include it as part of the "duration of the marriage".'[463]

He accordingly included the parties' 18 months of pre-marital cohabitation in his calculation of the duration of the marriage.[464] Aside from the difficulty of assessing whether any given period of cohabitation was 'seamless' with the marriage on the one hand, or a 'trial

---

[457] [2002] EWHC 3106 (Fam), [2003] 2 FLR 285.   [458] Known as a *Mesher* order: see below p 1053.

[459] See also *McFarlane v McFarlane; Parlour v Parlour*[[2004] EWCA Civ 872, [2005] Fam 171 and *Re G (Financial Provision: Liberty to Restore Application for Lump Sum)* [2004] EWHC 88 (Fam), [2004] 1 FLR 997 for a similar approach.

[460] See *Krystman v Krystman* [1973] 3 All ER 247, CA: no order made when the parties had cohabited for only a fortnight at the beginning of a marriage which had taken place 26 years earlier. See R Deech 'Financial Relief: The Retreat from Precedent and Principle' (1982) 98 LQR 621 at 630–2.

[461] See *Campbell v Campbell* [1976] Fam 347; *Foley v Foley* [1981] Fam 160; but cf *Kokosinski v Kokosinski* [1980] Fam 72, discussed below.

[462] [2003] EWHC 611 (Fam) [2003] 2 FLR 108. For a critique, see S Gilmore, 'Duration of Marriage *and* Seamless Preceding Cohabitation?' [2004] Fam Law 205. See also the useful survey of the case law by J Edwards, 'Duration of Marriage: From "I Do", "I Promise" or "I May"?' [2004] Fam Law 726.

[463] At para 33.

[464] In fact, he regarded it as cancelled out by the 18 months that followed from the issue of the divorce petition until the decree: para 34.

marriage' instead on the other, there is also the objection that the judge not only ignored clear earlier case law but also the plain words of the statute.

A better approach, it is submitted, is to consider pre-marital cohabitation either as part of 'all the circumstances of the case' to which the court must have regard under s 25(1), or as relevant to weighing a party's contribution to the welfare of the family under s 25(2)(f), or as 'conduct' under s25(2)(g). For example, in *Kokosinski v Kokosinski*[465] the husband was a Polish refugee who had lived in this country since the Second World War. He started to live with the petitioner in 1947 and a son was born in 1950. He could not marry her until his first wife (who was still living in Poland) divorced him, which she did not do until 1969. In the meantime the petitioner had been loving, faithful and hardworking, had brought up their child and had played a substantial part in building up the husband's business. The parties married in 1971 but separated in the following year. Wood J was of the opinion that in these circumstances it would offend a reasonable person's sense of justice to ignore this long period of cohabitation and took it into account in deciding what order to make, either as part of all the circumstances, or as 'conduct'.[466] More recently, in *Co v Co (Ancillary Relief: Pre-marital Cohabitation)*[467] Coleridge J took account of eight years' cohabitation prior to a four-year marriage, commenting that:

'Committed, settled relationships which often endure for years in the context of cohabitation (often but not always with children) outside marriage must, I think, be regarded as every bit as valid as those where parties have made the same degree of commitment but recorded it publicly by civil registration, ie by marriage. This has nothing to do with morality or religious belief and everything to do with striving to achieve financial fairness as between a couple at a particular stage in society's development. . . . Section 25 is concerned with taking into account the reality of a couple's circumstances and situation during their relationship. It is concerned with establishing fact not fiction in all areas including the financial. To ignore such a factor as cohabitation would lead the court to be considering the case on an untrue basis and almost inevitably lead to unfairness.'[468]

He therefore regarded it as part of the circumstances of the case or, if it were necessary to fit it within one of the specific factors, as part of 'contribution' or 'conduct'.

This issue may arise in particular in relation to civil partnerships. Just as was the case in *Kokosinski v Kokosinksi*[469] civil partners will have been prevented from obtaining legal recognition of their relationships and thus cannot build up a long duration post-registration for several years to come, but many may have lived together for a long time.

---

[465] [1980] Fam 72. The facts are not dissimilar from those which would entitle a cohabitant to an order under the Inheritance (Provision for Family and Dependants) Act 1975 after the man's death. See below, p 1108.

[466] See also *Gojkovic v Gojkovic* [1992] Fam 40, [1990] 2 All ER 84, where the substantial award to the wife was in large part based upon her outstanding contribution to the family business and much of her effort was made during pre-marital cohabitation.

[467] [2004] EWHC 287 (Fam), [2004] 1 FLR 1095.

[468] Ibid at paras 44–6. See also *M v M (Financial Relief: Substantial Earning Capacity)* [2004] EWHC 688 (Fam), [2004] 2 FLR 236: 'in modern society it is a couple's commitment to each other by cohabiting that is the relevant start date for consideration in most cases' *per* Baron J at para 55. Cf *Miller v Miller* (above), where the couple did not cohabit before the wedding. The Court of Appeal considered that the wife's 'commitment' to the marriage began when the parties became engaged and the length of that engagement was a relevant factor in determining the award to her. The House of Lords did not disagree with this view.

[469] [1980] Fam 72.

One would expect the courts to adopt Coleridge J's approach to ensure that a fair settlement is nonetheless achieved.[470]

A different problem arose in *Chaterjee v Chaterjee*,[471] where the parties lived together for 12 or 13 years *after* being divorced. Following their final separation the wife pursued a claim for financial relief. It was held that this cohabitation was akin to marriage for this purpose and consequently that the court could deal with property acquired since the divorce. In *Hill v Hill*[472] the Court of Appeal allowed a 'wife' to seek further financial relief, over 25 years after the parties had divorced, and during which period they had cohabited. Just as the court could take pre-marital cohabitation into account in the appropriate circumstances, so too could it consider a period of post-divorce cohabitation in arriving at a reasonable and just solution.

(e) 'Any physical or mental disability of either of the parties to the marriage'

In practice, these issues are subsumed under the other heads in s 25, especially, of course, that referring to the parties' needs. For example, in *C v C (Financial Provision: Personal Damages)*,[473] as noted above, a husband who was rendered paraplegic in a car accident was deemed to need all of the damages awarded to him in a structured settlement, and thus his wife and child received nothing, notwithstanding their dependence upon social security benefits.

(f) 'The contributions which each of the parties has made or is likely in the foreseeable future to make to the welfare of the family, including any contribution by looking after the home or caring for the family'

It is expressly provided that this is to include any contribution made by looking after the home or caring for the family, but it includes a financial contribution, such as by means of an inheritance, as well.[474] This principle enables the court to recognise the contribution of a spouse to the family business,[475] but it was primarily introduced to give the wife credit for her contribution in kind as housekeeper, wife and mother[476] and has been exceptionally important in this regard. This is first because it marks out a different approach to how provision should be made for a spouse as compared with the more rigid rules governing property law[477] and secondly because, since *White v White*[478] the evaluation of

---

[470] See M Harper et al, *Civil Partnership—The New Law* (2005) paras 5.19, 7.31.

[471] [1976] Fam 199, CA. See also *S v S (Financial Provision) (Post Divorce Cohabitation)* [1994] 2 FLR 228.

[472] [1998] 1 FLR 198, CA, doubted in *Hewitson v Hewitson* [1995] 1 FLR 241, CA. While noting 'as a matter of policy' that a cohabitant should not have the equivalent rights of a wife, or former wife, the court pointed to another policy issue—that of encouraging reconciliation—which (in this case) meant that the parties' children had been brought up by them both, in a settled home.

[473] [1995] 2 FLR 171. See above, p 1033 n 379.

[474] So held by Ormrod LJ in *P v P* [1978] 3 All ER 70 at 74, CA. See also *Norris v Norris* [2002] EWHC 2996 (Fam), [2003] 1 FLR 1142.

[475] *Gojkovic v Gojkovic* [1992] Fam 40, CA. See also *Conran v Conran* [1997] 2 FLR 615 discussed above at p 1038, where the wife's contribution to helping the husband's business to succeed was indirect but 'outstanding'.

[476] See eg *Duxbury v Duxbury* [1992] Fam 62n, CA (a wife who had done 'everything expected of her as a wife and mother' was entitled to have her contribution recognised by the court). See also *Vicary v Vicary* [1992] 2 FLR 271, CA, where the wife's lump sum was assessed by reference to her acting as an 'unimpeachable wife and mother', enabling the husband to concentrate on his business activities.

[477] See above pp 153–73.   [478] [2001] 1 AC 596.

'contributions' has become steadily more non-discriminatory towards women. It is important to trace this development.

Initially, after the House of Lords' decision, there was an attempt, at first by respondents, to justify a departure from the 'yardstick of equality' on the basis that one spouse had made a bigger contribution to the welfare of the family than the other. This might be shown by, for example, bringing money into the marriage, from which the family business was built up[479] or by the particular business acumen displayed by the husband. In *Cowan v Cowan*[480] for example, the husband spotted the potential of plastic bin liners in revolutionising waste collection and disposal and set up companies to supply and market these to local authorities and supermarkets. The Court of Appeal awarded the wife 38% of the combined assets, justifying their departure from equality by virtue of the husband's special business talent, described by his counsel as a 'stellar' contribution. This ruling led to a number of cases where the spouses argued over whether or not the husband could be said to have been exceptionally gifted in business.[481] In *L v L (Financial Provision: Contributions)*[482] the wife was awarded only 37% of the assets, the husband being characterised as having made a special or exceptional contribution through his business, although 'he was not a genius'. By contrast, in *H-J v H-J (Financial Provision: Equality)*[483] and *G v G (Financial Provision: Equal Division)*[484] Coleridge J declined to regard one spouse's contribution as greater than the other, regarding attempts to distinguish between the spouses as contrary to the principles underlying *White v White* and as opening 'a forensic Pandora's box'.[485] The matter was resolved when *L v L* went on appeal as *Lambert v Lambert*.[486] The Court of Appeal firmly attempted to close Pandora's box to forestall further attempts to distinguish, apart from in the most exceptional of cases, between the different contributions of the spouses. Thorpe LJ commented:

'the danger of gender discrimination resulting from a finding of special financial contribution is plain. If all that is regarded is the scale of the breadwinner's success then discrimination is almost bound to follow since there is no equal opportunity for the homemaker to demonstrate the scale of her comparable success. Examples cited of the mother who cares for a handicapped child seem to me both theoretical and distasteful. Such sacrifices and achievements are the product of love and commitment and are not to be counted in cash. The more driven the breadwinner the less available will he be physically and emotionally both as a husband and a father.'[487]

In awarding the wife 50% of the combined assets, the court held that, once the trial judge had rejected the argument that the husband was a business genius, and had accepted that

---

[479] As in *White v White* itself, where the husband's father lent the couple money to help acquire the first of their farms. See also *Dharamshi v Dharamshi* [2001] 1 FLR 736.

[480] [2001] EWCA Civ 679, [2002] Fam 97.

[481] Or, in *Norris v Norris* [2002] EWHC 2996 (Fam), [2003] 1 FLR 1142, whether the contribution of the wife, both in lending her inherited wealth to the husband's business and looking after the child of the marriage, could be regarded as exceptional.

[482] [2002] 1 FLR 642.   [483] [2002] 1 FLR 415.

[484] [2002] EWHC 1339 (Fam), [2002] 2 FLR 1143.   [485] Ibid at para 34.

[486] [2002] EWCA Civ 1685, [2003] 1 FLR 139. See D Hodson with M Green and N De Souza, '*Lambert—Shutting Pandora's Box*' [2003] Fam Law 37; DJ G Brasse, '*Lambert v Lambert*—Pandora's Hostage to Fortune' [2003] Fam Law 101; R Bailey-Harris, '*Lambert v Lambert*—Towards the recognition of marriage as a partnership of equals' [2003] CFLQ 417.

[487] Ibid at para 45.

the wife could not have done any more to contribute to the welfare of the family, he should not have elevated the husband's contribution above that of the wife. Since *Lambert*, it may be said that the spouses' contributions are more likely to be regarded as being of equal worth, regardless of the form they have taken, and an equal division of surplus assets is becoming more common.[488] In *Miller v Miller; McFarlane v McFarlane*[489] their Lordships agreed that the correct approach is to regard contribution as a factor pointing away from equality of division only when it would be inequitable to do otherwise. In so holding, they drew, as will be seen below, on the approach taken to 'conduct' under s 25(2)(g).

An example, perhaps, of this approach may be found in *Sorrell v Sorrell*.[490] There, the husband was an exceptionally talented businessman who had built up the family assets to over £100 million. The marriage had lasted for 32 years and the wife had brought up the three children. The court held that she should not receive half, but 40%, of the assets: in order to achieve fairness, recognition of the husband's exceptional and individual qualities must be given. Yet one may ask, how could a housewife and mother ever match the husband's opportunity to mark his worth? Does this ruling not fall into precisely the trap of gender discrimination identified by Thorpe LJ in *Lambert v Lambert*?

As noted above,[491] when civil partnerships come to be dissolved, it may be even harder to distinguish between the parties' respective contributions.

What of the case, however, where one spouse has *not* made a contribution (or any sufficient contribution) to the welfare of the family? Should he or she be penalised by being awarded a reduced settlement? In *H v H*[492] a wife who had left her husband for another man after 15 years of married life and bringing up four children was given a smaller award on the ground that she had 'left the job unfinished' and in *E v E (Financial Provision)*[493] it was said that the wife, who had committed adultery, had made a negative, or minimal, contribution. But in *W v W*[494] Wilson J held that such terms are unhelpful when weighing each spouse's contribution under s 25(2)(f) and should be raised, if at all, as 'conduct' under s 25(2)(g).[495] He accordingly attached no weight to the husband's allegation that the wife, who was a recovering alcoholic, had made a 'negative contribution' during her years of drinking.

Finally, it will be noted that the enjoinder to consider what contributions each party is likely to make in the foreseeable future was introduced as a result of the amendment by the Matrimonial and Family Proceedings Act 1984 s 3. It is intended to emphasise in particular the continuing role a parent (usually the mother) may have in looking after any children of the family although it will usually be counter-balanced by the other parent's ongoing duty to support the children financially so that the parties' contributions

---

[488] See eg *Norris v Norris* (above); *C v C (Variation of Post-Nuptial Settlement: Company Shares)* [2003] EWHC 1222 (Fam), [2003] 2 FLR 493. One would certainly expect a wife such as Lady Conran to obtain a significantly higher proportion of the assets than she did in *Conran v Conran* [1997] 2 FLR 615, discussed above at p 1038.

[489] [2006] UKHL 24, [2006] 3 All ER 1. See Lord Nicholls at para 68 and Baroness Hale at para 146.

[490] [2005] EWHC 1717 (Fam), [2006] 1 FLR 497.   [491] See p 1030.

[492] [1975] Fam 9; cf *West v West* [1978] Fam 1, CA.   [493] [1990] 2 FLR 233.

[494] [2001] Fam Law 656.   [495] See below pp 1047–51.

continue to be regarded as of equal worth. It may, however, be a useful counterweight to any contention that there should be an immediate clean break.[496]

(g) 'The conduct of each of the parties, if that conduct is such that it would in the opinion of the court be inequitable to disregard it'

The extent to which the court should take a spouse's conduct during the marriage into account when assessing what order should be made, is understandably an emotionally charged issue. Yet even before 1971, when the substantive law was based upon the concept of matrimonial fault, there had been a tendency by the courts, when hearing undefended cases, to place much less stress on the technical finding of innocence or guilt. When irretrievable breakdown became the sole ground for divorce in 1971, conduct arguably became of much less significance. The law was subject to further change in 1984 and again in 1996, although the latter amendment, contained in the Family Law Act, has not been implemented.[497]

The law before the 1984 reform

Under s 25 as originally enacted, the court was directed, inter alia, to exercise its powers so:

'. . . to place the parties, so far as it is practicable and, *having regard to their conduct just to do so*, in the financial position in which they would have been if the marriage had not broken down and each had properly discharged his or her financial obligation and responsibilities towards the other.'[498]

It soon became apparent that 'conduct' should not often be taken into account. The basic principle was established in the leading case, *Wachtel v Wachtel*,[499] in which Lord Denning MR, delivering the judgment of the court, said:[500]

'It has been suggested that there should be a "discount" or "reduction" in what the wife is to receive because of her supposed misconduct, guilt or blame (whatever word is used). We cannot accept this argument. In the vast majority of cases it is repugnant to the principles underlying the new legislation . . . There will be many cases in which a wife (though once considered guilty or blameworthy) will have cared for the home and looked after the family for many years. Is she to be deprived of the benefit otherwise to be accorded to her by s 25(1)(f) because she may share responsibility for the breakdown with her husband? There will no doubt be a residue of cases where the conduct of one of the parties is . . . "both obvious and gross", so much so that to order one party to support another whose conduct falls into this category is repugnant to anyone's sense of justice. In such a case the court remains free to decline to afford financial support or to reduce the support which it would otherwise have ordered. But, short of cases falling into this category, the court should not reduce its order for financial provision merely because of what was formerly regarded as guilt or blame. To do so would be to impose a fine for supposed misbehaviour in the course of an unhappy married life . . . In the financial adjustments consequent upon the dissolution of a marriage which has irretrievably broken down, the imposition of financial penalties ought seldom to find a place.'

---

[496] A deferred clean break may still be desirable, however.
[497] Family Law Act 1996, s 66(1), Sch 8, Pt I, para 9(2).   [498] Emphasis added.
[499] [1973] Fam 72, CA.   [500] At 90.

In brief, conduct would not affect the order made unless it would be offensive to one's sense of justice to ignore it.[501]

In view of the above, it is hardly surprising that conduct was rarely taken into account. Matrimonial misconduct such as adultery was usually ignored,[502] as were 'brief periods of callous unkindness or brutality'.[503] But of course there were some cases where conduct was held to be relevant.[504] Amongst reported cases, the wife's share was reduced where she had accepted a half-share of the matrimonial home whilst carrying on an adulterous affair,[505] where she had fired a shotgun at her husband,[506] and where she had twice wounded her husband and damaged his career by her behaviour.[507]

The law after the 1984 reform

In 1984, with the removal of the status quo ideal or minimal loss principle,[508] conduct was reintroduced as a new s 25(2)(g) of the Matrimonial Causes Act 1973.[509] The court was directed to have regard to 'the conduct of each of the parties, if that conduct is such that it would in the opinion of the court be inequitable to disregard it'.

It could have been said that, since conduct now stood as a separate circumstance to which the court had 'in particular' to have regard, not only did it have a higher profile (though that was the necessary drafting consequence of the removal of the 'tail piece' of the original s 25) but it had been given greater statutory emphasis. In the event, however, there was no change in practice. In one reported case, *Anthony v Anthony*,[510] where the trial judge took conduct into account because, in his view, the wife 'broke up the marriage', the Court of Appeal held that there was nothing in her conduct of such a serious nature as to justify any reliance upon it. In *Leadbeater v Leadbeater*,[511] conduct was again dismissed as an issue, in part because each spouse's conduct cancelled the other's out, but mainly because the judge did not think it inequitable to ignore it. In *Le Foe v Le Foe and Woolwich plc; Woolwich plc v Le Foe and Le Foe*[512] by contrast, the husband's conduct, in mortgaging the matrimonial home without the wife's knowledge in order to use the funds to put into another home in which he planned to move with his mistress, was taken into account, by leaving the husband to bear the debt and ensuring that the wife still received the amount (around £650,000) that she would have received were there no such liability.

---

[501] Per Orr LJ in *Jones v Jones* [1976] Fam 8 at 15, CA.

[502] See eg *Trippas v Trippas* [1973] Fam 134, CA, and *Harnett v Harnett* [1974] 1 All ER 764, CA.

[503] *Griffiths v Griffiths* [1974] 1 All ER 932.

[504] See also *Kokosinski v Kokosinski* [1980] Fam 72 where 'good' conduct was taken into account.

[505] *Cuzner v Underdown* [1974] 2 All ER 351, CA (wife ordered to transfer the half-share to husband).

[506] *Armstrong v Armstrong* (1974) 4 Fam Law 156, CA (wife's share reduced to a quarter). A comparison of this case with the last suggests that the courts look more leniently on a wife who intends to inflict serious injury on a husband than on one who is unfaithful!

[507] *Bateman v Bateman* [1979] Fam 25.　　　[508] See above, p 1020.

[509] As a result of an amendment made under the Matrimonial and Family Proceedings Act 1984 s 3.

[510] [1986] 2 FLR 353, CA.

[511] [1985] FLR 789; cf *Suter v Suter and Jones* [1987] Fam 111, CA, where there is some suggestion that introducing a lover into the former matrimonial home could be taken into account under s 25(2)(g); but contrast *Duxbury v Duxbury* [1992] Fam 62n, CA where Ackner LJ said that applying s 25 is essentially a 'financial not a moral exercise'.

[512] [2001] 2 FLR 970.

Perhaps the leading authority is *Kyte v Kyte*,[513] where the husband suffered from manic depression, which caused the wife suffering and unhappiness. On several occasions the husband tried, unsuccessfully, to commit suicide. The registrar found that on one of these occasions the wife (who knew she stood to inherit on the husband's death) did nothing to stop him. On another she provided drugs and alcohol to facilitate the attempt. The wife had also formed 'a deceitful relationship' with another man. In the Court of Appeal, Purchas LJ (giving the judgment of the court) said[514] that the court must look at the whole picture, including conduct during the marriage and after the marriage which might or might not have contributed to the breakdown. Although the parties may not each have been blameless, a spouse should only be penalised where the imbalance of conduct, one way or the other, would make it inequitable to ignore the comparative conduct of the parties. On this basis, the wife's behaviour (even when considered in the context of the husband's) was gross and obvious and so her lump sum award was reduced from £14,000 to just £5,000.

Where one spouse commits a criminal offence against the other, conduct, unsurprisingly, will be taken into account. In *Evans v Evans*,[515] for example, the Court of Appeal upheld the discharge of a periodical payments order in favour of a wife when she was convicted of inciting others to kill her husband. In *H v H (Financial Relief: Attempted Murder as Conduct)*[516] the husband stabbed the wife so severely that the trial judge regarded her survival as miraculous. She was granted the entire equity in the former matrimonial home and the rest of the parties' assets, apart from the husband's personal belongings, in exchange for his receiving a lump sum of £30,000, so that she could have a secure future free from financial worry or pressure.

A perhaps unduly merciful approach was taken, however, in *Clark v Clark*.[517] The wife, in her forties and in debt, married the husband, a wealthy man aged nearly 80. During the six-year marriage, which was never consummated, she induced the husband to purchase properties which were put in her name, introduced her lover into the house and confined the husband to a caravan in the grounds, and then a part of the house. The trial judge considered that, although the wife's conduct was inequitable to disregard, it would be unduly harsh to leave her with nothing and he also noted the husband's generosity to her during the marriage. He awarded her a lump sum of around £500,000 out of the husband's worth of £2.5 million. The Court of Appeal commented that it would be hard to conceive of a case of graver marital misconduct and noted that to have left the wife with nothing would not have exceeded the wide ambit of judicial discretion. They nonetheless awarded the wife £175,000, to which the husband had been prepared to agree.

The misconduct may be aimed at the spouse in his or her capacity as a parent of the children of the marriage, rather than directly against him or her. For example, abduction of the children of the marriage has also been held to be conduct that it would be

---

[513] [1988] Fam 145, CA.   [514] At 155.
[515] [1989] 1 FLR 351, CA. See also *H v H (Financial Provision: Conduct)* [1994] 2 FLR 801 (husband's conduct in brutally assaulting wife taken into account) and *A v A (Financial Provision: Conduct)* [1995] 1 FLR 345 (husband's assault upon wife was conduct which was taken into account but not so as to deprive the husband of all his capital).
[516] [2005] EWHC 2911 (Fam), [2006] 1 FLR 990.   [517] [1999] 2 FLR 498, CA.

inequitable to disregard. In *Al Khatib v Masry*[518] Munby J held that the husband's conduct in abducting the children and 'depriving them and the wife of that most basic human right, their mutual society, falls squarely within the class of case contemplated by Parliament when enacting s 25(2)(g) of the 1973 Act.'[519]

It should be noted that the conduct to which the court may have regard is not restricted to that in relation to the breakdown of the marriage: it also embraces conduct in the context of the ancillary relief proceedings themselves. Whilst misconduct in the proceedings is usually reflected in the court's order for costs,[520] on occasion it influences the amount of the award the court makes. For example, in *Al Khatib v Masry*[521] the husband also refused to file a Form E or any other formal evidence, would not answer questions and refused to attend court. Transactions purporting to transfer shares in properties were found to be shams. When he finally did file a Form E, the wife was able to identify a number of specific instances of non-disclosure and inconsistency. The husband's wealth was therefore estimated at comfortably in excess of £50 million, of which the wife was awarded £23 million.[522]

On numerous occasions in the debates on the Family Law Bill the concern was expressed that the courts were reluctant to take into account conduct in relation to the making of financial and property orders. An amendment to s 25(2)(g) was passed, in an attempt '. . . to emphasise that conduct of the parties of whatever nature, should it be inequitable for the court to disregard it, has to be considered and that it is not only conduct in the course of ancillary relief proceedings that is to be considered.'[523] It inserted the additional wording '. . . whatever the nature of the conduct and whether it occurred during the marriage or after the separation of the parties or (as the case may be) dissolution or annulment of the marriage'. The potential impact of this provision was difficult to assess. It sat uneasily with the greater emphasis in the Family Law Act on irretrievable breakdown as the sole criterion of the failure of the marriage, and on mediated settlements and compromise. With the decision not to implement Part II of the 1996 Act, such speculation has become irrelevant.

However, it seemed for a while that the courts themselves were recognising that 'conduct' may be a relevant factor, even if not 'obvious and gross'. In *Miller v Miller*[524] the Court of Appeal agreed with the trial judge that the husband's conduct in leaving the wife for another woman entitled the trial judge to attach less weight to the short duration of the marriage than he would have done otherwise.[525] The House of Lords firmly rejected

---

[518] [2002] EWHC 108 (Fam), [2002] 1 FLR 1053.

[519] Ibid at para 103. See also *B v B (Financial Provision: Welfare of Child and Conduct)* [2002] 1 FLR 555: husband had abducted child to Italy and been imprisoned for the offence.

[520] See eg *Tavoulareas v Tavoulareas* [1998] 2 FLR 418, CA, *Young v Young* [1998] 2 FLR 1131, CA.

[521] [2002] EWHC 108 (Fam), [2002] 1 FLR 1053.

[522] See also *B v B (Real Property: Assessment of Interests)* [1998] 2 FLR 490: wife's deceitful behaviour in relation to discovery was held to be conduct inequitable to ignore; *Beach v Beach* [1995] 2 FLR 160; *H v H (Financial Relief: Conduct)* [1998] 1 FLR 971—husband's misuse of family funds taken into account; *B v B (Financial Provision: Welfare of Child and Conduct)* [2002] 1 FLR 555: as well as abducting child, husband failed to disclose bank account and transferred funds to Italy.

[523] Standing Committee E, Official Report, 16 May 1996, Col 370.

[524] [2005] EWCA Civ 984, [2006] 1 FLR 151. See the discussion by A Meehan, '*Miller*: Practitioners' Expectations Disappointed' [2005] Fam Law 787.

[525] See also *G v G (Financial Provision: Separation Agreement)* [2004] 1 FLR 1011.

this[526] and endorsed the long-standing principle that only 'obvious and gross' conduct should be regarded as affecting the outcome.

(h) 'In the case of proceedings for divorce or nullity of marriage, the value to each of the parties to the marriage of any benefit (for example, a pension) which, by reason of the dissolution or annulment of the marriage, that party will lose the chance of acquiring'[527]

As we have seen, the court's power to make financial provision orders in relation to pensions has been the subject of legislative changes, discussed above.[528] But even where a pension sharing or attachment order is not made, the loss of the pension may still be 'offset' in determining the share of the available assets that the parties are to receive. It is common for the wife to receive the matrimonial home in return for not seeking a share of the husband's pension, for example.[529]

One additional right that a divorced wife loses is that of claiming certain social security benefits by virtue of her husband's contributions; another is the loss of an entitlement on the husband's intestacy. A further example of a lost benefit is to be seen in *Trippas v Trippas*.[530] After the parties had separated, the husband received a considerable sum from the sale of a family business. The court awarded the wife a lump sum of £10,000 on the ground that, had the marriage still been on foot, she would have received such a benefit either directly in cash or indirectly in kind; furthermore, the husband could have been expected to leave her a large sum if he had predeceased her, so that she had lost something analogous to a pension.

3 THE MATRIMONIAL HOME

The matrimonial home presents particular problems. In many cases (perhaps apart from accrued pension rights) it will be the only asset of any value owned by either spouse. It may be the only means of giving one of the spouses (whom, for the sake of argument, we shall assume to be the wife) the security of a home with the children in the future. Consequently the parties' interests will often be in direct conflict: the wife will wish to be given the right to occupy the house, whilst the husband will want an immediate sale so as to realise his capital, without which he may be unable to buy another home for his second family. Faced with this, and given that the court's first consideration must be the welfare of the children, it must seek to ensure that the children (and therefore the spouse with whom the children are living) have a home.[531]

Once the children's accommodation has been secured, the court will usually try to make an order which will give the other spouse a home as well. In *M v B (Ancillary Proceedings: Lump Sum)*[532] the Court of Appeal considered that in any case where, by stretch and

---

[526] *Miller v Miller; McFarlane v McFarlane* [2006] UKHL 24, [2006] 3 All ER 1 at paras 65, 145.

[527] As amended by Pensions Act 1995 s 166(2).   [528] At pp 999–1003.

[529] See A Perry et al, *How Parents Cope Financially on Separation and Divorce* (2000) p 31; J Ginn and D Price, 'Do divorced women catch up in pension building?' [2002] CFLQ 157 at 169–70.

[530] [1973] Fam 134, CA but was not the loss to the wife caused by the breakdown of the marriage, rather than by its dissolution? See also *Kokosinski v Kokosinski* [1980] Fam 72.

[531] *Browne v Pritchard* [1975] 3 All ER 721 at 724, CA; *Scott v Scott* [1978] 3 All ER 65, CA.

[532] [1998] 1 FLR 53, CA. See also *H v H (Financial Provision: Conduct)* [1998] 1 FLR 971.

risk-taking, there is the possibility of a division which will enable both parties to rehouse themselves, this is an important consideration and one which, almost invariably, will have a decisive impact on the outcome. This is so particularly where young children are involved; while the primary carer needs to make the main home for the children, it is also important (albeit to a lesser extent) that the other parent has a home where the children can enjoy contact. However, there is no principle or presumption that both spouses must be housed from the available assets.[533]

We must now consider the various ways in which the court may use the wide range of powers that it has at its disposal.

(a) Buying out the other spouse's share

The court may require the wife to buy out the husband's interest by ordering him to transfer his share to her and ordering her to pay him a lump sum equal to its value. This is the ideal solution because she retains a roof over her head and he gets the immediate use of his money. Obviously, however, such an order can be made only if the wife has sufficient capital or, alternatively, a large enough income to pay the sum in instalments, or to raise it by borrowing (perhaps secured by mortgage on the property). If, however, the husband does not need the capital immediately, the payment can be deferred until the house is sold.

(b) Outright transfer of share to other spouse with no compensation

The court can order the husband to transfer his share of the home to the wife without any compensating payment on her part. There are a number of quite dissimilar situations in which this may offer the best solution. If the house forms only part of the capital assets which have to be apportioned, it may be transferred to the wife in part or complete satisfaction of her claim for a lump sum or other capital settlement. Again, if the husband is wealthy, the wife might take the house as representing the capitalisation of part, or all of her claim for periodical payments which will be proportionately reduced or, in a suitable case, discharged altogether, thereby achieving an 'immediate' clean break. It might also be felt desirable to capitalise periodical payments if the husband's past behaviour indicated that any other order might prove to be ineffective.[534] At the other end of the economic scale, if the husband's earnings are so small that it will be impossible for him to make an adequate contribution towards the support of the wife and children of the family, the only possible solution might be to transfer the matrimonial home to her unconditionally and make no order, or only a minimal order, against him for periodical payments. This occurred, for example, in *S v S*,[535] where the husband was ordered to pay a total of £4 a week for his wife and daughter and to transfer his half-share in the matrimonial home to the former. This may prove to be much more valuable to the wife than a relatively greater order for periodical payments if she can claim income support, because the value of the house will not be taken into account in assessing the benefit payable. Even if the parties are not at either extreme of the economic spectrum, the particular circumstances may make it necessary to order a transfer of the matrimonial home without payment, but with a compensating reduction in periodical payments, as the only way of ensuring that either of

---

[533] See *Piglowska v Piglowski* [1999] 1 WLR 1360, HL.
[534] As in *Bryant v Bryant* (1976) 6 Fam Law 108, CA.   [535] [1976] Fam 18n.

them has a home. In *Hanlon v Hanlon*[536] the husband was a police officer who, since separating from his wife, was living rent-free in a police house. On his retirement he could expect a lump sum payment of up to £7,000. The wife was living in the matrimonial home with the two sons of the marriage (then both apprentices over the age of 18) and the two daughters, who were still at school. The most that the parties could expect from the sale of the house was £10,000[537] which, if divided equally, would give neither of them enough to buy any other accommodation. In these circumstances the Court of Appeal ordered the husband's half-share to be transferred to the wife, in return for which she was prepared to forgo any further periodical payments for the two girls. It will be appreciated that the effect of the Child Support Act 1991[538] means that such orders do not enable the non-resident parent to avoid his continuing maintenance liability towards the children, and hence such a trade-off could not now be made. However, a settlement in which the wife forgoes periodical payments for her own benefit (or a share in the husband's pension) in return for the matrimonial home is still common.

A transfer of the husband's interests without compensation might also be appropriate if his conduct justified the extinction of his share.[539] In conjunction with other factors such an order has also been made when the wife's earning capacity has been so seriously impaired that she is in greater need of security than usual: in *Jones v Jones*[540] this was the result of the husband's conduct in inflicting an injury on her, and in *S v S*[541] of having to nurse a young daughter suffering from kidney trouble.

Two further points should be borne in mind which may be of particular importance when dealing with the property of less affluent spouses. First, the court may make an order transferring a protected statutory, secure or assured tenancy from one spouse to the other.[542] Secondly, like any other lease, a council tenancy is 'property' for the purpose of s 24 of the Matrimonial Causes Act and the court may therefore make an order in relation to it.[543] In exercising its powers, the court is entitled to have regard to the local authority's housing policy, and its likely impact on the parties, and their separate prospects of re-housing.[544]

(c) Postponing sale of the home until a specified event

Mesher orders

The order may provide that both spouses shall keep or acquire an interest in the house as equitable tenants in common, which will involve settling it on them on trust (if it is not already so held), with sale of the home to take place at some specified time in the future. In the meantime the wife will be given exclusive possession. Such an order enables both

---

[536] [1978] 2 All ER 889, CA.

[537] In point of fact, because of (what was then) the Law Society's legal aid charge for costs (see above, p 1015, this expectation was considerably reduced: see the later case of *Hanlon v Law Society* [1981] AC 124, HL.

[538] See above, pp 929–51.

[539] See *Bryant v Bryant* (1976) 6 Fam Law 108, CA; *H v H (Financial Provision: Conduct)* [1994] 2 FLR 801.

[540] [1976] Fam 8, CA.   [541] [1975] 2 All ER 19n followed in *Jones v Jones* (above).

[542] Family Law Act 1996 Sch 7, discussed above, p 206.

[543] *Thompson v Thompson* [1976] Fam 25, CA; cf *Hale v Hale* [1975] 2 All ER 1090, CA. See also *Newlon Housing Trust v Al-Sulaimen* [1998] 3 WLR 451, HL.

[544] *Jones v Jones* [1997] 1 FLR 27, CA, reversing dicta in *Thompson v Thompson* (above) on the basis of changes in the relationship of council tenant and council in what is now Housing Act 1985.

spouses to keep their interest in the capital, but also resolves the immediate problem of accommodation for the wife and the children. For some years perhaps the commonest type of order made was referred to as a *Mesher* order.[545] Here, it was normal to order that the sale of the property should not take place until the youngest child reached a specified age (often 17) or, perhaps, until all the children completed their education, or until the wife died, or until further order.[546]

Although frequently made in practice, *Mesher* orders have a number of defects and have been criticised by the courts.[547] In the first place, the husband and wife will have to act together to effect the sale, perhaps many years after the divorce, and this may cause difficulties, particularly if their relationship is bitter.[548] Secondly, children often do not leave home until long after they have completed their education and may therefore still need the house as their home. Thirdly, being 'property transfer orders' they are not variable even if, for example, the husband reneges on his obligation to make periodical payments.[549] Finally, and perhaps most significantly, a *Mesher* order may lead to a wife being thrown on the housing market in middle age, after her children have left home, without the capital or income to secure adequate alternative accommodation for herself. There may be cases where the *Mesher* order continues to produce the best solution,[550] but, given the emphasis on the yardstick of equality in *White v White*,[551] if such an order will produce significant inequality of outcome between the parties as to their eventual capital positions when sale takes place, or there is doubt as to whether the wife will be able to re-house herself, then it should not be made.[552]

Martin orders

A different order, in effect, if not in form, is a *Martin* order. As with the *Mesher* order, the matrimonial home is settled upon the spouses on trust for themselves as beneficial tenants in common. However, the contingent events specified in the order as triggering a sale are designed to ensure that the wife remains in occupation of the house for as long as she needs a roof over her head. In *Martin v Martin*[553] the husband had left to live with another

---

[545] From the name of the case in which such an order was made, *Mesher v Mesher and Hall* (1973) reported [1980] 1 All ER 126n, CA.

[546] It is important that the court should retain the option of ordering an earlier sale in case the wife remarries or some unforeseen event occurs. See further below, p 1062.

[547] See eg *Hanlon v Hanlon* [1978] 2 All ER 889 at 892–3, CA, per Ormrod LJ; *Carson v Carson* [1983] 1 All ER 478 at 482–3, CA per Ormrod LJ; and *Harman v Glencross* [1986] 1 All ER 545 at 556, CA per Balcombe LJ; *Mortimer v Mortimer-Griffin* [1986] 2 FLR 315 at 319, CA per Parker LJ.

[548] For problems relating to the need for repairs to the house: see *Harvey v Harvey* [1987] 1 FLR 67. But see *Teschner v Teschner* [1985] FLR 627, CA.

[549] As in *Carson v Carson*, above. See also *Dinch v Dinch* [1987] 1 All ER 818, HL.

[550] See eg *Rushton v Rushton* (1978) 1 FLR 195, CA; *Dorney-Kingdom v Dorney-Kingdom* [2000] 2 FLR 855, CA.

[551] [2001] 1 AC 596, HL.

[552] *B v B (Mesher Order)* [2002] EWHC 316 (Fam) [2003] 2 FLR 285; *Clutton v Clutton* [1991] 1 All ER 340 at 346, CA (per Lloyd LJ). A similar approach can be seen, by way of analogy, in *Greenham v Greenham* [1989] 1 FLR 105, CA where it was said to be 'wrong' to order a husband to sell his home, and pay a lump sum to the wife, on his attaining the age of 70. The Court of Appeal varied the order to provide for a lump sum to be payable on the husband's death or on the earlier sale of the property.

[553] *Martin v Martin* [1978] Fam 12, CA cf *Eshak v Nowojewski* (1980) 11 Fam Law 115, CA (sale deferred until death of husband who had custody of children and was unable to work; wife had remarried and her second husband was catering for her needs).

woman in a council house of which the latter was the tenant and which would apparently be transferred to them both jointly. The wife was left alone in the former matrimonial home which belonged to both spouses beneficially in equal shares. The Court of Appeal affirmed the judge's order that the house should be held on trust for the wife during her life, or until her remarriage or such earlier date as she should cease to live there and thereafter on trust for them both in equal shares. The husband was already provided with another home and consequently had no need of the capital; the wife, on the other hand, would have been unable to purchase alternative accommodation with her half-share of the capital and so an immediate sale would have deprived her of the modest comfortable home that she had before the marriage broke down.[554]

In *Clutton v Clutton*[555] the Court of Appeal gave its approval to a *Martin* order in a slightly different form. The sale was to take place on the death, remarriage or cohabitation of the wife, whereupon the proceeds were to be divided, two-thirds to the wife and one-third to the husband. The court held that a *Martin* order in these terms did not suffer from the same disadvantages as a *Mesher* order as far as the occupying spouse was concerned. Nor did it offend against the clean break principle which ought not to mean that one of the spouses was to be deprived of any share in an asset acquired by the joint efforts of both. The wife had argued that the effect of the order would be to make her subject to 'perpetual supervision' by the husband, who would be anxious to establish cohabitation and trigger a sale. While accepting the force of this argument, Lloyd LJ[556] suggested that the bitterness the wife might feel on being 'spied on' was far outweighed by the bitterness the husband would feel if the wife, despite her present assertions, soon remarried or cohabited and continued to occupy the former matrimonial home.[557]

(d) Transfer with charge on the home

The court may order the husband to transfer his interest to the wife and give him a charge on the house equal to the value of his share.[558] The charge should not be realised until the wife no longer needs to live in the house and it can be sold. This solution is to be preferred because the husband will not have to concur in the sale and the spouses can make a clean break.[559] His charge should represent a given fraction of the value of the house at the time

---

[554] The implications for legally aided parties of the Legal Services Commission's statutory charge (discussed above, p 1015) must not be overlooked.

[555] [1991] 1 All ER 340, CA.   [556] Ibid at 344 and 345.

[557] For criticism of the *Clutton* Order, see M Hayes 'Cohabitation Clauses in Financial Provision and Property Adjustment Orders—Law, Policy and Justice' (1994) 110 LQR 124.

[558] Although such orders appear to be frequently made in practice there is no express statutory power in the Matrimonial Causes Act 1973, Pt II to *order* a spouse to execute a charge over the former matrimonial home, or *impose* a charge on property ordered to be transferred from one spouse to another. However, it appears such orders can be effected by imposing conditions on the exercise of the express powers in ss 21–4A (eg H can be ordered to *transfer* Whiteacre to W *upon condition* W executes a charge in favour of H) or, alternatively, they can be incorporated into consent orders formulated as undertakings given to the court following *Livesey (formerly Jenkins) v Jenkins* [1985] AC 424, HL. See further R Bird 'Problems in Ancillary Relief Orders' [1990] Fam Law 420.

[559] See *Schuller v Schuller* [1990] 2 FLR 193, CA where, on the facts, the court refused to order a deferred charge which was to be enforceable on the death of the elderly husband or on earlier sale of the property. Butler-Sloss LJ said (at 199) that such an order would 'fly in the face of the duty upon the court to try, wherever possible, to create a clean break'.

of the sale;[560] if it is fixed by reference to its present value, the sum which the husband will eventually receive will not have increased to take account of inflation.[561]

(e) Settlement on spouse and children

The possibility of settling the house for the benefit of the wife and children[562] appears to be little used in practice. It would usually involve giving the wife a life interest with remainder to children and consequently will rarely provide the best solution, because neither spouse will ever have the use of the capital and, save in exceptional circumstances, the court does not make an order providing for children after they have completed their education or training.[563]

(f) Immediate sale and division of proceeds

The court could order the house to be sold[564] and the proceeds to be divided in such proportions as it thinks fit. This might be the best way of dealing with the situation if there were no children living at home and the house was too big for either spouse to live in alone. The money should be sufficient to give at least one of them (and preferably both) enough to put down as a deposit on the purchase of a new house or flat. This solution is not appropriate if its effect would be to deprive both of them of a home.

If there is any danger that the husband will try to dispose of the home before an order is made, the wife's simplest remedy before the divorce takes effect is to register her home rights under the Land Registration Act 2002 or, in the case of unregistered land, as a Class F land charge under the Land Charges Act 1972. Alternatively she could apply to have the husband restrained from selling it on the ground that the disposition would defeat her claim for financial relief.[565] A further problem arises if the house is subject to a mortgage (as will frequently be the case).

4 COSTS AWARDS

In civil cases generally, the loser must usually pay the winner's costs, and this has also been the starting point in family cases,[566] but the courts in all cases have discretion not so to order. However, it became the common practice (strongly encouraged as an incentive to earlier settlement) to make written offers of settlement, known as 'Calderbank offers'.[567]

---

[560] As in *Browne v Pritchard* [1975] 3 All ER 721, CA. See also *H v H* [1975] Fam 9.

[561] Such an order was made in *Hector v Hector* [1973] 3 All ER 1070, CA but was regarded as out of line by Latey J in *S v S* [1976] Fam 18n at 21.

[562] See *Wachtel v Wachtel* [1973] Fam 72 at 96, CA, where Lord Denning MR referred to settling a lump sum.

[563] *Chamberlain v Chamberlain* [1974] 1 All ER 33, CA, allowing an appeal against such an order, and *Kiely v Kiely* [1988] 1 FLR 248, CA. But cf *H v H (Financial Provision: Conduct)* [1998] 1 FLR 971 where a lump sum to enable the husband to buy a house was settled on trust for him with reversion to the children.

[564] Under s 24A of the Matrimonial Causes Act 1973, discussed above at p 1007.

[565] See above p 187 and below, p 1072. But registration of a Class F land charge will be set aside as an abuse of process if the wife has no intention of occupying the house: *Barnett v Hassett* [1982] 1 All ER 80.

[566] *Gojkovc v Gojkovic (No 2)* [1992] Fam 40, CA. For consideration of the distinction between penalising a party in costs for litigation misconduct, and adjusting an award to take account of marital misconduct, see *Tavoulareas v Tavoulareas* [1998] 2 FLR 418, CA and *Young v Young* [1998] 2 FLR 1131, CA.

[567] *Calderbank v Calderbank* [1976] Fam 93, CA.

These resembled a payment into court,[568] with one party making an offer to the other 'without prejudice as to costs'. If the offer were rejected, no reference was made to it until after the court had made its order. If the order were more favourable to the offeree than the terms of the *Calderbank* offer, the court would usually award the offeree his or her costs; if not, the court might order the offeree to pay the costs of both sides from the date on which the *Calderbank* offer was made.[569] In *H v H (Financial Relief: Costs)*,[570] Holman J criticised the tactical 'poker' of *Calderbank* exchanges, and suggested that the time was fast approaching when it should be removed altogether. His Lordship noted[571] that the rules contained in the Ancillary Relief Procedure[572] force the parties into making 'open' proposals at an early stage, so that, in those cases which do not settle, the judge at final hearing has all the information necessary for him to do overall justice between the parties, instead of having to divide the available assets on two separate occasions, first substantively, and then in relation to costs.

In *Norris v Norris; Haskins v Haskins*,[573] the Court of Appeal reminded courts of their discretion to depart from the normal costs rule where appropriate, but called for the rules to be amended. In so doing, they took on board the serious criticisms that the existing regime promoted uncertainty as to the outcome of cases, and a sense of grievance amongst litigants.[574] The Costs Sub-Committee of the President's Ancillary Relief Advisory Group[575] made recommendations which were put forward for consultation by the Department for Constitutional Affairs[576] and new rules passed in 2006.[577] These Rules, inter alia, insert a new r 2.71 into the Family Proceedings Rules 1991, which provides that the:

'general rule in ancillary relief proceedings is that the court will not make an order requiring one party to pay the costs of another party; but . . . the court may make such an order at any stage of the proceedings where it considers it appropriate to do so because of the conduct of a party in relation to the proceedings (whether before or during them).'[578]

In deciding whether to make an order, the court must have regard to any failure by a party to comply with the Rules, a court order or any practice direction which the court considers relevant; any open offer to settle; whether it was reasonable for a party to raise, pursue or contest a particular allegation or issue; the manner in which a party pursued or responded to the application or allegation or issue; any other aspect of a party's conduct in relation to

---

[568] *Gojkovic v Gojkovic (No 2)* (above) at 237 (per Butler-Sloss LJ at 239).

[569] For a case where the court's order 'beat' the husband's '*Calderbank* offer' so the wife received her costs see *Thompson v Thompson* [1993] 2 FLR 464, CA.

[570] [1997] 2 FLR 57. See too *P v P (Financial Relief: Non Disclosure)* [1994] 2 FLR 381, although the court's order 'beat' the terms of the husband's *Calderbank* offer, the court declined to make a costs order in the wife's favour, to reflect the wife's serious misconduct, and culpability within the litigation.

[571] Ibid at 59.   [572] See above, p 986.   [573] [2003] EWCA Civ 1084, [2003] 2 FLR 1124.

[574] See P Watson-Lee, 'Ancillary Relief Costs—Time for Regime Change?' [2003] Fam Law 487; N Mostyn QC in *GW v RW (Financial Provision: Departure from Equality)* [2003] EWHC 611 (Fam), [2003] 2 FLR 108; Butler Sloss P in *Norris v Norris; Haskins v Haskins* (above) at paras 28, 29; Thorpe LJ at para 64.

[575] See the discussion of their proposals by the President and Thorpe LJ ibid.

[576] Department for Constitutional Affairs: *Costs in Ancillary Relief Proceedings and Appeals in Ancillary Relief Proceedings* (CP (L) 29/04).

[577] Family Proceedings Rules 2006 SI 2006/352 (L.1) in force in respect of applications made on or after 3 April 2006. See also *Practice Direction (Ancillary Relief: Costs)* 20 February 2006.

[578] Rule 2.71(4).

the proceedings which the court considers relevant; and the financial effect on the parties of any costs order. It has been suggested that it is uncertain whether this change in the Rules will lead to lower offers being made, thus reducing the chance of settlement, or more realistic ones.[579] At least the judge will be able to factor the costs that each party has incurred into determining what orders should be made.

5 APPEALS

Given the breadth of the court's powers and the width of its discretion, every case will turn on its particular facts, and there will frequently be a variety of outcomes that might be arrived at. The costs of matrimonial litigation may be extremely high and an appeal may do little to improve an outcome for a disappointed party, even if he or she 'wins'. The courts therefore take a restrictive approach to permitting appeals. In *Piglowska v Piglowski*,[580] the parties' costs equalled the value of the assets they were fighting over. The House of Lords applied its earlier ruling in *G v G*[581] to the effect that it is 'only where a lower court's decision exceeds the generous ambit within which reasonable disagreement is possible, and is, in fact, plainly wrong, that an appellate body is entitled to interfere.'[582] Lord Hoffmann noted that the parties' case had been heard by five differently constituted tribunals, and he commented:

'This cannot be right. To allow successive appeals in the hope of producing an answer which accords with perfect justice is to kill the parties with kindness.'

In *Cordle v Cordle*[583] the Court of Appeal reiterated that any appeal from a decision of a district judge in ancillary relief may only be allowed by the circuit judge if it is demonstrated that there has been some procedural irregularity or that in conducting the necessary balancing exercise the district judge has taken into account matters which are irrelevant, or ignored matters which are relevant, or has otherwise arrived at a conclusion that is plainly wrong. The appeal is limited to a review of the decision or order of the district judge, unless the judge considers that in the circumstances of the case it would be in the interests of justice to hold a rehearing.[584] We discuss below the question of appealing out of time.[585]

---

[579] See N Shepherd, 'Farewell to *Calderbanks*' [2005] Fam Law 933. But for a warning that litigation will then ensue regarding what amounts to 'unreasonable behaviour' see DJ M Segal, 'The *Calderbank* Procedure: New Developments' [2004] Fam Law 107 at 114.

[580] [1999] 1 WLR 1360, HL, discussed above at p 1036.

[581] [1985] 1 WLR 647, HL.

[582] Ibid at 228, per Lord Fraser of Tullybelton, quoting Asquith LJ in *Bellenden (formerly Satterthwaite) v Satterthwaite* [1948] 1 All ER 343 at 345.

[583] [2001] EWCA Civ 1791, [2002] 1 FLR 207. For criticism of the decision, see R Spon-Smith, 'Appeals in Ancillary Relief Proceedings—The New Rule' [2003] Fam Law 428.

[584] Family Proceedings Rules 1991 (SI 1991/1247) r 8.1(3) as amended by Family Proceedings (Amendment) Rules 2003 (SI 2003/184). For an example of the approach, see *B v B (Mesher Order)* [2002] EWHC 3106, [2003] 2 FLR 285.

[585] See pp 1064–9.

D VARIATION, DISCHARGE, SUSPENSION AND REVIVAL OF ORDERS

1 ORDERS THAT MAY BE VARIED

The court has power to vary, discharge or suspend any of the following orders and to revive any term suspended:[586]

— maintenance pending suit and any interim order for maintenance;
— periodical payments (secured and unsecured);
— an order relating to instalments in the case of lump sum payments;
— a deferred order made in relation to pensions;
— an order for the settlement (but not the transfer) of property made on or after the grant of a decree of judicial separation;
— an order for the variation of a marriage settlement made on or after the grant of a decree of judicial separation;
— any order for the sale of property;
— a pension sharing order made at a time before the decree has been made absolute.

Periodical payments are normally variable because if either party's needs or resources change, justice may demand a corresponding change in the amount payable. Accordingly, unless the fixed term for which the court may have ordered periodical payments to continue has expired,[587] an application may be made to vary an order. The principal exception is where the court has expressly added a s 28(1A) direction, ie that the period fixed for the order cannot be extended. As we have seen,[588] such orders are intended to provide for a 'deferred clean break' between the parties where it is thought that the parties can become financially independent of one another. On the other hand, once a lump sum has been paid, it cannot be discharged or varied; it would therefore be unfair to the payee if her right to a sum not yet paid could be prejudiced on the ground that the court had softened the blow to the payer by providing that he could pay the sum in question over a period of time. The same objection cannot be raised, however, to a change in the period or manner

---

[586] Matrimonial Causes Act 1973 s 31(1), (2), as amended by the Pensions Act 1995 s 166(3)(a) and the Welfare Reform and Pensions Act 1999 Sch 3 para 7(2). The court may also order any instrument to be varied etc: s 31(3).

[587] In *T v T (Financial Provision)* [1988] 1 FLR 480 a periodical payments order in favour of a wife was expressed to take effect until the wife remarried, or the husband retired or until further order. It was held that the wife could not apply for a variation after the husband retired. The words 'or further order' could be relied on for an earlier variation, ie before the happening of the specified event, but not afterwards. The same approach was adopted in *Richardson v Richardson* [1994] 1 FLR 286 and approved by the Court of Appeal in *G v G (Periodical Payments: Jurisdiction)* [1997] 1 FLR 368, CA. Here Ward LJ suggested that one way around the problem would be for a court to make a substantial periodical payments order for a fixed term followed by a nominal order. This, at least, would 'give a peg on which to hang a late variation application'. (This point appears not to be affected by the Court of Appeal's subsequent disapproval of Ward LJ's view in *G v G* that a fixed term order may only be extended if the order—and not just the application—to extend that term is made prior to its completion. See above p 1026.) See further J Harcus 'Periodical Payments Order—End of Term?' [1997] Fam Law 340.

[588] Above, p 1026. There is no power to vary an order dismissing an application for periodical payments made under s 25A(3).

in which the instalments are paid, and consequently these can be varied by an alteration of their size or frequency. In *Tilley v Tilley*[589] the Court of Appeal held that this power enables the court to suspend or to remit future instalments entirely: a decision endorsed in *Penrose v Penrose*,[590] where Balcombe LJ considered such power should be exercised 'with caution'. Bodey J went further, in *Westbury v Sampson* (a claim for professional negligence by the husband's solicitor) by holding that the court may also vary, suspend or discharge the principal sum itself. However, he made clear that the goal of finality means that courts should apply a similar approach to this question as when determining whether to re-open an order following supervening events, and that such power must be used 'particularly sparingly'.[591]

The reason that, generally speaking, orders relating to property cannot be varied is that they are designed to make a final adjustment of the spouses' rights, so that any subsequent change in their needs and resources is irrelevant. Settlements of property and variations of marriage settlements made on the making of separation orders will come into a different category, however, because a further adjustment may have to be made if the marriage is later dissolved, and the spouses themselves may wish to have the order varied if they become reconciled. Consequently, variations of these orders will be made only in proceedings on an application for rescission of a decree of judicial separation or for dissolution of the marriage.[592]

Section 31(7)(a) of the 1973 Act 1973[593] places the court's duty to consider making a 'clean break' on a variation application on the same footing as in relation to original orders. On applications to vary periodical payments (secured or unsecured) made in divorce or nullity proceedings, the court shall consider whether:

'. . . it would be appropriate to vary the order so that payments under the order are required to be made or secured only for such further period as will in the opinion of the court be sufficient . . . to enable the party in whose favour the order was made to adjust without undue hardship to the termination of those payments.'

The court has power[594] to direct that an order for variation or discharge of a periodical payments order shall not take effect until the expiry of a specified period, thus enabling the payee to adjust, in the interim, to a termination of the payments in her favour or a reduction in their amount. Where, on a variation application, the court imposes a 'clean break' (by either discharging a periodical payments order or directing it continues only for a fixed period), it also has power[595] to order a 'compensating' lump sum,[596] property

---

[589] (1979) 10 Fam Law 89, CA.   [590] [1994] 2 FLR 621, CA.

[591] [2001] EWCA Civ 407, [2002] 1 FLR 166 at para 18. Approved in *Shaw v Shaw* [2002] EWCA Civ 1298, [2002] 2 FLR 1204. See further below pp 1064–9.

[592] Matrimonial Causes Act 1973 s 31(4).

[593] As amended by Family Law Act 1996 Sch 8, para 16.

[594] Matrimonial Causes Act 1973 s 31(10).

[595] Ibid, s 31(7A) and (7B) as inserted by Family Law Act 1996 Sch 8, para 16. The provision came into force on 1 November 1998, but is applicable to divorces granted prior to that date: *Harris v Harris* [2001] 1 FCR 68, CA.

[596] Where a lump sum is ordered in these circumstances, it may be ordered to be paid by instalments, which may be secured: Matrimonial Causes Act 1973 s 31(7c).

adjustment order[597] or pension sharing order.[598] The court may also order that the payee under the original periodical payments order shall not be entitled to apply for a further order, or for an extension of its term.[599]

This power to order a spouse to make capital provision in substitution of future periodical payments was introduced following the recommendation of the Law Commission.[600] The court is not given any statutory guidance on calculating a fair level of capital commutation, but in *Pearce v Pearce*[601] the Court of Appeal held that:

'(i) On dismissing an entitlement to future periodical payments the court's function is not to reopen capital claims but to substitute for the periodical payments order such other order or orders as will both fairly compensate the payee and at the same time complete the clean break.

(ii) In surveying what substitute order or orders should be made first consideration should be given to the option of carving out of the payer's pension funds a pension for the payee equivalent to the discharged periodical payments order.'[602]

The court disapproved an earlier decision[603] where Charles J had considered that the court has a wide discretion to exercise its powers without being limited to capitalisation of the periodical payments figure (suitably adjusted to take account of the change in circumstances prompting the application). Rejecting this approach, it held that the court should first determine the application for variation applying s 31(7) and the relevant authorities.[604] It should then fix the date upon which periodical payments are to cease and, the order for lump sum and/or property adjustment in lieu. The final stage is to exercise a discretion to depart from the mathematics of the *Duxbury* tables 'to reflect special factors which individual cases will regularly generate.'[605] Thorpe LJ considered that:

'this discipline is necessary as a safeguard against the temptation to further adjust the capital division between the parties to reflect the factors which were not foreseen or which did not pertain at the date of the original division. This abstinence is required not only by authority but also as a matter of policy. Families with not inconsiderable assets are obliged to achieve division, by one means or another, once the marriage has foundered. They are entitled to know that that obligation once completed does not revive. In cases where a complete clean

---

[597] Where the court makes more than one property adjustment order in favour of the same party, it may only make a single order of each type: Matrimonial Causes Act 1973 s 31(7E).

[598] Matrimonial Causes Act 1973 s 31(7B)(ba) inserted by Welfare Reform and Pensions Act 1999 Sch 3 para 7(5), in force from 1 December 2000 unless marriage dissolved by decree granted in proceedings begun before that date: Welfare Reform and Pensions Act 1999 (Commencement No 5) Order 2000, SI 2000/1116, art 2(e) and the Welfare Reform and Pensions Act 1999, s 85(3)(b).

[599] Matrimonial Causes Act 1973 s 31(7B)(c).   [600] Law Com No 192, paragraphs 6.8–6.10.

[601] [2003] EWCA Civ 1054, [2004] 1 WLR 68.

[602] Ibid per Thorpe LJ at para 45, who, in preferring the substitution of a pension sharing order where possible thought that 'there is great attraction in a mechanism to achieve clean break by substituting for an income stream that locks the parties in continuing relationship an income stream that permits finality, severance and independence. Often the application for the exercise of the jurisdiction under s 31(7B) will not be opposed. The only issue is the nature and extent of the financial benefit to be substituted for the periodical payments order. The substitution of an alternative income stream in the shape of a pension involves a much simpler and less speculative exercise. Substituting like for like offers much less scope for debate, disagreement and ingenuity of argument.' At para 15.

[603] *Cornick v Cornick (No 3)* [2001] 2 FLR 1240.   [604] See below p 1062.

[605] [2003] EWCA Civ 1054, [2004] 1 WLR 68 at para 38.

break cannot be achieved at the date of redistribution of the family assets it is important that the parties should be encouraged to take advantage of any subsequent developments that permit the dismissal of the outstanding periodical payments order.'[606]

A *Mesher* order, being a property adjustment order, cannot be varied.[607] In *Norman v Norman*[608] a husband attempted to invoke the court's power of sale under s 24A to accelerate a sale following a *Mesher* order, but the court rejected this on the ground that such an order would in reality be a variation of the *Mesher* order. It was held that the proper procedure was to apply for a sale under what was then the Law of Property Act 1925 s 30.[609] In *Thompson v Thompson*,[610] however, it was held that, provided the sale was deferred inter alia 'until further order',[611] there was power to order an earlier sale under s 24A, at any rate on the application of the party in occupation, since in the court's view this would be to work out the terms of the original order rather than to amount to a substantive variation of its terms.[612] On the other hand, in *Taylor v Taylor*,[613] in which the matrimonial home was made subject to a charge in favour of the wife who retained exclusive right of occupation, the husband applied under s 24A for an earlier sale and the Court of Appeal seemed to take the view that this was a matter which went to the court's discretion rather than jurisdiction. In other words, there was power to order the sale under s 24A, but the question remained whether, on the merits, that power should be exercised.

In *Omielan v Omielan*,[614] the question raised was whether a sale could be ordered to be deferred on a subsequent variation application. A consent order had been made whereby the parties agreed to divide the proceeds of sale of the former matrimonial home, 75% to the children, 25% to the wife. The sale was to be postponed until the wife remarried, died or cohabited with another man for longer than six months. When it became known that the wife had been living with another man for six months, the husband applied for an order for sale; the wife applied for a variation, asking that the sale be postponed until the youngest child attained 18. The Court of Appeal held it had no jurisdiction to entertain the wife's application. The original order constituted a variation of settlement to which an ancillary order for sale was attached. The court's powers to vary orders for sale are limited to subsidiary matters of implementation, enforcement or procedure; they do not give jurisdiction to re-open primary property adjustment orders.[615]

2 FACTORS TO BE TAKEN INTO CONSIDERATION

The Act provides that, on hearing an application for variation, the court shall have regard to all the circumstances of the case, first consideration being given to the welfare while a

---

[606] Ibid at para 39.
[607] *Carson v Carson* [1983] 1 All ER 478. See the views of the Law Commission: Law Com 192 para 6.3.
[608] [1983] 1 All ER 486.   [609] Now Trusts of Land and Appointment of Trustees Act 1996 s 14.
[610] [1986] Fam 38, CA.
[611] Or words to similar effect. Express authority can be given to allow the parties to come back to the court to ask for an earlier sale: see eg *Anthony v Anthony* [1986] 2 FLR 353, CA at 359.
[612] Aliter if it was sought to *delay* the sale or if the party not in occupation sought the sale.
[613] [1987] 1 FLR 142, CA.
[614] [1996] 2 FLR 306, CA. See also *Harper v O'Reilly and Harper* [1997] 2 FLR 816.
[615] For the position concerning redemption of a charge over the matrimonial home, see *Popat v Popat* [1991] 2 FLR 163 and *Knibb v Knibb* [1987] 2 FLR 396.

minor of any child of the family who has not attained the age of 18, and the circumstances of the case shall include any change in the matters to which it was required to have regard when making the order in the first place.[616] If the application is made after the death of the party against whom the order was originally made, the court must also take into account the changed circumstances resulting from the death.[617] It should be noted that while it is important not to allow variation applications to be used as a disguised appeal against the terms of the original order, the court's discretion is generally unfettered.[618] However, the obligation to consider whether a clean break can be achieved between the parties will be 'much enhanced' where the periodical payments order was term-limited and the parties had expected that the payer's obligations were to terminate absolutely on the expiry of the term. 'In such circumstances, the exercise of a power to extend obligations requires some exceptional justification.'[619]

In *Flavell v Flavell*[620] the Court of Appeal held that jurisdiction to vary an order does not depend upon an exceptional or material change of circumstance, although the absence of such change may affect the exercise of the court's discretion. The court is not required to proceed from the starting point of the original order, but will consider the matter de novo.

Two judicial limitations have been placed on the court's power, however. First, the parties are still estopped per rem judicatem from raising matters inconsistent with a previous decree or order, and neither party may adduce evidence which could have been put before the court when the original order was made.[621] Secondly, a party who has led the other to act to his or her detriment on the assumption that he will continue to honour the order may not later apply to have it reduced or discharged.[622]

If the change of circumstances on which the application is based is not likely to be permanent (eg the husband's temporary unemployment), the order should be suspended rather than discharged, so that it can be revived later if necessary.[623]

3 VARIATION OF CONSENT ORDERS

The fact that a party has consented to an order being made against him cannot act as an estoppel or give the other party a contractual right to have the order kept in force indefinitely, and a consent order may generally be varied in the same circumstances as any other order.[624] This is so even though the order provides that the parties shall not apply for a

---

616 Matrimonial Causes Act 1973 s 31(7)(a).

617 Ibid s 31(7)(b). See *Jones v Jones* [1971] 3 All ER 1201 at 1206 and 1207.

618 *Lewis v Lewis* [1977] 3 All ER 992, CA; *Garner v Garner* [1992] 1 FLR 573, CA (a case concerning child maintenance); *Cornick v Cornick (No 2)* [1995] 2 FLR 490, CA. In *Pearce v Pearce* [2003] EWCA Civ 1054 [2004] 1 WLR 68 at para 25, Thorpe LJ considered that this line of authority does not apply to the orders defined in s 31(7B)(a) and (b), which are orders that the court has no power to vary; sed quaere? Section 31(7) states that it applies to a court exercising powers under the section; the fact that the order made under this section cannot itself subsequently be varied need not affect how the court takes the initial decisions *whether and how* to vary the original order, which clearly was capable of such variation.

619 Per Thorpe LJ in *Fleming v Fleming* [2003] EWCA Civ 1841, [2004] 1 FLR 667 at para 13.

620 [1997] 1 FLR 353, CA.   621 *Hall v Hall* (1914) 111 LT 403, CA.

622 *B (MAL) v B (NE)* [1968] 1 WLR 1109.   623 See *Mills v Mills* [1940] P 124, CA.

624 *B (GC) v B (BA)* [1970] 1 All ER 913.

variation: it is doubtful whether such a provision is valid[625] and, even if it is, it may itself be suspended along with the other provisions of the order.[626] Usually, however, the court should be slower to accede to an application to vary consent orders, because otherwise parties and their solicitors might be deterred from negotiating them altogether. Hence a variation sought on the ground that the applicant's consent was given as a result of a mistake (eg about the other party's income) should be made only if justice demands it and a substantially different order would be made.[627] The court might also exercise its power if the applicant had not been independently and competently advised[628] (although the Court of Appeal subsequently held[629] that only in the most exceptional case will bad legal advice be a ground for interfering with a consent order) or if, for whatever reason, the order was grossly unjust.[630] In any case, it is doubtful whether the court can vary or discharge an order which it has no power to make in the first place, eg an order for unsecured periodical payments for the payee's life.[631]

4 APPEALING OUT OF TIME

In exceptional circumstances it is possible to obtain leave to appeal out of time. This may be the only option in cases where, whether upon a consent order or a contested one, a clean break order has been made. Of course, the whole point of a clean break order or a property adjustment order is that there should be a final settlement between the parties. Nevertheless, circumstances may subsequently occur that so fundamentally change the position that in all justice the order should be reopened. It seems established, however, that, in the absence of fraud, misrepresentation or material non-disclosure,[632] or a fundamental mistake common to both parties, events occurring after the making of an order only give grounds for appeal in exceptional circumstances. The leading case is *Barder v Caluori*.[633] Here, in a full and final settlement made in a consent order the husband agreed

---

[625] See *N v N (Consent Order: Variation)* [1993] 2 FLR 868, CA where a consent order was made providing periodical payments to the wife for five years. Separate from the order, the wife entered into a 'side letter', agreeing not to apply for the extension of the term except '. . . for the protection of [the child] in circumstances of serious illness or disability'. When the wife decided to retrain for a new career, she applied for a three-year extension of maintenance. Although the Court of Appeal held the side letter void, it was nonetheless highly relevant and could not be disregarded. On the principles of *Edgar v Edgar* [1980] 3 All ER 887, CA (above p 1010) the court declined to allow the wife's variation application. The court doubted the suitability of a side letter of this sort in a 'child case' and suggested, in any event, such side letters should be shown to the judge.

[626] *Jessel v Jessel* [1979] 3 All ER 645, CA.   [627] *B (GC) v B (BA)* (above).

[628] Per Baker P in *Wilkins v Wilkins* [1969] 2 All ER 463; *Peacock v Peacock* [1991] 1 FLR 324 where Thorpe J said (at 328) that he would not hold the parties to any agreement that they may have concluded, since the area of negotiation was complicated, neither spouse had had the benefit of legal advice, and both were 'way out of their depth'.

[629] *Harris v Manahan* [1997] 1 FLR 205, CA.

[630] As in *Smethurst v Smethurst* [1978] Fam 52, where, for reasons which were not apparent, the sum originally ordered was about twice that which the husband could reasonably afford to pay.

[631] See *Mills v Mills* [1940] P 124, CA and *Hinde v Hinde* [1953] 1 All ER 171, CA. But they probably can be varied etc by consent, and an undertaking given to the court may be discharged: *Russell v Russell* [1956] P 283, CA.

[632] In such cases, as in those concerning supervening events, the application to appeal must be made promptly: *Shaw v Shaw* [2002] EWCA Civ 1298, [2002] 2 FLR 1204.

[633] [1988] AC 20, HL.

to transfer to his wife his half-interest in the matrimonial home subject to her undertaking responsibility for two outstanding mortgages. The order specified that the transfer should take place within 28 days. Neither party gave notice of appeal, but before the order was executed the wife killed both the children and committed suicide. It was held by the House of Lords that because the fundamental assumption on which the order had been made, namely that the wife and children would require a suitable home for a substantial period, had been totally invalidated within so short a time of the original order being made, leave to appeal should be granted. It was further held that the original order should be set aside.

The House of Lords laid down four conditions which must be satisfied if leave to appeal out of time is to be granted from an order for financial provision or property adjustment (whether or not made by consent):

(1) new events must have occurred since the making of the order which have invalidated the basis or assumption upon which the order was made so that the appeal would be certain, or very likely, to succeed;

(2) the new events should have occurred within a relatively short time of the order being made;

(3) the application for leave should be made reasonably promptly;

(4) the grant of leave should not prejudice third parties who have acquired interests in good faith and for value in the property which is the subject of the order.

In Lord Brandon's view, these conditions sought to reconcile two conflicting principles: on the one hand, that there should be finality in litigation and, on the other, that justice requires that cases be decided on their true facts rather than on assumptions or estimates which turn out to be erroneous.[634]

Cases applying the *Barder* criteria may be categorised into several broad groups.

(a) Unexpected death of one of the spouses

In the first group, as in *Barder v Caluori* itself, the supervening event has been the unexpected death of one of the spouses. In *Smith v Smith (Smith Intervening)*,[635] for example, the wife committed suicide six months after the making of a 'clean break' consent order, and the Court of Appeal set the original order aside. By contrast, in *Benson v Benson*[636] the court held that the wife's death 15 months after the making of the order was an event entitling the court to intervene but nonetheless dismissed the husband's application. The husband had delayed his application for over a year, and so had not proceeded with reasonable promptness. In deciding whether application for leave to appeal has been

---

[634] Ibid at 41.

[635] [1992] Fam 69, CA. See also *Passmore v Gill and Gill* [1987] 1 FLR 441, CA and *Barber v Barber* [1993] 1 FLR 476, CA where the order was set aside when the wife died intestate three months after the order. Cf *Amey v Amey* [1992] 2 FLR 89. The court refused to set aside a 'clean break' agreement under which the husband paid a £120,000 lump sum to the wife, and, just two months later, before the agreement could be approved by the court, the wife died of a heart attack. Scott Baker J held that, since the wife had died, it was no longer open to the court to affirm or vary the agreement under the Matrimonial Causes Act 1973. Nor was the agreement vitiated at common law by common mistake or frustration: the parties had divided their capital entitlements without making any assumption as to the wife's future health, so her unexpected death did not entitle the court to intervene.

[636] [1996] 1 FLR 692.

made reasonably promptly, account should be taken of the situation in which the individual finds himself; there should be no unreasonably inflexible rule of thumb.[637]

(b) Remarriage of other spouse

In the second category there are cases where a spouse has sought leave to appeal out of time where, subsequent to the making of the original order, the other spouse has remarried and vacated the former matrimonial home. In *Wells v Wells*[638] (a case which pre-dated *Barder*), just six months after the husband had been ordered to make a property transfer to provide a home for the wife and children, the wife remarried and began living with her second husband. The Court of Appeal held that these new events had invalidated the basis of the original order, and substituted an order for the sale of the property and the division of the proceeds of sale. In *Chaudhuri v Chaudhuri*[639] by contrast, the husband's application was dismissed where the wife had remarried and moved out of the former matrimonial home 15 months after the making of the property transfer order in her favour. The original order had expressly contemplated the possibility of the wife's remarriage,[640] and the change of circumstances was said to be much less drastic than that in *Wells v Wells*.

(c) Reconciliation of the spouses

In another group of cases, the unforeseen event has been the reconciliation of the spouses after their divorce, and their subsequent cohabitation. In *S v S (Financial Provision) (Post Divorce Cohabitation)*[641] a consent order was set aside, some 15 years after it was made, where the divorced couple had cohabited in the meanwhile. The judge considered that, in the highly unusual circumstances of the case, the wife had satisfied the *Barder* criteria, since she had applied to set aside the order with reasonable promptness when she realised the relationship had finally broken down. In *Hewitson v Hewitson*,[642] the Court of Appeal later doubted whether post-divorce cohabitation could amount to relevant circumstances entitling the court to set aside an order: 'There has to be finality and an end to litigation ... the umbrella of the dissolved marriage which covers the post-divorce period cannot remain open for ever.'[643]

---

[637] Cf *Reid v Reid* [2003] EWHC 2878 (Fam) [2004] 1 FLR 736: wife dying two months after consent order was not reasonably foreseeable and had it been foreseen, a different settlement would have been reached which gave more weight to the husband's needs rather than the wife's contributions after a long marriage. See further D Burrows, 'Permission to Appeal Out of Time' [2005] Fam Law 44. See also *Heard v Heard* [1995] 1 FLR 970, CA and see *S v S (Financial Provision) (Post-Divorce Cohabitation)* [1994] 2 FLR 228 and *Hill v Hill* [1998] 1 FLR 198, CA. In any event, in assessing if an individual has proceeded reasonably promptly, time will be taken to run from the date of the order, rather than from the date on which the order is implemented: *B v B (Financial Provision: Leave to Appeal)* [1994] 1 FLR 219.

[638] [1992] 2 FLR 66, CA (decided in 1980). See also *Williams v Lindley* [2005] EWCA Civ 103 [2005] 2 FLR 710: wife became engaged one month after order. Order set aside.

[639] [1992] 2 FLR 73, CA.

[640] The original order provided for the transfer of the property to the wife subject to a charge in favour of the husband enforceable upon the happening of the following events: the children ceasing full-time education, the death or remarriage of the wife, or her permanent cohabitation with another man.

[641] [1994] 2 FLR 228.   [642] [1995] 1 FLR 241, CA.

[643] Ibid at 244 (per Butler-Sloss LJ). Cf *Hill v Hill* [1998] 1 FLR 198, CA (discussed above at p 1044) where the court adopted a different approach. The parties had cohabited for a 25-year period following a divorce, and a consent order which had been made in 1969. At first instance, Holman J dismissed the wife's application to set aside the 1969 order, which she had made after the parties had separated in 1995. The wife's appeal

(d) Change in the law

A further basis upon which it has been argued that the *Barder* criteria apply to justify the setting aside of an earlier order is a change in the law. In *Crozier v Crozier*[644] this argument was rejected. A consent order had been made whereby the husband had transferred his interest in the former matrimonial home to the wife who, in return, had accepted nominal maintenance payments for herself and her child. Following the implementation of the Child Support Act 1991, the husband's maintenance payments for the child, as an absent parent, were substantially increased. Booth J rejected the husband's argument that the 1991 Act, and its new administrative machinery for the assessment and collection of child maintenance, constituted a 'new event' which invalidated the fundamental basis upon which the earlier consent order and capital settlement had been made. The 1991 Act did not alter the position which had existed previously – that parents could not, by agreement or otherwise, throw off their continuing legal liability to support their children. However, in *S v S (Ancillary Relief: Consent Order)*[645] Bracewell J held that the ruling in *White v White*[646] *was* capable of constituting a *Barder* event, because its effect on the outcome in 'big money' cases was very significant and the wife would very likely have received more capital after a long marriage than she had done under a consent order. Nonetheless, the wife failed because, by the time the consent order was made, argument had been heard and judgment reserved in *White v White* and it had been, or should have been, known to her advisers that the House of Lords was due to rule shortly. They could have suspended negotiations pending the House of Lords' judgment. Her Ladyship concluded that the ruling was thus 'foreseeable and the impact avoidable.'[647]

(e) Change in valuation of property

In a large group of cases, it has been argued that a property valuation, which was used by the court in making its original order, has turned out to be inaccurate and unreliable, thus invalidating the basis upon which the order was made. In *Hope-Smith v Hope-Smith*[648] the husband was ordered to pay to the wife £32,000 out of the proceeds of sale of the former matrimonial home, then valued at £116,000. As a result of the husband's 'wilful conduct and dilatory tactics' the house remained unsold some two years later when it was worth over £200,000. The Court of Appeal held that the *Barder* conditions were satisfied through no fault of the wife.[649] It substituted an order that the wife was to receive 40% of the ultimate net sale proceeds, which would be sufficient to enable her to re-house herself.[650]

---

was successful. While not setting aside the 1969 order on *Barder* principles, the Court of Appeal, on reviewing its terms, considered it had not constituted a comprehensive financial settlement of the wife's capital and property claims. The court therefore had jurisdiction to entertain the wife's application for further relief.

[644] [1994] 1 FLR 126.   [645] [2002] EWHC 223 (Fam), [2003] Fam 1.

[646] [2001] 1 AC 596, HL.   [647] [2002] EWHC 223 (Fam), [2003] Fam 1 at para 54.

[648] [1989] 2 FLR 56, CA.

[649] See also *Middleton v Middleton* [1998] 2 FLR 821, CA: value of premises used for sub-post office business dropped from around £54,000 to virtually nothing after husband transferred the business to other premises. Consent order set aside because entire basis upon which it had been made had been deliberately frustrated by the husband's actions. Cf *McGladdery v McGladdery* [1999] 2 FLR 1102: wife's refusal to comply with orders 'nowhere near the *Barder* territory'.

[650] See also *Heard v Heard* [1995] 1 FLR 970, CA, where an order was made that the wife receive £16,000 from the proceeds of the former matrimonial home, with the husband receiving the balance. The valuation before the judge suggested the house was worth £67,000. In the event no offer was received above

In contrast, in *Rooker v Rooker*,[651] on broadly similar facts, the court dismissed the wife's appeal because, although the husband had delayed the sale, the wife had not taken proper steps to enforce the original order. In *Edmonds v Edmonds*[652] the Court of Appeal refused to reopen a case where a house, valued by the judge at £70,000 and which the wife had claimed she intended to keep as her home, was sold by her for £110,000 six months later. Although the husband had asserted throughout his belief that the valuation should be higher, he had failed to produce any corroborative expert evidence to support his view. It was held that, since the husband had not taken the opportunity to challenge the false assumption upon which the judge had proceeded, he could not subsequently be heard to say that the new events had invalidated the judge's decision.[653] In a later decision, *Thompson v Thompson*,[654] the Court of Appeal granted leave to appeal out of time against a clean break order where the husband's business had been valued at £20,000, and just one week later was sold for £45,000. The circuit judge dismissed the wife's application for leave because she had agreed the valuation of £20,000, despite having previously received a valuation report of the business at £45,000. On appeal, however, Mustill LJ drew a distinction between the situation where a valuation was unsound when made and that where a reasonable estimate had been falsified by new events. In the first situation, the court must inquire whether the applicant was in some way responsible for the error. If she was, then, as in *Edmonds v Edmonds*, she may not succeed. The mere fact that a valuation report had been agreed, however, cannot be conclusive against an order being reopened, but deliberate fault on the part of the applicant would prevent leave being granted. The second situation is clearly a new event regardless of how the valuation came into existence. Provided that the other criteria in *Barder v Caluori* were satisfied, leave to appeal out of time would be given.

Mustill LJ, concerned lest his decision be seen as opening the floodgates and encouraging applicants to seek leave to appeal out of time, emphasised the severity of the requirements laid down in *Barder v Caluori*, adding:[655]

'. . . advisers must be alert, and the circuit judge will be alert if they are not, to make sure that the courts are not swamped with meritless applications for leave to appeal out of time.'

In subsequent cases the courts have adopted a restrictive approach, particularly where the substance of an application is based on little more than that property has turned out to be worth more, or less, than at the date of the court's order. In *Rundle v Rundle*,[656] for example, the Court of Appeal rejected the wife's application for leave to appeal where she argued that the value of the former matrimonial home had fallen by nearly 15% after the court order, but before its sale. Purchas LJ considered that fluctuations in the value of

---

£33,000. The Court of Appeal set aside the order, which had been invalidated by an unsound valuation: the judge had clearly intended that the husband was to be left with enough money to re-house himself. Contrast *B v B (Financial Provision: Leave to Appeal)* [1994] 1 FLR 219 where a fall in the value of a house from £340,000 to £250,000 was held not to justify re-opening an order.

[651] [1988] 1 FLR 219, CA.   [652] [1990] 2 FLR 202, CA.

[653] See to similar effect, *Kean v Kean* [2002] 2 FLR 28. Compare *Warren v Warren* [1982] 4 FLR 529, CA where there was a 'gross error' through no-one's fault of almost 100% in the agreed valuation. Since neither party had had the opportunity to correct the false assumption on which the order was made, it was held to be unfair to hold them to it, so the order was set aside.

[654] [1991] 2 FLR 530, CA.   [655] [1991] 2 FLR 530 at 539, CA.   [656] [1992] 2 FLR 80, CA.

assets, and particularly real property, are inevitable; to allow them on their own to form the basis of an appeal would deny the maxim that there should be finality in litigation. In *Cornick v Cornick*[657] there was a dramatic increase in the value of the husband's shareholdings, the effect of which was to reduce the wife's share of the family wealth from some 51%, at the date of the court order, to just 20% 18 months later. Hale J reviewed earlier authorities, and considered that for the *Barder* principles to apply, something unforeseen and unforeseeable[658] must have happened which dramatically affected the value of assets so as to bring about a substantial change in the balance of assets effected by the court order. This was not such a case, and the sharp increase in the value of the husband's shares was not a 'new event' within the scope of the *Barder* principles. The husband's shares had been properly valued at the date of the hearing and the case law showed that the property price fluctuations, however dramatic, did not of themselves entitle the court to intervene.

Where the court does grant leave to appeal out of time, it should reassess the order for financial provision or property adjustment afresh, and consider the criteria in s 25(2) of the Matrimonial Causes Act 1973 having regard to all the facts as they are known at the time of the appeal hearing.[659]

E ENFORCEMENT OF ORDERS

1 METHODS OF ENFORCEMENT

(a) Periodical payments

If periodical payments are secured, there is of course no question of enforcement. When arrears[660] of unsecured periodical payments accrue, the payee[661] has a number of means of enforcing the order at her disposal. But her position is basically different from that of a successful claimant in an action for damages for tort or breach of contract, for the order is not a final judgment and she does not have the full rights of a judgment creditor.

---

[657] [1994] 2 FLR 530. In *Worlock v Worlock* [1994] 2 FLR 689, CA the husband's wealth was greatly increased some two years after a consent order, where his family company's land gained the benefit of planning permission, and he took a transfer of shares from his mother. The Court of Appeal held this was not a *Barder* situation. The relevant circumstances (the husband's expectation to acquire the mother's shares and the landholding) were known at the time of the original order. It was only the scale of events, and their timing, which were different from originally envisaged. Contrast *Penrose v Penrose* [1994] 2 FLR 621, CA where the Court of Appeal accepted the husband's argument that an unexpectedly large tax liability could be a 'new event' under *Barder* principles. The Court, however, declined to set the order aside; the husband could have established his likely tax liability if he had made due and proper inquiry before the hearing.

[658] For another judgment focusing on foreseeability, see *Maskell v Maskell* [2001] EWCA Civ 858, [2003] 1 FLR 1138: husband's redundancy not unforeseeable: 'There is nothing permanent about employment of the sort that Mr Maskell held at the date of judgment before the district judge. There are hundreds of thousands of breadwinners who have to face the challenge of the loss of what seems to be secure employment as a result of all sorts of events' per Thorpe LJ at para 4.

[659] *Smith v Smith (Smith Intervening)* [1992] Fam 69, CA; *Garner v Garner* [1992] 1 FLR 573, CA.

[660] The court also has power to order the recovery of overpayments: see Matrimonial Causes Act 1973 s 33 and s 38.

[661] We assume for the purpose of discussion that this is the wife.

If the party in default applies to have the order varied or discharged, the court in effect has a discretion to remit the arrears in part or even entirely by making a retrospective order.[662] In order to prevent large sums from mounting up, arrears which have been due for twelve months or more may not be enforced without the leave of the court: this gives some protection to a party who has stopped paying the full sum ordered and has been mistakenly led to believe by the other's acquiescence that he will not enforce the rest.[663] The court can also give the debtor time to pay and, in particular, may order payment by instalments. Because of this discretion, the arrears do not constitute a legal debt and cannot be sued for as such,[664] nor may the payee institute bankruptcy proceedings as a means of execution or prove in the other party's bankruptcy for arrears.[665] But with these important exceptions she has available all the usual means of execution open to a judgment creditor in the High Court or a county court, as the case may be.[666]

One way of enforcing the payment of arrears is by issuing a judgment summons under the Debtors Act 1869, when the court can make an order for the payment by instalments and commit the payer for contempt if he wilfully fails to pay them.[667] Because the process subjects the respondent to the risk of imprisonment, it must comply with the rights conferred by Art 6 of the European Convention on Human Rights, including a presumption of innocence, precise articulation of the charge, adequate time to prepare a defence and examination of supporting evidence.[668] Since the crucial issue is whether the failure to pay is wilful, it has been held that the judge should consider whether the order might have been varied or suspended if the debtor had applied for that purpose, and if so, may make a new order for payment of the amount due together with the costs of the summons.[669] It has been suggested that the requirements of the Convention render the judgment summons largely obsolete as a means of enforcement, since the protections now given to the defendant mean that it is easier to hide assets and resist disclosure[670] and it seems that it is little used.

Alternatively, the payee may apply for an attachment of earnings order. The detailed provisions are mutatis mutandis the same as those relating to attachment orders made

---

[662] *MacDonald v MacDonald* [1964] P 1CA.

[663] Matrimonial Causes Act 1973 s 32. See further Law Com No 25, para 92.

[664] *Bailey v Bailey* (1884) 13 QBD 855, CA; *Robins v Robins* [1907] 2 KB 13.

[665] *Cartwright v Cartwright (No 2)* [2002] EWCA Civ 931, [2002] 1 FLR 919. Consequently the arrears are not affected by bankruptcy and may be enforced by other methods: *Linton v Linton* (1885) 15 QBD 239; *Re Henderson* (1888) 20 QBD 509, CA. For bankruptcy proceedings as a means of enforcing payment of a lump sum, see below.

[666] An undertaking to make payments given to the court may be enforced in the same way as an order (at least if the court would have had jurisdiction to make a similar order): *Gandolfo v Gandolfo* [1981] QB 359, CA. An order made by a divorce county court may be transferred to the High Court if it cannot be conveniently enforced in the county court. It is then enforceable as though it had been made by the High Court: Family Proceedings Rules 1991 r 7.3.

[667] For the procedure, see the Family Proceedings Rules 1991 r 7.2, r 7.4–7.6 as amended by the Family Proceedings (Amendment) Rules 2003 (SI 2003/184) r 11 and Sch 1.

[668] *Mubarak v Mubarak* [2001] 1 FLR 698, CA; *Corbett v Corbett* [2003] EWCA Civ 559, [2003] 2 FLR 385.

[669] *Corbett v Corbett* (above). Power to consider variation is contained in FPR 1991 r 7.4(9)(b).

[670] See Thorpe LJ at para 41 in *Mubarak v Mubarak* (above). See also P Rutter, 'Judgment Summonses: The Final Nail in the Coffin' [2003] Fam Law 433. But for a contrary view, see J Southgate, 'Judgment Summonses: Still Scope for a Comeback?' [2003] Fam Law 436.

in a magistrates' court.[671] The Maintenance Enforcement Act 1991 extended the enforcement powers of the High Court and county courts as regards maintenance orders (which include orders for periodical payments). These powers apply when the court makes a maintenance order, or in subsequent proceedings for its revocation or variation. The first is to order payment by standing order, or by other similar method.[672] A debtor who has unreasonably refused to open a bank account can be ordered to do so for this purpose.[673] The second is an unrestricted power to make an attachment of earnings order.[674]

(b) Other orders

An order for the payment of a lump sum is more in the nature of a judgment for damages and generally may be enforced in the same way. A lump sum (or costs) order is now provable on the bankruptcy of the payer spouse.[675] The payee may issue a judgment summons or apply for an attachment of earnings order.[676] As in the case of periodical payments, a lump sum payment (or any part payable by instalment) cannot be enforced more than 12 months after it falls due without the leave of the court.[677]

Failure to comply with an order to transfer or settle property may be enforced in the same way as any other similar order in the High Court or a county court. Once a property adjustment order in ancillary relief proceedings has taken effect (on decree absolute), it confers on the beneficiary an equitable interest in the property which may then be enforced, including in situations where the property has since vested in the payer's trustee in bankruptcy. Thus, in a case where the husband was made bankrupt before the order could be executed, his trustee took subject to the wife's interest in the husband's share in the matrimonial home, which he had been ordered to transfer to her.[678]

---

[671] See above, p 978. If the order is a High Court order, the collecting officer is the proper officer of the High Court or the appropriate officer of the county court specified in the order: Attachment of Earnings Act 1971 s 6 (7).

[672] Maintenance Enforcement Act 1991 s 1(5).   [673] Ibid, s 1(6).

[674] Ibid, s 1(4)(b). Previously, the latter could only be made if the debtor consented, or if he was guilty of wilful neglect or culpable default in failing to meet the order.

[675] Insolvency Rules 1986 (SI 1986/1925) r 12.3 as amended by Insolvency (Amendment) Rules 2005 (SI 2005/527) rr 44, 3.1, but only in relation to bankruptcy orders made on or after 1 April 2005. The bankrupt will be released from his obligation under the order when discharged. Cf *Woodley v Woodley (No 2)* [1993] 2 FLR 477, CA, where Balcombe LJ suggested the rules be changed to allow a lump sum order to be provable on a payer's bankruptcy and yet not to be released on his discharge. Note that the court has power to make a lump sum order against a bankrupt spouse, although it should have a clear picture of the assets and liabilities of the bankrupt and consider the effect the bankruptcy has on the debtor spouse's ability to pay: *Woodley v Woodley* [1992] 2 FLR 417, CA and *Hellyer v Hellyer* [1996] 2 FLR 579, CA. In *Russell v Russell* [1998] 1 FLR 936 it was held that a bankruptcy order could properly be made to enforce a lump sum even though (at that time) the sum was not provable in the bankruptcy, where the debtor had failed to comply with other orders of the court.

[676] See the definition of 'maintenance order' in the Administration of Justice Act 1970 s 28 and Sch 8, and the Attachment of Earnings Act 1971 Sch 1, para 3, as amended in each case by the Matrimonial Causes Act 1973 Sch 2, and the Domestic Proceedings and Magistrates' Courts Act 1978 Sch 2.

[677] Matrimonial Causes Act 1973 s 32 as amended by the Family Law Act 1996 Sch 8, para 17. Other useful methods of obtaining enforcement include freezing orders, oral examination, production appointments and sequestration: see Jacob J in *Mubarak v Mubarak* [2001] 1 FLR 698, CA. But for the limitations of these methods, see the next instalments of the litigation involving this divorce: *Mubarak v Mubarak* [2002] EWHC 2171 (Fam), [2003] 2 FLR 533 and [2004] EWHC 1158 (Fam), [2004] 2 FLR 932.

[678] *Mountney v Treharne* [2002] EWCA Civ 1174, [2002] 2 FLR 930.

2 ATTEMPTS TO DEFEAT CLAIMS FOR FINANCIAL RELIEF

A spouse might well try to defeat an application for financial relief by disposing of his property or transferring it out of the jurisdiction. He might do this beforehand in anticipation of an application or order or, alternatively, after an order has been made in order to reduce the property available to meet it. To prevent fraudulent dispositions of this kind, a measure of protection is given by the Matrimonial Causes Act 1973 s 37.[679] This applies to any order for maintenance pending suit, financial provision, property adjustment or pension sharing order, any order made under s 27 of the Act on the ground of failure to provide reasonable maintenance, the variation of any of these orders during the payer's lifetime, and the alteration of a maintenance agreement during the parties' joint lives. For the sake of convenience, it will be assumed throughout the following discussion that the wife (or former wife) is applying for or has obtained an order against the husband; it must be appreciated, however, that exactly the same principles apply if the husband is seeking financial provision from the wife or if anyone is seeking it for the children of the family.

If the court is satisfied that the husband is about to make any disposition or to transfer out of the jurisdiction or otherwise deal with any property with the intention of defeating the wife's claim, it may make such an order as it thinks fit to restrain him from doing so and to protect the claim.[680] It cannot, however, issue a mandatory injunction to require him to take steps in relation to assets in order to release these to the payee. In *Field v Field*, for example, it was held that the court could not order the husband to elect to take the maximum lump sum from his pension in order to pay the second instalment of a lump sum order to the wife.[681]

In *Crittenden v Crittenden*[682] the Court of Appeal held that, for the purpose of s 37, 'property' means property in which either or both spouses has or had a beneficial interest, in possession or reversion, while 'dealing with' refers to some *positive* dealing with property, and not to anything which is purely negative, such as failing to deal with property.[683]

---

[679] As amended by the Welfare Reform and Pensions Act 1999 Sch 3, para 9. The power was originally given by the Matrimonial Causes (Property and Maintenance) Act 1958 s 2. There is similar power under s 423 of the Insolvency Act 1986, and applications may be made under both Acts. For a useful comparison of these powers, see *Trowbridge v Trowbridge* [2003] 2 FLR 231 paras 49–61. Cf *Ram v Ram, Ram and Russell* [2004] EWCA Civ 1452, [2004] 3 FCR 425 where the wife succeeded in having a disposition set aside under s 423 but the property was then vested in the trustee in bankruptcy. The case preceded the entry into force of Insolvency (Amendment) Rules 2005 (SI 2005/527) rr 44, 3.1 which should ameliorate the position for others in the same position as the wife in future.

[680] It has been held that this power extends to restraining dispositions of property already situated abroad: *Hamlin v Hamlin* [1986] Fam 11, CA. However, the court will only make an order if it can be enforced.

[681] *Field v Field* [2003] 1 FLR 376: furthermore, the husband's pension rights did not give him a beneficial interest in the fund which could amount to 'property' for the purposes of s 37.

[682] [1990] 2 FLR 361, CA.

[683] On the other hand, 'dealing with' in s 37 does *not* require there to be a disposition in favour of the third party: *Shipman v Shipman* [1991] 1 FLR 250, where Anthony Lincoln J held that a husband's use of his funds as a deposit on the purchase of a house, to maintain himself and to pay off existing debts was caught by s 37. The judge also held, following *Roche v Roche* (1981) 11 Fam Law 243, CA, that the court has an inherent jurisdiction to grant injunctions freezing assets which might otherwise be put beyond reach of an applicant, notwithstanding the enhancement of s 37. Note also *Newlon Housing Trust v Al-Sulaimen* [1998] 3 WLR 451, HL where the House of Lords held that a concession by counsel that the service of a notice to quit by one of the spouses, who were joint tenants of a council tenancy (the effect of the notice being to terminate the

It followed that the court had no power, under s 37, to make orders relating to assets owned by a *company* in which the husband held the issued shares. Nor could the court make an order under s 37 requiring the husband to enter into a covenant not to compete with a proposed purchaser of the company's assets. *Crittenden v Crittenden* was not followed in *Green v Green*[684] (where Connell J preferred the earlier authority of *Nicholas v Nicholas*)[685] to the extent that the court held it may make an order against a limited company which may be regarded as a spouse's 'alter ego', ie where he owns or controls all its shares, or a majority of them in circumstances where minority shareholdings could be disregarded.

If the court is satisfied that the husband has already made a disposition with the intention of defeating the wife's claim, it may make an order setting the disposition aside.[686] In this case, however, a wife who has not yet obtained an order for financial relief must also show that, if the disposition were set aside, the court would make a different order from that which it would otherwise make. Defeating the wife's claim may take the form of preventing her from obtaining an order at all, reducing the amount that might be ordered, or impeding or frustrating the enforcement of any order that might be made or has been made. It seems, despite an earlier judicial suggestion to the contrary,[687] that where a husband declares himself bankrupt to avoid a claim for ancillary relief, the bankruptcy itself is not a reviewable disposition entitling the court to intervene under s 37. The correct procedure is for application to be made under s 282(1)(a) of the Insolvency Act 1986 to annul the bankruptcy order on the basis it ought not to have been made.[688]

In many cases it may be difficult to establish what the husband's intention was when he made a disposition. Consequently the Act introduced a compromise designed to protect the interests of the wife, the husband and the transferee. If the husband made the disposition three years or more before the application to set it aside, the wife must prove affirmatively that he had the intention to defeat her claim. If he made it less than three years before or is about to make it, this intention will be presumed if the effect of the transaction would be to defeat her claim or, where the disposition has already taken place and an order is in force, if it has had this effect: the burden then shifts on to him to prove that this was not his intention. In *Kemmis v Kemmis (Welland Intervening)*[689] it was held that the husband's intention to defeat the wife's claim has to be a subjective intention, but

---

tenancy), was a 'disposition' of property reviewable under s 37, had been wrongly made, following its earlier opinion in *Harrow London Borough Council v Johnstone* [1997] 1 All ER 929, HL at 940a (Lord Mustill) and 940h (Lord Hoffmann) and see *Bater and Bater v Greenwich London Borough Council* [1999] 2 FLR 993, CA.

[684] [1993] 1 FLR 326.   [685] [1984] FLR 285, CA.

[686] But it may be unnecessary to go to these lengths where it is clear that the husband retains control over the assets: the court may simply deal with the case on the basis that the property remains his: *Purba v Purba* [2000] 1 FLR 444, CA: husband transferred funds to accounts in names of relatives who were bare trustees.

[687] *Woodley v Woodley* [1992] 2 FLR 417 at 423F (per Ewbank J).

[688] *F v F (Divorce: Insolvency: Annulment of Bankruptcy Order)* [1994] 1 FLR 359; the bankruptcy proceedings may be transferred to the Family Division: see *Couvaras v Wolf* [2002] 2 FLR 107 where Wilson J had thoroughly investigated the husband's finances in the ancillary relief proceedings and determined that the bankruptcy petition was a sham and the proceedings an abuse of the process of the court. See also *F v F (S Intervening)(Financial Provision: Bankruptcy: Reviewable Disposition)* [2002] EWHC 2814 (Fam), [2003] 1 FLR 911: husband had assets exceeding his indebtedness by more than £300,000 when he petitioned for bankruptcy and the order should not have been made.

[689] [1988] 1 WLR 1307, CA. See also *F v F (S Intervening)(Financial Provision: Bankruptcy: Reviewable Disposition)* [2002] EWHC 2814 (Fam), [2003] 1 FLR 911.

does not have to be the husband's sole or even dominant intention. It suffices if it plays a *substantial* part in the husband's intention as a whole.

Certain transactions may not be upset at all. No order may be made after the husband's death with respect to any disposition made by him by will or codicil. A disposition inter vivos *already* made may not be set aside if it was made for valuable consideration (other than marriage) to a third party acting in good faith and without notice of the husband's intention to defeat the wife's claim.[690] Where a third party had *actual* knowledge of the husband's intention, it is difficult to see how he could claim to act in good faith, and so the transaction will be set aside. However, in *Kemmis v Kemmis (Welland Intervening)*[691] the Court of Appeal held the defence is also not available to a third party who has *constructive* notice of the husband's intentions.[692]

The disposition is voidable and not void, and consequently, even if it is set aside, this cannot affect any subsequent dealings with the property in good faith. Hence, if the husband's immediate transferee is not protected but disposes of the property to a bona fide purchaser for value without notice, the latter's title cannot be upset by the order. In *National Provincial Bank Ltd v Hastings Car Mart Ltd (No 3)*[693] the husband, who had deserted the wife, conveyed the matrimonial home to the defendant company, who immediately charged it to the plaintiff bank. Although the conveyance to the defendants was set aside on the ground that it was made with the intention of defeating the wife's claim to maintenance, it was held by the Court of Appeal that this did not extinguish the plaintiff's mortgage, which remained a valid charge.

3 REGISTRATION OF ORDERS IN OTHER COURTS

If the spouse ordered to pay money duly fulfils his or her obligations, orders made in magistrates' courts have the advantage that payment may be made through the justices' chief executive; conversely, if he fails to fulfil them, a spouse who has an order made in the High Court or a county court has superior means of enforcing it at his or her disposal. Consequently the Maintenance Orders Act of 1958 introduced the means of registering in one court a 'maintenance order'[694] made by another. Under this Act a person entitled to payments under a maintenance order made by the High Court or a county court may apply to the court that made the order to have it registered in a magistrates' court; whether or not the application is granted lies completely in the discretion of the court.[695] In the

---

[690] Section 37(4). A purchaser acts in good faith provided that he acts honestly: *Central Estates (Belgravia) Ltd v Woolgar* [1972] 1 QB 48, CA.

[691] [1988] 1 WLR 1307, CA.

[692] *Sherry v Sherry* [1991] 1 FLR 307, CA. See also *Trowbridge v Trowbridge* [2003] 2 FLR 231: second wife was ignorant of husband's intention of defeating first wife's enforcement action when he made her substantial regular monthly payments and could thus rely on s 37(4). However, the payments were capable of being set aside under the Insolvency Act 1986 s 423.

[693] [1964] Ch 665, CA. See further the same case in the House of Lords (*National Provincial Bank Ltd v Ainsworth*) above, p 185. There was no appeal on the point discussed here. Presumably in circumstances such as these the immediate transferee may be ordered to pay over the value of the property.

[694] As defined by the Maintenance Orders Act 1958 s 1(1A) added by the Administration of Justice Act 1970 s 27(3) and Sch 8, as subsequently amended. The statutory definition includes (inter alia) orders for periodical or other payments made, or having effect if made, under the Matrimonial Causes Act 1973 Pt III, the Domestic Proceedings and Magistrates' Courts Act 1978 and the Children Act 1989.

[695] Section 1(1)(a), s 2(1).

same way a person entitled to payments under a maintenance order made by the magistrates' court may apply to that court to have it registered in the High Court; again, the court has a discretion[696] whether or not to grant the application. County courts made 948 orders for registration in the magistrates' courts in 2004.[697]

If the application is granted, no proceedings may be begun or continued to enforce the order in the original court and any attachment of earnings order already in force ceases to have effect.[698] Once the order has been registered, it may be enforced only as though it had been made by the court in which it is registered.[699]

An order may be varied, revoked, suspended and revived only by the original court, except that, in the case of orders made by the High Court or a county court and registered in a magistrates' court, variation of rates of payment (as distinct from a variation of other provisions and complete revocation, suspension and revival of the order) may be made only by the magistrates' court in which it is registered[700] if both parties are in England or Wales.[701]

There are also provisions to register and enforce in this country maintenance orders made abroad.[702] Of particular importance are the Civil Jurisdiction and Judgments Act 1982 (as amended) and the Brussels I Regulation—Council Regulation (EC) No 44/2001 of 22 December 2000 on jurisdiction and the recognition and enforcement of judgments in civil and commercial matters.[703] Article 5(2) of the Regulation gives jurisdiction to courts to entertain proceedings regarding 'matters relating to maintenance' and s 5(4) of the Act provides that a 'maintenance order' duly registered may be enforced in the same way as if it had been made by the registering court. Maintenance (in the context of divorce) has been defined by the European Court as any 'financial obligations between former spouses after divorce which are fixed on the basis of their respective needs and resources'.[704] The Regulation does not, however, apply to 'rights in property arising out of a matrimonial relationship,'[705] and the question has arisen whether orders other than for periodical payments may be classed as 'maintenance' and hence enforceable in another contracting state. In *Van Den Boogaard v Laumen*[706] the European Court of Justice held

---

[696] Section 1(1)(b), s 2(3)(3A).   [697] *Judicial Statistics 2004* (2005) Table 5.8.

[698] Section 2(2), (4); Attachment of Earnings Act 1971 s 11(1)(a), (2).

[699] Section 3. This includes the power to remit the whole or any part of arrears due.

[700] Or any other magistrates' court having jurisdiction in the place where the complainant is for the time being: Magistrates' Court (Maintenance Orders Act 1958) Rules 1959 r 9. The magistrates are not obliged to provide reasons other than, if requested, written reasons for the purposes of appeal: *Hackshaw v Hackshaw* [1999] 2 FLR 876. See also *Stray v Stray* [1999] 2 FLR 610.

[701] Section 4, as amended by the Administration of Justice Act 1970 Sch 11. Hence an order for maintenance pending suit and an interim order made under s 27 of the Matrimonial Causes Act 1973 should normally not be registered in a magistrates' court because this removes control from the divorce court: *Armsby v Armsby* (1973) 118 Sol Jo 183; cf *Practice Direction* [1980] 1 All ER 1007. The magistrates' court has a discretion to remit the application to the original court and the original court may vary the order of payment in proceedings to vary other provisions of the order.

[702] Maintenance Orders (Reciprocal Enforcement) Act 1972. For full details see S Oliver and P Clements, *Enforcing Family Finance Orders* (2nd ed 2006).

[703] Discussed in Chapter 1 pp 29–30. The Regulation superseded, as far as the EU states apart from Denmark are concerned, the 1968 Brussels Convention on Jurisdiction and Enforcement of Judgments in Civil and Commercial Matters which was incorporated into English law by the Civil Jurisdiction and Judgments Act 1982.

[704] *De Cavel v De Cavel* [1980] 3 CMLR 1 at para 5.   [705] Art 2(a).

[706] [1997] QB 759, construing the Brussels Convention.

that they may do so if the purpose of making the order was to ensure the former spouse's maintenance. The court considering the question will have to determine this from the reasoning of the original court:

'If this shows that a provision awarded is designed to enable one spouse to provide for himself or herself or if the needs and resources of each of the spouses are taken into consideration in the determination of its amount, the decision will be concerned with maintenance. On the other hand, where the provision awarded is solely concerned with dividing property between the spouses, the decision will be concerned with rights in property arising out of a matrimonial relationship and will not therefore be enforceable under the Brussels Convention. A decision which does both these things may . . . be enforced in part if it clearly shows the aims to which the different parts of the judicial provision correspond.'[707]

The Court made clear that a lump sum, and even a property adjustment order, are capable of being orders 'for the provision of maintenance' so long as that is their purpose. Accordingly, in *Al-Khatib v Masry*[708] Munby J held that a *Duxbury* fund may constitute 'maintenance' for this purpose, and he provided that his order would expressly so state to facilitate the wife's enforcing the award under a *Duxbury* calculation of a lump sum of £5.5 million in another jurisdiction. He also stated that the order, when drawn, could, if she wished, provide that the obligation of meeting this maintenance liability should fall primarily upon properties in France, so that the transfer to the wife of title to these properties would be treated as being in commutation of her maintenance claim.[709]

F FINANCIAL RELIEF AFTER FOREIGN DIVORCE, DISSOLUTION, ANNULMENT OR LEGAL SEPARATION [710]

1 BACKGROUND TO THE LEGISLATION

Formerly, the court could only make financial provision or property adjustment orders under the Matrimonial Causes Act 1973 in the course of divorce, nullity or judicial separation proceedings instituted in England and Wales. This meant that spouses who had been divorced, or whose marriage had been annulled, abroad could not seek such relief from the English divorce courts.[711] Though logical, this rule could nevertheless cause hardship, particularly to those who were habitually resident in England and Wales and who, having been divorced abroad, sometimes without their knowledge,[712] had no other means of

---

[707] Ibid at para 22.   [708] [2002] 1 FLR 1053.   [709] At para 129.

[710] See generally C Canton 'The Matrimonial and Family Proceedings Act 1984: Financial Relief After Foreign Divorce' [1985] Fam Law 13 and Gordon 'Part III of the MFPA 1984: A Panacea for Foreign Divorcees?' [1986] JSWL 329. The Civil Partnership Act 2004 s 72(4) and Sch 7 Part 1 make equivalent provision for civil partnerships dissolved abroad.

[711] Similarly, since they were no longer married, they could not seek maintenance under the Matrimonial Causes Act 1973 s 27, or under the Domestic Proceedings and Magistrates' Courts Act 1978.

[712] As could happen, for example, where divorce by talaq is permitted. See also *Lamagni v Lamagni* [1995] 2 FLR 452, CA where an English wife obtained a divorce decree in England without knowledge that her Italian husband had earlier obtained a divorce in proceedings in Belgium.

redress.[713] Responding to calls for reform,[714] the Law Commission[715] recommended widening the jurisdiction of the divorce courts to give redress to such applicants. These recommendations were enacted in the Matrimonial and Family Proceedings Act 1984, Part III.[716]

2 WHEN RELIEF MAY BE SOUGHT

Under s 12(1) of the 1984 Act, where a marriage has been dissolved or annulled, or the parties to the marriage are legally separated, by means of judicial or other proceedings in an overseas country, and the divorce, annulment or legal separation is entitled to be recognised as valid in England and Wales,[717] then either party may apply to the court for financial relief. It will be noted that under this provision:

(1) The divorce etc must have been granted in an 'overseas country', which means a country or territory outside the British Islands.[718] Hence, for example, a spouse who has been divorced in Scotland cannot, under these provisions, subsequently seek financial relief in the English court.

(2) The divorce etc must have been by means of 'judicial or other proceedings'. The phrase 'other proceedings' is intended to cover cases where the marriage has been terminated extra-judicially, for example by talaq.[719]

(3) Provided the above criteria are satisfied, *either* party may apply for relief.

(4) A party who has been legally separated abroad can apply for relief even though he may be able to petition for divorce etc in an English court.

(5) A party who remarries (but not the other party) loses the right to apply for relief.[720]

3 APPLICANTS ARE REQUIRED TO OBTAIN LEAVE

(a) Procedure

Before any substantive claim may be made, applicants must first obtain the court's leave to make an application for a financial order. The court cannot grant leave unless it considers that there is a substantial ground for making the application and that there is jurisdiction

---

[713] See eg *Torok v Torok* [1973] 3 All ER 101 and *Quazi v Quazi* [1980] AC 744, HL.

[714] Not least by the Law Lords in *Quazi v Quazi*, above.

[715] Law Com No 117 *Financial Relief after Foreign Divorce* (1982).

[716] Jurisdiction is vested in the Family Division of the High Court and any county court designated by the Lord Chancellor: ss 27, 33(4) and 34(1)(b).

[717] For a discussion of the rules of recognition see eg Cheshire and North *Private International Law* (13th edn, 1999 by P North and J Fawcett). See *Emin v Yeldag (Attorney-General and Secretary of State for Foreign and Commonwealth Affairs Intervening)* [2001] 1 FLR 956: divorce granted in Turkish Republic of Northern Cyprus recognised, and hence application for leave under Part III could be made, notwithstanding non-recognition of the state of Northern Cyprus by the United Kingdom.

[718] Matrimonial and Family Proceedings Act 1984 s 27. British Islands means England and Wales, Scotland, Northern Ireland, the Isle of Man and the Channel Islands: Interpretation Act 1978 Sch 1.

[719] See Law Com, op cit, at p 21 in their explanatory notes on clause 1 of their draft Bill.

[720] Matrimonial and Family Proceedings Act 1984 s 12(2). The right is lost even if the subsequent marriage is void or voidable: s 12(3).

to make the order.[721] Applications for leave are made ex parte and should be accompanied by an affidavit stating the facts relied upon and the grounds upon which it is alleged the court has jurisdiction.[722] The requirement to obtain leave is intended to filter applications whilst at the same time providing maximum protection for all those concerned. The idea of the ex parte procedure is to save the potential respondent the time and expense of being involved in the case before the bona fides of the application have been tested. Given the one-sided nature of the application, there are those who doubt whether the potential respondent is well protected by this procedure.[723]

Leave may be granted notwithstanding that an order has been made by a court outside England and Wales requiring the respondent to make financial provision for, or to transfer property to, the applicant or a child of the family.[724] However, in *Hewitson v Hewitson*[725] the Court of Appeal held that the mischief the 1984 Act was designed to redress was a narrow one: to give the English courts power to entertain applications for financial provision where no, or no sufficient, relief had been awarded abroad. The Act is not intended to provide an applicant with 'two bites at the one cherry',[726] or to invite the English courts to act as a court of appeal from the courts of other countries. On the facts, the Court of Appeal found the parties' claims to ancillary relief had been settled by a final clean break order in California. The court refused leave, even though the wife argued that after the divorce the parties had resumed cohabitation as a result of which she was left in a parlous financial position. Similarly, in *Jordan v Jordan*[727] the court refused leave where the wife's avowed purpose in invoking the Part III jurisdiction was effectively to find a means of enforcing a consent order made by the California court against the husband's assets. The Court of Appeal held that leave should rarely be given where a foreign order had been made unless enforcement remedies in the foreign jurisdiction were manifestly inadequate and reciprocal enforcement remedies were ineffective. By contrast, in *M v L (Financial Relief after Overseas Divorce)*[728] where the parties had divorced in South Africa 30 years before the wife's application, and a maintenance order for the children was the sole order

---

[721] Ibid, s 13(1) and s 15. See *Holmes v Holmes* [1989] Fam 47, CA: court must take into account the criteria set out in s 16 and if it is clear that, were leave to be given, the application would founder 'at the first hurdle of s 16(1)' then leave should not be granted. The burden of showing that there are substantial grounds for granting leave falls on the applicant: *Z v Z (Financial Provision: Overseas Divorce)* [1992] 2 FLR 291. However, if leave is granted ex parte, it does not follow that the onus is then transferred to the other party to establish that leave should not have been granted or continued: *N v N (Foreign Divorce: Financial Relief)* [1997] 1 FLR 900.

[722] Family Proceedings Rules 1991 r 3.18. It seems that the court has a discretion to allow the potential respondent to be heard, at any rate, where objection is taken to jurisdiction: *Chebaro v Chebaro* [1986] Fam 71 at 72 per Sheldon J at first instance. The affidavit should pay particular reference to the matters set out in s 16(1) of the 1984 Act: see below.

[723] See eg Scot Law Com No 72, para 2.13. Quaere whether the procedure would be improved by allowing potential respondents to be heard if they so desired; see *Hewitson v Hewitson* [1995] 1 FLR 241, CA where, at 245, Butler-Sloss LJ considered '. . . the procedure for leave under s 13 might be usefully reviewed'.

[724] 1984 Act s 13(2), though this is a factor to be taken into account in deciding whether to make an order: s 16(2), discussed below. The reference to a court outside England and Wales means that there is jurisdiction even if a court in another part of the United Kingdom has made an order. This could happen, for example, where the divorce takes place abroad, the applicant is domiciled in Scotland and the matrimonial home is in England.

[725] [1995] 1 FLR 241, CA.

[726] *Lamagni v Lamagni* [1995] 2 FLR 452 at 454, CA per Butler-Sloss LJ.

[727] [1999] 2 FLR 1069, CA.   [728] [2003] EWHC 328 (Fam) [2003] 2 FLR 425.

made by the South African court, the wife was given leave, Coleridge J considering that 'this wife has scarcely had a first nibble let alone a bite of the cherry.'[729]

(b) Jurisdiction

Before leave may be granted, the court must be satisfied that there is jurisdiction to make the order.[730] Subject to the provisions governing EU member states,[731] the court has jurisdiction if:

(a) either party to the marriage was domiciled in England and Wales on the date of the application for leave or when the divorce, nullity or legal separation took effect; or

(b) either party was habitually resident there throughout the period of one year ending on the date of the application for leave or when the divorce etc took effect; or

(c) either or both parties had at the date of the application for leave a beneficial interest in possession[732] in a dwelling house[733] situated in England and Wales which was at some time during the marriage a matrimonial home of the parties to the marriage.[734]

If jurisdiction is taken on the last basis, the court's powers are more limited.[735]

(c) Interim orders

Once leave has been granted, then, save where jurisdiction has been taken solely upon the matrimonial home basis, and provided that it appears to the court that the applicant or any child of the family is in need of immediate financial assistance, the court may make an interim order for maintenance.[736]

4 APPLYING FOR AN ORDER

Once leave has been granted, application may be made for financial relief.[737] It should be stressed that the granting of leave does not ipso facto mean that an order will be made. Indeed, before an order will be made the court must consider whether in all the circumstances it is appropriate for an English court to do so.[738] In deciding that issue the court is directed[739] to have regard to a number of matters designed to test whether the parties have any real connection with England and Wales; whether adequate relief has been or could be

---

[729] At para 37. For another example of leave being given despite substantial delay, see *Lamagni v Lamagni* [1995] 2 FLR 452, CA.

[730] Pursuant to s 15(1) of the 1984 Act.   [731] See above pp 32–5.

[732] This includes the receipt of or the right to receive rent or profits: s 27.

[733] This includes any building or part thereof which is occupied as a dwelling, and any yard, garden, garage or outhouse belonging to the dwelling-house and occupied therewith: s 27.

[734] This latter requirement implies that the married parties must have lived together in the property in question.

[735] Under s 20: see below.

[736] Section 14 of the 1984 Act. Under this provision the court may order the respondent to make periodical payments to the applicant or any child of the family for such term as the court thinks fit but beginning no earlier than the date of the grant of leave and ending with the date of the determination of the application for the order.

[737] For the procedure, see the Family Proceedings Rules 1991 r 3.18.

[738] Section 16(1) of the 1984 Act.   [739] By s 16(2).

obtained elsewhere, and whether in any event it would be worthwhile making an order here.[740] Purchas LJ said in *Holmes v Holmes*[741] that the requirements in s 16 reflect the fundamental rule of comity as between competent courts dealing with matters of this kind. The Court of Appeal stressed that an English court must always be slow to interfere with the competent court seized of the matter, which has made orders which are clearly enforceable, and which has dealt with the matter on a reasonably careful assessment of all its features.[742] However, 'the ultimate objective of Part III is to provide for a very small residuum of cases where the English court, bearing in mind all the warnings and cautions set out in the authorities, nevertheless feels that the outcome achieved in the foreign jurisdiction is simply not a just one as between the parties'.[743] The desire to achieve fairness is well-illustrated by *A v S (Financial Relief After Overseas US Divorce and Financial Proceedings)*.[744] There, the wife was British and the husband a US citizen. The husband bought a house in England and allegedly promised to put it in joint names after the wife's divorce was finalised. The parties married and moved to Texas but separated after only a few months, the wife returning to the English house. The husband speedily obtained a divorce in Texas, under whose law the wife received no share of any property acquired in sole names before the marriage, and thus no share of the English property. The court held that, given the husband's alleged promise, which had not been ruled upon by the Texas court, the fact that the Texan rules fell hard on the wife, that this could be remedied without injustice to the husband and that the wife had a real need for financial help, it was appropriate, notwithstanding evidence that the wife had lied in both the Texan and English proceedings, to make a lump sum award of £60,000 in the wife's favour.

5 ORDERS THAT MAY BE MADE

Provided it is satisfied that it should make an order, the court has the same powers (save where jurisdiction is taken on the matrimonial home basis) as under the Matrimonial Causes Act 1973, Part II.[745] In deciding what orders to make the court must have regard to the same considerations as it would when dealing with a domestic application,[746] though in addition it must consider the extent to which any overseas order has been or is likely to be complied with.[747]

Where jurisdiction is assumed on the matrimonial home basis, the court's powers are confined to making orders concerning that property or to making lump sum orders not exceeding the paying party's interest in it.[748]

---

[740] See *N v N (Foreign Divorce: Financial Relief)* [1997] 1 FLR 900 where Cazalet J, in setting aside an ex parte leave obtained by the husband, considered that the parties, who were both Swedish nationals and had been divorced in Sweden, had their main connection with that country which '. . . would outweigh the other considerations arising under s 16 such that the court would not regard it as appropriate for an order to be made [in England]'.

[741] [1989] Fam 47 at 53.

[742] Which reflects the decisions in relation to the grant of leave referred to earlier (see above, p 1077).

[743] [2002] EWHC 1157 (Fam), [2003] 1 FLR 431 per Bodey J at para 76.   [744] Ibid.

[745] And under Sch 7 to the Family Law Act 1996 (transfer of tenancies). However, it does not have the same procedural powers: *Roker International Properties Inc and Another v Couvaras and Wolf* [2000] 2 FLR 976: no power under FPR 1991 r 2.62 to order 'production' (now 'inspection') appointment in Part III applications, but a subpoena duces tecum may be issued instead.

[746] Section 18(1)–(5).   [747] Section 18(6).   [748] Section 20.

There are also similar provisions to domestic proceedings for dealing with consent orders[749] and for variation and discharge.[750]

In addition to the above powers, the court may, provided leave has been given, make such orders as it thinks fit restraining any disposition about to be made with the intention of defeating the claim for financial relief or setting aside any such disposition already made.[751] This power can be exercised even where the jurisdictional requirements are not satisfied, provided the court is satisfied that the marriage has been dissolved etc abroad and that the applicant intends to apply for leave for financial relief as soon as he has been habitually resident in England and Wales for one year.[752]

G REFORM [753]

The legislation, case law and practice which we have discussed in this chapter are so immensely complex and important that, inevitably, the whole topic remains the subject of continuing proposals for reform. The high level of divorce in England and Wales means that substantial numbers of couples are caught up in the web of negotiation, settlement and litigation over finance and property post-divorce each year. Once the Civil Partnership Act 2004 has come fully into effect, there is no reason to expect a lower rate of separation and dissolution for civil partners than for spouses. The costs, for the parties themselves and the state through the Legal Services Commission and the Court Service, are high and, although the encouragement of settlement via the Ancillary Relief Procedure and mediation may have some effect in lowering them, it might be argued that greater certainty of outcome would reduce disputes and hence cut costs further.[754] We have noted judicial concern at the high cost of litigation in ancillary relief.[755] Indeed, Thorpe LJ has gone so far as to suggest that the courts should not make orders unless there is a manifest need to do so, with the parties relying instead upon negotiation and mediation to settle their affairs.[756]

It is not surprising, therefore, that the government established an Ancillary Relief Advisory Group, composed of legal practitioners, the judiciary, and academics, to advise the Lord Chancellor on all aspects of ancillary relief, and to consider ways of reforming the law. In particular, the Group was invited to consider whether the Scottish system

---

[749] Orders can be made in the terms agreed on the basis only of prescribed information furnished with the application: s 19.

[750] Section 21 as amended by Welfare Reform and Pensions Act 1999 Schs 12, 13.

[751] Section 23. Where jurisdiction is taken upon the matrimonial home basis, the court's powers are confined to restraining or setting aside dispositions of the property: s 23(4). See also s 37 of the 1973 Act, discussed above, pp 1072–4.

[752] Section 24.

[753] See J Eekelaar, 'Should Section 25 be Reformed?' [1998] Fam Law 469; R Bailey-Harris, 'Dividing the Assets on Family Breakdown' (2001) 54 Current Legal Problems 533.

[754] See Davis et al *Simple Quarrels: Negotiating Money and Property Disputes on Divorce* (1994) p 270. The Law Society have characterised the new procedure as 'one of the unsung legal successes of recent years', with improvements in speed though accompanied by some 'front loading' of costs. See P Watson-Lee, 'Financial Provision on Divorce: Clarity and Fairness: Part 1' [2004] Fam Law 182 at 183.

[755] See above, p 1058.

[756] *White v White* [1998] 2 FLR 310, CA, reiterating his view in *H v H (Financial Provision: Capital Allowance)* [1993] 2 FLR 335 at 347.

(which applies a presumption of equal sharing of family assets) might be applied in England and Wales and whether pre-nuptial agreements should be given greater weight.[757] The Group was unanimously against the introduction of a system of presumptive equal division, considering it inappropriate for the jurisdiction in England and Wales. Whilst agreeing that there is a strong case in principle for codification of the principles that are currently applied in the courts, the group was divided on whether it would be desirable to enact a fresh statutory objective. In sum, the group was unenthusiastic about any major reform in the absence of much more evidence as to its need and as to what would represent an improvement over the current position. The members rightly noted that they were drawn only from the legal community and that social and public policy issues required a wider research base and consultative forum for debate.[758]

The government accepted the Group's recommendation not to introduce a presumption of equal division of assets[759] but in its Green Paper, *Supporting Families*[760] did suggest that pre-nuptial agreements should be binding in certain circumstances,[761] and that 'an over-arching objective and a set of guiding principles' might provide greater certainty and clarity in the law. They accordingly proposed that the court should 'exercise its powers so as to endeavour to do that which is fair and reasonable between the parties and any child of the family' and that the following guiding principles, set out in order of precedence, should guide the court:

'First, to promote the welfare of any child of the family under the age of eighteen, by meeting the housing needs of any children and the primary carer, and of the secondary carer; both to facilitate contact and to recognise the continuing importance of the secondary carer's role.

Second, the court would take into account the existence and content of any written agreement about financial arrangements, reached before or during marriage, which has not been enforced . . . .

Third, having dealt with the needs of children and the housing needs of the couple, and having taken into account a nuptial agreement, the court would then divide any surplus so as to achieve a fair result, recognising that fairness will generally require the value of the assets to be divided equally between the parties.

Fourth, the court would try to terminate financial relationships between the parties at the earliest date practicable.'[762]

No legislation resulted from the Green Paper, but the impetus for reform has perhaps been strengthened by the House of Lords' ruling in *White v White*[763] which has undoubtedly brought the 'yardstick of equality'—in effect, equal shares—to the forefront of attention when parties are negotiating, in small as well as 'big money' cases. The courts are still working through the implications of the judgment and there is no large-scale empirical study charting its impact in practice.[764] Were such research to be undertaken, it might shed

---

[757] [1998] Fam Law 381.

[758] Lord Chancellor's Ancillary Relief Advisory Group, *Report to the Lord Chancellor* (1998).

[759] See [1998] Fam Law 654.   [760] Home Office (1998) Ch 4.

[761] Ibid para 4.23 and see the discussion above at p 1014.   [762] Ibid paras 4.48, 4.49.

[763] [2001] 1 AC 596.

[764] There is a reported study by L Fisher, 'The Unexpected Impact of *White*—Taking "Equality" Too Far?' [2002] Fam Law 108 but this was a small-scale study based on interviews with ten solicitors. The author reported that *White* had influenced settlements both at the big money and poor end of the scale, with a

light on how viable equal division actually is across the financial spectrum and thus help identify whether codification of *White* would be desirable. In the meantime, however, the Law Society's Family Law Committee[765] has stressed the difficulties faced by litigants and their advisers in dealing with the width of discretion open to different judges and the lack of predictability in outcomes even (or perhaps especially) after *White*.[766] In their own proposals for reform, the Family Law Committee's working party rejected the replacement of discretion by a formula, and also rejected a straightforward equal division of assets as potentially unfair where the parent with care needs to retain the former matrimonial home—the only significant asset in many cases—as a home for the children. They also considered that ignoring the length of the marriage could be unjust. The Committee concluded that a guideline, which would be readily understood by the lay public, is required. Their proposal was as follows:

(1) Different guidelines should apply to cases where assets exceed needs and those where they do not.

(2) In relation to cases where needs outweigh the assets, where there are minor children, the housing needs of the parent with care will normally be the first matter to resolve. This should be decided on what is in the best interests of the children. This may, but need not, result in the home being preserved for the carer and children: where existing resources enable the other parent to be housed without having a detrimental effect on the children the court may require the parent with care to move.

(3) Where assets remain after meeting the housing needs of the parties, they should be distributed in accordance with the parties' remaining needs and in proportion to their separate abilities to meet those needs.

(4) In relation to cases where assets exceed needs, those needs will first be (notionally) met. Such needs may include a capital fund to provide for maintenance of one party where continuing financial obligations are appropriate.

(5) The contributions of each party must be taken into account, with the non-financial contributions of the home maker and child carer given a weight and significance appropriate to the circumstances of the case and their significance relative to any financial contributions within the trial judge's discretion. Such financial contributions could include money or capital introduced into the marriage as a result of an inheritance.

(6) Having dealt with the needs of children, the housing and other needs of the couple, and having taken into account any pre-nuptial agreement, any surplus must be divided fairly—this may or may not result in an equal division depending upon the factors in s 25 such as length of the marriage, the parties' future obligations and their overall financial positions.

greater tendency toward 'equality' albeit falling short of a 50/50 split. The interviewees also reported a greater emphasis upon conduct and contributions as a means of justifying a departure from equality (but the study preceded *Lambert v Lambert* [2002] EWCA Civ 1685, [2003] 1 FLR 139), and confusion as to how *White* should affect periodical payments and pension sharing.

765 Law Society, *Financial Provision on Divorce: Clarity and Fairness—Proposals for Reform* (2003).
766 P Watson-Lee, 'Financial Provision on Divorce: Clarity and Fairness: Part 2' [2004] Fam Law 348.

Whether these proposals should be adopted is doubtful. Although they largely seek to codify existing practice, they provide ample scope for disagreement and litigation. There may be disagreement as to whether what might be termed the 'needs' or 'contributions' approach is applicable to cases where it is unclear whether assets in fact exceed needs or not. In a 'needs' case, how should matters be resolved if there are no children? The reinstatement of a discretion to value non-financial contributions 'relative to' financial ones could be regarded as retrograde both in relation to its potentially discriminatory effect and as being productive of more litigation concerning the parties' competing contributions which *Lambert v Lambert*[767] was intended to halt. The weight to be given to any pre-nuptial agreement is not clarified. When 'may' an inheritance be counted, and when should it be excluded as a contribution? And so on.

As such questions make clear, one of the many difficulties in producing reform proposals lies in reconciling competing interests and competing objectives. Should the law be based on a view of marriage (and now, civil partnership) as an equal partnership or a joint enterprise, and if so, as one which requires equality of outcome, or formal equality? Does a spouse or civil partner have to 'earn' a share of the assets or should the division of assets focus on compensating for loss incurred as a result of the relationship? Given that assets tend to be concentrated in the hands, and obtainable through the earning power, of men rather than women, does a contributions-based system inevitably favour the man? Where there are children, should greater weight be given to their interests than simply 'first consideration' and how can this be balanced with the needs of their parents? When, if at all, should spouses—in practice almost always only wives—receive continuing and indefinite maintenance from a person to whom they no longer have any legal ties?

Finally, how far should couples be encouraged to make pre-nuptial agreements? Should such agreements be binding where children have subsequently been born, contrary to the views of the Government in their Green Paper? If not, they would have little impact, since over half of divorces do involve couples with children and it must be doubted how readily many couples will enter into such agreements in any case. No doubt, valuable lessons can be learned by considering the experience of other jurisdictions where such approaches are already part of the law and the gradual encroachment of European law and European norms into the English forum should not be underestimated.[768] Whatever reforms are finally decided upon, it is to be hoped that they will be implemented slowly, after adequate consultation, and without retrospective effect, in order to avoid the worst features of the child support experiment.

[767] [2002] EWCA Civ 1685, [2003] 1 FLR 139.
[768] Consider the elucidation of common principles of European family law, as proposed by the Commission on Family Law, *Principles of European Family Law Regarding Divorce and Maintenance between Former Spouses* (2004).

H FINANCIAL PROVISION AFTER DIVORCE ETC OR DISSOLUTION: COMPARABLE PROVISIONS UNDER THE MATRIMONIAL CAUSES ACT 1973 AND CIVIL PARTNERSHIP ACT 2004 [769]

Matrimonial Causes Act 1973 Part II	Civil Partnership Act 2004 Schedule 5
S 22 maintenance pending suit	Part 8, para 38
S 23 financial provision orders	Part 1, paras 1, 2, 3, 4, 5
S 24 property adjustment orders	Part 2, paras 6, 7, 8, 9
S 24A orders for sale	Part 3, paras 10, 11, 12, 13, 14
S 24B pension sharing orders	Part 4, para 15
S 21A, S 25D	Para 16
S 24D	Para 17
S 24B	Paras 18, 19(1)
S 24C	Para 19
S 25 matters to which court is to have regard	Part 5, paras 20, 21, 22,
S 25A terminating financial obligations	Para 23
S 25B pensions	Part 6, paras 24, 25
S 25C pensions: lump sums	Para 26
S 25D pensions: supplementary	Paras 27, 28, 29
S 25E Pension Protection Fund	Part 7, paras 30, 31, 32, 33, 34, 35, 36, 37
S 26 commencement of proceedings	Part 10, para 46
S 28 duration of continuing financial provision orders for spouse	Paras 47, 48
S 28(1A)direction preventing application for extension	Para 47(5)
S 29 duration of continuing financial provision orders for children	Para 49
S 31 variation or discharge	Part 11, paras 50, 51, 52, 56, 57, 58, 60, 61, 62
S 31(7) matters to which court is to have regard	Para 59,
S 31(7A)–(7G) power to make supplemental provision on variation	Paras 53, 54
S 27 failure to maintain	Part 9, paras 39, 40, 41, 42, 43, 44, 45
S 27(6A), (6B) variation of order for child	Part 11, para 55
S 32 payment of arrears unenforceable without leave	Part 12, para 63
S 33 orders for repayment	Para 64

[769] Note that not all the provisions listed are discussed in this chapter.

19

THE LEGAL CONSEQUENCES
OF A DEATH IN THE FAMILY

When a person dies, there are various legal consequences, the most important of which will concern the status of his partner, if the deceased was married or had a civil partnership, and the distribution of any property the deceased owned. In this chapter we consider first the rare situation where a person's death must be legally presumed so that his spouse or civil partner can regard her or himself as free to remarry, and his relatives can deal with his estate. We then consider the law concerning succession and inheritance. Finally, we discuss the position where death is caused by a fatal accident and family members seek compensation.

A PRESUMPTION OF DEATH

The death of either party brings a marriage (or civil partnership) to an end. Before 1938, if a spouse disappeared in circumstances which led to the reasonable inference that he or she was dead, but the death could not be proved, the other could remarry without committing the crime of bigamy and the second marriage would be *presumptively* valid. But if it were later proved that the spouse was in fact alive when the other remarried, then the second marriage would be *conclusively* void, with all the legal consequences that this entailed. To deal with this problem, the Matrimonial Causes Act 1973 s 19[1] permits the court to make a decree[2] of presumption of death and of dissolution of the marriage if it is satisfied that there are reasonable grounds for supposing that the petitioner's spouse is dead. The general common law presumption of death which may be raised by seven years' absence[3] is specifically applied to these proceedings by s 19(3), which provides:

'. . . the fact that for a period of seven years or more the other party to the marriage has been continually absent from the petitioner and the petitioner has no reason to believe that the

---

[1] As amended by Domicile and Matrimonial Proceedings Act 1973 s 17(2) and Sch 6. The power was originally given by the Matrimonial Causes Act 1937. Proceedings must be commenced in a divorce county court but should normally be transferred to the High Court: Matrimonial and Family Proceedings Act 1984 s 33(3); *Practice Direction (Family Division: Distribution of Business)* [1992] 3 All ER 151.

[2] Note that, as with nullity and divorce, a decree nisi and decree absolute are granted. For the position regarding civil partners, see below.

[3] *Chard v Chard* [1956] P 259. See G Treitel 'Presumption of Death' (1954) 17 MLR 530; *Tweney v Tweney* [1946] P 180; *Re Watkins* [1953] 2 All ER 1113; *Bullock v Bullock* [1960] 2 All ER 307.

other party has been living within that time shall be evidence that the other party is dead until the contrary is proved.'

The petitioner is not bound to rely on this period of absence. The court may accept any satisfactory evidence from which it may be presumed that the spouse is dead:[4] the inference to be drawn from the seven years' absence is of particular importance when there is no evidence at all of what has happened since.

The statutory presumption is different from that which arises at common law after seven years' absence. What is important under the statute is the petitioner's (or applicant's) belief. In *Thompson v Thompson*[5] Sachs J held that nothing must have happened during the period of seven years from which the petitioner, as a reasonable person, would conclude that the other spouse was still alive. Although the point was left open, the court is hardly likely to accept that the belief is reasonably held unless the petitioner has made all appropriate enquiries. The jurisdiction is discretionary; consequently, even if the petitioner can claim the benefit of the presumption, the court will not pronounce a decree, contrary to the justice of the case, where there is a possibility that the other party is still alive.

A decree nisi must be rescinded if the other spouse is found to be still alive.[6] Once it has been made absolute, however, it dissolves the marriage irrevocably even though the other subsequently reappears.[7]

As in the case of divorce, the court has jurisdiction if the petitioner is domiciled in England and Wales when the proceedings are begun, or has been habitually resident here throughout the period of one year ending with that date.[8]

In the case of a civil partnership, s 55 of the Civil Partnership Act 2004 provides that a civil partner may apply (rather than petition) for a 'presumption of death order'[9] in the same circumstances, including the seven year presumption, as obtain under the Matrimonial Causes Act. The order will be a conditional order in the first instance, becoming final after a prescribed period.[10] Under s 222 of the 2004 Act, the court has jurisdiction if the applicant is domiciled in England and Wales or has been habitually resident for the past year when proceedings are begun, or 'the two people concerned registered as civil partners of each other in England and Wales and it appears to the court to be in the interests of justice to assume jurisdiction in the case.'[11]

---

[4] Such as disappearance following the Asian Tsunami in 2004.

[5] [1956] P 414. A pure speculation is insufficient. The petitioner must give evidence: *Parkinson v Parkinson* [1939] P 346. For the common law presumption, see the 8th edition of this work, pp 68–70.

[6] *Manser v Manser* [1940] P 224.

[7] But in that case the court has power to make orders for financial relief: *Deacock v Deacock* [1958] P 230, CA.

[8] Domicile and Matrimonial Proceedings Act 1973 s 5(4).

[9] Rather than a decree.

[10] Civil Partnership Act 2004 s 38. The period is six weeks unless otherwise prescribed by the Lord Chancellor.

[11] Ibid s 222(c). It will be recalled that a couple may register provided each has had a usual place of residence in England and Wales for at least seven days immediately before giving notice: s 8(1)(b), (4)(b) so that they might not otherwise satisfy the jurisdictional rules for seeking the presumption. See above p 96.

B SUCCESSION [12]

We discuss the rules governing the disposition of property in four different contexts. First, we examine the position where the deceased dies leaving a will. Secondly, we discuss the intestacy rules applying where no will (or valid will) has been made. Thirdly, we note the rules governing the statutory succession to tenancies. Finally, we consider the opportunities to challenge the disposition of property where a person considers that they have not been adequately provided for under either the will which was made, or under the intestacy rules. In all of these contexts, it will be seen that the rules make assumptions about what constitute family relationships and the appropriateness of recognising these through devolution on death.

1 TESTATE SUCCESSION [13]

The law relating to wills and testate succession generally presents few problems peculiar to family law. Until the beginning of the last century the most important question was the testamentary capacity of a married woman. At common law she had virtually no power to make a will, although she could always devise and bequeath property held to her separate use in equity even if it were subject to a restraint upon anticipation. When the equitable concept of separate property was extended to legal separate property by the Married Women's Property Act 1882, her power to dispose of it by will was likewise extended, so that her testamentary incapacity remained only with respect to property acquired by her before 1883. Under the Law Reform (Married Women and Tortfeasors) Act 1935 she was given full power to dispose of all her property as if she were a feme sole.

There are, however, still certain matters of particular importance to family members which we must note.

(a) Revocation of wills by marriage or civil partnership

By s 18 of the Wills Act 1837 every will made by a man or woman is revoked by his or her marriage.[14] The section does not apply if the marriage is void,[15] but does in the case of voidable marriages.[16] Equivalent provisions apply to civil partnerships[17] and one would expect these to be interpreted in the same way as they have been in relation to marriage.

There are, however, a number of exceptions to the general rule. First, a will is not to be

---

[12] See A Borkowski *Textbook on Succession* (2nd edn, 2002) for a concise and entertaining account of the law. For an empirical study of family wills, see J Finch et al *Wills, Inheritance and Families* (1996).

[13] See C Sherrin et al (eds) *Williams on Wills* (8th edn, 2002); R Kerridge, *Parry and Clark: The Law of Succession* (11th edn, 2002).

[14] As substituted by s 18 of the Administration of Justice Act 1982, implementing the recommendations of the 22nd Report of the Law Reform Committee (The Making and Revocation of Wills) 1980 (Cmnd 7902). The changes made by the Administration of Justice Act do not apply to wills *made* before 1 January 1983: s 73(3).

[15] *Mette v Mette* (1859) 1 Sw & Tr 416.   [16] *Re Roberts* [1978] 3 All ER 225, CA.

[17] Section 18B inserted by s 71 and Sch 4 para 2 to the Civil Partnership Act 2004.

revoked by marriage, insofar as it is made in exercise of a power of appointment, if the property thereby appointed would not pass in default of appointment to the testator's personal representatives.[18] The reason for this exception is obvious: the marriage cannot possibly affect the devolution of the property involved.

The other exceptions are designed to fulfil the intention of a testator who makes his will on the eve of his wedding. If it appears from a will that at the time it was made the testator was expecting to be married to a particular person and that he intended that the will should not be revoked by the marriage, the marriage to that person is not to revoke it. The same rule applies if it appears that the testator intended that a particular disposition should not be revoked by the marriage: in that case the disposition is to take effect, as are all other dispositions in the will, unless it appears that the testator intended that a particular disposition was to be revoked.[19]

The exceptions relating to wills made in contemplation of marriage replace an exception (couched in significantly different terms) contained in s 177 of the Law of Property Act 1925. This section was liberally construed. For example, in *In the Estate of Langston*[20] a will by which the testator left his whole estate to 'my fiancée MEB' was held not to have been revoked by his marriage to her two months later. Similarly, a will would now be saved if the testator made a bequest 'to my fiancée ABC' but gave the residue of his estate to others.[21] Difficulty arises because it is frequently impossible to tell whether, by making a gift to his fiancée, a testator was intending to provide for his future wife or was merely making a temporary arrangement in case he should die before the proposed marriage took place. It would appear that in many cases this problem is resolved by s 21 of the Administration of Justice Act 1982, which permits extrinsic evidence to be admitted to resolve ambiguities in the wording of a will.[22]

(b) Revocation of wills by dissolution or annulment

Whereas the entry into a marriage or civil partnership automatically revokes a will (unless one of the exceptions just considered applies), its dissolution used not to do so. Consequently, if the testator did not make another will, his estate might pass to a former wife

---

[18] Section 18(2). Hence the will may be revoked in part but not insofar as the power is exercised: *In the Goods of Russell* (1890) 15 PD 111. See also *In the Goods of Gilligan* [1950] P 32.

[19] Section 18(3), (4). This provision does not apply to wills made before 1 January 1983 (Administration of Justice Act 1982 s 73(7) and s 76(11)) which are still governed by s 177 of the Law of Property Act 1925.

[20] [1953] P 100. See also *Pilot v Gainfort* [1931] P 103, where the testator made a will by which he bequeathed his personalty to 'DFP my wife'. Although he was living with her at the time, he did not marry her until 18 months later. It was held that the will was not revoked by the marriage. Sed quaere? On the face of the will it appeared that the testator was *already* married. Contrast *In the Estate of Gray* (1963) 107 Sol Jo 156.

[21] Thus reversing *Re Coleman* [1976] Ch 1.

[22] In any case, the surviving spouse now needs less protection because of the substantial sums that she (or he) takes on intestacy and the court's wide powers to make financial provision for a dependant under the Inheritance (Provision for Family and Dependants) Act 1975 (see below p 1107 and 1113 et seq). Cf *Anthony and Another v Donges and Another* [1998] 2 FLR 775: testator provided that if wife survived him, she was to have 'such minimal part of my estate . . . as she may be entitled to under English law for maintenance purposes'. Held, the clause was void for uncertainty, there being no such entitlement, and the testator could not provide jurisdiction to the court to apply the 1975 Act in modified form. But other beneficiaries, with no alternative claim, may be deprived of their gifts by revocation. See J Tiley 'Wills and Revocation—Marriage and Contemplation' (1975) 34 CLJ 205.

from whom he had long been divorced and who might have remarried. To overcome this difficulty, s 18A of the Wills Act[23] was added to provide that,

'(a) provisions of the will appointing executors or trustees or conferring a power of appointment, if they appoint or confer the power on the former spouse, shall take effect as if the former spouse had died on the date on which the marriage is dissolved[24] or annulled, and

(b) any property which, or an interest in which, is devised or bequeathed to the former spouse shall pass as if the former spouse had died on that date,

except in so far as a contrary intention appears by the will.'[25]

The section operates if the marriage was dissolved or annulled by a court of civil jurisdiction in England and Wales or by a divorce or annulment obtained elsewhere and entitled to recognition in this country. It will not operate, however, if no proceedings are taken for the annulment of a void marriage. Section 18C[26] makes equivalent provision in relation to civil partnerships.

The 1995 Act also amended the law to provide that, where the spouse (and now civil partner) of the testator is appointed in his will as a guardian, the appointment is revoked if the marriage (or civil partnership) is subsequently dissolved or annulled.[27]

(c) Mutual wills

Although mutual wills are rare, they are still made occasionally, and they are of particular interest in family law as mutual testators are usually (although not invariably) husband and wife. The essence of mutual wills is that the parties agree to make wills in similar terms and to be bound to dispose of their estate in a specified manner. It is not sufficient that the testators agree to make identical wills: it must also be established that there is a contract enforceable at law to the effect that each party will give effect to the agreement between them and will not exercise his testamentary freedom to make a will with different provisions.[28] Although English law knows of no such thing as an irrevocable will, equity

---

[23] Added by the Administration of Justice Act 1982 s 18(2). The section was amended by s 3 of the Law Reform (Succession) Act 1995 to reverse the decision in *Re Sinclair* [1985] Ch 446, where the Court of Appeal held that, on a proper construction of the words in the section as it then stood, the testator's property would pass on intestacy and not, as he had intended, to charity, because the former spouse had not predeceased him. The Law Commission reviewed the decision (Law Com No 217, *Family Law, The Effect of Divorce on Wills* (1993)); see R Kerridge 'The Effect of Divorce on Wills' (1995) 59 Conv 12) and recommended that it should be replaced to provide that, in the event of a divorce or annulment, property should pass as if the former spouse had predeceased the testator.

[24] The relevant date is the date of decree absolute.

[25] This formulation applies where the testator dies on or after 1 January 1996, regardless of the date of the will or of the divorce or annulment. See C Barton and R Wells 'A Matter of Life and Death—the Law Reform (Succession) Act 1995' [1996] Fam Law 172; G Miller 'Intestacy, divorce and wills' (1995) 145 NLJ 1693.

[26] Inserted by s 71 and Sch 4 para 2 to the Civil Partnership Act 2004.

[27] Children Act 1989 s 6(3A) inserted by s 4 of the 1995 Act, and s 6(3B) inserted by s 76 of the Civil Partnership Act 2004. See further, p 441 above.

[28] For a case where it was held that there was insufficient evidence to prove an agreement, see *Birch v Curtis* [2002] EWHC 1158 (Ch) [2002] 2 FLR 847. Note that in *Re Dale* [1994] Ch 31, it was held that the mutual wills doctrine applied to parents who had made wills in favour of their children, even though they had left no property to each other. As Borkowski (op cit, p 46) points out, there is therefore no need for mutual wills to confer reciprocal benefits upon their makers.

takes the view that it would be inequitable to permit the survivor to take the benefits under the other's will[29] without giving effect to the agreement himself and it protects the other beneficiaries by attaching a trust to the property on the first testator's death.

Let us suppose that a husband, H, and wife, W, agree to make mutual wills in the following form: 'I devise and bequeath the whole of my estate to trustees on trust for my wife W (or my husband H) for life and then on trust for my son S absolutely' or alternatively '—to W (or H) provided that she (or he) survives me, and if she (or he) does not, to S'. The following illustrations will show how the equitable principle operates:

(1) H and W agree that they will no longer be bound by their agreement. Both are free to revoke their wills and no trust is created on the death of either.

(2) H revokes his will and tells W that he has done so. W is free to revoke her will and no trust is created.[30]

(3) H revokes his will without telling W. H dies first and W discovers the revocation. As she is still free to make other testamentary dispositions, she may do so and no trust is created.[31]

(4) W dies first without having revoked her will. As it would be unconscionable to permit H to take the interest given by W's will without adhering to the agreement which effectively gave it to him, equity imposes an obligation on him to observe it and regards him as holding both estates on trust to carry out its terms. Consequently, if he later revokes his will[32] (or revoked it before W's death without informing her), his personal representatives are bound to give effect to the agreement and take his estate with a trust impressed on it for the benefit of S.[33] There are conflicting dicta on whether H would still be bound by the agreement if he repudiated it by disclaiming the gift to himself, but since the trust arises from the prior agreement, the better view is that it is automatically impressed on the property on the first party's death and the survivor's accepting the gift is therefore immaterial.[34]

If these conditions are satisfied, the trust takes effect from the moment the first testator

---

[29] *Re Cleaver* [1981] 2 All ER 1018; *Re Oldham* [1925] Ch 75; *Gray v Perpetual Trustee Co Ltd* [1928] AC 391, PC; *Re Goodchild (Deceased)* [1997] 1 WLR 1216, CA.

[30] *Birmingham v Renfrew* (1936) 57 CLR 666 at 682 (Aust) cited with approval in *Re Cleaver* (above) at 1023.

[31] *Stone v Hoskins* [1905] P 194; a minor alteration will be sufficient to revoke the agreement: *Re Hobley, deceased, The Times*, 16 June 1997.

[32] Quaere if the will is revoked by operation of law if H remarries. In *Re Marsland* [1939] Ch 820, CA, it was held that this did not amount to a breach of an express covenant not to revoke a will. It is submitted that this principle should not be applied to mutual wills, because the trusts attach on the death of the first testator and, if it were applied, they would frequently fail; and see *Re Goodchild (Deceased)* [1996] 1 FLR 591 (upheld on appeal, [1997] 1 WLR 1216, CA) where it was held (obiter) that effect should be given to the original intention, and that it was immaterial that revocation was by operation of law. See Grattan 'Mutual wills and remarriage' (1997) 61 Conv 153.

[33] *Dufour v Pereira* (1769) 1 Dick 419.

[34] See the different interpretations placed on Lord Camden's judgment in *Dufour v Pereira* (above) by Lord Hailsham LC in *Gray v Perpetual Trustee Co Ltd* (above) at 399, and by Clauson J in *Re Hagger* [1930] 2 Ch 190 at 195. If this were not so and the survivor were the widow or widower of the other, he or she might disclaim the legacy and take the estate on intestacy, thus obtaining the benefit whilst going back on the agreement. *Re Dale* (above) supports this view: since neither testator was to benefit under the other's will, the trust could not be conditional upon acceptance of the gift.

dies.[35] Consequently the remaindermen have a vested interest from this time, and the gifts to them will not lapse if they die after this date but before the surviving testator.[36] But it is still not settled whether any property acquired by the survivor after the first party's death is also subject to the trust or whether this will attach only to the property which he has at that time. Nor is it clear, as Borkowski points out, whether the Contracts (Rights of Third Parties) Act 1999, applies to mutual wills so as to enable a beneficiary to sue under that Act to enforce his or her claim.[37] Whatever the answer, there are considerable problems. For example, may the survivor deal with his property as he wishes, including disposing of or dissipating it, or is he, as a trustee, bound to convert it into authorised investments?[38] If the wills appear to give an absolute interest to the survivor, the following practical solution was propounded by Dixon J in the Australian decision, *Birmingham v Renfrew*:[39]

'The object of the transaction is to put the survivor in a position to enjoy for his own benefit the full ownership so that, for instance, he may convert [the property passing under the will of the party first dying] and expend the proceeds if he choose—No doubt gifts and settlements, inter vivos, if calculated to defeat the intention of the compact, could not be made by the survivor and his right of disposition, inter vivos, is, therefore, not unqualified. But, substantially, the purpose of the arrangement will often be to allow full enjoyment for the survivor's own benefit and advantage upon condition that at his death the residue shall pass as arranged.'

An example of dealing which is 'calculated to defeat the compact' may be seen in *Healey v Brown*.[40] There, the spouses made mutual wills providing that their matrimonial home should be left to the wife's niece and the remainder of their estate to the husband's son by his earlier marriage. After the wife's death, the husband transferred the home from his sole name into joint names with his son. After the husband's death, the niece claimed all or part of the interest in the former matrimonial home. It was held that although the mutual wills doctrine should apply because the husband's action 'could scarcely run more directly and fully counter to the intention of the mutual will compact', the obligation it imposed could not be enforced because the property to be bequeathed was land and the spouses' agreement was not made in accordance with the requirements of s 2 of the Law Reform (Miscellaneous Provisions) Act 1989.[41] The court in fact found for the claimant, under constructive trusts doctrine. But the case also points up another difficulty with the mutual wills doctrine, which is determining what property is subject to the trust. The home was held in joint names under a joint tenancy at the time of the wife's death. Her share therefore passed to the husband under the right of survivorship. The court held that only this half share could be made subject to the trust imposed by the parties' agreement.[42]

---

[35] *Re Hagger* (above); *Re Green* [1951] Ch 148; *Re Goodchild* (above).   [36] *Re Hagger* (above).

[37] See Borkowski, op cit at pp 51–2.   [38] See Borkowski, op cit, pp 48–9.

[39] (1936) 57 CLR 666 at 689.   [40] Ch Div, 25 April 2002 (Lexis).

[41] Which require that a contract for the sale or other disposition of an interest in land can only be made in writing and only by incorporating all the terms which the parties have expressly agreed in one document or, where contracts are exchanged, in each.

[42] On the basis that, in *Re Goodchild* [1997] 1 WLR 1216, Morritt LJ had held that the constructive trust doctrine has no operation in the case of mutual wills in regard to property already owned both legally and beneficially by the second testator to die. Thus, it could not be used to impose a trust over the husband's own half share, which he already owned.

(d) Gifts to the testator's wife or husband

Provided it was obviously the testator's intention, a gift to the testator's 'wife' (or 'husband') will take effect in favour of a woman (or man) with whom he (or she) is living as husband and wife, even though they are not legally married.[43] Such a gift will even be valid if it is directed to be held on trust during widowhood: in this case it will be construed as being determinable upon the other's contracting a valid marriage after the testator's death.[44]

In a home-made will it is not uncommon for a testator to make a bequest in the form: 'I give my whole estate to my wife, W, and after her death to my children'. His probable intention was that she should have full power to dispose of capital and income but that anything that was left at her death should go to the children.[45] The effect, however, was to give her only a life interest, because an absolute interest would be incompatible with the gift over. To remedy this, Administration of Justice Act 1982 s 22[46] provides that, if a testator makes a gift to his or her spouse in terms which in themselves would confer an absolute interest and by the same instrument gives an interest in the same property to his or her issue, the gift to the spouse takes effect absolutely unless a contrary intention is shown. The section is not well drafted. The absolute gift to the spouse presumably destroys the gift to the issue: if, therefore, the wife predeceases the testator, the gift will fall into residue and may not pass to the issue, which will again defeat the testator's intention. Hart J has doubted the wisdom of the approach adopted in the section, and in *Re Harrison (Deceased)*[47] he held that the court should look at the words used by the testator in the context of the will as a whole to determine his true intention. In this case, the husband stated in his will 'The Bungalow I leave in trust to my wife . . . On her death the Bungalow is to be sold and cash raised is to be equally divided between [his four children].' Hart J concluded that the words 'in trust', coupled with the other provisions in the will relating to the children's interests, led to the conclusion that an absolute gift had not been intended.

It will also be observed that the section does not apply to a gift to an unmarried cohabitant, or if the gift over is to someone other than the testator's issue (as might be the case if he were childless).

A provision of similar type might also be inserted in an attempt to limit exposure to inheritance tax liability. The first £285,000 worth of an estate is exempt from inheritance tax,[48] and no inheritance tax is payable in relation to property passed to a surviving spouse or civil partner. If the husband, for example, leaves all his property to his widow, no tax is therefore payable on the husband's death, but when the widow dies, the total estate now passing under her will may be more vulnerable to inheritance tax liability because its value is more likely to exceed the exempt amount. In such a situation, the first spouse may therefore be advised not to leave all his estate to his spouse, but to ensure that the exempt

---

[43] *Re Brown* (1910) 26 TLR 257. A fortiori if he names her (eg 'to my wife EAS'): *Re Smalley* [1929] 2 Ch 112, CA.

[44] Even though the 'wife' is already married to another man: *Re Wagstaff* [1908] 1 Ch 162, CA; *Re Hammond* [1911] 2 Ch 342; cf *Re Lynch* [1943] 1 All ER 168.

[45] See the 19th Report of the Law Reform Committee (*Interpretation of Wills*) 1973 (Cmnd 5301), para 60.

[46] Implementing the recommendations of the Law Reform Committee: ibid, para 62. An equivalent provision applies to civil partners: Civil Partnership Act 2004 Sch 4 para 5.

[47] [2005] EWHC 2957 (Ch) [2006] 1 All ER 858.   [48] In 2006–7, rising to £300,000 in 2007–8.

amount goes to other beneficiaries such as his children. This means that property of less value will go to the widow or widower, who will therefore have less to pass on when he or she in turn dies and thus there will be less likelihood of having to pay inheritance tax. The problem with this solution is that if the bulk of the estate is the first spouse's interest in the matrimonial home, by passing that to the other beneficiaries, he will deprive his widow of the right to remain in the home without a potential claim from the others that a sale should take place. Various means of trying to protect the surviving spouse whilst limiting tax liability have been attempted but many have fallen foul of the tax rules. For example, in *IRC v Lloyds Private Banking Ltd*[49] the wife's will left her half share in the matrimonial home on trust to her daughter, subject to a provision requiring the trustee not to take any steps to disturb the husband's continuing occupation. The court upheld the Inland Revenue Commissioners' claim that the provision was a disposition giving the husband a life interest in the wife's half share, so that when he in turn died, tax was due on that interest. Specialist inheritance tax planning is needed to try to avoid such pitfalls.

Unlike the position on intestacy,[50] the surviving spouse cannot demand that the matrimonial home or personal chattels should be appropriated as part of a gift (eg a residuary bequest). If they have not been specifically disposed of by the will, the only thing a widow or widower wishing to retain such property can do is to ask the personal representatives to exercise their power of appropriation in this way.[51]

(e) Gifts to children

The common law presumption that the term 'children' in a will applied only to legitimate children was reversed by the Family Law Reform Act 1969 s 15.[52] The Legitimacy Act 1926, which enabled legitimated children to take under a disposition after their legitimation, was extended by the Children Act 1975 to wills taking effect after 1 January 1976, even where they came into operation before the parents' marriage.[53]

2 INTESTATE SUCCESSION[54]

(a) Intestate succession before 1926

Before the Administration of Estates Act 1925 came into force, there was a considerable difference between the descent of real and personal property. All inheritable estates of freehold descended to the heir at law subject to the husband's curtesy and the wife's dower.[55] The husband took all his wife's personalty (including her separate estate if she had not disposed of it by will). On the death of a married man his widow took one-third of his personalty if he left issue and one-half if he did not; the remainder of his estate was

49 [1999] 1 FLR 147.   50 See below, p 1098.
51 For the personal representatives' powers of appropriation, see the Administration of Estates Act 1925 s 41.
52 In respect of any disposition made on or after 1 January 1970.
53 Schedule 1, Pt III, re-enacted in Legitimacy Act 1976 s 5(3). For the position of adopted children, see above, p 871.
54 See C Sherrin and R Bonehill *The Law and Practice of Intestate Succession* (3rd edn, 2004); Law Commission Working Paper No 108 (1988), and Report No 186 (1989) *Distribution on Intestacy*. The rules apply equally to a partial intestacy; Administration of Estates Act 1925 s 49.
55 See above, p 128.

divided among his issue or, in default of issue, among his next-of-kin as defined by the Statutes of Distribution of 1670 and 1685. Under the Intestates' Estates Act 1890, which was passed to give a widow a larger provision if the estate was small and the intestate left no issue, she took the whole of the real and personal estate if the total value did not exceed £500; if it exceeded this sum, the estate was to stand charged with the payment to her of £500.

(b) Administration of Estates Act 1925

This Act radically overhauled the law relating to intestate succession in two respects. First, the law relating to realty and personalty was put on the same footing; and secondly the distribution of estates was completely changed. The principal effect of this Act, and subsequent amendments, was to give the surviving widow a much greater interest than she had before 1926 and to give the surviving widower the same rights as the surviving widow. The Civil Partnership Act 2004 further amends the Act to extend the rights of the surviving spouse to surviving civil partners.[56]

In 1989, the Law Commission recommended that the surviving spouse should receive the whole estate as the best means of ensuring her or him adequate provision. Furthermore, it would greatly simplify the rules. It also appeared to be in line with public opinion.[57] However, their view has been criticised as failing adequately to consider the needs of the deceased's minor children, and of unduly benefiting second or subsequent spouses,[58] and the government rejected it when enacting other reforms to the intestacy rules in the Law Reform (Succession) Act 1995. The Law Commission also considered, but rejected, the view that a surviving unmarried cohabitant should be treated like a surviving spouse, on the grounds that this would increase the complexity and cost of administration, and special rules would be needed to deal with the situation where both a spouse and a cohabitant survived. They considered that any hardship done to a cohabitant, or to a relative or dependant of the deceased by the intestacy rules is adequately remedied by a claim under the Inheritance (Provision for Family and Dependants) Act 1975,[59] and they proposed strengthening the claim of a cohabitant under that Act. It is also always open to all the beneficiaries under a will or an intestacy, if of full age and capacity, to agree to distribute the estate in any way they wish.[60]

(c) The rights of the surviving spouse or civil partner

The spouse (or civil partner) must survive the intestate by 28 days.[61] This requirement is to prevent 'the assets of both spouses going to the parents or relatives of the second to die, in cases of not quite simultaneous death, usually in accidents'[62] and echoes survivorship

---

[56] Civil Partnership Act 2004 s 71 and Sch 4 paras 7–12.

[57] Law Com No 187 *Distribution on Intestacy* paras 25, 29.

[58] S M Cretney 'Reform of Intestacy: The Best We Can Do?' (1995) 111 LQR 77; R Kerridge 'Distribution on Intestacy: The Law Commission's Report' (1990) 54 Conv 358; J Finch et al *Wills, Inheritance and Families* (1996) Ch 7. They reached the same provisional conclusion in the Law Com Consultation Paper No 179 (2006) paras 8.8–8.17.

[59] See below, pp 1105–24.   [60] Known as the rule in *Saunders v Vautier* (1841) Cr & Ph 240.

[61] Where the death occurs on or after 1 January 1996: Administration of Estates Act 1925 s 46(2A), inserted by Law Reform (Succession) Act 1995 s 1(1) as amended by the Civil Partnership Act 2004 Sch 4 para 7.

[62] Law Com No 187 para 57.

clauses usually inserted into wills. Where it is uncertain which spouse died first, the younger of the two is usually deemed to have survived the other,[63] but on intestacy the estate is to be distributed as though the intestate had survived.[64]

The surviving spouse or civil partner takes the following interests.[65]

Personal chattels

The surviving spouse or civil partner is always entitled to the personal chattels (provided that the estate is solvent). They are defined as:[66]

'Carriages, horses, stable furniture and effects (not used for business purposes), motor cars and accessories (not used for business purposes), garden effects, domestic animals, plate, plated articles, linen, china, glass, books, pictures, prints, furniture, jewellery,[67] articles of household or personal use or ornament, musical and scientific instruments and apparatus, wines, liquors and consumable stores, but [they] do not include any chattels used at the death of the intestate for business purposes[68] nor money or securities for money.'

Residuary interests

The interest which the surviving spouse or civil partner takes over and above the personal chattels depends upon what other relatives the intestate leaves surviving. The provisions are set out in s 46 of the Administration of Estates Act 1925.

If he leaves any children or remoter issue, the spouse takes what is usually termed a 'statutory legacy', currently of £125,000 with interest at 6% per annum until it is paid and a *life* interest in half the residue.

If he leaves no issue but a parent or a brother or sister of the whole blood or issue of such a brother or sister, the surviving spouse or civil partner takes a statutory legacy of £200,000 with interest at 6% per annum until it is paid and an *absolute* interest in half the residue.

If he leaves neither issue nor any of the above relations, the surviving spouse or civil partner takes the whole of the residue absolutely.

Redemption of life interest

The spouse or civil partner may, if he wishes to do so, insist on the personal representatives' redeeming his life interest by paying the capital value to him.[69] He must elect to do so within 12 months after representation is taken out, but the court may extend this period if it considers that the limit will operate unfairly because a previous will was revoked or invalid, or because the interest of some person in the estate had not been determined

---

63 Law of Property Act 1925 s 184.   64 Administration of Estates Act 1925 s 46(3) as amended.

65 Administration of Estates Act 1925 s 46 as amended; Family Provision (Intestate Succession) Order, SI 2906/1993. See DCA, *Administration of Estates: Review of the Statutory Legacy* (2005).

66 Ibid, s 55(1)(x). This section has been widely construed and has been held to include a 60-foot motor yacht (*Re Chaplin* [1950] Ch 507) and a collection of clocks and watches (*Re Crispin's Will Trusts* [1975] Ch 245, CA). The mere fact that the property might be regarded as an investment does not prevent it from being a personal chattel too: *Re Reynold's Will Trusts* [1965] 3 All ER 686 (valuable stamp collection, which was deceased's principal hobby, held to be an article of personal use).

67 Including cut but unmounted jewels: *Re Whitby* [1944] Ch 210, CA.

68 See *Re Ogilby* [1942] Ch 288.

69 Administration of Estates Act 1925 s 47A as amended by Civil Partnership Act 2004 Sch 4 para 9.

when representation was taken out, or because of any other circumstances affecting the administration or distribution of the estate.[70]

Rights with respect to the family home

The Intestates' Estates Act 1952 gives the surviving spouse or civil partner a right within certain limits to retain the matrimonial or civil partnership home.[71] Where the intestate's estate comprises an interest in a dwelling-house in which the surviving spouse or civil partner was resident at the time of the intestate's death, the survivor may require the personal representatives to appropriate the house in or towards satisfaction of any absolute interest that the survivor has in the estate,[72] and if the value of the house exceeds the value of the survivor's interest, he may exercise this option if he pays the excess value to the representatives.[73] He must exercise this option within 12 months of representation being taken out, but this period may be extended by the court, as in the case of an application to have a life interest redeemed.[74] Consequently the personal representatives are forbidden to sell the house within this period without the written consent of the surviving spouse or civil partner unless this is necessary for the payment of expenses or debts.[75]

There are two limitations upon this power. First, these provisions normally do not apply if the house is held upon a lease which had less than two years to run from the date of the intestate's death or which could be determined by the landlord within this period.[76] This means that many houses (eg those held on periodic tenancies) fall outside these provisions, but to offset this it must be remembered that there will usually be a statutory transmission to the surviving spouse or civil partner.[77] Secondly, the survivor cannot require the personal representatives to appropriate the house in certain specified instances except on an order of the court, which must be satisfied that the appropriation is not likely to diminish the value of assets in the residuary estate (other than the interest in the house) or make these assets more difficult to dispose of.[78]

Judicial separation or separation order in relation to a civil partnership

By s 18(2) of the Matrimonial Causes Act 1973, if either spouse dies intestate as respects any real or personal property whilst a judicial separation is in force and the parties remain separated, his or her property is to devolve as though the other were dead. A similar provision is contained in s 57 of the Civil Partnership Act 2004 in relation to civil partners who are subject to a separation order under that Act. The reason for these provisions is that the rules of intestate succession are intended to reflect the testamentary dispositions

---

[70] Ibid s 47A(5).   [71] Section 5 and Sch 2 as amended by Civil Partnership Act 2004 Sch 4 para 13.

[72] Ibid, para 1(1). 'Dwelling-house' includes part of a building occupied as a separate dwelling and an absolute interest includes a redeemed life interest: ibid, para 1(4)–(5).

[73] Ibid, para 5(2); Re Phelps [1980] Ch 275, CA. The value is to be assessed at the date of appropriation: Robinson v Collins [1975] 1 All ER 321.

[74] Ibid, para 3. It cannot be exercised after the surviving spouse's death by his or her personal representatives: ibid, para 3(1)(b).

[75] Ibid, para 4. But if they fail to observe this provision, the spouse has no right to claim the house from the purchaser: ibid, para 4(5).

[76] Ibid, para 1(2). But the personal representatives have a discretionary power to appropriate the lease under s 41 of the Administration of Estates Act 1925: ibid, para 5(2). For exceptional cases (where the surviving spouse would be entitled to acquire the freehold or an extended lease), see the Leasehold Reform Act 1967 s 7(8).

[77] See below, pp 1101–5.   [78] Intestates' Estates Act 1952 Sch 2 para 2.

the deceased might reasonably be expected to have made, and as separation almost always marks the de facto end of the relationship, it is highly unlikely that either would have left anything to the other.

(d) Interests taken by the intestate's children and remoter issue

If the intestate leaves a surviving spouse or civil partner, the personal representatives must hold one-half of the residue (after taking out the personal chattels and the £125,000 due to the survivor) on the statutory trusts for the intestate's issue and the other half on the same trusts subject to the surviving spouse's life interest. If the intestate leaves no surviving spouse or civil partner, the personal representatives must hold the whole of the residue on the statutory trusts for the issue.[79]

The statutory trusts

The property is to be held on trust in equal shares for all the children alive at the intestate's death who reach the age of 18 or marry or form a civil partnership under that age. But if any of his children has predeceased him, that child's share is held upon the same trusts for his own children or remoter issue.[80]

Until a beneficiary obtains a vested interest, the trustees may use the whole of the income of the part to which he is contingently entitled for his maintenance, education or benefit, and they may use one half of the capital to which he is contingently entitled for his advancement.[81] Subject to this they must accumulate the income at compound interest.[82] They may also at their discretion permit him to have the use of any personal chattels.[83]

(e) Children of unmarried parents

Originally, in accordance with the general rule at common law, only legitimate persons and those claiming a relationship through legitimate persons, could participate in intestate succession. Those who had been legitimated could claim after the passing of the Legitimacy Act 1926,[84] and the Family Law Reform Act 1969 permitted illegitimate children and their parents to succeed to each other.[85] In pursuance of the policy of removing the disadvantages flowing from birth outside marriage, s 18 of the Family Law Reform Act 1987 now provides that, for the purposes of the distribution of the estate of an intestate, any relationship shall be construed without regard to whether the parents of the deceased, the claimant or any person through whom the claimant is related to the deceased were

---

[79] Administration of Estates Act 1925 s 46(1) as amended by Civil Partnership Act 2004 Sch 4 para 7.

[80] Ibid, s 47(1)(i) (as amended by Civil Partnership Act 2004 Sch 4 para 8); Family Law Reform Act 1969 s 3(2). Under the forfeiture rule, a person is not to profit from his crime; thus, if the deceased were unlawfully killed by his or her child, the child could not inherit the deceased's property (under either a will or an intestacy). In *Re DWS (Deceased)* [2001] Ch 568, CA, the only son killed his parents. The Court of Appeal held that their grandson could not take under their intestacy because s 47(1)(i) of the Administration of Estates Act 1925 provides that the issue of a child of the intestate may only take where the child has predeceased the intestate. Instead, the estate passed to the grandfather's sister. The Law Commission (Law Com No 295) *The Forfeiture Rule and the Law of Succession* (2005) have recommended that the effect of *Re DWS* should be reversed so that in such circumstances the child should be treated as if he himself is dead, enabling the next closest in the list of those entitled to succeed to take.

[81] Administration of Estates Act 1925 s 47(1)(ii); Trustee Act 1925 s 31(1), s 32(1).

[82] Trustee Act 1925 s 31(2).   [83] Administration of Estates Act 1925 s 47(1)(iv).

[84] Now see the Legitimacy Act 1976 s 5.   [85] Section 14.

married to each other.[86] But because of the difficulty in tracing some fathers, whose identity might not be known, a person whose parents were not married to each other is to be presumed not to have been survived by his father or by anyone related to him through his father unless the contrary is shown.[87]

(f) Adopted children

An adopted child is treated as though he were the child of his adopters and of no other person.[88] If he was adopted by a couple, he will be in the position of a brother (or sister) of the whole blood of any other child or adopted child of both the adopters and a brother of the half blood of any child or adopted child of one of them; if he was adopted by one person only, he will be in the position of a brother of the half blood of any child or adopted child of his adopter. He has no claims on the death of his birth parents or anyone related to them.[89]

(g) Interests taken by other members of the family

If the intestate dies leaving a surviving spouse or civil partner but no issue, the other half of the residue (after taking out the personal chattels, the £200,000 and the half-interest which has gone to the survivor) is to be held on trust for the intestate's parents in equal shares (or for one parent absolutely if only one parent survives the intestate), and if neither of his parents survives him, on the statutory trusts for his brothers and sisters of the whole blood and their issue.[90]

If there is no surviving spouse or civil partner, nor issue, the whole estate must be held on trust for the persons coming into the first of the following classes that can be satisfied: the intestates' parents; his brothers and sisters of the whole blood (or their issue); his brothers and sisters of the half blood (or their issue); surviving grandparents; uncles and aunts of the whole blood (or their issue) and uncles and aunts of the half blood (or their issue). If none of these classes is filled, the whole estate will go to the Crown as bona vacantia.[91]

The statutory trusts are exactly the same in the above cases as the statutory trusts for the intestate's children and issue. All the interests are contingent upon the beneficiary's attaining his majority or marrying, and if no member of any class takes a vested interest, the members of the next class will take.[92]

---

[86] Applying s 1 of the 1987 Act (see above p 349). Any reference to statutory next of kin in an instrument taking effect on or after this date is to be construed likewise: s 18(3).

[87] Family Law Reform Act 1987 s 18(2). See G Miller 'The Family Law Reform Act 1987 and the Law of Succession' (1988) 52 Conv 410.

[88] Adoption and Children Act 2002 ss 67, 69 and 73(5). Hence a child adopted by one of his birth parents cannot claim on the death of the other: s 67(4).

[89] Except where he has an interest vested in possession in him before the adoption: see s 69(4), reversing *Staffordshire County Council v B* [1998] 1 FLR 261, discussed above at p 872.

[90] Administration of Estates Act 1925 s 46(1)(i).   [91] Ibid, s 46(1)(vi).

[92] If all the members of a particular class (apart from parents or grandparents) are dead, but one or more have left issue, the issue will take in preference to the members of a more remote class: *Re Lockwood* [1958] Ch 231. For example, issue of a brother or sister of the whole blood will take before a brother and sister of the half blood.

C THE STATUTORY TRANSMISSION OF TENANCIES

1 THE PRIVATE SECTOR

We have already seen that the Rent Act 1977 and Housing Act 1988 provide some protection to tenants from arbitrary eviction by the landlord.[93] The protection extends to members of the tenant's family so long as they are living with him, but this would be completely defeated if the landlord could evict them immediately the tenancy was ended by the tenant's death. It is open to the landlord to grant a fresh contractual tenancy to the person remaining in possession, but where this is not done, there may be a right to remain in the property by virtue of the statutory transmission of the tenancy. As with other aspects of housing law, the extent to which the tenant's family can benefit from these rules has been greatly reduced as part of the policy of freeing landlords from restrictive controls, and the protection will eventually wither away.

2 REGULATED TENANCIES UNDER THE RENT ACT 1977

(a) Surviving spouse or civil partner

On the tenant's death, a statutory tenancy automatically vests in his surviving spouse or civil partner[94] provided that the survivor was residing in the dwelling-house immediately before the death. The residence qualification prevents the spouse or civil partner from claiming the benefit of the Act if the parties had separated and the survivor left the premises before the tenant's death. The successor remains a statutory tenant so long as she occupies the dwelling-house as her residence, even though she subsequently remarries.[95]

(b) Surviving cohabitant

The same protection was extended to surviving *heterosexual* cohabitants by the Housing Act 1988,[96] giving statutory effect to the decision of the Court of Appeal in *Dyson Holdings Ltd v Fox*[97] in which the Court declined to follow its previous decision in *Gammans v Ekins*[98] and held that, whatever the position had been 25 years earlier, in 1975 a cohabitant could properly be regarded as a member of the deceased tenant's family. The provision originally provided that 'a person who was living with the original tenant as his or her wife or husband shall be treated as the spouse of the original tenant'. An attempt to widen the meaning of this phrase to include same sex couples failed in *Fitzpatrick v Sterling Housing Association Ltd*.[99] There, the applicant had lived with his male partner for 18 years in a flat of which the partner was a protected tenant. When the partner died, the applicant sought a declaration that he was entitled to succeed to the tenancy. The House of Lords considered

---

[93] See above, pp 196–203.

[94] Rent Act 1977 Sch 1 para 2(1) as amended by Civil Partnership Act 2004 Sch 8 para 13(2).

[95] Rent Act 1977 Sch 1, paras 1 and 2, as amended by the Housing Act 1980 s 76 and the Housing Act 1988 Sch 4, paras 1 and 2.

[96] Section 39 and Sch 4 para 2.   [97] [1976] QB 503.   [98] [1950] 2 KB 328.

[99] [2001] 1 AC 27, HL. See above p 102.

that the words used were gender-specific and thus could not be extended to cover couples of the same sex. However, they recognised that the matter might need to be revisited once the Human Rights Act 1998 came into force, and the opportunity to do so was taken in *Ghaidan v Godin-Mendoza*.[100] This time, the House ruled that restricting the ambit of the provision to heterosexual couples was discriminatory towards those of the same sex, and that such discrimination infringed Art 14 of the European Convention on Human Rights taken with the right to respect for one's home under Art 8. Finding no objective or reasonable justification for such discrimination,[101] the House held that the provision should be interpreted so as to give effect to the surviving partners' Convention rights. They thus held, agreeing with the Court of Appeal, that the words 'as his or her wife or husband' should be read as stating: 'as if they were' his or her wife or husband'. The effect of the decision has been given statutory form by the Civil Partnership Act 2004, which amends the Rent Act to provide that

'(a) a person who was living with the original tenant as his or her wife or husband shall be treated as the spouse of the original tenant, and

(b) a person who was living with the original tenant as if they were civil partners shall be treated as the civil partner of the original tenant.'[102]

(c) Member of the deceased's family

If the tenant leaves no spouse or partner who can succeed to the tenancy, then a member of his family may stay in the property, provided that this person resided in the dwelling-house immediately before the tenant's death and for a minimum period of two years immediately before then.[103] However, he will obtain, not a statutory tenancy under the Rent Act, but an assured periodic tenancy under the Housing Act.[104]

It is not sufficient that the claimant and the deceased were members of the same family; the claimant must show that he was a member of the *deceased*'s family.[105] In *Fitzpatrick v Sterling Housing Association Ltd*[106] the appellant argued that if he could not be treated as if he had lived 'as husband and wife' with the deceased, then in the alternative he should be regarded as a member of his partner's family. A majority of the House of Lords upheld his claim on this latter basis. Lord Slynn argued that the hallmarks of the family relationship intended by Parliament to be covered by the legislation:

---

[100] [2004] UKHL 30, [2004] 2 AC 557. Lord Millett dissented. See above p 102.

[101] See also the same conclusion reached by the European Court of Human Rights in *Karner v Austria* [2003] 2 FLR 623 in relation to the phrase 'life companion' used in the equivalent Austrian legislation.

[102] Rent Act 1977 Sch 2 para 2(2) as amended by Civil Partnership Act 2004 Sch 8 para 13(3). Note that the choice of wording suggests that the phrase 'living (together) as husband and wife' is a term of art: the provision for same sex couples keeps the House of Lords' formulation of 'living *as if* they were civil partners' rather than 'living *as* civil partners'. But cf the formulation used to amend the Inheritance (Provision for Family and Dependants) Act 1975, below at p 1108.

[103] Rent Act 1977 Sch 1, para 3. For deaths after 15 January 1989 the residence must be in the same house as the tenant, but it need not be shown that it was as part of the tenant's household (cf *Swanbrae Ltd v Elliott* (1986) 19 HLR 86, CA where a tenant's daughter continued to sleep at her own house three or four nights a week, her son still lived there, her post was sent there and she gave it as her usual address, it was held she was not residing with her mother).

[104] Housing Act 1988 s 39(5)–(6).   [105] *Langdon v Horton* [1951] 1 KB 666 at 669 and 671, CA.

[106] [2001] 1 AC 27, HL.

'were essentially that there should be a degree of mutual inter-dependence, of the sharing of lives, of caring and love, of commitment and support.'[107]

On this basis, he concluded that the appellant could demonstrate that the relationship with his partner was of this character and hence within the ambit of the provision. Lord Nicholls of Birkenhead, to similar effect, considered that once it was accepted (as Parliament had done in 1988) that a heterosexual couple could be regarded as member of a family, there was no rational basis on which to exclude a same sex couple in a similar situation. For him, the key point was that 'the concept underlying membership of a family for present purposes is the sharing of lives together in a single family unit living in one house.'[108] And Lord Clyde considered that:

'essentially the bond must be one of love and affection, not of a casual or transitory nature, but in a relationship which is permanent or at least intended to be so. As a result of that personal attachment to each other, other characteristics will follow, such as a readiness to support each other emotionally and financially, to care for and look after the other in times of need, and to provide a companionship in which mutual interests and activities can be shared and enjoyed together. It would be difficult to establish such a bond unless the couple were living together in the same house. It would also be difficult to establish it without an active sexual relationship between them or at least the potentiality of such a relationship. If they have or are caring for children whom they regard as their own, that would make the family designation more immediately obvious, but the existence of children is not a necessary element. Each case will require to depend eventually upon its own facts'.[109]

It is clear from these dicta that, as their Lordships themselves stressed, they were deciding on the meaning of 'family' for the purposes of the Rent Act only, and it may well be that in other contexts, an alternative meaning will be arrived at.

Even where the claimant and the deceased were blood relations, it does not follow that the claimant will necessarily be regarded as a member of the tenant's family. The parties' conduct must be taken into account as well, and the more remote the relationship, the more important this may become. In *Langdon v Horton*,[110] for example, the Court of Appeal held that two sisters, who had gone to live with their widowed cousin and stayed with her until she died 29 years later, were no more members of her family than would be two friends sharing a flat. In *Jones v Whitehill*,[111] on the other hand, it was held that a niece who had gone to look after her elderly aunt and uncle in their declining years was a member of their family as she had assumed 'out of love and natural affection the duties and offices peculiarly attributable to members of a family'.[112]

As Wikeley has pointed out,[113] judicial interpretation of the term 'family' has generally failed to take notice of the social policy objective of the Rent Act legislation. However, this objective has now changed from a primary concern to secure the tenant and his family in their home towards encouraging the flexible provision of rented sector accommodation by enabling landlords to regain possession of their property. Ironically, just as the courts, as evidenced in *Fitzpatrick* and *Ghaidan* may be prepared to show greater willingness

---

107 Ibid at p 38.   108 At p 44D.   109 At p 515F–H.   110 [1951] 1 KB 666, CA.
111 [1950] 2 KB 204, CA.   112 At 207.
113 N Wikeley, '*Fitzpatrick v Sterling Housing Association Ltd*: Same-sex partners and succession to Rent Act tenancies' [1998] CFLQ 191 at 196 (commenting on the Court of Appeal's decision).

to adopt an extended view of family relationships, the legislature has curtailed the opportunity to rely on these in this context.

(d) Death of the first successor

Where the first successor obtained a statutory tenancy on the tenant's death (ie as his surviving spouse, civil partner or cohabitant), then a person who was a member of the family, both of the original tenant and of the first successor, may succeed—but to an assured periodic tenancy only—provided that he resided in the dwelling-house with the first successor at the time of, and for the period of two years immediately before, the first successor's death.

No further successions are possible.

3 ASSURED TENANCIES

The surviving spouse, civil partner or cohabitant of a tenant holding an assured periodic (but not fixed-term) tenancy, may succeed to the tenancy provided that he or she occupied the dwelling-house as his or her only or principal home.[114] No right of succession is given to any other members of the tenant's family.

No succession at all is offered in the case of assured shortholds (now the primary form of private sector tenancy).

4 SECURE TENANCIES

A member of a secure tenant's family may succeed to a secure fixed-term, or periodic, tenancy provided that he is a *qualified successor*, that is, the tenant's spouse or civil partner, or a member of his family.[115] Section 113(1) defines a member of the tenant's family as follows:

'(a) he is the spouse or civil partner of that person, or he and that person live together as husband and wife or as if they were civil partners, or

(b) he is that person's parent, grandparent, child, grandchild, brother, sister, uncle, aunt, nephew or niece.'

And s 113(2) continues, for the purposes of subsection (1)(b):

'(a) a relationship by marriage or civil partnership shall be treated as a relationship by blood,

(b) a relationship of the half-blood shall be treated as a relationship of the whole blood,

---

[114] Housing Act 1988 s 17 as amended by Civil Partnership Act 2004 Sch 8 para 41. Para 41(3) provides the same definition for couples living together as has been incorporated into Rent Act 1977 Sch 2 para 2(2) (see above at p 1102 n 102). For the position prior to the entry into force of this provision, see *Nutting v Southern Housing Group Ltd* [2004] EWHC 2982 (Ch) [2005] 1 FLR 1066 where it was held that the principles applied by the House of Lords in *Ghaidan v Godin-Mendoza* [2004] UKHL 30 [2004] 2 AC 557 governed the construction of the reference in s 17(4) to a person 'living with the tenant as his or her wife or husband' (but the claim failed on its facts as it was held that the couple were not living with each other at the time of the death as they had not made a lifetime commitment to each other). See further above p 103.

[115] Housing Act 1985 s 87 as amended by Civil Partnership Act 2004 Sch 8 para 20.

(c) the stepchild of a person shall be treated as his child, and

(d) an illegitimate child shall be treated as the legitimate child of his mother and reputed father.'

Although the precise wording of the section avoids the mass of litigation to which the term has given rise under the Rent Act, it is not free from ambiguity. For example, does the term 'stepchild' include a child of the secure tenant's cohabitant?

If there is more than one person qualified to succeed, the surviving spouse or civil partner is preferred to any other member of the family; if there is no surviving spouse or civil partner and two or more persons are qualified, they must agree amongst themselves which of them is to succeed and, if they cannot agree, the landlord may select one of them.[116]

To be a qualified successor, the claimant must have occupied the dwelling-house as his only or principal home at the time of the tenant's death. In addition, if he is a member of the tenant's family other than a spouse or civil partner, he must have resided with the tenant throughout the period of 12 months ending with the tenant's death. Temporary absences will not necessarily break the chain of continuity of residence; thus, where the tenant's grandson was absent from her flat for some three months while 'house sitting' for friends, but retained his postal address at the tenancy and left his possessions there, the Court of Appeal held that continuity was not broken, even though he had hoped to avoid returning to the grandmother's flat by finding alternative permanent accommodation for himself and his wife.[117]

A child who satisfies the above criteria may succeed as a 'secure tenant in equity' even though she cannot hold the legal title. In *Kingston upon Thames Borough Council v Prince*[118] a 13-year-old girl had been living with her grandfather for three years; her mother had lived with them for six months prior to the grandfather's death. The mother could not take over the tenancy as she had not lived there long enough, but it was held that the child could do so with the legal estate held by her mother on trust for her until she reached her majority.

No further succession is possible after the first.

D PROVISION FOR MEMBERS OF THE FAMILY AND OTHER DEPENDANTS [119]

The Dower Act 1833 permitted a husband to extinguish his wife's right to dower, and in so doing, abolished the last vestige of family provision in English law.[120] After that there was nothing to stop a man (or a woman with respect to her separate property) from devising and bequeathing his whole estate to a charity or a complete stranger and leaving

---

[116] Section 89(2).

[117] *Camden London Borough Council v Goldenberg* [1997] 1 FLR 556, CA; cf *Swanbrae Ltd v Elliott* (1986) 19 HLR 86, CA noted above, where a similar test resulted in the claimant failing to establish residence with her mother, because she had retained links with another property of which she was tenant.

[118] [1999] 1 FLR 593, CA. [119] See R Oughton *Tyler's Family Provision* (3rd edn, 1998).

[120] See J Unger 'The Inheritance Act and the Family' (1943) 6 MLR 215.

his widow and children penniless. To prevent this evil, the Inheritance (Family Provision) Act 1938 was passed. This did not cast upon a testator any positive duty to make reasonable provision for his dependants—indeed, it would have been impossible to do so—but enacted that, if he failed to do so, the court might order such reasonable provision as it thought fit to be made out of his estate for the benefit of the surviving spouse and certain classes of children. In 1952 the principle underlying this Act was applied to cases of intestacy.[121] It is easy to see that the law of intestate succession might leave a child without adequate support: the whole estate might go to a widow who refused to make any provision for the children of a previous marriage or might be divided between a daughter married to a rich man and a minor son whose education was incomplete. In 1958 a similar power to apply for provision was given to a former spouse, that is, one whose marriage to the deceased had been dissolved or annulled and who had not remarried.[122] This, of course, was of particular value to a divorced wife who had obtained an order for unsecured periodical payments which would cease on her former husband's death.

Notwithstanding these extensions, there were still many gaps and deficiencies in the law. The term 'dependant' was so narrowly defined that it excluded many who had been supported by another during his lifetime and who had a moral, if not a legal, claim on his estate. No application could be made, for example, by a parent, brother or sister, another's children who had been treated as members of the deceased's family, or a person with whom he had been cohabiting outside marriage. Provision could be ordered only out of property which the deceased had power to dispose of by will, so that he could defeat the operation of the Act altogether by settling his property during his lifetime or by contracting to leave it to a third person after his death.[123] Furthermore, the court was limited to ordering reasonable provision for the dependant's maintenance and had no power to divide capital assets: the result was that a surviving wife could be in a worse position than a divorced wife who obtained a property adjustment order. When the Law Commission examined the whole question of family property law, they rejected the proposal that a surviving spouse should have a right to inherit a fixed proportion of the deceased's estate in favour of the more flexible approach of family provision. They added, however, that this would need strengthening, and in particular 'the surviving partner of a marriage should have a claim upon the family assets at least equivalent to that of a divorced person'.[124] Their detailed recommendations were published in 1974,[125] and led to the enactment of the Inheritance (Provision for Family and Dependants) Act 1975,[126] which replaced the existing relevant legislation with a new code. This, in turn, was further amended in the light of the Law Commission's recommendation that cohabitants should be given

---

[121] Intestates' Estates Act 1952.

[122] Matrimonial Causes (Property and Maintenance) Act 1958, subsequently re-enacted in the Matrimonial Causes Act 1965 ss 26–8.

[123] *Schaefer v Schuhmann* [1972] AC 572, PC. But the disposition might possibly have been set aside had it been fraudulent: see below, p 1120.

[124] Law Com No 52, *First Report on Family Property: a New Approach* (1973) paras 31–45.

[125] Law Com No 61, *Second Report on Family Property: Family Provision on Death* (1974).

[126] For an interesting analysis of the apparently different approaches taken to claims under the Act in the Family Division and Chancery Division, see F Cownie and A Bradney, 'Divided Justice, Different Voices: inheritance and family provision' (2003) 23 LS 566.

additional rights to claim family provision[127] and by the Civil Partnership Act 2004 to enable same-sex partners to have equivalent rights to spouses after a partner's death.[128]

The Act applies only if the person against whose estate the claim is being made died domiciled in England and Wales.[129]

1 WHO MAY APPLY FOR AN ORDER

Application for provision may be made only by the following persons.[130]

(a) Deceased's spouse[131] or civil partner

This category includes a person who had in good faith entered into a void marriage or civil partnership with the deceased. The reason is that such a person is de facto in the position of a surviving spouse or civil partner and may not discover that the union is void until after the other party's death, when it will be too late to apply for financial relief in nullity proceedings. Consequently, the survivor may not make an application under this head if during the deceased's lifetime the marriage or civil partnership has been dissolved or annulled by a decree recognised in England and Wales or he has entered into a later union and thus in effect treated the first as at an end.[132]

(b) A former spouse or civil partner of the deceased, who has not formed a subsequent marriage or civil partnership

A former spouse or civil partner of the deceased, whose union with the deceased was dissolved or annulled during his lifetime under the law of any part of the British Islands or recognised as valid in England and Wales and who, in either case, has not formed a subsequent marriage or civil partnership, may apply.[133] This enables the court to make or continue financial provision for those to whom it could award financial relief under the Matrimonial Causes Act 1973 or Civil Partnership Act 2004. An application by a former spouse or civil partner will, as the Court of Appeal pointed out in Re Fullard,[134] rarely be successful. In that case it refused to make an order in favour of the plaintiff who had

---

[127] Law Com No 187, *Distribution on Intestacy* (1989) paras 58–60. The recommendation was enacted by s 2 of the Law Reform (Succession) Act 1995, discussed further below, p 1108.

[128] Civil Partnership Act 2004 s 71 and Sch 4 paras 15–27.   [129] Section 1(1).

[130] An application may not be made more than six months after the date on which representation is first taken out without the permission of the court: ss 4 and 23. The personal representatives will not be personally liable for distribution after this time if no application is then pending, but property may be recovered from the beneficiaries to whom it has been transferred if it is needed to make provision for a dependant to whom the court gives leave to make a late application: s 20(1). For examples of permission being granted, see *Stock v Brown* [1994] 1 FLR 840 (applicant was elderly widow in financial difficulties—leave was given six years after grant of probate); *Re C (Deceased) (Leave to Apply for Provision)* [1995] 2 FLR 24 (applicant was an eight-year-old illegitimate child of the deceased: leave given two-and-a-half years after the death).

[131] A party to a polygamous marriage is a spouse for the purposes of the Act: *Re Sehota* [1978] 3 All ER 385.

[132] Section 25(4) (4A) as amended. A later marriage or civil partnership includes one which is void or voidable (because the person in question would have a claim against the other party to it): s 25(5) (5A) as amended.

[133] Section 25(1), as amended. Formation of a subsequent marriage or civil partnership includes one which is void or voidable: s 25(5) as amended.

[134] [1982] Fam 42, CA.

accepted a half-share of the matrimonial home (the parties' only asset) only a few months before her former husband's death. Normally, the court said, it would be appropriate to make an award in such circumstances only if the sole order made in previous proceedings had been for periodical payments, which had been running for a long time, and the deceased's estate could support their continuation,[135] or if the death had released a substantial capital sum, such as the payment of an insurance policy, of which the deceased was aware and which therefore should be taken into account in deciding whether he had made reasonable provision for the applicant.[136]

(c) A person who was cohabiting with the deceased when he or she died [137]

The Law Reform (Succession) Act 1995 s 2 added to the list of applicants a person who has lived as husband and wife with the deceased in the same household, for the whole of the period of two years ending immediately before the date of his death.[138] The aim of this reform, recommended by the Law Commission,[139] was to give greater recognition to the position of cohabitants who, previously, had to show dependence upon the deceased if they were to succeed in a claim.[140] The Civil Partnership Act 2004 has further amended the list to provide similarly for a person who lived with the deceased as his or her civil partner.[141]

The courts have adopted a broad view of what constitutes living together as husband and wife for the purposes of this provision. In *Re Watson (Deceased)*[142] the applicant and the deceased had known each other for thirty years, initially intimately, but had not married, each having to care for their elderly parents. After these died, the applicant moved in with the deceased but did not have a sexual relationship with him. On his death the question arose whether she had a claim on his estate which would otherwise go to the Crown as bona vacantia. It was held that

'the court should ask itself whether, in the opinion of a reasonable person with normal perceptions, it could be said that the two people in question were living together as husband and wife; but, when considering that question, one should not ignore the multifarious nature of marital relationships.'[143]

On this basis, the court concluded that the applicant satisfied the test, noting that

'It cannot be doubted but that it is not unusual for a happily married husband and wife in their mid-fifties (which was the age of the parties when they started living together in the present case) not merely to have separate bedrooms, but to abstain from sexual relations. [The parties] lived alone together for over 10 years in a house where they shared the bathroom and the living rooms. He went out to work and earnt the bulk of the household's

---

[135] As in *Re Crawford* (1982) 4 FLR 273.

[136] But not other accretions of wealth since the divorce: *Re Fullard* (above) at 52.

[137] See C Harrap 'Provision for Cohabitants on Death' [1997] Fam Law 422.

[138] Applies to deaths on or after 1 January 1996.

[139] Law Com No 187, paras 58–61.   [140] See further below, p 1110.

[141] Civil Partnership Act 2004 Sch 4 para 15(5). Cf the formulation used to amend the Housing legislation, which refers to couples living together 'as if' they were civil partners, not 'as civil partners'. See above p 1102. (In *Saunders v Garett* (2005) NLJ 1486, it was held, before the 2004 Act came into force, that the 1975 Act should be read as including same-sex cohabiting partners, although the applicant failed on the basis that reasonable provision had in fact been made for him in the deceased's will.)

[142] [1999] 1 FLR 878.   [143] At p 883G.

income, while she did the housekeeping (save three hours a week cleaning in the first four or five years), the shopping, the washing, the cooking and the gardening. No doubt, they ate together every day and that they enjoyed the living rooms jointly.'[144]

In *Watson* the deceased went into hospital about three weeks before he died, and the court was clear that no argument could be put that the couple were not living together 'immediately before the date of the death' on this account. However, in *Gully v Dix*[145] the claimant, who had cohabited with the deceased (who was alcoholic, incontinent and eventually diagnosed as suffering from Huntingdon's Chorea) for some 17 years, left him and moved in with her daughter three months before he died because she could not cope with his medical condition. She had left him on previous occasions and returned, and he phoned her frequently while she was away asking her to come back, but her daughter did not pass on his messages. The Court of Appeal upheld the trial judge's view that he should look at 'the settled state of affairs during the relationship between these parties and not the immediate de facto situation prevailing before the deceased's death'.[146] The couple's cohabitation was, in his view, only 'suspended' and had not been terminated, so that the claimant could proceed with her claim.

In *Kotke v Saffarini*[147] the issue was not whether the parties' cohabitation had come to an end, but whether it had ever begun. The claim was brought under the Fatal Accidents Act 1976[148] but is equally relevant to this provision. The parties had a sexual relationship but each owned a house. The deceased worked away from both his own house, which he rented out, and that of the claimant, staying with her at weekends. She became pregnant and their child was born shortly before the deceased was killed in a road accident. The Court of Appeal held that the trial judge had correctly determined that the relevant question was whether, at the requisite time (two years before the death) it could be demonstrated that, albeit retaining a separate domestic establishment in the house in which he had lived for some years, the deceased had effectively 'moved' to live under the same roof as the claimant, 'illness, holidays, work and other periodical absences' apart. The judge's view that there is a difference between wanting and intending to live in the same household, planning to do so, and actually doing so, was correct and his view that, on the evidence, the parties had not crossed the statutory threshold into the final stage could not be challenged.

It should be noted that either hetero- or same sex cohabitants may only receive provision based on his or her need for 'maintenance';[149] there is no entitlement to seek a capital share of the deceased's estate as there is for a surviving spouse or civil partner.

(d) A child of the deceased

This includes a child whose parents were not married to each other, an adopted child, and a child en ventre sa mère at the time of the death.[150] The age and marital status of the child are irrelevant.[151]

---

[144] At p 884B.   [145] [2004] EWCA Civ 139 [2004] 1 WLR 1399.   [146] Ibid para 15.

[147] [2005] EWCA Civ 221 [2005] 2 FLR 517.   [148] See below pp 1124–8.

[149] See below, p 1113.

[150] Section 25(1); Adoption and Children Act 2002 s 67. Conversely, if the deceased's natural child is adopted after the deceased's death, he cannot subsequently apply for an order under the Act as the deceased's child: *Re Collins (Deceased)* [1990] Fam 56.

[151] *Re Callaghan* [1985] Fam 1.

(e) Any other person whom the deceased treated as a child of the family

This corresponds to the court's power to award financial relief to a child of the family under the Matrimonial Causes Act or Civil Partnership Act. Obviously anyone who is a child of the family for the purpose of those Acts[152] will qualify as an applicant under the Inheritance Act. However, the category of persons able to apply for provision after death is wider, for only the deceased (and not his or her spouse or civil partner) need have treated the applicant as a child of the family, and children placed as foster children are not automatically excluded. The decision of the Court of Appeal in *Re Leach*[153] shows how wide the category can be. The applicant was a spinster aged 53 on her stepmother's death. She frequently visited her father after his remarriage and had a room in his bungalow. After his death she continued to visit her stepmother, who regarded her as a daughter rather than as a stepdaughter. The Court of Appeal held that it is not necessary for the applicant to have been treated as a child of the family by the deceased during the latter's marriage: as Slade LJ pointed out, a young child, who had lived with others during his father's second marriage and came to live with his stepmother after his father's death, would properly be regarded as a member of her family in relation to that marriage.[154] A display of affection, kindness or hospitality is not of itself sufficient to constitute treatment for this purpose: the question is whether 'the deceased has, *as wife or husband* (or widow or widower)[155] under the relevant marriage, expressly or impliedly, assumed the position of a parent towards the applicant, with the attendant *responsibilities and privileges* of that relationship'.[156] The deceased's privileges might well increase and his or her responsibilities diminish with age, and it follows from this approach that the applicant can qualify even though he was treated as a child of the family only when he was an adult[157] and the treatment ceased before the death. Applying this test, the court concluded that the applicant in this case had clearly been treated as a child of the family.

(f) Any other person who was being maintained, either wholly or in part, by the deceased immediately before his death

This provision, which was controversial when first introduced, gives an applicant a legal claim after the deceased's death whereas she (or he) may have had no claim at all during his lifetime. However anomalous this may be, it can be justified on the ground that the deceased would presumably have continued to provide for the applicant had he survived. In many cases there will be a clear moral claim, and the deceased's failure to provide for her after his death may be due to oversight or accident, eg the failure to make a will in time or the revocation of an earlier will by marriage.[158] Although in some cases the applicant and the deceased will have been members of the same family—eg two sisters who lived together—it is not necessary to establish such a relationship. What is essential is a de facto dependence, and the commonest example is still, notwithstanding the amendment made by the 1995 Act, likely to be that of a cohabitant.

'Maintained'

For the purpose of this provision, the applicant will be regarded as having been maintained

---

[152] See above, p 338.   [153] [1986] Ch 226, CA.   [154] At 234.
[155] Or, presumably now, civil partner.   [156] At 237.   [157] See also *Re Callaghan* [1985] Fam 1.
[158] See Law Com No 61, paras 85–94.

by the deceased only if the latter had been making a substantial contribution in money or money's worth towards his or her reasonable needs otherwise than for full valuable consideration.[159] Two classes of possible claimant are immediately seen to be outside this definition. The first are those who have not been in receipt of a *substantial* contribution. This means that the deceased's mistress may have a claim if he set her up in her own home and paid all her domestic bills,[160] but not if he did no more than make her casual payments and gifts. Secondly, the requirement that the contribution must have been made otherwise than for full valuable consideration clearly excludes claims by, for example, a housekeeper or companion who worked for an economic salary. It is not essential, however, that the consideration should have been provided under a contract between the applicant and the deceased.[161] According to Stephenson LJ in *Jelley v Iliffe*:[162]

'The court has to balance what [the deceased] was contributing against what [the applicant] was contributing, and if there is any doubt about the balance tipping in favour of [the deceased's] being the greater contribution, the matter must go to trial. If, however, the balance is bound to come down in favour of [the applicant's] being the greater contribution, or if the contributions are clearly equal, there is no dependency.'

Provided one is dealing with tangible matters such as the provision of accommodation or board and lodging, this is a relatively simple matter of assessment and accounting. Difficulty arises because Stephenson LJ added that the court must put a financial value on imponderables like companionship and weigh these against contributions of money and accommodation.[163] Bearing in mind that the Act speaks of contributions *in money or money's worth*, it is submitted that companionship and the like should be brought into account only insofar as they involve services which can and should be evaluated. The court would be put in an impossible position if it had to place a price on the emotional and other support which the two gave each other, and one would be forced to the absurd conclusion that, the more the applicant had offered the deceased, the less chance he would have of succeeding.[164]

If a claim is made by a relative or friend who lived with the deceased and performed domestic services for him in exchange for free board and lodging, the obvious approach is to assess what the latter would have had to pay for the benefit he received. But as Griffiths LJ stressed in *Jelley v Iliffe*,[165] it is essential to use common sense and ask whether the applicant could fairly be called a dependant: it would not be right to deprive a woman, with whom a man had been living as his wife, of a claim by arguing that she had been performing the duties of a housekeeper whom it would have cost more to employ.[166] Similarly, in *Bouette v Rose*[167] the Court of Appeal allowed a mother's claim to go forward

---

[159] Section 1(3); *Jelley v Iliffe* [1981] Fam 128, CA; *Bishop v Plumley* [1991] 1 All ER 236, CA; *Graham v Murphy* [1997] 1 FLR 860 (male cohabitant living in deceased's house at her expense); *Rees v Newbery and the Institute of Cancer Research* [1998] 1 FLR 1041 (applicant living in flat owned by the deceased at substantially below the market rent).

[160] As in *Malone v Harrison* [1979] 1 WLR 1353.   [161] *Jelley v Iliffe* (above) at 136, 141.

[162] At 138.   [163] Following *Re Wilkinson* [1978] Fam 22.

[164] *Bishop v Plumley* (above) at 242.   [165] At 141. Applied in *Bishop v Plumley* (above).

[166] See also *Churchill v Roach* [2004] 2 FLR 989: deceased bought property adjoining claimant's which was knocked through into hers. They lived together and he paid the bulk of the living expenses. He died before the titles to the two properties could be amalgamated as had been planned. Held, he had partially maintained her. See DJ M Cardinal, 'Inheritance or Estoppel—How the Cohabitant Succeeded' [2004] Fam Law 362.

[167] [2000] 1 FLR 363, CA.

after the death at the age of 14 of her daughter, who had been the beneficiary of a substantial damages award administered by the Court of Protection. The award had been used to purchase a home for the mother and daughter to live in and to provide income for the mother to see to the daughter's care. It was held that the daughter had made a substantial contribution, through the payments made by the Court, to the mother's financial and material needs.

'Immediately before the death of the deceased'

The applicant must also prove that the deceased was maintaining him (or her) immediately before his death. This requirement was subject to a detailed examination by the Court of Appeal in *Jelley v Iliffe*.[168] As Stephenson LJ said:[169]

'In considering whether a person is being maintained "immediately before the death of the deceased" it is the settled basis or general arrangement between the parties as regards maintenance during the lifetime of the deceased which has to be looked at, not the actual, perhaps fluctuating, variation of it which exists immediately before his or her death. It is, I think, not disputed that a relationship of dependence which has persisted for years will not be defeated by its termination during a few weeks of mortal sickness.'

On the other hand, if the deceased had clearly abandoned responsibility for the applicant's maintenance before his death, the latter will have no claim.[170] Nor will the applicant have one if he was being maintained on a purely temporary basis or by chance at the time of the death, eg if he was a friend whom the deceased had taken in for a few days whilst he recovered from an illness.

(g) Death of applicant

As the claim is essential for a dependant's provision, an application automatically abates if the applicant dies before an order is made.[171]

2 REASONABLE PROVISION

The applicant must also show that the provisions of the deceased's will or the law relating to intestacy (or the combination of both if there is a partial intestacy) are not such as to make reasonable financial provision for him.[172] This, of course, is a question of fact, but if the applicant cannot discharge the burden of proof, he has no claim at all. It is not the purpose of the Act merely to enable the court to provide legacies or rewards for meritorious conduct.[173]

---

[168] [1981] Fam 128, CA.

[169] At 136 following *Re Beaumont* [1980] Ch 444 at 456. Griffiths LJ expressed the same view at 141. Cumming-Bruce LJ agreed with both judgments.

[170] *Kourkgy v Lusher* (1981) 4 FLR 65 (claimant unsuccessful when deceased had stopped cohabiting with her and returned to his wife three weeks before his death).

[171] *Whytte v Ticehurst* [1986] Fam 64; *Re Bramwell* [1988] 2 FLR 263.

[172] Section 1(1) and s 2(1). For a clear example of failure to make *reasonable* provision, see *Hanbury v Hanbury* [1999] 2 FLR 255 (county court) where the deceased bequeathed his seriously disabled daughter by his first marriage only £10,000 whilst his second wife had assets of over £260,000 (see further below regarding dispositions intended to defeat the daughter's claim at p 1120 n 234).

[173] *Re Coventry* [1980] Ch 461 at 486 and 495; *Re Abram (Deceased)* [1996] 2 FLR 379 at 388H; cf *Re Christie* [1979] Ch 168, doubted in *Re Coventry* at 490.

(a) For a surviving spouse or civil partner [174]

In defining reasonable provision, the Act draws a significant distinction between surviving spouses or civil partners and all other applicants. If the application is made by a surviving spouse or civil partner (except where a decree of judicial separation or separation order was in force and the separation was continuing at the deceased's death), reasonable financial provision means such financial provision as it would be reasonable in all the circumstances of the case for a husband or wife (or civil partner) to receive, *whether or not that provision is required for his or her maintenance.*[175]

The reason for this is that a surviving spouse or civil partner would normally expect to receive a share of the deceased spouse's estate and it would be anomalous if the court could give her (or him) less after the other's death than it could on divorce or dissolution.[176] In other words, the Act has two distinct objects: to provide appropriate support for a dependant (including a surviving spouse or civil partner) and to make a fair division of assets between the two, although it is apparent that the courts do not always keep these two objects distinct.[177]

(b) Maintenance for any other applicant

In all other cases, the financial provision to be considered is that which it would be reasonable in all the circumstances of the case for the applicant to receive *for his maintenance.* When considering the provision of maintenance, the court is not limited to assessing the amount needed for bare necessities, nor must it take into account everything which the applicant might regard as reasonably desirable for his benefit or welfare. One must ask whether he will be able to maintain himself in a manner suitable to the circumstances.[178]

'Maintenance' means—

'... payments which, directly or indirectly, enable the applicant in the future to discharge the cost of his daily living ... The provision that is to be made is to meet recurring expenses, being expenses of living of an income nature.'[179]

Such payments may embrace the payment of debts, provided that these will enable the applicant to carry on his business or profession,[180] but not where they will simply be used to reduce liabilities in bankruptcy or an individual voluntary arrangement under the

---

[174] See JG Miller 'Provision for a Surviving Spouse' (1997) 61 Conv 442.

[175] Section 1(2) as amended by the Civil Partnership Act 2004 Sch 4 para 14(6).

[176] This accounts for the exception where a decree of judicial separation or separation order is in force, because the survivor will already have had an opportunity of applying to the court for a lump sum or property adjustment order. Hence, if the deceased's marriage or civil partnership had been dissolved or annulled and he died within 12 months of this (or if he died within 12 months of a separation decree or order) and no application for financial relief has been made or, if it has the proceedings have not been determined, the court may consider an application for an order under the Inheritance Act as though no order (or decree) had been made: s 14 and s 14A as inserted by the Civil Partnership Act 2004 Sch 4 para 20. Otherwise the applicant would lose the benefit of both statutes.

[177] See JG Miller 'Provision for a Surviving Spouse' (1986) 102 LQR 445.

[178] *Re Coventry* [1980] Ch 461, CA, at 485 (per Goff LJ), and 494 (per Buckley LJ) respectively. As it was put per Roach JA in *Re Duranceau* [1952] 3 DLR 714 (Canada) at 720, is 'the provision sufficient to enable the dependant to live neither luxuriously nor miserably but decently and comfortably according to his or her station in life?' cited by Goff LJ in *Re Coventry* (supra) at 485, and Slade LJ in *Re Leach* [1986] Ch 226 at 240.

[179] Per Browne-Wilkinson J in *Re Dennis (Deceased)* [1981] 2 All ER 140 at 145–6.

[180] Given as an example by Browne-Wilkinson J in *Re Dennis* (above).

Insolvency Act 1986.[181] A payment intended to relieve someone of income expenditure, eg to buy a house without taking on a mortgage, may be appropriate.[182]

3 FACTORS TO BE TAKEN INTO ACCOUNT

The Act specifically requires the court to have regard to the following matters when determining whether reasonable financial provision has been made for the applicant, and, if not, what orders it should make.[183]

(a) Factors relevant to all applications

'(a) the financial resources and financial needs which the applicant has or is likely to have in the foreseeable future;

(b) the financial resources and financial needs which any other applicant for an order . . . has or is likely to have in the foreseeable future;

(c) the financial resources and financial needs which any beneficiary of the estate of the deceased has or is likely to have in the foreseeable future;

(d) any obligations and responsibilities which the deceased had towards any applicant for an order . . . or towards any beneficiary of the estate of the deceased;

(e) the size and nature of the net estate of the deceased;

(f) any physical or mental disability of any applicant . . . or any beneficiary of the estate of the deceased;

(g) any other matter, including the conduct of the applicant or any other person, which in the circumstances of the case the court may consider relevant.'[184]

Financial resources and financial needs

The financial resources and needs[185] of the applicant, any other applicant for an order, and any beneficiary of the estate,[186] and any physical or mental disability from which any of them suffers, must be considered.

In this connection the court must take into account the individual's earning capacity, any resources and needs which he is likely to have in the foreseeable future, and his financial obligations and responsibilities.[187] It is, of course, necessary to consider the position of other applicants and beneficiaries, because any order made will limit the property available for them; consequently an applicant is more likely to succeed if an order in his favour can be made at the expense of a beneficiary towards whom the deceased had no obligations.[188] Generally speaking, the court must pay regard to similar matters when considering the question of financial relief on divorce, and they have already been

---

[181] *Re Abram (Deceased)* [1996] 2 FLR 379.   [182] *Re Callaghan* [1985] Fam 1.

[183] Section 3.   [184] Section 3(1).

[185] That is, reasonable requirements: *Harrington v Gill* (1983) 4 FLR 265, CA.

[186] Beneficiary includes not only a person claiming under the deceased's will or on his intestacy, but also anyone nominated by him to receive money or property after his death and any recipient of a donatio mortis causa, because all this property forms part of the net estate: s 25(1).

[187] Including his debts: *Re Goodchild (Deceased)* [1996] 1 All ER 670.

[188] As in *Re Besterman* [1984] Ch 458, CA, *Re Bunning* [1984] Ch 480, *Rees v Newbery and the Institute of Cancer Research* [1998] 1 FLR 1041. In each of these cases the residuary legatees were charities.

considered more fully in the discussion of that problem,[189] but in one or two respects the court's approach must be different. The standard at which the applicant lived whilst the deceased was alive is clearly relevant but cannot be conclusive in the changed circumstances brought about by the death. For example, money will no longer be needed to maintain the deceased,[190] and it will usually be more reasonable to expect a woman to make provision for her widower, particularly if his earning capacity is reduced, than to support her divorced husband.[191] In the case of a small estate it is particularly important to consider the extent to which an applicant can claim social security benefits or may be expected to make use of the NHS or community care provision. If an order for financial provision would be so small that it would merely reduce the amount payable to him out of public funds without giving him any advantage, it may be eminently reasonable to use the whole estate to give a benefit to another applicant or beneficiary.[192] Conversely, if the estate is large and the applicant is in later middle age or elderly, consideration should be given to his or her provision in later life or possible infirmity,[193] but this need not require the provision of an absolute interest in property where a life interest will suffice.[194]

Obligations and responsibilities of the deceased

Both legal and moral obligations are included in this provision, but they must have been in existence immediately before the deceased's death. Thus, a failure to support a child after the deceased's marriage broke down did not justify an award to the now adult child.[195] Since such an applicant, as distinct from a surviving spouse, may only receive an award constituting *maintenance*, this approach[196] is consistent with the general view of the courts that adult children should not generally expect to receive financial support from their parents.[197]

The cases on this issue seemed to establish that an adult child would have to show either that the deceased owed him a moral obligation, going beyond the mere fact of a blood relationship, to make provision for him out of his estate, or some other reason why, in the circumstances, it was unreasonable that no, or no more, provision had been made. In *Re Coventry*, for example, the plaintiff, who at the time of the application was aged 48 and divorced, had left the Royal Navy and lived with his father for the last 19 years of the latter's life. Shortly after he returned home, his mother left because of the way in which her husband and son treated her. The plaintiff ran the house and looked after his father, and sought an order under the Act on the latter's death intestate. His disposable income was

---

[189] Above, pp 1030–51.   [190] See below, p 1117.

[191] See *Re Clayton* [1966] 2 All ER 370 (widower disabled and earning only £10 a week); *Re Wilson* (1969) 113 Sol Jo 794 (widower aged 92).

[192] See *Re E, E v E* [1966] 2 All ER 44; *Re Clayton* (above); *Re Watkins* [1949] 1 All ER 695. Contrast *Re Collins (Deceased)* [1990] Fam 56, (lump sum ordered for applicant on income support). (It should be noted, however, that Hollings J seems (at 62) to have misstated Stamp LJ's conclusions in *Re E, E v E*.)

[193] *Re Besterman* (above). In *Espinosa v Bourke* [1999] 1 FLR 747, the Court of Appeal had regard in particular to the appellant's needs, as someone with limited prospects of employment at her age (55), in straightened financial circumstances with little chance of managing other than from a share of her father's estate.

[194] *Davis v Davis* [1993] 1 FLR 54, CA.   [195] *Re Jennings (Deceased)* [1994] Ch 256, CA.

[196] Which has been criticised as regrettable by D Chatterton 'Inheritance Act Claims by Children' [1994] Fam Law 330; Borkowski, op cit, p 298.

[197] See JG Miller 'Provision for Adult Children under the Inheritance (Provision for Family and Dependants) Act 1975' (1995) 59 Conv 22 and N Peart and A Borkowski, 'Provision for adult children on death—the lesson from New Zealand' [2000] CFLQ 333.

about £40 a week; his mother (who was the only other person interested in the estate, which was worth about £7,000) lived entirely on social security benefits. The Court of Appeal considered that it would be rare for a relatively young and able-bodied man in employment to succeed in a claim under the Act,[198] and upheld Oliver J's decision to dismiss his claim. In *Williams v Johns*[199] a judge dismissed an adult adoptive daughter's claim because the deceased had made a written statement, filed with her will, that she felt no obligation towards her daughter, who had caused her much distress. The judge specifically stated that the plaintiff had to establish a moral obligation on the part of the deceased to make provision for her.

However, in *Re Hancock (Deceased)*[200] the Court of Appeal held that this approach was wrong. The adult daughter, now in her seventies, had lived in precarious financial circumstances for many years. After her father's death, the land occupied by his family business (now run by several of her siblings), which had been valued at the time of probate at £100,000, was sold for some £650,000 for redevelopment. The Court of Appeal upheld the first instance decision to award her £3,000 per annum maintenance, and held that the Act imposes no express requirement to establish a moral obligation or special circumstances. Rather, *in the absence* of such factors, it may be difficult to make out a claim where the claimant is in employment, possibly in affluent circumstances, and with an earning capacity in the foreseeable future. By contrast, since the daughter was in modest financial circumstances, facing a future where she would not be working and thus could not improve her condition in life, and since the evidence showed that the father had recognised that some provision ought, if possible, to be made for her after his widow's death, her claim could be supported.[201] Similarly, where the claimant has health problems,[202] or has worked in the family business at a very low wage in the expectation that he will inherit,[203] or where the deceased previously made a will in favour of the applicant as part of a mutual understanding with his spouse,[204] then provision may be made.

The size and nature of the estate[205]

If, for example, the deceased had a large income but little capital, it might be reasonable for him to leave the whole of his estate to his widow to the total exclusion of others whom he had supported during his lifetime. Likewise the source of the deceased's capital may be

---

[198] Prima facie it is not unreasonable for the deceased not to make financial provision for any adult (other than his or her spouse) capable of maintaining himself: *Re Dennis* [1981] 2 All ER 140 at 145; *Williams v Johns* [1988] 2 FLR 475.

[199] [1988] 2 FLR 475.

[200] [1998] 2 FLR 346, CA, followed in *Re Pearce (Deceased)* [1998] 2 FLR 705, CA. See A Borkowski, 'Re Hancock (Deceased) and Espinosa v Bourke: Moral obligation and family provision' [1999] CFLQ 305; J Wilson and R Bailey-Harris, 'Family Provision: The Adult Child and Moral Obligation' [2005] Fam Law 555.

[201] See also *Espinosa v Bourke* [1999] 1 FLR 747: deceased had disapproved of daughter's lifestyle; she had left him to be cared for by her teenaged son while she lived in Spain and he considered he had made adequate provision for her during his lifetime. Nonetheless, the Court of Appeal held that although her conduct was a relevant factor, it was outweighed by her needs, and the deceased's promise to his wife that he would leave the shares he inherited from her to the daughter.

[202] *Millward v Shenton* [1972] 2 All ER 1025, CA; *Re Debenham* [1986] 1 FLR 404.

[203] *Re Abram (Deceased)* [1996] 2 FLR 379.   [204] *Re Goodchild (Deceased)* [1997] 2 FLR 644, CA.

[205] Including property forming part of an unsevered joint tenancy or a transaction or contract intended to defeat an application under the Act which may be made available for financial provision (see below, p 1120): *Kourkgy v Lusher* (1981) 4 FLR 65, *Hanbury v Hanbury* [1999] 2 FLR 255.

relevant; for example, if it came largely from a former spouse, the children of that spouse may have a stronger claim than the deceased's spouse or relations.[206] If the estate is small, the courts discourage applications altogether because of the danger that it will be entirely swallowed up by the costs of the action.[207]

Any other relevant matter, including the conduct of the applicant or any other person[208]

In the case of a former spouse the test should be the same whether the application is made on divorce or after the other party's death.[209] It is submitted that this should be applied if the applicant is a widow or widower, because he should be in no worse position than he would have been if the marriage had been dissolved.[210] The same should now be true for a (former) civil partner. It is accepted that the court should take into account the fact that a child has given up work to look after a parent,[211] but, on the other hand, it is not easy to see what weight should be given to a child's hurtful conduct. It is submitted that the test should be this: bearing in mind the deceased's treatment of the applicant, was the latter's conduct towards him such that a reasonable parent would have considered that he had forfeited any further claim to financial provision?[212]

(b) Factors relevant to applications by spouses or civil partners

If the applicant is a surviving or former spouse or civil partner, the court must also have regard to the duration of the marriage/ partnership, the applicant's age, and the contribution he or she made to the welfare of the deceased's family, including any contribution by looking after the home or caring for the family.[213] If the couple have been living apart, the length of their separation will also be relevant.[214] Again, the similarity with the law of divorce will be seen. Moreover (except when a decree of judicial separation or separation order was in force and the separation was continuing at the deceased's death), the court must also consider what provision the applicant might reasonably have expected to receive had the marriage or civil partnership been terminated by divorce or dissolution instead of death,[215] on the ground that it would be anomalous if the latter could expect less on death than she would have got on divorce or dissolution.

In *Fielden and Another v Cunliffe*[216] the wife worked as the deceased's housekeeper

[206] *Re Callaghan* [1985] Fam 1.

[207] See *Re Coventry* (above), at 486 (per Goff LJ); *Re Fullard* [1982] Fam 42 at 46 (per Ormrod LJ).

[208] But this does not include undertakings given by other beneficiaries not to claim their rights under the will, because the question is whether *the will* (or the law of intestacy) makes reasonable financial provision for the applicant: *Rajabally v Rajabally* [1987] 2 FLR 390, CA.

[209] *Re Snoek* (1983) 13 Fam Law 18.   [210] See above, p 1113.

[211] See *Re Coventry* [1980] Ch 461 at 489–90.

[212] See *Williams v Johns* [1988] 2 FLR 475, discussed above, p 1116.

[213] Section 3(2) as amended by Civil Partnership Act 2004 Sch 4 para 17.

[214] *Re Rowlands* [1984] FLR 813, CA.

[215] Section 3(2) as amended by Civil Partnership Act 2004 Sch 4 para 17(5). See *Re Besterman* ([1984] Ch 458, CA); *Re Bunning* ([1984] Ch 480); *Jessop v Jessop* [1992] 1 FLR 591, CA at 597.

[216] [2005] EWCA Civ 1508, [2006] 3 FCR 593. This decision appears to overrule the approach taken in *P v G, P and P (Family Provision: Relevance of Divorce Provision)* [2004] EWHC 2944 (Fam), [2006] 1 FLR 431. There, it was held that the divorce analogy represents the minimum that a widow should attain in Inheritance Act cases. The deceased husband's estate was worth about £5 million. He had reduced his bequests to the second wife in his will after they had contemplated divorce (although they had reconciled shortly before his death). She was granted a lump sum of £2 million, including the matrimonial home, on top of the pension income to which she was already entitled.

before marrying him a year before he died. At first instance, she was awarded a lump sum of £800,000 out of the estate valued at some £1.4 million. In reducing the award to £600,000, the Court of Appeal held that the correct approach for the court to adopt, following the decision of the House of Lords in *White v White*[217] is to apply the statutory provisions to the facts of the individual case with the objective of achieving a result which is fair, and non-discriminatory. This does not mean that an equal share may result, for the situation is not identical to that of a divorce. As Wall LJ put it:

'A marriage dissolved by divorce involves a conscious decision by one or both of the spouses to bring the marriage to an end. That process leaves two living former spouses, each of whom has resources, needs and responsibilities. In such a case the length of the marriage and the parties' respective contributions to it assume a particular importance when the court is striving to reach a fair financial outcome. However, where the marriage, as here, is dissolved by death, a widow is entitled to say that she entered into it on the basis that it would be of indefinite duration, and in the expectation that she would devote the remainder of the parties' joint lives to being his wife and caring for him. The fact that the marriage has been prematurely terminated by death after a short period may therefore render the length of the marriage a less critical factor than it would be in the case of a divorce.'[218]

However, the deceased is entitled to bequeath his estate to whomever he likes, and is only subject to the statutory obligation to make *reasonable* financial provision for the surviving spouse (or civil partner). In the context of securing such 'reasonable financial provision', the Court of Appeal concluded that the brevity of the marriage and the fact that the widow had made only a very small contribution to the family wealth were factors against equality of division in ensuring a *fair* outcome to the case.

(c) Factors relevant to applications by cohabitants

In such cases, the court must additionally have regard to the age of the applicant, the length of the period of cohabitation, and the contribution made by the applicant to the welfare of the family or of the deceased, including any contribution made by looking after the home or caring for the family.[219]

(d) Factors relevant to applications by a child, or child of the family, of the deceased

If the applicant is a child of the deceased or a person whom he treated as a child of the family, the court must also have regard to the manner in which he was being or might expect to be educated or trained. If he is a child of the family but not the deceased's own child, the court must also consider the same matters as it has to take into account when deciding whether to make an order in favour of such a child on divorce or dissolution.[220]

(e) Factors relevant to applications by dependants

If the applicant is relying on a de facto dependence during the deceased's lifetime, the court must specifically have regard to the extent to which the deceased had assumed

[217] [2001] 1 AC 596.   [218] *Fielden v Cunliffe* [2005] EWCA Civ 1508, [2006] 3 FCR 593 at para [30].
[219] Section 3(2A) as amended by Civil Partnership Act 2004 Sch 4 para 18.
[220] Section 3(3). For the matters to be taken into account, see the Matrimonial Causes Act 1973 s 25(4) (above, p 967) and Civil Partnership Act 2004 Sch 5 para 22.

responsibility for his maintenance, the basis upon which he had done so, and the length of time for which he had discharged it.[221] These are three of the matters which the court has to take into account when considering applications from persons who have been treated as children of the family, and the similarity of their position is obvious. The assumption of responsibility may be inferred from the fact of the deceased having maintained the applicant.[222]

(f) Objective test

In *Re Coventry* Goff LJ said:[223]

'The question is not whether it might have been reasonable for the deceased to assist . . . the plaintiff, but whether in all the circumstances, looked at objectively, it is unreasonable that the effective provisions governing the estate did not do so.'

Accordingly, the Act provides that the court shall take into account the facts as known at the hearing.[224] The injustice that could otherwise be worked can be seen by examining the facts of *Re Goodwin*.[225] A testator provided for his children by making specific bequests in their favour and for his widow, their stepmother, by a legacy and the bequest of the residue of his estate. He expected the residue to be worth over £8,000 whereas it turned out to be worth about £1,500. Megarry J concluded that in the event the provision for the widow was not reasonable and made an order in her favour. Similarly, in *Re Hancock (Deceased)*[226] the value of the deceased's estate had increased six-fold between probate and the date of the hearing some 10 years later. Since the delay was not the fault of the claimant, it was held that it was right to take the full value into account in assessing whether reasonable provision had been made for her.

4 PROPERTY AVAILABLE FOR FINANCIAL PROVISION

Except for the power to order the variation of an ante-nuptial or post-nuptial settlement or the equivalent in relation to a civil partnership (which will be considered later), the court can only make orders for the payment of money out of the deceased's net estate or affecting property comprised in that estate.[227] Basically, this means such property[228] as the deceased had power to dispose of by will (otherwise than by virtue of a special power of appointment), less the amount of funeral, testamentary and administration expenses and any liabilities.[229] Five other types of property are also comprised within the definition. First, property in respect of which the deceased had a general power of appointment not exercisable by will is included if the power was never exercised, for he could have exercised the power in his own favour and thus brought it within his estate.[230] Secondly, some

---

221 Section 3(4); *Graham v Murphy* [1997] 1 FLR 860; *Rees v Newbery and the Institute of Cancer Research* [1998] 1 FLR 1041.
222 *Jelley v Iliffe* [1981] Fam 128, CA overruling *Re Beaumont* [1980] Ch 444 on this point.
223 [1980] Ch 461 at 488–9.   224 Section 3(5).   225 [1969] 1 Ch 283.
226 Discussed above, p 1116.
227 Sections 2(1) (as amended by Civil Partnership Act 2004 Sch 4 para 16), 8(1). For net estate generally, see Law Com No 61, paras 127–43.
228 Including property situated abroad: *Bheekhun v Williams* [1999] 2 FLR 229.
229 Section 25(1), (2).   230 Section 25(1).

statutes enable a person to nominate another to take the benefit of a fund after his death. This is equivalent to a testamentary disposition, and such property is therefore part of his estate for this purpose notwithstanding any nomination.[231] Thirdly, for a similar reason donationes mortis causa made by the deceased are included.[232] Fourthly, the court may order the severance of a joint tenancy or joint interest (eg in a bank account) or any part of a joint tenancy or interest to which the deceased was entitled immediately before his death and which would therefore otherwise pass to the other joint tenants, for the same reason that he could have effected a severance himself and thus brought the property into his estate.[233] The undivided share will then form part of the net estate. Finally, the estate includes any money or property ordered to be restored or provided if a disposition or contract is set aside under the provisions noted next.

(a) Transactions intended to defeat applications

One of the weaknesses of earlier legislation was that the deceased could defeat an application by settling or disposing of his property during his lifetime so that it never formed part of his estate at all or, alternatively, could contract to leave it to a third person after his death.[234] The 1975 Act contains provisions designed to frustrate such transactions.[235]

5 ORDERS THAT MAY BE MADE

(a) Interim orders

If a dependant is in immediate need of financial assistance, and property forming part of the net estate can be made available to meet his needs but it is not yet possible to make a final order, the court may make an interim order. This may take the form of one payment or of periodical payments, and the court may later direct that any sum paid under an interim order shall be treated as having been paid on account of the final order. As far as possible, the same matters should be taken into account in making an interim order as in making a final order.[236]

(b) Final orders

If the court is satisfied that reasonable financial provision has not been made for the applicant, it may make a final order containing one or more of the provisions set out

---

[231] But not if the power arises purely under a contract or trust deed: *Re Cairnes* (1982) 4 FLR 225 (death benefits payable under occupational pension scheme). It might be possible to have such a nomination set aside as a transaction intended to defeat an application under the Act: see below.

[232] Section 8(2). In this case and the last, any person giving effect to the nomination or gift is protected.

[233] Section 9. See *Jessop v Jessop* [1992] 1 FLR 591, CA; *Hanbury v Hanbury* [1999] 2 FLR 255. This power can be exercised only if an application for an order for financial provision was made within six months from the date on which representation was first taken out. Any person dealing with the property before an order for severance is protected.

[234] See eg *Hanbury v Hanbury* [1999] 2 FLR 255 where the father sought (unsuccessfully) to prevent his estate being vulnerable to a claim by his adult (handicapped) daughter. If the transaction was effected fraudulently with intent to defeat the dependant's claim, it is arguable that it could be set aside under the court's general power to upset fraudulent transactions, or perhaps under s 423 of the Insolvency Act 1986: see *Cadogan v Cadogan* [1977] 3 All ER 831, CA. This might still be relevant eg if the transaction was made more than six years before the deceased's death.

[235] See ss 10 and 11.   [236] Section 5. For the protection of personal representatives, see s 20(2).

below.[237] In determining what order (if any) to make, the court must have regard to the same matters as it has when deciding whether reasonable provision has been made.[238]

Periodical payments

This may be for a specified amount or for an amount equal to the whole or any part of the income of the net estate or of such part of the estate as the court directs to be set aside or appropriated for this purpose, or it may be determined in any other way the court thinks fit.[239] The order may last for such term and be subject to such conditions as the court directs. Formation of a subsequent marriage or civil partnership of the deceased's spouse or civil partner will not automatically discharge the order (although it may be a ground for an application to have it discharged by the court). It would be anomalous, however, to give former and separated spouses or civil partners greater rights on the deceased's death than they had before, and consequently an order for periodical payments made in their favour will terminate automatically on remarriage or new civil partnership[240] In other cases it would normally be reasonable to direct that payment to a child should terminate on his ceasing to receive education or training, or that payment to a parent who is temporarily unable to work owing to illness should terminate on his ceasing to be under a disability.

An order may be varied, suspended or discharged on the application of anyone who has already applied for an order or would be entitled to apply if he were not time-barred.[241] The variation can only be made in respect of property being used for the making of such payments and, if in favour of another person, only at the expense of the recipient. The variation can take the form of a lump sum or the transfer of the property, as well as the provision of further periodical payments.

Lump sum

Such an order would be particularly valuable if the estate is so small that any periodical payments would be valueless. It could also enable, say, a claimant to purchase the goodwill of a business: indeed, if the estate is large enough, it is submitted that this will normally be the proper order to make in favour of a surviving spouse or civil partner. If the order is made at the expense of beneficiaries towards whom the deceased had no obligations, a spouse or civil partner will probably obtain more under the Inheritance Act than she (or he) would have obtained in divorce or dissolution proceedings, because the estate is no longer needed for the deceased's support and it may be reasonable to give the applicant a cushion to provide against future contingencies.[242]

---

[237] Section 2(1). See generally Law Com No 61, paras 109–26.

[238] Section 3(1). See above, pp 1112–19.   [239] Section 2(2), (3).

[240] Section 19(2) as amended by Civil Partnership Act Sch 4 para 26. This applies to separated spouses or civil partners only if the decree or order was in force and the separation continuing at the time of the deceased's death.

[241] Section 6.

[242] See *Re Besterman* [1984] Ch 458; *Re Bunning* [1984] Ch 480; JG Miller 'Provision for a Surviving Spouse' (1986) 102 LQR 445; T Prime 'Family Provision—The Spouse's Application' [1986] Fam Law 95. In *Fielden and Another v Cunliffe* [2005] EWCA Civ 1508, [2005] All ER (D) 80 (Dec), Wall LJ suggested (at para 77) that the view that such a 'cushion' should be given must be regarded with caution, since it pre-dated *White v White*. However, he saw it as still being 'authority for the proposition that the blameless widow of a wealthy man is entitled to look forward to financial security throughout her remaining life-time, and that "reasonable financial provision", which is not limited to maintenance, must be viewed accordingly'.

A lump sum in favour of a non-family dependant may be valuable if relationships in a family are so bitter that a clean break is desirable,[243] or to avoid embarrassment, or to achieve finality in the interests of the other beneficiaries.[244] The disadvantage of such an order is that it cannot be varied to take account of unforeseen changes in the circumstances of the applicant or a beneficiary and, if it represents the capitalisation of periodical payments, events may prove the estimate to have been wildly inaccurate. Consequently, the courts have been reluctant to order the payment of a lump sum to an applicant who is elderly or in poor health, because premature death would often result in the deceased's assets being vested in someone outside the family.[245]

As on divorce, the court may order that a lump sum be paid by instalments.[246]

The transfer or settlement of property comprised in the net estate

The court might well order that the former family home be transferred or settled for the benefit of a surviving partner[247] particularly if he or she has to bring up young children. In other cases it may be more convenient, as on divorce, to order the transfer of property than the payment of a lump sum.

The transfer or settlement of property to be acquired out of the estate

This has no counterpart in the Matrimonial Causes Act and is designed particularly to enable a home to be bought for the applicant.[248]

The variation of any ante-nuptial or post-nuptial settlement or settlement in relation to a civil partnership

This is strictly equivalent to the court's powers on divorce or dissolution and the variation may be made only for the benefit of the surviving party to the marriage or civil partnership or a child of the family in relation to that marriage or civil partnership.[249]

6 RELATIONSHIP TO EXISTING AGREEMENTS AND ORDERS

It must not be forgotten that other liabilities to support a dependant may survive the deceased's death. An order for secured periodical payments may have been made in his favour during previous proceedings or he may be a party to a maintenance agreement under which payments continue. Not only will the existence of the continuing right affect any order that may be made if he applies for financial relief under the Act but also, in the changed circumstances brought about by the death, it may make unfairly generous

---

[243] See *Re Collins (Deceased)* [1990] Fam 56 (need to achieve finality where defendant was violent man and applicant, his daughter, had been fostered).

[244] *Graham v Murphy* [1997] 1 FLR 860; *Rees v Newbery and the Institute of Cancer Research* [1998] 1 FLR 1041.

[245] See *Re Debenham* [1986] 1 FLR 404 (daughter aged 58, epileptic, given small lump sum and annuity). In *Stead v Stead* [1985] FLR 16, CA, the lump sum awarded to a widow, aged 82, was limited to the amount needed to cover certain eventualities, apparently on the ground that, if she were given more, she would merely save it. But this is not an invariable rule and a lump sum may be ordered in other circumstances: *Kusminow v Barclays Bank Trust Co Ltd* [1989] Fam Law 66, *Re Pearce (Deceased)* [1998] 2 FLR 705, CA.

[246] Section 7. The court may subsequently vary the number and amount of instalments and the dates on which they are to be paid, but not the total sum payable.

[247] As in *Harrington v Gill* (1983) 4 FLR 265, CA.   [248] See Law Com No 61, para 116.

[249] Section 2(1)(f), (g) inserted by Civil Partnership Act 2004 Sch 4 para 16.

provision for him compared with the amount left for other applicants. To prevent the unnecessary duplication of proceedings, the court may vary existing orders and agreements in proceedings under the 1975 Act.[250]

If the applicant for financial relief under the Inheritance Act continues to be entitled to secured periodical payments on an order made under the Matrimonial Causes Act 1973 or Sch 5 to the Civil Partnership Act 2004, the court may vary or discharge the order or revive the operation of any provision which has been previously suspended.[251] Similarly, if the applicant is still entitled to payments under a maintenance agreement, the court may vary or revoke the agreement.[252] The definition of a maintenance agreement is the same as that contained in s 34 of the Matrimonial Causes Act[253] except, importantly, that it need not be in writing.[254] The court has no power to reduce the sums payable if, in proceedings brought by another applicant under the Act, it comes to the conclusion that they are too large. This can be done only if the personal representatives themselves take proceedings to have the order or agreement varied under the Matrimonial Causes Act or Civil Partnership Act, which they may be unwilling to do.

Conversely, if the personal representatives, the recipient of secured periodical payments or a party to a maintenance agreement applies for a variation of the order or agreement under those Acts,[255] the court may deem the application to have been accompanied by an application for an order under the Inheritance Act and exercise all the powers it has under that Act.[256] This may be of particular importance to a party to an agreement, because under the other Acts there is no power to set aside a disposition intended to defeat an application for a variation of a maintenance agreement after the payer's death. By invoking this jurisdiction, the court can exercise its jurisdiction to set aside dispositions and contracts under s 10 and s 11.

Whether as part of an agreed financial settlement, or in pursuance of the principle that a clean break should be made wherever possible, the court dealing with financial provision on divorce, dissolution, nullity or separation may wish to exclude the possibility of a future application under the Inheritance Act. Accordingly it may make an order having this effect on the application of either party to the marriage or civil partnership if it is satisfied that it is just to do so.[257] However, the fact that such a clause has not been included does not, of itself, strengthen a claim.[258] The order will take effect only when a decree of nullity or divorce is made absolute or the nullity or dissolution order is made final or, in the case of a separation, if the decree or order is in force and the separation is

---

[250] See further Law Com No 61, Part VII.

[251] Section 16 as amended by Civil Partnership Act 2004 Sch 4 para 23. The court must have regard to all the circumstances, including any change in the matters to which it was required to have regard when making the order for secured periodical payments.

[252] Section 17 as amended by Civil Partnership Act 2004 Sch 4 para 24. The court must have regard to all the circumstances, including any change in the circumstances in the light of which the agreement was made.

[253] And Sch 5 para 67 to the Civil Partnership Act 2004. See above p 954.   [254] Section 17(4).

[255] In such a case, the agreement must be a maintenance agreement within the meaning of those Acts.

[256] Inheritance (Provision for Family and Dependants) Act 1975 ss 18 and 18A (inserted by Civil Partnership Act 2004 Sch 4 para 25).

[257] Sections 15, 15ZA as inserted by the Civil Partnership Act 2004 Sch 4 para 21.

[258] *Cameron v Treasury Solicitor* [1996] 2 FLR 716, CA (but note that there the divorce had taken place at a time when such a clause could only be added by consent and was not routine); cf *T v T (Financial Relief: Pensions)* [1998] 1 FLR 1072 where Singer J thought that such an application might be fairer than attempting to attach the husband's pension many years before he might be expected to die.

continuing on the death of one of the parties. The court has the same power if it makes an order for financial relief following a foreign dissolution, annulment or legal separation granted in an overseas country and recognised here.[259]

By analogy with applications for financial relief in matrimonial proceedings, a party presumably cannot contract out of his or her power to apply under the Inheritance Act except by way of a consent order.[260]

E COMPENSATION UNDER THE FATAL ACCIDENTS ACT[261]

1 BACKGROUND

It was a firm rule of tort that 'the death of a human being could not be complained of as an injury'.[262] Consequently the dependants of a person killed as the result of another's negligence could not claim damages from him. With the advent of heavy industry in the nineteenth century, the problem became more serious, and the Fatal Accidents Act 1846 (known as Lord Campbell's Act) was enacted to deal with it. The Act permitted certain dependants to recover the financial loss suffered as a result of a person's death caused by the defendant's wrongful act, neglect or default. The legislation was extensively amended, and is now contained in the Fatal Accidents Act 1976, which itself was amended by the Administration of Justice Act 1982 s 3. The Law Commission called for further reform of the Act in 1999[263] but apart from incorporating references to civil partners into its provisions where necessary, no further substantial reform has yet been enacted.

2 WHO MAY CLAIM

A claimant[264] must come within one of the categories laid down by the Act as follows:[265]

(a)   The deceased's wife or husband, or former wife or husband of the deceased, ie a person whose marriage to the deceased has been dissolved, annulled or declared void.

---

[259] Section 15A, inserted by the Matrimonial and Family Proceedings Act 1984 s 25(3) and s 15B, inserted by the Civil Partnership Act 2004 Sch 4 para 22. In this case, however, an order following a legal separation will have effect provided that the separation is in force on the party's death, whether or not the separation is continuing de facto.

[260] See *Re M (Deceased)* [1968] P 174.

[261] See M Duncan and C Marsh *Fatal Accident Claims* (1993); Law Commission Consultation Paper No 148, *Claims for Wrongful Death* (1997), Report No 263 *Claims for Wrongful Death* (1999).

[262] *Baker v Bolton* (1808) 1 Camp 493 per Lord Ellenborough CJ. The principle was affirmed by the House of Lords in *Admiralty Comrs v SS Amerika (owners)* [1917] AC 38.

[263] Report No 263 *Claims for Wrongful Death* (1999).

[264] The action must be brought by the personal representatives of the deceased on behalf of all the claimants, within six months of the death or, thereafter, by a claimant himself (again on behalf of all claimants): s 2.

[265] Section 1(3).

(aa) The deceased's civil partner or former civil partner.[266]

(b) Anyone who was living with the deceased in the same household immediately before the latter's death and had been so living for not less than two years as the deceased's husband or wife or civil partner.[267]

(c) A parent or other ascendant of the deceased.

(d) Anyone whom the deceased had treated as his parent.

(e) A child or other descendant of the deceased.[268]

(f) Anyone who was treated by the deceased as a child of the family[269] in relation to any marriage or civil partnership to which the deceased was a party.

(g) The deceased's brother, sister, uncle or aunt, or the issue of any of these.[270]

It will be seen that those coming within classes (a), (aa), (e) and (f) may all have had a claim or potential claim for maintenance against the deceased had he survived. With respect to cohabitants, it may be assumed that, if the survivor had been financially dependent on the deceased, that dependency would have continued. All the other cases consist of comparatively close relations who in certain circumstances might have received financial support from the deceased. The range of possible claimants is wider than under the intestacy rules, but is narrower than under the Inheritance (Provision for Family and Dependants) Act 1975 for, in contrast to that Act, if a person cannot bring himself within the categories listed, he has no claim even though he was financially dependent upon the deceased.

The claimant must establish a pecuniary loss as a result of the death,[271] unless the claim relates to damages for bereavement suffered by the spouse or civil partner of the deceased, or, where the deceased was a minor who never married or was a civil partner, by his parents (if he was legitimate), and by his mother (if he was not).[272] Thus, a former spouse, for example, whose claims for financial relief in the divorce suit have been dealt with by a clean break settlement, could not apply. But even though the deceased had made no contribution to the claimant's support before his death, an action will lie provided that the latter had a reasonable expectation of pecuniary advantage in the future if the other had survived.[273] This is particularly important in the case of a child who could have looked to the deceased to pay for her education or, conversely, of a parent who had reasonable hopes

---

[266] Inserted by Civil Partnership Act s 83(1). Partnerships that have been annulled are included: s 83(5) inserting s 1(4A).

[267] As amended by Civil Partnership Act s 83(3). Brief absences by the deceased from the claimant do not prevent a claim being brought: *Pounder v London Underground Ltd* [1995] PIQR P217.

[268] Including an unborn child conceived before the death, if born alive: *The George and Richard* (1871) LR 3 A & E 466.

[269] See above, p 338. As amended by Civil Partnership Act s 83(4).

[270] Fatal Accidents Act 1976 s 1(3) as amended by the Administration of Justice Act 1982 s 3(1). In deducing any of these relationships, '(a) any relationship by marriage or civil partnership shall be treated as a relationship by consanguinity, any relationship of the half blood as a relationship of the whole blood, and the stepchild of a person as his child, and (b) an illegitimate person shall be treated as the legitimate child of his mother and reputed father': s 1(5) as amended.

[271] *Duckworth v Johnson* (1859) 4 H & N 653.   [272] Section 1A as amended.

[273] There must be more than a 'mere speculative possibility of a benefit' per McCardie J in *Barnett v Cohen* [1921] 2 KB 461 at 471.

THE LEGAL CONSEQUENCES OF A DEATH IN THE FAMILY

of being supported by his child in his old age.[274] In any case, the financial benefit that the claimant has lost as a result of the death must derive from the relationship and must not be a mere business loss.[275]

3 AGAINST WHOM THE ACTION MAY BE BROUGHT

The action will lie against any person whom the deceased could himself have sued in respect of the fatal injury had he not died.[276]

4 ASSESSMENT OF DAMAGES

Damages are to be measured by reference to the material loss which the claimant has suffered as a result of the death.[277] Funeral expenses may also be recovered.[278] Where an action is brought on behalf of a cohabitant, the court is required to take into account the fact that the claimant had no enforceable right to be maintained by the deceased.[279] Difficult problems can arise in attempting to assess loss based on a quantification of the value of services provided by the deceased, rather than income brought into the household or paid to the claimant. For example, if a mother is killed in an accident, cash amounts can be attributed to her child-care, housekeeping, cooking etc, by comparing these with rates payable for a nanny or housekeeper, but commercial rates may distort the true measure of loss actually suffered, and consideration also needs to be given to the age of the children left behind and their diminishing need for care as they grow up. The courts therefore prefer to adopt a discretionary approach, and may reduce an award if the evidence establishes that the mother was unreliable.[280]

Section 4 of the Act provides that in 'assessing damages in respect of a person's death in an action under this Act, benefits which have accrued or will or may accrue to any person from his estate or otherwise as a result of his death shall be disregarded.' In *Laniyan v Barry May Haulage*[281] the unmarried father, who had no parental responsibility and had never financially supported his son, took over his care after the mother was killed. It was

---

[274] *Taff Vale Rly Co v Jenkins* [1913] AC 1, HL; *Kandalla v British Airways Board* [1981] QB 158.

[275] *Burgess v Florence Nightingale Hospital for Gentlewomen* [1955] 1 QB 349 (no claim for loss of income due to death of plaintiff's wife who had been his professional dancing partner). Contrast *Malyon v Plummer* [1964] 1 QB 330, CA—wife could recover for loss of value of directorship in company in which she and her deceased husband had been co-directors because her appointment was due to the relationship of husband and wife—applied in *Hack v Personal Representatives of Gangaram (Deceased)* (21 February 1996, unreported), QBD.

[276] Hence no action will lie if the deceased had already sued for his own injuries, and if he had received full compensation in his lifetime: *Read v Great Eastern Rly Co* (1868) LR 3 QB 555; or usually if his own claim was statute-barred: Limitation Act 1980 s 12(1) and s 33.

[277] Except in respect of bereavement damages, where a fixed sum of £10,000 is awarded: s 1A(3); Damages for Bereavement (Variation of Sum) (England and Wales) Order 2002, SI 2002/644. This amount (increased from £7,500) was recommended by the Law Commission in their Report No 263 at para 6.41

[278] Section 3(5).

[279] Section 3(4). Thus, in *Drew v Abassi and Packer* (24 May 1995, unreported) CA, cited by Law Commission, Consultation Paper No 148 at para 2.16 n 50), notwithstanding the finding by the trial judge that the relationship between the plaintiff and the deceased was one which 'would have survived as well as any marriage', he was held entitled to have discounted the appropriate multiplier by two years.

[280] *Stanley v Saddique* [1992] QB 1, CA.   [281] 19 July 2001, unreported.

held that the fact that the father *could have* supported him did not negate the fact that, in reality, he had not and would not have done so, and thus that his assumption of care was a benefit accrued as a result of the mother's death to be disregarded in calculating the measure of damages owed.[282]

Bizarrely, a widow's remarriage, or her prospects of remarriage, may not be taken into account when assessing her damages,[283] but the likelihood of she and the deceased having divorced if he had survived is to be considered.[284] This is anomalous, especially since the likelihood of remarriage may be taken into account when assessing compensation for a widower, (civil partner) or cohabitant. Even more illogically, a *widow's* prospect of remarrying will be a relevant factor when assessing her *child's* damages for loss of the child's father.

5 REFORM OF THE LEGISLATION

The Law Commission reviewed the working of the Fatal Accidents Act in a Consultation Paper issued in 1997 and Report published in 1999.[285] They considered the list of possible claimants too restrictive, drawing attention to the unfairness of excluding, for example, the survivor of a couple who have lived together for less than two years, or of children who have been treated as part of the deceased's family, but who fall outside the statutory definition of a 'child of the family' because he was a cohabitant.[286] The Commission's final recommendation was to add to the list of existing claimants, a category defined in the same way as under s 1(1)(e) of the Inheritance (Provision for Family and Dependants) Act 1975, that is, a person who immediately before the death was being maintained, either wholly or partly, by the deceased.

The Law Commission also criticised the inconsistent approach required under the current law to the question whether a claimant's future life prospects can be taken into account. They noted that the bar on considering a widow's chances of remarriage was introduced only in 1971, in response to criticisms that widows were being subjected to distressing and embarrassing questioning and assessment by lawyers and judges in court, and even to investigation by private detectives in attempts to determine whether they were likely to form new attachments. They concluded that no consideration should be given to the *prospects* of remarriage or financially supportive cohabitation of any relevant person (not just a widow) but that their *actual* engagement, remarriage or cohabitation at time of trial should be regarded as relevant factors.[287] (Presumably, forming a civil partnership would be treated similarly). Similarly, they recommended that the prospect of divorce or breakdown in the relationship should not be taken into account unless the couple were no longer living together or one of them had instituted divorce, nullity or separation proceedings.[288]

---

[282] The deputy High Court judge considered the position would have been different if the parents had been living together or there had been a financial order or actual support in place before the death or, also, if there had been a real prospect of the father providing future support: para 49.

[283] Section 3(3).   [284] *Owen v Martin* [1992] PIQR Q151.

[285] Consultation Paper No 148, Report No 263.   [286] Report para 3.15 et seq.

[287] See Law Com op cit para 4.53.   [288] At para 4.66.

The Law Commission's considerations on these matters, and the Parliamentary and judicial recognition of a broad range of 'family relationships' as deserving of legal significance, as discussed throughout this chapter, reflect the extent to which families are undergoing profound and rapid changes. The certainties of definition which could be applied a century ago by a society confident of its values have given way to a more questioning attitude as to which relationships in what circumstances should be given legal recognition, and what forms that recognition should take. Family law will continue to be shaped by the efforts of policy makers and legal practitioners to keep abreast of the social revolution which has so profoundly transformed family life. It will do so in the understanding that, while the form or structure of the 'family' may change, its essential characteristics will remain, in the words of Lord Slynn of Hadley in *Fitzpatrick v Sterling Housing Association Ltd* 'a degree of mutual inter-dependence, of the sharing of lives, of caring and love, of commitment and support.'[289]

---

[289] [2001] 1 AC 27, HL at p 38C–D.

INDEX

BROMLEY'S FAMILY LAW